# Presidential
# Inaugural
# Addresses

# Presidential Inaugural Addresses

**Word Cloud Classics**

San Diego

Canterbury Classics
An imprint of Printers Row Publishing Group
10350 Barnes Canyon Road, Suite 100, San Diego, CA 92121
www.canterburyclassicsbooks.com • mail@canterburyclassicsbooks.com

Printers Row Publishing Group is a division of Readerlink Distribution Services, LLC.
The Canterbury Classics and Word Cloud Classics names and logos are registered
trademarks of Readerlink Distribution Services, LLC.

All correspondence concerning the content of this book should be addressed to
Canterbury Classics, Editorial Department, at the above address.

Publisher: Peter Norton
Associate Publisher: Ana Parker
Publishing Team: April Farr, Kathryn C. Dalby
Editorial Team: JoAnn Padgett, Melinda Allman, Traci Douglas, Dan Mansfield
Production/Design Team: Jonathan Lopes, Rusty von Dyl,
Ray Caramanna

Spine art: Gettyimages/eyewave (statue), Gettyimages/clipartdotcom (flag)

ISBN: 978-1-64517-082-2
Printed in China
23 22 21 20 19   1 2 3 4 5

# CONTENTS

## GEORGE WASHINGTON
## FIRST INAUGURAL ADDRESS
## THURSDAY, APRIL 30, 1789

Fellow-Citizens of the Senate and of the House of Representatives:
Among the vicissitudes incident to life no event could have
filled me with greater anxieties than that of which the notification was
transmitted by your order, and received on the 14th day of the present
month. On the one hand, I was summoned by my country, whose
voice I can never hear but with veneration and love, from a retreat
which I had chosen with the fondest predilection, and, in my flattering
hopes, with an immutable decision, as the asylum of my declining
years—a retreat which was rendered every day more necessary as
well as more dear to me by the addition of habit to inclination, and of
frequent interruptions in my health to the gradual waste committed
on it by time. On the other hand, the magnitude and difficulty of the
trust to which the voice of my country called me, being sufficient
to awaken in the wisest and most experienced of her citizens a
distrustful scrutiny into his qualifications, could not but overwhelm
with despondence one who (inheriting inferior endowments from
nature and unpracticed in the duties of civil administration) ought
to be peculiarly conscious of his own deficiencies. In this conflict of
emotions all I dare aver is that it has been my faithful study to collect
my duty from a just appreciation of every circumstance by which it
might be affected. All I dare hope is that if, in executing this task, I
have been too much swayed by a grateful remembrance of former
instances, or by an affectionate sensibility to this transcendent proof
of the confidence of my fellow-citizens, and have thence too little
consulted my incapacity as well as disinclination for the weighty and
untried cares before me, my error will be palliated by the motives
which mislead me, and its consequences be judged by my country
with some share of the partiality in which they originated.

Such being the impressions under which I have, in obedience to the public summons, repaired to the present station, it would be peculiarly improper to omit in this first official act my fervent supplications to that Almighty Being who rules over the universe, who presides in the councils of nations, and whose providential aids can supply every human defect, that His benediction may consecrate to the liberties and happiness of the people of the United States a Government instituted by themselves for these essential purposes, and may enable every instrument employed in its administration to execute with success the functions allotted to his charge. In tendering this homage to the Great Author of every public and private good, I assure myself that it expresses your sentiments not less than my own, nor those of my fellow-citizens at large less than either. No people can be bound to acknowledge and adore the Invisible Hand which conducts the affairs of men more than those of the United States. Every step by which they have advanced to the character of an independent nation seems to have been distinguished by some token of providential agency; and in the important revolution just accomplished in the system of their united government the tranquil deliberations and voluntary consent of so many distinct communities from which the event has resulted can not be compared with the means by which most governments have been established without some return of pious gratitude, along with an humble anticipation of the future blessings which the past seem to presage. These reflections, arising out of the present crisis, have forced themselves too strongly on my mind to be suppressed. You will join with me, I trust, in thinking that there are none under the influence of which the proceedings of a new and free government can more auspiciously commence.

By the article establishing the executive department it is made the duty of the President "to recommend to your consideration such measures as he shall judge necessary and expedient." The circumstances under which I now meet you will acquit me from entering into that subject further than to refer to the great constitutional charter under which you are assembled, and which, in defining your powers, designates the objects to which your attention is to be given. It will be more consistent with those circumstances, and far more congenial with the feelings which actuate me, to substitute, in place of a recommendation of particular measures, the tribute that is due to the talents, the rectitude, and the patriotism which adorn the characters selected to devise and adopt them. In these honorable qualifications I behold the surest pledges that as on one side no local prejudices or attachments, no separate views nor party animosities, will misdirect the comprehensive and equal eye which ought to watch over this great assemblage of communities and interests, so, on another, that the foundation of our national policy will be laid in the pure and immutable principles of private morality, and the preeminence of free government be exemplified by all the attributes which can win the affections of its citizens and command the respect of the world. I dwell on this prospect with every satisfaction which an ardent love for my country can inspire, since there is no truth more thoroughly established than that there exists in the economy and course of nature an indissoluble union between virtue and happiness; between duty and advantage; between the genuine maxims of an honest and magnanimous policy and the solid rewards of public prosperity and felicity; since we ought to be no less persuaded that the propitious smiles of Heaven can never be expected on a nation that disregards the eternal rules of order and right which Heaven itself has ordained; and since the preservation of the sacred fire of liberty and the destiny of the republican model of government are justly considered, perhaps, as deeply, as finally, staked on the experiment entrusted to the hands of the American people.

Besides the ordinary objects submitted to your care, it will remain with your judgment to decide how far an exercise of the occasional power delegated by the fifth article of the Constitution is rendered expedient at the present juncture by the nature of objections which have been urged against the system, or by the degree of inquietude which has given birth to them. Instead of undertaking particular recommendations on this subject, in which I could be guided by no lights derived from official opportunities, I shall again give way to my entire confidence in your discernment and pursuit of the public good; for I assure myself that whilst you carefully avoid every alteration which might endanger the benefits of an united and effective government, or which ought to await the future lessons of experience, a reverence for the characteristic rights of freemen and a regard for the public harmony will sufficiently influence your deliberations on the question how far the former can be impregnably fortified or the latter be safely and advantageously promoted.

To the foregoing observations I have one to add, which will be most properly addressed to the House of Representatives. It concerns myself, and will therefore be as brief as possible. When I was first honored with a call into the service of my country, then on the eve of an arduous struggle for its liberties, the light in which I contemplated my duty required that I should renounce every pecuniary compensation. From this resolution I have in no instance departed; and being still under the impressions which produced it, I must decline as inapplicable to myself any share in the personal emoluments which may be indispensably included in a permanent provision for the executive department, and must accordingly pray that the pecuniary estimates for the station in which I am placed may during my continuance in it be limited to such actual expenditures as the public good may be thought to require.

Having thus imparted to you my sentiments as they have been awakened by the occasion which brings us together, I shall take my present leave; but not without resorting once more to the benign Parent of the Human Race in humble supplication that, since He has been pleased to favor the American people with opportunities for deliberating in perfect tranquillity, and dispositions for deciding with unparalleled unanimity on a form of government for the security of their union and the advancement of their happiness, so His divine blessing may be equally conspicuous in the enlarged views, the temperate consultations, and the wise measures on which the success of this Government must depend.

# GEORGE WASHINGTON
## SECOND INAUGURAL ADDRESS
### MONDAY, MARCH 4, 1793

Fellow Citizens:

I am again called upon by the voice of my country to execute the functions of its Chief Magistrate. When the occasion proper for it shall arrive, I shall endeavor to express the high sense I entertain of this distinguished honor, and of the confidence which has been reposed in me by the people of united America.

Previous to the execution of any official act of the President the Constitution requires an oath of office. This oath I am now about to take, and in your presence: That if it shall be found during my administration of the Government I have in any instance violated willingly or knowingly the injunctions thereof, I may (besides incurring constitutional punishment) be subject to the upbraidings of all who are now witnesses of the present solemn ceremony.

# JOHN ADAMS
# INAUGURAL ADDRESS
# SATURDAY, MARCH 4, 1797

When it was first perceived, in early times, that no middle course for America remained between unlimited submission to a foreign legislature and a total independence of its claims, men of reflection were less apprehensive of danger from the formidable power of fleets and armies they must determine to resist than from those contests and dissensions which would certainly arise concerning the forms of government to be instituted over the whole and over the parts of this extensive country. Relying, however, on the purity of their intentions, the justice of their cause, and the integrity and intelligence of the people, under an overruling Providence which had so signally protected this country from the first, the representatives of this nation, then consisting of little more than half its present number, not only broke to pieces the chains which were forging and the rod of iron that was lifted up, but frankly cut asunder the ties which had bound them, and launched into an ocean of uncertainty.

The zeal and ardor of the people during the Revolutionary war, supplying the place of government, commanded a degree of order sufficient at least for the temporary preservation of society. The Confederation which was early felt to be necessary was prepared from the models of the Batavian and Helvetic confederacies, the only examples which remain with any detail and precision in history, and certainly the only ones which the people at large had ever considered. But reflecting on the striking difference in so many particulars between this country and those where a courier may go from the seat of government to the frontier in a single day, it was then certainly foreseen by some who assisted in Congress at the formation of it that it could not be durable.

Negligence of its regulations, inattention to its recommendations, if not disobedience to its authority, not only in individuals but in

States, soon appeared with their melancholy consequences—universal languor, jealousies and rivalries of States, decline of navigation and commerce, discouragement of necessary manufactures, universal fall in the value of lands and their produce, contempt of public and private faith, loss of consideration and credit with foreign nations, and at length in discontents, animosities, combinations, partial conventions, and insurrection, threatening some great national calamity.

In this dangerous crisis the people of America were not abandoned by their usual good sense, presence of mind, resolution, or integrity. Measures were pursued to concert a plan to form a more perfect union, establish justice, insure domestic tranquillity, provide for the common defense, promote the general welfare, and secure the blessings of liberty. The public disquisitions, discussions, and deliberations issued in the present happy Constitution of Government.

Employed in the service of my country abroad during the whole course of these transactions, I first saw the Constitution of the United States in a foreign country. Irritated by no literary altercation, animated by no public debate, heated by no party animosity, I read it with great satisfaction, as the result of good heads prompted by good hearts, as an experiment better adapted to the genius, character, situation, and relations of this nation and country than any which had ever been proposed or suggested. In its general principles and great outlines it was conformable to such a system of government as I had ever most esteemed, and in some States, my own native State in particular, had contributed to establish. Claiming a right of suffrage, in common with my fellow-citizens, in the adoption or rejection of a constitution which was to rule me and my posterity, as well as them and theirs, I did not hesitate to express my approbation of it on all occasions, in public and in private. It was not then, nor has been since, any objection to it in my mind that the Executive and Senate were not more permanent. Nor have I ever entertained a thought of promoting any alteration in it but such as the people themselves, in the course of their experience, should see and feel to be necessary or expedient, and by their representatives in Congress and the State legislatures, according to the Constitution itself, adopt and ordain.

Returning to the bosom of my country after a painful separation from it for ten years, I had the honor to be elected to a station under the new order of things, and I have repeatedly laid myself under the most serious obligations to support the Constitution. The operation of it has equaled the most sanguine expectations of its friends, and from an habitual attention to it, satisfaction in its administration, and delight in its effects upon the peace, order, prosperity, and happiness of the nation I have acquired an habitual attachment to it and veneration for it.

What other form of government, indeed, can so well deserve our esteem and love?

There may be little solidity in an ancient idea that congregations of men into cities and nations are the most pleasing objects in the sight of superior intelligences, but this is very certain, that to a benevolent human mind there can be no spectacle presented by any nation more pleasing, more noble, majestic, or august, than an assembly like that which has so often been seen in this and the other Chamber of Congress, of a Government in which the Executive authority, as well as that of all the branches of the Legislature, are exercised by citizens selected at regular periods by their neighbors to make and execute laws for the general good. Can anything essential, anything more than mere ornament and decoration, be added to this by robes and diamonds? Can authority be more amiable and respectable when it descends from accidents or institutions established in remote antiquity than when it springs fresh from the hearts and judgments of an honest and enlightened people? For it is the people only that are represented. It is their power and majesty that is reflected, and only for their good, in every legitimate government, under whatever form it may appear. The existence of such a government as ours for any length of time is a full proof of a general dissemination of knowledge and virtue throughout the whole body of the people. And what object or consideration more pleasing than this can be presented to the human mind? If national pride is ever justifiable or excusable it is when it springs, not from power or riches, grandeur or glory, but from conviction of national innocence, information, and benevolence.

In the midst of these pleasing ideas we should be unfaithful to ourselves if we should ever lose sight of the danger to our liberties if anything partial or extraneous should infect the purity of our free, fair, virtuous, and independent elections. If an election is to be determined by a majority of a single vote, and that can be procured by a party through artifice or corruption, the Government may be the choice of a party for its own ends, not of the nation for the national good. If that solitary suffrage can be obtained by foreign nations by flattery or menaces, by fraud or violence, by terror, intrigue, or venality, the Government may not be the choice of the American people, but of foreign nations. It may be foreign nations who govern us, and not we, the people, who govern ourselves; and candid men will acknowledge that in such cases choice would have little advantage to boast of over lot or chance.

Such is the amiable and interesting system of government (and such are some of the abuses to which it may be exposed) which the people of America have exhibited to the admiration and anxiety of the wise and virtuous of all nations for eight years under the administration of a citizen who, by a long course of great actions, regulated by prudence, justice, temperance, and fortitude, conducting a people inspired with the same virtues and animated with the same ardent patriotism and love of liberty to independence and peace, to increasing wealth and unexampled prosperity, has merited the gratitude of his fellow-citizens, commanded the highest praises of foreign nations, and secured immortal glory with posterity.

In that retirement which is his voluntary choice may he long live to enjoy the delicious recollection of his services, the gratitude of mankind, the happy fruits of them to himself and the world, which are daily increasing, and that splendid prospect of the future fortunes of this country which is opening from year to year. His name may be still a rampart, and the knowledge that he lives a bulwark against all open or secret enemies of his country's peace. This example has been recommended to the imitation of his successors by both Houses of Congress and by the voice of the legislatures and the people throughout the nation.

On this subject it might become me better to be silent or to speak with diffidence; but as something may be expected, the occasion, I hope, will be admitted as an apology if I venture to say that if a preference, upon principle, of a free republican government formed upon long and serious reflection, after a diligent and impartial inquiry after truth; if an attachment to the Constitution of the United States, and a conscientious determination to support it until it shall be altered by the judgments and wishes of the people, expressed in the mode prescribed in it; if a respectful attention to the constitutions of the individual States and a constant caution and delicacy toward the State governments; if an equal and impartial regard to the rights, interest, honor, and happiness of all the States in the Union, without preference or regard to a northern or southern, an eastern or western, position, their various political opinions on unessential points or their personal attachments; if a love of virtuous men of all parties and denominations; if a love of science and letters and a wish to patronize every rational effort to encourage schools, colleges, universities, academies, and every institution for propagating knowledge, virtue, and religion among all classes of the people, not only for their benign influence on the happiness of life in all its stages and classes, and of society in all its forms, but as the only means of preserving our Constitution from its natural enemies, the spirit of sophistry, the spirit of party, the spirit of intrigue, the profligacy of corruption, and the pestilence of foreign influence, which is the angel of destruction to elective governments; if a love of equal laws, of justice, and humanity in the interior administration; if an inclination to improve agriculture, commerce, and manufacturers for necessity, convenience, and defense; if a spirit of equity and humanity toward the aboriginal nations of America, and a disposition to meliorate their condition by inclining them to be more friendly to us, and our citizens to be more friendly to them; if an inflexible determination to maintain peace and inviolable faith with all nations, and that system of neutrality and impartiality among the belligerent powers of Europe which has been adopted by this Government and so solemnly sanctioned by both Houses of Congress and applauded by the legislatures of the States and the public opinion, until it shall be otherwise ordained by Congress; if a personal esteem for the French nation, formed in a residence of seven years chiefly among them, and a sincere desire to preserve the friendship which has been so much for the honor and interest of both nations; if, while the conscious honor and integrity of the people of America and the internal sentiment of their own power and energies must be preserved, an earnest endeavor to investigate every just cause and remove every colorable pretense of complaint;

if an intention to pursue by amicable negotiation a reparation for the injuries that have been committed on the commerce of our fellow-citizens by whatever nation, and if success can not be obtained, to lay the facts before the Legislature, that they may consider what further measures the honor and interest of the Government and its constituents demand; if a resolution to do justice as far as may depend upon me, at all times and to all nations, and maintain peace, friendship, and benevolence with all the world; if an unshaken confidence in the honor, spirit, and resources of the American people, on which I have so often hazarded my all and never been deceived; if elevated ideas of the high destinies of this country and of my own duties toward it, founded on a knowledge of the moral principles and intellectual improvements of the people deeply engraven on my mind in early life, and not obscured but exalted by experience and age; and, with humble reverence, I feel it to be my duty to add, if a veneration for the religion of a people who profess and call themselves Christians, and a fixed resolution to consider a decent respect for Christianity among the best recommendations for the public service, can enable me in any degree to comply with your wishes, it shall be my strenuous endeavor that this sagacious injunction of the two Houses shall not be without effect.

With this great example before me, with the sense and spirit, the faith and honor, the duty and interest, of the same American people pledged to support the Constitution of the United States, I entertain no doubt of its continuance in all its energy, and my mind is prepared without hesitation to lay myself under the most solemn obligations to support it to the utmost of my power.

And may that Being who is supreme over all, the Patron of Order, the Fountain of Justice, and the Protector in all ages of the world of virtuous liberty, continue His blessing upon this nation and its Government and give it all possible success and duration consistent with the ends of His providence.

# THOMAS JEFFERSON
## FIRST INAUGURAL ADDRESS
## WEDNESDAY, MARCH 4, 1801

Friends and Fellow-Citizens:

Called upon to undertake the duties of the first executive office of our country, I avail myself of the presence of that portion of my fellow-citizens which is here assembled to express my grateful thanks for the favor with which they have been pleased to look toward me, to declare a sincere consciousness that the task is above my talents, and that I approach it with those anxious and awful presentiments which the greatness of the charge and the weakness of my powers so justly inspire. A rising nation, spread over a wide and fruitful land, traversing all the seas with the rich productions of their industry, engaged in commerce with nations who feel power and forget right, advancing rapidly to destinies beyond the reach of mortal eye—when I contemplate these transcendent objects, and see the honor, the happiness, and the hopes of this beloved country committed to the issue, and the auspices of this day, I shrink from the contemplation, and humble myself before the magnitude of the undertaking. Utterly, indeed, should I despair did not the presence of many whom I here see remind me that in the other high authorities provided by our Constitution I shall find resources of wisdom, of virtue, and of zeal on which to rely under all difficulties. To you, then, gentlemen, who are charged with the sovereign functions of legislation, and to those associated with you, I look with encouragement for that guidance and support which may enable us to steer with safety the vessel in which we are all embarked amidst the conflicting elements of a troubled world.

During the contest of opinion through which we have passed the animation of discussions and of exertions has sometimes worn an aspect which might impose on strangers unused to think freely and to speak and to write what they think; but this being now decided by the voice of the nation, announced according to the rules of the Constitution, all will, of course, arrange themselves under the will of the law, and unite in common efforts for the common good. All, too, will bear in mind this sacred principle, that though the will of the majority is in all cases to prevail, that will to be rightful must be reasonable; that the minority possess their equal rights, which equal law must protect, and to violate would be oppression. Let us, then, fellow-citizens, unite with one heart and one mind. Let us restore to social intercourse that harmony and affection without which liberty and even life itself are but dreary things. And let us reflect that, having banished from our land that religious intolerance under which mankind so long bled and suffered, we have yet gained little if we countenance a political intolerance as despotic, as wicked, and capable of as bitter and bloody persecutions. During the throes and convulsions of the ancient world, during the agonizing spasms of infuriated man, seeking through blood and slaughter his long-lost liberty, it was not wonderful that the agitation of the billows should reach even this distant and peaceful shore; that this should be more felt and feared by some and less by others, and should divide opinions as to measures of safety. But every difference of opinion is not a difference of principle. We have called by different names brethren of the same principle. We are all Republicans, we are all Federalists. If there be any among us who would wish to dissolve this Union or to change its republican form, let them stand undisturbed as monuments of the safety with which error of opinion may be tolerated where reason is left free to combat it. I know, indeed, that some honest men fear that a republican government can not be strong, that this Government is not strong enough; but would the honest patriot, in the full tide of successful experiment, abandon a government which has so far kept us free and firm on the theoretic and visionary fear that this Government, the world's best hope, may by possibility want energy to preserve itself? I trust not. I believe this, on the contrary, the strongest Government on earth. I believe it the only one where every man, at the call of the law, would fly to the standard of the law, and would meet invasions of the public order as his own personal concern. Sometimes it is said that man can not be trusted with the government of himself. Can he, then, be trusted with the government of others? Or have we found angels in the forms of kings to govern him? Let history answer this question.

Let us, then, with courage and confidence pursue our own Federal and Republican principles, our attachment to union and representative government. Kindly separated by nature and a wide ocean from the exterminating havoc of one quarter of the globe; too high-minded to endure the degradations of the others; possessing a chosen country, with room enough for our descendants to the thousandth and thousandth generation; entertaining a due sense of our equal right to the use of our own faculties, to the acquisitions of our own industry, to honor and confidence from our fellow-citizens, resulting not from birth, but from our actions and their sense of them; enlightened by a benign religion, professed, indeed, and practiced in various forms, yet all of them inculcating honesty, truth, temperance, gratitude, and the love of man; acknowledging and adoring an overruling Providence, which by all its dispensations proves that it delights in the happiness of man here and his greater happiness hereafter—with all these blessings, what more is necessary to make us a happy and a prosperous people? Still one thing more, fellow-citizens—a wise and frugal Government, which shall restrain men from injuring one another, shall leave them otherwise free to regulate their own pursuits of industry and improvement, and shall not take from the mouth of labor the bread it has earned. This is the sum of good government, and this is necessary to close the circle of our felicities.

About to enter, fellow-citizens, on the exercise of duties which comprehend everything dear and valuable to you, it is proper you should understand what I deem the essential principles of our Government, and consequently those which ought to shape its Administration. I will compress them within the narrowest compass they will bear, stating the general principle, but not all its limitations. Equal and exact justice to all men, of whatever state or persuasion, religious or political; peace, commerce, and honest friendship with all nations, entangling alliances with none; the support of the State governments in all their rights, as the most competent administrations for our domestic concerns and the surest bulwarks against antirepublican tendencies; the preservation of the General Government in its whole constitutional vigor, as the sheet anchor of our peace at home and safety abroad; a jealous care of the right of election by the people—a mild and safe corrective of abuses which are lopped by the sword of revolution where peaceable remedies are unprovided; absolute acquiescence in the decisions of the majority, the vital principle of republics, from which is no appeal but to force, the vital principle and immediate parent of despotism; a well disciplined militia, our best reliance in peace and for the first moments of war, till regulars may relieve them; the supremacy of the civil over the military authority; economy in the public expense, that labor may be lightly burthened; the honest payment of our debts and sacred preservation of the public faith; encouragement of agriculture, and of commerce as its handmaid; the diffusion of information and arraignment of all abuses at the bar of the public reason; freedom of religion; freedom of the press, and freedom of person under the protection of the habeas corpus, and trial by juries impartially selected. These principles form the bright constellation which has gone before us and guided our steps through an age of revolution and reformation. The wisdom of our sages and blood of our heroes have been devoted to their attainment. They should be the creed of our political faith, the text of civic instruction, the touchstone by which to try the services of those we trust; and should we wander from them in moments of error or of alarm, let us hasten to retrace our steps and to regain the road which alone leads to peace, liberty, and safety.

I repair, then, fellow-citizens, to the post you have assigned me. With experience enough in subordinate offices to have seen the difficulties of this the greatest of all, I have learnt to expect that it will rarely fall to the lot of imperfect man to retire from this station with the reputation and the favor which bring him into it. Without pretensions to that high confidence you reposed in our first and greatest revolutionary character, whose preeminent services had entitled him to the first place in his country's love and destined for him the fairest page in the volume of faithful history, I ask so much confidence only as may give firmness and effect to the legal administration of your affairs. I shall often go wrong through defect of judgment. When right, I shall often be thought wrong by those whose positions will not command a view of the whole ground. I ask your indulgence for my own errors, which will never be intentional, and your support against the errors of others, who may condemn what they would not if seen in all its parts. The approbation implied by your suffrage is a great consolation to me for the past, and my future solicitude will be to retain the good opinion of those who have bestowed it in advance, to conciliate that of others by doing them all the good in my power, and to be instrumental to the happiness and freedom of all.

Relying, then, on the patronage of your good will, I advance with obedience to the work, ready to retire from it whenever you become sensible how much better choice it is in your power to make. And may that Infinite Power which rules the destinies of the universe lead our councils to what is best, and give them a favorable issue for your peace and prosperity.

# THOMAS JEFFERSON
# SECOND INAUGURAL ADDRESS
# MONDAY, MARCH 4, 1805

Proceeding, fellow-citizens, to that qualification which the Constitution requires before my entrance on the charge again conferred on me, it is my duty to express the deep sense I entertain of this new proof of confidence from my fellow-citizens at large, and the zeal with which it inspires me so to conduct myself as may best satisfy their just expectations.

On taking this station on a former occasion I declared the principles on which I believed it my duty to administer the affairs of our Commonwealth. My conscience tells me I have on every occasion acted up to that declaration according to its obvious import and to the understanding of every candid mind.

In the transaction of your foreign affairs we have endeavored to cultivate the friendship of all nations, and especially of those with which we have the most important relations. We have done them justice on all occasions, favored where favor was lawful, and cherished mutual interests and intercourse on fair and equal terms. We are firmly convinced, and we act on that conviction, that with nations as with individuals our interests soundly calculated will ever be found inseparable from our moral duties, and history bears witness to the fact that a just nation is trusted on its word when recourse is had to armaments and wars to bridle others.

At home, fellow-citizens, you best know whether we have done well or ill. The suppression of unnecessary offices, of useless establishments and expenses, enabled us to discontinue our internal taxes. These, covering our land with officers and opening our doors to their intrusions, had already begun that process of domiciliary vexation which once entered is scarcely to be restrained from reaching successively every article of property and produce. If among these taxes some minor ones fell which had not been inconvenient, it was because their amount would not have paid the officers who collected them, and because, if they had any merit, the State authorities might adopt them instead of others less approved.

The remaining revenue on the consumption of foreign articles is paid chiefly by those who can afford to add foreign luxuries to domestic comforts, being collected on our seaboard and frontiers only, and incorporated with the transactions of our mercantile citizens, it may be the pleasure and the pride of an American to ask, What farmer, what mechanic, what laborer ever sees a tax-gatherer of the United States? These contributions enable us to support the current expenses of the Government, to fulfill contracts with foreign nations, to extinguish the native right of soil within our limits, to extend those limits, and to apply such a surplus to our public debts as places at a short day their final redemption, and that redemption once effected the revenue thereby liberated may, by a just repartition of it among the States and a corresponding amendment of the Constitution, be applied in time of peace to rivers, canals, roads, arts, manufactures, education, and other great objects within each State. In time of war, if injustice by ourselves or others must sometimes produce war, increased as the same revenue will be by increased population and consumption, and aided by other resources reserved for that crisis, it may meet within the year all the expenses of the year without encroaching on the rights of future generations by burthening them with the debts of the past. War will then be but a suspension of useful works, and a return to a state of peace, a return to the progress of improvement.

I have said, fellow-citizens, that the income reserved had enabled us to extend our limits, but that extension may possibly pay for itself before we are called on, and in the meantime may keep down the accruing interest; in all events, it will replace the advances we shall have made. I know that the acquisition of Louisiana had been disapproved by some from a candid apprehension that the enlargement of our territory would endanger its union. But who can limit the extent to which the federative principle may operate effectively? The larger our association the less will it be shaken by local passions; and in any view is it not better that the opposite bank of the Mississippi should be settled by our own brethren and children than by strangers of another family? With which should we be most likely to live in harmony and friendly intercourse?

In matters of religion I have considered that its free exercise is placed by the Constitution independent of the powers of the General Government. I have therefore undertaken on no occasion to prescribe the religious exercises suited to it, but have left them, as the Constitution found them, under the direction and discipline of the church or State authorities acknowledged by the several religious societies.

The aboriginal inhabitants of these countries I have regarded with the commiseration their history inspires. Endowed with the faculties and the rights of men, breathing an ardent love of liberty and independence, and occupying a country which left them no desire but to be undisturbed, the stream of overflowing population from other regions directed itself on these shores; without power to divert or habits to contend against it, they have been overwhelmed by the current or driven before it; now reduced within limits too narrow for the hunter's state, humanity enjoins us to teach them agriculture and the domestic arts; to encourage them to that industry which alone can enable them to maintain their place in existence and to prepare them in time for that state of society which to bodily comforts adds the improvement of the mind and morals. We have therefore liberally furnished them with the implements of husbandry and household use; we have placed among them instructors in the arts of first necessity, and they are covered with the aegis of the law against aggressors from among ourselves.

But the endeavors to enlighten them on the fate which awaits their present course of life, to induce them to exercise their reason, follow its dictates, and change their pursuits with the change of circumstances have powerful obstacles to encounter; they are combated by the habits of their bodies, prejudices of their minds, ignorance, pride, and the influence of interested and crafty individuals among them who feel themselves something in the present order of things and fear to become nothing in any other. These persons inculcate a sanctimonious reverence for the customs of their ancestors; that whatsoever they did must be done through all time; that reason is a false guide, and to advance under its counsel in their physical, moral, or political condition is perilous innovation; that their duty is to remain as their Creator made them, ignorance being safety and knowledge full of danger; in short, my friends, among them also is seen the action and counteraction of good sense and of bigotry; they too have their antiphilosophists who find an interest in keeping things in their present state, who dread reformation, and exert all their faculties to maintain the ascendancy of habit over the duty of improving our reason and obeying its mandates.

In giving these outlines I do not mean, fellow-citizens, to arrogate to myself the merit of the measures. That is due, in the first place, to the reflecting character of our citizens at large, who, by the weight of public opinion, influence and strengthen the public measures. It is due to the sound discretion with which they select from among themselves those to whom they confide the legislative duties. It is due to the zeal and wisdom of the characters thus selected, who lay the foundations of public happiness in wholesome laws, the execution of which alone remains for others, and it is due to the able and faithful auxiliaries, whose patriotism has associated them with me in the executive functions.

During this course of administration, and in order to disturb it, the artillery of the press has been leveled against us, charged with whatsoever its licentiousness could devise or dare. These abuses of an institution so important to freedom and science are deeply to be regretted, inasmuch as they tend to lessen its usefulness and to sap its safety. They might, indeed, have been corrected by the wholesome punishments reserved to and provided by the laws of the several States against falsehood and defamation, but public duties more urgent press on the time of public servants, and the offenders have therefore been left to find their punishment in the public indignation.

Nor was it uninteresting to the world that an experiment should be fairly and fully made, whether freedom of discussion, unaided by power, is not sufficient for the propagation and protection of truth—whether a government conducting itself in the true spirit of its constitution, with zeal and purity, and doing no act which it would be unwilling the whole world should witness, can be written down by falsehood and defamation. The experiment has been tried; you have witnessed the scene; our fellow-citizens looked on, cool and collected; they saw the latent source from which these outrages proceeded; they gathered around their public functionaries, and when the Constitution called them to the decision by suffrage, they pronounced their verdict, honorable to those who had served them and consolatory to the friend of man who believes that he may be trusted with the control of his own affairs.

No inference is here intended that the laws provided by the States against false and defamatory publications should not be enforced; he who has time renders a service to public morals and public tranquillity in reforming these abuses by the salutary coercions of the law; but the experiment is noted to prove that, since truth and reason have maintained their ground against false opinions in league with false facts, the press, confined to truth, needs no other legal restraint; the public judgment will correct false reasoning and opinions on a full hearing of all parties; and no other definite line can be drawn between the inestimable liberty of the press and its demoralizing licentiousness. If there be still improprieties which this rule would not restrain, its supplement must be sought in the censorship of public opinion.

Contemplating the union of sentiment now manifested so generally as auguring harmony and happiness to our future course, I offer to our country sincere congratulations. With those, too, not yet rallied to the same point the disposition to do so is gaining strength; facts are piercing through the veil drawn over them, and our doubting brethren will at length see that the mass of their fellow-citizens with whom they can not yet resolve to act as to principles and measures, think as they think and desire what they desire; that our wish as well as theirs is that the public efforts may be directed honestly to the public good, that peace be cultivated, civil and religious liberty unassailed, law and order preserved, equality of rights maintained, and that state of property, equal or unequal, which results to every man from his own industry or that of his father's. When satisfied of these views it is not in human nature that they should not approve and support them. In the meantime let us cherish them with patient affection, let us do them justice, and more than justice, in all competitions of interest; and we need not doubt that truth, reason, and their own interests will at length prevail, will gather them into the fold of their country, and will complete that entire union of opinion which gives to a nation the blessing of harmony and the benefit of all its strength.

I shall now enter on the duties to which my fellow-citizens have again called me, and shall proceed in the spirit of those principles which they have approved. I fear not that any motives of interest may lead me astray; I am sensible of no passion which could seduce me knowingly from the path of justice, but the weaknesses of human nature and the limits of my own understanding will produce errors of judgment sometimes injurious to your interests. I shall need, therefore, all the indulgence which I have heretofore experienced from my constituents; the want of it will certainly not lessen with increasing years. I shall need, too, the favor of that Being in whose hands we are, who led our fathers, as Israel of old, from their native land and planted them in a country flowing with all the necessaries and comforts of life; who has covered our infancy with His providence and our riper years with His wisdom and power, and to whose goodness I ask you to join in supplications with me that He will so enlighten the minds of your servants, guide their councils, and prosper their measures that whatsoever they do shall result in your good, and shall secure to you the peace, friendship, and approbation of all nations.

# JAMES MADISON
## FIRST INAUGURAL ADDRESS
## SATURDAY, MARCH 4, 1809

Unwilling to depart from examples of the most revered authority, I avail myself of the occasion now presented to express the profound impression made on me by the call of my country to the station to the duties of which I am about to pledge myself by the most solemn of sanctions. So distinguished a mark of confidence, proceeding from the deliberate and tranquil suffrage of a free and virtuous nation, would under any circumstances have commanded my gratitude and devotion, as well as filled me with an awful sense of the trust to be assumed. Under the various circumstances which give peculiar solemnity to the existing period, I feel that both the honor and the responsibility allotted to me are inexpressibly enhanced.

The present situation of the world is indeed without a parallel and that of our own country full of difficulties. The pressure of these, too, is the more severely felt because they have fallen upon us at a moment when the national prosperity being at a height not before attained, the contrast resulting from the change has been rendered the more striking. Under the benign influence of our republican institutions, and the maintenance of peace with all nations whilst so many of them were engaged in bloody and wasteful wars, the fruits of a just policy were enjoyed in an unrivaled growth of our faculties and resources. Proofs of this were seen in the improvements of agriculture, in the successful enterprises of commerce, in the progress of manufacturers and useful arts, in the increase of the public revenue and the use made of it in reducing the public debt, and in the valuable works and establishments everywhere multiplying over the face of our land.

It is a precious reflection that the transition from this prosperous condition of our country to the scene which has for some time been distressing us is not chargeable on any unwarrantable views, nor, as I trust, on any involuntary errors in the public councils. Indulging no passions which trespass on the rights or the repose of other nations, it has been the true glory of the United States to cultivate peace by observing justice, and to entitle themselves to the respect of the nations at war by fulfilling their neutral obligations with the most scrupulous impartiality. If there be candor in the world, the truth of these assertions will not be questioned; posterity at least will do justice to them.

This unexceptionable course could not avail against the injustice and violence of the belligerent powers. In their rage against each other, or impelled by more direct motives, principles of retaliation have been introduced equally contrary to universal reason and acknowledged law. How long their arbitrary edicts will be continued in spite of the demonstrations that not even a pretext for them has been given by the United States, and of the fair and liberal attempt to induce a revocation of them, can not be anticipated. Assuring myself that under every vicissitude the determined spirit and united councils of the nation will be safeguards to its honor and its essential interests, I repair to the post assigned me with no other discouragement than what springs from my own inadequacy to its high duties. If I do not sink under the weight of this deep conviction it is because I find some support in a consciousness of the purposes and a confidence in the principles which I bring with me into this arduous service.

To cherish peace and friendly intercourse with all nations having correspondent dispositions; to maintain sincere neutrality toward belligerent nations; to prefer in all cases amicable discussion and reasonable accommodation of differences to a decision of them by an appeal to arms; to exclude foreign intrigues and foreign partialities, so degrading to all countries and so baneful to free ones; to foster a spirit of independence too just to invade the rights of others, too proud to surrender our own, too liberal to indulge unworthy prejudices ourselves and too elevated not to look down upon them in others; to hold the union of the States as the basis of their peace and happiness; to support the Constitution, which is the cement of the Union, as well in its limitations as in its authorities; to respect the rights and authorities reserved to the States and to the people as equally incorporated with and essential to the success of the general system; to avoid the slightest interference with the right of conscience or the functions of religion, so wisely exempted from civil jurisdiction; to preserve in their full energy the other salutary provisions in behalf of private and personal rights, and of the freedom of the press; to observe economy in public expenditures; to liberate the public resources by an honorable discharge of the public debts; to keep within the requisite limits a standing military force, always remembering that an armed and trained militia is the firmest bulwark of republics—that without standing armies their liberty can never be in danger, nor with large ones safe; to promote by authorized means improvements friendly to agriculture, to manufactures, and to external as well as internal commerce; to favor in like manner the advancement of science and the diffusion of information as the best aliment to true liberty; to carry on the benevolent plans which have been so meritoriously applied to the conversion of our aboriginal neighbors from the degradation and wretchedness of savage life to a participation of the improvements of which the human mind and manners are susceptible in a civilized state—as far as sentiments and intentions such as these can aid the fulfillment of my duty, they will be a resource which can not fail me.

It is my good fortune, moreover, to have the path in which I am to tread lighted by examples of illustrious services successfully rendered in the most trying difficulties by those who have marched before me. Of those of my immediate predecessor it might least become me here to speak. I may, however, be pardoned for not suppressing the sympathy with which my heart is full in the rich reward he enjoys in the benedictions of a beloved country, gratefully bestowed or exalted talents zealously devoted through a long career to the advancement of its highest interest and happiness.

But the source to which I look or the aids which alone can supply my deficiencies is in the well-tried intelligence and virtue of my fellow-citizens, and in the counsels of those representing them in the other departments associated in the care of the national interests. In these my confidence will under every difficulty be best placed, next to that which we have all been encouraged to feel in the guardianship and guidance of that Almighty Being whose power regulates the destiny of nations, whose blessings have been so conspicuously dispensed to this rising Republic, and to whom we are bound to address our devout gratitude for the past, as well as our fervent supplications and best hopes for the future.

# JAMES MADISON
## SECOND INAUGURAL ADDRESS
### THURSDAY, MARCH 4, 1813

About to add the solemnity of an oath to the obligations imposed by a second call to the station in which my country heretofore placed me, I find in the presence of this respectable assembly an opportunity of publicly repeating my profound sense of so distinguished a confidence and of the responsibility united with it. The impressions on me are strengthened by such an evidence that my faithful endeavors to discharge my arduous duties have been favorably estimated, and by a consideration of the momentous period at which the trust has been renewed. From the weight and magnitude now belonging to it I should be compelled to shrink if I had less reliance on the support of an enlightened and generous people, and felt less deeply a conviction that the war with a powerful nation, which forms so prominent a feature in our situation, is stamped with that justice which invites the smiles of Heaven on the means of conducting it to a successful termination.

May we not cherish this sentiment without presumption when we reflect on the characters by which this war is distinguished?

It was not declared on the part of the United States until it had been long made on them, in reality though not in name; until arguments and postulations had been exhausted; until a positive declaration had been received that the wrongs provoking it would not be discontinued; nor until this last appeal could no longer be delayed without breaking down the spirit of the nation, destroying all confidence in itself and in its political institutions, and either perpetuating a state of disgraceful suffering or regaining by more costly sacrifices and more severe struggles our lost rank and respect among independent powers.

On the issue of the war are staked our national sovereignty on the high seas and the security of an important class of citizens whose occupations give the proper value to those of every other class. Not to contend for such a stake is to surrender our equality with other powers on the element common to all and to violate the sacred title which every member of the society has to its protection. I need not call into view the unlawfulness of the practice by which our mariners are forced at the will of every cruising officer from their own vessels into foreign ones, nor paint the outrages inseparable from it. The proofs are in the records of each successive Administration of our Government, and the cruel sufferings of that portion of the American people have found their way to every bosom not dead to the sympathies of human nature.

As the war was just in its origin and necessary and noble in its objects, we can reflect with a proud satisfaction that in carrying it on no principle of justice or honor, no usage of civilized nations, no precept of courtesy or humanity, have been infringed. The war has been waged on our part with scrupulous regard to all these obligations, and in a spirit of liberality which was never surpassed.

How little has been the effect of this example on the conduct of the enemy!

They have retained as prisoners of war citizens of the United States not liable to be so considered under the usages of war.

They have refused to consider as prisoners of war, and threatened to punish as traitors and deserters, persons emigrating without restraint to the United States, incorporated by naturalization into our political family, and fighting under the authority of their adopted country in open and honorable war for the maintenance of its rights and safety. Such is the avowed purpose of a Government which is in the practice of naturalizing by thousands citizens of other countries, and not only of permitting but compelling them to fight its battles against their native country.

They have not, it is true, taken into their own hands the hatchet and the knife, devoted to indiscriminate massacre, but they have let loose the savages armed with these cruel instruments; have allured them into their service, and carried them to battle by their sides, eager to glut their savage thirst with the blood of the vanquished and to finish the work of torture and death on maimed and defenseless captives. And, what was never before seen, British commanders have extorted victory over the unconquerable valor of our troops by presenting to the sympathy of their chief captives awaiting massacre from their savage associates. And now we find them, in further contempt of the modes of honorable warfare, supplying the place of a conquering force by attempts to disorganize our political society, to dismember our confederated Republic. Happily, like others, these will recoil on the authors; but they mark the degenerate counsels from which they emanate, and if they did not belong to a sense of unexampled inconsistencies might excite the greater wonder as proceeding from a Government which founded the very war in which it has been so long engaged on a charge against the disorganizing and insurrectional policy of its adversary.

To render the justice of the war on our part the more conspicuous, the reluctance to commence it was followed by the earliest and strongest manifestations of a disposition to arrest its progress. The sword was scarcely out of the scabbard before the enemy was apprised of the reasonable terms on which it would be resheathed. Still more precise advances were repeated, and have been received in a spirit forbidding every reliance not placed on the military resources of the nation.

These resources are amply sufficient to bring the war to an honorable issue. Our nation is in number more than half that of the British Isles. It is composed of a brave, a free, a virtuous, and an intelligent people. Our country abounds in the necessaries, the arts, and the comforts of life. A general prosperity is visible in the public countenance. The means employed by the British cabinet to undermine it have recoiled on themselves; have given to our national faculties a more rapid development, and, draining or diverting the precious metals from British circulation and British vaults, have poured them into those of the United States. It is a propitious consideration that an unavoidable war should have found this seasonable facility for the contributions required to support it. When the public voice called for war, all knew, and still know, that without them it could not be carried on through the period which it might last, and the patriotism, the good sense, and the manly spirit of our fellow-citizens are pledges for the cheerfulness with which they will bear each his share of the common burden. To render the war short and its success sure, animated and systematic exertions alone are necessary, and the success of our arms now may long preserve our country from the necessity of another resort to them. Already have the gallant exploits of our naval heroes proved to the world our inherent capacity to maintain our rights on one element. If the reputation of our arms has been thrown under clouds on the other, presaging flashes of heroic enterprise assure us that nothing is wanting to correspondent triumphs there also but the discipline and habits which are in daily progress.

# JAMES MONROE
## FIRST INAUGURAL ADDRESS
### TUESDAY, MARCH 4, 1817

I should be destitute of feeling if I was not deeply affected by the strong proof which my fellow-citizens have given me of their confidence in calling me to the high office whose functions I am about to assume. As the expression of their good opinion of my conduct in the public service, I derive from it a gratification which those who are conscious of having done all that they could to merit it can alone feel. My sensibility is increased by a just estimate of the importance of the trust and of the nature and extent of its duties, with the proper discharge of which the highest interests of a great and free people are intimately connected. Conscious of my own deficiency, I cannot enter on these duties without great anxiety for the result. From a just responsibility I will never shrink, calculating with confidence that in my best efforts to promote the public welfare my motives will always be duly appreciated and my conduct be viewed with that candor and indulgence which I have experienced in other stations.

In commencing the duties of the chief executive office it has been the practice of the distinguished men who have gone before me to explain the principles which would govern them in their respective Administrations. In following their venerated example my attention is naturally drawn to the great causes which have contributed in a principal degree to produce the present happy condition of the United States. They will best explain the nature of our duties and shed much light on the policy which ought to be pursued in future.

From the commencement of our Revolution to the present day almost forty years have elapsed, and from the establishment of this Constitution twenty-eight. Through this whole term the Government has been what may emphatically be called self-government. And what has been the effect? To whatever object we turn our attention, whether it relates to our foreign or domestic concerns, we find abundant cause to felicitate ourselves in the excellence of our institutions. During a period fraught with difficulties and marked by very extraordinary events the United States have flourished beyond example. Their citizens individually have been happy and the nation prosperous.

Under this Constitution our commerce has been wisely regulated with foreign nations and between the States; new States have been admitted into our Union; our territory has been enlarged by fair and honorable treaty, and with great advantage to the original States; the States, respectively protected by the National Government under a mild, parental system against foreign dangers, and enjoying within their separate spheres, by a wise partition of power, a just proportion of the sovereignty, have improved their police, extended their settlements, and attained a strength and maturity which are the best proofs of wholesome laws well administered. And if we look to the condition of individuals what a proud spectacle does it exhibit! On whom has oppression fallen in any quarter of our Union? Who has been deprived of any right of person or property? Who restrained from offering his vows in the mode which he prefers to the Divine Author of his being? It is well known that all these blessings have been enjoyed in their fullest extent; and I add with peculiar satisfaction that there has been no example of a capital punishment being inflicted on anyone for the crime of high treason.

Some who might admit the competency of our Government to these beneficent duties might doubt it in trials which put to the test its strength and efficiency as a member of the great community of nations. Here too experience has afforded us the most satisfactory proof in its favor. Just as this Constitution was put into action several of the principal States of Europe had become much agitated and some of them seriously convulsed. Destructive wars ensued, which have of late only been terminated. In the course of these conflicts the United States received great injury from several of the parties. It was their interest to stand aloof from the contest, to demand justice from the party committing the injury, and to cultivate by a fair and honorable conduct the friendship of all. War became at length inevitable, and the result has shown that our Government is equal to that, the greatest of trials, under the most unfavorable circumstances. Of the virtue of the people and of the heroic exploits of the Army, the Navy, and the militia I need not speak.

Such, then, is the happy Government under which we live—a Government adequate to every purpose for which the social compact is formed; a Government elective in all its branches, under which every citizen may by his merit obtain the highest trust recognized by the Constitution; which contains within it no cause of discord, none to put at variance one portion of the community with another; a Government which protects every citizen in the full enjoyment of his rights, and is able to protect the nation against injustice from foreign powers.

Other considerations of the highest importance admonish us to cherish our Union and to cling to the Government which supports it. Fortunate as we are in our political institutions, we have not been less so in other circumstances on which our prosperity and happiness essentially depend. Situated within the temperate zone, and extending through many degrees of latitude along the Atlantic, the United States enjoy all the varieties of climate, and every production incident to that portion of the globe. Penetrating internally to the Great Lakes and beyond the sources of the great rivers which communicate through our whole interior, no country was ever happier with respect to its domain. Blessed, too, with a fertile soil, our produce has always been very abundant, leaving, even in years the least favorable, a surplus for the wants of our fellow-men in other countries. Such is our peculiar felicity that there is not a part of our Union that is not particularly interested in preserving it. The great agricultural interest of the nation prospers under its protection. Local interests are not less fostered by it. Our fellow-citizens of the North engaged in navigation find great encouragement in being made the favored carriers of the vast productions of the other portions of the United States, while the inhabitants of these are amply recompensed, in their turn, by the nursery for seamen and naval force thus formed and reared up for the support of our common rights. Our manufactures find a generous encouragement by the policy which patronizes domestic industry, and the surplus of our produce a steady and profitable market by local wants in less-favored parts at home.

Such, then, being the highly favored condition of our country, it is the interest of every citizen to maintain it. What are the dangers which menace us? If any exist they ought to be ascertained and guarded against.

In explaining my sentiments on this subject it may be asked, What raised us to the present happy state? How did we accomplish the Revolution? How remedy the defects of the first instrument of our Union, by infusing into the National Government sufficient power for national purposes, without impairing the just rights of the States or affecting those of individuals? How sustain and pass with glory through the late war? The Government has been in the hands of the people. To the people, therefore, and to the faithful and able depositaries of their trust is the credit due. Had the people of the United States been educated in different principles, had they been less intelligent, less independent, or less virtuous, can it be believed that we should have maintained the same steady and consistent career or been blessed with the same success? While, then, the constituent body retains its present sound and healthful state everything will be safe. They will choose competent and faithful representatives for every department. It is only when the people become ignorant and corrupt, when they degenerate into a populace, that they are incapable of exercising the sovereignty. Usurpation is then an easy attainment, and an usurper soon found. The people themselves become the willing instruments of their own debasement and ruin. Let us, then, look to the great cause, and endeavor to preserve it in full force. Let us by all wise and constitutional measures promote intelligence among the people as the best means of preserving our liberties.

Dangers from abroad are not less deserving of attention. Experiencing the fortune of other nations, the United States may be again involved in war, and it may in that event be the object of the adverse party to overset our Government, to break our Union, and demolish us as a nation. Our distance from Europe and the just, moderate, and pacific policy of our Government may form some security against these dangers, but they ought to be anticipated and guarded against. Many of our citizens are engaged in commerce and navigation, and all of them are in a certain degree dependent on their prosperous state. Many are engaged in the fisheries. These interests are exposed to invasion in the wars between other powers, and we should disregard the faithful admonition of experience if we did not expect it. We must support our rights or lose our character, and with it, perhaps, our liberties. A people who fail to do it can scarcely be said to hold a place among independent nations. National honor is national property of the highest value. The sentiment in the mind of every citizen is national strength. It ought therefore to be cherished.

To secure us against these dangers our coast and inland frontiers should be fortified, our Army and Navy, regulated upon just principles as to the force of each, be kept in perfect order, and our militia be placed on the best practicable footing. To put our extensive coast in such a state of defense as to secure our cities and interior from invasion will be attended with expense, but the work when finished will be permanent, and it is fair to presume that a single campaign of invasion by a naval force superior to our own, aided by a few thousand land troops, would expose us to greater expense, without taking into the estimate the loss of property and distress of our citizens, than would be sufficient for this great work. Our land and naval forces should be moderate, but adequate to the necessary purposes—the former to garrison and preserve our fortifications and to meet the first invasions of a foreign foe, and, while constituting the elements of a greater force, to preserve the science as well as all the necessary implements of war in a state to be brought into activity in the event of war; the latter, retained within the limits proper in a state of peace, might aid in maintaining the neutrality of the United States with dignity in the wars of other powers and in saving the property of their citizens from spoliation. In time of war, with the enlargement of which the great naval resources of the country render it susceptible, and which should be duly fostered in time of peace, it would contribute essentially, both as an auxiliary of defense and as a powerful engine of annoyance, to diminish the calamities of war and to bring the war to a speedy and honorable termination.

But it ought always to be held prominently in view that the safety of these States and of everything dear to a free people must depend in an eminent degree on the militia. Invasions may be made too formidable to be resisted by any land and naval force which it would comport either with the principles of our Government or the circumstances of the United States to maintain. In such cases recourse must be had to the great body of the people, and in a manner to produce the best effect. It is of the highest importance, therefore, that they be so organized and trained as to be prepared for any emergency.

The arrangement should be such as to put at the command of the Government the ardent patriotism and youthful vigor of the country. If formed on equal and just principles, it can not be oppressive. It is the crisis which makes the pressure, and not the laws which provide a remedy for it. This arrangement should be formed, too, in time of peace, to be the better prepared for war. With such an organization of such a people the United States have nothing to dread from foreign invasion. At its approach an overwhelming force of gallant men might always be put in motion.

Other interests of high importance will claim attention, among which the improvement of our country by roads and canals, proceeding always with a constitutional sanction, holds a distinguished place. By thus facilitating the intercourse between the States we shall add much to the convenience and comfort of our fellow-citizens, much to the ornament of the country, and, what is of greater importance, we shall shorten distances, and, by making each part more accessible to and dependent on the other, we shall bind the Union more closely together. Nature has done so much for us by intersecting the country with so many great rivers, bays, and lakes, approaching from distant points so near to each other, that the inducement to complete the work seems to be peculiarly strong. A more interesting spectacle was perhaps never seen than is exhibited within the limits of the United States—a territory so vast and advantageously situated, containing objects so grand, so useful, so happily connected in all their parts!

Our manufacturers will likewise require the systematic and fostering care of the Government. Possessing as we do all the raw materials, the fruit of our own soil and industry, we ought not to depend in the degree we have done on supplies from other countries. While we are thus dependent the sudden event of war, unsought and unexpected, can not fail to plunge us into the most serious difficulties. It is important, too, that the capital which nourishes our manufacturers should be domestic, as its influence in that case instead of exhausting, as it may do in foreign hands, would be felt advantageously on agriculture and every other branch of industry. Equally important is it to provide at home a market for our raw materials, as by extending the competition it will enhance the price and protect the cultivator against the casualties incident to foreign markets.

With the Indian tribes it is our duty to cultivate friendly relations and to act with kindness and liberality in all our transactions. Equally proper is it to persevere in our efforts to extend to them the advantages of civilization.

The great amount of our revenue and the flourishing state of the Treasury are a full proof of the competency of the national resources for any emergency, as they are of the willingness of our fellow-citizens to bear the burdens which the public necessities require. The vast amount of vacant lands, the value of which daily augments, forms an additional resource of great extent and duration. These resources, besides accomplishing every other necessary purpose, put it completely in the power of the United States to discharge the national debt at an early period. Peace is the best time for improvement and preparation of every kind; it is in peace that our commerce flourishes most, that taxes are most easily paid, and that the revenue is most productive.

The Executive is charged officially in the Departments under it with the disbursement of the public money, and is responsible for the faithful application of it to the purposes for which it is raised. The Legislature is the watchful guardian over the public purse. It is its duty to see that the disbursement has been honestly made. To meet the requisite responsibility every facility should be afforded to the Executive to enable it to bring the public agents intrusted with the public money strictly and promptly to account. Nothing should be presumed against them; but if, with the requisite facilities, the public money is suffered to lie long and uselessly in their hands, they will not be the only defaulters, nor will the demoralizing effect be confined to them. It will evince a relaxation and want of tone in the Administration which will be felt by the whole community. I shall do all I can to secure economy and fidelity in this important branch of the Administration, and I doubt not that the Legislature will perform its duty with equal zeal. A thorough examination should be regularly made, and I will promote it.

It is particularly gratifying to me to enter on the discharge of these duties at a time when the United States are blessed with peace. It is a state most consistent with their prosperity and happiness. It will be my sincere desire to preserve it, so far as depends on the Executive, on just principles with all nations, claiming nothing unreasonable of any and rendering to each what is its due.

Equally gratifying is it to witness the increased harmony of opinion which pervades our Union. Discord does not belong to our system. Union is recommended as well by the free and benign principles of our Government, extending its blessings to every individual, as by the other eminent advantages attending it. The American people have encountered together great dangers and sustained severe trials with success. They constitute one great family with a common interest. Experience has enlightened us on some questions of essential importance to the country. The progress has been slow, dictated by a just reflection and a faithful regard to every interest connected with it. To promote this harmony in accord with the principles of our republican Government and in a manner to give them the most complete effect, and to advance in all other respects the best interests of our Union, will be the object of my constant and zealous exertions.

Never did a government commence under auspices so favorable, nor ever was success so complete. If we look to the history of other nations, ancient or modern, we find no example of a growth so rapid, so gigantic, of a people so prosperous and happy. In contemplating what we have still to perform, the heart of every citizen must expand with joy when he reflects how near our Government has approached to perfection; that in respect to it we have no essential improvement to make; that the great object is to preserve it in the essential principles and features which characterize it, and that is to be done by preserving the virtue and enlightening the minds of the people; and as a security against foreign dangers to adopt such arrangements as are indispensable to the support of our independence, our rights and liberties. If we persevere in the career in which we have advanced so far and in the path already traced, we can not fail, under the favor of a gracious Providence, to attain the high destiny which seems to await us.

In the Administrations of the illustrious men who have preceded me in this high station, with some of whom I have been connected by the closest ties from early life, examples are presented which will always be found highly instructive and useful to their successors. From these I shall endeavor to derive all the advantages which they may afford. Of my immediate predecessor, under whom so important a portion of this great and successful experiment has been made, I shall be pardoned for expressing my earnest wishes that he may long enjoy in his retirement the affections of a grateful country, the best reward of exalted talents and the most faithful and meritorious service. Relying on the aid to be derived from the other departments of the Government, I enter on the trust to which I have been called by the suffrages of my fellow-citizens with my fervent prayers to the Almighty that He will be graciously pleased to continue to us that protection which He has already so conspicuously displayed in our favor.

# JAMES MONROE
## SECOND INAUGURAL ADDRESS
### MONDAY, MARCH 5, 1821

Fellow-Citizens:

I shall not attempt to describe the grateful emotions which the new and very distinguished proof of the confidence of my fellow-citizens, evinced by my reelection to this high trust, has excited in my bosom. The approbation which it announces of my conduct in the preceding term affords me a consolation which I shall profoundly feel through life. The general accord with which it has been expressed adds to the great and never-ceasing obligations which it imposes. To merit the continuance of this good opinion, and to carry it with me into my retirement as the solace of advancing years, will be the object of my most zealous and unceasing efforts.

Having no pretensions to the high and commanding claims of my predecessors, whose names are so much more conspicuously identified with our Revolution, and who contributed so preeminently to promote its success, I consider myself rather as the instrument than the cause of the union which has prevailed in the late election. In surmounting, in favor of my humble pretensions, the difficulties which so often produce division in like occurrences, it is obvious that other powerful causes, indicating the great strength and stability of our Union, have essentially contributed to draw you together. That these powerful causes exist, and that they are permanent, is my fixed opinion; that they may produce a like accord in all questions touching, however remotely, the liberty, prosperity, and happiness of our country will always be the object of my most fervent prayers to the Supreme Author of All Good.

In a government which is founded by the people, who possess exclusively the sovereignty, it seems proper that the person who may be placed by their suffrages in this high trust should declare on commencing its duties the principles on which he intends to conduct the Administration. If the person thus elected has served the preceding term, an opportunity is afforded him to review its principal occurrences and to give such further explanation respecting them as in his judgment may be useful to his constituents. The events of one year have influence on those of another, and, in like manner, of a preceding on the succeeding Administration. The movements of a great nation are connected in all their parts. If errors have been committed they ought to be corrected; if the policy is sound it ought to be supported. It is by a thorough knowledge of the whole subject that our fellow-citizens are enabled to judge correctly of the past and to give a proper direction to the future.

Just before the commencement of the last term the United States had concluded a war with a very powerful nation on conditions equal and honorable to both parties. The events of that war are too recent and too deeply impressed on the memory of all to require a development from me. Our commerce had been in a great measure driven from the sea, our Atlantic and inland frontiers were invaded in almost every part; the waste of life along our coast and on some parts of our inland frontiers, to the defense of which our gallant and patriotic citizens were called, was immense, in addition to which not less than $120,000,000 were added at its end to the public debt.

As soon as the war had terminated, the nation, admonished by its events, resolved to place itself in a situation which should be better calculated to prevent the recurrence of a like evil, and, in case it should recur, to mitigate its calamities. With this view, after reducing our land force to the basis of a peace establishment, which has been further modified since, provision was made for the construction of fortifications at proper points through the whole extent of our coast and such an augmentation of our naval force as should be well adapted to both purposes. The laws making this provision were passed in 1815 and 1816, and it has been since the constant effort of the Executive to carry them into effect.

The advantage of these fortifications and of an augmented naval force in the extent contemplated, in a point of economy, has been fully illustrated by a report of the Board of Engineers and Naval Commissioners lately communicated to Congress, by which it appears that in an invasion by 20,000 men, with a correspondent naval force, in a campaign of six months only, the whole expense of the construction of the works would be defrayed by the difference in the sum necessary to maintain the force which would be adequate to our defense with the aid of those works and that which would be incurred without them. The reason of this difference is obvious. If fortifications are judiciously placed on our great inlets, as distant from our cities as circumstances will permit, they will form the only points of attack, and the enemy will be detained there by a small regular force a sufficient time to enable our militia to collect and repair to that on which the attack is made. A force adequate to the enemy, collected at that single point, with suitable preparation for such others as might be menaced, is all that would be requisite. But if there were no fortifications, then the enemy might go where he pleased, and, changing his position and sailing from place to place, our force must be called out and spread in vast numbers along the whole coast and on both sides of every bay and river as high up in each as it might be navigable for ships of war. By these fortifications, supported by our Navy, to which they would afford like support, we should present to other powers an armed front from St. Croix to the Sabine, which would protect in the event of war our whole coast and interior from invasion; and even in the wars of other powers, in which we were neutral, they would be found eminently useful, as, by keeping their public ships at a distance from our cities, peace and order in them would be preserved and the Government be protected from insult.

It need scarcely be remarked that these measures have not been resorted to in a spirit of hostility to other powers. Such a disposition does not exist toward any power. Peace and good will have been, and will hereafter be, cultivated with all, and by the most faithful regard to justice. They have been dictated by a love of peace, of economy, and an earnest desire to save the lives of our fellow-citizens from that destruction and our country from that devastation which are inseparable from war when it finds us unprepared for it. It is believed, and experience has shown, that such a preparation is the best expedient that can be resorted to prevent war. I add with much pleasure that considerable progress has already been made in these measures of defense, and that they will be completed in a few years, considering the great extent and importance of the object, if the plan be zealously and steadily persevered in.

The conduct of the Government in what relates to foreign powers is always an object of the highest importance to the nation. Its agriculture, commerce, manufactures, fisheries, revenue, in short, its peace, may all be affected by it. Attention is therefore due to this subject.

At the period adverted to the powers of Europe, after having been engaged in long and destructive wars with each other, had concluded a peace, which happily still exists. Our peace with the power with whom we had been engaged had also been concluded. The war between Spain and the colonies in South America, which had commenced many years before, was then the only conflict that remained unsettled. This being a contest between different parts of the same community, in which other powers had not interfered, was not affected by their accommodations.

This contest was considered at an early stage by my predecessor a civil war in which the parties were entitled to equal rights in our ports. This decision, the first made by any power, being formed on great consideration of the comparative strength and resources of the parties, the length of time, and successful opposition made by the colonies, and of all other circumstances on which it ought to depend, was in strict accord with the law of nations. Congress has invariably acted on this principle, having made no change in our relations with either party. Our attitude has therefore been that of neutrality between them, which has been maintained by the Government with the strictest impartiality. No aid has been afforded to either, nor has any privilege been enjoyed by the one which has not been equally open to the other party, and every exertion has been made in its power to enforce the execution of the laws prohibiting illegal equipments with equal rigor against both.

By this equality between the parties their public vessels have been received in our ports on the same footing; they have enjoyed an equal right to purchase and export arms, munitions of war, and every other supply, the exportation of all articles whatever being permitted under laws which were passed long before the commencement of the contest; our citizens have traded equally with both, and their commerce with each has been alike protected by the Government.

Respecting the attitude which it may be proper for the United States to maintain hereafter between the parties, I have no hesitation in stating it as my opinion that the neutrality heretofore observed should still be adhered to. From the change in the Government of Spain and the negotiation now depending, invited by the Cortes and accepted by the colonies, it may be presumed, that their differences will be settled on the terms proposed by the colonies. Should the war be continued, the United States, regarding its occurrences, will always have it in their power to adopt such measures respecting it as their honor and interest may require.

Shortly after the general peace a band of adventurers took advantage of this conflict and of the facility which it afforded to establish a system of buccaneering in the neighboring seas, to the great annoyance of the commerce of the United States, and, as was represented, of that of other powers. Of this spirit and of its injurious bearing on the United States strong proofs were afforded by the establishment at Amelia Island, and the purposes to which it was made instrumental by this band in 1817, and by the occurrences which took place in other parts of Florida in 1818, the details of which in both instances are too well known to require to be now recited. I am satisfied had a less decisive course been adopted that the worst consequences would have resulted from it. We have seen that these checks, decisive as they were, were not sufficient to crush that piratical spirit. Many culprits brought within our limits have been condemned to suffer death, the punishment due to that atrocious crime. The decisions of upright and enlightened tribunals fall equally on all whose crimes subject them, by a fair interpretation of the law, to its censure. It belongs to the Executive not to suffer the executions under these decisions to transcend the great purpose for which punishment is necessary. The full benefit of example being secured, policy as well as humanity equally forbids that they should be carried further. I have acted on this principle, pardoning those who appear to have been led astray by ignorance of the criminality of the acts they had committed, and suffering the law to take effect on those only in whose favor no extenuating circumstances could be urged.

Great confidence is entertained that the late treaty with Spain, which has been ratified by both the parties, and the ratifications whereof have been exchanged, has placed the relations of the two countries on a basis of permanent friendship. The provision made by it for such of our citizens as have claims on Spain of the character described will, it is presumed, be very satisfactory to them, and the boundary which is established between the territories of the parties westward of the Mississippi, heretofore in dispute, has, it is thought, been settled on conditions just and advantageous to both. But to the acquisition of Florida too much importance can not be attached. It secures to the United States a territory important in itself, and whose importance is much increased by its bearing on many of the highest interests of the Union. It opens to several of the neighboring States a free passage to the ocean, through the Province ceded, by several rivers, having their sources high up within their limits. It secures us against all future annoyance from powerful Indian tribes. It gives us several excellent harbors in the Gulf of Mexico for ships of war of the largest size. It covers by its position in the Gulf the Mississippi and other great waters within our extended limits, and thereby enables the United States to afford complete protection to the vast and very valuable productions of our whole Western country, which find a market through those streams.

By a treaty with the British Government, bearing date on the 20th of October, 1818, the convention regulating the commerce between the United States and Great Britain, concluded on the 3d of July, 1815, which was about expiring, was revived and continued for the term of ten years from the time of its expiration. By that treaty, also, the differences which had arisen under the treaty of Ghent respecting the right claimed by the United States for their citizens to take and cure fish on the coast of His Britannic Majesty's dominions in America, with other differences on important interests, were adjusted to the satisfaction of both parties. No agreement has yet been entered into respecting the commerce between the United States and the British dominions in the West Indies and on this continent. The restraints imposed on that commerce by Great Britain, and reciprocated by the United States on a principle of defense, continue still in force.

The negotiation with France for the regulation of the commercial relations between the two countries, which in the course of the last summer had been commenced at Paris, has since been transferred to this city, and will be pursued on the part of the United States in the spirit of conciliation, and with an earnest desire that it may terminate in an arrangement satisfactory to both parties.

Our relations with the Barbary Powers are preserved in the same state and by the same means that were employed when I came into this office. As early as 1801 it was found necessary to send a squadron into the Mediterranean for the protection of our commerce, and no period has intervened, a short term excepted, when it was thought advisable to withdraw it. The great interests which the United States have in the Pacific, in commerce and in the fisheries, have also made it necessary to maintain a naval force there. In disposing of this force in both instances the most effectual measures in our power have been taken, without interfering with its other duties, for the suppression of the slave trade and of piracy in the neighboring seas.

The situation of the United States in regard to their resources, the extent of their revenue, and the facility with which it is raised affords a most gratifying spectacle. The payment of nearly $67,000,000 of the public debt, with the great progress made in measures of defense and in other improvements of various kinds since the late war, are conclusive proofs of this extraordinary prosperity, especially when it is recollected that these expenditures have been defrayed without a burthen on the people, the direct tax and excise having been repealed soon after the conclusion of the late war, and the revenue applied to these great objects having been raised in a manner not to be felt. Our great resources therefore remain untouched for any purpose which may affect the vital interests of the nation. For all such purposes they are inexhaustible. They are more especially to be found in the virtue, patriotism, and intelligence of our fellow-citizens, and in the devotion with which they would yield up by any just measure of taxation all their property in support of the rights and honor of their country.

Under the present depression of prices, affecting all the productions of the country and every branch of industry, proceeding from causes explained on a former occasion, the revenue has considerably diminished, the effect of which has been to compel Congress either to abandon these great measures of defense or to resort to loans or internal taxes to supply the deficiency. On the presumption that this depression and the deficiency in the revenue arising from it would be temporary, loans were authorized for the demands of the last and present year. Anxious to relieve my fellow-citizens in 1817 from every burthen which could be dispensed with, and the state of the Treasury permitting it, I recommended the repeal of the internal taxes, knowing that such relief was then peculiarly necessary in consequence of the great exertions made in the late war. I made that recommendation under a pledge that should the public exigencies require a recurrence to them at any time while I remained in this trust, I would with equal promptitude perform the duty which would then be alike incumbent on me. By the experiment now making it will be seen by the next session of Congress whether the revenue shall have been so augmented as to be adequate to all these necessary purposes. Should the deficiency still continue, and especially should it be probable that it would be permanent, the course to be pursued appears to me to be obvious. I am satisfied that under certain circumstances loans may be resorted to with great advantage. I am equally well satisfied, as a general rule, that the demands of the current year, especially in time of peace, should be provided for by the revenue of that year.

I have never dreaded, nor have I ever shunned, in any situation in which I have been placed making appeals to the virtue and patriotism of my fellow-citizens, well knowing that they could never be made in vain, especially in times of great emergency or for purposes of high national importance. Independently of the exigency of the case, many considerations of great weight urge a policy having in view a provision of revenue to meet to a certain extent the demands of the nation, without relying altogether on the precarious resource of foreign commerce. I am satisfied that internal duties and excises, with corresponding imposts on foreign articles of the same kind, would, without imposing any serious burdens on the people, enhance the price of produce, promote our manufactures, and augment the revenue, at the same time that they made it more secure and permanent.

The care of the Indian tribes within our limits has long been an essential part of our system, but, unfortunately, it has not been executed in a manner to accomplish all the objects intended by it. We have treated them as independent nations, without their having any substantial pretensions to that rank. The distinction has flattered their pride, retarded their improvement, and in many instances paved the way to their destruction. The progress of our settlements westward, supported as they are by a dense population, has constantly driven them back, with almost the total sacrifice of the lands which they have been compelled to abandon. They have claims on the magnanimity and, I may add, on the justice of this nation which we must all feel. We should become their real benefactors; we should perform the office of their Great Father, the endearing title which they emphatically give to the Chief Magistrate of our Union. Their sovereignty over vast territories should cease, in lieu of which the right of soil should be secured to each individual and his posterity in competent portions; and for the territory thus ceded by each tribe some reasonable equivalent should be granted, to be vested in permanent funds for the support of civil government over them and for the education of their children, for their instruction in the arts of husbandry, and to provide sustenance for them until they could provide it for themselves. My earnest hope is that Congress will digest some plan, founded on these principles, with such improvements as their wisdom may suggest, and carry it into effect as soon as it may be practicable.

Europe is again unsettled and the prospect of war increasing. Should the flame light up in any quarter, how far it may extend it is impossible to foresee. It is our peculiar felicity to be altogether unconnected with the causes which produce this menacing aspect elsewhere. With every power we are in perfect amity, and it is our interest to remain so if it be practicable on just conditions. I see no reasonable cause to apprehend variance with any power, unless it proceed from a violation of our maritime rights. In these contests, should they occur, and to whatever extent they may be carried, we shall be neutral; but as a neutral power we have rights which it is our duty to maintain. For like injuries it will be incumbent on us to seek redress in a spirit of amity, in full confidence that, injuring none, none would knowingly injure us. For more imminent dangers we should be prepared, and it should always be recollected that such preparation adapted to the circumstances and sanctioned by the judgment and wishes of our constituents can not fail to have a good effect in averting dangers of every kind. We should recollect also that the season of peace is best adapted to these preparations.

If we turn our attention, fellow-citizens, more immediately to the internal concerns of our country, and more especially to those on which its future welfare depends, we have every reason to anticipate the happiest results. It is now rather more than forty-four years since we declared our independence, and thirty-seven since it was acknowledged. The talents and virtues which were displayed in that great struggle were a sure presage of all that has since followed. A people who were able to surmount in their infant state such great perils would be more competent as they rose into manhood to repel any which they might meet in their progress. Their physical strength would be more adequate to foreign danger, and the practice of self-government, aided by the light of experience, could not fail to produce an effect equally salutary on all those questions connected with the internal organization. These favorable anticipations have been realized.

In our whole system, national and State, we have shunned all the defects which unceasingly preyed on the vitals and destroyed the ancient Republics. In them there were distinct orders, a nobility and a people, or the people governed in one assembly. Thus, in the one instance there was a perpetual conflict between the orders in society for the ascendency, in which the victory of either terminated in the overthrow of the government and the ruin of the state; in the other, in which the people governed in a body, and whose dominions seldom exceeded the dimensions of a county in one of our States, a tumultuous and disorderly movement permitted only a transitory existence. In this great nation there is but one order, that of the people, whose power, by a peculiarly happy improvement of the representative principle, is transferred from them, without impairing in the slightest degree their sovereignty, to bodies of their own creation, and to persons elected by themselves, in the full extent necessary for all the purposes of free, enlightened and efficient government. The whole system is elective, the complete sovereignty being in the people, and every officer in every department deriving his authority from and being responsible to them for his conduct.

Our career has corresponded with this great outline. Perfection in our organization could not have been expected in the outset either in the National or State Governments or in tracing the line between their respective powers. But no serious conflict has arisen, nor any contest but such as are managed by argument and by a fair appeal to the good sense of the people, and many of the defects which experience had clearly demonstrated in both Governments have been remedied. By steadily pursuing this course in this spirit there is every reason to believe that our system will soon attain the highest degree of perfection of which human institutions are capable, and that the movement in all its branches will exhibit such a degree of order and harmony as to command the admiration and respect of the civilized world.

Our physical attainments have not been less eminent. Twenty-five years ago the river Mississippi was shut up and our Western brethren had no outlet for their commerce. What has been the progress since that time? The river has not only become the property of the United States from its source to the ocean, with all its tributary streams (with the exception of the upper part of the Red River only), but Louisiana, with a fair and liberal boundary on the western side and the Floridas on the eastern, have been ceded to us. The United States now enjoy the complete and uninterrupted sovereignty over the whole territory from St. Croix to the Sabine. New States, settled from among ourselves in this and in other parts, have been admitted into our Union in equal participation in the national sovereignty with the original States. Our population has augmented in an astonishing degree and extended in every direction. We now, fellow-citizens, comprise within our limits the dimensions and faculties of a great power under a Government possessing all the energies of any government ever known to the Old World, with an utter incapacity to oppress the people.

Entering with these views the office which I have just solemnly sworn to execute with fidelity and to the utmost of my ability, I derive great satisfaction from a knowledge that I shall be assisted in the several Departments by the very enlightened and upright citizens from whom I have received so much aid in the preceding term. With full confidence in the continuance of that candor and generous indulgence from my fellow-citizens at large which I have heretofore experienced, and with a firm reliance on the protection of Almighty God, I shall forthwith commence the duties of the high trust to which you have called me.

# JOHN QUINCY ADAMS
## INAUGURAL ADDRESS
### FRIDAY, MARCH 4, 1825

In compliance with an usage coeval with the existence of our Federal Constitution, and sanctioned by the example of my predecessors in the career upon which I am about to enter, I appear, my fellow-citizens, in your presence and in that of Heaven to bind myself by the solemnities of religious obligation to the faithful performance of the duties allotted to me in the station to which I have been called.

In unfolding to my countrymen the principles by which I shall be governed in the fulfillment of those duties my first resort will be to that Constitution which I shall swear to the best of my ability to preserve, protect, and defend. That revered instrument enumerates the powers and prescribes the duties of the Executive Magistrate, and in its first words declares the purposes to which these and the whole action of the Government instituted by it should be invariably and sacredly devoted—to form a more perfect union, establish justice, insure domestic tranquillity, provide for the common defense, promote the general welfare, and secure the blessings of liberty to the people of this Union in their successive generations. Since the adoption of this social compact one of these generations has passed away. It is the work of our forefathers. Administered by some of the most eminent men who contributed to its formation, through a most eventful period in the annals of the world, and through all the vicissitudes of peace and war incidental to the condition of associated man, it has not disappointed the hopes and aspirations of those illustrious benefactors of their age and nation. It has promoted the lasting welfare of that country so dear to us all; it has to an extent far beyond the ordinary lot of humanity secured the freedom and happiness of this people. We now receive it as a precious inheritance from those to whom we are indebted for its establishment, doubly bound by the examples which they have left us and by the blessings which we have enjoyed as the fruits of their labors to transmit the same unimpaired to the succeeding generation.

In the compass of thirty-six years since this great national covenant was instituted a body of laws enacted under its authority and in conformity with its provisions has unfolded its powers and carried into practical operation its effective energies. Subordinate departments have distributed the executive functions in their various relations to foreign affairs, to the revenue and expenditures, and to the military force of the Union by land and sea. A coordinate department of the judiciary has expounded the Constitution and the laws, settling in harmonious coincidence with the legislative will numerous weighty questions of construction which the imperfection of human language had rendered unavoidable. The year of jubilee since the first formation of our Union has just elapsed; that of the declaration of our independence is at hand. The consummation of both was effected by this Constitution.

Since that period a population of four millions has multiplied to twelve. A territory bounded by the Mississippi has been extended from sea to sea. New States have been admitted to the Union in numbers nearly equal to those of the first Confederation. Treaties of peace, amity, and commerce have been concluded with the principal dominions of the earth. The people of other nations, inhabitants of regions acquired not by conquest, but by compact, have been united with us in the participation of our rights and duties, of our burdens and blessings. The forest has fallen by the ax of our woodsmen; the soil has been made to teem by the tillage of our farmers; our commerce has whitened every ocean. The dominion of man over physical nature has been extended by the invention of our artists. Liberty and law have marched hand in hand. All the purposes of human association have been accomplished as effectively as under any other government on the globe, and at a cost little exceeding in a whole generation the expenditure of other nations in a single year.

Such is the unexaggerated picture of our condition under a Constitution founded upon the republican principle of equal rights. To admit that this picture has its shades is but to say that it is still the condition of men upon earth. From evil—physical, moral, and political—it is not our claim to be exempt. We have suffered sometimes by the visitation of Heaven through disease; often by the wrongs and injustice of other nations, even to the extremities of war; and, lastly, by dissensions among ourselves—dissensions perhaps inseparable from the enjoyment of freedom, but which have more than once appeared to threaten the dissolution of the Union, and with it the overthrow of all the enjoyments of our present lot and all our earthly hopes of the future. The causes of these dissensions have been various, founded upon differences of speculation in the theory of republican government; upon conflicting views of policy in our relations with foreign nations; upon jealousies of partial and sectional interests, aggravated by prejudices and prepossessions which strangers to each other are ever apt to entertain.

It is a source of gratification and of encouragement to me to observe that the great result of this experiment upon the theory of human rights has at the close of that generation by which it was formed been crowned with success equal to the most sanguine expectations of its founders. Union, justice, tranquillity, the common defense, the general welfare, and the blessings of liberty—all have been promoted by the Government under which we have lived. Standing at this point of time, looking back to that generation which has gone by and forward to that which is advancing, we may at once indulge in grateful exultation and in cheering hope. From the experience of the past we derive instructive lessons for the future. Of the two great political parties which have divided the opinions and feelings of our country, the candid and the just will now admit that both have contributed splendid talents, spotless integrity, ardent patriotism, and disinterested sacrifices to the formation and administration of this Government, and that both have required a liberal indulgence for a portion of human infirmity and error. The revolutionary wars of Europe, commencing precisely at the moment when the Government of the United States first went into operation under this Constitution, excited a collision of sentiments and of sympathies which kindled all the passions and imbittered the conflict of parties till the nation was involved in war and the Union was shaken to its center. This time of trial embraced a period of five and twenty years, during which the policy of the Union in its relations with Europe constituted the principal basis of our political divisions and the most arduous part of the action of our

Federal Government. With the catastrophe in which the wars of the French Revolution terminated, and our own subsequent peace with Great Britain, this baneful weed of party strife was uprooted. From that time no difference of principle, connected either with the theory of government or with our intercourse with foreign nations, has existed or been called forth in force sufficient to sustain a continued combination of parties or to give more than wholesome animation to public sentiment or legislative debate. Our political creed is, without a dissenting voice that can be heard, that the will of the people is the source and the happiness of the people the end of all legitimate government upon earth; that the best security for the beneficence and the best guaranty against the abuse of power consists in the freedom, the purity, and the frequency of popular elections; that the General Government of the Union and the separate governments of the States are all sovereignties of limited powers, fellow-servants of the same masters, uncontrolled within their respective spheres, uncontrollable by encroachments upon each other; that the firmest security of peace is the preparation during peace of the defenses of war; that a rigorous economy and accountability of public expenditures should guard against the aggravation and alleviate when possible the burden of taxation; that the military should be kept in strict subordination to the civil power; that the freedom of the press and of religious opinion should be inviolate; that the policy of our country is peace and the ark of our salvation union are articles of faith upon which we are all now agreed. If there have been those who doubted whether a confederated representative democracy were a government competent to the wise and orderly management of the common concerns of a mighty nation, those doubts have been dispelled; if there have been projects of partial confederacies to be erected upon the ruins of the Union, they have been scattered to the winds; if there have been dangerous attachments to one foreign nation and antipathies against another, they have been extinguished. Ten years of peace, at home and abroad, have assuaged the animosities of political contention and blended into harmony the most discordant elements of public opinion. There still remains one effort of magnanimity, one sacrifice of prejudice and passion, to be made by the individuals throughout the nation who have heretofore followed the standards of political party. It is that of discarding every remnant of rancor against each other, of embracing as countrymen and friends, and of yielding to talents and virtue alone that confidence which in times of contention for principle was bestowed only upon those who bore the badge of party communion.

The collisions of party spirit which originate in speculative opinions or in different views of administrative policy are in their nature transitory. Those which are founded on geographical divisions, adverse interests of soil, climate, and modes of domestic life are more permanent, and therefore, perhaps, more dangerous. It is this which gives inestimable value to the character of our Government, at once federal and national. It holds out to us a perpetual admonition to preserve alike and with equal anxiety the rights of each individual State in its own government and the rights of the whole nation in that of the Union. Whatsoever is of domestic concernment, unconnected with the other members of the Union or with foreign lands, belongs exclusively to the administration of the State governments. Whatsoever directly involves the rights and interests of the federative fraternity or of foreign powers is of the resort of this General Government. The duties of both are obvious in the general principle, though sometimes perplexed with difficulties in the detail. To respect the rights of the State governments is the inviolable duty of that of the Union; the government of every State will feel its own obligation to respect and preserve the rights of the whole. The prejudices everywhere too commonly entertained against distant strangers are worn away, and the jealousies of jarring interests are allayed by the composition and functions of the great national councils annually assembled from all quarters of the Union at this place. Here the distinguished men from every section of our country, while meeting to deliberate upon the great interests of those by whom they are deputed, learn to estimate the talents and do justice to the virtues of each other. The harmony of the nation is promoted and the whole Union is knit together by the sentiments of mutual respect, the habits of social intercourse, and the ties of personal friendship formed between the representatives of its several parts in the performance of their service at this metropolis.

Passing from this general review of the purposes and injunctions of the Federal Constitution and their results as indicating the first traces of the path of duty in the discharge of my public trust, I turn to the Administration of my immediate predecessor as the second. It has passed away in a period of profound peace, how much to the satisfaction of our country and to the honor of our country's name is known to you all. The great features of its policy, in general concurrence with the will of the Legislature, have been to cherish peace while preparing for defensive war; to yield exact justice to other nations and maintain the rights of our own; to cherish the principles of freedom and of equal rights wherever they were proclaimed; to discharge with all possible promptitude the national debt; to reduce within the narrowest limits of efficiency the military force; to improve the organization and discipline of the Army; to provide and sustain a school of military science; to extend equal protection to all the great interests of the nation; to promote the civilization of the Indian tribes, and to proceed in the great system of internal improvements within the limits of the constitutional power of the Union. Under the pledge of these promises, made by that eminent citizen at the time of his first induction to this office, in his career of eight years the internal taxes have been repealed; sixty millions of the public debt have been discharged; provision has been made for the comfort and relief of the aged and indigent among the surviving warriors of the Revolution; the regular armed force has been reduced and its constitution revised and perfected; the accountability for the expenditure of public moneys has been made more effective; the Floridas have been peaceably acquired, and our boundary has been extended to the Pacific Ocean; the independence of the southern nations of this hemisphere has been recognized, and recommended by example and by counsel to the potentates of Europe; progress has been made in the defense of the country by fortifications and the increase of the Navy, toward the effectual suppression of the African traffic in slaves; in alluring the aboriginal hunters of our land to the cultivation of the soil and of the mind, in exploring the interior regions of the Union, and in preparing by scientific researches and surveys for the further application of our national resources to the internal improvement of our country.

In this brief outline of the promise and performance of my immediate predecessor the line of duty for his successor is clearly delineated. To pursue to their consummation those purposes of improvement in our common condition instituted or recommended by him will embrace the whole sphere of my obligations. To the topic of internal improvement, emphatically urged by him at his inauguration, I recur with peculiar satisfaction. It is that from which I am convinced that the unborn millions of our posterity who are in future ages to people this continent will derive their most fervent gratitude to the founders of the Union; that in which the beneficent action of its Government will be most deeply felt and acknowledged. The magnificence and splendor of their public works are among the imperishable glories of the ancient republics. The roads and aqueducts of Rome have been the admiration of all after ages, and have survived thousands of years after all her conquests have been swallowed up in despotism or become the spoil of barbarians. Some diversity of opinion has prevailed with regard to the powers of Congress for legislation upon objects of this nature. The most respectful deference is due to doubts originating in pure patriotism and sustained by venerated authority. But nearly twenty years have passed since the construction of the first national road was commenced. The authority for its construction was then unquestioned. To how many thousands of our countrymen has it proved a benefit? To what single individual has it ever proved an injury? Repeated, liberal, and candid discussions in the Legislature have conciliated the sentiments and approximated the opinions of enlightened minds upon the question of constitutional power. I can not but hope that by the same process of friendly, patient, and persevering deliberation all constitutional objections will ultimately be removed. The extent and limitation of the powers of the General Government in relation to this transcendently important interest will be settled and acknowledged to the common satisfaction of all, and every speculative scruple will be solved by a practical public blessing.

Fellow-citizens, you are acquainted with the peculiar circumstances of the recent election, which have resulted in affording me the opportunity of addressing you at this time. You have heard the exposition of the principles which will direct me in the fulfillment of the high and solemn trust imposed upon me in this station. Less possessed of your confidence in advance than any of my predecessors, I am deeply conscious of the prospect that I shall stand more and oftener in need of your indulgence. Intentions upright and pure, a heart devoted to the welfare of our country, and the unceasing application of all the faculties allotted to me to her service are all the pledges that I can give for the faithful performance of the arduous duties I am to undertake. To the guidance of the legislative councils, to the assistance of the executive and subordinate departments, to the friendly cooperation of the respective State governments, to the candid and liberal support of the people so far as it may be deserved by honest industry and zeal, I shall look for whatever success may attend my public service; and knowing that "except the Lord keep the city the watchman waketh but in vain," with fervent supplications for His favor, to His overruling providence I commit with humble but fearless confidence my own fate and the future destinies of my country.

# ANDREW JACKSON
## FIRST INAUGURAL ADDRESS
## WEDNESDAY, MARCH 4, 1829

Fellow-Citizens:

About to undertake the arduous duties that I have been appointed to perform by the choice of a free people, I avail myself of this customary and solemn occasion to express the gratitude which their confidence inspires and to acknowledge the accountability which my situation enjoins. While the magnitude of their interests convinces me that no thanks can be adequate to the honor they have conferred, it admonishes me that the best return I can make is the zealous dedication of my humble abilities to their service and their good.

As the instrument of the Federal Constitution it will devolve on me for a stated period to execute the laws of the United States, to superintend their foreign and their confederate relations, to manage their revenue, to command their forces, and, by communications to the Legislature, to watch over and to promote their interests generally. And the principles of action by which I shall endeavor to accomplish this circle of duties it is now proper for me briefly to explain.

In administering the laws of Congress I shall keep steadily in view the limitations as well as the extent of the Executive power, trusting thereby to discharge the functions of my office without transcending its authority. With foreign nations it will be my study to preserve peace and to cultivate friendship on fair and honorable terms, and in the adjustment of any differences that may exist or arise to exhibit the forbearance becoming a powerful nation rather than the sensibility belonging to a gallant people.

In such measures as I may be called on to pursue in regard to the rights of the separate States I hope to be animated by a proper respect for those sovereign members of our Union, taking care not to confound the powers they have reserved to themselves with those they have granted to the Confederacy.

The management of the public revenue—that searching operation in all governments—is among the most delicate and important trusts in ours, and it will, of course, demand no inconsiderable share of my official solicitude. Under every aspect in which it can be considered it would appear that advantage must result from the observance of a strict and faithful economy. This I shall aim at the more anxiously both because it will facilitate the extinguishment of the national debt, the unnecessary duration of which is incompatible with real independence, and because it will counteract that tendency to public and private profligacy which a profuse expenditure of money by the Government is but too apt to engender. Powerful auxiliaries to the attainment of this desirable end are to be found in the regulations provided by the wisdom of Congress for the specific appropriation of public money and the prompt accountability of public officers.

With regard to a proper selection of the subjects of impost with a view to revenue, it would seem to me that the spirit of equity, caution, and compromise in which the Constitution was formed requires that the great interests of agriculture, commerce, and manufactures should be equally favored, and that perhaps the only exception to this rule should consist in the peculiar encouragement of any products of either of them that may be found essential to our national independence.

Internal improvement and the diffusion of knowledge, so far as they can be promoted by the constitutional acts of the Federal Government, are of high importance.

Considering standing armies as dangerous to free governments in time of peace, I shall not seek to enlarge our present establishment, nor disregard that salutary lesson of political experience which teaches that the military should be held subordinate to the civil power. The gradual increase of our Navy, whose flag has displayed in distant climes our skill in navigation and our fame in arms; the preservation of our forts, arsenals, and dockyards, and the introduction of progressive improvements in the discipline and science of both branches of our military service are so plainly prescribed by prudence that I should be excused for omitting their mention sooner than for enlarging on their importance. But the bulwark of our defense is the national militia, which in the present state of our intelligence and population must render us invincible. As long as our Government is administered for the good of the people, and is regulated by their will; as long as it secures to us the rights of person and of property, liberty of conscience and of the press, it will be worth defending; and so long as it is worth defending a patriotic militia will cover it with an impenetrable aegis. Partial injuries and occasional mortifications we may be subjected to, but a million of armed freemen, possessed of the means of war, can never be conquered by a foreign foe. To any just system, therefore, calculated to strengthen this natural safeguard of the country I shall cheerfully lend all the aid in my power.

It will be my sincere and constant desire to observe toward the Indian tribes within our limits a just and liberal policy, and to give that humane and considerate attention to their rights and their wants which is consistent with the habits of our Government and the feelings of our people.

The recent demonstration of public sentiment inscribes on the list of Executive duties, in characters too legible to be overlooked, the task of reform, which will require particularly the correction of those abuses that have brought the patronage of the Federal Government into conflict with the freedom of elections, and the counteraction of those causes which have disturbed the rightful course of appointment and have placed or continued power in unfaithful or incompetent hands.

In the performance of a task thus generally delineated I shall endeavor to select men whose diligence and talents will insure in their respective stations able and faithful cooperation, depending for the advancement of the public service more on the integrity and zeal of the public officers than on their numbers.

A diffidence, perhaps too just, in my own qualifications will teach me to look with reverence to the examples of public virtue left by my illustrious predecessors, and with veneration to the lights that flow from the mind that founded and the mind that reformed our system. The same diffidence induces me to hope for instruction and aid from the coordinate branches of the Government, and for the indulgence and support of my fellow-citizens generally. And a firm reliance on the goodness of that Power whose providence mercifully protected our national infancy, and has since upheld our liberties in various vicissitudes, encourages me to offer up my ardent supplications that He will continue to make our beloved country the object of His divine care and gracious benediction.

# ANDREW JACKSON
## SECOND INAUGURAL ADDRESS
## MONDAY, MARCH 4, 1833

Fellow-Citizens:

The will of the American people, expressed through their unsolicited suffrages, calls me before you to pass through the solemnities preparatory to taking upon myself the duties of President of the United States for another term. For their approbation of my public conduct through a period which has not been without its difficulties, and for this renewed expression of their confidence in my good intentions, I am at a loss for terms adequate to the expression of my gratitude. It shall be displayed to the extent of my humble abilities in continued efforts so to administer the Government as to preserve their liberty and promote their happiness.

So many events have occurred within the last four years which have necessarily called forth—sometimes under circumstances the most delicate and painful—my views of the principles and policy which ought to be pursued by the General Government that I need on this occasion but allude to a few leading considerations connected with some of them.

The foreign policy adopted by our Government soon after the formation of our present Constitution, and very generally pursued by successive Administrations, has been crowned with almost complete success, and has elevated our character among the nations of the earth. To do justice to all and to submit to wrong from none has been during my Administration its governing maxim, and so happy have been its results that we are not only at peace with all the world, but have few causes of controversy, and those of minor importance, remaining unadjusted.

In the domestic policy of this Government there are two objects which especially deserve the attention of the people and their representatives, and which have been and will continue to be the subjects of my increasing solicitude. They are the preservation of the rights of the several States and the integrity of the Union.

These great objects are necessarily connected, and can only be attained by an enlightened exercise of the powers of each within its appropriate sphere in conformity with the public will constitutionally expressed. To this end it becomes the duty of all to yield a ready and patriotic submission to the laws constitutionally enacted, and thereby promote and strengthen a proper confidence in those institutions of the several States and of the United States which the people themselves have ordained for their own government.

My experience in public concerns and the observation of a life somewhat advanced confirm the opinions long since imbibed by me, that the destruction of our State governments or the annihilation of their control over the local concerns of the people would lead directly to revolution and anarchy, and finally to despotism and military domination. In proportion, therefore, as the General Government encroaches upon the rights of the States, in the same proportion does it impair its own power and detract from its ability to fulfill the purposes of its creation. Solemnly impressed with these considerations, my countrymen will ever find me ready to exercise my constitutional powers in arresting measures which may directly or indirectly encroach upon the rights of the States or tend to consolidate all political power in the General Government. But of equal, and, indeed, of incalculable, importance is the union of these States, and the sacred duty of all to contribute to its preservation by a liberal support of the General Government in the exercise of its just powers. You have been wisely admonished to "accustom yourselves to think and speak of the Union as of the palladium of your political safety and prosperity, watching for its preservation with jealous anxiety, discountenancing whatever may suggest even a suspicion that it can in any event be abandoned, and indignantly frowning upon the first dawning of any attempt to alienate any portion of our country from the rest or to enfeeble the sacred ties which now link together the various parts." Without union our independence and liberty would never have been achieved; without union they never can be maintained. Divided into twenty-four, or even a smaller number, of separate communities, we shall see our internal trade burdened with numberless restraints and exactions; communication between distant points and sections obstructed or cut off; our sons made soldiers to deluge with blood the fields they now till in peace; the mass of our people borne down and impoverished by taxes to support armies and navies, and military leaders at the head of their victorious legions becoming our lawgivers and judges. The loss of liberty, of all good government, of peace, plenty, and happiness, must inevitably follow a dissolution of the Union. In supporting it, therefore, we support all that is dear to the freeman and the philanthropist.

The time at which I stand before you is full of interest. The eyes of all nations are fixed on our Republic. The event of the existing crisis will be decisive in the opinion of mankind of the practicability of our federal system of government. Great is the stake placed in our hands; great is the responsibility which must rest upon the people of the United States. Let us realize the importance of the attitude in which we stand before the world. Let us exercise forbearance and firmness. Let us extricate our country from the dangers which surround it and learn wisdom from the lessons they inculcate.

Deeply impressed with the truth of these observations, and under the obligation of that solemn oath which I am about to take, I shall continue to exert all my faculties to maintain the just powers of the Constitution and to transmit unimpaired to posterity the blessings of our Federal Union. At the same time, it will be my aim to inculcate by my official acts the necessity of exercising by the General Government those powers only that are clearly delegated; to encourage simplicity and economy in the expenditures of the Government; to raise no more money from the people than may be requisite for these objects, and in a manner that will best promote the interests of all classes of the community and of all portions of the Union. Constantly bearing in mind that in entering into society "individuals must give up a share of liberty to preserve the rest," it will be my desire so to discharge my duties as to foster with our brethren in all parts of the country a spirit of liberal concession and compromise, and, by reconciling our fellow-citizens to those partial sacrifices which they must unavoidably make for the preservation of a greater good, to recommend our invaluable Government and Union to the confidence and affections of the American people.

Finally, it is my most fervent prayer to that Almighty Being before whom I now stand, and who has kept us in His hands from the infancy of our Republic to the present day, that He will so overrule all my intentions and actions and inspire the hearts of my fellow-citizens that we may be preserved from dangers of all kinds and continue forever a united and happy people.

# MARTIN VAN BUREN
## INAUGURAL ADDRESS
## MONDAY, MARCH 4, 1837

Fellow-Citizens:

The practice of all my predecessors imposes on me an obligation I cheerfully fulfill—to accompany the first and solemn act of my public trust with an avowal of the principles that will guide me in performing it and an expression of my feelings on assuming a charge so responsible and vast. In imitating their example I tread in the footsteps of illustrious men, whose superiors it is our happiness to believe are not found on the executive calendar of any country. Among them we recognize the earliest and firmest pillars of the Republic— those by whom our national independence was first declared, him who above all others contributed to establish it on the field of battle, and those whose expanded intellect and patriotism constructed, improved, and perfected the inestimable institutions under which we live. If such men in the position I now occupy felt themselves overwhelmed by a sense of gratitude for this the highest of all marks of their country's confidence, and by a consciousness of their inability adequately to discharge the duties of an office so difficult and exalted, how much more must these considerations affect one who can rely on no such claims for favor or forbearance! Unlike all who have preceded me, the Revolution that gave us existence as one people was achieved at the period of my birth; and whilst I contemplate with grateful reverence that memorable event, I feel that I belong to a later age and that I may not expect my countrymen to weigh my actions with the same kind and partial hand.

So sensibly, fellow-citizens, do these circumstances press themselves upon me that I should not dare to enter upon my path of duty did I not look for the generous aid of those who will be associated with me in the various and coordinate branches of the Government; did I not repose with unwavering reliance on the patriotism, the intelligence, and the kindness of a people who never yet deserted a public servant honestly laboring their cause; and, above all, did I not permit myself humbly to hope for the sustaining support of an ever-watchful and beneficent Providence.

To the confidence and consolation derived from these sources it would be ungrateful not to add those which spring from our present fortunate condition. Though not altogether exempt from embarrassments that disturb our tranquillity at home and threaten it abroad, yet in all the attributes of a great, happy, and flourishing people we stand without a parallel in the world. Abroad we enjoy the respect and, with scarcely an exception, the friendship of every nation; at home, while our Government quietly but efficiently performs the sole legitimate end of political institutions—in doing the greatest good to the greatest number—we present an aggregate of human prosperity surely not elsewhere to be found.

How imperious, then, is the obligation imposed upon every citizen, in his own sphere of action, whether limited or extended, to exert himself in perpetuating a condition of things so singularly happy! All the lessons of history and experience must be lost upon us if we are content to trust alone to the peculiar advantages we happen to possess. Position and climate and the bounteous resources that nature has scattered with so liberal a hand—even the diffused intelligence and elevated character of our people—will avail us nothing if we fail sacredly to uphold those political institutions that were wisely and deliberately formed with reference to every circumstance that could preserve or might endanger the blessings we enjoy. The thoughtful framers of our Constitution legislated for our country as they found it. Looking upon it with the eyes of statesmen and patriots, they saw all the sources of rapid and wonderful prosperity; but they saw also that various habits, opinions and institutions peculiar to the various portions of so vast a region were deeply fixed. Distinct sovereignties were in actual existence, whose cordial union was essential to the welfare and happiness of all. Between many of them there was, at least to some extent, a real diversity of interests, liable to be exaggerated through sinister designs; they differed in size, in population, in wealth, and in actual and prospective resources and power; they varied in the character of their industry and staple productions, and [in some] existed domestic institutions which, unwisely disturbed, might endanger the harmony of the whole. Most carefully were all these circumstances weighed, and the foundations of the new Government laid upon principles of reciprocal concession and equitable compromise. The jealousies which the smaller States might entertain of the power of the rest were allayed by a rule of representation confessedly unequal at the time, and designed forever to remain so. A natural fear that the broad scope of general legislation might bear upon and unwisely control particular interests was counteracted by limits strictly drawn around the action of the Federal authority, and to the people and the States was left unimpaired their sovereign power over the innumerable subjects embraced in the internal government of a just republic, excepting such only as necessarily appertain to the concerns of the whole confederacy or its intercourse as a united community with the other nations of the world.

This provident forecast has been verified by time. Half a century, teeming with extraordinary events, and elsewhere producing astonishing results, has passed along, but on our institutions it has left no injurious mark. From a small community we have risen to a people powerful in numbers and in strength; but with our increase has gone hand in hand the progress of just principles. The privileges, civil and religious, of the humblest individual are still sacredly protected at home, and while the valor and fortitude of our people have removed far from us the slightest apprehension of foreign power, they have not yet induced us in a single instance to forget what is right. Our commerce has been extended to the remotest nations; the value and even nature of our productions have been greatly changed; a wide difference has arisen in the relative wealth and resources of every portion of our country; yet the spirit of mutual regard and of faithful adherence to existing compacts has continued to prevail in our councils and never long been absent from our conduct. We have learned by experience a fruitful lesson—that an implicit and undeviating adherence to the principles on which we set out can carry us prosperously onward through all the conflicts of circumstances and vicissitudes inseparable from the lapse of years.

The success that has thus attended our great experiment is in itself a sufficient cause for gratitude, on account of the happiness it has actually conferred and the example it has unanswerably given. But to me, my fellow-citizens, looking forward to the far-distant future with ardent prayers and confiding hopes, this retrospect presents a ground for still deeper delight. It impresses on my mind a firm belief that the perpetuity of our institutions depends upon ourselves; that if we maintain the principles on which they were established they are destined to confer their benefits on countless generations yet to come, and that America will present to every friend of mankind the cheering proof that a popular government, wisely formed, is wanting in no element of endurance or strength. Fifty years ago its rapid failure was boldly predicted. Latent and uncontrollable causes of dissolution were supposed to exist even by the wise and good, and not only did unfriendly or speculative theorists anticipate for us the fate of past republics, but the fears of many an honest patriot overbalanced his sanguine hopes. Look back on these forebodings, not hastily but reluctantly made, and see how in every instance they have completely failed.

An imperfect experience during the struggles of the Revolution was supposed to warrant the belief that the people would not bear the taxation requisite to discharge an immense public debt already incurred and to pay the necessary expenses of the Government. The cost of two wars has been paid, not only without a murmur, but with unequaled alacrity. No one is now left to doubt that every burden will be cheerfully borne that may be necessary to sustain our civil institutions or guard our honor or welfare. Indeed, all experience has shown that the willingness of the people to contribute to these ends in cases of emergency has uniformly outrun the confidence of their representatives.

In the early stages of the new Government, when all felt the imposing influence as they recognized the unequaled services of the first President, it was a common sentiment that the great weight of his character could alone bind the discordant materials of our Government together and save us from the violence of contending factions. Since his death nearly forty years are gone. Party exasperation has been often carried to its highest point; the virtue and fortitude of the people have sometimes been greatly tried; yet our system, purified and enhanced in value by all it has encountered, still preserves its spirit of free and fearless discussion, blended with unimpaired fraternal feeling.

The capacity of the people for self-government, and their willingness, from a high sense of duty and without those exhibitions of coercive power so generally employed in other countries, to submit to all needful restraints and exactions of municipal law, have also been favorably exemplified in the history of the American States. Occasionally, it is true, the ardor of public sentiment, outrunning the regular progress of the judicial tribunals or seeking to reach cases not denounced as criminal by the existing law, has displayed itself in a manner calculated to give pain to the friends of free government and to encourage the hopes of those who wish for its overthrow. These occurrences, however, have been far less frequent in our country than in any other of equal population on the globe, and with the diffusion of intelligence it may well be hoped that they will constantly diminish in frequency and violence. The generous patriotism and sound common sense of the great mass of our fellow-citizens will assuredly in time produce this result; for as every assumption of illegal power not only wounds the majesty of the law, but furnishes a pretext for abridging the liberties of the people, the latter have the most direct and permanent interest in preserving the landmarks of social order and maintaining on all occasions the inviolability of those constitutional and legal provisions which they themselves have made.

In a supposed unfitness of our institutions for those hostile emergencies which no country can always avoid their friends found a fruitful source of apprehension, their enemies of hope. While they foresaw less promptness of action than in governments differently formed, they overlooked the far more important consideration that with us war could never be the result of individual or irresponsible will, but must be a measure of redress for injuries sustained voluntarily resorted to by those who were to bear the necessary sacrifice, who would consequently feel an individual interest in the contest, and whose energy would be commensurate with the difficulties to be encountered. Actual events have proved their error; the last war, far from impairing, gave new confidence to our Government, and amid recent apprehensions of a similar conflict we saw that the energies of our country would not be wanting in ample season to vindicate its rights. We may not possess, as we should not desire to possess, the extended and ever-ready military organization of other nations; we may occasionally suffer in the outset for the want of it; but among ourselves all doubt upon this great point has ceased, while a salutary experience will prevent a contrary opinion from inviting aggression from abroad.

Certain danger was foretold from the extension of our territory, the multiplication of States, and the increase of population. Our system was supposed to be adapted only to boundaries comparatively narrow. These have been widened beyond conjecture; the members of our Confederacy are already doubled, and the numbers of our people are incredibly augmented. The alleged causes of danger have long surpassed anticipation, but none of the consequences have followed. The power and influence of the Republic have arisen to a height obvious to all mankind; respect for its authority was not more apparent at its ancient than it is at its present limits; new and inexhaustible sources of general prosperity have been opened; the effects of distance have been averted by the inventive genius of our people, developed and fostered by the spirit of our institutions; and the enlarged variety and amount of interests, productions, and pursuits have strengthened the chain of mutual dependence and formed a circle of mutual benefits too apparent ever to be overlooked.

In justly balancing the powers of the Federal and State authorities difficulties nearly insurmountable arose at the outset and subsequent collisions were deemed inevitable. Amid these it was scarcely believed possible that a scheme of government so complex in construction could remain uninjured. From time to time embarrassments have certainly occurred; but how just is the confidence of future safety imparted by the knowledge that each in succession has been happily removed! Overlooking partial and temporary evils as inseparable from the practical operation of all human institutions, and looking only to the general result, every patriot has reason to be satisfied. While the Federal Government has successfully performed its appropriate functions in relation to foreign affairs and concerns evidently national, that of every State has remarkably improved in protecting and developing local interests and individual welfare; and if the vibrations of authority have occasionally tended too much toward one or the other, it is unquestionably certain that the ultimate operation of the entire system has been to strengthen all the existing institutions and to elevate our whole country in prosperity and renown.

The last, perhaps the greatest, of the prominent sources of discord and disaster supposed to lurk in our political condition was the institution of domestic slavery. Our forefathers were deeply impressed with the delicacy of this subject, and they treated it with a forbearance so evidently wise that in spite of every sinister foreboding it never until the present period disturbed the tranquillity of our common country. Such a result is sufficient evidence of the justice and the patriotism of their course; it is evidence not to be mistaken that an adherence to it can prevent all embarrassment from this as well as from every other anticipated cause of difficulty or danger. Have not recent events made it obvious to the slightest reflection that the least deviation from this spirit of forbearance is injurious to every interest, that of humanity included? Amidst the violence of excited passions this generous and fraternal feeling has been sometimes disregarded; and standing as I now do before my countrymen, in this high place of honor and of trust, I can not refrain from anxiously invoking my fellow-citizens never to be deaf to its dictates. Perceiving before my election the deep interest this subject was beginning to excite, I believed it a solemn duty fully to make known my sentiments in regard to it, and now, when every motive for misrepresentation has passed away, I trust that they will be candidly weighed and understood. At least they will be my standard of conduct in the path before me. I then declared that if the desire of those of my countrymen who were favorable to my election was gratified "I must go into the Presidential chair the inflexible and uncompromising opponent of every attempt on the part of Congress to abolish slavery in the District of Columbia against the wishes of the slaveholding States, and also with a determination equally decided to resist the slightest interference with it in the States where it exists." I submitted also to my fellow-citizens, with fullness and frankness, the reasons which led me to this determination. The result authorizes me to believe that they have been approved and are confided in by a majority of the people of the United States, including those whom they most immediately affect. It now only remains to add that no bill conflicting with these views can ever receive my constitutional sanction. These opinions have been adopted in the firm belief that they are in accordance with the spirit that actuated the venerated fathers of the Republic, and that succeeding experience has proved them to be humane, patriotic, expedient, honorable, and just. If the agitation of this subject was intended to reach the stability of our institutions, enough has occurred to show that it has signally failed, and that in this as in every other instance the apprehensions of the timid and the hopes of the wicked for the destruction of our Government are again destined to be disappointed. Here and there, indeed, scenes of dangerous excitement have occurred, terrifying instances of local violence have been witnessed, and a reckless disregard of the consequences of their conduct has exposed individuals to popular indignation; but neither masses of the people nor sections of the country have been swerved from their devotion to the bond of union and the principles it has made sacred. It will be ever thus. Such attempts at dangerous agitation may periodically return, but with each the object will be better understood. That predominating affection for our political system which prevails throughout our territorial limits, that calm and enlightened judgment which ultimately governs our people as one vast body, will always be at hand to resist and control every effort, foreign or domestic, which aims or would lead to overthrow our institutions.

What can be more gratifying than such a retrospect as this? We look back on obstacles avoided and dangers overcome, on expectations more than realized and prosperity perfectly secured. To the hopes of the hostile, the fears of the timid, and the doubts of the anxious actual experience has given the conclusive reply. We have seen time gradually dispel every unfavorable foreboding and our Constitution surmount every adverse circumstance dreaded at the outset as beyond control. Present excitement will at all times magnify present dangers, but true philosophy must teach us that none more threatening than the past can remain to be overcome; and we ought (for we have just reason) to entertain an abiding confidence in the stability of our institutions and an entire conviction that if administered in the true form, character, and spirit in which they were established they are abundantly adequate to preserve to us and our children the rich blessings already derived from them, to make our beloved land for a thousand generations that chosen spot where happiness springs from a perfect equality of political rights.

For myself, therefore, I desire to declare that the principle that will govern me in the high duty to which my country calls me is a strict adherence to the letter and spirit of the Constitution as it was designed by those who framed it. Looking back to it as a sacred instrument carefully and not easily framed; remembering that it was throughout a work of concession and compromise; viewing it as limited to national objects; regarding it as leaving to the people and the States all power not explicitly parted with, I shall endeavor to preserve, protect, and defend it by anxiously referring to its provision for direction in every action. To matters of domestic concernment which it has intrusted to the Federal Government and to such as relate to our intercourse with foreign nations I shall zealously devote myself; beyond those limits I shall never pass.

To enter on this occasion into a further or more minute exposition of my views on the various questions of domestic policy would be as obtrusive as it is probably unexpected. Before the suffrages of my countrymen were conferred upon me I submitted to them, with great precision, my opinions on all the most prominent of these subjects. Those opinions I shall endeavor to carry out with my utmost ability.

Our course of foreign policy has been so uniform and intelligible as to constitute a rule of Executive conduct which leaves little to my discretion, unless, indeed, I were willing to run counter to the lights of experience and the known opinions of my constituents. We sedulously cultivate the friendship of all nations as the conditions most compatible with our welfare and the principles of our Government. We decline alliances as adverse to our peace. We desire commercial relations on equal terms, being ever willing to give a fair equivalent for advantages received. We endeavor to conduct our intercourse with openness and sincerity, promptly avowing our objects and seeking to establish that mutual frankness which is as beneficial in the dealings of nations as of men. We have no disposition and we disclaim all right to meddle in disputes, whether internal or foreign, that may molest other countries, regarding them in their actual state as social communities, and preserving a strict neutrality in all their controversies. Well knowing the tried valor of our people and our exhaustless resources, we neither anticipate nor fear any designed aggression; and in the consciousness of our own just conduct we feel a security that we shall never be called upon to exert our determination never to permit an invasion of our rights without punishment or redress.

In approaching, then, in the presence of my assembled countrymen, to make the solemn promise that yet remains, and to pledge myself that I will faithfully execute the office I am about to fill, I bring with me a settled purpose to maintain the institutions of my country, which I trust will atone for the errors I commit.

In receiving from the people the sacred trust twice confided to my illustrious predecessor, and which he has discharged so faithfully and so well, I know that I can not expect to perform the arduous task with equal ability and success. But united as I have been in his counsels, a daily witness of his exclusive and unsurpassed devotion to his country's welfare, agreeing with him in sentiments which his countrymen have warmly supported, and permitted to partake largely of his confidence, I may hope that somewhat of the same cheering approbation will be found to attend upon my path. For him I but express with my own the wishes of all, that he may yet long live to enjoy the brilliant evening of his well-spent life; and for myself, conscious of but one desire, faithfully to serve my country, I throw myself without fear on its justice and its kindness. Beyond that I only look to the gracious protection of the Divine Being whose strengthening support I humbly solicit, and whom I fervently pray to look down upon us all. May it be among the dispensations of His providence to bless our beloved country with honors and with length of days. May her ways be ways of pleasantness and all her paths be peace!

# WILLIAM HENRY HARRISON
## INAUGURAL ADDRESS
## THURSDAY, MARCH 4, 1841

Called from a retirement which I had supposed was to continue for the residue of my life to fill the chief executive office of this great and free nation, I appear before you, fellow-citizens, to take the oaths which the Constitution prescribes as a necessary qualification for the performance of its duties; and in obedience to a custom coeval with our Government and what I believe to be your expectations I proceed to present to you a summary of the principles which will govern me in the discharge of the duties which I shall be called upon to perform.

It was the remark of a Roman consul in an early period of that celebrated Republic that a most striking contrast was observable in the conduct of candidates for offices of power and trust before and after obtaining them, they seldom carrying out in the latter case the pledges and promises made in the former. However much the world may have improved in many respects in the lapse of upward of two thousand years since the remark was made by the virtuous and indignant Roman, I fear that a strict examination of the annals of some of the modern elective governments would develop similar instances of violated confidence.

Although the fiat of the people has gone forth proclaiming me the Chief Magistrate of this glorious Union, nothing upon their part remaining to be done, it may be thought that a motive may exist to keep up the delusion under which they may be supposed to have acted in relation to my principles and opinions; and perhaps there may be some in this assembly who have come here either prepared to condemn those I shall now deliver, or, approving them, to doubt the sincerity with which they are now uttered. But the lapse of a few months will confirm or dispel their fears. The outline of principles to govern and measures to be adopted by an Administration not yet begun will soon be exchanged for immutable history, and I shall stand either exonerated by my countrymen or classed with the mass of those who promised that they might deceive and flattered with the intention to betray. However strong may be my present purpose to realize the expectations of a magnanimous and confiding people, I too well understand the dangerous temptations to which I shall be exposed from the magnitude of the power which it has been the pleasure of the people to commit to my hands not to place my chief confidence upon the aid of that Almighty Power which has hitherto protected me and enabled me to bring to favorable issues other important but still greatly inferior trusts heretofore confided to me by my country.

The broad foundation upon which our Constitution rests being the people—a breath of theirs having made, as a breath can unmake, change, or modify it—it can be assigned to none of the great divisions of government but to that of democracy. If such is its theory, those who are called upon to administer it must recognize as its leading principle the duty of shaping their measures so as to produce the greatest good to the greatest number. But with these broad admissions, if we would compare the sovereignty acknowledged to exist in the mass of our people with the power claimed by other sovereignties, even by those which have been considered most purely democratic, we shall find a most essential difference. All others lay claim to power limited only by their own will. The majority of our citizens, on the contrary, possess a sovereignty with an amount of power precisely equal to that which has been granted to them by the parties to the national compact, and nothing beyond. We admit of no government by divine right, believing that so far as power is concerned the Beneficent Creator has made no distinction amongst men; that all are upon an equality, and that the only legitimate right to govern is an express grant of power from the governed. The Constitution of the United States is the instrument containing this grant of power to the several departments composing the Government. On an examination of that instrument it will be found to contain declarations of power granted and of power withheld. The latter is also susceptible of division into power which the majority had the right to grant, but which they do not think proper to intrust to their agents, and that which they could not have granted, not being possessed by themselves. In other words, there are certain rights possessed by each individual American citizen which in his compact with the others he has never surrendered. Some of them, indeed, he is unable to surrender, being, in the language of our system, unalienable. The boasted privilege of a Roman citizen was to him a shield only against a petty provincial ruler, whilst the proud democrat of Athens would console himself under a sentence of death for a supposed violation of the national faith—which no one understood and which at times was the subject of the mockery of all—or the banishment from his home, his family, and his country with or without an alleged cause, that it was the act not of a single tyrant or hated aristocracy, but of his assembled countrymen. Far different is the power of our sovereignty. It can interfere with no one's faith, prescribe forms of worship for no one's observance, inflict no punishment but after well-ascertained guilt, the result of investigation under rules prescribed by the Constitution itself. These precious privileges, and those scarcely less important of giving expression to his thoughts and opinions, either by writing or speaking, unrestrained but by the liability for injury to others, and that of a full participation in all the advantages which flow from the Government, the acknowledged property of all, the American citizen derives from no charter granted by his fellow-man. He claims them because he is himself a man, fashioned by the same Almighty hand as the rest of his species and entitled to a full share of the blessings with which He has endowed them. Notwithstanding the limited sovereignty possessed by the people of the United States and the restricted grant of power to the Government which they have adopted, enough has been given to accomplish all the objects for which it was created. It has been found powerful in war, and hitherto justice has been administered, and intimate union effected, domestic tranquillity preserved, and personal liberty secured to the citizen. As was to be expected, however, from the defect of language and the necessarily sententious manner in which the Constitution is written, disputes have arisen as to the amount of power which it has actually granted or was intended to grant.

This is more particularly the case in relation to that part of the instrument which treats of the legislative branch, and not only as regards the exercise of powers claimed under a general clause giving that body the authority to pass all laws necessary to carry into effect the specified powers, but in relation to the latter also. It is, however, consolatory to reflect that most of the instances of alleged departure from the letter or spirit of the Constitution have ultimately received the sanction of a majority of the people. And the fact that many of our statesmen most distinguished for talent and patriotism have been at one time or other of their political career on both sides of each of the most warmly disputed questions forces upon us the inference that the errors, if errors there were, are attributable to the intrinsic difficulty in many instances of ascertaining the intentions of the framers of the Constitution rather than the influence of any sinister or unpatriotic motive. But the great danger to our institutions does not appear to me to be in a usurpation by the Government of power not granted by the people, but by the accumulation in one of the departments of that which was assigned to others. Limited as are the powers which have been granted, still enough have been granted to constitute a despotism if concentrated in one of the departments. This danger is greatly heightened, as it has been always observable that men are less jealous of encroachments of one department upon another than upon their own reserved rights. When the Constitution of the United States first came from the hands of the Convention which formed it, many of the sternest republicans of the day were alarmed at the extent of the power which had been granted to the Federal Government, and more particularly of that portion which had been assigned to the executive branch. There were in it features which appeared not to be in harmony with their ideas of a simple representative democracy or republic, and knowing the tendency of power to increase itself, particularly when exercised by a single individual, predictions were made that at no very remote period the Government would terminate in virtual monarchy. It would not become me to say that the fears of these patriots have been already realized; but as I sincerely believe that the tendency of measures and of men's opinions for some years past has been in that direction, it is, I conceive, strictly proper that I should take this occasion to repeat the assurances I have heretofore given of my determination to arrest the progress of that tendency if it really exists and restore the Government to its pristine health and vigor, as far as this can be effected by any legitimate exercise of the power placed in my hands.

I proceed to state in as summary a manner as I can my opinion of the sources of the evils which have been so extensively complained of and the correctives which may be applied. Some of the former are unquestionably to be found in the defects of the Constitution; others, in my judgment, are attributable to a misconstruction of some of its provisions. Of the former is the eligibility of the same individual to a second term of the Presidency. The sagacious mind of Mr. Jefferson early saw and lamented this error, and attempts have been made, hitherto without success, to apply the amendatory power of the States to its correction. As, however, one mode of correction is in the power of every President, and consequently in mine, it would be useless, and perhaps invidious, to enumerate the evils of which, in the opinion of many of our fellow-citizens, this error of the sages who framed the Constitution may have been the source and the bitter fruits which we are still to gather from it if it continues to disfigure our system. It may be observed, however, as a general remark, that republics can commit no greater error than to adopt or continue any feature in their systems of government which may be calculated to create or increase the lover of power in the bosoms of those to whom necessity obliges them to commit the management of their affairs; and surely nothing is more likely to produce such a state of mind than the long continuance of an office of high trust. Nothing can be more corrupting, nothing more destructive of all those noble feelings which belong to the character of a devoted republican patriot. When this corrupting passion once takes possession of the human mind, like the love of gold it becomes insatiable. It is the never-dying worm in his bosom, grows with his growth and strengthens with the declining years of its victim. If this is true, it is the part of wisdom for a republic to limit the service of that officer at least to whom she has intrusted the management of her foreign relations, the execution of her laws, and the command of her armies and navies to a period so short as to prevent his forgetting that he is the accountable agent, not the principal; the servant, not the master. Until an amendment of the Constitution can be effected public opinion may secure the desired object. I give my aid to it by renewing the pledge heretofore given that under no circumstances will I consent to serve a second term.

But if there is danger to public liberty from the acknowledged defects of the Constitution in the want of limit to the continuance of the Executive power in the same hands, there is, I apprehend, not much less from a misconstruction of that instrument as it regards the powers actually given. I can not conceive that by a fair construction any or either of its provisions would be found to constitute the President a part of the legislative power. It can not be claimed from the power to recommend, since, although enjoined as a duty upon him, it is a privilege which he holds in common with every other citizen; and although there may be something more of confidence in the propriety of the measures recommended in the one case than in the other, in the obligations of ultimate decision there can be no difference. In the language of the Constitution, "all the legislative powers" which it grants "are vested in the Congress of the United States." It would be a solecism in language to say that any portion of these is not included in the whole.

It may be said, indeed, that the Constitution has given to the Executive the power to annul the acts of the legislative body by refusing to them his assent. So a similar power has necessarily resulted from that instrument to the judiciary, and yet the judiciary forms no part of the Legislature. There is, it is true, this difference between these grants of power: The Executive can put his negative upon the acts of the Legislature for other cause than that of want of conformity to the Constitution, whilst the judiciary can only declare void those which violate that instrument. But the decision of the judiciary is final in such a case, whereas in every instance where the veto of the Executive is applied it may be overcome by a vote of two-thirds of both Houses of Congress. The negative upon the acts of the legislative by the executive authority, and that in the hands of one individual, would seem to be an incongruity in our system. Like some others of a similar character, however, it appears to be highly expedient, and if used only with the forbearance and in the spirit which was intended by its authors it may be productive of great good and be found one of the best safeguards to the Union. At the period of the formation of the Constitution the principle does not appear to have enjoyed much favor in the State governments. It existed but in two, and in one of these there was a plural executive. If we would search for the motives which operated upon the purely patriotic and enlightened assembly which framed the Constitution for the adoption of a provision so apparently repugnant to the leading democratic principle that the majority should govern, we must reject the idea that they anticipated from it any benefit to the ordinary course of legislation. They knew too well the high degree of intelligence which existed among the people and the enlightened character of the State legislatures not to have the fullest confidence that the two bodies elected by them would be worthy representatives of such constituents, and, of course, that they would require no aid in conceiving and maturing the measures which the circumstances of the country might require. And it is preposterous to suppose that a thought could for a moment have been entertained that the President, placed at the capital, in the center of the country, could better understand the wants and wishes of the people than their own immediate representatives, who spend a part of every year among them, living with them, often laboring with them, and bound to them by the triple tie of interest, duty, and affection. To assist or control Congress, then, in its ordinary legislation could not, I conceive, have been the motive for conferring the veto power on the President. This argument acquires additional force from the fact of its never having been thus used by the first six Presidents—and two of them were members of the Convention, one presiding over its deliberations and the other bearing a larger share in consummating the labors of that august body than any other person. But if bills were never returned to Congress by either of the Presidents above referred to upon the ground of their being inexpedient or not as well adapted as they might be to the wants of the people, the veto was applied upon that of want of conformity to the Constitution or because errors had been committed from a too hasty enactment.

There is another ground for the adoption of the veto principle, which had probably more influence in recommending it to the Convention than any other. I refer to the security which it gives to the just and equitable action of the Legislature upon all parts of the Union. It could not but have occurred to the Convention that in a country so extensive, embracing so great a variety of soil and climate, and consequently of products, and which from the same causes must ever exhibit a great difference in the amount of the population of its various sections, calling for a great diversity in the employments of the people, that the legislation of the majority might not always justly regard the rights and interests of the minority, and that acts of this character might be passed under an express grant by the words of the Constitution, and therefore not within the competency of the judiciary to declare void; that however enlightened and patriotic they might suppose from past experience the members of Congress might be, and however largely partaking, in the general, of the liberal feelings of the people, it was impossible to expect that bodies so constituted should not sometimes be controlled by local interests and sectional feelings. It was proper, therefore, to provide some umpire from whose situation and mode of appointment more independence and freedom from such influences might be expected. Such a one was afforded by the executive department constituted by the Constitution. A person elected to that high office, having his constituents in every section, State, and subdivision of the Union, must consider himself bound by the most solemn sanctions to guard, protect, and defend the rights of all and of every portion, great or small, from the injustice and oppression of the rest. I consider the veto power, therefore, given by the Constitution to the Executive of the United States solely as a conservative power, to be used only first, to protect the Constitution from violation; secondly, the people from the effects of hasty legislation where their will has been probably disregarded or not well understood, and, thirdly, to prevent the effects of combinations violative of the rights of minorities. In reference to the second of these objects I may observe that I consider it the right and privilege of the people to decide disputed points of the Constitution arising from the general grant of power to Congress to carry into effect the powers expressly given; and I believe with Mr. Madison that "repeated recognitions under varied circumstances in acts of the legislative, executive, and judicial branches of the Government, accompanied by indications in different modes of the concurrence of the general will of the nation," as affording to the President sufficient authority for his considering such disputed points as settled.

Upward of half a century has elapsed since the adoption of the present form of government. It would be an object more highly desirable than the gratification of the curiosity of speculative statesmen if its precise situation could be ascertained, a fair exhibit

made of the operations of each of its departments, of the powers
which they respectively claim and exercise, of the collisions which
have occurred between them or between the whole Government and
those of the States or either of them. We could then compare our
actual condition after fifty years' trial of our system with what it was
in the commencement of its operations and ascertain whether the
predictions of the patriots who opposed its adoption or the confident
hopes of its advocates have been best realized. The great dread
of the former seems to have been that the reserved powers of the
States would be absorbed by those of the Federal Government and a
consolidated power established, leaving to the States the shadow only
of that independent action for which they had so zealously contended
and on the preservation of which they relied as the last hope of
liberty. Without denying that the result to which they looked with
so much apprehension is in the way of being realized, it is obvious
that they did not clearly see the mode of its accomplishment. The
General Government has seized upon none of the reserved rights
of the States. As far as any open warfare may have gone, the State
authorities have amply maintained their rights. To a casual observer
our system presents no appearance of discord between the different
members which compose it. Even the addition of many new ones has
produced no jarring. They move in their respective orbits in perfect
harmony with the central head and with each other. But there is still an
undercurrent at work by which, if not seasonably checked, the worst
apprehensions of our antifederal patriots will be realized, and not only
will the State authorities be overshadowed by the great increase of
power in the executive department of the General Government, but
the character of that Government, if not its designation, be essentially
and radically changed. This state of things has been in part effected
by causes inherent in the Constitution and in part by the never-failing
tendency of political power to increase itself. By making the President
the sole distributer of all the patronage of the Government the framers
of the Constitution do not appear to have anticipated at how short a
period it would become a formidable instrument to control the free
operations of the State governments. Of trifling importance at first, it
had early in Mr. Jefferson's Administration become so powerful as to
create great alarm in the mind of that patriot from the potent influence

it might exert in controlling the freedom of the elective franchise. If such could have then been the effects of its influence, how much greater must be the danger at this time, quadrupled in amount as it certainly is and more completely under the control of the Executive will than their construction of their powers allowed or the forbearing characters of all the early Presidents permitted them to make. But it is not by the extent of its patronage alone that the executive department has become dangerous, but by the use which it appears may be made of the appointing power to bring under its control the whole revenues of the country. The Constitution has declared it to be the duty of the President to see that the laws are executed, and it makes him the Commander in Chief of the Armies and Navy of the United States. If the opinion of the most approved writers upon that species of mixed government which in modern Europe is termed monarchy in contradistinction to despotism is correct, there was wanting no other addition to the powers of our Chief Magistrate to stamp a monarchical character on our Government but the control of the public finances; and to me it appears strange indeed that anyone should doubt that the entire control which the President possesses over the officers who have the custody of the public money, by the power of removal with or without cause, does, for all mischievous purposes at least, virtually subject the treasure also to his disposal. The first Roman Emperor, in his attempt to seize the sacred treasure, silenced the opposition of the officer to whose charge it had been committed by a significant allusion to his sword. By a selection of political instruments for the care of the public money a reference to their commissions by a President would be quite as effectual an argument as that of Caesar to the Roman knight. I am not insensible of the great difficulty that exists in drawing a proper plan for the safe-keeping and disbursement of the public revenues, and I know the importance which has been attached by men of great abilities and patriotism to the divorce, as it is called, of the Treasury from the banking institutions. It is not the divorce which is complained of, but the unhallowed union of the Treasury with the executive department, which has created such extensive alarm. To this danger to our republican institutions and that created by the influence given to the Executive through the instrumentality of the Federal officers I propose to apply all the remedies which may be at my command. It was certainly a great error in the framers of the Constitution not to have made the officer at the head of the Treasury Department entirely independent of the Executive. He should at least have been removable only upon the demand of the popular branch of the Legislature. I have determined never to remove a Secretary of the Treasury without communicating all the circumstances attending such removal to both Houses of Congress.

The influence of the Executive in controlling the freedom of the elective franchise through the medium of the public officers can be effectually checked by renewing the prohibition published by Mr. Jefferson forbidding their interference in elections further than giving their own votes, and their own independence secured by an assurance of perfect immunity in exercising this sacred privilege of freemen under the dictates of their own unbiased judgments. Never with my consent shall an officer of the people, compensated for his services out of their pockets, become the pliant instrument of Executive will.

There is no part of the means placed in the hands of the Executive which might be used with greater effect for unhallowed purposes than the control of the public press. The maxim which our ancestors derived from the mother country that "the freedom of the press is the great bulwark of civil and religious liberty" is one of the most precious legacies which they have left us. We have learned, too, from our own as well as the experience of other countries, that golden shackles, by whomsoever or by whatever pretense imposed, are as fatal to it as the iron bonds of despotism. The presses in the necessary employment of the Government should never be used "to clear the guilty or to varnish crime." A decent and manly examination of the acts of the Government should be not only tolerated, but encouraged.

Upon another occasion I have given my opinion at some length upon the impropriety of Executive interference in the legislation of Congress—that the article in the Constitution making it the duty of the President to communicate information and authorizing him to recommend measures was not intended to make him the source in legislation, and, in particular, that he should never be looked to for schemes of finance. It would be very strange, indeed, that the Constitution should have strictly forbidden one branch of the Legislature from interfering in the origination of such bills and that it should be considered proper that an altogether different department of the Government should be permitted to do so. Some of our best political maxims and opinions have been drawn from our parent isle. There are others, however, which can not be introduced in our system without singular incongruity and the production of much mischief, and this I conceive to be one. No matter in which of the houses of Parliament a bill may originate nor by whom introduced—a minister or a member of the opposition—by the fiction of law, or rather of constitutional principle, the sovereign is supposed to have prepared it agreeably to his will and then submitted it to Parliament for their advice and consent. Now the very reverse is the case here, not only with regard to the principle, but the forms prescribed by the Constitution. The principle certainly assigns to the only body constituted by the Constitution (the legislative body) the power to make laws, and the forms even direct that the enactment should be ascribed to them. The Senate, in relation to revenue bills, have the right to propose amendments, and so has the Executive by the power given him to return them to the House of Representatives with his objections. It is in his power also to propose amendments in the existing revenue laws, suggested by his observations upon their defective or injurious operation. But the delicate duty of devising schemes of revenue should be left where the Constitution has placed it—with the immediate representatives of the people. For similar reasons the mode of keeping the public treasure should be prescribed by them, and the further removed it may be from the control of the Executive the more wholesome the arrangement and the more in accordance with republican principle.

Connected with this subject is the character of the currency. The idea of making it exclusively metallic, however well intended, appears to me to be fraught with more fatal consequences than any other scheme having no relation to the personal rights of the citizens that has ever been devised. If any single scheme could produce the effect of arresting at once that mutation of condition by which thousands of our most indigent fellow-citizens by their industry and enterprise are raised to the possession of wealth, that is the one. If there is one measure better calculated than another to produce that state of things so much deprecated by all true republicans, by which the rich are daily adding to their hoards and the poor sinking deeper into penury, it is an exclusive metallic currency. Or if there is a process by which the character of the country for generosity and nobleness of feeling may be destroyed by the great increase and neck toleration of usury, it is an exclusive metallic currency.

Amongst the other duties of a delicate character which the President is called upon to perform is the supervision of the government of the Territories of the United States. Those of them which are destined to become members of our great political family are compensated by their rapid progress from infancy to manhood for the partial and temporary deprivation of their political rights. It is in this District only where American citizens are to be found who under a settled policy are deprived of many important political privileges without any inspiring hope as to the future. Their only consolation under circumstances of such deprivation is that of the devoted exterior guards of a camp—that their sufferings secure tranquillity and safety within. Are there any of their countrymen, who would subject them to greater sacrifices, to any other humiliations than those essentially necessary to the security of the object for which they were thus separated from their fellow-citizens? Are their rights alone not to be guaranteed by the application of those great principles upon which all our constitutions are founded? We are told by the greatest of British orators and statesmen that at the commencement of the War of the Revolution the most stupid men in England spoke of "their American subjects." Are there, indeed, citizens of any of our States who have dreamed of their subjects in the District of Columbia? Such dreams can never be realized by any agency of mine. The people of the District of Columbia are not the subjects of the people of the States, but free American citizens. Being in the latter condition when the Constitution was formed, no words used in that instrument could have been intended to deprive them of that character. If there is anything in the great principle of unalienable rights so emphatically insisted upon in our Declaration of Independence, they could neither make nor the United States accept a surrender of their liberties and become the subjects—in other words, the slaves—of their former fellow-citizens. If this be true—and it will scarcely be denied by anyone who has a correct idea of his own rights as an American citizen—the grant to Congress of exclusive jurisdiction in the District of Columbia can be interpreted, so far as respects the aggregate people of the United

States, as meaning nothing more than to allow to Congress the controlling power necessary to afford a free and safe exercise of the functions assigned to the General Government by the Constitution. In all other respects the legislation of Congress should be adapted to their peculiar position and wants and be conformable with their deliberate opinions of their own interests.

I have spoken of the necessity of keeping the respective departments of the Government, as well as all the other authorities of our country, within their appropriate orbits. This is a matter of difficulty in some cases, as the powers which they respectively claim are often not defined by any distinct lines. Mischievous, however, in their tendencies as collisions of this kind may be, those which arise between the respective communities which for certain purposes compose one nation are much more so, for no such nation can long exist without the careful culture of those feelings of confidence and affection which are the effective bonds to union between free and confederated states. Strong as is the tie of interest, it has been often found ineffectual. Men blinded by their passions have been known to adopt measures for their country in direct opposition to all the suggestions of policy. The alternative, then, is to destroy or keep down a bad passion by creating and fostering a good one, and this seems to be the corner stone upon which our American political architects have reared the fabric of our Government. The cement which was to bind it and perpetuate its existence was the affectionate attachment between all its members. To insure the continuance of this feeling, produced at first by a community of dangers, of sufferings, and of interests, the advantages of each were made accessible to all. No participation in any good possessed by any member of our extensive Confederacy, except in domestic government, was withheld from the citizen of any other member. By a process attended with no difficulty, no delay, no expense but that of removal, the citizen of one might become the citizen of any other, and successively of the whole. The lines, too, separating powers to be exercised by the citizens of one State from those of another seem to be so distinctly drawn as to leave no room for misunderstanding. The citizens of each State unite in their persons all the privileges which that character confers and all that they may claim as citizens of the United States, but in no case can the same persons at the same time act as the citizen of two separate States, and he is therefore positively precluded from any interference with the reserved powers of any State but that of which he is for the time being a citizen. He may, indeed, offer to the citizens of other States his advice as to their management, and the form in which it is tendered is left to his own discretion and sense of propriety. It may be observed, however, that organized associations of citizens requiring compliance with their wishes too much resemble the recommendations of Athens to her allies, supported by an armed and powerful fleet. It was, indeed, to the ambition of the leading States of Greece to control the domestic concerns of the others that the destruction of that celebrated Confederacy, and subsequently of all its members, is mainly to be attributed, and it is owing to the absence of that spirit that the Helvetic Confederacy has for so many years been preserved. Never has there been seen in the institutions of the separate members of any confederacy more elements of discord. In the principles and forms of government and religion, as well as in the circumstances of the several Cantons, so marked a discrepancy was observable as to promise anything but harmony in their intercourse or permanency in their alliance, and yet for ages neither has been interrupted. Content with the positive benefits which their union produced, with the independence and safety from foreign aggression which it secured, these sagacious people respected the institutions of each other, however repugnant to their own principles and prejudices.

Our Confederacy, fellow-citizens, can only be preserved by the same forbearance. Our citizens must be content with the exercise of the powers with which the Constitution clothes them. The attempt of those of one State to control the domestic institutions of another can only result in feelings of distrust and jealousy, the certain harbingers of disunion, violence, and civil war, and the ultimate destruction of our free institutions. Our Confederacy is perfectly illustrated by the terms and principles governing a common copartnership. There is a fund of power to be exercised under the direction of the joint councils of the allied members, but that which has been reserved by the individual members is intangible by the common Government or the individual members composing it. To attempt it finds no support in the principles of our Constitution.

It should be our constant and earnest endeavor mutually to cultivate a spirit of concord and harmony among the various parts of our Confederacy. Experience has abundantly taught us that the agitation by citizens of one part of the Union of a subject not confided to the General Government, but exclusively under the guardianship of the local authorities, is productive of no other consequences than bitterness, alienation, discord, and injury to the very cause which is intended to be advanced. Of all the great interests which appertain to our country, that of union—cordial, confiding, fraternal union—is by far the most important, since it is the only true and sure guaranty of all others.

In consequence of the embarrassed state of business and the currency, some of the States may meet with difficulty in their financial concerns. However deeply we may regret anything imprudent or excessive in the engagements into which States have entered for purposes of their own, it does not become us to disparage the States governments, nor to discourage them from making proper efforts for their own relief. On the contrary, it is our duty to encourage them to the extent of our constitutional authority to apply their best means and cheerfully to make all necessary sacrifices and submit to all necessary burdens to fulfill their engagements and maintain their credit, for the character and credit of the several States form a part of the character and credit of the whole country. The resources of the country are abundant, the enterprise and activity of our people proverbial, and we may well hope that wise legislation and prudent administration by the respective governments, each acting within its own sphere, will restore former prosperity.

Unpleasant and even dangerous as collisions may sometimes be between the constituted authorities of the citizens of our country in relation to the lines which separate their respective jurisdictions, the results can be of no vital injury to our institutions if that ardent patriotism, that devoted attachment to liberty, that spirit of moderation and forbearance for which our countrymen were once distinguished, continue to be cherished. If this continues to be the ruling passion of our souls, the weaker feeling of the mistaken enthusiast will be corrected, the Utopian dreams of the scheming politician dissipated, and the complicated intrigues of the demagogue rendered harmless.

The spirit of liberty is the sovereign balm for every injury which our institutions may receive. On the contrary, no care that can be used in the construction of our Government, no division of powers, no distribution of checks in its several departments, will prove effectual to keep us a free people if this spirit is suffered to decay; and decay it will without constant nurture. To the neglect of this duty the best historians agree in attributing the ruin of all the republics with whose existence and fall their writings have made us acquainted. The same causes will ever produce the same effects, and as long as the love of power is a dominant passion of the human bosom, and as long as the understandings of men can be warped and their affections changed by operations upon their passions and prejudices, so long will the liberties of a people depend on their own constant attention to its preservation. The danger to all well-established free governments arises from the unwillingness of the people to believe in its existence or from the influence of designing men diverting their attention from the quarter whence it approaches to a source from which it can never come. This is the old trick of those who would usurp the government of their country. In the name of democracy they speak, warning the people against the influence of wealth and the danger of aristocracy. History, ancient and modern, is full of such examples. Caesar became the master of the Roman people and the senate under the pretense of supporting the democratic claims of the former against the aristocracy of the latter; Cromwell, in the character of protector of the liberties of the people, became the dictator of England, and Bolivar possessed himself of unlimited power with the title of his country's liberator. There is, on the contrary, no instance on record of an extensive and well-established republic being changed into an aristocracy. The tendencies of all such governments in their decline is to monarchy, and the antagonist principle to liberty there is the spirit of faction—a spirit which assumes the character and in times of great excitement imposes itself upon the people as the genuine spirit of freedom, and, like the false Christs whose coming was foretold by the Savior, seeks to, and were it possible would, impose upon the true and most faithful disciples of liberty. It is in periods like this that it behooves the people to be most watchful of those to whom they have intrusted power. And although there is at times much difficulty in distinguishing the false from the true spirit, a calm and dispassionate investigation will detect the counterfeit, as well by the character of its operations as the results that are produced. The true spirit of liberty, although devoted, persevering, bold, and uncompromising in principle, that secured is mild and tolerant and scrupulous as to the means it employs, whilst the spirit of party, assuming to be that of liberty, is harsh, vindictive, and intolerant, and totally reckless as to the character of the allies which it brings to the aid of its cause. When the genuine spirit of liberty animates the body of a people to a thorough examination of their affairs, it leads to the excision of every excrescence which may have fastened itself upon any of the departments of the government, and restores the system to its pristine health and beauty. But the reign of an intolerant spirit of party amongst a free people seldom fails to result in a dangerous accession to the executive power introduced and established amidst unusual professions of devotion to democracy.

The foregoing remarks relate almost exclusively to matters connected with our domestic concerns. It may be proper, however, that I should give some indications to my fellow-citizens of my proposed course of conduct in the management of our foreign relations. I assure them, therefore, that it is my intention to use every means in my power to preserve the friendly intercourse which now so happily subsists with every foreign nation, and that although, of course, not well informed as to the state of pending negotiations with any of them, I see in the personal characters of the sovereigns, as well as in the mutual interests of our own and of the governments with which our relations are most intimate, a pleasing guaranty that the harmony so important to the interests of their subjects as well as of our citizens will not be interrupted by the advancement of any claim or pretension upon their part to which our honor would not permit us to yield. Long the defender of my country's rights in the field, I trust that my fellow-citizens will not see in my earnest desire to preserve peace with foreign powers any indication that their rights will ever be sacrificed or the honor of the nation tarnished by any admission on the part of their Chief Magistrate unworthy of their former glory. In our intercourse with our aboriginal neighbors the same liberality and justice which marked the course prescribed to me by two of my illustrious predecessors when acting under their direction in the discharge of the duties of superintendent and commissioner shall be strictly observed. I can conceive of no more sublime spectacle, none more likely to propitiate an impartial and common Creator, than a rigid adherence to the principles of justice on the part of a powerful nation in its transactions with a weaker and uncivilized people whom circumstances have placed at its disposal.

Before concluding, fellow-citizens, I must say something to you on the subject of the parties at this time existing in our country. To me it appears perfectly clear that the interest of that country requires that the violence of the spirit by which those parties are at this time governed must be greatly mitigated, if not entirely extinguished, or consequences will ensue which are appalling to be thought of.

If parties in a republic are necessary to secure a degree of vigilance sufficient to keep the public functionaries within the bounds of law and duty, at that point their usefulness ends. Beyond that they become destructive of public virtue, the parent of a spirit antagonist to that of liberty, and eventually its inevitable conqueror. We have examples of republics where the love of country and of liberty at one time were the dominant passions of the whole mass of citizens, and yet, with the continuance of the name and forms of free government, not a vestige of these qualities remaining in the bosoms of any one of its citizens. It was the beautiful remark of a distinguished English writer that "in the Roman senate Octavius had a party and Anthony a party, but the Commonwealth had none." Yet the senate continued to meet in the temple of liberty to talk of the sacredness and beauty of the Commonwealth and gaze at the statues of the elder Brutus and of the Curtii and Decii, and the people assembled in the forum, not, as in the days of Camillus and the Scipios, to cast their free votes for annual magistrates or pass upon the acts of the senate, but to receive from the hands of the leaders of the respective parties their share of the spoils and to shout for one or the other, as those collected in Gaul or Egypt and the lesser Asia would furnish the larger dividend. The spirit of liberty had fled, and, avoiding the abodes of civilized man, had sought protection in the wilds of Scythia or Scandinavia; and so under the operation of the same causes and influences it will fly from our Capitol and our forums. A calamity so awful, not only to our country, but to the world, must be deprecated by every patriot and every tendency to a state of things likely to produce it immediately checked. Such a tendency has existed—does exist. Always the friend of my countrymen, never their flatterer, it becomes my duty to say to them from this high place to which their partiality has exalted me that there exists in the land a spirit hostile to their best interests—hostile to liberty itself. It is a spirit contracted in its views, selfish in its objects. It looks to the aggrandizement of a few even to the destruction of the interests of the whole. The entire remedy is with the people. Something, however, may be effected by the means which they have placed in my hands. It is union that we want, not of a party for the sake of that party, but a union of the whole country for the sake of the whole country, for the defense of its interests and its honor against foreign aggression, for the defense of those principles for which our ancestors so gloriously contended. As far as it depends upon me it shall be accomplished. All the influence that I possess shall be exerted to prevent the formation at least of an Executive party in the halls of the legislative body. I wish for the support of no member of that body to any measure of mine that does not satisfy his judgment and his sense of duty to those from whom he holds his appointment, nor any confidence in advance from the people but that asked for by Mr. Jefferson, "to give firmness and effect to the legal administration of their affairs."

I deem the present occasion sufficiently important and solemn to justify me in expressing to my fellow-citizens a profound reverence for the Christian religion and a thorough conviction that sound morals, religious liberty, and a just sense of religious responsibility are essentially connected with all true and lasting happiness; and to that good Being who has blessed us by the gifts of civil and religious freedom, who watched over and prospered the labors of our fathers and has hitherto preserved to us institutions far exceeding in excellence those of any other people, let us unite in fervently commending every interest of our beloved country in all future time.

Fellow-citizens, being fully invested with that high office to which the partiality of my countrymen has called me, I now take an affectionate leave of you. You will bear with you to your homes the remembrance of the pledge I have this day given to discharge all the high duties of my exalted station according to the best of my ability, and I shall enter upon their performance with entire confidence in the support of a just and generous people.

# JOHN TYLER
## ADDRESS UPON ASSUMING
## THE OFFICE OF PRESIDENT
## FRIDAY, APRIL 9, 1841

Fellow-citizens:

Before my arrival at the seat of Government the painful communication was made to you by the officers presiding over the several Departments of the deeply regretted death of William Henry Harrison, late President of the United States. Upon him you had conferred your suffrages for the first office in your gift, and had selected him as your chosen instrument to correct and reform all such errors and abuses as had manifested themselves from time to time in the practical operation of the Government. While standing at the threshold of this great work he has by the dispensation of an all-wise Providence been removed from amongst us, and by the provisions of the Constitution the efforts to be directed to the accomplishing of this vitally important task have devolved upon myself. This same occurrence has subjected the wisdom and sufficiency of our institutions to a new test. For the first time in our history the person elected to the Vice-Presidency of the United States, by the happening of a contingency provided for in the Constitution, has had devolved upon him the Presidential office. The spirit of faction, which is directly opposed to the spirit of a lofty patriotism, may find in this occasion for assaults upon my Administration; and in succeeding, under circumstances so sudden and unexpected and to responsibilities so greatly augmented, to the administration of public affairs I shall place in the intelligence and patriotism of the people my only sure reliance. My earnest prayer shall be constantly addressed to the all-wise and all-powerful Being who made me, and by whose dispensation I am called to the high office of President of this Confederacy, understandingly to carry out the principles of that Constitution which I have sworn "to protect, preserve, and defend."

The usual opportunity which is afforded to a Chief Magistrate upon his induction to office of presenting to his countrymen an exposition of the policy which would guide his Administration, in the form of an inaugural address, not having, under the peculiar circumstances which have brought me to the discharge of the high duties of President of the United States, been afforded to me, a brief exposition of the principles which will govern me in the general course of my administration of public affairs would seem to be due as well to myself as to you.

In regard to foreign nations, the groundwork of my policy will be justice on our part to all, submitting to injustice from none. While I shall sedulously cultivate the relations of peace and amity with one and all, it will be my most imperative duty to see that the honor of the country shall sustain no blemish. With a view to this, the condition of our military defenses will become a matter of anxious solicitude. The Army, which has in other days covered itself with renown, and the Navy, not inappropriately termed the right arm of the public defense, which has spread a light of glory over the American standard in all the waters of the earth, should be rendered replete with efficiency.

In view of the fact, well avouched by history, that the tendency of all human institutions is to concentrate power in the hands of a single man, and that their ultimate downfall has proceeded from this cause, I deem it of the most essential importance that a complete separation should take place between the sword and the purse. No matter where or how the public moneys shall be deposited, so long as the President can exert the power of appointing and removing at his pleasure the agents selected for their custody the Commander in Chief of the Army and Navy is in fact the treasurer. A permanent and radical change should therefore be decreed. The patronage incident to the Presidential office, already great, is constantly increasing. Such increase is destined to keep pace with the growth of our population, until, without a figure of speech, an army of officeholders may be spread over the land. The unrestrained power exerted by a selfishly ambitious man in order either to perpetuate his authority or to hand it over to some favorite as his successor may lead to the employment of all the means within his control to accomplish his object. The right to remove from office, while subjected to no just restraint, is inevitably destined to produce a spirit of crouching servility with the official corps, which, in order to uphold the hand which feeds them, would lead to direct and active interference in the elections, both State and Federal, thereby subjecting the course of State legislation to the dictation of the chief executive officer and making the will of that officer absolute and supreme. I will at a proper time invoke the action of Congress upon this subject, and shall readily acquiesce in the adoption of all proper measures which are calculated to arrest these evils, so full of danger in their tendency. I will remove no incumbent from office who has faithfully and honestly acquitted himself of the duties of his office, except in such cases where such officer has been guilty of an active partisanship or by secret means—the less manly, and therefore the more objectionable has given his official influence to the purposes of party, thereby bringing the patronage of the Government in conflict with the freedom of elections. Numerous removals may become necessary under this rule. These will be made by me through no acerbity of feeling—I have had no cause to cherish or indulge unkind feelings toward any—but my conduct will be regulated by a profound sense of what is due to the country and its institutions; nor shall I neglect to apply the same unbending rule to those of my own appointment. Freedom of opinion will be tolerated, the full enjoyment of the right of suffrage will be maintained as the birthright of every American citizen; but I say emphatically to the official corps, "Thus far and no farther." I have dwelt the longer upon this subject because removals from office are likely often to arise, and I would have my countrymen to understand the principle of the Executive action.

In all public expenditures the most rigid economy should be resorted to, and, as one of its results, a public debt in time of peace be sedulously avoided. A wise and patriotic constituency will never object to the imposition of necessary burdens for useful ends, and true wisdom dictates the resort to such means in order to supply deficiencies in the revenue, rather than to those doubtful expedients which, ultimating in a public debt, serve to embarrass the resources of the country and to lessen its ability to meet any great emergency which may arise. All sinecures should be abolished. The appropriations should be direct and explicit, so as to leave as limited a share of discretion to the disbursing agents as may be found compatible with the public service. A strict responsibility on the part of all the agents of the Government should be maintained and peculation or defalcation visited with immediate expulsion from office and the most condign punishment.

The public interest also demands that if any war has existed between the Government and the currency it shall cease. Measures of a financial character now having the sanction of legal enactment shall be faithfully enforced until repealed by the legislative authority. But I owe it to myself to declare that I regard existing enactments as unwise and impolitic and in a high degree oppressive. I shall promptly give my sanction to any constitutional measure which, originating in Congress, shall have for its object the restoration of a sound circulating medium, so essentially necessary to give confidence in all the transactions of life, to secure to industry its just and adequate rewards, and to reestablish the public prosperity. In deciding upon the adaptation of any such measure to the end proposed, as well as its conformity to the Constitution, I shall resort to the fathers of the great republican school for advice and instruction, to be drawn from their sage views of our system of government and the light of their ever-glorious example.

The institutions under which we live, my countrymen, secure each person in the perfect enjoyment of all his rights. The spectacle is exhibited to the world of a government deriving its powers from the consent of the governed and having imparted to it only so much power as is necessary for its successful operation. Those who are charged with its administration should carefully abstain from all attempts to enlarge the range of powers thus granted to the several departments of the Government other than by an appeal to the people for additional grants, lest by so doing they disturb that balance which the patriots and statesmen who framed the Constitution designed to establish between the Federal Government and the States composing the Union. The observance of these rules is enjoined upon us by that feeling of reverence and affection which finds a place in the heart of every patriot for the preservation of union and the blessings of union—for the good of our children and our children's children through countless generations. An opposite course could not fail to generate factions intent upon the gratification of their selfish ends, to give birth to local and sectional jealousies, and to ultimate either in breaking asunder the bonds of union or in building up a central system which would inevitably end in a bloody scepter and an iron crown.

In conclusion I beg you to be assured that I shall exert myself to carry the foregoing principles into practice during my administration of the Government, and, confiding in the protecting care of an everwatchful and overruling Providence, it shall be my first and highest duty to preserve unimpaired the free institutions under which we live and transmit them to those who shall succeed me in their full force and vigor.

# JAMES K. POLK
## INAUGURAL ADDRESS
### TUESDAY, MARCH 4, 1845

Fellow-Citizens:

Without solicitation on my part, I have been chosen by the free and voluntary suffrages of my countrymen to the most honorable and most responsible office on earth. I am deeply impressed with gratitude for the confidence reposed in me. Honored with this distinguished consideration at an earlier period of life than any of my predecessors, I can not disguise the diffidence with which I am about to enter on the discharge of my official duties.

If the more aged and experienced men who have filled the office of President of the United States even in the infancy of the Republic distrusted their ability to discharge the duties of that exalted station, what ought not to be the apprehensions of one so much younger and less endowed now that our domain extends from ocean to ocean, that our people have so greatly increased in numbers, and at a time when so great diversity of opinion prevails in regard to the principles and policy which should characterize the administration of our Government? Well may the boldest fear and the wisest tremble when incurring responsibilities on which may depend our country's peace and prosperity, and in some degree the hopes and happiness of the whole human family.

In assuming responsibilities so vast I fervently invoke the aid of that Almighty Ruler of the Universe in whose hands are the destinies of nations and of men to guard this Heaven-favored land against the mischiefs which without His guidance might arise from an unwise public policy. With a firm reliance upon the wisdom of Omnipotence to sustain and direct me in the path of duty which I am appointed to pursue, I stand in the presence of this assembled multitude of my countrymen to take upon myself the solemn obligation "to the best of my ability to preserve, protect, and defend the Constitution of the United States."

A concise enumeration of the principles which will guide me in the administrative policy of the Government is not only in accordance with the examples set me by all my predecessors, but is eminently befitting the occasion.

The Constitution itself, plainly written as it is, the safeguard of our federative compact, the offspring of concession and compromise, binding together in the bonds of peace and union this great and increasing family of free and independent States, will be the chart by which I shall be directed.

It will be my first care to administer the Government in the true spirit of that instrument, and to assume no powers not expressly granted or clearly implied in its terms. The Government of the United States is one of delegated and limited powers, and it is by a strict adherence to the clearly granted powers and by abstaining from the exercise of doubtful or unauthorized implied powers that we have the only sure guaranty against the recurrence of those unfortunate collisions between the Federal and State authorities which have occasionally so much disturbed the harmony of our system and even threatened the perpetuity of our glorious Union.

"To the States, respectively, or to the people" have been reserved "the powers not delegated to the United States by the Constitution nor prohibited by it to the States." Each State is a complete sovereignty within the sphere of its reserved powers. The Government of the Union, acting within the sphere of its delegated authority, is also a complete sovereignty. While the General Government should abstain from the exercise of authority not clearly delegated to it, the States should be equally careful that in the maintenance of their rights they do not overstep the limits of powers reserved to them. One of the most distinguished of my predecessors attached deserved importance to "the support of the State governments in all their rights, as the most competent administration for our domestic concerns and the surest bulwark against antirepublican tendencies," and to the "preservation of the General Government in its whole constitutional vigor, as the sheet anchor of our peace at home and safety abroad."

To the Government of the United States has been intrusted the exclusive management of our foreign affairs. Beyond that it wields a few general enumerated powers. It does not force reform on the

States. It leaves individuals, over whom it casts its protecting influence, entirely free to improve their own condition by the legitimate exercise of all their mental and physical powers. It is a common protector of each and all the States; of every man who lives upon our soil, whether of native or foreign birth; of every religious sect, in their worship of the Almighty according to the dictates of their own conscience; of every shade of opinion, and the most free inquiry; of every art, trade, and occupation consistent with the laws of the States. And we rejoice in the general happiness, prosperity, and advancement of our country, which have been the offspring of freedom, and not of power.

This most admirable and wisest system of well-regulated self-government among men ever devised by human minds has been tested by its successful operation for more than half a century, and if preserved from the usurpations of the Federal Government on the one hand and the exercise by the States of powers not reserved to them on the other, will, I fervently hope and believe, endure for ages to come and dispense the blessings of civil and religious liberty to distant generations. To effect objects so dear to every patriot I shall devote myself with anxious solicitude. It will be my desire to guard against that most fruitful source of danger to the harmonious action of our system which consists in substituting the mere discretion and caprice of the Executive or of majorities in the legislative department of the Government for powers which have been withheld from the Federal Government by the Constitution. By the theory of our Government majorities rule, but this right is not an arbitrary or unlimited one. It is a right to be exercised in subordination to the Constitution and in conformity to it. One great object of the Constitution was to restrain majorities from oppressing minorities or encroaching upon their just rights. Minorities have a right to appeal to the Constitution as a shield against such oppression.

That the blessings of liberty which our Constitution secures may be enjoyed alike by minorities and majorities, the Executive has been wisely invested with a qualified veto upon the acts of the Legislature. It is a negative power, and is conservative in its character. It arrests for the time hasty, inconsiderate, or unconstitutional legislation, invites reconsideration, and transfers questions at issue between the legislative and executive departments to the tribunal of the people.

Like all other powers, it is subject to be abused. When judiciously and properly exercised, the Constitution itself may be saved from infraction and the rights of all preserved and protected.

The inestimable value of our Federal Union is felt and acknowledged by all. By this system of united and confederated States our people are permitted collectively and individually to seek their own happiness in their own way, and the consequences have been most auspicious. Since the Union was formed the number of the States has increased from thirteen to twenty-eight; two of these have taken their position as members of the Confederacy within the last week. Our population has increased from three to twenty millions. New communities and States are seeking protection under its aegis, and multitudes from the Old World are flocking to our shores to participate in its blessings. Beneath its benign sway peace and prosperity prevail. Freed from the burdens and miseries of war, our trade and intercourse have extended throughout the world. Mind, no longer tasked in devising means to accomplish or resist schemes of ambition, usurpation, or conquest, is devoting itself to man's true interests in developing his faculties and powers and the capacity of nature to minister to his enjoyments. Genius is free to announce its inventions and discoveries, and the hand is free to accomplish whatever the head conceives not incompatible with the rights of a fellow-being. All distinctions of birth or of rank have been abolished. All citizens, whether native or adopted, are placed upon terms of precise equality. All are entitled to equal rights and equal protection. No union exists between church and state, and perfect freedom of opinion is guaranteed to all sects and creeds.

These are some of the blessings secured to our happy land by our Federal Union. To perpetuate them it is our sacred duty to preserve it. Who shall assign limits to the achievements of free minds and free hands under the protection of this glorious Union? No treason to mankind since the organization of society would be equal in atrocity to that of him who would lift his hand to destroy it. He would overthrow the noblest structure of human wisdom, which protects himself and his fellow-man. He would stop the progress of free government and involve his country either in anarchy or despotism. He would extinguish the fire of liberty, which warms and animates the hearts of happy millions and invites all the nations of the earth to imitate our example. If he say that error and wrong are committed in the administration of the Government, let him remember that nothing human can be perfect, and that under no other system of government revealed by Heaven or devised by man has reason been allowed so free and broad a scope to combat error. Has the sword of despots proved to be a safer or surer instrument of reform in government than enlightened reason? Does he expect to find among the ruins of this Union a happier abode for our swarming millions than they now have under it? Every lover of his country must shudder at the thought of the possibility of its dissolution, and will be ready to adopt the patriotic sentiment, "Our Federal Union—it must be preserved." To preserve it the compromises which alone enabled our fathers to form a common constitution for the government and protection of so many States and distinct communities, of such diversified habits, interests, and domestic institutions, must be sacredly and religiously observed. Any attempt to disturb or destroy these compromises, being terms of the compact of union, can lead to none other than the most ruinous and disastrous consequences.

It is a source of deep regret that in some sections of our country misguided persons have occasionally indulged in schemes and agitations whose object is the destruction of domestic institutions existing in other sections—institutions which existed at the adoption of the Constitution and were recognized and protected by it. All must see that if it were possible for them to be successful in attaining their object the dissolution of the Union and the consequent destruction of our happy form of government must speedily follow.

I am happy to believe that at every period of our existence as a nation there has existed, and continues to exist, among the great mass of our people a devotion to the Union of the States which will shield and protect it against the moral treason of any who would seriously contemplate its destruction. To secure a continuance of that devotion the compromises of the Constitution must not only be preserved, but sectional jealousies and heartburnings must be discountenanced, and all should remember that they are members of the same political family, having a common destiny. To increase the attachment of our people to the Union, our laws should be just. Any policy which shall tend to favor monopolies or the peculiar interests of sections or classes must operate to the prejudice of the interest of their fellow-citizens, and should be avoided. If the compromises of the Constitution be preserved, if sectional jealousies and heartburnings be discountenanced, if our laws be just and the Government be practically administered strictly within the limits of power prescribed to it, we may discard all apprehensions for the safety of the Union.

With these views of the nature, character, and objects of the Government and the value of the Union, I shall steadily oppose the creation of those institutions and systems which in their nature tend to pervert it from its legitimate purposes and make it the instrument of sections, classes, and individuals. We need no national banks or other extraneous institutions planted around the Government to control or strengthen it in opposition to the will of its authors. Experience has taught us how unnecessary they are as auxiliaries of the public authorities—how impotent for good and how powerful for mischief.

Ours was intended to be a plain and frugal government, and I shall regard it to be my duty to recommend to Congress and, as far as the Executive is concerned, to enforce by all the means within my power the strictest economy in the expenditure of the public money which may be compatible with the public interests.

A national debt has become almost an institution of European monarchies. It is viewed in some of them as an essential prop to existing governments. Melancholy is the condition of that people whose government can be sustained only by a system which periodically transfers large amounts from the labor of the many to the coffers of the few. Such a system is incompatible with the ends for which our republican Government was instituted. Under a wise policy the debts contracted in our Revolution and during the War of 1812 have been happily extinguished. By a judicious application of the revenues not required for other necessary purposes, it is not doubted that the debt which has grown out of the circumstances of the last few years may be speedily paid off.

I congratulate my fellow-citizens on the entire restoration of the credit of the General Government of the Union and that of many of the States. Happy would it be for the indebted States if they were freed from their liabilities, many of which were incautiously contracted. Although the Government of the Union is neither in a legal nor a moral sense bound for the debts of the States, and it would be a violation of our compact of union to assume them, yet we can not but feel a deep interest in seeing all the States meet their public liabilities and pay off their just debts at the earliest practicable period. That they will do so as soon as it can be done without imposing too heavy burdens on their citizens there is no reason to doubt. The sound moral and honorable feeling of the people of the indebted States can not be questioned, and we are happy to perceive a settled disposition on their part, as their ability returns after a season of unexampled pecuniary embarrassment, to pay off all just demands and to acquiesce in any reasonable measures to accomplish that object.

One of the difficulties which we have had to encounter in the practical administration of the Government consists in the adjustment of our revenue laws and the levy of the taxes necessary for the support of Government. In the general proposition that no more money shall be collected than the necessities of an economical administration shall require all parties seem to acquiesce. Nor does there seem to be any material difference of opinion as to the absence of right in the Government to tax one section of country, or one class of citizens, or one occupation, for the mere profit of another. "Justice and sound policy forbid the Federal Government to foster one branch of industry to the detriment of another, or to cherish the interests of one portion to the injury of another portion of our common country." I have heretofore declared to my fellow-citizens that "in my judgment it is the duty of the Government to extend, as far as it may be practicable to do so, by its revenue laws and all other means within its power, fair and just protection to all of the great interests of the whole Union, embracing agriculture, manufactures, the mechanic arts, commerce, and navigation." I have also declared my opinion to be "in favor of a tariff for revenue," and that "in adjusting the details of such a tariff I have sanctioned such moderate discriminating duties as would produce the amount of revenue needed and at the same time afford reasonable incidental protection to our home industry," and that I was "opposed to a tariff for protection merely, and not for revenue."

The power "to lay and collect taxes, duties, imposts, and excises" was an indispensable one to be conferred on the Federal Government, which without it would possess no means of providing for its own support. In executing this power by levying a tariff of duties for the support of Government, the raising of revenue should be the object and protection the incident. To reverse this principle and make protection the object and revenue the incident would be to inflict manifest injustice upon all other than the protected interests. In levying duties for revenue it is doubtless proper to make such discriminations within the revenue principle as will afford incidental protection to our home interests. Within the revenue limit there is a discretion to discriminate; beyond that limit the rightful exercise of the power is not conceded. The incidental protection afforded to our home interests by discriminations within the revenue range it is believed will be ample. In making discriminations all our home interests should as far as practicable be equally protected. The largest portion of our people are agriculturists. Others are employed in manufactures, commerce, navigation, and the mechanic arts. They are all engaged in their respective pursuits and their joint labors constitute the national or home industry. To tax one branch of this home industry for the benefit of another would be unjust. No one of these interests can rightfully claim an advantage over the others, or to be enriched by impoverishing the others. All are equally entitled to the fostering care and protection of the Government. In exercising a sound discretion in levying discriminating duties within the limit prescribed, care should be taken that it be done in a manner not to benefit the wealthy few at the expense of the toiling millions by taxing lowest the luxuries of life, or articles of superior quality and high price, which can only be consumed by the wealthy, and highest the necessaries of life, or articles of coarse quality and low price, which the poor and great mass of our people must consume. The burdens of government should as far as practicable be distributed justly and equally among all classes of our population. These general views, long entertained on this subject, I have deemed it proper to reiterate. It is a subject upon which conflicting interests of sections and occupations are supposed to exist, and a spirit of mutual concession and compromise in adjusting its details should be cherished by every part of our widespread country as the only means of preserving harmony and a cheerful acquiescence of all in the operation of our revenue laws. Our patriotic citizens in every part of the Union will readily submit to the payment of such taxes as shall be needed for the support of their Government, whether in peace or in war, if they are so levied as to distribute the burdens as equally as possible among them.

The Republic of Texas has made known her desire to come into our Union, to form a part of our Confederacy and enjoy with us the blessings of liberty secured and guaranteed by our Constitution. Texas was once a part of our country—was unwisely ceded away to a foreign power—is now independent, and possesses an undoubted right to dispose of a part or the whole of her territory and to merge her sovereignty as a separate and independent state in ours. I congratulate my country that by an act of the late Congress of the United States the assent of this Government has been given to the reunion, and it only remains for the two countries to agree upon the terms to consummate an object so important to both.

I regard the question of annexation as belonging exclusively to the United States and Texas. They are independent powers competent to contract, and foreign nations have no right to interfere with them or to take exceptions to their reunion. Foreign powers do not seem to appreciate the true character of our Government. Our Union is a confederation of independent States, whose policy is peace with each other and all the world. To enlarge its limits is to extend the dominions of peace over additional territories and increasing millions. The world has nothing to fear from military ambition in our Government. While the Chief Magistrate and the popular branch of Congress are elected for short terms by the suffrages of those millions who must in their own persons bear all the burdens and miseries of war, our Government can not be otherwise than pacific. Foreign powers should therefore look on the annexation of Texas to the United States not as the conquest of a nation seeking to extend her dominions by arms and violence, but as the peaceful acquisition of a territory once her own, by adding another member to our confederation, with the consent of that member, thereby diminishing the chances of war and opening to them new and ever-increasing markets for their products.

To Texas the reunion is important, because the strong protecting arm of our Government would be extended over her, and the vast resources of her fertile soil and genial climate would be speedily developed, while the safety of New Orleans and of our whole southwestern frontier against hostile aggression, as well as the interests of the whole Union, would be promoted by it.

In the earlier stages of our national existence the opinion prevailed with some that our system of confederated States could not operate successfully over an extended territory, and serious objections have at different times been made to the enlargement of our boundaries. These objections were earnestly urged when we acquired Louisiana. Experience has shown that they were not well founded. The title of numerous Indian tribes to vast tracts of country has been extinguished; new States have been admitted into the Union; new Territories have been created and our jurisdiction and laws extended over them. As our population has expanded, the Union has been cemented and strengthened. As our boundaries have been enlarged and our agricultural population has been spread over a large surface, our federative system has acquired additional strength and security. It may well be doubted whether it would not be in greater danger of overthrow if our present population were confined to the comparatively narrow limits of the original thirteen States than it is now that they are sparsely settled over a more expanded territory. It is confidently believed that our system may be safely extended to the utmost bounds of our territorial limits, and that as it shall be extended the bonds of our Union, so far from being weakened, will become stronger.

None can fail to see the danger to our safety and future peace if Texas remains an independent state or becomes an ally or dependency of some foreign nation more powerful than herself. Is there one among our citizens who would not prefer perpetual peace with Texas to occasional wars, which so often occur between bordering independent nations? Is there one who would not prefer free intercourse with her to high duties on all our products and manufactures which enter her ports or cross her frontiers? Is there one who would not prefer an unrestricted communication with her citizens to the frontier obstructions which must occur if she remains out of the Union? Whatever is good or evil in the local institutions of Texas will remain her own whether annexed to the United States or not. None of the present States will be responsible for them any more than they are for the local institutions of each other. They have confederated together for certain specified objects. Upon the same principle that they would refuse to form a perpetual union with Texas because of her local institutions our forefathers would have been prevented from forming our present Union. Perceiving no valid objection to the measure and many reasons for its adoption vitally affecting the peace, the safety, and the prosperity of both countries, I shall on the broad principle which formed the basis and produced the adoption of our Constitution, and not in any narrow spirit of sectional policy, endeavor by all constitutional, honorable, and appropriate means to consummate the expressed will of the people and Government of the United States by the reannexation of Texas to our Union at the earliest practicable period.

Nor will it become in a less degree my duty to assert and maintain by all constitutional means the right of the United States to that portion of our territory which lies beyond the Rocky Mountains. Our title to the country of the Oregon is "clear and unquestionable," and already are our people preparing to perfect that title by occupying it with their wives and children. But eighty years ago our population was confined on the west by the ridge of the Alleghanies. Within that period—within the lifetime, I might say, of some of my hearers— our people, increasing to many millions, have filled the eastern valley of the Mississippi, adventurously ascended the Missouri to its headsprings, and are already engaged in establishing the blessings of self-government in valleys of which the rivers flow to the Pacific. The world beholds the peaceful triumphs of the industry of our emigrants. To us belongs the duty of protecting them adequately wherever they may be upon our soil. The jurisdiction of our laws and the benefits of our republican institutions should be extended over them in the distant regions which they have selected for their homes. The increasing facilities of intercourse will easily bring the States, of which the formation in that part of our territory can not be long delayed, within the sphere of our federative Union. In the meantime every obligation imposed by treaty or conventional stipulations should be sacredly respected.

In the management of our foreign relations it will be my aim to observe a careful respect for the rights of other nations, while our own will be the subject of constant watchfulness. Equal and exact justice should characterize all our intercourse with foreign countries. All alliances having a tendency to jeopard the welfare and honor of our country or sacrifice any one of the national interests will be studiously avoided, and yet no opportunity will be lost to cultivate a favorable understanding with foreign governments by which our navigation and commerce may be extended and the ample products of our fertile soil, as well as the manufactures of our skillful artisans, find a ready market and remunerating prices in foreign countries.

In taking "care that the laws be faithfully executed," a strict performance of duty will be exacted from all public officers. From those officers, especially, who are charged with the collection and disbursement of the public revenue will prompt and rigid accountability be required. Any culpable failure or delay on their part to account for the moneys intrusted to them at the times and in the manner required by law will in every instance terminate the official connection of such defaulting officer with the Government.

Although in our country the Chief Magistrate must almost of necessity be chosen by a party and stand pledged to its principles and measures, yet in his official action he should not be the President of a part only, but of the whole people of the United States. While he executes the laws with an impartial hand, shrinks from no proper responsibility, and faithfully carries out in the executive department of the Government the principles and policy of those who have chosen him, he should not be unmindful that our fellow-citizens who have differed with him in opinion are entitled to the full and free exercise of their opinions and judgments, and that the rights of all are entitled to respect and regard.

Confidently relying upon the aid and assistance of the coordinate departments of the Government in conducting our public affairs, I enter upon the discharge of the high duties which have been assigned me by the people, again humbly supplicating that Divine Being who has watched over and protected our beloved country from its infancy to the present hour to continue His gracious benedictions upon us, that we may continue to be a prosperous and happy people.

## ZACHARY TAYLOR
## INAUGURAL ADDRESS
## MONDAY, MARCH 5, 1849

E lected by the American people to the highest office known to our laws, I appear here to take the oath prescribed by the Constitution, and, in compliance with a time-honored custom, to address those who are now assembled.

The confidence and respect shown by my countrymen in calling me to be the Chief Magistrate of a Republic holding a high rank among the nations of the earth have inspired me with feelings of the most profound gratitude; but when I reflect that the acceptance of the office which their partiality has bestowed imposes the discharge of the most arduous duties and involves the weightiest obligations, I am conscious that the position which I have been called to fill, though sufficient to satisfy the loftiest ambition, is surrounded by fearful responsibilities. Happily, however, in the performance of my new duties I shall not be without able cooperation. The legislative and judicial branches of the Government present prominent examples of distinguished civil attainments and matured experience, and it shall be my endeavor to call to my assistance in the Executive Departments individuals whose talents, integrity, and purity of character will furnish ample guaranties for the faithful and honorable performance of the trusts to be committed to their charge. With such aids and an honest purpose to do whatever is right, I hope to execute diligently, impartially, and for the best interests of the country the manifold duties devolved upon me.

In the discharge of these duties my guide will be the Constitution, which I this day swear to "preserve, protect, and defend." For the interpretation of that instrument I shall look to the decisions of the judicial tribunals established by its authority and to the practice of the Government under the earlier Presidents, who had so large a share in its formation. To the example of those illustrious patriots I shall always defer with reverence, and especially to his example who was by so many titles "the Father of his Country."

To command the Army and Navy of the United States; with the advice and consent of the Senate, to make treaties and to appoint ambassadors and other officers; to give to Congress information of the state of the Union and recommend such measures as he shall judge to be necessary; and to take care that the laws shall be faithfully executed—these are the most important functions intrusted to the President by the Constitution, and it may be expected that I shall briefly indicate the principles which will control me in their execution.

Chosen by the body of the people under the assurance that my Administration would be devoted to the welfare of the whole country, and not to the support of any particular section or merely local interest, I this day renew the declarations I have heretofore made and proclaim my fixed determination to maintain to the extent of my ability the Government in its original purity and to adopt as the basis of my public policy those great republican doctrines which constitute the strength of our national existence.

In reference to the Army and Navy, lately employed with so much distinction on active service, care shall be taken to insure the highest condition of efficiency, and in furtherance of that object the military and naval schools, sustained by the liberality of Congress, shall receive the special attention of the Executive.

As American freemen we can not but sympathize in all efforts to extend the blessings of civil and political liberty, but at the same time we are warned by the admonitions of history and the voice of our own beloved Washington to abstain from entangling alliances with foreign nations. In all disputes between conflicting governments it is our interest not less than our duty to remain strictly neutral, while our geographical position, the genius of our institutions and our people, the advancing spirit of civilization, and, above all, the dictates of religion direct us to the cultivation of peaceful and friendly relations with all other powers. It is to be hoped that no international question can now arise which a government confident in its own strength and resolved to protect its own just rights may not settle by wise negotiation; and it eminently becomes a government like our own, founded on the morality and intelligence of its citizens and upheld by their affections, to exhaust every resort of honorable diplomacy before appealing to arms. In the conduct of our foreign relations I shall conform to these views, as I believe them essential to the best interests and the true honor of the country.

The appointing power vested in the President imposes delicate and onerous duties. So far as it is possible to be informed, I shall make honesty, capacity, and fidelity indispensable prerequisites to the bestowal of office, and the absence of either of these qualities shall be deemed sufficient cause for removal.

It shall be my study to recommend such constitutional measures to Congress as may be necessary and proper to secure encouragement and protection to the great interests of agriculture, commerce, and manufactures, to improve our rivers and harbors, to provide for the speedy extinguishment of the public debt, to enforce a strict accountability on the part of all officers of the Government and the utmost economy in all public expenditures; but it is for the wisdom of Congress itself, in which all legislative powers are vested by the Constitution, to regulate these and other matters of domestic policy. I shall look with confidence to the enlightened patriotism of that body to adopt such measures of conciliation as may harmonize conflicting interests and tend to perpetuate that Union which should be the paramount object of our hopes and affections. In any action calculated to promote an object so near the heart of everyone who truly loves his country I will zealously unite with the coordinate branches of the Government.

In conclusion I congratulate you, my fellow-citizens, upon the high state of prosperity to which the goodness of Divine Providence has conducted our common country. Let us invoke a continuance of the same protecting care which has led us from small beginnings to the eminence we this day occupy, and let us seek to deserve that continuance by prudence and moderation in our councils, by well-directed attempts to assuage the bitterness which too often marks unavoidable differences of opinion, by the promulgation and practice of just and liberal principles, and by an enlarged patriotism, which shall acknowledge no limits but those of our own widespread Republic.

# MILLARD FILLMORE
## FIRST ANNUAL MESSAGE
### MONDAY, DECEMBER 2, 1850

Fellow-Citizens of the Senate and of the House of Representatives: Being suddenly called in the midst of the last session of Congress by a painful dispensation of Divine Providence to the responsible station which I now hold, I contented myself with such communications to the Legislature as the exigency of the moment seemed to require. The country was shrouded in mourning for the loss of its venerable Chief Magistrate and all hearts were penetrated with grief. Neither the time nor the occasion appeared to require or to justify on my part any general expression of political opinions or any announcement of the principles which would govern me in the discharge of the duties to the performance of which I had been so unexpectedly called. I trust, therefore, that it may not be deemed inappropriate if I avail myself of this opportunity of the reassembling of Congress to make known my sentiments in a general manner in regard to the policy which ought to be pursued by the Government both in its intercourse with foreign nations and its management and administration of internal affairs.

Nations, like individuals in a state of nature, are equal and independent, possessing certain rights and owing certain duties to each other, arising from their necessary and unavoidable relations; which rights and duties there is no common human authority to protect and enforce. Still, they are rights and duties, binding in morals, in conscience, and in honor, although there is no tribunal to which an injured party can appeal but the disinterested judgment of mankind, and ultimately the arbitrament of the sword.

Among the acknowledged rights of nations is that which each possesses of establishing that form of government which it may deem most conducive to the happiness and prosperity of its own citizens, of changing that form as circumstances may require, and of managing its internal affairs according to its own will. The people of the United States claim this right for themselves, and they readily concede it to others. Hence it becomes an imperative duty not to interfere in the government or internal policy of other nations; and although we may sympathize with the unfortunate or the oppressed everywhere in their struggles for freedom, our principles forbid us from taking any part in such foreign contests. We make no wars to promote or to prevent successions to thrones, to maintain any theory of a balance of power, or to suppress the actual government which any country chooses to establish for itself. We instigate no revolutions, nor suffer any hostile military expeditions to be fitted out in the United States to invade the territory or provinces of a friendly nation. The great law of morality ought to have a national as well as a personal and individual application. We should act toward other nations as we wish them to act toward us, and justice and conscience should form the rule of conduct between governments, instead of mere power, self interest, or the desire of aggrandizement. To maintain a strict neutrality in foreign wars, to cultivate friendly relations, to reciprocate every noble and generous act, and to perform punctually and scrupulously every treaty obligation—these are the duties which we owe to other states, and by the performance of which we best entitle ourselves to like treatment from them; or, if that, in any case, be refused, we can enforce our own rights with justice and a clear conscience.

In our domestic policy the Constitution will be my guide, and in questions of doubt I shall look for its interpretation to the judicial decisions of that tribunal which was established to expound it and to the usage of the Government, sanctioned by the acquiescence of the country. I regard all its provisions as equally binding. In all its parts it is the will of the people expressed in the most solemn form, and the constituted authorities are but agents to carry that will into effect. Every power which it has granted is to be exercised for the public good; but no pretense of utility, no honest conviction, even, of what might be expedient, can justify the assumption of any power not granted. The powers conferred upon the Government and their distribution to the several departments are as clearly expressed in that sacred instrument as the imperfection of human language will allow, and I deem it my first duty not to question its wisdom, add to its provisions, evade its requirements, or nullify its commands.

Upon you, fellow-citizens, as the representatives of the States and the people, is wisely devolved the legislative power. I shall comply with my duty in laying before you from time to time any information calculated to enable you to discharge your high and responsible trust for the benefit of our common constituents.

My opinions will be frankly expressed upon the leading subjects of legislation; and if—which I do not anticipate—any act should pass the two Houses of Congress which should appear to me unconstitutional, or an encroachment on the just powers of other departments, or with provisions hastily adopted and likely to produce consequences injurious and unforeseen, I should not shrink from the duty of returning it to you, with my reasons, for your further consideration. Beyond the due performance of these constitutional obligations, both my respect for the Legislature and my sense of propriety will restrain me from any attempt to control or influence your proceedings. With you is the power, the honor, and the responsibility of the legislation of the country.

The Government of the United States is a limited Government. It is confined to the exercise of powers expressly granted and such others as may be necessary for carrying those powers into effect; and it is at all times an especial duty to guard against any infringement on the just rights of the States. Over the objects and subjects intrusted to Congress its legislative authority is supreme. But here that authority ceases, and every citizen who truly loves the Constitution and desires the continuance of its existence and its blessings will resolutely and firmly resist any interference in those domestic affairs which the Constitution has dearly and unequivocally left to the exclusive authority of the States. And every such citizen will also deprecate useless irritation among the several members of the Union and all reproach and crimination tending to alienate one portion of the country from another. The beauty of our system of government consists, and its safety and durability must consist, in avoiding mutual collisions and encroachments and in the regular separate action of all, while each is revolving in its own distinct orbit.

The Constitution has made it the duty of the President to take care that the laws be faithfully executed. In a government like ours, in which all laws are passed by a majority of the representatives of the people, and these representatives are chosen for such short periods that any injurious or obnoxious law can very soon be repealed, it would appear unlikely that any great numbers should be found ready to resist the execution of the laws. But it must be borne in mind that the country is extensive; that there may be local interests or prejudices rendering a law odious in one part which is not so in another, and that the thoughtless and inconsiderate, misled by their passions or their imaginations, may be induced madly to resist such laws as they disapprove. Such persons should recollect that without law there can be no real practical liberty; that when law is trampled under foot tyranny rules, whether it appears in the form of a military despotism or of popular violence. The law is the only sure protection of the weak and the only efficient restraint upon the strong. When impartially and faithfully administered, none is beneath its protection and none above its control. You, gentlemen, and the country may be assured that to the utmost of my ability and to the extent of the power vested in me I shall at all times and in all places take care that the laws be faithfully executed. In the discharge of this duty, solemnly imposed upon me by the Constitution and by my oath of office, I shall shrink from no responsibility, and shall endeavor to meet events as they may arise with firmness, as well as with prudence and discretion.

The appointing power is one of the most delicate with which the Executive is invested. I regard it as a sacred trust, to be exercised with the sole view of advancing the prosperity and happiness of the people. It shall be my effort to elevate the standard of official employment by selecting for places of importance individuals fitted for the posts to which they are assigned by their known integrity, talents, and virtues. In so extensive a country, with so great a population, and where few persons appointed to office can be known to the appointing power, mistakes will sometimes unavoidably happen and unfortunate appointments be made notwithstanding the greatest care. In such cases the power of removal may be properly exercised; and neglect of duty or malfeasance in office will be no more tolerated in individuals appointed by myself than in those appointed by others.

I am happy in being able to say that no unfavorable change in our foreign relations has taken place since the message at the opening of the last session of Congress. We are at peace with all nations and we enjoy in an eminent degree the blessings of that peace in a prosperous and growing commerce and in all the forms of amicable national intercourse. The unexampled growth of the country, the present amount of its population, and its ample means of self-protection assure for it the respect of all nations, while it is trusted that its character for justice and a regard to the rights of other States will cause that respect to be readily and cheerfully paid.

A convention was negotiated between the United States and Great Britain in April last for facilitating and protecting the construction of a ship canal between the Atlantic and Pacific oceans and for other purposes. The instrument has since been ratified by the contracting parties, the exchange of ratifications has been effected, and proclamation thereof has been duly made.

In addition to the stipulations contained in this convention, two other objects remain to be accomplished between the contracting powers: First. The designation and establishment of a free port at each end of the canal.

Second. An agreement fixing the distance from the shore within which belligerent maritime operations shall not be carried on. On these points there is little doubt that the two Governments will come to an understanding.

The company of citizens of the United States who have acquired from the State of Nicaragua the privilege of constructing a ship canal between the two oceans through the territory of that State have made progress in their preliminary arrangements. The treaty between the United States and Great Britain of the 19th of April last, above referred to, being now in operation, it is to be hoped that the guaranties which it offers will be sufficient to secure the completion of the work with all practicable expedition. It is obvious that this result would be indefinitely postponed if any other than peaceful measures for the purpose of harmonizing conflicting claims to territory in that quarter should be adopted. It will consequently be my endeavor to cause any further negotiations on the part of this Government which may be requisite for this purpose to be so conducted as to bring them to a speedy and successful close.

Some unavoidable delay has occurred, arising from distance and the difficulty of intercourse between this Government and that of Nicaragua, but as intelligence has just been received of the appointment of an envoy extraordinary and minister plenipotentiary of that Government to reside at Washington, whose arrival may soon be expected, it is hoped that no further impediments will be experienced in the prompt transaction of business between the two Governments.

Citizens of the United States have undertaken the connection of the two oceans by means of a railroad across the Isthmus of Tehuantepec, under grants of the Mexican Government to a citizen of that Republic. It is understood that a thorough survey of the course of the communication is in preparation, and there is every reason to expect that it will be prosecuted with characteristic energy, especially when that Government shall have consented to such stipulations with the Government of the United States as may be necessary to impart a feeling of security to those who may embark their property in the enterprise. Negotiations are pending for the accomplishment of that object, and a hope is confidently entertained that when the Government of Mexico shall become duly sensible of the advantages which that country can not fail to derive from the work, and learn that the Government of the United States desires that the right of sovereignty of Mexico in the Isthmus shall remain unimpaired, the stipulations referred to will be agreed to with alacrity.

By the last advices from Mexico it would appear, however, that that Government entertains strong objections to some of the stipulations which the parties concerned in the project of the railroad deem necessary for their protection and security. Further consideration, it is to be hoped, or some modification of terms, may yet reconcile the differences existing between the two Governments in this respect.

Fresh instructions have recently been given to the minister of the United States in Mexico, who is prosecuting the subject with promptitude and ability.

Although the negotiations with Portugal for the payment of claims of citizens of the United States against that Government have not yet resulted in a formal treaty, yet a proposition, made by the Government of Portugal for the final adjustment and payment of those claims, has recently been accepted on the part of the United States. It gives me pleasure to say that Mr. Clay, to whom the negotiation on the part of the United States had been intrusted, discharged the duties of his appointment with ability and discretion, acting always within the instructions of his Government.

It is expected that a regular convention will be immediately negotiated for carrying the agreement between the two Governments into effect. The commissioner appointed under the act of Congress for carrying into effect the convention with Brazil of the 27th of January, 1849, has entered upon the performance of the duties imposed upon him by that act. It is hoped that those duties may be completed within the time which it prescribes. The documents, however, which the Imperial Government, by the third article of the convention, stipulates to furnish to the Government of the United States have not yet been received. As it is presumed that those documents will be essential for the correct disposition of the claims, it may become necessary for Congress to extend the period limited for the duration of the commission. The sum stipulated by the fourth article of the convention to be paid to this Government has been received.

The collection in the ports of the United States of discriminating duties upon the vessels of Chili and their cargoes has been suspended, pursuant to the provisions of the act of Congress of the 24th of May, 1828. It is to be hoped that this measure will impart a fresh impulse to the commerce between the two countries, which of late, and especially since our acquisition of California, has, to the mutual advantage of the parties, been much augmented.

Peruvian guano has become so desirable an article to the agricultural interest of the United States that it is the duty of the Government to employ all the means properly in its power for the purpose of causing that article to be imported into the country at a reasonable price. Nothing will be omitted on my part toward accomplishing this desirable end. I am persuaded that in removing any restraints on this traffic the Peruvian Government will promote its own best interests, while it will afford a proof of a friendly disposition toward this country, which will be duly appreciated.

The treaty between the United States and His Majesty the King of the Hawaiian Islands, which has recently been made public, will, it is believed, have a beneficial effect upon the relations between the two countries.

The relations between those parts of the island of St. Domingo which were formerly colonies of Spain and France, respectively, are still in an unsettled condition. The proximity of that island to the United States and the delicate questions involved in the existing controversy there render it desirable that it should be permanently and speedily adjusted. The interests of humanity and of general commerce also demand this; and as intimations of the same sentiment have been received from other governments, it is hoped that some plan may soon be devised to effect the object in a manner likely to give general satisfaction. The Government of the United States will not fail, by the exercise of all proper friendly offices, to do all in its power to put an end to the destructive war which has raged between the different parts of the island and to secure to them both the benefits of peace and commerce.

I refer you to the report of the Secretary of the Treasury for a detailed statement of the finances.

The total receipts into the Treasury for the year ending 30th of June last were $47,421,748.90. The total expenditures during the same period were $43,002,168.90. The public debt has been reduced since the last annual report from the Treasury Department $495,276.79.

By the nineteenth section of the act of 28th January, 1847, the proceeds of the sales of the public lands were pledged for the interest and principal of the public debt. The great amount of those lands subsequently granted by Congress for military bounties will, it is believed, very nearly supply the public demand for several years to come, and but little reliance can, therefore, be placed on that hitherto fruitful source of revenue. Aside from the permanent annual expenditures, which have necessarily largely increased, a portion of the public debt, amounting to $8,075,986.59, must be provided for within the next two fiscal years. It is most desirable that these accruing demands should be met without resorting to new loans.

All experience has demonstrated the wisdom and policy of raising a large portion of revenue for the support of Government from duties on goods imported. The power to lay these duties is unquestionable, and its chief object, of course, is to replenish the Treasury. But if in doing this an incidental advantage may be gained by encouraging the industry of our own citizens, it is our duty to avail ourselves of that advantage.

A duty laid upon an article which can not be produced in this country, such as tea or coffee, adds to the cost of the article, and is chiefly or wholly paid by the consumer. But a duty laid upon an article which may be produced here stimulates the skill and industry of our own country to produce the same article, which is brought into the market in competition with the foreign article, and the importer is thus compelled to reduce his price to that at which the domestic article can be sold, thereby throwing a part of the duty upon the producer of the foreign article. The continuance of this process creates the skill and invites the capital which finally enable us to produce the article much cheaper than it could have been procured from abroad, thereby benefiting both the producer and the consumer at home. The consequence of this is that the artisan and the agriculturist are brought together, each affords a ready market for the produce of the other, the whole country becomes prosperous, and the ability to produce every necessary of life renders us independent in war as well as in peace.

A high tariff can never be permanent. It will cause dissatisfaction, and will be changed. It excludes competition, and thereby invites the investment of capital in manufactures to such excess that when changed it brings distress, bankruptcy, and ruin upon all who have been misled by its faithless protection. What the manufacturer wants is uniformity and permanency, that he may feel a confidence that he is not to be ruined by sudden exchanges. But to make a tariff uniform and permanent it is not only necessary that the laws should not be altered, but that the duty should not fluctuate. To effect this all duties should be specific wherever the nature of the article is such as to admit of it. Ad valorem duties fluctuate with the price and offer strong temptations to fraud and perjury. Specific duties, on the contrary, are equal and uniform in all ports and at all times, and offer a strong inducement to the importer to bring the best article, as he pays no more duty upon that than upon one of inferior quality. I therefore strongly recommend a modification of the present tariff, which has prostrated some of our most important and necessary manufactures, and that specific duties be imposed sufficient to raise the requisite revenue, making such discriminations in favor of the industrial pursuits of our own country as to encourage home production without excluding foreign competition. It is also important that an unfortunate provision in the present tariff, which imposes a much higher duty upon the raw material that enters into our manufactures than upon the manufactured article, should be remedied.

The papers accompanying the report of the Secretary of the Treasury will disclose frauds attempted upon the revenue, in variety and amount so great as to justify the conclusion that it is impossible under any system of ad valorem duties levied upon the foreign cost or value of the article to secure an honest observance and an effectual administration of the laws. The fraudulent devices to evade the law which have been detected by the vigilance of the appraisers leave no room to doubt that similar impositions not discovered, to a large amount, have been successfully practiced since the enactment of the law now in force. This state of things has already had a prejudicial influence upon those engaged in foreign commerce. It has a tendency to drive the honest trader from the business of importing and to throw that important branch of employment into the hands of unscrupulous and dishonest men, who are alike regardless of law and the obligations of an oath. By these means the plain intentions of Congress, as expressed in the law, are daily defeated. Every motive of policy and duty, therefore, impels me to ask the earnest attention of Congress to this subject. If Congress should deem it unwise to attempt any important changes in the system of levying duties at this session, it will become indispensable to the protection of the revenue that such remedies as in the judgment of Congress may mitigate the evils complained of should be at once applied.

As before stated, specific duties would, in my opinion, afford the most perfect remedy for this evil; but if you should not concur in this view, then, as a partial remedy, I beg leave respectfully to recommend that instead of taking the invoice of the article abroad as a means of determining its value here, the correctness of which invoice it is in many cases impossible to verify, the law be so changed as to require a home valuation or appraisal, to be regulated in such manner as to give, as far as practicable, uniformity in the several ports.

There being no mint in California, I am informed that the laborers in the mines are compelled to dispose of their gold dust at a large discount. This appears to me to be a heavy and unjust tax upon the labor of those employed in extracting this precious metal, and I doubt not you will be disposed at the earliest period possible to relieve them from it by the establishment of a mint. In the meantime, as an assayer's office is established there, I would respectfully submit for your consideration the propriety of authorizing gold bullion which has been assayed and stamped to be received in payment of Government dues. I can not conceive that the Treasury would suffer any less by such a provision, which will at once raise bullion to its par value, and thereby save (if I am rightly informed) many millions of dollars to the laborers which are now paid in brokerage to convert this precious metal into available funds. This discount upon their hard earnings is a heavy tax, and every effort should be made by the Government to relieve them from so great a burden.

More than three-fourths of our population are engaged in the cultivation of the soil. The commercial, manufacturing, and navigating interests are all to a great extent dependent on the agricultural. It is therefore the most important interest of the nation, and has a just claim to the fostering care and protection of the Government so far as they can be extended consistently with the provisions of the Constitution. As this can not be done by the ordinary modes of legislation, I respectfully recommend the establishment of an agricultural bureau, to be charged with the duty of giving to this leading branch of American industry the encouragement which it so well deserves. In view of the immense mineral resources of our country, provision should also be made for the employment of a competent mineralogist and chemist, who should be required, under the direction of the head of the bureau, to collect specimens of the various minerals of our country and to ascertain by careful analysis their respective elements and properties and their adaptation to useful purposes. He should also be required to examine and report upon the qualities of different soils and the manures best calculated to improve their productiveness. By publishing the results of such experiments, with suitable explanations, and by the collection and distribution of rare seeds and plants, with instructions as to the best system of cultivation, much may be done to promote this great national interest.

In compliance with the act of Congress passed on the 23d of May, 1850, providing, among other things, for taking the Seventh Census, a superintendent was appointed and all other measures adopted which were deemed necessary to insure the prompt and faithful performance of that duty. The appropriation already made will, it is believed, be sufficient to defray the whole expense of the work, but further legislation may be necessary in regard to the compensation of some of the marshals of the Territories. It will also be proper to make provision by law at an early day for the publication of such abstracts of the returns as the public interests may require.

The unprecedented growth of our territories on the Pacific in wealth and population and the consequent increase of their social and commercial relations with the Atlantic States seem to render it the duty of the Government to use all its constitutional power to improve the means of intercourse with them. The importance of opening "a line of communication, the best and most expeditious of which the nature of the country will admit," between the Valley of the Mississippi and the Pacific was brought to your notice by my predecessor in his annual message; and as the reasons which he presented in favor of the measure still exist in full force, I beg leave to call your attention to them and to repeat the recommendations then made by him.

The uncertainty which exists in regard to the validity of land titles in California is a subject which demands your early consideration. Large bodies of land in that State are claimed under grants said to have been made by authority of the Spanish and Mexican Governments. Many of these have not been perfected, others have been revoked, and some are believed to be fraudulent. But until they shall have been judicially investigated they will continue to retard the settlement and improvement of the country. I therefore respectfully recommend that provision be made by law for the appointment of commissioners to examine all such claims with a view to their final adjustment.

I also beg leave to call your attention to the propriety of extending at an early day our system of land laws, with such modifications as may be necessary, over the State of California and the Territories of Utah and New Mexico. The mineral lands of California will, of course, form an exception to any general system which may be adopted. Various methods of disposing of them have been suggested. I was at first inclined to favor the system of leasing, as it seemed to promise the largest revenue to the Government and to afford the best security against monopolies; but further reflection and our experience in leasing the lead mines and selling lands upon credit have brought my mind to the conclusion that there would be great difficulty in collecting the rents, and that the relation of debtor and creditor between the citizens and the Government would be attended with many mischievous consequences. I therefore recommend that instead of retaining the mineral lands under the permanent control of the Government they be divided into small parcels and sold, under such restrictions as to quantity and time as will insure the best price and guard most effectually against combinations of capitalists to obtain monopolies.

The annexation of Texas and the acquisition of California and New Mexico have given increased importance to our Indian relations. The various tribes brought under our jurisdiction by these enlargements of our boundaries are estimated to embrace a population of 124,000. Texas and New Mexico are surrounded by powerful tribes of Indians, who are a source of constant terror and annoyance to the inhabitants. Separating into small predatory bands, and always mounted, they overrun the country, devastating farms, destroying crops, driving off whole herds of cattle, and occasionally murdering the inhabitants or carrying them into captivity. The great roads leading into the country are infested with them, whereby traveling is rendered extremely dangerous and immigration is almost entirely arrested. The Mexican frontier, which by the eleventh article of the treaty of Guadalupe Hidalgo we are bound to protect against the Indians within our border, is exposed to these incursions equally with our own. The military force stationed in that country, although forming a large proportion of the Army, is represented as entirely inadequate to our own protection and the fulfillment of our treaty stipulations with Mexico. The principal deficiency is in cavalry, and I recommend that Congress should, at as early a period as practicable, provide for the raising of one or more regiments of mounted men.

For further suggestions on this subject and others connected with our domestic interests and the defense of our frontier, I refer you to the reports of the Secretary of the Interior and of the Secretary of War.

I commend also to your favorable consideration the suggestion contained in the last-mentioned report and in the letter of the General in Chief relative to the establishment of an asylum for the relief of disabled and destitute soldiers. This subject appeals so strongly to your sympathies that it would be superfluous in me to say anything more than barely to express my cordial approbation of the proposed object.

The Navy continues to give protection to our commerce and other national interests in the different quarters of the globe, and, with the exception of a single steamer on the Northern lakes, the vessels in commission are distributed in six different squadrons.

The report of the head of that Department will exhibit the services of these squadrons and of the several vessels employed in each during the past year. It is a source of gratification that, while they have been constantly prepared for any hostile emergency, they have everywhere met with the respect and courtesy due as well to the dignity as to the peaceful dispositions and just purposes of the nation.

The two brigantines accepted by the Government from a generous citizen of New York and placed under the command of an officer of the Navy to proceed to the Arctic Seas in quest of the British commander Sir John Franklin and his companions, in compliance with the act of Congress approved in May last, had when last heard from penetrated into a high northern latitude; but the success of this noble and humane enterprise is yet uncertain.

I invite your attention to the view of our present naval establishment and resources presented in the report of the Secretary of the Navy, and the suggestions therein made for its improvement, together with the naval policy recommended for the security of our Pacific Coast and the protection and extension of our commerce with eastern Asia. Our facilities for a larger participation in the trade of the East, by means of our recent settlements on the shores of the Pacific, are too obvious to be overlooked or disregarded.

The questions in relation to rank in the Army and Navy and relative rank between officers of the two branches of the service, presented to the Executive by certain resolutions of the House of Representatives at the last session of Congress, have been submitted to a board of officers in each branch of the service, and their report may be expected at an early day.

I also earnestly recommend the enactment of a law authorizing officers of the Army and Navy to be retired from the service when incompetent for its vigorous and active duties, taking care to make suitable provision for those who have faithfully served their country and awarding distinctions by retaining in appropriate commands those who have been particularly conspicuous for gallantry and good conduct. While the obligation of the country to maintain and honor those who, to the exclusion of other pursuits, have devoted themselves to its arduous service is acknowledged, this obligation should not be permitted to interfere with the efficiency of the service itself.

I am gratified in being able to state that the estimates of expenditure for the Navy in the ensuing year are less by more than $1,000,000 than those of the present, excepting the appropriation which may become necessary for the construction of a dock on the coast of the Pacific, propositions for which are now being considered and on which a special report may be expected early in your present session.

There is an evident justness in the suggestion of the same report that appropriations for the naval service proper should be separated from those for fixed and permanent objects, such as building docks and navy yards and the fixtures attached, and from the extraordinary objects under the care of the Department which, however important, are not essentially naval.

A revision of the code for the government of the Navy seems to require the immediate consideration of Congress. Its system of crimes and punishments had undergone no change for half a century until the last session, though its defects have been often and ably pointed out; and the abolition of a particular species of corporal punishment, which then took place, without providing any substitute, has left the service in a state of defectiveness which calls for prompt correction. I therefore recommend that the whole subject be revised without delay and such a system established for the enforcement of discipline as shall be at once humane and effectual.

The accompanying report of the Postmaster-General presents a satisfactory view of the operations and condition of that Department. At the close of the last fiscal year the length of the inland mail routes in the United States (not embracing the service in Oregon and California) was 178,672 miles, the annual transportation thereon 46,541,423 miles, and the annual cost of such transportation $2,724,426. The increase of the annual transportation over that of the preceding year was 3,997,354 miles and the increase in cost was $342,440. The number of post-offices in the United States on the 1st day of July last was 18,417, being an increase of 1,670 during the preceding year.

The gross revenues of the Department for the fiscal year ending June 30, 1850, amounted to $5,552,971.48, including the annual appropriation of $200,000 for the franked matter of the Departments and excluding the foreign postages collected for and payable to the British Government.

The expenditures for the same period were $5,212,953.43, leaving a balance of revenue over expenditures of $340,018.05.

I am happy to find that the fiscal condition of the Department is such as to justify the Postmaster-General in recommending the reduction of our inland letter postage to 3 cents the single letter when prepaid and 5 cents when not prepaid. He also recommends that the prepaid rate shall be reduced to 2 cents whenever the revenues of the Department, after the reduction, shall exceed its expenditures by more than 5 per cent for two consecutive years; that the postage upon California and other letters sent by our ocean steamers shall be much reduced, and that the rates of postage on newspapers, pamphlets, periodicals, and other printed matter shall be modified and some reduction thereon made.

It can not be doubted that the proposed reductions will for the present diminish the revenues of the Department. It is believed that the deficiency, after the surplus already accumulated shall be exhausted, may be almost wholly met either by abolishing the existing privileges of sending free matter through the mails or by paying out of the Treasury to the Post-Office Department a sum equivalent to the postage of which it is deprived by such privileges. The last is supposed to be the preferable mode, and will, if not entirely, so nearly supply that deficiency as to make any further appropriation that may be found necessary so inconsiderable as to form no obstacle to the proposed reductions.

I entertain no doubt of the authority of Congress to make appropriations for leading objects in that class of public works comprising what are usually called works of internal improvement. This authority I suppose to be derived chiefly from the power of regulating commerce with foreign nations and among the States and the power of laying and collecting imposts. Where commerce is to be carried on and imposts collected there must be ports and harbors as well as wharves and custom-houses. If ships laden with valuable cargoes approach the shore or sail along the coast, light-houses are necessary at suitable points for the protection of life and property. Other facilities and securities for commerce and navigation are hardly less important; and those clauses of the Constitution, therefore, to which I have referred have received from the origin of the Government a liberal and beneficial construction. Not only have light-houses, buoys, and beacons been established and floating lights maintained, but harbors have been cleared and improved, piers constructed, and even breakwaters for the safety of shipping and sea walls to protect harbors from being filled up and rendered useless by the action of the ocean, have been erected at very great expense. And this construction of the Constitution appears the more reasonable from the consideration that if these works, of such evident importance and utility, are not to be accomplished by Congress they can not be accomplished at all. By the adoption of the Constitution the several States voluntarily parted with the power of collecting duties of imposts in their own ports, and it is not to be expected that they should raise money by internal taxation, direct or indirect, for the benefit of that commerce the revenues derived from which do not, either in whole or in part, go into their own treasuries. Nor do I perceive any difference between the power of Congress to make appropriations for objects of this kind on the ocean and the power to make appropriations for similar objects on lakes and rivers, wherever they are large enough to bear on their waters an extensive traffic. The magnificent Mississippi and its tributaries and the vast lakes of the North and Northwest appear to me to fall within the exercise of the power as justly and as clearly as the ocean and the Gulf of Mexico. It is a mistake to regard expenditures judiciously made for these objects as expenditures for local purposes. The position or sight of the work is necessarily local, but its utility is general. A ship canal around the Falls of St. Mary of less than a mile in length, though local in its construction, would yet be national in its purpose and its benefits, as it would remove the only obstruction to a navigation of more than 1,000 miles, affecting several States, as well as our commercial relations with Canada. So, too, the breakwater at the mouth of the Delaware is erected, not for the exclusive benefit of the States bordering on the bay and river of that name, but for that of the whole coastwise navigation of the United States and, to a considerable extent, also of foreign commerce. If a ship be lost on the bar at the entrance of a Southern port for want of sufficient depth of water, it is very likely to be a Northern ship; and if a steamboat be sunk in any part of the Mississippi on account of its channel not having been properly cleared of obstructions, it may be a boat belonging to either of eight or ten States. I may add, as somewhat remarkable, that among all the thirty-one States there is none that is not to a greater or less extent bounded on the ocean, or the Gulf of Mexico, or one of the Great Lakes, or some navigable river.

In fulfilling our constitutional duties, fellow-citizens, on this subject, as in carrying into effect all other powers conferred by the Constitution, we should consider ourselves as deliberating and acting for one and the same country, and bear constantly in mind that our regard and our duty are due not to a particular part only, but to the whole.

I therefore recommend that appropriations be made for completing such works as have been already begun and for commencing such others as may seem to the wisdom of Congress to be of public and general importance.

The difficulties and delays incident to the settlement of private claims by Congress amount in many cases to a denial of justice. There is reason to apprehend that many unfortunate creditors of the Government have thereby been unavoidably ruined. Congress has so much business of a public character that it is impossible it should give much attention to mere private claims, and their accumulation is now so great that many claimants must despair of ever being able to obtain a hearing. It may well be doubted whether Congress, from the nature of its organization, is properly constituted to decide upon such cases. It is impossible that each member should examine the merits of every claim on which he is compelled to vote, and it is preposterous to ask a judge to decide a case which he has never heard. Such decisions may, and frequently must, do injustice either to the claimant or the

Government, and I perceive no better remedy for this growing evil than the establishment of some tribunal to adjudicate upon such claims. I beg leave, therefore, most respectfully to recommend that provision be made by law for the appointment of a commission to settle all private claims against the United States; and as an ex parte hearing must in all contested cases be very unsatisfactory, I also recommend the appointment of a solicitor, whose duty it shall be to represent the Government before such commission and protect it against all illegal, fraudulent, or unjust claims which may be presented for their adjudication. This District, which has neither voice nor vote in your deliberations, looks to you for protection and aid, and I commend all its wants to your favorable consideration, with a full confidence that you will meet them not only with justice, but with liberality. It should be borne in mind that in this city, laid out by Washington and consecrated by his name, is located the Capitol of our nation, the emblem of our Union and the symbol of our greatness. Here also are situated all the public buildings necessary for the use of the Government, and all these are exempt from taxation. It should be the pride of Americans to render this place attractive to the people of the whole Republic and convenient and safe for the transaction of the public business and the preservation of the public records. The Government should therefore bear a liberal proportion of the burdens of all necessary and useful improvements. And as nothing could contribute more to the health, comfort, and safety of the city and the security of the public buildings and records than an abundant supply of pure water, I respectfully recommend that you make such provisions for obtaining the same as in your wisdom you may deem proper.

The act, passed at your last session, making certain propositions to Texas for settling the disputed boundary between that State and the Territory of New Mexico was, immediately on its passage, transmitted by express to the governor of Texas, to be laid by him before the general assembly for its agreement thereto. Its receipt was duly acknowledged, but no official information has yet been received of the action of the general assembly thereon. It may, however, be very soon expected, as, by the terms of the propositions submitted they were to have been acted upon on or before the first day of the present month.

It was hardly to have been expected that the series of measures passed at your last session with the view of healing the sectional differences which had sprung from the slavery and territorial questions should at once have realized their beneficent purpose. All mutual concession in the nature of a compromise must necessarily be unwelcome to men of extreme opinions. And though without such concessions our Constitution could not have been formed, and can not be permanently sustained, yet we have seen them made the subject of bitter controversy in both sections of the Republic. It required many months of discussion and deliberation to secure the concurrence of a majority of Congress in their favor. It would be strange if they had been received with immediate approbation by people and States prejudiced and heated by the exciting controversies of their representatives. I believe those measures to have been required by the circumstances and condition of the country. I believe they were necessary to allay asperities and animosities that were rapidly alienating one section of the country from another and destroying those fraternal sentiments which are the strongest supports of the Constitution. They were adopted in the spirit of conciliation and for the purpose of conciliation. I believe that a great majority of our fellow citizens sympathize in that spirit and that purpose, and in the main approve and are prepared in all respects to sustain these enactments. I can not doubt that the American people, bound together by kindred blood and common traditions, still cherish a paramount regard for the Union of their fathers, and that they are ready to rebuke any attempt to violate its integrity, to disturb the compromises on which it is based, or to resist the laws which have been enacted under its authority.

The series of measures to which I have alluded are regarded by me as a settlement in principle and substance—a final settlement of the dangerous and exciting subjects which they embraced. Most of these subjects, indeed, are beyond your reach, as the legislation which disposed of them was in its character final and irrevocable. It may be presumed from the opposition which they all encountered that none of those measures was free from imperfections, but in their mutual dependence and connection they formed a system of compromise the most conciliatory and best for the entire country that could be obtained from conflicting sectional interests and opinions.

For this reason I recommend your adherence to the adjustment established by those measures until time and experience shall demonstrate the necessity of further legislation to guard against evasion or abuse.

By that adjustment we have been rescued from the wide and boundless agitation that surrounded us, and have a firm, distinct, and legal ground to rest upon. And the occasion, I trust, will justify me in exhorting my countrymen to rally upon and maintain that ground as the best, if not the only, means of restoring peace and quiet to the country and maintaining inviolate the integrity of the Union.

And now, fellow-citizens, I can not bring this communication to a close without invoking you to join me in humble and devout thanks to the Great Ruler of Nations for the multiplied blessings which He has graciously bestowed upon us. His hand, so often visible in our preservation, has stayed the pestilence, saved us from foreign wars and domestic disturbances, and scattered plenty throughout the land.

Our liberties, religions and civil, have been maintained, the fountains of knowledge have all been kept open, and means of happiness widely spread and generally enjoyed greater than have fallen to the lot of any other nation. And while deeply penetrated with gratitude for the past, let us hope that His all-wise providence will so guide our counsels as that they shall result in giving satisfaction to our constituents, securing the peace of the country, and adding new strength to the united Government under which we live.

# FRANKLIN PIERCE
## INAUGURAL ADDRESS
### FRIDAY, MARCH 4, 1853

My Countrymen:

It is a relief to feel that no heart but my own can know the personal regret and bitter sorrow over which I have been borne to a position so suitable for others rather than desirable for myself.

The circumstances under which I have been called for a limited period to preside over the destinies of the Republic fill me with a profound sense of responsibility, but with nothing like shrinking apprehension. I repair to the post assigned me not as to one sought, but in obedience to the unsolicited expression of your will, answerable only for a fearless, faithful, and diligent exercise of my best powers. I ought to be, and am, truly grateful for the rare manifestation of the nation's confidence; but this, so far from lightening my obligations, only adds to their weight. You have summoned me in my weakness; you must sustain me by your strength. When looking for the fulfillment of reasonable requirements, you will not be unmindful of the great changes which have occurred, even within the last quarter of a century, and the consequent augmentation and complexity of duties imposed in the administration both of your home and foreign affairs.

Whether the elements of inherent force in the Republic have kept pace with its unparalleled progression in territory, population, and wealth has been the subject of earnest thought and discussion on both sides of the ocean. Less than sixty-four years ago the Father of his Country made "the" then "recent accession of the important State of North Carolina to the Constitution of the United States" one of the subjects of his special congratulation. At that moment, however, when the agitation consequent upon the Revolutionary struggle had hardly subsided, when we were just emerging from the weakness and embarrassments of the Confederation, there was an evident consciousness of vigor equal to the great mission so wisely and bravely fulfilled by our fathers. It was not a presumptuous assurance, but a calm faith, springing from a clear view of the sources of power in a government constituted like ours. It is no paradox to say that although comparatively weak the new-born nation was intrinsically strong. Inconsiderable in population and apparent resources, it was upheld by a broad and intelligent comprehension of rights and an all-pervading purpose to maintain them, stronger than armaments. It came from the furnace of the Revolution, tempered to the necessities of the times. The thoughts of the men of that day were as practical as their sentiments were patriotic. They wasted no portion of their energies upon idle and delusive speculations, but with a firm and fearless step advanced beyond the governmental landmarks which had hitherto circumscribed the limits of human freedom and planted their standard, where it has stood against dangers which have threatened from abroad, and internal agitation, which has at times fearfully menaced at home. They proved themselves equal to the solution of the great problem, to understand which their minds had been illuminated by the dawning lights of the Revolution. The object sought was not a thing dreamed of; it was a thing realized. They had exhibited only the power to achieve, but, what all history affirms to be so much more unusual, the capacity to maintain. The oppressed throughout the world from that day to the present have turned their eyes hitherward, not to find those lights extinguished or to fear lest they should wane, but to be constantly cheered by their steady and increasing radiance.

In this our country has, in my judgment, thus far fulfilled its highest duty to suffering humanity. It has spoken and will continue to speak, not only by its words, but by its acts, the language of sympathy, encouragement, and hope to those who earnestly listen to tones which pronounce for the largest rational liberty. But after all, the most animating encouragement and potent appeal for freedom will be its own history—its trials and its triumphs. Preeminently, the power of our advocacy reposes in our example; but no example, be it remembered, can be powerful for lasting good, whatever apparent advantages may be gained, which is not based upon eternal principles of right and justice. Our fathers decided for themselves, both upon the hour to declare and the hour to strike. They were their own judges of the circumstances under which it became them to pledge to each other "their lives, their fortunes, and their sacred honor" for the acquisition of the priceless inheritance transmitted to us. The energy with which that great conflict was opened and, under the guidance of a manifest and beneficent Providence the uncomplaining endurance with which it was prosecuted to its consummation were only surpassed by the wisdom and patriotic spirit of concession which characterized all the counsels of the early fathers.

One of the most impressive evidences of that wisdom is to be found in the fact that the actual working of our system has dispelled a degree of solicitude which at the outset disturbed bold hearts and far-reaching intellects. The apprehension of dangers from extended territory, multiplied States, accumulated wealth, and augmented population has proved to be unfounded. The stars upon your banner have become nearly threefold their original number; your densely populated possessions skirt the shores of the two great oceans; and yet this vast increase of people and territory has not only shown itself compatible with the harmonious action of the States and Federal Government in their respective constitutional spheres, but has afforded an additional guaranty of the strength and integrity of both.

With an experience thus suggestive and cheering, the policy of my Administration will not be controlled by any timid forebodings of evil from expansion. Indeed, it is not to be disguised that our attitude as a nation and our position on the globe render the acquisition of certain possessions not within our jurisdiction eminently important for our protection, if not in the future essential for the preservation of the rights of commerce and the peace of the world. Should they be obtained, it will be through no grasping spirit, but with a view to obvious national interest and security, and in a manner entirely consistent with the strictest observance of national faith. We have nothing in our history or position to invite aggression; we have everything to beckon us to the cultivation of relations of peace and amity with all nations. Purposes, therefore, at once just and pacific will be significantly marked in the conduct of our foreign affairs. I intend that my Administration shall leave no blot upon our fair record, and trust I may safely give the assurance that no act within the legitimate scope of my constitutional control will be tolerated on the part of any portion of our citizens which can not challenge a ready justification before the tribunal of the civilized world. An Administration would be unworthy of confidence at home or respect abroad should it cease to be influenced by the conviction that no apparent advantage can be purchased at a price so dear as that of national wrong or dishonor. It is not your privilege as a nation to speak of a distant past. The striking incidents of your history, replete with instruction and furnishing abundant grounds for hopeful confidence, are comprised in a period comparatively brief. But if your past is limited, your future is boundless. Its obligations throng the unexplored pathway of advancement, and will be limitless as duration. Hence a sound and comprehensive policy should embrace not less the distant future than the urgent present.

The great objects of our pursuit as a people are best to be attained by peace, and are entirely consistent with the tranquillity and interests of the rest of mankind. With the neighboring nations upon our continent we should cultivate kindly and fraternal relations. We can desire nothing in regard to them so much as to see them consolidate their strength and pursue the paths of prosperity and happiness. If in the course of their growth we should open new channels of trade and create additional facilities for friendly intercourse, the benefits realized will be equal and mutual. Of the complicated European systems of national polity we have heretofore been independent. From their wars, their tumults, and anxieties we have been, happily, almost entirely exempt. Whilst these are confined to the nations which gave them existence, and within their legitimate jurisdiction, they can not affect us except as they appeal to our sympathies in the cause of human freedom and universal advancement. But the vast interests of commerce are common to all mankind, and the advantages of trade and international intercourse must always present a noble field for the moral influence of a great people.

With these views firmly and honestly carried out, we have a right to expect, and shall under all circumstances require, prompt reciprocity. The rights which belong to us as a nation are not alone to be regarded, but those which pertain to every citizen in his individual capacity, at home and abroad, must be sacredly maintained. So long as he can discern every star in its place upon that ensign, without wealth to purchase for him preferment or title to secure for him place, it will be his privilege, and must be his acknowledged right, to stand unabashed even in the presence of princes, with a proud consciousness that he is himself one of a nation of sovereigns and that he can not in legitimate pursuit wander so far from home that the agent whom he shall leave behind in the place which I now occupy will not see that no rude hand of power or tyrannical passion is laid upon him with impunity. He must realize that upon every sea and on every soil where our enterprise may rightfully seek the protection of our flag American citizenship is an inviolable panoply for the security of American rights. And in this connection it can hardly be necessary to reaffirm a principle which should now be regarded as fundamental. The rights, security, and repose of this Confederacy reject the idea of interference or colonization on this side of the ocean by any foreign power beyond present jurisdiction as utterly inadmissible.

The opportunities of observation furnished by my brief experience as a soldier confirmed in my own mind the opinion, entertained and acted upon by others from the formation of the Government, that the maintenance of large standing armies in our country would be not only dangerous, but unnecessary. They also illustrated the importance—I might well say the absolute necessity—of the military science and practical skill furnished in such an eminent degree by the institution which has made your Army what it is, under the discipline and instruction of officers not more distinguished for their solid attainments, gallantry, and devotion to the public service than for unobtrusive bearing and high moral tone. The Army as organized must be the nucleus around which in every time of need the strength of your military power, the sure bulwark of your defense—a national militia—may be readily formed into a well-disciplined and efficient organization. And the skill and self-devotion of the Navy assure you that you may take the performance of the past as a pledge for the future, and may confidently expect that the flag which has waved its untarnished folds over every sea will still float in undiminished honor. But these, like many other subjects, will be appropriately brought at a future time to the attention of the coordinate branches of the Government, to which I shall always look with profound respect and with trustful confidence that they will accord to me the aid and support which I shall so much need and which their experience and wisdom will readily suggest.

In the administration of domestic affairs you expect a devoted integrity in the public service and an observance of rigid economy in all departments, so marked as never justly to be questioned. If this reasonable expectation be not realized, I frankly confess that one of your leading hopes is doomed to disappointment, and that my efforts in a very important particular must result in a humiliating failure. Offices can be properly regarded only in the light of aids for the accomplishment of these objects, and as occupancy can confer no prerogative nor importunate desire for preferment any claim, the public interest imperatively demands that they be considered with sole reference to the duties to be performed. Good citizens may well claim the protection of good laws and the benign influence of good government, but a claim for office is what the people of a republic should never recognize. No reasonable man of any party will expect the Administration to be so regardless of its responsibility and of the obvious elements of success as to retain persons known to be under the influence of political hostility and partisan prejudice in positions which will require not only severe labor, but cordial cooperation. Having no implied engagements to ratify, no rewards to bestow, no resentments to remember, and no personal wishes to consult in selections for official station, I shall fulfill this difficult and delicate trust, admitting no motive as worthy either of my character or position which does not contemplate an efficient discharge of duty and the best interests of my country. I acknowledge my obligations to the masses of my countrymen, and to them alone. Higher objects than personal aggrandizement gave direction and energy to their exertions in the late canvass, and they shall not be disappointed. They require at my hands diligence, integrity, and capacity wherever there are duties to be performed. Without these qualities in their public servants, more stringent laws for the prevention or punishment of fraud, negligence, and peculation will be vain. With them they will be unnecessary.

But these are not the only points to which you look for vigilant watchfulness. The dangers of a concentration of all power in the general government of a confederacy so vast as ours are too obvious to be disregarded. You have a right, therefore, to expect your agents in every department to regard strictly the limits imposed upon them by the Constitution of the United States. The great scheme of our constitutional liberty rests upon a proper distribution of power between the State and Federal authorities, and experience has shown that the harmony and happiness of our people must depend upon a just discrimination between the separate rights and responsibilities of the States and your common rights and obligations under the General Government; and here, in my opinion, are the considerations which should form the true basis of future concord in regard to the questions which have most seriously disturbed public tranquillity. If the Federal Government will confine itself to the exercise of powers clearly granted by the Constitution, it can hardly happen that its action upon any question should endanger the institutions of the States or interfere with their right to manage matters strictly domestic according to the will of their own people.

In expressing briefly my views upon an important subject which has recently agitated the nation to almost a fearful degree, I am moved by no other impulse than a most earnest desire for the perpetuation of that Union which has made us what we are, showering upon us blessings and conferring a power and influence which our fathers could hardly have anticipated, even with their most sanguine hopes directed to a far-off future. The sentiments I now announce were not unknown before the expression of the voice which called me here. My own position upon this subject was clear and unequivocal, upon the record of my words and my acts, and it is only recurred to at this time because silence might perhaps be misconstrued. With the Union my best and dearest earthly hopes are entwined. Without it what are we individually or collectively? What becomes of the noblest field ever opened for the advancement of our race in religion, in government, in the arts, and in all that dignifies and adorns mankind? From that radiant constellation which both illumines our own way and points out to struggling nations their course, let but a single star be lost, and, if these be not utter darkness, the luster of the whole is dimmed. Do my countrymen need any assurance that such a catastrophe is not to overtake them while I possess the power to stay it? It is with me an earnest and vital belief that as the Union has been the source, under Providence, of our prosperity to this time, so it is the surest pledge of a continuance of the blessings we have enjoyed, and which we are sacredly bound to transmit undiminished to our children. The field of calm and free discussion in our country is open, and will always be so, but never has been and never can be traversed for good in a spirit of sectionalism and uncharitableness. The founders of the Republic dealt with things as they were presented to them, in a spirit of self-sacrificing patriotism, and, as time has proved, with a comprehensive wisdom which it will always be safe for us to consult. Every measure tending to strengthen the fraternal feelings of all the members of our Union has had my heartfelt approbation. To every theory of society or government, whether the offspring of feverish ambition or of morbid enthusiasm, calculated to dissolve the bonds of law and affection which unite us, I shall interpose a ready and stern resistance. I believe that involuntary servitude, as it exists in different States of this Confederacy, is recognized by the Constitution. I believe that it stands like any other admitted right, and that the States where it exists are entitled to efficient remedies to enforce the constitutional provisions. I hold that the laws of 1850, commonly called the "compromise measures," are strictly constitutional and to be unhesitatingly carried into effect. I believe that the constituted authorities of this Republic are bound to regard the rights of the South in this respect as they would view any other legal and constitutional right, and that the laws to enforce them should be respected and obeyed, not with a reluctance encouraged by abstract opinions as to their propriety in a different state of society, but cheerfully and according to the decisions of the tribunal to which their exposition belongs. Such have been, and are, my convictions, and upon them I shall act. I fervently hope that the question is at rest, and that no sectional or ambitious or fanatical excitement may again threaten the durability of our institutions or obscure the light of our prosperity.

But let not the foundation of our hope rest upon man's wisdom. It will not be sufficient that sectional prejudices find no place in the public deliberations. It will not be sufficient that the rash counsels of human passion are rejected. It must be felt that there is no national security but in the nation's humble, acknowledged dependence upon God and His overruling providence.

We have been carried in safety through a perilous crisis. Wise counsels, like those which gave us the Constitution, prevailed to uphold it. Let the period be remembered as an admonition, and not as an encouragement, in any section of the Union, to make experiments where experiments are fraught with such fearful hazard. Let it be impressed upon all hearts that, beautiful as our fabric is, no earthly power or wisdom could ever reunite its broken fragments. Standing, as I do, almost within view of the green slopes of Monticello, and, as it were, within reach of the tomb of Washington, with all the cherished memories of the past gathering around me like so many eloquent voices of exhortation from heaven, I can express no better hope for my country than that the kind Providence which smiled upon our fathers may enable their children to preserve the blessings they have inherited.

# JAMES BUCHANAN
# INAUGURAL ADDRESS
# WEDNESDAY, MARCH 4, 1857

Fellow-Citizens:

I appear before you this day to take the solemn oath "that I will faithfully execute the office of President of the United States and will to the best of my ability preserve, protect, and defend the Constitution of the United States."

In entering upon this great office I must humbly invoke the God of our fathers for wisdom and firmness to execute its high and responsible duties in such a manner as to restore harmony and ancient friendship among the people of the several States and to preserve our free institutions throughout many generations. Convinced that I owe my election to the inherent love for the Constitution and the Union which still animates the hearts of the American people, let me earnestly ask their powerful support in sustaining all just measures calculated to perpetuate these, the richest political blessings which Heaven has ever bestowed upon any nation. Having determined not to become a candidate for reelection, I shall have no motive to influence my conduct in administering the Government except the desire ably and faithfully to serve my country and to live in grateful memory of my countrymen.

We have recently passed through a Presidential contest in which the passions of our fellow-citizens were excited to the highest degree by questions of deep and vital importance; but when the people proclaimed their will the tempest at once subsided and all was calm.

The voice of the majority, speaking in the manner prescribed by the Constitution, was heard, and instant submission followed. Our own country could alone have exhibited so grand and striking a spectacle of the capacity of man for self-government.

What a happy conception, then, was it for Congress to apply this simple rule, that the will of the majority shall govern, to the settlement of the question of domestic slavery in the Territories. Congress is neither "to legislate slavery into any Territory or State nor to exclude it therefrom, but to leave the people thereof perfectly free to form and regulate their domestic institutions in their own way, subject only to the Constitution of the United States."

As a natural consequence, Congress has also prescribed that when the Territory of Kansas shall be admitted as a State it "shall be received into the Union with or without slavery, as their constitution may prescribe at the time of their admission."

A difference of opinion has arisen in regard to the point of time when the people of a Territory shall decide this question for themselves.

This is, happily, a matter of but little practical importance. Besides, it is a judicial question, which legitimately belongs to the Supreme Court of the United States, before whom it is now pending, and will, it is understood, be speedily and finally settled. To their decision, in common with all good citizens, I shall cheerfully submit, whatever this may be, though it has ever been my individual opinion that under the Nebraska-Kansas act the appropriate period will be when the number of actual residents in the Territory shall justify the formation of a constitution with a view to its admission as a State into the Union. But be this as it may, it is the imperative and indispensable duty of the Government of the United States to secure to every resident inhabitant the free and independent expression of his opinion by his vote. This sacred right of each individual must be preserved. That being accomplished, nothing can be fairer than to leave the people of a Territory free from all foreign interference to decide their own destiny for themselves, subject only to the Constitution of the United States.

The whole Territorial question being thus settled upon the principle of popular sovereignty—a principle as ancient as free government itself—everything of a practical nature has been decided. No other question remains for adjustment, because all agree that under the Constitution slavery in the States is beyond the reach of any human power except that of the respective States themselves wherein it exists. May we not, then, hope that the long agitation on this subject is approaching its end, and that the geographical parties to which it has given birth, so much dreaded by the Father of his Country, will speedily become extinct? Most happy will it be for the country when the public mind shall be diverted from this question to others of more pressing and practical importance. Throughout the whole progress of this agitation, which has scarcely known any intermission for more than twenty years, whilst it has been productive of no positive good to any human being it has been the prolific source of great evils to the master, to the slave, and to the whole country. It has alienated and estranged the people of the sister States from each other, and has even seriously endangered the very existence of the Union. Nor has the danger yet entirely ceased. Under our system there is a remedy for all mere political evils in the sound sense and sober judgment of the people. Time is a great corrective. Political subjects which but a few years ago excited and exasperated the public mind have passed away and are now nearly forgotten. But this question of domestic slavery is of far graver importance than any mere political question, because should the agitation continue it may eventually endanger the personal safety of a large portion of our countrymen where the institution exists. In that event no form of government, however admirable in itself and however productive of material benefits, can compensate for the loss of peace and domestic security around the family altar. Let every Union-loving man, therefore, exert his best influence to suppress this agitation, which since the recent legislation of Congress is without any legitimate object.

It is an evil omen of the times that men have undertaken to calculate the mere material value of the Union. Reasoned estimates have been presented of the pecuniary profits and local advantages which would result to different States and sections from its dissolution and of the comparative injuries which such an event would inflict on other States and sections. Even descending to this low and narrow view of the mighty question, all such calculations are at fault. The bare reference to a single consideration will be conclusive on this point. We at present enjoy a free trade throughout our extensive and expanding country such as the world has never witnessed. This trade is conducted on railroads and canals, on noble rivers and arms of the sea, which bind together the North and the South, the East and the West, of our Confederacy. Annihilate this trade, arrest its free progress by the geographical lines of jealous and hostile States, and you destroy the prosperity and onward march of the whole and every part and involve all in one common ruin. But such considerations, important as they are in themselves, sink into insignificance when we reflect on the terrific evils which would result from disunion to every portion of the Confederacy—to the North, not more than to the South, to the East not more than to the West. These I shall not attempt to portray, because I feel an humble confidence that the kind Providence which inspired our fathers with wisdom to frame the most perfect form of government and union ever devised by man will not suffer it to perish until it shall have been peacefully instrumental by its example in the extension of civil and religious liberty throughout the world.

Next in importance to the maintenance of the Constitution and the Union is the duty of preserving the Government free from the taint or even the suspicion of corruption. Public virtue is the vital spirit of republics, and history proves that when this has decayed and the love of money has usurped its place, although the forms of free government may remain for a season, the substance has departed forever.

Our present financial condition is without a parallel in history. No nation has ever before been embarrassed from too large a surplus in its treasury. This almost necessarily gives birth to extravagant legislation. It produces wild schemes of expenditure and begets a race of speculators and jobbers, whose ingenuity is exerted in contriving and promoting expedients to obtain public money. The purity of official agents, whether rightfully or wrongfully, is suspected, and the character of the government suffers in the estimation of the people. This is in itself a very great evil.

The natural mode of relief from this embarrassment is to appropriate the surplus in the Treasury to great national objects for which a clear warrant can be found in the Constitution. Among these I might mention the extinguishment of the public debt, a reasonable increase of the Navy, which is at present inadequate to the protection of our vast tonnage afloat, now greater than that of any other nation, as well as to the defense of our extended seacoast.

It is beyond all question the true principle that no more revenue ought to be collected from the people than the amount necessary to defray the expenses of a wise, economical, and efficient administration of the Government. To reach this point it was necessary to resort to a modification of the tariff, and this has, I trust, been accomplished in such a manner as to do as little injury as may have been practicable to our domestic manufactures, especially those necessary for the defense of the country. Any discrimination against a particular branch for the purpose of benefiting favored corporations, individuals, or interests would have been unjust to the rest of the community and inconsistent with that spirit of fairness and equality which ought to govern in the adjustment of a revenue tariff.

But the squandering of the public money sinks into comparative insignificance as a temptation to corruption when compared with the squandering of the public lands.

No nation in the tide of time has ever been blessed with so rich and noble an inheritance as we enjoy in the public lands. In administering this important trust, whilst it may be wise to grant portions of them for the improvement of the remainder, yet we should never forget that it is our cardinal policy to reserve these lands, as much as may be, for actual settlers, and this at moderate prices. We shall thus not only best promote the prosperity of the new States and Territories, by furnishing them a hardy and independent race of honest and industrious citizens, but shall secure homes for our children and our children's children, as well as for those exiles from foreign shores who may seek in this country to improve their condition and to enjoy the blessings of civil and religious liberty. Such emigrants have done much to promote the growth and prosperity of the country. They have proved faithful both in peace and in war. After becoming citizens they are entitled, under the Constitution and laws, to be placed on a perfect equality with native-born citizens, and in this character they should ever be kindly recognized.

The Federal Constitution is a grant from the States to Congress of certain specific powers, and the question whether this grant should be liberally or strictly construed has more or less divided political parties from the beginning. Without entering into the argument, I desire to state at the commencement of my Administration that long experience and observation have convinced me that a strict construction of the powers of the Government is the only true, as well as the only safe, theory of the Constitution. Whenever in our past history doubtful powers have been exercised by Congress, these have never failed to produce injurious and unhappy consequences. Many such instances might be adduced if this were the proper occasion. Neither is it necessary for the public service to strain the language of the Constitution, because all the great and useful powers required for a successful administration of the Government, both in peace and in war, have been granted, either in express terms or by the plainest implication.

Whilst deeply convinced of these truths, I yet consider it clear that under the war-making power Congress may appropriate money toward the construction of a military road when this is absolutely necessary for the defense of any State or Territory of the Union against foreign invasion. Under the Constitution Congress has power "to declare war," "to raise and support armies," "to provide and maintain a navy," and to call forth the militia to "repel invasions." Thus endowed, in an ample manner, with the war-making power, the corresponding duty is required that "the United States shall protect each of them [the States] against invasion." Now, how is it possible to afford this protection to California and our Pacific possessions except by means of a military road through the Territories of the United States, over which men and munitions of war may be speedily transported from the Atlantic States to meet and to repel the invader? In the event of a war with a naval power much stronger than our own we should then have no other available access to the Pacific Coast, because such a power would instantly close the route across the isthmus of Central America. It is impossible to conceive that whilst the Constitution has expressly required Congress to defend all the States it should yet deny to them, by any fair construction, the only possible means by which one of these States can be defended. Besides, the Government, ever since its origin, has been in the constant practice of constructing military roads. It might also be wise to consider whether the love for the Union which now animates our fellow-citizens on the Pacific Coast may not be impaired by our neglect or refusal to provide for them, in their remote and isolated condition, the only means by which the power of the States on this side of the Rocky Mountains can reach them in sufficient time to "protect" them "against invasion." I forbear for the present from expressing an opinion as to the wisest and most economical mode in which the Government can lend its aid in accomplishing this great and necessary work. I believe that many of the difficulties in the way, which now appear formidable, will in a great degree vanish as soon as the nearest and best route shall have been satisfactorily ascertained.

It may be proper that on this occasion I should make some brief remarks in regard to our rights and duties as a member of the great family of nations. In our intercourse with them there are some plain principles, approved by our own experience, from which we should never depart. We ought to cultivate peace, commerce, and friendship with all nations, and this not merely as the best means of promoting our own material interests, but in a spirit of Christian benevolence toward our fellow-men, wherever their lot may be cast. Our diplomacy should be direct and frank, neither seeking to obtain more nor accepting less than is our due. We ought to cherish a sacred regard for the independence of all nations, and never attempt to interfere in the domestic concerns of any unless this shall be imperatively required by the great law of self-preservation. To avoid entangling alliances has been a maxim of our policy ever since the days of Washington, and its wisdom no one will attempt to dispute. In short, we ought to do justice in a kindly spirit to all nations and require justice from them in return.

It is our glory that whilst other nations have extended their dominions by the sword we have never acquired any territory except by fair purchase or, as in the case of Texas, by the voluntary determination of a brave, kindred, and independent people to blend their destinies with our own. Even our acquisitions from Mexico form no exception. Unwilling to take advantage of the fortune of war against a sister republic, we purchased these possessions under the treaty of peace for a sum which was considered at the time a fair equivalent. Our past history forbids that we shall in the future acquire territory unless this be sanctioned by the laws of justice and honor. Acting on this principle, no nation will have a right to interfere or to complain if in the progress of events we shall still further extend our possessions. Hitherto in all our acquisitions the people, under the protection of the American flag, have enjoyed civil and religious liberty, as well as equal and just laws, and have been contented, prosperous, and happy. Their trade with the rest of the world has rapidly increased, and thus every commercial nation has shared largely in their successful progress.

I shall now proceed to take the oath prescribed by the Constitution, whilst humbly invoking the blessing of Divine Providence on this great people.

# ABRAHAM LINCOLN
## FIRST INAUGURAL ADDRESS
### MONDAY, MARCH 4, 1861

Fellow-Citizens of the United States:

In compliance with a custom as old as the Government itself, I appear before you to address you briefly and to take in your presence the oath prescribed by the Constitution of the United States to be taken by the President "before he enters on the execution of this office."

I do not consider it necessary at present for me to discuss those matters of administration about which there is no special anxiety or excitement.

Apprehension seems to exist among the people of the Southern States that by the accession of a Republican Administration their property and their peace and personal security are to be endangered. There has never been any reasonable cause for such apprehension. Indeed, the most ample evidence to the contrary has all the while existed and been open to their inspection. It is found in nearly all the published speeches of him who now addresses you. I do but quote from one of those speeches when I declare that—

I have no purpose, directly or indirectly, to interfere with the institution of slavery in the States where it exists. I believe I have no lawful right to do so, and I have no inclination to do so.

Those who nominated and elected me did so with full knowledge that I had made this and many similar declarations and had never recanted them; and more than this, they placed in the platform for my acceptance, and as a law to themselves and to me, the clear and emphatic resolution which I now read:

Resolved, That the maintenance inviolate of the rights of the States, and especially the right of each State to order and control its own domestic institutions according to its own judgment exclusively, is essential to that balance of power on which the perfection and endurance of our political fabric depend; and we denounce the lawless invasion by armed force of the soil of any State or Territory, no matter what pretext, as among the gravest of crimes.

I now reiterate these sentiments, and in doing so I only press upon the public attention the most conclusive evidence of which the case is susceptible that the property, peace, and security of no section are to be in any wise endangered by the now incoming Administration. I add, too, that all the protection which, consistently with the Constitution and the laws, can be given will be cheerfully given to all the States when lawfully demanded, for whatever cause—as cheerfully to one section as to another.

There is much controversy about the delivering up of fugitives from service or labor. The clause I now read is as plainly written in the Constitution as any other of its provisions:

No person held to service or labor in one State, under the laws thereof, escaping into another, shall in consequence of any law or regulation therein be discharged from such service or labor, but shall be delivered up on claim of the party to whom such service or labor may be due.

It is scarcely questioned that this provision was intended by those who made it for the reclaiming of what we call fugitive slaves; and the intention of the lawgiver is the law. All members of Congress swear their support to the whole Constitution—to this provision as much as to any other. To the proposition, then, that slaves whose cases come within the terms of this clause "shall be delivered up" their oaths are unanimous. Now, if they would make the effort in good temper, could they not with nearly equal unanimity frame and pass a law by means of which to keep good that unanimous oath?

There is some difference of opinion whether this clause should be enforced by national or by State authority, but surely that difference is not a very material one. If the slave is to be surrendered, it can be of but little consequence to him or to others by which authority it is done. And should anyone in any case be content that his oath shall go unkept on a merely unsubstantial controversy as to how it shall be kept?

Again: In any law upon this subject ought not all the safeguards of liberty known in civilized and humane jurisprudence to be introduced, so that a free man be not in any case surrendered as a slave? And might it not be well at the same time to provide by law for the enforcement of that clause in the Constitution which guarantees that "the citizens of each State shall be entitled to all privileges and immunities of citizens in the several States"?

I take the official oath today with no mental reservations and with no purpose to construe the Constitution or laws by any hypercritical rules; and while I do not choose now to specify particular acts of Congress as proper to be enforced, I do suggest that it will be much safer for all, both in official and private stations, to conform to and abide by all those acts which stand unrepealed than to violate any of them trusting to find impunity in having them held to be unconstitutional.

It is seventy-two years since the first inauguration of a President under our National Constitution. During that period fifteen different and greatly distinguished citizens have in succession administered the executive branch of the Government. They have conducted it through many perils, and generally with great success. Yet, with all this scope of precedent, I now enter upon the same task for the brief constitutional term of four years under great and peculiar difficulty. A disruption of the Federal Union, heretofore only menaced, is now formidably attempted.

I hold that in contemplation of universal law and of the Constitution the Union of these States is perpetual. Perpetuity is implied, if not expressed, in the fundamental law of all national governments. It is safe to assert that no government proper ever had a provision in its organic law for its own termination. Continue to execute all the express provisions of our National Constitution, and the Union will endure forever, it being impossible to destroy it except by some action not provided for in the instrument itself.

Again: If the United States be not a government proper, but an association of States in the nature of contract merely, can it, as a contract, be peaceably unmade by less than all the parties who made it? One party to a contract may violate it—break it, so to speak—but does it not require all to lawfully rescind it?

Descending from these general principles, we find the proposition that in legal contemplation the Union is perpetual confirmed by the history of the Union itself. The Union is much older than the Constitution. It was formed, in fact, by the Articles of Association in 1774. It was matured and continued by the Declaration of Independence in 1776. It was further matured, and the faith of all the then thirteen States expressly plighted and engaged that it should be perpetual, by the Articles of Confederation in 1778. And finally, in 1787, one of the declared objects for ordaining and establishing the Constitution was "to form a more perfect Union."

But if destruction of the Union by one or by a part only of the States be lawfully possible, the Union is less perfect than before the Constitution, having lost the vital element of perpetuity.

It follows from these views that no State upon its own mere motion can lawfully get out of the Union; that resolves and ordinances to that effect are legally void, and that acts of violence within any State or States against the authority of the United States are insurrectionary or revolutionary, according to circumstances.

I therefore consider that in view of the Constitution and the laws the Union is unbroken, and to the extent of my ability, I shall take care, as the Constitution itself expressly enjoins upon me, that the laws of the Union be faithfully executed in all the States. Doing this I deem to be only a simple duty on my part, and I shall perform it so far as practicable unless my rightful masters, the American people, shall withhold the requisite means or in some authoritative manner direct the contrary. I trust this will not be regarded as a menace, but only as the declared purpose of the Union that it will constitutionally defend and maintain itself.

In doing this there needs to be no bloodshed or violence, and there shall be none unless it be forced upon the national authority. The power confided to me will be used to hold, occupy, and possess the property and places belonging to the Government and to collect the duties and imposts; but beyond what may be necessary for these objects, there will be no invasion, no using of force against or among the people anywhere. Where hostility to the United States in any interior locality shall be so great and universal as to prevent competent resident citizens from holding the Federal offices, there will be no attempt to force obnoxious strangers among the people for that object. While the strict legal right may exist in the Government to enforce the exercise of these offices, the attempt to do so would be so irritating and so nearly impracticable withal that I deem it better to forego for the time the uses of such offices.

The mails, unless repelled, will continue to be furnished in all parts of the Union. So far as possible the people everywhere shall have that sense of perfect security which is most favorable to calm thought and reflection. The course here indicated will be followed unless current events and experience shall show a modification or change to be proper, and in every case and exigency my best discretion will be exercised, according to circumstances actually existing and with a view and a hope of a peaceful solution of the national troubles and the restoration of fraternal sympathies and affections.

That there are persons in one section or another who seek to destroy the Union at all events and are glad of any pretext to do it I will neither affirm nor deny; but if there be such, I need address no word to them. To those, however, who really love the Union may I not speak?

Before entering upon so grave a matter as the destruction of our national fabric, with all its benefits, its memories, and its hopes, would it not be wise to ascertain precisely why we do it? Will you hazard so desperate a step while there is any possibility that any portion of the ills you fly from have no real existence? Will you, while the certain ills you fly to are greater than all the real ones you fly from, will you risk the commission of so fearful a mistake?

All profess to be content in the Union if all constitutional rights can be maintained. Is it true, then, that any right plainly written in the Constitution has been denied? I think not. Happily, the human mind is so constituted that no party can reach to the audacity of doing this. Think, if you can, of a single instance in which a plainly written provision of the Constitution has ever been denied. If by the mere force of numbers a majority should deprive a minority of any clearly written constitutional right, it might in a moral point of view justify revolution; certainly would if such right were a vital one. But such is not our case. All the vital rights of minorities and of individuals are so plainly assured to them by affirmations and negations, guaranties and prohibitions, in the Constitution that controversies never arise concerning them. But no organic law can ever be framed with a provision specifically applicable to every question which may occur in practical administration. No foresight can anticipate nor any document of reasonable length contain express provisions for all possible questions. Shall fugitives from labor be surrendered by national or by State authority? The Constitution does not expressly say. May Congress prohibit slavery in the Territories? The Constitution does not expressly say. Must Congress protect slavery in the Territories? The Constitution does not expressly say.

From questions of this class spring all our constitutional controversies, and we divide upon them into majorities and minorities. If the minority will not acquiesce, the majority must, or the Government must cease. There is no other alternative, for continuing the Government is acquiescence on one side or the other. If a minority in such case will secede rather than acquiesce, they make a precedent which in turn will divide and ruin them, for a minority of their own will secede from them whenever a majority refuses to be controlled by such minority. For instance, why may not any portion of a new confederacy a year or two hence arbitrarily secede again, precisely as portions of the present Union now claim to secede from it? All who cherish disunion sentiments are now being educated to the exact temper of doing this.

Is there such perfect identity of interests among the States to compose a new union as to produce harmony only and prevent renewed secession?

Plainly the central idea of secession is the essence of anarchy. A majority held in restraint by constitutional checks and limitations, and always changing easily with deliberate changes of popular opinions and sentiments, is the only true sovereign of a free people. Whoever rejects it does of necessity fly to anarchy or to despotism. Unanimity is impossible. The rule of a minority, as a permanent arrangement, is wholly inadmissible; so that, rejecting the majority principle, anarchy or despotism in some form is all that is left.

I do not forget the position assumed by some that constitutional questions are to be decided by the Supreme Court, nor do I deny that such decisions must be binding in any case upon the parties to a suit as to the object of that suit, while they are also entitled to very high respect and consideration in all parallel cases by all other departments of the Government. And while it is obviously possible that such decision may be erroneous in any given case, still the evil effect following it, being limited to that particular case, with the chance that it may be overruled and never become a precedent for other cases, can better be borne than could the evils of a different practice. At the same time, the candid citizen must confess that if the policy of the Government upon vital questions affecting the whole people is to be irrevocably fixed by decisions of the Supreme Court, the instant they are made in ordinary litigation between parties in personal actions the people will have ceased to be their own rulers, having to that extent practically resigned their Government into the hands of that eminent tribunal. Nor is there in this view any assault upon the court or the judges. It is a duty from which they may not shrink to decide cases properly brought before them, and it is no fault of theirs if others seek to turn their decisions to political purposes.

One section of our country believes slavery is right and ought to be extended, while the other believes it is wrong and ought not to be extended. This is the only substantial dispute. The fugitive-slave clause of the Constitution and the law for the suppression of the foreign slave trade are each as well enforced, perhaps, as any law can ever be in a community where the moral sense of the people imperfectly supports the law itself. The great body of the people abide by the dry legal obligation in both cases, and a few break over in each. This, I think, can not be perfectly cured, and it would be worse in both cases after the separation of the sections than before. The foreign slave trade, now imperfectly suppressed, would be ultimately revived without restriction in one section, while fugitive slaves, now only partially surrendered, would not be surrendered at all by the other.

Physically speaking, we can not separate. We can not remove our respective sections from each other nor build an impassable wall between them. A husband and wife may be divorced and go out of the presence and beyond the reach of each other, but the different parts of our country can not do this. They can not but remain face to face, and intercourse, either amicable or hostile, must continue between them. Is it possible, then, to make that intercourse more advantageous or more satisfactory after separation than before? Can aliens make treaties easier than friends can make laws? Can treaties be more faithfully enforced between aliens than laws can among friends? Suppose you go to war, you can not fight always; and when, after much loss on both sides and no gain on either, you cease fighting, the identical old questions, as to terms of intercourse, are again upon you.

This country, with its institutions, belongs to the people who inhabit it. Whenever they shall grow weary of the existing Government, they can exercise their constitutional right of amending it or their revolutionary right to dismember or overthrow it. I can not be ignorant of the fact that many worthy and patriotic citizens are desirous of having the National Constitution amended. While I make no recommendation of amendments, I fully recognize the rightful authority of the people over the whole subject, to be exercised in either of the modes prescribed in the instrument itself; and I should, under existing circumstances, favor rather than oppose a fair opportunity being afforded the people to act upon it. I will venture to add that to me the convention mode seems preferable, in that it allows amendments to originate with the people themselves, instead of only permitting them to take or reject propositions originated by others, not especially chosen for the purpose, and which might not be precisely such as they would wish to either accept or refuse. I understand a proposed amendment to the Constitution—which amendment, however, I have not seen—has passed Congress, to the effect that the Federal Government shall never interfere with the domestic institutions of the States, including that of persons held to service. To avoid misconstruction of what I have said, I depart from my purpose not to speak of particular amendments so far as to say that, holding such a provision to now be implied constitutional law, I have no objection to its being made express and irrevocable.

The Chief Magistrate derives all his authority from the people, and they have referred none upon him to fix terms for the separation of the States. The people themselves can do this if also they choose, but the Executive as such has nothing to do with it. His duty is to administer the present Government as it came to his hands and to transmit it unimpaired by him to his successor.

Why should there not be a patient confidence in the ultimate justice of the people? Is there any better or equal hope in the world? In our present differences, is either party without faith of being in the right?

If the Almighty Ruler of Nations, with His eternal truth and justice, be on your side of the North, or on yours of the South, that truth and that justice will surely prevail by the judgment of this great tribunal of the American people.

By the frame of the Government under which we live this same people have wisely given their public servants but little power for mischief, and have with equal wisdom provided for the return of that little to their own hands at very short intervals. While the people retain their virtue and vigilance no Administration by any extreme of wickedness or folly can very seriously injure the Government in the short space of four years.

My countrymen, one and all, think calmly and well upon this whole subject. Nothing valuable can be lost by taking time. If there be an object to hurry any of you in hot haste to a step which you would never take deliberately, that object will be frustrated by taking time; but no good object can be frustrated by it. Such of you as are now dissatisfied still have the old Constitution unimpaired, and, on the sensitive point, the laws of your own framing under it; while the new Administration will have no immediate power, if it would, to change either. If it were admitted that you who are dissatisfied hold the right side in the dispute, there still is no single good reason for precipitate action. Intelligence, patriotism, Christianity, and a firm reliance on Him who has never yet forsaken this favored land are still competent to adjust in the best way all our present difficulty.

In your hands, my dissatisfied fellow-countrymen, and not in mine, is the momentous issue of civil war. The Government will not assail you. You can have no conflict without being yourselves the aggressors. You have no oath registered in heaven to destroy the Government, while I shall have the most solemn one to "preserve, protect, and defend it."

I am loath to close. We are not enemies, but friends. We must not be enemies. Though passion may have strained it must not break our bonds of affection. The mystic chords of memory, stretching from every battlefield and patriot grave to every living heart and hearthstone all over this broad land, will yet swell the chorus of the Union, when again touched, as surely they will be, by the better angels of our nature.

# ABRAHAM LINCOLN
## SECOND INAUGURAL ADDRESS
## SATURDAY, MARCH 4, 1865

Fellow-Countrymen:

At this second appearing to take the oath of the Presidential office there is less occasion for an extended address than there was at the first. Then a statement somewhat in detail of a course to be pursued seemed fitting and proper. Now, at the expiration of four years, during which public declarations have been constantly called forth on every point and phase of the great contest which still absorbs the attention and engrosses the energies of the nation, little that is new could be presented. The progress of our arms, upon which all else chiefly depends, is as well known to the public as to myself, and it is, I trust, reasonably satisfactory and encouraging to all. With high hope for the future, no prediction in regard to it is ventured.

On the occasion corresponding to this four years ago all thoughts were anxiously directed to an impending civil war. All dreaded it, all sought to avert it. While the inaugural address was being delivered from this place, devoted altogether to saving the Union without war, urgent agents were in the city seeking to destroy it without war—seeking to dissolve the Union and divide effects by negotiation. Both parties deprecated war, but one of them would make war rather than let the nation survive, and the other would accept war rather than let it perish, and the war came.

One-eighth of the whole population were colored slaves, not distributed generally over the Union, but localized in the southern part of it. These slaves constituted a peculiar and powerful interest. All knew that this interest was somehow the cause of the war. To strengthen, perpetuate, and extend this interest was the object for which the insurgents would rend the Union even by war, while the Government claimed no right to do more than to restrict the territorial enlargement of it. Neither party expected for the war the magnitude or the duration which it has already attained. Neither anticipated that the cause of the conflict might cease with or even before the conflict itself should cease. Each looked for an easier triumph, and a result less fundamental and astounding. Both read the same Bible and pray to the same God, and each invokes His aid against the other. It may seem strange that any men should dare to ask a just God's assistance in wringing their bread from the sweat of other men's faces, but let us judge not, that we be not judged. The prayers of both could not be answered. That of neither has been answered fully. The Almighty has His own purposes. "Woe unto the world because of offenses; for it must needs be that offenses come, but woe to that man by whom the offense cometh." If we shall suppose that American slavery is one of those offenses which, in the providence of God, must needs come, but which, having continued through His appointed time, He now wills to remove, and that He gives to both North and South this terrible war as the woe due to those by whom the offense came, shall we discern therein any departure from those divine attributes which the believers in a living God always ascribe to Him? Fondly do we hope, fervently do we pray, that this mighty scourge of war may speedily pass away. Yet, if God wills that it continue until all the wealth piled by the bondsman's two hundred and fifty years of unrequited toil shall be sunk, and until every drop of blood drawn with the lash shall be paid by another drawn with the sword, as was said three thousand years ago, so still it must be said "the judgments of the Lord are true and righteous altogether." With malice toward none, with charity for all, with firmness in the right as God gives us to see the right, let us strive on to finish the work we are in, to bind up the nation's wounds, to care for him who shall have borne the battle and for his widow and his orphan, to do all which may achieve and cherish a just and lasting peace among ourselves and with all nations.

# ANDREW JOHNSON
## ADDRESS UPON ASSUMING
## THE OFFICE OF PRESIDENT
## MONDAY, APRIL 17, 1865

Gentlemen: I must be permitted to say that I have been almost overwhelmed by the announcement of the sad event which has so recently occurred. I feel incompetent to perform duties so important and responsible as those which have been so unexpectedly thrown upon me. As to an indication of any policy which may be pursued by me in the administration of the Government, I have to say that that must be left for development as the Administration progresses. The message or declaration must be made by the acts as they transpire. The only assurance that I can now give of the future is reference to the past. The course which I have taken in the past in connection with this rebellion must be regarded as a guaranty of the future. My past public life, which has been long and laborious, has been founded, as I in good conscience believe, upon a great principle of right, which lies at the basis of all things. The best energies of my life have been spent in endeavoring to establish and perpetuate the principles of free government, and I believe that the Government in passing through its present perils will settle down upon principles consonant with popular rights more permanent and enduring than heretofore. I must be permitted to say, if I understand the feelings of my own heart, that I have long labored to ameliorate and elevate the condition of the great mass of the American people. Toil and an honest advocacy of the great principles of free government have been my lot. Duties have been mine; consequences are God's. This has been the foundation of my political creed, and I feel that in the end the Government will triumph and that these great principles will be permanently established.

In conclusion, gentlemen, let me say that I want your

encouragement and countenance. I shall ask and rely upon you and others in carrying the Government through its present perils. I feel in making this request that it will be heartily responded to by you and all other patriots and lovers of the rights and interests of a free people.

# ULYSSES S. GRANT
## FIRST INAUGURAL ADDRESS
## THURSDAY, MARCH 4, 1869

Citizens of the United States:

Your suffrages having elected me to the office of President of the United States, I have, in conformity to the Constitution of our country, taken the oath of office prescribed therein. I have taken this oath without mental reservation and with the determination to do to the best of my ability all that is required of me. The responsibilities of the position I feel, but accept them without fear. The office has come to me unsought; I commence its duties untrammeled. I bring to it a conscious desire and determination to fill it to the best of my ability to the satisfaction of the people.

On all leading questions agitating the public mind I will always express my views to Congress and urge them according to my judgment, and when I think it advisable will exercise the constitutional privilege of interposing a veto to defeat measures which I oppose; but all laws will be faithfully executed, whether they meet my approval or not.

I shall on all subjects have a policy to recommend, but none to enforce against the will of the people. Laws are to govern all alike— those opposed as well as those who favor them. I know no method to secure the repeal of bad or obnoxious laws so effective as their stringent execution.

The country having just emerged from a great rebellion, many questions will come before it for settlement in the next four years which preceding Administrations have never had to deal with. In meeting these it is desirable that they should be approached calmly, without prejudice, hate, or sectional pride, remembering that the greatest good to the greatest number is the object to be attained.

This requires security of person, property, and free religious and political opinion in every part of our common country, without regard to local prejudice. All laws to secure these ends will receive my best efforts for their enforcement.

A great debt has been contracted in securing to us and our posterity the Union. The payment of this, principal and interest, as well as the return to a specie basis as soon as it can be accomplished without material detriment to the debtor class or to the country at large, must be provided for. To protect the national honor, every dollar of Government indebtedness should be paid in gold, unless otherwise expressly stipulated in the contract. Let it be understood that no repudiator of one farthing of our public debt will be trusted in public place, and it will go far toward strengthening a credit which ought to be the best in the world, and will ultimately enable us to replace the debt with bonds bearing less interest than we now pay. To this should be added a faithful collection of the revenue, a strict accountability to the Treasury for every dollar collected, and the greatest practicable retrenchment in expenditure in every department of Government.

When we compare the paying capacity of the country now, with the ten States in poverty from the effects of war, but soon to emerge, I trust, into greater prosperity than ever before, with its paying capacity twenty-five years ago, and calculate what it probably will be twenty-five years hence, who can doubt the feasibility of paying every dollar then with more ease than we now pay for useless luxuries? Why, it looks as though Providence had bestowed upon us a strong box in the precious metals locked up in the sterile mountains of the far West, and which we are now forging the key to unlock, to meet the very contingency that is now upon us.

Ultimately it may be necessary to insure the facilities to reach these riches and it may be necessary also that the General Government should give its aid to secure this access; but that should only be when a dollar of obligation to pay secures precisely the same sort of dollar to use now, and not before. Whilst the question of specie payments is in abeyance the prudent business man is careful about contracting debts payable in the distant future. The nation should follow the same rule. A prostrate commerce is to be rebuilt and all industries encouraged.

The young men of the country—those who from their age must be its rulers twenty-five years hence—have a peculiar interest in maintaining the national honor. A moment's reflection as to what will be our commanding influence among the nations of the earth in their day, if they are only true to themselves, should inspire them with national pride. All divisions—geographical, political, and religious— can join in this common sentiment. How the public debt is to be paid or specie payments resumed is not so important as that a plan should be adopted and acquiesced in. A united determination to do is worth more than divided counsels upon the method of doing. Legislation upon this subject may not be necessary now, or even advisable, but it will be when the civil law is more fully restored in all parts of the country and trade resumes its wonted channels.

It will be my endeavor to execute all laws in good faith, to collect all revenues assessed, and to have them properly accounted for and economically disbursed. I will to the best of my ability appoint to office those only who will carry out this design.

In regard to foreign policy, I would deal with nations as equitable law requires individuals to deal with each other, and I would protect the law-abiding citizen, whether of native or foreign birth, wherever his rights are jeopardized or the flag of our country floats. I would respect the rights of all nations, demanding equal respect for our own. If others depart from this rule in their dealings with us, we may be compelled to follow their precedent.

The proper treatment of the original occupants of this land—the Indians one deserving of careful study. I will favor any course toward them which tends to their civilization and ultimate citizenship.

The question of suffrage is one which is likely to agitate the public so long as a portion of the citizens of the nation are excluded from its privileges in any State. It seems to me very desirable that this question should be settled now, and I entertain the hope and express the desire that it may be by the ratification of the fifteenth article of amendment to the Constitution.

In conclusion I ask patient forbearance one toward another throughout the land, and a determined effort on the part of every citizen to do his share toward cementing a happy union; and I ask the prayers of the nation to Almighty God in behalf of this consummation.

# ULYSSES S. GRANT
## SECOND INAUGURAL ADDRESS
## TUESDAY, MARCH 4, 1873

Fellow-Citizens:

Under Providence I have been called a second time to act as Executive over this great nation. It has been my endeavor in the past to maintain all the laws, and, so far as lay in my power, to act for the best interests of the whole people. My best efforts will be given in the same direction in the future, aided, I trust, by my four years' experience in the office.

When my first term of the office of Chief Executive began, the country had not recovered from the effects of a great internal revolution, and three of the former States of the Union had not been restored to their Federal relations.

It seemed to me wise that no new questions should be raised so long as that condition of affairs existed. Therefore the past four years, so far as I could control events, have been consumed in the effort to restore harmony, public credit, commerce, and all the arts of peace and progress. It is my firm conviction that the civilized world is tending toward republicanism, or government by the people through their chosen representatives, and that our own great Republic is destined to be the guiding star to all others.

Under our Republic we support an army less than that of any European power of any standing and a navy less than that of either of at least five of them. There could be no extension of territory on the continent which would call for an increase of this force, but rather might such extension enable us to diminish it.

The theory of government changes with general progress. Now that the telegraph is made available for communicating thought, together with rapid transit by steam, all parts of a continent are made contiguous for all purposes of government, and communication between the extreme limits of the country made easier than it was throughout the old thirteen States at the beginning of our national existence.

The effects of the late civil strife have been to free the slave and make him a citizen. Yet he is not possessed of the civil rights which citizenship should carry with it. This is wrong, and should be corrected. To this correction I stand committed, so far as Executive influence can avail.

Social equality is not a subject to be legislated upon, nor shall I ask that anything be done to advance the social status of the colored man, except to give him a fair chance to develop what there is good in him, give him access to the schools, and when he travels let him feel assured that his conduct will regulate the treatment and fare he will receive.

The States lately at war with the General Government are now happily rehabilitated, and no Executive control is exercised in any one of them that would not be exercised in any other State under like circumstances.

In the first year of the past Administration the proposition came up for the admission of Santo Domingo as a Territory of the Union. It was not a question of my seeking, but was a proposition from the people of Santo Domingo, and which I entertained. I believe now, as I did then, that it was for the best interest of this country, for the people of Santo Domingo, and all concerned that the proposition should be received favorably. It was, however, rejected constitutionally, and therefore the subject was never brought up again by me.

In future, while I hold my present office, the subject of acquisition of territory must have the support of the people before I will recommend any proposition looking to such acquisition. I say here, however, that I do not share in the apprehension held by many as to the danger of governments becoming weakened and destroyed by reason of their extension of territory. Commerce, education, and rapid transit of thought and matter by telegraph and steam have changed all this. Rather do I believe that our Great Maker is preparing the world, in His own good time, to become one nation, speaking one language, and when armies and navies will be no longer required.

My efforts in the future will be directed to the restoration of good feeling between the different sections of our common country; to the restoration of our currency to a fixed value as compared with the world's standard of values—gold—and, if possible, to a par with it; to the construction of cheap routes of transit throughout the land, to the end that the products of all may find a market and leave a living remuneration to the producer; to the maintenance of friendly relations with all our neighbors and with distant nations; to the reestablishment of our commerce and share in the carrying trade upon the ocean; to the encouragement of such manufacturing industries as can be economically pursued in this country, to the end that the exports of home products and industries may pay for our imports—the only sure method of returning to and permanently maintaining a specie basis; to the elevation of labor; and, by a humane course, to bring the aborigines of the country under the benign influences of education and civilization. It is either this or war of extermination: Wars of extermination, engaged in by people pursuing commerce and all industrial pursuits, are expensive even against the weakest people, and are demoralizing and wicked. Our superiority of strength and advantages of civilization should make us lenient toward the Indian. The wrong inflicted upon him should be taken into account and the balance placed to his credit. The moral view of the question should be considered and the question asked, Can not the Indian be made a useful and productive member of society by proper teaching and treatment? If the effort is made in good faith, we will stand better before the civilized nations of the earth and in our own consciences for having made it.

All these things are not to be accomplished by one individual, but they will receive my support and such recommendations to Congress as will in my judgment best serve to carry them into effect. I beg your support and encouragement.

It has been, and is, my earnest desire to correct abuses that have grown up in the civil service of the country. To secure this reformation rules regulating methods of appointment and promotions were established and have been tried. My efforts for such reformation shall be continued to the best of my judgment. The spirit of the rules adopted will be maintained.

I acknowledge before this assemblage, representing, as it does, every section of our country, the obligation I am under to my countrymen for the great honor they have conferred on me by returning me to the highest office within their gift, and the further obligation resting on me to render to them the best services within my power. This I promise, looking forward with the greatest anxiety to the day when I shall be released from responsibilities that at times are almost overwhelming, and from which I have scarcely had a respite since the eventful firing upon Fort Sumter, in April, 1861, to the present day. My services were then tendered and accepted under the first call for troops growing out of that event.

I did not ask for place or position, and was entirely without influence or the acquaintance of persons of influence, but was resolved to perform my part in a struggle threatening the very existence of the nation. I performed a conscientious duty, without asking promotion or command, and without a revengeful feeling toward any section or individual.

Notwithstanding this, throughout the war, and from my candidacy for my present office in 1868 to the close of the last Presidential campaign, I have been the subject of abuse and slander scarcely ever equaled in political history, which today I feel that I can afford to disregard in view of your verdict, which I gratefully accept as my vindication.

# RUTHERFORD B. HAYES
## INAUGURAL ADDRESS
## MONDAY, MARCH 5, 1877

Fellow-Citizens:

We have assembled to repeat the public ceremonial, begun by Washington, observed by all my predecessors, and now a time-honored custom, which marks the commencement of a new term of the Presidential office. Called to the duties of this great trust, I proceed, in compliance with usage, to announce some of the leading principles, on the subjects that now chiefly engage the public attention, by which it is my desire to be guided in the discharge of those duties. I shall not undertake to lay down irrevocably principles or measures of administration, but rather to speak of the motives which should animate us, and to suggest certain important ends to be attained in accordance with our institutions and essential to the welfare of our country.

At the outset of the discussions which preceded the recent Presidential election it seemed to me fitting that I should fully make known my sentiments in regard to several of the important questions which then appeared to demand the consideration of the country. Following the example, and in part adopting the language, of one of my predecessors, I wish now, when every motive for misrepresentation has passed away, to repeat what was said before the election, trusting that my countrymen will candidly weigh and understand it, and that they will feel assured that the sentiments declared in accepting the nomination for the Presidency will be the standard of my conduct in the path before me, charged, as I now am, with the grave and difficult task of carrying them out in the practical administration of the Government so far as depends, under the Constitution and laws on the Chief Executive of the nation.

The permanent pacification of the country upon such principles and by such measures as will secure the complete protection of all its citizens in the free enjoyment of all their constitutional rights is now the one subject in our public affairs which all thoughtful and patriotic citizens regard as of supreme importance.

Many of the calamitous efforts of the tremendous revolution which has passed over the Southern States still remain. The immeasurable benefits which will surely follow, sooner or later, the hearty and generous acceptance of the legitimate results of that revolution have not yet been realized. Difficult and embarrassing questions meet us at the threshold of this subject. The people of those States are still impoverished, and the inestimable blessing of wise, honest, and peaceful local self-government is not fully enjoyed. Whatever difference of opinion may exist as to the cause of this condition of things, the fact is clear that in the progress of events the time has come when such government is the imperative necessity required by all the varied interests, public and private, of those States. But it must not be forgotten that only a local government which recognizes and maintains inviolate the rights of all is a true self-government.

With respect to the two distinct races whose peculiar relations to each other have brought upon us the deplorable complications and perplexities which exist in those States, it must be a government which guards the interests of both races carefully and equally. It must be a government which submits loyally and heartily to the Constitution and the laws—the laws of the nation and the laws of the States themselves—accepting and obeying faithfully the whole Constitution as it is.

Resting upon this sure and substantial foundation, the superstructure of beneficent local governments can be built up, and not otherwise. In furtherance of such obedience to the letter and the spirit of the Constitution, and in behalf of all that its attainment implies, all so-called party interests lose their apparent importance, and party lines may well be permitted to fade into insignificance. The question we have to consider for the immediate welfare of those States of the Union is the question of government or no government; of social order and all the peaceful industries and the happiness that belongs to it, or a return to barbarism. It is a question in which every citizen of the nation is deeply interested, and with respect to which we ought not to be, in a partisan sense, either Republicans or Democrats, but fellow-citizens and fellowmen, to whom the interests of a common country and a common humanity are dear.

The sweeping revolution of the entire labor system of a large portion of our country and the advance of 4,000,000 people from a condition of servitude to that of citizenship, upon an equal footing with their former masters, could not occur without presenting problems of the gravest moment, to be dealt with by the emancipated race, by their former masters, and by the General Government, the author of the act of emancipation. That it was a wise, just, and providential act, fraught with good for all concerned, is not generally conceded throughout the country. That a moral obligation rests upon the National Government to employ its constitutional power and influence to establish the rights of the people it has emancipated, and to protect them in the enjoyment of those rights when they are infringed or assailed, is also generally admitted.

The evils which afflict the Southern States can only be removed or remedied by the united and harmonious efforts of both races, actuated by motives of mutual sympathy and regard; and while in duty bound and fully determined to protect the rights of all by every constitutional means at the disposal of my Administration, I am sincerely anxious to use every legitimate influence in favor of honest and efficient local self-government as the true resource of those States for the promotion of the contentment and prosperity of their citizens. In the effort I shall make to accomplish this purpose I ask the cordial cooperation of all who cherish an interest in the welfare of the country, trusting that party ties and the prejudice of race will be freely surrendered in behalf of the great purpose to be accomplished. In the important work of restoring the South it is not the political situation alone that merits attention. The material development of that section of the country has been arrested by the social and political revolution through which it has passed, and now needs and deserves the considerate care of the National Government within the just limits prescribed by the Constitution and wise public economy.

But at the basis of all prosperity, for that as well as for every other part of the country, lies the improvement of the intellectual and moral condition of the people. Universal suffrage should rest upon universal education. To this end, liberal and permanent provision should be made for the support of free schools by the State governments, and, if need be, supplemented by legitimate aid from national authority.

Let me assure my countrymen of the Southern States that it is my earnest desire to regard and promote their truest interest—the interests of the white and of the colored people both and equally—and to put forth my best efforts in behalf of a civil policy which will forever wipe out in our political affairs the color line and the distinction between North and South, to the end that we may have not merely a united North or a united South, but a united country.

I ask the attention of the public to the paramount necessity of reform in our civil service—a reform not merely as to certain abuses and practices of so-called official patronage which have come to have the sanction of usage in the several Departments of our Government, but a change in the system of appointment itself; a reform that shall be thorough, radical, and complete; a return to the principles and practices of the founders of the Government. They neither expected nor desired from public officers any partisan service. They meant that public officers should owe their whole service to the Government and to the people. They meant that the officer should be secure in his tenure as long as his personal character remained untarnished and the performance of his duties satisfactory. They held that appointments to office were not to be made nor expected merely as rewards for partisan services, nor merely on the nomination of members of Congress, as being entitled in any respect to the control of such appointments.

The fact that both the great political parties of the country, in declaring their principles prior to the election, gave a prominent place to the subject of reform of our civil service, recognizing and strongly urging its necessity, in terms almost identical in their specific import with those I have here employed, must be accepted as a conclusive argument in behalf of these measures. It must be regarded as the expression of the united voice and will of the whole country upon this subject, and both political parties are virtually pledged to give it their unreserved support.

The President of the United States of necessity owes his election to office to the suffrage and zealous labors of a political party, the members of which cherish with ardor and regard as of essential importance the principles of their party organization; but he should strive to be always mindful of the fact that he serves his party best who serves the country best.

In furtherance of the reform we seek, and in other important respects a change of great importance, I recommend an amendment to the Constitution prescribing a term of six years for the Presidential office and forbidding a reelection.

With respect to the financial condition of the country, I shall not attempt an extended history of the embarrassment and prostration which we have suffered during the past three years. The depression in all our varied commercial and manufacturing interests throughout the country, which began in September, 1873, still continues. It is very gratifying, however, to be able to say that there are indications all around us of a coming change to prosperous times.

Upon the currency question, intimately connected, as it is, with this topic, I may be permitted to repeat here the statement made in my letter of acceptance, that in my judgment the feeling of uncertainty inseparable from an irredeemable paper currency, with its fluctuation of values, is one of the greatest obstacles to a return to prosperous times. The only safe paper currency is one which rests upon a coin basis and is at all times and promptly convertible into coin.

I adhere to the views heretofore expressed by me in favor of Congressional legislation in behalf of an early resumption of specie payments, and I am satisfied not only that this is wise, but that the interests, as well as the public sentiment, of the country imperatively demand it.

Passing from these remarks upon the condition of our own country to consider our relations with other lands, we are reminded by the international complications abroad, threatening the peace of Europe, that our traditional rule of noninterference in the affairs of foreign nations has proved of great value in past times and ought to be strictly observed.

The policy inaugurated by my honored predecessor, President Grant, of submitting to arbitration grave questions in dispute between ourselves and foreign powers points to a new, and incomparably the best, instrumentality for the preservation of peace, and will, as I believe, become a beneficent example of the course to be pursued in similar emergencies by other nations.

If, unhappily, questions of difference should at any time during the period of my Administration arise between the United States and any foreign government, it will certainly be my disposition and my hope to aid in their settlement in the same peaceful and honorable way, thus securing to our country the great blessings of peace and mutual good offices with all the nations of the world.

Fellow-citizens, we have reached the close of a political contest marked by the excitement which usually attends the contests between great political parties whose members espouse and advocate with earnest faith their respective creeds. The circumstances were, perhaps, in no respect extraordinary save in the closeness and the consequent uncertainty of the result.

For the first time in the history of the country it has been deemed best, in view of the peculiar circumstances of the case, that the objections and questions in dispute with reference to the counting of the electoral votes should be referred to the decision of a tribunal appointed for this purpose.

That tribunal—established by law for this sole purpose; its members, all of them, men of long-established reputation for integrity and intelligence, and, with the exception of those who are also members of the supreme judiciary, chosen equally from both political parties; its deliberations enlightened by the research and the arguments of able counsel—was entitled to the fullest confidence of the American people. Its decisions have been patiently waited for, and accepted as legally conclusive by the general judgment of the public. For the present, opinion will widely vary as to the wisdom of the several conclusions announced by that tribunal. This is to be anticipated in every instance where matters of dispute are made the subject of arbitration under the forms of law. Human judgment is never unerring, and is rarely regarded as otherwise than wrong by the unsuccessful party in the contest.

The fact that two great political parties have in this way settled a dispute in regard to which good men differ as to the facts and the law no less than as to the proper course to be pursued in solving the question in controversy is an occasion for general rejoicing.

Upon one point there is entire unanimity in public sentiment—that conflicting claims to the Presidency must be amicably and peaceably adjusted, and that when so adjusted the general acquiescence of the nation ought surely to follow.

It has been reserved for a government of the people, where the right of suffrage is universal, to give to the world the first example in history of a great nation, in the midst of the struggle of opposing parties for power, hushing its party tumults to yield the issue of the contest to adjustment according to the forms of law.

Looking for the guidance of that Divine Hand by which the destinies of nations and individuals are shaped, I call upon you, Senators, Representatives, judges, fellow-citizens, here and everywhere, to unite with me in an earnest effort to secure to our country the blessings, not only of material prosperity, but of justice, peace, and union—a union depending not upon the constraint of force, but upon the loving devotion of a free people; "and that all things may be so ordered and settled upon the best and surest foundations that peace and happiness, truth and justice, religion and piety, may be established among us for all generations."

## JAMES A. GARFIELD
## INAUGURAL ADDRESS
## FRIDAY, MARCH 4, 1881

Fellow-Citizens:

We stand today upon an eminence which overlooks a hundred years of national life—a century crowded with perils, but crowned with the triumphs of liberty and law. Before continuing the onward march let us pause on this height for a moment to strengthen our faith and renew our hope by a glance at the pathway along which our people have traveled.

It is now three days more than a hundred years since the adoption of the first written constitution of the United States—the Articles of Confederation and Perpetual Union. The new Republic was then beset with danger on every hand. It had not conquered a place in the family of nations. The decisive battle of the war for independence, whose centennial anniversary will soon be gratefully celebrated at Yorktown, had not yet been fought. The colonists were struggling not only against the armies of a great nation, but against the settled opinions of mankind; for the world did not then believe that the supreme authority of government could be safely intrusted to the guardianship of the people themselves.

We can not overestimate the fervent love of liberty, the intelligent courage, and the sum of common sense with which our fathers made the great experiment of self-government. When they found, after a short trial, that the confederacy of States, was too weak to meet the necessities of a vigorous and expanding republic, they boldly set it aside, and in its stead established a National Union, founded directly upon the will of the people, endowed with full power of self-preservation and ample authority for the accomplishment of its great object.

Under this Constitution the boundaries of freedom have been enlarged, the foundations of order and peace have been strengthened, and the growth of our people in all the better elements of national life has indicated the wisdom of the founders and given new hope to their descendants. Under this Constitution our people long ago made themselves safe against danger from without and secured for their mariners and flag equality of rights on all the seas. Under this Constitution twenty-five States have been added to the Union, with constitutions and laws, framed and enforced by their own citizens, to secure the manifold blessings of local self-government.

The jurisdiction of this Constitution now covers an area fifty times greater than that of the original thirteen States and a population twenty times greater than that of 1780.

The supreme trial of the Constitution came at last under the tremendous pressure of civil war. We ourselves are witnesses that the Union emerged from the blood and fire of that conflict purified and made stronger for all the beneficent purposes of good government.

And now, at the close of this first century of growth, with the inspirations of its history in their hearts, our people have lately reviewed the condition of the nation, passed judgment upon the conduct and opinions of political parties, and have registered their will concerning the future administration of the Government. To interpret and to execute that will in accordance with the Constitution is the paramount duty of the Executive.

Even from this brief review it is manifest that the nation is resolutely facing to the front, resolved to employ its best energies in developing the great possibilities of the future. Sacredly preserving whatever has been gained to liberty and good government during the century, our people are determined to leave behind them all those bitter controversies concerning things which have been irrevocably settled, and the further discussion of which can only stir up strife and delay the onward march.

The supremacy of the nation and its laws should be no longer a subject of debate. That discussion, which for half a century threatened the existence of the Union, was closed at last in the high court of war by a decree from which there is no appeal—that the Constitution and the laws made in pursuance thereof are and shall continue to be the supreme law of the land, binding alike upon the States and the people. This decree does not disturb the autonomy of the States nor interfere with any of their necessary rights of local self-government, but it does fix and establish the permanent supremacy of the Union.

The will of the nation, speaking with the voice of battle and through the amended Constitution, has fulfilled the great promise of 1776 by proclaiming "liberty throughout the land to all the inhabitants thereof."

The elevation of the negro race from slavery to the full rights of citizenship is the most important political change we have known since the adoption of the Constitution of 1787. NO thoughtful man can fail to appreciate its beneficent effect upon our institutions and people. It has freed us from the perpetual danger of war and dissolution. It has added immensely to the moral and industrial forces of our people. It has liberated the master as well as the slave from a relation which wronged and enfeebled both. It has surrendered to their own guardianship the manhood of more than 5,000,000 people, and has opened to each one of them a career of freedom and usefulness. It has given new inspiration to the power of self-help in both races by making labor more honorable to the one and more necessary to the other. The influence of this force will grow greater and bear richer fruit with the coming years.

No doubt this great change has caused serious disturbance to our Southern communities. This is to be deplored, though it was perhaps unavoidable. But those who resisted the change should remember that under our institutions there was no middle ground for the negro race between slavery and equal citizenship. There can be no permanent disfranchised peasantry in the United States. Freedom can never yield its fullness of blessings so long as the law or its administration places the smallest obstacle in the pathway of any virtuous citizen.

The emancipated race has already made remarkable progress. With unquestioning devotion to the Union, with a patience and gentleness not born of fear, they have "followed the light as God gave them to see the light." They are rapidly laying the material foundations of self-support, widening their circle of intelligence, and beginning to enjoy the blessings that gather around the homes of the industrious poor. They deserve the generous encouragement of all good men. So far as my authority can lawfully extend they shall enjoy the full and equal protection of the Constitution and the laws.

The free enjoyment of equal suffrage is still in question, and a frank statement of the issue may aid its solution. It is alleged that in many communities negro citizens are practically denied the freedom of the ballot. In so far as the truth of this allegation is admitted, it is answered that in many places honest local government is impossible if the mass of uneducated negroes are allowed to vote. These are grave allegations. So far as the latter is true, it is the only palliation that can be offered for opposing the freedom of the ballot. Bad local government is certainly a great evil, which ought to be prevented; but to violate the freedom and sanctities of the suffrage is more than an evil. It is a crime which, if persisted in, will destroy the Government itself. Suicide is not a remedy. If in other lands it be high treason to compass the death of the king, it shall be counted no less a crime here to strangle our sovereign power and stifle its voice.

It has been said that unsettled questions have no pity for the repose of nations. It should be said with the utmost emphasis that this question of the suffrage will never give repose or safety to the States or to the nation until each, within its own jurisdiction, makes and keeps the ballot free and pure by the strong sanctions of the law.

But the danger which arises from ignorance in the voter can not be denied. It covers a field far wider than that of negro suffrage and the present condition of the race. It is a danger that lurks and hides in the sources and fountains of power in every state. We have no standard by which to measure the disaster that may be brought upon us by ignorance and vice in the citizens when joined to corruption and fraud in the suffrage.

The voters of the Union, who make and unmake constitutions, and upon whose will hang the destinies of our governments, can transmit their supreme authority to no successors save the coming generation of voters, who are the sole heirs of sovereign power. If that generation comes to its inheritance blinded by ignorance and corrupted by vice, the fall of the Republic will be certain and remediless.

The census has already sounded the alarm in the appalling figures which mark how dangerously high the tide of illiteracy has risen among our voters and their children.

To the South this question is of supreme importance. But the responsibility for the existence of slavery did not rest upon the South alone. The nation itself is responsible for the extension of the suffrage, and is under special obligations to aid in removing the illiteracy which it has added to the voting population. For the North and South alike there is but one remedy. All the constitutional power of the nation and of the States and all the volunteer forces of the people should be surrendered to meet this danger by the savory influence of universal education.

It is the high privilege and sacred duty of those now living to educate their successors and fit them, by intelligence and virtue, for the inheritance which awaits them.

In this beneficent work sections and races should be forgotten and partisanship should be unknown. Let our people find a new meaning in the divine oracle which declares that "a little child shall lead them," for our own little children will soon control the destinies of the Republic.

My countrymen, we do not now differ in our judgment concerning the controversies of past generations, and fifty years hence our children will not be divided in their opinions concerning our controversies. They will surely bless their fathers and their fathers' God that the Union was preserved, that slavery was overthrown, and that both races were made equal before the law. We may hasten or we may retard, but we can not prevent, the final reconciliation. Is it not possible for us now to make a truce with time by anticipating and accepting its inevitable verdict?

Enterprises of the highest importance to our moral and material well-being unite us and offer ample employment of our best powers. Let all our people, leaving behind them the battlefields of dead issues, move forward and in their strength of liberty and the restored Union win the grander victories of peace.

The prosperity which now prevails is without parallel in our history. Fruitful seasons have done much to secure it, but they have not done all. The preservation of the public credit and the resumption of specie payments, so successfully attained by the Administration of my predecessors, have enabled our people to secure the blessings which the seasons brought.

By the experience of commercial nations in all ages it has been found that gold and silver afford the only safe foundation for a monetary system. Confusion has recently been created by variations in the relative value of the two metals, but I confidently believe that arrangements can be made between the leading commercial nations which will secure the general use of both metals. Congress should provide that the compulsory coinage of silver now required by law may not disturb our monetary system by driving either metal out of circulation. If possible, such an adjustment should be made that the purchasing power of every coined dollar will be exactly equal to its debt-paying power in all the markets of the world.

The chief duty of the National Government in connection with the currency of the country is to coin money and declare its value. Grave doubts have been entertained whether Congress is authorized by the Constitution to make any form of paper money legal tender. The present issue of United States notes has been sustained by the necessities of war; but such paper should depend for its value and currency upon its convenience in use and its prompt redemption in coin at the will of the holder, and not upon its compulsory circulation. These notes are not money, but promises to pay money. If the holders demand it, the promise should be kept.

The refunding of the national debt at a lower rate of interest should be accomplished without compelling the withdrawal of the national-bank notes, and thus disturbing the business of the country.

I venture to refer to the position I have occupied on financial questions during a long service in Congress, and to say that time and experience have strengthened the opinions I have so often expressed on these subjects.

The finances of the Government shall suffer no detriment which it may be possible for my Administration to prevent.

The interests of agriculture deserve more attention from the Government than they have yet received. The farms of the United States afford homes and employment for more than one-half our people, and furnish much the largest part of all our exports. As the Government lights our coasts for the protection of mariners and the benefit of commerce, so it should give to the tillers of the soil the best lights of practical science and experience.

Our manufacturers are rapidly making us industrially independent, and are opening to capital and labor new and profitable fields of employment. Their steady and healthy growth should still be matured. Our facilities for transportation should be promoted by the continued improvement of our harbors and great interior waterways and by the increase of our tonnage on the ocean.

The development of the world's commerce has led to an urgent demand for shortening the great sea voyage around Cape Horn by constructing ship canals or railways across the isthmus which unites the continents. Various plans to this end have been suggested and will need consideration, but none of them has been sufficiently matured to warrant the United States in extending pecuniary aid. The subject, however, is one which will immediately engage the attention of the Government with a view to a thorough protection to American interests. We will urge no narrow policy nor seek peculiar or exclusive privileges in any commercial route; but, in the language of my predecessor, I believe it to be the right "and duty of the United States to assert and maintain such supervision and authority over any interoceanic canal across the isthmus that connects North and South America as will protect our national interest."

The Constitution guarantees absolute religious freedom. Congress is prohibited from making any law respecting an establishment of religion or prohibiting the free exercise thereof. The Territories of the United States are subject to the direct legislative authority of Congress, and hence the General Government is responsible for any violation of the Constitution in any of them. It is therefore a reproach to the Government that in the most populous of the Territories the constitutional guaranty is not enjoyed by the people and the authority of Congress is set at naught. The Mormon Church not only offends the moral sense of manhood by sanctioning polygamy, but prevents the administration of justice through ordinary instrumentalities of law.

In my judgment it is the duty of Congress, while respecting to the uttermost the conscientious convictions and religious scruples of every citizen, to prohibit within its jurisdiction all criminal practices, especially of that class which destroy the family relations and endanger social order. Nor can any ecclesiastical organization be safely permitted to usurp in the smallest degree the functions and powers of the National Government.

The civil service can never be placed on a satisfactory basis until it is regulated by law. For the good of the service itself, for the protection of those who are intrusted with the appointing power against the waste of time and obstruction to the public business caused by the inordinate pressure for place, and for the protection of incumbents against intrigue and wrong, I shall at the proper time ask Congress to fix the tenure of the minor offices of the several Executive Departments and prescribe the grounds upon which removals shall be made during the terms for which incumbents have been appointed.

Finally, acting always within the authority and limitations of the Constitution, invading neither the rights of the States nor the reserved rights of the people, it will be the purpose of my Administration to maintain the authority of the nation in all places within its jurisdiction; to enforce obedience to all the laws of the Union in the interests of the people; to demand rigid economy in all the expenditures of the Government, and to require the honest and faithful service of all executive officers, remembering that the offices were created, not for the benefit of incumbents or their supporters, but for the service of the Government.

And now, fellow-citizens, I am about to assume the great trust which you have committed to my hands. I appeal to you for that earnest and thoughtful support which makes this Government in fact, as it is in law, a government of the people.

I shall greatly rely upon the wisdom and patriotism of Congress and of those who may share with me the responsibilities and duties of administration, and, above all, upon our efforts to promote the welfare of this great people and their Government I reverently invoke the support and blessings of Almighty God.

# CHESTER A. ARTHUR
## ADDRESS UPON ASSUMING
## THE OFFICE OF PRESIDENT
## THURSDAY, SEPTEMBER 22, 1881

For the fourth time in the history of the Republic its Chief Magistrate has been removed by death. All hearts are filled with grief and horror at the hideous crime which has darkened our land, and the memory of the murdered President, his protracted sufferings, his unyielding fortitude, the example and achievements of his life, and the pathos of his death will forever illumine the pages of our history.

For the fourth time the officer elected by the people and ordained by the Constitution to fill a vacancy so created is called to assume the Executive chair. The wisdom of our fathers, foreseeing even the most dire possibilities, made sure that the Government should never be imperiled because of the uncertainty of human life. Men may die, but the fabrics of our free institutions remain unshaken. No higher or more assuring proof could exist of the strength and permanence of popular government than the fact that though the chosen of the people be struck down his constitutional successor is peacefully installed without shock or strain except the sorrow which mourns the bereavement. All the noble aspirations of my lamented predecessor which found expression in his life, the measures devised and suggested during his brief Administration to correct abuses, to enforce economy, to advance prosperity, and to promote the general welfare, to Insure domestic security and maintain friendly and honorable relations with the nations of the earth, will be garnered in the hearts of the people; and it will be my earnest endeavor to profit, and to see that the nation shall profit, by his example and experience.

Prosperity blesses our country. Our fiscal policy is fixed by law, is well grounded and generally approved. No threatening issue mars our foreign intercourse, and the wisdom, integrity, and thrift of our people may be trusted to continue undisturbed the present assured career of peace, tranquilly, and welfare. The gloom and anxiety which have enshrouded the country must make repose especially welcome now. No demand for speedy legislation has been heard; no adequate occasion is apparent for an unusual session of Congress. The Constitution defines the functions and powers of the executive as clearly as those of either of the other two departments of the Government, and he must answer for the just exercise of the discretion it permits and the performance of the duties it imposes. Summoned to these high duties and responsibilities and profoundly conscious of their magnitude and gravity, I assume the trust imposed by the Constitution, relying for aid on divine guidance and the virtue, patriotism, and intelligence of the American people.

# GROVER CLEVELAND
## FIRST INAUGURAL ADDRESS
### WEDNESDAY, MARCH 4, 1885

Fellow-Citizens:

In the presence of this vast assemblage of my countrymen I am about to supplement and seal by the oath which I shall take the manifestation of the will of a great and free people. In the exercise of their power and right of self-government they have committed to one of their fellow-citizens a supreme and sacred trust, and he here consecrates himself to their service.

This impressive ceremony adds little to the solemn sense of responsibility with which I contemplate the duty I owe to all the people of the land. Nothing can relieve me from anxiety lest by any act of mine their interests may suffer, and nothing is needed to strengthen my resolution to engage every faculty and effort in the promotion of their welfare.

Amid the din of party strife the people's choice was made, but its attendant circumstances have demonstrated anew the strength and safety of a government by the people. In each succeeding year it more clearly appears that our democratic principle needs no apology, and that in its fearless and faithful application is to be found the surest guaranty of good government.

But the best results in the operation of a government wherein every citizen has a share largely depend upon a proper limitation of purely partisan zeal and effort and a correct appreciation of the time when the heat of the partisan should be merged in the patriotism of the citizen.

Today the executive branch of the Government is transferred to new keeping. But this is still the Government of all the people, and it should be none the less an object of their affectionate solicitude. At this hour the animosities of political strife, the bitterness of partisan defeat, and the exultation of partisan triumph should be supplanted by an ungrudging acquiescence in the popular will and a sober, conscientious concern for the general weal. Moreover, if from this hour we cheerfully and honestly abandon all sectional prejudice and distrust, and determine, with manly confidence in one another, to work out harmoniously the achievements of our national destiny, we shall deserve to realize all the benefits which our happy form of government can bestow.

On this auspicious occasion we may well renew the pledge of our devotion to the Constitution, which, launched by the founders of the Republic and consecrated by their prayers and patriotic devotion, has for almost a century borne the hopes and the aspirations of a great people through prosperity and peace and through the shock of foreign conflicts and the perils of domestic strife and vicissitudes.

By the Father of his Country our Constitution was commended for adoption as "the result of a spirit of amity and mutual concession." In that same spirit it should be administered, in order to promote the lasting welfare of the country and to secure the full measure of its priceless benefits to us and to those who will succeed to the blessings of our national life. The large variety of diverse and competing interests subject to Federal control, persistently seeking the recognition of their claims, need give us no fear that "the greatest good to the greatest number" will fail to be accomplished if in the halls of national legislation that spirit of amity and mutual concession shall prevail in which the Constitution had its birth. If this involves the surrender or postponement of private interests and the abandonment of local advantages, compensation will be found in the assurance that the common interest is subserved and the general welfare advanced.

In the discharge of my official duty I shall endeavor to be guided by a just and unstrained construction of the Constitution, a careful observance of the distinction between the powers granted to the Federal Government and those reserved to the States or to the people, and by a cautious appreciation of those functions which by the Constitution and laws have been especially assigned to the executive branch of the Government.

But he who takes the oath today to preserve, protect, and defend the Constitution of the United States only assumes the solemn obligation which every patriotic citizen—on the farm, in the workshop, in the busy marts of trade, and everywhere—should share with him. The Constitution which prescribes his oath, my countrymen, is yours; the Government you have chosen him to administer for a time is yours; the suffrage which executes the will of freemen is yours; the laws and the entire scheme of our civil rule, from the town meeting to the State capitals and the national capital, is yours. Your every voter, as surely as your Chief Magistrate, under the same high sanction, though in a different sphere, exercises a public trust. Nor is this all. Every citizen owes to the country a vigilant watch and close scrutiny of its public servants and a fair and reasonable estimate of their fidelity and usefulness. Thus is the people's will impressed upon the whole framework of our civil polity—municipal, State, and Federal; and this is the price of our liberty and the inspiration of our faith in the Republic.

It is the duty of those serving the people in public place to closely limit public expenditures to the actual needs of the Government economically administered, because this bounds the right of the Government to exact tribute from the earnings of labor or the property of the citizen, and because public extravagance begets extravagance among the people. We should never be ashamed of the simplicity and prudential economies which are best suited to the operation of a republican form of government and most compatible with the mission of the American people. Those who are selected for a limited time to manage public affairs are still of the people, and may do much by their example to encourage, consistently with the dignity of their official functions, that plain way of life which among their fellow-citizens aids integrity and promotes thrift and prosperity.

The genius of our institutions, the needs of our people in their home life, and the attention which is demanded for the settlement and development of the resources of our vast territory dictate the scrupulous avoidance of any departure from that foreign policy commended by the history, the traditions, and the prosperity of our Republic. It is the policy of independence, favored by our position and defended by our known love of justice and by our power. It is the policy of peace suitable to our interests. It is the policy of neutrality, rejecting any share in foreign broils and ambitions upon other continents and repelling their intrusion here. It is the policy of

Monroe and of Washington and Jefferson—"Peace, commerce, and honest friendship with all nations; entangling alliance with none."

A due regard for the interests and prosperity of all the people demands that our finances shall be established upon such a sound and sensible basis as shall secure the safety and confidence of business interests and make the wage of labor sure and steady, and that our system of revenue shall be so adjusted as to relieve the people of unnecessary taxation, having a due regard to the interests of capital invested and workingmen employed in American industries, and preventing the accumulation of a surplus in the Treasury to tempt extravagance and waste.

Care for the property of the nation and for the needs of future settlers requires that the public domain should be protected from purloining schemes and unlawful occupation.

The conscience of the people demands that the Indians within our boundaries shall be fairly and honestly treated as wards of the Government and their education and civilization promoted with a view to their ultimate citizenship, and that polygamy in the Territories, destructive of the family relation and offensive to the moral sense of the civilized world, shall be repressed.

The laws should be rigidly enforced which prohibit the immigration of a servile class to compete with American labor, with no intention of acquiring citizenship, and bringing with them and retaining habits and customs repugnant to our civilization.

The people demand reform in the administration of the Government and the application of business principles to public affairs. As a means to this end, civil-service reform should be in good faith enforced. Our citizens have the right to protection from the incompetency of public employees who hold their places solely as the reward of partisan service, and from the corrupting influence of those who promise and the vicious methods of those who expect such rewards; and those who worthily seek public employment have the right to insist that merit and competency shall be recognized instead of party subserviency or the surrender of honest political belief.

In the administration of a government pledged to do equal and exact justice to all men there should be no pretext for anxiety touching the protection of the freedmen in their rights or their security in the enjoyment of their privileges under the Constitution and its amendments. All discussion as to their fitness for the place accorded to them as American citizens is idle and unprofitable except as it suggests the necessity for their improvement. The fact that they are citizens entitles them to all the rights due to that relation and charges them with all its duties, obligations, and responsibilities.

These topics and the constant and ever-varying wants of an active and enterprising population may well receive the attention and the patriotic endeavor of all who make and execute the Federal law. Our duties are practical and call for industrious application, an intelligent perception of the claims of public office, and, above all, a firm determination, by united action, to secure to all the people of the land the full benefits of the best form of government ever vouchsafed to man. And let us not trust to human effort alone, but humbly acknowledging the power and goodness of Almighty God, who presides over the destiny of nations, and who has at all times been revealed in our country's history, let us invoke His aid and His blessings upon our labors.

# BENJAMIN HARRISON
## INAUGURAL ADDRESS
## MONDAY, MARCH 4, 1889

Fellow-Citizens:

There is no constitutional or legal requirement that the President shall take the oath of office in the presence of the people, but there is so manifest an appropriateness in the public induction to office of the chief executive officer of the nation that from the beginning of the Government the people, to whose service the official oath consecrates the officer, have been called to witness the solemn ceremonial. The oath taken in the presence of the people becomes a mutual covenant. The officer covenants to serve the whole body of the people by a faithful execution of the laws, so that they may be the unfailing defense and security of those who respect and observe them, and that neither wealth, station, nor the power of combinations shall be able to evade their just penalties or to wrest them from a beneficent public purpose to serve the ends of cruelty or selfishness.

My promise is spoken; yours unspoken, but not the less real and solemn. The people of every State have here their representatives. Surely I do not misinterpret the spirit of the occasion when I assume that the whole body of the people covenant with me and with each other today to support and defend the Constitution and the Union of the States, to yield willing obedience to all the laws and each to every other citizen his equal civil and political rights. Entering thus solemnly into covenant with each other, we may reverently invoke and confidently expect the favor and help of Almighty God—that He will give to me wisdom, strength, and fidelity, and to our people a spirit of fraternity and a love of righteousness and peace.

This occasion derives peculiar interest from the fact that the Presidential term which begins this day is the twenty-sixth under our Constitution. The first inauguration of President Washington took place in New York, where Congress was then sitting, on the 30th day of April, 1789, having been deferred by reason of delays attending the organization of the Congress and the canvass of the electoral vote. Our people have already worthily observed the centennials of the Declaration of Independence, of the battle of Yorktown, and of the adoption of the Constitution, and will shortly celebrate in New York the institution of the second great department of our constitutional scheme of government. When the centennial of the institution of the judicial department, by the organization of the Supreme Court, shall have been suitably observed, as I trust it will be, our nation will have fully entered its second century.

I will not attempt to note the marvelous and in great part happy contrasts between our country as it steps over the threshold into its second century of organized existence under the Constitution and that weak but wisely ordered young nation that looked undauntedly down the first century, when all its years stretched out before it.

Our people will not fail at this time to recall the incidents which accompanied the institution of government under the Constitution, or to find inspiration and guidance in the teachings and example of Washington and his great associates, and hope and courage in the contrast which thirty-eight populous and prosperous States offer to the thirteen States, weak in everything except courage and the love of liberty, that then fringed our Atlantic seaboard.

The Territory of Dakota has now a population greater than any of the original States (except Virginia) and greater than the aggregate of five of the smaller States in 1790. The center of population when our national capital was located was east of Baltimore, and it was argued by many well-informed persons that it would move eastward rather than westward; yet in 1880 it was found to be near Cincinnati, and the new census about to be taken will show another stride to the westward. That which was the body has come to be only the rich fringe of the nation's robe. But our growth has not been limited to territory, population and aggregate wealth, marvelous as it has been in each of those directions. The masses of our people are better fed, clothed, and housed than their fathers were. The facilities for popular education have been vastly enlarged and more generally diffused.

The virtues of courage and patriotism have given recent proof of their continued presence and increasing power in the hearts and over the lives of our people. The influences of religion have been multiplied and strengthened. The sweet offices of charity have greatly increased. The virtue of temperance is held in higher estimation. We have not attained an ideal condition. Not all of our people are happy and prosperous; not all of them are virtuous and law-abiding. But on the whole the opportunities offered to the individual to secure the comforts of life are better than are found elsewhere and largely better than they were here one hundred years ago.

The surrender of a large measure of sovereignty to the General Government, effected by the adoption of the Constitution, was not accomplished until the suggestions of reason were strongly reenforced by the more imperative voice of experience. The divergent interests of peace speedily demanded a "more perfect union." The merchant, the shipmaster, and the manufacturer discovered and disclosed to our statesmen and to the people that commercial emancipation must be added to the political freedom which had been so bravely won. The commercial policy of the mother country had not relaxed any of its hard and oppressive features. To hold in check the development of our commercial marine, to prevent or retard the establishment and growth of manufactures in the States, and so to secure the American market for their shops and the carrying trade for their ships, was the policy of European statesmen, and was pursued with the most selfish vigor.

Petitions poured in upon Congress urging the imposition of discriminating duties that should encourage the production of needed things at home. The patriotism of the people, which no longer found afield of exercise in war, was energetically directed to the duty of equipping the young Republic for the defense of its independence by making its people self-dependent. Societies for the promotion of home manufactures and for encouraging the use of domestics in the dress of the people were organized in many of the States. The revival at the end of the century of the same patriotic interest in the preservation and development of domestic industries and the defense of our working people against injurious foreign competition is an incident worthy of attention. It is not a departure but a return that we have witnessed. The protective policy had then its opponents. The argument was made, as now, that its benefits inured to particular classes or sections.

If the question became in any sense or at any time sectional, it was only because slavery existed in some of the States. But for this there was no reason why the cotton-producing States should not have led or walked abreast with the New England States in the production of cotton fabrics. There was this reason only why the States that divide with Pennsylvania the mineral treasures of the great southeastern and central mountain ranges should have been so tardy in bringing to the smelting furnace and to the mill the coal and iron from their near opposing hillsides. Mill fires were lighted at the funeral pile of slavery. The emancipation proclamation was heard in the depths of the earth as well as in the sky; men were made free, and material things became our better servants.

The sectional element has happily been eliminated from the tariff discussion. We have no longer States that are necessarily only planting States. None are excluded from achieving that diversification of pursuits among the people which brings wealth and contentment. The cotton plantation will not be less valuable when the product is spun in the country town by operatives whose necessities call for diversified crops and create a home demand for garden and agricultural products. Every new mine, furnace, and factory is an extension of the productive capacity of the State more real and valuable than added territory.

Shall the prejudices and paralysis of slavery continue to hang upon the skirts of progress? How long will those who rejoice that slavery no longer exists cherish or tolerate the incapacities it put upon their communities? I look hopefully to the continuance of our protective system and to the consequent development of manufacturing and mining enterprises in the States hitherto wholly given to agriculture as a potent influence in the perfect unification of our people. The men who have invested their capital in these enterprises, the farmers who have felt the benefit of their neighborhood, and the men who work in shop or field will not fail to find and to defend a community of interest.

Is it not quite possible that the farmers and the promoters of the great mining and manufacturing enterprises which have recently been established in the South may yet find that the free ballot of the workingman, without distinction of race, is needed for their defense as well as for his own? I do not doubt that if those men in the South who now accept the tariff views of Clay and the constitutional exposition of Webster would courageously avow and defend their real convictions they would not find it difficult, by friendly instruction and cooperation, to make the black man their efficient and safe ally, not only in establishing correct principles in our national administration, but in preserving for their local communities the benefits of social order and economical and honest government. At least until the good offices of kindness and education have been fairly tried the contrary conclusion can not be plausibly urged.

I have altogether rejected the suggestion of a special Executive policy for any section of our country. It is the duty of the Executive to administer and enforce in the methods and by the instrumentalities pointed out and provided by the Constitution all the laws enacted by Congress. These laws are general and their administration should be uniform and equal. As a citizen may not elect what laws he will obey, neither may the Executive eject which he will enforce. The duty to obey and to execute embraces the Constitution in its entirety and the whole code of laws enacted under it. The evil example of permitting individuals, corporations, or communities to nullify the laws because they cross some selfish or local interest or prejudices is full of danger, not only to the nation at large, but much more to those who use this pernicious expedient to escape their just obligations or to obtain an unjust advantage over others. They will presently themselves be compelled to appeal to the law for protection, and those who would use the law as a defense must not deny that use of it to others.

If our great corporations would more scrupulously observe their legal limitations and duties, they would have less cause to complain of the unlawful limitations of their rights or of violent interference with their operations. The community that by concert, open or secret, among its citizens denies to a portion of its members their plain rights under the law has severed the only safe bond of social order and prosperity. The evil works from a bad center both ways. It demoralizes those who practice it and destroys the faith of those who suffer by it in the efficiency of the law as a safe protector. The man in whose breast that faith has been darkened is naturally the subject of dangerous and uncanny suggestions. Those who use unlawful methods, if moved by no higher motive than the selfishness that prompted them, may well stop and inquire what is to be the end of this.

An unlawful expedient can not become a permanent condition of government. If the educated and influential classes in a community either practice or connive at the systematic violation of laws that seem to them to cross their convenience, what can they expect when the lesson that convenience or a supposed class interest is a sufficient cause for lawlessness has been well learned by the ignorant classes? A community where law is the rule of conduct and where courts, not mobs, execute its penalties is the only attractive field for business investments and honest labor.

Our naturalization laws should be so amended as to make the inquiry into the character and good disposition of persons applying for citizenship more careful and searching. Our existing laws have been in their administration an unimpressive and often an unintelligible form. We accept the man as a citizen without any knowledge of his fitness, and he assumes the duties of citizenship without any knowledge as to what they are. The privileges of American citizenship are so great and its duties so grave that we may well insist upon a good knowledge of every person applying for citizenship and a good knowledge by him of our institutions. We should not cease to be hospitable to immigration, but we should cease to be careless as to the character of it. There are men of all races, even the best, whose coming is necessarily a burden upon our public revenues or a threat to social order. These should be identified and excluded.

We have happily maintained a policy of avoiding all interference with European affairs. We have been only interested spectators of their contentions in diplomacy and in war, ready to use our friendly offices to promote peace, but never obtruding our advice and never attempting unfairly to coin the distresses of other powers into commercial advantage to ourselves. We have a just right to expect that our European policy will be the American policy of European courts.

It is so manifestly incompatible with those precautions for our peace and safety which all the great powers habitually observe and enforce in matters affecting them that a shorter waterway between our eastern and western seaboards should be dominated by any European Government that we may confidently expect that such a purpose will not be entertained by any friendly power.

We shall in the future, as in the past, use every endeavor to maintain and enlarge our friendly relations with all the great powers, but they will not expect us to look kindly upon any project that would leave us subject to the dangers of a hostile observation or environment. We have not sought to dominate or to absorb any of our weaker neighbors, but rather to aid and encourage them to establish free and stable governments resting upon the consent of their own people. We have a clear right to expect, therefore, that no European Government will seek to establish colonial dependencies upon the territory of these independent American States. That which a sense of justice restrains us from seeking they may be reasonably expected willingly to forego.

It must not be assumed, however, that our interests are so exclusively American that our entire inattention to any events that may transpire elsewhere can be taken for granted. Our citizens domiciled for purposes of trade in all countries and in many of the islands of the sea demand and will have our adequate care in their personal and commercial rights. The necessities of our Navy require convenient coaling stations and dock and harbor privileges. These and other trading privileges we will feel free to obtain only by means that do not in any degree partake of coercion, however feeble the government from which we ask such concessions. But having fairly obtained them by methods and for purposes entirely consistent with the most friendly disposition toward all other powers, our consent will be necessary to any modification or impairment of the concession.

We shall neither fail to respect the flag of any friendly nation or the just rights of its citizens, nor to exact the like treatment for our own. Calmness, justice, and consideration should characterize our diplomacy. The offices of an intelligent diplomacy or of friendly arbitration in proper cases should be adequate to the peaceful adjustment of all international difficulties. By such methods we will make our contribution to the world's peace, which no nation values more highly, and avoid the opprobrium which must fall upon the nation that ruthlessly breaks it.

The duty devolved by law upon the President to nominate and, by and with the advice and consent of the Senate, to appoint all public officers whose appointment is not otherwise provided for in the Constitution or by act of Congress has become very burdensome and its wise and efficient discharge full of difficulty. The civil list is so large that a personal knowledge of any large number of the applicants is impossible. The President must rely upon the representations of others, and these are often made inconsiderately and without any just sense of responsibility. I have a right, I think, to insist that those who volunteer or are invited to give advice as to appointments shall exercise consideration and fidelity. A high sense of duty and an ambition to improve the service should characterize all public officers.

There are many ways in which the convenience and comfort of those who have business with our public offices may be promoted by a thoughtful and obliging officer, and I shall expect those whom I may appoint to justify their selection by a conspicuous efficiency in the discharge of their duties. Honorable party service will certainly not be esteemed by me a disqualification for public office, but it will in no case be allowed to serve as a shield of official negligence, incompetency, or delinquency. It is entirely creditable to seek public office by proper methods and with proper motives, and all applicants will be treated with consideration; but I shall need, and the heads of Departments will need, time for inquiry and deliberation. Persistent importunity will not, therefore, be the best support of an application for office. Heads of Departments, bureaus, and all other public officers having any duty connected therewith will be expected to enforce the civil-service law fully and without evasion. Beyond this obvious duty I hope to do something more to advance the reform of the civil service. The ideal, or even my own ideal, I shall probably not attain. Retrospect will be a safer basis of judgment than promises. We shall not, however, I am sure, be able to put our civil service upon a nonpartisan basis until we have secured an incumbency that fair-minded men of the opposition will approve for impartiality and integrity. As the number of such in the civil list is increased removals from office will diminish.

While a Treasury surplus is not the greatest evil, it is a serious evil. Our revenue should be ample to meet the ordinary annual demands upon our Treasury, with a sufficient margin for those extraordinary but scarcely less imperative demands which arise now and then. Expenditure should always be made with economy and only upon public necessity. Wastefulness, profligacy, or favoritism in public expenditures is criminal. But there is nothing in the condition of our country or of our people to suggest that anything presently necessary to the public prosperity, security, or honor should be unduly postponed.

It will be the duty of Congress wisely to forecast and estimate these extraordinary demands, and, having added them to our ordinary expenditures, to so adjust our revenue laws that no considerable annual surplus will remain. We will fortunately be able to apply to the redemption of the public debt any small and unforeseen excess of revenue. This is better than to reduce our income below our necessary expenditures, with the resulting choice between another change of our revenue laws and an increase of the public debt. It is quite possible, I am sure, to effect the necessary reduction in our revenues without breaking down our protective tariff or seriously injuring any domestic industry.

The construction of a sufficient number of modern war ships and of their necessary armament should progress as rapidly as is consistent with care and perfection in plans and workmanship. The spirit, courage, and skill of our naval officers and seamen have many times in our history given to weak ships and inefficient guns a rating greatly beyond that of the naval list. That they will again do so upon occasion I do not doubt; but they ought not, by premeditation or neglect, to be left to the risks and exigencies of an unequal combat. We should encourage the establishment of American steamship lines. The exchanges of commerce demand stated, reliable, and rapid means of communication, and until these are provided the development of our trade with the States lying south of us is impossible.

Our pension laws should give more adequate and discriminating relief to the Union soldiers and sailors and to their widows and orphans. Such occasions as this should remind us that we owe everything to their valor and sacrifice.

It is a subject of congratulation that there is a near prospect of the admission into the Union of the Dakotas and Montana and Washington Territories. This act of justice has been unreasonably delayed in the case of some of them. The people who have settled these Territories are intelligent, enterprising, and patriotic, and the accession these new States will add strength to the nation. It is due to the settlers in the Territories who have availed themselves of the invitations of our land laws to make homes upon the public domain that their titles should be speedily adjusted and their honest entries confirmed by patent.

It is very gratifying to observe the general interest now being manifested in the reform of our election laws. Those who have been for years calling attention to the pressing necessity of throwing about the ballot box and about the elector further safeguards, in order that our elections might not only be free and pure, but might clearly appear to be so, will welcome the accession of any who did not so soon discover the need of reform. The National Congress has not as yet taken control of elections in that case over which the Constitution gives it jurisdiction, but has accepted and adopted the election laws of the several States, provided penalties for their violation and a method of supervision. Only the inefficiency of the State laws or an unfair partisan administration of them could suggest a departure from this policy.

It was clearly, however, in the contemplation of the framers of the Constitution that such an exigency might arise, and provision was wisely made for it. The freedom of the ballot is a condition of our national life, and no power vested in Congress or in the Executive to secure or perpetuate it should remain unused upon occasion. The people of all the Congressional districts have an equal interest that the election in each shall truly express the views and wishes of a majority of the qualified electors residing within it. The results of such elections are not local, and the insistence of electors residing in other districts that they shall be pure and free does not savor at all of impertinence.

If in any of the States the public security is thought to be threatened by ignorance among the electors, the obvious remedy is education. The sympathy and help of our people will not be withheld from any community struggling with special embarrassments or difficulties connected with the suffrage if the remedies proposed proceed upon lawful lines and are promoted by just and honorable methods. How shall those who practice election frauds recover that respect for the sanctity of the ballot which is the first condition and obligation of good citizenship? The man who has come to regard the ballot box as a juggler's hat has renounced his allegiance.

Let us exalt patriotism and moderate our party contentions. Let those who would die for the flag on the field of battle give a better proof of their patriotism and a higher glory to their country by promoting fraternity and justice. A party success that is achieved by unfair methods or by practices that partake of revolution is hurtful and evanescent even from a party standpoint. We should hold our differing opinions in mutual respect, and, having submitted them to the arbitrament of the ballot, should accept an adverse judgment with the same respect that we would have demanded of our opponents if the decision had been in our favor.

No other people have a government more worthy of their respect and love or a land so magnificent in extent, so pleasant to look upon, and so full of generous suggestion to enterprise and labor. God has placed upon our head a diadem and has laid at our feet power and wealth beyond definition or calculation. But we must not forget that we take these gifts upon the condition that justice and mercy shall hold the reins of power and that the upward avenues of hope shall be free to all the people.

I do not mistrust the future. Dangers have been in frequent ambush along our path, but we have uncovered and vanquished them all. Passion has swept some of our communities, but only to give us a new demonstration that the great body of our people are stable, patriotic, and law-abiding. No political party can long pursue advantage at the expense of public honor or by rude and indecent methods without protest and fatal disaffection in its own body. The peaceful agencies of commerce are more fully revealing the necessary unity of all our communities, and the increasing intercourse of our people is promoting mutual respect. We shall find unalloyed pleasure in the revelation which our next census will make of the swift development of the great resources of some of the States. Each State will bring its generous contribution to the great aggregate of the nation's increase. And when the harvests from the fields, the cattle from the hills, and the ores of the earth shall have been weighed, counted, and valued, we will turn from them all to crown with the highest honor the State that has most promoted education, virtue, justice, and patriotism among its people.

# GROVER CLEVELAND
## SECOND INAUGURAL ADDRESS
### SATURDAY, MARCH 4, 1893

My Fellow-Citizens:

In obedience of the mandate of my countrymen I am about to dedicate myself to their service under the sanction of a solemn oath. Deeply moved by the expression of confidence and personal attachment which has called me to this service, I am sure my gratitude can make no better return than the pledge I now give before God and these witnesses of unreserved and complete devotion to the interests and welfare of those who have honored me.

I deem it fitting on this occasion, while indicating the opinion I hold concerning public questions of present importance, to also briefly refer to the existence of certain conditions and tendencies among our people which seem to menace the integrity and usefulness of their Government.

While every American citizen must contemplate with the utmost pride and enthusiasm the growth and expansion of our country, the sufficiency of our institutions to stand against the rudest shocks of violence, the wonderful thrift and enterprise of our people, and the demonstrated superiority of our free government, it behooves us to constantly watch for every symptom of insidious infirmity that threatens our national vigor.

The strong man who in the confidence of sturdy health courts the sternest activities of life and rejoices in the hardihood of constant labor may still have lurking near his vitals the unheeded disease that dooms him to sudden collapse.

It can not be doubted that our stupendous achievements as a people and our country's robust strength have given rise to heedlessness of those laws governing our national health which we can no more evade than human life can escape the laws of God and nature.

Manifestly nothing is more vital to our supremacy as a nation and to the beneficent purposes of our Government than a sound and stable currency. Its exposure to degradation should at once arouse to activity the most enlightened statesmanship, and the danger of depreciation in the purchasing power of the wages paid to toil should furnish the strongest incentive to prompt and conservative precaution.

In dealing with our present embarrassing situation as related to this subject we will be wise if we temper our confidence and faith in our national strength and resources with the frank concession that even these will not permit us to defy with impunity the inexorable laws of finance and trade. At the same time, in our efforts to adjust differences of opinion we should be free from intolerance or passion, and our judgments should be unmoved by alluring phrases and unvexed by selfish interests.

I am confident that such an approach to the subject will result in prudent and effective remedial legislation. In the meantime, so far as the executive branch of the Government can intervene, none of the powers with which it is invested will be withheld when their exercise is deemed necessary to maintain our national credit or avert financial disaster.

Closely related to the exaggerated confidence in our country's greatness which tends to a disregard of the rules of national safety, another danger confronts us not less serious. I refer to the prevalence of a popular disposition to expect from the operation of the Government especial and direct individual advantages.

The verdict of our voters which condemned the injustice of maintaining protection for protection's sake enjoins upon the people's servants the duty of exposing and destroying the brood of kindred evils which are the unwholesome progeny of paternalism. This is the bane of republican institutions and the constant peril of our government by the people. It degrades to the purposes of wily craft the plan of rule our fathers established and bequeathed to us as an object of our love and veneration. It perverts the patriotic sentiments of our countrymen and tempts them to pitiful calculation of the sordid gain to be derived from their Government's maintenance. It undermines the self-reliance of our people and substitutes in its place dependence upon governmental favoritism. It stifles the spirit of true Americanism and stupefies every ennobling trait of American citizenship.

The lessons of paternalism ought to be unlearned and the better lesson taught that while the people should patriotically and cheerfully support their Government its functions do not include the support of the people.

The acceptance of this principle leads to a refusal of bounties and subsidies, which burden the labor and thrift of a portion of our citizens to aid ill-advised or languishing enterprises in which they have no concern. It leads also to a challenge of wild and reckless pension expenditure, which overleaps the bounds of grateful recognition of patriotic service and prostitutes to vicious uses the people's prompt and generous impulse to aid those disabled in their country's defense.

Every thoughtful American must realize the importance of checking at its beginning any tendency in public or private station to regard frugality and economy as virtues which we may safely outgrow. The toleration of this idea results in the waste of the people's money by their chosen servants and encourages prodigality and extravagance in the home life of our countrymen.

Under our scheme of government the waste of public money is a crime against the citizen, and the contempt of our people for economy and frugality in their personal affairs deplorably saps the strength and sturdiness of our national character.

It is a plain dictate of honesty and good government that public expenditures should be limited by public necessity, and that this should be measured by the rules of strict economy; and it is equally clear that frugality among the people is the best guaranty of a contented and strong support of free institutions.

One mode of the misappropriation of public funds is avoided when appointments to office, instead of being the rewards of partisan activity, are awarded to those whose efficiency promises a fair return of work for the compensation paid to them. To secure the fitness and competency of appointees to office and remove from political action the demoralizing madness for spoils, civil-service reform has found a place in our public policy and laws. The benefits already gained through this instrumentality and the further usefulness it promises entitle it to the hearty support and encouragement of all who desire to see our public service well performed or who hope for the elevation of political sentiment and the purification of political methods.

The existence of immense aggregations of kindred enterprises and combinations of business interests formed for the purpose of limiting production and fixing prices is inconsistent with the fair field which ought to be open to every independent activity. Legitimate strife in business should not be superseded by an enforced concession to the demands of combinations that have the power to destroy, nor should the people to be served lose the benefit of cheapness which usually results from wholesome competition. These aggregations and combinations frequently constitute conspiracies against the interests of the people, and in all their phases they are unnatural and opposed to our American sense of fairness. To the extent that they can be reached and restrained by Federal power the General Government should relieve our citizens from their interference and exactions.

Loyalty to the principles upon which our Government rests positively demands that the equality before the law which it guarantees to every citizen should be justly and in good faith conceded in all parts of the land. The enjoyment of this right follows the badge of citizenship wherever found, and, unimpaired by race or color, it appeals for recognition to American manliness and fairness.

Our relations with the Indians located within our border impose upon us responsibilities we can not escape. Humanity and consistency require us to treat them with forbearance and in our dealings with them to honestly and considerately regard their rights and interests. Every effort should be made to lead them, through the paths of civilization and education, to self-supporting and independent citizenship. In the meantime, as the nation's wards, they should be promptly defended against the cupidity of designing men and shielded from every influence or temptation that retards their advancement.

The people of the United States have decreed that on this day the control of their Government in its legislative and executive branches shall be given to a political party pledged in the most positive terms to the accomplishment of tariff reform. They have thus determined in favor of a more just and equitable system of Federal taxation. The agents they have chosen to carry out their purposes are bound by their promises not less than by the command of their masters to devote themselves unremittingly to this service.

While there should be no surrender of principle, our task must be undertaken wisely and without heedless vindictiveness. Our mission is not punishment, but the rectification of wrong. If in lifting burdens from the daily life of our people we reduce inordinate and unequal advantages too long enjoyed, this is but a necessary incident of our return to right and justice. If we exact from unwilling minds acquiescence in the theory of an honest distribution of the fund of the governmental beneficence treasured up for all, we but insist upon a principle which underlies our free institutions. When we tear aside the delusions and misconceptions which have blinded our countrymen to their condition under vicious tariff laws, we but show them how far they have been led away from the paths of contentment and prosperity. When we proclaim that the necessity for revenue to support the Government furnishes the only justification for taxing the people, we announce a truth so plain that its denial would seem to indicate the extent to which judgment may be influenced by familiarity with perversions of the taxing power. And when we seek to reinstate the self-confidence and business enterprise of our citizens by discrediting an abject dependence upon governmental favor, we strive to stimulate those elements of American character which support the hope of American achievement.

Anxiety for the redemption of the pledges which my party has made and solicitude for the complete justification of the trust the people have reposed in us constrain me to remind those with whom I am to cooperate that we can succeed in doing the work which has been especially set before us only by the most sincere, harmonious, and disinterested effort. Even if insuperable obstacles and opposition prevent the consummation of our task, we shall hardly be excused; and if failure can be traced to our fault or neglect we may be sure the people will hold us to a swift and exacting accountability.

The oath I now take to preserve, protect, and defend the Constitution of the United States not only impressively defines the great responsibility I assume, but suggests obedience to constitutional commands as the rule by which my official conduct must be guided. I shall to the best of my ability and within my sphere of duty preserve the Constitution by loyally protecting every grant of Federal power it contains, by defending all its restraints when attacked by impatience and restlessness, and by enforcing its limitations and reservations in favor of the States and the people.

Fully impressed with the gravity of the duties that confront me and mindful of my weakness, I should be appalled if it were my lot to bear unaided the responsibilities which await me. I am, however, saved from discouragement when I remember that I shall have the support and the counsel and cooperation of wise and patriotic men who will stand at my side in Cabinet places or will represent the people in their legislative halls.

I find also much comfort in remembering that my countrymen are just and generous and in the assurance that they will not condemn those who by sincere devotion to their service deserve their forbearance and approval.

Above all, I know there is a Supreme Being who rules the affairs of men and whose goodness and mercy have always followed the American people, and I know He will not turn from us now if we humbly and reverently seek His powerful aid.

# WILLIAM MCKINLEY
## FIRST INAUGURAL ADDRESS
## THURSDAY, MARCH 4, 1897

Fellow-Citizens:

In obedience to the will of the people, and in their presence, by the authority vested in me by this oath, I assume the arduous and responsible duties of President of the United States, relying upon the support of my countrymen and invoking the guidance of Almighty God. Our faith teaches that there is no safer reliance than upon the God of our fathers, who has so singularly favored the American people in every national trial, and who will not forsake us so long as we obey His commandments and walk humbly in His footsteps.

The responsibilities of the high trust to which I have been called—always of grave importance—are augmented by the prevailing business conditions entailing idleness upon willing labor and loss to useful enterprises. The country is suffering from industrial disturbances from which speedy relief must be had. Our financial system needs some revision; our money is all good now, but its value must not further be threatened. It should all be put upon an enduring basis, not subject to easy attack, nor its stability to doubt or dispute. Our currency should continue under the supervision of the Government. The several forms of our paper money offer, in my judgment, a constant embarrassment to the Government and a safe balance in the Treasury. Therefore I believe it necessary to devise a system which, without diminishing the circulating medium or offering a premium for its contraction, will present a remedy for those arrangements which, temporary in their nature, might well in the years of our prosperity have been displaced by wiser provisions. With adequate revenue secured, but not until then, we can enter upon such changes in our fiscal laws as will, while insuring safety and volume to our money, no longer impose upon the Government the necessity of maintaining so large a gold reserve, with its attendant and inevitable temptations to speculation. Most of our financial laws are the outgrowth of experience and trial, and should not be amended without investigation and demonstration of the wisdom of the proposed changes. We must be both "sure we are right" and "make haste slowly." If, therefore, Congress, in its wisdom, shall deem it expedient to create a commission to take under early consideration the revision of our coinage, banking and currency laws, and give them that exhaustive, careful and dispassionate examination that their importance demands, I shall cordially concur in such action. If such power is vested in the President, it is my purpose to appoint a commission of prominent, well-informed citizens of different parties, who will command public confidence, both on account of their ability and special fitness for the work. Business experience and public training may thus be combined, and the patriotic zeal of the friends of the country be so directed that such a report will be made as to receive the support of all parties, and our finances cease to be the subject of mere partisan contention. The experiment is, at all events, worth a trial, and, in my opinion, it can but prove beneficial to the entire country.

The question of international bimetallism will have early and earnest attention. It will be my constant endeavor to secure it by co-operation with the other great commercial powers of the world. Until that condition is realized when the parity between our gold and silver money springs from and is supported by the relative value of the two metals, the value of the silver already coined and of that which may hereafter be coined, must be kept constantly at par with gold by every resource at our command. The credit of the Government, the integrity of its currency, and the inviolability of its obligations must be preserved. This was the commanding verdict of the people, and it will not be unheeded.

Economy is demanded in every branch of the Government at all times, but especially in periods, like the present, of depression in business and distress among the people. The severest economy must be observed in all public expenditures, and extravagance stopped wherever it is found, and prevented wherever in the future it may be developed. If the revenues are to remain as now, the only relief that can come must be from decreased expenditures. But the present

PRESIDENTIAL INAUGURAL ADDRESSES

must not become the permanent condition of the Government. It has been our uniform practice to retire, not increase our outstanding obligations, and this policy must again be resumed and vigorously enforced. Our revenues should always be large enough to meet with ease and promptness not only our current needs and the principal and interest of the public debt, but to make proper and liberal provision for that most deserving body of public creditors, the soldiers and sailors and the widows and orphans who are the pensioners of the United States.

The Government should not be permitted to run behind or increase its debt in times like the present. Suitably to provide against this is the mandate of duty—the certain and easy remedy for most of our financial difficulties. A deficiency is inevitable so long as the expenditures of the Government exceed its receipts. It can only be met by loans or an increased revenue. While a large annual surplus of revenue may invite waste and extravagance, inadequate revenue creates distrust and undermines public and private credit. Neither should be encouraged. Between more loans and more revenue there ought to be but one opinion. We should have more revenue, and that without delay, hindrance, or postponement. A surplus in the Treasury created by loans is not a permanent or safe reliance. It will suffice while it lasts, but it can not last long while the outlays of the Government are greater than its receipts, as has been the case during the past two years. Nor must it be forgotten that however much such loans may temporarily relieve the situation, the Government is still indebted for the amount of the surplus thus accrued, which it must ultimately pay, while its ability to pay is not strengthened, but weakened by a continued deficit. Loans are imperative in great emergencies to preserve the Government or its credit, but a failure to supply needed revenue in time of peace for the maintenance of either has no justification.

The best way for the Government to maintain its credit is to pay as it goes—not by resorting to loans, but by keeping out of debt—through an adequate income secured by a system of taxation, external or internal, or both. It is the settled policy of the Government, pursued from the beginning and practiced by all parties and Administrations, to raise the bulk of our revenue from taxes upon foreign productions entering the United States for sale and consumption, and avoiding, for the most part, every form of direct taxation, except in time of war. The country is clearly opposed to any needless additions to the subject of internal taxation, and is committed by its latest popular utterance to the system of tariff taxation. There can be no misunderstanding, either, about the principle upon which this tariff taxation shall be levied. Nothing has ever been made plainer at a general election than that the controlling principle in the raising of revenue from duties on imports is zealous care for American interests and American labor. The people have declared that such legislation should be had as will give ample protection and encouragement to the industries and the development of our country. It is, therefore, earnestly hoped and expected that Congress will, at the earliest practicable moment, enact revenue legislation that shall be fair, reasonable, conservative, and just, and which, while supplying sufficient revenue for public purposes, will still be signally beneficial and helpful to every section and every enterprise of the people. To this policy we are all, of whatever party, firmly bound by the voice of the people—a power vastly more potential than the expression of any political platform. The paramount duty of Congress is to stop deficiencies by the restoration of that protective legislation which has always been the firmest prop of the Treasury. The passage of such a law or laws would strengthen the credit of the Government both at home and abroad, and go far toward stopping the drain upon the gold reserve held for the redemption of our currency, which has been heavy and well-nigh constant for several years.

In the revision of the tariff especial attention should be given to the re-enactment and extension of the reciprocity principle of the law of 1890, under which so great a stimulus was given to our foreign trade in new and advantageous markets for our surplus agricultural and manufactured products. The brief trial given this legislation amply justifies a further experiment and additional discretionary power in the making of commercial treaties, the end in view always to be the opening up of new markets for the products of our country, by granting concessions to the products of other lands that we need and cannot produce ourselves, and which do not involve any loss of labor to our own people, but tend to increase their employment.

The depression of the past four years has fallen with especial severity upon the great body of toilers of the country, and upon none more than the holders of small farms. Agriculture has languished and labor suffered. The revival of manufacturing will be a relief to both. No portion of our population is more devoted to the institution of free government nor more loyal in their support, while none bears more cheerfully or fully its proper share in the maintenance of the Government or is better entitled to its wise and liberal care and protection. Legislation helpful to producers is beneficial to all. The depressed condition of industry on the farm and in the mine and factory has lessened the ability of the people to meet the demands upon them, and they rightfully expect that not only a system of revenue shall be established that will secure the largest income with the least burden, but that every means will be taken to decrease, rather than increase, our public expenditures. Business conditions are not the most promising. It will take time to restore the prosperity of former years. If we cannot promptly attain it, we can resolutely turn our faces in that direction and aid its return by friendly legislation. However troublesome the situation may appear, Congress will not, I am sure, be found lacking in disposition or ability to relieve it as far as legislation can do so. The restoration of confidence and the revival of business, which men of all parties so much desire, depend more largely upon the prompt, energetic, and intelligent action of Congress than upon any other single agency affecting the situation.

It is inspiring, too, to remember that no great emergency in the one hundred and eight years of our eventful national life has ever arisen that has not been met with wisdom and courage by the American people, with fidelity to their best interests and highest destiny, and to the honor of the American name. These years of glorious history have exalted mankind and advanced the cause of freedom throughout the world, and immeasurably strengthened the precious free institutions which we enjoy. The people love and will sustain these institutions. The great essential to our happiness and prosperity is that we adhere to the principles upon which the Government was established and insist upon their faithful observance. Equality of rights must prevail, and our laws be always and everywhere respected and obeyed. We may have failed in the discharge of our full duty as citizens of the great Republic, but it is consoling and encouraging to realize that free speech, a free press, free thought, free schools, the free and unmolested right of religious liberty and worship, and free and fair elections are dearer and more universally enjoyed today than ever before. These guaranties must be sacredly preserved and wisely strengthened. The constituted authorities must be cheerfully and vigorously upheld. Lynchings must not be tolerated in a great and civilized country like the United States; courts, not mobs, must execute the penalties of the law. The preservation of public order, the right of discussion, the integrity of courts, and the orderly administration of justice must continue forever the rock of safety upon which our Government securely rests.

One of the lessons taught by the late election, which all can rejoice in, is that the citizens of the United States are both law-respecting and law-abiding people, not easily swerved from the path of patriotism and honor. This is in entire accord with the genius of our institutions, and but emphasizes the advantages of inculcating even a greater love for law and order in the future. Immunity should be granted to none who violate the laws, whether individuals, corporations, or communities; and as the Constitution imposes upon the President the duty of both its own execution, and of the statutes enacted in pursuance of its provisions, I shall endeavor carefully to carry them into effect. The declaration of the party now restored to power has been in the past that of "opposition to all combinations of capital organized in trusts, or otherwise, to control arbitrarily the condition of trade among our citizens," and it has supported "such legislation as will prevent the execution of all schemes to oppress the people by undue charges on their supplies, or by unjust rates for the transportation of their products to the market." This purpose will be steadily pursued, both by the enforcement of the laws now in existence and the recommendation and support of such new statutes as may be necessary to carry it into effect.

Our naturalization and immigration laws should be further improved to the constant promotion of a safer, a better, and a higher citizenship. A grave peril to the Republic would be a citizenship too ignorant to understand or too vicious to appreciate the great value and beneficence of our institutions and laws, and against all who come here to make war upon them our gates must be promptly and tightly closed. Nor must we be unmindful of the need of improvement among our own citizens, but with the zeal of our forefathers encourage the spread of knowledge and free education. Illiteracy must be banished from the land if we shall attain that high destiny as the foremost of the enlightened nations of the world which, under Providence, we ought to achieve.

Reforms in the civil service must go on; but the changes should be real and genuine, not perfunctory, or prompted by a zeal in behalf of any party simply because it happens to be in power. As a member of Congress I voted and spoke in favor of the present law, and I shall attempt its enforcement in the spirit in which it was enacted. The purpose in view was to secure the most efficient service of the best men who would accept appointment under the Government, retaining faithful and devoted public servants in office, but shielding none, under the authority of any rule or custom, who are inefficient, incompetent, or unworthy. The best interests of the country demand this, and the people heartily approve the law wherever and whenever it has been thus administrated.

Congress should give prompt attention to the restoration of our American merchant marine, once the pride of the seas in all the great ocean highways of commerce. To my mind, few more important subjects so imperatively demand its intelligent consideration. The United States has progressed with marvelous rapidity in every field of enterprise and endeavor until we have become foremost in nearly all the great lines of inland trade, commerce, and industry. Yet, while this is true, our American merchant marine has been steadily declining until it is now lower, both in the percentage of tonnage and the number of vessels employed, than it was prior to the Civil War. Commendable progress has been made of late years in the upbuilding of the American Navy, but we must supplement these efforts by providing as a proper consort for it a merchant marine amply sufficient for our own carrying trade to foreign countries. The question is one that appeals both to our business necessities and the patriotic aspirations of a great people.

It has been the policy of the United States since the foundation of the Government to cultivate relations of peace and amity with all the nations of the world, and this accords with my conception of our duty now. We have cherished the policy of non-interference with affairs of foreign governments wisely inaugurated by Washington, keeping ourselves free from entanglement, either as allies or foes, content to leave undisturbed with them the settlement of their own domestic concerns. It will be our aim to pursue a firm and dignified foreign policy, which shall be just, impartial, ever watchful of our national honor, and always insisting upon the enforcement of the lawful rights of American citizens everywhere. Our diplomacy should seek nothing more and accept nothing less than is due us. We want no wars of conquest; we must avoid the temptation of territorial aggression. War should never be entered upon until every agency of peace has failed; peace is preferable to war in almost every contingency. Arbitration is the true method of settlement of international as well as local or individual differences. It was recognized as the best means of adjustment of differences between employers and employees by the Forty-ninth Congress, in 1886, and its application was extended to our diplomatic relations by the unanimous concurrence of the Senate and House of the Fifty-first Congress in 1890. The latter resolution was accepted as the basis of negotiations with us by the British House of Commons in 1893, and upon our invitation a treaty of arbitration between the United States and Great Britain was signed at Washington and transmitted to the Senate for its ratification in January last. Since this treaty is clearly the result of our own initiative; since it has been recognized as the leading feature of our foreign policy throughout our entire national history—the adjustment of difficulties by judicial methods rather than force of arms—and since it presents to the world the glorious example of reason and peace, not passion and war, controlling the relations between two of the greatest nations in the world, an example certain to be followed by others, I respectfully urge the early action of the Senate thereon, not merely as a matter of policy, but as a duty to mankind. The importance and moral influence of the ratification of such a treaty can hardly be overestimated in the cause of advancing civilization. It may well engage the best thought of the statesmen and people of every country, and I cannot but consider it fortunate that it was reserved to the United States to have the leadership in so grand a work.

It has been the uniform practice of each President to avoid, as far as possible, the convening of Congress in extraordinary session. It is an example which, under ordinary circumstances and in the absence of a public necessity, is to be commended. But a failure to convene the representatives of the people in Congress in extra session when it involves neglect of a public duty places the responsibility of such neglect upon the Executive himself. The condition of the public Treasury, as has been indicated, demands the immediate consideration of Congress. It alone has the power to provide revenues for the Government. Not to convene it under such circumstances I can view in no other sense than the neglect of a plain duty. I do not sympathize with the sentiment that Congress in session is dangerous to our general business interests. Its members are the agents of the people, and their presence at the seat of Government in the execution of the sovereign will should not operate as an injury, but a benefit. There could be no better time to put the Government upon a sound financial and economic basis than now. The people have only recently voted that this should be done, and nothing is more binding upon the agents of their will than the obligation of immediate action. It has always seemed to me that the postponement of the meeting of Congress until more than a year after it has been chosen deprived Congress too often of the inspiration of the popular will and the country of the corresponding benefits. It is evident, therefore, that to postpone action in the presence of so great a necessity would be unwise on the part of the Executive because unjust to the interests of the people. Our action now will be freer from mere partisan consideration than if the question of tariff revision was postponed until the regular session of Congress. We are nearly two years from a Congressional election, and politics cannot so greatly distract us as if such contest was immediately pending. We can approach the problem calmly and patriotically, without fearing its effect upon an early election.

Our fellow-citizens who may disagree with us upon the character of this legislation prefer to have the question settled now, even against their preconceived views, and perhaps settled so reasonably, as I trust and believe it will be, as to insure great permanence, than to have further uncertainty menacing the vast and varied business interests of the United States. Again, whatever action Congress may take will be given a fair opportunity for trial before the people are called to pass judgment upon it, and this I consider a great essential to the rightful and lasting settlement of the question. In view of these considerations, I shall deem it my duty as President to convene Congress in extraordinary session on Monday, the 15th day of March, 1897.

In conclusion, I congratulate the country upon the fraternal spirit of the people and the manifestations of good will everywhere so apparent. The recent election not only most fortunately demonstrated the obliteration of sectional or geographical lines, but to some extent also the prejudices which for years have distracted our councils and marred our true greatness as a nation. The triumph of the people, whose verdict is carried into effect today, is not the triumph of one section, nor wholly of one party, but of all sections and all the people. The North and the South no longer divide on the old lines, but upon principles and policies; and in this fact surely every lover of the country can find cause for true felicitation.

Let us rejoice in and cultivate this spirit; it is ennobling and will be both a gain and a blessing to our beloved country. It will be my constant aim to do nothing, and permit nothing to be done, that will arrest or disturb this growing sentiment of unity and cooperation, this revival of esteem and affiliation which now animates so many thousands in both the old antagonistic sections, but I shall cheerfully do everything possible to promote and increase it.

Let me again repeat the words of the oath administered by the Chief Justice which, in their respective spheres, so far as applicable, I would have all my countrymen observe: "I will faithfully execute the office of President of the United States, and will, to the best of my ability, preserve, protect, and defend the Constitution of the United States." This is the obligation I have reverently taken before the Lord Most High. To keep it will be my single purpose, my constant prayer; and I shall confidently rely upon the forbearance and assistance of all the people in the discharge of my solemn responsibilities.

# WILLIAM MCKINLEY
## SECOND INAUGURAL ADDRESS
## MONDAY, MARCH 4, 1901

My Fellow-Citizens:

When we assembled here on the 4th of March, 1897, there was great anxiety with regard to our currency and credit. None exists now. Then our Treasury receipts were inadequate to meet the current obligations of the Government. Now they are sufficient for all public needs, and we have a surplus instead of a deficit. Then I felt constrained to convene the Congress in extraordinary session to devise revenues to pay the ordinary expenses of the Government. Now I have the satisfaction to announce that the Congress just closed has reduced taxation in the sum of $41,000,000. Then there was deep solicitude because of the long depression in our manufacturing, mining, agricultural, and mercantile industries and the consequent distress of our laboring population. Now every avenue of production is crowded with activity, labor is well employed, and American products find good markets at home and abroad.

Our diversified productions, however, are increasing in such unprecedented volume as to admonish us of the necessity of still further enlarging our foreign markets by broader commercial relations. For this purpose reciprocal trade arrangements with other nations should in liberal spirit be carefully cultivated and promoted.

The national verdict of 1896 has for the most part been executed. Whatever remains unfulfilled is a continuing obligation resting with undiminished force upon the Executive and the Congress. But fortunate as our condition is, its permanence can only be assured by sound business methods and strict economy in national administration and legislation. We should not permit our great prosperity to lead us to reckless ventures in business or profligacy in public expenditures. While the Congress determines the objects and the sum of appropriations, the officials of the executive departments are responsible for honest and faithful disbursement, and it should be their constant care to avoid waste and extravagance.

Honesty, capacity, and industry are nowhere more indispensable than in public employment. These should be fundamental requisites to original appointment and the surest guaranties against removal.

Four years ago we stood on the brink of war without the people knowing it and without any preparation or effort at preparation for the impending peril. I did all that in honor could be done to avert the war, but without avail. It became inevitable; and the Congress at its first regular session, without party division, provided money in anticipation of the crisis and in preparation to meet it. It came. The result was signally favorable to American arms and in the highest degree honorable to the Government. It imposed upon us obligations from which we cannot escape and from which it would be dishonorable to seek escape. We are now at peace with the world, and it is my fervent prayer that if differences arise between us and other powers they may be settled by peaceful arbitration and that hereafter we may be spared the horrors of war.

Intrusted by the people for a second time with the office of President, I enter upon its administration appreciating the great responsibilities which attach to this renewed honor and commission, promising unreserved devotion on my part to their faithful discharge and reverently invoking for my guidance the direction and favor of Almighty God. I should shrink from the duties this day assumed if I did not feel that in their performance I should have the co-operation of the wise and patriotic men of all parties. It encourages me for the great task which I now undertake to believe that those who voluntarily committed to me the trust imposed upon the Chief Executive of the Republic will give to me generous support in my duties to "preserve, protect, and defend, the Constitution of the United States" and to "care that the laws be faithfully executed." The national purpose is indicated through a national election. It is the constitutional method of ascertaining the public will. When once it is registered it is a law to us all, and faithful observance should follow its decrees.

Strong hearts and helpful hands are needed, and, fortunately, we have them in every part of our beloved country. We are reunited. Sectionalism has disappeared. Division on public questions can no longer be traced by the war maps of 1861. These old differences less and less disturb the judgment. Existing problems demand the thought and quicken the conscience of the country, and the responsibility for their presence, as well as for their righteous settlement, rests upon us all—no more upon me than upon you. There are some national questions in the solution of which patriotism should exclude partisanship. Magnifying their difficulties will not take them off our hands nor facilitate their adjustment. Distrust of the capacity, integrity, and high purposes of the American people will not be an inspiring theme for future political contests. Dark pictures and gloomy forebodings are worse than useless. These only becloud, they do not help to point the way of safety and honor. "Hope maketh not ashamed." The prophets of evil were not the builders of the Republic, nor in its crises since have they saved or served it. The faith of the fathers was a mighty force in its creation, and the faith of their descendants has wrought its progress and furnished its defenders. They are obstructionists who despair, and who would destroy confidence in the ability of our people to solve wisely and for civilization the mighty problems resting upon them. The American people, intrenched in freedom at home, take their love for it with them wherever they go, and they reject as mistaken and unworthy the doctrine that we lose our own liberties by securing the enduring foundations of liberty to others. Our institutions will not deteriorate by extension, and our sense of justice will not abate under tropic suns in distant seas. As heretofore, so hereafter will the nation demonstrate its fitness to administer any new estate which events devolve upon it, and in the fear of God will "take occasion by the hand and make the bounds of freedom wider yet." If there are those among us who would make our way more difficult, we must not be disheartened, but the more earnestly dedicate ourselves to the task upon which we have rightly entered. The path of progress is seldom smooth. New things are often found hard to do. Our fathers found them so. We find them so. They are inconvenient. They cost us something. But are we not made better for the effort and sacrifice, and are not those we serve lifted up and blessed?

We will be consoled, too, with the fact that opposition has confronted every onward movement of the Republic from its opening hour until now, but without success. The Republic has marched on and on, and its step has exalted freedom and humanity. We are undergoing the same ordeal as did our predecessors nearly a century ago. We are following the course they blazed. They triumphed. Will their successors falter and plead organic impotency in the nation? Surely after 125 years of achievement for mankind we will not now surrender our equality with other powers on matters fundamental and essential to nationality. With no such purpose was the nation created. In no such spirit has it developed its full and independent sovereignty. We adhere to the principle of equality among ourselves, and by no act of ours will we assign to ourselves a subordinate rank in the family of nations.

My fellow-citizens, the public events of the past four years have gone into history. They are too near to justify recital. Some of them were unforeseen; many of them momentous and far-reaching in their consequences to ourselves and our relations with the rest of the world. The part which the United States bore so honorably in the thrilling scenes in China, while new to American life, has been in harmony with its true spirit and best traditions, and in dealing with the results its policy will be that of moderation and fairness.

We face at this moment a most important question that of the future relations of the United States and Cuba. With our near neighbors we must remain close friends. The declaration of the purposes of this Government in the resolution of April 20, 1898, must be made good. Ever since the evacuation of the island by the army of Spain, the Executive, with all practicable speed, has been assisting its people in the successive steps necessary to the establishment of a free and independent government prepared to assume and perform the obligations of international law which now rest upon the United States under the treaty of Paris. The convention elected by the people to frame a constitution is approaching the completion of its labors. The transfer of American control to the new government is of such great importance, involving an obligation resulting from our intervention and the treaty of peace, that I am glad to be advised by the recent act of Congress of the policy which the legislative branch of the Government deems essential to the best interests of Cuba and the United States. The principles which led to our intervention require that the fundamental law upon which the new government rests should be adapted to secure a government capable of performing the duties and discharging the functions of a separate nation, of observing its international obligations of protecting life and property, insuring order, safety, and liberty, and conforming to the established and historical policy of the United States in its relation to Cuba.

The peace which we are pledged to leave to the Cuban people must carry with it the guaranties of permanence. We became sponsors for the pacification of the island, and we remain accountable to the Cubans, no less than to our own country and people, for the reconstruction of Cuba as a free commonwealth on abiding foundations of right, justice, liberty, and assured order. Our enfranchisement of the people will not be completed until free Cuba shall "be a reality, not a name; a perfect entity, not a hasty experiment bearing within itself the elements of failure."

While the treaty of peace with Spain was ratified on the 6th of February, 1899, and ratifications were exchanged nearly two years ago, the Congress has indicated no form of government for the Philippine Islands. It has, however, provided an army to enable the Executive to suppress insurrection, restore peace, give security to the inhabitants, and establish the authority of the United States throughout the archipelago. It has authorized the organization of native troops as auxiliary to the regular force. It has been advised from time to time of the acts of the military and naval officers in the islands, of my action in appointing civil commissions, of the instructions with which they were charged, of their duties and powers, of their recommendations, and of their several acts under executive commission, together with the very complete general information they have submitted. These reports fully set forth the conditions, past and present, in the islands, and the instructions clearly show the principles which will guide the Executive until the Congress shall, as it is required to do by the treaty, determine "the civil rights and political status of the native inhabitants." The Congress having added the sanction of its authority to the powers already possessed and exercised by the Executive under the Constitution, thereby leaving with the Executive the responsibility for the government of the Philippines, I shall continue the efforts already begun until order shall be restored throughout the islands, and as fast as conditions permit will establish local governments, in the formation of which the full co-operation of the people has been already invited, and when established will encourage the people to administer them. The settled purpose, long ago proclaimed, to afford the inhabitants of the islands self-government as fast as they were ready for it will be pursued with earnestness and fidelity. Already something has been accomplished in this direction. The Government's representatives, civil and military, are doing faithful and noble work in their mission of emancipation and merit the approval and support of their countrymen. The most liberal terms of amnesty have already been communicated to the insurgents, and the way is still open for those who have raised their arms against the Government for honorable submission to its authority. Our countrymen should not be deceived. We are not waging war against the inhabitants of the Philippine Islands. A portion of them are making war against the United States. By far the greater part of the inhabitants recognize American sovereignty and welcome it as a guaranty of order and of security for life, property, liberty, freedom of conscience, and the pursuit of happiness. To them full protection will be given. They shall not be abandoned. We will not leave the destiny of the loyal millions the islands to the disloyal thousands who are in rebellion against the United States. Order under civil institutions will come as soon as those who now break the peace shall keep it. Force will not be needed or used when those who make war against us shall make it no more. May it end without further bloodshed, and there be ushered in the reign of peace to be made permanent by a government of liberty under law!

## THEODORE ROOSEVELT
## INAUGURAL ADDRESS
## SATURDAY, MARCH 4, 1905

My fellow-citizens, no people on earth have more cause to be thankful than ours, and this is said reverently, in no spirit of boastfulness in our own strength, but with gratitude to the Giver of Good who has blessed us with the conditions which have enabled us to achieve so large a measure of well-being and of happiness. To us as a people it has been granted to lay the foundations of our national life in a new continent. We are the heirs of the ages, and yet we have had to pay few of the penalties which in old countries are exacted by the dead hand of a bygone civilization. We have not been obliged to fight for our existence against any alien race; and yet our life has called for the vigor and effort without which the manlier and hardier virtues wither away. Under such conditions it would be our own fault if we failed; and the success which we have had in the past, the success which we confidently believe the future will bring, should cause in us no feeling of vainglory, but rather a deep and abiding realization of all which life has offered us; a full acknowledgment of the responsibility which is ours; and a fixed determination to show that under a free government a mighty people can thrive best, alike as regards the things of the body and the things of the soul.

Much has been given us, and much will rightfully be expected from us. We have duties to others and duties to ourselves; and we can shirk neither. We have become a great nation, forced by the fact of its greatness into relations with the other nations of the earth, and we must behave as beseems a people with such responsibilities. Toward all other nations, large and small, our attitude must be one of cordial and sincere friendship. We must show not only in our words, but in our deeds, that we are earnestly desirous of securing their good will by acting toward them in a spirit of just and generous recognition of all their rights. But justice and generosity in a nation, as in an individual, count most when shown not by the weak but by the strong. While ever careful to refrain from wrongdoing others, we must be no less insistent that we are not wronged ourselves. We wish peace, but we wish the peace of justice, the peace of righteousness. We wish it because we think it is right and not because we are afraid. No weak nation that acts manfully and justly should ever have cause to fear us, and no strong power should ever be able to single us out as a subject for insolent aggression.

Our relations with the other powers of the world are important; but still more important are our relations among ourselves. Such growth in wealth, in population, and in power as this nation has seen during the century and a quarter of its national life is inevitably accompanied by a like growth in the problems which are ever before every nation that rises to greatness. Power invariably means both responsibility and danger. Our forefathers faced certain perils which we have outgrown. We now face other perils, the very existence of which it was impossible that they should foresee. Modern life is both complex and intense, and the tremendous changes wrought by the extraordinary industrial development of the last half century are felt in every fiber of our social and political being. Never before have men tried so vast and formidable an experiment as that of administering the affairs of a continent under the forms of a Democratic republic. The conditions which have told for our marvelous material well-being, which have developed to a very high degree our energy, self-reliance, and individual initiative, have also brought the care and anxiety inseparable from the accumulation of great wealth in industrial centers. Upon the success of our experiment much depends, not only as regards our own welfare, but as regards the welfare of mankind. If we fail, the cause of free self-government throughout the world will rock to its foundations, and therefore our responsibility is heavy, to ourselves, to the world as it is today, and to the generations yet unborn. There is no good reason why we should fear the future, but there is every reason why we should face it seriously, neither hiding from ourselves the gravity of the problems before us nor fearing to approach these problems with the unbending, unflinching purpose to solve them aright.

Yet, after all, though the problems are new, though the tasks set before us differ from the tasks set before our fathers who founded and preserved this Republic, the spirit in which these tasks must be undertaken and these problems faced, if our duty is to be well done, remains essentially unchanged. We know that self-government is difficult. We know that no people needs such high traits of character as that people which seeks to govern its affairs aright through the freely expressed will of the freemen who compose it. But we have faith that we shall not prove false to the memories of the men of the mighty past. They did their work, they left us the splendid heritage we now enjoy. We in our turn have an assured confidence that we shall be able to leave this heritage unwasted and enlarged to our children and our children's children. To do so we must show, not merely in great crises, but in the everyday affairs of life, the qualities of practical intelligence, of courage, of hardihood, and endurance, and above all the power of devotion to a lofty ideal, which made great the men who founded this Republic in the days of Washington, which made great the men who preserved this Republic in the days of Abraham Lincoln.

# WILLIAM HOWARD TAFT
## INAUGURAL ADDRESS
## THURSDAY, MARCH 4, 1909

My Fellow-Citizens:

Anyone who has taken the oath I have just taken must feel a heavy weight of responsibility. If not, he has no conception of the powers and duties of the office upon which he is about to enter, or he is lacking in a proper sense of the obligation which the oath imposes.

The office of an inaugural address is to give a summary outline of the main policies of the new administration, so far as they can be anticipated. I have had the honor to be one of the advisers of my distinguished predecessor, and, as such, to hold up his hands in the reforms he has initiated. I should be untrue to myself, to my promises, and to the declarations of the party platform upon which I was elected to office, if I did not make the maintenance and enforcement of those reforms a most important feature of my administration. They were directed to the suppression of the lawlessness and abuses of power of the great combinations of capital invested in railroads and in industrial enterprises carrying on interstate commerce. The steps which my predecessor took and the legislation passed on his recommendation have accomplished much, have caused a general halt in the vicious policies which created popular alarm, and have brought about in the business affected a much higher regard for existing law.

To render the reforms lasting, however, and to secure at the same time freedom from alarm on the part of those pursuing proper and progressive business methods, further legislative and executive action are needed. Relief of the railroads from certain restrictions of the antitrust law have been urged by my predecessor and will be urged by me. On the other hand, the administration is pledged to legislation looking to a proper federal supervision and restriction to prevent excessive issues of bonds and stock by companies owning and operating interstate commerce railroads.

Then, too, a reorganization of the Department of Justice, of the Bureau of Corporations in the Department of Commerce and Labor, and of the Interstate Commerce Commission, looking to effective cooperation of these agencies, is needed to secure a more rapid and certain enforcement of the laws affecting interstate railroads and industrial combinations.

I hope to be able to submit at the first regular session of the incoming Congress, in December next, definite suggestions in respect to the needed amendments to the antitrust and the interstate commerce law and the changes required in the executive departments concerned in their enforcement.

It is believed that with the changes to be recommended American business can be assured of that measure of stability and certainty in respect to those things that may be done and those that are prohibited which is essential to the life and growth of all business. Such a plan must include the right of the people to avail themselves of those methods of combining capital and effort deemed necessary to reach the highest degree of economic efficiency, at the same time differentiating between combinations based upon legitimate economic reasons and those formed with the intent of creating monopolies and artificially controlling prices.

The work of formulating into practical shape such changes is creative word of the highest order, and requires all the deliberation possible in the interval. I believe that the amendments to be proposed are just as necessary in the protection of legitimate business as in the clinching of the reforms which properly bear the name of my predecessor.

A matter of most pressing importance is the revision of the tariff. In accordance with the promises of the platform upon which I was elected, I shall call Congress into extra session to meet on the 15th day of March, in order that consideration may be at once given to a bill revising the Dingley Act. This should secure an adequate revenue and adjust the duties in such a manner as to afford to labor and to all industries in this country, whether of the farm, mine or factory, protection by tariff equal to the difference between the cost of production abroad and the cost of production here, and have a provision which shall put into force, upon executive determination of certain facts, a higher or maximum tariff against those countries whose trade policy toward us equitably requires such discrimination. It is thought that there has been such a change in conditions since the enactment of the Dingley Act, drafted on a similarly protective principle, that the measure of the tariff above stated will permit the reduction of rates in certain schedules and will require the advancement of few, if any.

The proposal to revise the tariff made in such an authoritative way as to lead the business community to count upon it necessarily halts all those branches of business directly affected; and as these are most important, it disturbs the whole business of the country. It is imperatively necessary, therefore, that a tariff bill be drawn in good faith in accordance with promises made before the election by the party in power, and as promptly passed as due consideration will permit. It is not that the tariff is more important in the long run than the perfecting of the reforms in respect to antitrust legislation and interstate commerce regulation, but the need for action when the revision of the tariff has been determined upon is more immediate to avoid embarrassment of business. To secure the needed speed in the passage of the tariff bill, it would seem wise to attempt no other legislation at the extra session. I venture this as a suggestion only, for the course to be taken by Congress, upon the call of the Executive, is wholly within its discretion.

In the mailing of a tariff bill the prime motive is taxation and the securing thereby of a revenue. Due largely to the business depression which followed the financial panic of 1907, the revenue from customs and other sources has decreased to such an extent that the expenditures for the current fiscal year will exceed the receipts by $100,000,000. It is imperative that such a deficit shall not continue, and the framers of the tariff bill must, of course, have in mind the total revenues likely to be produced by it and so arrange the duties as to secure an adequate income. Should it be impossible to do so by import duties, new kinds of taxation must be adopted, and among these I recommend a graduated inheritance tax as correct in principle and as certain and easy of collection.

The obligation on the part of those responsible for the expenditures made to carry on the Government, to be as economical as possible, and to make the burden of taxation as light as possible, is plain, and should be affirmed in every declaration of government policy. This is especially true when we are face to face with a heavy deficit. But when the desire to win the popular approval leads to the cutting off of expenditures really needed to make the Government effective and to enable it to accomplish its proper objects, the result is as much to be condemned as the waste of government funds in unnecessary expenditure. The scope of a modern government in what it can and ought to accomplish for its people has been widened far beyond the principles laid down by the old "laissez faire" school of political writers, and this widening has met popular approval.

In the Department of Agriculture the use of scientific experiments on a large scale and the spread of information derived from them for the improvement of general agriculture must go on.

The importance of supervising business of great railways and industrial combinations and the necessary investigation and prosecution of unlawful business methods are another necessary tax upon Government which did not exist half a century ago.

The putting into force of laws which shall secure the conservation of our resources, so far as they may be within the jurisdiction of the Federal Government, including the most important work of saving and restoring our forests and the great improvement of waterways, are all proper government functions which must involve large expenditure if properly performed. While some of them, like the reclamation of arid lands, are made to pay for themselves, others are of such an indirect benefit that this cannot be expected of them. A permanent improvement, like the Panama Canal, should be treated as a distinct enterprise, and should be paid for by the proceeds of bonds, the issue of which will distribute its cost between the present and future generations in accordance with the benefits derived. It may well be submitted to the serious consideration of Congress whether the deepening and control of the channel of a great river system, like that of the Ohio or of the Mississippi, when definite and practical plans for the enterprise have been approved and determined upon, should not be provided for in the same way.

Then, too, there are expenditures of Government absolutely necessary if our country is to maintain its proper place among the nations of the world, and is to exercise its proper influence in defense of its own trade interests in the maintenance of traditional American policy against the colonization of European monarchies in this hemisphere, and in the promotion of peace and international morality. I refer to the cost of maintaining a proper army, a proper navy, and suitable fortifications upon the mainland of the United States and in its dependencies.

We should have an army so organized and so officered as to be capable in time of emergency, in cooperation with the national militia and under the provisions of a proper national volunteer law, rapidly to expand into a force sufficient to resist all probable invasion from abroad and to furnish a respectable expeditionary force if necessary in the maintenance of our traditional American policy which bears the name of President Monroe.

Our fortifications are yet in a state of only partial completeness, and the number of men to man them is insufficient. In a few years however, the usual annual appropriations for our coast defenses, both on the mainland and in the dependencies, will make them sufficient to resist all direct attack, and by that time we may hope that the men to man them will be provided as a necessary adjunct. The distance of our shores from Europe and Asia of course reduces the necessity for maintaining under arms a great army, but it does not take away the requirement of mere prudence—that we should have an army sufficiently large and so constituted as to form a nucleus out of which a suitable force can quickly grow.

What has been said of the army may be affirmed in even a more emphatic way of the navy. A modern navy can not be improvised. It must be built and in existence when the emergency arises which calls for its use and operation. My distinguished predecessor has in many speeches and messages set out with great force and striking language the necessity for maintaining a strong navy commensurate with the coast line, the governmental resources, and the foreign trade of our Nation; and I wish to reiterate all the reasons which he has presented in favor of the policy of maintaining a strong navy as the best conservator of our peace with other nations, and the best means of securing respect for the assertion of our rights, the defense of our interests, and the exercise of our influence in international matters.

Our international policy is always to promote peace. We shall enter into any war with a full consciousness of the awful consequences that it always entails, whether successful or not, and we, of course, shall make every effort consistent with national honor and the highest national interest to avoid a resort to arms. We favor every instrumentality, like that of the Hague Tribunal and arbitration treaties made with a view to its use in all international controversies, in order to maintain peace and to avoid war. But we should be blind to existing conditions and should allow ourselves to become foolish idealists if we did not realize that, with all the nations of the world armed and prepared for war, we must be ourselves in a similar condition, in order to prevent other nations from taking advantage of us and of our inability to defend our interests and assert our rights with a strong hand.

In the international controversies that are likely to arise in the Orient growing out of the question of the open door and other issues the United States can maintain her interests intact and can secure respect for her just demands. She will not be able to do so, however, if it is understood that she never intends to back up her assertion of right and her defense of her interest by anything but mere verbal protest and diplomatic note. For these reasons the expenses of the army and navy and of coast defenses should always be considered as something which the Government must pay for, and they should not be cut off through mere consideration of economy. Our Government is able to afford a suitable army and a suitable navy. It may maintain them without the slightest danger to the Republic or the cause of free institutions, and fear of additional taxation ought not to change a proper policy in this regard.

The policy of the United States in the Spanish war and since has given it a position of influence among the nations that it never had before, and should be constantly exerted to securing to its bona fide citizens, whether native or naturalized, respect for them as such in foreign countries. We should make every effort to prevent humiliating and degrading prohibition against any of our citizens wishing temporarily to sojourn in foreign countries because of race or religion.

The admission of Asiatic immigrants who cannot be amalgamated with our population has been made the subject either of prohibitory clauses in our treaties and statutes or of strict administrative regulation secured by diplomatic negotiation. I sincerely hope that we may continue to minimize the evils likely to arise from such immigration without unnecessary friction and by mutual concessions between self-respecting governments. Meantime we must take every precaution to prevent, or failing that, to punish outbursts of race feeling among our people against foreigners of whatever nationality who have by our grant a treaty right to pursue lawful business here and to be protected against lawless assault or injury.

This leads me to point out a serious defect in the present federal jurisdiction, which ought to be remedied at once. Having assured to other countries by treaty the protection of our laws for such of their subjects or citizens as we permit to come within our jurisdiction, we now leave to a state or a city, not under the control of the Federal Government, the duty of performing our international obligations in this respect. By proper legislation we may, and ought to, place in the hands of the Federal Executive the means of enforcing the treaty rights of such aliens in the courts of the Federal Government. It puts our Government in a pusillanimous position to make definite engagements to protect aliens and then to excuse the failure to perform those engagements by an explanation that the duty to keep them is in States or cities, not within our control. If we would promise we must put ourselves in a position to perform our promise. We cannot permit the possible failure of justice, due to local prejudice in any State or municipal government, to expose us to the risk of a war which might be avoided if federal jurisdiction was asserted by suitable legislation by Congress and carried out by proper proceedings instituted by the Executive in the courts of the National Government.

One of the reforms to be carried out during the incoming administration is a change of our monetary and banking laws, so as to secure greater elasticity in the forms of currency available for trade and to prevent the limitations of law from operating to increase the embarrassment of a financial panic. The monetary commission, lately appointed, is giving full consideration to existing conditions and to all proposed remedies, and will doubtless suggest one that will meet the requirements of business and of public interest.

We may hope that the report will embody neither the narrow view of those who believe that the sole purpose of the new system should be to secure a large return on banking capital or of those who would have greater expansion of currency with little regard to provisions for its immediate redemption or ultimate security. There is no subject of economic discussion so intricate and so likely to evoke differing views and dogmatic statements as this one. The commission, in studying the general influence of currency on business and of business on currency, have wisely extended their investigations in European banking and monetary methods. The information that they have derived from such experts as they have found abroad will undoubtedly be found helpful in the solution of the difficult problem they have in hand.

The incoming Congress should promptly fulfill the promise of the Republican platform and pass a proper postal savings bank bill. It will not be unwise or excessive paternalism. The promise to repay by the Government will furnish an inducement to savings deposits which private enterprise can not supply and at such a low rate of interest as not to withdraw custom from existing banks. It will substantially increase the funds available for investment as capital in useful enterprises. It will furnish absolute security which makes the proposed scheme of government guaranty of deposits so alluring, without its pernicious results.

I sincerely hope that the incoming Congress will be alive, as it should be, to the importance of our foreign trade and of encouraging it in every way feasible. The possibility of increasing this trade in the Orient, in the Philippines, and in South America are known to everyone who has given the matter attention. The direct effect of free trade between this country and the Philippines will be marked upon our sales of cottons, agricultural machinery, and other manufactures. The necessity of the establishment of direct lines of steamers between North and South America has been brought to the attention of Congress by my predecessor and by Mr. Root before and after his noteworthy visit to that continent, and I sincerely hope that Congress may be induced to see the wisdom of a tentative effort to establish such lines by the use of mail subsidies.

The importance of the part which the Departments of Agriculture and of Commerce and Labor may play in ridding the markets of Europe of prohibitions and discriminations against the importation of our products is fully understood, and it is hoped that the use of the maximum and minimum feature of our tariff law to be soon passed will be effective to remove many of those restrictions.

The Panama Canal will have a most important bearing upon the trade between the eastern and far western sections of our country, and will greatly increase the facilities for transportation between the eastern and the western seaboard, and may possibly revolutionize the transcontinental rates with respect to bulky merchandise. It will also have a most beneficial effect to increase the trade between the eastern seaboard of the United States and the western coast of South America, and, indeed, with some of the important ports on the east coast of South America reached by rail from the west coast.

The work on the canal is making most satisfactory progress. The type of the canal as a lock canal was fixed by Congress after a full consideration of the conflicting reports of the majority and minority of the consulting board, and after the recommendation of the War Department and the Executive upon those reports. Recent suggestion that something had occurred on the Isthmus to make the lock type of the canal less feasible than it was supposed to be when the reports were made and the policy determined on led to a visit to the Isthmus of a board of competent engineers to examine the Gatun dam and locks, which are the key of the lock type. The report of that board shows nothing has occurred in the nature of newly revealed evidence which should change the views once formed in the original discussion. The construction will go on under a most effective organization controlled by Colonel Goethals and his fellow army engineers associated with him, and will certainly be completed early in the next administration, if not before.

Some type of canal must be constructed. The lock type has been selected. We are all in favor of having it built as promptly as possible. We must not now, therefore, keep up a fire in the rear of the agents whom we have authorized to do our work on the Isthmus. We must hold up their hands, and speaking for the incoming administration I wish to say that I propose to devote all the energy possible and under my control to pushing of this work on the plans which have been adopted, and to stand behind the men who are doing faithful, hard work to bring about the early completion of this, the greatest constructive enterprise of modern times.

The governments of our dependencies in Porto Rico and the Philippines are progressing as favorably as could be desired. The prosperity of Porto Rico continues unabated. The business conditions in the Philippines are not all that we could wish them to be, but with the passage of the new tariff bill permitting free trade between the United States and the archipelago, with such limitations on sugar and tobacco as shall prevent injury to domestic interests in those products, we can count on an improvement in business conditions in the Philippines and the development of a mutually profitable trade between this country and the islands. Meantime our Government in each dependency is upholding the traditions of civil liberty and increasing popular control which might be expected under American auspices. The work which we are doing there redounds to our credit as a nation.

I look forward with hope to increasing the already good feeling between the South and the other sections of the country. My chief purpose is not to effect a change in the electoral vote of the Southern States. That is a secondary consideration. What I look forward to is an increase in the tolerance of political views of all kinds and their advocacy throughout the South, and the existence of a respectable political opposition in every State; even more than this, to an increased feeling on the part of all the people in the South that this Government is their Government, and that its officers in their states are their officers.

The consideration of this question can not, however, be complete and full without reference to the negro race, its progress and its present condition. The thirteenth amendment secured them freedom; the fourteenth amendment due process of law, protection of property, and the pursuit of happiness; and the fifteenth amendment attempted to secure the negro against any deprivation of the privilege to vote because he was a negro. The thirteenth and fourteenth amendments have been generally enforced and have secured the objects for which they are intended. While the fifteenth amendment has not been generally observed in the past, it ought to be observed, and the tendency of Southern legislation today is toward the enactment of electoral qualifications which shall square with that amendment. Of course, the mere adoption of a constitutional law is only one step in the right direction. It must be fairly and justly enforced as well. In time both will come. Hence it is clear to all that the domination of an ignorant, irresponsible element can be prevented by constitutional laws which shall exclude from voting both negroes and whites not having education or other qualifications thought to be necessary for a proper electorate. The danger of the control of an ignorant electorate has therefore passed. With this change, the interest which many of the Southern white citizens take in the welfare of the negroes has increased. The colored men must base their hope on the results of their own industry, self-restraint, thrift, and business success, as well as upon the aid and comfort and sympathy which they may receive from their white neighbors of the South.

There was a time when Northerners who sympathized with the negro in his necessary struggle for better conditions sought to give him the suffrage as a protection to enforce its exercise against the prevailing sentiment of the South. The movement proved to be a failure. What remains is the fifteenth amendment to the Constitution and the right to have statutes of States specifying qualifications for electors subjected to the test of compliance with that amendment. This is a great protection to the negro. It never will be repealed, and it never ought to be repealed. If it had not passed, it might be difficult now to adopt it; but with it in our fundamental law, the policy of Southern legislation must and will tend to obey it, and so long as the statutes of the States meet the test of this amendment and are not otherwise in conflict with the Constitution and laws of the United States, it is not the disposition or within the province of the Federal Government to interfere with the regulation by Southern States of their domestic affairs. There is in the South a stronger feeling than ever among the intelligent well-to-do, and influential element in favor of the industrial education of the negro and the encouragement of the race to make themselves useful members of the community. The progress which the negro has made in the last fifty years, from slavery, when its statistics are reviewed, is marvelous, and it furnishes every reason to hope that in the next twenty-five years a still greater improvement in his condition as a productive member of society, on the farm, and in the shop, and in other occupations may come.

The negroes are now Americans. Their ancestors came here

years ago against their will, and this is their only country and their only flag. They have shown themselves anxious to live for it and to die for it. Encountering the race feeling against them, subjected at times to cruel injustice growing out of it, they may well have our profound sympathy and aid in the struggle they are making. We are charged with the sacred duty of making their path as smooth and easy as we can. Any recognition of their distinguished men, any appointment to office from among their number, is properly taken as an encouragement and an appreciation of their progress, and this just policy should be pursued when suitable occasion offers.

But it may well admit of doubt whether, in the case of any race, an appointment of one of their number to a local office in a community in which the race feeling is so widespread and acute as to interfere with the ease and facility with which the local government business can be done by the appointee is of sufficient benefit by way of encouragement to the race to outweigh the recurrence and increase of race feeling which such an appointment is likely to engender. Therefore the Executive, in recognizing the negro race by appointments, must exercise a careful discretion not thereby to do it more harm than good. On the other hand, we must be careful not to encourage the mere pretense of race feeling manufactured in the interest of individual political ambition.

Personally, I have not the slightest race prejudice or feeling, and recognition of its existence only awakens in my heart a deeper sympathy for those who have to bear it or suffer from it, and I question the wisdom of a policy which is likely to increase it. Meantime, if nothing is done to prevent it, a better feeling between the negroes and the whites in the South will continue to grow, and more and more of the white people will come to realize that the future of the South is to be much benefited by the industrial and intellectual progress of the negro. The exercise of political franchises by those of this race who are intelligent and well to do will be acquiesced in, and the right to vote will be withheld only from the ignorant and irresponsible of both races.

There is one other matter to which I shall refer. It was made the subject of great controversy during the election and calls for at least a passing reference now. My distinguished predecessor has given much attention to the cause of labor, with whose struggle for better things he has shown the sincerest sympathy. At his instance Congress has passed the bill fixing the liability of interstate carriers to their employees for injury sustained in the course of employment, abolishing the rule of fellow-servant and the common-law rule as to contributory negligence, and substituting therefor the so-called rule of "comparative negligence." It has also passed a law fixing the compensation of government employees for injuries sustained in the employ of the Government through the negligence of the superior. It has also passed a model child-labor law for the District of Columbia. In previous administrations an arbitration law for interstate commerce railroads and their employees, and laws for the application of safety devices to save the lives and limbs of employees of interstate railroads had been passed. Additional legislation of this kind was passed by the outgoing Congress.

I wish to say that insofar as I can I hope to promote the enactment of further legislation of this character. I am strongly convinced that the Government should make itself as responsible to employees injured in its employ as an interstate-railway corporation is made responsible by federal law to its employees; and I shall be glad, whenever any additional reasonable safety device can be invented to reduce the loss of life and limb among railway employees, to urge Congress to require its adoption by interstate railways.

Another labor question has arisen which has awakened the most excited discussion. That is in respect to the power of the federal courts to issue injunctions in industrial disputes. As to that, my convictions are fixed. Take away from the courts, if it could be taken away, the power to issue injunctions in labor disputes, and it would create a privileged class among the laborers and save the lawless among their number from a most needful remedy available to all men for the protection of their business against lawless invasion. The proposition that business is not a property or pecuniary right which can be protected by equitable injunction is utterly without foundation in precedent or reason. The proposition is usually linked with one to make the secondary boycott lawful. Such a proposition is at variance with the American instinct, and will find no support, in my judgment, when submitted to the American people. The secondary boycott is an instrument of tyranny, and ought not to be made legitimate.

The issue of a temporary restraining order without notice has in several instances been abused by its inconsiderate exercise, and to remedy this the platform upon which I was elected recommends the formulation in a statute of the conditions under which such a temporary restraining order ought to issue. A statute can and ought to be framed to embody the best modern practice, and can bring the subject so closely to the attention of the court as to make abuses of the process unlikely in the future. The American people, if I understand them, insist that the authority of the courts shall be sustained, and are opposed to any change in the procedure by which the powers of a court may be weakened and the fearless and effective administration of justice be interfered with.

Having thus reviewed the questions likely to recur during my administration, and having expressed in a summary way the position which I expect to take in recommendations to Congress and in my conduct as an Executive, I invoke the considerate sympathy and support of my fellow-citizens and the aid of the Almighty God in the discharge of my responsible duties.

# WOODROW WILSON
## FIRST INAUGURAL ADDRESS
## TUESDAY, MARCH 4, 1913

There has been a change of government. It began two years ago, when the House of Representatives became Democratic by a decisive majority. It has now been completed. The Senate about to assemble will also be Democratic. The offices of President and Vice-President have been put into the hands of Democrats. What does the change mean? That is the question that is uppermost in our minds today. That is the question I am going to try to answer, in order, if I may, to interpret the occasion.

It means much more than the mere success of a party. The success of a party means little except when the Nation is using that party for a large and definite purpose. No one can mistake the purpose for which the Nation now seeks to use the Democratic Party. It seeks to use it to interpret a change in its own plans and point of view. Some old things with which we had grown familiar, and which had begun to creep into the very habit of our thought and of our lives, have altered their aspect as we have latterly looked critically upon them, with fresh, awakened eyes; have dropped their disguises and shown themselves alien and sinister. Some new things, as we look frankly upon them, willing to comprehend their real character, have come to assume the aspect of things long believed in and familiar, stuff of our own convictions. We have been refreshed by a new insight into our own life.

We see that in many things that life is very great. It is incomparably great in its material aspects, in its body of wealth, in the diversity and sweep of its energy, in the industries which have been conceived and built up by the genius of individual men and the limitless enterprise of groups of men. It is great, also, very great, in its moral force. Nowhere else in the world have noble men and women exhibited in more striking forms the beauty and the energy of sympathy and helpfulness and counsel in their efforts to rectify wrong, alleviate suffering, and set the weak in the way of strength and hope. We have built up, moreover, a great system of government, which has stood through a long age as in many respects a model for those who seek to set liberty upon foundations that will endure against fortuitous change, against storm and accident. Our life contains every great thing, and contains it in rich abundance.

But the evil has come with the good, and much fine gold has been corroded. With riches has come inexcusable waste. We have squandered a great part of what we might have used, and have not stopped to conserve the exceeding bounty of nature, without which our genius for enterprise would have been worthless and impotent, scorning to be careful, shamefully prodigal as well as admirably efficient. We have been proud of our industrial achievements, but we have not hitherto stopped thoughtfully enough to count the human cost, the cost of lives snuffed out, of energies overtaxed and broken, the fearful physical and spiritual cost to the men and women and children upon whom the dead weight and burden of it all has fallen pitilessly the years through. The groans and agony of it all had not yet reached our ears, the solemn, moving undertone of our life, coming up out of the mines and factories, and out of every home where the struggle had its intimate and familiar seat. With the great Government went many deep secret things which we too long delayed to look into and scrutinize with candid, fearless eyes. The great Government we loved has too often been made use of for private and selfish purposes, and those who used it had forgotten the people.

At last a vision has been vouchsafed us of our life as a whole. We see the bad with the good, the debased and decadent with the sound and vital. With this vision we approach new affairs. Our duty is to cleanse, to reconsider, to restore, to correct the evil without impairing the good, to purify and humanize every process of our common life without weakening or sentimentalizing it. There has been something crude and heartless and unfeeling in our haste to succeed and be great. Our thought has been "Let every man look out for himself, let every generation look out for itself," while we reared giant machinery which made it impossible that any but those who stood at the levers of control should have a chance to look out for themselves. We had not forgotten our morals. We remembered well enough that we had set up a policy which was meant to serve the humblest as well as the most powerful, with an eye single to the standards of justice and fair play, and remembered it with pride. But we were very heedless and in a hurry to be great.

We have come now to the sober second thought. The scales of heedlessness have fallen from our eyes. We have made up our minds to square every process of our national life again with the standards we so proudly set up at the beginning and have always carried at our hearts. Our work is a work of restoration.

We have itemized with some degree of particularity the things that ought to be altered and here are some of the chief items: A tariff which cuts us off from our proper part in the commerce of the world, violates the just principles of taxation, and makes the Government a facile instrument in the hand of private interests; a banking and currency system based upon the necessity of the Government to sell its bonds fifty years ago and perfectly adapted to concentrating cash and restricting credits; an industrial system which, take it on all its sides, financial as well as administrative, holds capital in leading strings, restricts the liberties and limits the opportunities of labor, and exploits without renewing or conserving the natural resources of the country; a body of agricultural activities never yet given the efficiency of great business undertakings or served as it should be through the instrumentality of science taken directly to the farm, or afforded the facilities of credit best suited to its practical needs; watercourses undeveloped, waste places unreclaimed, forests untended, fast disappearing without plan or prospect of renewal, unregarded waste heaps at every mine. We have studied as perhaps no other nation has the most effective means of production, but we have not studied cost or economy as we should either as organizers of industry, as statesmen, or as individuals.

Nor have we studied and perfected the means by which government may be put at the service of humanity, in safeguarding the health of the Nation, the health of its men and its women and its children, as well as their rights in the struggle for existence. This is no sentimental duty. The firm basis of government is justice, not pity. These are matters of justice. There can be no equality or opportunity, the first essential of justice in the body politic, if men and women and children be not shielded in their lives, their very vitality, from the consequences of great industrial and social processes which they can not alter, control, or singly cope with. Society must see to it that it does not itself crush or weaken or damage its own constituent parts. The first duty of law is to keep sound the society it serves. Sanitary laws, pure food laws, and laws determining conditions of labor which individuals are powerless to determine for themselves are intimate parts of the very business of justice and legal efficiency.

These are some of the things we ought to do, and not leave the others undone, the old-fashioned, never-to-be-neglected, fundamental safeguarding of property and of individual right. This is the high enterprise of the new day: To lift everything that concerns our life as a Nation to the light that shines from the hearthfire of every man's conscience and vision of the right. It is inconceivable that we should do this as partisans; it is inconceivable we should do it in ignorance of the facts as they are or in blind haste. We shall restore, not destroy. We shall deal with our economic system as it is and as it may be modified, not as it might be if we had a clean sheet of paper to write upon; and step by step we shall make it what it should be, in the spirit of those who question their own wisdom and seek counsel and knowledge, not shallow self-satisfaction or the excitement of excursions whither they can not tell. Justice, and only justice, shall always be our motto.

And yet it will be no cool process of mere science. The Nation has been deeply stirred, stirred by a solemn passion, stirred by the knowledge of wrong, of ideals lost, of government too often debauched and made an instrument of evil. The feelings with which we face this new age of right and opportunity sweep across our heartstrings like some air out of God's own presence, where justice and mercy are reconciled and the judge and the brother are one. We know our task to be no mere task of politics but a task which shall search us through and through, whether we be able to understand our time and the need of our people, whether we be indeed their spokesmen and interpreters, whether we have the pure heart to comprehend and the rectified will to choose our high course of action.

This is not a day of triumph; it is a day of dedication. Here muster, not the forces of party, but the forces of humanity. Men's hearts wait upon us; men's lives hang in the balance; men's hopes call upon us to say what we will do. Who shall live up to the great trust? Who dares fail to try? I summon all honest men, all patriotic, all forward-looking men, to my side. God helping me, I will not fail them, if they will but counsel and sustain me!

# WOODROW WILSON
## SECOND INAUGURAL ADDRESS
## MONDAY, MARCH 5, 1917

My Fellow Citizens:

The four years which have elapsed since last I stood in this place have been crowded with counsel and action of the most vital interest and consequence. Perhaps no equal period in our history has been so fruitful of important reforms in our economic and industrial life or so full of significant changes in the spirit and purpose of our political action. We have sought very thoughtfully to set our house in order, correct the grosser errors and abuses of our industrial life, liberate and quicken the processes of our national genius and energy, and lift our politics to a broader view of the people's essential interests.

It is a record of singular variety and singular distinction. But I shall not attempt to review it. It speaks for itself and will be of increasing influence as the years go by. This is not the time for retrospect. It is time rather to speak our thoughts and purposes concerning the present and the immediate future.

Although we have centered counsel and action with such unusual concentration and success upon the great problems of domestic legislation to which we addressed ourselves four years ago, other matters have more and more forced themselves upon our attention— matters lying outside our own life as a nation and over which we had no control, but which, despite our wish to keep free of them, have drawn us more and more irresistibly into their own current and influence.

It has been impossible to avoid them. They have affected the life of the whole world. They have shaken men everywhere with a passion and an apprehension they never knew before. It has been hard to preserve calm counsel while the thought of our own people swayed this way and that under their influence. We are a composite and cosmopolitan people. We are of the blood of all the nations that are at war. The currents of our thoughts as well as the currents of our trade run quick at all seasons back and forth between us and them. The war inevitably set its mark from the first alike upon our minds, our industries, our commerce, our politics and our social action. To be indifferent to it, or independent of it, was out of the question.

And yet all the while we have been conscious that we were not part of it. In that consciousness, despite many divisions, we have drawn closer together. We have been deeply wronged upon the seas, but we have not wished to wrong or injure in return; have retained throughout the consciousness of standing in some sort apart, intent upon an interest that transcended the immediate issues of the war itself.

As some of the injuries done us have become intolerable we have still been clear that we wished nothing for ourselves that we were not ready to demand for all mankind—fair dealing, justice, the freedom to live and to be at ease against organized wrong.

It is in this spirit and with this thought that we have grown more and more aware, more and more certain that the part we wished to play was the part of those who mean to vindicate and fortify peace. We have been obliged to arm ourselves to make good our claim to a certain minimum of right and of freedom of action. We stand firm in armed neutrality since it seems that in no other way we can demonstrate what it is we insist upon and cannot forget. We may even be drawn on, by circumstances, not by our own purpose or desire, to a more active assertion of our rights as we see them and a more immediate association with the great struggle itself. But nothing will alter our thought or our purpose. They are too clear to be obscured. They are too deeply rooted in the principles of our national life to be altered. We desire neither conquest nor advantage. We wish nothing that can be had only at the cost of another people. We always professed unselfish purpose and we covet the opportunity to prove our professions are sincere.

There are many things still to be done at home, to clarify our own politics and add new vitality to the industrial processes of our own life, and we shall do them as time and opportunity serve, but we realize that the greatest things that remain to be done must be done with the whole world for stage and in cooperation with the wide and universal forces of mankind, and we are making our spirits ready for those things.

We are provincials no longer. The tragic events of the thirty months of vital turmoil through which we have just passed have made us citizens of the world. There can be no turning back. Our own fortunes as a nation are involved whether we would have it so or not.

And yet we are not the less Americans on that account. We shall be the more American if we but remain true to the principles in which we have been bred. They are not the principles of a province or of a single continent. We have known and boasted all along that they were the principles of a liberated mankind. These, therefore, are the things we shall stand for, whether in war or in peace:

That all nations are equally interested in the peace of the world and in the political stability of free peoples, and equally responsible for their maintenance; that the essential principle of peace is the actual equality of nations in all matters of right or privilege; that peace cannot securely or justly rest upon an armed balance of power; that governments derive all their just powers from the consent of the governed and that no other powers should be supported by the common thought, purpose or power of the family of nations; that the seas should be equally free and safe for the use of all peoples, under rules set up by common agreement and consent, and that, so far as practicable, they should be accessible to all upon equal terms; that national armaments shall be limited to the necessities of national order and domestic safety; that the community of interest and of power upon which peace must henceforth depend imposes upon each nation the duty of seeing to it that all influences proceeding from its own citizens meant to encourage or assist revolution in other states should be sternly and effectually suppressed and prevented.

I need not argue these principles to you, my fellow countrymen; they are your own part and parcel of your own thinking and your own motives in affairs. They spring up native amongst us. Upon this as a platform of purpose and of action we can stand together. And it is imperative that we should stand together. We are being forged into a new unity amidst the fires that now blaze throughout the world. In their ardent heat we shall, in God's Providence, let us hope, be purged of faction and division, purified of the errant humors of party and of private interest, and shall stand forth in the days to come with a new dignity of national pride and spirit. Let each man see to it that the dedication is in his own heart, the high purpose of the nation in his own mind, ruler of his own will and desire.

I stand here and have taken the high and solemn oath to which you have been audience because the people of the United States have chosen me for this august delegation of power and have by their gracious judgment named me their leader in affairs.

I know now what the task means. I realize to the full the responsibility which it involves. I pray God I may be given the wisdom and the prudence to do my duty in the true spirit of this great people. I am their servant and can succeed only as they sustain and guide me by their confidence and their counsel. The thing I shall count upon, the thing without which neither counsel nor action will avail, is the unity of America—an America united in feeling, in purpose and in its vision of duty, of opportunity and of service.

We are to beware of all men who would turn the tasks and the necessities of the nation to their own private profit or use them for the building up of private power.

United alike in the conception of our duty and in the high resolve to perform it in the face of all men, let us dedicate ourselves to the great task to which we must now set our hand. For myself I beg your tolerance, your countenance and your united aid.

The shadows that now lie dark upon our path will soon be dispelled, and we shall walk with the light all about us if we be but true to ourselves—to ourselves as we have wished to be known in the counsels of the world and in the thought of all those who love liberty and justice and the right exalted.

# WARREN G. HARDING
## INAUGURAL ADDRESS
### FRIDAY, MARCH 4, 1921

M y Countrymen:

When one surveys the world about him after the great storm, noting the marks of destruction and yet rejoicing in the ruggedness of the things which withstood it, if he is an American he breathes the clarified atmosphere with a strange mingling of regret and new hope. We have seen a world passion spend its fury, but we contemplate our Republic unshaken, and hold our civilization secure. Liberty—liberty within the law—and civilization are inseparable, and though both were threatened we find them now secure; and there comes to Americans the profound assurance that our representative government is the highest expression and surest guaranty of both.

Standing in this presence, mindful of the solemnity of this occasion, feeling the emotions which no one may know until he senses the great weight of responsibility for himself, I must utter my belief in the divine inspiration of the founding fathers. Surely there must have been God's intent in the making of this new-world Republic. Ours is an organic law which had but one ambiguity, and we saw that effaced in a baptism of sacrifice and blood, with union maintained, the Nation supreme, and its concord inspiring. We have seen the world rivet its hopeful gaze on the great truths on which the founders wrought. We have seen civil, human, and religious liberty verified and glorified. In the beginning the Old World scoffed at our experiment; today our foundations of political and social belief stand unshaken, a precious inheritance to ourselves, an inspiring example of freedom and civilization to all mankind. Let us express renewed and strengthened devotion, in grateful reverence for the immortal beginning, and utter our confidence in the supreme fulfillment.

The recorded progress of our Republic, materially and spiritually, in itself proves the wisdom of the inherited policy of noninvolvement in Old World affairs. Confident of our ability to work out our own destiny, and jealously guarding our right to do so, we seek no part in directing the destinies of the Old World. We do not mean to be entangled. We will accept no responsibility except as our own conscience and judgment, in each instance, may determine.

Our eyes never will be blind to a developing menace, our ears never deaf to the call of civilization. We recognize the new order in the world, with the closer contacts which progress has wrought. We sense the call of the human heart for fellowship, fraternity, and cooperation. We crave friendship and harbor no hate. But America, our America, the America builded on the foundation laid by the inspired fathers, can be a party to no permanent military alliance. It can enter into no political commitments, nor assume any economic obligations which will subject our decisions to any other than our own authority.

I am sure our own people will not misunderstand, nor will the world misconstrue. We have no thought to impede the paths to closer relationship. We wish to promote understanding. We want to do our part in making offensive warfare so hateful that Governments and peoples who resort to it must prove the righteousness of their cause or stand as outlaws before the bar of civilization.

We are ready to associate ourselves with the nations of the world, great and small, for conference, for counsel; to seek the expressed views of world opinion; to recommend a way to approximate disarmament and relieve the crushing burdens of military and naval establishments. We elect to participate in suggesting plans for mediation, conciliation, and arbitration, and would gladly join in that expressed conscience of progress, which seeks to clarify and write the laws of international relationship, and establish a world court for the disposition of such justiciable questions as nations are agreed to submit thereto. In expressing aspirations, in seeking practical plans, in translating humanity's new concept of righteousness and justice and its hatred of war into recommended action we are ready most heartily to unite, but every commitment must be made in the exercise of our national sovereignty. Since freedom impelled, and independence inspired, and nationality exalted, a world supergovernment is contrary to everything we cherish and can have no sanction by our Republic. This is not selfishness, it is sanctity. It is not aloofness, it is security. It is not suspicion of others, it is patriotic adherence to the things which made us what we are.

Today, better than ever before, we know the aspirations of humankind, and share them. We have come to a new realization of our place in the world and a new appraisal of our Nation by the world. The unselfishness of these United States is a thing proven; our devotion to peace for ourselves and for the world is well established; our concern for preserved civilization has had its impassioned and heroic expression. There was no American failure to resist the attempted reversion of civilization; there will be no failure today or tomorrow.

The success of our popular government rests wholly upon the correct interpretation of the deliberate, intelligent, dependable popular will of America. In a deliberate questioning of a suggested change of national policy, where internationality was to supersede nationality, we turned to a referendum, to the American people. There was ample discussion, and there is a public mandate in manifest understanding.

America is ready to encourage, eager to initiate, anxious to participate in any seemly program likely to lessen the probability of war, and promote that brotherhood of mankind which must be God's highest conception of human relationship. Because we cherish ideals of justice and peace, because we appraise international comity and helpful relationship no less highly than any people of the world, we aspire to a high place in the moral leadership of civilization, and we hold a maintained America, the proven Republic, the unshaken temple of representative democracy, to be not only an inspiration and example, but the highest agency of strengthening good will and promoting accord on both continents.

Mankind needs a world-wide benediction of understanding. It is needed among individuals, among peoples, among governments, and it will inaugurate an era of good feeling to make the birth of a new order. In such understanding men will strive confidently for the promotion of their better relationships and nations will promote the comities so essential to peace.

We must understand that ties of trade bind nations in closest intimacy, and none may receive except as he gives. We have not strengthened ours in accordance with our resources or our genius, notably on our own continent, where a galaxy of Republics reflects the glory of new-world democracy, but in the new order of finance and trade we mean to promote enlarged activities and seek expanded confidence.

Perhaps we can make no more helpful contribution by example than prove a Republic's capacity to emerge from the wreckage of war. While the world's embittered travail did not leave us devastated lands nor desolated cities, left no gaping wounds, no breast with hate, it did involve us in the delirium of expenditure, in expanded currency and credits, in unbalanced industry, in unspeakable waste, and disturbed relationships. While it uncovered our portion of hateful selfishness at home, it also revealed the heart of America as sound and fearless, and beating in confidence unfailing.

Amid it all we have riveted the gaze of all civilization to the unselfishness and the righteousness of representative democracy, where our freedom never has made offensive warfare, never has sought territorial aggrandizement through force, never has turned to the arbitrament of arms until reason has been exhausted. When the Governments of the earth shall have established a freedom like our own and shall have sanctioned the pursuit of peace as we have practiced it, I believe the last sorrow and the final sacrifice of international warfare will have been written.

Let me speak to the maimed and wounded soldiers who are present today, and through them convey to their comrades the gratitude of the Republic for their sacrifices in its defense. A generous country will never forget the services you rendered, and you may hope for a policy under Government that will relieve any maimed successors from taking your places on another such occasion as this.

Our supreme task is the resumption of our onward, normal way. Reconstruction, readjustment, restoration all these must follow. I would like to hasten them. If it will lighten the spirit and add to the resolution with which we take up the task, let me repeat for our Nation, we shall give no people just cause to make war upon us; we hold no national prejudices; we entertain no spirit of revenge; we do not hate; we do not covet; we dream of no conquest, nor boast of armed prowess.

If, despite this attitude, war is again forced upon us, I earnestly hope a way may be found which will unify our individual and collective strength and consecrate all America, materially and spiritually, body and soul, to national defense. I can envision the ideal republic, where every man and woman is called under the flag for assignment to duty for whatever service, military or civic, the individual is best fitted; where we may call to universal service every plant, agency, or facility, all in the sublime sacrifice for country, and not one penny of war profit shall inure to the benefit of private individual, corporation, or combination, but all above the normal shall flow into the defense chest of the Nation. There is something inherently wrong, something out of accord with the ideals of representative democracy, when one portion of our citizenship turns its activities to private gain amid defensive war while another is fighting, sacrificing, or dying for national preservation.

Out of such universal service will come a new unity of spirit and purpose, a new confidence and consecration, which would make our defense impregnable, our triumph assured. Then we should have little or no disorganization of our economic, industrial, and commercial systems at home, no staggering war debts, no swollen fortunes to flout the sacrifices of our soldiers, no excuse for sedition, no pitiable slackerism, no outrage of treason. Envy and jealousy would have no soil for their menacing development, and revolution would be without the passion which engenders it.

A regret for the mistakes of yesterday must not, however, blind us to the tasks of today. War never left such an aftermath. There has been staggering loss of life and measureless wastage of materials. Nations are still groping for return to stable ways. Discouraging indebtedness confronts us like all the war-torn nations, and these obligations must be provided for. No civilization can survive repudiation.

We can reduce the abnormal expenditures, and we will. We can strike at war taxation, and we must. We must face the grim necessity, with full knowledge that the task is to be solved, and we must proceed with a full realization that no statute enacted by man can repeal the inexorable laws of nature. Our most dangerous tendency is to expect too much of government, and at the same time do for it too little. We contemplate the immediate task of putting our public household in order. We need a rigid and yet sane economy, combined with fiscal justice, and it must be attended by individual prudence and thrift, which are so essential to this trying hour and reassuring for the future.

The business world reflects the disturbance of war's reaction. Herein flows the lifeblood of material existence. The economic mechanism is intricate and its parts interdependent, and has suffered the shocks and jars incident to abnormal demands, credit inflations, and price upheavals. The normal balances have been impaired, the channels of distribution have been clogged, the relations of labor and management have been strained. We must seek the readjustment with care and courage. Our people must give and take. Prices must reflect the receding fever of war activities. Perhaps we never shall know the old levels of wages again, because war invariably readjusts compensations, and the necessaries of life will show their inseparable relationship, but we must strive for normalcy to reach stability. All the penalties will not be light, nor evenly distributed. There is no way of making them so. There is no instant step from disorder to order. We must face a condition of grim reality, charge off our losses and start afresh. It is the oldest lesson of civilization. I would like government to do all it can to mitigate; then, in understanding, in mutuality of interest, in concern for the common good, our tasks will be solved. No altered system will work a miracle. Any wild experiment will only add to the confusion. Our best assurance lies in efficient administration of our proven system.

The forward course of the business cycle is unmistakable. Peoples are turning from destruction to production. Industry has sensed the changed order and our own people are turning to resume their normal, onward way. The call is for productive America to go on. I know that Congress and the Administration will favor every wise Government policy to aid the resumption and encourage continued progress.

I speak for administrative efficiency, for lightened tax burdens, for sound commercial practices, for adequate credit facilities, for sympathetic concern for all agricultural problems, for the omission of unnecessary interference of Government with business, for an end to Government's experiment in business, and for more efficient business in Government administration. With all of this must attend a mindfulness of the human side of all activities, so that social, industrial, and economic justice will be squared with the purposes of a righteous people.

With the nation-wide induction of womanhood into our political life, we may count upon her intuitions, her refinements, her intelligence, and her influence to exalt the social order. We count upon her exercise of the full privileges and the performance of the duties of citizenship to speed the attainment of the highest state.

I wish for an America no less alert in guarding against dangers from within than it is watchful against enemies from without. Our fundamental law recognizes no class, no group, no section; there must be none in legislation or administration. The supreme inspiration is the common weal. Humanity hungers for international peace, and we crave it with all mankind. My most reverent prayer for America is for industrial peace, with its rewards, widely and generally distributed, amid the inspirations of equal opportunity. No one justly may deny the equality of opportunity which made us what we are. We have mistaken unpreparedness to embrace it to be a challenge of the reality, and due concern for making all citizens fit for participation will give added strength of citizenship and magnify our achievement.

If revolution insists upon overturning established order, let other peoples make the tragic experiment. There is no place for it in America. When World War threatened civilization we pledged our resources and our lives to its preservation, and when revolution threatens we unfurl the flag of law and order and renew our consecration. Ours is a constitutional freedom where the popular will is the law supreme and minorities are sacredly protected. Our revisions, reformations, and evolutions reflect a deliberate judgment and an orderly progress, and we mean to cure our ills, but never destroy or permit destruction by force.

I had rather submit our industrial controversies to the conference table in advance than to a settlement table after conflict and suffering. The earth is thirsting for the cup of good will, understanding is its fountain source. I would like to acclaim an era of good feeling amid dependable prosperity and all the blessings which attend.

It has been proved again and again that we cannot, while throwing our markets open to the world, maintain American standards of living and opportunity, and hold our industrial eminence in such unequal competition. There is a luring fallacy in the theory of banished barriers of trade, but preserved American standards require our higher production costs to be reflected in our tariffs on imports. Today, as never before, when peoples are seeking trade restoration and expansion, we must adjust our tariffs to the new order. We seek participation in the world's exchanges, because therein lies our way to widened influence and the triumphs of peace. We know full well we cannot sell where we do not buy, and we cannot sell successfully where we do not carry. Opportunity is calling not alone for the restoration, but for a new era in production, transportation and trade. We shall answer it best by meeting the demand of a surpassing home market, by promoting self-reliance in production, and by bidding enterprise, genius, and efficiency to carry our cargoes in American bottoms to the marts of the world.

We would not have an America living within and for herself alone, but we would have her self-reliant, independent, and ever nobler, stronger, and richer. Believing in our higher standards, reared through constitutional liberty and maintained opportunity, we invite the world to the same heights. But pride in things wrought is no reflex of a completed task. Common welfare is the goal of our national endeavor. Wealth is not inimical to welfare; it ought to be its friendliest agency. There never can be equality of rewards or possessions so long as the human plan contains varied talents and differing degrees of industry and thrift, but ours ought to be a country free from the great blotches of distressed poverty. We ought to find a way to guard against the perils and penalties of unemployment. We want an America of homes, illumined with hope and happiness, where mothers, freed from the necessity for long hours of toil beyond their own doors, may preside as befits the hearthstone of American citizenship. We want the cradle of American childhood rocked under conditions so wholesome and so hopeful that no blight may touch it in its development, and we want to provide that no selfish interest, no material necessity, no lack of opportunity shall prevent the gaining of that education so essential to best citizenship.

There is no short cut to the making of these ideals into glad realities. The world has witnessed again and again the futility and the mischief of ill-considered remedies for social and economic disorders. But we are mindful today as never before of the friction of modern industrialism, and we must learn its causes and reduce its evil consequences by sober and tested methods. Where genius has made for great possibilities, justice and happiness must be reflected in a greater common welfare.

Service is the supreme commitment of life. I would rejoice to acclaim the era of the Golden Rule and crown it with the autocracy of service. I pledge an administration wherein all the agencies of Government are called to serve, and ever promote an understanding of Government purely as an expression of the popular will.

One cannot stand in this presence and be unmindful of the tremendous responsibility. The world upheaval has added heavily to our tasks. But with the realization comes the surge of high resolve, and there is reassurance in belief in the God-given destiny of our Republic. If I felt that there is to be sole responsibility in the Executive for the America of tomorrow I should shrink from the burden. But here are a hundred millions, with common concern and shared responsibility, answerable to God and country. The Republic summons them to their duty, and I invite co-operation.

I accept my part with single-mindedness of purpose and humility of spirit, and implore the favor and guidance of God in His Heaven. With these I am unafraid, and confidently face the future.

I have taken the solemn oath of office on that passage of Holy Writ wherein it is asked: "What doth the Lord require of thee but to do justly, and to love mercy, and to walk humbly with thy God?" This I plight to God and country.

## CALVIN COOLIDGE
## INAUGURAL ADDRESS
## WEDNESDAY, MARCH 4, 1925

My Countrymen:

No one can contemplate current conditions without finding much that is satisfying and still more that is encouraging. Our own country is leading the world in the general readjustment to the results of the great conflict. Many of its burdens will bear heavily upon us for years, and the secondary and indirect effects we must expect to experience for some time. But we are beginning to comprehend more definitely what course should be pursued, what remedies ought to be applied, what actions should be taken for our deliverance, and are clearly manifesting a determined will faithfully and conscientiously to adopt these methods of relief. Already we have sufficiently rearranged our domestic affairs so that confidence has returned, business has revived, and we appear to be entering an era of prosperity which is gradually reaching into every part of the Nation. Realizing that we can not live unto ourselves alone, we have contributed of our resources and our counsel to the relief of the suffering and the settlement of the disputes among the European nations. Because of what America is and what America has done, a firmer courage, a higher hope, inspires the heart of all humanity.

These results have not occurred by mere chance. They have been secured by a constant and enlightened effort marked by many sacrifices and extending over many generations. We can not continue these brilliant successes in the future, unless we continue to learn from the past. It is necessary to keep the former experiences of our country both at home and abroad continually before us, if we are to have any science of government. If we wish to erect new structures, we must have a definite knowledge of the old foundations. We must realize that human nature is about the most constant thing in the universe and that the essentials of human relationship do not change. We must frequently take our bearings from these fixed stars of our political firmament if we expect to hold a true course. If we examine carefully what we have done, we can determine the more accurately what we can do.

We stand at the opening of the one hundred and fiftieth year since our national consciousness first asserted itself by unmistakable action with an array of force. The old sentiment of detached and dependent colonies disappeared in the new sentiment of a united and independent Nation. Men began to discard the narrow confines of a local charter for the broader opportunities of a national constitution. Under the eternal urge of freedom we became an independent Nation. A little less than 50 years later that freedom and independence were reasserted in the face of all the world, and guarded, supported, and secured by the Monroe doctrine. The narrow fringe of States along the Atlantic seaboard advanced its frontiers across the hills and plains of an intervening continent until it passed down the golden slope to the Pacific. We made freedom a birthright. We extended our domain over distant islands in order to safeguard our own interests and accepted the consequent obligation to bestow justice and liberty upon less favored peoples. In the defense of our own ideals and in the general cause of liberty we entered the Great War. When victory had been fully secured, we withdrew to our own shores unrecompensed save in the consciousness of duty done.

Throughout all these experiences we have enlarged our freedom, we have strengthened our independence. We have been, and propose to be, more and more American. We believe that we can best serve our own country and most successfully discharge our obligations to humanity by continuing to be openly and candidly, intensely and scrupulously, American. If we have any heritage, it has been that. If we have any destiny, we have found it in that direction.

But if we wish to continue to be distinctively American, we must continue to make that term comprehensive enough to embrace the legitimate desires of a civilized and enlightened people determined in all their relations to pursue a conscientious and religious life. We can not permit ourselves to be narrowed and dwarfed by slogans and phrases. It is not the adjective, but the substantive, which is of real importance. It is not the name of the action, but the result of the action, which is the chief concern. It will be well not to be too much disturbed by the thought of either isolation or entanglement of pacifists and militarists. The physical configuration of the earth has separated us from all of the Old World, but the common brotherhood of man, the highest law of all our being, has united us by inseparable bonds with all humanity. Our country represents nothing but peaceful intentions toward all the earth, but it ought not to fail to maintain such a military force as comports with the dignity and security of a great people. It ought to be a balanced force, intensely modern, capable of defense by sea and land, beneath the surface and in the air. But it should be so conducted that all the world may see in it, not a menace, but an instrument of security and peace.

This Nation believes thoroughly in an honorable peace under which the rights of its citizens are to be everywhere protected. It has never found that the necessary enjoyment of such a peace could be maintained only by a great and threatening array of arms. In common with other nations, it is now more determined than ever to promote peace through friendliness and good will, through mutual understandings and mutual forbearance. We have never practiced the policy of competitive armaments. We have recently committed ourselves by covenants with the other great nations to a limitation of our sea power. As one result of this, our Navy ranks larger, in comparison, than it ever did before. Removing the burden of expense and jealousy, which must always accrue from a keen rivalry, is one of the most effective methods of diminishing that unreasonable hysteria and misunderstanding which are the most potent means of fomenting war. This policy represents a new departure in the world. It is a thought, an ideal, which has led to an entirely new line of action. It will not be easy to maintain. Some never moved from their old positions, some are constantly slipping back to the old ways of thought and the old action of seizing a musket and relying on force. America has taken the lead in this new direction, and that lead America must continue to hold. If we expect others to rely on our fairness and justice we must show that we rely on their fairness and justice.

If we are to judge by past experience, there is much to be hoped for in international relations from frequent conferences and consultations. We have before us the beneficial results of the Washington conference and the various consultations recently held upon European affairs, some of which were in response to our suggestions and in some of which we were active participants. Even the failures can not but be accounted useful and an immeasurable advance over threatened or actual warfare. I am strongly in favor of continuation of this policy, whenever conditions are such that there is even a promise that practical and favorable results might be secured.

In conformity with the principle that a display of reason rather than a threat of force should be the determining factor in the intercourse among nations, we have long advocated the peaceful settlement of disputes by methods of arbitration and have negotiated many treaties to secure that result. The same considerations should lead to our adherence to the Permanent Court of International Justice. Where great principles are involved, where great movements are under way which promise much for the welfare of humanity by reason of the very fact that many other nations have given such movements their actual support, we ought not to withhold our own sanction because of any small and inessential difference, but only upon the ground of the most important and compelling fundamental reasons. We can not barter away our independence or our sovereignty, but we ought to engage in no refinements of logic, no sophistries, and no subterfuges, to argue away the undoubted duty of this country by reason of the might of its numbers, the power of its resources, and its position of leadership in the world, actively and comprehensively to signify its approval and to bear its full share of the responsibility of a candid and disinterested attempt at the establishment of a tribunal for the administration of even-handed justice between nation and nation. The weight of our enormous influence must be cast upon the side of a reign not of force but of law and trial, not by battle but by reason.

We have never any wish to interfere in the political conditions of any other countries. Especially are we determined not to become implicated in the political controversies of the Old World. With a great deal of hesitation, we have responded to appeals for help to maintain order, protect life and property, and establish responsible government in some of the small countries of the Western Hemisphere. Our private citizens have advanced large sums of money to assist in the necessary financing and relief of the Old World. We have not failed, nor shall we fail to respond, whenever necessary to mitigate human suffering and assist in the rehabilitation of distressed nations. These, too, are requirements which must be met by reason of our vast powers and the place we hold in the world.

Some of the best thought of mankind has long been seeking for a formula for permanent peace. Undoubtedly the clarification of the principles of international law would be helpful, and the efforts of scholars to prepare such a work for adoption by the various nations should have our sympathy and support. Much may be hoped for from the earnest studies of those who advocate the outlawing of aggressive war. But all these plans and preparations, these treaties and covenants, will not of themselves be adequate. One of the greatest dangers to peace lies in the economic pressure to which people find themselves subjected. One of the most practical things to be done in the world is to seek arrangements under which such pressure may be removed, so that opportunity may be renewed and hope may be revived. There must be some assurance that effort and endeavor will be followed by success and prosperity. In the making and financing of such adjustments there is not only an opportunity, but a real duty, for America to respond with her counsel and her resources. Conditions must be provided under which people can make a living and work out of their difficulties. But there is another element, more important than all, without which there can not be the slightest hope of a permanent peace. That element lies in the heart of humanity. Unless the desire for peace be cherished there, unless this fundamental and only natural source of brotherly love be cultivated to its highest degree, all artificial efforts will be in vain. Peace will come when there is realization that only under a reign of law, based on righteousness and supported by the religious conviction of the brotherhood of man, can there be any hope of a complete and satisfying life. Parchment will fail, the sword will fail, it is only the spiritual nature of man that can be triumphant.

It seems altogether probable that we can contribute most to these important objects by maintaining our position of political detachment and independence. We are not identified with any Old World interests. This position should be made more and more clear in our relations with all foreign countries. We are at peace with all of them. Our program is never to oppress, but always to assist. But while we do justice to others, we must require that justice be done to us. With us a treaty of peace means peace, and a treaty of amity means amity. We have made great contributions to the settlement of contentious differences in both Europe and Asia. But there is a very definite point beyond which we can not go. We can only help those who help themselves. Mindful of these limitations, the one great duty that stands out requires us to use our enormous powers to trim the balance of the world.

While we can look with a great deal of pleasure upon what we have done abroad, we must remember that our continued success in that direction depends upon what we do at home. Since its very outset, it has been found necessary to conduct our Government by means of political parties. That system would not have survived from generation to generation if it had not been fundamentally sound and provided the best instrumentalities for the most complete expression of the popular will. It is not necessary to claim that it has always worked perfectly. It is enough to know that nothing better has been devised. No one would deny that there should be full and free expression and an opportunity for independence of action within the party. There is no salvation in a narrow and bigoted partisanship. But if there is to be responsible party government, the party label must be something more than a mere device for securing office. Unless those who are elected under the same party designation are willing to assume sufficient responsibility and exhibit sufficient loyalty and coherence, so that they can cooperate with each other in the support of the broad general principles, of the party platform, the election is merely a mockery, no decision is made at the polls, and there is no representation of the popular will. Common honesty and good faith with the people who support a party at the polls require that party, when it enters office, to assume the control of that portion of the Government to which it has been elected. Any other course is bad faith and a violation of the party pledges.

When the country has bestowed its confidence upon a party by making it a majority in the Congress, it has a right to expect such unity of action as will make the party majority an effective instrument of government. This Administration has come into power with a very clear and definite mandate from the people. The expression of the popular will in favor of maintaining our constitutional guarantees was overwhelming and decisive. There was a manifestation of such faith in the integrity of the courts that we can consider that issue rejected for some time to come. Likewise, the policy of public ownership of railroads and certain electric utilities met with unmistakable defeat. The people declared that they wanted their rights to have not a political but a judicial determination, and their independence and freedom continued and supported by having the ownership and control of their property, not in the Government, but in their own hands. As they always do when they have a fair chance, the people demonstrated that they are sound and are determined to have a sound government.

When we turn from what was rejected to inquire what was accepted, the policy that stands out with the greatest clearness is that of economy in public expenditure with reduction and reform of taxation. The principle involved in this effort is that of conservation. The resources of this country are almost beyond computation. No mind can comprehend them. But the cost of our combined governments is likewise almost beyond definition. Not only those who are now making their tax returns, but those who meet the enhanced cost of existence in their monthly bills, know by hard experience what this great burden is and what it does. No matter what others may want, these people want a drastic economy. They are opposed to waste. They know that extravagance lengthens the hours and diminishes the rewards of their labor. I favor the policy of economy, not because I wish to save money, but because I wish to save people. The men and women of this country who toil are the ones who bear the cost of the Government. Every dollar that we carelessly waste means that their life will be so much the more meager. Every dollar that we prudently save means that their life will be so much the more abundant. Economy is idealism in its most practical form.

If extravagance were not reflected in taxation, and through taxation both directly and indirectly injuriously affecting the people, it would not be of so much consequence. The wisest and soundest method of solving our tax problem is through economy. Fortunately, of all the great nations this country is best in a position to adopt that simple remedy. We do not any longer need wartime revenues. The collection of any taxes which are not absolutely required, which do not beyond reasonable doubt contribute to the public welfare, is only a species of legalized larceny. Under this republic the rewards of industry belong to those who earn them. The only constitutional tax is the tax which ministers to public necessity. The property of the country belongs to the people of the country. Their title is absolute. They do not support any privileged class; they do not need to maintain great military forces; they ought not to be burdened with a great array of public employees. They are not required to make any contribution to Government expenditures except that which they voluntarily assess upon themselves through the action of their own representatives. Whenever taxes become burdensome a remedy can be applied by the people; but if they do not act for themselves, no one can be very successful in acting for them.

The time is arriving when we can have further tax reduction, when, unless we wish to hamper the people in their right to earn a living, we must have tax reform. The method of raising revenue ought not to impede the transaction of business; it ought to encourage it. I am opposed to extremely high rates, because they produce little or no revenue, because they are bad for the country, and, finally, because they are wrong. We can not finance the country, we can not improve social conditions, through any system of injustice, even if we attempt to inflict it upon the rich. Those who suffer the most harm will be the poor. This country believes in prosperity. It is absurd to suppose that it is envious of those who are already prosperous. The wise and correct course to follow in taxation and all other economic legislation is not to destroy those who have already secured success but to create conditions under which every one will have a better chance to be successful. The verdict of the country has been given on this question. That verdict stands. We shall do well to heed it.

These questions involve moral issues. We need not concern ourselves much about the rights of property if we will faithfully observe the rights of persons. Under our institutions their rights are supreme. It is not property but the right to hold property, both great and small, which our Constitution guarantees. All owners of property are charged with a service. These rights and duties have been revealed, through the conscience of society, to have a divine sanction. The very stability of our society rests upon production and conservation. For individuals or for governments to waste and squander their resources is to deny these rights and disregard these obligations. The result of economic dissipation to a nation is always moral decay.

These policies of better international understandings, greater economy, and lower taxes have contributed largely to peaceful and prosperous industrial relations. Under the helpful influences of restrictive immigration and a protective tariff, employment is plentiful, the rate of pay is high, and wage earners are in a state of contentment seldom before seen. Our transportation systems have been gradually recovering and have been able to meet all the requirements of the service. Agriculture has been very slow in reviving, but the price of cereals at last indicates that the day of its deliverance is at hand.

We are not without our problems, but our most important problem is not to secure new advantages but to maintain those which we already possess. Our system of government made up of three separate and independent departments, our divided sovereignty composed of Nation and State, the matchless wisdom that is enshrined in our Constitution, all these need constant effort and tireless vigilance for their protection and support.

In a republic the first rule for the guidance of the citizen is obedience to law. Under a despotism the law may be imposed upon the subject. He has no voice in its making, no influence in its administration, it does not represent him. Under a free government the citizen makes his own laws, chooses his own administrators, which do represent him. Those who want their rights respected under the Constitution and the law ought to set the example themselves of observing the Constitution and the law. While there may be those of high intelligence who violate the law at times, the barbarian and the defective always violate it. Those who disregard the rules of society are not exhibiting a superior intelligence, are not promoting freedom and independence, are not following the path of civilization, but are displaying the traits of ignorance, of servitude, of savagery, and treading the way that leads back to the jungle.

The essence of a republic is representative government. Our Congress represents the people and the States. In all legislative affairs it is the natural collaborator with the President. In spite of all the criticism which often falls to its lot, I do not hesitate to say that there is no more independent and effective legislative body in the world. It is, and should be, jealous of its prerogative. I welcome its cooperation, and expect to share with it not only the responsibility, but the credit, for our common effort to secure beneficial legislation.

These are some of the principles which America represents. We have not by any means put them fully into practice, but we have strongly signified our belief in them. The encouraging feature of our country is not that it has reached its destination, but that it has overwhelmingly expressed its determination to proceed in the right direction. It is true that we could, with profit, be less sectional and more national in our thought. It would be well if we could replace much that is only a false and ignorant prejudice with a true and enlightened pride of race. But the last election showed that appeals to class and nationality had little effect. We were all found loyal to a common citizenship. The fundamental precept of liberty is toleration. We can not permit any inquisition either within or without the law or apply any religious test to the holding of office. The mind of America must be forever free.

It is in such contemplations, my fellow countrymen, which are not exhaustive but only representative, that I find ample warrant for satisfaction and encouragement. We should not let the much that is to do obscure the much which has been done. The past and present show faith and hope and courage fully justified. Here stands our country, an example of tranquillity at home, a patron of tranquillity abroad. Here stands its Government, aware of its might but obedient to its conscience. Here it will continue to stand, seeking peace and prosperity, solicitous for the welfare of the wage earner, promoting enterprise, developing waterways and natural resources, attentive to the intuitive counsel of womanhood, encouraging education, desiring the advancement of religion, supporting the cause of justice and honor among the nations. America seeks no earthly empire built on blood and force. No ambition, no temptation, lures her to thought of foreign dominions. The legions which she sends forth are armed, not with the sword, but with the cross. The higher state to which she seeks the allegiance of all mankind is not of human, but of divine origin. She cherishes no purpose save to merit the favor of Almighty God.

## *HERBERT HOOVER*
## *INAUGURAL ADDRESS*
## *MONDAY, MARCH 4, 1929*

M y Countrymen:

This occasion is not alone the administration of the most sacred oath which can be assumed by an American citizen. It is a dedication and consecration under God to the highest office in service of our people. I assume this trust in the humility of knowledge that only through the guidance of Almighty Providence can I hope to discharge its ever-increasing burdens.

It is in keeping with tradition throughout our history that I should express simply and directly the opinions which I hold concerning some of the matters of present importance.

### OUR PROGRESS

If we survey the situation of our Nation both at home and abroad, we find many satisfactions; we find some causes for concern. We have emerged from the losses of the Great War and the reconstruction following it with increased virility and strength. From this strength we have contributed to the recovery and progress of the world. What America has done has given renewed hope and courage to all who have faith in government by the people. In the large view, we have reached a higher degree of comfort and security than ever existed before in the history of the world. Through liberation from widespread poverty we have reached a higher degree of individual freedom than ever before. The devotion to and concern for our institutions are deep and sincere. We are steadily building a new race—a new civilization great in its own attainments. The influence and high purposes of our Nation are respected among the peoples of the world. We aspire to distinction in the world, but to a distinction based upon confidence in our sense of justice as well as our accomplishments within our own borders and in our own lives.

For wise guidance in this great period of recovery the Nation is deeply indebted to Calvin Coolidge.

But all this majestic advance should not obscure the constant dangers from which self-government must be safeguarded. The strong man must at all times be alert to the attack of insidious disease.

## THE FAILURE OF OUR
## SYSTEM OF CRIMINAL JUSTICE

The most malign of all these dangers today is disregard and disobedience of law. Crime is increasing. Confidence in rigid and speedy justice is decreasing. I am not prepared to believe that this indicates any decay in the moral fiber of the American people. I am not prepared to believe that it indicates an impotence of the Federal Government to enforce its laws.

It is only in part due to the additional burdens imposed upon our judicial system by the eighteenth amendment. The problem is much wider than that. Many influences had increasingly complicated and weakened our law enforcement organization long before the adoption of the eighteenth amendment.

To reestablish the vigor and effectiveness of law enforcement we must critically consider the entire Federal machinery of justice, the redistribution of its functions, the simplification of its procedure, the provision of additional special tribunals, the better selection of juries, and the more effective organization of our agencies of investigation and prosecution that justice may be sure and that it may be swift. While the authority of the Federal Government extends to but part of our vast system of national, State, and local justice, yet the standards which the Federal Government establishes have the most profound influence upon the whole structure.

We are fortunate in the ability and integrity of our Federal judges and attorneys. But the system which these officers are called upon to administer is in many respects ill adapted to present-day conditions. Its intricate and involved rules of procedure have become the refuge of both big and little criminals. There is a belief abroad that by invoking technicalities, subterfuge, and delay, the ends of justice may be thwarted by those who can pay the cost.

Reform, reorganization and strengthening of our whole judicial and enforcement system, both in civil and criminal sides, have been advocated for years by statesmen, judges, and bar associations. First steps toward that end should not longer be delayed. Rigid and expeditious justice is the first safeguard of freedom, the basis of all ordered liberty, the vital force of progress. It must not come to be in our Republic that it can be defeated by the indifference of the citizen, by exploitation of the delays and entanglements of the law, or by combinations of criminals. Justice must not fail because the agencies of enforcement are either delinquent or inefficiently organized. To consider these evils, to find their remedy, is the most sore necessity of our times.

## ENFORCEMENT OF
## THE EIGHTEENTH AMENDMENT

Of the undoubted abuses which have grown up under the eighteenth amendment, part are due to the causes I have just mentioned; but part are due to the failure of some States to accept their share of responsibility for concurrent enforcement and to the failure of many State and local officials to accept the obligation under their oath of office zealously to enforce the laws. With the failures from these many causes has come a dangerous expansion in the criminal elements who have found enlarged opportunities in dealing in illegal liquor.

But a large responsibility rests directly upon our citizens. There would be little traffic in illegal liquor if only criminals patronized it. We must awake to the fact that this patronage from large numbers of law-abiding citizens is supplying the rewards and stimulating crime.

I have been selected by you to execute and enforce the laws of the country. I propose to do so to the extent of my own abilities, but the measure of success that the Government shall attain will depend upon the moral support which you, as citizens, extend. The duty of citizens to support the laws of the land is coequal with the duty of their Government to enforce the laws which exist. No greater national service can be given by men and women of good will—who, I know, are not unmindful of the responsibilities of citizenship—than that they should, by their example, assist in stamping out crime and outlawry by refusing participation in and condemning all transactions with illegal liquor. Our whole system of self-government will crumble either if officials elect what laws they will enforce or citizens elect what laws they will support. The worst evil of disregard for some law is that it destroys respect for all law. For our citizens to patronize the violation of a particular law on the ground that they are opposed to it is destructive of the very basis of all that protection of life, of homes and property which they rightly claim under other laws. If citizens do not like a law, their duty as honest men and women is to discourage its violation; their right is openly to work for its repeal.

To those of criminal mind there can be no appeal but vigorous enforcement of the law. Fortunately they are but a small percentage of our people. Their activities must be stopped.

## A NATIONAL INVESTIGATION

I propose to appoint a national commission for a searching investigation of the whole structure of our Federal system of jurisprudence, to include the method of enforcement of the eighteenth amendment and the causes of abuse under it. Its purpose will be to make such recommendations for reorganization of the administration of Federal laws and court procedure as may be found desirable. In the meantime it is essential that a large part of the enforcement activities be transferred from the Treasury Department to the Department of Justice as a beginning of more effective organization.

## THE RELATION OF GOVERNMENT TO BUSINESS

The election has again confirmed the determination of the American people that regulation of private enterprise and not Government ownership or operation is the course rightly to be pursued in our relation to business. In recent years we have established a differentiation in the whole method of business regulation between the industries which produce and distribute commodities on the one hand and public utilities on the other. In the former, our laws insist upon effective competition; in the latter, because we substantially confer a monopoly by limiting competition, we must regulate their services and rates. The rigid enforcement of the laws applicable to both groups is the very base of equal opportunity and freedom from domination for all our people, and it is just as essential for the stability and prosperity of business itself as for the protection of the public at large. Such regulation should be extended by the Federal Government within the limitations of the Constitution and only when the individual States are without power to protect their citizens through their own authority. On the other hand, we should be fearless when the authority rests only in the Federal Government.

## COOPERATION BY THE GOVERNMENT

The larger purpose of our economic thought should be to establish more firmly stability and security of business and employment and thereby remove poverty still further from our borders. Our people have in recent years developed a new-found capacity for cooperation among themselves to effect high purposes in public welfare. It is an advance toward the highest conception of self-government. Self-government does not and should not imply the use of political agencies alone. Progress is born of cooperation in the community— not from governmental restraints. The Government should assist and encourage these movements of collective self-help by itself cooperating with them. Business has by cooperation made great progress in the advancement of service, in stability, in regularity of employment and in the correction of its own abuses. Such progress, however, can continue only so long as business manifests its respect for law.

There is an equally important field of cooperation by the Federal Government with the multitude of agencies, State, municipal and private, in the systematic development of those processes which directly affect public health, recreation, education, and the home. We have need further to perfect the means by which Government can be adapted to human service.

## EDUCATION

Although education is primarily a responsibility of the States and local communities, and rightly so, yet the Nation as a whole is vitally concerned in its development everywhere to the highest standards and to complete universality. Self-government can succeed only through an instructed electorate. Our objective is not simply to overcome illiteracy. The Nation has marched far beyond that. The more complex the problems of the Nation become, the greater is the need for more and more advanced instruction. Moreover, as our numbers increase and as our life expands with science and invention, we must discover more and more leaders for every walk of life. We can not hope to succeed in directing this increasingly complex civilization unless we can draw all the talent of leadership from the whole people. One civilization after another has been wrecked upon the attempt to secure sufficient leadership from a single group or class. If we would prevent the growth of class distinctions and would constantly refresh our leadership with the ideals of our people, we must draw constantly from the general mass. The full opportunity for every boy and girl to rise through the selective processes of education can alone secure to us this leadership.

## PUBLIC HEALTH

In public health the discoveries of science have opened a new era. Many sections of our country and many groups of our citizens suffer from diseases the eradication of which are mere matters of administration and moderate expenditure. Public health service should be as fully organized and as universally incorporated into our governmental system as is public education. The returns are a thousand fold in economic benefits, and infinitely more in reduction of suffering and promotion of human happiness.

## WORLD PEACE

The United States fully accepts the profound truth that our own progress, prosperity, and peace are interlocked with the progress, prosperity, and peace of all humanity. The whole world is at peace. The dangers to a continuation of this peace today are largely the fear and suspicion which still haunt the world. No suspicion or fear can be rightly directed toward our country.

Those who have a true understanding of America know that we have no desire for territorial expansion, for economic or other domination of other peoples. Such purposes are repugnant to our ideals of human freedom. Our form of government is ill adapted to the responsibilities which inevitably follow permanent limitation of the independence of other peoples. Superficial observers seem to find no destiny for our abounding increase in population, in wealth and power except that of imperialism. They fail to see that the American people are engrossed in the building for themselves of a new economic system, a new social system, a new political system all of which are characterized by aspirations of freedom of opportunity and thereby are the negation of imperialism. They fail to realize that because of our abounding prosperity our youth are pressing more and more into our institutions of learning; that our people are seeking a larger vision through art, literature, science, and travel; that they are moving toward stronger moral and spiritual life—that from these things our sympathies are broadening beyond the bounds of our Nation and race toward their true expression in a real brotherhood of man. They fail to see that the idealism of America will lead it to no narrow or selfish channel, but inspire it to do its full share as a nation toward the advancement of civilization. It will do that not by mere declaration but by taking a practical part in supporting all useful international undertakings. We not only desire peace with the world, but to see peace maintained throughout the world. We wish to advance the reign of justice and reason toward the extinction of force.

The recent treaty for the renunciation of war as an instrument of national policy sets an advanced standard in our conception of the relations of nations. Its acceptance should pave the way to greater limitation of armament, the offer of which we sincerely extend to the world. But its full realization also implies a greater and greater perfection in the instrumentalities for pacific settlement of controversies between nations. In the creation and use of these instrumentalities we should support every sound method of conciliation, arbitration, and judicial settlement. American statesmen were among the first to propose and they have constantly urged upon the world, the establishment of a tribunal for the settlement of controversies of a justiciable character. The Permanent Court of International Justice in its major purpose is thus peculiarly identified with American ideals and with American statesmanship. No more potent instrumentality for this purpose has ever been conceived and no other is practicable of establishment. The reservations placed upon our adherence should not be misinterpreted. The United States seeks by these reservations no special privilege or advantage but only to clarify our relation to advisory opinions and other matters which are subsidiary to the major purpose of the court. The way should, and I believe will, be found by which we may take our proper place in a movement so fundamental to the progress of peace.

Our people have determined that we should make no political engagements such as membership in the League of Nations, which may commit us in advance as a nation to become involved in the settlements of controversies between other countries. They adhere to the belief that the independence of America from such obligations increases its ability and availability for service in all fields of human progress.

I have lately returned from a journey among our sister Republics of the Western Hemisphere. I have received unbounded hospitality and courtesy as their expression of friendliness to our country. We are held by particular bonds of sympathy and common interest with them. They are each of them building a racial character and a culture which is an impressive contribution to human progress. We wish only for the maintenance of their independence, the growth of their stability, and their prosperity. While we have had wars in the Western Hemisphere, yet on the whole the record is in encouraging contrast with that of other parts of the world. Fortunately the New World is largely free from the inheritances of fear and distrust which have so troubled the Old World. We should keep it so.

It is impossible, my countrymen, to speak of peace without profound emotion. In thousands of homes in America, in millions of homes around the world, there are vacant chairs. It would be a shameful confession of our unworthiness if it should develop that we have abandoned the hope for which all these men died. Surely civilization is old enough, surely mankind is mature enough so that we ought in our own lifetime to find a way to permanent peace. Abroad, to west and east, are nations whose sons mingled their blood with the blood of our sons on the battlefields. Most of these nations have contributed to our race, to our culture, our knowledge, and our progress. From one of them we derive our very language and from many of them much of the genius of our institutions. Their desire for peace is as deep and sincere as our own.

Peace can be contributed to by respect for our ability in defense. Peace can be promoted by the limitation of arms and by the creation of the instrumentalities for peaceful settlement of controversies. But it will become a reality only through self-restraint and active effort in friendliness and helpfulness. I covet for this administration a record of having further contributed to advance the cause of peace.

## PARTY RESPONSIBILITIES

In our form of democracy the expression of the popular will can be effected only through the instrumentality of political parties. We maintain party government not to promote intolerant partisanship but because opportunity must be given for expression of the popular will, and organization provided for the execution of its mandates and for accountability of government to the people. It follows that the government both in the executive and the legislative branches must carry out in good faith the platforms upon which the party was entrusted with power. But the government is that of the whole people; the party is the instrument through which policies are determined and men chosen to bring them into being. The animosities of elections should have no place in our Government, for government must concern itself alone with the common weal.

## SPECIAL SESSION OF THE CONGRESS

Action upon some of the proposals upon which the Republican Party was returned to power, particularly further agricultural relief and limited changes in the tariff, cannot in justice to our farmers, our labor, and our manufacturers be postponed. I shall therefore request a special session of Congress for the consideration of these two questions. I shall deal with each of them upon the assembly of the Congress.

## OTHER MANDATES FROM THE ELECTION

It appears to me that the more important further mandates from the recent election were the maintenance of the integrity of the Constitution; the vigorous enforcement of the laws; the continuance of economy in public expenditure; the continued regulation of business to prevent domination in the community; the denial of ownership or operation of business by the Government in competition with its citizens; the avoidance of policies which would involve us in the controversies of foreign nations; the more effective reorganization of the departments of the Federal Government; the expansion of public works; and the promotion of welfare activities affecting education and the home.

These were the more tangible determinations of the election, but beyond them was the confidence and belief of the people that we would not neglect the support of the embedded ideals and aspirations of America. These ideals and aspirations are the touchstones upon which the day-today administration and legislative acts of government must be tested. More than this, the Government must, so far as lies within its proper powers, give leadership to the realization of these ideals and to the fruition of these aspirations. No one can adequately reduce these things of the spirit to phrases or to a catalogue of definitions. We do know what the attainments of these ideals should be: The preservation of self-government and its full foundations in local government; the perfection of justice whether in economic or in social fields; the maintenance of ordered liberty; the denial of domination by any group or class; the building up and preservation of equality of opportunity; the stimulation of initiative and individuality; absolute integrity in public affairs; the choice of officials for fitness to office; the direction of economic progress toward prosperity for the further lessening of poverty; the freedom of public opinion; the sustaining of education and of the advancement of knowledge; the growth of religious spirit and the tolerance of all faiths; the strengthening of the home; the advancement of peace.

There is no short road to the realization of these aspirations. Ours is a progressive people, but with a determination that progress must be based upon the foundation of experience. Ill-considered remedies for our faults bring only penalties after them. But if we hold the faith of the men in our mighty past who created these ideals, we shall leave them heightened and strengthened for our children.

## CONCLUSION

This is not the time and place for extended discussion. The questions before our country are problems of progress to higher standards; they are not the problems of degeneration. They demand thought and they serve to quicken the conscience and enlist our sense of responsibility for their settlement. And that responsibility rests upon you, my countrymen, as much as upon those of us who have been selected for office.

Ours is a land rich in resources; stimulating in its glorious beauty; filled with millions of happy homes; blessed with comfort and opportunity. In no nation are the institutions of progress more advanced. In no nation are the fruits of accomplishment more secure. In no nation is the government more worthy of respect. No country is more loved by its people. I have an abiding faith in their capacity, integrity and high purpose. I have no fears for the future of our country. It is bright with hope.

In the presence of my countrymen, mindful of the solemnity of this occasion, knowing what the task means and the responsibility which it involves, I beg your tolerance, your aid, and your cooperation. I ask the help of Almighty God in this service to my country to which you have called me.

# FRANKLIN D. ROOSEVELT
## FIRST INAUGURAL ADDRESS
## SATURDAY, MARCH 4, 1933

I am certain that my fellow Americans expect that on my induction into the Presidency I will address them with a candor and a decision which the present situation of our Nation impels. This is preeminently the time to speak the truth, the whole truth, frankly and boldly. Nor need we shrink from honestly facing conditions in our country today. This great Nation will endure as it has endured, will revive and will prosper. So, first of all, let me assert my firm belief that the only thing we have to fear is fear itself—nameless, unreasoning, unjustified terror which paralyzes needed efforts to convert retreat into advance. In every dark hour of our national life a leadership of frankness and vigor has met with that understanding and support of the people themselves which is essential to victory. I am convinced that you will again give that support to leadership in these critical days.

In such a spirit on my part and on yours we face our common difficulties. They concern, thank God, only material things. Values have shrunken to fantastic levels; taxes have risen; our ability to pay has fallen; government of all kinds is faced by serious curtailment of income; the means of exchange are frozen in the currents of trade; the withered leaves of industrial enterprise lie on every side; farmers find no markets for their produce; the savings of many years in thousands of families are gone.

More important, a host of unemployed citizens face the grim problem of existence, and an equally great number toil with little return. Only a foolish optimist can deny the dark realities of the moment.

Yet our distress comes from no failure of substance. We are stricken by no plague of locusts. Compared with the perils which our forefathers conquered because they believed and were not afraid, we have still much to be thankful for. Nature still offers her bounty and human efforts have multiplied it. Plenty is at our doorstep, but a generous use of it languishes in the very sight of the supply. Primarily this is because the rulers of the exchange of mankind's goods have failed, through their own stubbornness and their own incompetence, have admitted their failure, and abdicated. Practices of the unscrupulous money changers stand indicted in the court of public opinion, rejected by the hearts and minds of men.

True they have tried, but their efforts have been cast in the pattern of an outworn tradition. Faced by failure of credit they have proposed only the lending of more money. Stripped of the lure of profit by which to induce our people to follow their false leadership, they have resorted to exhortations, pleading tearfully for restored confidence. They know only the rules of a generation of self-seekers. They have no vision, and when there is no vision the people perish.

The money changers have fled from their high seats in the temple of our civilization. We may now restore that temple to the ancient truths. The measure of the restoration lies in the extent to which we apply social values more noble than mere monetary profit.

Happiness lies not in the mere possession of money; it lies in the joy of achievement, in the thrill of creative effort. The joy and moral stimulation of work no longer must be forgotten in the mad chase of evanescent profits. These dark days will be worth all they cost us if they teach us that our true destiny is not to be ministered unto but to minister to ourselves and to our fellow men.

Recognition of the falsity of material wealth as the standard of success goes hand in hand with the abandonment of the false belief that public office and high political position are to be valued only by the standards of pride of place and personal profit; and there must be an end to a conduct in banking and in business which too often has given to a sacred trust the likeness of callous and selfish wrongdoing. Small wonder that confidence languishes, for it thrives only on honesty, on honor, on the sacredness of obligations, on faithful protection, on unselfish performance; without them it cannot live.

Restoration calls, however, not for changes in ethics alone. This Nation asks for action, and action now.

Our greatest primary task is to put people to work. This is no unsolvable problem if we face it wisely and courageously. It can be accomplished in part by direct recruiting by the Government itself, treating the task as we would treat the emergency of a war, but at the same time, through this employment, accomplishing greatly needed projects to stimulate and reorganize the use of our natural resources.

Hand in hand with this we must frankly recognize the overbalance of population in our industrial centers and, by engaging on a national scale in a redistribution, endeavor to provide a better use of the land for those best fitted for the land. The task can be helped by definite efforts to raise the values of agricultural products and with this the power to purchase the output of our cities. It can be helped by preventing realistically the tragedy of the growing loss through foreclosure of our small homes and our farms. It can be helped by insistence that the Federal, State, and local governments act forthwith on the demand that their cost be drastically reduced. It can be helped by the unifying of relief activities which today are often scattered, uneconomical, and unequal. It can be helped by national planning for and supervision of all forms of transportation and of communications and other utilities which have a definitely public character. There are many ways in which it can be helped, but it can never be helped merely by talking about it. We must act and act quickly.

Finally, in our progress toward a resumption of work we require two safeguards against a return of the evils of the old order; there must be a strict supervision of all banking and credits and investments; there must be an end to speculation with other people's money, and there must be provision for an adequate but sound currency.

There are the lines of attack. I shall presently urge upon a new Congress in special session detailed measures for their fulfillment, and I shall seek the immediate assistance of the several States.

Through this program of action we address ourselves to putting our own national house in order and making income balance outgo. Our international trade relations, though vastly important, are in point of time and necessity secondary to the establishment of a sound national economy. I favor as a practical policy the putting of first things first. I shall spare no effort to restore world trade by international economic readjustment, but the emergency at home cannot wait on that accomplishment.

The basic thought that guides these specific means of national recovery is not narrowly nationalistic. It is the insistence, as a first consideration, upon the interdependence of the various elements in all parts of the United States—a recognition of the old and permanently important manifestation of the American spirit of the pioneer. It is the way to recovery. It is the immediate way. It is the strongest assurance that the recovery will endure.

In the field of world policy I would dedicate this Nation to the policy of the good neighbor—the neighbor who resolutely respects himself and, because he does so, respects the rights of others—the neighbor who respects his obligations and respects the sanctity of his agreements in and with a world of neighbors.

If I read the temper of our people correctly, we now realize as we have never realized before our interdependence on each other; that we can not merely take but we must give as well; that if we are to go forward, we must move as a trained and loyal army willing to sacrifice for the good of a common discipline, because without such discipline no progress is made, no leadership becomes effective. We are, I know, ready and willing to submit our lives and property to such discipline, because it makes possible a leadership which aims at a larger good. This I propose to offer, pledging that the larger purposes will bind upon us all as a sacred obligation with a unity of duty hitherto evoked only in time of armed strife.

With this pledge taken, I assume unhesitatingly the leadership of this great army of our people dedicated to a disciplined attack upon our common problems.

Action in this image and to this end is feasible under the form of government which we have inherited from our ancestors. Our Constitution is so simple and practical that it is possible always to meet extraordinary needs by changes in emphasis and arrangement without loss of essential form. That is why our constitutional system has proved itself the most superbly enduring political mechanism the modern world has produced. It has met every stress of vast expansion of territory, of foreign wars, of bitter internal strife, of world relations.

It is to be hoped that the normal balance of executive and legislative authority may be wholly adequate to meet the unprecedented task before us. But it may be that an unprecedented demand and need for undelayed action may call for temporary departure from that normal balance of public procedure.

I am prepared under my constitutional duty to recommend the measures that a stricken nation in the midst of a stricken world may require. These measures, or such other measures as the Congress may build out of its experience and wisdom, I shall seek, within my constitutional authority, to bring to speedy adoption.

But in the event that the Congress shall fail to take one of these two courses, and in the event that the national emergency is still critical, I shall not evade the clear course of duty that will then confront me. I shall ask the Congress for the one remaining instrument to meet the crisis—broad Executive power to wage a war against the emergency, as great as the power that would be given to me if we were in fact invaded by a foreign foe.

For the trust reposed in me I will return the courage and the devotion that befit the time. I can do no less.

We face the arduous days that lie before us in the warm courage of the national unity; with the clear consciousness of seeking old and precious moral values; with the clean satisfaction that comes from the stern performance of duty by old and young alike. We aim at the assurance of a rounded and permanent national life.

We do not distrust the future of essential democracy. The people of the United States have not failed. In their need they have registered a mandate that they want direct, vigorous action. They have asked for discipline and direction under leadership. They have made me the present instrument of their wishes. In the spirit of the gift I take it.

In this dedication of a Nation we humbly ask the blessing of God. May He protect each and every one of us. May He guide me in the days to come.

# FRANKLIN D. ROOSEVELT
## SECOND INAUGURAL ADDRESS
## WEDNESDAY, JANUARY 20, 1937

When four years ago we met to inaugurate a President, the Republic, single-minded in anxiety, stood in spirit here. We dedicated ourselves to the fulfillment of a vision—to speed the time when there would be for all the people that security and peace essential to the pursuit of happiness. We of the Republic pledged ourselves to drive from the temple of our ancient faith those who had profaned it; to end by action, tireless and unafraid, the stagnation and despair of that day. We did those first things first.

Our covenant with ourselves did not stop there. Instinctively we recognized a deeper need—the need to find through government the instrument of our united purpose to solve for the individual the ever-rising problems of a complex civilization. Repeated attempts at their solution without the aid of government had left us baffled and bewildered. For, without that aid, we had been unable to create those moral controls over the services of science which are necessary to make science a useful servant instead of a ruthless master of mankind. To do this we knew that we must find practical controls over blind economic forces and blindly selfish men.

We of the Republic sensed the truth that democratic government has innate capacity to protect its people against disasters once considered inevitable, to solve problems once considered unsolvable. We would not admit that we could not find a way to master economic epidemics just as, after centuries of fatalistic suffering, we had found a way to master epidemics of disease. We refused to leave the problems of our common welfare to be solved by the winds of chance and the hurricanes of disaster.

In this we Americans were discovering no wholly new truth; we were writing a new chapter in our book of self-government.

This year marks the one hundred and fiftieth anniversary of

the Constitutional Convention which made us a nation. At that Convention our forefathers found the way out of the chaos which followed the Revolutionary War; they created a strong government with powers of united action sufficient then and now to solve problems utterly beyond individual or local solution. A century and a half ago they established the Federal Government in order to promote the general welfare and secure the blessings of liberty to the American people.

Today we invoke those same powers of government to achieve the same objectives.

Four years of new experience have not belied our historic instinct. They hold out the clear hope that government within communities, government within the separate States, and government of the United States can do the things the times require, without yielding its democracy. Our tasks in the last four years did not force democracy to take a holiday.

Nearly all of us recognize that as intricacies of human relationships increase, so power to govern them also must increase—power to stop evil; power to do good. The essential democracy of our Nation and the safety of our people depend not upon the absence of power, but upon lodging it with those whom the people can change or continue at stated intervals through an honest and free system of elections. The Constitution of 1787 did not make our democracy impotent.

In fact, in these last four years, we have made the exercise of all power more democratic; for we have begun to bring private autocratic powers into their proper subordination to the public's government. The legend that they were invincible—above and beyond the processes of a democracy—has been shattered. They have been challenged and beaten.

Our progress out of the depression is obvious. But that is not all that you and I mean by the new order of things. Our pledge was not merely to do a patchwork job with secondhand materials. By using the new materials of social justice we have undertaken to erect on the old foundations a more enduring structure for the better use of future generations.

In that purpose we have been helped by achievements of mind and spirit. Old truths have been relearned; untruths have been unlearned.

We have always known that heedless self-interest was bad morals; we know now that it is bad economics. Out of the collapse of a prosperity whose builders boasted their practicality has come the conviction that in the long run economic morality pays. We are beginning to wipe out the line that divides the practical from the ideal; and in so doing we are fashioning an instrument of unimagined power for the establishment of a morally better world.

This new understanding undermines the old admiration of worldly success as such. We are beginning to abandon our tolerance of the abuse of power by those who betray for profit the elementary decencies of life.

In this process evil things formerly accepted will not be so easily condoned. Hard-headedness will not so easily excuse hardheartedness. We are moving toward an era of good feeling. But we realize that there can be no era of good feeling save among men of good will.

For these reasons I am justified in believing that the greatest change we have witnessed has been the change in the moral climate of America.

Among men of good will, science and democracy together offer an ever-richer life and ever-larger satisfaction to the individual. With this change in our moral climate and our rediscovered ability to improve our economic order, we have set our feet upon the road of enduring progress.

Shall we pause now and turn our back upon the road that lies ahead? Shall we call this the promised land? Or, shall we continue on our way? For "each age is a dream that is dying, or one that is coming to birth."

Many voices are heard as we face a great decision. Comfort says, "Tarry a while." Opportunism says, "This is a good spot." Timidity asks, "How difficult is the road ahead?"

True, we have come far from the days of stagnation and despair. Vitality has been preserved. Courage and confidence have been restored. Mental and moral horizons have been extended.

But our present gains were won under the pressure of more than ordinary circumstances. Advance became imperative under the goad of fear and suffering. The times were on the side of progress.

To hold to progress today, however, is more difficult. Dulled conscience, irresponsibility, and ruthless self-interest already reappear. Such symptoms of prosperity may become portents of disaster! Prosperity already tests the persistence of our progressive purpose.

Let us ask again: Have we reached the goal of our vision of that fourth day of March 1933? Have we found our happy valley?

I see a great nation, upon a great continent, blessed with a great wealth of natural resources. Its hundred and thirty million people are at peace among themselves; they are making their country a good neighbor among the nations. I see a United States which can demonstrate that, under democratic methods of government, national wealth can be translated into a spreading volume of human comforts hitherto unknown, and the lowest standard of living can be raised far above the level of mere subsistence.

But here is the challenge to our democracy: In this nation I see tens of millions of its citizens—a substantial part of its whole population—who at this very moment are denied the greater part of what the very lowest standards of today call the necessities of life.

I see millions of families trying to live on incomes so meager that the pall of family disaster hangs over them day by day.

I see millions whose daily lives in city and on farm continue under conditions labeled indecent by a so-called polite society half a century ago.

I see millions denied education, recreation, and the opportunity to better their lot and the lot of their children.

I see millions lacking the means to buy the products of farm and factory and by their poverty denying work and productiveness to many other millions.

I see one-third of a nation ill-housed, ill-clad, ill-nourished.

It is not in despair that I paint you that picture. I paint it for you in hope—because the Nation, seeing and understanding the injustice in it, proposes to paint it out. We are determined to make every American citizen the subject of his country's interest and concern; and we will never regard any faithful law-abiding group within our borders as superfluous. The test of our progress is not whether we add more to the abundance of those who have much; it is whether we provide enough for those who have too little.

If I know aught of the spirit and purpose of our Nation, we will not listen to Comfort, Opportunism, and Timidity. We will carry on.

Overwhelmingly, we of the Republic are men and women of good will; men and women who have more than warm hearts of dedication; men and women who have cool heads and willing hands of practical purpose as well. They will insist that every agency of popular government use effective instruments to carry out their will.

Government is competent when all who compose it work as trustees for the whole people. It can make constant progress when it keeps abreast of all the facts. It can obtain justified support and legitimate criticism when the people receive true information of all that government does.

If I know aught of the will of our people, they will demand that these conditions of effective government shall be created and maintained. They will demand a nation uncorrupted by cancers of injustice and, therefore, strong among the nations in its example of the will to peace.

Today we reconsecrate our country to long-cherished ideals in a suddenly changed civilization. In every land there are always at work forces that drive men apart and forces that draw men together. In our personal ambitions we are individualists. But in our seeking for economic and political progress as a nation, we all go up, or else we all go down, as one people.

To maintain a democracy of effort requires a vast amount of patience in dealing with differing methods, a vast amount of humility. But out of the confusion of many voices rises an understanding of dominant public need. Then political leadership can voice common ideals, and aid in their realization.

In taking again the oath of office as President of the United States, I assume the solemn obligation of leading the American people forward along the road over which they have chosen to advance.

While this duty rests upon me I shall do my utmost to speak their purpose and to do their will, seeking Divine guidance to help us each and every one to give light to them that sit in darkness and to guide our feet into the way of peace.

# FRANKLIN D. ROOSEVELT
## THIRD INAUGURAL ADDRESS
### MONDAY, JANUARY 20, 1941

On each national day of inauguration since 1789, the people have renewed their sense of dedication to the United States.

In Washington's day the task of the people was to create and weld together a nation.

In Lincoln's day the task of the people was to preserve that Nation from disruption from within.

In this day the task of the people is to save that Nation and its institutions from disruption from without.

To us there has come a time, in the midst of swift happenings, to pause for a moment and take stock—to recall what our place in history has been, and to rediscover what we are and what we may be. If we do not, we risk the real peril of inaction.

Lives of nations are determined not by the count of years, but by the lifetime of the human spirit. The life of a man is three-score years and ten: a little more, a little less. The life of a nation is the fullness of the measure of its will to live.

There are men who doubt this. There are men who believe that democracy, as a form of Government and a frame of life, is limited or measured by a kind of mystical and artificial fate that, for some unexplained reason, tyranny and slavery have become the surging wave of the future—and that freedom is an ebbing tide.

But we Americans know that this is not true.

Eight years ago, when the life of this Republic seemed frozen by a fatalistic terror, we proved that this is not true. We were in the midst of shock—but we acted. We acted quickly, boldly, decisively.

These later years have been living years—fruitful years for the people of this democracy. For they have brought to us greater security and, I hope, a better understanding that life's ideals are to be measured in other than material things. Most vital to our present and our future is this experience of a democracy which successfully survived crisis at home; put away many evil things; built new structures on enduring lines; and, through it all, maintained the fact of its democracy.

For action has been taken within the three-way framework of the Constitution of the United States. The coordinate branches of the Government continue freely to function. The Bill of Rights remains inviolate. The freedom of elections is wholly maintained. Prophets of the downfall of American democracy have seen their dire predictions come to naught.

Democracy is not dying.

We know it because we have seen it revive—and grow.

We know it cannot die—because it is built on the unhampered initiative of individual men and women joined together in a common enterprise—an enterprise undertaken and carried through by the free expression of a free majority.

We know it because democracy alone, of all forms of government, enlists the full force of men's enlightened will.

We know it because democracy alone has constructed an unlimited civilization capable of infinite progress in the improvement of human life.

We know it because, if we look below the surface, we sense it still spreading on every continent—for it is the most humane, the most advanced, and in the end the most unconquerable of all forms of human society.

A nation, like a person, has a body—a body that must be fed and clothed and housed, invigorated and rested, in a manner that measures up to the objectives of our time.

A nation, like a person, has a mind—a mind that must be kept informed and alert, that must know itself, that understands the hopes and the needs of its neighbors—all the other nations that live within the narrowing circle of the world.

And a nation, like a person, has something deeper, something more permanent, something larger than the sum of all its parts. It is that something which matters most to its future—which calls forth the most sacred guarding of its present.

It is a thing for which we find it difficult—even impossible—to hit upon a single, simple word.

And yet we all understand what it is—the spirit—the faith of America. It is the product of centuries. It was born in the multitudes of those who came from many lands—some of high degree, but mostly plain people, who sought here, early and late, to find freedom more freely.

The democratic aspiration is no mere recent phase in human history. It is human history. It permeated the ancient life of early peoples. It blazed anew in the middle ages. It was written in Magna Charta.

In the Americas its impact has been irresistible. America has been the New World in all tongues, to all peoples, not because this continent was a new-found land, but because all those who came here believed they could create upon this continent a new life—a life that should be new in freedom.

Its vitality was written into our own Mayflower Compact, into the Declaration of Independence, into the Constitution of the United States, into the Gettysburg Address.

Those who first came here to carry out the longings of their spirit, and the millions who followed, and the stock that sprang from them—all have moved forward constantly and consistently toward an ideal which in itself has gained stature and clarity with each generation.

The hopes of the Republic cannot forever tolerate either undeserved poverty or self-serving wealth.

We know that we still have far to go; that we must more greatly build the security and the opportunity and the knowledge of every citizen, in the measure justified by the resources and the capacity of the land.

But it is not enough to achieve these purposes alone. It is not enough to clothe and feed the body of this Nation, and instruct and inform its mind. For there is also the spirit. And of the three, the greatest is the spirit.

Without the body and the mind, as all men know, the Nation could not live.

But if the spirit of America were killed, even though the Nation's body and mind, constricted in an alien world, lived on, the America we know would have perished.

That spirit—that faith—speaks to us in our daily lives in ways often unnoticed, because they seem so obvious. It speaks to us here in the Capital of the Nation. It speaks to us through the processes of governing in the sovereignties of 48 States. It speaks to us in our counties, in our cities, in our towns, and in our villages. It speaks to us from the other nations of the hemisphere, and from those across the seas—the enslaved, as well as the free. Sometimes we fail to hear or heed these voices of freedom because to us the privilege of our freedom is such an old, old story.

The destiny of America was proclaimed in words of prophecy spoken by our first President in his first inaugural in 1789—words almost directed, it would seem, to this year of 1941: "The preservation of the sacred fire of liberty and the destiny of the republican model of government are justly considered... deeply,... finally, staked on the experiment intrusted to the hands of the American people."

If we lose that sacred fire—if we let it be smothered with doubt and fear—then we shall reject the destiny which Washington strove so valiantly and so triumphantly to establish. The preservation of the spirit and faith of the Nation does, and will, furnish the highest justification for every sacrifice that we may make in the cause of national defense.

In the face of great perils never before encountered, our strong purpose is to protect and to perpetuate the integrity of democracy.

For this we muster the spirit of America, and the faith of America.

We do not retreat. We are not content to stand still. As Americans, we go forward, in the service of our country, by the will of God.

# FRANKLIN D. ROOSEVELT
## FOURTH INAUGURAL ADDRESS
## SATURDAY, JANUARY 20, 1945

Mr. Chief Justice, Mr. Vice President, my friends, you will understand and, I believe, agree with my wish that the form of this inauguration be simple and its words brief.

We Americans of today, together with our allies, are passing through a period of supreme test. It is a test of our courage—of our resolve—of our wisdom—our essential democracy.

If we meet that test—successfully and honorably—we shall perform a service of historic importance which men and women and children will honor throughout all time.

As I stand here today, having taken the solemn oath of office in the presence of my fellow countrymen—in the presence of our God—I know that it is America's purpose that we shall not fail.

In the days and in the years that are to come we shall work for a just and honorable peace, a durable peace, as today we work and fight for total victory in war.

We can and we will achieve such a peace.

We shall strive for perfection. We shall not achieve it immediately—but we still shall strive. We may make mistakes—but they must never be mistakes which result from faintness of heart or abandonment of moral principle.

I remember that my old schoolmaster, Dr. Peabody, said, in days that seemed to us then to be secure and untroubled: "Things in life will not always run smoothly. Sometimes we will be rising toward the heights—then all will seem to reverse itself and start downward. The great fact to remember is that the trend of civilization itself is forever upward; that a line drawn through the middle of the peaks and the valleys of the centuries always has an upward trend."

Our Constitution of 1787 was not a perfect instrument; it is not perfect yet. But it provided a firm base upon which all manner of men, of all races and colors and creeds, could build our solid structure of democracy.

And so today, in this year of war, 1945, we have learned lessons— at a fearful cost—and we shall profit by them.

We have learned that we cannot live alone, at peace; that our own well-being is dependent on the well-being of other nations far away. We have learned that we must live as men, not as ostriches, nor as dogs in the manger.

We have learned to be citizens of the world, members of the human community.

We have learned the simple truth, as Emerson said, that "The only way to have a friend is to be one."

We can gain no lasting peace if we approach it with suspicion and mistrust or with fear. We can gain it only if we proceed with the understanding, the confidence, and the courage which flow from conviction.

The Almighty God has blessed our land in many ways. He has given our people stout hearts and strong arms with which to strike mighty blows for freedom and truth. He has given to our country a faith which has become the hope of all peoples in an anguished world.

So we pray to Him now for the vision to see our way clearly—to see the way that leads to a better life for ourselves and for all our fellow men—to the achievement of His will to peace on earth.

# HARRY S. TRUMAN
## INAUGURAL ADDRESS
## THURSDAY, JANUARY 20, 1949

Mr. Vice President, Mr. Chief Justice, and fellow citizens, I accept with humility the honor which the American people have conferred upon me. I accept it with a deep resolve to do all that I can for the welfare of this Nation and for the peace of the world.

In performing the duties of my office, I need the help and prayers of every one of you. I ask for your encouragement and your support. The tasks we face are difficult, and we can accomplish them only if we work together.

Each period of our national history has had its special challenges. Those that confront us now are as momentous as any in the past. Today marks the beginning not only of a new administration, but of a period that will be eventful, perhaps decisive, for us and for the world.

It may be our lot to experience, and in large measure to bring about, a major turning point in the long history of the human race. The first half of this century has been marked by unprecedented and brutal attacks on the rights of man, and by the two most frightful wars in history. The supreme need of our time is for men to learn to live together in peace and harmony.

The peoples of the earth face the future with grave uncertainty, composed almost equally of great hopes and great fears. In this time of doubt, they look to the United States as never before for good will, strength, and wise leadership.

It is fitting, therefore, that we take this occasion to proclaim to the world the essential principles of the faith by which we live, and to declare our aims to all peoples.

The American people stand firm in the faith which has inspired this Nation from the beginning. We believe that all men have a right to equal justice under law and equal opportunity to share in the common good. We believe that all men have the right to freedom of thought and expression. We believe that all men are created equal because they are created in the image of God.

From this faith we will not be moved.

The American people desire, and are determined to work for, a world in which all nations and all peoples are free to govern themselves as they see fit, and to achieve a decent and satisfying life. Above all else, our people desire, and are determined to work for, peace on earth—a just and lasting peace—based on genuine agreement freely arrived at by equals.

In the pursuit of these aims, the United States and other like-minded nations find themselves directly opposed by a regime with contrary aims and a totally different concept of life.

That regime adheres to a false philosophy which purports to offer freedom, security, and greater opportunity to mankind. Misled by this philosophy, many peoples have sacrificed their liberties only to learn to their sorrow that deceit and mockery, poverty and tyranny, are their reward.

That false philosophy is communism.

Communism is based on the belief that man is so weak and inadequate that he is unable to govern himself, and therefore requires the rule of strong masters.

Democracy is based on the conviction that man has the moral and intellectual capacity, as well as the inalienable right, to govern himself with reason and justice.

Communism subjects the individual to arrest without lawful cause, punishment without trial, and forced labor as the chattel of the state. It decrees what information he shall receive, what art he shall produce, what leaders he shall follow, and what thoughts he shall think.

Democracy maintains that government is established for the benefit of the individual, and is charged with the responsibility of protecting the rights of the individual and his freedom in the exercise of his abilities.

Communism maintains that social wrongs can be corrected only by violence.

Democracy has proved that social justice can be achieved through peaceful change.

Communism holds that the world is so deeply divided into opposing classes that war is inevitable.

Democracy holds that free nations can settle differences justly and maintain lasting peace.

These differences between communism and democracy do not concern the United States alone. People everywhere are coming to realize that what is involved is material well-being, human dignity, and the right to believe in and worship God.

I state these differences, not to draw issues of belief as such, but because the actions resulting from the Communist philosophy are a threat to the efforts of free nations to bring about world recovery and lasting peace.

Since the end of hostilities, the United States has invested its substance and its energy in a great constructive effort to restore peace, stability, and freedom to the world.

We have sought no territory and we have imposed our will on none. We have asked for no privileges we would not extend to others.

We have constantly and vigorously supported the United Nations and related agencies as a means of applying democratic principles to international relations. We have consistently advocated and relied upon peaceful settlement of disputes among nations.

We have made every effort to secure agreement on effective international control of our most powerful weapon, and we have worked steadily for the limitation and control of all armaments.

We have encouraged, by precept and example, the expansion of world trade on a sound and fair basis.

Almost a year ago, in company with 16 free nations of Europe, we launched the greatest cooperative economic program in history. The purpose of that unprecedented effort is to invigorate and strengthen democracy in Europe, so that the free people of that continent can resume their rightful place in the forefront of civilization and can contribute once more to the security and welfare of the world.

Our efforts have brought new hope to all mankind. We have beaten back despair and defeatism. We have saved a number of countries from losing their liberty. Hundreds of millions of people all over the world now agree with us, that we need not have war—that we can have peace.

The initiative is ours.

We are moving on with other nations to build an even stronger structure of international order and justice. We shall have as our partners countries which, no longer solely concerned with the problem of national survival, are now working to improve the standards of living of all their people. We are ready to undertake new projects to strengthen the free world.

In the coming years, our program for peace and freedom will emphasize four major courses of action.

First, we will continue to give unfaltering support to the United Nations and related agencies, and we will continue to search for ways to strengthen their authority and increase their effectiveness. We believe that the United Nations will be strengthened by the new nations which are being formed in lands now advancing toward self-government under democratic principles.

Second, we will continue our programs for world economic recovery.

This means, first of all, that we must keep our full weight behind the European recovery program. We are confident of the success of this major venture in world recovery. We believe that our partners in this effort will achieve the status of self-supporting nations once again.

In addition, we must carry out our plans for reducing the barriers to world trade and increasing its volume. Economic recovery and peace itself depend on increased world trade.

Third, we will strengthen freedom-loving nations against the dangers of aggression.

We are now working out with a number of countries a joint agreement designed to strengthen the security of the North Atlantic area. Such an agreement would take the form of a collective defense arrangement within the terms of the United Nations Charter.

We have already established such a defense pact for the Western Hemisphere by the treaty of Rio de Janeiro.

The primary purpose of these agreements is to provide unmistakable proof of the joint determination of the free countries to resist armed attack from any quarter. Each country participating in these arrangements must contribute all it can to the common defense.

If we can make it sufficiently clear, in advance, that any armed attack affecting our national security would be met with overwhelming force, the armed attack might never occur.

I hope soon to send to the Senate a treaty respecting the North Atlantic security plan.

In addition, we will provide military advice and equipment to free nations which will cooperate with us in the maintenance of peace and security.

Fourth, we must embark on a bold new program for making the benefits of our scientific advances and industrial progress available for the improvement and growth of underdeveloped areas.

More than half the people of the world are living in conditions approaching misery. Their food is inadequate. They are victims of disease. Their economic life is primitive and stagnant. Their poverty is a handicap and a threat both to them and to more prosperous areas.

For the first time in history, humanity possesses the knowledge and the skill to relieve the suffering of these people.

The United States is pre-eminent among nations in the development of industrial and scientific techniques. The material resources which we can afford to use for the assistance of other peoples are limited. But our imponderable resources in technical knowledge are constantly growing and are inexhaustible.

I believe that we should make available to peace-loving peoples the benefits of our store of technical knowledge in order to help them realize their aspirations for a better life. And, in cooperation with other nations, we should foster capital investment in areas needing development.

Our aim should be to help the free peoples of the world, through their own efforts, to produce more food, more clothing, more materials for housing, and more mechanical power to lighten their burdens.

We invite other countries to pool their technological resources in this undertaking. Their contributions will be warmly welcomed. This should be a cooperative enterprise in which all nations work together through the United Nations and its specialized agencies wherever practicable. It must be a worldwide effort for the achievement of peace, plenty, and freedom.

With the cooperation of business, private capital, agriculture, and labor in this country, this program can greatly increase the industrial activity in other nations and can raise substantially their standards of living.

Such new economic developments must be devised and controlled to benefit the peoples of the areas in which they are established. Guarantees to the investor must be balanced by guarantees in the interest of the people whose resources and whose labor go into these developments.

The old imperialism—exploitation for foreign profit—has no place in our plans. What we envisage is a program of development based on the concepts of democratic fair-dealing.

All countries, including our own, will greatly benefit from a constructive program for the better use of the world's human and natural resources. Experience shows that our commerce with other countries expands as they progress industrially and economically.

Greater production is the key to prosperity and peace. And the key to greater production is a wider and more vigorous application of modern scientific and technical knowledge.

Only by helping the least fortunate of its members to help themselves can the human family achieve the decent, satisfying life that is the right of all people.

Democracy alone can supply the vitalizing force to stir the peoples of the world into triumphant action, not only against their human oppressors, but also against their ancient enemies—hunger, misery, and despair.

On the basis of these four major courses of action we hope to help create the conditions that will lead eventually to personal freedom and happiness for all mankind.

If we are to be successful in carrying out these policies, it is clear that we must have continued prosperity in this country and we must keep ourselves strong.

Slowly but surely we are weaving a world fabric of international security and growing prosperity.

We are aided by all who wish to live in freedom from fear—even by those who live today in fear under their own governments.

We are aided by all who want relief from the lies of propaganda— who desire truth and sincerity.

We are aided by all who desire self-government and a voice in deciding their own affairs.

We are aided by all who long for economic security—for the security and abundance that men in free societies can enjoy.

We are aided by all who desire freedom of speech, freedom of religion, and freedom to live their own lives for useful ends.

Our allies are the millions who hunger and thirst after righteousness.

In due time, as our stability becomes manifest, as more and more nations come to know the benefits of democracy and to participate in growing abundance, I believe that those countries which now oppose us will abandon their delusions and join with the free nations of the world in a just settlement of international differences.

Events have brought our American democracy to new influence and new responsibilities. They will test our courage, our devotion to duty, and our concept of liberty.

But I say to all men, what we have achieved in liberty, we will surpass in greater liberty.

Steadfast in our faith in the Almighty, we will advance toward a world where man's freedom is secure.

To that end we will devote our strength, our resources, and our firmness of resolve. With God's help, the future of mankind will be assured in a world of justice, harmony, and peace.

# DWIGHT D. EISENHOWER
## FIRST INAUGURAL ADDRESS
## TUESDAY, JANUARY 20, 1953

M y friends, before I begin the expression of those thoughts that
I deem appropriate to this moment, would you permit me the
privilege of uttering a little private prayer of my own. And I ask that
you bow your heads:

Almighty God, as we stand here at this moment my future associates
in the executive branch of government join me in beseeching that
Thou will make full and complete our dedication to the service of the
people in this throng, and their fellow citizens everywhere.

Give us, we pray, the power to discern clearly right from wrong,
and allow all our words and actions to be governed thereby, and by
the laws of this land. Especially we pray that our concern shall be for
all the people regardless of station, race, or calling.

May cooperation be permitted and be the mutual aim of those who,
under the concepts of our Constitution, hold to differing political
faiths; so that all may work for the good of our beloved country and
Thy glory. Amen.

My fellow citizens:

The world and we have passed the midway point of a century of
continuing challenge. We sense with all our faculties that forces of good
and evil are massed and armed and opposed as rarely before in history.

This fact defines the meaning of this day. We are summoned by
this honored and historic ceremony to witness more than the act of
one citizen swearing his oath of service, in the presence of God. We
are called as a people to give testimony in the sight of the world to our
faith that the future shall belong to the free.

Since this century's beginning, a time of tempest has seemed to
come upon the continents of the earth. Masses of Asia have awakened
to strike off shackles of the past. Great nations of Europe have fought

their bloodiest wars. Thrones have toppled and their vast empires have disappeared. New nations have been born.

For our own country, it has been a time of recurring trial. We have grown in power and in responsibility. We have passed through the anxieties of depression and of war to a summit unmatched in man's history. Seeking to secure peace in the world, we have had to fight through the forests of the Argonne, to the shores of Iwo Jima, and to the cold mountains of Korea.

In the swift rush of great events, we find ourselves groping to know the full sense and meaning of these times in which we live. In our quest of understanding, we beseech God's guidance. We summon all our knowledge of the past and we scan all signs of the future. We bring all our wit and all our will to meet the question:

How far have we come in man's long pilgrimage from darkness toward light? Are we nearing the light—a day of freedom and of peace for all mankind? Or are the shadows of another night closing in upon us?

Great as are the preoccupations absorbing us at home, concerned as we are with matters that deeply affect our livelihood today and our vision of the future, each of these domestic problems is dwarfed by, and often even created by, this question that involves all humankind.

This trial comes at a moment when man's power to achieve good or to inflict evil surpasses the brightest hopes and the sharpest fears of all ages. We can turn rivers in their courses, level mountains to the plains. Oceans and land and sky are avenues for our colossal commerce. Disease diminishes and life lengthens.

Yet the promise of this life is imperiled by the very genius that has made it possible. Nations amass wealth. Labor sweats to create—and turns out devices to level not only mountains but also cities. Science seems ready to confer upon us, as its final gift, the power to erase human life from this planet.

At such a time in history, we who are free must proclaim anew our faith. This faith is the abiding creed of our fathers. It is our faith in the deathless dignity of man, governed by eternal moral and natural laws.

This faith defines our full view of life. It establishes, beyond debate, those gifts of the Creator that are man's inalienable rights, and that make all men equal in His sight.

In the light of this equality, we know that the virtues most cherished by free people—love of truth, pride of work, devotion to country—all are treasures equally precious in the lives of the most humble and of the most exalted. The men who mine coal and fire furnaces and balance ledgers and turn lathes and pick cotton and heal the sick and plant corn—all serve as proudly, and as profitably, for America as the statesmen who draft treaties and the legislators who enact laws.

This faith rules our whole way of life. It decrees that we, the people, elect leaders not to rule but to serve. It asserts that we have the right to choice of our own work and to the reward of our own toil. It inspires the initiative that makes our productivity the wonder of the world. And it warns that any man who seeks to deny equality among all his brothers betrays the spirit of the free and invites the mockery of the tyrant.

It is because we, all of us, hold to these principles that the political changes accomplished this day do not imply turbulence, upheaval or disorder. Rather this change expresses a purpose of strengthening our dedication and devotion to the precepts of our founding documents, a conscious renewal of faith in our country and in the watchfulness of a Divine Providence.

The enemies of this faith know no god but force, no devotion but its use. They tutor men in treason. They feed upon the hunger of others. Whatever defies them, they torture, especially the truth.

Here, then, is joined no argument between slightly differing philosophies. This conflict strikes directly at the faith of our fathers and the lives of our sons. No principle or treasure that we hold, from the spiritual knowledge of our free schools and churches to the creative magic of free labor and capital, nothing lies safely beyond the reach of this struggle.

Freedom is pitted against slavery; lightness against the dark.

The faith we hold belongs not to us alone but to the free of all the world. This common bond binds the grower of rice in Burma and the planter of wheat in Iowa, the shepherd in southern Italy and the mountaineer in the Andes. It confers a common dignity upon the French soldier who dies in Indo-China, the British soldier killed in Malaya, the American life given in Korea.

We know, beyond this, that we are linked to all free peoples not merely by a noble idea but by a simple need. No free people can for long cling to any privilege or enjoy any safety in economic solitude. For all our own material might, even we need markets in the world for the surpluses of our farms and our factories. Equally, we need for these same farms and factories vital materials and products of distant lands. This basic law of interdependence, so manifest in the commerce of peace, applies with thousand-fold intensity in the event of war.

So we are persuaded by necessity and by belief that the strength of all free peoples lies in unity; their danger, in discord.

To produce this unity, to meet the challenge of our time, destiny has laid upon our country the responsibility of the free world's leadership.

So it is proper that we assure our friends once again that, in the discharge of this responsibility, we Americans know and we observe the difference between world leadership and imperialism; between firmness and truculence; between a thoughtfully calculated goal and spasmodic reaction to the stimulus of emergencies.

We wish our friends the world over to know this above all: we face the threat—not with dread and confusion—but with confidence and conviction.

We feel this moral strength because we know that we are not helpless prisoners of history. We are free men. We shall remain free, never to be proven guilty of the one capital offense against freedom, a lack of staunch faith.

In pleading our just cause before the bar of history and in pressing our labor for world peace, we shall be guided by certain fixed principles.

These principles are:

(1) Abhorring war as a chosen way to balk the purposes of those who threaten us, we hold it to be the first task of statesmanship to develop the strength that will deter the forces of aggression and promote the conditions of peace. For, as it must be the supreme purpose of all free men, so it must be the dedication of their leaders, to save humanity from preying upon itself.

In the light of this principle, we stand ready to engage with any and all others in joint effort to remove the causes of mutual fear and distrust among nations, so as to make possible drastic reduction of armaments. The sole requisites for undertaking such effort are that—in their purpose—they be aimed logically and honestly toward secure peace for all; and that—in their result—they provide methods by which every participating nation will prove good faith in carrying out its pledge.

(2) Realizing that common sense and common decency alike dictate the futility of appeasement, we shall never try to placate an aggressor by the false and wicked bargain of trading honor for security. Americans, indeed all free men, remember that in the final choice a soldier's pack is not so heavy a burden as a prisoner's chains.

(3) Knowing that only a United States that is strong and immensely productive can help defend freedom in our world, we view our Nation's strength and security as a trust upon which rests the hope of free men everywhere. It is the firm duty of each of our free citizens and of every free citizen everywhere to place the cause of his country before the comfort, the convenience of himself.

(4) Honoring the identity and the special heritage of each nation in the world, we shall never use our strength to try to impress upon another people our own cherished political and economic institutions.

(5) Assessing realistically the needs and capacities of proven friends of freedom, we shall strive to help them to achieve their own security and well-being. Likewise, we shall count upon them to assume, within the limits of their resources, their full and just burdens in the common defense of freedom.

(6) Recognizing economic health as an indispensable basis of military strength and the free world's peace, we shall strive to foster everywhere, and to practice ourselves, policies that encourage productivity and profitable trade. For the impoverishment of any single people in the world means danger to the well-being of all other peoples.

(7) Appreciating that economic need, military security and political wisdom combine to suggest regional groupings of free peoples, we hope, within the framework of the United Nations, to help strengthen such special bonds the world over. The nature of these ties must vary with the different problems of different areas.

In the Western Hemisphere, we enthusiastically join with all our neighbors in the work of perfecting a community of fraternal trust and common purpose.

In Europe, we ask that enlightened and inspired leaders of the Western nations strive with renewed vigor to make the unity of their peoples a reality. Only as free Europe unitedly marshals its strength can it effectively safeguard, even with our help, its spiritual and cultural heritage.

(8) Conceiving the defense of freedom, like freedom itself, to be one and indivisible, we hold all continents and peoples in equal regard and honor. We reject any insinuation that one race or another, one people or another, is in any sense inferior or expendable.

(9) Respecting the United Nations as the living sign of all people's hope for peace, we shall strive to make it not merely an eloquent symbol but an effective force. And in our quest for an honorable peace, we shall neither compromise, nor tire, nor ever cease.

By these rules of conduct, we hope to be known to all peoples.

By their observance, an earth of peace may become not a vision but a fact.

This hope—this supreme aspiration—must rule the way we live.

We must be ready to dare all for our country. For history does not long entrust the care of freedom to the weak or the timid. We must acquire proficiency in defense and display stamina in purpose.

We must be willing, individually and as a Nation, to accept whatever sacrifices may be required of us. A people that values its privileges above its principles soon loses both.

These basic precepts are not lofty abstractions, far removed from matters of daily living. They are laws of spiritual strength that generate and define our material strength. Patriotism means equipped forces and a prepared citizenry. Moral stamina means more energy and more productivity, on the farm and in the factory. Love of liberty means the guarding of every resource that makes freedom possible— from the sanctity of our families and the wealth of our soil to the genius of our scientists.

And so each citizen plays an indispensable role. The productivity of our heads, our hands, and our hearts is the source of all the strength we can command, for both the enrichment of our lives and the winning of the peace.

No person, no home, no community can be beyond the reach of this call. We are summoned to act in wisdom and in conscience, to work with industry, to teach with persuasion, to preach with conviction, to weigh our every deed with care and with compassion. For this truth must be clear before us: whatever America hopes to bring to pass in the world must first come to pass in the heart of America.

The peace we seek, then, is nothing less than the practice and fulfillment of our whole faith among ourselves and in our dealings with others. This signifies more than the stilling of guns, easing the sorrow of war. More than escape from death, it is a way of life. More than a haven for the weary, it is a hope for the brave.

This is the hope that beckons us onward in this century of trial. This is the work that awaits us all, to be done with bravery, with charity, and with prayer to Almighty God.

## DWIGHT D. EISENHOWER
## SECOND INAUGURAL ADDRESS
## MONDAY, JANUARY 21, 1957

Mr. Chairman, Mr. Vice President, Mr. Chief Justice, Mr. Speaker, members of my family and friends, my countrymen, and the friends of my country, wherever they may be, we meet again, as upon a like moment four years ago, and again you have witnessed my solemn oath of service to you.

I, too, am a witness, today testifying in your name to the principles and purposes to which we, as a people, are pledged.

Before all else, we seek, upon our common labor as a nation, the blessings of Almighty God. And the hopes in our hearts fashion the deepest prayers of our whole people.

May we pursue the right—without self-righteousness.

May we know unity—without conformity.

May we grow in strength—without pride in self.

May we, in our dealings with all peoples of the earth, ever speak truth and serve justice.

And so shall America—in the sight of all men of good will— prove true to the honorable purposes that bind and rule us as a people in all this time of trial through which we pass.

We live in a land of plenty, but rarely has this earth known such peril as today.

In our nation work and wealth abound. Our population grows. Commerce crowds our rivers and rails, our skies, harbors, and highways. Our soil is fertile, our agriculture productive. The air rings with the song of our industry—rolling mills and blast furnaces, dynamos, dams, and assembly lines—the chorus of America the bountiful.

This is our home—yet this is not the whole of our world. For our world is where our full destiny lies—with men, of all people, and all nations, who are or would be free. And for them—and so for us—this is no time of ease or of rest.

In too much of the earth there is want, discord, danger. New forces and new nations stir and strive across the earth, with power to bring, by their fate, great good or great evil to the free world's future. From the deserts of North Africa to the islands of the South Pacific one third of all mankind has entered upon an historic struggle for a new freedom; freedom from grinding poverty. Across all continents, nearly a billion people seek, sometimes almost in desperation, for the skills and knowledge and assistance by which they may satisfy from their own resources, the material wants common to all mankind.

No nation, however old or great, escapes this tempest of change and turmoil. Some, impoverished by the recent World War, seek to restore their means of livelihood. In the heart of Europe, Germany still stands tragically divided. So is the whole continent divided. And so, too, is all the world.

The divisive force is International Communism and the power that it controls.

The designs of that power, dark in purpose, are clear in practice. It strives to seal forever the fate of those it has enslaved. It strives to break the ties that unite the free. And it strives to capture—to exploit for its own greater power—all forces of change in the world, especially the needs of the hungry and the hopes of the oppressed.

Yet the world of International Communism has itself been shaken by a fierce and mighty force: the readiness of men who love freedom to pledge their lives to that love. Through the night of their bondage, the unconquerable will of heroes has struck with the swift, sharp thrust of lightning. Budapest is no longer merely the name of a city; henceforth it is a new and shining symbol of man's yearning to be free.

Thus across all the globe there harshly blow the winds of change. And, we—though fortunate be our lot—know that we can never turn our backs to them.

We look upon this shaken earth, and we declare our firm and fixed purpose—the building of a peace with justice in a world where moral law prevails.

The building of such a peace is a bold and solemn purpose. To proclaim it is easy. To serve it will be hard. And to attain it, we must be aware of its full meaning—and ready to pay its full price.

We know clearly what we seek, and why.

We seek peace, knowing that peace is the climate of freedom. And now, as in no other age, we seek it because we have been warned, by the power of modern weapons, that peace may be the only climate possible for human life itself.

Yet this peace we seek cannot be born of fear alone: it must be rooted in the lives of nations. There must be justice, sensed and shared by all peoples, for, without justice the world can know only a tense and unstable truce. There must be law, steadily invoked and respected by all nations, for without law, the world promises only such meager justice as the pity of the strong upon the weak. But the law of which we speak, comprehending the values of freedom, affirms the equality of all nations, great and small.

Splendid as can be the blessings of such a peace, high will be its cost: in toil patiently sustained, in help honorably given, in sacrifice calmly borne.

We are called to meet the price of this peace.

To counter the threat of those who seek to rule by force, we must pay the costs of our own needed military strength, and help to build the security of others.

We must use our skills and knowledge and, at times, our substance, to help others rise from misery, however far the scene of suffering may be from our shores. For wherever in the world a people knows desperate want, there must appear at least the spark of hope, the hope of progress—or there will surely rise at last the flames of conflict.

We recognize and accept our own deep involvement in the destiny of men everywhere. We are accordingly pledged to honor, and to strive to fortify, the authority of the United Nations. For in that body rests the best hope of our age for the assertion of that law by which all nations may live in dignity.

And, beyond this general resolve, we are called to act a responsible role in the world's great concerns or conflicts—whether they touch upon the affairs of a vast region, the fate of an island in the Pacific, or the use of a canal in the Middle East. Only in respecting the hopes and cultures of others will we practice the equality of all nations. Only as we show willingness and wisdom in giving counsel—in receiving counsel—and in sharing burdens, will we wisely perform the work of peace.

For one truth must rule all we think and all we do. No people can live to itself alone. The unity of all who dwell in freedom is their only sure defense. The economic need of all nations—in mutual dependence—makes isolation an impossibility; not even America's prosperity could long survive if other nations did not also prosper. No nation can longer be a fortress, lone and strong and safe. And any people, seeking such shelter for themselves, can now build only their own prison.

Our pledge to these principles is constant, because we believe in their rightness.

We do not fear this world of change. America is no stranger to much of its spirit. Everywhere we see the seeds of the same growth that America itself has known. The American experiment has, for generations, fired the passion and the courage of millions elsewhere seeking freedom, equality, and opportunity. And the American story of material progress has helped excite the longing of all needy peoples for some satisfaction of their human wants. These hopes that we have helped to inspire, we can help to fulfill.

In this confidence, we speak plainly to all peoples.

We cherish our friendship with all nations that are or would be free. We respect, no less, their independence. And when, in time of want or peril, they ask our help, they may honorably receive it; for we no more seek to buy their sovereignty than we would sell our own. Sovereignty is never bartered among freemen.

We honor the aspirations of those nations which, now captive, long for freedom. We seek neither their military alliance nor any artificial imitation of our society. And they can know the warmth of the welcome that awaits them when, as must be, they join again the ranks of freedom.

We honor, no less in this divided world than in a less tormented time, the people of Russia. We do not dread, rather do we welcome, their progress in education and industry. We wish them success in their demands for more intellectual freedom, greater security before their own laws, fuller enjoyment of the rewards of their own toil. For as such things come to pass, the more certain will be the coming of that day when our peoples may freely meet in friendship.

So we voice our hope and our belief that we can help to heal this divided world. Thus may the nations cease to live in trembling before the menace of force. Thus may the weight of fear and the weight of arms be taken from the burdened shoulders of mankind.

This, nothing less, is the labor to which we are called and our strength dedicated.

And so the prayer of our people carries far beyond our own frontiers, to the wide world of our duty and our destiny.

May the light of freedom, coming to all darkened lands, flame brightly—until at last the darkness is no more.

May the turbulence of our age yield to a true time of peace, when men and nations shall share a life that honors the dignity of each, the brotherhood of all.

# JOHN F. KENNEDY
## INAUGURAL ADDRESS
### FRIDAY, JANUARY 20, 1961

Vice President Johnson, Mr. Speaker, Mr. Chief Justice, President Eisenhower, Vice President Nixon, President Truman, reverend clergy, fellow citizens, we observe today not a victory of party, but a celebration of freedom—symbolizing an end, as well as a beginning—signifying renewal, as well as change. For I have sworn before you and Almighty God the same solemn oath our forebears prescribed nearly a century and three quarters ago.

The world is very different now. For man holds in his mortal hands the power to abolish all forms of human poverty and all forms of human life. And yet the same revolutionary beliefs for which our forebears fought are still at issue around the globe—the belief that the rights of man come not from the generosity of the state, but from the hand of God.

We dare not forget today that we are the heirs of that first revolution. Let the word go forth from this time and place, to friend and foe alike, that the torch has been passed to a new generation of Americans—born in this century, tempered by war, disciplined by a hard and bitter peace, proud of our ancient heritage—and unwilling to witness or permit the slow undoing of those human rights to which this Nation has always been committed, and to which we are committed today at home and around the world.

Let every nation know, whether it wishes us well or ill, that we shall pay any price, bear any burden, meet any hardship, support any friend, oppose any foe, in order to assure the survival and the success of liberty.

This much we pledge—and more.

To those old allies whose cultural and spiritual origins we share, we pledge the loyalty of faithful friends. United, there is little we cannot do in a host of cooperative ventures. Divided, there is little we can do—for we dare not meet a powerful challenge at odds and split asunder.

To those new States whom we welcome to the ranks of the free, we pledge our word that one form of colonial control shall not have passed away merely to be replaced by a far more iron tyranny. We shall not always expect to find them supporting our view. But we shall always hope to find them strongly supporting their own freedom— and to remember that, in the past, those who foolishly sought power by riding the back of the tiger ended up inside.

To those peoples in the huts and villages across the globe struggling to break the bonds of mass misery, we pledge our best efforts to help them help themselves, for whatever period is required—not because the Communists may be doing it, not because we seek their votes, but because it is right. If a free society cannot help the many who are poor, it cannot save the few who are rich.

To our sister republics south of our border, we offer a special pledge—to convert our good words into good deeds—in a new alliance for progress—to assist free men and free governments in casting off the chains of poverty. But this peaceful revolution of hope cannot become the prey of hostile powers. Let all our neighbors know that we shall join with them to oppose aggression or subversion anywhere in the Americas. And let every other power know that this Hemisphere intends to remain the master of its own house.

To that world assembly of sovereign states, the United Nations, our last best hope in an age where the instruments of war have far outpaced the instruments of peace, we renew our pledge of support— to prevent it from becoming merely a forum for invective—to strengthen its shield of the new and the weak—and to enlarge the area in which its writ may run.

Finally, to those nations who would make themselves our adversary, we offer not a pledge but a request: that both sides begin anew the quest for peace, before the dark powers of destruction unleashed by science engulf all humanity in planned or accidental self-destruction.

We dare not tempt them with weakness. For only when our arms are sufficient beyond doubt can we be certain beyond doubt that they will never be employed.

But neither can two great and powerful groups of nations take comfort from our present course—both sides overburdened by the cost of modern weapons, both rightly alarmed by the steady spread of the deadly atom, yet both racing to alter that uncertain balance of terror that stays the hand of mankind's final war.

So let us begin anew—remembering on both sides that civility is not a sign of weakness, and sincerity is always subject to proof. Let us never negotiate out of fear. But let us never fear to negotiate.

Let both sides explore what problems unite us instead of belaboring those problems which divide us.

Let both sides, for the first time, formulate serious and precise proposals for the inspection and control of arms—and bring the absolute power to destroy other nations under the absolute control of all nations.

Let both sides seek to invoke the wonders of science instead of its terrors. Together let us explore the stars, conquer the deserts, eradicate disease, tap the ocean depths, and encourage the arts and commerce.

Let both sides unite to heed in all corners of the earth the command of Isaiah—to "undo the heavy burdens...and to let the oppressed go free."

And if a beachhead of cooperation may push back the jungle of suspicion, let both sides join in creating a new endeavor, not a new balance of power, but a new world of law, where the strong are just and the weak secure and the peace preserved.

All this will not be finished in the first 100 days. Nor will it be finished in the first 1,000 days, nor in the life of this Administration, nor even perhaps in our lifetime on this planet. But let us begin.

In your hands, my fellow citizens, more than in mine, will rest the final success or failure of our course. Since this country was founded, each generation of Americans has been summoned to give testimony to its national loyalty. The graves of young Americans who answered the call to service surround the globe.

Now the trumpet summons us again—not as a call to bear arms, though arms we need; not as a call to battle, though embattled we are— but a call to bear the burden of a long twilight struggle, year in and year out, "rejoicing in hope, patient in tribulation"—a struggle against the common enemies of man: tyranny, poverty, disease, and war itself.

Can we forge against these enemies a grand and global alliance, North and South, East and West, that can assure a more fruitful life for all mankind? Will you join in that historic effort?

In the long history of the world, only a few generations have been granted the role of defending freedom in its hour of maximum danger. I do not shrink from this responsibility—I welcome it. I do not believe that any of us would exchange places with any other people or any other generation. The energy, the faith, the devotion which we bring to this endeavor will light our country and all who serve it—and the glow from that fire can truly light the world.

And so, my fellow Americans: ask not what your country can do for you—ask what you can do for your country.

My fellow citizens of the world: ask not what America will do for you, but what together we can do for the freedom of man.

Finally, whether you are citizens of America or citizens of the world, ask of us the same high standards of strength and sacrifice which we ask of you. With a good conscience our only sure reward, with history the final judge of our deeds, let us go forth to lead the land we love, asking His blessing and His help, but knowing that here on earth God's work must truly be our own.

# LYNDON BAINES JOHNSON
## INAUGURAL ADDRESS
## WEDNESDAY, JANUARY 20, 1965

My fellow countrymen, on this occasion, the oath I have taken before you and before God is not mine alone, but ours together. We are one nation and one people. Our fate as a nation and our future as a people rest not upon one citizen, but upon all citizens.

This is the majesty and the meaning of this moment.

For every generation, there is a destiny. For some, history decides. For this generation, the choice must be our own.

Even now, a rocket moves toward Mars. It reminds us that the world will not be the same for our children, or even for ourselves in a short span of years. The next man to stand here will look out on a scene different from our own, because ours is a time of change—rapid and fantastic change bearing the secrets of nature, multiplying the nations, placing in uncertain hands new weapons for mastery and destruction, shaking old values, and uprooting old ways.

Our destiny in the midst of change will rest on the unchanged character of our people, and on their faith.

### THE AMERICAN COVENANT

They came here—the exile and the stranger, brave but frightened—to find a place where a man could be his own man. They made a covenant with this land. Conceived in justice, written in liberty, bound in union, it was meant one day to inspire the hopes of all mankind; and it binds us still. If we keep its terms, we shall flourish.

### JUSTICE AND CHANGE

First, justice was the promise that all who made the journey would share in the fruits of the land.

In a land of great wealth, families must not live in hopeless poverty. In a land rich in harvest, children just must not go hungry. In a land of healing miracles, neighbors must not suffer and die unattended. In a great land of learning and scholars, young people must be taught to read and write.

For the more than 30 years that I have served this Nation, I have believed that this injustice to our people, this waste of our resources, was our real enemy. For 30 years or more, with the resources I have had, I have vigilantly fought against it. I have learned, and I know, that it will not surrender easily.

But change has given us new weapons. Before this generation of Americans is finished, this enemy will not only retreat—it will be conquered.

Justice requires us to remember that when any citizen denies his fellow, saying, "His color is not mine," or "His beliefs are strange and different," in that moment he betrays America, though his forebears created this Nation.

## LIBERTY AND CHANGE

Liberty was the second article of our covenant. It was self-government. It was our Bill of Rights. But it was more. America would be a place where each man could be proud to be himself: stretching his talents, rejoicing in his work, important in the life of his neighbors and his nation.

This has become more difficult in a world where change and growth seem to tower beyond the control and even the judgment of men. We must work to provide the knowledge and the surroundings which can enlarge the possibilities of every citizen.

The American covenant called on us to help show the way for the liberation of man. And that is today our goal. Thus, if as a nation there is much outside our control, as a people no stranger is outside our hope.

Change has brought new meaning to that old mission. We can never again stand aside, prideful in isolation. Terrific dangers and troubles that we once called "foreign" now constantly live among us. If American lives must end, and American treasure be spilled, in countries we barely know, that is the price that change has demanded of conviction and of our enduring covenant.

Think of our world as it looks from the rocket that is heading toward Mars. It is like a child's globe, hanging in space, the continents stuck to its side like colored maps. We are all fellow passengers on a dot of earth. And each of us, in the span of time, has really only a moment among our companions.

How incredible it is that in this fragile existence, we should hate and destroy one another. There are possibilities enough for all who will abandon mastery over others to pursue mastery over nature. There is world enough for all to seek their happiness in their own way.

Our Nation's course is abundantly clear. We aspire to nothing that belongs to others. We seek no dominion over our fellow man, but man's dominion over tyranny and misery.

But more is required. Men want to be a part of a common enterprise—a cause greater than themselves. Each of us must find a way to advance the purpose of the Nation, thus finding new purpose for ourselves. Without this, we shall become a nation of strangers.

## UNION AND CHANGE

The third article was union. To those who were small and few against the wilderness, the success of liberty demanded the strength of union. Two centuries of change have made this true again.

No longer need capitalist and worker, farmer and clerk, city and countryside, struggle to divide our bounty. By working shoulder to shoulder, together we can increase the bounty of all. We have discovered that every child who learns, every man who finds work, every sick body that is made whole—like a candle added to an altar—brightens the hope of all the faithful.

So let us reject any among us who seek to reopen old wounds and to rekindle old hatreds. They stand in the way of a seeking nation.

Let us now join reason to faith and action to experience, to transform our unity of interest into a unity of purpose. For the hour and the day and the time are here to achieve progress without strife, to achieve change without hatred—not without difference of opinion, but without the deep and abiding divisions which scar the union for generations.

## THE AMERICAN BELIEF

Under this covenant of justice, liberty, and union we have become a nation—prosperous, great, and mighty. And we have kept our freedom. But we have no promise from God that our greatness will endure. We have been allowed by Him to seek greatness with the sweat of our hands and the strength of our spirit.

I do not believe that the Great Society is the ordered, changeless, and sterile battalion of the ants. It is the excitement of becoming—always becoming, trying, probing, falling, resting, and trying again—but always trying and always gaining.

In each generation, with toil and tears, we have had to earn our heritage again.

If we fail now, we shall have forgotten in abundance what we learned in hardship: that democracy rests on faith, that freedom asks more than it gives, and that the judgment of God is harshest on those who are most favored.

If we succeed, it will not be because of what we have, but it will be because of what we are; not because of what we own, but, rather because of what we believe.

For we are a nation of believers. Underneath the clamor of building and the rush of our day's pursuits, we are believers in justice and liberty and union, and in our own Union. We believe that every man must someday be free. And we believe in ourselves.

Our enemies have always made the same mistake. In my lifetime—in depression and in war—they have awaited our defeat. Each time, from the secret places of the American heart, came forth the faith they could not see or that they could not even imagine. It brought us victory. And it will again.

For this is what America is all about. It is the uncrossed desert and the unclimbed ridge. It is the star that is not reached and the harvest sleeping in the unplowed ground. Is our world gone? We say "Farewell." Is a new world coming? We welcome it—and we will bend it to the hopes of man.

To these trusted public servants and to my family and those close friends of mine who have followed me down a long, winding road, and to all the people of this Union and the world, I will repeat today what I said on that sorrowful day in November 1963: "I will lead and I will do the best I can."

But you must look within your own hearts to the old promises and to the old dream. They will lead you best of all.

For myself, I ask only, in the words of an ancient leader: "Give me now wisdom and knowledge, that I may go out and come in before this people: for who can judge this thy people, that is so great?"

# RICHARD MILHOUS NIXON
## FIRST INAUGURAL ADDRESS
## MONDAY, JANUARY 20, 1969

Senator Dirksen, Mr. Chief Justice, Mr. Vice President, President Johnson, Vice President Humphrey, my fellow Americans—and my fellow citizens of the world community:

I ask you to share with me today the majesty of this moment. In the orderly transfer of power, we celebrate the unity that keeps us free.

Each moment in history is a fleeting time, precious and unique. But some stand out as moments of beginning, in which courses are set that shape decades or centuries.

This can be such a moment.

Forces now are converging that make possible, for the first time, the hope that many of man's deepest aspirations can at last be realized. The spiraling pace of change allows us to contemplate, within our own lifetime, advances that once would have taken centuries.

In throwing wide the horizons of space, we have discovered new horizons on earth.

For the first time, because the people of the world want peace, and the leaders of the world are afraid of war, the times are on the side of peace.

Eight years from now America will celebrate its 200th anniversary as a nation. Within the lifetime of most people now living, mankind will celebrate that great new year which comes only once in a thousand years—the beginning of the third millennium.

What kind of nation we will be, what kind of world we will live in, whether we shape the future in the image of our hopes, is ours to determine by our actions and our choices.

The greatest honor history can bestow is the title of peacemaker. This honor now beckons America—the chance to help lead the world at last out of the valley of turmoil, and onto that high ground of peace that man has dreamed of since the dawn of civilization.

If we succeed, generations to come will say of us now living that we mastered our moment, that we helped make the world safe for mankind.

This is our summons to greatness.

I believe the American people are ready to answer this call.

The second third of this century has been a time of proud achievement. We have made enormous strides in science and industry and agriculture. We have shared our wealth more broadly than ever. We have learned at last to manage a modern economy to assure its continued growth.

We have given freedom new reach, and we have begun to make its promise real for black as well as for white.

We see the hope of tomorrow in the youth of today. I know America's youth. I believe in them. We can be proud that they are better educated, more committed, more passionately driven by conscience than any generation in our history.

No people has ever been so close to the achievement of a just and abundant society, or so possessed of the will to achieve it. Because our strengths are so great, we can afford to appraise our weaknesses with candor and to approach them with hope.

Standing in this same place a third of a century ago, Franklin Delano Roosevelt addressed a Nation ravaged by depression and gripped in fear. He could say in surveying the Nation's troubles: "They concern, thank God, only material things."

Our crisis today is the reverse. We have found ourselves rich in goods, but ragged in spirit; reaching with magnificent precision for the moon, but falling into raucous discord on earth.

We are caught in war, wanting peace. We are torn by division, wanting unity. We see around us empty lives, wanting fulfillment. We see tasks that need doing, waiting for hands to do them.

To a crisis of the spirit, we need an answer of the spirit.

To find that answer, we need only look within ourselves.

When we listen to "the better angels of our nature," we find that they celebrate the simple things, the basic things—such as goodness, decency, love, kindness.

Greatness comes in simple trappings.

The simple things are the ones most needed today if we are to surmount what divides us, and cement what unites us.

To lower our voices would be a simple thing.

In these difficult years, America has suffered from a fever of words; from inflated rhetoric that promises more than it can deliver; from angry rhetoric that fans discontents into hatreds; from bombastic rhetoric that postures instead of persuading.

We cannot learn from one another until we stop shouting at one another—until we speak quietly enough so that our words can be heard as well as our voices.

For its part, government will listen. We will strive to listen in new ways—to the voices of quiet anguish, the voices that speak without words, the voices of the heart—to the injured voices, the anxious voices, the voices that have despaired of being heard.

Those who have been left out, we will try to bring in.

Those left behind, we will help to catch up.

For all of our people, we will set as our goal the decent order that makes progress possible and our lives secure.

As we reach toward our hopes, our task is to build on what has gone before—not turning away from the old, but turning toward the new.

In this past third of a century, government has passed more laws, spent more money, initiated more programs, than in all our previous history.

In pursuing our goals of full employment, better housing, excellence in education; in rebuilding our cities and improving our rural areas; in protecting our environment and enhancing the quality of life—in all these and more, we will and must press urgently forward.

We shall plan now for the day when our wealth can be transferred from the destruction of war abroad to the urgent needs of our people at home.

The American dream does not come to those who fall asleep.

But we are approaching the limits of what government alone can do.

Our greatest need now is to reach beyond government, and to enlist the legions of the concerned and the committed.

What has to be done, has to be done by government and people together or it will not be done at all. The lesson of past agony is that without the people we can do nothing; with the people we can do everything.

To match the magnitude of our tasks, we need the energies of our people—enlisted not only in grand enterprises, but more importantly in those small, splendid efforts that make headlines in the neighborhood newspaper instead of the national journal.

With these, we can build a great cathedral of the spirit—each of us raising it one stone at a time, as he reaches out to his neighbor, helping, caring, doing.

I do not offer a life of uninspiring ease. I do not call for a life of grim sacrifice. I ask you to join in a high adventure—one as rich as humanity itself, and as exciting as the times we live in.

The essence of freedom is that each of us shares in the shaping of his own destiny.

Until he has been part of a cause larger than himself, no man is truly whole.

The way to fulfillment is in the use of our talents; we achieve nobility in the spirit that inspires that use.

As we measure what can be done, we shall promise only what we know we can produce, but as we chart our goals we shall be lifted by our dreams.

No man can be fully free while his neighbor is not. To go forward at all is to go forward together.

This means black and white together, as one nation, not two. The laws have caught up with our conscience. What remains is to give life to what is in the law: to ensure at last that as all are born equal in dignity before God, all are born equal in dignity before man.

As we learn to go forward together at home, let us also seek to go forward together with all mankind.

Let us take as our goal: where peace is unknown, make it welcome; where peace is fragile, make it strong; where peace is temporary, make it permanent.

After a period of confrontation, we are entering an era of negotiation.

Let all nations know that during this administration our lines of communication will be open.

We seek an open world—open to ideas, open to the exchange of goods and people—a world in which no people, great or small, will live in angry isolation.

We cannot expect to make everyone our friend, but we can try to make no one our enemy.

Those who would be our adversaries, we invite to a peaceful competition—not in conquering territory or extending dominion, but in enriching the life of man.

As we explore the reaches of space, let us go to the new worlds together—not as new worlds to be conquered, but as a new adventure to be shared.

With those who are willing to join, let us cooperate to reduce the burden of arms, to strengthen the structure of peace, to lift up the poor and the hungry.

But to all those who would be tempted by weakness, let us leave no doubt that we will be as strong as we need to be for as long as we need to be.

Over the past twenty years, since I first came to this Capital as a freshman Congressman, I have visited most of the nations of the world.

I have come to know the leaders of the world, and the great forces, the hatreds, the fears that divide the world.

I know that peace does not come through wishing for it—that there is no substitute for days and even years of patient and prolonged diplomacy.

I also know the people of the world.

I have seen the hunger of a homeless child, the pain of a man wounded in battle, the grief of a mother who has lost her son. I know these have no ideology, no race.

I know America. I know the heart of America is good.

I speak from my own heart, and the heart of my country, the deep concern we have for those who suffer, and those who sorrow.

I have taken an oath today in the presence of God and my countrymen to uphold and defend the Constitution of the United States. To that oath I now add this sacred commitment: I shall consecrate my office, my energies, and all the wisdom I can summon, to the cause of peace among nations.

Let this message be heard by strong and weak alike:

The peace we seek to win is not victory over any other people, but the peace that comes "with healing in its wings"; with compassion for those who have suffered; with understanding for those who have opposed us; with the opportunity for all the peoples of this earth to choose their own destiny.

Only a few short weeks ago, we shared the glory of man's first sight of the world as God sees it, as a single sphere reflecting light in the darkness.

As the Apollo astronauts flew over the moon's gray surface on Christmas Eve, they spoke to us of the beauty of earth—and in that voice so clear across the lunar distance, we heard them invoke God's blessing on its goodness.

In that moment, their view from the moon moved poet Archibald MacLeish to write:

"To see the earth as it truly is, small and blue and beautiful in that eternal silence where it floats, is to see ourselves as riders on the earth together, brothers on that bright loveliness in the eternal cold— brothers who know now they are truly brothers."

In that moment of surpassing technological triumph, men turned their thoughts toward home and humanity—seeing in that far perspective that man's destiny on earth is not divisible; telling us that however far we reach into the cosmos, our destiny lies not in the stars but on Earth itself, in our own hands, in our own hearts.

We have endured a long night of the American spirit. But as our eyes catch the dimness of the first rays of dawn, let us not curse the remaining dark. Let us gather the light.

Our destiny offers, not the cup of despair, but the chalice of opportunity. So let us seize it, not in fear, but in gladness—and, "riders on the earth together," let us go forward, firm in our faith, steadfast in our purpose, cautious of the dangers; but sustained by our confidence in the will of God and the promise of man.

# RICHARD MILHOUS NIXON
## SECOND INAUGURAL ADDRESS
### SATURDAY, JANUARY 20, 1973

Mr. Vice President, Mr. Speaker, Mr. Chief Justice, Senator Cook, Mrs. Eisenhower, and my fellow citizens of this great and good country we share together:

When we met here four years ago, America was bleak in spirit, depressed by the prospect of seemingly endless war abroad and of destructive conflict at home.

As we meet here today, we stand on the threshold of a new era of peace in the world.

The central question before us is: How shall we use that peace? Let us resolve that this era we are about to enter will not be what other postwar periods have so often been: a time of retreat and isolation that leads to stagnation at home and invites new danger abroad.

Let us resolve that this will be what it can become: a time of great responsibilities greatly borne, in which we renew the spirit and the promise of America as we enter our third century as a nation.

This past year saw far-reaching results from our new policies for peace. By continuing to revitalize our traditional friendships, and by our missions to Peking and to Moscow, we were able to establish the base for a new and more durable pattern of relationships among the nations of the world. Because of America's bold initiatives, 1972 will be long remembered as the year of the greatest progress since the end of World War II toward a lasting peace in the world.

The peace we seek in the world is not the flimsy peace which is merely an interlude between wars, but a peace which can endure for generations to come.

It is important that we understand both the necessity and the limitations of America's role in maintaining that peace.

Unless we in America work to preserve the peace, there will be no peace.

Unless we in America work to preserve freedom, there will be no freedom.

But let us clearly understand the new nature of America's role, as a result of the new policies we have adopted over these past four years.

We shall respect our treaty commitments.

We shall support vigorously the principle that no country has the right to impose its will or rule on another by force.

We shall continue, in this era of negotiation, to work for the limitation of nuclear arms, and to reduce the danger of confrontation between the great powers.

We shall do our share in defending peace and freedom in the world. But we shall expect others to do their share.

The time has passed when America will make every other nation's conflict our own, or make every other nation's future our responsibility, or presume to tell the people of other nations how to manage their own affairs.

Just as we respect the right of each nation to determine its own future, we also recognize the responsibility of each nation to secure its own future.

Just as America's role is indispensable in preserving the world's peace, so is each nation's role indispensable in preserving its own peace.

Together with the rest of the world, let us resolve to move forward from the beginnings we have made. Let us continue to bring down the walls of hostility which have divided the world for too long, and to build in their place bridges of understanding—so that despite profound differences between systems of government, the people of the world can be friends.

Let us build a structure of peace in the world in which the weak are as safe as the strong—in which each respects the right of the other to live by a different system—in which those who would influence others will do so by the strength of their ideas, and not by the force of their arms.

Let us accept that high responsibility not as a burden, but gladly—gladly because the chance to build such a peace is the noblest endeavor in which a nation can engage; gladly, also, because only if we act greatly in meeting our responsibilities abroad will we remain a great

Nation, and only if we remain a great Nation will we act greatly in meeting our challenges at home.

We have the chance today to do more than ever before in our history to make life better in America—to ensure better education, better health, better housing, better transportation, a cleaner environment—to restore respect for law, to make our communities more livable—and to insure the God-given right of every American to full and equal opportunity.

Because the range of our needs is so great—because the reach of our opportunities is so great—let us be bold in our determination to meet those needs in new ways.

Just as building a structure of peace abroad has required turning away from old policies that failed, so building a new era of progress at home requires turning away from old policies that have failed.

Abroad, the shift from old policies to new has not been a retreat from our responsibilities, but a better way to peace.

And at home, the shift from old policies to new will not be a retreat from our responsibilities, but a better way to progress.

Abroad and at home, the key to those new responsibilities lies in the placing and the division of responsibility. We have lived too long with the consequences of attempting to gather all power and responsibility in Washington.

Abroad and at home, the time has come to turn away from the condescending policies of paternalism—of "Washington knows best."

A person can be expected to act responsibly only if he has responsibility. This is human nature. So let us encourage individuals at home and nations abroad to do more for themselves, to decide more for themselves. Let us locate responsibility in more places. Let us measure what we will do for others by what they will do for themselves.

That is why today I offer no promise of a purely governmental solution for every problem. We have lived too long with that false promise. In trusting too much in government, we have asked of it more than it can deliver. This leads only to inflated expectations, to reduced individual effort, and to a disappointment and frustration that erode confidence both in what government can do and in what people can do.

Government must learn to take less from people so that people can do more for themselves.

Let us remember that America was built not by government, but by people—not by welfare, but by work—not by shirking responsibility, but by seeking responsibility.

In our own lives, let each of us ask—not just what will government do for me, but what can I do for myself?

In the challenges we face together, let each of us ask—not just how can government help, but how can I help?

Your National Government has a great and vital role to play. And I pledge to you that where this Government should act, we will act boldly and we will lead boldly. But just as important is the role that each and every one of us must play, as an individual and as a member of his own community.

From this day forward, let each of us make a solemn commitment in his own heart: to bear his responsibility, to do his part, to live his ideals—so that together, we can see the dawn of a new age of progress for America, and together, as we celebrate our 200th anniversary as a nation, we can do so proud in the fulfillment of our promise to ourselves and to the world.

As America's longest and most difficult war comes to an end, let us again learn to debate our differences with civility and decency. And let each of us reach out for that one precious quality government cannot provide—a new level of respect for the rights and feelings of one another, a new level of respect for the individual human dignity which is the cherished birthright of every American.

Above all else, the time has come for us to renew our faith in ourselves and in America.

In recent years, that faith has been challenged.

Our children have been taught to be ashamed of their country, ashamed of their parents, ashamed of America's record at home and of its role in the world.

At every turn, we have been beset by those who find everything wrong with America and little that is right. But I am confident that this will not be the judgment of history on these remarkable times in which we are privileged to live.

America's record in this century has been unparalleled in the world's history for its responsibility, for its generosity, for its creativity and for its progress.

Let us be proud that our system has produced and provided more freedom and more abundance, more widely shared, than any other system in the history of the world.

Let us be proud that in each of the four wars in which we have been engaged in this century, including the one we are now bringing to an end, we have fought not for our selfish advantage, but to help others resist aggression.

Let us be proud that by our bold, new initiatives, and by our steadfastness for peace with honor, we have made a break-through toward creating in the world what the world has not known before—a structure of peace that can last, not merely for our time, but for generations to come.

We are embarking here today on an era that presents challenges great as those any nation, or any generation, has ever faced.

We shall answer to God, to history, and to our conscience for the way in which we use these years.

As I stand in this place, so hallowed by history, I think of others who have stood here before me. I think of the dreams they had for America, and I think of how each recognized that he needed help far beyond himself in order to make those dreams come true.

Today, I ask your prayers that in the years ahead I may have God's help in making decisions that are right for America, and I pray for your help so that together we may be worthy of our challenge.

Let us pledge together to make these next four years the best four years in America's history, so that on its 200th birthday America will be as young and as vital as when it began, and as bright a beacon of hope for all the world.

Let us go forward from here confident in hope, strong in our faith in one another, sustained by our faith in God who created us, and striving always to serve His purpose.

# GERALD FORD
## REMARKS ON TAKING
## THE OATH OF OFFICE
## WEDNESDAY, AUGUST 9, 1974

Mr. Chief Justice, my dear friends, my fellow Americans:
The oath that I have taken is the same oath that was taken by
George Washington and by every President under the Constitution.
But I assume the Presidency under extraordinary circumstances
never before experienced by Americans. This is an hour of history
that troubles our minds and hurts our hearts.

Therefore, I feel it is my first duty to make an unprecedented
compact with my countrymen. Not an inaugural address, not a
fireside chat, not a campaign speech—just a little straight talk among
friends. And I intend it to be the first of many.

I am acutely aware that you have not elected me as your President
by your ballots, and so I ask you to confirm me as your President with
your prayers. And I hope that such prayers will also be the first of
many.

If you have not chosen me by secret ballot, neither have I gained
office by any secret promises. I have not campaigned either for the
Presidency or the Vice Presidency. I have not subscribed to any
partisan platform. I am indebted to no man, and only to one woman—
my dear wife—as I begin this very difficult job.

I have not sought this enormous responsibility, but I will not shirk
it. Those who nominated and confirmed me as Vice President were
my friends and are my friends. They were of both parties, elected by
all the people and acting under the Constitution in their name. It is
only fitting then that I should pledge to them and to you that I will be
the President of all the people.

Thomas Jefferson said the people are the only sure reliance for the
preservation of our liberty. And down the years, Abraham Lincoln

renewed this American article of faith asking, "Is there any better way or equal hope in the world?"

I intend, on Monday next, to request of the Speaker of the House of Representatives and the President pro tempore of the Senate the privilege of appearing before the Congress to share with my former colleagues and with you, the American people, my views on the priority business of the Nation and to solicit your views and their views. And may I say to the Speaker and the others, if I could meet with you right after these remarks, I would appreciate it.

Even though this is late in an election year, there is no way we can go forward except together and no way anybody can win except by serving the people's urgent needs. We cannot stand still or slip backwards. We must go forward now together.

To the peoples and the governments of all friendly nations, and I hope that could encompass the whole world, I pledge an uninterrupted and sincere search for peace. America will remain strong and united, but its strength will remain dedicated to the safety and sanity of the entire family of man, as well as to our own precious freedom.

I believe that truth is the glue that holds government together, not only our Government but civilization itself. That bond, though strained, is unbroken at home and abroad.

In all my public and private acts as your President, I expect to follow my instincts of openness and candor with full confidence that honesty is always the best policy in the end.

My fellow Americans, our long national nightmare is over.

Our Constitution works; our great Republic is a government of laws and not of men. Here the people rule. But there is a higher Power, by whatever name we honor Him, who ordains not only righteousness but love, not only justice but mercy.

As we bind up the internal wounds of Watergate, more painful and more poisonous than those of foreign wars, let us restore the golden rule to our political process, and let brotherly love purge our hearts of suspicion and of hate.

In the beginning, I asked you to pray for me. Before closing, I ask again your prayers, for Richard Nixon and for his family. May our former President, who brought peace to millions, find it for himself. May God bless and comfort his wonderful wife and daughters, whose love and loyalty will forever be a shining legacy to all who bear the lonely burdens of the White House.

I can only guess at those burdens, although I have witnessed at close hand the tragedies that befell three Presidents and the lesser trials of others.

With all the strength and all the good sense I have gained from life, with all the confidence my family, my friends, and my dedicated staff impart to me, and with the good will of countless Americans I have encountered in recent visits to 40 States, I now solemnly reaffirm my promise I made to you last December 6: to uphold the Constitution, to do what is right as God gives me to see the right, and to do the very best I can for America.

God helping me, I will not let you down.

Thank you.

# JAMES E. CARTER
## INAUGURAL ADDRESS
## THURSDAY, JANUARY 20, 1977

For myself and for our Nation, I want to thank my predecessor for all he has done to heal our land.

In this outward and physical ceremony we attest once again to the inner and spiritual strength of our Nation. As my high school teacher, Miss Julia Coleman, used to say: "We must adjust to changing times and still hold to unchanging principles."

Here before me is the Bible used in the inauguration of our first President, in 1789, and I have just taken the oath of office on the Bible my mother gave me a few years ago, opened to a timeless admonition from the ancient prophet Micah:

"He hath showed thee, O man, what is good; and what doth the Lord require of thee, but to do justly, and to love mercy, and to walk humbly with thy God." (Micah 6:8)

This inauguration ceremony marks a new beginning, a new dedication within our Government, and a new spirit among us all. A President may sense and proclaim that new spirit, but only a people can provide it.

Two centuries ago our Nation's birth was a milestone in the long quest for freedom, but the bold and brilliant dream which excited the founders of this Nation still awaits its consummation. I have no new dream to set forth today, but rather urge a fresh faith in the old dream.

Ours was the first society openly to define itself in terms of both spirituality and of human liberty. It is that unique self-definition which has given us an exceptional appeal, but it also imposes on us a special obligation, to take on those moral duties which, when assumed, seem invariably to be in our own best interests.

You have given me a great responsibility—to stay close to you, to be worthy of you, and to exemplify what you are. Let us create together a new national spirit of unity and trust. Your strength can compensate for my weakness, and your wisdom can help to minimize my mistakes.

Let us learn together and laugh together and work together and pray together, confident that in the end we will triumph together in the right.

The American dream endures. We must once again have full faith in our country—and in one another. I believe America can be better. We can be even stronger than before.

Let our recent mistakes bring a resurgent commitment to the basic principles of our Nation, for we know that if we despise our own government we have no future. We recall in special times when we have stood briefly, but magnificently, united. In those times no prize was beyond our grasp.

But we cannot dwell upon remembered glory. We cannot afford to drift. We reject the prospect of failure or mediocrity or an inferior quality of life for any person. Our Government must at the same time be both competent and compassionate.

We have already found a high degree of personal liberty, and we are now struggling to enhance equality of opportunity. Our commitment to human rights must be absolute, our laws fair, our natural beauty preserved; the powerful must not persecute the weak, and human dignity must be enhanced.

We have learned that "more" is not necessarily "better," that even our great Nation has its recognized limits, and that we can neither answer all questions nor solve all problems. We cannot afford to do everything, nor can we afford to lack boldness as we meet the future. So, together, in a spirit of individual sacrifice for the common good, we must simply do our best.

Our Nation can be strong abroad only if it is strong at home. And we know that the best way to enhance freedom in other lands is to demonstrate here that our democratic system is worthy of emulation.

To be true to ourselves, we must be true to others. We will not behave in foreign places so as to violate our rules and standards here at home, for we know that the trust which our Nation earns is essential to our strength.

The world itself is now dominated by a new spirit. Peoples more numerous and more politically aware are craving and now demanding their place in the sun—not just for the benefit of their own physical condition, but for basic human rights.

The passion for freedom is on the rise. Tapping this new spirit, there can be no nobler nor more ambitious task for America to undertake on this day of a new beginning than to help shape a just and peaceful world that is truly humane.

We are a strong nation, and we will maintain strength so sufficient that it need not be proven in combat—a quiet strength based not merely on the size of an arsenal, but on the nobility of ideas.

We will be ever vigilant and never vulnerable, and we will fight our wars against poverty, ignorance, and injustice—for those are the enemies against which our forces can be honorably marshaled.

We are a purely idealistic Nation, but let no one confuse our idealism with weakness.

Because we are free we can never be indifferent to the fate of freedom elsewhere. Our moral sense dictates a clearcut preference for these societies which share with us an abiding respect for individual human rights. We do not seek to intimidate, but it is clear that a world which others can dominate with impunity would be inhospitable to decency and a threat to the well-being of all people.

The world is still engaged in a massive armaments race designed to ensure continuing equivalent strength among potential adversaries. We pledge perseverance and wisdom in our efforts to limit the world's armaments to those necessary for each nation's own domestic safety. And we will move this year a step toward ultimate goal—the elimination of all nuclear weapons from this Earth. We urge all other people to join us, for success can mean life instead of death.

Within us, the people of the United States, there is evident a serious and purposeful rekindling of confidence. And I join in the hope that when my time as your President has ended, people might say this about our Nation:

—that we had remembered the words of Micah and renewed our search for humility, mercy, and justice;

—that we had torn down the barriers that separated those of different race and region and religion, and where there had been mistrust, built unity, with a respect for diversity;

—that we had found productive work for those able to perform it;

—that we had strengthened the American family, which is the basis of our society;

—that we had ensured respect for the law, and equal treatment under the law, for the weak and the powerful, for the rich and the poor;

—and that we had enabled our people to be proud of their own Government once again.

I would hope that the nations of the world might say that we had built a lasting peace, built not on weapons of war but on international policies which reflect our own most precious values.

These are not just my goals, and they will not be my accomplishments, but the affirmation of our Nation's continuing moral strength and our belief in an undiminished, ever-expanding American dream.

# RONALD REAGAN
## FIRST INAUGURAL ADDRESS
## TUESDAY, JANUARY 20, 1981

Senator Hatfield, Mr. Chief Justice, Mr. President, Vice President Bush, Vice President Mondale, Senator Baker, Speaker O'Neill, Reverend Moomaw, and my fellow citizens:

To a few of us here today, this is a solemn and most momentous occasion; and yet, in the history of our Nation, it is a commonplace occurrence. The orderly transfer of authority as called for in the Constitution routinely takes place as it has for almost two centuries and few of us stop to think how unique we really are. In the eyes of many in the world, this every-four-years ceremony we accept as normal is nothing less than a miracle.

Mr. President, I want our fellow citizens to know how much you did to carry on this tradition. By your gracious cooperation in the transition process, you have shown a watching world that we are a united people pledged to maintaining a political system which guarantees individual liberty to a greater degree than any other, and I thank you and your people for all your help in maintaining the continuity which is the bulwark of our Republic.

The business of our nation goes forward. These United States are confronted with an economic affliction of great proportions. We suffer from the longest and one of the worst sustained inflations in our national history. It distorts our economic decisions, penalizes thrift, and crushes the struggling young and the fixed-income elderly alike. It threatens to shatter the lives of millions of our people.

Idle industries have cast workers into unemployment, causing human misery and personal indignity. Those who do work are denied a fair return for their labor by a tax system which penalizes successful achievement and keeps us from maintaining full productivity.

But great as our tax burden is, it has not kept pace with public spending. For decades, we have piled deficit upon deficit, mortgaging our future and our children's future for the temporary convenience of the present. To continue this long trend is to guarantee tremendous social, cultural, political, and economic upheavals.

You and I, as individuals, can, by borrowing, live beyond our means, but for only a limited period of time. Why, then, should we think that collectively, as a nation, we are not bound by that same limitation?

We must act today in order to preserve tomorrow. And let there be no misunderstanding—we are going to begin to act, beginning today.

The economic ills we suffer have come upon us over several decades. They will not go away in days, weeks, or months, but they will go away. They will go away because we, as Americans, have the capacity now, as we have had in the past, to do whatever needs to be done to preserve this last and greatest bastion of freedom.

In this present crisis, government is not the solution to our problem.

From time to time, we have been tempted to believe that society has become too complex to be managed by self-rule, that government by an elite group is superior to government for, by, and of the people. But if no one among us is capable of governing himself, then who among us has the capacity to govern someone else? All of us together, in and out of government, must bear the burden. The solutions we seek must be equitable, with no one group singled out to pay a higher price.

We hear much of special interest groups. Our concern must be for a special interest group that has been too long neglected. It knows no sectional boundaries or ethnic and racial divisions, and it crosses political party lines. It is made up of men and women who raise our food, patrol our streets, man our mines and our factories, teach our children, keep our homes, and heal us when we are sick—professionals, industrialists, shopkeepers, clerks, cabbies, and truckdrivers. They are, in short, "We the people," this breed called Americans.

Well, this administration's objective will be a healthy, vigorous, growing economy that provides equal opportunity for all Americans, with no barriers born of bigotry or discrimination. Putting America back to work means putting all Americans back to work. Ending inflation means freeing all Americans from the terror of runaway living costs. All must share in the productive work of this "new beginning" and all must share in the bounty of a revived economy. With the idealism and fair play which are the core of our system and our strength, we can have a strong and prosperous America at peace with itself and the world.

So, as we begin, let us take inventory. We are a nation that has a government—not the other way around. And this makes us special among the nations of the Earth. Our Government has no power except that granted it by the people. It is time to check and reverse the growth of government which shows signs of having grown beyond the consent of the governed.

It is my intention to curb the size and influence of the Federal establishment and to demand recognition of the distinction between the powers granted to the Federal Government and those reserved to the States or to the people. All of us need to be reminded that the Federal Government did not create the States; the States created the Federal Government.

Now, so there will be no misunderstanding, it is not my intention to do away with government. It is, rather, to make it work—work with us, not over us; to stand by our side, not ride on our back. Government can and must provide opportunity, not smother it; foster productivity, not stifle it.

If we look to the answer as to why, for so many years, we achieved so much, prospered as no other people on Earth, it was because here, in this land, we unleashed the energy and individual genius of man to a greater extent than has ever been done before. Freedom and the dignity of the individual have been more available and assured here than in any other place on Earth. The price for this freedom at times has been high, but we have never been unwilling to pay that price.

It is no coincidence that our present troubles parallel and are proportionate to the intervention and intrusion in our lives that result from unnecessary and excessive growth of government. It is time for us to realize that we are too great a nation to limit ourselves to small dreams. We are not, as some would have us believe, doomed to an inevitable decline. I do not believe in a fate that will fall on us no matter what we do. I do believe in a fate that will fall on us if we do nothing. So, with all the creative energy at our command, let us begin an era of national renewal. Let us renew our determination, our courage, and our strength. And let us renew our faith and our hope.

We have every right to dream heroic dreams. Those who say that we are in a time when there are no heroes just don't know where to look. You can see heroes every day going in and out of factory gates. Others, a handful in number, produce enough food to feed all of us and then the world beyond. You meet heroes across a counter—and they are on both sides of that counter. There are entrepreneurs with faith in themselves and faith in an idea who create new jobs, new wealth and opportunity. They are individuals and families whose taxes support the Government and whose voluntary gifts support church, charity, culture, art, and education. Their patriotism is quiet but deep. Their values sustain our national life.

I have used the words "they" and "their" in speaking of these heroes. I could say "you" and "your" because I am addressing the heroes of whom I speak—you, the citizens of this blessed land. Your dreams, your hopes, your goals are going to be the dreams, the hopes, and the goals of this administration, so help me God.

We shall reflect the compassion that is so much a part of your makeup. How can we love our country and not love our countrymen, and loving them, reach out a hand when they fall, heal them when they are sick, and provide opportunities to make them self-sufficient so they will be equal in fact and not just in theory?

Can we solve the problems confronting us? Well, the answer is an unequivocal and emphatic "yes." To paraphrase Winston Churchill, I did not take the oath I have just taken with the intention of presiding over the dissolution of the world's strongest economy.

In the days ahead I will propose removing the roadblocks that have slowed our economy and reduced productivity. Steps will be taken aimed at restoring the balance between the various levels of government. Progress may be slow—measured in inches and feet, not miles—but we will progress. It is time to reawaken this industrial giant, to get government back within its means, and to lighten our punitive tax burden. And these will be our first priorities, and on these principles, there will be no compromise.

On the eve of our struggle for independence a man who might have been one of the greatest among the Founding Fathers, Dr.

Joseph Warren, President of the Massachusetts Congress, said to his fellow Americans, "Our country is in danger, but not to be despaired of.... On you depend the fortunes of America. You are to decide the important questions upon which rests the happiness and the liberty of millions yet unborn. Act worthy of yourselves."

Well, I believe we, the Americans of today, are ready to act worthy of ourselves, ready to do what must be done to ensure happiness and liberty for ourselves, our children and our children's children.

And as we renew ourselves here in our own land, we will be seen as having greater strength throughout the world. We will again be the exemplar of freedom and a beacon of hope for those who do not now have freedom.

To those neighbors and allies who share our freedom, we will strengthen our historic ties and assure them of our support and firm commitment. We will match loyalty with loyalty. We will strive for mutually beneficial relations. We will not use our friendship to impose on their sovereignty, for our own sovereignty is not for sale.

As for the enemies of freedom, those who are potential adversaries, they will be reminded that peace is the highest aspiration of the American people. We will negotiate for it, sacrifice for it; we will not surrender for it—now or ever.

Our forbearance should never be misunderstood. Our reluctance for conflict should not be misjudged as a failure of will. When action is required to preserve our national security, we will act. We will maintain sufficient strength to prevail if need be, knowing that if we do so we have the best chance of never having to use that strength.

Above all, we must realize that no arsenal, or no weapon in the arsenals of the world, is so formidable as the will and moral courage of free men and women. It is a weapon our adversaries in today's world do not have. It is a weapon that we as Americans do have. Let that be understood by those who practice terrorism and prey upon their neighbors.

I am told that tens of thousands of prayer meetings are being held on this day, and for that I am deeply grateful. We are a nation under God, and I believe God intended for us to be free. It would be fitting and good, I think, if on each Inauguration Day in future years it should be declared a day of prayer.

This is the first time in history that this ceremony has been held, as you have been told, on this West Front of the Capitol. Standing here, one faces a magnificent vista, opening up on this city's special beauty and history. At the end of this open mall are those shrines to the giants on whose shoulders we stand.

Directly in front of me, the monument to a monumental man: George Washington, Father of our country. A man of humility who came to greatness reluctantly. He led America out of revolutionary victory into infant nationhood. Off to one side, the stately memorial to Thomas Jefferson. The Declaration of Independence flames with his eloquence.

And then beyond the Reflecting Pool the dignified columns of the Lincoln Memorial. Whoever would understand in his heart the meaning of America will find it in the life of Abraham Lincoln.

Beyond those monuments to heroism is the Potomac River, and on the far shore the sloping hills of Arlington National Cemetery with its row on row of simple white markers bearing crosses or Stars of David. They add up to only a tiny fraction of the price that has been paid for our freedom.

Each one of those markers is a monument to the kinds of hero I spoke of earlier. Their lives ended in places called Belleau Wood, The Argonne, Omaha Beach, Salerno and halfway around the world on Guadalcanal, Tarawa, Pork Chop Hill, the Chosin Reservoir, and in a hundred rice paddies and jungles of a place called Vietnam.

Under one such marker lies a young man—Martin Treptow—who left his job in a small town barber shop in 1917 to go to France with the famed Rainbow Division. There, on the western front, he was killed trying to carry a message between battalions under heavy artillery fire.

We are told that on his body was found a diary. On the flyleaf under the heading, "My Pledge," he had written these words: "America must win this war. Therefore, I will work, I will save, I will sacrifice, I will endure, I will fight cheerfully and do my utmost, as if the issue of the whole struggle depended on me alone."

The crisis we are facing today does not require of us the kind of sacrifice that Martin Treptow and so many thousands of others were called upon to make. It does require, however, our best effort, and our willingness to believe in ourselves and to believe in our capacity to perform great deeds; to believe that together, with God's help, we can and will resolve the problems which now confront us.

And, after all, why shouldn't we believe that? We are Americans. God bless you, and thank you.

# RONALD REAGAN
## SECOND INAUGURAL ADDRESS
### MONDAY, JANUARY 21, 1985

Senator Mathias, Chief Justice Burger, Vice President Bush, Speaker O'Neill, Senator Dole, Reverend Clergy, members of my family and friends, and my fellow citizens:

This day has been made brighter with the presence here of one who, for a time, has been absent—Senator John Stennis.

God bless you and welcome back.

There is, however, one who is not with us today: Representative Gillis Long of Louisiana left us last night. I wonder if we could all join in a moment of silent prayer. (Moment of silent prayer.) Amen.

There are no words adequate to express my thanks for the great honor that you have bestowed on me. I will do my utmost to be deserving of your trust.

This is, as Senator Mathias told us, the 50th time that we the people have celebrated this historic occasion. When the first President, George Washington, placed his hand upon the Bible, he stood less than a single day's journey by horseback from raw, untamed wilderness. There were 4 million Americans in a union of 13 States. Today we are 60 times as many in a union of 50 States. We have lighted the world with our inventions, gone to the aid of mankind wherever in the world there was a cry for help, journeyed to the Moon and safely returned. So much has changed. And yet we stand together as we did two centuries ago.

When I took this oath four years ago, I did so in a time of economic stress. Voices were raised saying we had to look to our past for the greatness and glory. But we, the present-day Americans, are not given to looking backward. In this blessed land, there is always a better tomorrow.

Four years ago, I spoke to you of a new beginning and we have accomplished that. But in another sense, our new beginning is a continuation of that beginning created two centuries ago when, for the first time in history, government, the people said, was not our master, it is our servant; its only power that which we the people allow it to have.

That system has never failed us, but, for a time, we failed the system. We asked things of government that government was not equipped to give. We yielded authority to the National Government that properly belonged to States or to local governments or to the people themselves. We allowed taxes and inflation to rob us of our earnings and savings and watched the great industrial machine that had made us the most productive people on Earth slow down and the number of unemployed increase.

By 1980, we knew it was time to renew our faith, to strive with all our strength toward the ultimate in individual freedom consistent with an orderly society.

We believed then and now there are no limits to growth and human progress when men and women are free to follow their dreams.

And we were right to believe that. Tax rates have been reduced, inflation cut dramatically, and more people are employed than ever before in our history.

We are creating a nation once again vibrant, robust, and alive. But there are many mountains yet to climb. We will not rest until every American enjoys the fullness of freedom, dignity, and opportunity as our birthright. It is our birthright as citizens of this great Republic, and we'll meet this challenge.

These will be years when Americans have restored their confidence and tradition of progress; when our values of faith, family, work, and neighborhood were restated for a modern age; when our economy was finally freed from government's grip; when we made sincere efforts at meaningful arms reduction, rebuilding our defenses, our economy, and developing new technologies, and helped preserve peace in a troubled world; when Americans courageously supported the struggle for liberty, self-government, and free enterprise throughout the world, and turned the tide of history away from totalitarian darkness and into the warm sunlight of human freedom.

My fellow citizens, our Nation is poised for greatness. We must do what we know is right and do it with all our might. Let history say of us, "These were golden years—when the American Revolution was reborn, when freedom gained new life, when America reached for her best."

Our two-party system has served us well over the years, but never better than in those times of great challenge when we came together not as Democrats or Republicans, but as Americans united in a common cause.

Two of our Founding Fathers, a Boston lawyer named Adams and a Virginia planter named Jefferson, members of that remarkable group who met in Independence Hall and dared to think they could start the world over again, left us an important lesson. They had become political rivals in the Presidential election of 1800. Then years later, when both were retired, and age had softened their anger, they began to speak to each other again through letters. A bond was reestablished between those two who had helped create this government of ours.

In 1826, the 50th anniversary of the Declaration of Independence, they both died. They died on the same day, within a few hours of each other, and that day was the Fourth of July.

In one of those letters exchanged in the sunset of their lives, Jefferson wrote: "It carries me back to the times when, beset with difficulties and dangers, we were fellow laborers in the same cause, struggling for what is most valuable to man, his right to self-government. Laboring always at the same oar, with some wave ever ahead threatening to overwhelm us, and yet passing harmless...we rode through the storm with heart and hand."

Well, with heart and hand, let us stand as one today: One people under God determined that our future shall be worthy of our past. As we do, we must not repeat the well-intentioned errors of our past. We must never again abuse the trust of working men and women, by sending their earnings on a futile chase after the spiraling demands of a bloated Federal Establishment. You elected us in 1980 to end this prescription for disaster, and I don't believe you reelected us in 1984 to reverse course.

At the heart of our efforts is one idea vindicated by 25 straight months of economic growth: Freedom and incentives unleash the drive and entrepreneurial genius that are the core of human progress. We have begun to increase the rewards for work, savings, and investment; reduce the increase in the cost and size of government and its interference in people's lives.

We must simplify our tax system, make it more fair, and bring the rates down for all who work and earn. We must think anew and move with a new boldness, so every American who seeks work can find work; so the least among us shall have an equal chance to achieve the greatest things—to be heroes who heal our sick, feed the hungry, protect peace among nations, and leave this world a better place.

The time has come for a new American emancipation—a great national drive to tear down economic barriers and liberate the spirit of enterprise in the most distressed areas of our country. My friends, together we can do this, and do it we must, so help me God.

From new freedom will spring new opportunities for growth, a more productive, fulfilled and united people, and a stronger America—an America that will lead the technological revolution, and also open its mind and heart and soul to the treasures of literature, music, and poetry, and the values of faith, courage, and love.

A dynamic economy, with more citizens working and paying taxes, will be our strongest tool to bring down budget deficits. But an almost unbroken 50 years of deficit spending has finally brought us to a time of reckoning. We have come to a turning point, a moment for hard decisions. I have asked the Cabinet and my staff a question, and now I put the same question to all of you: If not us, who? And if not now, when? It must be done by all of us going forward with a program aimed at reaching a balanced budget. We can then begin reducing the national debt.

I will shortly submit a budget to the Congress aimed at freezing government program spending for the next year. Beyond that, we must take further steps to permanently control Government's power to tax and spend. We must act now to protect future generations from Government's desire to spend its citizens' money and tax them into servitude when the bills come due. Let us make it unconstitutional for the Federal Government to spend more than the Federal Government takes in.

We have already started returning to the people and to State and local governments responsibilities better handled by them. Now, there is a place for the Federal Government in matters of social compassion.

But our fundamental goals must be to reduce dependency and upgrade the dignity of those who are infirm or disadvantaged. And here a growing economy and support from family and community offer our best chance for a society where compassion is a way of life, where the old and infirm are cared for, the young and, yes, the unborn protected, and the unfortunate looked after and made self-sufficient.

And there is another area where the Federal Government can play a part. As an older American, I remember a time when people of different race, creed, or ethnic origin in our land found hatred and prejudice installed in social custom and, yes, in law. There is no story more heartening in our history than the progress that we have made toward the "brotherhood of man" that God intended for us. Let us resolve there will be no turning back or hesitation on the road to an America rich in dignity and abundant with opportunity for all our citizens.

Let us resolve that we the people will build an American opportunity society in which all of us—white and black, rich and poor, young and old—will go forward together arm in arm. Again, let us remember that though our heritage is one of blood lines from every corner of the Earth, we are all Americans pledged to carry on this last, best hope of man on Earth.

I have spoken of our domestic goals and the limitations which we should put on our National Government. Now let me turn to a task which is the primary responsibility of National Government—the safety and security of our people.

Today, we utter no prayer more fervently than the ancient prayer for peace on Earth. Yet history has shown that peace will not come, nor will our freedom be preserved, by good will alone. There are those in the world who scorn our vision of human dignity and freedom. One nation, the Soviet Union, has conducted the greatest military buildup in the history of man, building arsenals of awesome offensive weapons.

We have made progress in restoring our defense capability. But much remains to be done. There must be no wavering by us, nor any doubts by others, that America will meet her responsibilities to remain free, secure, and at peace.

There is only one way safely and legitimately to reduce the cost of national security, and that is to reduce the need for it. And this we are trying to do in negotiations with the Soviet Union. We are not just discussing limits on a further increase of nuclear weapons. We seek, instead, to reduce their number. We seek the total elimination one day of nuclear weapons from the face of the Earth.

Now, for decades, we and the Soviets have lived under the threat of mutual assured destruction; if either resorted to the use of nuclear weapons, the other could retaliate and destroy the one who had started it. Is there either logic or morality in believing that if one side threatens to kill tens of millions of our people, our only recourse is to threaten killing tens of millions of theirs?

I have approved a research program to find, if we can, a security shield that would destroy nuclear missiles before they reach their target. It wouldn't kill people, it would destroy weapons. It wouldn't militarize space, it would help demilitarize the arsenals of Earth. It would render nuclear weapons obsolete. We will meet with the Soviets, hoping that we can agree on a way to rid the world of the threat of nuclear destruction.

We strive for peace and security, heartened by the changes all around us. Since the turn of the century, the number of democracies in the world has grown fourfold. Human freedom is on the march, and nowhere more so than our own hemisphere. Freedom is one of the deepest and noblest aspirations of the human spirit. People, worldwide, hunger for the right of self-determination, for those inalienable rights that make for human dignity and progress.

America must remain freedom's staunchest friend, for freedom is our best ally.

And it is the world's only hope, to conquer poverty and preserve peace. Every blow we inflict against poverty will be a blow against its dark allies of oppression and war. Every victory for human freedom will be a victory for world peace.

So we go forward today, a nation still mighty in its youth and powerful in its purpose. With our alliances strengthened, with our economy leading the world to a new age of economic expansion, we look forward to a world rich in possibilities. And all this because we have worked and acted together, not as members of political parties, but as Americans.

My friends, we live in a world that is lit by lightning. So much is changing and will change, but so much endures, and transcends time.

History is a ribbon, always unfurling; history is a journey. And as we continue our journey, we think of those who traveled before us. We stand together again at the steps of this symbol of our democracy— or we would have been standing at the steps if it hadn't gotten so cold. Now we are standing inside this symbol of our democracy. Now we hear again the echoes of our past: a general falls to his knees in the hard snow of Valley Forge; a lonely President paces the darkened halls, and ponders his struggle to preserve the Union; the men of the Alamo call out encouragement to each other; a settler pushes west and sings a song, and the song echoes out forever and fills the unknowing air.

It is the American sound. It is hopeful, big-hearted, idealistic, daring, decent, and fair. That's our heritage; that is our song. We sing it still. For all our problems, our differences, we are together as of old, as we raise our voices to the God who is the Author of this most tender music. And may He continue to hold us close as we fill the world with our sound—sound in unity, affection, and love—one people under God, dedicated to the dream of freedom that He has placed in the human heart, called upon now to pass that dream on to a waiting and hopeful world.

God bless you and may God bless America.

# GEORGE H. W. BUSH
## INAUGURAL ADDRESS
### FRIDAY, JANUARY 20, 1989

Mr. Chief Justice, Mr. President, Vice President Quayle, Senator Mitchell, Speaker Wright, Senator Dole, Congressman Michel, and fellow citizens, neighbors, and friends:

There is a man here who has earned a lasting place in our hearts and in our history. President Reagan, on behalf of our Nation, I thank you for the wonderful things that you have done for America.

I have just repeated word for word the oath taken by George Washington 200 years ago, and the Bible on which I placed my hand is the Bible on which he placed his. It is right that the memory of Washington be with us today, not only because this is our Bicentennial Inauguration, but because Washington remains the Father of our Country. And he would, I think, be gladdened by this day; for today is the concrete expression of a stunning fact: our continuity these 200 years since our government began.

We meet on democracy's front porch, a good place to talk as neighbors and as friends. For this is a day when our nation is made whole, when our differences, for a moment, are suspended.

And my first act as President is a prayer. I ask you to bow your heads:

Heavenly Father, we bow our heads and thank You for Your love. Accept our thanks for the peace that yields this day and the shared faith that makes its continuance likely. Make us strong to do Your work, willing to heed and hear Your will, and write on our hearts these words: "Use power to help people." For we are given power not to advance our own purposes, nor to make a great show in the world, nor a name. There is but one just use of power, and it is to serve people. Help us to remember it, Lord. Amen.

I come before you and assume the Presidency at a moment rich with promise. We live in a peaceful, prosperous time, but we can make it better. For a new breeze is blowing, and a world refreshed by freedom seems reborn; for in man's heart, if not in fact, the day of the dictator is over. The totalitarian era is passing, its old ideas blown away like leaves from an ancient, lifeless tree. A new breeze is blowing, and a nation refreshed by freedom stands ready to push on. There is new ground to be broken, and new action to be taken. There are times when the future seems thick as a fog; you sit and wait, hoping the mists will lift and reveal the right path. But this is a time when the future seems a door you can walk right through into a room called tomorrow.

Great nations of the world are moving toward democracy through the door to freedom. Men and women of the world move toward free markets through the door to prosperity. The people of the world agitate for free expression and free thought through the door to the moral and intellectual satisfactions that only liberty allows.

We know what works: Freedom works. We know what's right: Freedom is right. We know how to secure a more just and prosperous life for man on Earth: through free markets, free speech, free elections, and the exercise of free will unhampered by the state.

For the first time in this century, for the first time in perhaps all history, man does not have to invent a system by which to live. We don't have to talk late into the night about which form of government is better. We don't have to wrest justice from the kings. We only have to summon it from within ourselves. We must act on what we know. I take as my guide the hope of a saint: In crucial things, unity; in important things, diversity; in all things, generosity.

America today is a proud, free nation, decent and civil, a place we cannot help but love. We know in our hearts, not loudly and proudly, but as a simple fact, that this country has meaning beyond what we see, and that our strength is a force for good. But have we changed as a nation even in our time? Are we enthralled with material things, less appreciative of the nobility of work and sacrifice?

My friends, we are not the sum of our possessions. They are not the measure of our lives. In our hearts we know what matters. We cannot hope only to leave our children a bigger car, a bigger bank account. We must hope to give them a sense of what it means to be a loyal friend, a loving parent, a citizen who leaves his home, his neighborhood and town better than he found it. What do we want the men and women who work with us to say when we are no longer there? That we were more driven to succeed than anyone around us? Or that we stopped to ask if a sick child had gotten better, and stayed a moment there to trade a word of friendship?

No President, no government, can teach us to remember what is best in what we are. But if the man you have chosen to lead this government can help make a difference; if he can celebrate the quieter, deeper successes that are made not of gold and silk, but of better hearts and finer souls; if he can do these things, then he must.

America is never wholly herself unless she is engaged in high moral principle. We as a people have such a purpose today. It is to make kinder the face of the Nation and gentler the face of the world. My friends, we have work to do. There are the homeless, lost and roaming. There are the children who have nothing, no love, no normalcy. There are those who cannot free themselves of enslavement to whatever addiction—drugs, welfare, the demoralization that rules the slums. There is crime to be conquered, the rough crime of the streets. There are young women to be helped who are about to become mothers of children they can't care for and might not love. They need our care, our guidance, and our education, though we bless them for choosing life.

The old solution, the old way, was to think that public money alone could end these problems. But we have learned that is not so. And in any case, our funds are low. We have a deficit to bring down. We have more will than wallet; but will is what we need. We will make the hard choices, looking at what we have and perhaps allocating it differently, making our decisions based on honest need and prudent safety. And then we will do the wisest thing of all: We will turn to the only resource we have that in times of need always grows—the goodness and the courage of the American people.

I am speaking of a new engagement in the lives of others, a new activism, hands-on and involved, that gets the job done. We must bring in the generations, harnessing the unused talent of the elderly and the unfocused energy of the young. For not only leadership is passed from generation to generation, but so is stewardship. And the generation born after the Second World War has come of age.

I have spoken of a thousand points of light, of all the community organizations that are spread like stars throughout the Nation, doing good. We will work hand in hand, encouraging, sometimes leading, sometimes being led, rewarding. We will work on this in the White House, in the Cabinet agencies. I will go to the people and the programs that are the brighter points of light, and I will ask every member of my government to become involved. The old ideas are new again because they are not old, they are timeless: duty, sacrifice, commitment, and a patriotism that finds its expression in taking part and pitching in.

We need a new engagement, too, between the Executive and the Congress. The challenges before us will be thrashed out with the House and the Senate. We must bring the Federal budget into balance. And we must ensure that America stands before the world united, strong, at peace, and fiscally sound. But, of course, things may be difficult. We need compromise; we have had dissension. We need harmony; we have had a chorus of discordant voices.

For Congress, too, has changed in our time. There has grown a certain divisiveness. We have seen the hard looks and heard the statements in which not each other's ideas are challenged, but each other's motives. And our great parties have too often been far apart and untrusting of each other. It has been this way since Vietnam. That war cleaves us still. But, friends, that war began in earnest a quarter of a century ago; and surely the statute of limitations has been reached. This is a fact: The final lesson of Vietnam is that no great nation can long afford to be sundered by a memory. A new breeze is blowing, and the old bipartisanship must be made new again.

To my friends—and yes, I do mean friends—in the loyal opposition—and yes, I mean loyal: I put out my hand. I am putting out my hand to you, Mr. Speaker. I am putting out my hand to you Mr. Majority Leader. For this is the thing: This is the age of the offered hand. We can't turn back clocks, and I don't want to. But when our fathers were young, Mr. Speaker, our differences ended at the water's edge. And we don't wish to turn back time, but when our mothers were young, Mr. Majority Leader, the Congress and the Executive were capable of working together to produce a budget on which this nation could live. Let us negotiate soon and hard. But in the end, let us produce. The American people await action. They didn't send us here to bicker. They ask us to rise above the merely partisan. "In crucial things, unity"—and this, my friends, is crucial.

To the world, too, we offer new engagement and a renewed vow: We will stay strong to protect the peace. The "offered hand" is a reluctant fist; but once made, strong, and can be used with great effect. There are today Americans who are held against their will in foreign lands, and Americans who are unaccounted for. Assistance can be shown here, and will be long remembered. Good will begets good will. Good faith can be a spiral that endlessly moves on.

Great nations like great men must keep their word. When America says something, America means it, whether a treaty or an agreement or a vow made on marble steps. We will always try to speak clearly, for candor is a compliment, but subtlety, too, is good and has its place. While keeping our alliances and friendships around the world strong, ever strong, we will continue the new closeness with the Soviet Union, consistent both with our security and with progress. One might say that our new relationship in part reflects the triumph of hope and strength over experience. But hope is good, and so are strength and vigilance.

Here today are tens of thousands of our citizens who feel the understandable satisfaction of those who have taken part in democracy and seen their hopes fulfilled. But my thoughts have been turning the past few days to those who would be watching at home, to an older fellow who will throw a salute by himself when the flag goes by, and the women who will tell her sons the words of the battle hymns. I don't mean this to be sentimental. I mean that on days like this, we remember that we are all part of a continuum, inescapably connected by the ties that bind.

Our children are watching in schools throughout our great land. And to them I say, thank you for watching democracy's big day. For democracy belongs to us all, and freedom is like a beautiful kite that can go higher and higher with the breeze. And to all I say: No matter what your circumstances or where you are, you are part of this day, you are part of the life of our great nation.

A President is neither prince nor pope, and I don't seek a window on men's souls. In fact, I yearn for a greater tolerance, an easy-goingness about each other's attitudes and way of life.

There are few clear areas in which we as a society must rise up united and express our intolerance. The most obvious now is drugs. And when that first cocaine was smuggled in on a ship, it may as well have been a deadly bacteria, so much has it hurt the body, the soul of our country. And there is much to be done and to be said, but take my word for it: This scourge will stop.

And so, there is much to do; and tomorrow the work begins. I do not mistrust the future; I do not fear what is ahead. For our problems are large, but our heart is larger. Our challenges are great, but our will is greater. And if our flaws are endless, God's love is truly boundless.

Some see leadership as high drama, and the sound of trumpets calling, and sometimes it is that. But I see history as a book with many pages, and each day we fill a page with acts of hopefulness and meaning. The new breeze blows, a page turns, the story unfolds. And so today a chapter begins, a small and stately story of unity, diversity, and generosity—shared, and written, together.

Thank you. God bless you and God bless the United States of America.

# WILLIAM J. CLINTON
## FIRST INAUGURAL ADDRESS
## WEDNESDAY, JANUARY 21, 1993

My fellow citizens:
Today we celebrate the mystery of American renewal.

This ceremony is held in the depth of winter, but by the words we speak and the faces we show the world, we force the spring. A spring reborn in the world's oldest democracy, that brings forth the vision and courage to reinvent America. When our founders boldly declared America's independence to the world, and our purposes to the Almighty, they knew that America, to endure, would have to change. Not change for change sake, but change to preserve America's ideals: life, liberty, the pursuit of happiness.

Though we march to the music of our time, our mission is timeless. Each generation of Americans must define what it means to be an American. On behalf of our nation, I salute my predecessor, President Bush, for his half-century of service to America...and I thank the millions of men and women whose steadfastness and sacrifice triumphed over depression, fascism and communism.

Today, a generation raised in the shadows of the Cold War assumes new responsibilities in a world warmed by the sunshine of freedom, but threatened still by ancient hatreds and new plagues. Raised in unrivalled prosperity, we inherit an economy that is still the world's strongest, but is weakened by business failures, stagnant wages, increasing inequality, and deep divisions among our people.

When George Washington first took the oath I have just sworn to uphold, news travelled slowly across the land by horseback, and across the ocean by boat. Now, the sights and sounds of this ceremony are broadcast instantaneously to billions around the world. Communications and commerce are global. Investment is mobile. Technology is almost magical, and ambition for a better life is now universal.

We earn our livelihood in America today in peaceful competition with people all across the Earth. Profound and powerful forces are shaking and remaking our world, and the urgent question of our time is whether we can make change our friend and not our enemy. This new world has already enriched the lives of millions of Americans who are able to compete and win in it. But when most people are working harder for less, when others cannot work at all, when the cost of health care devastates families and threatens to bankrupt our enterprises, great and small; when the fear of crime robs law-abiding citizens of their freedom; and when millions of poor children cannot even imagine the lives we are calling them to lead, we have not made change our friend.

We know we have to face hard truths and take strong steps, but we have not done so. Instead we have drifted, and that drifting has eroded our resources, fractured our economy, and shaken our confidence. Though our challenges are fearsome, so are our strengths. Americans have ever been a restless, questing, hopeful people, and we must bring to our task today the vision and will of those who came before us. From our Revolution to the Civil War, to the Great Depression, to the Civil Rights movement, our people have always mustered the determination to construct from these crises the pillars of our history. Thomas Jefferson believed that to preserve the very foundations of our nation we would need dramatic change from time to time. Well, my fellow Americans, this is *our* time. Let us embrace it.

Our democracy must be not only the envy of the world but the engine of our own renewal. There is nothing wrong with America that cannot be cured by what is right with America.

And so today we pledge an end to the era of deadlock and drift, and a new season of American renewal has begun.

To renew America we must be bold. We must do what no generation has had to do before. We must invest more in our own people, in their jobs, and in their future, and at the same time cut our massive debt... and we must do so in a world in which we must compete for every opportunity. It will not be easy. It will require sacrifice, but it can be done, and done fairly. Not choosing sacrifice for its own sake, but for our own sake. We must provide for our nation the way a family provides for its children. Our Founders saw themselves in the light of posterity. We can do no less. Anyone who has ever watched a child's eyes wander into sleep knows what posterity is. Posterity is the world to come, the world for whom we hold our ideals, from whom we have borrowed our planet, and to whom we bear sacred responsibilities. We must do what America does best, offer more opportunity to all and demand more responsibility from all.

It is time to break the bad habit of expecting something for nothing: from our government, or from each other. Let us all take more responsibility, not only for ourselves and our families, but for our communities and our country. To renew America we must revitalize our democracy. This beautiful capitol, like every capitol since the dawn of civilization, is often a place of intrigue and calculation. Powerful people maneuver for position and worry endlessly about who is in and who is out, who is up and who is down, forgetting those people whose toil and sweat sends us here and paves our way.

Americans deserve better, and in this city today there are people who want to do better, and so I say to all of you here, let us resolve to reform our politics, so that power and privilege no longer shout down the voice of the people. Let us put aside personal advantage, so that we can feel the pain and see the promise of America. Let us resolve to make our government a place for what Franklin Roosevelt called "bold, persistent experimentation, a government for our tomorrows, not our yesterdays." Let us give this capitol back to the people to whom it belongs.

To renew America we must meet challenges abroad, as well as at home. There is no longer a clear division between what is foreign and what is domestic. The world economy, the world environment, the world AIDS crisis, the world arms race: they affect us all. Today as an old order passes, the new world is more free, but less stable. Communism's collapse has called forth old animosities, and new dangers. Clearly, America must continue to lead the world we did so much to make. While America rebuilds at home, we will not shrink from the challenges nor fail to seize the opportunities of this new world. Together with our friends and allies, we will work together to shape change, lest it engulf us. When our vital interests are challenged, or the will and conscience of the international community is defied, we will act; with peaceful diplomacy whenever possible, with force when necessary. The brave Americans serving our nation today in the Persian Gulf, in Somalia, and wherever else they stand, are testament to our resolve. But our greatest strength is the power of our ideas, which are still new in many lands. Across the world, we see them embraced and we rejoice. Our hopes, our hearts, our hands, are with those on every continent, who are building democracy and freedom. Their cause is America's cause. The American people have summoned the change we celebrate today. You have raised your voices in an unmistakable chorus, you have cast your votes in historic numbers, you have changed the face of Congress, the presidency, and the political process itself. Yes, you, my fellow Americans, have forced the spring. Now we must do the work the season demands. To that work I now turn with all the authority of my office. I ask the Congress to join with me; but no president, no Congress, no government can undertake this mission alone.

My fellow Americans, you, too, must play your part in our renewal. I challenge a new generation of young Americans to a season of service, to act on your idealism, by helping troubled children, keeping company with those in need, reconnecting our torn communities. There is so much to be done. Enough, indeed, for millions of others who are still young in spirit, to give of themselves in service, too. In serving we recognize a simple, but powerful, truth: we need each other, and we must care for one another.

Today we do more than celebrate America, we rededicate ourselves to the very idea of America, an idea born in revolution, and renewed through two centuries of challenge, an idea tempered by the knowledge that but for fate, we, the fortunate and the unfortunate, might have been each other; an idea ennobled by the faith that our nation can summon from its myriad diversity, the deepest measure of unity; an idea infused with the conviction that America's journey long, heroic journey must go forever upward.

And so, my fellow Americans, as we stand at the edge of the 21st Century, let us begin anew, with energy and hope, with faith and discipline, and let us work until our work is done. The Scripture says: "And let us not be weary in well-doing, for in due season we shall reap, if we faint not." From this joyful mountaintop of celebration we hear a call to service in the valley. We have heard the trumpets, we have changed the guard, and now each in our own way, and with God's help, we must answer the call. Thank you and God bless you all.

# WILLIAM J. CLINTON
## SECOND INAUGURAL ADDRESS
## MONDAY, JANUARY 20, 1997

My fellow citizens:

At this last presidential inauguration of the 20th century, let us lift our eyes toward the challenges that await us in the next century. It is our great good fortune that time and chance have put us not only at the edge of a new century, in a new millennium, but on the edge of a bright new prospect in human affairs—a moment that will define our course, and our character, for decades to come. We must keep our old democracy forever young. Guided by the ancient vision of a promised land, let us set our sights upon a land of new promise.

The promise of America was born in the 18th century out of the bold conviction that we are all created equal. It was extended and preserved in the 19th century, when our nation spread across the continent, saved the union, and abolished the awful scourge of slavery.

Then, in turmoil and triumph, that promise exploded onto the world stage to make this the American Century.

And what a century it has been. America became the world's mightiest industrial power; saved the world from tyranny in two world wars and a long cold war; and time and again, reached out across the globe to millions who, like us, longed for the blessings of liberty.

Along the way, Americans produced a great middle class and security in old age; built unrivaled centers of learning and opened public schools to all; split the atom and explored the heavens; invented the computer and the microchip; and deepened the wellspring of justice by making a revolution in civil rights for African Americans and all minorities, and extending the circle of citizenship, opportunity and dignity to women.

Now, for the third time, a new century is upon us, and another time to choose. We began the 19th century with a choice, to spread our nation from coast to coast. We began the 20th century with a choice, to harness the Industrial Revolution to our values of free enterprise, conservation, and human decency. Those choices made all the difference. At the dawn of the 21st century a free people must now choose to shape the forces of the Information Age and the global society, to unleash the limitless potential of all our people, and, yes, to form a more perfect union.

When last we gathered, our march to this new future seemed less certain than it does today. We vowed then to set a clear course to renew our nation.

In these four years, we have been touched by tragedy, exhilarated by challenge, strengthened by achievement. America stands alone as the world's indispensable nation. Once again, our economy is the strongest on Earth. Once again, we are building stronger families, thriving communities, better educational opportunities, a cleaner environment. Problems that once seemed destined to deepen now bend to our efforts: our streets are safer and record numbers of our fellow citizens have moved from welfare to work.

And once again, we have resolved for our time a great debate over the role of government. Today we can declare: Government is not the problem, and government is not the solution. We—the American people—we are the solution. Our founders understood that well and gave us a democracy strong enough to endure for centuries, flexible enough to face our common challenges and advance our common dreams in each new day.

As times change, so government must change. We need a new government for a new century—humble enough not to try to solve all our problems for us, but strong enough to give us the tools to solve our problems for ourselves; a government that is smaller, lives within its means, and does more with less. Yet where it can stand up for our values and interests in the world, and where it can give Americans the power to make a real difference in their everyday lives, government should do more, not less. The preeminent mission of our new government is to give all Americans an opportunity—not a guarantee, but a real opportunity—to build better lives.

Beyond that, my fellow citizens, the future is up to us. Our founders taught us that the preservation of our liberty and our union depends upon responsible citizenship. And we need a new sense of responsibility for a new century. There is work to do, work that government alone cannot do: teaching children to read; hiring people off welfare rolls; coming out from behind locked doors and shuttered windows to help reclaim our streets from drugs and gangs and crime; taking time out of our own lives to serve others.

Each and every one of us, in our own way, must assume personal responsibility—not only for ourselves and our families, but for our neighbors and our nation. Our greatest responsibility is to embrace a new spirit of community for a new century. For any one of us to succeed, we must succeed as one America.

The challenge of our past remains the challenge of our future— will we be one nation, one people, with one common destiny, or not? Will we all come together, or come apart?

The divide of race has been America's constant curse. And each new wave of immigrants gives new targets to old prejudices. Prejudice and contempt, cloaked in the pretense of religious or political conviction are no different. These forces have nearly destroyed our nation in the past. They plague us still. They fuel the fanaticism of terror. And they torment the lives of millions in fractured nations all around the world.

These obsessions cripple both those who hate and, of course, those who are hated, robbing both of what they might become. We cannot, we will not, succumb to the dark impulses that lurk in the far regions of the soul everywhere. We shall overcome them. And we shall replace them with the generous spirit of a people who feel at home with one another.

Our rich texture of racial, religious and political diversity will be a Godsend in the 21st century. Great rewards will come to those who can live together, learn together, work together, forge new ties that bind together.

As this new era approaches we can already see its broad outlines. Ten years ago, the Internet was the mystical province of physicists; today, it is a commonplace encyclopedia for millions of schoolchildren. Scientists now are decoding the blueprint of human life. Cures for our most feared illnesses seem close at hand.

The world is no longer divided into two hostile camps. Instead, now we are building bonds with nations that once were our adversaries. Growing connections of commerce and culture give us a chance to lift the fortunes and spirits of people the world over. And for the very first time in all of history, more people on this planet live under democracy than dictatorship.

My fellow Americans, as we look back at this remarkable century, we may ask, can we hope not just to follow, but even to surpass the achievements of the 20th century in America and to avoid the awful bloodshed that stained its legacy? To that question, every American here and every American in our land today must answer a resounding "Yes."

This is the heart of our task. With a new vision of government, a new sense of responsibility, a new spirit of community, we will sustain America's journey. The promise we sought in a new land we will find again in a land of new promise.

In this new land, education will be every citizen's most prized possession. Our schools will have the highest standards in the world, igniting the spark of possibility in the eyes of every girl and every boy. And the doors of higher education will be open to all. The knowledge and power of the Information Age will be within reach not just of the few, but of every classroom, every library, every child. Parents and children will have time not only to work, but to read and play together. And the plans they make at their kitchen table will be those of a better home, a better job, the certain chance to go to college.

Our streets will echo again with the laughter of our children, because no one will try to shoot them or sell them drugs anymore. Everyone who can work, will work, with today's permanent under class part of tomorrow's growing middle class. New miracles of medicine at last will reach not only those who can claim care now, but the children and hardworking families too long denied.

We will stand mighty for peace and freedom, and maintain a strong defense against terror and destruction. Our children will sleep free from the threat of nuclear, chemical or biological weapons. Ports and airports, farms and factories will thrive with trade and innovation and ideas. And the world's greatest democracy will lead a whole world of democracies.

Our land of new promise will be a nation that meets its obligations—a nation that balances its budget, but never loses the balance of its values. A nation where our grandparents have secure retirement and health care, and their grandchildren know we have made the reforms necessary to sustain those benefits for their time. A nation that fortifies the world's most productive economy even as it protects the great natural bounty of our water, air, and majestic land.

And in this land of new promise, we will have reformed our politics so that the voice of the people will always speak louder than the din of narrow interests—regaining the participation and deserving the trust of all Americans.

Fellow citizens, let us build that America, a nation ever moving forward toward realizing the full potential of all its citizens. Prosperity and power—yes, they are important, and we must maintain them. But let us never forget: The greatest progress we have made, and the greatest progress we have yet to make, is in the human heart. In the end, all the world's wealth and a thousand armies are no match for the strength and decency of the human spirit.

Thirty-four years ago, the man whose life we celebrate today spoke to us down there, at the other end of this Mall, in words that moved the conscience of a nation. Like a prophet of old, he told of his dream that one day America would rise up and treat all its citizens as equals before the law and in the heart. Martin Luther King's dream was the American Dream. His quest is our quest: the ceaseless striving to live out our true creed. Our history has been built on such dreams and labors. And by our dreams and labors we will redeem the promise of America in the 21st century.

To that effort I pledge all my strength and every power of my office. I ask the members of Congress here to join in that pledge. The American people returned to office a President of one party and a Congress of another. Surely, they did not do this to advance the politics of petty bickering and extreme partisanship they plainly deplore. No, they call on us instead to be repairers of the breach, and to move on with America's mission.

America demands and deserves big things from us—and nothing

big ever came from being small. Let us remember the timeless wisdom of Cardinal Bernardin, when facing the end of his own life. He said:

"It is wrong to waste the precious gift of time, on acrimony and division."

Fellow citizens, we must not waste the precious gift of this time. For all of us are on that same journey of our lives, and our journey, too, will come to an end. But the journey of our America must go on.

And so, my fellow Americans, we must be strong, for there is much to dare. The demands of our time are great and they are different. Let us meet them with faith and courage, with patience and a grateful and happy heart. Let us shape the hope of this day into the noblest chapter in our history. Yes, let us build our bridge. A bridge wide enough and strong enough for every American to cross over to a blessed land of new promise.

May those generations whose faces we cannot yet see, whose names we may never know, say of us here that we led our beloved land into a new century with the American Dream alive for all her children; with the American promise of a more perfect union a reality for all her people; with America's bright flame of freedom spreading throughout all the world.

From the height of this place and the summit of this century, let us go forth. May God strengthen our hands for the good work ahead—and always, always bless our America.

# GEORGE W. BUSH
## FIRST INAUGURAL ADDRESS
## SATURDAY, JANUARY 20, 2001

President Clinton, distinguished guests and my fellow citizens:
The peaceful transfer of authority is rare in history, yet common in our country. With a simple oath, we affirm old traditions and make new beginnings.

As I begin, I thank President Clinton for his service to our nation; and I thank Vice President Gore for a contest conducted with spirit and ended with grace.

I am honored and humbled to stand here, where so many of America's leaders have come before me, and so many will follow.

We have a place, all of us, in a long story—a story we continue, but whose end we will not see. It is the story of a new world that became a friend and liberator of the old, a story of a slave-holding society that became a servant of freedom, the story of a power that went into the world to protect but not possess, to defend but not to conquer.

It is the American story—a story of flawed and fallible people, united across the generations by grand and enduring ideals. The grandest of these ideals is an unfolding American promise that everyone belongs, that everyone deserves a chance, that no insignificant person was ever born. Americans are called to enact this promise in our lives and in our laws. And though our nation has sometimes halted, and sometimes delayed, we must follow no other course.

Through much of the last century, America's faith in freedom and democracy was a rock in a raging sea. Now it is a seed upon the wind, taking root in many nations. Our democratic faith is more than the creed of our country, it is the inborn hope of our humanity, an ideal we carry but do not own, a trust we bear and pass along. And even after nearly 225 years, we have a long way yet to travel.

While many of our citizens prosper, others doubt the promise, even the justice, of our own country. The ambitions of some

Americans are limited by failing schools and hidden prejudice and the circumstances of their birth. And sometimes our differences run so deep, it seems we share a continent, but not a country.

We do not accept this, and we will not allow it. Our unity, our union, is the serious work of leaders and citizens in every generation. And this is my solemn pledge: I will work to build a single nation of justice and opportunity. I know this is in our reach because we are guided by a power larger than ourselves who creates us equal in His image. And we are confident in principles that unite and lead us onward.

America has never been united by blood or birth or soil. We are bound by ideals that move us beyond our backgrounds, lift us above our interests and teach us what it means to be citizens. Every child must be taught these principles. Every citizen must uphold them. And every immigrant, by embracing these ideals, makes our country more, not less, American.

Today, we affirm a new commitment to live out our nation's promise through civility, courage, compassion and character. America, at its best, matches a commitment to principle with a concern for civility. A civil society demands from each of us good will and respect, fair dealing and forgiveness.

Some seem to believe that our politics can afford to be petty because, in a time of peace, the stakes of our debates appear small. But the stakes for America are never small. If our country does not lead the cause of freedom, it will not be led. If we do not turn the hearts of children toward knowledge and character, we will lose their gifts and undermine their idealism. If we permit our economy to drift and decline, the vulnerable will suffer most. We must live up to the calling we share. Civility is not a tactic or a sentiment. It is the determined choice of trust over cynicism, of community over chaos. And this commitment, if we keep it, is a way to shared accomplishment.

America, at its best, is also courageous. Our national courage has been clear in times of depression and war, when defending common dangers defined our common good. Now we must choose if the example of our fathers and mothers will inspire us or condemn us. We must show courage in a time of blessing by confronting problems instead of passing them on to future generations.

Together, we will reclaim America's schools, before ignorance and apathy claim more young lives. We will reform Social Security and Medicare, sparing our children from struggles we have the power to prevent. And we will reduce taxes, to recover the momentum of our economy and reward the effort and enterprise of working Americans. We will build our defenses beyond challenge, lest weakness invite challenge. We will confront weapons of mass destruction, so that a new century is spared new horrors.

The enemies of liberty and our country should make no mistake: America remains engaged in the world by history and by choice, shaping a balance of power that favors freedom. We will defend our allies and our interests. We will show purpose without arrogance. We will meet aggression and bad faith with resolve and strength. And to all nations, we will speak for the values that gave our nation birth.

America, at its best, is compassionate. In the quiet of American conscience, we know that deep, persistent poverty is unworthy of our nation's promise. And whatever our views of its cause, we can agree that children at risk are not at fault. Abandonment and abuse are not acts of God, they are failures of love. And the proliferation of prisons, however necessary, is no substitute for hope and order in our souls. Where there is suffering, there is duty. Americans in need are not strangers, they are citizens, not problems, but priorities. And all of us are diminished when any are hopeless.

Government has great responsibilities for public safety and public health, for civil rights and common schools. Yet compassion is the work of a nation, not just a government. And some needs and hurts are so deep they will only respond to a mentor's touch or a pastor's prayer. Church and charity, synagogue and mosque lend our communities their humanity, and they will have an honored place in our plans and in our laws. Many in our country do not know the pain of poverty, but we can listen to those who do. And I can pledge our nation to a goal: When we see that wounded traveler on the road to Jericho, we will not pass to the other side.

America, at its best, is a place where personal responsibility is valued and expected. Encouraging responsibility is not a search for scapegoats, it is a call to conscience. And though it requires sacrifice, it brings a deeper fulfillment. We find the fullness of life not only in options, but in commitments. And we find that children and community are the commitments that set us free. Our public interest depends on private character, on civic duty and family bonds and basic fairness, on uncounted, unhonored acts of decency which give direction to our freedom. Sometimes in life we are called to do great things. But as a saint of our times has said, every day we are called to do small things with great love. The most important tasks of a democracy are done by everyone.

I will live and lead by these principles: to advance my convictions with civility, to pursue the public interest with courage, to speak for greater justice and compassion, to call for responsibility and try to live it as well. In all these ways, I will bring the values of our history to the care of our times.

What you do is as important as anything government does. I ask you to seek a common good beyond your comfort; to defend needed reforms against easy attacks; to serve your nation, beginning with your neighbor. I ask you to be citizens: citizens, not spectators; citizens, not subjects; responsible citizens, building communities of service and a nation of character.

Americans are generous and strong and decent, not because we believe in ourselves, but because we hold beliefs beyond ourselves. When this spirit of citizenship is missing, no government program can replace it. When this spirit is present, no wrong can stand against it.

After the Declaration of Independence was signed, Virginia statesman John Page wrote to Thomas Jefferson: "We know the race is not to the swift nor the battle to the strong. Do you not think an angel rides in the whirlwind and directs this storm?" Much time has passed since Jefferson arrived for his inauguration. The years and changes accumulate. But the themes of this day he would know: our nation's grand story of courage and its simple dream of dignity.

We are not this story's author, who fills time and eternity with His purpose. Yet His purpose is achieved in our duty, and our duty is fulfilled in service to one another. Never tiring, never yielding, never finishing, we renew that purpose today, to make our country more just and generous, to affirm the dignity of our lives and every life.

This work continues. This story goes on. And an angel still rides in the whirlwind and directs this storm.

God bless you all, and God bless America.

# GEORGE W. BUSH
## SECOND INAUGURAL ADDRESS
### THURSDAY, JANUARY 20, 2005

Vice President Cheney, Mr. Chief Justice, President Carter, President Bush, President Clinton, reverend clergy, distinguished guests, fellow citizens:

On this day, prescribed by law and marked by ceremony, we celebrate the durable wisdom of our Constitution, and recall the deep commitments that unite our country. I am grateful for the honor of this hour, mindful of the consequential times in which we live, and determined to fulfill the oath that I have sworn and you have witnessed.

At this second gathering, our duties are defined not by the words I use, but by the history we have seen together. For a half century, America defended our own freedom by standing watch on distant borders. After the shipwreck of communism came years of relative quiet, years of repose, years of sabbatical—and then there came a day of fire.

We have seen our vulnerability—and we have seen its deepest source. For as long as whole regions of the world simmer in resentment and tyranny—prone to ideologies that feed hatred and excuse murder—violence will gather, and multiply in destructive power, and cross the most defended borders, and raise a mortal threat. There is only one force of history that can break the reign of hatred and resentment, and expose the pretensions of tyrants, and reward the hopes of the decent and tolerant, and that is the force of human freedom.

We are led, by events and common sense, to one conclusion: The survival of liberty in our land increasingly depends on the success of liberty in other lands. The best hope for peace in our world is the expansion of freedom in all the world.

America's vital interests and our deepest beliefs are now one. From the day of our Founding, we have proclaimed that every man and woman on this earth has rights, and dignity, and matchless value, because they bear the image of the Maker of Heaven and earth. Across the generations we have proclaimed the imperative of self-government, because no one is fit to be a master, and no one deserves to be a slave. Advancing these ideals is the mission that created our Nation. It is the honorable achievement of our fathers. Now it is the urgent requirement of our nation's security, and the calling of our time.

So it is the policy of the United States to seek and support the growth of democratic movements and institutions in every nation and culture, with the ultimate goal of ending tyranny in our world.

This is not primarily the task of arms, though we will defend ourselves and our friends by force of arms when necessary. Freedom, by its nature, must be chosen, and defended by citizens, and sustained by the rule of law and the protection of minorities. And when the soul of a nation finally speaks, the institutions that arise may reflect customs and traditions very different from our own. America will not impose our own style of government on the unwilling. Our goal instead is to help others find their own voice, attain their own freedom, and make their own way.

The great objective of ending tyranny is the concentrated work of generations. The difficulty of the task is no excuse for avoiding it. America's influence is not unlimited, but fortunately for the oppressed, America's influence is considerable, and we will use it confidently in freedom's cause.

My most solemn duty is to protect this nation and its people against further attacks and emerging threats. Some have unwisely chosen to test America's resolve, and have found it firm.

We will persistently clarify the choice before every ruler and every nation: The moral choice between oppression, which is always wrong, and freedom, which is eternally right. America will not pretend that jailed dissidents prefer their chains, or that women welcome humiliation and servitude, or that any human being aspires to live at the mercy of bullies.

We will encourage reform in other governments by making clear that success in our relations will require the decent treatment of their own people. America's belief in human dignity will guide our policies, yet rights must be more than the grudging concessions of dictators; they are secured by free dissent and the participation of the governed. In the long run, there is no justice without freedom, and there can be no human rights without human liberty.

Some, I know, have questioned the global appeal of liberty—though this time in history, four decades defined by the swiftest advance of freedom ever seen, is an odd time for doubt. Americans, of all people, should never be surprised by the power of our ideals. Eventually, the call of freedom comes to every mind and every soul. We do not accept the existence of permanent tyranny because we do not accept the possibility of permanent slavery. Liberty will come to those who love it.

Today, America speaks anew to the peoples of the world:

All who live in tyranny and hopelessness can know: the United States will not ignore your oppression, or excuse your oppressors. When you stand for your liberty, we will stand with you.

Democratic reformers facing repression, prison, or exile can know: America sees you for who you are: the future leaders of your free country.

The rulers of outlaw regimes can know that we still believe as Abraham Lincoln did: "Those who deny freedom to others deserve it not for themselves; and, under the rule of a just God, cannot long retain it."

The leaders of governments with long habits of control need to know: To serve your people you must learn to trust them. Start on this journey of progress and justice, and America will walk at your side.

And all the allies of the United States can know: we honor your friendship, we rely on your counsel, and we depend on your help. Division among free nations is a primary goal of freedom's enemies. The concerted effort of free nations to promote democracy is a prelude to our enemies' defeat.

Today, I also speak anew to my fellow citizens:

From all of you, I have asked patience in the hard task of securing America, which you have granted in good measure. Our country has accepted obligations that are difficult to fulfill, and would be dishonorable to abandon. Yet because we have acted in the great liberating tradition of this nation, tens of millions have achieved their freedom. And as hope kindles hope, millions more will find it. By our efforts, we have lit a fire as well—a fire in the minds of men. It warms those who feel its power, it burns those who fight its progress, and one day this untamed fire of freedom will reach the darkest corners of our world.

A few Americans have accepted the hardest duties in this cause—in the quiet work of intelligence and diplomacy . . . the idealistic work of helping raise up free governments . . . the dangerous and necessary work of fighting our enemies. Some have shown their devotion to our country in deaths that honored their whole lives—and we will always honor their names and their sacrifice.

All Americans have witnessed this idealism, and some for the first time. I ask our youngest citizens to believe the evidence of your eyes. You have seen duty and allegiance in the determined faces of our soldiers. You have seen that life is fragile, and evil is real, and courage triumphs. Make the choice to serve in a cause larger than your wants, larger than yourself—and in your days you will add not just to the wealth of our country, but to its character.

America has need of idealism and courage, because we have essential work at home—the unfinished work of American freedom. In a world moving toward liberty, we are determined to show the meaning and promise of liberty.

In America's ideal of freedom, citizens find the dignity and security of economic independence, instead of laboring on the edge of subsistence. This is the broader definition of liberty that motivated the Homestead Act, the Social Security Act, and the G.I. Bill of Rights. And now we will extend this vision by reforming great institutions to serve the needs of our time. To give every American a stake in the promise and future of our country, we will bring the highest standards to our schools, and build an ownership society. We will widen the ownership of homes and businesses, retirement savings and health insurance—preparing our people for the challenges of life in a free society. By making every citizen an agent of his or her own destiny, we will give our fellow Americans greater freedom from want and fear, and make our society more prosperous and just and equal.

In America's ideal of freedom, the public interest depends on private character—on integrity, and tolerance toward others, and the rule of conscience in our own lives. Self-government relies, in the end, on the governing of the self. That edifice of character is built in families, supported by communities with standards, and sustained in our national life by the truths of Sinai, the Sermon on the Mount, the words of the Koran, and the varied faiths of our people. Americans move forward in every generation by reaffirming all that is good and true that came before—ideals of justice and conduct that are the same yesterday, today, and forever.

In America's ideal of freedom, the exercise of rights is ennobled by service, and mercy, and a heart for the weak. Liberty for all does not mean independence from one another. Our nation relies on men and women who look after a neighbor and surround the lost with love. Americans, at our best, value the life we see in one another, and must always remember that even the unwanted have worth. And our country must abandon all the habits of racism, because we cannot carry the message of freedom and the baggage of bigotry at the same time.

From the perspective of a single day, including this day of dedication, the issues and questions before our country are many. From the viewpoint of centuries, the questions that come to us are narrowed and few. Did our generation advance the cause of freedom? And did our character bring credit to that cause?

These questions that judge us also unite us, because Americans of every party and background, Americans by choice and by birth, are bound to one another in the cause of freedom. We have known divisions, which must be healed to move forward in great purposes— and I will strive in good faith to heal them. Yet those divisions do not define America. We felt the unity and fellowship of our nation when freedom came under attack, and our response came like a single hand over a single heart. And we can feel that same unity and pride whenever America acts for good, and the victims of disaster are given hope, and the unjust encounter justice, and the captives are set free.

We go forward with complete confidence in the eventual triumph of freedom. Not because history runs on the wheels of inevitability; it is human choices that move events. Not because we consider ourselves a chosen nation; God moves and chooses as He wills. We have confidence because freedom is the permanent hope of mankind, the hunger in dark places, the longing of the soul. When our Founders declared a new order of the ages; when soldiers died in wave upon wave for a union based on liberty; when citizens marched in peaceful outrage under the banner "Freedom Now"—they were acting on an ancient hope that is meant to be fulfilled. History has an ebb and flow of justice, but history also has a visible direction, set by liberty and the Author of Liberty.

When the Declaration of Independence was first read in public and the Liberty Bell was sounded in celebration, a witness said, "It rang as if it meant something." In our time it means something still. America, in this young century, proclaims liberty throughout all the world, and to all the inhabitants thereof. Renewed in our strength— tested, but not weary—we are ready for the greatest achievements in the history of freedom.

May God bless you, and may He watch over the United States of America.

# BARACK OBAMA
## FIRST INAUGURAL ADDRESS
## TUESDAY, JANUARY 20, 2009

My fellow citizens:

I stand here today humbled by the task before us, grateful for the trust you have bestowed, mindful of the sacrifices borne by our ancestors. I thank President Bush for his service to our nation, as well as the generosity and cooperation he has shown throughout this transition.

Forty-four Americans have now taken the presidential oath. The words have been spoken during rising tides of prosperity and the still waters of peace. Yet, every so often the oath is taken amidst gathering clouds and raging storms. At these moments, America has carried on not simply because of the skill or vision of those in high office, but because we the people have remained faithful to the ideals of our forebears, and true to our founding documents.

So it has been. So it must be with this generation of Americans.

That we are in the midst of crisis is now well understood. Our nation is at war, against a far-reaching network of violence and hatred. Our economy is badly weakened, a consequence of greed and irresponsibility on the part of some, but also our collective failure to make hard choices and prepare the nation for a new age. Homes have been lost; jobs shed; businesses shuttered. Our health care is too costly; our schools fail too many; and each day brings further evidence that the ways we use energy strengthen our adversaries and threaten our planet.

These are the indicators of crisis, subject to data and statistics. Less measurable but no less profound is a sapping of confidence across our land—a nagging fear that America's decline is inevitable, and that the next generation must lower its sights.

Today I say to you that the challenges we face are real. They are serious and they are many. They will not be met easily or in a short span of time. But know this, America—they will be met.

On this day, we gather because we have chosen hope over fear, unity of purpose over conflict and discord.

On this day, we come to proclaim an end to the petty grievances and false promises, the recriminations and worn out dogmas, that for far too long have strangled our politics.

We remain a young nation, but in the words of scripture, the time has come to set aside childish things. The time has come to reaffirm our enduring spirit; to choose our better history; to carry forward that precious gift, that noble idea, passed on from generation to generation: the God-given promise that all are equal, all are free and all deserve a chance to pursue their full measure of happiness.

In reaffirming the greatness of our nation, we understand that greatness is never a given. It must be earned. Our journey has never been one of shortcuts or settling for less. It has not been the path for the faint-hearted—for those who prefer leisure over work, or seek only the pleasures of riches and fame. Rather, it has been the risk-takers, the doers, the makers of things—some celebrated but more often men and women obscure in their labor, who have carried us up the long, rugged path towards prosperity and freedom.

For us, they packed up their few worldly possessions and traveled across oceans in search of a new life.

For us, they toiled in sweatshops and settled the West; endured the lash of the whip and plowed the hard earth.

For us, they fought and died, in places like Concord and Gettysburg; Normandy and Khe Sahn.

Time and again these men and women struggled and sacrificed and worked till their hands were raw so that we might live a better life. They saw America as bigger than the sum of our individual ambitions; greater than all the differences of birth or wealth or faction.

This is the journey we continue today. We remain the most prosperous, powerful nation on Earth. Our workers are no less productive than when this crisis began. Our minds are no less inventive, our goods and services no less needed than they were last week or last month or last year. Our capacity remains undiminished. But our time of standing pat, of protecting narrow interests and putting off unpleasant decisions—that time has surely passed. Starting today, we must pick ourselves up, dust ourselves off, and begin again the work of remaking America.

For everywhere we look, there is work to be done. The state of the economy calls for action, bold and swift, and we will act—not only to create new jobs, but to lay a new foundation for growth. We will build the roads and bridges, the electric grids and digital lines that feed our commerce and bind us together. We will restore science to its rightful place, and wield technology's wonders to raise health care's quality and lower its cost. We will harness the sun and the winds and the soil to fuel our cars and run our factories. And we will transform our schools and colleges and universities to meet the demands of a new age. All this we can do. And all this we will do.

Now, there are some who question the scale of our ambitions— who suggest that our system cannot tolerate too many big plans. Their memories are short. For they have forgotten what this country has already done; what free men and women can achieve when imagination is joined to common purpose, and necessity to courage.

What the cynics fail to understand is that the ground has shifted beneath them—that the stale political arguments that have consumed us for so long no longer apply. The question we ask today is not whether our government is too big or too small, but whether it works—whether it helps families find jobs at a decent wage, care they can afford, a retirement that is dignified. Where the answer is yes, we intend to move forward. Where the answer is no, programs will end. And those of us who manage the public's dollars will be held to account—to spend wisely, reform bad habits, and do our business in the light of day—because only then can we restore the vital trust between a people and their government.

Nor is the question before us whether the market is a force for good or ill. Its power to generate wealth and expand freedom is unmatched, but this crisis has reminded us that without a watchful eye, the market can spin out of control—and that a nation cannot prosper long when it favors only the prosperous. The success of our economy has always depended not just on the size of our gross domestic product, but on the reach of our prosperity; on our ability to extend opportunity to every willing heart—not out of charity, but because it is the surest route to our common good.

As for our common defense, we reject as false the choice between our safety and our ideals. Our founding fathers, faced with perils we can scarcely imagine, drafted a charter to assure the rule of law and the rights of man, a charter expanded by the blood of generations. Those ideals still light the world, and we will not give them up for expedience's sake. And so to all other peoples and governments who are watching today, from the grandest capitals to the small village where my father was born: know that America is a friend of each nation and every man, woman, and child who seeks a future of peace and dignity, and that we are ready to lead once more.

Recall that earlier generations faced down fascism and communism not just with missiles and tanks, but with sturdy alliances and enduring convictions. They understood that our power alone cannot protect us, nor does it entitle us to do as we please. Instead, they knew that our power grows through its prudent use; our security emanates from the justness of our cause, the force of our example, the tempering qualities of humility and restraint.

We are the keepers of this legacy. Guided by these principles once more, we can meet those new threats that demand even greater effort—even greater cooperation and understanding between nations. We will begin to responsibly leave Iraq to its people, and forge a hard-earned peace in Afghanistan. With old friends and former foes, we will work tirelessly to lessen the nuclear threat, and roll back the specter of a warming planet. We will not apologize for our way of life, nor will we waver in its defense, and for those who seek to advance their aims by inducing terror and slaughtering innocents, we say to you now that our spirit is stronger and cannot be broken; you cannot outlast us, and we will defeat you.

For we know that our patchwork heritage is a strength, not a weakness. We are a nation of Christians and Muslims, Jews and Hindus—and non-believers. We are shaped by every language and culture, drawn from every end of this Earth; and because we have tasted the bitter swill of civil war and segregation, and emerged from that dark chapter stronger and more united, we cannot help but believe that the old hatreds shall someday pass; that the lines of tribe shall soon dissolve; that as the world grows smaller, our common humanity shall reveal itself; and that America must play its role in ushering in a new era of peace.

To the Muslim world, we seek a new way forward, based on mutual interest and mutual respect. To those leaders around the globe who seek to sow conflict, or blame their society's ills on the West—know that your people will judge you on what you can build, not what you destroy. To those who cling to power through corruption and deceit and the silencing of dissent, know that you are on the wrong side of history; but that we will extend a hand if you are willing to unclench your fist.

To the people of poor nations, we pledge to work alongside you to make your farms flourish and let clean waters flow; to nourish starved bodies and feed hungry minds. And to those nations like ours that enjoy relative plenty, we say we can no longer afford indifference to suffering outside our borders; nor can we consume the world's resources without regard to effect. For the world has changed, and we must change with it.

As we consider the road that unfolds before us, we remember with humble gratitude those brave Americans who, at this very hour, patrol far-off deserts and distant mountains. They have something to tell us today, just as the fallen heroes who lie in Arlington whisper through the ages. We honor them not only because they are guardians of our liberty, but because they embody the spirit of service; a willingness to find meaning in something greater than themselves. And yet, at this moment—a moment that will define a generation—it is precisely this spirit that must inhabit us all.

For as much as government can do and must do, it is ultimately the faith and determination of the American people upon which this nation relies. It is the kindness to take in a stranger when the levees break, the selflessness of workers who would rather cut their hours than see a friend lose their job which sees us through our darkest hours. It is the firefighter's courage to storm a stairway filled with smoke, but also a parent's willingness to nurture a child, that finally decides our fate.

Our challenges may be new. The instruments with which we meet them may be new. But those values upon which our success depends—hard work and honesty, courage and fair play, tolerance and curiosity, loyalty and patriotism—these things are old. These things are true. They have been the quiet force of progress throughout our history. What is demanded then is a return to these truths. What is required of us now is a new era of responsibility—a recognition, on the part of every American, that we have duties to ourselves, our nation, and the world, duties that we do not grudgingly accept but rather seize gladly, firm in the knowledge that there is nothing so satisfying to the spirit, so defining of our character, than giving our all to a difficult task.

This is the price and the promise of citizenship.

This is the source of our confidence—the knowledge that God calls on us to shape an uncertain destiny.

This is the meaning of our liberty and our creed—why men and women and children of every race and every faith can join in celebration across this magnificent mall, and why a man whose father less than sixty years ago might not have been served at a local restaurant can now stand before you to take a most sacred oath.

So let us mark this day with remembrance, of who we are and how far we have traveled. In the year of America's birth, in the coldest of months, a small band of patriots huddled by dying campfires on the shores of an icy river. The capital was abandoned. The enemy was advancing. The snow was stained with blood. At a moment when the outcome of our revolution was most in doubt, the father of our nation ordered these words be read to the people:

"Let it be told to the future world...that in the depth of winter, when nothing but hope and virtue could survive...that the city and the country, alarmed at one common danger, came forth to meet (it)."

America, in the face of our common dangers, in this winter of our hardship, let us remember these timeless words. With hope and virtue, let us brave once more the icy currents, and endure what storms may come. Let it be said by our children's children that when we were tested we refused to let this journey end, that we did not turn back nor did we falter; and with eyes fixed on the horizon and God's grace upon us, we carried forth that great gift of freedom and delivered it safely to future generations.

# BARACK OBAMA
## SECOND INAUGURAL ADDRESS
## MONDAY, JANUARY 21, 2013

Vice President Biden, Mr. Chief Justice, members of the United States Congress, distinguished guests, and fellow citizens:

Each time we gather to inaugurate a President we bear witness to the enduring strength of our Constitution. We affirm the promise of our democracy. We recall that what binds this nation together is not the colors of our skin or the tenets of our faith or the origins of our names. What makes us exceptional—what makes us American—is our allegiance to an idea articulated in a declaration made more than two centuries ago: "We hold these truths to be self-evident, that all men are created equal; that they are endowed by their Creator with certain unalienable rights; that among these are life, liberty, and the pursuit of happiness."

Today we continue a never-ending journey to bridge the meaning of those words with the realities of our time. For history tells us that while these truths may be self-evident, they've never been self-executing; that while freedom is a gift from God, it must be secured by His people here on Earth. The patriots of 1776 did not fight to replace the tyranny of a king with the privileges of a few or the rule of a mob. They gave to us a republic, a government of, and by, and for the people, entrusting each generation to keep safe our founding creed.

And for more than two hundred years, we have.

Through blood drawn by lash and blood drawn by sword, we learned that no union founded on the principles of liberty and equality could survive half-slave and half-free. We made ourselves anew, and vowed to move forward together.

Together, we determined that a modern economy requires railroads and highways to speed travel and commerce, schools and colleges to train our workers.

Together, we discovered that a free market only thrives when there are rules to ensure competition and fair play.

Together, we resolved that a great nation must care for the vulnerable, and protect its people from life's worst hazards and misfortune.

Through it all, we have never relinquished our skepticism of central authority, nor have we succumbed to the fiction that all society's ills can be cured through government alone. Our celebration of initiative and enterprise, our insistence on hard work and personal responsibility, these are constants in our character.

But we have always understood that when times change, so must we; that fidelity to our founding principles requires new responses to new challenges; that preserving our individual freedoms ultimately requires collective action. For the American people can no more meet the demands of today's world by acting alone than American soldiers could have met the forces of fascism or communism with muskets and militias. No single person can train all the math and science teachers we'll need to equip our children for the future, or build the roads and networks and research labs that will bring new jobs and businesses to our shores. Now, more than ever, we must do these things together, as one nation and one people.

This generation of Americans has been tested by crises that steeled our resolve and proved our resilience. A decade of war is now ending. An economic recovery has begun. America's possibilities are limitless, for we possess all the qualities that this world without boundaries demands: youth and drive; diversity and openness; an endless capacity for risk and a gift for reinvention. My fellow Americans, we are made for this moment, and we will seize it—so long as we seize it together.

For we, the people, understand that our country cannot succeed when a shrinking few do very well and a growing many barely make it. We believe that America's prosperity must rest upon the broad shoulders of a rising middle class. We know that America thrives when every person can find independence and pride in their work; when the wages of honest labor liberate families from the brink of hardship. We are true to our creed when a little girl born into the bleakest poverty knows that she has the same chance to succeed as anybody else, because she is an American; she is free, and she is equal, not just in the eyes of God but also in our own.

We understand that outworn programs are inadequate to the needs of our time. So we must harness new ideas and technology to remake our government, revamp our tax code, reform our schools, and empower our citizens with the skills they need to work harder, learn more, reach higher. But while the means will change, our purpose endures: a nation that rewards the effort and determination of every single American. That is what this moment requires. That is what will give real meaning to our creed.

We, the people, still believe that every citizen deserves a basic measure of security and dignity. We must make the hard choices to reduce the cost of health care and the size of our deficit. But we reject the belief that America must choose between caring for the generation that built this country and investing in the generation that will build its future. For we remember the lessons of our past, when twilight years were spent in poverty and parents of a child with a disability had nowhere to turn.

We do not believe that in this country freedom is reserved for the lucky, or happiness for the few. We recognize that no matter how responsibly we live our lives, any one of us at any time may face a job loss, or a sudden illness, or a home swept away in a terrible storm. The commitments we make to each other through Medicare and Medicaid and Social Security, these things do not sap our initiative, they strengthen us. They do not make us a nation of takers; they free us to take the risks that make this country great.

We, the people, still believe that our obligations as Americans are not just to ourselves, but to all posterity. We will respond to the threat of climate change, knowing that the failure to do so would betray our children and future generations. Some may still deny the overwhelming judgment of science, but none can avoid the devastating impact of raging fires and crippling drought and more powerful storms.

The path towards sustainable energy sources will be long and sometimes difficult. But America cannot resist this transition, we must lead it. We cannot cede to other nations the technology that will power new jobs and new industries, we must claim its promise. That's how we will maintain our economic vitality and our national treasure— our forests and waterways, our crop lands and snow-capped peaks.

That is how we will preserve our planet, commanded to our care by God. That's what will lend meaning to the creed our fathers once declared.

We, the people, still believe that enduring security and lasting peace do not require perpetual war. Our brave men and women in uniform, tempered by the flames of battle, are unmatched in skill and courage. Our citizens, seared by the memory of those we have lost, know too well the price that is paid for liberty. The knowledge of their sacrifice will keep us forever vigilant against those who would do us harm. But we are also heirs to those who won the peace and not just the war; who turned sworn enemies into the surest of friends—and we must carry those lessons into this time as well.

We will defend our people and uphold our values through strength of arms and rule of law. We will show the courage to try and resolve our differences with other nations peacefully—not because we are naive about the dangers we face, but because engagement can more durably lift suspicion and fear.

America will remain the anchor of strong alliances in every corner of the globe. And we will renew those institutions that extend our capacity to manage crisis abroad, for no one has a greater stake in a peaceful world than its most powerful nation. We will support democracy from Asia to Africa, from the Americas to the Middle East, because our interests and our conscience compel us to act on behalf of those who long for freedom. And we must be a source of hope to the poor, the sick, the marginalized, the victims of prejudice—not out of mere charity, but because peace in our time requires the constant advance of those principles that our common creed describes: tolerance and opportunity, human dignity and justice.

We, the people, declare today that the most evident of truths—that all of us are created equal—is the star that guides us still; just as it guided our forebears through Seneca Falls, and Selma, and Stonewall; just as it guided all those men and women, sung and unsung, who left footprints along this great Mall, to hear a preacher say that we cannot walk alone; to hear a King proclaim that our individual freedom is inextricably bound to the freedom of every soul on Earth.

It is now our generation's task to carry on what those pioneers began. For our journey is not complete until our wives, our mothers and daughters can earn a living equal to their efforts. Our journey is not complete until our gay brothers and sisters are treated like anyone else under the law—for if we are truly created equal, then surely the love we commit to one another must be equal as well. Our journey is not complete until no citizen is forced to wait for hours to exercise the right to vote. Our journey is not complete until we find a better way to welcome the striving, hopeful immigrants who still see America as a land of opportunity—until bright young students and engineers are enlisted in our workforce rather than expelled from our country. Our journey is not complete until all our children, from the streets of Detroit to the hills of Appalachia, to the quiet lanes of Newtown, know that they are cared for and cherished and always safe from harm.

That is our generation's task—to make these words, these rights, these values of life and liberty and the pursuit of happiness real for every American. Being true to our founding documents does not require us to agree on every contour of life. It does not mean we all define liberty in exactly the same way or follow the same precise path to happiness. Progress does not compel us to settle centuries-long debates about the role of government for all time, but it does require us to act in our time.

For now decisions are upon us and we cannot afford delay. We cannot mistake absolutism for principle, or substitute spectacle for politics, or treat name-calling as reasoned debate. We must act, knowing that our work will be imperfect. We must act, knowing that today's victories will be only partial and that it will be up to those who stand here in four years and 40 years and 400 years hence to advance the timeless spirit once conferred to us in a spare Philadelphia hall.

My fellow Americans, the oath I have sworn before you today, like the one recited by others who serve in this Capitol, was an oath to God and country, not party or faction. And we must faithfully execute that pledge during the duration of our service. But the words I spoke today are not so different from the oath that is taken each time a soldier signs up for duty or an immigrant realizes her dream. My oath is not so different from the pledge we all make to the flag that waves above and that fills our hearts with pride.

They are the words of citizens and they represent our greatest hope. You and I, as citizens, have the power to set this country's course. You and I, as citizens, have the obligation to shape the debates of our time—not only with the votes we cast, but with the voices we lift in defense of our most ancient values and enduring ideals.

Let us, each of us, now embrace with solemn duty and awesome joy what is our lasting birthright. With common effort and common purpose, with passion and dedication, let us answer the call of history and carry into an uncertain future that precious light of freedom.

Thank you. God bless you, and may He forever bless these United States of America.

# DONALD J. TRUMP
## INAUGURAL ADDRESS
### FRIDAY, JANUARY 20, 2017

Chief Justice Roberts, President Carter, President Clinton, President Bush, President Obama, fellow Americans, and people of the world: thank you.

We, the citizens of America, are now joined in a great national effort to rebuild our country and to restore its promise for all of our people.

Together, we will determine the course of America and the world for years to come.

We will face challenges. We will confront hardships. But we will get the job done.

Every four years, we gather on these steps to carry out the orderly and peaceful transfer of power, and we are grateful to President Obama and First Lady Michelle Obama for their gracious aid throughout this transition. They have been magnificent.

Today's ceremony, however, has very special meaning. Because today we are not merely transferring power from one Administration to another, or from one party to another—but we are transferring power from Washington, D.C. and giving it back to you, the American People.

For too long, a small group in our nation's Capital has reaped the rewards of government while the people have borne the cost.

Washington flourished—but the people did not share in its wealth.

Politicians prospered—but the jobs left, and the factories closed.

The establishment protected itself, but not the citizens of our country.

Their victories have not been your victories; their triumphs have not been your triumphs; and while they celebrated in our nation's Capital, there was little to celebrate for struggling families all across our land.

That all changes—starting right here, and right now, because this moment is your moment: it belongs to you.

It belongs to everyone gathered here today and everyone watching all across America.

This is your day. This is your celebration.

And this, the United States of America, is your country.

What truly matters is not which party controls our government, but whether our government is controlled by the people.

January 20th 2017, will be remembered as the day the people became the rulers of this nation again.

The forgotten men and women of our country will be forgotten no longer.

Everyone is listening to you now.

You came by the tens of millions to become part of a historic movement the likes of which the world has never seen before.

At the center of this movement is a crucial conviction: that a nation exists to serve its citizens.

Americans want great schools for their children, safe neighborhoods for their families, and good jobs for themselves.

These are the just and reasonable demands of a righteous public.

But for too many of our citizens, a different reality exists: Mothers and children trapped in poverty in our inner cities; rusted-out factories scattered like tombstones across the landscape of our nation; an education system, flush with cash, but which leaves our young and beautiful students deprived of knowledge; and the crime and gangs and drugs that have stolen too many lives and robbed our country of so much unrealized potential.

This American carnage stops right here and stops right now.

We are one nation—and their pain is our pain. Their dreams are our dreams; and their success will be our success. We share one heart, one home, and one glorious destiny.

The oath of office I take today is an oath of allegiance to all Americans.

For many decades, we've enriched foreign industry at the expense of American industry;

Subsidized the armies of other countries while allowing for the very sad depletion of our military;

We've defended other nation's borders while refusing to defend our own;

And spent trillions of dollars overseas while America's infrastructure has fallen into disrepair and decay.

We've made other countries rich while the wealth, strength, and confidence of our country has disappeared over the horizon.

One by one, the factories shuttered and left our shores, with not even a thought about the millions upon millions of American workers left behind.

The wealth of our middle class has been ripped from their homes and then redistributed across the entire world.

But that is the past. And now we are looking only to the future.

We assembled here today are issuing a new decree to be heard in every city, in every foreign capital, and in every hall of power.

From this day forward, a new vision will govern our land.

From this moment on, it's going to be America First.

Every decision on trade, on taxes, on immigration, on foreign affairs, will be made to benefit American workers and American families.

We must protect our borders from the ravages of other countries making our products, stealing our companies, and destroying our jobs. Protection will lead to great prosperity and strength.

I will fight for you with every breath in my body—and I will never, ever let you down.

America will start winning again, winning like never before.

We will bring back our jobs. We will bring back our borders. We will bring back our wealth. And we will bring back our dreams.

We will build new roads, and highways, and bridges, and airports, and tunnels, and railways all across our wonderful nation.

We will get our people off of welfare and back to work—rebuilding our country with American hands and American labor.

We will follow two simple rules: Buy American and Hire American.

We will seek friendship and goodwill with the nations of the world—but we do so with the understanding that it is the right of all nations to put their own interests first.

We do not seek to impose our way of life on anyone, but rather to let it shine as an example for everyone to follow.

We will reinforce old alliances and form new ones—and unite the civilized world against Radical Islamic Terrorism, which we will eradicate completely from the face of the Earth.

At the bedrock of our politics will be a total allegiance to the United States of America, and through our loyalty to our country, we will rediscover our loyalty to each other.

When you open your heart to patriotism, there is no room for prejudice.

The Bible tells us, "how good and pleasant it is when God's people live together in unity."

We must speak our minds openly, debate our disagreements honestly, but always pursue solidarity.

When America is united, America is totally unstoppable.

There should be no fear—we are protected, and we will always be protected.

We will be protected by the great men and women of our military and law enforcement and, most importantly, we are protected by God.

Finally, we must think big and dream even bigger.

In America, we understand that a nation is only living as long as it is striving.

We will no longer accept politicians who are all talk and no action—constantly complaining but never doing anything about it.

The time for empty talk is over.

Now arrives the hour of action.

Do not let anyone tell you it cannot be done. No challenge can match the heart and fight and spirit of America.

We will not fail. Our country will thrive and prosper again.

We stand at the birth of a new millennium, ready to unlock the mysteries of space, to free the Earth from the miseries of disease, and to harness the energies, industries and technologies of tomorrow.

A new national pride will stir our souls, lift our sights, and heal our divisions.

It is time to remember that old wisdom our soldiers will never forget: that whether we are black or brown or white, we all bleed the same red blood of patriots, we all enjoy the same glorious freedoms, and we all salute the same great American Flag.

And whether a child is born in the urban sprawl of Detroit or the windswept plains of Nebraska, they look up at the same night sky, they fill their heart with the same dreams, and they are infused with the breath of life by the same almighty Creator.

So to all Americans, in every city near and far, small and large, from mountain to mountain, and from ocean to ocean, hear these words:

You will never be ignored again.

Your voice, your hopes, and your dreams, will define our American destiny. And your courage and goodness and love will forever guide us along the way.

Together, We Will Make America Strong Again.

We Will Make America Wealthy Again.

We Will Make America Proud Again.

We Will Make America Safe Again.

And, Yes, Together, We Will Make America Great Again. Thank you, God Bless You, And God Bless America.

# Word Cloud Classics

*Adventures of Huckleberry Finn*

*The Adventures of Sherlock Holmes*

*Aesop's Fables*

*The Age of Innocence*

*Alice's Adventures in Wonderland and Through the Looking-Glass*

*Anna Karenina*

*Anne of Green Gables*

*The Art of War*

*The Autobiography of Benjamin Franklin and Other Writings*

*The Awakening and Other Stories*

*The Beautiful and Damned and Other Stories*

*Black Beauty*

*The Brothers Grimm 101 Fairy Tales*

*The Brothers Grimm Volume II: 110 Grimmer Fairy Tales*

*Bulfinch's Mythology: Stories of Gods and Heroes*

*The Call of the Wild and Other Stories*

*A Christmas Carol and Other Holiday Treasures*

*Classic Horror Tales*

*Classic Westerns: Zane Grey*

*Common Sense and Selected Works of Thomas Paine*

*The Count of Monte Cristo*

*Crime and Punishment*

*Don Quixote*

*Dracula*

*Dubliners & A Portrait of the Artist as a Young Man and Other Works*

*Emma*

*Frankenstein*

*Great Expectations*

*Hans Christian Andersen Tales*

*H. P. Lovecraft Cthulhu Mythos Tales*

*Inferno*

*The Inventions, Researches, and Writings of Nikola Tesla*

*Jane Eyre*

*The Jungle Book*

*Lady Chatterley's Lover*

*Leaves of Grass*

*The Legend of Sleepy Hollow and Other Tales*

# Word Cloud Classics

*Les Misérables*

*Little Women*

*Madame Bovary*

*Mansfield Park*

*The Merry Adventures of Robin Hood*

*Moby-Dick*

*My Ántonia*

*Narrative of the Life of Frederick Douglass and Other Works*

*Northanger Abbey*

*Odyssey*

*Persuasion*

*Peter Pan*

*The Phantom of the Opera*

*The Picture of Dorian Gray*

*The Poetry of Emily Dickinson*

*Presidential Inaugural Addresses*

*Pride and Prejudice*

*The Prince and Other Writings*

*The Red Badge of Courage and Other Stories*

*The Romantic Poets*

*The Scarlet Letter*

*The Secret Garden*

*Selected Works of Alexander Hamilton*

*Sense and Sensibility*

*Shakespeare's Sonnets and Other Poems*

*Strange Case of Dr. Jekyll and Mr. Hyde & Other Stories*

*Tarzan of the Apes & The Return of Tarzan*

*The Three Musketeers*

*Treasure Island*

*12 Years a Slave*

*Twenty Thousand Leagues Under the Sea*

*Uncle Tom's Cabin, or Life Among the Lowly*

*The U.S. Constitution and Other Key American Writings*

*Walden and Civil Disobedience*

*The Wind in the Willows and Other Stories*

*The Wizard of Oz*

*Wuthering Heights*

# Narrative of the Life of Frederick Douglass and Other Works

# Word Cloud Classics

*A Christmas Carol
and Other Holiday Treasures*

*Adventures of
Huckleberry Finn*

*The Adventures of
Sherlock Holmes*

*Aesop's Fables*

*The Age of Innocence*

*Anna Karenina*

*Anne of Green Gables*

*The Art of War*

*The Brothers Grimm:
101 Fairy Tales*

*The Brothers Grimm
Volume II:
110 Grimmer Fairy Tales*

*Common Sense and Selected
Works of Thomas Paine*

*The Count of Monte Cristo*

*Don Quixote*

*Dracula*

*Frankenstein*

*Great Expectations*

*Inferno*

*Jane Eyre*

*Lady Chatterley's Lover*

*Les Misérables*

*Little Women*

*Madame Bovary*

*Moby-Dick*

*Persuasion*

*The Picture of Dorian Gray*

*Pride and Prejudice*

*The Prince and Other Writings*

*The Red Badge of Courage
and Other Stories*

*The Scarlet Letter*

*The Secret Garden*

*Sense and Sensibility*

*The Three Musketeers*

*Twenty Thousand Leagues
Under the Sea*

*Uncle Tom's Cabin*

*Walden and
Civil Disobedience*

*The Wizard of Oz*

# Narrative of the Life of Frederick Douglass and Other Works

CANTERBURY CLASSICS

San Diego

Canterbury Classics
An imprint of Printers Row Publishing Group
10350 Barnes Canyon Road, Suite 100, San Diego, CA 92121
www.canterburyclassicsbooks.com • mail@canterburyclassicsbooks.com

Printers Row Publishing Group is a division of
Readerlink Distribution Services, LLC.
The Canterbury Classics and Word Cloud Classics names and logos
are trademarks of Readerlink Distribution Services, LLC.

All correspondence regarding the content of this book should be addressed to
Canterbury Classics, Editorial Department, at the above address.

Publisher: Peter Norton
Associate Publisher: Ana Parker
Publishing Team: April Farr, Kathryn C. Dalby
Production/Design Team: Jonathan Lopes, Rusty von Dyl

Spine art: Gettyimages/eyewave (statue), Gettyimages/clipartdotcom (flag)

ISBN: 978-1-64517-086-0
Printed in China
23 22 21 20 19   1 2 3 4 5

# CONTENTS

*Appendix, Containing Extracts from Speeches, Etc.*

# Narrative of the Life of Frederick Douglass, an American Slave, Written by Himself

*Boston*

*Published at the Anti-Slavery Office, No. 25 Cornhill, 1845*

*Entered, according to Act of Congress, in the year 1845
by Frederick Douglass, in the clerk's office of the
District Court of Massachusetts*

# PREFACE

In the month of August, 1841, I attended an anti-slavery convention in Nantucket, at which it was my happiness to become acquainted with Frederick Douglass, the writer of the following Narrative. He was a stranger to nearly every member of that body; but, having recently made his escape from the southern prison-house of bondage, and feeling his curiosity excited to ascertain the principles and measures of the abolitionists—of whom he had heard a somewhat vague description while he was a slave—he was induced to give his attendance, on the occasion alluded to, though at that time a resident in New Bedford.

Fortunate, most fortunate occurrence! Fortunate for the millions of his manacled brethren, yet panting for deliverance from their awful thraldom! Fortunate for the cause of Negro emancipation, and of universal liberty! Fortunate for the land of his birth, which he has already done so much to save and bless! Fortunate for a large circle of friends and acquaintances, whose sympathy and affection he has strongly secured by the many sufferings he has endured, by his virtuous traits of character, by his ever-abiding remembrance of those who are in bonds, as being bound with them! Fortunate for the multitudes, in various parts of our republic, whose minds he has enlightened on the subject of slavery, and who have been melted to tears by his pathos, or roused to virtuous indignation by his stirring eloquence against the enslavers of men! Fortunate for himself, as it at once brought him into the field of public usefulness, "gave the world assurance of a *man*," quickened the slumbering energies of his soul, and consecrated him to the great work of breaking the rod of the oppressor, and letting the oppressed go free!

I shall never forget his first speech at the convention—the extraordinary emotion it excited in my own mind—the powerful impression it created upon a crowded auditory, completely taken by surprise—the applause which followed from the beginning to the end of his felicitous remarks. I think I never hated slavery so intensely as at that moment; certainly, my perception of the enormous outrage which is inflicted by it, on the godlike nature of its victims, was rendered far more clear than ever. There stood one, in physical proportion and stature commanding and exact—in intellect richly endowed—in natural eloquence a prodigy—in soul manifestly "created but a little lower than the angels"—yet a slave, ay, a fugitive slave—trembling for his safety, hardly daring to believe that on the American soil, a single white person could be found who would befriend him at all hazards, for the love of God and humanity! Capable of high attainments as an intellectual and moral being—needing nothing but a comparatively small amount of cultivation to make him an ornament to society and a blessing to his race—by the law of the land, by the voice of the people, by the terms of the slave code, he was only a piece of property, a beast of burden, a chattel personal, nevertheless!

A beloved friend from New Bedford prevailed on Mr. Douglass to address the convention: He came forward to the platform with a hesitancy and embarrassment, necessarily the attendants of a sensitive mind in such a novel position. After apologizing for his ignorance, and reminding the audience that slavery was a poor school for the human intellect and heart, he proceeded to narrate some of the facts in his own history as a slave, and in the course of his speech gave utterance to many noble thoughts and thrilling reflections. As soon as he had taken his seat, filled with hope and admiration, I rose, and declared that Patrick Henry, of revolutionary fame, never made a speech more eloquent in the cause of liberty, than the one we had just listened to from the lips of that hunted fugitive. So I believed at that time—such is my belief now. I reminded the audience of the peril which surrounded this self-emancipated young man at the North—even in Massachusetts, on the soil of the Pilgrim Fathers, among the descendants of revolutionary sires; and I appealed to them, whether they would ever allow him to be carried back into slavery—law or no law, constitution or no constitution. The response was unanimous and in thunder-tones— "No!" "Will you succor and protect him as a brother-man—a resident of the old Bay State?" "Yes!" shouted the whole mass, with an energy so startling, that the ruthless tyrants south of Mason and Dixon's line might almost have heard the mighty burst of feeling, and recognized it as the pledge of an invincible determination, on the part of those who gave it, never to betray him that wanders, but to hide the outcast, and firmly to abide the consequences.

It was at once deeply impressed upon my mind, that, if Mr. Douglass could be persuaded to consecrate his time and talents to the promotion of the anti-slavery enterprise, a powerful impetus would be given to it, and a stunning blow at the same time inflicted on northern prejudice against a colored complexion. I therefore endeavored to instil hope and courage into his mind, in order that he might dare to engage in a vocation so anomalous and responsible for a person in his situation; and I was seconded in this effort by warm-hearted friends, especially by the late General Agent of the Massachusetts Anti-Slavery Society, Mr. John A. Collins, whose judgment in this instance entirely coincided with my own. At first, he could give no encouragement; with unfeigned diffidence, he expressed his conviction that he was not adequate to the performance of so great a task; the path marked out was wholly an untrodden one; he was sincerely apprehensive that he should do more harm than good. After much deliberation, however, he consented to make a trial; and ever since that period, he has acted as a lecturing agent, under the auspices either of the American or the Massachusetts Anti-Slavery Society. In labors he has been most abundant; and his success in combating prejudice, in gaining proselytes, in agitating the public mind, has far surpassed the most sanguine expectations that were raised at the commencement of his brilliant career. He has borne himself with gentleness and meekness, yet with true manliness of character. As a public speaker, he excels in pathos, wit, comparison, imitation, strength of reasoning, and fluency of language. There is in him that union of head and heart, which is indispensable to an enlightenment of the heads and a winning of the hearts of others. May his strength continue to be equal to his day! May he continue to "grow in grace, and in the knowledge of God," that he may be increasingly serviceable in the cause of bleeding humanity, whether at home or abroad!

It is certainly a very remarkable fact, that one of the most efficient advocates of the slave population, now before the public, is a fugitive slave, in the person of Frederick Douglass; and that the free colored population of the United States are as ably represented by one of their own number, in the person of Charles Lenox Remond, whose eloquent appeals have extorted the highest applause of multitudes on both sides of the Atlantic. Let the calumniators of the colored race despise themselves for their baseness and illiberality of spirit, and henceforth cease to talk of the natural inferiority of those who require nothing but time and opportunity to attain to the highest point of human excellence.

It may, perhaps, be fairly questioned, whether any other portion of the population of the earth could have endured the privations, sufferings and horrors of slavery, without having become more degraded in the scale of humanity than the slaves of African descent. Nothing has been left undone to cripple their intellects, darken their minds, debase their moral nature, obliterate all traces of their relationship to mankind; and yet how wonderfully they have sustained the mighty load of a most frightful bondage, under which they have been groaning for centuries! To illustrate the effect of slavery on the white man—to show that he has no powers of endurance, in such a condition, superior to those of his black brother—Daniel O'Connell, the distinguished advocate of universal emancipation, and the mightiest champion of prostrate but not conquered Ireland, relates the following anecdote in a speech delivered by him in the Conciliation Hall, Dublin, before the Loyal National Repeal Association, March 31, 1845. "No matter," said Mr. O'Connell, "under what specious term it may disguise itself, slavery is still hideous. *It has a natural, an inevitable tendency to brutalize every noble faculty of man.* An American sailor, who was cast away on the shore of Africa, where he was kept in slavery for three years, was, at the expiration of that period, found to be imbruted and stultified—he had lost all reasoning power; and having forgotten his native language, could only utter some savage gibberish between Arabic and English, which nobody could understand, and which even he himself found difficulty in pronouncing. So much for the humanizing influence of *the domestic institution*!" Admitting this to have been an extraordinary case of mental deterioration, it proves at least that the white slave can sink as low in the scale of humanity as the black one.

Mr. Douglass has very properly chosen to write his own Narrative, in his own style, and according to the best of his ability, rather than to employ some one else. It is, therefore, entirely his own production; and, considering how long and dark was the career he had to run as a slave—how few have been his opportunities to improve his mind since he broke his iron fetters—it is, in my judgment, highly creditable to his head and heart. He who can peruse it without a tearful eye, a heaving breast, an afflicted spirit—without being filled with an unutterable abhorrence of slavery and all its abettors, and animated with a determination to seek the immediate overthrow of that execrable system—without trembling for the fate of this country in the hands of a righteous God, who is ever on the side of the oppressed, and whose arm is not shortened that it cannot save—must have a flinty heart, and be qualified to act the part of a trafficker "in slaves and the souls of men." I am confident that it is essentially true in all its statements; that nothing has been set down in malice, nothing exaggerated, nothing drawn from the imagination; that it comes short of the reality, rather than overstates a single fact in regard to *slavery as it is*. The experience of Frederick Douglass, as a slave, was not a peculiar one; his lot was not especially a hard one; his case may be regarded as a very fair specimen of the treatment of slaves in Maryland, in which state it is conceded that they are better fed and less cruelly treated than in Georgia, Alabama, or Louisiana. Many have suffered incomparably more, while very few on the plantations have suffered less, than himself. Yet how deplorable was his situation! What terrible chastisements were inflicted upon his person! What still more shocking outrages were perpetrated upon his mind! With all his noble powers and sublime aspirations, how like a brute was he treated, even by those professing to have the same mind in them that was in Christ Jesus! To what dreadful liabilities was he continually subjected! How destitute of friendly counsel and aid, even in his greatest extremities! How heavy was the midnight of woe which shrouded in blackness the last ray of hope, and filled the future with terror and gloom! What longings after freedom took possession of his breast, and how his misery augmented, in proportion as he grew reflective and intelligent,—thus demonstrating that a happy slave is an extinct man! How he thought, reasoned, felt, under the lash of the driver, with the chains upon his limbs! What perils he encountered in his endeavors to escape from his horrible doom! And how signal have been his deliverance and preservation in the midst of a nation of pitiless enemies!

This Narrative contains many affecting incidents, many passages of great eloquence and power; but I think the most thrilling one of them all is the description Douglass gives of his feelings, as he stood soliloquizing respecting his fate, and the chances of his one day being a freeman, on the banks of the Chesapeake Bay—viewing the receding vessels as they flew with their white wings before the breeze, and apostrophizing them as animated by the living spirit of freedom. Who can read that passage, and be insensible to its pathos and sublimity? Compressed into it is a whole Alexandrian library of thought, feeling, and sentiment—all that can, all that need be urged, in the form of expostulation, entreaty, rebuke, against that crime of crimes—making man the property of his fellow-man! O, how accursed is that system, which entombs the godlike mind of man, defaces the divine image, reduces those who by creation were crowned with glory and honor to a level with four-footed beasts, and exalts the dealer in human flesh above all that is called God! Why should its existence be prolonged one hour? Is it not evil, only evil, and that continually? What does its presence imply but the absence of all fear of God, all regard for man, on the part of the people of the United States? Heaven speed its eternal overthrow!

So profoundly ignorant of the nature of slavery are many persons, that they are stubbornly incredulous whenever they read or listen to any recital of the cruelties which are daily inflicted on its victims. They do not deny that the slaves are held as property; but that terrible fact seems to convey to their minds no idea of injustice, exposure to outrage, or savage barbarity. Tell them of cruel scourgings, of mutilations and brandings, of scenes of pollution and blood, of the banishment of all light and knowledge, and they affect to be greatly indignant at such enormous exaggerations, such wholesale misstatements, such abominable libels on the character of the southern planters! As if all these direful outrages were not the natural results of slavery! As if it were less cruel to reduce a human being to the condition of a thing, than to give him a severe flagellation, or to deprive him of necessary food and clothing! As if whips, chains, thumb-screws, paddles, blood-hounds, overseers, drivers, patrols, were not all indispensable to keep the slaves down, and to give protection to their ruthless oppressors! As if, when the marriage institution is abolished, concubinage, adultery, and incest, must not necessarily abound; when all the rights of humanity are annihilated, any barrier remains to protect the victim from the fury of the spoiler; when absolute power is assumed over life and liberty, it will not be wielded with destructive sway! Skeptics of this character abound in society. In some few instances, their incredulity arises from a want of reflection; but, generally, it indicates a hatred of the light, a desire to shield slavery from the assaults of its foes, a contempt of the colored race, whether bond or free. Such will try to discredit the shocking tales of slaveholding cruelty which are recorded in this truthful Narrative; but they will labor in vain. Mr. Douglass has frankly disclosed the place of his birth, the names of those who claimed ownership in his body and soul, and the names also of those who committed the crimes which he has alleged against them. His statements, therefore, may easily be disproved, if they are untrue.

In the course of his Narrative, he relates two instances of murderous cruelty—in one of which a planter deliberately shot a slave belonging to a neighboring plantation, who had unintentionally gotten within his lordly domain in quest of fish; and in the other, an overseer blew out the brains of a slave who had fled to a stream of water to escape a bloody scourging. Mr. Douglass states that in neither of these instances was any thing done by way of legal arrest or judicial investigation. The *Baltimore American*, of March 17, 1845, relates a similar case of atrocity, perpetrated with similar impunity—as follows: "Shooting a slave.—We learn, upon the authority of a letter from Charles County, Maryland, received by a gentleman of this city, that a young man, named Matthews, a nephew of General Matthews, and whose father, it is believed, holds an office at Washington, killed one of the slaves upon his father's farm by shooting him. The letter states that young Matthews had been left in charge of the farm; that he gave an order to the servant, which was disobeyed, when he proceeded to the house, obtained a gun, and, returning, shot the servant. He immediately, the letter continues, fled to his father's residence, where he still remains unmolested." Let it never be forgotten, that no slaveholder or overseer can be convicted of any outrage perpetrated on the person of a slave, however diabolical it may be, on the testimony of colored witnesses, whether bond or free. By the slave code, they are adjudged to be as incompetent to testify against a white man, as though they were indeed a part of the brute creation. Hence, there is no legal protection in fact, whatever there may be in form, for the slave population; and any amount of cruelty may be inflicted on them with impunity. Is it possible for the human mind to conceive of a more horrible state of society?

The effect of a religious profession on the conduct of southern masters is vividly described in the following Narrative, and shown to be any thing but salutary. In the nature of the case, it must be in the highest degree pernicious. The testimony of Mr. Douglass, on this point, is sustained by a cloud of witnesses, whose veracity is unimpeachable. "A slaveholder's profession of Christianity is a palpable imposture. He is a felon of the highest grade. He is a man-stealer. It is of no importance what you put in the other scale."

Reader! Are you with the man-stealers in sympathy and purpose, or on the side of their down-trodden victims? If with the former, then are you the foe of God and man. If with the latter, what are you prepared to do and dare in their behalf? Be faithful, be vigilant, be untiring in your efforts to break every yoke, and let the oppressed go free. Come what may—cost what it may—inscribe on the banner which you unfurl to the breeze, as your religious and political motto—"*No compromise with slavery! No union with slaveholders!*"

Wm. Lloyd Garrison*, Boston
May 1, 1845

---

\* William Lloyd Garrison, one of the most prominent white abolitionists of the 19th century, was the editor of *The Liberator*, a famous abolitionist newspaper, and a founder of the American Anti-Slavery Society.

# LETTER FROM WENDELL
# PHILLIPS, ESQ.

Boston, April 22, 1845

My Dear Friend:
You remember the old fable of "The Man and the Lion," where the lion complained that he should not be so misrepresented "when the lions wrote history."

I am glad the time has come when the "lions write history." We have been left long enough to gather the character of slavery from the involuntary evidence of the masters. One might, indeed, rest sufficiently satisfied with what, it is evident, must be, in general, the results of such a relation, without seeking farther to find whether they have followed in every instance. Indeed, those who stare at the half-peck of corn a week, and love to count the lashes on the slave's back, are seldom the "stuff" out of which reformers and abolitionists are to be made. I remember that, in 1838, many were waiting for the results of the West India experiment, before they could come into our ranks. Those "results" have come long ago; but, alas! few of that number have come with them, as converts. A man must be disposed to judge of emancipation by other tests than whether it has increased the produce of sugar—and to hate slavery for other reasons than because it starves men and whips women—before he is ready to lay the first stone of his anti-slavery life.

I was glad to learn, in your story, how early the most neglected of God's children waken to a sense of their rights, and of the injustice done them. Experience is a keen teacher; and long before you had mastered your A B C, or knew where the "white sails" of the Chesapeake were bound, you began, I see, to gauge the wretchedness of the slave, not by his hunger and want, not by his lashes and toil, but by the cruel and blighting death which gathers over his soul.

In connection with this, there is one circumstance which makes your recollections peculiarly valuable, and renders your early insight the more remarkable. You come from that part of the country where we are told slavery appears with its fairest features. Let us hear, then, what it is at its best estate—gaze on its bright side, if it has one; and then imagination may task her powers to add dark lines to the picture, as she travels southward to that (for the colored man) Valley of the Shadow of Death, where the Mississippi sweeps along.

Again, we have known you long, and can put the most entire confidence in your truth, candor, and sincerity. Every one who has heard you speak has felt, and, I am confident, every one who reads your book will feel, persuaded that you give them a fair specimen of the whole truth. No one-sided portrait—no wholesale complaints—but strict justice done, whenever individual kindliness has neutralized, for a moment, the deadly system with which it was strangely allied. You have been with us, too, some years, and can fairly compare the twilight of rights, which your race enjoy at the North, with that "noon of night" under which they labor south of Mason and Dixon's line. Tell us whether, after all, the half-free colored man of Massachusetts is worse off than the pampered slave of the rice swamps!

In reading your life, no one can say that we have unfairly picked out some rare specimens of cruelty. We know that the bitter drops, which even you have drained from the cup, are no incidental aggravations, no individual ills, but such as must mingle always and necessarily in the lot of every slave. They are the essential ingredients, not the occasional results, of the system.

After all, I shall read your book with trembling for you. Some years ago, when you were beginning to tell me your real name and birthplace, you may remember I stopped you, and preferred to remain ignorant of all. With the exception of a vague description, so I continued, till the other day, when you read me your memoirs. I hardly knew, at the time, whether to thank you or not for the sight of them, when I reflected that it was still dangerous, in Massachusetts, for honest men to tell their names! They say the fathers, in 1776, signed the Declaration of Independence with the halter about their necks. You, too, publish your declaration of freedom with danger compassing you around. In all the broad lands which the Constitution of the United States overshadows, there is no single spot—however narrow or desolate—where a fugitive slave can plant himself and say, "I am safe." The whole armory of Northern Law has no shield for you. I am free to say that, in your place, I should throw the MS into the fire.

You, perhaps, may tell your story in safety, endeared as you are to so many warm hearts by rare gifts, and a still rarer devotion of them to the service of others. But it will be owing only to your labors, and the fearless efforts of those who, trampling the laws and Constitution of the country under their feet, are determined that they will "hide the outcast," and that their hearths shall be, spite of the law, an asylum for the oppressed, if, some time or other, the humblest may stand in our streets, and bear witness in safety against the cruelties of which he has been the victim.

Yet it is sad to think, that these very throbbing hearts which welcome your story, and form your best safeguard in telling it, are all beating contrary to the "statute in such case made and provided." Go on, my dear friend, till you, and those who, like you, have been saved, so as by fire, from the dark prison-house, shall stereotype these free, illegal pulses into statutes; and New England, cutting loose from a blood-stained Union, shall glory in being the house of refuge for the oppressed—till we no longer merely "hide the outcast," or make a merit of standing idly by while he is hunted in our midst; but, consecrating anew the soil of the Pilgrims as an asylum for the oppressed, proclaim our *welcome* to the slave so loudly, that the tones shall reach every hut in the Carolinas, and make the broken-hearted bondman leap up at the thought of old Massachusetts.

God speed the day!
Till then, and ever,
Yours truly,
Wendell Phillips *

---

* Wendell Phillips was a 19th century abolitionist, orator, lawyer, and friend of William Lloyd Garrison. Phillips also advocated on behalf of Native Americans and supported the women's rights movement.

# FREDERICK DOUGLASS

Frederick Douglass was born in slavery as Frederick Augustus Washington Bailey near Easton in Talbot County, Maryland. He was not sure of the exact year of his birth, but he knew that it was 1817 or 1818. As a young boy he was sent to Baltimore, to be a house servant, where he learned to read and write, with the assistance of his master's wife. In 1838 he escaped from slavery and went to New York City, where he married Anna Murray, a free colored woman whom he had met in Baltimore. Soon thereafter he changed his name to Frederick Douglass. In 1841 he addressed a convention of the Massachusetts Anti-Slavery Society in Nantucket and so greatly impressed the group that they immediately employed him as an agent. He was such an impressive orator that numerous persons doubted if he had ever been a slave, so he wrote *Narrative of the Life of Frederick Douglass*. During the Civil War he assisted in the recruiting of colored men for the 54th and 55th Massachusetts Regiments and consistently argued for the emancipation of slaves. After the war he was active in securing and protecting the rights of the freemen. In his later years, at different times, he was secretary of the Santo Domingo Commission, marshall and recorder of deeds of the District of Columbia, and United States Minister to Haiti. His other autobiographical works are *My Bondage and My Freedom* and *Life and Times of Frederick Douglass*, published in 1855 and 1881 respectively. He died in 1895.

# *CHAPTER I*

I was born in Tuckahoe, near Hillsborough, and about twelve miles from Easton, in Talbot County, Maryland. I have no accurate knowledge of my age, never having seen any authentic record containing it. By far the larger part of the slaves know as little of their ages as horses know of theirs, and it is the wish of most masters within my knowledge to keep their slaves thus ignorant. I do not remember to have ever met a slave who could tell of his birthday. They seldom come nearer to it than planting-time, harvest-time, cherry-time, spring-time, or fall-time. A want of information concerning my own was a source of unhappiness to me even during childhood. The white children could tell their ages. I could not tell why I ought to be deprived of the same privilege. I was not allowed to make any inquiries of my master concerning it. He deemed all such inquiries on the part of a slave improper and impertinent, and evidence of a restless spirit. The nearest estimate I can give makes me now between twenty-seven and twenty-eight years of age. I come to this, from hearing my master say, some time during 1835, I was about seventeen years old.

My mother was named Harriet Bailey. She was the daughter of Isaac and Betsey Bailey, both colored, and quite dark. My mother was of a darker complexion than either my grandmother or grandfather.

My father was a white man. He was admitted to be such by all I ever heard speak of my parentage. The opinion was also whispered that my master was my father; but of the correctness of this opinion, I know nothing; the means of knowing was withheld from me. My mother and I were separated when I was but an infant—before I knew her as my mother. It is a common custom, in the part of Maryland from which I ran away, to part children from their mothers at a very early age. Frequently, before the child has reached its twelfth month, its mother is taken from it, and hired out on some farm a considerable distance off, and the child is placed under the care of an old woman, too old for field labor. For what this separation is done, I do not know, unless it be to hinder the development of the child's affection toward its mother, and to blunt and destroy the natural affection of the mother for the child. This is the inevitable result.

I never saw my mother, to know her as such, more than four or five times in my life; and each of these times was very short in duration, and at night. She was hired by a Mr. Stewart, who lived about twelve miles from my home. She made her journeys to see me in the night, travelling the whole distance on foot, after the performance of her day's work. She was a field hand, and a whipping is the penalty of not being in the field at sunrise, unless a slave has special permission from his or her master to the contrary—a permission which they seldom get, and one that gives to him that gives it the proud name of being a kind master. I do not recollect of ever seeing my mother by the light of day. She was with me in the night. She would lie down with me, and get me to sleep, but long before I waked she was gone. Very little communication ever took place between us. Death soon ended what little we could have while she lived, and with it her hardships and suffering. She died when I was about seven years old, on one of my master's farms, near Lee's Mill. I was not allowed to be present during her illness, at her death, or burial. She was gone long before I knew any thing about it. Never having enjoyed, to any considerable extent, her soothing presence, her tender and watchful care, I received the tidings of her death with much the same emotions I should have probably felt at the death of a stranger.

Called thus suddenly away, she left me without the slightest intimation of who my father was. The whisper that my master was my father, may or may not be true; and, true or false, it is of but little consequence to my purpose whilst the fact remains, in all its glaring odiousness, that slaveholders have ordained, and by law established, that the children of slave-women shall in all cases follow the condition of their mothers; and this is done too obviously to administer to their own lusts, and make a gratification of their wicked desires profitable as well as pleasurable; for by this cunning arrangement, the slaveholder, in cases not a few, sustains to his slaves the double relation of master and father.

I know of such cases; and it is worthy of remark that such slaves invariably suffer greater hardships, and have more to contend with, than others. They are, in the first place, a constant offense to their mistress. She is ever disposed to find fault with them; they can seldom do any thing to please her; she is never better pleased than when she sees them under the lash, especially when she suspects her husband of showing to his mulatto children favors which he withholds from his black slaves. The master is frequently compelled to sell this class of his slaves, out of deference to the feelings of his white wife; and, cruel as the deed may strike any one to be, for a man to sell his own children to human flesh-mongers, it is often the dictate of humanity for him to do so; for, unless he does this, he must not only whip them himself, but must stand by and see one white son tie up his brother, of but few shades darker complexion than himself, and ply the gory lash to his naked back; and if he lisp one word of disapproval, it is set down to his parental partiality, and only makes a bad matter worse, both for himself and the slave whom he would protect and defend.

Every year brings with it multitudes of this class of slaves. It was doubtless in consequence of a knowledge of this fact, that one great statesman of the south predicted the downfall of slavery by the inevitable laws of population. Whether this prophecy is ever fulfilled or not, it is nevertheless plain that a very different-looking class of people are springing up at the south, and are now held in slavery, from those originally brought to this country from Africa; and if their increase do no other good, it will do away the force of the argument, that God cursed Ham, and therefore American slavery is right. If the lineal descendants of Ham are alone to be scripturally enslaved, it is certain that slavery at the south must soon become unscriptural; for thousands are ushered into the world, annually, who, like myself, owe their existence to white fathers, and those fathers most frequently their own masters.

I have had two masters. My first master's name was Anthony. I do not remember his first name. He was generally called Captain Anthony—a title which, I presume, he acquired by sailing a craft on the Chesapeake Bay. He was not considered a rich slaveholder. He owned two or three farms, and about thirty slaves. His farms and slaves were under the care of an overseer. The overseer's name was Plummer. Mr. Plummer was a miserable drunkard, a profane swearer, and a savage monster. He always went armed with a cowskin and a heavy cudgel. I have known him to cut and slash the women's heads so horribly, that even master would be enraged at his cruelty, and would threaten to whip him if he did not mind himself. Master, however, was not a humane slaveholder. It required extraordinary barbarity on the part of an overseer to affect him. He was a cruel man, hardened by a long life of slaveholding. He would at times seem to take great pleasure in whipping a slave. I have often been awakened at the dawn of day by the most heart-rending shrieks of an own aunt of mine, whom he used to tie up to a joist, and whip upon her naked back till she was literally covered with blood. No words, no tears, no prayers, from his gory victim, seemed to move his iron heart from its bloody purpose. The louder she screamed, the harder he whipped; and where the blood ran fastest, there he whipped longest. He would whip her to make her scream, and whip her to make her hush; and not until overcome by fatigue, would he cease to swing the blood-clotted cowskin. I remember the first time I ever witnessed this horrible exhibition. I was quite a child, but I well remember it. I never shall forget it whilst I remember any thing. It was the first of a long series of such outrages, of which I was doomed to be a witness and a participant. It struck me with awful force. It was the blood-stained gate, the entrance to the hell of slavery, through which I was about to pass. It was a most terrible spectacle. I wish I could commit to paper the feelings with which I beheld it.

This occurrence took place very soon after I went to live with my old master, and under the following circumstances. Aunt Hester went out one night—where or for what I do not know—and happened to be absent when my master desired her presence. He had ordered her not to go out evenings, and warned her that she must never let him catch her in company with a young man, who was paying attention to her belonging to Colonel Lloyd. The young man's name was Ned Roberts, generally called Lloyd's Ned. Why master was so careful of her, may be safely left to conjecture. She was a woman of noble form, and of graceful proportions, having very few equals, and fewer superiors, in personal appearance, among the colored or white women of our neighborhood.

Aunt Hester had not only disobeyed his orders in going out, but had been found in company with Lloyd's Ned; which circumstance, I found, from what he said while whipping her, was the chief offense. Had he been a man of pure morals himself, he might have been thought interested in protecting the innocence of my aunt; but those who knew him will not suspect him of any such virtue. Before he commenced whipping Aunt Hester, he took her into the kitchen, and stripped her from neck to waist, leaving her neck, shoulders, and back, entirely naked. He then told her to cross her hands, calling her at the same time a d——d b——h. After crossing her hands, he tied them with a strong rope, and led her to a stool under a large hook in the joist, put in for the purpose. He made her get upon the stool, and tied her hands to the hook. She now stood fair for his infernal purpose. Her arms were stretched up at their full length, so that she stood upon the ends of her toes. He then said to her, "Now, you d——d b——h, I'll learn you how to disobey my orders!" and after rolling up his sleeves, he commenced to lay on the heavy cowskin, and soon the warm, red blood (amid heart-rending shrieks from her, and horrid oaths from him) came dripping to the floor. I was so terrified and horror-stricken at the sight, that I hid myself in a closet, and dared not venture out till long after the bloody transaction was over. I expected it would be my turn next. It was all new to me. I had never seen any thing like it before. I had always lived with my grandmother on the outskirts of the plantation, where she was put to raise the children of the younger women. I had therefore been, until now, out of the way of the bloody scenes that often occurred on the plantation.

# CHAPTER II

My master's family consisted of two sons, Andrew and Richard; one daughter, Lucretia, and her husband, Captain Thomas Auld. They lived in one house, upon the home plantation of Colonel Edward Lloyd. My master was Colonel Lloyd's clerk and superintendent. He was what might be called the overseer of the overseers. I spent two years of childhood on this plantation in my old master's family. It was here that I witnessed the bloody transaction recorded in the first chapter; and as I received my first impressions of slavery on this plantation, I will give some description of it, and of slavery as it there existed. The plantation is about twelve miles north of Easton, in Talbot County, and is situated on the border of Miles River. The principal products raised upon it were tobacco, corn, and wheat. These were raised in great abundance; so that, with the products of this and the other farms belonging to him, he was able to keep in almost constant employment a large sloop, in carrying them to market at Baltimore. This sloop was named *Sally Lloyd*, in honor of one of the colonel's daughters. My master's son-in-law, Captain Auld, was master of the vessel; she was otherwise manned by the colonel's own slaves. Their names were Peter, Isaac, Rich, and Jake. These were esteemed very highly by the other slaves, and looked upon as the privileged ones of the plantation; for it was no small affair, in the eyes of the slaves, to be allowed to see Baltimore.

Colonel Lloyd kept from three to four hundred slaves on his home plantation, and owned a large number more on the neighboring farms belonging to him. The names of the farms nearest to the home plantation were Wye Town and New Design. "Wye Town" was under the overseership of a man named Noah Willis. New Design was under the overseership of a Mr. Townsend. The overseers of these, and all the rest of the farms, numbering over twenty, received advice and direction from the managers of the home plantation. This was the great business place. It was the seat of government for the whole twenty farms. All disputes among the overseers were settled here. If a slave was convicted of any high misdemeanor, became unmanageable, or evinced a determination to run away, he was brought immediately here, severely whipped, put on board the sloop, carried to Baltimore, and sold to Austin Woldfolk, or some other slave-trader, as a warning to the slaves remaining.

Here, too, the slaves of all the other farms received their monthly allowance of food, and their yearly clothing. The men and women slaves received, as their monthly allowance of food, eight pounds of pork, or its equivalent in fish, and one bushel of cornmeal. Their yearly clothing consisted of two coarse linen shirts, one pair of linen trousers, like the shirts, one jacket, one pair of trousers for winter, made of coarse Negro cloth, one pair of stockings, and one pair of shoes; the whole of which could not have cost more than seven dollars. The allowance of the slave children was given to their mothers, or the old women having the care of them. The children unable to work in the field had neither shoes, stockings, jackets, nor trousers, given to them; their clothing consisted of two coarse linen shirts per year. When these failed them, they went naked until the next allowance day. Children from seven to ten years old, of both sexes, almost naked, might be seen at all seasons of the year.

There were no beds given the slaves, unless one coarse blanket be considered such, and none but the men and women had these. This, however, is not considered a very great privation. They find less difficulty from the want of beds, than from the want of time to sleep; for when their day's work in the field is done, the most of them having their washing, mending, and cooking to do, and having few or none of the ordinary facilities for doing either of these, very many of their sleeping hours are consumed in preparing for the field the coming day; and when this is done, old and young, male and female, married and single, drop down side by side, on one common bed—the cold, damp floor,—each covering himself or herself with their miserable blankets; and here they sleep till they are summoned to the field by the driver's horn. At the sound of this, all must rise, and be off to the field. There must be no halting; every one must be at his or her post; and woe betides them who hear not this morning summons to the field; for if they are not awakened by the sense of hearing, they are by the sense of feeling: no age nor sex finds any favor. Mr. Severe, the overseer, used to stand by the door of the quarter, armed with a large hickory stick and heavy cowskin, ready to whip any one who was so unfortunate as not to hear, or, from any other cause, was prevented from being ready to start for the field at the sound of the horn.

Mr. Severe was rightly named: he was a cruel man. I have seen him whip a woman, causing the blood to run half an hour at the time; and this, too, in the midst of her crying children, pleading for their mother's release. He seemed to take pleasure in manifesting his fiendish barbarity. Added to his cruelty, he was a profane swearer. It was enough to chill the blood and stiffen the hair of an ordinary man to hear him talk. Scarce a sentence escaped him but that was commenced or concluded by some horrid oath. The field was the place to witness his cruelty and profanity. His presence made it both the field of blood and of blasphemy. From the rising till the going down of the sun, he was cursing, raving, cutting, and slashing among the slaves of the field, in the most frightful manner. His career was short. He died very soon after I went to Colonel Lloyd's; and he died as he lived, uttering, with his dying groans, bitter curses and horrid oaths. His death was regarded by the slaves as the result of a merciful providence.

Mr. Severe's place was filled by a Mr. Hopkins. He was a very different man. He was less cruel, less profane, and made less noise, than Mr. Severe. His course was characterized by no extraordinary demonstrations of cruelty. He whipped, but seemed to take no pleasure in it. He was called by the slaves a good overseer.

The home plantation of Colonel Lloyd wore the appearance of a country village. All the mechanical operations for all the farms were performed here. The shoemaking and mending, the blacksmithing, cartwrighting, coopering, weaving, and grain-grinding, were all performed by the slaves on the home plantation. The whole place wore a business-like aspect very unlike the neighboring farms. The number of houses, too, conspired to give it advantage over the neighboring farms. It was called by the slaves the Great House Farm. Few privileges were esteemed higher, by the slaves of the out-farms, than that of being selected to do errands at the Great House Farm. It was associated in their minds with greatness. A representative could not be prouder of his election to a seat in the American Congress, than a slave on one of the out-farms would be of his election to do errands at the Great House Farm. They regarded it as evidence of great confidence reposed in them by their overseers; and it was on this account, as well as a constant desire to be out of the field from under the driver's lash, that they esteemed it a high privilege, one worth careful living for. He was called the smartest and most trusty fellow, who had this honor conferred upon him the most frequently. The competitors for this office sought as diligently to please their overseers, as the office-seekers in the political parties seek to please and deceive the people. The same traits of character might be seen in Colonel Lloyd's slaves, as are seen in the slaves of the political parties.

The slaves selected to go to the Great House Farm, for the monthly allowance for themselves and their fellow-slaves, were peculiarly enthusiastic. While on their way, they would make the dense old woods, for miles around, reverberate with their wild songs, revealing at once the highest joy and the deepest sadness. They would compose and sing as they went along, consulting neither time nor tune. The thought that came up, came out—if not in the word, in the sound—and as frequently in the one as in the other. They would sometimes sing the most pathetic sentiment in the most rapturous tone, and the most rapturous sentiment in the most pathetic tone. Into all of their songs they would manage to weave something of the Great House Farm. Especially would they do this, when leaving home. They would then sing most exultingly the following words:

> I am going away to the Great House Farm!
> O, yea! O, yea! O!

This they would sing, as a chorus, to words which to many would seem unmeaning jargon, but which, nevertheless, were full of meaning to themselves. I have sometimes thought that the mere hearing of those songs would do more to impress some minds with the horrible character of slavery, than the reading of whole volumes of philosophy on the subject could do.

I did not, when a slave, understand the deep meaning of those rude and apparently incoherent songs. I was myself within the circle; so that I neither saw nor heard as those without might see and hear. They told a tale of woe which was then altogether beyond my feeble comprehension; they were tones loud, long, and deep; they breathed the prayer and complaint of souls boiling over with the bitterest anguish. Every tone was a testimony against slavery, and a prayer to God for deliverance from chains. The hearing of those wild notes always depressed my spirit, and filled me with ineffable sadness. I have frequently found myself in tears while hearing them. The mere recurrence to those songs, even now, afflicts me; and while I am writing these lines, an expression of feeling has already found its way down my cheek. To those songs I trace my first glimmering conception of the dehumanizing character of slavery. I can never get rid of that conception. Those songs still follow me, to deepen my hatred of slavery, and quicken my sympathies for my brethren in bonds. If any one wishes to be impressed with the soul-killing effects of slavery, let him go to Colonel Lloyd's plantation, and, on allowance day, place himself in the deep pine woods, and there let him, in silence, analyze the sounds that shall pass through the chambers of his soul—and if he is not thus impressed, it will only be because "there is no flesh in his obdurate heart."

I have often been utterly astonished, since I came to the north, to find persons who could speak of the singing, among slaves, as evidence of their contentment and happiness. It is impossible to conceive of a greater mistake. Slaves sing most when they are most unhappy. The songs of the slave represent the sorrows of his heart; and he is relieved by them, only as an aching heart is relieved by its tears. At least, such is my experience. I have often sung to drown my sorrow, but seldom to express my happiness. Crying for joy, and singing for joy, were alike uncommon to me while in the jaws of slavery. The singing of a man cast away upon a desolate island might be as appropriately considered as evidence of contentment and happiness, as the singing of a slave; the songs of the one and of the other are prompted by the same emotion.

# CHAPTER III

Colonel Lloyd kept a large and finely cultivated garden, which afforded almost constant employment for four men, besides the chief gardener, (Mr. M'Durmond.) This garden was probably the greatest attraction of the place. During the summer months, people came from far and near—from Baltimore, Easton, and Annapolis—to see it. It abounded in fruits of almost every description, from the hardy apple of the north to the delicate orange of the south. This garden was not the least source of trouble on the plantation. Its excellent fruit was quite a temptation to the hungry swarms of boys, as well as the older slaves, belonging to the colonel, few of whom had the virtue or the vice to resist it. Scarcely a day passed, during the summer, but that some slave had to take the lash for stealing fruit. The colonel had to resort to all kinds of stratagems to keep his slaves out of the garden. The last and most successful one was that of tarring his fence all around; after which, if a slave was caught with any tar upon his person, it was deemed sufficient proof that he had either been into the garden, or had tried to get in. In either case, he was severely whipped by the chief gardener. This plan worked well; the slaves became as fearful of tar as of the lash. They seemed to realize the impossibility of touching *tar* without being defiled.

The colonel also kept a splendid riding equipage. His stable and carriage-house presented the appearance of some of our large city livery establishments. His horses were of the finest form and noblest blood. His carriage-house contained three splendid coaches, three or four gigs, besides dearborns and barouches of the most fashionable style.

This establishment was under the care of two slaves—old Barney and young Barney—father and son. To attend to this establishment was their sole work. But it was by no means an easy employment; for in nothing was Colonel Lloyd more particular than in the management of his horses. The slightest inattention to these was unpardonable, and was visited upon those, under whose care they were placed, with the severest punishment; no excuse could shield them, if the colonel only suspected any want of attention to his horses—a supposition which he frequently indulged, and one which, of course, made the office of old and young Barney a very trying one. They never knew when they were safe from punishment. They were frequently whipped when least deserving, and escaped whipping when most deserving it. Every thing depended upon the looks of the horses, and the state of Colonel Lloyd's own mind when his horses were brought to him for use. If a horse did not move fast enough, or hold his head high enough, it was owing to some fault of his keepers. It was painful to stand near the stable-door, and hear the various complaints against the keepers when a horse was taken out for use. "This horse has not had proper attention. He has not been sufficiently rubbed and curried, or he has not been properly fed; his food was too wet or too dry; he got it too soon or too late; he was too hot or too cold; he had too much hay, and not enough of grain; or he had too much grain, and not enough of hay; instead of old Barney's attending to the horse, he had very improperly left it to his son." To all these complaints, no matter how unjust, the slave must answer never a word. Colonel Lloyd could not brook any contradiction from a slave. When he spoke, a slave must stand, listen, and tremble; and such was literally the case. I have seen Colonel Lloyd make old Barney, a man between fifty and sixty years of age, uncover his bald head, kneel down upon the cold, damp ground, and receive upon his naked and toil-worn shoulders more than thirty lashes at the time. Colonel Lloyd had three sons—Edward, Murray, and Daniel—and three sons-in-law, Mr. Winder, Mr. Nicholson, and Mr. Lowndes. All of these lived at the Great House Farm, and enjoyed the luxury of whipping the servants when they pleased, from old Barney down to William Wilkes, the coach-driver. I have seen Winder make one of the house-servants stand off from him a suitable distance to be touched with the end of his whip, and at every stroke raise great ridges upon his back.

To describe the wealth of Colonel Lloyd would be almost equal to describing the riches of Job. He kept from ten to fifteen house-servants. He was said to own a thousand slaves, and I think this estimate quite within the truth. Colonel Lloyd owned so many that he did not know them when he saw them; nor did all the slaves of the out-farms know him. It is reported of him, that, while riding along the road one day, he met a colored man, and addressed him in the usual manner of speaking to colored people on the public highways of the south: "Well, boy, whom do you belong to?" "To Colonel Lloyd," replied the slave.

"Well, does the colonel treat you well?" "No, sir," was the ready reply. "What, does he work you too hard?" "Yes, sir." "Well, don't he give you enough to eat?" "Yes, sir, he gives me enough, such as it is."

The colonel, after ascertaining where the slave belonged, rode on; the man also went on about his business, not dreaming that he had been conversing with his master. He thought, said, and heard nothing more of the matter, until two or three weeks afterwards. The poor man was then informed by his overseer that, for having found fault with his master, he was now to be sold to a Georgia trader. He was immediately chained and handcuffed; and thus, without a moment's warning, he was snatched away, and forever sundered, from his family and friends, by a hand more unrelenting than death. This is the penalty of telling the truth, of telling the simple truth, in answer to a series of plain questions.

It is partly in consequence of such facts, that slaves, when inquired of as to their condition and the character of their masters, almost universally say they are contented, and that their masters are kind. The slaveholders have been known to send in spies among their slaves, to ascertain their views and feelings in regard to their condition. The frequency of this has had the effect to establish among the slaves the maxim, that a still tongue makes a wise head. They suppress the truth rather than take the consequences of telling it, and in so doing prove themselves a part of the human family. If they have any thing to say of their masters, it is generally in their masters' favor, especially when speaking to an untried man. I have been frequently asked, when a slave, if I had a kind master, and do not remember ever to have given a negative answer; nor did I, in pursuing this course, consider myself as uttering what was absolutely false; for I always measured the kindness of my master by the standard of kindness set up among slaveholders around us. Moreover, slaves are like other people, and imbibe prejudices quite common to others. They think their own better than that of others. Many, under the influence of this prejudice, think their own masters are better than the masters of other slaves; and this, too, in some cases, when the very reverse is true. Indeed, it is not uncommon for slaves even to fall out and quarrel among themselves about the relative goodness of their masters, each contending for the superior goodness of his own over that of the others. At the very same time, they mutually execrate their masters when viewed separately. It was so on our plantation. When Colonel Lloyd's slaves met the slaves of Jacob Jepson, they seldom parted without a quarrel about their masters; Colonel Lloyd's slaves contending that he was the richest, and Mr. Jepson's slaves that he was the smartest, and most of a man. Colonel Lloyd's slaves would boast his ability to buy and sell Jacob Jepson. Mr. Jepson's slaves would boast his ability to whip Colonel Lloyd. These quarrels would almost always end in a fight between the parties, and those that whipped were supposed to have gained the point at issue. They seemed to think that the greatness of their masters was transferable to themselves. It was considered as being bad enough to be a slave; but to be a poor man's slave was deemed a disgrace indeed!

# CHAPTER IV

M r. Hopkins remained but a short time in the office of overseer.
Why his career was so short, I do not know, but suppose he
lacked the necessary severity to suit Colonel Lloyd. Mr. Hopkins
was succeeded by Mr. Austin Gore, a man possessing, in an eminent
degree, all those traits of character indispensable to what is called a
first-rate overseer. Mr. Gore had served Colonel Lloyd, in the capacity
of overseer, upon one of the out-farms, and had shown himself worthy
of the high station of overseer upon the home or Great House Farm.

Mr. Gore was proud, ambitious, and persevering. He was artful,
cruel, and obdurate. He was just the man for such a place, and it was
just the place for such a man. It afforded scope for the full exercise of
all his powers, and he seemed to be perfectly at home in it. He was one
of those who could torture the slightest look, word, or gesture, on
the part of the slave, into impudence, and would treat it accordingly.
There must be no answering back to him; no explanation was allowed
a slave, showing himself to have been wrongfully accused. Mr. Gore
acted fully up to the maxim laid down by slaveholders—"It is better
that a dozen slaves should suffer under the lash, than that the overseer
should be convicted, in the presence of the slaves, of having been
at fault." No matter how innocent a slave might be—it availed him
nothing, when accused by Mr. Gore of any misdemeanor. To be
accused was to be convicted, and to be convicted was to be punished;
the one always following the other with immutable certainty. To escape
punishment was to escape accusation; and few slaves had the fortune
to do either, under the overseership of Mr. Gore. He was just proud
enough to demand the most debasing homage of the slave, and quite
servile enough to crouch, himself, at the feet of the master. He was
ambitious enough to be contented with nothing short of the highest
rank of overseers, and persevering enough to reach the height of his
ambition. He was cruel enough to inflict the severest punishment,
artful enough to descend to the lowest trickery, and obdurate enough
to be insensible to the voice of a reproving conscience. He was, of
all the overseers, the most dreaded by the slaves. His presence was
painful; his eye flashed confusion; and seldom was his sharp, shrill

voice heard, without producing horror and trembling in their ranks.

Mr. Gore was a grave man, and, though a young man, he indulged in no jokes, said no funny words, seldom smiled. His words were in perfect keeping with his looks, and his looks were in perfect keeping with his words. Overseers will sometimes indulge in a witty word, even with the slaves; not so with Mr. Gore. He spoke but to command, and commanded but to be obeyed; he dealt sparingly with his words, and bountifully with his whip, never using the former where the latter would answer as well. When he whipped, he seemed to do so from a sense of duty, and feared no consequences. He did nothing reluctantly, no matter how disagreeable; always at his post, never inconsistent. He never promised but to fulfill. He was, in a word, a man of the most inflexible firmness and stone-like coolness.

His savage barbarity was equaled only by the consummate coolness with which he committed the grossest and most savage deeds upon the slaves under his charge. Mr. Gore once undertook to whip one of Colonel Lloyd's slaves, by the name of Demby. He had given Demby but few stripes, when, to get rid of the scourging, he ran and plunged himself into a creek, and stood there at the depth of his shoulders, refusing to come out. Mr. Gore told him that he would give him three calls, and that, if he did not come out at the third call, he would shoot him. The first call was given. Demby made no response, but stood his ground. The second and third calls were given with the same result. Mr. Gore then, without consultation or deliberation with any one, not even giving Demby an additional call, raised his musket to his face, taking deadly aim at his standing victim, and in an instant poor Demby was no more. His mangled body sank out of sight, and blood and brains marked the water where he had stood.

A thrill of horror flashed through every soul upon the plantation, excepting Mr. Gore. He alone seemed cool and collected. He was asked by Colonel Lloyd and my old master, why he resorted to this extraordinary expedient. His reply was, (as well as I can remember), that Demby had become unmanageable. He was setting a dangerous example to the other slaves—one which, if suffered to pass without some such demonstration on his part, would finally lead to the total subversion of all rule and order upon the plantation. He argued that if one slave refused to be corrected, and escaped with his life, the other slaves would soon copy the example; the result of which would be, the freedom of the slaves, and the enslavement of the whites. Mr. Gore's defense was satisfactory. He was continued in his station as overseer upon the home plantation. His fame as an overseer went abroad. His horrid crime was not even submitted to judicial investigation. It was committed in the presence of slaves, and they of course could neither institute a suit, nor testify against him; and thus the guilty perpetrator of one of the bloodiest and most foul murders goes unwhipped of justice, and uncensured by the community in which he lives. Mr. Gore lived in St. Michael's, Talbot County, Maryland, when I left there; and if he is still alive, he very probably lives there now; and if so, he is now, as he was then, as highly esteemed and as much respected as though his guilty soul had not been stained with his brother's blood.

I speak advisedly when I say this—that killing a slave, or any colored person, in Talbot County, Maryland, is not treated as a crime, either by the courts or the community. Mr. Thomas Lanman, of St. Michael's, killed two slaves, one of whom he killed with a hatchet, by knocking his brains out. He used to boast of the commission of the awful and bloody deed. I have heard him do so laughingly, saying, among other things, that he was the only benefactor of his country in the company, and that when others would do as much as he had done, we should be relieved of "the d———d niggers."

The wife of Mr. Giles Hicks, living but a short distance from where I used to live, murdered my wife's cousin, a young girl between fifteen and sixteen years of age, mangling her person in the most horrible manner, breaking her nose and breastbone with a stick, so that the poor girl expired in a few hours afterward. She was immediately buried, but had not been in her untimely grave but a few hours before she was taken up and examined by the coroner, who decided that she had come to her death by severe beating. The offense for which this girl was thus murdered was this: She had been set that night to mind Mrs. Hicks's baby, and during the night she fell asleep, and the baby cried. She, having lost her rest for several nights previous, did not hear the crying. They were both in the room with Mrs. Hicks. Mrs. Hicks, finding the girl slow to move, jumped from her bed, seized an oak stick of wood by the fireplace, and with it broke the girl's nose and breastbone, and thus ended her life. I will not say that this most horrid murder produced no sensation in the community. It did produce sensation, but not enough to bring the murderess to punishment. There was a warrant issued for her arrest, but it was never served. Thus she escaped not only punishment, but even the pain of being arraigned before a court for her horrid crime.

Whilst I am detailing bloody deeds which took place during my stay on Colonel Lloyd's plantation, I will briefly narrate another, which occurred about the same time as the murder of Demby by Mr. Gore.

Colonel Lloyd's slaves were in the habit of spending a part of their nights and Sundays in fishing for oysters, and in this way made up the deficiency of their scanty allowance. An old man belonging to Colonel Lloyd, while thus engaged, happened to get beyond the limits of Colonel Lloyd's, and on the premises of Mr. Beal Bondly. At this trespass, Mr. Bondly took offense, and with his musket came down to the shore, and blew its deadly contents into the poor old man.

Mr. Bondly came over to see Colonel Lloyd the next day, whether to pay him for his property, or to justify himself in what he had done, I know not. At any rate, this whole fiendish transaction was soon hushed up. There was very little said about it at all, and nothing done. It was a common saying, even among little white boys, that it was worth a half-cent to kill a "nigger," and a half-cent to bury one.

# CHAPTER V

As to my own treatment while I lived on Colonel Lloyd's plantation, it was very similar to that of the other slave children. I was not old enough to work in the field, and there being little else than field work to do, I had a great deal of leisure time. The most I had to do was to drive up the cows at evening, keep the fowls out of the garden, keep the front yard clean, and run of errands for my old master's daughter, Mrs. Lucretia Auld. The most of my leisure time I spent in helping Master Daniel Lloyd in finding his birds, after he had shot them. My connection with Master Daniel was of some advantage to me. He became quite attached to me, and was a sort of protector of me. He would not allow the older boys to impose upon me, and would divide his cakes with me.

I was seldom whipped by my old master, and suffered little from any thing else than hunger and cold. I suffered much from hunger, but much more from cold. In hottest summer and coldest winter, I was kept almost naked—no shoes, no stockings, no jacket, no trousers, nothing on but a coarse tow linen shirt, reaching only to my knees. I had no bed. I must have perished with cold, but that, the coldest nights, I used to steal a bag which was used for carrying corn to the mill. I would crawl into this bag, and there sleep on the cold, damp, clay floor, with my head in and feet out. My feet have been so cracked with the frost, that the pen with which I am writing might be laid in the gashes.

We were not regularly allowanced. Our food was coarse cornmeal boiled. This was called *mush*. It was put into a large wooden tray or trough, and set down upon the ground. The children were then called, like so many pigs, and like so many pigs they would come and devour the mush; some with oyster-shells, others with pieces of shingle, some with naked hands, and none with spoons. He that ate fastest got most; he that was strongest secured the best place; and few left the trough satisfied.

I was probably between seven and eight years old when I left Colonel Lloyd's plantation. I left it with joy. I shall never forget the ecstasy with which I received the intelligence that my old master (Anthony) had determined to let me go to Baltimore, to live with Mr.

Hugh Auld, brother to my old master's son-in-law, Captain Thomas Auld. I received this information about three days before my departure. They were three of the happiest days I ever enjoyed. I spent the most part of all these three days in the creek, washing off the plantation scurf, and preparing myself for my departure.

The pride of appearance which this would indicate was not my own. I spent the time in washing, not so much because I wished to, but because Mrs. Lucretia had told me I must get all the dead skin off my feet and knees before I could go to Baltimore; for the people in Baltimore were very cleanly, and would laugh at me if I looked dirty. Besides, she was going to give me a pair of trousers, which I should not put on unless I got all the dirt off me. The thought of owning a pair of trousers was great indeed! It was almost a sufficient motive, not only to make me take off what would be called by pig-drovers the mange, but the skin itself. I went at it in good earnest, working for the first time with the hope of reward.

The ties that ordinarily bind children to their homes were all suspended in my case. I found no severe trial in my departure. My home was charmless; it was not home to me; on parting from it, I could not feel that I was leaving any thing which I could have enjoyed by staying. My mother was dead, my grandmother lived far off, so that I seldom saw her. I had two sisters and one brother, that lived in the same house with me; but the early separation of us from our mother had well nigh blotted the fact of our relationship from our memories. I looked for home elsewhere, and was confident of finding none which I should relish less than the one which I was leaving. If, however, I found in my new home hardship, hunger, whipping, and nakedness, I had the consolation that I should not have escaped any one of them by staying. Having already had more than a taste of them in the house of my old master, and having endured them there, I very naturally inferred my ability to endure them elsewhere, and especially at Baltimore; for I had something of the feeling about Baltimore that is expressed in the proverb, that "being hanged in England is preferable to dying a natural death in Ireland." I had the strongest desire to see Baltimore. Cousin Tom, though not fluent in speech, had inspired me with that desire by his eloquent description of the place. I could never point out any thing at the Great House, no matter how beautiful or powerful, but that he had seen something at Baltimore far exceeding, both in beauty and strength, the object which I pointed out to him. Even the Great House itself, with all its pictures, was far inferior to many buildings in Baltimore. So strong was my desire, that I thought a gratification of it would fully compensate for whatever loss of comforts I should sustain by the exchange. I left without a regret, and with the highest hopes of future happiness.

We sailed out of Miles River for Baltimore on a Saturday morning. I remember only the day of the week, for at that time I had no knowledge of the days of the month, nor the months of the year. On setting sail, I walked aft, and gave to Colonel Lloyd's plantation what I hoped would be the last look. I then placed myself in the bows of the sloop, and there spent the remainder of the day in looking ahead, interesting myself in what was in the distance rather than in things near by or behind.

In the afternoon of that day, we reached Annapolis, the capital of the state. We stopped but a few moments, so that I had no time to go on shore. It was the first large town that I had ever seen, and though it would look small compared with some of our New England factory villages, I thought it a wonderful place for its size—more imposing even than the Great House Farm!

We arrived at Baltimore early on Sunday morning, landing at Smith's Wharf, not far from Bowley's Wharf. We had on board the sloop a large flock of sheep; and after aiding in driving them to the slaughterhouse of Mr. Curtis on Louden Slater's Hill, I was conducted by Rich, one of the hands belonging on board of the sloop, to my new home in Alliciana Street, near Mr. Gardner's ship-yard, on Fells Point.

Mr. and Mrs. Auld were both at home, and met me at the door with their little son Thomas, to take care of whom I had been given. And here I saw what I had never seen before; it was a white face beaming with the most kindly emotions; it was the face of my new mistress, Sophia Auld. I wish I could describe the rapture that flashed through my soul as I beheld it. It was a new and strange sight to me, brightening up my pathway with the light of happiness. Little Thomas was told, there was his Freddy—and I was told to take care of little Thomas; and thus I entered upon the duties of my new home with the most cheering prospect ahead.

I look upon my departure from Colonel Lloyd's plantation as one of the most interesting events of my life. It is possible, and even quite probable, that but for the mere circumstance of being removed from that plantation to Baltimore, I should have today, instead of being here seated by my own table, in the enjoyment of freedom and the happiness of home, writing this Narrative, been confined in the galling chains of slavery. Going to live at Baltimore laid the foundation, and opened the gateway, to all my subsequent prosperity. I have ever regarded it as the first plain manifestation of that kind providence which has ever since attended me, and marked my life with so many favors. I regarded the selection of myself as being somewhat remarkable. There were a number of slave children that might have been sent from the plantation to Baltimore. There were those younger, those older, and those of the same age. I was chosen from among them all, and was the first, last, and only choice.

I may be deemed superstitious, and even egotistical, in regarding this event as a special interposition of divine Providence in my favor. But I should be false to the earliest sentiments of my soul, if I suppressed the opinion. I prefer to be true to myself, even at the hazard of incurring the ridicule of others, rather than to be false, and incur my own abhorrence. From my earliest recollection, I date the entertainment of a deep conviction that slavery would not always be able to hold me within its foul embrace; and in the darkest hours of my career in slavery, this living word of faith and spirit of hope departed not from me, but remained like ministering angels to cheer me through the gloom. This good spirit was from God, and to him I offer thanksgiving and praise.

# CHAPTER VI

My new mistress proved to be all she appeared when I first met her at the door—a woman of the kindest heart and finest feelings. She had never had a slave under her control previously to myself, and prior to her marriage she had been dependent upon her own industry for a living. She was by trade a weaver; and by constant application to her business, she had been in a good degree preserved from the blighting and dehumanizing effects of slavery. I was utterly astonished at her goodness. I scarcely knew how to behave towards her. She was entirely unlike any other white woman I had ever seen. I could not approach her as I was accustomed to approach other white ladies. My early instruction was all out of place. The crouching servility, usually so acceptable a quality in a slave, did not answer when manifested toward her. Her favor was not gained by it; she seemed to be disturbed by it. She did not deem it impudent or unmannerly for a slave to look her in the face. The meanest slave was put fully at ease in her presence, and none left without feeling better for having seen her. Her face was made of heavenly smiles, and her voice of tranquil music.

But, alas! this kind heart had but a short time to remain such. The fatal poison of irresponsible power was already in her hands, and soon commenced its infernal work. That cheerful eye, under the influence of slavery, soon became red with rage; that voice, made all of sweet accord, changed to one of harsh and horrid discord; and that angelic face gave place to that of a demon.

Very soon after I went to live with Mr. and Mrs. Auld, she very kindly commenced to teach me the A B C. After I had learned this, she assisted me in learning to spell words of three or four letters. Just at this point of my progress, Mr. Auld found out what was going on, and at once forbade Mrs. Auld to instruct me further, telling her, among other things, that it was unlawful, as well as unsafe, to teach a slave to read. To use his own words, further, he said, "If you give a nigger an inch, he will take an ell. A nigger should know nothing but to obey his master— to do as he is told to do. Learning would *spoil* the best nigger in the world. Now," said he, "if you teach that nigger (speaking of myself) how to read, there would be no keeping him. It would forever unfit him to be a slave. He would at once become unmanageable, and of no value to his master. As to himself, it could do him no good, but a great deal of harm. It would make him discontented and unhappy." These words sank deep into my heart, stirred up sentiments within that lay slumbering, and called into existence an entirely new train of thought. It was a new and special revelation, explaining dark and mysterious things, with which my youthful understanding had struggled, but struggled in vain. I now understood what had been to me a most perplexing difficulty—to wit, the white man's power to enslave the black man. It was a grand achievement, and I prized it highly. From that moment, I understood the pathway from slavery to freedom. It was just what I wanted, and I got it at a time when I the least expected it. Whilst I was saddened by the thought of losing the aid of my kind mistress, I was gladdened by the invaluable instruction which, by the merest accident, I had gained from my master. Though conscious of the difficulty of learning without a teacher, I set out with high hope, and a fixed purpose, at whatever cost of trouble, to learn how to read. The very decided manner with which he spoke, and strove to impress his wife with the evil consequences of giving me instruction, served to convince me that he was deeply sensible of the truths he was uttering. It gave me the best assurance that I might rely with the utmost confidence on the results which, he said, would flow from teaching me to read. What he most dreaded, that I most desired. What he most loved, that I most hated. That which to him was a great evil, to be carefully shunned, was to me a great good, to be diligently sought; and the argument which he so warmly urged, against my learning to read, only served to inspire me with a desire and determination to learn. In learning to read, I owe almost as much to the bitter opposition of my master, as to the kindly aid of my mistress. I acknowledge the benefit of both.

I had resided but a short time in Baltimore before I observed a marked difference, in the treatment of slaves, from that which I had witnessed in the country. A city slave is almost a freeman, compared with a slave on the plantation. He is much better fed and clothed, and enjoys privileges altogether unknown to the slave on the plantation. There is a vestige of decency, a sense of shame, that does much to curb and check those outbreaks of atrocious cruelty so commonly enacted upon the plantation. He is a desperate slaveholder, who will shock the humanity of his non-slaveholding neighbors with the cries of his lacerated slave. Few are willing to incur the odium attaching to the reputation of being a cruel master; and above all things, they would not be known as not giving a slave enough to eat. Every city slaveholder is anxious to have it known of him, that he feeds his slaves well; and it is due to them to say, that most of them do give their slaves enough to eat. There are, however, some painful exceptions to this rule. Directly opposite to us, on Philpot Street, lived Mr. Thomas Hamilton. He owned two slaves. Their names were Henrietta and Mary. Henrietta was about twenty-two years of age, Mary was about fourteen; and of all the mangled and emaciated creatures I ever looked upon, these two were the most so. His heart must be harder than stone, that could look upon these unmoved. The head, neck, and shoulders of Mary were literally cut to pieces. I have frequently felt her head, and found it nearly covered with festering sores, caused by the lash of her cruel mistress. I do not know that her master ever whipped her, but I have been an eye-witness to the cruelty of Mrs. Hamilton. I used to be in Mr. Hamilton's house nearly every day. Mrs. Hamilton used to sit in a large chair in the middle of the room, with a heavy cowskin always by her side, and scarce an hour passed during the day but was marked by the blood of one of these slaves. The girls seldom passed her without her saying, "Move faster, you black gip!" at the same time giving them a blow with the cowskin over the head or shoulders, often drawing the blood. She would then say, "Take that, you black gip!" continuing, "If you don't move faster, I'll move you!" Added to the cruel lashings to which these slaves were subjected, they were kept nearly half-starved. They seldom knew what it was to eat a full meal. I have seen Mary contending with the pigs for the offal thrown into the street. So much was Mary kicked and cut to pieces, that she was oftener called "pecked" than by her name.

# CHAPTER VII

I lived in Master Hugh's family about seven years. During this time, I succeeded in learning to read and write. In accomplishing this, I was compelled to resort to various stratagems. I had no regular teacher. My mistress, who had kindly commenced to instruct me, had, in compliance with the advice and direction of her husband, not only ceased to instruct, but had set her face against my being instructed by any one else. It is due, however, to my mistress to say of her, that she did not adopt this course of treatment immediately. She at first lacked the depravity indispensable to shutting me up in mental darkness. It was at least necessary for her to have some training in the exercise of irresponsible power, to make her equal to the task of treating me as though I were a brute.

My mistress was, as I have said, a kind and tender-hearted woman; and in the simplicity of her soul she commenced, when I first went to live with her, to treat me as she supposed one human being ought to treat another. In entering upon the duties of a slaveholder, she did not seem to perceive that I sustained to her the relation of a mere chattel, and that for her to treat me as a human being was not only wrong, but dangerously so. Slavery proved as injurious to her as it did to me. When I went there, she was a pious, warm, and tender-hearted woman. There was no sorrow or suffering for which she had not a tear. She had bread for the hungry, clothes for the naked, and comfort for every mourner that came within her reach. Slavery soon proved its ability to divest her of these heavenly qualities. Under its influence, the tender heart became stone, and the lamblike disposition gave way to one of tiger-like fierceness. The first step in her downward course was in her ceasing to instruct me. She now commenced to practice her husband's precepts. She finally became even more violent in her opposition than her husband himself. She was not satisfied with simply doing as well as he had commanded; she seemed anxious to do better. Nothing seemed to make her more angry than to see me with a newspaper. She seemed to think that here lay the danger. I have had her rush at me with a face made all up of fury, and snatch from me a newspaper, in a manner that fully revealed her apprehension. She was an apt woman; and a little experience soon demonstrated, to her satisfaction, that education and slavery were incompatible with each other.

From this time I was most narrowly watched. If I was in a separate room any considerable length of time, I was sure to be suspected of having a book, and was at once called to give an account of myself. All this, however, was too late. The first step had been taken. Mistress, in teaching me the alphabet, had given me the inch, and no precaution could prevent me from taking the ell.

The plan which I adopted, and the one by which I was most successful, was that of making friends of all the little white boys whom I met in the street. As many of these as I could, I converted into teachers. With their kindly aid, obtained at different times and in different places, I finally succeeded in learning to read. When I was sent of errands, I always took my book with me, and by doing one part of my errand quickly, I found time to get a lesson before my return. I used also to carry bread with me, enough of which was always in the house, and to which I was always welcome; for I was much better off in this regard than many of the poor white children in our neighborhood. This bread I used to bestow upon the hungry little urchins, who, in return, would give me that more valuable bread of knowledge. I am strongly tempted to give the names of two or three of those little boys, as a testimonial of the gratitude and affection I bear them; but prudence forbids;—not that it would injure me, but it might embarrass them; for it is almost an unpardonable offense to teach slaves to read in this Christian country. It is enough to say of the dear little fellows, that they lived on Philpot Street, very near Durgin & Bailey's ship-yard. I used to talk this matter of slavery over with them. I would sometimes say to them, I wished I could be as free as they would be when they got to be men. "You will be free as soon as you are twenty-one, *but I am a slave for life*! Have not I as good a right to be free as you have?" These words used to trouble them; they would express for me the liveliest sympathy, and console me with the hope that something would occur by which I might be free.

I was now about twelve years old, and the thought of being *a slave for life* began to bear heavily upon my heart. Just about this time, I got hold of a book entitled *The Columbian Orator*. Every opportunity I got, I used to read this book. Among much of other interesting matter, I found in it a dialogue between a master and his slave. The slave was represented as having run away from his master three times. The dialogue represented the conversation which took place between them, when the slave was retaken the third time. In this dialogue, the whole argument in behalf of slavery was brought forward by the master, all of which was disposed of by the slave. The slave was made to say some very smart as well as impressive things in reply to his master—things which had the desired though unexpected effect; for the conversation resulted in the voluntary emancipation of the slave on the part of the master.

In the same book, I met with one of Sheridan's mighty speeches on and in behalf of Catholic emancipation. These were choice documents to me. I read them over and over again with unabated interest. They gave tongue to interesting thoughts of my own soul, which had frequently flashed through my mind, and died away for want of utterance. The moral which I gained from the dialogue was the power of truth over the conscience of even a slaveholder. What I got from Sheridan was a bold denunciation of slavery, and a powerful vindication of human rights. The reading of these documents enabled me to utter my thoughts, and to meet the arguments brought forward to sustain slavery; but while they relieved me of one difficulty, they brought on another even more painful than the one of which I was relieved. The more I read, the more I was led to abhor and detest my enslavers. I could regard them in no other light than a band of successful robbers, who left their homes, and gone to Africa, and stolen us from our homes, and in a strange land reduced us to slavery. I loathed them as being the meanest as well as the most wicked of men. As I read and contemplated the subject, behold! that very discontentment which Master Hugh had predicted would follow my learning to read had already come, to torment and sting my soul to unutterable anguish. As I writhed under it, I would at times feel that learning to read had been a curse rather than a blessing. It had given me a view of my wretched condition, without the remedy. It opened my eyes to the horrible pit, but to no ladder upon which to get out. In moments of agony, I envied my fellow-slaves for their stupidity. I have often wished myself a beast. I preferred the condition of the meanest reptile to my own. Any thing, no matter what, to get rid of thinking! It was this everlasting thinking of my condition that tormented me. There was no getting rid of it. It was pressed upon me by every object within sight or hearing, animate or inanimate. The silver trump of freedom had roused my soul to eternal wakefulness.

Freedom now appeared, to disappear no more forever. It was heard in every sound, and seen in every thing. It was ever present to torment me with a sense of my wretched condition. I saw nothing without seeing it, I heard nothing without hearing it, and felt nothing without feeling it. It looked from every star, it smiled in every calm, breathed in every wind, and moved in every storm.

I often found myself regretting my own existence, and wishing myself dead; and but for the hope of being free, I have no doubt but that I should have killed myself, or done something for which I should have been killed. While in this state of mind, I was eager to hear any one speak of slavery. I was a ready listener. Every little while, I could hear something about the abolitionists. It was some time before I found what the word meant. It was always used in such connections as to make it an interesting word to me. If a slave ran away and succeeded in getting clear, or if a slave killed his master, set fire to a barn, or did any thing very wrong in the mind of a slaveholder, it was spoken of as the fruit of abolition. Hearing the word in this connection very often, I set about learning what it meant. The dictionary afforded me little or no help. I found it was "the act of abolishing"; but then I did not know what was to be abolished. Here I was perplexed. I did not dare to ask any one about its meaning, for I was satisfied that it was something they wanted me to know very little about. After a patient waiting, I got one of our city papers, containing an account of the number of petitions from the north, praying for the abolition of slavery in the District of Columbia, and of the slave trade between the states. From this time I understood the words abolition and abolitionist, and always drew near when that word was spoken, expecting to hear something of importance to myself and fellow-slaves. The light broke in upon me by degrees. I went one day down on the wharf of Mr. Waters; and seeing two Irishmen unloading a scow of stone, I went, unasked, and helped them. When we had finished, one of them came to me and asked me if I were a slave. I told him I was. He asked, "Are ye a slave for life?" I told him that I was. The good Irishman seemed to be deeply affected by the statement. He said to the other that it was a pity so fine a little fellow as myself should be a slave for life. He said it was a shame to hold me. They both advised me to run away to the north; that I should find friends there, and that I should be free. I pretended not to be interested in what they said, and treated them as if I did not understand them; for

I feared they might be treacherous. White men have been known to encourage slaves to escape, and then, to get the reward, catch them and return them to their masters. I was afraid that these seemingly good men might use me so; but I nevertheless remembered their advice, and from that time I resolved to run away. I looked forward to a time at which it would be safe for me to escape. I was too young to think of doing so immediately; besides, I wished to learn how to write, as I might have occasion to write my own pass. I consoled myself with the hope that I should one day find a good chance. Meanwhile, I would learn to write.

The idea as to how I might learn to write was suggested to me by being in Durgin & Bailey's ship-yard, and frequently seeing the ship carpenters, after hewing, and getting a piece of timber ready for use, write on the timber the name of that part of the ship for which it was intended. When a piece of timber was intended for the larboard side, it would be marked thus—"L." When a piece was for the starboard side, it would be marked thus—"S." A piece for the larboard side forward, would be marked thus—"L. F." When a piece was for starboard side forward, it would be marked thus—"S. F." For larboard aft, it would be marked thus—"L. A." For starboard aft, it would be marked thus— "S. A." I soon learned the names of these letters, and for what they were intended when placed upon a piece of timber in the ship-yard. I immediately commenced copying them, and in a short time was able to make the four letters named. After that, when I met with any boy who I knew could write, I would tell him I could write as well as he. The next word would be, "I don't believe you. Let me see you try it." I would then make the letters which I had been so fortunate as to learn, and ask him to beat that. In this way I got a good many lessons in writing, which it is quite possible I should never have gotten in any other way. During this time, my copybook was the board fence, brick wall, and pavement; my pen and ink was a lump of chalk. With these, I learned mainly how to write. I then commenced and continued copying the Italics in *Webster's Spelling Book*, until I could make them all without looking on the book. By this time, my little Master Thomas had gone to school, and learned how to write, and had written over a number of copybooks. These had been brought home, and shown to some of our near neighbors, and then laid aside. My mistress used to go to class meeting at the Wilk Street meeting-house every Monday afternoon, and leave me to take care of the house. When left thus, I used to spend the time in writing in the spaces left in Master Thomas's copybook, copying what he had written. I continued to do this until I could write a hand very similar to that of Master Thomas. Thus, after a long, tedious effort for years, I finally succeeded in learning how to write.

# CHAPTER VIII

In a very short time after I went to live at Baltimore, my old master's youngest son Richard died; and in about three years and six months after his death, my old master, Captain Anthony, died, leaving only his son, Andrew, and daughter, Lucretia, to share his estate. He died while on a visit to see his daughter at Hillsborough. Cut off thus unexpectedly, he left no will as to the disposal of his property. It was therefore necessary to have a valuation of the property, that it might be equally divided between Mrs. Lucretia and Master Andrew. I was immediately sent for, to be valued with the other property. Here again my feelings rose up in detestation of slavery. I had now a new conception of my degraded condition. Prior to this, I had become, if not insensible to my lot, at least partly so. I left Baltimore with a young heart overborne with sadness, and a soul full of apprehension. I took passage with Captain Rowe, in the schooner *Wild Cat*, and, after a sail of about twenty-four hours, I found myself near the place of my birth. I had now been absent from it almost, if not quite, five years. I, however, remembered the place very well. I was only about five years old when I left it, to go and live with my old master on Colonel Lloyd's plantation; so that I was now between ten and eleven years old.

We were all ranked together at the valuation. Men and women, old and young, married and single, were ranked with horses, sheep, and swine. There were horses and men, cattle and women, pigs and children, all holding the same rank in the scale of being, and were all subjected to the same narrow examination. Silvery-headed age and sprightly youth, maids and matrons, had to undergo the same indelicate inspection. At this moment, I saw more clearly than ever the brutalizing effects of slavery upon both slave and slaveholder.

After the valuation, then came the division. I have no language to express the high excitement and deep anxiety which were felt among us poor slaves during this time. Our fate for life was now to be decided. We had no more voice in that decision than the brutes among whom we were ranked. A single word from the white men was enough—against all our wishes, prayers, and entreaties—to sunder forever the dearest friends, dearest kindred, and strongest ties known to human beings. In addition to the pain of separation, there was the horrid dread of falling into the hands of Master Andrew. He was known to us all as being a most cruel wretch—a common drunkard, who had, by his reckless mismanagement and profligate dissipation, already wasted a large portion of his father's property. We all felt that we might as well be sold at once to the Georgia traders, as to pass into his hands; for we knew that that would be our inevitable condition—a condition held by us all in the utmost horror and dread.

I suffered more anxiety than most of my fellow-slaves. I had known what it was to be kindly treated; they had known nothing of the kind. They had seen little or nothing of the world. They were in very deed men and women of sorrow, and acquainted with grief. Their backs had been made familiar with the bloody lash, so that they had become callous; mine was yet tender; for while at Baltimore I got few whippings, and few slaves could boast of a kinder master and mistress than myself; and the thought of passing out of their hands into those of Master Andrew—a man who, but a few days before, to give me a sample of his bloody disposition, took my little brother by the throat, threw him on the ground, and with the heel of his boot stamped upon his head till the blood gushed from his nose and ears—was well calculated to make me anxious as to my fate. After he had committed this savage outrage upon my brother, he turned to me, and said that was the way he meant to serve me one of these days—meaning, I suppose, when I came into his possession.

Thanks to a kind Providence, I fell to the portion of Mrs. Lucretia, and was sent immediately back to Baltimore, to live again in the family of Master Hugh. Their joy at my return equaled their sorrow at my departure. It was a glad day to me. I had escaped a worse than lion's jaws. I was absent from Baltimore, for the purpose of valuation and division, just about one month, and it seemed to have been six.

Very soon after my return to Baltimore, my mistress, Lucretia, died, leaving her husband and one child, Amanda; and in a very short time after her death, Master Andrew died. Now all the property of my old master, slaves included, was in the hands of strangers—strangers who had had nothing to do with accumulating it. Not a slave was left free. All remained slaves, from the youngest to the oldest. If any one thing in my experience, more than another, served to deepen my conviction of the infernal character of slavery, and to fill me with unutterable loathing of slaveholders, it was their base ingratitude to my poor old grandmother. She had served my old master faithfully from youth to old age. She had been the source of all his wealth; she had peopled his plantation with slaves; she had become a great grandmother in his service. She had rocked him in infancy, attended him in childhood, served him through life, and at his death wiped from his icy brow the cold death-sweat, and closed his eyes forever. She was nevertheless left a slave—a slave for life—a slave in the hands of strangers; and in their hands she saw her children, her grandchildren, and her great-grandchildren, divided, like so many sheep, without being gratified with the small privilege of a single word, as to their or her own destiny. And, to cap the climax of their base ingratitude and fiendish barbarity, my grandmother, who was now very old, having outlived my old master and all his children, having seen the beginning and end of all of them, and her present owners finding she was of but little value, her frame already racked with the pains of old age, and complete helplessness fast stealing over her once active limbs, they took her to the woods, built her a little hut, put up a little mud-chimney, and then made her welcome to the privilege of supporting herself there in perfect loneliness; thus virtually turning her out to die! If my poor old grandmother now lives, she lives to suffer in utter loneliness; she lives to remember and mourn over the loss of children, the loss of grandchildren, and the loss of great-grandchildren. They are, in the language of the slave's poet, Whittier,

> Gone, gone, sold and gone
> To the rice swamp dank and lone,
> Where the slave-whip ceaseless swings,
> Where the noisome insect stings,
> Where the fever-demon strews
> Poison with the falling dews,
> Where the sickly sunbeams glare
> Through the hot and misty air—
>   Gone, gone, sold and gone
>   To the rice swamp dank and lone,
>   From Virginia hills and waters—
>   Woe is me, my stolen daughters!*

---

* From "The Farewell of a Virginia Slave Mother of Her Daughters Sold into Southern Bondage" by John Greenleaf Whittier

The hearth is desolate. The children, the unconscious children, who once sang and danced in her presence, are gone. She gropes her way, in the darkness of age, for a drink of water. Instead of the voices of her children, she hears by day the moans of the dove, and by night the screams of the hideous owl. All is gloom. The grave is at the door. And now, when weighed down by the pains and aches of old age, when the head inclines to the feet, when the beginning and ending of human existence meet, and helpless infancy and painful old age combine together—at this time, this most needful time, the time for the exercise of that tenderness and affection which children only can exercise towards a declining parent—my poor old grandmother, the devoted mother of twelve children, is left all alone, in yonder little hut, before a few dim embers. She stands—she sits—she staggers—she falls—she groans—she dies—and there are none of her children or grandchildren present, to wipe from her wrinkled brow the cold sweat of death, or to place beneath the sod her fallen remains. Will not a righteous God visit for these things?

In about two years after the death of Mrs. Lucretia, Master Thomas married his second wife. Her name was Rowena Hamilton. She was the eldest daughter of Mr. William Hamilton. Master now lived in St. Michael's. Not long after his marriage, a misunderstanding took place between himself and Master Hugh; and as a means of punishing his brother, he took me from him to live with himself at St. Michael's. Here I underwent another most painful separation. It, however, was not so severe as the one I dreaded at the division of property; for, during this interval, a great change had taken place in Master Hugh and his once kind and affectionate wife. The influence of brandy upon him, and of slavery upon her, had effected a disastrous change in the characters of both; so that, as far as they were concerned, I thought I had little to lose by the change. But it was not to them that I was attached. It was to those little Baltimore boys that I felt the strongest attachment. I had received many good lessons from them, and was still receiving them, and the thought of leaving them was painful indeed. I was leaving, too, without the hope of ever being allowed to return. Master Thomas had said he would never let me return again. The barrier betwixt himself and brother he considered impassable.

I then had to regret that I did not at least make the attempt to carry out my resolution to run away; for the chances of success are tenfold greater from the city than from the country.

I sailed from Baltimore for St. Michael's in the sloop *Amanda*, Captain Edward Dodson. On my passage, I paid particular attention to the direction which the steamboats took to go to Philadelphia. I found, instead of going down, on reaching North Point they went up the bay, in a north-easterly direction. I deemed this knowledge of the utmost importance. My determination to run away was again revived. I resolved to wait only so long as the offering of a favorable opportunity. When that came, I was determined to be off.

# CHAPTER IX

I have now reached a period of my life when I can give dates. I left Baltimore, and went to live with Master Thomas Auld, at St. Michael's, in March, 1832. It was now more than seven years since I lived with him in the family of my old master, on Colonel Lloyd's plantation. We of course were now almost entire strangers to each other. He was to me a new master, and I to him a new slave. I was ignorant of his temper and disposition; he was equally so of mine. A very short time, however, brought us into full acquaintance with each other. I was made acquainted with his wife not less than with himself. They were well matched, being equally mean and cruel. I was now, for the first time during a space of more than seven years, made to feel the painful gnawings of hunger—a something which I had not experienced before since I left Colonel Lloyd's plantation. It went hard enough with me then, when I could look back to no period at which I had enjoyed a sufficiency. It was tenfold harder after living in Master Hugh's family, where I had always had enough to eat, and of that which was good. I have said Master Thomas was a mean man. He was so. Not to give a slave enough to eat, is regarded as the most aggravated development of meanness even among slaveholders. The rule is, no matter how coarse the food, only let there be enough of it. This is the theory; and in the part of Maryland from which I came, it is the general practice—though there are many exceptions. Master Thomas gave us enough of neither coarse nor fine food. There were four slaves of us in the kitchen—my sister Eliza, my aunt Priscilla, Henny, and myself; and we were allowed less than a half of a bushel of cornmeal per week, and very little else, either in the shape of meat or vegetables. It was not enough for us to subsist upon. We were therefore reduced to the wretched necessity of living at the expense of our neighbors. This we did by begging and stealing, whichever came handy in the time of need, the one being considered as legitimate as the other. A great many times have we poor creatures been nearly perishing with hunger, when food in abundance lay mouldering in the safe and smoke-house, and our pious mistress was aware of the fact; and yet that mistress and her husband would kneel every morning, and pray that God would bless them in basket and store!

Bad as all slaveholders are, we seldom meet one destitute of every element of character commanding respect. My master was one of this rare sort. I do not know of one single noble act ever performed by him. The leading trait in his character was meanness; and if there were any other element in his nature, it was made subject to this. He was mean; and, like most other mean men, he lacked the ability to conceal his meanness. Captain Auld was not born a slaveholder. He had been a poor man, master only of a Bay craft. He came into possession of all his slaves by marriage; and of all men, adopted slaveholders are the worst. He was cruel, but cowardly. He commanded without firmness. In the enforcement of his rules, he was at times rigid, and at times lax. At times, he spoke to his slaves with the firmness of Napoleon and the fury of a demon; at other times, he might well be mistaken for an inquirer who had lost his way. He did nothing of himself. He might have passed for a lion, but for his ears. In all things noble which he attempted, his own meanness shone most conspicuous. His airs, words, and actions, were the airs, words, and actions of born slaveholders, and, being assumed, were awkward enough. He was not even a good imitator. He possessed all the disposition to deceive, but wanted the power. Having no resources within himself, he was compelled to be the copyist of many, and being such, he was forever the victim of inconsistency; and of consequence he was an object of contempt, and was held as such even by his slaves. The luxury of having slaves of his own to wait upon him was something new and unprepared for. He was a slaveholder without the ability to hold slaves. He found himself incapable of managing his slaves either by force, fear, or fraud. We seldom called him "master"; we generally called him "Captain Auld," and were hardly disposed to title him at all. I doubt not that our conduct had much to do with making him appear awkward, and of consequence fretful. Our want of reverence for him must have perplexed him greatly. He wished to have us call him master, but lacked the firmness necessary to command us to do so. His wife used to insist upon our calling him so, but to no purpose. In August, 1832, my master attended a Methodist camp-meeting held in the Bay-side, Talbot County, and there experienced religion. I indulged a faint hope that his conversion would lead him to emancipate his slaves, and that, if he did not do this, it would, at any rate, make him more kind and humane. I was disappointed in both these respects. It neither made him to be humane to his slaves, nor to emancipate them. If it had any effect on his character, it made him more cruel and hateful in all his ways; for I believe him to have been a much worse man after his conversion than before. Prior to his conversion, he relied upon his own depravity to shield and sustain him in his savage barbarity; but after his conversion, he found religious sanction and support for his slaveholding cruelty. He made the greatest pretensions to piety. His house was the house of prayer. He prayed morning, noon, and night. He very soon distinguished himself among his brethren, and was soon made a class-leader and exhorter. His activity in revivals was great, and he proved himself an instrument in the hands of the church in converting many souls. His house was the preachers' home. They used to take great pleasure in coming there to put up; for while he starved us, he stuffed them. We have had three or four preachers there at a time. The names of those who used to come most frequently while I lived there, were Mr. Storks, Mr. Ewery, Mr. Humphry, and Mr. Hickey. I have also seen Mr. George Cookman at our house. We slaves loved Mr. Cookman. We believed him to be a good man. We thought him instrumental in getting Mr. Samuel Harrison, a very rich slaveholder, to emancipate his slaves; and by some means got the impression that he was laboring to effect the emancipation of all the slaves. When he was at our house, we were sure to be called in to prayers. When the others were there, we were sometimes called in and sometimes not. Mr. Cookman took more notice of us than either of the other ministers. He could not come among us without betraying his sympathy for us, and, stupid as we were, we had the sagacity to see it.

While I lived with my master in St. Michael's, there was a white young man, a Mr. Wilson, who proposed to keep a Sabbath school for the instruction of such slaves as might be disposed to learn to read the New Testament. We met but three times, when Mr. West and Mr. Fairbanks, both class-leaders, with many others, came upon us with sticks and other missiles, drove us off, and forbade us to meet again. Thus ended our little Sabbath school in the pious town of St. Michael's.

I have said my master found religious sanction for his cruelty. As an example, I will state one of many facts going to prove the charge. I have seen him tie up a lame young woman, and whip her with a heavy cowskin upon her naked shoulders, causing the warm red blood to drip;

and, in justification of the bloody deed, he would quote this passage of Scripture—"He that knoweth his master's will, and doeth it not, shall be beaten with many stripes."

Master would keep this lacerated young woman tied up in this horrid situation four or five hours at a time. I have known him to tie her up early in the morning, and whip her before breakfast; leave her, go to his store, return at dinner, and whip her again, cutting her in the places already made raw with his cruel lash. The secret of master's cruelty toward "Henny" is found in the fact of her being almost helpless. When quite a child, she fell into the fire, and burned herself horribly. Her hands were so burnt that she never got the use of them. She could do very little but bear heavy burdens. She was to master a bill of expense; and as he was a mean man, she was a constant offense to him. He seemed desirous of getting the poor girl out of existence. He gave her away once to his sister; but, being a poor gift, she was not disposed to keep her. Finally, my benevolent master, to use his own words, "set her adrift to take care of herself." Here was a recently-converted man, holding on upon the mother, and at the same time turning out her helpless child, to starve and die! Master Thomas was one of the many pious slaveholders who hold slaves for the very charitable purpose of taking care of them.

My master and myself had quite a number of differences. He found me unsuitable to his purpose. My city life, he said, had had a very pernicious effect upon me. It had almost ruined me for every good purpose, and fitted me for every thing which was bad. One of my greatest faults was that of letting his horse run away, and go down to his father-in-law's farm, which was about five miles from St. Michael's. I would then have to go after it. My reason for this kind of carelessness, or carefulness, was, that I could always get something to eat when I went there. Master William Hamilton, my master's father-in-law, always gave his slaves enough to eat. I never left there hungry, no matter how great the need of my speedy return. Master Thomas at length said he would stand it no longer. I had lived with him nine months, during which time he had given me a number of severe whippings, all to no good purpose. He resolved to put me out, as he said, to be broken; and, for this purpose, he let me for one year to a man named Edward Covey. Mr. Covey was a poor man, a farm-renter. He rented the place upon which he lived, as also the hands with which he tilled it. Mr. Covey had acquired a very high reputation for breaking young slaves, and this reputation was of immense value to him. It enabled him to get his farm tilled with much less expense to himself than he could have had it done without such a reputation. Some slaveholders thought it not much loss to allow Mr. Covey to have their slaves one year, for the sake of the training to which they were subjected, without any other compensation. He could hire young help with great ease, in consequence of this reputation. Added to the natural good qualities of Mr. Covey, he was a professor of religion—a pious soul—a member and a class-leader in the Methodist church. All of this added weight to his reputation as a "nigger-breaker." I was aware of all the facts, having been made acquainted with them by a young man who had lived there. I nevertheless made the change gladly; for I was sure of getting enough to eat, which is not the smallest consideration to a hungry man.

# CHAPTER X

I had left Master Thomas's house, and went to live with Mr. Covey, on the 1st of January, 1833. I was now, for the first time in my life, a field hand. In my new employment, I found myself even more awkward than a country boy appeared to be in a large city. I had been at my new home but one week before Mr. Covey gave me a very severe whipping, cutting my back, causing the blood to run, and raising ridges on my flesh as large as my little finger. The details of this affair are as follows: Mr. Covey sent me, very early in the morning of one of our coldest days in the month of January, to the woods, to get a load of wood. He gave me a team of unbroken oxen. He told me which was the in-hand ox, and which the off-hand one. He then tied the end of a large rope around the horns of the in-hand ox, and gave me the other end of it, and told me, if the oxen started to run, that I must hold on upon the rope. I had never driven oxen before, and of course I was very awkward. I, however, succeeded in getting to the edge of the woods with little difficulty; but I had got a very few rods into the woods, when the oxen took fright, and started full tilt, carrying the cart against trees, and over stumps, in the most frightful manner. I expected every moment that my brains would be dashed out against the trees. After running thus for a considerable distance, they finally upset the cart, dashing it with great force against a tree, and threw themselves into a dense thicket. How I escaped death, I do not know. There I was, entirely alone, in a thick wood, in a place new to me. My cart was upset and shattered, my oxen were entangled among the young trees, and there was none to help me. After a long spell of effort, I succeeded in getting my cart righted, my oxen disentangled, and again yoked to the cart. I now proceeded with my team to the place where I had, the day before, been chopping wood, and loaded my cart pretty heavily, thinking in this way to tame my oxen. I then proceeded on my way home. I had now consumed one half of the day. I got out of the woods safely, and now felt out of danger. I stopped my oxen to open the woods gate; and just as I did so, before I could get hold of my ox-rope, the oxen again started, rushed through the gate, catching it between the wheel and the body of the cart, tearing it to pieces, and coming within a few inches of crushing me against the gate-post. Thus twice, in one short day, I escaped death by the merest chance. On my return, I told Mr. Covey what had happened, and how it happened. He ordered me to return to the woods again immediately. I did so, and he followed on after me. Just as I got into the woods, he came up and told me to stop my cart, and that he would teach me how to trifle away my time, and break gates. He then went to a large gum-tree, and with his ax cut three large switches, and, after trimming them up neatly with his pocketknife, he ordered me to take off my clothes. I made him no answer, but stood with my clothes on. He repeated his order. I still made him no answer, nor did I move to strip myself. Upon this he rushed at me with the fierceness of a tiger, tore off my clothes, and lashed me till he had worn out his switches, cutting me so savagely as to leave the marks visible for a long time after. This whipping was the first of a number just like it, and for similar offenses.

I lived with Mr. Covey one year. During the first six months, of that year, scarce a week passed without his whipping me. I was seldom free from a sore back. My awkwardness was almost always his excuse for whipping me. We were worked fully up to the point of endurance. Long before day we were up, our horses fed, and by the first approach of day we were off to the field with our hoes and plowing teams. Mr. Covey gave us enough to eat, but scarce time to eat it. We were often less than five minutes taking our meals. We were often in the field from the first approach of day till its last lingering ray had left us; and at saving-fodder time, midnight often caught us in the field binding blades.

Covey would be out with us. The way he used to stand it, was this. He would spend the most of his afternoons in bed. He would then come out fresh in the evening, ready to urge us on with his words, example, and frequently with the whip. Mr. Covey was one of the few slaveholders who could and did work with his hands. He was a hard-working man. He knew by himself just what a man or a boy could do. There was no deceiving him. His work went on in his absence almost as well as in his presence; and he had the faculty of making us feel that he was ever present with us. This he did by surprising us. He seldom approached the spot where we were at work openly, if he could do it secretly. He always aimed at taking us by surprise. Such was his cunning, that we used to call him, among ourselves, "the snake." When we were at work in the cornfield, he would sometimes crawl on his hands and knees to avoid detection, and all at once he would rise nearly in our midst, and scream out, "Ha, ha! Come, come! Dash on, dash on!" This being his mode of attack, it was never safe to stop a single minute. His comings were like a thief in the night. He appeared to us as being ever at hand. He was under every tree, behind every stump, in every bush, and at every window, on the plantation. He would sometimes mount his horse, as if bound to St. Michael's, a distance of seven miles, and in half an hour afterwards you would see him coiled up in the corner of the wood-fence, watching every motion of the slaves. He would, for this purpose, leave his horse tied up in the woods. Again, he would sometimes walk up to us, and give us orders as though he was upon the point of starting on a long journey, turn his back upon us, and make as though he was going to the house to get ready; and, before he would get half way thither, he would turn short and crawl into a fence-corner, or behind some tree, and there watch us till the going down of the sun.

Mr. Covey's forte consisted in his power to deceive. His life was devoted to planning and perpetrating the grossest deceptions. Every thing he possessed in the shape of learning or religion, he made conform to his disposition to deceive. He seemed to think himself equal to deceiving the Almighty. He would make a short prayer in the morning, and a long prayer at night; and, strange as it may seem, few men would at times appear more devotional than he. The exercises of his family devotions were always commenced with singing; and, as he was a very poor singer himself, the duty of raising the hymn generally came upon me. He would read his hymn, and nod at me to commence. I would at times do so; at others, I would not. My non-compliance would almost always produce much confusion. To show himself independent of me, he would start and stagger through with his hymn in the most discordant manner. In this state of mind, he prayed with more than ordinary spirit. Poor man! Such was his disposition, and success at deceiving, I do verily believe that he sometimes deceived himself into the solemn belief, that he was a sincere worshipper of the most high God; and this, too, at a time when he may be said to have been guilty of compelling his woman slave to commit the sin of adultery. The facts in the case are these: Mr. Covey was a poor man; he was just commencing in life; he was only able to buy one slave; and, shocking as is the fact, he bought her, as he said, for *a breeder*. This woman was named Caroline. Mr. Covey bought her from Mr. Thomas Lowe, about six miles from St. Michael's. She was a large, able-bodied woman, about twenty years old. She had already given birth to one child, which proved her to be just what he wanted. After buying her, he hired a married man of Mr. Samuel Harrison, to live with him one year; and him he used to fasten up with her every night! The result was, that, at the end of the year, the miserable woman gave birth to twins. At this result Mr. Covey seemed to be highly pleased, both with the man and the wretched woman. Such was his joy, and that of his wife, that nothing they could do for Caroline during her confinement was too good, or too hard, to be done. The children were regarded as being quite an addition to his wealth.

If at any one time of my life more than another, I was made to drink the bitterest dregs of slavery, that time was during the first six months of my stay with Mr. Covey. We were worked in all weathers. It was never too hot or too cold; it could never rain, blow, hail, or snow, too hard for us to work in the field. Work, work, work, was scarcely more the order of the day than of the night. The longest days were too short for him, and the shortest nights too long for him. I was somewhat unmanageable when I first went there, but a few months of this discipline tamed me. Mr. Covey succeeded in breaking me. I was broken in body, soul, and spirit. My natural elasticity was crushed, my intellect languished, the disposition to read departed, the cheerful spark that lingered about my eye died; the dark night of slavery closed in upon me; and behold a man transformed into a brute!

Sunday was my only leisure time. I spent this in a sort of beast-like stupor, between sleep and wake, under some large tree. At times I would rise up, a flash of energetic freedom would dart through my soul, accompanied with a faint beam of hope, that flickered for a moment, and then vanished. I sank down again, mourning over my wretched condition. I was sometimes prompted to take my life, and that of Covey, but was prevented by a combination of hope and fear. My sufferings on this plantation seem now like a dream rather than a stern reality.

Our house stood within a few rods of the Chesapeake Bay, whose broad bosom was ever white with sails from every quarter of the habitable globe. Those beautiful vessels, robed in purest white, so delightful to the eye of freemen, were to me so many shrouded ghosts, to terrify and torment me with thoughts of my wretched condition. I have often, in the deep stillness of a summer's Sabbath, stood all alone upon the lofty banks of that noble bay, and traced, with saddened heart and tearful eye, the countless number of sails moving off to the mighty ocean. The sight of these always affected me powerfully. My thoughts would compel utterance; and there, with no audience but the Almighty, I would pour out my soul's complaint, in my rude way, with an apostrophe to the moving multitude of ships:

"You are loosed from your moorings, and are free; I am fast in my chains, and am a slave! You move merrily before the gentle gale, and I sadly before the bloody whip! You are freedom's swift-winged angels, that fly round the world; I am confined in bands of iron! O that I were free! O, that I were on one of your gallant decks, and under your protecting wing! Alas! Betwixt me and you, the turbid waters roll. Go on, go on. O that I could also go! Could I but swim! If I could fly! O, why was I born a man, of whom to make a brute! The glad ship is gone; she hides in the dim distance. I am left in the hottest hell of unending slavery. O God, save me! God, deliver me! Let me be free! Is there any God? Why am I a slave? I will run away. I will not stand it. Get caught, or get clear, I'll try it. I had as well die with ague as the fever. I have only one life to lose. I had as well be killed running as die standing. Only think of it; one hundred miles straight north, and I am free! Try it? Yes! God helping me, I will. It cannot be that I shall live and die a slave. I will take to the water. This very bay shall yet bear me into freedom. The steamboats steered in a north-east course from North Point. I will do the same; and when I get to the head of the bay, I will turn my canoe adrift, and walk straight through Delaware into Pennsylvania. When I get there, I shall not be required to have a pass; I can travel without being disturbed. Let but the first opportunity offer, and, come what will, I am off. Meanwhile, I will try to bear up under the yoke. I am not the only slave in the world. Why should I fret? I can bear as much as any of them. Besides, I am but a boy, and all boys are bound to some one. It may be that my misery in slavery will only increase my happiness when I get free. There is a better day coming."

Thus I used to think, and thus I used to speak to myself; goaded almost to madness at one moment, and at the next reconciling myself to my wretched lot.

I have already intimated that my condition was much worse, during the first six months of my stay at Mr. Covey's, than in the last six. The circumstances leading to the change in Mr. Covey's course toward me form an epoch in my humble history. You have seen how a man was made a slave; you shall see how a slave was made a man. On one of the hottest days of the month of August, 1833, Bill Smith, William Hughes, a slave named Eli, and myself, were engaged in fanning wheat. Hughes was clearing the fanned wheat from before the fan. Eli was turning, Smith was feeding, and I was carrying wheat to the fan. The work was simple, requiring strength rather than intellect; yet, to one entirely unused to such work, it came very hard. About three o'clock of that day, I broke down; my strength failed me; I was seized with a violent aching of the head, attended with extreme dizziness; I trembled in every limb. Finding what was coming, I nerved myself up, feeling it would never do to stop work. I stood as long as I could stagger to the hopper with grain. When I could stand no longer, I fell, and felt as if held down by an immense weight. The fan of course stopped; every one had his own work to do; and no one could do the work of the other, and have his own go on at the same time.

Mr. Covey was at the house, about one hundred yards from the treading-yard where we were fanning. On hearing the fan stop, he left immediately, and came to the spot where we were. He hastily inquired what the matter was. Bill answered that I was sick, and there was no one to bring wheat to the fan. I had by this time crawled away under the side of the post and rail-fence by which the yard was enclosed, hoping to find relief by getting out of the sun. He then asked where I was. He was told by one of the hands. He came to the spot, and, after looking at me awhile, asked me what was the matter. I told him as well as I could, for I scarce had strength to speak. He then gave me a savage kick in the side, and told me to get up. I tried to do so, but fell back in the attempt. He gave me another kick, and again told me to rise. I again tried, and succeeded in gaining my feet; but, stooping to get the tub with which I was feeding the fan, I again staggered and fell. While down in this situation, Mr. Covey took up the hickory slat with which Hughes had been striking off the half-bushel measure, and with it gave me a heavy blow upon the head, making a large wound, and the blood ran freely; and with this again told me to get up. I made no effort to comply, having now made up my mind to let him do his worst. In a short time after receiving this blow, my head grew better. Mr. Covey had now left me to my fate. At this moment I resolved, for the first time, to go to my master, enter a complaint, and ask his protection. In order to do this, I must that afternoon walk seven miles; and this, under the circumstances, was truly a severe undertaking. I was exceedingly feeble; made so as much by the kicks and blows which I received, as by the severe fit of sickness to which I had been subjected. I, however, watched my chance, while Covey was looking in an opposite direction, and started for St. Michael's. I succeeded in getting a considerable distance on my way to the woods, when Covey discovered me, and called after me to come back, threatening what he would do if I did not come. I disregarded both his calls and his threats, and made my way to the woods as fast as my feeble state would allow; and thinking I might be overhauled by him if I kept the road, I walked through the woods, keeping far enough from the road to avoid detection, and near enough to prevent losing my way. I had not gone far before my little strength again failed me. I could go no farther. I fell down, and lay for a considerable time. The blood was yet oozing from the wound on my head. For a time I thought I should bleed to death; and think now that I should have done so, but that the blood so matted my hair as to stop the wound. After lying there about three quarters of an hour, I nerved myself up again, and started on my way, through bogs and briers, bare-footed and bare-headed, tearing my feet sometimes at nearly every step; and after a journey of about seven miles, occupying some five hours to perform it, I arrived at master's store. I then presented an appearance enough to affect any but a heart of iron. From the crown of my head to my feet, I was covered with blood. My hair was all clotted with dust and blood; my shirt was stiff with blood. I suppose I looked like a man who had escaped a den of wild beasts, and barely escaped them. In this state I appeared before my master, humbly entreating him to interpose his authority for my protection. I told him all the circumstances as well as I could, and it seemed, as I spoke, at times to affect him. He would then walk the floor, and seek to justify Covey by saying he expected I deserved it. He asked me what I wanted. I told him, to let me get a new home; that as sure as I lived with Mr. Covey again, I should live with but to die with him; that Covey would surely kill me; he was in a fair way for it. Master Thomas ridiculed the idea that there was any danger of Mr. Covey's killing me, and said that he knew Mr. Covey; that he was a good man, and that he could not think of taking me from him; that, should he do so, he would lose the whole year's wages; that I belonged to Mr. Covey for one year, and that I must go back to him, come what might; and that I must not trouble him with any more stories, or that he would himself *get hold of me*. After threatening me thus, he gave me a very large dose of salts, telling me that I might remain in St. Michael's that night, (it being quite late), but that I must be off back to Mr. Covey's early in the morning; and that if I did not, he would *get hold of me*, which meant that he would whip me. I remained all night, and, according to his orders, I started off to Covey's in the morning, (Saturday morning), wearied in body and broken in spirit. I got no supper that night, or breakfast that morning. I reached Covey's about nine o'clock; and just as I was getting over the fence that divided Mrs. Kemp's fields from ours, out ran Covey with his cowskin, to give me another whipping. Before he could reach me, I succeeded in getting to the cornfield; and as the corn was very high, it afforded me the means of hiding. He seemed very angry, and searched for me a long time. My behavior was altogether unaccountable. He finally gave up the chase, thinking, I suppose, that I must come home for something to eat; he would give himself no further trouble in looking for me. I spent that day mostly in the woods, having the alternative before me—to go home and be whipped to death, or stay in the woods and be starved to death. That night, I fell in with Sandy Jenkins, a slave with whom I was somewhat acquainted. Sandy had a free wife who lived about four miles from Mr. Covey's; and it being Saturday, he was on his way to see her. I told him my circumstances, and he very kindly invited me to go home with him. I went home with him, and talked this whole matter over, and got his advice as to what course it was best for me to pursue. I found Sandy an old adviser. He told me, with great solemnity, I must go back to Covey; but that before I went, I must go with him into another part of the woods, where there was a certain *root*, which, if I would take some of it with me, carrying it *always on my right side*, would render it impossible for Mr. Covey, or any other white man, to whip me. He said he had carried it for years; and since he had done so, he had never received a blow, and never expected to while he carried it. I at first rejected the idea, that the simple carrying of a root in my pocket would have any such effect as he had said, and was not disposed to take it; but Sandy impressed the necessity with much earnestness, telling me it could do no harm, if it did no good. To please him, I at length took the *root*, and, according to his direction, carried it upon my right side. This was Sunday morning. I immediately started for home; and upon entering the yard gate, out came Mr. Covey on his way to meeting. He spoke to me very kindly, bade me drive the pigs from a lot near by, and passed on towards the church. Now, this singular conduct of Mr. Covey really made me begin to think that there was something in the *root* which Sandy had given me; and had it been on any other day than Sunday, I could have attributed the conduct to no other cause than the influence of that root; and as it was, I was half inclined to think the root to be something more than I at first had taken it to be. All went well till Monday morning. On this morning, the virtue of the *root* was fully tested. Long before daylight, I was called to go and rub, curry, and feed, the horses. I obeyed, and was glad to obey. But whilst thus engaged, whilst in the act of throwing down some blades from the loft, Mr. Covey entered the stable with a long rope; and just as I was half out of the loft, he caught hold of my legs, and was about tying me. As soon as I found what he was up to, I gave a sudden spring, and as I did so, he holding to my legs, I was brought sprawling on the stable floor. Mr. Covey seemed now to think he had me, and could do what he pleased; but at this moment—from whence came the spirit I don't know—I resolved to fight; and, suiting my action to the resolution, I seized Covey hard by the throat; and as I did so, I rose. He held on to me, and I to him. My resistance was so entirely unexpected that Covey seemed taken all aback. He trembled like a leaf. This gave me assurance, and I held him uneasy, causing the blood to run where I touched him with the ends of my fingers. Mr. Covey soon called out to Hughes for help. Hughes came, and, while Covey held me, attempted to tie my right hand. While he was in the act of doing so, I watched my chance, and gave him a heavy kick close under the ribs. This kick fairly sickened Hughes, so that he left me in the hands of Mr. Covey. This kick had the effect of not only weakening Hughes, but Covey also. When he saw Hughes bending over with pain, his courage quailed. He asked me if I meant to persist in my resistance. I told him I did, come what might; that he had used me like a brute for six months, and that I was determined to be used so no longer. With that, he strove to drag me to a stick that was lying just out of the stable door. He meant to knock me down. But just as he was leaning over to get the stick, I seized him with both hands by his collar, and brought him by a sudden snatch to the ground. By this time, Bill came. Covey called upon him for assistance. Bill wanted to know what he could do. Covey said, "Take hold of him, take hold of him!" Bill said his master hired him out to work, and not to help to whip me; so he left Covey and myself to fight our own battle out. We were at it for nearly two hours.

Covey at length let me go, puffing and blowing at a great rate, saying that if I had not resisted, he would not have whipped me half so much. The truth was, that he had not whipped me at all. I considered him as getting entirely the worst end of the bargain; for he had drawn no blood from me, but I had from him. The whole six months afterwards, that I spent with Mr. Covey, he never laid the weight of his finger upon me in anger. He would occasionally say, he didn't want to get hold of me again. "No," thought I, "you need not; for you will come off worse than you did before."

This battle with Mr. Covey was the turning-point in my career as a slave. It rekindled the few expiring embers of freedom, and revived within me a sense of my own manhood. It recalled the departed self-confidence, and inspired me again with a determination to be free. The gratification afforded by the triumph was a full compensation for whatever else might follow, even death itself. He only can understand the deep satisfaction which I experienced, who has himself repelled by force the bloody arm of slavery. I felt as I never felt before. It was a glorious resurrection, from the tomb of slavery, to the heaven of freedom. My long-crushed spirit rose, cowardice departed, bold defiance took its place; and I now resolved that, however long I might remain a slave in form, the day had passed forever when I could be a slave in fact. I did not hesitate to let it be known of me, that the white man who expected to succeed in whipping, must also succeed in killing me.

From this time I was never again what might be called fairly whipped, though I remained a slave four years afterwards. I had several fights, but was never whipped.

It was for a long time a matter of surprise to me why Mr. Covey did not immediately have me taken by the constable to the whipping-post, and there regularly whipped for the crime of raising my hand against a white man in defense of myself. And the only explanation I can now think of does not entirely satisfy me; but such as it is, I will give it. Mr. Covey enjoyed the most unbounded reputation for being a first-rate overseer and Negro-breaker. It was of considerable importance to him. That reputation was at stake; and had he sent me—a boy about sixteen years old—to the public whipping-post, his reputation would have been lost; so, to save his reputation, he suffered me to go unpunished.

My term of actual service to Mr. Edward Covey ended on Christmas day, 1833. The days between Christmas and New Year's day are allowed as holidays; and, accordingly, we were not required to perform any labor, more than to feed and take care of the stock. This time we regarded as our own, by the grace of our masters; and we therefore used or abused it nearly as we pleased. Those of us who had families at a distance, were generally allowed to spend the whole six days in their society. This time, however, was spent in various ways. The staid, sober, thinking and industrious ones of our number would employ themselves in making corn-brooms, mats, horse-collars, and baskets; and another class of us would spend the time in hunting opossums, hares, and coons. But by far the larger part engaged in such sports and merriments as playing ball, wrestling, running foot-races, fiddling, dancing, and drinking whisky; and this latter mode of spending the time was by far the most agreeable to the feelings of our masters. A slave who would work during the holidays was considered by our masters as scarcely deserving them. He was regarded as one who rejected the favor of his master. It was deemed a disgrace not to get drunk at Christmas; and he was regarded as lazy indeed, who had not provided himself with the necessary means, during the year, to get whisky enough to last him through Christmas.

From what I know of the effect of these holidays upon the slave, I believe them to be among the most effective means in the hands of the slaveholder in keeping down the spirit of insurrection. Were the slaveholders at once to abandon this practice, I have not the slightest doubt it would lead to an immediate insurrection among the slaves. These holidays serve as conductors, or safety-valves, to carry off the rebellious spirit of enslaved humanity. But for these, the slave would be forced up to the wildest desperation; and woe betide the slaveholder, the day he ventures to remove or hinder the operation of those conductors! I warn him that, in such an event, a spirit will go forth in their midst, more to be dreaded than the most appalling earthquake.

The holidays are part and parcel of the gross fraud, wrong, and inhumanity of slavery. They are professedly a custom established by the benevolence of the slaveholders; but I undertake to say, it is the result of selfishness, and one of the grossest frauds committed upon the down-trodden slave. They do not give the slaves this time because they would not like to have their work during its continuance, but because they know it would be unsafe to deprive them of it. This will be seen by the fact, that the slaveholders like to have their slaves spend those days just in such a manner as to make them as glad of their ending as of their beginning. Their object seems to be, to disgust their slaves with freedom, by plunging them into the lowest depths of dissipation. For instance, the slaveholders not only like to see the slave drink of his own accord, but will adopt various plans to make him drunk. One plan is, to make bets on their slaves, as to who can drink the most whisky without getting drunk; and in this way they succeed in getting whole multitudes to drink to excess. Thus, when the slave asks for virtuous freedom, the cunning slaveholder, knowing his ignorance, cheats him with a dose of vicious dissipation, artfully labelled with the name of liberty. The most of us used to drink it down, and the result was just what might be supposed; many of us were led to think that there was little to choose between liberty and slavery. We felt, and very properly too, that we had almost as well be slaves to man as to rum. So, when the holidays ended, we staggered up from the filth of our wallowing, took a long breath, and marched to the field—feeling, upon the whole, rather glad to go, from what our master had deceived us into a belief was freedom, back to the arms of slavery.

I have said that this mode of treatment is a part of the whole system of fraud and inhumanity of slavery. It is so. The mode here adopted to disgust the slave with freedom, by allowing him to see only the abuse of it, is carried out in other things. For instance, a slave loves molasses; he steals some. His master, in many cases, goes off to town, and buys a large quantity; he returns, takes his whip, and commands the slave to eat the molasses, until the poor fellow is made sick at the very mention of it. The same mode is sometimes adopted to make the slaves refrain from asking for more food than their regular allowance. A slave runs through his allowance, and applies for more. His master is enraged at him; but, not willing to send him off without food, gives him more than is necessary, and compels him to eat it within a given time. Then, if he complains that he cannot eat it, he is said to be satisfied neither full nor fasting, and is whipped for being hard to please! I have an abundance of such illustrations of the same principle, drawn from my own observation, but think the cases I have cited sufficient. The practice is a very common one.

On the first of January, 1834, I left Mr. Covey, and went to live with Mr. William Freeland, who lived about three miles from St. Michael's. I soon found Mr. Freeland a very different man from Mr. Covey. Though not rich, he was what would be called an educated southern gentleman. Mr. Covey, as I have shown, was a well-trained Negro-breaker and slave-driver. The former (slaveholder though he was) seemed to possess some regard for honor, some reverence for justice, and some respect for humanity. The latter seemed totally insensible to all such sentiments. Mr. Freeland had many of the faults peculiar to slaveholders, such as being very passionate and fretful; but I must do him the justice to say, that he was exceedingly free from those degrading vices to which Mr. Covey was constantly addicted. The one was open and frank, and we always knew where to find him. The other was a most artful deceiver, and could be understood only by such as were skillful enough to detect his cunningly-devised frauds. Another advantage I gained in my new master was, he made no pretensions to, or profession of, religion; and this, in my opinion, was truly a great advantage. I assert most unhesitatingly, that the religion of the south is a mere covering for the most horrid crimes—a justifier of the most appalling barbarity—a sanctifier of the most hateful frauds—and a dark shelter under which the darkest, foulest, grossest, and most infernal deeds of slaveholders find the strongest protection. Were I to be again reduced to the chains of slavery, next to that enslavement, I should regard being the slave of a religious master the greatest calamity that could befall me. For of all slaveholders with whom I have ever met, religious slaveholders are the worst. I have ever found them the meanest and basest, the most cruel and cowardly, of all others. It was my unhappy lot not only to belong to a religious slaveholder, but to live in a community of such religionists. Very near Mr. Freeland lived the Rev. Daniel Weeden, and in the same neighborhood lived the Rev. Rigby Hopkins. These were members and ministers in the Reformed Methodist Church. Mr. Weeden owned, among others, a woman slave, whose name I have forgotten. This woman's back, for weeks, was kept literally raw, made so by the lash of this merciless, *religious* wretch. He used to hire hands. His maxim was, Behave well or behave ill, it is the duty of a master occasionally to whip a slave, to remind him of his master's authority. Such was his theory, and such his practice.

Mr. Hopkins was even worse than Mr. Weeden. His chief boast was his ability to manage slaves. The peculiar feature of his government was that of whipping slaves in advance of deserving it. He always managed to have one or more of his slaves to whip every Monday morning. He did this to alarm their fears, and strike terror into those who escaped. His plan was to whip for the smallest offenses, to prevent the commission of large ones. Mr. Hopkins could always find some excuse for whipping a slave. It would astonish one, unaccustomed to a slaveholding life, to see with what wonderful ease a slaveholder can find things, of which to make occasion to whip a slave. A mere look, word, or motion—a mistake, accident, or want of power—are all matters for which a slave may be whipped at any time. Does a slave look dissatisfied? It is said, he has the devil in him, and it must be whipped out. Does he speak loudly when spoken to by his master? Then he is getting high-minded, and should be taken down a button-hole lower. Does he forget to pull off his hat at the approach of a white person? Then he is wanting in reverence, and should be whipped for it. Does he ever venture to vindicate his conduct, when censured for it? Then he is guilty of impudence—one of the greatest crimes of which a slave can be guilty. Does he ever venture to suggest a different mode of doing things from that pointed out by his master? He is indeed presumptuous, and getting above himself; and nothing less than a flogging will do for him. Does he, while plowing, break a plow—or, while hoeing, break a hoe? It is owing to his carelessness, and for it a slave must always be whipped. Mr. Hopkins could always find something of this sort to justify the use of the lash, and he seldom failed to embrace such opportunities. There was not a man in the whole county, with whom the slaves who had the getting their own home, would not prefer to live, rather than with this Rev. Mr. Hopkins. And yet there was not a man any where round, who made higher professions of religion, or was more active in revivals—more attentive to the class, love-feast, prayer and preaching meetings, or more devotional in his family—that prayed earlier, later, louder, and longer—than this same reverend slave-driver, Rigby Hopkins.

But to return to Mr. Freeland, and to my experience while in his employment. He, like Mr. Covey, gave us enough to eat; but, unlike Mr. Covey, he also gave us sufficient time to take our meals. He worked us hard, but always between sunrise and sunset. He required a good deal of work to be done, but gave us good tools with which to work. His farm was large, but he employed hands enough to work it, and with ease, compared with many of his neighbors. My treatment, while in his employment, was heavenly, compared with what I experienced at the hands of Mr. Edward Covey.

Mr. Freeland was himself the owner of but two slaves. Their names were Henry Harris and John Harris. The rest of his hands he hired. These consisted of myself, Sandy Jenkins,* and Handy Caldwell. Henry and John were quite intelligent, and in a very little while after I went there, I succeeded in creating in them a strong desire to learn how to read. This desire soon sprang up in the others also. They very soon mustered up some old spelling books, and nothing would do but that I must keep a Sabbath school. I agreed to do so, and accordingly devoted my Sundays to teaching these my loved fellow-slaves how to read. Neither of them knew his letters when I went there. Some of the slaves of the neighboring farms found what was going on, and also availed themselves of this little opportunity to learn to read. It was understood, among all who came, that there must be as little display about it as possible. It was necessary to keep our religious masters at St. Michael's unacquainted with the fact, that, instead of spending the Sabbath in wrestling, boxing, and drinking whisky, we were trying to learn how to read the will of God; for they had much rather see us engaged in those degrading sports, than to see us behaving like intellectual, moral, and accountable beings. My blood boils as I think of the bloody manner in which Messrs. Wright Fairbanks and Garrison West, both class-leaders, in connection with many others, rushed in upon us with sticks and stones, and broke up our virtuous little Sabbath school, at St. Michael's—all calling themselves Christians! Humble followers of the Lord Jesus Christ! But I am again digressing.

I held my Sabbath school at the house of a free colored man, whose name I deem it imprudent to mention; for should it be known, it might embarrass him greatly, though the crime of holding the school was committed ten years ago. I had at one time over forty scholars, and those of the right sort, ardently desiring to learn. They were of all ages, though mostly men and women. I look back to those Sundays with an amount of pleasure not to be expressed. They were great days to my soul. The work of instructing my dear fellow-slaves was the sweetest

---

* This is the same man who gave me the roots to prevent my being whipped by Mr. Covey. He was "a clever soul." We used frequently to talk about the fight with Covey, and as often as we did so, he would claim my success as the result of the roots which he gave me. This superstition is very common among the more ignorant slaves. A slave seldom dies but that his death is attributed to trickery. (Original note)

engagement with which I was ever blessed. We loved each other, and to leave them at the close of the Sabbath was a severe cross indeed. When I think that these precious souls are today shut up in the prison-house of slavery, my feelings overcome me, and I am almost ready to ask, "Does a righteous God govern the universe? And for what does he hold the thunders in his right hand, if not to smite the oppressor, and deliver the spoiled out of the hand of the spoiler?" These dear souls came not to Sabbath school because it was popular to do so, nor did I teach them because it was reputable to be thus engaged. Every moment they spent in that school, they were liable to be taken up, and given thirty-nine lashes. They came because they wished to learn. Their minds had been starved by their cruel masters. They had been shut up in mental darkness. I taught them, because it was the delight of my soul to be doing something that looked like bettering the condition of my race. I kept up my school nearly the whole year I lived with Mr. Freeland; and, beside my Sabbath school, I devoted three evenings in the week, during the winter, to teaching the slaves at home. And I have the happiness to know, that several of those who came to Sabbath school learned how to read; and that one, at least, is now free through my agency.

The year passed off smoothly. It seemed only about half as long as the year which preceded it. I went through it without receiving a single blow. I will give Mr. Freeland the credit of being the best master I ever had, *till I became my own master*. For the ease with which I passed the year, I was, however, somewhat indebted to the society of my fellow-slaves. They were noble souls; they not only possessed loving hearts, but brave ones. We were linked and interlinked with each other. I loved them with a love stronger than any thing I have experienced since. It is sometimes said that we slaves do not love and confide in each other. In answer to this assertion, I can say, I never loved any or confided in any people more than my fellow-slaves, and especially those with whom I lived at Mr. Freeland's. I believe we would have died for each other. We never undertook to do any thing, of any importance, without a mutual consultation. We never moved separately. We were one; and as much so by our tempers and dispositions, as by the mutual hardships to which we were necessarily subjected by our condition as slaves.

At the close of the year 1834, Mr. Freeland again hired me of my master, for the year 1835. But, by this time, I began to want to live *upon free land* as well as *with Freeland*; and I was no longer content, therefore, to live with him or any other slaveholder. I began, with the commencement of the year, to prepare myself for a final struggle, which should decide my fate one way or the other. My tendency was upward. I was fast approaching manhood, and year after year had passed, and I was still a slave. These thoughts roused me—I must do something. I therefore resolved that 1835 should not pass without witnessing an attempt, on my part, to secure my liberty. But I was not willing to cherish this determination alone. My fellow-slaves were dear to me. I was anxious to have them participate with me in this, my life-giving determination. I therefore, though with great prudence, commenced early to ascertain their views and feelings in regard to their condition, and to imbue their minds with thoughts of freedom. I bent myself to devising ways and means for our escape, and meanwhile strove, on all fitting occasions, to impress them with the gross fraud and inhumanity of slavery. I went first to Henry, next to John, then to the others. I found, in them all, warm hearts and noble spirits. They were ready to hear, and ready to act when a feasible plan should be proposed. This was what I wanted. I talked to them of our want of manhood, if we submitted to our enslavement without at least one noble effort to be free. We met often, and consulted frequently, and told our hopes and fears, recounted the difficulties, real and imagined, which we should be called on to meet. At times we were almost disposed to give up, and try to content ourselves with our wretched lot; at others, we were firm and unbending in our determination to go. Whenever we suggested any plan, there was shrinking—the odds were fearful. Our path was beset with the greatest obstacles; and if we succeeded in gaining the end of it, our right to be free was yet questionable—we were yet liable to be returned to bondage. We could see no spot, this side of the ocean, where we could be free. We knew nothing about Canada. Our knowledge of the north did not extend farther than New York; and to go there, and be forever harassed with the frightful liability of being returned to slavery—with the certainty of being treated tenfold worse than before—the thought was truly a horrible one, and one which it was not easy to overcome. The case sometimes stood thus: At every gate through which we were to pass, we saw a watchman— at every ferry a guard—on every bridge a sentinel—and in every wood a patrol. We were hemmed in upon every side. Here were the difficulties, real or imagined—the good to be sought, and the evil to be shunned. On the one hand, there stood slavery, a stern reality, glaring frightfully upon us,—its robes already crimsoned with the blood of millions, and even now feasting itself greedily upon our own flesh. On the other hand, away back in the dim distance, under the flickering light of the north star, behind some craggy hill or snow-covered mountain, stood a doubtful freedom—half frozen—beckoning us to come and share its hospitality. This in itself was sometimes enough to stagger us; but when we permitted ourselves to survey the road, we were frequently appalled. Upon either side we saw grim death, assuming the most horrid shapes. Now it was starvation, causing us to eat our own flesh—now we were contending with the waves, and were drowned— now we were overtaken, and torn to pieces by the fangs of the terrible bloodhound. We were stung by scorpions, chased by wild beasts, bitten by snakes, and finally, after having nearly reached the desired spot— after swimming rivers, encountering wild beasts, sleeping in the woods, suffering hunger and nakedness—we were overtaken by our pursuers, and, in our resistance, we were shot dead upon the spot! I say, this picture sometimes appalled us, and made us

> rather bear those ills we had,
> Than fly to others, that we knew not of.[*]

In coming to a fixed determination to run away, we did more than Patrick Henry, when he resolved upon liberty or death. With us it was a doubtful liberty at most, and almost certain death if we failed. For my part, I should prefer death to hopeless bondage.

Sandy, one of our number, gave up the notion, but still encouraged us. Our company then consisted of Henry Harris, John Harris, Henry Bailey, Charles Roberts, and myself. Henry Bailey was my uncle, and belonged to my master. Charles married my aunt: he belonged to my master's father-in-law, Mr. William Hamilton.

The plan we finally concluded upon was, to get a large canoe belonging to Mr. Hamilton, and upon the Saturday night previous to Easter holidays, paddle directly up the Chesapeake Bay. On our arrival at the head of the bay, a distance of seventy or eighty miles from where we lived, it was our purpose to turn our canoe adrift, and follow the guidance of the north star till we got beyond the limits of Maryland.

---

[*] From *Hamlet* by William Shakespeare.

Our reason for taking the water route was, that we were less liable to be suspected as runaways; we hoped to be regarded as fishermen; whereas, if we should take the land route, we should be subjected to interruptions of almost every kind. Any one having a white face, and being so disposed, could stop us, and subject us to examination.

The week before our intended start, I wrote several protections, one for each of us. As well as I can remember, they were in the following words, to wit:

> *This is to certify that I, the undersigned, have given the bearer, my servant, full liberty to go to Baltimore, and spend the Easter holidays. Written with mine own hand, etc., 1835.*
>
> *William Hamilton,*
> *Near St. Michael's, in Talbot County, Maryland*

We were not going to Baltimore; but, in going up the bay, we went toward Baltimore, and these protections were only intended to protect us while on the bay.

As the time drew near for our departure, our anxiety became more and more intense. It was truly a matter of life and death with us. The strength of our determination was about to be fully tested. At this time, I was very active in explaining every difficulty, removing every doubt, dispelling every fear, and inspiring all with the firmness indispensable to success in our undertaking; assuring them that half was gained the instant we made the move; we had talked long enough; we were now ready to move; if not now, we never should be; and if we did not intend to move now, we had as well fold our arms, sit down, and acknowledge ourselves fit only to be slaves. This, none of us were prepared to acknowledge. Every man stood firm; and at our last meeting, we pledged ourselves afresh, in the most solemn manner, that, at the time appointed, we would certainly start in pursuit of freedom. This was in the middle of the week, at the end of which we were to be off. We went, as usual, to our several fields of labor, but with bosoms highly agitated with thoughts of our truly hazardous undertaking. We tried to conceal our feelings as much as possible; and I think we succeeded very well.

After a painful waiting, the Saturday morning, whose night was to witness our departure, came. I hailed it with joy, bring what of sadness it might. Friday night was a sleepless one for me. I probably felt more anxious than the rest, because I was, by common consent, at the head of the whole affair. The responsibility of success or failure lay heavily upon me. The glory of the one, and the confusion of the other, were alike mine. The first two hours of that morning were such as I never experienced before, and hope never to again. Early in the morning, we went, as usual, to the field. We were spreading manure; and all at once, while thus engaged, I was overwhelmed with an indescribable feeling, in the fullness of which I turned to Sandy, who was near by, and said, "We are betrayed!" "Well," said he, "that thought has this moment struck me." We said no more. I was never more certain of any thing.

The horn was blown as usual, and we went up from the field to the house for breakfast. I went for the form, more than for want of any thing to eat that morning. Just as I got to the house, in looking out at the lane gate, I saw four white men, with two colored men. The white men were on horseback, and the colored ones were walking behind, as if tied. I watched them a few moments till they got up to our lane gate. Here they halted, and tied the colored men to the gate-post. I was not yet certain as to what the matter was. In a few moments, in rode Mr. Hamilton, with a speed betokening great excitement. He came to the door, and inquired if Master William was in. He was told he was at the barn. Mr. Hamilton, without dismounting, rode up to the barn with extraordinary speed. In a few moments, he and Mr. Freeland returned to the house. By this time, the three constables rode up, and in great haste dismounted, tied their horses, and met Master William and Mr. Hamilton returning from the barn; and after talking awhile, they all walked up to the kitchen door. There was no one in the kitchen but myself and John. Henry and Sandy were up at the barn. Mr. Freeland put his head in at the door, and called me by name, saying, there were some gentlemen at the door who wished to see me. I stepped to the door, and inquired what they wanted. They at once seized me, and, without giving me any satisfaction, tied me—lashing my hands closely together. I insisted upon knowing what the matter was. They at length said, that they had learned I had been in a "scrape," and that I was to be examined before my master; and if their information proved false, I should not be hurt.

In a few moments, they succeeded in tying John. They then turned to Henry, who had by this time returned, and commanded him to cross his hands. "I won't!" said Henry, in a firm tone, indicating his readiness to meet the consequences of his refusal. "Won't you?" said Tom Graham, the constable. "No, I won't!" said Henry, in a still stronger tone. With this, two of the constables pulled out their shining pistols, and swore, by their Creator, that they would make him cross his hands or kill him. Each cocked his pistol, and, with fingers on the trigger, walked up to Henry, saying, at the same time, if he did not cross his hands, they would blow his damned heart out. "Shoot me, shoot me!" said Henry; "you can't kill me but once. Shoot, shoot—and be damned! *I won't be tied!*" This he said in a tone of loud defiance; and at the same time, with a motion as quick as lightning, he with one single stroke dashed the pistols from the hand of each constable. As he did this, all hands fell upon him, and, after beating him some time, they finally overpowered him, and got him tied.

During the scuffle, I managed, I know not how, to get my pass out, and, without being discovered, put it into the fire. We were all now tied; and just as we were to leave for Easton jail, Betsy Freeland, mother of William Freeland, came to the door with her hands full of biscuits, and divided them between Henry and John. She then delivered herself of a speech, to the following effect: addressing herself to me, she said, "*You devil! You yellow devil!* It was you that put it into the heads of Henry and John to run away. But for you, you long-legged mulatto devil! Henry nor John would never have thought of such a thing." I made no reply, and was immediately hurried off towards St. Michael's. Just a moment previous to the scuffle with Henry, Mr. Hamilton suggested the propriety of making a search for the protections which he had understood Frederick had written for himself and the rest. But, just at the moment he was about carrying his proposal into effect, his aid was needed in helping to tie Henry; and the excitement attending the scuffle caused them either to forget, or to deem it unsafe, under the circumstances, to search. So we were not yet convicted of the intention to run away.

When we got about half way to St. Michael's, while the constables having us in charge were looking ahead, Henry inquired of me what he should do with his pass. I told him to eat it with his biscuit, and own nothing; and we passed the word around, "*Own nothing*"; and "*Own nothing!*" said we all. Our confidence in each other was unshaken. We were resolved to succeed or fail together, after the calamity had befallen us as much as before. We were now prepared for any thing. We were to be dragged that morning fifteen miles behind horses, and then to be placed in the Easton jail. When we reached St. Michael's, we underwent a sort of examination. We all denied that we ever intended to run away. We did this more to bring out the evidence against us, than from any hope of getting clear of being sold; for, as I have said, we were ready for that. The fact was, we cared but little where we went, so we went together. Our greatest concern was about separation. We dreaded that more than any thing this side of death. We found the evidence against us to be the testimony of one person; our master would not tell who it was; but we came to a unanimous decision among ourselves as to who their informant was. We were sent off to the jail at Easton. When we got there, we were delivered up to the sheriff, Mr. Joseph Graham, and by him placed in jail. Henry, John, and myself, were placed in one room together—Charles, and Henry Bailey, in another. Their object in separating us was to hinder concert.

We had been in jail scarcely twenty minutes, when a swarm of slave-traders, and agents for slave-traders, flocked into jail to look at us, and to ascertain if we were for sale. Such a set of beings I never saw before! I felt myself surrounded by so many fiends from perdition. A band of pirates never looked more like their father, the devil. They laughed and grinned over us, saying, "Ah, my boys! We have got you, haven't we?" And after taunting us in various ways, they one by one went into an examination of us, with intent to ascertain our value. They would impudently ask us if we would not like to have them for our masters. We would make them no answer, and leave them to find out as best they could. Then they would curse and swear at us, telling us that they could take the devil out of us in a very little while, if we were only in their hands.

While in jail, we found ourselves in much more comfortable quarters than we expected when we went there. We did not get much to eat, nor that which was very good; but we had a good clean room, from the windows of which we could see what was going on in the street, which was very much better than though we had been placed in one of the dark, damp cells. Upon the whole, we got along very well, so far as the jail and its keeper were concerned. Immediately after the holidays were over, contrary to all our expectations, Mr. Hamilton and Mr. Freeland came up to Easton, and took Charles, the two Henrys, and John, out of jail, and carried them home, leaving me alone. I regarded this separation as a final one. It caused me more pain than any thing else in the whole transaction. I was ready for any thing rather than separation. I supposed that they had consulted together, and had decided that, as I was the whole cause of the intention of the others to run away, it was hard to make the innocent suffer with the guilty; and that they had, therefore, concluded to take the others home, and sell me, as a warning to the others that remained. It is due to the noble Henry to say, he seemed almost as reluctant at leaving the prison as at leaving home to come to the prison. But we knew we should, in all probability, be separated, if we were sold; and since he was in their hands, he concluded to go peaceably home.

I was now left to my fate. I was all alone, and within the walls of a stone prison. But a few days before, and I was full of hope. I expected to have been safe in a land of freedom; but now I was covered with gloom, sunk down to the utmost despair. I thought the possibility of freedom was gone. I was kept in this way about one week, at the end of which, Captain Auld, my master, to my surprise and utter astonishment, came up, and took me out, with the intention of sending me, with a gentleman of his acquaintance, into Alabama. But, from some cause or other, he did not send me to Alabama, but concluded to send me back to Baltimore, to live again with his brother Hugh, and to learn a trade.

Thus, after an absence of three years and one month, I was once more permitted to return to my old home at Baltimore. My master sent me away, because there existed against me a very great prejudice in the community, and he feared I might be killed.

In a few weeks after I went to Baltimore, Master Hugh hired me to Mr. William Gardner, an extensive ship-builder, on Fell's Point. I was put there to learn how to calk. It, however, proved a very unfavorable place for the accomplishment of this object. Mr. Gardner was engaged that spring in building two large man-of-war brigs, professedly for the Mexican government. The vessels were to be launched in the July of that year, and in failure thereof, Mr. Gardner was to lose a considerable sum; so that when I entered, all was hurry. There was no time to learn any thing. Every man had to do that which he knew how to do. In entering the ship-yard, my orders from Mr. Gardner were, to do whatever the carpenters commanded me to do. This was placing me at the beck and call of about seventy-five men. I was to regard all these as masters. Their word was to be my law. My situation was a most trying one. At times I needed a dozen pair of hands. I was called a dozen ways in the space of a single minute. Three or four voices would strike my ear at the same moment. It was—"Fred., come help me to cant this timber here." "Fred., come carry this timber yonder." "Fred., bring that roller here." "Fred., go get a fresh can of water." "Fred., come help saw off the end of this timber." "Fred., go quick, and get the crowbar." "Fred., hold on the end of this fall." "Fred., go to the blacksmith's shop, and get a new punch." "Hurra, Fred! Run and bring me a cold chisel." "I say, Fred., bear a hand, and get up a fire as quick as lightning under that steam-box." "Halloo, nigger! come, turn this grindstone." "Come, come! Move, move! And bowse this timber forward." "I say, darky, blast your eyes, why don't you heat up some pitch?" "Halloo! Halloo! Halloo!" (Three voices at the same time.) "Come here! Go there! Hold on where you are! Damn you, if you move, I'll knock your brains out!"

This was my school for eight months; and I might have remained there longer, but for a most horrid fight I had with four of the white apprentices, in which my left eye was nearly knocked out, and I was horribly mangled in other respects. The facts in the case were these: Until a very little while after I went there, white and black ship carpenters worked side by side, and no one seemed to see any impropriety in it. All hands seemed to be very well satisfied. Many of the black carpenters were freemen. Things seemed to be going on very well. All at once, the white carpenters knocked off, and said they would not work with free colored workmen. Their reason for this, as alleged, was, that if free colored carpenters were encouraged, they would soon take the trade into their own hands, and poor white men would be thrown out of employment. They therefore felt called upon at once to put a stop to it. And, taking advantage of Mr. Gardner's necessities, they broke off, swearing they would work no longer, unless he would discharge his black carpenters. Now, though this did not extend to me in form, it did reach me in fact. My fellow-apprentices very soon began to feel it degrading to them to work with me. They began to put on airs, and talk about the "niggers" taking the country, saying we all ought to be killed; and, being encouraged by the journeymen, they commenced making my condition as hard as they could, by hectoring me around, and sometimes striking me. I, of course, kept the vow I made after the fight with Mr. Covey, and struck back again, regardless of consequences; and while I kept them from combining, I succeeded very well; for I could whip the whole of them, taking them separately. They, however, at length combined, and came upon me, armed with sticks, stones, and heavy handspikes. One came in front with a half brick. There was one at each side of me, and one behind me. While I was attending to those in front, and on either side, the one behind ran up with the handspike, and struck me a heavy blow upon the head. It stunned me. I fell, and with this they all ran upon me, and fell to beating me with their fists. I let them lay on for a while, gathering strength. In an instant, I gave a sudden surge, and rose to my hands and knees. Just as I did that, one of their number gave me, with his heavy boot, a powerful kick in the left eye. My eyeball seemed to have burst. When they saw my eye closed, and badly swollen, they left me. With this I seized the handspike, and for a time pursued them. But here the carpenters interfered, and I thought I might as well give it up. It was impossible to stand my hand against so many. All this took place in sight of not less than fifty white ship carpenters, and not one interposed a friendly word; but some cried, "Kill the damned nigger! Kill him! Kill him! He struck a white person." I found my only chance for life was in flight. I succeeded in getting away without an additional blow, and barely so; for to strike a white man is death by Lynch law—and that was the law in Mr. Gardner's ship-yard; nor is there much of any other out of Mr. Gardner's ship-yard.

I went directly home, and told the story of my wrongs to Master Hugh; and I am happy to say of him, irreligious as he was, his conduct was heavenly, compared with that of his brother Thomas under similar circumstances. He listened attentively to my narration of the circumstances leading to the savage outrage, and gave many proofs of his strong indignation at it. The heart of my once overkind mistress was again melted into pity. My puffed-out eye and blood-covered face moved her to tears. She took a chair by me, washed the blood from my face, and, with a mother's tenderness, bound up my head, covering the wounded eye with a lean piece of fresh beef. It was almost compensation for my suffering to witness, once more, a manifestation of kindness from this, my once affectionate old mistress. Master Hugh was very much enraged. He gave expression to his feelings by pouring out curses upon the heads of those who did the deed. As soon as I got a little the better of my bruises, he took me with him to Esquire Watson's, on Bond Street, to see what could be done about the matter. Mr. Watson inquired who saw the assault committed. Master Hugh told him it was done in Mr. Gardner's ship-yard at midday, where there were a large company of men at work. "As to that," he said, "the deed was done, and there was no question as to who did it." His answer was, he could do nothing in the case, unless some white man would come forward and testify. He could issue no warrant on my word. If I had been killed in the presence of a thousand colored people, their testimony combined would have been insufficient to have arrested one of the murderers. Master Hugh, for once, was compelled to say this state of things was too bad. Of course, it was impossible to get any white man to volunteer his testimony in my behalf, and against the white young men. Even those who may have sympathized with me were not prepared to do this. It required a degree of courage unknown to them to do so; for just at that time, the slightest manifestation of humanity toward a colored person was denounced as abolitionism, and that name subjected its bearer to frightful liabilities. The watchwords of the bloody-minded in that region, and in those days, were, "Damn the abolitionists!" and "Damn the niggers!" There was nothing done, and probably nothing would have been done if I had been killed. Such was, and such remains, the state of things in the Christian city of Baltimore.

Master Hugh, finding he could get no redress, refused to let me go back again to Mr. Gardner. He kept me himself, and his wife dressed my wound till I was again restored to health. He then took me into the ship-yard of which he was foreman, in the employment of Mr. Walter Price. There I was immediately set to calking, and very soon learned the art of using my mallet and irons. In the course of one year from the time I left Mr. Gardner's, I was able to command the highest wages given to the most experienced calkers. I was now of some importance to my master. I was bringing him from six to seven dollars per week. I sometimes brought him nine dollars per week: my wages were a dollar and a half a day. After learning how to calk, I sought my own employment, made my own contracts, and collected the money which I earned. My pathway became much more smooth than before; my condition was now much more comfortable. When I could get no calking to do, I did nothing. During these leisure times, those old notions about freedom would steal over me again. When in Mr. Gardner's employment, I was kept in such a perpetual whirl of excitement, I could think of nothing, scarcely, but my life; and in thinking of my life, I almost forgot my liberty. I have observed this in my experience of slavery—that whenever my condition was improved, instead of its increasing my contentment, it only increased my desire to be free, and set me to thinking of plans to gain my freedom. I have found that, to make a contented slave, it is necessary to make a thoughtless one. It is necessary to darken his moral and mental vision, and, as far as possible, to annihilate the power of reason. He must be able to detect no inconsistencies in slavery; he must be made to feel that slavery is right; and he can be brought to that only when he ceases to be a man.

I was now getting, as I have said, one dollar and fifty cents per day. I contracted for it; I earned it; it was paid to me; it was rightfully my own; yet, upon each returning Saturday night, I was compelled to deliver every cent of that money to Master Hugh. And why? Not because he earned it—not because he had any hand in earning it—not because I owed it to him—nor because he possessed the slightest shadow of a right to it; but solely because he had the power to compel me to give it up. The right of the grim-visaged pirate upon the high seas is exactly the same.

# CHAPTER XI

I now come to that part of my life during which I planned, and finally succeeded in making, my escape from slavery. But before narrating any of the peculiar circumstances, I deem it proper to make known my intention not to state all the facts connected with the transaction. My reasons for pursuing this course may be understood from the following: First, were I to give a minute statement of all the facts, it is not only possible, but quite probable, that others would thereby be involved in the most embarrassing difficulties. Secondly, such a statement would most undoubtedly induce greater vigilance on the part of slaveholders than has existed heretofore among them; which would, of course, be the means of guarding a door whereby some dear brother bondman might escape his galling chains. I deeply regret the necessity that impels me to suppress any thing of importance connected with my experience in slavery. It would afford me great pleasure indeed, as well as materially add to the interest of my narrative, were I at liberty to gratify a curiosity, which I know exists in the minds of many, by an accurate statement of all the facts pertaining to my most fortunate escape. But I must deprive myself of this pleasure, and the curious of the gratification which such a statement would afford. I would allow myself to suffer under the greatest imputations which evil-minded men might suggest, rather than exculpate myself, and thereby run the hazard of closing the slightest avenue by which a brother slave might clear himself of the chains and fetters of slavery.

I have never approved of the very public manner in which some of our western friends have conducted what they call the *underground railroad*, but which I think, by their open declarations, has been made most emphatically the *upperground railroad*. I honor those good men and women for their noble daring, and applaud them for willingly subjecting themselves to bloody persecution, by openly avowing their participation in the escape of slaves. I, however, can see very little good resulting from such a course, either to themselves or the slaves escaping; while, upon the other hand, I see and feel assured that those open declarations are a positive evil to the slaves remaining, who are seeking to escape. They do nothing towards enlightening the slave, whilst they do much towards enlightening the master. They stimulate him to greater watchfulness, and enhance his power to capture his slave. We owe something to the slave south of the line as well as to those north of it; and in aiding the latter on their way to freedom, we should be careful to do nothing which would be likely to hinder the former from escaping from slavery. I would keep the merciless slaveholder profoundly ignorant of the means of flight adopted by the slave. I would leave him to imagine himself surrounded by myriads of invisible tormentors, ever ready to snatch from his infernal grasp his trembling prey. Let him be left to feel his way in the dark; let darkness commensurate with his crime hover over him; and let him feel that at every step he takes, in pursuit of the flying bondman, he is running the frightful risk of having his hot brains dashed out by an invisible agency. Let us render the tyrant no aid; let us not hold the light by which he can trace the footprints of our flying brother. But enough of this. I will now proceed to the statement of those facts, connected with my escape, for which I am alone responsible, and for which no one can be made to suffer but myself.

In the early part of the year 1838, I became quite restless. I could see no reason why I should, at the end of each week, pour the reward of my toil into the purse of my master. When I carried to him my weekly wages, he would, after counting the money, look me in the face with a robber-like fierceness, and ask, "Is this all?" He was satisfied with nothing less than the last cent. He would, however, when I made him six dollars, sometimes give me six cents, to encourage me. It had the opposite effect. I regarded it as a sort of admission of my right to the whole. The fact that he gave me any part of my wages was proof, to my mind, that he believed me entitled to the whole of them. I always felt worse for having received any thing; for I feared that the giving me a few cents would ease his conscience, and make him feel himself to be a pretty honorable sort of robber. My discontent grew upon me. I was ever on the look-out for means of escape; and, finding no direct means, I determined to try to hire my time, with a view of getting money with which to make my escape. In the spring of 1838, when Master Thomas came to Baltimore to purchase his spring goods, I got an opportunity, and applied to him to allow me to hire my time. He unhesitatingly refused my request, and told me this was another stratagem by which to escape. He told me I could go nowhere but that he could get me;

and that, in the event of my running away, he should spare no pains in his efforts to catch me. He exhorted me to content myself, and be obedient. He told me, if I would be happy, I must lay out no plans for the future. He said, if I behaved myself properly, he would take care of me. Indeed, he advised me to complete thoughtlessness of the future, and taught me to depend solely upon him for happiness. He seemed to see fully the pressing necessity of setting aside my intellectual nature, in order to contentment in slavery. But in spite of him, and even in spite of myself, I continued to think, and to think about the injustice of my enslavement, and the means of escape.

About two months after this, I applied to Master Hugh for the privilege of hiring my time. He was not acquainted with the fact that I had applied to Master Thomas, and had been refused. He too, at first, seemed disposed to refuse; but, after some reflection, he granted me the privilege, and proposed the following terms: I was to be allowed all my time, make all contracts with those for whom I worked, and find my own employment; and, in return for this liberty, I was to pay him three dollars at the end of each week; find myself in calking tools, and in board and clothing. My board was two dollars and a half per week. This, with the wear and tear of clothing and calking tools, made my regular expenses about six dollars per week. This amount I was compelled to make up, or relinquish the privilege of hiring my time. Rain or shine, work or no work, at the end of each week the money must be forthcoming, or I must give up my privilege. This arrangement, it will be perceived, was decidedly in my master's favor. It relieved him of all need of looking after me. His money was sure. He received all the benefits of slaveholding without its evils; while I endured all the evils of a slave, and suffered all the care and anxiety of a freeman. I found it a hard bargain. But, hard as it was, I thought it better than the old mode of getting along. It was a step towards freedom to be allowed to bear the responsibilities of a freeman, and I was determined to hold on upon it. I bent myself to the work of making money. I was ready to work at night as well as day, and by the most untiring perseverance and industry, I made enough to meet my expenses, and lay up a little money every week. I went on thus from May till August. Master Hugh then refused to allow me to hire my time longer. The ground for his refusal was a failure on my part, one Saturday night, to pay him for my week's time. This failure was occasioned by my attending a camp-meeting about ten miles from Baltimore. During the week, I had entered into an engagement with a number of young friends to start from Baltimore to the camp-ground early Saturday evening; and being detained by my employer, I was unable to get down to Master Hugh's without disappointing the company. I knew that Master Hugh was in no special need of the money that night. I therefore decided to go to camp-meeting, and upon my return pay him the three dollars. I staid at the camp-meeting one day longer than I intended when I left. But as soon as I returned, I called upon him to pay him what he considered his due. I found him very angry; he could scarce restrain his wrath. He said he had a great mind to give me a severe whipping. He wished to know how I dared go out of the city without asking his permission. I told him I hired my time and while I paid him the price which he asked for it, I did not know that I was bound to ask him when and where I should go. This reply troubled him; and, after reflecting a few moments, he turned to me, and said I should hire my time no longer; that the next thing he should know of, I would be running away. Upon the same plea, he told me to bring my tools and clothing home forthwith. I did so; but instead of seeking work, as I had been accustomed to do previously to hiring my time, I spent the whole week without the performance of a single stroke of work. I did this in retaliation. Saturday night, he called upon me as usual for my week's wages. I told him I had no wages; I had done no work that week. Here we were upon the point of coming to blows. He raved, and swore his determination to get hold of me. I did not allow myself a single word; but was resolved, if he laid the weight of his hand upon me, it should be blow for blow. He did not strike me, but told me that he would find me in constant employment in future. I thought the matter over during the next day, Sunday, and finally resolved upon the third day of September, as the day upon which I would make a second attempt to secure my freedom. I now had three weeks during which to prepare for my journey. Early on Monday morning, before Master Hugh had time to make any engagement for me, I went out and got employment of Mr. Butler, at his ship-yard near the drawbridge, upon what is called the City Block, thus making it unnecessary for him to seek employment for me. At the end of the week, I brought him between eight and nine dollars. He seemed very well pleased, and asked why I did not do the same the week before. He little knew what my plans were. My object in working steadily was to remove any suspicion he might entertain of my intent to run away; and in this I succeeded admirably. I suppose he thought I was never better satisfied with my condition than at the very time during which I was planning my escape. The second week passed, and again I carried him my full wages; and so well pleased was he, that he gave me twenty-five cents, (quite a large sum for a slaveholder to give a slave), and bade me to make a good use of it. I told him I would.

Things went on without very smoothly indeed, but within there was trouble. It is impossible for me to describe my feelings as the time of my contemplated start drew near. I had a number of warm-hearted friends in Baltimore—friends that I loved almost as I did my life—and the thought of being separated from them forever was painful beyond expression. It is my opinion that thousands would escape from slavery, who now remain, but for the strong cords of affection that bind them to their friends. The thought of leaving my friends was decidedly the most painful thought with which I had to contend. The love of them was my tender point, and shook my decision more than all things else. Besides the pain of separation, the dread and apprehension of a failure exceeded what I had experienced at my first attempt. The appalling defeat I then sustained returned to torment me. I felt assured that, if I failed in this attempt, my case would be a hopeless one—it would seal my fate as a slave forever. I could not hope to get off with any thing less than the severest punishment, and being placed beyond the means of escape. It required no very vivid imagination to depict the most frightful scenes through which I should have to pass, in case I failed. The wretchedness of slavery, and the blessedness of freedom, were perpetually before me. It was life and death with me. But I remained firm, and, according to my resolution, on the third day of September, 1838, I left my chains, and succeeded in reaching New York without the slightest interruption of any kind. How I did so—what means I adopted—what direction I travelled, and by what mode of conveyance—I must leave unexplained, for the reasons before mentioned.

I have been frequently asked how I felt when I found myself in a Free State. I have never been able to answer the question with any satisfaction to myself. It was a moment of the highest excitement I ever experienced. I suppose I felt as one may imagine the unarmed mariner to feel when he is rescued by a friendly man-of-war from the pursuit of a pirate. In writing to a dear friend, immediately after my arrival at

New York, I said I felt like one who had escaped a den of hungry lions. This state of mind, however, very soon subsided; and I was again seized with a feeling of great insecurity and loneliness. I was yet liable to be taken back, and subjected to all the tortures of slavery. This in itself was enough to damp the ardor of my enthusiasm. But the loneliness overcame me. There I was in the midst of thousands, and yet a perfect stranger; without home and without friends, in the midst of thousands of my own brethren—children of a common Father, and yet I dared not to unfold to any one of them my sad condition. I was afraid to speak to any one for fear of speaking to the wrong one, and thereby falling into the hands of money-loving kidnappers, whose business it was to lie in wait for the panting fugitive, as the ferocious beasts of the forest lie in wait for their prey. The motto which I adopted when I started from slavery was this—"Trust no man!" I saw in every white man an enemy, and in almost every colored man cause for distrust. It was a most painful situation; and, to understand it, one must needs experience it, or imagine himself in similar circumstances. Let him be a fugitive slave in a strange land—a land given up to be the hunting-ground for slaveholders—whose inhabitants are legalized kidnappers—where he is every moment subjected to the terrible liability of being seized upon by his fellow-men, as the hideous crocodile seizes upon his prey!—I say, let him place himself in my situation—without home or friends—without money or credit—wanting shelter, and no one to give it—wanting bread, and no money to buy it—and at the same time let him feel that he is pursued by merciless men-hunters, and in total darkness as to what to do, where to go, or where to stay—perfectly helpless both as to the means of defense and means of escape—in the midst of plenty, yet suffering the terrible gnawings of hunger—in the midst of houses, yet having no home—among fellow-men, yet feeling as if in the midst of wild beasts, whose greediness to swallow up the trembling and half-famished fugitive is only equaled by that with which the monsters of the deep swallow up the helpless fish upon which they subsist,I say, let him be placed in this most trying situation,the situation in which I was placed,then, and not till then, will he fully appreciate the hardships of, and know how to sympathize with, the toil-worn and whip-scarred fugitive slave.

Thank Heaven, I remained but a short time in this distressed situation. I was relieved from it by the humane hand of Mr. David

Ruggles, whose vigilance, kindness, and perseverance, I shall never forget. I am glad of an opportunity to express, as far as words can, the love and gratitude I bear him. Mr. Ruggles is now afflicted with blindness, and is himself in need of the same kind offices which he was once so forward in the performance of toward others. I had been in New York but a few days, when Mr. Ruggles sought me out, and very kindly took me to his boarding-house at the corner of Church and Lespenard Streets. Mr. Ruggles was then very deeply engaged in the memorable Darg case,* as well as attending to a number of other fugitive slaves, devising ways and means for their successful escape; and, though watched and hemmed in on almost every side, he seemed to be more than a match for his enemies.

Very soon after I went to Mr. Ruggles, he wished to know of me where I wanted to go; as he deemed it unsafe for me to remain in New York. I told him I was a calker, and should like to go where I could get work. I thought of going to Canada; but he decided against it, and in favor of my going to New Bedford, thinking I should be able to get work there at my trade. At this time, Anna†, my intended wife, came on; for I wrote to her immediately after my arrival at New York, (notwithstanding my homeless, houseless, and helpless condition), informing her of my successful flight, and wishing her to come on forthwith. In a few days after her arrival, Mr. Ruggles called in the Rev. J. W. C. Pennington, who, in the presence of Mr. Ruggles, Mrs. Michaels, and two or three others, performed the marriage ceremony, and gave us a certificate, of which the following is an exact copy:

*This may certify, that I joined together in holy matrimony Frederick Johnson‡ and Anna Murray, as man and wife, in the presence of Mr. David Ruggles and Mrs. Michaels.*

*James W. C. Pennington*
*New York, Sept. 15, 1838*

Upon receiving this certificate, and a five-dollar bill from Mr. Ruggles, I shouldered one part of our baggage, and Anna took up

---

* In 1838, Virginia slaveowner John P. Darg brought his slave Thomas Hughes with him to New York City. Hughes ultimately escaped Darg's control, and the famous African American abolitionist David Ruggles helped him to find asylum. When Ruggles refused to return Hughes, Darg had him arrested for grand larceny.

† She was free. (Original note)

‡ I had changed my name from Frederick *Bailey* to that of *Johnson*. (Original note)

the other, and we set out forthwith to take passage on board of the steamboat *John W. Richmond* for Newport, on our way to New Bedford. Mr. Ruggles gave me a letter to a Mr. Shaw in Newport, and told me, in case my money did not serve me to New Bedford, to stop in Newport and obtain further assistance; but upon our arrival at Newport, we were so anxious to get to a place of safety, that, notwithstanding we lacked the necessary money to pay our fare, we decided to take seats in the stage, and promise to pay when we got to New Bedford. We were encouraged to do this by two excellent gentlemen, residents of New Bedford, whose names I afterward ascertained to be Joseph Ricketson and William C. Taber. They seemed at once to understand our circumstances, and gave us such assurance of their friendliness as put us fully at ease in their presence.

It was good indeed to meet with such friends, at such a time. Upon reaching New Bedford, we were directed to the house of Mr. Nathan Johnson, by whom we were kindly received, and hospitably provided for. Both Mr. and Mrs. Johnson took a deep and lively interest in our welfare. They proved themselves quite worthy of the name of abolitionists. When the stage-driver found us unable to pay our fare, he held on upon our baggage as security for the debt. I had but to mention the fact to Mr. Johnson, and he forthwith advanced the money.

We now began to feel a degree of safety, and to prepare ourselves for the duties and responsibilities of a life of freedom. On the morning after our arrival at New Bedford, while at the breakfast-table, the question arose as to what name I should be called by. The name given me by my mother was, "Frederick Augustus Washington Bailey." I, however, had dispensed with the two middle names long before I left Maryland so that I was generally known by the name of "Frederick Bailey." I started from Baltimore bearing the name of "Stanley." When I got to New York, I again changed my name to "Frederick Johnson," and thought that would be the last change. But when I got to New Bedford, I found it necessary again to change my name. The reason of this necessity was, that there were so many Johnsons in New Bedford, it was already quite difficult to distinguish between them. I gave Mr. Johnson the privilege of choosing me a name, but told him he must not take from me the name of "Frederick." I must hold on to that, to preserve a sense of my identity. Mr. Johnson had just been reading the *Lady of the Lake*, and at once suggested that my name be "Douglass."

From that time until now I have been called "Frederick Douglass"; and as I am more widely known by that name than by either of the others, I shall continue to use it as my own.

I was quite disappointed at the general appearance of things in New Bedford. The impression which I had received respecting the character and condition of the people of the north, I found to be singularly erroneous. I had very strangely supposed, while in slavery, that few of the comforts, and scarcely any of the luxuries, of life were enjoyed at the north, compared with what were enjoyed by the slaveholders of the south. I probably came to this conclusion from the fact that northern people owned no slaves. I supposed that they were about upon a level with the non-slaveholding population of the south. I knew they were exceedingly poor, and I had been accustomed to regard their poverty as the necessary consequence of their being non-slaveholders. I had somehow imbibed the opinion that, in the absence of slaves, there could be no wealth, and very little refinement. And upon coming to the north, I expected to meet with a rough, hard-handed, and uncultivated population, living in the most Spartan-like simplicity, knowing nothing of the ease, luxury, pomp, and grandeur of southern slaveholders. Such being my conjectures, any one acquainted with the appearance of New Bedford may very readily infer how palpably I must have seen my mistake.

In the afternoon of the day when I reached New Bedford, I visited the wharves, to take a view of the shipping. Here I found myself surrounded with the strongest proofs of wealth. Lying at the wharves, and riding in the stream, I saw many ships of the finest model, in the best order, and of the largest size. Upon the right and left, I was walled in by granite warehouses of the widest dimensions, stowed to their utmost capacity with the necessaries and comforts of life. Added to this, almost every body seemed to be at work, but noiselessly so, compared with what I had been accustomed to in Baltimore. There were no loud songs heard from those engaged in loading and unloading ships. I heard no deep oaths or horrid curses on the laborer. I saw no whipping of men; but all seemed to go smoothly on. Every man appeared to understand his work, and went at it with a sober, yet cheerful earnestness, which betokened the deep interest which he felt in what he was doing, as well as a sense of his own dignity as a man. To me this looked exceedingly strange. From the wharves I strolled around and over the town, gazing with wonder and admiration at the splendid churches, beautiful dwellings, and finely-cultivated gardens; evincing an amount of wealth, comfort, taste, and refinement, such as I had never seen in any part of slaveholding Maryland.

Every thing looked clean, new, and beautiful. I saw few or no dilapidated houses, with poverty-stricken inmates; no half-naked children and bare-footed women, such as I had been accustomed to see in Hillsborough, Easton, St. Michael's, and Baltimore. The people looked more able, stronger, healthier, and happier, than those of Maryland. I was for once made glad by a view of extreme wealth, without being saddened by seeing extreme poverty. But the most astonishing as well as the most interesting thing to me was the condition of the colored people, a great many of whom, like myself, had escaped thither as a refuge from the hunters of men. I found many, who had not been seven years out of their chains, living in finer houses, and evidently enjoying more of the comforts of life, than the average of slaveholders in Maryland. I will venture to assert, that my friend Mr. Nathan Johnson (of whom I can say with a grateful heart, "I was hungry, and he gave me meat; I was thirsty, and he gave me drink; I was a stranger, and he took me in") lived in a neater house; dined at a better table; took, paid for, and read, more newspapers; better understood the moral, religious, and political character of the nation—than nine tenths of the slaveholders in Talbot County Maryland. Yet Mr. Johnson was a working man. His hands were hardened by toil, and not his alone, but those also of Mrs. Johnson. I found the colored people much more spirited than I had supposed they would be. I found among them a determination to protect each other from the blood-thirsty kidnapper, at all hazards. Soon after my arrival, I was told of a circumstance which illustrated their spirit. A colored man and a fugitive slave were on unfriendly terms. The former was heard to threaten the latter with informing his master of his whereabouts. Straightway a meeting was called among the colored people, under the stereotyped notice, "Business of importance!" The betrayer was invited to attend. The people came at the appointed hour, and organized the meeting by appointing a very religious old gentleman as president, who, I believe, made a prayer, after which he addressed the meeting as follows: *"Friends, we have got him here, and I would recommend that you young men just take him outside the door, and kill him!"* With this, a number of them bolted at him; but they were intercepted by some more timid than themselves, and the betrayer escaped their vengeance, and has not been seen in New Bedford since. I believe there have been no more such threats, and should there be hereafter, I doubt not that death would be the consequence.

I found employment, the third day after my arrival, in stowing a sloop with a load of oil. It was new, dirty, and hard work for me; but I went at it with a glad heart and a willing hand. I was now my own master. It was a happy moment, the rapture of which can be understood only by those who have been slaves. It was the first work, the reward of which was to be entirely my own. There was no Master Hugh standing ready, the moment I earned the money, to rob me of it. I worked that day with a pleasure I had never before experienced. I was at work for myself and newly-married wife. It was to me the starting-point of a new existence. When I got through with that job, I went in pursuit of a job of calking; but such was the strength of prejudice against color, among the white calkers, that they refused to work with me, and of course I could get no employment.* Finding my trade of no immediate benefit, I threw off my calking habiliments, and prepared myself to do any kind of work I could get to do. Mr. Johnson kindly let me have his wood-horse and saw, and I very soon found myself a plenty of work. There was no work too hard—none too dirty. I was ready to saw wood, shovel coal, carry wood, sweep the chimney, or roll oil casks—all of which I did for nearly three years in New Bedford, before I became known to the anti-slavery world.

In about four months after I went to New Bedford, there came a young man to me, and inquired if I did not wish to take the *Liberator*. I told him I did; but, just having made my escape from slavery, I remarked that I was unable to pay for it then. I, however, finally became a subscriber to it. The paper came, and I read it from week to week with such feelings as it would be quite idle for me to attempt to describe. The paper became my meat and my drink. My soul was set all on fire. Its sympathy for my brethren in bonds—its scathing denunciations of slaveholders—its faithful exposures of slavery—and its powerful attacks upon the upholders of the institution—sent a thrill of joy through my soul, such as I had never felt before!

I had not long been a reader of the *Liberator*, before I got a pretty

---

* I am told that colored persons can now get employment at calking in New Bedford—a result of anti-slavery effort. (Original note)

correct idea of the principles, measures and spirit of the anti-slavery reform. I took right hold of the cause. I could do but little; but what I could, I did with a joyful heart, and never felt happier than when in an anti-slavery meeting. I seldom had much to say at the meetings, because what I wanted to say was said so much better by others. But, while attending an anti-slavery convention at Nantucket, on the 11th of August, 1841, I felt strongly moved to speak, and was at the same time much urged to do so by Mr. William C. Coffin, a gentleman who had heard me speak in the colored people's meeting at New Bedford. It was a severe cross, and I took it up reluctantly. The truth was, I felt myself a slave, and the idea of speaking to white people weighed me down. I spoke but a few moments, when I felt a degree of freedom, and said what I desired with considerable ease. From that time until now, I have been engaged in pleading the cause of my brethren—with what success, and with what devotion, I leave those acquainted with my labors to decide.

# *APPENDIX*

I find, since reading over the foregoing Narrative, that I have, in several instances, spoken in such a tone and manner, respecting religion, as may possibly lead those unacquainted with my religious views to suppose me an opponent of all religion. To remove the liability of such misapprehension, I deem it proper to append the following brief explanation. What I have said respecting and against religion, I mean strictly to apply to the *slaveholding religion* of this land, and with no possible reference to Christianity proper; for, between the Christianity of this land, and the Christianity of Christ, I recognize the widest possible difference—so wide, that to receive the one as good, pure, and holy, is of necessity to reject the other as bad, corrupt, and wicked. To be the friend of the one, is of necessity to be the enemy of the other. I love the pure, peaceable, and impartial Christianity of Christ: I therefore hate the corrupt, slaveholding, women-whipping, cradle-plundering, partial and hypocritical Christianity of this land. Indeed, I can see no reason, but the most deceitful one, for calling the religion of this land Christianity. I look upon it as the climax of all misnomers, the boldest of all frauds, and the grossest of all libels. Never was there a clearer case of "stealing the livery of the court of heaven to serve the devil in." I am filled with unutterable loathing when I contemplate the religious pomp and show, together with the horrible inconsistencies, which every where surround me. We have men-stealers for ministers, women-whippers for missionaries, and cradle-plunderers for church members. The man who wields the blood-clotted cowskin during the week fills the pulpit on Sunday, and claims to be a minister of the meek and lowly Jesus. The man who robs me of my earnings at the end of each week meets me as a class-leader on Sunday morning, to show me the way of life, and the path of salvation. He who sells my sister, for purposes of prostitution, stands forth as the pious advocate of purity. He who proclaims it a religious duty to read the Bible denies me the right of learning to read the name of the God who made me. He who is the religious advocate of marriage robs whole millions of its sacred influence, and leaves them to the ravages of wholesale pollution. The warm defender of the sacredness of the family relation is the same that scatters whole families—sundering husbands and wives, parents and children, sisters and brothers—leaving the hut vacant, and the hearth desolate. We see the thief preaching against theft, and the adulterer against adultery. We have men sold to build churches, women sold to support the gospel, and babes sold to purchase Bibles for the *poor heathen! all for the glory of God and the good of souls!* The slave auctioneer's bell and the church-going bell chime in with each other, and the bitter cries of the heart-broken slave are drowned in the religious shouts of his pious master. Revivals of religion and revivals in the slave trade go hand in hand together. The slave prison and the church stand near each other. The clanking of fetters and the rattling of chains in the prison, and the pious psalm and solemn prayer in the church, may be heard at the same time. The dealers in the bodies and souls of men erect their stand in the presence of the pulpit, and they mutually help each other. The dealer gives his blood-stained gold to support the pulpit, and the pulpit, in return, covers his infernal business with the garb of Christianity. Here we have religion and robbery the allies of each other—devils dressed in angels' robes, and hell presenting the semblance of paradise.

> Just God! and these are they,
> Who minister at thine altar, God of right!
> Men who their hands, with prayer and blessing, lay
> On Israel's ark of light.
>
> What! preach, and kidnap men?
> Give thanks, and rob thy own afflicted poor?
> Talk of thy glorious liberty, and then
> Bolt hard the captive's door?
>
> What! servants of thy own
> Merciful Son, who came to seek and save
> The homeless and the outcast, fettering down
> The tasked and plundered slave!
>
> Pilate and Herod friends!
> Chief priests and rulers, as of old, combine!
> Just God and holy! is that church which lends
> Strength to the spoiler thine?*

* From "Clerical Oppressors" by John Greenleaf Whittier.

The Christianity of America is a Christianity, of whose votaries it may be as truly said, as it was of the ancient scribes and Pharisees, "They bind heavy burdens, and grievous to be borne, and lay them on men's shoulders, but they themselves will not move them with one of their fingers. All their works they do for to be seen of men.—They love the uppermost rooms at feasts, and the chief seats in the synagogues, . . . . and to be called of men, Rabbi, Rabbi.—But woe unto you, scribes and Pharisees, hypocrites! For ye shut up the kingdom of heaven against men; for ye neither go in yourselves, neither suffer ye them that are entering to go in. Ye devour widows' houses, and for a pretence make long prayers; therefore ye shall receive the greater damnation. Ye compass sea and land to make one proselyte, and when he is made, ye make him twofold more the child of hell than yourselves.—Woe unto you, scribes and Pharisees, hypocrites! For ye pay tithe of mint, and anise, and cumin, and have omitted the weightier matters of the law, judgment, mercy, and faith; these ought ye to have done, and not to leave the other undone. Ye blind guides! which strain at a gnat, and swallow a camel. Woe unto you, scribes and Pharisees, hypocrites! For ye make clean the outside of the cup and of the platter; but within, they are full of extortion and excess.—Woe unto you, scribes and Pharisees, hypocrites! For ye are like unto whited sepulchres, which indeed appear beautiful outward, but are within full of dead men's bones, and of all uncleanness. Even so ye also outwardly appear righteous unto men, but within ye are full of hypocrisy and iniquity."

Dark and terrible as is this picture, I hold it to be strictly true of the overwhelming mass of professed Christians in America. They strain at a gnat, and swallow a camel. Could any thing be more true of our churches? They would be shocked at the proposition of fellowshipping a *sheep*-stealer; and at the same time they hug to their communion a *man*-stealer, and brand me with being an infidel, if I find fault with them for it. They attend with Pharisaical strictness to the outward forms of religion, and at the same time neglect the weightier matters of the law, judgment, mercy, and faith. They are always ready to sacrifice, but seldom to show mercy. They are they who are represented as professing to love God whom they have not seen, whilst they hate their brother whom they have seen. They love the heathen on the other side of the globe. They can pray for him, pay money to have the Bible put into his hand, and missionaries to instruct him; while they despise and totally neglect the heathen at their own doors.

Such is, very briefly, my view of the religion of this land; and to avoid any misunderstanding, growing out of the use of general terms, I mean by the religion of this land, that which is revealed in the words, deeds, and actions, of those bodies, north and south, calling themselves Christian churches, and yet in union with slaveholders. It is against religion, as presented by these bodies, that I have felt it my duty to testify.

I conclude these remarks by copying the following portrait of the religion of the south, (which is, by communion and fellowship, the religion of the north), which I soberly affirm is "true to the life," and without caricature or the slightest exaggeration. It is said to have been drawn, several years before the present anti-slavery agitation began, by a northern Methodist preacher, who, while residing at the south, had an opportunity to see slaveholding morals, manners, and piety, with his own eyes. "Shall I not visit for these things? saith the Lord. Shall not my soul be avenged on such a nation as this?"

# A PARODY

Come, saints and sinners, hear me tell
How pious priests whip Jack and Nell,
And women buy and children sell,
And preach all sinners down to hell,
And sing of heavenly union.

They'll bleat and baa, dona like goats,
Gorge down black sheep, and strain at motes,
Array their backs in fine black coats,
Then seize their Negroes by their throats,
And choke, for heavenly union.

They'll church you if you sip a dram,
And damn you if you steal a lamb;
Yet rob old Tony, Doll, and Sam,
Of human rights, and bread and ham;
Kidnapper's heavenly union.

They'll loudly talk of Christ's reward,
And bind his image with a cord,
And scold, and swing the lash abhorred,
And sell their brother in the Lord
To handcuffed heavenly union.

They'll read and sing a sacred song,
And make a prayer both loud and long,
And teach the right and do the wrong,
Hailing the brother, sister throng,
With words of heavenly union.

We wonder how such saints can sing,
Or praise the Lord upon the wing,
Who roar, and scold, and whip, and sting,

And to their slaves and mammon cling,
    In guilty conscience union.

They'll raise tobacco, corn, and rye,
And drive, and thieve, and cheat, and lie,
    And lay up treasures in the sky,
    By making switch and cowskin fly,
    In hope of heavenly union.

They'll crack old Tony on the skull,
And preach and roar like Bashan bull,
    Or braying ass, of mischief full,
    Then seize old Jacob by the wool,
    And pull for heavenly union.

A roaring, ranting, sleek man-thief,
Who lived on mutton, veal, and beef,
    Yet never would afford relief
    To needy, sable sons of grief,
    Was big with heavenly union.

"Love not the world," the preacher said,
And winked his eye, and shook his head;
He seized on Tom, and Dick, and Ned,
Cut short their meat, and clothes, and bread,
    Yet still loved heavenly union.

Another preacher whining spoke
Of One whose heart for sinners broke:
    He tied old Nanny to an oak,
    And drew the blood at every stroke,
    And prayed for heavenly union.

Two others oped their iron jaws,
And waved their children-stealing paws;
    There sat their children in gewgaws;
    By stinting Negroes' backs and maws,
    They kept up heavenly union.

> All good from Jack another takes,
> And entertains their flirts and rakes,
> Who dress as sleek as glossy snakes,
> And cram their mouths with sweetened cakes;
> And this goes down for union.

Sincerely and earnestly hoping that this little book may do something toward throwing light on the American slave system, and hastening the glad day of deliverance to the millions of my brethren in bonds—faithfully relying upon the power of truth, love, and justice, for success in my humble efforts—and solemnly pledging my self anew to the sacred cause—I subscribe myself,

*Frederick Douglass*
*Lynn, Mass., April 28, 1845*

THE END

# My Bondage and My Freedom

*"By a principle essential to Christianity, a person is eternally differenced from a thing; so that the idea of a human being, necessarily excludes the idea of property in that being."*

—Coleridge

Entered according to Act of Congress in 1855 by
Frederick Douglass in the Clerk's Office of the
District Court of the Northern District of New York

To Honorable Gerrit Smith,* as a slight token of esteem for his characer, admiration for his genius and benevolence, affection for his person, and gratitude for his friendship, and as a small but most sincere acknowledgment of his preeminent services in behalf of the rights and liberties of an afflicted, despised, and deeply outraged people, by ranking slavery with piracy and murder, and by denying it either a legal or constitutional existence, this volume is respectfully dedicated.

By his faithful and firmly atttached friend,
Frederick Douglass
Rochester, N.Y.

---

* Gerrit Smith was a 19th century abolitionist and politician, who served in Congress as a member of the Free Soil Party, which advocated for the end of slavery in the United States.

# EDITOR'S PREFACE

If the volume now presented to the public were a mere work of *art*, the history of its misfortune might be written in two very simple words— *too late*. The nature and character of slavery have been subjects of an almost endless variety of artistic representation; and after the brilliant achievements in that field, and while those achievements are yet fresh in the memory of the million, he who would add another to the legion, must possess the charm of transcendent excellence, or apologize for something worse than rashness. The reader is, therefore, assured, with all due promptitude, that his attention is not invited to a work of *art*, but to a work of *facts—facts*, terrible and almost incredible, it may be—yet *facts*, nevertheless.

I am authorized to say that there is not a fictitious name nor place in the whole volume; but that names and places are literally given, and that every transaction therein described actually transpired.

Perhaps the best Preface to this volume is furnished in the following letter of Mr. Douglass, written in answer to my urgent solicitation for such a work:

Rochester, NY, July 2, 1855.

Dear Friend:
I have long entertained, as you very well know, a somewhat positive repugnance to writing or speaking anything for the public, which could, with any degree of plausibility, make me liable to the imputation of seeking personal notoriety, for its own sake. Entertaining that feeling very sincerely, and permitting its control, perhaps, quite unreasonably, I have often refused to narrate my personal experience in public anti-slavery meetings, and in sympathizing circles, when urged to do so by friends, with whose views and wishes, ordinarily, it were a pleasure to comply. In my letters and speeches, I have generally aimed to discuss the question of Slavery in the light of fundamental principles, and upon facts, notorious and open to all; making, I trust, no more of the fact of my own former enslavement, than

circumstances seemed absolutely to require. I have never placed my opposition to slavery on a basis so narrow as my own enslavement, but rather upon the indestructible and unchangeable laws of human nature, every one of which is perpetually and flagrantly violated by the slave system. I have also felt that it was best for those having histories worth the writing—or supposed to be so—to commit such work to hands other than their own. To write of one's self, in such a manner as not to incur the imputation of weakness, vanity, and egotism, is a work within the ability of but few; and I have little reason to believe that I belong to that fortunate few.

These considerations caused me to hesitate, when first you kindly urged me to prepare for publication a full account of my life as a slave, and my life as a freeman.

Nevertheless, I see, with you, many reasons for regarding my autobiography as exceptional in its character, and as being, in some sense, naturally beyond the reach of those reproaches which honorable and sensitive minds dislike to incur. It is not to illustrate any heroic achievements of a man, but to vindicate a just and beneficent principle, in its application to the whole human family, by letting in the light of truth upon a system, esteemed by some as a blessing, and by others as a curse and a crime. I agree with you, that this system is now at the bar of public opinion—not only of this country, but of the whole civilized world—for judgment. Its friends have made for it the usual plea—"not guilty"; the case must, therefore, proceed. Any facts, either from slaves, slaveholders, or by-standers, calculated to enlighten the public mind, by revealing the true nature, character, and tendency of the slave system, are in order, and can scarcely be innocently withheld.

I see, too, that there are special reasons why I should write my own biography, in preference to employing another to do it. Not only is slavery on trial, but unfortunately, the enslaved people are also on trial. It is alleged, that they are, naturally, inferior; that they are *so low* in the scale of humanity, and so utterly stupid, that they are unconscious of their wrongs, and do not apprehend their rights. Looking, then, at your request, from this stand-point, and wishing everything of which you think me capable to go to the benefit of my afflicted people, I part with my doubts and hesitation, and proceed to furnish you the desired manuscript; hoping that you may be able to make such arrangements for its publication as shall be best adapted to accomplish that good which you so enthusiastically anticipate.

*Frederick Douglass*

There was little necessity for doubt and hesitation on the part of Mr. Douglass, as to the propriety of his giving to the world a full account of himself. A man who was born and brought up in slavery, a living witness of its horrors; who often himself experienced its cruelties; and who, despite the depressing influences surrounding his birth, youth and manhood, has risen, from a dark and almost absolute obscurity, to the distinguished position which he now occupies, might very well assume the existence of a commendable curiosity, on the part of the public, to know the facts of his remarkable history.

*Editor*

# INTRODUCTION

When a man raises himself from the lowest condition in society to the highest, mankind pay him the tribute of their admiration; when he accomplishes this elevation by native energy, guided by prudence and wisdom, their admiration is increased; but when his course, onward and upward, excellent in itself, furthermore proves a possible, what had hitherto been regarded as an impossible, reform, then he becomes a burning and a shining light, on which the aged may look with gladness, the young with hope, and the down-trodden, as a representative of what they may themselves become. To such a man, dear reader, it is my privilege to introduce you.

The life of Frederick Douglass, recorded in the pages which follow, is not merely an example of self-elevation under the most adverse circumstances; it is, moreover, a noble vindication of the highest aims of the American anti-slavery movement. The real object of that movement is not only to disenthrall, it is, also, to bestow upon the Negro the exercise of all those rights, from the possession of which he has been so long debarred.

But this full recognition of the colored man to the right, and the entire admission of the same to the full privileges, political, religious and social, of manhood, requires powerful effort on the part of the enthralled, as well as on the part of those who would disenthrall them. The people at large must feel the conviction, as well as admit the abstract logic, of human equality; the Negro, for the first time in the world's history, brought in full contact with high civilization, must prove his title first to all that is demanded for him; in the teeth of unequal chances, he must prove himself equal to the mass of those who oppress him—therefore, absolutely superior to his apparent fate, and to their relative ability. And it is most cheering to the friends of freedom, today, that evidence of this equality is rapidly accumulating, not from the ranks of the half-freed colored people of the free states, but from the very depths of slavery itself; the indestructible equality of man to man is demonstrated by the ease with which black men, scarce one remove from barbarism—if slavery can be honored with such a distinction—vault into the high places of the most advanced and painfully acquired civilization. Ward and Garnett, Wells Brown and Pennington, Loguen and Douglass, are banners on the outer wall, under which abolition is fighting its most successful battles, because they are living exemplars of the practicability of the most radical abolitionism; for, they were all of them born to the doom of slavery, some of them remained slaves until adult age, yet they all have not only won equality to their white fellow citizens, in civil, religious, political and social rank, but they have also illustrated and adorned our common country by their genius, learning and eloquence.

The characteristics whereby Mr. Douglass has won first rank among these remarkable men, and is still rising toward highest rank among living Americans, are abundantly laid bare in the book before us. Like the autobiography of Hugh Miller, it carries us so far back into early childhood, as to throw light upon the question, "when positive and persistent memory begins in the human being." And, like Hugh Miller, he must have been a shy old-fashioned child, occasionally oppressed by what he could not well account for, peering and poking about among the layers of right and wrong, of tyrant and thrall, and the wonderfulness of that hopeless tide of things which brought power to one race, and unrequited toil to another, until, finally, he stumbled upon his "first-found Ammonite," hidden away down in the depths of his own nature, and which revealed to him the fact that liberty and right, for all men, were anterior to slavery and wrong. When his knowledge of the world was bounded by the visible horizon on Col. Lloyd's plantation, and while every thing around him bore a fixed, iron stamp, as if it had always been so, this was, for one so young, a notable discovery.

To his uncommon memory, then, we must add a keen and accurate insight into men and things; an original breadth of common sense which enabled him to see, and weigh, and compare whatever passed before him, and which kindled a desire to search out and define their relations to other things not so patent, but which never succumbed to the marvelous nor the supernatural; a sacred thirst for liberty and for learning, first as a means of attaining liberty, then as an end in itself most desirable; a will; an unfaltering energy and determination to obtain what his soul pronounced desirable; a majestic self-hood; determined courage; a deep and agonizing sympathy with his embruted, crushed and bleeding fellow-slaves, and an extraordinary depth of passion, together with that rare alliance between passion and intellect, which enables the former, when deeply roused, to excite, develop and sustain the latter.

With these original gifts in view, let us look at his schooling; the fearful discipline through which it pleased God to prepare him for the high calling on which he has since entered—the advocacy of emancipation by the people who are not slaves. And for this special mission, his plantation education was better than any he could have acquired in any lettered school. What he needed, was facts and experiences, welded to acutely wrought up sympathies, and these he could not elsewhere have obtained, in a manner so peculiarly adapted to his nature. His physical being was well trained, also, running wild until advanced into boyhood; hard work and light diet, thereafter, and a skill in handicraft in youth.

For his special mission, then, this was, considered in connection with his natural gifts, a good schooling; and, for his special mission, he doubtless "left school" just at the proper moment. Had he remained longer in slavery—had he fretted under bonds until the ripening of manhood and its passions, until the drear agony of slave-wife and slave-children had been piled upon his already bitter experiences—then, not only would his own history have had another termination, but the drama of American slavery would have been essentially varied; for I cannot resist the belief, that the boy who learned to read and write as he did, who taught his fellow-slaves these precious acquirements as he did, who plotted for their mutual escape as he did, would, when a man at bay, strike a blow which would make slavery reel and stagger. Furthermore, blows and insults he bore, at the moment, without resentment; deep but suppressed emotion rendered him insensible to their sting; but it was afterward, when the memory of them went seething through his brain, breeding a fiery indignation at his injured self-hood, that the resolve came to resist, and the time fixed when to resist, and the plot laid, how to resist; and he always kept his self-pledged word. In what he undertook, in this line, he looked fate in the face, and had a cool, keen look at the relation of means to ends. Henry Bibb, to avoid chastisement, strewed his master's bed with charmed leaves and *was whipped*. Frederick Douglass quietly pocketed a like *fetiche*, compared his muscles with those of Covey—and *whipped him*.

In the history of his life in bondage, we find, well developed, that inherent and continuous energy of character which will ever render him distinguished. What his hand found to do, he did with his might; even while conscious that he was wronged out of his daily earnings, he worked, and worked hard. At his daily labor he went with a will; with keen, well set eye, brawny chest, lithe figure, and fair sweep of arm, he would have been king among calkers, had that been his mission.

It must not be overlooked, in this glance at his education, that Mr. Douglass lacked one aid to which so many men of mark have been deeply indebted—he had neither a mother's care, nor a mother's culture, save that which slavery grudgingly meted out to him. Bitter nurse! may not even her features relax with human feeling, when she gazes at such offspring! How susceptible he was to the kindly influences of mother-culture, may be gathered from his own words: "It has been a life-long standing grief to me, that I know so little of my mother, and that I was so early separated from her. The counsels of her love must have been beneficial to me. The side view of her face is imaged on my memory, and I take few steps in life, without feeling her presence; but the image is mute, and I have no striking words of hers treasured up."

From the depths of chattel slavery in Maryland, our author escaped into the caste-slavery of the north, in New Bedford, Massachusetts. Here he found oppression assuming another, and hardly less bitter, form; of that very handicraft which the greed of slavery had taught him, his half-freedom denied him the exercise for an honest living; he found himself one of a class—free colored men—whose position he has described in the following words:

"Aliens are we in our native land. The fundamental principles of the republic, to which the humblest white man, whether born here or elsewhere, may appeal with confidence, in the hope of awakening a favorable response, are held to be inapplicable to us. The glorious doctrines of your revolutionary fathers, and the more glorious teachings of the Son of God, are construed and applied against us. We are literally scourged beyond the beneficent range of both authorities, human and divine . . . American humanity hates us, scorns us, disowns and denies, in a thousand ways, our very personality. The outspread wing of American Christianity, apparently broad enough to give shelter to a perishing world, refuses to cover us. To us, its bones are brass, and its features iron. In running thither for shelter and succor, we have only fled from the hungry blood-hound to the devouring wolf—

from a corrupt and selfish world, to a hollow and hypocritical church."
—*Speech before American and Foreign Anti-Slavery Society, May, 1854.*

Four years or more, from 1837 to 1841, he struggled on, in New Bedford, sawing wood, rolling casks, or doing what labor he might, to support himself and young family; four years he brooded over the scars which slavery and semi-slavery had inflicted upon his body and soul; and then, with his wounds yet unhealed, he fell among the Garrisonians—a glorious waif to those most ardent reformers. It happened one day, at Nantucket, that he, diffidently and reluctantly, was led to address an anti-slavery meeting. He was about the age when the younger Pitt entered the House of Commons;* like Pitt, too, he stood up a born orator.

William Lloyd Garrison, who was happily present, writes thus of Mr. Douglass's maiden effort; "I shall never forget his first speech at the convention—the extraordinary emotion it excited in my own mind—the powerful impression it created upon a crowded auditory, completely taken by surprise . . . I think I never hated slavery so intensely as at that moment; certainly, my perception of the enormous outrage which is inflicted by it on the godlike nature of its victims, was rendered far more clear than ever. There stood one in physical proportions and stature commanding and exact—in intellect richly endowed—in natural eloquence a prodigy."

It is of interest to compare Mr. Douglass's account of this meeting with Mr. Garrison's. Of the two, I think the latter the most correct. It must have been a grand burst of eloquence! The pent up agony, indignation and pathos of an abused and harrowed boyhood and youth, bursting out in all their freshness and overwhelming earnestness!

This unique introduction to its great leader, led immediately to the employment of Mr. Douglass as an agent by the American Anti-Slavery Society. So far as his self-relying and independent character would permit, he became, after the strictest sect, a Garrisonian. It is not too much to say, that he formed a complement which they needed, and they were a complement equally necessary to his "make-up." With his deep and keen sensitiveness to wrong, and his wonderful memory, he came from the land of bondage full of its woes and its evils, and painting them in characters of living light; and, on his part, he found, told out in sound Saxon phrase, all those principles of justice and right

---

* British politician William Pitt the Younger became prime minister in 1783 at the age of 24.

and liberty, which had dimly brooded over the dreams of his youth, seeking definite forms and verbal expression. It must have been an electric flashing of thought, and a knitting of soul, granted to but few in this life, and will be a life-long memory to those who participated in it. In the society, moreover, of Wendell Phillips, Edmund Quincy, William Lloyd Garrison, and other men of earnest faith and refined culture, Mr. Douglass enjoyed the high advantage of their assistance and counsel in the labor of self-culture, to which he now addressed himself with wonted energy. Yet, these gentlemen, although proud of Frederick Douglass, failed to fathom, and bring out to the light of day, the highest qualities of his mind; the force of their own education stood in their own way: they did not delve into the mind of a colored man for capacities which the pride of race led them to believe to be restricted to their own Saxon blood. Bitter and vindictive sarcasm, irresistible mimicry, and a pathetic narrative of his own experiences of slavery, were the intellectual manifestations which they encouraged him to exhibit on the platform or in the lecture desk.

A visit to England, in 1845, threw Mr. Douglass among men and women of earnest souls and high culture, and who, moreover, had never drank of the bitter waters of American caste. For the first time in his life, he breathed an atmosphere congenial to the longings of his spirit, and felt his manhood free and unrestricted. The cordial and manly greetings of the British and Irish audiences in public, and the refinement and elegance of the social circles in which he mingled, not only as an equal, but as a recognized man of genius, were, doubtless, genial and pleasant resting places in his hitherto thorny and troubled journey through life. There are joys on the earth, and, to the wayfaring fugitive from American slavery or American caste, this is one of them.

But his sojourn in England was more than a joy to Mr. Douglass. Like the platform at Nantucket, it awakened him to the consciousness of new powers that lay in him. From the pupilage of Garrisonism he rose to the dignity of a teacher and a thinker; his opinions on the broader aspects of the great American question were earnestly and incessantly sought, from various points of view, and he must, perforce, bestir himself to give suitable answer. With that prompt and truthful perception which has led their sisters in all ages of the world to gather at the feet and support the hands of reformers, the gentlewomen of

England* were foremost to encourage and strengthen him to carve out for himself a path fitted to his powers and energies, in the life-battle against slavery and caste to which he was pledged. And one stirring thought, inseparable from the British idea of the evangel of freedom, must have smote his ear from every side—

> Hereditary bondmen! know ye not
> Who would be free, themselves must strike the blow?†

The result of this visit was, that on his return to the United States, he established a newspaper. This proceeding was sorely against the wishes and the advice of the leaders of the American Anti-Slavery Society, but our author had fully grown up to the conviction of a truth which they had once promulged, but now forgotten, to wit: that in their own elevation—self-elevation—colored men have a blow to strike "on their own hook," against slavery and caste. Differing from his Boston friends in this matter, diffident in his own abilities, reluctant at their dissuadings, how beautiful is the loyalty with which he still clung to their principles in all things else, and even in this.

Now came the trial hour. Without cordial support from any large body of men or party on this side the Atlantic, and too far distant in space and immediate interest to expect much more, after the much already done, on the other side, he stood up, almost alone, to the arduous labor and heavy expenditure of editor and lecturer. The Garrison party, to which he still adhered, did not want a colored newspaper— there was an odor of *caste* about it; the Liberty party could hardly be expected to give warm support to a man who smote their principles as with a hammer; and the wide gulf which separated the free colored people from the Garrisonians, also separated them from their brother, Frederick Douglass.

The arduous nature of his labors, from the date of the establishment of his paper, may be estimated by the fact, that anti-slavery papers in the United States, even while organs of, and when supported by, anti-slavery parties, have, with a single exception, failed to pay expenses.

---

* One of these ladies, impelled by the same noble spirit which carried Miss Nightingale to Scutari [Turkey], has devoted her time, her untiring energies, to a great extent her means, and her high literary abilities, to the advancement and support of Frederick Douglass's Paper, the only organ of the down-trodden, edited and published by one of themselves, in the United States. (Original note)
† From *Childe Harold's Pilgrimage* by George Gordon, Lord Byron.

Mr. Douglass has maintained, and does maintain, his paper without the support of any party, and even in the teeth of the opposition of those from whom he had reason to expect counsel and encouragement. He has been compelled, at one and the same time, and almost constantly, during the past seven years, to contribute matter to its columns as editor, and to raise funds for its support as lecturer. It is within bounds to say, that he has expended twelve thousand dollars of his own hard earned money, in publishing this paper, a larger sum than has been contributed by any one individual for the general advancement of the colored people. There had been many other papers published and edited by colored men, beginning as far back as 1827, when the Rev. Samuel E. Cornish and John B. Russworm (a graduate of Bowdoin college, and afterward Governor of Cape Palmas) published the *Freedom's Journal*, in New York City; probably not less than one hundred newspaper enterprises have been started in the United States, by free colored men, born free, and some of them of liberal education and fair talents for this work; but, one after another, they have fallen through, although, in several instances, anti-slavery friends contributed to their support.[*] It had almost been given up, as an impracticable thing, to maintain a colored newspaper, when Mr. Douglass, with fewest early advantages of all his competitors, essayed, and has proved the thing perfectly practicable, and, moreover, of great public benefit. This paper, in addition to its power in holding up the hands of those to whom it is especially devoted, also affords irrefutable evidence of the justice, safety and practicability of Immediate Emancipation; it further proves the immense loss which slavery inflicts on the land while it dooms such energies as his to the hereditary degradation of slavery.

It has been said in this Introduction, that Mr. Douglass had raised himself by his own efforts to the highest position in society. As a successful editor, in our land, he occupies this position. Our editors rule the land, and he is one of them. As an orator and thinker, his position is equally high, in the opinion of his countrymen. If a stranger in the United States would seek its most distinguished men—the movers of public opinion—he will find their names mentioned, and their movements chronicled, under the head of *"By Magnetic Telegraph,"* in the daily papers. The keen caterers for the public attention, set down, in

---

[*] Mr. Stephen Myers, of Albany, deserves mention as one of the most persevering among the colored editorial fraternity.

this column, such men only as have won high mark in the public esteem. During the past winter—1854-5—very frequent mention of Frederick Douglass was made under this head in the daily papers; his name glided as often—this week from Chicago, next week from Boston—over the lightning wires, as the name of any other man, of whatever note. To no man did the people more widely nor more earnestly say, "*Tell me thy thought!*" And, somehow or other, revolution seemed to follow in his wake. His were not the mere words of eloquence which Kossuth speaks of, that delight the ear and then pass away. No! They were *work*-able, *do*-able words, that brought forth fruits in the revolution in Illinois, and in the passage of the franchise resolutions by the Assembly of New York.

And the secret of his power, what is it? He is a Representative American man—a type of his countrymen. Naturalists tell us that a full grown man is a resultant or representative of all animated nature on this globe; beginning with the early embryo state, then representing the lowest forms of organic life,* and passing through every subordinate grade or type, until he reaches the last and highest—manhood. In like manner, and to the fullest extent, has Frederick Douglass passed through every gradation of rank comprised in our national make-up, and bears upon his person and upon his soul every thing that is American. And he has not only full sympathy with every thing American; his proclivity or bent, to active toil and visible progress, are in the strictly national direction, delighting to outstrip "all creation."

Nor have the natural gifts, already named as his, lost anything by his severe training. When unexcited, his mental processes are probably slow, but singularly clear in perception, and wide in vision, the unfailing memory bringing up all the facts in their every aspect; incongruities he lays hold of incontinently, and holds up on the edge of his keen and telling wit. But this wit never descends to frivolity; it is rigidly in the keeping of his truthful common sense, and always used in illustration or proof of some point which could not so readily be reached any other way. "Beware of a Yankee when he is feeding," is a shaft that strikes home in a matter never so laid bare by satire before. "The Garrisonian views of disunion, if carried to a successful issue, would only place the people of the north in the same relation to American slavery which

---

* The German physiologists have even discovered vegetable matter—starch—in the human body. See Med. Chirurgical Rev., Oct., 1854, p. 339.

they now bear to the slavery of Cuba or the Brazils," is a statement, in a few words, which contains the result and the evidence of an argument which might cover pages, but could not carry stronger conviction, nor be stated in less pregnable form. In proof of this, I may say, that having been submitted to the attention of the Garrisonians in print, in March, it was repeated before them at their business meeting in May—the platform, *par excellence*, on which they invite free fight, *a l'outrance*, to all comers. It was given out in the clear, ringing tones, wherewith the hall of shields was wont to resound of old, yet neither Garrison, nor Phillips, nor May, nor Remond, nor Foster, nor Burleigh, with his subtle steel of "the ice brook's temper," ventured to break a lance upon it! The doctrine of the dissolution of the Union, as a means for the abolition of American slavery, was silenced upon the lips that gave it birth, and in the presence of an array of defenders who compose the keenest intellects in the land.

"*The man who is right is a majority*" is an aphorism struck out by Mr. Douglass in that great gathering of the friends of freedom, at Pittsburgh, in 1852, where he towered among the highest, because, with abilities inferior to none, and moved more deeply than any, there was neither policy nor party to trammel the outpourings of his soul. Thus we find, opposed to all disadvantages which a black man in the United States labors and struggles under, is this one vantage ground—when the chance comes, and the audience where he may have a say, he stands forth the freest, most deeply moved and most earnest of all men.

It has been said of Mr. Douglass, that his descriptive and declamatory powers, admitted to be of the very highest order, take precedence of his logical force. Whilst the schools might have trained him to the exhibition of the formulas of deductive logic, nature and circumstances forced him into the exercise of the higher faculties required by induction. The first ninety pages of this "Life in Bondage," afford specimens of observing, comparing, and careful classifying, of such superior character, that it is difficult to believe them the results of a child's thinking; he questions the earth, and the children and the slaves around him again and again, and finally looks to "*God in the sky*" for the why and the wherefore of the unnatural thing, slavery. "*Yes, if indeed thou art, wherefore dost thou suffer us to be slain?*" is the only prayer and worship of the God-forsaken Dodos in the heart of Africa. Almost the same was his prayer. One of his earliest observations was that white children should know their ages, while the colored children were ignorant of theirs; and the songs of the slaves grated on his inmost soul, because a something told him that harmony in sound, and music of the spirit, could not consociate with miserable degradation.

To such a mind, the ordinary processes of logical deduction are like proving that two and two make four. Mastering the intermediate steps by an intuitive glance, or recurring to them as Ferguson resorted to geometry, it goes down to the deeper relation of things, and brings out what may seem, to some, mere statements, but which are new and brilliant generalizations, each resting on a broad and stable basis. Thus, Chief Justice Marshall gave his decisions, and then told Brother Story to look up the authorities—and they never differed from him. Thus, also, in his "Lecture on the Anti-Slavery Movement," delivered before the Rochester Ladies' Anti-Slavery Society, Mr. Douglass presents a mass of thought, which, without any showy display of logic on his part, requires an exercise of the reasoning faculties of the reader to keep pace with him. And his "Claims of the Negro Ethnologically Considered," is full of new and fresh thoughts on the dawning science of race-history.

If, as has been stated, his intellection is slow, when unexcited, it is most prompt and rapid when he is thoroughly aroused. Memory, logic, wit, sarcasm, invective pathos and bold imagery of rare structural beauty, well up as from a copious fountain, yet each in its proper place, and contributing to form a whole, grand in itself, yet complete in the minutest proportions. It is most difficult to hedge him in a corner, for his positions are taken so deliberately, that it is rare to find a point in them undefended aforethought. Professor Reason tells me the following: "On a recent visit of a public nature, to Philadelphia, and in a meeting composed mostly of his colored brethren, Mr. Douglass proposed a comparison of views in the matters of the relations and duties of 'our people;' he holding that prejudice was the result of condition, and could be conquered by the efforts of the degraded themselves. A gentleman present, distinguished for logical acumen and subtlety, and who had devoted no small portion of the last twenty-five years to the study and elucidation of this very question, held the opposite view, that prejudice is innate and unconquerable. He terminated a series of well dove-tailed, Socratic questions to Mr. Douglass, with the following: 'If the legislature at Harrisburgh should awaken, tomorrow morning, and find each man's skin turned black and his hair woolly, what could they do to remove prejudice?' 'Immediately pass laws entitling black men to all civil, political and social privileges,' was the instant reply—and the questioning ceased."

The most remarkable mental phenomenon in Mr. Douglass, is his style in writing and speaking. In March, 1855, he delivered an address in the assembly chamber before the members of the legislature of the state of New York. An eye witness[*] describes the crowded and most intelligent audience, and their rapt attention to the speaker, as the grandest scene he ever witnessed in the capitol. Among those whose eyes were riveted on the speaker full two hours and a half, were Thurlow Weed and Lieutenant Governor Raymond; the latter, at the conclusion of the address, exclaimed to a friend, "I would give twenty thousand dollars, if I could deliver that address in that manner." Mr. Raymond is a first class graduate of Dartmouth, a rising politician, ranking foremost in the legislature; of course, his ideal of oratory must be of the most polished and finished description.

The style of Mr. Douglass in writing, is to me an intellectual puzzle. The strength, affluence and terseness may easily be accounted for, because the style of a man is the man; but how are we to account for that rare polish in his style of writing, which, most critically examined, seems the result of careful early culture among the best classics of our language; it equals if it does not surpass the style of Hugh Miller, which was the wonder of the British literary public, until he unraveled the mystery in the most interesting of autobiographies. But Frederick Douglass was still calking the seams of Baltimore clippers, and had only written a "pass," at the age when Miller's style was already formed.

I asked William Whipper, of Pennsylvania, the gentleman alluded to above, whether he thought Mr. Douglass's power inherited from the Negroid, or from what is called the Caucasian side of his make up? After some reflection, he frankly answered, "I must admit, although sorry to do so, that the Caucasian predominates." At that time, I almost agreed with him; but, facts narrated in the first part of this work, throw a different light on this interesting question.

[*] Mr. Wm. H. Topp, of Albany.

We are left in the dark as to who was the paternal ancestor of our author; a fact which generally holds good of the Romuluses and Remuses who are to inaugurate the new birth of our republic. In the absence of testimony from the Caucasian side, we must see what evidence is given on the other side of the house.

"My grandmother, though advanced in years, was yet a woman of power and spirit. She was marvelously straight in figure, elastic and muscular."

After describing her skill in constructing nets, her perseverance in using them, and her wide-spread fame in the agricultural way he adds, "It happened to her—as it will happen to any careful and thrifty person residing in an ignorant and improvident neighborhood—to enjoy the reputation of being born to good luck." And his grandmother was a black woman.

"My mother was tall, and finely proportioned; of deep black, glossy complexion; had regular features; and among other slaves was remarkably sedate in her manners." "Being a field hand, she was obliged to walk twelve miles and return, between nightfall and daybreak, to see her children." "I shall never forget the indescribable expression of her countenance when I told her that I had had no food since morning . . . There was pity in her glance at me, and a fiery indignation at Aunt Katy at the same time; . . . she read Aunt Katy a lecture which she never forgot." "I learned after my mother's death, that she could read, and that she was the only one of all the slaves and colored people in Tuckahoe who enjoyed that advantage. How she acquired this knowledge, I know not, for Tuckahoe is the last place in the world where she would be apt to find facilities for learning." "There is, in *Prichard's Natural History of Man*, the head of a figurethe features of which so resemble those of my mother, that I often recur to it with something of the feeling which I suppose others experience when looking upon the pictures of dear departed ones."

The head alluded to is copied from the statue of Ramses the Great, an Egyptian king of the nineteenth dynasty. The authors of the *Types of Mankind* give a side view of the same, remarking that the profile, "like Napoleon's, is superbly European!" The nearness of its resemblance to Mr. Douglass's mother rests upon the evidence of his memory, and judging from his almost marvelous feats of recollection of forms and outlines recorded in this book, this testimony may be admitted.

These facts show that for his energy, perseverance, eloquence, invective, sagacity, and wide sympathy, he is indebted to his Negro blood. The very marvel of his style would seem to be a development of that other marvel—how his mother learned to read. The versatility of talent which he wields, in common with Dumas, Ira Aldridge, and Miss Greenfield, would seem to be the result of the grafting of the Anglo-Saxon on good, original, Negro stock. If the friends of "Caucasus" choose to claim, for that region, what remains after this analysis—to wit: combination—they are welcome to it. They will forgive me for reminding them that the term "Caucasian" is cropped by recent writers on Ethnology; for the people about Mount Caucasus, are, and have ever been, Mongols. The great "white race" now seek paternity, according to Dr. Pickering, in Arabia—"Arida Nutrix" of the best breed of horses etc. Keep on, gentlemen; you will find yourselves in Africa, by-and-by. The Egyptians, like the Americans, were a *mixed race*, with some Negro blood circling around the throne, as well as in the mud hovels.

This is the proper place to remark of our author, that the same strong self-hood, which led him to measure strength with Mr. Covey, and to wrench himself from the embrace of the Garrisonians, and which has borne him through many resistances to the personal indignities offered him as a colored man, sometimes becomes a hyper-sensitiveness to such assaults as men of his mark will meet with, on paper. Keen and unscrupulous opponents have sought, and not unsuccessfully, to pierce him in this direction; for well they know, that if assailed, he will smite back.

It is not without a feeling of pride, dear reader, that I present you with this book. The son of a self-emancipated bond-woman, I feel joy in introducing to you my brother, who has rent his own bonds, and who, in his every relation—as a public man, as a husband and as a father—is such as does honor to the land which gave him birth. I shall place this book in the hands of the only child spared me, bidding him to strive and emulate its noble example. You may do likewise. It is an American book, for Americans, in the fullest sense of the idea. It shows that the worst of our institutions, in its worst aspect, cannot keep down energy, truthfulness, and earnest struggle for the right. It proves the justice and practicability of Immediate Emancipation. It shows that any man in our land, "no matter in what battle his liberty may have been cloven down, . . . no matter what complexion an Indian or an African sun may have burned upon him," not only may "stand forth redeemed and disenthralled," but may also stand up a candidate for the highest suffrage of a great people—the tribute of their honest, hearty admiration. Reader, *Vale!*

New York
*James M'Cune Smith**

---

* Nineteenth-century abolitionist, James M'Cune Smith was the first African American hold a medical degree.

# LIFE AS A SLAVE

## CHAPTER I

### CHILDHOOD

*Place of birth—Character of the District—Tuckahoe—Origin
of the Name—Choptank River—Time of Birth—Genealogical
Trees—Mode of Counting Time—Names of Grandparents—
Their Position—Grandmother Especially Esteemed—"Born
to Good Luck"—Sweet Potatoes—Superstition—The Log
Cabin—Its Charms—Separating Children—My Aunts—Their
Names—First Knowledge of Being a Slave—Old Master—
Griefs and Joys of Childhood—Comparative Happiness of the
Slave-Boy and the Son of a Slaveholder.*

In Talbot County, Eastern Shore, Maryland, near Easton, the county town of that county, there is a small district of country, thinly populated, and remarkable for nothing that I know of more than for the worn-out, sandy, desert-like appearance of its soil, the general dilapidation of its farms and fences, the indigent and spiritless character of its inhabitants, and the prevalence of ague and fever.

The name of this singularly unpromising and truly famine stricken district is Tuckahoe, a name well known to all Marylanders, black and white. It was given to this section of country probably, at the first, merely in derision; or it may possibly have been applied to it, as I have heard, because some one of its earlier inhabitants had been guilty of the petty meanness of stealing a hoe—or taking a hoe that did not belong to him. Eastern Shore men usually pronounce the word *took*, as *tuck*; *Took-a-hoe*, therefore, is, in Maryland parlance, *Tuckahoe*. But, whatever may have been its origin—and about this I will not be positive—that name has stuck to the district in question; and it is seldom mentioned but with contempt and derision, on account of the barrenness of its soil, and the ignorance, indolence, and poverty of its people. Decay and ruin are everywhere visible, and the thin population of the place would have quitted it long ago, but for the Choptank River, which runs through it, from which they take abundance of shad and herring, and plenty of ague and fever.

It was in this dull, flat, and unthrifty district, or neighborhood, surrounded by a white population of the lowest order, indolent and drunken to a proverb, and among slaves, who seemed to ask, "*Oh! What's the use?*" every time they lifted a hoe, that I—without any fault of mine—was born, and spent the first years of my childhood.

The reader will pardon so much about the place of my birth, on the score that it is always a fact of some importance to know where a man is born, if, indeed, it be important to know anything about him. In regard to the *time* of my birth, I cannot be as definite as I have been respecting the *place*. Nor, indeed, can I impart much knowledge concerning my parents. Genealogical trees do not flourish among slaves. A person of some consequence here in the north, sometimes designated *father*, is literally abolished in slave law and slave practice. It is only once in a while that an exception is found to this statement. I never met with a slave who could tell me how old he was. Few slave-mothers know anything of the months of the year, nor of the days of the month. They keep no family records, with marriages, births, and deaths. They measure the ages of their children by spring-time, winter-time, harvest-time, planting-time, and the like; but these soon become undistinguishable and forgotten. Like other slaves, I cannot tell how old I am. This destitution was among my earliest troubles. I learned when I grew up, that my master—and this is the case with masters generally— allowed no questions to be put to him, by which a slave might learn his age. Such questions deemed evidence of impatience, and even of impudent curiosity. From certain events, however, the dates of which I have since learned, I suppose myself to have been born about the year 1817.

The first experience of life with me that I now remember—and I remember it but hazily—began in the family of my grandmother and grandfather, Betsey and Isaac Baily. They were quite advanced in life, and had long lived on the spot where they then resided. They were considered old settlers in the neighborhood, and, from certain circumstances, I infer that my grandmother, especially, was held in high esteem, far higher than is the lot of most colored persons in the slave states. She was a good nurse, and a capital hand at making nets for catching shad and herring; and these nets were in great demand, not only in Tuckahoe, but at Denton and Hillsborough, neighboring villages. She was not only good at making the nets, but was also somewhat famous for her good fortune in taking the fishes referred to. I have known her to be in the water half the day. Grandmother was likewise more provident than most of her neighbors in the preservation of seedling sweet potatoes, and it happened to her—as it will happen to any careful and thrifty person residing in an ignorant and improvident community—to enjoy the reputation of having been born to "good luck." Her "good luck" was owing to the exceeding care which she took in preventing the succulent root from getting bruised in the digging, and in placing it beyond the reach of frost, by actually burying it under the hearth of her cabin during the winter months. In the time of planting sweet potatoes, "Grandmother Betty," as she was familiarly called, was sent for in all directions, simply to place the seedling potatoes in the hills; for superstition had it, that if "Grandmamma Betty but touches them at planting, they will be sure to grow and flourish." This high reputation was full of advantage to her, and to the children around her. Though Tuckahoe had but few of the good things of life, yet of such as it did possess grandmother got a full share, in the way of presents. If good potato crops came after her planting, she was not forgotten by those for whom she planted; and as she was remembered by others, so she remembered the hungry little ones around her.

The dwelling of my grandmother and grandfather had few pretensions. It was a log hut, or cabin, built of clay, wood, and straw. At a distance it resembled—though it was smaller, less commodious and less substantial—the cabins erected in the western states by the first settlers. To my child's eye, however, it was a noble structure, admirably adapted to promote the comforts and conveniences of its inmates. A few rough, Virginia fence-rails, flung loosely over the rafters above, answered the triple purpose of floors, ceilings, and bedsteads. To be sure, this upper apartment was reached only by a ladder—but what in the world for climbing could be better than a ladder? To me, this ladder was really a high invention, and possessed a sort of charm as I played with delight upon the rounds of it. In this little hut there was a large family of children: I dare not say how many. My grandmother—whether because too old for field service, or because she had so faithfully discharged the duties of her station in early life, I know not—enjoyed the high privilege of living in a cabin, separate from the quarter, with no other burden than her own support, and the necessary care of the little children, imposed. She evidently esteemed it a great fortune to live so. The children were not her own, but her grandchildren—the children of her daughters. She took delight in having them around her, and in attending to their few wants. The practice of separating children from their mother, and hiring the latter out at distances too great to admit of their meeting, except at long intervals, is a marked feature of the cruelty and barbarity of the slave system. But it is in harmony with the grand aim of slavery, which, always and everywhere, is to reduce man to a level with the brute. It is a successful method of obliterating from the mind and heart of the slave, all just ideas of the sacredness of *the family*, as an institution.

Most of the children, however, in this instance, being the children of my grandmother's daughters, the notions of family, and the reciprocal duties and benefits of the relation, had a better chance of being understood than where children are placed—as they often are in the hands of strangers, who have no care for them, apart from the wishes of their masters. The daughters of my grandmother were five in number. Their names were *Jenny, Esther, Milly, Priscilla*, and *Harriet*. The daughter last named was my mother, of whom the reader shall learn more by-and-by.

Living here, with my dear old grandmother and grandfather, it was a long time before I knew myself to be a *slave*. I knew many other things before I knew that. Grandmother and grandfather were the greatest people in the world to me; and being with them so snugly in their own little cabin—I supposed it be their own—knowing no higher authority over me or the other children than the authority of grandmamma, for a time there was nothing to disturb me; but, as I grew larger and older, I learned by degrees the sad fact, that the "little hut," and the lot on which it stood, belonged not to my dear old grandparents, but to some person who lived a great distance off, and who was called, by grandmother, "*Old Master*." I further learned the sadder fact, that not only the house and lot, but that grandmother herself, (grandfather was free), and all the little children around her, belonged to this mysterious personage, called by grandmother, with every mark of reverence, "Old Master." Thus early did clouds and shadows begin to fall upon my path. Once on the track—troubles never come singly—I was not long in finding out another fact, still more grievous to my childish heart. I was told that this "old master," whose name seemed ever to be mentioned with fear and shuddering, only allowed the children to live with grandmother for a limited time, and that in fact as soon as they were big enough, they were promptly taken away, to live with the said "old master." These were distressing revelations indeed; and though I was quite too young to comprehend the full import of the intelligence, and mostly spent my childhood days in gleesome sports with the other children, a shade of disquiet rested upon me.

The absolute power of this distant "old master" had touched my young spirit with but the point of its cold, cruel iron, and left me something to brood over after the play and in moments of repose. Grandmammy was, indeed, at that time, all the world to me; and the thought of being separated from her, in any considerable time, was more than an unwelcome intruder. It was intolerable.

Children have their sorrows as well as men and women; and it would be well to remember this in our dealings with them. *Slave*-children *are* children, and prove no exceptions to the general rule. The liability to be separated from my grandmother, seldom or never to see her again, haunted me. I dreaded the thought of going to live with that mysterious "old master," whose name I never heard mentioned with affection, but always with fear. I look back to this as among the heaviest of my childhood's sorrows. My grandmother! My grandmother! And the little hut, and the joyous circle under her care, but especially *she*, who made us sorry when she left us but for an hour, and glad on her return—how could I leave her and the good old home?

But the sorrows of childhood, like the pleasures of after life, are transient. It is not even within the power of slavery to write *indelible* sorrow, at a single dash, over the heart of a child.

> The tear down childhood's cheek that flows,
> Is like the dew-drop on the rose—
> When next the summer breeze comes by,
> And waves the bush—the flower is dry.*

There is, after all, but little difference in the measure of contentment

---

* From *Rokeby* by Walter Scott.

felt by the slave-child neglected and the slaveholder's child cared for and petted. The spirit of the All Just mercifully holds the balance for the young.

The slaveholder, having nothing to fear from impotent childhood, easily affords to refrain from cruel inflictions; and if cold and hunger do not pierce the tender frame, the first seven or eight years of the slave-boy's life are about as full of sweet content as those of the most favored and petted white children of the slaveholder. The slave-boy escapes many troubles which befall and vex his white brother. He seldom has to listen to lectures on propriety of behavior, or on anything else. He is never chided for handling his little knife and fork improperly or awkwardly, for he uses none. He is never reprimanded for soiling the table-cloth, for he takes his meals on the clay floor. He never has the misfortune, in his games or sports, of soiling or tearing his clothes, for he has almost none to soil or tear. He is never expected to act like a nice little gentleman, for he is only a rude little slave. Thus, freed from all restraint, the slave-boy can be, in his life and conduct, a genuine boy, doing whatever his boyish nature suggests; enacting, by turns, all the strange antics and freaks of horses, dogs, pigs, and barn-door fowls, without in any manner compromising his dignity, or incurring reproach of any sort. He literally runs wild; has no pretty little verses to learn in the nursery; no nice little speeches to make for aunts, uncles, or cousins, to show how smart he is; and, if he can only manage to keep out of the way of the heavy feet and fists of the older slave-boys, he may trot on, in his joyous and roguish tricks, as happy as any little heathen under the palm trees of Africa. To be sure, he is occasionally reminded, when he stumbles in the path of his master—and this he early learns to avoid—that he is eating his "*white bread*," and that he will be made to "*see sights*" by-and-by. The threat is soon forgotten; the shadow soon passes, and our sable boy continues to roll in the dust, or play in the mud, as bests suits him, and in the veriest freedom. If he feels uncomfortable, from mud or from dust, the coast is clear; he can plunge into the river or the pond, without the ceremony of undressing, or the fear of wetting his clothes; his little tow-linen shirt—for that is all he has on—is easily dried; and it needed ablution as much as did his skin. His food is of the coarsest kind, consisting for the most part of cornmeal mush, which often finds its way from the wooden tray to his mouth in an oyster shell. His days, when the weather is warm, are spent in the pure, open air, and in the bright sunshine. He always sleeps in airy apartments; he seldom has to take powders, or to be paid to swallow pretty little sugar-coated pills, to cleanse his blood, or to quicken his appetite. He eats no candies; gets no lumps of loaf sugar; always relishes his food; cries but little, for nobody cares for his crying; learns to esteem his bruises but slight, because others so esteem them. In a word, he is, for the most part of the first eight years of his life, a spirited, joyous, uproarious, and happy boy, upon whom troubles fall only like water on a duck's back. And such a boy, so far as I can now remember, was the boy whose life in slavery I am now narrating.

# CHAPTER II

## REMOVED FROM MY FIRST HOME

*The Name "Old Master" a Terror—Colonel Lloyd's
Plantation—Wye River—Whence Its Name—Position of the
Lloyds—Home Attraction—Meet Offering—Journey From
Tuckahoe to Wye River—Scene on Reaching Old Master's—
Departure of Grandmother—Strange Meeting of Sisters and
Brothers—Refusal to Be Comforted—Sweet Sleep.*

That mysterious individual referred to in the first chapter as an object of terror among the inhabitants of our little cabin, under the ominous title of "old master," was really a man of some consequence. He owned several farms in Tuckahoe; was the chief clerk and butler on the home plantation of Col. Edward Lloyd; had overseers on his own farms; and gave directions to overseers on the farms belonging to Col. Lloyd. This plantation is situated on Wye River—the river receiving its name, doubtless, from Wales, where the Lloyds originated. They (the Lloyds) are an old and honored family in Maryland, exceedingly wealthy. The home plantation, where they have resided, perhaps for a century or more, is one of the largest, most fertile, and best appointed, in the state.

About this plantation, and about that queer old master—who must be something more than a man, and something worse than an angel—the reader will easily imagine that I was not only curious, but eager, to know all that could be known. Unhappily for me, however, all the information I could get concerning him increased my great dread of being carried thither—of being separated from and deprived of the protection of my grandmother and grandfather. It was, evidently, a great thing to go to Col. Lloyd's; and I was not without a little curiosity to see the place; but no amount of coaxing could induce in me the wish to remain there. The fact is, such was my dread of leaving the little cabin, that I wished to remain little forever, for I knew the taller I grew the shorter my stay. The old cabin, with its rail floor and rail bedsteads upstairs, and its clay floor downstairs, and its dirt chimney, and windowless sides, and that most curious piece of workmanship dug in front of the fireplace, beneath which grandmammy placed the sweet potatoes to keep them from the frost, *was my home*—the only home I ever had; and I loved it, and all connected with it. The old fences around it, and the stumps in the edge of the woods near it, and the squirrels that ran, skipped, and played upon them, were objects of interest and affection. There, too, right at the side of the hut, stood the old well, with its stately and skyward-pointing beam, so aptly placed between the limbs of what had once been a tree, and so nicely balanced that I could move it up and down with only one hand, and could get a drink myself without calling for help. Where else in the world could such a well be found, and where could such another home be met with? Nor were these all the attractions of the place. Down in a little valley, not far from grandmammy's cabin, stood Mr. Lee's mill, where the people came often in large numbers to get their corn ground. It was a watermill; and I never shall be able to tell the many things thought and felt, while I sat on the bank and watched that mill, and the turning of that ponderous wheel. The mill-pond, too, had its charms; and with my pinhook, and thread line, I could get *nibbles*, if I could catch no fish. But, in all my sports and plays, and in spite of them, there would, occasionally, come the painful foreboding that I was not long to remain there, and that I must soon be called away to the home of old master.

I was *a slave*—born a slave and though the fact was incomprehensible to me, it conveyed to my mind a sense of my entire dependence on the will of *somebody* I had never seen; and, from some cause or other, I had been made to fear this somebody above all else on earth. Born for another's benefit, as the *firstling* of the cabin flock I was soon to be selected as a meet offering to the fearful and inexorable demigod, whose huge image on so many occasions haunted my childhood's imagination. When the time of my departure was decided upon, my grandmother, knowing my fears, and in pity for them, kindly kept me ignorant of the dreaded event about to transpire. Up to the morning (a beautiful summer morning) when we were to start, and, indeed, during the whole journey—a journey which, child as I was, I remember as well as if it were yesterday—she kept the sad fact hidden from me. This reserve was necessary; for, could I have known all, I should have given grandmother some trouble in getting me started. As it was, I was helpless, and she—dear woman!—led me along by the hand, resisting, with the reserve and solemnity of a priestess, all my inquiring looks to the last.

The distance from Tuckahoe to Wye River—where my old master lived—was full twelve miles, and the walk was quite a severe test of the endurance of my young legs. The journey would have proved too severe for me, but that my dear old grandmother—blessings on her memory!—afforded occasional relief by "toting" me (as Marylanders have it) on her shoulder. My grandmother, though advanced in years—as was evident from more than one gray hair, which peeped from between the ample and graceful folds of her newly-ironed bandana turban—was yet a woman of power and spirit. She was marvelously straight in figure, elastic, and muscular. I seemed hardly to be a burden to her. She would have "toted" me farther, but that I felt myself too much of a man to allow it, and insisted on walking. Releasing dear grandmamma from carrying me, did not make me altogether independent of her, when we happened to pass through portions of the somber woods which lay between Tuckahoe and Wye River. She often found me increasing the energy of my grip, and holding her clothing, lest something should come out of the woods and eat me up. Several old logs and stumps imposed upon me, and got themselves taken for wild beasts. I could see their legs, eyes, and ears, or I could see something like eyes, legs, and ears, till I got close enough to them to see that the eyes were knots, washed white with rain, and the legs were broken limbs, and the ears, only ears owing to the point from which they were seen. Thus early I learned that the point from which a thing is viewed is of some importance.

As the day advanced the heat increased; and it was not until the afternoon that we reached the much dreaded end of the journey. I found myself in the midst of a group of children of many colors; black, brown, copper colored, and nearly white. I had not seen so many children before. Great houses loomed up in different directions, and a great many men and women were at work in the fields. All this hurry, noise, and singing was very different from the stillness of Tuckahoe. As a new comer, I was an object of special interest; and, after laughing and yelling around me, and playing all sorts of wild tricks, they (the children) asked me to go out and play with them. This I refused to do, preferring to stay with grandmamma. I could not help feeling that our being there boded no good to me. Grandmamma looked sad. She was soon to lose another object of affection, as she had lost many before. I knew she was unhappy, and the shadow fell from her brow on me, though I knew not the cause.

All suspense, however, must have an end; and the end of mine, in this instance, was at hand. Affectionately patting me on the head, and exhorting me to be a good boy, grandmamma told me to go and play with the little children. "They are kin to you," said she; "go and play with them." Among a number of cousins were Phil, Tom, Steve, and Jerry, Nance and Betty.

Grandmother pointed out my brother Perry, my sister Sarah, and my sister Eliza, who stood in the group. I had never seen my brother nor my sisters before; and, though I had sometimes heard of them, and felt a curious interest in them, I really did not understand what they were to me, or I to them. We were brothers and sisters, but what of that? Why should they be attached to me, or I to them? Brothers and sisters we were by blood; but slavery had made us strangers. I heard the words brother and sisters, and knew they must mean something; but slavery had robbed these terms of their true meaning. The experience through which I was passing, they had passed through before. They had already been initiated into the mysteries of old master's domicile, and they seemed to look upon me with a certain degree of compassion; but my heart clave to my grandmother. Think it not strange, dear reader, that so little sympathy of feeling existed between us. The conditions of brotherly and sisterly feeling were wanting—we had never nestled and played together. My poor mother, like many other slave-women, had *many children*, but *no family*! The domestic hearth, with its holy lessons and precious endearments, is abolished in the case of a slave-mother and her children. "Little children, love one another," are words seldom heard in a slave cabin.

I really wanted to play with my brother and sisters, but they were strangers to me, and I was full of fear that grandmother might leave without taking me with her. Entreated to do so, however, and that, too, by my dear grandmother, I went to the back part of the house, to play with them and the other children. *Play*, however, I did not, but stood with my back against the wall, witnessing the playing of the others. At last, while standing there, one of the children, who had been in the kitchen, ran up to me, in a sort of roguish glee, exclaiming, "Fed, Fed!

Grandmammy gone! Grandmammy gone!" I could not believe it; yet, fearing the worst, I ran into the kitchen, to see for myself, and found it even so. Grandmammy had indeed gone, and was now far away, "clean" out of sight. I need not tell all that happened now. Almost heart-broken at the discovery, I fell upon the ground, and wept a boy's bitter tears, refusing to be comforted. My brother and sisters came around me, and said, "Don't cry," and gave me peaches and pears, but I flung them away, and refused all their kindly advances. I had never been deceived before; and I felt not only grieved at parting—as I supposed forever— with my grandmother, but indignant that a trick had been played upon me in a matter so serious.

It was now late in the afternoon. The day had been an exciting and wearisome one, and I knew not how or where, but I suppose I sobbed myself to sleep. There is a healing in the angel wing of sleep, even for the slave-boy; and its balm was never more welcome to any wounded soul than it was to mine, the first night I spent at the domicile of old master. The reader may be surprised that I narrate so minutely an incident apparently so trivial, and which must have occurred when I was not more than seven years old; but as I wish to give a faithful history of my experience in slavery, I cannot withhold a circumstance which, at the time, affected me so deeply. Besides, this was, in fact, my first introduction to the realities of slavery.

# CHAPTER III

## PARENTAGE

*My Father Shrouded in Mystery—My Mother—Her Personal
Appearance—Interference of Slavery with the Natural
Affections of Mother and Children—Situation of My
Mother—Her Nightly Visits to Her Boy—Striking Incident—
Her Death—Her Place of Burial.*

If the reader will now be kind enough to allow me time to grow
bigger, and afford me an opportunity for my experience to become
greater, I will tell him something, by-and-by, of slave life, as I saw, felt,
and heard it, on Col. Edward Lloyd's plantation, and at the house of
old master, where I had now, despite of myself, most suddenly, but not
unexpectedly, been dropped. Meanwhile, I will redeem my promise to
say something more of my dear mother.

I say nothing of *father*, for he is shrouded in a mystery I have never
been able to penetrate. Slavery does away with fathers, as it does away
with families. Slavery has no use for either fathers or families, and its
laws do not recognize their existence in the social arrangements of the
plantation. When they *do* exist, they are not the outgrowths of slavery,
but are antagonistic to that system. The order of civilization is reversed
here. The name of the child is not expected to be that of its father, and
his condition does not necessarily affect that of the child. He may be
the slave of Mr. Tilgman; and his child, when born, may be the slave
of Mr. Gross. He may be a *freeman*; and yet his child may be a *chattel.*
He may be white, glorying in the purity of his Anglo-Saxon blood; and
his child may be ranked with the blackest slaves. Indeed, he *may be*, and
often is, master and father to the same child. He can be father without
being a husband, and may sell his child without incurring reproach, if
the child be by a woman in whose veins courses one thirty-second part
of African blood. My father was a white man, or nearly white. It was
sometimes whispered that my master was my father.

But to return, or rather, to begin. My knowledge of my mother is very scanty, but very distinct. Her personal appearance and bearing are ineffaceably stamped upon my memory. She was tall, and finely proportioned; of deep black, glossy complexion; had regular features, and, among the other slaves, was remarkably sedate in her manners. There is in *Prichard's Natural History of Man*, the head of a figure—on page 157—the features of which so resemble those of my mother, that I often recur to it with something of the feeling which I suppose others experience when looking upon the pictures of dear departed ones.

Yet I cannot say that I was very deeply attached to my mother; certainly not so deeply as I should have been had our relations in childhood been different. We were separated, according to the common custom, when I was but an infant, and, of course, before I knew my mother from any one else.

The germs of affection with which the Almighty, in his wisdom and mercy, arms the hopeless infant against the ills and vicissitudes of his lot, had been directed in their growth toward that loving old grandmother, whose gentle hand and kind deportment it was in the first effort of my infantile understanding to comprehend and appreciate. Accordingly, the tenderest affection which a beneficent Father allows, as a partial compensation to the mother for the pains and lacerations of her heart, incident to the maternal relation, was, in my case, diverted from its true and natural object, by the envious, greedy, and treacherous hand of slavery. The slave-mother can be spared long enough from the field to endure all the bitterness of a mother's anguish, when it adds another name to a master's ledger, but not long enough to receive the joyous reward afforded by the intelligent smiles of her child. I never think of this terrible interference of slavery with my infantile affections, and its diverting them from their natural course, without feelings to which I can give no adequate expression.

I do not remember to have seen my mother at my grandmother's at any time. I remember her only in her visits to me at Col. Lloyd's plantation, and in the kitchen of my old master. Her visits to me there were few in number, brief in duration, and mostly made in the night. The pains she took, and the toil she endured, to see me, tells me that a true mother's heart was hers, and that slavery had difficulty in paralyzing it with unmotherly indifference.

My mother was hired out to a Mr. Stewart, who lived about twelve miles from old master's, and, being a field hand, she seldom had leisure, by day, for the performance of the journey. The nights and the distance were both obstacles to her visits. She was obliged to walk, unless chance flung into her way an opportunity to ride; and the latter was sometimes her good luck. But she always had to walk one way or the other. It was a greater luxury than slavery could afford, to allow a black slave-mother a horse or a mule, upon which to travel twenty-four miles, when she could walk the distance. Besides, it is deemed a foolish whim for a slave-mother to manifest concern to see her children, and, in one point of view, the case is made out—she can do nothing for them. She has no control over them; the master is even more than the mother, in all matters touching the fate of her child. Why, then, should she give herself any concern? She has no responsibility. Such is the reasoning, and such the practice. The iron rule of the plantation, always passionately and violently enforced in that neighborhood, makes flogging the penalty of failing to be in the field before sunrise in the morning, unless special permission be given to the absenting slave. "I went to see my child," is no excuse to the ear or heart of the overseer.

One of the visits of my mother to me, while at Col. Lloyd's, I remember very vividly, as affording a bright gleam of a mother's love, and the earnestness of a mother's care.

I had on that day offended "Aunt Katy," (called "Aunt" by way of respect), the cook of old master's establishment. I do not now remember the nature of my offense in this instance, for my offenses were numerous in that quarter, greatly depending, however, upon the mood of Aunt Katy, as to their heinousness; but she had adopted, that day, her favorite mode of punishing me, namely, making me go without food all day—that is, from after breakfast. The first hour or two after dinner, I succeeded pretty well in keeping up my spirits; but though I made an excellent stand against the foe, and fought bravely during the afternoon, I knew I must be conquered at last, unless I got the accustomed reenforcement of a slice of corn bread, at sundown. Sundown came, but *no bread*, and, in its stead, there came the threat, with a scowl well suited to its terrible import, that she "meant to *starve the life out of me!*" Brandishing her knife, she chopped off the heavy slices for the other children, and put the loaf away, muttering, all the while, her savage designs upon myself. Against this disappointment, for I was expecting that her heart would relent at last, I made an extra effort to maintain my dignity; but when I saw all the other children around me with merry and satisfied faces, I could stand it no longer. I went out behind the house, and cried like a fine fellow! When tired of this, I returned to the kitchen, sat by the fire, and brooded over my hard lot. I was too hungry to sleep. While I sat in the corner, I caught sight of an ear of Indian corn on an upper shelf of the kitchen. I watched my chance, and got it, and, shelling off a few grains, I put it back again. The grains in my hand, I quickly put in some ashes, and covered them with embers, to roast them. All this I did at the risk of getting a brutal thumping, for Aunt Katy could beat, as well as starve me. My corn was not long in roasting, and, with my keen appetite, it did not matter even if the grains were not exactly done. I eagerly pulled them out, and placed them on my stool, in a clever little pile. Just as I began to help myself to my very dry meal, in came my dear mother. And now, dear reader, a scene occurred which was altogether worth beholding, and to me it was instructive as well as interesting. The friendless and hungry boy, in his extremest need—and when he did not dare to look for succor—found himself in the strong, protecting arms of a mother; a mother who was, at the moment (being endowed with high powers of manner as well as matter) more than a match for all his enemies. I shall never forget the indescribable expression of her countenance, when I told her that I had had no food since morning; and that Aunt Katy said she "meant to starve the life out of me." There was pity in her glance at me, and a fiery indignation at Aunt Katy at the same time; and, while she took the corn from me, and gave me a large ginger cake, in its stead, she read Aunt Katy a lecture which she never forgot. My mother threatened her with complaining to old master in my behalf; for the latter, though harsh and cruel himself, at times, did not sanction the meanness, injustice, partiality and oppressions enacted by Aunt Katy in the kitchen. That night I learned the fact, that I was, not only a child, but *somebody's* child. The "sweet cake" my mother gave me was in the shape of a heart, with a rich, dark ring glazed upon the edge of it. I was victorious, and well off for the moment; prouder, on my mother's knee, than a king upon his throne. But my triumph was short. I dropped off to sleep, and waked in the morning only to find my mother gone, and myself left at the mercy of the sable virago, dominant in my old master's kitchen, whose fiery wrath was my constant dread.

I do not remember to have seen my mother after this occurrence. Death soon ended the little communication that had existed between us; and with it, I believe, a life judging from her weary, sad, down-cast countenance and mute demeanor—full of heartfelt sorrow. I was not allowed to visit her during any part of her long illness; nor did I see her for a long time before she was taken ill and died. The heartless and ghastly form of *slavery* rises between mother and child, even at the bed of death. The mother, at the verge of the grave, may not gather her children, to impart to them her holy admonitions, and invoke for them her dying benediction. The bond-woman lives as a slave, and is left to die as a beast; often with fewer attentions than are paid to a favorite horse. Scenes of sacred tenderness, around the death-bed, never forgotten, and which often arrest the vicious and confirm the virtuous during life, must be looked for among the free, though they sometimes occur among the slaves. It has been a life-long, standing grief to me, that I knew so little of my mother; and that I was so early separated from her. The counsels of her love must have been beneficial to me. The side view of her face is imaged on my memory, and I take few steps in life, without feeling her presence; but the image is mute, and I have no striking words of hers treasured up.

I learned, after my mother's death, that she could read, and that she was the only one of all the slaves and colored people in Tuckahoe who enjoyed that advantage. How she acquired this knowledge, I know not, for Tuckahoe is the last place in the world where she would be apt to find facilities for learning. I can, therefore, fondly and proudly ascribe to her an earnest love of knowledge. That a "field hand" should learn to read, in any slave state, is remarkable; but the achievement of my mother, considering the place, was very extraordinary; and, in view of that fact, I am quite willing, and even happy, to attribute any love of letters I possess, and for which I have got—despite of prejudices only too much credit, *not* to my admitted Anglo-Saxon paternity, but to the native genius of my sable, unprotected, and uncultivated *mother*—a woman, who belonged to a race whose mental endowments it is, at present, fashionable to hold in disparagement and contempt.

Summoned away to her account, with the impassable gulf of slavery between us during her entire illness, my mother died without leaving me a single intimation of *who* my father was. There was a whisper, that my master was my father; yet it was only a whisper, and I cannot say that I ever gave it credence. Indeed, I now have reason to think he was not; nevertheless, the fact remains, in all its glaring odiousness, that, by the laws of slavery, children, in all cases, are reduced to the condition of their mothers. This arrangement admits of the greatest license to brutal slaveholders, and their profligate sons, brothers, relations and friends, and gives to the pleasure of sin, the additional attraction of profit. A whole volume might be written on this single feature of slavery, as I have observed it.

One might imagine, that the children of such connections, would fare better, in the hands of their masters, than other slaves. The rule is quite the other way; and a very little reflection will satisfy the reader that such is the case. A man who will enslave his own blood, may not be safely relied on for magnanimity. Men do not love those who remind them of their sins unless they have a mind to repent—and the mulatto child's face is a standing accusation against him who is master and father to the child. What is still worse, perhaps, such a child is a constant offense to the wife. She hates its very presence, and when a slaveholding woman hates, she wants not means to give that hate telling effect. Women—white women, I mean—are *idols* at the south, not *wives*, for the slave-women are preferred in many instances; and if these *idols* but nod, or lift a finger, woe to the poor victim: kicks, cuffs and stripes are sure to follow. Masters are frequently compelled to sell this class of their slaves, out of deference to the feelings of their white wives; and shocking and scandalous as it may seem for a man to sell his own blood to the traffickers in human flesh, it is often an act of humanity toward the slave-child to be thus removed from his merciless tormentors.

It is not within the scope of the design of my simple story, to comment upon every phase of slavery not within my experience as a slave.

But, I may remark, that, if the lineal descendants of Ham are only to be enslaved, according to the scriptures, slavery in this country will soon become an unscriptural institution; for thousands are ushered into the world, annually, who—like myself—owe their existence to white fathers, and, most frequently, to their masters, and master's sons. The slave-woman is at the mercy of the fathers, sons or brothers of her master. The thoughtful know the rest.

After what I have now said of the circumstances of my mother, and my relations to her, the reader will not be surprised, nor be disposed to censure me, when I tell but the simple truth, viz: that I received the tidings of her death with no strong emotions of sorrow for her, and with very little regret for myself on account of her loss. I had to learn the value of my mother long after her death, and by witnessing the devotion of other mothers to their children.

There is not, beneath the sky, an enemy to filial affection so destructive as slavery. It had made my brothers and sisters strangers to me; it converted the mother that bore me, into a myth; it shrouded my father in mystery, and left me without an intelligible beginning in the world.

My mother died when I could not have been more than eight or nine years old, on one of old master's farms in Tuckahoe, in the neighborhood of Hillsborough. Her grave is, as the grave of the dead at sea, unmarked, and without stone or stake.

# CHAPTER IV

## A GENERAL SURVEY OF THE SLAVE PLANTATION

*Isolation of Lloyd's Plantation—Public Opinion There No Protection to the Slave—Absolute Power of the Overseer—Natural and Artificial Charms of the Place—Its Business-like Appearance—Superstition About the Burial Ground—Great ideas of Col. Lloyd—Etiquette Among Slaves—The Comic Slave Doctor—Praying and Flogging—"Old Master" Losing Its Terrors—His Business—Character of Aunt Katy—Sufferings from Hunger—Old Master's Home—Jargon of the Plantation—Guinea Slaves—Master Daniel—Family of Col. Lloyd—Family of Capt. Anthony—His Social Position—Notions of Rank and Station.*

It is generally supposed that slavery, in the state of Maryland, exists in its mildest form, and that it is totally divested of those harsh and terrible peculiarities, which mark and characterize the slave system, in the southern and south-western states of the American union. The argument in favor of this opinion, is the contiguity of the free states, and the exposed condition of slavery in Maryland to the moral, religious and humane sentiment of the free states.

I am not about to refute this argument, so far as it relates to slavery in that state, generally; on the contrary, I am willing to admit that, to this general point, the argument is well grounded. Public opinion is, indeed, an unfailing restraint upon the cruelty and barbarity of masters, overseers, and slave-drivers, whenever and wherever it can reach them; but there are certain secluded and out-of-the-way places, even in the state of Maryland, seldom visited by a single ray of healthy public sentiment—where slavery, wrapt in its own congenial, midnight darkness, *can*, and *does*, develop all its malign and shocking characteristics; where it can be indecent without shame, cruel without shuddering, and murderous without apprehension or fear of exposure.

Just such a secluded, dark, and out-of-the-way place, is the "home plantation" of Col. Edward Lloyd, on the Eastern Shore, Maryland. It is far away from all the great thoroughfares, and is proximate to no town or village. There is neither school-house, nor town-house in its neighborhood. The school-house is unnecessary, for there are no children to go to school. The children and grandchildren of Col. Lloyd were taught in the house, by a private tutor—a Mr. Page—a tall, gaunt sapling of a man, who did not speak a dozen words to a slave in a whole year. The overseers' children go off somewhere to school; and they, therefore, bring no foreign or dangerous influence from abroad, to embarrass the natural operation of the slave system of the place. Not even the mechanics—through whom there is an occasional outburst of honest and telling indignation, at cruelty and wrong on other plantations—are white men, on this plantation. Its whole public is made up of, and divided into, three classes—*slaveholders*, *slaves*, and *overseers*. Its blacksmiths, wheelwrights, shoemakers, weavers, and coopers, are slaves. Not even commerce, selfish and iron-hearted as it is, and ready, as it ever is, to side with the strong against the weak—the rich against the poor—is trusted or permitted within its secluded precincts. Whether with a view of guarding against the escape of its secrets, I know not, but it is a fact, the every leaf and grain of the produce of this plantation, and those of the neighboring farms belonging to Col. Lloyd, are transported to Baltimore in Col. Lloyd's own vessels; every man and boy on board of which—except the captain—are owned by him. In return, everything brought to the plantation, comes through the same channel. Thus, even the glimmering and unsteady light of trade, which sometimes exerts a civilizing influence, is excluded from this "tabooed" spot.

Nearly all the plantations or farms in the vicinity of the "home plantation" of Col. Lloyd, belong to him; and those which do not, are owned by personal friends of his, as deeply interested in maintaining the slave system, in all its rigor, as Col. Lloyd himself. Some of his neighbors are said to be even more stringent than he. The Skinners, the Peakers, the Tilgmans, the Lockermans, and the Gipsons, are in the same boat; being slaveholding neighbors, they may have strengthened each other in their iron rule. They are on intimate terms, and their interests and tastes are identical.

Public opinion in such a quarter, the reader will see, is not likely to be very efficient in protecting the slave from cruelty. On the contrary, it must increase and intensify his wrongs. Public opinion seldom differs very widely from public practice. To be a restraint upon cruelty and vice, public opinion must emanate from a humane and virtuous community. To no such humane and virtuous community, is Col. Lloyd's plantation exposed. That plantation is a little nation of its own, having its own language, its own rules, regulations and customs. The laws and institutions of the state, apparently touch it nowhere. The troubles arising here, are not settled by the civil power of the state. The overseer is generally accuser, judge, jury, advocate and executioner. The criminal is always dumb. The overseer attends to all sides of a case.

There are no conflicting rights of property, for all the people are owned by one man; and they can themselves own no property. Religion and politics are alike excluded. One class of the population is too high to be reached by the preacher; and the other class is too low to be cared for by the preacher. The poor have the gospel preached to them, in this neighborhood, only when they are able to pay for it. The slaves, having no money, get no gospel. The politician keeps away, because the people have no votes, and the preacher keeps away, because the people have no money. The rich planter can afford to learn politics in the parlor, and to dispense with religion altogether.

In its isolation, seclusion, and self-reliant independence, Col. Lloyd's plantation resembles what the baronial domains were during the middle ages in Europe. Grim, cold, and unapproachable by all genial influences from communities without, *there it stands*; full three hundred years behind the age, in all that relates to humanity and morals.

This, however, is not the only view that the place presents. Civilization is shut out, but nature cannot be. Though separated from the rest of the world; though public opinion, as I have said, seldom gets a chance to penetrate its dark domain; though the whole place is stamped with its own peculiar, ironlike individuality; and though crimes, high-handed and atrocious, may there be committed, with almost as much impunity as upon the deck of a pirate ship—it is, nevertheless, altogether, to outward seeming, a most strikingly interesting place, full of life, activity, and spirit; and presents a very favorable contrast to the indolent monotony and languor of Tuckahoe. Keen as was my regret and great as was my sorrow at leaving the latter, I was not long in adapting myself to this, my new home. A man's troubles are always half disposed of, when he finds endurance his only remedy. I found myself here; there was no getting away; and what remained for me, but to make the best of it? Here were plenty of children to play with, and plenty of places of pleasant resort for boys of my age, and boys older. The little tendrils of affection, so rudely and treacherously broken from around the darling objects of my grandmother's hut, gradually began to extend, and to entwine about the new objects by which I now found myself surrounded.

There was a windmill (always a commanding object to a child's eye) on Long Point—a tract of land dividing Miles River from the Wye a mile or more from my old master's house. There was a creek to swim in, at the bottom of an open flat space, of twenty acres or more, called "the Long Green"—a very beautiful play-ground for the children.

In the river, a short distance from the shore, lying quietly at anchor, with her small boat dancing at her stern, was a large sloop—the *Sally Lloyd*; called by that name in honor of a favorite daughter of the colonel. The sloop and the mill were wondrous things, full of thoughts and ideas. A child cannot well look at such objects without *thinking*.

Then here were a great many houses; human habitations, full of the mysteries of life at every stage of it. There was the little red house, up the road, occupied by Mr. Sevier, the overseer. A little nearer to my old master's, stood a very long, rough, low building, literally alive with slaves, of all ages, conditions and sizes. This was called "the Long Quarter." Perched upon a hill, across the Long Green, was a very tall, dilapidated, old brick building—the architectural dimensions of which proclaimed its erection for a different purpose—now occupied by slaves, in a similar manner to the Long Quarter. Besides these, there were numerous other slave houses and huts, scattered around in the neighborhood, every nook and corner of which was completely occupied. Old master's house, a long, brick building, plain, but substantial, stood in the center of the plantation life, and constituted one independent establishment on the premises of Col. Lloyd.

Besides these dwellings, there were barns, stables, store-houses, and tobacco-houses; blacksmiths' shops, wheelwrights' shops, coopers' shops—all objects of interest; but, above all, there stood the grandest building my eyes had then ever beheld, called, by every one on the plantation, the "Great House." This was occupied by Col. Lloyd and his family. They occupied it; *I* enjoyed it. The great house was surrounded by numerous and variously shaped out-buildings. There were kitchens, wash-houses, dairies, summer-house, green-houses, hen-houses, turkey-houses, pigeon-houses, and arbors, of many sizes and devices, all neatly painted, and altogether interspersed with grand old trees, ornamental and primitive, which afforded delightful shade in summer, and imparted to the scene a high degree of stately beauty. The great house itself was a large, white, wooden building, with wings on three sides of it. In front, a large portico, extending the entire length of the building, and supported by a long range of columns, gave to the whole establishment an air of solemn grandeur. It was a treat to my young and gradually opening mind, to behold this elaborate exhibition of wealth, power, and vanity. The carriage entrance to the house was a large gate, more than a quarter of a mile distant from it; the intermediate space was a beautiful lawn, very neatly trimmed, and watched with the greatest care. It was dotted thickly over with delightful trees, shrubbery, and flowers. The road, or lane, from the gate to the great house, was richly paved with white pebbles from the beach, and, in its course, formed a complete circle around the beautiful lawn. Carriages going in and retiring from the great house, made the circuit of the lawn, and their passengers were permitted to behold a scene of almost Eden-like beauty. Outside this select inclosure, were parks, where—as about the residences of the English nobility—rabbits, deer, and other wild game, might be seen, peering and playing about, with none to molest them or make them afraid. The tops of the stately poplars were often covered with the red-winged black-birds, making all nature vocal with the joyous life and beauty of their wild, warbling notes. These all belonged to me, as well as to Col. Edward Lloyd, and for a time I greatly enjoyed them.

A short distance from the great house, were the stately mansions of the dead, a place of somber aspect. Vast tombs, embowered beneath the weeping willow and the fir tree, told of the antiquities of the Lloyd family, as well as of their wealth. Superstition was rife among the slaves about this family burying ground. Strange sights had been seen there by some of the older slaves. Shrouded ghosts, riding on great black horses, had been seen to enter; balls of fire had been seen to fly there at midnight, and horrid sounds had been repeatedly heard. Slaves know enough of the rudiments of theology to believe that those go to hell who die slaveholders; and they often fancy such persons wishing themselves back again, to wield the lash. Tales of sights and sounds, strange and terrible, connected with the huge black tombs, were a very great security to the grounds about them, for few of the slaves felt like approaching them even in the day time. It was a dark, gloomy and forbidding place, and it was difficult to feel that the spirits of the sleeping dust there deposited, reigned with the blest in the realms of eternal peace.

The business of twenty or thirty farms was transacted at this, called, by way of eminence, "great house farm." These farms all belonged to Col. Lloyd, as did, also, the slaves upon them. Each farm was under the management of an overseer. As I have said of the overseer of the home plantation, so I may say of the overseers on the smaller ones; they stand between the slave and all civil constitutions—their word is law, and is implicitly obeyed.

The colonel, at this time, was reputed to be, and he apparently was, very rich. His slaves, alone, were an immense fortune. These, small and great, could not have been fewer than one thousand in number, and though scarcely a month passed without the sale of one or more lots to the Georgia traders, there was no apparent diminution in the number of his human stock: the home plantation merely groaned at a removal of the young increase, or human crop, then proceeded as lively as ever. Horse-shoeing, cart-mending, plow-repairing, coopering, grinding, and weaving, for all the neighboring farms, were performed here, and slaves were employed in all these branches. "Uncle Tony" was the blacksmith; "Uncle Harry" was the cartwright; "Uncle Abel" was the shoemaker; and all these had hands to assist them in their several departments.

These mechanics were called "uncles" by all the younger slaves, not because they really sustained that relationship to any, but according to plantation *etiquette*, as a mark of respect, due from the younger to the older slaves. Strange, and even ridiculous as it may seem, among a people so uncultivated, and with so many stern trials to look in the face, there is not to be found, among any people, a more rigid enforcement of the law of respect to elders, than they maintain. I set this down as partly constitutional with my race, and partly conventional. There is no better material in the world for making a gentleman, than is furnished in the African. He shows to others, and exacts for himself, all the tokens of respect which he is compelled to manifest toward his master. A young slave must approach the company of the older with hat in hand, and woe betide him, if he fails to acknowledge a favor, of any sort, with the accustomed "tank'ee," etc. So uniformly are good manners enforced among slaves, I can easily detect a "bogus" fugitive by his manners.

Among other slave notabilities of the plantation, was one called by everybody Uncle Isaac Copper. It is seldom that a slave gets a surname from anybody in Maryland; and so completely has the south shaped the manners of the north, in this respect, that even abolitionists make very little of the surname of a Negro. The only improvement on the "Bills," "Jacks," "Jims," and "Neds" of the south, observable here is, that "William," "John," "James," "Edward," are substituted. It goes against the grain to treat and address a Negro precisely as they would treat and address a white man. But, once in a while, in slavery as in the free states, by some extraordinary circumstance, the Negro has a surname fastened to him, and holds it against all conventionalities. This was the case with Uncle Isaac Copper. When the "uncle" was dropped, he generally had the prefix "doctor," in its stead. He was our doctor of medicine, and doctor of divinity as well. Where he took his degree I am unable to say, for he was not very communicative to inferiors, and I was emphatically such, being but a boy seven or eight years old. He was too well established in his profession to permit questions as to his native skill, or his attainments. One qualification he undoubtedly had—he was a confirmed *cripple*; and he could neither work, nor would he bring anything if offered for sale in the market. The old man, though lame, was no sluggard. He was a man that made his crutches do him good service. He was always on the alert, looking up the sick, and all such as were supposed to need his counsel. His remedial prescriptions embraced four articles. For diseases of the body, *Epsom salts* and *castor oil*; for those of the soul, *the Lord's Prayer*, and *hickory switches!*

I was not long at Col. Lloyd's before I was placed under the care of Doctor Issac Copper. I was sent to him with twenty or thirty other children, to learn the "Lord's Prayer." I found the old gentleman seated on a huge three-legged oaken stool, armed with several large hickory switches; and, from his position, he could reach—lame as he was—any boy in the room. After standing awhile to learn what was expected of us, the old gentleman, in any other than a devotional tone, commanded us to kneel down. This done, he commenced telling us to say everything he said. "Our Father"—this was repeated after him with promptness and uniformity; "Who art in heaven"—was less promptly and uniformly repeated; and the old gentleman paused in the prayer, to give us a short lecture upon the consequences of inattention, both immediate and future, and especially those more immediate. About these he was absolutely certain, for he held in his right hand the means of bringing all his predictions and warnings to pass. On he proceeded with the prayer; and we with our thick tongues and unskilled ears, followed him to the best of our ability. This, however, was not sufficient to please the old gentleman. Everybody, in the south, wants the privilege of whipping somebody else. Uncle Isaac shared the common passion of his country, and, therefore, seldom found any means of keeping his disciples in order short of flogging. "Say everything I say"; and bang would come the switch on some poor boy's undevotional head. "*What you looking at there*"—"*Stop that pushing*"—and down again would come the lash.

The whip is all in all. It is supposed to secure obedience to the slaveholder, and is held as a sovereign remedy among the slaves themselves, for every form of disobedience, temporal or spiritual. Slaves, as well as slaveholders, use it with an unsparing hand. Our devotions at Uncle Isaac's combined too much of the tragic and comic, to make them very salutary in a spiritual point of view; and it is due to truth to say, I was often a truant when the time for attending the praying and flogging of Doctor Isaac Copper came on.

The windmill under the care of Mr. Kinney, a kind-hearted old Englishman, was to me a source of infinite interest and pleasure. The old man always seemed pleased when he saw a troop of darkey little urchins, with their tow-linen shirts fluttering in the breeze, approaching to view and admire the whirling wings of his wondrous machine. From the mill we could see other objects of deep interest. These were, the vessels from St. Michael's, on their way to Baltimore. It was a source of much amusement to view the flowing sails and complicated rigging, as the little crafts dashed by, and to speculate upon Baltimore, as to the kind and quality of the place. With so many sources of interest around me, the reader may be prepared to learn that I began to think very highly of Col. L.'s plantation. It was just a place to my boyish taste. There were fish to be caught in the creek, if one only had a hook and line; and crabs, clams and oysters were to be caught by wading, digging and raking for them. Here was a field for industry and enterprise, strongly inviting; and the reader may be assured that I entered upon it with spirit.

Even the much dreaded old master, whose merciless fiat had brought me from Tuckahoe, gradually, to my mind, parted with his terrors. Strange enough, his reverence seemed to take no particular notice of me, nor of my coming. Instead of leaping out and devouring me, he scarcely seemed conscious of my presence. The fact is, he was occupied with matters more weighty and important than either looking after or vexing me. He probably thought as little of my advent, as he would have thought of the addition of a single pig to his stock!

As the chief butler on Col. Lloyd's plantation, his duties were numerous and perplexing. In almost all important matters he answered in Col. Lloyd's stead. The overseers of all the farms were in some sort under him, and received the law from his mouth. The colonel himself seldom addressed an overseer, or allowed an overseer to address him. Old master carried the keys of all store-houses; measured out the allowance for each slave at the end of every month; superintended the storing of all goods brought to the plantation; dealt out the raw material to all the handicraftsmen; shipped the grain, tobacco, and all saleable produce of the plantation to market, and had the general oversight of the coopers' shop, wheelwrights' shop, blacksmiths' shop, and shoemakers' shop. Besides the care of these, he often had business for the plantation which required him to be absent two and three days.

Thus largely employed, he had little time, and perhaps as little disposition, to interfere with the children individually. What he was to Col. Lloyd, he made Aunt Katy to him. When he had anything to say or do about us, it was said or done in a wholesale manner; disposing of us in classes or sizes, leaving all minor details to Aunt Katy, a person of whom the reader has already received no very favorable impression. Aunt Katy was a woman who never allowed herself to act greatly within the margin of power granted to her, no matter how broad that authority might be. Ambitious, ill-tempered and cruel, she found in her present position an ample field for the exercise of her ill-omened qualities. She had a strong hold on old master—she was considered a first rate cook, and she really was very industrious. She was, therefore, greatly favored by old master, and as one mark of his favor, she was the only mother who was permitted to retain her children around her. Even to these children she was often fiendish in her brutality. She pursued her son Phil, one day, in my presence, with a huge butcher knife, and dealt a blow with its edge which left a shocking gash on his arm, near the wrist. For this, old master did sharply rebuke her, and threatened that if she ever should do the like again, he would take the skin off her back. Cruel, however, as Aunt Katy was to her own children, at times she was not destitute of maternal feeling, as I often had occasion to know, in the bitter pinches of hunger I had to endure. Differing from the practice of Col. Lloyd, old master, instead of allowing so much for each slave, committed the allowance for all to the care of Aunt Katy, to be divided after cooking it, amongst us. The allowance, consisting of coarse cornmeal, was not very abundant—indeed, it was very slender; and in passing through Aunt Katy's hands, it was made more slender still, for some of us. William, Phil and Jerry were her children, and it is not to accuse her too severely, to allege that she was often guilty of starving myself and the other children, while she was literally cramming her own. Want of food was my chief trouble the first summer at my old master's. Oysters and clams would do very well, with an occasional supply of bread, but they soon failed in the absence of bread. I speak but the simple truth, when I say, I have often been so pinched with hunger, that I have fought with the dog—"Old Nep"—for the smallest crumbs that fell from the kitchen table, and have been glad when I won a single crumb in the combat. Many times have I followed, with eager step, the waiting-girl when she went out to shake the table cloth, to get the crumbs and small bones flung out for the cats. The water, in which meat had been boiled, was as eagerly sought for by me. It was a great thing to get the privilege of dipping a piece of bread in such water; and the skin taken from rusty bacon, was a positive luxury. Nevertheless, I sometimes got full meals and kind words from sympathizing old slaves, who knew my sufferings, and received the comforting assurance that I should be a man some day. "Never mind, honey—better day comin'," was even then a solace, a cheering consolation to me in my troubles. Nor were all the kind words I received from slaves. I had a friend in the parlor, as well, and one to whom I shall be glad to do justice, before I have finished this part of my story.

I was not long at old master's, before I learned that his surname was Anthony, and that he was generally called "Captain Anthony"—a title which he probably acquired by sailing a craft in the Chesapeake Bay. Col. Lloyd's slaves never called Capt. Anthony "old master," but always Capt. Anthony; and me they called "Captain Anthony Fred." There is not, probably, in the whole south, a plantation where the

English language is more imperfectly spoken than on Col. Lloyd's. It is a mixture of Guinea and everything else you please. At the time of which I am now writing, there were slaves there who had been brought from the coast of Africa. They never used the "s" in indication of the possessive case. "Cap'n Ant'ney Tom," "Lloyd Bill," "Aunt Rose Harry," means "Captain Anthony's Tom," "Lloyd's Bill," etc. "*Oo you dem long to?*" means, "Whom do you belong to?" "*Oo dem got any peachy?*" means, "Have you got any peaches?" I could scarcely understand them when I first went among them, so broken was their speech; and I am persuaded that I could not have been dropped anywhere on the globe, where I could reap less, in the way of knowledge, from my immediate associates, than on this plantation. Even "*Mas' Daniel*," by his association with his father's slaves, had measurably adopted their dialect and their ideas, so far as they had ideas to be adopted. The equality of nature is strongly asserted in childhood, and childhood requires children for associates. *Color* makes no difference with a child. Are you a child with wants, tastes and pursuits common to children, not put on, but natural? Then, were you black as ebony you would be welcome to the child of alabaster whiteness. The law of compensation holds here, as well as elsewhere. Mas' Daniel could not associate with ignorance without sharing its shade; and he could not give his black playmates his company, without giving them his intelligence, as well. Without knowing this, or caring about it, at the time, I, for some cause or other, spent much of my time with Mas' Daniel, in preference to spending it with most of the other boys.

Mas' Daniel was the youngest son of Col. Lloyd; his older brothers were Edward and Murray—both grown up, and fine looking men. Edward was especially esteemed by the children, and by me among the rest; not that he ever said anything to us or for us, which could be called especially kind; it was enough for us, that he never looked nor acted scornfully toward us. There were also three sisters, all married; one to Edward Winder; a second to Edward Nicholson; a third to Mr. Lownes.

The family of old master consisted of two sons, Andrew and Richard; his daughter, Lucretia, and her newly married husband, Capt. Auld. This was the house family. The kitchen family consisted of Aunt Katy, Aunt Esther, and ten or a dozen children, most of them older than myself. Capt. Anthony was not considered a rich slaveholder, but was pretty well off in the world. He owned about thirty "*head*" of slaves, and three farms in Tuckahoe. The most valuable part of his property was his slaves, of whom he could afford to sell one every year. This crop, therefore, brought him seven or eight hundred dollars a year, besides his yearly salary, and other revenue from his farms.

The idea of rank and station was rigidly maintained on Col. Lloyd's plantation. Our family never visited the great house, and the Lloyds never came to our home. Equal non-intercourse was observed between Capt. Anthony's family and that of Mr. Sevier, the overseer.

Such, kind reader, was the community, and such the place, in which my earliest and most lasting impressions of slavery, and of slave-life, were received; of which impressions you will learn more in the coming chapters of this book.

# CHAPTER V

## GRADUAL INITIATION TO THE MYSTERIES OF SLAVERY

*Growing Acquaintance with Old Master—His Character—
Evils of Unrestrained Passion—Apparent Tenderness—Old
Master a Man of Trouble—Custom of Muttering to Himself—
Necessity of Being Aware of His Words—The Supposed
Obtuseness of Slave-Children—Brutal Outrage—Drunken
Overseer—Slaveholder's Impatience—Wisdom of Appealing
to Superiors—The Slaveholder's Wrath Bad as That of
the Overseer—A Base and Selfish Attempt to Break Up a
Courtship—A Harrowing Scene.*

Although my old master—Capt. Anthony—gave me at first, (as the reader will have already seen) very little attention, and although that little was of a remarkably mild and gentle description, a few months only were sufficient to convince me that mildness and gentleness were not the prevailing or governing traits of his character. These excellent qualities were displayed only occasionally. He could, when it suited him, appear to be literally insensible to the claims of humanity, when appealed to by the helpless against an aggressor, and he could himself commit outrages, deep, dark and nameless. Yet he was not by nature worse than other men. Had he been brought up in a free state, surrounded by the just restraints of free society—restraints which are necessary to the freedom of all its members, alike and equally— Capt. Anthony might have been as humane a man, and every way as respectable, as many who now oppose the slave system; certainly as humane and respectable as are members of society generally. The slaveholder, as well as the slave, is the victim of the slave system. A man's character greatly takes its hue and shape from the form and color of things about him. Under the whole heavens there is no relation more unfavorable to the development of honorable character, than that sustained by the slaveholder to the slave. Reason is imprisoned here, and passions run wild. Like the fires of the prairie, once lighted, they are at the mercy of every wind, and must burn, till they have consumed all that is combustible within their remorseless grasp. Capt. Anthony could be kind, and, at times, he even showed an affectionate disposition. Could the reader have seen him gently leading me by the hand—as he sometimes did—patting me on the head, speaking to me in soft, caressing tones and calling me his "little Indian boy," he would have deemed him a kind old man, and really, almost fatherly. But the pleasant moods of a slaveholder are remarkably brittle; they are easily snapped; they neither come often, nor remain long. His temper is subjected to perpetual trials; but, since these trials are never borne patiently, they add nothing to his natural stock of patience.

Old master very early impressed me with the idea that he was an unhappy man. Even to my child's eye, he wore a troubled, and at times, a haggard aspect. His strange movements excited my curiosity, and awakened my compassion. He seldom walked alone without muttering to himself; and he occasionally stormed about, as if defying an army of invisible foes. "He would do this, that, and the other; he'd be d——d if he did not,"—was the usual form of his threats. Most of his leisure was spent in walking, cursing and gesticulating, like one possessed by a demon. Most evidently, he was a wretched man, at war with his own soul, and with all the world around him. To be overheard by the children, disturbed him very little. He made no more of *our* presence, than of that of the ducks and geese which he met on the green. He little thought that the little black urchins around him, could see, through those vocal crevices, the very secrets of his heart. Slaveholders ever underrate the intelligence with which they have to grapple. I really understood the old man's mutterings, attitudes and gestures, about as well as he did himself. But slaveholders never encourage that kind of communication, with the slaves, by which they might learn to measure the depths of his knowledge. Ignorance is a high virtue in a human chattel; and as the master studies to keep the slave ignorant, the slave is cunning enough to make the master think he succeeds. The slave fully appreciates the saying, "where ignorance is bliss, 'tis folly to be wise."* When old master's gestures were violent, ending with a threatening shake of the head, and a sharp snap of his middle finger and thumb, I

* From "Ode on a Distant Prospect of Eton College" by Thomas Grey.

deemed it wise to keep at a respectable distance from him; for, at such times, trifling faults stood, in his eyes, as momentous offenses; and, having both the power and the disposition, the victim had only to be near him to catch the punishment, deserved or undeserved.

One of the first circumstances that opened my eyes to the cruelty and wickedness of slavery, and the heartlessness of my old master, was the refusal of the latter to interpose his authority, to protect and shield a young woman, who had been most cruelly abused and beaten by his overseer in Tuckahoe. This overseer—a Mr. Plummer—was a man like most of his class, little better than a human brute; and, in addition to his general profligacy and repulsive coarseness, the creature was a miserable drunkard. He was, probably, employed by my old master, less on account of the excellence of his services, than for the cheap rate at which they could be obtained. He was not fit to have the management of a drove of mules. In a fit of drunken madness, he committed the outrage which brought the young woman in question down to my old master's for protection. This young woman was the daughter of Milly, an own aunt of mine. The poor girl, on arriving at our house, presented a pitiable appearance. She had left in haste, and without preparation; and, probably, without the knowledge of Mr. Plummer. She had traveled twelve miles, bare-footed, bare-necked and bare-headed. Her neck and shoulders were covered with scars, newly made; and not content with marring her neck and shoulders, with the cowhide, the cowardly brute had dealt her a blow on the head with a hickory club, which cut a horrible gash, and left her face literally covered with blood. In this condition, the poor young woman came down, to implore protection at the hands of my old master. I expected to see him boil over with rage at the revolting deed, and to hear him fill the air with curses upon the brutal Plummer; but I was disappointed. He sternly told her, in an angry tone, he "believed she deserved every bit of it," and, if she did not go home instantly, he would himself take the remaining skin from her neck and back. Thus was the poor girl compelled to return, without redress, and perhaps to receive an additional flogging for daring to appeal to old master against the overseer.

Old master seemed furious at the thought of being troubled by such complaints. I did not, at that time, understand the philosophy of his treatment of my cousin. It was stern, unnatural, violent. Had the man no bowels of compassion? Was he dead to all sense of humanity? No. I think I now understand it. This treatment is a part of the system, rather than a part of the man. Were slaveholders to listen to complaints of this sort against the overseers, the luxury of owning large numbers of slaves, would be impossible. It would do away with the office of overseer, entirely; or, in other words, it would convert the master himself into an overseer. It would occasion great loss of time and labor, leaving the overseer in fetters, and without the necessary power to secure obedience to his orders. A privilege so dangerous as that of appeal, is, therefore, strictly prohibited; and any one exercising it, runs a fearful hazard. Nevertheless, when a slave has nerve enough to exercise it, and boldly approaches his master, with a well-founded complaint against an overseer, though he may be repulsed, and may even have that of which he complains repeated at the time, and, though he may be beaten by his master, as well as by the overseer, for his temerity, in the end the policy of complaining is, generally, vindicated by the relaxed rigor of the overseer's treatment. The latter becomes more careful, and less disposed to use the lash upon such slaves thereafter. It is with this final result in view, rather than with any expectation of immediate good, that the outraged slave is induced to meet his master with a complaint. The overseer very naturally dislikes to have the ear of the master disturbed by complaints; and, either upon this consideration, or upon advice and warning privately given him by his employers, he generally modifies the rigor of his rule, after an outbreak of the kind to which I have been referring.

Howsoever the slaveholder may allow himself to act toward his slave, and, whatever cruelty he may deem it wise, for example's sake, or for the gratification of his humor, to inflict, he cannot, in the absence of all provocation, look with pleasure upon the bleeding wounds of a defenseless slave-woman. When he drives her from his presence without redress, or the hope of redress, he acts, generally, from motives of policy, rather than from a hardened nature, or from innate brutality. Yet, let but his own temper be stirred, his own passions get loose, and the slave-owner will *go far beyond* the overseer in cruelty. He will convince the slave that his wrath is far more terrible and boundless, and vastly more to be dreaded, than that of the underling overseer. What may have been mechanically and heartlessly done by the overseer, is now done with a will. The man who now wields the lash is irresponsible. He may, if he pleases, cripple or kill, without fear of consequences; except in so far as it may concern profit or loss. To a man of violent temper—as my old master was—this was but a very slender and inefficient restraint. I have seen him in a tempest of passion, such as I have just described—a passion into which entered all the bitter ingredients of pride, hatred, envy, jealousy, and the thirst for revenge.

The circumstances which I am about to narrate, and which gave rise to this fearful tempest of passion, are not singular nor isolated in slave life, but are common in every slaveholding community in which I have lived. They are incidental to the relation of master and slave, and exist in all sections of slave-holding countries.

The reader will have noticed that, in enumerating the names of the slaves who lived with my old master, *Esther* is mentioned. This was a young woman who possessed that which is ever a curse to the slave-girl; namely—personal beauty. She was tall, well formed, and made a fine appearance. The daughters of Col. Lloyd could scarcely surpass her in personal charms. Esther was courted by Ned Roberts, and he was as fine looking a young man, as she was a woman. He was the son of a favorite slave of Col. Lloyd. Some slaveholders would have been glad to promote the marriage of two such persons; but, for some reason or other, my old master took it upon him to break up the growing intimacy between Esther and Edward. He strictly ordered her to quit the company of said Roberts, telling her that he would punish her severely if he ever found her again in Edward's company. This unnatural and heartless order was, of course, broken. A woman's love is not to be annihilated by the peremptory command of any one, whose breath is in his nostrils. It was impossible to keep Edward and Esther apart. Meet they would, and meet they did. Had old master been a man of honor and purity, his motives, in this matter, might have been viewed more favorably. As it was, his motives were as abhorrent, as his methods were foolish and contemptible. It was too evident that he was not concerned for the girl's welfare. It is one of the damning characteristics of the slave system, that it robs its victims of every earthly incentive to a holy life. The fear of God, and the hope of heaven, are found sufficient to sustain many slave-women, amidst the snares and dangers of their strange lot; but, this side of God and heaven, a slave-woman is at the mercy of the power, caprice and passion of her owner. Slavery provides no means for the honorable continuance of the race. Marriage—as imposing obligations on the parties to it—has no existence here, except in such hearts as are purer and higher than the standard morality around them. It is one of the consolations of my life, that I know of many honorable instances of persons who maintained their honor, where all around was corrupt.

Esther was evidently much attached to Edward, and abhorred—as she had reason to do—the tyrannical and base behavior of old master. Edward was young, and fine looking, and he loved and courted her. He might have been her husband, in the high sense just alluded to; but *who* and what was this old master? His attentions were plainly brutal and selfish, and it was as natural that Esther should loathe him, as that she should love Edward. Abhorred and circumvented as he was, old master, having the power, very easily took revenge. I happened to see this exhibition of his rage and cruelty toward Esther. The time selected was singular. It was early in the morning, when all besides was still, and before any of the family, in the house or kitchen, had left their beds. I saw but few of the shocking preliminaries, for the cruel work had begun before I awoke. I was probably awakened by the shrieks and piteous cries of poor Esther. My sleeping place was on the floor of a little, rough closet, which opened into the kitchen; and through the cracks of its unplaned boards, I could distinctly see and hear what was going on, without being seen by old master. Esther's wrists were firmly tied, and the twisted rope was fastened to a strong staple in a heavy wooden joist above, near the fireplace. Here she stood, on a bench, her arms tightly drawn over her breast. Her back and shoulders were bare to the waist. Behind her stood old master, with cowskin in hand, preparing his barbarous work with all manner of harsh, coarse, and tantalizing epithets. The screams of his victim were most piercing. He was cruelly deliberate, and protracted the torture, as one who was delighted with the scene. Again and again he drew the hateful whip through his hand, adjusting it with a view of dealing the most pain-giving blow. Poor Esther had never yet been severely whipped, and her shoulders were plump and tender. Each blow, vigorously laid on, brought screams as well as blood. "*Have mercy; Oh! Have mercy*" she cried; "*I won't do so no more*"; but her piercing cries seemed only to increase his fury. His answers to them are too coarse and blasphemous to be produced here. The whole scene, with all its attendants, was revolting and shocking, to the last degree; and when the motives of this brutal castigation are considered—language has no power to convey a just sense of its awful criminality. After laying on some thirty or forty stripes, old master untied his suffering victim, and let her get down. She could scarcely stand, when untied. From my heart I pitied her, and—child though I was—the outrage kindled in me a feeling far from peaceful; but I was hushed, terrified, stunned, and could do nothing, and the fate of Esther might be mine next. The scene here described was often repeated in the case of poor Esther, and her life, as I knew it, was one of wretchedness.

# CHAPTER VI

## TREATMENT OF SLAVES ON
## LLOYD'S PLANTATION

*Early Reflections on Slavery—Presentiment of One Day
Being a Freeman—Combat Between an Overseer and a
Slave-Woman—The Advantages of Resistance—Allowance
Day on the Home Plantation—The Singing of Slaves—An
Explanation—The Slaves' Food and Clothing—Naked
Children—Life in the Quarter—Deprivation of Sleep—
Nursing Children Carried to the Field—Description of the
Cowskin—The Ash Cake—Manner of Making It—The
Dinner Hour—The Contrast.*

The heart-rending incidents, related in the foregoing chapter, led
me, thus early, to inquire into the nature and history of slavery.
*Why am I a slave? Why are some people slaves, and others masters? Was
there ever a time this was not so? How did the relation commence?* These
were the perplexing questions which began now to claim my thoughts,
and to exercise the weak powers of my mind, for I was still but a child,
and knew less than children of the same age in the free states. As my
questions concerning these things were only put to children a little
older, and little better informed than myself, I was not rapid in reaching
a solid footing. By some means I learned from these inquiries that
"*God, up in the sky,*" made every body; and that he made *white* people
to be masters and mistresses, and *black* people to be slaves. This did not
satisfy me, nor lessen my interest in the subject. I was told, too, that
God was good, and that He knew what was best for me, and best for
everybody. This was less satisfactory than the first statement; because it
came, point blank, against all my notions of goodness. It was not good
to let old master cut the flesh off Esther, and make her cry so. Besides,
how did people know that God made black people to be slaves? Did
they go up in the sky and learn it? Or, did He come down and tell them

so? All was dark here. It was some relief to my hard notions of the goodness of God, that, although he made white men to be slaveholders, he did not make them to be *bad* slaveholders, and that, in due time, he would punish the bad slaveholders; that he would, when they died, send them to the bad place, where they would be "burnt up." Nevertheless, I could not reconcile the relation of slavery with my crude notions of goodness.

Then, too, I found that there were puzzling exceptions to this theory of slavery on both sides, and in the middle. I knew of blacks who were *not* slaves; I knew of whites who were *not* slaveholders; and I knew of persons who were *nearly* white, who were slaves. *Color*, therefore, was a very unsatisfactory basis for slavery.

Once, however, engaged in the inquiry, I was not very long in finding out the true solution of the matter. It was not *color*, but *crime*, not *God*, but *man*, that afforded the true explanation of the existence of slavery; nor was I long in finding out another important truth, viz: what man can make, man can unmake. The appalling darkness faded away, and I was master of the subject. There were slaves here, direct from Guinea; and there were many who could say that their fathers and mothers were stolen from Africa—forced from their homes, and compelled to serve as slaves. This, to me, was knowledge; but it was a kind of knowledge which filled me with a burning hatred of slavery, increased my suffering, and left me without the means of breaking away from my bondage. Yet it was knowledge quite worth possessing. I could not have been more than seven or eight years old, when I began to make this subject my study. It was with me in the woods and fields; along the shore of the river, and wherever my boyish wanderings led me; and though I was, at that time, quite ignorant of the existence of the free states, I distinctly remember being, *even then*, most strongly impressed with the idea of being a freeman some day. This cheering assurance was an inborn dream of my human nature—a constant menace to slavery—and one which all the powers of slavery were unable to silence or extinguish.

Up to the time of the brutal flogging of my Aunt Esther—for she was my own aunt—and the horrid plight in which I had seen my cousin from Tuckahoe, who had been so badly beaten by the cruel Mr. Plummer, my attention had not been called, especially, to the gross features of slavery. I had, of course, heard of whippings and of savage *rencontres* between overseers and slaves, but I had always been out of the way at the times and places of their occurrence. My plays and sports, most of the time, took me from the corn and tobacco fields, where the great body of the hands were at work, and where scenes of cruelty were enacted and witnessed. But, after the whipping of Aunt Esther, I saw many cases of the same shocking nature, not only in my master's house, but on Col. Lloyd's plantation. One of the first which I saw, and which greatly agitated me, was the whipping of a woman belonging to Col. Lloyd, named Nelly. The offense alleged against Nelly, was one of the commonest and most indefinite in the whole catalogue of offenses usually laid to the charge of slaves, viz: "impudence." This may mean almost anything, or nothing at all, just according to the caprice of the master or overseer, at the moment. But, whatever it is, or is not, if it gets the name of "impudence," the party charged with it is sure of a flogging. This offense may be committed in various ways; in the tone of an answer; in answering at all; in not answering; in the expression of countenance; in the motion of the head; in the gait, manner and bearing of the slave. In the case under consideration, I can easily believe that, according to all slaveholding standards, here was a genuine instance of impudence. In Nelly there were all the necessary conditions for committing the offense. She was a bright mulatto, the recognized wife of a favorite "hand" on board Col. Lloyd's sloop, and the mother of five sprightly children. She was a vigorous and spirited woman, and one of the most likely, on the plantation, to be guilty of impudence. My attention was called to the scene, by the noise, curses and screams that proceeded from it; and, on going a little in that direction, I came upon the parties engaged in the skirmish. Mr. Siever, the overseer, had hold of Nelly, when I caught sight of them; he was endeavoring to drag her toward a tree, which endeavor Nelly was sternly resisting; but to no purpose, except to retard the progress of the overseer's plans. Nelly—as I have said—was the mother of five children; three of them were present, and though quite small (from seven to ten years old, I should think) they gallantly came to their mother's defense, and gave the overseer an excellent pelting with stones. One of the little fellows ran up, seized the overseer by the leg and bit him; but the monster was too busily engaged with Nelly, to pay any attention to the assaults of the children. There were numerous bloody marks on Mr. Sevier's face, when I first saw him, and they increased as the struggle went on. The imprints of Nelly's fingers were visible, and I was glad to see them. Amidst the wild screams of the children—"*Let my mammy go*"—"*let my mammy go*"—there escaped, from between the teeth of the bullet-headed overseer, a few bitter curses, mingled with threats, that "he would teach the d——d b——h how to give a white man impudence." There is no doubt that Nelly felt herself superior, in some respects, to the slaves around her. She was a wife and a mother; her husband was a valued and favorite slave. Besides, he was one of the first hands on board of the sloop, and the sloop hands—since they had to represent the plantation abroad—were generally treated tenderly. The overseer never was allowed to whip Harry; why then should he be allowed to whip Harry's wife? Thoughts of this kind, no doubt, influenced her; but, for whatever reason, she nobly resisted, and, unlike most of the slaves, seemed determined to make her whipping cost Mr. Sevier as much as possible. The blood on his (and her) face, attested her skill, as well as her courage and dexterity in using her nails. Maddened by her resistance, I expected to see Mr. Sevier level her to the ground by a stunning blow; but no; like a savage bull-dog—which he resembled both in temper and appearance—he maintained his grip, and steadily dragged his victim toward the tree, disregarding alike her blows, and the cries of the children for their mother's release. He would, doubtless, have knocked her down with his hickory stick, but that such act might have cost him his place. It is often deemed advisable to knock a man-slave down, in order to tie him, but it is considered cowardly and inexcusable, in an overseer, thus to deal with a *woman*. He is expected to tie her up, and to give her what is called, in southern parlance, a "genteel flogging," without any very great outlay of strength or skill. I watched, with palpitating interest, the course of the preliminary struggle, and was saddened by every new advantage gained over her by the ruffian. There were times when she seemed likely to get the better of the brute, but he finally overpowered her, and succeeded in getting his rope around her arms, and in firmly tying her to the tree, at which he had been aiming. This done, and Nelly was at the mercy of his merciless lash; and now, what followed, I have no heart to describe. The cowardly creature made good his every threat; and wielded the lash with all the hot zest of furious revenge. The cries of the woman, while undergoing the terrible infliction, were mingled with those of the children, sounds which I hope the reader may never be called upon to hear. When Nelly was untied, her back was covered with blood. The red stripes were all over her shoulders. She was whipped—severely whipped; but she was not subdued, for she continued to denounce the overseer, and to call him every vile name. He had bruised her flesh, but had left her invincible spirit undaunted. Such floggings are seldom repeated by the same overseer. They prefer to whip those who are most easily whipped. The old doctrine that submission is the very best cure for outrage and wrong, does not hold good on the slave plantation. He is whipped oftenest, who is whipped easiest; and that slave who has the courage to stand up for himself against the overseer, although he may have many hard stripes at the first, becomes, in the end, a freeman, even though he sustain the formal relation of a slave. "You can shoot me but you can't whip me," said a slave to Rigby Hopkins; and the result was that he was neither whipped nor shot. If the latter had been his fate, it would have been less deplorable than the living and lingering death to which cowardly and slavish souls are subjected. I do not know that Mr. Sevier ever undertook to whip Nelly again. He probably never did, for it was not long after his attempt to subdue her, that he was taken sick, and died. The wretched man died as he had lived, unrepentant; and it was said—with how much truth I know not—that in the very last hours of his life, his ruling passion showed itself, and that when wrestling with death, he was uttering horrid oaths, and flourishing the cowskin, as though he was tearing the flesh off some helpless slave. One thing is certain, that when he was in health, it was enough to chill the blood, and to stiffen the hair of an ordinary man, to hear Mr. Sevier talk. Nature, or his cruel habits, had given to his face an expression of unusual savageness, even for a slave-driver. Tobacco and rage had worn his teeth short, and nearly every sentence that escaped their compressed grating, was commenced or concluded with some outburst of profanity. His presence made the field alike the field of blood, and of blasphemy. Hated for his cruelty, despised for his cowardice, his death was deplored by no one outside his own house—if indeed it was deplored there; it was regarded by the slaves as a merciful interposition of Providence. Never went there a man to the grave loaded with heavier curses. Mr. Sevier's place was promptly taken by a Mr. Hopkins, and the change was quite a relief, he being a very different man. He was, in all respects, a better man than his predecessor; as good as any man can be, and yet be an overseer. His course was characterized by no extraordinary cruelty; and when he whipped a slave, as he sometimes did, he seemed to take no especial pleasure in it, but, on the contrary, acted as though he felt it to be a mean business. Mr. Hopkins stayed but a short time; his place—much to the regret of the slaves generally—was taken by a Mr. Gore, of whom more will be said hereafter. It is enough, for the present, to say, that he was no improvement on Mr. Sevier, except that he was less noisy and less profane.

I have already referred to the business-like aspect of Col. Lloyd's plantation. This business-like appearance was much increased on the two days at the end of each month, when the slaves from the different farms came to get their monthly allowance of meal and meat. These were gala days for the slaves, and there was much rivalry among them as to who should be elected to go up to the great house farm for the allowance, and, indeed, to attend to any business at this (for them) the capital. The beauty and grandeur of the place, its numerous slave population, and the fact that Harry, Peter and Jake—the sailors of the sloop—almost always kept, privately, little trinkets which they bought at Baltimore, to sell, made it a privilege to come to the great house farm. Being selected, too, for this office, was deemed a high honor. It was taken as a proof of confidence and favor; but, probably, the chief motive of the competitors for the place, was, a desire to break the dull monotony of the field, and to get beyond the overseer's eye and lash. Once on the road with an ox team, and seated on the tongue of his cart, with no overseer to look after him, the slave was comparatively free; and, if thoughtful, he had time to think. Slaves are generally expected to sing as well as to work. A silent slave is not liked by masters or overseers. "*Make a noise*," "*make a noise*," and "*bear a hand*," are the words usually addressed to the slaves when there is silence amongst them. This may account for the almost constant singing heard in the southern states. There was, generally, more or less singing among the teamsters, as it was one means of letting the overseer know where they were, and that they were moving on with the work. But, on allowance day, those who visited the great house farm were peculiarly excited and noisy. While on their way, they would make the dense old woods, for miles around, reverberate with their wild notes. These were not always merry because they were wild. On the contrary, they were mostly of a plaintive cast, and told a tale of grief and sorrow. In the most boisterous outbursts of rapturous sentiment, there was ever a tinge of deep melancholy. I have never heard any songs like those anywhere since I left slavery, except when in Ireland. There I heard the same *wailing notes*, and was much affected by them. It was during the famine of 1845–6. In all the songs of the slaves, there was ever some expression in praise of the great house farm; something which would flatter the pride of the owner, and, possibly, draw a favorable glance from him.

> I am going away to the great house farm,
>    O yea! O yea! O yea!
> My old master is a good old master,
>    O yea! O yea! O yea!

This they would sing, with other words of their own improvising— jargon to others, but full of meaning to themselves. I have sometimes thought, that the mere hearing of those songs would do more to impress truly spiritual-minded men and women with the soul-crushing and death-dealing character of slavery, than the reading of whole volumes of its mere physical cruelties. They speak to the heart and to the soul of the thoughtful. I cannot better express my sense of them now, than ten years ago, when, in sketching my life, I thus spoke of this feature of my plantation experience:*

> I did not, when a slave, understand the deep meanings of those rude, and apparently incoherent songs. I was myself within the circle, so that I neither saw nor heard as those without might see and hear. They told a tale which was then altogether beyond my feeble comprehension; they were tones, loud, long and deep, breathing the prayer and complaint of souls boiling over with the bitterest anguish. Every tone was a testimony against slavery, and a prayer to God for deliverance from chains. The hearing of those wild notes always depressed my spirits, and filled my heart with ineffable sadness. The mere recurrence, even now, afflicts my spirit, and while I am writing these lines, my tears are falling. To those songs I trace my first glimmering conceptions of the dehumanizing character of slavery. I can never get rid of that conception. Those songs still follow me, to deepen my hatred of slavery, and quicken my sympathies

---

* From *The Narrative of the Life of Frederick Douglass.*

for my brethren in bonds. If any one wishes to be impressed
with a sense of the soul-killing power of slavery, let him
go to Col. Lloyd's plantation, and, on allowance day, place
himself in the deep, pine woods, and there let him, in silence,
thoughtfully analyze the sounds that shall pass through the
chambers of his soul, and if he is not thus impressed, it will
only be because "there is no flesh in his obdurate heart."*

The remark is not unfrequently made, that slaves are the most
contented and happy laborers in the world. They dance and sing,
and make all manner of joyful noises—so they do; but it is a great
mistake to suppose them happy because they sing. The songs of the
slave represent the sorrows, rather than the joys, of his heart; and he is
relieved by them, only as an aching heart is relieved by its tears. Such is
the constitution of the human mind, that, when pressed to extremes, it
often avails itself of the most opposite methods. Extremes meet in mind
as in matter. When the slaves on board of the *Pearl* †were overtaken,
arrested, and carried to prison—their hopes for freedom blasted—as
they marched in chains they sang, and found (as Emily Edmonson tells
us) a melancholy relief in singing. The singing of a man cast away on
a desolate island, might be as appropriately considered an evidence of
his contentment and happiness, as the singing of a slave. Sorrow and
desolation have their songs, as well as joy and peace. Slaves sing more
to *make* themselves happy, than to express their happiness.

It is the boast of slaveholders, that their slaves enjoy more of the
physical comforts of life than the peasantry of any country in the
world. My experience contradicts this. The men and the women slaves
on Col. Lloyd's farm, received, as their monthly allowance of food,
eight pounds of pickled pork, or their equivalent in fish. The pork was
often tainted, and the fish was of the poorest quality—herrings, which
would bring very little if offered for sale in any northern market. With
their pork or fish, they had one bushel of Indian meal—unbolted—of
which quite fifteen percent was fit only to feed pigs. With this, one pint
of salt was given; and this was the entire monthly allowance of a full
grown slave, working constantly in the open field, from morning until

---

* From *The Task*, book 2, "The Time Piece" by William Cowper.

† In April 1848, a group of about seventy slaves boarded a ship called the *Pearl* in Washington,
D.C. Their goal was to sail up the Potomac River to the Chesapeake Bay and then to freedom in
the North. But they were caught in Maryland, and most were sold back into slavery in the Deep
South. It was the largest slave escape attempt in the United States.

night, every day in the month except Sunday, and living on a fraction more than a quarter of a pound of meat per day, and less than a peck of cornmeal per week. There is no kind of work that a man can do which requires a better supply of food to prevent physical exhaustion, than the field-work of a slave. So much for the slave's allowance of food; now for his raiment. The yearly allowance of clothing for the slaves on this plantation, consisted of two tow-linen shirts—such linen as the coarsest crash towels are made of; one pair of trowsers of the same material, for summer, and a pair of trowsers and a jacket of woolen, most slazily put together, for winter; one pair of yarn stockings, and one pair of shoes of the coarsest description. The slave's entire apparel could not have cost more than eight dollars per year. The allowance of food and clothing for the little children, was committed to their mothers, or to the older slave-women having the care of them. Children who were unable to work in the field, had neither shoes, stockings, jackets nor trowsers given them. Their clothing consisted of two coarse tow-linen shirts—already described—per year; and when these failed them, as they often did, they went naked until the next allowance day. Flocks of little children from five to ten years old, might be seen on Col. Lloyd's plantation, as destitute of clothing as any little heathen on the west coast of Africa; and this, not merely during the summer months, but during the frosty weather of March. The little girls were no better off than the boys; all were nearly in a state of nudity.

As to beds to sleep on, they were known to none of the field hands; nothing but a coarse blanket—not so good as those used in the north to cover horses—was given them, and this only to the men and women. The children stuck themselves in holes and corners, about the quarters; often in the corner of the huge chimneys, with their feet in the ashes to keep them warm. The want of beds, however, was not considered a very great privation. Time to sleep was of far greater importance, for, when the day's work is done, most of the slaves have their washing, mending and cooking to do; and, having few or none of the ordinary facilities for doing such things, very many of their sleeping hours are consumed in necessary preparations for the duties of the coming day.

The sleeping apartments—if they may be called such—have little regard to comfort or decency. Old and young, male and female, married and single, drop down upon the common clay floor, each covering up with his or her blanket—the only protection they have from cold or exposure. The night, however, is shortened at both ends. The slaves work often as long as they can see, and are late in cooking and mending for the coming day; and, at the first gray streak of morning, they are summoned to the field by the driver's horn.

More slaves are whipped for oversleeping than for any other fault. Neither age nor sex finds any favor. The overseer stands at the quarter door, armed with stick and cowskin, ready to whip any who may be a few minutes behind time. When the horn is blown, there is a rush for the door, and the hindermost one is sure to get a blow from the overseer. Young mothers who worked in the field, were allowed an hour, about ten o'clock in the morning, to go home to nurse their children. Sometimes they were compelled to take their children with them, and to leave them in the corner of the fences, to prevent loss of time in nursing them. The overseer generally rides about the field on horseback. A cowskin and a hickory stick are his constant companions. The cowskin is a kind of whip seldom seen in the northern states. It is made entirely of untanned, but dried, ox hide, and is about as hard as a piece of well-seasoned live oak. It is made of various sizes, but the usual length is about three feet. The part held in the hand is nearly an inch in thickness; and, from the extreme end of the butt or handle, the cowskin tapers its whole length to a point. This makes it quite elastic and springy. A blow with it, on the hardest back, will gash the flesh, and make the blood start. Cowskins are painted red, blue and green, and are the favorite slave whip. I think this whip worse than the "cat-o'nine-tails." It condenses the whole strength of the arm to a single point, and comes with a spring that makes the air whistle. It is a terrible instrument, and is so handy, that the overseer can always have it on his person, and ready for use. The temptation to use it is ever strong; and an overseer can, if disposed, always have cause for using it. With him, it is literally a word and a blow, and, in most cases, the blow comes first.

As a general rule, slaves do not come to the quarters for either breakfast or dinner, but take their "ash cake" with them, and eat it in the field. This was so on the home plantation; probably, because the distance from the quarter to the field, was sometimes two, and even three miles.

The dinner of the slaves consisted of a huge piece of ash cake, and a small piece of pork, or two salt herrings. Not having ovens, nor any suitable cooking utensils, the slaves mixed their meal with a little water, to such thickness that a spoon would stand erect in it; and, after the wood had burned away to coals and ashes, they would place the dough between oak leaves and lay it carefully in the ashes, completely covering it; hence, the bread is called ash cake. The surface of this peculiar bread is covered with ashes, to the depth of a sixteenth part of an inch, and the ashes, certainly, do not make it very grateful to the teeth, nor render it very palatable. The bran, or coarse part of the meal, is baked with the fire, and bright scales run through the bread. This bread, with its ashes and bran, would disgust and choke a northern man, but it is quite liked by the slaves. They eat it with avidity, and are more concerned about the quantity than about the quality. They are far too scantily provided for, and are worked too steadily, to be much concerned for the quality of their food. The few minutes allowed them at dinner time, after partaking of their coarse repast, are variously spent. Some lie down on the "turning row," and go to sleep; others draw together, and talk; and others are at work with needle and thread, mending their tattered garments. Sometimes you may hear a wild, hoarse laugh arise from a circle, and often a song. Soon, however, the overseer comes dashing through the field. "*Tumble up! Tumble up*, and to *work, work*," is the cry; and, now, from twelve o'clock (midday) till dark, the human cattle are in motion, wielding their clumsy hoes; hurried on by no hope of reward, no sense of gratitude, no love of children, no prospect of bettering their condition; nothing, save the dread and terror of the slave-driver's lash. So goes one day, and so comes and goes another.

But, let us now leave the rough usage of the field, where vulgar coarseness and brutal cruelty spread themselves and flourish, rank as weeds in the tropics; where a vile wretch, in the shape of a man, rides, walks, or struts about, dealing blows, and leaving gashes on broken-spirited men and helpless women, for thirty dollars per month—a business so horrible, hardening and disgraceful, that, rather than engage in it, a decent man would blow his own brains out—and let the reader view with me the equally wicked, but less repulsive aspects of slave life; where pride and pomp roll luxuriously at ease; where the toil of a thousand men supports a single family in easy idleness and sin. This is the great house; it is the home of the *Lloyds*! Some idea of its splendor has already been given—and, it is here that we shall find that height of luxury which is the opposite of that depth of poverty and physical wretchedness that we have just now been contemplating. But, there is this difference in the two extremes; viz: that in the case of the slave, the miseries and hardships of his lot are imposed by others, and, in the master's case, they are imposed by himself. The slave is a subject, subjected by others; the slaveholder is a subject, but he is the author of his own subjection. There is more truth in the saying, that slavery is a greater evil to the master than to the slave, than many, who utter it, suppose. The self-executing laws of eternal justice follow close on the heels of the evil-doer here, as well as elsewhere; making escape from all its penalties impossible. But, let others philosophize; it is my province here to relate and describe; only allowing myself a word or two, occasionally, to assist the reader in the proper understanding of the facts narrated.

# CHAPTER VII

## LIFE IN THE GREAT HOUSE

*Comforts and Luxuries—Elaborate Expenditure—House Servants—Men Servants and Maid Servants—Appearances— Slave Aristocracy—Stable and Carriage House—Boundless Hospitality—Fragrance of Rich Dishes—The Deceptive Character of Slavery—Slaves Seem Happy—Slaves and Slaveholders Alike Wretched—Fretful Discontent of Slaveholders—Fault-Finding—Old Barney—His Profession—Whipping—Humiliating Spectacle—Case Exceptional—William Wilks—Supposed Son of Col. Lloyd— Curious Incident—Slaves Prefer Rich Masters to Poor Ones.*

The close-fisted stinginess that fed the poor slave on coarse cornmeal and tainted meat; that clothed him in crashy tow-linen, and hurried him to toil through the field, in all weathers, with wind and rain beating through his tattered garments; that scarcely gave even the young slave-mother time to nurse her hungry infant in the fence corner; wholly vanishes on approaching the sacred precincts of the great house, the home of the Lloyds. There the scriptural phrase finds an exact illustration; the highly favored inmates of this mansion are literally arrayed "in purple and fine linen,"* and fare sumptuously every day! The table groans under the heavy and blood-bought luxuries gathered with painstaking care, at home and abroad. Fields, forests, rivers and seas, are made tributary here. Immense wealth, and its lavish expenditure, fill the great house with all that can please the eye, or tempt the taste. Here, appetite, not food, is the great *desideratum.* Fish, flesh and fowl, are here in profusion. Chickens, of all breeds; ducks, of all kinds, wild and tame, the common, and the huge Muscovite; Guinea fowls, turkeys, geese, and pea fowls, are in their several pens, fat and fatting for the destined vortex. The graceful swan, the mongrels, the black-necked wild goose; partridges, quails, pheasants and pigeons;

---

* Biblical reference, Luke 16:19.

choice water fowl, with all their strange varieties, are caught in this huge family net. Beef, veal, mutton and venison, of the most select kinds and quality, roll bounteously to this grand consumer. The teeming riches of the Chesapeake Bay, its rock, perch, drums, crocus, trout, oysters, crabs, and terrapin, are drawn hither to adorn the glittering table of the great house. The dairy, too, probably the finest on the Eastern Shore of Maryland—supplied by cattle of the best English stock, imported for the purpose, pours its rich donations of fragant cheese, golden butter, and delicious cream, to heighten the attraction of the gorgeous, unending round of feasting. Nor are the fruits of the earth forgotten or neglected. The fertile garden, many acres in size, constituting a separate establishment, distinct from the common farm—with its scientific gardener, imported from Scotland (a Mr. McDermott) with four men under his direction, was not behind, either in the abundance or in the delicacy of its contributions to the same full board. The tender asparagus, the succulent celery, and the delicate cauliflower; egg plants, beets, lettuce, parsnips, peas, and French beans, early and late; radishes, cantelopes, melons of all kinds; the fruits and flowers of all climes and of all descriptions, from the hardy apple of the north, to the lemon and orange of the south, culminated at this point. Baltimore gathered figs, raisins, almonds and juicy grapes from Spain. Wines and brandies from France; teas of various flavor, from China; and rich, aromatic coffee from Java, all conspired to swell the tide of high life, where pride and indolence rolled and lounged in magnificence and satiety.

Behind the tall-backed and elaborately wrought chairs, stand the servants, men and maidens—fifteen in number—discriminately selected, not only with a view to their industry and faithfulness, but with special regard to their personal appearance, their graceful agility and captivating address. Some of these are armed with fans, and are fanning reviving breezes toward the over-heated brows of the alabaster ladies; others watch with eager eye, and with fawn-like step anticipate and supply wants before they are sufficiently formed to be announced by word or sign.

These servants constituted a sort of black aristocracy on Col. Lloyd's plantation. They resembled the field hands in nothing, except in color, and in this they held the advantage of a velvet-like glossiness, rich and beautiful. The hair, too, showed the same advantage. The delicate colored maid rustled in the scarcely worn silk of her young mistress, while the servant men were equally well attired from the over-flowing wardrobe of their young masters; so that, in dress, as well as in form and feature, in manner and speech, in tastes and habits, the distance between these favored few, and the sorrow and hunger-smitten multitudes of the quarter and the field, was immense; and this is seldom passed over.

Let us now glance at the stables and the carriage house, and we shall find the same evidences of pride and luxurious extravagance. Here are three splendid coaches, soft within and lustrous without. Here, too, are gigs, phaetons, barouches, sulkeys and sleighs. Here are saddles and harnesses—beautifully wrought and silver mounted—kept with every care. In the stable you will find, kept only for pleasure, full thirty-five horses, of the most approved blood for speed and beauty. There are two men here constantly employed in taking care of these horses. One of these men must be always in the stable, to answer every call from the great house. Over the way from the stable, is a house built expressly for the hounds—a pack of twenty-five or thirty—whose fare would have made glad the heart of a dozen slaves. Horses and hounds are not the only consumers of the slave's toil. There was practiced, at the Lloyd's, a hospitality which would have astonished and charmed any health-seeking northern divine or merchant, who might have chanced to share it. Viewed from his own table, and *not* from the field, the colonel was a model of generous hospitality. His house was, literally, a hotel, for weeks during the summer months. At these times, especially, the air was freighted with the rich fumes of baking, boiling, roasting and broiling. The odors I shared with the winds; but the meats were under a more stringent monopoly except that, occasionally, I got a cake from Mas' Daniel. In Mas' Daniel I had a friend at court, from whom I learned many things which my eager curiosity was excited to know. I always knew when company was expected, and who they were, although I was an outsider, being the property, not of Col. Lloyd, but of a servant of the wealthy colonel. On these occasions, all that pride, taste and money could do, to dazzle and charm, was done.

Who could say that the servants of Col. Lloyd were not well clad and cared for, after witnessing one of his magnificent entertainments? Who could say that they did not seem to glory in being the slaves of such a master? Who, but a fanatic, could get up any sympathy for persons whose every movement was agile, easy and graceful, and who evinced a consciousness of high superiority? And who would ever venture to suspect that Col. Lloyd was subject to the troubles of ordinary mortals? Master and slave seem alike in their glory here? Can it all be seeming? Alas! It may only be a sham at last! This immense wealth; this gilded splendor; this profusion of luxury; this exemption from toil; this life of ease; this sea of plenty; aye, what of it all? Are the pearly gates of happiness and sweet content flung open to such suitors? *Far from it!* The poor slave, on his hard, pine plank, but scantily covered with his thin blanket, sleeps more soundly than the feverish voluptuary who reclines upon his feather bed and downy pillow. Food, to the indolent lounger, is poison, not sustenance. Lurking beneath all their dishes, are invisible spirits of evil, ready to feed the self-deluded gormandizers with aches, pains, fierce temper, uncontrolled passions, dyspepsia, rheumatism, lumbago and gout; and of these the Lloyds got their full share. To the pampered love of ease, there is no resting place. What is pleasant today, is repulsive tomorrow; what is soft now, is hard at another time; what is sweet in the morning, is bitter in the evening. Neither to the wicked, nor to the idler, is there any solid peace: "*Troubled, like the restless sea.*"

I had excellent opportunities of witnessing the restless discontent and the capricious irritation of the Lloyds. My fondness for horses— not peculiar to me more than to other boys—attracted me, much of the time, to the stables. This establishment was especially under the care of "old" and "young" Barney—father and son. Old Barney was a fine looking old man, of a brownish complexion, who was quite portly, and wore a dignified aspect for a slave. He was, evidently, much devoted to his profession, and held his office an honorable one. He was a farrier as well as an ostler; he could bleed, remove lampers from the mouths of the horses, and was well instructed in horse medicines. No one on the farm knew, so well as Old Barney, what to do with a sick horse. But his gifts and acquirements were of little advantage to him. His office was by no means an enviable one. He often got presents, but he got stripes as well; for in nothing was Col. Lloyd more unreasonable and exacting, than in respect to the management of his pleasure horses. Any supposed inattention to these animals were sure to be visited with degrading punishment. His horses and dogs fared better than his men. Their beds must be softer and cleaner than those of his human cattle. No excuse could shield Old Barney, if the colonel only suspected something wrong about his horses; and, consequently, he was often punished when faultless. It was absolutely painful to listen to the many unreasonable and fretful scoldings, poured out at the stable, by Col. Lloyd, his sons and sons-in-law. Of the latter, he had three—Messrs. Nicholson, Winder and Lownes. These all lived at the great house a portion of the year, and enjoyed the luxury of whipping the servants when they pleased, which was by no means unfrequently. A horse was seldom brought out of the stable to which no objection could be raised. "There was dust in his hair"; "there was a twist in his reins"; "his mane did not lie straight"; "he had not been properly grained"; "his head did not look well"; "his fore-top was not combed out"; "his fetlocks had not been properly trimmed"; something was always wrong. Listening to complaints, however groundless, Barney must stand, hat in hand, lips sealed, never answering a word. He must make no reply, no explanation; the judgment of the master must be deemed infallible, for his power is absolute and irresponsible. In a free state, a master, thus complaining without cause, of his ostler, might be told—"Sir, I am sorry I cannot please you, but, since I have done the best I can, your remedy is to dismiss me." Here, however, the ostler must stand, listen and tremble. One of the most heart-saddening and humiliating scenes I ever witnessed, was the whipping of Old Barney, by Col. Lloyd himself. Here were two men, both advanced in years; there were the silvery locks of Col. L., and there was the bald and toil-worn brow of Old Barney; master and slave; superior and inferior here, but *equals* at the bar of God; and, in the common course of events, they must both soon meet in another world, in a world where all distinctions, except those based on obedience and disobedience, are blotted out forever. "Uncover your head!" said the imperious master; he was obeyed. "Take off your jacket, you old rascal!" and off came Barney's jacket. "Down on your knees!" Down knelt the old man, his shoulders bare, his bald head glistening in the sun, and his aged knees on the cold, damp ground. In his humble and debasing attitude, the master—that master to whom he had given the best years and the best strength of his life—came forward, and laid on thirty lashes, with his horse whip. The old man bore it patiently, to the last, answering each blow with a slight shrug of the shoulders, and a groan. I cannot think that Col. Lloyd succeeded in marring the flesh of Old Barney very seriously, for the whip was a light, riding whip; but the spectacle of an aged man—a husband and a father—humbly kneeling before a worm of the dust, surprised and shocked me at the time; and since I have grown old enough to think on the wickedness of slavery, few facts have been of more value to me than this, to which I was a witness. It reveals slavery in its true color, and in its maturity of repulsive hatefulness. I owe it to truth, however, to say, that this was the first and the last time I ever saw Old Barney, or any other slave, compelled to kneel to receive a whipping.

I saw, at the stable, another incident, which I will relate, as it is illustrative of a phase of slavery to which I have already referred in another connection. Besides two other coachmen, Col. Lloyd owned one named William, who, strangely enough, was often called by his surname, Wilks, by white and colored people on the home plantation. Wilks was a very fine looking man. He was about as white as anybody on the plantation; and in manliness of form, and comeliness of features, he bore a very striking resemblance to Mr. Murray Lloyd. It was whispered, and pretty generally admitted as a fact, that William Wilks was a son of Col. Lloyd, by a highly favored slave-woman, who was still on the plantation. There were many reasons for believing this whisper, not only in William's appearance, but in the undeniable freedom which he enjoyed over all others, and his apparent consciousness of being something more than a slave to his master. It was notorious, too, that William had a deadly enemy in Murray Lloyd, whom he so much resembled, and that the latter greatly worried his father with importunities to sell William. Indeed, he gave his father no rest until he did sell him, to Austin Woldfolk, the great slave-trader at that time. Before selling him, however, Mr. L. tried what giving William a whipping would do, toward making things smooth; but this was a failure. It was a compromise, and defeated itself; for, immediately after the infliction, the heart-sickened colonel atoned to William for the abuse, by giving him a gold watch and chain. Another fact, somewhat curious, is, that though sold to the remorseless *Woldfolk*, taken in irons to Baltimore and cast into prison, with a view to being driven to the south, William, by some means—always a mystery to me—outbid all his purchasers, paid for himself, *and now resides in Baltimore, a freeman.* Is there not room to suspect, that, as the gold watch was presented to atone for the whipping, a purse of gold was given him by the same hand, with which to effect his purchase, as an atonement for the indignity involved in selling his own flesh and blood. All the circumstances of William, on the great house farm, show him to have occupied a different position from the other slaves, and, certainly, there is nothing in the supposed hostility of slaveholders to amalgamation, to forbid the supposition that William Wilks was the son of Edward Lloyd. *Practical* amalgamation is common in every neighborhood where I have been in slavery.

Col. Lloyd was not in the way of knowing much of the real opinions and feelings of his slaves respecting him. The distance between him and them was far too great to admit of such knowledge. His slaves were so numerous, that he did not know them when he saw them. Nor, indeed, did all his slaves know him. In this respect, he was inconveniently rich. It is reported of him, that, while riding along the road one day, he met a colored man, and addressed him in the usual way of speaking to colored people on the public highways of the south: "Well, boy, who do you belong to?" "To Col. Lloyd," replied the slave. "Well, does the colonel treat you well?" "No, sir," was the ready reply. "What? Does he work you too hard?" "Yes, sir." "Well, don't he give enough to eat?" "Yes, sir, he gives me enough, such as it is." The colonel, after ascertaining where the slave belonged, rode on; the slave also went on about his business, not dreaming that he had been conversing with his master. He thought, said and heard nothing more of the matter, until two or three weeks afterwards. The poor man was then informed by his overseer, that, for having found fault with his master, he was now to be sold to a Georgia trader. He was immediately chained and handcuffed; and thus, without a moment's warning he was snatched away, and forever sundered from his family and friends, by a hand more unrelenting than that of death. *This* is the penalty of telling the simple truth, in answer to a series of plain questions. It is partly in consequence of such facts, that slaves, when inquired of as to their condition and the character of their masters, almost invariably say they are contented, and that their masters are kind. Slaveholders have been known to send spies among their slaves, to ascertain, if possible, their views and feelings in regard to their condition. The frequency of this had the effect to establish among the slaves the maxim, that a still tongue makes a wise head. They suppress the truth rather than take the consequence of telling it, and, in so doing, they prove themselves a part of the human family. If they have anything to say of their master, it is, generally, something in his favor, especially when speaking to strangers. I was frequently asked, while a slave, if I had a kind master, and I do not remember ever to have given a negative reply. Nor did I, when pursuing this course, consider myself as uttering what was utterly false; for I always measured the kindness of my master by the standard of kindness set up by slaveholders around us. However, slaves are like other people, and imbibe similar prejudices. They are apt to think *their condition* better than that of others. Many, under the influence of this prejudice, think their own masters are better than the masters of other slaves; and this, too, in some cases, when the very reverse is true. Indeed, it is not uncommon for slaves even to fall out and quarrel among themselves about the relative kindness of their masters, contending for the superior goodness of his own over that of others. At the very same time, they mutually execrate their masters, when viewed separately. It was so on our plantation. When Col. Lloyd's slaves met those of Jacob Jepson, they seldom parted without a quarrel about their masters; Col. Lloyd's slaves contending that he was the richest, and Mr. Jepson's slaves that he was the smartest, man of the two. Col. Lloyd's slaves would boast his ability to buy and sell Jacob Jepson; Mr. Jepson's slaves would boast his ability to whip Col. Lloyd. These quarrels would almost always end in a fight between the parties; those that beat were supposed to have gained the point at issue. They seemed to think that the greatness of their masters was transferable to themselves. To be a *slave*, was thought to be bad enough; but to be a *poor man's* slave, was deemed a disgrace, indeed.

# CHAPTER VIII

## A CHAPTER OF HORRORS

*Austin Gore—A Sketch of His Character—Overseers as a Class—Their Peculiar Characteristics—The Marked Individuality of Austin Gore—His Sense of Duty—How He Whipped—Murder of Poor Denby—How It Occurred— Sensation—How Gore Made Peace with Col. Lloyd—The Murder Unpunished—Another Dreadful Murder Narrated— No Laws for the Protection of Slaves Can Be Enforced in the Southern States.*

As I have already intimated elsewhere, the slaves on Col. Lloyd's plantation, whose hard lot, under Mr. Sevier, the reader has already noticed and deplored, were not permitted to enjoy the comparatively moderate rule of Mr. Hopkins. The latter was succeeded by a very different man. The name of the new overseer was Austin Gore. Upon this individual I would fix particular attention; for under his rule there was more suffering from violence and bloodshed than had—according to the older slaves—ever been experienced before on this plantation. I confess, I hardly know how to bring this man fitly before the reader. He was, it is true, an overseer, and possessed, to a large extent, the peculiar characteristics of his class; yet, to call him merely an overseer, would not give the reader a fair notion of the man. I speak of overseers as a class. They are such. They are as distinct from the slaveholding gentry of the south, as are the fish-women of Paris, and the coal-heavers of London, distinct from other members of society. They constitute a separate fraternity at the south, not less marked than is the fraternity of Park Lane bullies in New York. They have been arranged and classified by that great law of attraction, which determines the spheres and affinities of men; which ordains, that men, whose malign and brutal propensities predominate over their moral and intellectual endowments, shall, naturally, fall into those employments which promise the largest gratification to those predominating instincts or propensities. The office of overseer takes this raw material of vulgarity and brutality, and stamps it as a distinct class of southern society. But, in this class, as in all other classes, there are characters of marked individuality, even while they bear a general resemblance to the mass. Mr. Gore was one of those, to whom a general characterization would do no manner of justice. He was an overseer; but he was something more. With the malign and tyrannical qualities of an overseer, he combined something of the lawful master. He had the artfulness and the mean ambition of his class; but he was wholly free from the disgusting swagger and noisy bravado of his fraternity. There was an easy air of independence about him; a calm self-possession, and a sternness of glance, which might well daunt hearts less timid than those of poor slaves, accustomed from childhood and through life to cower before a driver's lash. The home plantation of Col. Lloyd afforded an ample field for the exercise of the qualifications for overseership, which he possessed in such an eminent degree.

Mr. Gore was one of those overseers, who could torture the slightest word or look into impudence; he had the nerve, not only to resent, but to punish, promptly and severely. He never allowed himself to be answered back, by a slave. In this, he was as lordly and as imperious as Col. Edward Lloyd, himself; acting always up to the maxim, practically maintained by slaveholders, that it is better that a dozen slaves suffer under the lash, without fault, than that the master or the overseer should *seem* to have been wrong in the presence of the slave. *Everything must be absolute here.* Guilty or not guilty, it is enough to be accused, to be sure of a flogging. The very presence of this man Gore was painful, and I shunned him as I would have shunned a rattlesnake. His piercing, black eyes, and sharp, shrill voice, ever awakened sensations of terror among the slaves. For so young a man (I describe him as he was, twenty-five or thirty years ago), Mr. Gore was singularly reserved and grave in the presence of slaves. He indulged in no jokes, said no funny things, and kept his own counsels. Other overseers, how brutal soever they might be, were, at times, inclined to gain favor with the slaves, by indulging a little pleasantry; but Gore was never known to be guilty of any such weakness. He was always the cold, distant, unapproachable *overseer* of Col. Edward Lloyd's plantation, and needed no higher pleasure than was involved in a faithful discharge of the duties of his office. When he whipped, he seemed to do so from a sense of duty, and feared no consequences. What Hopkins did reluctantly, Gore did with alacrity. There was a stern will, an iron-like reality, about this Gore, which would have easily made him the chief of a band of pirates, had his environments been favorable to such a course of life. All the coolness, savage barbarity and freedom from moral restraint, which are necessary in the character of a pirate-chief, centered, I think, in this man Gore. Among many other deeds of shocking cruelty which he perpetrated, while I was at Mr. Lloyd's, was the murder of a young colored man, named Denby. He was sometimes called Bill Denby, or Demby; (I write from sound, and the sounds on Lloyd's plantation are not very certain.) I knew him well. He was a powerful young man, full of animal spirits, and, so far as I know, he was among the most valuable of Col. Lloyd's slaves. In something—I know not what—he offended this Mr. Austin Gore, and, in accordance with the custom of the latter, he under took to flog him. He gave Denby but few stripes; the latter broke away from him and plunged into the creek, and, standing there to the depth of his neck in water, he refused to come out at the order of the overseer; whereupon, for this refusal, *Gore shot him dead!* It is said that Gore gave Denby three calls, telling him that if he did not obey the last call, he would shoot him. When the third call was given, Denby stood his ground firmly; and this raised the question, in the minds of the by-standing slaves—"Will he dare to shoot?" Mr. Gore, without further parley, and without making any further effort to induce Denby to come out of the water, raised his gun deliberately to his face, took deadly aim at his standing victim, and, in an instant, poor Denby was numbered with the dead. His mangled body sank out of sight, and only his warm, red blood marked the place where he had stood.

This devilish outrage, this fiendish murder, produced, as it was well calculated to do, a tremendous sensation. A thrill of horror flashed through every soul on the plantation, if I may except the guilty wretch who had committed the hell-black deed. While the slaves generally were panic-struck, and howling with alarm, the murderer himself was calm and collected, and appeared as though nothing unusual had happened. The atrocity roused my old master, and he spoke out, in reprobation of it; but the whole thing proved to be less than a nine days' wonder. Both Col. Lloyd and my old master arraigned Gore for his cruelty in the matter, but this amounted to nothing. His reply, or explanation—as I remember to have heard it at the time—was, that the extraordinary expedient was demanded by necessity; that Denby had become unmanageable; that he had set a dangerous example to the other slaves; and that, without some such prompt measure as that to which he had resorted, were adopted, there would be an end to all rule and order on the plantation. That very convenient covert for all manner of cruelty and outrage—that cowardly alarm-cry, that the slaves would "*take the place*," was pleaded, in extenuation of this revolting crime, just as it had been cited in defense of a thousand similar ones. He argued, that if one slave refused to be corrected, and was allowed to escape with his life, when he had been told that he should lose it if he persisted in his course, the other slaves would soon copy his example; the result of which would be, the freedom of the slaves, and the enslavement of the whites. I have every reason to believe that Mr. Gore's defense, or explanation, was deemed satisfactory—at least to Col. Lloyd. He was continued in his office on the plantation. His fame as an overseer went abroad, and his horrid crime was not even submitted to judicial investigation. The murder was committed in the presence of slaves, and they, of course, could neither institute a suit, nor testify against the murderer. His bare word would go further in a court of law, than the united testimony of ten thousand black witnesses.

All that Mr. Gore had to do, was to make his peace with Col. Lloyd. This done, and the guilty perpetrator of one of the most foul murders goes unwhipped of justice, and uncensured by the community in which he lives. Mr. Gore lived in St. Michael's, Talbot County, when I left Maryland; if he is still alive he probably yet resides there; and I have no reason to doubt that he is now as highly esteemed, and as greatly respected, as though his guilty soul had never been stained with innocent blood. I am well aware that what I have now written will by some be branded as false and malicious. It will be denied, not only that such a thing ever did transpire, as I have now narrated, but that such a thing could happen in *Maryland*. I can only say—believe it or not— that I have said nothing but the literal truth, gainsay it who may.

I speak advisedly when I say this—that killing a slave, or any colored person, in Talbot County, Maryland, is not treated as a crime, either by the courts or the community. Mr. Thomas Lanman, ship carpenter, of St. Michael's, killed two slaves, one of whom he butchered with a hatchet, by knocking his brains out. He used to boast of the commission of the awful and bloody deed. I have heard him do so, laughingly, saying, among other things, that he was the only benefactor of his country in the company, and that when "others would do as much as he had done, we should be relieved of the d—d niggers."

As an evidence of the reckless disregard of human life where the life is that of a slave I may state the notorious fact, that the wife of Mr. Giles Hicks, who lived but a short distance from Col. Lloyd's, with her own hands murdered my wife's cousin, a young girl between fifteen and sixteen years of age—mutilating her person in a most shocking manner. The atrocious woman, in the paroxysm of her wrath, not content with murdering her victim, literally mangled her face, and broke her breast-bone. Wild, however, and infuriated as she was, she took the precaution to cause the slave-girl to be buried; but the facts of the case coming abroad, very speedily led to the disinterment of the remains of the murdered slave-girl. A coroner's jury was assembled, who decided that the girl had come to her death by severe beating. It was ascertained that the offense for which this girl was thus hurried out of the world, was this: she had been set that night, and several preceding nights, to mind Mrs. Hicks's baby, and having fallen into a sound sleep, the baby cried, waking Mrs. Hicks, but not the slave-girl. Mrs. Hicks, becoming infuriated at the girl's tardiness, after calling several times, jumped from her bed and seized a piece of fire-wood from the fireplace; and then, as she lay fast asleep, she deliberately pounded in her skull and breast-bone, and thus ended her life. I will not say that this most horrid murder produced no sensation in the community. It *did* produce a sensation; but, incredible to tell, the moral sense of the community was blunted too entirely by the ordinary nature of slavery horrors, to bring the murderess to punishment. A warrant was issued for her arrest, but, for some reason or other, that warrant was never served. Thus did Mrs. Hicks not only escape condign punishment, but even the pain and mortification of being arraigned before a court of justice.

Whilst I am detailing the bloody deeds that took place during my stay on Col. Lloyd's plantation, I will briefly narrate another dark transaction, which occurred about the same time as the murder of Denby by Mr. Gore.

On the side of the river Wye, opposite from Col. Lloyd's, there lived a Mr. Beal Bondley, a wealthy slaveholder. In the direction of his land, and near the shore, there was an excellent oyster fishing ground, and to this, some of the slaves of Col. Lloyd occasionally resorted in their little canoes, at night, with a view to make up the deficiency of their scanty allowance of food, by the oysters that they could easily get there. This, Mr. Bondley took it into his head to regard as a trespass, and while an old man belonging to Col. Lloyd was engaged in catching a few of the many millions of oysters that lined the bottom of that creek, to satisfy his hunger, the villainous Mr. Bondley, lying in ambush, without the slightest ceremony, discharged the contents of his musket into the back and shoulders of the poor old man. As good fortune would have it, the shot did not prove mortal, and Mr. Bondley came over, the next day, to see Col. Lloyd—whether to pay him for his property, or to justify himself for what he had done, I know not; but this I *can* say, the cruel and dastardly transaction was speedily hushed up; there was very little said about it at all, and nothing was publicly done which looked like the application of the principle of justice to the man whom *chance*, only, saved from being an actual murderer. One of the commonest sayings to which my ears early became accustomed, on Col. Lloyd's plantation and elsewhere in Maryland, was, that it was *"worth but half a cent to kill a nigger, and a half a cent to bury him"*; and the facts of my experience go far to justify the practical truth of this strange proverb. Laws for the protection of the lives of the slaves, are, as they must needs be, utterly incapable of being enforced, where the very parties who are nominally protected, are not permitted to give evidence, in courts of law, against the only class of persons from whom abuse, outrage and murder might be reasonably apprehended. While I heard of numerous murders committed by slaveholders on the Eastern Shores of Maryland, I never knew a solitary instance in which a slaveholder was either hung or imprisoned for having murdered a slave. The usual pretext for killing a slave is, that the slave has offered resistance. Should a slave, when assaulted, but raise his hand in self defense, the white assaulting party is fully justified by southern, or Maryland, public opinion, in shooting the slave down. Sometimes this is done, simply because it is alleged that the slave has been saucy. But here I leave this phase of the society of my early childhood, and will relieve the kind reader of these heart-sickening details.

# CHAPTER IX

## PERSONAL TREATMENT

*Miss Lucretia—Her Kindness—How It Was Manifested—
"Ike"—A Battle with Him—The Consequences Thereof—Miss
Lucretia's Balsam—Bread—How I Obtained It—Beams
of Sunlight Amidst the General Darkness—Suffering from
Cold—How We Took Our Meals—Orders to Prepare for
Baltimore—Overjoyed at the Thought of Quitting the
Plantation—Extraordinary Cleansing—Cousin Tom's Version
of Baltimore—Arrival There—Kind Reception Given Me by
Mrs. Sophia Auld—Little Tommy—My New Position—My
New Duties—A Turning Point in My History.*

I have nothing cruel or shocking to relate of my own personal experience, while I remained on Col. Lloyd's plantation, at the home of my old master. An occasional cuff from Aunt Katy, and a regular whipping from old master, such as any heedless and mischievous boy might get from his father, is all that I can mention of this sort. I was not old enough to work in the field, and, there being little else than field work to perform, I had much leisure. The most I had to do, was, to drive up the cows in the evening, to keep the front yard clean, and to perform small errands for my young mistress, Lucretia Auld. I have reasons for thinking this lady was very kindly disposed toward me, and, although I was not often the object of her attention, I constantly regarded her as my friend, and was always glad when it was my privilege to do her a service. In a family where there was so much that was harsh, cold and indifferent, the slightest word or look of kindness passed, with me, for its full value. Miss Lucretia—as we all continued to call her long after her marriage—had bestowed upon me such words and looks as taught me that she pitied me, if she did not love me. In addition to words and looks, she sometimes gave me a piece of bread and butter; a thing not set down in the bill of fare, and which must have been an extra ration, planned aside from either Aunt Katy or old master, solely out of the tender regard and friendship she had for me. Then, too, I one day got into the wars with Uncle Able's son, "Ike," and had got sadly worsted; in fact, the little rascal had struck me directly in the forehead with a sharp piece of cinder, fused with iron, from the old blacksmith's forge, which made a cross in my forehead very plainly to be seen now. The gash bled very freely, and I roared very loudly and betook myself home. The cold-hearted Aunt Katy paid no attention either to my wound or my roaring, except to tell me it served me right; I had no business with Ike; it was good for me; I would now keep away *"from dem Lloyd niggers."* Miss Lucretia, in this state of the case, came forward; and, in quite a different spirit from that manifested by Aunt Katy, she called me into the parlor (an extra privilege of itself) and, without using toward me any of the hard-hearted and reproachful epithets of my kitchen tormentor, she quietly acted the good Samaritan. With her own soft hand she washed the blood from my head and face, fetched her own balsam bottle, and with the balsam wetted a nice piece of white linen, and bound up my head. The balsam was not more healing to the wound in my head, than her kindness was healing to the wounds in my spirit, made by the unfeeling words of Aunt Katy. After this, Miss Lucretia was my friend. I felt her to be such; and I have no doubt that the simple act of binding up my head, did much to awaken in her mind an interest in my welfare. It is quite true, that this interest was never very marked, and it seldom showed itself in anything more than in giving me a piece of bread when I was hungry; but this was a great favor on a slave plantation, and I was the only one of the children to whom such attention was paid. When very hungry, I would go into the back yard and play under Miss Lucretia's window. When pretty severely pinched by hunger, I had a habit of singing, which the good lady very soon came to understand as a petition for a piece of bread. When I sung under Miss Lucretia's window, I was very apt to get well paid for my music. The reader will see that I now had two friends, both at important points—Mas' Daniel at the great house, and Miss Lucretia at home. From Mas' Daniel I got protection from the bigger boys; and from Miss Lucretia I got bread, by singing when I was hungry, and sympathy when I was abused by that termagant, who had the reins of government in the kitchen. For such friendship I felt deeply grateful, and bitter as are my recollections of slavery, I love to recall any instances of kindness, any sunbeams of humane treatment, which found way to my soul through the iron grating of my house of bondage. Such beams seem all the brighter from the general darkness into which they penetrate, and the impression they make is vividly distinct and beautiful.

As I have before intimated, I was seldom whipped—and never severely—by my old master. I suffered little from the treatment I received, except from hunger and cold. These were my two great physical troubles. I could neither get a sufficiency of food nor of clothing; but I suffered less from hunger than from cold. In hottest summer and coldest winter, I was kept almost in a state of nudity; no shoes, no stockings, no jacket, no trowsers; nothing but coarse sackcloth or tow-linen, made into a sort of shirt, reaching down to my knees. This I wore night and day, changing it once a week. In the day time I could protect myself pretty well, by keeping on the sunny side of the house; and in bad weather, in the corner of the kitchen chimney. The great difficulty was, to keep warm during the night. I had no bed. The pigs in the pen had leaves, and the horses in the stable had straw, but the children had no beds. They lodged anywhere in the ample kitchen. I slept, generally, in a little closet, without even a blanket to cover me. In very cold weather, I sometimes got down the bag in which cornmeal was usually carried to the mill, and crawled into that. Sleeping there, with my head in and feet out, I was partly protected, though not comfortable. My feet have been so cracked with the frost, that the pen with which I am writing might be laid in the gashes. The manner of taking our meals at old master's, indicated but little refinement. Our cornmeal mush, when sufficiently cooled, was placed in a large wooden tray, or trough, like those used in making maple sugar here in the north. This tray was set down, either on the floor of the kitchen, or out of doors on the ground; and the children were called, like so many pigs; and like so many pigs they would come, and literally devour the mush—some with oyster shells, some with pieces of shingles, and none with spoons. He that eat fastest got most, and he that was strongest got the best place; and few left the trough really satisfied. I was the most unlucky of any, for Aunt Katy had no good feeling for me; and if I pushed any of the other children, or if they told her anything unfavorable of me, she always believed the worst, and was sure to whip me.

As I grew older and more thoughtful, I was more and more filled with a sense of my wretchedness. The cruelty of Aunt Katy, the hunger and cold I suffered, and the terrible reports of wrong and outrage which came to my ear, together with what I almost daily witnessed, led me, when yet but eight or nine years old, to wish I had never been born. I used to contrast my condition with the black-birds, in whose wild and sweet songs I fancied them so happy! Their apparent joy only deepened the shades of my sorrow. There are thoughtful days in the lives of children—at least there were in mine when they grapple with all the great, primary subjects of knowledge, and reach, in a moment, conclusions which no subsequent experience can shake. I was just as well aware of the unjust, unnatural and murderous character of slavery, when nine years old, as I am now. Without any appeal to books, to laws, or to authorities of any kind, it was enough to accept God as a father, to regard slavery as a crime.

I was not ten years old when I left Col. Lloyd's plantation for Baltimore. I left that plantation with inexpressible joy. I never shall forget the ecstacy with which I received the intelligence from my friend, Miss Lucretia, that my old master had determined to let me go to Baltimore to live with Mr. Hugh Auld, a brother to Mr. Thomas Auld, my old master's son-in-law. I received this information about three days before my departure. They were three of the happiest days of my childhood. I spent the largest part of these three days in the creek, washing off the plantation scurf, and preparing for my new home. Mrs. Lucretia took a lively interest in getting me ready. She told me I must get all the dead skin off my feet and knees, before I could go to Baltimore, for the people there were very cleanly, and would laugh at me if I looked dirty; and, besides, she was intending to give me a pair of trowsers, which I should not put on unless I got all the dirt off. This was a warning to which I was bound to take heed; for the thought of owning a pair of trowsers, was great, indeed. It was almost a sufficient motive, not only to induce me to scrub off the *mange* (as pig drovers would call it) but the skin as well. So I went at it in good earnest, working for the first time in the hope of reward. I was greatly excited, and could hardly consent to sleep, lest I should be left. The ties that, ordinarily, bind children to their homes, were all severed, or they never had any existence in my case, at least so far as the home plantation of Col. L. was concerned. I therefore found no severe trial at the moment of my departure, such as I had experienced when separated from my home in Tuckahoe. My home at my old master's was charmless to me; it was not home, but a prison to me; on parting from it, I could not feel that I was leaving anything which I could have enjoyed by staying. My mother was now long dead; my grandmother was far away, so that I seldom saw her; Aunt Katy was my unrelenting tormentor; and my two sisters and brothers, owing to our early separation in life, and the family-destroying power of slavery, were, comparatively, strangers to me. The fact of our relationship was almost blotted out. I looked for *home* elsewhere, and was confident of finding none which I should relish less than the one I was leaving. If, however, I found in my new home—to which I was going with such blissful anticipations—hardship, whipping and nakedness, I had the questionable consolation that I should not have escaped any one of these evils by remaining under the management of Aunt Katy. Then, too, I thought, since I had endured much in this line on Lloyd's plantation, I could endure as much elsewhere, and especially at Baltimore; for I had something of the feeling about that city which is expressed in the saying, that being "hanged in England, is better than dying a natural death in Ireland." I had the strongest desire to see Baltimore. My cousin Tom—a boy two or three years older than I—had been there, and though not fluent (he stuttered immoderately) in speech, he had inspired me with that desire, by his eloquent description of the place. Tom was, sometimes, Capt. Auld's cabin boy; and when he came from Baltimore, he was always a sort of hero amongst us, at least till his Baltimore trip was forgotten. I could never tell him of anything, or point out anything that struck me as beautiful or powerful, but that he had seen something in Baltimore far surpassing it. Even the great house itself, with all its pictures within, and pillars without, he had the hardihood to say "was nothing to Baltimore." He bought a trumpet (worth six pence) and brought it home; told what he had seen in the windows of stores; that he had heard shooting crackers, and seen soldiers; that he had seen a steamboat; that there were ships in Baltimore that could carry four such sloops as the *Sally Lloyd*. He said a great deal about the market-house; he spoke of the bells ringing; and of many other things which roused my curiosity very much; and, indeed, which heightened my hopes of happiness in my new home.

We sailed out of Miles River for Baltimore early on a Saturday morning. I remember only the day of the week; for, at that time, I had no knowledge of the days of the month, nor, indeed, of the months of the year. On setting sail, I walked aft, and gave to Col. Lloyd's plantation what I hoped would be the last look I should ever give to it, or to any place like it. My strong aversion to the great farm, was not owing to my own personal suffering, but the daily suffering of others, and to the certainty that I must, sooner or later, be placed under the barbarous rule of an overseer, such as the accomplished Gore, or the brutal and drunken Plummer. After taking this last view, I quitted the quarter deck, made my way to the bow of the sloop, and spent the remainder of the day in looking ahead; interesting myself in what was in the distance, rather than what was near by or behind. The vessels, sweeping along the bay, were very interesting objects. The broad bay opened like a shoreless ocean on my boyish vision, filling me with wonder and admiration.

Late in the afternoon, we reached Annapolis, the capital of the state, stopping there not long enough to admit of my going ashore. It was the first large town I had ever seen; and though it was inferior to many a factory village in New England, my feelings, on seeing it, were excited to a pitch very little below that reached by travelers at the first view of Rome. The dome of the state house was especially imposing, and surpassed in grandeur the appearance of the great house. The great world was opening upon me very rapidly, and I was eagerly acquainting myself with its multifarious lessons.

We arrived in Baltimore on Sunday morning, and landed at Smith's wharf, not far from Bowly's wharf. We had on board the sloop a large flock of sheep, for the Baltimore market; and, after assisting in driving them to the slaughter house of Mr. Curtis, on Loudon Slater's Hill, I was speedily conducted by Rich—one of the hands belonging to the sloop—to my new home in Alliciana Street, near Gardiner's ship-yard, on Fell's Point. Mr. and Mrs. Hugh Auld, my new mistress and master, were both at home, and met me at the door with their rosy cheeked little son, Thomas, to take care of whom was to constitute my future occupation. In fact, it was to "little Tommy," rather than to his parents, that old master made a present of me; and though there was no *legal* form or arrangement entered into, I have no doubt that Mr. and Mrs. Auld felt that, in due time, I should be the legal property of their bright-eyed and beloved boy, Tommy. I was struck with the appearance, especially, of my new mistress. Her face was lighted with the kindliest emotions; and the reflex influence of her countenance, as well as the tenderness with which she seemed to regard me, while asking me sundry little questions, greatly delighted me, and lit up, to my fancy, the pathway of my future. Miss Lucretia was kind; but my new mistress, "Miss Sophy," surpassed her in kindness of manner. Little Thomas was affectionately told by his mother, that "*there was his Freddy,*" and that "Freddy would take care of him"; and I was told to "be kind to little Tommy"—an injunction I scarcely needed, for I had already fallen in love with the dear boy; and with these little ceremonies I was initiated into my new home, and entered upon my peculiar duties, with not a cloud above the horizon.

I may say here, that I regard my removal from Col. Lloyd's plantation as one of the most interesting and fortunate events of my life. Viewing it in the light of human likelihoods, it is quite probable that, but for the mere circumstance of being thus removed before the rigors of slavery had fastened upon me; before my young spirit had been crushed under the iron control of the slave-driver, instead of being, today, a *freeman*, I might have been wearing the galling chains of slavery. I have sometimes felt, however, that there was something more intelligent than *chance*, and something more certain than *luck*, to be seen in the circumstance. If I have made any progress in knowledge; if I have cherished any honorable aspirations, or have, in any manner, worthily discharged the duties of a member of an oppressed people; this little circumstance must be allowed its due weight in giving my life that direction. I have ever regarded it as the first plain manifestation of that

> Divinity that shapes our ends,
> Rough hew them as we will.[*]

I was not the only boy on the plantation that might have been sent to live in Baltimore. There was a wide margin from which to select. There were boys younger, boys older, and boys of the same age, belonging to my old master—some at his own house, and some at his farm—but the high privilege fell to my lot.

I may be deemed superstitious and egotistical, in regarding this event as a special interposition of Divine Providence in my favor; but the thought is a part of my history, and I should be false to the earliest and most cherished sentiments of my soul, if I suppressed, or hesitated to avow that opinion, although it may be characterized as irrational by

---

[*] From *Hamlet* by William Shakespeare.

the wise, and ridiculous by the scoffer. From my earliest recollections of serious matters, I date the entertainment of something like an ineffaceable conviction, that slavery would not always be able to hold me within its foul embrace; and this conviction, like a word of living faith, strengthened me through the darkest trials of my lot. This good spirit was from God; and to him I offer thanksgiving and praise.

# CHAPTER X

## LIFE IN BALTIMORE

*City Annoyances—Plantation Regrets—My Mistress, Miss
Sophia—Her Kindness to Me—My Master, Hugh Auld—His
Sourness—My Increased Sensitiveness—My Comforts—My
Occupation—The Baneful Effects of Slaveholding on My
Dear and Good Mistress—How She Commenced Teaching Me
to Read—Why She Ceased Teaching Me—Clouds Gathering
Over My Bright Prospects—Master Auld's Exposition of
the True Philosophy of Slavery—City Slaves—Plantation
Slaves—The Contrast—Exceptions—Mr. Hamilton's Two
Slaves, Henrietta and Mary—Mrs. Hamilton's Cruel Treatment
of Them—The Piteous Aspect They Presented—No Power
Must Come Between the Slave and Slaveholder.*

Once in Baltimore, with hard brick pavements under my feet, which almost raised blisters, by their very heat, for it was in the height of summer; walled in on all sides by towering brick buildings; with troops of hostile boys ready to pounce upon me at every street corner; with new and strange objects glaring upon me at every step, and with startling sounds reaching my ears from all directions, I for a time thought that, after all, the home plantation was a more desirable place of residence than my home on Alliciana Street, in Baltimore. My country eyes and ears were confused and bewildered here; but the boys were my chief trouble. They chased me, and called me "*Eastern Shore man*," till really I almost wished myself back on the Eastern Shore. I had to undergo a sort of moral acclimation, and when that was over, I did much better. My new mistress happily proved to be all she *seemed* to be, when, with her husband, she met me at the door, with a most beaming, benignant countenance. She was, naturally, of an excellent disposition, kind, gentle and cheerful. The supercilious contempt for the rights and feelings of the slave, and the petulance and bad humor which generally characterize slaveholding ladies, were all quite absent from kind "Miss" Sophia's manner and bearing toward me. She had, in truth, never been a slaveholder, but had—a thing quite unusual in the south—depended almost entirely upon her own industry for a living. To this fact the dear lady, no doubt, owed the excellent preservation of her natural goodness of heart, for slavery can change a saint into a sinner, and an angel into a demon. I hardly knew how to behave toward "Miss Sopha," as I used to call Mrs. Hugh Auld. I had been treated as a *pig* on the plantation; I was treated as a *child* now. I could not even approach her as I had formerly approached Mrs. Thomas Auld. How could I hang down my head, and speak with bated breath, when there was no pride to scorn me, no coldness to repel me, and no hatred to inspire me with fear? I therefore soon learned to regard her as something more akin to a mother, than a slaveholding mistress. The crouching servility of a slave, usually so acceptable a quality to the haughty slaveholder, was not understood nor desired by this gentle woman. So far from deeming it impudent in a slave to look her straight in the face, as some slaveholding ladies do, she seemed ever to say, "look up, child; don't be afraid; see, I am full of kindness and good will toward you." The hands belonging to Col. Lloyd's sloop, esteemed it a great privilege to be the bearers of parcels or messages to my new mistress; for whenever they came, they were sure of a most kind and pleasant reception. If little Thomas was her son, and her most dearly beloved child, she, for a time, at least, made me something like his half-brother in her affections. If dear Tommy was exalted to a place on his mother's knee, "Feddy" was honored by a place at his mother's side. Nor did he lack the caressing strokes of her gentle hand, to convince him that, though *motherless*, he was not *friendless*. Mrs. Auld was not only a kind-hearted woman, but she was remarkably pious; frequent in her attendance of public worship, much given to reading the Bible, and to chanting hymns of praise, when alone. Mr. Hugh Auld was altogether a different character. He cared very little about religion, knew more of the world, and was more of the world, than his wife. He set out, doubtless to be—as the world goes—a respectable man, and to get on by becoming a successful ship-builder, in that city of ship-building. This was his ambition, and it fully occupied him. I was, of course, of very little consequence to him, compared with what I was to good Mrs. Auld; and, when he smiled upon me, as he sometimes did, the smile was borrowed from his lovely wife, and, like all borrowed light, was transient, and vanished with the source whence it was derived. While I must characterize Master Hugh as being a very sour man, and of forbidding appearance, it is due to him to acknowledge, that he was never very cruel to me, according to the notion of cruelty in Maryland. The first year or two which I spent in his house, he left me almost exclusively to the management of his wife. She was my law-giver. In hands so tender as hers, and in the absence of the cruelties of the plantation, I became, both physically and mentally, much more sensitive to good and ill treatment; and, perhaps, suffered more from a frown from my mistress, than I formerly did from a cuff at the hands of Aunt Katy. Instead of the cold, damp floor of my old master's kitchen, I found myself on carpets; for the corn bag in winter, I now had a good straw bed, well furnished with covers; for the coarse cornmeal in the morning, I now had good bread, and mush occasionally; for my poor tow-linen shirt, reaching to my knees, I had good, clean clothes. I was really well off. My employment was to run errands, and to take care of Tommy; to prevent his getting in the way of carriages, and to keep him out of harm's way generally. Tommy, and I, and his mother, got on swimmingly together, for a time. I say *for a time*, because the fatal poison of irresponsible power, and the natural influence of slavery customs, were not long in making a suitable impression on the gentle and loving disposition of my excellent mistress. At first, Mrs. Auld evidently regarded me simply as a child, like any other child; she had not come to regard me as *property*. This latter thought was a thing of conventional growth. The first was natural and spontaneous. A noble nature, like hers, could not, instantly, be wholly perverted; and it took several years to change the natural sweetness of her temper into fretful bitterness. In her worst estate, however, there were, during the first seven years I lived with her, occasional returns of her former kindly disposition.

The frequent hearing of my mistress reading the Bible—for she often read aloud when her husband was absent—soon awakened my curiosity in respect to this *mystery* of reading, and roused in me the desire to learn. Having no fear of my kind mistress before my eyes, (she had then given me no reason to fear), I frankly asked her to teach me to read; and, without hesitation, the dear woman began the task, and very soon, by her assistance, I was master of the alphabet, and could spell words of three or four letters. My mistress seemed almost as proud of my progress, as if I had been her own child; and, supposing that her husband would be as well pleased, she made no secret of what she was doing for me. Indeed, she exultingly told him of the aptness of her pupil, of her intention to persevere in teaching me, and of the duty which she felt it to teach me, at least to read *the Bible*. Here arose the first cloud over my Baltimore prospects, the precursor of drenching rains and chilling blasts.

Master Hugh was amazed at the simplicity of his spouse, and, probably for the first time, he unfolded to her the true philosophy of slavery, and the peculiar rules necessary to be observed by masters and mistresses, in the management of their human chattels. Mr. Auld promptly forbade continuance of her instruction; telling her, in the first place, that the thing itself was unlawful; that it was also unsafe, and could only lead to mischief. To use his own words, further, he said, "If you give a nigger an inch, he will take an ell"; "he should know nothing but the will of his master, and learn to obey it." "If you teach that nigger—speaking of myself—how to read the Bible, there will be no keeping him"; "it would forever unfit him for the duties of a slave"; and "as to himself, learning would do him no good, but probably, a great deal of harm—making him disconsolate and unhappy." "If you learn him now to read, he'll want to know how to write; and, this accomplished, he'll be running away with himself." Such was the tenor of Master Hugh's oracular exposition of the true philosophy of training a human chattel; and it must be confessed that he very clearly comprehended the nature and the requirements of the relation of master and slave. His discourse was the first decidedly anti-slavery lecture to which it had been my lot to listen. Mrs. Auld evidently felt the force of his remarks; and, like an obedient wife, began to shape her course in the direction indicated by her husband. The effect of his words, *on me*, was neither slight nor transitory. His iron sentences—cold and harsh—sunk deep into my heart, and stirred up not only my feelings into a sort of rebellion, but awakened within me a slumbering train of vital thought. It was a new and special revelation, dispelling a painful mystery, against which my youthful understanding had struggled, and struggled in vain, to wit: the *white* man's power to perpetuate the enslavement of the black man. "Very well," thought I; "knowledge unfits a child to be a slave." I instinctively assented to the proposition; and from that moment I understood the direct pathway from slavery to freedom. This was just what I needed; and I got it at a time, and from a source, whence I least expected it. I was saddened at the thought of losing the assistance of my kind mistress; but the information, so instantly derived, to some extent compensated me for the loss I had sustained in this direction. Wise as Mr. Auld was, he evidently underrated my comprehension, and had little idea of the use to which I was capable of putting the impressive lesson he was giving to his wife. *He* wanted me to be a *slave*; I had already voted against that on the home plantation of Col. Lloyd. That which he most loved I most hated; and the very determination which he expressed to keep me in ignorance, only rendered me the more resolute in seeking intelligence. In learning to read, therefore, I am not sure that I do not owe quite as much to the opposition of my master, as to the kindly assistance of my amiable mistress. I acknowledge the benefit rendered me by the one, and by the other; believing, that but for my mistress, I might have grown up in ignorance.

I had resided but a short time in Baltimore, before I observed a marked difference in the manner of treating slaves, generally, from which I had witnessed in that isolated and out-of-the-way part of the country where I began life. A city slave is almost a free citizen, in Baltimore, compared with a slave on Col. Lloyd's plantation. He is much better fed and clothed, is less dejected in his appearance, and enjoys privileges altogether unknown to the whip-driven slave on the plantation. Slavery dislikes a dense population, in which there is a majority of non-slaveholders. The general sense of decency that must pervade such a population, does much to check and prevent those outbreaks of atrocious cruelty, and those dark crimes without a name, almost openly perpetrated on the plantation. He is a desperate slaveholder who will shock the humanity of his non-slaveholding neighbors, by the cries of the lacerated slaves; and very few in the city are willing to incur the odium of being cruel masters. I found, in Baltimore, that no man was more odious to the white, as well as to the colored people, than he, who had the reputation of starving his slaves. Work them, flog them, if need be, but don't starve them. There are, however, some painful exceptions to this rule. While it is quite true that most of the slaveholders in Baltimore feed and clothe their slaves well, there are others who keep up their country cruelties in the city.

An instance of this sort is furnished in the case of a family who lived directly opposite to our house, and were named Hamilton. Mrs. Hamilton owned two slaves. Their names were Henrietta and Mary.

They had always been house slaves. One was aged about twenty-two, and the other about fourteen. They were a fragile couple by nature, and the treatment they received was enough to break down the constitution of a horse. Of all the dejected, emaciated, mangled and excoriated creatures I ever saw, those two girls—in the refined, church going and Christian city of Baltimore were the most deplorable. Of stone must that heart be made, that could look upon Henrietta and Mary, without being sickened to the core with sadness. Especially was Mary a heart-sickening object. Her head, neck and shoulders, were literally cut to pieces. I have frequently felt her head, and found it nearly covered over with festering sores, caused by the lash of her cruel mistress. I do not know that her master ever whipped her, but I have often been an eye witness of the revolting and brutal inflictions by Mrs. Hamilton; and what lends a deeper shade to this woman's conduct, is the fact, that, almost in the very moments of her shocking outrages of humanity and decency, she would charm you by the sweetness of her voice and her seeming piety. She used to sit in a large rocking chair, near the middle of the room, with a heavy cowskin, such as I have elsewhere described; and I speak within the truth when I say, that these girls seldom passed that chair, during the day, without a blow from that cowskin, either upon their bare arms, or upon their shoulders. As they passed her, she would draw her cowskin and give them a blow, saying, "*Move faster, you black jip!*" and, again, "*Take that, you black jip!*" continuing, "*If you don't move faster, I will give you more.*" Then the lady would go on, singing her sweet hymns, as though her *righteous* soul were sighing for the holy realms of paradise.

Added to the cruel lashings to which these poor slave-girls were subjected—enough in themselves to crush the spirit of men—they were, really, kept nearly half starved; they seldom knew what it was to eat a full meal, except when they got it in the kitchens of neighbors, less mean and stingy than the psalm-singing Mrs. Hamilton. I have seen poor Mary contending for the offal, with the pigs in the street. So much was the poor girl pinched, kicked, cut and pecked to pieces, that the boys in the street knew her only by the name of "*pecked*," a name derived from the scars and blotches on her neck, head and shoulders.

It is some relief to this picture of slavery in Baltimore, to say—what is but the simple truth—that Mrs. Hamilton's treatment of her slaves was generally condemned, as disgraceful and shocking; but while I say this, it must also be remembered, that the very parties who censured the cruelty of Mrs. Hamilton, would have condemned and promptly punished any attempt to interfere with Mrs. Hamilton's *right* to cut and slash her slaves to pieces. There must be no force between the slave and the slaveholder, to restrain the power of the one, and protect the weakness of the other; and the cruelty of Mrs. Hamilton is as justly chargeable to the upholders of the slave system, as drunkenness is chargeable on those who, by precept and example, or by indifference, uphold the drinking system.

# CHAPTER XI

## "A CHANGE CAME O'ER THE
## SPIRIT OF MY DREAM"*

*How I Learned to Read—My Mistress—Her Slaveholding
Duties—Their Deplorable Effects Upon Her Originally Noble
Nature—The Conflict in Her Mind—Her Final Opposition
to My Learning to Read—Too Late—She Had Given Me
the Inch, I Was Resolved to Take the Ell—How I Pursued
My Education—My Tutors—How I Compensated Them—
What Progress I Made—Slavery—What I Heard Said About
It—Thirteen Years Old—The Columbian Orator—A Rich
Scene—A Dialogue—Speeches of Chatham, Sheridan,
Pitt and Fox—Knowledge Ever Increasing—My Eyes
Opened—Liberty—How I Pined for It—My Sadness—
The Dissatisfaction of My Poor Mistress—My Hatred of
Slavery—One Upas Tree Overshadowed Us Both.*

I lived in the family of Master Hugh, at Baltimore, seven years, during which time—as the almanac makers say of the weather—my condition was variable. The most interesting feature of my history here, was my learning to read and write, under somewhat marked disadvantages. In attaining this knowledge, I was compelled to resort to indirections by no means congenial to my nature, and which were really humiliating to me. My mistress—who, as the reader has already seen, had begun to teach me—was suddenly checked in her benevolent design, by the strong advice of her husband. In faithful compliance with this advice, the good lady had not only ceased to instruct me, herself, but had set her face as a flint against my learning to read by any means. It is due, however, to my mistress to say, that she did not adopt this course in all its stringency at the first. She either thought it unnecessary, or she lacked the depravity indispensable to shutting me up in mental darkness. It was, at least, necessary for her to have some training, and

* From "The Dream" by George Gordon, Lord Byron.

some hardening, in the exercise of the slaveholder's prerogative, to make her equal to forgetting my human nature and character, and to treating me as a thing destitute of a moral or an intellectual nature. Mrs. Auld—my mistress—was, as I have said, a most kind and tender-hearted woman; and, in the humanity of her heart, and the simplicity of her mind, she set out, when I first went to live with her, to treat me as she supposed one human being ought to treat another.

It is easy to see, that, in entering upon the duties of a slaveholder, some little experience is needed. Nature has done almost nothing to prepare men and women to be either slaves or slaveholders. Nothing but rigid training, long persisted in, can perfect the character of the one or the other. One cannot easily forget to love freedom; and it is as hard to cease to respect that natural love in our fellow-creatures. On entering upon the career of a slaveholding mistress, Mrs. Auld was singularly deficient; nature, which fits nobody for such an office, had done less for her than any lady I had known. It was no easy matter to induce her to think and to feel that the curly-headed boy, who stood by her side, and even leaned on her lap; who was loved by little Tommy, and who loved little Tommy in turn; sustained to her only the relation of a chattel. I was *more* than that, and she felt me to be more than that. I could talk and sing; I could laugh and weep; I could reason and remember; I could love and hate. I was human, and she, dear lady, knew and felt me to be so. How could she, then, treat me as a brute, without a mighty struggle with all the noble powers of her own soul. That struggle came, and the will and power of the husband was victorious. Her noble soul was overthrown; but, he that overthrew it did not, himself, escape the consequences. He, not less than the other parties, was injured in his domestic peace by the fall.

When I went into their family, it was the abode of happiness and contentment. The mistress of the house was a model of affection and tenderness. Her fervent piety and watchful uprightness made it impossible to see her without thinking and feeling—"*that woman is a Christian.*" There was no sorrow nor suffering for which she had not a tear, and there was no innocent joy for which she had not a smile. She had bread for the hungry, clothes for the naked, and comfort for every mourner that came within her reach. Slavery soon proved its ability to divest her of these excellent qualities, and her home of its early happiness. Conscience cannot stand much violence. Once thoroughly broken down, *who* is he that can repair the damage? It may be broken toward the slave, on Sunday, and toward the master on Monday. It cannot endure such shocks. It must stand entire, or it does not stand at all. If my condition waxed bad, that of the family waxed not better. The first step, in the wrong direction, was the violence done to nature and to conscience, in arresting the benevolence that would have enlightened my young mind. In ceasing to instruct me, she must begin to justify herself *to* herself; and, once consenting to take sides in such a debate, she was riveted to her position. One needs very little knowledge of moral philosophy, to see *where* my mistress now landed. She finally became even more violent in her opposition to my learning to read, than was her husband himself. She was not satisfied with simply doing as *well* as her husband had commanded her, but seemed resolved to better his instruction. Nothing appeared to make my poor mistress— after her turning toward the downward path—more angry, than seeing me, seated in some nook or corner, quietly reading a book or a newspaper. I have had her rush at me, with the utmost fury, and snatch from my hand such newspaper or book, with something of the wrath and consternation which a traitor might be supposed to feel on being discovered in a plot by some dangerous spy.

Mrs. Auld was an apt woman, and the advice of her husband, and her own experience, soon demonstrated, to her entire satisfaction, that education and slavery are incompatible with each other. When this conviction was thoroughly established, I was most narrowly watched in all my movements. If I remained in a separate room from the family for any considerable length of time, I was sure to be suspected of having a book, and was at once called upon to give an account of myself. All this, however, was entirely *too late*. The first, and never to be retraced, step had been taken. In teaching me the alphabet, in the days of her simplicity and kindness, my mistress had given me the "*inch*," and now, no ordinary precaution could prevent me from taking the "*ell*."

Seized with a determination to learn to read, at any cost, I hit upon many expedients to accomplish the desired end. The plea which I mainly adopted, and the one by which I was most successful, was that of using my young white playmates, with whom I met in the streets, as teachers. I used to carry, almost constantly, a copy of *Webster's Spelling Book* in my pocket; and, when sent of errands, or when play time was allowed me, I would step, with my young friends, aside, and take a lesson in spelling. I generally paid my *tuition fee* to the boys, with bread, which I also carried in my pocket. For a single biscuit, any of my hungry little comrades would give me a lesson more valuable to me than bread. Not every one, however, demanded this consideration, for there were those who took pleasure in teaching me, whenever I had a chance to be taught by them. I am strongly tempted to give the names of two or three of those little boys, as a slight testimonial of the gratitude and affection I bear them, but prudence forbids; not that it would injure me, but it might, possibly, embarrass them; for it is almost an unpardonable offense to do any thing, directly or indirectly, to promote a slave's freedom, in a slave state. It is enough to say, of my warm-hearted little play fellows, that they lived on Philpot Street, very near Durgin & Bailey's ship-yard.

Although slavery was a delicate subject, and very cautiously talked about among grown up people in Maryland, I frequently talked about it—and that very freely—with the white boys. I would, sometimes, say to them, while seated on a curb stone or a cellar door, "I wish I could be free, as you will be when you get to be men." "You will be free, you know, as soon as you are twenty-one, and can go where you like, but I am a slave for life. Have I not as good a right to be free as you have?" Words like these, I observed, always troubled them; and I had no small satisfaction in wringing from the boys, occasionally, that fresh and bitter condemnation of slavery, that springs from nature, unseared and unperverted. Of all consciences let me have those to deal with which have not been bewildered by the cares of life. I do not remember ever to have met with a *boy*, while I was in slavery, who defended the slave system; but I have often had boys to console me, with the hope that something would yet occur, by which I might be made free. Over and over again, they have told me, that "they believed *I* had as good a right to be free as *they* had"; and that "they did not believe God ever made any one to be a slave." The reader will easily see, that such little conversations with my play fellows, had no tendency to weaken my love of liberty, nor to render me contented with my condition as a slave.

When I was about thirteen years old, and had succeeded in learning to read, every increase of knowledge, especially respecting the *free states*, added something to the almost intolerable burden of the thought—*I am a slave for life*. To my bondage I saw no end. It was a terrible reality, and I shall never be able to tell how sadly that thought chafed my young spirit. Fortunately, or unfortunately, about this time in my life, I had made enough money to buy what was then a very popular school book, viz: the *Columbian Orator*. I bought this addition to my library, of Mr. Knight, on Thames Street, Fell's Point, Baltimore, and paid him fifty cents for it. I was first led to buy this book, by hearing some little boys say they were going to learn some little pieces out of it for the Exhibition. This volume was, indeed, a rich treasure, and every opportunity afforded me, for a time, was spent in diligently perusing it. Among much other interesting matter, that which I had perused and reperused with unflagging satisfaction, was a short dialogue between a master and his slave. The slave is represented as having been recaptured, in a second attempt to run away; and the master opens the dialogue with an upbraiding speech, charging the slave with ingratitude, and demanding to know what he has to say in his own defense. Thus upbraided, and thus called upon to reply, the slave rejoins, that he knows how little anything that he can say will avail, seeing that he is completely in the hands of his owner; and with noble resolution, calmly says, "I submit to my fate." Touched by the slave's answer, the master insists upon his further speaking, and recapitulates the many acts of kindness which he has performed toward the slave, and tells him he is permitted to speak for himself. Thus invited to the debate, the quondam slave made a spirited defense of himself, and thereafter the whole argument, for and against slavery, was brought out. The master was vanquished at every turn in the argument; and seeing himself to be thus vanquished, he generously and meekly emancipates the slave, with his best wishes for his prosperity. It is scarcely necessary to say, that a dialogue, with such an origin, and such an ending—read when the fact of my being a slave was a constant burden of grief—powerfully affected me; and I could not help feeling that the day might come, when the well-directed answers made by the slave to the master, in this instance, would find their counterpart in myself.

This, however, was not all the fanaticism which I found in this *Columbian Orator*. I met there one of Sheridan's mighty speeches, on the subject of Catholic Emancipation, Lord Chatham's speech on the American war, and speeches by the great William Pitt and by Fox. These were all choice documents to me, and I read them, over and over again, with an interest that was ever increasing, because it was ever gaining in intelligence; for the more I read them, the better I understood them.

The reading of these speeches added much to my limited stock of language, and enabled me to give tongue to many interesting thoughts, which had frequently flashed through my soul, and died away for want of utterance. The mighty power and heart-searching directness of truth, penetrating even the heart of a slaveholder, compelling him to yield up his earthly interests to the claims of eternal justice, were finely illustrated in the dialogue, just referred to; and from the speeches of Sheridan, I got a bold and powerful denunciation of oppression, and a most brilliant vindication of the rights of man. Here was, indeed, a noble acquisition. If I ever wavered under the consideration, that the Almighty, in some way, ordained slavery, and willed my enslavement for his own glory, I wavered no longer. I had now penetrated the secret of all slavery and oppression, and had ascertained their true foundation to be in the pride, the power and the avarice of man. The dialogue and the speeches were all redolent of the principles of liberty, and poured floods of light on the nature and character of slavery. With a book of this kind in my hand, my own human nature, and the facts of my experience, to help me, I was equal to a contest with the religious advocates of slavery, whether among the whites or among the colored people, for blindness, in this matter, is not confined to the former. I have met many religious colored people, at the south, who are under the delusion that God requires them to submit to slavery, and to wear their chains with meekness and humility. I could entertain no such nonsense as this; and I almost lost my patience when I found any colored man weak enough to believe such stuff. Nevertheless, the increase of knowledge was attended with bitter, as well as sweet results. The more I read, the more I was led to abhor and detest slavery, and my enslavers. "Slaveholders," thought I, "are only a band of successful robbers, who left their homes and went into Africa for the purpose of stealing and reducing my people to slavery." I loathed them as the meanest and the most wicked of men. As I read, behold! The very discontent so graphically pre dicted by Master Hugh, had already come upon me. I was no longer the light-hearted, gleesome boy, full of mirth and play, as when I landed first at Baltimore. Knowledge had come; light had penetrated the moral dungeon where I dwelt; and, behold! There lay the bloody whip, for my back, and here was the iron chain; and my good, *kind master*, he was the author of my situation. The revelation haunted me, stung me, and made me gloomy and miserable. As I writhed under the sting and torment of this knowledge, I almost envied my fellow-slaves their stupid contentment. This knowledge opened my eyes to the horrible pit, and revealed the teeth of the frightful dragon that was ready to pounce upon me, but it opened no way for my escape. I have often wished myself a beast, or a bird—anything, rather than a slave. I was wretched and gloomy, beyond my ability to describe. I was too thoughtful to be happy. It was this everlasting thinking which distressed and tormented me; and yet there was no getting rid of the subject of my thoughts. All nature was redolent of it. Once awakened by the silver trump of knowledge, my spirit was roused to eternal wakefulness. Liberty! The inestimable birthright of every man, had, for me, converted every object into an asserter of this great right. It was heard in every sound, and beheld in every object. It was ever present, to torment me with a sense of my wretched condition. The more beautiful and charming were the smiles of nature, the more horrible and desolate was my condition. I saw nothing without seeing it, and I heard nothing without hearing it. I do not exaggerate, when I say, that it looked from every star, smiled in every calm, breathed in every wind, and moved in every storm.

I have no doubt that my state of mind had something to do with the change in the treatment adopted, by my once kind mistress toward me. I can easily believe, that my leaden, downcast, and discontented look, was very offensive to her. Poor lady! She did not know my trouble, and I dared not tell her. Could I have freely made her acquainted with the real state of my mind, and given her the reasons therefor, it might have been well for both of us. Her abuse of me fell upon me like the blows of the false prophet upon his ass; she did not know that an *angel* stood in the way; and—such is the relation of master and slave—I could not tell her. Nature had made us *friends*; slavery made us *enemies*. My interests were in a direction opposite to hers, and we both had our private thoughts and plans. She aimed to keep me ignorant; and I resolved to know, although knowledge only increased my discontent. My feelings were not the result of any marked cruelty in the treatment I received; they sprung from the consideration of my being a slave at all. It was *slavery*—not its mere *incidents*—that I hated. I had been cheated. I saw through the attempt to keep me in ignorance; I saw that slaveholders would have gladly made me believe that they were merely acting under the authority of God, in making a slave of me, and in making slaves of others; and I treated them as robbers and deceivers. The feeding and clothing me well, could not atone for taking my liberty from me. The smiles of my mistress could not remove the deep sorrow that dwelt in my young bosom. Indeed, these, in time, came only to deepen my sorrow. She had changed; and the reader will see that I had changed, too. We were both victims to the same overshadowing evil— *she*, as mistress, *I*, as slave. I will not censure her harshly; she cannot censure me, for she knows I speak but the truth, and have acted in my opposition to slavery, just as she herself would have acted, in a reverse of circumstances.

# CHAPTER XII

## RELIGIOUS NATURE AWAKENED

*Abolitionists Spoken Of—My Eagerness to Know What
This Word Meant—My Consultation of the Dictionary—
Incendiary Information—How and Where Derived—The
Enigma Solved—Nathaniel Turner's Insurrection—The
Cholera—Religion—First Awakened by a Methodist Minister
Named Hanson—My Dear and Good Old Colored Friend,
Lawson—His Character and Occupation—His Influence Over
Me—Our Mutual Attachment—The Comfort I Derived from
His Teaching—New Hopes and Aspirations—Heavenly Light
Amidst Earthly Darkness—The Two Irishmen on the Wharf—
Their Conversation—How I Learned to Write—What Were
My Aims.*

Whilst in the painful state of mind described in the foregoing chapter, almost regretting my very existence, because doomed to a life of bondage, so goaded and so wretched, at times, that I was even tempted to destroy my own life, I was keenly sensitive and eager to know any, and every thing that transpired, having any relation to the subject of slavery. I was all ears, all eyes, whenever the words *slave*, *slavery*, dropped from the lips of any white person, and the occasions were not unfrequent when these words became leading ones, in high, social debate, at our house. Every little while, I could hear Master Hugh, or some of his company, speaking with much warmth and excitement about "*abolitionists*." Of *who* or *what* these were, I was totally ignorant. I found, however, that whatever they might be, they were most cordially hated and soundly abused by slaveholders, of every grade. I very soon discovered, too, that slavery was, in some sort, under consideration, whenever the abolitionists were alluded to. This made the term a very interesting one to me. If a slave, for instance, had made good his escape from slavery, it was generally alleged, that he had been persuaded and assisted by the abolitionists. If, also, a slave killed his master—as was sometimes the case—or struck down his overseer, or set fire to his master's dwelling, or committed any violence or crime, out of the common way, it was certain to be said, that such a crime was the legitimate fruits of the abolition movement. Hearing such charges often repeated, I, naturally enough, received the impression that abolition—whatever else it might be—could not be unfriendly to the slave, nor very friendly to the slaveholder. I therefore set about finding out, if possible, *who* and *what* the abolitionists were, and why they were so obnoxious to the slaveholders. The dictionary afforded me very little help. It taught me that abolition was the "act of abolishing"; but it left me in ignorance at the very point where I most wanted information— and that was, as to the *thing* to be abolished. A city newspaper, the *Baltimore American*, gave me the incendiary information denied me by the dictionary. In its columns I found, that, on a certain day, a vast number of petitions and memorials had been presented to congress, praying for the abolition of slavery in the District of Columbia, and for the abolition of the slave trade between the states of the Union. This was enough. The vindictive bitterness, the marked caution, the studied reverse, and the cumbrous ambiguity, practiced by our white folks, when alluding to this subject, was now fully explained. Ever, after that, when I heard the words "abolition," or "abolition movement," mentioned, I felt the matter one of a personal concern; and I drew near to listen, when I could do so, without seeming too solicitous and prying. There was *hope* in those words. Ever and anon, too, I could see some terrible denunciation of slavery, in our papers—copied from abolition papers at the north—and the injustice of such denunciation commented on. These I read with avidity. I had a deep satisfaction in the thought, that the rascality of slaveholders was not concealed from the eyes of the world, and that I was not alone in abhorring the cruelty and brutality of slavery. A still deeper train of thought was stirred. I saw that there was *fear*, as well as *rage*, in the manner of speaking of the abolitionists. The latter, therefore, I was compelled to regard as having some power in the country; and I felt that they might, possibly, succeed in their designs. When I met with a slave to whom I deemed it safe to talk on the subject, I would impart to him so much of the mystery as I had been able to penetrate. Thus, the light of this grand movement broke in upon my mind, by degrees; and I must say, that, ignorant as I then was of the philosophy of that movement, I believed in it from the first—and I believed in it, partly, because I saw that it alarmed the consciences of slaveholders. The insurrection of Nathaniel Turner* had been quelled, but the alarm and terror had not subsided. The cholera was on its way, and the thought was present, that God was angry with the white people because of their slaveholding wickedness, and, therefore, his judgments were abroad in the land. It was impossible for me not to hope much from the abolition movement, when I saw it supported by the Almighty, and armed with *death*!

Previous to my contemplation of the anti-slavery movement, and its probable results, my mind had been seriously awakened to the subject of religion. I was not more than thirteen years old, when I felt the need of God, as a father and protector. My religious nature was awakened by the preaching of a white Methodist minister, named Hanson. He thought that all men, great and small, bond and free, were sinners in the sight of God; that they were, by nature, rebels against His government; and that they must repent of their sins, and be reconciled to God, through Christ. I cannot say that I had a very distinct notion of what was required of me; but one thing I knew very well—I was wretched, and had no means of making myself otherwise. Moreover, I knew that I could pray for light. I consulted a good colored man, named Charles Johnson; and, in tones of holy affection, he told me to pray, and what to pray for. I was, for weeks, a poor, broken-hearted mourner, traveling through the darkness and misery of doubts and fears. I finally found that change of heart which comes by "casting all one's care" upon God, and by having faith in Jesus Christ, as the Redeemer, Friend, and Savior of those who diligently seek Him.

After this, I saw the world in a new light. I seemed to live in a new world, surrounded by new objects, and to be animated by new hopes and desires. I loved all mankind—slaveholders not excepted; though I abhorred slavery more than ever. My great concern was, now, to have the world converted. The desire for knowledge increased, and especially did I want a thorough acquaintance with the contents of the Bible. I have gathered scattered pages from this holy book, from the filthy street gutters of Baltimore, and washed and dried them, that in the moments of my leisure, I might get a word or two of wisdom from them. While thus religiously seeking knowledge, I became acquainted with a good

---

* Nat Turner led a violent slave rebellion in Virginia in August 1831, killing more than 50 white people and freeing their slaves. Although he lived on the run for a couple of months, he was ultimately captured and executed in November 1831.

old colored man, named Lawson. A more devout man than he, I never saw. He drove a dray for Mr. James Ramsey, the owner of a rope-walk on Fell's Point, Baltimore. This man not only prayed three times a day, but he prayed as he walked through the streets, at his work—on his dray—everywhere. His life was a life of prayer, and his words (when he spoke to his friends), were about a better world. Uncle Lawson lived near Master Hugh's house; and, becoming deeply attached to the old man, I went often with him to prayer-meeting, and spent much of my leisure time with him on Sunday. The old man could read a little, and I was a great help to him, in making out the hard words, for I was a better reader than he. I could teach him "*the letter*," but he could teach me "*the spirit*"; and high, refreshing times we had together, in singing, praying and glorifying God. These meetings with Uncle Lawson went on for a long time, without the knowledge of Master Hugh or my mistress. Both knew, however, that I had become religious, and they seemed to respect my conscientious piety. My mistress was still a professor of religion, and belonged to class. Her leader was no less a person than the Rev. Beverly Waugh, the presiding elder, and now one of the bishops of the Methodist Episcopal church. Mr. Waugh was then stationed over Wilk Street church. I am careful to state these facts, that the reader may be able to form an idea of the precise influences which had to do with shaping and directing my mind.

In view of the cares and anxieties incident to the life she was then leading, and, especially, in view of the separation from religious associations to which she was subjected, my mistress had, as I have before stated, become lukewarm, and needed to be looked up by her leader. This brought Mr. Waugh to our house, and gave me an opportunity to hear him exhort and pray. But my chief instructor, in matters of religion, was Uncle Lawson. He was my spiritual father; and I loved him intensely, and was at his house every chance I got.

This pleasure was not long allowed me. Master Hugh became averse to my going to Father Lawson's, and threatened to whip me if I ever went there again. I now felt myself persecuted by a wicked man; and I *would* go to Father Lawson's, notwithstanding the threat. The good old man had told me, that the "Lord had a great work for me to do"; and I must prepare to do it; and that he had been shown that I must preach the gospel. His words made a deep impression on my mind, and I verily felt that some such work was before me, though I could not see how

I should ever engage in its performance. "The good Lord," he said, "would bring it to pass in his own good time," and that I must go on reading and studying the scriptures. The advice and the suggestions of Uncle Lawson, were not without their influence upon my character and destiny. He threw my thoughts into a channel from which they have never entirely diverged. He fanned my already intense love of knowledge into a flame, by assuring me that I was to be a useful man in the world. When I would say to him, "How can these things be and what can I do?" his simple reply was, "*Trust in the Lord.*" When I told him that "I was a slave, and a slave *for life*," he said, "The Lord can make you free, my dear. All things are possible* with him, only *have faith in God.*" "Ask, and it shall be given."† "If you want liberty," said the good old man, "ask the Lord for it, *in faith, and he will give it to you.*"

Thus assured, and cheered on, under the inspiration of hope, I worked and prayed with a light heart, believing that my life was under the guidance of a wisdom higher than my own. With all other blessings sought at the mercy seat, I always prayed that God would, of His great mercy, and in His own good time, deliver me from my bondage.

I went, one day, on the wharf of Mr. Waters; and seeing two Irishmen unloading a large scow of stone, or ballast, I went on board, unasked, and helped them. When we had finished the work, one of the men came to me, aside, and asked me a number of questions, and among them, if I were a slave. I told him "I was a slave, and a slave for life." The good Irishman gave his shoulders a shrug, and seemed deeply affected by the statement. He said, "it was a pity so fine a little fellow as myself should be a slave for life." They both had much to say about the matter, and expressed the deepest sympathy with me, and the most decided hatred of slavery. They went so far as to tell me that I ought to run away, and go to the north; that I should find friends there, and that I would be as free as anybody. I, however, pretended not to be interested in what they said, for I feared they might be treacherous. White men have been known to encourage slaves to escape, and then—to get the reward—they have kidnapped them, and returned them to their masters. And while I mainly inclined to the notion that these men were honest and meant me no ill, I feared it might be otherwise.

---

* From the Bible, Matthew 19:26 and Mark 9:23.
† From the Bible, Matthew 7:7.

I nevertheless remembered their words and their advice, and looked forward to an escape to the north, as a possible means of gaining the liberty for which my heart panted. It was not my enslavement, at the then present time, that most affected me; the being a slave *for life*, was the saddest thought. I was too young to think of running away immediately; besides, I wished to learn how to write, before going, as I might have occasion to write my own pass. I now not only had the hope of freedom, but a foreshadowing of the means by which I might, some day, gain that inestimable boon. Meanwhile, I resolved to add to my educational attainments the art of writing.

After this manner I began to learn to write: I was much in the ship-yard—Master Hugh's, and that of Durgan & Bailey—and I observed that the carpenters, after hewing and getting a piece of timber ready for use, wrote on it the initials of the name of that part of the ship for which it was intended. When, for instance, a piece of timber was ready for the starboard side, it was marked with a capital "S." A piece for the larboard side was marked "L"; larboard forward, "L. F."; larboard aft, was marked "L. A."; starboard aft, "S. A."; and starboard forward "S. F." I soon learned these letters, and for what they were placed on the timbers.

My work was now, to keep fire under the steam box, and to watch the ship-yard while the carpenters had gone to dinner. This interval gave me a fine opportunity for copying the letters named. I soon astonished myself with the ease with which I made the letters; and the thought was soon present, "if I can make four, I can make more." But having made these easily, when I met boys about Bethel church, or any of our play-grounds, I entered the lists with them in the art of writing, and would make the letters which I had been so fortunate as to learn, and ask them to "beat that if they could." With playmates for my teachers, fences and pavements for my copybooks, and chalk for my pen and ink, I learned the art of writing. I, however, afterward adopted various methods of improving my hand. The most successful, was copying the *italics* in *Webster's Spelling Book*, until I could make them all without looking on the book. By this time, my little "Master Tommy" had grown to be a big boy, and had written over a number of copybooks, and brought them home. They had been shown to the neighbors, had elicited due praise, and were now laid carefully away. Spending my time between the ship-yard and house, I was as often the lone keeper of the latter as of the former. When my mistress left me in charge of the house, I had a grand time; I got Master Tommy's copybooks and a pen and ink, and, in the ample spaces between the lines, I wrote other lines, as nearly like his as possible. The process was a tedious one, and I ran the risk of getting a flogging for marring the highly prized copybooks of the oldest son. In addition to those opportunities, sleeping, as I did, in the kitchen loft—a room seldom visited by any of the family—I got a flour barrel up there, and a chair; and upon the head of that barrel I have written (or endeavored to write) copying from the Bible and the Methodist hymn book, and other books which had accumulated on my hands, till late at night, and when all the family were in bed and asleep. I was supported in my endeavors by renewed advice, and by holy promises from the good Father Lawson, with whom I continued to meet, and pray, and read the scriptures. Although Master Hugh was aware of my going there, I must say, for his credit, that he never executed his threat to whip me, for having thus, innocently, employed my leisure time.

# CHAPTER XIII

## THE VICISSITUDES OF SLAVE LIFE

*Death of Old Master's Son Richard, Speedily Followed by That of Old Master—Valuation and Division of All the Property, Including the Slaves—My Presence Required at Hillsborough to be Appraised and Allotted to a New Owner—My Sad Prospects and Grief—Parting—The Utter Powerlessness of the Slaves to Decide Their Own Destiny—A General Dread of Master Andrew—His Wickedness and Cruelty—Miss Lucretia My New Owner—My Return to Baltimore—Joy Under the Roof of Master Hugh—Death of Mrs. Lucretia—My Poor Old Grandmother—Her Sad Fate—The Lone Cot in the Woods— Master Thomas Auld's Second Marriage—Again Removed from Master Hugh's—Reasons for Regretting the Change—A Plan of Escape Entertained.*

I must now ask the reader to go with me a little back in point of time, in my humble story, and to notice another circumstance that entered into my slavery experience, and which, doubtless, has had a share in deepening my horror of slavery, and increasing my hostility toward those men and measures that practically uphold the slave system.

It has already been observed, that though I was, after my removal from Col. Lloyd's plantation, in *form* the slave of Master Hugh, I was, in *fact*, and in *law*, the slave of my old master, Capt. Anthony. Very well.

In a very short time after I went to Baltimore, my old master's youngest son, Richard, died; and, in three years and six months after his death, my old master himself died, leaving only his son, Andrew, and his daughter, Lucretia, to share his estate. The old man died while on a visit to his daughter, in Hillsborough, where Capt. Auld and Mrs. Lucretia now lived. The former, having given up the command of Col. Lloyd's sloop, was now keeping a store in that town.

Cut off, thus unexpectedly, Capt. Anthony died intestate; and his property must now be equally divided between his two children, Andrew and Lucretia.

The valuation and the division of slaves, among contending heirs, is an important incident in slave life. The character and tendencies of the heirs, are generally well understood among the slaves who are to be divided, and all have their aversions and preferences. But, neither their aversions nor their preferences avail them anything.

On the death of old master, I was immediately sent for, to be valued and divided with the other property. Personally, my concern was, mainly, about my possible removal from the home of Master Hugh, which, after that of my grandmother, was the most endeared to me. But, the whole thing, as a feature of slavery, shocked me. It furnished me anew insight into the unnatural power to which I was subjected. My detestation of slavery, already great, rose with this new conception of its enormity.

That was a sad day for me, a sad day for little Tommy, and a sad day for my dear Baltimore mistress and teacher, when I left for the Eastern Shore, to be valued and divided. We, all three, wept bitterly that day; for we might be parting, and we feared we were parting, forever. No one could tell among which pile of chattels I should be flung. Thus early, I got a foretaste of that painful uncertainty which slavery brings to the ordinary lot of mortals. Sickness, adversity and death may interfere with the plans and purposes of all; but the slave has the added danger of changing homes, changing hands, and of having separations unknown to other men. Then, too, there was the intensified degradation of the spectacle. What an assemblage! Men and women, young and old, married and single; moral and intellectual beings, in open contempt of their humanity, level at a blow with horses, sheep, horned cattle and swine! Horses and men—cattle and women—pigs and children—all holding the same rank in the scale of social existence; and all subjected to the same narrow inspection, to ascertain their value in gold and silver—the only standard of worth applied by slaveholders to slaves! How vividly, at that moment, did the brutalizing power of slavery flash before me! Personality swallowed up in the sordid idea of property! Manhood lost in chattelhood!

After the valuation, then came the division. This was an hour of high excitement and distressing anxiety. Our destiny was now to be *fixed for life*, and we had no more voice in the decision of the question, than the oxen and cows that stood chewing at the haymow. One word from the appraisers, against all preferences or prayers, was enough to sunder all the ties of friendship and affection, and even to separate husbands and wives, parents and children. We were all appalled before that power, which, to human seeming, could bless or blast us in a moment. Added to the dread of separation, most painful to the majority of the slaves, we all had a decided horror of the thought of falling into the hands of Master Andrew. He was distinguished for cruelty and intemperance.

Slaves generally dread to fall into the hands of drunken owners. Master Andrew was almost a confirmed sot, and had already, by his reckless mismanagement and profligate dissipation, wasted a large portion of old master's property. To fall into his hands, was, therefore, considered merely as the first step toward being sold away to the far south. He would spend his fortune in a few years, and his farms and slaves would be sold, we thought, at public outcry; and we should be hurried away to the cotton fields, and rice swamps, of the sunny south. This was the cause of deep consternation.

The people of the north, and free people generally, I think, have less attachment to the places where they are born and brought up, than have the slaves. Their freedom to go and come, to be here and there, as they list, prevents any extravagant attachment to any one particular place, in their case. On the other hand, the slave is a fixture; he has no choice, no goal, no destination; but is pegged down to a single spot, and must take root here, or nowhere. The idea of removal elsewhere, comes, generally, in the shape of a threat, and in punishment of crime. It is, therefore, attended with fear and dread. A slave seldom thinks of bettering his condition by being sold, and hence he looks upon separation from his native place, with none of the enthusiasm which animates the bosoms of young freemen, when they contemplate a life in the far west, or in some distant country where they intend to rise to wealth and distinction. Nor can those from whom they separate, give them up with that cheerfulness with which friends and relations yield each other up, when they feel that it is for the good of the departing one that he is removed from his native place. Then, too, there is correspondence, and there is, at least, the hope of reunion, because reunion is *possible*. But, with the slave, all these mitigating circumstances are wanting. There is no improvement in his condition *probable*—no correspondence *possible*—no reunion attainable. His going out into the world, is like a living man going into the tomb, who, with open eyes, sees himself buried out of sight and hearing of wife, children and friends of kindred tie.

In contemplating the likelihoods and possibilities of our circumstances, I probably suffered more than most of my fellow-servants. I had known what it was to experience kind, and even tender treatment; they had known nothing of the sort. Life, to them, had been rough and thorny, as well as dark. They had—most of them—lived on my old master's farm in Tuckahoe, and had felt the reign of Mr. Plummer's rule. The overseer had written his character on the living parchment of most of their backs, and left them callous; my back (thanks to my early removal from the plantation to Baltimore) was yet tender. I had left a kind mistress at Baltimore, who was almost a mother to me. She was in tears when we parted, and the probabilities of ever seeing her again, trembling in the balance as they did, could not be viewed without alarm and agony. The thought of leaving that kind mistress forever, and, worse still, of being the slave of Andrew Anthony—a man who, but a few days before the division of the property, had, in my presence, seized my brother Perry by the throat, dashed him on the ground, and with the heel of his boot stamped him on the head, until the blood gushed from his nose and ears—was terrible! This fiendish proceeding had no better apology than the fact, that Perry had gone to play, when Master Andrew wanted him for some trifling service. This cruelty, too, was of a piece with his general character. After inflicting his heavy blows on my brother, on observing me looking at him with intense astonishment, he said, "*That* is the way I will serve you, one of these days"; meaning, no doubt, when I should come into his possession. This threat, the reader may well suppose, was not very tranquilizing to my feelings. I could see that he really thirsted to get hold of me. But I was there only for a few days. I had not received any orders, and had violated none, and there was, therefore, no excuse for flogging me.

At last, the anxiety and suspense were ended; and they ended, thanks to a kind Providence, in accordance with my wishes. I fell to the portion of Mrs. Lucretia—the dear lady who bound up my head, when the savage Aunt Katy was adding to my sufferings her bitterest maledictions.

Capt. Thomas Auld and Mrs. Lucretia at once decided on my return to Baltimore. They knew how sincerely and warmly Mrs. Hugh Auld was attached to me, and how delighted Mr. Hugh's son would be to have me back; and, withal, having no immediate use for one so young, they willingly let me off to Baltimore.

I need not stop here to narrate my joy on returning to Baltimore, nor that of little Tommy; nor the tearful joy of his mother; nor the evident satisfaction of Master Hugh. I was just one month absent from Baltimore, before the matter was decided; and the time really seemed full six months.

One trouble over, and on comes another. The slave's life is full of uncertainty. I had returned to Baltimore but a short time, when the tidings reached me, that my friend, Mrs. Lucretia, who was only second in my regard to Mrs. Hugh Auld, was dead, leaving her husband and only one child—a daughter, named Amanda.

Shortly after the death of Mrs. Lucretia, strange to say, Master Andrew died, leaving his wife and one child. Thus, the whole family of Anthonys was swept away; only two children remained. All this happened within five years of my leaving Col. Lloyd's.

No alteration took place in the condition of the slaves, in consequence of these deaths, yet I could not help feeling less secure, after the death of my friend, Mrs. Lucretia, than I had done during her life. While she lived, I felt that I had a strong friend to plead for me in any emergency. Ten years ago, while speaking of the state of things in our family, after the events just named, I used this language*:

> Now all the property of my old master, slaves included,
> was in the hands of strangers—strangers who had nothing
> to do in accumulating it. Not a slave was left free. All
> remained slaves, from youngest to oldest. If any one thing
> in my experience, more than another, served to deepen my
> conviction of the infernal character of slavery, and to fill me
> with unutterable loathing of slaveholders, it was their base
> ingratitude to my poor old grandmother. She had served my
> old master faithfully from youth to old age. She had been the
> source of all his wealth; she had peopled his plantation with
> slaves; she had become a great-grandmother in his service.
> She had rocked him in infancy, attended him in childhood,
> served him through life, and at his death wiped from his
> icy brow the cold death-sweat, and closed his eyes forever.
> She was nevertheless left a slave—a slave for life—a slave

---

* From *Narrative of the Life of Frederick Douglass.*

in the hands of strangers; and in their hands she saw her children, her grandchildren, and her great-grandchildren, divided, like so many sheep, without being gratified with the small privilege of a single word, as to their or her own destiny. And, to cap the climax of their base ingratitude and fiendish barbarity, my grandmother, who was now very old, having outlived my old master and all his children, having seen the beginning and end of all of them, and her present owners finding she was of but little value, her frame already racked with the pains of old age, and complete helplessness fast stealing over her once active limbs, they took her to the woods, built her a little hut, put up a little mud-chimney, and then made her welcome to the privilege of supporting herself there in perfect loneliness; thus virtually turning her out to die! If my poor old grandmother now lives, she lives to suffer in utter loneliness; she lives to remember and mourn over the loss of children, the loss of grandchildren, and the loss of great-grandchildren. They are, in the language of the slave's poet, Whittier—

> "Gone, gone, sold and gone,
> To the rice swamp dank and lone,
> Where the slave-whip ceaseless swings,
> Where the noisome insect stings,
> Where the fever-demon strews
> Poison with the falling dews,
> Where the sickly sunbeams glare
> Through the hot and misty air:—
> > Gone, gone, sold and gone
> > To the rice swamp dank and lone,
> > From Virginia hills and waters—
> > Woe is me, my stolen daughters!"*

The hearth is desolate. The children, the unconscious children, who once sang and danced in her presence, are gone. She gropes her way, in the darkness of age, for a drink of water. Instead of the voices of her children, she hears by day the moans of the dove, and by night the screams of the hideous owl. All is gloom. The grave is at the door. And now, when weighed down by the pains and aches of old age,

---

* From "The Farewell of a Virginia Slave Mother to Her Daughters Sold into Southern Bondage" by John Greenleaf Whittier.

when the head inclines to the feet, when the beginning and ending of human existence meet, and helpless infancy and painful old age combine together—at this time, this most needful time, the time for the exercise of that tenderness and affection which children only can exercise toward a declining parent—my poor old grandmother, the devoted mother of twelve children, is left all alone, in yonder little hut, before a few dim embers.

Two years after the death of Mrs. Lucretia, Master Thomas married his second wife. Her name was Rowena Hamilton, the eldest daughter of Mr. William Hamilton, a rich slaveholder on the Eastern Shore of Maryland, who lived about five miles from St. Michael's, the then place of my master's residence.

Not long after his marriage, Master Thomas had a misunderstanding with Master Hugh, and, as a means of punishing his brother, he ordered him to send me home.

As the ground of misunderstanding will serve to illustrate the character of southern chivalry, and humanity, I will relate it.

Among the children of my Aunt Milly, was a daughter, named Henny. When quite a child, Henny had fallen into the fire, and burnt her hands so bad that they were of very little use to her. Her fingers were drawn almost into the palms of her hands. She could make out to do something, but she was considered hardly worth the having—of little more value than a horse with a broken leg. This unprofitable piece of human property, ill shapen, and disfigured, Capt. Auld sent off to Baltimore, making his brother Hugh welcome to her services.

After giving poor Henny a fair trial, Master Hugh and his wife came to the conclusion, that they had no use for the crippled servant, and they sent her back to Master Thomas. Thus, the latter took as an act of ingratitude, on the part of his brother; and, as a mark of his displeasure, he required him to send me immediately to St. Michael's, saying, if he cannot keep "*Hen*," he shall not have "*Fred.*"

Here was another shock to my nerves, another breaking up of my plans, and another severance of my religious and social alliances. I was now a big boy. I had become quite useful to several young colored men, who had made me their teacher. I had taught some of them to read, and was accustomed to spend many of my leisure hours with them. Our attachment was strong, and I greatly dreaded the separation. But regrets, especially in a slave, are unavailing. I was only a slave; my wishes were nothing, and my happiness was the sport of my masters.

My regrets at now leaving Baltimore, were not for the same reasons as when I before left that city, to be valued and handed over to my proper owner. My home was not now the pleasant place it had formerly been. A change had taken place, both in Master Hugh, and in his once pious and affectionate wife. The influence of brandy and bad company on him, and the influence of slavery and social isolation upon her, had wrought disastrously upon the characters of both. Thomas was no longer "little Tommy," but was a big boy, and had learned to assume the airs of his class toward me. My condition, therefore, in the house of Master Hugh, was not, by any means, so comfortable as in former years. My attachments were now outside of our family. They were felt to those to whom I *imparted* instruction, and to those little white boys from whom I *received* instruction. There, too, was my dear old father, the pious Lawson, who was, in Christian graces, the very counterpart of "Uncle" Tom. The resemblance is so perfect, that he might have been the original of Mrs. Stowe's* Christian hero. The thought of leaving these dear friends, greatly troubled me, for I was going without the hope of ever returning to Baltimore again; the feud between Master Hugh and his brother being bitter and irreconcilable, or, at least, supposed to be so.

In addition to thoughts of friends from whom I was parting, as I supposed, *forever*, I had the grief of neglected chances of escape to brood over. I had put off running away, until now I was to be placed where the opportunities for escaping were much fewer than in a large city like Baltimore.

On my way from Baltimore to St. Michael's, down the Chesapeake Bay, our sloop—the *Amanda*—was passed by the steamers plying between that city and Philadelphia, and I watched the course of those steamers, and, while going to St. Michael's, I formed a plan to escape from slavery; of which plan, and matters connected therewith the kind reader shall learn more hereafter.

---

* Harriet Beecher Stowe published the first installment of what became *Uncle Tom's Cabin* in 1851. The book was the best-selling novel of the 19th century and fueled the abolitionist cause by changing the way most Americans viewed slavery.

# CHAPTER XIV

## EXPERIENCE IN ST. MICHAEL'S

*The Village—Its Inhabitants—Their Occupation and Low
Propensities —Captain Thomas Auld—His Character—His
Second Wife, Rowena—Well Matched—Sufferings from
Hunger—Obliged to Take Food—Mode of Argument in
Vindication Thereof—No Moral Code of Free Society Can
Apply to Slave Society—Southern Camp-Meeting—What
Master Thomas Did There—Hopes—Suspicions About
His Conversion—The Result—Faith and Works Entirely
at Variance—His Rise and Progress in the Church—Poor
Cousin "Henny"—His Treatment of Her—The Methodist
Preachers—Their Utter Disregard of Us—One Excellent
Exception—Rev. George Cookman—Sabbath School—How
Broken Up and by Whom—A Funeral Pall Cast Over All My
Prospects—Covey the Negro-Breaker.*

St. Michael's, the village in which was now my new home, compared favorably with villages in slave states, generally. There were a few comfortable dwellings in it, but the place, as a whole, wore a dull, slovenly, enterprise-forsaken aspect. The mass of the buildings were wood; they had never enjoyed the artificial adornment of paint, and time and storms had worn off the bright color of the wood, leaving them almost as black as buildings charred by a conflagration.

St. Michael's had, in former years, (previous to 1833, for that was the year I went to reside there), enjoyed some reputation as a ship-building community, but that business had almost entirely given place to oyster fishing, for the Baltimore and Philadelphia markets—a course of life highly unfavorable to morals, industry, and manners. Miles River was broad, and its oyster fishing grounds were extensive; and the fishermen were out, often, all day, and a part of the night, during autumn, winter and spring. This exposure was an excuse for carrying with them, in considerable quantities, spirituous liquors, the then supposed best antidote for cold. Each canoe was supplied with its jug of rum; and tippling, among this class of the citizens of St. Michael's, became general. This drinking habit, in an ignorant population, fostered coarseness, vulgarity and an indolent disregard for the social improvement of the place, so that it was admitted, by the few sober, thinking people who remained there, that St. Michael's had become a very *unsaintly*, as well as unsightly place, before I went there to reside.

I left Baltimore for St. Michael's in the month of March, 1833. I know the year, because it was the one succeeding the first cholera in Baltimore, and was the year, also, of that strange phenomenon, when the heavens seemed about to part with its starry train. I witnessed this gorgeous spectacle, and was awe-struck. The air seemed filled with bright, descending messengers from the sky. It was about daybreak when I saw this sublime scene. I was not without the suggestion, at the moment, that it might be the harbinger of the coming of the Son of Man; and, in my then state of mind, I was prepared to hail Him as my friend and deliverer. I had read, that the "stars shall fall from heaven";* and they were now falling. I was suffering much in my mind. It did seem that every time the young tendrils of my affection became attached, they were rudely broken by some unnatural outside power; and I was beginning to look away to heaven for the rest denied me on earth.

But, to my story. It was now more than seven years since I had lived with Master Thomas Auld, in the family of my old master, on Col. Lloyd's plantation. We were almost entire strangers to each other; for, when I knew him at the house of my old master, it was not as a master, but simply as "Captain Auld," who had married old master's daughter. All my lessons concerning his temper and disposition, and the best methods of pleasing him, were yet to be learnt. Slaveholders, however, are not very ceremonious in approaching a slave; and my ignorance of the new material in shape of a master was but transient. Nor was my mistress long in making known her animus. She was not a "Miss Lucretia," traces of whom I yet remembered, and the more especially, as I saw them shining in the face of little Amanda, her daughter, now living under a step-mother's government. I had not forgotten the soft hand, guided by a tender heart, that bound up with healing balsam the gash made in my head by Ike, the son of Abel. Thomas and Rowena,

---

* From the Bible, Matthew 24:29.

I found to be a well-matched pair. *He* was stingy, and *she* was cruel; and—what was quite natural in such cases—she possessed the ability to make him as cruel as herself, while she could easily descend to the level of his meanness. In the house of Master Thomas, I was made—for the first time in seven years—to feel the pinchings of hunger, and this was not very easy to bear.

For, in all the changes of Master Hugh's family, there was no change in the bountifulness with which they supplied me with food. Not to give a slave enough to eat, is meanness intensified, and it is so recognized among slaveholders generally, in Maryland. The rule is, no matter how coarse the food, only let there be enough of it. This is the theory, and—in the part of Maryland I came from—the general practice accords with this theory. Lloyd's plantation was an exception, as was, also, the house of Master Thomas Auld.

All know the lightness of Indian cornmeal, as an article of food, and can easily judge from the following facts whether the statements I have made of the stinginess of Master Thomas, are borne out. There were four slaves of us in the kitchen, and four whites in the great house—Thomas Auld, Mrs. Auld, Hadaway Auld (brother of Thomas Auld) and little Amanda. The names of the slaves in the kitchen, were Eliza, my sister; Priscilla, my aunt; Henny, my cousin; and myself. There were eight persons in the family. There was, each week, one half bushel of cornmeal brought from the mill; and in the kitchen, cornmeal was almost our exclusive food, for very little else was allowed us. Out of this bushel of cornmeal, the family in the great house had a small loaf every morning; thus leaving us, in the kitchen, with not quite a half a peck per week, apiece. This allowance was less than half the allowance of food on Lloyd's plantation. It was not enough to subsist upon; and we were, therefore, reduced to the wretched necessity of living at the expense of our neighbors. We were compelled either to beg, or to steal, and we did both. I frankly confess, that while I hated everything like stealing, *as such*, I nevertheless did not hesitate to take food, when I was hungry, wherever I could find it. Nor was this practice the mere result of an unreasoning instinct; it was, in my case, the result of a clear apprehension of the claims of morality. I weighed and considered the matter closely, before I ventured to satisfy my hunger by such means. Considering that my labor and person were the property of Master Thomas, and that I was by him deprived of the necessaries of life—

necessaries obtained by my own labor—it was easy to deduce the right to supply myself with what was my own. It was simply appropriating what was my own to the use of my master, since the health and strength derived from such food were exerted in *his* service. To be sure, this was stealing, according to the law and gospel I heard from St. Michael's pulpit; but I had already begun to attach less importance to what dropped from that quarter, on that point, while, as yet, I retained my reverence for religion. It was not always convenient to steal from master, and the same reason why I might, innocently, steal from him, did not seem to justify me in stealing from others. In the case of my master, it was only a question of *removal*—the taking his meat out of one tub, and putting it into another; the ownership of the meat was not affected by the transaction. At first, he owned it in the *tub*, and last, he owned it in *me*. His meat house was not always open. There was a strict watch kept on that point, and the key was on a large bunch in Rowena's pocket. A great many times have we, poor creatures, been severely pinched with hunger, when meat and bread have been moulding under the lock, while the key was in the pocket of our mistress. This had been so when she knew we were nearly half starved; and yet, that mistress, with saintly air, would kneel with her husband, and pray each morning that a merciful God would bless them in basket and in store, and save them, at last, in his kingdom. But I proceed with the argument.

It was necessary that the right to steal from *others* should be established; and this could only rest upon a wider range of generalization than that which supposed the right to steal from my master.

It was sometime before I arrived at this clear right. The reader will get some idea of my train of reasoning, by a brief statement of the case. "I am," thought I, "not only the slave of Thomas, but I am the slave of society at large. Society at large has bound itself, in form and in fact, to assist Master Thomas in robbing me of my rightful liberty, and of the just reward of my labor; therefore, whatever rights I have against Master Thomas, I have, equally, against those confederated with him in robbing me of liberty. As society has marked me out as privileged plunder, on the principle of self-preservation I am justified in plundering in turn. Since each slave belongs to all; all must, therefore, belong to each."

I shall here make a profession of faith which may shock some, offend others, and be dissented from by all. It is this: Within the bounds of his just earnings, I hold that the slave is fully justified in helping himself to *the gold and silver, and the best apparel of his master, or that of any other slaveholder; and that such taking is not stealing in any just sense of that word.*

The morality of *free* society can have no application to *slave* society. Slaveholders have made it almost impossible for the slave to commit any crime, known either to the laws of God or to the laws of man. If he steals, he takes his own; if he kills his master, he imitates only the heroes of the revolution. Slaveholders I hold to be individually and collectively responsible for all the evils which grow out of the horrid relation, and I believe they will be so held at the judgment, in the sight of a just God. Make a man a slave, and you rob him of moral responsibility. Freedom of choice is the essence of all accountability. But my kind readers are, probably, less concerned about my opinions, than about that which more nearly touches my personal experience; albeit, my opinions have, in some sort, been formed by that experience.

Bad as slaveholders are, I have seldom met with one so entirely destitute of every element of character capable of inspiring respect, as was my present master, Capt. Thomas Auld.

When I lived with him, I thought him incapable of a noble action. The leading trait in his character was intense selfishness. I think he was fully aware of this fact himself, and often tried to conceal it. Capt. Auld was not a *born* slaveholder—not a birthright member of the slaveholding oligarchy. He was only a slaveholder by *marriage-right*; and, of all slaveholders, these latter are, *by far*, the most exacting. There was in him all the love of domination, the pride of mastery, and the swagger of authority, but his rule lacked the vital element of consistency. He could be cruel; but his methods of showing it were cowardly, and evinced his meanness rather than his spirit. His commands were strong, his enforcement weak.

Slaves are not insensible to the whole-souled characteristics of a generous, dashing slaveholder, who is fearless of consequences; and they prefer a master of this bold and daring kind—even with the risk of being shot down for impudence—to the fretful, little soul, who never uses the lash but at the suggestion of a love of gain.

Slaves, too, readily distinguish between the birthright bearing of the original slaveholder and the assumed attitudes of the accidental slaveholder; and while they cannot respect either, they certainly despise the latter more than the former.

The luxury of having slaves wait upon him was something new to Master Thomas; and for it he was wholly unprepared. He was a slaveholder, without the ability to hold or manage his slaves. We seldom called him "master," but generally addressed him by his "bay craft" title—"*Capt. Auld.*" It is easy to see that such conduct might do much to make him appear awkward, and, consequently, fretful. His wife was especially solicitous to have us call her husband "*master.*" "Is your *master* at the store?"—"Where is your *master?*"—"Go and tell your *master*"—"I will make your *master* acquainted with your conduct"— she would say; but we were inapt scholars. Especially were I and my sister Eliza inapt in this particular. Aunt Priscilla was less stubborn and defiant in her spirit than Eliza and myself; and, I think, her road was less rough than ours.

In the month of August, 1833, when I had almost become desperate under the treatment of Master Thomas, and when I entertained more strongly than ever the oft-repeated determination to run away, a circumstance occurred which seemed to promise brighter and better days for us all. At a Methodist camp-meeting, held in the Bay Side (a famous place for camp-meetings) about eight miles from St. Michael's, Master Thomas came out with a profession of religion. He had long been an object of interest to the church, and to the ministers, as I had seen by the repeated visits and lengthy exhortations of the latter. He was a fish quite worth catching, for he had money and standing. In the community of St. Michael's he was equal to the best citizen. He was strictly temperate; *perhaps*, from principle, but most likely, from interest. There was very little to do for him, to give him the appearance of piety, and to make him a pillar in the church. Well, the camp-meeting continued a week; people gathered from all parts of the county, and two steamboat loads came from Baltimore. The ground was happily chosen; seats were arranged; a stand erected; a rude altar fenced in, fronting the preachers' stand, with straw in it for the accommodation of mourners. This latter would hold at least one hundred persons. In front, and on the sides of the preachers' stand, and outside the long rows of seats, rose the first class of stately tents, each vieing with the other in strength, neatness, and capacity for accommodating its inmates. Behind this first circle of tents was another, less imposing, which reached round the camp-ground to the speakers' stand. Outside this second class of tents were covered wagons, ox carts, and vehicles of every shape and size. These served as tents to their owners. Outside of these, huge fires were burning, in all directions, where roasting, and boiling, and frying, were going on, for the benefit of those who were attending to their own spiritual welfare within the circle. *Behind* the preachers' stand, a narrow space was marked out for the use of the colored people. There were no seats provided for this class of persons; the preachers addressed them, "*over the left*," if they addressed them at all. After the preaching was over, at every service, an invitation was given to mourners to come into the pen; and, in some cases, ministers went out to persuade men and women to come in. By one of these ministers, Master Thomas Auld was persuaded to go inside the pen. I was deeply interested in that matter, and followed; and, though colored people were not allowed either in the pen or in front of the preachers' stand, I ventured to take my stand at a sort of half-way place between the blacks and whites, where I could distinctly see the movements of mourners, and especially the progress of Master Thomas.

"If he has got religion," thought I, "he will emancipate his slaves; and if he should not do so much as this, he will, at any rate, behave toward us more kindly, and feed us more generously than he has heretofore done." Appealing to my own religious experience, and judging my master by what was true in my own case, I could not regard him as soundly converted, unless some such good results followed his profession of religion.

But in my expectations I was doubly disappointed; Master Thomas was *Master Thomas* still. The fruits of his righteousness were to show themselves in no such way as I had anticipated. His conversion was not to change his relation toward men—at any rate not toward *black* men—but toward God. My faith, I confess, was not great. There was something in his appearance that, in my mind, cast a doubt over his conversion. Standing where I did, I could see his every movement. I watched narrowly while he remained in the little pen; and although I saw that his face was extremely red, and his hair disheveled, and though I heard him groan, and saw a stray tear halting on his cheek, as if inquiring "which way shall I go?"—I could not wholly confide in the genuineness of his conversion. The hesitating behavior of that tear-drop, and its loneliness, distressed me, and cast a doubt upon the whole transaction, of which it was a part. But people said, "*Capt. Auld had come through,*" and it was for me to hope for the best. I was bound to do this, in charity, for I, too, was religious, and had been in the church full three years, although now I was not more than sixteen years old. Slaveholders may, sometimes, have confidence in the piety of some of their slaves; but the slaves seldom have confidence in the piety of their masters. *"He can't go to heaven with our blood in his skirts,"* is a settled point in the creed of every slave; rising superior to all teaching to the contrary, and standing forever as a fixed fact. The highest evidence the slaveholder can give the slave of his acceptance with God, is the emancipation of his slaves. This is proof that he is willing to give up all to God, and for the sake of God. Not to do this, was, in my estimation, and in the opinion of all the slaves, an evidence of half-heartedness, and wholly inconsistent with the idea of genuine conversion. I had read, also, somewhere in the Methodist Discipline, the following question and answer:

"*Question.* What shall be done for the extirpation of slavery?

"*Answer.* We declare that we are as much as ever convinced of the great evil of slavery; therefore, no slaveholder shall be eligible to any official station in our church."

These words sounded in my ears for a long time, and encouraged me to hope. But, as I have before said, I was doomed to disappointment. Master Thomas seemed to be aware of my hopes and expectations concerning him. I have thought, before now, that he looked at me in answer to my glances, as much as to say, "I will teach you, young man, that, though I have parted with my sins, I have not parted with my sense. I shall hold my slaves, and go to heaven too."

Possibly, to convince us that we must not presume *too much* upon his recent conversion, he became rather more rigid and stringent in his exactions. There always was a scarcity of good nature about the man; but now his whole countenance was *soured* over with the seemings of piety. His religion, therefore, neither made him emancipate his slaves, nor caused him to treat them with greater humanity. If religion had any effect on his character at all, it made him more cruel and hateful in all his ways. The natural wickedness of his heart had not been removed, but only reinforced, by the profession of religion. Do I judge him harshly? God forbid. Facts are facts. Capt. Auld made the greatest profession of piety. His house was, literally, a house of prayer. In the morning, and in the evening, loud prayers and hymns were heard there, in which both himself and his wife joined; *yet, no more meal* was brought from the mill, *no more attention* was paid to the moral welfare of the kitchen; and nothing was done to make us feel that the heart of Master Thomas was one whit better than it was before he went into the little pen, opposite to the preachers' stand, on the camp-ground.

Our hopes (founded on the discipline) soon vanished; for the authorities let him into the church *at once*, and before he was out of his term of *probation*, I heard of his leading class! He distinguished himself greatly among the brethren, and was soon an exhorter. His progress was almost as rapid as the growth of the fabled vine of Jack's bean. No man was more active than he, in revivals. He would go many miles to assist in carrying them on, and in getting outsiders interested in religion. His house being one of the holiest, if not the happiest in St. Michael's, became the "preachers' home." These preachers evidently liked to share Master Thomas's hospitality; for while he *starved* us, he *stuffed* them. Three or four of these ambassadors of the gospel—according to slavery—have been there at a time; all living on the fat of the land, while we, in the kitchen, were nearly starving. Not often did we get a smile of recognition from these holy men. They seemed almost as unconcerned about our getting to heaven, as they were about our getting out of slavery. To this general charge there was one exception—the Rev. George Cookman. Unlike Rev. Messrs. Storks, Ewry, Hickey, Humphrey and Cooper (all whom were on the St. Michael's circuit) he kindly took an interest in our temporal and spiritual welfare. Our souls and our bodies were all alike sacred in his sight; and he really had a good deal of genuine anti-slavery feeling mingled with his colonization ideas. There was not a slave in our neighborhood that did not love, and almost venerate, Mr. Cookman. It was pretty generally believed that he had been chiefly instrumental in bringing one of the largest slaveholders—Mr. Samuel Harrison—in that neighborhood, to emancipate all his slaves, and, indeed, the general impression was, that Mr. Cookman had labored faithfully with slaveholders, whenever he met them, to induce them to emancipate their bondmen, and that he did this as a religious duty. When this good man was at our house, we were all sure to be called in to prayers in the morning; and he was not slow in making inquiries as to the state of our minds, nor in giving us a word of exhortation and of encouragement. Great was the sorrow of all the slaves, when this faithful preacher of the gospel was removed from the Talbot County circuit. He was an eloquent preacher, and possessed what few ministers, south of Mason Dixon's line, possess, or *dare* to show, viz: a warm and philanthropic heart. The Mr. Cookman, of whom I speak, was an Englishman by birth, and perished while on his way to England, on board the ill-fated *President*. Could the thousands of slaves in Maryland know the fate of the good man, to whose words of comfort they were so largely indebted, they would thank me for dropping a tear on this page, in memory of their favorite preacher, friend and benefactor.

But, let me return to Master Thomas, and to my experience, after his conversion. In Baltimore, I could, occasionally, get into a Sabbath school, among the free children, and receive lessons, with the rest; but, having already learned both to read and to write, I was more of a teacher than a pupil, even there. When, however, I went back to the Eastern Shore, and was at the house of Master Thomas, I was neither allowed to teach, nor to be taught. The whole community—with but a single exception, among the whites—frowned upon everything like imparting instruction either to slaves or to free colored persons. That single exception, a pious young man, named Wilson, asked me, one day, if I would like to assist him in teaching a little Sabbath school, at the house of a free colored man in St. Michael's, named James Mitchell. The idea was to me a delightful one, and I told him I would gladly devote as much of my Sabbath as I could command, to that most laudable work. Mr. Wilson soon mustered up a dozen old spelling books, and a few testaments; and we commenced operations, with some twenty scholars, in our Sunday school. Here, thought I, is something worth living for; here is an excellent chance for usefulness; and I shall soon have a company of young friends, lovers of knowledge, like some of my Baltimore friends, from whom I now felt parted forever.

Our first Sabbath passed delightfully, and I spent the week after very joyously. I could not go to Baltimore, but I could make a little Baltimore here. At our second meeting, I learned that there was some objection to the existence of the Sabbath school; and, sure enough, we had scarcely got at work—*good work*, simply teaching a few colored children how to read the gospel of the Son of God—when in rushed a mob, headed by Mr. Wright Fairbanks and Mr. Garrison West—two class-leaders — and Master Thomas; who, armed with sticks and other missiles, drove us off, and commanded us never to meet for such a purpose again. One of this pious crew told me, that as for my part, I wanted to be another Nat Turner; and if I did not look out, I should get as many balls into me, as Nat did into him. Thus ended the infant Sabbath school, in the town of St. Michael's. The reader will not be surprised when I say, that the breaking up of my Sabbath school, by these class-leaders, and professedly holy men, did not serve to strengthen my religious convictions. The cloud over my St. Michael's home grew heavier and blacker than ever.

It was not merely the agency of Master Thomas, in breaking up and destroying my Sabbath school, that shook my confidence in the power of southern religion to make men wiser or better; but I saw in him all the cruelty and meanness, *after* his conversion, which he had exhibited before he made a profession of religion. His cruelty and meanness were especially displayed in his treatment of my unfortunate cousin, Henny, whose lameness made her a burden to him. I have no extraordinary personal hard usage toward myself to complain of, against him, but I have seen him tie up the lame and maimed woman, and whip her in a manner most brutal, and shocking; and then, with blood-chilling blasphemy, he would quote the passage of scripture, "That servant which knew his lord's will, and prepared not himself, neither did according to his will, shall be beaten with many stripes."* Master would keep this lacerated woman tied up by her wrists, to a bolt in the joist, three, four and five hours at a time. He would tie her up early in the morning, whip her with a cowskin before breakfast; leave her tied up; go to his store, and, returning to his dinner, repeat the castigation; laying on the rugged lash, on flesh already made raw by repeated blows. He seemed desirous to get the poor girl out of existence, or, at any rate, off his hands. In proof of this, he afterwards gave her away to his sister Sarah (Mrs. Cline) but, as in the case of Master Hugh, Henny was soon returned on his hands. Finally, upon a pretense that he could do nothing with her (I use his own words) he "set her adrift, to take care of herself." Here was a recently converted man, holding, with tight grasp, the well-framed, and able bodied slaves left him by old master—the persons, who, in freedom, could have taken care of themselves; yet, turning loose the only cripple among them, virtually to starve and die.

No doubt, had Master Thomas been asked, by some pious northern brother, why he continued to sustain the relation of a slaveholder, to those whom he retained, his answer would have been precisely the same

---

* From the Bible, Luke 12:47.

as many other religious slaveholders have returned to that inquiry, viz: "I hold my slaves for their own good."

Bad as my condition was when I lived with Master Thomas, I was soon to experience a life far more goading and bitter. The many differences springing up between myself and Master Thomas, owing to the clear perception I had of his character, and the boldness with which I defended myself against his capricious complaints, led him to declare that I was unsuited to his wants; that my city life had affected me perniciously; that, in fact, it had almost ruined me for every good purpose, and had fitted me for everything that was bad. One of my greatest faults, or offenses, was that of letting his horse get away, and go down to the farm belonging to his father-in-law. The animal had a liking for that farm, with which I fully sympathized. Whenever I let it out, it would go dashing down the road to Mr. Hamilton's, as if going on a grand frolic. My horse gone, of course I must go after it. The explanation of our mutual attachment to the place is the same; the horse found there good pasturage, and I found there plenty of bread. Mr. Hamilton had his faults, but starving his slaves was not among them. He gave food, in abundance, and that, too, of an excellent quality. In Mr. Hamilton's cook—Aunt Mary—I found a most generous and considerate friend. She never allowed me to go there without giving me bread enough to make good the deficiencies of a day or two. Master Thomas at last resolved to endure my behavior no longer; he could neither keep me, nor his horse, we liked so well to be at his father-in-law's farm. I had now lived with him nearly nine months, and he had given me a number of severe whippings, without any visible improvement in my character, or my conduct; and now he was resolved to put me out—as he said—*"to be broken."*

There was, in the Bay Side, very near the camp-ground, where my master got his religious impressions, a man named Edward Covey, who enjoyed the execrated reputation, of being a first rate hand at breaking young Negroes. This Covey was a poor man, a farm renter; and this reputation (hateful as it was to the slaves and to all good men) was, at the same time, of immense advantage to him. It enabled him to get his farm tilled with very little expense, compared with what it would have cost him without this most extraordinary reputation. Some slaveholders thought it an advantage to let Mr. Covey have the government of their slaves a year or two, almost free of charge, for the sake of the excellent training such slaves got under his happy management! Like some horse breakers, noted for their skill, who ride the best horses in the country without expense, Mr. Covey could have under him, the most fiery bloods of the neighborhood, for the simple reward of returning them to their owners, well broken. Added to the natural fitness of Mr. Covey for the duties of his profession, he was said to "enjoy religion," and was as strict in the cultivation of piety, as he was in the cultivation of his farm. I was made aware of his character by some who had been under his hand; and while I could not look forward to going to him with any pleasure, I was glad to get away from St. Michael's. I was sure of getting enough to eat at Covey's, even if I suffered in other respects. *This*, to a hungry man, is not a prospect to be regarded with indifference.

# CHAPTER XV

## COVEY, THE NEGRO BREAKER

*Journey to My New Master's—Meditations by the Way—View of Covey's Residence—The Family—My Awkwardness as a Field Hand—A Cruel Beating—Why It Was Given—Description of Covey—First Adventure at Ox Driving—Hair Breadth Escapes—Ox and Man Alike Property—Covey's Manner of Proceeding to Whip—Hard Labor Better Than the Whip for Breaking Down the Spirit—Cunning and Trickery of Covey—Family Worship—Shocking Contempt for Chastity—I Am Broken Down—Great Mental Agitation in Contrasting the Freedom of the Ships with His Own Slavery—Anguish Beyond Description.*

The morning of the first of January, 1834, with its chilling wind and pinching frost, quite in harmony with the winter in my own mind, found me, with my little bundle of clothing on the end of a stick, swung across my shoulder, on the main road, bending my way toward Covey's, whither I had been imperiously ordered by Master Thomas. The latter had been as good as his word, and had committed me, without reserve, to the mastery of Mr. Edward Covey. Eight or ten years had now passed since I had been taken from my grandmother's cabin, in Tuckahoe; and these years, for the most part, I had spent in Baltimore, where—as the reader has already seen—I was treated with comparative tenderness. I was now about to sound profounder depths in slave life. The rigors of a field, less tolerable than the field of battle, awaited me. My new master was notorious for his fierce and savage disposition, and my only consolation in going to live with him was, the certainty of finding him precisely as represented by common fame. There was neither joy in my heart, nor elasticity in my step, as I started in search of the tyrant's home. Starvation made me glad to leave Thomas Auld's, and the cruel lash made me dread to go to Covey's. Escape was impossible; so, heavy and sad, I paced the seven miles, which separated Covey's house from

St. Michael's—thinking much by the solitary way—averse to my condition; but *thinking* was all I could do. Like a fish in a net, allowed to play for a time, I was now drawn rapidly to the shore, secured at all points. "I am," thought I, "but the sport of a power which makes no account, either of my welfare or of my happiness. By a law which I can clearly comprehend, but cannot evade nor resist, I am ruthlessly snatched from the hearth of a fond grandmother, and hurried away to the home of a mysterious 'old master;' again I am removed from there, to a master in Baltimore; thence am I snatched away to the Eastern Shore, to be valued with the beasts of the field, and, with them, divided and set apart for a possessor; then I am sent back to Baltimore; and by the time I have formed new attachments, and have begun to hope that no more rude shocks shall touch me, a difference arises between brothers, and I am again broken up, and sent to St. Michael's; and now, from the latter place, I am footing my way to the home of a new master, where, I am given to understand, that, like a wild young working animal, I am to be broken to the yoke of a bitter and life-long bondage."

With thoughts and reflections like these, I came in sight of a small wood-colored building, about a mile from the main road, which, from the description I had received, at starting, I easily recognized as my new home. The Chesapeake Bay—upon the jutting banks of which the little wood-colored house was standing—white with foam, raised by the heavy north-west wind; Poplar Island, covered with a thick, black pine forest, standing out amid this half ocean; and Kent Point, stretching its sandy, desert-like shores out into the foam-crested bay—were all in sight, and deepened the wild and desolate aspect of my new home.

The good clothes I had brought with me from Baltimore were now worn thin, and had not been replaced; for Master Thomas was as little careful to provide us against cold, as against hunger. Met here by a north wind, sweeping through an open space of forty miles, I was glad to make any port; and, therefore, I speedily pressed on to the little wood-colored house. The family consisted of Mr. and Mrs. Covey; Miss Kemp (a broken-backed woman), a sister of Mrs. Covey; William Hughes, cousin to Edward Covey; Caroline, the cook; Bill Smith, a hired man; and myself. Bill Smith, Bill Hughes, and myself, were the working force of the farm, which consisted of three or four hundred acres. I was now, for the first time in my life, to be a field hand; and in my new employment I found myself even more awkward than a green country boy may be supposed to be, upon his first entrance into the bewildering scenes of city life; and my awkwardness gave me much trouble. Strange and unnatural as it may seem, I had been at my new home but three days, before Mr. Covey (my brother in the Methodist church) gave me a bitter foretaste of what was in reserve for me. I presume he thought, that since he had but a single year in which to complete his work, the sooner he began, the better. Perhaps he thought that by coming to blows at once, we should mutually better understand our relations. But to whatever motive, direct or indirect, the cause may be referred, I had not been in his possession three whole days, before he subjected me to a most brutal chastisement. Under his heavy blows, blood flowed freely, and wales were left on my back as large as my little finger. The sores on my back, from this flogging, continued for weeks, for they were kept open by the rough and coarse cloth which I wore for shirting. The occasion and details of this first chapter of my experience as a field hand, must be told, that the reader may see how unreasonable, as well as how cruel, my new master, Covey, was. The whole thing I found to be characteristic of the man; and I was probably treated no worse by him than scores of lads who had previously been committed to him, for reasons similar to those which induced my master to place me with him. But, here are the facts connected with the affair, precisely as they occurred.

On one of the coldest days of the whole month of January, 1834, I was ordered, at day break, to get a load of wood, from a forest about two miles from the house. In order to perform this work, Mr. Covey gave me a pair of unbroken oxen, for, it seems, his breaking abilities had not been turned in this direction; and I may remark, in passing, that working animals in the south, are seldom so well trained as in the north. In due form, and with all proper ceremony, I was introduced to this huge yoke of unbroken oxen, and was carefully told which was "Buck," and which was "Darby"—which was the "in hand," and which was the "off hand" ox. The master of this important ceremony was no less a person than Mr. Covey, himself; and the introduction was the first of the kind I had ever had. My life, hitherto, had led me away from horned cattle, and I had no knowledge of the art of managing them. What was meant by the "in ox," as against the "off ox," when both were equally fastened to one cart, and under one yoke, I could not very easily divine; and the difference, implied by the names, and the peculiar duties of each, were alike Greek to me. Why was not the "off ox" called the "in ox?" Where and what is the reason for this distinction in names, when there is none in the things themselves? After initiating me into the "*woa*," "*back*" "*gee*," "*hither*"—the entire spoken language between oxen and driver—Mr. Covey took a rope, about ten feet long and one inch thick, and placed one end of it around the horns of the "in hand ox," and gave the other end to me, telling me that if the oxen started to run away, as the scamp knew they would, I must hold on to the rope and stop them. I need not tell any one who is acquainted with either the strength of the disposition of an untamed ox, that this order was about as unreasonable as a command to shoulder a mad bull! I had never driven oxen before, and I was as awkward, as a driver, as it is possible to conceive. It did not answer for me to plead ignorance, to Mr. Covey; there was something in his manner that quite forbade that. He was a man to whom a slave seldom felt any disposition to speak. Cold, distant, morose, with a face wearing all the marks of captious pride and malicious sternness, he repelled all advances. Covey was not a large man; he was only about five feet ten inches in height, I should think; short necked, round shoulders; of quick and wiry motion, of thin and wolfish visage; with a pair of small, greenish-gray eyes, set well back under a forehead without dignity, and constantly in motion, and floating his passions, rather than his thoughts, in sight, but denying them utterance in words. The creature presented an appearance altogether ferocious and sinister, disagreeable and forbidding, in the extreme. When he spoke, it was from the corner of his mouth, and in a sort of light growl, like a dog, when an attempt is made to take a bone from him. The fellow had already made me believe him even *worse* than he had been presented. With his directions, and without stopping to question, I started for the woods, quite anxious to perform my first exploit in driving, in a creditable manner. The distance from the house to the woods gate—a full mile, I should think—was passed over with very little difficulty; for although the animals ran, I was fleet enough, in the open field, to keep pace with them; especially as they pulled me along at the end of the rope; but, on reaching the woods, I was speedily thrown into a distressing plight. The animals took fright, and started off ferociously into the woods, carrying the cart, full tilt, against trees, over stumps, and dashing from side to side, in a manner altogether frightful. As I held the rope, I expected every moment to be crushed between the cart and the huge trees, among which they were so furiously dashing. After running thus for several minutes, my oxen were, finally, brought to a stand, by a tree, against which they dashed themselves with great violence, upsetting the cart, and entangling themselves among sundry young saplings. By the shock, the body of the cart was flung in one direction, and the wheels and tongue in another, and all in the greatest confusion. There I was, all alone, in a thick wood, to which I was a stranger; my cart upset and shattered; my oxen entangled, wild, and enraged; and I, poor soul! but a green hand, to set all this disorder right. I knew no more of oxen than the ox driver is supposed to know of wisdom. After standing a few moments surveying the damage and disorder, and not without a presentiment that this trouble would draw after it others, even more distressing, I took one end of the cart body, and, by an extra outlay of strength, I lifted it toward the axle-tree, from which it had been violently flung; and after much pulling and straining, I succeeded in getting the body of the cart in its place. This was an important step out of the difficulty, and its performance increased my courage for the work which remained to be done. The cart was provided with an ax, a tool with which I had become pretty well acquainted in the ship-yard at Baltimore. With this, I cut down the saplings by which my oxen were entangled, and again pursued my journey, with my heart in my mouth, lest the oxen should again take it into their senseless heads to cut up a caper. My fears were groundless. Their spree was over for the present, and the rascals now moved off as soberly as though their behavior had been natural and exemplary. On reaching the part of the forest where I had been, the day before, chopping wood, I filled the cart with a heavy load, as a security against another running away. But, the neck of an ox is equal in strength to iron. It defies all ordinary burdens, when excited. Tame and docile to a proverb, when *well* trained, the ox is the most sullen and intractable of animals when but half broken to the yoke.

I now saw, in my situation, several points of similarity with that of the oxen. They were property, so was I; they were to be broken, so was I. Covey was to break me, I was to break them; break and be broken— such is life.

Half the day already gone, and my face not yet homeward! It required only two day's experience and observation to teach me, that such apparent waste of time would not be lightly overlooked by Covey.

I therefore hurried toward home; but, on reaching the lane gate, I met with the crowning disaster for the day. This gate was a fair specimen of southern handicraft. There were two huge posts, eighteen inches in diameter, rough hewed and square, and the heavy gate was so hung on one of these, that it opened only about half the proper distance. On arriving here, it was necessary for me to let go the end of the rope on the horns of the "in hand ox"; and now as soon as the gate was open, and I let go of it to get the rope, again, off went my oxen—making nothing of their load—full tilt; and in doing so they caught the huge gate between the wheel and the cart body, literally crushing it to splinters, and coming only within a few inches of subjecting me to a similar crushing, for I was just in advance of the wheel when it struck the left gate post. With these two hair-breadth escapes, I thought I could successfully explain to Mr. Covey the delay, and avert apprehended punishment. I was not without a faint hope of being commended for the stern resolution which I had displayed in accomplishing the difficult task—a task which, I afterwards learned, even Covey himself would not have undertaken, without first driving the oxen for some time in the open field, preparatory to their going into the woods. But, in this I was disappointed. On coming to him, his countenance assumed an aspect of rigid displeasure, and, as I gave him a history of the casualties of my trip, his wolfish face, with his greenish eyes, became intensely ferocious. "Go back to the woods again," he said, muttering something else about wasting time. I hastily obeyed; but I had not gone far on my way, when I saw him coming after me. My oxen now behaved themselves with singular propriety, opposing their present conduct to my representation of their former antics. I almost wished, now that Covey was coming, they would do something in keeping with the character I had given them; but no, they had already had their spree, and they could afford now to be extra good, readily obeying my orders, and seeming to understand them quite as well as I did myself. On reaching the woods, my tormentor—who seemed all the way to be remarking upon the good behavior of his oxen—came up to me, and ordered me to stop the cart, accompanying the same with the threat that he would now teach me how to break gates, and idle away my time, when he sent me to the woods. Suiting the action to the word, Covey paced off, in his own wiry fashion, to a large, black gum tree, the young shoots of which are generally used for *ox goads*, they being exceedingly tough. Three of these *goads*, from four to six feet long, he cut off, and trimmed up, with his large jack-knife. This done, he ordered me to take off my clothes. To this unreasonable order I made no reply, but sternly refused to take off my clothing. "If you will beat me," thought I, "you shall do so over my clothes." After many threats, which made no impression on me, he rushed at me with something of the savage fierceness of a wolf, tore off the few and thinly worn clothes I had on, and proceeded to wear out, on my back, the heavy goads which he had cut from the gum tree. This flogging was the first of a series of floggings; and though very severe, it was less so than many which came after it, and these, for offenses far lighter than the gate breaking.

I remained with Mr. Covey one year (I cannot say I *lived* with him) and during the first six months that I was there, I was whipped, either with sticks or cowskins, every week. Aching bones and a sore back were my constant companions. Frequent as the lash was used, Mr. Covey thought less of it, as a means of breaking down my spirit, than that of hard and long continued labor. He worked me steadily, up to the point of my powers of endurance. From the dawn of day in the morning, till the darkness was complete in the evening, I was kept at hard work, in the field or the woods. At certain seasons of the year, we were all kept in the field till eleven and twelve o'clock at night. At these times, Covey would attend us in the field, and urge us on with words or blows, as it seemed best to him. He had, in his life, been an overseer, and he well understood the business of slave-driving. There was no deceiving him. He knew just what a man or boy could do, and he held both to strict account. When he pleased, he would work himself, like a very Turk, making everything fly before him. It was, however, scarcely necessary for Mr. Covey to be really present in the field, to have his work go on industriously. He had the faculty of making us feel that he was always present. By a series of adroitly managed surprises, which he practiced, I was prepared to expect him at any moment. His plan was, never to approach the spot where his hands were at work, in an open, manly and direct manner. No thief was ever more artful in his devices than this man Covey. He would creep and crawl, in ditches and gullies; hide behind stumps and bushes, and practice so much of the cunning of the serpent, that Bill Smith and I—between ourselves— never called him by any other name than "*the snake*." We fancied that in his eyes and his gait we could see a snakish resemblance. One half of his proficiency in the art of Negro breaking, consisted, I should think, in this species of cunning. We were never secure. He could see or hear us nearly all the time. He was, to us, behind every stump, tree, bush and fence on the plantation. He carried this kind of trickery so far, that he would sometimes mount his horse, and make believe he was going to St. Michael's; and, in thirty minutes afterward, you might find his horse tied in the woods, and the snake-like Covey lying flat in the ditch, with his head lifted above its edge, or in a fence corner, watching every movement of the slaves! I have known him walk up to us and give us special orders, as to our work, in advance, as if he were leaving home with a view to being absent several days; and before he got half way to the house, he would avail himself of our inattention to his movements, to turn short on his heels, conceal himself behind a fence corner or a tree, and watch us until the going down of the sun. Mean and contemptible as is all this, it is in keeping with the character which the life of a slaveholder is calculated to produce. There is no earthly inducement, in the slave's condition, to incite him to labor faithfully. The fear of punishment is the sole motive for any sort of industry, with him. Knowing this fact, as the slaveholder does, and judging the slave by himself, he naturally concludes the slave will be idle whenever the cause for this fear is absent. Hence, all sorts of petty deceptions are practiced, to inspire this fear.

But, with Mr. Covey, trickery was natural. Everything in the shape of learning or religion, which he possessed, was made to conform to this semi-lying propensity. He did not seem conscious that the practice had anything unmanly, base or contemptible about it. It was a part of an important system, with him, essential to the relation of master and slave. I thought I saw, in his very religious devotions, this controlling element of his character. A long prayer at night made up for the short prayer in the morning; and few men could seem more devotional than he, when he had nothing else to do.

Mr. Covey was not content with the cold style of family worship, adopted in these cold latitudes, which begin and end with a simple prayer. No! The voice of praise, as well as of prayer, must be heard in his house, night and morning. At first, I was called upon to bear some part in these exercises; but the repeated flogging given me by Covey, turned the whole thing into mockery. He was a poor singer, and mainly relied on me for raising the hymn for the family, and when I failed to do so, he was thrown into much confusion. I do not think that he ever abused me on account of these vexations. His religion was a thing altogether apart from his worldly concerns. He knew nothing of it as a holy principle, directing and controlling his daily life, making the latter conform to the requirements of the gospel. One or two facts will illustrate his character better than a volume of generalities.

I have already said, or implied, that Mr. Edward Covey was a poor man. He was, in fact, just commencing to lay the foundation of his fortune, as fortune is regarded in a slave state. The first condition of wealth and respectability there, being the ownership of human property, every nerve is strained, by the poor man, to obtain it, and very little regard is had to the manner of obtaining it. In pursuit of this object, pious as Mr. Covey was, he proved himself to be as unscrupulous and base as the worst of his neighbors. In the beginning, he was only able—as he said—"to buy one slave"; and, scandalous and shocking as is the fact, he boasted that he bought her simply "*as a breeder.*" But the worst is not told in this naked statement. This young woman (Caroline was her name) was virtually compelled by Mr. Covey to abandon herself to the object for which he had purchased her; and the result was, the birth of twins at the end of the year. At this addition to his human stock, both Edward Covey and his wife, Susan, were ecstatic with joy. No one dreamed of reproaching the woman, or of finding fault with the hired man—Bill Smith—the father of the children, for Mr. Covey himself had locked the two up together every night, thus inviting the result.

But I will pursue this revolting subject no further. No better illustration of the unchaste and demoralizing character of slavery can be found, than is furnished in the fact that this professedly Christian slaveholder, amidst all his prayers and hymns, was shamelessly and boastfully encouraging, and actually compelling, in his own house, undisguised and unmitigated fornication, as a means of increasing his human stock. I may remark here, that, while this fact will be read with disgust and shame at the north, it will be *laughed* at, as smart and praiseworthy in Mr. Covey, at the south; for a man is no more condemned there for buying a woman and devoting her to this life of dishonor, than for buying a cow, and raising stock from her. The same rules are observed, with a view to increasing the number and quality of the former, as of the latter.

I will here reproduce what I said of my own experience in this wretched place, more than ten years ago:[*]

If at any one time of my life, more than another, I was made to drink the bitterest dregs of slavery, that time was during the first six months of my stay with Mr. Covey. We were worked all weathers. It was never too hot or too cold; it could never rain, blow, snow, or hail too hard for us to work in the field. Work, work, work, was scarcely more the order of the day than the night. The longest days were too short for him, and the shortest nights were too long for him. I was somewhat unmanageable when I first went there; but a few months of his discipline tamed me. Mr. Covey succeeded in breaking me. I was broken in body, soul and spirit. My natural elasticity was crushed; my intellect languished; the disposition to read departed; the cheerful spark that lingered about my eye died; the dark night of slavery closed in upon me; and behold a man transformed into a brute!

Sunday was my only leisure time. I spent this in a sort of beast-like stupor, between sleep and wake, under some large tree. At times, I would rise up, a flash of energetic freedom would dart through my soul, accompanied with a faint beam of hope, flickered for a moment, and then vanished. I sank down again, mourning over my wretched condition. I was sometimes prompted to take my life, and that of Covey, but was prevented by a combination of hope and fear. My sufferings on this plantation seem now like a dream rather than a stern reality.

Our house stood within a few rods of the Chesapeake Bay, whose broad bosom was ever white with sails from every quarter of the habitable globe. Those beautiful vessels, robed in purest white, so delightful to the eye of freemen, were to me so many shrouded ghosts, to terrify and torment me with thoughts of my wretched condition. I have often, in the deep stillness of a summer's Sabbath, stood all alone upon the banks of that noble bay, and traced, with saddened heart and tearful eye, the countless number of sails moving off to the mighty ocean. The sight of these always affected me powerfully. My thoughts would compel utterance; and there, with no audience but the Almighty, I would pour out

[*] From *Narrative of the Life of Frederick Douglass.*

my soul's complaint in my rude way, with an apostrophe to the moving multitude of ships:

"You are loosed from your moorings, and free; I am fast in my chains, and am a slave! You move merrily before the gentle gale, and I sadly before the bloody whip! You are freedom's swift-winged angels, that fly around the world; I am confined in bands of iron! O, that I were free! O, that I were on one of your gallant decks, and under your protecting wing! Alas! Betwixt me and you the turbid waters roll. Go on, go on. O that I could also go! Could I but swim! If I could fly! O, why was I born a man, of whom to make a brute! The glad ship is gone; she hides in the dim distance. I am left in the hottest hell of unending slavery. O God, save me! God, deliver me! Let me be free! Is there any God? Why am I a slave? I will run away. I will not stand it. Get caught, or get clear, I'll try it. I had as well die with ague as with fever. I have only one life to lose. I had as well be killed running as die standing. Only think of it; one hundred miles straight north, and I am free! Try it? Yes! God helping me, I will. It cannot be that I shall live and die a slave. I will take to the water. This very bay shall yet bear me into freedom. The steamboats steered in a north-east coast from North Point. I will do the same; and when I get to the head of the bay, I will turn my canoe adrift, and walk straight through Delaware into Pennsylvania. When I get there, I shall not be required to have a pass; I will travel without being disturbed. Let but the first opportunity offer, and come what will, I am off. Meanwhile, I will try to bear up under the yoke. I am not the only slave in the world. Why should I fret? I can bear as much as any of them. Besides, I am but a boy, and all boys are bound to some one. It may be that my misery in slavery will only increase my happiness when I get free. There is a better day coming.'"

I shall never be able to narrate the mental experience through which it was my lot to pass during my stay at Covey's. I was completely wrecked, changed and bewildered; goaded almost to madness at one time, and at another reconciling myself to my wretched condition. Everything in the way of kindness, which I had experienced at Baltimore; all my former hopes and aspirations for usefulness in the world, and the happy moments spent in the exercises of religion, contrasted with my then present lot, but increased my anguish.

I suffered bodily as well as mentally. I had neither sufficient time in which to eat or to sleep, except on Sundays. The overwork, and the brutal chastisements of which I was the victim, combined with that ever-gnawing and soul-devouring thought—"*I am a slave—a slave for life—a slave with no rational ground to hope for freedom*"—rendered me a living embodiment of mental and physical wretchedness.

# CHAPTER XVI

## ANOTHER PRESSURE OF THE TYRANT'S VICE

*Experience at Covey's Summed Up—First Six Months Severer Than the Second—Preliminaries to the Chance—Reasons for Narrating the Circumstances—Scene in Treading-Yard—Taken Ill—Unusual Brutality of Covey—Escape to St. Michael's— The Pursuit—Suffering in the Woods—Driven Back Again to Covey's—Bearing of Master Thomas—The Slave Is Never Sick—Natural to Expect Slaves to Feign Sickness—Laziness of Slaveholders.*

The foregoing chapter, with all its horrid incidents and shocking features, may be taken as a fair representation of the first six months of my life at Covey's. The reader has but to repeat, in his own mind, once a week, the scene in the woods, where Covey subjected me to his merciless lash, to have a true idea of my bitter experience there, during the first period of the breaking process through which Mr. Covey carried me. I have no heart to repeat each separate transaction, in which I was victim of his violence and brutality. Such a narration would fill a volume much larger than the present one. I aim only to give the reader a truthful impression of my slave life, without unnecessarily affecting him with harrowing details.

As I have elsewhere intimated that my hardships were much greater during the first six months of my stay at Covey's, than during the remainder of the year, and as the change in my condition was owing to causes which may help the reader to a better understanding of human nature, when subjected to the terrible extremities of slavery, I will narrate the circumstances of this change, although I may seem thereby to applaud my own courage. You have, dear reader, seen me humbled, degraded, broken down, enslaved, and brutalized, and you understand how it was done; now let us see the converse of all this, and how it was brought about; and this will take us through the year 1834.

On one of the hottest days of the month of August, of the year just mentioned, had the reader been passing through Covey's farm, he might have seen me at work, in what is there called the "treading-yard"—a yard upon which wheat is trodden out from the straw, by the horses' feet. I was there, at work, feeding the "fan," or rather bringing wheat to the fan, while Bill Smith was feeding. Our force consisted of Bill Hughes, Bill Smith, and a slave by the name of Eli; the latter having been hired for this occasion. The work was simple, and required strength and activity, rather than any skill or intelligence, and yet, to one entirely unused to such work, it came very hard. The heat was intense and overpowering, and there was much hurry to get the wheat, trodden out that day, through the fan; since, if that work was done an hour before sundown, the hands would have, according to a promise of Covey, that hour added to their night's rest. I was not behind any of them in the wish to complete the day's work before sundown, and, hence, I struggled with all my might to get the work forward. The promise of one hour's repose on a week day, was sufficient to quicken my pace, and to spur me on to extra endeavor. Besides, we had all planned to go fishing, and I certainly wished to have a hand in that. But I was disappointed, and the day turned out to be one of the bitterest I ever experienced. About three o'clock, while the sun was pouring down his burning rays, and not a breeze was stirring, I broke down; my strength failed me; I was seized with a violent aching of the head, attended with extreme dizziness, and trembling in every limb. Finding what was coming, and feeling it would never do to stop work, I nerved myself up, and staggered on until I fell by the side of the wheat fan, feeling that the earth had fallen upon me. This brought the entire work to a dead stand. There was work for four; each one had his part to perform, and each part depended on the other, so that when one stopped, all were compelled to stop. Covey, who had now become my dread, as well as my tormentor, was at the house, about a hundred yards from where I was fanning, and instantly, upon hearing the fan stop, he came down to the treading-yard, to inquire into the cause of our stopping. Bill Smith told him I was sick, and that I was unable longer to bring wheat to the fan.

I had, by this time, crawled away, under the side of a post-and-rail fence, in the shade, and was exceeding ill. The intense heat of the sun, the heavy dust rising from the fan, the stooping, to take up the wheat from the yard, together with the hurrying, to get through, had caused a rush of blood to my head. In this condition, Covey finding out where I was, came to me; and, after standing over me a while, he asked me what the matter was. I told him as well as I could, for it was with difficulty that I could speak. He then gave me a savage kick in the side, which jarred my whole frame, and commanded me to get up. The man had obtained complete control over me; and if he had commanded me to do any possible thing, I should, in my then state of mind, have endeavored to comply. I made an effort to rise, but fell back in the attempt, before gaining my feet. The brute now gave me another heavy kick, and again told me to rise. I again tried to rise, and succeeded in gaining my feet; but upon stooping to get the tub with which I was feeding the fan, I again staggered and fell to the ground; and I must have so fallen, had I been sure that a hundred bullets would have pierced me, as the consequence. While down, in this sad condition, and perfectly helpless, the merciless Negro breaker took up the hickory slab, with which Hughes had been striking off the wheat to a level with the sides of the half bushel measure (a very hard weapon) and with the sharp edge of it, he dealt me a heavy blow on my head which made a large gash, and caused the blood to run freely, saying, at the same time, "*If you have got the headache, I'll cure you.*" This done, he ordered me again to rise, but I made no effort to do so; for I had made up my mind that it was useless, and that the heartless monster might now do his worst; he could but kill me, and that might put me out of my misery. Finding me unable to rise, or rather despairing of my doing so, Covey left me, with a view to getting on with the work without me. I was bleeding very freely, and my face was soon covered with my warm blood. Cruel and merciless as was the motive that dealt that blow, dear reader, the wound was fortunate for me. Bleeding was never more efficacious. The pain in my head speedily abated, and I was soon able to rise. Covey had, as I have said, now left me to my fate; and the question was, shall I return to my work, or shall I find my way to St. Michael's, and make Capt. Auld acquainted with the atrocious cruelty of his brother Covey, and beseech him to get me another master? Remembering the object he had in view, in placing me under the management of Covey, and further, his cruel treatment of my poor crippled cousin, Henny, and his meanness in the matter of feeding and clothing his slaves, there was little ground to hope for a favorable reception at the hands of Capt. Thomas Auld. Nevertheless, I resolved to go straight to Capt. Auld, thinking that, if not animated by motives of humanity, he might be induced to interfere on my behalf from selfish considerations. "He cannot," thought I, "allow his property to be thus bruised and battered, marred and defaced; and I will go to him, and tell him the simple truth about the matter." In order to get to St. Michael's, by the most favorable and direct road, I must walk seven miles; and this, in my sad condition, was no easy performance. I had already lost much blood; I was exhausted by over exertion; my sides were sore from the heavy blows planted there by the stout boots of Mr. Covey; and I was, in every way, in an unfavorable plight for the journey. I however watched my chance, while the cruel and cunning Covey was looking in an opposite direction, and started off, across the field, for St. Michael's. This was a daring step; if it failed, it would only exasperate Covey, and increase the rigors of my bondage, during the remainder of my term of service under him; but the step was taken, and I must go forward. I succeeded in getting nearly half way across the broad field, toward the woods, before Mr. Covey observed me. I was still bleeding, and the exertion of running had started the blood afresh. "*Come back! Come back!*" vociferated Covey, with threats of what he would do if I did not return instantly. But, disregarding his calls and his threats, I pressed on toward the woods as fast as my feeble state would allow. Seeing no signs of my stopping, Covey caused his horse to be brought out and saddled, as if he intended to pursue me. The race was now to be an unequal one; and, thinking I might be overhauled by him, if I kept the main road, I walked nearly the whole distance in the woods, keeping far enough from the road to avoid detection and pursuit. But, I had not gone far, before my little strength again failed me, and I laid down. The blood was still oozing from the wound in my head; and, for a time, I suffered more than I can describe. There I was, in the deep woods, sick and emaciated, pursued by a wretch whose character for revolting cruelty beggars all opprobrious speech—bleeding, and almost bloodless. I was not without the fear of bleeding to death. The thought of dying in the woods, all alone, and of being torn to pieces by the buzzards, had not yet been rendered tolerable by my many troubles and hardships, and I was glad when the shade of the trees, and the cool evening breeze, combined with my matted hair to stop the flow of blood. After lying there about three quarters of an hour, brooding over the singular and mournful lot to which I was doomed, my mind passing over the whole scale or circle of belief and unbelief, from faith in the overruling providence of God, to the blackest atheism, I again took up my journey toward St. Michael's, more weary and sad than in the morning when I left Thomas Auld's for the home of Mr. Covey. I was bare-footed and bare-headed, and in my shirt sleeves. The way was through bogs and briers, and I tore my feet often during the journey. I was full five hours in going the seven or eight miles; partly, because of the difficulties of the way, and partly, because of the feebleness induced by my illness, bruises and loss of blood. On gaining my master's store, I presented an appearance of wretchedness and woe, fitted to move any but a heart of stone. From the crown of my head to the sole of my feet, there were marks of blood. My hair was all clotted with dust and blood, and the back of my shirt was literally stiff with the same. Briers and thorns had scarred and torn my feet and legs, leaving blood marks there. Had I escaped from a den of tigers, I could not have looked worse than I did on reaching St. Michael's. In this unhappy plight, I appeared before my professedly *Christian* master, humbly to invoke the interposition of his power and authority, to protect me from further abuse and violence. I had begun to hope, during the latter part of my tedious journey toward St. Michael's, that Capt. Auld would now show himself in a nobler light than I had ever before seen him. I was disappointed. I had jumped from a sinking ship into the sea; I had fled from the tiger to something worse. I told him all the circumstances, as well as I could; how I was endeavoring to please Covey; how hard I was at work in the present instance; how unwilling I sunk down under the heat, toil and pain; the brutal manner in which Covey had kicked me in the side; the gash cut in my head; my hesitation about troubling him (Capt. Auld) with complaints; but, that now I felt it would not be best longer to conceal from him the outrages committed on me from time to time by Covey. At first, Master Thomas seemed somewhat affected by the story of my wrongs, but he soon repressed his feelings and became cold as iron. It was impossible—as I stood before him at the first—for him to seem indifferent. I distinctly saw his human nature asserting its conviction against the slave system, which made cases like mine *possible*; but, as I have said, humanity fell before the systematic tyranny of slavery. He first walked the floor, apparently much agitated by my story, and the sad spectacle I presented; but, presently, it was *his* turn to talk. He began moderately, by finding excuses for Covey, and ending with a full justification of him, and a passionate condemnation of me. "He had no doubt I deserved the flogging. He did not believe I was sick; I was only endeavoring to get rid of work. My dizziness was laziness, and Covey did right to flog me, as he had done." After thus fairly annihilating me, and rousing himself by his own eloquence, he fiercely demanded what I wished *him* to do in the case!

With such a complete knock-down to all my hopes, as he had given me, and feeling, as I did, my entire subjection to his power, I had very little heart to reply. I must not affirm my innocence of the allegations which he had piled up against me; for that would be impudence, and would probably call down fresh violence as well as wrath upon me. The guilt of a slave is always, and everywhere, presumed; and the innocence of the slaveholder or the slave employer, is always asserted. The word of the slave, against this presumption, is generally treated as impudence, worthy of punishment. "Do you contradict me, you rascal?" is a final silencer of counter statements from the lips of a slave.

Calming down a little in view of my silence and hesitation, and, perhaps, from a rapid glance at the picture of misery I presented, he inquired again, "what I would have him do?" Thus invited a second time, I told Master Thomas I wished him to allow me to get a new home and to find a new master; that, as sure as I went back to live with Mr. Covey again, I should be killed by him; that he would never forgive my coming to him (Capt. Auld) with a complaint against him (Covey); that, since I had lived with him, he almost crushed my spirit, and I believed that he would ruin me for future service; that my life was not safe in his hands. This, Master Thomas (*my brother in the church*) regarded as "nonsense." "There was no danger of Mr. Covey's killing me; he was a good man, industrious and religious, and he would not think of removing me from that home; besides," said he and this I found was the most distressing thought of all to him—"if you should leave Covey now, that your year has but half expired, I should lose your wages for the entire year. You belong to Mr. Covey for one year, and you *must go back* to him, come what will. You must not trouble me with any more stories about Mr. Covey; and if you do not go immediately home, I will get hold of you myself." This was just what I expected, when I found he had *prejudged* the case against me. "But, Sir," I said, "I am sick and tired, and I cannot get home tonight." At this, he again relented, and finally he allowed me to remain all night at St. Michael's; but said I must be off early in the morning, and concluded his directions by making me swallow a huge dose of *epsom salt*s—about the only medicine ever administered to slaves.

It was quite natural for Master Thomas to presume I was feigning sickness to escape work, for he probably thought that were *he* in the place of a slave with no wages for his work, no praise for well doing, no motive for toil but the lash—he would try every possible scheme by which to escape labor. I say I have no doubt of this; the reason is, that there are not, under the whole heavens, a set of men who cultivate such an intense dread of labor as do the slaveholders. The charge of laziness against the slave is ever on their lips, and is the standing apology for every species of cruelty and brutality. These men literally "bind heavy burdens, grievous to be borne, and lay them on men's shoulders; but they, themselves, will not move them with one of their fingers."*

My kind readers shall have, in the next chapter—what they were led, perhaps, to expect to find in this—namely: an account of my partial disenthrallment from the tyranny of Covey, and the marked change which it brought about.

---

* From the Bible, Matthew 23:4.

# CHAPTER XVII

## THE LAST FLOGGING

*A Sleepless Night—Return to Covey's—Pursued by Covey—
The Chase Defeated—Vengeance Postpones—Musings in the
Woods—The Alternative—Deplorable Spectacle—Night in the
Woods—Expected Attack—Accosted by Sandy, A Friend, Not
a Hunter—Sandy's Hospitality—The "Ash Cake" Supper—
The Interview with Sandy—His Advice—Sandy a Conjurer As
Well As a Christian—The Magic Root—Strange Meeting with
Covey—His Manner—Covey's Sunday Face—My Defensive
Resolve—The Fight—The Victory, and Its Results.*

Sleep itself does not always come to the relief of the weary in
body, and the broken in spirit; especially when past troubles only
foreshadow coming disasters. The last hope had been extinguished. My
master, who I did not venture to hope would protect me as *a man*, had
even now refused to protect me as *his property*; and had cast me back,
covered with reproaches and bruises, into the hands of a stranger to
that mercy which was the soul of the religion he professed. May the
reader never spend such a night as that allotted to me, previous to the
morning which was to herald my return to the den of horrors from
which I had made a temporary escape.

I remained all night—sleep I did not—at St. Michael's; and in the
morning (Saturday) I started off, according to the order of Master
Thomas, feeling that I had no friend on earth, and doubting if I had one
in heaven. I reached Covey's about nine o'clock; and just as I stepped
into the field, before I had reached the house, Covey, true to his snakish
habits, darted out at me from a fence corner, in which he had secreted
himself, for the purpose of securing me. He was amply provided with a
cowskin and a rope; and he evidently intended to *tie me up*, and to wreak
his vengeance on me to the fullest extent. I should have been an easy
prey, had he succeeded in getting his hands upon me, for I had taken no
refreshment since noon on Friday; and this, together with the pelting,

excitement, and the loss of blood, had reduced my strength. I, however, darted back into the woods, before the ferocious hound could get hold of me, and buried myself in a thicket, where he lost sight of me. The cornfield afforded me cover, in getting to the woods. But for the tall corn, Covey would have overtaken me, and made me his captive. He seemed very much chagrined that he did not catch me, and gave up the chase, very reluctantly; for I could see his angry movements, toward the house from which he had sallied, on his foray.

Well, now I am clear of Covey, and of his wrathful lash, for present. I am in the wood, buried in its somber gloom, and hushed in its solemn silence; hid from all human eyes; shut in with nature and nature's God, and absent from all human contrivances. Here was a good place to pray; to pray for help for deliverance—a prayer I had often made before. But how could I pray? Covey could pray—Capt. Auld could pray—I would fain pray; but doubts (arising partly from my own neglect of the means of grace, and partly from the sham religion which everywhere prevailed, cast in my mind a doubt upon all religion, and led me to the conviction that prayers were unavailing and delusive) prevented my embracing the opportunity, as a religious one. Life, in itself, had almost become burdensome to me. All my outward relations were against me; I must stay here and starve (I was already hungry) or go home to Covey's, and have my flesh torn to pieces, and my spirit humbled under the cruel lash of Covey. This was the painful alternative presented to me. The day was long and irksome. My physical condition was deplorable. I was weak, from the toils of the previous day, and from the want of food and rest; and had been so little concerned about my appearance, that I had not yet washed the blood from my garments. I was an object of horror, even to myself. Life, in Baltimore, when most oppressive, was a paradise to this. What had I done, what had my parents done, that such a life as this should be mine? That day, in the woods, I would have exchanged my manhood for the brutehood of an ox.

Night came. I was still in the woods, unresolved what to do. Hunger had not yet pinched me to the point of going home, and I laid myself down in the leaves to rest; for I had been watching for hunters all day, but not being molested during the day, I expected no disturbance during the night. I had come to the conclusion that Covey relied upon hunger to drive me home; and in this I was quite correct—the facts showed that he had made no effort to catch me, since morning.

During the night, I heard the step of a man in the woods. He was coming toward the place where I lay. A person lying still has the advantage over one walking in the woods, in the day time, and this advantage is much greater at night. I was not able to engage in a physical struggle, and I had recourse to the common resort of the weak. I hid myself in the leaves to prevent discovery. But, as the night rambler in the woods drew nearer, I found him to be a *friend*, not an enemy; it was a slave of Mr. William Groomes, of Easton, a kind-fellow, named "Sandy." Sandy lived with Mr. Kemp that year, about four miles from St. Michael's. He, like myself, had been hired out by the year; but, unlike myself, had not been hired out to be broken. Sandy was the husband of a free woman, who lived in the lower part of *"Pot-pie Neck,"* and he was now on his way through the woods, to see her, and to spend the Sabbath with her.

As soon as I had ascertained that the disturber of my solitude was not an enemy, but the good-hearted Sandy—a man as famous among the slaves of the neighborhood for his good nature, as for his good sense—I came out from my hiding place, and made myself known to him. I explained the circumstances of the past two days, which had driven me to the woods, and he deeply compassionated my distress. It was a bold thing for him to shelter me, and I could not ask him to do so; for, had I been found in his hut, he would have suffered the penalty of thirty-nine lashes on his bare back, if not something worse. But Sandy was too generous to permit the fear of punishment to prevent his relieving a brother bondman from hunger and exposure; and, therefore, on his own motion, I accompanied him to his home, or rather to the home of his wife—for the house and lot were hers. His wife was called up—for it was now about midnight—a fire was made, some Indian meal was soon mixed with salt and water, and an ash cake was baked in a hurry to relieve my hunger. Sandy's wife was not behind him in kindness—both seemed to esteem it a privilege to succor me; for, although I was hated by Covey and by my master, I was loved by the colored people, because *they* thought I was hated for my knowledge, and persecuted because I was feared. I was the *only* slave *now* in that region who could read and write. There had been one other man, belonging to Mr. Hugh Hamilton, who could read (his name was "Jim"), but he, poor fellow, had, shortly after my coming into the neighborhood, been sold off to the far south. I saw Jim ironed, in the cart, to be carried to Easton for sale—pinioned like a yearling for the slaughter. My knowledge was now the pride of my brother slaves; and, no doubt, Sandy felt something of the general interest in me on that account. The supper was soon ready, and though I have feasted since, with honorables, lord mayors and aldermen, over the sea, my supper on ash cake and cold water, with Sandy, was the meal, of all my life, most sweet to my taste, and now most vivid in my memory.

Supper over, Sandy and I went into a discussion of what was *possible* for me, under the perils and hardships which now overshadowed my path. The question was, must I go back to Covey, or must I now tempt to run away? Upon a careful survey, the latter was found to be impossible; for I was on a narrow neck of land, every avenue from which would bring me in sight of pursuers. There was the Chesapeake Bay to the right, and "Pot-pie" river to the left, and St. Michael's and its neighborhood occupying the only space through which there was any retreat.

I found Sandy an old advisor. He was not only a religious man, but he professed to believe in a system for which I have no name. He was a genuine African, and had inherited some of the so-called magical powers, said to be possessed by African and eastern nations. He told me that he could help me; that, in those very woods, there was an herb, which in the morning might be found, possessing all the powers required for my protection (I put his thoughts in my own language); and that, if I would take his advice, he would procure me the root of the herb of which he spoke. He told me further, that if I would take that root and wear it on my right side, it would be impossible for Covey to strike me a blow; that with this root about my person, no white man could whip me. He said he had carried it for years, and that he had fully tested its virtues. He had never received a blow from a slaveholder since he carried it; and he never expected to receive one, for he always meant to carry that root as a protection. He knew Covey well, for Mrs. Covey was the daughter of Mr. Kemp; and he (Sandy) had heard of the barbarous treatment to which I was subjected, and he wanted to do something for me.

Now all this talk about the root, was to me, very absurd and ridiculous, if not positively sinful. I at first rejected the idea that the simple carrying a root on my right side (a root, by the way, over which I walked every time I went into the woods) could possess any such magic power as he ascribed to it, and I was, therefore, not disposed to cumber my pocket with it. I had a positive aversion to all pretenders to "*divination.*" It was beneath one of my intelligence to countenance such dealings with the devil, as this power implied. But, with all my learning—it was really precious little—Sandy was more than a match for me. "My book learning," he said, "had not kept Covey off me" (a powerful argument just then) and he entreated me, with flashing eyes, to try this. If it did me no good, it could do me no harm, and it would cost me nothing, any way. Sandy was so earnest, and so confident of the good qualities of this weed, that, to please him, rather than from any conviction of its excellence, I was induced to take it. He had been to me the good Samaritan, and had, almost providentially, found me, and helped me when I could not help myself; how did I know but that the hand of the Lord was in it? With thoughts of this sort, I took the roots from Sandy, and put them in my right hand pocket.

This was, of course, Sunday morning. Sandy now urged me to go home, with all speed, and to walk up bravely to the house, as though nothing had happened. I saw in Sandy too deep an insight into human nature, with all his superstition, not to have some respect for his advice; and perhaps, too, a slight gleam or shadow of his superstition had fallen upon me. At any rate, I started off toward Covey's, as directed by Sandy. Having, the previous night, poured my griefs into Sandy's ears, and got him enlisted in my behalf, having made his wife a sharer in my sorrows, and having, also, become well refreshed by sleep and food, I moved off, quite courageously, toward the much dreaded Covey's. Singularly enough, just as I entered his yard gate, I met him and his wife, dressed in their Sunday best—looking as smiling as angels—on their way to church. The manner of Covey astonished me. There was something really benignant in his countenance. He spoke to me as never before; told me that the pigs had got into the lot, and he wished me to drive them out; inquired how I was, and seemed an altered man. This extraordinary conduct of Covey, really made me begin to think that Sandy's herb had more virtue in it than I, in my pride, had been willing to allow; and, had the day been other than Sunday, I should have attributed Covey's altered manner solely to the magic power of the root. I suspected, however, that the *Sabbath*, and not the *root*, was the real explanation of Covey's manner. His religion hindered him from breaking the Sabbath, but not from breaking my skin. He had more respect for the *day* than for the *man*, for whom the day was mercifully given; for while he would cut and slash my body during the week, he would not hesitate, on Sunday, to teach me the value of my soul, or the way of life and salvation by Jesus Christ.

All went well with me till Monday morning; and then, whether the root had lost its virtue, or whether my tormentor had gone deeper into the black art than myself (as was sometimes said of him), or whether he had obtained a special indulgence, for his faithful Sabbath day's worship, it is not necessary for me to know, or to inform the reader; but, this I *may* say—the pious and benignant smile which graced Covey's face on *Sunday*, wholly disappeared on *Monday*. Long before daylight, I was called up to go and feed, rub, and curry the horses. I obeyed the call, and would have so obeyed it, had it been made at an earlier hour, for I had brought my mind to a firm resolve, during that Sunday's reflection, viz: to obey every order, however unreasonable, if it were possible, and, if Mr. Covey should then undertake to beat me, to defend and protect myself to the best of my ability. My religious views on the subject of resisting my master, had suffered a serious shock, by the savage persecution to which I had been subjected, and my hands were no longer tied by my religion. Master Thomas's indifference had served the last link. I had now to this extent "backslidden" from this point in the slave's religious creed; and I soon had occasion to make my fallen state known to my Sunday-pious brother, Covey.

Whilst I was obeying his order to feed and get the horses ready for the field, and when in the act of going up the stable loft for the purpose of throwing down some blades, Covey sneaked into the stable, in his peculiar snake-like way, and seizing me suddenly by the leg, he brought me to the stable floor, giving my newly mended body a fearful jar. I now forgot my *roots*, and remembered my pledge to *stand up in my own defense*. The brute was endeavoring skillfully to get a slip-knot on my legs, before I could draw up my feet. As soon as I found what he was up to, I gave a sudden spring (my two day's rest had been of much service to me), and by that means, no doubt, he was able to bring me to the floor so heavily. He was defeated in his plan of tying me. While down, he seemed to think he had me very securely in his power. He little thought he was—as the rowdies say—"in" for a "rough and tumble" fight; but such was the fact. Whence came the daring spirit necessary to grapple with a man who, eight-and-forty hours before, could, with his slightest word have made me tremble like a leaf in a storm, I do not know; at any rate, *I was resolved to fight*, and, what was better still, I was actually hard at it. The fighting madness had come upon me, and I found my strong fingers firmly attached to the throat of my cowardly tormentor; as heedless of consequences, at the moment, as though we stood as equals before the law. The very color of the man was forgotten. I felt as supple as a cat, and was ready for the snakish creature at every turn. Every blow of his was parried, though I dealt no blows in turn. I was strictly on the *defensive*, preventing him from injuring me, rather than trying to injure him. I flung him on the ground several times, when he meant to have hurled me there. I held him so firmly by the throat, that his blood followed my nails. He held me, and I held him.

All was fair, thus far, and the contest was about equal. My resistance was entirely unexpected, and Covey was taken all aback by it, for he trembled in every limb. "*Are you going to resist*, you scoundrel?" said he. To which, I returned a polite "*Yes sir*"; steadily gazing my interrogator in the eye, to meet the first approach or dawning of the blow, which I expected my answer would call forth. But, the conflict did not long remain thus equal. Covey soon cried out lustily for help; not that I was obtaining any marked advantage over him, or was injuring him, but because he was gaining none over me, and was not able, single handed, to conquer me. He called for his cousin Hughes, to come to his assistance, and now the scene was changed. I was compelled to give blows, as well as to parry them; and, since I was, in any case, to suffer for resistance, I felt (as the musty proverb goes) that "I might as well be hanged for an old sheep as a lamb." I was still *defensive* toward Covey, but *aggressive* toward Hughes; and, at the first approach of the latter, I dealt a blow, in my desperation, which fairly sickened my youthful assailant. He went off, bending over with pain, and manifesting no disposition to come within my reach again. The poor fellow was in the act of trying to catch and tie my right hand, and while flattering himself with success, I gave him the kick which sent him staggering away in pain, at the same time that I held Covey with a firm hand.

Taken completely by surprise, Covey seemed to have lost his usual strength and coolness. He was frightened, and stood puffing and blowing, seemingly unable to command words or blows. When he saw that poor Hughes was standing half bent with pain—his courage quite gone—the cowardly tyrant asked if I "meant to persist in my resistance." I told him "I *did mean to resist, come what might*"; that I had been by him treated like a *brute*, during the last six months; and that I should stand it *no longer*. With that, he gave me a shake, and attempted to drag me toward a stick of wood, that was lying just outside the stable door. He meant to knock me down with it; but, just as he leaned over to get the stick, I seized him with both hands by the collar, and, with a vigorous and sudden snatch, I brought my assailant harmlessly, his full length, on the *not over* clean ground—for we were now in the cow yard. He had selected the place for the fight, and it was but right that he should have all the advantages of his own selection.

By this time, Bill, the hired man, came home. He had been to Mr. Hemsley's, to spend the Sunday with his nominal wife, and was coming home on Monday morning, to go to work. Covey and I had been skirmishing from before daybreak, till now, that the sun was almost shooting his beams over the eastern woods, and we were still at it. I could not see where the matter was to terminate. He evidently was afraid to let me go, lest I should again make off to the woods; otherwise, he would probably have obtained arms from the house, to frighten me. Holding me, Covey called upon Bill for assistance. The scene here, had something comic about it. "Bill," who knew *precisely* what Covey wished him to do, affected ignorance, and pretended he did not know what to do. "What shall I do, Mr. Covey," said Bill. "Take hold of him—take hold of him!" said Covey. With a toss of his head, peculiar to Bill, he said, "Indeed, Mr. Covey I want to go to work." "*This* is your work," said Covey; "take hold of him." Bill replied, with spirit, "My master hired me here, to work, and *not* to help you whip Frederick." It was now my turn to speak. "Bill," said I, "don't put your hands on me." To which he replied, "My god! Frederick, I ain't goin' to tech ye," and Bill walked off, leaving Covey and myself to settle our matters as best we might.

But, my present advantage was threatened when I saw Caroline (the slave-woman of Covey) coming to the cow yard to milk, for she was a powerful woman, and could have mastered me very easily, exhausted as I now was. As soon as she came into the yard, Covey attempted to rally her to his aid. Strangely—and, I may add, fortunately—Caroline was in no humor to take a hand in any such sport. We were all in open rebellion, that morning. Caroline answered the command of her master to "*take hold of me,*" precisely as Bill had answered, but in her, it was at greater peril so to answer; she was the slave of Covey, and he could do what he pleased with her. It was not so with Bill, and Bill knew it. Samuel Harris, to whom Bill belonged, did not allow his slaves to be beaten, unless they were guilty of some crime which the law would punish. But, poor Caroline, like myself, was at the mercy of the merciless Covey; nor did she escape the dire effects of her refusal. He gave her several sharp blows.

Covey at length (two hours had elapsed) gave up the contest. Letting me go, he said—puffing and blowing at a great rate—"Now, you scoundrel, go to your work; I would not have whipped you half so much as I have had you not resisted." The fact was, *he had not whipped me at all*. He had not, in all the scuffle, drawn a single drop of blood from me. I had drawn blood from him; and, even without this satisfaction, I should have been victorious, because my aim had not been to injure him, but to prevent his injuring me.

During the whole six months that I lived with Covey, after this transaction, he never laid on me the weight of his finger in anger. He would, occasionally, say he did not want to have to get hold of me again—a declaration which I had no difficulty in believing; and I had a secret feeling, which answered, "You need not wish to get hold of me again, for you will be likely to come off worse in a second fight than you did in the first."

Well, my dear reader, this battle with Mr. Covey—undignified as it was, and as I fear my narration of it is—was the turning point in my "*life as a slave*." It rekindled in my breast the smouldering embers of liberty; it brought up my Baltimore dreams, and revived a sense of my own manhood. I was a changed being after that fight. I was nothing before; *I was a man now*. It recalled to life my crushed self-respect and my self-confidence, and inspired me with a renewed determination to be *a freeman*. A man, without force, is without the essential dignity of humanity. Human nature is so constituted, that it cannot *honor* a helpless man, although it can *pity* him; and even this it cannot do long, if the signs of power do not arise.

He can only understand the effect of this combat on my spirit, who has himself incurred something, hazarded something, in repelling the unjust and cruel aggressions of a tyrant. Covey was a tyrant, and a cowardly one, withal. After resisting him, I felt as I had never felt before. It was a resurrection from the dark and pestiferous tomb of slavery, to the heaven of comparative freedom. I was no longer a servile coward, trembling under the frown of a brother worm of the dust, but, my long-cowed spirit was roused to an attitude of manly independence. I had reached the point, at which I was *not afraid to die.* This spirit made me a freeman in *fact*, while I remained a slave in *form.* When a slave cannot be flogged he is more than half free. He has a domain as broad as his own manly heart to defend, and he is really *"a power on earth."* While slaves prefer their lives, with flogging, to instant death, they will always find Christians enough, like unto Covey, to accommodate that preference. From this time, until that of my escape from slavery, I was never fairly whipped. Several attempts were made to whip me, but they were always unsuccessful. Bruises I did get, as I shall hereafter inform the reader; but the case I have been describing, was the end of the brutification to which slavery had subjected me.

The reader will be glad to know why, after I had so grievously offended Mr. Covey, he did not have me taken in hand by the authorities; indeed, why the law of Maryland, which assigns hanging to the slave who resists his master, was not put in force against me; at any rate, why I was not taken up, as is usual in such cases, and publicly whipped, for an example to other slaves, and as a means of deterring me from committing the same offense again. I confess, that the easy manner in which I got off, was for a long time, a surprise to me, and I cannot, even now, fully explain the cause.

The only explanation I can venture to suggest, is the fact, that Covey was, probably, ashamed to have it known and confessed that he had been mastered by a boy of sixteen. Mr. Covey enjoyed the unbounded and very valuable reputation, of being a first rate overseer and *Negro breaker.* By means of this reputation, he was able to procure his hands for *very trifling* compensation, and with very great ease. His interest and his pride mutually suggested the wisdom of passing the matter by, in silence. The story that he had undertaken to whip a lad, and had been resisted, was, of itself, sufficient to damage him; for his bearing should, in the estimation of slaveholders, be of that imperial order that should make such an occurrence *impossible.* I judge from these circumstances, that Covey deemed it best to give me the go-by. It is, perhaps, not altogether creditable to my natural temper, that, after this conflict with Mr. Covey, I did, at times, purposely aim to provoke him to an attack, by refusing to keep with the other hands in the field, but I could never bully him to another battle. I had made up my mind to do him serious damage, if he ever again attempted to lay violent hands on me.

> Hereditary bondmen, know ye not
> Who would be free, themselves must strike the blow?

K*

---

* From *Childe Harold's Pilgrimage* by George Gordon, Lord Byron.

# CHAPTER XVIII

## NEW RELATIONS AND DUTIES

*Change of Master—Benefits Derived by the Change—Fame of the Fight with Covey—Reckless Unconcern—My Abhorrence of Slavery—Ability to Read a Cause of Prejudice—The Holidays—How Spent—Sharp Hit at Slavery—Effects of Holidays—A Device of Slavery—Difference Between Covey and Freeland—An Irreligious Master Preferred to a Religious One—Catalogue of Floggable Offenses—Hard Life at Covey's Useful—Improved Condition Not Followed by Contentment—Congenial Society at Freeland's—Sabbath School Instituted—Secrecy Necessary—Affectionate Relations of Tutor and Pupils—Confidence and Friendship Among Slaves—I Decline Publishing Particulars of Conversations with My Friends—Slavery the Inviter of Vengeance.*

My term of actual service to Mr. Edward Covey ended on Christmas day, 1834. I gladly left the snakish Covey, although he was now as gentle as a lamb. My home for the year 1835 was already secured—my next master was already selected. There is always more or less excitement about the matter of changing hands, but I had become somewhat reckless. I cared very little into whose hands I fell—I meant to fight my way. Despite of Covey, too, the report got abroad, that I was hard to whip; that I was guilty of kicking back; that though generally a good tempered Negro, I sometimes "*got the devil in me.*" These sayings were rife in Talbot County, and they distinguished me among my servile brethren. Slaves, generally, will fight each other, and die at each other's hands; but there are few who are not held in awe by a white man. Trained from the cradle up, to think and feel that their masters are superior, and invested with a sort of sacredness, there are few who can outgrow or rise above the control which that sentiment exercises. I had now got free from it, and the thing was known. One bad sheep will spoil a whole flock. Among the slaves, I was a bad sheep.

I hated slavery, slaveholders, and all pertaining to them; and I did not fail to inspire others with the same feeling, wherever and whenever opportunity was presented. This made me a marked lad among the slaves, and a suspected one among the slaveholders. A knowledge of my ability to read and write, got pretty widely spread, which was very much against me.

The days between Christmas day and New Year's, are allowed the slaves as holidays. During these days, all regular work was suspended, and there was nothing to do but to keep fires, and look after the stock. This time was regarded as our own, by the grace of our masters, and we, therefore used it, or abused it, as we pleased. Those who had families at a distance, were now expected to visit them, and to spend with them the entire week. The younger slaves, or the unmarried ones, were expected to see to the cattle, and attend to incidental duties at home. The holidays were variously spent. The sober, thinking and industrious ones of our number, would employ themselves in manufacturing corn brooms, mats, horse collars and baskets, and some of these were very well made. Another class spent their time in hunting opossums, coons, rabbits, and other game. But the majority spent the holidays in sports, ball playing, wrestling, boxing, running foot races, dancing, and drinking whisky; and this latter mode of spending the time was generally most agreeable to their masters. A slave who would work during the holidays, was thought, by his master, undeserving of holidays. Such an one had rejected the favor of his master. There was, in this simple act of continued work, an accusation against slaves; and a slave could not help thinking, that if he made three dollars during the holidays, he might make three hundred during the year. Not to be drunk during the holidays, was disgraceful; and he was esteemed a lazy and improvident man, who could not afford to drink whisky during Christmas.

The fiddling, dancing and "*jubilee beating*," was going on in all directions. This latter performance is strictly southern. It supplies the place of a violin, or of other musical instruments, and is played so easily, that almost every farm has its "Juba" beater. The performer improvises as he beats, and sings his merry songs, so ordering the words as to have them fall pat with the movement of his hands. Among a mass of nonsense and wild frolic, once in a while a sharp hit is given to the meanness of slaveholders. Take the following, for an example:

We raise de wheat,
Dey gib us de corn;
We bake de bread,
Dey gib us de cruss;
We sif de meal,
Dey gib us de huss;
We peal de meat,
Dey gib us de skin,
And dat's de way
Dey takes us in.
We skim de pot,
Dey gib us the liquor,
And say dat's good enough for nigger.
    Walk over! Walk over!
    Tom butter and de fat;
    Poor nigger you can't get over dat;
                Walk over!

This is not a bad summary of the palpable injustice and fraud of slavery, giving—as it does—to the lazy and idle, the comforts which God designed should be given solely to the honest laborer. But to the holidays.

Judging from my own observation and experience, I believe these holidays to be among the most effective means, in the hands of slaveholders, of keeping down the spirit of insurrection among the slaves.

To enslave men, successfully and safely, it is necessary to have their minds occupied with thoughts and aspirations short of the liberty of which they are deprived. A certain degree of attainable good must be kept before them. These holidays serve the purpose of keeping the minds of the slaves occupied with prospective pleasure, within the limits of slavery. The young man can go wooing; the married man can visit his wife; the father and mother can see their children; the industrious and money loving can make a few dollars; the great wrestler can win laurels; the young people can meet, and enjoy each other's society; the drunken man can get plenty of whisky; and the religious man can hold prayer meetings, preach, pray and exhort during the holidays. Before the holidays, these are pleasures in prospect; after the holidays, they become pleasures of memory, and they serve to keep out thoughts and wishes of a more dangerous character. Were slaveholders at once to abandon the practice of allowing their slaves these liberties, periodically, and to keep them, the year round, closely confined to the narrow circle of their homes, I doubt not that the south would blaze with insurrections. These holidays are conductors or safety valves to carry off the explosive elements inseparable from the human mind, when reduced to the condition of slavery. But for these, the rigors of bondage would become too severe for endurance, and the slave would be forced up to dangerous desperation. Woe to the slaveholder when he undertakes to hinder or to prevent the operation of these electric conductors. A succession of earthquakes would be less destructive, than the insurrectionary fires which would be sure to burst forth in different parts of the south, from such interference.

Thus, the holidays, became part and parcel of the gross fraud, wrongs and inhumanity of slavery. Ostensibly, they are institutions of benevolence, designed to mitigate the rigors of slave life, but, practically, they are a fraud, instituted by human selfishness, the better to secure the ends of injustice and oppression. The slave's happiness is not the end sought, but, rather, the master's safety. It is not from a generous unconcern for the slave's labor that this cessation from labor is allowed, but from a prudent regard to the safety of the slave system. I am strengthened in this opinion, by the fact, that most slaveholders like to have their slaves spend the holidays in such a manner as to be of no real benefit to the slaves. It is plain, that everything like rational enjoyment among the slaves, is frowned upon; and only those wild and low sports, peculiar to semi-civilized people, are encouraged. All the license allowed, appears to have no other object than to disgust the slaves with their temporary freedom, and to make them as glad to return to their work, as they were to leave it. By plunging them into exhausting depths of drunkenness and dissipation, this effect is almost certain to follow. I have known slaveholders resort to cunning tricks, with a view of getting their slaves deplorably drunk. A usual plan is, to make bets on a slave, that he can drink more whisky than any other; and so to induce a rivalry among them, for the mastery in this degradation. The scenes, brought about in this way, were often scandalous and loathsome in the extreme. Whole multitudes might be found stretched out in brutal drunkenness, at once helpless and disgusting. Thus, when the slave asks for a few hours of virtuous freedom, his cunning master takes advantage of his ignorance, and cheers him with a dose of vicious and revolting dissipation, artfully labeled with the name of *liberty*. We were induced to drink, I among the rest, and when the holidays were over, we all staggered up from our filth and wallowing, took a long breath, and went away to our various fields of work; feeling, upon the whole, rather glad to go from that which our masters artfully deceived us into the belief was freedom, back again to the arms of slavery. It was not what we had taken it to be, nor what it might have been, had it not been abused by us. It was about as well to be a slave to *master*, as to be a slave to *rum* and *whisky*.

I am the more induced to take this view of the holiday system, adopted by slaveholders, from what I know of their treatment of slaves, in regard to other things. It is the commonest thing for them to try to disgust their slaves with what they do not want them to have, or to enjoy. A slave, for instance, likes molasses; he steals some; to cure him of the taste for it, his master, in many cases, will go away to town, and buy a large quantity of the *poorest* quality, and set it before his slave, and, with whip in hand, compel him to eat it, until the poor fellow is made to sicken at the very thought of molasses. The same course is often adopted to cure slaves of the disagreeable and inconvenient practice of asking for more food, when their allowance has failed them. The same disgusting process works well, too, in other things, but I need not cite them. When a slave is drunk, the slaveholder has no fear that he will plan an insurrection; no fear that he will escape to the north. It is the sober, thinking slave who is dangerous, and needs the vigilance of his master, to keep him a slave. But, to proceed with my narrative.

On the first of January, 1835, I proceeded from St. Michael's to Mr. William Freeland's, my new home. Mr. Freeland lived only three miles from St. Michael's, on an old worn out farm, which required much labor to restore it to anything like a self-supporting establishment.

I was not long in finding Mr. Freeland to be a very different man from Mr. Covey. Though not rich, Mr. Freeland was what may be called a well-bred southern gentleman, as different from Covey, as a well-trained and hardened Negro breaker is from the best specimen of the first families of the south. Though Freeland was a slaveholder, and shared many of the vices of his class, he seemed alive to the sentiment of honor. He had some sense of justice, and some feelings of humanity. He was fretful, impulsive and passionate, but I must do him the justice to say, he was free from the mean and selfish characteristics which distinguished the creature from which I had now, happily, escaped. He was open, frank, imperative, and practiced no concealments, disdaining to play the spy. In all this, he was the opposite of the crafty Covey.

Among the many advantages gained in my change from Covey's to Freeland's—startling as the statement may be—was the fact that the latter gentleman made no profession of religion. I assert *most unhesitatingly*, that the religion of the south—as I have observed it and proved it—is a mere covering for the most horrid crimes; the justifier of the most appalling barbarity; a sanctifier of the most hateful frauds; and a secure shelter, under which the darkest, foulest, grossest, and most infernal abominations fester and flourish. Were I again to be reduced to the condition of a slave, *next* to that calamity, I should regard the fact of being the slave of a religious slaveholder, the greatest that could befall me. For all slaveholders with whom I have ever met, religious slaveholders are the worst. I have found them, almost invariably, the vilest, meanest and basest of their class. Exceptions there may be, but this is true of religious slaveholders, *as a class*. It is not for me to explain the fact. Others may do that; I simply state it as a fact, and leave the theological, and psychological inquiry, which it raises, to be decided by others more competent than myself. Religious slaveholders, like religious persecutors, are ever extreme in their malice and violence. Very near my new home, on an adjoining farm, there lived the Rev. Daniel Weeden, who was both pious and cruel after the real Covey pattern. Mr. Weeden was a local preacher of the Protestant Methodist persuasion, and a most zealous supporter of the ordinances of religion, generally. This Weeden owned a woman called "Ceal," who was a standing proof of his mercilessness. Poor Ceal's back, always scantily clothed, was kept literally raw, by the lash of this religious man and gospel minister. The most notoriously wicked man—so called in distinction from church members—could hire hands more easily than this brute. When sent out to find a home, a slave would never enter the gates of the preacher Weeden, while a sinful sinner needed a hand. Behave ill, or behave well, it was the known maxim of Weeden, that it is the duty of a master to use the lash. If, for no other reason, he contended that this was essential to remind a slave of his condition, and of his master's authority. The good slave must be whipped, to be *kept* good, and the bad slave must be whipped, to be *made* good. Such was Weeden's theory, and such was his practice. The back of his slave-woman will, in the judgment, be the swiftest witness against him.

While I am stating particular cases, I might as well immortalize another of my neighbors, by calling him by name, and putting him in print. He did not think that a "chiel" was near, "taking notes," and will, doubtless, feel quite angry at having his character touched off in the ragged style of a slave's pen. I beg to introduce the reader to Rev. Rigby Hopkins. Mr. Hopkins resides between Easton and St. Michael's, in Talbot County, Maryland. The severity of this man made him a perfect terror to the slaves of his neighborhood. The peculiar feature of his government, was, his system of whipping slaves, as he said, *in advance* of deserving it. He always managed to have one or two slaves to whip on Monday morning, so as to start his hands to their work, under the inspiration of a new assurance on Monday, that his preaching about kindness, mercy, brotherly love, and the like, on Sunday, did not interfere with, or prevent him from establishing his authority, by the cowskin. He seemed to wish to assure them, that his tears over poor, lost and ruined sinners, and his pity for them, did not reach to the blacks who tilled his fields. This saintly Hopkins used to boast, that he was the best hand to manage a Negro in the county. He whipped for the smallest offenses, by way of preventing the commission of large ones.

The reader might imagine a difficulty in finding faults enough for such frequent whipping. But this is because you have no idea how easy a matter it is to offend a man who is on the look-out for offenses. The man, unaccustomed to slaveholding, would be astonished to observe how many *floggable* offenses there are in the slaveholder's catalogue of crimes; and how easy it is to commit any one of them, even when the slave least intends it. A slaveholder, bent on finding fault, will hatch up a dozen a day, if he chooses to do so, and each one of these shall be of a punishable description. A mere look, word, or motion, a mistake, accident, or want of power, are all matters for which a slave may be whipped at any time. Does a slave look dissatisfied with his condition? It is said, that he has the devil in him, and it must be whipped out. Does he answer *loudly*, when spoken to by his master, with an air of self-consciousness? Then, must he be taken down a button-hole lower, by the lash, well laid on. Does he forget, and omit to pull off his hat, when approaching a white person? Then, he must, or may be, whipped for his bad manners. Does he ever venture to vindicate his conduct, when harshly and unjustly accused? Then, he is guilty of impudence, one of the greatest crimes in the social catalogue of southern society. To allow a slave to escape punishment, who has impudently attempted to exculpate himself from unjust charges, preferred against him by some white person, is to be guilty of great dereliction of duty. Does a slave ever venture to suggest a better way of doing a thing, no matter what? He is, altogether, too officious—wise above what is written—and he deserves, even if he does not get, a flogging for his presumption. Does he, while plowing, break a plow, or while hoeing, break a hoe, or while chopping, break an ax? No matter what were the imperfections of the implement broken, or the natural liabilities for breaking, the slave can be whipped for carelessness. The *reverend* slaveholder could always find something of this sort, to justify him in using the lash several times during the week. Hopkins—like Covey and Weeden—were shunned by slaves who had the privilege (as many had) of finding their own masters at the end of each year; and yet, there was not a man in all that section of country, who made a louder profession of religion, than did Mr. Rigby Hopkins.

But, to continue the thread of my story, through my experience when at Mr. William Freeland's.

My poor, weather-beaten bark now reached smoother water, and gentler breezes. My stormy life at Covey's had been of service to me. The things that would have seemed very hard, had I gone direct to Mr. Freeland's, from the home of Master Thomas, were now (after the hardships at Covey's) "trifles light as air."* I was still a field hand, and had come to prefer the severe labor of the field, to the enervating duties of a house servant. I had become large and strong; and had begun to take pride in the fact, that I could do as much hard work as some of the older men. There is much rivalry among slaves, at times, as to which can do the most work, and masters generally seek to promote such rivalry. But some of us were too wise to race with each other very long. Such racing, we had the sagacity to see, was not likely to pay. We had our times for measuring each other's strength, but we knew too much to keep up the competition so long as to produce an extraordinary day's work. We knew that if, by extraordinary exertion, a large quantity of work was done in one day, the fact, becoming known to the master, might lead him to require the same amount every day. This thought

---

* From *Othello* by William Shakespeare.

was enough to bring us to a dead halt when ever so much excited for the race.

At Mr. Freeland's, my condition was every way improved. I was no longer the poor scape-goat that I was when at Covey's, where every wrong thing done was saddled upon me, and where other slaves were whipped over my shoulders. Mr. Freeland was too just a man thus to impose upon me, or upon any one else.

It is quite usual to make one slave the object of especial abuse, and to beat him often, with a view to its effect upon others, rather than with any expectation that the slave whipped will be improved by it, but the man with whom I now was, could descend to no such meanness and wickedness. Every man here was held individually responsible for his own conduct.

This was a vast improvement on the rule at Covey's. There, I was the general pack horse. Bill Smith was protected, by a positive prohibition made by his rich master, and the command of the rich slaveholder is *law* to the poor one; Hughes was favored, because of his relationship to Covey; and the hands hired temporarily, escaped flogging, except as they got it over my poor shoulders. Of course, this comparison refers to the time when Covey *could* whip me.

Mr. Freeland, like Mr. Covey, gave his hands enough to eat, but, unlike Mr. Covey, he gave them time to take their meals; he worked us hard during the day, but gave us the night for rest—another advantage to be set to the credit of the sinner, as against that of the saint. We were seldom in the field after dark in the evening, or before sunrise in the morning. Our implements of husbandry were of the most improved pattern, and much superior to those used at Covey's.

Notwithstanding the improved condition which was now mine, and the many advantages I had gained by my new home, and my new master, I was still restless and discontented. I was about as hard to please by a master, as a master is by slave. The freedom from bodily torture and unceasing labor, had given my mind an increased sensibility, and imparted to it greater activity. I was not yet exactly in right relations. "How be it, that was not first which is spiritual, but that which is natural, and afterward that which is spiritual."* When entombed at Covey's, shrouded in darkness and physical wretchedness, temporal well-being was the grand *desideratum*; but, temporal wants supplied,

---

* From the Bible, I Corinthians 15:46.

the spirit puts in its claims. Beat and cuff your slave, keep him hungry and spiritless, and he will follow the chain of his master like a dog; but, feed and clothe him well—work him moderately—surround him with physical comfort—and dreams of freedom intrude. Give him a *bad* master, and he aspires to a *good* master; give him a good master, and he wishes to become his *own* master. Such is human nature. You may hurl a man so low, beneath the level of his kind, that he loses all just ideas of his natural position; but elevate him a little, and the clear conception of rights arises to life and power, and leads him onward. Thus elevated, a little, at Freeland's, the dreams called into being by that good man, Father Lawson, when in Baltimore, began to visit me; and shoots from the tree of liberty began to put forth tender buds, and dim hopes of the future began to dawn.

I found myself in congenial society, at Mr. Freeland's. There were Henry Harris, John Harris, Handy Caldwell, and Sandy Jenkins.*

Henry and John were brothers, and belonged to Mr. Freeland. They were both remarkably bright and intelligent, though neither of them could read. Now for mischief! I had not been long at Freeland's before I was up to my old tricks. I early began to address my companions on the subject of education, and the advantages of intelligence over ignorance, and, as far as I dared, I tried to show the agency of ignorance in keeping men in slavery. *Webster's Spelling Book* and the *Columbian Orator* were looked into again. As summer came on, and the long Sabbath days stretched themselves over our idleness, I became uneasy, and wanted a Sabbath school, in which to exercise my gifts, and to impart the little knowledge of letters which I possessed, to my brother slaves. A house was hardly necessary in the summer time; I could hold my school under the shade of an old oak tree, as well as any where else. The thing was, to get the scholars, and to have them thoroughly imbued with the desire to learn. Two such boys were quickly secured, in Henry and John, and from them the contagion spread. I was not long bringing around me twenty or thirty young men, who enrolled themselves, gladly, in my Sabbath school, and were willing to meet me regularly, under the trees or elsewhere, for the purpose of learning to read. It was surprising with

---

* This is the same man who gave me the roots to prevent my being whipped by Mr. Covey. He was "a clever soul." We used frequently to talk about the fight with Covey, and as often as we did so, he would claim my success as the result of the roots which he gave me. This superstition is very common among the more ignorant slaves. A slave seldom dies, but that his death is attributed to trickery. (Original note)

what ease they provided themselves with spelling books. These were mostly the cast off books of their young masters or mistresses. I taught, at first, on our own farm. All were impressed with the necessity of keeping the matter as private as possible, for the fate of the St. Michael's attempt was notorious, and fresh in the minds of all. Our pious masters, at St. Michael's, must not know that a few of their dusky brothers were learning to read the word of God, lest they should come down upon us with the lash and chain. We might have met to drink whisky, to wrestle, fight, and to do other unseemly things, with no fear of interruption from the saints or sinners of St. Michael's.

But, to meet for the purpose of improving the mind and heart, by learning to read the sacred scriptures, was esteemed a most dangerous nuisance, to be instantly stopped. The slaveholders of St. Michael's, like slaveholders elsewhere, would always prefer to see the slaves engaged in degrading sports, rather than to see them acting like moral and accountable beings.

Had any one asked a religious white man, in St. Michael's, twenty years ago, the names of three men in that town, whose lives were most after the pattern of our Lord and Master, Jesus Christ, the first three would have been as follows:

> Garrison West, *Class-Leader*.
> Wright Fairbanks, *Class-Leader*.
> Thomas Auld, *Class-Leader*.

And yet, these were men who ferociously rushed in upon my Sabbath school, at St. Michael's, armed with mob-like missiles, and forbade our meeting again, on pain of having our backs made bloody by the lash. This same Garrison West was my class-leader, and I must say, I thought him a Christian, until he took part in breaking up my school. He led me no more after that. The plea for this outrage was then, as it is now and at all times—the danger to good order. If the slaves learnt to read, they would learn something else, and something worse. The peace of slavery would be disturbed; slave rule would be endangered. I leave the reader to characterize a system which is endangered by such causes. I do not dispute the soundness of the reasoning. It is perfectly sound; and, if slavery be *right*, Sabbath schools for teaching slaves to read the Bible are *wrong*, and ought to be put down. These Christian class-leaders were, to this extent, consistent. They had settled the question, that slavery is *right*, and, by that standard, they determined that Sabbath schools are wrong. To be sure, they were Protestant, and held to the great Protestant right of every man to *"search the scriptures"* for himself; but, then, to all general rules, there are *exceptions*. How convenient! What crimes may not be committed under the doctrine of the last remark. But, my dear, class leading Methodist brethren, did not condescend to give me a reason for breaking up the Sabbath school at St. Michael's; it was enough that they had determined upon its destruction. I am, however, digressing.

After getting the school cleverly into operation, the second time—holding it in the woods, behind the barn, and in the shade of trees—I succeeded in inducing a free colored man, who lived several miles from our house, to permit me to hold my school in a room at his house. He, very kindly, gave me this liberty; but he incurred much peril in doing so, for the assemblage was an unlawful one. I shall not mention, here, the name of this man; for it might, even now, subject him to persecution, although the offenses were committed more than twenty years ago. I had, at one time, more than forty scholars, all of the right sort; and many of them succeeded in learning to read. I have met several slaves from Maryland, who were once my scholars; and who obtained their freedom, I doubt not, partly in consequence of the ideas imparted to them in that school. I have had various employments during my short life; but I look back to *none* with more satisfaction, than to that afforded by my Sunday school. An attachment, deep and lasting, sprung up between me and my persecuted pupils, which made parting from them intensely grievous; and, when I think that most of these dear souls are yet shut up in this abject thralldom, I am overwhelmed with grief.

Besides my Sunday school, I devoted three evenings a week to my fellow-slaves, during the winter. Let the reader reflect upon the fact, that, in this Christian country, men and women are hiding from professors of religion, in barns, in the woods and fields, in order to learn to read the *Holy Bible*. Those dear souls, who came to my Sabbath school, came not because it was popular or reputable to attend such a place, for they came under the liability of having forty stripes laid on their naked backs. Every moment they spent in my school, they were under this terrible liability; and, in this respect, I was a sharer with them. Their minds had been cramped and starved by their cruel masters; the light of education had been completely excluded; and their hard earnings had been taken to educate their master's children. I felt a delight in circumventing the tyrants, and in blessing the victims of their curses.

The year at Mr. Freeland's passed off very smoothly, to outward seeming. Not a blow was given me during the whole year. To the credit of Mr. Freeland—irreligious though he was—it must be stated, that he was the best master I ever had, until I became my own master, and assumed for myself, as I had a right to do, the responsibility of my own existence and the exercise of my own powers. For much of the happiness—or absence of misery—with which I passed this year with Mr. Freeland, I am indebted to the genial temper and ardent friendship of my brother-slaves. They were, every one of them, manly, generous and brave, yes; I say they were brave, and I will add, fine looking. It is seldom the lot of mortals to have truer and better friends than were the slaves on this farm. It is not uncommon to charge slaves with great treachery toward each other, and to believe them incapable of confiding in each other; but I must say, that I never loved, esteemed, or confided in men, more than I did in these. They were as true as steel, and no band of brothers could have been more loving. There were no mean advantages taken of each other, as is sometimes the case where slaves are situated as we were; no tattling; no giving each other bad names to Mr. Freeland; and no elevating one at the expense of the other. We never undertook to do any thing, of any importance, which was likely to affect each other, without mutual consultation. We were generally a unit, and moved together. Thoughts and sentiments were exchanged between us, which might well be called very incendiary, by oppressors and tyrants; and perhaps the time has not even now come, when it is safe to unfold all the flying suggestions which arise in the minds of intelligent slaves. Several of my friends and brothers, if yet alive, are still in some part of the house of bondage; and though twenty years have passed away, the suspicious malice of slavery might punish them for even listening to my thoughts.

The slaveholder, kind or cruel, is a slaveholder still—the every hour violator of the just and inalienable rights of man; and he is, therefore, every hour silently whetting the knife of vengeance for his own throat. He never lisps a syllable in commendation of the fathers of this republic, nor denounces any attempted oppression of himself, without inviting the knife to his own throat, and asserting the rights of rebellion for his own slaves.

The year is ended, and we are now in the midst of the Christmas holidays, which are kept this year as last, according to the general description previously given.

# CHAPTER XIX

## THE RUN-AWAY PLOT

*New Year's Thoughts and Meditations—Again Bought
by Freeland—No Ambition to Be a Slave—Kindness No
Compensation for Slavery—Incipient Steps Toward Escape—
Considerations Leading Thereto—Irreconcilable Hostility
to Slavery—Solemn Vow Taken—Plan Divulged to the
Slaves—*Columbian Orator*—Scheme Gains Favor, Despite
Pro-Slavery Preaching—Danger of Discovery—Skill of
Slaveholders in Reading the Minds of Their Slaves—Suspicion
and Coercion—Hymns with Double Meaning—Value, in
Dollars, of Our Company—Preliminary Consulation—
Pass-word—Conflicts of Hope and Fear—Difficulties
to Be Overcome—Ignorance of Geography—Survey of
Imaginary Difficulties—Effect on Our Minds—Patrick
Henry—Sandy Becomes a Dreamer—Route to the North
Laid Out—Objections Considered—Frauds Practiced on
Freemen—Passes Written—Anxieties as the Time Drew
Near—Dread of Failure—Appeals to Comrades—Strange
Presentiment—Coincidence—The Betrayal Discovered—The
Manner of Arresting Us—Resistance Made by Henry Harris—
Its Effect—The Unique Speech of Mrs. Freeland—Our Sad
Procession to Prison—Brutal Jeers By the Multitude Along the
Road—Passes Eaten—The Denial—Sandy Too Well Loved to
Be Suspected—Dragged Behind Horses—The Jail a Relief—A
New Set of Tormentors—Slave-Traders—John, Charles and
Henry Released—Alone in Prison—I Am Taken Out, and Sent
to Baltimore.*

I am now at the beginning of the year 1836, a time favorable for serious
thoughts. The mind naturally occupies itself with the mysteries of
life in all its phases—the ideal, the real and the actual. Sober people
look both ways at the beginning of the year, surveying the errors of
the past, and providing against possible errors of the future. I, too,

was thus exercised. I had little pleasure in retrospect, and the prospect was not very brilliant. "Notwithstanding," thought I, "the many resolutions and prayers I have made, in behalf of freedom, I am, this first day of the year 1836, still a slave, still wandering in the depths of spirit-devouring thralldom. My faculties and powers of body and soul are not my own, but are the property of a fellow-mortal, in no sense superior to me, except that he has the physical power to compel me to be owned and controlled by him. By the combined physical force of the community, I am his slave—a slave for life." With thoughts like these, I was perplexed and chafed; they rendered me gloomy and disconsolate. The anguish of my mind may not be written.

At the close of the year 1835, Mr. Freeland, my temporary master, had bought me of Capt. Thomas Auld, for the year 1836. His promptness in securing my services, would have been flattering to my vanity, had I been ambitious to win the reputation of being a valuable slave. Even as it was, I felt a slight degree of complacency at the circumstance. It showed he was as well pleased with me as a slave, as I was with him as a master. I have already intimated my regard for Mr. Freeland, and I may say here, in addressing northern readers—where there is no selfish motive for speaking in praise of a slaveholder—that Mr. Freeland was a man of many excellent qualities, and to me quite preferable to any master I ever had.

But the kindness of the slave-master only gilds the chain of slavery, and detracts nothing from its weight or power. The thought that men are made for other and better uses than slavery, thrives best under the gentle treatment of a kind master. But the grim visage of slavery can assume no smiles which can fascinate the partially enlightened slave, into a forgetfulness of his bondage, nor of the desirableness of liberty.

I was not through the first month of this, my second year with the kind and gentlemanly Mr. Freeland, before I was earnestly considering and advising plans for gaining that freedom, which, when I was but a mere child, I had ascertained to be the natural and inborn right of every member of the human family. The desire for this freedom had been benumbed, while I was under the brutalizing dominion of Covey; and it had been postponed, and rendered inoperative, by my truly pleasant Sunday school engagements with my friends, during the year 1835, at Mr. Freeland's. It had, however, never entirely subsided. I hated slavery, always, and the desire for freedom only needed a favorable breeze, to fan it into a blaze, at any moment. The thought of only being a creature of the *present* and the *past*, troubled me, and I longed to have a *future*—a future with hope in it. To be shut up entirely to the past and present, is abhorrent to the human mind; it is to the soul—whose life and happiness is unceasing progress—what the prison is to the body; a blight and mildew, a hell of horrors. The dawning of this, another year, awakened me from my temporary slumber, and roused into life my latent, but long cherished aspirations for freedom. I was now not only ashamed to be contented in slavery, but ashamed to *seem* to be contented, and in my present favorable condition, under the mild rule of Mr. F., I am not sure that some kind reader will not condemn me for being over ambitious, and greatly wanting in proper humility, when I say the truth, that I now drove from me all thoughts of making the best of my lot, and welcomed only such thoughts as led me away from the house of bondage. The intense desires, now felt, *to be free*, quickened by my present favorable circumstances, brought me to the determination to *act*, as well as to think and speak. Accordingly, at the beginning of this year 1836, I took upon me a solemn vow, that the year which had now dawned upon me should not close, without witnessing an earnest attempt, on my part, to gain my liberty. This vow only bound me to make my escape individually; but the year spent with Mr. Freeland had attached me, as with "hooks of steel," to my brother slaves. The most affectionate and confiding friendship existed between us; and I felt it my duty to give them an opportunity to share in my virtuous determination by frankly disclosing to them my plans and purposes. Toward Henry and John Harris, I felt a friendship as strong as one man can feel for another; for I could have died with and for them. To them, therefore, with a suitable degree of caution, I began to disclose my sentiments and plans; sounding them, the while, on the subject of running away, provided a good chance should offer. I scarcely need tell the reader, that I did my *very best* to imbue the minds of my dear friends with my own views and feelings. Thoroughly awakened, now, and with a definite vow upon me, all my little reading, which had any bearing on the subject of human rights, was rendered available in my communications with my friends. That (to me) gem of a book, the *Columbian Orator*, with its eloquent orations and spicy dialogues, denouncing oppression and slavery—telling of what had been dared, done and suffered by men, to obtain the inestimable boon of liberty—was still fresh in my memory, and whirled into the ranks of my speech with the aptitude of well trained soldiers, going through the drill. The fact is, I here began my public speaking. I canvassed, with Henry and John, the subject of slavery, and dashed against it the condemning brand of God's eternal justice, which it every hour violates. My fellow-servants were neither indifferent, dull, nor inapt. Our feelings were more alike than our opinions. All, however, were ready to act, when a feasible plan should be proposed. "Show us *how* the thing is to be done," said they, "and all is clear."

We were all, except Sandy, quite free from slaveholding priestcraft. It was in vain that we had been taught from the pulpit at St. Michael's, the duty of obedience to our masters; to recognize God as the author of our enslavement; to regard running away an offense, alike against God and man; to deem our enslavement a merciful and beneficial arrangement; to esteem our condition, in this country, a paradise to that from which we had been snatched in Africa; to consider our hard hands and dark color as God's mark of displeasure, and as pointing us out as the proper subjects of slavery; that the relation of master and slave was one of reciprocal benefits; that our work was not more serviceable to our masters, than our master's thinking was serviceable to us. I say, it was in vain that the pulpit of St. Michael's had constantly inculcated these plausible doctrine. Nature laughed them to scorn. For my own part, I had now become altogether too big for my chains. Father Lawson's solemn words, of what I ought to be, and might be, in the providence of God, had not fallen dead on my soul. I was fast verging toward manhood, and the prophecies of my childhood were still unfulfilled. The thought, that year after year had passed away, and my resolutions to run away had failed and faded—that I was *still a slave*, and a slave, too, with chances for gaining my freedom diminished and still diminishing—was not a matter to be slept over easily: nor did I easily sleep over it.

But here came a new trouble. Thoughts and purposes so incendiary as those I now cherished, could not agitate the mind long, without danger of making themselves manifest to scrutinizing and unfriendly beholders. I had reason to fear that my sable face might prove altogether too transparent for the safe concealment of my hazardous enterprise. Plans of greater moment have leaked through stone walls, and revealed their projectors. But, here was no stone wall to hide my purpose. I would have given my poor, tell tale face for the immoveable countenance of an Indian, for it was far from being proof against the daily, searching glances of those with whom I met.

It is the interest and business of slaveholders to study human nature, with a view to practical results, and many of them attain astonishing proficiency in discerning the thoughts and emotions of slaves. They have to deal not with earth, wood, or stone, but with men; and, by every regard they have for their safety and prosperity, they must study to know the material on which they are at work. So much intellect as the slaveholder has around him, requires watching. Their safety depends upon their vigilance. Conscious of the injustice and wrong they are every hour perpetrating, and knowing what they themselves would do if made the victims of such wrongs, they are looking out for the first signs of the dread retribution of justice. They watch, therefore, with skilled and practiced eyes, and have learned to read, with great accuracy, the state of mind and heart of the slaves, through his sable face. These uneasy sinners are quick to inquire into the matter, where the slave is concerned. Unusual sobriety, apparent abstraction, sullenness and indifference—indeed, any mood out of the common way—afford ground for suspicion and inquiry. Often relying on their superior position and wisdom, they hector and torture the slave into a confession, by affecting to know the truth of their accusations. "You have got the devil in you," say they, "and we will whip him out of you." I have often been put thus to the torture, on bare suspicion. This system has its disadvantages as well as their opposite. The slave is sometimes whipped into the confession of offenses which he never committed. The reader will see that the good old rule—"a man is to be held innocent until proved to be guilty"—does not hold good on the slave plantation. Suspicion and torture are the approved methods of getting at the truth, here. It was necessary for me, therefore, to keep a watch over my deportment, lest the enemy should get the better of me.

But with all our caution and studied reserve, I am not sure that Mr. Freeland did not suspect that all was not right with us. It did seem that he watched us more narrowly, after the plan of escape had been conceived and discussed amongst us. Men seldom see themselves as others see them; and while, to ourselves, everything connected with our contemplated escape appeared concealed, Mr. Freeland may have, with the peculiar prescience of a slaveholder, mastered the huge thought which was disturbing our peace in slavery.

I am the more inclined to think that he suspected us, because, prudent as we were, as I now look back, I can see that we did many silly things, very well calculated to awaken suspicion. We were, at times, remarkably buoyant, singing hymns and making joyous exclamations, almost as triumphant in their tone as if we reached a land of freedom and safety. A keen observer might have detected in our repeated singing of

> O Canaan, sweet Canaan,
> I am bound for the land of Canaan,

something more than a hope of reaching heaven. We meant to reach the *north*—and the north was our Canaan.

> I thought I heard them say,
> There were lions in the way,
> I don't expect to stay
>     Much longer here.
>
> Run to Jesus—shun the danger—
> I don't expect to stay
>     Much longer here.

was a favorite air, and had a double meaning. In the lips of some, it meant the expectation of a speedy summons to a world of spirits; but, in the lips of *our* company, it simply meant, a speedy pilgrimage toward a free state, and deliverance from all the evils and dangers of slavery.

I had succeeded in winning to my (what slaveholders would call wicked) scheme, a company of five young men, the very flower of the neighborhood, each one of whom would have commanded one thousand dollars in the home market. At New Orleans, they would have brought fifteen hundred dollars a piece, and, perhaps, more. The names of our party were as follows: Henry Harris; John Harris, brother to Henry; Sandy Jenkins, of root memory; Charles Roberts, and Henry Bailey. I was the youngest, but one, of the party. I had, however, the advantage of them all, in experience, and in a knowledge of letters. This gave me great influence over them. Perhaps not one of them, left to himself, would have dreamed of escape as a possible thing. Not one of them was self-moved in the matter. They all wanted to be free; but the serious thought of running away, had not entered into their minds, until I won them to the undertaking. They all were tolerably well off—for slaves—and had dim hopes of being set free, some day, by their masters. If any one is to blame for disturbing the quiet of the slaves and slave-masters of the neighborhood of St. Michael's, *I am the man*. I claim to be the instigator of the high crime (as the slaveholders regard it) and I kept life in it, until life could be kept in it no longer.

Pending the time of our contemplated departure out of our Egypt, we met often by night, and on every Sunday. At these meetings we talked the matter over; told our hopes and fears, and the difficulties discovered or imagined; and, like men of sense, we counted the cost of the enterprise to which we were committing ourselves.

These meetings must have resembled, on a small scale, the meetings of revolutionary conspirators, in their primary condition. We were plotting against our (so called) lawful rulers; with this difference that we sought our own good, and not the harm of our enemies. We did not seek to overthrow them, but to escape from them. As for Mr. Freeland, we all liked him, and would have gladly remained with him, *as freemen*. *Liberty* was our aim; and we had now come to think that we had a right to liberty, against every obstacle even against the lives of our enslavers.

We had several words, expressive of things, important to us, which we understood, but which, even if distinctly heard by an outsider, would convey no certain meaning. I have reasons for suppressing these *pass-words*, which the reader will easily divine. I hated the secrecy; but where slavery is powerful, and liberty is weak, the latter is driven to concealment or to destruction.

The prospect was not always a bright one. At times, we were almost tempted to abandon the enterprise, and to get back to that comparative peace of mind, which even a man under the gallows might feel, when all hope of escape had vanished. Quiet bondage was felt to be better than the doubts, fears and uncertainties, which now so sadly perplexed and disturbed us.

The infirmities of humanity, generally, were represented in our little band. We were confident, bold and determined, at times; and, again, doubting, timid and wavering; whistling, like the boy in the graveyard, to keep away the spirits.

To look at the map, and observe the proximity of Eastern Shore, Maryland, to Delaware and Pennsylvania, it may seem to the reader quite absurd, to regard the proposed escape as a formidable undertaking. But to *understand*, some one has said a man must *stand under*. The real distance was great enough, but the imagined distance was, to our ignorance, even greater. Every slaveholder seeks to impress his slave with a belief in the boundlessness of slave territory, and of his own almost illimitable power. We all had vague and indistinct notions of the geography of the country.

The distance, however, is not the chief trouble. The nearer are the lines of a slave state and the borders of a free one, the greater the peril. Hired kidnappers infest these borders. Then, too, we knew that merely reaching a free state did not free us; that, wherever caught, we could be returned to slavery. We could see no spot on this side the ocean, where we could be free. We had heard of Canada, the real Canaan of the American bondmen, simply as a country to which the wild goose and the swan repaired at the end of winter, to escape the heat of summer, but not as the home of man. I knew something of theology, but nothing of geography. I really did not, at that time, know that there was a state of New York, or a state of Massachusetts. I had heard of Pennsylvania, Delaware and New Jersey, and all the southern states, but was ignorant of the free states, generally. New York city was our northern limit, and to go there, and be forever harassed with the liability of being hunted down and returned to slavery—with the certainty of being treated ten times worse than we had ever been treated before—was a prospect far from delightful, and it might well cause some hesitation about engaging in the enterprise. The case, sometimes, to our excited visions, stood thus: At every gate through which we had to pass, we saw a watchman; at every ferry, a guard; on every bridge, a sentinel; and in every wood, a patrol or slave-hunter. We were hemmed in on every side. The good to be sought, and the evil to be shunned, were flung in the balance, and weighed against each other. On the one hand, there stood slavery; a stern reality, glaring frightfully upon us, with the blood of millions in his polluted skirts—terrible to behold—greedily devouring our hard earnings and feeding himself upon our flesh. Here was the evil from which to escape. On the other hand, far away, back in the hazy distance, where all forms seemed but shadows, under the flickering light of the north star—behind some craggy hill or snow-covered mountain—

stood a doubtful freedom, half frozen, beckoning us to her icy domain. This was the good to be sought. The inequality was as great as that between certainty and uncertainty. This, in itself, was enough to stagger us; but when we came to survey the untrodden road, and conjecture the many possible difficulties, we were appalled, and at times, as I have said, were upon the point of giving over the struggle altogether.

The reader can have little idea of the phantoms of trouble which flit, in such circumstances, before the uneducated mind of the slave. Upon either side, we saw grim death assuming a variety of horrid shapes. Now, it was starvation, causing us, in a strange and friendless land, to eat our own flesh. Now, we were contending with the waves (for our journey was in part by water) and were drowned. Now, we were hunted by dogs, and overtaken and torn to pieces by their merciless fangs. We were stung by scorpions—chased by wild beasts—bitten by snakes; and, worst of all, after having succeeded in swimming rivers—encountering wild beasts—sleeping in the woods—suffering hunger, cold, heat and nakedness—we supposed ourselves to be overtaken by hired kidnappers, who, in the name of the law, and for their thrice accursed reward, would, perchance, fire upon us—kill some, wound others, and capture all. This dark picture, drawn by ignorance and fear, at times greatly shook our determination, and not unfrequently caused us to

> Rather bear those ills we had
> Than fly to others which we knew not of.*

I am not disposed to magnify this circumstance in my experience, and yet I think I shall seem to be so disposed, to the reader. No man can tell the intense agony which is felt by the slave, when wavering on the point of making his escape. All that he has is at stake; and even that which he has not, is at stake, also. The life which he has, may be lost, and the liberty which he seeks, may not be gained.

Patrick Henry, to a listening senate, thrilled by his magic eloquence, and ready to stand by him in his boldest flights, could say, *give me liberty or give me death*, and this saying was a sublime one, even for a freeman; but, incomparably more sublime, is the same sentiment, when *practically* asserted by men accustomed to the lash and chain—men

---

* From *Hamlet* by William Shakespeare.

whose sensibilities must have become more or less deadened by their bondage. With us it was a *doubtful* liberty, at best, that we sought; and a certain, lingering death in the rice swamps and sugar fields, if we failed. Life is not lightly regarded by men of sane minds. It is precious, alike to the pauper and to the prince—to the slave, and to his master; and yet, I believe there was not one among us, who would not rather have been shot down, than pass away life in hopeless bondage.

In the progress of our preparations, Sandy, the root man, became troubled. He began to have dreams, and some of them were very distressing. One of these, which happened on a Friday night, was, to him, of great significance; and I am quite ready to confess, that I felt somewhat damped by it myself. He said, "I dreamed, last night, that I was roused from sleep, by strange noises, like the voices of a swarm of angry birds, that caused a roar as they passed, which fell upon my ear like a coming gale over the tops of the trees. Looking up to see what it could mean," said Sandy, "I saw you, Frederick, in the claws of a huge bird, surrounded by a large number of birds, of all colors and sizes. These were all picking at you, while you, with your arms, seemed to be trying to protect your eyes. Passing over me, the birds flew in a south-westerly direction, and I watched them until they were clean out of sight. Now, I saw this as plainly as I now see you; and furder, honey, watch de Friday night dream; dare is sumpon in it, shose you born; dare is, indeed, honey."

I confess I did not like this dream; but I threw off concern about it, by attributing it to the general excitement and perturbation consequent upon our contemplated plan of escape. I could not, however, shake off its effect at once. I felt that it boded me no good. Sandy was unusually emphatic and oracular, and his manner had much to do with the impression made upon me.

The plan of escape which I recommended, and to which my comrades assented, was to take a large canoe, owned by Mr. Hamilton, and, on the Saturday night previous to the Easter holidays, launch out into the Chesapeake Bay, and paddle for its head—a distance of seventy miles—with all our might. Our course, on reaching this point, was, to turn the canoe adrift, and bend our steps toward the north star, till we reached a free state.

There were several objections to this plan. One was, the danger from gales on the bay. In rough weather, the waters of the Chesapeake are much agitated, and there is danger, in a canoe, of being swamped by the waves. Another objection was, that the canoe would soon be missed; the absent persons would, at once, be suspected of having taken it; and we should be pursued by some of the fast sailing bay craft out of St. Michael's. Then, again, if we reached the head of the bay, and turned the canoe adrift, she might prove a guide to our track, and bring the land hunters after us.

These and other objections were set aside, by the stronger ones which could be urged against every other plan that could then be suggested. On the water, we had a chance of being regarded as fishermen, in the service of a master. On the other hand, by taking the land route, through the counties adjoining Delaware, we should be subjected to all manner of interruptions, and many very disagreeable questions, which might give us serious trouble. Any white man is authorized to stop a man of color, on any road, and examine him, and arrest him, if he so desires.

By this arrangement, many abuses (considered such even by slaveholders) occur. Cases have been known, where freemen have been called upon to show their free papers, by a pack of ruffians—and, on the presentation of the papers, the ruffians have torn them up, and seized their victim, and sold him to a life of endless bondage.

The week before our intended start, I wrote a pass for each of our party, giving them permission to visit Baltimore, during the Easter holidays. The pass ran after this manner:

> This is to certify, that I, the undersigned, have given the bearer, my servant, John, full liberty to go to Baltimore, to spend the Easter holidays.
>
> W.H.<br>Near St. Michael's,<br>Talbot County, Maryland

Although we were not going to Baltimore, and were intending to land east of North Point, in the direction where I had seen the Philadelphia steamers go, these passes might be made useful to us in the lower part of the bay, while steering toward Baltimore. These were not, however, to be shown by us, until all other answers failed to satisfy the inquirer. We were all fully alive to the importance of being calm and self-possessed, when accosted, if accosted we should be; and we more times than one rehearsed to each other how we should behave in the hour of trial.

These were long, tedious days and nights. The suspense was painful, in the extreme. To balance probabilities, where life and liberty hang on the result, requires steady nerves. I panted for action, and was glad when the day, at the close of which we were to start, dawned upon us. Sleeping, the night before, was out of the question. I probably felt more deeply than any of my companions, because I was the instigator of the movement. The responsibility of the whole enterprise rested on my shoulders. The glory of success, and the shame and confusion of failure, could not be matters of indifference to me. Our food was prepared; our clothes were packed up; we were all ready to go, and impatient for Saturday morning—considering that the last morning of our bondage.

I cannot describe the tempest and tumult of my brain, that morning. The reader will please to bear in mind, that, in a slave state, an unsuccessful runaway is not only subjected to cruel torture, and sold away to the far south, but he is frequently execrated by the other slaves. He is charged with making the condition of the other slaves intolerable, by laying them all under the suspicion of their masters—subjecting them to greater vigilance, and imposing greater limitations on their privileges. I dreaded murmurs from this quarter. It is difficult, too, for a slave-master to believe that slaves escaping have not been aided in their flight by some one of their fellow-slaves. When, therefore, a slave is missing, every slave on the place is closely examined as to his knowledge of the undertaking; and they are sometimes even tortured, to make them disclose what they are suspected of knowing of such escape.

Our anxiety grew more and more intense, as the time of our intended departure for the north drew nigh. It was truly felt to be a matter of life and death with us; and we fully intended to *fight* as well as *run*, if necessity should occur for that extremity. But the trial hour was not yet to come. It was easy to resolve, but not so easy to act. I expected there might be some drawing back, at the last. It was natural that there should be; therefore, during the intervening time, I lost no opportunity to explain away difficulties, to remove doubts, to dispel fears, and to inspire all with firmness. It was too late to look back; and *now* was the time to go forward. Like most other men, we had done the talking part of our work, long and well; and the time had come to *act* as if we were in earnest, and meant to be as true in action as in words. I did not forget to appeal to the pride of my comrades, by telling them that, if after having solemnly promised to go, as they had done, they now failed to make the attempt, they would, in effect, brand themselves with cowardice, and might as well sit down, fold their arms, and acknowledge themselves as fit only to be *slaves*. This detestable character, all were unwilling to assume. Every man except Sandy (he, much to our regret, withdrew) stood firm; and at our last meeting we pledged ourselves afresh, and in the most solemn manner, that, at the time appointed, we *would* certainly start on our long journey for a free country. This meeting was in the middle of the week, at the end of which we were to start.

Early that morning we went, as usual, to the field, but with hearts that beat quickly and anxiously. Any one intimately acquainted with us, might have seen that all was not well with us, and that some monster lingered in our thoughts. Our work that morning was the same as it had been for several days past—drawing out and spreading manure. While thus engaged, I had a sudden presentiment, which flashed upon me like lightning in a dark night, revealing to the lonely traveler the gulf before, and the enemy behind. I instantly turned to Sandy Jenkins, who was near me, and said to him, "*Sandy, we are betrayed*; something has just told me so." I felt as sure of it, as if the officers were there in sight. Sandy said, "Man, dat is strange; but I feel just as you do." If my mother—then long in her grave—had appeared before me, and told me that we were betrayed, I could not, at that moment, have felt more certain of the fact.

In a few minutes after this, the long, low and distant notes of the horn summoned us from the field to breakfast. I felt as one may be supposed to feel before being led forth to be executed for some great offense. I wanted no breakfast; but I went with the other slaves toward the house, for form's sake. My feelings were not disturbed as to the right of running away; on that point I had no trouble, whatever. My anxiety arose from a sense of the consequences of failure.

In thirty minutes after that vivid presentiment came the apprehended crash. On reaching the house, for breakfast, and glancing my eye toward the lane gate, the worst was at once made known. The lane gate off Mr. Freeland's house, is nearly a half mile from the door, and shaded by the heavy wood which bordered the main road. I was, however, able to descry four white men, and two colored men, approaching. The white men were on horseback, and the colored men were walking behind, and seemed to be tied. "*It is all over with us*," thought I, "*we are surely betrayed.*" I now became composed, or at least comparatively so, and calmly awaited the result. I watched the ill-omened company, till I saw them enter the gate. Successful flight was impossible, and I made up my mind to stand, and meet the evil, whatever it might be; for I was not without a slight hope that things might turn differently from what I at first expected. In a few moments, in came Mr. William Hamilton, riding very rapidly, and evidently much excited. He was in the habit of riding very slowly, and was seldom known to gallop his horse. This time, his horse was nearly at full speed, causing the dust to roll thick behind him. Mr. Hamilton, though one of the most resolute men in the whole neighborhood, was, nevertheless, a remarkably mild spoken man; and, even when greatly excited, his language was cool and circumspect. He came to the door, and inquired if Mr. Freeland was in. I told him that Mr. Freeland was at the barn. Off the old gentleman rode, toward the barn, with unwonted speed. Mary, the cook, was at a loss to know what was the matter, and I did not profess any skill in making her understand. I knew she would have united, as readily as any one, in cursing me for bringing trouble into the family; so I held my peace, leaving matters to develop themselves, without my assistance. In a few moments, Mr. Hamilton and Mr. Freeland came down from the barn to the house; and, just as they made their appearance in the front yard, three men (who proved to be constables) came dashing into the lane, on horseback, as if summoned by a sign requiring quick work. A few seconds brought them into the front yard, where they hastily dismounted, and tied their horses. This done, they joined Mr. Freeland and Mr. Hamilton, who were standing a short distance from the kitchen. A few moments were spent, as if in consulting how to proceed, and then the whole party walked up to the kitchen door. There was now no one in the kitchen but myself and John Harris. Henry and Sandy were yet at the barn. Mr. Freeland came inside the kitchen door, and with an agitated voice, called me by name, and told me to come forward; that there were some gentlemen who wished to see me. I stepped toward them, at the door, and asked what they wanted, when the constables grabbed me, and told me that I had better not resist; that I had been in a scrape, or was said to have been in one; that they were merely going to take me where I could be examined; that they were going to carry me to St. Michael's, to have me brought before my master. They further said, that, in case the evidence against me was not true, I should be acquitted. I was now firmly tied, and completely at the mercy of my captors. Resistance was idle. They were five in number, armed to the very teeth. When they had secured me, they next turned to John Harris, and, in a few moments, succeeded in tying him as firmly as they had already tied me. They next turned toward Henry Harris, who had now returned from the barn. "Cross your hands," said the constables, to Henry. "I *won't*," said Henry, in a voice so firm and clear, and in a manner so determined, as for a moment to arrest all proceedings. "Won't you cross your hands?" said Tom Graham, the constable. "*No I won't,*" said Henry, with increasing emphasis. Mr. Hamilton, Mr. Freeland, and the officers, now came near to Henry. Two of the constables drew out their shining pistols, and swore by the name of God, that he should cross his hands, or they would shoot him down. Each of these hired ruffians now cocked their pistols, and, with fingers apparently on the triggers, presented their deadly weapons to the breast of the unarmed slave, saying, at the same time, if he did not cross his hands, they would "blow his d——d heart out of him."

"*Shoot! Shoot me!*" said Henry. "*You can't kill me but once.* Shoot!— shoot! and be d——d. *I won't be tied.*" This, the brave fellow said in a voice as defiant and heroic in its tone, as was the language itself; and, at the moment of saying this, with the pistols at his very breast, he quickly raised his arms, and dashed them from the puny hands of his assassins, the weapons flying in opposite directions. Now came the struggle. All hands was now rushed upon the brave fellow, and, after beating him for some time, they succeeded in overpowering and tying him. Henry put me to shame; he fought, and fought bravely. John and I had made no resistance. The fact is, I never see much use in fighting, unless there is a reasonable probability of whipping somebody. Yet there was something almost providential in the resistance made by the gallant Henry. But for that resistance, every soul of us would have been hurried off to the far south. Just a moment previous to the trouble with Henry, Mr. Hamilton *mildly* said—and this gave me the unmistakable clue to the cause of our arrest—"Perhaps we had now better make a search for those protections, which we understand Frederick has written for himself and the rest." Had these passes been found, they would have been point blank proof against us, and would have confirmed all the statements of our betrayer. Thanks to the resistance of Henry, the excitement produced by the scuffle drew all attention in that direction, and I succeeded in flinging my pass, unobserved, into the fire. The confusion attendant upon the scuffle, and the apprehension of further trouble, perhaps, led our captors to forego, for the present, any search for "*those protections*" *which Frederick was said to have written for his companions*; so we were not yet convicted of the purpose to run away; and it was evident that there was some doubt, on the part of all, whether we had been guilty of such a purpose.

Just as we were all completely tied, and about ready to start toward St. Michael's, and thence to jail, Mrs. Betsey Freeland (mother to William, who was very much attached—after the southern fashion—to Henry and John, they having been reared from childhood in her house) came to the kitchen door, with her hands full of biscuits—for we had not had time to take our breakfast that morning—and divided them between Henry and John. This done, the lady made the following parting address to me, looking and pointing her bony finger at me. "You devil! You yellow devil! It was you that put it into the heads of Henry and John to run away. But for *you*, you *long legged yellow devil*, Henry and John would never have thought of running away." I gave the lady a look, which called forth a scream of mingled wrath and terror, as she slammed the kitchen door, and went in, leaving me, with the rest, in hands as harsh as her own broken voice.

Could the kind reader have been quietly riding along the main road to or from Easton, that morning, his eye would have met a painful sight. He would have seen five young men, guilty of no crime, save that of preferring *liberty* to a life of *bondage*, drawn along the public highway—firmly bound together—tramping through dust and heat, bare-footed and bare-headed—fastened to three strong horses, whose riders were armed to the teeth, with pistols and daggers—on their way to prison, like felons, and suffering every possible insult from the crowds of idle, vulgar people, who clustered around, and heartlessly made their failure the occasion for all manner of ribaldry and sport. As I looked upon this crowd of vile persons, and saw myself and friends thus assailed and persecuted, I could not help seeing the fulfillment of Sandy's dream. I was in the hands of moral vultures, and firmly held in their sharp talons, and was hurried away toward Easton, in a south-easterly direction, amid the jeers of new birds of the same feather, through every neighborhood we passed. It seemed to me (and this shows the good understanding between the slaveholders and their allies) that every body we met knew the cause of our arrest, and were out, awaiting our passing by, to feast their vindictive eyes on our misery and to gloat over our ruin. Some said, *I ought to be hanged*, and others, *I ought to be burnt*, others, I ought to have the "*hide*" taken from my back; while no one gave us a kind word or sympathizing look, except the poor slaves, who were lifting their heavy hoes, and who cautiously glanced at us through the post-and-rail fences, behind which they were at work. Our sufferings, that morning, can be more easily imagined than described. Our hopes were all blasted, at a blow. The cruel injustice, the victorious crime, and the helplessness of innocence, led me to ask, in my ignorance and weakness, "Where now is the God of justice and mercy? And why have these wicked men the power thus to trample upon our rights, and to insult our feelings?" And yet, in the next moment, came the consoling thought, "*The day of oppressor will come at last.*" Of one thing I could be glad—not one of my dear friends, upon whom I had brought this great calamity, either by word or look, reproached me for having led them into it. We were a band of brothers, and never dearer to each other than now. The thought which gave us the most pain, was the probable separation which would now take place, in case we were sold off to the far south, as we were likely to be. While the constables were looking forward, Henry and I, being fastened together, could occasionally exchange a word, without being observed by the kidnappers who had us in charge. "What shall I do with my pass?" said Henry. "Eat it with your biscuit," said I; "it won't do to tear it up." We were now near St. Michael's. The direction concerning the passes was passed around, and executed. "*Own nothing!*" said I. "*Own nothing!*" was passed around and enjoined, and assented to. Our confidence in each other was unshaken; and we were quite resolved to succeed or fail together—as much after the calamity which had befallen us, as before.

On reaching St. Michael's, we underwent a sort of examination at my master's store, and it was evident to my mind, that Master Thomas suspected the truthfulness of the evidence upon which they had acted in arresting us; and that he only affected, to some extent, the positiveness with which he asserted our guilt. There was nothing said by any of our company, which could, in any manner, prejudice our cause; and there was hope, yet, that we should be able to return to our homes—if for nothing else, at least to find out the guilty man or woman who had betrayed us.

To this end, we all denied that we had been guilty of intended flight. Master Thomas said that the evidence he had of our intention to run away, was strong enough to hang us, in a case of murder. "But," said I, "the cases are not equal. If murder were committed, some one must have committed it—the thing is done! In our case, nothing has been done! We have not run away. Where is the evidence against us? We were quietly at our work." I talked thus, with unusual freedom, to bring out the evidence against us, for we all wanted, above all things, to know the guilty wretch who had betrayed us, that we might have something tangible upon which to pour the execrations. From something which dropped, in the course of the talk, it appeared that there was but one witness against us—and that that witness could not be produced. Master Thomas would not tell us *who* his informant was; but we suspected, and suspected *one* person *only*. Several circumstances seemed to point Sandy out, as our betrayer. His entire knowledge of our plans—his participation in them—his withdrawal from us—his dream, and his simultaneous presentiment that we were betrayed—the taking us, and the leaving him—were calculated to turn suspicion toward him; and yet, we could not suspect him. We all loved him too well to think it *possible* that he could have betrayed us. So we rolled the guilt on other shoulders.

We were literally dragged, that morning, behind horses, a distance of fifteen miles, and placed in the Easton jail. We were glad to reach the end of our journey, for our pathway had been the scene of insult and mortification. Such is the power of public opinion, that it is hard, even for the innocent, to feel the happy consolations of innocence, when they fall under the maledictions of this power. How could we regard ourselves as in the right, when all about us denounced us as criminals, and had the power and the disposition to treat us as such.

In jail, we were placed under the care of Mr. Joseph Graham, the sheriff of the county. Henry, and John, and myself, were placed in one room, and Henry Bailey and Charles Roberts, in another, by themselves. This separation was intended to deprive us of the advantage of concert, and to prevent trouble in jail.

Once shut up, a new set of tormentors came upon us. A swarm of imps, in human shape the slave-traders, deputy slave-traders, and agents of slave-traders—that gather in every country town of the state, watching for chances to buy human flesh (as buzzards to eat carrion) flocked in upon us, to ascertain if our masters had placed us in jail to be sold. Such a set of debased and villainous creatures, I never saw before, and hope never to see again. I felt myself surrounded as by a pack of *fiends*, fresh from *perdition*. They laughed, leered, and grinned at us; saying, "Ah! Boys, we've got you, havn't we? So you were about to make your escape? Where were you going to?" After taunting us, and peering at us, as long as they liked, they one by one subjected us to an examination, with a view to ascertain our value; feeling our arms and legs, and shaking us by the shoulders to see if we were sound and healthy; impudently asking us, "how we would like to have them for masters?" To such questions, we were, very much to their annoyance, quite dumb, disdaining to answer them. For one, I detested the whisky-bloated gamblers in human flesh; and I believe I was as much detested by them in turn. One fellow told me, "if he had me, he would cut the devil out of me pretty quick."

These Negro buyers are very offensive to the genteel southern Christian public. They are looked upon, in respectable Maryland society, as necessary, but detestable characters. As a class, they are hardened ruffians, made such by nature and by occupation. Their ears are made quite familiar with the agonizing cry of outraged and woe-smitten humanity. Their eyes are forever open to human misery. They walk amid desecrated affections, insulted virtue, and blasted hopes. They have grown intimate with vice and blood; they gloat over the wildest illustrations of their soul-damning and earth-polluting business, and are moral pests. Yes; they are a legitimate fruit of slavery; and it is a puzzle to make out a case of greater villainy for them, than for the slaveholders, who make such a class *possible*. They are mere hucksters of the surplus slave produce of Maryland and Virginia—coarse, cruel, and swaggering bullies, whose very breathing is of blasphemy and blood.

Aside from these slave-buyers, who infested the prison, from time to time, our quarters were much more comfortable than we had any right to expect they would be. Our allowance of food was small and coarse, but our room was the best in the jail—neat and spacious, and with nothing about it necessarily reminding us of being in prison, but its heavy locks and bolts and the black, iron lattice-work at the windows. We were prisoners of state, compared with most slaves who are put into that Easton jail. But the place was not one of contentment. Bolts, bars and grated windows are not acceptable to freedom-loving people of any color. The suspense, too, was painful. Every step on the stairway was listened to, in the hope that the comer would cast a ray of light on our fate. We would have given the hair off our heads for half a dozen words with one of the waiters in Sol. Lowe's hotel. Such waiters were in the way of hearing, at the table, the probable course of things. We could see them flitting about in their white jackets in front of this hotel, but could speak to none of them.

Soon after the holidays were over, contrary to all our expectations, Messrs. Hamilton and Freeland came up to Easton; not to make a bargain with the "Georgia traders," nor to send us up to Austin Woldfolk, as is usual in the case of runaway slaves, but to release Charles, Henry Harris, Henry Bailey and John Harris, from prison, and this, too, without the infliction of a single blow. I was now left entirely alone in prison. The innocent had been taken, and the guilty left. My friends were separated from me, and apparently forever. This circumstance caused me more pain than any other incident connected with our capture and imprisonment. Thirty-nine lashes on my naked and bleeding back, would have been joyfully borne, in preference to this separation from these, the friends of my youth. And yet, I could not but feel that I was the victim of something like justice. Why should these young men, who were led into this scheme by me, suffer as much as the instigator? I felt glad that they were released from prison, and from the dread prospect of a life (or death I should rather say) in the rice swamps. It is due to the noble Henry, to say, that he seemed almost as reluctant to leave the prison with me in it, as he was to be tied and dragged to prison. But he and the rest knew that we should, in all the likelihoods of the case, be separated, in the event of being sold; and since we were now completely in the hands of our owners, we all concluded it would be best to go peaceably home.

Not until this last separation, dear reader, had I touched those profounder depths of desolation, which it is the lot of slaves often to reach. I was solitary in the world, and alone within the walls of a stone prison, left to a fate of life-long misery. I had hoped and expected much, for months before, but my hopes and expectations were now withered and blasted. The ever dreaded slave life in Georgia, Louisiana and Alabama—from which escape is next to impossible—now, in my loneliness, stared me in the face. The possibility of ever becoming anything but an abject slave, a mere machine in the hands of an owner, had now fled, and it seemed to me it had fled forever. A life of living death, beset with the innumerable horrors of the cotton field, and the sugar plantation, seemed to be my doom. The fiends, who rushed into the prison when we were first put there, continued to visit me, and to ply me with questions and with their tantalizing remarks. I was insulted, but helpless; keenly alive to the demands of justice and liberty, but with no means of asserting them. To talk to those imps about justice and mercy, would have been as absurd as to reason with bears and tigers. Lead and steel are the only arguments that they understand.

After remaining in this life of misery and despair about a week, which, by the way, seemed a month, Master Thomas, very much to my surprise, and greatly to my relief, came to the prison, and took me out, for the purpose, as he said, of sending me to Alabama, with a friend of his, who would emancipate me at the end of eight years. I was glad enough to get out of prison; but I had no faith in the story that this friend of Capt. Auld would emancipate me, at the end of the time indicated. Besides, I never had heard of his having a friend in Alabama, and I took the announcement, simply as an easy and comfortable method of shipping me off to the far south. There was a little scandal, too, connected with the idea of one Christian selling another to the Georgia traders, while it was deemed every way proper for them to sell to others. I thought this friend in Alabama was an invention, to meet this difficulty, for Master Thomas was quite jealous of his Christian reputation, however unconcerned he might be about his real Christian character. In these remarks, however, it is possible that I do Master Thomas Auld injustice. He certainly did not exhaust his power upon me, in the case, but acted, upon the whole, very generously, considering the nature of my offense. He had the power and the provocation to send me, without reserve, into the very everglades of Florida, beyond the remotest hope of emancipation; and his refusal to exercise that power, must be set down to his credit.

After lingering about St. Michael's a few days, and no friend from Alabama making his appearance, to take me there, Master Thomas decided to send me back again to Baltimore, to live with his brother Hugh, with whom he was now at peace; possibly he became so by his profession of religion, at the camp-meeting in the Bay Side. Master Thomas told me that he wished me to go to Baltimore, and learn a trade; and that, if I behaved myself properly, he would *emancipate me at twenty-five*! Thanks for this one beam of hope in the future. The promise had but one fault; it seemed too good to be true.

# CHAPTER XX

## APPRENTICESHIP LIFE

*Nothing Lost by the Attempt to Run Away—Comrades in Their Old Homes—Reasons for Sending Me Away—Return to Baltimore—Contrast Between Tommy and That of His Colored Companion—Trials in Gardiner's Ship-Yard—Desperate Fight—Its Causes—Conflict Between White and Black Labor—Description of the Outrage—Colored Testimony Nothing—Conduct of Master Hugh—Spirit of Slavery in Baltimore—My Condition Improves—New Associations—Slaveholder's Right to Take His Wages—How to Make a Contented Slave.*

Well! Dear reader, I am not, as you may have already inferred, a loser by the general upstir, described in the foregoing chapter. The little domestic revolution, notwithstanding the sudden snub it got by the treachery of somebody—I dare not say or think *who*—did not, after all, end so disastrously, as when in the iron cage at Easton, I conceived it would. The prospect, from that point, did look about as dark as any that ever cast its gloom over the vision of the anxious, out-looking, human spirit. "All is well that ends well." My affectionate comrades, Henry and John Harris, are still with Mr. William Freeland. Charles Roberts and Henry Bailey are safe at their homes. I have not, therefore, any thing to regret on their account. Their masters have mercifully forgiven them, probably on the ground suggested in the spirited little speech of Mrs. Freeland, made to me just before leaving for the jail—namely: that they had been allured into the wicked scheme of making their escape, by me; and that, but for me, they would never have dreamed of a thing so shocking! My friends had nothing to regret, either; for while they were watched more closely on account of what had happened, they were, doubtless, treated more kindly than before, and got new assurances that they would be legally emancipated, some day, provided their behavior should make them deserving, from that time forward. Not a blow, as I learned, was struck any one of them. As for Master William Freeland, good, unsuspecting soul, he did not believe that we were intending to run away at all. Having given—as he thought—no occasion to his boys to leave him, he could not think it probable that they had entertained a design so grievous. This, however, was not the view taken of the matter by "Mas' Billy," as we used to call the soft spoken, but crafty and resolute Mr. William Hamilton. He had no doubt that the crime had been meditated; and regarding me as the instigator of it, he frankly told Master Thomas that he must remove me from that neighborhood, or he would shoot me down. He would not have one so dangerous as "Frederick" tampering with his slaves. William Hamilton was not a man whose threat might be safely disregarded. I have no doubt that he would have proved as good as his word, had the warning given not been promptly taken. He was furious at the thought of such a piece of high-handed *theft*, as we were about to perpetrate—the stealing of our own bodies and souls! The feasibility of the plan, too, could the first steps have been taken, was marvelously plain. Besides, this was a *new* idea, this use of the bay. Slaves escaping, until now, had taken to the woods; they had never dreamed of profaning and abusing the waters of the noble Chesapeake, by making them the highway from slavery to freedom. Here was a broad road of destruction to slavery, which, before, had been looked upon as a wall of security by slaveholders. But Master Billy could not get Mr. Freeland to see matters precisely as he did; nor could he get Master Thomas so excited as he was himself. The latter—I must say it to his credit—showed much humane feeling in his part of the transaction, and atoned for much that had been harsh, cruel and unreasonable in his former treatment of me and others. His clemency was quite unusual and unlooked for. "Cousin Tom" told me that while I was in jail, Master Thomas was very unhappy; and that the night before his going up to release me, he had walked the floor nearly all night, evincing great distress; that very tempting offers had been made to him, by the Negro-traders, but he had rejected them all, saying that *money could not tempt him to sell me to the far south*. All this I can easily believe, for he seemed quite reluctant to send me away, at all. He told me that he only consented to do so, because of the very strong prejudice against me in the neighborhood, and that he feared for my safety if I remained there.

Thus, after three years spent in the country, roughing it in the field, and experiencing all sorts of hardships, I was again permitted to return to Baltimore, the very place, of all others, short of a free state, where I most desired to live. The three years spent in the country, had made some difference in me, and in the household of Master Hugh. "Little Tommy" was no longer *little* Tommy; and I was not the slender lad who had left for the Eastern Shore just three years before. The loving relations between me and Mas' Tommy were broken up. He was no longer dependent on me for protection, but felt himself a *man*, with other and more suitable associates. In childhood, he scarcely considered me inferior to himself certainly, as good as any other boy with whom he played; but the time had come when his *friend* must become his *slave*. So we were cold, and we parted. It was a sad thing to me, that, loving each other as we had done, we must now take different roads. To him, a thousand avenues were open. Education had made him acquainted with all the treasures of the world, and liberty had flung open the gates thereunto; but I, who had attended him seven years, and had watched over him with the care of a big brother, fighting his battles in the street, and shielding him from harm, to an extent which had induced his mother to say, "Oh! Tommy is always safe, when he is with Freddy," must be confined to a single condition. He could grow, and become a *man*; I could grow, though I could *not* become a man, but must remain, all my life, a minor—a mere boy. Thomas Auld, Junior, obtained a situation on board the brig *Tweed*, and went to sea. I know not what has become of him; he certainly has my good wishes for his welfare and prosperity. There were few persons to whom I was more sincerely attached than to him, and there are few in the world I would be more pleased to meet.

Very soon after I went to Baltimore to live, Master Hugh succeeded in getting me hired to Mr. William Gardiner, an extensive ship-builder on Fell's Point. I was placed here to learn to calk, a trade of which I already had some knowledge, gained while in Mr. Hugh Auld's ship-yard, when he was a master builder. Gardiner's, however, proved a very unfavorable place for the accomplishment of that object. Mr. Gardiner was, that season, engaged in building two large man-of-war vessels, professedly for the Mexican government. These vessels were to be launched in the month of July, of that year, and, in failure thereof, Mr. G. would forfeit a very considerable sum of money. So, when I entered the ship-yard, all was hurry and driving. There were in the yard about one hundred men; of these about seventy or eighty were regular carpenters—privileged men. Speaking of my condition here I wrote, years ago—and I have now no reason to vary the picture as follows:*

> There was no time to learn any thing. Every man had to do that which he knew how to do. In entering the ship-yard, my orders from Mr. Gardiner were, to do whatever the carpenters commanded me to do. This was placing me at the beck and call of about seventy-five men. I was to regard all these as masters. Their word was to be my law. My situation was a most trying one. At times I needed a dozen pair of hands. I was called a dozen ways in the space of a single minute. Three or four voices would strike my ear at the same moment. It was—"Fred., come help me to cant this timber here." "Fred., come carry this timber yonder." "Fred., bring that roller here." "Fred., go get a fresh can of water." "Fred., come help saw off the end of this timber." "Fred., go quick and get the crow bar." "Fred., hold on the end of this fall." "Fred., go to the blacksmith's shop, and get a new punch." "Hurra, Fred.! Run and bring me a cold chisel." "I say, Fred., bear a hand, and get up a fire as quick as lightning under that steam-box." "Halloo, nigger! Come, turn this grindstone." "Come, come! Move, move! And bowse this timber forward." "I say, darkey, blast your eyes, why don't you heat up some pitch?" "Halloo! Halloo! Halloo!" (Three voices at the same time.) "Come here!—Go there!—Hold on where you are! D——n you, if you move, I'll knock your brains out!"

Such, dear reader, is a glance at the school which was mine, during the first eight months of my stay at Baltimore. At the end of the eight months, Master Hugh refused longer to allow me to remain with Mr. Gardiner. The circumstance which led to his taking me away, was a brutal outrage, committed upon me by the white apprentices of the ship-yard. The fight was a desperate one, and I came out of it most shockingly mangled. I was cut and bruised in sundry places, and my left eye was nearly knocked out of its socket. The facts, leading to this barbarous outrage upon me, illustrate a phase of slavery destined to become an important element in the overthrow of the slave system,

---

* From *Narrative of the Life of Frederick Douglass.*

and I may, therefore state them with some minuteness. That phase is this: *the conflict of slavery with the interests of the white mechanics and laborers of the south.* In the country, this conflict is not so apparent; but, in cities, such as Baltimore, Richmond, New Orleans, Mobile, etc., it is seen pretty clearly. The slaveholders, with a craftiness peculiar to themselves, by encouraging the enmity of the poor, laboring white man against the blacks, succeed in making the said white man almost as much a slave as the black slave himself. The difference between the white slave, and the black slave, is this: the latter belongs to *one* slaveholder, and the former belongs to all the slaveholders, collectively. The white slave has taken from him, by indirection, what the black slave has taken from him, directly, and without ceremony. Both are plundered, and by the same plunderers. The slave is robbed, by his master, of all his earnings, above what is required for his bare physical necessities; and the white man is robbed by the slave system, of the just results of his labor, because he is flung into competition with a class of laborers who work without wages. The competition, and its injurious consequences, will, one day, array the non-slaveholding white people of the slave states, against the slave system, and make them the most effective workers against the great evil. At present, the slaveholders blind them to this competition, by keeping alive their prejudice against the slaves, *as men*—not against them *as slaves.* They appeal to their pride, often denouncing emancipation, as tending to place the white man, on an equality with Negroes, and, by this means, they succeed in drawing off the minds of the poor whites from the real fact, that, by the rich slave-master, they are already regarded as but a single remove from equality with the slave. The impression is cunningly made, that slavery is the only power that can prevent the laboring white man from falling to the level of the slave's poverty and degradation. To make this enmity deep and broad, between the slave and the poor white man, the latter is allowed to abuse and whip the former, without hinderance. But—as I have suggested—this state of facts prevails *mostly* in the country. In the city of Baltimore, there are not unfrequent murmurs, that educating the slaves to be mechanics may, in the end, give slave-masters power to dispense with the services of the poor white man altogether. But, with characteristic dread of offending the slaveholders, these poor, white mechanics in Mr. Gardiner's ship-yard—instead of applying the natural, honest remedy for the apprehended evil, and objecting at once to work there by the side of slaves—made a cowardly attack upon the free colored mechanics, saying *they* were eating the bread which should be eaten by American freemen, and swearing that they would not work with them. The feeling was, *really*, against having their labor brought into competition with that of the colored people at all; but it was too much to strike directly at the interest of the slaveholders; and, therefore proving their servility and cowardice they dealt their blows on the poor, colored freeman, and aimed to prevent *him* from serving himself, in the evening of life, with the trade with which he had served his master, during the more vigorous portion of his days. Had they succeeded in driving the black freemen out of the ship-yard, they would have determined also upon the removal of the black slaves. The feeling was very bitter toward all colored people in Baltimore, about this time (1836), and they—free and slave—suffered all manner of insult and wrong.

Until a very little before I went there, white and black ship carpenters worked side by side, in the ship-yards of Mr. Gardiner, Mr. Duncan, Mr. Walter Price, and Mr. Robb. Nobody seemed to see any impropriety in it. To outward seeming, all hands were well satisfied. Some of the blacks were first rate workmen, and were given jobs requiring the highest skill. All at once, however, the white carpenters knocked off, and swore that they would no longer work on the same stage with free Negroes. Taking advantage of the heavy contract resting upon Mr. Gardiner, to have the war vessels for Mexico ready to launch in July, and of the difficulty of getting other hands at that season of the year, they swore they would not strike another blow for him, unless he would discharge his free colored workmen.

Now, although this movement did not extend to me, *in form*, it did reach me, *in fact*. The spirit which it awakened was one of malice and bitterness, toward colored people *generally*, and I suffered with the rest, and suffered severely. My fellow-apprentices very soon began to feel it to be degrading to work with me. They began to put on high looks, and to talk contemptuously and maliciously of *"the niggers"*; saying, that "they would take the country," that "they ought to be killed." Encouraged by the cowardly workmen, who, knowing me to be a slave, made no issue with Mr. Gardiner about my being there, these young men did their utmost to make it impossible for me to stay. They seldom called me to do any thing, without coupling the call with a curse, and

Edward North, the biggest in every thing, rascality included, ventured to strike me, whereupon I picked him up, and threw him into the dock. Whenever any of them struck me, I struck back again, regardless of consequences. I could manage any of them *singly*, and, while I could keep them from combining, I succeeded very well. In the conflict which ended my stay at Mr. Gardiner's, I was beset by four of them at once—Ned North, Ned Hays, Bill Stewart, and Tom Humphreys. Two of them were as large as myself, and they came near killing me, in broad day light. The attack was made suddenly, and simultaneously. One came in front, armed with a brick; there was one at each side, and one behind, and they closed up around me. I was struck on all sides; and, while I was attending to those in front, I received a blow on my head, from behind, dealt with a heavy hand-spike. I was completely stunned by the blow, and fell, heavily, on the ground, among the timbers. Taking advantage of my fall, they rushed upon me, and began to pound me with their fists. I let them lay on, for a while, after I came to myself, with a view of gaining strength. They did me little damage, so far; but, finally, getting tired of that sport, I gave a sudden surge, and, despite their weight, I rose to my hands and knees. Just as I did this, one of their number (I know not which) planted a blow with his boot in my left eye, which, for a time, seemed to have burst my eyeball. When they saw my eye completely closed, my face covered with blood, and I staggering under the stunning blows they had given me, they left me. As soon as I gathered sufficient strength, I picked up the hand-spike, and, madly enough, attempted to pursue them; but here the carpenters interfered, and compelled me to give up my frenzied pursuit. It was impossible to stand against so many.

Dear reader, you can hardly believe the statement, but it is true, and, therefore, I write it down: not fewer than fifty white men stood by, and saw this brutal and shameless outrage committed, and not a man of them all interposed a single word of mercy. There were four against one, and that one's face was beaten and battered most horribly, and no one said, "That is enough"; but some cried out, "Kill him—kill him—kill the d——d nigger! Knock his brains out—he struck a white person." I mention this inhuman outcry, to show the character of the men, and the spirit of the times, at Gardiner's ship-yard, and, indeed, in Baltimore generally, in 1836. As I look back to this period, I am almost amazed that I was not murdered outright, in that ship-yard, so murderous was the spirit which prevailed there. On two occasions, while there, I came near losing my life. I was driving bolts in the hold, through the keelson, with Hays. In its course, the bolt bent. Hays cursed me, and said that it was my blow which bent the bolt. I denied this, and charged it upon him. In a fit of rage he seized an adze, and darted toward me. I met him with a maul, and parried his blow, or I should have then lost my life. A son of old Tom Lanman (the latter's double murder I have elsewhere charged upon him), in the spirit of his miserable father, made an assault upon me, but the blow with his maul missed me. After the united assault of North, Stewart, Hays and Humphreys, finding that the carpenters were as bitter toward me as the apprentices, and that the latter were probably set on by the former, I found my only chances for life was in flight. I succeeded in getting away, without an additional blow. To strike a white man, was death, by Lynch law, in Gardiner's ship-yard; nor was there much of any other law toward colored people, at that time, in any other part of Maryland. The whole sentiment of Baltimore was murderous.

After making my escape from the ship-yard, I went straight home, and related the story of the outrage to Master Hugh Auld; and it is due to him to say, that his conduct—though he was not a religious man—was every way more humane than that of his brother, Thomas, when I went to the latter in a somewhat similar plight, from the hands of "*Brother Edward Covey*." He listened attentively to my narration of the circumstances leading to the ruffianly outrage, and gave many proofs of his strong indignation at what was done. Hugh was a rough, but manly-hearted fellow, and, at this time, his best nature showed itself.

The heart of my once almost over-kind mistress, Sophia, was again melted in pity toward me. My puffed-out eye, and my scarred and blood-covered face, moved the dear lady to tears. She kindly drew a chair by me, and with friendly, consoling words, she took water, and washed the blood from my face. No mother's hand could have been more tender than hers. She bound up my head, and covered my wounded eye with a lean piece of fresh beef. It was almost compensation for the murderous assault, and my suffering, that it furnished an occasion for the manifestation, once more, of the originally characteristic kindness of my mistress. Her affectionate heart was not yet dead, though much hardened by time and by circumstances.

As for Master Hugh's part, as I have said, he was furious about it; and he gave expression to his fury in the usual forms of speech in that locality. He poured curses on the heads of the whole ship-yard company, and swore that he would have satisfaction for the outrage. His indignation was really strong and healthy; but, unfortunately, it resulted from the thought that his rights of property, in my person, had not been respected, more than from any sense of the outrage committed on me as a man. I inferred as much as this, from the fact that he could, himself, beat and mangle when it suited him to do so. Bent on having satisfaction, as he said, just as soon as I got a little the better of my bruises, Master Hugh took me to Esquire Watson's office, on Bond Street, Fell's Point, with a view to procuring the arrest of those who had assaulted me. He related the outrage to the magistrate, as I had related it to him, and seemed to expect that a warrant would, at once, be issued for the arrest of the lawless ruffians.

Mr. Watson heard it all, and instead of drawing up his warrant, he inquired—

"Mr. Auld, who saw this assault of which you speak?"

"It was done, sir, in the presence of a ship-yard full of hands."

"Sir," said Watson, "I am sorry, but I cannot move in this matter except upon the oath of white witnesses."

"But here's the boy; look at his head and face," said the excited Master Hugh; "*they* show *what* has been done."

But Watson insisted that he was not authorized to do anything, unless white witnesses of the transaction would come forward, and testify to what had taken place. He could issue no warrant on my word, against white persons; and, if I had been killed in the presence of a *thousand blacks*, their testimony, combined, would have been insufficient to arrest a single murderer. Master Hugh, for once, was compelled to say, that this state of things was *too bad*; and he left the office of the magistrate, disgusted.

Of course, it was impossible to get any white man to testify against my assailants. The carpenters saw what was done; but the actors were but the agents of their malice, and only what the carpenters sanctioned. They had cried, with one accord, "*Kill the nigger!*" "*Kill the nigger!*" Even those who may have pitied me, if any such were among them, lacked the moral courage to come and volunteer their evidence. The slightest manifestation of sympathy or justice toward a person of color, was denounced as abolitionism; and the name of abolitionist, subjected its bearer to frightful liabilities. "D——n *abolitionists*," and "*Kill the niggers*," were the watch-words of the foul-mouthed ruffians of those days. Nothing was done, and probably there would not have been any thing done, had I been killed in the affray. The laws and the morals of the Christian city of Baltimore, afforded no protection to the sable denizens of that city.

Master Hugh, on finding he could get no redress for the cruel wrong, withdrew me from the employment of Mr. Gardiner, and took me into his own family, Mrs. Auld kindly taking care of me, and dressing my wounds, until they were healed, and I was ready to go again to work.

While I was on the Eastern Shore, Master Hugh had met with reverses, which overthrew his business; and he had given up ship-building in his own yard, on the City Block, and was now acting as foreman of Mr. Walter Price. The best he could now do for me, was to take me into Mr. Price's yard, and afford me the facilities there, for completing the trade which I had began to learn at Gardiner's. Here I rapidly became expert in the use of my calking tools; and, in the course of a single year, I was able to command the highest wages paid to journeymen calkers in Baltimore.

The reader will observe that I was now of some pecuniary value to my master. During the busy season, I was bringing six and seven dollars per week. I have, sometimes, brought him as much as nine dollars a week, for the wages were a dollar and a half per day.

After learning to calk, I sought my own employment, made my own contracts, and collected my own earnings; giving Master Hugh no trouble in any part of the transactions to which I was a party.

Here, then, were better days for the Eastern Shore *slave*. I was now free from the vexatious assaults of the apprentices at Mr. Gardiner's; and free from the perils of plantation life, and once more in a favorable condition to increase my little stock of education, which had been at a dead stand since my removal from Baltimore. I had, on the Eastern Shore, been only a teacher, when in company with other slaves, but now there were colored persons who could instruct me. Many of the young calkers could read, write and cipher. Some of them had high notions about mental improvement; and the free ones, on Fell's Point, organized what they called the "*East Baltimore Mental Improvement Society*." To this society, notwithstanding it was intended that only free persons should attach themselves, I was admitted, and was, several times, assigned a prominent part in its debates. I owe much to the society of these young men.

The reader already knows enough of the *ill* effects of good treatment on a slave, to anticipate what was now the case in my improved condition. It was not long before I began to show signs of disquiet with slavery, and to look around for means to get out of that condition by the shortest route. I was living among *free men*; and was, in all respects, equal to them by nature and by attainments. *Why should I be a slave?* There was no reason why I should be the thrall of any man.

Besides, I was now getting—as I have said—a dollar and fifty cents per day. I contracted for it, worked for it, earned it, collected it; it was paid to me, and it was *rightfully* my own; and yet, upon every returning Saturday night, this money—my own hard earnings, every cent of it—was demanded of me, and taken from me by Master Hugh. He did not earn it; he had no hand in earning it; why, then, should he have it? I owed him nothing. He had given me no schooling, and I had received from him only my food and raiment; and for these, my services were supposed to pay, from the first. The right to take my earnings, was the right of the robber. He had the power to compel me to give him the fruits of my labor, and this power was his only right in the case. I became more and more dissatisfied with this state of things; and, in so becoming, I only gave proof of the same human nature which every reader of this chapter in my life—slaveholder, or non-slaveholder—is conscious of possessing.

To make a contented slave, you must make a thoughtless one. It is necessary to darken his moral and mental vision, and, as far as possible, to annihilate his power of reason. He must be able to detect no inconsistencies in slavery. The man that takes his earnings, must be able to convince him that he has a perfect right to do so. It must not depend upon mere force; the slave must know no Higher Law than his master's will. The whole relationship must not only demonstrate, to his mind, its necessity, but its absolute rightfulness. If there be one crevice through which a single drop can fall, it will certainly rust off the slave's chain.

# CHAPTER XXI

## MY ESCAPE FROM SLAVERY

*Closing Incidents of "My Life as a Slave"—Reasons Why
Full Particulars of the Manner of My Escape Will Not Be
Given—Craftiness and Malice of Slaveholders—Suspicion
of Aiding a Slave's Escape About as Dangerous as Positive
Evidence—Want of Wisdom Shown in Publishing Details of
the Escape of the Fugitives—Published Accounts Reach the
Masters, Not the Slaves—Slaveholders Stimulated to Greater
Watchfulness—My Condition—Discontent—Suspicions
Implied By Master Hugh's Manner, When Receiving My
Wages—His Occasional Generosity!—Difficulties in the
Way of Escape—Every Avenue Guarded—Plan to Obtain
Money—I Am Allowed to Hire My Time—A Gleam of
Hope—Attends Camp-Meeting, Without Permission—Anger
of Master Hugh Thereat—The Result—My Plans of
Escape Accelerated Thereby—The Day for My Departure
Fixed—Harassed By Doubts and Fears—Painful Thoughts of
Separation From Friends—The Attempt Made—Its Success.*

I will now make the kind reader acquainted with the closing incidents
of my "Life as a Slave," having already trenched upon the limit
allotted to my "Life as a Freeman." Before, however, proceeding
with this narration, it is, perhaps, proper that I should frankly state,
in advance, my intention to withhold a part of the facts connected
with my escape from slavery. There are reasons for this suppression,
which I trust the reader will deem altogether valid. It may be easily
conceived, that a full and complete statement of all facts pertaining to
the flight of a bondman, might implicate and embarrass some who may
have, wittingly or unwittingly, assisted him; and no one can wish me to
involve any man or woman who has befriended me, even in the liability
of embarrassment or trouble.

Keen is the scent of the slaveholder; like the fangs of the rattlesnake,
his malice retains its poison long; and, although it is now nearly

seventeen years since I made my escape, it is well to be careful, in dealing with the circumstances relating to it. Were I to give but a shadowy outline of the process adopted, with characteristic aptitude, the crafty and malicious among the slaveholders might, possibly, hit upon the track I pursued, and involve some one in suspicion which, in a slave state, is about as bad as positive evidence. The colored man, there, must not only shun evil, but shun the very *appearance* of evil, or be condemned as a criminal. A slaveholding community has a peculiar taste for ferreting out offenses against the slave system, justice there being more sensitive in its regard for the peculiar rights of this system, than for any other interest or institution. By stringing together a train of events and circumstances, even if I were not very explicit, the means of escape might be ascertained, and, possibly, those means be rendered, thereafter, no longer available to the liberty-seeking children of bondage I have left behind me. No anti-slavery man can wish me to do anything favoring such results, and no slaveholding reader has any right to expect the impartment of such information.

While, therefore, it would afford me pleasure, and perhaps would materially add to the interest of my story, were I at liberty to gratify a curiosity which I know to exist in the minds of many, as to the manner of my escape, I must deprive myself of this pleasure, and the curious of the gratification, which such a statement of facts would afford. I would allow myself to suffer under the greatest imputations that evil minded men might suggest, rather than exculpate myself by explanation, and thereby run the hazards of closing the slightest avenue by which a brother in suffering might clear himself of the chains and fetters of slavery.

The practice of publishing every new invention by which a slave is known to have escaped from slavery, has neither wisdom nor necessity to sustain it. Had not Henry Box Brown and his friends attracted slaveholding attention to the manner of his escape, we might have had a thousand Box Browns per annum. The singularly original plan adopted by William and Ellen Crafts, perished with the first using, because every slaveholder in the land was apprised of it. The *salt water slave* who hung in the guards of a steamer, being washed three days and three nights—like another Jonah—by the waves of the sea, has, by the publicity given to the circumstance, set a spy on the guards of every steamer departing from southern ports.

I have never approved of the very public manner, in which some of our western friends have conducted what *they* call the "*Underground Railroad*," but which, I think, by their open declarations, has been made, most emphatically, the "*Upperground* Railroad." Its stations are far better known to the slaveholders than to the slaves. I honor those good men and women for their noble daring, in willingly subjecting themselves to persecution, by openly avowing their participation in the escape of slaves; nevertheless, the good resulting from such avowals, is of a very questionable character. It may kindle an enthusiasm, very pleasant to inhale; but that is of no practical benefit to themselves, nor to the slaves escaping. Nothing is more evident, than that such disclosures are a positive evil to the slaves remaining, and seeking to escape. In publishing such accounts, the anti-slavery man addresses the slaveholder, *not the slave*; he stimulates the former to greater watchfulness, and adds to his facilities for capturing his slave. We owe something to the slaves, south of Mason and Dixon's line, as well as to those north of it; and, in discharging the duty of aiding the latter, on their way to freedom, we should be careful to do nothing which would be likely to hinder the former, in making their escape from slavery. Such is my detestation of slavery, that I would keep the merciless slaveholder profoundly ignorant of the means of flight adopted by the slave. He should be left to imagine himself surrounded by myriads of invisible tormentors, ever ready to snatch, from his infernal grasp, his trembling prey. In pursuing his victim, let him be left to feel his way in the dark; let shades of darkness, commensurate with his crime, shut every ray of light from his pathway; and let him be made to feel, that, at every step he takes, with the hellish purpose of reducing a brother man to slavery, he is running the frightful risk of having his hot brains dashed out by an invisible hand.

But, enough of this. I will now proceed to the statement of those facts, connected with my escape, for which I am alone responsible, and for which no one can be made to suffer but myself.

My condition in the year (1838) of my escape, was, comparatively, a free and easy one, so far, at least, as the wants of the physical man were concerned; but the reader will bear in mind, that my troubles from the beginning, have been less physical than mental, and he will thus be prepared to find, after what is narrated in the previous chapters, that slave life was adding nothing to its charms for me, as I grew older, and became better acquainted with it. The practice, from week to week, of openly robbing me of all my earnings, kept the nature and character of slavery constantly before me. I could be robbed by *indirection*, but this was *too* open and barefaced to be endured. I could see no reason why I should, at the end of each week, pour the reward of my honest toil into the purse of any man. The thought itself vexed me, and the manner in which Master Hugh received my wages, vexed me more than the original wrong. Carefully counting the money and rolling it out, dollar by dollar, he would look me in the face, as if he would search my heart as well as my pocket, and reproachfully ask me, "*Is that all?*"— implying that I had, perhaps, kept back part of my wages; or, if not so, the demand was made, possibly, to make me feel, that, after all, I was an "unprofitable servant." Draining me of the last cent of my hard earnings, he would, however, occasionally—when I brought home an extra large sum—dole out to me a sixpence or a shilling, with a view, perhaps, of kindling up my gratitude; but this practice had the opposite effect—it was an admission of *my right to the whole sum*. The fact, that he gave me any part of my wages, was proof that he suspected that I had a right *to the whole of them*. I always felt uncomfortable, after having received anything in this way, for I feared that the giving me a few cents, might, possibly, ease his conscience, and make him feel himself a pretty honorable robber, after all!

Held to a strict account, and kept under a close watch—the old suspicion of my running away not having been entirely removed— escape from slavery, even in Baltimore, was very difficult. The railroad from Baltimore to Philadelphia was under regulations so stringent, that even *free* colored travelers were almost excluded. They must have *free* papers; they must be measured and carefully examined, before they were allowed to enter the cars; they only went in the day time, even when so examined. The steamboats were under regulations equally stringent. All the great turnpikes, leading northward, were beset with kidnappers, a class of men who watched the newspapers for advertisements for runaway slaves, making their living by the accursed reward of slave hunting.

My discontent grew upon me, and I was on the look-out for means of escape. With money, I could easily have managed the matter, and, therefore, I hit upon the plan of soliciting the privilege of hiring my time. It is quite common, in Baltimore, to allow slaves this privilege, and it is the practice, also, in New Orleans. A slave who is considered trustworthy, can, by paying his master a definite sum regularly, at the end of each week, dispose of his time as he likes. It so happened that I was not in very good odor, and I was far from being a trustworthy slave. Nevertheless, I watched my opportunity when Master Thomas came to Baltimore (for I was still his property, Hugh only acted as his agent) in the spring of 1838, to purchase his spring supply of goods, and applied to him, directly, for the much-coveted privilege of hiring my time. This request Master Thomas unhesitatingly refused to grant; and he charged me, with some sternness, with inventing this stratagem to make my escape. He told me, "I could go *nowhere* but he could catch me; and, in the event of my running away, I might be assured he should spare no pains in his efforts to recapture me." He recounted, with a good deal of eloquence, the many kind offices he had done me, and exhorted me to be contented and obedient. "Lay out no plans for the future," said he. "If you behave yourself properly, I will take care of you." Now, kind and considerate as this offer was, it failed to soothe me into repose. In spite of Master Thomas, and, I may say, in spite of myself, also, I continued to think, and worse still, to think almost exclusively about the injustice and wickedness of slavery. No effort of mine or of his could silence this trouble-giving thought, or change my purpose to run away.

About two months after applying to Master Thomas for the privilege of hiring my time, I applied to Master Hugh for the same liberty, supposing him to be unacquainted with the fact that I had made a similar application to Master Thomas, and had been refused. My boldness in making this request, fairly astounded him at the first. He gazed at me in amazement. But I had many good reasons for pressing the matter; and, after listening to them awhile, he did not absolutely refuse, but told me he would think of it. Here, then, was a gleam of hope. Once master of my own time, I felt sure that I could make, over and above my obligation to him, a dollar or two every week. Some slaves have made enough, in this way, to purchase their freedom. It is a sharp spur to industry; and some of the most enterprising colored men in Baltimore hire themselves in this way. After mature reflection— as I must suppose it was—Master Hugh granted me the privilege in question, on the following terms: I was to be allowed all my time; to make all bargains for work; to find my own employment, and to collect my own wages; and, in return for this liberty, I was required, or obliged, to pay him three dollars at the end of each week, and to board and clothe myself, and buy my own calking tools. A failure in any of these particulars would put an end to my privilege. This was a hard bargain. The wear and tear of clothing, the losing and breaking of tools, and the expense of board, made it necessary for me to earn at least six dollars per week, to keep even with the world. All who are acquainted with calking, know how uncertain and irregular that employment is. It can be done to advantage only in dry weather, for it is useless to put wet oakum into a seam. Rain or shine, however, work or no work, at the end of each week the money must be forthcoming.

Master Hugh seemed to be very much pleased, for a time, with this arrangement; and well he might be, for it was decidedly in his favor. It relieved him of all anxiety concerning me. His money was sure. He had armed my love of liberty with a lash and a driver, far more efficient than any I had before known; and, while he derived all the benefits of slaveholding by the arrangement, without its evils, I endured all the evils of being a slave, and yet suffered all the care and anxiety of a responsible freeman. "Nevertheless," thought I, "it is a valuable privilege another step in my career toward freedom." It was something even to be permitted to stagger under the disadvantages of liberty, and I was determined to hold on to the newly gained footing, by all proper industry. I was ready to work by night as well as by day; and being in the enjoyment of excellent health, I was able not only to meet my current expenses, but also to lay by a small sum at the end of each week. All went on thus, from the month of May till August; then—for reasons which will become apparent as I proceed—my much valued liberty was wrested from me.

During the week previous to this (to me) calamitous event, I had made arrangements with a few young friends, to accompany them, on Saturday night, to a camp-meeting, held about twelve miles from Baltimore. On the evening of our intended start for the camp-ground, something occurred in the ship-yard where I was at work, which detained me unusually late, and compelled me either to disappoint my young friends, or to neglect carrying my weekly dues to Master Hugh. Knowing that I had the money, and could hand it to him on another day, I decided to go to camp-meeting, and to pay him the three dollars, for the past week, on my return. Once on the camp-ground, I was induced to remain one day longer than I had intended, when I left home. But, as soon as I returned, I went straight to his house on Fell Street, to hand him his (my) money. Unhappily, the fatal mistake had been committed. I found him exceedingly angry. He exhibited all the signs of apprehension and wrath, which a slaveholder may be surmised to exhibit on the supposed escape of a favorite slave. "You rascal! I have a great mind to give you a severe whipping. How dare you go out of the city without first asking and obtaining my permission?" "Sir," said I, "I hired my time and paid you the price you asked for it. I did not know that it was any part of the bargain that I should ask you when or where I should go."

"You did not know, you rascal! You are bound to show yourself here every Saturday night." After reflecting, a few moments, he became somewhat cooled down; but, evidently greatly troubled, he said. "Now, you scoundrel! You have done for yourself; you shall hire your time no longer. The next thing I shall hear of, will be your running away. Bring home your tools and your clothes, at once. I'll teach you how to go off in this way."

Thus ended my partial freedom. I could hire my time no longer; and I obeyed my master's orders at once. The little taste of liberty which I had had—although as the reader will have seen, it was far from being unalloyed—by no means enhanced my contentment with slavery. Punished thus by Master Hugh, it was now my turn to punish him. "Since," thought I, "you *will* make a slave of me, I will await your orders in all things"; and, instead of going to look for work on Monday morning, as I had formerly done, I remained at home during the entire week, without the performance of a single stroke of work. Saturday night came, and he called upon me, as usual, for my wages. I, of course, told him I had done no work, and had no wages. Here we were at the point of coming to blows. His wrath had been accumulating during the whole week; for he evidently saw that I was making no effort to get work, but was most aggravatingly awaiting his orders, in all things. As I look back to this behavior of mine, I scarcely know what possessed me, thus to trifle with those who had such unlimited power to bless or to blast me. Master Hugh raved and swore his determination to *"get hold of me"*; but, wisely for *him*, and happily for *me*, his wrath only employed those very harmless, impalpable missiles, which roll from a limber tongue. In my desperation, I had fully made up my mind to measure strength with Master Hugh, in case he should undertake to execute his threats. I am glad there was no necessity for this; for resistance to him could not have ended so happily for me, as it did in the case of Covey. He was not a man to be safely resisted by a slave; and I freely own, that in my conduct toward him, in this instance, there was more folly than wisdom. Master Hugh closed his reproofs, by telling me that, hereafter, I need give myself no uneasiness about getting work; that he "would, himself, see to getting work for me, and enough of it, at that." This threat I confess had some terror in it; and, on thinking the matter over, during the Sunday, I resolved, not only to save him the trouble of getting me work, but that, upon the third day of September, I would attempt to make my escape from slavery. The refusal to allow me to hire my time, therefore, hastened the period of flight. I had three weeks, now, in which to prepare for my journey.

Once resolved, I felt a certain degree of repose, and on Monday, instead of waiting for Master Hugh to seek employment for me, I was up by break of day, and off to the ship-yard of Mr. Butler, on the City Block, near the draw-bridge. I was a favorite with Mr. B., and, young as I was, I had served as his foreman on the float stage, at calking. Of course, I easily obtained work, and, at the end of the week—which by the way was exceedingly fine—I brought Master Hugh nearly nine dollars. The effect of this mark of returning good sense, on my part, was excellent. He was very much pleased; he took the money, commended me, and told me I might have done the same thing the week before. It is a blessed thing that the tyrant may not always know the thoughts and purposes of his victim. Master Hugh little knew what my plans were. The going to camp-meeting without asking his permission— the insolent answers made to his reproaches—the sulky deportment the week after being deprived of the privilege of hiring my time— had awakened in him the suspicion that I might be cherishing disloyal purposes. My object, therefore, in working steadily, was to remove suspicion, and in this I succeeded admirably. He probably thought I was never better satisfied with my condition, than at the very time I was planning my escape. The second week passed, and again I carried him my full week's wages—*nine dollars*; and so well pleased was he, that he gave me *twenty-five cents*! and "bade me make good use of it!" I told him I would, for one of the uses to which I meant to put it, was to pay my fare on the underground railroad.

Things without went on as usual; but I was passing through the same internal excitement and anxiety which I had experienced two years and a half before. The failure, in that instance, was not calculated to increase my confidence in the success of this, my second attempt; and I knew that a second failure could not leave me where my first did—I must either get to the *far north*, or be sent to the far south. Besides the exercise of mind from this state of facts, I had the painful sensation of being about to separate from a circle of honest and warm-hearted friends, in Baltimore. The thought of such a separation, where the hope of ever meeting again is excluded, and where there can be no correspondence, is very painful. It is my opinion, that thousands would escape from slavery who now remain there, but for the strong cords of affection that bind them to their families, relatives and friends. The daughter is hindered from escaping, by the love she bears her mother, and the father, by the love he bears his children; and so, to the end of the chapter. I had no relations in Baltimore, and I saw no probability of ever living in the neighborhood of sisters and brothers; but the thought of leaving my friends, was among the strongest obstacles to my running away. The last two days of the week—Friday and Saturday—were spent mostly in collecting my things together, for my journey. Having worked four days that week, for my master, I handed him six dollars, on Saturday night. I seldom spent my Sundays at home; and, for fear that something might be discovered in my conduct, I kept up my custom, and absented myself all day. On Monday, the third day of September, 1838, in accordance with my resolution, I bade farewell to the city of Baltimore, and to that slavery which had been my abhorrence from childhood.

How I got away—in what direction I traveled—whether by land or by water; whether with or without assistance—must, for reasons already mentioned, remain unexplained.

# LIFE AS A FREEMAN

## CHAPTER XXII

### LIBERTY ATTAINED

*Transition from Slavery to Freedom—A Wanderer in New York—Feelings on Reaching That City—An Old Acquaintance Met—Unfavorable Impressions—Loneliness and Insecurity—Apology for Slaves Who Return to Their Masters—Compelled to Tell My Condition—Succored By a Sailor—David Ruggles—The Underground Railroad—Marriage—Baggage Taken From Me—Kindness of Nathan Johnson—My Change of Name—Dark Notions of Northern Civilization—The Contrast—Colored People in New Bedford—An Incident Illustrating Their Spirit—A Common Laborer—Denied Work at My Trade—The First Winter at the North—Repulse at the Doors of the Church—Sanctified Hate—The* Liberator *and Its Editor.*

There is no necessity for any extended notice of the incidents of this part of my life. There is nothing very striking or peculiar about my career as a freeman, when viewed apart from my life as a slave. The relation subsisting between my early experience and that which I am now about to narrate, is, perhaps, my best apology for adding another chapter to this book.

Disappearing from the kind reader, in a flying cloud or balloon (pardon the figure), driven by the wind, and knowing not where I should land—whether in slavery or in freedom—it is proper that I should remove, at once, all anxiety, by frankly making known where I alighted. The flight was a bold and perilous one; but here I am, in the great city of New York, safe and sound, without loss of blood or bone. In less than a week after leaving Baltimore, I was walking amid the hurrying throng, and gazing upon the dazzling wonders of Broadway.

The dreams of my childhood and the purposes of my manhood were now fulfilled. A free state around me, and a free earth under my feet! What a moment was this to me! A whole year was pressed into a single day. A new world burst upon my agitated vision. I have often been asked, by kind friends to whom I have told my story, how I felt when first I found myself beyond the limits of slavery; and I must say here, as I have often said to them, there is scarcely anything about which I could not give a more satisfactory answer. It was a moment of joyous excitement, which no words can describe. In a letter to a friend, written soon after reaching New York, I said I felt as one might be supposed to feel, on escaping from a den of hungry lions. But, in a moment like that, sensations are too intense and too rapid for words. Anguish and grief, like darkness and rain, may be described, but joy and gladness, like the rainbow of promise, defy alike the pen and pencil.

For ten or fifteen years I had been dragging a heavy chain, with a huge block attached to it, cumbering my every motion. I had felt myself doomed to drag this chain and this block through life. All efforts, before, to separate myself from the hateful encumbrance, had only seemed to rivet me the more firmly to it. Baffled and discouraged at times, I had asked myself the question, "May not this, after all, be God's work? May He not, for wise ends, have doomed me to this lot?" A contest had been going on in my mind for years, between the clear consciousness of right and the plausible errors of superstition; between the wisdom of manly courage, and the foolish weakness of timidity. The contest was now ended; the chain was severed; God and right stood vindicated. *I was a freeman*, and the voice of peace and joy thrilled my heart.

Free and joyous, however, as I was, joy was not the only sensation I experienced. It was like the quick blaze, beautiful at the first, but which subsiding, leaves the building charred and desolate. I was soon taught that I was still in an enemy's land. A sense of loneliness and insecurity oppressed me sadly. I had been but a few hours in New York, before I was met in the streets by a fugitive slave, well known to me, and the information I got from him respecting New York, did nothing to lessen my apprehension of danger. The fugitive in question was "Allender's Jake," in Baltimore; but, said he, I am "William Dixon," in New York! I knew Jake well, and knew when Tolly Allender and Mr. Price (for the latter employed Master Hugh as his foreman, in his ship-yard on Fell's Point) made an attempt to recapture Jake, and failed. Jake told me all about his circumstances, and how narrowly he escaped being taken back to slavery; that the city was now full of southerners, returning from the springs; that the black people in New York were not to be trusted; that there were hired men on the look-out for fugitives from slavery, and who, for a few dollars, would betray me into the hands of the slave-catchers; that I must trust no man with my secret; that I must not think of going either on the wharves to work, or to a boarding-house to board; and, worse still, this same Jake told me it was not in his power to help me. He seemed, even while cautioning me, to be fearing lest, after all, I might be a party to a second attempt to recapture him. Under the inspiration of this thought, I must suppose it was, he gave signs of a wish to get rid of me, and soon left me—his whitewash brush in hand—as he said, for his work. He was soon lost to sight among the throng, and I was alone again, an easy prey to the kidnappers, if any should happen to be on my track.

New York, seventeen years ago, was less a place of safety for a runaway slave than now, and all know how unsafe it now is, under the new fugitive slave bill.* I was much troubled. I had very little money enough to buy me a few loaves of bread, but not enough to pay board, outside a lumber yard. I saw the wisdom of keeping away from the ship-yards, for if Master Hugh pursued me, he would naturally expect to find me looking for work among the calkers. For a time, every door seemed closed against me. A sense of my loneliness and helplessness crept over me, and covered me with something bordering on despair. In the midst of thousands of my fellow-men, and yet a perfect stranger! In the midst of human brothers, and yet more fearful of them than of hungry wolves! I was without home, without friends, without work, without money, and without any definite knowledge of which way to go, or where to look for succor.

Some apology can easily be made for the few slaves who have, after making good their escape, turned back to slavery, preferring the actual rule of their masters, to the life of loneliness, apprehension, hunger, and anxiety, which meets them on their first arrival in a free state. It is difficult for a freeman to enter into the feelings of such fugitives. He cannot see things in the same light with the slave, because he does not, and cannot, look from the same point from which the slave does.

---

* The Fugitive Slave Law of 1850 declared that any escaped slaves found in free states had to be returned to their masters.

"Why do you tremble," he says to the slave—"you are in a free state";
but the difficulty is, in realizing that he is in a free state, the slave might
reply. A freeman cannot understand why the slave-master's shadow
is bigger, to the slave, than the might and majesty of a free state; but
when he reflects that the slave knows more about the slavery of his
master than he does of the might and majesty of the free state, he has
the explanation. The slave has been all his life learning the power of his
master—being trained to dread his approach—and only a few hours
learning the power of the state. The master is to him a stern and flinty
reality, but the state is little more than a dream. He has been accustomed
to regard every white man as the friend of his master, and every colored
man as more or less under the control of his master's friends—the
white people. It takes stout nerves to stand up, in such circumstances.
A man, homeless, shelterless, breadless, friendless, and moneyless, is
not in a condition to assume a very proud or joyous tone; and in just
this condition was I, while wandering about the streets of New York
city and lodging, at least one night, among the barrels on one of its
wharves. I was not only free from slavery, but I was free from home,
as well. The reader will easily see that I had something more than the
simple fact of being free to think of, in this extremity.

I kept my secret as long as I could, and at last was forced to go in
search of an honest man—a man sufficiently human not to betray me
into the hands of slave-catchers. I was not a bad reader of the human
face, nor long in selecting the right man, when once compelled to
disclose the facts of my condition to some one.

I found my man in the person of one who said his name was Stewart.
He was a sailor, warm-hearted and generous, and he listened to my story
with a brother's interest. I told him I was running for my freedom—
knew not where to go—money almost gone—was hungry—thought
it unsafe to go the ship-yards for work, and needed a friend. Stewart
promptly put me in the way of getting out of my trouble. He took
me to his house, and went in search of the late David Ruggles, who
was then the secretary of the New York Vigilance Committee, and a
very active man in all anti-slavery works. Once in the hands of Mr.
Ruggles, I was comparatively safe. I was hidden with Mr. Ruggles
several days. In the meantime, my intended wife, Anna, came on from
Baltimore—to whom I had written, informing her of my safe arrival at
New York—and, in the presence of Mrs. Mitchell and Mr. Ruggles, we

were married, by Rev. James W. C. Pennington.

Mr. Ruggles* was the first officer on the underground railroad with whom I met after reaching the north, and, indeed, the first of whom I ever heard anything. Learning that I was a calker by trade, he promptly decided that New Bedford was the proper place to send me. "Many ships," said he, "are there fitted out for the whaling business, and you may there find work at your trade, and make a good living." Thus, in one fortnight after my flight from Maryland, I was safe in New Bedford, regularly entered upon the exercise of the rights, responsibilities, and duties of a freeman.

I may mention a little circumstance which annoyed me on reaching New Bedford. I had not a cent of money, and lacked two dollars toward paying our fare from Newport, and our baggage—not very costly— was taken by the stage driver, and held until I could raise the money to redeem it. This difficulty was soon surmounted. Mr. Nathan Johnson, to whom we had a line from Mr. Ruggles, not only received us kindly and hospitably, but, on being informed about our baggage, promptly loaned me two dollars with which to redeem my little property. I shall ever be deeply grateful, both to Mr. and Mrs. Nathan Johnson, for the lively interest they were pleased to take in me, in this hour of my extremest need. They not only gave myself and wife bread and shelter, but taught us how to begin to secure those benefits for ourselves. Long may they live, and may blessings attend them in this life and in that which is to come!

Once initiated into the new life of freedom, and assured by Mr. Johnson that New Bedford was a safe place, the comparatively unimportant matter, as to what should be my name, came up for consideration. It was necessary to have a name in my new relations. The name given me by my beloved mother was no less pretentious than "Frederick Augustus Washington Bailey." I had, however, before leaving Maryland, dispensed with the *Augustus Washington*, and retained the name *Frederick Bailey*. Between Baltimore and New

---

* He was a whole-souled man, fully imbued with a love of his afflicted and hunted people, and took pleasure in being to me, as was his wont, "Eyes to the blind, and legs to the lame." This brave and devoted man suffered much from the persecutions common to all who have been prominent benefactors. He at last became blind, and needed a friend to guide him, even as he had been a guide to others. Even in his blindness, he exhibited his manly character. In search of health, he became a physician. When hope of gaining his own was gone, he had hope for others. Believing in hydropathy, he established, at Northampton, Massachusetts, a large "Water Cure," and became one of the most successful of all engaged in that mode of treatment. (Original note)

Bedford, however, I had several different names, the better to avoid being overhauled by the hunters, which I had good reason to believe would be put on my track. Among honest men an honest man may well be content with one name, and to acknowledge it at all times and in all places; but toward fugitives, Americans are not honest. When I arrived at New Bedford, my name was Johnson; and finding that the Johnson family in New Bedford were already quite numerous—sufficiently so to produce some confusion in attempts to distinguish one from another—there was the more reason for making another change in my name. In fact, "Johnson" had been assumed by nearly every slave who had arrived in New Bedford from Maryland, and this, much to the annoyance of the original "Johnsons" (of whom there were many) in that place. Mine host, unwilling to have another of his own name added to the community in this unauthorized way, after I spent a night and a day at his house, gave me my present name. He had been reading the *Lady of the Lake*, and was pleased to regard me as a suitable person to wear this, one of Scotland's many famous names. Considering the noble hospitality and manly character of Nathan Johnson, I have felt that he, better than I, illustrated the virtues of the great Scottish chief. Sure I am, that had any slave-catcher entered his domicile, with a view to molest any one of his household, he would have shown himself like him of the "stalwart hand."

The reader will be amused at my ignorance, when I tell the notions I had of the state of northern wealth, enterprise, and civilization. Of wealth and refinement, I supposed the north had none. My *Columbian Orator*, which was almost my only book, had not done much to enlighten me concerning northern society. The impressions I had received were all wide of the truth. New Bedford, especially, took me by surprise, in the solid wealth and grandeur there exhibited. I had formed my notions respecting the social condition of the free states, by what I had seen and known of free, white, non-slaveholding people in the slave states. Regarding slavery as the basis of wealth, I fancied that no people could become very wealthy without slavery. A free white man, holding no slaves, in the country, I had known to be the most ignorant and poverty-stricken of men, and the laughing stock even of slaves themselves—called generally by them, in derision, *"poor white trash."* Like the non-slaveholders at the south, in holding no slaves, I suppose the northern people like them, also, in poverty and degradation. Judge, then, of my amazement and joy, when I found—as I did find—the very laboring population of New Bedford living in better houses, more elegantly furnished—surrounded by more comfort and refinement—than a majority of the slaveholders on the Eastern Shore of Maryland. There was my friend, Mr. Johnson, himself a colored man (who at the south would have been regarded as a proper marketable commodity), who lived in a better house—dined at a richer board—was the owner of more books—the reader of more newspapers—was more conversant with the political and social condition of this nation and the world—than nine-tenths of all the slaveholders of Talbot County, Maryland. Yet Mr. Johnson was a working man, and his hands were hardened by honest toil. Here, then, was something for observation and study. Whence the difference? The explanation was soon furnished, in the superiority of mind over simple brute force. Many pages might be given to the contrast, and in explanation of its causes. But an incident or two will suffice to show the reader as to how the mystery gradually vanished before me.

My first afternoon, on reaching New Bedford, was spent in visiting the wharves and viewing the shipping. The sight of the broad brim and the plain, Quaker dress, which met me at every turn, greatly increased my sense of freedom and security. "I am among the Quakers," thought I, "and am safe." Lying at the wharves and riding in the stream, were full-rigged ships of finest model, ready to start on whaling voyages. Upon the right and the left, I was walled in by large granite-fronted warehouses, crowded with the good things of this world. On the wharves, I saw industry without bustle, labor without noise, and heavy toil without the whip. There was no loud singing, as in southern ports, where ships are loading or unloading—no loud cursing or swearing—but everything went on as smoothly as the works of a well adjusted machine. How different was all this from the nosily fierce and clumsily absurd manner of labor-life in Baltimore and St. Michael's! One of the first incidents which illustrated the superior mental character of northern labor over that of the south, was the manner of unloading a ship's cargo of oil. In a southern port, twenty or thirty hands would have been employed to do what five or six did here, with the aid of a single ox attached to the end of a fall. Main strength, unassisted by skill, is slavery's method of labor. An old ox, worth eighty dollars, was doing, in New Bedford, what would have required fifteen thousand dollars worth of human bones and muscles to have performed in a southern port. I found that everything was done here with a scrupulous regard to economy, both in regard to men and things, time and strength. The maid servant, instead of spending at least a tenth part of her time in bringing and carrying water, as in Baltimore, had the pump at her elbow. The wood was dry, and snugly piled away for winter. Wood-houses, in-door pumps, sinks, drains, self-shutting gates, washing machines, pounding barrels, were all new things, and told me that I was among a thoughtful and sensible people. To the ship-repairing dock I went, and saw the same wise prudence. The carpenters struck where they aimed, and the calkers wasted no blows in idle flourishes of the mallet. I learned that men went from New Bedford to Baltimore, and bought old ships, and brought them here to repair, and made them better and more valuable than they ever were before. Men talked here of going whaling on a four *years'* voyage with more coolness than sailors where I came from talked of going a four *months'* voyage.

I now find that I could have landed in no part of the United States, where I should have found a more striking and gratifying contrast to the condition of the free people of color in Baltimore, than I found here in New Bedford. No colored man is really free in a slaveholding state. He wears the badge of bondage while nominally free, and is often subjected to hardships to which the slave is a stranger; but here in New Bedford, it was my good fortune to see a pretty near approach to freedom on the part of the colored people. I was taken all aback when Mr. Johnson—who lost no time in making me acquainted with the fact—told me that there was nothing in the constitution of Massachusetts to prevent a colored man from holding any office in the state. There, in New Bedford, the black man's children—although anti-slavery was then far from popular—went to school side by side with the white children, and apparently without objection from any quarter. To make me at home, Mr. Johnson assured me that no slaveholder could take a slave from New Bedford; that there were men there who would lay down their lives, before such an outrage could be perpetrated. The colored people themselves were of the best metal, and would fight for liberty to the death.

Soon after my arrival in New Bedford, I was told the following story, which was said to illustrate the spirit of the colored people in that goodly town: A colored man and a fugitive slave happened to have a little quarrel, and the former was heard to threaten the latter with informing his master of his whereabouts. As soon as this threat became known, a notice was read from the desk of what was then the only colored church in the place, stating that business of importance was to be then and there transacted. Special measures had been taken to secure the attendance of the would-be Judas, and had proved successful. Accordingly, at the hour appointed, the people came, and the betrayer also. All the usual formalities of public meetings were scrupulously gone through, even to the offering prayer for Divine direction in the duties of the occasion. The president himself performed this part of the ceremony, and I was told that he was unusually fervent. Yet, at the close of his prayer, the old man (one of the numerous family of Johnsons) rose from his knees, deliberately surveyed his audience, and then said, in a tone of solemn resolution, "*Well, friends, we have got him here, and I would now recommend that you young men should just take him outside the door and kill him.*" With this, a large body of the congregation, who well understood the business they had come there to transact, made a rush at the villain, and doubtless would have killed him, had he not availed himself of an open sash, and made good his escape. He has never shown his head in New Bedford since that time. This little incident is perfectly characteristic of the spirit of the colored people in New Bedford. A slave could not be taken from that town seventeen years ago, any more than he could be so taken away now. The reason is, that the colored people in that city are educated up to the point of fighting for their freedom, as well as speaking for it.

Once assured of my safety in New Bedford, I put on the habiliments of a common laborer, and went on the wharf in search of work. I had no notion of living on the honest and generous sympathy of my colored brother, Johnson, or that of the abolitionists. My cry was like that of Hood's laborer, "Oh! Only give me work." Happily for me, I was not long in searching. I found employment, the third day after my arrival in New Bedford, in stowing a sloop with a load of oil for the New York market. It was new, hard, and dirty work, even for a calker, but I went at it with a glad heart and a willing hand. I was now my own master—a tremendous fact—and the rapturous excitement with which I seized the job, may not easily be understood, except by some one with an experience like mine. The thoughts—"I can work! I can work for a living; I am not afraid of work; I have no Master Hugh to rob me of my earnings"—placed me in a state of independence, beyond seeking friendship or support of any man. That day's work I considered the real starting point of something like a new existence. Having finished this job and got my pay for the same, I went next in pursuit of a job at calking. It so happened that Mr. Rodney French, late mayor of the city of New Bedford, had a ship fitting out for sea, and to which there was a large job of calking and coppering to be done. I applied to that noble-hearted man for employment, and he promptly told me to go to work; but going on the float stage for the purpose, I was informed that every white man would leave the ship if I struck a blow upon her. "Well, well," thought I, "this is a hardship, but yet not a very serious one for me." The difference between the wages of a calker and that of a common day laborer, was an hundred percent in favor of the former; but then I was free, and free to work, though not at my trade. I now prepared myself to do anything which came to hand in the way of turning an honest penny; sawed wood—dug cellars—shoveled coal—swept chimneys with Uncle Lucas Debuty—rolled oil casks on the wharves—helped to load and unload vessels—worked in Ricketson's candle works—in Richmond's brass foundery, and elsewhere; and thus supported myself and family for three years.

The first winter was unusually severe, in consequence of the high prices of food; but even during that winter we probably suffered less than many who had been free all their lives. During the hardest of the winter, I hired out for nine dollars a month; and out of this rented two rooms for nine dollars per quarter, and supplied my wife—who was unable to work—with food and some necessary articles of furniture. We were closely pinched to bring our wants within our means; but the jail stood over the way, and I had a wholesome dread of the consequences of running in debt. This winter past, and I was up with the times—got plenty of work—got well paid for it—and felt that I had not done a foolish thing to leave Master Hugh and Master Thomas. I was now living in a new world, and was wide awake to its advantages. I early began to attend the meetings of the colored people of New Bedford, and to take part in them. I was somewhat amazed to see colored men drawing up resolutions and offering them for consideration. Several colored young men of New Bedford, at that period, gave promise of great usefulness. They were educated, and possessed what seemed to me, at the time, very superior talents. Some of them have been cut down by death, and others have removed to different parts of the world, and some remain there now, and justify, in their present activities, my early impressions of them.

Among my first concerns on reaching New Bedford, was to become united with the church, for I had never given up, in reality, my religious faith. I had become lukewarm and in a backslidden state, but I was still convinced that it was my duty to join the Methodist church. I was not then aware of the powerful influence of that religious body in favor of the enslavement of my race, nor did I see how the northern churches could be responsible for the conduct of southern churches; neither did I fully understand how it could be my duty to remain separate from the church, because bad men were connected with it. The slaveholding church, with its Coveys, Weedens, Aulds, and Hopkins, I could see through at once, but I could not see how Elm Street church, in New Bedford, could be regarded as sanctioning the Christianity of these characters in the church at St. Michael's. I therefore resolved to join the Methodist church in New Bedford, and to enjoy the spiritual advantage of public worship. The minister of the Elm Street Methodist church, was the Rev. Mr. Bonney; and although I was not allowed a seat in the body of the house, and was proscribed on account of my color, regarding this proscription simply as an accommodation of the unconverted congregation who had not yet been won to Christ and his brotherhood, I was willing thus to be proscribed, lest sinners should be driven away from the saving power of the gospel. Once converted, I thought they would be sure to treat me as a man and a brother. "Surely," thought I, "these Christian people have none of this feeling against color. They, at least, have renounced this unholy feeling." Judge, then, dear reader, of my astonishment and mortification, when I found, as soon I did find, all my charitable assumptions at fault.

An opportunity was soon afforded me for ascertaining the exact position of Elm Street church on that subject. I had a chance of seeing the religious part of the congregation by themselves; and although they disowned, in effect, their black brothers and sisters, before the world, I did think that where none but the saints were assembled, and no offense could be given to the wicked, and the gospel could not be "blamed," they would certainly recognize us as children of the same Father, and heirs of the same salvation, on equal terms with themselves.

The occasion to which I refer, was the sacrament of the Lord's

Supper, that most sacred and most solemn of all the ordinances of the Christian church. Mr. Bonney had preached a very solemn and searching discourse, which really proved him to be acquainted with the inmost secrets of the human heart. At the close of his discourse, the congregation was dismissed, and the church remained to partake of the sacrament. I remained to see, as I thought, this holy sacrament celebrated in the spirit of its great Founder.

There were only about a half dozen colored members attached to the Elm Street church, at this time. After the congregation was dismissed, these descended from the gallery, and took a seat against the wall most distant from the altar. Brother Bonney was very animated, and sung very sweetly, "Salvation 'tis a joyful sound," and soon began to administer the sacrament. I was anxious to observe the bearing of the colored members, and the result was most humiliating. During the whole ceremony, they looked like sheep without a shepherd. The white members went forward to the altar by the bench full; and when it was evident that all the whites had been served with the bread and wine, Brother Bonney— pious Brother Bonney—after a long pause, as if inquiring whether all the white members had been served, and fully assuring himself on that important point, then raised his voice to an unnatural pitch, and looking to the corner where his black sheep seemed penned, beckoned with his hand, exclaiming, "Come forward, colored friends! Come forward! You, too, have an interest in the blood of Christ. God is no respecter of persons. Come forward, and take this holy sacrament to your comfort." The colored members—poor, slavish souls—went forward, as invited. I went *out*, and have never been in that church since, although I honestly went there with a view to joining that body. I found it impossible to respect the religious profession of any who were under the dominion of this wicked prejudice, and I could not, therefore, feel that in joining them, I was joining a Christian church, at all. I tried other churches in New Bedford, with the same result, and finally, I attached myself to a small body of colored Methodists, known as the Zion Methodists. Favored with the affection and confidence of the members of this humble communion, I was soon made a class-leader and a local preacher among them. Many seasons of peace and joy I experienced among them, the remembrance of which is still precious, although I could not see it to be my duty to remain with that body, when I found that it consented to the same spirit which held my brethren in chains.

In four or five months after reaching New Bedford, there came a young man to me, with a copy of the *Liberator*, the paper edited by William Lloyd Garrison, and published by Isaac Knapp, and asked me to subscribe for it. I told him I had but just escaped from slavery, and was of course very poor, and remarked further, that I was unable to pay for it then; the agent, however, very willingly took me as a subscriber, and appeared to be much pleased with securing my name to his list. From this time I was brought in contact with the mind of William Lloyd Garrison. His paper took its place with me next to the Bible.

The *Liberator* was a paper after my own heart. It detested slavery— exposed hypocrisy and wickedness in high places—made no truce with the traffickers in the bodies and souls of men; it preached human brotherhood, denounced oppression, and, with all the solemnity of God's word, demanded the complete emancipation of my race. I not only liked—I *loved* this paper, and its editor. He seemed a match for all the opponents of emancipation, whether they spoke in the name of the law, or the gospel. His words were few, full of holy fire, and straight to the point. Learning to love him, through his paper, I was prepared to be pleased with his presence. Something of a hero worshipper, by nature, here was one, on first sight, to excite my love and reverence.

Seventeen years ago, few men possessed a more heavenly countenance than William Lloyd Garrison, and few men evinced a more genuine or a more exalted piety. The Bible was his text book— held sacred, as the word of the Eternal Father—sinless perfection— complete submission to insults and injuries—literal obedience to the injunction, if smitten on one side to turn the other also. Not only was Sunday a Sabbath, but all days were Sabbaths, and to be kept holy. All sectarism false and mischievous—the regenerated, throughout the world, members of one body, and the *head* Christ Jesus. Prejudice against color was rebellion against God. Of all men beneath the sky, the slaves, because most neglected and despised, were nearest and dearest to his great heart. Those ministers who defended slavery from the Bible, were of their "father the devil"; and those churches which fellowshipped slaveholders as Christians, were synagogues of Satan, and our nation was a nation of liars. Never loud or noisy—calm and serene as a summer sky, and as pure. "You are the man, the Moses, raised up by God, to deliver his modern Israel from bondage," was the spontaneous feeling of my heart, as I sat away back in the hall and listened to his mighty words; mighty in truth—mighty in their simple earnestness.

I had not long been a reader of the *Liberator*, and listener to its editor, before I got a clear apprehension of the principles of the anti-slavery movement. I had already the spirit of the movement, and only needed to understand its principles and measures. These I got from the *Liberator*, and from those who believed in that paper. My acquaintance with the movement increased my hope for the ultimate freedom of my race, and I united with it from a sense of delight, as well as duty.

Every week the *Liberator* came, and every week I made myself master of its contents. All the anti-slavery meetings held in New Bedford I promptly attended, my heart burning at every true utterance against the slave system, and every rebuke of its friends and supporters. Thus passed the first three years of my residence in New Bedford. I had not then dreamed of the possibility of my becoming a public advocate of the cause so deeply imbedded in my heart. It was enough for me to listen—to receive and applaud the great words of others, and only whisper in private, among the white laborers on the wharves, and elsewhere, the truths which burned in my breast.

# CHAPTER XXIII

## INTRODUCED TO THE ABOLITIONISTS

*First Speech at Nantucket—Much Sensation—Extraordinary Speech of Mr. Garrison—Author Becomes a Public Lecturer— Fourteen Years' Experience—Youthful Enthusiasm—A Brand New Fact—Matter of My Speech—Could Not Follow the Program—Fugitive Slaveship Doubted—To Settle All Doubt I Write My Experience of Slavery—Danger of Recapture Increased.*

In the summer of 1841, a grand anti-slavery convention was held in Nantucket, under the auspices of Mr. Garrison and his friends. Until now, I had taken no holiday since my escape from slavery. Having worked very hard that spring and summer, in Richmond's brass foundery—sometimes working all night as well as all day— and needing a day or two of rest, I attended this convention, never supposing that I should take part in the proceedings. Indeed, I was not aware that any one connected with the convention even so much as knew my name. I was, however, quite mistaken. Mr. William C. Coffin, a prominent abolitionist in those days of trial, had heard me speaking to my colored friends, in the little school-house on Second Street, New Bedford, where we worshiped. He sought me out in the crowd, and invited me to say a few words to the convention. Thus sought out, and thus invited, I was induced to speak out the feelings inspired by the occasion, and the fresh recollection of the scenes through which I had passed as a slave. My speech on this occasion is about the only one I ever made, of which I do not remember a single connected sentence. It was with the utmost difficulty that I could stand erect, or that I could command and articulate two words without hesitation and stammering. I trembled in every limb. I am not sure that my embarrassment was not the most effective part of my speech, if speech it could be called. At any rate, this is about the only part of my performance that I now distinctly remember. But excited and convulsed as I was, the audience, though remarkably quiet before, became as much excited as myself. Mr. Garrison followed me, taking me as his text; and now, whether I had made an eloquent speech in behalf of freedom or not, his was one never to be forgotten by those who heard it. Those who had heard Mr. Garrison oftenest, and had known him longest, were astonished. It was an effort of unequaled power, sweeping down, like a very tornado, every opposing barrier, whether of sentiment or opinion. For a moment, he possessed that almost fabulous inspiration, often referred to but seldom attained, in which a public meeting is transformed, as it were, into a single individuality—the orator wielding a thousand heads and hearts at once, and by the simple majesty of his all controlling thought, converting his hearers into the express image of his own soul. That night there were at least one thousand Garrisonians in Nantucket! At the close of this great meeting, I was duly waited on by Mr. John A. Collins—then the general agent of the Massachusetts anti-slavery society—and urgently solicited by him to become an agent of that society, and to publicly advocate its anti-slavery principles. I was reluctant to take the proffered position. I had not been quite three years from slavery—was honestly distrustful of my ability—wished to be excused; publicity exposed me to discovery and arrest by my master; and other objections came up, but Mr. Collins was not to be put off, and I finally consented to go out for three months, for I supposed that I should have got to the end of my story and my usefulness, in that length of time.

Here opened upon me a new life—a life for which I had had no preparation. I was a "graduate from the peculiar institution," Mr. Collins used to say, when introducing me, "*with my diploma written on my back!*" The three years of my freedom had been spent in the hard school of adversity. My hands had been furnished by nature with something like a solid leather coating, and I had bravely marked out for myself a life of rough labor, suited to the hardness of my hands, as a means of supporting myself and rearing my children.

Now what shall I say of this fourteen years' experience as a public advocate of the cause of my enslaved brothers and sisters? The time is but as a speck, yet large enough to justify a pause for retrospection— and a pause it must only be.

Young, ardent, and hopeful, I entered upon this new life in the full gush of unsuspecting enthusiasm. The cause was good; the men engaged in it were good; the means to attain its triumph, good; Heaven's blessing must attend all, and freedom must soon be given to the pining millions under a ruthless bondage. My whole heart went with the holy cause, and my most fervent prayer to the Almighty Disposer of the hearts of men, were continually offered for its early triumph. "Who or what," thought I, "can withstand a cause so good, so holy, so indescribably glorious. The God of Israel is with us. The might of the Eternal is on our side. Now let but the truth be spoken, and a nation will start forth at the sound!" In this enthusiastic spirit, I dropped into the ranks of freedom's friends, and went forth to the battle. For a time I was made to forget that my skin was dark and my hair crisped. For a time I regretted that I could not have shared the hardships and dangers endured by the earlier workers for the slave's release. I soon, however, found that my enthusiasm had been extravagant; that hardships and dangers were not yet passed; and that the life now before me, had shadows as well as sunbeams.

Among the first duties assigned me, on entering the ranks, was to travel, in company with Mr. George Foster, to secure subscribers to the *Anti-Slavery Standard* and the *Liberator*. With him I traveled and lectured through the eastern counties of Massachusetts. Much interest was awakened—large meetings assembled. Many came, no doubt, from curiosity to hear what a Negro could say in his own cause. I was generally introduced as a "*chattel*"—a "*thing*"—a piece of southern "*property*"—the chairman assuring the audience that it could speak. Fugitive slaves, at that time, were not so plentiful as now; and as a fugitive slave lecturer, I had the advantage of being a "*brand new fact*"—the first one out. Up to that time, a colored man was deemed a fool who confessed himself a runaway slave, not only because of the danger to which he exposed himself of being retaken, but because it was a confession of a very *low* origin! Some of my colored friends in New Bedford thought very badly of my wisdom for thus exposing and degrading myself. The only precaution I took, at the beginning, to prevent Master Thomas from knowing where I was, and what I was about, was the withholding my former name, my master's name, and the name of the state and county from which I came. During the first three or four months, my speeches were almost exclusively made up of narrations of my own personal experience as a slave. "Let us have the facts," said the people. So also said Friend George Foster, who always wished to pin me down to my simple narrative. "Give us the facts," said Collins, "we will take care of the philosophy." Just here arose some embarrassment. It was impossible for me to repeat the same old story month after month, and to keep up my interest in it. It was new to the people, it is true, but it was an old story to me; and to go through with it night after night, was a task altogether too mechanical for my nature. "Tell your story, Frederick," would whisper my then revered friend, William Lloyd Garrison, as I stepped upon the platform. I could not always obey, for I was now reading and thinking. New views of the subject were presented to my mind. It did not entirely satisfy me to *narrate* wrongs; I felt like *denouncing* them. I could not always curb my moral indignation for the perpetrators of slaveholding villainy, long enough for a circumstantial statement of the facts which I felt almost everybody must know. Besides, I was growing, and needed room. "People won't believe you ever was a slave, Frederick, if you keep on this way," said Friend Foster. "Be yourself," said Collins, "and tell your story." It was said to me, "Better have a *little* of the plantation manner of speech than not; 'tis not best that you seem too learned." These excellent friends were actuated by the best of motives, and were not altogether wrong in their advice; and still I must speak just the word that seemed to *me* the word to be spoken *by* me.

At last the apprehended trouble came. People doubted if I had ever been a slave. They said I did not talk like a slave, look like a slave, nor act like a slave, and that they believed I had never been south of Mason and Dixon's line. "He don't tell us where he came from— what his master's name was—how he got away—nor the story of his experience. Besides, he is educated, and is, in this, a contradiction of all the facts we have concerning the ignorance of the slaves." Thus, I was in a pretty fair way to be denounced as an impostor. The committee of the Massachusetts anti-slavery society knew all the facts in my case, and agreed with me in the prudence of keeping them private. They, therefore, never doubted my being a genuine fugitive; but going down the aisles of the churches in which I spoke, and hearing the free spoken Yankees saying, repeatedly, "*He's never been a slave, I'll warrant ye,*" I resolved to dispel all doubt, at no distant day, by such a revelation of facts as could not be made by any other than a genuine fugitive.

In a little less than four years, therefore, after becoming a public lecturer, I was induced to write out the leading facts connected with my experience in slavery, giving names of persons, places, and dates—thus putting it in the power of any who doubted, to ascertain the truth or falsehood of my story of being a fugitive slave. This statement soon became known in Maryland, and I had reason to believe that an effort would be made to recapture me.

It is not probable that any open attempt to secure me as a slave could have succeeded, further than the obtainment, by my master, of the money value of my bones and sinews. Fortunately for me, in the four years of my labors in the abolition cause, I had gained many friends, who would have suffered themselves to be taxed to almost any extent to save me from slavery. It was felt that I had committed the double offense of running away, and exposing the secrets and crimes of slavery and slaveholders. There was a double motive for seeking my reenslavement—avarice and vengeance; and while, as I have said, there was little probability of successful recapture, if attempted openly, I was constantly in danger of being spirited away, at a moment when my friends could render me no assistance. In traveling about from place to place—often alone—I was much exposed to this sort of attack. Any one cherishing the design to betray me, could easily do so, by simply tracing my whereabouts through the anti-slavery journals, for my meetings and movements were promptly made known in advance. My true friends, Mr. Garrison and Mr. Phillips, had no faith in the power of Massachusetts to protect me in my right to liberty. Public sentiment and the law, in their opinion, would hand me over to the tormentors. Mr. Phillips, especially, considered me in danger, and said, when I showed him the manuscript of my story, if in my place, he would throw it into the fire. Thus, the reader will observe, the settling of one difficulty only opened the way for another; and that though I had reached a free state, and had attained position for public usefulness, I was still tormented with the liability of losing my liberty. How this liability was dispelled, will be related, with other incidents, in the next chapter.

# CHAPTER XXIV

## TWENTY-ONE MONTHS IN GREAT BRITAIN

*Good Arising Out of Unpropitious Events—Denied Cabin
Passage—Proscription Turned to Good Account—The
Hutchinson Family—The Mob on Board the* Cambria—
*Happy Introduction to the British Public—Letter Addressed to
William Lloyd Garrison—Time and Labors While Abroad—
Freedom Purchased—Mrs. Henry Richardson—Free Papers—
Abolitionists Displeased with the Ransom—How My Energies
Were Directed—Reception Speech in London—Character of
the Speech Defended—Circumstances Explained—Causes
Contributing to the Success of My Mission—Free Church of
Scotland—Testimonial.*

The allotments of Providence, when coupled with trouble and anxiety, often conceal from finite vision the wisdom and goodness in which they are sent; and, frequently, what seemed a harsh and invidious dispensation, is converted by after experience into a happy and beneficial arrangement. Thus, the painful liability to be returned again to slavery, which haunted me by day, and troubled my dreams by night, proved to be a necessary step in the path of knowledge and usefulness. The writing of my pamphlet, in the spring of 1845, endangered my liberty, and led me to seek a refuge from republican slavery in monarchical England. A rude, uncultivated fugitive slave was driven, by stern necessity, to that country to which young American gentlemen go to increase their stock of knowledge, to seek pleasure, to have their rough, democratic manners softened by contact with English aristocratic refinement. On applying for a passage to England, on board the *Cambria*, of the Cunard line, my friend, James N. Buffum, of Lynn, Massachusetts, was informed that I could not be received on board as a cabin passenger. American prejudice against color triumphed over British liberality and civilization, and erected a color test and condition for crossing the sea in the cabin of a British vessel. The insult was keenly felt by my white friends, but to me, it was common, expected, and therefore, a thing of no great consequence, whether I went in the cabin or in the steerage. Moreover, I felt that if I could not go into the first cabin, first-cabin passengers could come into the second cabin, and the result justified my anticipations to the fullest extent. Indeed, I soon found myself an object of more general interest than I wished to be; and so far from being degraded by being placed in the second cabin, that part of the ship became the scene of as much pleasure and refinement, during the voyage, as the cabin itself. The Hutchinson Family, celebrated vocalists—fellow-passengers—often came to my rude forecastle deck, and sung their sweetest songs, enlivening the place with eloquent music, as well as spirited conversation, during the voyage. In two days after leaving Boston, one part of the ship was about as free to me as another. My fellow-passengers not only visited me, but invited me to visit them, on the saloon deck. My visits there, however, were but seldom. I preferred to live within my privileges, and keep upon my own premises. I found this quite as much in accordance with good policy, as with my own feelings. The effect was, that with the majority of the passengers, all color distinctions were flung to the winds, and I found myself treated with every mark of respect, from the beginning to the end of the voyage, except in a single instance; and in that, I came near being mobbed, for complying with an invitation given me by the passengers, and the captain of the *Cambria*, to deliver a lecture on slavery. Our New Orleans and Georgia passengers were pleased to regard my lecture as an insult offered to them, and swore I should not speak. They went so far as to threaten to throw me overboard, and but for the firmness of Captain Judkins, probably would have (under the inspiration of *slavery* and *brandy*) attempted to put their threats into execution. I have no space to describe this scene, although its tragic and comic peculiarities are well worth describing. An end was put to the *melee*, by the captain's calling the ship's company to put the salt water mobocrats in irons. At this determined order, the gentlemen of the lash scampered, and for the rest of the voyage conducted themselves very decorously.

This incident of the voyage, in two days after landing at Liverpool, brought me at once before the British public, and that by no act of my own. The gentlemen so promptly snubbed in their meditated violence, flew to the press to justify their conduct, and to denounce me as a worthless and insolent Negro. This course was even less wise than the conduct it was intended to sustain; for, besides awakening something like a national interest in me, and securing me an audience, it brought out counter statements, and threw the blame upon themselves, which they had sought to fasten upon me and the gallant captain of the ship.

Some notion may be formed of the difference in my feelings and circumstances, while abroad, from the following extract from one of a series of letters addressed by me to Mr. Garrison, and published in the *Liberator*. It was written on the first day of January, 1846:

> *My Dear Friend Garrison:*
>
> Up to this time, I have given no direct expression of the views, feelings, and opinions which I have formed, respecting the character and condition of the people of this land. I have refrained thus, purposely. I wish to speak advisedly, and in order to do this, I have waited till, I trust, experience has brought my opinions to an intelligent maturity. I have been thus careful, not because I think what I say will have much effect in shaping the opinions of the world, but because whatever of influence I may possess, whether little or much, I wish it to go in the right direction, and according to truth. I hardly need say that, in speaking of Ireland, I shall be influenced by no prejudices in favor of America. I think my circumstances all forbid that. I have no end to serve, no creed to uphold, no government to defend; and as to nation, I belong to none. I have no protection at home, or resting-place abroad. The land of my birth welcomes me to her shores only as a slave, and spurns with contempt the idea of treating me differently; so that I am an outcast from the society of my childhood, and an outlaw in the land of my birth. "I am a stranger with thee, and a sojourner, as all my fathers were." That men should be patriotic, is to me perfectly natural; and as a philosophical fact, I am able to give it an *intellectual* recognition. But no further can I go. If ever I had any patriotism, or any capacity for the feeling, it was whipped out of me long since, by the lash of the American soul-drivers.
>
> In thinking of America, I sometimes find myself admiring her bright blue sky, her grand old woods, her fertile fields, her beautiful rivers, her mighty lakes, and star-

crowned mountains. But my rapture is soon checked, my joy is soon turned to mourning. When I remember that all is cursed with the infernal spirit of slaveholding, robbery, and wrong; when I remember that with the waters of her noblest rivers, the tears of my brethren are borne to the ocean, disregarded and forgotten, and that her most fertile fields drink daily of the warm blood of my outraged sisters; I am filled with unutterable loathing, and led to reproach myself that anything could fall from my lips in praise of such a land. America will not allow her children to love her. She seems bent on compelling those who would be her warmest friends, to be her worst enemies. May God give her repentance, before it is too late, is the ardent prayer of my heart. I will continue to pray, labor, and wait, believing that she cannot always be insensible to the dictates of justice, or deaf to the voice of humanity.

My opportunities for learning the character and condition of the people of this land have been very great. I have traveled almost from the Hill of Howth to the Giant's Causeway, and from the Giant's Causeway, to Cape Clear. During these travels, I have met with much in the character and condition of the people to approve, and much to condemn; much that has thrilled me with pleasure, and very much that has filled me with pain. I will not, in this letter, attempt to give any description of those scenes which have given me pain. This I will do hereafter. I have enough, and more than your subscribers will be disposed to read at one time, of the bright side of the picture. I can truly say, I have spent some of the happiest moments of my life since landing in this country. I seem to have undergone a transformation. I live a new life. The warm and generous cooperation extended to me by the friends of my despised race; the prompt and liberal manner with which the press has rendered me its aid; the glorious enthusiasm with which thousands have flocked to hear the cruel wrongs of my down-trodden and long-enslaved fellow-countrymen portrayed; the deep sympathy for the slave, and the strong abhorrence of the slaveholder, everywhere evinced; the cordiality with which members and ministers of various religious bodies, and of various shades of religious opinion, have embraced me, and lent me their aid; the kind of hospitality constantly proffered to me by persons of the highest rank in society;

the spirit of freedom that seems to animate all with whom I come in contact, and the entire absence of everything that looked like prejudice against me, on account of the color of my skin—contrasted so strongly with my long and bitter experience in the United States, that I look with wonder and amazement on the transition. In the southern part of the United States, I was a slave, thought of and spoken of as property; in the language of the law, "*held, taken, reputed, and adjudged to be a chattel in the hands of my owners and possessors, and their executors, administrators, and assigns, to all intents, constructions, and purposes whatsoever.*" (Brev. Digest, 224). In the northern states, a fugitive slave, liable to be hunted at any moment, like a felon, and to be hurled into the terrible jaws of slavery—doomed by an inveterate prejudice against color to insult and outrage on every hand (Massachusetts out of the question)—denied the privileges and courtesies common to others in the use of the most humble means of conveyance—shut out from the cabins on steamboats—refused admission to respectable hotels— caricatured, scorned, scoffed, mocked, and maltreated with impunity by any one (no matter how black his heart), so he has a white skin. But now behold the change! Eleven days and a half gone, and I have crossed three thousand miles of the perilous deep. Instead of a democratic government, I am under a monarchical government. Instead of the bright, blue sky of America, I am covered with the soft, grey fog of the Emerald Isle. I breathe, and lo! the chattel becomes a man. I gaze around in vain for one who will question my equal humanity, claim me as his slave, or offer me an insult. I employ a cab—I am seated beside white people—I reach the hotel—I enter the same door—I am shown into the same parlor—I dine at the same table and no one is offended. No delicate nose grows deformed in my presence. I find no difficulty here in obtaining admission into any place of worship, instruction, or amusement, on equal terms with people as white as any I ever saw in the United States. I meet nothing to remind me of my complexion. I find myself regarded and treated at every turn with the kindness and deference paid to white people. When I go to church, I am met by no upturned nose and scornful lip to tell me, "*We don't allow niggers in here!*"

I remember, about two years ago, there was in Boston, near the south-west corner of Boston Common, a menagerie. I had long desired to see such a collection as I understood was being exhibited there. Never having had an opportunity while a slave, I resolved to seize this, my first, since my escape. I went, and as I approached the entrance to gain admission, I was met and told by the door-keeper, in a harsh and contemptuous tone, "*We don't allow niggers in here.*" I also remember attending a revival meeting in the Rev. Henry Jackson's meeting-house, at New Bedford, and going up the broad aisle to find a seat, I was met by a good deacon, who told me, in a pious tone, "*We don't allow niggers in here!*" Soon after my arrival in New Bedford, from the south, I had a strong desire to attend the Lyceum, but was told, "*They don't allow niggers in here!*" While passing from New York to Boston, on the steamer Massachusetts, on the night of the 9th of December, 1843, when chilled almost through with the cold, I went into the cabin to get a little warm. I was soon touched upon the shoulder, and told, "*We don't allow niggers in here!*" On arriving in Boston, from an anti-slavery tour, hungry and tired, I went into an eating-house, near my friend, Mr. Campbell's, to get some refreshments. I was met by a lad in a white apron, "*We don't allow niggers in here!*" A week or two before leaving the United States, I had a meeting appointed at Weymouth, the home of that glorious band of true abolitionists, the Weston family, and others. On attempting to take a seat in the omnibus to that place, I was told by the driver (and I never shall forget his fiendish hate). "*I don't allow niggers in here!*" Thank heaven for the respite I now enjoy! I had been in Dublin but a few days, when a gentleman of great respectability kindly offered to conduct me through all the public buildings of that beautiful city; and a little afterward, I found myself dining with the lord mayor of Dublin. What a pity there was not some American democratic Christian at the door of his splendid mansion, to bark out at my approach, "*They don't allow niggers in here!*" The truth is, the people here know nothing of the republican Negro hate prevalent in our glorious land. They measure and esteem men according to their moral and intellectual worth, and not according to the color of their skin. Whatever may be said of the aristocracies here, there is none based on the color of a man's skin. This species of aristocracy belongs preeminently to "the land of the free, and the home of the brave." I have never found it abroad, in any but Americans. It sticks to them wherever they go. They find it almost as hard to get rid of, as to get rid of their skins.

The second day after my arrival at Liverpool, in company with my friend, Buffum, and several other friends, I went to Eaton Hall, the residence of the Marquis of Westminster, one of the most splendid buildings in England. On approaching the door, I found several of our American passengers, who came out with us in the *Cambria*, waiting for admission, as but one party was allowed in the house at a time. We all had to wait till the company within came out. And of all the faces, expressive of chagrin, those of the Americans were preeminent. They looked as sour as vinegar, and as bitter as gall, when they found I was to be admitted on equal terms with themselves. When the door was opened, I walked in, on an equal footing with my white fellow-citizens, and from all I could see, I had as much attention paid me by the servants that showed us through the house, as any with a paler skin. As I walked through the building, the statuary did not fall down, the pictures did not leap from their places, the doors did not refuse to open, and the servants did not say, "*We don't allow niggers in here!*"

A happy new-year to you, and all the friends of freedom.[*]

My time and labors, while abroad, were divided between England, Ireland, Scotland, and Wales. Upon this experience alone, I might write a book twice the size of this, *My Bondage and My Freedom.* I visited and lectured in nearly all the large towns and cities in the United Kingdom, and enjoyed many favorable opportunities for observation and information. But books on England are abundant, and the public may, therefore, dismiss any fear that I am meditating another infliction in that line; though, in truth, I should like much to write a book on those countries, if for nothing else, to make grateful mention of the many dear friends, whose benevolent actions toward me are ineffaceably stamped upon my memory, and warmly treasured in my heart. To these friends I owe my freedom in the United States. On their own motion, without any solicitation from me (Mrs. Henry Richardson, a clever

---

[*] Letter first published in the January 30, 1846, edition of the *Liberator*.

lady, remarkable for her devotion to every good work, taking the lead), they raised a fund sufficient to purchase my freedom, and actually paid it over, and placed the papers* of my manumission in my hands, before they would tolerate the idea of my returning to this, my native country. To this commercial transaction I owe my exemption from the democratic operation of the Fugitive Slave Bill of 1850. But for this, I might at any time become a victim of this most cruel and scandalous enactment, and be doomed to end my life, as I began it, a slave. The sum paid for my freedom was one hundred and fifty pounds sterling.

Some of my uncompromising anti-slavery friends in this country failed to see the wisdom of this arrangement, and were not pleased that I consented to it, even by my silence. They thought it a violation of anti-slavery principles—conceding a right of property in man—and a wasteful expenditure of money. On the other hand, viewing it simply in the light of a ransom, or as money extorted by a robber, and my liberty

---

* The following is a copy of these curious papers, both of my transfer from Thomas to Hugh Auld, and from Hugh to myself:

"Know all men by these Presents, That I, Thomas Auld, of Talbot County, and state of Maryland, for and in consideration of the sum of one hundred dollars, current money, to me paid by Hugh Auld, of the city of Baltimore, in the said state, at and before the sealing and delivery of these presents, the receipt whereof, I, the said Thomas Auld, do hereby acknowledge, have granted, bargained, and sold, and by these presents do grant, bargain, and sell unto the said Hugh Auld, his executors, administrators, and assigns, *one Negro man*, by the name of Frederick Baily, or Douglass, as he calls himself—he is now about twenty-eight years of age—to have and to hold the said Negro man for life. And I, the said Thomas Auld, for myself, my heirs, executors, and administrators, all and singular, the said Frederick Baily alias Douglass, unto the said Hugh Auld, his executors, administrators, and assigns against me, the said Thomas Auld, my executors, and administrators, and against all and every other person or persons whatsoever, shall and will warrant and forever defend by these presents. In witness whereof, I set my hand and seal, this thirteenth day of November, eighteen hundred and forty-six.          Thomas Auld

"Signed, sealed, and delivered in presence of Wrightson Jones.
     "John C. Leas."
The authenticity of this bill of sale is attested by N. Harrington, a justice of the peace of the state of Maryland, and for the county of Talbot, dated same day as above.

"To all whom it may concern: Be it known, that I, Hugh Auld, of the city of Baltimore, in Baltimore County, in the state of Maryland, for divers good causes and considerations, me thereunto moving, have released from slavery, liberated, manumitted, and set free, and by these presents do hereby release from slavery, liberate, manumit, and set free, *my Negro man*, named Frederick Baily, otherwise called Douglass, being of the age of twenty-eight years, or thereabouts, and able to work and gain a sufficient livelihood and maintenance; and him the said Negro man named Frederick Baily, otherwise called Frederick Douglass, I do declare to be henceforth free, manumitted, and discharged from all manner of servitude to me, my executors, and administrators forever.

"In witness whereof, I, the said Hugh Auld, have hereunto set my hand and seal the fifth of December, in the year one thousand eight hundred and forty-six.

Hugh Auld

"Sealed and delivered in presence of T. Hanson Belt.
"James N. S. T. Wright" (Original note)

of more value than one hundred and fifty pounds sterling, I could not see either a violation of the laws of morality, or those of economy, in the transaction.

It is true, I was not in the possession of my claimants, and could have easily remained in England, for the same friends who had so generously purchased my freedom, would have assisted me in establishing myself in that country. To this, however, I could not consent. I felt that I had a duty to perform—and that was, to labor and suffer with the oppressed in my native land. Considering, therefore, all the circumstances—the fugitive slave bill included—I think the very best thing was done in letting Master Hugh have the hundred and fifty pounds sterling, and leaving me free to return to my appropriate field of labor. Had I been a private person, having no other relations or duties than those of a personal and family nature, I should never have consented to the payment of so large a sum for the privilege of living securely under our glorious republican form of government. I could have remained in England, or have gone to some other country; and perhaps I could even have lived unobserved in this. But to this I could not consent. I had already become somewhat notorious, and withal quite as unpopular as notorious; and I was, therefore, much exposed to arrest and recapture.

The main object to which my labors in Great Britain were directed, was the concentration of the moral and religious sentiment of its people against American slavery. England is often charged with having established slavery in the United States, and if there were no other justification than this, for appealing to her people to lend their moral aid for the abolition of slavery, I should be justified. My speeches in Great Britain were wholly extemporaneous, and I may not always have been so guarded in my expressions, as I otherwise should have been. I was ten years younger then than now, and only seven years from slavery. I cannot give the reader a better idea of the nature of my discourses, than by republishing one of them, delivered in Finsbury chapel, London, to an audience of about two thousand persons, and which was published in the *London Universe*, at the time.

Those in the United States who may regard this speech as being harsh in its spirit and unjust in its statements, because delivered before an audience supposed to be anti-republican in their principles and feelings, may view the matter differently, when they learn that the case supposed did not exist. It so happened that the great mass of the people in England who attended and patronized my anti-slavery meetings, were, in truth, about as good republicans as the mass of Americans, and with this decided advantage over the latter—they are lovers of republicanism for all men, for black men as well as for white men. They are the people who sympathize with Louis Kossuth and Mazzini,* and with the oppressed and enslaved, of every color and nation, the world over. They constitute the democratic element in British politics, and are as much opposed to the union of church and state as we, in America, are to such an union. At the meeting where this speech was delivered, Joseph Sturge—a world-wide philanthropist, and a member of the society of Friends—presided, and addressed the meeting. George William Alexander, another Friend, who has spent more than an American fortune in promoting the anti-slavery cause in different sections of the world, was on the platform; and also Dr. Campbell (now of the *British Banner*) who combines all the humane tenderness of Melanchthon, with the directness and boldness of Luther. He is in the very front ranks of non-conformists, and looks with no unfriendly eye upon America. George Thompson, too, was there; and America will yet own that he did a true man's work in relighting the rapidly dying-out fire of true republicanism in the American heart, and be ashamed of the treatment he met at her hands. Coming generations in this country will applaud the spirit of this much abused republican friend of freedom. There were others of note seated on the platform, who would gladly ingraft upon English institutions all that is purely republican in the institutions of America. Nothing, therefore, must be set down against this speech on the score that it was delivered in the presence of those who cannot appreciate the many excellent things belonging to our system of government, and with a view to stir up prejudice against republican institutions.

Again, let it also be remembered—for it is the simple truth—that neither in this speech, nor in any other which I delivered in England, did I ever allow myself to address Englishmen as against Americans. I took my stand on the high ground of human brotherhood, and spoke to Englishmen as men, in behalf of men. Slavery is a crime, not against Englishmen, but against God, and all the members of the human family; and it belongs to the whole human family to seek its suppression. In a

---

* Louis Kossuth (Hungary) and Giuseppe Mazzini (Italy) were 19th century politicians who advocated for democracy.

letter to Mr. Greeley, of the *New York Tribune*, written while abroad, I said:

> I am, nevertheless, aware that the wisdom of exposing the sins of one nation in the ear of another, has been seriously questioned by good and clear-sighted people, both on this and on your side of the Atlantic. And the thought is not without weight on my own mind. I am satisfied that there are many evils which can be best removed by confining our efforts to the immediate locality where such evils exist. This, however, is by no means the case with the system of slavery. It is such a giant sin—such a monstrous aggregation of iniquity—so hardening to the human heart—so destructive to the moral sense, and so well calculated to beget a character, in every one around it, favorable to its own continuance—that I feel not only at liberty, but abundantly justified, in appealing to the whole world to aid in its removal.

But, even if I had—as has been often charged—labored to bring American institutions generally into disrepute, and had not confined my labors strictly within the limits of humanity and morality, I should not have been without illustrious examples to support me. Driven into semi-exile by civil and barbarous laws, and by a system which cannot be thought of without a shudder, I was fully justified in turning, if possible, the tide of the moral universe against the heaven-daring outrage.

Four circumstances greatly assisted me in getting the question of American slavery before the British public. First, the mob on board the *Cambria*, already referred to, which was a sort of national announcement of my arrival in England. Secondly, the highly reprehensible course pursued by the Free Church of Scotland, in soliciting, receiving, and retaining money in its sustentation fund for supporting the gospel in Scotland, which was evidently the ill-gotten gain of slaveholders and slave-traders. Third, the great Evangelical Alliance—or rather the attempt to form such an alliance, which should include slaveholders of a certain description—added immensely to the interest felt in the slavery question. About the same time, there was the World's Temperance Convention, where I had the misfortune to come in collision with sundry American doctors of divinity—Dr. Cox among the number—with whom I had a small controversy.

It has happened to me—as it has happened to most other men engaged in a good cause—often to be more indebted to my enemies than to my own skill or to the assistance of my friends, for whatever success has attended my labors. Great surprise was expressed by American newspapers, north and south, during my stay in Great Britain, that a person so illiterate and insignificant as myself could awaken an interest so marked in England. These papers were not the only parties surprised. I was myself not far behind them in surprise. But the very contempt and scorn, the systematic and extravagant disparagement of which I was the object, served, perhaps, to magnify my few merits, and to render me of some account, whether deserving or not. A man is sometimes made great, by the greatness of the abuse a portion of mankind may think proper to heap upon him. Whether I was of as much consequence as the English papers made me out to be, or not, it was easily seen, in England, that I could not be the ignorant and worthless creature, some of the American papers would have them believe I was. Men, in their senses, do not take bowie-knives to kill mosquitoes, nor pistols to shoot flies; and the American passengers who thought proper to get up a mob to silence me, on board the *Cambria*, took the most effective method of telling the British public that I had something to say.

But to the second circumstance, namely, the position of the Free Church of Scotland, with the great Doctors Chalmers, Cunningham, and Candlish at its head. That church, with its leaders, put it out of the power of the Scotch people to ask the old question, which we in the north have often most wickedly asked—"*What have we to do with slavery?*" That church had taken the price of blood into its treasury, with which to build *free* churches, and to pay *free* church ministers for preaching the gospel; and, worse still, when honest John Murray, of Bowlien Bay—now gone to his reward in heaven—with William Smeal, Andrew Paton, Frederick Card, and other sterling anti-slavery men in Glasgow, denounced the transaction as disgraceful and shocking to the religious sentiment of Scotland, this church, through its leading divines, instead of repenting and seeking to mend the mistake into which it had fallen, made it a flagrant sin, by undertaking to defend, in the name of God and the Bible, the principle not only of taking the money of slave-dealers to build churches, but of holding fellowship with the holders and traffickers in human flesh. This, the reader will see, brought up the whole question of slavery, and opened the way to its full discussion, without any agency of mine. I have never seen a people more deeply moved than were the people of Scotland, on this very question. Public meeting succeeded public meeting. Speech after speech, pamphlet after pamphlet, editorial after editorial, sermon after sermon, soon lashed the conscientious Scotch people into a perfect *furore*. "*Send back the money*!" was indignantly cried out, from Greenock to Edinburgh, and from Edinburgh to Aberdeen. George Thompson, of London, Henry C. Wright, of the United States, James N. Buffum, of Lynn, Massachusetts, and myself were on the anti-slavery side; and Doctors Chalmers, Cunningham, and Candlish on the other. In a conflict where the latter could have had even the show of right, the truth, in our hands as against them, must have been driven to the wall; and while I believe we were able to carry the conscience of the country against the action of the Free Church, the battle, it must be confessed, was a hard-fought one. Abler defenders of the doctrine of fellowshipping slaveholders as Christians, have not been met with. In defending this doctrine, it was necessary to deny that slavery is a sin. If driven from this position, they were compelled to deny that slaveholders were responsible for the sin; and if driven from both these positions, they must deny that it is a sin in such a sense, and that slaveholders are sinners in such a sense, as to make it wrong, in the circumstances in which they were placed, to recognize them as Christians. Dr. Cunningham was the most powerful debater on the slavery side of the question; Mr. Thompson was the ablest on the anti-slavery side. A scene occurred between these two men, a parallel to which I think I never witnessed before, and I know I never have since. The scene was caused by a single exclamation on the part of Mr. Thompson.

The general assembly of the Free Church was in progress at Cannon Mills, Edinburgh. The building would hold about twenty-five hundred persons; and on this occasion it was densely packed, notice having been given that Doctors Cunningham and Candlish would speak, that day, in defense of the relations of the Free Church of Scotland to slavery in America. Messrs. Thompson, Buffum, myself, and a few anti-slavery friends, attended, but sat at such a distance, and in such a position, that, perhaps, we were not observed from the platform. The excitement was intense, having been greatly increased by a series of meetings held by Messrs. Thompson, Wright, Buffum, and myself, in the most splendid hall in that most beautiful city, just previous to the meetings of the general assembly. "*Send back the money!*" stared at us from every street corner; "*Send back the money!*" in large capitals, adorned the broad flags of the pavement; "*Send back the money!*" was the chorus of the popular street songs; "*Send back the money!*" was the heading of leading editorials in the daily newspapers. This day, at Cannon Mills, the great doctors of the church were to give an answer to this loud and stern demand. Men of all parties and all sects were most eager to hear. Something great was expected. The occasion was great, the men great, and great speeches were expected from them.

In addition to the outside pressure upon Doctors Cunningham and Candlish, there was wavering in their own ranks. The conscience of the church itself was not at ease. A dissatisfaction with the position of the church touching slavery, was sensibly manifest among the members, and something must be done to counteract this untoward influence. The great Dr. Chalmers was in feeble health, at the time. His most potent eloquence could not now be summoned to Cannon Mills, as formerly. He whose voice was able to rend asunder and dash down the granite walls of the established church of Scotland, and to lead a host in solemn procession from it, as from a doomed city, was now old and enfeebled. Besides, he had said his word on this very question; and his word had not silenced the clamor without, nor stilled the anxious heavings within. The occasion was momentous, and felt to be so. The church was in a perilous condition. A change of some sort must take place in her condition, or she must go to pieces. To stand where she did, was impossible. The whole weight of the matter fell on Cunningham and Candlish. No shoulders in the church were broader than theirs; and I must say, badly as I detest the principles laid down and defended by them, I was compelled to acknowledge the vast mental endowments of the men. Cunningham rose; and his rising was the signal for almost tumultous applause. You will say this was scarcely in keeping with the solemnity of the occasion, but to me it served to increase its grandeur and gravity. The applause, though tumultuous, was not joyous. It seemed to me, as it thundered up from the vast audience, like the fall of an immense shaft, flung from shoulders already galled by its crushing weight. It was like saying, "Doctor, we have borne this burden long enough, and willingly fling it upon you. Since it was you who brought it upon us, take it now, and do what you will with it, for we are too weary to bear it."

Doctor Cunningham proceeded with his speech, abounding in logic, learning, and eloquence, and apparently bearing down all opposition; but at the moment—the fatal moment—when he was just bringing all his arguments to a point, and that point being, that neither Jesus Christ nor his holy apostles regarded slaveholding as a sin, George Thompson, in a clear, sonorous, but rebuking voice, broke the deep stillness of the audience, exclaiming, *Hear! Hear! Hear!* The effect of this simple and common exclamation is almost incredible. It was as if a granite wall had been suddenly flung up against the advancing current of a mighty river. For a moment, speaker and audience were brought to a dead silence. Both the doctor and his hearers seemed appalled by the audacity, as well as the fitness of the rebuke. At length a shout went up to the cry of "Put him out!" Happily, no one attempted to execute this cowardly order, and the doctor proceeded with his discourse. Not, however, as before, did the learned doctor proceed. The exclamation of Thompson must have reechoed itself a thousand times in his memory, during the remainder of his speech, for the doctor never recovered from the blow.

The deed was done, however; the pillars of the church—*the proud, Free Church of Scotland*—were committed and the humility of repentance was absent. The Free Church held on to the blood-stained money, and continued to justify itself in its position—and of course to apologize for slavery—and does so till this day. She lost a glorious opportunity for giving her voice, her vote, and her example to the cause of humanity; and today she is staggering under the curse of the enslaved, whose blood is in her skirts. The people of Scotland are, to this day, deeply grieved at the course pursued by the Free Church, and would hail, as a relief from a deep and blighting shame, the "sending back the money" to the slaveholders from whom it was gathered.

One good result followed the conduct of the Free Church; it furnished an occasion for making the people of Scotland thoroughly acquainted with the character of slavery, and for arraying against the system the moral and religious sentiment of that country. Therefore, while we did not succeed in accomplishing the specific object of our mission, namely—procure the sending back of the money—we were amply justified by the good which really did result from our labors.

Next comes the Evangelical Alliance. This was an attempt to form a union of all evangelical Christians throughout the world. Sixty or seventy American divines attended, and some of them went there merely to weave a world-wide garment with which to clothe evangelical slaveholders. Foremost among these divines, was the Rev. Samuel Hanson Cox, moderator of the New School Presbyterian General Assembly. He and his friends spared no pains to secure a platform broad enough to hold American slaveholders, and in this partly succeeded. But the question of slavery is too large a question to be finally disposed of, even by the Evangelical Alliance. We appealed from the judgment of the Alliance, to the judgment of the people of Great Britain, and with the happiest effect. This controversy with the Alliance might be made the subject of extended remark, but I must forbear, except to say, that this effort to shield the Christian character of slaveholders greatly served to open a way to the British ear for anti-slavery discussion, and that it was well improved.

The fourth and last circumstance that assisted me in getting before the British public, was an attempt on the part of certain doctors of divinity to silence me on the platform of the World's Temperance Convention. Here I was brought into point blank collison with Rev. Dr. Cox, who made me the subject not only of bitter remark in the convention, but also of a long denunciatory letter published in the *New York Evangelist* and other American papers. I replied to the doctor as well as I could, and was successful in getting a respectful hearing before the British public, who are by nature and practice ardent lovers of fair play, especially in a conflict between the weak and the strong.

Thus did circumstances favor me, and favor the cause of which I strove to be the advocate. After such distinguished notice, the public in both countries was compelled to attach some importance to my labors. By the very ill usage I received at the hands of Dr. Cox and his party, by the mob on board the *Cambria*, by the attacks made upon me in the American newspapers, and by the aspersions cast upon me through the organs of the Free Church of Scotland, I became one of that class of men, who, for the moment, at least, "have greatness forced upon them."* People became the more anxious to hear for themselves, and to judge for themselves, of the truth which I had to unfold. While, therefore, it is by no means easy for a stranger to get fairly before the British public, it was my lot to accomplish it in the easiest manner possible.

---

\* From *Twelfth Night* by William Shakespeare.

Having continued in Great Britain and Ireland nearly two years, and being about to return to America—not as I left it, a slave, but a freeman—leading friends of the cause of emancipation in that country intimated their intention to make me a testimonial, not only on grounds of personal regard to myself, but also to the cause to which they were so ardently devoted. How far any such thing could have succeeded, I do not know; but many reasons led me to prefer that my friends should simply give me the means of obtaining a printing press and printing materials, to enable me to start a paper, devoted to the interests of my enslaved and oppressed people. I told them that perhaps the greatest hinderance to the adoption of abolition principles by the people of the United States, was the low estimate, everywhere in that country, placed upon the Negro, as a man; that because of his assumed natural inferiority, people reconciled themselves to his enslavement and oppression, as things inevitable, if not desirable. The grand thing to be done, therefore, was to change the estimation in which the colored people of the United States were held; to remove the prejudice which depreciated and depressed them; to prove them worthy of a higher consideration; to disprove their alleged inferiority, and demonstrate their capacity for a more exalted civilization than slavery and prejudice had assigned to them. I further stated, that, in my judgment, a tolerably well conducted press, in the hands of persons of the despised race, by calling out the mental energies of the race itself; by making them acquainted with their own latent powers; by enkindling among them the hope that for them there is a future; by developing their moral power; by combining and reflecting their talents—would prove a most powerful means of removing prejudice, and of awakening an interest in them. I further informed them—and at that time the statement was true—that there was not, in the United States, a single newspaper regularly published by the colored people; that many attempts had been made to establish such papers; but that, up to that time, they had all failed. These views I laid before my friends. The result was, nearly two thousand five hundred dollars were speedily raised toward starting my paper. For this prompt and generous assistance, rendered upon my bare suggestion, without any personal efforts on my part, I shall never cease to feel deeply grateful; and the thought of fulfilling the noble expectations of the dear friends who gave me this evidence of their confidence, will never cease to be a motive for persevering exertion.

Proposing to leave England, and turning my face toward America, in the spring of 1847, I was met, on the threshold, with something which painfully reminded me of the kind of life which awaited me in my native land. For the first time in the many months spent abroad, I was met with proscription on account of my color. A few weeks before departing from England, while in London, I was careful to purchase a ticket, and secure a berth for returning home, in the *Cambria*—the steamer in which I left the United States—paying therefor the round sum of forty pounds and nineteen shillings sterling. This was first cabin fare. But on going aboard the *Cambria*, I found that the Liverpool agent had ordered my berth to be given to another, and had forbidden my entering the saloon! This contemptible conduct met with stern rebuke from the British press. For, upon the point of leaving England, I took occasion to expose the disgusting tyranny, in the columns of the *London Times*. That journal, and other leading journals throughout the United Kingdom, held up the outrage to unmitigated condemnation. So good an opportunity for calling out a full expression of British sentiment on the subject, had not before occurred, and it was most fully embraced. The result was, that Mr. Cunard came out in a letter to the public journals, assuring them of his regret at the outrage, and promising that the like should never occur again on board his steamers; and the like, we believe, has never since occurred on board the steamships of the Cunard line.

It is not very pleasant to be made the subject of such insults; but if all such necessarily resulted as this one did, I should be very happy to bear, patiently, many more than I have borne, of the same sort. Albeit, the lash of proscription, to a man accustomed to equal social position, even for a time, as I was, has a sting for the soul hardly less severe than that which bites the flesh and draws the blood from the back of the plantation slave. It was rather hard, after having enjoyed nearly two years of equal social privileges in England, often dining with gentlemen of great literary, social, political, and religious eminence—never, during the whole time, having met with a single word, look, or gesture, which gave me the slightest reason to think my color was an offense to anybody—now to be cooped up in the stern of the *Cambria*, and denied the right to enter the saloon, lest my dark presence should be deemed an offense to some of my democratic fellow-passengers. The reader will easily imagine what must have been my feelings.

# CHAPTER XXV

## VARIOUS INCIDENTS

I have now given the reader an imperfect sketch of nine years' experience in freedom—three years as a common laborer on the wharves of New Bedford, four years as a lecturer in New England, and two years of semi-exile in Great Britain and Ireland. A single ray of light remains to be flung upon my life during the last eight years, and my story will be done.

A trial awaited me on my return from England to the United States, for which I was but very imperfectly prepared. My plans for my then future usefulness as an anti-slavery advocate were all settled. My friends in England had resolved to raise a given sum to purchase for me a press and printing materials; and I already saw myself wielding my pen, as well as my voice, in the great work of renovating the public mind, and building up a public sentiment which should, at least, send slavery and oppression to the grave, and restore to "liberty and the pursuit of happiness" the people with whom I had suffered, both as a slave and as a freeman. Intimation had reached my friends in Boston of what I intended to do, before my arrival, and I was prepared to find them favorably disposed toward my much cherished enterprise. In this I was mistaken. I found them very earnestly opposed to the idea of my starting a paper, and for several reasons. First, the paper was not needed; secondly, it would interfere with my usefulness as a lecturer; thirdly, I was better fitted to speak than to write; fourthly, the paper could not succeed. This opposition, from a quarter so highly esteemed, and to which I had been accustomed to look for advice and direction, caused me not only to hesitate, but inclined me to abandon the enterprise. All previous attempts to establish such a journal having failed, I felt that probably I should but add another to the list of failures, and thus contribute another proof of the mental and moral deficiencies of my race. Very much that was said to me in respect to my imperfect literary acquirements, I felt to be most painfully true. The unsuccessful projectors of all the previous colored newspapers were my superiors in point of education, and if they failed, how could I hope for success? Yet I did hope for success, and persisted in the undertaking. Some of my English friends greatly encouraged me to go forward, and I shall never cease to be grateful for their words of cheer and generous deeds.

I can easily pardon those who have denounced me as ambitious and presumptuous, in view of my persistence in this enterprise. I was but nine years from slavery. In point of mental experience, I was but nine years old. That one, in such circumstances, should aspire to establish a printing press, among an educated people, might well be considered, if not ambitious, quite silly. My American friends looked at me with astonishment! "A wood-sawyer" offering himself to the public as an editor! A slave, brought up in the very depths of ignorance, assuming to instruct the highly civilized people of the north in the principles of liberty, justice, and humanity! The thing looked absurd. Nevertheless, I persevered. I felt that the want of education, great as it was, could be overcome by study, and that knowledge would come by experience; and further (which was perhaps the most controlling consideration), I thought that an intelligent public, knowing my early history, would easily pardon a large share of the deficiencies which I was sure that my paper would exhibit. The most distressing thing, however, was the offense which I was about to give my Boston friends, by what seemed to them a reckless disregard of their sage advice. I am not sure that I was not under the influence of something like a slavish adoration of my Boston friends, and I labored hard to convince them of the wisdom of my undertaking, but without success. Indeed, I never expect to succeed, although time has answered all their original objections. The paper has been successful. It is a large sheet, costing eighty dollars per week—has three thousand subscribers—has been published regularly nearly eight years—and bids fair to stand eight years longer. At any rate, the eight years to come are as full of promise as were the eight that are past.

It is not to be concealed, however, that the maintenance of such a journal, under the circumstances, has been a work of much difficulty; and could all the perplexity, anxiety, and trouble attending it, have been clearly foreseen, I might have shrunk from the undertaking. As it is, I rejoice in having engaged in the enterprise, and count it joy to have been able to suffer, in many ways, for its success, and for the success of the cause to which it has been faithfully devoted. I look upon the time, money, and labor bestowed upon it, as being amply rewarded, in the development of my own mental and moral energies, and in the corresponding development of my deeply injured and oppressed people.

From motives of peace, instead of issuing my paper in Boston, among my New England friends, I came to Rochester, western New York, among strangers, where the circulation of my paper could not interfere with the local circulation of the *Liberator* and the *Standard*; for at that time I was, on the anti-slavery question, a faithful disciple of William Lloyd Garrison, and fully committed to his doctrine touching the pro-slavery character of the constitution of the United States, and the *non-voting principle*, of which he is the known and distinguished advocate. With Mr. Garrison, I held it to be the first duty of the non-slaveholding states to dissolve the union with the slaveholding states; and hence my cry, like his, was, "No union with slaveholders." With these views, I came into western New York; and during the first four years of my labor here, I advocated them with pen and tongue, according to the best of my ability.

About four years ago, upon a reconsideration of the whole subject, I became convinced that there was no necessity for dissolving the "union between the northern and southern states"; that to seek this dissolution was no part of my duty as an abolitionist; that to abstain from voting, was to refuse to exercise a legitimate and powerful means for abolishing slavery; and that the constitution of the United States not only contained no guarantees in favor of slavery, but, on the contrary, it is, in its letter and spirit, an anti-slavery instrument, demanding the abolition of slavery as a condition of its own existence, as the supreme law of the land.

Here was a radical change in my opinions, and in the action logically resulting from that change. To those with whom I had been in agreement and in sympathy, I was now in opposition. What they held to be a great and important truth, I now looked upon as a dangerous error. A very painful, and yet a very natural, thing now happened. Those who could not see any honest reasons for changing their views, as I had done, could not easily see any such reasons for my change, and the common punishment of apostates was mine.

The opinions first entertained were naturally derived and honestly entertained, and I trust that my present opinions have the same claims to respect. Brought directly, when I escaped from slavery, into contact with a class of abolitionists regarding the constitution as a slaveholding instrument, and finding their views supported by the united and entire history of every department of the government, it is not strange that I assumed the constitution to be just what their interpretation made it. I was bound, not only by their superior knowledge, to take their opinions as the true ones, in respect to the subject, but also because I had no means of showing their unsoundness. But for the responsibility of conducting a public journal, and the necessity imposed upon me of meeting opposite views from abolitionists in this state, I should in all probability have remained as firm in my disunion views as any other disciple of William Lloyd Garrison.

My new circumstances compelled me to re-think the whole subject, and to study, with some care, not only the just and proper rules of legal interpretation, but the origin, design, nature, rights, powers, and duties of civil government, and also the relations which human beings sustain to it. By such a course of thought and reading, I was conducted to the conclusion that the constitution of the United States—inaugurated "to form a more perfect union, establish justice, insure domestic tranquillity, provide for the common defense, promote the general welfare, and secure the blessing of liberty"—could not well have been designed at the same time to maintain and perpetuate a system of rapine and murder, like slavery; especially, as not one word can be found in the constitution to authorize such a belief. Then, again, if the declared purposes of an instrument are to govern the meaning of all its parts and details, as they clearly should, the constitution of our country is our warrant for the abolition of slavery in every state in the American Union. I mean, however, not to argue, but simply to state my views.

It would require very many pages of a volume like this, to set forth the arguments demonstrating the unconstitutionality and the complete illegality of slavery in our land; and as my experience, and not my arguments, is within the scope and contemplation of this volume, I omit the latter and proceed with the former.

I will now ask the kind reader to go back a little in my story, while I bring up a thread left behind for convenience sake, but which, small as it is, cannot be properly omitted altogether; and that thread is American prejudice against color, and its varied illustrations in my own experience.

When I first went among the abolitionists of New England, and began to travel, I found this prejudice very strong and very annoying. The abolitionists themselves were not entirely free from it, and I could see that they were nobly struggling against it. In their eagerness, sometimes, to show their contempt for the feeling, they proved that they had not entirely recovered from it; often illustrating the saying, in their conduct, that a man may "stand up so straight as to lean backward." When it was said to me, "Mr. Douglass, I will walk to meeting with you; I am not afraid of a black man," I could not help thinking—seeing nothing very frightful in my appearance—"And why should you be?" The children at the north had all been educated to believe that if they were bad, the old *black* man—not the old devil—would get them; and it was evidence of some courage, for any so educated to get the better of their fears.

The custom of providing separate cars for the accommodation of colored travelers, was established on nearly all the railroads of New England, a dozen years ago. Regarding this custom as fostering the spirit of caste, I made it a rule to seat myself in the cars for the accommodation of passengers generally. Thus seated, I was sure to be called upon to betake myself to the "*Jim Crow car.*" Refusing to obey, I was often dragged out of my seat, beaten, and severely bruised, by conductors and brakemen. Attempting to start from Lynn, one day, for Newburyport, on the Eastern railroad, I went, as my custom was, into one of the best railroad carriages on the road. The seats were very luxuriant and beautiful. I was soon waited upon by the conductor, and ordered out; whereupon I demanded the reason for my invidious removal. After a good deal of parleying, I was told that it was because I was black. This I denied, and appealed to the company to sustain my denial; but they were evidently unwilling to commit themselves, on a point so delicate, and requiring such nice powers of discrimination, for they remained as dumb as death. I was soon waited on by half a dozen fellows of the baser sort (just such as would volunteer to take a bull-dog out of a meeting-house in time of public worship), and told that I must move out of that seat, and if I did not, they would drag me out. I refused to move, and they clutched me, head, neck, and shoulders. But, in anticipation of the stretching to which I was about to be subjected, I had interwoven myself among the seats. In dragging me out, on this occasion, it must have cost the company twenty-five or thirty dollars, for I tore up seats and all. So great was the excitement in Lynn, on the subject, that the superintendent, Mr. Stephen A. Chase, ordered the trains to run through Lynn without stopping, while I remained in that town; and this ridiculous farce was enacted. For several days the trains went dashing through Lynn without stopping. At the same time that they excluded a free colored man from their cars, this same company allowed slaves, in company with their masters and mistresses, to ride unmolested.

After many battles with the railroad conductors, and being roughly handled in not a few instances, proscription was at last abandoned; and the "Jim Crow car"—set up for the degradation of colored people—is nowhere found in New England. This result was not brought about without the intervention of the people, and the threatened enactment of a law compelling railroad companies to respect the rights of travelers. Hon. Charles Francis Adams performed signal service in the Massachusetts legislature, in bringing this reformation; and to him the colored citizens of that state are deeply indebted.

Although often annoyed, and sometimes outraged, by this prejudice against color, I am indebted to it for many passages of quiet amusement. A half-cured subject of it is sometimes driven into awkward straits, especially if he happens to get a genuine specimen of the race into his house.

In the summer of 1843, I was traveling and lecturing, in company with William A. White, Esq., through the state of Indiana. Anti-slavery friends were not very abundant in Indiana, at that time, and beds were not more plentiful than friends. We often slept out, in preference to sleeping in the houses, at some points. At the close of one of our meetings, we were invited home with a kindly-disposed old farmer, who, in the generous enthusiasm of the moment, seemed to have forgotten that he had but one spare bed, and that his guests were an ill-matched pair. All went on pretty well, till near bed time, when signs of uneasiness began to show themselves, among the unsophisticated sons and daughters. White is remarkably fine looking, and very evidently a born gentleman; the idea of putting us in the same bed was hardly to be tolerated; and yet, there we were, and but the one bed for us, and that, by the way, was in the same room occupied by the other members of the family. White, as well as I, perceived the difficulty, for yonder slept the old folks, there the sons, and a little farther along slept the daughters; and but one other bed remained. Who should have this bed, was the puzzling question. There was some whispering between the old folks, some confused looks among the young, as the time for going to bed approached. After witnessing the confusion as long as I liked, I relieved the kindly-disposed family by playfully saying, "Friend White, having got entirely rid of my prejudice against color, I think, as a proof of it, I must allow you to sleep with me tonight." White kept up the joke, by seeming to esteem himself the favored party, and thus the difficulty was removed. If we went to a hotel, and called for dinner, the landlord was sure to set one table for White and another for me, always taking him to be master, and me the servant. Large eyes were generally made when the order was given to remove the dishes from my table to that of White's. In those days, it was thought strange that a white man and a colored man could dine peaceably at the same table, and in some parts the strangeness of such a sight has not entirely subsided.

Some people will have it that there is a natural, an inherent, and an invincible repugnance in the breast of the white race toward dark-colored people; and some very intelligent colored men think that their proscription is owing solely to the color which nature has given them. They hold that they are rated according to their color, and that it is impossible for white people ever to look upon dark races of men, or men belonging to the African race, with other than feelings of aversion. My experience, both serious and mirthful, combats this conclusion. Leaving out of sight, for a moment, grave facts, to this point, I will state one or two, which illustrate a very interesting feature of American character as well as American prejudice. Riding from Boston to Albany, a few years ago, I found myself in a large car, well filled with passengers. The seat next to me was about the only vacant one. At every stopping place we took in new passengers, all of whom, on reaching the seat next to me, cast a disdainful glance upon it, and passed to another car, leaving me in the full enjoyment of a whole form. For a time, I did not know but that my riding there was prejudicial to the interest of the railroad company. A circumstance occurred, however, which gave me an elevated position at once. Among the passengers on this train was Gov. George N. Briggs. I was not acquainted with him, and had no idea that I was known to him. Known to him, however, I was, for upon observing me, the governor left his place, and making his way toward me, respectfully asked the privilege of a seat by my side; and upon introducing himself, we entered into a conversation very pleasant and instructive to me. The despised seat now became honored. His excellency had removed all the prejudice against sitting by the side of a Negro; and upon his leaving it, as he did, on reaching Pittsfield, there were at least one dozen applicants for the place. The governor had, without changing my skin a single shade, made the place respectable which before was despicable.

A similar incident happened to me once on the Boston and New Bedford railroad, and the leading party to it has since been governor of the state of Massachusetts. I allude to Col. John Henry Clifford. Lest the reader may fancy I am aiming to elevate myself, by claiming too much intimacy with great men, I must state that my only acquaintance with Col. Clifford was formed while I was *his hired servant*, during the first winter of my escape from slavery. I owe it him to say, that in that relation I found him always kind and gentlemanly. But to the incident. I entered a car at Boston, for New Bedford, which, with the exception of a single seat was full, and found I must occupy this, or stand up, during the journey. Having no mind to do this, I stepped up to the man having the next seat, and who had a few parcels on the seat, and gently asked leave to take a seat by his side. My fellow-passenger gave me a look made up of reproach and indignation, and asked me why I should come to that particular seat. I assured him, in the gentlest manner, that of all others this was the seat for me. Finding that I was actually about to sit down, he sang out, "O! Stop, stop! And let me get out!" Suiting the action to the word, up the agitated man got, and sauntered to the other end of the car, and was compelled to stand for most of the way thereafter. Halfway to New Bedford, or more, Col. Clifford, recognizing me, left his seat, and not having seen me before since I had ceased to wait on him (in everything except hard arguments against his pro-slavery position), apparently forgetful of his rank, manifested, in greeting me, something of the feeling of an old friend. This demonstration was not lost on the gentleman whose dignity I had, an hour before, most seriously offended. Col. Clifford was known to be about the most aristocratic gentleman in Bristol County; and it was evidently thought that I must be somebody, else I should not have been thus noticed, by a person so distinguished. Sure enough, after Col. Clifford left me, I found myself surrounded with friends; and among the number, my offended friend stood nearest, and with an apology for his rudeness, which I could not resist, although it was one of the lamest ever offered. With such facts as these before me—and I have many of them—I am inclined to think that pride and fashion have much to do with the treatment commonly extended to colored people in the United States. I once heard a very plain man say (and he was cross-eyed, and awkwardly flung together in other respects) that he should be a handsome man when public opinion shall be changed.

Since I have been editing and publishing a journal devoted to the cause of liberty and progress, I have had my mind more directed to the condition and circumstances of the free colored people than when I was the agent of an abolition society. The result has been a corresponding change in the disposition of my time and labors. I have felt it to be a part of my mission—under a gracious Providence—to impress my sable brothers in this country with the conviction that, notwithstanding the ten thousand discouragements and the powerful hinderances, which beset their existence in this country—notwithstanding the blood-written history of Africa, and her children, from whom we have descended, or the clouds and darkness (whose stillness and gloom are made only more awful by wrathful thunder and lightning) now overshadowing them—progress is yet possible, and bright skies shall yet shine upon their pathway; and that "Ethiopia shall yet reach forth her hand unto God."

Believing that one of the best means of emancipating the slaves of the south is to improve and elevate the character of the free colored people of the north I shall labor in the future, as I have labored in the past, to promote the moral, social, religious, and intellectual elevation of the free colored people; never forgetting my own humble origin, nor refusing, while Heaven lends me ability, to use my voice, my pen, or my vote, to advocate the great and primary work of the universal and unconditional emancipation of my entire race.

# Appendix,
# Containing Extracts
# from Speeches, Etc. [*]

* Mr. Douglass's published speeches alone, would fill two volumes of the size of this. Our space will only permit the insertion of the extracts which follow; and which, for originality of thought, beauty and force of expression, and for impassioned, indignatory eloquence, have seldom been equaled. (Original editor's note)

# *RECEPTION SPEECH*

## AT FINSBURY CHAPEL, MOORFIELDS,
## ENGLAND, MAY 12, 1846

M<sup>r</sup>. Douglass rose amid loud cheers, and said: I feel exceedingly glad of the opportunity now afforded me of presenting the claims of my brethren in bonds in the United States, to so many in London and from various parts of Britain, who have assembled here on the present occasion. I have nothing to commend me to your consideration in the way of learning, nothing in the way of education, to entitle me to your attention; and you are aware that slavery is a very bad school for rearing teachers of morality and religion. Twenty-one years of my life have been spent in slavery—personal slavery—surrounded by degrading influences, such as can exist nowhere beyond the pale of slavery; and it will not be strange, if under such circumstances, I should betray, in what I have to say to you, a deficiency of that refinement which is seldom or ever found, except among persons that have experienced superior advantages to those which I have enjoyed. But I will take it for granted that you know something about the degrading influences of slavery, and that you will not expect great things from me this evening, but simply such facts as I may be able to advance immediately in connection with my own experience of slavery.

Now, what is this system of slavery? This is the subject of my lecture this evening—what is the character of this institution? I am about to answer the inquiry, what is American slavery? I do this the more readily, since I have found persons in this country who have identified the term slavery with that which I think it is not, and in some instances, I have feared, in so doing, have rather (unwittingly, I know) detracted much from the horror with which the term slavery is contemplated. It is common in this country to distinguish every bad thing by the name of slavery. Intemperance is slavery; to be deprived of the right to vote is slavery, says one; to have to work hard is slavery, says another; and I do not know but that if we should let them go on, they would say that to eat when we are hungry, to walk when we desire to have exercise, or to minister to our necessities, or have necessities at all, is slavery. I do not wish for a moment to detract from the horror with which the evil of intemperance is contemplated—not at all; nor do I wish to throw the slightest obstruction in the way of any political freedom that any class of persons in this country may desire to obtain. But I am here to say that I think the term slavery is sometimes abused by identifying it with that which it is not. Slavery in the United States is the granting of that power by which one man exercises and enforces a right of property in the body and soul of another. The condition of a slave is simply that of the brute beast. He is a piece of property—a marketable commodity, in the language of the law, to be bought or sold at the will and caprice of the master who claims him to be his property; he is spoken of, thought of, and treated as property. His own good, his conscience, his intellect, his affections, are all set aside by the master. The will and the wishes of the master are the law of the slave. He is as much a piece of property as a horse. If he is fed, he is fed because he is property. If he is clothed, it is with a view to the increase of his value as property. Whatever of comfort is necessary to him for his body or soul that is inconsistent with his being property, is carefully wrested from him, not only by public opinion, but by the law of the country. He is carefully deprived of everything that tends in the slightest degree to detract from his value as property. He is deprived of education. God has given him an intellect; the slaveholder declares it shall not be cultivated. If his moral perception leads him in a course contrary to his value as property, the slaveholder declares he shall not exercise it. The marriage institution cannot exist among slaves, and one-sixth of the population of democratic America is denied its privileges by the law of the land. What is to be thought of a nation boasting of its liberty, boasting of its humanity, boasting of its Christianity, boasting of its love of justice and purity, and yet having within its own borders three millions of persons denied by law the right of marriage?—what must be the condition of that people? I need not lift up the veil by giving you any experience of my own. Every one that can put two ideas together, must see the most fearful results from such a state of things as I have just mentioned. If any of these three millions find for themselves companions, and prove themselves honest, upright, virtuous persons to each other, yet in these cases—few as I am bound to confess they are—the virtuous live in constant apprehension of being torn asunder by the merciless men-stealers that claim them as their property. This is American slavery; no marriage—no education—the light of the gospel shut out from the dark mind of the bondman—and he forbidden by law to learn to read. If a mother shall teach her children to read, the law in Louisiana proclaims that she may be hanged by the neck. If the father attempt to give his son a knowledge of letters, he may be punished by the whip in one instance, and in another be killed, at the discretion of the court. Three millions of people shut out from the light of knowledge! It is easy for you to conceive the evil that must result from such a state of things.

I now come to the physical evils of slavery. I do not wish to dwell at length upon these, but it seems right to speak of them, not so much to influence your minds on this question, as to let the slaveholders of America know that the curtain which conceals their crimes is being lifted abroad; that we are opening the dark cell, and leading the people into the horrible recesses of what they are pleased to call their domestic institution. We want them to know that a knowledge of their whippings, their scourgings, their brandings, their chainings, is not confined to their plantations, but that some Negro of theirs has broken loose from his chains—has burst through the dark incrustation of slavery, and is now exposing their deeds of deep damnation to the gaze of the Christian people of England.

The slaveholders resort to all kinds of cruelty. If I were disposed, I have matter enough to interest you on this question for five or six evenings, but I will not dwell at length upon these cruelties. Suffice it to say, that all of the peculiar modes of torture that were resorted to in the West India islands, are resorted to, I believe, even more frequently, in the United States of America. Starvation, the bloody whip, the chain, the gag, the thumb-screw, cat-hauling, the cat-o'-nine-tails, the dungeon, the blood-hound, are all in requisition to keep the slave in his condition as a slave in the United States. If any one has a doubt upon this point, I would ask him to read the chapter on slavery in Dickens's *Notes on America*.* If any man has a doubt upon it, I have here the "testimony of a thousand witnesses," which I can give at any length, all going to prove the truth of my statement. The blood-hound is regularly trained in the United States, and advertisements are to be found in the southern papers of the Union, from persons advertising

---

* From *American Notes for General Circulation* by Charles Dickens.

themselves as blood-hound trainers, and offering to hunt down slaves at fifteen dollars a piece, recommending their hounds as the fleetest in the neighborhood, never known to fail. Advertisements are from time to time inserted, stating that slaves have escaped with iron collars about their necks, with bands of iron about their feet, marked with the lash, branded with red-hot irons, the initials of their master's name burned into their flesh; and the masters advertise the fact of their being thus branded with their own signature, thereby proving to the world, that, however damning it may appear to non-slavers, such practices are not regarded discreditable among the slaveholders themselves. Why, I believe if a man should brand his horse in this country—burn the initials of his name into any of his cattle, and publish the ferocious deed here—that the united execrations of Christians in Britain would descend upon him. Yet in the United States, human beings are thus branded. As Whittier says—

> Our countrymen in chains,
>   The whip on woman's shrinking flesh,
> Our soil yet reddening with the stains
>   Caught from her scourgings warm and fresh.*

The slave-dealer boldly publishes his infamous acts to the world. Of all things that have been said of slavery to which exception has been taken by slaveholders, this, the charge of cruelty, stands foremost, and yet there is no charge capable of clearer demonstration, than that of the most barbarous inhumanity on the part of the slaveholders toward their slaves. And all this is necessary; it is necessary to resort to these cruelties, in order to *make the slave a slave*, and *to keep him a slave*. Why, my experience all goes to prove the truth of what you will call a marvelous proposition, that the better you treat a slave, the more you destroy his value *as a slave*, and enhance the probability of his eluding the grasp of the slaveholder; the more kindly you treat him, the more wretched you make him, while you keep him in the condition of a slave. My experience, I say, confirms the truth of this proposition. When I was treated exceedingly ill; when my back was being scourged daily; when I was whipped within an inch of my life—*life* was all I cared for. "Spare my life," was my continual prayer. When I was looking

---

* From "Expostulation" by John Greenleaf Whittier.

for the blow about to be inflicted upon my head, I was not thinking of my liberty; it was my life. But, as soon as the blow was not to be feared, then came the longing for liberty. If a slave has a bad master, his ambition is to get a better; when he gets a better, he aspires to have the best; and when he gets the best, he aspires to be his own master. But the slave must be brutalized to keep him as a slave. The slaveholder feels this necessity. I admit this necessity. If it be right to hold slaves at all, it is right to hold them in the only way in which they can be held; and this can be done only by shutting out the light of education from their minds, and brutalizing their persons. The whip, the chain, the gag, the thumb-screw, the blood-hound, the stocks, and all the other bloody paraphernalia of the slave system, are indispensably necessary to the relation of master and slave. The slave must be subjected to these, or he ceases to be a slave. Let him know that the whip is burned; that the fetters have been turned to some useful and profitable employment; that the chain is no longer for his limbs; that the blood-hound is no longer to be put upon his track; that his master's authority over him is no longer to be enforced by taking his life—and immediately he walks out from the house of bondage and asserts his freedom as a man. The slaveholder finds it necessary to have these implements to keep the slave in bondage; finds it necessary to be able to say, "Unless you do so and so; unless you do as I bid you—I will take away your life!"

Some of the most awful scenes of cruelty are constantly taking place in the middle states of the Union. We have in those states what are called the slave-breeding states. Allow me to speak plainly. Although it is harrowing to your feelings, it is necessary that the facts of the case should be stated. We have in the United States slave-breeding states. The very state from which the minister from our court to yours comes, is one of these states—Maryland, where men, women, and children are reared for the market, just as horses, sheep, and swine are raised for the market. Slave-rearing is there looked upon as a legitimate trade; the law sanctions it, public opinion upholds it, the church does not condemn it. It goes on in all its bloody horrors, sustained by the auctioneer's block. If you would see the cruelties of this system, hear the following narrative. Not long since the following scene occurred. A slave-woman and a slave-man had united themselves as man and wife in the absence of any law to protect them as man and wife. They had lived together by the permission, not by right, of their master, and they had reared a family. The master found it expedient, and for his interest, to sell them. He did not ask them their wishes in regard to the matter at all; they were not consulted. The man and woman were brought to the auctioneer's block, under the sound of the hammer. The cry was raised, "Here goes; who bids cash?" Think of it—a man and wife to be sold! The woman was placed on the auctioneer's block; her limbs, as is customary, were brutally exposed to the purchasers, who examined her with all the freedom with which they would examine a horse. There stood the husband, powerless; no right to his wife; the master's right preeminent. She was sold. He was next brought to the auctioneer's block. His eyes followed his wife in the distance; and he looked beseechingly, imploringly, to the man that had bought his wife, to buy him also. But he was at length bid off to another person. He was about to be separated forever from her he loved. No word of his, no work of his, could save him from this separation. He asked permission of his new master to go and take the hand of his wife at parting. It was denied him. In the agony of his soul he rushed from the man who had just bought him, that he might take a farewell of his wife; but his way was obstructed, he was struck over the head with a loaded whip, and was held for a moment; but his agony was too great. When he was let go, he fell a corpse at the feet of his master. His heart was broken. Such scenes are the everyday fruits of American slavery. Some two years since, the Hon. Seth. M. Gates, an anti-slavery gentleman of the state of New York, a representative in the congress of the United States, told me he saw with his own eyes the following circumstances. In the national District of Columbia, over which the star-spangled emblem is constantly waving, where orators are ever holding forth on the subject of American liberty, American democracy, American republicanism, there are two slave prisons. When going across a bridge, leading to one of these prisons, he saw a young woman run out, bare-footed and bare-headed, and with very little clothing on. She was running with all speed to the bridge he was approaching. His eye was fixed upon her, and he stopped to see what was the matter. He had not paused long before he saw three men run out after her. He now knew what the nature of the case was; a slave escaping from her chains—a young woman, a sister— escaping from the bondage in which she had been held. She made her way to the bridge, but had not reached it, ere from the Virginia side there came two slaveholders. As soon as they saw them, her pursuers called out, "Stop her!" True to their Virginian instincts, they came to the rescue of their brother-kidnappers, across the bridge. The poor girl now saw that there was no chance for her. It was a trying time. She knew if she went back, she must be a slave forever—she must be dragged down to the scenes of pollution which the slaveholders continually provide for most of the poor, sinking, wretched young women, whom they call their property. She formed her resolution; and just as those who were about to take her, were going to put hands upon her, to drag her back, she leaped over the balustrades of the bridge, and down she went to rise no more. She chose death, rather than to go back into the hands of those Christian slaveholders from whom she had escaped.

Can it be possible that such things as these exist in the United States? Are not these the exceptions? Are any such scenes as this general? Are not such deeds condemned by the law and denounced by public opinion? Let me read to you a few of the laws of the slaveholding states of America. I think no better exposure of slavery can be made than is made by the laws of the states in which slavery exists. I prefer reading the laws to making any statement in confirmation of what I have said myself; for the slaveholders cannot object to this testimony, since it is the calm, the cool, the deliberate enactment of their wisest heads, of their most clear-sighted, their own constituted representatives. "If more than seven slaves together are found in any road without a white person, twenty lashes a piece; for visiting a plantation without a written pass, ten lashes; for letting loose a boat from where it is made fast, thirty-nine lashes for the first offense; and for the second, shall have cut off from his head one ear; for keeping or carrying a club, thirty-nine lashes; for having any article for sale, without a ticket from his master, ten lashes; for traveling in any other than the most usual and accustomed road, when going alone to any place, forty lashes; for traveling in the night without a pass, forty lashes." I am afraid you do not understand the awful character of these lashes. You must bring it before your mind. A human being in a perfect state of nudity, tied hand and foot to a stake, and a strong man standing behind with a heavy whip, knotted at the end, each blow cutting into the flesh, and leaving the warm blood dripping to the feet; and for these trifles. "For being found in another person's Negro-quarters, forty lashes; for hunting with dogs in the woods, thirty lashes; for being on horseback without the written permission of his master, twenty-five lashes; for riding or going abroad in the night, or riding horses in the day time, without leave, a slave may be whipped, cropped, or branded in the cheek with the letter R. or otherwise punished, such punishment not extending to life, or so as to render him unfit for labor." The laws referred to, may be found by consulting Brevard's Digest; Haywood's Manual; Virginia Revised Code; Prince's Digest; Missouri Laws; Mississippi Revised Code. A man, for going to visit his brethren, without the permission of his master—and in many instances he may not have that permission; his master, from caprice or other reasons, may not be willing to allow it— may be caught on his way, dragged to a post, the branding-iron heated, and the name of his master or the letter R branded into his cheek or on his forehead. They treat slaves thus, on the principle that they must punish for light offenses, in order to prevent the commission of larger ones. I wish you to mark that in the single state of Virginia there are seventy-one crimes for which a colored man may be executed; while there are only three of these crimes, which, when committed by a white man, will subject him to that punishment. There are many of these crimes which if the white man did not commit, he would be regarded as a scoundrel and a coward. In the state of Maryland, there is a law to this effect: that if a slave shall strike his master, he may be hanged, his head severed from his body, his body quartered, and his head and quarters set up in the most prominent places in the neighborhood. If a colored woman, in the defense of her own virtue, in defense of her own person, should shield herself from the brutal attacks of her tyrannical master, or make the slightest resistance, she may be killed on the spot. No law whatever will bring the guilty man to justice for the crime.

But you will ask me, can these things be possible in a land professing Christianity? Yes, they are so; and this is not the worst. No; a darker feature is yet to be presented than the mere existence of these facts. I have to inform you that the religion of the southern states, at this time, is the great supporter, the great sanctioner of the bloody atrocities to which I have referred. While America is printing tracts and Bibles; sending missionaries abroad to convert the heathen; expending her money in various ways for the promotion of the gospel in foreign lands—the slave not only lies forgotten, uncared for, but is trampled under foot by the very churches of the land. What have we in America? Why, we have slavery made part of the religion of the land. Yes, the pulpit there stands up as the great defender of this cursed *institution*, as it is called. Ministers of religion come forward and torture the hallowed pages of inspired wisdom to sanction the bloody deed. They stand forth as the foremost, the strongest defenders of this "institution." As a proof of this, I need not do more than state the general fact, that slavery has existed under the droppings of the sanctuary of the south for the last two hundred years, and there has not been any war between the *religion* and the *slavery* of the south. Whips, chains, gags, and thumb-screws have all lain under the droppings of the sanctuary, and instead of rusting from off the limbs of the bondman, those droppings have served to preserve them in all their strength. Instead of preaching the gospel against this tyranny, rebuke, and wrong, ministers of religion have sought, by all and every means, to throw in the back-ground whatever in the Bible could be construed into opposition to slavery, and to bring forward that which they could torture into its support. This I conceive to be the darkest feature of slavery, and the most difficult to attack, because it is identified with religion, and exposes those who denounce it to the charge of infidelity. Yes, those with whom I have been laboring, namely, the old organization anti-slavery society of America, have been again and again stigmatized as infidels, and for what reason? Why, solely in consequence of the faithfulness of their attacks upon the slaveholding religion of the southern states, and the northern religion that sympathizes with it. I have found it difficult to speak on this matter without persons coming forward and saying, "Douglass, are you not afraid of injuring the cause of Christ? You do not desire to do so, we know; but are you not undermining religion?" This has been said to me again and again, even since I came to this country, but I cannot be induced to leave off these exposures. I love the religion of our blessed Savior. I love that religion that comes from above, in the "wisdom of God," which is first pure, then peaceable, gentle, and easy to be entreated, full of mercy and good fruits, without partiality and without hypocrisy. I love that religion that sends its votaries to bind up the wounds of him that has fallen among thieves. I love that religion that makes it the duty of its disciples to visit the fatherless and the widow in their affliction. I love that religion that is based upon the glorious principle, of love to God and love to man; which makes its followers do unto others as they themselves would be done by. If you demand liberty to yourself, it says, grant it to your neighbors. If you claim a right to think for yourself, it says, allow your neighbors the same right.

If you claim to act for yourself, it says, allow your neighbors the same right. It is because I love this religion that I hate the slaveholding, the woman-whipping, the mind-darkening, the soul-destroying religion that exists in the southern states of America. It is because I regard the one as good, and pure, and holy, that I cannot but regard the other as bad, corrupt, and wicked. Loving the one I must hate the other; holding to the one I must reject the other.

I may be asked, why I am so anxious to bring this subject before the British public—why I do not confine my efforts to the United States? My answer is, first, that slavery is the common enemy of mankind, and all mankind should be made acquainted with its abominable character. My next answer is, that the slave is a man, and, as such, is entitled to your sympathy as a brother. All the feelings, all the susceptibilities, all the capacities, which you have, he has. He is a part of the human family. He has been the prey—the common prey—of Christendom for the last three hundred years, and it is but right, it is but just, it is but proper, that his wrongs should be known throughout the world. I have another reason for bringing this matter before the British public, and it is this: slavery is a system of wrong, so blinding to all around, so hardening to the heart, so corrupting to the morals, so deleterious to religion, so sapping to all the principles of justice in its immediate vicinity, that the community surrounding it lack the moral stamina necessary to its removal. It is a system of such gigantic evil, so strong, so overwhelming in its power, that no one nation is equal to its removal. It requires the humanity of Christianity, the morality of the world to remove it. Hence, I call upon the people of Britain to look at this matter, and to exert the influence I am about to show they possess, for the removal of slavery from America. I can appeal to them, as strongly by their regard for the slaveholder as for the slave, to labor in this cause. I am here, because you have an influence on America that no other nation can have. You have been drawn together by the power of steam to a marvelous extent; the distance between London and Boston is now reduced to some twelve or fourteen days, so that the denunciations against slavery, uttered in London this week, may be heard in a fortnight in the streets of Boston, and reverberating amidst the hills of Massachusetts. There is nothing said here against slavery that will not be recorded in the United States. I am here, also, because the slaveholders do not want me to be here; they would rather that I were not here. I have adopted a maxim laid down by Napoleon, never to occupy ground which the enemy would like me to occupy. The slaveholders would much rather have me, if I will denounce slavery, denounce it in the northern states, where their friends and supporters are, who will stand by and mob me for denouncing it. They feel something as the man felt, when he uttered his prayer, in which he made out a most horrible case for himself, and one of his neighbors touched him and said, "My friend, I always had the opinion of you that you have now expressed for yourself—that you are a very great sinner." Coming from himself, it was all very well, but coming from a stranger it was rather cutting. The slaveholders felt that when slavery was denounced among themselves, it was not so bad; but let one of the slaves get loose, let him summon the people of Britain, and make known to them the conduct of the slaveholders toward their slaves, and it cuts them to the quick, and produces a sensation such as would be produced by nothing else. The power I exert now is something like the power that is exerted by the man at the end of the lever; my influence now is just in proportion to the distance that I am from the United States. My exposure of slavery abroad will tell more upon the hearts and consciences of slaveholders, than if I was attacking them in America; for almost every paper that I now receive from the United States, comes teeming with statements about this fugitive Negro, calling him a "glib-tongued scoundrel," and saying that he is running out against the institutions and people of America. I deny the charge that I am saying a word against the institutions of America, or the people, as such. What I have to say is against slavery and slaveholders. I feel at liberty to speak on this subject. I have on my back the marks of the lash; I have four sisters and one brother now under the galling chain. I feel it my duty to cry aloud and spare not. I am not averse to having the good opinion of my fellow-creatures. I am not averse to being kindly regarded by all men; but I am bound, even at the hazard of making a large class of religionists in this country hate me, oppose me, and malign me as they have done—I am bound by the prayers, and tears, and entreaties of three millions of kneeling bondsmen, to have no compromise with men who are in any shape or form connected with the slaveholders of America. I expose slavery in this country, because to expose it is to kill it. Slavery is one of those monsters of darkness to whom the light of truth is death. Expose slavery, and it dies. Light is to slavery what the heat of the sun is to the root of a tree; it must die under it. All the slaveholder asks of me is silence. He does not ask me to go abroad and preach in favor of slavery; he does not ask any one to do that. He would not say that slavery is a good thing, but the best under the circumstances. The slaveholders want total darkness on the subject. They want the hatchway shut down, that the monster may crawl in his den of darkness, crushing human hopes and happiness, destroying the bondman at will, and having no one to reprove or rebuke him. Slavery shrinks from the light; it hateth the light, neither cometh to the light, lest its deeds should be reproved. To tear off the mask from this abominable system, to expose it to the light of heaven, aye, to the heat of the sun, that it may burn and wither it out of existence, is my object in coming to this country. I want the slaveholder surrounded, as by a wall of anti-slavery fire, so that he may see the condemnation of himself and his system glaring down in letters of light. I want him to feel that he has no sympathy in England, Scotland, or Ireland; that he has none in Canada, none in Mexico, none among the poor wild Indians; that the voice of the civilized, aye, and savage world is against him. I would have condemnation blaze down upon him in every direction, till, stunned and overwhelmed with shame and confusion, he is compelled to let go the grasp he holds upon the persons of his victims, and restore them to their long-lost rights.

### Dr. Campbell's Reply

*From Rev. Dr. Campbell's brilliant reply we extract the following:*

Frederick Douglass, "the beast of burden," the portion of "goods and chattels," the representative of three millions of men, has been raised up! Shall I say the *man*? If there is a man on earth, he is a man. My blood boiled within me when I heard his address tonight, and thought that he had left behind him three millions of such men.

We must see more of this man; we must have more of this man. One would have taken a voyage round the globe some forty years back—especially since the introduction of steam—to have heard such an exposure of slavery from the lips of a slave. It will be an era in the individual history of the present assembly. Our children—our boys and girls—I have tonight seen the delightful sympathy of their hearts evinced by their heaving breasts, while their eyes sparkled with wonder and admiration, that this black man—this slave—had so much logic, so much wit, so much fancy, so much eloquence. He was something more than a man, according to their little notions. Then, I say, we must hear him again. We have got a purpose to accomplish. He has appealed to the pulpit of England. The English pulpit is with him. He has appealed to the press of England; the press of England is conducted by English hearts, and that press will do him justice. About ten days hence, and his second master, who may well prize "such a piece of goods," will have the pleasure of reading his burning words, and his first master will bless himself that he has got quit of him. We have to create public opinion, or rather, not to create it, for it is created already; but we have to foster it; and when tonight I heard those magnificent words—the words of Curran,* by which my heart, from boyhood, has ofttimes been deeply moved—I rejoice to think that they embody an instinct of an Englishman's nature. I heard, with inexpressible delight, how they told on this mighty mass of the citizens of the metropolis.

Britain has now no slaves; we can therefore talk to the other nations now, as we could not have talked a dozen years ago. I want the whole of the London ministry to meet Douglass. For as his appeal is to England, and throughout England, I should rejoice in the idea of churchmen and dissenters merging all sectional distinctions in this cause. Let us have a public breakfast. Let the ministers meet him; let them hear him; let them grasp his hand; and let him enlist their sympathies on behalf of the slave. Let him inspire them with abhorrence of the man-stealer—the slaveholder. No slaveholding American shall ever cross my door. No slaveholding or slavery-supporting minister shall ever pollute my pulpit. While I have a tongue to speak, or a hand to write, I will, to the utmost of my power, oppose these slaveholding men. We must have Douglass amongst us to aid in fostering public opinion.

The great conflict with slavery must now take place in America; and while they are adding other slave states to the Union, our business is to step forward and help the abolitionists there. It is a pleasing circumstance that such

---

* Irish politician, orator, and wit John Philpot Curran (1750–1817).

a body of men has risen in America, and whilst we hurl our thunders against her slavers, let us make a distinction between those who advocate slavery and those who oppose it. George Thompson has been there. This man, Frederick Douglass, has been there, and has been compelled to flee. I wish, when he first set foot on our shores, he had made a solemn vow, and said, "Now that I am free, and in the sanctuary of freedom, I will never return till I have seen the emancipation of my country completed." He wants to surround these men, the slaveholders, as by a wall of fire; and he himself may do much toward kindling it. Let him travel over the island—east, west, north, and south— everywhere diffusing knowledge and awakening principle, till the whole nation become a body of petitioners to America. He will, he must, do it. He must for a season make England his home. He must send for his wife. He must send for his children. I want to see the sons and daughters of such a sire. We, too, must do something for him and them worthy of the English name. I do not like the idea of a man of such mental dimensions, such moral courage, and all but incomparable talent, having his own small wants, and the wants of a distant wife and children, supplied by the poor profits of his publication, the sketch of his life. Let the pamphlet be bought by tens of thousands. But we will do something more for him, shall we not?

It only remains that we pass a resolution of thanks to Frederick Douglass, the slave that was, the man that is! He that was covered with chains, and that is now being covered with glory, and whom we will send back a gentleman.

# LETTER TO HIS OLD MASTER[*]

*To My Old Master, Thomas Auld*

Sir—The long and intimate, though by no means friendly, relation which unhappily subsisted between you and myself, leads me to hope that you will easily account for the great liberty which I now take in addressing you in this open and public manner. The same fact may remove any disagreeable surprise which you may experience on again finding your name coupled with mine, in any other way than in an advertisement, accurately describing my person, and offering a large sum for my arrest. In thus dragging you again before the public, I am aware that I shall subject myself to no inconsiderable amount of censure. I shall probably be charged with an unwarrantable, if not a wanton and reckless disregard of the rights and properties of private life. There are those north as well as south who entertain a much higher respect for rights which are merely conventional, than they do for rights which are personal and essential. Not a few there are in our country, who, while they have no scruples against robbing the laborer of the hard earned results of his patient industry, will be shocked by the extremely indelicate manner of bringing your name before the public. Believing this to be the case, and wishing to meet every reasonable or plausible objection to my conduct, I will frankly state the ground upon which I justify myself in this instance, as well as on former occasions when I have thought proper to mention your name in public. All will agree that a man guilty of theft, robbery, or murder, has forfeited the right to concealment and private life; that the community have a right to subject such persons to the most complete exposure. However much they may desire retirement, and aim to conceal themselves and their movements from the popular gaze, the public have a right to ferret them out, and bring their conduct before the proper tribunals of the country for investigation. Sir, you will undoubtedly make the proper application of these generally admitted principles, and will easily see

---

[*]It is not often that chattels address their owners. The following letter is unique; and probably the only specimen of the kind extant. It was written while in England. (Original note)

the light in which you are regarded by me; I will not therefore manifest ill temper, by calling you hard names. I know you to be a man of some intelligence, and can readily determine the precise estimate which I entertain of your character. I may therefore indulge in language which may seem to others indirect and ambiguous, and yet be quite well understood by yourself.

I have selected this day on which to address you, because it is the anniversary of my emancipation; and knowing no better way, I am led to this as the best mode of celebrating that truly important event. Just ten years ago this beautiful September morning, yon bright sun beheld me a slave—a poor degraded chattel—trembling at the sound of your voice, lamenting that I was a man, and wishing myself a brute. The hopes which I had treasured up for weeks of a safe and successful escape from your grasp, were powerfully confronted at this last hour by dark clouds of doubt and fear, making my person shake and my bosom to heave with the heavy contest between hope and fear. I have no words to describe to you the deep agony of soul which I experienced on that never-to-be-forgotten morning—for I left by daylight. I was making a leap in the dark. The probabilities, so far as I could by reason determine them, were stoutly against the undertaking. The preliminaries and precautions I had adopted previously, all worked badly. I was like one going to war without weapons—ten chances of defeat to one of victory. One in whom I had confided, and one who had promised me assistance, appalled by fear at the trial hour, deserted me, thus leaving the responsibility of success or failure solely with myself. You, sir, can never know my feelings. As I look back to them, I can scarcely realize that I have passed through a scene so trying. Trying, however, as they were, and gloomy as was the prospect, thanks be to the Most High, who is ever the God of the oppressed, at the moment which was to determine my whole earthly career, His grace was sufficient; my mind was made up. I embraced the golden opportunity, took the morning tide at the flood, and a free man, young, active, and strong, is the result.

I have often thought I should like to explain to you the grounds upon which I have justified myself in running away from you. I am almost ashamed to do so now, for by this time you may have discovered them yourself. I will, however, glance at them. When yet but a child about six years old, I imbibed the determination to run away. The very first mental effort that I now remember on my part, was an attempt to solve the mystery—why am I a slave? and with this question my youthful mind was troubled for many days, pressing upon me more heavily at times than others. When I saw the slave-driver whip a slave-woman, cut the blood out of her neck, and heard her piteous cries, I went away into the corner of the fence, wept and pondered over the mystery. I had, through some medium, I know not what, got some idea of God, the Creator of all mankind, the black and the white, and that he had made the blacks to serve the whites as slaves. How he could do this and be *good*, I could not tell. I was not satisfied with this theory, which made God responsible for slavery, for it pained me greatly, and I have wept over it long and often. At one time, your first wife, Mrs. Lucretia, heard me sighing and saw me shedding tears, and asked of me the matter, but I was afraid to tell her. I was puzzled with this question, till one night while sitting in the kitchen, I heard some of the old slaves talking of their parents having been stolen from Africa by white men, and were sold here as slaves. The whole mystery was solved at once. Very soon after this, my Aunt Jinny and Uncle Noah ran away, and the great noise made about it by your father-in-law, made me for the first time acquainted with the fact, that there were free states as well as slave states. From that time, I resolved that I would some day run away. The morality of the act I dispose of as follows: I am myself; you are yourself; we are two distinct persons, equal persons. What you are, I am. You are a man, and so am I. God created both, and made us separate beings. I am not by nature bond to you, or you to me. Nature does not make your existence depend upon me, or mine to depend upon yours. I cannot walk upon your legs, or you upon mine. I cannot breathe for you, or you for me; I must breathe for myself, and you for yourself. We are distinct persons, and are each equally provided with faculties necessary to our individual existence. In leaving you, I took nothing but what belonged to me, and in no way lessened your means for obtaining an *honest* living. Your faculties remained yours, and mine became useful to their rightful owner. I therefore see no wrong in any part of the transaction. It is true, I went off secretly; but that was more your fault than mine. Had I let you into the secret, you would have defeated the enterprise entirely; but for this, I should have been really glad to have made you acquainted with my intentions to leave.

You may perhaps want to know how I like my present condition. I am free to say, I greatly prefer it to that which I occupied in Maryland.

I am, however, by no means prejudiced against the state as such. Its geography, climate, fertility, and products, are such as to make it a very desirable abode for any man; and but for the existence of slavery there, it is not impossible that I might again take up my abode in that state. It is not that I love Maryland less, but freedom more. You will be surprised to learn that people at the north labor under the strange delusion that if the slaves were emancipated at the south, they would flock to the north. So far from this being the case, in that event, you would see many old and familiar faces back again to the south. The fact is, there are few here who would not return to the south in the event of emancipation. We want to live in the land of our birth, and to lay our bones by the side of our fathers; and nothing short of an intense love of personal freedom keeps us from the south. For the sake of this, most of us would live on a crust of bread and a cup of cold water.

Since I left you, I have had a rich experience. I have occupied stations which I never dreamed of when a slave. Three out of the ten years since I left you, I spent as a common laborer on the wharves of New Bedford, Massachusetts. It was there I earned my first free dollar. It was mine. I could spend it as I pleased. I could buy hams or herring with it, without asking any odds of anybody. That was a precious dollar to me. You remember when I used to make seven, or eight, or even nine dollars a week in Baltimore, you would take every cent of it from me every Saturday night, saying that I belonged to you, and my earnings also. I never liked this conduct on your part—to say the best, I thought it a little mean. I would not have served you so. But let that pass. I was a little awkward about counting money in New England fashion when I first landed in New Bedford. I came near betraying myself several times. I caught myself saying phip, for fourpence; and at one time a man actually charged me with being a runaway, whereupon I was silly enough to become one by running away from him, for I was greatly afraid he might adopt measures to get me again into slavery, a condition I then dreaded more than death.

I soon learned, however, to count money, as well as to make it, and got on swimmingly. I married soon after leaving you; in fact, I was engaged to be married before I left you; and instead of finding my companion a burden, she was truly a helpmate. She went to live at service, and I to work on the wharf, and though we toiled hard the first winter, we never lived more happily. After remaining in New

Bedford for three years, I met with William Lloyd Garrison, a person of whom you have *possibly* heard, as he is pretty generally known among slaveholders. He put it into my head that I might make myself serviceable to the cause of the slave, by devoting a portion of my time to telling my own sorrows, and those of other slaves, which had come under my observation. This was the commencement of a higher state of existence than any to which I had ever aspired. I was thrown into society the most pure, enlightened, and benevolent, that the country affords. Among these I have never forgotten you, but have invariably made you the topic of conversation—thus giving you all the notoriety I could do. I need not tell you that the opinion formed of you in these circles is far from being favorable. They have little respect for your honesty, and less for your religion.

But I was going on to relate to you something of my interesting experience. I had not long enjoyed the excellent society to which I have referred, before the light of its excellence exerted a beneficial influence on my mind and heart. Much of my early dislike of white persons was removed, and their manners, habits, and customs, so entirely unlike what I had been used to in the kitchen-quarters on the plantations of the south, fairly charmed me, and gave me a strong disrelish for the coarse and degrading customs of my former condition. I therefore made an effort so to improve my mind and deportment, as to be somewhat fitted to the station to which I seemed almost providentially called. The transition from degradation to respectability was indeed great, and to get from one to the other without carrying some marks of one's former condition, is truly a difficult matter. I would not have you think that I am now entirely clear of all plantation peculiarities, but my friends here, while they entertain the strongest dislike to them, regard me with that charity to which my past life somewhat entitles me, so that my condition in this respect is exceedingly pleasant. So far as my domestic affairs are concerned, I can boast of as comfortable a dwelling as your own. I have an industrious and neat companion, and four dear children—the oldest a girl of nine years, and three fine boys, the oldest eight, the next six, and the youngest four years old. The three oldest are now going regularly to school—two can read and write, and the other can spell, with tolerable correctness, words of two syllables. Dear fellows! They are all in comfortable beds, and are sound asleep, perfectly secure under my own roof. There are no slaveholders here to rend my heart by snatching them from my arms, or blast a mother's dearest hopes by tearing them from her bosom. These dear children are ours—not to work up into rice, sugar, and tobacco, but to watch over, regard, and protect, and to rear them up in the nurture and admonition of the gospel—to train them up in the paths of wisdom and virtue, and, as far as we can, to make them useful to the world and to themselves. Oh! Sir, a slaveholder never appears to me so completely an agent of hell, as when I think of and look upon my dear children. It is then that my feelings rise above my control. I meant to have said more with respect to my own prosperity and happiness, but thoughts and feelings which this recital has quickened, unfit me to proceed further in that direction. The grim horrors of slavery rise in all their ghastly terror before me; the wails of millions pierce my heart and chill my blood. I remember the chain, the gag, the bloody whip; the death-like gloom overshadowing the broken spirit of the fettered bondman; the appalling liability of his being torn away from wife and children, and sold like a beast in the market. Say not that this is a picture of fancy. You well know that I wear stripes on my back, inflicted by your direction; and that you, while we were brothers in the same church, caused this right hand, with which I am now penning this letter, to be closely tied to my left, and my person dragged, at the pistol's mouth, fifteen miles, from the Bay Side to Easton, to be sold like a beast in the market, for the alleged crime of intending to escape from your possession. All this, and more, you remember, and know to be perfectly true, not only of yourself, but of nearly all of the slaveholders around you.

At this moment, you are probably the guilty holder of at least three of my own dear sisters, and my only brother, in bondage. These you regard as your property. They are recorded on your ledger, or perhaps have been sold to human flesh-mongers, with a view to filling your own ever-hungry purse. Sir, I desire to know how and where these dear sisters are. Have you sold them? Or are they still in your possession? What has become of them? Are they living or dead? And my dear old grandmother, whom you turned out like an old horse to die in the woods—is she still alive? Write and let me know all about them. If my grandmother be still alive, she is of no service to you, for by this time she must be nearly eighty years old—too old to be cared for by one to whom she has ceased to be of service; send her to me at Rochester, or bring her to Philadelphia, and it shall be the crowning happiness of my life to take care of her in her old age. Oh! She was to me a mother and a father, so far as hard toil for my comfort could make her such. Send me my grandmother! that I may watch over and take care of her in her old age. And my sisters—let me know all about them. I would write to them, and learn all I want to know of them, without disturbing you in any way, but that, through your unrighteous conduct, they have been entirely deprived of the power to read and write. You have kept them in utter ignorance, and have therefore robbed them of the sweet enjoyments of writing or receiving letters from absent friends and relatives. Your wickedness and cruelty, committed in this respect on your fellow-creatures, are greater than all the stripes you have laid upon my back or theirs. It is an outrage upon the soul, a war upon the immortal spirit, and one for which you must give account at the bar of our common Father and Creator.

The responsibility which you have assumed in this regard is truly awful, and how you could stagger under it these many years is marvelous. Your mind must have become darkened, your heart hardened, your conscience seared and petrified, or you would have long since thrown off the accursed load, and sought relief at the hands of a sin-forgiving God. How, let me ask, would you look upon me, were I, some dark night, in company with a band of hardened villains, to enter the precincts of your elegant dwelling, and seize the person of your own lovely daughter, Amanda, and carry her off from your family, friends, and all the loved ones of her youth—make her my slave—compel her to work, and I take her wages—place her name on my ledger as property—disregard her personal rights—fetter the powers of her immortal soul by denying her the right and privilege of learning to read and write—feed her coarsely—clothe her scantily, and whip her on the naked back occasionally; more, and still more horrible, leave her unprotected—a degraded victim to the brutal lust of fiendish overseers, who would pollute, blight, and blast her fair soul—rob her of all dignity—destroy her virtue, and annihilate in her person all the graces that adorn the character of virtuous womanhood? I ask, how would you regard me, if such were my conduct? Oh! The vocabulary of the damned would not afford a word sufficiently infernal to express your idea of my God-provoking wickedness. Yet, sir, your treatment of my beloved sisters is in all essential points precisely like the case I have now supposed. Damning as would be such a deed on my part, it would be no more so than that which you have committed against me and my sisters.

I will now bring this letter to a close; you shall hear from me again unless you let me hear from you. I intend to make use of you as a weapon with which to assail the system of slavery—as a means of concentrating public attention on the system, and deepening the horror of trafficking in the souls and bodies of men. I shall make use of you as a means of exposing the character of the American church and clergy—and as a means of bringing this guilty nation, with yourself, to repentance. In doing this, I entertain no malice toward you personally. There is no roof under which you would be more safe than mine, and there is nothing in my house which you might need for your comfort, which I would not readily grant. Indeed, I should esteem it a privilege to set you an example as to how mankind ought to treat each other.

*I am your fellow-man, but not your slave.*

# THE NATURE OF SLAVERY

## EXTRACT FROM A LECTURE ON SLAVERY, AT ROCHESTER, DECEMBER 1, 1850.

More than twenty years of my life were consumed in a state of slavery. My childhood was environed by the baneful peculiarities of the slave system. I grew up to manhood in the presence of this hydra headed monster—not as a master—not as an idle spectator—not as the guest of the slaveholder—but as *a slave*, eating the bread and drinking the cup of slavery with the most degraded of my brother-bondmen, and sharing with them all the painful conditions of their wretched lot. In consideration of these facts, I feel that I have a right to speak, and to speak *strongly*. Yet, my friends, I feel bound to speak truly.

Goading as have been the cruelties to which I have been subjected—bitter as have been the trials through which I have passed—exasperating as have been, and still are, the indignities offered to my manhood—I find in them no excuse for the slightest departure from truth in dealing with any branch of this subject.

First of all, I will state, as well as I can, the legal and social relation of master and slave. A master is one—to speak in the vocabulary of the southern states—who claims and exercises a right of property in the person of a fellow-man. This he does with the force of the law and the sanction of southern religion. The law gives the master absolute power over the slave. He may work him, flog him, hire him out, sell him, and, in certain contingencies, *kill* him, with perfect impunity. The slave is a human being, divested of all rights—reduced to the level of a brute—a mere "chattel" in the eye of the law—placed beyond the circle of human brotherhood—cut off from his kind—his name, which the "recording angel" may have enrolled in heaven, among the blest, is impiously inserted in a *master's ledger*, with horses, sheep, and swine. In law, the slave has no wife, no children, no country, and no home.

He can own nothing, possess nothing, acquire nothing, but what must belong to another. To eat the fruit of his own toil, to clothe his person with the work of his own hands, is considered stealing. He toils that another may reap the fruit; he is industrous that another may live in idleness; he eats unbolted meal that another may eat the bread of fine flour; he labors in chains at home, under a burning sun and biting lash, that another may ride in ease and splendor abroad; he lives in ignorance that another may be educated; he is abused that another may be exalted; he rests his toil-worn limbs on the cold, damp ground that another may repose on the softest pillow; he is clad in coarse and tattered raiment that another may be arrayed in purple and fine linen; he is sheltered only by the wretched hovel that a master may dwell in a magnificent mansion; and to this condition he is bound down as by an arm of iron.

From this monstrous relation there springs an unceasing stream of most revolting cruelties. The very accompaniments of the slave system stamp it as the offspring of hell itself. To ensure good behavior, the slaveholder relies on the whip; to induce proper humility, he relies on the whip; to rebuke what he is pleased to term insolence, he relies on the whip; to supply the place of wages as an incentive to toil, he relies on the whip; to bind down the spirit of the slave, to imbrute and destroy his manhood, he relies on the whip, the chain, the gag, the thumb-screw, the pillory, the bowie-knife, the pistol, and the blood-hound. These are the necessary and unvarying accompaniments of the system. Wherever slavery is found, these horrid instruments are also found. Whether on the coast of Africa, among the savage tribes, or in South Carolina, among the refined and civilized, slavery is the same, and its accompaniments one and the same. It makes no difference whether the slaveholder worships the God of the Christians, or is a follower of Mahomet, he is the minister of the same cruelty, and the author of the same misery. *Slavery* is always *slavery*; always the same foul, haggard, and damning scourge, whether found in the eastern or in the western hemisphere.

There is a still deeper shade to be given to this picture. The physical cruelties are indeed sufficiently harassing and revolting; but they are as a few grains of sand on the sea shore, or a few drops of water in the great ocean, compared with the stupendous wrongs which it inflicts upon the mental, moral, and religious nature of its hapless victims. It is only when we contemplate the slave as a moral and intellectual being, that we can adequately comprehend the unparalleled enormity of slavery, and the intense criminality of the slaveholder. I have said that the slave was a man. "What a piece of work is man! How noble in reason! How infinite in faculties! In form and moving how express and admirable! In action how like an angel! In apprehension how like a God! The beauty of the world! The paragon of animals!"*

The slave is a man, "the image of God," but "a little lower than the angels"; possessing a soul, eternal and indestructible; capable of endless happiness, or immeasurable woe; a creature of hopes and fears, of affections and passions, of joys and sorrows, and he is endowed with those mysterious powers by which man soars above the things of time and sense, and grasps, with undying tenacity, the elevating and sublimely glorious idea of a God. It is *such* a being that is smitten and blasted. The first work of slavery is to mar and deface those characteristics of its victims which distinguish *men* from *things*, and *persons* from *property*. Its first aim is to destroy all sense of high moral and religious responsibility. It reduces man to a mere machine. It cuts him off from his Maker, it hides from him the laws of God, and leaves him to grope his way from time to eternity in the dark, under the arbitrary and despotic control of a frail, depraved, and sinful fellow-man. As the serpent-charmer of India is compelled to extract the deadly teeth of his venomous prey before he is able to handle him with impunity, so the slaveholder must strike down the conscience of the slave before he can obtain the entire mastery over his victim.

It is, then, the first business of the enslaver of men to blunt, deaden, and destroy the central principle of human responsibility. Conscience is, to the individual soul, and to society, what the law of gravitation is to the universe. It holds society together; it is the basis of all trust and confidence; it is the pillar of all moral rectitude. Without it, suspicion would take the place of trust; vice would be more than a match for virtue; men would prey upon each other, like the wild beasts of the desert; and earth would become a *hell*.

Nor is slavery more adverse to the conscience than it is to the mind. This is shown by the fact, that in every state of the American Union, where slavery exists, except the state of Kentucky, there are laws absolutely prohibitory of education among the slaves. The crime of teaching a slave to read is punishable with severe fines and imprisonment, and, in some instances, with *death itself.*

---

* From *Hamlet* by William Shakespeare.

Nor are the laws respecting this matter a dead letter. Cases may occur in which they are disregarded, and a few instances may be found where slaves may have learned to read; but such are isolated cases, and only prove the rule. The great mass of slaveholders look upon education among the slaves as utterly subversive of the slave system. I well remember when my mistress first announced to my master that she had discovered that I could read. His face colored at once with surprise and chagrin. He said that "I was ruined, and my value as a slave destroyed; that a slave should know nothing but to obey his master; that to give a Negro an inch would lead him to take an ell; that having learned how to read, I would soon want to know how to write; and that by-and-by I would be running away." I think my audience will bear witness to the correctness of this philosophy, and to the literal fulfillment of this prophecy.

It is perfectly well understood at the south, that to educate a slave is to make him discontented with slavery, and to invest him with a power which shall open to him the treasures of freedom; and since the object of the slaveholder is to maintain complete authority over his slave, his constant vigilance is exercised to prevent everything which militates against, or endangers, the stability of his authority. Education being among the menacing influences, and, perhaps, the most dangerous, is, therefore, the most cautiously guarded against.

It is true that we do not often hear of the enforcement of the law, punishing as a crime the teaching of slaves to read, but this is not because of a want of disposition to enforce it. The true reason or explanation of the matter is this: there is the greatest unanimity of opinion among the white population in the south in favor of the policy of keeping the slave in ignorance. There is, perhaps, another reason why the law against education is so seldom violated. The slave is too poor to be able to offer a temptation sufficiently strong to induce a white man to violate it; and it is not to be supposed that in a community where the moral and religious sentiment is in favor of slavery, many martyrs will be found sacrificing their liberty and lives by violating those prohibitory enactments.

As a general rule, then, darkness reigns over the abodes of the enslaved, and "how great is that darkness!"*

We are sometimes told of the contentment of the slaves, and are

---

* From the Bible, Matthew 6:23.

entertained with vivid pictures of their happiness. We are told that they often dance and sing; that their masters frequently give them wherewith to make merry; in fine, that they have little of which to complair.. I admit that the slave does sometimes sing, dance, and appear to be merry. But what does this prove? It only proves to my mind, that though slavery is armed with a thousand stings, it is not able entirely to kill the elastic spirit of the bondman. That spirit will rise and walk abroad, despite of whips and chains, and extract from the cup of nature occasional drops of joy and gladness. No thanks to the slaveholder, nor to slavery, that the vivacious captive may sometimes dance in his chains; his very mirth in such circumstances stands before God as an accusing angel against his enslaver.

It is often said, by the opponents of the anti-slavery cause, that the condition of the people of Ireland is more deplorable than that of the American slaves. Far be it from me to underrate the sufferings of the Irish people. They have been long oppressed; and the same heart that prompts me to plead the cause of the American bondman, makes it impossible for me not to sympathize with the oppressed of all lands. Yet I must say that there is no analogy between the two cases. The Irishman is poor, but he is not a slave. He may be in rags, but he is not a slave. He is still the master of his own body, and can say with the poet, "The hand of Douglass is his own."* "The world is all before him, where to choose";† and poor as may be my opinion of the British parliament, I cannot believe that it will ever sink to such a depth of infamy as to pass a law for the recapture of fugitive Irishmen! The shame and scandal of kidnapping will long remain wholly monopolized by the American congress. The Irishman has not only the liberty to emigrate from his country, but he has liberty at home. He can write, and speak, and cooperate for the attainment of his rights and the redress of his wrongs.

The multitude can assemble upon all the green hills and fertile plains of the Emerald Isle; they can pour out their grievances, and proclaim their wants without molestation; and the press, that "swift-winged messenger," can bear the tidings of their doings to the extreme bounds of the civilized world. They have their "Conciliation Hall," on the banks of the Liffey, their reform clubs, and their newspapers; they pass resolutions, send forth addresses, and enjoy the right of petition. But

---

* Reference to *Marmion* by Walter Scott.
† Reference to *Paradise Lost* by John Milton.

how is it with the American slave? Where may he assemble? Where is his Conciliation Hall? Where are his newspapers? Where is his right of petition? Where is his freedom of speech? his liberty of the press? and his right of locomotion? He is said to be happy; happy men can speak. But ask the slave what is his condition—what his state of mind—what he thinks of enslavement? and you had as well address your inquiries to the *silent dead*. There comes no voice from the enslaved. We are left to gather his feelings by imagining what ours would be, were our souls in his soul's stead.

If there were no other fact descriptive of slavery, than that the slave is dumb, this alone would be sufficient to mark the slave system as a grand aggregation of human horrors.

Most who are present, will have observed that leading men in this country have been putting forth their skill to secure quiet to the nation. A system of measures to promote this object was adopted a few months ago in congress. The result of those measures is known. Instead of quiet, they have produced alarm; instead of peace, they have brought us war; and so it must ever be.

While this nation is guilty of the enslavement of three millions of innocent men and women, it is as idle to think of having a sound and lasting peace, as it is to think there is no God to take cognizance of the affairs of men. There can be no peace to the wicked while slavery continues in the land. It will be condemned; and while it is condemned there will be agitation. Nature must cease to be nature; men must become monsters; humanity must be transformed; Christianity must be exterminated; all ideas of justice and the laws of eternal goodness must be utterly blotted out from the human soul—ere a system so foul and infernal can escape condemnation, or this guilty republic can have a sound, enduring peace.

# INHUMANITY OF SLAVERY

## EXTRACT FROM A LECTURE ON SLAVERY, AT ROCHESTER, DECEMBER 8, 1850.

The relation of master and slave has been called patriarchal, and only second in benignity and tenderness to that of the parent and child. This representation is doubtless believed by many northern people; and this may account, in part, for the lack of interest which we find among persons whom we are bound to believe to be honest and humane. What, then, are the facts? Here I will not quote my own experience in slavery; for this you might call one-sided testimony. I will not cite the declarations of abolitionists; for these you might pronounce exaggerations. I will not rely upon advertisements cut from newspapers; for these you might call isolated cases. But I will refer you to the laws adopted by the legislatures of the slave states. I give you such evidence, because it cannot be invalidated nor denied. I hold in my hand sundry extracts from the slave codes of our country, from which I will quote . . .

Now, if the foregoing be an indication of kindness, *what is cruelty?* If this be parental affection, *what is bitter malignity?* A more atrocious and blood-thirsty string of laws could not well be conceived of. And yet I am bound to say that they fall short of indicating the horrible cruelties constantly practiced in the slave states.

I admit that there are individual slaveholders less cruel and barbarous than is allowed by law; but these form the exception. The majority of slaveholders find it necessary, to insure obedience, at times, to avail themselves of the utmost extent of the law, and many go beyond it. If kindness were the rule, we should not see advertisements filling the columns of almost every southern newspaper, offering large rewards for fugitive slaves, and describing them as being branded with irons, loaded with chains, and scarred by the whip. One of the most telling testimonies against the pretended kindness of slaveholders, is the fact that uncounted numbers of fugitives are now inhabiting the Dismal Swamp, preferring the untamed wilderness to their cultivated homes—choosing rather to encounter hunger and thirst, and to roam with the wild beasts of the forest, running the hazard of being hunted and shot down, than to submit to the authority of *kind* masters.

I tell you, my friends, humanity is never driven to such an unnatural course of life, without great wrong. The slave finds more of the milk of human kindness in the bosom of the savage Indian, than in the heart of his *Christian* master. He leaves the man of the *Bible*, and takes refuge with the man of the *tomahawk*. He rushes from the praying slaveholder into the paws of the bear. He quits the homes of men for the haunts of wolves. He prefers to encounter a life of trial, however bitter, or death, however terrible, to dragging out his existence under the dominion of these *kind* masters.

The apologists for slavery often speak of the abuses of slavery; and they tell us that they are as much opposed to those abuses as we are; and that they would go as far to correct those abuses and to ameliorate the condition of the slave as anybody. The answer to that view is, that slavery is *itself* an abuse; that it lives by abuse; and dies by the absence of abuse. Grant that slavery is right; grant that the relations of master and slave may innocently exist; and there is not a single outrage which was ever committed against the slave but what finds an apology in the very necessity of the case. As we said by a slaveholder (the Rev. A. G. Few) to the Methodist conference, "If the relation be right, the means to maintain it are also right"; for without those means slavery could not exist. Remove the dreadful scourge—the plaited thong—the galling fetter—the accursed chain—and let the slaveholder rely solely upon moral and religious power, by which to secure obedience to his orders, and how long do you suppose a slave would remain on his plantation? The case only needs to be stated; it carries its own refutation with it.

Absolute and arbitrary power can never be maintained by one man over the body and soul of another man, without brutal chastisement and enormous cruelty.

To talk of *kindness* entering into a relation in which one party is robbed of wife, of children, of his hard earnings, of home, of friends, of society, of knowledge, and of all that makes this life desirable, is most absurd, wicked, and preposterous.

I have shown that slavery is wicked—wicked, in that it violates the great law of liberty, written on every human heart—wicked, in that it violates the first command of the decalogue—wicked, in that it fosters the most disgusting licentiousness—wicked, in that it mars and defaces the image of God by cruel and barbarous inflictions—wicked, in that it contravenes the laws of eternal justice, and tramples in the dust all the humane and heavenly precepts of the New Testament.

The evils resulting from this huge system of iniquity are not confined to the states south of Mason and Dixon's line. Its noxious influence can easily be traced throughout our northern borders. It comes even as far north as the state of New York. Traces of it may be seen even in Rochester; and travelers have told me it casts its gloomy shadows across the lake, approaching the very shores of Queen Victoria's dominions.

The presence of slavery may be explained by—as it is the explanation of—the mobocratic violence which lately disgraced New York, and which still more recently disgraced the city of Boston. These violent demonstrations, these outrageous invasions of human rights, faintly indicate the presence and power of slavery here. It is a significant fact, that while meetings for almost any purpose under heaven may be held unmolested in the city of Boston, that in the same city, a meeting cannot be peaceably held for the purpose of preaching the doctrine of the American Declaration of Independence, "that all men are created equal." The pestiferous breath of slavery taints the whole moral atmosphere of the north, and enervates the moral energies of the whole people.

The moment a foreigner ventures upon our soil, and utters a natural repugnance to oppression, that moment he is made to feel that there is little sympathy in this land for him. If he were greeted with smiles before, he meets with frowns now; and it shall go well with him if he be not subjected to that peculiarly fitting method of showing fealty to slavery, the assaults of a mob.

Now, will any man tell me that such a state of things is natural, and that such conduct on the part of the people of the north, springs from a consciousness of rectitude? No! Every fiber of the human heart unites in detestation of tyranny, and it is only when the human mind has become familiarized with slavery, is accustomed to its injustice, and corrupted by its selfishness, that it fails to record its abhorrence of slavery, and does not exult in the triumphs of liberty.

The northern people have been long connected with slavery; they have been linked to a decaying corpse, which has destroyed the moral health. The union of the government; the union of the north and south, in the political parties; the union in the religious organizations of the land, have all served to deaden the moral sense of the northern people, and to impregnate them with sentiments and ideas forever in conflict with what as a nation we call *genius of American institutions*. Rightly viewed, this is an alarming fact, and ought to rally all that is pure, just, and holy in one determined effort to crush the monster of corruption, and to scatter "its guilty profits" to the winds. In a high moral sense, as well as in a national sense, the whole American people are responsible for slavery, and must share, in its guilt and shame, with the most obdurate men-stealers of the south.

While slavery exists, and the union of these states endures, every American citizen must bear the chagrin of hearing his country branded before the world as a nation of liars and hypocrites; and behold his cherished flag pointed at with the utmost scorn and derision. Even now an American *abroad* is pointed out in the crowd, as coming from a land where men gain their fortunes by "the blood of souls," from a land of slave markets, of blood-hounds, and slave-hunters; and, in some circles, such a man is shunned altogether, as a moral pest. Is it not time, then, for every American to awake, and inquire into his duty with respect to this subject?

Wendell Phillips—the eloquent New England orator—on his return from Europe, in 1842, said, "As I stood upon the shores of Genoa, and saw floating on the placid waters of the Mediterranean, the beautiful American war ship *Ohio*, with her masts tapering proportionately aloft, and an eastern sun reflecting her noble form upon the sparkling waters, attracting the gaze of the multitude, my first impulse was of pride, to think myself an American; but when I thought that the first time that gallant ship would gird on her gorgeous apparel, and wake from beneath her sides her dormant thunders, it would be in defense of the African slave trade, I blushed in utter *shame* for my country."

Let me say again, *slavery is alike the sin and the shame of the American people*; it is a blot upon the American name, and the only national reproach which need make an American hang his head in shame, in the presence of monarchical governments.

With this gigantic evil in the land, we are constantly told to look at home; if we say aught against crowned heads, we are pointed to our enslaved millions; if we talk of sending missionaries and Bibles abroad, we are pointed to three millions now lying in worse than heathen darkness; if we express a word of sympathy for Kossuth and his Hungarian fugitive brethren, we are pointed to that horrible and hell-black enactment, "the fugitive slave bill."

Slavery blunts the edge of all our rebukes of tyranny abroad—the criticisms that we make upon other nations, only call forth ridicule, contempt, and scorn. In a word, we are made a reproach and a by-word to a mocking earth, and we must continue to be so made, so long as slavery continues to pollute our soil.

We have heard much of late of the virtue of patriotism, the love of country, etc., and this sentiment, so natural and so strong, has been impiously appealed to, by all the powers of human selfishness, to cherish the viper which is stinging our national life away. In its name, we have been called upon to deepen our infamy before the world, to rivet the fetter more firmly on the limbs of the enslaved, and to become utterly insensible to the voice of human woe that is wafted to us on every southern gale. We have been called upon, in its name, to desecrate our whole land by the footprints of slave-hunters, and even to engage ourselves in the horrible business of kidnapping.

I, too, would invoke the spirit of patriotism; not in a narrow and restricted sense, but, I trust, with a broad and manly signification; not to cover up our national sins, but to inspire us with sincere repentance; not to hide our shame from the world's gaze, but utterly to abolish the cause of that shame; not to explain away our gross inconsistencies as a nation, but to remove the hateful, jarring, and incongruous elements from the land; not to sustain an egregious wrong, but to unite all our energies in the grand effort to remedy that wrong.

I would invoke the spirit of patriotism, in the name of the law of the living God, natural and revealed, and in the full belief that "righteousness exalteth a nation, while sin is a reproach to any people."* "He that walketh righteously, and speaketh uprightly; he that despiseth the gain of oppressions, that shaketh his hands from the holding of bribes, he shall dwell on high, his place of defense shall be the munitions of rocks, bread shall be given him, his water shall be sure."†

---

* Reference to the Bible, Proverbs 14:34.
† From the Bible, Isaiah 33:15–16.

We have not only heard much lately of patriotism, and of its aid being invoked on the side of slavery and injustice, but the very prosperity of this people has been called in to deafen them to the voice of duty, and to lead them onward in the pathway of sin. Thus has the blessing of God been converted into a curse. In the spirit of genuine patriotism, I warn the American people, by all that is just and honorable, to *beware!*

I warn them that, strong, proud, and prosperous though we be, there is a power above us that can "bring down high looks; at the breath of whose mouth our wealth may take wings; and before whom every knee shall bow"; and who can tell how soon the avenging angel may pass over our land, and the sable bondmen now in chains, may become the instruments of our nation's chastisement! Without appealing to any higher feeling, I would warn the American people, and the American government, to be wise in their day and generation. I exhort them to remember the history of other nations; and I remind them that America cannot always sit "as a queen," in peace and repose; that prouder and stronger governments than this have been shattered by the bolts of a just God; that the time *may* come when those they now despise and hate, may be needed; when those whom they now compel by oppression to be enemies, may be wanted as friends. What has been, may be again. There is a point beyond which human endurance cannot go. The crushed worm may yet turn under the heel of the oppressor. I warn them, then, with all solemnity, and in the name of retributive justice, *to look to their ways*; for in an evil hour, those sable arms that have, for the last two centuries, been engaged in cultivating and adorning the fair fields of our country, may yet become the instruments of terror, desolation, and death, throughout our borders.

It was the sage of the Old Dominion that said—while speaking of the possibility of a conflict between the slaves and the slaveholders—"God has no attribute that could take sides with the oppressor in such a contest. I tremble for my country when I reflect that God *is just*, and that his justice cannot sleep forever." Such is the warning voice of Thomas Jefferson; and every day's experience since its utterance until now, confirms its wisdom, and commends its truth.

# WHAT TO THE SLAVE IS THE FOURTH OF JULY?

## EXTRACT FROM AN ORATION, AT ROCHESTER, JULY 5, 1852

Fellow-citizens—Pardon me, and allow me to ask, why am I called upon to speak here today? What have I, or those I represent, to do with your national independence? Are the great principles of political freedom and of natural justice, embodied in that Declaration of Independence, extended to us? And am I, therefore, called upon to bring our humble offering to the national altar, and to confess the benefits, and express devout gratitude for the blessings, resulting from your independence to us?

Would to God, both for your sakes and ours, that an affirmative answer could be truthfully returned to these questions! Then would my task be light, and my burden easy and delightful. For who is there so cold that a nation's sympathy could not warm him? Who so obdurate and dead to the claims of gratitude, that would not thankfully acknowledge such priceless benefits? Who so stolid and selfish, that would not give his voice to swell the hallelujahs of a nation's jubilee, when the chains of servitude had been torn from his limbs? I am not that man. In a case like that, the dumb might eloquently speak, and the "lame man leap as an hart."*

But, such is not the state of the case. I say it with a sad sense of the disparity between us. I am not included within the pale of this glorious anniversary! Your high independence only reveals the immeasurable distance between us. The blessings in which you this day rejoice, are not enjoyed in common. The rich inheritance of justice, liberty, prosperity, and independence, bequeathed by your fathers, is shared by you, not by me. The sunlight that brought life and healing to you, has brought stripes and death to me. This Fourth of July is *yours*, not *mine*.

---

* From the Bible, Isaiah 35:6.

*You* may rejoice, *I* must mourn. To drag a man in fetters into the grand illuminated temple of liberty, and call upon him to join you in joyous anthems, were inhuman mockery and sacrilegious irony. Do you mean, citizens, to mock me, by asking me to speak today? If so, there is a parallel to your conduct. And let me warn you that it is dangerous to copy the example of a nation whose crimes, towering up to heaven, were thrown down by the breath of the Almighty, burying that nation in irrecoverable ruin! I can today take up the plaintive lament of a peeled and woe-smitten people.

"By the rivers of Babylon, there we sat down. Yea! We wept when we remembered Zion. We hanged our harps upon the willows in the midst thereof. For there, they that carried us away captive, required of us a song; and they who wasted us required of us mirth, saying, Sing us one of the songs of Zion. How can we sing the Lord's song in a strange land? If I forget thee, O Jerusalem, let my right hand forget her cunning. If I do not remember thee, let my tongue cleave to the roof of my mouth."*

Fellow-citizens, above your national, tumultous joy, I hear the mournful wail of millions, whose chains, heavy and grievous yesterday, are today rendered more intolerable by the jubilant shouts that reach them. If I do forget, if I do not faithfully remember those bleeding children of sorrow this day, "may my right hand forget her cunning, and may my tongue cleave to the roof of my mouth!" To forget them, to pass lightly over their wrongs, and to chime in with the popular theme, would be treason most scandalous and shocking, and would make me a reproach before God and the world. My subject, then, fellow-citizens, is *American slavery*. I shall see this day and its popular characteristics from the slave's point of view. Standing there, identified with the American bondman, making his wrongs mine, I do not hesitate to declare, with all my soul, that the character and conduct of this nation never looked blacker to me than on this Fourth of July. Whether we turn to the declarations of the past, or to the professions of the present, the conduct of the nation seems equally hideous and revolting. America is false to the past, false to the present, and solemnly binds herself to be false to the future. Standing with God and the crushed and bleeding slave on this occasion, I will, in the name of humanity which is outraged, in the name of liberty which is fettered, in the name of the

---

* From the Bible, Psalm 137:1–6.

constitution and the Bible, which are disregarded and trampled upon, dare to call in question and to denounce, with all the emphasis I can command, everything that serves to perpetuate slavery—the great sin and shame of America! "I will not equivocate; I will not excuse";* I will use the severest language I can command; and yet not one word shall escape me that any man, whose judgment is not blinded by prejudice, or who is not at heart a slaveholder, shall not confess to be right and just.

But I fancy I hear some one of my audience say, it is just in this circumstance that you and your brother abolitionists fail to make a favorable impression on the public mind. Would you argue more, and denounce less, would you persuade more and rebuke less, your cause would be much more likely to succeed. But, I submit, where all is plain there is nothing to be argued. What point in the anti-slavery creed would you have me argue? On what branch of the subject do the people of this country need light? Must I undertake to prove that the slave is a man? That point is conceded already. Nobody doubts it. The slaveholders themselves acknowledge it in the enactment of laws for their government. They acknowledge it when they punish disobedience on the part of the slave. There are seventy-two crimes in the state of Virginia, which, if committed by a black man (no matter how ignorant he be), subject him to the punishment of death; while only two of these same crimes will subject a white man to the like punishment. What is this but the acknowledgment that the slave is a moral, intellectual, and responsible being. The manhood of the slave is conceded. It is admitted in the fact that southern statute books are covered with enactments forbidding, under severe fines and penalties, the teaching of the slave to read or write. When you can point to any such laws, in reference to the beasts of the field, then I may consent to argue the manhood of the slave. When the dogs in your streets, when the fowls of the air, when the cattle on your hills, when the fish of the sea, and the reptiles that crawl, shall be unable to distinguish the slave from a brute, then will I argue with you that the slave is a man!

For the present, it is enough to affirm the equal manhood of the Negro race. Is it not astonishing that, while we are plowing, planting, and reaping, using all kinds of mechanical tools, erecting houses, constructing bridges, building ships, working in metals of brass, iron, copper, silver, and gold; that, while we are reading, writing,

---

* William Lloyd Garrison, published in the *Liberator* in January 1831.

and cyphering, acting as clerks, merchants, and secretaries, having among us lawyers, doctors, ministers, poets, authors, editors, orators, and teachers; that, while we are engaged in all manner of enterprises common to other men—digging gold in California, capturing the whale in the Pacific, feeding sheep and cattle on the hillside, living, moving, acting, thinking, planning, living in families as husbands, wives, and children, and, above all, confessing and worshipping the Christian's God, and looking hopefully for life and immortality beyond the grave—we are called upon to prove that we are men!

Would you have me argue that man is entitled to liberty? That he is the rightful owner of his own body? You have already declared it. Must I argue the wrongfulness of slavery? Is that a question for republicans? Is it to be settled by the rules of logic and argumentation, as a matter beset with great difficulty, involving a doubtful application of the principle of justice, hard to be understood? How should I look today in the presence of Americans, dividing and subdividing a discourse, to show that men have a natural right to freedom, speaking of it relatively and positively, negatively and affirmatively? To do so, would be to make myself ridiculous, and to offer an insult to your understanding. There is not a man beneath the canopy of heaven that does not know that slavery is wrong for him.

What! am I to argue that it is wrong to make men brutes, to rob them of their liberty, to work them without wages, to keep them ignorant of their relations to their fellow-men, to beat them with sticks, to flay their flesh with the lash, to load their limbs with irons, to hunt them with dogs, to sell them at auction, to sunder their families, to knock out their teeth, to burn their flesh, to starve them into obedience and submission to their masters? Must I argue that a system, thus marked with blood and stained with pollution, is wrong? No; I will not. I have better employment for my time and strength than such arguments would imply.

What, then, remains to be argued? Is it that slavery is not divine; that God did not establish it; that our doctors of divinity are mistaken? There is blasphemy in the thought. That which is inhuman cannot be divine. Who can reason on such a proposition! They that can, may! I cannot. The time for such argument is past.

At a time like this, scorching irony, not convincing argument, is needed. Oh! Had I the ability, and could I reach the nation's ear, I would today pour out a fiery stream of biting ridicule, blasting reproach, withering sarcasm, and stern rebuke. For it is not light that is needed, but fire; it is not the gentle shower, but thunder. We need the storm, the whirlwind, and the earthquake. The feeling of the nation must be quickened; the conscience of the nation must be roused; the propriety of the nation must be startled; the hypocrisy of the nation must be exposed; and its crimes against God and man must be proclaimed and denounced.

What to the American slave is your Fourth of July? I answer, a day that reveals to him, more than all other days in the year, the gross injustice and cruelty to which he is the constant victim. To him, your celebration is a sham; your boasted liberty, an unholy license; your national greatness, swelling vanity; your sounds of rejoicing are empty and heartless; your denunciations of tyrants, brass-fronted impudence; your shouts of liberty and equality, hollow mockery; your prayers and hymns, your sermons and thanksgivings, with all your religious parade and solemnity, are to him mere bombast, fraud, deception, impiety, and hypocrisy—a thin veil to cover up crimes which would disgrace a nation of savages. There is not a nation on the earth guilty of practices more shocking and bloody, than are the people of these United States, at this very hour.

Go where you may, search where you will, roam through all the monarchies and despotisms of the old world, travel through South America, search out every abuse, and when you have found the last, lay your facts by the side of the everyday practices of this nation, and you will say with me, that, for revolting barbarity and shameless hypocrisy, America reigns without a rival.

# THE INTERNAL SLAVE TRADE

## EXTRACT FROM AN ORATION, AT ROCHESTER, JULY 5, 1852

Take the American slave trade, which, we are told by the papers, is especially prosperous just now. Ex-senator Benton tells us that the price of men was never higher than now. He mentions the fact to show that slavery is in no danger. This trade is one of the peculiarities of American institutions. It is carried on in all the large towns and cities in one-half of this confederacy; and millions are pocketed every year by dealers in this horrid traffic. In several states this trade is a chief source of wealth. It is called (in contradistinction to the foreign slave trade) "*the internal slave trade.*" It is, probably, called so, too, in order to divert from it the horror with which the foreign slave trade is contemplated. That trade has long since been denounced by this government as piracy. It has been denounced with burning words, from the high places of the nation, as an execrable traffic. To arrest it, to put an end to it, this nation keeps a squadron, at immense cost, on the coast of Africa. Everywhere in this country, it is safe to speak of this foreign slave trade as a most inhuman traffic, opposed alike to the laws of God and of man. The duty to extirpate and destroy it is admitted even by our *doctors of divinity*. In order to put an end to it, some of these last have consented that their colored brethren (nominally free) should leave this country, and establish themselves on the western coast of Africa. It is, however, a notable fact, that, while so much execration is poured out by Americans, upon those engaged in the foreign slave trade, the men engaged in the slave trade between the states pass without condemnation, and their business is deemed honorable.

Behold the practical operation of this internal slave trade—the American slave trade sustained by American politics and American religion! Here you will see men and women reared like swine for the market. You know what is a swine-drover? I will show you a man-drover. They inhabit all our southern states. They perambulate the country, and crowd the highways of the nation with droves of human stock. You will see one of these human-flesh-jobbers, armed with pistol, whip, and bowie-knife, driving a company of a hundred men, women, and children, from the Potomac to the slave market at New Orleans. These wretched people are to be sold singly, or in lots, to suit purchasers. They are food for the cotton field and the deadly sugar-mill. Mark the sad procession as it moves wearily along, and the inhuman wretch who drives them. Hear his savage yells and his blood-chilling oaths, as he hurries on his affrighted captives. There, see the old man, with locks thinned and gray. Cast one glance, if you please, upon that young mother, whose shoulders are bare to the scorching sun, her briny tears falling on the brow of the babe in her arms. See, too, that girl of thirteen, weeping, yes, weeping, as she thinks of the mother from whom she has been torn. The drove moves tardily. Heat and sorrow have nearly consumed their strength. Suddenly you hear a quick snap, like the discharge of a rifle; the fetters clank, and the chain rattles simultaneously; your ears are saluted with a scream that seems to have torn its way to the center of your soul. The crack you heard was the sound of the slave whip; the scream you heard was from the woman you saw with the babe. Her speed had faltered under the weight of her child and her chains; that gash on her shoulder tells her to move on. Follow this drove to New Orleans. Attend the auction; see men examined like horses; see the forms of women rudely and brutally exposed to the shocking gaze of American slave-buyers. See this drove sold and separated forever; and never forget the deep, sad sobs that arose from that scattered multitude. Tell me, citizens, where, under the sun, can you witness a spectacle more fiendish and shocking. Yet this is but a glance at the American slave trade, as it exists at this moment, in the ruling part of the United States.

I was born amid such sights and scenes. To me the American slave trade is a terrible reality. When a child, my soul was often pierced with a sense of its horrors. I lived on Philpot Street, Fell's Point, Baltimore, and have watched from the wharves the slave ships in the basin, anchored from the shore, with their cargoes of human flesh, waiting for favorable winds to waft them down the Chesapeake. There was, at that time, a grand slave mart kept at the head of Pratt Street, by Austin Woldfolk. His agents were sent into every town and county in Maryland, announcing their arrival through the papers, and on flaming hand-bills, headed, "cash for Negroes." These men were generally well dressed, and very captivating in their manners; ever ready to drink, to treat, and to gamble. The fate of many a slave has depended upon the turn of a single card; and many a child has been snatched from the arms of its mother by bargains arranged in a state of brutal drunkenness.

The flesh-mongers gather up their victims by dozens, and drive them, chained, to the general depot at Baltimore. When a sufficient number have been collected here, a ship is chartered, for the purpose of conveying the forlorn crew to Mobile or to New Orleans. From the slave prison to the ship, they are usually driven in the darkness of night; for since the anti-slavery agitation a certain caution is observed.

In the deep, still darkness of midnight, I have been often aroused by the dead, heavy footsteps and the piteous cries of the chained gangs that passed our door. The anguish of my boyish heart was intense; and I was often consoled, when speaking to my mistress in the morning, to hear her say that the custom was very wicked; that she hated to hear the rattle of the chains, and the heart-rending cries. I was glad to find one who sympathized with me in my horror.

Fellow-citizens, this murderous traffic is today in active operation in this boasted republic. In the solitude of my spirit, I see clouds of dust raised on the highways of the south; I see the bleeding footsteps; I hear the doleful wail of fettered humanity, on the way to the slave markets, where the victims are to be sold like horses, sheep, and swine, knocked off to the highest bidder. There I see the tenderest ties ruthlessly broken, to gratify the lust, caprice, and rapacity of the buyers and sellers of men. My soul sickens at the sight.

> Is this the land your fathers loved?
>     The freedom which they toiled to win?
> Is this the earth whereon they moved?
>     Are these the graves they slumber in?*

But a still more inhuman, disgraceful, and scandalous state of things remains to be presented. By an act of the American congress, not yet two years old, slavery has been nationalized in its most horrible and revolting form. By that act, Mason and Dixon's line has been

---

* From "Stanzas for the Times" by John Greenleaf Whittier.

obliterated; New York has become as Virginia; and the power to hold, hunt, and sell men, women, and children as slaves, remains no longer a mere state institution, but is now an institution of the whole United States. The power is coextensive with the star-spangled banner and American Christianity. Where these go, may also go the merciless slave-hunter. Where these are, man is not sacred. He is a bird for the sportsman's gun. By that most foul and fiendish of all human decrees, the liberty and person of every man are put in peril. Your broad republican domain is a hunting-ground for men. Not for thieves and robbers, enemies of society, merely, but for men guilty of no crime. Your law-makers have commanded all good citizens to engage in this hellish sport. Your president, your secretary of state, your lords, nobles, and ecclesiastics, enforce as a duty you owe to your free and glorious country and to your God, that you do this accursed thing. Not fewer than forty Americans have within the past two years been hunted down, and without a moment's warning, hurried away in chains, and consigned to slavery and excruciating torture. Some of these have had wives and children dependent on them for bread; but of this no account was made. The right of the hunter to his prey, stands superior to the right of marriage, and to all rights in this republic, the rights of God included! For black men there are neither law, justice, humanity, nor religion. The fugitive slave law makes *mercy to them a crime*; and bribes the judge who tries them. An American judge *gets ten dollars for every victim he consigns* to slavery, and five, when he fails to do so. The oath of two villains is sufficient, under this hell-black enactment, to send the most pious and exemplary black man into the remorseless jaws of slavery! His own testimony is nothing. He can bring no witnesses for himself. The minister of American justice is bound by the law to hear but *one side*, and that side is the side of the oppressor. Let this damning fact be perpetually told. Let it be thundered around the world, that, in tyrant-killing, king-hating, people-loving, democratic, Christian America, the seats of justice are filled with judges, who hold their office under an open and palpable *bribe*, and are bound, in deciding in the case of a man's liberty, *to hear only his accusers*!

In glaring violation of justice, in shameless disregard of the forms of administering law, in cunning arrangement to entrap the defenseless, and in diabolical intent, this fugitive slave law stands alone in the annals of tyrannical legislation. I doubt if there be another nation on the globe having the brass and the baseness to put such a law on the statute-book. If any man in this assembly thinks differently from me in this matter, and feels able to disprove my statements, I will gladly confront him at any suitable time and place he may select.

# THE SLAVERY PARTY.

## EXTRACT FROM A SPEECH DELIVERED BEFORE THE A. A. S. SOCIETY, IN NEW YORK, MAY, 1853.

Sir, it is evident that there is in this country a purely slavery party—a party which exists for no other earthly purpose but to promote the interests of slavery. The presence of this party is felt everywhere in the republic. It is known by no particular name, and has assumed no definite shape; but its branches reach far and wide in the church and in the state. This shapeless and nameless party is not intangible in other and more important respects. That party, sir, has determined upon a fixed, definite, and comprehensive policy toward the whole colored population of the United States. What that policy is, it becomes us as abolitionists, and especially does it become the colored people themselves, to consider and to understand fully. We ought to know who our enemies are, where they are, and what are their objects and measures. Well, sir, here is my version of it—not original with me—but mine because I hold it to be true.

I understand this policy to comprehend five cardinal objects. They are these: 1st. The complete suppression of all anti-slavery discussion. 2nd. The expatriation of the entire free people of color from the United States. 3rd. The unending perpetuation of slavery in this republic. 4th. The nationalization of slavery to the extent of making slavery respected in every state of the Union. 5th. The extension of slavery over Mexico and the entire South American states.

Sir, these objects are forcibly presented to us in the stern logic of passing events; in the facts which are and have been passing around us during the last three years. The country has been and is now dividing on these grand issues. In their magnitude, these issues cast all others into the shade, depriving them of all life and vitality. Old party ties are broken. Like is finding its like on either side of these great issues, and the great battle is at hand. For the present, the best representative of the slavery party in politics is the democratic party. Its great head for the present is President Pierce, whose boast it was, before his election, that his whole life had been consistent with the interests of slavery, that he is above reproach on that score. In his inaugural address, he reassures the south on this point. Well, the head of the slave power being in power, it is natural that the pro-slavery elements should cluster around the administration, and this is rapidly being done. A fraternization is going on. The stringent protectionists and the free-traders strike hands. The supporters of Fillmore are becoming the supporters of Pierce. The silver-gray whig shakes hands with the hunker democrat; the former only differing from the latter in name. They are of one heart, one mind, and the union is natural and perhaps inevitable. Both hate Negroes; both hate progress; both hate the "higher law"; both hate William H. Seward; both hate the free democratic party; and upon this hateful basis they are forming a union of hatred. "Pilate and Herod are thus made friends." Even the central organ of the whig party is extending its beggar hand for a morsel from the table of slavery democracy, and when spurned from the feast by the more deserving, it pockets the insult; when kicked on one side it turns the other, and perseveres in its importunities. The fact is, that paper comprehends the demands of the times; it understands the age and its issues; it wisely sees that slavery and freedom are the great antagonistic forces in the country, and it goes to its own side. Silver grays and hunkers all understand this. They are, therefore, rapidly sinking all other questions to nothing, compared with the increasing demands of slavery. They are collecting, arranging, and consolidating their forces for the accomplishment of their appointed work.

The keystone to the arch of this grand union of the slavery party of the United States, is the compromise of 1850. In that compromise we have all the objects of our slaveholding policy specified. It is, sir, favorable to this view of the designs of the slave power, that both the whig and the democratic party bent lower, sunk deeper, and strained harder, in their conventions, preparatory to the late presidential election, to meet the demands of the slavery party than at any previous time in their history. Never did parties come before the northern people with propositions of such undisguised contempt for the moral sentiment and the religious ideas of that people. They virtually asked them to unite in a war upon free speech, and upon conscience, and to drive the Almighty presence from the councils of the nation. Resting their platforms upon the fugitive slave bill, they boldly asked the people for political power to execute the horrible and hell-black provisions of that bill. The history of that election reveals, with great clearness, the extent to which slavery has shot its leprous distillment through the life-blood of the nation. The party most thoroughly opposed to the cause of justice and humanity, triumphed; while the party suspected of a leaning toward liberty, was overwhelmingly defeated, some say annihilated.

But here is a still more important fact, illustrating the designs of the slave power. It is a fact full of meaning, that no sooner did the democratic slavery party come into power, than a system of legislation was presented to the legislatures of the northern states, designed to put the states in harmony with the fugitive slave law, and the malignant bearing of the national government toward the colored inhabitants of the country. This whole movement on the part of the states, bears the evidence of having one origin, emanating from one head, and urged forward by one power. It was simultaneous, uniform, and general, and looked to one end. It was intended to put thorns under feet already bleeding; to crush a people already bowed down; to enslave a people already but half free; in a word, it was intended to discourage, dishearten, and drive the free colored people out of the country. In looking at the recent black law of Illinois,* one is struck dumb with its enormity. It would seem that the men who enacted that law, had not only banished from their minds all sense of justice, but all sense of shame. It coolly proposes to sell the bodies and souls of the blacks to increase the intelligence and refinement of the whites; to rob every black stranger who ventures among them, to increase their literary fund.

While this is going on in the states, a pro-slavery, political board of health is established at Washington. Senators Hale, Chase, and Sumner are robbed of a part of their senatorial dignity and consequence as representing sovereign states, because they have refused to be inoculated with the slavery virus. Among the services which a senator is expected by his state to perform, are many that can only be done efficiently on committees; and, in saying to these honorable senators, you shall not serve on the committees of this body, the slavery party

---

* The Illinois Black Code of 1853 prohibited African Americans from moving into the state.

took the responsibility of robbing and insulting the states that sent them. It is an attempt at Washington to decide for the states who shall be sent to the senate. Sir, it strikes me that this aggression on the part of the slave power did not meet at the hands of the proscribed senators the rebuke which we had a right to expect would be administered. It seems to me that an opportunity was lost, that the great principle of senatorial equality was left undefended, at a time when its vindication was sternly demanded. But it is not to the purpose of my present statement to criticize the conduct of our friends. I am persuaded that much ought to be left to the discretion of anti-slavery men in congress, and charges of recreancy should never be made but on the most sufficient grounds. For, of all the places in the world where an anti-slavery man needs the confidence and encouragement of friends, I take Washington to be that place.

Let me now call attention to the social influences which are operating and cooperating with the slavery party of the country, designed to contribute to one or all of the grand objects aimed at by that party. We see here the black man attacked in his vital interests; prejudice and hate are excited against him; enmity is stirred up between him and other laborers. The Irish people, warm-hearted, generous, and sympathizing with the oppressed everywhere, when they stand upon their own green island, are instantly taught, on arriving in this Christian country, to hate and despise the colored people. They are taught to believe that we eat the bread which of right belongs to them. The cruel lie is told the Irish, that our adversity is essential to their prosperity. Sir, the Irish-American will find out his mistake one day. He will find that in assuming our avocation he also has assumed our degradation. But for the present we are sufferers. The old employments by which we have heretofore gained our livelihood, are gradually, and it may be inevitably, passing into other hands. Every hour sees us elbowed out of some employment to make room perhaps for some newly-arrived emigrants, whose hunger and color are thought to give them a title to especial favor. White men are becoming house-servants, cooks, and stewards, common laborers, and flunkeys to our gentry, and, for aught I see, they adjust themselves to their stations with all becoming obsequiousness. This fact proves that if we cannot rise to the whites, the whites can fall to us. Now, sir, look once more. While the colored people are thus elbowed out of employment; while the enmity of emigrants is being excited against us;

while state after state enacts laws against us; while we are hunted down, like wild game, and oppressed with a general feeling of insecurity—the American colonization society—that old offender against the best interests and slanderer of the colored people—awakens to new life, and vigorously presses its scheme upon the consideration of the people and the government. New papers are started—some for the north and some for the south—and each in its tone adapting itself to its latitude. Government, state and national, is called upon for appropriations to enable the society to send us out of the country by steam! They want steamers to carry letters and Negroes to Africa. Evidently, this society looks upon our "extremity as its opportunity," and we may expect that it will use the occasion well. They do not deplore, but glory, in our misfortunes.

But, sir, I must hasten. I have thus briefly given my view of one aspect of the present condition and future prospects of the colored people of the United States. And what I have said is far from encouraging to my afflicted people. I have seen the cloud gather upon the sable brows of some who hear me. I confess the case looks black enough. Sir, I am not a hopeful man. I think I am apt even to undercalculate the benefits of the future. Yet, sir, in this seemingly desperate case, I do not despair for my people. There is a bright side to almost every picture of this kind; and ours is no exception to the general rule. If the influences against us are strong, those for us are also strong. To the inquiry, will our enemies prevail in the execution of their designs. In my God and in my soul, I believe they *will not*. Let us look at the first object sought for by the slavery party of the country, viz: the suppression of anti-slavery discussion. They desire to suppress discussion on this subject, with a view to the peace of the slaveholder and the security of slavery. Now, sir, neither the principle nor the subordinate objects here declared, can be at all gained by the slave power, and for this reason: It involves the proposition to padlock the lips of the whites, in order to secure the fetters on the limbs of the blacks. The right of speech, precious and priceless, *cannot*, *will not*, be surrendered to slavery. Its suppression is asked for, as I have said, to give peace and security to slaveholders. Sir, that thing cannot be done. God has interposed an insuperable obstacle to any such result. "There can be *no peace*, saith my God, to the wicked."* Suppose it were possible to put down this discussion, what would it

---

* From the Bible, Isaiah 57:21.

avail the guilty slaveholder, pillowed as he is upon heaving bosoms of ruined souls? He could not have a peaceful spirit. If every anti-slavery tongue in the nation were silent—every anti-slavery organization dissolved—every anti-slavery press demolished—every anti-slavery periodical, paper, book, pamphlet, or what not, were searched out, gathered, deliberately burned to ashes, and their ashes given to the four winds of heaven, still, still the slaveholder could have "*no peace.*" In every pulsation of his heart, in every throb of his life, in every glance of his eye, in the breeze that soothes, and in the thunder that startles, would be waked up an accuser, whose cause is, "Thou art, verily, guilty concerning thy brother."

# THE ANTI-SLAVERY MOVEMENT

## EXTRACTS FROM A LECTURE BEFORE VARIOUS ANTI-SLAVERY BODIES, IN THE WINTER OF 1855.

A grand movement on the part of mankind, in any direction, or for any purpose, moral or political, is an interesting fact, fit and proper to be studied. It is such, not only for those who eagerly participate in it, but also for those who stand aloof from it—even for those by whom it is opposed. I take the anti-slavery movement to be such an one, and a movement as sublime and glorious in its character, as it is holy and beneficent in the ends it aims to accomplish. At this moment, I deem it safe to say, it is properly engrossing more minds in this country than any other subject now before the American people. The late John C. Calhoun—one of the mightiest men that ever stood up in the American senate—did not deem it beneath him; and he probably studied it as deeply, though not as honestly, as Gerrit Smith, or William Lloyd Garrison. He evinced the greatest familiarity with the subject; and the greatest efforts of his last years in the senate had direct reference to this movement. His eagle eye watched every new development connected with it; and he was ever prompt to inform the south of every important step in its progress. He never allowed himself to make light of it; but always spoke of it and treated it as a matter of grave import; and in this he showed himself a master of the mental, moral, and religious constitution of human society. Daniel Webster, too, in the better days of his life, before he gave his assent to the fugitive slave bill, and trampled upon all his earlier and better convictions—when his eye was yet single—he clearly comprehended the nature of the elements involved in this movement; and in his own majestic eloquence, warned the south, and the country, to have a care how they attempted to put it down. He is an illustration that it is easier to give, than to take, good advice. To these two men—the greatest men to whom the nation has yet given birth—may be traced the two great facts of the present—the south triumphant, and the north humbled. Their names may stand thus—Calhoun and domination—Webster and degradation. Yet again. If to the enemies of liberty this subject is one of engrossing interest, vastly more so should it be such to freedom's friends. The latter, it leads to the gates of all valuable knowledge—philanthropic, ethical, and religious; for it brings them to the study of man, wonderfully and fearfully made—the proper study of man through all time—the open book, in which are the records of time and eternity.

Of the existence and power of the anti-slavery movement, as a fact, you need no evidence. The nation has seen its face, and felt the controlling pressure of its hand. You have seen it moving in all directions, and in all weathers, and in all places, appearing most where desired least, and pressing hardest where most resisted. No place is exempt. The quiet prayer meeting, and the stormy halls of national debate, share its presence alike. It is a common intruder, and of course has the name of being ungentlemanly. Brethren who had long sung, in the most affectionate fervor, and with the greatest sense of security,

> Together let us sweetly live—together let us die,

have been suddenly and violently separated by it, and ranged in hostile attitude toward each other. The Methodist, one of the most powerful religious organizations of this country, has been rent asunder, and its strongest bolts of denominational brotherhood started at a single surge. It has changed the tone of the northern pulpit, and modified that of the press. A celebrated divine, who, four years ago, was for flinging his own mother, or brother, into the remorseless jaws of the monster slavery, lest he should swallow up the Union, now recognizes anti-slavery as a characteristic of future civilization. Signs and wonders follow this movement; and the fact just stated is one of them. Party ties are loosened by it; and men are compelled to take sides for or against it, whether they will or not. Come from where he may, or come for what he may, he is compelled to show his hand. What is this mighty force? What is its history? And what is its destiny? Is it ancient or modern, transient or permanent? Has it turned aside, like a stranger and a sojourner, to tarry for a night? Or has it come to rest with us forever?

Excellent chances are here for speculation; and some of them are quite profound. We might, for instance, proceed to inquire not only into the philosophy of the anti-slavery movement, but into the philosophy of the law, in obedience to which that movement started into existence. We might demand to know what is that law or power, which, at different times, disposes the minds of men to this or that particular object—now for peace, and now for war—now for freedom, and now for slavery; but this profound question I leave to the abolitionists of the superior class to answer. The speculations which must precede such answer, would afford, perhaps, about the same satisfaction as the learned theories which have rained down upon the world, from time to time, as to the origin of evil. I shall, therefore, avoid water in which I cannot swim, and deal with anti-slavery as a fact, like any other fact in the history of mankind, capable of being described and understood, both as to its internal forces, and its external phases and relations.

*[After an eloquent, a full, and highly interesting exposition of the nature, character, and history of the anti-slavery movement, from the insertion of which want of space precludes us, he concluded in the following happy manner.]*

Present organizations may perish, but the cause will go on. That cause has a life, distinct and independent of the organizations patched up from time to time to carry it forward. Looked at, apart from the bones and sinews and body, it is a thing immortal. It is the very essence of justice, liberty, and love. The moral life of human society, it cannot die while conscience, honor, and humanity remain. If but one be filled with it, the cause lives. Its incarnation in any one individual man, leaves the whole world a priesthood, occupying the highest moral eminence— even that of disinterested benevolence. Whoso has ascended his height, and has the grace to stand there, has the world at his feet, and is the world's teacher, as of divine right. He may set in judgment on the age, upon the civilization of the age, and upon the religion of the age; for he has a test, a sure and certain test, by which to try all institutions, and to measure all men. I say, he may do this, but this is not the chief business for which he is qualified. The great work to which he is called is not that of judgment. Like the Prince of Peace, he may say, if I judge, I judge righteous judgment; still mainly, like him, he may say, this is not his work. The man who has thoroughly embraced the principles of justice, love, and liberty, like the true preacher of Christianity, is less anxious to reproach the world of its sins, than to win it to repentance. His great work on earth is to exemplify, and to illustrate, and to ingraft those principles upon the living and practical understandings of all men within the reach of his influence. This is his work; long or short his years, many or few his adherents, powerful or weak his instrumentalities, through good report, or through bad report, this is his work. It is to snatch from the bosom of nature the latent facts of each individual man's experience, and with steady hand to hold them up fresh and glowing, enforcing, with all his power, their acknowledgment and practical adoption. If there be but one such man in the land, no matter what becomes of abolition societies and parties, there will be an anti-slavery cause, and an anti-slavery movement. Fortunately for that cause, and fortunately for him by whom it is espoused, it requires no extraordinary amount of talent to preach it or to receive it when preached. The grand secret of its power is, that each of its principles is easily rendered appreciable to the faculty of reason in man, and that the most unenlightened conscience has no difficulty in deciding on which side to register its testimony. It can call its preachers from among the fishermen, and raise them to power. In every human breast, it has an advocate which can be silent only when the heart is dead. It comes home to every man's understanding, and appeals directly to every man's conscience. A man that does not recognize and approve for himself the rights and privileges contended for, in behalf of the American slave, has not yet been found. In whatever else men may differ, they are alike in the apprehension of their natural and personal rights. The difference between abolitionists and those by whom they are opposed, is not as to principles. All are agreed in respect to these. The manner of applying them is the point of difference.

The slaveholder himself, the daily robber of his equal brother, discourses eloquently as to the excellency of justice, and the man who employs a brutal driver to flay the flesh of his Negroes, is not offended when kindness and humanity are commended. Every time the abolitionist speaks of justice, the anti-abolitionist assents—says, yes, I wish the world were filled with a disposition to render to every man what is rightfully due him; I should then get what is due me. That's right; let us have justice. By all means, let us have justice. Every time the abolitionist speaks in honor of human liberty, he touches a chord in the heart of the anti-abolitionist, which responds in harmonious vibrations. Liberty—yes, that is evidently my right, and let him beware who attempts to invade or abridge that right. Every time he speaks of love, of human brotherhood, and the reciprocal duties of man and man, the anti-abolitionist assents—says, yes, all right—all true—we cannot have such ideas too often, or too fully expressed. So he says, and so he feels, and only shows thereby that he is a man as well as an anti-abolitionist. You have only to keep out of sight the manner of applying your principles, to get them endorsed every time. Contemplating himself, he sees truth with absolute clearness and distinctness. He only blunders when asked to lose sight of himself. In his own cause he can beat a Boston lawyer, but he is dumb when asked to plead the cause of others. He knows very well whatsoever he would have done unto himself, but is quite in doubt as to having the same thing done unto others. It is just here, that lions spring up in the path of duty, and the battle once fought in heaven is refought on the earth. So it is, so hath it ever been, and so must it ever be, when the claims of justice and mercy make their demand at the door of human selfishness. Nevertheless, there is that within which ever pleads for the right and the just.

In conclusion, I have taken a sober view of the present anti-slavery movement. I am sober, but not hopeless. There is no denying, for it is everywhere admitted, that the anti-slavery question is the great moral and social question now before the American people. A state of things has gradually been developed, by which that question has become the first thing in order. It must be met. Herein is my hope. The great idea of impartial liberty is now fairly before the American people. Anti-slavery is no longer a thing to be prevented. The time for prevention is past. This is great gain. When the movement was younger and weaker—when it wrought in a Boston garret to human apprehension, it might have been silently put out of the way. Things are different now. It has grown too large—its friends are too numerous—its facilities too abundant—its ramifications too extended—its power too omnipotent, to be snuffed out by the contingencies of infancy. A thousand strong men might be struck down, and its ranks still be invincible. One flash from the heart-supplied intellect of Harriet Beecher Stowe could light a million camp fires in front of the embattled host of slavery, which not all the waters of the Mississippi, mingled as they are with blood, could extinguish.

The present will be looked to by after coming generations, as the age of anti-slavery literature—when supply on the gallop could not keep pace with the ever growing demand—when a picture of a Negro on the cover was a help to the sale of a book—when conservative lyceums and other American literary associations began first to select their orators for distinguished occasions from the ranks of the previously despised abolitionists. If the anti-slavery movement shall fail now, it will not be from outward opposition, but from inward decay. Its auxiliaries are everywhere. Scholars, authors, orators, poets, and statesmen give it their aid. The most brilliant of American poets volunteer in its service. Whittier speaks in burning verse to more than thirty thousand, in the *National Era*. Your own Longfellow whispers, in every hour of trial and disappointment, "labor and wait." James Russell Lowell is reminding us that "men are more than institutions." Pierpont cheers the heart of the pilgrim in search of liberty, by singing the praises of "the north star." Bryant, too, is with us; and though chained to the car of party, and dragged on amidst a whirl of political excitement, he snatches a moment for letting drop a smiling verse of sympathy for the man in chains. The poets are with us. It would seem almost absurd to say it, considering the use that has been made of them, that we have allies in the Ethiopian songs; those songs that constitute our national music, and without which we have no national music. They are heart songs, and the finest feelings of human nature are expressed in them. "Lucy Neal," "Old Kentucky Home," and "Uncle Ned," can make the heart sad as well as merry, and can call forth a tear as well as a smile. They awaken the sympathies for the slave, in which anti-slavery principles take root, grow, and flourish. In addition to authors, poets, and scholars at home, the moral sense of the civilized world is with us. England, France, and Germany, the three great lights of modern civilization, are with us, and every American traveler learns to regret the existence of slavery in his country. The growth of intelligence, the influence of commerce, steam, wind, and lightning are our allies. It would be easy to amplify this summary, and to swell the vast conglomeration of our material forces; but there is a deeper and truer method of measuring the power of our cause, and of comprehending its vitality. This is to be found in its accordance with the best elements of human nature. It is beyond the power of slavery to annihilate affinities recognized and established by the Almighty. The slave is bound to mankind by the powerful and inextricable net-work of human brotherhood. His voice is the voice of a man, and his cry is the cry of a man in distress, and man must cease to be man before he can become insensible to that cry. It is the righteous of the cause—the humanity of the cause—which constitutes its potency. As one genuine bankbill is worth more than a thousand counterfeits, so is one man, with right on his side, worth more than a thousand in the wrong. "One may chase a thousand, and put ten thousand to flight."* It is, therefore, upon the goodness of our cause, more than upon all other auxiliaries, that we depend for its final triumph.

Another source of congratulations is the fact that, amid all the efforts made by the church, the government, and the people at large, to stay the onward progress of this movement, its course has been onward, steady, straight, unshaken, and unchecked from the beginning. Slavery has gained victories large and numerous; but never as against this movement—against a temporizing policy, and against northern timidity, the slave power has been victorious; but against the spread and prevalence in the country, of a spirit of resistance to its aggression, and of sentiments favorable to its entire overthrow, it has yet accomplished nothing. Every measure, yet devised and executed, having for its object the suppression of anti-slavery, has been as idle and fruitless as pouring oil to extinguish fire. A general rejoicing took place on the passage of "the compromise measures" of 1850. Those measures were called peace measures, and were afterward termed by both the great parties of the country, as well as by leading statesmen, a final settlement of the whole question of slavery; but experience has laughed to scorn the wisdom of pro-slavery statesmen; and their final settlement of agitation seems to be the final revival, on a broader and grander scale than ever before, of the question which they vainly attempted to suppress forever. The fugitive slave bill has especially been of positive service to the anti-slavery movement. It has illustrated before all the people the horrible character of slavery toward the slave, in hunting him down in a free state, and tearing him away from wife and children, thus setting its claims higher than marriage or parental claims. It has revealed the arrogant and overbearing spirit of the slave states toward the free states; despising their principles—shocking their feelings of humanity, not only by bringing before them the abominations of slavery, but by attempting to make them parties to the crime. It has called into exercise among

---

* Reference to the Bible, Deuteronomy 32:30.

the colored people, the hunted ones, a spirit of manly resistance well calculated to surround them with a bulwark of sympathy and respect hitherto unknown. For men are always disposed to respect and defend rights, when the victims of oppression stand up manfully for themselves.

There is another element of power added to the anti-slavery movement, of great importance; it is the conviction, becoming every day more general and universal, that slavery must be abolished at the south, or it will demoralize and destroy liberty at the north. It is the nature of slavery to beget a state of things all around it favorable to its own continuance. This fact, connected with the system of bondage, is beginning to be more fully realized. The slave-holder is not satisfied to associate with men in the church or in the state, unless he can thereby stain them with the blood of his slaves. To be a slave-holder is to be a propagandist from necessity; for slavery can only live by keeping down the under-growth morality which nature supplies. Every new-born white babe comes armed from the Eternal presence, to make war on slavery. The heart of pity, which would melt in due time over the brutal chastisements it sees inflicted on the helpless, must be hardened. And this work goes on every day in the year, and every hour in the day.

What is done at home is being done also abroad here in the north. And even now the question may be asked, have we at this moment a single free state in the Union? The alarm at this point will become more general. The slave power must go on in its career of exactions. Give, give, will be its cry, till the timidity which concedes shall give place to courage, which shall resist. Such is the voice of experience, such has been the past, such is the present, and such will be that future, which, so sure as man is man, will come. Here I leave the subject; and I leave off where I began, consoling myself and congratulating the friends of freedom upon the fact that the anti-slavery cause is not a new thing under the sun; not some moral delusion which a few years' experience may dispel. It has appeared among men in all ages, and summoned its advocates from all ranks. Its foundations are laid in the deepest and holiest convictions, and from whatever soul the demon, selfishness, is expelled, there will this cause take up its abode. Old as the everlasting hills; immovable as the throne of God; and certain as the purposes of eternal power, against all hinderances, and against all delays, and despite all the mutations of human instrumentalities, it is the faith of my soul, that this anti-slavery cause will triumph.

*Department of the Interior.*
*Washington D.C. Aug.* 10. 1863

*To whom it may concern,*

*The bearer of this, Frederick Douglass, is known to us as a loyal, free, man, and is, hence, entitled to travel, unmolested.—*

*We trust he will be recognized everywhere, as a free man, and a gentleman.*

*Respectfully*

# The Autobiography of Benjamin Franklin

# The Autobiography of Benjamin Franklin

**Word Cloud Classics**
San Diego

Canterbury Classics
An imprint of Printers Row Publishing Group
10350 Barnes Canyon Road, Suite 100, San Diego, CA 92121
www.canterburyclassicsbooks.com • mail@canterburyclassicsbooks.com

Printers Row Publishing Group is a division of Readerlink Distribution Services, LLC. The Canterbury Classics and Word Cloud Classics names and logos are trademarks of Readerlink Distribution Services, LLC.

All correspondence concerning the content of this book should be addressed to Canterbury Classics, Editorial Department, at the above address.

Publisher: Peter Norton
Associate Publisher: Ana Parker
Publishing/Editorial Team: April Farr, Kathryn C. Dalby, Aaron Guzman
Editorial Team: JoAnn Padgett, Melinda Allman, Traci Douglas
Production/Design Team: Jonathan Lopes, Rusty von Dyl,
Ray Caramanna

Spine art: Gettyimages/eyewave (statue), Gettyimages/clipartdotcom (flag)

ISBN: 978-1-64517-087-7
Printed in China
23 22 21 20 19  1 2 3 4 5

# Contents

# The Autobiography of Benjamin Franklin

WITH ILLUSTRATIONS BY
E. BOYD SMITH

EDITED BY
FRANK WOODWORTH PINE

# Introduction

We Americans devour eagerly any piece of writing that purports to tell us the secret of success in life; yet how often we are disappointed to find nothing but commonplace statements, or receipts that we know by heart but never follow. Most of the life stories of our famous and successful men fail to inspire because they lack the human element that makes the record real and brings the story within our grasp. While we are searching far and near for some Aladdin's Lamp to give coveted fortune, there is ready at our hand if we will only reach out and take it, like the charm in Milton's *Comus*,

> "Unknown, and like esteemed, and the dull swain
> Treads on it daily with his clouted shoon;"

the interesting, human, and vividly told story of one of the wisest and most useful lives in our own history, and perhaps in any history. In Franklin's *Autobiography* is offered not so much a ready-made formula for success, as the companionship of a real flesh and blood man of extraordinary mind and quality, whose daily walk and conversation will help us to meet our own difficulties, much as does the example of a wise and strong friend. While we are fascinated by the story, we absorb the human experience through which a strong and helpful character is building.

The thing that makes Franklin's *Autobiography* different from every other life story of a great and successful man is just this human aspect of the account. Franklin told the story of his life, as he himself says, for the benefit of his posterity. He wanted to help them by the relation of his own rise from obscurity and poverty to eminence and wealth. He is not unmindful of the importance of his public services and their recognition, yet his accounts of these achievements are given only as a part of the story, and the vanity displayed is incidental and in keeping with the honesty of the recital. There is nothing of the impossible in the method and practice of Franklin as he sets them forth. The youth who reads the fascinating story is astonished to find that Franklin in his early years struggled with the same everyday passions and difficulties that he himself experiences, and he loses the sense of discouragement that comes from a realization of his own shortcomings and inability to attain.

There are other reasons why the *Autobiography* should be an intimate friend of American young people. Here they may establish a close relationship with one of the foremost Americans as well as one of the wisest men of his age.

The life of Benjamin Franklin is of importance to every American primarily because of the part he played in securing the independence of the United States and in establishing it as a nation. Franklin shares with Washington the honors of the Revolution, and of the events leading to the birth of the new nation. While Washington was the animating spirit of the struggle in the colonies, Franklin was its ablest champion abroad. To Franklin's cogent reasoning and keen satire, we owe the clear and forcible presentation of the American case in England and France; while to his personality and diplomacy as well as to his facile pen, we are indebted for the foreign alliance and the funds without which Washington's work must have failed. His patience, fortitude, and practical wisdom, coupled with self-sacrificing devotion to the cause of his country, are hardly less noticeable than similar qualities displayed by Washington. In fact, Franklin as a public man was much like Washington, especially in the entire disinterestedness of his public service.

Franklin is also interesting to us because by his life and teachings he has done more than any other American to advance the material prosperity of his countrymen. It is said that his widely and faithfully read maxims made Philadelphia and Pennsylvania wealthy, while Poor Richard's pithy sayings, translated into many languages, have had a world-wide influence.

Franklin is a good type of our American manhood. Although not the wealthiest or the most powerful, he is undoubtedly, in the versatility of his genius and achievements, the greatest of our self-made men. The simple yet graphic story in the *Autobiography* of his steady rise from humble boyhood in a tallow-chandler shop, by industry, economy, and perseverance in self-improvement, to eminence, is the most remarkable of all the remarkable histories of our self-made men. It is in itself a wonderful illustration of the results possible to be attained in a land of unequaled opportunity by following Franklin's maxims.

Franklin's fame, however, was not confined to his own country. Although he lived in a century notable for the rapid evolution of scientific and political thought and activity, yet no less a keen judge and critic than Lord Jeffrey, the famous editor of the *Edinburgh Review*, a century ago said that "in one point of view the name of Franklin must be considered as standing higher than any of the others which illustrated the eighteenth century. Distinguished as a statesman, he was equally great as a philosopher, thus uniting in himself a rare degree of excellence in both these pursuits, to excel in either of which is deemed the highest praise."

Franklin has indeed been aptly called "many-sided." He was eminent in science and public service, in diplomacy and in literature. He was the Edison of his day, turning his scientific discoveries to the benefit of his fellow-men. He perceived the identity of lightning and electricity and set up the lightning rod. He invented the Franklin stove, still widely used, and refused to patent it. He possessed a masterly shrewdness in business and practical affairs. Carlyle called him the father of all the Yankees. He founded a fire company, assisted in founding a hospital, and improved the cleaning and lighting of streets. He developed journalism, established the American Philosophical Society, the public library in Philadelphia, and the University of Pennsylvania. He organized a postal system for the colonies, which was the basis of the present United States Post Office. Bancroft, the eminent historian, called him "the greatest diplomatist of his century." He perfected the Albany Plan of Union for the colonies. He is the only statesman who signed the Declaration of Independence, the Treaty of Alliance with France, the Treaty of Peace with England, and the Constitution. As a writer, he has produced, in his *Autobiography* and in *Poor Richard's Almanac*, two works that are not surpassed by similar writing. He received honorary degrees from Harvard and Yale, from Oxford and St. Andrews, and was made a fellow of the Royal Society, which awarded him the Copley gold medal for improving natural knowledge. He was one of the eight foreign associates of the French Academy of Science.

The careful study of the *Autobiography* is also valuable because of the style in which it is written. If Robert Louis Stevenson is right in believing that his remarkable style was acquired by imitation then the youth who would gain the power to express his ideas clearly, forcibly, and interestingly cannot do better than to study Franklin's method.

Franklin's fame in the scientific world was due almost as much to his modest, simple, and sincere manner of presenting his discoveries and to the precision and clearness of the style in which he described his experiments, as to the results he was able to announce. Sir Humphry Davy, the celebrated English chemist, himself an excellent literary critic as well as a great scientist, said: "A singular felicity guided all Franklin's researches, and by very small means he established very grand truths. The style and manner of his publication on electricity are almost as worthy of admiration as the doctrine it contains."

Franklin's place in literature is hard to determine because he was not primarily a literary man. His aim in his writings as in his life work was to be helpful to his fellow-men. For him writing was never an end in itself, but always a means to an end. Yet his success as a scientist, a statesman, and a diplomat, as well as socially, was in no little part due to his ability as a writer. "His letters charmed all, and made his correspondence eagerly sought. His political arguments were the joy of his party and the dread of his opponents. His scientific discoveries were explained in language at once so simple and so clear that plow-boy and exquisite could follow his thought or his experiment to its conclusion."[*]

As far as American literature is concerned, Franklin has no contemporaries. Before the *Autobiography* only one literary work of importance had been produced in this country—Cotton Mather's *Magnalia*, a church history of New England in a ponderous, stiff style. Franklin was the first American author to gain a wide and permanent reputation in Europe. The *Autobiography*, *Poor Richard*, *Father Abraham's Speech* or *The Way to Wealth*, as well as some of the *Bagatelles*, are as widely known abroad as any American writings. Franklin must also be classed as the first American humorist.

English literature of the eighteenth century was characterized by the development of prose. Periodical literature reached its perfection early in the century in *The Tatler* and *The Spectator* of Addison and Steele. Pamphleteers flourished throughout the period. The homelier prose of Bunyan and Defoe gradually gave place to the more elegant and artificial language of Samuel Johnson, who set the standard for prose writing from 1745 onward. This century saw the beginnings of the modern novel, in Fielding's *Tom Jones*, Richardson's *Clarissa Harlowe*,

---

[*] *The Many-Sided Franklin.* Paul L. Ford.

Sterne's *Tristram Shandy*, and Goldsmith's *Vicar of Wakefield*. Gibbon wrote *The Decline and Fall of the Roman Empire*, Hume his *History of England*, and Adam Smith the *Wealth of Nations*.

In the simplicity and vigor of his style Franklin more nearly resembles the earlier group of writers. In his first essays he was not an inferior imitator of Addison. In his numerous parables, moral allegories, and apologues he showed Bunyan's influence. But Franklin was essentially a journalist. In his swift, terse style, he is most like Defoe, who was the first great English journalist and master of the newspaper narrative. The style of both writers is marked by homely, vigorous expression, satire, burlesque, repartee. Here the comparison must end. Defoe and his contemporaries were authors. Their vocation was writing and their success rests on the imaginative or creative power they displayed. To authorship Franklin laid no claim. He wrote no work of the imagination. He developed only incidentally a style in many respects as remarkable as that of his English contemporaries. He wrote the best autobiography in existence, one of the most widely known collections of maxims, and an unsurpassed series of political and social satires, because he was a man of unusual scope of power and usefulness, who knew how to tell his fellow-men the secrets of that power and that usefulness.

## THE STORY OF THE AUTOBIOGRAPHY

The account of how Franklin's *Autobiography* came to be written and of the adventures of the original manuscript forms in itself an interesting story. The *Autobiography* is Franklin's longest work, and yet it is only a fragment. The first part, written as a letter to his son, William Franklin, was not intended for publication; and the composition is more informal and the narrative more personal than in the second part, from 1730 on, which was written with a view to publication. The entire manuscript shows little evidence of revision. In fact, the expression is so homely and natural that his grandson, William Temple Franklin, in editing the work changed some of the phrases because he thought them inelegant and vulgar.

Franklin began the story of his life while on a visit to his friend, Bishop Shipley, at Twyford, in Hampshire, southern England, in 1771. He took the manuscript, completed to 1731, with him when he returned to Philadelphia in 1775. It was left there with his other papers when he went to France in the following year, and disappeared during the confusion incident to the Revolution. Twenty-three pages of closely written manuscript fell into the hands of Abel James, an old friend, who sent a copy to Franklin at Passy, near Paris, urging him to complete the story. Franklin took up the work at Passy in 1784 and carried the narrative forward a few months. He changed the plan to meet his new purpose of writing to benefit the young reader. His work was soon interrupted and was not resumed until 1788, when he was at home in Philadelphia. He was now old, infirm, and suffering, and was still engaged in public service. Under these discouraging conditions the work progressed slowly. It finally stopped when the narrative reached the year 1757. Copies of the manuscript were sent to friends of Franklin in England and France, among others to Monsieur Le Veillard at Paris.

The first edition of the *Autobiography* was published in French at Paris in 1791. It was clumsily and carelessly translated, and was imperfect and unfinished. Where the translator got the manuscript is not known. Le Veillard disclaimed any knowledge of the publication. From this faulty French edition many others were printed, some in Germany, two in England, and another in France, so great was the demand for the work.

In the meantime the original manuscript of the *Autobiography* had started on a varied and adventurous career. It was left by Franklin with his other works to his grandson, William Temple Franklin, whom Franklin designated as his literary executor. When Temple Franklin came to publish his grandfather's works in 1817, he sent the original manuscript of the *Autobiography* to the daughter of Le Veillard in exchange for her father's copy, probably thinking the clearer transcript would make better printer's copy. The original manuscript thus found its way to the Le Veillard family and connections, where it remained until sold in 1867 to Mr. John Bigelow, United States Minister to France. By him it was later sold to Mr. E. Dwight Church of New York, and passed with the rest of Mr. Church's library into the possession of Mr. Henry E. Huntington. The original manuscript of Franklin's *Autobiography* now rests in the vault in Mr. Huntington's residence at Fifth Avenue and Fifty-seventh Street, New York City.

When Mr. Bigelow came to examine his purchase, he was astonished to find that what people had been reading for years as the authentic *Life* *of Benjamin Franklin by Himself*, was only a garbled and incomplete version of the real *Autobiography*. Temple Franklin had taken unwarranted liberties with the original. Mr. Bigelow says he found more than twelve hundred changes in the text. In 1868, therefore, Mr. Bigelow published the standard edition of Franklin's *Autobiography*. It corrected errors in the previous editions and was the first English edition to contain the short fourth part, comprising the last few pages of the manuscript, written during the last year of Franklin's life. Mr. Bigelow republished the *Autobiography*, with additional interesting matter, in three volumes in 1875, in 1905, and in 1910. The text in this volume is that of Mr. Bigelow's editions.[*]

The *Autobiography* has been reprinted in the United States many scores of times and translated into all the languages of Europe. It has never lost its popularity and is still in constant demand at circulating libraries. The reason for this popularity is not far to seek. For in this work Franklin told in a remarkable manner the story of a remarkable life. He displayed hard common sense and a practical knowledge of the art of living. He selected and arranged his material, perhaps unconsciously, with the unerring instinct of the journalist for the best effects. His success is not a little due to his plain, clear, vigorous English. He used short sentences and words, homely expressions, apt illustrations, and pointed allusions. Franklin had a most interesting, varied, and unusual life. He was one of the greatest conversationalists of his time.

His book is the record of that unusual life told in Franklin's own unexcelled conversational style. It is said that the best parts of Boswell's famous biography of Samuel Johnson are those parts where Boswell permits Johnson to tell his own story. In the *Autobiography* a no less remarkable man and talker than Samuel Johnson is telling his own story throughout.

F. W. P.

The Gilman Country School, Baltimore, September, 1916.

---

[*] For the division into chapters and the chapter titles, however, the present editor is responsible.

# I

## Ancestry and Early Youth in Boston

Twyford,* *at the Bishop of St. Asaph's,* 1771.

Dear son: I have ever had pleasure in obtaining any little anecdotes of my ancestors. You may remember the inquiries I made among the remains of my relations when you were with me in England, and the journey I undertook for that purpose. Imagining it may be equally agreeable to you to know the circumstances of my life, many of which you are yet unacquainted with, and expecting the enjoyment of a week's uninterrupted leisure in my present country retirement, I sit down to write them for you. To which I have besides some other inducements. Having emerged from the poverty and obscurity in which I was born and bred, to a state of affluence and some degree of reputation in the world, and having gone so far through life with a considerable share of felicity, the conducing means I made use of, which with the blessing of God so well succeeded, my posterity may like to know, as they may find some of them suitable to their own situations, and therefore fit to be imitated.

That felicity, when I reflected on it, has induced me sometimes to say, that were it offered to my choice, I should have no objection to a repetition of the same life from its beginning, only asking the advantages authors have in a second edition to correct some faults of the first. So I might, besides correcting the faults, change some sinister accidents and events of it for others more favourable. But though this were denied, I should still accept the offer. Since such a repetition is not to be expected, the next thing most like living one's life over again seems to be a recollection of that life, and to make that recollection as durable as possible by putting it down in writing.

---

* A small village not far from Winchester in Hampshire, southern England. Here was the country seat of the Bishop of St. Asaph, Dr. Jonathan Shipley, the "good Bishop," as Dr. Franklin used to style him. Their relations were intimate and confidential. In his pulpit, and in the House of Lords, as well as in society, the bishop always opposed the harsh measures of the Crown toward the Colonies.—Bigelow.

Hereby, too, I shall indulge the inclination so natural in old men, to be talking of themselves and their own past actions; and I shall indulge it without being tiresome to others, who, through respect to age, might conceive themselves obliged to give me a hearing, since this may be read or not as anyone pleases. And, lastly (I may as well confess it, since my denial of it will be believed by nobody), perhaps I shall a good deal gratify my own *vanity*.[*] Indeed, I scarce ever heard or saw the introductory words, "*Without vanity I may say*," etc., but some vain thing immediately followed. Most people dislike vanity in others, whatever share they have of it themselves; but I give it fair quarter wherever I meet with it, being persuaded that it is often productive of good to the possessor, and to others that are within his sphere of action; and therefore, in many cases, it would not be altogether absurd if a man were to thank God for his vanity among the other comforts of life.

And now I speak of thanking God, I desire with all humility to acknowledge that I owe the mentioned happiness of my past life to His kind providence, which led me to the means I used and gave them success. My belief of this induces me to *hope*, though I must not *presume*, that the same goodness will still be exercised toward me, in continuing that happiness, or enabling me to bear a fatal reverse, which I may experience as others have done; the complexion of my future fortune being known to Him only in whose power it is to bless to us even our afflictions.

The notes one of my uncles (who had the same kind of curiosity in collecting family anecdotes) once put into my hands, furnished me with several particulars relating to our ancestors. From these notes I learned that the family had lived in the same village, Ecton, in Northamptonshire,[†] for three hundred years, and how much longer he knew not (perhaps from the time when the name of Franklin, that before was the name of an order of people,[‡] was assumed by them as a surname when others took surnames all over the kingdom), on a freehold of about thirty acres, aided by the smith's business, which had continued in the family till his time, the eldest son being always

---

[*] In this connection Woodrow Wilson says, "And yet the surprising and delightful thing about this book (the *Autobiography*) is that, take it all in all, it has not the low tone of conceit, but is a staunch man's sober and unaffected assessment of himself and the circumstances of his career."

[†] See *Introduction*.

[‡] A small landowner.

bred to that business; a custom which he and my father followed as to their eldest sons. When I searched the registers at Ecton, I found an account of their births, marriages and burials from the year 1555 only, there being no registers kept in that parish at any time preceding. By that register I perceived that I was the youngest son of the youngest son for five generations back. My grandfather Thomas, who was born in 1598, lived at Ecton till he grew too old to follow business longer, when he went to live with his son John, a dyer at Banbury, in Oxfordshire, with whom my father served an apprenticeship. There my grandfather died and lies buried. We saw his gravestone in 1758. His eldest son Thomas lived in the house at Ecton, and left it with the land to his only child, a daughter, who, with her husband, one Fisher, of Wellingborough, sold it to Mr. Isted, now lord of the manor there. My grandfather had four sons that grew up, viz.: Thomas, John, Benjamin and Josiah. I will give you what account I can of them at this distance from my papers, and if these are not lost in my absence, you will among them find many more particulars.

Thomas was bred a smith under his father; but, being ingenious, and encouraged in learning (as all my brothers were) by an Esquire Palmer, then the principal gentleman in that parish, he qualified himself for the business of scrivener; became a considerable man in the county; was a chief mover of all public-spirited undertakings for the county or town of Northampton, and his own village, of which many instances were related of him; and much taken notice of and patronized by the then Lord Halifax. He died in 1702, January 6, old style,<sup>*</sup> just four years to a day before I was born. The account we received of his life and character from some old people at Ecton, I remember, struck you as something extraordinary, from its similarity to what you knew of mine. "Had he died on the same day," you said, "one might have supposed a transmigration."

John was bred a dyer, I believe of woollens, Benjamin was bred a silk dyer, serving an apprenticeship at London. He was an ingenious

---

* January 17, new style. This change in the calendar was made in 1582 by Pope Gregory XIII, and adopted in England in 1752. Every year whose number in the common reckoning since Christ is not divisible by 4, as well as every year whose number is divisible by 100 but not by 400, shall have 365 days, and all other years shall have 366 days. In the eighteenth century there was a difference of eleven days between the old and the new style of reckoning, which the English Parliament canceled by making the 3rd of September, 1752, the 14th. The Julian calendar, or "old style," is still retained in Russia and Greece, whose dates consequently are now 13 days behind those of other Christian countries.

man. I remember him well, for when I was a boy he came over to my father in Boston, and lived in the house with us some years. He lived to a great age. His grandson, Samuel Franklin, now lives in Boston. He left behind him two quarto volumes, MS., of his own poetry, consisting of little occasional pieces addressed to his friends and relations, of which the following, sent to me, is a specimen.* He had formed a short-hand of his own, which he taught me, but, never practising it, I have now forgot it. I was named after this uncle, there being a particular affection between him and my father. He was very pious, a great attender of sermons of the best preachers, which he took down in his short-hand, and had with him many volumes of them. He was also much of a politician; too much, perhaps, for his station. There fell lately into my hands, in London, a collection he had made of all the principal pamphlets relating to public affairs, from 1641 to 1717; many of the volumes are wanting as appears by the numbering, but there still remain eight volumes in folio, and twenty-four in quarto and in octavo. A dealer in old books met with them, and knowing me by my sometimes buying of him, he brought them to me. It seems my uncle must have left them here when he went to America, which was about fifty years since. There are many of his notes in the margins.

This obscure family of ours was early in the Reformation, and continued Protestants through the reign of Queen Mary, when they were sometimes in danger of trouble on account of their zeal against popery. They had got an English Bible, and to conceal and secure it, it was fastened open with tapes under and within the cover of a joint-stool. When my great-great-grandfather read it to his family, he turned up the joint-stool upon his knees, turning over the leaves then under the tapes. One of the children stood at the door to give notice if he saw the apparitor coming, who was an officer of the spiritual court. In that case the stool was turned down again upon its feet, when the Bible remained concealed under it as before. This anecdote I had from my uncle Benjamin. The family continued all of the Church of England till about the end of Charles the Second's reign, when some of the ministers that had been outed for non-conformity, holding conventicles† in Northamptonshire, Benjamin and Josiah adhered to them, and so continued all their lives: the rest of the family remained with the Episcopal Church.

---

* The specimen is not in the manuscript of the *Autobiography*.

† Secret gatherings of dissenters from the established Church.

*Birthplace of Franklin. Milk Street, Boston.*

Josiah, my father, married young, and carried his wife with three children into New England, about 1682. The conventicles having been forbidden by law, and frequently disturbed, induced some considerable men of his acquaintance to remove to that country, and he was prevailed with to accompany them thither, where they expected to enjoy their mode of religion with freedom. By the same wife he had four children more born there, and by a second wife ten more, in all seventeen; of which I remember thirteen sitting at one time at his table, who all grew up to be men and women, and married; I was the youngest son, and the youngest child but two, and was born in Boston, New England.[*] My mother, the second wife, was Abiah Folger, daughter of Peter Folger, one of the first settlers of New England, of whom honorable mention is made by Cotton Mather,[†] in his church history of that country, entitled *Magnalia Christi Americana*, as "*a godly, learned Englishman,*" if I remember the words rightly. I have heard that he wrote sundry small occasional pieces, but only one of them was printed, which I saw now many years since. It was written in 1675, in the home-spun verse of that time and people, and addressed

---

[*] Franklin was born on Sunday, January 6, old style, 1706, in a house on Milk Street, opposite the Old South Meeting House, where he was baptized on the day of his birth, during a snowstorm. The house where he was born was burned in 1810.—Griffin.

[†] Cotton Mather (1663-1728), clergyman, author, and scholar. Pastor of the North Church, Boston. He took an active part in the persecution of witchcraft.

to those then concerned in the government there. It was in favour of liberty of conscience, and in behalf of the Baptists, Quakers, and other sectaries that had been under persecution, ascribing the Indian wars, and other distresses that had befallen the country, to that persecution, as so many judgments of God to punish so heinous an offense, and exhorting a repeal of those uncharitable laws. The whole appeared to me as written with a good deal of decent plainness and manly freedom. The six concluding lines I remember, though I have forgotten the two first of the stanza; but the purport of them was, that his censures proceeded from good-will, and, therefore, he would be known to be the author.

> "Because to be a libeller (says he)
>   I hate it with my heart;
> From Sherburne town,* where now I dwell
>   My name I do put here;
> Without offense your real friend,
>   It is Peter Folgier."

My elder brothers were all put apprentices to different trades. I was put to the grammar-school at eight years of age, my father intending to devote me, as the tithe† of his sons, to the service of the Church. My early readiness in learning to read (which must have been very early, as I do not remember when I could not read), and the opinion of all his friends, that I should certainly make a good scholar, encouraged him in this purpose of his. My uncle Benjamin, too, approved of it, and proposed to give me all his short-hand volumes of sermons, I suppose as a stock to set up with, if I would learn his character.‡ I continued, however, at the grammar-school not quite one year, though in that time I had risen gradually from the middle of the class of that year to be the head of it, and farther was removed into the next class above it, in order to go with that into the third at the end of the year. But my father, in the meantime, from a view of the expense of a college education, which having so large a family he could not well afford, and the mean living many so educated were afterwards able to obtain— reasons that he gave to his friends in my hearing—altered his first

---

* Nantucket.
† Tenth.
‡ System of short-hand.

intention, took me from the grammar-school, and sent me to a school for writing and arithmetic, kept by a then famous man, Mr. George Brownell, very successful in his profession generally, and that by mild, encouraging methods. Under him I acquired fair writing pretty soon, but I failed in the arithmetic, and made no progress in it. At ten years old I was taken home to assist my father in his business, which was that of a tallow-chandler and sope-boiler; a business he was not bred to, but had assumed on his arrival in New England, and on finding his dyeing trade would not maintain his family, being in little request. Accordingly, I was employed in cutting wick for the candles, filling the dipping mould and the moulds for cast candles, attending the shop, going of errands, etc.

I disliked the trade, and had a strong inclination for the sea, but my father declared against it; however, living near the water, I was much in and about it, learnt early to swim well, and to manage boats; and when in a boat or canoe with other boys, I was commonly allowed to govern, especially in any case of difficulty; and upon other occasions I was generally a leader among the boys, and sometimes led them into scrapes, of which I will mention one instance, as it shows an early projecting public spirit, tho' not then justly conducted.

There was a salt-marsh that bounded part of the mill-pond, on the edge of which, at high water, we used to stand to fish for minnows. By much trampling, we had made it a mere quagmire. My proposal was to build a wharf there fit for us to stand upon, and I showed my comrades a large heap of stones, which were intended for a new house near the marsh, and which would very well suit our purpose. Accordingly, in the evening, when the workmen were gone, I assembled a number of my playfellows, and working with them diligently like so many emmets, sometimes two or three to a stone, we brought them all away and built our little wharf. The next morning the workmen were surprised at missing the stones, which were found in our wharf. Inquiry was made after the removers; we were discovered and complained of; several of us were corrected by our fathers; and, though I pleaded the usefulness of the work, mine convinced me that nothing was useful which was not honest.

I think you may like to know something of his person and character. He had an excellent constitution of body, was of middle stature, but well set, and very strong; he was ingenious, could draw prettily, was skilled a little in music, and had a clear, pleasing voice, so that when he played psalm tunes on his violin and sung withal, as he sometimes did in an evening after the business of the day was over, it was extremely agreeable to hear. He had a mechanical genius too, and, on occasion, was very handy in the use of other tradesmen's tools; but his great excellence lay in a sound understanding and solid judgment in prudential matters, both in private and publick affairs. In the latter, indeed, he was never employed, the numerous family he had to educate and the straitness of his circumstances keeping him close to his trade; but I remember well his being frequently visited by leading people, who consulted him for his opinion in affairs of the town or of the church he belonged to, and showed a good deal of respect for his judgment and advice: he was also much consulted by private persons about their affairs when any difficulty occurred, and frequently chosen an arbitrator between contending parties. At his table he liked to have, as often as he could, some sensible friend or neighbor to converse with, and always took care to start some ingenious or useful topic for discourse, which might tend to improve the minds of his children. By this means he turned our attention to what was good, just, and prudent in the conduct of life; and little or no notice was ever taken of what related to the victuals on the table, whether it was well or ill dressed, in or out of season, of good or bad flavor, preferable or inferior to this or that other thing of the kind, so that I was bro't up in such a perfect inattention to those matters as to be quite indifferent what kind of food was set before me, and so unobservant of it, that to this day if I am asked I can scarce tell a few hours after dinner what I dined upon. This has been a convenience to me in traveling, where my companions have been sometimes very unhappy for want of a suitable gratification of their more delicate, because better instructed, tastes and appetites.

My mother had likewise an excellent constitution: she suckled all her ten children. I never knew either my father or mother to have any sickness but that of which they dy'd, he at 89, and she at 85 years of age. They lie buried together at Boston, where I some years since placed a marble over their grave,* with this inscription:

---

* This marble having decayed, the citizens of Boston in 1827 erected in its place a granite obelisk, twenty-one feet high, bearing the original inscription quoted in the text and another explaining the erection of the monument.

Josiah Franklin,
and
Abiah his wife,
lie here interred.
They lived lovingly together in wedlock
fifty-five years.
Without an estate, or any gainful employment,
By constant labor and industry,
with God's blessing,
They maintained a large family
comfortably,
and brought up thirteen children
and seven grandchildren
reputably.
From this instance, reader,
Be encouraged to diligence in thy calling,
And distrust not Providence.
He was a pious and prudent man;
She, a discreet and virtuous woman.
Their youngest son,
In filial regard to their memory,
Places this stone.
J. F. born 1655, died 1744, Ætat 89.
A. F. born 1667, died 1752,—— —85.

By my rambling digressions I perceive myself to be grown old. I us'd to write more methodically. But one does not dress for private company as for a publick ball. 'Tis perhaps only negligence.

To return: I continued thus employed in my father's business for two years, that is, till I was twelve years old; and my brother John, who was bred to that business, having left my father, married, and set up for himself at Rhode Island, there was all appearance that I was destined to supply his place, and become a tallow-chandler. But my dislike to the trade continuing, my father was under apprehensions that if he did not find one for me more agreeable, I should break away and get to sea, as his son Josiah had done, to his great vexation. He therefore sometimes took me to walk with him, and see joiners, bricklayers, turners, braziers, etc., at their work, that he might observe my inclination, and endeavor to fix it on some trade or other on land. It has ever since been a pleasure to me to see good workmen handle their tools; and it has been useful to me, having learnt so much by it as to be able to do little jobs myself in my house when a workman could not readily be got, and to construct little machines for my experiments, while the intention of making the experiment was fresh and warm in my mind. My father at last fixed upon the cutler's trade, and my uncle Benjamin's son Samuel, who was bred to that business in London, being about that time established in Boston, I was sent to be with him some time on liking. But his expectations of a fee with me displeasing my father, I was taken home again.

## II

## *Beginning Life as a Printer*

From a child I was fond of reading, and all the little money that came into my hands was ever laid out in books. Pleased with the *Pilgrim's Progress*, my first collection was of John Bunyan's works in separate little volumes. I afterward sold them to enable me to buy R. Burton's *Historical Collections*; they were small chapmen's books,[*] and cheap, 40 or 50 in all. My father's little library consisted chiefly of books in polemic divinity, most of which I read, and have since often regretted that, at a time when I had such a thirst for knowledge, more proper books had not fallen in my way, since it was now resolved I should not be a clergyman. Plutarch's *Lives* there was in which I read abundantly, and I still think that time spent to great advantage. There was also a book of DeFoe's, called an *Essay on Projects*, and another of Dr. Mather's, called *Essays to do Good*, which perhaps gave me a turn of thinking that had an influence on some of the principal future events of my life.

This bookish inclination at length determined my father to make me a printer, though he had already one son (James) of that profession. In 1717 my brother James returned from England with a press and letters to set up his business in Boston. I liked it much better than that of my father, but still had a hankering for the sea. To prevent the apprehended effect of such an inclination, my father was impatient to have me bound to my brother. I stood out some time, but at last was persuaded, and signed the indentures when I was yet but twelve years old. I was to serve as an apprentice till I was twenty-one years of age, only I was to be allowed journeyman's wages during the last year. In a little time I made great proficiency in the business, and became a useful hand to my brother. I now had access to better books. An acquaintance with the apprentices of booksellers enabled me sometimes to borrow a small one, which I was careful to return soon and clean.

---

[*] Small books, sold by chapmen or peddlers.

Often I sat up in my room reading the greatest part of the night, when the book was borrowed in the evening and to be returned early in the morning, lest it should be missed or wanted.

And after some time an ingenious tradesman, Mr. Matthew Adams, who had a pretty collection of books, and who frequented our printing-house, took notice of me, invited me to his library, and very kindly lent me such books as I chose to read. I now took a fancy to poetry, and made some little pieces; my brother, thinking it might turn to account, encouraged me, and put me on composing occasional ballads. One was called *The Lighthouse Tragedy*, and contained an account of the drowning of Captain Worthilake, with his two daughters: the other was a sailor's song, on the taking of *Teach* (or Blackbeard) the pirate. They were wretched stuff, in the Grub-street-ballad style;[*] and when they were printed he sent me about the town to sell them. The first sold wonderfully, the event being recent, having made a great noise. This flattered my vanity; but my father discouraged me by ridiculing my performances, and telling me verse-makers were generally beggars. So I escaped being a poet, most probably a very bad one; but as prose writing has been of great use to me in the course of my life, and was a principal means of my advancement, I shall tell you how, in such a situation, I acquired what little ability I have in that way.

There was another bookish lad in the town, John Collins by name, with whom I was intimately acquainted. We sometimes disputed, and very fond we were of argument, and very desirous of confuting one another, which disputatious turn, by the way, is apt to become a very bad habit, making people often extremely disagreeable in company by the contradiction that is necessary to bring it into practice; and thence, besides souring and spoiling the conversation, is productive of disgusts and, perhaps enmities where you may have occasion for friendship. I had caught it by reading my father's books of dispute about religion. Persons of good sense, I have since observed, seldom fall into it, except lawyers, university men, and men of all sorts that have been bred at Edinborough.

A question was once, somehow or other, started between Collins and me, of the propriety of educating the female sex in learning, and their abilities for study. He was of opinion that it was improper, and that they

---

[*] Grub-street: famous in English literature as the home of poor writers.

were naturally unequal to it. I took the contrary side, perhaps a little for dispute's sake. He was naturally more eloquent, had a ready plenty of words, and sometimes, as I thought, bore me down more by his fluency than by the strength of his reasons. As we parted without settling the point, and were not to see one another again for some time, I sat down to put my arguments in writing, which I copied fair and sent to him. He answered, and I replied. Three or four letters of a side had passed, when my father happened to find my papers and read them. Without entering into the discussion, he took occasion to talk to me about the manner of my writing; observed that, though I had the advantage of my antagonist in correct spelling and pointing (which I ow'd to the printing-house), I fell far short in elegance of expression, in method and in perspicuity, of which he convinced me by several instances. I saw the justice of his remarks, and thence grew more attentive to the manner in writing, and determined to endeavor at improvement.

About this time I met with an odd volume of the *Spectator*.[*] It was the third. I had never before seen any of them. I bought it, read it over and over, and was much delighted with it. I thought the writing excellent, and wished, if possible, to imitate it. With this view I took some of the papers, and, making short hints of the sentiment in each sentence, laid them by a few days, and then, without looking at the book, try'd to compleat the papers again, by expressing each hinted sentiment at length, and as fully as it had been expressed before, in any suitable words that should come to hand. Then I compared my *Spectator* with the original, discovered some of my faults, and corrected them. But I found I wanted a stock of words, or a readiness in recollecting and using them, which I thought I should have acquired before that time if I had gone on making verses; since the continual occasion for words of the same import, but of different length, to suit the measure, or of different sound for the rhyme, would have laid me under a constant necessity of searching for variety, and also have tended to fix that variety in my mind, and make me master of it. Therefore I took some of the tales and turned them into verse; and, after a time, when I had pretty well forgotten the prose, turned them back again. I also sometimes jumbled my collections of hints into confusion, and after some weeks endeavored to reduce them into

---

[*] A daily London journal, comprising satirical essays on social subjects, published by Addison and Steele in 1711–1712. The *Spectator* and its predecessor, the *Tatler* (1709), marked the beginning of periodical literature.

the best order, before I began to form the full sentences and compleat the paper. This was to teach me method in the arrangement of thoughts. By comparing my work afterwards with the original, I discovered many faults and amended them; but I sometimes had the pleasure of fancying that, in certain particulars of small import, I had been lucky enough to improve the method of the language, and this encouraged me to think I might possibly in time come to be a tolerable English writer, of which I was extremely ambitious. My time for these exercises and for reading was at night, after work or before it began in the morning, or on Sundays, when I contrived to be in the printing-house alone, evading as much as I could the common attendance on public worship which my father used to exact of me when I was under his care, and which indeed I still thought a duty, thought I could not, as it seemed to me, afford time to practise it.

When about 16 years of age I happened to meet with a book, written by one Tryon, recommending a vegetable diet. I determined to go into it. My brother, being yet unmarried, did not keep house, but boarded himself and his apprentices in another family. My refusing to eat flesh occasioned an inconveniency, and I was frequently chid for my singularity. I made myself acquainted with Tryon's manner of preparing some of his dishes, such as boiling potatoes or rice, making hasty pudding, and a few others, and then proposed to my brother, that if he would give me, weekly, half the money he paid for my board, I would board myself. He instantly agreed to it, and I presently found that I could save half what he paid me. This was an additional fund for buying books. But I had another advantage in it. My brother and the rest going from the printing-house to their meals, I remained there alone, and, dispatching presently my light repast, which often was no more than a bisket or a slice of bread, a handful of raisins or a tart from the pastry-cook's, and a glass of water, had the rest of the time till their return for study, in which I made the greater progress, from that greater clearness of head and quicker apprehension which usually attend temperance in eating and drinking.

And now it was that, being on some occasion made asham'd of my ignorance in figures, which I had twice failed in learning when at school, I took Cocker's book of Arithmetick, and went through the whole by myself with great ease. I also read Seller's and Shermy's books of Navigation, and became acquainted with the little geometry they contain; but never proceeded far in that science. And I read about this time Locke *On Human Understanding*,* and the *Art of Thinking*, by Messrs. du Port Royal.†

While I was intent on improving my language, I met with an English grammar (I think it was Greenwood's), at the end of which there were two little sketches of the arts of rhetoric and logic, the latter finishing with a specimen of a dispute in the Socratic‡ method; and soon after I procur'd Xenophon's Memorable Things of Socrates, wherein there are many instances of the same method. I was charm'd with it, adopted it, dropt my abrupt contradiction and positive argumentation, and put on the humble inquirer and doubter. And being then, from reading Shaftesbury and Collins, become a real doubter in many points of our religious doctrine, I found this method safest for myself and very embarrassing to those against whom I used it; therefore I took a delight in it, practis'd it continually, and grew very artful and expert in drawing people, even of superior knowledge, into concessions, the consequences of which they did not foresee, entangling them in difficulties out of which they could not extricate themselves, and so obtaining victories that neither myself nor my cause always deserved. I continu'd this method some few years, but gradually left it, retaining only the habit of expressing myself in terms of modest diffidence; never using, when I advanced anything that may possibly be disputed, the words *certainly*, *undoubtedly*, or any others that give the air of positiveness to an opinion; but rather say, I conceive or apprehend a thing to be so and so; it appears to me, or *I should think it so or so*, for such and such reasons; or *I imagine it to be so*; or *it is so, if I am not mistaken*. This habit, I believe, has been of great advantage to me when I have had occasion to inculcate my opinions, and persuade men into measures that I have been from time to time engaged in promoting; and, as the chief ends of conversation are to *inform* or to be *informed*, to *please* or to *persuade*, I wish well-meaning, sensible men would not lessen their power of doing good by a positive, assuming manner, that seldom fails to disgust, tends to create opposition, and to defeat everyone of those purposes for which speech was given to us, to wit,

---

* John Locke (1632–1704), a celebrated English philosopher, founder of the so-called "common-sense" school of philosophers. He drew up a constitution for the colonists of Carolina.

† A noted society of scholarly and devout men occupying the abbey of Port Royal near Paris, who published learned works, among them the one here referred to, better known as the *Port Royal Logic*.

‡ Socrates confuted his opponents in argument by asking questions so skillfully devised that the answers would confirm the questioner's position or show the error of the opponent.

giving or receiving information or pleasure. For, if you would inform, a positive and dogmatical manner in advancing your sentiments may provoke contradiction and prevent a candid attention. If you wish information and improvement from the knowledge of others, and yet at the same time express yourself as firmly fix'd in your present opinions, modest, sensible men, who do not love disputation, will probably leave you undisturbed in the possession of your error. And by such a manner, you can seldom hope to recommend yourself in *pleasing* your hearers, or to persuade those whose concurrence you desire.

Pope[*] says, judiciously:

> "*Men should be taught as if you taught them not,*
> *And things unknown propos'd as things forgot;*"

farther recommending to us

> "To speak, tho' sure, with seeming diffidence."

And he might have coupled with this line that which he has coupled with another, I think, less properly,

> "For want of modesty is want of sense."

If you ask, Why less properly? I must repeat the lines,

> "Immodest words admit of no defense,
> For want of modesty is want of sense."

Now, is not *want of sense* (where a man is so unfortunate as to want it) some apology for his *want of modesty*? and would not the lines stand more justly thus?

> "Immodest words admit *but* this defense,
> That want of modesty is want of sense."

This, however, I should submit to better judgments.

My brother had, in 1720 or 1721, begun to print a newspaper. It was the second that appeared in America,[†] and was called the New

---

* Alexander Pope (1688–1744), the greatest English poet of the first half of the eighteenth century.

† Franklin's memory does not serve him correctly here. The *Courant* was really the fifth newspaper established in America, although generally called the fourth, because the first, *Public Occurrences*, published in Boston in 1690, was suppressed after the first issue. Following is the order in which the other four papers were published: *Boston News Letter*, 1704; *Boston Gazette*, December 21, 1719; *The American Weekly Mercury*, Philadelphia, December 22, 1719; *The New England Courant*, 1721.

England Courant. The only one before it was the Boston News-Letter. I remember his being dissuaded by some of his friends from the undertaking, as not likely to succeed, one newspaper being, in their judgment, enough for America. At this time (1771) there are not less than five-and-twenty. He went on, however, with the undertaking, and after having worked in composing the types and printing off the sheets, I was employed to carry the papers thro' the streets to the customers.

*First page of* The New England Courant *of Dec. 4–11, 1721.*

*From a copy in the Library of the Massachusetts Historical Society.*

He had some ingenious men among his friends, who amus'd themselves by writing little pieces for this paper, which gain'd it credit and made it more in demand, and these gentlemen often visited us. Hearing their conversations, and their accounts of the approbation their papers were received with, I was excited to try my hand among them; but, being still a boy, and suspecting that my brother would object to printing anything of mine in his paper if he knew it to be mine, I contrived to disguise my hand, and, writing an anonymous paper, I put it in at night under the door of the printing-house. It was found in the morning, and communicated to his writing friends when they call'd in as usual. They read it, commented on it in my hearing, and I had the exquisite pleasure of finding it met with their approbation, and that, in their different guesses at the author, none were named but men of some character among us for learning and ingenuity. I suppose now that I was rather lucky in my judges, and that perhaps they were not really so very good ones as I then esteem'd them.

Encourag'd, however, by this, I wrote and conveyed in the same way to the press several more papers which were equally approv'd; and I kept my secret till my small fund of sense for such performances was pretty well exhausted, and then I discovered* it, when I began to be considered a little more by my brother's acquaintance, and in a manner that did not quite please him, as he thought, probably with reason, that it tended to make me too vain. And, perhaps, this might be one occasion of the differences that we began to have about this time. Though a brother, he considered himself as my master, and me as his apprentice, and, accordingly, expected the same services from me as he would from another, while I thought he demean'd me too much in some he requir'd of me, who from a brother expected more indulgence. Our disputes were often brought before our father, and I fancy I was either generally in the right, or else a better pleader, because the judgment was generally in my favor. But my brother was passionate, and had often beaten me, which I took extreamly amiss; and, thinking my apprenticeship very tedious, I was continually wishing for some opportunity of shortening it, which at length offered in a manner unexpected.

One of the pieces in our newspaper on some political point, which I have now forgotten, gave offense to the Assembly. He was taken

---

* Disclosed.

up, censur'd, and imprison'd for a month, by the speaker's warrant, I suppose, because he would not discover his author. I too was taken up and examin'd before the council; but, tho' I did not give them any satisfaction, they contented themselves with admonishing me, and dismissed me, considering me, perhaps, as an apprentice, who was bound to keep his master's secrets.

During my brother's confinement, which I resented a good deal, notwithstanding our private differences, I had the management of the paper; and I made bold to give our rulers some rubs in it, which my brother took very kindly, while others began to consider me in an unfavorable light, as a young genius that had a turn for libeling and satyr. My brother's discharge was accompany'd with an order of the House (a very odd one), that *"James Franklin should no longer print the paper called the* New England Courant."

There was a consultation held in our printing-house among his friends, what he should do in this case. Some proposed to evade the order by changing the name of the paper; but my brother, seeing inconveniences in that, it was finally concluded on as a better way, to let it be printed for the future under the name of Benjamin Franklin; and to avoid the censure of the Assembly, that might fall on him as still printing it by his apprentice, the contrivance was that my old indenture should be return'd to me, with a full discharge on the back of it, to be shown on occasion, but to secure to him the benefit of my service, I was to sign new indentures for the remainder of the term, which were to be kept private. A very flimsy scheme it was; however, it was immediately executed, and the paper went on accordingly, under my name for several months.

At length, a fresh difference arising between my brother and me, I took upon me to assert my freedom, presuming that he would not venture to produce the new indentures. It was not fair in me to take this advantage, and this I therefore reckon one of the first errata of my life; but the unfairness of it weighed little with me, when under the impressions of resentment for the blows his passion too often urged him to bestow upon me, though he was otherwise not an ill-natur'd man: perhaps I was too saucy and provoking.

When he found I would leave him, he took care to prevent my getting employment in any other printing-house of the town, by going round and speaking to every master, who accordingly refus'd to give me work. I then thought of going to New York, as the nearest place where there was a printer; and I was rather inclin'd to leave Boston when I reflected that I had already made myself a little obnoxious to the governing party, and, from the arbitrary proceedings of the Assembly in my brother's case, it was likely I might, if I stay'd, soon bring myself into scrapes; and farther, that my indiscreet disputations about religion began to make me pointed at with horror by good people as an infidel or atheist. I determin'd on the point, but my father now siding with my brother, I was sensible that, if I attempted to go openly, means would be used to prevent me. My friend Collins, therefore, undertook to manage a little for me. He agreed with the captain of a New York sloop for my passage, under the notion of my being a young acquaintance of his. So I sold some of my books to raise a little money, was taken on board privately, and as we had a fair wind, in three days I found myself in New York, near 300 miles from home, a boy of but 17, without the least recommendation to, or knowledge of, any person in the place, and with very little money in my pocket.

# III
## Arrival in Philadelphia

M y inclinations for the sea were by this time worne out, or I might now have gratify'd them. But, having a trade, and supposing myself a pretty good workman, I offer'd my service to the printer in the place, old Mr. William Bradford, who had been the first printer in Pennsylvania, but removed from thence upon the quarrel of George Keith. He could give me no employment, having little to do, and help enough already; but says he, "My son at Philadelphia has lately lost his principal hand, Aquilla Rose, by death; if you go thither, I believe he may employ you." Philadelphia was a hundred miles further; I set out, however, in a boat for Amboy, leaving my chest and things to follow me round by sea.

In crossing the bay, we met with a squall that tore our rotten sails to pieces, prevented our getting into the Kill,* and drove us upon Long Island. In our way, a drunken Dutchman, who was a passenger too, fell overboard; when he was sinking, I reached through the water to his shock pate, and drew him up, so that we got him in again. His ducking sobered him a little, and he went to sleep, taking first out of his pocket a book, which he desir'd I would dry for him. It proved to be my old favorite author, Bunyan's Pilgrim's Progress, in Dutch, finely printed on good paper, with copper cuts, a dress better than I had ever seen it wear in its own language. I have since found that it has been translated into most of the languages of Europe, and suppose it has been more generally read than any other book, except perhaps the Bible. Honest John was the first that I know of who mix'd narration and dialogue; a method of writing very engaging to the reader, who in the most interesting parts finds himself, as it were, brought into the company and present at the discourse. De Foe in his Cruso, his Moll Flanders, Religious Courtship, Family Instructor, and other pieces, has imitated

---

* Kill van Kull, the channel separating Staten Island from New Jersey on the north.

it with success; and Richardson* has done the same in his Pamela, etc.

When we drew near the island, we found it was at a place where there could be no landing, there being a great surff on the stony beach. So we dropt anchor, and swung round towards the shore. Some people came down to the water edge and hallow'd to us, as we did to them; but the wind was so high, and the surff so loud, that we could not hear so as to understand each other. There were canoes on the shore, and we made signs, and hallow'd that they should fetch us; but they either did not understand us, or thought it impracticable, so they went away, and night coming on, we had no remedy but to wait till the wind should abate; and, in the meantime, the boatman and I concluded to sleep, if we could; and so crowded into the scuttle, with the Dutchman, who was still wet, and the spray beating over the head of our boat, leak'd thro' to us, so that we were soon almost as wet as he. In this manner we lay all night, with very little rest; but, the wind abating the next day, we made a shift to reach Amboy before night, having been thirty hours on the water, without victuals, or any drink but a bottle of filthy rum, and the water we sail'd on being salt.

In the evening I found myself very feverish, and went in to bed; but, having read somewhere that cold water drank plentifully was good for a fever, I follow'd the prescription, sweat plentifully most of the night, my fever left me, and in the morning, crossing the ferry, I proceeded on my journey on foot, having fifty miles to Burlington, where I was told I should find boats that would carry me the rest of the way to Philadelphia.

It rained very hard all the day; I was thoroughly soak'd, and by noon a good deal tired; so I stopt at a poor inn, where I staid all night, beginning now to wish that I had never left home. I cut so miserable a figure, too, that I found, by the questions ask'd me, I was suspected to be some runaway servant, and in danger of being taken up on that suspicion. However, I proceeded the next day, and got in the evening to an inn, within eight or ten miles of Burlington, kept by one Dr. Brown. He entered into conversation with me while I took some refreshment, and, finding I had read a little, became very sociable and friendly. Our acquaintance continu'd as long as he liv'd. He had been, I imagine, an itinerant doctor, for there was no town in England, or country in

---

* Samuel Richardson, the father of the English novel, wrote *Pamela, Clarissa Harlowe*, and the *History of Sir Charles Grandison*, novels published in the form of letters.

Europe, of which he could not give a very particular account. He had some letters, and was ingenious, but much of an unbeliever, and wickedly undertook, some years after, to travesty the Bible in doggrel verse, as Cotton had done Virgil. By this means he set many of the facts in a very ridiculous light, and might have hurt weak minds if his work had been published; but it never was.

At his house I lay that night, and the next morning reach'd Burlington, but had the mortification to find that the regular boats were gone a little before my coming, and no other expected to go before Tuesday, this being Saturday; wherefore I returned to an old woman in the town, of whom I had bought gingerbread to eat on the water, and ask'd her advice. She invited me to lodge at her house till a passage by water should offer; and being tired with my foot traveling, I accepted the invitation. She understanding I was a printer, would have had me stay at that town and follow my business, being ignorant of the stock necessary to begin with. She was very hospitable, gave me a dinner of ox-cheek with great good will, accepting only of a pot of ale in return; and I thought myself fixed till Tuesday should come. However, walking in the evening by the side of the river, a boat came by, which I found was going towards Philadelphia, with several people in her. They took me in, and, as there was no wind, we row'd all the way; and about midnight, not having yet seen the city, some of the company were confident we must have passed it, and would row no farther; the others knew not where we were; so we put toward the shore, got into a creek, landed near an old fence, with the rails of which we made a fire, the night being cold, in October, and there we remained till daylight. Then one of the company knew the place to be Cooper's Creek, a little above Philadelphia, which we saw as soon as we got out of the creek, and arriv'd there about eight or nine o'clock on the Sunday morning, and landed at the Market-street wharf.

I have been the more particular in this description of my journey, and shall be so of my first entry into that city, that you may in your mind compare such unlikely beginnings with the figure I have since made there. I was in my working dress, my best clothes being to come round by sea. I was dirty from my journey; my pockets were stuff'd out with shirts and stockings, and I knew no soul nor where to look for lodging. I was fatigued with traveling, rowing, and want of rest, I was very hungry; and my whole stock of cash consisted of a Dutch dollar, and about a shilling in copper. The latter I gave the people of the boat for my passage, who at first refus'd it, on account of my rowing; but I insisted on their taking it. A man being sometimes more generous when he has but a little money than when he has plenty, perhaps thro' fear of being thought to have but little.

Then I walked up the street, gazing about till near the market-house I met a boy with bread. I had made many a meal on bread, and, inquiring where he got it, I went immediately to the baker's he directed me to, in Second-street, and ask'd for bisket, intending such as we had in Boston; but they, it seems, were not made in Philadelphia. Then I asked for a three-penny loaf, and was told they had none such. So not considering or knowing the difference of money, and the greater cheapness nor the names of his bread, I bade him give me three-penny worth of any sort. He gave me, accordingly, three great puffy rolls. I was surpris'd at the quantity, but took it, and, having no room in my pockets, walk'd off with a roll under each arm, and eating the other. Thus I went up Market-street as far as Fourth-street, passing by the door of Mr. Read, my future wife's father; when she, standing at the door, saw me, and thought I made, as I certainly did, a most awkward, ridiculous appearance. Then I turned and went down Chestnut-street and part of Walnut-street, eating my roll all the way, and, coming round, found myself again at Market-street wharf, near the boat I came in, to which I went for a draught of the river water; and, being filled with one of my rolls, gave the other two to a woman and her child that came down the river in the boat with us, and were waiting to go farther.

Thus refreshed, I walked again up the street, which by this time had many clean-dressed people in it, who were all walking the same way. I joined them, and thereby was led into the great meeting-house of the Quakers near the market. I sat down among them, and, after looking round awhile and hearing nothing said, being very drowsy thro' labour and want of rest the preceding night, I fell fast asleep, and continu'd so till the meeting broke up, when one was kind enough to rouse me. This was, therefore, the first house I was in, or slept in, in Philadelphia.

Walking down again toward the river, and, looking in the faces of people, I met a young Quaker man, whose countenance I lik'd, and, accosting him, requested he would tell me where a stranger could get lodging. We were then near the sign of the Three Mariners. "Here," says he, "is one place that entertains strangers, but it is not a reputable house; if thee wilt walk with me, I'll show thee a better." He brought me to the Crooked Billet in Water-street. Here I got a dinner; and, while I was eating it, several sly questions were asked me, as it seemed to be suspected from my youth and appearance, that I might be some runaway.

After dinner, my sleepiness return'd, and being shown to a bed, I lay down without undressing, and slept till six in the evening, was call'd to supper, went to bed again very early, and slept soundly till next morning. Then I made myself as tidy as I could, and went to Andrew Bradford the printer's. I found in the shop the old man his father, whom

I had seen at New York, and who, traveling on horseback, had got to Philadelphia before me. He introduc'd me to his son, who receiv'd me civilly, gave me a breakfast, but told me he did not at present want a hand, being lately suppli'd with one; but there was another printer in town, lately set up, one Keimer, who, perhaps, might employ me; if not, I should be welcome to lodge at his house, and he would give me a little work to do now and then till fuller business should offer.

The old gentleman said he would go with me to the new printer; and when we found him, "Neighbour," says Bradford, "I have brought to see you a young man of your business; perhaps you may want such a one." He ask'd me a few questions, put a composing stick in my hand to see how I work'd, and then said he would employ me soon, though he had just then nothing for me to do; and, taking old Bradford, whom he had never seen before, to be one of the town's people that had a good will for him, enter'd into a conversation on his present undertaking and prospects; while Bradford, not discovering that he was the other printer's father, on Keimer's saying he expected soon to get the greatest part of the business into his own hands, drew him on by artful questions, and starting little doubts, to explain all his views, what interest he reli'd on, and in what manner he intended to proceed. I, who stood by and heard all, saw immediately that one of them was a crafty old sophister, and the other a mere novice. Bradford left me with Keimer, who was greatly surpris'd when I told him who the old man was.

Keimer's printing-house, I found, consisted of an old shatter'd press, and one small, worn-out font of English, which he was then using himself, composing an Elegy on Aquilla Rose, before mentioned, an ingenious young man, of excellent character, much respected in the town, clerk of the Assembly, and a pretty poet. Keimer made verses too, but very indifferently. He could not be said to write them, for his manner was to compose them in the types directly out of his head. So there being no copy,[*] but one pair of cases, and the Elegy likely to require all the letter, no one could help him. I endeavour'd to put his press (which he had not yet us'd, and of which he understood nothing) into order fit to be work'd with; and, promising to come and print off his Elegy as soon as he should have got it ready, I return'd to Bradford's, who gave me a little job to do for the present, and there I lodged and dieted. A

---

[*] Manuscript.

few days after, Keimer sent for me to print off the Elegy. And now he had got another pair of cases,* and a pamphlet to reprint, on which he set me to work.

These two printers I found poorly qualified for their business. Bradford had not been bred to it, and was very illiterate; and Keimer, tho' something of a scholar, was a mere compositor, knowing nothing of presswork. He had been one of the French prophets,† and could act their enthusiastic agitations. At this time he did not profess any particular religion, but something of all on occasion; was very ignorant of the world, and had, as I afterward found, a good deal of the knave in his composition. He did not like my lodging at Bradford's while I work'd with him. He had a house, indeed, but without furniture, so he could not lodge me; but he got me a lodging at Mr. Read's before mentioned, who was the owner of his house; and, my chest and clothes being come by this time, I made rather a more respectable appearance in the eyes of Miss Read than I had done when she first happen'd to see me eating my roll in the street.

I began now to have some acquaintance among the young people of the town, that were lovers of reading, with whom I spent my evenings very pleasantly; and gaining money by my industry and frugality, I lived very agreeably, forgetting Boston as much as I could, and not desiring that any there should know where I resided, except my friend Collins, who was in my secret, and kept it when I wrote to him. At length, an incident happened that sent me back again much sooner than I had intended. I had a brother-in-law, Robert Holmes, master of a sloop that traded between Boston and Delaware. He being at Newcastle, forty miles below Philadelphia, heard there of me, and wrote me a letter mentioning the concern of my friends in Boston at my abrupt departure, assuring me of their good will to me, and that everything would be accommodated to my mind if I would return, to which he exhorted me very earnestly. I wrote an answer to his letter, thank'd him for his advice, but stated my reasons for quitting Boston fully and in such a light as to convince him I was not so wrong as he had apprehended.

---

* The frames for holding type are in two sections, the upper for capitals and the lower for small letters.

† Protestants of the South of France, who became fanatical under the persecutions of Louis XIV, and thought they had the gift of prophecy. They had as mottoes "No Taxes" and "Liberty of Conscience."

# IV

## First Visit to Boston

Sir William Keith, governor of the province, was then at Newcastle, and Captain Holmes, happening to be in company with him when my letter came to hand, spoke to him of me, and show'd him the letter. The governor read it, and seem'd surpris'd when he was told my age. He said I appear'd a young man of promising parts, and therefore should be encouraged; the printers at Philadelphia were wretched ones; and, if I would set up there, he made no doubt I should succeed; for his part, he would procure me the public business, and do me every other service in his power. This my brother-in-law afterwards told me in Boston, but I knew as yet nothing of it; when, one day, Keimer and I being at work together near the window, we saw the governor and another gentleman (which proved to be Colonel French, of Newcastle), finely dress'd, come directly across the street to our house, and heard them at the door.

Keimer ran down immediately, thinking it a visit to him; but the governor inquir'd for me, came up, and with a condescension and politeness I had been quite unus'd to, made me many compliments, desired to be acquainted with me, blam'd me kindly for not having made myself known to him when I first came to the place, and would have me away with him to the tavern, where he was going with Colonel French to taste, as he said, some excellent Madeira. I was not a little surprised, and Keimer star'd like a pig poison'd.* I went, however, with the governor and Colonel French to a tavern, at the corner of Third-street, and over the Madeira he propos'd my setting up my business, laid before me the probabilities of success, and both he and Colonel French assur'd me I should have their interest and influence in procuring the public business of both governments.† On my doubting whether my father would assist me in it, Sir William said he would give

---

* Temple Franklin considered this specific figure vulgar and changed it to "stared with astonishment."

† Pennsylvania and Delaware.

me a letter to him, in which he would state the advantages, and he did not doubt of prevailing with him. So it was concluded I should return to Boston in the first vessel, with the governor's letter recommending me to my father. In the meantime the intention was to be kept a secret, and I went on working with Keimer as usual, the governor sending for me now and then to dine with him, a very great honour I thought it, and conversing with me in the most affable, familiar, and friendly manner imaginable.

About the end of April, 1724, a little vessel offer'd for Boston. I took leave of Keimer as going to see my friends. The governor gave me an ample letter, saying many flattering things of me to my father, and strongly recommending the project of my setting up at Philadelphia as a thing that must make my fortune. We struck on a shoal in going down the bay, and sprung a leak; we had a blustering time at sea, and were oblig'd to pump almost continually, at which I took my turn. We arriv'd safe, however, at Boston in about a fortnight. I had been absent seven months, and my friends had heard nothing of me; for my br. Holmes was not yet return'd, and had not written about me. My unexpected appearance surpris'd the family; all were, however, very glad to see me, and made me welcome, except my brother. I went to see him at his printing-house. I was better dress'd than ever while in his service, having a genteel new suit from head to foot, a watch, and my pockets

lin'd with near five pounds sterling in silver. He receiv'd me not very frankly, look'd me all over, and turn'd to his work again.

The journeymen were inquisitive where I had been, what sort of a country it was, and how I lik'd it. I prais'd it much, and the happy life I led in it, expressing strongly my intention of returning to it; and, one of them asking what kind of money we had there, I produc'd a handful of silver, and spread it before them, which was a kind of raree-show* they had not been us'd to, paper being the money of Boston.† Then I took an opportunity of letting them see my watch; and, lastly (my brother still grum and sullen), I gave them a piece of eight‡ to drink, and took my leave. This visit of mine offended him extreamly; for, when my mother some time after spoke to him of a reconciliation, and of her wishes to see us on good terms together, and that we might live for the future as brothers, he said I had insulted him in such a manner before his people that he could never forget or forgive it. In this, however, he was mistaken.

My father received the governor's letter with some apparent surprise, but said little of it to me for some days, when Capt. Holmes returning he show'd it to him, asked him if he knew Keith, and what kind of man he was; adding his opinion that he must be of small discretion to think of setting a boy up in business who wanted yet three years of being at man's estate. Holmes said what he could in favour of the project, but my father was clear in the impropriety of it, and at last, gave a flat denial to it. Then he wrote a civil letter to Sir William, thanking him for the patronage he had so kindly offered me, but declining to assist me as yet in setting up, I being, in his opinion, too young to be trusted with the management of a business so important, and for which the preparation must be so expensive.

My friend and companion Collins, who was a clerk in the post-office, pleas'd with the account I gave him of my new country, determined to go thither also; and, while I waited for my father's determination, he set out before me by land to Rhode Island, leaving his books, which were a pretty collection of mathematicks and natural philosophy, to come with mine and me to New York, where he propos'd to wait for me.

---

* A peep-show in a box.

† There were no mints in the colonies, so the metal money was of foreign coinage and not nearly so common as paper money, which was printed in large quantities in America, even in small denominations

‡ Spanish dollar about equivalent to our dollar.

My father, tho' he did not approve Sir William's proposition, was yet pleas'd that I had been able to obtain so advantageous a character from a person of such note where I had resided, and that I had been so industrious and careful as to equip myself so handsomely in so short a time; therefore, seeing no prospect of an accommodation between my brother and me, he gave his consent to my returning again to Philadelphia, advis'd me to behave respectfully to the people there, endeavour to obtain the general esteem, and avoid lampooning and libeling, to which he thought I had too much inclination; telling me, that by steady industry and a prudent parsimony I might save enough by the time I was one-and-twenty to set me up; and that, if I came near the matter, he would help me out with the rest. This was all I could obtain, except some small gifts as tokens of his and my mother's love, when I embark'd again for New York, now with their approbation and their blessing.

The sloop putting in at Newport, Rhode Island, I visited my brother John, who had been married and settled there some years. He received me very affectionately, for he always lov'd me. A friend of his, one Vernon, having some money due to him in Pennsylvania, about thirty-five pounds currency, desired I would receive it for him, and keep it till I had his directions what to remit it in. Accordingly, he gave me an order. This afterwards occasion'd me a good deal of uneasiness.

At Newport we took in a number of passengers for New York, among which were two young women, companions, and a grave, sensible, matronlike Quaker woman, with her attendants. I had shown an obliging readiness to do her some little services, which impress'd her I suppose with a degree of good will toward me; therefore, when she saw a daily growing familiarity between me and the two young women, which they appear'd to encourage, she took me aside, and said, "Young man, I am concern'd for thee, as thou hast no friend with thee, and seems not to know much of the world, or of the snares youth is expos'd to; depend upon it, those are very bad women; I can see it in all their actions; and if thee art not upon thy guard, they will draw thee into some danger; they are strangers to thee, and I advise thee, in a friendly concern for thy welfare, to have no acquaintance with them." As I seem'd at first not to think so ill of them as she did, she mentioned some things she had observ'd and heard that had escap'd my notice, but now convinc'd me she was right. I thank'd her for her kind advice, and promis'd to follow it. When we arriv'd at New York, they told me where they liv'd, and invited me to come and see them; but I avoided it, and it was well I did; for the next day the captain miss'd a silver spoon and some other things, that had been taken out of his cabin, and, knowing that these were a couple of strumpets, he got a warrant to search their lodgings, found the stolen goods, and had the thieves punish'd. So, tho' we had escap'd a sunken rock, which we scrap'd upon in the passage, I thought this escape of rather more importance to me.

At New York I found my friend Collins, who had arriv'd there some time before me. We had been intimate from children, and had read the same books together; but he had the advantage of more time for reading and studying, and a wonderful genius for mathematical learning, in which he far outstript me. While I liv'd in Boston, most of my hours of leisure for conversation were spent with him, and he continu'd a sober as well as an industrious lad; was much respected for his learning by several of the clergy and other gentlemen, and seemed to promise making a good figure in life. But, during my absence, he had acquir'd a habit of sotting with brandy; and I found by his own account, and what I heard from others, that he had been drunk every day since his arrival at New York, and behav'd very oddly. He had gam'd, too, and lost his money, so that I was oblig'd to discharge his lodgings, and defray his expenses to and at Philadelphia, which prov'd extremely inconvenient to me.

The then governor of New York, Burnet (son of Bishop Burnet), hearing from the captain that a young man, one of his passengers, had a great many books, desir'd he would bring me to see him. I waited upon him accordingly, and should have taken Collins with me but that he was not sober. The gov'r. treated me with great civility, show'd me his library, which was a very large one, and we had a good deal of conversation about books and authors. This was the second governor who had done me the honour to take notice of me; which, to a poor boy like me, was very pleasing.

We proceeded to Philadelphia. I received on the way Vernon's money, without which we could hardly have finish'd our journey. Collins wished to be employ'd in some counting-house; but, whether they discover'd his dramming by his breath, or by his behaviour, tho' he had some recommendations, he met with no success in any application, and continu'd lodging and boarding at the same house with me, and at my expense. Knowing I had that money of Vernon's, he was continually borrowing of me, still promising repayment as soon as he should be in business. At length he had got so much of it that I was distress'd to think what I should do in case of being call'd on to remit it.

His drinking continu'd, about which we sometimes quarrel'd; for, when a little intoxicated, he was very fractious. Once, in a boat on the Delaware with some other young men, he refused to row in his turn. "I will be row'd home," says he. "We will not row you," says I. "You must, or stay all night on the water," says he, "just as you please." The others said, "Let us row; what signifies it?" But, my mind being soured with his other conduct, I continu'd to refuse. So he swore he would make me row, or throw me overboard; and coming along, stepping on the thwarts, toward me, when he came up and struck at me, I clapped my hand under his crutch, and, rising, pitched him head-foremost into the river. I knew he was a good swimmer, and so was under little concern about him; but before he could get round to lay hold of the boat, we had with a few strokes pull'd her out of his reach; and ever when he drew near the boat, we ask'd if he would row, striking a few strokes to slide her away from him. He was ready to die with vexation, and obstinately would not promise to row. However, seeing him at last beginning to tire, we lifted him in and brought him home dripping wet in the evening. We hardly exchang'd a civil word afterwards, and a West India captain, who had a commission to procure a tutor for the sons of a gentleman at Barbados, happening to meet with him, agreed to carry him thither. He left me then, promising to remit me the first money he should receive in order to discharge the debt; but I never heard of him after.

The breaking into this money of Vernon's was one of the first great errata of my life; and this affair show'd that my father was not much out in his judgment when he suppos'd me too young to manage business of importance. But Sir William, on reading his letter, said he was too prudent. There was great difference in persons; and discretion did not always accompany years, nor was youth always without it. "And since he will not set you up," says he, "I will do it myself. Give me an inventory of the things necessary to be had from England, and I will send for them. You shall repay me when you are able; I am resolv'd to have a good printer here, and I am sure you must succeed." This was spoken with such an appearance of cordiality, that I had not the least doubt of his meaning what he said. I had hitherto kept the proposition of my setting up, a secret in Philadelphia, and I still kept it. Had it been known that I depended on the governor, probably some friend, that knew him better, would have advis'd me not to rely on him, as I afterwards heard it as his known character to be liberal of promises which he never meant to keep. Yet, unsolicited as he was by me, how could I think his generous offers insincere? I believ'd him one of the best men in the world.

I presented him an inventory of a little print'-house, amounting by my computation to about one hundred pounds sterling. He lik'd it, but ask'd me if my being on the spot in England to chuse the types, and see that everything was good of the kind, might not be of some advantage. "Then," says he, "when there, you may make acquaintances, and establish correspondences in the bookselling and stationery way." I agreed that this might be advantageous. "Then," says he, "get yourself ready to go with Annis;" which was the annual ship, and the only one at that time usually passing between London and Philadelphia. But it would be some months before Annis sail'd, so I continued working with Keimer, fretting about the money Collins had got from me, and in daily apprehensions of being call'd upon by Vernon, which, however, did not happen for some years after.

I believe I have omitted mentioning that, in my first voyage from Boston, being becalm'd off Block Island, our people set about catching cod, and hauled up a great many. Hitherto I had stuck to my resolution of not eating animal food, and on this occasion I consider'd, with my master Tryon, the taking every fish as a kind of unprovoked murder, since none of them had, or ever could do us any injury that might justify the slaughter. All this seemed very reasonable. But I had formerly been a great lover of fish, and, when this came hot out of the frying-pan, it smelt admirably well. I balanc'd some time between principle and inclination, till I recollected that, when the fish were opened, I saw smaller fish taken out of their stomachs; then thought I, "If you eat one another, I don't see why we mayn't eat you." So I din'd upon cod very heartily, and continued to eat with other people, returning only now and then occasionally to a vegetable diet. So convenient a thing is it to be a *reasonable creature*, since it enables one to find or make a reason for everything one has a mind to do.

# V

## Early Friends in Philadelphia

Keimer and I liv'd on a pretty good familiar footing, and agreed tolerably well, for he suspected nothing of my setting up. He retained a great deal of his old enthusiasms and lov'd argumentation. We therefore had many disputations. I used to work him so with my Socratic method, and had trepann'd him so often by questions apparently so distant from any point we had in hand, and yet by degrees led to the point, and brought him into difficulties and contradictions, that at last he grew ridiculously cautious, and would hardly answer me the most common question, without asking first, "*What do you intend to infer from that?*" However, it gave him so high an opinion of my abilities in the confuting way, that he seriously proposed my being his colleague in a project he had of setting up a new sect. He was to preach the doctrines, and I was to confound all opponents. When he came to explain with me upon the doctrines, I found several conundrums which I objected to, unless I might have my way a little too, and introduce some of mine.

Keimer wore his beard at full length, because somewhere in the Mosaic law it is said, "*Thou shalt not mar the corners of thy beard.*" He likewise kept the Seventh day, Sabbath; and these two points were essentials with him. I dislik'd both; but agreed to admit them upon condition of his adopting the doctrine of using no animal food. "I doubt," said he, "my constitution will not bear that." I assur'd him it would, and that he would be the better for it. He was usually a great glutton, and I promised myself some diversion in half starving him. He agreed to try the practice, if I would keep him company. I did so, and we held it for three months. We had our victuals dress'd, and brought to us regularly by a woman in the neighborhood, who had from me a list of forty dishes, to be prepar'd for us at different times, in all which there was neither fish, flesh, nor fowl, and the whim suited me the better at this time from the cheapness of it, not costing us above eighteenpence sterling each per week. I have since kept several Lents most strictly, leaving the common diet for that, and that for the common, abruptly, without the least inconvenience, so that I think there is little in the advice of making those changes by easy gradations. I went on pleasantly, but poor Keimer suffered grievously, tired of the project, long'd for the flesh-pots of Egypt, and order'd a roast pig. He invited me and two women friends to dine with him; but, it being brought too soon upon table, he could not resist the temptation, and ate the whole before we came.

I had made some courtship during this time to Miss Read. I had a great respect and affection for her, and had some reason to believe she had the same for me; but, as I was about to take a long voyage, and we were both very young, only a little above eighteen, it was thought most prudent by her mother to prevent our going too far at present, as a marriage, if it was to take place, would be more convenient after my return, when I should be, as I expected, set up in my business. Perhaps, too, she thought my expectations not so well founded as I imagined them to be.

My chief acquaintances at this time were Charles Osborne, Joseph Watson, and James Ralph, all lovers of reading. The two first were clerks to an eminent scrivener or conveyancer in the town, Charles Brockden; the other was clerk to a merchant. Watson was a pious, sensible young man, of great integrity; the others rather more lax in their principles of religion, particularly Ralph, who, as well as Collins, had been unsettled by me, for which they both made me suffer. Osborne was sensible, candid, frank; sincere and affectionate to his friends; but, in literary matters, too fond of criticizing. Ralph was ingenious, genteel in his manners, and extremely eloquent; I think I never knew a prettier talker. Both of them were great admirers of poetry, and began to try their hands in little pieces. Many pleasant walks we four had together on Sundays into the woods, near Schuylkill, where we read to one another, and conferr'd on what we read.

Ralph was inclin'd to pursue the study of poetry, not doubting but he might become eminent in it, and make his fortune by it, alleging that the best poets must, when they first began to write, make as many faults as he did. Osborne dissuaded him, assur'd him he had no genius for poetry, and advis'd him to think of nothing beyond the business he was bred to; that, in the mercantile way, tho' he had no stock, he might, by his diligence and punctuality, recommend himself to employment as

a factor, and in time acquire wherewith to trade on his own account. I approv'd the amusing one's self with poetry now and then, so far as to improve one's language, but no farther.

On this it was propos'd that we should each of us, at our next meeting, produce a piece of our own composing, in order to improve by our mutual observations, criticisms, and corrections. As language and expression were what we had in view, we excluded all considerations of invention by agreeing that the task should be a version of the eighteenth Psalm, which describes the descent of a Deity. When the time of our meeting drew nigh, Ralph called on me first, and let me know his piece was ready. I told him I had been busy, and, having little inclination, had done nothing. He then show'd me his piece for my opinion, and I much approv'd it, as it appear'd to me to have great merit. "Now," says he, "Osborne never will allow the least merit in anything of mine, but makes 1000 criticisms out of mere envy. He is not so jealous of you; I wish, therefore, you would take this piece, and produce it as yours; I will pretend not to have had time, and so produce nothing. We shall then see what he will say to it." It was agreed, and I immediately transcrib'd it, that it might appear in my own hand.

We met; Watson's performance was read; there were some beauties in it, but many defects. Osborne's was read; it was much better; Ralph did it justice; remarked some faults, but applauded the beauties. He himself had nothing to produce. I was backward; seemed desirous of being excused; had not had sufficient time to correct, etc.; but no excuse could be admitted; produce I must. It was read and repeated; Watson and Osborne gave up the contest, and join'd in applauding it. Ralph only made some criticisms, and propos'd some amendments; but I defended my text. Osborne was against Ralph, and told him he was no better a critic than poet, so he dropt the argument. As they two went home together, Osborne expressed himself still more strongly in favor of what he thought my production; having restrain'd himself before, as he said, lest I should think it flattery. "But who would have imagin'd," said he, "that Franklin had been capable of such a performance; such painting, such force, such fire! He has even improv'd the original. In his common conversation he seems to have no choice of words; he hesitates and blunders; and yet, good God! how he writes!" When we next met, Ralph discovered the trick we had plaid him, and Osborne was a little laughed at.

This transaction fixed Ralph in his resolution of becoming a poet. I did all I could to dissuade him from it, but he continued scribbling verses till *Pope* cured him.* He became, however, a pretty good prose writer. More of him hereafter. But, as I may not have occasion again to mention the other two, I shall just remark here, that Watson died in my arms a few years after, much lamented, being the best of our set. Osborne went to the West Indies, where he became an eminent lawyer and made money, but died young. He and I had made a serious agreement, that the one who happen'd first to die should, if possible, make a friendly visit to the other, and acquaint him how he found things in that separate state. But he never fulfill'd his promise.

---

* "In one of the later editions of the *Dunciad* occur the following lines:
'Silence, ye wolves! while Ralph to Cynthia howls,
And makes night hideous—answer him, ye owls.'
To this the poet adds the following note:
'James Ralph, a name inserted after the first editions,
not known till he writ a swearing-piece called *Sawney*,
very abusive of Dr. Swift, Mr. Gay, and myself.'"

# VI
## First Visit to London

The governor, seeming to like my company, had me frequently to his house, and his setting me up was always mention'd as a fixed thing. I was to take with me letters recommendatory to a number of his friends, besides the letter of credit to furnish me with the necessary money for purchasing the press and types, paper, etc. For these letters I was appointed to call at different times, when they were to be ready; but a future time was still named. Thus he went on till the ship, whose departure too had been several times postponed, was on the point of sailing. Then, when I call'd to take my leave and receive the letters, his secretary, Dr. Bard, came out to me and said the governor was extremely busy in writing, but would be down at Newcastle, before the ship, and there the letters would be delivered to me.

Ralph, though married, and having one child, had determined to accompany me in this voyage. It was thought he intended to establish a correspondence, and obtain goods to sell on commission; but I found afterwards, that, thro' some discontent with his wife's relations, he purposed to leave her on their hands, and never return again. Having taken leave of my friends, and interchang'd some promises with Miss Read, I left Philadelphia in the ship, which anchor'd at Newcastle. The governor was there; but when I went to his lodging, the secretary came to me from him with the civillest message in the world, that he could not then see me, being engaged in business of the utmost importance, but should send the letters to me on board, wished me heartily a good voyage and a speedy return, etc. I returned on board a little puzzled, but still not doubting.

Mr. Andrew Hamilton, a famous lawyer of Philadelphia, had taken passage in the same ship for himself and son, and with Mr. Denham, a Quaker merchant, and Messrs. Onion and Russel, masters of an iron work in Maryland, had engaged the great cabin; so that Ralph and I were forced to take up with a berth in the steerage, and none on board knowing us, were considered as ordinary persons. But Mr. Hamilton and his son (it was James, since governor) return'd from Newcastle to Philadelphia, the father being recall'd by a great fee to plead for a seized ship; and, just before we sail'd, Colonel French coming on board, and showing me great respect, I was more taken notice of, and, with my friend Ralph, invited by the other gentlemen to come into the cabin, there being now room. Accordingly, we remov'd thither.

Understanding that Colonel French had brought on board the governor's despatches, I ask'd the captain for those letters that were to be under my care. He said all were put into the bag together and he could not then come at them; but, before we landed in England, I should have an opportunity of picking them out; so I was satisfied for the present, and we proceeded on our voyage. We had a sociable company in the cabin, and lived uncommonly well, having the addition of all Mr. Hamilton's stores, who had laid in plentifully. In this passage Mr. Denham contracted a friendship for me that continued during his life. The voyage was otherwise not a pleasant one, as we had a great deal of bad weather.

When we came into the Channel, the captain kept his word with me, and gave me an opportunity of examining the bag for the governor's letters. I found none upon which my name was put as under my care. I picked out six or seven, that, by the handwriting, I thought might be the promised letters, especially as one of them was directed to Basket, the king's printer, and another to some stationer. We arriv'd in London the 24th of December, 1724. I waited upon the stationer, who came first in my way, delivering the letter as from Governor Keith. "I don't know such a person," says he; but, opening the letter, "O! this is from Riddlesden. I have lately found him to be a compleat rascal, and I will have nothing to do with him, nor receive any letters from him." So, putting the letter into my hand, he turn'd on his heel and left me to serve some customer. I was surprized to find these were not the governor's letters; and, after recollecting and comparing circumstances, I began to doubt his sincerity. I found my friend Denham, and opened the whole affair to him. He let me into Keith's character; told me there was not the least probability that he had written any letters for me; that no one, who knew him, had the smallest dependence on him; and he laught at the notion of the governor's giving me a letter of credit, having, as he said, no credit to give. On my expressing some concern about what I should do, he advised me to endeavour getting some employment in

the way of my business. "Among the printers here," said he, "you will improve yourself, and when you return to America, you will set up to greater advantage."

We both of us happen'd to know, as well as the stationer, that Riddlesden, the attorney, was a very knave. He had half ruin'd Miss Read's father by persuading him to be bound for him. By this letter it appear'd there was a secret scheme on foot to the prejudice of Hamilton (suppos'd to be then coming over with us); and that Keith was concerned in it with Riddlesden. Denham, who was a friend of Hamilton's, thought he ought to be acquainted with it; so, when he arriv'd in England, which was soon after, partly from resentment and ill-will to Keith and Riddlesden, and partly from good-will to him, I waited on him, and gave him the letter. He thank'd me cordially, the information being of importance to him; and from that time he became my friend, greatly to my advantage afterwards on many occasions.

But what shall we think of a governor's playing such pitiful tricks, and imposing so grossly on a poor ignorant boy! It was a habit he had acquired. He wish'd to please everybody; and, having little to give, he gave expectations. He was otherwise an ingenious, sensible man, a pretty good writer, and a good governor for the people, tho' not for his constituents, the proprietaries, whose instructions he sometimes disregarded. Several of our best laws were of his planning and passed during his administration.

Ralph and I were inseparable companions. We took lodgings together in Little Britain* at three shillings and sixpence a week—as much as we could then afford. He found some relations, but they were poor, and unable to assist him. He now let me know his intentions of remaining in London, and that he never meant to return to Philadelphia. He had brought no money with him, the whole he could muster having been expended in paying his passage. I had fifteen pistoles;† so he borrowed occasionally of me to subsist, while he was looking out for business. He first endeavoured to get into the play-house, believing himself qualify'd for an actor; but Wilkes,‡ to whom he apply'd, advis'd him candidly not to think of that employment, as it was impossible he should succeed in it. Then he propos'd to Roberts, a publisher in Paternoster Row,§ to write for him a weekly paper like the Spectator, on certain conditions, which Roberts did not approve. Then he endeavoured to get employment as a hackney writer, to copy for the stationers and lawyers about the Temple,¶ but could find no vacancy.

I immediately got into work at Palmer's, then a famous printing-house in Bartholomew Close, and here I continu'd near a year. I was pretty diligent, but spent with Ralph a good deal of my earnings in going to plays and other places of amusement. We had together consumed all my pistoles, and now just rubbed on from hand to mouth. He seem'd quite to forget his wife and child, and I, by degrees, my engagements with Miss Read, to whom I never wrote more than one letter, and that was to let her know I was not likely soon to return. This was another of the great errata of my life, which I should wish to correct if I were to live it over again. In fact, by our expenses, I was constantly kept unable to pay my passage.

At Palmer's I was employed in composing for the second edition of Wollaston's "Religion of Nature." Some of his reasonings not appearing to me well founded, I wrote a little metaphysical piece in which I made remarks on them. It was entitled "A Dissertation on Liberty and Necessity, Pleasure and Pain." I inscribed it to my

---

* One of the oldest parts of London, north of St. Paul's Cathedral, called "Little Britain" because the Dukes of Brittany used to live there. See the essay entitled "Little Britain" in Washington Irving's *Sketch Book*.
† A gold coin worth about four dollars in our money.
‡ A popular comedian, manager of Drury Lane Theater.
§ Street north of St. Paul's, occupied by publishing houses.
¶ Law schools and lawyers' residences situated southwest of St. Paul's, between Fleet Street and the Thames.

friend Ralph; I printed a small number. It occasion'd my being more consider'd by Mr. Palmer as a young man of some ingenuity, tho' he seriously expostulated with me upon the principles of my pamphlet, which to him appear'd abominable. My printing this pamphlet was another erratum.

While I lodg'd in Little Britain, I made an acquaintance with one Wilcox, a bookseller, whose shop was at the next door. He had an immense collection of second-hand books. Circulating libraries were not then in use; but we agreed that, on certain reasonable terms, which I have now forgotten, I might take, read, and return any of his books. This I esteem'd a great advantage, and I made as much use of it as I could.

My pamphlet by some means falling into the hands of one Lyons, a surgeon, author of a book entitled *The Infallibility of Human Judgment*, it occasioned an acquaintance between us. He took great notice of me, called on me often to converse on those subjects, carried me to the Horns, a pale alehouse in Lane, Cheapside, and introduced me to Dr. Mandeville, author of the *Fable of the Bees*, who had a club there, of which he was the soul, being a most facetious, entertaining companion. Lyons, too, introduced me to Dr. Pemberton, at Batson's Coffee-house, who promis'd to give me an opportunity, sometime or other, of seeing Sir Isaac Newton, of which I was extreamly desirous; but this never happened.

I had brought over a few curiosities, among which the principal was a purse made of the asbestos, which purifies by fire. Sir Hans Sloane heard of it, came to see me, and invited me to his house in Bloomsbury Square, where he show'd me all his curiosities, and persuaded me to let him add that to the number, for which he paid me handsomely.

In our house there lodg'd a young woman, a milliner, who, I think, had a shop in the Cloisters. She had been genteelly bred, was sensible and lively, and of most pleasing conversation. Ralph read plays to her in the evenings, they grew intimate, she took another lodging, and he followed her. They liv'd together some time; but, he being still out of business, and her income not sufficient to maintain them with her child, he took a resolution of going from London, to try for a country school, which he thought himself well qualified to undertake, as he wrote an excellent hand, and was a master of arithmetic and accounts. This, however, he deemed a business below him, and confident of future better fortune, when he should be unwilling to have it known that he once was so meanly employed, he changed his name, and did me the honour to assume mine; for I soon after had a letter from him, acquainting me that he was settled in a small village (in Berkshire, I think it was, where he taught reading and writing to ten or a dozen boys, at sixpence each per week), recommending Mrs. T— to my care, and desiring me to write to him, directing for Mr. Franklin, schoolmaster, at such a place.

He continued to write frequently, sending me large specimens of an epic poem which he was then composing, and desiring my remarks and corrections. These I gave him from time to time, but endeavour'd rather to discourage his proceeding. One of Young's Satires* was then just published. I copy'd and sent him a great part of it, which set in a strong light the folly of pursuing the Muses with any hope of advancement by them. All was in vain; sheets of the poem continued to come by every post. In the meantime, Mrs. T—, having on his account lost her friends and business, was often in distresses, and us'd to send for me and borrow what I could spare to help her out of them. I grew fond of her company, and, being at that time under no religious restraint, and presuming upon my importance to her, I attempted familiarities (another erratum) which she repuls'd with a proper resentment, and acquainted him with my behaviour. This made a breach between us; and, when he returned again to London, he let me know he thought I had cancell'd all the obligations he had been under to me. So I found I was never to expect his repaying me what I lent to him or advanc'd for him. This, however, was not then of much consequence, as he was totally unable; and in the loss of his friendship I found myself relieved from a burthen. I now began to think of getting a little money beforehand, and, expecting better work, I left Palmer's to work at Watts's, near Lincoln's Inn Fields, a still greater printing-house.† Here I continued all the rest of my stay in London.

At my first admission into this printing-house I took to working at press, imagining I felt a want of the bodily exercise I had been us'd to in America, where presswork is mix'd with composing. I drank only water; the other workmen, near fifty in number, were great guzzlers of beer. On occasion, I carried up and down stairs a large form of types in each hand, when others carried but one in both hands. They wondered to see, from

---

* Edward Young (1681–1765), an English poet. See his satires, Vol. III, Epist. ii, page 70.
† The printing press at which Franklin worked is preserved in the Patent Office at Washington.

this and several instances, that the *Water-American*, as they called me, was *stronger* than themselves, who drank *strong* beer! We had an alehouse boy who attended always in the house to supply the workmen. My companion at the press drank every day a pint before breakfast, a pint at breakfast with his bread and cheese, a pint between breakfast and dinner, a pint at dinner, a pint in the afternoon about six o'clock, and another when he had done his day's work. I thought it a detestable custom; but it was necessary, he suppos'd, to drink *strong* beer, that he might be *strong* to labour. I endeavoured to convince him that the bodily strength afforded by beer could only be in proportion to the grain or flour of the barley dissolved in the water of which it was made; that there was more flour in a pennyworth of bread; and therefore, if he would eat that with a pint of water, it would give him more strength than a quart of beer. He drank on, however, and had four or five shillings to pay out of his wages every Saturday

night for that muddling liquor; an expense I was free from. And thus these poor devils keep themselves always under.

Watts, after some weeks, desiring to have me in the composing-room,[*] I left the pressmen; a new bien venu or sum for drink, being five shillings, was demanded of me by the compositors. I thought it an imposition, as I had paid below; the master thought so too, and forbade my paying it. I stood out two or three weeks, was accordingly considered as an excommunicate, and had so many little pieces of

---

[*] Franklin now left the work of operating the printing presses, which was largely a matter of manual labor, and began setting type, which required more skill and intelligence.

private mischief done me, by mixing my sorts, transposing my pages, breaking my matter, etc., etc., if I were ever so little out of the room, and all ascribed to the chappel ghost, which they said ever haunted those not regularly admitted, that, notwithstanding the master's protection, I found myself oblig'd to comply and pay the money, convinc'd of the folly of being on ill terms with those one is to live with continually.

I was now on a fair footing with them, and soon acquir'd considerable influence. I propos'd some reasonable alterations in their chappel laws,* and carried them against all opposition. From my example, a great part of them left their muddling breakfast of beer, and bread, and cheese, finding they could with me be supply'd from a neighbouring house with a large porringer of hot water-gruel, sprinkled with pepper, crumb'd with bread, and a bit of butter in it, for the price of a pint of beer, viz., three half-pence. This was a more comfortable as well as cheaper breakfast, and keep their heads clearer. Those who continued sotting with beer all day, were often, by not paying, out of credit at the alehouse, and us'd to make interest with me to get beer; their *light*, as they phrased it, *being out*. I watch'd the pay-table on Saturday night, and collected what I stood engag'd for them, having to pay sometimes near thirty shillings a week on their accounts. This, and my being esteem'd a pretty good *riggite*, that is, a jocular verbal satirist, supported my consequence in the society. My constant attendance (I never making a St. Monday)† recommended me to the master; and my uncommon quickness at composing occasioned my being put upon all work of dispatch, which was generally better paid. So I went on now very agreeably.

My lodging in Little Britain being too remote, I found another in Duke-street, opposite to the Romish Chapel. It was two pair of stairs backwards, at an Italian warehouse. A widow lady kept the house; she had a daughter, and a maid servant, and a journeyman who attended the warehouse, but lodg'd abroad. After sending to inquire my character at the house where I last lodg'd she agreed to take me in at the same rate, 3s. 6d. per week; cheaper, as she said, from the protection she expected in having a man lodge in the house. She was a widow, an elderly woman; had been bred a Protestant, being a clergyman's daughter, but

---

* A printing house is called a chapel because Caxton, the first English printer, did his printing in a chapel connected with Westminster Abbey.

† A holiday taken to prolong the dissipation of Saturday's wages.

was converted to the Catholic religion by her husband, whose memory she much revered; had lived much among people of distinction, and knew a thousand anecdotes of them as far back as the times of Charles the Second. She was lame in her knees with the gout, and, therefore, seldom stirred out of her room, so sometimes wanted company; and hers was so highly amusing to me, that I was sure to spend an evening with her whenever she desired it. Our supper was only half an anchovy each, on a very little strip of bread and butter, and half a pint of ale between us; but the entertainment was in her conversation. My always keeping good hours, and giving little trouble in the family, made her unwilling to part with me, so that, when I talk'd of a lodging I had heard of, nearer my business, for two shillings a week, which, intent as I now was on saving money, made some difference, she bid me not think of it, for she would abate me two shillings a week for the future; so I remained with her at one shilling and sixpence as long as I staid in London.

In a garret of her house there lived a maiden lady of seventy, in the most retired manner, of whom my landlady gave me this account: that she was a Roman Catholic, had been sent abroad when young, and lodg'd in a nunnery with an intent of becoming a nun; but, the country not agreeing with her, she returned to England, where, there being no nunnery, she had vow'd to lead the life of a nun, as near as might be done in those circumstances. Accordingly, she had given all her estate to charitable uses, reserving only twelve pounds a year to live on, and out of this sum she still gave a great deal in charity, living herself on water-gruel only, and using no fire but to boil it. She had lived many years in that garret, being permitted to remain there gratis by successive Catholic tenants of the house below, as they deemed it a blessing to have her there. A priest visited her to confess her every day. "I have ask'd her," says my landlady, "how she, as she liv'd, could possibly find so much employment for a confessor?" "Oh," said she, "it is impossible to avoid *vain thoughts*." I was permitted once to visit her. She was cheerful and polite, and convers'd pleasantly. The room was clean, but had no other furniture than a matras, a table with a crucifix and book, a stool which she gave me to sit on, and a picture over the chimney of Saint Veronica displaying her handkerchief, with the miraculous figure of Christ's bleeding face on it,[*] which she explained to me with great seriousness. She look'd pale, but was never sick; and I give it as another instance on how small an income, life and health may be supported.

At Watts's printing-house I contracted an acquaintance with an ingenious young man, one Wygate, who, having wealthy relations, had been better educated than most printers; was a tolerable Latinist, spoke French, and lov'd reading. I taught him and a friend of his to swim at twice going into the river, and they soon became good swimmers. They introduc'd me to some gentlemen from the country, who went to Chelsea by water to see the College and Don Saltero's curiosities.[†] In our return, at the request of the company, whose curiosity Wygate had excited, I stripped and leaped into the river, and swam from near Chelsea to Blackfriar's,[‡] performing on the way many feats of activity, both upon and under water, that surpris'd and pleas'd those to whom they were novelties.

I had from a child been ever delighted with this exercise, had studied and practis'd all Thevenot's motions and positions, added some of my own, aiming at the graceful and easy as well as the useful. All these I took this occasion of exhibiting to the company, and was much flatter'd by their admiration; and Wygate, who was desirous of becoming a master, grew more and more attach'd to me on that account, as well as from the similarity of our studies. He at length proposed to me traveling all over Europe together, supporting ourselves everywhere by working at our business. I was once inclined to it; but, mentioning it to my good friend Mr. Denham, with whom I often spent an hour when I had leisure, he dissuaded me from it, advising me to think only of returning to Pennsylvania, which he was now about to do.

I must record one trait of this good man's character. He had formerly been in business at Bristol, but failed in debt to a number of people, compounded and went to America. There, by a close application to business as a merchant, he acquired a plentiful fortune in a few years.

---

[*] The story is that she met Christ on His way to crucifixion and offered Him her handkerchief to wipe the blood from His face, after which the handkerchief always bore the image of Christ's bleeding face.

[†] James Salter, a former servant of Hans Sloane, lived in Cheyne Walk, Chelsea. "His house, a barber-shop, was known as 'Don Saltero's Coffee-House.' The curiosities were in glass cases and constituted an amazing and motley collection—a petrified crab from China, a 'lignified hog,' Job's tears, Madagascar lances, William the Conqueror's flaming sword, and Henry the Eighth's coat of mail."—Smyth.

[‡] About three miles.

Returning to England in the ship with me, he invited his old creditors to an entertainment, at which he thank'd them for the easy composition they had favoured him with, and, when they expected nothing but the treat, every man at the first remove found under his plate an order on a banker for the full amount of the unpaid remainder with interest.

He now told me he was about to return to Philadelphia, and should carry over a great quantity of goods in order to open a store there. He propos'd to take me over as his clerk, to keep his books, in which he would instruct me, copy his letters, and attend the store. He added, that, as soon as I should be acquainted with mercantile business, he would promote me by sending me with a cargo of flour and bread, etc., to the West Indies, and procure me commissions from others which would be profitable; and, if I manag'd well, would establish me handsomely. The thing pleas'd me; for I was grown tired of London, remembered with pleasure the happy months I had spent in Pennsylvania, and wish'd again to see it; therefore I immediately agreed on the terms of fifty pounds a year,[*] Pennsylvania money; less, indeed, than my present gettings as a compositor, but affording a better prospect.

I now took leave of printing, as I thought, forever, and was daily employed in my new business, going about with Mr. Denham among the tradesmen to purchase various articles, and seeing them pack'd up, doing errands, calling upon workmen to dispatch, etc.; and, when all was on board, I had a few days' leisure. On one of these days, I was, to my surprise, sent for by a great man I knew only by name, a Sir William Wyndham, and I waited upon him. He had heard by some means or other of my swimming from Chelsea to Blackfriars, and of my teaching Wygate and another young man to swim in a few hours. He had two sons, about to set out on their travels; he wish'd to have them first taught swimming, and proposed to gratify me handsomely if I would teach them. They were not yet come to town, and my stay was uncertain, so I could not undertake it; but, from this incident, I thought it likely that, if I were to remain in England and open a swimming-school, I might get a good deal of money; and it struck me so strongly, that, had the overture been sooner made me, probably I should not so soon have returned to America. After many years, you and I had something of more importance to do with one of these sons of Sir

---

[*] About $167.

William Wyndham, become Earl of Egremont, which I shall mention in its place.

Thus I spent about eighteen months in London; most part of the time I work'd hard at my business, and spent but little upon myself except in seeing plays and in books. My friend Ralph had kept me poor; he owed me about twenty-seven pounds, which I was now never likely to receive; a great sum out of my small earnings! I lov'd him, notwithstanding, for he had many amiable qualities. I had by no means improv'd my fortune; but I had picked up some very ingenious acquaintance, whose conversation was of great advantage to me; and I had read considerably.

# VII

## Beginning Business in Philadelphia

We sail'd from Gravesend on the 23rd of July, 1726. For the incidents of the voyage, I refer you to my Journal, where you will find them all minutely related. Perhaps the most important part of that journal is the *plan** to be found in it, which I formed at sea, for regulating my future conduct in life. It is the more remarkable, as being formed when I was so young, and yet being pretty faithfully adhered to quite thro' to old age.

We landed in Philadelphia on the 11th of October, where I found sundry alterations. Keith was no longer governor, being superseded by Major Gordon. I met him walking the streets as a common citizen. He seem'd a little asham'd at seeing me, but pass'd without saying anything. I should have been as much asham'd at seeing Miss Read, had not her friends, despairing with reason of my return after the receipt of my letter, persuaded her to marry another, one Rogers, a potter, which was done in my absence. With him, however, she was never happy, and soon parted from him, refusing to cohabit with him or bear his name, it being now said that he had another wife. He was a worthless fellow, tho' an excellent workman, which was the temptation to her friends. He got into debt, ran away in 1727 or 1728, went to the West Indies, and died there. Keimer had got a better house, a shop well supply'd with stationery, plenty of new types, a number of hands, tho' none good, and seem'd to have a great deal of business.

Mr. Denham took a store in Water-street, where we open'd our goods; I attended the business diligently, studied accounts, and grew, in a little time, expert at selling. We lodg'd and boarded together; he counsell'd me as a father, having a sincere regard for me. I respected and loved him, and we might have gone on together very happy; but, in the beginning of February, 1726/7, when I had just pass'd my twenty-first year, we both were taken ill. My distemper was a pleurisy, which

---

* "Not found in the manuscript journal, which was left among Franklin's papers."—Bigelow.

very nearly carried me off. I suffered a good deal, gave up the point in my own mind, and was rather disappointed when I found myself recovering, regretting, in some degree, that I must now, some time or other, have all that disagreeable work to do over again. I forget what his distemper was; it held him a long time, and at length carried him off. He left me a small legacy in a nuncupative will, as a token of his kindness for me, and he left me once more to the wide world; for the store was taken into the care of his executors, and my employment under him ended.

My brother-in-law, Holmes, being now at Philadelphia, advised my return to my business; and Keimer tempted me, with an offer of large wages by the year, to come and take the management of his printing-house, that he might better attend his stationer's shop. I had heard a bad character of him in London from his wife and her friends, and was not fond of having any more to do with him. I tri'd for farther employment as a merchant's clerk; but, not readily meeting with any, I clos'd again with Keimer. I found in his house these hands: Hugh Meredith, a Welsh Pennsylvanian, thirty years of age, bred to country work; honest, sensible, had a great deal of solid observation, was something of a reader, but given to drink. Stephen Potts, a young countryman of full age, bred to the same, of uncommon natural parts, and great wit and humor, but a little idle. These he had agreed with at extream low wages per week to be rais'd a shilling every three months, as they would deserve by improving in their business; and the expectation of these high wages, to come on hereafter, was what he had drawn them in with. Meredith was to work at press, Potts at book-binding, which he, by agreement, was to teach them, though he knew neither one nor t'other. John—, a wild Irishman, brought up to no business, whose service, for four years, Keimer had purchased from the captain of a ship; he, too, was to be made a pressman. George Webb, an Oxford scholar, whose time for four years he had likewise bought, intending him for a compositor, of whom more presently; and David Harry, a country boy, whom he had taken apprentice.

I soon perceiv'd that the intention of engaging me at wages so much higher than he had been us'd to give, was, to have these raw, cheap hands form'd thro' me; and, as soon as I had instructed them, then they being all articled to him, he should be able to do without me. I went on, however, very chearfully, put his printing-house in order, which had been in great confusion, and brought his hands by degrees to mind their business and to do it better.

It was an odd thing to find an Oxford scholar in the situation of a bought servant. He was not more than eighteen years of age, and gave me this account of himself; that he was born in Gloucester, educated at a grammar-school there, had been distinguish'd among the scholars for some apparent superiority in performing his part, when they exhibited plays; belong'd to the Witty Club there, and had written some pieces in prose and verse, which were printed in the Gloucester newspapers; thence he was sent to Oxford; where he continued about a year, but not well satisfi'd, wishing of all things to see London, and become a player. At length, receiving his quarterly allowance of fifteen guineas, instead of discharging his debts he walk'd out of town, hid his gown in a furze bush, and footed it to London, where, having no friend to advise him, he fell into bad company, soon spent his guineas, found no means of being introduc'd among the players, grew necessitous, pawn'd his cloaths, and wanted bread. Walking the street very hungry, and not knowing what to do with himself, a crimp's bill* was put into

---

* A crimp was the agent of a shipping company. Crimps were sometimes employed to decoy men into such service as is here mentioned.

his hand, offering immediate entertainment and encouragement to such as would bind themselves to serve in America. He went directly, sign'd the indentures, was put into the ship, and came over, never writing a line to acquaint his friends what was become of him. He was lively, witty, good-natur'd, and a pleasant companion, but idle, thoughtless, and imprudent to the last degree.

John, the Irishman, soon ran away; with the rest I began to live very agreeably, for they all respected me the more, as they found Keimer incapable of instructing them, and that from me they learned something daily. We never worked on Saturday, that being Keimer's Sabbath, so I had two days for reading. My acquaintance with ingenious people in the town increased. Keimer himself treated me with great civility and apparent regard, and nothing now made me uneasy but my debt to Vernon, which I was yet unable to pay, being hitherto but a poor æconomist. He, however, kindly made no demand of it.

Our printing-house often wanted sorts, and there was no letter-founder in America; I had seen types cast at James's in London, but without much attention to the manner; however, I now contrived a mould, made use of the letters we had as puncheons, struck the mattrices in lead, and thus supply'd in a pretty tolerable way all deficiencies. I also engrav'd several things on occasion; I made the ink; I was warehouseman, and everything, and, in short, quite a factotum.

But, however serviceable I might be, I found that my services became every day of less importance, as the other hands improv'd in the business; and, when Keimer paid my second quarter's wages, he let me know that he felt them too heavy, and thought I should make an abatement. He grew by degrees less civil, put on more of the master, frequently found fault, was captious, and seem'd ready for an outbreaking. I went on, nevertheless, with a good deal of patience, thinking that his encumber'd circumstances were partly the cause. At length a trifle snapt our connections; for, a great noise happening near the court-house, I put my head out of the window to see what was the matter. Keimer, being in the street, look'd up and saw me, call'd out to me in a loud voice and angry tone to mind my business, adding some reproachful words, that nettled me the more for their publicity, all the neighbours who were looking out on the same occasion being witnesses how I was treated. He came up immediately into the printing-house, continu'd the quarrel, high words pass'd on both sides, he gave me the quarter's warning we had stipulated, expressing a wish that he had not been oblig'd to so long a warning. I told him his wish was unnecessary, for I would leave him that instant; and so, taking my hat, walk'd out of doors, desiring Meredith, whom I saw below, to take care of some things I left, and bring them to my lodgings.

Meredith came accordingly in the evening, when we talked my affair over. He had conceiv'd a great regard for me, and was very unwilling that I should leave the house while he remain'd in it. He dissuaded me from returning to my native country, which I began to think of; he reminded me that Keimer was in debt for all he possess'd; that his creditors began to be uneasy; that he kept his shop miserably, sold often without profit for ready money, and often trusted without keeping accounts; that he must therefore fail, which would make a vacancy I might profit of. I objected my want of money. He then let me know that his father had a high opinion of me, and, from some discourse that had pass'd between them, he was sure would advance money to set us up, if I would enter into partnership with him. "My time," says he, "will be out with Keimer in the spring; by that time we may have our press and types in from London. I am sensible I am no workman; if you like it, your skill in the business shall be set against the stock I furnish, and we will share the profits equally."

The proposal was agreeable, and I consented; his father was in town and approv'd of it; the more as he saw I had great influence with his son, had prevailed on him to abstain long from dram-drinking, and he hop'd might break him of that wretched habit entirely, when we came to be so closely connected. I gave an inventory to the father, who carry'd it to a merchant; the things were sent for, the secret was to be kept till they should arrive, and in the meantime I was to get work, if I could, at the other printing-house. But I found no vacancy there, and so remained idle a few days, when Keimer, on a prospect of being employ'd to print some paper money in New Jersey, which would require cuts and various types that I only could supply, and apprehending Bradford might engage me and get the jobb from him, sent me a very civil message, that old friends should not part for a few words, the effect of sudden passion, and wishing me to return. Meredith persuaded me to comply, as it would give more opportunity for his improvement under my daily instructions; so I return'd, and we went on more smoothly than for some time before. The New Jersey jobb was obtained, I contriv'd a copperplate press for it, the first that had been seen in the country; I cut several ornaments and checks for the bills. We went together to Burlington, where I executed the whole to satisfaction; and he received so large a sum for the work as to be enabled thereby to keep his head much longer above water.

At Burlington I made an acquaintance with many principal people of the province. Several of them had been appointed by the Assembly a committee to attend the press, and take care that no more bills were printed than the law directed. They were therefore, by turns, constantly with us, and generally he who attended, brought with him a friend or two for company. My mind having been much more improv'd by reading than Keimer's, I suppose it was for that reason my conversation seem'd to be more valu'd. They had me to their houses, introduced me to their friends, and show'd me much civility; while he, tho' the master, was a little neglected. In truth, he was an odd fish; ignorant of common life, fond of rudely opposing receiv'd opinions, slovenly to extream dirtiness, enthusiastic in some points of religion, and a little knavish withal.

We continu'd there near three months; and by that time I could reckon among my acquired friends, Judge Allen, Samuel Bustill, the secretary of the Province, Isaac Pearson, Joseph Cooper, and several of the Smiths, members of Assembly, and Isaac Decow, the surveyor-general. The latter was a shrewd, sagacious old man, who told me that he began for himself, when young, by wheeling clay for brick-makers, learned to write after he was of age, carri'd the chain for surveyors, who taught him surveying, and he had now by his industry, acquir'd a good estate; and says he, "I foresee that you will soon work this man out of his business, and make a fortune in it at Philadelphia." He had not then the least intimation of my intention to set up there or anywhere. These friends were afterwards of great use to me, as I occasionally was to some of them. They all continued their regard for me as long as they lived.

Before I enter upon my public appearance in business, it may be well to let you know the then state of my mind with regard to my principles and morals, that you may see how far those influenc'd the future events of my life. My parents had early given me religious impressions, and brought me through my childhood piously in the Dissenting way. But I was scarce fifteen, when, after doubting by turns of several points, as I found them disputed in the different books I read, I began to doubt of Revelation itself. Some books against Deism* fell into my hands; they were said to be the substance of sermons preached at Boyle's Lectures. It happened that they wrought an effect on me quite contrary to what was intended by them; for the arguments of the Deists, which were quoted to be refuted, appeared to me much stronger than the refutations; in short, I soon became a thorough Deist. My arguments perverted some others, particularly Collins and Ralph; but, each of them having afterwards wrong'd me greatly without the least compunction, and recollecting Keith's conduct towards me (who was another free-thinker), and my own towards Vernon and Miss Read, which at times gave me great trouble, I began to suspect that this doctrine, tho' it might be true, was not very useful. My London pamphlet, which had for its motto these lines of Dryden:†

> "Whatever is, is right. Though purblind man
> Sees but a part o' the chain, the nearest link:
> His eyes not carrying to the equal beam,
> That poises all above;"

and from the attributes of God, his infinite wisdom, goodness and power, concluded that nothing could possibly be wrong in the world, and that vice and virtue were empty distinctions, no such things existing, appear'd now not so clever a performance as I once thought it; and I doubted whether some error had not insinuated itself unperceiv'd into my argument, so as to infect all that follow'd, as is common in metaphysical reasonings.

I grew convinc'd that *truth*, *sincerity* and *integrity* in dealings between man and man were of the utmost importance to the felicity of life; and I form'd written resolutions, which still remain in my journal book, to practice them ever while I lived. Revelation had indeed no weight with me, as such; but I entertain'd an opinion that, though certain actions might not be bad *because* they were forbidden by it, or good *because* it commanded them, yet probably these actions might be forbidden *because* they were bad for us, or commanded *because* they were beneficial to us, in their own natures, all the circumstances of things considered. And

---

\* The creed of an eighteenth century theological sect which, while believing in God refused to credit the possibility of miracles and to acknowledge the validity of revelation.

† A great English poet, dramatist, and critic (1631–1700). The lines are inaccurately quoted from Dryden's Œdipus, Act III, Scene I, line 293.

this persuasion, with the kind hand of Providence, or some guardian angel, or accidental favourable circumstances and situations, or all together, preserved me, thro' this dangerous time of youth, and the hazardous situations I was sometimes in among strangers, remote from the eye and advice of my father, without any willful gross immorality or injustice, that might have been expected from my want of religion. I say willful, because the instances I have mentioned had something of *necessity* in them, from my youth, inexperience, and the knavery of others. I had therefore a tolerable character to begin the world with; I valued it properly, and determin'd to preserve it.

We had not been long return'd to Philadelphia before the new types arriv'd from London. We settled with Keimer, and left him by his consent before he heard of it. We found a house to hire near the market, and took it. To lessen the rent, which was then but twenty-four pounds a year, tho' I have since known it to let for seventy, we took in Thomas Godfrey, a glazier, and his family, who were to pay a considerable part of it to us, and we to board with them. We had scarce opened our letters and put our press in order, before George House, an acquaintance of mine, brought a countryman to us, whom he had met in the street inquiring for a printer. All our cash was now expended in the variety of particulars we had been obliged to procure, and this countryman's five shillings, being our first-fruits, and coming so seasonably, gave me more pleasure than any crown I have since earned; and the gratitude I felt toward House has made me often more ready than perhaps I should otherwise have been to assist young beginners.

There are croakers in every country, always boding its ruin. Such a one then lived in Philadelphia; a person of note, an elderly man, with a wise look and a very grave manner of speaking; his name was Samuel Mickle. This gentleman, a stranger to me, stopt one day at my door, and asked me if I was the young man who had lately opened a new printing-house. Being answered in the affirmative, he said he was sorry for me, because it was an expensive undertaking, and the expense would be lost; for Philadelphia was a sinking place, the people already half-bankrupts, or near being so; all appearances to the contrary, such as new buildings and the rise of rents, being to his certain knowledge fallacious; for they were, in fact, among the things that would soon ruin us. And he gave me such a detail of misfortunes now existing, or that were soon to exist, that he left me half melancholy. Had I known him before I engaged in this business, probably I never should have done it. This man continued to live in this decaying place, and to declaim in the same strain, refusing for many years to buy a house there, because all was going to destruction; and at last I had the pleasure of seeing him give five times as much for one as he might have bought it for when he first began his croaking.

I should have mentioned before, that, in the autumn of the preceding year, I had form'd most of my ingenious acquaintance into a club of mutual improvement, which was called the Junto;* we met on Friday evenings. The rules that I drew up required that every member, in his turn, should produce one or more queries on any point of Morals, Politics, or Natural Philosophy, to be discuss'd by the company; and once in three months produce and read an essay of his own writing, on any subject he pleased. Our debates were to be under the direction of a president, and to be conducted in the sincere spirit of inquiry after truth, without fondness for dispute, or desire of victory; and, to prevent warmth, all expressions of positiveness in opinions, or direct contradiction, were after some time made contraband, and prohibited under small pecuniary penalties.

The first members were Joseph Breintnal, a copyer of deeds for the scriveners, a good-natur'd, friendly middle-ag'd man, a great lover of poetry, reading all he could meet with, and writing some that was tolerable; very ingenious in many little Nicknackeries, and of sensible conversation.

Thomas Godfrey, a self-taught mathematician, great in his way, and afterward inventor of what is now called Hadley's Quadrant. But he knew little out of his way, and was not a pleasing companion; as, like most great mathematicians I have met with, he expected universal precision in everything said, or was forever denying or distinguishing upon trifles, to the disturbance of all conversation. He soon left us.

Nicholas Scull, a surveyor, afterwards surveyor-general, who lov'd books, and sometimes made a few verses.

William Parsons, bred a shoemaker, but, loving reading, had acquir'd a considerable share of mathematics, which he first studied with a view to astrology, that he afterwards laught at it. He also became surveyor-general.

---

* A Spanish term meaning a combination for political intrigue; here a club or society.

William Maugridge, a joiner, a most exquisite mechanic, and a solid, sensible man.

Hugh Meredith, Stephen Potts, and George Webb I have characteriz'd before.

Robert Grace, a young gentleman of some fortune, generous, lively, and witty; a lover of punning and of his friends.

And William Coleman, then a merchant's clerk, about my age, who had the coolest, clearest head, the best heart, and the exactest morals of almost any man I ever met with. He became afterwards a merchant of great note, and one of our provincial judges. Our friendship continued without interruption to his death, upwards of forty years; and the club continued almost as long, and was the best school of philosophy, morality, and politics that then existed in the province; for our queries, which were read the week preceding their discussion, put us upon reading with attention upon the several subjects, that we might speak more to the purpose; and here, too, we acquired better habits of conversation, everything being studied in our rules which might prevent our disgusting each other. From hence the long continuance of the club, which I shall have frequent occasion to speak further of hereafter.

But my giving this account of it here is to show something of the interest I had, everyone of these exerting themselves in recommending business to us. Breintnal particularly procur'd us from the Quakers the printing forty sheets of their history, the rest being to be done by Keimer; and upon this we work'd exceedingly hard, for the price was low. It was a folio, pro patria size, in pica, with long primer notes.* I compos'd of it a sheet a day, and Meredith worked it off at press; it was often eleven at night, and sometimes later, before I had finished my distribution for the next day's work, for the little jobbs sent in by our other friends now and then put us back. But so determin'd I was to continue doing a sheet a day of the folio, that one night, when, having impos'd† my forms, I thought my day's work over, one of them by accident was broken, and two pages reduced to pi,‡ I immediately distribut'd and composed it over again before I went to bed; and this

---

\* A sheet 8-1/2 by 13-1/2 inches, having the words *pro patria* in translucent letters in the body of the paper. Pica—a size of type; as, A B C D: Long Primer—a smaller size of type; as, A B C D.

† To arrange and lock up pages or columns of type in a rectangular iron frame, ready for printing.

‡ Reduced to complete disorder.

industry, visible to our neighbors, began to give us character and credit; particularly, I was told, that mention being made of the new printing-office at the merchants' Every-night club, the general opinion was that it must fail, there being already two printers in the place, Keimer and Bradford; but Dr. Baird (whom you and I saw many years after at his native place, St. Andrew's in Scotland) gave a contrary opinion: "For the industry of that Franklin," says he, "is superior to anything I ever saw of the kind; I see him still at work when I go home from club, and he is at work again before his neighbors are out of bed." This struck the rest, and we soon after had offers from one of them to supply us with stationery; but as yet we did not chuse to engage in shop business.

I mention this industry the more particularly and the more freely, tho' it seems to be talking in my own praise, that those of my posterity, who shall read it, may know the use of that virtue, when they see its effects in my favour throughout this relation.

George Webb, who had found a female friend that lent him wherewith to purchase his time of Keimer, now came to offer himself as a journeyman to us. We could not then employ him; but I foolishly let him know as a secret that I soon intended to begin a newspaper, and might then have work for him. My hopes of success, as I told him, were founded on this, that the then only newspaper, printed by Bradford, was a paltry thing, wretchedly manag'd, no way entertaining, and yet was profitable to him; I therefore thought a good paper would scarcely fail of good encouragement. I requested Webb not to mention it; but he told it to Keimer, who immediately, to be beforehand with me, published proposals for printing one himself, on which Webb was to be employ'd. I resented this; and, to counteract them, as I could not yet begin our paper, I wrote several pieces of entertainment for Bradford's paper, under the title of the Busy Body, which Breintnal continu'd some months. By this means the attention of the publick was fixed on that paper, and Keimer's proposals, which we burlesqu'd and ridicul'd, were disregarded. He began his paper, however, and, after carrying it on three quarters of a year, with at most only ninety subscribers, he offered it to me for a trifle; and I, having been ready some time to go on with it, took it in hand directly; and it prov'd in a few years extremely profitable to me.

I perceive that I am apt to speak in the singular number, though our partnership still continu'd; the reason may be that, in fact, the whole management of the business lay upon me. Meredith was no compositor, a poor pressman, and seldom sober. My friends lamented my connection with him, but I was to make the best of it.

Our first papers made a quite different appearance from any before in the province; a better type, and better printed; but some spirited remarks of my writing, on the dispute then going on between Governor Burnet and the Massachusetts Assembly, struck the principal people, occasioned the paper and the manager of it to be much talk'd of, and in a few weeks brought them all to be our subscribers.

Their example was follow'd by many, and our number went on growing continually. This was one of the first good effects of my having learnt a little to scribble; another was, that the leading men, seeing a newspaper now in the hands of one who could also handle a pen, thought it convenient to oblige and encourage me. Bradford still printed the votes, and laws, and other publick business. He had printed an address of the House to the governor, in a coarse, blundering manner; we reprinted it elegantly and correctly, and sent one to every member. They were sensible of the difference: it strengthened the hands of our friends in the House, and they voted us their printers for the year ensuing.

Among my friends in the House I must not forget Mr. Hamilton, before mentioned, who was then returned from England, and had a seat in it. He interested himself for me strongly in that instance, as he did in many others afterward, continuing his patronage till his death.*

---

* I got his son once £500.—*Marg. note.*

Mr. Vernon, about this time, put me in mind of the debt I ow'd him, but did not press me. I wrote him an ingenuous letter of acknowledgment, crav'd his forbearance a little longer, which he allow'd me, and as soon as I was able, I paid the principal with interest, and many thanks; so that erratum was in some degree corrected.

But now another difficulty came upon me which I had never the least reason to expect. Mr. Meredith's father, who was to have paid for our printing-house, according to the expectations given me, was able to advance only one hundred pounds currency, which had been paid; and a hundred more was due to the merchant, who grew impatient, and su'd us all. We gave bail, but saw that, if the money could not be rais'd in time, the suit must soon come to a judgment and execution, and our hopeful prospects must, with us, be ruined, as the press and letters must be sold for payment, perhaps at half price.

In this distress two true friends, whose kindness I have never forgotten, nor ever shall forget while I can remember any thing, came to me separately, unknown to each other, and, without any application from me, offering each of them to advance me all the money that should be necessary to enable me to take the whole business upon myself, if that should be practicable; but they did not like my continuing the partnership with Meredith, who, as they said, was often seen drunk in the streets, and playing at low games in alehouses, much to our discredit. These two friends were William Coleman and Robert Grace. I told them I could not propose a separation while any prospect remain'd of the Meredith's fulfilling their part of our agreement, because I thought myself under great obligations to them for what they had done, and would do if they could; but, if they finally fail'd in their performance, and our partnership must be dissolv'd, I should then think myself at liberty to accept the assistance of my friends.

Thus the matter rested for some time, when I said to my partner, "Perhaps your father is dissatisfied at the part you have undertaken in this affair of ours, and is unwilling to advance for you and me what he would for you alone. If that is the case, tell me, and I will resign the whole to you, and go about my business." "No," said he, "my father has really been disappointed, and is really unable; and I am unwilling to distress him farther. I see this is a business I am not fit for. I was bred a farmer, and it was a folly in me to come to town, and put myself, at thirty years of age, an apprentice to learn a new trade. Many of our

Welsh people are going to settle in North Carolina, where land is cheap. I am inclin'd to go with them, and follow my old employment. You may find friends to assist you. If you will take the debts of the company upon you; return to my father the hundred pounds he has advanced; pay my little personal debts, and give me thirty pounds and a new saddle, I will relinquish the partnership, and leave the whole in your hands." I agreed to this proposal: it was drawn up in writing, sign'd, and seal'd immediately. I gave him what he demanded, and he went soon after to Carolina, from whence he sent me next year two long letters, containing the best account that had been given of that country, the climate, the soil, husbandry, etc., for in those matters he was very judicious. I printed them in the papers, and they gave great satisfaction to the publick.

As soon as he was gone, I recurr'd to my two friends; and because I would not give an unkind preference to either, I took half of what each had offered and I wanted of one, and half of the other; paid off the company's debts, and went on with the business in my own name, advertising that the partnership was dissolved. I think this was in or about the year 1729.

# VIII

## Business Success and First Public Service

About this time there was a cry among the people for more paper money, only fifteen thousand pounds being extant in the province, and that soon to be sunk.* The wealthy inhabitants oppos'd any addition, being against all paper currency, from an apprehension that it would depreciate, as it had done in New England, to the prejudice of all creditors. We had discuss'd this point in our Junto, where I was on the side of an addition, being persuaded that the first small sum struck in 1723 had done much good by increasing the trade, employment, and number of inhabitants in the province, since I now saw all the old houses inhabited, and many new ones building: whereas I remembered well, that when I first walk'd about the streets of Philadelphia, eating my roll, I saw most of the houses in Walnut Street, between Second and Front streets,† with bills on their doors, "To be let"; and many likewise in Chestnut-street and other streets, which made me then think the inhabitants of the city were deserting it one after another.

Our debates possess'd me so fully of the subject, that I wrote and printed an anonymous pamphlet on it, entitled "The Nature and Necessity of a Paper Currency." It was well receiv'd by the common people in general; but the rich men dislik'd it, for it increas'd and strengthen'd the clamor for more money, and they happening to have no writers among them that were able to answer it, their opposition slacken'd, and the point was carried by a majority in the House. My friends there, who conceiv'd I had been of some service, thought fit to reward me by employing me in printing the money; a very profitable jobb and a great help to me. This was another advantage gain'd by my being able to write.

The utility of this currency became by time and experience so evident as never afterwards to be much disputed; so that it grew soon to fifty-five thousand pounds, and in 1739 to eighty thousand pounds,

---

* Recalled to be redeemed.

† This part of Philadelphia is now the center of the wholesale business district.

since which it arose during war to upwards of three hundred and fifty thousand pounds, trade, building, and inhabitants all the while increasing, tho' I now think there are limits beyond which the quantity may be hurtful.[*]

I soon after obtain'd, thro' my friend Hamilton, the printing of the Newcastle paper money, another profitable jobb as I then thought it; small things appearing great to those in small circumstances; and these, to me, were really great advantages, as they were great encouragements. He procured for me, also, the printing of the laws and votes of that government, which continu'd in my hands as long as I follow'd the business.

I now open'd a little stationer's shop. I had in it blanks of all sorts, the correctest that ever appear'd among us, being assisted in that by my friend Breintnal. I had also paper, parchment, chapmen's books, etc. One Whitemash, a compositor I had known in London, an excellent workman, now came to me, and work'd with me constantly and diligently; and I took an apprentice, the son of Aquilla Rose.

I began now gradually to pay off the debt I was under for the printing-house. In order to secure my credit and character as a tradesman, I took care not only to be in *reality* industrious and frugal, but to avoid all appearances to the contrary. I drest plainly; I was seen at no places of idle diversion. I never went out a fishing or shooting; a book, indeed, sometimes debauch'd me from my work, but that was seldom, snug, and gave no scandal; and, to show that I was not above my business, I sometimes brought home the paper I purchas'd at the stores thro' the streets on a wheelbarrow. Thus being esteem'd an industrious, thriving young man, and paying duly for what I bought, the merchants who imported stationery solicited my custom; others proposed supplying me with books, and I went on swimmingly. In the meantime, Keimer's credit and business declining daily, he was at last forc'd to sell his printing-house to satisfy his creditors. He went to Barbadoes, and there lived some years in very poor circumstances.

His apprentice, David Harry, whom I had instructed while I work'd with him, set up in his place at Philadelphia, having bought his materials.

---

[*] Paper money is a promise to pay its face value in gold or silver. When a state or nation issues more such promises than there is a likelihood of its being able to redeem, the paper representing the promises depreciates in value. Before the success of the Colonies in the Revolution was assured, it took hundreds of dollars of their paper money to buy a pair of boots.

I was at first apprehensive of a powerful rival in Harry, as his friends were very able, and had a good deal of interest. I therefore propos'd a partnership to him, which he, fortunately for me, rejected with scorn. He was very proud, dress'd like a gentleman, liv'd expensively, took much diversion and pleasure abroad, ran in debt, and neglected his business; upon which, all business left him; and, finding nothing to do, he followed Keimer to Barbadoes, taking the printing-house with him. There this apprentice employ'd his former master as a journeyman; they quarrell'd often; Harry went continually behindhand, and at length was forc'd to sell his types and return to his country work in Pennsylvania. The person that bought them employ'd Keimer to use them, but in a few years he died.

There remained now no competitor with me at Philadelphia but the old one, Bradford; who was rich and easy, did a little printing now and then by straggling hands, but was not very anxious about the business. However, as he kept the post-office, it was imagined he had better opportunities of obtaining news; his paper was thought a better distributer of advertisements than mine, and therefore had many more, which was a profitable thing to him, and a disadvantage to me; for, tho' I did indeed receive and send papers by the post, yet the publick opinion was otherwise, for what I did send was by bribing the riders, who took them privately, Bradford being unkind enough to forbid it, which occasion'd some resentment on my part; and I thought so meanly of him for it, that, when I afterward came into his situation, I took care never to imitate it.

I had hitherto continu'd to board with Godfrey, who lived in part of my house with his wife and children, and had one side of the shop for his glazier's business, tho' he worked little, being always absorbed in his mathematics. Mrs. Godfrey projected a match for me with a relation's daughter, took opportunities of bringing us often together, till a serious courtship on my part ensu'd, the girl being in herself very deserving. The old folks encourag'd me by continual invitations to supper, and by leaving us together, till at length it was time to explain. Mrs. Godfrey manag'd our little treaty. I let her know that I expected as much money with their daughter as would pay off my remaining debt for the printing-house, which I believe was not then above a hundred pounds. She brought me word they had no such sum to spare; I said they might mortgage their house in the loan-office. The answer to this, after some days, was, that they did not approve the match; that, on inquiry of Bradford, they had been informed the printing business was not a profitable one; the types would soon be worn out, and more wanted; that S. Keimer and D. Harry had failed one after the other, and I should probably soon follow them; and, therefore, I was forbidden the house, and the daughter shut up.

Whether this was a real change of sentiment or only artifice, on a supposition of our being too far engaged in affection to retract, and therefore that we should steal a marriage, which would leave them at liberty to give or withhold what they pleas'd, I know not; but I suspected the latter, resented it, and went no more. Mrs. Godfrey brought me afterward some more favorable accounts of their disposition, and would have drawn me on again; but I declared absolutely my resolution to have nothing more to do with that family. This was resented by the Godfreys; we differed, and they removed, leaving me the whole house, and I resolved to take no more inmates.

But this affair having turned my thoughts to marriage, I look'd round me and made overtures of acquaintance in other places; but soon found that, the business of a printer being generally thought a poor one, I was not to expect money with a wife, unless with such a one as I should not otherwise think agreeable. A friendly correspondence as neighbours and old acquaintances had continued between me and Mrs. Read's family, who all had a regard for me from the time of my first lodging in their house. I was often invited there and consulted in their affairs, wherein I sometimes was of service. I piti'd poor Miss Read's unfortunate situation, who was generally dejected, seldom chearful, and avoided company. I considered my giddiness and inconstancy when in London as in a great degree the cause of her unhappiness, tho' the mother was good enough to think the fault more her own than mine, as she had prevented our marrying before I went thither, and persuaded the other match in my absence. Our mutual affection was revived, but there were now great objections to our union. The match was indeed looked upon as invalid, a preceding wife being said to be living in England; but this could not easily be prov'd, because of the distance; and, tho' there was a report of his death, it was not certain. Then, tho' it should be true, he had left many debts, which his successor might be call'd upon to pay. We ventured, however, over all these difficulties, and I took her to wife, September 1st, 1730. None of the inconveniences happened that we had apprehended; she proved a good and faithful helpmate,[*] assisted me much by attending the shop; we throve together, and have ever mutually endeavour'd to make each other happy. Thus I corrected that great *erratum* as well as I could.

About this time, our club meeting, not at a tavern, but in a little room of Mr. Grace's, set apart for that purpose, a proposition was made by me, that, since our books were often referr'd to in our disquisitions upon the queries, it might be convenient to us to have them altogether where we met, that upon occasion they might be consulted; and by thus clubbing our books to a common library, we should, while we lik'd to keep them together, have each of us the advantage of using the books of all the other members, which would be nearly as beneficial as if each owned the whole. It was lik'd and agreed to, and we fill'd one end of the room with such books as we could best spare. The number was not so great as we expected; and tho' they had been of great use, yet some inconveniences occurring for want of due care of them, the collection, after about a year, was separated, and each took his books home again.

And now I set on foot my first project of a public nature, that for a subscription library. I drew up the proposals, got them put into form

---

[*] Mrs. Franklin survived her marriage over forty years. Franklin's correspondence abounds with evidence that their union was a happy one. "We are grown old together, and if she has any faults, I am so used to them that I don't perceive them." The following is a stanza from one of Franklin's own songs written for the Junto:

"Of their Chloes and Phyllises poets may prate,
I sing my plain country Joan,
These twelve years my wife, still the joy of my life,
Blest day that I made her my own."

by our great scrivener, Brockden, and, by the help of my friends in the Junto, procured fifty subscribers of forty shillings each to begin with, and ten shillings a year for fifty years, the term our company was to continue. We afterwards obtain'd a charter, the company being increased to one hundred: this was the mother of all the North American subscription libraries, now so numerous. It is become a great thing itself, and continually increasing. These libraries have improved the general conversation of the Americans, made the common tradesmen and farmers as intelligent as most gentlemen from other countries, and perhaps have contributed in some degree to the stand so generally made throughout the colonies in defense of their privileges.[*]

*Mem°.* Thus far was written with the intention express'd in the beginning and therefore contains several little family anecdotes of no importance to others. What follows was written many years after in compliance with the advice contain'd in these letters, and accordingly intended for the public. The affairs of the Revolution occasion'd the interruption.[†]

It is some time since I receiv'd the above letters, but I have been too busy till now to think of complying with the request they contain. It might, too, be much better done if I were at home among my papers, which would aid my memory, and help to ascertain dates; but my return being uncertain, and having just now a little leisure, I will endeavour to recollect and write what I can; if I live to get home, it may there be corrected and improv'd.

Not having any copy here of what is already written, I know not whether an account is given of the means I used to establish the Philadelphia public library, which, from a small beginning, is now become so considerable, though I remember to have come down to near the time of that transaction (1730). I will therefore begin here with an account of it, which may be struck out if found to have been already given.

At the time I establish'd myself in Pennsylvania, there was not a good bookseller's shop in any of the colonies to the southward of Boston. In New York and Philad'a the printers were indeed stationers;

---

[*] Here the first part of the *Autobiography*, written at Twyford in 1771, ends. The second part, which follows, was written at Passy in 1784.

[†] After this memorandum, Franklin inserted letters from Abel James and Benjamin Vaughan, urging him to continue his *Autobiography*. [*Continuation of the Account of my Life, begun at Passy, near Paris, 1784.*]

they sold only paper, etc., almanacs, ballads, and a few common school-books. Those who lov'd reading were obliged to send for their books from England; the members of the Junto had each a few. We had left the alehouse, where we first met, and hired a room to hold our club in. I propos'd that we should all of us bring our books to that room, where they would not only be ready to consult in our conferences, but become a common benefit, each of us being at liberty to borrow such as he wish'd to read at home. This was accordingly done, and for some time contented us.

Finding the advantage of this little collection, I propos'd to render the benefit from books more common, by commencing a public subscription library. I drew a sketch of the plan and rules that would be necessary, and got a skilful conveyancer, Mr. Charles Brockden, to put the whole in form of articles of agreement to be subscribed, by which each subscriber engag'd to pay a certain sum down for the first purchase of books, and an annual contribution for increasing them. So few were the readers at that time in Philadelphia, and the majority of us so poor, that I was not able, with great industry, to find more than fifty persons, mostly young tradesmen, willing to pay down for this purpose forty shillings each, and ten shillings per annum. On this little fund we began. The books were imported; the library was opened one day in the week for lending to the subscribers, on their promissory notes to pay double the value if not duly returned. The institution soon manifested its utility, was imitated by other towns, and in other provinces. The libraries were augmented by donations; reading became fashionable; and our people, having no publick amusements to divert their attention from study, became better acquainted with books, and in a few years were observ'd by strangers to be better instructed and more intelligent than people of the same rank generally are in other countries.

When we were about to sign the above mentioned articles, which were to be binding on us, our heirs, etc., for fifty years, Mr. Brockden, the scrivener, said to us, "You are young men, but it is scarcely probable that any of you will live to see the expiration of the term fix'd in the instrument." A number of us, however, are yet living; but the instrument was after a few years rendered null by a charter that incorporated and gave perpetuity to the company.

The objections and reluctances I met with in soliciting the subscriptions, made me soon feel the impropriety of presenting one's self as the proposer of any useful project, that might be suppos'd to raise one's reputation in the smallest degree above that of one's neighbours, when one has need of their assistance to accomplish that project. I therefore put myself as much as I could out of sight, and stated it as a scheme of a *number of friends*, who had requested me to go about and propose it to such as they thought lovers of reading. In this way my affair went on more smoothly, and I ever after practis'd it on such occasions; and, from my frequent successes, can heartily recommend it. The present little sacrifice of your vanity will afterwards be amply repaid. If it remains a while uncertain to whom the merit belongs, someone more vain than yourself will be encouraged to claim it, and then even envy will be disposed to do you justice by plucking those assumed feathers, and restoring them to their right owner.

This library afforded me the means of improvement by constant study, for which I set apart an hour or two each day, and thus repair'd in some degree the loss of the learned education my father once intended for me. Reading was the only amusement I allow'd myself. I spent no time in taverns, games, or frolicks of any kind; and my industry in my business continu'd as indefatigable as it was necessary. I was indebted for my printing-house; I had a young family coming on to be educated, and I had to contend with for business two printers, who were established in the place before me. My circumstances, however, grew daily easier. My original habits of frugality continuing, and my father having, among his instructions to me when a boy, frequently repeated a proverb of Solomon, "Seest thou a man diligent in his calling, he shall stand before kings, he shall not stand before mean men," I from thence considered industry as a means of obtaining wealth and distinction, which encourag'd me, tho' I did not think that I should ever literally *stand before kings*, which, however, has since happened; for I have stood before *five*, and even had the honor of sitting down with one, the King of Denmark, to dinner.

We have an English proverb that says, "*He that would thrive, must ask his wife.*" It was lucky for me that I had one as much dispos'd to industry and frugality as myself. She assisted me chearfully in my business, folding and stitching pamphlets, tending shop, purchasing old linen rags for the paper-makers, etc., etc. We kept no idle servants, our table was plain and simple, our furniture of the cheapest. For instance, my breakfast was a long time break and milk (no tea), and I ate it out of a twopenny earthen porringer, with a pewter spoon. But mark how luxury will enter families, and make a progress, in spite of principle: being call'd one morning to breakfast, I found it in a China bowl, with a spoon of silver! They had been bought for me without my knowledge by my wife, and had cost her the enormous sum of three-and-twenty shillings, for which she had no other excuse or apology to make, but that she thought *her* husband deserv'd a silver spoon and China bowl as well as any of his neighbors. This was the first appearance of plate and China in our house, which afterward, in a course of years, as our wealth increas'd, augmented gradually to several hundred pounds in value.

I had been religiously educated as a Presbyterian; and though some of the dogmas of that persuasion, such as the *eternal decrees of God*, *election, reprobation, etc.*, appeared to me unintelligible, others doubtful, and I early absented myself from the public assemblies of the sect, Sunday being my studying day, I never was without some religious principles. I never doubted, for instance, the existence of the Deity; that he made the world, and govern'd it by his Providence; that the most acceptable service of God was the doing good to man; that our souls are immortal; and that all crime will be punished, and virtue rewarded, either here or hereafter. These I esteem'd the essentials of every religion; and, being to be found in all the religions we had in our country, I respected them all, tho' with different degrees of respect, as I found them more or less mix'd with other articles, which, without any tendency to inspire, promote, or confirm morality, serv'd principally to divide us, and make us unfriendly to one another. This respect to all, with an opinion that the worst had some good effects, induc'd me to avoid all discourse that might tend to lessen the good opinion another might have of his own religion; and as our province increas'd in people, and new places of worship were continually wanted, and generally erected by voluntary contribution, my mite for such purpose, whatever might be the sect, was never refused.

Tho' I seldom attended any public worship, I had still an opinion of its propriety, and of its utility when rightly conducted, and I regularly paid my annual subscription for the support of the only Presbyterian minister or meeting we had in Philadelphia. He us'd to visit me sometimes as a friend, and admonished me to attend his administrations, and I was now and then prevail'd on to do so, once for five Sundays successively. Had he been in my opinion a good preacher, perhaps

I might have continued,* notwithstanding the occasion I had for the Sunday's leisure in my course of study; but his discourses were chiefly either polemic arguments, or explications of the peculiar doctrines of our sect, and were all to me very dry, uninteresting, and unedifying, since not a single moral principle was inculcated or enforc'd, their aim seeming to be rather to make us Presbyterians than good citizens.

At length he took for his text that verse of the fourth chapter of Philippians, *"Finally, brethren, whatsoever things are true, honest, just, pure, lovely, or of good report, if there be any virtue, or any praise, think on these things."* And I imagin'd, in a sermon on such a text, we could not miss of having some morality. But he confin'd himself to five points only, as meant by the apostle, viz.: 1. Keeping holy the Sabbath day. 2. Being diligent in reading the holy Scriptures. 3. Attending duly the publick worship. 4. Partaking of the Sacrament. 5. Paying a due respect to God's ministers. These might be all good things; but, as they were not the kind of good things that I expected from that text, I despaired of ever meeting with them from any other, was disgusted, and attended his preaching no more. I had some years before compos'd a little Liturgy, or form of prayer, for my own private use (viz., in 1728), entitled, *Articles of Belief and Acts of Religion.* I return'd to the use of this, and went no more to the public assemblies. My conduct might be blameable, but I leave it, without attempting further to excuse it; my present purpose being to relate facts, and not to make apologies for them.

---

* Franklin expressed a different view about the duty of attending church later.

# IX

## Plan for Attaining Moral Perfection

I t was about this time I conceived the bold and arduous project of arriving at moral perfection. I wish'd to live without committing any fault at any time; I would conquer all that either natural inclination, custom, or company might lead me into. As I knew, or thought I knew, what was right and wrong, I did not see why I might not always do the one and avoid the other. But I soon found I had undertaken a task of more difficulty than I had imagined.* While my care was employ'd in guarding against one fault, I was often surprised by another; habit took the advantage of inattention; inclination was sometimes too strong for reason. I concluded, at length, that the mere speculative conviction that it was our interest to be completely virtuous, was not sufficient to prevent our slipping; and that the contrary habits must be broken, and good ones acquired and established, before we can have any dependence on a steady, uniform rectitude of conduct. For this purpose I therefore contrived the following method.

In the various enumerations of the moral virtues I had met with in my reading, I found the catalogue more or less numerous, as different writers included more or fewer ideas under the same name. Temperance, for example, was by some confined to eating and drinking, while by others it was extended to mean the moderating every other pleasure, appetite, inclination, or passion, bodily or mental, even to our avarice and ambition. I propos'd to myself, for the sake of clearness, to use rather more names, with fewer ideas annex'd to each, than a few names with more ideas; and I included under thirteen names of virtues all that at that time occurr'd to me as necessary or desirable, and annexed to each a short precept, which fully express'd the extent I gave to its meaning.

These names of virtues, with their precepts, were:

---

* Compare Philippians iv, 8.

1. TEMPERANCE.
Eat not to dullness; drink not to elevation.

2. SILENCE.
Speak not but what may benefit others or yourself; avoid trifling conversation.

3. ORDER.
Let all your things have their places; let each part of your business have its time.

4. RESOLUTION.
Resolve to perform what you ought; perform without fail what you resolve.

5. FRUGALITY.
Make no expense but to do good to others or yourself; *i. e.*, waste nothing.

6. INDUSTRY.
Lose no time; be always employ'd in something useful; cut off all unnecessary actions.

7. SINCERITY.
Use no hurtful deceit; think innocently and justly; and, if you speak, speak accordingly.

8. JUSTICE.
Wrong none by doing injuries, or omitting the benefits that are your duty.

9. MODERATION.
Avoid extreams; forbear resenting injuries so much as you think they deserve.

10. CLEANLINESS.
Tolerate no uncleanliness in body, cloaths, or habitation.

11. TRANQUILLITY.
Be not disturbed at trifles, or at accidents common or unavoidable.

12. CHASTITY.

13. HUMILITY.
Imitate Jesus and Socrates.

My intention being to acquire the *habitude* of all these virtues, I judg'd it would be well not to distract my attention by attempting the whole at once, but to fix it on one of them at a time; and, when I should be master of that, then to proceed to another, and so on, till I should have gone thro' the thirteen; and, as the previous acquisition of some might facilitate the acquisition of certain others, I arrang'd them with that view, as they stand above. Temperance first, as it tends to procure that coolness and clearness of head, which is so necessary where constant vigilance was to be kept up, and guard maintained against the unremitting attraction of ancient habits, and the force of perpetual temptations. This being acquir'd and establish'd, Silence would be more easy; and my desire being to gain knowledge at the same time that I improv'd in virtue, and considering that in conversation it was obtain'd rather by the use of the ears than of the tongue, and therefore wishing to break a habit I was getting into of prattling, punning, and joking, which only made me acceptable to trifling company, I gave *Silence* the second place. This and the next, *Order*, I expected would allow me more time for attending to my project and my studies. *Resolution*, once become habitual, would keep me firm in my endeavours to obtain all the subsequent virtues; *Frugality* and Industry freeing me from my remaining debt, and producing affluence and independence, would make more easy the practice of Sincerity and Justice, etc., etc. Conceiving then, that, agreeably to the advice of Pythagoras[*] in his Golden Verses, daily examination would be necessary, I contrived the following method for conducting that examination.

I made a little book, in which I allotted a page for each of the virtues.[†]

---

[*] A famous Greek philosopher, who lived about 582–500 B. C. The *Golden Verses* here ascribed to him are probably of later origin. "The time which he recommends for this work is about even or bed-time, that we may conclude the action of the day with the judgment of conscience, making the examination of our conversation an evening song to God."

[†] This "little book" is dated July 1, 1733.—W. T. F.

I rul'd each page with red ink, so as to have seven columns, one for
each day of the week, marking each column with a letter for the day. I
cross'd these columns with thirteen red lines, marking the beginning of
each line with the first letter of one of the virtues, on which line, and
in its proper column, I might mark, by a little black spot, every fault I
found upon examination to have been committed respecting that virtue
upon that day.

I determined to give a week's strict attention to each of the virtues
successively. Thus, in the first week, my great guard was to avoid every
the least offense against *Temperance*, leaving the other virtues to their
ordinary chance, only marking every evening the faults of the day.
Thus, if in the first week I could keep my first line, marked T, clear
of spots, I suppos'd the habit of that virtue so much strengthen'd, and
its opposite weaken'd, that I might venture extending my attention to
include the next, and for the following week keep both lines clear of
spots. Proceeding thus to the last, I could go thro' a course compleat in
thirteen weeks, and four courses in a year. And like him who, having a
garden to weed, does not attempt to eradicate all the bad herbs at once,

*Form of the pages.*

| TEMPERANCE. | | | | | | |
|---|---|---|---|---|---|---|
| EAT NOT TO DULLNESS DRINK NOT TO ELEVATION. | | | | | | |
| | S. | M. | T. | W. | T. | F. | S. |
| T. | | | | | | | |
| S. | * | * | | * | | * | |
| O. | * * | * | * | | * | * | * |
| R. | | | * | | | * | |
| F. | | * | | | * | | |
| I. | | | * | | | | |
| S. | | | | | | | |
| J. | | | | | | | |
| M. | | | | | | | |
| C. | | | | | | | |
| T. | | | | | | | |
| C. | | | | | | | |
| H. | | | | | | | |
| J. | | | | | | | |

which would exceed his reach and his strength, but works on one of the beds at a time, and, having accomplish'd the first, proceeds to a second, so I should have, I hoped, the encouraging pleasure of seeing on my pages the progress I made in virtue, by clearing successively my lines of their spots, till in the end, by a number of courses, I should be happy in viewing a clean book, after a thirteen weeks' daily examination.

This my little book had for its motto these lines from Addison's *Cato*:

> "Here will I hold. If there's a power above us
> (And that there is, all nature cries aloud
> Thro' all her works), He must delight in virtue;
> And that which he delights in must be happy."

Another from Cicero,

> "O vitæ Philosophia dux! O virtutum indagatrix
> expultrixque vitiorum! Unus dies, bene et ex præceptis
> tuis actus, peccanti immortalitati est anteponendus."*

Another from the Proverbs of Solomon, speaking of wisdom or virtue:

> "Length of days is in her right hand, and in her
> left hand riches and honour. Her ways are ways of
> pleasantness, and all her paths are peace." iii. 16, 17.

And conceiving God to be the fountain of wisdom, I thought it right and necessary to solicit his assistance for obtaining it; to this end I formed the following little prayer, which was prefix'd to my tables of examination, for daily use.

> "*O powerful Goodness! bountiful Father! merciful Guide!
> Increase in me that wisdom which discovers my truest
> interest. Strengthen my resolutions to perform what that
> wisdom dictates. Accept my kind offices to thy other children
> as the only return in my power for thy continual favours
> to me.*"

---

* "O philosophy, guide of life! O searcher out of virtue and exterminator of vice! One day spent well and in accordance with thy precepts is worth an immortality of sin."—*Tusculan Inquiries*, Book V.

I used also sometimes a little prayer which I took from Thomson's Poems, viz.:

> "Father of light and life, thou Good Supreme!
> O teach me what is good; teach me Thyself!
> Save me from folly, vanity, and vice,
> From every low pursuit; and fill my soul
> With knowledge, conscious peace, and virtue pure;
> Sacred, substantial, never-fading bliss!"

The precept of *Order* requiring that *every part of my business should have its allotted time*, one page in my little book contain'd the following scheme of employment for the twenty-four hours of a natural day.

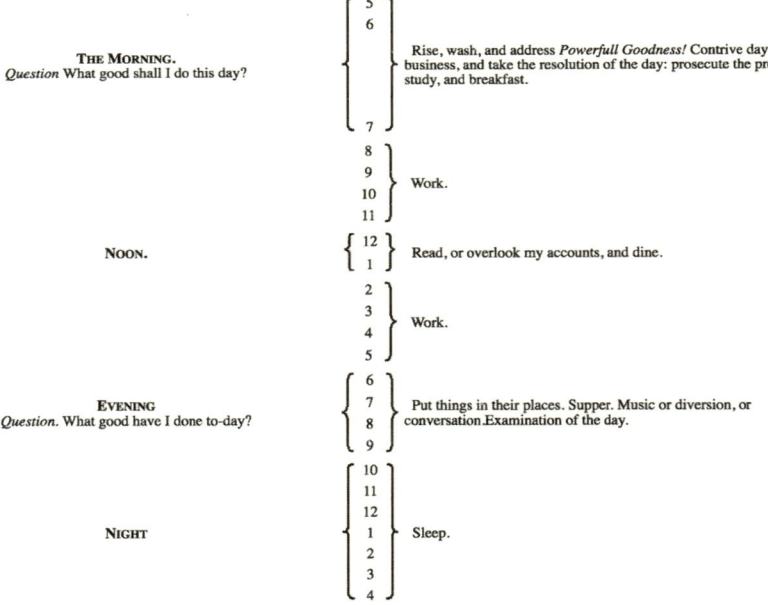

| | | |
|---|---|---|
| **THE MORNING.**<br>*Question* What good shall I do this day? | 5<br>6<br><br><br>7 | Rise, wash, and address *Powerfull Goodness!* Contrive day's business, and take the resolution of the day: prosecute the present study, and breakfast. |
| | 8<br>9<br>10<br>11 | Work. |
| **NOON.** | 12<br>1 | Read, or overlook my accounts, and dine. |
| | 2<br>3<br>4<br>5 | Work. |
| **EVENING**<br>*Question.* What good have I done to-day? | 6<br>7<br>8<br>9 | Put things in their places. Supper. Music or diversion, or conversation.Examination of the day. |
| **NIGHT** | 10<br>11<br>12<br>1<br>2<br>3<br>4 | Sleep. |

I enter'd upon the execution of this plan for self-examination, and continu'd it with occasional intermissions for some time. I was surpris'd to find myself so much fuller of faults than I had imagined; but I had the satisfaction of seeing them diminish. To avoid the trouble of renewing now and then my little book, which, by scraping out the marks on the paper of old faults to make room for new ones in a new course, became full of holes, I transferr'd my tables and precepts to the ivory leaves of a memorandum book, on which the lines were drawn with red ink, that made a durable stain, and on those lines I mark'd my faults with a black-lead pencil, which marks I could easily wipe out with a wet sponge. After a while I went thro' one course only in a year, and afterward only one in several years, till at length I omitted them entirely, being employ'd in voyages and business abroad, with a multiplicity of affairs that interfered; but I always carried my little book with me.

My scheme of Order gave me the most trouble;[*] and I found that, tho' it might be practicable where a man's business was such as to leave him the disposition of his time, that of a journeyman printer, for instance, it was not possible to be exactly observed by a master, who must mix with the world, and often receive people of business at their own hours. *Order*, too, with regard to places for things, papers, etc., I found extreamly difficult to acquire. I had not been early accustomed to it, and, having an exceeding good memory, I was not so sensible of the inconvenience attending want of method. This article, therefore, cost me so much painful attention, and my faults in it vexed me so much, and I made so little progress in amendment, and had such frequent relapses, that I was almost ready to give up the attempt, and content myself with a faulty character in that respect, like the man who, in buying an ax of a smith, my neighbour, desired to have the whole of its surface as bright as the edge. The smith consented to grind it bright for him if he would turn the wheel; he turn'd, while the smith press'd the broad face of the ax hard and heavily on the stone, which made the turning of it very fatiguing. The man came every now and then from the wheel to see how the work went on, and at length would take his ax as it was, without farther grinding. "No," said the smith, "turn on, turn on; we shall have it bright by-and-by; as yet, it is only speckled." "Yes," says the man, "*but I think I like a speckled ax best.*" And I believe this may have been the case with many, who, having, for want of some such means as I employ'd, found the difficulty of obtaining good and

---

[*] Professor McMaster tells us that when Franklin was American Agent in France, his lack of business order was a source of annoyance to his colleagues and friends. "Strangers who came to see him were amazed to behold papers of the greatest importance scattered in the most careless way over the table and floor."

breaking bad habits in other points of vice and virtue, have given up the struggle, and concluded that *"a speckled ax was best"*; for something, that pretended to be reason, was every now and then suggesting to me that such extream nicety as I exacted of myself might be a kind of foppery in morals, which, if it were known, would make me ridiculous; that a perfect character might be attended with the inconvenience of being envied and hated; and that a benevolent man should allow a few faults in himself, to keep his friends in countenance.

In truth, I found myself incorrigible with respect to Order; and now I am grown old, and my memory bad, I feel very sensibly the want of it. But, on the whole, tho' I never arrived at the perfection I had been so ambitious of obtaining, but fell far short of it, yet I was, by the endeavour, a better and a happier man than I otherwise should have been if I had not attempted it; as those who aim at perfect writing by imitating the engraved copies, tho' they never reach the wish'd-for excellence of those copies, their hand is mended by the endeavour, and is tolerable while it continues fair and legible.

It may be well my posterity should be informed that to this little artifice, with the blessing of God, their ancestor ow'd the constant felicity of his life, down to his 79th year, in which this is written. What reverses may attend the remainder is in the hand of Providence; but, if they arrive, the reflection on past happiness enjoy'd ought to help his bearing them with more resignation. To Temperance he ascribes his long-continued health, and what is still left to him of a good constitution; to Industry and Frugality, the early easiness of his circumstances and acquisition of his fortune, with all that knowledge that enabled him to be a useful citizen, and obtained for him some degree of reputation among the learned; to Sincerity and Justice, the confidence of his country, and the honorable employs it conferred upon him; and to the joint influence of the whole mass of the virtues,* even in the imperfect state he was able to acquire them, all that evenness of temper, and that cheerfulness in conversation, which makes his company still sought for, and agreeable even to his younger acquaintance. I hope, therefore, that some of my descendants may follow the example and reap the benefit.

It will be remark'd that, tho' my scheme was not wholly without religion, there was in it no mark of any of the distinguishing tenets of any particular sect. I had purposely avoided them; for, being fully persuaded of the utility and excellency of my method, and that it might be serviceable to people in all religions, and intending some time or other to publish it, I would not have anything in it that should prejudice anyone, of any sect, against it. I purposed writing a little comment on each virtue, in which I would have shown the advantages of possessing it, and the mischiefs attending its opposite vice; and I should have called my book The Art of Virtue,† because it would have shown the means and manner of obtaining virtue, which would have distinguished it from the mere exhortation to be good, that does not instruct and indicate the means, but is like the apostle's man of verbal charity, who only without

---

* While there can be no question that Franklin's moral improvement and happiness were due to the practice of these virtues, yet most people will agree that we shall have to go back of his plan for the impelling motive to a virtuous life. Franklin's own suggestion that the scheme smacks of "foppery in morals" seems justified. Woodrow Wilson well puts it: "Men do not take fire from such thoughts, unless something deeper, which is missing here, shine through them. What may have seemed to the eighteenth century a system of morals seems to us nothing more vital than a collection of the precepts of good sense and sound conduct. What redeems it from pettiness in this book is the scope of power and of usefulness to be seen in Franklin himself, who set these standards up in all seriousness and candor for his own life." See *Galatians*, chapter V, for the Christian plan of moral perfection.

† Nothing so likely to make a man's fortune as virtue.—*Marg. note.*

showing to the naked and hungry how or where they might get clothes or victuals, exhorted them to be fed and clothed.—James ii. 15, 16.

But it so happened that my intention of writing and publishing this comment was never fulfilled. I did, indeed, from time to time, put down short hints of the sentiments, reasonings, etc., to be made use of in it, some of which I have still by me; but the necessary close attention to private business in the earlier part of my life, and public business since, have occasioned my postponing it; for, it being connected in my mind with *a great and extensive project*, that required the whole man to execute, and which an unforeseen succession of employs prevented my attending to, it has hitherto remain'd unfinish'd.

In this piece it was my design to explain and enforce this doctrine, that vicious actions are not hurtful because they are forbidden, but forbidden because they are hurtful, the nature of man alone considered; that it was, therefore, everyone's interest to be virtuous who wish'd to be happy even in this world; and I should, from this circumstance (there being always in the world a number of rich merchants, nobility, states, and princes, who have need of honest instruments for the management of their affairs, and such being so rare), have endeavoured to convince young persons that no qualities were so likely to make a poor man's fortune as those of probity and integrity.

My list of virtues contain'd at first but twelve; but a Quaker friend having kindly informed me that I was generally thought proud; that my pride show'd itself frequently in conversation; that I was not content with being in the right when discussing any point, but was overbearing, and rather insolent, of which he convinc'd me by mentioning several instances; I determined endeavouring to cure myself, if I could, of this vice or folly among the rest, and I added *Humility* to my list, giving an extensive meaning to the word.

I cannot boast of much success in acquiring the *reality* of this virtue, but I had a good deal with regard to the *appearance* of it. I made it a rule to forbear all direct contradiction to the sentiments of others, and all positive assertion of my own. I even forbid myself, agreeably to the old laws of our Junto, the use of every word or expression in the language that imported a fix'd opinion, such as *certainly, undoubtedly*, etc., and I adopted, instead of them, *I conceive, I apprehend*, or *I imagine* a thing to be so or so; or it *so appears to me at present*. When another asserted something that I thought an error, I deny'd myself the pleasure of contradicting him abruptly, and of showing immediately some absurdity in his proposition; and in answering I began by observing that in certain cases or circumstances his opinion would be right, but in the present case there *appear'd* or *seem'd* to me some difference, etc. I soon found the advantage of this change in my manner; the conversations I engag'd in went on more pleasantly. The modest way in which I propos'd my opinions procur'd them a readier reception and less contradiction; I had less mortification when I was found to be in the wrong, and I more easily prevail'd with others to give up their mistakes and join with me when I happened to be in the right.

And this mode, which I at first put on with some violence to natural inclination, became at length so easy, and so habitual to me, that perhaps for these fifty years past no one has ever heard a dogmatical expression escape me. And to this habit (after my character of integrity) I think it principally owing that I had early so much weight with my fellow-citizens when I proposed new institutions, or alterations in the old, and so much influence in public councils when I became a member; for I was but a bad speaker, never eloquent, subject to much hesitation in my choice of words, hardly correct in language, and yet I generally carried my points.

In reality, there is, perhaps, no one of our natural passions so hard to subdue as *pride*. Disguise it, struggle with it, beat it down, stifle it, mortify it as much as one pleases, it is still alive, and will every now and then peep out and show itself; you will see it, perhaps, often in this history; for, even if I could conceive that I had compleatly overcome it, I should probably be proud of my humility.

[Thus far written at Passy, 1784.]

[*"I am now about to write at home, August, 1788, but cannot have the help expected from my papers, many of them being lost in the war. I have, however, found the following."*]*

Having mentioned *a great and extensive project* which I had conceiv'd, it seems proper that some account should be here given of that project and its object. Its first rise in my mind appears in the following little paper, accidentally preserv'd, viz.:

*Observations* on my reading history, in Library, May 19th, 1731.

"That the great affairs of the world, the wars, revolutions, etc., are carried on and effected by parties.

---

* This is a marginal memorandum.—B.

"That the view of these parties is their present general interest, or what they take to be such.

"That the different views of these different parties occasion all confusion.

"That while a party is carrying on a general design, each man has his particular private interest in view.

"That as soon as a party has gain'd its general point, each member becomes intent upon his particular interest; which, thwarting others, breaks that party into divisions, and occasions more confusion.

"That few in public affairs act from a mere view of the good of their country, whatever they may pretend; and, tho' their actings bring real good to their country, yet men primarily considered that their own and their country's interest was united, and did not act from a principle of benevolence.

"That fewer still, in public affairs, act with a view to the good of mankind.

"There seems to me at present to be great occasion for raising a United Party for Virtue, by forming the virtuous and good men of all nations into a regular body, to be govern'd by suitable good and wise rules, which good and wise men may probably be more unanimous in their obedience to, than common people are to common laws.

"I at present think that whoever attempts this aright, and is well qualified, cannot fail of pleasing God, and of meeting with success.

B. F."

Revolving this project in my mind, as to be undertaken hereafter, when my circumstances should afford me the necessary leisure, I put down from time to time, on pieces of paper, such thoughts as occurr'd to me respecting it. Most of these are lost; but I find one purporting to be the substance of an intended creed, containing, as I thought, the essentials of every known religion, and being free of everything that might shock the professors of any religion. It is express'd in these words, viz.:

"That there is one God, who made all things.

"That he governs the world by his providence.

"That he ought to be worshiped by adoration, prayer, and thanksgiving.

"But that the most acceptable service of God is doing good to man.

"That the soul is immortal.

"And that God will certainly reward virtue and punish vice, either here or hereafter."

My ideas at that time were, that the sect should be begun and spread at first among young and single men only; that each person to be initiated should not only declare his assent to such creed, but should have exercised himself with the thirteen weeks' examination and practice of the virtues, as in the beforemention'd model; that the existence of such a society should be kept a secret, till it was become considerable, to prevent solicitations for the admission of improper persons, but that the members should each of them search among his acquaintance for ingenuous, well-disposed youths, to whom, with prudent caution, the scheme should be gradually communicated; that the members should engage to afford their advice, assistance, and support to each other in promoting one another's interests, business, and advancement in life; that, for distinction, we should be call'd *The Society of the Free and Easy*: free, as being, by the general practice and habit of the virtues, free from the dominion of vice; and particularly by the practice of industry and frugality, free from debt, which exposes a man to confinement, and a species of slavery to his creditors.

This is as much as I can now recollect of the project, except that I communicated it in part to two young men, who adopted it with some enthusiasm; but my then narrow circumstances, and the necessity I was under of sticking close to my business, occasioned my postponing the further prosecution of it at that time; and my multifarious occupations, public and private, induc'd me to continue postponing, so that it has been omitted till I have no longer strength or activity left sufficient for such an enterprise; though I am still of opinion that it was a practicable scheme, and might have been very useful, by forming a great number of good citizens; and I was not discourag'd by the seeming magnitude of the undertaking, as I have always thought that one man of tolerable abilities may work great changes, and accomplish great affairs among mankind, if he first forms a good plan, and, cutting off all amusements or other employments that would divert his attention, makes the execution of that same plan his sole study and business.

# X

## Poor Richard's Almanac
## and Other Activities

In 1732 I first publish'd my Almanack, under the name of *Richard Saunders*; it was continu'd by me about twenty-five years, commonly call'd *Poor Richard's Almanac.** I endeavour'd to make it both entertaining and useful, and it accordingly came to be in such demand, that I reap'd considerable profit from it, vending annually near ten thousand. And observing that it was generally read, scarce any neighborhood in the province being without it, I consider'd it as a proper vehicle for conveying instruction among the common people, who bought scarcely any other books; I therefore filled all the little spaces that occurr'd between the remarkable days in the calendar with proverbial sentences, chiefly such as inculcated industry and frugality, as the means of procuring wealth, and thereby securing virtue; it being more difficult for a man in want, to act always honestly, as, to use here one of those proverbs, *it is hard for an empty sack to stand upright.*

These proverbs, which contained the wisdom of many ages and nations, I assembled and form'd into a connected discourse prefix'd to the Almanack of 1757, as the harangue of a wise old man to the people attending an auction. The bringing all these scatter'd councils thus into a focus enabled them to make greater impression. The piece, being universally approved, was copied in all the newspapers of the Continent; reprinted in Britain on a broadside, to be stuck up in houses; two translations were made of it in French, and great numbers bought by the clergy and gentry, to distribute gratis among their poor parishioners and tenants. In Pennsylvania, as it discouraged useless expense in foreign superfluities, some thought it had its share

---

* The almanac at that time was a kind of periodical as well as a guide to natural phenomena and the weather. Franklin took his title from *Poor Robin*, a famous English almanac, and from Richard Saunders, a well-known almanac publisher.

of influence in producing that growing plenty of money which was observable for several years after its publication.

I considered my newspaper, also, as another means of communicating instruction, and in that view frequently reprinted in it extracts from the Spectator, and other moral writers; and sometimes publish'd little pieces of my own, which had been first composed for reading in our Junto. Of these are a Socratic dialogue, tending to prove that, whatever might be his parts and abilities, a vicious man could not properly be called a man of sense; and a discourse on self-denial, showing that virtue was not secure till its practice became a habitude, and was free from the opposition of contrary inclinations. These may be found n the papers about the beginning of 1735.*

In the conduct of my newspaper, I carefully excluded all libeling and personal abuse, which is of late years become so disgraceful to our country. Whenever I was solicited to insert anything of that kind, and the writers pleaded, as they generally did, the liberty of the press, and that a newspaper was like a stage-coach, in which anyone who would pay had a right to a place, my answer was, that I would print the piece separately if desired, and the author might have as many copies as he pleased to distribute himself, but that I would not take upon me to spread his detraction; and that, having contracted with my subscribers to furnish them with what might be either useful or entertaining I could not fill their papers with private altercation, in which they had no concern, without doing them manifest injustice. Now, many of our printers make no scruple of gratifying the malice of individuals by false accusations of the fairest characters among ourselves, augmenting animosity even to the producing of duels; and are, moreover, so indiscreet as to print scurrilous reflections on the government of neighboring states, and even on the conduct of our best national allies, which may be attended with the most pernicious consequences. These things I mention as a caution to young printers, and that they may be encouraged not to pollute their presses and disgrace their profession by such infamous practices, but refuse steadily, as they may see by my example that such a course of conduct will not, on the whole, be injurious to their interests.

In 1733 I sent one of my journeymen to Charleston, South Carolina,

---

* June 23 and July 7, 1730.—Smyth.

## IV Mon. June hath xxx days.

Things that are bitter, bitterrer than Gall
Phyſicians ſay are always phyſical :
Now Women's Tongues if into Powder beaten,
May in a Potion or a Pill be eaten,
And as there's nought more bitter, I do muſe,
That Women's Tongues in Phyſick they ne'er uſe.
My ſelf and others who lead reſtleſs Lives,
Would ſpare that bitter Member of our Wives.

| | | | | | | | |
|---|---|---|---|---|---|---|---|
| 1 | 3 | *fine weather,* | 4 | ♌ | 4 | 36 | 8 | ☽ ſet 10 12 aft |
| 2 | 4 | Aſcenſion Day | 5 | 19 | 4 | 35 | 8 | *He that can have* |
| 3 | 5 | ☌ ♄ ♀ *ſudden* | 6 | ♍ | 4 | 35 | 8 | *Patience, can* |
| 4 | 6 | *ſhowers* | 6h | 19 | 4 | 35 | 8 | *have what he* |
| 5 | 7 | *of Rain.* | 7 | ♎ | 4 | 35 | 8 | Firſt Quarter. |
| 6 | C | Exaudi | 8 | 19 | 4 | 35 | 8 | *will.* |
| 7 | 2 | △ ♂ ☿ *thunder,* | 9 | ♏ | 4 | 35 | 8 | ☊ 5 ♎ |
| 8 | 3 | *perhaps hail.* | 10 | 17 | 4 | 35 | 8 | ☉ent. ♋ 10 day |
| 9 | 4 | 7* riſe 2 15 | 10 | ♐ | 4 | 34 | 8 | making longeſt |
| 10 | 5 | *very hot,* | 11 | 13 | 4 | 34 | 8 | day 14 h. 51 m. |
| 11 | 6 | St. Barnabas. | 12 | 26 | 4 | 34 | 8 | Full ● 12 day, |
| 12 | 7 | *then rain.* | 1 | ♑ | 4 | 34 | 8 | at 1 morn. |
| 13 | C | Whitſunday. | 2 | 20 | 4 | 35 | 8 | ☽ riſe 8 20 aft. |
| 14 | 2 | | 2h | ♒ | 4 | 35 | 8 | *Now I've a ſheep* |
| 15 | 3 | K. Geo. II. procl | 3 | 15 | 4 | 35 | 8 | *and a cow, every* |
| 16 | 4 | ſ. ☉ ♄ *wind, rain,* | 4 | 27 | 4 | 35 | 8 | *body bids me good* |
| 17 | 5 | ✱ ♄ ☿ *hail and* | 5 | ♓ | 4 | 35 | 8 | *morrow.* |
| 18 | 6 | *thunder.* | 6 | 21 | 4 | 35 | 8 | ☽ riſe 11 10 af. |
| 19 | 7 | Day ſhorter 2 m. | 6h | ♈ | 4 | 35 | 8 | |
| 20 | C | Trinity Sund. | 7 | 15 | 4 | 36 | 8 | Laſt Quarter. |
| 21 | 2 | *If we have rain a-* | 8 | 27 | 4 | 36 | 8 | *God helps them* |
| 22 | 3 | *bout the Change,* | 9 | ♉ | 4 | 36 | 8 | *that help them-* |
| 23 | 4 | *Let not my reader* | 10 | 22 | 4 | 36 | 8 | *ſelves.* |
| 24 | 5 | St. John Bap. | 10 | ♊ | 4 | 36 | 8 | ☽ riſe 2 morn. |
| 25 | 6 | 7* riſe 1 8 | 11 | 18 | 4 | 37 | 8 | *Why does the* |
| 26 | 7 | vc. ☉ ♃ *think it* | 12 | ♋ | 4 | 37 | 8 | *blind man's wife* |
| 27 | C | *ſtrange.* | 1 | 16 | 4 | 38 | 8 | New ☽ 27 day, |
| 28 | 2 | ✱ ♄ ♂ *hail and* | 2 | ♌ | 4 | 38 | 8 | near noon. |
| 29 | 3 | St. Peter & Paul | 2h | 15 | 4 | 39 | 8 | *paint herſelf.* |
| 30 | 4 | □ ♂ ♀ *rain.* | 3 | ♍ | 4 | 40 | 8 | ☽ ſets 9 30 |

*Two pages from* Poor Richard's Almanac *for 1736.*
*Reproduced from a copy at the New York Public Library.*

Who can charge *Ebrio* with Thirst of Wealth?
See he consumes his Money, Time and Health,
In drunken Frolicks which will all confound,
Neglects his Farm, forgets to till his Ground,
His Stock grows less that might be kept with ease;
In nought but Guts and Debts he finds Encrease.
In Town reels as if he'd shove down each Wall,
Yet Walls must stand, poor Soul, or he must fall.

| | | | | | | |
|---|---|---|---|---|---|---|
| 1 | 5 | Day short. 11 m | 3 | 15 | 4 40 | New preaches |
| 2 | 6 | 7* rise 12 32 | 5 | ♎ | 4 41 | better than the |
| 3 | 7 | twindy weather. | 6 | 15 | 4 41 | Sant, and she says |
| 4 | ☾ 2 Sund. p Trinit | 6h | ♏ | 4 42 | First Quarter. |
| 5 | 2 | Ve ♃ ♀ xow | 7 | 14 | 4 43 | Soothing. |
| 6 | 3 | pleasant weather | 8 | 27 | 4 44 | ) sets 12 30 m |
| 7 | 4 | some days | 9 | ♐ | 4 45 | The absent are |
| 8 | 5 | together, | 10 | 23 | 4 46 | never without |
| 9 | 6 | but inclines to | 10 | ♑ | 4 47 | fault, nor the |
| 10 | 7 | falling | 11 | 18 | 4 48 | present without |
| 11 | ☾ 3 Sund. p. Trin. | 12 | ♒ | 4 49 | Full ● 11 day, |
| 12 | 2 | ✳ ♄ ♀ weather. | 1 | 13 | 4 50 | 2 afternoon. |
| 13 | 3 | Dog-days begin | 2 | 27 | 4 50 | ⊙ in ♌ |
| 14 | 4 | Days 14 h. 20 m | 2h | ♓ | 4 51 | ) rise 8 35 aft. |
| 15 | 5 | St. Swithin. | 3 | 19 | 4 52 | excuse. |
| 16 | 6 | ♌ 1 ♋ | 4 | ♈ | 4 53 | |
| 17 | 7 | ♂ ⊙ ♀ rain | 5 | 13 | 4 54 | Gifts burst |
| 18 | ☾ 7* rise 11 40 | 6 | 25 | 4 55 | rocks. |
| 19 | 2 | hail or rain, | 6h | ♉ | 4 56 | Last Quarter. |
| 20 | 3 | ✳ ⊙ ♄ thunder. | 7 | 19 | 4 57 | ) rise 11 52 at |
| 21 | 4 | 7* rise 11 38 | 8 | ♊ | 4 57 | If wind blows you |
| 22 | 5 | then high | 9 | 14 | 4 58 | you thro' a hole, |
| 23 | 6 | wind. | 10 | 27 | 4 59 | Make your will |
| 24 | 7 | ♂ ⊙ ♃ | 10 | ♋ | 4 59 | and take care of |
| 25 | ☾ St. James. | 11 | 25 | 5 0 | 7 | your soul. |
| 26 | 2 | hot | 12 | ♌ | 5 1 | 7 New ) 26 day, |
| 27 | 3 | ) near cor ♌ | 1 | 24 | 5 2 | 7 next 8 aftern |
| 28 | 4 | ♂ ♃ ♀ a clear | 2 | ♍ | 5 3 | 7 ) sets 8 aftern. |
| 29 | 5 | aire and fine | 2h | 24 | 5 4 | 7 The rotten Apple |
| 30 | 6 | weather | 3 | ♎ | 5 5 | 7 spoils his Com- |
| 31 | 7 | 7* rise 10 40 | 4 | 23 | 5 6 | 7 panion. |

where a printer was wanting. I furnish'd him with a press and letters, on an agreement of partnership, by which I was to receive one-third of the profits of the business, paying one-third of the expense. He was a man of learning, and honest but ignorant in matters of account; and, tho' he sometimes made me remittances, I could get no account from him, nor any satisfactory state of our partnership while he lived. On his decease, the business was continued by his widow, who, being born and bred in Holland, where, as I have been inform'd, the knowledge of accounts makes a part of female education, she not only sent me as clear a state as she could find of the transactions past, but continued to account with the greatest regularity and exactness every quarter afterwards, and managed the business with such success, that she not only brought up reputably a family of children, but, at the expiration of the term, was able to purchase of me the printing-house, and establish her son in it.

I mention this affair chiefly for the sake of recommending that branch of education for our young females, as likely to be of more use to them and their children, in case of widowhood, than either music or dancing, by preserving them from losses by imposition of crafty men, and enabling them to continue, perhaps, a profitable mercantile house, with establish'd correspondence, till a son is grown up fit to undertake and go on with it, to the lasting advantage and enriching of the family.

About the year 1734 there arrived among us from Ireland a young Presbyterian preacher, named Hemphill, who delivered with a good voice, and apparently extempore, most excellent discourses, which drew together considerable numbers of different persuasions, who join'd in admiring them. Among the rest, I became one of his constant hearers, his sermons pleasing me, as they had little of the dogmatical kind, but inculcated strongly the practice of virtue, or what in the religious stile are called good works. Those, however, of our congregation, who considered themselves as orthodox Presbyterians, disapprov'd his doctrine, and were join'd by most of the old clergy, who arraign'd him of heterodoxy before the synod, in order to have him silenc'd. I became his zealous partisan, and contributed all I could to raise a party in his favour, and we combated for him awhile with some hopes of success. There was much scribbling pro and con upon the occasion; and finding that, tho' an elegant preacher, he was but a poor writer, I lent him my pen and wrote for him two or three pamphlets, and one piece in the Gazette of April, 1735. Those pamphlets, as is generally the case with controversial writings, tho' eagerly read at the time, were soon out of vogue, and I question whether a single copy of them now exists.[*]

During the contest an unlucky occurrence hurt his cause exceedingly. One of our adversaries having heard him preach a sermon that was much admired, thought he had somewhere read the sermon before, or at least a part of it. On search, he found that part quoted at length, in one of the British Reviews, from a discourse of Dr. Foster's.[†] This detection gave many of our party disgust, who accordingly abandoned his cause, and occasion'd our more speedy discomfiture in the synod. I stuck by him, however, as I rather approv'd his giving us good sermons composed by others, than bad ones of his own manufacture, tho' the latter was the practice of our common teachers. He afterward acknowledg'd to me that none of those he preach'd were his own; adding, that his memory was such as enabled him to retain and repeat any sermon after one reading only. On our defeat, he left us in search elsewhere of better fortune, and I quitted the congregation, never joining it after, tho' I continu'd many years my subscription for the support of its ministers.

I had begun in 1733 to study languages; I soon made myself so much a master of the French as to be able to read the books with ease. I then undertook the Italian. An acquaintance, who was also learning it, us'd often to tempt me to play chess with him. Finding this took up too much of the time I had to spare for study, I at length refus'd to play any more, unless on this condition, that the victor in every game should have a right to impose a task, either in parts of the grammar to be got by heart, or in translations, etc., which tasks the vanquish'd was to perform upon honour, before our next meeting. As we play'd pretty equally, we thus beat one another into that language. I afterwards with a little painstaking, acquir'd as much of the Spanish as to read their books also.

I have already mention'd that I had only one year's instruction in a Latin school, and that when very young, after which I neglected that language entirely. But, when I had attained an acquaintance with the French, Italian, and Spanish, I was surpris'd to find, on looking over

* See "A List of Books written by, or relating to Benjamin Franklin," by Paul Leicester Ford. 1889. p. 15.—Smyth.

† Dr. James Foster (1697–1753):—
  "Let modest Foster, if he will excel
  Ten metropolitans in preaching well."
—Pope (Epilogue to the Satires, I, 132).
"Those who had not heard Farinelli sing and Foster preach were not qualified to appear in genteel company," Hawkins. "History of Music."—Smyth.

a Latin Testament, that I understood so much more of that language than I had imagined, which encouraged me to apply myself again to the study of it, and I met with more success, as those preceding languages had greatly smooth'd my way.

From these circumstances, I have thought that there is some inconsistency in our common mode of teaching languages. We are told that it is proper to begin first with the Latin, and, having acquir'd that, it will be more easy to attain those modern languages which are deriv'd from it; and yet we do not begin with the Greek, in order more easily to acquire the Latin. It is true that, if you can clamber and get to the top of a staircase without using the steps, you will more easily gain them in descending; but certainly, if you begin with the lowest you will with more ease ascend to the top; and I would therefore offer it to the consideration of those who superintend the education of our youth, whether, since many of those who begin with the Latin quit the same after spending some years without having made any great proficiency, and what they have learnt becomes almost useless, so that their time has been lost, it would not have been better to have begun with the French, proceeding to the Italian, etc.; for, tho', after spending the same time, they should quit the study of languages and never arrive at the Latin, they would, however, have acquired another tongue or two, that, being in modern use, might be serviceable to them in common life.[*]

After ten years' absence from Boston, and having become easy in my circumstances, I made a journey thither to visit my relations, which I could not sooner well afford. In returning, I call'd at Newport to see my brother, then settled there with his printing-house. Our former differences were forgotten, and our meeting was very cordial and affectionate. He was fast declining in his health, and requested of me that, in case of his death, which he apprehended not far distant, I would take home his son, then but ten years of age, and bring him up to the printing business. This I accordingly perform'd, sending him a few years to school before I took him into the office. His mother

---

[*] "The authority of Franklin, the most eminently practical man of his age, in favor of reserving the study of the dead languages until the mind has reached a certain maturity, is confirmed by the confession of one of the most eminent scholars of any age. "'Our seminaries of learning,' says Gibbon, 'do not exactly correspond with the precept of a Spartan king, that the child should be instructed in the arts which will be useful to the man; since a finished scholar may emerge from the head of Westminster or Eton, in total ignorance of the business and conversation of English gentlemen in the latter end of the eighteenth century. But these schools may assume the merit of teaching all that they pretend to teach, the Latin and Greek languages.'"—Bigelow.

carried on the business till he was grown up, when I assisted him with an assortment of new types, those of his father being in a manner worn out. Thus it was that I made my brother ample amends for the service I had depriv'd him of by leaving him so early.

In 1736 I lost one of my sons, a fine boy of four years old, by the small-pox, taken in the common way. I long regretted bitterly, and still regret that I had not given it to him by inoculation. This I mention for the sake of parents who omit that operation, on the supposition that they should never forgive themselves if a child died under it; my example showing that the regret may be the same either way, and that, therefore, the safer should be chosen.

Our club, the Junto, was found so useful, and afforded such satisfaction to the members, that several were desirous of introducing their friends, which could not well be done without exceeding what we had settled as a convenient number, viz., twelve. We had from the beginning made it a rule to keep our institution a secret, which was pretty well observ'd; the intention was to avoid applications of improper persons for admittance, some of whom, perhaps, we might find it difficult to refuse. I was one of those who were against any addition to our number, but, instead of it, made in writing a proposal, that every member separately should endeavour to form a subordinate club, with the same rules respecting queries, etc., and without informing them of the connection with the Junto. The advantages proposed were, the improvement of so many more young citizens by the use of our institutions; our better acquaintance with the general sentiments of the inhabitants on any occasion, as the Junto member might propose what queries we should desire, and was to report to the Junto what pass'd in his separate club; the promotion of our particular interests in business by more extensive recommendation, and the increase of our influence in public affairs, and our power of doing good by spreading thro' the several clubs the sentiments of the Junto.

The project was approv'd, and every member undertook to form his club, but they did not all succeed. Five or six only were compleated, which were called by different names, as the Vine, the Union, the Band, etc. They were useful to themselves, and afforded us a good deal of amusement, information, and instruction, besides answering, in some considerable degree, our views of influencing the public opinion on particular occasions, of which I shall give some instances in course of time as they happened.

My first promotion was my being chosen, in 1736, clerk of the General Assembly. The choice was made that year without opposition; but the year following, when I was again propos'd (the choice, like that of the members, being annual), a new member made a long speech against me, in order to favour some other candidate. I was, however, chosen, which was the more agreeable to me, as, besides the pay for the immediate service as clerk, the place gave me a better opportunity of keeping up an interest among the members, which secur'd to me the business of printing the votes, laws, paper money, and other occasional jobbs for the public, that, on the whole, were very profitable.

I therefore did not like the opposition of this new member, who was a gentleman of fortune and education, with talents that were likely to give him, in time, great influence in the House, which, indeed, afterwards happened. I did not, however, aim at gaining his favour by paying any servile respect to him, but, after some time, took this other method. Having heard that he had in his library a certain very scarce and curious book, I wrote a note to him, expressing my desire of perusing that book, and requesting he would do me the favour of lending it to me for a few days. He sent it immediately, and I return'd it in about a week with another note, expressing strongly my sense of the favour. When we next met in the House, he spoke to me (which he had never done before), and with great civility; and he ever after manifested a readiness to serve me on all occasions, so that we became great friends, and our friendship continued to his death. This is another instance of the truth of an old maxim I had learned, which says, *"He that has once done you a kindness will be more ready to do you another, than he whom you yourself have obliged."* And it shows how much more profitable it is prudently to remove, than to resent, return, and continue inimical proceedings.

In 1737, Colonel Spotswood, late governor of Virginia, and then postmaster-general, being dissatisfied with the conduct of his deputy at Philadelphia, respecting some negligence in rendering, and inexactitude of his accounts, took from him the commission and offered it to me. I accepted it readily, and found it of great advantage; for, tho' the salary was small, it facilitated the correspondence that improv'd my newspaper, increas'd the number demanded, as well as the advertisements to be inserted, so that it came to afford me a considerable income. My old competitor's newspaper declin'd proportionately, and I was satisfy'd without retaliating his refusal, while postmaster, to permit my papers being carried by the riders. Thus he suffer'd greatly from his neglect in due accounting; and I mention it as a lesson to those young men who may be employ'd in managing affairs for others, that they should always render accounts, and make remittances, with great clearness and punctuality. The character of observing such a conduct is the most powerful of all recommendations to new employments and increase of business.

# XI

## *Interest in Public Affairs*

---

I began now to turn my thoughts a little to public affairs, beginning, however, with small matters. The city watch was one of the first things that I conceiv'd to want regulation. It was managed by the constables of the respective wards in turn; the constable warned a number of housekeepers to attend him for the night. Those who chose never to attend, paid him six shillings a year to be excus'd, which was suppos'd to be for hiring substitutes, but was, in reality, much more than was necessary for that purpose, and made the constableship a place of profit; and the constable, for a little drink, often got such ragamuffins about him as a watch, that respectable housekeepers did not choose to mix with. Walking the rounds, too, was often neglected, and most of the nights spent in tippling. I thereupon wrote a paper to be read in Junto, representing these irregularities, but insisting more particularly on the inequality of this six-shilling tax of the constables, respecting the circumstances of those who paid it, since a poor widow housekeeper, all whose property to be guarded by the watch did not perhaps exceed the value of fifty pounds, paid as much as the wealthiest merchant, who had thousands of pounds' worth of goods in his stores.

On the whole, I proposed as a more effectual watch, the hiring of proper men to serve constantly in that business; and as a more equitable way of supporting the charge, the levying a tax that should be proportion'd to the property. This idea, being approv'd by the Junto, was communicated to the other clubs, but as arising in each of them; and though the plan was not immediately carried into execution, yet, by preparing the minds of people for the change, it paved the way for the law obtained a few years after, when the members of our clubs were grown into more influence.

About this time I wrote a paper (first to be read in Junto, but it was afterward publish'd) on the different accidents and carelessnesses by which houses were set on fire, with cautions against them, and means proposed of avoiding them. This was much spoken of as a useful piece, and gave rise to a project, which soon followed it, of forming a company for the more ready extinguishing of fires, and mutual assistance in removing and securing of goods when in danger. Associates in this scheme were presently found, amounting to thirty. Our articles of agreement oblig'd every member to keep always in good order, and fit for use, a certain number of leather buckets, with strong bags and baskets (for packing and transporting of goods), which were to be brought to every fire; and we agreed to meet once a month and spend a social evening together, in discoursing and communicating such ideas as occurred to us upon the subjects of fires, as might be useful in our conduct on such occasions.

The utility of this institution soon appeared, and many more desiring to be admitted than we thought convenient for one company, they were advised to form another, which was accordingly done; and this went on, one new company being formed after another, till they became so numerous as to include most of the inhabitants who were men of property; and now, at the time of my writing this, tho' upward of fifty years since its establishment, that which I first formed, called the Union Fire Company, still subsists and flourishes, tho' the first members are all deceas'd but myself and one, who is older by a year than I am. The small fines that have been paid by members for absence at the monthly meetings have been apply'd to the purchase of fire-engines, ladders, fire-hooks, and other useful implements for each company, so that I question whether there is a city in the world better provided with the means of putting a stop to beginning conflagrations; and, in fact, since these institutions, the city has never lost by fire more than one or two

houses at a time, and the flames have often been extinguished before the house in which they began has been half consumed.

In 1739 arrived among us from Ireland the Reverend Mr. Whitefield,[*] who had made himself remarkable there as an itinerant preacher. He was at first permitted to preach in some of our churches; but the clergy, taking a dislike to him, soon refus'd him their pulpits, and he was oblig'd to preach in the fields. The multitudes of all sects and denominations that attended his sermons were enormous, and it was matter of speculation to me, who was one of the number, to observe the extraordinary influence of his oratory on his hearers, and how much they admir'd and respected him, notwithstanding his common abuse of them, by assuring them they were naturally *half beasts and half devils*. It was wonderful to see the change soon made in the manners of our inhabitants. From being thoughtless or indifferent about religion, it seem'd as if all the world were growing religious, so that one could not walk thro' the town in an evening without hearing psalms sung in different families of every street.

And it being found inconvenient to assemble in the open air, subject to its inclemencies, the building of a house to meet in was no sooner propos'd, and persons appointed to receive contributions, but sufficient sums were soon receiv'd to procure the ground and erect the building, which was one hundred feet long and seventy broad, about the size of Westminster Hall;[†] and the work was carried on with such spirit as to be finished in a much shorter time than could have been expected. Both house and ground were vested in trustees, expressly for the use of any preacher of any religious persuasion who might desire to say something to the people at Philadelphia; the design in building not being to accommodate any particular sect, but the inhabitants in general; so that even if the Mufti of Constantinople were to send a missionary to preach Mohammedanism to us, he would find a pulpit at his service.

Mr. Whitefield, in leaving us, went preaching all the way thro' the colonies to Georgia. The settlement of that province had lately been begun, but, instead of being made with hardy, industrious husbandmen, accustomed to labour, the only people fit for such an enterprise, it was

---

[*] George Whitefield, pronounced Hwit'field (1714–1770), a celebrated English clergyman and pulpit orator, one of the founders of Methodism.

[†] A part of the palace of Westminster, now forming the vestibule to the Houses of Parliament in London.

with families of broken shop-keepers and other insolvent debtors, many of indolent and idle habits, taken out of the jails, who, being set down in the woods, unqualified for clearing land, and unable to endure the hardships of a new settlement, perished in numbers, leaving many helpless children unprovided for. The sight of their miserable situation inspir'd the benevolent heart of Mr. Whitefield with the idea of building an Orphan House there, in which they might be supported and educated. Returning northward, he preach'd up this charity, and made large collections, for his eloquence had a wonderful power over the hearts and purses of his hearers, of which I myself was an instance.

I did not disapprove of the design, but, as Georgia was then destitute of materials and workmen, and it was proposed to send them from Philadelphia at a great expense, I thought it would have been better to have built the house here, and brought the children to it. This I advis'd; but he was resolute in his first project, rejected my counsel, and I therefore refus'd to contribute. I happened soon after to attend one of his sermons, in the course of which I perceived he intended to finish with a collection, and I silently resolved he should get nothing from me. I had in my pocket a handful of copper money, three or four silver dollars, and five pistoles in gold. As he proceeded I began to soften, and concluded to give the coppers. Another stroke of his oratory made me asham'd of that, and determin'd me to give the silver; and he finish'd so admirably, that I empty'd my pocket wholly into the collector's dish, gold and all. At this sermon there was also one of our club, who, being of my sentiments respecting the building in Georgia, and suspecting a collection might be intended, had, by precaution, emptied his pockets before he came from home. Towards the conclusion of the discourse, however, he felt a strong desire to give, and apply'd to a neighbour who stood near him, to borrow some money for the purpose. The application was unfortunately [made] to perhaps the only man in the company who had the firmness not to be affected by the preacher. His answer was, "*At any other time, Friend Hopkinson, I would lend to thee freely; but not now, for thee seems to be out of thy right senses.*"

Some of Mr. Whitefield's enemies affected to suppose that he would apply these collections to his own private emolument; but I, who was intimately acquainted with him (being employed in printing his Sermons and Journals, etc.), never had the least suspicion of his integrity, but am to this day decidedly of opinion that he was in all his conduct a perfectly *honest man*; and methinks my testimony in his favour ought to have the more weight, as we had no religious connection. He us'd, indeed, sometimes to pray for my conversion, but never had the satisfaction of believing that his prayers were heard. Ours was a mere civil friendship, sincere on both sides, and lasted to his death.

The following instance will show something of the terms on which we stood. Upon one of his arrivals from England at Boston, he wrote to me that he should come soon to Philadelphia, but knew not where he could lodge when there, as he understood his old friend and host, Mr. Benezet was removed to Germantown. My answer was, "You know my house; if you can make shift with its scanty accommodations, you will be most heartily welcome." He reply'd, that if I made that kind offer for Christ's sake, I should not miss of a reward. And I returned, "*Don't let me be mistaken; it was not for Christ's sake, but for your sake.*" One of our common acquaintance jocosely remark'd, that, knowing it to be the custom of the saints, when they received any favour, to shift the burden of the obligation from off their own shoulders, and place it in heaven, I had contriv'd to fix it on earth.

The last time I saw Mr. Whitefield was in London, when he consulted me about his Orphan House concern, and his purpose of appropriating it to the establishment of a college.

He had a loud and clear voice, and articulated his words and sentences so perfectly, that he might be heard and understood at a great distance, especially as his auditories, however numerous, observ'd the most exact silence. He preach'd one evening from the top of the Courthouse steps, which are in the middle of Market-street, and on the west side of Second-street, which crosses it at right angles. Both streets were fill'd with his hearers to a considerable distance. Being among the hindmost in Market-street, I had the curiosity to learn how far he could be heard, by retiring backwards down the street towards the river; and I found his voice distinct till I came near Front-street, when some noise in that street obscur'd it. Imagining then a semicircle, of which my distance should be the radius, and that it were fill'd with auditors, to each of whom I allow'd two square feet, I computed that he might well be heard by more than thirty thousand. This reconcil'd me to the newspaper accounts of his having preach'd to twenty-five thousand people in the fields, and to the ancient histories of generals haranguing whole armies, of which I had sometimes doubted.

By hearing him often, I came to distinguish easily between sermons newly compos'd, and those which he had often preach'd in the course of his travels. His delivery of the latter was so improv'd by frequent repetitions that every accent, every emphasis, every modulation of voice, was so perfectly well turn'd and well plac'd, that, without being interested in the subject, one could not help being pleas'd with the discourse; a pleasure of much the same kind with that receiv'd from an excellent piece of musick. This is an advantage itinerant preachers have over those who are stationary, as the latter cannot well improve their delivery of a sermon by so many rehearsals.

His writing and printing from time to time gave great advantage to his enemies; unguarded expressions, and even erroneous opinions, delivered in preaching, might have been afterwards explain'd or qualifi'd by supposing others that might have accompani'd them, or they might have been deny'd; but *litera scripta manet*. Critics attack'd his writings violently, and with so much appearance of reason as to diminish the number of his votaries and prevent their increase; so that I am of opinion if he had never written anything, he would have left behind him a much more numerous and important sect, and his reputation might in that case have been still growing, even after his death, as there being nothing of his writing on which to found a censure and give him a lower character, his proselytes would be left at liberty to feign for him as great a variety of excellences as their enthusiastic admiration might wish him to have possessed.

My business was now continually augmenting, and my circumstances growing daily easier, my newspaper having become very profitable, as being for a time almost the only one in this and the neighbouring provinces. I experienced, too, the truth of the observation, "*that after getting the first hundred pound, it is more easy to get the second*," money itself being of a prolific nature.

The partnership at Carolina having succeeded, I was encourag'd to engage in others, and to promote several of my workmen, who had behaved well, by establishing them with printing-houses in different colonies, on the same terms with that in Carolina. Most of them did well, being enabled at the end of our term, six years, to purchase the types of me and go on working for themselves, by which means several families were raised. Partnerships often finish in quarrels; but I was happy in this, that mine were all carried on and ended amicably, owing, I think, a good deal to the precaution of having very explicitly settled, in our articles, everything to be done by or expected from each partner, so that there was nothing to dispute, which precaution I would therefore recommend to all who enter into partnerships; for, whatever esteem partners may have for, and confidence in each other at the time of the contract, little jealousies and disgusts may arise, with ideas of inequality in the care and burden of the business, etc., which are attended often with breach of friendship and of the connection, perhaps with lawsuits and other disagreeable consequences.

# XII
## Defense of the Province

I had, on the whole, abundant reason to be satisfied with my being established in Pennsylvania. There were, however, two, things that I regretted, there being no provision for defense, nor for a compleat education of youth; no militia, nor any college. I therefore, in 1743, drew up a proposal for establishing an academy; and at that time, thinking the Reverend Mr. Peters, who was out of employ, a fit person to superintend such an institution, I communicated the project to him; but he, having more profitable views in the service of the proprietaries, which succeeded, declin'd the undertaking; and, not knowing another at that time suitable for such a trust, I let the scheme lie awhile dormant. I succeeded better the next year, 1744, in proposing and establishing a Philosophical Society. The paper I wrote for that purpose will be found among my writings, when collected.

With respect to defense, Spain having been several years at war against Great Britain, and being at length join'd by France, which brought us into great danger; and the laboured and long-continued endeavour of our governor, Thomas, to prevail with our Quaker Assembly to pass a militia law, and make other provisions for the security of the province, having proved abortive, I determined to try what might be done by a voluntary association of the people. To promote this, I first wrote and published a pamphlet, entitled "Plain Truth," in which I stated our defenceless situation in strong lights, with the necessity of union and discipline for our defense, and promis'd to propose in a few days an association, to be generally signed for that purpose. The pamphlet had a sudden and surprising effect. I was call'd upon for the instrument of association, and having settled the draft of it with a few friends, I appointed a meeting of the citizens in the large building before mentioned. The house was pretty full; I had prepared a number of printed copies, and provided pens and ink dispers'd all over the room. I harangued them a little on the subject, read the paper, and explained it, and then distributed the copies, which were eagerly signed, not the least objection being made.

When the company separated, and the papers were collected, we found above twelve hundred hands; and, other copies being dispersed in the country, the subscribers amounted at length to upward of ten thousand. These all furnished themselves as soon as they could with arms, formed themselves into companies and regiments, chose their own officers, and met every week to be instructed in the manual exercise, and other parts of military discipline. The women, by subscriptions among themselves, provided silk colours, which they presented to the companies, painted with different devices and mottos, which I supplied.

The officers of the companies composing the Philadelphia regiment, being met, chose me for their colonel; but, conceiving myself unfit, I declin'd that station, and recommended Mr. Lawrence, a fine person, and man of influence, who was accordingly appointed. I then propos'd a lottery to defray the expense of building a battery below the town, and furnishing it with cannon. It filled expeditiously, and the

*One of the flags of the Pennsylvania Association, 1747. Designed by Franklin and made by the women of Philadelphia.*

battery was soon erected, the merlons being fram'd of logs and fill'd with earth. We bought some old cannon from Boston, but, these not being sufficient, we wrote to England for more, soliciting, at the same time, our proprietaries for some assistance, tho' without much expectation of obtaining it.

Meanwhile, Colonel Lawrence, William Allen, Abram Taylor, Esqr., and myself were sent to New York by the associators, commission'd to borrow some cannon of Governor Clinton. He at first refus'd us peremptorily; but at dinner with his council, where there was great drinking of Madeira wine, as the custom of that place then was, he softened by degrees, and said he would lend us six. After a few more bumpers he advanc'd to ten; and at length he very good-naturedly conceded eighteen. They were fine cannon, eighteen-pounders, with their carriages, which we soon transported and mounted on our battery, where the associators kept a nightly guard while the war lasted, and among the rest I regularly took my turn of duty there as a common soldier.

My activity in these operations was agreeable to the governor and council; they took me into confidence, and I was consulted by them in every measure wherein their concurrence was thought useful to the association. Calling in the aid of religion, I propos'd to them the proclaiming a fast, to promote reformation, and implore the blessing of Heaven on our undertaking. They embrac'd the motion; but, as it was the first fast ever thought of in the province, the secretary had no precedent from which to draw the proclamation. My education in New England, where a fast is proclaimed every year, was here of some advantage: I drew it in the accustomed stile, it was translated into German,* printed in both languages, and divulg'd thro' the province. This gave the clergy of the different sects an opportunity of influencing their congregations to join in the association, and it would probably have been general among all but Quakers if the peace had not soon interven'd.

It was thought by some of my friends that, by my activity in these affairs, I should offend that sect, and thereby lose my interest in the Assembly of the province, where they formed a great majority. A young gentleman who had likewise some friends in the House, and wished to succeed me as their clerk, acquainted me that it was decided to displace me at the next election; and he, therefore, in good will, advis'd me to resign, as more consistent with my honour than being turn'd out. My answer to him was, that I had read or heard of some public man who made it a rule never to ask for an office, and never to refuse one when offer'd to him. "I approve," says I, "of his rule, and will practice it with a small addition; I shall never *ask*, never *refuse*, nor ever *resign* an office. If they will have my office of clerk to dispose of to another, they shall take it from me. I will not, by giving it up, lose my right of some time or other making reprisals on my adversaries." I heard, however, no more of this; I was chosen again unanimously as usual at the next election. Possibly, as they dislik'd my late intimacy with the members of council, who had join'd the governors in all the disputes about military preparations, with which the House had long been harass'd, they might have been pleas'd if I would voluntarily have left them; but they did not care to displace me on account merely of my zeal for the association, and they could not well give another reason.

Indeed I had some cause to believe that the defense of the country was not disagreeable to any of them, provided they were not requir'd to assist in it. And I found that a much greater number of them than I could have imagined, tho' against offensive war, were clearly for the defensive. Many pamphlets *pro and con* were publish'd on the subject, and some by good Quakers, in favour of defense, which I believe convinc'd most of their younger people.

A transaction in our fire company gave me some insight into their prevailing sentiments. It had been propos'd that we should encourage

---

* Wm. Penn's agents sought recruits for the colony of Pennsylvania in the low countries of Germany, and there are still in eastern Pennsylvania many Germans, inaccurately called Pennsylvania Dutch. Many of them use a Germanized English.

the scheme for building a battery by laying out the present stock, then about sixty pounds, in tickets of the lottery. By our rules, no money could be dispos'd of till the next meeting after the proposal. The company consisted of thirty members, of which twenty-two were Quakers, and eight only of other persuasions. We eight punctually attended the meeting; but, tho' we thought that some of the Quakers would join us, we were by no means sure of a majority. Only one Quaker, Mr. James Morris, appear'd to oppose the measure. He expressed much sorrow that it had ever been propos'd, as he said *Friends* were all against it, and it would create such discord as might break up the company. We told him that we saw no reason for that; we were the minority, and if *Friends* were against the measure, and outvoted us, we must and should, agreeably to the usage of all societies, submit. When the hour for business arriv'd it was mov'd to put the vote; he allow'd we might then do it by the rules, but, as he could assure us that a number of members intended to be present for the purpose of opposing it, it would be but candid to allow a little time for their appearing.

While we were disputing this, a waiter came to tell me two gentlemen below desir'd to speak with me. I went down, and found they were two of our Quaker members. They told me there were eight of them assembled at a tavern just by; that they were determin'd to come and vote with us if there should be occasion, which they hop'd would not be the case, and desir'd we would not call for their assistance if we could do without it, as their voting for such a measure might embroil them with their elders and friends. Being thus secure of a majority, I went up, and after a little seeming hesitation, agreed to a delay of another hour. This Mr. Morris allow'd to be extreamly fair. Not one of his opposing friends appear'd, at which he express'd great surprize; and, at the expiration of the hour, we carri'd the resolution eight to one; and as, of the twenty-two Quakers, eight were ready to vote with us, and thirteen, by their absence, manifested that they were not inclin'd to oppose the measure, I afterward estimated the proportion of Quakers sincerely against defense as one to twenty-one only; for these were all regular members of that society, and in good reputation among them, and had due notice of what was propos'd at that meeting.

The honorable and learned Mr. Logan, who had always been of that sect, was one who wrote an address to them, declaring his approbation of defensive war, and supporting his opinion by many strong arguments.

He put into my hands sixty pounds to be laid out in lottery tickets for the battery, with directions to apply what prizes might be drawn wholly to that service. He told me the following anecdote of his old master, William Penn, respecting defense. He came over from England, when a young man, with that proprietary, and as his secretary. It was war-time, and their ship was chas'd by an armed vessel, suppos'd to be an enemy. Their captain prepar'd for defense; but told William Penn, and his company of Quakers, that he did not expect their assistance, and they might retire into the cabin, which they did, except James Logan,[*] who chose to stay upon deck, and was quarter'd to a gun. The suppos'd enemy prov'd a friend, so there was no fighting; but when the secretary went down to communicate the intelligence, William Penn rebuk'd him severely for staying upon deck, and undertaking to assist in defending the vessel, contrary to the principles of *Friends*, especially as it had not been required by the captain. This reproof, being before all the company, piqu'd the secretary, who answer'd, *"I being thy servant, why did thee not order me to come down? But thee was willing enough that I should stay and help to fight the ship when thee thought there was danger."*

My being many years in the Assembly, the majority of which were constantly Quakers, gave me frequent opportunities of seeing the embarrassment given them by their principle against war, whenever application was made to them, by order of the crown, to grant aids for military purposes. They were unwilling to offend government, on the one hand, by a direct refusal; and their friends, the body of the Quakers, on the other, by compliance contrary to their principles; hence a variety of evasions to avoid complying, and modes of disguising the compliance when it became unavoidable. The common mode at last was, to grant money under the phrase of its being *"for the king's use,"* and never to inquire how it was applied.

But, if the demand was not directly from the crown, that phrase was found not so proper, and some other was to be invented. As, when powder was wanting (I think it was for the garrison at Louisburg), and the government of New England solicited a grant of some from Pennsylvania, which was much urg'd on the House by Governor Thomas, they could not grant money to buy powder, because that

---

[*] James Logan (1674–1751) came to America with William Penn in 1699, and was the business agent for the Penn family. He bequeathed his valuable library, preserved at his country seat, "Senton", to the city of Philadelphia.—Smyth.

was an ingredient of war; but they voted an aid to New England of three thousand pounds, to be put into the hands of the governor, and appropriated it for the purchasing of bread, flour, wheat or *other grain*. Some of the council, desirous of giving the House still further embarrassment, advis'd the governor not to accept provision, as not being the thing he had demanded; but he repli'd, "I shall take the money, for I understand very well their meaning; other grain is gunpowder," which he accordingly bought, and they never objected to it.*

It was in allusion to this fact that, when in our fire company we feared the success of our proposal in favour of the lottery, and I had said to my friend Mr. Syng, one of our members, "If we fail, let us move the purchase of a fire-engine with the money; the Quakers can have no objection to that; and then, if you nominate me and I you as a committee for that purpose, we will buy a great gun, which is certainly a *fire-engine*." "I see," says he, "you have improv'd by being so long in the Assembly; your equivocal project would be just a match for their wheat or *other grain*."

These embarrassments that the Quakers suffer'd from having establish'd and published it as one of their principles that no kind of war was lawful, and which, being once published, they could not afterwards, however they might change their minds, easily get rid of, reminds me of what I think a more prudent conduct in another sect among us, that of the Dunkers. I was acquainted with one of its founders, Michael Welfare, soon after it appear'd. He complain'd to me that they were grievously calumniated by the zealots of other persuasions, and charg'd with abominable principles and practices to which they were utter strangers. I told him this had always been the case with new sects, and that, to put a stop to such abuse, I imagin'd it might be well to publish the articles of their belief, and the rules of their discipline. He said that it had been propos'd among them, but not agreed to, for this reason: "When we were first drawn together as a society," says he, "it had pleased God to enlighten our minds so far as to see that some doctrines, which we once esteemed truths, were errors; and that others, which we had esteemed errors, were real truths. From time to time He has been pleased to afford us farther light, and our principles have been improving, and our errors diminishing. Now we

---

* See the votes.—*Marg. note.*

are not sure that we are arrived at the end of this progression, and at the perfection of spiritual or theological knowledge; and we fear that, if we should once print our confession of faith, we should feel ourselves as if bound and confin'd by it, and perhaps be unwilling to receive further improvement, and our successors still more so, as conceiving what we their elders and founders had done, to be something sacred, never to be departed from."

This modesty in a sect is perhaps a singular instance in the history of mankind, every other sect supposing itself in possession of all truth, and that those who differ are so far in the wrong; like a man traveling in foggy weather, those at some distance before him on the road he sees wrapped up in the fog, as well as those behind him, and also the people in the fields on each side, but near him all appears clear, tho' in truth he is as much in the fog as any of them. To avoid this kind of embarrassment, the Quakers have of late years been gradually declining the public service in the Assembly and in the magistracy, choosing rather to quit their power than their principle.

In order of time, I should have mentioned before, that having, in 1742, invented an open stove* for the better warming of rooms, and at the same time saving fuel, as the fresh air admitted was warmed in entering, I made a present of the model to Mr. Robert Grace, one of my early friends, who, having an iron-furnace,† found the casting of the plates for these stoves a profitable thing, as they were growing in demand. To promote that demand, I wrote and published a pamphlet, entitled "*An Account of the new-invented Pennsylvania Fireplaces; wherein their Construction and Manner of Operation is particularly explained; their Advantages above every other Method of warming Rooms demonstrated; and all Objections that have been raised against the Use of them answered and obviated,*" etc. This pamphlet had a good effect. Gov'r. Thomas was so pleas'd with the construction of this stove, as described in it, that he offered to give me a patent for the sole vending of them for a term of years; but I declin'd it from a principle which has ever weighed with me on such occasions, viz., *That, as we enjoy great advantages from the inventions of others, we should be glad of an opportunity to serve others by any invention of ours; and this we should do freely and generously.*

An ironmonger in London however, assuming a good deal of my

---

\* The Franklin stove is still in use.
† Warwick Furnace, Chester County, Pennsylvania, across the Schuylkill River from Pottstown.

pamphlet, and working it up into his own, and making some small changes in the machine, which rather hurt its operation, got a patent for it there, and made, as I was told, a little fortune by it. And this is not the only instance of patents taken out for my inventions by others, tho' not always with the same success, which I never contested, as having no desire of profiting by patents myself, and hating disputes. The use of these fireplaces in very many houses, both of this and the neighbouring colonies, has been, and is, a great saving of wood to the inhabitants.

# XIII
## Public Services and Duties
### (1749–1753)

Peace being concluded, and the association business therefore at an end, I turn'd my thoughts again to the affair of establishing an academy. The first step I took was to associate in the design a number of active friends, of whom the Junto furnished a good part; the next was to write and publish a pamphlet, entitled "Proposals Relating to the Education of Youth in Pennsylvania." This I distributed among the principal inhabitants gratis; and as soon as I could suppose their minds a little prepared by the perusal of it, I set on foot a subscription for opening and supporting an academy; it was to be paid in quotas yearly for five years; by so dividing it, I judg'd the subscription might be larger, and I believe it was so, amounting to no less, if I remember right, than five thousand pounds.

In the introduction to these proposals, I stated their publication, not as an act of mine, but of some *publick-spirited gentlemen*, avoiding as much as I could, according to my usual rule, the presenting myself to the publick as the author of any scheme for their benefit.

The subscribers, to carry the project into immediate execution, chose out of their number twenty-four trustees, and appointed Mr. Francis,[*] then attorney-general, and myself to draw up constitutions for the government of the academy; which being done and signed, a house was hired, masters engag'd, and the schools opened, I think, in the same year, 1749.

The scholars increasing fast, the house was soon found too small, and we were looking out for a piece of ground, properly situated, with intention to build, when Providence threw into our way a large house ready built, which, with a few alterations, might well serve our purpose.

---

[*] Tench Francis, uncle of Sir Philip Francis, emigrated from England to Maryland, and became attorney for Lord Baltimore. He removed to Philadelphia and was attorney-general of Pennsylvania from 1741 to 1755. He died in Philadelphia August 16, 1758.—Smyth.

This was the building before mentioned, erected by the hearers of Mr. Whitefield, and was obtained for us in the following manner.

It is to be noted that the contributions to this building being made by people of different sects, care was taken in the nomination of trustees, in whom the building and ground was to be vested, that a predominancy should not be given to any sect, lest in time that predominancy might be a means of appropriating the whole to the use of such sect, contrary to the original intention. It was therefore that one of each sect was appointed, viz., one Church-of-England man, one Presbyterian, one Baptist, one Moravian, etc., those, in case of vacancy by death, were to fill it by election from among the contributors. The Moravian happen'd not to please his colleagues, and on his death they resolved to have no other of that sect. The difficulty then was, how to avoid having two of some other sect, by means of the new choice.

Several persons were named, and for that reason not agreed to. At length one mention'd me, with the observation that I was merely an honest man, and of no sect at all, which prevailed with them to chuse me. The enthusiasm which existed when the house was built had long since abat'd, and its trustees had not been able to procure fresh contributions for paying the ground-rent, and discharging some other debts the building had occasion'd, which embarrass'd them greatly. Being now a member of both sets of trustees, that for the building and that for the academy, I had a good opportunity of negotiating with both, and brought them finally to an agreement, by which the trustees for the building were to cede it to those of the academy, the latter undertaking to discharge the debt, to keep forever open in the building a large hall for occasional preachers, according to the original intention, and maintain a free-school for the instruction of poor children. Writings were accordingly drawn, and on paying the debts the trustees of the academy were put in possession of the premises; and by dividing the great and lofty hall into stories, and different rooms above and below for the several schools, and purchasing some additional ground, the whole was soon made fit for our purpose, and the scholars remov'd into the building. The care and trouble of agreeing with the workmen, purchasing materials, and superintending the work, fell upon me; and I went thro' it the more cheerfully, as it did not then interfere with my private business, having the year before taken a very able, industrious, and honest partner, Mr. David Hall, with whose character I was well acquainted, as he had work'd for me four years. He took off my hands all care of the printing-office, paying me punctually my share of the profits. The partnership continued eighteen years, successfully for us both.

The trustees of the academy, after a while, were incorporated by a charter from the governor; their funds were increas'd by contributions in Britain and grants of land from the proprietaries, to which the Assembly has since made considerable addition; and thus was established the present University of Philadelphia.* I have been continued one of its trustees from the beginning, now near forty years, and have had the very great pleasure of seeing a number of the youth who have receiv'd their education in it, distinguish'd by their improv'd abilities, serviceable in public stations, and ornaments to their country.

When I disengaged myself, as above mentioned, from private business, I flatter'd myself that, by the sufficient tho' moderate fortune I had acquir'd, I had secured leisure during the rest of my life for philosophical studies and amusements. I purchased all Dr. Spence's apparatus, who had come from England to lecture here, and I proceeded in my electrical experiments with great alacrity; but the publick, now considering me as a man of leisure, laid hold of me for their purposes, every part of our civil government, and almost at the same time, imposing some duty upon me. The governor put me into the commission of the peace; the corporation of the city chose me of the common council, and soon after an alderman; and the citizens at large chose me a burgess to represent them in Assembly. This latter station was the more agreeable to me, as I was at length tired with sitting there to hear debates, in which, as clerk, I could take no part, and which were often so unentertaining that I was induc'd to amuse myself with making magic squares or circles, or anything to avoid weariness; and I conceiv'd my becoming a member would enlarge my power of doing good. I would not, however, insinuate that my ambition was not flatter'd by all these promotions; it certainly was; for, considering my low beginning, they were great things to me; and they were still more pleasing, as being so many spontaneous testimonies of the public good opinion, and by me entirely unsolicited.

The office of justice of the peace I try'd a little, by attending a few

---

* Later called the University of Pennsylvania.

courts, and sitting on the bench to hear causes; but finding that more knowledge of the common law than I possess'd was necessary to act in that station with credit, I gradually withdrew from it, excusing myself by my being oblig'd to attend the higher duties of a legislator in the Assembly. My election to this trust was repeated every year for ten years, without my ever asking any elector for his vote, or signifying, either directly or indirectly, any desire of being chosen. On taking my seat in the House, my son was appointed their clerk.

The year following, a treaty being to be held with the Indians at Carlisle, the governor sent a message to the House, proposing that they should nominate some of their members, to be join'd with some members of council, as commissioners for that purpose.* The House named the speaker (Mr. Norris) and myself; and, being commission'd, we went to Carlisle, and met the Indians accordingly.

As those people are extreamly apt to get drunk, and, when so, are very quarrelsome and disorderly, we strictly forbade the selling any liquor to them; and when they complain'd of this restriction, we told them that if they would continue sober during the treaty, we would give them plenty of rum when business was over. They promis'd this, and they kept their promise, because they could get no liquor, and the treaty was conducted very orderly, and concluded to mutual satisfaction. They then claim'd and received the rum; this was in the afternoon: they were near one hundred men, women, and children, and were lodg'd in temporary cabins, built in the form of a square, just without the town. In the evening, hearing a great noise among them, the commissioners walk'd out to see what was the matter. We found they had made a great bonfire in the middle of the square; they were all drunk, men and women, quarreling and fighting. Their dark-colour'd bodies, half naked, seen only by the gloomy light of the bonfire, running after and beating one another with firebrands, accompanied by their horrid yellings, form'd a scene the most resembling our ideas of hell that could well be imagin'd; there was no appeasing the tumult, and we retired to our lodging. At midnight a number of them came thundering at our door, demanding more rum, of which we took no notice.

The next day, sensible they had misbehav'd in giving us that disturbance, they sent three of their old counselors to make their apology.

---

* See the votes to have this more correctly.—*Marg. note.*

The orator acknowledg'd the fault, but laid it upon the rum; and then endeavoured to excuse the rum by saying, "*The Great Spirit, who made all things, made everything for some use, and whatever use he design'd*

*anything for, that use it should always be put to. Now, when he made rum, he said, 'Let this be for the Indians to get drunk with,' and it must be so.*" And, indeed, if it be the design of Providence to extirpate these savages in order to make room for cultivators of the earth, it seems not improbable that rum may be the appointed means. It has already annihilated all the tribes who formerly inhabited the sea-coast.

In 1751, Dr. Thomas Bond, a particular friend of mine, conceived the idea of establishing a hospital in Philadelphia (a very beneficent design, which has been ascrib'd to me, but was originally his), for the reception and cure of poor sick persons, whether inhabitants of the province or strangers. He was zealous and active in endeavouring to procure subscriptions for it, but the proposal being a novelty in America, and at first not well understood, he met but with small success.

At length he came to me with the compliment that he found there was no such thing as carrying a public-spirited project through without my being concern'd in it. "For," says he, "I am often ask'd by those to whom I propose subscribing, Have you consulted Franklin upon this business? And what does he think of it? And when I tell them that I have not (supposing it rather out of your line), they do not subscribe, but say they will consider of it." I enquired into the nature and probable utility of his scheme, and receiving from him a very satisfactory explanation, I not only subscrib'd to it myself, but engag'd heartily in the design of procuring subscriptions from others. Previously, however, to the solicitation, I endeavoured to prepare the minds of the people by writing on the subject in the newspapers, which was my usual custom in such cases, but which he had omitted.

The subscriptions afterwards were more free and generous; but, beginning to flag, I saw they would be insufficient without some assistance from the Assembly, and therefore propos'd to petition for it, which was done. The country members did not at first relish the project; they objected that it could only be serviceable to the city, and therefore the citizens alone should be at the expense of it; and they doubted whether the citizens themselves generally approv'd of it. My allegation on the contrary, that it met with such approbation as to leave no doubt of our being able to raise two thousand pounds by voluntary donations, they considered as a most extravagant supposition, and utterly impossible.

On this I form'd my plan; and, asking leave to bring in a bill for incorporating the contributors according to the prayer of their petition, and granting them a blank sum of money, which leave was obtained chiefly on the consideration that the House could throw the bill out if they did not like it, I drew it so as to make the important clause a conditional one, viz., "And be it enacted, by the authority aforesaid, that when the said contributors shall have met and chosen their managers and treasurer, *and shall have raised by their contributions a capital stock of two thousand pounds value* (the yearly interest of which is to be applied to the accommodating of the sick poor in the said hospital, free of charge for diet, attendance, advice, and medicines), *and shall make the same appear to the satisfaction of the speaker of the Assembly for the time being*, that *then* it shall and may be lawful for the said speaker, and he is hereby required, to sign an order on the provincial treasurer for the payment of two thousand pounds, in two yearly payments, to the treasurer of the said hospital, to be applied to the founding, building, and finishing of the same."

This condition carried the bill through; for the members, who had oppos'd the grant, and now conceiv'd they might have the credit of being charitable without the expense, agreed to its passage; and then, in soliciting subscriptions among the people, we urg'd the conditional promise of the law as an additional motive to give, since every man's donation would be doubled; thus the clause work'd both ways. The subscriptions accordingly soon exceeded the requisite sum, and we claim'd and receiv'd the public gift, which enabled us to carry the design into execution. A convenient and handsome building was soon erected; the institution has by constant experience been found useful, and flourishes to this day; and I do not remember any of my political manoeuvers, the success of which gave me at the time more pleasure, or wherein, after thinking of it, I more easily excus'd myself for having made some use of cunning.

It was about this time that another projector, the Rev. Gilbert Tennent,* came to me with a request that I would assist him in procuring a subscription for erecting a new meeting-house. It was to be for the use of a congregation he had gathered among the Presbyterians, who were originally disciples of Mr. Whitefield. Unwilling to make myself disagreeable to my fellow-citizens by too frequently soliciting their contributions, I absolutely refus'd. He then desired I would furnish him with a list of the names of persons I knew by experience to be generous and public-spirited. I thought it would be unbecoming in me, after their kind compliance with my solicitations, to mark them out to be worried by other beggars, and therefore refus'd also to give such a list. He then desir'd I would at least give him my advice. "That I will readily do," said I; "and, in the first place, I advise you to apply to all those whom you know will give something; next, to those whom you are uncertain whether they will give anything or not, and show them the list of those who have given; and, lastly, do not neglect those who you are sure will give nothing, for in some of them you may be mistaken." He laugh'd and thank'd me, and said he would take my advice. He did so, for he ask'd of *everybody*, and he obtain'd a much larger sum than he expected, with which he erected the capacious and very elegant meeting-house that stands in Arch-street.

Our city, tho' laid out with a beautiful regularity, the streets large, straight, and crossing each other at right angles, had the disgrace of suffering those streets to remain long unpav'd, and in wet weather the wheels of heavy carriages plough'd them into a quagmire, so that it

---

* Gilbert Tennent (1703–1764) came to America with his father, Rev. William Tennent, and taught for a time in the "Log College," from which sprang the College of New Jersey.—Smyth.

was difficult to cross them; and in dry weather the dust was offensive. I had liv'd near what was call'd the Jersey Market, and saw with pain the inhabitants wading in mud while purchasing their provisions. A strip of ground down the middle of that market was at length pav'd with brick, so that, being once in the market, they had firm footing, but were often over shoes in dirt to get there. By talking and writing on the subject, I was at length instrumental in getting the street pav'd with stone between the market and the brick'd foot-pavement, that was on each side next the houses. This, for some time, gave an easy access to the market dry-shod; but, the rest of the street not being pav'd, whenever a carriage came out of the mud upon this pavement, it shook off and left its dirt upon it, and it was soon cover'd with mire, which was not remov'd, the city as yet having no scavengers.

After some inquiry, I found a poor, industrious man, who was willing to undertake keeping the pavement clean, by sweeping it twice a week, carrying off the dirt from before all the neighbours' doors, for the sum of sixpence per month, to be paid by each house. I then wrote and printed a paper setting forth the advantages to the neighbourhood that might be obtain'd by this small expense; the greater ease in keeping our houses clean, so much dirt not being brought in by people's feet; the benefit to the shops by more custom, etc., etc., as buyers could more easily get at them; and by not having, in windy weather, the dust blown in upon their goods, etc., etc. I sent one of these papers to each house, and in a day or two went round to see who would subscribe an agreement to pay these sixpences; it was unanimously sign'd, and for a time well executed. All the inhabitants of the city were delighted with the cleanliness of the pavement that surrounded the market, it being a convenience to all, and this rais'd a general desire to have all the streets paved, and made the people more willing to submit to a tax for that purpose.

After some time I drew a bill for paving the city, and brought it into the Assembly. It was just before I went to England, in 1757, and did not pass till I was gone,* and then with an alteration in the mode of assessment, which I thought not for the better, but with an additional provision for lighting as well as paving the streets, which was a great improvement. It was by a private person, the late Mr. John Clifton,

---

* See votes.

his giving a sample of the utility of lamps, by placing one at his door, that the people were first impress'd with the idea of enlighting all the city. The honour of this public benefit has also been ascrib'd to me, but it belongs truly to that gentleman. I did but follow his example, and have only some merit to claim respecting the form of our lamps, as differing from the globe lamps we were at first supply'd with from London. Those we found inconvenient in these respects: they admitted no air below; the smoke, therefore, did not readily go out above, but circulated in the globe, lodg'd on its inside, and soon obstructed the light they were intended to afford; giving, besides, the daily trouble of wiping them clean; and an accidental stroke on one of them would demolish it, and render it totally useless. I therefore suggested the composing them of four flat panes, with a long funnel above to draw up the smoke, and crevices admitting air below, to facilitate the ascent of the smoke; by this means they were kept clean, and did not grow dark in a few hours, as the London lamps do, but continu'd bright till morning, and an accidental stroke would generally break but a single pane, easily repair'd.

I have sometimes wonder'd that the Londoners did not, from the effect holes in the bottom of the globe lamps us'd at Vauxhall* have in keeping them clean, learn to have such holes in their street lamps. But, these holes being made for another purpose, viz., to communicate flame more suddenly to the wick by a little flax hanging down thro' them, the other use, of letting in air, seems not to have been thought of; and therefore, after the lamps have been lit a few hours, the streets of London are very poorly illuminated.

The mention of these improvements puts me in mind of one I propos'd, when in London, to Dr. Fothergill, who was among the best men I have known, and a great promoter of useful projects. I had observ'd that the streets, when dry, were never swept, and the light dust carried away; but it was suffer'd to accumulate till wet weather reduc'd it to mud, and then, after lying some days so deep on the pavement that there was no crossing but in paths kept clean by poor people with brooms, it was with great labour rak'd together and thrown up into

---

* Vauxhall Gardens, once a popular and fashionable London resort, situated on the Thames above Lambeth. The Gardens were closed in 1859, but they will always be remembered because of Sir Roger de Coverley's visit to them in the *Spectator* and from the descriptions in Smollett's *Humphry Clinker* and Thackeray's *Vanity Fair*.

carts open above, the sides of which suffered some of the slush at every jolt on the pavement to shake out and fall, sometimes to the annoyance of foot-passengers. The reason given for not sweeping the dusty streets was that the dust would fly into the windows of shops and houses.

An accidental occurrence had instructed me how much sweeping might be done in a little time. I found at my door in Craven-street,* one morning, a poor woman sweeping my pavement with a birch broom; she appeared very pale and feeble, as just come out of a fit of sickness. I ask'd who employ'd her to sweep there; she said, "Nobody, but I am very poor and in distress, and I sweeps before gentle-folkses doors, and hopes they will give me something." I bid her sweep the whole street clean, and I would give her a shilling; this was at nine o'clock; at 12 she came for the shilling. From the slowness I saw at first in her working, I could scarce believe that the work was done so soon, and sent my servant to examine it, who reported that the whole street was swept perfectly clean, and all the dust plac'd in the gutter, which was in the middle; and the next rain wash'd it quite away, so that the pavement and even the kennel were perfectly clean.

I then judg'd that, if that feeble woman could sweep such a street in three hours, a strong, active man might have done it in half the time. And here let me remark the convenience of having but one gutter in

---

* A short street near Charing Cross, London.

such a narrow street, running down its middle, instead of two, one on each side, near the footway; for where all the rain that falls on a street runs from the sides and meets in the middle, it forms there a current strong enough to wash away all the mud it meets with; but when divided into two channels, it is often too weak to cleanse either, and only makes the mud it finds more fluid, so that the wheels of carriages and feet of horses throw and dash it upon the foot-pavement, which is thereby rendered foul and slippery, and sometimes splash it upon those who are walking. My proposal, communicated to the good doctor, was as follows:

"For the more effectual cleaning and keeping clean the streets of London and Westminster, it is proposed that the several watchmen be contracted with to have the dust swept up in dry seasons, and the mud rak'd up at other times, each in the several streets and lanes of his round; that they be furnish'd with brooms and other proper instruments for these purposes, to be kept at their respective stands, ready to furnish the poor people they may employ in the service.

"That in the dry summer months the dust be all swept up into heaps at proper distances, before the shops and windows of houses are usually opened, when the scavengers, with close-covered carts, shall also carry it all away.

"That the mud, when rak'd up, be not left in heaps to be spread abroad again by the wheels of carriages and trampling of horses, but that the scavengers be provided with bodies of carts, not plac'd high upon wheels, but low upon sliders, with lattice bottoms, which, being cover'd with straw, will retain the mud thrown into them, and permit the water to drain from it, whereby it will become much lighter, water making the greatest part of its weight; these bodies of carts to be plac'd at convenient distances, and the mud brought to them in wheelbarrows; they remaining where plac'd till the mud is drain'd, and then horses brought to draw them away."

I have since had doubts of the practicability of the latter part of this proposal, on account of the narrowness of some streets, and the difficulty of placing the draining-sleds so as not to encumber too much the passage; but I am still of opinion that the former, requiring the dust to be swept up and carry'd away before the shops are open, is very practicable in the summer, when the days are long; for, in walking thro' the Strand and Fleet-street one morning at seven o'clock, I observ'd there was not one shop open, tho' it had been daylight and the sun up above three hours; the inhabitants of London chusing voluntarily to live much by candle-light, and sleep by sunshine, and yet often complain, a little absurdly, of the duty on candles, and the high price of tallow.

Some may think these trifling matters not worth minding or relating; but when they consider that tho' dust blown into the eyes of a single person, or into a single shop on a windy day, is but of small importance, yet the great number of the instances in a populous city, and its frequent repetitions give it weight and consequence, perhaps they will not censure very severely those who bestow some attention to affairs of this seemingly low nature. Human felicity is produced not so much by great pieces of good fortune that seldom happen, as by little advantages that occur every day. Thus, if you teach a poor young man to shave himself, and keep his razor in order, you may contribute more to the happiness of his life than in giving him a thousand guineas. The money may be soon spent, the regret only remaining of having foolishly consumed it; but in the other case, he escapes the frequent vexation of waiting for barbers, and of their sometimes dirty fingers, offensive breaths, and dull razors; he shaves when most convenient to him, and enjoys daily the pleasure of its being done with a good instrument. With these sentiments I have hazarded the few preceding pages, hoping they may afford hints which some time or other may be useful to a city I love, having lived many years in it very happily, and perhaps to some of our towns in America.

Having been for some time employed by the postmaster-general of America as his comptroller in regulating several offices, and bringing the officers to account, I was, upon his death in 1753, appointed, jointly with Mr. William Hunter, to succeed him, by a commission from the postmaster-general in England. The American office never had hitherto paid anything to that of Britain. We were to have six hundred pounds a year between us, if we could make that sum out of the profits of the office. To do this, a variety of improvements were necessary; some of these were inevitably at first expensive, so that in the first four years the office became above nine hundred pounds in debt to us. But it soon after began to repay us; and before I was displac'd by a freak of the ministers, of which I shall speak hereafter, we had brought it to yield *three times* as much clear revenue to the crown as the post-office of Ireland. Since that imprudent transaction, they have receiv'd from it—not one farthing!

The business of the post-office occasion'd my taking a journey this year to New England, where the College of Cambridge, of their own motion, presented me with the degree of Master of Arts. Yale College, in Connecticut, had before made me a similar compliment. Thus, without studying in any college, I came to partake of their honours. They were conferr'd in consideration of my improvements and discoveries in the electric branch of natural philosophy.

# XIV
## *Albany Plan of Union*

In 1754, war with France being again apprehended, a congress of commissioners from the different colonies was, by an order of the Lords of Trade, to be assembled at Albany, there to confer with the chiefs of the Six Nations concerning the means of defending both their country and ours. Governor Hamilton, having receiv'd this order, acquainted the House with it, requesting they would furnish proper presents for the Indians, to be given on this occasion; and naming the speaker (Mr. Norris) and myself to join Mr. Thomas Penn and Mr. Secretary Peters as commissioners to act for Pennsylvania. The House approv'd the nomination, and provided the goods for the present, and tho' they did not much like treating out of the provinces; and we met the other commissioners at Albany about the middle of June.

In our way thither, I projected and drew a plan for the union of all the colonies under one government, so far as might be necessary for defense, and other important general purposes. As we pass'd thro' New York, I had there shown my project to Mr. James Alexander and Mr. Kennedy, two gentlemen of great knowledge in public affairs, and, being fortified by their approbation, I ventur'd to lay it before the Congress. It then appeared that several of the commissioners had form'd plans of the same kind. A previous question was first taken, whether a union should be established, which pass'd in the affirmative unanimously. A committee was then appointed, one member from each colony, to consider the several plans and report. Mine happen'd to be preferr'd, and, with a few amendments, was accordingly reported.

By this plan the general government was to be administer'd by a president-general, appointed and supported by the crown, and a grand council was to be chosen by the representatives of the people of the several colonies, met in their respective assemblies. The debates upon it in Congress went on daily, hand in hand with the Indian business. Many objections and difficulties were started, but at length they were all overcome, and the plan was unanimously agreed to, and copies ordered

to be transmitted to the Board of Trade and to the assemblies of the several provinces. Its fate was singular; the assemblies did not adopt it, as they all thought there was too much *prerogative* in it, and in England it was judg'd to have too much of the *democratic*. The Board of Trade therefore did not approve of it, nor recommend it for the approbation of his majesty; but another scheme was form'd, supposed to answer the same purpose better, whereby the governors of the provinces, with some members of their respective councils, were to meet and order the raising of troops, building of forts, etc., and to draw on the treasury of Great Britain for the expense, which was afterwards to be refunded by an act of Parliament laying a tax on America. My plan, with my reasons in support of it, is to be found among my political papers that are printed.

Being the winter following in Boston, I had much conversation with Governor Shirley upon both the plans. Part of what passed between us on the occasion may also be seen among those papers. The different and contrary reasons of dislike to my plan makes me suspect that it was really the true medium; and I am still of opinion it would have been happy for both sides the water if it had been adopted. The colonies, so united, would have been sufficiently strong to have defended themselves; there would then have been no need of troops from England; of course, the subsequent pretence for taxing America, and the bloody contest it occasioned, would have been avoided. But such mistakes are not new; history is full of the errors of states and princes.

> "Look round the habitable world, how few
> Know their own good, or, knowing it, pursue!"

Those who govern, having much business on their hands, do not generally like to take the trouble of considering and carrying into execution new projects. The best public measures are therefore seldom *adopted from previous wisdom, but forc'd by the occasion.*

The Governor of Pennsylvania, in sending it down to the Assembly, expressed his approbation of the plan, "as appearing to him to be drawn up with great clearness and strength of judgment, and therefore recommended it as well worthy of their closest and most serious attention." The House, however, by the management of a certain member, took it up when I happen'd to be absent, which I thought not very fair, and reprobated it without paying any attention to it at all, to my no small mortification.

# XV
## Quarrels with the Proprietary Governors

I n my journey to Boston this year, I met at New York with our new governor, Mr. Morris, just arriv'd there from England, with whom I had been before intimately acquainted. He brought a commission to supersede Mr. Hamilton, who, tir'd with the disputes his proprietary instructions subjected him to, had resign'd. Mr. Morris ask'd me if I thought he must expect as uncomfortable an administration. I said, "No; you may, on the contrary, have a very comfortable one, if you will only take care not to enter into any dispute with the Assembly." "My dear friend," says he, pleasantly, "how can you advise my avoiding disputes? You know I love disputing; it is one of my greatest pleasures; however, to show the regard I have for your counsel, I promise you I will, if possible, avoid them." He had some reason for loving to dispute, being eloquent, an acute sophister, and, therefore, generally successful in argumentative conversation. He had been brought up to it from a boy, his father, as I have heard, accustoming his children to dispute with one another for his diversion, while sitting at table after dinner; but I think the practice was not wise; for, in the course of my observation, these disputing, contradicting, and confuting people are generally unfortunate in their affairs. They get victory sometimes, but they never get good will, which would be of more use to them. We parted, he going to Philadelphia, and I to Boston.

In returning, I met at New York with the votes of the Assembly, by which it appear'd that, notwithstanding his promise to me, he and the House were already in high contention; and it was a continual battle between them as long as he retain'd the government. I had my share of it; for, as soon as I got back to my seat in the Assembly, I was put on every committee for answering his speeches and messages, and by the committees always desired to make the drafts. Our answers, as well as his messages, were often tart, and sometimes indecently abusive; and, as he knew I wrote for the Assembly, one might have imagined that, when we met, we could hardly avoid cutting throats; but he was so

good-natur'd a man that no personal difference between him and me was occasion'd by the contest, and we often din'd together.

One afternoon, in the height of this public quarrel, we met in the street. "Franklin," says he, "you must go home with me and spend the evening; I am to have some company that you will like;" and, taking me by the arm, he led me to his house. In gay conversation over our wine, after supper, he told us, jokingly, that he much admir'd the idea of Sancho Panza,* who, when it was proposed to give him a government, requested it might be a government of *blacks*, as then, if he could not agree with his people, he might sell them. One of his friends, who sat next to me, says, "Franklin, why do you continue to side with these damn'd Quakers? Had not you better sell them? The proprietor would give you a good price." "The governor," says I, "has not yet *blacked* them enough." He, indeed, had laboured hard to blacken the Assembly in all his messages, but they wip'd off his colouring as fast as he laid it on, and plac'd it, in return, thick upon his own face; so that, finding he

---

* The "round, selfish, and self-important" squire of Don Quixote in Cervantes' romance of that name.

was likely to be negrofied himself, he, as well as Mr. Hamilton, grew tir'd of the contest, and quitted the government.

These public quarrels* were all at bottom owing to the proprietaries, our hereditary governors, who, when any expense was to be incurred for the defense of their province, with incredible meanness instructed their deputies to pass no act for levying the necessary taxes, unless their vast estates were in the same act expressly excused; and they had even taken bonds of these deputies to observe such instructions. The Assemblies for three years held out against this injustice, tho' constrained to bend at last. At length Captain Denny, who was Governor Morris's successor, ventured to disobey those instructions; how that was brought about I shall show hereafter.

But I am got forward too fast with my story: there are still some transactions to be mention'd that happened during the administration of Governor Morris.

War being in a manner commenced with France, the government of Massachusetts Bay projected an attack upon Crown Point,† and sent Mr. Quincy to Pennsylvania, and Mr. Pownall, afterward Governor Pownall, to New York, to solicit assistance. As I was in the Assembly, knew its temper, and was Mr. Quincy's countryman, he appli'd to me for my influence and assistance. I dictated his address to them, which was well received. They voted an aid of ten thousand pounds, to be laid out in provisions. But the governor refusing his assent to their bill (which included this with other sums granted for the use of the crown), unless a clause were inserted exempting the proprietary estate from bearing any part of the tax that would be necessary, the Assembly, tho' very desirous of making their grant to New England effectual, were at a loss how to accomplish it. Mr. Quincy labored hard with the governor to obtain his assent, but he was obstinate.

I then suggested a method of doing the business without the governor, by orders on the trustees of the Loan office, which, by law, the Assembly had the right of drawing. There was, indeed, little or no money at that time in the office, and therefore I propos'd that the orders should be payable in a year, and to bear an interest of five per cent.

---

* My acts in Morris's time, military, etc.—*Marg. note.*

† On Lake Champlain, ninety miles north of Albany. It was captured by the French in 1731, attacked by the English in 1755 and 1756, and abandoned by the French in 1759. It was finally captured from the English by the Americans in 1775.

With these orders I suppos'd the provisions might easily be purchas'd. The Assembly, with very little hesitation, adopted the proposal. The orders were immediately printed, and I was one of the committee directed to sign and dispose of them. The fund for paying them was the interest of all the paper currency then extant in the province upon loan, together with the revenue arising from the excise, which being known to be more than sufficient, they obtain'd instant credit, and were not only receiv'd in payment for the provisions, but many money'd people, who had cash lying by them, vested it in those orders, which they found advantageous, as they bore interest while upon hand, and might on any occasion be used as money; so that they were eagerly all bought up, and in a few weeks none of them were to be seen. Thus this important affair was by my means completed. Mr. Quincy return'd thanks to the Assembly in a handsome memorial, went home highly pleas'd with this success of his embassy, and ever after bore for me the most cordial and affectionate friendship.

# XVI
## Braddock's Expedition
---

The British government, not chusing to permit the union of the
colonies as propos'd at Albany, and to trust that union with their
defense, lest they should thereby grow too military, and feel their
own strength, suspicions and jealousies at this time being entertain'd
of them, sent over General Braddock with two regiments of regular
English troops for that purpose. He landed at Alexandria, in Virginia,
and thence march'd to Frederictown, in Maryland, where he halted
for carriages. Our Assembly apprehending, from some information,
that he had conceived violent prejudices against them, as averse to
the service, wish'd me to wait upon him, not as from them, but as
postmaster-general, under the guise of proposing to settle with him the
mode of conducting with most celerity and certainty the despatches
between him and the governors of the several provinces, with whom
he must necessarily have continual correspondence, and of which they
propos'd to pay the expense. My son accompanied me on this journey.

We found the general at Frederictown, waiting impatiently for
the return of those he had sent thro' the back parts of Maryland and
Virginia to collect waggons. I stayed with him several days, din'd with
him daily, and had full opportunity of removing all his prejudices, by
the information of what the Assembly had before his arrival actually
done, and were still willing to do, to facilitate his operations. When
I was about to depart, the returns of waggons to be obtained were
brought in, by which it appear'd that they amounted only to twenty-
five, and not all of those were in serviceable condition. The general and
all the officers were surpris'd, declar'd the expedition was then at an end,
being impossible, and exclaim'd against the ministers for ignorantly
landing them in a country destitute of the means of conveying their
stores, baggage, etc., not less than one hundred and fifty waggons being
necessary.

I happen'd to say I thought it was pity they had not been landed
rather in Pennsylvania, as in that country almost every farmer had his

waggon. The general eagerly laid hold of my words, and said, "Then you, sir, who are a man of interest there, can probably procure them for us; and I beg you will undertake it." I ask'd what terms were to be offer'd the owners of the waggons, and I was desir'd to put on paper the terms that appeared to me necessary. This I did, and they were agreed to, and a commission and instructions accordingly prepar'd immediately. What those terms were will appear in the advertisement I publish'd as soon as I arriv'd at Lancaster, which being, from the great and sudden effect it produc'd, a piece of some curiosity, I shall insert it at length, as follows:

"Advertisement.

"Lancaster, *April* 26, 1755.

"Whereas, one hundred and fifty waggons, with four horses to each waggon, and fifteen hundred saddle or pack horses, are wanted for the service of his majesty's forces now about to rendezvous at Will's Creek, and his excellency General Braddock having been pleased to empower me to contract for the hire of the same, I hereby give notice that I shall attend for that purpose at Lancaster from this day to next Wednesday evening, and at York from next Thursday morning till Friday evening, where I shall be ready to agree for waggons and teams, or single horses, on the following terms, viz.: 1. That there shall be paid for each waggon, with four good horses and a driver, fifteen shillings per diem; and for each able horse with a pack-saddle, or other saddle and furniture, two shillings per diem; and for each able horse without a saddle, eighteen pence per diem. 2. That the pay commence from the time of their joining the forces at Will's Creek, which must be on or before the 20th of May ensuing, and that a reasonable allowance be paid over and above for the time necessary for their travelling to Will's Creek and home again after their discharge. 3. Each waggon and team, and every saddle or pack horse, is to be valued by indifferent persons chosen between me and the owner; and in case of the loss of any waggon, team, or other horse in the service, the price according to such valuation is to be allowed and paid. 4. Seven days' pay is to be advanced and paid in hand by me to the owner of each waggon and team, or horse, at the time of contracting, if required, and the remainder to be paid by General Braddock, or by the paymaster of the army, at the time of their discharge, or from time to time, as it shall be demanded. 5. No drivers of waggons, or persons taking care of the hired horses, are on any account to be called upon to do the duty of soldiers, or be otherwise employed than in conducting or taking care of their carriages or horses. 6. All oats, Indian corn, or other forage that waggons or horses bring to the camp, more than is necessary for the subsistence of the horses, is to be taken for the use of the army, and a reasonable price paid for the same.

"Note.—My son, William Franklin, is empowered to enter into like contracts with any person in Cumberland county.

B. Franklin."

*"To the inhabitants of the Counties of Lancaster, York, and Cumberland.*

"Friends and Countrymen,

"Being occasionally[*] at the camp at Frederic a few days since, I found the general and officers extremely exasperated on account of their not being supplied with horses and carriages, which had been expected from this province, as most able to furnish them; but, through the dissensions between our governor and Assembly, money had not been provided, nor any steps taken for that purpose.

---

* By chance.

"It was proposed to send an armed force immediately into these counties, to seize as many of the best carriages and horses as should be wanted, and compel as many persons into the service as would be necessary to drive and take care of them.

"I apprehended that the progress of British soldiers through these counties on such an occasion, especially considering the temper they are in, and their resentment against us, would be attended with many and great inconveniences to the inhabitants, and therefore more willingly took the trouble of trying first what might be done by fair and equitable means. The people of these back counties have lately complained to the Assembly that a sufficient currency was wanting; you have an opportunity of receiving and dividing among you a very considerable sum; for, if the service of this expedition should continue, as it is more than probable it will, for one hundred and twenty days, the hire of these waggons and horses will amount to upward of thirty thousand pounds, which will be paid you in silver and gold of the king's money.

"The service will be light and easy, for the army will scarce march above twelve miles per day, and the waggons and baggage-horses, as they carry those things that are absolutely necessary to the welfare of the army, must march with the army, and no faster; and are, for the army's sake, always placed where they can be most secure, whether in a march or in a camp.

"If you are really, as I believe you are, good and loyal subjects to his majesty, you may now do a most acceptable service, and make it easy to yourselves; for three or four of such as cannot separately spare from the business of their plantations a waggon and four horses and a driver, may do it together, one furnishing the waggon, another one or two horses, and another the driver, and divide the pay proportionately between you; but if you do not this service to your king and country voluntarily, when such good pay and reasonable terms are offered to you, your loyalty will be strongly suspected. The king's business must be done; so many brave troops, come so far for your defense, must not stand idle through your backwardness to do what may be reasonably expected from you; waggons and horses must be had; violent measures will probably be used, and you will be left to seek for a recompense where you can find it, and your case, perhaps, be little pitied or regarded.

"I have no particular interest in this affair, as, except the satisfaction of endeavouring to do good, I shall have only my labour for my pains. If this method of obtaining the waggons and horses is not likely to succeed, I am obliged to send word to the general in fourteen days; and I suppose Sir John St. Clair, the hussar, with a body of soldiers, will immediately enter the province for the purpose, which I shall be sorry to hear, because I am very sincerely and truly your friend and well-wisher,

B. FRANKLIN."

I received of the general about eight hundred pounds, to be disbursed in advance-money to the waggon owners, etc.; but that sum being insufficient, I advanc'd upward of two hundred pounds more, and in two weeks the one hundred and fifty waggons, with two hundred and fifty-nine carrying horses, were on their march for the camp. The advertisement promised payment according to the valuation, in case any waggon or horse should be lost. The owners, however, alleging they did not know General Braddock, or what dependence might be had on his promise, insisted on my bond for the performance, which I accordingly gave them.

While I was at the camp, supping one evening with the officers of Colonel Dunbar's regiment, he represented to me his concern for the subalterns, who, he said, were generally not in affluence, and could ill afford, in this dear country, to lay in the stores that might be necessary in so long a march, thro' a wilderness, where nothing was to be purchas'd. I commiserated their case, and resolved to endeavour procuring them some relief. I said nothing, however, to him of my intention, but wrote the next morning to the committee of the Assembly, who had the disposition of some public money, warmly recommending the case of these officers to their consideration, and proposing that a present should be sent them of necessaries and refreshments. My son, who had some experience of a camp life, and of its wants, drew up a list for me, which I enclos'd in my letter. The committee approv'd, and used such diligence that, conducted by my son, the stores arrived at the camp as soon as the waggons. They consisted of twenty parcels, each containing

| | |
|---|---|
| 6 lbs. loaf sugar. | 1 Gloucester cheese. |
| 6 lbs. good Muscovado do. | 1 kegg containing 20 lbs. |
| 1 lb. good green tea. | good butter. |
| 1 lb. good bohea do. | 2 doz. old Madeira wine. |
| 6 lbs. good ground coffee. | 2 gallons Jamaica spirits. |
| 6 lbs. chocolate. | 1 bottle flour of mustard. |
| 1-2 cwt. best white biscuit. | 2 well-cur'd hams. |
| 1-2 lb. pepper. | 1-2 dozen dry'd tongues. |
| 1 quart best white wine | 6 lbs. rice. |
| vinegar. | 6 lbs. raisins. |

These twenty parcels, well pack'd, were placed on as many horses, each parcel, with the horse, being intended as a present for one officer. They were very thankfully receiv'd, and the kindness acknowledg'd by letters to me from the colonels of both regiments, in the most grateful terms. The general, too, was highly satisfied with my conduct in procuring him the waggons, etc., and readily paid my account of disbursements, thanking me repeatedly, and requesting my farther assistance in sending provisions after him. I undertook this also, and was busily employ'd in it till we heard of his defeat, advancing for the service of my own money, upwards of one thousand pounds sterling, of which I sent him an account. It came to his hands, luckily for me, a few days before the battle, and he return'd me immediately an order on the paymaster for the round sum of one thousand pounds, leaving the remainder to the next account. I consider this payment as good luck, having never been able to obtain that remainder, of which more hereafter.

This general was, I think, a brave man, and might probably have made a figure as a good officer in some European war. But he had too much self-confidence, too high an opinion of the validity of regular troops, and too mean a one of both Americans and Indians. George Croghan, our Indian interpreter, join'd him on his march with one hundred of those people, who might have been of great use to his army as guides, scouts, etc., if he had treated them kindly; but he slighted and neglected them, and they gradually left him. In conversation with him one day, he was giving me some account of his intended progress. "After taking Fort Duquesne,"* says he, "I am to proceed to Niagara; and, having taken that, to Frontenac,† if the season will allow time; and I suppose it will, for Duquesne can hardly detain me above three or four days; and then I see nothing that can obstruct my march to Niagara." Having before revolv'd in my mind the long line his army must make in their march by a very narrow road, to be cut for them thro' the woods and bushes, and also what I had read of a former defeat of fifteen hundred French, who invaded the Iroquois country, I had conceiv'd some doubts and some fears for the event of the campaign. But I ventur'd only to say, "To be sure, sir, if you arrive well before Duquesne, with these fine troops, so well provided with artillery, that place not yet completely fortified, and as we hear with no very strong garrison, can probably make but a short resistance. The only danger I apprehend of obstruction to your march is from ambuscades of Indians, who, by constant practice, are dexterous in laying and executing them; and the slender line, near four miles long, which your army must make, may expose it to be attack'd by surprise in its flanks, and to be cut like a thread into several pieces, which, from their distance, cannot come up in time to support each other."

He smil'd at my ignorance, and reply'd, "These savages may, indeed, be a formidable enemy to your raw American militia, but upon the king's regular and disciplin'd troops, sir, it is impossible they should make any impression." I was conscious of an impropriety in my disputing with a military man in matters of his profession, and said no more. The enemy, however, did not take the advantage of his army which I apprehended its long line of march expos'd it to, but let it advance without interruption till within nine miles of the place; and

---

* Pittsburg.
† Kingston, at the eastern end of Lake Ontario.

then, when more in a body (for it had just passed a river, where the front had halted till all were come over), and in a more open part of the woods than any it had pass'd, attack'd its advanced guard by heavy fire from behind trees and bushes, which was the first intelligence the general had of an enemy's being near him. This guard being disordered, the general hurried the troops up to their assistance, which was done in great confusion, thro' waggons, baggage, and cattle; and presently the fire came upon their flank: the officers, being on horseback, were more easily distinguish'd, pick'd out as marks, and fell very fast; and the soldiers were crowded together in a huddle, having or hearing no orders, and standing to be shot at till two-thirds of them were killed; and then, being seiz'd with a panick, the whole fled with precipitation.

The waggoners took each a horse out of his team and scamper'd; their example was immediately followed by others; so that all the waggons, provisions, artillery, and stores were left to the enemy. The general, being wounded, was brought off with difficulty; his secretary, Mr. Shirley, was killed by his side; and out of eighty-six officers, sixty-three were killed or wounded, and seven hundred and fourteen men killed out of eleven hundred. These eleven hundred had been picked men from the whole army; the rest had been left behind with Colonel Dunbar, who was to follow with the heavier part of the stores, provisions, and baggage. The flyers, not being pursu'd, arriv'd at Dunbar's camp, and the panick they brought with them instantly seiz'd him and all his people; and, tho' he had now above one thousand men, and the enemy who had beaten Braddock did not at most exceed four hundred Indians and French together, instead of proceeding, and endeavouring to recover some of the lost honour, he ordered all the stores, ammunition, etc., to be destroy'd, that he might have more horses to assist his flight towards the settlements, and less lumber to remove. He was there met with requests from the governors of Virginia, Maryland, and Pennsylvania, that he would post his troops on the frontier, so as to afford some protection to the inhabitants; but he continued his hasty march thro' all the country, not thinking himself safe till he arrived at Philadelphia, where the inhabitants could protect him. This whole transaction gave us Americans the first suspicion that our exalted ideas of the prowess of British regulars had not been well founded.[*]

In their first march, too, from their landing till they got beyond the settlements, they had plundered and stripped the inhabitants, totally ruining some poor families, besides insulting, abusing, and confining the people if they remonstrated. This was enough to put us out of conceit of such defenders, if we had really wanted any. How different was the conduct of our French friends in 1781, who, during a march thro' the most inhabited part of our country from Rhode Island to Virginia, near seven hundred miles, occasioned not the smallest complaint for the loss of a pig, a chicken, or even an apple.

Captain Orme, who was one of the general's aids-de-camp, and, being grievously wounded, was brought off with him, and continu'd with him to his death, which happen'd in a few days, told me that he was totally silent all the first day, and at night only said, "*Who would have thought it?*" That he was silent again the following day, saying only at last, "*We shall better know how to deal with them another time*"; and dy'd in a few minutes after.

The secretary's papers, with all the general's orders, instructions, and correspondence, falling into the enemy's hands, they selected and translated into French a number of the articles, which they printed, to prove the hostile intentions of the British court before the declaration of war. Among these I saw some letters of the general to the ministry, speaking highly of the great service I had rendered the army, and

[*] Other accounts of this expedition and defeat may be found in Fiske's *Washington and His Country*, or Lodge's *George Washington*, Vol. 1.

recommending me to their notice. David Hume,[*] too, who was some years after secretary to Lord Hertford, when minister in France, and afterward to General Conway, when secretary of state, told me he had seen among the papers in that office, letters from Braddock highly recommending me. But, the expedition having been unfortunate, my service, it seems, was not thought of much value, for those recommendations were never of any use to me.

As to rewards from himself, I ask'd only one, which was, that he would give orders to his officers not to enlist any more of our bought servants, and that he would discharge such as had been already enlisted. This he readily granted, and several were accordingly return'd to their masters, on my application. Dunbar, when the command devolv'd on him, was not so generous. He being at Philadelphia, on his retreat, or rather flight, I apply'd to him for the discharge of the servants of three poor farmers of Lancaster county that he had enlisted, reminding him of the late general's orders on that head. He promised me that, if the masters would come to him at Trenton, where he should be in a few days on his march to New York, he would there deliver their men to them. They accordingly were at the expense and trouble of going to Trenton, and there he refus'd to perform his promise, to their great loss and disappointment.

As soon as the loss of the waggons and horses was generally known, all the owners came upon me for the valuation which I had given bond to pay. Their demands gave me a great deal of trouble, my acquainting them that the money was ready in the paymaster's hands, but that orders for paying it must first be obtained from General Shirley,[†] and my assuring them that I had apply'd to that general by letter; but, he being at a distance, an answer could not soon be receiv'd, and they must have patience, all this was not sufficient to satisfy, and some began to sue me. General Shirley at length relieved me from this terrible situation by appointing commissioners to examine the claims, and ordering payment. They amounted to near twenty thousand pound, which to pay would have ruined me.

Before we had the news of this defeat, the two Doctors Bond came to me with a subscription paper for raising money to defray the expense of a grand firework, which it was intended to exhibit at a rejoicing on

---

[*] A famous Scotch philosopher and historian (1711–1776).

[†] Governor of Massachusetts and commander of the British forces in America.

receipt of the news of our taking Fort Duquesne. I looked grave, and said it would, I thought, be time enough to prepare for the rejoicing when we knew we should have occasion to rejoice. They seem'd surpris'd that I did not immediately comply with their proposal. "Why the d——l!" says one of them, "you surely don't suppose that the fort will not be taken?" "I don't know that it will not be taken, but I know that the events of war are subject to great uncertainty." I gave them the reasons of my doubting; the subscription was dropt, and the projectors thereby missed the mortification they would have undergone if the firework had been prepared. Dr. Bond, on some other occasion afterward, said that he did not like Franklin's forebodings.

Governor Morris, who had continually worried the Assembly with message after message before the defeat of Braddock, to beat them into the making of acts to raise money for the defense of the province, without taxing, among others, the proprietary estates, and had rejected all their bills for not having such an exempting clause, now redoubled his attacks with more hope of success, the danger and necessity being greater. The Assembly, however, continu'd firm, believing they had justice on their side, and that it would be giving up an essential right if they suffered the governor to amend their money-bills. In one of the last, indeed, which was for granting fifty thousand pounds, his propos'd amendment was only of a single word. The bill express'd "that all estates, real and personal, were to be taxed, those of the proprietaries *not* excepted." His amendment was, for *not* read *only*: a small, but very material alteration. However, when the news of this disaster reached England, our friends there whom we had taken care to furnish with all the Assembly's answers to the governor's messages, rais'd a clamor against the proprietaries for their meanness and injustice in giving their governor such instructions; some going so far as to say that, by obstructing the defense of their province, they forfeited their right to it. They were intimidated by this, and sent orders to their receiver-general to add five thousand pounds of their money to whatever sum might be given by the Assembly for such purpose.

This, being notified to the House, was accepted in lieu of their share of a general tax, and a new bill was form'd, with an exempting clause, which passed accordingly. By this act I was appointed one of the commissioners for disposing of the money, sixty thousand pounds. I had been active in modelling the bill and procuring its passage, and had, at the same time, drawn a bill for establishing and disciplining a voluntary militia, which I carried thro' the House without much difficulty, as care was taken in it to leave the Quakers at their liberty. To promote the association necessary to form the militia, I wrote a dialogue,* stating and answering all the objections I could think of to such a militia, which was printed, and had, as I thought, great effect.

---

* This dialogue and the militia act are in the Gentleman's Magazine for February and March, 1756.—*Marg. note.*

# XVII
## Franklin's Defense of the Frontier

While the several companies in the city and country were forming, and learning their exercise, the governor prevail'd with me to take charge of our North-western frontier, which was infested by the enemy, and provide for the defense of the inhabitants by raising troops and building a line of forts. I undertook this military business, tho' I did not conceive myself well qualified for it. He gave me a commission with full powers, and a parcel of blank commissions for officers, to be given to whom I thought fit. I had but little difficulty in raising men, having soon five hundred and sixty under my command. My son, who had in the preceding war been an officer in the army rais'd against Canada, was my aid-de-camp, and of great use to me. The Indians had burned Gnadenhut,* a village settled by the Moravians, and massacred the inhabitants; but the place was thought a good situation for one of the forts.

In order to march thither, I assembled the companies at Bethlehem, the chief establishment of those people. I was surprised to find it in so good a posture of defense; the destruction of Gnadenhut had made them apprehend danger. The principal buildings were defended by a stockade; they had purchased a quantity of arms and ammunition from New York, and had even plac'd quantities of small paving stones between the windows of their high stone houses, for their women to throw down upon the heads of any Indians that should attempt to force into them. The armed brethren, too, kept watch, and reliev'd as methodically as in any garrison town. In conversation with the bishop, Spangenberg, I mention'd this my surprise; for, knowing they had obtained an act of Parliament exempting them from military duties in the colonies, I had suppos'd they were conscientiously scrupulous of bearing arms. He answer'd me that it was not one of their established principles, but that, at the time of their obtaining that act, it was

---

* Pronounced Gna´-den-hoot.

thought to be a principle with many of their people. On this occasion, however, they, to their surprise, found it adopted by but a few. It seems they were either deceiv'd in themselves, or deceiv'd the Parliament; but common sense, aided by present danger, will sometimes be too strong for whimsical opinions.

It was the beginning of January when we set out upon this business of building forts. I sent one detachment toward the Minisink, with instructions to erect one for the security of that upper part of the country, and another to the lower part, with similar instructions; and I concluded to go myself with the rest of my force to Gnadenhut, where a fort was tho't more immediately necessary. The Moravians procur'd me five waggons for our tools, stores, baggage, etc.

Just before we left Bethlehem, eleven farmers, who had been driven from their plantations by the Indians, came to me requesting a supply of firearms, that they might go back and fetch off their cattle. I gave them each a gun with suitable ammunition. We had not march'd many miles before it began to rain, and it continued raining all day; there were no habitations on the road to shelter us, till we arriv'd near night at the house of a German, where, and in his barn, we were all huddled together, as wet as water could make us. It was well we were not attack'd in our march, for our arms were of the most ordinary sort, and our men could not keep their gun locks* dry. The Indians are dexterous

---

* Flint-lock guns, discharged by means of a spark struck from flint and steel into powder (priming) in an open pan.

in contrivances for that purpose, which we had not. They met that day the eleven poor farmers above mentioned, and killed ten of them. The one who escap'd inform'd that his and his companions' guns would not go off, the priming being wet with the rain.

The next day being fair, we continu'd our march, and arriv'd at the desolated Gnadenhut. There was a saw-mill near, round which were left several piles of boards, with which we soon hutted ourselves; an operation the more necessary at that inclement season, as we had no tents. Our first work was to bury more effectually the dead we found there, who had been half interr'd by the country people.

The next morning our fort was plann'd and mark'd out, the circumference measuring four hundred and fifty-five feet, which would require as many palisades to be made of trees, one with another, of a foot diameter each. Our axes, of which we had seventy, were immediately set to work to cut down trees, and, our men being dexterous in the use of them, great despatch was made. Seeing the trees fall so fast, I

had the curiosity to look at my watch when two men began to cut at a pine; in six minutes they had it upon the ground, and I found it of fourteen inches diameter. Each pine made three palisades of eighteen feet long, pointed at one end. While these were preparing, our other men dug a trench all round, of three feet deep, in which the palisades were to be planted; and, our waggons, the bodies being taken off, and the fore and hind wheels separated by taking out the pin which united the two parts of the perch,* we had ten carriages,

---

\* Here the pole connecting the front and rear wheels of a wagon.

with two horses each, to bring the palisades from the woods to the spot. When they were set up, our carpenters built a stage of boards all round within, about six feet high, for the men to stand on when to fire thro' the loopholes. We had one swivel gun, which we mounted on one of the angles, and fir'd it as soon as fix'd, to let the Indians know, if any were within hearing, that we had such pieces; and thus our fort, if such a magnificent name may be given to so miserable a stockade, was finish'd in a week, though it rain'd so hard every other day that the men could not work.

This gave me occasion to observe, that, when men are employ'd, they are best content'd; for on the days they worked they were good-natur'd and cheerful, and, with the consciousness of having done a good day's work, they spent the evening jollily; but on our idle days they were mutinous and quarrelsome, finding fault with their pork, the bread, etc., and in continual ill-humour, which put me in mind of a sea-captain, whose rule it was to keep his men constantly at work; and, when his mate once told him that they had done everything, and there was nothing further to employ them about, *"Oh,"* says he, *"make them scour the anchor."*

This kind of fort, however contemptible, is a sufficient defense against Indians, who have no cannon. Finding ourselves now posted securely, and having a place to retreat to on occasion, we ventur'd out in parties to scour the adjacent country. We met with no Indians, but we found the places on the neighbouring hills where they had lain to watch our proceedings. There was an art in their contrivance of those places that seems worth mention. It being winter, a fire was necessary for them; but a common fire on the surface of the ground would by its light have discover'd their position at a distance. They had therefore dug holes in the ground about three feet diameter, and somewhat deeper; we saw where they had with their hatchets cut off the charcoal from the sides of burnt logs lying in the woods. With these coals they had made small fires in the bottom of the holes, and we observ'd among the weeds and grass the prints of their bodies, made by their laying all round, with their legs hanging down in the holes to keep their feet warm, which, with them, is an essential point. This kind of fire, so manag'd, could not discover them, either by its light, flame, sparks, or even smoke: it appear'd that their number was not great, and it seems they saw we were too many to be attacked by them with prospect of advantage.

We had for our chaplain a zealous Presbyterian minister, Mr. Beatty, who complained to me that the men did not generally attend his prayers and exhortations. When they enlisted, they were promised, besides pay and provisions, a gill of rum a day, which was punctually serv'd out to them, half in the morning, and the other half in the evening; and I observed they were as punctual in attending to receive it; upon which I said to Mr. Beatty, "It is, perhaps, below the dignity of your profession to act as steward of the rum, but if you were to deal it out and only just after prayers, you would have them all about you." He liked the tho't, undertook the office, and, with the help of a few hands to measure out the liquor, executed it to satisfaction, and never were prayers more generally and more punctually attended; so that I thought this method preferable to the punishment inflicted by some military laws for non-attendance on divine service.

I had hardly finish'd this business, and got my fort well stor'd with provisions, when I receiv'd a letter from the governor, acquainting me that he had call'd the Assembly, and wished my attendance there, if the posture of affairs on the frontiers was such that my remaining there was no longer necessary. My friends, too, of the Assembly, pressing me by their letters to be, if possible, at the meeting, and my three intended forts being now compleated, and the inhabitants contented to remain on their farms under that protection, I resolved to return; the more willingly, as a New England officer, Colonel Clapham, experienced in Indian war, being on a visit to our establishment, consented to accept the command. I gave him a commission, and, parading the garrison, had it read before them, and introduc'd him to them as an officer who, from his skill in military affairs, was much more fit to command them than myself; and, giving them a little exhortation, took my leave. I was escorted as far as Bethlehem, where I rested a few days to recover from the fatigue I had undergone. The first night, being in a good bed, I could hardly sleep, it was so different from my hard lodging on the floor of our hut at Gnaden wrapt only in a blanket or two.

While at Bethlehem, I inquir'd a little into the practice of the Moravians: some of them had accompanied me, and all were very kind to me. I found they work'd for a common stock, ate at common tables, and slept in common dormitories, great numbers together. In the dormitories I observed loopholes, at certain distances all along just under the ceiling, which I thought judiciously placed for change of air. I was at their church, where I was entertain'd with good musick, the organ being accompanied with violins, hautboys, flutes, clarinets, etc. I understood that their sermons were not usually preached to mixed congregations of men, women, and children, as is our common practice, but that they assembled sometimes the married men, at other times their wives, then the young men, the young women, and the little children, each division by itself. The sermon I heard was to the latter, who came in and were plac'd in rows on benches; the boys under the conduct of a young man, their tutor, and the girls conducted by a young woman. The discourse seem'd well adapted to their capacities, and was delivered in a pleasing, familiar manner, coaxing them, as it were, to be good. They behav'd very orderly, but looked pale and unhealthy, which made me suspect they were kept too much within doors, or not allow'd sufficient exercise.

I inquir'd concerning the Moravian marriages, whether the report was true that they were by lot. I was told that lots were us'd only in particular cases; that generally, when a young man found himself dispos'd to marry, he inform'd the elders of his class, who consulted the elder ladies that govern'd the young women. As these elders of the different sexes were well acquainted with the tempers and dispositions of their respective pupils, they could best judge what matches were suitable, and their judgments were generally acquiesc'd in; but if, for example, it should happen that two or three young women were found to be equally proper for the young man, the lot was then recurred to. I objected, if the matches are not made by the mutual choice of the parties, some of them may chance to be very unhappy. "And so they may," answer'd my informer, "if you let the parties chuse for themselves;" which, indeed, I could not deny.

Being returned to Philadelphia, I found the association went on swimmingly, the inhabitants that were not Quakers having pretty generally come into it, formed themselves into companies, and chose their captains, lieutenants, and ensigns, according to the new law. Dr. B. visited me, and gave me an account of the pains he had taken to spread a general good liking to the law, and ascribed much to those endeavours. I had had the vanity to ascribe all to my *Dialogue*; however, not knowing but that he might be in the right, I let him enjoy his opinion, which I take to be generally the best way in such cases. The officers, meeting, chose me to be colonel of the regiment, which I this time accepted.

I forget how many companies we had, but we paraded about twelve hundred well-looking men, with a company of artillery, who had been furnished with six brass field-pieces, which they had become so expert in the use of as to fire twelve times in a minute. The first time I reviewed my regiment they accompanied me to my house, and would salute me with some rounds fired before my door, which shook down and broke several glasses of my electrical apparatus. And my new honour proved not much less brittle; for all our commissions were soon after broken by a repeal of the law in England.

During this short time of my colonelship, being about to set out on a journey to Virginia, the officers of my regiment took it into their heads that it would be proper for them to escort me out of town, as far as the Lower Ferry. Just as I was getting on horseback they came to my door, between thirty and forty, mounted, and all in their uniforms. I had not been previously acquainted with the project, or I should have prevented it, being naturally averse to the assuming of state on any occasion; and I was a good deal chagrin'd at their appearance, as I could not avoid their accompanying me. What made it worse was, that, as soon as we began to move, they drew their swords and rode with them naked all the way. Somebody wrote an account of this to the proprietor, and it gave him great offense. No such honour had been paid him when in the province, nor to any of his governors; and he said it was only proper to princes of the blood royal, which may be true for aught I know, who was, and still am, ignorant of the etiquette in such cases.

This silly affair, however, greatly increased his rancour against me, which was before not a little, on account of my conduct in the Assembly respecting the exemption of his estate from taxation, which I had always oppos'd very warmly, and not without severe reflections on his meanness and injustice of contending for it. He accused me to the ministry as being the great obstacle to the King's service, preventing, by my influence in the House, the proper form of the bills for raising money, and he instanced this parade with my officers as a proof of my having an intention to take the government of the province out of his hands by force. He also applied to Sir Everard Fawkener, the postmaster-general, to deprive me of my office; but it had no other effect than to procure from Sir Everard a gentle admonition.

Notwithstanding the continual wrangle between the governor and the House, in which I, as a member, had so large a share, there still subsisted a civil intercourse between that gentleman and myself, and we never had any personal difference. I have sometimes since thought that his little or no resentment against me, for the answers it was known I drew up to his messages, might be the effect of professional habit, and that, being bred a lawyer, he might consider us both as merely advocates for contending clients in a suit, he for the proprietaries and I for the Assembly. He would, therefore, sometimes call in a friendly way to advise with me on difficult points, and sometimes, tho' not often, take my advice.

We acted in concert to supply Braddock's army with provisions; and, when the shocking news arrived of his defeat, the governor sent in haste for me, to consult with him on measures for preventing the desertion of the back counties. I forget now the advice I gave; but I think it was, that Dunbar should be written to, and prevail'd with, if possible, to post his troops on the frontiers for their protection, till, by reinforcements from the colonies, he might be able to proceed on the expedition. And, after my return from the frontier, he would have had me undertake the conduct of such an expedition with provincial troops, for the reduction of Fort Duquesne, Dunbar and his men being otherwise employed; and he proposed to commission me as general. I had not so good an opinion of my military abilities as he profess'd to have, and I believe his professions must have exceeded his real sentiments; but probably he might think that my popularity would facilitate the raising of the men, and my influence in Assembly, the grant of money to pay them, and that, perhaps, without taxing the proprietary estate. Finding me not so forward to engage as he expected, the project was dropt, and he soon after left the government, being superseded by Captain Denny.

# XVIII
## Scientific Experiments

Before I proceed in relating the part I had in public affairs under this new governor's administration, it may not be amiss here to give some account of the rise and progress of my philosophical reputation.

In 1746, being at Boston, I met there with a Dr. Spence, who was lately arrived from Scotland, and show'd me some electric experiments. They were imperfectly perform'd, as he was not very expert; but, being on a subject quite new to me, they equally surpris'd and pleased me. Soon after my return to Philadelphia, our library company receiv'd from Mr. P. Collinson, Fellow of the Royal Society[*] of London, a present of a glass tube, with some account of the use of it in making such experiments. I eagerly seized the opportunity of repeating what I had seen at Boston; and, by much practice, acquired great readiness in performing those, also, which we had an account of from England, adding a number of new ones. I say much practice, for my house was continually full, for some time, with people who came to see these new wonders.

To divide a little this incumbrance among my friends, I caused a number of similar tubes to be blown at our glass-house, with which they furnish'd themselves, so that we had at length several performers. Among these, the principal was Mr. Kinnersley, an ingenious neighbour, who, being out of business, I encouraged to undertake showing the experiments for money, and drew up for him two lectures, in which the experiments were rang'd in such order, and accompanied with such explanations in such method, as that the foregoing should assist in comprehending the following. He procur'd an elegant apparatus for the purpose, in which all the little machines that I had roughly made for myself were nicely form'd by instrument-makers. His lectures were well attended, and gave great satisfaction; and after some time he went thro' the colonies, exhibiting them in every capital town, and pick'd up

---

[*] The Royal Society of London for Improving Natural Knowledge was founded in 1660 and holds the foremost place among English societies for the advancement of science.

some money. In the West India islands, indeed, it was with difficulty the experiments could be made, from the general moisture of the air.

Oblig'd as we were to Mr. Collinson for his present of the tube, etc., I thought it right he should be inform'd of our success in using it, and wrote him several letters containing accounts of our experiments. He got them read in the Royal Society, where they were not at first thought worth so much notice as to be printed in their Transactions. One paper, which I wrote for Mr. Kinnersley, on the sameness of lightning with electricity,* I sent to Dr. Mitchel, an acquaintance of mine, and one of the members also of that society, who wrote me word that it had been read, but was laughed at by the connoisseurs. The papers, however, being shown to Dr. Fothergill, he thought them of too much value to be stifled, and advis'd the printing of them. Mr. Collinson then gave them to *Cave* for publication in his Gentleman's Magazine; but he chose to print them separately in a pamphlet, and Dr. Fothergill wrote the preface. Cave, it seems, judged rightly for his profit, for by the additions that arrived afterward, they swell'd to a quarto volume, which has had five editions, and cost him nothing for copy-money.

It was, however, some time before those papers were much taken notice of in England. A copy of them happening to fall into the hands of the Count de Buffon,† a philosopher deservedly of great reputation in France, and, indeed, all over Europe, he prevailed with M. Dalibard‡ to translate them into French, and they were printed at Paris. The publication offended the Abbé Nollet, preceptor in Natural Philosophy to the royal family, and an able experimenter, who had form'd and publish'd a theory of electricity, which then had the general vogue. He could not at first believe that such a work came from America, and said it must have been fabricated by his enemies at Paris, to decry his system. Afterwards, having been assur'd that there really existed such a person as Franklin at Philadelphia, which he had doubted, he wrote and published a volume of Letters, chiefly address'd to me, defending his theory, and denying the verity of my experiments, and of the positions deduc'd from them.

---

\* See page 327.

† A celebrated French naturalist (1707–1788).

‡ Dalibard, who had translated Franklin's letters to Collinson into French, was the first to demonstrate, in a practical application of Franklin's experiment, that lightning and electricity are the same. "This was May 10th, 1752, one month before Franklin flew his famous kite at Philadelphia and proved the fact himself."—McMaster.

I once purpos'd answering the abbé, and actually began the answer; but, on consideration that my writings contained a description of experiments which anyone might repeat and verify, and if not to be verifi'd, could not be defended; or of observations offer'd as conjectures, and not delivered dogmatically, therefore not laying me under any obligation to defend them; and reflecting that a dispute between two persons, writing in different languages, might be lengthened greatly by mistranslations, and thence misconceptions of one another's meaning, much of one of the abbé's letters being founded on an error in the translation, I concluded to let my papers shift for themselves, believing it was better to spend what time I could spare from public business in making new experiments, than in disputing about those already made. I therefore never answered M. Nollet, and the event gave me no cause to repent my silence; for my friend M. le Roy, of the Royal Academy of Sciences, took up my cause and refuted him; my book was translated into the Italian, German, and Latin languages; and the doctrine it contain'd was by degrees universally adopted by the philosophers of Europe, in preference to that of the abbé; so that he lived to see himself the last of his sect, except Monsieur B——, of Paris, his *élève* and immediate disciple.

What gave my book the more sudden and general celebrity, was the success of one of its proposed experiments, made by Messrs. Dalibard and De Lor at Marly, for drawing lightning from the clouds. This engag'd the public attention everywhere. M. de Lor, who had an apparatus for experimental philosophy, and lectur'd in that branch of science, undertook to repeat what he called the *Philadelphia Experiments*; and, after they were performed before the king and court, all the curious of Paris flocked to see them. I will not swell this narrative with an account of that capital experiment, nor of the infinite pleasure I receiv'd in the success of a similar one I made soon after with a kite at Philadelphia, as both are to be found in the histories of electricity.

Dr. Wright, an English physician, when at Paris, wrote to a friend, who was of the Royal Society, an account of the high esteem my experiments were in among the learned abroad, and of their wonder that my writings had been so little noticed in England. The society, on this, resum'd the consideration of the letters that had been read to them; and the celebrated Dr. Watson drew up a summary account of them, and of all I had afterwards sent to England on the subject, which he accompanied with some praise of the writer. This summary was then printed in their Transactions; and some members of the society in London, particularly the very ingenious Mr. Canton, having verified the experiment of procuring lightning from the clouds by a pointed rod, and acquainting them with the success, they soon made me more than amends for the slight with which they had before treated me. Without my having made any application for that honour, they chose me a member, and voted that I should be excus'd the customary payments, which would have amounted to twenty-five guineas; and ever since have given me their Transactions gratis. They also presented me with the gold medal of Sir Godfrey Copley[*] for the year 1753, the delivery of which was accompanied by a very handsome speech of the president, Lord Macclesfield, wherein I was highly honoured.

---

[*] An English baronet (died in 1709), donator of a fund of £100, "in trust for the Royal Society of London for improving natural knowledge."

# XIX
## Agent of Pennsylvania in London

Our new governor, Captain Denny, brought over for me the before mentioned medal from the Royal Society, which he presented to me at an entertainment given him by the city. He accompanied it with very polite expressions of his esteem for me, having, as he said, been long acquainted with my character. After dinner, when the company, as was customary at that time, were engag'd in drinking, he took me aside into another room, and acquainted me that he had been advis'd by his friends in England to cultivate a friendship with me, as one who was capable of giving him the best advice, and of contributing most effectually to the making his administration easy; that he therefore desired of all things to have a good understanding with me, and he begged me to be assured of his readiness on all occasions to render me every service that might be in his power. He said much to me, also, of the proprietor's good disposition towards the province, and of the advantage it might be to us all, and to me in particular, if the opposition that had been so long continu'd to his measures was dropt, and harmony restor'd between him and the people; in effecting which, it was thought no one could be more serviceable than myself; and I might depend on adequate acknowledgments and recompenses, etc., etc. The drinkers, finding we did not return immediately to the table, sent us a decanter of Madeira, which the governor made liberal use of, and in proportion became more profuse of his solicitations and promises.

My answers were to this purpose: that my circumstances, thanks to God, were such as to make proprietary favours unnecessary to me; and that, being a member of the Assembly, I could not possibly accept of any; that, however, I had no personal enmity to the proprietary, and that, whenever the public measures he propos'd should appear to be for the good of the people, no one should espouse and forward them more zealously than myself; my past opposition having been founded on this, that the measures which had been urged were evidently intended to serve the proprietary interest, with great prejudice to that of the people;

that I was much obliged to him (the governor) for his professions of regard to me, and that he might rely on everything in my power to make his administration as easy as possible, hoping at the same time that he had not brought with him the same unfortunate instruction his predecessor had been hampered with.

On this he did not then explain himself; but when he afterwards came to do business with the Assembly, they appear'd again, the disputes were renewed, and I was as active as ever in the opposition, being the penman, first, of the request to have a communication of the instructions, and then of the remarks upon them, which may be found in the votes of the time, and in the Historical Review I afterward publish'd. But between us personally no enmity arose; we were often together; he was a man of letters, had seen much of the world, and was very entertaining and pleasing in conversation. He gave me the first information that my old friend Jas. Ralph was still alive; that he was esteem'd one of the best political writers in England; had been employed in the dispute* between Prince Frederic and the king, and had obtain'd a pension of three hundred a year; that his reputation was indeed small as a poet, Pope having damned his poetry in the *Dunciad*,† but his prose was thought as good as any man's.

The Assembly finally finding the proprietary obstinately persisted in manacling their deputies with instructions inconsistent not only with the privileges of the people, but with the service of the crown, resolv'd to petition the king against them, and appointed me their agent to go over to England, to present and support the petition. The House had sent up a bill to the governor, granting a sum of sixty thousand pounds for the king's use (ten thousand pounds of which was subjected to the orders of the then general, Lord Loudoun), which the governor absolutely refus'd to pass, in compliance with his instructions.

I had agreed with Captain Morris, of the packet at New York, for my passage, and my stores were put on board, when Lord Loudoun arriv'd at Philadelphia, expressly, as he told me, to endeavour an accommodation between the governor and Assembly, that his majesty's service might not be obstructed by their dissensions. Accordingly, he desir'd the governor and myself to meet him, that he might hear what was to be said on both sides. We met and discussed the business. In

---

* Quarrel between George II and his son, Frederick, Prince of Wales, who died before his father.

† A satirical poem by Alexander Pope directed against various contemporary writers.

behalf of the Assembly, I urged all the various arguments that may be found in the public papers of that time, which were of my writing, and are printed with the minutes of the Assembly; and the governor pleaded his instructions, the bond he had given to observe them, and his ruin if he disobey'd, yet seemed not unwilling to hazard himself if Lord Loudoun would advise it. This his lordship did not chuse to do, though I once thought I had nearly prevail'd with him to do it; but finally he rather chose to urge the compliance of the Assembly; and he entreated me to use my endeavours with them for that purpose, declaring that he would spare none of the king's troops for the defense of our frontiers, and that, if we did not continue to provide for that defense ourselves, they must remain expos'd to the enemy.

I acquainted the House with what had pass'd, and, presenting them with a set of resolutions I had drawn up, declaring our rights, and that we did not relinquish our claim to those rights, but only suspended the exercise of them on this occasion thro' *force*, against which we protested, they at length agreed to drop that bill, and frame another conformable to the proprietary instructions. This of course the governor pass'd, and I was then at liberty to proceed on my voyage. But, in the meantime, the packet had sailed with my sea-stores, which was some loss to me, and my only recompense was his lordship's thanks for my service, all the credit of obtaining the accommodation falling to his share.

He set out for New York before me; and, as the time for dispatching the packet-boats was at his disposition, and there were two then remaining there, one of which, he said, was to sail very soon, I requested to know the precise time, that I might not miss her by any delay of mine. His answer was, "I have given out that she is to sail on Saturday next; but I may let you know, *entre nous*, that if you are there by Monday morning, you will be in time, but do not delay longer." By some accidental hindrance at a ferry, it was Monday noon before I arrived, and I was much afraid she might have sailed, as the wind was fair; but I was soon made easy by the information that she was still in the harbor, and would not move till the next day. One would imagine that I was now on the very point of departing for Europe. I thought so; but I was not then so well acquainted with his lordship's character, of which *indecision* was one of the strongest features. I shall give some instances. It was about the beginning of April that I came to New York, and I think it was near the end of June before we sail'd. There were then two of the packet-boats, which had been long in port, but were detained for the general's letters, which were always to be ready to-morrow. Another packet arriv'd; she too was detain'd; and, before we sail'd, a fourth was expected. Ours was the first to be dispatch'd, as having been there longest. Passengers were engaged in all, and some extremely impatient to be gone, and the merchants uneasy about their letters, and the orders they had given for insurance (it being war time) for fall goods; but their anxiety avail'd nothing; his lordship's letters were not ready; and yet whoever waited on him found him always at his desk, pen in hand, and concluded he must needs write abundantly.

Going myself one morning to pay my respects, I found in his antechamber one Innis, a messenger of Philadelphia, who had come from thence express with a packet from Governor Denny for the general. He delivered to me some letters from my friends there, which occasion'd my inquiring when he was to return, and where he lodg'd, that I might send some letters by him. He told me he was order'd to call to-morrow at nine for the general's answer to the governor, and should set off immediately. I put my letters into his hands the same day. A fortnight after I met him again in the same place. "So, you are soon return'd, Innis?" "*Return'd!* no, I am not *gone* yet." "How so?" "I have called here by order every morning these two weeks past for his lordship's letter, and it is not yet ready." "Is it possible, when he is so great a writer? for I see him constantly at his escritoire." "Yes," says Innis, "but he is like St. George on the signs, *always on horseback, and never rides on.*" This observation of the messenger was, it seems, well founded; for, when in England, I understood that Mr. Pitt[*] gave it as one reason for removing this general, and sending Generals Amherst and Wolfe, *that the minister never heard from him, and could not know what he was doing.*

This daily expectation of sailing, and all the three packets going down to Sandy Hook, to join the fleet there, the passengers thought it best to be on board, lest by a sudden order the ships should sail, and they be left behind. There, if I remember right, we were about six weeks, consuming our sea-stores, and oblig'd to procure more. At length the fleet sail'd, the general and all his army on board, bound

---

[*] William Pitt, first Earl of Chatham (1708–1778), a great English statesman and orator. Under his able administration, England won Canada from France. He was a friend of America at the time of our Revolution.

to Louisburg, with the intent to besiege and take that fortress; all the packet-boats in company ordered to attend the general's ship, ready to receive his dispatches when they should be ready. We were out five days before we got a letter with leave to part, and then our ship quitted the fleet and steered for England. The other two packets he still detained, carried them with him to Halifax, where he stayed some time to exercise the men in sham attacks upon sham forts, then altered his mind as to besieging Louisburg, and returned to New York, with all his troops, together with the two packets above mentioned, and all their passengers! During his absence the French and savages had taken Fort George, on the frontier of that province, and the savages had massacred many of the garrison after capitulation.

I saw afterwards in London Captain Bonnell, who commanded one of those packets. He told me that, when he had been detain'd a month, he acquainted his lordship that his ship was grown foul, to a degree that must necessarily hinder her fast sailing, a point of consequence for a packet-boat, and requested an allowance of time to heave her down and clean her bottom. He was asked how long time that would require. He answered, three days. The general replied, "If you can do it in one day, I give leave; otherwise not; for you must certainly sail the day after to-morrow." So he never obtain'd leave, though detained afterwards from day to day during full three months.

I saw also in London one of Bonnell's passengers, who was so enrag'd against his lordship for deceiving and detaining him so long at New York, and then carrying him to Halifax and back again, that he swore he would sue him for damages. Whether he did or not, I never heard; but, as he represented the injury to his affairs, it was very considerable.

On the whole, I wonder'd much how such a man came to be intrusted* with so important a business as the conduct of a great army; but, having since seen more of the great world, and the means of obtaining, and motives for giving places, my wonder is diminished. General Shirley, on whom the command of the army devolved upon the death of Braddock, would, in my opinion, if continued in place, have made a much better campaign than that of Loudoun in 1757, which was frivolous, expensive, and disgraceful to our nation beyond conception; for, tho' Shirley was not a bred soldier, he was sensible and

---

* This relation illustrates the corruption that characterized English public life in the eighteenth century. It was gradually overcome in the early part of the next century.

sagacious in himself, and attentive to good advice from others, capable of forming judicious plans, and quick and active in carrying them into execution. Loudoun, instead of defending the colonies with his great army, left them totally expos'd while he paraded idly at Halifax, by which means Fort George was lost, besides, he derang'd all our mercantile operations, and distress'd our trade, by a long embargo on the exportation of provisions, on pretence of keeping supplies from being obtain'd by the enemy, but in reality for beating down their price in favour of the contractors, in whose profits, it was said, perhaps from suspicion only, he had a share. And, when at length the embargo was taken off, by neglecting to send notice of it to Charlestown, the Carolina fleet was detain'd near three months longer, whereby their bottoms were so much damaged by the worm that a great part of them foundered in their passage home.

Shirley was, I believe, sincerely glad of being relieved from so burdensome a charge as the conduct of an army must be to a man unacquainted with military business. I was at the entertainment given by the city of New York to Lord Loudoun, on his taking upon him the command. Shirley, tho' thereby superseded, was present also. There was a great company of officers, citizens, and strangers, and, some chairs having been borrowed in the neighborhood, there was one among them very low, which fell to the lot of Mr. Shirley. Perceiving it as I sat by him, I said, "They have given you, sir, too low a seat." "No matter," says he, "Mr. Franklin, I find *a low seat* the easiest."

While I was, as afore mention'd, detain'd at New York, I receiv'd all the accounts of the provisions, etc., that I had furnish'd to Braddock, some of which accounts could not sooner be obtain'd from the different persons I had employ'd to assist in the business. I presented them to Lord Loudoun, desiring to be paid the balance. He caus'd them to be regularly examined by the proper officer, who, after comparing every article with its voucher, certified them to be right; and the balance due for which his lordship promis'd to give me an order on the paymaster. This was, however, put off from time to time; and tho' I call'd often for it by appointment, I did not get it. At length, just before my departure, he told me he had, on better consideration, concluded not to mix his accounts with those of his predecessors. "And you," says he, "when in England, have only to exhibit your accounts at the treasury, and you will be paid immediately."

I mention'd, but without effect, the great and unexpected expense I had been put to by being detain'd so long at New York, as a reason for my desiring to be presently paid; and on my observing that it was not right I should be put to any further trouble or delay in obtaining the money I had advanc'd, as I charged no commission for my service, "O, Sir," says he, "you must not think of persuading us that you are no gainer; we understand better those affairs, and know that every one concerned in supplying the army finds means, in the doing it, to fill his own pockets." I assur'd him that was not my case, and that I had not pocketed a farthing; but he appear'd clearly not to believe me; and, indeed, I have since learnt that immense fortunes are often made in such employments. As to my balance, I am not paid it to this day, of which more hereafter.

Our captain of the packet had boasted much, before we sailed, of the swiftness of his ship; unfortunately, when we came to sea, she proved the dullest of ninety-six sail, to his no small mortification. After many conjectures respecting the cause, when we were near another ship almost as dull as ours, which, however, gain'd upon us, the captain ordered all hands to come aft, and stand as near the ensign staff as possible. We were, passengers included, about forty persons. While we stood there, the ship mended her pace, and soon left her neighbour far behind, which prov'd clearly what our captain suspected, that she was loaded too much by the head. The casks of water, it seems, had been all plac'd forward; these he therefore order'd to be mov'd further aft, on which the ship recover'd her character, and proved the best sailer in the fleet.

The captain said she had once gone at the rate of thirteen knots, which is accounted thirteen miles per hour. We had on board, as a passenger, Captain Kennedy, of the Navy, who contended that it was impossible, and that no ship ever sailed so fast, and that there must have been some error in the division of the log-line, or some mistake in heaving the log.* A wager ensu'd between the two captains, to be decided when there should be sufficient wind. Kennedy thereupon examin'd rigorously the log-line, and, being satisfi'd with that, he determin'd to throw the log himself. Accordingly some days after, when the wind blew very fair and fresh, and the captain of the packet,

---

* A piece of wood shaped and weighted so as to keep it stable when in the water. To this is attached a line knotted at regular distances. By these devices it is possible to tell the speed of a ship.

Lutwidge, said he believ'd she then went at the rate of thirteen knots, Kennedy made the experiment, and own'd his wager lost.

The above fact I give for the sake of the following observation. It has been remark'd, as an imperfection in the art of ship-building, that it can never be known, till she is tried, whether a new ship will or will not be a good sailer; for that the model of a good-sailing ship has been exactly follow'd in a new one, which has prov'd, on the contrary, remarkably dull. I apprehend that this may partly be occasion'd by the different opinions of seamen respecting the modes of lading, rigging, and sailing of a ship; each has his system; and the same vessel, laden by the judgment and orders of one captain, shall sail better or worse than when by the orders of another. Besides, it scarce ever happens that a ship is form'd, fitted for the sea, and sail'd by the same person. One man builds the hull, another rigs her, a third lades and sails her. No one of these has the advantage of knowing all the ideas and experience of the others, and, therefore, cannot draw just conclusions from a combination of the whole.

Even in the simple operation of sailing when at sea, I have often observ'd different judgments in the officers who commanded the successive watches, the wind being the same. One would have the sails trimm'd sharper or flatter than another, so that they seem'd to have no certain rule to govern by. Yet I think a set of experiments might be instituted; first, to determine the most proper form of the hull for swift sailing; next, the best dimensions and properest place for the masts; then the form and quantity of sails, and their position, as the wind may be; and, lastly, the disposition of the lading. This is an age of experiments, and I think a set accurately made and combin'd would be of great use. I am persuaded, therefore, that ere long some ingenious philosopher will undertake it, to whom I wish success.

We were several times chas'd in our passage, but out-sail'd every thing, and in thirty days had soundings. We had a good observation, and the captain judg'd himself so near our port, Falmouth, that, if we made a good run in the night, we might be off the mouth of that harbor in the morning, and by running in the night might escape the notice of the enemy's privateers, who often cruis'd near the entrance of the channel. Accordingly, all the sail was set that we could possibly make, and the wind being very fresh and fair, we went right before it, and made great way. The captain, after his observation, shap'd his

course, as he thought, so as to pass wide of the Scilly Isles; but it seems there is sometimes a strong indraught setting up St. George's Channel, which deceives seamen and caused the loss of Sir Cloudesley Shovel's squadron. This indraught was probably the cause of what happened to us.

We had a watchman plac'd in the bow, to whom they often called, "*Look well out before there*," and he as often answered, "*Ay, ay*"; but perhaps had his eyes shut, and was half asleep at the time, they sometimes answering, as is said, mechanically; for he did not see a light just before us, which had been hid by the studding-sails from the man at the helm, and from the rest of the watch, but by an accidental yaw of the ship was discover'd, and occasion'd a great alarm, we being very near it, the light appearing to me as big as a cartwheel. It was midnight, and our captain fast asleep; but Captain Kennedy, jumping upon deck, and seeing the danger, ordered the ship to wear round, all sails standing; an operation dangerous to the masts, but it carried us clear, and we escaped shipwreck, for we were running right upon the rocks on which the lighthouse was erected. This deliverance impressed me strongly with the utility of lighthouses, and made me resolve to encourage the building more of them in America if I should live to return there.

In the morning it was found by the soundings, etc., that we were near our port, but a thick fog hid the land from our sight. About nine o'clock the fog began to rise, and seem'd to be lifted up from the water like the curtain at a play-house, discovering underneath, the town of Falmouth, the vessels in its harbor, and the fields that surrounded it. This was a most pleasing spectacle to those who had been so long without any other prospects than the uniform view of a vacant ocean, and it gave us the more pleasure as we were now free from the anxieties which the state of war occasion'd.

I set out immediately, with my son, for London, and we only stopt a little by the way to view Stonehenge* on Salisbury Plain, and Lord Pembroke's house and gardens, with his very curious antiquities at Wilton. We arrived in London the 27th of July, 1757.[†]

As soon as I was settled in a lodging Mr. Charles had provided for me, I went to visit Dr. Fothergill, to whom I was strongly recommended, and whose counsel respecting my proceedings I was advis'd to obtain. He was against an immediate complaint to government, and thought the proprietaries should first be personally appli'd to, who might possibly be induc'd by the interposition and persuasion of some private friends, to accommodate matters amicably. I then waited on my old friend and correspondent, Mr. Peter Collinson, who told me that John Hanbury, the great Virginia merchant, had requested to be informed when I should arrive, that he might carry me to Lord Granville's,[‡] who was then President of the Council and wished to see me as soon as possible. I agreed to go with him the next morning. Accordingly Mr. Hanbury called for me and took me in his carriage to that nobleman's, who receiv'd me with great civility; and after some questions respecting the present state of affairs in America and discourse thereupon, he said to me: "You Americans have wrong ideas of the nature of your constitution; you contend that the king's instructions to his governors are not laws, and think yourselves at liberty to regard or disregard them at your own discretion. But those instructions are not like the pocket instructions given to a minister going abroad, for regulating his conduct in some trifling point of ceremony. They are first drawn up by judges learned in the laws; they are then considered, debated, and perhaps

---

* A celebrated prehistoric ruin, probably of a temple built by the early Britons, near Salisbury, England. It consists of inner and outer circles of enormous stones, some of which are connected by stone slabs.

† "Here terminates the *Autobiography*, as published by Wm. Temple Franklin and his successors. What follows was written in the last year of Dr. Franklin's life, and was never before printed in English."—Mr. Bigelow's note in his edition of 1868.

‡ George Granville or Grenville (1712–1770). As English premier from 1763 to 1765, he introduced the direct taxation of the American Colonies and has sometimes been called the immediate cause of the Revolution.

amended in Council, after which they are signed by the king. They are then, so far as they relate to you, the *law of the land*, for the king is the Legislator of the Colonies,"* I told his lordship this was new doctrine to me. I had always understood from our charters that our laws were to be made by our Assemblies, to be presented indeed to the king for his royal assent, but that being once given the king could not repeal or alter them. And as the Assemblies could not make permanent laws without his assent, so neither could he make a law for them without theirs. He assur'd me I was totally mistaken. I did not think so, however, and his lordship's conversation having a little alarm'd me as to what might be the sentiments of the court concerning us, I wrote it down as soon as I return'd to my lodgings. I recollected that about 20 years before, a clause in a bill brought into Parliament by the ministry had propos'd to make the king's instructions laws in the colonies, but the clause was thrown out by the Commons, for which we adored them as our friends and friends of liberty, till by their conduct towards us in 1765 it seem'd that they had refus'd that point of sovereignty to the king only that they might reserve it for themselves.

After some days, Dr. Fothergill having spoken to the proprietaries, they agreed to a meeting with me at Mr. T. Penn's house in Spring Garden. The conversation at first consisted of mutual declarations of disposition to reasonable accommodations, but I suppose each party had its own ideas of what should be meant by *reasonable*. We then went into consideration of our several points of complaint, which I enumerated. The proprietaries justify'd their conduct as well as they could, and I the Assembly's. We now appeared very wide, and so far from each other in our opinions as to discourage all hope of agreement. However, it was concluded that I should give them the heads of our complaints in writing, and they promis'd then to consider them. I did so soon after, but they put the paper into the hands of their solicitor, Ferdinand John Paris, who managed for them all their law business in their great suit with the neighbouring proprietary of Maryland, Lord Baltimore, which

---

* This whole passage shows how hopelessly divergent were the English and American views on the relations between the mother country and her colonies. Grenville here made clear that the Americans were to have no voice in making or amending their laws. Parliament and the king were to have absolute power over the colonies. No wonder Franklin was alarmed by this new doctrine. With his keen insight into human nature and his consequent knowledge of American character, he foresaw the inevitable result of such an attitude on the part of England. This conversation with Grenville makes these last pages of the *Autobiography* one of its most important parts.

had subsisted 70 years, and wrote for them all their papers and messages in their dispute with the Assembly. He was a proud, angry man, and as I had occasionally in the answers of the Assembly treated his papers with some severity, they being really weak in point of argument and haughty in expression, he had conceived a mortal enmity to me, which discovering itself whenever we met, I declin'd the proprietary's proposal that he and I should discuss the heads of complaint between our two selves, and refus'd treating with anyone but them. They then by his advice put the paper into the hands of the Attorney and Solicitor-General for their opinion and counsel upon it, where it lay unanswered a year wanting eight days, during which time I made frequent demands of an answer from the proprietaries, but without obtaining any other

than that they had not yet received the opinion of the Attorney and Solicitor-General. What it was when they did receive it I never learnt, for they did not communicate it to me, but sent a long message to the Assembly drawn and signed by Paris, reciting my paper, complaining of its want of formality, as a rudeness on my part, and giving a flimsy justification of their conduct, adding that they should be willing to accommodate matters if the Assembly would send out *some person of candour* to treat with them for that purpose, intimating thereby that I was not such.

The want of formality or rudeness was, probably, my not having address'd the paper to them with their assum'd titles of True and Absolute Proprietaries of the Province of Pennsylvania, which I omitted as not thinking it necessary in a paper, the intention of which was only to reduce to a certainty by writing, what in conversation I had delivered *viva voce*.

But during this delay, the Assembly having prevailed with Gov'r Denny to pass an act taxing the proprietary estate in common with the estates of the people, which was the grand point in dispute, they omitted answering the message.

When this act however came over, the proprietaries, counselled by Paris, determined to oppose its receiving the royal assent. Accordingly they petitioned the king in Council, and a hearing was appointed in which two lawyers were employ'd by them against the act, and two by me in support of it. They alledg'd that the act was intended to load the proprietary estate in order to spare those of the people, and that if it were suffer'd to continue in force, and the proprietaries, who were in odium with the people, left to their mercy in proportioning the taxes, they would inevitably be ruined. We reply'd that the act had no such intention, and would have no such effect. That the assessors were honest and discreet men under an oath to assess fairly and equitably, and that any advantage each of them might expect in lessening his own tax by augmenting that of the proprietaries was too trifling to induce them to perjure themselves. This is the purport of what I remember as urged by both sides, except that we insisted strongly on the mischievous consequences that must attend a repeal, for that the money, £100,000, being printed and given to the king's use, expended in his service, and now spread among the people, the repeal would strike it dead in their hands to the ruin of many, and the total discouragement of future grants, and the selfishness of the proprietors in soliciting such a general catastrophe, merely from a groundless fear of their estate being taxed too highly, was insisted on in the strongest terms. On this, Lord Mansfield, one of the counsel, rose, and beckoning me took me into the clerk's chamber, while the lawyers were pleading, and asked me if I was really of opinion that no injury would be done the proprietary estate in the execution of the act. I said certainly. "Then," says he, "you can have little objection to enter into an engagement to assure that point." I answer'd, "None at all." He then call'd in Paris, and after some discourse, his lordship's proposition was accepted on both sides; a paper to the purpose was drawn up by the Clerk of the Council, which I sign'd with Mr. Charles, who was also an Agent of the Province for their ordinary affairs, when Lord Mansfield returned to the Council

Chamber, where finally the law was allowed to pass. Some changes were however recommended and we also engaged they should be made by a subsequent law, but the Assembly did not think them necessary; for one year's tax having been levied by the act before the order of Council arrived, they appointed a committee to examine the proceedings of the assessors, and on this committee they put several particular friends of the proprietaries. After a full enquiry, they unanimously sign'd a report that they found the tax had been assess'd with perfect equity.

The Assembly looked into my entering into the first part of the engagement, as an essential service to the Province, since it secured the credit of the paper money then spread over all the country. They gave me their thanks in form when I return'd. But the proprietaries were enraged at Governor Denny for having pass'd the act, and turn'd him out with threats of suing him for breach of instructions which he had given bond to observe. He, however, having done it at the instance of the General, and for His Majesty's service, and having some powerful interest at court, despis'd the threats and they were never put in execution.... [unfinished]

# The Way to Wealth

# INTRODUCTION.

*Dr. Franklin, wishing to collect into one piece all the sayings upon the following subjects, which he had dropped in the course of publishing the Almanacks called "Poor Richard," introduces Father Abraham for this purpose. Hence it is, that Poor Richard is so often quoted, and that, in the present title, he is said to be improved. Notwithstanding the stroke of humour in the concluding paragraph of this address, Poor Richard (Saunders) and Father Abraham have proved, in America, that they are no common preachers. And shall we, brother Englishmen, refuse good sense and saving knowledge, because it comes from the other side of the water?*

# THE WAY TO WEALTH.

COURTEOUS READER,

I have heard that nothing gives an author so great pleasure, as to find his works respectfully quoted by others. Judge, then, how much I must have been gratified by an incident I am going to relate to you. I stopped my horse, lately, where a great number of people were collected at an auction of merchants' goods. The hour of the sale not being come, they were conversing on the badness of the times; and one of the company called to a plain, clean, old man, with white locks, "Pray, Father Abraham, what think you of the times? Will not those heavy taxes quite ruin the country! How shall we be ever able to pay them? What would you advise us to?" Father Abraham stood up, and replied, "If you would have my advice, I will give it you in short; 'for a word to the wise is enough,' as Poor Richard says." They joined in desiring him to speak his mind, and, gathering round him, he proceeded as follows:

"Friends," says he, "the taxes are indeed very heavy; and, if those laid on by the government were the only ones we had to pay, we might more easily discharge them; but we have many others, and much more grievous to some of us. We are taxed twice as much by our idleness, three times as much by our pride, and four times as much by our folly; and from these taxes the commissioners cannot ease or deliver us by allowing an abatement. However, let us hearken to good advice, and something may be done for us; 'God helps them that help themselves,' as Poor Richard says.

"I. It would be thought a hard government that should tax its people one-tenth part of their time to be employed in its service: but idleness taxes many of us much more; sloth, by bringing on diseases, absolutely shortens life.

" 'Sloth, like rust, consumes faster than labour wears, while the used key is always bright,' as Poor Richard says. 'But, dost thou love life? then do not squander time, for that is the stuff life is made of,' as Poor Richard says. How much more than is necessary do we spend in sleep! forgetting that, 'the sleeping fox catches no poultry, and that there will be sleeping enough in the grave,' as Poor Richard says.

"If time be of all things the most precious, 'wasting time must be' as Poor Richard says, 'the greatest prodigality;' since, as he elsewhere tells us, 'Lost time is never found again; and what we call time enough, always proves little enough.' Let us then up and be doing, and doing to the purpose: so by diligence shall we do more with less perplexity. 'Sloth makes all things difficult, but industry all easy; and he that riseth late, must trot all day, and shall scarce overtake his business at night; while laziness travels so slowly, that poverty soon overtakes him. Drive thy business, let not that drive thee; and early to bed, and early to rise, makes a man healthy, wealthy, and wise,' as Poor Richard says.

"So what signifies wishing and hoping for better times? We may make these times better, if we bestir ourselves. 'Industry need not wish, and he that lives upon hope will die fasting. There are no gains without pains; then help hands, for I have no lands;' or if I have, they are smartly taxed. 'He that hath a trade, hath an estate; and he that hath a calling, hath an office of profit and honour,' as Poor Richard says; but then the trade must be worked at, and the calling well followed, or neither the estate nor the office will enable us to pay our taxes. If we are industrious, we shall never starve; for 'at the working man's house hunger looks in, but dares not enter.' Nor will the bailiff or the constable enter, for 'industry pays debts, while despair increaseth them.' What, enough you have found no treasure, nor has any rich relation left you a legacy; 'Diligence is the mother of good luck, and God gives all things to industry. Then plow deep, while sluggards sleep, and you shall have corn to sell and to keep.' Work while it is called to-day, for you know not how much you may be hindered to-morrow. 'One to-day is worth two to-morrows,' as Poor Richard says, and farther, 'Never leave that till to-morrow, which you can do to-day.' If you were a servant, would you not be ashamed that a good master should catch you idle? Are you then your own master? Be ashamed to catch yourself idle, when there is so much to be done for yourself, your family, your country, and your king. Handle your tools without mittens; remember, that 'The cat in gloves catches no mice,' as Poor Richard says. It is true, there is much to be done, and, perhaps, you are weak-handed: but stick to it steadily, and you will see great effects; for "Constant dropping wears away stone; and by diligence and patience the mouse ate in two the cable; and little strokes fell great oaks.'

"Methinks I hear some of you say, 'Must a man afford himself no leisure?' I will tell thee, my friend, what Poor Richard says, 'Employ thy time well, if thou meanest to gain leisure; and, since thou art not sure of a minute, throw not away an hour.' Leisure is time for doing something useful; this leisure the diligent man will obtain, but the lazy man never; for 'A life of leisure and a life of laziness are two things. Many, without labour, would live by their wits only, but they break for want of stock;' whereas industry gives comfort, and plenty, and respect. 'Fly pleasures and they will follow you. The diligent spinner has a large shift; and now I have a sheep and a cow, every body bids me good-morrow.'

"II. But with our industry we must likewise be steady, settled, and careful, and oversee our own affairs with our own eyes, and not trust too much to others: for, as Poor Richard says:

> 'I never saw an oft-removed tree,
> Nor yet an oft-removed family,
> That throve so well as those that settled be.'

And again, 'Three removes are as bad as a fire,' and again, 'Keep thy shop, and thy shop will keep thee:' and again, 'If you would have your business done, go; if not, send.' And again,

'He that by the plow would thrive,
Himself must either hold or drive.'

And again, 'The eye of the master will do more work than both his hands:' and again, 'Want of care does us more damage than want of knowledge;' and again, 'Not to oversee workmen is to leave them your purse open.'

"Trusting too much to others' care is the ruin of many; for, 'In the affairs of this world, men are saved, not by faith, but by the want of it. But a man's own care is profitable; for, if you would have a faithful servant, and one that you like, serve yourself. A little neglect may breed great mischief; for want of a nail the shoe was lost; for want of a shoe the horse was lost; and for want of a horse the rider was lost;' being overtaken and slain by the enemy; all for want of a little care about a horse-shoe nail.

"III. So much for industry, my friends, and attention to one's own business; but to these we must add frugality, if we would make our industry more certainly successful. A man may if he knows not how to save as he gets, 'keep his nose all his life to the grindstone, and die not worth a groat at last. A fat kitchen makes a lean will;' and,

'Many estates are spent in the getting,
Since women for tea forsook spinning and knitting,
And men for punch forsook hewing and splitting.'

'If you would be wealthy, think of saving, as well as of getting. The Indies have not made Spain rich, because her out-goes are greater than her incomes.'

"Away, then, with your expensive follies, and you will not then have so much cause to complain of hard times, heavy taxes, and chargeable families; for,

'Women and wine, game and deceit,
Make the wealth small, and the want great.'

And farther, 'What maintains one vice, would bring up two children.' You may think perhaps, that a little tea, or a little punch now and then, diet a little more costly, clothes a little finer, and a little entertainment now and then, can be no great matter; but remember, 'Many a little makes a mickle.' Beware of little expences; 'A small leak will sink a great ship,' as Poor Richard says; and again, 'Who dainties love shall beggars prove;' and moreover, 'Fools make feasts, and wise men eat them.' Here you are all got together to this sale of fineries and nic-nacs. You call them goods; but, if you do not take care, they will prove evils to some of you. You expect they will be sold cheap, and, perhaps, they may for less than they cost; but, if you have no occasion for them, they may be dear to you. Remember what poor Richard says, 'Buy what thou hast no need of, and ere long thou shalt sell thy necessaries.' And again, 'At a great pennyworth pause a while:' he means, that perhaps the cheapness is apparent only, and not real; or the bargain, by straitening thee in thy business, may do thee more harm than good. For, in another place, he says, 'Many have been ruined by buying good pennyworths.' Again, 'It is foolish to lay out money in a purchase of repentance;' and yet this folly is practised every day at auctions, for want of minding the Almanack. Many a one, for the sake of finery on the back, have gone with a hungry belly, and half starved their families; 'Silks and satins, scarlet and velvets, put out the kitchen fire,' as Poor Richard says. These are not the necessaries of life; they can scarcely be called the conveniences; and yet only because they look pretty, how many want to have them! By these, and other extravagancies, the genteel are reduced to poverty, and forced to borrow of those whom they formerly despised, but who, through industry and frugality, have maintained their standing; in which case it appears plainly, that 'A ploughman on his legs is higher than a gentleman on his knees,' as Poor Richard says. Perhaps they have had a small estate left them, which they knew not the getting of; they think 'it is day, and will never be night:' that a little to be spent out of so much is not worth minding; but 'Always taking out of the meal-tub, and never putting in, soon comes to the bottom,' as Poor Richard says; and then, 'When the well is dry, they know the worth of water.' But this they might have known before, if they had taken his advice. 'If you would know the value of money, go and try to borrow some; for he that goes a borrowing, goes a sorrowing,' as Poor Richard says; and, indeed, so does he that lends to such people, when he goes to get it in again. Poor Dick farther advises, and says,

> 'Fond pride of dress is sure a very curse,
> Ere fancy you consult, consult your purse.'

And again, 'Pride is as loud a beggar as Want, and a great deal more saucy.' When you have bought one fine thing, you must buy ten more, that your appearance may be all of a piece; but Poor Dick says, 'It is easier to suppress the first desire, than to satisfy all that follow it.' And it is as truly folly for the poor to ape the rich, as for the frog to swell, in order to equal the ox.

> 'Vessels large may venture more,
> But little boats should keep near shore.'

"It is, however, a folly soon punished: for, as Poor Richard says, 'Pride that dines on vanity, sups on contempt; Pride breakfasted with Plenty, dined with Poverty and supped with Infamy.' And, after all, of what use is this pride of appearance, for which so much is risked, so much is suffered? It cannot promote health, nor ease pain; it makes no increase of merit in the person, it creates envy, it hastens misfortune.

"But what madness it must be to run in debt for these superfluities? We are offered, by the terms of this sale, six months credit; and that, perhaps, has induced some of us to attend it, because we cannot spare the ready money, and hope now to be fine without it. But, ah! think what you do when you run in debt: you give to another power over your liberty. If you cannot pay at the time, you will be ashamed to see your creditor; you will be in fear when you speak to him; you will make poor pitiful sneaking excuses, and, by degrees, come to lose your veracity, and sink into base, downright lying; for, 'The second vice is lying, the first is running in debt,' as Poor Richard says; and again, to the same purpose, 'Lying rides upon Debt's back:' whereas a free-born man ought not to be ashamed nor afraid to see or speak to any man living. But poverty often deprives a man of all spirit and virtue. 'It is hard for an empty bag to stand upright.' What would you think of that prince, or of that government, who should issue an edict forbidding you to dress like a gentleman or gentlewoman, on pain of imprisonment or servitude? Would you not say that you were free, have a right to dress as you please, and that such an edict would be a breach of your privileges, and such a government tyrannical? And yet you are about to put yourself under that tyranny, when you run in debt for such dress! Your creditor has authority, at his pleasure, to deprive you of your liberty, by confining you in gaol for life, or by selling you for a servant, if you should not be able to pay him. When you have got your bargain, you may, perhaps, think little of payment; but, as Poor Richard says, 'Creditors have better memories than debtors; creditors

are a superstitious sect, great observers of set days and times.' The day
comes round before you are aware, and the demand is made before you
are prepared to satisfy it; or, if you bear your debt in mind, the term,
which at first seemed so long, will, as it lessens, appear extremely short:
Time will seem to have added wings to his heels as well as his shoulders.
'Those have a short Lent, who owe money to be paid at Easter.' At
present, perhaps, you may think yourselves in thriving circumstances,
and that you can bear a little extravagance without injury; but

> 'For age and want save while you may,
> No morning sun lasts a whole day.'

"Gain may be temporary and uncertain; but ever, while you live,
expense is constant and certain; and 'It is easier to build two chimneys,
than to keep one in fuel,' as Poor Richard says: so, 'Rather go to bed
supper-less, than rise in debt,'

> 'Get what you can, and what you get hold,
> 'Tis the stone that will turn all your lead into gold.'

And when you have got the Philosopher's stone, sure you will no longer
complain of bad times, or the difficulty of paying taxes.

"IV. This doctrine, my friends, is reason and wisdom; but, after all,
do not depend too much upon your own industry, and frugality, and
prudence, though excellent things; for they may all be blasted without
the blessing of Heaven; and therefore, ask that blessing humbly, and be
not uncharitable to those that at present seem to want it, but comfort and
help them. Remember, Job suffered, and was afterwards prosperous.

"And now to conclude, 'Experience keeps a dear school, but fools
will learn in no other,' as Poor Richard says, and scarce in that; for it
is true, 'We may give advice, but we cannot give conduct.' However,
remember this, 'They that will not be counselled cannot be helped;'
and farther, that 'If you will not hear Reason, she will surely rap your
knuckles,' as Poor Richard says.'

Thus the old gentleman ended his harangue. The people heard it,
and approved the doctrine, and immediately practised the contrary,
just as if it had been a common sermon; for the auction opened, and
they began to buy extravagantly. I found the good man had thoroughly
studied my Almanacks, and digested all I had dropt on those topics
during the course of twenty-five years. The frequent mention he made

of me must have tired any one else; but my vanity was wonderfully delighted with it, though I was conscious that not a tenth part of the wisdom was my own, which he ascribed to me; but rather the gleanings that I had made of the sense of all ages and nations. However, I resolved to be the better for the echo of it; and, though I had at first determined to buy stuff for a new coat, I went away, resolved to wear my old one a little longer. Reader, if thou wilt do the same, thy profit will be as great as mine. I am, as ever, thine to serve thee,

RICHARD SAUNDERS.

# Common Sense
# and The Rights of Man

# Word Cloud Classics

A Christmas Carol
and Other Holiday Treasures

Adventures of
Huckleberry Finn

The Adventures of
Sherlock Holmes

Aesop's Fables

The Age of Innocence

Anna Karenina

Anne of Green Gables

The Art of War

The Brothers Grimm:
101 Fairy Tales

The Brothers Grimm
Volume II:
110 Grimmer Fairy Tales

The Count of Monte Cristo

Don Quixote

Dracula

Frankenstein

Great Expectations

Inferno

Jane Eyre

Lady Chatterley's Lover

Les Misérables

Little Women

Madame Bovary

Moby-Dick

Narrative of the Life
of Frederick Douglass
and Other Works

Persuasion

The Picture of Dorian Gray

Pride and Prejudice

The Prince and Other Writings

The Red Badge of Courage
and Other Stories

The Scarlet Letter

The Secret Garden

Sense and Sensibility

The Three Musketeers

Twenty Thousand Leagues
Under the Sea

Uncle Tom's Cabin

Walden and
Civil Disobedience

The Wizard of Oz

# Common Sense and The Rights of Man

*THOMAS PAINE*

**Word Cloud Classics**

San Diego

Canterbury Classics
An imprint of Printers Row Publishing Group
10350 Barnes Canyon Road, Suite 100, San Diego, CA 92121
www.canterburyclassicsbooks.com • mail@canterburyclassicsbooks.com

Printers Row Publishing Group is a division of Readerlink Distribution Services, LLC. The Canterbury Classics and Word Cloud Classics names and logos are registered trademarks of Readerlink Distribution Services, LLC.

All correspondence concerning the content of this book should be addressed to Canterbury Classics, Editorial Department, at the above address.

Publisher: Peter Norton
Associate Publisher: Ana Parker
Publishing/Editorial Team: April Farr, Kathryn C. Dalby
Editorial Team: JoAnn Padgett, Melinda Allman
Production/Design Team: Jonathan Lopes, Rusty von Dyl

Spine art: Gettyimages/eyewave (statue), Gettyimages/clipartdotcom (flag)

Inconsistencies in spelling and punctuation throughout remain in order to preserve the original flavor of Thomas Paine's text.

ISBN: 978-1-64517-085-3
Printed in China
23 22 21 20 19  1 2 3 4 5

# CONTENTS

# Common Sense
## (1776)

# INTRODUCTION

Perhaps the sentiments contained in the following pages, are not *yet* sufficiently fashionable to procure them general Favour; a long Habit of not thinking a Thing *wrong*, gives it a superficial appearance of being *right*, and raises at first a formidable outcry in defense of Custom. But the Tumult soon subsides. Time makes more Converts than Reason.

As a long and violent abuse of power, is generally the Means of calling the right of it in question (and in Matters too which might never have been thought of, had not the Sufferers been aggravated into the inquiry) and as the King of England hath undertaken in his *own right*, to support the Parliament in what he calls *Theirs*, and as the good People of this Country are grievously oppressed by the Combination, they have an undoubted privilege to inquire into the Pretensions of both, and equally to reject the Usurpation of *either*.

In the following Sheets, the Author hath studiously avoided every thing which is personal among ourselves. Compliments as well as censure to individuals make no part thereof. The wise and the worthy, need not the triumph of a Pamphlet; and those whose sentiments are injudicious, or unfriendly, will cease of themselves unless too much pains are bestowed upon their conversion.

The cause of America is in a great measure the cause of all mankind. Many circumstances hath, and will arise, which are not local, but universal, and through which the principles of all Lovers of Mankind are affected, and in the Event of which, their Affections are interested. The laying a Country desolate with Fire and Sword, declaring War against the natural rights of all Mankind, and extirpating the Defenders thereof from the Face of the Earth, is the Concern of every Man to whom Nature hath given the Power of feeling; of which Class, regardless of Party Censure, is

*The Author.*

P.S. The Publication of this new Edition hath been delayed, with a view of taking notice (had it been necessary) of any attempt to refute the Doctrine of Independence: As no answer hath yet appeared, it is now presumed that none will, the time needful for getting such a Performance ready for the Public being considerably past.

Who the Author of this Production is, is wholly unnecessary to the Public, as the Object for Attention is the *Doctrine itself*, not the *Man*. Yet it may not be unnecessary to say, That he is unconnected with any Party, and under no sort of Influence public or private, but the influence of reason and principle.

Philadelphia, February 14, 1776

# I. OF THE ORIGIN AND DESIGN OF GOVERNMENT IN GENERAL, WITH CONCISE REMARKS ON THE ENGLISH CONSTITUTION

Some writers have so confounded society with government, as to leave little or no distinction between them; whereas they are not only different, but have different origins. Society is produced by our wants, and government by our wickedness; the former promotes our happiness *positively* by uniting our affections, the latter *negatively* by restraining our vices. The one encourages intercourse, the other creates distinctions. The first a patron, the last a punisher.

Society in every state is a blessing, but Government even in its best state is but a necessary evil; in its worst state an intolerable one; for when we suffer, or are exposed to the same miseries *by a Government*, which we might expect in a country *without Government*, our calamity is heightened by reflecting that we furnish the means by which we suffer. Government, like dress, is the badge of lost innocence; the palaces of kings are built on the ruins of the bowers of paradise. For were the impulses of conscience clear, uniform, and irresistibly obeyed, man would need no other lawgiver; but that not being the case, he finds it necessary to surrender up a part of his property to furnish means for the protection of the rest; and this he is induced to do by the same prudence which in every other case advises him out of two evils to choose the least. *Wherefore*, security being the true design and end of government, it unanswerably follows, that whatever *form* thereof appears most likely to ensure it to us, with the least expense and greatest benefit, is preferable to all others.

In order to gain a clear and just idea of the design and end of government, let us suppose a small number of persons settled in some sequestered part of the earth, unconnected with the rest, they will then represent the first peopling of any country, or of the world. In this state of natural liberty, society will be their first thought. A thousand motives will excite them thereto, the strength of one man is so unequal to his wants, and his mind so unfitted for perpetual solitude, that he is soon obliged to seek assistance and relief of another, who in his turn requires the same. Four or five united would be able to raise a tolerable dwelling in the midst of a wilderness, but one man might labour out of the common period of life without accomplishing any thing; when he had felled his timber he could not remove it, nor erect it after it was removed; hunger in the mean time would urge him from his work, and every different want call him a different way. Disease, nay even misfortune would be death, for though neither might be mortal, yet either would disable him from living, and reduce him to a state in which he might rather be said to perish than to die.

Thus necessity, like a gravitating power, would soon form our newly arrived emigrants into society, the reciprocal blessings of which, would supersede, and render the obligations of law and government unnecessary while they remained perfectly just to each other; but as nothing but heaven is impregnable to vice, it will unavoidably happen, that in proportion as they surmount the first difficulties of emigration, which bound them together in a common cause, they will begin to relax in their duty and attachment to each other; and this remissness will point out the necessity of establishing some form of government to supply the defect of moral virtue.

Some convenient tree will afford them a State-House, under the branches of which, the whole colony may assemble to deliberate on public matters. It is more than probable that their first laws will have the title only of *regulations*, and be enforced by no other penalty than public disesteem. In this first parliament every man, by natural right, will have a seat.

But as the colony increases, the public concerns will increase likewise, and the distance at which the members may be separated, will render it too inconvenient for all of them to meet on every occasion as at first, when their number was small, their habitations near, and the public concerns few and trifling. This will point out the convenience of their consenting to leave the legislative part to be managed by a select number chosen from the whole body, who are supposed to have the same concerns at stake which those who appointed them, and who will act in the same manner as the whole body would act, were they present. If the colony continues increasing, it will become necessary to augment the number of the representatives, and that the interest of every part of the colony may be attended to, it will be found best to divide the whole into convenient parts, each part sending its proper number; and that the *elected* might never form to themselves an interest separate from the *electors*, prudence will point out the propriety of having elections often: because as the *elected* might by that means return and mix again with the general body of the *electors* in a few months, their fidelity to the public will be secured by the prudent reflection of not making a rod for themselves. And as this frequent interchange will establish a common interest with every part of the community, they will mutually and naturally support each other, and on this (not on the unmeaning name of king) depends *the strength of government, and the happiness of the governed*.

Here then is the origin and rise of government; namely, a mode rendered necessary by the inability of moral virtue to govern the world; here too is the design and end of government, viz. freedom and security. And however our eyes may be dazzled with show, or our ears deceived by sound; however prejudice may warp our wills, or interest darken our understanding, the simple voice of nature and of reason will say, 'tis right.

I draw my idea of the form of government from a principle in nature, which no art can overturn, viz. that the more simple any thing is, the less liable it is to be disordered; and the easier repaired when disordered; and with this maxim in view, I offer a few remarks on the so much boasted constitution of England. That it was noble for the dark and slavish times in which it was erected, is granted. When the world was overrun with tyranny the least remove therefrom was a glorious rescue. But that it is imperfect, subject to convulsions, and incapable of producing what it seems to promise, is easily demonstrated.

Absolute governments (tho' the disgrace of human nature) have this advantage with them, that they are simple; if the people suffer, they know the head from which their suffering springs, know likewise the remedy, and are not bewildered by a variety of causes and cures. But the constitution of England is so exceedingly complex, that the nation may suffer for years together without being able to discover in which part the fault lies; some will say in one and some in another, and every political physician will advise a different medicine.

I know it is difficult to get over local or long standing prejudices, yet if we will suffer ourselves to examine the component parts of the

English constitution, we shall find them to be the base remains of two ancient tyrannies, compounded with some new republican materials.

*First*—The remains of Monarchial tyranny in the person of the King.

*Secondly*—The remains of Aristocratical tyranny in the persons of the Peers.

*Thirdly*—The new Republican materials in the persons of the Commons, on whose virtue depends the freedom of England.

The two first, by being hereditary, are independent of the People; wherefore in a *constitutional sense* they contribute nothing towards the freedom of the State.

To say that the constitution of England is a *union* of three powers reciprocally *checking* each other, is farcical, either the words have no meaning, or they are flat contradictions.

To say that the Commons is a check upon the King, presupposes two things:

*First*—That the King is not to be trusted without being looked after, or in other words, that a thirst for absolute power is the natural disease of monarchy.

*Secondly*—That the Commons, by being appointed for that purpose, are either wiser or more worthy of confidence than the Crown.

But as the same constitution which gives the Commons a power to check the King by withholding the supplies, gives afterwards the King a power to check the Commons, by empowering him to reject their other bills; it again supposes that the King is wiser than those whom it has already supposed to be wiser than him. A mere absurdity!

There is something exceedingly ridiculous in the composition of Monarchy; it first excludes a man from the means of information, yet empowers him to act in cases where the highest judgment is required. The state of a king shuts him from the World, yet the business of a king requires him to know it thoroughly; wherefore the different parts, by unnaturally opposing and destroying each other, prove the whole character to be absurd and useless.

Some writers have explained the English constitution thus: The King, say they, is one, the people another; the Peers are a house in behalf of the King, the commons in behalf of the people; but this hath all the distinctions of a house divided against itself; and though the expressions be pleasantly arranged, yet when examined, they appear idle and ambiguous; and it will always happen, that the nicest construction that words are capable of, when applied to the description of something which either cannot exist, or is too incomprehensible to be within the compass of description, will be words of sound only, and though they may amuse the ear, they cannot inform the mind, for this explanation includes a previous question, viz. *how came the king by a power which the people are afraid to trust, and always obliged to check?* Such a power could not be the gift of a wise people, neither can any power, *which needs checking*, be from God; yet the provision, which the constitution makes, supposes such a power to exist.

But the provision is unequal to the task; the means either cannot or will not accomplish the end, and the whole affair is a *felo de se;*[*] for as the greater weight will always carry up the less, and as all the wheels of a machine are put in motion by one, it only remains to know which power in the constitution has the most weight, for that will govern; and though the others, or a part of them, may clog, or, as the phrase is, check the rapidity of its motion, yet so long as they cannot stop it, their endeavours will be ineffectual; the first moving power will at last have its way, and what it wants in speed, is supplied by time.

That the crown is this overbearing part in the English constitution, needs not be mentioned, and that it derives its whole consequence merely from being the giver of places and pensions, is self-evident, wherefore, though we have been wise enough to shut and lock a door against absolute Monarchy, we at the same time have been foolish enough to put the Crown in possession of the key.

The prejudice of Englishmen in favour of their own government by king, lords, and commons, arises as much or more from national pride than reason. Individuals are undoubtedly safer in England than in some other countries, but the *will* of the king is as much the *law* of the land in Britain as in France, with this difference, that instead of proceeding directly from his mouth, it is handed to the people under the more formidable shape of an act of parliament. For the fate of Charles the First hath only made kings more subtle—not more just.

Wherefore, laying aside all national pride and prejudice in favour of modes and forms, the plain truth is, that *it is wholly owing to the constitution of the people, and not to the constitution of the government*, that the crown is not as oppressive in England as in Turkey.

An inquiry into the *constitutional errors* in the English form of

---

[*] Suicide.

government is at this time highly necessary; for as we are never in a proper condition of doing justice to others, while we continue under the influence of some leading partiality, so neither are we capable of doing it to ourselves while we remain fettered by any obstinate prejudice. And as a man, who is attached to a prostitute, is unfitted to choose or judge a wife, so any prepossession in favour of a rotten constitution of government will disable us from discerning a good one.

## II. OF MONARCHY AND
## HEREDITARY SUCCESSION

Mankind being originally equals in the order of creation, the equality could only be destroyed by some subsequent circumstance; the distinctions of rich, and poor, may in a great measure be accounted for, and that without having recourse to the harsh, ill-sounding names of oppression and avarice. Oppression is often the *consequence*, but seldom or never the *means* of riches; and though avarice will preserve a man from being necessitously poor, it generally makes him too timorous to be wealthy.

But there is another and greater distinction, for which no truly natural or religious reason can be assigned, and that is, the distinction of men into *Kings* and *Subjects*. Male and female are the distinctions of nature, good and bad the distinctions of heaven; but how a race of men came into the world so exalted above the rest, and distinguished like some new species, is worth inquiring into, and whether they are the means of happiness or of misery to mankind.

In the early ages of the world, according to the scripture chronology, there were no kings; the consequence of which was, there were no wars; it is the pride of kings which throw mankind into confusion. Holland without a king hath enjoyed more peace for this last century than any of the monarchial governments in Europe. Antiquity favours the same remark; for the quiet and rural lives of the first patriarchs hath a happy something in them, which vanishes away when we come to the history of Jewish royalty.

Government by kings was first introduced into the world by the Heathens, from whom the children of Israel copied the custom. It was the most prosperous invention the Devil ever set on foot for the promotion of idolatry. The Heathens paid divine honours to their deceased kings, and the Christian World hath improved on the plan, by doing the same to their living ones. How impious is the title of sacred majesty applied to a worm, who in the midst of his splendor is crumbling into dust!

As the exalting one man so greatly above the rest cannot be justified on the equal rights of nature, so neither can it be defended on the authority of scripture; for the will of the Almighty, as declared by Gideon and the prophet Samuel, expressly disapproves of government by Kings. All anti-monarchical parts of scripture have been very smoothly glossed over in monarchical governments, but they undoubtedly merit the attention of countries which have their governments yet to form. *Render unto Caesar the things which are Caesar's* is the scripture doctrine of courts, yet it is no support of monarchical government, for the Jews at that time were without a king, and in a state of vassalage to the Romans.

Near three thousand years passed away from the Mosaic account of the creation, till the Jews under a national delusion requested a king. Till then their form of government (except in extraordinary cases, where the Almighty interposed) was a kind of Republic administered by a judge and the elders of the tribes. Kings they had none, and it was held sinful to acknowledge any being under that title but the Lord of Hosts. And when a man seriously reflects on the idolatrous homage which is paid to the persons of kings, he need not wonder that the Almighty, ever jealous of his honour, should disapprove of a form of government which so impiously invades the prerogative of heaven.

Monarchy is ranked in scripture as one of the sins of the Jews, for which a curse in reserve is denounced against them. The history of that transaction is worth attending to.

The children of Israel being oppressed by the Midianites, Gideon marched against them with a small army, and victory, through the divine interposition, decided in his favour. The Jews, elate with success, and attributing it to the generalship of Gideon, proposed making him a king, saying, *Rule thou over us, thou and thy son and thy son's son.* Here was temptation in its fullest extent; not a kingdom only, but an hereditary one, but Gideon in the piety of his soul replied, *I will not rule over you, neither shall my son rule over you.* THE LORD SHALL RULE OVER YOU. Words need not be more explicit; Gideon doth not decline the honour, but denieth their right to give it; neither doth he compliment them with invented declarations of his thanks, but in the positive style of a prophet charges them with disaffection to their proper Sovereign, the King of heaven.

About one hundred and thirty years after this, they fell again into the same error. The hankering which the Jews had for the idolatrous customs of the Heathens, is something exceedingly unaccountable; but so it was, that laying hold of the misconduct of Samuel's two sons, who were entrusted with some secular concerns, they came in an abrupt and clamorous manner to Samuel, saying, *Behold thou art old, and thy sons walk not in thy ways, now make us a king to judge us, like all other nations.* And here we cannot but observe that their motives were bad, viz. that they might be *like* unto other nations, *i.e.* the Heathens, whereas their true glory laid in being as much *unlike* them as possible. *But the thing displeased Samuel when they said, Give us a King to judge us; and Samuel prayed unto the Lord, and the Lord said unto Samuel, Hearken unto the voice of the people in all that they say unto thee, for they have not rejected thee, but they have rejected me,* THAT I SHOULD NOT REIGN OVER THEM. *According to all the works which they have since the day that I brought them up out of Egypt, even unto this day; wherewith they have forsaken me and served other Gods: so do they also unto thee. Now therefore hearken unto their voice, howbeit, protest solemnly unto them and show them the manner of the King that shall reign over them,* i.e. not of any particular king, but the general manner of the Kings of the earth, whom Israel was so eagerly copying after. And notwithstanding the great distance of time and difference of manners, the character is still in fashion. *And Samuel told all the words of the Lord unto the people, that asked of him a King. And he said, This shall be the manner of the King that shall reign over you. He will take your sons and appoint them for himself for his chariots and to be his horsemen, and some shall run before his chariots* (this description agrees with the present mode of impressing men) *and he will appoint him captains over thousands and captains over fifties, and will set them to ear his ground and to reap his harvest, and to make his instruments of war, and instruments of his chariots. And he will take your daughters to be confectionaries, and to be cooks, and to be bakers* (this describes the expense and luxury as well as the oppression of Kings) *and he will take your fields, and your vineyards, and your olive yards, even the best of them, and give them to his servants. And he will take the tenth of your seed, and of your vineyards, and give them to his officers and to his servants* (by which we see that bribery, corruption, and favouritism are the standing vices of Kings) *and he will take the tenth of your men servants, and your maid servants, and your goodliest young men and your asses, and put them to his work; and he will take the tenth of your sheep, and ye shall be his servants, and ye shall cry out in that day because of your king which ye shall have chosen*, AND THE LORD WILL NOT HEAR YOU IN THAT DAY. This accounts for the continuation of Monarchy; neither do the characters of the few good kings which have lived since, either sanctify the title, or blot out the sinfulness of the origin; the high encomium given of David takes no notice of him *officially as a King*, but only as a *Man* after God's own heart. *Nevertheless the people refused to obey the voice of Samuel, and they said, Nay but we will have a king over us, that we may be like all the nations, and that our king may judge us, and go out before us and fight our battles.* Samuel continued to reason with them, but to no purpose; he set before them their ingratitude, but all would not avail; and seeing them fully bent on their folly, he cried out, *I will call unto the Lord, and he shall send thunder and rain* (which then was a punishment, being in the time of wheat harvest) *that ye may perceive and see that your wickedness is great which ye have done in the sight of the Lord*, IN ASKING YOU A KING. *So Samuel called unto the Lord, and the Lord sent thunder and rain that day, and all the people greatly feared the Lord and Samuel. And all the people said unto Samuel, Pray for thy servants unto the Lord thy God that we die not, for* WE HAVE ADDED UNTO OUR SINS THIS EVIL, TO ASK A KING. These portions of scripture are direct and positive. They admit of no equivocal construction. That the Almighty hath here entered his protest against monarchical government, is true, or the scripture is false. And a man hath good reason to believe that there is as much of kingcraft, as priestcraft, in withholding the scripture from the public in Popish countries. For monarchy in every instance is the Popery of government.

To the evil of monarchy we have added that of hereditary succession; and as the first is a degradation and lessening of ourselves, so the second, claimed as a matter of right, is an insult and an imposition on posterity. For all men being originally equals, no *one* by *birth* could have a right to set up his own family in perpetual preference to all others for ever, and though himself might deserve *some* decent degree of honours of his contemporaries, yet his descendants might be far too unworthy to inherit them. One of the strongest natural proofs of the folly of hereditary right in Kings, is, that nature disapproves it, otherwise she would not so frequently turn it into ridicule by giving mankind an *Ass for a Lion*.

Secondly, as no man at first could possess any other public honours than were bestowed upon him, so the givers of those honours could have no power to give away the right of posterity. And though they might say, "We choose you for *our* head," they could not, without manifest injustice to their children, say, "that your children and your children's children shall reign over *ours* for ever." Because such an unwise, unjust, unnatural compact might (perhaps) in the next succession put them under the government of a rogue or a fool. Most wise men, in their private sentiments, have ever treated hereditary right with contempt; yet it is one of those evils, which when once established is not easily removed; many submit from fear, others from superstition, and the more powerful part shares with the king the plunder of the rest.

This is supposing the present race of kings in the world to have had an honourable origin; whereas it is more than probable, that could we take off the dark covering of antiquity, and trace them to their first rise, that we should find the first of them nothing better than the principal ruffian of some restless gang, whose savage manners or preeminence in subtlety obtained the title of chief among plunderers; and who by increasing in power, and extending his depredations, overawed the quiet and defenseless to purchase their safety by frequent contributions. Yet his electors could have no idea of giving hereditary right to his descendants, because such a perpetual exclusion of themselves was incompatible with the free and unrestrained principles they professed to live by. Wherefore, hereditary succession in the early ages of monarchy could not take place as a matter of claim, but as something casual or complemental; but as few or no records were extant in those days, and traditional history stuffed with fables, it was very easy, after the lapse of a few generations, to trump up some superstitious tale, conveniently timed, Mahomet-like, to cram hereditary right down the throats of the vulgar. Perhaps the disorders which threatened, or seemed to threaten, on the decease of a leader and the choice of a new one (for elections among ruffians could not be very orderly) induced many at first to favour hereditary pretensions; by which means it happened, as it hath happened since, that what at first was submitted to as a convenience, was afterwards claimed as a right.

England, since the conquest, hath known some few good monarchs, but groaned beneath a much larger number of bad ones; yet no man in his senses can say that their claim under William the Conqueror is a very honourable one. A French bastard landing with an armed banditti, and establishing himself king of England against the consent of the natives, is in plain terms a very paltry rascally original. It certainly hath no divinity in it. However, it is needless to spend much time in exposing the folly of hereditary right; if there are any so weak as to believe it, let them promiscuously worship the ass and lion, and welcome. I shall neither copy their humility, nor disturb their devotion.

Yet I should be glad to ask how they suppose kings came at first? The question admits but of three answers, viz. either by lot, by election, or by usurpation. If the first king was taken by lot, it establishes a precedent for the next, which excludes hereditary succession. Saul was by lot, yet the succession was not hereditary, neither does it appear from that transaction there was any intention it ever should be. If the first king of any country was by election, that likewise establishes a precedent for the next; for to say, that the *right* of all future generations is taken away, by the act of the first electors, in their choice not only of a king, but of a family of kings for ever, hath no parallel in or out of scripture but the doctrine of original sin, which supposes the free will of all men lost in Adam; and from such comparison, and it will admit of no other, hereditary succession can derive no glory. For as in Adam all sinned, and as in the first electors all men obeyed; as in the one all mankind were subjected to Satan, and in the other to Sovereignty; as our innocence was lost in the first, and our authority in the last; and as both disable us from reassuming some former state and privilege, it unanswerably follows that original sin and hereditary succession are parallels. Dishonourable rank! Inglorious connection! Yet the most subtle sophist cannot produce a juster simile.

As to usurpation, no man will be so hardy as to defend it; and that William the Conqueror was an usurper is a fact not to be contradicted. The plain truth is, that the antiquity of English monarchy will not bear looking into.

But it is not so much the absurdity as the evil of hereditary succession which concerns mankind. Did it ensure a race of good and wise men it would have the seal of divine authority, but as it opens a door to the *foolish*, the *wicked*, and the *improper*, it hath in it the nature of oppression. Men who look upon themselves born to reign, and others to obey, soon grow insolent; selected from the rest of mankind their minds are early poisoned by importance; and the world they act in differs so materially from the world at large, that they have but little opportunity of knowing its true interests, and when they succeed to the government are frequently the most ignorant and unfit of any throughout the dominions.

Another evil which attends hereditary succession is, that the throne is subject to be possessed by a minor at any age; all which time the regency, acting under the cover of a king, have every opportunity and inducement to betray their trust. The same national misfortune happens, when a king, worn out with age and infirmity, enters the last stage of human weakness. In both these cases the public becomes a prey to every miscreant, who can tamper successfully with the follies either of age or infancy.

The most plausible plea, which hath ever been offered in favour of hereditary succession, is, that it preserves a nation from civil wars; and were this true, it would be weighty; whereas, it is the most barefaced falsity ever imposed upon mankind. The whole history of England disowns the fact. Thirty kings and two minors have reigned in that distracted kingdom since the conquest, in which time there have been (including the Revolution) no less than eight civil wars and nineteen rebellions. Wherefore instead of making for peace, it makes against it, and destroys the very foundation it seems to stand on.

The contest for monarchy and succession, between the houses of York and Lancaster, laid England in a scene of blood for many years. Twelve pitched battles, besides skirmishes and sieges, were fought between Henry and Edward. Twice was Henry prisoner to Edward, who in his turn was prisoner to Henry. And so uncertain is the fate of war and the temper of a nation, when nothing but personal matters are the ground of a quarrel, that Henry was taken in triumph from a prison to a palace, and Edward obliged to fly from a palace to a foreign land; yet, as sudden transitions of temper are seldom lasting, Henry in his turn was driven from the throne, and Edward recalled to succeed him. The parliament always following the strongest side.

This contest began in the reign of Henry the Sixth, and was not entirely extinguished till Henry the Seventh, in whom the families were united. Including a period of 67 years, viz. from 1422 to 1489.

In short, monarchy and succession have laid (not this or that kingdom only) but the world in blood and ashes. 'Tis a form of government which the word of God bears testimony against, and blood will attend it.

If we inquire into the business of a king, we shall find that in some countries they have none; and after sauntering away their lives without pleasure to themselves or advantage to the nation, withdraw from the scene, and leave their successors to tread the same idle ground. In absolute monarchies the whole weight of business, civil and military, lies on the King; the children of Israel in their request for a king, urged this plea "that he may judge us, and go out before us and fight our battles." But in countries where he is neither a judge nor a general, as in England, a man would be puzzled to know what *is* his business.

The nearer any government approaches to a Republic the less business there is for a king. It is somewhat difficult to find a proper name for the government of England. Sir William Meredith calls it a Republic; but in its present state it is unworthy of the name, because the corrupt influence of the Crown, by having all the places in its disposal, hath so effectually swallowed up the power, and eaten out the virtue of the House of Commons (the Republican part in the constitution) that the government of England is nearly as monarchical as that of France or Spain. Men fall out with names without understanding them. For it is the Republican and not the monarchical part of the constitution of England which Englishmen glory in, viz. the liberty of choosing an House of Commons from out of their own body—and it is easy to see that when Republican virtue fails, slavery ensues. Why is the constitution of England sickly, but because monarchy hath poisoned the Republic, the Crown hath engrossed the Commons?

In England a king hath little more to do than to make war and give away places; which in plain terms, is to impoverish the nation and set it together by the ears. A pretty business indeed for a man to be allowed eight hundred thousand sterling a year for, and worshipped into the bargain! Of more worth is one honest man to society and in the sight of God, than all the crowned ruffians that ever lived.

# III. THOUGHTS ON THE PRESENT STATE OF AMERICAN AFFAIRS

In the following pages I offer nothing more than simple facts, plain arguments, and common sense; and have no other preliminaries to settle with the reader, than that he will divest himself of prejudice and prepossession, and suffer his reason and his feelings to determine for themselves; that he will put *on*, or rather that he will not put *off* the true character of a man, and generously enlarge his views beyond the present day.

Volumes have been written on the subject of the struggle between England and America. Men of all ranks have embarked in the controversy, from different motives, and with various designs; but all have been ineffectual, and the period of debate is closed. Arms, as the last resource, decide this contest; the appeal was the choice of the king, and the continent hath accepted the challenge.

It hath been reported of the late Mr. Pelham (who tho' an able minister was not without his faults) that on his being attacked in the House of Commons, on the score, that his measures were only of a temporary kind, replied *"They will last my time."* Should a thought so fatal and unmanly possess the colonies in the present contest, the name of ancestors will be remembered by future generations with detestation.

The Sun never shined on a cause of greater worth. 'Tis not the affair of a City, a County, a Province, or a Kingdom, but of a Continent—of at least one eighth part of the habitable Globe. 'Tis not the concern of a day, a year, or an age; posterity are virtually involved in the contest, and will be more or less affected, even to the end of time, by the proceedings now. Now is the seed-time of Continental union, faith and honour. The least fracture now will be like a name engraved with the point of a pin on the tender rind of a young oak; the wound will enlarge with the tree, and posterity read it in full grown characters.

By referring the matter from argument to arms, a new æra for politics is struck—a new method of thinking hath arisen. All plans, proposals, etc. prior to the nineteenth of April, *i.e.* to the commencement of hostilities, are like the almanacks of the last year; which, tho' proper then are superseded and useless now. Whatever was advanced by the advocates on either side of the question then, terminated in one and the same point, viz. a union with Great Britain: the only difference between the parties was the method of effecting it; the one proposing force, the other friendship; but it hath so far happened that the first hath failed, and the second hath withdrawn her influence.

As much hath been said of the advantages of reconciliation which, like an agreeable dream, hath passed away and left us as we were, it is but right, that we should examine the contrary side of the argument, and inquire into some of the many material injuries which these Colonies sustain, and always will sustain, by being connected with, and dependent on Great Britain: To examine that connection and dependence, on the principles of nature and common sense, to see what we have to trust to, if separated, and what we are to expect, if dependent.

I have heard it asserted by some, that as America hath flourished under her former connection with Great Britain that the same connection is necessary towards her future happiness, and will always have the same effect. Nothing can be more fallacious than this kind of argument. We may as well assert that because a child has thrived upon milk that it is never to have meat, or that the first twenty years of our lives is to become a precedent for the next twenty. But even this is admitting more than is true, for I answer roundly, that America would have flourished as much, and probably much more, had no European power had any thing to do with her. The commerce, by which she hath enriched herself, are the necessaries of life, and will always have a market while eating is the custom of Europe.

But she has protected us, say some. That she has engrossed us is true, and defended the continent at our expense as well as her own is admitted, and she would have defended Turkey from the same motive, viz. for the sake of trade and dominion.

Alas, we have been long led away by ancient prejudices, and made large sacrifices to superstition. We have boasted the protection of Great Britain, without considering, that her motive was *interest* not *attachment*; that she did not protect us from *our enemies* on *our account*, but from *her enemies* on *her own account*, from those who had no quarrel with us on any *other account*, and who will always be our enemies on the *same account*. Let Britain wave her pretensions to the Continent, or the Continent throw off the dependence, and we should be at peace with France and Spain were they at war with Britain. The miseries of Hanover last war ought to warn us against connections.

It has lately been asserted in parliament, that the Colonies have no relation to each other but through the Parent Country, *i.e.* that Pennsylvania and the Jerseys, and so on for the rest, are sister colonies by the way of England; this is certainly a very roundabout way of proving relationship, but it is the nearest and only true way of proving enemyship, if I may so call it. France and Spain never were, nor perhaps ever will be, our enemies as *Americans*, but as our being the *subjects of Great Britain.*

But Britain is the parent country, say some. Then the more shame upon her conduct. Even brutes do not devour their young, nor savages make war upon their families; wherefore the assertion, if true, turns to her reproach; but it happens not to be true, or only partly so and the phrase *parent* or *mother country* hath been jesuitically adopted by the King and his parasites, with a low papistical design of gaining an unfair bias on the credulous weakness of our minds. Europe, and not England, is the parent country of America. This new World hath been the asylum for the persecuted lovers of civil and religious liberty from *every part* of Europe. Hither have they fled, not from the tender embraces of the mother, but from the cruelty of the monster; and it is so far true of England, that the same tyranny which drove the first emigrants from home, pursues their descendants still.

In this extensive quarter of the globe, we forget the narrow limits of three hundred and sixty miles (the extent of England) and carry our friendship on a larger scale; we claim brotherhood with every European Christian, and triumph in the generosity of the sentiment.

It is pleasant to observe by what regular gradations we surmount the force of local prejudice, as we enlarge our acquaintance with the World. A man born in any town in England divided into parishes, will naturally associate most with his fellow-parishioners (because their interests in many cases will be common) and distinguish him by the name of *neighbour*; if he meet him but a few miles from home, he drops the narrow idea of a street, and salutes him by the name of *townsman*; if he travel out of the county, and meet him in any other, he forgets the minor divisions of street and town, and calls him *countryman, i.e. countyman*; but if in their foreign excursions they should associate in

France or any other part of *Europe*, their local remembrance would be enlarged into that of *Englishmen*. And by a just parity of reasoning, all Europeans meeting in America, or any other quarter of the globe, are *countrymen*; for England, Holland, Germany, or Sweden, when compared with the whole, stand in the same places on the larger scale, which the divisions of street, town, and county do on the smaller ones; distinctions too limited for Continental minds. Not one third of the inhabitants, even of this province, are of English descent. Wherefore I reprobate the phrase of Parent or Mother Country applied to England only, as being false, selfish, narrow and ungenerous.

But admitting, that we were all of English descent, what does it amount to? Nothing. Britain, being now an open enemy, extinguishes every other name and title: And to say that reconciliation is our duty, is truly farcical. The first king of England, of the present line (William the Conqueror) was a Frenchman, and half the Peers of England are descendants from the same country; therefore, by the same method of reasoning, England ought to be governed by France.

Much hath been said of the united strength of Britain and the colonies, that in conjunction they might bid defiance to the world. But this is mere presumption; the fate of war is uncertain, neither do the expressions mean any thing; for this continent would never suffer itself to be drained of inhabitants, to support the British arms in either Asia, Africa, or Europe.

Besides what have we to do with setting the world at defiance? Our plan is commerce, and that, well attended to, will secure us the peace and friendship of all Europe; because, it is the interest of all Europe to have America a *free port*. Her trade will always be a protection, and her barrenness of gold and silver secure her from invaders.

I challenge the warmest advocate for reconciliation, to show a single advantage that this continent can reap, by being connected with Great Britain. I repeat the challenge; not a single advantage is derived. Our corn will fetch its price in any market in Europe, and our imported goods must be paid for, buy them where we will.

But the injuries and disadvantages we sustain by that connection, are without number; and our duty to mankind at large, as well as to ourselves, instruct us to renounce the alliance: because, any submission to, or dependence on Great Britain, tends directly to involve this Continent in European wars and quarrels, and sets us at variance with nations, who would otherwise seek our friendship, and against whom we have neither anger nor complaint. As Europe is our market for trade, we ought to form no partial connection with any part of it. It is the true interest of America to steer clear of European contentions, which she never can do, while by her dependence on Britain, she is made the make-weight in the scale of British politics.

Europe is too thickly planted with kingdoms to be long at peace, and whenever a war breaks out between England and any foreign power, the trade of America goes to ruin, *because of her connection with England*. The next war may not turn out like the last, and should it not, the advocates for reconciliation now, will be wishing for separation then, because neutrality in that case would be a safer convoy than a man of war. Every thing that is right or natural pleads for separation. The blood of the slain, the weeping voice of nature cries, *'Tis time to part*. Even the distance at which the Almighty hath placed England and America is a strong and natural proof, that the authority of the one over the other was never the design of Heaven. The time likewise at which the Continent was discovered, adds weight to the argument, and the manner in which it was peopled increases the force of it. The Reformation was preceded by the discovery of America, as if the Almighty graciously meant to open a sanctuary to the persecuted in future years, when home should afford neither friendship nor safety.

The authority of Great Britain over this continent, is a form of government, which sooner or later must have an end: And a serious mind can draw no true pleasure by looking forward under the painful and positive conviction that what he calls "the present constitution" is merely temporary. As parents, we can have no joy, knowing that this government is not sufficiently lasting to ensure any thing which we may bequeath to posterity: And by a plain method of argument, as we are running the next generation into debt, we ought to do the work of it, otherwise we use them meanly and pitifully. In order to discover the line of our duty rightly, we should take our children in our hand, and fix our station a few years farther into life; that eminence will present a prospect which a few present fears and prejudices conceal from our sight.

Though I would carefully avoid giving unnecessary offense, yet I am inclined to believe, that all those who espouse the doctrine of reconciliation, may be included within the following descriptions.

Interested men, who are not to be trusted; weak men, who *cannot* see; prejudiced men, who *will not* see; and a certain set of moderate men who think better of the European world than it deserves; and this last class, by an ill-judged deliberation, will be the cause of more calamities to this continent than all the other three.

It is the good fortune of many to live distant from the scene of present sorrow; the evil is not sufficiently brought to their doors to make *them* feel the precariousness with which all American property is possessed. But let our imaginations transport us for a few moments to Boston; that seat of wretchedness will teach us wisdom, and instruct us for ever to renounce a power in whom we can have no trust. The inhabitants of that unfortunate city, who but a few months ago were in ease and affluence, have now no other alternative than to stay and starve, or turn and beg. Endangered by the fire of their friends if they continue within the city, and plundered by the soldiery if they leave it, in their present condition they are prisoners without the hope of redemption, and in a general attack for their relief, they would be exposed to the fury of both armies.

Men of passive tempers look somewhat lightly over the offenses of Britain, and, still hoping for the best, are apt to call out, *Come, come, we shall be friends again for all this*. But examine the passions and feelings of mankind: Bring the doctrine of reconciliation to the touchstone of nature, and then tell me whether you can hereafter love, honour, and faithfully serve the power that hath carried fire and sword into your land? If you cannot do all these, then are you only deceiving yourselves, and by your delay bringing ruin upon posterity. Your future connection with Britain, whom you can neither love nor honour, will be forced and unnatural, and being formed only on the plan of present convenience, will in a little time fall into a relapse more wretched than the first. But if you say, you can still pass the violations over, then I ask, Hath your house been burnt? Hath your property been destroyed before your face? Are your wife and children destitute of a bed to lie on, or bread to live on? Have you lost a parent or a child by their hands, and yourself the ruined and wretched survivor? If you have not, then are you not a judge of those who have. But if you have, and still can shake hands with the murderers, then are you unworthy of the name of husband, father, friend, or lover, and whatever may be your rank or title in life, you have the heart of a coward, and the spirit of a sycophant.

This is not inflaming or exaggerating matters, but trying them by those feelings and affections which nature justifies, and without which, we should be incapable of discharging the social duties of life, or enjoying the felicities of it. I mean not to exhibit horror for the purpose of provoking revenge, but to awaken us from fatal and unmanly slumbers, that we may pursue determinately some fixed object. It is not in the power of Britain or of Europe to conquer America, if she do not conquer herself by *delay* and *timidity*. The present winter is worth an age if rightly employed, but if lost or neglected, the whole Continent will partake of the misfortune; and there is no punishment which that man will not deserve, be he who, or what, or where he will, that may be the means of sacrificing a season so precious and useful.

It is repugnant to reason, to the universal order of things, to all examples from former ages, to suppose, that this Continent can longer remain subject to any external power. The most sanguine in Britain doth not think so. The utmost stretch of human wisdom cannot, at this time, compass a plan short of separation, which can promise the continent even a year's security. Reconciliation is *now* a fallacious dream. Nature hath deserted the connection, and Art cannot supply her place. For, as Milton wisely expresses, "never can true reconcilement grow where wounds of deadly hate have pierced so deep."

Every quiet method for peace hath been ineffectual. Our prayers have been rejected with disdain; and only tended to convince us, that nothing flatters vanity, or confirms obstinacy in Kings more than repeated petitioning—and nothing hath contributed more than that very measure to make the Kings of Europe absolute: Witness Denmark and Sweden. Wherefore, since nothing but blows will do, for God's sake let us come to a final separation, and not leave the next generation to be cutting throats, under the violated unmeaning names of parent and child.

To say they will never attempt it again is idle and visionary, we thought so at the repeal of the stamp act, yet a year or two undeceived us; as well may we suppose that nations, which have been once defeated, will never renew the quarrel.

As to government matters, it is not in the power of Britain to do this continent justice: The business of it will soon be too weighty, and intricate, to be managed with any tolerable degree of convenience, by a power so distant from us, and so very ignorant of us; for if they cannot conquer us, they cannot govern us. To be always running three or four thousand miles with a tale or a petition, waiting four or five months for an answer, which when obtained requires five or six more to explain it in, will in a few years be looked upon as folly and childishness. There was a time when it was proper, and there is a proper time for it to cease.

Small islands not capable of protecting themselves are the proper objects for kingdoms to take under their care; but there is something very absurd, in supposing a Continent to be perpetually governed by an island. In no instance hath nature made the satellite larger than its primary planet, and as England and America, with respect to each other, reverses the common order of nature, it is evident they belong to different systems; England to Europe, America to itself.

I am not induced by motives of pride, party, or resentment to espouse the doctrine of separation and independence; I am clearly, positively, and conscientiously persuaded that it is the true interest of this Continent to be so; that every thing short of *that* is mere patchwork, that it can afford no lasting felicity,—that it is leaving the sword to our children, and shrinking back at a time, when, a little more, a little farther, would have rendered this Continent the glory of the earth.

As Britain hath not manifested the least inclination towards a compromise, we may be assured that no terms can be obtained worthy the acceptance of the Continent, or any ways equal to the expense of blood and treasure we have been already put to.

The object, contended for, ought always to bear some just proportion to the expense. The removal of North, or the whole detestable junto, is a matter unworthy the millions we have expended. A temporary stoppage of trade was an inconvenience, which would have sufficiently balanced the repeal of all the acts complained of, had such repeals been obtained; but if the whole Continent must take up arms, if every man must be a soldier, it is scarcely worth our while to fight against a contemptible ministry only. Dearly, dearly, do we pay for the repeal of the acts, if that is all we fight for; for in a just estimation, it is as great a folly to pay a Bunker-hill price for law, as for land. As I have always considered the independency of this continent, as an event, which sooner or later must arrive, so from the late rapid progress of the Continent to maturity, the event could not be far off. Wherefore, on the breaking out of hostilities, it was not worth while to have disputed a matter, which time would have finally redressed, unless we meant to be in earnest; otherwise, it is like wasting an estate on a suit at law, to regulate the trespasses of a tenant, whose lease is just expiring. No man was a warmer wisher for reconciliation than myself, before the fatal nineteenth of April 1775, but the moment the event of that day was made known, I rejected the hardened, sullen-tempered Pharaoh of England for ever; and disdain the wretch, that with the pretended title of *Father of His People* can unfeelingly hear of their slaughter, and composedly sleep with their blood upon his soul.

But admitting that matters were now made up, what would be the event? I answer, the ruin of the Continent. And that for several reasons.

*First.* The powers of governing still remaining in the hands of the King, he will have a negative over the whole legislation of this Continent. And as he hath shown himself such an inveterate enemy to liberty, and discovered such a thirst for arbitrary power; is he, or is he not, a proper man to say to these colonies, *You shall make no laws but what I please*. And is there any inhabitant in America so ignorant as not to know, that according to what is called the *present constitution*, that this Continent can make no laws but what the king gives leave to; and is there any man so unwise, as not to see, that (considering what has happened) he will suffer no law to be made here, but such as suit *his* purpose. We may be as effectually enslaved by the want of laws in America, as by submitting to laws made for us in England. After matters are made up (as it is called) can there be any doubt, but the whole power of the crown will be exerted, to keep this continent as low and humble as possible? Instead of going forward we shall go backward, or be perpetually quarrelling or ridiculously petitioning. We are already greater than the King wishes us to be, and will he not hereafter endeavour to make us less? To bring the matter to one point, Is the power who is jealous of our prosperity, a proper power to govern us? Whoever says *No* to this question, is an *Independent*, for independency means no more, than, whether we shall make our own laws, or whether the King, the greatest enemy this Continent hath, or can have, shall tell us *There shall be no laws but such as I like*.

But the King you will say has a negative in England; the people there can make no laws without his consent. In point of right and good order, there is something very ridiculous, that a youth of twenty-one (which hath often happened) shall say to several millions of people, older and wiser than himself, "I forbid this or that act of yours to be law." But in this place I decline this sort of reply, though I will never cease to expose the absurdity of it, and only answer, that England being the King's residence, and America not so, makes quite another case. The King's negative *here* is ten times more dangerous and fatal than it can be in England, for *there* he will scarcely refuse his consent to a bill for putting England into as strong a state of defense as possible, and in America he would never suffer such a bill to be passed.

America is only a secondary object in the system of British politics. England consults the good of *this* country, no farther than it answers her *own* purpose. Wherefore, her own interest leads her to suppress the growth of *ours* in every case which doth not promote her advantage, or in the least interferes with it. A pretty state we should soon be in under such a second-hand government, considering what has happened! Men do not change from enemies to friends by the alteration of a name: And in order to show that reconciliation now is a dangerous doctrine, I affirm, *that it would be policy in the King at this time to repeal the acts, for the sake of reinstating himself in the government of the provinces*; in order that *he may accomplish by craft and subtlety, in the long run, what he cannot do by force and violence in the short one*. Reconciliation and ruin are nearly related.

*Secondly.* That as even the best terms which we can expect to obtain can amount to no more than a temporary expedient, or a kind of government by guardianship, which can last no longer than till the Colonies come of age, so the general face and state of things, in the interim, will be unsettled and unpromising. Emigrants of property will not choose to come to a country whose form of government hangs but by a thread, and who is every day tottering on the brink of commotion and disturbance; and numbers of the present inhabitants would lay hold of the interval, to dispense of their effects, and quit the Continent.

But the most powerful of all arguments, is, that nothing but independence, *i.e.* a Continental form of government, can keep the peace of the Continent and preserve it inviolate from civil wars. I dread the event of a reconciliation with Britain now, as it is more than probable that it will be followed by a revolt somewhere or other, the consequences of which may be far more fatal than all the malice of Britain.

Thousands are already ruined by British barbarity;(thousands more will probably suffer the same fate). Those men have other feelings than us who have nothing suffered. All they *now* possess is liberty; what they before enjoyed is sacrificed to its service, and having nothing more to lose, they disdain submission. Besides, the general temper of the Colonies, towards a British government, will be like that of a youth, who is nearly out of his time; they will care very little about her. And a government which cannot preserve the peace is no government at all, and in that case we pay our money for nothing; and pray what is it that Britain can do, whose power will be wholly on paper, should a civil tumult break out the very day after reconciliation? I have heard some men say, many of whom I believe spoke without thinking, that they dreaded an independence, fearing that it would produce civil wars. It is but seldom that our first thoughts are truly correct, and that is the case here; for there are ten times more to dread from a patched up connection than from independence. I make the sufferers' case my own, and I protest, that were I driven from house and home, my property destroyed, and my circumstances ruined, that as man, sensible of injuries, I could never relish the doctrine of reconciliation, or consider myself bound thereby.

The Colonies have manifested such a spirit of good order and obedience to Continental government, as is sufficient to make every reasonable person easy and happy on that head. No man can assign the least pretence for his fears, on any other grounds, than such as are truly childish and ridiculous, viz. that one colony will be striving for superiority over another.

Where there are no distinctions there can be no superiority, perfect equality affords no temptation. The Republics of Europe are all (and we may say always) in peace. Holland and Switzerland are without wars, foreign or domestic: Monarchical governments, it is true, are never long at rest; the crown itself is a temptation to enterprising ruffians at home; and that degree of pride and insolence ever attendant on regal authority, swells into a rupture with foreign powers, in instances where a republican government, by being formed on more natural principles, would negotiate the mistake.

If there is any true cause of fear respecting independence, it is because no plan is yet laid down. Men do not see their way out. Wherefore, as an opening into that business, I offer the following hints; at the same time modestly affirming, that I have no other opinion of them myself, than that they may be the means of giving rise to something better. Could the straggling thoughts of individuals be collected, they would frequently form materials for wise and able men to improve into useful matter.

Let the assemblies be annual, with a president only. The representation more equal. Their business wholly domestic, and subject to the authority of a Continental Congress.

Let each Colony be divided into six, eight, or ten, convenient districts, each district to send a proper number of Delegates to Congress, so that each Colony send at least thirty. The whole number in Congress will be at least 390. Each Congress to sit and to choose a president by the following method. When the Delegates are met, let a Colony be taken from the whole thirteen Colonies by lot, after which, let the whole Congress choose (by ballot) a president from out of the Delegates of that Province. In the next Congress, let a Colony be taken by lot from twelve only, omitting that Colony from which the president was taken in the former Congress, and so proceeding on till the whole thirteen shall have had their proper rotation. And in order that nothing may pass into a law but what is satisfactorily just, not less than three fifths of the Congress to be called a majority. He that will promote discord, under a government so equally formed as this, would have joined Lucifer in his revolt.

But as there is a peculiar delicacy, from whom, or in what manner, this business must first arise, and as it seems most agreeable and consistent, that it should come from some intermediate body between the governed and the governors, that is, between the Congress and the People. Let a Continental Conference be held, in the following manner, and for the following purpose.

A Committee of twenty-six members of Congress, viz. two for each colony. Two Members from each House of Assembly, or Provincial Convention; and five Representatives of the people at large, to be chosen in the capital city or town of each Province, for and in behalf of the whole Province, by as many qualified voters as shall think proper to attend from all parts of the Province for that purpose; or, if more convenient, the Representatives may be chosen in two or three of the most populous parts thereof. In this conference, thus assembled, will be united, the two grand principles of business, *knowledge* and *power*. The members of Congress, Assemblies, or Conventions, by having had experience in national concerns, will be able and useful counsellors, and the whole, being empowered by the people, will have a truly legal authority.

The conferring members being met, let their business be to frame a Continental Charter, or Charter of the United Colonies; (answering to what is called the Magna Carta of England) fixing the number and manner of choosing Members of Congress, Members of Assembly, with their date of sitting; and drawing the line of business and jurisdiction between them: Always remembering, that our strength is continental, not provincial. Securing freedom and property to all men, and above all things, the free exercise of religion, according to the dictates of conscience; with such other matter as is necessary for a charter to contain. Immediately after which, the said Conference to dissolve, and the bodies which shall be chosen comformable to the said charter, to be the Legislators and Governors of this Continent for the time being: Whose peace and happiness may God preserve, Amen.

Should any body of men be hereafter delegated for this or some similar purpose, I offer them the following extracts from that wise observer on governments, Dragonetti. "The science," says he, "of the Politician consists in fixing the true point of happiness and freedom. Those men would deserve the gratitude of ages, who should discover a mode of government that contained the greatest sum of individual happiness, with the least national expense."*

But where, says some, is the King of America? I'll tell you, Friend, he reigns above, and doth not make havoc of mankind like the Royal Brute of Britain. Yet that we may not appear to be defective even in earthly honours, let a day be solemnly set apart for proclaiming the Charter; let it be brought forth placed on the Divine Law, the Word of God; let a crown be placed thereon, by which the world may know, that so far as we approve of monarchy, that in America *the law is king*. For as in absolute governments the King is law, so in free countries the law *ought* to be King; and there ought to be no other. But lest any ill use should afterwards arise, let the Crown at the conclusion of the ceremony be demolished, and scattered among the people whose right it is.

A government of our own is our natural right: And when a man seriously reflects on the precariousness of human affairs, he will become convinced, that it is infinitely wiser and safer, to form a constitution of our own in a cool deliberate manner, while we have it in our power,

---

* From "Of Virtue and Rewards," by Italian lawyer and author Giacinto Dragonetti, published in 1766.

than to trust such an interesting event to time and chance. If we omit it now, some Massanello* may hereafter arise, who laying hold of popular disquietudes, may collect together the desperate and the discontented, and by assuming to themselves the powers of government, may sweep away the liberties of the Continent like a deluge. Should the government of America return again into the hands of Britain, the tottering situation of things will be a temptation for some desperate adventurer to try his fortune; and in such a case, that relief can Britain give? Ere she could hear the news, the fatal business might be done; and ourselves suffering like the wretched Britons under the oppression of the Conqueror. Ye that oppose independence now, ye know not what ye do; ye are opening a door to eternal tyranny, by keeping vacant the seat of government. There are thousands, and tens of thousands, who would think it glorious to expel from the Continent that barbarous and hellish power, which hath stirred up the Indians and Negroes to destroy us; the cruelty hath a double guilt, it is dealing brutally by us, and treacherously by them.

To talk of friendship with those in whom our reason forbids us to have faith, and our affections wounded through a thousand pores instruct us to detest, is madness and folly. Every day wears out the little remains of kindred between us and them, and can there be any reason to hope, that as the relationship expires, the affection will increase, or that we shall agree better, when we have ten times more and greater concerns to quarrel over than ever?

Ye that tell us of harmony and reconciliation, can ye restore to us the time that is past? Can ye give to prostitution its former innocence? Neither can ye reconcile Britain and America. The last cord now is broken, the people of England are presenting addresses against us. There are injuries which nature cannot forgive; she would cease to be nature if she did. As well can the lover forgive the ravisher of his mistress, as the Continent forgive the murders of Britain. The Almighty hath implanted in us these unextinguishable feelings for good and wise purposes. They are the Guardians of his Image in our hearts. They distinguish us from the herd of common animals. The social compact would dissolve, and justice be extirpated from the earth, or have only a

*Thomas Anello, otherwise Massanello, a fisherman of Naples, who after spiriting up his countrymen in the public marketplace, against the oppressions of the Spaniards, to whom the place was then subject, prompted them to revolt, and in the space of a day became King. (Author's note)

casual existence were we callous to the touches of affection. The robber and the murderer would often escape unpunished, did not the injuries which our tempers sustain, provoke us into justice.

O ye that love mankind! Ye that dare oppose, not only the tyranny, but the tyrant, stand forth! Every spot of the old world is overrun with oppression. Freedom hath been hunted round the Globe. Asia and Africa have long expelled her. Europe regards her like a stranger, and England hath given her warning to depart. O! receive the fugitive, and prepare in time an asylum for mankind.

# IV. OF THE PRESENT ABILITY
## OF AMERICA, WITH SOME
### MISCELLANEOUS REFLECTIONS

I have never met with a man, either in England or America, who hath not confessed his opinion that a separation between the countries would take place one time or other: And there is no instance in which we have shown less judgment, than in endeavouring to describe, what we call the ripeness or fitness of the Continent for independence.

As all men allow the measure, and vary only in their opinion of the time, let us, in order to remove mistakes, take a general survey of things, and endeavour, if possible, to find out the *very* time. But we need not go far, the inquiry ceases at once, for, the *time hath found us*. The general concurrence, the glorious union of all things prove the fact.

'Tis not in numbers but in unity that our great strength lies; yet our present numbers are sufficient to repel the force of all the world. The Continent hath at this time the largest body of armed and disciplined men of any power under Heaven; and is just arrived at that pitch of strength, in which no single colony is able to support itself, and the whole, when united, can accomplish the matter, and either more, or, less than this, might be fatal in its effects. Our land force is already sufficient, and as to Naval affairs, we cannot be insensible that Britain would never suffer an American man of war to be built, while the Continent remained in her hands. Wherefore, we should be no forwarder an hundred years hence in that branch than we are now; but the truth is, we should be less so, because the timber of the Country is every day diminishing, and that, which will remain at last, will be far off and difficult to procure.

Were the Continent crowded with inhabitants, her sufferings under the present circumstances would be intolerable. The more seaport towns we had, the more should we have both to defend and to lose. Our present numbers are so happily proportioned to our wants, that no man need be idle. The diminution of trade affords an army, and the necessities of an army create a new trade.

Debts we have none; and whatever we may contract on this account will serve as a glorious memento of our virtue. Can we but leave posterity with a settled form of government, an independent constitution of its own, the purchase at any price will be cheap. But to expend millions for the sake of getting a few vile acts repealed, and routing the present ministry only, is unworthy the charge, and is using posterity with the utmost cruelty; because it is leaving them the great work to do, and a debt upon their backs, from which they derive no advantage. Such a thought is unworthy of a man of honour, and is the true characteristic of a narrow heart and a piddling politician.

The debt we may contract doth not deserve our regard, if the work be but accomplished. No nation ought to be without a debt. A national debt is a national bond; and when it bears no interest, is in no case a grievance. Britain is oppressed with a debt of upwards of one hundred and forty millions sterling, for which she pays upwards of four millions interest. And as a compensation for her debt, she has a large navy; America is without a debt, and without a navy; yet for the twentieth part of the English national debt, could have a navy as large again. The navy of England is not worth, at this time, more than three millions and an half sterling.

The first and second editions of this pamphlet were published without the following calculations, which are now given as a proof that the above estimation of the navy is just.*

The charge of building a ship of each rate, and furnishing her with masts, yards, sails and rigging, together with a proportion of eight months boatswain's and carpenter's sea-stores, as calculated by Mr. Burchett, Secretary to the navy.

* From *Naval History*, by English writer John Entic, published in 1757.

| | | | |
|---|---|---|---|
| For a ship of 100 guns | - | - | 35,553 pounds Sterling |
| 90 | - | - | 29,886 |
| 80 | - | - | 23,638 |
| 70 | - | - | 17,795 |
| 60 | - | - | 14,197 |
| 50 | - | - | 10,606 |
| 40 | - | - | 7,558 |
| 30 | - | - | 5,846 |
| 20 | - | - | 3,710 |

And from hence it is easy to sum up the value, or cost rather, of the whole British navy, which in the year 1757, when it was at its greatest glory consisted of the following ships and guns:

| Ships | Guns | | Cost of one | | Cost of all |
|---|---|---|---|---|---|
| 6 | - | 100 | - | 35,553 | - 213,318 |
| 12 | - | 90 | - | 29,886 | - 358,632 |
| 12 | - | 80 | - | 23,638 | - 283,656 |
| 43 | - | 70 | - | 17,785 | - 764,755 |
| 35 | - | 60 | - | 14,197 | - 496,895 |
| 40 | - | 50 | - | 10,606 | - 424,240 |
| 45 | - | 40 | - | 7,558 | - 340,110 |
| 58 | - | 20 | - | 3,710 | - 215,180 |
| 85 | Sloops, bombs, and fireships, one with another, at | | 2,000 | - | 170,000 |
| | | | | Cost | 3,266,786 |
| Remains for guns | - | | | - | 233,214 |
| | | | | Total | 3,500,000 |

No country on the globe is so happily situated, or so internally capable of raising a fleet as America. Tar, timber, iron, and cordage are her natural produce. We need go abroad for nothing. Whereas the Dutch, who make large profits by hiring out their ships of war to the Spaniards and Portuguese, are obliged to import most of the materials they use. We ought to view the building a fleet as an article of commerce, it being the natural manufactory of this country. It is the best money we can lay out. A navy when finished is worth more than it cost. And is that nice point in national policy, in which commerce and protection are united. Let us build; if we want them not, we can sell; and by that means replace our paper currency with ready gold and silver.

In point of manning a fleet, people in general run into great errors; it is not necessary that one fourth part should be sailors. The Terrible privateer, Captain Death, stood the hottest engagement of any ship last war, yet had not twenty sailors on board, though her complement of men was upwards of two hundred. A few able and social sailors will soon instruct a sufficient number of active landmen in the common work of a ship. Wherefore, we never can be more capable to begin on maritime matters than now, while our timber is standing, our fisheries blocked up, and our sailors and shipwrights out of employ. Men of war of seventy and eighty guns were built forty years ago in New England, and why not the same now? Ship-building is America's greatest pride, and in which she will in time excel the whole world. The great empires of the east are mostly inland, and consequently excluded from the possibility of rivalling her. Africa is in a state of barbarism; and no power in Europe hath either such an extent of coast, or such an internal supply of materials. Where nature hath given the one, she has withheld the other; to America only hath she been liberal of both. The vast empire of Russia is almost shut out from the sea: wherefore, her boundless forests, her tar, iron, and cordage are only articles of commerce.

In point of safety, ought we to be without a fleet? We are not the little people now, which we were sixty years ago; at that time we might have trusted our property in the streets, or fields rather; and slept securely without locks or bolts to our doors or windows. The case now is altered, and our methods of defense ought to improve with our increase of property. A common pirate, twelve months ago, might have come up the Delaware, and laid the city of Philadelphia under instant contribution, for what sum he pleased; and the same might have happened to other places. Nay, any daring fellow, in a brig of fourteen or sixteen guns might have robbed the whole Continent, and carried off half a million of money. These are circumstances which demand our attention, and point out the necessity of naval protection.

Some, perhaps, will say that after we have made it up with Britain, she will protect us. Can we be so unwise as to mean, that she shall keep a navy in our harbours for that purpose? Common sense will tell us, that the power which hath endeavoured to subdue us, is of all others the most improper to defend us. Conquest may be effected under the pretence of friendship; and ourselves after a long and brave resistance, be at last cheated into slavery. And if her ships are not to be admitted into our harbours, I would ask, how is she to protect us? A navy three or four thousand miles off can be of little use, and on sudden emergencies, none at all. Wherefore, if we must hereafter protect ourselves, why not do it for ourselves?

The English list of ships of war, is long and formidable, but not a tenth part of them are at any one time fit for service, numbers of them not in being; yet their names are pompously continued in the list, if only a plank be left of the ship: and not a fifth part of such as are fit for service, can be spared on any one station at one time. The East and West Indies, Mediterranean, Africa, and other parts over which Britain extends her claim, make large demands upon her navy. From a mixture of prejudice and inattention, we have contracted a false notion respecting the navy of England, and have talked as if we should have the whole of it to encounter at once, and for that reason, supposed, that we must have one as large; which not being instantly practicable, have been made use of by a set of disguised Tories to discourage our beginning thereon. Nothing can be farther from truth than this; for if America had only a twentieth part of the naval force of Britain, she would be by far an overmatch for her; because, as we neither have, nor claim any foreign dominion, our whole force would be employed on our own coast, where we should, in the long run, have two to one the advantage of those who had three or four thousand miles to sail over, before they could attack us, and the same distance to return in order to refit and recruit. And although Britain, by her fleet, hath a check over our trade to Europe, we have as large a one over her trade to the West Indies, which, by laying in the neighbourhood of the continent, is entirely at its mercy.

Some method might be fallen on to keep up a naval force in time of peace, if we should not judge it necessary to support a constant navy. If premiums were to be given to merchants, to build and employ in their service ships mounted with twenty, thirty, forty or fifty guns (the premiums to be in proportion to the loss of bulk to the merchants), fifty or sixty of those ships, with a few guardships on constant duty, would keep up a sufficient navy, and that without burdening ourselves with the evil so loudly complained of in England, of suffering their fleet, in time of peace to lie rotting in the docks. To unite the sinews of commerce and defense is sound policy; for when our strength and our riches play into each other's hand, we need fear no external enemy.

In almost every article of defense we abound. Hemp flourishes even to rankness, so that we need not want cordage. Our iron is superior to that of other countries. Our small arms equal to any in the world. Cannon we can cast at pleasure. Saltpetre and gunpowder we are every day producing. Our knowledge is hourly improving. Resolution is our inherent character, and courage hath never yet forsaken us. Wherefore, what is it that we want? Why is it that we hesitate? From Britain we can expect nothing but ruin. If she is once admitted to the government of America again, this Continent will not be worth living in. Jealousies will be always arising; insurrections will be constantly happening; and who will go forth to quell them? Who will venture his life to reduce his own countrymen to a foreign obedience? The difference between Pennsylvania and Connecticut, respecting some unlocated lands, shows the insignificance of a British government, and fully proves that nothing but Continental authority can regulate Continental matters.

Another reason why the present time is preferable to all others, is, that the fewer our numbers are, the more land there is yet unoccupied, which instead of being lavished by the king on his worthless dependents, may be hereafter applied, not only to the discharge of the present debt, but to the constant support of government. No nation under Heaven hath such an advantage at this.

The infant state of the Colonies, as it is called, so far from being against, is an argument in favour of independence. We are sufficiently numerous, and were we more so, we might be less united. It is a matter worthy of observation, that the more a country is peopled, the smaller their armies are. In military numbers, the ancients far exceeded the moderns: and the reason is evident. For trade being the consequence of population, men become too much absorbed thereby to attend to anything else. Commerce diminishes the spirit, both of patriotism and military defence. And history sufficiently informs us, that the bravest achievements were always accomplished in the non-age of a nation. With the increase of commerce, England hath lost its spirit. The city of London, notwithstanding its numbers, submits to continued insults with the patience of a coward. The more men have to lose, the less willing are they to venture. The rich are in general slaves to fear, and submit to courtly power with the trembling duplicity of a spaniel.

Youth is the seed time of good habits, as well in nations as in individuals. It might be difficult, if not impossible, to form the Continent into one government half a century hence. The vast variety of interests, occasioned by an increase of trade and population, would create confusion. Colony would be against Colony. Each being able might scorn each other's assistance: and while the proud and foolish gloried in their little distinctions, the wise would lament, that the union had not been formed before. Wherefore, the *present time* is the *true time* for establishing it. The intimacy which is contracted in infancy, and the friendship which is formed in misfortune, are, of all others, the most lasting and unalterable. Our present union is marked with both these characters: we are young and we have been distressed; but our concord hath withstood our troubles, and fixes a memorable area for posterity to glory in.

The present time, likewise, is that peculiar time, which never happens to a nation but once, viz. the time of forming itself into a government. Most nations have let slip the opportunity, and by that means have been compelled to receive laws from their conquerors, instead of making laws for themselves. First, they had a king, and then a form of government; whereas, the articles or charter of government, should be formed first, and men delegated to execute them afterward but from the errors of other nations, let us learn wisdom, and lay hold of the present opportunity —*to begin government at the right end.*

When William the Conqueror subdued England, he gave them law at the point of the sword; and until we consent that the seat of government in America, be legally and authoritatively occupied, we shall be in danger of having it filled by some fortunate ruffian, who may treat us in the same manner, and then, where will be our freedom? where our property?

As to religion, I hold it to be the indispensable duty of all government to protect all conscientious professors thereof, and I know of no other business which government hath to do therewith. Let a man throw aside that narrowness of soul, that selfishness of principle, which the niggards of all professions are so unwilling to part with, and he will be at delivered of his fears on that head. Suspicion is the companion of mean souls, and the bane of all good society. For myself, I fully and conscientiously believe, that it is the will of the Almighty, that there should be diversity of religious opinions among us: It affords a larger field for our Christian kindness. Were we all of one way of thinking, our religious dispositions would want matter for probation; and on this liberal principle, I look on the various denominations among us, to be like children of the same family, differing only, in what is called, their Christian names.

Earlier in this work, I threw out a few thoughts on the propriety of a Continental Charter, (for I only presume to offer hints, not plans) and in this place, I take the liberty of rementioning the subject, by observing, that a charter is to be understood as a bond of solemn obligation, which the whole enters into, to support the right of every separate part, whether of religion, personal freedom, or property. A firm bargain and a right reckoning make long friends.

In a former page I likewise mentioned the necessity of a large and equal representation; and there is no political matter which more deserves our attention. A small number of electors, or a small number of representatives, are equally dangerous. But if the number of the representatives be not only small, but unequal, the danger is increased. As an instance of this, I mention the following; when the Associators petition was before the House of Assembly of Pennsylvania; twenty-eight members only were present, all the Bucks county members, being eight, voted against it, and had seven of the Chester members done the same, this whole province had been governed by two counties only, and this danger it is always exposed to. The unwarrantable stretch likewise, which that house made in their last sitting, to gain an undue authority over the Delegates of that Province, ought to warn the people at large, how they trust power out of their own hands. A set of instructions for the Delegates were put together, which in point of sense and business would have dishonoured a schoolboy, and after being approved by a *few*, a *very few*, without doors, were carried into the House, and there passed *in behalf of the whole Colony*; whereas, did the whole Colony know, with what ill-will that House hath entered on some necessary public measures, they would not hesitate a moment to think them unworthy of such a trust.

Immediate necessity makes many things convenient, which if continued would grow into oppressions. Expedience and right are different things. When the calamities of America required a consultation, there was no method so ready, or at that time so proper, as to appoint persons from the several Houses of Assembly for that purpose; and the wisdom with which they have proceeded hath preserved this Continent from ruin. But as it is more than probable that we shall never be without a Congress, every well wisher to good order, must own, that the mode for choosing members of that body, deserves consideration. And I put it as a question to those, who make a study of mankind, whether representation and election is not too great a power for one and the same body of men to possess? When we are planning for posterity, we ought to remember, that virtue is not hereditary.

It is from our enemies that we often gain excellent maxims, and are frequently surprised into reason by their mistakes, Mr. Cornwall (one of the Lords of the Treasury) treated the petition of the New York Assembly with contempt, because *that* House, he said, consisted but of twenty-six members, which trifling number, he argued, could not with decency be put for the whole. We thank him for his involuntary honesty.*

To conclude, however strange it may appear to some, or however unwilling they may be to think so, matters not, but many strong and striking reasons may be given, to show, that nothing can settle our affairs so expeditiously as an open and determined declaration for independence. Some of which are,

*First*—It is the custom of nations, when any two are at war, for some other powers, not engaged in the quarrel, to step in as mediators, and bring about the preliminaries of a peace: but while America calls herself the Subject of Great Britain, no power, however well disposed she may be, can offer her mediation. Wherefore, in our present state we may quarrel on for ever.

*Secondly*—It is unreasonable to suppose, that France or Spain will

---

*Those who would fully understand of what great consequence a large and equal representation is to a state, should read Burgh's *Political Disquisitions*. (Author's note)

give us any kind of assistance, if we mean only, to make use of that assistance for the purpose of repairing the breach, and strengthening the connection between Britain and America; because, those powers would be sufferers by the consequences.

*Thirdly*—While we profess ourselves the subjects of Britain, we must, in the eye of foreign nations, be considered as rebels. The precedent is somewhat dangerous to *their peace*, for men to be in arms under the name of subjects; we, on the spot, can solve the paradox: but to unite resistance and subjection, requires an idea much too refined for common understanding.

*Fourthly*—Were a manifesto to be published, and despatched to foreign courts, setting forth the miseries we have endured, and the peaceable methods we have ineffectually used for redress; declaring, at the same time, that not being able, any longer, to live happily or safely under the cruel disposition of the British court, we had been driven to the necessity of breaking off all connections with her; at the same time, assuring all such courts of our peaceable disposition towards them, and of our desire of entering into trade with them: Such a memorial would produce more good effects to this Continent, than if a ship were freighted with petitions to Britain.

Under our present denomination of British subjects, we can neither be received nor heard abroad: The custom of all courts is against us, and will be so, until, by an independence, we take rank with other nations.

These proceedings may at first appear strange and difficult; but, like all other steps which we have already passed over, will in a little time become familiar and agreeable; and, until an independence is declared, the Continent will feel itself like a man who continues putting off some unpleasant business from day to day, yet knows it must be done, hates to set about it, wishes it over, and is continually haunted with the thoughts of its necessity.

# *APPENDIX*

$S$ ince the publication of the first edition of this pamphlet, or rather, on the same day on which it came out, the King's Speech made its appearance in this city. Had the spirit of prophecy directed the birth of this production, it could not have brought it forth, at a more seasonable juncture, or a more necessary time. The bloody mindedness of the one, show the necessity of pursuing the doctrine of the other. Men read by way of revenge. And the Speech, instead of terrifying, prepared a way for the manly principles of Independence.

Ceremony, and even, silence, from whatever motive they may arise, have a hurtful tendency, when they give the least degree of countenance to base and wicked performances; wherefore, if this maxim be admitted, it naturally follows, that the King's Speech, as being a piece of finished villany, deserved, and still deserves, a general execration both by the Congress and the people. Yet, as the domestic tranquillity of a nation, depends greatly, on the *chastity* of what may properly be called National Manners, it is often better, to pass some things over in silent disdain, than to make use of such new methods of dislike, as might introduce the least innovation, on that guardian of our peace and safety. And, perhaps, it is chiefly owing to this prudent delicacy, that the King's Speech, hath not, before now, suffered a public execution. The Speech if it may be called one, is nothing better than a wilful audacious libel against the truth, the common good, and the existence of mankind; and is a formal and pompous method of offering up human sacrifices to the pride of tyrants. But this general massacre of mankind is one of the privileges, and the certain consequence of Kings; for as nature knows them *not*, they know *not her*, and although they are beings of our *own* creating, they know not *us*, and are become the gods of their creators. The Speech hath one good quality, which is, that it is not calculated to deceive, neither can we, even if we would, be deceived by it. Brutality and tyranny appear on the face of it. It leaves us at no loss: And every line convinces, even in the moment of reading, that He, who hunts the woods for prey, the naked and untutored Indian, is less a Savage than the King of Britain.

Sir John Dalrymple, the putative father of a whining jesuitical piece, fallaciously called, "The Address of the People of *England* to the Inhabitants of *America*," hath, perhaps, from a vain supposition, that the people *here* were to be frightened at the pomp and description of a king, given, (though very unwisely on his part) the real character of the present one: "But" says this writer, "if you are inclined to pay compliments to an administration, which we do not complain of," (meaning the Marquis of Rockingham's at the repeal of the Stamp Act) "it is very unfair in you to withhold them from that prince *by whose* NOD ALONE *they were permitted to do any thing.*" This is Toryism with a witness! Here is idolatry even without a mask: And he who can calmly hear, and digest such doctrine, hath forfeited his claim to rationality—an apostate from the order of manhood; and ought to be considered—as one, who hath not only given up the proper dignity of man, but sunk himself beneath the rank of animals, and contemptibly crawl through the world like a worm.

However, it matters very little now, what the king of England either says or does; he hath wickedly broken through every moral and human obligation, trampled nature and conscience beneath his feet; and by a steady and constitutional spirit of insolence and cruelty, procured for himself an universal hatred. It is *now* the interest of America to provide for herself. She hath already a large and young family, whom it is more her duty to take care of, than to be granting away her property, to support a power who is become a reproach to the names of men and Christians—ye, whose office it is to watch over the morals of a nation, of whatsoever sect or denomination ye are of, as well as ye, who, are more immediately the guardians of the public liberty, if ye wish to preserve your native country uncontaminated by European corruption, ye must in secret wish a separation—But leaving the moral part to private reflection, I shall chiefly confine my farther remarks to the following heads.

First. That it is the interest of America to be separated from Britain.

Secondly. Which is the easiest and most practicable plan, *reconciliation* or *independence?* with some occasional remarks.

In support of the first, I could, if I judged it proper, produce the opinion of some of the ablest and most experienced men on this continent; and whose sentiments, on that head, are not yet publicly known. It is in reality a self-evident position: For no nation in a state of foreign dependence, limited in its commerce, and cramped and fettered in its legislative powers, can ever arrive at any material eminence. America doth not yet know what opulence is; and although the progress which she hath made stands unparalleled in the history of other nations, it is but childhood, compared with what she would be capable of arriving at, had she, as she ought to have, the legislative powers in her own hands. England is, at this time, proudly coveting what would do her no good, were she to accomplish it; and the Continent hesitating on a matter, which will be her final ruin if neglected. It is the commerce and not the conquest of America, by which England is to be benefited, and that would in a great measure continue, were the countries as independent of each other as France and Spain; because in many articles, neither can go to a better market. But it is the independence of this country of Britain or any other, which is now the main and only object worthy of contention, and which, like all other truths discovered by necessity, will appear clearer and stronger every day.

First. Because it will come to that one time or other.

Secondly. Because, the longer it is delayed the harder it will be to accomplish.

I have frequently amused myself both in public and private companies, with silently remarking, the specious errors of those who speak without reflecting. And among the many which I have heard, the following seems the most general, viz. that had this rupture happened forty or fifty years hence, instead of *now*, the Continent would have been more able to have shaken off the dependence. To which I reply, that our military ability, *at this time*, arises from the experience gained in the last war, and which in forty or fifty years time, would have been totally extinct. The Continent, would not, by that time, have had a General, or even a military officer left; and we, or those who may succeed us, would have been as ignorant of martial matters as the ancient Indians: And this single position, closely attended to, will unanswerably prove, that the present time is preferable to all others. The argument turns thus—at the conclusion of the last war, we had experience, but wanted numbers; and forty or fifty years hence, we should have numbers, without experience; wherefore, the proper point of time, must be some particular point between the two extremes, in which a sufficiency of the former remains, and a proper increase of the latter is obtained: And that point of time is the present time.

The reader will pardon this digression, as it does not properly come under the head I first set out with, and to which I again return by the following position, viz.

Should affairs be patched up with Britain, and she to remain the governing and sovereign power of America, (which, as matters are now circumstanced, is giving up the point entirely) we shall deprive ourselves of the very means of sinking the debt we have, or may contract. The value of the back lands which some of the provinces are clandestinely deprived of, by the unjust extension of the limits of Canada, valued only at five pounds sterling per hundred acres, amount to upwards of twenty-five millions, Pennsylvania currency; and the quit-rents at one penny sterling per acre, to two millions yearly.

It is by the sale of those lands that the debt may be sunk, without burthen to any, and the quit-rent reserved thereon, will always lessen, and in time, will wholly support the yearly expence of government. It matters not how long the debt is in paying, so that the lands when sold be applied to the discharge of it, and for the execution of which, the Congress for the time being, will be the continental trustees.

I proceed now to the second head, viz. Which is the easiest and most practicable plan, *reconciliation* or *independence*; with some occasional remarks.

He who takes nature for his guide is not easily beaten out of his argument, and on that ground, I answer *generally—That INDEPENDENCE being a SINGLE SIMPLE LINE, contained within ourselves; and reconciliation, a matter exceedingly perplexed and complicated, and in which, a treacherous capricious court is to interfere, gives the answer without a doubt.*

The present state of America is truly alarming to every man who is capable of reflexion. Without law, without government, without any other mode of power than what is founded on, and granted by courtesy. Held together by an unexampled concurrence of sentiment, which, is nevertheless subject to change, and which, every secret enemy is endeavouring to dissolve. Our present condition, is, Legislation without law; wisdom without a plan; a constitution without a name; and, what is strangely astonishing, perfect Independence contending for dependence. The instance is without a precedent; the case never existed before; and who can tell what may be the event? The property of no man is secure in the present unbraced system of things. The mind of the multitude is left at random, and seeing no fixed object before them, they pursue such as fancy or opinion starts. Nothing is criminal; there is no such thing as treason; wherefore, every one thinks himself at liberty to act as he pleases. The Tories dared not have assembled offensively, had they known that their lives, by that act, were forfeited to the laws of the state. A line of distinction should be drawn, between, English soldiers taken in battle, and inhabitants of America taken in arms. The first are prisoners, but the latter traitors. The one forfeits his liberty, the other his head.

Notwithstanding our wisdom, there is a visible feebleness in some of our proceedings which gives encouragement to dissensions. The Continental belt is too loosely buckled. And if something is not done in time, it will be too late to do any thing, and we shall fall into a state, in which, neither *reconciliation* nor *independence* will be practicable. The king and his worthless adherents are got at their old game of dividing the Continent, and there are not wanting among us, Printers, who will be busy in spreading specious falsehoods. The artful and hypocritical letter which appeared a few months ago in two of the New York papers, and likewise in two others, is an evidence that there are men who want either judgment or honesty.

It is easy getting into holes and corners and talking of reconciliation: But do such men seriously consider, how difficult the task is, and how dangerous it may prove, should the Continent divide thereon. Do they take within their view, all the various orders of men whose situation and circumstances, as well as their own, are to be considered therein. Do they put themselves in the place of the sufferer whose *all* is *already* gone, and of the soldier, who hath quitted *all* for the defence of his country. If their ill judged moderation be suited to their own private situations *only*, regardless of others, the event will convince them, that "they are reckoning without their Host."

Put us, says some, on the footing we were on in sixty-three: To which I answer, the request is not *now* in the power of Britain to comply with, neither will she propose it; but if it were, and even should be granted, I ask, as a reasonable question, By what means is such a corrupt and faithless court to be kept to its engagements? Another parliament, nay, even the present, may hereafter repeal the obligation, on the pretense, of its being violently obtained, or unwisely granted; and in that case, Where is our redress?——No going to law with nations; cannon are the barristers of Crowns; and the sword, not of justice, but of war, decides the suit. To be on the footing of sixty-three, it is not sufficient, that the laws only be put on the same state, but, that our circumstances, likewise, be put on the same state; Our burnt and destroyed towns repaired or built up, our private losses made good, our public debts (contracted for defence) discharged; otherwise, we shall be millions worse than we were at that enviable period. Such a request, had it been complied with a year ago, would have won the heart and soul of the Continent—but now it is too late, "The Rubicon is passed."

Besides, the taking up arms, merely to enforce the repeal of a pecuniary law, seems as unwarrantable by the divine law, and as repugnant to human feelings, as the taking up arms to enforce obedience thereto. The object, on either side, doth not justify the means; for the lives of men are too valuable to be cast away on such trifles. It is the violence which is done and threatened to our persons; the destruction of our property by an armed force; the invasion of our country by fire and sword, which conscientiously qualifies the use of arms: And the instant, in which such a mode of defence became necessary, all subjection to Britain ought to have ceased; and the independency of America, should have been considered, as dating its æra from, and published by, *the first musket that was fired against her*. This line is a line of consistency; neither drawn by caprice, nor extended by ambition; but produced by a chain of events, of which the Colonies were not the authors.

I shall conclude these remarks with the following timely and well intended hints. We ought to reflect, that there are three different ways by which an independency may hereafter be effected; and that *one* of those *three*, will one day or other, be the fate of America, viz. By the legal voice of the people in Congress; by a military power; or by a mob—It may not always happen that *our* soldiers are citizens, and the multitude a body of reasonable men; virtue, as I have already remarked, is not hereditary, neither is it perpetual. Should an independency be brought about by the first of those means, we have every opportunity and every encouragement before us, to form the noblest purest constitution on the face of the earth. We have it in our power to begin the world over again. A situation, similar to the present, hath not happened since the days of Noah until now. The birthday of a new world is at hand, and a race of men, perhaps as numerous as all Europe contains, are to receive their portion of freedom from the event of a few months. The Reflexion is awful—and in this point of view, How trifling, how ridiculous, do the little, paltry cavillings, of a few weak or interested men appear, when weighed against the business of a world.

Should we neglect the present favourable and inviting period, and an Independence be hereafter effected by any other means, we must charge the consequence to ourselves, or to those rather, whose narrow and prejudiced souls, are habitually opposing the measure, without either inquiring or reflecting. There are reasons to be given in support of Independence, which men should rather privately think of, than be publicly told of. We ought not now to be debating whether we shall be independent or not, but, anxious to accomplish it on a firm, secure, and honourable basis, and uneasy rather that it is not yet began upon. Every day convinces us of its necessity. Even the Tories (if such beings yet remain among us) should, of all men, be the most solicitous to promote it; for, as the appointment of committees at first, protected them from popular rage, so, a wise and well established form of government, will be the only certain means of continuing it securely to them. *Wherefore*, if they have not virtue enough to be *Whigs*, they ought to have prudence enough to wish for Independence.

In short, Independence is the only *bond* that can tye and keep us together. We shall then see our object, and our ears will be legally shut against the schemes of an intriguing, as well, as a cruel enemy. We shall then too, be on a proper footing, to treat with Britain; for there is reason to conclude, that the pride of that court, will be less hurt by treating with the American states for terms of peace, than with those, whom she denominates, "rebellious subjects," for terms of accommodation. It is our delaying it that encourages her to hope for conquest, and our backwardness tends only to prolong the war. As we have, without any good effect therefrom, withheld our trade to obtain a redress of our grievances, let us *now* try the alternative, by *independently* redressing them ourselves, and then offering to open the trade. The mercantile and reasonable part in England, will be still with us; because, peace *with* trade, is preferable to war *without* it. And if this offer be not accepted, other courts may be applied to.

On these grounds I rest the matter. And as no offer hath yet been made to refute the doctrine contained in the former editions of this pamphlet, it is a negative proof, that either the doctrine cannot be refuted, or, that the party in favour of it are too numerous to be opposed. *Wherefore*, instead of gazing at each other with suspicious or doubtful curiosity, let each of us, hold out to his neighbour the hearty hand of friendship, and unite in drawing a line, which, like an act of oblivion shall bury in forgetfulness every former dissension. Let the names of Whig and Tory be extinct; and let none other be heard among us, than those of *a good citizen, an open and resolute friend, and a virtuous supporter of the* RIGHTS of MANKIND *and of the* FREE AND INDEPENDENT STATES OF AMERICA.

\* \* \* \*

*To the Representatives of the Religious Society of the People called Quakers, or to so many of them as were concerned in publishing the late piece, entitled "The Ancient Testimony and Principles of the People called Quakers renewed, with Respect to the King and Government, and touching the Commotions now prevailing in these and other parts of America addressed to the people in general."*

The Writer of this, is one of those few, who never dishonours religion either by ridiculing, or cavilling at any denomination whatsoever. To God, and not to man, are all men accountable on the score of religion. Wherefore, this epistle is not so properly addressed to you as a religious, but as a political body, dabbling in matters, which the professed Quietude of your Principles instruct you not to meddle with.

As you have, without a proper authority for so doing, put yourselves in the place of the whole body of the Quakers, so, the writer of this, in order to be on an equal rank with yourselves, is under the necessity, of putting himself in the place of all those, who, approve the very writings and principles, against which, your testimony is directed: And he hath chosen this singular situation, in order, that you might discover in him that presumption of character which you cannot see in yourselves. For neither he nor you can have any claim or title to *Political Representation*.

When men have departed from the right way, it is no wonder that they stumble and fall. And it is evident from the manner in which ye have managed your testimony, that politics, (as a religious body of men) is not your proper Walk; for however well adapted it might appear to you, it is, nevertheless, a jumble of good and bad put unwisely together, and the conclusion drawn therefrom, both unnatural and unjust.

The two first pages, (and the whole doth not make four) we give you credit for, and expect the same civility from you, because the love and desire of peace is not confined to Quakerism, it is the *natural*, as well the religious wish of all denominations of men. And on this ground, as men labouring to establish an Independent Constitution of our own, do we exceed all others in our hope, end, and aim. *Our plan is peace for ever.* We are tired of contention with Britain, and can see no real end to it but in a final separation. We act consistently, because for the sake of introducing an endless and uninterrupted peace, do we bear the evils and burthens of the present day. We are endeavouring, and will steadily continue to endeavour, to separate and dissolve a connexion which hath already filled our land with blood; and which, while the name of it remains, will be the fatal cause of future mischiefs to both countries.

We fight neither for revenge nor conquest; neither from pride nor passion; we are not insulting the world with our fleets and armies, nor ravaging the globe for plunder. Beneath the shade of our own vines are we attacked; in our own houses, and on our own lands, is the violence committed against us. We view our enemies in the character of Highwaymen and Housebreakers, and having no defence for ourselves in the civil law, are obliged to punish them by the military one, and apply the sword, in the very case, where you have before now, applied the halter.——Perhaps we feel for the ruined and insulted sufferers in all and every part of the continent, with a degree of tenderness which hath not yet made its way into some of your bosoms. But be ye sure that ye mistake not the cause and ground of your Testimony. Call not coldness of soul, religion; nor put the *Bigot* in the place of the *Christian*.

O ye partial ministers of your own acknowledged principles. If the bearing arms be sinful, the first going to war must be more so, by all the difference between wilful attack, and unavoidable defence. Wherefore, if ye really preach from conscience, and mean not to make a political hobbyhorse of your religion convince the world thereof, by proclaiming your doctrine to our enemies, *for they likewise bear arms.* Give us proof of your sincerity by publishing it at St. James's, to the commanders in chief at Boston, to the Admirals and Captains who are piratically ravaging our coasts, and to all the murdering miscreants who are acting in authority under Him whom ye profess to serve. Had ye the honest soul of *Barclay** ye would preach repentance to *your* king; Ye would tell the Royal Wretch his sins, and warn him of eternal ruin. Ye would not spend your partial invectives against the injured and the insulted only, but, like faithful ministers, would cry aloud and *spare none*. Say not that ye are persecuted, neither endeavour to make us the authors of that reproach, which, ye are bringing upon yourselves; for we testify unto all men, that we do not complain against you because ye are *Quakers*, but because ye pretend to *be* and are *not* Quakers.

Alas! it seems by the particular tendency of some part of your testimony, and other parts of your conduct, as if, all sin was reduced to, and comprehended in, *the act of bearing arms*, and that by the *people only*. Ye appear to us, to have mistaken party for conscience; because, the general tenor of your actions wants uniformity——And it is exceedingly difficult to us to give credit to many of your pretended scruples; because we see them made by the same men, who, in the very instant that they are exclaiming against the mammon of this world, are nevertheless, hunting after it with a step as steady as Time, and an appetite as keen as Death.

The quotation which ye have made from Proverbs, in the third page of your testimony, that, "when a man's ways please the Lord, he maketh even his enemies to be at peace with him"; is very unwisely chosen on your part; because, it amounts to a proof, that the king's ways (whom ye are desirous of supporting) do *not* please the Lord, otherwise, his reign would be in peace.

I now proceed to the latter part of your testimony, and that, for which all the foregoing seems only an introduction, viz.

"It hath ever been our judgment and principle, since we were called to profess the light of Christ Jesus, manifested in our

---

*"Thou hast tasted of prosperity and adversity; thou knowest what it is to be banished thy native country, to be over-ruled as well as to rule, and set upon the throne; and being *oppressed* thou hast reason to know how *hateful* the *oppressor* is both to God and man: If after all these warnings and advertisements, thou dost not turn unto the Lord with all thy heart, but forget him who remembered thee in thy distress, and give up thyself to follow lust and vanity, surely great will be thy condemnation.—— Against which snare, as well as the temptation of those who may or do feed thee, and prompt thee to evil, the most excellent and prevalent remedy will be, to apply thyself to that light of Christ which shineth in thy conscience, and which neither can, nor will flatter thee, nor suffer thee to be at ease in thy sins."——*Barclay's Address to Charles II.* (Author's note)

consciences unto this day, that the setting up and putting down kings and governments, is God's peculiar prerogative; for causes best known to himself: And that it is not our business to have any hand or contrivance therein; nor to be busy bodies above our station, much less to plot and contrive the ruin, or overturn of any of them, but to pray for the king, and safety of our nation, and good of all men: That we may live a peaceable and quiet life, in all godliness and honesty; *under the government which God is pleased to set over us.*"—If these are *really* your principles why do ye not abide by them? Why do ye not leave that, which ye call God's Work, to be managed by himself? These very principles instruct you to wait with patience and humility, for the event of all public measures, and to receive *that event* as the divine will towards you. *Wherefore*, what occasion is there for your *political testimony* if you fully believe what it contains? And the very publishing it proves, that either, ye do not believe what ye profess, or have not virtue enough to practise what ye believe.

The principles of Quakerism have a direct tendency to make a man the quiet and inoffensive subject of any, and every government *which is set over him*. And if the setting up and putting down of kings and governments is God's peculiar prerogative, he most certainly will not be robbed thereof by us: wherefore, the principle itself leads you to approve of every thing, which ever happened, or may happen to kings as being his work. *Oliver Cromwell* thanks you. *Charles*, then, died not by the hands of man; and should the present Proud Imitator of him, come to the same untimely end, the writers and publishers of the Testimony, are bound, by the doctrine it contains, to applaud the fact. Kings are not taken away by miracles, neither are changes in governments brought about by any other means than such as are common and human; and such as we are now using. Even the dispersion of the Jews, though foretold by our Saviour, was effected by arms. Wherefore, as ye refuse to be the means on one side, ye ought not to be meddlers on the other; but to wait the issue in silence; and unless ye can produce divine authority, to prove, that the Almighty who hath created and placed this *new* world, at the greatest distance it could possibly stand, east and west, from every part of the old, doth, nevertheless, disapprove of its being independent of the corrupt and abandoned court of Britain, unless I say, ye can show this, how can ye on the ground of your principles, justify the exciting and stirring up the people "firmly to unite in the *abhorrence* of all such *writings*, and *measures*, as evidence a desire and design to break off the *happy* connexion we have hitherto enjoyed, with the kingdom of Great-Britain, and our just and necessary subordination to the king, and those who are lawfully placed in authority under him." What a slap of the face is here! the men, who in the very paragraph before, have quietly and passively resigned up the ordering, altering, and disposal of kings and governments, into the hands of God, are now, recalling their principles, and putting in for a share of the business. Is it possible, that the conclusion, which is here justly quoted, can any ways follow from the doctrine laid down? The inconsistency is too glaring not to be seen; the absurdity too great not to be laughed at; and such as could only have been made by those, whose understandings were darkened by the narrow and crabby spirit of a despairing political party; for ye are not to be considered as the whole body of the Quakers but only as a factional and fractional part thereof.

Here ends the examination of your testimony; (which I call upon no man to abhor, as ye have done, but only to read and judge of fairly;) to which I subjoin the following remark; "That the setting up and putting down of kings," most certainly mean, the making him a king, who is yet not so, and the making him no king who is already one. And pray what hath this to do in the present case? We neither mean to *set up* nor to *pull down*, neither to *make* nor to *unmake*, but to have nothing to *do* with them. Wherefore, your testimony in whatever light it is viewed serves only to dishonour your judgment, and for many other reasons had better have been let alone than published.

First. Because it tends to the decrease and reproach of all religion whatever, and is of the utmost danger to society to make it a party in political disputes.

Secondly. Because it exhibits a body of men, numbers of whom disavow the publishing political testimonies, as being concerned therein and approvers thereof.

Thirdly. Because it hath a tendency to undo that continental harmony and friendship which yourselves by your late liberal and charitable donations hath lent a hand to establish; and the preservation of which, is of the utmost consequence to us all.

And here without anger or resentment I bid you farewell. Sincerely wishing, that as men and Christians, ye may always fully and uninterruptedly enjoy every civil and religious right; and be, in your turn, the means of securing it to others; but that the example which ye have unwisely set, of mingling religion with politics, *may be disavowed and reprobated by every inhabitant of America.*

*FINIS.*

# The Rights of Man (1794–95)

## PART I AND PART II

*By Thomas Paine*
*Secretary for Foreign Affairs to Congress in the American War, and*
*Author of the Works Entitled* Common Sense
*and "A Letter To Abbé Raynal"*

## EDITOR'S INTRODUCTION

When Thomas Paine sailed from America for France, in April, 1787, he was perhaps as happy a man as any in the world. His most intimate friend, Jefferson, was Minister at Paris, and his friend Lafayette was the idol of France. His fame had preceded him, and he at once became, in Paris, the centre of the same circle of savants and philosophers that had surrounded Franklin. His main reason for proceeding at once to Paris was that he might submit to the Academy of Sciences his invention of an iron bridge, and with its favorable verdict he came to England, in September. He at once went to his aged mother at Thetford, leaving with a publisher (Ridgway), his "Prospects on the Rubicon." He next made arrangements to patent his bridge, and to construct at Rotherham the large model of it exhibited on Paddington Green, London. He was welcomed in England by leading statesmen, such as Lansdowne and Fox, and above all by Edmund Burke, who for some time had him as a guest at Beaconsfield, and drove him about in various parts of the country. He had not the slightest revolutionary purpose, either as regarded England or France. Towards Louis XVI he felt only gratitude for the services he had rendered America, and towards George III he felt no animosity whatever. His four months' sojourn in Paris had convinced him that there was approaching a reform of that country after the American model, except that the Crown would be preserved, a compromise he approved, provided the throne should not be hereditary. Events in France travelled more swiftly than he had anticipated, and Paine was summoned by Lafayette, Condorcet, and others, as an adviser in the formation of a new constitution.

Such was the situation immediately preceding the political and literary duel between Paine and Burke, which in the event turned out a tremendous war between Royalism and Republicanism in Europe. Paine was, both in France and in England, the inspirer of moderate counsels. Samuel Rogers relates that in early life he dined at a friend's house in London with Thomas Paine, when one of the toasts given was the "memory of Joshua,"—in allusion to the Hebrew leader's conquest of the kings of Canaan, and execution of them. Paine observed that he would not treat kings like Joshua. "I'm of the Scotch parson's opinion," he said, "when he prayed against Louis XIV—'Lord, shake him over the mouth of hell, but don't let him drop!'" Paine then gave as his toast, "The Republic of the World,"—which Samuel Rogers, aged twenty-nine, noted as a sublime idea. This was Paine's faith and hope, and with it he confronted the revolutionary storms which presently burst over France and England.

Until Burke's arraignment of France in his parliamentary speech (February 9, 1790), Paine had no doubt whatever that he would sympathize with the movement in France, and wrote to him from that country as if conveying glad tidings. Burke's "Reflections on the Revolution in France" appeared November 1, 1790, and Paine at once set himself to answer it. He was then staying at the Angel Inn, Islington. The inn has been twice rebuilt since that time, and from its contents there is preserved only a small image, which perhaps was meant to represent "Liberty,"—possibly brought from Paris by Paine as an ornament for his study. From the Angel he removed to a house in Harding Street, Fetter Lane. Rickman says Part First of *Rights of Man* was finished at Versailles, but probably this has reference to the preface only, as I cannot find Paine in France that year until April 8. The book had been printed by Johnson, in time for the opening of Parliament, in February; but this publisher became frightened after a few copies were out (there is one in the British Museum), and the work was transferred to J. S. Jordan, 166 Fleet Street, with a preface sent from Paris (not contained in Johnson's edition, nor in the American editions). The pamphlet, though sold at the same price as Burke's, three shillings, had a vast circulation, and Paine gave the proceeds to the Constitutional Societies which sprang up under his teachings in various parts of the country.

Soon after appeared Burke's "Appeal from the New to the Old Whigs." In this Burke quoted a good deal from *Rights of Man*, but replied to it only with exclamation points, saying that the only answer such ideas merited was "criminal justice." Paine's Part Second followed, published February 17, 1792. In Part First Paine had mentioned a rumor that Burke was a masked pensioner (a charge that will be noticed in connection with its detailed statement in a further publication); and as Burke had been formerly arraigned in Parliament, while Paymaster, for a very questionable proceeding, this charge no doubt hurt a good deal. Although the government did not follow Burke's suggestion of a prosecution at that time, there is little doubt that it was he who induced the prosecution of Part Second. Before the trial came on, December 18, 1792, Paine was occupying his seat in the French Convention, and could only be outlawed.

Burke humorously remarked to a friend of Paine and himself, "We hunt in pairs." The severally representative character and influence of these two men in the revolutionary era, in France and England, deserve more adequate study than they have received. While Paine maintained freedom of discussion, Burke first proposed criminal prosecution for sentiments by no means libellous (such as Paine's Part First). While Paine was endeavoring to make the movement in France peaceful, Burke fomented the league of monarchs against France which maddened its people, and brought on the Reign of Terror. While Paine was endeavoring to preserve the French throne ("phantom" though he believed it), to prevent bloodshed, Burke was secretly writing to the Queen of France, entreating her not to compromise, and to "trust to the support of foreign armies" ("Histoire de France depuis 1789." Henri Martin, i., 151). While Burke thus helped to bring the King and Queen to the guillotine, Paine pleaded for their lives to the last moment. While Paine maintained the right of mankind to improve their condition, Burke held that "the awful Author of our being is the author of our place in the order of existence; and that, having disposed and marshalled us by a divine tactick, not according to our will, but according to his, he has, in and by that disposition, virtually subjected us to act the part which belongs to the place assigned us." Paine was a religious believer in eternal principles; Burke held that "political problems do not primarily concern truth or falsehood. They relate to good or evil. What in the result is likely to produce evil is politically false, that which is productive of good politically is true." Assuming thus the visionary's right to decide before the result what was "likely to produce evil," Burke vigorously sought to kindle war against the French Republic which might have developed itself peacefully, while Paine was striving for an international Congress in Europe in the interest of peace. Paine had faith in the people, and believed that, if allowed to choose representatives, they would select their best and wisest men; and that while reforming government the people would remain orderly, as they had generally remained in America during the transition from

British rule to self-government. Burke maintained that if the existing political order were broken up there would be no longer a people, but "a number of vague, loose individuals, and nothing more." "Alas!" he exclaims, "they little know how many a weary step is to be taken before they can form themselves into a mass, which has a true personality." For the sake of peace Paine wished the revolution to be peaceful as the advance of summer; he used every endeavor to reconcile English radicals to some *modus vivendi* with the existing order, as he was willing to retain Louis XVI as head of the executive in France: Burke resisted every tendency of English statesmanship to reform at home, or to negotiate with the French Republic, and was mainly responsible for the King's death and the war that followed between England and France in February, 1793. Burke became a royal favorite, Paine was outlawed by a prosecution originally proposed by Burke. While Paine was demanding religious liberty, Burke was opposing the removal of penal statutes from Unitarians, on the ground that but for those statutes Paine might some day set up a church in England. When Burke was retiring on a large royal pension, Paine was in prison, through the devices of Burke's confederate, the American Minister in Paris. So the two men, as Burke said, "hunted in pairs."

So far as Burke attempts to affirm any principle he is fairly quoted in Paine's work, and nowhere misrepresented. As for Paine's own ideas, the reader should remember that "Rights of Man" was the earliest complete statement of republican principles. They were pronounced to be the fundamental principles of the American Republic by Jefferson, Madison, and Jackson, the three Presidents who above all others represented the republican idea which Paine first allied with American Independence. Those who suppose that Paine did but reproduce the principles of Rousseau and Locke will find by careful study of his well-weighed language that such is not the case. Paine's political principles were evolved out of his early Quakerism. He was potential in George Fox. The belief that every human soul was the child of God, and capable of direct inspiration from the Father of all, without mediator or priestly intervention, or sacramental instrumentality, was fatal to all privilege and rank. The universal Fatherhood implied universal Brotherhood, or human equality. But the fate of the Quakers proved the necessity of protecting the individual spirit from oppression by the majority as well as by privileged classes. For this purpose Paine insisted on surrounding the individual right with the security of the Declaration of Rights, not to be invaded by any government; and would reduce government to an association limited in its operations to the defence of those rights which the individual is unable, alone, to maintain.

From the preceding chapter it will be seen that Part Second of *Rights of Man* was begun by Paine in the spring of 1791. At the close of that year, or early in 1792, he took up his abode with his friend Thomas "Clio" Rickman, at No. 7 Upper Marylebone Street. Rickman was a radical publisher; the house remains still a book-binding establishment, and seems little changed since Paine therein revised the proofs of Part Second on a table which Rickman marked with a plate, and which is now in possession of Mr. Edward Truelove. As the plate states, Paine wrote on the same table other works which appeared in England in 1792.

In 1795 D. I. Eaton published an edition of *Rights of Man*, with a preface purporting to have been written by Paine while in Luxembourg prison. It is manifestly spurious. The genuine English and French prefaces are given.

*Author Unknown*

# THE RIGHTS OF MAN

## PART THE FIRST

# *DEDICATION*

## GEORGE WASHINGTON,
## PRESIDENT OF THE UNITED STATES
## OF AMERICA.

Sir,

I present you a small treatise in defence of those principles of freedom which your exemplary virtue hath so eminently contributed to establish. That the Rights of Man may become as universal as your benevolence can wish, and that you may enjoy the happiness of seeing the New World regenerate the Old, is the prayer of

Sir,

Your much obliged, and

Obedient humble Servant,

*Thomas Paine*

# PAINE'S PREFACE
## TO THE ENGLISH EDITION

From the part Mr. Burke took in the American Revolution, it was natural that I should consider him a friend to mankind; and as our acquaintance commenced on that ground, it would have been more agreeable to me to have had cause to continue in that opinion than to change it.

At the time Mr. Burke made his violent speech last winter in the English Parliament against the French Revolution and the National Assembly, I was in Paris, and had written to him but a short time before to inform him how prosperously matters were going on. Soon after this I saw his advertisement of the Pamphlet he intended to publish: As the attack was to be made in a language but little studied, and less understood in France, and as everything suffers by translation, I promised some of the friends of the Revolution in that country that whenever Mr. Burke's Pamphlet came forth, I would answer it. This appeared to me the more necessary to be done, when I saw the flagrant misrepresentations which Mr. Burke's Pamphlet contains; and that while it is an outrageous abuse on the French Revolution, and the principles of Liberty, it is an imposition on the rest of the world.

I am the more astonished and disappointed at this conduct in Mr. Burke, as (from the circumstances I am going to mention) I had formed other expectations.

I had seen enough of the miseries of war, to wish it might never more have existence in the world, and that some other mode might be found out to settle the differences that should occasionally arise in the neighbourhood of nations. This certainly might be done if Courts were disposed to set honesty about it, or if countries were enlightened enough not to be made the dupes of Courts. The people of America had been bred up in the same prejudices against France, which at that time characterised the people of England; but experience and an acquaintance with the French Nation have most effectually shown to the Americans the falsehood of those prejudices; and I do not believe that a more cordial and confidential intercourse exists between any two countries than between America and France.

When I came to France, in the spring of 1787, the Archbishop of Thoulouse was then Minister, and at that time highly esteemed. I became much acquainted with the private Secretary of that Minister, a man of an enlarged benevolent heart; and found that his sentiments and my own perfectly agreed with respect to the madness of war, and the wretched impolicy of two nations, like England and France, continually worrying each other, to no other end than that of a mutual increase of burdens and taxes. That I might be assured I had not misunderstood him, nor he me, I put the substance of our opinions into writing and sent it to him; subjoining a request, that if I should see among the people of England, any disposition to cultivate a better understanding between the two nations than had hitherto prevailed, how far I might be authorised to say that the same disposition prevailed on the part of France? He answered me by letter in the most unreserved manner, and that not for himself only, but for the Minister, with whose knowledge the letter was declared to be written.

I put this letter into the, hands of Mr. Burke almost three years ago, and left it with him, where it still remains; hoping, and at the same time naturally expecting, from the opinion I had conceived of him, that he would find some opportunity of making good use of it, for the purpose of removing those errors and prejudices which two neighbouring nations, from the want of knowing each other, had entertained, to the injury of both.

When the French Revolution broke out, it certainly afforded to Mr. Burke an opportunity of doing some good, had he been disposed to it; instead of which, no sooner did he see the old prejudices wearing away, than he immediately began sowing the seeds of a new inveteracy, as if he were afraid that England and France would cease to be enemies. That there are men in all countries who get their living by war, and by keeping up the quarrels of Nations, is as shocking as it is true; but when those who are concerned in the government of a country, make it their study to sow discord and cultivate prejudices between Nations, it becomes the more unpardonable.

With respect to a paragraph in this work alluding to Mr. Burke's having a pension, the report has been some time in circulation, at least two months; and as a person is often the last to hear what concerns him the most to know, I have mentioned it, that Mr. Burke may have an opportunity of contradicting the rumour, if he thinks proper.

*Thomas Paine*

# PAINE'S PREFACE
## TO THE FRENCH EDITION

The astonishment which the French Revolution has caused throughout Europe should be considered from two different points of view: first as it affects foreign peoples, secondly as it affects their governments.

The cause of the French people is that of all Europe, or rather of the whole world; but the governments of all those countries are by no means favorable to it. It is important that we should never lose sight of this distinction. We must not confuse the peoples with their governments; especially not the English people with its government.

The government of England is no friend of the revolution of France. Of this we have sufficient proofs in the thanks given by that weak and witless person, the Elector of Hanover, sometimes called the King of England, to Mr. Burke for the insults heaped on it in his book, and in the malevolent comments of the English Minister, Mr. Pitt, in his speeches in Parliament.

In spite of the professions of sincerest friendship found in the official correspondence of the English government with that of France, its conduct gives the lie to all its declarations, and shows us clearly that it is not a court to be trusted, but an insane court, plunging in all the quarrels and intrigues of Europe, in quest of a war to satisfy its folly and countenance its extravagance.

The English nation, on the contrary, is very favorably disposed towards the French Revolution, and to the progress of liberty in the whole world; and this feeling will become more general in England as the intrigues and artifices of its government are better known, and the principles of the revolution better understood. The French should know that most English newspapers are directly in the pay of government, or, if indirectly connected with it, always under its orders; and that those papers constantly distort and attack the revolution in France in order to deceive the nation. But, as it is impossible long to prevent the prevalence of truth, the daily falsehoods of those papers no longer have the desired effect.

To be convinced that the voice of truth has been stifled in England, the world needs only to be told that the government regards and prosecutes as a libel that which it should protect.* This outrage on morality is called *law*, and judges are found wicked enough to inflict penalties on truth.

The English government presents, just now, a curious phenomenon. Seeing that the French and English nations are getting rid of the prejudices and false notions formerly entertained against each other, and which have cost them so much money, that government seems to be placarding its need of a foe; for unless it finds one somewhere, no pretext exists for the enormous revenue and taxation now deemed necessary.

Therefore it seeks in Russia the enemy it has lost in France, and appears to say to the universe, or to say to itself. "If nobody will be so kind as to become my foe, I shall need no more fleets nor armies, and shall be forced to reduce my taxes. The American war enabled me to double the taxes; the Dutch business to add more; the Nootka humbug gave me a pretext for raising three millions sterling more; but unless I can make an enemy of Russia the harvest from wars will end. I was the first to incite Turk against Russian, and now I hope to reap a fresh crop of taxes."

If the miseries of war, and the flood of evils it spreads over a country, did not check all inclination to mirth, and turn laughter into grief, the frantic conduct of the government of England would only excite ridicule. But it is impossible to banish from one's mind the images of suffering which the contemplation of such vicious policy presents. To reason with governments, as they have existed for ages, is to argue with brutes. It is only from the nations themselves that reforms can be expected. There ought not now to exist any doubt that the peoples of France, England, and America, enlightened and enlightening each other, shall henceforth be able, not merely to give the world an example of good government, but by their united influence enforce its practice.

(Translated from French)

---

* The main and uniform maxim of the judges is, the greater the truth the greater the libel. (Author's note)

# *PART THE FIRST*

## BEING AN ANSWER TO
## MR. BURKE'S ATTACK ON THE
## FRENCH REVOLUTION

Among the incivilities by which nations or individuals provoke and irritate each other, Mr. Burke's pamphlet on the French Revolution is an extraordinary instance. Neither the People of France, nor the National Assembly, were troubling themselves about the affairs of England, or the English Parliament; and that Mr. Burke should commence an unprovoked attack upon them, both in Parliament and in public, is a conduct that cannot be pardoned on the score of manners, nor justified on that of policy.

There is scarcely an epithet of abuse to be found in the English language, with which Mr. Burke has not loaded the French Nation and the National Assembly. Everything which rancour, prejudice, ignorance or knowledge could suggest, is poured forth in the copious fury of near four hundred pages. In the strain and on the plan Mr. Burke was writing, he might have written on to as many thousands. When the tongue or the pen is let loose in a frenzy of passion, it is the man, and not the subject, that becomes exhausted.

Hitherto Mr. Burke has been mistaken and disappointed in the opinions he had formed of the affairs of France; but such is the ingenuity of his hope, or the malignancy of his despair, that it furnishes him with new pretences to go on. There was a time when it was impossible to make Mr. Burke believe there would be any Revolution in France. His opinion then was, that the French had neither spirit to undertake it nor fortitude to support it; and now that there is one, he seeks an escape by condemning it.

Not sufficiently content with abusing the National Assembly, a great part of his work is taken up with abusing Dr. Price* (one of the best-hearted

---

* British philosopher, writer, and activist Richard Price (1723–97).

men that lives) and the two societies in England known by the name of the Revolution Society and the Society for Constitutional Information.

Dr. Price had preached a sermon on the 4th of November, 1789, being the anniversary of what is called in England the Revolution, which took place 1688. Mr. Burke, speaking of this sermon, says: "The political Divine proceeds dogmatically to assert, that by the principles of the Revolution, the people of England have acquired three fundamental rights:

1. To choose our own governors.
2. To cashier them for misconduct.
3. To frame a government for ourselves."

Dr. Price does not say that the right to do these things exists in this or in that person, or in this or in that description of persons, but that it exists in the *whole*; that it is a right resident in the nation. Mr. Burke, on the contrary, denies that such a right exists in the nation, either in whole or in part, or that it exists anywhere; and, what is still more strange and marvellous, he says: "that the people of England utterly disclaim such a right, and that they will resist the practical assertion of it with their lives and fortunes." That men should take up arms and spend their lives and fortunes, *not* to maintain their rights, but to maintain they have *not* rights, is an entirely new species of discovery, and suited to the paradoxical genius of Mr. Burke.

The method which Mr. Burke takes to prove that the people of England have no such rights, and that such rights do not now exist in the nation, either in whole or in part, or anywhere at all, is of the same marvellous and monstrous kind with what he has already said; for his arguments are that the persons, or the generation of persons, in whom they did exist, are dead, and with them the right is dead also. To prove this, he quotes a declaration made by Parliament about a hundred years ago, to William and Mary, in these words: "The Lords Spiritual and Temporal, and Commons, do, in the name of the people aforesaid" (meaning the people of England then living) "most humbly and faithfully *submit* themselves, their *heirs* and *posterities*, for *ever*." He quotes a clause of another Act of Parliament made in the same reign, the terms of which he says, "bind us" (meaning the people of their day), "our *heirs* and our posterity, to *them*, their *heirs* and *posterity*, to the end of time."

Mr. Burke conceives his point sufficiently established by producing those clauses, which he enforces by saying that they exclude the right of the nation for *ever*. And not yet content with making such declarations, repeated over and over again, he farther says, "that if the people of England possessed such a right before the Revolution" (which he acknowledges to have been the case, not only in England, but throughout Europe, at an early period), "yet that the *English Nation* did, at the time of the Revolution, most solemnly renounce and abdicate it, for themselves, and for *all their posterity, for ever*."

As Mr. Burke occasionally applies the poison drawn from his horrid principles, not only to the English nation, but to the French Revolution and the National Assembly, and charges that august, illuminated and illuminating body of men with the epithet of *usurpers*, I shall, *sans cérémonie*, place another system of principles in opposition to his.

The English Parliament of 1688 did a certain thing, which, for themselves and their constituents, they had a right to do, and which it appeared right should be done. But, in addition to this right, which they possessed by delegation, *they set up another right by assumption*, that of binding and controlling posterity to the end of time. The case, therefore, divides itself into two parts; the right which they possessed by delegation, and the right which they set up by assumption. The first is admitted; but with respect to the second, I reply:

There never did, there never will, and there never can, exist a Parliament, or any description of men, or any generation of men, in any country, possessed of the right or the power of binding and controlling posterity to the "*end of time*," or of commanding for ever how the world shall be governed, or who shall govern it; and therefore all such clauses, acts or declarations by which the makers of them attempt to do what they have neither the right nor the power to do, nor the power to execute, are in themselves null and void. Every age and generation must be as free to act for itself *in all cases* as the age and generations which preceded it. The vanity and presumption of governing beyond the grave is the most ridiculous and insolent of all tyrannies. Man has no property in man; neither has any generation a property in the generations which are to follow. The Parliament or the people of 1688, or of any other period, had no more right to dispose of the people of the present day, or to bind or to control them *in any shape whatever*, than the parliament or the people of the present day have to dispose of, bind or control those who are to live a hundred or a thousand years hence. Every generation is, and must be, competent to all the purposes which its occasions require. It is the living, and not the dead, that are to be accommodated. When man ceases to be, his power and his wants cease with him; and having no longer any participation in the concerns of this world, he has no longer any authority in directing who shall be its governors, or how its government shall be organised, or how administered.

I am not contending for nor against any form of government, nor for nor against any party, here or elsewhere. That which a whole nation chooses to do it has a right to do. Mr. Burke says, No. Where, then, does the right exist? I am contending for the rights of the *living*, and against their being willed away and controlled and contracted for by the manuscript assumed authority of the dead, and Mr. Burke is contending for the authority of the dead over the rights and freedom of the living. There was a time when kings disposed of their crowns by will upon their death-beds, and consigned the people, like beasts of the field, to whatever successor they appointed. This is now so exploded as scarcely to be remembered, and so monstrous as hardly to be believed. But the Parliamentary clauses upon which Mr. Burke builds his political church are of the same nature.

The laws of every country must be analogous to some common principle. In England no parent or master, nor all the authority of Parliament, omnipotent as it has called itself, can bind or control the personal freedom even of an individual beyond the age of twenty-one years. On what ground of right, then, could the Parliament of 1688, or any other Parliament, bind all posterity for ever?

Those who have quitted the world, and those who have not yet arrived at it, are as remote from each other as the utmost stretch of mortal imagination can conceive. What possible obligation, then, can exist between them—what rule or principle can be laid down that of two nonentities, the one out of existence and the other not in, and who never can meet in this world, the one should control the other to the end of time?

In England it is said that money cannot be taken out of the pockets of the people without their consent. But who authorised, or who could authorise, the Parliament of 1688 to control and take away the freedom of posterity (who were not in existence to give or to withhold their consent) and limit and confine their right of acting in certain cases for ever?

A greater absurdity cannot present itself to the understanding of man than what Mr. Burke offers to his readers. He tells them, and he tells the world to come, that a certain body of men who existed a hundred years ago made a law, and that there does not exist in the nation, nor ever will, nor ever can, a power to alter it. Under how many subtilties or absurdities has the divine right to govern been imposed on the credulity of mankind? Mr. Burke has discovered a new one, and he has shortened his journey to Rome by appealing to the power of this infallible Parliament of former days, and he produces what it has done as of divine authority, for that power must certainly be more than human which no human power to the end of time can alter.

But Mr. Burke has done some service—not to his cause, but to his country—by bringing those clauses into public view. They serve to demonstrate how necessary it is at all times to watch against the attempted encroachment of power, and to prevent its running to excess. It is somewhat extraordinary that the offence for which James II. was expelled, that of setting up power by *assumption*, should be re-acted, under another shape and form, by the Parliament that expelled him. It shows that the Rights of Man were but imperfectly understood at the Revolution, for certain it is that the right which that Parliament set up by *assumption* (for by the delegation it had not, and could not have it, because none could give it) over the persons and freedom of posterity for ever was of the same tyrannical unfounded kind which James attempted to set up over the Parliament and the nation, and for which he was expelled. The only difference is (for in principle they differ not) that the one was an usurper over living, and the other over the unborn; and as the one has no better authority to stand upon than the other, both of them must be equally null and void, and of no effect.

From what, or from whence, does Mr. Burke prove the right of any human power to bind posterity for ever? He has produced his clauses, but he must produce also his proofs that such a right existed, and show how it existed. If it ever existed it must now exist, for whatever appertains to the nature of man cannot be annihilated by man. It is the nature of man to die, and he will continue to die as long as he continues to be born. But Mr. Burke has set up a sort of political Adam, in whom all posterity are bound for ever. He must, therefore, prove that his Adam possessed such a power, or such a right.

The weaker any cord is, the less will it bear to be stretched, and the worse is the policy to stretch it, unless it is intended to break it. Had anyone proposed the overthrow of Mr. Burke's positions, he would have proceeded as Mr. Burke has done. He would have magnified the authorities, on purpose to have called the *right* of them into question; and the instant the question of right was started, the authorities must have been given up.

It requires but a very small glance of thought to perceive that although laws made in one generation often continue in force through succeeding generations, yet they continue to derive their force from the consent of the living. A law not repealed continues in force, not because it *cannot* be repealed, but because it is *not* repealed; and the non-repealing passes for consent.

But Mr. Burke's clauses have not even this qualification in their favour. They become null, by attempting to become immortal. The nature of them precludes consent. They destroy the right which they *might* have, by grounding it on a right which they *cannot* have. Immortal power is not a human right, and therefore cannot be a right of Parliament. The Parliament of 1688 might as well have passed an act to have authorised themselves to live for ever, as to make their authority live for ever. All, therefore, that can be said of those clauses is that they are a formality of words, of as much import as if those who used them had addressed a congratulation to themselves, and in the oriental style of antiquity had said: O Parliament, live for ever!

The circumstances of the world are continually changing, and the opinions of men change also; and as government is for the living, and not for the dead, it is the living only that has any right in it. That which may be thought right and found convenient in one age may be thought wrong and found inconvenient in another. In such cases, who is to decide, the living or the dead?

As almost one hundred pages of Mr. Burke's book are employed upon these clauses, it will consequently follow that if the clauses themselves, so far as they set up an *assumed usurped* dominion over posterity for ever, are unauthoritative, and in their nature null and void; that all his voluminous inferences, and declamation drawn therefrom, or founded thereon, are null and void also; and on this ground I rest the matter.

We now come more particularly to the affairs of France. Mr. Burke's book has the appearance of being written as instruction to the French nation; but if I may permit myself the use of an extravagant metaphor, suited to the extravagance of the case, it is darkness attempting to illuminate light.

While I am writing this there are accidentally before me some proposals for a declaration of rights by the Marquis de la Fayette* (I ask his pardon for using his former address, and do it only for distinction's sake) to the National Assembly, on the 11th of July, 1789, three days before the taking of the Bastille, and I cannot but remark with astonishment how opposite the sources are from which that gentleman and Mr. Burke draw their principles. Instead of referring to musty records and mouldy parchments to prove that the rights of the living are lost, "renounced and abdicated for ever," by those who are now no more, as Mr. Burke has done, M. de la Fayette applies to the living world, and emphatically says: "Call to mind the sentiments which nature has engraved on the heart of every citizen, and which take a new force when they are solemnly recognised by all:—For a nation to love liberty, it is sufficient that she knows it; and to be free, it is sufficient that she wills it." How dry, barren, and obscure is the source from which Mr. Burke labors! and how ineffectual, though gay with flowers, are all his declamation and his arguments compared with these clear, concise, and soul-animating sentiments! Few and short as they are, they lead on to a vast field of generous and manly thinking, and do not finish, like Mr. Burke's periods, with music in the ear, and nothing in the heart.

As I have introduced M. de la Fayette, I will take the liberty of adding an anecdote respecting his farewell address to the Congress of America in 1783, and which occurred fresh to my mind, when I saw Mr. Burke's thundering attack on the French Revolution. M. de la Fayette went to America at the early period of the war, and continued a volunteer in her service to the end. His conduct through the whole of that enterprise is one of the most extraordinary that is to be found in the history of a young man, scarcely twenty years of age. Situated in a country that was like the lap of sensual pleasure, and with the means of enjoying it, how few are there to be found who would exchange such a scene for the woods and wildernesses of America, and pass the flowery

---

* French general Gilbert du Motier, Marquis de Lafayette (1757–1834).

years of youth in unprofitable danger and hardship! but such is the fact. When the war ended, and he was on the point of taking his final departure, he presented himself to Congress, and contemplating in his affectionate farewell the Revolution he had seen, expressed himself in these words: "May this great monument raised to liberty serve as a lesson to the oppressor, and an example to the oppressed!" When this address came to the hands of Dr. Franklin, who was then in France, he applied to Count Vergennes to have it inserted in the French Gazette, but never could obtain his consent. The fact was that Count Vergennes* was an aristocratical despot at home, and dreaded the example of the American Revolution in France, as certain other persons now dread the example of the French Revolution in England, and Mr. Burke's tribute of fear (for in this light his book must be considered) runs parallel with Count Vergennes' refusal. But to return more particularly to his work.

"We have seen," says Mr. Burke, "the French rebel against a mild and lawful monarch, with more fury, outrage, and insult, than any people has been known to rise against the most illegal usurper, or the most sanguinary tyrant." This is one among a thousand other instances, in which Mr. Burke shows that he is ignorant of the springs and principles of the French Revolution.

It was not against Louis XVI but against the despotic principles of the Government, that the nation revolted. These principles had not their origin in him, but in the original establishment, many centuries back: and they were become too deeply rooted to be removed, and the Augean stables of parasites and plunderers too abominably filthy to be cleansed by anything short of a complete and universal Revolution. When it becomes necessary to do anything, the whole heart and soul should go into the measure, or not attempt it. That crisis was then arrived, and there remained no choice but to act with determined vigor, or not to act at all. The king was known to be the friend of the nation, and this circumstance was favorable to the enterprise. Perhaps no man bred up in the style of an absolute king, ever possessed a heart so little disposed to the exercise of that species of power as the present King of France. But the principles of the Government itself still remained the same. The Monarch and the Monarchy were distinct and separate things; and it was against the established despotism of the latter, and

---

*French statesman Charles Gravier, comte de Vergennes (1717–87).

not against the person or principles of the former, that the revolt commenced, and the Revolution has been carried.

Mr. Burke does not attend to the distinction between men and principles, and, therefore, he does not see that a revolt may take place against the despotism of the latter, while there lies no charge of despotism against the former.

The natural moderation of Louis XVI contributed nothing to alter the hereditary despotism of the monarchy. All the tyrannies of former reigns, acted under that hereditary despotism, were still liable to be revived in the hands of a successor. It was not the respite of a reign that would satisfy France, enlightened as she was then become. A casual discontinuance of the *practice* of despotism, is not a discontinuance of its *principles*: the former depends on the virtue of the individual who is in immediate possession of the power; the latter, on the virtue and fortitude of the nation. In the case of Charles I and James II of England, the revolt was against the personal despotism of the men; whereas in France, it was against the hereditary despotism of the established Government. But men who can consign over the rights of posterity for ever on the authority of a mouldy parchment, like Mr. Burke, are not qualified to judge of this Revolution. It takes in a field too vast for their views to explore, and proceeds with a mightiness of reason they cannot keep pace with.

But there are many points of view in which this Revolution may be considered. When despotism has established itself for ages in a country, as in France, it is not in the person of the king only that it resides. It has the appearance of being so in show, and in nominal authority; but it is not so in practice and in fact. It has its standard everywhere. Every office and department has its despotism, founded upon custom and usage. Every place has its Bastille, and every Bastille its despot. The original hereditary despotism resident in the person of the king, divides and sub-divides itself into a thousand shapes and forms, till at last the whole of it is acted by deputation. This was the case in France; and against this species of despotism, proceeding on through an endless labyrinth of office till the source of it is scarcely perceptible, there is no mode of redress. It strengthens itself by assuming the appearance of duty, and tyrannies under the pretence of obeying.

When a man reflects on the condition which France was in from the nature of her government, he will see other causes for revolt than those which immediately connect themselves with the person or character of Louis XVI. There were, if I may so express it, a thousand despotisms to be reformed in France, which had grown up under the hereditary despotism of the monarchy, and became so rooted as to be in a great measure independent of it. Between the Monarchy, the Parliament, and the Church there was a *rivalship* of despotism; besides the feudal despotism operating locally, and the ministerial despotism operating everywhere. But Mr. Burke, by considering the king as the only possible object of a revolt, speaks as if France was a village, in which everything that passed must be known to its commanding officer, and no oppression could be acted but what he could immediately control. Mr. Burke might have been in the Bastille his whole life, as well under Louis XVI as Louis XIV, and neither the one nor the other have known that such a man as Burke existed. The despotic principles of the government were the same in both reigns, though the dispositions of the men were as remote as tyranny and benevolence.

What Mr. Burke considers as a reproach to the French Revolution (that of bringing it forward under a reign more mild than the preceding ones) is one of its highest honours. The Revolutions that have taken place in other European countries, have been excited by personal hatred. The rage was against the man, and he became the victim. But, in the instance of France we see a Revolution generated in the rational contemplation of the Rights of Man, and distinguishing from the beginning between persons and principles.

But Mr. Burke appears to have no idea of principles when he is contemplating Governments. "Ten years ago," says he, "I could have felicitated France on her having a Government, without inquiring what the nature of that Government was, or how it was administered." Is this the language of a rational man? Is it the language of a heart feeling as it ought to feel for the rights and happiness of the human race? On this ground, Mr. Burke must compliment all the Governments in the world, while the victims who suffer under them, whether sold into slavery, or tortured out of existence, are wholly forgotten. It is power, and not principles, that Mr. Burke venerates; and under this abominable depravity he is disqualified to judge between them. Thus much for his opinion as to the occasions of the French Revolution. I now proceed to other considerations.

I know a place in America called Point-no-Point, because as you proceed along the shore, gay and flowery as Mr. Burke's language, it continually recedes and presents itself at a distance before you; but when you have got as far as you can go, there is no point at all. Just thus it is with Mr. Burke's three hundred and sixty-six pages. It is therefore difficult to reply to him. But as the points he wishes to establish may be inferred from what he abuses, it is in his paradoxes that we must look for his arguments.

As to the tragic paintings by which Mr. Burke has outraged his own imagination, and seeks to work upon that of his readers, they are very well calculated for theatrical representation, where facts are manufactured for the sake of show, and accommodated to produce, through the weakness of sympathy, a weeping effect. But Mr. Burke should recollect that he is writing history, and not *plays*, and that his readers will expect truth, and not the spouting rant of high-toned exclamation.

When we see a man dramatically lamenting in a publication intended to be believed that "*The age of chivalry* is gone! that *The glory of Europe is extinguished for ever*! that *The unbought grace of life* (if anyone knows what it is), *the cheap defence of nations, the nurse of manly sentiment and heroic enterprise is gone*!" and all this because the Quixot age of chivalry nonsense is gone, what opinion can we form of his judgment, or what regard can we pay to his facts? In the rhapsody of his imagination he has discovered a world of wind mills, and his sorrows are that there are no Quixots to attack them. But if the age of aristocracy, like that of chivalry, should fall (and they had originally some connection) Mr. Burke, the trumpeter of the Order, may continue his parody to the end, and finish with exclaiming: "*Othello's occupation's gone*!"

Notwithstanding Mr. Burke's horrid paintings, when the French Revolution is compared with the Revolutions of other countries, the astonishment will be that it is marked with so few sacrifices; but this astonishment will cease when we reflect that *principles*, and not *persons*, were the meditated objects of destruction. The mind of the nation was acted upon by a higher stimulus than what the consideration of persons could inspire, and sought a higher conquest than could be produced by the downfall of an enemy. Among the few who fell there do not appear to be any that were intentionally singled out. They all of them had their fate in the circumstances of the moment, and were not pursued with that long, cold-blooded unabated revenge which pursued the unfortunate Scotch in the affair of 1745.

Through the whole of Mr. Burke's book I do not observe that the Bastille is mentioned more than once, and that with a kind of implication as if he were sorry it was pulled down, and wished it were built up again. "We have rebuilt Newgate," says he, "and tenanted the mansion; and we have prisons almost as strong as the Bastille for those who dare to libel the queens of France."\* As to what a madman like the person called Lord George Gordon might say, and to whom Newgate is rather a bedlam than a prison, it is unworthy a rational consideration. It was a madman that libelled, and that is sufficient apology; and it afforded an opportunity for confining him, which was the thing that was wished for. But certain it is that Mr. Burke, who does not call himself a madman (whatever other people may do), has libelled in the most unprovoked manner, and in the grossest style of the most vulgar abuse, the whole representative authority of France, and yet Mr. Burke takes his seat in the British House of Commons! From his violence and his grief, his silence on some points and his excess on others, it is difficult not to believe that Mr. Burke is sorry, extremely sorry, that arbitrary power, the power of the Pope and the Bastille, are pulled down.

Not one glance of compassion, not one commiserating reflection that I can find throughout his book, has he bestowed on those who lingered out the most wretched of lives, a life without hope in the most miserable of prisons. It is painful to behold a man employing his talents to corrupt himself. Nature has been kinder to Mr. Burke than he is to her. He is not affected by the reality of distress touching his heart, but by the showy resemblance of it striking his imagination. He pities the plumage, but forgets the dying bird. Accustomed to kiss the aristocratical hand that hath purloined him from himself, he degenerates into a composition of art, and the genuine soul of nature forsakes him. His hero or his

---

\* Since writing the above, two other places occur in Mr. Burke's pamphlet in which the name of the Bastille is mentioned, but in the same manner. In the one he introduces it in a sort of obscure question, and asks: "Will any ministers who now serve such a king, with but a decent appearance of respect, cordially obey the orders of those whom but the other day, *in his name*, they had committed to the Bastille?" In the other the taking it is mentioned as implying criminality in the French guards, who assisted in demolishing it. "They have not," says he, "forgot the taking the king's castles at Paris." This is Mr. Burke, who pretends to write on constitutional freedom. (Author's note)

heroine must be a tragedy-victim expiring in show, and not the real prisoner of misery, sliding into death in the silence of a dungeon.

As Mr. Burke has passed over the whole transaction of the Bastille (and his silence is nothing in his favour), and has entertained his readers with refections on supposed facts distorted into real falsehoods, I will give, since he has not, some account of the circumstances which preceded that transaction. They will serve to show that less mischief could scarcely have accompanied such an event when considered with the treacherous and hostile aggravations of the enemies of the Revolution.

The mind can hardly picture to itself a more tremendous scene than what the city of Paris exhibited at the time of taking the Bastille, and for two days before and after, nor perceive the possibility of its quieting so soon. At a distance this transaction has appeared only as an act of heroism standing on itself, and the close political connection it had with the Revolution is lost in the brilliancy of the achievement. But we are to consider it as the strength of the parties brought man to man, and contending for the issue. The Bastille was to be either the prize or the prison of the assailants. The downfall of it included the idea of the downfall of despotism, and this compounded image was become as figuratively united as Bunyan's Doubting Castle and Giant Despair.

The National Assembly, before and at the time of taking the Bastille, was sitting at Versailles, twelve miles distant from Paris. About a week before the rising of the Parisians, and their taking the Bastille, it was discovered that a plot was forming, at the head of which was the Count D'Artois, the king's youngest brother, for demolishing the National Assembly, seizing its members, and thereby crushing, by a *coup de main*, all hopes and prospects of forming a free government. For the sake of humanity, as well as freedom, it is well this plan did not succeed. Examples are not wanting to show how dreadfully vindictive and cruel are all old governments, when they are successful against what they call a revolt.

This plan must have been some time in contemplation; because, in order to carry it into execution, it was necessary to collect a large military force round Paris, and cut off the communication between that city and the National Assembly at Versailles. The troops destined for this service were chiefly the foreign troops in the pay of France, and who, for this particular purpose, were drawn from the distant provinces where they were then stationed. When they were collected to the amount of between twenty-five and thirty thousand, it was judged time to put the plan into execution. The ministry who were then in office, and who were friendly to the Revolution, were instantly dismissed and a new ministry formed of those who had concerted the project, among whom was Count de Broglio, and to his share was given the command of those troops. The character of this man as described to me in a letter which I communicated to Mr. Burke before he began to write his book, and from an authority which Mr. Burke well knows was good, was that of "a high-flying aristocrat, cool, and capable of every mischief."

While these matters were agitating, the National Assembly stood in the most perilous and critical situation that a body of men can be supposed to act in. They were the devoted victims, and they knew it. They had the hearts and wishes of their country on their side, but military authority they had none. The guards of Broglio surrounded the hall where the Assembly sat, ready, at the word of command, to seize their persons, as had been done the year before to the Parliament of Paris. Had the National Assembly deserted their trust, or had they exhibited signs of weakness or fear, their enemies had been encouraged and their country depressed. When the situation they stood in, the cause they were engaged in, and the crisis then ready to burst, which should determine their personal and political fate and that of their country, and probably of Europe, are taken into one view, none but a heart callous with prejudice or corrupted by dependence can avoid interesting itself in their success.

The Archbishop of Vienne was at this time President of the National Assembly—a person too old to undergo the scene that a few days or a few hours might bring forth. A man of more activity and bolder fortitude was necessary, and the National Assembly chose (under the form of a Vice-President, for the Presidency still resided in the Archbishop) M. de la Fayette; and this is the only instance of a Vice-President being chosen. It was at the moment that this storm was pending (July 11th) that a declaration of rights was brought forward by M. de la Fayette, and is the same which is alluded to earlier. It was hastily drawn up, and makes only a part of the more extensive declaration of rights agreed upon and adopted afterwards by the National Assembly. The particular reason for bringing it forward at this moment (M. de la Fayette has since informed me) was that, if the National Assembly should fall in the threatened destruction that then surrounded it, some trace of its principles might have the chance of surviving the wreck.

Everything now was drawing to a crisis. The event was freedom or slavery. On one side, an army of nearly thirty thousand men; on the other, an unarmed body of citizens—for the citizens of Paris, on whom the National Assembly must then immediately depend, were as unarmed and as undisciplined as the citizens of London are now. The French guards had given strong symptoms of their being attached to the national cause; but their numbers were small, not a tenth part of the force that Broglio commanded, and their officers were in the interest of Broglio.

Matters being now ripe for execution, the new ministry made their appearance in office. The reader will carry in his mind that the Bastille was taken the 14th July; the point of time I am now speaking of is the 12th. Immediately on the news of the change of ministry reaching Paris, in the afternoon, all the playhouses and places of entertainment, shops and houses, were shut up. The change of ministry was considered as the prelude of hostilities, and the opinion was rightly founded.

The foreign troops began to advance towards the city. The Prince de Lambesc, who commanded a body of German cavalry, approached by the Place of Louis XV, which connects itself with some of the streets. In his march, he insulted and struck an old man with a sword. The French are remarkable for their respect to old age; and the insolence with which it appeared to be done, uniting with the general fermentation they were in, produced a powerful effect, and a cry of "To arms! to arms!" spread itself in a moment over the city.

Arms they had none, nor scarcely anyone who knew the use of them; but desperate resolution, when every hope is at stake, supplies, for a while, the want of arms. Near where the Prince de Lambesc was drawn up, were large piles of stones collected for building the new bridge, and with these the people attacked the cavalry. A party of French guards upon hearing the firing, rushed from their quarters and joined the people; and night coming on, the cavalry retreated.

The streets of Paris, being narrow, are favourable for defence, and the loftiness of the houses, consisting of many stories, from which great annoyance might be given, secured them against nocturnal enterprises; and the night was spent in providing themselves with every sort of weapon they could make or procure: guns, swords, blacksmiths' hammers, carpenters' axes, iron crows, pikes, halberts, pitchforks, spits, clubs, etc., etc. The incredible numbers in which they assembled the next morning, and the still more incredible resolution they exhibited, embarrassed and astonished their enemies. Little did the new ministry expect such a salute. Accustomed to slavery themselves, they had no idea that liberty was capable of such inspiration, or that a body of unarmed citizens would dare to face the military force of thirty thousand men. Every moment of this day was employed in collecting arms, concerting plans, and arranging themselves into the best order which such an instantaneous movement could afford. Broglio continued lying round the city, but made no further advances this day, and the succeeding night passed with as much tranquility as such a scene could possibly produce.

But defence only was not the object of the citizens. They had a cause at stake, on which depended their freedom or their slavery. They every moment expected an attack, or to hear of one made on the National Assembly; and in such a situation, the most prompt measures are sometimes the best. The object that now presented itself was the Bastille; and the *éclat* of carrying such a fortress in the face of such an army, could not fail to strike terror into the new ministry, who had scarcely yet had time to meet. By some intercepted correspondence this morning, it was discovered that the Mayor of Paris, M. Defflesselles, who appeared to be in the interest of the citizens, was betraying them; and from this discovery, there remained no doubt that Broglio would reinforce the Bastille the ensuing evening. It was therefore necessary to attack it that day; but before this could be done, it was first necessary to procure a better supply of arms than they were then possessed of.

There was, adjoining to the city a large magazine of arms deposited at the Hospital of the Invalids, which the citizens summoned to surrender; and as the place was neither defensible, nor attempted much defence, they soon succeeded. Thus supplied, they marched to attack the Bastille; a vast mixed multitude of all ages, and of all degrees, armed with all sorts of weapons. Imagination would fail in describing to itself the appearance of such a procession, and of the anxiety of the events which a few hours or a few minutes might produce. What plans the ministry were forming, were as unknown to the people within the city, as what the citizens were doing was unknown to the ministry; and what movements Broglio might make for the support or relief of the place, were to the citizens equally as unknown. All was mystery and hazard.

That the Bastille was attacked with an enthusiasm of heroism, such only as the highest animation of liberty could inspire, and carried in the space of a few hours, is an event which the world is fully possessed of. I am not undertaking the detail of the attack, but bringing into view the conspiracy against the nation which provoked it, and which fell with the Bastille. The prison to which the new ministry were dooming the National Assembly, in addition to its being the high altar and castle of despotism, became the proper object to begin with. This enterprise broke up the new ministry, who began now to fly from the ruin they had prepared for others. The troops of Broglio dispersed, and himself fled also.

Mr. Burke has spoken a great deal about plots, but he has never once spoken of this plot against the National Assembly, and the liberties of the nation; and that he might not, he has passed over all the circumstances that might throw it in his way. The exiles who have fled from France, whose case he so much interests himself in, and from whom he has had his lesson, fled in consequence of the miscarriage of this plot. No plot was formed against them; they were plotting against others; and those who fell, met, not unjustly, the punishment they were preparing to execute. But will Mr. Burke say that if this plot, contrived with the subtilty of an ambuscade, had succeeded, the successful party would have restrained their wrath so soon? Let the history of all governments answer the question.

Whom has the National Assembly brought to the scaffold? None. They were themselves the devoted victims of this plot, and they have not retaliated; why, then, are they charged with revenge they have not acted? In the tremendous breaking forth of a whole people, in which all degrees, tempers and characters are confounded, delivering themselves, by a miracle of exertion, from the destruction meditated against them, is it to be expected that nothing will happen? When men are sore with the sense of oppressions, and menaced with the prospects of new ones, is the calmness of philosophy or the palsy of insensibility to be looked for? Mr. Burke exclaims against outrage; yet the greatest is that which himself has committed. His book is a volume of outrage, not apologised for by the impulse of a moment, but cherished through a space of ten months; yet Mr. Burke had no provocation—no life, no interest, at stake.

More of the citizens fell in this struggle than of their opponents: but four or five persons were seized by the populace, and instantly put to death; the Governor of the Bastille, and the Mayor of Paris, who was detected in the act of betraying them; and afterwards Foulon, one of the new ministry, and Berthier, his son-in-law, who had accepted the office of intendant of Paris. Their heads were stuck upon spikes, and carried about the city; and it is upon this mode of punishment that Mr. Burke builds a great part of his tragic scene. Let us therefore examine how men came by the idea of punishing in this manner.

They learn it from the governments they live under; and retaliate the punishments they have been accustomed to behold. The heads stuck upon spikes, which remained for years upon Temple Bar, differed nothing in the horror of the scene from those carried about upon spikes at Paris; yet this was done by the English Government. It may perhaps be said that it signifies nothing to a man what is done to him after he is dead; but it signifies much to the living; it either tortures their feelings or hardens their hearts, and in either case it instructs them how to punish when power falls into their hands.

Lay then the axe to the root, and teach governments humanity. It is their sanguinary punishments which corrupt mankind. In England the punishment in certain cases is by *hanging*, *drawing* and *quartering*; the heart of the sufferer is cut out and held up to the view of the populace. In France, under the former Government, the punishments were not less barbarous. Who does not remember the execution of Damien, torn to pieces by horses? The effect of those cruel spectacles exhibited to the populace is to destroy tenderness or excite revenge; and by the base and false idea of governing men by terror, instead of reason, they become precedents. It is over the lowest class of mankind that government by terror is intended to operate, and it is on them that it operates to the worst effect. They have sense enough to feel they are the objects aimed at; and they inflict in their turn the examples of terror they have been instructed to practise.

There is in all European countries a large class of people of that description, which in England is called the "mob." Of this class were those who committed the burnings and devastations in London in 1780, and of this class were those who carried the heads on iron spikes in Paris. Foulon and Berthier were taken up in the country, and sent to Paris, to undergo their examination at the Hôtel de Ville; for the National Assembly, immediately on the new ministry coming into office, passed a decree, which they communicated to the King and Cabinet, that they (the National Assembly) would hold the ministry, of which Foulon was one, responsible for the measures they were advising and pursuing; but the mob, incensed at the appearance of Foulon and Berthier, tore them from their conductors before they were carried to the Hôtel de Ville, and executed them on the spot. Why then does Mr. Burke charge outrages of this kind on a whole people? As well may he charge the riots and outrages of 1780 on all the people of London, or those in Ireland on all his countrymen.

But everything we see or hear offensive to our feelings and derogatory to the human character should lead to other reflections than those of reproach. Even the beings who commit them have some claim to our consideration. How then is it that such vast classes of mankind as are distinguished by the appellation of the vulgar, or the ignorant mob, are so numerous in all old countries? The instant we ask ourselves this question, reflection feels an answer. They rise, as an unavoidable consequence, out of the ill construction of all old governments in Europe, England included with the rest. It is by distortedly exalting some men, that others are distortedly debased, till the whole is out of nature. A vast mass of mankind are degradedly thrown into the background of the human picture, to bring forward, with greater glare, the puppet-show of state and aristocracy. In the commencement of a revolution, those men are rather the followers of the *camp* than of the *standard* of liberty, and have yet to be instructed how to reverence it.

I give to Mr. Burke all his theatrical exaggerations for facts, and I then ask him if they do not establish the certainty of what I here lay down? Admitting them to be true, they show the necessity of the French Revolution, as much as any one thing he could have asserted. These outrages were not the effect of the principles of the Revolution, but of the degraded mind that existed before the Revolution, and which the Revolution is calculated to reform. Place them then to their proper cause, and take the reproach of them to your own side.

It is the honour of the National Assembly and the city of Paris that, during such a tremendous scene of arms and confusion, beyond the control of all authority, they have been able, by the influence of example and exhortation, to restrain so much. Never were more pains taken to instruct and enlighten mankind, and to make them see that their interest consisted in their virtue, and not in their revenge, than have been displayed in the Revolution of France. I now proceed to make some remarks on Mr. Burke's account of the expedition to Versailles, October the 5th and 6th.

I can consider Mr. Burke's book in scarcely any other light than a dramatic performance; and he must, I think, have considered it in the same light himself, by the poetical liberties he has taken of omitting some facts, distorting others, and making the whole machinery bend to produce a stage effect. Of this kind is his account of the expedition to Versailles. He begins this account by omitting the only facts which as causes are known to be true; everything beyond these is conjecture, even in Paris; and he then works up a tale accommodated to his own passions and prejudices.

It is to be observed throughout Mr. Burke's book that he never speaks of plots *against* the Revolution; and it is from those plots that all the mischiefs have arisen. It suits his purpose to exhibit the consequences without their causes. It is one of the arts of the drama to do so. If the crimes of men were exhibited with their sufferings, stage effect would sometimes be lost, and the audience would be inclined to approve where it was intended they should commiserate.

After all the investigations that have been made into this intricate affair (the expedition to Versailles), it still remains enveloped in all that kind of mystery which ever accompanies events produced more from a concurrence of awkward circumstances than from fixed design. While the characters of men are forming, as is always the case in revolutions, there is a reciprocal suspicion, and a disposition to misinterpret each other; and even parties directly opposite in principle will sometimes concur in pushing forward the same movement with very different views, and with the hopes of its producing very different consequences. A great deal of this may be discovered in this embarrassed affair, and yet the issue of the whole was what nobody had in view.

The only things certainly known are that considerable uneasiness was at this time excited at Paris by the delay of the King in not sanctioning and forwarding the decrees of the National Assembly, particularly that of the *Declaration of the Rights of Man*, and the decrees of the *fourth of August*, which contained the foundation principles on which the constitution was to be erected. The kindest, and perhaps the fairest conjecture upon this matter is, that some of the ministers intended to make remarks and observations upon certain parts of them before they were finally sanctioned and sent to the provinces; but be this as it may, the enemies of the Revolution derived hope from the delay, and the friends of the Revolution uneasiness.

During this state of suspense, the Garde du Corps, which was composed as such regiments generally are, of persons much connected with the Court, gave an entertainment at Versailles (October 1) to some foreign regiments then arrived; and when the entertainment was at the height, on a signal given, the Garde du Corps tore the national cockade from their hats, trampled it under foot, and replaced it with a counter-cockade prepared for the purpose. An indignity of this kind amounted to defiance. It was like declaring war; and if men will give challenges they must expect consequences. But all this Mr. Burke has carefully kept out of sight. He begins his account by saying: "History will record that on the morning of the 6th October, 1789, the King and Queen of France, after a day of confusion, alarm, dismay, and slaughter, lay down under the pledged security of public faith to indulge nature in a few hours of respite, and troubled melancholy repose." This is neither the sober style of history, nor the intention of it. It leaves everything to be guessed at and mistaken. One would at least think there had been a battle; and a battle there probably would have been had it not been for the moderating prudence of those whom Mr. Burke involves in his censures. By his keeping the Garde du Corps out of sight Mr. Burke has afforded himself the dramatic licence of putting the King and Queen in their places, as if the object of the expedition was against them. But to return to my account this conduct of the Garde du Corps, as might well be expected, alarmed and enraged the Partisans. The colors of the cause, and the cause itself, were become too united to mistake the intention of the insult, and the Partisans were determined to call the Garde du Corps to an account. There was certainly nothing of the cowardice of assassination in marching in the face of the day to demand satisfaction, if such a phrase may be used, of a body of armed men who had voluntarily given defiance. But the circumstance which serves to throw this affair into embarrassment is, that the enemies of the Revolution appear to have encouraged it as well as its friends. The one hoped to prevent a civil war by checking it in time, and the other to make one. The hopes of those opposed to the Revolution rested in making the King of their party, and getting him from Versailles to Metz, where they expected to collect a force and set up a standard. We have, therefore, two different objects presenting themselves at the same time, and to be accomplished by the same means: the one to chastise the Garde du Corps, which was the object of the Partisans; the other to render the confusion of such a scene an inducement to the King to set off for Metz.

On the 5th of October a very numerous body of women, and men in the disguise of women, collected around the Hôtel de Ville or town-hall at Paris, and set off for Versailles. Their professed object was the Garde du Corps; but prudent men readily recollect that mischief is more easily begun than ended; and this impressed itself with the more force from the suspicions already stated, and the irregularity of such a cavalcade. As soon, therefore, as a sufficient force could be collected, M. de la Fayette, by orders from the civil authority of Paris, set off after them at the head of twenty thousand of the Paris militia. The Revolution could derive no benefit from confusion, and its opposers might. By an amiable and spirited manner of address he had hitherto been fortunate in calming disquietudes, and in this he was extraordinarily successful; to frustrate, therefore, the hopes of those who might seek to improve this scene into a sort of justifiable necessity for the King's quitting Versailles and withdrawing to Metz, and to prevent at the same time the consequences that might ensue between the Garde du Corps and this phalanx of men and women, he forwarded expresses to the King, that he was on his march to Versailles, by the orders of the civil authority of Paris, for the purpose of peace and protection, expressing at the same time the necessity of restraining the Garde du Corps from firing upon the people.*

He arrived at Versailles between ten and eleven at night. The Garde du Corps was drawn up, and the people had arrived some time before, but everything had remained suspended. Wisdom and policy now consisted in changing a scene of danger into a happy event. M. de la Fayette became the mediator between the enraged parties; and the King, to remove the uneasiness which had arisen from the delay already stated, sent for the President of the National Assembly, and signed the Declaration of the Rights of Man, and such other parts of the constitution as were in readiness.

It was now about one in the morning. Everything appeared to be composed, and a general congratulation took place. By the beat of a drum a proclamation was made that the citizens of Versailles would give the hospitality of their houses to their fellow-citizens of Paris.

* I am warranted in asserting this, as I had it personally from M. de la Fayette, with whom I lived in habits of friendship for fourteen years. (Author's note)

Those who could not be accommodated in this manner remained in the streets, or took up their quarters in the churches; and at two o'clock the King and Queen retired.

In this state matters passed till the break of day, when a fresh disturbance arose from the censurable conduct of some of both parties, for such characters there will be in all such scenes. One of the Garde du Corps appeared at one of the windows of the palace, and the people who had remained during the night in the streets accosted him with reviling and provocative language. Instead of retiring, as in such a case prudence would have dictated, he presented his musket, fired, and killed one of the Paris militia. The peace being thus broken, the people rushed into the palace in quest of the offender. They attacked the quarters of the Garde du Corps within the palace, and pursued them throughout the avenues of it, and to the apartments of the King. On this tumult, not the Queen only, as Mr. Burke has represented it, but every person in the palace, was awakened and alarmed; and M. de la Fayette had a second time to interpose between the parties, the event of which was that the Garde du Corps put on the national cockade, and the matter ended as by oblivion, after the loss of two or three lives.

During the latter part of the time in which this confusion was acting, the King and Queen were in public at the balcony, and neither of them concealed for safety's sake, as Mr. Burke insinuates. Matters being thus appeased, and tranquility restored, a general acclamation broke forth of Le Roi a Paris—Le Roi a Paris—The King to Paris. It was the shout of peace, and immediately accepted on the part of the King. By this measure all future projects of trapanning the King to Metz, and setting up the standard of opposition to the constitution, were prevented, and the suspicions extinguished. The King and his family reached Paris in the evening, and were congratulated on their arrival by M. Bailly, the Mayor of Paris, in the name of the citizens. Mr. Burke, who throughout his book confounds things, persons, and principles, as in his remarks on M. Bailly's address, confounded time also. He censures M. Bailly for calling it "un bon jour," a good day. Mr. Burke should have informed himself that this scene took up the space of two days, the day on which it began with every appearance of danger and mischief, and the day on which it terminated without the mischiefs that threatened; and that it is to this peaceful termination that M. Bailly alludes, and to the arrival of the King at Paris. Not less than three hundred thousand persons arranged themselves in the procession from Versailles to Paris, and not an act of molestation was committed during the whole march.

Mr. Burke on the authority of M. Lally Tollendal, a deserter from the National Assembly, says that on entering Paris, the people shouted "Tous les eveques a la lanterne." All Bishops to be hanged at the lanthorn or lamp-posts. It is surprising that nobody could hear this but Lally Tollendal, and that nobody should believe it but Mr. Burke. It has not the least connection with any part of the transaction, and is totally foreign to every circumstance of it. The Bishops had never been introduced before into any scene of Mr. Burke's drama: why then are they, all at once, and altogether, tout a coup, et tous ensemble, introduced now? Mr. Burke brings forward his Bishops and his lanthorn-like figures in a magic lanthorn, and raises his scenes by contrast instead of connection. But it serves to show, with the rest of his book what little credit ought to be given where even probability is set at defiance, for the purpose of defaming; and with this reflection, instead of a soliloquy in praise of chivalry, as Mr. Burke has done, I close the account of the expedition to Versailles.*

I have now to follow Mr. Burke through a pathless wilderness of rhapsodies, and a sort of descant upon governments, in which he asserts whatever he pleases, on the presumption of its being believed, without offering either evidence or reasons for so doing.

Before anything can be reasoned upon to a conclusion, certain facts, principles, or data, to reason from, must be established, admitted, or denied. Mr. Burke with his usual outrage, abused the *Declaration of the Rights of Man*, published by the National Assembly of France, as the basis on which the constitution of France is built. This he calls "paltry and blurred sheets of paper about the rights of man." Does Mr. Burke mean to deny that *man* has any rights? If he does, then he must mean that there are no such things as rights anywhere, and that he has none himself; for who is there in the world but man? But if Mr. Burke means to admit that man has rights, the question then will be: What are those rights, and how man came by them originally?

The error of those who reason by precedents drawn from antiquity, respecting the rights of man, is that they do not go far enough into antiquity. They do not go the whole way. They stop in some of the

---

* An account of the expedition to Versailles may be seen in No. 13 of the Revolution de Paris containing the events from the 3rd to the 10th of October, 1789. (Author's note)

intermediate stages of an hundred or a thousand years, and produce what was then done, as a rule for the present day. This is no authority at all. If we travel still farther into antiquity, we shall find a direct contrary opinion and practice prevailing; and if antiquity is to be authority, a thousand such authorities may be produced, successively contradicting each other; but if we proceed on, we shall at last come out right; we shall come to the time when man came from the hand of his Maker. What was he then? Man. Man was his high and only title, and a higher cannot be given him. But of titles I shall speak hereafter.

We are now got at the origin of man, and at the origin of his rights. As to the manner in which the world has been governed from that day to this, it is no farther any concern of ours than to make a proper use of the errors or the improvements which the history of it presents. Those who lived an hundred or a thousand years ago, were then moderns, as we are now. They had *their* ancients, and those ancients had others, and we also shall be ancients in our turn. If the mere name of antiquity is to govern in the affairs of life, the people who are to live an hundred or a thousand years hence, may as well take us for a precedent, as we make a precedent of those who lived an hundred or a thousand years ago. The fact is, that portions of antiquity, by proving everything, establish nothing. It is authority against authority all the way, till we come to the divine origin of the rights of man at the creation. Here our enquiries find a resting-place, and our reason finds a home. If a dispute about the rights of man had arisen at the distance of an hundred years from the creation, it is to this source of authority they must have referred, and it is to this same source of authority that we must now refer.

Though I mean not to touch upon any sectarian principle of religion, yet it may be worth observing, that the genealogy of Christ is traced to Adam. Why then not trace the rights of man to the creation of man? I will answer the question. Because there have been upstart governments, thrusting themselves between, and presumptuously working to *un-make* man.

If any generation of men ever possessed the right of dictating the mode by which the world should be governed for ever, it was the first generation that existed; and if that generation did it not, no succeeding generation can show any authority for doing it, nor can set any up. The illuminating and divine principle of the equal rights of man (for it has its origin from the Maker of man) relates, not only to the living individuals, but to generations of men succeeding each other. Every generation is equal in rights to generations which preceded it, by the same rule that every individual is born equal in rights with his contemporary.

Every history of the creation, and every traditionary account, whether from the lettered or unlettered world, however they may vary in their opinion or belief of certain particulars, all agree in establishing one point, *the unity of man*; by which I mean that men are all of *one degree*, and consequently that all men are born equal, and with equal natural right, in the same manner as if posterity had been continued by *creation* instead of *generation*, the latter being the only mode by which the former is carried forward; and consequently every child born into the world must be considered as deriving its existence from God. The world is as new to him as it was to the first man that existed, and his natural right in it is of the same kind.

The Mosaic account of the creation, whether taken as divine authority or merely historical, is full to this point, *the unity or equality of man*. The expression admits of no controversy. "And God said, Let us make man in our own image. In the image of God created he him; male and female created he them." The distinction of sexes is pointed out, but no other distinction is even implied. If this be not divine authority, it is at least historical authority, and shows that the equality of man, so far from being a modern doctrine, is the oldest upon record.

It is also to be observed that all the religions known in the world are founded, so far as they relate to man, on the *unity of man*, as being all of one degree. Whether in heaven or in hell, or in whatever state man may be supposed to exist hereafter, the good and the bad are the only distinctions. Nay, even the laws of governments are obliged to slide into this principle, by making degrees to consist in crimes and not in persons.

It is one of the greatest of all truths, and of the highest advantage to cultivate. By considering man in this light, and by instructing him to consider himself in this light, it places him in a close connection with all his duties, whether to his Creator or to the creation, of which he is a part; and it is only when he forgets his origin, or, to use a more fashionable phrase, his *birth and family*, that he becomes dissolute. It is not among the least of the evils of the present existing governments in all parts of Europe that man, considered as man, is thrown back to a vast distance from his Maker, and the artificial chasm filled up with a succession of barriers, or sort of turnpike gates, through which he has to pass. I will quote Mr. Burke's catalogue of barriers that he has set up between man and his Maker. Putting himself in the character of a herald, he says: "We fear God—we look with *awe* to kings—with affection to Parliaments with duty to magistrates—with reverence to priests, and with respect to nobility." Mr. Burke has forgotten to put in "*chivalry*." He has also forgotten to put in Peter.

The duty of man is not a wilderness of turnpike gates, through which he is to pass by tickets from one to the other. It is plain and simple, and consists but of two points. His duty to God, which every man must feel; and with respect to his neighbor, to do as he would be done by. If those to whom power is delegated do well, they will be respected: if not, they will be despised; and with regard to those to whom no power is delegated, but who assume it, the rational world can know nothing of them.

Hitherto we have spoken only (and that but in part) of the natural rights of man. We have now to consider the civil rights of man, and to show how the one originates from the other. Man did not enter into society to become worse than he was before, nor to have fewer rights than he had before, but to have those rights better secured. His natural rights are the foundation of all his civil rights. But in order to pursue this distinction with more precision, it will be necessary to mark the different qualities of natural and civil rights.

A few words will explain this. Natural rights are those which appertain to man in right of his existence. Of this kind are all the intellectual rights, or rights of the mind, and also all those rights of acting as an individual for his own comfort and happiness, which are not injurious to the natural rights of others. Civil rights are those which appertain to man in right of his being a member of society. Every civil right has for its foundation some natural right pre-existing in the individual, but to the enjoyment of which his individual power is not, in all cases, sufficiently competent. Of this kind are all those which relate to security and protection.

From this short review it will be easy to distinguish between that class of natural rights which man retains after entering into society and those which he throws into the common stock as a member of society.

The natural rights which he retains are all those in which the *power* to execute is as perfect in the individual as the right itself. Among this class, as is before mentioned, are all the intellectual rights, or rights of the mind; consequently religion is one of those rights. The natural rights which are not retained, are all those in which, though the right is perfect in the individual, the power to execute them is defective. They answer not his purpose. A man, by natural right, has a right to judge in his own cause; and so far as the right of the mind is concerned, he never surrenders it. But what availeth it him to judge, if he has not power to redress? He therefore deposits this right in the common stock of society, and takes the arm of society, of which he is a part, in preference and in addition to his own. Society *grants* him nothing. Every man is a proprietor in society, and draws on the capital as a matter of right.

From these premises two or three certain conclusions will follow:

First, That every civil right grows out of a natural right; or, in other words, is a natural right exchanged.

Secondly, That civil power properly considered as such is made up of the aggregate of that class of the natural rights of man, which becomes defective in the individual in point of power, and answers not his purpose, but when collected to a focus becomes competent to the purpose of every one.

Thirdly, That the power produced from the aggregate of natural rights, imperfect in power in the individual, cannot be applied to invade the natural rights which are retained in the individual, and in which the power to execute is as perfect as the right itself.

We have now, in a few words, traced man from a natural individual to a member of society, and shown, or endeavoured to show, the quality of the natural rights retained, and of those which are exchanged for civil rights. Let us now apply these principles to governments.

In casting our eyes over the world, it is extremely easy to distinguish the governments which have arisen out of society, or out of the social compact, from those which have not; but to place this in a clearer light than what a single glance may afford, it will be proper to take a review of the several sources from which governments have arisen and on which they have been founded.

They may be all comprehended under three heads.

First, Superstition.

Secondly, Power.

Thirdly, The common interest of society and the common rights of man.

The first was a government of priestcraft, the second of conquerors, and the third of reason.

When a set of artful men pretended, through the medium of oracles, to hold intercourse with the Deity, as familiarly as they now march up the back-stairs in European courts, the world was completely under the government of superstition. The oracles were consulted, and whatever they were made to say became the law; and this sort of government lasted as long as this sort of superstition lasted.

After these a race of conquerors arose, whose government, like that of William the Conqueror, was founded in power, and the sword assumed the name of a sceptre. Governments thus established last as long as the power to support them lasts; but that they might avail themselves of every engine in their favor, they united fraud to force, and set up an idol which they called *Divine Right*, and which, in imitation of the Pope, who affects to be spiritual and temporal, and in contradiction to the Founder of the Christian religion, twisted itself afterwards into an idol of another shape, called *Church and State*. The key of St. Peter and the key of the Treasury became quartered on one another, and the wondering cheated multitude worshipped the invention.

When I contemplate the natural dignity of man, when I feel (for Nature has not been kind enough to me to blunt my feelings) for the honour and happiness of its character, I become irritated at the attempt to govern mankind by force and fraud, as if they were all knaves and fools, and can scarcely avoid disgust at those who are thus imposed upon.

We have now to review the governments which arise out of society, in contradistinction to those which arose out of superstition and conquest.

It has been thought a considerable advance towards establishing the principles of Freedom to say that Government is a compact between those who govern and those who are governed; but this cannot be true, because it is putting the effect before the cause; for as man must have existed before governments existed, there necessarily was a time when governments did not exist, and consequently there could originally exist no governors to form such a compact with.

The fact therefore must be that the *individuals themselves*, each in his own personal and sovereign right, *entered into a compact with each other* to produce a government: and this is the only mode in which governments have a right to arise, and the only principle on which they have a right to exist.

To possess ourselves of a clear idea of what government is, or ought to be, we must trace it to its origin. In doing this we shall easily discover that governments must have arisen either *out* of the people or *over* the people. Mr. Burke has made no distinction. He investigates nothing to its source, and therefore he confounds everything; but he has signified his intention of undertaking, at some future opportunity, a comparison between the constitution of England and France. As he thus renders it a subject of controversy by throwing the gauntlet, I take him upon his own ground. It is in high challenges that high truths have the right of appearing; and I accept it with the more readiness because it affords me, at the same time, an opportunity of pursuing the subject with respect to governments arising out of society.

But it will be first necessary to define what is meant by a *Constitution*. It is not sufficient that we adopt the word; we must fix also a standard signification to it.

A constitution is not a thing in name only, but in fact. It has not an ideal, but a real existence; and wherever it cannot be produced in a visible form, there is none. A constitution is a thing *antecedent* to a government, and a government is only the creature of a constitution. The constitution of a country is not the act of its government, but of the people constituting its government. It is the body of elements, to which you can refer, and quote article by article; and which contains the principles on which the government shall be established, the manner in which it shall be organised, the powers it shall have, the mode of elections, the duration of Parliaments, or by what other name such bodies may be called; the powers which the executive part of the government shall have; and in fine, everything that relates to the complete organisation of a civil government, and the principles on which it shall act, and by which it shall be bound. A constitution, therefore, is to a government what the laws made afterwards by that government are to a court of judicature. The court of judicature does not make the laws, neither can it alter them; it only acts in conformity to the laws made: and the government is in like manner governed by the constitution.

Can, then, Mr. Burke produce the English Constitution? If he cannot, we may fairly conclude that though it has been so much talked about, no such thing as a constitution exists, or ever did exist, and consequently that the people have yet a constitution to form.

Mr. Burke will not, I presume, deny the position I have already advanced—namely, that governments arise either *out* of the people or *over* the people. The English Government is one of those which arose out of a conquest, and not out of society, and consequently it arose over the people; and though it has been much modified from the opportunity of circumstances since the time of William the Conqueror, the country has never yet regenerated itself, and is therefore without a constitution.

I readily perceive the reason why Mr. Burke declined going into the comparison between the English and French constitutions, because he could not but perceive, when he sat down to the task, that no such a thing as a constitution existed on his side the question. His book is certainly bulky enough to have contained all he could say on this subject, and it would have been the best manner in which people could have judged of their separate merits. Why then has he declined the only thing that was worth while to write upon? It was the strongest ground he could take, if the advantages were on his side, but the weakest if they were not; and his declining to take it is either a sign that he could not possess it or could not maintain it.

Mr. Burke said, in a speech last winter in Parliament, "that when the National Assembly first met in three Orders (the *Tiers Etat*, the Clergy, and the Noblesse), France had then a good constitution." This shows, among numerous other instances, that Mr. Burke does not understand what a constitution is. The persons so met were not a *constitution*, but a *convention*, to make a constitution.

The present National Assembly of France is, strictly speaking, the personal social compact. The members of it are the delegates of the nation in its *original* character; future assemblies will be the delegates of the nation in its *organised* character. The authority of the present Assembly is different from what the authority of future Assemblies will be. The authority of the present one is to form a constitution; the authority of future assemblies will be to legislate according to the principles and forms prescribed in that constitution; and if experience should hereafter show that alterations, amendments, or additions are necessary, the constitution will point out the mode by which such things shall be done, and not leave it to the discretionary power of the future government.

A government on the principles on which constitutional governments arising out of society are established, cannot have the right of altering itself. If it had, it would be arbitrary. It might make itself what it pleased; and wherever such a right is set up, it shows there is no constitution. The act by which the English Parliament empowered itself to sit seven years, shows there is no constitution in England. It might, by the same self-authority, have sat any great number of years, or for life. The bill which the present Mr. Pitt brought into Parliament some years ago, to reform Parliament, was on the same erroneous principle. The right of reform is in the nation in its original character, and the constitutional method would be by a general convention elected for the purpose. There is, moreover, a paradox in the idea of vitiated bodies reforming themselves.

From these preliminaries I proceed to draw some comparisons. I have already spoken of the declaration of rights; and as I mean to be as concise as possible, I shall proceed to other parts of the French Constitution.

The constitution of France says that every man who pays a tax of sixty sous per annum (2s. 6d. English) is an elector. What article will Mr. Burke place against this? Can anything be more limited, and at the same time more capricious, than the qualification of electors is in England? Limited—because not one man in an hundred (I speak much within compass) is admitted to vote. Capricious—because the lowest character that can be supposed to exist, and who has not so much as the visible means of an honest livelihood, is an elector in some places: while in other places, the man who pays very large taxes, and has a known fair character, and the farmer who rents to the amount of three or four hundred pounds a year, with a property on that farm to three or four times that amount, is not admitted to be an elector. Everything is out of nature, as Mr. Burke says on another occasion, in this strange chaos, and all sorts of follies are blended with all sorts of crimes. William the Conqueror and his descendants parcelled out the country in this manner, and bribed some parts of it by what they call charters to hold the other parts of it the better subjected to their will. This is the reason why so many of those charters abound in Cornwall; the people were averse to the Government established at the Conquest, and the towns were garrisoned and bribed to enslave the country. All the old charters are the badges of this conquest, and it is from this source that the capriciousness of election arises.

The French Constitution says that the number of representatives for any place shall be in a ratio to the number of taxable inhabitants or electors. What article will Mr. Burke place against this? The county of York, which contains nearly a million of souls, sends two county members; and so does the county of Rutland, which contains not an hundredth part of that number. The old town of Sarum, which contains not three houses, sends two members; and the town of Manchester, which contains upward of sixty thousand souls, is not admitted to send any. Is there any principle in these things? It is admitted that all this is altered, but there is much to be done yet, before we have a fair representation of the people. Is there anything by which you can trace the marks of freedom, or discover those of wisdom? No wonder then Mr. Burke has declined the comparison, and endeavored to lead his readers from the point by a wild, unsystematical display of paradoxical rhapsodies.

The French Constitution says that the National Assembly shall be elected every two years. What article will Mr. Burke place against this? Why, that the nation has no right at all in the case; that the government is perfectly arbitrary with respect to this point; and he can quote for his authority the precedent of a former Parliament.

The French Constitution says there shall be no game laws, that the farmer on whose lands wild game shall be found (for it is by the produce of his lands they are fed) shall have a right to what he can take; that there shall be no monopolies of any kind—that all trades shall be free and every man free to follow any occupation by which he can procure an honest livelihood, and in any place, town, or city throughout the nation. What will Mr. Burke say to this? In England, game is made the property of those at whose expense it is not fed; and with respect to monopolies, the country is cut up into monopolies. Every chartered town is an aristocratical monopoly in itself, and the qualification of electors proceeds out of those chartered monopolies. Is this freedom? Is this what Mr. Burke means by a constitution?

In these chartered monopolies, a man coming from another part of the country is hunted from them as if he were a foreign enemy. An Englishman is not free of his own country; every one of those places presents a barrier in his way, and tells him he is not a freeman—that he has no rights. Within these monopolies are other monopolies. In a city, such for instance as Bath, which contains between twenty and thirty thousand inhabitants, the right of electing representatives to Parliament is monopolised by about thirty-one persons. And within these monopolies are still others. A man even of the same town, whose parents were not in circumstances to give him an occupation, is debarred, in many cases, from the natural right of acquiring one, be his genius or industry what it may.

Are these things examples to hold out to a country regenerating itself from slavery, like France? Certainly they are not, and certain am I, that when the people of England come to reflect upon them they will, like France, annihilate those badges of ancient oppression, those traces of a conquered nation. Had Mr. Burke possessed talents similar to the author of "On the Wealth of Nations." he would have comprehended all the parts which enter into, and, by assemblage, form a constitution. He would have reasoned from minutiae to magnitude. It is not from his prejudices only, but from the disorderly cast of his genius, that he is unfitted for the subject he writes upon. Even his genius is without a constitution. It is a genius at random, and not a genius constituted. But he must say something. He has therefore mounted in the air like a balloon, to draw the eyes of the multitude from the ground they stand upon.

Much is to be learned from the French Constitution. Conquest and tyranny transplanted themselves with William the Conqueror from Normandy into England, and the country is yet disfigured with the marks. May, then, the example of all France contribute to regenerate the freedom which a province of it destroyed!

The French Constitution says that to preserve the national representation from being corrupt, no member of the National Assembly shall be an officer of the government, a placeman or a pensioner. What will Mr. Burke place against this? I will whisper his answer: *Loaves and Fishes*. Ah! this government of loaves and fishes has more mischief in it than people have yet reflected on. The National Assembly has made the discovery, and it holds out the example to the world. Had governments agreed to quarrel on purpose to fleece their countries by taxes, they could not have succeeded better than they have done.

Everything in the English government appears to me the reverse of what it ought to be, and of what it is said to be. The Parliament, imperfectly and capriciously elected as it is, is nevertheless *supposed* to hold the national purse in *trust* for the nation; but in the manner in which an English Parliament is constructed it is like a man being both mortgagor and mortgagee, and in the case of misapplication of trust it is the criminal sitting in judgment upon himself. If those who vote the supplies are the same persons who receive the supplies when voted, and are to account for the expenditure of those supplies to those who voted them, it is *themselves accountable to themselves*, and the Comedy of Errors concludes with the pantomime of *Hush*. Neither the Ministerial party nor the Opposition will touch upon this case. The national purse is the common hack which each mounts upon. It is like what the country people call "Ride and tie—you ride a little way, and then I."* They order these things better in France.

The French Constitution says that the right of war and peace is in the nation. Where else should it reside but in those who are to pay the expense?

In England this right is said to reside in a *metaphor* shown at the Tower for sixpence or a shilling a piece: so are the lions; and it would be a step nearer to reason to say it resided in them, for any inanimate metaphor is no more than a hat or a cap. We can all see the absurdity of worshipping Aaron's molten calf, or Nebuchadnezzar's golden image; but why do men continue to practise themselves the absurdities they despise in others?

It may with reason be said that in the manner the English nation is represented it signifies not where the right resides, whether in the Crown or in the Parliament. War is the common harvest of all those who participate in the division and expenditure of public money, in all countries. It is the art of *conquering at home*; the object of it is an increase of revenue; and as revenue cannot be increased without taxes, a pretence must be made for expenditure. In reviewing the history of the English Government, its wars and its taxes, a bystander, not blinded by prejudice nor warped by interest, would declare that taxes were not raised to carry on wars, but that wars were raised to carry on taxes.

Mr. Burke, as a member of the House of Commons, is a part of the English Government; and though he professes himself an enemy to

---

* It is a practice in some parts of the country, when two travellers have but one horse, which, like the national purse, will not carry double, that the one mounts and rides two or three miles ahead, and then ties the horse to a gate and walks on. When the second traveller arrives he takes the horse, rides on, and passes his companion a mile or two, and ties again, and so on—*Ride and tie*. (Author's note)

war, he abuses the French Constitution, which seeks to explode it. He holds up the English Government as a model, in all its parts, to France; but he should first know the remarks which the French make upon it. They contend in favor of their own, that the portion of liberty enjoyed in England is just enough to enslave a country more productively than by despotism, and that as the real object of all despotism is revenue, a government so formed obtains more than it could do either by direct despotism, or in a full state of freedom, and is, therefore on the ground of interest, opposed to both. They account also for the readiness which always appears in such governments for engaging in wars by remarking on the different motives which produced them. In despotic governments wars are the effect of pride; but in those governments in which they become the means of taxation, they acquire thereby a more permanent promptitude.

The French Constitution, therefore, to provide against both these evils, has taken away the power of declaring war from kings and ministers, and placed the right where the expense must fall.

When the question of the right of war and peace was agitating in the National Assembly, the people of England appeared to be much interested in the event, and highly to applaud the decision. As a principle it applies as much to one country as another. William the Conqueror, *as a conqueror*, held this power of war and peace in himself, and his descendants have ever since claimed it under him as a right.

Although Mr. Burke has asserted the right of the Parliament at the Revolution to bind and control the nation and posterity for ever, he denies at the same time that the Parliament or the nation had any right to alter what he calls the succession of the crown in anything but in part, or by a sort of modification. By his taking this ground he throws the case back to the *Norman Conquest*, and by thus running a line of succession springing from William the Conqueror to the present day, he makes it necessary to enquire who and what William the Conqueror was, and where he came from, and into the origin, history and nature of what are called prerogatives. Everything must have had a beginning, and the fog of time and antiquity should be penetrated to discover it. Let, then, Mr. Burke bring forward his William of Normandy, for it is to this origin that his argument goes. It also unfortunately happens, in running this line of succession, that another line parallel thereto presents itself, which is that if the succession runs in the line of the conquest, the nation runs in the line of being conquered, and it ought to rescue itself from this reproach.

But it will perhaps be said that though the power of declaring war descends in the heritage of the conquest, it is held in check by the right of Parliament to withhold the supplies. It will always happen when a thing is originally wrong that amendments do not make it right, and it often happens that they do as much mischief one way as good the other, and such is the case here, for if the one rashly declares war as a matter of right, and the other peremptorily withholds the supplies as a matter of right, the remedy becomes as bad, or worse, than the disease. The one forces the nation to a combat, and the other ties its hands; but the more probable issue is that the contest will end in a collusion between the parties, and be made a screen to both.

On this question of war, three things are to be considered. First, the right of declaring it: secondly, the expense of supporting it: thirdly, the mode of conducting it after it is declared. The French Constitution places the *right* where the *expense* must fall, and this union can only be in the nation. The mode of conducting it after it is declared, it consigns to the executive department. Were this the case in all countries, we should hear but little more of wars.

Before I proceed to consider other parts of the French Constitution, and by way of relieving the fatigue of argument, I will introduce an anecdote which I had from Dr. Franklin.

While the Doctor resided in France as Minister from America, during the war, he had numerous proposals made to him by projectors of every country and of every kind, who wished to go to the land that floweth with milk and honey, America; and among the rest, there was one who offered himself to be king. He introduced his proposal to the Doctor by letter, which is now in the hands of M. Beaumarchais, of Paris—stating, first, that as the Americans had dismissed or sent away[*] their King, that they would want another. Secondly, that himself was a Norman. Thirdly, that he was of a more ancient family than the Dukes of Normandy, and of a more honourable descent, his line having never been bastardised. Fourthly, that there was already a precedent in England of kings coming out of Normandy, and on these grounds he rested his offer, enjoining that the Doctor would forward it to America. But as the

---

* The word he used was *renvoye*, dismissed or sent away. (Author's note)

Doctor neither did this, nor yet sent him an answer, the projector wrote a second letter, in which he did not, it is true, threaten to go over and conquer America, but only with great dignity proposed that if his offer was not accepted, an acknowledgment of about £30,000 might be made to him for his generosity! Now, as all arguments respecting succession must necessarily connect that succession with some beginning, Mr. Burke's arguments on this subject go to show that there is no English origin of kings, and that they are descendants of the Norman line in right of the Conquest. It may, therefore, be of service to his doctrine to make this story known, and to inform him, that in case of that natural extinction to which all mortality is subject, Kings may again be had from Normandy, on more reasonable terms than William the Conqueror; and consequently, that the good people of England, at the revolution of 1688, might have done much better, had such a generous Norman as *this* known *their* wants, and they had known *his*. The chivalric character which Mr. Burke so much admires, is certainly much easier to make a bargain with than a hard dealing Dutchman. But to return to the matters of the constitution: The French Constitution says, *There shall be no titles*; and, of consequence, all that class of equivocal generation which in some countries is called "aristocracy" and in others "nobility," is done away, and the *peer* is exalted into the *Man*.

Titles are but nicknames, and every nickname is a title. The thing is perfectly harmless in itself, but it marks a sort of foppery in the human character, which degrades it. It reduces man into the diminutive of man in things which are great, and the counterfeit of women in things which are little. It talks about its fine blue ribbon like a girl, and shows its new garter like a child. A certain writer, of some antiquity, says: "When I was a child, I thought as a child; but when I became a man, I put away childish things."

It is, properly, from the elevated mind of France that the folly of titles has fallen. It has outgrown the baby clothes of *Count* and *Duke*, and breeched itself in manhood. France has not levelled, it has exalted. It has put down the dwarf, to set up the man. The punyism of a senseless word like *Duke*, *Count* or *Earl* has ceased to please. Even those who possessed them have disowned the gibberish, and as they outgrew the rickets, have despised the rattle. The genuine mind of man, thirsting for its native home, society, contemns the gewgaws that separate him from it. Titles are like circles drawn by the magician's wand, to contract the sphere of man's felicity. He lives immured within the Bastille of a word, and surveys at a distance the envied life of man.

Is it, then, any wonder that titles should fall in France? Is it not a greater wonder that they should be kept up anywhere? What are they? What is their worth, and "what is their amount?" When we think or speak of a Judge or a General, we associate with it the ideas of office and character; we think of gravity in one and bravery in the other; but when we use the word merely as a title, no ideas associate with it. Through all the vocabulary of Adam there is not such an animal as a Duke or a Count; neither can we connect any certain ideas with the words. Whether they mean strength or weakness, wisdom or folly, a child or a man, or the rider or the horse, is all equivocal. What respect then can be paid to that which describes nothing, and which means nothing? Imagination has given figure and character to centaurs, satyrs, and down to all the fairy tribe; but titles baffle even the powers of fancy, and are a chimerical nondescript.

But this is not all. If a whole country is disposed to hold them in contempt, all their value is gone, and none will own them. It is common opinion only that makes them anything, or nothing, or worse than nothing. There is no occasion to take titles away, for they take themselves away when society concurs to ridicule them. This species of imaginary consequence has visibly declined in every part of Europe, and it hastens to its exit as the world of reason continues to rise. There was a time when the lowest class of what are called nobility was more thought of than the highest is now, and when a man in armour riding throughout Christendom in quest of adventures was more stared at than a modern Duke. The world has seen this folly fall, and it has fallen by being laughed at, and the farce of titles will follow its fate. The patriots of France have discovered in good time that rank and dignity in society must take a new ground. The old one has fallen through. It must now take the substantial ground of character, instead of the chimerical ground of titles; and they have brought their titles to the altar, and made of them a burnt-offering to Reason.

If no mischief had annexed itself to the folly of titles they would not have been worth a serious and formal destruction, such as the National Assembly have decreed them; and this makes it necessary to enquire farther into the nature and character of aristocracy.

That, then, which is called aristocracy in some countries and nobility in others arose out of the governments founded upon conquest. It was originally a military order for the purpose of supporting military government (for such were all governments founded in conquest); and to keep up a succession of this order for the purpose for which it was established, all the younger branches of those families were disinherited and the law of *primogenitureship* set up.

The nature and character of aristocracy shows itself to us in this law. It is the law against every other law of nature, and Nature herself calls for its destruction. Establish family justice, and aristocracy falls. By the aristocratical law of primogenitureship, in a family of six children five are exposed. Aristocracy has never more than *one* child. The rest are begotten to be devoured. They are thrown to the cannibal for prey, and the natural parent prepares the unnatural repast.

As everything which is out of nature in man affects, more or less, the interest of society, so does this. All the children which the aristocracy disowns (which are all except the eldest) are, in general, cast like orphans on a parish, to be provided for by the public, but at a greater charge. Unnecessary offices and places in governments and courts are created at the expense of the public to maintain them.

With what kind of parental reflections can the father or mother contemplate their younger offspring? By nature they are children, and by marriage they are heirs; but by aristocracy they are bastards and orphans. They are the flesh and blood of their parents in the one line, and nothing akin to them in the other. To restore, therefore, parents to their children, and children to their parents relations to each other, and man to society—and to exterminate the monster aristocracy, root and branch—the French Constitution has destroyed the law of Primogenitureship. Here then lies the monster; and Mr. Burke, if he pleases, may write its epitaph.

Hitherto we have considered aristocracy chiefly in one point of view. We have now to consider it in another. But whether we view it before or behind, or sideways, or any way else, domestically or publicly, it is still a monster.

In France aristocracy had one feature less in its countenance than what it has in some other countries. It did not compose a body of hereditary legislators. It was not "*a corporation of aristocracy*," for such I have heard M. de la Fayette describe an English House of Peers. Let us then examine the grounds upon which the French Constitution has resolved against having such a House in France.

Because, in the first place, as is already mentioned, aristocracy is kept up by family tyranny and injustice.

Secondly. Because there is an unnatural unfitness in an aristocracy to be legislators for a nation. Their ideas of *distributive justice* are corrupted at the very source. They begin life by trampling on all their younger brothers and sisters, and relations of every kind, and are taught and educated so to do. With what ideas of justice or honour can that man enter a house of legislation, who absorbs in his own person the inheritance of a whole family of children or doles out to them some pitiful portion with the insolence of a gift?

Thirdly. Because the idea of hereditary legislators is as inconsistent as that of hereditary judges, or hereditary juries; and as absurd as an hereditary mathematician, or an hereditary wise man; and as ridiculous as an hereditary poet laureate.

Fourthly. Because a body of men, holding themselves accountable to nobody, ought not to be trusted by anybody.

Fifthly. Because it is continuing the uncivilised principle of governments founded in conquest, and the base idea of man having property in man, and governing him by personal right.

Sixthly. Because aristocracy has a tendency to deteriorate the human species. By the universal economy of nature it is known, and by the instance of the Jews it is proved, that the human species has a tendency to degenerate, in any small number of persons, when separated from the general stock of society, and inter-marrying constantly with each other. It defeats even its pretended end, and becomes in time the opposite of what is noble in man. Mr. Burke talks of nobility; let him show what it is. The greatest characters the world have known have arisen on the democratic floor. Aristocracy has not been able to keep a proportionate pace with democracy. The artificial *noble* shrinks into a dwarf before the *noble* of Nature; and in the few instances of those (for there are some in all countries) in whom nature, as by a miracle, has survived in aristocracy, *those men despise it.*——But it is time to proceed to a new subject.

The French Constitution has reformed the condition of the clergy. It has raised the income of the lower and middle classes, and taken from the higher. None are now less than twelve hundred livres (fifty pounds sterling), nor any higher than two or three thousand pounds. What will Mr. Burke place against this? Hear what he says.

He says: "That the people of England can see without pain or grudging, an archbishop precede a duke; they can see a Bishop of Durham, or a Bishop of Winchester in possession of £10,000 a-year; and cannot see why it is in worse hands than estates to a like amount, in the hands of this earl or that squire." And Mr. Burke offers this as an example to France.

As to the first part, whether the archbishop precedes the duke, or the duke the bishop, it is, I believe, to the people in general, somewhat like *Sternhold* and *Hopkins*, or *Hopkins* and *Sternhold*; you may put which you please first; and as I confess that I do not understand the merits of this case, I will not contest it with Mr. Burke.

But with respect to the latter, I have something to say. Mr. Burke has not put the case right. The comparison is out of order, by being put between the bishop and the earl or the squire. It ought to be put between the bishop and the curate, and then it will stand thus:—"*The people of England can see without pain or grudging, a Bishop of Durham, or a Bishop of Winchester, in possession of ten thousand pounds a-year, and a curate on thirty or forty pounds a-year, or less.*" No, sir, they certainly do not see those things without great pain or grudging. It is a case that applies itself to every man's sense of justice, and is one among many that calls aloud for a constitution.

In France the cry of "*the church! the church!*" was repeated as often as in Mr. Burke's book, and as loudly as when the Dissenters' Bill was before the English Parliament; but the generality of the French clergy were not to be deceived by this cry any longer. They knew that whatever the pretence might be, it was they who were one of the principal objects of it. It was the cry of the high beneficed clergy, to prevent any regulation of income taking place between those of ten thousand pounds a-year and the parish priest. They therefore joined their case to those of every other oppressed class of men, and by this union obtained redress.

The French Constitution has abolished tythes, that source of perpetual discontent between the tythe-holder and the parishioner. When land is held on tythe, it is in the condition of an estate held between two parties; the one receiving one-tenth, and the other nine-tenths of the produce: and consequently, on principles of equity, if the estate can be improved, and made to produce by that improvement double or treble what it did before, or in any other ratio, the expense of such improvement ought to be borne in like proportion between the parties who are to share the produce. But this is not the case in tythes: the farmer bears the whole expense, and the tythe-holder takes a tenth of the improvement, in addition to the original tenth, and by this means gets the value of two-tenths instead of one. This is another case that calls for a constitution.

The French Constitution hath abolished or renounced Toleration, and Intolerance also, and hath established *Universal Right Of Conscience*.

Toleration is not the *opposite* of Intolerance, but is the *counterfeit* of it. Both are despotisms. The one assumes to itself the right of withholding Liberty of Conscience, and the other of granting it. The one is the Pope armed with fire and faggot, and the other is the Pope selling or granting indulgences. The former is church and state, and the latter is church and traffic.

But Toleration may be viewed in a much stronger light. Man worships not himself, but his Maker; and the liberty of conscience which he claims is not for the service of himself, but of his God. In this case, therefore, we must necessarily have the associated idea of two things; the mortal who renders the worship, and the Immortal Being who is worshipped. Toleration, therefore, places itself, not between man and man, nor between church and church, nor between one denomination of religion and another, but between God and man; between the being who worships, and the Being who is worshipped; and by the same act of assumed authority which it tolerates man to pay his worship, it presumptuously and blasphemously sets itself up to tolerate the Almighty to receive it.

Were a bill brought into any Parliament, entitled, "An Act to tolerate or grant liberty to the Almighty to receive the worship of a Jew or Turk," or "to prohibit the Almighty from receiving it," all men would startle and call it blasphemy. There would be an uproar. The presumption of toleration in religious matters would then present itself unmasked; but the presumption is not the less because the name of "Man" only appears to those laws, for the associated idea of the *worshipper* and the *worshipped* cannot be separated. Who then art thou, vain dust and ashes! by whatever name thou art called, whether a King, a Bishop, a Church, or a State, a Parliament, or anything else, that obtrudest thine insignificance between the soul of man and its Maker? Mind thine own concerns. If he believes not as thou believest, it is a proof that thou believest not as he believes, and there is no earthly power can determine between you.

With respect to what are called denominations of religion, if every one is left to judge of its own religion, there is no such thing as a religion that is wrong; but if they are to judge of each other's religion, there is no such thing as a religion that is right; and therefore all the world is right, or all the world is wrong. But with respect to religion itself, without regard to names, and as directing itself from the universal family of mankind to the Divine object of all adoration, *it is man bringing to his Maker the fruits of his heart*; and though those fruits may differ from each other like the fruits of the earth, the grateful tribute of every one is accepted.

A Bishop of Durham, or a Bishop of Winchester, or the archbishop who heads the dukes, will not refuse a tythe-sheaf of wheat because it is not a cock of hay, nor a cock of hay because it is not a sheaf of wheat; nor a pig, because it is neither one nor the other; but these same persons, under the figure of an established church, will not permit their Maker to receive the varied tythes of man's devotion.

One of the continual choruses of Mr. Burke's book is "Church and State." He does not mean some one particular church, or some one particular state, but any church and state; and he uses the term as a general figure to hold forth the political doctrine of always uniting the church with the state in every country, and he censures the National Assembly for not having done this in France. Let us bestow a few thoughts on this subject.

All religions are in their nature kind and benign, and united with principles of morality. They could not have made proselytes at first by professing anything that was vicious, cruel, persecuting, or immoral. Like everything else, they had their beginning; and they proceeded by persuasion, exhortation, and example. How then is it that they lose their native mildness, and become morose and intolerant?

It proceeds from the connection which Mr. Burke recommends. By engendering the church with the state, a sort of mule-animal, capable only of destroying, and not of breeding up, is produced, called *the Church established by Law*. It is a stranger, even from its birth, to any parent mother, on whom it is begotten, and whom in time it kicks out and destroys.

The inquisition in Spain does not proceed from the religion originally professed, but from this mule-animal, engendered between the church and the state. The burnings in Smithfield proceeded from the same heterogeneous production; and it was the regeneration of this strange animal in England afterwards, that renewed rancour and irreligion among the inhabitants, and that drove the people called Quakers and Dissenters to America. Persecution is not an original feature in *any* religion; but it is alway the strongly-marked feature of all law-religions, or religions established by law. Take away the law-establishment, and every religion re-assumes its original benignity. In America, a Catholic priest is a good citizen, a good character, and a good neighbour; an Episcopalian minister is of the same description: and this proceeds independently of the men, from there being no law-establishment in America.

If also we view this matter in a temporal sense, we shall see the ill effects it has had on the prosperity of nations. The union of church and state has impoverished Spain. The revoking the edict of Nantes drove the silk manufacture from that country into England; and church and state are now driving the cotton manufacture from England to America and France. Let then Mr. Burke continue to preach his antipolitical doctrine of Church and State. It will do some good. The National Assembly will not follow his advice, but will benefit by his folly. It was by observing the ill effects of it in England, that America has been warned against it; and it is by experiencing them in France, that the National Assembly have abolished it, and, like America, have established Universal Right Of Conscience, and Universal Right Of Citizenship.*

I will here cease the comparison with respect to the principles of the French Constitution, and conclude this part of the subject with a few

---

* When in any country we see extraordinary circumstances taking place, they naturally lead any man who has a talent for observation and investigation, to enquire into the causes. The manufacturers of Manchester, Birmingham, and Sheffield, are the principal manufacturers in England. From whence did this arise? A little observation will explain the case. The principal, and the generality of the inhabitants of those places, are not of what is called in England, *the church established by law*: and they, or their fathers, (for it is within but a few years) withdrew from the persecution of the chartered towns, where test-laws more particularly operate, and established a sort of asylum for themselves in those places. It was the only asylum that then offered, for the rest of Europe was worse.——But the case is now changing. France and America bid all comers welcome, and initiate them into all the rights of citizenship. Policy and interest, therefore, will, but perhaps too late, dictate in England, what reason and justice could not. Those manufacturers are withdrawing, and arising in other places. There is now erecting in Passey, three miles from Paris, a large cotton manufactory, and several are already erected in America. Soon after the rejecting the Bill for repealing the test-law, one of the richest manufacturers in England said in my hearing, "England, Sir, is not a country for a dissenter to live in,—we must go to France." These are truths, and it is doing justice to both parties to tell them. It is chiefly the dissenters that have carried English manufactures to the height they are now at, and the same men have it in their power to carry them away; and though those manufactures would afterwards continue in those places, the foreign market will be lost. There frequently appear in the *London Gazette*, extracts from certain acts to prevent machines and persons, as far as they can extend to persons, from going out of the country. It appears from these that the ill effects of the test-laws and church-establishment begin to be much suspected; but the remedy of force can never supply the remedy of reason. In the progress of less than a century, all the unrepresented part of England, of all denominations, which is at least an hundred times the most numerous, may begin to feel the necessity of a constitution, and then all those matters will come regularly before them. (Author's note)

observations on the organisation of the formal parts of the French and English governments.

The executive power in each country is in the hands of a person styled the King; but the French Constitution distinguishes between the King and the Sovereign: It considers the station of King as official, and places Sovereignty in the nation.

The representatives of the nation, who compose the National Assembly, and who are the legislative power, originate in and from the people by election, as an inherent right in the people.—In England it is otherwise; and this arises from the original establishment of what is called its monarchy; for, as by the conquest all the rights of the people or the nation were absorbed into the hands of the Conqueror, and who added the title of King to that of Conqueror, those same matters which in France are now held as rights in the people, or in the nation, are held in England as grants from what is called the crown. The Parliament in England, in both its branches, was erected by patents from the descendants of the Conqueror. The House of Commons did not originate as a matter of right in the people to delegate or elect, but as a grant or boon.

By the French Constitution the nation is always named before the king. The third article of the declaration of rights says: "The nation is essentially the source (or fountain) of all sovereignty." Mr. Burke argues that in England a king is the fountain—that he is the fountain of all honour. But as this idea is evidently descended from the conquest I shall make no other remark upon it, than that it is the nature of conquest to turn everything upside down; and as Mr. Burke will not be refused the privilege of speaking twice, and as there are but two parts in the figure, the fountain and the spout, he will be right the second time.

The French Constitution puts the legislative before the executive, the law before the king; *la loi, le roi.* This also is in the natural order of things, because laws must have existence before they can have execution.

A king in France does not, in addressing himself to the National Assembly, say, "My Assembly," similar to the phrase used in England of *"my* Parliament"; neither can he use it consistently with the constitution, nor could it be admitted. There may be propriety in the use of it in England, because as is before mentioned, both Houses of Parliament originated from what is called the crown by patent or boon—and not from the inherent rights of the people, as the National Assembly does in France, and whose name designates its origin.

The President of the National Assembly does not ask the King *to grant to the Assembly liberty of speech*, as is the case with the English House of Commons. The constitutional dignity of the National Assembly cannot debase itself. Speech is, in the first place, one of the natural rights of man always retained; and with respect to the National Assembly the use of it is their *duty*, and the nation is their *authority*. They were elected by the greatest body of men exercising the right of election the European world ever saw. They sprung not from the filth of rotten boroughs, nor are they the vassal representatives of aristocratical ones. Feeling the proper dignity of their character they support it. Their Parliamentary language, whether for or against a question, is free, bold and manly, and extends to all the parts and circumstances of the case. If any matter or subject respecting the executive department or the person who presides in it (the king) comes before them it is debated on with the spirit of men, and in the language of gentlemen; and their answer or their address is returned in the same style. They stand not aloof with the gaping vacuity of vulgar ignorance, nor bend with the cringe of sycophantic insignificance. The graceful pride of truth knows no extremes, and preserves, in every latitude of life, the right-angled character of man.

Let us now look to the other side of the question. In the addresses of the English Parliaments to their kings we see neither the intrepid spirit of the old Parliaments of France, nor the serene dignity of the present National Assembly; neither do we see in them anything of the style of English manners, which border somewhat on bluntness. Since then they are neither of foreign extraction, nor naturally of English production, their origin must be sought for elsewhere, and that origin is the Norman Conquest. They are evidently of the vassalage class of manners, and emphatically mark the prostrate distance that exists in no other condition of men than between the conqueror and the conquered. That this vassalage idea and style of speaking was not got rid of even at the Revolution of 1688, is evident from the declaration of Parliament to William and Mary in these words: "We do most humbly and faithfully *submit* ourselves, our heirs and posterities, for ever." Submission is wholly a vassalage term, repugnant to the dignity of freedom, and an echo of the language used at the Conquest.

As the estimation of all things is given by comparison, the Revolution of 1688, however from circumstances it may have been exalted beyond its value, will find its level. It is already on the wane, eclipsed by the enlarging orb of reason, and the luminous revolutions of America and France. In less than another century it will go, as well as Mr. Burke's labours, "to the family vault of all the Capulets." Mankind will then scarcely believe that a country calling itself free would send to Holland for a man, and clothe him with power on purpose to put themselves in fear of him, and give him almost a million sterling a year for leave to *submit* themselves and their posterity, like bondmen and bondwomen, for ever.

But there is a truth that ought to be made known; I have had the opportunity of seeing it; which is, *that notwithstanding appearances, there is not any description of men that despise monarchy so much as courtiers.* But they well know, that if it were seen by others, as it is seen by them, the juggle could not be kept up; they are in the condition of men who get their living by a show, and to whom the folly of that show is so familiar that they ridicule it; but were the audience to be made as wise in this respect as themselves, there would be an end to the show and the profits with it. The difference between a republican and a courtier with respect to monarchy, is that the one opposes monarchy, believing it to be something; and the other laughs at it, knowing it to be nothing.

As I used sometimes to correspond with Mr. Burke believing him then to be a man of sounder principles than his book shows him to be, I wrote to him last winter from Paris, and gave him an account how prosperously matters were going on. Among other subjects in that letter, I referred to the happy situation the National Assembly were placed in; that they had taken ground on which their moral duty and their political interest were united. They have not to hold out a language which they do not themselves believe, for the fraudulent purpose of making others believe it. Their station requires no artifice to support it, and can only be maintained by enlightening mankind. It is not their interest to cherish ignorance, but to dispel it. They are not in the case of a ministerial or an opposition party in England, who, though they are opposed, are still united to keep up the common mystery. The National Assembly must throw open a magazine of light. It must show man the proper character of man; and the nearer it can bring him to that standard, the stronger the National Assembly becomes.

In contemplating the French Constitution, we see in it a rational order of things. The principles harmonise with the forms, and both with their origin. It may perhaps be said as an excuse for bad forms, that they are nothing more than forms; but this is a mistake. Forms grow out of principles, and operate to continue the principles they grow from. It is impossible to practise a bad form on anything but a bad principle. It cannot be ingrafted on a good one; and wherever the forms in any government are bad, it is a certain indication that the principles are bad also.

I will here finally close this subject. I began it by remarking that Mr. Burke had *voluntarily* declined going into a comparison of the English and French Constitutions. He apologises (in page 241) for not doing it, by saying that he had not time. Mr. Burke's book was upwards of eight months in hand, and is extended to a volume of three hundred and sixty-six pages. As his omission does injury to his cause, his apology makes it worse; and men on the English side of the water will begin to consider, whether there is not some radical defect in what is called the English constitution, that made it necessary for Mr. Burke to suppress the comparison, to avoid bringing it into view.

As Mr. Burke has not written on constitutions so neither has he written on the French Revolution. He gives no account of its commencement or its progress. He only expresses his wonder. "It looks," says he, "to me, as if I were in a great crisis, not of the affairs of France alone, but of all Europe, perhaps of more than Europe. All circumstances taken together, the French Revolution is the most astonishing that has hitherto happened in the world."

As wise men are astonished at foolish things, and other people at wise ones, I know not on which ground to account for Mr. Burke's astonishment; but certain it is, that he does not understand the French Revolution. It has apparently burst forth like a creation from a chaos, but it is no more than the consequence of a mental revolution priorily existing in France. The mind of the nation had changed beforehand, and the new order of things has naturally followed the new order of thoughts. I will here, as concisely as I can, trace out the growth of the French Revolution, and mark the circumstances that have contributed to produce it.

The despotism of Louis XIV, united with the gaiety of his Court, and the gaudy ostentation of his character, had so humbled, and at the same time so fascinated the mind of France, that the people appeared to have lost all sense of their own dignity, in contemplating that of their Grand Monarch; and the whole reign of Louis XV, remarkable only for weakness and effeminacy, made no other alteration than that of spreading a sort of lethargy over the nation, from which it showed no disposition to rise.

The only signs which appeared to the spirit of Liberty during those periods, are to be found in the writings of the French philosophers. Montesquieu, President of the Parliament of Bordeaux, went as far as a writer under a despotic government could well proceed; and being obliged to divide himself between principle and prudence, his mind often appears under a veil, and we ought to give him credit for more than he has expressed.

Voltaire, who was both the flatterer and the satirist of despotism, took another line. His forte lay in exposing and ridiculing the superstitions which priest-craft, united with state-craft, had interwoven with governments. It was not from the purity of his principles, or his love of mankind (for satire and philanthropy are not naturally concordant), but from his strong capacity of seeing folly in its true shape, and his irresistible propensity to expose it, that he made those attacks. They were, however, as formidable as if the motive had been virtuous; and he merits the thanks rather than the esteem of mankind.

On the contrary, we find in the writings of Rousseau, and the Abbé Raynal, a loveliness of sentiment in favour of liberty, that excites respect, and elevates the human faculties; but having raised this animation, they do not direct its operation, and leave the mind in love with an object, without describing the means of possessing it.

The writings of Quesnay, Turgot, and the friends of those authors, are of the serious kind; but they laboured under the same disadvantage with Montesquieu; their writings abound with moral maxims of government, but are rather directed to economise and reform the administration of the government, than the government itself.

But all those writings and many others had their weight; and by the different manner in which they treated the subject of government, Montesquieu by his judgment and knowledge of laws, Voltaire by his wit, Rousseau and Raynal by their animation, and Quesnay and Turgot by their moral maxims and systems of economy, readers of every class met with something to their taste, and a spirit of political inquiry began to diffuse itself through the nation at the time the dispute between England and the then colonies of America broke out.

In the war which France afterwards engaged in, it is very well known that the nation appeared to be before-hand with the French ministry. Each of them had its view; but those views were directed to different objects; the one sought liberty, and the other retaliation on England. The French officers and soldiers who after this went to America, were eventually placed in the school of Freedom, and learned the practice as well as the principles of it by heart.

As it was impossible to separate the military events which took place in America from the principles of the American Revolution, the publication of those events in France necessarily connected themselves with the principles which produced them. Many of the facts were in themselves principles; such as the declaration of American Independence, and the treaty of alliance between France and America, which recognised the natural rights of man, and justified resistance to oppression.

The then Minister of France, Count Vergennes, was not the friend of America; and it is both justice and gratitude to say, that it was the Queen of France who gave the cause of America a fashion at the French Court. Count Vergennes was the personal and social friend of Dr. Franklin; and the Doctor had obtained, by his sensible gracefulness, a sort of influence over him; but with respect to principles Count Vergennes was a despot.

The situation of Dr. Franklin, as Minister from America to France, should be taken into the chain of circumstances. The diplomatic character is of itself the narrowest sphere of society that man can act in. It forbids intercourse by the reciprocity of suspicion; and a diplomatic is a sort of unconnected atom, continually repelling and repelled. But this was not the case with Dr. Franklin. He was not the diplomatic of a Court, but of *Man*. His character as a philosopher had been long established, and his circle of society in France was universal.

Count Vergennes resisted for a considerable time the publication in France of American constitutions, translated into the French language: but even in this he was obliged to give way to public opinion, and a sort of propriety in admitting to appear what he had undertaken to defend. The American constitutions were to liberty what a grammar is to language: they define its parts of speech, and practically construct them into syntax.

The peculiar situation of the then Marquis de la Fayette is another link in the great chain. He served in America as an American officer under a commission of Congress, and by the universality of his acquaintance was in close friendship with the civil government of America, as well as with the military line. He spoke the language of the country, entered into the discussions on the principles of government, and was always a welcome friend at any election.

When the war closed, a vast reinforcement to the cause of Liberty spread itself over France, by the return of the French officers and soldiers. A knowledge of the practice was then joined to the theory; and all that was wanting to give it real existence was opportunity. Man cannot, properly speaking, make circumstances for his purpose, but he always has it in his power to improve them when they occur, and this was the case in France.

M. Neckar was displaced in May, 1781; and by the ill-management of the finances afterwards, and particularly during the extravagant administration of M. Calonne, the revenue of France, which was nearly twenty-four millions sterling per year, was become unequal to the expenditure, not because the revenue had decreased, but because the expenses had increased; and this was a circumstance which the nation laid hold of to bring forward a Revolution. The English Minister, Mr. Pitt, has frequently alluded to the state of the French finances in his budgets, without understanding the subject. Had the French Parliaments been as ready to register edicts for new taxes as an English Parliament is to grant them, there had been no derangement in the finances, nor yet any Revolution; but this will better explain itself as I proceed.

It will be necessary here to show how taxes were formerly raised in France. The King, or rather the Court or Ministry acting under the use of that name, framed the edicts for taxes at their own discretion, and sent them to the Parliaments to be registered; for until they were registered by the Parliaments they were not operative. Disputes had long existed between the Court and the Parliaments with respect to the extent of the Parliament's authority on this head. The Court insisted that the authority of Parliaments went no farther than to remonstrate or show reasons against the tax, reserving to itself the right of determining whether the reasons were well or ill-founded; and in consequence thereof, either to withdraw the edict as a matter of choice, or to *order* it to be unregistered as a matter of authority. The Parliaments on their part insisted that they had not only a right to remonstrate, but to reject; and on this ground they were always supported by the nation.

But to return to the order of my narrative. M. Calonne wanted money: and as he knew the sturdy disposition of the Parliaments with respect to new taxes, he ingeniously sought either to approach them by a more gentle means than that of direct authority, or to get over their heads by a manoeuvre; and for this purpose he revived the project of assembling a body of men from the several provinces, under the style of an "Assembly of the Notables," or men of note, who met in 1787, and who were either to recommend taxes to the Parliaments, or to act as a Parliament themselves. An Assembly under this name had been called in 1617.

As we are to view this as the first practical step towards the Revolution, it will be proper to enter into some particulars respecting it. The Assembly of the Notables has in some places been mistaken for the States-General, but was wholly a different body, the States-General being always by election. The persons who composed the Assembly of the Notables were all nominated by the king, and consisted of one hundred and forty members. But as M. Calonne could not depend upon a majority of this Assembly in his favour, he very ingeniously arranged them in such a manner as to make forty-four a majority of one hundred and forty; to effect this he disposed of them into seven separate committees, of twenty members each. Every general question was to be decided, not by a majority of persons, but by a majority of committee, and as eleven votes would make a majority in a committee, and four committees a majority of seven, M. Calonne had good reason to conclude that as forty-four would determine any general question he could not be outvoted. But all his plans deceived him, and in the event became his overthrow.

The then Marquis de la Fayette was placed in the second committee, of which the Count D'Artois was president, and as money matters were the object, it naturally brought into view every circumstance connected with it. M. de la Fayette made a verbal charge against Calonne for selling crown lands to the amount of two millions of livres, in a manner that appeared to be unknown to the king. The Count D'Artois (as if to intimidate, for the Bastille was then in being) asked the Marquis if he would render the charge in writing? He replied that he would. The Count D'Artois did not demand it, but brought a message from the king to that purport. M. de la Fayette then delivered in his charge in writing, to be given to the king, undertaking to support it. No farther proceedings were had upon this affair, but M. Calonne was soon after dismissed by the king and set off to England.

As M. de la Fayette, from the experience of what he had seen in America, was better acquainted with the science of civil government than the generality of the members who composed the Assembly of the Notables could then be, the brunt of the business fell considerably to his share. The plan of those who had a constitution in view was to contend with the Court on the ground of taxes, and some of them openly professed their object. Disputes frequently arose between Count D'Artois and M. de la Fayette upon various subjects. With respect to the arrears already incurred the latter proposed to remedy them by accommodating the expenses to the revenue instead of the revenue to the expenses; and as objects of reform he proposed to abolish the Bastille and all the State prisons throughout the nation (the keeping of which was attended with great expense), and to suppress *Lettres de Cachet*; but those matters were not then much attended to, and *with respect to Lettres de Cachet, a majority of the Nobles appeared to be in favour of them.*

On the subject of supplying the Treasury by new taxes the Assembly declined taking the matter on themselves, concurring in the opinion that they had not authority. In a debate on this subject M. de la Fayette said that raising money by taxes could only be done by a National Assembly, freely elected by the people, and acting as their representatives. Do you mean, said the Count D'Artois, the States-General? M. de la Fayette replied that he did. Will you, said the Count D'Artois, sign what you say to be given to the king? The other replied that he would not only do this but that he would go farther, and say that the effectual mode would be for the king to agree to the establishment of a constitution.

As one of the plans had thus failed, that of getting the Assembly to act as a Parliament, the other came into view, that of recommending. On this subject the Assembly agreed to recommend two new taxes to be unregistered by the Parliament: the one a stamp-tax and the other a territorial tax, or sort of land-tax. The two have been estimated at about five millions sterling per annum. We have now to turn our attention to the Parliaments, on whom the business was again devolving.

The Archbishop of Thoulouse (since Archbishop of Sens, and now a Cardinal), was appointed to the administration of the finances soon after the dismission of Calonne. He was also made Prime Minister, an office that did not always exist in France. When this office did not exist, the chief of each of the principal departments transacted business immediately with the King, but when a Prime Minister was appointed they did business only with him. The Archbishop arrived to more state authority than any minister since the Duke de Choiseul, and the nation was strongly disposed in his favour; but by a line of conduct scarcely to be accounted for he perverted every opportunity, turned out a despot, and sunk into disgrace, and a Cardinal.

The Assembly of the Notables having broken up, the minister sent the edicts for the two new taxes recommended by the Assembly to the Parliaments to be unregistered. They of course came first before the Parliament of Paris, who returned for answer: *That with such a revenue as the nation then supported the name of taxes ought not to be mentioned but for the purpose of reducing them*; and threw both the edicts out.[*] On this refusal the Parliament was ordered to Versailles, where, in the usual form, the King held what under the old government was called a Bed of justice; and the two edicts were unregistered in presence of the Parliament by an order of State, in the manner mentioned, earlier. On this the Parliament immediately returned to Paris, renewed their session in form, and ordered the enregistering to be struck out, declaring that everything done at Versailles was illegal. All the members of the Parliament were then served with *Lettres de Cachet*, and exiled to Troyes; but as they continued as inflexible in exile as before, and as vengeance did not supply the place of taxes, they were after a short time recalled to Paris.

The edicts were again tendered to them, and the Count D'Artois undertook to act as representative of the King. For this purpose he came from Versailles to Paris, in a train of procession; and the Parliament were assembled to receive him. But show and parade had lost their influence in France; and whatever ideas of importance he might set off with, he had to return with those of mortification and disappointment. On alighting from his carriage to ascend the steps of the Parliament House, the crowd (which was numerously collected)

---

* When the English Minister, Mr. Pitt, mentions the French finances again in the English Parliament, it would be well that he noticed this as an example. (Author's note)

threw out trite expressions, saying: "This is Monsieur D'Artois, who wants more of our money to spend." The marked disapprobation which he saw impressed him with apprehensions, and the word *Aux armes*! (*To arms*!) was given out by the officer of the guard who attended him. It was so loudly vociferated, that it echoed through the avenues of the house, and produced a temporary confusion. I was then standing in one of the apartments through which he had to pass, and could not avoid reflecting how wretched was the condition of a disrespected man.

He endeavoured to impress the Parliament by great words, and opened his authority by saying, "The King, our Lord and Master." The Parliament received him very coolly, and with their usual determination not to register the taxes: and in this manner the interview ended.

After this a new subject took place: In the various debates and contests which arose between the Court and the Parliaments on the subject of taxes, the Parliament of Paris at last declared that although it had been customary for Parliaments to enregister edicts for taxes as a matter of convenience, the right belonged only to the States-General; and that, therefore, the Parliament could no longer with propriety continue to debate on what it had not authority to act. The King after this came to Paris and held a meeting with the Parliament, in which he continued from ten in the morning till about six in the evening, and, in a manner that appeared to proceed from him as if unconsulted upon with the Cabinet or Ministry, gave his word to the Parliament that the States-General should be convened.

But after this another scene arose, on a ground different from all the former. The Minister and the Cabinet were averse to calling the States-General. They well knew that if the States-General were assembled, themselves must fall; and as the King had not mentioned *any time*, they hit on a project calculated to elude, without appearing to oppose.

For this purpose, the Court set about making a sort of constitution itself. It was principally the work of M. Lamoignon, the Keeper of the Seals, who afterwards shot himself. This new arrangement consisted in establishing a body under the name of a *Cour Plenière*, or Full Court, in which were invested all the powers that the Government might have occasion to make use of. The persons composing this Court were to be nominated by the King; the contended right of taxation was given up on the part of the King, and a new criminal code of laws and law proceedings was substituted in the room of the former. The thing, in many points, contained better principles than those upon which the Government had hitherto been administered; but with respect to the *Cour Plenière*, it was no other than a medium through which despotism was to pass, without appearing to act directly from itself.

The Cabinet had high expectations from their new contrivance. The people who were to compose the *Cour Plenière* were already nominated; and as it was necessary to carry a fair appearance, many of the best characters in the nation were appointed among the number. It was to commence on May 8, 1788; but an opposition arose to it on two grounds the one as to principle, the other as to form.

On the ground of Principle it was contended that Government had not a right to alter itself, and that if the practice was once admitted it would grow into a principle and be made a precedent for any future alterations the Government might wish to establish: that the right of altering the Government was a national right, and not a right of Government. And on the ground of form it was contended that the *Cour Plenière* was nothing more than a larger Cabinet.

The then Duke de la Rochefoucault, Luxembourg, De Noailles, and many others, refused to accept the nomination, and strenuously opposed the whole plan. When the edict for establishing this new court was sent to the Parliaments to be unregistered and put into execution, they resisted also. The Parliament of Paris not only refused, but denied the authority; and the contest renewed itself between the Parliament and the Cabinet more strongly than ever. While the Parliament were sitting in debate on this subject, the Ministry ordered a regiment of soldiers to surround the House and form a blockade. The members sent out for beds and provisions, and lived as in a besieged citadel: and as this had no effect, the commanding officer was ordered to enter the Parliament House and seize them, which he did, and some of the principal members were shut up in different prisons. About the same time a deputation of persons arrived from the province of Brittany to remonstrate against the establishment of the *Cour Plenière*, and those the archbishop sent to the Bastille. But the spirit of the nation was not to be overcome, and it was so fully sensible of the strong ground it had taken—that of withholding taxes—that it contented itself with keeping up a sort of quiet resistance, which effectually overthrew all the plans at that time formed against it. The project of the *Cour Plenière* was at last obliged to be given up, and the Prime Minister not long afterwards followed its fate, and M. Neckar was recalled into office.

The attempt to establish the *Cour Plenière* had an effect upon the nation which itself did not perceive. It was a sort of new form of government that insensibly served to put the old one out of sight and to unhinge it from the superstitious authority of antiquity. It was Government dethroning Government; and the old one, by attempting to make a new one, made a chasm.

The failure of this scheme renewed the subject of convening the State-General; and this gave rise to a new series of politics. There was no settled form for convening the States-General: all that it positively meant was a deputation from what was then called the Clergy, the Noblesse, and the Commons; but their numbers or their proportions had not been always the same. They had been convened only on extraordinary occasions, the last of which was in 1614; their numbers were then in equal proportions, and they voted by orders.

It could not well escape the sagacity of M. Neckar, that the mode of 1614 would answer neither the purpose of the then government nor of the nation. As matters were at that time circumstanced it would have been too contentious to agree upon anything. The debates would have been endless upon privileges and exemptions, in which neither the wants of the Government nor the wishes of the nation for a Constitution would have been attended to. But as he did not choose to take the decision upon himself, he summoned again the Assembly of the Notables and referred it to them. This body was in general interested in the decision, being chiefly of aristocracy and high-paid clergy, and they decided in favor of the mode of 1614. This decision was against the sense of the Nation, and also against the wishes of the Court; for the aristocracy opposed itself to both and contended for privileges independent of either. The subject was then taken up by the Parliament, who recommended that the number of the Commons should be equal to the other two: and they should all sit in one house and vote in one body. The number finally determined on was 1,200; 600 to be chosen by the Commons (and this was less than their proportion ought to have been when their worth and consequence is considered on a national scale), 300 by the Clergy, and 300 by the Aristocracy; but with respect to the mode of assembling themselves, whether together or apart, or the manner in which they should vote, those matters were referred.*

The election that followed was not a contested election, but an animated one. The candidates were not men, but principles. Societies were formed in Paris, and committees of correspondence and communication established throughout the nation, for the purpose of enlightening the people, and explaining to them the principles of civil government; and so orderly was the election conducted, that it did not give rise even to the rumour of tumult.

The States-General were to meet at Versailles in April 1789, but did not assemble till May. They situated themselves in three separate chambers, or rather the Clergy and Aristocracy withdrew each into a separate chamber. The majority of the Aristocracy claimed what they called the privilege of voting as a separate body, and of giving their consent or their negative in that manner; and many of the bishops and the high-beneficed clergy claimed the same privilege on the part of their Order.

The *Tiers Etat* (as they were then called) disowned any knowledge of artificial orders and artificial privileges; and they were not only resolute on this point, but somewhat disdainful. They began to consider the Aristocracy as a kind of fungus growing out of the corruption of society, that could not be admitted even as a branch of it; and from the disposition the Aristocracy had shown by upholding *Lettres de Cachet*, and in sundry other instances, it was manifest that no constitution could be formed by admitting men in any other character than as National Men.

---

* Mr. Burke, (and I must take the liberty of telling him that he is very unacquainted with French affairs), speaking upon this subject, says, "The first thing that struck me in calling the States-General, was a great departure from the ancient course"; and he soon after says, "From the moment I read the list, I saw distinctly, and very nearly as it has happened, all that was to follow."—Mr. Burke certainly did not see all that was to follow. I endeavoured to impress him, as well before as after the States-General met, that there would be a *revolution*; but was not able to make him see it, neither would he believe it. How then he could distinctly see all the parts, when the whole was out of sight, is beyond my comprehension. And with respect to the "departure from the ancient course," besides the natural weakness of the remark, it shows that he is unacquainted with circumstances. The departure was necessary, from the experience had upon it, that the ancient course was a bad one. The States-General of 1614 were called at the commencement of the civil war in the minority of Louis XIII: but by the class of arranging them by orders, they increased the confusion they were called to compose. The author of *L'Intrigue du Cabinet*, (Intrigue of the Cabinet), who wrote before any revolution was thought of in France, speaking of the States-General of 1614, says, "They held the public in suspense five months; and by the questions agitated therein, and the heat with which they were put, it appears that the great (*les grands*) thought more to satisfy their *particular* passions, than to procure the goods of the nation; and the whole time passed away in altercations, ceremonies and parade."—*L'Intrigue du Cabinet*, vol. i. p. 329. (Author's note)

After various altercations on this head, the *Tiers Etat* or Commons (as they were then called) declared themselves (on a motion made for that purpose by the Abbé Sieyes) "The Representatives Of The Nation; and that the two Orders could be considered but as deputies of corporations, and could only have a deliberate voice when they assembled in a national character with the national representatives." This proceeding extinguished the style of *Etats Generaux*, or States-General, and erected it into the style it now bears, that of *L'Assemblee Nationale*, or National Assembly.

This motion was not made in a precipitate manner. It was the result of cool deliberation, and concerned between the national representatives and the patriotic members of the two chambers, who saw into the folly, mischief, and injustice of artificial privileged distinctions. It was become evident, that no constitution, worthy of being called by that name, could be established on anything less than a national ground. The Aristocracy had hitherto opposed the despotism of the Court, and affected the language of patriotism; but it opposed it as its rival (as the English Barons opposed King John) and it now opposed the nation from the same motives.

On carrying this motion, the national representatives, as had been concerted, sent an invitation to the two chambers, to unite with them in a national character, and proceed to business. A majority of the clergy, chiefly of the parish priests, withdrew from the clerical chamber, and joined the nation; and forty-five from the other chamber joined in like manner. There is a sort of secret history belonging to this last circumstance, which is necessary to its explanation; it was not judged prudent that all the patriotic members of the chamber styling itself the Nobles, should quit it at once; and in consequence of this arrangement, they drew off by degrees, always leaving some, as well to reason the case, as to watch the suspected. In a little time the numbers increased from forty-five to eighty, and soon after to a greater number; which, with the majority of the clergy, and the whole of the national representatives, put the malcontents in a very diminutive condition.

The King, who, very different from the general class called by that name, is a man of a good heart, showed himself disposed to recommend a union of the three chambers, on the ground the National Assembly had taken; but the malcontents exerted themselves to prevent it, and began now to have another project in view. Their numbers consisted of a majority of the aristocratical chamber, and the minority of the clerical chamber, chiefly of bishops and high-beneficed clergy; and these men were determined to put everything to issue, as well by strength as by stratagem. They had no objection to a constitution; but it must be such a one as themselves should dictate, and suited to their own views and particular situations. On the other hand, the Nation disowned knowing anything of them but as citizens, and was determined to shut out all such up-start pretensions. The more aristocracy appeared, the more it was despised; there was a visible imbecility and want of intellects in the majority, a sort of *je ne sais quoi*, that while it affected to be more than citizen, was less than man. It lost ground from contempt more than from hatred; and was rather jeered at as an ass, than dreaded as a lion. This is the general character of aristocracy, or what are called Nobles or Nobility, or rather No-ability, in all countries.

The plan of the malcontents consisted now of two things; either to deliberate and vote by chambers (or orders), more especially on all questions respecting a Constitution (by which the aristocratical chamber would have had a negative on any article of the Constitution); or, in case they could not accomplish this object, to overthrow the National Assembly entirely.

To effect one or other of these objects they began to cultivate a friendship with the despotism they had hitherto attempted to rival, and the Count D'Artois became their chief. The king (who has since declared himself deceived into their measures) held, according to the old form, *a Bed of Justice*, in which he accorded to the deliberation and vote *par tete* (by head) upon several subjects; but reserved the deliberation and vote upon all questions respecting a constitution to the three chambers separately. This declaration of the king was made against the advice of M. Neckar, who now began to perceive that he was growing out of fashion at Court, and that another minister was in contemplation.

As the form of sitting in separate chambers was yet apparently kept up, though essentially destroyed, the national representatives immediately after this declaration of the King resorted to their own chambers to consult on a protest against it; and the minority of the chamber (calling itself the Nobles), who had joined the national cause, retired to a private house to consult in like manner. The malcontents had by this time concerted their measures with the court, which the Count

D'Artois undertook to conduct; and as they saw from the discontent which the declaration excited, and the opposition making against it, that they could not obtain a control over the intended constitution by a separate vote, they prepared themselves for their final object—that of conspiring against the National Assembly, and overthrowing it.

The next morning the door of the chamber of the National Assembly was shut against them, and guarded by troops; and the members were refused admittance. On this they withdrew to a tennis-ground in the neighbourhood of Versailles, as the most convenient place they could find, and, after renewing their session, took an oath never to separate from each other, under any circumstance whatever, death excepted, until they had established a constitution. As the experiment of shutting up the house had no other effect than that of producing a closer connection in the members, it was opened again the next day, and the public business recommenced in the usual place.

We are now to have in view the forming of the new ministry, which was to accomplish the overthrow of the National Assembly. But as force would be necessary, orders were issued to assemble thirty thousand troops, the command of which was given to Broglio, one of the intended new ministry, who was recalled from the country for this purpose. But as some management was necessary to keep this plan concealed till the moment it should be ready for execution, it is to this policy that a declaration made by Count D'Artois must be attributed, and which is here proper to be introduced.

It could not but occur while the malcontents continued to resort to their chambers separate from the National Assembly, more jealousy would be excited than if they were mixed with it, and that the plot might be suspected. But as they had taken their ground, and now wanted a pretence for quitting it, it was necessary that one should be devised. This was effectually accomplished by a declaration made by the Count D'Artois: "That if they took not a Part in the National Assembly, the life of the king would be endangered": on which they quitted their chambers, and mixed with the Assembly, in one body.

At the time this declaration was made, it was generally treated as a piece of absurdity in Count D'Artois calculated merely to relieve the outstanding members of the two chambers from the diminutive situation they were put in; and if nothing more had followed, this conclusion would have been good. But as things best explain themselves by their events, this apparent union was only a cover to the machinations which were secretly going on; and the declaration accommodated itself to answer that purpose. In a little time the National Assembly found itself surrounded by troops, and thousands more were daily arriving. On this a very strong declaration was made by the National Assembly to the King, remonstrating on the impropriety of the measure, and demanding the reason. The King, who was not in the secret of this business, as himself afterwards declared, gave substantially for answer, that he had no other object in view than to preserve the public tranquility, which appeared to be much disturbed.

But in a few days from this time the plot unravelled itself M. Neckar and the ministry were displaced, and a new one formed of the enemies of the Revolution; and Broglio, with between twenty-five and thirty thousand foreign troops, was arrived to support them. The mask was now thrown off, and matters were come to a crisis. The event was that in a space of three days the new ministry and their abettors found it prudent to fly the nation; the Bastille was taken, and Broglio and his foreign troops dispersed, as is already related in the former part of this work.

There are some curious circumstances in the history of this short-lived ministry, and this short-lived attempt at a counter-revolution. The Palace of Versailles, where the Court was sitting, was not more than four hundred yards distant from the hall where the National Assembly was sitting. The two places were at this moment like the separate headquarters of two combatant armies; yet the Court was as perfectly ignorant of the information which had arrived from Paris to the National Assembly, as if it had resided at an hundred miles distance. The then Marquis de la Fayette, who (as has been already mentioned) was chosen to preside in the National Assembly on this particular occasion, named by order of the Assembly three successive deputations to the king, on the day and up to the evening on which the Bastille was taken, to inform and confer with him on the state of affairs; but the ministry, who knew not so much as that it was attacked, precluded all communication, and were solacing themselves how dextrously they had succeeded; but in a few hours the accounts arrived so thick and fast that they had to start from their desks and run. Some set off in one disguise, and some in another, and none in their own character. Their anxiety now was to outride the news, lest they should be stopt, which, though it flew fast, flew not so fast as themselves.

It is worth remarking that the National Assembly neither pursued those fugitive conspirators, nor took any notice of them, nor sought to retaliate in any shape whatever. Occupied with establishing a constitution founded on the Rights of Man and the Authority of the People, the only authority on which Government has a right to exist in any country, the National Assembly felt none of those mean passions which mark the character of impertinent governments, founding themselves on their own authority, or on the absurdity of hereditary succession. It is the faculty of the human mind to become what it contemplates, and to act in unison with its object.

The conspiracy being thus dispersed, one of the first works of the National Assembly, instead of vindictive proclamations, as has been the case with other governments, was to publish a declaration of the Rights of Man, as the basis on which the new constitution was to be built, and which is here subjoined:

# DECLARATION OF THE RIGHTS
# OF MAN AND OF CITIZENS

## BY THE NATIONAL ASSEMBLY
## OF FRANCE

The representatives of the people of France, formed into a National Assembly, considering that ignorance, neglect, or contempt of human rights, are the sole causes of public misfortunes and corruptions of Government, have resolved to set forth in a solemn declaration, these natural, imprescriptible, and inalienable rights: that this declaration being constantly present to the minds of the members of the body social, they may be forever kept attentive to their rights and their duties; that the acts of the legislative and executive powers of Government, being capable of being every moment compared with the end of political institutions, may be more respected; and also, that the future claims of the citizens, being directed by simple and incontestable principles, may always tend to the maintenance of the Constitution, and the general happiness.

For these reasons the National Assembly doth recognize and declare, in the presence of the Supreme Being, and with the hope of his blessing and favour, the following *sacred* rights of men and of citizens:

One: Men are born, and always continue, free and equal in respect of their Rights. Civil distinctions, therefore, can be founded only on Public Utility.

Two: The end of all Political associations is the Preservation of the Natural and Imprescriptible Rights of Man; and these rights are Liberty, Property, Security, and Resistance of Oppression.

Three: The Nation is essentially the source of all Sovereignty; nor can any *individual*, or any *body of Men*, be entitled to any authority which is not expressly derived from it.

Four: Political Liberty consists in the power of doing whatever does not Injure another. The exercise of the Natural Rights of every Man, has no other limits than those which are necessary to secure to every *other* Man the Free exercise of the same Rights; and these limits are determinable only by the Law.

Five: The Law ought to Prohibit only actions hurtful to Society. What is not Prohibited by the Law should not be hindered; nor should anyone be compelled to that which the Law does not Require.

Six: the Law is an expression of the Will of the Community. All Citizens have a right to concur, either personally or by their Representatives, in its formation. It Should be the same to all, whether it protects or punishes; and all being equal in its sight, are equally eligible to all Honours, Places, and employments, according to their different abilities, without any other distinction than that created by their Virtues and talents.

Seven: No Man should be accused, arrested, or held in confinement, except in cases determined by the Law, and according to the forms which it has prescribed. All who promote, solicit, execute, or cause to be executed, arbitrary orders, ought to be punished, and every Citizen called upon, or apprehended by virtue of the Law, ought immediately to obey, and renders himself culpable by resistance.

Eight: The Law ought to impose no other penalties but such as are absolutely and evidently necessary; and no one ought to be punished, but in virtue of a Law promulgated before the offence, and Legally applied.

Nine: Every Man being presumed innocent till he has been convicted, whenever his detention becomes indispensable, all rigour to him, more than is necessary to secure his person, ought to be provided against by the Law.

Ten: No Man ought to be molested on account of his opinions, not even on account of his Religious opinions, provided his avowal of them does not disturb the Public Order established by the Law.

Eleven: The unrestrained communication of thoughts and opinions being one of the Most Precious Rights of Man, every Citizen may speak, write, and publish freely, provided he is responsible for the abuse of this Liberty, in cases determined by the Law.

Twelve: A Public force being necessary to give security to the Rights of Men and of Citizens, that force is instituted for the benefit of the Community and not for the particular benefit of the persons to whom it is intrusted.

Thirteen: A common contribution being necessary for the support of the Public force, and for defraying the other expenses of Government, it ought to be divided equally among the Members of the Community, according to their abilities.

Fourteen: every Citizen has a Right, either by himself or his Representative, to a free voice in determining the necessity of Public Contributions, the appropriation of them, and their amount, mode of assessment, and duration.

Fifteen: every Community has a Right to demand of all its agents an account of their conduct.

Sixteen: every Community in which a Separation of Powers and a Security of Rights is not Provided for, wants a Constitution.

Seventeen: The Right to Property being inviolable and sacred, no one ought to be deprived of it, except in cases of evident Public necessity, legally ascertained, and on condition of a previous just Indemnity.

# *OBSERVATIONS ON THE*
# *DECLARATION OF RIGHTS*

The first three articles comprehend in general terms the whole of a Declaration of Rights, all the succeeding articles either originate from them or follow as elucidations. The 4th, 5th, and 6th define more particularly what is only generally expressed in the 1st, 2nd, and 3rd.

The 7th, 8th, 9th, 10th, and 11th articles are declaratory of *principles* upon which laws shall be constructed, conformable to *rights* already declared. But it is questioned by some very good people in France, as well as in other countries, whether the 10th article sufficiently guarantees the right it is intended to accord with; besides which it takes off from the divine dignity of religion, and weakens its operative force upon the mind, to make it a subject of human laws. It then presents itself to man like light intercepted by a cloudy medium, in which the source of it is obscured from his sight, and he sees nothing to reverence in the dusky ray.*

The remaining articles, beginning with the twelfth, are substantially contained in the principles of the preceding articles; but in the particular situation in which France then was, having to undo what was wrong, as well as to set up what was right, it was proper to be more particular than what in another condition of things would be necessary.

While the Declaration of Rights was before the National Assembly some of its members remarked that if a declaration of rights were published it should be accompanied by a Declaration of Duties. The observation discovered a mind that reflected, and it only erred by not reflecting far enough. A Declaration of Rights is, by reciprocity, a

---

* There is a single idea, which, if it strikes rightly upon the mind, either in a legal or a religious sense, will prevent any man or any body of men, or any government, from going wrong on the subject of religion; which is, that before any human institutions of government were known in the world, there existed, if I may so express it, a compact between God and man, from the beginning of time: and that as the relation and condition which man in his *individual person* stands in towards his Maker cannot be changed by any human laws or human authority, that religious devotion, which is a part of this compact, cannot so much as be made a subject of human laws; and that all laws must conform themselves to this prior existing compact, and not assume to make the compact conform to the laws, which, besides being human, are subsequent thereto. The first act of man, when he looked around and saw himself a creature which he did not make, and a world furnished for his reception, must have been devotion; and devotion must ever continue sacred to every individual man, *as it appears right to him*; and governments do mischief by interfering. (Author's note)

Declaration of Duties also. Whatever is my right as a man is also the right of another; and it becomes my duty to guarantee as well as to possess.

The three first articles are the base of Liberty, as well individual as national; nor can any country be called free whose government does not take its beginning from the principles they contain, and continue to preserve them pure; and the whole of the Declaration of Rights is of more value to the world, and will do more good, than all the laws and statutes that have yet been promulgated.

In the declaratory exordium which prefaces the Declaration of Rights we see the solemn and majestic spectacle of a nation opening its commission, under the auspices of its Creator, to establish a Government, a scene so new, and so transcendantly unequalled by anything in the European world, that the name of a Revolution is diminutive of its character, and it rises into a Regeneration of man. What are the present Governments of Europe but a scene of iniquity and oppression? What is that of England? Do not its own inhabitants say it is a market where every man has his price, and where corruption is common traffic at the expense of a deluded people? No wonder, then, that the French Revolution is traduced. Had it confined itself merely to the destruction of flagrant despotism perhaps Mr. Burke and some others had been silent. Their cry now is, "It has gone too far"—that is, it has gone too far for them. It stares corruption in the face, and the venal tribe are all alarmed. Their fear discovers itself in their outrage, and they are but publishing the groans of a wounded vice. But from such opposition the French Revolution, instead of suffering, receives an homage. The more it is struck the more sparks it will emit; and the fear is it will not be struck enough. It has nothing to dread from attacks; truth has given it an establishment, and time will record it with a name as lasting as his own.

Having now traced the progress of the French Revolution through most of its principal stages, from its commencement to the taking of the Bastille, and its establishment by the Declaration of Rights, I will close the subject with the energetic apostrophe of M. de la Fayette, "May this great monument, raised to Liberty, serve as a lesson to the oppressor, and an example to the oppressed!"

# MISCELLANEOUS CHAPTER

To prevent interrupting the argument in the preceding part of this work, or the narrative that follows it, I reserved some observations to be thrown together in a Miscellaneous Chapter; by which variety might not be censured for confusion. Mr. Burke's book is *all* Miscellany. His intention was to make an attack on the French Revolution; but instead of proceeding with an orderly arrangement, he has stormed it with a mob of ideas tumbling over and destroying one another.

But this confusion and contradiction in Mr. Burke's Book is easily accounted for.——When a man in a wrong cause attempts to steer his course by anything else than some polar truth or principle, he is sure to be lost. It is beyond the compass of his capacity to keep all the parts of an argument together, and make them unite in one issue, by any other means than having this guide always in view. Neither memory nor invention will supply the want of it. The former fails him, and the latter betrays him.

Notwithstanding the nonsense, for it deserves no better name, that Mr. Burke has asserted about hereditary rights, and hereditary succession, and that a Nation has not a right to form a Government of itself; it happened to fall in his way to give some account of what Government is. "*Government*," says he, "*is a contrivance of human wisdom.*"

Admitting that government is a contrivance of human *wisdom*, it must necessarily follow, that hereditary succession, and hereditary rights (as they are called), can make no part of it, because it is impossible to make wisdom hereditary; and on the other hand, *that* cannot be a wise contrivance, which in its operation may commit the government of a nation to the wisdom of an idiot. The ground which Mr. Burke now takes is fatal to every part of his cause. The argument changes from hereditary rights to hereditary wisdom; and the question is, Who is the wisest man? He must now show that every one in the line of hereditary succession was a Solomon, or his title is not good to be a king. What a stroke has Mr. Burke now made! To use a sailor's phrase, he has *swabbed the deck*, and scarcely left a name legible in the list of Kings; and he has mowed down and thinned the House of Peers, with a scythe as formidable as Death and Time.

But Mr. Burke appears to have been aware of this retort; and he has taken care to guard against it, by making government to be not only a *contrivance* of human wisdom, but a *monopoly* of wisdom. He puts the nation as fools on one side, and places his government of wisdom, all wise men of Gotham, on the other side; and he then proclaims, and says that "Men have a *right* that their *wants* should be provided for by this wisdom." Having thus made proclamation, he next proceeds to explain to them what their wants are, and also what their *rights* are. In this he has succeeded dextrously, for he makes their wants to be a *want* of wisdom; but as this is cold comfort, he then informs them, that they have a *right* (not to any of the wisdom) but to be governed by it; and in order to impress them with a solemn reverence for this monopoly-government of wisdom, and of its vast capacity for all purposes, possible or impossible, right or wrong, he proceeds with astrological mysterious importance, to tell to them its powers in these words: "The rights of men in government are their advantages; and these are often in balance between differences of good; and in compromises sometimes between *good* and *evil*, and sometimes between *evil* and *evil*. Political reason is a *computing principle*; adding—subtracting—multiplying—and dividing, morally and not metaphysically or mathematically, true moral denominations."

As the wondering audience, whom Mr. Burke supposes himself talking to, may not understand all this learned jargon, I will undertake to be its interpreter. The meaning, then, good people, of all this, is: *That government is governed by no principle whatever; that it can make evil good, or good evil, just as it pleases. In short, that government is arbitrary power.*

But there are some things which Mr. Burke has forgotten. First, he has not shown where the wisdom originally came from: and secondly, he has not shown by what authority it first began to act. In the manner he introduces the matter, it is either government stealing wisdom, or wisdom stealing government. It is without an origin, and its powers without authority. In short, it is usurpation.

Whether it be from a sense of shame, or from a consciousness of some radical defect in a government necessary to be kept out of sight, or from both, or from any other cause, I undertake not to determine, but so it is, that a monarchical reasoner never traces government to its source, or from its source. It is one of the *shibboleths* by which he may be known. A thousand years hence, those who shall live in America or

France, will look back with contemplative pride on the origin of their government, and say, *This was the work of our glorious ancestors*! But what can a monarchical talker say? What has he to exult in? Alas he has nothing. A certain something forbids him to look back to a beginning, lest some robber, or some Robin Hood, should rise from the long obscurity of time and say, *I am the origin*. Hard as Mr. Burke laboured at the Regency Bill and Hereditary Succession two years ago, and much as he dived for precedents, he still had not boldness enough to bring up William of Normandy, and say, *There is the head of the list! there is the fountain of honour*! the son of a prostitute, and the plunderer of the English nation.

The opinions of men with respect to government are changing fast in all countries. The Revolutions of America and France have thrown a beam of light over the world, which reaches into man. The enormous expense of governments has provoked people to think, by making them feel; and when once the veil begins to rend, it admits not of repair. Ignorance is of a peculiar nature: once dispelled, it is impossible to re-establish it. It is not originally a thing of itself, but is only the absence of knowledge; and though man may be *kept* ignorant, he cannot be *made* ignorant. The mind, in discovering truth, acts in the same manner as it acts through the eye in discovering objects; when once any object has been seen, it is impossible to put the mind back to the same condition it was in before it saw it. Those who talk of a counter-revolution in France, show how little they understand of man. There does not exist in the compass of language an arrangement of words to express so much as the means of effecting a counter-revolution. The means must be an obliteration of knowledge; and it has never yet been discovered how to make man *unknow* his knowledge, or *unthink* his thoughts.

Mr. Burke is labouring in vain to stop the progress of knowledge; and it comes with the worse grace from him, as there is a certain transaction known in the city which renders him suspected of being a pensioner in a fictitious name. This may account for some strange doctrine he has advanced in his book, which though he points it at the Revolution Society, is effectually directed against the whole nation.

"The King of England," says he, "holds *his* crown (for it does not belong to the Nation, according to Mr. Burke) in *contempt* of the choice of the Revolution Society, who have not a single vote for a king among them either *individually* or *collectively*; and his Majesty's heirs each in their time and order, will come to the Crown *with the same contempt* of their choice, with which his Majesty has succeeded to that which he now wears."

As to who is King in England, or elsewhere, or whether there is any King at all, or whether the people choose a Cherokee chief, or a Hessian hussar for a King, it is not a matter that I trouble myself about—be that to themselves; but with respect to the doctrine, so far as it relates to the Rights of Men and Nations, it is as abominable as anything ever uttered in the most enslaved country under heaven. Whether it sounds worse to my ear, by not being accustomed to hear such despotism, than what it does to another person, I am not so well a judge of; but of its abominable principle I am at no loss to judge.

It is not the Revolution Society that Mr. Burke means; it is the Nation, as well in its *original* as in its *representative* character; and he has taken care to make himself understood, by saying that they have not a vote either *collectively* or *individually*. The Revolution Society is composed of citizens of all denominations, and of members of both the Houses of Parliament; and consequently, if there is not a right to a vote in any of the characters, there can be no right to any either in the nation or in its Parliament. This ought to be a caution to every country how to import foreign families to be kings. It is somewhat curious to observe, that although the people of England had been in the habit of talking about kings, it is always a Foreign House of Kings; hating Foreigners yet governed by them.——It is now the House of Brunswick, one of the petty tribes of Germany.

It has hitherto been the practice of the English Parliaments to regulate what was called the succession (taking it for granted that the Nation then continued to accord to the form of annexing a monarchical branch of its government; for without this the Parliament could not have had authority to have sent either to Holland or to Hanover, or to impose a king upon the nation against its will). And this must be the utmost limit to which Parliament can go upon this case; but the right of the Nation goes to the *whole* case, because it has the right of changing its *whole* form of government. The right of a Parliament is only a right in trust, a right by delegation, and that but from a very small part of the Nation; and one of its Houses has not even this. But the right of the Nation is an original right, as universal as taxation. The nation is the paymaster of everything, and everything must conform to its general will.

I remember taking notice of a speech in what is called the English House of Peers, by the then Earl of Shelburne, and I think it was at the time he was Minister, which is applicable to this case. I do not directly charge my memory with every particular; but the words and the purport, as nearly as I remember, were these: *"That the form of a Government was a matter wholly at the will of the Nation at all times, that if it chose a monarchical form, it had a right to have it so; and if it afterwards chose to be a Republic, it had a right to be a Republic, and to say to a King, 'We have no longer any occasion for you.'"*

When Mr. Burke says that "His Majesty's heirs and successors, each in their time and order, will come to the crown with the *same contempt* of their choice with which His Majesty had succeeded to that he wears," it is saying too much even to the humblest individual in the country; part of whose daily labour goes towards making up the million sterling a-year, which the country gives the person it styles a king. Government with insolence is despotism; but when contempt is added it becomes worse; and to pay for contempt is the excess of slavery. This species of government comes from Germany; and reminds me of what one of the Brunswick soldiers told me, who was taken prisoner by, the Americans in the late war: "Ah!" said he, "America is a fine free country, it is worth the people's fighting for; I know the difference by knowing my own: in my country, if the prince says eat straw, we eat straw." God help that country, thought I, be it England or elsewhere, whose liberties are to be protected by German principles of government, and Princes of Brunswick!

As Mr. Burke sometimes speaks of England, sometimes of France, and sometimes of the world, and of government in general, it is difficult to answer his book without apparently meeting him on the same ground. Although principles of Government are general subjects, it is next to impossible, in many cases, to separate them from the idea of place and circumstance, and the more so when circumstances are put for arguments, which is frequently the case with Mr. Burke.

In the former part of his book, addressing himself to the people of France, he says: "No experience has taught us (meaning the English), that in any other course or method than that of a *hereditary crown*, can our liberties be regularly perpetuated and preserved sacred as our *hereditary right*." I ask Mr. Burke, who is to take them away? M. de la Fayette, in speaking to France, says: *"For a Nation to be free, it is sufficient that she wills it.*" But Mr. Burke represents England as wanting capacity to take care of itself, and that its liberties must be taken care of by a King holding it in "contempt." If England is sunk to this, it is preparing itself to eat straw, as in Hanover, or in Brunswick. But besides the folly of the declaration, it happens that the facts are all against Mr. Burke. It was by the government *being hereditary*, that the liberties of the people were endangered. Charles I and James II are instances of this truth; yet neither of them went so far as to hold the Nation in contempt.

As it is sometimes of advantage to the people of one country to hear what those of other countries have to say respecting it, it is possible that the people of France may learn something from Mr. Burke's book, and that the people of England may also learn something from the answers it will occasion. When Nations fall out about freedom, a wide field of debate is opened. The argument commences with the rights of war, without its evils, and as knowledge is the object contended for, the party that sustains the defeat obtains the prize.

Mr. Burke talks about what he calls an hereditary crown, as if it were some production of Nature; or as if, like Time, it had a power to operate, not only independently, but in spite of man; or as if it were a thing or a subject universally consented to. Alas! it has none of those properties, but is the reverse of them all. It is a thing in imagination, the propriety of which is more than doubted, and the legality of which in a few years will be denied.

But, to arrange this matter in a clearer view than what general expression can heads under which (what is called) an hereditary crown, or more properly speaking, an hereditary succession to the Government of a Nation, can be considered; which are:

First, The right of a particular Family to establish itself.

Secondly, The right of a Nation to establish a particular Family.

With respect to the *first* of these heads, that of a Family establishing itself with hereditary powers on its own authority, and independent of the consent of a Nation, all men will concur in calling it despotism; and it would be trespassing on their understanding to attempt to prove it.

But the *second* head, that of a Nation establishing a particular Family with *hereditary powers*, does not present itself as despotism on the first reflection; but if men will permit it a second reflection to take place, and carry that reflection forward but one remove out of their own persons to that of their offspring, they will then see that hereditary succession becomes in its consequences the same despotism to others, which they reprobated for themselves. It operates to preclude the consent of the succeeding generations; and the preclusion of consent is despotism. When the person who at any time shall be in possession of a Government, or those who stand in succession to him, shall say to a Nation, I hold this power in "contempt" of you, it signifies not on what authority he pretends to say it. It is no relief, but an aggravation to a person in slavery, to reflect that he was sold by his parent; and as that which heightens the criminality of an act cannot be produced to prove the legality of it, hereditary succession cannot be established as a legal thing.

In order to arrive at a more perfect decision on this head, it will be proper to consider the generation which undertakes to establish a Family with *hereditary powers*, apart and separate from the generations which are to follow; and also to consider the character in which the first generation acts with respect to succeeding generations.

The generation which first selects a person, and puts him at the head of its Government, either with the title of King, or any other distinction, acts on its *own choice*, be it wise or foolish, as a free agent for itself The person so set up is not hereditary, but selected and appointed; and the generation who sets him up, does not live under a hereditary government, but under a government of its own choice and establishment. Were the generation who sets him up, and the person so set up, to live for ever, it never could become hereditary succession; and of consequence hereditary succession can only follow on the death of the first parties.

As, therefore, hereditary succession is out of the question with respect to the *first* generation, we have now to consider the character in which *that* generation acts with respect to the commencing generation, and to all succeeding ones.

It assumes a character, to which it has neither right nor title. It changes itself from a *Legislator* to a *Testator*, and effects to make its Will, which is to have operation after the demise of the makers, to bequeath the Government; and it not only attempts to bequeath, but to establish on the succeeding generation, a new and different form of Government under which itself lived. Itself, as already observed, lived not under a hereditary Government but under a Government of its own choice and establishment; and it now attempts, by virtue of a will and testament (and which it has not authority to make), to take from the commencing generation, and all future ones, the rights and free agency by which itself acted.

But, exclusive of the right which any generation has to act collectively as a testator, the objects to which it applies itself in this case, are not within the compass of any law, or of any will or testament.

The rights of men in society, are neither devisable or transferable, nor annihilable, but are descendable only, and it is not in the power of any generation to intercept finally, and cut off the descent. If the present generation, or any other, are disposed to be slaves, it does not lessen the right of the succeeding generation to be free. Wrongs cannot have a legal descent. When Mr. Burke attempts to maintain that the *English nation did at the Revolution of 1688, most solemnly renounce and abdicate their rights for themselves, and for all their posterity for ever*, he speaks a language that merits not reply, and which can only excite contempt for his prostitute principles, or pity for his ignorance.

In whatever light hereditary succession, as growing out of the will and testament of some former generation, presents itself, it is an absurdity. A cannot make a will to take from B the property of B, and give it to C; yet this is the manner in which (what is called) hereditary succession by law operates. A certain former generation made a will, to take away the rights of the commencing generation, and all future ones, and convey those rights to a third person, who afterwards comes forward, and tells them, in Mr. Burke's language, that they have *no rights*, that their rights are already bequeathed to him and that he will govern in *contempt* of them. From such principles, and such ignorance, good Lord deliver the world!

But, after all, what is this metaphor called a crown, or rather what is monarchy? Is it a thing, or is it a name, or is it a fraud? Is it a "contrivance of human wisdom," or of human craft to obtain money from a nation under specious pretences? Is it a thing necessary to a nation? If it is, in what does that necessity consist, what service does it perform, what is its business, and what are its merits? Does the virtue consist in the metaphor, or in the man? Doth the goldsmith that makes the crown, make the virtue also? Doth it operate like Fortunatus's wishing-cap, or Harlequin's wooden sword? Doth it make a man a conjurer? In fine, what is it? It appears to be something going much out of fashion, falling into ridicule, and rejected in some countries, both as unnecessary and expensive. In America it is considered as an absurdity; and in France it has so far declined, that the goodness of the man, and the respect for his personal character, are the only things that preserve the appearance of its existence.

If government be what Mr. Burke describes it, "a contrivance of human wisdom" I might ask him, if wisdom was at such a low ebb in England, that it was become necessary to import it from Holland and from Hanover? But I will do the country the justice to say, that was not the case; and even if it was it mistook the cargo. The wisdom of every country, when properly exerted, is sufficient for all its purposes; and there could exist no more real occasion in England to have sent for a Dutch Stadtholder, or a German Elector, than there was in America to have done a similar thing. If a country does not understand its own affairs, how is a foreigner to understand them, who knows neither its laws, its manners, nor its language? If there existed a man so transcendently wise above all others, that his wisdom was necessary to instruct a nation, some reason might be offered for monarchy; but when we cast our eyes about a country, and observe how every part understands its own affairs; and when we look around the world, and see that of all men in it, the race of kings are the most insignificant in capacity, our reason cannot fail to ask us—What are those men kept for?

If there is anything in monarchy which we people of America do not understand, I wish Mr. Burke would be so kind as to inform us. I see in America, a government extending over a country ten times as large as England, and conducted with regularity, for a fortieth part of the expense which Government costs in England. If I ask a man in America if he wants a King, he retorts, and asks me if I take him for an idiot? How is it that this difference happens? are we more or less wise than others? I see in America the generality of people living in a style of plenty unknown in monarchical countries; and I see that the principle of its government, which is that of the *equal Rights of Man*, is making a rapid progress in the world.

If monarchy is a useless thing, why is it kept up anywhere? and if a necessary thing, how can it be dispensed with? That *civil government* is necessary, all civilized nations will agree; but civil government is republican government. All that part of the government of England which begins with the office of constable, and proceeds through the department of magistrate, quarter-sessions, and general assize, including trial by jury, is republican government. Nothing of monarchy appears in any part of it, except in the name which William the Conqueror imposed upon the English, that of obliging them to call him "Their Sovereign Lord the King."

It is easy to conceive that a band of interested men, such as Placemen, Pensioners, Lords of the bed-chamber, Lords of the kitchen, Lords of the necessary-house, and the Lord knows what besides, can find as many reasons for monarchy as their salaries, paid at the expense of the country, amount to; but if I ask the farmer, the manufacturer, the merchant, the tradesman, and down through all the occupations of life to the common labourer, what service monarchy is to him? he can give me no answer. If I ask him what monarchy is, he believes it is something like a sinecure.

Notwithstanding the taxes of England amount to almost seventeen millions a year, said to be for the expenses of Government, it is still evident that the sense of the Nation is left to govern itself, and does govern itself, by magistrates and juries, almost at its own charge, on republican principles, exclusive of the expense of taxes. The salaries of the judges are almost the only charge that is paid out of the revenue. Considering that all the internal government is executed by the people, the taxes of England ought to be the lightest of any nation in Europe; instead of which, they are the contrary. As this cannot be accounted for on the score of civil government, the subject necessarily extends itself to the monarchical part.

When the people of England sent for George the First (and it would puzzle a wiser man than Mr. Burke to discover for what he could be wanted, or what service he could render), they ought at least to have conditioned for the abandonment of Hanover. Besides the endless German intrigues that must follow from a German Elector being King of England, there is a natural impossibility of uniting in the same person the principles of Freedom and the principles of Despotism, or as it is usually called in England Arbitrary Power. A German Elector is in his electorate a despot; how then could it be expected that he should be attached to principles of liberty in one country, while his interest in another was to be supported by despotism? The union cannot exist; and it might easily have been foreseen that German Electors would make German Kings, or in Mr. Burke's words, would assume government with "contempt." The English have been in the habit of considering a King of England only in the character in which he appears to them; whereas the same person, while the connection lasts, has a home-seat in another country, the interest of which is different to their own, and the principles of the governments in opposition to each other. To such a person England will appear as a town-residence, and the Electorate as the estate. The English may wish, as I believe they do, success to the principles of liberty in France, or in Germany; but a German Elector trembles for the fate of despotism in his electorate; and the Duchy of Mecklenburgh, where the present Queen's family governs, is under the same wretched state of arbitrary power, and the people in slavish vassalage.

There never was a time when it became the English to watch continental intrigues more circumspectly than at the present moment, and to distinguish the politics of the Electorate from the politics of the Nation. The Revolution of France has entirely changed the ground with respect to England and France, as nations; but the German despots, with Prussia at their head, are combining against liberty; and the fondness of Mr. Pitt for office, and the interest which all his family connections have obtained, do not give sufficient security against this intrigue.

As everything which passes in the world becomes matter for history, I will now quit this subject, and take a concise review of the state of parties and politics in England, as Mr. Burke has done in France.

Whether the present reign commenced with contempt, I leave to Mr. Burke: certain, however, it is, that it had strongly that appearance. The animosity of the English nation, it is very well remembered, ran high; and, had the true principles of Liberty been as well understood then as they now promise to be, it is probable the Nation would not have patiently submitted to so much. George the First and Second were sensible of a rival in the remains of the Stuarts; and as they could not but consider themselves as standing on their good behaviour, they had prudence to keep their German principles of government to themselves; but as the Stuart family wore away, the prudence became less necessary.

The contest between rights, and what were called prerogatives, continued to heat the nation till some time after the conclusion of the American War, when all at once it fell a calm—Execration exchanged itself for applause, and Court popularity sprung up like a mushroom in a night.

To account for this sudden transition, it is proper to observe that there are two distinct species of popularity; the one excited by merit, and the other by resentment. As the Nation had formed itself into two parties, and each was extolling the merits of its parliamentary champions for and against prerogative, nothing could operate to give a more general shock than an immediate coalition of the champions themselves. The partisans of each being thus suddenly left in the lurch, and mutually heated with disgust at the measure, felt no other relief than uniting in a common execration against both. A higher stimulus or resentment being thus excited than what the contest on prerogatives occasioned, the nation quitted all former objects of rights and wrongs, and sought only that of gratification. The indignation at the Coalition so effectually superseded the indignation against the Court as to extinguish it; and without any change of principles on the part of the Court, the same people who had reprobated its despotism united with it to revenge themselves on the Coalition Parliament. The case was not, which they liked best, but which they hated most; and the least hated passed for love. The dissolution of the Coalition Parliament, as it afforded the means of gratifying the resentment of the Nation, could not fail to be popular; and from hence arose the popularity of the Court.

Transitions of this kind exhibit a Nation under the government of temper, instead of a fixed and steady principle; and having once committed itself, however rashly, it feels itself urged along to justify by continuance its first proceeding. Measures which at other times it would censure it now approves, and acts persuasion upon itself to suffocate its judgment.

On the return of a new Parliament, the new Minister, Mr. Pitt, found himself in a secure majority; and the Nation gave him credit, not out of regard to himself, but because it had resolved to do it out of resentment to another. He introduced himself to public notice by a proposed Reform of Parliament, which in its operation would have amounted to a public justification of corruption. The Nation was to be at the expense of buying up the rotten boroughs, whereas it ought to punish the persons who deal in the traffic.

Passing over the two bubbles of the Dutch business and the million a-year to sink the national debt, the matter which most presents itself, is the affair of the Regency. Never, in the course of my observation, was delusion more successfully acted, nor a nation more completely deceived. But, to make this appear, it will be necessary to go over the circumstances.

Mr. Fox had stated in the House of Commons, that the Prince of Wales, as heir in succession, had a right in himself to assume the Government. This was opposed by Mr. Pitt; and, so far as the opposition was confined to the doctrine, it was just. But the principles which Mr. Pitt maintained on the contrary side were as bad, or worse in their extent, than those of Mr. Fox; because they went to establish an aristocracy over the Nation, and over the small representation it has in the House of Commons.

Whether the English form of Government be good or bad, is not in this case the question; but, taking it as it stands, without regard to its merits or demerits, Mr. Pitt was farther from the point than Mr. Fox.

It is supposed to consist of three parts:—while therefore the Nation is disposed to continue this form, the parts have a *national standing*, independent of each other, and are not the creatures of each other. Had Mr. Fox passed through Parliament, and said that the person alluded to claimed on the ground of the Nation, Mr. Pitt must then have contended what he called the right of the Parliament against the right of the Nation.

By the appearance which the contest made, Mr. Fox took the hereditary ground, and Mr. Pitt the Parliamentary ground; but the fact is, they both took hereditary ground, and Mr. Pitt took the worst of the two.

What is called the Parliament is made up of two Houses, one of which is more hereditary, and more beyond the control of the Nation than what the Crown (as it is called) is supposed to be. It is an hereditary aristocracy, assuming and asserting indefeasible, irrevocable rights and authority, wholly independent of the Nation. Where, then, was the merited popularity of exalting this hereditary power over another hereditary power less independent of the Nation than what itself assumed to be, and of absorbing the rights of the Nation into a House over which it has neither election nor control?

The general impulse of the Nation was right; but it acted without reflection. It approved the opposition made to the right set up by Mr. Fox, without perceiving that Mr. Pitt was supporting another indefeasible right more remote from the Nation, in opposition to it.

With respect to the House of Commons, it is elected but by a small part of the Nation; but were the election as universal as taxation, which it ought to be, it would still be only the organ of the Nation, and cannot possess inherent rights.—When the National Assembly of France resolves a matter, the resolve is made in right of the Nation; but Mr. Pitt, on all national questions, so far as they refer to the House of Commons, absorbs the rights of the Nation into the organ, and makes the organ into a Nation, and the Nation itself into a cypher.

In a few words, the question on the Regency was a question of a million a-year, which is appropriated to the executive department: and Mr. Pitt could not possess himself of any management of this sum, without setting up the supremacy of Parliament; and when this was accomplished, it was indifferent who should be Regent, as he must be Regent at his own cost. Among the curiosities which this contentious debate afforded, was that of making the Great Seal into a King, the affixing of which to an act was to be royal authority. If, therefore, Royal Authority is a Great Seal, it consequently is in itself nothing; and a good Constitution would be of infinitely more value to the Nation than what the three Nominal Powers, as they now stand, are worth.

The continual use of the word *Constitution* in the English Parliament shows there is none; and that the whole is merely a form of government without a Constitution, and constituting itself with what powers it pleases. If there were a Constitution, it certainly could be referred to; and the debate on any constitutional point would terminate by producing the Constitution. One member says this is Constitution, and another says that is Constitution—To-day it is one thing; and to-morrow something else—while the maintaining of the debate proves there is none. Constitution is now the cant word of Parliament, tuning itself to the ear of the Nation. Formerly it was the *universal supremacy of Parliament—the omnipotence of Parliament*: But since the progress of Liberty in France, those phrases have a despotic harshness in their note; and the English Parliament have catched the fashion from the National Assembly, but without the substance, of speaking of *Constitution*.

As the present generation of the people in England did not make the Government, they are not accountable for any of its defects; but, that sooner or later, it must come into their hands to undergo a constitutional reformation, is as certain as that the same thing has happened in France. If France, with a revenue of nearly twenty-four millions sterling, with an extent of rich and fertile country above four times larger than England, with a population of twenty-four millions of inhabitants to support taxation, with upwards of ninety millions sterling of gold and silver circulating in the nation, and with a debt less than the present debt of England—still found it necessary, from whatever cause, to come to a settlement of its affairs, it solves the problem of funding for both countries.

It is out of the question to say how long what is called the English constitution has lasted, and to argue from thence how long it is to last; the question is, how long can the funding system last? It is a thing but of modern invention, and has not yet continued beyond the life of a man; yet in that short space it has so far accumulated, that, together with the current expenses, it requires an amount of taxes at least equal to the whole landed rental of the nation in acres to defray the annual expenditure. That a government could not have always gone on by the same system which has been followed for the last seventy years, must be evident to every man; and for the same reason it cannot always go on.

The funding system is not money; neither is it, properly speaking, credit. It, in effect, creates upon paper the sum which it appears to borrow, and lays on a tax to keep the imaginary capital alive by the payment of interest and sends the annuity to market, to be sold for paper already in circulation. If any credit is given, it is to the disposition of the people to pay the tax, and not to the government, which lays it on. When this disposition expires, what is supposed to be the credit of Government expires with it. The instance of France under the former Government shows that it is impossible to compel the payment of taxes by force, when a whole nation is determined to take its stand upon that ground.

Mr. Burke, in his review of the finances of France, states the quantity of gold and silver in France, at about eighty-eight millions sterling. In doing this, he has, I presume, divided by the difference of exchange, instead of the standard of twenty-four livres to a pound sterling; for M. Neckar's statement, from which Mr. Burke's is taken, is *two thousand two hundred millions of livres*, which is upwards of ninety-one millions and a half sterling.

M. Neckar in France, and Mr. George Chalmers at the Office of Trade and Plantation in England, of which Lord Hawkesbury is president, published nearly about the same time (1786) an account of the quantity of money in each nation, from the returns of the Mint of each nation. Mr. Chalmers, from the returns of the English Mint at the

Tower of London, states the quantity of money in England, including Scotland and Ireland, to be twenty millions sterling.*

M. Neckar† says that the amount of money in France, recoined from the old coin which was called in, was two thousand five hundred millions of livres (upwards of one hundred and four millions sterling); and, after deducting for waste, and what may be in the West Indies and other possible circumstances, states the circulation quantity at home to be ninety-one millions and a half sterling; but, taking it as Mr. Burke has put it, it is sixty-eight millions more than the national quantity in England.

That the quantity of money in France cannot be under this sum, may at once be seen from the state of the French Revenue, without referring to the records of the French Mint for proofs. The revenue of France, prior to the Revolution, was nearly twenty-four millions sterling; and as paper had then no existence in France the whole revenue was collected upon gold and silver; and it would have been impossible to have collected such a quantity of revenue upon a less national quantity than M. Neckar has stated. Before the establishment of paper in England, the revenue was about a fourth part of the national amount of gold and silver, as may be known by referring to the revenue prior to King William, and the quantity of money stated to be in the nation at that time, which was nearly as much as it is now.

It can be of no real service to a nation, to impose upon itself, or to permit itself to be imposed upon; but the prejudices of some, and the imposition of others, have always represented France as a nation possessing but little money—whereas the quantity is not only more than four times what the quantity is in England, but is considerably greater on a proportion of numbers. To account for this deficiency on the part of England, some reference should be had to the English system of funding. It operates to multiply paper, and to substitute it in the room of money, in various shapes; and the more paper is multiplied, the more opportunities are offered to export the specie; and it admits of a possibility (by extending it to small notes) of increasing paper till there is no money left.

I know this is not a pleasant subject to English readers; but the matters I am going to mention, are so important in themselves, as to require the attention of men interested in money transactions of a public

* See "Estimate of the Comparative Strength of Great Britain," by G. Chalmers. (Author's note)
† See "Administration of the Finances of France," vol. iii, by M. Neckar. (Author's note)

nature. There is a circumstance stated by M. Neckar, in his treatise on the administration of the finances, which has never been attended to in England, but which forms the only basis whereon to estimate the quantity of money (gold and silver) which ought to be in every nation in Europe, to preserve a relative proportion with other nations.

Lisbon and Cadiz are the two ports into which (money) gold and silver from South America are imported, and which afterwards divide and spread themselves over Europe by means of commerce, and increase the quantity of money in all parts of Europe. If, therefore, the amount of the annual importation into Europe can be known, and the relative proportion of the foreign commerce of the several nations by which it can be distributed can be ascertained, they give a rule sufficiently true, to ascertain the quantity of money which ought to be found in any nation, at any given time.

M. Neckar shows from the registers of Lisbon and Cadiz, that the importation of gold and silver into Europe, is five millions sterling annually. He has not taken it on a single year, but on an average of fifteen succeeding years, from 1763 to 1777, both inclusive; in which time, the amount was one thousand eight hundred million livres, which is seventy-five millions sterling.[*]

From the commencement of the Hanover succession in 1714 to the time Mr. Chalmers published, is seventy-two years; and the quantity imported into Europe, in that time, would be three hundred and sixty millions sterling.

If the foreign commerce of Great Britain be stated at a sixth part of what the whole foreign commerce of Europe amounts to (which is probably an inferior estimation to what the gentlemen at the Exchange would allow) the proportion which Britain should draw by commerce of this sum, to keep herself on a proportion with the rest of Europe, would be also a sixth part which is sixty millions sterling; and if the same allowance for waste and accident be made for England which M. Neckar makes for France, the quantity remaining after these deductions would be fifty-two millions; and this sum ought to have been in the nation (at the time Mr. Chalmers published), in addition to the sum which was in the nation at the commencement of the Hanover succession, and to have made in the whole at least sixty-six millions sterling; instead of

---

[*] "Administration of the Finances of France," vol. iii. (Author's note)

which there were but twenty millions, which is forty-six millions below its proportionate quantity.

As the quantity of gold and silver imported into Lisbon and Cadiz is more exactly ascertained than that of any commodity imported into England, and as the quantity of money coined at the Tower of London is still more positively known, the leading facts do not admit of controversy. Either, therefore, the commerce of England is unproductive of profit, or the gold and silver which it brings in leak continually away by unseen means at the average rate of about three-quarters of a million a year, which, in the course of seventy-two years, accounts for the deficiency; and its absence is supplied by paper.*

The Revolution of France is attended with many novel circumstances, not only in the political sphere, but in the circle of money

---

* Whether the English commerce does not bring in money, or whether the government sends it out after it is brought in, is a matter which the parties concerned can best explain; but that the deficiency exists, is not in the power of either to disprove. While Dr. Price, Mr. Eden, (now Auckland), Mr. Chalmers, and others, were debating whether the quantity of money in England was greater or less than at the Revolution, the circumstance was not adverted to, that since the Revolution, there cannot have been less than four hundred millions sterling imported into Europe; and therefore the quantity in England ought at least to have been four times greater than it was at the Revolution, to be on a proportion with Europe. What England is now doing by paper, is what she would have been able to do by solid money, if gold and silver had come into the nation in the proportion it ought, or had not been sent out; and she is endeavouring to restore by paper, the balance she has lost by money. It is certain, that the gold and silver which arrive annually in the register-ships to Spain and Portugal, do not remain in those countries. Taking the value half in gold and half in silver, it is about four hundred tons annually; and from the number of ships and galloons employed in the trade of bringing those metals from South-America to Portugal and Spain, the quantity sufficiently proves itself, without referring to the registers.

In the situation England now is, it is impossible she can increase in money. High taxes not only lessen the property of the individuals, but they lessen also the money capital of the nation, by inducing smuggling, which can only be carried on by gold and silver. By the politics which the British Government have carried on with the Inland Powers of Germany and the Continent, it has made an enemy of all the Maritime Powers, and is therefore obliged to keep up a large navy; but though the navy is built in England, the naval stores must be purchased from abroad, and that from countries where the greatest part must be paid for in gold and silver. Some fallacious rumours have been set afloat in England to induce a belief in money, and, among others, that of the French refugees bringing great quantities. The idea is ridiculous. The general part of the money in France is silver; and it would take upwards of twenty of the largest broad wheel wagons, with ten horses each, to remove one million sterling of silver. Is it then to be supposed, that a few people fleeing on horse-back or in post-chaises, in a secret manner, and having the French Custom-House to pass, and the sea to cross, could bring even a sufficiency for their own expenses?

When millions of money are spoken of, it should be recollected, that such sums can only accumulate in a country by slow degrees, and a long procession of time. The most frugal system that England could now adopt, would not recover in a century the balance she has lost in money since the commencement of the Hanover succession. She is seventy millions behind France, and she must be in some considerable proportion behind every country in Europe, because the returns of the English mint do not show an increase of money, while the registers of Lisbon and Cadiz show an European increase of between three and four hundred millions sterling. (Author's note)

transactions. Among others, it shows that a government may be in a state of insolvency and a nation rich. So far as the fact is confined to the late Government of France, it was insolvent; because the nation would no longer support its extravagance, and therefore it could no longer support itself—but with respect to the nation all the means existed. A government may be said to be insolvent every time it applies to the Nation to discharge its arrears. The insolvency of the late Government of France and the present of England differed in no other respect than as the dispositions of the people differ. The people of France refused their aid to the old Government; and the people of England submit to taxation without inquiry. What is called the Crown in England has been insolvent several times; the last of which, publicly known, was in May, 1777, when it applied to the Nation to discharge upwards of £600,000 private debts, which otherwise it could not pay.

It was the error of Mr. Pitt, Mr. Burke, and all those who were unacquainted with the affairs of France to confound the French Nation with the French Government. The French Nation, in effect, endeavoured to render the late Government insolvent for the purpose of taking government into its own hands: and it reserved its means for the support of the new Government. In a country of such vast extent and population as France the natural means cannot be wanting, and the political means appear the instant the nation is disposed to permit them. When Mr. Burke, in a speech last winter in the British Parliament, "cast his eyes over the map of Europe, and saw a chasm that once was France," he talked like a dreamer of dreams. The same natural France existed as before, and all the natural means existed with it. The only chasm was that the extinction of despotism had left, and which was to be filled up with the Constitution more formidable in resources than the power which had expired.

Although the French Nation rendered the late Government insolvent, it did not permit the insolvency to act towards the creditors; and the creditors, considering the Nation as the real pay-master, and the Government only as the agent, rested themselves on the Nation, in preference to the Government. This appears greatly to disturb Mr. Burke, as the precedent is fatal to the policy by which governments have supposed themselves secure. They have contracted debts, with a view of attaching what is called the monied interest of a Nation to their support; but the example in France shows that the permanent security of the creditor is in the Nation, and not in the Government; and that in all possible revolutions that may happen in Governments, the means are always with the Nation, and the Nation always in existence. Mr. Burke argues that the creditors ought to have abided the fate of the Government which they trusted; but the National Assembly considered them as the creditors of the Nation, and not of the Government—of the master, and not of the steward.

Notwithstanding the late government could not discharge the current expenses, the present government has paid off a great part of the capital. This has been accomplished by two means; the one by lessening the expenses of government, and the other by the sale of the monastic and ecclesiastical landed estates. The devotees and penitent debauchees, extortioners and misers of former days, to ensure themselves a better world than that they were about to leave, had bequeathed immense property in trust to the priesthood for *pious uses*; and the priesthood kept it for themselves. The National Assembly has ordered it to be sold for the good of the whole nation, and the priesthood to be decently provided for.

In consequence of the revolution, the annual interest of the debt of France will be reduced at least six millions sterling, by paying off upwards of one hundred millions of the capital; which, with lessening the former expenses of government at least three millions, will place France in a situation worthy the imitation of Europe.

Upon a whole review of the subject, how vast is the contrast! While Mr. Burke has been talking of a general bankruptcy in France, the National Assembly has been paying off the capital of its debt; and while taxes have increased near a million a year in England, they have lowered several millions a year in France. Not a word has either Mr. Burke or Mr. Pitt said about the French affairs, or the state of the French finances, in the present Session of Parliament. The subject begins to be too well understood, and imposition serves no longer.

There is a general enigma running through the whole of Mr. Burke's book. He writes in a rage against the National Assembly; but what is he enraged about? If his assertions were as true as they are groundless, and that France by her Revolution, had annihilated her power, and become what he calls a *chasm*, it might excite the grief of a Frenchman (considering himself as a national man), and provoke his rage against the National Assembly; but why should it excite the rage of Mr. Burke?

Alas! it is not the Nation of France that Mr. Burke means, but the Court; and every Court in Europe, dreading the same fate, is in mourning. He writes neither in the character of a Frenchman nor an Englishman, but in the fawning character of that creature known in all countries, and a friend to none—a courtier. Whether it be the Court of Versailles, or the Court of St. James, or Carlton-House, or the Court in expectation, signifies not; for the caterpillar principle of all Courts and Courtiers are alike. They form a common policy throughout Europe, detached and separate from the interest of Nations: and while they appear to quarrel, they agree to plunder. Nothing can be more terrible to a Court or Courtier than the Revolution of France. That which is a blessing to Nations is bitterness to them: and as their existence depends on the duplicity of a country, they tremble at the approach of principles, and dread the precedent that threatens their overthrow.

# CONCLUSION

Reason and Ignorance, the opposites of each other, influence the great bulk of mankind. If either of these can be rendered sufficiently extensive in a country, the machinery of Government goes easily on. Reason obeys itself; and Ignorance submits to whatever is dictated to it.

The two modes of the Government which prevail in the world, are:

*First*, Government by election and representation.

*Secondly*, Government by hereditary succession.

The former is generally known by the name of republic; the latter by that of monarchy and aristocracy.

Those two distinct and opposite forms erect themselves on the two distinct and opposite bases of Reason and Ignorance.—As the exercise of Government requires talents and abilities, and as talents and abilities cannot have hereditary descent, it is evident that hereditary succession requires a belief from man to which his reason cannot subscribe, and which can only be established upon his ignorance; and the more ignorant any country is, the better it is fitted for this species of Government.

On the contrary, Government, in a well-constituted republic, requires no belief from man beyond what his reason can give. He sees the *rationale* of the whole system, its origin and its operation; and as it is best supported when best understood, the human faculties act with boldness, and acquire, under this form of government, a gigantic manliness.

As, therefore, each of those forms acts on a different base, the one moving freely by the aid of reason, the other by ignorance; we have next to consider, what it is that gives motion to that species of Government which is called mixed Government, or, as it is sometimes ludicrously styled, a Government of *this, that* and *t'other*.

The moving power in this species of Government is, of necessity, Corruption. However imperfect election and representation may be in mixed Governments, they still give exercise to a greater portion of reason than is convenient to the hereditary Part; and therefore it becomes necessary to buy the reason up. A mixed Government is an imperfect everything, cementing and soldering the discordant parts together by corruption, to act as a whole. Mr. Burke appears highly disgusted that France, since she had resolved on a revolution, did not adopt what he calls "A British Constitution"; and the regretful manner in which he expresses himself on this occasion implies a suspicion that the British Constitution needed something to keep its defects in countenance.

In mixed Governments there is no responsibility: the parts cover each other till responsibility is lost; and the corruption which moves the machine, contrives at the same time its own escape. When it is laid down as a maxim, that *a King can do no wrong*, it places him in a state of similar security with that of idiots and persons insane, and responsibility is out of the question with respect to himself. It then descends upon the Minister, who shelters himself under a majority in Parliament, which, by places, pensions, and corruption, he can always command; and that majority justifies itself by the same authority with which it protects the Minister. In this rotatory motion, responsibility is thrown off from the parts, and from the whole.

When there is a Part in a Government which can do no wrong, it implies that it does nothing; and is only the machine of another power, by whose advice and direction it acts. What is supposed to be the King in the mixed Governments, is the Cabinet; and as the Cabinet is always a part of the Parliament, and the members justifying in one character what they advise and act in another, a mixed Government becomes a continual enigma; entailing upon a country by the quantity of corruption necessary to solder the parts, the expense of supporting all the forms of government at once, and finally resolving itself into a Government by Committee; in which the advisers, the actors, the approvers, the justifiers, the persons responsible, and the persons not responsible, are the same persons.

By this pantomimical contrivance, and change of scene and character, the parts help each other out in matters which neither of them singly would assume to act. When money is to be obtained, the mass of variety apparently dissolves, and a profusion of parliamentary praises passes between the parts. Each admires with astonishment, the wisdom, the liberality, the disinterestedness of the other: and all of them breathe a pitying sigh at the burthens of the Nation.

But in a well-constituted republic, nothing of this soldering, praising, and pitying, can take place; the representation being equal throughout the country, and complete in itself, however it may be arranged into legislative and executive, they have all one and the same natural source. The parts are not foreigners to each other, like democracy, aristocracy, and monarchy. As there are no discordant distinctions, there is nothing to corrupt by compromise, nor confound by contrivance. Public measures appeal of themselves to the understanding of the Nation, and, resting on their own merits, disown any flattering applications to vanity. The continual whine of lamenting the burden of taxes, however successfully it may be practised in mixed Governments, is inconsistent with the sense and spirit of a republic. If taxes are necessary, they are of course advantageous; but if they require an apology, the apology itself implies an impeachment. Why, then, is man thus imposed upon, or why does he impose upon himself?

When men are spoken of as kings and subjects, or when Government is mentioned under the distinct and combined heads of monarchy, aristocracy, and democracy, what is it that *reasoning* man is to understand by the terms? If there really existed in the world two or more distinct and separate *elements* of human power, we should then see the several origins to which those terms would descriptively apply; but as there is but one species of man, there can be but one element of human power; and that element is man himself. Monarchy, aristocracy, and democracy, are but creatures of imagination; and a thousand such may be contrived as well as three.

\* \* \* \*

From the Revolutions of America and France, and the symptoms that have appeared in other countries, it is evident that the opinion of the world is changing with respect to systems of Government, and that revolutions are not within the compass of political calculations. The progress of time and circumstances, which men assign to the accomplishment of great changes, is too mechanical to measure the force of the mind, and the rapidity of reflection, by which revolutions are generated: All the old governments have received a shock from those that already appear, and which were once more improbable, and are a greater subject of wonder, than a general revolution in Europe would be now.

When we survey the wretched condition of man, under the monarchical and hereditary systems of Government, dragged from his home by one power, or driven by another, and impoverished by taxes more than by enemies, it becomes evident that those systems are bad, and that a general revolution in the principle and construction of Governments is necessary.

What is government more than the management of the affairs of a Nation? It is not, and from its nature cannot be, the property of any particular man or family, but of the whole community, at whose expense it is supported; and though by force and contrivance it has been usurped into an inheritance, the usurpation cannot alter the right of things. Sovereignty, as a matter of right, appertains to the Nation only, and not to any individual; and a Nation has at all times an inherent indefeasible right to abolish any form of Government it finds inconvenient, and to establish such as accords with its interest, disposition and happiness. The romantic and barbarous distinction of men into Kings and subjects, though it may suit the condition of courtiers, cannot that of citizens; and is exploded by the principle upon which Governments are now founded. Every citizen is a member of the Sovereignty, and, as such, can acknowledge no personal subjection; and his obedience can be only to the laws.

When men think of what Government is, they must necessarily suppose it to possess a knowledge of all the objects and matters upon which its authority is to be exercised. In this view of Government, the republican system, as established by America and France, operates to embrace the whole of a Nation; and the knowledge necessary to the interest of all the parts, is to be found in the center, which the parts by representation form: But the old Governments are on a construction that excludes knowledge as well as happiness; government by Monks, who knew nothing of the world beyond the walls of a Convent, is as consistent as government by Kings.

What were formerly called Revolutions, were little more than a change of persons, or an alteration of local circumstances. They rose and fell like things of course, and had nothing in their existence or their fate that could influence beyond the spot that produced them. But what we now see in the world, from the Revolutions of America and France, are a renovation of the natural order of things, a system of principles as universal as truth and the existence of man, and combining moral with political happiness and national prosperity.

"I. Men are born, and always continue, free and equal in respect of their rights. Civil distinctions, therefore, can be founded only on public utility.

"II. The end of all political associations is the preservation of the natural and imprescriptible rights of man; and these rights are liberty, property, security, and resistance of oppression.

"III. The nation is essentially the source of all sovereignty; nor can any *individual*, or *any body of Men*, be entitled to any authority which is not expressly derived from it."

In these principles, there is nothing to throw a Nation into confusion by inflaming ambition. They are calculated to call forth wisdom and abilities, and to exercise them for the public good, and not for the emolument or aggrandisement of particular descriptions of men or families. Monarchical sovereignty, the enemy of mankind, and the source of misery, is abolished; and the sovereignty itself is restored to its natural and original place, the Nation. Were this the case throughout Europe, the cause of wars would be taken away.

It is attributed to Henry the Fourth of France, a man of enlarged and benevolent heart, that he proposed, about the year 1610, a plan for abolishing war in Europe. The plan consisted in constituting an European Congress, or as the French authors style it, a Pacific Republic; by appointing delegates from the several Nations who were to act as a Court of arbitration in any disputes that might arise between Nation and Nation.

Had such a plan been adopted at the time it was proposed, the taxes of England and France, as two of the parties, would have been at least ten millions sterling annually to each Nation less than they were at the commencement of the French Revolution.

To conceive a cause why such a plan has not been adopted (and that instead of a Congress for the purpose of *preventing* war, it has been called only to *terminate* a war, after a fruitless expense of several years) it will be necessary to consider the interest of Governments as a distinct interest to that of Nations.

Whatever is the cause of taxes to a Nation, becomes also the means of revenue to Government. Every war terminates with an addition of taxes, and consequently with an addition of revenue; and in any event of war, in the manner they are now commenced and concluded, the power and interest of Governments are increased. War, therefore, from its productiveness, as it easily furnishes the pretence of necessity for taxes and appointments to places and offices, becomes a principal part of the system of old Governments; and to establish any mode to abolish war, however advantageous it might be to Nations, would be to take from such Government the most lucrative of its branches. The frivolous matters upon which war is made, show the disposition and avidity of Governments to uphold the system of war, and betray the motives upon which they act.

Why are not Republics plunged into war, but because the nature of their Government does not admit of an interest distinct from that of the Nation? Even Holland, though an ill-constructed Republic, and with a commerce extending over the world, existed nearly a century without war: and the instant the form of Government was changed in France, the republican principles of peace and domestic prosperity and economy arose with the new Government; and the same consequences would follow the cause in other Nations.

As war is the system of Government on the old construction, the animosity which Nations reciprocally entertain, is nothing more than what the policy of their Governments excites to keep up the spirit of the system. Each Government accuses the other of perfidy, intrigue, and ambition, as a means of heating the imagination of their respective Nations, and incensing them to hostilities. Man is not the enemy of man, but through the medium of a false system of Government. Instead, therefore, of exclaiming against the ambition of Kings, the exclamation should be directed against the principle of such Governments; and instead of seeking to reform the individual, the wisdom of a Nation should apply itself to reform the system.

Whether the forms and maxims of Governments which are still in practice, were adapted to the condition of the world at the period they were established, is not in this case the question. The older they are, the less correspondence can they have with the present state of things. Time, and change of circumstances and opinions, have the same progressive effect in rendering modes of Government obsolete as they have upon customs and manners.—Agriculture, commerce, manufactures, and the tranquil arts, by which the prosperity of Nations is best promoted, require a different system of Government, and a different species of knowledge to direct its operations, than what might have been required in the former condition of the world.

As it is not difficult to perceive, from the enlightened state of mankind, that hereditary Governments are verging to their decline, and that Revolutions on the broad basis of national sovereignty and Government by representation, are making their way in Europe, it would be an act of wisdom to anticipate their approach, and produce Revolutions by reason and accommodation, rather than commit them to the issue of convulsions.

From what we now see, nothing of reform in the political world ought to be held improbable. It is an age of Revolutions, in which everything may be looked for. The intrigue of Courts, by which the system of war is kept up, may provoke a confederation of Nations to abolish it: and an European Congress to patronise the progress of free Government, and promote the civilisation of Nations with each other, is an event nearer in probability, than once were the revolutions and alliance of France and America.

## THE RIGHTS OF MAN

## PART THE SECOND, COMBINING
## PRINCIPLE AND PRACTICE

# FRENCH TRANSLATOR'S
# PREFACE
## *(1792)*

The work of which we offer a translation to the public has created the greatest sensation in England. Paine, that man of freedom, who seems born to preach "Common Sense" to the whole world with the same success as in America, explains in it to the people of England the theory of the practice of the Rights of Man.

Owing to the prejudices that still govern that nation, the author has been obliged to condescend to answer Mr. Burke. He has done so more especially in an extended preface which is nothing but a piece of very tedious controversy, in which he shows himself very sensitive to criticisms that do not really affect him. To translate it seemed an insult to the *free French people*, and similar reasons have led the editors to suppress also a dedicatory epistle addressed by Paine to Lafayette.

The French can no longer endure dedicatory epistles. A man should write privately to those he esteems: when he publishes a book his thoughts should be offered to the public alone. Paine, that uncorrupted friend of freedom, believed too in the sincerity of Lafayette. So easy is it to deceive men of single-minded purpose! Bred at a distance from courts, that austere American does not seem any more on his guard against the artful ways and speech of courtiers than some Frenchmen who resemble him.

# TO M. DE LA FAYETTE

After an acquaintance of nearly fifteen years in difficult situations in America, and various consultations in Europe, I feel a pleasure in presenting to you this small treatise, in gratitude for your services to my beloved America, and as a testimony of my esteem for the virtues, public and private, which I know you to possess.

The only point upon which I could ever discover that we differed was not as to principles of government, but as to time. For my own part I think it equally as injurious to good principles to permit them to linger, as to push them on too fast. That which you suppose accomplishable in fourteen or fifteen years, I may believe practicable in a much shorter period. Mankind, as it appears to me, are always ripe enough to understand their true interest, provided it be presented clearly to their understanding, and that in a manner not to create suspicion by anything like self-design, nor offend by assuming too much. Where we would wish to reform we must not reproach.

When the American revolution was established I felt a disposition to sit serenely down and enjoy the calm. It did not appear to me that any object could afterwards arise great enough to make me quit tranquility and feel as I had felt before. But when principle, and not place, is the energetic cause of action, a man, I find, is everywhere the same.

I am now once more in the public world; and as I have not a right to contemplate on so many years of remaining life as you have, I have resolved to labour as fast as I can; and as I am anxious for your aid and your company, I wish you to hasten your principles and overtake me.

If you make a campaign the ensuing spring, which it is most probable there will be no occasion for, I will come and join you. Should the campaign commence, I hope it will terminate in the extinction of German despotism, and in establishing the freedom of all Germany. When France shall be surrounded with revolutions she will be in peace and safety, and her taxes, as well as those of Germany, will consequently become less.

Your sincere,

Affectionate Friend,

*Thomas Paine*

London, Feb. 9, 1792

# PREFACE

When I began the chapter entitled the "Conclusion" in the former part of the *Rights of Man*, published last year, it was my intention to have extended it to a greater length; but in casting the whole matter in my mind, which I wish to add, I found that it must either make the work too bulky, or contract my plan too much. I therefore brought it to a close as soon as the subject would admit, and reserved what I had further to say to another opportunity.

Several other reasons contributed to produce this determination. I wished to know the manner in which a work, written in a style of thinking and expression different to what had been customary in England, would be received before I proceeded farther. A great field was opening to the view of mankind by means of the French Revolution. Mr. Burke's outrageous opposition thereto brought the controversy into England. He attacked principles which he knew (from information) I would contest with him, because they are principles I believe to be good, and which I have contributed to establish, and conceive myself bound to defend. Had he not urged the controversy, I had most probably been a silent man.

Another reason for deferring the remainder of the work was, that Mr. Burke promised in his first publication to renew the subject at another opportunity, and to make a comparison of what he called the English and French Constitutions. I therefore held myself in reserve for him. He has published two works since, without doing this: which he certainly would not have omitted, had the comparison been in his favour.

In his last work, his *"Appeal from the New to the Old Whigs,"* he has quoted about ten pages from the *Rights of Man*, and having given himself the trouble of doing this, says he "shall not attempt in the smallest degree to refute them," meaning the principles therein contained. I am enough acquainted with Mr. Burke to know that he would if he could. But instead of contesting them, he immediately after consoles himself with saying that "he has done his part."—He has not done his part. He has not performed his promise of a comparison of constitutions. He started the controversy, he gave the challenge, and has fled from it; and he is now a case in point with his own opinion that "*the age of chivalry is gone!*"

The title, as well as the substance of his last work, his "*Appeal,*" is his condemnation. Principles must stand on their own merits, and if they are good they certainly will. To put them under the shelter of other men's authority, as Mr. Burke has done, serves to bring them into suspicion. Mr. Burke is not very fond of dividing his honours, but in this case he is artfully dividing the disgrace.

But who are those to whom Mr. Burke has made his appeal? A set of childish thinkers, and half-way politicians born in the last century, men who went no farther with any principle than as it suited their purposes as a party; the nation was always left out of the question; and this has been the character of every party from that day to this. The nation sees nothing of such works, or such politics, worthy its attention. A little matter will move a party, but it must be something great that moves a nation.

Though I see nothing in Mr. Burke's "Appeal" worth taking much notice of, there is, however, one expression upon which I shall offer a few remarks. After quoting largely from the *Rights of Man*, and declining to contest the principles contained in that work, he says: "This will most probably be done (*if such writings shall be thought to deserve any other refutation than that of criminal justice*) by others, who may think with Mr. Burke and with the same zeal."

In the first place, it has not yet been done by anybody. Not less, I believe, than eight or ten pamphlets intended as answers to the former part of the *Rights of Man* have been published by different persons, and not one of them to my knowledge, has extended to a second edition, nor are even the titles of them so much as generally remembered. As I am averse to unnecessary multiplying publications, I have answered none of them. And as I believe that a man may write himself out of reputation when nobody else can do it, I am careful to avoid that rock.

But as I would decline unnecessary publications on the one hand, so would I avoid everything that might appear like sullen pride on the other. If Mr. Burke, or any person on his side the question, will produce an answer to the *Rights of Man* that shall extend to a half, or even to a fourth part of the number of copies to which the *Rights of Man* extended, I will reply to his work. But until this be done, I shall so far take the sense of the public for my guide (and the world knows I am not a flatterer) that what they do not think worth while to read, is not worth mine to answer. I suppose the number of copies to which the first part of the *Rights of Man* extended, taking England, Scotland, and Ireland, is not less than between forty and fifty thousand.

I now come to remark on the remaining part of the quotation I have made from Mr. Burke.

"If," says he, "such writings shall be thought to deserve any other refutation than that of *criminal* justice."

Pardoning the pun, it must be *criminal* justice indeed that should condemn a work as a substitute for not being able to refute it. The greatest condemnation that could be passed upon it would be a refutation. But in proceeding by the method Mr. Burke alludes to, the condemnation would, in the final event, pass upon the criminality of the process and not upon the work, and in this case, I had rather be the author, than be either the judge or the jury that should condemn it.

But to come at once to the point. I have differed from some professional gentlemen on the subject of prosecutions, and I since find they are falling into my opinion, which I will here state as fully, but as concisely as I can.

I will first put a case with respect to any law, and then compare it with a government, or with what in England is, or has been, called a constitution.

It would be an act of despotism, or what in England is called arbitrary power, to make a law to prohibit investigating the principles, good or bad, on which such a law, or any other is founded.

If a law be bad it is one thing to oppose the practice of it, but it is quite a different thing to expose its errors, to reason on its defects, and to show cause why it should be repealed, or why another ought to be substituted in its place. I have always held it an opinion (making it also my practice) that it is better to obey a bad law, making use at the same time of every argument to show its errors and procure its repeal, than forcibly to violate it; because the precedent of breaking a bad law might weaken the force, and lead to a discretionary violation, of those which are good.

The case is the same with respect to principles and forms of government, or to what are called constitutions and the parts of which they are, composed.

It is for the good of nations and not for the emolument or aggrandisement of particular individuals, that government ought to be established, and that mankind are at the expense of supporting it. The defects of every government and constitution both as to principle and form, must, on a parity of reasoning, be as open to discussion as the defects of a law, and it is a duty which every man owes to society to point them out. When those defects, and the means of remedying them, are generally seen by a Nation, that Nation will reform its government or its constitution in the one case, as the government repealed or reformed the law in the other. The operation of government is restricted to the making and the administering of laws; but it is to a Nation that the right of forming or reforming, generating or regenerating constitutions and governments belong; and consequently those subjects, as subjects of investigation, are always before a country *as a matter of right*, and cannot, without invading the general rights of that country, be made subjects for prosecution. On this ground I will meet Mr. Burke whenever he please. It is better that the whole argument should come out than to seek to stifle it. It was himself that opened the controversy, and he ought not to desert it.

I do not believe that monarchy and aristocracy will continue seven years longer in any of the enlightened countries in Europe. If better reasons can be shown for them than against them, they will stand; if the contrary, they will not. Mankind are not now to be told they shall not think, or they shall not read; and publications that go no farther than to investigate principles of government, to invite men to reason and to reflect, and to show the errors and excellences of different systems, have a right to appear. If they do not excite attention, they are not worth the trouble of a prosecution; and if they do, the prosecution will amount to nothing, since it cannot amount to a prohibition of reading. This would be a sentence on the public, instead of the author, and would also be the most effectual mode of making or hastening revolution.

On all cases that apply universally to a nation, with respect to systems of government, a jury of *twelve* men is not competent to decide. Where there are no witnesses to be examined, no facts to be proved, and where the whole matter is before the whole public, and the merits or demerits of it resting on their opinion; and where there is nothing to be known in a court, but what every body knows out of it, every twelve men is equally as good a jury as the other, and would most probably reverse each other's verdict; or, from the variety of their opinions, not be able to form one. It is one case, whether a Nation approve a work, or a plan; but it is quite another case, whether it will commit to any such jury the power of determining whether that Nation have a right to, or shall reform its government or not. I mention those cases that Mr. Burke may see I have not written on Government without reflecting on what is Law, as well as on what are Rights.——The only effectual jury in such cases would be a convention of the whole Nation fairly elected; for in all such cases the whole Nation is the vicinage. If Mr. Burke will propose such a jury, I will waive all privileges of being the citizen of another country, and, defending its principles, abide the issue, provided he will do the same; for my opinion is, that his work and his principles would be condemned instead of mine.

As to the prejudices which men have from education and habit, in favour of any particular form or system of government, those prejudices have yet to stand the test of reason and reflection. In fact, such prejudices are nothing. No man is prejudiced in favour of a thing, knowing it to be wrong. He is attached to it on the belief of its being right; and when he sees it is not so, the prejudice will be gone. We have but a defective idea of what prejudice is. It *might be said*, that until men think for themselves the whole is prejudice, and *not opinion*; for that only is opinion which is the result of reason and reflection. I offer this remark, that Mr. Burke may not confide too much in what have been the customary prejudices of the country.

I do not believe that the people of England have ever been fairly and candidly dealt by. They have been imposed upon by parties, and by men assuming the character of leaders. It is time that the Nation should rise above those trifles. It is time to dismiss that inattention which has so long been the encouraging cause of stretching taxation to excess. It is time to dismiss all those songs and toasts which are calculated to enslave, and operate to suffocate reflection. On all such subjects men have but to think, and they will neither act wrong nor be misled. To say that any people are not fit for freedom, is to make poverty their choice, and to say they had rather be loaded with taxes than not. If such a case could be proved, it would equally prove that those who govern are not fit to govern them, for they are a part of the same national mass.

But admitting governments to be changed all over Europe; it certainly may be done without convulsion or revenge. It is not worth making changes or revolutions, unless it be for some great national benefit: and when this shall appear to a Nation, the danger will be, as in America and France, to those who oppose; and with this reflection I close my Preface.

*Thomas Paine*
London, Feb. 9, 1792

# INTRODUCTION

What Archimedes said of the mechanical powers, may be applied to Reason and Liberty. *"Had we,"* said he, *"a place to stand upon, we might raise the world."*

The revolution of America presented in politics what was only theory in mechanics. So deeply rooted were all the governments of the old world, and so effectually had the tyranny and the antiquity of habit established itself over the mind, that no beginning could be made in Asia, Africa, or Europe, to reform the political condition of man. Freedom had been hunted round the globe; reason was considered as rebellion; and the slavery of fear had made men afraid to think.

But such is the irresistible nature of truth, that all it asks—and all it wants—is the liberty of appearing. The sun needs no inscription to distinguish him from darkness; and no sooner did the American governments display themselves to the world, than despotism felt a shock and man began to contemplate redress.

The independence of America, considered merely as a separation from England, would have been a matter but of little importance, had it not been accompanied by a revolution in the principles and practice of governments. She made a stand, not for herself only, but for the world, and looked beyond the advantages herself could receive. Even the Hessian, though hired to fight against her, may live to bless his defeat; and England, condemning the viciousness of its government, rejoice in its miscarriage.

As America was the only spot in the political world where the principle of universal reformation could begin, so also was it the best in the natural world. An assemblage of circumstances conspired, not only to give birth, but to add gigantic maturity to its principles. The scene which that country presents to the eye of a spectator, has something in it which generates and encourages great ideas. Nature appears to him in magnitude. The mighty objects he beholds, act upon his mind by enlarging it, and he partakes of the greatness he contemplates.— Its first settlers were emigrants from different European Nations, and of diversified professions of religion, retiring from the governmental persecutions of the old world, and meeting in the new, not as enemies, but as brothers. The wants which necessarily accompany the cultivation of a wilderness produced among them a state of society, which countries long harassed by the quarrels and intrigues of governments, had neglected to cherish. In such a situation man becomes what he ought. He sees his species, not with the inhuman idea of a natural enemy, but as kindred; and the example shows to the artificial world, that man must go back to Nature for information.

From the rapid progress which America makes in every species of improvement, it is rational to conclude that, if the governments of Asia, Africa, and Europe had begun on a principle similar to that of America, or had not been very early corrupted therefrom, those countries must by this time have been in a far superior condition to what they are. Age after age has passed away, for no other purpose than to behold their wretchedness. Could we suppose a spectator who knew nothing of the world, and who was put into it merely to make his observations, he would take a great part of the old world to be new, just struggling with the difficulties and hardships of an infant settlement. He could not suppose that the hordes of miserable poor with which old countries abound could be any other than those who had not yet had time to provide for themselves. Little would he think they were the consequence of what in such countries they call government.

If, from the more wretched parts of the old world, we look at those which are in an advanced stage of improvement we still find the greedy hand of government thrusting itself into every corner and crevice of industry, and grasping the spoil of the multitude. Invention is continually exercised to furnish new pretences for revenue and taxation. It watches prosperity as its prey, and permits none to escape without a tribute.

As revolutions have begun (and as the probability is always greater against a thing beginning, than of proceeding after it has begun), it is natural to expect that other revolutions will follow. The amazing and still increasing expenses with which old governments are conducted, the numerous wars they engage in or provoke, the embarrassments they throw in the way of universal civilisation and commerce, and the oppression and usurpation acted at home, have wearied out the patience, and exhausted the property of the world. In such a situation, and with such examples already existing, revolutions are to be looked for. They are become subjects of universal conversation, and may be considered as the *Order of the day*.

If systems of government can be introduced less expensive and more productive of general happiness than those which have existed, all attempts to oppose their progress will in the end be fruitless. Reason, like time, will make its own way, and prejudice will fall in a combat with interest. If universal peace, civilisation, and commerce are ever to be the happy lot of man, it cannot be accomplished but by a revolution in the system of governments. All the monarchical governments are military. War is their trade, plunder and revenue their objects. While such governments continue, peace has not the absolute security of a day. What is the history of all monarchical governments but a disgustful picture of human wretchedness, and the accidental respite of a few years' repose? Wearied with war, and tired with human butchery, they sat down to rest, and called it peace. This certainly is not the condition that heaven intended for man; and if *this be monarchy*, well might monarchy be reckoned among the sins of the Jews.

The revolutions which formerly took place in the world had nothing in them that interested the bulk of mankind. They extended only to a change of persons and measures, but not of principles, and rose or fell among the common transactions of the moment. What we now behold may not improperly be called a *"counter-revolution."* Conquest and tyranny, at some earlier period, dispossessed man of his rights, and he is now recovering them. And as the tide of all human affairs has its ebb and flow in directions contrary to each other, so also is it in this. Government founded on a moral *theory, on a system of universal peace, on the indefeasible hereditary Rights of Man*, is now revolving from west to east by a stronger impulse than the government of the sword revolved from east to west. It interests not particular individuals, but nations in its progress, and promises a new era to the human race.

The danger to which the success of revolutions is most exposed is that of attempting them before the principles on which they proceed, and the advantages to result from them, are sufficiently seen and understood. Almost everything appertaining to the circumstances of a nation, has been absorbed and confounded under the general and mysterious word *government*. Though it avoids taking to its account the errors it commits, and the mischiefs it occasions, it fails not to arrogate to itself whatever has the appearance of prosperity. It robs industry of its honours, by pedantically making itself the cause of its effects; and purloins from the general character of man, the merits that appertain to him as a social being.

It may therefore be of use in this day of revolutions to discriminate between those things which are the effect of government, and those which are not. This will best be done by taking a review of society and civilisation, and the consequences resulting therefrom, as things distinct from what are called governments. By beginning with this investigation, we shall be able to assign effects to their proper causes and analyse the mass of common errors.

# CHAPTER I.

## OF SOCIETY AND CIVILISATION

Great part of that order which reigns among mankind is not the effect of government. It has its origin in the principles of society and the natural constitution of man. It existed prior to government, and would exist if the formality of government was abolished. The mutual dependence and reciprocal interest which man has upon man, and all the parts of civilised community upon each other, create that great chain of connection which holds it together. The landholder, the farmer, the manufacturer, the merchant, the tradesman, and every occupation, prospers by the aid which each receives from the other, and from the whole. Common interest regulates their concerns, and forms their law; and the laws which common usage ordains, have a greater influence than the laws of government. In fine, society performs for itself almost everything which is ascribed to government.

To understand the nature and quantity of government proper for man, it is necessary to attend to his character. As Nature created him for social life, she fitted him for the station she intended. In all cases she made his natural wants greater than his individual powers. No one man is capable, without the aid of society, of supplying his own wants, and those wants, acting upon every individual, impel the whole of them into society, as naturally as gravitation acts to a centre.

But she has gone further. She has not only forced man into society by a diversity of wants which the reciprocal aid of each other can supply, but she has implanted in him a system of social affections, which, though not necessary to his existence, are essential to his happiness. There is no period in life when this love for society ceases to act. It begins and ends with our being.

If we examine with attention into the composition and constitution of man, the diversity of his wants, and the diversity of talents in different men for reciprocally accommodating the wants of each other, his propensity to society, and consequently to preserve the advantages resulting from it, we shall easily discover, that a great part of what is called government is mere imposition.

Government is no farther necessary than to supply the few cases to which society and civilisation are not conveniently competent; and instances are not wanting to show, that everything which government can usefully add thereto, has been performed by the common consent of society, without government.

For upwards of two years from the commencement of the American War, and to a longer period in several of the American States, there were no established forms of government. The old governments had been abolished, and the country was too much occupied in defence to employ its attention in establishing new governments; yet during this interval order and harmony were preserved as inviolate as in any country in Europe. There is a natural aptness in man, and more so in society, because it embraces a greater variety of abilities and resource, to accommodate itself to whatever situation it is in. The instant formal government is abolished, society begins to act: a general association takes place, and common interest produces common security.

So far is it from being true, as has been pretended, that the abolition of any formal government is the dissolution of society, that it acts by a contrary impulse, and brings the latter the closer together. All that part of its organisation which it had committed to its government, devolves again upon itself, and acts through its medium. When men, as well from natural instinct as from reciprocal benefits, have habituated themselves to social and civilised life, there is always enough of its principles in practice to carry them through any changes they may find necessary or convenient to make in their government. In short, man is so naturally a creature of society that it is almost impossible to put him out of it.

Formal government makes but a small part of civilised life; and when even the best that human wisdom can devise is established, it is a thing more in name and idea than in fact. It is to the great and fundamental principles of society and civilisation—to the common usage universally consented to, and mutually and reciprocally maintained—to the unceasing circulation of interest, which, passing through its million channels, invigorates the whole mass of civilised man—it is to these things, infinitely more than to anything which even the best instituted government can perform, that the safety and prosperity of the individual and of the whole depends.

The more perfect civilisation is, the less occasion has it for government, because the more does it regulate its own affairs, and govern itself; but so contrary is the practice of old governments to the reason of the case, that the expenses of them increase in the proportion they ought to diminish. It is but few general laws that civilised life requires, and those of such common usefulness, that whether they are enforced by the forms of government or not, the effect will be nearly the same. If we consider what the principles are that first condense men into society, and what are the motives that regulate their mutual intercourse afterwards, we shall find, by the time we arrive at what is called government, that nearly the whole of the business is performed by the natural operation of the parts upon each other.

Man, with respect to all those matters, is more a creature of consistency than he is aware, or than governments would wish him to believe. All the great laws of society are laws of nature. Those of trade and commerce, whether with respect to the intercourse of individuals or of nations, are laws of mutual and reciprocal interest. They are followed and obeyed, because it is the interest of the parties so to do, and not on account of any formal laws their governments may impose or interpose.

But how often is the natural propensity to society disturbed or destroyed by the operations of government! When the latter, instead of being ingrafted on the principles of the former, assumes to exist for itself, and acts by partialities of favour and oppression, it becomes the cause of the mischiefs it ought to prevent.

If we look back to the riots and tumults which at various times have happened in England, we shall find that they did not proceed from the want of a government, but that government was itself the generating cause; instead of consolidating society it divided it; it deprived it of its natural cohesion, and engendered discontents and disorders which otherwise would not have existed. In those associations which men promiscuously form for the purpose of trade, or of any concern in which government is totally out of the question, and in which they act merely on the principles of society, we see how naturally the various parties unite; and this shows, by comparison, that governments, so far from being always the cause or means of order, are often the destruction of it. The riots of 1780 had no other source than the remains of those prejudices which the government itself had encouraged. But with respect to England there are also other causes.

Excess and inequality of taxation, however disguised in the means, never fail to appear in their effects. As a great mass of the community are thrown thereby into poverty and discontent, they are constantly on the brink of commotion; and deprived, as they unfortunately are, of the means of information, are easily heated to outrage. Whatever the apparent cause of any riots may be, the real one is always want of happiness. It shows that something is wrong in the system of government that injures the felicity by which society is to be preserved.

But as a fact is superior to reasoning, the instance of America presents itself to confirm these observations. If there is a country in the world where concord, according to common calculation, would be least expected, it is America. Made up as it is of people from different nations,* accustomed to different forms and habits of government, speaking different languages, and more different in their modes of worship, it would appear that the union of such a people was impracticable; but by the simple operation of constructing government on the principles of society and the rights of man, every difficulty retires, and all the parts are brought into cordial unison. There the poor are not oppressed, the rich are not privileged. Industry is not mortified by the splendid extravagance of a court rioting at its expense. Their taxes are few, because their government is just: and as there is nothing to render them wretched, there is nothing to engender riots and tumults.

A metaphysical man, like Mr. Burke, would have tortured his invention to discover how such a people could be governed. He would have supposed that some must be managed by fraud, others by force, and all by some contrivance; that genius must be hired to impose upon ignorance, and show and parade to fascinate the vulgar. Lost in the abundance of his researches, he would have resolved and re-resolved, and finally overlooked the plain and easy road that lay directly before him.

---

* That part of America which is generally called New-England, including New-Hampshire, Massachusetts, Rhode-Island, and Connecticut, is peopled chiefly by English descendants. In the state of New-York about half are Dutch, the rest English, Scotch, and Irish. In New-Jersey, a mixture of English and Dutch, with some Scotch and Irish. In Pennsylvania about one third are English, another Germans, and the remainder Scotch and Irish, with some Swedes. The States to the southward have a greater proportion of English than the middle States, but in all of them there is a mixture; and besides those enumerated, there are a considerable number of French, and some few of all the European nations, lying on the coast. The most numerous religious denomination are the Presbyterians; but no one sect is established above another, and all men are equally citizens. (Author's note)

One of the great advantages of the American Revolution has been, that it led to a discovery of the principles, and laid open the imposition, of governments. All the revolutions till then had been worked within the atmosphere of a court, and never on the grand floor of a nation. The parties were always of the class of courtiers; and whatever was their rage for reformation, they carefully preserved the fraud of the profession.

In all cases they took care to represent government as a thing made up of mysteries, which only themselves understood; and they hid from the understanding of the nation the only thing that was beneficial to know, namely, *That government is nothing more than a national association adding on the principles of society.*

Having thus endeavoured to show that the social and civilised state of man is capable of performing within itself almost everything necessary to its protection and government, it will be proper, on the other hand, to take a review of the present old governments, and examine whether their principles and practice are correspondent thereto.

# CHAPTER II.

## OF THE ORIGIN OF THE
## PRESENT OLD GOVERNMENTS

It is impossible that such governments as have hitherto existed in the world, could have commenced by any other means than a total violation of every principle sacred and moral. The obscurity in which the origin of all the present old governments is buried, implies the iniquity and disgrace with which they began. The origin of the present government of America and France will ever be remembered, because it is honourable to record it; but with respect to the rest, even Flattery has consigned them to the tomb of time, without an inscription.

It could have been no difficult thing in the early and solitary ages of the world, while the chief employment of men was that of attending flocks and herds, for a banditti of ruffians to overrun a country, and lay it under contributions. Their power being thus established, the chief of the band contrived to lose the name of Robber in that of Monarch; and hence the origin of Monarchy and Kings.

The origin of the Government of England, so far as relates to what is called its line of monarchy, being one of the latest, is perhaps the best recorded. The hatred which the Norman invasion and tyranny begat, must have been deeply rooted in the nation, to have outlived the contrivance to obliterate it. Though not a courtier will talk of the curfew-bell, not a village in England has forgotten it.

Those bands of robbers having parcelled out the world, and divided it into dominions, began, as is naturally the case, to quarrel with each other. What at first was obtained by violence was considered by others as lawful to be taken, and a second plunderer succeeded the first. They alternately invaded the dominions which each had assigned to himself, and the brutality with which they treated each other explains the original character of monarchy. It was ruffian torturing ruffian. The conqueror considered the conquered, not as his prisoner, but his property. He led him in triumph rattling in chains, and doomed him, at pleasure, to slavery or death. As time obliterated the history of their beginning, their successors assumed new appearances, to cut off the entail of their disgrace, but their principles and objects remained the same. What at first was plunder, assumed the softer name of revenue; and the power originally usurped, they affected to inherit.

From such beginning of governments, what could be expected but a continued system of war and extortion? It has established itself into a trade. The vice is not peculiar to one more than to another, but is the common principle of all. There does not exist within such governments sufficient stamina whereon to engraft reformation; and the shortest and most effectual remedy is to begin anew on the ground of the nation.

What scenes of horror, what perfection of iniquity, present themselves in contemplating the character and reviewing the history of such governments! If we would delineate human nature with a baseness of heart and hypocrisy of countenance that reflection would shudder at and humanity disown, it is kings, courts and cabinets that must sit for the portrait. Man, naturally as he is, with all his faults about him, is not up to the character.

Can we possibly suppose that if governments had originated in a right principle, and had not an interest in pursuing a wrong one, the world could have been in the wretched and quarrelsome condition we have seen it? What inducement has the farmer, while following the plough, to lay aside his peaceful pursuit, and go to war with the farmer of another country? or what inducement has the manufacturer? What is dominion to them, or to any class of men in a nation? Does it add an acre to any man's estate, or raise its value? Are not conquest and defeat each of the same price, and taxes the never-failing consequence?—Though this reasoning may be good to a nation, it is not so to a government. War is the Pharo-table of governments, and nations the dupes of the game.

If there is anything to wonder at in this miserable scene of governments more than might be expected, it is the progress which the peaceful arts of agriculture, manufacture and commerce have made beneath such a long accumulating load of discouragement and oppression. It serves to show that instinct in animals does not act with stronger impulse than the principles of society and civilisation operate in man. Under all discouragements, he pursues his object, and yields to nothing but impossibilities.

# CHAPTER III.

## OF THE OLD AND NEW SYSTEMS OF GOVERNMENT

Nothing can appear more contradictory than the principles on which the old governments began, and the condition to which society, civilisation and commerce are capable of carrying mankind. Government, on the old system, is an assumption of power, for the aggrandisement of itself; on the new, a delegation of power for the common benefit of society. The former supports itself by keeping up a system of war; the latter promotes a system of peace, as the true means of enriching a nation. The one encourages national prejudices; the other promotes universal society, as the means of universal commerce. The one measures its prosperity, by the quantity of revenue it extorts; the other proves its excellence, by the small quantity of taxes it requires.

Mr. Burke has talked of old and new Whigs. If he can amuse himself with childish names and distinctions, I shall not interrupt his pleasure. It is not to him, but to the Abbé Sieyes, that I address this chapter. I am already engaged to the latter gentleman to discuss the subject of monarchical government; and as it naturally occurs in comparing the old and new systems, I make this the opportunity of presenting to him my observations. I shall occasionally take Mr. Burke in my way.

Though it might be proved that the system of government now called the *new*, is the most ancient in principle of all that have existed, being founded on the original, inherent Rights of Man: yet, as tyranny and the sword have suspended the exercise of those rights for many centuries past, it serves better the purpose of distinction to call it the *new*, than to claim the right of calling it the old.

The first general distinction between those two systems, is, that the one now called the old is *hereditary*, either in whole or in part; and the new is entirely *representative*. It rejects all hereditary government:

First, As being an imposition on mankind.

Secondly, As inadequate to the purposes for which government is necessary.

With respect to the first of these heads—It cannot be proved by what right hereditary government could begin; neither does there exist within the compass of mortal power a right to establish it. Man has no authority over posterity in matters of personal right; and, therefore, no man, or body of men, had, or can have, a right to set up hereditary government. Were even ourselves to come again into existence, instead of being succeeded by posterity, we have not now the right of taking from ourselves the rights which would then be ours. On what ground, then, do we pretend to take them from others?

All hereditary government is in its nature tyranny. An heritable crown, or an heritable throne, or by what other fanciful name such things may be called, have no other significant explanation than that mankind are heritable property. To inherit a government, is to inherit the people, as if they were flocks and herds.

With respect to the second head, that of being inadequate to the purposes for which government is necessary, we have only to consider what government essentially is, and compare it with the circumstances to which hereditary succession is subject.

Government ought to be a thing always in full maturity. It ought to be so constructed as to be superior to all the accidents to which individual man is subject; and, therefore, hereditary succession, by being *subject to them all*, is the most irregular and imperfect of all the systems of government.

We have heard the *Rights of Man* called a levelling system; but the only system to which the word *levelling* is truly applicable, is the hereditary monarchical system. It is a system of *mental levelling*. It indiscriminately admits every species of character to the same authority. Vice and virtue, ignorance and wisdom, in short, every quality good or bad, is put on the same level. Kings succeed each other, not as rationals, but as animals. It signifies not what their mental or moral characters are. Can we then be surprised at the abject state of the human mind in monarchical countries, when the government itself is formed on such an abject levelling system?—It has no fixed character. To-morrow it is one thing; to-morrow it is something else. It changes with the temper of every succeeding individual, and is subject to all the varieties of each. It is government through the medium of passions and accidents. It appears under all the various characters of childhood, decrepitude, dotage, a thing at nurse, in leading-strings, or in crutches. It reverses the wholesome order of nature. It occasionally puts children over men, and the conceits of nonage over wisdom and experience. In short, we cannot conceive a more ridiculous figure of government, than hereditary succession, in all its cases, presents.

Could it be made a decree in nature, or an edict registered in heaven, and man could know it, that virtue and wisdom should invariably appertain to hereditary succession, the objection to it would be removed; but when we see that nature acts as if she disowned and sported with the hereditary system; that the mental character of successors, in all countries, is below the average of human understanding; that one is a tyrant, another an idiot, a third insane, and some all three together, it is impossible to attach confidence to it, when reason in man has power to act.

It is not to the Abbé Sieyes that I need apply this reasoning; he has already saved me that trouble by giving his own opinion upon the case. "If it be asked," says he, "what is my opinion with respect to hereditary right, I answer without hesitation, That in good theory, an hereditary transmission of any power of office, can never accord with the laws of a true representation. Hereditaryship is, in this sense, as much an attaint upon principle, as an outrage upon society. But let us," continues he, "refer to the history of all elective monarchies and principalities: is there one in which the elective mode is not worse than the hereditary succession?"

As to debating on which is the worst of the two, it is admitting both to be bad; and herein we are agreed. The preference which the Abbé has given, is a condemnation of the thing that he prefers. Such a mode of reasoning on such a subject is inadmissible, because it finally amounts to an accusation upon Providence, as if she had left to man no other choice with respect to government than between two evils, the best of which he admits to be *"an attaint upon principle, and an outrage upon society."*

Passing over, for the present, all the evils and mischiefs which monarchy has occasioned in the world, nothing can more effectually prove its uselessness in a state of *civil government*, than making it hereditary. Would we make any office hereditary that required wisdom and abilities to fill it? And where wisdom and abilities are not necessary, such an office, whatever it may be, is superfluous or insignificant.

Hereditary succession is a burlesque upon monarchy. It puts it in the most ridiculous light, by presenting it as an office which any child or idiot may fill. It requires some talents to be a common mechanic; but to be a king requires only the animal figure of man—a sort of breathing automaton. This sort of superstition may last a few years more, but it cannot long resist the awakened reason and interest of man.

As to Mr. Burke, he is a stickler for monarchy, not altogether as a pensioner, if he is one, which I believe, but as a political man. He has taken up a contemptible opinion of mankind, who, in their turn, are taking up the same of him. He considers them as a herd of beings that must be governed by fraud, effigy, and show; and an idol would be as good a figure of monarchy with him, as a man. I will, however, do him the justice to say that, with respect to America, he has been very complimentary. He always contended, at least in my hearing, that the people of America were more enlightened than those of England, or of any country in Europe; and that therefore the imposition of show was not necessary in their governments.

Though the comparison between hereditary and elective monarchy, which the Abbé has made, is unnecessary to the case, because the representative system rejects both: yet, were I to make the comparison, I should decide contrary to what he has done.

The civil wars which have originated from contested hereditary claims, are more numerous, and have been more dreadful, and of longer continuance, than those which have been occasioned by election. All the civil wars in France arose from the hereditary system; they were either produced by hereditary claims, or by the imperfection of the hereditary form, which admits of regencies or monarchy at nurse. With respect to England, its history is full of the same misfortunes. The contests for succession between the houses of York and Lancaster lasted a whole century; and others of a similar nature have renewed themselves since that period. Those of 1715 and 1745 were of the same kind. The succession war for the crown of Spain embroiled almost half Europe. The disturbances of Holland are generated from the hereditaryship of the Stadtholder. A government calling itself free, with an hereditary office, is like a thorn in the flesh, that produces a fermentation which endeavours to discharge it.

But I might go further, and place also foreign wars, of whatever kind, to the same cause. It is by adding the evil of hereditary succession to that of monarchy, that a permanent family interest is created, whose constant objects are dominion and revenue. Poland, though an elective monarchy, has had fewer wars than those which are hereditary; and it is the only government that has made a voluntary essay, though but a small one, to reform the condition of the country.

Having thus glanced at a few of the defects of the old, or hereditary systems of government, let us compare it with the new, or representative system.

The representative system takes society and civilisation for its basis; nature, reason, and experience, for its guide.

Experience, in all ages, and in all countries, has demonstrated that it is impossible to control Nature in her distribution of mental powers. She gives them as she pleases. Whatever is the rule by which she, apparently to us, scatters them among mankind, that rule remains a secret to man. It would be as ridiculous to attempt to fix the hereditaryship of human beauty, as of wisdom. Whatever wisdom constituently is, it is like a seedless plant; it may be reared when it appears, but it cannot be voluntarily produced. There is always a sufficiency somewhere in the general mass of society for all purposes; but with respect to the parts of society, it is continually changing its place. It rises in one to-day, in another to-morrow, and has most probably visited in rotation every family of the earth, and again withdrawn.

As this is in the order of nature, the order of government must necessarily follow it, or government will, as we see it does, degenerate into ignorance. The hereditary system, therefore, is as repugnant to human wisdom as to human rights; and is as absurd as it is unjust.

As the republic of letters brings forward the best literary productions, by giving to genius a fair and universal chance; so the representative system of government is calculated to produce the wisest laws, by collecting wisdom from where it can be found. I smile to myself when I contemplate the ridiculous insignificance into which literature and all the sciences would sink, were they made hereditary; and I carry the same idea into governments. An hereditary governor is as inconsistent as an hereditary author. I know not whether Homer or Euclid had sons; but I will venture an opinion that if they had, and had left their works unfinished, those sons could not have completed them.

Do we need a stronger evidence of the absurdity of hereditary government than is seen in the descendants of those men, in any line of life, who once were famous? Is there scarcely an instance in which there is not a total reverse of the character? It appears as if the tide of mental faculties flowed as far as it could in certain channels, and then forsook its course, and arose in others. How irrational then is the hereditary system, which establishes channels of power, in company with which wisdom refuses to flow! By continuing this absurdity, man is perpetually in contradiction with himself; he accepts, for a king, or a chief magistrate, or a legislator, a person whom he would not elect for a constable.

It appears to general observation, that revolutions create genius and talents; but those events do no more than bring them forward. There is existing in man, a mass of sense lying in a dormant state, and which, unless something excites it to action, will descend with him, in that condition, to the grave. As it is to the advantage of society that the whole of its faculties should be employed, the construction of government ought to be such as to bring forward, by a quiet and regular operation, all that extent of capacity which never fails to appear in revolutions.

This cannot take place in the insipid state of hereditary government, not only because it prevents, but because it operates to benumb. When the mind of a nation is bowed down by any political superstition in its government, such as hereditary succession is, it loses a considerable portion of its powers on all other subjects and objects. Hereditary succession requires the same obedience to ignorance, as to wisdom; and when once the mind can bring itself to pay this indiscriminate reverence, it descends below the stature of mental manhood. It is fit to be great only in little things. It acts a treachery upon itself, and suffocates the sensations that urge the detection.

Though the ancient governments present to us a miserable picture of the condition of man, there is one which above all others exempts itself from the general description. I mean the democracy of the Athenians. We see more to admire, and less to condemn, in that great, extraordinary people, than in anything which history affords.

Mr. Burke is so little acquainted with constituent principles of government, that he confounds democracy and representation together. Representation was a thing unknown in the ancient democracies. In those the mass of the people met and enacted laws (grammatically speaking) in the first person. Simple democracy was no other than the common hall of the ancients. It signifies the *form*, as well as the public principle of the government. As those democracies increased in population, and the territory extended, the simple democratical form became unwieldy and impracticable; and as the system of representation was not known, the consequence was, they either degenerated convulsively into monarchies, or became absorbed into such as then existed. Had the system of representation been then understood, as it now is, there is no reason to believe that those forms of government, now called monarchical or aristocratical, would ever have taken place. It was the want of some method to consolidate the parts of society, after it became too populous, and too extensive for the simple democratical form, and also the lax and solitary condition of shepherds and herdsmen in other parts of the world, that afforded opportunities to those unnatural modes of government to begin.

As it is necessary to clear away the rubbish of errors, into which the subject of government has been thrown, I will proceed to remark on some others.

It has always been the political craft of courtiers and court-governments, to abuse something which they called republicanism; but what republicanism was, or is, they never attempt to explain. Let us examine a little into this case.

The only forms of government are the democratical, the aristocratical, the monarchical, and what is now called the representative.

What is called a *republic* is not any *particular form* of government. It is wholly characteristical of the purport, matter or object for which government ought to be instituted, and on which it is to be employed, *Res-Publica*, the public affairs, or the public good; or, literally translated, the *public thing*. It is a word of a good original, referring to what ought to be the character and business of government; and in this sense it is naturally opposed to the word *monarchy*, which has a base original signification. It means arbitrary power in an individual person; in the exercise of which, *himself*, and not the *res-publica*, is the object.

Every government that does not act on the principle of a *Republic*, or in other words, that does not make the *res-publica* its whole and sole object, is not a good government. Republican government is no other than government established and conducted for the interest of the public, as well individually as collectively. It is not necessarily connected with any particular form, but it most naturally associates with the representative form, as being best calculated to secure the end for which a nation is at the expense of supporting it.

Various forms of government have affected to style themselves a republic. Poland calls itself a republic, which is an hereditary aristocracy, with what is called an elective monarchy. Holland calls itself a republic, which is chiefly aristocratical, with an hereditary stadtholdership. But the government of America, which is wholly on the system of representation, is the only real Republic, in character and in practice, that now exists. Its government has no other object than the public business of the nation, and therefore it is properly a republic; and the Americans have taken care that This, and no other, shall always be the object of their government, by their rejecting everything hereditary, and establishing governments on the system of representation only. Those who have said that a republic is not a *form* of government calculated for countries of great extent, mistook, in the first place, the *business* of a government, for a *form* of government; for the *res-publica* equally appertains to every extent of territory and population. And, in the second place, if they meant anything with respect to *form*, it was the simple democratical form, such as was the mode of government in the ancient democracies, in which there was no representation. The case, therefore, is not, that a republic cannot be extensive, but that it cannot be extensive on the simple democratical form; and the question naturally presents itself, What is the best form of government for conducting the *Res-Publica*, or the *Public Business* of a nation, after it becomes too extensive and populous for the simple democratical form? It cannot be monarchy, because monarchy is subject to an objection of the same amount to which the simple democratical form was subject.

It is possible that an individual may lay down a system of principles, on which government shall be constitutionally established to any extent of territory. This is no more than an operation of the mind, acting by its own powers. But the practice upon those principles, as applying to the various and numerous circumstances of a nation, its agriculture, manufacture, trade, commerce, etc., etc., a knowledge of a different kind, and which can be had only from the various parts of society. It is an assemblage of practical knowledge, which no individual can possess; and therefore the monarchical form is as much limited, in useful practice, from the incompetency of knowledge, as was the democratical form, from the multiplicity of population. The one degenerates, by extension, into confusion; the other, into ignorance and incapacity, of which all the great monarchies are an evidence. The monarchical form, therefore, could not be a substitute for the democratical, because it has equal inconveniences.

Much less could it when made hereditary. This is the most effectual of all forms to preclude knowledge. Neither could the high democratical mind have voluntarily yielded itself to be governed by children and idiots, and all the motley insignificance of character, which attends such a mere animal system, the disgrace and the reproach of reason and of man.

As to the aristocratical form, it has the same vices and defects with the monarchical, except that the chance of abilities is better from the proportion of numbers, but there is still no security for the right use and application of them.*

Referring them to the original simple democracy, it affords the true data from which government on a large scale can begin. It is incapable of extension, not from its principle, but from the inconvenience of its form; and monarchy and aristocracy, from their incapacity. Retaining, then, democracy as the ground, and rejecting the corrupt systems of monarchy and aristocracy, the representative system naturally presents itself; remedying at once the defects of the simple democracy as to form, and the incapacity of the other two with respect to knowledge.

Simple democracy was society governing itself without the aid of secondary means. By ingrafting representation upon democracy, we arrive at a system of government capable of embracing and confederating all the various interests and every extent of territory and population; and that also with advantages as much superior to hereditary government, as the republic of letters is to hereditary literature.

It is on this system that the American government is founded. It is representation ingrafted upon democracy. It has fixed the form by a scale parallel in all cases to the extent of the principle. What Athens was in miniature America will be in magnitude. The one was the wonder of the ancient world; the other is becoming the admiration of the present. It is the easiest of all the forms of government to be understood and the most eligible in practice; and excludes at once the ignorance and insecurity of the hereditary mode, and the inconvenience of the simple democracy.

---

* For a character of aristocracy, the reader is referred to *Rights of Man*, Part I. (Author's note)

It is impossible to conceive a system of government capable of acting over such an extent of territory, and such a circle of interests, as is immediately produced by the operation of representation. France, great and populous as it is, is but a spot in the capaciousness of the system. It is preferable to simple democracy even in small territories. Athens, by representation, would have outrivalled her own democracy.

That which is called government, or rather that which we ought to conceive government to be, is no more than some common center in which all the parts of society unite. This cannot be accomplished by any method so conducive to the various interests of the community, as by the representative system. It concentrates the knowledge necessary to the interest of the parts, and of the whole. It places government in a state of constant maturity. It is, as has already been observed, never young, never old. It is subject neither to nonage, nor dotage. It is never in the cradle, nor on crutches. It admits not of a separation between knowledge and power, and is superior, as government always ought to be, to all the accidents of individual man, and is therefore superior to what is called monarchy.

A nation is not a body, the figure of which is to be represented by the human body; but is like a body contained within a circle, having a common center, in which every radius meets; and that center is formed by representation. To connect representation with what is called monarchy, is eccentric government. Representation is of itself the delegated monarchy of a nation, and cannot debase itself by dividing it with another.

Mr. Burke has two or three times, in his parliamentary speeches, and in his publications, made use of a jingle of words that convey no ideas. Speaking of government, he says, "It is better to have monarchy for its basis, and republicanism for its corrective, than republicanism for its basis, and monarchy for its corrective."—If he means that it is better to correct folly with wisdom, than wisdom with folly, I will no otherwise contend with him, than that it would be much better to reject the folly entirely.

But what is this thing which Mr. Burke calls monarchy? Will he explain it? All men can understand what representation is; and that it must necessarily include a variety of knowledge and talents. But what security is there for the same qualities on the part of monarchy? or, when the monarchy is a child, where then is the wisdom? What does it know about government? Who then is the monarch, or where is the monarchy? If it is to be performed by regency, it proves to be a farce. A regency is a mock species of republic, and the whole of monarchy deserves no better description. It is a thing as various as imagination can paint. It has none of the stable character that government ought to possess. Every succession is a revolution, and every regency a counter-revolution. The whole of it is a scene of perpetual court cabal and intrigue, of which Mr. Burke is himself an instance. To render monarchy consistent with government, the next in succession should not be born a child, but a man at once, and that man a Solomon. It is ridiculous that nations are to wait and government be interrupted till boys grow to be men.

Whether I have too little sense to see, or too much to be imposed upon; whether I have too much or too little pride, or of anything else, I leave out of the question; but certain it is, that what is called monarchy, always appears to me a silly, contemptible thing. I compare it to something kept behind a curtain, about which there is a great deal of bustle and fuss, and a wonderful air of seeming solemnity; but when, by any accident, the curtain happens to be open—and the company see what it is, they burst into laughter.

In the representative system of government, nothing of this can happen. Like the nation itself, it possesses a perpetual stamina, as well of body as of mind, and presents itself on the open theatre of the world in a fair and manly manner. Whatever are its excellences or defects, they are visible to all. It exists not by fraud and mystery; it deals not in cant and sophistry; but inspires a language that, passing from heart to heart, is felt and understood.

We must shut our eyes against reason, we must basely degrade our understanding, not to see the folly of what is called monarchy. Nature is orderly in all her works; but this is a mode of government that counteracts nature. It turns the progress of the human faculties upside down. It subjects age to be governed by children, and wisdom by folly.

On the contrary, the representative system is always parallel with the order and immutable laws of nature, and meets the reason of man in every part. For example:

In the American Federal Government, more power is delegated to the President of the United States than to any other individual member of Congress. He cannot, therefore, be elected to this office under the age of thirty-five years. By this time the judgment of man becomes more matured, and he has lived long enough to be acquainted with men and things, and the country with him.——But on the monarchial plan (exclusive of the numerous chances there are against every man born into the world, of drawing a prize in the lottery of human faculties), the next in succession, whatever he may be, is put at the head of a nation, and of a government, at the age of eighteen years. Does this appear like an action of wisdom? Is it consistent with the proper dignity and the manly character of a nation? Where is the propriety of calling such a lad the father of the people?——In all other cases, a person is a minor until the age of twenty-one years. Before this period, he is not trusted with the management of an acre of land, or with the heritable property of a flock of sheep, or an herd of swine; but, wonderful to tell! he may, at the age of eighteen years, be trusted with a nation.

That monarchy is all a bubble, a mere court artifice to procure money, is evident (at least to me) in every character in which it can be viewed. It would be impossible, on the rational system of representative government, to make out a bill of expenses to such an enormous amount as this deception admits. Government is not of itself a very chargeable institution. The whole expense of the federal government of America, founded, as I have already said, on the system of representation, and extending over a country nearly ten times as large as England, is but six hundred thousand dollars, or one hundred and thirty-five thousand pounds sterling.

I presume that no man in his sober senses will compare the character of any of the kings of Europe with that of General Washington. Yet, in France, and also in England, the expense of the civil list only, for the support of one man, is eight times greater than the whole expense of the federal government in America. To assign a reason for this, appears almost impossible. The generality of people in America, especially the poor, are more able to pay taxes, than the generality of people either in France or England.

But the case is, that the representative system diffuses such a body of knowledge throughout a nation, on the subject of government, as to explode ignorance and preclude imposition. The craft of courts cannot be acted on that ground. There is no place for mystery; nowhere for it to begin. Those who are not in the representation, know as much of the nature of business as those who are. An affectation of mysterious importance would there be scouted. Nations can have no secrets; and the secrets of courts, like those of individuals, are always their defects.

In the representative system, the reason for everything must publicly appear. Every man is a proprietor in government, and considers it a necessary part of his business to understand. It concerns his interest, because it affects his property. He examines the cost, and compares it with the advantages; and above all, he does not adopt the slavish custom of following what in other governments are called *leaders*.

It can only be by blinding the understanding of man, and making him believe that government is some wonderful mysterious thing, that excessive revenues are obtained. Monarchy is well calculated to ensure this end. It is the popery of government; a thing kept up to amuse the ignorant, and quiet them into taxes.

The government of a free country, properly speaking, is not in the persons, but in the laws. The enacting of those requires no great expense; and when they are administered, the whole of civil government is performed—the rest is all court contrivance.

# CHAPTER IV.

## OF CONSTITUTIONS

That men mean distinct and separate things when they speak of constitutions and of governments, is evident; or why are those terms distinctly and separately used? A constitution is not the act of a government, but of a people constituting a government; and government without a constitution, is power without a right.

All power exercised over a nation, must have some beginning. It must either be delegated or assumed. There are no other sources. All delegated power is trust, and all assumed power is usurpation. Time does not alter the nature and quality of either.

In viewing this subject, the case and circumstances of America present themselves as in the beginning of a world; and our enquiry into the origin of government is shortened, by referring to the facts that have arisen in our own day. We have no occasion to roam for information into the obscure field of antiquity, nor hazard ourselves upon conjecture. We are brought at once to the point of seeing government begin, as if we had lived in the beginning of time. The real volume, not of history, but of facts, is directly before us, unmutilated by contrivance, or the errors of tradition.

I will here concisely state the commencement of the American constitutions; by which the difference between constitutions and governments will sufficiently appear.

It may not appear improper to remind the reader that the United States of America consist of thirteen separate states, each of which established a government for itself, after the declaration of independence, done the 4th of July, 1776. Each state acted independently of the rest, in forming its governments; but the same general principle pervades the whole. When the several state governments were formed, they proceeded to form the federal government, that acts over the whole in all matters which concern the interest of the whole, or which relate to the intercourse of the several states with each other, or with foreign nations. I will begin with giving an instance from one of the state governments (that of Pennsylvania) and then proceed to the federal government.

The state of Pennsylvania, though nearly of the same extent of territory as England, was then divided into only twelve counties. Each of those counties had elected a committee at the commencement of the dispute with the English government; and as the city of Philadelphia, which also had its committee, was the most central for intelligence, it became the center of communication to the several country committees. When it became necessary to proceed to the formation of a government, the committee of Philadelphia proposed a conference of all the committees, to be held in that city, and which met the latter end of July, 1776.

Though these committees had been duly elected by the people, they were not elected expressly for the purpose, nor invested with the authority of forming a constitution; and as they could not, consistently with the American idea of rights, assume such a power, they could only confer upon the matter, and put it into a train of operation. The conferees, therefore, did no more than state the case, and recommend to the several counties to elect six representatives for each county, to meet in convention at Philadelphia, with powers to form a constitution, and propose it for public consideration.

This convention, of which Benjamin Franklin was president, having met and deliberated, and agreed upon a constitution, they next ordered it to be published, not as a thing established, but for the consideration of the whole people, their approbation or rejection, and then adjourned to a stated time. When the time of adjournment was expired, the convention re-assembled; and as the general opinion of the people in approbation of it was then known, the constitution was signed, sealed, and proclaimed on the *authority of the people* and the original instrument deposited as a public record. The convention then appointed a day for the general election of the representatives who were to compose the government, and the time it should commence; and having done this they dissolved, and returned to their several homes and occupations.

In this constitution were laid down, first, a declaration of rights; then followed the form which the government should have, and the powers it should possess—the authority of the courts of judicature, and of juries—the manner in which elections should be conducted, and the proportion of representatives to the number of electors—the time which each succeeding assembly should continue, which was one year—the mode of levying, and of accounting for the expenditure, of public money—of appointing public officers, etc., etc., etc.

No article of this constitution could be altered or infringed at the discretion of the government that was to ensue. It was to that government a law. But as it would have been unwise to preclude the benefit of experience, and in order also to prevent the accumulation of errors, if any should be found, and to preserve an unison of government with the circumstances of the state at all times, the constitution provided that, at the expiration of every seven years, a convention should be elected, for the express purpose of revising the constitution, and making alterations, additions, or abolitions therein, if any such should be found necessary.

Here we see a regular process—a government issuing out of a constitution, formed by the people in their original character; and that constitution serving, not only as an authority, but as a law of control to the government. It was the political bible of the state. Scarcely a family was without it. Every member of the government had a copy; and nothing was more common, when any debate arose on the principle of a bill, or on the extent of any species of authority, than for the members to take the printed constitution out of their pocket, and read the chapter with which such matter in debate was connected.

Having thus given an instance from one of the states, I will show the proceedings by which the federal constitution of the United States arose and was formed.

Congress, at its two first meetings, in September 1774, and May 1775, was nothing more than a deputation from the legislatures of the several provinces, afterwards states; and had no other authority than what arose from common consent, and the necessity of its acting as a public body. In everything which related to the internal affairs of America, congress went no further than to issue recommendations to the several provincial assemblies, who at discretion adopted them or not. Nothing on the part of congress was compulsive; yet, in this situation, it was more faithfully and affectionately obeyed than was any government in Europe. This instance, like that of the national assembly in France, sufficiently shows, that the strength of government does not consist in any thing *within* itself, but in the attachment of a nation, and the interest which a people feel in supporting it. When this is lost, government is but a child in power; and though, like the old government in France, it may harass individuals for a while, it but facilitates its own fall.

After the declaration of independence, it became consistent with the principle on which representative government is founded, that the authority of congress should be defined and established. Whether that authority should be more or less than congress then discretionarily exercised was not the question. It was merely the rectitude of the measure.

For this purpose, the act, called the act of confederation (which was a sort of imperfect federal constitution), was proposed, and, after long deliberation, was concluded in the year 1781. It was not the act of congress, because it is repugnant to the principles of representative government that a body should give power to itself. Congress first informed the several states, of the powers which it conceived were necessary to be invested in the union, to enable it to perform the duties and services required from it; and the states severally agreed with each other, and concentrated in congress those powers.

It may not be improper to observe that in both those instances (the one of Pennsylvania, and the other of the United States), there is no such thing as the idea of a compact between the people on one side, and the government on the other. The compact was that of the people with each other, to produce and constitute a government. To suppose that any government can be a party in a compact with the whole people, is to suppose it to have existence before it can have a right to exist. The only instance in which a compact can take place between the people and those who exercise the government, is, that the people shall pay them, while they choose to employ them.

Government is not a trade which any man, or any body of men, has a right to set up and exercise for his own emolument, but is altogether a trust, in right of those by whom that trust is delegated, and by whom it is always resumeable. It has of itself no rights; they are altogether duties.

Having thus given two instances of the original formation of a constitution, I will show the manner in which both have been changed since their first establishment.

The powers vested in the governments of the several states, by the state constitutions, were found, upon experience, to be too great; and those vested in the federal government, by the act of confederation, too little. The defect was not in the principle, but in the distribution of power.

Numerous publications, in pamphlets and in the newspapers, appeared, on the propriety and necessity of new modelling the federal government. After some time of public discussion, carried on through the channel of the press, and in conversations, the state of Virginia, experiencing some inconvenience with respect to commerce, proposed holding a continental conference; in consequence of which, a deputation from five or six state assemblies met at Annapolis, in Maryland, in 1786. This meeting, not conceiving itself sufficiently authorised to go into the business of a reform, did no more than state their general opinions of the propriety of the measure, and recommend that a convention of all the states should be held the year following.

The convention met at Philadelphia in May, 1787, of which General Washington was elected president. He was not at that time connected with any of the state governments, or with congress. He delivered up his commission when the war ended, and since then had lived a private citizen.

The convention went deeply into all the subjects; and having, after a variety of debate and investigation, agreed among themselves upon the several parts of a federal constitution, the next question was, the manner of giving it authority and practice.

For this purpose they did not, like a cabal of courtiers, send for a Dutch Stadtholder, or a German Elector; but they referred the whole matter to the sense and interest of the country.

They first directed that the proposed constitution should be published. Secondly, that each state should elect a convention, expressly for the purpose of taking it into consideration, and of ratifying or rejecting it; and that as soon as the approbation and ratification of any nine states should be given, that those states shall proceed to the election of their proportion of members to the new federal government; and that the operation of it should then begin, and the former federal government cease.

The several states proceeded accordingly to elect their conventions. Some of those conventions ratified the constitution by very large majorities, and two or three unanimously. In others there were much debate and division of opinion. In the Massachusetts convention, which met at Boston, the majority was not above nineteen or twenty, in about three hundred members; but such is the nature of representative government, that it quietly decides all matters by majority. After the debate in the Massachusetts convention was closed, and the vote taken, the objecting members rose and declared, "*That though they had argued and voted against it, because certain parts appeared to them in a different light to what they appeared to other members; yet, as the vote had decided in favour of the constitution as proposed, they should give it the same practical support as if they had for it.*"

As soon as nine states had concurred (and the rest followed in the order their conventions were elected), the old fabric of the federal government was taken down, and the new one erected, of which General Washington is president.—In this place I cannot help remarking, that the character and services of this gentleman are sufficient to put all those men called kings to shame. While they are receiving from the sweat and labours of mankind, a prodigality of pay, to which neither their abilities nor their services can entitle them, he is rendering every service in his power, and refusing every pecuniary reward. He accepted no pay as commander-in-chief; he accepts none as president of the United States.

After the new federal constitution was established, the state of Pennsylvania, conceiving that some parts of its own constitution required to be altered, elected a convention for that purpose. The proposed alterations were published, and the people concurring therein, they were established.

In forming those constitutions, or in altering them, little or no inconvenience took place. The ordinary course of things was not interrupted, and the advantages have been much. It is always the interest of a far greater number of people in a nation to have things right, than to let them remain wrong; and when public matters are open to debate, and the public judgment free, it will not decide wrong, unless it decides too hastily.

In the two instances of changing the constitutions, the governments then in being were not actors either way. Government has no right to make itself a party in any debate respecting the principles or modes of forming, or of changing, constitutions. It is not for the benefit of those who exercise the powers of government that constitutions, and the governments issuing from them, are established. In all those matters the right of judging and acting are in those who pay, and not in those who receive.

A constitution is the property of a nation, and not of those who exercise the government. All the constitutions of America are declared to be established on the authority of the people. In France, the word nation is used instead of the people; but in both cases, a constitution is a thing antecedent to the government, and always distinct there from.

In England it is not difficult to perceive that everything has a constitution, except the nation. Every society and association that is established, first agreed upon a number of original articles, digested into form, which are its constitution. It then appointed its officers, whose powers and authorities are described in that constitution, and the government of that society then commenced. Those officers, by whatever name they are called, have no authority to add to, alter, or abridge the original articles. It is only to the constituting power that this right belongs.

From the want of understanding the difference between a constitution and a government, Dr. Johnson, and all writers of his description, have always bewildered themselves. They could not but perceive, that there must necessarily be a *controlling* power existing somewhere, and they placed this power in the discretion of the persons exercising the government, instead of placing it in a constitution formed by the nation. When it is in a constitution, it has the nation for its support, and the natural and the political controlling powers are together. The laws which are enacted by governments, control men only as individuals, but the nation, through its constitution, controls the whole government, and has a natural ability to do so. The final controlling power, therefore, and the original constituting power, are one and the same power.

Dr. Johnson could not have advanced such a position in any country where there was a constitution; and he is himself an evidence that no such thing as a constitution exists in England. But it may be put as a question, not improper to be investigated, that if a constitution does not exist, how came the idea of its existence so generally established?

In order to decide this question, it is necessary to consider a constitution in both its cases: First, as creating a government and giving it powers. Secondly, as regulating and restraining the powers so given.

If we begin with William of Normandy, we find that the government of England was originally a tyranny, founded on an invasion and conquest of the country. This being admitted, it will then appear, that the exertion of the nation, at different periods, to abate that tyranny, and render it less intolerable, has been credited for a constitution.

Magna Charta, as it was called (it is now like an almanack of the same date), was no more than compelling the government to renounce a part of its assumptions. It did not create and give powers to government in a manner a constitution does; but was, as far as it went, of the nature of a re-conquest, and not a constitution; for could the nation have totally expelled the usurpation, as France has done its despotism, it would then have had a constitution to form.

The history of the Edwards and the Henries, and up to the commencement of the Stuarts, exhibits as many instances of tyranny as could be acted within the limits to which the nation had restricted it. The Stuarts endeavoured to pass those limits, and their fate is well known. In all those instances we see nothing of a constitution, but only of restrictions on assumed power.

After this, another William, descended from the same stock, and claiming from the same origin, gained possession; and of the two evils, *James* and *William*, the nation preferred what it thought the least; since, from circumstances, it must take one. The act, called the Bill of Rights, comes here into view. What is it, but a bargain, which the parts of the government made with each other to divide powers, profits, and privileges? You shall have so much, and I will have the rest; and with respect to the nation, it said, for *your share*, YOU *shall have the right of petitioning*. This being the case, the bill of rights is more properly a bill of wrongs, and of insult. As to what is called the convention parliament, it was a thing that made itself, and then made the authority by which it acted. A few persons got together, and called themselves by that name. Several of them had never been elected, and none of them for the purpose.

From the time of William a species of government arose, issuing out of this coalition bill of rights; and more so, since the corruption introduced at the Hanover succession by the agency of Walpole; that can be described by no other name than a despotic legislation. Though the parts may embarrass each other, the whole has no bounds; and the only right it acknowledges out of itself, is the right of petitioning. Where then is the constitution either that gives or restrains power?

It is not because a part of the government is elective, that makes it less a despotism, if the persons so elected possess afterwards, as a parliament, unlimited powers. Election, in this case, becomes separated from representation, and the candidates are candidates for despotism.

I cannot believe that any nation, reasoning on its own rights, would have thought of calling these things *a constitution*, if the cry of constitution had not been set up by the government. It has got into circulation like the words *bore* and *quoȝ* [quiz], by being chalked up in the speeches of parliament, as those words were on window shutters and doorposts; but whatever the constitution may be in other respects, it has undoubtedly been *the most productive machine of taxation that was ever invented*. The taxes in France, under the new constitution, are not quite thirteen shillings per head,* and the taxes in England, under what is called its present constitution, are forty-eight shillings and sixpence per head—men, women, and children—amounting to nearly seventeen millions sterling, besides the expense of collecting, which is upwards of a million more.

In a country like England, where the whole of the civil Government is executed by the people of every town and county, by means of parish officers, magistrates, quarterly sessions, juries, and assize; without any trouble to what is called the government or any other expense to the revenue than the salary of the judges, it is astonishing how such a mass of taxes can be employed. Not even the internal defence of the country is paid out of the revenue. On all occasions, whether real or contrived, recourse is continually had to new loans and new taxes. No wonder, then, that a machine of government so advantageous to the advocates of a court, should be so triumphantly extolled! No wonder, that St. James's or St. Stephen's should echo with the continual cry of constitution; no wonder, that the French revolution should be reprobated, and the *res-publica* treated with reproach! The *red book* of England, like the red book of France, will explain the reason.†

I will now, by way of relaxation, turn a thought or two to Mr. Burke. I ask his pardon for neglecting him so long.

---

* The whole amount of the assessed taxes of France, for the present year, is three hundred millions of francs, which is twelve millions and a half sterling; and the incidental taxes are estimated at three millions, making in the whole fifteen millions and a half; which among twenty-four millions of people, is not quite thirteen shillings per head. France has lessened her taxes since the revolution, nearly nine millions sterling annually. Before the revolution, the city of Paris paid a duty of upwards of thirty per cent on all articles brought into the city. This tax was collected at the city gates. It was taken off on the first of last May, and the gates taken down. (Author's note)

† What was called the *livre rouge*, or the red book, in France, was not exactly similar to the Court Calendar in England; but it sufficiently showed how a great part of the taxes was lavished. (Author's note)

"America," says he (in his speech on the Canada Constitution bill), "never dreamed of such absurd doctrine as the *Rights of Man*."

Mr. Burke is such a bold presumer, and advances his assertions and his premises with such a deficiency of judgment, that, without troubling ourselves about principles of philosophy or politics, the mere logical conclusions they produce, are ridiculous. For instance,

If governments, as Mr. Burke asserts, are not founded on the Rights of *Man*, and are founded on *any rights* at all, they consequently must be founded on the right of *something* that is *not man*. What then is that something?

Generally speaking, we know of no other creatures that inhabit the earth than man and beast; and in all cases, where only two things offer themselves, and one must be admitted, a negation proved on any one, amounts to an affirmative on the other; and therefore, Mr. Burke, by proving against the Rights of *Man*, proves in behalf of the *beast*; and consequently, proves that government is a beast; and as difficult things sometimes explain each other, we now see the origin of keeping wild beasts in the Tower; for they certainly can be of no other use than to show the origin of the government. They are in the place of a constitution. O John Bull, what honours thou hast lost by not being a wild beast. Thou mightest, on Mr. Burke's system, have been in the Tower for life.

If Mr. Burke's arguments have not weight enough to keep one serious, the fault is less mine than his; and as I am willing to make an apology to the reader for the liberty I have taken, I hope Mr. Burke will also make his for giving the cause.

Having thus paid Mr. Burke the compliment of remembering him, I return to the subject.

From the want of a constitution in England to restrain and regulate the wild impulse of power, many of the laws are irrational and tyrannical, and the administration of them vague and problematical.

The attention of the government of England (for I rather choose to call it by this name than the English government) appears, since its political connection with Germany, to have been so completely engrossed and absorbed by foreign affairs, and the means of raising taxes, that it seems to exist for no other purposes. Domestic concerns are neglected; and with respect to regular law, there is scarcely such a thing.

Almost every case must now be determined by some precedent, be that precedent good or bad, or whether it properly applies or not; and the practice is become so general as to suggest a suspicion, that it proceeds from a deeper policy than at first sight appears.

Since the revolution of America, and more so since that of France, this preaching up the doctrines of precedents, drawn from times and circumstances antecedent to those events, has been the studied practice of the English government. The generality of those precedents are founded on principles and opinions, the reverse of what they ought; and the greater distance of time they are drawn from, the more they are to be suspected. But by associating those precedents with a superstitious reverence for ancient things, as monks show relics and call them holy, the generality of mankind are deceived into the design. Governments now act as if they were afraid to awaken a single reflection in man. They are softly leading him to the sepulchre of precedents, to deaden his faculties and call attention from the scene of revolutions. They feel that he is arriving at knowledge faster than they wish, and their policy of precedents is the barometer of their fears. This political popery, like the ecclesiastical popery of old, has had its day, and is hastening to its exit. The ragged relic and the antiquated precedent, the monk and the monarch, will moulder together.

Government by precedent, without any regard to the principle of the precedent, is one of the vilest systems that can be set up. In numerous instances, the precedent ought to operate as a warning, and not as an example, and requires to be shunned instead of imitated; but instead of this, precedents are taken in the lump, and put at once for constitution and for law.

Either the doctrine of precedents is policy to keep a man in a state of ignorance, or it is a practical confession that wisdom degenerates in governments as governments increase in age, and can only hobble along by the stilts and crutches of precedents. How is it that the same persons who would proudly be thought wiser than their predecessors, appear at the same time only as the ghosts of departed wisdom? How strangely is antiquity treated! To some purposes it is spoken of as the times of darkness and ignorance, and to answer others, it is put for the light of the world.

If the doctrine of precedents is to be followed, the expenses of government need not continue the same. Why pay men extravagantly, who have but little to do? If everything that can happen is already in precedent, legislation is at an end, and precedent, like a dictionary, determines every case. Either, therefore, government has arrived at its dotage, and requires to be renovated, or all the occasions for exercising its wisdom have occurred.

We now see all over Europe, and particularly in England, the curious phenomenon of a nation looking one way, and the government the other—the one forward and the other backward. If governments are to go on by precedent, while nations go on by improvement, they must at last come to a final separation; and the sooner, and the more civilly they determine this point, the better.*

Having thus spoken of constitutions generally, as things distinct from actual governments, let us proceed to consider the parts of which a constitution is composed.

Opinions differ more on this subject than with respect to the whole. That a nation ought to have a constitution, as a rule for the conduct of its government, is a simple question in which all men, not directly courtiers, will agree. It is only on the component parts that questions and opinions multiply.

But this difficulty, like every other, will diminish when put into a train of being rightly understood.

The first thing is, that a nation has a right to establish a constitution.

Whether it exercises this right in the most judicious manner at first is quite another case. It exercises it agreeably to the judgment it possesses; and by continuing to do so, all errors will at last be exploded.

When this right is established in a nation, there is no fear that it will be employed to its own injury. A nation can have no interest in being wrong.

Though all the constitutions of America are on one general principle, yet no two of them are exactly alike in their component parts, or in the distribution of the powers which they give to the actual governments. Some are more, and others less complex.

---

* In England the improvements in agriculture, useful arts, manufactures, and commerce, have been made in opposition to the genius of its government, which is that of following precedents. It is from the enterprise and industry of the individuals, and their numerous associations, in which, tritely speaking, government is neither pillow nor bolster, that these improvements have proceeded. No man thought about government, or who was *in*, or who was *out*, when he was planning or executing those things; and all he had to hope, with respect to government, was, *that it would let him alone*. Three or four very silly ministerial newspapers are continually offending against the spirit of national improvement, by ascribing it to a minister. They may with as much truth ascribe this book to a minister. (Author's note)

In forming a constitution, it is first necessary to consider what are the ends for which government is necessary? Secondly, what are the best means, and the least expensive, for accomplishing those ends?

Government is nothing more than a national association; and the object of this association is the good of all, as well individually as collectively. Every man wishes to pursue his occupation, and to enjoy the fruits of his labours and the produce of his property in peace and safety, and with the least possible expense. When these things are accomplished, all the objects for which government ought to be established are answered.

It has been customary to consider government under three distinct general heads. The legislative, the executive, and the judicial.

But if we permit our judgment to act unincumbered by the habit of multiplied terms, we can perceive no more than two divisions of power, of which civil government is composed, namely, that of legislating or enacting laws, and that of executing or administering them. Everything, therefore, appertaining to civil government, classes itself under one or other of these two divisions.

So far as regards the execution of the laws, that which is called the judicial power, is strictly and properly the executive power of every country. It is that power to which every individual has appeal, and which causes the laws to be executed; neither have we any other clear idea with respect to the official execution of the laws. In England, and also in America and France, this power begins with the magistrate, and proceeds up through all the courts of judicature.

I leave to courtiers to explain what is meant by calling monarchy the executive power. It is merely a name in which acts of government are done; and any other, or none at all, would answer the same purpose. Laws have neither more nor less authority on this account. It must be from the justness of their principles, and the interest which a nation feels therein, that they derive support; if they require any other than this, it is a sign that something in the system of government is imperfect. Laws difficult to be executed cannot be generally good.

With respect to the organization of the *legislative power*, different modes have been adopted in different countries. In America it is generally composed of two houses. In France it consists but of one, but in both countries, it is wholly by representation.

The case is, that mankind (from the long tyranny of assumed power) have had so few opportunities of making the necessary trials on modes and principles of government, in order to discover the best, *that government is but now beginning to be known*, and experience is yet wanting to determine many particulars.

The objections against two houses are, first, that there is an inconsistency in any part of a whole legislature, coming to a final determination by vote on any matter, whilst *that matter*, with respect to *that whole*, is yet only in a train of deliberation, and consequently open to new illustrations.

Secondly, That by taking the vote on each, as a separate body, it always admits of the possibility, and is often the case in practice, that the minority governs the majority, and that, in some instances, to a degree of great inconsistency.

Thirdly, That two houses arbitrarily checking or controlling each other is inconsistent; because it cannot be proved on the principles of just representation, that either should be wiser or better than the other. They may check in the wrong as well as in the right therefore to give the power where we cannot give the wisdom to use it, nor be assured of its being rightly used, renders the hazard at least equal to the precaution.*

The objection against a single house is, that it is always in a condition of committing itself too soon.—But it should at the same time be remembered, that when there is a constitution which defines the power, and establishes the principles within which a legislature shall act, there is already a more effectual check provided, and more powerfully operating, than any other check can be. For example,

---

* With respect to the two houses, of which the English parliament is composed, they appear to be effectually influenced into one, and, as a legislature, to have no temper of its own. The minister, whoever he at any time may be, touches it as with an opium wand, and it sleeps obedience.

But if we look at the distinct abilities of the two houses, the difference will appear so great, as to show the inconsistency of placing power where there can be no certainty of the judgment to use it. Wretched as the state of representation is in England, it is manhood compared with what is called the house of Lords; and so little is this nick-named house regarded, that the people scarcely enquire at any time what it is doing. It appears also to be most under influence, and the furthest removed from the general interest of the nation. In the debate on engaging in the Russian and Turkish war, the majority in the house of peers in favor of it was upwards of ninety, when in the other house, which was more than double its numbers, the majority was sixty-three.

The proceedings on Mr. Fox's bill, respecting the rights of juries, merits also to be noticed. The persons called the peers were not the objects of that bill. They are already in possession of more privileges than that bill gave to others. They are their own jury, and if any one of that house were prosecuted for a libel, he would not suffer, even upon conviction, for the first offense. Such inequality in laws ought not to exist in any country. The French constitution says, that *the law is the same to every individual, whether to Protect or to punish. All are equal in its sight.* (Author's note)

Were a Bill to be brought into any of the American legislatures similar to that which was passed into an act by the English parliament, at the commencement of George the First, to extend the duration of the assemblies to a longer period than they now sit, the check is in the constitution, which in effect says, Thus far shalt thou go and no further.

But in order to remove the objection against a single house (that of acting with too quick an impulse), and at the same time to avoid the inconsistencies, in some cases absurdities, arising from two houses, the following method has been proposed as an improvement upon both.

First, To have but one representation.

Secondly, To divide that representation, by lot, into two or three parts.

Thirdly, That every proposed bill shall be first debated in those parts by succession, that they may become the hearers of each other, but without taking any vote. After which the whole representation to assemble for a general debate and determination by vote.

To this proposed improvement has been added another, for the purpose of keeping the representation in the state of constant renovation; which is, that one-third of the representation of each county, shall go out at the expiration of one year, and the number be replaced by new elections. Another third at the expiration of the second year replaced in like manner, and every third year to be a general election.*

But in whatever manner the separate parts of a constitution may be arranged, there is *one* general principle that distinguishes freedom from slavery, which is, that all *hereditary government over a people is to them a species of slavery, and representative government is freedom.*

Considering government in the only light in which it should be considered, that of a *National Association*, it ought to be so constructed as not to be disordered by any accident happening among the parts: and, therefore, no extraordinary power, capable of producing such an effect, should be lodged in the hands of any individual. The death, sickness, absence or defection, of any one individual in a government, ought to be a matter of no more consequence, with respect to the nation, than if the same circumstance had taken place in a member of the English Parliament, or the French National Assembly.

---

* As to the state of representation in England, it is too absurd to be reasoned upon. Almost all the represented parts are decreasing in population, and the unrepresented parts are increasing. A general convention of the nation is necessary to take the whole form of government into consideration. (Author's note)

Scarcely anything presents a more degrading character of national greatness, than its being thrown into confusion, by anything happening to or acted by any individual; and the ridiculousness of the scene is often increased by the natural insignificance of the person by whom it is occasioned. Were a government so constructed, that it could not go on unless a goose or a gander were present in the senate, the difficulties would be just as great and as real, on the flight or sickness of the goose, or the gander, as if it were called a King. We laugh at individuals for the silly difficulties they make to themselves, without perceiving that the greatest of all ridiculous things are acted in governments.*

All the constitutions of America are on a plan that excludes the childish embarrassments which occur in monarchical countries. No suspension of government can there take place for a moment, from any circumstances whatever. The system of representation provides for everything, and is the only system in which nations and governments can always appear in their proper character.

As extraordinary power ought not to be lodged in the hands of any individual, so ought there to be no appropriations of public money to any person, beyond what his services in a state may be worth. It signifies not whether a man be called a president, a king, an emperor, a senator, or by any other name which propriety or folly may devise or arrogance assume; it is only a certain service he can perform in the state; and the service of any such individual in the routine of office, whether such office be called monarchical, presidential, senatorial, or by any other name or title, can never exceed the value of ten thousand pounds a year. All the great services that are done in the world are performed by volunteer characters, who accept nothing for them; but the routine of office is always regulated to such a general standard of abilities as to be within the compass of numbers in every country to perform, and

---

* It is related that in the canton of Berne, in Switzerland, it has been customary, from time immemorial, to keep a bear at the public expense, and the people had been taught to believe that if they had not a bear they should all be undone. It happened some years ago that the bear, then in being, was taken sick, and died too suddenly to have his place immediately supplied with another. During this interregnum the people discovered that the corn grew, and the vintage flourished, and the sun and moon continued to rise and set, and everything went on the same as before, and taking courage from these circumstances, they resolved not to keep any more bears; for, said they, "a bear is a very voracious expensive animal, and we were obliged to pull out his claws, lest he should hurt the citizens." The story of the bear of Berne was related in some of the French newspapers, at the time of the flight of Louis XVI, and the application of it to monarchy could not be mistaken in France; but it seems that the aristocracy of Berne applied it to themselves, and have since prohibited the reading of French newspapers. (Author's note)

therefore cannot merit very extraordinary recompense. *Government*, says Swift, *is a Plain thing, and fitted to the capacity of many heads.*

It is inhuman to talk of a million sterling a year, paid out of the public taxes of any country, for the support of any individual, whilst thousands who are forced to contribute thereto, are pining with want, and struggling with misery. Government does not consist in a contrast between prisons and palaces, between poverty and pomp; it is not instituted to rob the needy of his mite, and increase the wretchedness of the wretched.——But on this part of the subject I shall speak hereafter, and confine myself at present to political observations.

When extraordinary power and extraordinary pay are allotted to any individual in a government, he becomes the center, round which every kind of corruption generates and forms. Give to any man a million a year, and add thereto the power of creating and disposing of places, at the expense of a country, and the liberties of that country are no longer secure. What is called the splendour of a throne is no other than the corruption of the state. It is made up of a band of parasites, living in luxurious indolence, out of the public taxes.

When once such a vicious system is established it becomes the guard and protection of all inferior abuses. The man who is in the receipt of a million a year is the last person to promote a spirit of reform, lest, in the event, it should reach to himself. It is always his interest to defend inferior abuses, as so many outworks to protect the citadel; and on this species of political fortification, all the parts have such a common dependence that it is never to be expected they will attack each other.*

---

* It is scarcely possible to touch on any subject, that will not suggest an allusion to some corruption in governments. The simile of "*fortifications*," unfortunately involves with it a circumstance, which is directly in point with the matter above alluded to.

Among the numerous instances of abuse which have been acted or protected by governments, ancient or modern, there is not a greater than that of quartering a man and his heirs upon the public, to be maintained at its expense.

Humanity dictates a provision for the poor; but by what right, moral or political, does any government assume to say, that the person called the Duke of Richmond, shall be maintained by the public? Yet, if common report is true, not a beggar in London can purchase his wretched pittance of coal, without paying towards the civil list of the Duke of Richmond. Were the whole produce of this imposition but a shilling a year, the iniquitous principle would be still the same; but when it amounts, as it is said to do, to no less than twenty thousand pounds per annum, the enormity is too serious to be permitted to remain. This is one of the effects of monarchy and aristocracy.

In stating this case I am led by no personal dislike. Though I think it mean in any man to live upon the public, the vice originates in the government; and so general is it become, that whether the parties are in the ministry or in the opposition, it makes no difference: they are sure of the guarantee of each other. (Author's note)

Monarchy would not have continued so many ages in the world, had it not been for the abuses it protects. It is the master-fraud, which shelters all others. By admitting a participation of the spoil, it makes itself friends; and when it ceases to do this it will cease to be the idol of courtiers.

As the principle on which constitutions are now formed rejects all hereditary pretensions to government, it also rejects all that catalogue of assumptions known by the name of prerogatives.

If there is any government where prerogatives might with apparent safety be entrusted to any individual, it is in the federal government of America. The president of the United States of America is elected only for four years. He is not only responsible in the general sense of the word, but a particular mode is laid down in the constitution for trying him. He cannot be elected under thirty-five years of age; and he must be a native of the country.

In a comparison of these cases with the Government of England, the difference when applied to the latter amounts to an absurdity. In England the person who exercises prerogative is often a foreigner; always half a foreigner, and always married to a foreigner. He is never in full natural or political connection with the country, is not responsible for anything, and becomes of age at eighteen years; yet such a person is permitted to form foreign alliances, without even the knowledge of the nation, and to make war and peace without its consent.

But this is not all. Though such a person cannot dispose of the government in the manner of a testator, he dictates the marriage connections, which, in effect, accomplish a great part of the same end. He cannot directly bequeath half the government to Prussia, but he can form a marriage partnership that will produce almost the same thing. Under such circumstances, it is happy for England that she is not situated on the Continent, or she might, like Holland, fall under the dictatorship of Prussia. Holland, by marriage, is as effectually governed by Prussia, as if the old tyranny of bequeathing the government had been the means.

The presidency in America (or, as it is sometimes called, the executive) is the only office from which a foreigner is excluded, and in England it is the only one to which he is admitted. A foreigner cannot be a member of Parliament, but he may be what is called a king. If there is any reason for excluding foreigners, it ought to be from those offices where mischief can most be acted, and where, by uniting every bias of interest and attachment, the trust is best secured. But as nations proceed in the great business of forming constitutions, they will examine with more precision into the nature and business of that department which is called the executive. What the legislative and judicial departments are every one can see; but with respect to what, in Europe, is called the executive, as distinct from those two, it is either a political superfluity or a chaos of unknown things.

Some kind of official department, to which reports shall be made from the different parts of a nation, or from abroad, to be laid before the national representatives, is all that is necessary; but there is no consistency in calling this the executive; neither can it be considered in any other light than as inferior to the legislative. The sovereign authority in any country is the power of making laws, and everything else is an official department.

Next to the arrangement of the principles and the organization of the several parts of a constitution, is the provision to be made for the support of the persons to whom the nation shall confide the administration of the constitutional powers.

A nation can have no right to the time and services of any person at his own expense, whom it may choose to employ or entrust in any department whatever; neither can any reason be given for making provision for the support of any one part of a government and not for the other.

But admitting that the honour of being entrusted with any part of a government is to be considered a sufficient reward, it ought to be so to every person alike. If the members of the legislature of any country are to serve at their own expense that which is called the executive, whether monarchical or by any other name, ought to serve in like manner. It is inconsistent to pay the one, and accept the service of the other gratis.

In America, every department in the government is decently provided for; but no one is extravagantly paid. Every member of Congress, and of the Assemblies, is allowed a sufficiency for his expenses. Whereas in England, a most prodigal provision is made for the support of one part of the Government, and none for the other, the consequence of which is that the one is furnished with the means of corruption and the other is put into the condition of being corrupted. Less than a fourth part of such expense, applied as it is in America, would remedy a great part of the corruption.

Another reform in the American constitution is the exploding all oaths of personality. The oath of allegiance in America is to the nation only. The putting any individual as a figure for a nation is improper. The happiness of a nation is the superior object, and therefore the intention of an oath of allegiance ought not to be obscured by being figuratively taken, to, or in the name of, any person. The oath, called the civic oath, in France, viz., "*the nation, the law, and the king*," is improper. If taken at all, it ought to be as in America, to the nation only. The law may or may not be good; but, in this place, it can have no other meaning, than as being conducive to the happiness of a nation, and therefore is included in it. The remainder of the oath is improper, on the ground, that all personal oaths ought to be abolished. They are the remains of tyranny on one part and slavery on the other; and the name of the Creator ought not to be introduced to witness the degradation of his creation; or if taken, as is already mentioned, as figurative of the nation, it is in this place redundant. But whatever apology may be made for oaths at the first establishment of a government, they ought not to be permitted afterwards. If a government requires the support of oaths, it is a sign that it is not worth supporting, and ought not to be supported. Make government what it ought to be, and it will support itself.

To conclude this part of the subject:——One of the greatest improvements that have been made for the perpetual security and progress of constitutional liberty, is the provision which the new constitutions make for occasionally revising, altering, and amending them.

The principle upon which Mr. Burke formed his political creed, that of "*binding and controlling posterity to the end of time, and of renouncing and abdicating the rights of all posterity, for ever*," is now become too detestable to be made a subject of debate; and therefore, I pass it over with no other notice than exposing it.

Government is but now beginning to be known. Hitherto it has been the mere exercise of power, which forbade all effectual enquiry into rights, and grounded itself wholly on possession. While the enemy of liberty was its judge, the progress of its principles must have been small indeed.

The constitutions of America, and also that of France, have either affixed a period for their revision, or laid down the mode by which improvement shall be made. It is perhaps impossible to establish anything that combines principles with opinions and practice, which the progress of circumstances, through a length of years, will not in some measure derange, or render inconsistent; and, therefore, to prevent inconveniences accumulating, till they discourage reformations or provoke revolutions, it is best to provide the means of regulating them as they occur. The Rights of Man are the rights of all generations of men, and cannot be monopolised by any. That which is worth following, will be followed for the sake of its worth, and it is in this that its security lies, and not in any conditions with which it may be encumbered. When a man leaves property to his heirs, he does not connect it with an obligation that they shall accept it. Why, then, should we do otherwise with respect to constitutions? The best constitution that could now be devised, consistent with the condition of the present moment, may be far short of that excellence which a few years may afford. There is a morning of reason rising upon man on the subject of government, that has not appeared before. As the barbarism of the present old governments expires, the moral conditions of nations with respect to each other will be changed. Man will not be brought up with the savage idea of considering his species as his enemy, because the accident of birth gave the individuals existence in countries distinguished by different names; and as constitutions have always some relation to external as well as to domestic circumstances, the means of benefitting by every change, foreign or domestic, should be a part of every constitution. We already see an alteration in the national disposition of England and France towards each other, which, when we look back to only a few years, is itself a Revolution. Who could have foreseen, or who could have believed, that a French National Assembly would ever have been a popular toast in England, or that a friendly alliance of the two nations should become the wish of either? It shows that man, were he not corrupted by governments, is naturally the friend of man, and that human nature is not of itself vicious. That spirit of jealousy and ferocity, which the governments of the two countries inspired, and which they rendered subservient to the purpose of taxation, is now yielding to the dictates of reason, interest, and humanity. The trade of courts is beginning to be understood, and the affectation of mystery, with all the artificial sorcery by which they imposed upon mankind, is on the decline. It has received its death-wound; and though it may linger, it will expire. Government ought to be as much open to improvement as anything which appertains to man, instead of which it has been monopolised from age to age, by the most ignorant and vicious of the human race. Need we any other proof of their wretched management, than the excess of debts and taxes with which every nation groans, and the quarrels into which they have precipitated the world? Just emerging from such a barbarous condition, it is too soon to determine to what extent of improvement government may yet be carried. For what we can foresee, all Europe may form but one great Republic, and man be free of the whole.

# CHAPTER V.

## WAYS AND MEANS OF IMPROVING THE CONDITION OF EUROPE, INTERSPERSED WITH MISCELLANEOUS OBSERVATIONS

In contemplating a subject that embraces with equatorial magnitude the whole region of humanity it is impossible to confine the pursuit in one single direction. It takes ground on every character and condition that appertains to man, and blends the individual, the nation, and the world. From a small spark, kindled in America, a flame has arisen not to be extinguished. Without consuming, like the *Ultima Ratio Regum*, it winds its progress from nation to nation, and conquers by a silent operation. Man finds himself changed, he scarcely perceives how. He acquires a knowledge of his rights by attending justly to his interest, and discovers in the event that the strength and powers of despotism consist wholly in the fear of resisting it, and that, in order "*to be free, it is sufficient that he wills it.*"

Having in all the preceding parts of this work endeavoured to establish a system of principles as a basis on which governments ought to be erected, I shall proceed in this, to the ways and means of rendering them into practice. But in order to introduce this part of the subject with more propriety, and stronger effect, some preliminary observations, deducible from, or connected with, those principles, are necessary.

Whatever the form or constitution of government may be, it ought to have no other object than the *general* happiness. When, instead of this, it operates to create and increase wretchedness in any of the parts of society, it is on a wrong system, and reformation is necessary. Customary language has classed the condition of man under the two descriptions of civilised and uncivilised life. To the one it has ascribed felicity and affluence; to the other hardship and want. But, however our imagination may be impressed by painting and comparison, it is nevertheless true, that a great portion of mankind, in what are called civilised countries, are in a state of poverty and wretchedness, far below the condition of an Indian. I speak not of one country, but of all. It is so in England, it is so all over Europe. Let us enquire into the cause.

It lies not in any natural defect in the principles of civilisation, but in preventing those principles having a universal operation; the consequence of which is, a perpetual system of war and expense, that drains the country, and defeats the general felicity of which civilisation is capable. All the European governments (France now excepted) are constructed not on the principle of universal civilisation, but on the reverse of it. So far as those governments relate to each other, they are in the same condition as we conceive of savage uncivilised life; they put themselves beyond the law as well of God as of man, and are, with respect to principle and reciprocal conduct, like so many individuals in a state of nature. The inhabitants of every country, under the civilisation of laws, easily civilise together, but governments being yet in an uncivilised state, and almost continually at war, they pervert the abundance which civilised life produces to carry on the uncivilised part to a greater extent. By thus engrafting the barbarism of government upon the internal civilisation of a country, it draws from the latter, and more especially from the poor, a great portion of those earnings, which should be applied to their own subsistence and comfort. Apart from all reflections of morality and philosophy, it is a melancholy fact that more than one-fourth of the labour of mankind is annually consumed by this barbarous system. What has served to continue this evil, is the pecuniary advantage which all the governments of Europe have found in keeping up this state of uncivilisation. It affords to them pretences for power, and revenue, for which there would be neither occasion nor apology, if the circle of civilisation were rendered complete. Civil government alone, or the government of laws, is not productive of pretences for many taxes; it operates at home, directly under the eye of the country, and precludes the possibility of much imposition. But when the scene is laid in the uncivilised contention of governments, the field of pretences is enlarged, and the country, being no longer a judge, is open to every imposition, which governments please to act. Not a thirtieth, scarcely a fortieth, part of the taxes which are raised in England are either occasioned by, or applied to, the purpose of civil government. It is not difficult to see, that the whole which the actual government does in this respect, is to enact laws, and that the country administers and executes them, at its own expense, by means of magistrates, juries, sessions, and assize, over and above the taxes which it pays. In this view of the case, we have two distinct characters of government; the one the civil government, or the government of laws, which operates at home, the other the court or cabinet government, which operates abroad, on the rude plan of uncivilised life; the one attended with little charge, the other with boundless extravagance; and so distinct are the two, that if the latter were to sink, as it were, by a sudden opening of the earth, and totally disappear, the former would not be deranged. It would still proceed, because it is the common interest of the nation that it should, and all the means are in practice. Revolutions, then, have for their object a change in the moral condition of governments, and with this change the burthen of public taxes will lessen, and civilisation will be left to the enjoyment of that abundance, of which it is now deprived. In contemplating the whole of this subject, I extend my views into the department of commerce. In all my publications, where the matter would admit, I have been an advocate for commerce, because I am a friend to its effects. It is a pacific system, operating to cordialise mankind, by rendering nations, as well as individuals, useful to each other. As to the mere theoretical reformation, I have never preached it up. The most effectual process is that of improving the condition of man by means of his interest; and it is on this ground that I take my stand. If commerce were permitted to act to the universal extent it is capable, it would extirpate the system of war, and produce a revolution in the uncivilised state of governments. The invention of commerce has arisen since those governments began, and is the greatest approach towards universal civilisation that has yet been made by any means not immediately flowing from moral principles. Whatever has a tendency to promote the civil intercourse of nations by an exchange of benefits, is a subject as worthy of philosophy as of politics. Commerce is no other than the traffic of two individuals, multiplied on a scale of numbers; and by the same rule that nature intended for the intercourse of two, she intended that of all. For this purpose she has distributed the materials of manufactures and commerce, in various and distant parts of a nation and of the world; and as they cannot be procured by war so cheaply or so commodiously as by commerce, she has rendered the latter the means of extirpating the former. As the two are nearly the opposite of each other, consequently, the uncivilised state of the European governments is injurious to commerce. Every kind of destruction or embarrassment serves to lessen the quantity, and it matters but little in what part of the commercial world the reduction begins. Like blood, it cannot be taken from any of the parts, without being taken from the whole mass in circulation, and all partake of the loss. When the ability in any nation to buy is destroyed, it equally involves the seller. Could the government of England destroy the commerce of all other nations, she would most effectually ruin her own. It is possible that a nation may be the carrier for the world, but she cannot be the merchant. She cannot be the seller and buyer of her own merchandise. The ability to buy must reside out of herself; and, therefore, the prosperity of any commercial nation is regulated by the prosperity of the rest. If they are poor she cannot be rich, and her condition, be what it may, is an index of the height of the commercial tide in other nations. That the principles of commerce, and its universal operation may be understood, without understanding the practice, is a position that reason will not deny; and it is on this ground only that I argue the subject. It is one thing in the counting-house, in the world it is another. With respect to its operation it must necessarily be contemplated as a reciprocal thing; that only one-half its powers resides within the nation, and that the whole is as effectually destroyed by the destroying the half that resides without, as if the destruction had been committed on that which is within; for neither can act without the other. When in the last, as well as in former wars, the commerce of England sunk, it was because the quantity was lessened everywhere; and it now rises, because commerce is in a rising state in every nation. If England, at this day, imports and exports more than at any former period, the nations with which she trades must necessarily do the same; her imports are their exports, and *vice versa*. There can be no such thing as a nation flourishing alone in commerce: she can only participate; and the destruction of it in any part must necessarily affect all. When, therefore, governments are at war, the attack is made upon a common stock of commerce, and the consequence is the same as if each had attacked his own. The present increase of commerce is not to be attributed to ministers, or to any political contrivances, but to its own natural operation in consequence of peace. The regular markets had been destroyed, the channels of trade broken up, the high road of the seas infested with robbers of every nation, and the attention of the world called to other objects. Those interruptions have ceased, and peace has restored the deranged condition of things to their proper order.* It is worth remarking that every nation reckons the balance of trade in its own favour; and therefore something must be irregular in the common ideas upon this subject. The fact, however, is true, according to what is called a balance; and it is from this cause that commerce is universally supported. Every nation feels the advantage, or it would abandon the practice: but the deception lies in the mode of making up the accounts, and in attributing what are called profits to a wrong cause. Mr. Pitt has sometimes amused himself, by showing what he called a balance of trade from the custom-house books. This mode of calculating not only affords no rule that is true, but one that is false.

In the first place, Every cargo that departs from the custom-house appears on the books as an export; and, according to the custom-house balance, the losses at sea, and by foreign failures, are all reckoned on the side of profit because they appear as exports.

Secondly, Because the importation by the smuggling trade does not appear on the custom-house books, to arrange against the exports.

No balance, therefore, as applying to superior advantages, can be drawn from these documents; and if we examine the natural operation of commerce, the idea is fallacious; and if true, would soon be injurious. The great support of commerce consists in the balance being a level of benefits among all nations.

Two merchants of different nations trading together, will both become rich, and each makes the balance in his own favour; consequently, they do not get rich of each other; and it is the same with respect to the nations in which they reside. The case must be, that each nation must get rich out of its own means, and increases that riches by something which it procures from another in exchange.

If a merchant in England sends an article of English manufacture abroad which costs him a shilling at home, and imports something which sells for two, he makes a balance of one shilling in his favour; but this is not gained out of the foreign nation or the foreign merchant,

---

* In America the increase of commerce is greater in proportion than in England. It is, at this time, at least one half more than at any period prior to the revolution. The greatest number of vessels cleared out of the port of Philadelphia, before the commencement of the war, was between eight and nine hundred. In the year 1788, the number was upwards of twelve hundred. As the State of Pennsylvania is estimated at an eighth part of the United States in population, the whole number of vessels must now be nearly ten thousand. (Author's note)

for he also does the same by the articles he receives, and neither has the advantage upon the other. The original value of the two articles in their proper countries was but two shillings; but by changing their places, they acquire a new idea of value, equal to double what they had first, and that increased value is equally divided.

There is no otherwise a balance on foreign than on domestic commerce. The merchants of London and Newcastle trade on the same principles, as if they resided in different nations, and make their balances in the same manner: yet London does not get rich out of Newcastle, any more than Newcastle out of London: but coals, the merchandize of Newcastle, have an additional value at London, and London merchandize has the same at Newcastle.

Though the principle of all commerce is the same, the domestic, in a national view, is the part the most beneficial; because the whole of the advantages, an both sides, rests within the nation; whereas, in foreign commerce, it is only a participation of one-half.

The most unprofitable of all commerce is that connected with foreign dominion. To a few individuals it may be beneficial, merely because it is commerce; but to the nation it is a loss. The expense of maintaining dominion more than absorbs the profits of any trade. It does not increase the general quantity in the world, but operates to lessen it; and as a greater mass would be afloat by relinquishing dominion, the participation without the expense would be more valuable than a greater quantity with it.

But it is impossible to engross commerce by dominion; and therefore it is still more fallacious. It cannot exist in confined channels, and necessarily breaks out by regular or irregular means, that defeat the attempt: and to succeed would be still worse. France, since the Revolution, has been more indifferent as to foreign possessions, and other nations will become the same when they investigate the subject with respect to commerce.

To the expense of dominion is to be added that of navies, and when the amounts of the two are subtracted from the profits of commerce, it will appear, that what is called the balance of trade, even admitting it to exist, is not enjoyed by the nation, but absorbed by the Government.

The idea of having navies for the protection of commerce is delusive. It is putting means of destruction for the means of protection. Commerce needs no other protection than the reciprocal interest which every nation feels in supporting it—it is common stock—it exists by a balance of advantages to all; and the only interruption it meets, is from the present uncivilised state of governments, and which it is its common interest to reform.*

Quitting this subject, I now proceed to other matters.—As it is necessary to include England in the prospect of a general reformation, it is proper to inquire into the defects of its government. It is only by each nation reforming its own, that the whole can be improved, and the full benefit of reformation enjoyed. Only partial advantages can flow from partial reforms.

France and England are the only two countries in Europe where a reformation in government could have successfully begun. The one secure by the ocean, and the other by the immensity of its internal strength, could defy the malignancy of foreign despotism. But it is with revolutions as with commerce, the advantages increase by their becoming general, and double to either what each would receive alone.

As a new system is now opening to the view of the world, the European courts are plotting to counteract it. Alliances, contrary to all former systems, are agitating, and a common interest of courts is forming against the common interest of man. This combination draws a line that runs throughout Europe, and presents a cause so entirely new as to exclude all calculations from former circumstances. While despotism warred with despotism, man had no interest in the contest; but in a cause that unites the soldier with the citizen, and nation with nation, the despotism of courts, though it feels the danger and meditates revenge, is afraid to strike.

No question has arisen within the records of history that pressed with the importance of the present. It is not whether this or that party shall be in or not, or Whig or Tory, high or low shall prevail; but whether man shall inherit his rights, and universal civilisation take place? Whether the fruits of his labours shall be enjoyed by himself or consumed by the profligacy of governments? Whether robbery shall be banished from courts, and wretchedness from countries?

---

* When I saw Mr. Pitt's mode of estimating the balance of trade, in one of his parliamentary speeches, he appeared to me to know nothing of the nature and interest of commerce; and no man has more wantonly tortured it than himself. During a period of peace it has been havocked with the calamities of war. Three times has it been thrown into stagnation, and the vessels unmanned by impressing, within less than four years of peace. (Author's note)

When, in countries that are called civilised, we see age going to the workhouse and youth to the gallows, something must be wrong in the system of government. It would seem, by the exterior appearance of such countries, that all was happiness; but there lies hidden from the eye of common observation, a mass of wretchedness, that has scarcely any other chance, than to expire in poverty or infamy. Its entrance into life is marked with the presage of its fate; and until this is remedied, it is in vain to punish.

Civil government does not exist in executions; but in making such provision for the instruction of youth and the support of age, as to exclude, as much as possible, profligacy from the one and despair from the other. Instead of this, the resources of a country are lavished upon kings, upon courts, upon hirelings, impostors and prostitutes; and even the poor themselves, with all their wants upon them, are compelled to support the fraud that oppresses them.

Why is it that scarcely any are executed but the poor? The fact is a proof, among other things, of a wretchedness in their condition. Bred up without morals, and cast upon the world without a prospect, they are the exposed sacrifice of vice and legal barbarity. The millions that are superfluously wasted upon governments are more than sufficient to reform those evils, and to benefit the condition of every man in a nation, not included within the purlieus of a court. This I hope to make appear in the progress of this work.

It is the nature of compassion to associate with misfortune. In taking up this subject I seek no recompense—I fear no consequence. Fortified with that proud integrity, that disdains to triumph or to yield, I will advocate the Rights of Man.

It is to my advantage that I have served an apprenticeship to life. I know the value of moral instruction, and I have seen the danger of the contrary.

At an early period—little more than sixteen years of age, raw and adventurous, and heated with the false heroism of a master* who had served in a man-of-war—I began the carver of my own fortune, and entered on board the Terrible Privateer, Captain Death. From this adventure I was happily prevented by the affectionate and moral remonstrance of a good father, who, from his own habits of life, being

---

* Rev. William Knowle, master of the grammar school of Thetford, in Norfolk. (Author's note)

of the Quaker profession, must begin to look upon me as lost. But the impression, much as it effected at the time, began to wear away, and I entered afterwards in the King of Prussia Privateer, Captain Mendez, and went with her to sea. Yet, from such a beginning, and with all the inconvenience of early life against me, I am proud to say, that with a perseverance undismayed by difficulties, a disinterestedness that compelled respect, I have not only contributed to raise a new empire in the world, founded on a new system of government, but I have arrived at an eminence in political literature, the most difficult of all lines to succeed and excel in, which aristocracy with all its aids has not been able to reach or to rival.\*

---

\* Politics and self-interest have been so uniformly connected that the world, from being so often deceived, has a right to be suspicious of public characters, but with regard to myself I am perfectly easy on this head. I did not, at my first setting out in public life, nearly seventeen years ago, turn my thoughts to subjects of government from motives of interest, and my conduct from that moment to this proves the fact. I saw an opportunity in which I thought I could do some good, and I followed exactly what my heart dictated. I neither read books, nor studied other people's opinion. I thought for myself. The case was this:

During the suspension of the old governments in America, both prior to and at the breaking out of hostilities, I was struck with the order and decorum with which everything was conducted, and impressed with the idea that a little more than what society naturally performed was all the government that was necessary, and that monarchy and aristocracy were frauds and impositions upon mankind. On these principles I published the pamphlet *Common Sense*. The success it met with was beyond anything since the invention of printing. I gave the copyright to every state in the Union, and the demand ran to not less than one hundred thousand copies. I continued the subject in the same manner, under the title of the *Crisis*, till the complete establishment of the Revolution.

After the declaration of independence Congress unanimously, and unknown to me, appointed me Secretary in the Foreign Department. This was agreeable to me, because it gave me the opportunity of seeing into the abilities of foreign courts, and their manner of doing business. But a misunderstanding arising between Congress and me, respecting one of their commissioners then in Europe, Mr. Silas Deane, I resigned the office, and declined at the same time the pecuniary offers made by the Ministers of France and Spain, M. Gerald and Don Juan Mirralles.

I had by this time so completely gained the ear and confidence of America, and my own independence was become so visible, as to give me a range in political writing beyond, perhaps, what any man ever possessed in any country, and, what is more extraordinary, I held it undiminished to the end of the war, and enjoy it in the same manner to the present moment. As my object was not myself, I set out with the determination, and happily with the disposition, of not being moved by praise or censure, friendship or calumny, nor of being drawn from my purpose by any personal altercation, and the man who cannot do this is not fit for a public character.

When the war ended I went from Philadelphia to Borden-Town, on the east bank of the Delaware, where I have a small place. Congress was at this time at Prince-Town, fifteen miles distant, and General Washington had taken his headquarters at Rocky Hill, within the neighbourhood of Congress, for the purpose of resigning up his commission (the object for which he accepted it being accomplished), and of retiring to private life. While he was on this business he wrote me the letter which I here subjoin:

"Rocky-Hill, Sept. 10, 1783.

"I have learned since I have been at this place that you are at Borden-Town. Whether for the sake of retirement or economy I know not. Be it for either, for both, or whatever it may, if you will come to this place, and partake with me, I shall be exceedingly happy to see you at it.

Knowing my own heart and feeling myself as I now do, superior to all the skirmish of party, the inveteracy of interested or mistaken opponents, I answer not to falsehood or abuse, but proceed to the defects of the English Government.

I begin with charters and corporations.

It is a perversion of terms to say that a charter gives rights. It operates by a contrary effect—that of taking rights away. Rights are inherently in all the inhabitants; but charters, by annulling those rights, in the majority, leave the right, by exclusion, in the hands of a few. If charters were constructed so as to express in direct terms, "that every inhabitant, who is not a member of a corporation, shall not exercise the right of voting," such charters would, in the face, be charters not of rights, but of exclusion. The effect is the same under the form they now stand; and the only persons on whom they operate are the persons

---

"Your presence may remind Congress of your past services to this country, and if it is in my power to impress them, command my best exertions with freedom, as they will be rendered cheerfully by one who entertains a lively sense of the importance of your works, and who, with much pleasure, subscribes himself,

Your sincere friend, G. Washington."

During the war, in the latter end of the year 1780, I formed to myself a design of coming over to England, and communicated it to General Greene, who was then in Philadelphia on his route to the southward, General Washington being then at too great a distance to communicate with immediately. I was strongly impressed with the idea that if I could get over to England without being known, and only remain in safety till I could get out a publication, that I could open the eyes of the country with respect to the madness and stupidity of its Government. I saw that the parties in Parliament had pitted themselves as far as they could go, and could make no new impressions on each other. General Greene entered fully into my views, but the affair of Arnold and Andre happening just after, he changed his mind, under strong apprehensions for my safety, wrote very pressingly to me from Annapolis, in Maryland, to give up the design, which, with some reluctance, I did. Soon after this I accompanied Colonel Lawrens, son of Mr. Lawrens, who was then in the Tower, to France on business from Congress. We landed at L'orient, and while I remained there, he being gone forward, a circumstance occurred that renewed my former design. An English packet from Falmouth to New York, with the Government dispatches on board, was brought into L'orient. That a packet should be taken is no extraordinary thing, but that the dispatches should be taken with it will scarcely be credited, as they are always slung at the cabin window in a bag loaded with cannon-ball, and ready to be sunk at a moment. The fact, however, is as I have stated it, for the dispatches came into my hands, and I read them. The capture, as I was informed, succeeded by the following stratagem: The captain of the *Madame* privateer, who spoke English, on coming up with the packet, passed himself for the captain of an English frigate, and invited the captain of the packet on board, which, when done, he sent some of his own hands back, and he secured the mail. But be the circumstance of the capture what it may, I speak with certainty as to the Government dispatches. They were sent up to Paris to Count Vergennes, and when Colonel Lawrens and myself returned to America we took the originals to Congress.

By these dispatches I saw into the stupidity of the English Cabinet far more than I otherwise could have done, and I renewed my former design. But Colonel Lawrens was so unwilling to return alone, more especially as, among other matters, we had a charge of upwards of two hundred thousand pounds sterling in money, that I gave in to his wishes, and finally gave up my plan. But I am now certain that if I could have executed it that it would not have been altogether unsuccessful. (Author's note)

whom they exclude. Those whose rights are guaranteed, by not being taken away, exercise no other rights than as members of the community they are entitled to without a charter; and, therefore, all charters have no other than an indirect negative operation. They do not give rights to A, but they make a difference in favour of A by taking away the right of B, and consequently are instruments of injustice.

But charters and corporations have a more extensive evil effect than what relates merely to elections. They are sources of endless contentions in the places where they exist, and they lessen the common rights of national society. A native of England, under the operation of these charters and corporations, cannot be said to be an Englishman in the full sense of the word. He is not free of the nation, in the same manner that a Frenchman is free of France, and an American of America. His rights are circumscribed to the town, and, in some cases, to the parish of his birth; and all other parts, though in his native land, are to him as a foreign country. To acquire a residence in these, he must undergo a local naturalisation by purchase, or he is forbidden or expelled the place. This species of feudality is kept up to aggrandise the corporations at the ruin of towns; and the effect is visible.

The generality of corporation towns are in a state of solitary decay, and prevented from further ruin only by some circumstance in their situation, such as a navigable river, or a plentiful surrounding country. As population is one of the chief sources of wealth (for without it land itself has no value), everything which operates to prevent it must lessen the value of property; and as corporations have not only this tendency, but directly this effect, they cannot but be injurious. If any policy were to be followed, instead of that of general freedom, to every person to settle where he chose (as in France or America) it would be more consistent to give encouragement to new comers than to preclude their admission by exacting premiums from them.*

---

* It is difficult to account for the origin of charter and corporation towns, unless we suppose them to have arisen out of, or been connected with, some species of garrison service. The times in which they began justify this idea. The generality of those towns have been garrisons, and the corporations were charged with the care of the gates of the towns, when no military garrison was present. Their refusing or granting admission to strangers, which has produced the custom of giving, selling, and buying freedom, has more of the nature of garrison authority than civil government. Soldiers are free of all corporations throughout the nation, by the same propriety that every soldier is free of every garrison, and no other persons are. He can follow any employment, with the permission of his officers, in any corporation towns throughout the nation. (Author's note)

The persons most immediately interested in the abolition of corporations are the inhabitants of the towns where corporations are established. The instances of Manchester, Birmingham, and Sheffield show, by contrast, the injuries which those Gothic institutions are to property and commerce. A few examples may be found, such as that of London, whose natural and commercial advantage, owing to its situation on the Thames, is capable of bearing up against the political evils of a corporation; but in almost all other cases the fatality is too visible to be doubted or denied.

Though the whole nation is not so directly affected by the depression of property in corporation towns as the inhabitants themselves, it partakes of the consequence. By lessening the value of property, the quantity of national commerce is curtailed. Every man is a customer in proportion to his ability; and as all parts of a nation trade with each other, whatever affects any of the parts must necessarily communicate to the whole.

As one of the Houses of the English Parliament is, in a great measure, made up of elections from these corporations; and as it is unnatural that a pure stream should flow from a foul fountain, its vices are but a continuation of the vices of its origin. A man of moral honour and good political principles cannot submit to the mean drudgery and disgraceful arts, by which such elections are carried. To be a successful candidate, he must be destitute of the qualities that constitute a just legislator; and being thus disciplined to corruption by the mode of entering into Parliament, it is not to be expected that the representative should be better than the man.

Mr. Burke, in speaking of the English representation, has advanced as bold a challenge as ever was given in the days of chivalry. "Our representation," says he, "has been found *perfectly adequate to all the purposes* for which a representation of the people can be desired or devised." "I defy," continues he, "the enemies of our constitution to show the contrary."—This declaration from a man who has been in constant opposition to all the measures of parliament the whole of his political life, a year or two excepted, is most extraordinary; and, comparing him with himself, admits of no other alternative, than that he acted against his judgment as a member, or has declared contrary to it as an author.

But it is not in the representation only that the defects lie, and therefore I proceed in the next place to the aristocracy.

What is called the House of Peers, is constituted on a ground very similar to that, against which there is no law in other cases. It amounts to a combination of persons in one common interest. No better reason can be given, why a house of legislation should be composed entirely of men whose occupation consists in letting landed property, than why it should be composed of those who hire, or of brewers, or bakers, or any other separate class of men. Mr. Burke calls this house *"the great ground and pillar of security to the landed interest."* Let us examine this idea.

What pillar of security does the landed interest require more than any other interest in the state, or what right has it to a distinct and separate representation from the general interest of a nation? The only use to be made of this power (and which it always has made), is to ward off taxes from itself, and throw the burthen upon those articles of consumption by which itself would be least affected.

That this has been the consequence (and will always be the consequence) of constructing governments on combinations, is evident with respect to England, from the history of its taxes.

Notwithstanding taxes have increased and multiplied upon every article of common consumption, the land-tax, which more particularly affects this "pillar," has diminished. In 1778 the amount of the land-tax was £1,950,000, which is half-a-million less than it produced almost a hundred years ago,* notwithstanding the rentals are in many instances doubled since that period.

Before the coming of the Hanoverians, the taxes were divided in nearly equal proportions between the land and articles of consumption, the land bearing rather the largest share: but since that era nearly thirteen millions annually of new taxes have been thrown upon consumption. The consequence of which has been a constant increase in the number and wretchedness of the poor, and in the amount of the poor-rates. Yet here again the burthen does not fall in equal proportions on the aristocracy with the rest of the community. Their residences, whether in town or country, are not mixed with the habitations of the poor. They live apart from distress, and the expense of relieving it. It is in manufacturing towns and labouring villages that those burthens press the heaviest; in many of which it is one class of poor supporting another.

* See Sir John Sinclair's History of the Revenue. The land-tax in 1646 was £2,473,499. (Author's note)

Several of the most heavy and productive taxes are so contrived, as to give an exemption to this pillar, thus standing in its own defence. The tax upon beer brewed for sale does not affect the aristocracy, who brew their own beer free from this duty. It falls only on those who have not conveniency or ability to brew, and who must purchase it in small quantities. But what will mankind think of the justice of taxation, when they know that this tax alone, from which the aristocracy are from circumstances exempt, is nearly equal to the whole of the land-tax, being in the year 1788, and it is not less now, £1,666,152, and with its proportion of the taxes on malt and hops, it exceeds it.—That a single article, thus partially consumed, and that chiefly by the working part, should be subject to a tax, equal to that on the whole rental of a nation, is, perhaps, a fact not to be paralleled in the histories of revenues.

This is one of the circumstances resulting from a house of legislation, composed on the ground of a combination of common interest; for whatever their separate politics as to parties may be, in this they are united. Whether a combination acts to raise the price of any article for sale, or rate of wages; or whether it acts to throw taxes from itself upon another class of the community, the principle and the effect are the same; and if the one be illegal, it will be difficult to show that the other ought to exist.

It is no use to say that taxes are first proposed in the House of Commons; for as the other house has always a negative, it can always defend itself; and it would be ridiculous to suppose that its acquiescence in the measures to be proposed were not understood before hand. Besides which, it has obtained so much influence by borough-traffic, and so many of its relations and connections are distributed on both sides the commons, as to give it, besides an absolute negative in one house, a preponderancy in the other, in all matters of common concern.

It is difficult to discover what is meant by the *landed interest*, if it does not mean a combination of aristocratical landholders, opposing their own pecuniary interest to that of the farmer, and every branch of trade, commerce, and manufacture. In all other respects it is the only interest that needs no partial protection. It enjoys the general protection of the world. Every individual, high or low, is interested in the fruits of the earth; men, women, and children, of all ages and degrees, will turn out to assist the farmer, rather than a harvest should not be got in; and they will not act thus by any other property. It is the only one for which the common prayer of mankind is put up, and the only one that can never fail from the want of means. It is the interest, not of the policy, but of the existence of man, and when it ceases, he must cease to be.

No other interest in a nation stands on the same united support. Commerce, manufactures, arts, sciences, and everything else, compared with this, are supported but in parts. Their prosperity or their decay has not the same universal influence. When the valleys laugh and sing, it is not the farmer only, but all creation that rejoice. It is a prosperity that excludes all envy; and this cannot be said of anything else.

Why then, does Mr. Burke talk of his house of peers as the pillar of the landed interest? Were that pillar to sink into the earth, the same landed property would continue, and the same ploughing, sowing, and reaping would go on. The aristocracy are not the farmers who work the land, and raise the produce, but are the mere consumers of the rent; and when compared with the active world are the drones, a seraglio of males, who neither collect the honey nor form the hive, but exist only for lazy enjoyment.

Mr. Burke, in his first essay, called aristocracy "the Corinthian capital of polished society." Towards completing the figure, he has now added the *pillar*; but still the base is wanting; and whenever a nation choose to act a Samson, not blind, but bold, down will go the temple of Dagon, the Lords and the Philistines.

If a house of legislation is to be composed of men of one class, for the purpose of protecting a distinct interest, all the other interests should have the same. The inequality, as well as the burthen of taxation, arises from admitting it in one case, and not in all. Had there been a house of farmers, there had been no game laws; or a house of merchants and manufacturers, the taxes had neither been so unequal nor so excessive. It is from the power of taxation being in the hands of those who can throw so great a part of it from their own shoulders, that it has raged without a check.

Men of small or moderate estates are more injured by the taxes being thrown on articles of consumption, than they are eased by warding it from landed property, for the following reasons:

First, They consume more of the productive taxable articles, in proportion to their property, than those of large estates.

Secondly, Their residence is chiefly in towns, and their property in houses; and the increase of the poor-rates, occasioned by taxes on consumption, is in much greater proportion than the land-tax has been favoured. In Birmingham, the poor-rates are not less than seven shillings in the pound. From this, as is already observed, the aristocracy are in a great measure exempt.

These are but a part of the mischiefs flowing from the wretched scheme of an house of peers.

As a combination, it can always throw a considerable portion of taxes from itself; and as an hereditary house, accountable to nobody, it resembles a rotten borough, whose consent is to be courted by interest. There are but few of its members, who are not in some mode or other participators, or disposers of the public money. One turns a candle-holder, or a lord in waiting; another a lord of the bed-chamber, a groom of the stole, or any insignificant nominal office to which a salary is annexed, paid out of the public taxes, and which avoids the direct appearance of corruption. Such situations are derogatory to the character of man; and where they can be submitted to, honour cannot reside.

To all these are to be added the numerous dependents, the long list of younger branches and distant relations, who are to be provided for at the public expense: in short, were an estimation to be made of the charge of aristocracy to a nation, it will be found nearly equal to that of supporting the poor. The Duke of Richmond alone (and there are cases similar to his) takes away as much for himself as would maintain two thousand poor and aged persons. Is it, then, any wonder, that under such a system of government, taxes and rates have multiplied to their present extent?

In stating these matters, I speak an open and disinterested language, dictated by no passion but that of humanity. To me, who have not only refused offers, because I thought them improper, but have declined rewards I might with reputation have accepted, it is no wonder that meanness and imposition appear disgustful. Independence is my happiness, and I view things as they are, without regard to place or person; my country is the world, and my religion is to do good.

Mr. Burke, in speaking of the aristocratical law of primogeniture, says, "it is the standing law of our landed inheritance; and which, without question, has a tendency, and I think," continues he, "a happy tendency, to preserve a character of weight and consequence."

Mr. Burke may call this law what he pleases, but humanity and impartial reflection will denounce it as a law of brutal injustice. Were we not accustomed to the daily practice, and did we only hear of it as the law of some distant part of the world, we should conclude that the legislators of such countries had not arrived at a state of civilisation.

As to its preserving a character of *weight and consequence*, the case appears to me directly the reverse. It is an attaint upon character; a sort of privateering on family property. It may have weight among dependent tenants, but it gives none on a scale of national, and much less of universal character. Speaking for myself, my parents were not able to give me a shilling, beyond what they gave me in education; and to do this they distressed themselves: yet, I possess more of what is called consequence, in the world, than any one in Mr. Burke's catalogue of aristocrats.

Having thus glanced at some of the defects of the two houses of parliament, I proceed to what is called the crown, upon which I shall be very concise.

It signifies a nominal office of a million sterling a year, the business of which consists in receiving the money. Whether the person be wise or foolish, sane or insane, a native or a foreigner, matters not. Every ministry acts upon the same idea that Mr. Burke writes, namely, that the people must be hood-winked, and held in superstitious ignorance by some bugbear or other; and what is called the crown answers this purpose, and therefore it answers all the purposes to be expected from it. This is more than can be said of the other two branches.

The hazard to which this office is exposed in all countries, is not from anything that can happen to the man, but from what may happen to the nation—the danger of its coming to its senses.

It has been customary to call the crown the executive power, and the custom is continued, though the reason has ceased.

It was called the *executive*, because the person whom it signified used, formerly, to act in the character of a judge, in administering or executing the laws. The tribunals were then a part of the court. The power, therefore, which is now called the judicial, is what was called the executive and, consequently, one or other of the terms is redundant, and one of the offices useless. When we speak of the crown now, it means nothing; it signifies neither a judge nor a general: besides which it is the laws that govern, and not the man. The old terms are kept up, to give an appearance of consequence to empty forms; and the only effect they have is that of increasing expenses.

Before I proceed to the means of rendering governments more conducive to the general happiness of mankind, than they are at present, it will not be improper to take a review of the progress of taxation in England.

It is a general idea, that when taxes are once laid on, they are never taken off. However true this may have been of late, it was not always so. Either, therefore, the people of former times were more watchful over government than those of the present, or government was administered with less extravagance.

It is now seven hundred years since the Norman conquest, and the establishment of what is called the crown. Taking this portion of time in seven separate periods of one hundred years each, the amount of the annual taxes, at each period, will be as follows:

| | | | |
|---|---|---|---|
| Annual taxes levied by William the Conqueror, beginning in the year 1066 | - | - | £400,000 |
| Annual taxes at 100 years from the conquest (1166) | - | - | 200,000 |
| Annual taxes at 200 years from the conquest (1266) | - | - | 150,000 |
| Annual taxes at 300 years from the conquest (1366) | - | - | 130,000 |
| Annual taxes at 400 years from the conquest (1466) | - | - | 100,000 |

These statements and those which follow, are taken from Sir John Sinclair's History of the Revenue; by which it appears, that taxes continued decreasing for four hundred years, at the expiration of which time they were reduced three-fourths, viz., from four hundred thousand pounds to one hundred thousand. The people of England of the present day, have a traditionary and historical idea of the bravery of their ancestors; but whatever their virtues or their vices might have been, they certainly were a people who would not be imposed upon, and who kept governments in awe as to taxation, if not as to principle. Though they were not able to expel the monarchical usurpation, they restricted it to a republican economy of taxes.

Let us now review the remaining three hundred years:

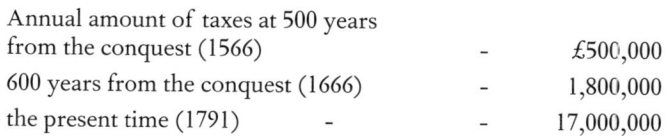

| Annual amount of taxes at 500 years from the conquest (1566) | - | £500,000 |
|---|---|---|
| 600 years from the conquest (1666) | - | 1,800,000 |
| the present time (1791) - | - | 17,000,000 |

The difference between the first four hundred years and the last three, is so astonishing, as to warrant an opinion, that the national character of the English has changed. It would have been impossible to have dragooned the former English, into the excess of taxation that now exists; and when it is considered that the pay of the army, the navy, and of all the revenue officers, is the same now as it was about a hundred years ago, when the taxes were not above a tenth part of what they are at present, it appears impossible to account for the enormous increase and expenditure on any other ground, than extravagance, corruption, and intrigue.*

---

* Several of the court newspapers have of late made frequent mention of Wat Tyler. That his memory should be traduced by court sycophants and those who live on the spoil of a public is not to be wondered at. He was, however, the means of checking the rage and injustice of taxation in his time, and the nation owed much to his valour. The history is concisely this: In the time of Richard II a poll tax was levied of one shilling per head upon every person in the nation of whatever estate or condition, on poor as well as rich, above the age of fifteen years. If any favour was shown in the law it was to the rich rather than to the poor, as no person could be charged more than twenty shillings for himself, family and servants, though ever so numerous; while all other families, under the number of twenty were charged per head. Poll taxes had always been odious, but this being also oppressive and unjust, it excited as it naturally must, universal detestation among the poor and middle classes. The person known by the name of Wat Tyler, whose proper name was Walter, and a tiler by trade, lived at Deptford. The gatherer of the poll tax, on coming to his house, demanded tax for one of his daughters, whom Tyler declared was under the age of fifteen. The tax-gatherer insisted on satisfying himself, and began an indecent examination of the girl, which, enraging the father, he struck him with a hammer that brought him to the ground, and was the cause of his death.

This circumstance served to bring the discontent to an issue. The inhabitants of the neighbourhood espoused the cause of Tyler, who in a few days was joined, according to some histories, by upwards of fifty thousand men, and chosen their chief. With this force he marched to London, to demand an abolition of the tax and a redress of other grievances. The Court, finding itself in a forlorn condition, and, unable to make resistance, agreed, with Richard at its head, to hold a conference with Tyler in Smithfield, making many fair professions, courtier-like, of its dispositions to redress the oppressions. While Richard and Tyler were in conversation on these matters, each being on horseback, Walworth, then Mayor of London, and one of the creatures of the Court, watched an opportunity, and like a cowardly assassin, stabbed Tyler with a dagger, and two or three others falling upon him, he was instantly sacrificed. Tyler appears to have been an intrepid disinterested man with respect to himself. All his proposals made to Richard were on a more just and public ground than those which had been made to John by the Barons, and notwithstanding the sycophancy of historians and men like Mr. Burke, who seek to gloss over a base action of the Court by traducing Tyler, his fame will outlive their falsehood. If the Barons merited a monument to be erected at Runnymede, Tyler merited one in Smithfield. (Author's note)

With the Revolution of 1688, and more so since the Hanover succession, came the destructive system of continental intrigues, and the rage for foreign wars and foreign dominion; systems of such secure mystery that the expenses admit of no accounts; a single line stands for millions. To what excess taxation might have extended had not the French revolution contributed to break up the system, and put an end to pretences, is impossible to say. Viewed, as that revolution ought to be, as the fortunate means of lessening the load of taxes of both countries, it is of as much importance to England as to France; and, if properly improved to all the advantages of which it is capable, and to which it leads, deserves as much celebration in one country as the other.

In pursuing this subject, I shall begin with the matter that first presents itself, that of lessening the burthen of taxes; and shall then add such matter and propositions, respecting the three countries of England, France, and America, as the present prospect of things appears to justify: I mean, an alliance of the three, for the purposes that will be mentioned in their proper place.

What has happened may happen again. By the statement before shown of the progress of taxation, it is seen that taxes have been lessened to a fourth part of what they had formerly been. Though the present circumstances do not admit of the same reduction, yet they admit of such a beginning, as may accomplish that end in less time than in the former case.

The amount of taxes for the year ending at Michaelmas 1788, was as follows:

| | | | | |
|---|---|---|---|---|
| Land-tax | - | - | - | £1,950,000 |
| Customs | - | - | - | 3,789,274 |
| Excise (including old and new malt) | | - | | 6,751,727 |
| Stamps | - | - | - | 1,278,214 |
| Miscellaneous taxes and incidents | - | | - | 1,803,755 |
| | | | | £15,572,755 |

Since the year 1788, upwards of one million new taxes have been laid on, besides the produce of the lotteries; and as the taxes have in general been more productive since than before, the amount may be taken, in round numbers, at £17,000,000. (The expense of collection and the drawbacks, which together amount to nearly two millions, are paid out of the gross amount; and the above is the net sum paid into the exchequer.) This sum of seventeen millions is applied to two different purposes; the one to pay the interest of the National Debt, the other to the current expenses of each year. About nine millions are appropriated to the former; and the remainder, being nearly eight millions, to the latter. As to the million, said to be applied to the reduction of the debt, it is so much like paying with one hand and taking out with the other, as not to merit much notice.

It happened, fortunately for France, that she possessed national domains for paying off her debt, and thereby lessening her taxes; but as this is not the case with England, her reduction of taxes can only take place by reducing the current expenses, which may now be done to the amount of four or five millions annually, as will hereafter appear. When this is accomplished it will more than counter-balance the enormous charge of the American war; and the saving will be from the same source from whence the evil arose.

As to the national debt, however heavy the interest may be in taxes, yet, as it serves to keep alive a capital useful to commerce, it balances by its effects a considerable part of its own weight; and as the quantity of gold and silver is, by some means or other, short of its proper proportion, being not more than twenty millions, whereas it should be sixty (foreign intrigue, foreign wars, foreign dominions, will in a great measure account for the deficiency), it would, besides the injustice, be bad policy to extinguish a capital that serves to supply that defect. But with respect to the current expense, whatever is saved therefrom is gain. The excess may serve to keep corruption alive, but it has no re-action on credit and commerce, like the interest of the debt.

It is now very probable that the English Government (I do not mean the nation) is unfriendly to the French Revolution. Whatever serves to expose the intrigue and lessen the influence of courts, by lessening taxation, will be unwelcome to those who feed upon the spoil. Whilst the clamour of French intrigue, arbitrary power, popery, and wooden shoes could be kept up, the nation was easily allured and alarmed into taxes. Those days are now past: deception, it is to be hoped, has reaped its last harvest, and better times are in prospect for both countries, and for the world.

Taking it for granted that an alliance may be formed between England, France, and America for the purposes hereafter to be mentioned, the national expenses of France and England may consequently be lessened. The same fleets and armies will no longer be necessary to either, and the reduction can be made ship for ship on each side. But to accomplish these objects the governments must necessarily be fitted to a common and correspondent principle. Confidence can never take place while an hostile disposition remains in either, or where mystery and secrecy on one side is opposed to candour and openness on the other.

These matters admitted, the national expenses might be put back, *for the sake of a precedent*, to what they were at some period when France and England were not enemies. This, consequently, must be prior to the Hanover succession, and also to the Revolution of 1688.* The first instance that presents itself, antecedent to those dates, is in the very wasteful and profligate times of Charles the Second; at which time England and France acted as allies. If I have chosen a period of great extravagance, it will serve to show modern extravagance in a still worse light; especially as the pay of the navy, the army, and the revenue officers has not increased since that time.

The peace establishment was then as follows (see Sir John Sinclair's History of the Revenue):

| | | | |
|---|---|---|---|
| Navy | - | - | £300,000 |
| Army | - | - | 212,000 |
| Ordnance | - | - | 40,000 |
| Civil List | - | - | 462,115 |
| | | | £1,014,115 |

---

* I happened to be in England at the celebration of the centenary of the Revolution of 1688. The characters of William and Mary have always appeared to be detestable; the one seeking to destroy his uncle, and the other her father, to get possession of power themselves; yet, as the nation was disposed to think something of that event, I felt hurt at seeing it ascribe the whole reputation of it to a man who had undertaken it as a job and who, besides what he otherwise got, charged six hundred thousand pounds for the expense of the fleet that brought him from Holland. George the First acted the same close-fisted part as William had done, and bought the Duchy of Bremen with the money he got from England, two hundred and fifty thousand pounds over and above his pay as king, and having thus purchased it at the expense of England, added it to his Hanoverian dominions for his own private profit. In fact, every nation that does not govern itself is governed as a job. England has been the prey of jobs ever since the Revolution. (Author's note)

The parliament, however, settled the whole annual peace establishment at $1,200,000.* If we go back to the time of Elizabeth the amount of all the taxes was but half a million, yet the nation sees nothing during that period that reproaches it with want of consequence.

All circumstances, then, taken together, arising from the French revolution, from the approaching harmony and reciprocal interest of the two nations, the abolition of the court intrigue on both sides, and the progress of knowledge in the science of government, the annual expenditure might be put back to one million and a half, viz.:

| | | | |
|---|---|---|---|
| Navy | - | - | £500,000 |
| Army | - | - | 500,000 |
| Expenses of Government | | - | 500,000 |
| | | | £1,500,000 |

Even this sum is six times greater than the expenses of government are in America, yet the civil internal government in England (I mean that administered by means of quarter sessions, juries and assize, and which, in fact, is nearly the whole, and performed by the nation), is less expense upon the revenue, than the same species and portion of government is in America.

It is time that nations should be rational, and not be governed like animals, for the pleasure of their riders. To read the history of kings, a man would be almost inclined to suppose that government consisted in stag-hunting, and that every nation paid a million a-year to a huntsman. Man ought to have pride, or shame enough to blush at being thus imposed upon, and when he feels his proper character he will. Upon all subjects of this nature, there is often passing in the mind, a train of ideas he has not yet accustomed himself to encourage and communicate. Restrained by something that puts on the character of prudence, he acts the hypocrite upon himself as well as to others. It is, however, curious to observe how soon this spell can be dissolved. A single expression, boldly conceived and uttered, will sometimes put a whole company into their proper feelings: and whole nations are acted on in the same manner.

---

* Charles, like his predecessors and successors, finding that war was the harvest of governments, engaged in a war with the Dutch, the expense of which increased the annual expenditure to £1,800,000 as stated under the date of 1666; but the peace establishment was but £1,200,000. (Author's note)

As to the offices of which any civil government may be composed, it matters but little by what names they are described. In the routine of business, as before observed, whether a man be styled a president, a king, an emperor, a senator, or anything else, it is impossible that any service he can perform, can merit from a nation more than ten thousand pounds a year; and as no man should be paid beyond his services, so every man of a proper heart will not accept more. Public money ought to be touched with the most scrupulous consciousness of honour. It is not the produce of riches only, but of the hard earnings of labour and poverty. It is drawn even from the bitterness of want and misery. Not a beggar passes, or perishes in the streets, whose mite is not in that mass.

Were it possible that the Congress of America could be so lost to their duty, and to the interest of their constituents, as to offer General Washington, as president of America, a million a year, he would not, and he could not, accept it. His sense of honour is of another kind. It has cost England almost seventy millions sterling, to maintain a family imported from abroad, of very inferior capacity to thousands in the nation; and scarcely a year has passed that has not produced some new mercenary application. Even the physicians' bills have been sent to the public to be paid. No wonder that jails are crowded, and taxes and poor-rates increased. Under such systems, nothing is to be looked for but what has already happened; and as to reformation, whenever it come, it must be from the nation, and not from the government.

To show that the sum of five hundred thousand pounds is more than sufficient to defray all the expenses of the government, exclusive of navies and armies, the following estimate is added, for any country, of the same extent as England.

In the first place, three hundred representatives fairly elected, are sufficient for all the purposes to which legislation can apply, and preferable to a larger number. They may be divided into two or three houses, or meet in one, as in France, or in any manner a constitution shall direct.

As representation is always considered, in free countries, as the most honourable of all stations, the allowance made to it is merely to defray the expense which the representatives incur by that service, and not to it as an office.

| | |
|---|---:|
| If an allowance, at the rate of five hundred pounds per annum, be made to every representative, deducting for non-attendance, the expense, if the whole number attended for six months, each year, would be | £75,000 |
| The official departments cannot reasonably exceed the following number, with the salaries annexed: | |
| Three offices at ten thousand pounds each | £30,000 |
| Ten ditto, at five thousand pounds each | 50,000 |
| Twenty ditto, at two thousand pounds each | 40,000 |
| Forty ditto, at one thousand pounds each | 40,000 |
| Two hundred ditto, at five hundred pounds each | 100,000 |
| Three hundred ditto, at two hundred pounds each | 60,000 |
| Five hundred ditto, at one hundred pounds each | 50,000 |
| Seven hundred ditto, at seventy-five pounds each | 52,500 |
| | £497,500 |

If a nation choose, it can deduct four per cent from all offices, and make one of twenty thousand per annum.

All revenue officers are paid out of the monies they collect, and therefore, are not in this estimation.

The foregoing is not offered as an exact detail of offices, but to show the number of rate of salaries which five hundred thousand pounds will support; and it will, on experience, be found impracticable to find business sufficient to justify even this expense. As to the manner in which office business is now performed, the Chiefs, in several offices, such as the post-office, and certain offices in the exchequer, etc., do little more than sign their names three or four times a year; and the whole duty is performed by under-clerks.

Taking, therefore, one million and a half as a sufficient peace establishment for all the honest purposes of government, which is three hundred thousand pounds more than the peace establishment in the profligate and prodigal times of Charles the Second (notwithstanding, as has been already observed, the pay and salaries of the army, navy, and revenue officers, continue the same as at that period), there will remain a surplus of upwards of six millions out of the present current expenses. The question then will be, how to dispose of this surplus.

Whoever has observed the manner in which trade and taxes twist themselves together, must be sensible of the impossibility of separating them suddenly.

First. Because the articles now on hand are already charged with the duty, and the reduction cannot take place on the present stock.

Secondly. Because, on all those articles on which the duty is charged in the gross, such as per barrel, hogshead, hundred weight, or ton, the abolition of the duty does not admit of being divided down so as fully to relieve the consumer, who purchases by the pint, or the pound. The last duty laid on strong beer and ale was three shillings per barrel, which, if taken off, would lessen the purchase only half a farthing per pint, and consequently, would not reach to practical relief.

This being the condition of a great part of the taxes, it will be necessary to look for such others as are free from this embarrassment and where the relief will be direct and visible, and capable of immediate operation.

In the first place, then, the poor-rates are a direct tax which every house-keeper feels, and who knows also, to a farthing, the sum which he pays. The national amount of the whole of the poor-rates is not positively known, but can be procured. Sir John Sinclair, in his History of the Revenue has stated it at £2,100,587. A considerable part of which is expended in litigations, in which the poor, instead of being relieved, are tormented. The expense, however, is the same to the parish from whatever cause it arises.

In Birmingham, the amount of poor-rates is fourteen thousand pounds a year. This, though a large sum, is moderate, compared with the population. Birmingham is said to contain seventy thousand souls, and on a proportion of seventy thousand to fourteen thousand pounds poor-rates, the national amount of poor-rates, taking the population of England as seven millions, would be but one million four hundred thousand pounds. It is, therefore, most probable, that the population of Birmingham is over-rated. Fourteen thousand pounds is the proportion upon fifty thousand souls, taking two millions of poor-rates, as the national amount.

Be it, however, what it may, it is no other than the consequence of excessive burthen of taxes, for, at the time when the taxes were very low, the poor were able to maintain themselves; and there were no poor-rates.[*] In the present state of things a labouring man, with a wife or two or three children, does not pay less than between seven and eight pounds a year in

---

[*] Poor-rates began about the time of Henry VIII, when the taxes began to increase, and they have increased as the taxes increased ever since. (Author's note)

taxes. He is not sensible of this, because it is disguised to him in the articles which he buys, and he thinks only of their dearness; but as the taxes take from him, at least, a fourth part of his yearly earnings, he is consequently disabled from providing for a family, especially, if himself, or any of them, are afflicted with sickness.

The first step, therefore, of practical relief, would be to abolish the poor-rates entirely, and in lieu thereof, to make a remission of taxes to the poor of double the amount of the present poor-rates, viz., four millions annually out of the surplus taxes. By this measure, the poor would be benefited two millions, and the house-keepers two millions. This alone would be equal to a reduction of one hundred and twenty millions of the National Debt, and consequently equal to the whole expense of the American War.

It will then remain to be considered, which is the most effectual mode of distributing this remission of four millions.

It is easily seen, that the poor are generally composed of large families of children, and old people past their labour. If these two classes are provided for, the remedy will so far reach to the full extent of the case, that what remains will be incidental, and, in a great measure, fall within the compass of benefit clubs, which, though of humble invention, merit to be ranked among the best of modern institutions.

Admitting England to contain seven millions of souls; if one-fifth thereof are of that class of poor which need support, the number will be one million four hundred thousand. Of this number, one hundred and forty thousand will be aged poor, as will be hereafter shown, and for which a distinct provision will be proposed.

There will then remain one million two hundred and sixty thousand which, at five souls to each family, amount to two hundred and fifty-two thousand families, rendered poor from the expense of children and the weight of taxes.

The number of children under fourteen years of age, in each of those families, will be found to be about five to every two families; some having two, and others three; some one, and others four: some none, and others five; but it rarely happens that more than five are under fourteen years of age, and after this age they are capable of service or of being apprenticed.

Allowing five children (under fourteen years) to every two families,

| | |
|---|---|
| The number of children will be | 630,000 |
| The number of parents, were they all living, would be | 504,000 |

It is certain, that if the children are provided for, the parents are relieved of consequence, because it is from the expense of bringing up children that their poverty arises.

Having thus ascertained the greatest number that can be supposed to need support on account of young families, I proceed to the mode of relief or distribution, which is,

To pay as a remission of taxes to every poor family, out of the surplus taxes, and in room of poor-rates, four pounds a year for every child under fourteen years of age; enjoining the parents of such children to send them to school, to learn reading, writing, and common arithmetic; the ministers of every parish, of every denomination to certify jointly to an office, for that purpose, that this duty is performed.

The amount of this expense will be, for six hundred and thirty thousand children,

at four pounds per annum each                    £2,520,000

By adopting this method, not only the poverty of the parents will be relieved, but ignorance will be banished from the rising generation, and the number of poor will hereafter become less, because their abilities, by the aid of education, will be greater. Many a youth, with good natural genius, who is apprenticed to a mechanical trade, such as a carpenter, joiner, millwright, shipwright, blacksmith, etc., is prevented getting forward the whole of his life from the want of a little common education when a boy.

I now proceed to the case of the aged.

I divide age into two classes. First, the approach of age, beginning at fifty. Secondly, old age commencing at sixty.

At fifty, though the mental faculties of man are in full vigour, and his judgment better than at any preceding date, the bodily powers for laborious life are on the decline. He cannot bear the same quantity of fatigue as at an earlier period. He begins to earn less, and is less capable of enduring wind and weather; and in those more retired employments where much sight is required, he fails apace, and sees himself, like an old horse, beginning to be turned adrift.

At sixty his labour ought to be over, at least from direct necessity. It is painful to see old age working itself to death, in what are called civilised countries, for daily bread.

To form some judgment of the number of those above fifty years of age, I have several times counted the persons I met in the streets of London, men, women, and children, and have generally found that the average is about one in sixteen or seventeen. If it be said that aged persons do not come much into the streets, so neither do infants; and a great proportion of grown children are in schools and in work-shops as apprentices. Taking, then, sixteen for a divisor, the whole number of persons in England of fifty years and upwards, of both sexes, rich and poor, will be four hundred and twenty thousand.

The persons to be provided for out of this gross number will be husbandmen, common labourers, journeymen of every trade and their wives, sailors, and disbanded soldiers, worn out servants of both sexes, and poor widows.

There will be also a considerable number of middling tradesmen, who having lived decently in the former part of life, begin, as age approaches, to lose their business, and at last fall to decay.

Besides these there will be constantly thrown off from the revolutions of that wheel which no man can stop nor regulate, a number from every class of life connected with commerce and adventure.

To provide for all those accidents, and whatever else may befall, I take the number of persons who, at one time or other of their lives, after fifty years of age, may feel it necessary or comfortable to be better supported, than they can support themselves, and that not as a matter of grace and favour, but of right, at one-third of the whole number, which is one hundred and forty thousand, as stated in a previous page, and for whom a distinct provision was proposed to be made. If there be more, society, notwithstanding the show and pomposity of government, is in a deplorable condition in England.

Of this one hundred and forty thousand, I take one half, seventy thousand, to be of the age of fifty and under sixty, and the other half to be sixty years and upwards. Having thus ascertained the probable proportion of the number of aged persons, I proceed to the mode of rendering their condition comfortable, which is:

To pay to every such person of the age of fifty years, and until he shall arrive at the age of sixty, the sum of six pounds per annum out of the surplus taxes, and ten pounds per annum during life after the age of sixty. The expense of which will be,

| Seventy thousand persons, at £6 per annum | £420,000 |
|---|---|
| Seventy thousand persons, at £10 per annum | 700,000 |
| | £1,120,000 |

This support, as already remarked, is not of the nature of a charity but of a right. Every person in England, male and female, pays on an average in taxes two pounds eight shillings and sixpence per annum from the day of his (or her) birth; and, if the expense of collection be added, he pays two pounds eleven shillings and sixpence; consequently, at the end of fifty years he has paid one hundred and twenty-eight pounds fifteen shillings; and at sixty one hundred and fifty-four pounds ten shillings. Converting, therefore, his (or her) individual tax in a tontine, the money he shall receive after fifty years is but little more than the legal interest of the net money he has paid; the rest is made up from those whose circumstances do not require them to draw such support, and the capital in both cases defrays the expenses of government. It is on this ground that I have extended the probable claims to one-third of the number of aged persons in the nation.——Is it, then, better that the lives of one hundred and forty thousand aged persons be rendered comfortable, or that a million a year of public money be expended on any one individual, and him often of the most worthless or insignificant character? Let reason and justice, let honour and humanity, let even hypocrisy, sycophancy and Mr. Burke, let George, let Louis, Leopold, Frederic, Catherine, Cornwallis, or Tippoo Saib, answer the question.*

* Reckoning the taxes by families, five to a family, each family pays on an average £12 7s. 6d. per annum. To this sum are to be added the poor-rates. Though all pay taxes in the articles they consume, all do not pay poor-rates. About two millions are exempted: some as not being house-keepers, others as not being able, and the poor themselves who receive the relief. The average, therefore, of poor-rates on the remaining number, is forty shillings for every family of five persons, which make the whole average amount of taxes and rates £14 17s. 6d. For six persons £17 17s. For seven persons £20 16s. 6d.

The average of taxes in America, under the new or representative system of government, including the interest of the debt contracted in the war, and taking the population at four millions of souls, which it now amounts to, and it is daily increasing, is five shillings per head, men, women, and children. The difference, therefore, between the two governments is as under: (Author's note)

| | England | | | America | | |
|---|---|---|---|---|---|---|
| For a family of five persons | £14 | 17s. | 6d. | £1 | 5s. | 0d. |
| For a family of six persons | 17 | 17 | 0 | 1 | 10 | 0 |
| For a family of seven persons | 20 | 16 | 6 | 1 | 15 | 0 |

The sum thus remitted to the poor will be,

| | |
|---|---|
| To two hundred and fifty-two thousand poor families, containing six hundred and thirty thousand children | £2,520,000 |
| To one hundred and forty thousand aged persons | 1,120,000 |
| | £3,640,000 |

There will then remain three hundred and sixty thousand pounds out of the four millions, part of which may be applied as follows:—

After all the above cases are provided for there will still be a number of families who, though not properly of the class of poor, yet find it difficult to give education to their children; and such children, under such a case, would be in a worse condition than if their parents were actually poor. A nation under a well-regulated government should permit none to remain uninstructed. It is monarchical and aristocratical government only that requires ignorance for its support.

Suppose, then, four hundred thousand children to be in this condition, which is a greater number than ought to be supposed after the provisions already made, the method will be:

To allow for each of those children ten shillings a year for the expense of schooling for six years each, which will give them six months schooling each year, and half a crown a year for paper and spelling books.

The expense of this will be annually £250,000.*

There will then remain one hundred and ten thousand pounds.

Notwithstanding the great modes of relief which the best instituted and best principled government may devise, there will be a number of smaller cases, which it is good policy as well as beneficence in a nation to consider.

Were twenty shillings to be given immediately on the birth of a child, to every woman who should make the demand, and none will

---

* Public schools do not answer the general purpose of the poor. They are chiefly in corporation towns from which the country towns and villages are excluded, or, if admitted, the distance occasions a great loss of time. Education, to be useful to the poor, should be on the spot, and the best method, I believe, to accomplish this is to enable the parents to pay the expenses themselves. There are always persons of both sexes to be found in every village, especially when growing into years, capable of such an undertaking. Twenty children at ten shillings each (and that not more than six months each year) would be as much as some livings amount to in the remotest parts of England, and there are often distressed clergymen's widows to whom such an income would be acceptable. Whatever is given on this account to children answers two purposes. To them it is education—to those who educate them it is a livelihood. (Author's note)

make it whose circumstances do not require it, it might relieve a great deal of instant distress.

There are about two hundred thousand births yearly in England; and if claimed by one fourth,

The amount would be £50,000.

And twenty shillings to every new-married couple who should claim in like manner.

This would not exceed the sum of £20,000.

Also twenty thousand pounds to be appropriated to defray the funeral expenses of persons, who, travelling for work, may die at a distance from their friends. By relieving parishes from this charge, the sick stranger will be better treated.

I shall finish this part of the subject with a plan adapted to the particular condition of a metropolis, such as London.

Cases are continually occurring in a metropolis, different from those which occur in the country, and for which a different, or rather an additional, mode of relief is necessary. In the country, even in large towns, people have a knowledge of each other, and distress never rises to that extreme height it sometimes does in a metropolis. There is no such thing in the country as persons, in the literal sense of the word, starved to death, or dying with cold from the want of a lodging. Yet such cases, and others equally as miserable, happen in London.

Many a youth comes up to London full of expectations, and with little or no money, and unless he get immediate employment he is already half undone; and boys bred up in London without any means of a livelihood, and as it often happens of dissolute parents, are in a still worse condition; and servants long out of place are not much better off. In short, a world of little cases is continually arising, which busy or affluent life knows not of, to open the first door to distress. Hunger is not among the postponable wants, and a day, even a few hours, in such a condition is often the crisis of a life of ruin.

These circumstances which are the general cause of the little thefts and pilferings that lead to greater, may be prevented. There yet remain twenty thousand pounds out of the four millions of surplus taxes, which with another fund hereafter to be mentioned, amounting to about twenty thousand pounds more, cannot be better applied than to this purpose. The plan will then be:

First, To erect two or more buildings, or take some already erected, capable of containing at least six thousand persons, and to have in each of these places as many kinds of employment as can be contrived, so that every person who shall come may find something which he or she can do.

Secondly, To receive all who shall come, without enquiring who or what they are. The only condition to be, that for so much, or so many hours' work, each person shall receive so many meals of wholesome food, and a warm lodging, at least as good as a barrack. That a certain portion of what each person's work shall be worth shall be reserved, and given to him or her, on their going away; and that each person shall stay as long or as short a time, or come as often as he choose, on these conditions.

If each person stayed three months, it would assist by rotation twenty-four thousand persons annually, though the real number, at all times, would be but six thousand. By establishing an asylum of this kind, such persons to whom temporary distresses occur, would have an opportunity to recruit themselves, and be enabled to look out for better employment.

Allowing that their labour paid but one half the expense of supporting them, after reserving a portion of their earnings for themselves, the sum of forty thousand pounds additional would defray all other charges for even a greater number than six thousand.

The fund very properly convertible to this purpose, in addition to the twenty thousand pounds, remaining of the former fund, will be the produce of the tax upon coals, so iniquitously and wantonly applied to the support of the Duke of Richmond. It is horrid that any man, more especially at the price coals now are, should live on the distresses of a community; and any government permitting such an abuse, deserves to be dismissed. This fund is said to be about twenty thousand pounds per annum.

I shall now conclude this plan with enumerating the several particulars, and then proceed to other matters.

The enumeration is as follows:

First, Abolition of two millions poor-rates.

Secondly, Provision for two hundred and fifty thousand poor families.

Thirdly, Education for one million and thirty thousand children.

Fourthly, Comfortable provision for one hundred and forty thousand aged persons.

Fifthly, Donation of twenty shillings each for fifty thousand births.

Sixthly, Donation of twenty shillings each for twenty thousand marriages.

Seventhly, Allowance of twenty thousand pounds for the funeral expenses of persons travelling for work, and dying at a distance from their friends.

Eighthly, Employment, at all times, for the casual poor in the cities of London and Westminster.

By the operation of this plan, the poor laws, those instruments of civil torture, will be superseded, and the wasteful expense of litigation prevented. The hearts of the humane will not be shocked by ragged and hungry children, and persons of seventy and eighty years of age, begging for bread. The dying poor will not be dragged from place to place to breathe their last, as a reprisal of parish upon parish. Widows will have a maintenance for their children, and not be carted away, on the death of their husbands, like culprits and criminals; and children will no longer be considered as increasing the distresses of their parents. The haunts of the wretched will be known, because it will be to their advantage; and the number of petty crimes, the offspring of distress and poverty, will be lessened. The poor, as well as the rich, will then be interested in the support of government, and the cause and apprehension of riots and tumults will cease.—Ye who sit in ease, and solace yourselves in plenty, and such there are in Turkey and Russia, as well as in England, and who say to yourselves, "Are we not well off?" have ye thought of these things? When ye do, ye will cease to speak and feel for yourselves alone.

The plan is easy in practice. It does not embarrass trade by a sudden interruption in the order of taxes, but effects the relief by changing the application of them; and the money necessary for the purpose can be drawn from the excise collections, which are made eight times a year in every market town in England.

Having now arranged and concluded this subject, I proceed to the next.

Taking the present current expenses at seven millions and an half, which is the least amount they are now at, there will remain (after the sum of one million and an half be taken for the new current expenses and four millions for the before-mentioned service) the sum of two millions; part of which to be applied as follows:

Though fleets and armies, by an alliance with France, will, in a great measure, become useless, yet the persons who have devoted themselves to those services, and have thereby unfitted themselves for other lines of life, are not to be sufferers by the means that make others happy. They are a different description of men from those who form or hang about a court.

A part of the army will remain, at least for some years, and also of the navy, for which a provision is already made in the former part of this plan of one million, which is almost half a million more than the peace establishment of the army and navy in the prodigal times of Charles the Second.

Suppose, then, fifteen thousand soldiers to be disbanded, and that an allowance be made to each of three shillings a week during life, clear of all deductions, to be paid in the same manner as the Chelsea College pensioners are paid, and for them to return to their trades and their friends; and also that an addition of fifteen thousand sixpences per week be made to the pay of the soldiers who shall remain; the annual expenses will be to the pay of:

| | |
|---|---:|
| Fifteen thousand disbanded soldiers at three shillings per week | £117,000 |
| Additional pay to the remaining soldiers | 19,500 |
| Suppose that the pay to the officers of the disbanded corps be the same amount as sum allowed to the men | 117,000 |
| | £253,500 |
| To prevent bulky estimations, admit the same sum to the disbanded navy as to the army, and the same increase of pay | 253,500 |
| Total | £507,000 |

Every year some part of this sum of half a million (I omit the odd seven thousand pounds for the purpose of keeping the account unembarrassed) will fall in, and the whole of it in time, as it is on the ground of life annuities, except the increased pay of twenty-nine thousand pounds. As it falls in, part of the taxes may be taken off; and as, for instance, when thirty thousand pounds fall in, the duty on hops may be wholly taken off; and as other parts fall in, the duties on candles and soap may be lessened, till at last they will totally cease. There now remains at least one million and a half of surplus taxes.

The tax on houses and windows is one of those direct taxes, which, like the poor-rates, is not confounded with trade; and, when taken off, the relief will be instantly felt. This tax falls heavy on the middle class of people. The amount of this tax, by the returns of 1788, was:

|  | £ | s. | d. |
|---|---|---|---|
| Houses and windows by the act of 1766 | 385,459 | 11 | 7 |
| Houses and windows by the act of 1779 | 130,739 | 14 | 5 ½ |
| Total | £516,199 | 6 | ½ |

If this tax be struck off, there will then remain about one million of surplus taxes; and as it is always proper to keep a sum in reserve, for incidental matters, it may be best not to extend reductions further in the first instance, but to consider what may be accomplished by other modes of reform.

Among the taxes most heavily felt is the commutation tax. I shall therefore offer a plan for its abolition, by substituting another in its place, which will effect three objects at once: 1, that of removing the burthen to where it can best be borne; 2, restoring justice among families by a distribution of property; 3, extirpating the overgrown influence arising from the unnatural law of primogeniture, which is one of the principal sources of corruption at elections. The amount of commutation tax by the returns of 1788, was £771,657.

When taxes are proposed, the country is amused by the plausible language of taxing luxuries. One thing is called a luxury at one time, and something else at another; but the real luxury does not consist in the article, but in the means of procuring it, and this is always kept out of sight.

I know not why any plant or herb of the field should be a greater luxury in one country than another; but an overgrown estate in either is a luxury at all times, and, as such, is the proper object of taxation.

It is, therefore, right to take those kind tax-making gentlemen up on their own word, and argue on the principle themselves have laid down, that of *taxing luxuries*. If they or their champion, Mr. Burke, who, I fear, is growing out of date, like the man in armour, can prove that an estate of twenty, thirty, or forty thousand pounds a year is not a luxury, I will give up the argument.

Admitting that any annual sum, say, for instance, one thousand pounds, is necessary or sufficient for the support of a family, consequently the second thousand is of the nature of a luxury, the third still more so, and by proceeding on, we shall at last arrive at a sum that may not improperly be called a prohibitable luxury. It would be impolitic to set bounds to property acquired by industry, and therefore it is right to place the prohibition beyond the probable acquisition to which industry can extend; but there ought to be a limit to property or the accumulation of it by bequest. It should pass in some other line. The richest in every nation have poor relations, and those often very near in consanguinity.

The following table of progressive taxation is constructed on the above principles, and as a substitute for the commutation tax. It will reach the point of prohibition by a regular operation, and thereby supersede the aristocratical law of primogeniture.

## TABLE I

A tax on all estates of the clear yearly value of £50, after deducting the land tax, and up

| | | 0s. | 3d. | per pound |
|---|---|---|---|---|
| To £500 | | 0s. | 3d. | per pound |
| From £500 to £1,000 | | 0 | 6 | |
| On the second thousand | | 0 | 9 | |
| On the third | " | 1 | 0 | |
| On the fourth | " | 1 | 6 | |
| On the fifth | " | 2 | 0 | |
| On the sixth | " | 3 | 0 | |
| On the seventh | " | 4 | 0 | |
| On the eighth | " | 5 | 0 | |
| On the ninth | " | 6 | 0 | |
| On the tenth | " | 7 | 0 | |
| On the eleventh | " | 8 | 0 | |
| On the twelfth | " | 9 | 0 | |
| On the thirteenth | " | 10 | 0 | |
| On the fourteenth | " | 11 | 0 | |
| On the fifteenth | " | 12 | 0 | |
| On the sixteenth | " | 13 | 0 | |
| On the seventeenth | " | 14 | 0 | |
| On the eighteenth | " | 15 | 0 | |
| On the nineteenth | " | 16 | 0 | |
| On the twentieth | " | 17 | 0 | |
| On the twenty-first | " | 18 | 0 | |
| On the twenty-second | " | 19 | 0 | |
| On the twenty-third | " | 20 | 0 | |

The foregoing table shows the progression per pound on every progressive thousand. The following table shows the amount of the tax on every thousand separately, and in the last column the total amount of all the separate sums collected.

## TABLE II

An estate of:

| | | | £ | s. | d. |
|---|---|---|---|---|---|
| £50 per annum, at 3d per pound, pays | | | £0 | 12s. | 6d. |
| 100 | " | " | 1 | 5 | 0 |
| 200 | " | " | 2 | 10 | 0 |
| 300 | " | " | 3 | 15 | 0 |
| 400 | " | " | 5 | 0 | 0 |
| 500 | " | " | 7 | 5 | 0 |

After £500, the tax of 6d. per pound takes place on the second £500; consequently an estate of £1,000 per annum pays £2l, 15s., and so on.

| £ | s. | d. | £ | s. | Total £ | s. |
|---|---|---|---|---|---|---|
| 1st 500 at | 0 | 3 per pound | 7 | 5 | 7 | 5 |
| 500 to 1000 | 0 | 6 | 14 | 10 | 21 | 5 |
| 2nd 1000 at | 0 | 9 | 37 | 11 | 59 | 5 |
| 3rd " | 1 | 0 | 50 | 0 | 109 | 5 |
| 4th " | 1 | 6 | 75 | 0 | 184 | 5 |
| 5th " | 2 | 0 | 100 | 0 | 284 | 5 |
| 6th " | 3 | 0 | 150 | 0 | 434 | 5 |
| 7th " | 4 | 0 | 200 | 0 | 634 | 5 |
| 8th " | 5 | 0 | 250 | 0 | 880 | 5 |
| 9th " | 6 | 0 | 300 | 0 | 1100 | 5 |
| 10th " | 7 | 0 | 350 | 0 | 1530 | 5 |
| 11th " | 8 | 0 | 400 | 0 | 1930 | 5 |
| 12th " | 9 | 0 | 450 | 0 | 2380 | 5 |
| 13th " | 10 | 0 | 500 | 0 | 2880 | 5 |
| 14th " | 11 | 0 | 550 | 0 | 3430 | 5 |
| 15th " | 12 | 0 | 600 | 0 | 4030 | 5 |
| 16th " | 13 | 0 | 650 | 0 | 4680 | 5 |
| 17th " | 14 | 0 | 700 | 0 | 5380 | 5 |
| 18th " | 15 | 0 | 750 | 0 | 6130 | 5 |
| 19th " | 16 | 0 | 800 | 0 | 6930 | 5 |
| 20th " | 17 | 0 | 850 | 0 | 7780 | 5 |
| 21st " | 18 | 0 | 900 | 0 | 8680 | 5 |
| 22nd " | 19 | 0 | 950 | 0 | 9630 | 5 |
| 23rd " | 20 | 0 | 1000 | 0 | 10630 | 5 |

At the twenty-third thousand the tax becomes 20s. in the pound, and consequently every thousand beyond that sum can produce no profit but by dividing the estate. Yet formidable as this tax appears, it will not, I believe, produce so much as the commutation tax; should it produce more, it ought to be lowered to that amount upon estates under two or three thousand a year.

On small and middling estates it is lighter (as it is intended to be) than the commutation tax. It is not till after seven or eight thousand a year that it begins to be heavy. The object is not so much the produce of the tax as the justice of the measure. The aristocracy has screened itself too much, and this serves to restore a part of the lost equilibrium.

As an instance of its screening itself, it is only necessary to look back to the first establishment of the excise laws, at what is called the Restoration, or the coming of Charles the Second. The aristocratical interest then in power, commuted the feudal services itself was under, by laying a tax on beer brewed for sale; that is, they compounded with Charles for an exemption from those services for themselves and their heirs, by a tax to be paid by other people. The aristocracy do not purchase beer brewed for sale, but brew their own beer free of the duty, and if any commutation at that time were necessary, it ought to have been at the expense of those for whom the exemptions from those services were intended;* instead of which, it was thrown on an entirely different class of men.

But the chief object of this progressive tax (besides the justice of rendering taxes more equal than they are) is, as already stated, to extirpate the overgrown influence arising from the unnatural law of primogeniture, and which is one of the principal sources of corruption at elections.

It would be attended with no good consequences to enquire how such vast estates as thirty, forty, or fifty thousand a year could commence, and that at a time when commerce and manufactures were not in a state to admit of such acquisitions. Let it be sufficient to remedy the evil by putting them in a condition of descending again to the community by the quiet means of apportioning them among all the heirs and heiresses

---

* The tax on beer brewed for sale, from which the aristocracy are exempt, is almost one million more than the present commutation tax, being by the returns of 1788, £1,666,152—and, consequently, they ought to take on themselves the amount of the commutation tax, as they are already exempted from one which is almost a million greater. (Author's note)

of those families. This will be the more necessary, because hitherto the aristocracy have quartered their younger children and connections upon the public in useless posts, places and offices, which when abolished will leave them destitute, unless the law of primogeniture be also abolished or superseded.

A progressive tax will, in a great measure, effect this object, and that as a matter of interest to the parties most immediately concerned, as will be seen by the following table; which shows the net produce upon every estate, after subtracting the tax. By this it will appear that after an estate exceeds thirteen or fourteen thousand a year, the remainder produces but little profit to the holder, and consequently, will pass either to the younger children, or to other kindred.

## TABLE III

Showing the net produce of every estate from one thousand to twenty-three thousand pounds a year.

| No. of thousands per ann. | Total tax subtracted | Net produce |
|---|---|---|
| £1000 | £21 | £979 |
| 2000 | 59 | 1941 |
| 3000 | 109 | 2891 |
| 4000 | 184 | 3816 |
| 5000 | 284 | 4716 |
| 6000 | 434 | 5566 |
| 7000 | 634 | 6366 |
| 8000 | 880 | 7120 |
| 9000 | 1100 | 7900 |
| 10,000 | 1530 | 8470 |
| 11,000 | 1930 | 9070 |
| 12,000 | 2380 | 9620 |
| 13,000 | 2880 | 10,120 |
| 14,000 | 3430 | 10,570 |
| 15,000 | 4030 | 10,970 |
| 16,000 | 4680 | 11,320 |
| 17,000 | 5380 | 11,620 |
| 18,000 | 6130 | 11,870 |
| 19,000 | 6930 | 12,170 |
| 20,000 | 7780 | 12,220 |
| 21,000 | 8680 | 12,320 |
| 22,000 | 9630 | 12,370 |
| 23,000 | 10,630 | 12,370 |

N.B. The odd shillings are dropped in this table.

According to this table, an estate cannot produce more than £12,370 clear of the land tax and the progressive tax, and therefore the dividing such estates will follow as a matter of family interest. An estate of £23,000 a year, divided into five estates of four thousand each and one of three, will be charged only £1,129 which is but five per cent, but if held by one possessor, will be charged £10,630.

Although an enquiry into the origin of those estates be unnecessary, the continuation of them in their present state is another subject. It is a matter of national concern. As hereditary estates, the law has created the evil, and it ought also to provide the remedy. Primogeniture ought to be abolished, not only because it is unnatural and unjust, but because the country suffers by its operation. By cutting off (as before observed) the younger children from their proper portion of inheritance, the public is loaded with the expense of maintaining them; and the freedom of elections violated by the overbearing influence which this unjust monopoly of family property produces. Nor is this all. It occasions a waste of national property. A considerable part of the land of the country is rendered unproductive, by the great extent of parks and chases which this law serves to keep up, and this at a time when the annual production of grain is not equal to the national consumption.*—In short, the evils of the aristocratical system are so great and numerous, so inconsistent with every thing that is just, wise, natural, and beneficent, that when they are considered, there ought not to be a doubt that many, who are now classed under that description, will wish to see such a system abolished.

What pleasure can they derive from contemplating the exposed condition, and almost certain beggary of their younger offspring? Every aristocratical family has an appendage of family beggars hanging round it, which in a few ages, or a few generations, are shook off, and console themselves with telling their tale in almshouses, workhouses, and prisons. This is the natural consequence of aristocracy. The peer and the beggar are often of the same family. One extreme produces the other: to make one rich many must be made poor; neither can the system be supported by other means.

There are two classes of people to whom the laws of England are particularly hostile, and those the most helpless; younger children, and

---

* See the Reports on the Corn Trade. (Author's note)

the poor. Of the former I have just spoken; of the latter I shall mention one instance out of the many that might be produced, and with which I shall close this subject.

Several laws are in existence for regulating and limiting work-men's wages. Why not leave them as free to make their own bargains, as the law-makers are to let their farms and houses? Personal labour is all the property they have. Why is that little, and the little freedom they enjoy, to be infringed? But the injustice will appear stronger, if we consider the operation and effect of such laws. When wages are fixed by what is called a law, the legal wages remain stationary, while every thing else is in progression; and as those who make that law still continue to lay on new taxes by other laws, they increase the expense of living by one law, and take away the means by another.

But if these gentlemen law-makers and tax-makers thought it right to limit the poor pittance which personal labour can produce, and on which a whole family is to be supported, they certainly must feel themselves happily indulged in a limitation on their own part, of not less than twelve thousand a-year, and that of property they never acquired (nor probably any of their ancestors), and of which they have made never acquire so ill a use.

Having now finished this subject, I shall bring the several particulars into one view, and then proceed to other matters.

The first EIGHT ARTICLES, mentioned earlier, are;

1. Abolition of two millions poor-rates.

2. Provision for two hundred and fifty-two thousand poor families, at the rate of four pounds per head for each child under fourteen years of age; which, with the addition of two hundred and fifty thousand pounds, provides also education for one million and thirty thousand children.

3. Annuity of six pounds (per annum) each for all poor persons, decayed tradesmen, and others (supposed seventy thousand) of the age of fifty years, and until sixty.

4. Annuity of ten pounds each for life for all poor persons, decayed tradesmen, and others (supposed seventy thousand) of the age of sixty years.

5. Donation of twenty shillings each for fifty thousand births.

6. Donation of twenty shillings each for twenty thousand marriages.

7. Allowance of twenty thousand pounds for the funeral expenses of persons travelling for work, and dying at a distance from their friends.

8. Employment at all times for the casual poor in the cities of London and Westminster.

SECOND ENUMERATION

9. Abolition of the tax on houses and windows.

10. Allowance of three shillings per week for life to fifteen thousand disbanded soldiers, and a proportionate allowance to the officers of the disbanded corps.

11. Increase of pay to the remaining soldiers of £19,500 annually.

12. The same allowance to the disbanded navy, and the same increase of pay, as to the army.

13. Abolition of the commutation tax.

14. Plan of a progressive tax, operating to extirpate the unjust and unnatural law of primogeniture, and the vicious influence of the aristocratical system.*

There yet remains, as already stated, one million of surplus taxes. Some part of this will be required for circumstances that do not immediately present themselves, and such part as shall not be wanted, will admit of a further reduction of taxes equal to that amount.

Among the claims that justice requires to be made, the condition of the inferior revenue-officers will merit attention. It is a reproach to any government to waste such an immensity of revenue in sinecures

---

* When enquiries are made into the condition of the poor, various degrees of distress will most probably be found, to render a different arrangement preferable to that which is already proposed. Widows with families will be in greater want than where there are husbands living. There is also a difference in the expense of living in different counties: and more so in fuel.

| | | |
|---|---|---:|
| Suppose then fifty thousand extraordinary cases, at the rate of ten pounds per family per annum | - - | £500,000 |
| 100,000 families, at £8 per family per annum | - - | 800,000 |
| 100,000 families, at £7 | - - | 700,000 |
| 104,000 families, at £5 | - - | 520,000 |
| And instead of ten shillings per head for the education of other children, to allow fifty shillings per family for that purpose to fifty thousand families - | - - | 250,000 |
| | | £2,770,000 |
| 140,000 aged persons as before | - - | 1,120,000 |
| | | £3,890,000 |

This arrangement amounts to the same sum as stated in this work, Part II, line number 1068, including the £250,000 for education; but it provides (including the aged people) for four hundred and four thousand families, which is almost one third of all the families in England. (Author's note)

and nominal and unnecessary places and officers, and not allow even a decent livelihood to those on whom the labour falls. The salary of the inferior officers of the revenue has stood at the petty pittance of less than fifty pounds a year for upwards of one hundred years. It ought to be seventy. About one hundred and twenty thousand pounds applied to this purpose, will put all those salaries in a decent condition.

This was proposed to be done almost twenty years ago, but the treasury-board then in being, startled at it, as it might lead to similar expectations from the army and navy; and the event was, that the King, or somebody for him, applied to parliament to have his own salary raised an hundred thousand pounds a year, which being done, every thing else was laid aside.

With respect to another class of men, the inferior clergy, I forbear to enlarge on their condition; but all partialities and prejudices for, or against, different modes and forms of religion aside, common justice will determine, whether there ought to be an income of twenty or thirty pounds a year to one man, and of ten thousand to another. I speak on this subject with the more freedom, because I am known not to be a Presbyterian; and therefore the cant cry of court sycophants, about church and meeting, kept up to amuse and bewilder the nation, cannot be raised against me.

Ye simple men on both sides the question, do you not see through this courtly craft? If ye can be kept disputing and wrangling about church and meeting, ye just answer the purpose of every courtier, who lives the while on the spoils of the taxes, and laughs at your credulity. Every religion is good that teaches man to be good; and I know of none that instructs him to be bad.

All the before-mentioned calculations suppose only sixteen millions and an half of taxes paid into the exchequer, after the expense of collection and drawbacks at the custom-house and excise-office are deducted; whereas the sum paid into the exchequer is very nearly, if not quite, seventeen millions. The taxes raised in Scotland and Ireland are expended in those countries, and therefore their savings will come out of their own taxes; but if any part be paid into the English exchequer, it might be remitted. This will not make one hundred thousand pounds a year difference.

There now remains only the national debt to be considered. In the year 1789, the interest, exclusive of the tontine, was £9,150,138. How much the capital has been reduced since that time the minister best knows. But after paying the interest, abolishing the tax on houses and windows, the commutation tax, and the poor-rates; and making all the provisions for the poor, for the education of children, the support of the aged, the disbanded part of the army and navy, and increasing the pay of the remainder, there will be a surplus of one million.

The present scheme of paying off the national debt appears to me, speaking as an indifferent person, to be an ill-concerted, if not a fallacious job. The burthen of the national debt consists not in its being so many millions, or so many hundred millions, but in the quantity of taxes collected every year to pay the interest. If this quantity continues the same, the burthen of the national debt is the same to all intents and purposes, be the capital more or less. The only knowledge which the public can have of the reduction of the debt, must be through the reduction of taxes for paying the interest. The debt, therefore, is not reduced one farthing to the public by all the millions that have been paid; and it would require more money now to purchase up the capital, than when the scheme began.

Digressing for a moment at this point, to which I shall return again, I look back to the appointment of Mr. Pitt, as minister.

I was then in America. The war was over; and though resentment had ceased, memory was still alive.

When the news of the coalition arrived, though it was a matter of no concern to I felt it as a man. It had something in it which shocked, by publicly sporting with decency, if not with principle. It was impudence in Lord North; it was a want of firmness in Mr. Fox.

Mr. Pitt was, at that time, what may be called a maiden character in politics. So far from being hackneyed, he appeared not to be initiated into the first mysteries of court intrigue. Everything was in his favour. Resentment against the coalition served as friendship to him, and his ignorance of vice was credited for virtue. With the return of peace, commerce and prosperity would rise of itself; yet even this increase was thrown to his account.

When he came to the helm, the storm was over, and he had nothing to interrupt his course. It required even ingenuity to be wrong, and he succeeded. A little time showed him the same sort of man as his predecessors had been. Instead of profiting by those errors which had accumulated a burthen of taxes unparalleled in the world, he sought,

I might almost say, he advertised for enemies, and provoked means to increase taxation. Aiming at something, he knew not what, he ransacked Europe and India for adventures, and abandoning the fair pretensions he began with, he became the knight-errant of modern times.

It is unpleasant to see character throw itself away. It is more so to see one's-self deceived. Mr. Pitt had merited nothing, but he promised much. He gave symptoms of a mind superior to the meanness and corruption of courts. His apparent candour encouraged expectations; and the public confidence, stunned, wearied, and confounded by a chaos of parties, revived and attached itself to him. But mistaking, as he has done, the disgust of the nation against the coalition, for merit in himself, he has rushed into measures which a man less supported would not have presumed to act.

All this seems to show that change of ministers amounts to nothing. One goes out, another comes in, and still the same measures, vices, and extravagance are pursued. It signifies not who is minister. The defect lies in the system. The foundation and the superstructure of the government is bad. Prop it as you please, it continually sinks into court government, and ever will.

I return, as I promised, to the subject of the national debt, that offspring of the Dutch-Anglo revolution, and its handmaid the Hanover succession.

But it is now too late to enquire how it began. Those to whom it is due have advanced the money; and whether it was well or ill spent, or pocketed, is not their crime. It is, however, easy to see, that as the nation proceeds in contemplating the nature and principles of government, and to understand taxes, and make comparisons between those of America, France, and England, it will be next to impossible to keep it in the same torpid state it has hitherto been. Some reform must, from the necessity of the case, soon begin. It is not whether these principles press with little or much force in the present moment. They are out. They are abroad in the world, and no force can stop them. Like a secret told, they are beyond recall; and he must be blind indeed that does not see that a change is already beginning.

Nine millions of dead taxes is a serious thing; and this not only for bad, but in a great measure for foreign government. By putting the power of making war into the hands of the foreigners who came for what they could get, little else was to be expected than what has happened.

Reasons are already advanced in this work, showing that whatever the reforms in the taxes may be, they ought to be made in the current expenses of government, and not in the part applied to the interest of the national debt. By remitting the taxes of the poor, *they* will be totally relieved, and all discontent will be taken away; and by striking off such of the taxes as are already mentioned, the nation will more than recover the whole expense of the mad American war.

There will then remain only the national debt as a subject of discontent; and in order to remove, or rather to prevent this, it would be good policy in the stockholders themselves to consider it as property, subject like all other property, to bear some portion of the taxes. It would give to it both popularity and security, and as a great part of its present inconvenience is balanced by the capital which it keeps alive, a measure of this kind would so far add to that balance as to silence objections.

This may be done by such gradual means as to accomplish all that is necessary with the greatest ease and convenience.

Instead of taxing the capital, the best method would be to tax the interest by some progressive ratio, and to lessen the public taxes in the same proportion as the interest diminished.

Suppose the interest was taxed one halfpenny in the pound the first year, a penny more the second, and to proceed by a certain ratio to be determined upon, always less than any other tax upon property. Such a tax would be subtracted from the interest at the time of payment, without any expense of collection.

One halfpenny in the pound would lessen the interest and consequently the taxes, twenty thousand pounds. The tax on wagons amounts to this sum, and this tax might be taken off the first year. The second year the tax on female servants, or some other of the like amount might also be taken off, and by proceeding in this manner, always applying the tax raised from the property of the debt toward its extinction, and not carry it to the current services, it would liberate itself.

The stockholders, notwithstanding this tax, would pay less taxes than they do now. What they would save by the extinction of the poor-rates, and the tax on houses and windows, and the commutation tax, would be considerably greater than what this tax, slow, but certain in its operation, amounts to.

It appears to me to be prudence to look out for measures that may apply under any circumstances that may approach. There is, at this moment, a crisis in the affairs of Europe that requires it. Preparation now is wisdom. If taxation be once let loose, it will be difficult to reinstate it; neither would the relief be so effectual, as if it proceeded by some certain and gradual reduction.

The fraud, hypocrisy, and imposition of governments, are now beginning to be too well understood to promise them any long career. The farce of monarchy and aristocracy, in all countries, is following that of chivalry, and Mr. Burke is dressing aristocracy, in all countries, is following that of chivalry, and Mr. Burke is dressing for the funeral. Let it then pass quietly to the tomb of all other follies, and the mourners be comforted.

The time is not very distant when England will laugh at itself for sending to Holland, Hanover, Zell, or Brunswick for men, at the expense of a million a year, who understood neither her laws, her language, nor her interest, and whose capacities would scarcely have fitted them for the office of a parish constable. If government could be trusted to such hands, it must be some easy and simple thing indeed, and materials fit for all the purposes may be found in every town and village in England.

When it shall be said in any country in the world, my poor are happy; neither ignorance nor distress is to be found among them; my jails are empty of prisoners, my streets of beggars; the aged are not in want, the taxes are not oppressive; the rational world is my friend, because I am the friend of its happiness: when these things can be said, then may that country boast its constitution and its government.

Within the space of a few years we have seen two revolutions, those of America and France. In the former, the contest was long, and the conflict severe; in the latter, the nation acted with such a consolidated impulse, that having no foreign enemy to contend with, the revolution was complete in power the moment it appeared. From both those instances it is evident, that the greatest forces that can be brought into the field of revolutions, are reason and common interest. Where these can have the opportunity of acting, opposition dies with fear, or crumbles away by conviction. It is a great standing which they have now universally obtained; and we may hereafter hope to see revolutions, or changes in governments, produced with the same quiet operation by which any measure, determinable by reason and discussion, is accomplished.

When a nation changes its opinion and habits of thinking, it is no longer to be governed as before; but it would not only be wrong, but bad policy, to attempt by force what ought to be accomplished by reason. Rebellion consists in forcibly opposing the general will of a nation, whether by a party or by a government. There ought, therefore, to be in every nation a method of occasionally ascertaining the state of public opinion with respect to government. On this point the old government of France was superior to the present government of England, because, on extraordinary occasions, recourse could be had what was then called the States General. But in England there are no such occasional bodies; and as to those who are now called Representatives, a great part of them are mere machines of the court, placemen, and dependents.

I presume, that though all the people of England pay taxes, not an hundredth part of them are electors, and the members of one of the houses of parliament represent nobody but themselves. There is, therefore, no power but the voluntary will of the people that has a right to act in any matter respecting a general reform; and by the same right that two persons can confer on such a subject, a thousand may. The object, in all such preliminary proceedings, is to find out what the general sense of a nation is, and to be governed by it. If it prefer a bad or defective government to a reform or choose to pay ten times more taxes than there is any occasion for, it has a right so to do; and so long as the majority do not impose conditions on the minority, different from what they impose upon themselves, though there may be much error, there is no injustice. Neither will the error continue long. Reason and discussion will soon bring things right, however wrong they may begin. By such a process no tumult is to be apprehended. The poor, in all countries, are naturally both peaceable and grateful in all reforms in which their interest and happiness is included. It is only by neglecting and rejecting them that they become tumultuous.

The objects that now press on the public attention are, the French revolution, and the prospect of a general revolution in governments. Of all nations in Europe there is none so much interested in the French revolution as England. Enemies for ages, and that at a vast expense, and without any national object, the opportunity now presents itself of amicably closing the scene, and joining their efforts to reform the rest of Europe. By doing this they will not only prevent the further effusion of blood, and increase of taxes, but be in a condition of getting rid of a considerable part of their present burthens, as has been already stated. Long experience however has shown, that reforms of this kind are not those which old governments wish to promote, and therefore it is to nations, and not to such governments, that these matters present themselves.

In the preceding part of this work, I have spoken of an alliance between England, France, and America, for purposes that were to be afterwards mentioned. Though I have no direct authority on the part of America, I have good reason to conclude, that she is disposed to enter into a consideration of such a measure, provided, that the governments with which she might ally, acted as national governments, and not as courts enveloped in intrigue and mystery. That France as a nation, and a national government, would prefer an alliance with England, is a matter of certainty. Nations, like individuals, who have long been enemies, without knowing each other, or knowing why, become the better friends when they discover the errors and impositions under which they had acted.

Admitting, therefore, the probability of such a connection, I will state some matters by which such an alliance, together with that of Holland, might render service, not only to the parties immediately concerned, but to all Europe.

It is, I think, certain, that if the fleets of England, France, and Holland were confederated, they could propose, with effect, a limitation to, and a general dismantling of, all the navies in Europe, to a certain proportion to be agreed upon.

First, That no new ship of war shall be built by any power in Europe, themselves included.

Second, That all the navies now in existence shall be put back, suppose to one-tenth of their present force. This will save to France and England, at least two millions sterling annually to each, and their relative force be in the same proportion as it is now. If men will permit themselves to think, as rational beings ought to think, nothing can appear more ridiculous and absurd, exclusive of all moral reflections, than to be at the expense of building navies, filling them with men, and then hauling them into the ocean, to try which can sink each other fastest. Peace, which costs nothing, is attended with infinitely more advantage, than any victory with all its expense. But this, though it best answers the purpose of nations, does not that of court governments, whose habited policy is pretence for taxation, places, and offices.

It is, I think, also certain, that the above confederated powers, together with that of the United States of America, can propose with effect, to Spain, the independence of South America, and the opening those countries of immense extent and wealth to the general commerce of the world, as North America now is.

With how much more glory, and advantage to itself, does a nation act, when it exerts its powers to rescue the world from bondage, and to create itself friends, than when it employs those powers to increase ruin, desolation, and misery. The horrid scene that is now acting by the English government in the East-Indies, is fit only to be told of Goths and Vandals, who, destitute of principle, robbed and tortured the world they were incapable of enjoying.

The opening of South America would produce an immense field of commerce, and a ready money market for manufactures, which the eastern world does not. The East is already a country full of manufactures, the importation of which is not only an injury to the manufactures of England, but a drain upon its specie. The balance against England by this trade is regularly upwards of half a million annually sent out in the East-India ships in silver; and this is the reason, together with German intrigue, and German subsidies, that there is so little silver in England.

But any war is harvest to such governments, however ruinous it may be to a nation. It serves to keep up deceitful expectations which prevent people from looking into the defects and abuses of government. It is the *lo here*! and the *lo there*! that amuses and cheats the multitude.

Never did so great an opportunity offer itself to England, and to all Europe, as is produced by the two Revolutions of America and France. By the former, freedom has a national champion in the western world; and by the latter, in Europe. When another nation shall join France, despotism and bad government will scarcely dare to appear. To use a trite expression, the iron is becoming hot all over Europe. The insulted German and the enslaved Spaniard, the Russ and the Pole, are beginning to think. The present age will hereafter merit to be called the Age of Reason, and the present generation will appear to the future as the Adam of a new world.

When all the governments of Europe shall be established on the representative system, nations will become acquainted, and the animosities and prejudices fomented by the intrigue and artifice of courts, will cease. The oppressed soldier will become a freeman; and the tortured sailor, no longer dragged through the streets like a felon, will pursue his mercantile voyage in safety. It would be better that nations should continue the pay of their soldiers during their lives, and give them their discharge and restore them to freedom and their friends, and cease recruiting, than retain such multitudes at the same expense, in a condition useless to society and to themselves. As soldiers have hitherto been treated in most countries, they might be said to be without a friend. Shunned by the citizen on an apprehension of their being enemies to liberty, and too often insulted by those who commanded them, their condition was a double oppression. But where genuine principles of liberty pervade a people, every thing is restored to order; and the soldier civilly treated, returns the civility.

In contemplating revolutions, it is easy to perceive that they may arise from two distinct causes; the one, to avoid or get rid of some great calamity; the other, to obtain some great and positive good; and the two may be distinguished by the names of active and passive revolutions. In those which proceed from the former cause, the temper becomes incensed and soured; and the redress, obtained by danger, is too often sullied by revenge. But in those which proceed from the latter, the heart, rather animated than agitated, enters serenely upon the subject. Reason and discussion, persuasion and conviction, become the weapons in the contest, and it is only when those are attempted to be suppressed that recourse is had to violence. When men unite in agreeing that a *thing is good*, could it be obtained, such for instance as relief from a burden of taxes and the extinction of corruption, the object is more than half accomplished. What they approve as the end, they will promote in the means.

Will any man say, in the present excess of taxation, falling so heavily on the poor, that a remission of five pounds annually of taxes to one hundred and four thousand poor families is not a *good thing*? Will he say that a remission of seven pounds annually to one hundred thousand other poor families—of eight pounds annually to another hundred thousand poor families, and of ten pounds annually to fifty thousand poor and widowed families, are not *good things*? And, to proceed a step further in this climax, will he say that to provide against the misfortunes to which all human life is subject, by securing six pounds annually for all poor, distressed, and reduced persons of the age of fifty and until sixty, and of ten pounds annually after sixty, is not a *good thing*?

Will he say that an abolition of two millions of poor-rates to the house-keepers, and of the whole of the house and window-light tax and of the commutation tax is not a *good thing*? Or will he say that to abolish corruption is a *bad thing*?

If, therefore, the good to be obtained be worthy of a passive, rational, and costless revolution, it would be bad policy to prefer waiting for a calamity that should force a violent one. I have no idea, considering the reforms which are now passing and spreading throughout Europe, that England will permit herself to be the last; and where the occasion and the opportunity quietly offer, it is better than to wait for a turbulent necessity. It may be considered as an honour to the animal faculties of man to obtain redress by courage and danger, but it is far greater honour to the rational faculties to accomplish the same object by reason, accommodation, and general consent.*

As reforms, or revolutions, call them which you please, extend themselves among nations, those nations will form connections and conventions, and when a few are thus confederated, the progress will be rapid, till despotism and corrupt government be totally expelled, at least out of two quarters of the world, Europe and America. The Algerine piracy may then be commanded to cease, for it is only by the malicious policy of old governments, against each other, that it exists.

Throughout this work, various and numerous as the subjects are, which I have taken up and investigated, there is only a single paragraph upon religion, viz. *"that every religion is good that teaches man to be good."*

I have carefully avoided to enlarge upon the subject, because I am inclined to believe that what is called the present ministry, wish to see

---

* I know it is the opinion of many of the most enlightened characters in France (there always will be those who see further into events than others), not only among the general mass of citizens, but of many of the principal members of the former National Assembly, that the monarchical plan will not continue many years in that country. They have found out, that as wisdom cannot be made hereditary, power ought not; and that, for a man to merit a million sterling a year from a nation, he ought to have a mind capable of comprehending from an atom to a universe, which, if he had, he would be above receiving the pay. But they wished not to appear to lead the nation faster than its own reason and interest dictated. In all the conversations where I have been present upon this subject, the idea always was, that when such a time, from the general opinion of the nation, shall arrive, that the honourable and liberal method would be, to make a handsome present in fee simple to the person, whoever he may be, that shall then be in the monarchical office, and for him to retire to the enjoyment of private life, possessing his share of general rights and privileges, and to be no more accountable to the public for his time and his conduct than any other citizen. (Author's note)

contentions about religion kept up, to prevent the nation turning its attention to subjects of government. It is as if they were to say, "Look that way, or any way, but this."

But as religion is very improperly made a political machine, and the reality of it is thereby destroyed, I will conclude this work with stating in what light religion appears to me.

If we suppose a large family of children, who, on any particular day, or particular circumstance, made it a custom to present to their parents some token of their affection and gratitude, each of them would make a different offering, and most probably in a different manner. Some would pay their congratulations in themes of verse and prose, by some little devices, as their genius dictated, or according to what they thought would please; and, perhaps, the least of all, not able to do any of those things, would ramble into the garden, or the field, and gather what it thought the prettiest flower it could find, though, perhaps, it might be but a simple weed. The parent would be more gratified by such a variety, than if the whole of them had acted on a concerted plan, and each had made exactly the same offering. This would have the cold appearance of contrivance, or the harsh one of control. But of all unwelcome things, nothing could more afflict the parent than to know, that the whole of them had afterwards gotten together by the ears, boys and girls, fighting, scratching, reviling, and abusing each other about which was the best or the worst present.

Why may we not suppose, that the great Father of all is pleased with variety of devotion; and that the greatest offence we can act, is that by which we seek to torment and render each other miserable? For my own part, I am fully satisfied that what I am now doing, with an endeavour to conciliate mankind, to render their condition happy, to unite nations that have hitherto been enemies, and to extirpate the horrid practice of war, and break the chains of slavery and oppression is acceptable in his sight, and being the best service I can perform, I act it cheerfully.

I do not believe that any two men, on what are called doctrinal points, think alike who think at all. It is only those who have not thought that appear to agree. It is in this case as with what is called the British constitution. It has been taken for granted to be good, and encomiums have supplied the place of proof. But when the nation comes to examine into its principles and the abuses it admits, it will be found to have more defects than I have pointed out in this work and the former.

As to what are called national religions, we may, with as much propriety, talk of national Gods. It is either political craft or the remains of the Pagan system, when every nation had its separate and particular deity. Among all the writers of the English church clergy, who have treated on the general subject of religion, the present Bishop of Llandaff has not been excelled, and it is with much pleasure that I take this opportunity of expressing this token of respect.

I have now gone through the whole of the subject, at least, as far as it appears to me at present. It has been my intention for the five years I have been in Europe, to offer an address to the people of England on the subject of government, if the opportunity presented itself before I returned to America. Mr. Burke has thrown it in my way, and I thank him. On a certain occasion, three years ago, I pressed him to propose a national convention, to be fairly elected, for the purpose of taking the state of the nation into consideration; but I found, that however strongly the parliamentary current was then setting against the party he acted with, their policy was to keep every thing within that field of corruption, and trust to accidents. Long experience had shown that parliaments would follow any change of ministers, and on this they rested their hopes and their expectations.

Formerly, when divisions arose respecting governments, recourse was had to the sword, and a civil war ensued. That savage custom is exploded by the new system, and reference is had to national conventions. Discussion and the general will arbitrates the question, and to this, private opinion yields with a good grace, and order is preserved uninterrupted.

Some gentlemen have affected to call the principles upon which this work and the former part of *Rights of Man* are founded, "a new-fangled doctrine." The question is not whether those principles are new or old, but whether they are right or wrong. Suppose the former, I will show their effect by a figure easily understood.

It is now towards the middle of February. Were I to take a turn into the country, the trees would present a leafless, wintery appearance. As people are apt to pluck twigs as they walk along, I perhaps might do the same, and by chance might observe, that a *single bud* on that twig had begun to swell. I should reason very unnaturally, or rather not reason at all, to suppose *this* was the *only* bud in England which had this appearance. Instead of deciding thus, I should instantly conclude, that the same appearance was beginning, or about to begin, every where; and though the vegetable sleep will continue longer on some trees and plants than on others, and though some of them may not *blossom* for two or three years, all will be in leaf in the summer, except those which are *rotten*. What pace the political summer may keep with the natural, no human foresight can determine. It is, however, not difficult to perceive that the spring is begun.—Thus wishing, as I sincerely do, freedom and happiness to all nations, I close the Second Part.

# *APPENDIX*

As the publication of this work has been delayed beyond the time intended, I think it not improper, all circumstances considered, to state the causes that have occasioned delay.

The reader will probably observe, that some parts in the plan contained in this work for reducing the taxes, and certain parts in Mr. Pitt's speech at the opening of the present session, Tuesday, January 31, are so much alike as to induce a belief, that either the author had taken the hint from Mr. Pitt, or Mr. Pitt from the author.—I will first point out the parts that are similar, and then state such circumstances as I am acquainted with, leaving the reader to make his own conclusion.

Considering it as almost an unprecedented case, that taxes should be proposed to be taken off, it is equally extraordinary that such a measure should occur to two persons at the same time; and still more so (considering the vast variety and multiplicity of taxes) that they should hit on the same specific taxes. Mr. Pitt has mentioned, in his speech, the tax on *carts and wagons*—that on *female servants*; the lowering the tax on *candles* and the taking off the tax of three shillings on *houses* having under seven windows.

Every one of those specific taxes are a part of the plan contained in this work, and proposed also to be taken off. Mr. Pitt's plan, it is true, goes no further than to a reduction of three hundred and twenty thousand pounds; and the reduction proposed in this work, to nearly six millions. I have made my calculations on only sixteen millions and an half of revenue, still asserting that it was "very nearly, if not quite, seventeen millions." Mr. Pitt states it at 16,690,000. I know enough of the matter to say, that he has not *over*stated it. Having thus given the particulars, which correspond in this work and his speech, I will state a chain of circumstances that may lead to some explanation.

The first hint for lessening the taxes, and that as a consequence flowing from the French revolution, is to be found in the Address and Declaration of the Gentlemen who met at the Thatched-House Tavern, August 20, 1791. Among many other particulars stated in that Address, is the following, put as an interrogation to the government opposers of the French Revolution. *"Are they sorry that the pretence for new oppressive taxes, and the occasion for continuing many old taxes will be at an end?"*

It is well known that the persons who chiefly frequent the Thatched-House Tavern, are men of court connections, and so much did they take this Address and Declaration respecting the French Revolution, and the reduction of taxes in disgust, that the Landlord was under the necessity of informing the Gentlemen, who composed the meeting of the 20th of August, and who proposed holding another meeting, that he could not receive them.*

What was only hinted in the Address and Declaration respecting taxes and principles of government, will be found reduced to a regular system in this work. But as Mr. Pitt's speech contains some of the same things respecting taxes, I now come to give the circumstances before alluded to.

The case is: This work was intended to be published just before the meeting of Parliament, and for that purpose a considerable part of the copy was put into the printer's hands in September, and all the remaining copy, which contains the part to which Mr. Pitt's speech is similar, was given to him full six weeks before the meeting of Parliament, and he was informed of the time at which it was to appear. He had composed nearly the whole about a fortnight before the time of Parliament meeting, and had given me a proof of the next sheet. It was then in sufficient forwardness to be out at the time proposed, as two other sheets were ready for striking off. I had before told him, that if he thought he should be straitened for time, I could get part of the work done at another press, which he desired me not to do. In this manner the work stood on the Tuesday fortnight preceding the meeting of Parliament, when all at once, without any previous intimation,

* The gentleman who signed the address and declaration as chairman of the meeting, Mr. Horne Tooke, being generally supposed to be the person who drew it up, and having spoken much in commendation of it, has been jocularly accused of praising his own work. To free him from this embarrassment, and to save him the repeated trouble of mentioning the author, as he has not failed to do, I make no hesitation in saying, that as the opportunity of benefiting by the French Revolution easily occurred to me, I drew up the publication in question, and showed it to him and some other gentlemen, who, fully approving it, held a meeting for the purpose of making it public, and subscribed to the amount of fifty guineas to defray the expense of advertising. I believe there are at this time, in England, a greater number of men acting on disinterested principles, and determined to look into the nature and practices of government themselves, and not blindly trust, as has hitherto been the case, either to government generally, or to parliaments, or to parliamentary opposition, than at any former period. Had this been done a century ago, corruption and taxation had not arrived to the height they are now at. (Author's note)

though I had been with him the evening before, he sent me, by one of his workmen, all the remaining copy, declining to go on with the work *on any consideration.*

To account for this extraordinary conduct I was totally at a loss, as he stopped at the part where the arguments on systems and principles of government closed, and where the plan for the reduction of taxes, the education of children, and the support of the poor and the aged begins; and still more especially, as he had, at the time of his beginning to print, and before he had seen the whole copy, offered a thousand pounds for the copy-right, together with the future copy-right of the former part of the *Rights of Man.* I told the person who brought me this offer that I should not accept it, and wished it not to be renewed, giving him as my reason, that though I believed the printer to be an honest man, I would never put it in the power of any printer or publisher to suppress or alter a work of mine, by making him master of the copy, or give to him the right of selling it to any minister, or to any other person, or to treat as a mere matter of traffic, that which I intended should operate as a principle.

His refusal to complete the work (which he could not purchase) obliged me to seek for another printer, and this of consequence would throw the publication back till after the meeting of Parliament, otherways it would have appeared that Mr. Pitt had only taken up a part of the plan which I had more fully stated.

Whether that gentleman, or any other, had seen the work, or any part of it, is more than I have authority to say. But the manner in which the work was returned, and the particular time at which this was done, and that after the offers he had made, are suspicious circumstances. I know what the opinion of booksellers and publishers is upon such a case, but as to my own opinion, I choose to make no declaration. There are many ways by which proof sheets may be procured by other persons before a work publicly appears; to which I shall add a certain circumstance, which is,

A ministerial bookseller in Piccadilly who has been employed, as common report says, by a clerk of one of the boards closely connected with the ministry (the board of trade and plantation, of which Hawkesbury is president) to publish what he calls my Life, (I wish his own life and those of the cabinet were as good), used to have his books printed at the same printing-office that I employed; but when the former part of *Rights of Man* came out, he took his work away in dudgeon; and about a week or ten days before the printer returned my copy, he came to make him an offer of his work again, which was accepted. This would consequently give him admission into the printing-office where the sheets of this work were then lying; and as booksellers and printers are free with each other, he would have the opportunity of seeing what was going on.——Be the case, however, as it may, Mr. Pitt's plan, little and diminutive as it is, would have made a very awkward appearance, had this work appeared at the time the printer had engaged to finish it.

I have now stated the particulars which occasioned the delay, from the proposal to purchase, to the refusal to print. If all the Gentlemen are innocent, it is very unfortunate for them that such a variety of suspicious circumstances should, without any design, arrange themselves together.

Having now finished this part, I will conclude with stating another circumstance.

About a fortnight or three weeks before the meeting of Parliament, a small addition, amounting to about twelve shillings and sixpence a year, was made to the pay of the soldiers, or rather their pay was docked so much less. Some Gentlemen who knew, in part, that this work would contain a plan of reforms respecting the oppressed condition of soldiers, wished me to add a note to the work, signifying that the part upon that subject had been in the printer's hands some weeks before that addition of pay was proposed. I declined doing this, lest it should be interpreted into an air of vanity, or an endeavour to excite suspicion (for which perhaps there might be no grounds) that some of the government gentlemen had, by some means or other, made out what this work would contain: and had not the printing been interrupted so as to occasion a delay beyond the time fixed for publication, nothing contained in this appendix would have appeared.

*Thomas Paine*

sition to the pleasure of doing

the state of your mind

ervice. It was not that there

r acceptance, upon the disposal

d have had any influence,

d what would be agreeable

progress of affairs. If we are

military operations, tis not a

, that you are one of those

field. With such an enemy

will not barely do their duty

ngy equal to all dangers

with very great regard.

I am dear Sir

Your obed Servant

A Hamilton

# Selected Works of
# Alexander Hamilton

# Selected Works of Alexander Hamilton

**Word Cloud Classics**

San Diego

Canterbury Classics
An imprint of Printers Row Publishing Group
10350 Barnes Canyon Road, Suite 100, San Diego, CA 92121
www.canterburyclassicsbooks.com • mail@canterburyclassicsbooks.com

Printers Row Publishing Group is a division of Readerlink Distribution Services, LLC. The Canterbury Classics and Word Cloud Classics names and logos are registered trademarks of Readerlink Distribution Services, LLC.

All correspondence concerning the content of this book should be addressed to Canterbury Classics, Editorial Department, at the above address.

Publisher: Peter Norton
Associate Publisher: Ana Parker
Publishing/Editorial Team: April Farr, Kathryn C. Dalby
Editorial Team: JoAnn Padgett, Melinda Allman, Dan Mansfield
Production Team: Jonathan Lopes, Rusty von Dyl

Cover and endpaper design: Rusty von Dyl

Spine art: Gettyimages/eyewave (statue), Gettyimages/clipartdotcom (flag)

ISBN: 978-1-64517-083-9
Printed in China
23 22 21 20 19  1 2 3 4 5

# CONTENTS

# A Note on the Text

The writings included in *Selected Works of Alexander Hamilton* are printed here as they originally appeared, with any inconsistencies in spelling, punctuation, and style retained to preserve the original flavor of Hamilton's words.

In places, portions of Hamilton's handwriting and archival copies of printed materials contained missing or indecipherable text; these instances are indicated by bracketed blank spaces: [      ].

The works included in this volume were obtained from the Alexander Hamilton Papers at Founders Online, a digital resource from the National Archives that provides the public with access to the collected writings of the founders of the United States of America.

# Chronology

1755    Alexander Hamilton is born on January 11 in the British West Indies, possibly on the island of Nevis. He is the second child of Rachel Lavien and James Hamilton.

1765    James Hamilton leaves his wife and family on the island of St. Croix, and is never heard from again. Rachel Lavien opens a store in Christiansted.

1768    Rachel Lavien becomes ill and dies on February 19; her entire estate is inherited by Peter Lavien, her only legitimate child from a previous marriage. Alexander Hamilton begins work as a clerk at a mercantile firm.

1772    With the help of Hugh Knox, a minister in Christiansted, Hamilton sails to the United States to begin his education. He enrolls at a Presbyterian academy in Elizabethtown, New Jersey.

1773    Enters King's College (now Columbia University) in New York City, and begins lifelong friendships with Robert Troup and John Jay. Writes *A Full Vindication of the Measures of Congress*, a pamphlet published on December 15.

1775    Sees his first action in the Revolutionary War in August when he comes under fire from a British ship in New York Harbor.

1776    Leaves King's College without completing his studies, in order to serve as a commander in an artillery company, with the rank of captain.

1777    Becomes aide-de-camp to General George Washington, with the rank of lieutenant colonel. Forms a friendship with the Marquis de Lafayette, who joins Washington's camp in August. Spends the winter with the Continental army at Valley Forge.

1780    Begins a courtship of Elizabeth Schuyler, daughter of New York landowner Philip Schuyler. Is denied a field command by General Washington. Marries Elizabeth Schuyler on December 14.

1781    Resigns his position with General Washington during a dispute in February, but remains on the staff until April. Publishes the first of his "Continentalist" papers, outlining his plan for the powers to be given to the United States Congress. Commands a New York battalion and participates in the siege of Yorktown in September. Leaves active military service after the British surrender on October 19.

1782    The Hamiltons' first child, Philip, is born on January 22. Hamilton begins his study of the law, and is appointed a delegate to Congress by the New York state legislature.

1783    Moves with his family to New York City, where he establishes his law office.

1787    Attends the Philadelphia constitutional convention as a delegate from New York. His speech advocating for a stronger central government modeled on the British system causes his political opponents to label him as a monarchist. Publishes (anonymously) the first of the *Federalist* papers advocating for the ratification of the new U.S. Constitution.

1788    Elected as a delegate to the New York ratifying convention, where he engages in debate with Antifederalists; the Constitution is ratified by a narrow margin on July 26.

1789    Becomes the first Secretary of the Treasury, and is assigned by the House of Representatives to organize the new nation's finances.

1790    Submits a report to the House of Representatives, urging support for the establishment of a national bank.

1791    Engages in an affair with Marisa Reynolds while his wife and family are at the Schuyler home in Albany; Hamilton ends up paying blackmail to Marisa's husband James in an attempt to preserve his reputation.

1792    Hamilton's management of the U.S. Treasury is called into question when James Reynolds accuses him of misusing funds to speculate. Under questioning by other representatives, Hamilton confesses to the affair with Marisa Reynolds and to making blackmail payments with his own money.

1793    Informs President George Washington that he will resign from his position as Secretary of the Treasury in June 1794.

1794    Hamilton postpones his resignation due to the ongoing conflict between Great Britain and France, and then informs Washington in December that he will resign in early 1795.

1795    Resigns as Secretary of the Treasury on January 31, and moves with his family to New York. Resumes his law practice in New York City, but maintains unofficial role as President Washington's adviser.

1796    Continues to advise Washington, and writes the first drafts of the president's farewell address. Urges members of the Federalist Party to support John Adams and Thomas Pickney in the presidential election; Adams wins the election, and Thomas Jefferson, who finished second, is elected vice president.

1797    Publishes the "Reynolds Pamphlet," in which he details his account of the affair with Marisa Reynolds, refuting claims that he made payments to James Reynolds in order to speculate in public funds. Remains occupied with his law practice in New York City.

1798    An undeclared naval conflict breaks out between the United States and France; George Washington is appointed commander in chief by President Adams, and Hamilton agrees to serve as inspector general. Supervises the fortification of New York City and is named second in command of the army in October.

1799    Continues reorganization of the army, and drafts a plan for a national military academy. George Washington dies on December 14.

1800    Attempts to rally support among members of the Federalist Party for presidential candidate Charles Cotesworth Pinckney. Writes a pamphlet for the Federalists that claims John Adams is unfit for the presidency; when the pamphlet is leaked to the press, Hamilton's reputation is damaged and support for the Federalist Party is diminished. Presidential election results in a tie between Republican candidates Thomas Jefferson and Aaron Burr, leaving the election in the hands of the House of Representatives, which is controlled by the Federalists. Hamilton urges the Federalists to support Jefferson over Burr.

1801    Jefferson is elected president on the thirty-sixth ballot in the House of Representatives on February 17. Hamilton helps establish the New-York Evening Post newspaper, and publishes several articles critical of the Jefferson administration. His eldest son, Philip, dies after a duel fought in defense of his father's policies.

1802    Drafts a resolution for the New York legislature calling for separate ballots to elect the president and vice president, and that electors be chosen according to popular vote in districts established by Congress; this system is eventually adopted as part of the Twelfth Amendment in 1804.

1803    Helps found the Merchants' Bank in New York City, and remains involved in his private law practice.

1804   Hamilton denounces the qualifications of Aaron Burr, who had been gaining support among Republicans as a candidate for governor of New York. Burr loses the election and demands explanations from Hamilton for his conduct; Hamilton offers no apologies. On June 27, Burr challenges Hamilton to a duel, which he accepts. The duel is conducted on July 11 at Weehawken, New Jersey. Burr's pistol ball hits Hamilton, puncturing his liver and lodging in his spine. After seeing his wife and children and receiving communion, Hamilton dies on the afternoon of July 12.

## To Edward Stevens

*St Croix Novemr. 11th 1769*

DEAR EDWARD

This just serves to acknowledge receipt of yours per Cap Lowndes which was delivered me Yesterday. The truth of Cap Lightbourn & Lowndes information is now verifyd by the Presence of your Father and Sister for whose safe arrival I Pray, and that they may convey that Satisfaction to your Soul that must naturally flow from the sight of Absent Friends in health, and shall for news this way refer you to them. As to what you say respecting your having soon the happiness of seeing us all, I wish, for an accomplishment of your hopes provided they are Concomitant with your welfare, otherwise not, tho doubt whether I shall be Present or not for to confess my weakness, Ned, my Ambition is prevalent that I contemn the grov'ling and condition of a Clerk or the like, to which my Fortune &c. condemns me and would willingly risk my life tho' not my Character to exalt my Station. Im confident, Ned that my Youth excludes me from any hopes of immediate Preferment nor do I desire it, but I mean to prepare the way for futurity. Im no Philosopher you see and may be jusly said to Build Castles in the Air. My Folly makes me ashamd and beg youll Conceal it, yet Neddy we have seen such Schemes successfull when the Projector is Constant I shall Conclude saying I wish there was a War.

I am  Dr Edward  Yours

ALEX HAMILTON

PS    I this moment receivd yours by William Smith and am pleasd to see you Give such Close Application to Study.

# *To* The Royal Danish American Gazette

*St. Croix, Sept. 6, 1772*

HONOURED SIR,

I take up my pen just to give you an imperfect account of one of the most dreadful Hurricanes that memory or any records whatever can trace, which happened here on the 31st ultimo at night.

It began about dusk, at North, and raged very violently till ten o'clock. Then ensued a sudden and unexpected interval, which lasted about an hour. Meanwhile the wind was shifting round to the South West point, from whence it returned with redoubled fury and continued so 'till near three o'clock in the morning. Good God! what horror and destruction. Its impossible for me to describe or you to form any idea of it. It seemed as if a total dissolution of nature was taking place. The roaring of the sea and wind, fiery meteors flying about it in the air, the prodigious glare of almost perpetual lightning, the crash of the falling houses, and the ear-piercing shrieks of the distressed, were sufficient to strike astonishment into Angels. A great part of the buildings throughout the Island are levelled to the ground, almost all the rest very much shattered; several persons killed and numbers utterly ruined; whole families running about the streets, unknowing where to find a place of shelter; the sick exposed to the keeness of water and air without a bed to lie upon, or a dry covering to their bodies; and our harbours entirely bare. In a word, misery, in all its most hideous shapes, spread over the whole face of the country. A strong smell of gunpowder added somewhat to the terrors of the night; and it was observed that the rain was surprizingly salt. Indeed the water is so brackish and full of sulphur that there is hardly any drinking it.

My reflections and feelings on this frightful and melancholy occasion, are set forth in the following self-discourse.

Where now, oh! vile worm, is all thy boasted fortitude and resolution? What is become of thine arrogance and self sufficiency? Why dost thou tremble and stand aghast? How humble, how helpless, how contemptible you now appear. And for why? The jarring of elements—the discord of clouds? Oh! impotent presumptuous fool! how durst thou offend that Omnipotence, whose nod alone were sufficient to quell the destruction that hovers over thee, or crush thee into atoms? See thy wretched helpless state, and learn to know thyself. Learn to know thy best support. Despise thyself, and adore thy God. How sweet, how unutterably sweet were now, the voice of an approving conscience; Then couldst thou say, hence ye idle alarms, why do I shrink? What have I to fear? A pleasing calm suspense! A short repose from calamity to end in eternal bliss? Let the Earth rend. Let the planets forsake their course. Let the Sun be extinguished and the Heavens burst asunder. Yet what have I to dread? My staff can never be broken—in Omnipotence I trusted.

He who gave the winds to blow, and the lightnings to rage—even him have I always loved and served. His precepts have I observed. His commandments have I obeyed—and his perfections have I adored. He will snatch me from ruin. He will exalt me to the fellowship of Angels and Seraphs, and to the fullness of never ending joys.

But alas! how different, how deplorable, how gloomy the prospect! Death comes rushing on in triumph veiled in a mantle of tenfold darkness. His unrelenting scythe, pointed, and ready for the stroke. On his right hand sits destruction, hurling the winds and belching forth flames: Calamity on his left threatening famine disease and distress of all kinds. And Oh! thou wretch, look still a little further; see the gulph of eternal misery open. There mayest thou shortly plunge—the just reward of thy vileness. Alas! whither canst thou fly? Where hide thyself? Thou canst not call upon thy God; thy life has been a continual warfare with him.

Hark—ruin and confusion on every side. 'Tis thy turn next; but one short moment, even now, Oh Lord help. Jesus be merciful!

Thus did I reflect, and thus at every gust of the wind, did I conclude, 'till it pleased the Almighty to allay it. Nor did my emotions proceed either from the suggestions of too much natural fear, or a conscience over-burthened with crimes of an uncommon cast. I thank God, this was not the case. The scenes of horror exhibited around us, naturally awakened such ideas in every thinking breast, and aggravated the deformity of every failing of our lives. It were a lamentable insensibility indeed, not to have had such feelings, and I think inconsistent with human nature.

Our distressed, helpless condition taught us humility and contempt of ourselves. The horrors of the night, the prospect of an immediate, cruel death—or, as one may say, of being crushed by the Almighty in his anger—filled us with terror. And every thing that had tended to weaken our interest with him, upbraided us in the strongest colours, with our baseness and folly. That which, in a calm unruffled temper, we call a natural cause, seemed then like the correction of the Deity. Our imagination represented him as an incensed master, executing vengeance on the crimes of his servants. The father and benefactor were forgot, and in that view, a consciousness of our guilt filled us with despair.

But see, the Lord relents. He hears our prayer. The Lightning ceases. The winds are appeased. The warring elements are reconciled and all things promise peace. The darkness is dispell'd and drooping nature revives at the approaching dawn. Look back Oh! my soul, look back and tremble. Rejoice at thy deliverance, and humble thyself in the presence of thy deliverer.

Yet hold, Oh vain mortal! Check thy ill timed joy. Art thou so selfish to exult because thy lot is happy in a season of universal woe? Hast thou no feelings for the miseries of thy fellow-creatures? And art thou incapable of the soft pangs of sympathetic sorrow? Look around thee and shudder at the view. See desolation and ruin where'er thou turnest thine eye! See thy fellow-creatures pale and lifeless; their bodies mangled, their souls snatched into eternity, unexpecting. Alas! perhaps unprepared! Hark the bitter groans of distress. See sickness and infirmities exposed to the inclemencies of wind and water! See tender infancy pinched with hunger and hanging on the mothers knee for food! See the unhappy mothers anxiety. Her poverty denies relief, her breast heaves with pangs of maternal pity, her heart is bursting, the tears gush down her cheeks. Oh sights of woe! Oh distress unspeakable! My heart bleeds, but I have no power to solace! O ye, who revel in affluence, see the afflictions of humanity and bestow your superfluity to ease them. Say not, we have suffered also, and thence withold your compassion. What are your sufferings compared to those? Ye have still more than enough left. Act wisely. Succour the miserable and lay up a treasure in Heaven.

I am afraid, Sir, you will think this description more the effort of imagination than a true picture of realities. But I can affirm with the greatest truth, that there is not a single circumstance touched upon, which I have not absolutely been an eye witness to.

Our General has issued several very salutary and humane regulations, and both in his publick and private measures, has shewn himself *the Man.*

## *A Full Vindication of the Measures of the Congress, &c.*

*New-York 1774*

FRIENDS AND COUNTRYMEN,

It was hardly to be expected that any man could be so presumptuous, as openly to controvert the equity, wisdom, and authority of the measures, adopted by the congress: an assembly truly respectable on every account! Whether we consider the characters of the men, who composed it; the number, and dignity of their constituents, or the important ends for which they were appointed. But, however improbable such a degree of presumption might have seemed, we find there are some, in whom it exists. Attempts are daily making to diminish the influence of their decisions, and prevent the salutary effects, intended by them. The impotence of such insidious efforts is evident from the general indignation they are treated with; so that no material ill-consequences can be dreaded from them. But lest they should have a tendency to mislead, and prejudice the minds of a few; it cannot be deemed altogether useless to bestow some notice upon them.

And first, let me ask these restless spirits, whence arises that violent antipathy they seem to entertain, not only to the natural rights of mankind; but to common sense and common modesty. That they are enemies to the natural rights of mankind is manifest, because they wish to see one part of their species enslaved by another. That they have an invincible aversion to common sense is apparent in many respects: They endeavour to persuade us, that the absolute sovereignty of parliament does not imply our absolute slavery; that it is a Christian duty to submit to be plundered of all we have, merely because some of our fellow-subjects are wicked enough to require it of us, that slavery, so far from being a great evil, is a great blessing; and even, that our contest with Britain is founded entirely upon the petty duty of 3 pence per pound on East India tea; whereas the whole world knows, it is built upon this interesting question, whether the inhabitants of Great-Britain have a right to dispose of the lives and properties of the inhabitants of America, or not? And lastly, that these men have discarded all pretension to common modesty, is clear from hence, first, because they, in the plainest terms, call an august body of men, famed for their patriotism and abilities, fools or knaves, and of course the people whom they represented cannot be exempt from the same opprobrious appellations; and secondly, because they set themselves up as standards of wisdom and probity, by contradicting and censuring the public voice in favour of those men.

A little consideration will convince us, that the congress instead of having "ignorantly misunderstood, carelessly neglected, or basely betrayed the interests of the colonies," have, on the contrary, devised and recommended the only effectual means to secure the freedom, and establish the future prosperity of America upon a solid basis. If we are not free and happy hereafter, it must proceed from the want of integrity and resolution, in executing what they have concerted; not from the temerity or impolicy of their determinations.

Before I proceed to confirm this assertion by the most obvious arguments, I will premise a few brief remarks. The only distinction between freedom and slavery consists in this: In the former state, a man is governed by the laws to which he has given his consent, either in person, or by his representative: In the latter, he is governed by the will of another. In the one case his life and property are his own, in the other, they depend upon the pleasure of a master. It is easy to discern which of these two states is preferable. No man in his senses can hesitate in choosing to be free, rather than a slave.

That Americans are intitled to freedom, is incontestible upon every rational principle. All men have one common original: they participate in one common nature, and consequently have one common right. No reason can be assigned why one man should exercise any power, or pre-eminence over his fellow creatures more than another; unless they have voluntarily vested him with it. Since then, Americans have not by any act of their's impowered the British Parliament to make laws for them, it follows they can have no just authority to do it.

Besides the clear voice of natural justice in this respect, the fundamental principles of the English constitution are in our favour. It has been repeatedly demonstrated, that the idea of legislation, or taxation, when the subject is not represented, is inconsistent with *that*. Nor is this all, our charters, the express conditions on which our progenitors relinquished their native countries, and came to settle in this, preclude every claim of ruling and taxing us without our assent.

Every subterfuge that sophistry has been able to invent, to evade or obscure this truth, has been refuted by the most conclusive reasonings; so that we may pronounce it a matter of undeniable certainty, that the pretensions of Parliament are contradictory to the law of nature, subversive of the British constitution, and destructive of the faith of the most solemn compacts.

What then is the subject of our controversy with the mother country? It is this, whether we shall preserve that security to our lives and properties, which the law of nature, the genius of the British constitution, and our charters afford us; or whether we shall resign them into the hands of the British House of Commons, which is no more privileged to dispose of them than the Grand Mogul? What can actuate those men, who labour to delude any of us into an opinion, that the object of contention between the parent state and the colonies is only three pence duty upon tea? or that the commotions in America originate in a plan, formed by some turbulent men to erect it into a republican government? The parliament claims a right to tax us in all cases whatsoever: Its late acts are in virtue of that claim. How ridiculous then is it to affirm, that we are quarrelling for the trifling sum of three pence a pound on tea; when it is evidently the principle against which we contend.

The design of electing members to represent us in general congress, was, that the wisdom of America might be collected in devising the most proper and expedient means to repel this atrocious invasion of our rights. It has been accordingly done. Their decrees are binding upon all, and demand a religious observance.

We did not, especially in this province, circumscribe them by any fixed boundary, and therefore as they cannot be said to have exceeded the limits of their authority, their act must be esteemed the act of their constituents. If it should be objected, that they have not answered the end of their election; but have fallen upon an improper and ruinous mode of proceeding: I reply, by asking, Who shall be the judge? Shall any individual oppose his private sentiment to the united counsels of men, in whom America has reposed so high a confidence? The attempt must argue no small degree of arrogance and self-sufficiency.

Yet this attempt has been made, and it is become in some measure necessary to vindicate the conduct of this venerable assembly from the aspersions of men, who are their adversaries, only because they are foes to America.

When the political salvation of any community is depending, it is incumbent upon those who are set up as its guardians, to embrace such measures, as have justice, vigour, and a probabilty of success to recommend them: If instead of this, they take those methods which are in themselves feeble, and little likely to succeed; and may, through a defect in vigour, involve the community in still greater danger; they may be justly considered as its betrayers. It is not enough in times of eminent peril to use only possible means of preservation: Justice and sound policy dictate the use of probable means.

The only scheme of opposition, suggested by those, who have been, and are averse from a non-importation and non-exportation agreement, is, by REMONSTRANCE and PETITION. The authors and abettors of this scheme, have never been able to *invent* a single argument to prove the likelihood of its succeeding. On the other hand, there are many standing facts, and valid considerations against it.

In the infancy of the present dispute, we had recourse to this method only. We addressed the throne in the most loyal and respectful manner, in a legislative capacity; but what was the consequence? Our address was treated with contempt and neglect. The first American congress did the same, and met with similar treatment. The total repeal of the stamp act, and the partial repeal of the revenue acts took place, not because the complaints of America were deemed just and reasonable; but because these acts were found to militate against the commercial interests of Great Britain: This was the declared motive of the repeal.

These instances are sufficient for our purpose; but they derive greater validity and force from the following:

The legal assembly of Massachusetts Bay, presented, not long since, a most humble, dutiful, and earnest petition to his Majesty, requesting the dismission of a governor, highly odious to the people, and whose misrepresentations they regarded as one chief source of all their calamities. Did they succeed in their request? No, it was treated with the greatest indignity, and stigmatized as "a seditious, vexatious, and scandalous libel."

I know the men I have to deal with will acquiesce in this stigma.

Will they also dare to calumniate the noble and spirited petition that came from the Mayor and Aldermen of the city of London? Will they venture to justify that unparalelled stride of power, by which popery and arbitrary dominion were established in Canada? The citizens of London remonstrated against it; they signified its repugnancy to the principles of the revolution; but like ours, their complaints were unattended to. From thence we may learn how little dependence ought to be placed on this method of obtaining the redress of grievances.

There is less reason now than ever to expect deliverance, in this way, from the hand of oppression. The system of slavery, fabricated against America, cannot at this time be considered as the effect of inconsideration and rashness. It is the offspring of mature deliberation. It has been fostered by time, and strengthened by every artifice human subtilty is capable of. After the claims of parliament had lain dormant for awhile, they are again resumed and prosecuted with more than common ardour. The Premier has advanced too far to recede with safety: He is deeply interested to execute his purpose, if possible: we know he has declared, that he will never desist, till he has brought America to his feet; and we may conclude, nothing but necessity will induce him to abandon his aims. In common life, to retract an error even in the beginning, is no easy task. Perseverance confirms us in it, and rivets the difficulty; but in a public station, to have been in an error, and to have persisted in it, when it is detected, ruins both reputation and fortune. To this we may add, that disappointment and opposition inflame the minds of men, and attach them, still more, to their mistakes.

What can we represent which has not already been represented? what petitions can we offer, that have not already been offered? The rights of America, and the injustice of parliamentary pretensions have been clearly and repeatedly stated, both in and out of parliament. No new arguments can be framed to operate in our favour. Should we even resolve the errors of the ministry and parliament into the fallibility of human understanding, if they have not yet been convinced, we have no prospect of being able to do it by any thing further we can say. But if we impute their conduct to a wicked thirst of domination and disregard to justice, we have no hope of prevailing with them to alter it, by expatiating on our rights, and suing to their compassion for relief; especially since we have found, by various experiments, the inefficacy of such methods.

Upon the whole, it is morally certain, this mode of opposition would be fruitless and defective. The exigency of the times requires vigorous and probable remedies; not weak and improbable. It would therefore be the extreme of folly to place any confidence in, much less, confine ourselves wholly to it.

This being the case, we can have no resource but in a restriction of our trade, or in a resistance *vi & armis*. It is impossible to conceive any other alternative. Our congress, therefore, have imposed what restraint they thought necessary. Those, who condemn or clamour against it, do nothing more, nor less, than advise us to be slaves.

I shall now examine the principal measures of the congress, and vindicate them fully from the charge of injustice or impolicy.

Were I to argue in a philosophical manner, I might say, the obligation to a mutual intercourse in the way of trade with the inhabitants of Great-Britain, Ireland and the West-Indies is of the *imperfect* kind. There is no law, either of nature, or of the civil society in which we live, that obliges us to purchase, and make use of the products and manufactures of a different land, or people. It is indeed a dictate of humanity to contribute to the support and happiness of our fellow creatures and more especially those who are allied to us by the ties of blood, interest, and mutual protection; but humanity does not require us to sacrifice our own security and welfare to the convenience, or advantage of others. Self preservation is the first principle of our nature. When our lives and properties are at stake, it would be foolish and unnatural to refrain from such measures as might preserve them, because they would be detrimental to others.

But we are justified upon another principle besides this. Though the manufacturers of Great Britain and Ireland, and the Inhabitants of the West Indies are not chargeable with any actual crime towards America, they may, in a political view, be esteemed criminal. In a civil society, it is the duty of each particular branch to promote, not only the good of the whole community, but the good of every other particular branch: If one part endeavours to violate the rights of another, the rest ought to assist in preventing the injury: When they do not, but remain neutral, they are deficient in their duty, and may be regarded, in some measure, as accomplices.

The reason of this is obvious, from the design of civil society, which is, that the united strength of the several members might give stability and security to the whole body, and each respective member; so that one part cannot encroach upon another, without becoming a common enemy, and eventually endangering the safety and happiness of all the other parts.

Since then the persons who will be distressed by the methods we are using for our own protection, have by their neutrality first committed a breach of an obligation, similar to that which bound us to consult their emolument, it is plain, the obligation upon us is annulled, and we are blameless in what we are about to do.

With respect to the manufacturers of Great Britain, they are criminal in a more particular sense. Our oppression arises from that member of the great body politic, of which they compose a considerable part. So far as their influence has been wanting to counteract the iniquity of their rulers, so far they acquiesced in it, and are to be deemed confederates in their guilt. It is impossible to exculpate a people, that suffers its rulers to abuse and tyrannize over others.

It may not be amiss to add, that we are ready to receive with open arms, any who may be sufferers by the operation of our measures, and recompense them with every blessing our country affords to honest industry. We will receive them as brethren, and make them sharers with us in all the advantages we are struggling for.

From these plain and indisputable principles, the mode of opposition we have chosen is reconcileable to the strictest maxims of Justice. It remains now to be examined, whether it has also the sanction of good policy.

To render it agreeable to good policy, three things are requisite. First, that the necessity of the times require it: Secondly, that it be not the probable source of greater evils, than those it pretends to remedy: And lastly, that it have a probability of success.

That the necessity of the times demands it needs but little elucidation. We are threatened with absolute slavery; it has been proved, that resistance by means of REMONSTRANCE and PETITION, would not be efficacious, and of course, that a restriction on our trade, is the only peaceable method, in our power, to avoid the impending mischief: It follows therefore, that such a restriction is necessary.

That it is not the probable source of greater evils than those it pretends to remedy, may easily be determined. The most abject slavery, which comprehends almost every species of human misery, is what it is designed to prevent.

The consequences of the means are a temporary stagnation of commerce, and thereby a deprivation of the luxuries and some of the conveniencies of life. The necessaries, and many of the conveniencies, our own fertile and propitious soil affords us.

No person, that has enjoyed the sweets of liberty, can be insensible of its infinite value, or can reflect on its reverse, without horror and detestation. No person, that is not lost to every generous feeling of humanity, or that is not stupidly blind to his own interest, could bear to offer himself and posterity as victims at the shrine of despotism, in preference to enduring the short lived inconveniencies that may result from an abridgment, or even entire suspension of commerce.

Were not the disadvantages of slavery too obvious to stand in need of it, I might enumerate and describe the tedious train of calamities, inseparable from it. I might shew that it is fatal to religion and morality; that it tends to debase the mind, and corrupt its noblest springs of action. I might shew, that it relaxes the sinews of industry, clips the wings of commerce, and introduces misery and indigence in every shape.

Under the auspices of tyranny, the life of the subject is often sported with; and the fruits of his daily toil are consumed in oppressive taxes, that serve to gratify the ambition, avarice and lusts of his superiors. Every court minion riots in the spoils of the honest labourer, and despises the hand by which he is fed. The page of history is replete with instances that loudly warn us to beware of slavery.

Rome was the nurse of freedom. She was celebrated for her justice and lenity; but in what manner did she govern her dependent provinces? They were made the continual scene of rapine and cruelty. From thence let us learn, how little confidence is due to the wisdom and equity of the most exemplary nations.

Should Americans submit to become the vassals of their fellow-subjects in Great Britain, their yoke will be peculiarly grievous and intolerable. A vast majority of mankind is intirely biassed by motives of self-interest. Most men are glad to remove any burthens off themselves, and place them upon the necks of their neighbours. We cannot therefore doubt, but that the British Parliament, with a view to the ease and advantage of itself, and its constituents, would oppress and grind the Americans as much as possible. Jealousy would concur with selfishness; and for fear of the future independence of America, if it should be permitted to rise to too great a height of splendor and opulence, every method would be taken to drain it of its wealth and restrain its prosperity. We are already suspected of aiming at independence, and that is one principal cause of the severity we experience. The same cause will always operate against us, and produce an uniform severity of treatment.

The evils which may flow from the execution of our measures, if we consider them with respect to their extent and duration, are comparatively nothing. In all human probability they will scarcely be felt. Reason and experience teach us, that the consequences would be too fatal to Great Britain to admit of delay. There is an immense trade between her and the colonies. The revenues arising from thence are prodigious. The consumption of her manufactures in these colonies supplies the means of subsistence to a vast number of her most useful inhabitants. The experiment we have made heretofore, shews us of how much importance our commercial connexion is to her; and gives us the highest assurance of obtaining immediate redress by suspending it.

From these considerations it is evident, she must do something decisive. She must either listen to our complaints, and restore us to a peaceful enjoyment of our violated rights; or she must exert herself to enforce her despotic claims by fire and sword. To imagine she would prefer the latter, implies a charge of the grossest infatuation of madness itself. Our numbers are very considerable; the courage of Americans has been tried and proved. Contests for liberty have ever been found the most bloody, implacable and obstinate. The disciplined troops Great Britain could send against us, would be but few, Our superiority in number would over balance our inferiority in discipline. It would be a hard, if not an impracticable task to subjugate us by force.

Besides, while Great Britain was engaged in carrying on an unnatural war against us, her commerce would be in a state of decay. Her revenues would be decreasing. An armament, sufficient to enslave America, would put her to an insupportable expence.

She would be laid open to the attacks of foreign enemies. Ruin, like a deluge, would pour in from every quarter. After lavishing her blood and treasure to reduce us to a state of vassalage, she would herself become a prey to some triumphant neighbour.

These are not imaginary mischiefs. The colonies contain above three millions of people. Commerce flourshes with the most rapid progress throughout them. This commerce Great-Britain has hitherto regulated to her own advantage. Can we think the annihilation of so exuberant a source of wealth, a matter of trifling import. On the contrary, must it not be productive of the most disastrous effects? It is evident it must. It is equally evident, that the conquest of so numerous a people, armed in the animating cause of liberty could not be accomplished without an inconceivable expence of blood and treasure.

We cannot therefore suspect Great-Britain to be capable of such frantic extravagance as to hazard these dreadful consequences; without which she must necessarily desist from her unjust pretensions, and leave us in the undisturbed possession of our privileges.

Those, who affect to ridicule the resistance America might make to the military force of Great-Britain, and represent its humiliation as a matter the most easily to be achieved, betray, either a mind clouded by the most irrational prejudices, or a total ignorance of human nature. However, it must be the wish of every honest man never to see a trial.

But should we admit a possibility of a third course, as our pamphleteer supposes, that is, the endeavouring to bring us to a compliance by putting a stop to our whole trade: Even this would not be so terrible as he pretends. We can live without trade of any kind. Food and clothing we have within ourselves. Our climate produces cotton, wool, flax and hemp, which, with proper cultivation would furnish us with summer apparel in abundance. The article of cotton indeed would do more, it would contribute to defend us from the inclemency of winter. We have sheep, which, with due care in improving and increasing them, would soon yield a sufficiency of wool. The large quantity of skins, we have among us, would never let us want a warm and comfortable suit. It would be no unbecoming employment for our daughters to provide silks of their own country. The silk-worm answers as well here as in any part of the world. Those hands, which may be deprived of business by the cessation of commerce, may be occupied in various kinds of manufactures and other internal improvements. If by the necessity of the thing, manufactures should once be established and take root among us, they will pave the way, still more, to the future grandeur and glory of America, and by lessening its need of external commerce, will render it still securer against the encroachments of tyranny.

It is however, chimerical to imagine that the circumstances of Great-Britain will admit of such a tardy method of subjecting us, for reasons, which have been already given, and which shall be corroborated by others equally forcible.

I come now to consider the last and principal ingredient that constitutes the policy of a measure, which is a probability of success. I have been obliged to anticipate this part of my subject, in considering the second requisite, and indeed what I have already said seems to me to leave no room for doubting, that the means we have used will be successful, but I shall here examine the matter more thoroughly, and endeavour to evince it more fully.

The design of the Congress in their proceedings, it cannot, and need not be desired, was either, by a prospect of the evil consequences, to influence the ministry to give up their enterprize; or should they prove inflexible, to affect the inhabitants of Great-Britain, Ireland and the West-Indies in such a manner, as to rouse them from their state of neutrality, and engage them to unite with us in opposing the lawless hand of tyranny, which is extended to ravish our liberty from us, and might soon be extended for the same purpose against them.

The FARMER mentions, as one probable consequence of our measures, "clamours, discord, confusion, mobs, riots, insurrections, rebellions in Great-Britain, Ireland and the West-Indies;" though at the same time that he thinks *it is*, he also thinks *it is not* a probable consequence. For my part, without hazarding any such seeming contradictions, I shall, in a plain way, assert, that I verily believe a non-importation and non-exportation will effect all the purposes they are intended for.

It is no easy matter to make any tolerably exact estimate of the advantages that acrue to Great-Britain, Ireland and the West-Indies from their commercial intercourse with the colonies, nor indeed is it necessary. Every man, the least acquainted with the state and extent of our trade, must be convinced, it is the source of immense revenues to the parent state, and gives employment and bread to a vast number of his Majesty's subjects. It is impossible but that a suspension of it for any time, must introduce beggary and wretchedness in an eminent degree, both in England and Ireland; and as to the West-India plantations, they could not possibly subsist without us. I am the more confident of this, because I have a pretty general acquaintance with their circumstances and dependencies.

We are told, "that it is highly improbable, we shall succeed in distressing the people of Great-Britain, Ireland and the West-Indies, so far as to oblige them to join with us in getting the acts of Parliament, which we complain of, repealed: The first distress (it is said) will fall on ourselves; it will be more severely felt by us, than any part of all his Majesty's dominions, and will affect us the longest. The fleets of Great-Britain command respect throughout the globe. Her influence extends to every part of the earth. Her manufactures are equal to any: Superior to most in the world. Her wealth is great. Her people enterprizing and persevering in their attempts to extend, and enlarge, and protect her trade. The total loss of our trade will be felt only for a time. Her merchants would turn their attention another way: New sources of trade and wealth would be opened: New schemes pursued. She would soon find a vent for all her manufactures in spite of all we could do. Our malice would hurt only ourselves. Should our schemes distress some branches of her trade, it would be only for a time; and there is ability and humanity enough in the nation to relieve those, that are distressed by us, and put them in some other way of getting their living."

The omnipotence and all sufficiency of Great-Britain may be pretty good topics for her passionate admirers to exercise their declamatory powers upon, for amusement and trial of skill; but they ought not to be proposed to the world as matters of truth and reality. In the calm, unprejudiced eye of reason, they are altogether visionary. As to her wealth, it is notorious that she is oppressed with a heavy national debt, which it requires the utmost policy and œconomy ever to discharge. Luxury has arrived to a great pitch; and it is an universal maxim that luxury indicates the declension of a state. Her subjects are loaded with the most enormous taxes: All circumstances agree in declaring their distress. The continual emigrations, from Great-Britain and Ireland, to the continent, are a glaring symptom, that those kingdoms are a good deal impoverished.

The attention of Great-Britain has hitherto been constantly awake to expand her commerce. She has been vigilant to explore every region, with which it might be her interest to trade. One of the principal branches of her commerce is with the colonies. These colonies, as they are now settled and peopled, have been the work of near two centuries: They are blessed with every advantage of soil, climate and situation. They have advanced with an almost incredible rapidity. It is therefore an egregious piece of absurdity to affirm, that the loss of our trade would be felt for a time (which must signify a short time.) No new schemes could be pursued that would not require, at least, as much time to repair the loss of our trade, as was spent in bringing it to its present degree of perfection, which is near two centuries. Nor can it be reasonably imagined, that the total and sudden loss of so extensive and lucrative a branch, would not produce the most violent effects to a nation that subsists entirely upon its commerce.

It is said, "there is ability and humanity enough in the nation to relieve those that are distressed by us; and to put them into some other way of getting their living." I wish the gentleman had obliged his readers so much, as to have pointed out this other way; I must confess, I have racked my brains to no purpose to discover it, and am fully of opinion it is purely ideal. Besides the common mechanic arts, which are subservient to the ordinary uses of life, and which are the instruments of commerce; know no other ways in time of peace, in which men can be employed, except in agriculture and the liberal arts. Persons employed in the mechanic arts, are those, whom the abridgment of commerce would immediately affect, and as to such branches as might be less affected, they are already sufficiently stocked with workmen, and could give bread to no more; not only so, but I can't see by what legerdemain, a weaver, or clothier could be at once converted into a carpenter or black-smith. With respect to agriculture, the lands of Great Britain and Ireland have been long ago distributed and taken up; nor do they require any additional labourers to till them; so that there could be no employment in this way. The liberal arts cannot maintain those who are already devoted to them; not to say, it is more than probable, the generality of mechanics, would make but indifferent philosophers, poets, painters and musicians.

What poor shifts is sophistry obliged to have recourse to! we are threatened with the resentment of those against whom our measures will operate. It is said, that "instead of conciliating, we shall alienate the affections of the people of Great-Britain, of friends, we shall make them our enemies;" and further, that "we shall excite the resentment of the government at home against us, which will do us no good, but, on the contrary, much harm."

Soon after, we are told that "we shall probably raise the resentment of the Irish and West-Indians: The passions of human nature" it is said, "are much the same in all countries. If they find us disposed wantonly to distress them, to serve our own purposes, they will look out for some method to do without us: will they not look elsewhere for a supply of those articles, they used to take from us? They would deserve to be despised for their meanness did they not."

To these objections I reply, first with respect to the inhabitants of Great-Britain, that if they are our friends, as is supposed, and as we have reason to believe; they cannot, without being destitute of rationality, be incensed against us for using the only peaceable and probable means, in our power, to preserve our invaded rights: They know by their own experience how fruitless remonstrances and petitions are: They know, we have tried them over and over to no purpose: They know also, how dangerous to their liberties, the loss of ours must be. What then could exite their resentment if they have the least regard to common justice? The calamities, that threaten them, proceed from the weakness, or wickedness of their own rulers; which compels us to take the measures we do. The insinuation, that we *wantonly* distress them to serve our own purposes, is futile and unsupported by a single argument. I have shewn, we could have no other resource; nor can they think our conduct such, without a degree of infatuation, that it would be impossible to provide against, and therefore useless to consult. It is most reasonable to believe, they will revenge the evils they may feel on the true authors of them, on an aspiring and ill-judging ministry; not on us, who act out of a melancholy necessity, and are the innocent causes in self-defence.

With respect to the ministry, it is certain, that any thing, which has a tendency to frustrate their designs, will not fail to excite their displeasure; but since we have nothing to expect from their justice and lenity, it can be no objection to a measure, that it tends to stir up their resentment. But their resentment (it is often said) may ruin us. The impossibility of doing that, without at the same time, ruining Great-Britain, is a sufficient security.

The same may be said with regard to the Irish and the West-Indians, which has been said concerning the people of Great-Britain. The Irish, in particular, by their own circumstances will be taught to sympathise with us, and commend our conduct. Justice will direct their resentment to its proper objects.

It is true self-love will prompt both the Irish and the West-Indians to take every method in their power, to escape the miseries they are in danger of; but what methods can they take? "The Irish (it is said) may be supplied with flax-seed from Holland, the Baltic, and the river St.

Lawrence: Canada produces no inconsiderable quantity already." And as to the West-Indies, "they produce now many of the necessaries of life. The quantity may be easily increased. Canada will furnish them with many articles they now take from us; flour, lumber, horses, &c. Georgia, the Floridas, and the Mississippi abound in lumber: Nova Scotia in fish."

The Dutch are rivals to the English in their commerce. They make large quantities of fine linens, gause, laces, &c. which require the flax to be picked before it comes to seed; for which reason, it is not in their power to raise much more seed than they want for their own use. Ireland has always had the surplus from them. They could, if they were ever so willing, enlarge their usual supplies but very little. It is indeed probable they may withold them. They may choose to improve the occasion for the advancement of their own trade: They may take advantage of the scarcity of materials in Ireland, to increase and put off their own manufactures.

The Baltic has ever supplied Ireland with its flax, and she has been able to consume that, with all she could derive from other quarters.

As to Canada, I am well informed it could at present afford, but a very inconsiderable quantity. It has had little encouragement, hitherto, to raise that article, and of course has not much attended to it. The instances mentioned, of seed being "bought up there at a low price, brought to New-York, and sold to the Irish factors at a great advance," does not prove there is any quantity raised there. Its cheapness proceeds from there being no demand for it; and where there was no demand, there was no inducement to cultivate it.

Upon the whole, it appears, that the supplies of flax-seed, which Ireland might draw elsewhere, could be trifling in comparison with those received from us, and not at all equivalent to her wants. But if this were not the case, if she might procure a sufficiency without our help, yet could she not do without us. She would want purchasers for her linens after they were manufactured; and where could she find any so numerous and wealthy as we are? I must refer it to the profound sagacity of Mr. A. W. Farmer, to explore them, it is too arduous a task for me.

Much less could the West-Indies subsist independent of us. Notwithstanding the continual imports from hence, there is seldom or ever, in any of the islands, a sufficient stock of provisions to last six months, which may give us an idea, how great the consumption is. The necessaries they produce within themselves, when compared with the consumption, are scarcely worth mentioning. Very small portions of the lands are appropriated to the productions of such necessaries, indeed it is too valuable to admit of it. Nor could the quantity be increased to any material degree, without applying the whole of the land to it. It is alledged, that Canada will furnish them with "flour, lumber, horses, &c. and that Georgia, the Floridas and Mississipi abound in lumber; Nova Scotia in fish." These countries have been all-along carrying on a trade to the West-Indies, as well as we; and can it be imagined that alone, they will be able to supply them tolerably? The Canadians have been indolent, and have not improved their country as they ought to have done. The wheat they raise at present, over and above what they have occasion for themselves, would be found to go but little way among the islands. Those, who think the contrary, must have mistaken notions of them. They must be unapprized of the number of souls they contain: Almost every 150 or 200 acres of land, exclusive of populous towns, comprehend a hundred people. It is not a small quantity of food that will suffice for so many. Ten or fifteen years diligence, I grant, might enable Canada to perform what is now expected from her; but, in the mean time, the West-Indians might have the satisfaction of starving.

To suppose the best, which is, that by applying their canelands to the purpose of procuring sustenance, they may preserve themselves from starving: still the consequences must be very serious or pernicious. The wealthy planters would but ill relish the loss of their crops, and such of them as were considerably in debt would be ruined. At any rate, the revenues of Great-Britain would suffer a vast diminution.

The FARMER, I am inclined to hope, builds too much upon the present disunion of Canada, Georgia, the Floridas, the Mississippi, and Nova Scotia from other colonies. A little time, I trust, will awaken them from their slumber, and bring them to a proper sense of their indiscretion. I please myself with the flattering prospect, that they will, ere long, unite in one indissoluble chain with the rest of the colonies. I cannot believe they will persist in such a conduct as must exclude them from the secure enjoyment of those heaven-descended immunities we are contending for.

There is one argument I have frequently heard urged, which it may be of some use to invalidate. It is this, that if the mother country should be inclined to an accommodation of our disputes, we have by our rash procedure thrown an insurmountable obstacle in her way; we have made it disgraceful to her to comply with our requisitions, because they are proposed in a hostile manner.

Our present measures, I have proved, are the only peaceable ones we could place the least confidence in. They are the least exceptionable, upon the score of irritating Great-Britain, of any our circumstances would permit. The congress have petitioned his Majesty for the redress of grievances. They have, no doubt, addressed him in the most humble, respectful and affectionate terms; assured him, of their own loyalty, and fidelity and of the loyalty and fidelity of his American subjects in general; endeavoured to convince him, that we have been misrepresented and abused; and expressed an earnest desire to see an amicable termination of the unhappy differences now existing. Can a pretext be wanting, in this case, to preserve the dignity of this parent state, and yet remove the complaints of the colonies? How easy would it be to overlook our particular agreements, and grant us redress in consequence of our petitions? It is easy to perceive there would be no difficulty in this respect.

I have omitted many considerations, which might be adduced to shew the impolicy of Great-Britains, delaying to accommodate matters, and attempting to enforce submission by cutting off all external sources of trade. To say all the subject allows, would spin out this piece to an immoderate length; I shall, therefore, content myself with mentioning only three things more. First, it would be extremely hurtful to the commerce of Great-Britain to drive us to the necessity of laying a regular foundation for manufactories of our own; which, if once established, could not easily, if at all, be undermined, or abolished. Secondly, it would be very expensive to the nation to maintain a fleet for the purpose of blocking up our ports, and destroying our trade: nor could she interrupt our intercourse with foreign climes without, at the same time, retrenching her own revenues; for she must then lose the duties and customs upon the articles we are wont to export to, and import from them. Added to this, it would not be prudent to risk the displeasure of those nations, to whom our trade is useful and beneficial. And lastly, a perseverance in ill-treatment would naturally beget such deep-rooted animosities in America, as might never be eradicated; and which might operate to the prejudice of the empire to the latest period.

Thus have I clearly proved, that the plan of opposition concerted by our congress is perfectly consonant with justice and sound policy; and will, in all human probability, secure our freedom against the assaults of our enemies.

But, after all, it may be demanded why they have adopted a non-exportation; seeing many arguments tend to shew that a non-importation alone would accomplish the end desired?

I answer, that the continuance of our exports is the only thing which could lessen, or retard the efficacy of a non-importation. It is not indeed probable it should do that to any great degree; but it was adviseable to provide against every possible obstruction. Besides this, the prospect of its taking place, and of the evils attendant upon it, will be a prevailing motive with the ministry to abandon their malignant schemes. It will also serve to convince them, that we are not afraid of putting ourselves to any inconveniencies, sooner than be the victims of their lawless ambition.

The execution of this measure has been wisely deferred to a future time, because we have the greatest reason to think affairs will be settled without it, and because its consequences would be too fatal to be justified by any thing but absolute necessity. This necessity there will be, should not our disputes terminate before the time allotted for its commencement.

Before I conclude this part of my address, I will answer two very singular interrogatories proposed by the Farmer, "Can we think (says he) to threaten, and bully, and frighten the supreme government of the nation into a compliance with our demands? Can we expect to force submission to our peevish and petulant humours, by exciting clamours and riots in England?" No, gentle Sir. We neither desire, nor endeavour to threaten, bully, or frighten any persons into a compliance with our demands. We have no peevish and petulant humours to be submitted to. All we aim at, is to convince your high and mighty masters, the ministry, that we are not such asses as to let them ride us as they please. We are determined to shew them, that we know the value of freedom; nor shall their rapacity extort, that inestimable jewel from us, without a manly and virtuous struggle. But for your part, sweet Sir! tho' we cannot much applaud your wisdom, yet we are compelled to admire your valour, which leads you to hope you may be able to *swear*, threaten, bully and frighten all America into a compliance with your sinister designs.

When properly accoutered and armed with your formidable hiccory cudgel, what may not the ministry expect from such a champion? alas! for the poor committee gentlemen, how I tremble when I reflect on the many wounds and scars they must receive from your tremendous arm! Alas! for their supporters and abettors; a very large part indeed of the continent; but what of that? they must all be soundly drubbed with that confounded hiccory cudgel; for surely you would not undertake to drub one of them, without knowing yourself able to treat all their friends and adherents in the same manner; since 'tis plain you would bring them all upon your back.

I am now to address myself in particular to the Farmers of New-York.

MY GOOD COUNTRYMEN,

The reason I address myself to you, in particular, is, because I am one of your number, or connected with you in interest more than with any other branch of the community. I love to speak the truth, and would scorn to prejudice you in favour of what I have to say, by taking upon me a fictitious character as other people have done. I can venture to assure you, the true writer of the piece signed A. W. FARMER, is not in reality a Farmer. He is some ministerial emissary, that has assumed the name to deceive you, and make you swallow the intoxicating potion he has prepared for you. But I have a better opinion of you than to think he will be able to succeed. I am persuaded you love yourselves and children better than to let any designing men cheat you out of your liberty and property, to serve their own purposes. You would be a disgrace to your ancestors, and the bitterest enemies to yourselves and to your posterity, if you did not act like men, in protecting and defending those rights you have hitherto enjoyed.

I say, my friends, I do not address you in particular, because I have any greater connexion with you, than with other people. I despise all false pretentions, and mean arts. Let those have recourse to dissimulation and falshood, who can't defend their cause without it. 'Tis my maxim to let the plain naked truth speak for itself; and if men won't listen to it, 'tis their own fault: they must be contented to suffer for it. I am neither merchant, nor farmer. I address you, because I wish well to my country, and of course to you, who are one chief support of it; and because an attempt has been made to lead you astray in particular. You are the men too who would lose most should you be foolish enough to counteract the prudent measures our worthy congress has taken for the preservation of our liberties. Those, who advise you to do it, are not your friends, but your greatest foes. They would have you made slaves, that they may pamper themselves with the fruits of your honest labour. 'Tis the Farmer who is most oppressed in all countries where slavery prevails.

You have seen how clearly I have proved, that a non-importation and non-exportation are the only peaceable means in our power to save ourselves from the most dreadful state of slavery. I have shewn there is not the least hope, to be placed in any thing else. I have confuted all the principal cavils raised by the pretended Farmer, and I hope, before I finish, to satisfy you, that he has attempted to frighten you with the prospect of evils, which will never happen. This indeed I have, in a great measure, done already, by making appear the great probability, I may almost say certainty, that our measures will procure us the most speedy redress.

Are you willing then to be slaves without a single struggle? Will you give up your freedom, or, which is the same thing, will you resign all security for your life and property, rather than endure some small present inconveniencies? Will you not take a little trouble to transmit the advantages you now possess to those, who are to come after you? I cannot doubt it. I would not suspect you of so much baseness and stupidity, as to suppose the contrary.

Pray who can tell me why a farmer in America, is not as honest and good a man, as a farmer in England? or why has not the one as good a right to what he has earned by his labour, as the other? I can't, for my life, see any distinction between them. And yet it seems the English farmers are to be governed and taxed by their own Assembly, or Parliament; and the American farmers are not. The former are to choose their own Representatives from among themselves, whose interest is connected with theirs, and over whom they have proper controul. The latter are to be loaded with taxes by men three thousand miles off; by men, who have no interest, or connexions among them; but whose interest it will be to burden them as much as possible; and over whom they cannot have the least restraint. How do you like this doctrine my friends? Are you ready to own the English farmers for your masters? Are you willing to acknowledge their right to take your property from you, and when they please? I know you scorn the thought. You had rather die, than submit to it.

But some people try to make you believe, we are disputing about the foolish trifle of three pence duty upon tea. They may as well tell you, that black is white. Surely you can judge for yourselves. Is a dispute, whether the Parliament of Great-Britain shall make what laws, and impose what taxes they please upon us, or not; I say, is this a dispute about three pence duty upon tea? The man that affirms it, deserves to be laughed at.

It is true, we are denying to pay the duty upon tea; but it is not for the value of the thing itself. It is because we cannot submit to that, without acknowledging the principle upon which it is founded, and that principle is *a right to tax us in all cases whatsoever*.

You have, heretofore experienced the benefit of being taxed by your own Assemblies only. Your burdens are so light, that you scarcely feel them. You'd soon find the difference if you were once to let the Parliament have the management of these matters.

How would you like to pay four shillings a year, out of every pound your farms are worth, to be squandered, (at least a great part of it) upon ministerial tools and court sycophants? What would you think of giving a tenth part of the yearly products of your lands to the clergy? Would you not think it very hard to pay 10s. sterling per annum, for every wheel of your waggons and other carriages, a shilling or two for every pane of glass in your houses, and two or three shillings for every one of your hearths? I might mention taxes upon your mares, cows, and many other things; but those I have already mentioned are sufficient. Methinks I see you stare, and hear you ask how you could live, if you were to pay such heavy taxes? Indeed my friends I can't tell you. You are to look out for that, and take care you do not run yourselves in the way of danger, by following the advice of those, who want to betray you. This you may depend upon, if ever you let the Parliament carry its point, you will have these and more to pay. Perhaps before long, your tables, and chairs, and platters, and dishes, and knives and forks, and every thing else would be taxed. Nay, I don't know but they would find means to tax you for every child you got, and for every kiss your daughters received from their sweet-hearts, and God knows, that would soon ruin you. The people of England would pull down the Parliament House, if their present heavy burdens were not transferred from them to you. Indeed there is no reason to think the Parliament would have any inclination to spare you: The contrary is evident.

But being ruined by taxes is not the worst you have to fear. What security would you have for your lives? How can any of you be sure you would have the free enjoyment of your religion long? would you put your religion in the power of any set of men living? Remember civil and religious liberty always go together, if the foundation of the one be sapped, the other will fall of course.

Call to mind one of our sister colonies, Boston. Reflect upon the situation of Canada, and then tell me whether you are inclined to place any confidence in the justice and humanity of the parliament. The port of Boston is blocked up, and an army planted in the town. An act has been passed to alter its charter, to prohibit its assemblies, to license the murder of its inhabitants, and to convey them from their own country to Great Britain, to be tried for their lives. What was all this for? Just because a small number of people, provoked by an open and dangerous attack upon their liberties, destroyed a parcel of Tea belonging to the East India Company. It was not public but private property they destroyed. It was not the act of the whole province, but the act of a part of the citizens; instead of trying to discover the perpetrators, and commencing a legal prosecution against them; the parliament of Great-Britain interfered in an unprecedented manner, and inflicted a punishment upon a whole province, "untried, unheard, unconvicted of any crime." This may be justice, but it looks so much like cruelty, that a man of a humane heart would be more apt to call it by the latter, than the former name.

The affair of Canada, if possible, is still worse. The English laws have been superceded by the French laws. The Romish faith is made the established religion of the land, and his Majesty is placed at the head of it. The free exercise of the protestant faith depends upon the pleasure of the Governor and Council. The subject is divested of the right of trial by jury, and an innocent man may be imprisoned his whole life, without being able to obtain any trial at all. The parliament was not contented with introducing arbitrary power and popery in Canada, with its former limits, but they have annexed to it the vast tracts of land that surround all the colonies.

Does not your blood run cold, to think an English parliament should pass an act for the establishment of arbitrary power and popery in such an extensive country? If they had had any regard to the freedom and happiness of mankind, they would never have done it. If they had been friends to the protestant cause, they would never have provided such a nursery for its great enemy: They would not have given such encouragement to popery. The thought of their conduct, in this particular shocks me. It must shock you too my friends. Beware of trusting yourselves to men, who are capable of such an action! They may as well establish popery in New-York and the other colonies as they did in Canada. They had no more right to do it there than here.

Is it not better, I ask, to suffer a few present inconveniencies, than to put yourselves in the way of losing every thing that is precious. Your lives, your property, your religion are all at stake. I do my duty. I warn you of your danger. If you should still be so mad, as to bring destruction upon yourselves; if you should still neglect what you owe to God and man, you cannot plead ignorance in your excuse. Your consciences will reproach you for your folly, and your children's children will curse you.

You are told, the schemes of our Congress will ruin you. You are told, they have not considered your interest; but have neglected, or betrayed you. It is endeavoured to make you look upon some of the wisest and best men in the America, as rogues and rebels. What will not wicked men attempt! They will scruple nothing, that may serve their purposes. In truth, my friends, it is very unlikely any of us shall suffer much; but let the worst happen, the farmers will be better off, than other people.

Many of those that made up the Congress have large possessions in land, and may, therefore be looked upon as farmers themselves. Can it be supposed, they would be careless about the farmer's interest, when they could not injure that, without injuring themselves? You see the absurdity of such a supposition.

The merchants and a great part of the tradesmen get their living by commerce. These are the people that would be hurt most, by putting a stop to it. As to the farmers, "they furnish food for the merchant and mechanic; the raw materials for most manufactures are the produce of their industry." The merchants and mechanics are already dependent upon the farmers for their food, and if the non-importation should continue any time, they would be dependent upon them for their cloaths also.

It is a false assertion, that the merchants have imported more than usual this year. That report has been raised by your enemies to poison your minds with evil suspicions. If our disputes be not settled within eighteen months, the goods we have among us will be consumed; and then the materials for making cloaths must be had from you. Manufactures must be promoted with vigour, and a high price will be given for your wool, flax and hemp. It will be your interest to pay the greatest care and attention to your sheep. Increase and improve the breed as much as possible: *Kill them sparingly*, and such only as will not be of use towards the increase and improvement of them. In a few months we shall know what we have to trust to. If matters be not accommodated by spring, enlarge the quantity of your flax and hemp. You will experience the benefit of it. All those articles will be very much wanted: They will bring a great deal higher price than they used to do. And while you are supplying the wants of the community, you will be enriching yourselves.

Should we hereafter, find it necessary to stop our exports, you can apply more of your land to raising flax and hemp, and less of it to wheat, rye, &c. By which means, you will not have any of those latter articles to lie upon hand. There will be a consumption for as much of the former as you can raise, and the great demand they will be in, will make them very profitable to you.

Patience good Mr. Critic! *Kill them sparingly, I said*, what objection have you to the phrase? You'll tell me, it is not *classical*; but I affirm it is, and if you will condescend to look into Mr. Johnson's dictionary, you will find I have his authority for it. Pray then, for the future, *spare* your wit, upon such occasions, otherwise the world will not be disposed to *spare* its ridicule. And though the man that *spares* nobody does not deserve to be *spared* himself, yet will I *spare* you, for the present, and proceed to things of more importance.

Pardon me, my friends, for taking up your time with this digression; but I could not forbear stepping out of the way a little, to shew the world, I am as able a critic, and as good a punster as Mr. Farmer. I now return to the main point with pleasure.

It is insinuated, "That the bustle about non-importation, &c. has its rise, not from patriotism, but selfishness;" and is only made by the merchants, that they may get a high price for their goods.

By this time, I flatter myself you are convinced, that we are not disputing about trifles. It has been clearly proved to you, that we are contending for every thing dear in life, and that the measures adopted by the congress, are the only ones which can save us from ruin. This is sufficient to confute that insinuation. But to confirm it, let me observe to you, that the merchants have not been the foremost to bring about a non-importation. All the members of the congress were unanimous in it; and *many* of them were not merchants. The warmest advocates for it, every where, are not concerned in trade, and, as I before remarked, the traders will be the principal sufferers, if it should continue any time.

But it is said it will not continue, because, "when the stores are like to become empty, they will have weight enough to break up the agreement." I don't think they would attempt it; but if they should, it is impossible a few mercenary men could have influence enough to make the whole body of people give up the only plan their circumstances admit of for the preservation of their rights, and, of course, to forfeit all they have been so long striving to secure. The making of a non-importation agreement did not depend upon the merchants; neither will the breaking of it depend upon them. The congress have provided against the breach of the non-importation, by the non-consumption agreement. They have resolved for themselves and us their constituents, "not to purchase, or use any East-India Tea whatsoever; nor any goods, wares, or merchandize, from Great-Britain or Ireland, imported after the first of December, nor molasses, &c. from the West Indies, nor wine from Madeira, or the Western Islands, nor foreign Indigo." If we do not purchase or use these things, the merchant will have no inducement to import them.

Hence you may perceive the reason of a non-consumption agreement. It is to put it out of the power of dishonest men, to break the non importation. *Is this a slavish regulation?* Or is it a hardship upon us to submit to it? Surely not. Every sensible, every good man must approve of it. Whoever tries to disaffect you to it, ought to meet with your contempt.

Take notice, my friends, how these men are obliged to contradict themselves. In one place you are told, that all the bustle about non-importation, &c. has its rise, not from patriotism, but from selfishness, "or, in other words, that it is made by the merchants to get a higher price for their goods." In another place it is said, that all we are doing is instigated by some turbulent men, who want to establish a republican form of government among us.

The Congress is censured for appointing committees to carry their measures into execution, and directing them "to establish such further regulations, as they may think proper for that purpose." Pray, did we not appoint our Delegates to make regulations for us? What signified making them, if they did not provide some persons to see them executed? Must a few bad men be left to do what they please, contrary to the general sense of the people, without any persons to controul them, or to look into their behaviour and mark them out to the public? The man that desires to screen his knavery from the public eye, will answer yes; but the honest man, that is determined to do nothing hurtful to his country, and who is conscious his actions will bear the light, will heartily answer no.

The high prices of goods are held up to make you dissatisfied with the non-importation. If the argument on this head were true, it would be much better to subject yourselves to that disadvantage, for a time, than to bring upon yourselves all the mischiefs I have pointed out to you. Should you submit to claims of the Parliament, you will not only be oppressed with the taxes upon your lands, &c. which I have already mentioned; but you will have to pay heavy taxes upon all the goods we import from Great-Britain. Large duties will be laid upon them at home; and the merchants, of course, will have a greater price for them, or it would not be worth their while to carry on trade. The duty laid upon paper, glass, painter's colours, &c. was a beginning of this kind. The present duty upon tea is preparatory to the imposition of duties upon all other articles. Do you think the Parliament would make such a serious matter of three pence a pound upon tea, if it intended to stop there? It is absurd to imagine it. You would soon find your mistake if you did. For fear of paying somewhat a higher price to the merchants for a year or two, you would have to pay an endless list of taxes, within and without, as long as you live, and your children after you.

But I trust, there is no danger that the prices of goods will rise much, if at all. The same congress that put a stop to the importation of them, has also forbid raising the prices of them. The same committee that is to regulate the one, is also to regulate the other. All care will be taken to give no cause of dissatisfaction. Confide in the men whom you, and the rest of the continent have chosen the guardians of our common liberties. They are men of sense and virtue. They will do nothing but what is really necessary for the security of your lives and properties.

A sad pother is made too about prohibiting the exportation of sheep, without excepting weathers. The poor Farmer is at a mighty loss to know how weathers can improve, or increase the breed. Truly I am not such a conjurer, as to be able to inform him; but if you please, my friends, I can give you two pretty good reasons, why the congress has not excepted weathers. One is, that for some time, we shall have occasion for all the wool we can raise; so that it would be imprudent to export sheep of any kind: and the other is, that, if you confine yourself chiefly to killing weathers, as you ought to do, you will have none to export. The gentleman who made the objection, must have known these things, as well as myself; but he loves to crack a jest, and could not pass by so fair an opportunity.

He takes notice of the first of these reasons himself; but in order to weaken its force, cries, "let me ask you, brother farmers, which of you would keep a flock of sheep, barely, for the sake of their wool?" To this he answers, "not one of you. If you cannot sell your sheep to advantage, at a certain age, you cannot keep them to any profit." He thinks, because he calls you brother farmers, that he can cajole you into believing what he pleases; but you are not the fools he takes you for. You know what is for your own interest better than he can tell you. And we all know, that in a little time, if our affairs be not settled, the demand for wool will be very great. You will be able to obtain such a price, as will make it worth your while to bestow the greatest attention upon your sheep.

In another place, this crafty writer tells you, that, "from the day our exports, from this province are stopped, the farmers may date the commencement of their ruin." He asks, "will the shop-keeper give you his goods? will the weaver, shoe-maker, black-smith, carpenter work for you without pay?" I make no doubt, you are satisfied, from what I have said, that we shall never have occasion to stop our exports; but if things turn out contrary to our expectation, and it should become necessary to take that step, you will find no difficulty in getting what you want from the merchants and mechanics. They will not be able to do without you, and, consequently, they cannot refuse to supply you with what you stand in need of from them. Where will the merchants and mechanics get food and materials for clothing, if not from the farmer? And if they are dependent upon you, for those two grand supports of life, how can they withold what they have from you?

I repeat it (my friends) we shall know, how matters are like to be settled by the spring. If our disputes be not terminated to our satisfaction by that time, it will be your business to plant large parts of your lands with flax and hemp. Those articles will be wanted for manufactures, and they will yield you a greater profit than any thing else. In the interim, take good care of your sheep.

I heartily concur with the farmer, in condemning all illicit trade. Perjury is, no doubt, a most heineous and detestable crime; and for my part, I had rather suffer any thing, than have my wants relieved at the expence of truth and integrity. I know, there are many pretended friends to liberty, who will take offence at this declaration; but I speak the sentiments of my heart without reserve. I do not write for a party. I should scorn to be of any. All I say, is from a disinterested regard to the public weal.

The congress, I am persuaded, were of the same opinion: They, like honest men, have, as much as was in their power, provided against this kind of trade, by agreeing to use no East-India tea whatever, after the first day of March next.

I shall now consider what has been said, with respect to the payment of debts, and stopping of the courts of justice. Let what will happen, it will be your own faults, if you are not able to pay your debts. I have told you, in what manner you may make as much out of your lands as ever: by bestowing more of your attention upon raising flax and hemp, and less upon other things. Those articles (as I have more than once observed) will be in the highest demand: There will be no doing without them; and, of course, you will be able to get a very profitable price for them. How can it be, that the farmers should be at a loss for money to pay their debts, at a time, when the whole community must buy, not only their food, but all the materials for their cloaths from them? You have no reason to be uneasy on that account.

As to the courts of justice, no violence can, or will be used to shut them up; but, if it should be found necessary, we may enter into solemn agreement to cease from all litigations at law, except in particular cases. We may regulate law suits, in such a manner, as to prevent any mischief that might arise from them. Restrictions may be laid on to hinder merciless creditors, from taking advantage of the times, to oppress and ruin their debtors but, at the same time, not to put it in the power of the debtors, *wantonly*, to withold their just dues from their creditors, when they are able to pay them. The law ruins many a good honest family. Disputes may be settled in a more friendly way; one or two virtuous neighbours may be chosen by each party to decide them. If the next congress should think any regulations concerning the courts of justice requisite, they will make them; and proper persons will be appointed to carry them into execution, and to see, that no individuals deviate from them. It will be your duty to elect persons, whose fidelity and zeal for your interest you can depend upon, to represent you in *that* congress; which is to meet at Philadelphia, in May ensuing.

The Farmer cries, "tell me not of delegates, congresses committees, mobs, riots, insurrections, associations; a plague on them all. Give me the steady, uniform, unbiassed influence of the courts of justice. I have been happy under their protection, and I trust in God, I shall be so again."

I say, tell me not of the British Commons, Lords, ministry, ministerial tools, placemen, pensioners, parasites. I scorn to let my life and property depend upon the pleasure of any of them. Give me the steady, uniform, unshaken security of constitutional freedom; give me the right to be tried by a jury of my own neighbours, and to be taxed by my own representatives only. What will become of the law and courts of justice without this? The shadow may remain, but the substance will be gone. I would die to preserve the law upon a solid foundation; but take away liberty, and the foundation is destroyed.

The last thing I shall take notice of, is the complaint of the Farmer, that the congress will not allow you "a dish of tea to please your wives with, nor a glass of Madeira to cheer your spirits, nor a spoonful of molasses, to sweeten your butter milk with." You would have a right to complain, if the use of these things had been forbidden to you alone; but it has been equally forbidden to all sorts of people. The members of the congress themselves are no more permitted to please their wives with a dish of tea, or to cheer their spirits with a glass of wine, or to sweeten their butter milk with a spoonful of molasses, than you are. They are upon a footing with you in this respect.

By him! but, with your leave, my friends, we'll try, if we can, to do without swearing. I say, it is enough to make a man mad, to hear such ridiculous quibbles offered instead of sound argument; but so it is, the piece I am writing against contains nothing else.

When a man grows warm, he has a confounded itch for swearing. I have been going, above twenty times, to rap out an oath, *by him that made me*, but I have checked myself, with this reflection, that it is rather *unmannerly*, to treat him that made us with so much freedom.

Thus have I examined and confuted, all the cavils and objections, of any consequence, stated by this Farmer. I have only passed over such things, as are of little weight, the fallacy of which will easily appear. I have shewn, that the congress have neither "ignorantly misunderstood, carelessly neglected, nor basely betrayed you;" but that they have desired and recommended the *only* effectual means to preserve your invaluable privileges. I have proved, that their measures cannot fail of success; but will procure the most speedy relief for us. I have also proved, that the farmers are the people who would suffer least, should we be obliged to carry all our measures into execution.

Will you then, my friends, allow yourselves, to be duped by this artful enemy? will you follow his advices, disregard the authority of your congress, and bring ruin on yourselves and posterity? will you act in such a manner as to deserve the hatred and resentment of all the rest of America? I am sure you will not. I should be sorry to think, any of my countrymen would be so mean, so blind to their own interest, so lost to every generous and manly feeling.

The sort of men I am opposing give you fair words, to persuade you to serve their own turns; but they think and speak of you in common in a very disrespectful manner. I have heard some of their party talk of you, as the most ignorant and mean-spirited set of people in the world. They say, that you have no sense of honour or generosity; that you don't care a farthing about your country, children or any body else, but yourselves; and that you are so ignorant, as not to be able to look beyond the present; so that if you can once be persuaded to believe the measures of your congress will involve you in some little present perplexities, you will be glad to do any thing to avoid them; without considering the much greater miseries that await you at a little distance off. This is the character they give of you. Bad men are apt to paint others like themselves. For my part, I will never entertain such an opinion of you, unless you should verify their words, by wilfully falling into the pit they have prepared for you. I flatter myself you will convince them of their error, by shewing the world, you are capable of judging what is right and left, and have resolution to pursue it.

All I ask is, that you will judge for yourselves. I don't desire you to take my opinion or any man's opinion, as the guide of your actions. I have stated a number of plain arguments; I have supported them with several well-known facts: It is your business to draw a conclusion and act accordingly.

I caution you, again and again, to beware of the men who advise you to forsake the plain path, marked out for you by the congress. They only mean to deceive and betray you. Our representatives in general assembly cannot take any wiser or better course to settle our differences, than our representatives in the continental congress have taken. If you join with the rest of America in the same common measure, you will be sure to preserve your liberties inviolate; but if you separate from them, and seek for redress alone, and unseconded, you will certainly fall a prey to your enemies, and repent your folly as long as you live.

May God give you wisdom to see what is your true interest, and inspire you with becoming zeal for the cause of virtue and mankind.

A FRIEND TO AMERICA.

## To John Jay

*New York Novem 26. 1775*

DEAR SIR

I take the liberty to trouble you with some remarks on a matter which to me appears of not a little importance; doubting not that you will use your influence in Congress to procure a remedy for the evil I shall mention, if you think the considerations I shall urge are of that weight they seem in my judgment to possess.

You will probably ere this reaches you have heard of the late incursion made into this city by a number of horsemen from New England under the command of Capt Sears, who took away Mr. Rivington's types, and a Couteau or two. Though I am fully sensible how dangerous and pernicious Rivington's press has been, and how detestable the character of the man is in every respect, yet I cannot help disapproving and condemning this step.

In times of such commotion as the present, while the passions of men are worked up to an uncommon pitch there is great danger of fatal extremes. The same state of the passions which fits the multitude, who have not a sufficient stock of reason and knowlege to guide them, for opposition to tyranny and oppression, very naturally leads them to a contempt and disregard of all authority. The due medium is hardly to be found among the more intelligent, it is almost impossible among the unthinking populace. When the minds of these are loosened from their attachment to ancient establishments and courses, they seem to grow giddy and are apt more or less to run into anarchy. These principles, too true in themselves, and confirmed to me both by reading and my own experience, deserve extremely the attention of those, who have the direction of public affairs. In such tempestuous times, it requires the greatest skill in the political pilots to keep men steady and within proper bounds, on which account I am always more or less alarmed at every thing which is done of mere will and pleasure, without any proper authority. Irregularities I know are to be expected, but they are nevertheless dangerous and ought to be checked, by every prudent and moderate mean. From these general maxims, I disapprove of the irruption in question, as serving to cherish a spirit of disorder at a season when men are too prone to it of themselves.

Moreover, New England is very populous and powerful. It is not safe to trust to the virtue of any people. Such proceedings will serve to produce and encourage a spirit of encroachment and arrogance in them. I like not to see potent neighbours indulged in the practice of making inroads at pleasure into this or any other province.

You well know too, sir, that antipathies and prejudices have long subsisted between this province and New England. To this may be attributed a principal part of the disaffection now prevalent among us. Measures of the present nature, however they may serve to intimidate, will secretly revive and increase those ancient animosities, which though smothered for a while will break out when there is a favorable opportunity.

Besides this, men coming from a neighbouring province to chastise the notorious friends of the ministry here, will hold up an idea to our ennemies not very advantageous to our affairs. They will imagine that the New Yorkers are totally, or a majority of them, disaffected to the American cause, which makes the interposal of their neighbours necessary: or that such violences will breed differences and effect that which they have been so eagerly wishing, a division and qurrelling among ourselves. Every thing of such an aspect must encourage their hopes.

Upon the whole the measure is condemned, by all the cautious and prudent among the whigs, and will evidently be productive of secret jealousy and ill blood if a stop is not put to things of the kind for the future.

All the good purposes that could be expected from such a step will be answered; and many ill consequences will be prevented if your body gently interposes a check for the future. Rivington will be intimidated & the tories will be convinced that the other colonies will not tamely see the general cause betrayed by the Yorkers. A favourable idea will be impressed of your justice & impartiality in discouraging the encroachments of any one province on another; and the apprehensions of prudent men respecting the ill-effects of an ungoverned spirit in the people of New England will be quieted. Believe me sir it is a matter of consequence and deserves serious attention

The tories it is objected by some are growing insolent and clamorous: It is necessary to repress and overawe them. There is truth in this; but the present remedy is a bad one. Let your body station in different parts of the province most tainted, with the ministerial infection, a few regiments of troops, raised in Philadelphia the Jerseys or any other province except New England. These will suffice to strengthen and support the Whigs who are still I flatter myself a large majority and to suppress the efforts of the tories. The pretence for this would be plausible. There is no knowing how soon the Ministry may make an attempt upon New York. There is reason to believe they will not be long before they turn their attention to it. In this there will be some order & regularity, and no grounds of alarm to our friends.

I am sir with very great Esteem— Your most hum servant

A. HAMILTON

## To John Jay

DEAR SIR,

Col Laurens, who will have the honor of delivering you this letter, is on his way to South Carolina, on a project, which I think, in the present situation of affairs there, is a very good one and deserves every kind of support and encouragement. This is to raise two three or four batalions of negroes; with the assistance of the government of that state, by contributions from the owners in proportion to the number they possess. If you should think proper to enter upon the subject with him, he will give you a detail of his plan. He wishes to have it recommended by Congress to the state; and, as an inducement, that they would engage to take those batalions into Continental pay.

It appears to me, that an expedient of this kind, in the present state of Southern affairs, is the most rational, that can be adopted, and promises very important advantages. Indeed, I hardly see how a sufficient force can be collected in that quarter without it; and the enemy's operations there are growing infinitely serious and formidable. I have not the least doubt, that the negroes will make very excellent soldiers, with proper management; and I will venture to pronounce, that they cannot be put in better hands than those of Mr. Laurens. He has all the zeal, intelligence, enterprise, and every other qualification requisite to succeed in such an undertaking. It is a maxim with some great military judges, that with sensible officers soldiers can hardly be too stupid; and on this principle it is thought that the Russians would make the best troops in the world, if they were under other officers than their own. The King of Prussia is among the number who maintain this doctrine and has a very emphatical saying on the occasion, which I do not exactly recollect. I mention this, because I frequently hear it objected to the scheme of embodying negroes that they are too stupid to make soldiers. This is so far from appearing to me a valid objection that I think their want of cultivation (for their natural faculties are probably as good as ours) joined to that habit of subordination which they acquire from a life of servitude, will make them sooner became soldiers than our White inhabitants. Let officers be men of sense and sentiment, and the nearer the soldiers approach to machines perhaps the better.

I foresee that this project will have to combat much opposition from prejudice and self-interest. The contempt we have been taught to entertain for the blacks, makes us fancy many things that are founded neither in reason nor experience; and an unwillingness to part with property of so valuable a kind will furnish a thousand arguments to show the impracticability or pernicious tendency of a scheme which requires such a sacrifice. But it should be considered, that if we do not make use of them in this way, the enemy probably will; and that the best way to counteract the temptations they will hold out will be to offer them ourselves. An essential part of the plan is to give them their freedom with their muskets. This will secure their fidelity, animate their courage, and I believe will have a good influence upon those who remain, by opening a door to their emancipation. This circumstance, I confess, has no small weight in inducing me to wish the success of the project; for the dictates of humanity and true policy equally interest me in favour of this unfortunate class of men.

When I am on the subject of Southern affairs, you will excuse the liberty I take, in saying, that I do not think measures sufficiently vigorous are persuing for our defence in that quarter. Except the few regular troops of South Carolina, we seem to be relying wholly on the militia of that and the two neighbouring states. These will soon grow impatient of service and leave our affairs in a very miserable situation. No considerable force can be uniformly kept up by militia—to say nothing of many obvious and well known inconveniences, that attend this kind of troops. I would beg leave to suggest, Sir, that no time ought to be lost in making a draft of militia to serve a twelve month from the States of North and South Carolina and Virginia. But South Carolina being very weak in her population of whites may be excused from the draft on condition of furnishing the black batalions. The two others may furnish about 3,500 men and be exempted on that account from sending any succours to this army. The states to the Northward of Virginia will be fully able to give competent supplies to the army here; and it will require all the force and exertions of the three states I have mentioned to withstand the storm which has arisen and is increasing in the South.

The troops drafted must be thrown into batalions and officered in the best manner we can. The supernumerary officers may be made use of as far as they will go.

If arms are wanted for these troops and no better way of supplying them is to be found, we should endeavour to levy a contribution of arms upon the militia at large. Extraordinary exigencies demand extraordinary means. I fear this Southern business will become a very *grave* one.

With the truest respect & esteem I am Sir Your most Obed servant
ALEX HAMILTON

Want of time to copy it, will apologise for sending this letter in its present state.

Head Quarters March 14th. 79

## To John Laurens

Cold in my professions, warm in my friendships, I wish, my Dear Laurens, it might be in my power, by action rather than words, to convince you that I love you. I shall only tell you that 'till you bade us Adieu, I hardly knew the value you had taught my heart to set upon you. Indeed, my friend, it was not well done. You know the opinion I entertain of mankind, and how much it is my desire to preserve myself free from particular attachments, and to keep my happiness independent on the caprice of others. You should not have taken advantage of my sensibility to steal into my affections without my consent. But as you have done it and as we are generally indulgent to those we love, I shall not scruple to pardon the fraud you have committed, on condition that for my sake, if not for your own, you will always continue to merit the partiality, which you have so artfully instilled into me.

I have received your two letters one from Philadelphia the other from Chester. I am pleased with your success, so far, and I hope the favourable omens, that precede your application to the Assembly may have as favourable an issue, provided the situation of affairs should require it which I fear will be the case. But both for your country's sake and for my own I wish the enemy may be gone from Georgia before you arrive and that you may be obliged to return and share the fortunes of your old friends. In respect to the Commission, which you received from Congress, all the world must think your conduct perfectly right. Indeed your ideas upon this occasion seem not to have their wonted accuracy; and you have had scruples, in a great measure, without foundation. By your appointment as Aide De Camp to the Commander in Chief, you had as much the rank of Lieutenant Colonel, as any officer in the line—your receiving a commission as Lieutenant Colonel from the date of that appointment, does not in the least injure or interfere with one of them; unless by virtue of it you are introduced into a particular regiment in violation of the right of succession; which is not the case at present neither is it a necessary consequence. As you were going to command a batalion, it was proper you should have a commission; and if this commission had been dated posterior to your appointment as Aide De Camp, I should have considered it as derogatory to your former rank, to mine, and to that of the whole corps. The only thing I see wrong in the affair is this—Congress by their conduct, both on the former and present occasion, appear to have intended to confer a privilege, an honor, a mark of distinction, a something upon you; which they withold from other Gentlemen in the family. This carries with it an air of preference, which, though we can all truly say, we love your character, and admire your military merit, cannot fail to give some of us uneasy sensations. But in this, my Dear J I wish you to understand me well. The blame, if there is any, falls wholly upon Congress. I repeat it, your conduct has been perfectly right and even laudable; you rejected the offer when you ought to have rejected it; and you accepted it when you ought to have accepted it; and let me add with a degree of overscrupulous delicacy. It was necessary to your project; your project was the public good; and *I* should have done the same. In hesitating, you have refined upon the refinements of generosity.

There is a total stagnation of news here, political and military. Gates has refused the Indian command. Sullivan is come to take it. The former has lately given a fresh proof of his impudence, his folly and his rascality. *'Tis no great matter;* but a peculiarity in the case prevents my saying *what.*

I anticipate by sympathy the pleasure you must feel from the sweet converse of your dearer self in the inclosed letters. I hope they may be recent. They were brought out of New York by General Thompson delivered to him there by a Mrs. Moore not long from England, *soi-disante parente de Madame votre épouse.* She speaks of a daughter of yours, well when she left England, perhaps [      ].

And Now my Dear as we are upon the subject of wife, I empower and command you to get me one in Carolina. Such a wife as I want will, I know, be difficult to be found, but if you succeed, it will be the stronger proof of your zeal and dexterity. Take her description—She must be young, handsome (I lay most stress upon a good shape) sensible (a little learning will do), well bred (but she must have an aversion to the word *ton*) chaste and tender (I am an enthusiast in my notions of fidelity and fondness) of some good nature, a great deal of generosity (she must neither love money nor scolding, for I dislike equally a termagent and an œconomist). In politics, I am indifferent what side she may be of; I think I have arguments that will easily convert her to mine. As to religion a moderate stock will satisfy me. She must believe in god and hate a saint. But as to fortune, the larger stock of that the better. You know my temper and circumstances and will therefore pay special attention to this article in the treaty. Though I run no risk of going to Purgatory for my avarice; yet as money is an essential ingredient to happiness in this world—as I have not much of my own and as I am very little calculated to get more either by my address or industry; it must needs be, that my wife, if I get one, bring at least a sufficiency to administer to her own extravagancies. NB You will be pleased to recollect in your negotiations that I have no invincible antipathy to the *maidenly beauties* & that I am willing to take the *trouble* of them upon myself.

If you should not readily meet with a lady that you think answers my description you can only advertise in the public papers and doubtless you will hear of many competitors for most of the qualifications required, who will be glad to become candidates for such a prize as I am. To excite their emulation, it will be necessary for you to give an account of the lover—his *size*, make, quality of mind and *body*, achievements, expectations, fortune, &c. In drawing my picture, you will no doubt be civil to your friend; mind you do justice to the length of my nose and don't forget, that I [      ].

After reviewing what I have written, I am ready to ask myself what could have put it into my head to hazard this Jeu *de follie*. Do I want a wife? No—I have plagues enough without desiring to add to the number that *greatest of all;* and if I were silly enough to do it, I should take care how I employ a proxy. Did I mean to show my wit? If I did, I am sure I have missed my aim. Did I only intend to frisk? In this I have succeeded, but I have done more. I have gratified my feelings, by lengthening out the only kind of intercourse now in my power with my friend. Adieu

Yours.

A HAMILTON

P.S—Fleury shall be taken care of. All the family send their love. In this join the General & Mrs. Washington & what is best, tis not in the stile of ceremony but sincerity.

*April 1779*

## *To John Laurens*

*Jany 8t.*

I had written the enclosed and was called off. Some ruffian hand has treated it in the manner you see. I have no time to copy it. I shall take up the story where I left it.

Another reason for believing the destination is your way, is that Governor Martin and divers others refugees of Georgia South and North Carolina are said to have gone in the fleet. You will have a busy time; acquit yourselves well. We hope however that some late violent winds will drown them all on their way. There is no other military news.

Believe me my Dr Laurens I am not insensible of the first mark of your affection in recommending me to your friends for a certain commission. However your partiality may have led you to overrate my qualifications that very partiality must endear you to me; and all the world will allow that your struggles and scruples upon the occasion deserve the envy of men of vertue. I am happy you placed the matter upon the footing you did, because I hope it will ultimately engage you to accept the appointment. Had it fallen to my lot, I should have been flattered by such a distinction but I should have felt all your embarrassments.

Of this however I need have no apprehension. Not one of the four in nomination but would stand a better chance than myself; and yet my vanity tells me they do not all merit a preference. But I am a stranger in this country. I have no property here, no connexions. If I have talents and integrity, (as you say I have) these are justly deemed very spurious titles in these enlightened days, when unsupported by others more solid; and were it not for your example, I should be inclined in considering the composition of a certain body, to suppose that three fourths of them are mortal enemies to the first and three fourths of the other fourth have a laudable contempt for the last.

Adieu God preserve and prosper you

A HAMILTON

I have strongly sollicited leave to go to the Southward. It could not be refused; but arguments have been used to dissuade me from it, which however little weight they may have had in my judgment gave law to my feelings. I am chagrined and unhappy but I submit. In short Laurens I am disgusted with every thing in this world but yourself and *very* few more honest fellows and I have no other wish than as soon as possible to make a brilliant exit. 'Tis a weakness; but I feel I am not fit for this terrestreal Country.

All the Lads embrace you. The General sends his love. Write to him as often as you can.

*1780*

## To Elizabeth Schuyler

Impatiently My Dearest have I been expecting the return of your father to bring me a letter from my charmer with the answers you have been good enough to promise me to the little questions asked in mine by him. I long to see the workings of my Betseys heart, and I promise my self I shall have ample gratification to my fondness in the sweet familiarity of her pen. She will there I hope paint me her feelings without reserve—even in those tender moments of pillowed retirement, when her soul abstracted from every other object, delivers itself up to Love and to me—yet with all that delicacy which suits the purity of her mind and which is so conspicuous in whatever she does.

It is now a week my Betsey since I have heard from you. In that time I have written you twice. I think it will be adviseable in future to number our letters, for I have reason to suspect they do not all meet with fair play. This is number one.

Meade just comes in and interrupts me by sending his love to you. He tells you he has written a long letter to his widow asking her opinion of the propriety of quitting the service; and that if she does not disapprove it, he will certainly take his final leave after the campaign. You see what a fine opportunity she has to be enrolled in the catalogue of heroines, and I dare say she will set you an example of fortitude and patriotism. I know too you have so much of the Portia in you, that you will not be out done in this line by any of your sex, and that if you saw me inclined to quit the service of your country, you would dissuade me from it. I have promised you, you recollect, to conform to your wishes, and I persist in this intention. It remains with you to show whether you are a *Roman* or an *American wife*.

Though I am not sanguine in expecting it, I am not without hopes this Winter will produce a peace and then you must submit to the mortification of enjoying more domestic happiness and less fame. This I know you will not like, but we cannot always have things as we wish.

The affairs of England are in so bad a plight that if no fortunate events attend her this campaign, it would seem impossible for her to proceed in the war. But she is an obstinate old dame, and seems determined to ruin her whole family, rather than to let Miss America go on flirting it with her new lovers, with whom, as giddy young girls often do, she eloped in contempt of her mothers authority. I know you will be ready to justify her conduct and to tell me the ill treatment she received was enough to make any girl of spirit act in the same manner. But I will one day cure you of these refractory notions about the right of resistance, (of which I foresee you will be apt to make a very dangerous application), and teach you the great advantage and absolute necessity of implicit obedience.

But now we are talking of times to come, tell me my pretty damsel have you made up your mind upon the subject of housekeeping? Do you soberly relish the pleasure of being a poor mans wife? Have you learned to think a home spun preferable to a brocade and the rumbling of a waggon wheel to the musical rattling of a coach and six? Will you be able to see with perfect composure your old acquaintances flaunting it in gay life, tripping it along in elegance and splendor, while you hold an humble station and have no other enjoyments than the sober comforts of a good wife? Can you in short be an Aquileia and chearfully plant turnips with me, if fortune should so order it? If you cannot my Dear we are playing a comedy of all in the wrong, and you should correct the mistake before we begin to act the tragedy of the unhappy couple.

I propose you a set of new questions my lovely girl; but though they are asked with an air of levity, they merit a very serious consideration, for on their being resolved in the affirmative stripped of all the colorings of a fond imagination our happiness may absolutely depend. I have not concealed my circumstances from my Betsey; they are far from splendid; they may possibly even be worse than I expect, for every day brings me fresh proof of the knavery of those to whom my little affairs are entrusted. They have already filed down what was in their hands more than one half, and I am told they go on diminishing it, 'till I *fear* they will reduce it below my *former fears*. An indifference to property enters into my character too much, and what affects me now as my Betsey is concerned in it, I should have laughed at or not thought of at all a year ago. But I have thoroughly examined my own heart. Beloved by you, I can be happy in any situation, and can struggle with every embarrassment of fortune with patience and firmness. I cannot however forbear entreating you to realize our union on the dark side and satisfy, without deceiving yourself, how far your affection for me can make you happy in a privation of those elegancies to which you have been accustomed. If fortune should smile upon us, it will do us no harm to have been prepared for adversity; if she frowns upon us, by being prepared, we shall encounter it without the chagrin of disappointment. Your future rank in life is a perfect lottery; you may move in an exalted you may move in a very humble sphere; the last is most probable; examine well your heart. And in doing it, don't figure to yourself a cottage in romance, with the spontaneous bounties of nature courting you to enjoyment. Don't imagine yourself a shepherdess, your hair embroidered with flowers a crook in your hand tending your flock under a shady tree, by the side of a cool fountain, your faithful shepherd sitting near and entertaining you with gentle tales of love. These are pretty dreams and very apt to enter into the heads of lovers when they think of a connection without the advantages of fortune. But they must not be indulged. You must apply your situation to real life, and think how you should feel in scenes of which you may find examples every day. So far My Dear Betsey as the tenderest affection can compensate for other inconveniences in making your estimate, you cannot give too large a credit for this article. My heart overflows with every thing for you, that admiration, esteem and love can inspire. *I would this moment give the world to be near you only to kiss your sweet hand.* Believe what I say to be truth and imagine what are my feelings when I say it. Let it awake your sympathy and let our hearts melt in a prayer to be soon united, never more to be separated.

Adieu loveliest of your sex

AH

Instead of inclosing your letter to your father I inclose his to you because I do not know whether he may not be on his way here. If he is at home he will tell you the military news. If he has set out for camp, you may open and read my letters to him. The one from Mr. Mathews you will return by the first opportunity.

*August 1780*

## To James Duane

Dr. Sir

Agreeably to your request and my promise I sit down to give you my ideas of the defects of our present system, and the changes necessary to save us from ruin. They may perhaps be the reveries of a projector rather than the sober views of a politician. You will judge of them, and make what use you please of them.

The fundamental defect is a want of power in Congress. It is hardly worth while to show in what this consists, as it seems to be universally acknowleged, or to point out how it has happened, as the only question is how to remedy it. It may however be said that it has originated from three causes—an excess of the spirit of liberty which has made the particular states show a jealousy of all power not in their own hands; and this jealousy has led them to exercise a right of judging in the last resort of the measures recommended by Congress, and of acting according to their own opinions of their propriety or necessity, a diffidence in Congress of their own powers, by which they have been timid and indecisive in their resolutions, constantly making concessions to the states, till they have scarcely left themselves the shadow of power; a want of sufficient means at their disposal to answer the public exigencies and of vigor to draw forth those means; which have occasioned them to depend on the states individually to fulfil their engagements with the army, and the consequence of which has been to ruin their influence and credit with the army, to establish its dependence on each state separately rather than on them, that is rather than on the whole collectively.

It may be pleaded, that Congress had never any definitive powers granted them and of course could exercise none—could do nothing more than recommend. The manner in which Congress was appointed would warrant, and the public good required, that they should have considered themselves as vested with full power *to preserve the republic from harm.* They have done many of the highest acts of sovereignty, which were always chearfully submitted to—the declaration of independence, the declaration of war, the levying an army, creating a navy, emitting money, making alliances with foreign powers, appointing a dictator &c. &c.—all these implications of a complete sovereignty were never disputed, and ought to have been a standard for the whole conduct of Administration. Undefined powers are discretionary powers, limited only by the object for which they were given—in the present case, the independence and freedom of America. The confederation made no difference; for as it has not been generally adopted, it had no operation. But from what I recollect of it, Congress have even descended from the authority which the spirit of that act gives them, while the particular states have no further attended to it than as it suited their pretensions and convenience. It would take too much time to enter into particular instances, each of which separately might appear inconsiderable; but united are of serious import. I only mean to remark, not to censure.

But the confederation itself is defective and requires to be altered; it is neither fit for war, nor peace. The idea of an uncontrolable sovereignty in each state, over its internal police, will defeat the other powers given to Congress, and make our union feeble and precarious. There are instances without number, where acts necessary for the general good, and which rise out of the powers given to Congress must interfere with the internal police of the states, and there are as many instances in which the particular states by arrangements of internal police can effectually though indirectly counteract the arrangements of Congress. You have already had examples of this for which I refer you to your own memory.

The confederation gives the states individually too much influence in the affairs of the army; they should have nothing to do with it. The entire formation and disposal of our military forces ought to belong to Congress. It is an essential cement of the union; and it ought to be the policy of Congress to destroy all ideas of state attachments in the army and make it look up wholly to them. For this purpose all appointments promotions and provisions whatsoever ought to be made by them. It may be apprehended that this may be dangerous to liberty. But nothing appears more evident to me, than that we run much greater risk of having a weak and disunited federal government, than one which will be able to usurp upon the rights of the people. Already some of the lines of the army would obey their states in opposition to Congress notwithstanding the pains we have taken to preserve the unity of the army—if any thing would hinder this it would be the personal influence of the General, a melancholy and mortifying consideration.

The forms of our state constitutions must always give them great weight in our affairs and will make it too difficult to bend them to the persuit of a common interest, too easy to oppose whatever they do not like and to form partial combinations subversive of the general one. There is a wide difference between our situation and that of an empire under one simple form of government, distributed into counties provinces or districts, which have no legislatures but merely magistratical bodies to execute the laws of a common sovereign. Here the danger is that the sovereign will have too much power to oppress the parts of which it is composed. In our case, that of an empire composed of confederated states each with a government completely organised within itself, having all the means to draw its subjects to a close dependence on itself—the danger is directly the reverse. It is that the common sovereign will not have power sufficient to unite the different members together, and direct the common forces to the interest and happiness of the whole.

The leagues among the old Grecian republics are a proof of this. They were continually at war with each other, and for want of union fell a prey to their neighbours. They frequently held general councils, but their resolutions were no further observed than as they suited the interests and inclinations of all the parties and at length, they sunk intirely into contempt.

The Swiss-cantons are another proof of the doctrine. They have had wars with each other which would have been fatal to them, had not the different powers in their neighbourhood been too jealous of one-another and too equally matched to suffer either to take advantage of their quarrels. That they have remained so long united at all is to be attributed to their weakness, to their poverty, and to the cause just mentioned. These ties will not exist in America; a little time hence, some of the states will be powerful empires, and we are so remote from other nations that we shall have all the leisure and opportunity we can wish to cut each others throats.

The Germanic corps might also be cited as an example in favour of the position.

The United provinces may be thought to be one against it. But the family of the stadtholders whose authority is interwoven with the whole government has been a strong link of union between them. Their physical necessities and the habits founded upon them have contributed to it. Each province is too inconsiderable by itself to undertake any thing. An analysis of their present constitutions would show that they have many ties which would not exist in ours; and that they are by no means a proper mode for us.

Our own experience should satisfy us. We have felt the difficulty of drawing out the resources of the country and inducing the states to combine in equal exertions for the common cause. The ill success of our last attempt is striking. Some have done a great deal, others little or scarcely any thing. The disputes about boundaries &c. testify how flattering a prospect we have of future tranquillity, if we do not frame in time a confederacy capable of deciding the differences and compelling the obedience of the respective members.

The confederation too gives the power of the purse too intirely to the state legislatures. It should provide perpetual funds in the disposal of Congress—by a land tax, poll tax, or the like. All imposts upon commerce ought to be laid by Congress and appropriated to their use, for without certain revenues, a government can have no power; that power, which holds the purse strings absolutely, must rule. This seems to be a medium, which without making Congress altogether independent will tend to give reality to its authority.

Another defect in our system is want of method and energy in the administration. This has partly resulted from the other defect, but in a great degree from prejudice and the want of a proper executive. Congress have kept the power too much into their own hands and have meddled too much with details of every sort. Congress is properly a deliberative corps and it forgets itself when it attempts to play the executive. It is impossible such a body, numerous as it is, constantly fluctuating, can ever act with sufficient decision, or with system. Two thirds of the members, one half the time, cannot know what has gone before them or what connection the subject in hand has to what has been transacted on former occasions. The members, who have been more permanent, will only give information, that promotes the side they espouse, in the present case, and will as often mislead as enlighten. The variety of business must distract, and the proneness of every assembly to debate must at all times delay.

Lately Congress, convinced of these inconveniences, have gone into the measure of appointing boards. But this is in my opinion a bad plan. A single man, in each department of the administration, would be greatly preferable. It would give us a chance of more knowlege, more activity, more responsibility and of course more zeal and attention. Boards partake of a part of the inconveniencies of larger assemblies. Their decisions are slower their energy less their responsibility more diffused. They will not have the same abilities and knowlege as an administration by single men. Men of the first pretensions will not so readily engage in them, because they will be less conspicuous, of less importance, have less opportunity of distinguishing themselves. The members of boards will take less pains to inform themselves and arrive to eminence, because they have fewer motives to do it. All these reasons conspire to give a preference to the plan of vesting the great executive departments of the state in the hands of individuals. As these men will be of course at all times under the direction of Congress, we shall blend the advantages of a monarchy and republic in our constitution.

A question has been made, whether single men could be found to undertake these offices. I think they could, because there would be then every thing to excite the ambition of candidates. But in order to this Congress by their manner of appointing them and the line of duty marked out must show that they are in earnest in making these offices, offices of real trust and importance.

I fear a little vanity has stood in the way of these arrangements, as though they would lessen the importance of Congress and leave them nothing to do. But they would have precisely the same rights and powers as heretofore, happily disencumbered of the detail. They would have to inspect the conduct of their ministers, deliberate upon their plans, originate others for the public good—only observing this rule that they ought to consult their ministers, and get all the information and advice they could from them, before they entered into any new measures or made changes in the old.

A third defect is the fluctuating constitution of our army. This has been a pregnant source of evil; all our military misfortunes, three fourths of our civil embarrassments are to be ascribed to it. The General has so fully enumerated the mischief of it in a late letter of the [     ] to Congress that I could only repeat what he has said, and will therefore refer you to that letter.

The imperfect and unequal provision made for the army is a fourth defect which you will find delineated in the same letter. Without a speedy change the army must dissolve; it is now a mob, rather than an army, without cloathing, without pay, without provision, without morals, without discipline. We begin to hate the country for its neglect of us; the country begins to hate us for our oppressions of them. Congress have long been jealous of us; we have now lost all confidence in them, and give the worst construction to all they do. Held together by the slenderest ties we are ripening for a dissolution.

The present mode of supplying the army—by state purchases—is not one of the least considerable defects of our system. It is too precarious a dependence, because the states will never be sufficiently impressed with our necessities. Each will make its own ease a primary object, the supply of the army a secondary one. The variety of channels through which the business is transacted will multiply the number of persons employed and the opportunities of embezzling public money. From the popular spirit on which most of the governments turn, the state agents, will be men of less character and ability, nor will there be so rigid a responsibility among them as there might easily be among those in the employ of the continent, of course not so much diligence care or economy. Very little of the money raised in the several states will go into the Continental treasury, on pretence, that it is all exhausted in providing the quotas of supplies, and the public will be without funds for the other demands of governments. The expence will be ultimately much greater and the advantages much smaller. We actually feel the insufficiency of this plan and have reason to dread under it a ruinous extremity of want.

These are the principal defects in the present system that now occur to me. There are many inferior ones in the organization of particular departments and many errors of administration which might be pointed out; but the task would be troublesome and tedious, and if we had once remedied those I have mentioned the others would not be attended with much difficulty.

I shall now propose the remedies, which appear to me applicable to our circumstances, and necessary to extricate our affairs from their present deplorable situation.

The first step must be to give Congress powers competent to the public exigencies. This may happen in two ways, one by resuming and exercising the discretionary powers I suppose to have been originally vested in them for the safety of the states and resting their conduct on the candor of their country men and the necessity of the conjuncture: the other by calling immediately a convention of all the states with full authority to conclude finally upon a general confederation, stating to them beforehand explicity the evils arising from a want of power in Congress, and the impossibily of supporting the contest on its present footing, that the delegates may come possessed of proper sentiments as well as proper authority to give to the meeting. Their commission should include a right of vesting Congress with the whole or a proportion of the unoccupied lands, to be employed for the purpose of raising a revenue, reserving the jurisdiction to the states by whom they are granted.

The first plan, I expect will be thought too bold an expedient by the generality of Congress; and indeed their practice hitherto has so rivetted the opinion of their want of power, that the success of this experiment may very well be doubted.

I see no objection to the other mode, that has any weight in competition with the reasons for it. The Convention should assemble the 1st of November next, the sooner, the better; our disorders are too violent to admit of a common or lingering remedy. The reasons for which I require them to be vested with plenipotentiary authority are that the business may suffer no delay in the execution, and may in reality come to effect. A convention may agree upon a confederation; the states individually hardly ever will. We must have one at all events, and a vigorous one if we mean to succeed in the contest and be happy hereafter. As I said before, to engage the states to comply with this mode, Congress ought to confess to them plainly and unanimously the impracticability of supporting our affairs on the present footing and without a solid coercive union. I ask that the Convention should have a power of vesting the whole or a part of the unoccupied land in Congress, because it is necessary that body should have some property as a fund for the arrangements of finance; and I know of no other kind that can be given them.

The confederation in my opinion should give Congress complete sovereignty; except as to that part of internal police, which relates to the rights of property and life among individuals and to raising money by internal taxes. It is necessary, that every thing, belonging to this, should be regulated by the state legislatures. Congress should have complete sovereignty in all that relates to war, peace, trade, finance, and to the management of foreign affairs, the right of declaring war of raising armies, officering, paying them, directing their motions in every respect, of equipping fleets and doing the same with them, of building fortifications arsenals magazines &c. &c., of making peace on such conditions as they think proper, of regulating trade, determining with what countries it shall be carried on, granting indulgencies laying prohibitions on all the articles of export or import, imposing duties granting bounties & premiums for raising exporting importing and applying to their own use the product of these duties, only giving credit to the states on whom they are raised in the general account of revenues and expences, instituting Admiralty courts &c., of coining money, establishing banks on such terms, and with such privileges as they think proper, appropriating funds and doing whatever else relates to the operations of finance, transacting every thing with foreign nations, making alliances offensive and defensive, treaties of commerce, &c. &c.

The confederation should provide certain perpetual revenues, productive and easy of collection, a land tax, poll tax or the like, which together with the duties on trade and the unlocated lands would give Congress a substantial existence, and a stable foundation for their schemes of finance. What more supplies were necessary should be occasionally demanded of the states, in the present mode of quotas.

The second step I would recommend is that Congress should instantly appoint the following great officers of state—A secretary for foreign affairs—a President of war—A President of Marine—A Financier—A President of trade; instead of this last a board of Trade may be preferable as the regulations of trade are slow and gradual and require prudence and experience (more than other qualities), for which boards are very well adapted.

Congress should choose for these offices, men of the first abilities, property and character in the continent—and such as have had the best opportunities of being acquainted with the several branches. General Schuyler (whom you mentioned) would make an excellent President of War, General McDougall a very good President of Marine. Mr. Robert Morris would have many things in his favour for the department of finance. He could by his own personal influence give great weight to the measures he should adopt. I dare say men equally capable may be found for the other departments.

I know not, if it would not be a good plan to let the Financier be President of the Board of trade; but he should only have a casting voice in determining questions there. There is a connection between trade and finance, which ought to make the director of one acquainted with the other; but the Financier should not direct the affairs of trade, because for the sake of acquiring reputation by increasing the revenues, he might adopt measures that would depress trade. In what relates to finance he should be alone.

These offices should have nearly the same powers and functions as those in France analogous to them, and each should be chief in his department, with subordinate boards composed of assistant clerks &c. to execute his orders.

In my opinion a plan of this kind would be of inconceivable utility to our affairs; its benefits would be very speedily felt. It would give new life and energy to the operations of government. Business would be conducted with dispatch method and system. A million of abuses now existing would be corrected, and judicious plans would be formed and executed for the public good.

Another step of immediate necessity is to recruit the army for the war, or at least for three years. This must be done by a mode similar to that which is practiced in Sweeden. There the inhabitants are thrown into classes of sixteen, and when the sovereign wants men each of these classes must furnish one. They raise a fixed sum of money, and if one of the class is willing to become a soldier, he receives the money and offers himself a volunteer; if none is found to do this, a draft is made and he on whom the lot falls receives the money and is obliged to serve. The minds of the people are prepared for a thing of this kind; the heavy bounties they have been obliged to pay for men to serve a few months must have disgusted them with this mode, and made them desirous of another, that will once for all answer the public purposes, and obviate a repetition of the demand. It ought by all means to be attempted, and Congress should frame a general plan and press the execution upon the states. When the confederation comes to be framed, it ought to provide for this by a fundamental law, and hereafter there would be no doubt of the success. But we cannot now wait for this; we want to replace the men whose times of service will expire the 1st of January, for then, without this, we shall have no army remaining and the enemy may do what they please. The General in his letter already quoted has assigned the most substantial reasons for paying immediate attention to this point.

Congress should endeavour, both upon their credit in Europe, and by every possible exertion in this country, to provide cloathing for their officers, and should abolish the whole system of state supplies. The making good the depreciation of the currency and all other compensations to the army should be immediately taken up by Congress, and not left to the states; if they would have the accounts of depreciation liquidated, and governmental certificates given for what is due in specie or an equivalent to specie, it would give satisfaction; appointing periodical settlements for future depreciation.

The placing the officers upon half pay during life would be a great stroke of policy, and would give Congress a stronger tie upon them, than any thing else they can do. No man, that reflects a moment, but will prefer a permanent provision of this kind to any temporary compensation, nor is it opposed to economy; the difference between this and between what has been already done will be insignificant. The benefit of it to the widows should be confined to those whose husbands die during the war. As to the survivors, not more than one half on the usual calculation of mens lives will exceed the seven years for which the half pay is already established. Besides this whatever may be the visionary speculations of some men at this time, we shall find it indispensable after the war to keep on foot a considerable body of troops; and all the officers retained for this purpose must be deducted out of the half pay list. If any one will take the pains to calculate the expence on these principles, I am persuaded he will find the addition of expence from the establishment proposed, by no means a national object.

The advantages of securing the attachment of the army to Congress, and binding them to the service by substantial ties are immense. We should then have discipline, an army in reality, as well as in name. Congress would then have a solid basis of authority and consequence, for to me it is an axiom that in our constitution an army is essential to the American union.

The providing of supplies is the pivot of every thing else (though a well constituted army would not in a small degree conduce to this, by giving consistency and weight to government). There are four ways all which must be united—a foreign loan, heavy pecuniary taxes, a tax in kind, a bank founded on public and private credit.

As to a foreign loan I dare say, Congress are doing every thing in their power to obtain it. The most effectual way will be to tell France that without it, we must make terms with great Britain. This must be done with plainness and firmness, but with respect and without petulance, not as a menace, but as a candid declaration of our circumstances. We need not fear to be deserted by France. Her interest and honor are too deeply involved in our fate; and she can make no possible compromise. She can assist us, if she is convinced it is absolutely necessary, either by lending us herself or by becoming our surety or by influencing Spain. It has been to me astonishing how any man could have doubted at any period of our affairs of the necessity of a foreign loan. It was self evident, that we had not a fund of wealth in this country, capable of affording revenues equal to the expences. We must then create artificial revenues, or borrow; the first was done, but it ought to have been foreseen, that the expedient could not last; and we should have provided in time for its failure.

Here was an error of Congress. I have good reason to believe, that measures were not taken in earnest early enough, to procure a loan abroad. I give you my honor that from our first outset, I thought as I do now and wished for a foreign loan not only because I foresaw it would be essential but because I considered it as a tie upon the nation from which it was derived and as a mean to prop our cause in Europe.

Concerning the necessity of heavy pecuniary taxes I need say nothing, as it is a point in which everybody is agreed; nor is there any danger, that the product of any taxes raised in this way will over burthen the people, or exceed the wants of the public. Indeed if all the paper in circulation were drawn annually into the treasury, it would neither do one, nor the other.

As to a tax in kind, the necessity of it results from this principle—that the money in circulation is not a sufficient representative of the productions of the country, and consequently no revenues raised from it as a medium can be a competent representative of that part of the products of the country, which it is bound to contribute to the support of the public. The public therefore to obtain its due or satisfy its just demands and its wants must call for a part of those products themselves. This is done in all those countries which are not commercial, in Russia, Prussia, Denmark Sweden &c. and is peculiarly necessary in our case.

Congress in calling for specific supplies seem to have had this in view; but their intention has not been answered. The states in general have undertaken to furnish the supplies by purchase, a mode as I have observed, attended with every inconvenience and subverting the principle on which the supplies were demanded—the insufficiency of our circulating medium as a representative for the labour and commodities of the Country. It is therefore necessary that Congress should be more explicit, should form the outlines of a plan for a tax in kind, and recommend it to the states, as a measure of absolute necessity.

The general idea I have of a plan, is that a respectable man should be appointed by the state in each county to collect the taxes and form magazines, that Congress should have in each state an officer to superintend the whole and that the state collectors should be subordinate and responsible to them. This Continental superintendent might be subject to the general direction of the Quarter Master General, or not, as might be deemed best; but if not subject to him, he should be obliged to make monthly returns to the President at War, who should instruct him what proportion to deliver to the Quarter Master General. It may be necessary that the superintendents should sometimes have power to dispose of the articles in their possession on public account; for it would happen that the contributions in places remote from the army could not be transported to the theatre of operations without too great expence, in which case it would be eligible to dispose of them and purchase with the money so raised in the countries near the immediate scene of war.

I know the objections which may be raised to this plan—its tendency to discourage industry and the like; but necessity calls for it; we cannot proceed without it, and less evils must give place to greater. It is besides practiced with success in other countries, and why not in this? It may be said, the examples cited are from nations under despotic governments and that the same would not be practicable with us; but I contend where the public good is evidently the object more may be effected in governments like ours than in any other. It has been a constant remark that free countries have ever paid the heaviest taxes. The obedience of a free people to general laws however hard they bear is ever more perfect than that of slaves to the arbitrary will of a prince. To this it may be added that Sweden was always a free government, and is so now in a great degree, notwithstanding the late revolution.

How far it may be practicable to erect a bank on the joint credit of the public and of individuals can only be certainly determined by the experiment; but it is of so much importance that the experiment ought to be fully tried. When I saw the subscriptions going on to the bank established for supplying the army, I was in hopes it was only the embryo of a more permanent and extensive establishment. But I have reason to believe I shall be disappointed. It does not seem to be at all conducted on the true principles of a bank. The directors of it are purchasing with their stock instead of bank notes as I expected; in consequence of which it must turn out to be a mere subscription of a particular sum of money for a particular purpose.

Paper credit never was long supported in any country, on a national scale, where it was not founded on the joint basis of public and private credit. An attempt to establish it on public credit alone in France under the auspices of Mr. Law had nearly ruined the kingdom; we have seen the effects of it in America, and every successive experiment proves the futility of the attempt. Our new money is depreciating almost as fast as the old, though it has in some states as real funds as paper money ever had. The reason is, that the monied men have not an immediate interest to uphold its credit. They may even in many ways find it their interest to undermine it. The only certain manner to obtain a permanent paper credit is to engage the monied interest immediately in it by making them contribute the whole or part of the stock and giving them the whole or part of the profits.

The invention of banks on the modern principle originated in Venice. There the public and a company of monied men are mutually concerned. The Bank of England unites public authority and faith with private credit; and hence we see what a vast fabric of paper credit is raised on a visionary basis. Had it not been for this, England would never have found sufficient funds to carry on her wars; but with the help of this she has done, and is doing wonders. The bank of Amsterdam is on a similar foundation.

And why can we not have an American bank? Are our monied men less enlightened to their own interest or less enterprising in the persuit? I believe the fault is in our government which does not exert itself to engage them in such a scheme. It is true, the individuals in America are not very rich, but this would not prevent their instituting a bank; it would only prevent its being done with such ample funds as in other countries. Have they not sufficient confidence in the government and in the issue of the cause? Let the Government endeavour to inspire that confidence, by adopting the measures I have recommended or others equivalent to them. Let it exert itself to procure a solid confederation, to establish a good plan of executive administration, to form a permanent military force, to obtain at all events a foreign loan. If these things were in a train of vigorous execution, it would give a new spring to our affairs; government would recover its respectability and individuals would renounce their diffidence.

The object I should propose to myself in the first instance from a bank would be an auxiliary mode of supplies; for which purpose contracts should be made between Government and the bank on terms liberal and advantageous to the latter. Every thing should be done in the first instance to encourage the bank; after it gets well established it will take care of itself and government may make the best terms it can for itself.

The first step to establishing the bank will be to engage a number of monied men of influence to relish the project and make it a business. The subscribers to that lately established are the fittest persons that can be found; and their plan may be interwoven.

The outlines of my plan would be to open subscriptions in all the states for the stock, which we will suppose to be one million of pounds. Real property of every kind, as well as specie should be deemed good stock, but at least a fourth part of the subscription should be in specie or plate. There should be one great company in three divisions in Virginia, Philadelphia, and at Boston or two at Philadelphia and Boston. The bank should have a right to issue bank notes bearing two per Cent interest for the whole of their stock; but not to exceed it. These notes may be payable every three months or oftener, and the faith of government must be pledged for the support of the bank. It must therefore have a right from time to time to inspect its operations, and must appoint inspectors for the purpose.

The advantages of the bank may consist in this, in the profits of the contracts made with government, which should bear interest to be annually paid in specie, in the loan of money at interest say six per Cent, in purchasing lives by annuities as practiced in England &c. The benefit resulting to the company is evident from the consideration, that they may employ in circulation a great deal more money than they have specie in stock, on the credit of the real property which they will have in other use; this money will be employed either in fulfilling their contracts with the public by which also they will gain a profit, or in loans at an advantageous interest or in annuities.

The bank may be allowed to purchase plate and bullion and coin money allowing government a part of the profit. I make the bank notes bear interest to obtain a readie currency and to induce the holders to prefer them to specie to prevent too great a run upon the bank at any time beyond its ability to pay.

If Government can obtain a foreign loan it should lend to the bank on easy terms to extend its influence and facilitate a compliance with its engagements. If government could engage the states to raise a sum of money in specie to be deposited in bank in the same manner, it would be of the greatest consequence. If government could prevail on the enthusiasm of the people to make a contribution in plate for the same purpose it would be a master stroke. Things of this kind sometimes succeed in popular contests; and if undertaken with address; I should not despair of its success; but I should not be sanguine.

The bank may be instituted for a term of years by way of trial and the particular privilege of coining money be for a term still shorter. A temporary transfer of it to a particular company can have no inconvenience as the government are in no condition to improve this resource nor could it in our circumstances be an object to them, though with the industry of a knot of individuals it might be.

A bank of this kind even in its commencement would answer the most valuable purposes to government and to the proprietors; in its progress the advantages will exceed calculation. It will promote commerce by furnishing a more extensive medium which we greatly want in our circumstances. I mean a more extensive valuable medium. We have an enormous nominal one at this time; but it is only a name.

In the present unsettled state of things in this country, we can hardly draw inferences from what has happened in others, otherwise I should be certain of the success of this scheme; but I think it has enough in its favour to be worthy of trial.

I have only skimmed the surface of the different subjects I have introduced. Should the plans recommended come into contemplation in earnest and you desire my further thoughts, I will endeavour to give them more form and particularity. I am persuaded a solid confederation a permanent army a reasonable prospect of subsisting it would give us treble consideration in Europe and produce a peace this winter.

If a Convention is called the minds of all the states and the people ought to be prepared to receive its determinations by sensible and popular writings, which should conform to the views of Congress. There are epochs in human affairs, when *novelty* even is useful. If a general opinion prevails that the old way is bad, whether true or false, and this obstructs or relaxes the operation of the public service, a change is necessary if it be but for the sake of change. This is exactly the case now. 'Tis an universal sentiment that our present system is a bad one, and that things do not go right on this account. The measure of a Convention would revive the hopes of the people and give a new direction to their passions, which may be improved in carrying points of substantial utility. The Eastern states have already pointed out this mode to Congress; they ought to take the hint and anticipate the others.

And, in future, My Dear Sir, two things let me recommend, as fundamental rules for the conduct of Congress—to attach the army to them by every motive, to maintain an air of authority (not domineering) in all their measures with the states. The manner in which a thing is done has more influence than is commonly imagined. Men are governed by opinion; this opinion is as much influenced by appearances as by realities; if a Government appears to be confident of its own powers, it is the surest way to inspire the same confidence in others; if it is diffident, it may be certain, there will be a still greater diffidence in others, and that its authority will not only be distrusted, controverted, but contemned.

I wish too Congress would always consider that a kindness consists as much in the manner as in the thing: the best things done hesitatingly and with an ill grace lose their effect, and produce disgust rather than satisfaction or gratitude. In what Congress have at any time done for the army, they have commonly been too late: They have seemed to yield to importunity rather than to sentiments of justice or to a regard to the accommodation of their troops. An attention to this idea is of more importance than it may be thought. I who have seen all the workings and progress of the present discontents, am convinced, that a want of this has not been among the most inconsiderable causes.

You will perceive My Dear Sir this letter is hastily written and with a confidential freedom, not as to a member of Congress, whose feelings may be sore at the prevailing clamours; but as to a friend who is in a situation to remedy public disorders, who wishes for nothing so much as truth, and who is desirous of information, even from those less capable of judging than himself. I have not even time to correct and copy and only enough to add that I am very truly and affectionately D Sir  Your most Obed ser

A. HAMILTON

*Liberty Pole*
*Sept. 3d 1780*

## *To Elizabeth Schuyler*

*Sepr 25*

In the midst of my letter, I was interrupted by a scene that shocked me more than any thing I have met with—the discovery of a treason of the deepest dye. The object was to sacrifice West Point. General Arnold had sold himself to André for this purpose. The latter came but in disguise and in returning to New York was detected. Arnold hearing of it immediately fled to the enemy. I went in persuit of him but was much too late, and I could hardly regret the disappointment, when on my return, I saw an amiable woman frantic with distress for the loss of a husband she tenderly loved—a traitor to his country and to his fame, a disgrace to his connections. It was the most affecting scene I ever was witness to. She for a considerable time intirely lost her senses. The General went up to see her and she upbraided him with being in a plot to murder her child; one moment she raved; another she melted into tears; sometimes she pressed her infant to her bosom and lamented its fate occasioned by the imprudence of its father in a manner that would have pierced insensibility itself. All the sweetness of beauty, all the loveliness of innocence, all the tenderness of a wife and all the fondness of a mother showed themselves in her appearance and conduct. We have every reason to believe she was intirely unacquainted with the plan, and that her first knowlege of it was when Arnold went to tell her he must banish himself from his Country and from her forever. She instantly fell into a convulsion and he left her in that situation.

This morning she is more composed. I paid her a visit and endeavoured to sooth her by every method in my power, though you may imagine she is not easily to be consoled. Added to her other distresses, She is very apprehensive the resentment of her country will fall upon her (who is only unfortunate) for the guilt of her husband. I have tried to persuade her, her apprehensions are ill founded; but she has too many proofs of the illiberality of the state to which she belongs to be convinced. She received us in bed, with every circumstance that could interest our sympathy. Her sufferings were so eloquent that I wished myself her brother, to have a right to become her defender. As it is, I have entreated her to enable me to give her proofs of my friendship.

Could I forgive Arnold for sacrificing his honor reputation and duty I could not forgive him for acting a part that must have forfieted the esteem of so fine a woman. At present she almost forgets his crime in his misfortune, and her horror at the guilt of the traitor is lost in her love of the man. But a virtuous mind cannot long esteem a base one, and time will make her despise, if it cannot make her hate.

Indeed my angelic Betsey, I would not for the world do any thing that would hazard your esteem. 'Tis to me a jewel of inestimable price & I think you may rely I shall never make you blush.

I thank you for all the goodness of which your letters are expressive, and I entreat you my lovely girl to believe that my tenderness for you every day increases and that no time or circumstances can abate it. I quarrel with the hours that they do not fly more rapidly and give us to each other.

*1780*

## To Elizabeth Schuyler

Since my last to you, I have received your letters No. 3 & 4; the others are yet on the way. Though it is too late to have the advantage of novelty, to comply with my promise, I send you my account of Arnold's affair; and to justify myself to your sentiments, I must inform you that I urged a compliance with Andre's request to be shot and I do not think it would have had an ill effect; but some people are only sensible to motives of policy, and sometimes from a narrow disposition mistake it. When André's tale comes to be told, and present resentment is over, the refusing him the privilege of choosing the manner of death will be branded with too much obduracy.

It was proposed to me to suggest to him the idea of an exchange for Arnold; but I knew I should have forfieted his esteem by doing it, and therefore declined it. As a man of honor he could not but reject it and I would not for the world have proposed to him a thing, which must have placed me in the unamiable light of supposing him capable of a meanness, or of not feeling myself the impropriety of the measure. I confess to you I had the weakness to value the esteem of a *dying* man; because I reverenced his merit.

I fear you will admire the picture so much as to forget the painter. I wished myself possessed of André's accomplishments for your sake; for I would wish to charm you in every sense. You cannot conceive my avidity for every thing that would endear me more to you. I shall never be satisfied with giving you pleasure, and I am mortified that I do not unite in myself every valuable and agreeable qualification. I do not my love affect modesty. I am conscious of the advantages I possess. I know I have talents and a good heart; but why am I not handsome? Why have I not every acquirement that can embellish human nature? Why have I not fortune, that I might hereafter have more leisure than I shall have to cultivate those improvements for which I am not entirely unfit?

Tis not the vanity of excelling others, but the desire of pleasing my Betsey that dictates these wishes. In her eyes I should wish to be the first the most amiable the most accomplished of my sex; but I will make up all I want in love.

Two days since, the bundle directed to your papa was delivered to me. I beg you to present my affectionate compliments with it to your mama.

I am in very good health and shall be in very good spirits when I meet my Betsey.

Adieu

A HAMILTON

How is your little sister? Is she as sprightly as ever? Does she set so much value upon a certain kiss as she seemed to do when we entered the carriage at Hartford? I forgot to tell you that she fell in love there with an old man of fifty.

*October 2, 1780*

## *To Margarita Schuyler*

Because your sister has the talent of growing more amiable every day, or because I am a fanatic in love, or both—or if you prefer another interpretation, because I have address enough to be a good dissembler, she fancies herself the happiest woman in the world, and would need persuade all her friends to embark with her in the matrimonial voyage. But I pray you do not let her advice have so much influence as to make you matrimony-mad. 'Tis a very good thing when their stars unite two people who are fit for each other, who have souls capable of relishing the sweets of friendship, and sensibilities. The conclusion of the sentence I trust to your fancy. But its a dog of life when two dissonant tempers meet, and 'tis ten to one but this is the case. When therefore I join her in advising you to marry, I add be cautious in the choice. Get a man of sense, not ugly enough to be pointed at—with some good-nature—a few grains of feeling—a little taste—a little imagination—and above all a good deal of decision to keep you in order; for that I foresee will be no easy task. If you can find one with all these qualities, willing to marry you, marry him as soon as you please.

I must tell you in confidence that I think I have been very fortunate.

*January 21, 1781*

## *To Philip Schuyler*

*Head Quarters New Windsor Feby 18, 81*

MY DEAR SIR.

Since I had the pleasure of writing you last an unexpected change has taken place in my situation. I am no longer a member of the General's family. This information will surprise you , and the manner of the change will surprise you more.—Two day ago The General and I passed each other on the stairs. He told me he wanted to speak to me, I answered that I would wait upon him immediately. I went below and delivered Mr. Tilghman a letter to be sent to The Commissary containing an order of a pressing and interesting nature, Returning to The General, I was stopped in the way Marquis De la Fayette and we conversed together about a minute on a matter of business. He can testify how impatient I was to get back and that I left him in a manner which but for our intimacy would have been more than abrupt. Instead of finding the General as usual in his room, I met him at the head of the stairs, where accosting me in a very angry tone, "Col Hamilton (said he), you have kept me waiting at the head of the stairs these ten minutes. I must tell you Sir you treat me with disrespect." I replied without petulancy, but with decision "I am not conscious of it Sir, but since you have thought it necessary to tell me so we part" "Very well Sir (said he) if it be your choice" or something to this effect and we separated.

I sincerely believe my absence which gave so much umbrage did not last two minutes.

In less than an hour after, Tilghman came to me in the Generals name assuring me of his great confidence in my abilities, integrity usefulness &c, and of his desire in a candid conversation to heal, a difference which could not have happened but in a moment of passion. I requested Mr. Tilghman to tell him 1. that I had taken my resolution in a manner not to be revoked: 2. that as a conversation could serve no other purpose than to produce explanations mutually disagreeable, though I certainly would not refuse an interview if he desired it yet I should be happy he would permit me to decline it 4. that however I did not wish to distress him or the public business, by quitting him before he could derive other assistance by the return of some of the Gentlemen who were absent: 3. that though determined to leave the family, the same principles which had kept me so long in it would continue to direct my conduct towards him when out of it. 5. And that in the mean time it depended on him to let our behaviour to each other be the same as if nothing had happened.

He consented to decline the conversation and thanked me for my offer of continuing my aid, in the manner I had mentioned.

Thus we stand. I wait Mr. Humphrey's return from the Eastward and may perhaps be induced to wait the return of Mr. Harrison from Virginia.

I have given you so particular a detail of our difference from the desire I have to justify myself in your opinion.

Perhaps you may think I was precipitate in rejecting the overture made by the general to an accommodation. I assure you My Dr Sir it was not the effect of resentment, it was the deliberate result of maxims I had long formed for the government of my own conduct.

I always disliked the office of an Aide de Camp as having in it a kind of personal dependance. I refused to serve in this capacity with two Major General's at an early period of the war. Infected however with the enthusiasm of the times, an idea of the Generals character which experience soon taught me to be unfounded overcame my scruples and induced me to *accept his invitation* to enter into his family. I believe you know the place I held in The Generals confidence and councils of which will make it the more extraordinary to you to learn that for three years past I have felt no friendship for him and have professed none. The truth is our own dispositions are the opposites of each other & the pride of my temper would not suffer me to profess what I did not feel. Indeed when advances of this kind have been made to me on his part, they were received in a manner that showed at least I had no inclination to court them, and that I wished to stand rather upon a footing of military confidence than of private attachment. You are too good a judge of human nature not to be sensible how this conduct in me must have operated on a man to whom all the world is offering incense. With this key you will easily unlock the present mystery. At the end of the war I may say many things to you concerning which I shall impose upon myself 'till then inviolable silence.

The General is a very honest man. His competitors have slender abilities and less integrity. His popularity has often been essential to the safety of America, and is still of great importance to it. These considerations have influenced my past conduct respecting him, and will influence my future. I think it is necessary he should be supported.

His estimation in your mind, whatever may be its amounts, I am persuaded has been formed on principles which a circumstance like this cannot materially affect; but if I thought it could diminish your friendship for him, I should almost forego the motives that urge me to justify myself to you. I wish what I have said to make no other impression than to satisfy you I have not been in the wrong. It is also said in confidence, for as a public knowlege of the breach would in many ways have an ill effect. it will probably be the policy of both sides to conceal it and cover the separation with some plausible pretext. I am importuned by such friends as are privy to the affair, to listen to a reconciliation: but my resolution is unalterable.

As I cannot think of quitting the army during the war, I have a project of re-entering into the artillery, by taking Lieutenant-Colonel Forrest's place, who is desirous of retiring on half pay. I have not however made up my mind upon this head, as I should be obliged to come in the youngest Lt Col instead of the eldest, which I ought to have been by natural succession had I remained in the corps; and at the same time to resume studies relative to the profession which, to avoid inferiority, must be laborious.

If a handsome command for the campaign in the light infantry should offer itself, I shall ballance between this and the artillery. My situation in the latter would be more solid and permanent; but as I hope the war will not last long enough to make it progressive, this consideration has the less force. A command for the campaign would leave me the winter to prosecute studies relative to my future career in life. With respect to the former, I have been materially the worse for going into his family.

I have written to you on this subject with all the freedom and confidence to which you have a right and with an assurance of the interest you take in all that concerns me.

Very sincerely & Affectionately I am Dr Sir Yr. most Obed

A HAMILTON

## *To Major James McHenry*

I have, Dear Mac, several of your letters. I shall soon have time enough to write my friends as often as they please.

The Great man and I have come to an open rupture. Proposals of accomodation have been made on his part but rejected. I pledge my honor to you that he will find me inflexible. He shall for once at least repent his ill-humour. Without a shadow of reason and on the slightest ground, he charged me in the most affrontive manner with treating him with disrespect. I answered very decisively—"Sir I am not conscious of it but since you have thought it necessary to tell me so, we part." I wait till more help arrives. At present there is besides myself only Tilghman, who is just recovering from a fit of illness the consequence of too close application to business.

We have often spoken freely our sentiments to each other. Except to a very few friends our difference will be a secret; therefore be silent. I shall continue to support a popularity that has been essential, is still useful.

Adieu my friend. May the time come when characters may be known in their true light.

AH

Madame sends her friendship to you.

*February 18, 1781*

## *The Continentalist No. III*

*Fishkill, New York, August 9, 1781*

The situation of these states is very unlike that of the United Provinces. Remote as we are from Europe, in a little time, we should fancy ourselves out of the reach of attempts from abroad, and in full liberty, at our leisure and convenience, to try our strength at home. This might not happen at once; but if the FOEDERAL GOVERNMENT SHOULD LOSE ITS AUTHORITY, it would CERTAINLY FOLLOW. Political societies, in close neighbourhood, must either be strongly united under one government, or there will infallibly exist emulations and quarrels. This is in human nature; and we have no reason to think ourselves wiser, or better, than other men. Some of the larger states, a small number of years hence, will be in themselves populous, rich and powerful, in all those circumstances calculated to inspire ambition and nourish ideas of separation and independence. Though it will ever be their true interest to preserve the union, their vanity and self importance, will be very likely to overpower that motive, and make them seek to place themselves at the head of particular confederacies independent of the general one. A schism once introduced, competitions of boundary and rivalships of commerce will easily afford pretexts for war. European powers may have inducements for fomenting these divisions and playing us off against each other. But without such a disposition in them, if separations once take place, we shall, of course, embrace different interests and connections. The particular confederacies, leaguing themselves with rival nations, will naturally be involved in their disputes; into which they will be the more readily tempted by the hope of making acquisitions upon each other, and upon the colonies of the powers with whom they are respectively at enmity.

WE ALREADY SEE SYMPTOMS OF THE EVILS TO BE APPREHENDED. In the midst of a war for our existence as a nation; in the midst of dangers too serious to be trifled with, some of the states have evaded, or refused, compliance with the demands of Congress in points of the greatest moment to the common safety. If they act such a part at this perilous juncture, what are we to expect in a time of peace and security? Is it not to be feared, that the resolutions of Congress would soon become like the decisions of the Greek amphyctions, or like the edicts of a German diet?

But as these evils are at a little distance, we may perhaps be insensible and short sighted enough to disregard them. There are others that threaten our immediate safety. Our whole system is in disorder; our currency depreciated, till in many places it will hardly obtain a circulation at all, public credit at its lowest ebb, our army deficient in numbers, and unprovided with every thing, the government, in its present condition, unable to command the means to pay, clothe, or feed their troops, the enemy making an alarming progress in the southern states, lately in complete possession of two of them, though now in part rescued by the genius and exertions of a General without an army, a force under Cornwallis still formidable to Virginia.

We ought to blush to acknowledge, that this is a true picture of our situation, when we reflect, that the enemy's whole force in the United States, including their American levies and the late reinforcement, is little more than fourteen thousand effective men; that our population, by recent examination, has been found to be greater, than at the commencement of the war; that the quantity of our specie has also increased, that the country abounds with all the necessaries of life, and has a sufficiency of foreign commodities, with a considerable and progressive commerce; that we have beyond comparison a better stock of warlike materials, than when we began the contest, and an ally as willing as able to supply our further wants: And that we have, on the spot, five thousand auxiliary troops, paid and subsisted by that ally, to assist in our defence.

Nothing but a GENERAL DISAFFECTION of the PEOPLE, or MISMANAGEMENT in their RULERS, can account for the figure we make, and for the distresses and perplexities we experience, contending against so small a force.

Our enemies themselves must now be persuaded, that the first is not the cause; and WE KNOW it is not. The most decided attachment of the people could alone have made them endure, without a convulsion, the successive shocks in our currency, added to the unavoidable inconveniences of war. There is perhaps not another nation in the world, that would have shown equal patience and perseverance in similar circumstances. The enemy have now tried the temper of almost every part of America; and they can hardly produce in their ranks a thousand men, who without their arts and seductions have voluntarily joined their standard. The miseries of a rigorous captivity, may perhaps have added half as many more to the number of the American levies, at this time in their armies. This small accession of force is the more extraordinary, as they have at some periods, been apparently in the full tide of success, while every thing wore an aspect tending to infuse despondency into the people of this country. This has been remarkably the case in the southern states. They for a time had almost undisturbed possession of two of them; and Cornwallis, after overruning a great part of a third; after two victorious battles, only brought with him into Virginia, about two hundred tories. In the state where he thought himself so well established, that he presumptuously ventured to assure the minister, there was not a rebel left, a small body of Continental troops, have been so effectually seconded by the militia of that vanquished country, as to have been able to capture a number of his troops more than equal to their own, and to repossess the principal part of the state.

As in the explanation of our embarrassments nothing can be alledged to the disaffection of the people, we must have recourse to the other cause of IMPOLICY and MISMANAGEMENT in their RULERS.

Where the blame of this may lie is not so much the question as what are the proper remedies; yet it may not be amiss to remark, that too large a share has fallen upon Congress. That body is no doubt chargeable with mistakes; but perhaps its greatest has been too much readiness to make concessions of the powers implied in its original trust. This is partly to be attributed to an excessive complaisance to the spirit, which has evidently actuated a majority of the states, a desire of monopolizing all power in themselves. Congress have been responsible for the administration of affairs, without the means of fulfilling that responsibility.

It would be too severe a reflection upon us to suppose, that a disposition to make the most of the friendship of others, and to exempt ourselves from a full share of the burthens of the war has had any part in the backwardness, which has appeared in many of the states, to confer powers and adopt measures adequate to the exigency. Such a sentiment would neither be wise, just, generous, nor honorable; nor do I believe the accusation would be well founded, yet our conduct makes us liable to a suspicion of this sort. It is certain, however, that too sanguine expectations from Europe have unintentionally relaxed our efforts, by diverting a sense of danger, and begetting an opinion, that the inequality of the contest would make every campaign the last.

We did not consider how difficult it must be to exhaust the resources of a nation circumstanced like that of Great Britain; whose government has always been distinguished for energy, and its people for enthusiasm. Nor did we, in estimating the superiority of our friends make sufficient allowance for that want of concert, which will ever characterise the operations of allies, or for the immense advantage to the enemy, of having their forces, though inferior, under a single direction. Finding the rest of Europe either friendly, or pacific, we never calculated the contingencies, which might alter that disposition; nor reflected that the death* of a single prince, the change or caprice of a single minister, was capable of giving a new face to the whole system.

We are at this time more sanguine than ever. The war with the Dutch, we believe, will give such an addition of force to our side, as will make the superiority irresistible. No person can dispute this, if things remain in their present state; but the extreme disparity of the contest is the very reason, why this cannot be the case. The neutral powers will either effect a particular, or a general accommodation, or they will take their sides. There are three suppositions to be made: one, that there will be a compromise between the united provinces and England; for which we are certain the mediation of Austria and Russia have been offered; another, a pacification between all the belligerent powers, for which we have reason to believe the same mediation has been offered; the third, a rejection of the terms of mediation and a more general war.

---

* The death of the Empress Queen has actually produced a change: Her politics, if not friendly to our connections, were at least pacific: and while she lived no hostile interference of the House of Austria was to be expected. The Emperor, her son, by her death, left more at liberty to pursue his inclinations, averse to the aggrandisement of France, of course afraid of the abasement of England, has given several indications of an unfriendly disposition. It should be a weighty consideration with us, that among the potentates which we look upon as amicable, three of the principal ones are at a very advanced stage of life. The King of Spain, the King of Prussia, and the Empress of Russia. We know not what may be the politics of successors.

Either of these suppositions is a motive for exertion. The first will place things in the same, probably in a worse situation, than before the declaration of the war against Holland. The composing of present differences may be accompanied with a revival of ancient connections; and at least would be productive of greater caution and restraint in a future intercourse with us.

The second, it is much to be dreaded, would hazard a dismemberment of a part of these states; and we are bound in honor, in duty and in interest, to employ every effort to dispossess the enemy of what they hold. A natural basis of the negociation, with respect to this continent, will be, that each party shall retain what it possesses at the conclusion of the treaty, qualified perhaps by a cession of particular points for an equivalent elsewhere. It is too delicate to dwell on the motives to this apprehension; but if such a compromise sometimes terminates the disputes of nations originally independent, it will be less extraordinary where one party was originally under the dominion of the other.

If we are determined, as we ought to be with the concurrence of our allies, not to accept such a condition, then we ought to prepare for the third event, a more general and more obstinate war.

Should this take place, a variety of new interests will be involved, and the affairs of America MAY CEASE TO BE OF PRIMARY IMPORTANCE. In proportion as the objects and operations of the war become complicated and extensive, the final success must become uncertain; and in proportion as the interests of others in our concerns may be weakened, or supplanted by more immediate interests of their own, ought our attention to ourselves, and exertions in our own behalf to be awakened and augmented.

We ought therefore, not only to strain every nerve for complying with the requisitions, to render the present campaign as decisive as possible; but we ought without delay, to ENLARGE THE POWERS OF CONGRESS. Every plan of which, this is not the foundation, will be illusory. The separate exertions of the states will never suffice. Nothing but a well-proportioned exertion of the resources of the whole, under the direction of a Common Council, with power sufficient to give efficacy to their resolutions, can preserve us from being a CONQUERED PEOPLE now, or can make us a HAPPY PEOPLE hereafter.

*The New-York Packet, and the American Advertiser, August 9, 1781*

## *To George Washington*

Sir

Flattering myself that your knowledge of me will induce you to receive the observations I make as dictated by a regard to the public good, I take the liberty to suggest to you my ideas on some matters of delicacy and importance. I view the present juncture as a very interesting one. I need not observe how far the temper and situation of the army make it so. The state of our finances was perhaps never more critical. I am under injunctions which will not permit me to disclose some facts that would at once demonstrate this position, but I think it probable you will be possessed of them through another channel. It is however certain that there has scarcely been a period of the revolution which called more for wisdom and decision in Congress. Unfortunately for us we are a body not governed by reason or foresight but by circumstances. It is probable we shall not take the proper measures, and if we do not a few months may open an embarrassing scene. This will be the case whether we have peace or a continuance of the war.

If the war continues it would seem that the army must in June subsist itself to *defend the* country; if peace should take place it *will* subsist itself to *procure justice to itself*. It appears to be a prevailing opinion in the army that the disposition to recompence their services will cease with the necessity for them, and that if they once lay down their arms, they will part with the means of obtaining justice. It is to be lamented that appearances afford too much ground for their distrust.

It becomes a serious inquiry what will be the true line of policy. The claims of the army urged with moderation, but with firmness, may operate on those weak minds which are influenced by their apprehensions more than their judgments; so as to produce a concurrence in the measures which the exigencies of affairs demand. They may add weight to the applications of Congress to the several states. So far an useful turn may be given to them. But the difficulty will be to keep a *complaining* and *suffering* army within the bounds of moderation.

This Your Excellency's influence must effect. In order to it, it will be adviseable not to discountenance their endeavours to procure redress, but rather by the intervention of confidential and prudent persons, *to take the direction of them*. This however must not appear: it is of moment to the public tranquillity that Your Excellency should preserve the confidence of the army without losing that of the people. This will enable you in case of extremity to guide the torrent, and bring order perhaps even good, out of confusion. 'Tis a part that requires address; but 'tis one which your own situation as well as the welfare of the community points out.

I will not conceal from Your Excellency a truth which it is necessary you should know. An idea is propagated in the army that delicacy carried to an extreme prevents your espousing its interests with sufficient warmth. The falsehood of this opinion no one can be better acquainted with than myself; but it is not the less mischievous for being false. Its tendency is to impair that influence, which you may exert with advantage, should any commotions unhappily ensue, to moderate the pretensions of the army and make their conduct correspond with their duty.

The great *desideratum* at present is the establishment of general funds, which alone can do justice to the Creditors of the United States (of whom the army forms the most meritorious class), restore public credit and supply the future wants of government. This is the object of all men of sense; in this the influence of the army, properly directed, may cooperate.

The intimations I have thrown out will suffice to give Your Excellency a proper conception of my sentiments. You will judge of their reasonableness or fallacy; but I persuade myself you will do justice to my motives.

I have the honor to be With great respect Your Excellencys Most Obedt servt.

ALEX HAMILTON

General Knox has the confidence of the army & is a man of sense. I think he may be safely made use of. Situated as I am Your Excellency will feel the confidential nature of these observations.

Philadelphia
Feby. 13th, 1783

# *To James Hamilton*

*New York, June 22, 1785.*

MY DEAR BROTHER:

I have received your letter of the 31st of May last, which, and one other, are the only letters I have received from you in many years. I am a little surprised you did not receive one which I wrote to you about six months ago. The situation you describe yourself to be in gives me much pain, and nothing will make me happier than, as far as may be in my power, to contribute to your relief. I will cheerfully pay your draft upon me for fifty pounds sterling, whenever it shall appear. I wish it was in my power to desire you to enlarge the sum; but though my future prospects are of the most flattering kind my present engagements would render it inconvenient to me to advance you a larger sum. My affection for you, however, will not permit me to be inattentive to your welfare, and I hope time will prove to you that I feel all the sentiment of a brother. Let me only request of you to exert your industry for a year or two more where you are, and at the end of that time I promise myself to be able to invite you to a more comfortable settlement in this Country. Allow me only to give you one caution, which is to avoid if possible getting in debt. Are you *married* or *single*? If the *latter*, it is my wish for many reasons it may be agreeable to you to continue in that state.

But what has become of our dear father? It is an age since I have heared from him or of him, though I have written him several letters. Perhaps, alas! he is no more, and I shall not have the pleasing opportunity of contributing to render the close of his life more happy than the progress of it. My heart bleeds at the recollection of his misfortunes and embarrassments. Sometimes I flatter myself his brothers have extended their support to him, and that he now enjoys tranquillity and ease. At other times I fear he is suffering in indigence. I entreat you, if you can, to relieve me from my doubts, and let me know how or where he is, if alive, if dead, how and where he died. Should he be alive inform him of my inquiries, beg him to write to me, and tell him how ready I shall be to devote myself and all I have to his accommodation and happiness.

I do not advise your coming to this country at present, for the war has also put things out of order here, and people in your business find a subsistence difficult enough. My object will be, by-and-by, to get you settled on a farm.

Believe me always your affectionate friend and brother,

ALEX. HAMILTON.

## Constitutional Convention: Plan of Government

I   The Supreme Legislative Power of the United States of America to be vested in two distinct bodies of men—the one to be called the *Assembly* the other the *senate;* who together shall form the Legislature of the United States, with power to pass all *laws whatsoever*, subject to the *negative* hereafter mentioned.

II   The Assembly to consist of persons elected *by the People* to serve for three years.

III   The Senate to consist of persons elected to serve during *good behaviour*. Their election to be made by *Electors* chosen for that purpose by the People. In order to this The States to be divided into election districts. On the death removal or resignation of any senator his place to be filled out of the district from which he came.

IV   The Supreme Executive authority of the United States to be vested in a *governor* to be elected to serve *during good behaviour*. His election to be made by *Electors* chosen by *electors* chosen by the people in the election districts aforesaid or by electors chosen for that purpose by the respective legislatures—provided that if an election be not made within a limited time the President of the Senate shall be the Governor. The Governor to have *a negative* upon all laws about to be passed and to have the execution of all laws passed—to be the Commander in Chief of the land and naval forces and of the Militia of the United States—to have the direction of war, when authorised or began—to have with the *advice* and *approbation* of the Senate the power of making all treaties—to have the appointment of the *heads or chief* officers of the departments of finance war and foreign affairs—to have the *nomination* of all other officers (ambassadors to foreign nations included) subject to the approbation or rejection of the Senate—to have the power of pardoning all offences but *treason*, which he shall not pardon without the approbation of the Senate.

V   On the death resignation or removal of the Governor his authorities to be exercised by the President of the Senate.

VI   The Senate to have the sole power of *declaring war*—the power of advising and approving all treaties—the power of approving or rejecting all appointments of officers except the heads or chiefs of the departments of finance war and foreign affairs.

VII   The Supreme Judicial authority of the United States to be vested in twelve Judges, to hold their offices during good behaviour with adequate and permanent salaries. This Court to have original jurisdiction in all causes of capture and an appellative jurisdiction (from the Courts of the several states) in all causes in which the revenues of the general government or the citizens of foreign nations are concerned.

VIII   The Legislature of the United States to have power to institute Courts in each state for the determination of all causes of capture and of all matters relating to their revenues, or in which the citizens of foreign nations are concerned.

IX   The Governor Senators and all Officers of the United States to be liable to impeachment for mal and corrupt conduct, and upon conviction to be removed from office and disqualified for holding any place of trust or profit. All impeachments to be tried by a Court to consist of the judges of the Supreme Court chief or Senior Judge of the superior Court of law of each state—provided that such judge hold his place during good behaviour and have a permanent salary.

X   All laws of the particular states contrary to the constitution or laws of the United States to be utterly void. And the better to prevent such laws being passed the Governor or President of each state shall *be appointed by the general government* and shall have a *negative* upon the laws about to be passed in the state of which he is governor or President.

XI   No state to have any forces land or naval—and the *Militia* of all the states to be under the sole and *exclusive direction* of the United States *the officers* of which to be appointed and commissioned by them.

*c. June 18, 1787*

## Speech in the Constitutional Convention on a Plan of Government

*James Madison's Version*

MR. HAMILTON, had been hitherto silent on the business before the Convention, partly from respect to others whose superior abilities age & experience rendered him unwilling to bring forward ideas dissimilar to theirs, and partly from his delicate situation with respect to his own State, to whose sentiments as expressed by his Colleagues, he could by no means accede. The crisis however which now marked our affairs, was too serious to permit any scruples whatever to prevail over the duty imposed on every man to contribute his efforts for the public safety & happiness. He was obliged therefore to declare himself unfriendly to both plans. He was particularly opposed to that from N. Jersey, being fully convinced, that no amendment of the Confederation, leaving the States in possession of their Sovereignty could possibly answer the purpose. On the other hand he confessed he was much discouraged by the amazing extent of Country in expecting the desired blessings from any general sovereignty that could be substituted. As to the powers of the Convention, he thought the doubts started on that subject had arisen from distinctions & reasonings too subtle. A *federal* Govt. he conceived to mean an association of independent Communities into one. Different Confederacies have different powers, and exercise them in different ways. In some instances the powers are exercised over collective bodies; in others over individuals, as in the German Diet—&

among ourselves in cases of piracy. Great latitude therefore must be given to the signification of the term. The plan last proposed departs itself from the *federal* idea, as understood by some, since it is to operate eventually on individuals. He agreed moreover with the Honble gentleman from Va. (Mr. R.) that we owed it to our Country, to do on this emergency whatever we should deem essential to its happiness. The States sent us here to provide for the exigences of the Union. To rely on & propose any plan not adequate to these exigences, merely because it was not clearly within our powers, would be to sacrifice the means to the end. It may be said that the *States* can not *ratify* a plan not within the purview of the article of Confederation providing for alterations & amendments. But may not the States themselves in which no constitutional authority equal to this purpose exists in the Legislatures, have had in view a reference to the people at large. In the Senate of N. York, a proviso was moved, that no act of the Convention should be binding untill it should be referred to the people & ratified; and the motion was lost by a single voice only, the reason assigned agst. it being, that it might possibly be found an inconvenient shackle.

The great question is what provision shall we make for the happiness of our Country? He would first make a comparative examination of the two plans—prove that there were essential defects in both—and point out such changes as might render a *national one*, efficacious. The great & essential principles necessary for the support of Government are 1. an active & constant interest in supporting it. This principle does not exist in the States in favor of the federal Govt. They have evidently in a high degree, the esprit de corps. They constantly pursue internal interests adverse to those of the whole. They have their particular debts—their particular plans of finance &c. All these when opposed to, invariably prevail over the requisitions & plans of Congress. 2. The love of power. Men love power. The same remarks are applicable to this principle. The States have constantly shewn a disposition rather to regain the powers delegated by them than to part with more, or to give effect to what they had parted with. The ambition of their demagogues is known to hate the controul of the Genl. Government. It may be remarked too that the Citizens have not that anxiety to prevent a dissolution of the Genl. Govt. as of the particular Govts. A dissolution of the latter would be fatal; of the former would still leave the purposes of Govt. attainable to a considerable degree. Consider what such a State as Virga. will be in a few years, a few compared with the life of nations. How strongly will it feel its importance & self-sufficiency? 3. An habitual attachment of the people. The whole force of this tie is on the side of the State Govt. Its sovereignty is immediately before the eyes of the people: its protection is immediately enjoyed by them. From its hand distributive justice, and all those acts which familiarize & endear Govt. to a people, are dispensed to them. 4. *Force* by which may be understood a *coertion of laws* or *coertion of arms*. Congs. have not the former except in few cases. In particular States, this coercion is nearly sufficient; tho' he held it in most cases, not entirely so. A certain portion of military force is absolutely necessary in large communities. Masss. is now feeling this necessity & making provision for it. But how can this force be exerted on the States collectively. It is impossible. It amounts to a war between the parties. Foreign powers also will not be idle spectators. They will interpose, the confusion will increase, and a dissolution of the Union will ensue. 5. *influence*. he did not mean corruption, but a dispensation of those regular honors & emoluments, which produce an attachment to the Govt. Almost all the weight of these is on the side of the States; and must continue so as long as the States continue to exist. All the passions then we see, of avarice, ambition, interest, which govern most individuals, and all public bodies, fall into the current of the States, and do not flow in the stream of the Genl. Govt. The former therefore will generally be an overmatch for the Genl. Govt. and render any confederacy, in its very nature precarious. Theory is in this case fully confirmed by experience. The Amphyctionic Council had it would seem ample powers for general purposes. It had in particular the power of fining and using force agst. delinquent members. What was the consequence. Their decrees were mere signals of war. The Phocian war is a striking example of it. Philip at length taking advantage of their disunion, and insinuating himself into their Councils, made himself master of their fortunes. The German Confederacy affords another lesson. The authority of Charlemagne seemed to be as great as could be necessary. The great feudal chiefs however, exercising their local sovereignties, soon felt the spirit & found the means of, encroachments, which reduced the imperial authority to a nominal sovereignty. The Diet has succeeded, which tho' aided by a Prince at its head, of great authority independently of his imperial attributes, is a striking illustration of the weakness of

Confederated Governments. Other examples instruct us in the same truth. The Swiss cantons have scarce any Union at all, and have been more than once at war with one another. How then are all these evils to be avoided? only by such a compleat sovereignty in the general Governmt. as will turn all the strong principles & passions above mentioned on its side. Does the scheme of N. Jersey produce this effect? does it afford any substantial remedy whatever? On the contrary it labors under great defects, and the defect of some of its provisions will destroy the efficacy of others. It gives a direct revenue to Congs. but this will not be sufficient. The balance can only be supplied by requisitions: which experience proves can not be relied on. If States are to deliberate on the mode, they will also deliberate on the object of the supplies, and will grant or not grant as they approve or disapprove of it. The delinquency of one will invite and countenance it in others. Quotas too must in the nature of things be so unequal as to produce the same evil. To what standard will you resort? Land is a fallacious one. Compare Holland with Russia: France or Engd. with other countries of Europe. Pena. with N. Carola. will the relative pecuniary abilities in those instances, correspond with the relative value of land. Take numbers of inhabitants for the rule and make like comparison of different countries, and you will find it to be equally unjust. The different degrees of industry and improvement in different Countries render the first object a precarious measure of wealth. Much depends too on *situation*. Cont. N. Jersey & N. Carolina, not being commercial States & contributing to the wealth of the commercial ones, can never bear quotas assessed by the ordinary rules of proportion. They will & must fail in their duty, their example will be followed, and the Union itself be dissolved. Whence then is the national revenue to be drawn? from Commerce? even from exports which notwithstanding the common opinion are fit objects of moderate taxation, from excise, &c &c. These tho' not equal, are less unequal than quotas. Another destructive ingredient in the plan, is that equality of suffrage which is so much desired by the small States. It is not in human nature that Va. & the large States should consent to it, or if they did that they shd. long abide by it. It shocks too much the ideas of Justice, and every human feeling. Bad principles in a Govt. tho slow are sure in their operation, and will gradually destroy it. A doubt has been raised whether Congs. at present have a right to keep Ships or troops in time of peace. He leans to the negative. Mr. Ps. plan provides no remedy. If the powers proposed were adequate, the organization of Congs. is such that they could never be properly & effectually exercised. The members of Congs. being chosen by the States & subject to recall, represent all the local prejudices. Should the powers be found effectual, they will from time to time be heaped on them, till a tyrannic sway shall be established. The general power whatever be its form if it preserves itself, must swallow up the State powers. Otherwise it will be swallowed up by them. It is agst. all the principles of a good Government to vest the requisite powers in such a body as Congs. Two Sovereignties can not co-exist within the same limits. Giving powers to Congs. must eventuate in a bad Govt. or in no Govt. The plan of N. Jersey therefore will not do. What then is to be done? Here he was embarrassed. The extent of the Country to be governed, discouraged him. The expence of a general Govt. was also formidable; unless there were such a diminution of expence on the side of the State Govts. as the case would admit. If they were extinguished, he was persuaded that great œconomy might be obtained by substituting a general Govt. He did not mean however to shock the public opinion by proposing such a measure. On the other hand he saw no *other* necessity for declining it. They are not necessary for any of the great purposes of commerce, revenue, or agriculture. Subordinate authorities he was aware would be necessary. There must be district tribunals: corporations for local purposes. But cui bono, the vast & expensive apparatus now appertaining to the States. The only difficulty of a serious nature which occurred to him, was that of drawing representatives from the extremes to the center of the Community. What inducements can be offered that will suffice? The moderate wages for the 1st. branch would only be a bait to little demagogues. Three dollars or thereabouts he supposed would be the utmost. The Senate he feared from a similar cause, would be filled by certain undertakers who wish for particular offices under the Govt. This view of the subject almost led him to despair that a Republican Govt. could be established over so great an extent. He was sensible at the same time that it would be unwise to propose one of any other form. In his private opinion he had no scruple in declaring, supported as he was by the opinions of so many of the wise & good, that the British Govt. was the best in the world: and that he doubted much whether any thing short of it would do in America. He hoped Gentlemen of different opinions would bear with him in this, and begged them to recollect the change of opinion on this subject which had taken place and was still going on. It was once thought that the power of Congs. was amply sufficient to secure the end of their institution. The error was now seen by every one. The members most tenacious of republicanism, he observed, were as loud as any in declaiming agst. the vices of democracy. This progress of the public mind led him to anticipate the time, when others as well as himself would join in the praise bestowed by Mr. Neckar on the British Constitution, namely, that it is the only Govt. in the world "which unites public strength with individual security." In every community where industry is encouraged, there will be a division of it into the few & the many. Hence separate interests will arise. There will be debtors & creditors &c. Give all power to the many, they will oppress the few. Give all power to the few, they will oppress the many. Both therefore ought to have power, that each may defend itself agst. the other. To the want of this check we owe our paper money, instalment laws &c. To the proper adjustment of it the British owe the excellence of their Constitution. Their house of Lords is a most noble institution. Having nothing to hope for by a change, and a sufficient interest by means of their property, in being faithful to the national interest, they form a permanent barrier agst. every pernicious innovation, whether attempted on the part of the Crown or of the Commons. No temporary Senate will have the firmness eno' to answer the purpose. The Senate (of Maryland) which seems to be so much appealed to, has not yet been sufficiently tried. Had the people been unanimous & eager, in the late appeal to them on the subject of a paper emission they would have yielded to the torrent. Their acquiescing in such an appeal is a proof of it. Gentlemen differ in their opinions concerning the necessary checks, from the different estimates they form of the human passions. They suppose seven years a sufficient period to give the senate an adequate firmness, from not duly considering the amazing violence & turbulence of the democratic spirit. When a great object of Govt. is pursued, which seizes the popular passions, they spread like wild fire, and become irresistable. He appealed to the gentlemen from the N. England States whether experience had not there verified the remark. As to the Executive, it seemed to be admitted that no good one could be established on Republican principles. Was not this giving up the merits of the question: for can there be a good Govt. without a good Executive.

The English model was the only good one on this subject. The Hereditary interest of the King was so interwoven with that of the Nation, and his personal emoluments so great, that he was placed above the danger of being corrupted from abroad—and at the same time was both sufficiently independent and sufficiently controuled, to answer the purpose of the institution at home. one of the weak sides of Republics was their being liable to foreign influence & corruption. Men of little character, acquiring great power become easily the tools of intermedling Neibours. Sweeden was a striking instance. The French & English had each their parties during the late Revolution which was effected by the predominant influence of the former. What is the inference from all these observations? That we ought to go as far in order to attain stability and permanency, as republican principles will admit. Let one branch of the Legislature hold their places for life or at least during good behaviour. Let the Executive also be for life. He appealed to the feelings of the members present whether a term of seven years, would induce the sacrifices of private affairs which an acceptance of public trust would require, so so as to ensure the services of the best Citizens. On this plan we should have in the Senate a permanent will, a weighty interest, which would answer essential purposes. But is this a Republican Govt., it will be asked? Yes if all the Magistrates are appointed, and vacancies are filled, by the people, or a process of election originating with the people. He was sensible that an Executive constituted as he proposed would have in fact but little of the power and independence that might be necessary. On the other plan of appointing him for 7 years, he thought the Executive ought to have but little power. He would be ambitious, with the means of making creatures; and as the object of his ambition wd. be to *prolong* his power, it is probable that in case of a war, he would avail himself of the emergence, to evade or refuse a degradation from his place. An Executive for life has not this motive for forgetting his fidelity, and will therefore be a safer depository of power. It will be objected probably, that such an Executive will be an *elective Monarch*, and will give birth to the tumults which characterize that form of Govt. He wd. reply that *Monarch* is an indefinite term. It marks not either the degree or duration of power. If this Executive Magistrate wd. be a monarch for life—the other propd. by the Report from the Comtte of the whole, wd. be a monarch for seven years. The circumstance of being elective was also applicable to both. It had been observed by judicious writers that elective monarchies wd. be the best if they could be guarded agst. the *tumults* excited by the ambition and intrigues of competitors. He was not sure that tumults were an inseparable evil. He rather thought this character of Elective Monarchies had been taken rather from particular cases than from general principles. The election of Roman Emperors was made by the *Army*. In *Poland* the election is made by great rival *princes* with independent power, and ample means, of raising commotions. In the German Empire, the appointment is made by the Electors & Princes, who have equal motives & means, for exciting cabals & parties. Might not such a mode of election be devised among ourselves as will defend the community agst. these effects in any dangerous degree? Having made these observations he would read to the Committee a sketch of a plan which he shd. prefer to either of those under consideration. He was aware that it went beyond the ideas of most members. But will such a plan be adopted out of doors? In return he would ask will the people adopt the other plan? At present they will adopt neither. But he sees the Union dissolving or already dissolved—he sees evils operating in the States which must soon cure the people of their fondness for democracies—he sees that a great progress has been already made & is still going on in the public mind. He thinks therefore that the people will in time be unshackled from their prejudices; and whenever that happens, they will themselves not be satisfied at stopping where the plan of Mr. R. wd. place them, but be ready to go as far at least as he proposes. He did not mean to offer the paper he had sketched as a proposition to the Committee. It was meant only to give a more correct view of his ideas, and to suggest the amendments which he should probably propose to the plan of Mr. R. in the proper stages of its future discussion. He read his sketch in the words following: towit . . ."

On these several articles he entered into explanatory observations corresponding with the principles of his introductory reasoning.

### Robert Yates's Version

MR. HAMILTON. To deliver my sentiments on so important a subject, when the first characters in the union have gone before me, inspires me with the greatest diffidence, especially when my own ideas are so materially dissimilar to the plans now before the committee. My situation is disagreeable, but it would be criminal not to come forward on a question of such magnitude. I have well considered the subject, and am convinced that no amendment of the confederation can answer the purpose of a good government, so long as state sovereignties do, in any shape, exist; and I have great doubts whether a national government on the Virginia plan can be made effectual. What is federal? An association of several independent states into one. How or in what manner this association is formed, is not so clearly distinguishable. We find the diet of Germany has in some instances the power of legislation on individuals. We find the United States of America have it in an extensive degree in the cases of piracies.

Let us now review the powers with which we are invested. We are appointed for the *sole* and *express* purpose of revising the confederation, and to *alter* or *amend* it, so as to render it effectual for the purposes of a good government. Those who suppose it must be federal, lay great stress on the terms *sole* and *express*, as if these words intended a confinement to a federal government; when the manifest import is no more than that the institution of a good government must be the *sole* and *express* object of your deliberations. Nor can we suppose an annihilation of our powers by forming a national government, as many of the states have made in their constitutions no provision for any alteration; and thus much I can say for the state I have the honor to represent, that when our credentials were under consideration in the senate, some members were for inserting a restriction in the powers, to prevent an encroachment on the constitution: it was answered by others, and thereupon the resolve carried on the credentials, that it might abridge some of the constitutional powers of the state, and that possibly in the formation of a new union it would be found necessary. This appears reasonable, and therefore leaves us at liberty to form such a national government as we think best adapted for the good of the whole. I have therefore no difficulty as to the extent of our powers, nor do I feel myself restrained in the exercise of my judgment under them. We can only propose and recommend—the power of ratifying or rejecting is still in the states. But on this great question I am still greatly embarrassed. I have before observed my apprehension of the inefficacy of either plan, and I have great doubts whether a more energetic government can pervade this wide and extensive country. I shall now show, that both plans are materially defective.

1. A good government ought to be constant, and ought to contain an active principle.

2. Utility and necessity.

3. An habitual sense of obligation.

4. Force.

5. Influence.

I hold it, that different societies have all different views and interests to pursue, and always prefer local to general concerns. For example: New-York legislature made an external compliance lately to a requisition of congress; but do they not at the same time counteract their compliance by gratifying the local objects of the state so as to defeat their concession? And this will ever be the case. Men always love power, and states will prefer their particular concerns to the general welfare; and as the states become large and important, will they not be less attentive to the general government? What, in process of time will Virginia be? She contains now half a million inhabitants—in twenty-five years she will double the number. Feeling her own weight and importance, must she not become indifferent to the concerns of the union? And where, in such a situation, will be found national attachment to the general government?

By *force*, I mean the *coercion* of law and the coercion of arms. Will this remark apply to the power intended to be vested in the government to be instituted by either plan? A delinquent must be compelled to obedience by force of arms. How is this to be done? If you are unsuccessful, a dissolution of your government must be the consequence; and in that case the individual legislatures will reassume their powers; nay, will not the interest of the states be thrown into the state governments?

By *influence*, I mean the regular weight and support it will receive from those who will find it their interest to support a government intended to preserve the peace and happiness of the community of the whole. The state governments, by either plan, will exert the means to counteract it. They have their state judges and militia all combined to support their state interests; and these will be influenced to oppose a national government. Either plan is therefore precarious. The national government cannot long exist when opposed by such a weighty rival. The experience of ancient and modern confederacies evince this point, and throw considerable light on the subject. The amphyctionic council of Greece had a right to require of its members troops, money and the force of the country. Were they obeyed in the exercise of those powers? Could they preserve the peace of the greater states and republics? or where were they obeyed? History shows that their decrees were disregarded, and that the stronger states, regardless of their power, gave law to the lesser.

Let us examine the federal institution of Germany. It was instituted upon the laudable principle of securing the independency of the several states of which it was composed, and to protect them against foreign invasion. Has it answered these good intentions? Do we not see that their councils are weak and distracted, and that it cannot prevent the wars and confusions which the respective electors carry on against each other? The Swiss cantons, or the Helvetic union, are equally inefficient.

Such are the lessons which the experience of others affords us, and from whence results the evident conclusion that all federal governments are weak and distracted. To avoid the evils deducible from these observations, we must establish a general and national government, completely sovereign, and annihilate the state distinctions and state operations; and unless we do this, no good purpose can be answered. What does the Jersey plan propose? It surely has not this for its object. By this we grant the regulation of trade and a more effectual collection of the revenue, and some partial duties. These, at five or ten per cent, would only perhaps amount to a fund to discharge the debt of the corporation.

Let us take a review of the variety of important objects, which must necessarily engage the attention of a national government. You have to protect your rights against Canada on the north, Spain on the south, and your western frontier against the savages. You have to adopt necessary plans for the settlement of your frontiers, and to institute the mode in which settlements and good government are to be made.

How is the expense of supporting and regulating these important matters to be defrayed? By requisition on the states, according to the Jersey plan? Will this do it? We have already found it ineffectual. Let one state prove delinquent, and it will encourage others to follow the example; and thus the whole will fail. And what is the standard to quota among the states their respective proportions? Can lands be the standard? How would that apply between Russia and Holland? Compare Pennsylvania with North-Carolina, or Connecticut with

New-York. Does not commerce or industry in the one or other make a great disparity between these different countries, and may not the comparative value of the states from these circumstances, make an unequal disproportion when the data is numbers? I therefore conclude that either system would ultimately destroy the confederation, or any other government which is established on such fallacious principles. Perhaps imposts, taxes on specific articles, would produce a more equal system of drawing a revenue.

Another objection against the Jersey plan is, the unequal representation. Can the great States consent to this? If they did it would eventually work its own destruction. How are forces to be raised by the Jersey plan? By quotas? Will the states comply with the requisition? As much as they will with the taxes.

Examine the present confederation, and it is evident they can raise no troops nor equip vessels before war is actually declared. They cannot therefore take any preparatory measure before an enemy is at your door. How unwise and inadequate their powers! and this must ever be the case when you attempt to define powers. Something will always be wanting. Congress, by being annually elected, and subject to recall, will ever come with the prejudices of their states rather than the good of the union. Add therefore additional powers to a body thus organized, and you establish a *sovereignty* of the worst kind, consisting of a single body. Where are the checks? None. They must either prevail over the state governments, or the prevalence of the state governments must end in their dissolution. This is a conclusive objection to the Jersey plan.

Such are the insuperable objections to both plans: and what is to be done on this occasion? I confess I am at a loss. I foresee the difficulty on a consolidated plan of drawing a representation from so extensive a continent to one place. What can be the inducements for gentlemen to come 600 miles to a national legislature? The expense would at least amount to £100,000. This however can be no conclusive objection if it eventuates in an extinction of state governments. The burthen of the latter would be saved, and the expense then would not be great. State distinctions would be found unnecessary, and yet I confess, to carry government to the extremities, the state governments reduced to corporations, and with very limited powers, might be necessary, and the expense of the national government become less burthensome.

Yet, I confess, I see great difficulty of drawing forth a good representation. What, for example, will be the inducements for gentlemen of fortune and abilities to leave their houses and business to attend annually and long? It cannot be the wages; for these, I presume, must be small. Will not the power, therefore, be thrown into the hands of the demagogue or middling politician, who, for the sake of a small stipend and the hopes of advancement, will offer himself as a candidate, and the real men of weight and influence, by remaining at home, add strength to the state governments? I am at a loss to know what must be done; I despair that a republican form of government can remove the difficulties. Whatever may be my opinion, I would hold it however unwise to change that form of government. I believe the British government forms the best model the world ever produced, and such has been its progress in the minds of the many, that this truth gradually gains ground. This government has for its object *public strength* and *individual security*. It is said with us to be unattainable. If it was once formed it would maintain itself. All communities divide themselves into the few and the many. The first are the rich and well born, the other the mass of the people. The voice of the people has been said to be the voice of God; and however generally this maxim has been quoted and believed, it is not true in fact. The people are turbulent and changing; they seldom judge or determine right. Give therefore to the first class a distinct, permanent share in the government. They will check the unsteadiness of the second, and as they cannot receive any advantage by a change, they therefore will ever maintain good government. Can a democratic assembly, who annually revolve in the mass of the people, be supposed steadily to pursue the public good? Nothing but a permanent body can check the imprudence of democracy. Their turbulent and uncontrouling disposition requires checks. The senate of New-York, although chosen for four years, we have found to be inefficient. Will, on the Virginia plan, a continuance of seven years do it? It is admitted, that you cannot have a good executive upon a democratic plan. See the excellency of the British executive. He is placed above temptation. He can have no distinct interests from the public welfare. Nothing short of such an executive can be efficient. The weak side of a republican government is the danger of foreign influence. This is unavoidable, unless it is so constructed as to bring forward its first characters in its support. I am therefore for a general government, yet would wish to go the full length of republican principles.

Let one body of the legislature be constituted during good behaviour or life.

Let one executive be appointed who dares execute his powers.

It may be asked is this a republican system? It is strictly so, as long as they remain elective.

And let me observe, that an executive is less dangerous to the liberties of the people when in office during life, than for seven years.

It may be said, this constitutes an elective monarchy? Pray, what is a monarchy? May not the governors of the respective states be considered in that light? But by making the executive subject to impeachment, the term monarchy cannot apply. These elective monarchs have produced tumults in Rome, and are equally dangerous to peace in Poland; but this cannot apply to the mode in which I would propose the election. Let electors be appointed in each of the states to elect the executive— (*Here Mr. H. produced his plan, a copy whereof is hereunto annexed,*) to consist of two branches—and I would give them the unlimited power of passing all laws without exception. The assembly to be elected for three years by the people in districts—the senate to be elected by the electors to be chosen for that purpose by the people, and to remain in office during life. The executive to have the power of negativing all laws—to make war or peace, with the advice of the senate—to make treaties with their advice, but to have the sole direction of all military operations, and to send ambassadors and appoint all military officers, and to pardon all offenders, treason excepted, unless by advice of the senate. On his death or removal, the president of the senate to officiate, with the same powers, until another is elected. Supreme judicial officers to be appointed by the executive and the senate. The legislature to appoint courts in each state, so as to make the state governments unnecessary to it.

All state laws to be absolutely void which contravene the general laws. An officer to be appointed in each state to have a negative on all state laws. All the militia and the appointment of officers to be under the national government.

I confess that this plan and that from Virginia are very remote from the idea of the people. Perhaps the Jersey plan is nearest their expectation. But the people are gradually ripening in their opinions of government— they begin to be tired of an excess of democracy—and what even is the Virginia plan, but *pork still, with a little change of the sauce.*

*June 18, 1787*

## *To George Washington*

D<small>R</small>. S<small>IR</small>.

In my passage through the Jerseys and since my arrival here I have taken particular pains to discover the public sentiment and I am more and more convinced that this is the critical opportunity for establishing the prosperity of this country on a solid foundation. I have conversed with men of information not only of this City but from different parts of the state; and they agree that there has been an astonishing revolution for the better in the minds of the people. The prevailing apprehension among thinking men is that the Convention, from a fear of shocking the popular opinion, will not go far enough. They seem to be convinced that a strong well mounted government will better suit the popular palate than one of a different complexion. Men in office are indeed taking all possible pains to give an unfavourable impression of the Convention; but the current seems to be running strongly the other way.

A plain but sensible man, in a conversation I had with him yesterday, expressed himself nearly in this manner. The people begin to be convinced that their "excellent form of government" as they have been used to call it, will not answer their purpose; and that they must substitute something not very remote from that which they have lately quitted.

These appearances though they will not warrant a conclusion that the people are yet ripe for such a plan as I advocate, yet serve to prove that there is no reason to despair of their adopting one equally energetic, if the Convention should think proper to propose it. They serve to prove that we ought not to allow too much weight to objections drawn from the supposed repugnancy of the people to an efficient constitution. I confess I am more and more inclined to believe that former habits of thinking are regaining their influence with more rapidity than is generally imagined.

Not having compared ideas with you, Sir, I cannot judge how far our sentiments agree; but as I persuade myself the genuineness of my representations will receive credit with you, my anxiety for the event of the deliberations of the Convention induces me to make this communication of what appears to be the tendency of the public mind. I own to you Sir that I am seriously and deeply distressed at the aspect of the Councils which prevailed when I left Philadelphia. I fear that we shall let slip the golden opportunity of rescuing the American empire from disunion anarchy and misery. No motley or feeble measure can answer the end or will finally receive the public support. Decision is true wisdom and will be not less reputable to the Convention than salutary to the community.

I shall of necessity remain here ten or twelve days; if I have reason to believe that my attendance at Philadelphia will not be mere waste of time, I shall after that period rejoin the Convention.

I remain with sincere esteem Dr Sir Yr. Obed serv

A HAMILTON

July 3d. 87

## *Conjectures About the New Constitution*

The new constitution has in favour of its success these circumstances—a very great weight of influence of the persons who framed it, particularly in the universal popularity of General Washington—the good will of the commercial interest throughout the states which will give all its efforts to the establishment of a government capable of regulating protecting and extending the commerce of the Union—the good will of most men of property in the several states who wish a government of the union able to protect them against domestic violence and the depredations which the democratic spirit is apt to make on property; and who are besides anxious for the respectability of the nation—the hopes of the Creditors of the United States that a general government possessing the means of doing it will pay the debt of the Union—a strong belief in the people at large of the insufficiency of the present confederation to preserve the existence of the Union and of the necessity of the union to their safety and prosperity; of course a strong desire of a change and a predisposition to receive well the propositions of the Convention.

Against its success is to be put the dissent of two or three important men in the Convention; who will think their characters pleged to defeat the plan—the influence of many *inconsiderable* men in possession of considerable offices under the state governments who will fear a diminution of their consequence, power and emolument by the establishment of the general government and who can hope for nothing there—the influence of some *considerable* men in office possessed of talents and popularity who partly from the same motives and partly from a desire of *playing a part* in a convulsion for their own aggrandisement will oppose the quiet adoption of the new government—(some considerable men out of office, from motives of ambition may be disposed to act the same part)—add to these causes the disinclination of the people to taxes, and of course to a strong government—the opposition of all men much in debt who will not wish to see a government established one object of which is to restrain the means of cheating Creditors—the democratical jealousy of the people which may be alarmed at the appearance of institutions that may seem calculated to place the power of the community in few hands and to raise a few individuals to stations of great preeminence—and the influence of some foreign powers who from different motives will not wish to see an energetic government established throughout the states.

In this view of the subject it is difficult to form any judgment whether the plan will be adopted or rejected. It must be essentially a matter of conjecture. The present appearances and all other circumstances considered the probability seems to be on the side of its adoption.

But the causes operating against its adoption are powerful and there will be nothing astonishing in the Contrary.

If it do not finally obtain, it is probable the discussion of the question will beget such struggles animosities and heats in the community that this circumstance conspiring with the *real necessity* of an essential change in our present situation will produce civil war. Should this happen, whatever parties prevail it is probable governments very different from the present in their principles will be established. A dismemberment of the Union and monarchies in different portions of it may be expected. It may however happen that no civil war will take place; but several republican confederacies be established between different combinations of the particular states.

A reunion with Great Britain, from universal disgust at a state of commotion, is not impossible, though not much to be feared. The most plausible shape of such a business would be the establishment of a son of the present monarch in the supreme government of this country with a family compact.

If the government be adopted, it is probable general Washington will be the President of the United States. This will insure a wise choice of men to administer the government and a good administration. A good administration will conciliate the confidence and affection of the people and perhaps enable the government to acquire more consistency than the proposed constitution seems to promise for so great a Country. It may then triumph altogether over the state governments and reduce them to an intire subordination, dividing the larger states into smaller districts. The *organs* of the general government may also acquire additional strength.

If this should not be the case, in the course of a few years, it is probable that the contests about the boundaries of power between the particular governments and the general government and the *momentum* of the larger states in such contests will produce a dissolution of the Union. This after all seems to be the most likely result.

But it is almost arrogance in so complicated a subject, depending so intirely on the incalculable fluctuations of the human passions, to attempt even a conjecture about the event.

It will be Eight or Nine months before any certain judgment can be formed respecting the adoption of the Plan.

*c. late September 1787*

## *The Federalist No. 1*

To the People of the State of New York.

After an unequivocal experience of the inefficacy of the subsisting Fœderal Government, you are called upon to deliberate on a new Constitution for the United States of America. The subject speaks its own importance; comprehending in its consequences, nothing less than the existence of the UNION, the safety and welfare of the parts of which it is composed, the fate of an empire, in many respects, the most interesting the world. It has been frequently remarked, that it seems to have been reserved to the people of this country, by their conduct and example, to decide the important question, whether societies of men are really capable or not, of establishing good government from reflection and choice, or whether they are forever destined to depend, for their political constitutions, on accident and force. If there be any truth in the remark, the crisis, at which we are arrived, may with propriety be regarded as the æra in which that decision is to be made; and a wrong election of the part we shall act, may, in this view, deserve to be considered as the general misfortune of mankind.

This idea will add the inducements of philanthropy to those of patriotism to heighten the sollicitude, which all considerate and good men must feel for the event. Happy will it be if our choice should be directed by a judicous estimate of our true interests, unperplexed and unbiassed by considerations not connected with the public good. But this is a thing more ardently to be wished, than seriously to be expected. The plan offered to our deliberations, affects too many particular interests, innovates upon too many local institutions, not to involve in its discussion a variety of objects foreign to its merits, and of views, passions and prejudices little favourable to the discovery of truth.

Among the most formidable of the obstacles which the new Constitution will have to encounter, may readily be distinguished the obvious interest of a certain class of men in every State to resist all changes which may hazard a diminution of the power, emolument and consequence of the offices they hold under the State-establishments— and the perverted ambition of another class of men, who will either hope to aggrandise themselves by the confusions of their country, or will flatter themselves with fairer prospects of elevation from the subdivision of the empire into several partial confederacies, than from its union under one government.

It is not, however, my design to dwell upon observations of this nature. I am well aware that it would be disingenuous to resolve indiscriminately the opposition of any set of men (merely because their situations might subject them to suspicion) into interested or ambitious views: Candour will oblige us to admit, that even such men may be actuated by upright intentions; and it cannot be doubted, that much of the opposition which has made its appearance, or may hereafter make its appearance, will spring from sources, blameless at least, if not respectable, the honest errors of minds led astray by preconceived jealousies and fears. So numerous indeed and so powerful are the causes, which serve to give a false bias to the judgment, that we upon many occasions, see wise and good men on the wrong as well as on the right side of questions, of the first magnitude to society. This circumstance, if duly attended to, would furnish a lesson of moderation of those, who are ever so much persuaded of their being in the right, in any controversy. And a further reason for caution, in this respect, might be drawn from the reflection, that we are not always sure, that those who advocate the truth are influenced by purer principles than their antagonists. Ambition, avarice, personal animosity, party opposition, and many other motives, not more laudable than these, are apt to operate as well upon those who support as upon those who oppose the right side of a question. Were there not even these inducements to moderation, nothing could be more illjudged than that intolerant spirit, which has, at all times, characterised political parties. For, in politics as in religion, it is equally absurd to aim at making proselytes by fire and sword. Heresies in either can rarely be cured by persecution.

And yet however just these sentiments will be allowed to be, we have already sufficient indications, that it will happen in this as in all former cases of great national discussion. A torrent of angry and malignant passions will be let loose. To judge from the conduct of the opposite parties, we shall be led to conclude, that they will mutually hope to evince the justness of their opinions, and to increase the number of their converts by the loudness of their declamations, and by the bitterness of their invectives. An enlightened zeal for the energy and efficiency of government will be stigmatised, as the off-spring of a temper fond of despotic power and hostile to the principles of liberty. An overscrupulous jealousy of danger to the rights of the people, which is more commonly the fault of the head than of the heart, will be represented as mere pretence and artifice; the bait for popularity at the expence of public good. It will be forgotten, on the one hand, that jealousy is the usual concomitant of violent love, and that the noble enthusiasm of liberty is too apt to be infected with a spirit of narrow and illiberal distrust. On the other hand, it will be equally forgotten, that the vigour of government is essential to the security of liberty; that, in the contemplation of a sound and well informed judgment, their interest can never be separated; and that a dangerous ambition more often lurks behind the specious mask of zeal for the rights of the people, than under the forbidding appearance of zeal for the firmness and efficiency of government. History will teach us, that the former has been found a much more certain road to the introduction of despotism, than the latter, and that of those men who have overturned the liberties of republics the greatest number have begun their carreer, by paying an obsequious court to the people, commencing Demagogues and ending Tyrants.

In the course of the preceeding observations I have had an eye, my Fellow Citizens, to putting you upon your guard against all attempts, from whatever quarter, to influence your decision in a matter of the utmost moment to your welfare by any impressions other than those which may result from the evidence of truth. You will, no doubt, at the same time, have collected from the general scope of them that they proceed from a source not unfriendly to the new Constitution. Yes, my Countrymen, I own to you, that, after having given it an attentive consideration, I am clearly of opinion, it is your interest to adopt it. I am convinced, that this is the safest course for your liberty, your dignity, and your happiness. I effect not reserves, which I do not feel. I will not amuse you with an appearance of deliberation, when I have decided. I frankly acknowledge to you my convictions, and I will freely lay before you the reasons on which they are founded. The consciousness of good intentions disdains ambiguity. I shall not however multiply professions on this head. My motives must remain in the depository of my own breast: My arguments will be open to all, and may be judged of by all. They shall at least be offered in a spirit, which will not disgrace the cause of truth.

I propose in a series of papers to discuss the following interesting particulars—*The utility of the UNION to your political prosperity—The insufficiency of the present Confederation to preserve that Union—The necessity of a government at least equally energetic with the one proposed to the attainment of this object—The conformity of the proposed constitution to the true principles of republican government—Its analogy to your own state constitution*—and lastly, *The additional security, which its adoption will afford to the preservation of that species of government, to liberty and to property.*

In the progress of this discussion I shall endeavour to give a satisfactory answer to all the objections which shall have made their appearance that may seem to have any claim to your attention.

It may perhaps be thought superfluous to offer arguments to prove the utility of the UNION, a point, no doubt, deeply engraved on the hearts of the great body of the people in every state, and one, which it may be imagined has no adversaries. But the fact is, that we already hear it whispered in the private circles of those who oppose the new constitution, that the Thirteen States are of too great extent for any general system, and that we must of necessity resort to separate confederacies of distinct portions of the whole.* This doctrine will, in all probability, be gradually propagated, till it has votaries enough to countenance an open avowal of it. For nothing can be more evident, to those who are able to take an enlarged view of the subject than the alternative of an adoption of the new Constitution, or a dismemberment of the Union. It will therefore be of use to begin by examining the advantages of that Union, the certain evils and the probable dangers, to which every State will be exposed from its dissolution. This shall accordingly constitute the subject of my next address.

PUBLIUS.

*The Independent Journal, October 27, 1787*

## The Federalist No. 15

TO THE PEOPLE OF THE STATE OF NEW-YORK.

In the course of the preceding papers, I have endeavoured, my Fellow Citizens, to place before you in a clear and convincing light, the importance of Union to your political safety and happiness. I have unfolded to you a complication of dangers to which you would be exposed should you permit that sacred knot which binds the people of America together to be severed or dissolved by ambition or by avarice, by jealousy or by misrepresentation. In the sequel of the inquiry, through which I propose to accompany you, the truths intended to be inculcated will receive further confirmation from facts and arguments hitherto unnoticed. If the road, over which you will still have to pass, should in some places appear to you tedious or irksome, you will recollect, that you are in quest of information on a subject the most momentous which can engage the attention of a free people: that the field through which you have to travel is in itself spacious, and that the difficulties of the journey have been unnecessarily increased by the mazes with which sophistry has beset the way. It will be my aim to

* The same idea, tracing the arguments to their consequences, is held out in several of the late publications against the New Constitution.

remove the obstacles to your progress in as compendious a manner, as it can be done, without sacrificing utility to dispatch.

In pursuance of the plan, which I have laid down for the discussion of the subject, the point next in order to be examined is the "insufficiency of the present confederation to the preservation of the Union." It may perhaps be asked, what need is there of reasoning or proof to illustrate a position, which is not either controverted or doubted; to which the understandings and feelings of all classes of men assent; and which in substance is admitted by the opponents as well as by the friends of the New Constitution? It must in truth be acknowledged that however these may differ in other respects, they in general appear to harmonise in this sentiment at least, that there are material imperfections in our national system, and that something is necessary to be done to rescue us from impending anarchy. The facts that support this opinion are no longer objects of speculation. They have forced themselves upon the sensibility of the people at large, and have at length extorted from those, whose mistaken policy has had the principal share in precipitating the extremity, at which we are arrived, a reluctant confession of the reality of those defects in the scheme of our Fœderal Government, which have been long pointed out and regretted by the intelligent friends of the Union.

We may indeed with propriety be said to have reached almost the last stage of national humiliation. There is scarcely any thing that can wound the pride, or degrade the character of an independent nation, which we do not experience. Are there engagements to the performance of which we are held by every tie respectable among men? These are the subjects of constant and unblushing violation. Do we owe debts to foreigners and to our own citizens contracted in a time of imminent peril, for the preservation of our political existence? These remain without any proper or satisfactory provision for their discharge. Have we valuable territories and important posts in the possession of a foreign power, which by express stipulations ought long since to have been surrendered? These are still retained, to the prejudice of our interests not less than of our rights. Are we in a condition to resent, or to repel the aggression? We have neither troops nor treasury nor government.* Are we even in a condition to remonstrate with dignity? The just imputations on our own faith, in respect to the same treaty,

* I mean for the Union.

ought first to be removed. Are we entitled by nature and compact to a free participation in the navigation of the Mississippi? Spain excludes us from it. Is public credit an indispensable resource in time of public danger? We seem to have abandoned its cause as desperate and irretrievable. Is commerce of importance to national wealth? Ours is at the lowest point of declension. Is respectability in the eyes of foreign powers a safe guard against foreign encroachments? The imbecility of our Government even forbids them to treat with us: Our ambassadors abroad are the mere pageants of mimic sovereignty. Is a violent and unnatural decrease in the value of land a symptom of national distress? The price of improved land in most parts of the country is much lower than can be accounted for by the quantity of waste land at market, and can only be fully explained by that want of private and public confidence, which are so alarmingly prevalent among all ranks and which have a direct tendency to depreciate property of every kind. Is private credit the friend and patron of industry? That most useful kind which relates to borrowing and lending is reduced within the narrowest limits, and this still more from an opinion of insecurity than from the scarcity of money. To shorten an enumeration of particulars which can afford neither pleasure nor instruction it may in general be demanded, what indication is there of national disorder, poverty and insignificance that could befal a community so peculiarly blessed with natural advantages as we are, which does not form a part of the dark catalogue of our public misfortunes?

This is the melancholy situation, to which we have been brought by those very maxims and councils, which would now deter us from adopting the proposed constitution; and which not content with having conducted us to the brink of a precipice, seem resolved to plunge us into the abyss, that awaits us below. Here, my Countrymen, impelled by every motive that ought to influence an enlightened people, let us make a firm stand for our safety, our tranquillity, our dignity, our reputation. Let us at last break the fatal charm which has too long seduced us from the paths of felicity and prosperity.

It is true, as has been before observed, that facts too stubborn to be resisted have produced a species of general assent to the abstract proposition that there exist material defects in our national system; but the usefulness of the concession, on the part of the old adversaries of fœderal measures, is destroyed by a strenuous opposition to a remedy, upon the only principles, that can give it a chance of success. While they admit that the Government of the United States is destitute of energy; they contend against conferring upon it those powers which are requisite to supply that energy: They seem still to aim at things repugnant and irreconcilable—at an augmentation of Fœderal authority without a diminution of State authority—at sovereignty in the Union and complete independence in the members. They still in fine seem to cherish with blind devotion the political monster of an *imperium in imperio*. This renders a full display of the principal defects of the confederation necessary, in order to shew, that the evils we experience do not proceed from minute or partial imperfections, but from fundamental errors in the structure of the building which cannot be amended otherwise than by an alteration in the first principles and main pillars of the fabric.

The great and radical vice in the construction of the existing Confederation is in the principle of LEGISLATION for STATES or GOVERNMENTS, in their CORPORATE or COLLECTIVE CAPACITIES and as contradistinguished from the INDIVIDUALS of whom they consist. Though this principle does not run through all the powers delegated to the Union; yet it pervades and governs those, on which the efficacy of the rest depends. Except as to the rule of apportionment, the United States have an indefinite discretion to make requisitions for men and money; but they have no authority to raise either by regulations extending to the individual citizens of America. The consequence of this is, that though in theory their resolutions concerning those objects are laws, constitutionally binding on the members of the Union, yet in practice they are mere recommendations, which the States observe or disregard at their option.

It is a singular instance of the capriciousness of the human mind, that after all the admonitions we have had from experience on this head, there should still be found men, who object to the New Constitution for deviating from a principle which has been found the bane of the old; and which is in itself evidently incompatible with the idea of GOVERNMENT; a principle in short which if it is to be executed at all must substitute the violent and sanguinary agency of the sword to the mild influence of the Magistracy.

There is nothing absurd or impracticable in the idea of a league or alliance between independent nations, for certain defined purposes precisely stated in a treaty; regulating all the details of time, place, circumstance and quantity; leaving nothing to future discretion; and depending for its execution on the good faith of the parties. Compacts of this kind exist among all civilized nations subject to the usual vicissitudes of peace and war, of observance and non observance, as the interests or passions of the contracting powers dictate. In the early part of the present century, there was an epidemical rage in Europe for this species of compacts; from which the politicians of the times fondly hoped for benefits which were never realised. With a view to establishing the equilibrium of power and the peace of that part of the world, all the resources of negotiation were exhausted, and triple and quadruple alliances were formed; but they were scarcely formed before they were broken, giving an instructive but afflicting lesson to mankind how little dependence is to be placed on treaties which have no other sanction than the obligations of good faith; and which oppose general considerations of peace and justice to the impulse of any immediate interest and passion.

If the particular States in this country are disposed to stand in a similar relation to each other, and to drop the project of a general DISCRETIONARY SUPERINTENDENCE, the scheme would indeed be pernicious, and would entail upon us all the mischiefs that have been enumerated under the first head; but it would have the merit of being at least consistent and practicable. Abandoning all views towards a confederate Government, this would bring us to a simple alliance offensive and defensive; and would place us in a situation to be alternately friends and enemies of each other as our mutual jealousies and rivalships nourished by the intrigues of foreign nations should prescribe to us.

But if we are unwilling to be placed in this perilous situation; if we will still adhere to the design of a national government, or which is the same thing of a superintending power under the direction of a common Council, we must resolve to incorporate into our plan those ingredients which may be considered as forming the characteristic difference between a league and a government; we must extend the authority of the union to the persons of the citizens,—the only proper objects of government.

Government implies the power of making laws. It is essential to the idea of a law, that it be attended with a sanction; or, in other words, a penalty or punishment for disobedience. If there be no penalty annexed to disobedience, the resolutions or commands which pretend to be laws will in fact amount to nothing more than advice or recommendation. This penalty, whatever it may be, can only be inflicted in two ways; by the agency of the Courts and Ministers of Justice, or by military force; by the COERTION of the magistracy, or by the COERTION of arms. The first kind can evidently apply only to men—the last kind must of necessity be employed against bodies politic, or communities or States. It is evident, that there is no process of a court by which their observance of the laws can in the last resort be enforced. Sentences may be denounced against them for violations of their duty; but these sentences can only be carried into execution by the sword. In an association where the general authority is confined to the collective bodies of the communities that compose it, every breach of the laws must involve a state of war, and military execution must become the only instrument of civil obedience. Such a state of things can certainly not deserve the name of government, nor would any prudent man choose to commit his happiness to it.

There was a time when we were told that breaches, by the States, of the regulations of the fœderal authority were not to be expected— that a sense of common interest would preside over the conduct of the respective members, and would beget a full compliance with all the constitutional requisitions of the Union. This language at the present day would appear as wild as a great part of what we now hear from the same quarter will be thought, when we shall have received further lessons from that best oracle of wisdom, experience. It at all times betrayed an ignorance of the true springs by which human conduct is actuated, and belied the original inducements to the establishment of civil power. Why has government been instituted at all? Because the passions of men will not conform to the dictates of reason and justice, without constraint. Has it been found that bodies of men act with more rectitude or greater disinterestedness than individuals? The contrary of this has been inferred by all accurate observers of the conduct of mankind; and the inference is founded upon obvious reasons. Regard to reputation has a less active influence, when the infamy of a bad action is to be divided among a number, than when it is to fall singly upon one. A spirit of faction which is apt to mingle its poison in the deliberations of all bodies of men, will often hurry the persons of whom they are composed into improprieties and excesses, for which they would blush in a private capacity.

In addition to all this, there is in the nature of sovereign power an impatience of controul, that disposes those who are invested with the exercise of it, to look with an evil eye upon all external attempts to restrain or direct its operations. From this spirit it happens that in every political association which is formed upon the principle of uniting in a common interest a number of lesser sovereignties, there will be found a kind of excentric tendency in the subordinate or inferior orbs, by the operation of which there will be a perpetual effort in each to fly off from the common center. This tendency is not difficult to be accounted for. It has its origin in the love of power. Power controuled or abridged is almost always the rival and enemy of that power by which it is controuled or abriged. This simple proposition will teach us how little reason there is to expect, that the persons, entrusted with the administration of the affairs of the particular members of a confederacy, will at all times be ready, with perfect good humour, and an unbiassed regard to the public weal, to execute the resolutions or decrees of the general authority. The reverse of this results from the constitution of human nature.

If therefore the measures of the confederacy cannot be executed, without the intervention of the particular administrations, there will be little prospect of their being executed at all. The rulers of the respective members, whether they have a constitutional right to do it or not, will undertake to judge of the propriety of the measures themselves. They will consider the conformity of the thing proposed or required to their immediate interests or aims, the momentary conveniences or inconveniences that would attend its adoption. All this will be done, and in a spirit of interested and suspicious scrutiny, without that knowledge of national circumstances and reasons of state, which is essential to a right judgment, and with that strong predilection in favour of local objects, which can hardly fail to mislead the decision. The same process must be repeated in every member of which the body is constituted; and the execution of the plans, framed by the councils of the whole, will always fluctuate on the discretion of the ill-informed and prejudiced opinion of every part. Those who have been conversant in the proceedings of popular assemblies; who have seen how difficult it often is, when there is no exterior pressure of circumstances, to bring them to harmonious resolutions on important points, will readily conceive how impossible it must be to induce a number of such assemblies, deliberating at a distance from each other, at different times, and under different impressions, long to cooperate in the same views and pursuits.

In our case, the concurrence of thirteen distinct sovereign wills is requisite under the confederation to the complete execution of every important measure, that proceeds from the Union. It has happened as was to have been foreseen. The measures of the Union have not been executed; and the delinquencies of the States have step by step matured themselves to an extreme; which has at length arrested all the wheels of the national government, and brought them to an awful stand. Congress at this time scarcely possess the means of keeping up the forms of administration; 'till the States can have time to agree upon a more substantial substitute for the present shadow of a fœderal government. Things did not come to this desperate extremity at once. The causes which have been specified produced at first only unequal and disproportionate degrees of compliance with the requisitions of the Union. The greater deficiencies of some States furnished the pretext of example and the temptation of interest to the complying, or to the least delinquent States. Why should we do more in proportion than those who are embarked with us in the same political voyage? Why should we consent to bear more than our proper share of the common burthen? These were suggestions which human selfishness could not withstand, and which even speculative men, who looked forward to remote consequences, could not, without hesitation, combat. Each State yielding to the persuasive voice of immediate interest and convenience has successively withdrawn its support, 'till the frail and tottering edifice seems ready to fall upon our heads and to crush us beneath its ruins.

PUBLIUS.

*The Independent Journal, December 1, 1787*

## The Federalist No. 35

To the People of the State of New-York.

Before we proceed to examine any other objections to an indefinite power of taxation in the Union, I shall make one general remark; which is, that if the jurisdiction of the national government in the article of revenue should be restricted to particular objects, it would naturally occasion an undue proportion of the public burthens to fall upon those objects. Two evils would spring from this source, the oppression of particular branches of industry, and an unequal distribution of the taxes, as well among the several States as among the citizens of the same State.

Suppose, as has been contended for, the fœderal power of taxation were to be confined to duties on imports, it is evident that the government, for want of being able to command other resources, would frequently be tempted to extend these duties to an injurious excess. There are persons who imagine that this can never be carried to too great a length; since the higher they are, the more it is alleged they will tend to discourage an extravagant consumption, to produce a favourable balance of trade, and to promote domestic manufactures. But all extremes are pernicious in various ways. Exorbitant duties on imported articles would beget a general spirit of smuggling; which is always prejudicial to the fair trader, and eventually to the revenue itself: They tend to render other classes of the community tributary in an improper degree to the manufacturing classes to whom they give a premature monopoly of the markets: They sometimes force industry out of its more natural channels into others in which it flows with less advantage. And in the last place they oppress the merchant, who is often obliged to pay them himself without any retribution from the consumer. When the demand is equal to the quantity of goods at market, the consumer generally pays the duty; but when the markets happen to be overstocked, a great proportion falls upon the merchant, and sometimes not only exhausts his profits, but breaks in upon his capital. I am apt to think that a division of the duty between the seller and the buyer more often happens than is commonly imagined. It is not always possible to raise the price of a commodity, in exact proportion to every additional imposition laid upon it. The merchant especially, in a country of small commercial capital, is often under a necessity of keeping prices down, in order to a more expeditious sale.

The maxim that the consumer is the payer, is so much oftener true than the reverse of the proposition, that it is far more equitable the duties on imports should go into a common stock, than that they should redound to the exclusive benefit of the importing States. But it is not so generally true as to render it equitable that those duties should form the only national fund. When they are paid by the merchant, they operate as an additional tax upon the importing State; whose citizens pay their proportion of them in the character of consumers. In this view they are productive of inequality among the States; which inequality would be encreased with the encreased extent of the duties. The confinement of the national revenues to this species of imposts, would be attended with inequality, from a different cause between the manufacturing and the non-manufacturing States. The States which can go furthest towards the supply of their own wants, by their own manufactures, will not, according to their numbers of wealth, consume so great a proportion of imported articles, as those States which are not in the same favourable situation; they would not therefore in this mode alone contribute to the public treasury in a ratio to their abilities. To make them do this, it is necessary that recourse be had to excises; the proper objects of which are particular kinds of manufactures. New-York is more deeply interested in these considerations than such of her citizens as contend for limiting the power of the Union to external taxation can be aware of—New-York is an importing State, and is not likely speedily to be to any great extent a manufacturing State. She would of course suffer in a double light from restraining the jurisdiction of the Union to commercial imposts.

So far as these observations tend to inculcate a danger of the import duties being extended to an injurious extreme it may be observed, conformably to a remark made in another part of these papers, that the interest of the revenue itself would be a sufficient guard against such an extreme. I readily admit that this would be the case as long as other resources were open; but if the avenues to them were closed HOPE stimulated by necessity would beget experiments fortified by rigorous precautions and additional penalties; which for a time would have the intended effect, till there had been leisure to contrive expedients to elude these new precautions. The first success would be apt to inspire false opinions; which it might require a long course of subsequent experience to correct. Necessity, especially in politics, often occasions false hopes, false reasonings and a system of measures, correspondently erroneous. But even if this supposed excess should not be a consequence of the limitation of the fœderal power of taxation the inequalities spoken of would still ensue, though not in the same degree, from the other causes that have been noticed. Let us now return to the examination of objections—

One, which if we may judge from the frequency of its repetition seems most to be relied on, is that the house of representatives is not sufficiently numerous for the reception of all the different classes of citizens; in order to combine the interests and feelings of every part of the community, and to produce a due sympathy between the representative body and its constituents. This argument presents itself under a very specious and seducing form; and is well calculated to lay hold of the prejudices to those to whom it is addressed. But when we come to dissect it with attention it will appear to be made up of nothing but fair sounding words. The object it seems to aim at is in the first place impracticable, and in the sense in which it is contended for is unnecessary. I reserve for another place the discussion of the question which relates to the sufficiency of the representative body in respect to numbers; and shall content myself with examining here the particular use which has been made of a contrary supposition in reference to the immediate subject of our inquiries.

The idea of an actual representation of all classes of the people by persons of each class is altogether visionary. Unless it were expressly provided in the Constitution that each different occupation should send one or more members the thing would never take place in practice. Mechanics and manufacturers will always be inclined with few exceptions to give their votes to merchants in preference to persons of their own professions or trades. Those discerning citizens are well aware that the mechanic and manufacturing arts furnish the materials of mercantile enterprise and industry. Many of them indeed are immediately connected with the operations of commerce. They know that the merchant is their natural patron and friend; and they are aware that however great the confidence they may justly feel in their own good sense, their interests can be more effectually promoted by the merchant than by themselves. They are sensible that their habits in life have not been such as to give them those acquired endowments, without which in a deliberative assembly the greatest natural abilities are for the most part useless; and that the influence and weight and superior acquirements of the merchants render them more equal to a contest with any spirit which might happen to infuse itself into the public councils unfriendly to the manufacturing and trading interests. These considerations and many others that might be mentioned prove, and experience confirms it, that artisans and manufacturers will commonly be disposed to bestow their votes upon merchants and those whom they recommend. We must therefore consider merchants as the natural representatives of all these classes of the community.

With regard to the learned professions, little need be observed; they truly form no distinct interest in society; and according to their situation and talents will be indiscriminately the objects of the confidence and choice of each other and of other parts of the community.

Nothing remains but the landed interest; and this in a political view and particularly in relation to taxes I take to be perfectly united from the wealthiest landlord to the poorest tenant. No tax can be laid on land which will not affect the proprietor of millions of acres as well as the proprietor of a single acre. Every land-holder will therefore have a common interest to keep the taxes on land as low as possible; and common interest may always be reckoned upon as the surest bond of sympathy. But if we even could suppose a distinction of interest between the opulent land-holder and the middling farmer, what reason is there to conclude that the first would stand a better chance of being deputed to the national legislature than the last? If we take fact as our guide and look into our own senate and assembly we shall find that moderate proprietors of land prevail in both; nor is this less the case in the senate which consists of a smaller number than in the Assembly, which is composed of a greater number. Where the qualifications of the electors are the same, whether they have to choose a small or a large number their votes will fall upon those in whom they have most confidence; whether these happen to be men of large fortunes or of moderate property or of no property at all.

It is said to be necessary that all classes of citizens should have some of their own number in the representative body, in order that their feelings and interests may be the better understood and attended to. But we have seen that this will never happen under any arrangement that leaves the votes of the people free. Where this is the case, the representative body, with too few exceptions to have any influence on the spirit of the government, will be composed of land-holders, merchants, and men of the learned professions. But where is the danger that the interests and feelings of the different classes of citizens will not be understood or attended to by these three descriptions of men? Will not the land-holder know and feel whatever will promote or injure the interests of landed property? and will he not from his own interest in that species of property be sufficiently prone to resist every attempt to prejudice or incumber it? Will not the merchant understand and be disposed to cultivate as far as may be proper the interests of the mechanic and manufacturing arts to which his commerce is so nearly allied? Will not the man of the learned profession, who will feel a neutrality to the rivalships between the different branches of industry, be likely to prove an impartial arbiter between them, ready to promote either, so far as it shall appear to him conducive to the general interests of the society?

If we take into the account the momentary humors or dispositions which may happen to prevail in particular parts of the society, and to which a wise administration will never be inattentive, is the man whose situation leads to extensive inquiry and information less likely to be a competent judge of their nature, extent and foundation than one whose observation does not travel beyond the circle of his neighbours and acquaintances? Is it not natural that a man who is a candidate for the favour of the people and who is dependent on the suffrages of his fellow-citizens for the continuance of his public honors should take care to inform himself of their dispositions and inclinations and should be willing to allow them their proper degree of influence upon his conduct. This dependence, and the necessity of being bound himself and his posterity by the laws to which he gives his assent are the true, and they are the strong chords of sympathy between the representatives and the constituent.

There is no part of the administration of government that requires extensive information and a thorough knowledge of the principles of political economy so much as the business of taxation. The man who understands those principles best will be least likely to resort to oppressive expedients, or to sacrifice any particular class of citizens to the procurement of revenue. It might be demonstrated that the most productive system of finance will always be the least burthensome. There can be no doubt that in order to a judicious exercise of the power of taxation it is necessary that the person in whose hands it is should be acquainted with the general genius, habits and modes of thinking of the people at large and with the resources of the country. And this is all that can be reasonably meant by a knowledge of the interests and feelings of the people. In any other sense the proposition has either no meaning, or an absurd one. And in that sense let every considerate citizen judge for himself where the requisite qualification is most likely to be found.

PUBLIUS.

*The Independent Journal, January 5, 1788*

## The Federalist No. 70

To the People of the State of New-York.

There is an idea, which is not without its advocates, that a vigorous executive is inconsistent with the genius of republican government. The enlightened well wishers to this species of government must at least hope that the supposition is destitute of foundation; since they can never admit its truth, without at the same time admitting the condemnation of their own principles. Energy in the executive is a leading character in the definition of good government. It is essential to the protection of the community against foreign attacks: It is not less essential to the steady administration of the laws, to the protection of property against those irregular and high handed combinations, which sometimes interrupt the ordinary course of justice to the security of liberty against the enterprises and assaults of ambition, of faction and of anarchy. Every man the least conversant in Roman story knows how often that republic was obliged to take refuge in the absolute power of a single man, under the formidable title of dictator, as well against the intrigues of ambitious individuals, who aspired to the tyranny, and the seditions of whole classes of the community, whose conduct threatened the existence of all government, as against the invasions of external enemies, who menaced the conquest and destruction of Rome.

There can be no need however to multiply arguments or examples on this head. A feeble executive implies a feeble execution of the government. A feeble execution is but another phrase for a bad execution: And a government ill executed, whatever it may be in theory, must be in practice a bad government.

Taking it for granted, therefore, that all men of sense will agree in the necessity of an energetic executive; it will only remain to inquire, what are the ingredients which constitute this energy—how far can they be combined with those other ingredients which constitute safety in the republican sense? And how far does this combination characterise the plan, which has been reported by the convention?

The ingredients, which constitute energy in the executive, are first unity, secondly duration, thirdly an adequate provision for its support, fourthly competent powers.

The circumstances which constitute safety in the republican sense are, Ist. a due dependence on the people, secondly a due responsibility.

Those politicians and statesmen, who have been the most celebrated for the soundness of their principles, and for the justness of their views, have declared in favor of a single executive and a numerous legislature. They have with great propriety considered energy as the most necessary qualification of the former, and have regarded this as most applicable to power in a single hand; while they have with equal propriety considered the latter as best adapted to deliberation and wisdom, and best calculated to conciliate the confidence of the people and to secure their privileges and interests.

That unity is conducive to energy will not be disputed. Decision, activity, secrecy, and dispatch will generally characterise the proceedings of one man, in a much more eminent degree, than the proceedings of any greater number; and in proportion as the number is increased, these qualities will be diminished.

This unity may be destroyed in two ways; either by vesting the power in two or more magistrates of equal dignity and authority; or by vesting it ostensibly in one man, subject in whole or in part to the controul and co-operation of others, in the capacity of counsellors to him. Of the first the two consuls of Rome may serve as an example; of the last we shall find examples in the constitutions of several of the states. New-York and New-Jersey, if I recollect right, are the only states, which have entrusted the executive authority wholly to single men.* Both these methods of destroying the unity of the executive have their partisans; but the votaries of an executive council are the most

---

* New-York has no council except for the single purpose of appointing to offices; New-Jersey has a council, whom the governor may consult. But I think from the terms of the constitution their resolutions do not bind him.

numerous. They are both liable, if not to equal, to similar objections; and may in most lights be examined in conjunction.

The experience of other nations will afford little instruction on this head. As far however as it teaches any thing, it teaches us not to be inamoured of plurality in the executive. We have seen that the Achæans on an experiment of two Præetors, were induced to abolish one. The Roman history records many instances of mischiefs to the republic from the dissentions between the consuls, and between the military tribunes, who were at times substituted to the consuls. But it gives us no specimens of any peculiar advantages derived to the state, from the circumstance of the plurality of those magistrates. That the dissentions between them were not more frequent, or more fatal, is matter of astonishment; until we advert to the singular position in which the republic was almost continually placed and to the prudent policy pointed out by the circumstances of the state, and pursued by the consuls, of making a division of the government between them. The Patricians engaged in a perpetual struggle with the Plebeians for the preservation of their antient authorities and dignities; the consuls, who were generally chosen out of the former body, were commonly united by the personal interest they had in the defence of the privileges of their order. In addition to this motive of union, after the arms of the republic had considerably expanded the bounds of its empire, it became an established custom with the consuls to divide the administration between themselves by lot; one of them remaining at Rome to govern the city and its environs; the other taking the command in the more distant provinces. This expedient must no doubt have had great influence in preventing those collisions and rivalships, which might otherwise have embroiled the peace of the republic.

But quitting the dim light of historical research, and attaching ourselves purely to the dictates of reason and good sense, we shall discover much greater cause to reject than to approve the idea of plurality in the executive, under any modification whatever.

Wherever two or more persons are engaged in any common enterprize or pursuit, there is always danger of difference of opinion. If it be a public trust or office in which they are cloathed with equal dignity and authority, there is peculiar danger of personal emulation and even animosity. From either and especially from all these causes, the most bitter dissentions are apt to spring. Whenever these happen, they lessen the respectability, weaken the authority, and distract the plans and operations of those whom they divide. If they should unfortunately assail the supreme executive magistracy of a country, consisting of a plurality of persons, they might impede or frustrate the most important measures of the government, in the most critical emergencies of the state. And what is still worse, they might split the community into the most violent and irreconcilable factions, adhering differently to the different individuals who composed the magistracy.

Men often oppose a thing merely because they have had no agency in planning it, or because it may have been planned by those whom they dislike. But if they have been consulted and have happened to disapprove, opposition then becomes in their estimation an indispensable duty of self love. They seem to think themselves bound in honor, and by all the motives of personal infallibility to defeat the success of what has been resolved upon, contrary to their sentiments. Men of upright, benevolent tempers have too many opportunities of remarking with horror, to what desperate lengths this disposition is sometimes carried, and how often the great interests of society are sacrificed to the vanity, to the conceit and to the obstinacy of individuals, who have credit enough to make their passions and their caprices interesting to mankind. Perhaps the question now before the public may in its consequences afford melancholy proofs of the effects of this despicable frailty, or rather detestable vice in the human character.

Upon the principles of a free government, inconveniencies from the source just mentioned must necessarily be submitted to in the formation of the legislature; but it is unnecessary and therefore unwise to introduce them into the constitution of the executive. It is here too that they may be most pernicious. In the legislature, promptitude of decision is oftener an evil than a benefit. The differences of opinion, and the jarrings of parties in that department of the government, though they may sometimes obstruct salutary plans, yet often promote deliberations and circumspection; and serve to check excesses in the majority. When a resolution too is once taken, the opposition must be at an end. That resolution is a law, and resistance to it punishable. But no favourable circumstances palliate or atone for the disadvantages of dissention in the executive department. Here they are pure and unmixed. There is no point at which they cease to operate. They serve to embarrass and weaken the execution of the plan or measure, to which they relate, from the first step to the final conclusion of it. They constantly counteract those qualities in the executive, which are the most necessary ingredients in its composition, vigour and expedition, and this without any counterballancing good. In the conduct of war, in which the energy of the executive is the bulwark of the national security, every thing would be to be apprehended from its plurality.

It must be confessed that these observations apply with principal weight to the first case supposed, that is to a plurality of magistrates of equal dignity and authority; a scheme the advocates for which are not likely to form a numerous sect: But they apply, though not with equal, yet with considerable weight, to the project of a council, whose concurrence is made constitutionally necessary to the operations of the ostensible executive. An artful cabal in that council would be able to distract and to enervate the whole system of administration. If no such cabal should exist, the mere diversity of views and opinions would alone be sufficient to tincture the exercise of the executive authority with a spirit of habitual feebleness and delatoriness.

But one of the weightiest objections to a plurality in the executive, and which lies as much against the last as the first plan, is that it tends to conceal faults, and destroy responsibility. Responsibility is of two kinds, to censure and to punishment. The first is the most important of the two; especially in an elective office. Man, in public trust, will much oftener act in such a manner as to render him unworthy of being any longer trusted, than in such a manner as to make him obnoxious to legal punishment. But the multiplication of the executive adds to the difficulty of detection in either case. It often becomes impossible, amidst mutual accusations, to determine on whom the blame or the punishment of a pernicious measure, or series of pernicious measures ought really to fall. It is shifted from one to another with so much dexterity, and under such plausible appearances, that the public opinion is left in suspense about the real author. The circumstances which may have led to any national miscarriage or misfortune are sometimes so complicated, that where there are a number of actors who may have had different degrees and kinds of agency, though we may clearly see upon the whole that there has been mismanagement, yet it may be impracticable to pronounce to whose account the evil which may have been incurred is truly chargeable.

"I was overruled by my council. The council were so divided in their opinions, that it was impossible to obtain any better resolution on the point." These and similar pretexts are constantly at hand, whether true or false. And who is there that will either take the trouble or incur the odium of a strict scrutiny into the secret springs of the transaction? Should there be found a citizen zealous enough to undertake the unpromising task, if there happen to be a collusion between the parties concerned, how easy is it to cloath the circumstances with so much ambiguity, as to render it uncertain what was the precise conduct of any of those parties?

In the single instance in which the governor of this state is coupled with a council, that is in the appointment to offices, we have seen the mischiefs of it in the view now under consideration. Scandalous appointments to important offices have been made. Some cases indeed have been so flagrant, that ALL PARTIES have agreed in the impropriety of the thing. When enquiry has been made, the blame has been laid by the governor on the members of the council; who on their part have charged it upon his nomination: While the people remain altogether at a loss to determine by whose influence their interests have been committed to hands so unqualified, and so manifestly improper. In tenderness to individuals, I forbear to descend to particulars.

It is evident from these considerations, that the plurality of the executive tends to deprive the people of the two greatest securities they can have for the faithful exercise of any delegated power; first, the restraints of public opinion, which lose their efficacy as well on account of the division of the censure attendant on bad measures among a number, as on account of the uncertainty on whom it ought to fall; and secondly, the opportunity of discovering with facility and clearness the misconduct of the persons they trust, in order either to their removal from office, or to their actual punishment, in cases which admit of it.

In England the king is a perpetual magistrate; and it is a maxim, which has obtained for the sake of the public peace, that he is unaccountable for his administration, and his person sacred. Nothing therefore can be wiser in that kingdom than to annex to the king a constitutional council, who may be responsible to the nation for the advice they give. Without this there would be no responsibility whatever in the executive department; an idea inadmissible in a free government. But even there the king is not bound by the resolutions of his council, though they are answerable for the advice they give. He is the absolute master of his own conduct, in the exercise of his office; and may observe or disregard the council given to him at his sole discretion.

But in a republic, where every magistrate ought to be personally responsible for his behaviour in office, the reason which in the British constitution dictates the propriety of a council not only ceases to apply, but turns against the institution. In the monarchy of Great-Britain, it furnishes a substitute for the prohibited responsibility of the chief magistrate; which serves in some degree as a hostage to the national justice for his good behaviour. In the American republic it would serve to destroy, or would greatly diminish the intended and necessary responsibility of the chief magistrate himself.

The idea of a council to the executive, which has so generally obtained in the state constitutions, has been derived from that maxim of republican jealousy, which considers power as safer in the hands of a number of men than of a single man. If the maxim should be admitted to be applicable to the case, I should contend that the advantage on that side would not counterballance the numerous disadvantages on the opposite side. But I do not think the rule at all applicable to the executive power. I clearly concur in opinion in this particular with a writer whom the celebrated Junius pronounces to be "deep, solid and ingenious," that, "the executive power is more easily confined when it is one:"* That it is far more safe there should be a single object for the jealousy and watchfulness of the people; and in a word that all multiplication of the executive is rather dangerous than friendly to liberty.

A little consideration will satisfy us, that the species of security sought for in the multiplication of the executive is unattainable. Numbers must be so great as to render combination difficult; or they are rather a source of danger than of security. The united credit and influence of several individuals must be more formidable to liberty than the credit and influence of either of them separately. When power therefore is placed in the hands of so small a number of men, as to admit of their interests and views being easily combined in a common enterprise, by an artful leader, it becomes more liable to abuse and more dangerous when abused, than if it be lodged in the hands of one man; who from the very circumstance of his being alone will be more narrowly watched and more readily suspected, and who cannot unite so great a mass of influence as when he is associated with others. The Decemvirs of Rome,

* De Lome.

whose name denotes their number,* were more to be dreaded in their usurpation than any ONE of them would have been. No person would think of proposing an executive much more numerous than that body, from six to a dozen have been suggested for the number of the council. The extreme of these numbers is not too great for an easy combination; and from such a combination America would have more to fear, than from the ambition of any single individual. A council to a magistrate, who is himself responsible for what he does, are generally nothing better than a clog upon his good intentions; are often the instruments and accomplices of his bad, and are almost always a cloak to his faults.

I forbear to dwell upon the subject of expence; though it be evident that if the council should be numerous enough to answer the principal end, aimed at by the institution, the salaries of the members, who must be drawn from their homes to reside at the seat of government, would form an item in the catalogue of public expenditures, too serious to be incurred for an object of equivocal utility.

I will only add, that prior to the appearance of the constitution, I rarely met with an intelligent man from any of the states, who did not admit as the result of experience, that the UNITY of the Executive of this state was one of the best of the distinguishing features of our constitution.

PUBLIUS.
*The Independent Journal, March 15, 1788*

## *To James Madison*

Some days since I wrote to you, My Dear Sir, inclosing a letter from a Mr. V Der Kemp &c.

I then mentioned to you that the question of a majority for or against the constitution would depend upon the County of Albany. By the latter accounts from that quarter I fear much that the issue there has been against us.

As Clinton is truly the leader of his party, and is inflexibly obstinate I count little on overcoming opposition by reason. Our only chances will be the previous ratification by nine states, which may shake the firmness of his followers; and a change in the sentiments of the people

* Ten.

which have been for some time travelling towards the constitution, though the first impressions made by every species of influence and artifice were too strong to be eradicated in time to give a decisive turn to the elections. We shall leave nothing undone to cultivate a favourable disposition in the citizens at large.

The language of the Antifœderalists is that if all the other states adopt, New York ought still to hold out. I have the most direct intelligence, but in a manner, which forbids a public use being made of it, that Clinton has in several conversations declared his opinion of the *inutility* of the UNION. Tis an unhappy reflection, that the friends to it should by quarrelling for straws among themselves promote the designs of its adversaries.

We think here that the situation of your state is critical. Let me know what you now think of it. I believe you meet nearly at the time we do. It will be of vast importance that an exact communication should be kept up between us at that period; and the moment *any decisive* question is taken, if favourable, I request you to dispatch an express to me with pointed orders to make all possible diligence, by changing horses &c. All expences shall be thankfully and liberally paid.

I executed your commands respecting the first vol of the Fœderalist. I sent 40 of the common copies & twelve of the finer ones addressed to the care of Governor Randolph. The Printer announces the second vol in a day or two, when an equal number of the two kinds shall also be forwarded. He informs that the Judicial department trial by jury bill of rights &c. is discussed in some additional papers which have not yet appeared in the Gazettes.

I remain with great sincerity & attachment

New York May 19. 1788

## *The Federalist No. 78*

To the People of the State of New-York.

We proceed now to an examination of the judiciary department of the proposed government.

In unfolding the defects of the existing confederation, the utility and necessity of a federal judicature have been clearly pointed out. It is the less necessary to recapitulate the considerations there urged; as the propriety of the institution in the abstract is not disputed: The only questions which have been raised being relative to the manner of constituting it, and to its extent. To these points therefore our observations shall be confined.

The manner of constituting it seems to embrace these several objects—1st. The mode of appointing the judges—2d. The tenure by which they are to hold their places—3d. The partition of the judiciary authority between different courts, and their relations to each other.

*First*. As to the mode of appointing the judges: This is the same with that of appointing the officers of the union in general, and has been so fully discussed in the two last numbers, that nothing can be said here which would not be useless repetition.

*Second*. As to the tenure by which the judges are to hold their places: This chiefly concerns their duration in office; the provisions for their support; and the precautions for their responsibility.

According to the plan of the convention, all the judges who may be appointed by the United States are to hold their offices *during good behaviour*, which is conformable to the most approved of the state constitutions; and among the rest, to that of this state. Its propriety having been drawn into question by the adversaries of that plan, is no light symptom of the rage for objection which disorders their imaginations and judgments. The standard of good behaviour for the continuance in office of the judicial magistracy is certainly one of the most valuable of the modern improvements in the practice of government. In a monarchy it is an excellent barrier to the despotism of the prince: In a republic it is a no less excellent barrier to the encroachments and oppressions of the representative body. And it is the best expedient which can be devised in any government, to secure a steady, upright and impartial administration of the laws.

Whoever attentively considers the different departments of power must perceive, that in a government in which they are separated from each other, the judiciary, from the nature of its functions, will always be the least dangerous to the political rights of the constitution; because it will be least in a capacity to annoy or injure them. The executive not only dispenses the honors, but holds the sword of the community. The legislature not only commands the purse, but prescribes the rules by which the duties and rights of every citizen are to be regulated. The judiciary on the contrary has no influence over either the sword or the purse, no direction either of the strength or of the wealth of the society, and can take no active resolution whatever. It may truly be said to have neither force nor will, but merely judgment; and must ultimately depend upon the aid of the executive arm even for the efficacy of its judgments.

This simple view of the matter suggests several important consequences. It proves incontestibly that the judiciary is beyond comparison the weakest of the three departments of power;* that it can never attack with success either of the other two; and that all possible care is requisite to enable it to defend itself against their attacks. It equally proves, that though individual oppression may now and then proceed from the courts of justice, the general liberty of the people can never be endangered from that quarter; I mean, so long as the judiciary remains truly distinct from both the legislative and executive. For I agree that "there is no liberty, if the power of judging be not separated from the legislative and executive powers."† And it proves, in the last place, that as liberty can have nothing to fear from the judiciary alone, but would have every thing to fear from its union with either of the other departments; that as all the effects of such an union must ensue from a dependence of the former on the latter, notwithstanding a nominal and apparent separation; that as from the natural feebleness of the judiciary, it is in continual jeopardy of being overpowered, awed or influenced by its coordinate branches; and that as nothing can contribute so much to its firmness and independence, as permanency in office, this quality may therefore be justly regarded as an indispensable ingredient in its constitution; and in a great measure as the citadel of the public justice and the public security.

The complete independence of the courts of justice is peculiarly essential in a limited constitution. By a limited constitution I understand one which contains certain specified exceptions to the legislative authority; such for instance as that it shall pass no bills of attainder, no *ex post facto* laws, and the like. Limitations of this kind can be preserved in practice no other way than through the medium of the courts of justice; whose duty it must be to declare all acts contrary to the manifest tenor

---

* The celebrated Montesquieu speaking of them says, "of the three powers above mentioned, the JUDICIARY is next to nothing." Spirit of Laws, vol. I, page 186.
† Idem. page 181.

of the constitution void. Without this, all the reservations of particular rights or privileges would amount to nothing.

Some perplexity respecting the right of the courts to pronounce legislative acts void, because contrary to the constitution, has arisen from an imagination that the doctrine would imply a superiority of the judiciary to the legislative power. It is urged that the authority which can declare the acts of another void, must necessarily be superior to the one whose acts may be declared void. As this doctrine is of great importance in all the American constitutions, a brief discussion of the grounds on which it rests cannot be unacceptable.

There is no position which depends on clearer principles, than that every act of a delegated authority, contrary to the tenor of the commission under which it is exercised, is void. No legislative act therefore contrary to the constitution can be valid. To deny this would be to affirm that the deputy is greater than his principal; that the servant is above his master; that the representatives of the people are superior to the people themselves; that men acting by virtue of powers may do not only what their powers do not authorise, but what they forbid.

If it be said that the legislative body are themselves the constitutional judges of their own powers, and that the construction they put upon them is conclusive upon the other departments, it may be answered, that this cannot be the natural presumption, where it is not to be collected from any particular provision in the constitution. It is not otherwise to be supposed that the constitution could intend to enable the representatives of the people to substitute their *will* to that of their constituents. It is far more rational to suppose that the courts were designed to be an intermediate body between the people and the legislature, in order, among other things, to keep the latter within the limits assigned to their authority. The interpretation of the laws is the proper and peculiar province of the courts. A constitution is in fact, and must be, regarded by the judges as a fundamental law. It therefore belongs to them to ascertain its meaning as well as the meaning of any particular act proceeding from the legislative body. If there should happen to be an irreconcileable variance between the two, that which has the superior obligation and validity ought of course to be preferred; or in other words, the constitution ought to be preferred to the statute, the intention of the people to the intention of their agents.

Nor does this conclusion by any means suppose a superiority of the judicial to the legislative power. It only supposes that the power of the people is superior to both; and that where the will of the legislature declared in its statutes, stands in opposition to that of the people declared in the constitution, the judges ought to be governed by the latter, rather than the former. They ought to regulate their decisions by the fundamental laws, rather than by those which are not fundamental.

This exercise of judicial discretion in determining between two contradictory laws, is exemplified in a familiar instance. It not uncommonly happens, that there are two statutes existing at one time, clashing in whole or in part with each other, and neither of them containing any repealing clause or expression. In such a case, it is the province of the courts to liquidate and fix their meaning and operation: So far as they can by any fair construction be reconciled to each other; reason and law conspire to dictate that this should be done: Where this is impracticable, it becomes a matter of necessity to give effect to one, in exclusion of the other. The rule which has obtained in the courts for determining their relative validity is that the last in order of time shall be preferred to the first. But this is mere rule of construction, not derived from any positive law, but from the nature and reason of the thing. It is a rule not enjoined upon the courts by legislative provision, but adopted by themselves, as consonant to truth and propriety, for the direction of their conduct as interpreters of the law. They thought it reasonable, that between the interfering acts of an *equal* authority, that which was the last indication of its will, should have the preference.

But in regard to the interfering acts of a superior and subordinate authority, of an original and derivative power, the nature and reason of the thing indicate the converse of that rule as proper to be followed. They teach us that the prior act of a superior ought to be prefered to the subsequent act of an inferior and subordinate authority; and that, accordingly, whenever a particular statute contravenes the constitution, it will be the duty of the judicial tribunals to adhere to the latter, and disregard the former.

It can be of no weight to say, that the courts on the pretence of a repugnancy, may substitute their own pleasure to the constitutional intentions of the legislature. This might as well happen in the case of two contradictory statutes; or it might as well happen in every adjudication upon any single statute. The courts must declare the sense of the law; and if they should be disposed to exercise *will* instead of *judgment*, the consequence would equally be the substitution of their pleasure to that of the legislative body. The observation, if it proved any thing, would prove that there ought to be no judges distinct from that body.

If then the courts of justice are to be considered as the bulwarks of a limited constitution against legislative encroachments, this consideration will afford a strong argument for the permanent tenure of judicial offices, since nothing will contribute so much as this to that independent spirit in the judges, which must be essential to the faithful performance of so arduous a duty.

This independence of the judges is equally requisite to guard the constitution and the rights of individuals from the effects of those ill humours which the arts of designing men, or the influence of particular conjunctures, sometimes disseminate among the people themselves, and which, though they speedily give place to better information and more deliberate reflection, have a tendency in the mean time to occasion dangerous innovations in the government, and serious oppressions of the minor party in the community. Though I trust the friends of the proposed constitution will never concur with its enemies* in questioning that fundamental principle of republican government, which admits the right of the people to alter or abolish the established constitution whenever they find it inconsistent with their happiness; yet it is not to be inferred from this principle, that the representatives of the people, whenever a momentary inclination happens to lay hold of a majority of their constituents incompatible with the provisions in the existing constitution, would on that account be justifiable in a violation of those provisions; or that the courts would be under a greater obligation to connive at infractions in this shape, than when they had proceeded wholly from the cabals of the representative body. Until the people have by some solemn and authoritative act annulled or changed the established form, it is binding upon themselves collectively, as well as individually; and no presumption, or even knowledge of their sentiments, can warrant their representatives in a departure from it, prior to such an act. But it is easy to see that it would require an uncommon portion of fortitude in the judges to do their duty as faithful guardians of the constitution, where legislative invasions of it had been instigated by the major voice of the community.

But it is not with a view to infractions of the constitution only that

* Vide Protest of the minority of the convention of Pennsylvania, Martin's speech, &c.

the independence of the judges may be an essential safeguard against the effects of occasional ill humours in the society. These sometimes extend no farther than to the injury of the private rights of particular classes of citizens, by unjust and partial laws. Here also the firmness of the judicial magistracy is of vast importance in mitigating the severity, and confining the operation of such laws. It not only serves to moderate the immediate mischiefs of those which may have been passed, but it operates as a check upon the legislative body in passing them; who, perceiving that obstacles to the success of an iniquitous intention are to be expected from the scruples of the courts, are in a manner compelled by the very motives of the injustice they meditate, to qualify their attempts. This is a circumstance calculated to have more influence upon the character of our governments, than but few may be aware of. The benefits of the integrity and moderation of the judiciary have already been felt in more states than one; and though they may have displeased those whose sinister expectations they may have disappointed, they must have commanded the esteem and applause of all the virtuous and disinterested. Considerate men of every description ought to prize whatever will tend to beget or fortify that temper in the courts; as no man can be sure that he may not be to-morrow the victim of a spirit of injustice, by which he may be a gainer to-day. And every man must now feel that the inevitable tendency of such a spirit is to sap the foundations of public and private confidence, and to introduce in its stead, universal distrust and distress.

That inflexible and uniform adherence to the rights of the constitution and of individuals, which we perceive to be indispensable in the courts of justice, can certainly not be expected from judges who hold their offices by a temporary commission. Periodical appointments, however regulated, or by whomsoever made, would in some way or other be fatal to their necessary independence. If the power of making them was committed either to the executive or legislature, there would be danger of an improper complaisance to the branch which possessed it; if to both, there would be an unwillingness to hazard the displeasure of either; if to the people, or to persons chosen by them for the special purpose, there would be too great a disposition to consult popularity, to justify a reliance that nothing would be consulted but the constitution and the laws.

There is yet a further and a weighty reason for the permanency of the judicial offices; which is deducible from the nature of the qualifications they require. It has been frequently remarked with great propriety, that a voluminous code of laws is one of the inconveniences necessarily connected with the advantages of a free government. To avoid an arbitrary discretion in the courts, it is indispensable that they should be bound down by strict rules and precedents, which serve to define and point out their duty in every particular case that comes before them; and it will readily be conceived from the variety of controversies which grow out of the folly and wickedness of mankind, that the records of those precedents must unavoidably swell to a very considerable bulk, and must demand long and laborious study to acquire a competent knowledge of them. Hence it is that there can be but few men in the society, who will have sufficient skill in the laws to qualify them for the stations of judges. And making the proper deductions for the ordinary depravity of human nature, the number must be still smaller of those who unite the requisite integrity with the requisite knowledge. These considerations apprise us, that the government can have no great option between fit characters; and that a temporary duration in office, which would naturally discourage such characters from quitting a lucrative line of practice to accept a seat on the bench, would have a tendency to throw the administration of justice into hands less able, and less well qualified to conduct it with utility and dignity. In the present circumstances of this country, and in those in which it is likely to be for a long time to come, the disadvantages on this score would be greater than they may at first sight appear; but it must be confessed that they are far inferior to those which present themselves under the other aspects of the subject.

Upon the whole there can be no room to doubt that the convention acted wisely in copying from the models of those constitutions which have established *good behaviour* as the tenure of their judicial offices in point of duration; and that so far from being blameable on this account, their plan would have been inexcuseably defective if it had wanted this important feature of good government. The experience of Great Britain affords an illustrious comment on the excellence of the institution.

PUBLIUS.
*The Federalist, May 28, 1788*

# The Federalist No. 84

In the course of the foregoing review of the constitution I have taken notice of, and endeavoured to answer, most of the objections which have appeared against it. There however remain a few which either did not fall naturally under any particular head, or were forgotten in their proper places. These shall now be discussed; but as the subject has been drawn into great length, I shall so far consult brevity as to comprise all my observations on these miscellaneous points in a single paper.

The most considerable of these remaining objections is, that the plan of the convention contains no bill of rights. Among other answers given to this, it has been upon different occasions remarked, that the constitutions of several of the states are in a similar predicament. I add, that New-York is of this number. And yet the opposers of the new system in this state, who profess an unlimited admiration for its constitution, are among the most intemperate partizans of a bill of rights. To justify their zeal in this matter, they alledge two things; one is, that though the constitution of New-York has no bill of rights prefixed to it, yet it contains in the body of it various provisions in favour of particular privileges and rights, which in substance amount to the same thing; the other is, that the constitution adopts in their full extent the common and statute law of Great-Britain, by which many other rights not expressed in it are equally secured.

To the first I answer, that the constitution proposed by the convention contains, as well as the constitution of this state, a number of such provisions.

Independent of those, which relate to the structure of the government, we find the following: Article I. section 3. clause 7. "Judgment in cases of impeachment shall not extend further than to removal from office, and disqualification to hold and enjoy any office of honour, trust or profit under the United States; but the party convicted shall nevertheless be liable and subject to indictment, trial, judgment and punishment, according to law." Section 9. of the same article, clause 2. "The privilege of the writ of *habeas corpus* shall not be suspended, unless when in cases of rebellion or invasion the public safety may require it." Clause 3. "No bill of attainder or *ex post facto* law shall be passed." Clause 7. "No title of nobility shall be granted by the United States: And no person holding any office of profit or trust under them, shall, without the consent of congress, accept of any present, emolument, office or title, of any kind whatever, from any king, prince or foreign state." Article III. section 2. clause 3. "The trial of all crimes, except in cases of impeachment, shall be by jury; and such trial shall be held in the state where the said crimes shall have been committed; but when not committed within any state, the trial shall be at such place or places as the congress may by law have directed." Section 3, of the same article, "Treason against the United States shall consist only in levying war against them, or in adhering to their enemies, giving them aid and comfort. No person shall be convicted of treason unless on the testimony of two witness to the same overt act, or on confession in open court." And clause 3, of the same section. "The congress shall have power to declare the punishment of treason, but no attainder of treason shall work corruption of blood, or forfeiture, except during the life of the person attainted."

It may well be a question whether these are not upon the whole, of equal importance with any which are to be found in the constitution of this state. The establishment of the writ of *habeas corpus*, the prohibition of *ex post facto* laws, and of TITLES OF NOBILITY, *to which we have no corresponding provisions in our constitution*, are perhaps greater securities to liberty and republicanism than any it contains. The creation of crimes after the commission of the fact, or in other words, the subjecting of men to punishment for things which, when they were done, were breaches of no law, and the practice of arbitrary imprisonments have been in all ages the favourite and most formidable instruments of tyranny. The observations of the judicious Blackstone* in reference to the latter, are well worthy of recital. "To bereave a man of life (says he) or by violence to confiscate his estate, without accusation or trial, would be so gross and notorious an act of despotism, as must at once convey the alarm of tyranny throughout the whole nation; but confinement of the person by secretly hurrying to goal, where his sufferings are unknown or forgotten, is a less public, a less striking, and therefore *a more dangerous engine* of arbitrary government." And as a remedy for this fatal evil, he is every where peculiarly emphatical in his

* Vide Blackstone's Commentaries, vol. I, page 136.

encomiums on the *habeas corpus* act, which in one place he calls "the BULWARK of the British constitution."*

Nothing need be said to illustrate the importance of the prohibition of titles of nobility. This may truly be denominated the corner stone of republican government; for so long as they are excluded, there can never be serious danger that the government will be any other than that of the people.

To the second, that is, to the pretended establishment of the common and statute law by the constitution, I answer, that they are expressly made subject "to such alterations and provisions as the legislature shall from time to time make concerning the same." They are therefore at any moment liable to repeal by the ordinary legislative power, and of course have no constitutional sanction. The only use of the declaration was to recognize the ancient law, and to remove doubts which might have been occasioned by the revolution. This consequently can be considered as no part of a declaration of rights, which under our constitutions must be intended as limitations of the power of the government itself.

It has been several times truly remarked, that bills of rights are in their origin, stipulations between kings and their subjects, abridgments of prerogative in favor of privilege, reservations of rights not surrendered to the prince. Such was MAGNA CHARTA, obtained by the Barons, sword in hand, from king John. Such were the subsequent confirmations of that charter by subsequent princes. Such was the *petition of right* assented to by Charles the First, in the beginning of his reign. Such also was the declaration of right presented by the lords and commons to the prince of Orange in 1688, and afterwards thrown into the form of an act of parliament, called the bill of rights. It is evident, therefore, that according to their primitive signification, they have no application to constitutions professedly founded upon the power of the people, and executed by their immediate representatives and servants. Here, in strictness, the people surrender nothing, and as they retain every thing, they have no need of particular reservations. "WE THE PEOPLE of the United States, to secure the blessings of liberty to ourselves and our posterity, do *ordain* and *establish* this constitution for the United States of America." Here is a better recognition of popular rights than volumes of those aphorisms which make the principal figure in several of our

* Vide Blackstone's Commentaries, vol. IV, page 438.

state bills of rights, and which would sound much better in a treatise of ethics than in a constitution of government.

But a minute detail of particular rights is certainly far less applicable to a constitution like that under consideration, which is merely intended to regulate the general political interests of the nation, than to a constitution which has the regulation of every species of personal and private concerns. If therefore the loud clamours against the plan of the convention on this score, are well founded, no epithets of reprobation will be too strong for the constitution of this state. But the truth is, that both of them contain all, which in relation to their objects, is reasonably to be desired.

I go further, and affirm that bills of rights, in the sense and in the extent in which they are contended for, are not only unnecessary in the proposed constitution, but would even be dangerous. They would contain various exceptions to powers which are not granted; and on this very account, would afford a colourable pretext to claim more than were granted. For why declare that things shall not be done which there is no power to do? Why for instance, should it be said, that the liberty of the press shall not be restrained, when no power is given by which restrictions may be imposed? I will not contend that such a provision would confer a regulating power; but it is evident that it would furnish, to men disposed to usurp, a plausible pretence for claiming that power. They might urge with a semblance of reason, that the constitution ought not to be charged with the absurdity of providing against the abuse of an authority, which was not given, and that the provision against restraining the liberty of the press afforded a clear implication, that a power to prescribe proper regulations concerning it, was intended to be vested in the national government. This may serve as a specimen of the numerous handles which would be given to the doctrine of constructive powers, by the indulgence of an injudicious zeal for bills of rights.

On the subject of the liberty of the press, as much has been said, I cannot forbear adding a remark or two: In the first place, I observe that there is not a syllable concerning it in the constitution of this state, and in the next, I contend that whatever has been said about it in that of any other state, amounts to nothing. What signifies a declaration that "the liberty of the press shall be inviolably preserved?" What is the liberty of the press? Who can give it any definition which would not leave the utmost latitude for evasion? I hold it to be impracticable;

and from this, I infer, that its security, whatever fine declarations may be inserted in any constitution respecting it, must altogether depend on public opinion, and on the general spirit of the people and of the government.* And here, after all, as intimated upon another occasion, must we seek for the only solid basis of all our rights.

There remains but one other view of this matter to conclude the point. The truth is, after all the declamation we have heard, that the constitution is itself in every rational sense, and to every useful purpose, A BILL OF RIGHTS. The several bills of rights, in Great Britain, form its constitution, and conversely the constitution of each state is its bill of rights. And the proposed constitution, if adopted, will be the bill of rights of the union. Is it one object of a bill of rights to declare and specify the political privileges of the citizens in the structure and administration of the government? This is done in the most ample and precise manner in the plan of the convention, comprehending various precautions for the public security, which are not to be found in any of the state constitutions. Is another object of a bill of rights to define certain immunities and modes of proceeding, which are relative to personal and private concerns? This we have seen has also been attended to, in a variety of cases, in the same plan. Adverting therefore to the substantial meaning of a bill of rights, it as absurd to allege that it is not to be found in the work of the convention. It may be said that it does not go far enough, though it will not be easy to make this appear; but it can with no propriety be contended that there is no such thing. It certainly must be immaterial what mode is observed as to the order of declaring the rights of the citizens, if they are to be found in any part of the instrument which establishes the government. And hence it must

---

* To show that there is a power in the constitution by which the liberty of the press may be affected, recourse has been had to the power of taxation. It is said that duties may be laid upon the publications so high as to amount to a prohibition. I know not by what logic it could be maintained that the declarations in the state constitutions, in favour of the freedom of the press, would be a constitutional impediment to the imposition of duties upon publications by the state legislatures. It cannot certainly be pretended that any degree of duties, however low, would be an abridgment of the liberty of the press. We know that newspapers are taxed in Great-Britain, and yet it is notorious that the press nowhere enjoys greater liberty than in that country. And if duties of any kind may be laid without a violation of that liberty, it is evident that the extent must depend on legislative discretion, regulated by public opinion; so that after all, general declarations respecting the liberty of the press will give it no greater security than it will have without them. The same invasions of it may be effected under the state constitutions which contain those declarations through the means of taxation, as under the proposed constitution which has nothing of the kind. It would be quite as significant to declare that government ought to be free, that taxes ought not to be excessive, &c., as that the liberty of the press ought not to be restrained.

be apparent that much of what has been said on this subject rests merely on verbal and nominal distinctions, which are entirely foreign from the substance of the thing.

Another objection, which has been made, and which from the frequency of its repetition it is to be presumed is relied on, is of this nature: It is improper (say the objectors) to confer such large powers, as are proposed, upon the national government; because the seat of that government must of necessity be too remote from many of the states to admit of a proper knowledge on the part of the constituent, of the conduct of the representative body. This argument, if it proves any thing, proves that there ought to be no general government whatever. For the powers which it seems to be agreed on all hands, ought to be vested in the union, cannot be safely intrusted to a body which is not under every requisite controul. But there are satisfactory reasons to shew that the objection is in reality not well founded. There is in most of the arguments which relate to distance a palpable illusion of the imagination. What are the sources of information by which the people in Montgomery county must regulate their judgment of the conduct of their representatives in the state legislature? Of personal observation they can have no benefit. This is confined to the citizens on the spot. They must therefore depend on the information of intelligent men, in whom they confide—and how must these men obtain their information? Evidently from the complection of public measures, from the public prints, from correspondences with their representatives, and with other persons who reside at the place of their deliberation. This does not apply to Montgomery county only, but to all the counties, at any considerable distance from the seat of government.

It is equally evident that the same sources of information would be open to the people, in relation to the conduct of their representatives in the general government; and the impediments to a prompt communication which distance may be supposed to create, will be overballanced by the effects of the vigilance of the state governments. The executive and legislative bodies of each state will be so many centinels over the persons employed in every department of the national administration; and as it will be in their power to adopt and pursue a regular and effectual system of intelligence, they can never be at a loss to know the behaviour of those who represent their constituents in the national councils, and can readily communicate the same knowledge to the people. Their disposition to apprise the community of whatever may prejudice its interests from another quarter, may be relied upon, if it were only from the rivalship of power. And we may conclude with the fullest assurance, that the people, through that channel, will be better informed of the conduct of their national representatives, than they can be by any means they now possess of that of their state representatives.

It ought also to be remembered, that the citizens who inhabit the country at and near the seat of government, will in all questions that affect the general liberty and prosperity, have the same interest with those who are at a distance; and that they will stand ready to sound the alarm when necessary, and to point out the actors in any pernicious project. The public papers will be expeditious messengers of intelligence to the most remote inhabitants of the union.

Among the many extraordinary objections which have appeared against the proposed constitution, the most extraordinary and the least colourable one, is derived from the want of some provision respecting the debts due to the United States. This has been represented as a tacit relinquishment of those debts, and as a wicked contrivance to screen public defaulters. The newspapers have teemed with the most inflammatory railings on this head; and yet there is nothing clearer than that the suggestion is entirely void of foundation, and is the offspring of extreme ignorance or extreme dishonesty. In addition to the remarks I have made upon the subject in another place, I shall only observe, that as it is a plain dictate of common sense, so it is also an established doctrine of political law, that *"States neither lose any of their rights, nor are discharged from any of their obligations by a change in the form of their civil government."*

The last objection of any consequence which I at present recollect, turns upon the article of expence. If it were even true that the adoption of the proposed government would occasion a considerable increase of expence, it would be an objection that ought to have no weight against the plan. The great bulk of the citizens of America, are with reason convinced that union is the basis of their political happiness. Men of sense of all parties now, with few exceptions, agree that it cannot be preserved under the present system, nor without radical alterations; that new and extensive powers ought to be granted

---

* Vide Rutherford's Institutes, vol. 2. book II. chap. x. sec. xiv, and xv.—Vide also Grotius, book II, chap. ix, sect. viii, and ix.

to the national head, and that these require a different organization of the federal government, a single body being an unsafe depository of such ample authorities. In conceding all this, the question of expence must be given up, for it is impossible, with any degree of safety, to narrow the foundation upon which the system is to stand. The two branches of the legislature are in the first instance, to consist of only sixty-five persons, which is the same number of which congress, under the existing confederation, may be composed. It is true that this number is intended to be increased; but this is to keep pace with the increase of the population and resources of the country. It is evident, that a less number would, even in the first instance, have been unsafe; and that a continuance of the present number would, in a more advanced stage of population, be a very inadequate representation of the people.

Whence is the dreaded augmentation of expence to spring? One source pointed out, is the multiplication of offices under the new government. Let us examine this a little.

It is evident that the principal departments of the administration under the present government, are the same which will be required under the new. There are now a secretary at war, a secretary for foreign affairs, a secretary for domestic affairs, a board of treasury consisting of three persons, a treasurer, assistants, clerks, &c. These offices are indispensable under any system, and will suffice under the new as well as under the old. As to ambassadors and other ministers and agents in foreign countries, the proposed constitution can make no other difference, than to render their characters, where they reside, more respectable, and their services more useful. As to persons to be employed in the collection of the revenues, it is unquestionably true that these will form a very considerable addition to the number of federal officers; but it will not follow, that this will occasion an increase of public expence. It will be in most cases nothing more than an exchange of state officers for national officers. In the collection of all duties, for instance, the persons employed will be wholly of the latter description. The states individually will stand in no need of any for this purpose. What difference can it make in point of expence, to pay officers of the customs appointed by the state, or those appointed by the United States? There is no good reason to suppose, that either the number or the salaries of the latter, will be greater than those of the former.

Where then are we to seek for those additional articles of expence which are to swell the account to the enormous size that has been represented to us? The chief item which occurs to me, respects the support of the judges of the United States. I do not add the president, because there is now a president of congress, whose expences may not be far, if any thing, short of those which will be incurred on account of the president of the United States. The support of the judges will clearly be an extra expence, but to what extent will depend on the particular plan which may be adopted in practice in regard to this matter. But it can upon no reasonable plan amount to a sum which will be an object of material consequence.

Let us now see what there is to counterballance any extra expences that may attend the establishment of the proposed government. The first thing that presents itself is, that a great part of the business, which now keeps congress sitting through the year, will be transacted by the president. Even the management of foreign negociations will naturally devolve upon him according to general principles concerted with the senate, and subject to their final concurrence. Hence it is evident, that a portion of the year will suffice for the session of both the senate and the house of representatives: We may suppose about a fourth for the latter, and a third or perhaps a half for the former. The extra business of treaties and appointments may give this extra occupation to the senate. From this circumstance we may infer, that until the house of representatives shall be increased greatly beyond its present number, there will be a considerable saving of expence from the difference between the constant session of the present, and the temporary session of the future congress.

But there is another circumstance, of great importance in the view of the economy. The business of the United States has hitherto occupied the state legislatures as well as congress. The latter has made requisitions which the former have had to provide for. Hence it has happened that the sessions of the state legislatures have been protracted greatly beyond what was necessary for the execution of the mere local business of the states. More than half their time has been frequently employed in matters which related to the United States. Now the members who compose the legislatures of the several states amount to two thousand and upwards; which number has hitherto performed what under the new system will be done in the first instance by sixty-five persons, and probably at no future period by above a fourth or a fifth of that number. The congress under the proposed government will do all the business of the United

States themselves, without the intervention of the state legislatures, who thenceforth will have only to attend to the affairs of their particular states, and will not have to sit in any proportion as long as they have heretofore done. This difference, in the time of the sessions of the state legislatures, will be all clear gain, and will alone form an article of saving, which may be regarded as an equivalent for any additional objects of expence that may be occasioned by the adoption of the new system.

The result from these observations is, that the sources of additional expence from the establishment of the proposed constitution are much fewer than may have been imagined, that they are counterbalanced by considerable objects of saving, and that while it is questionable on which side the scale will preponderate, it is certain that a government less expensive would be incompetent to the purposes of the union.

PUBLIUS.

*The Federalist, May 28, 1788*

## *New York Ratifying Convention: Third Speech of June 21*

### *Francis Child's Version*

THE HON. MR. HAMILTON. Mr. Chairman I rise to take notice of the observations of the hon. member from Ulster. I imagine the objections he has stated, are susceptible of a complete and satisfactory refutation. But before I proceed to this, I shall attend to the arguments advanced by the gentlemen from Albany and Dutchess. These arguments have been frequently urged, and much confidence has been placed in their strength: The danger of corruption has been dwelt upon with peculiar emphasis, and presented to our view in the most heightened and unnatural colouring: Events, merely possible have been magnified by distempered imagination into inevitable realities; and the most distant and doubtful conjectures have been formed into a serious and infallible prediction. In the same spirit, the most fallacious calculations have been made: The lowest possible quorum has been contemplated as the number to transact important business; and a majority of these to decide in all cases on questions of infinite moment. Allowing, for the present, the propriety and truth of these apprehensions, it would be easy, in comparing the two constitutions, to prove that the chances of corruption under the new, are much fewer that those to which the old one is exposed. Under the old confederation, the important powers of declaring war, making peace, &c. can be exercised by nine states. On the presumption that the smallest constitutional number will deliberate and decide, those interesting powers will be committed to fewer men, under the ancient than under the new government. In the former, eighteen members, in the latter, not less than twenty-four may determine all great questions. Thus on the principles of the gentlemen, the fairer prospect of safety is clearly visible in the new government. That we may have the fullest conviction of the truth of this position, it ought to be suggested, as a decisive argument, that it will ever be the interest of the several states to maintain, under the new government, an ample representation: For, as every member has a vote, the relative influence and authority of each state will be in proportion to the number of representatives she has in Congress. There is not therefore a shadow of probability, that the number of acting members in the general legislature, will be ever reduced to a bare quorum; especially as the expence of their support is to be defrayed from a federal treasury: But under the existing confederation, as each state has but one vote, it will be a matter of indifference, on the score of influence, whether she delegates two or six representatives: And the maintenance of them forming a striking article in the state expenditures, will forever prove a capital inducement to retain or withdraw from the federal legislature, those delegates which her selfishness may too often consider as superfluous.

There is another source of corruption, in the old government, which the proposed plan is happily calculated to remedy. The concurrence of nine states, as has been observed, is necessary to pass resolves the most important, and on which, the safety of the republic may depend. If these nine states are at any time assembled, a foreign enemy, by dividing a state and gaining over and silencing a single member, may frustrate the most indispensible plan of national policy, and totally prevent a measure, essential to the welfare or existence of the empire. Here, then, we find a radical, dangerous defect, which will forever embarrass and obstruct the machine of government; and suspend our fate on the uncertain virtue of an individual. What a difference between the old and new constitution strikes our view! In the one, corruption must embrace a majority; in the other, her poison administered to a single man, may render the efforts of a majority totally vain. This mode of corruption is still more dangerous, as its operations are more secret and imperceptible: The exertions of active villainy are commonly accompanied with circumstances, which tend to its own exposure: But this negative kind of guilt has so many plausible apologies as almost to elude suspicion.

In all reasonings on the subject of corruption, much use has been made of the examples furnished by the British house of commons. Many mistakes have arisen from fallacious comparisons between our government and theirs. It is time, that the real state of this matter should be explained. By far the greatest part of the house of commons is composed of representatives of towns or boroughs: These towns had antiently no voice in parliament; but on the extension of commercial wealth and influence, they were admitted to a seat. Many of them are in the possession and gift of the king; and from their dependence on him, and the destruction of the right of free election, they are stigmatized with the appellation of rotten boroughs. This is the true source of the corruption, which has so long excited the severe animadversion of zealous politicians and patriots. But the knights of the shire, who form another branch of the house of commons, and who are chosen from the body of the counties they represent, have been generally esteemed a virtuous and incorruptible set of men. I appeal, Sir, to the history of that house: This will shew us, that the rights of the people have been ever very safely trusted to their protection; that they have been the ablest bulwarks of the British commons; and that in the conflict of parties, by throwing their weight into one scale or the other, they have uniformly supported and strengthened the constitutional claims of the people. Notwithstanding the cry of corruption that has been perpetually raised against the house of commons, it has been found, that that house, sitting at first without any constitutional authority, became, at length, an essential member of the legislature, and have since, by regular gradations, acquired new and important accessions of privilege: That they have, on numerous occasions, impaired the overgrown prerogative, and limited the incroachments of monarchy.

An honorable member from Dutchess, (*Mr. Smith*) has observed, that the delegates from New-York, (for example) can have very little information of the local circumstances of Georgia or South Carolina, except from the representatives of those states; and on this ground, insists upon the expediency of an enlargment of the representation; since, otherwise, the majority must rely too much on the information of a few. In order to determine whether there is any weight in this reasoning, let us consider the powers of the national government, and compare them with the objects of state legislation. The powers of the new government are general, and calculated to embrace the aggregate interest of the Union, and the general interest of each state, so far as it stands in relation to the whole. The object of the state governments is to provide for their internal interests, as unconnected with the United States, and as composed of minute parts or districts. A particular knowledge, therefore, of the local circumstances of any state, as they may vary in different districts, is unnecessary for the federal representative. As he is not to represent the interests or local wants of the county of Dutchess or Montgomery; neither is it necessary that he should be acquainted with their particular resources: But in the state governments, as the laws regard the interests of the people, in all their various minute divisions; it is necessary, that the smallest interests should be represented. Taking these distinctions into view, I think it must appear evident, that one discerning and intelligent man will be as capable of understanding and representing the general interests of a state, as twenty; because, one man can be as fully acquainted with the general state of the commerce, manufactures, population, production and common resources of a state, which are the proper objects of federal legislation. It is to be presumed, that few men originally possess a complete knowledge of the circumstances of other states; They must rely, therefore, on the information, to be collected from the representatives of those states: And if the above reasoning be just, it appears evident, I imagine, that this reliance will be as secure as can be desired.

Sir, in my experience of public affairs, I have constantly remarked, in the conduct of members of Congress, a strong and uniform attachment to the interests of their own state: These interests have, on many occasions, been adhered to, with an undue and illiberal pertinacity; and have too often been preferred to the welfare of the Union. This attachment has given birth to an unaccommodating spirit of party, which has frequently embarrassed the best measures: It is by no means, however, an object of surprize. The early connections we have formed;

the habits and prejudices in which we have been bred, fix our affection so strongly, that no future objects of association can easily eradicate them: This, together with the entire and immediate dependence the representative feels on his constituent, will generally incline him to prefer the particular before the public good.

The subject, on which this argument of a small representation has been most plausibly used, is taxation. As to internal taxation, in which the difficulty principally rests, it is not probable, that any general regulation will originate in the national legislature. If Congress in times of great danger and distress, should be driven to this resource, they will undoubtedly adopt such measures, as are most conformable to the laws and customs of each state: They will take up your own codes and consult your own systems: This is a source of information which cannot mislead, and which will be equally accessible to every member. It will teach them the most certain, safe and expeditious mode of laying and collecting taxes in each state. They will appoint the officers of revenue agreeably to the spirit of your particular establishments; or they will make use of your own.

Sir, the most powerful obstacle to the members of Congress betraying the interests of their constituents, is the state legislatures themselves; who will be standing bodies of observation, possessing the confidence of the people, jealous of federal encroachments, and armed with every power to check the first essays of treachery. They will institute regular modes of enquiry: The complicated domestic attachments, which subsist between the state legislators and their electors, will ever make them vigilant guardians of the people's rights: Possessed of the means, and the disposition of resistance, the spirit of opposition will be easily communicated to the people; and under the conduct of an organized body of leaders, will act with weight and system. Thus it appears, that the very structure of the confederacy affords the surest preventives from error, and the most powerful checks to misconduct.

Sir, there is something in an argument, that has been urged, which, if it proves any thing, concludes against all union and all government; it goes to prove, that no powers should be entrusted to any body of men, because they may be abused. This is an argument of possibility and chance; one that would render useless all reasonings upon the probable operation of things, and defeat the established principles of natural and moral causes. It is a species of reasoning, sometimes used to excite popular jealousies, but is generally discarded by wise and discerning men. I do not suppose that the honorable member who advanced the idea, had any such design: He, undoubtedly, would not wish to extend his argument to the destruction of union or government; but this, Sir, is its real tendency. It has been asserted, that the interests, habits and manners of the Thirteen States are different; and hence it is inferred, that no general free government can suit them. This diversity of habits, &c. has been a favorite theme with those who are disposed for a division of our empire; and like many other popular objections, seems to be founded on fallacy. I acknowledge, that the local interests of the states are in some degree various; and that there is some difference in their habits and manners: But this I will presume to affirm; that, from New-Hampshire to Georgia, the people of America are as uniform in their interests and manners, as those of any established in Europe. This diversity, to the eye of a speculatist, may afford some marks of characteristic discrimination, but cannot form an impediment to the regular operation of those general powers, which the Constitution gives to the united government. Were the laws of the union to new-model the internal police of any state; were they to alter, or abrogate at a blow, the whole of its civil and criminal institutions; were they to penetrate the recesses of domestic life, and controul, in all respects, the private conduct of individuals, there might be more force in the objection: And the same constitution, which was happily calculated for one state, might sacrifice the wellfare of another. Though the difference of interests may create some difficulty and apparent partiality, in the first operations of government, yet the same spirit of accommodation, which produced the plan under discussion, would be exercised in lessening the weight of unequal burthens. Add to this that, under the regular and gentle influence of general laws, these varying interests will be constantly assimilating, till they embrace each other, and assume the same complexion.

*June 21, 1788*

## To George Washington

*New York September 1788*

DEAR SIR

Your Excellency's friendly and obliging letter of the 28th Ulto. came safely to hand. I thank you for your assurance of seconding my application to General Morgan. The truth of that affair is, that he purchased the watch for a trifle of a British soldier, who plundered Major Cochran at the moment of his fall at York Town.

I should be deeply pained my Dear Sir if your scruples in regard to a certain station should be matured into a resolution to decline it; though I am neither surprised at their existence nor can I but agree in opinion that the caution you observe in deferring an ultimate determination is prudent. I have however reflected maturely on the subject and have come to a conclusion, (in which I feel no hesitation) that every public and personal consideration will demand from you an acquiescence in what will *certainly* be the unanimous wish of your country. The absolute retreat which you meditated at the close of the late war was natural and proper. Had the government produced by the revolution gone on in a *tolerable* train, it would have been most adviseable to have persisted in that retreat. But I am clearly of opinion that the crisis which brought you again into public view left you no alterative but to comply—and I am equally clear in the opinion that you are by that act *pledged* to take a part in the execution of the government. I am not less convinced that the impression of this necessity of your filling the station in question is so universal that you run no risk of any uncandid imputation, by submitting to it. But even if this were not the case, a regard to your own reputation as well as to the public good, calls upon you in the strongest manner to run that risk.

It cannot be considered as a compliment to say that on your acceptance of the office of President the success of the new government in its commencement may materially depend. Your agency and influence will be not less important in preserving it from the future attacks of its enemies than they have been in recommending it in the first instance to the adoption of the people. Independent of all considerations drawn from this source the point of light in which you stand at home and abroad will make an infinite difference in the respectability with which the government will begin its operations in the alternative of your being or not being at the head of it. I forbear to urge considerations which might have a more personal application. What I have said will suffice for the inferences I mean to draw.

First—In a matter so essential to the well being of society as the prosperity of a newly instituted government a citizen of so much consequence as yourself to its success has no option but to lend his services if called for. Permit me to say it would be inglorious in such a situation not to hazard the glory however great, which he might have previously acquired.

Secondly. Your signature to the proposed system pledges your judgment for its being such an one as upon the whole was worthy of the public approbation. If it should miscarry (as men commonly decide from success or the want of it) the blame will in all probability be laid on the system itself. And the framers of it will have to encounter the disrepute of having brought about a revolution in government, without substituting any thing that was worthy of the effort. They pulled down one Utopia, it will be said, to build up another. This view of the subject, if I mistake not my dear Sir will suggest to your mind greater hazard to that fame, which must be and ought to be dear to you, in refusing your future aid to the system than in affording it. I will only add that in my estimate of the matter that aid is indispensable.

I have taken the liberty to express these sentiments to lay before you my view of the subject. I doubt not the considerations mentioned have fully occurred to you, and I trust they will finally produce in your mind the same result, which exists in mine. I flatter myself the frankness with which I have delivered myself will not be displeasing to you. It has been prompted by motives which you would not disapprove.

I remain My Dear Sir With the sincerest respect and regard  Your Obd & hum serv

A HAMILTON

The letter inclosed in yours was immediately forwarded.

## *To George Washington*

D<small>R.</small> S<small>IR</small>

In conformity to the intimation you were pleased to honor me with on [     ] evening last I have reflected on the etiquette proper to be observed by the President and now submit the ideas which have occurred to me on the subject.

The public good requires as a primary object that the dignity of the office should be supported. Whatever is essential to this ought to be pursued though at the risk of partial or momentary dissatisfaction. But care will be necessary to avoid extensive disgust or discontent. Men's minds are prepared for a pretty high tone in the demeanour of the Executive; but I doubt whether for so high a tone as in the abstract might be desireable. The notions of equality are yet in my opinion too general and too strong to admit of such a distance being placed between the President and other branches of the government as might even be consistent with a due proportion. The following plan will I think steer clear of extremes and involve no very material inconveniences.

I The President to have a levee day once a week for receiving visits. An hour to be fixed at which it shall be understood that he will appear and consequently that the visitors are previously to be assembled. The President to remain half an hour, in which time he may converse cursorily on indifferent subjects with such persons as shall strike his attention, and at the end of that half hour disappear. Some regulation will be hereafter necessary to designate those who may visit. A mode of introduction through particular officers will be indispensable. No visits to be returned.

II The President to accept no invitations: and to give formal entertainments only twice or four times a year on the anniversaries of important events in the revolution. If twice, the day of the declaration of Independence, and that of the inauguration of the President, which completed the organization of the Constitution, to be preferred; if four times, the day of the treaty of alliance with france & that of the definitive treaty with Britain to be added. The members of the two houses of the legislature Principal officers of the Government Foreign ministers and other distinguished strangers only to be invited. The numbers form in my mind an objection—

But there may be separate tables in separate rooms. This is practiced in some European Courts. I see no other method in which foreign Ministers can with propriety be included in any attentions of the table which the President may think fit to pay.

III The President on the levée days either by himself or some Gentleman of his household to give informal invitations to family dinners on the days of invitation. Not more than six or eight to be invited at a time & the matter to be confined essentially to members of the legislature and other official characters. The President never to remain long at table.

I think it probable that the last article will not correspond with the ideas of most of those with whom Your Excellency may converse but on pretty mature reflection I believe it will be necessary to remove the idea of too immense an inequality, which I fear would excite dissatisfaction and cabal. The thing may be so managed as neither to occasion much waste of time, nor to infringe on dignity.

It is an important point to consider what persons may have access to Your Excellency on business. The heads of departments will of course have this privilege. Foreign Ministers of some descriptions will also be intitled to it. In Europe I am informed ambassadors only have direct access to the Chief Magistrate. Something very *near* what prevails there would in my opinion be right. The distinction of rank between diplomatic characters requires attention and the door of access ought not to be too wide to that class of persons. I have thought that the members of the Senate should also have a right of *individual* access on matters relative to the *public administration*. In England & France Peers of the realm have this right. We have none such in this Country, but I believe that it will be satisfactory to the people to know that there is some body of men in the state who have a right of continual communication with the President. It will be considered as a safeguard against secret combinations to deceive him.

I have asked myself—will not the representatives expect the same privilege and be offended if they are not allowed to participate with the Senate? There is sufficient danger of this, to merit consideration. But there is a reason for the distinction in the constitution. The Senate are coupled with the President in certain executive functions; treaties and appointments. This makes them in a degree his constitutional counsellors and gives them a *peculiar* claim to the right of access.

On the whole, I think the discrimination will be proper & may be hazarded.

I have chosen this method of communication, because I understood Your Excellency, that it would be most convenient to you. The unstudied and unceremonious manner of it will I hope not render it the less acceptable. And if in the execution of your commands at any time I consult frankness and simplicity more than ceremony or profession, I flatter myself you will not on that account distrust the sincerity of the assurance I now give of my cordial wishes for your personal happiness and the success of your administration. I have the honor to be with the highest respect

Your Excellency's Most Obedient & humble servant

*May 5, 1789*

## *To Marquis de Lafayette*

*New York October 6th. 1789*

MY DEAR MARQUIS

I have seen with a mixture of Pleasure and apprehension the Progress of the events which have lately taken Place in your Country. As a friend to mankind and to liberty I rejoice in the efforts which you are making to establish it while I fear much for the final success of the attempts, for the fate of those I esteem who are engaged in it, and for the danger in case of success of innovations greater than will consist with the real felicity of your Nation. If your affairs still go well, when this reaches you, you will ask why this foreboding of ill, when all the appearences have been so much in your favor. I will tell you; I dread disagreements among those who are now united (which will be likely to be improved by the adverse party) about the nature of your constitution; I dread the vehement character of your people, whom I fear you may find it more easy to bring on, than to keep within Proper bounds, after you have put them in motion; I dread the interested refractoriness of your nobles, who cannot all be gratified and who may be unwilling to submit to the requisite sacrifices. And I dread the reveries of your Philosophic politicians who appear in the moment to have great influence and who being mere speculatists may aim at more refinement than suits either with human nature or the composition of your Nation.

These my dear Marquis are my apprehensions. My wishes for your personal success and that of the cause of liberty are incessant. Be virtuous amidst the Seductions of ambition, and you can hardly in any event be unhappy. You are combined with a great and good man; you will anticipate the name of Neckar. I trust you and he will never cease to harmonize.

You will, I presume, have heard before this gets to hand, that I have been appointed to the head of the Finances of this Country: this event I am sure will give you Pleasure. In undertaking the task, I hazard much, but I thought it an occasion that called upon me to hazard. I have no doubt that the reasonable expectation of the public may be satisfied, if I am properly supported by the Legislature, and in this respect, I stand at present on the most encouraging footing.

The debt due to France will be among the first objects of my attention. Hitherto it has been from necessity neglected. The Session of Congress is now over. It has been exhausted in the organization of the Government, and in a few laws of immediate urgency respecting navigation and commercial Imposts. The subject of the debt foreign and domestic has been referred to the next session which will commence the first Monday in January with an instruction to me to prepare and report a Plan comprehending an adequate Provision for the support of the Public Credit. There were many good reasons for a temporary adjournment.

From this sketch you will perceive that I am not in a situation to address any thing officially to your administration; but I venture to say to you, as my friend, that if the installments of the Principal of the debt could be suspended for a few years, it would be a valuable accommodation to the United States. In this suggestion I contemplate a speedy payment of the arrears of *interest* now due, and effectual Provision for the punctual payment of future interest as it arises. Could an arrangement of this sort meet the approbation of your Government, it would be best on every account that the offer should come unsolicited as a fresh mark of good will.

I wrote you last by Mr. De Warville. I presume you received my letter. As it touched some delicate issues I should be glad to know its fate.

Your with unalterable    esteem and affection

ALEXANDER HAMILTON

P. S. The latest accounts from France have abated some of my apprehensions. The abdications of priviledges patronised by your Nobility in the States General are truly noble, and bespeak a Patriotic and magnanimous policy, which promises good both to them and their Country.

## *To Henry Lee*

My Dear Friend

I have just received your letter of the 16th instant.

I am sure you are sincere when you say, you would not subject me to an impropriety. Nor do I know that there would be any in my answering your queries. But you remember the saying with regard to Caesar's Wife. I think the spirit of it applicable to every man concerned in the administration of the finances of a Country. With respect to the Conduct of such men—*Suspicion* is ever eagle eyed, And the most innocent things are apt to be misinterpreted.

Be assured of the affection & friendship of Yr.

A Hamilton

New York December 1st 1789

## *Report Relative to a Provision for the Support of Public Credit*

*Treasury Department, January 9, 1790.*

The Secretary of the Treasury, in obedience to the resolution of the House of Representatives, of the twenty-first day of September last, has, during the recess of Congress, applied himself to the consideration of a proper plan for the support of the Public Credit, with all the attention which was due to the authority of the House, and to the magnitude of the object.

In the discharge of this duty, he has felt, in no small degree, the anxieties which naturally flow from a just estimate of the difficulty of the task, from a well-founded diffidence of his own qualifications for executing it with success, and from a deep and solemn conviction of the momentous nature of the truth contained in the resolution under which his investigations have been conducted, "That an *adequate* provision for the support of the Public Credit, is a matter of high importance to the honor and prosperity of the United States."

With an ardent desire that his well-meant endeavors may be conducive to the real advantage of the nation, and with the utmost deference to the superior judgment of the House, he now respectfully submits the result of his enquiries and reflections, to their indulgent construction.

In the opinion of the Secretary, the wisdom of the House, in giving their explicit sanction to the proposition which has been stated, cannot but be applauded by all, who will seriously consider, and trace through their obvious consequences, these plain and undeniable truths.

That exigencies are to be expected to occur, in the affairs of nations, in which there will be a necessity for borrowing.

That loans in times of public danger, especially from foreign war, are found an indispensable resource, even to the wealthiest of them.

And that in a country, which, like this, is possessed of little active wealth, or in other words, little monied capital, the necessity for that resource, must, in such emergencies, be proportionably urgent.

And as on the one hand, the necessity for borrowing in particular emergencies cannot be doubted, so on the other, it is equally evident, that to be able to borrow upon *good terms*, it is essential that the credit of a nation should be well established.

For when the credit of a country is in any degree questionable, it never fails to give an extravagant premium, in one shape or another, upon all the loans it has occasion to make. Nor does the evil end here; the same disadvantage must be sustained upon whatever is to be bought on terms of future payment.

From this constant necessity of *borrowing* and *buying dear*, it is easy to conceive how immensely the expences of a nation, in a course of time, will be augmented by an unsound state of the public credit.

To attempt to enumerate the complicated variety of mischiefs in the whole system of the social œconomy, which proceed from a neglect of the maxims that uphold public credit, and justify the solicitude manifested by the House on this point, would be an improper intrusion on their time and patience.

In so strong a light nevertheless do they appear to the Secretary, that on their due observance at the present critical juncture, materially depends, in his judgment, the individual and aggregate prosperity of the citizens of the United States; their relief from the embarrassments they now experience; their character as a People; the cause of good government.

If the maintenance of public credit, then, be truly so important, the next enquiry which suggests itself is, by what means it is to be effected? The ready answer to which question is, by good faith, by a punctual performance of contracts. States, like individuals, who observe their engagements, are respected and trusted: while the reverse is the fate of those, who pursue an opposite conduct.

Every breach of the public engagements, whether from choice or necessity, is in different degrees hurtful to public credit. When such a necessity does truly exist, the evils of it are only to be palliated by a scrupulous attention, on the part of the government, to carry the violation no farther than the necessity absolutely requires, and to manifest, if the nature of the case admits of it, a sincere disposition to make reparation, whenever circumstances shall permit. But with every possible mitigation, credit must suffer, and numerous mischiefs ensue. It is therefore highly important, when an appearance of necessity seems to press upon the public councils, that they should examine well its reality, and be perfectly assured, that there is no method of escaping from it, before they yield to its suggestions. For though it cannot safely be affirmed, that occasions have never existed, or may not exist, in which violations of the public faith, in this respect, are inevitable; yet there is great reason to believe, that they exist far less frequently than precedents indicate; and are oftenest either pretended through levity, or want of firmness, or supposed through want of knowledge. Expedients might often have been devised to effect, consistently with good faith, what has been done in contravention of it. Those who are most commonly creditors of a nation, are, generally speaking, enlightened men; and there are signal examples to warrant a conclusion, that when a candid and fair appeal is made to them, they will understand their true interest too well to refuse their concurrence in such modifications of their claims, as any real necessity may demand.

While the observance of that good faith, which is the basis of public credit, is recommended by the strongest inducements of political expediency, it is enforced by considerations of still greater authority. There are arguments for it, which rest on the immutable principles of moral obligation. And in proportion as the mind is disposed to contemplate, in the order of Providence, an intimate connection between public virtue and public happiness, will be its repugnancy to a violation of those principles.

This reflection derives additional strength from the nature of the debt of the United States. It was the price of liberty. The faith of America has been repeatedly pledged for it, and with solemnities, that give peculiar force to the obligation. There is indeed reason to regret that it has not hitherto been kept; that the necessities of the war, conspiring with inexperience in the subjects of finance, produced direct infractions; and that the subsequent period has been a continued scene of negative violation, or non-compliance. But a diminution of this regret arises from the reflection, that the last seven years have exhibited an earnest and uniform effort, on the part of the government of the union, to retrieve the national credit, by doing justice to the creditors of the nation; and that the embarrassments of a defective constitution, which defeated this laudable effort, have ceased.

From this evidence of a favorable disposition, given by the former government, the institution of a new one, cloathed with powers competent to calling forth the resources of the community, has excited correspondent expectations. A general belief, accordingly, prevails, that the credit of the United States will quickly be established on the firm foundation of an effectual provision for the existing debt. The influence, which this has had at home, is witnessed by the rapid increase, that has taken place in the market value of the public securities. From January to November, they rose thirty-three and a third per cent, and from that period to this time, they have risen fifty per cent more. And the intelligence from abroad announces effects proportionably favourable to our national credit and consequence.

It cannot but merit particular attention, that among ourselves the most enlightened friends of good government are those, whose expectations are the highest.

To justify and preserve their confidence; to promote the encreasing respectability of the American name; to answer the calls of justice; to restore landed property to its due value; to furnish new resources both to agriculture and commerce; to cement more closely the union of the states; to add to their security against foreign attack; to establish public order on the basis of an upright and liberal policy. These are the great and invaluable ends to be secured, by a proper and adequate provision, at the present period, for the support of public credit.

To this provision we are invited, not only by the general considerations, which have been noticed, but by others of a more particular nature. It will procure to every class of the community some important advantages, and remove some no less important disadvantages.

The advantage to the public creditors from the increased value of that part of their property which constitutes the public debt, needs no explanation.

But there is a consequence of this, less obvious, though not less true, in which every other citizen is interested. It is a well known fact, that in countries in which the national debt is properly funded, and an object of established confidence, it answers most of the purposes of money. Transfers of stock or public debt are there equivalent to payments in specie; or in other words, stock, in the principal transactions of business, passes current as specie. The same thing would, in all probability happen here, under the like circumstances.

The benefits of this are various and obvious.

First. Trade is extended by it; because there is a larger capital to carry it on, and the merchant can at the same time, afford to trade for smaller profits; as his stock, which, when unemployed, brings him in an interest from the government, serves him also as money, when he has a call for it in his commercial operations.

Secondly. Agriculture and manufactures are also promoted by it: For the like reason, that more capital can be commanded to be employed in both; and because the merchant, whose enterprize in foreign trade, gives to them activity and extension, has greater means for enterprize.

Thirdly. The interest of money will be lowered by it, for this is always in a ratio, to the quantity of money, and to the quickness of circulation. This circumstance will enable both the public and individuals to borrow on easier and cheaper terms.

And from the combination of these effects, additional aids will be furnished to labour, to industry, and to arts of every kind.

But these good effects of a public debt are only to be looked for, when, by being well funded, it has acquired an *adequate* and *stable* value. Till then, it has rather a contrary tendency. The fluctuation and insecurity incident to it in an unfunded state, render it a mere commodity, and a precarious one. As such, being only an object of occasional and particular speculation, all the money applied to it is so much diverted from the more useful channels of circulation, for which the thing itself affords no substitute: So that, in fact, one serious inconvenience of an unfunded debt is, that it contributes to the scarcity of money.

This distinction which has been little if at all attended to, is of the greatest moment. It involves a question immediately interesting to every part of the community; which is no other than this—Whether the public debt, by a provision for it on true principles, shall be rendered a *substitute* for money; or whether, by being left as it is, or by being provided for in such a manner as will wound those principles, and destroy confidence, it shall be suffered to continue, as it is, a pernicious drain of our cash from the channels of productive industry.

The effect, which the funding of the public debt, on right principles, would have upon landed property, is one of the circumstances attending such an arrangement, which has been least adverted to, though it deserves the most particular attention. The present depreciated state of that species of property is a serious calamity. The value of cultivated lands, in most of the states, has fallen since the revolution from 25 to 50 per cent. In those farthest south, the decrease is still more considerable. Indeed, if the representations, continually received from that quarter, may be credited, lands there will command no price, which may not be deemed an almost total sacrifice.

This decrease, in the value of lands, ought, in a great measure, to be attributed to the scarcity of money. Consequently whatever produces an augmentation of the monied capital of the country, must have a proportional effect in raising that value. The beneficial tendency of a funded debt, in this respect, has been manifested by the most decisive experience in Great-Britain.

The proprietors of lands would not only feel the benefit of this increase in the value of their property, and of a more prompt and better sale, when they had occasion to sell; but the necessity of selling would be, itself, greatly diminished. As the same cause would contribute to the facility of loans, there is reason to believe, that such of them as are indebted, would be able through that resource, to satisfy their more urgent creditors.

It ought not however to be expected, that the advantages, described as likely to result from funding the public debt, would be instantaneous.

It might require some time to bring the value of stock to its natural level, and to attach to it that fixed confidence, which is necessary to its quality as money. Yet the late rapid rise of the public securities encourages an expectation, that the progress of stock to the desireable point, will be much more expeditious than could have been foreseen. And as in the mean time it will be increasing in value, there is room to conclude, that it will, from the outset, answer many of the purposes in contemplation. Particularly it seems to be probable, that from creditors, who are not themselves necessitous, it will early meet with a ready reception in payment of debts, at its current price.

Having now taken a concise view of the inducements to a proper provision for the public debt, the next enquiry which presents itself is, what ought to be the nature of such a provision? This requires some preliminary discussions.

It is agreed on all hands, that that part of the debt which has been contracted abroad, and is denominated the foreign debt, ought to be provided for, according to the precise terms of the contracts relating to it. The discussions, which can arise, therefore, will have reference essentially to the domestic part of it, or to that which has been contracted at home. It is to be regretted, that there is not the same unanimity of sentiment on this part, as on the other.

The Secretary has too much deference for the opinions of every part of the community, not to have observed one, which has, more than once, made its appearance in the public prints, and which is occasionally to be met with in conversation. It involves this question, whether a discrimination ought not to be made between original holders of the public securities, and present possessors, by purchase. Those who advocate a discrimination are for making a full provision for the securities of the former, at their nominal value; but contend, that the latter ought to receive no more than the cost to them, and the interest: And the idea is sometimes suggested of making good the difference to the primitive possessor.

In favor of this scheme, it is alledged, that it would be unreasonable to pay twenty shillings in the pound, to one who had not given more for it than three or four. And it is added, that it would be hard to aggravate the misfortune of the first owner, who, probably through necessity, parted with his property at so great a loss, by obliging him to contribute to the profit of the person, who had speculated on his distresses.

The Secretary, after the most mature reflection on the force of this argument, is induced to reject the doctrine it contains, as equally unjust and impolitic, as highly injurious, even to the original holders of public securities; as ruinous to public credit.

It is inconsistent with justice, because in the first place, it is a breach of contract; in violation of the rights of a fair purchaser.

The nature of the contract in its origin, is, that the public will pay the sum expressed in the security, to the first holder, or his *assignee*. The *intent*, in making the security assignable, is, that the proprietor may be able to make use of his property, by selling it for as much as it *may be worth in the market*, and that the buyer may be *safe* in the purchase.

Every buyer therefore stands exactly in the place of the seller, has the same right with him to the identical sum expressed in the security, and having acquired that right, by fair purchase, and in conformity to the original *agreement* and *intention* of the government, his claim cannot be disputed, without manifest injustice.

That he is to be considered as a fair purchaser, results from this: Whatever necessity the seller may have been under, was occasioned by the government, in not making a proper provision for its debts. The buyer had no agency in it, and therefore ought not to suffer. He is not even chargeable with having taken an undue advantage. He paid what the commodity was worth in the market, and took the risks of reimbursement upon himself. He of course gave a fair equivalent, and ought to reap the benefit of his hazard; a hazard which was far from inconsiderable, and which, perhaps, turned on little less than a revolution in government.

That the case of those, who parted with their securities from necessity, is a hard one, cannot be denied. But whatever complaint of injury, or claim of redress, they may have, respects the government solely. They have not only nothing to object to the persons who relieved their necessities, by giving them the current price of their property, but they are even under an implied condition to contribute to the reimbursement of those persons. They knew, that by the terms of the contract with themselves, the public were bound to pay to those, to whom they should convey their title, the sums stipulated to be paid to them; and, that as citizens of the United States, they were to bear their proportion of the contribution for that purpose. This, by the act of assignment, they tacitly engage to do; and if they had an option, they could not, with integrity or good faith, refuse to do it, without the consent of those to whom they sold.

But though many of the original holders sold from necessity, it does not follow, that this was the case with all of them. It may well be supposed, that some of them did it either through want of confidence in an eventual provision, or from the allurements of some profitable speculation. How shall these different classes be discriminated from each other? How shall it be ascertained, in any case, that the money, which the original holder obtained for his security, was not more beneficial to him, than if he had held it to the pressent time, to avail himself of the provision which shall be made? How shall it be known, whether if the purchaser had employed his money in some other way, he would not be in a better situation, than by having applied it in the purchase of securities, though he should now receive their full amount? And if neither of these things can be known, how shall it be determined whether a discrimination, independent of the breach of contract, would not do a real injury to purchasers; and if it included a compensation to the primitive proprietors, would not give them an advantage, to which they had no equitable pretension.

It may well be imagined, also, that there are not wanting instances, in which individuals, urged by a present necessity, parted with the securities received by them from the public, and shortly after replaced them with others, as an indemnity for their first loss. Shall they be deprived of the indemnity which they have endeavoured to secure by so provident an arrangement?

Questions of this sort, on a close inspection, multiply themselves without end, and demonstrate the injustice of a discrimination, even on the most subtile calculations of equity, abstracted from the obligation of contract.

The difficulties too of regulating the details of a plan for that purpose, which would have even the semblance of equity, would be found immense. It may well be doubted whether they would not be insurmountable, and replete with such absurd, as well as inequitable consequences, as to disgust even the proposers of the measure.

As a specimen of its capricious operation, it will be sufficient to notice the effect it would have upon two persons, who may be supposed two years ago to have purchased, each, securities at three shillings in the pound, and one of them to retain those bought by him, till the discrimination should take place; the other to have parted with those bought by him, within a month past, at nine shillings. The former, who had had most confidence in the government, would in this case only receive at the rate of three shillings and the interest; while the latter, who had had less confidence would receive *for what cost him the same money* at the rate of nine shillings, and his representative, *standing in his place*, would be entitled to a like rate.

The impolicy of a discrimination results from two considerations; one, that it proceeds upon a principle destructive of that *quality* of the public debt, or the stock of the nation, which is essential to its capacity for answering the purposes of money—that is the *security* of *transfer*; the other, that as well on this account, as because it includes a breach of faith, it renders property in the funds less valuable; consequently induces lenders to demand a higher premium for what they lend, and produces every other inconvenience of a bad state of public credit.

It will be perceived at first sight, that the transferable quality of stock is essential to its operation as money, and that this depends on the idea of complete security to the transferree, and a firm persuasion, that no distinction can in any circumstances be made between him and the original proprietor.

The precedent of an invasion of this fundamental principle, would of course tend to deprive the community of an advantage, with which no temporary saving could bear the least comparison.

And it will as readily be perceived, that the same cause would operate a diminution of the value of stock in the hands of the first, as well as of every other holder. The price, which any man, who should incline to purchase, would be willing to give for it, would be in a compound ratio to the immediate profit it afforded, and to the chance of the continuance of his profit. If there was supposed to be any hazard of the latter, the risk would be taken into the calculation, and either there would be no purchase at all, or it would be at a proportionably less price.

For this diminution of the value of stock, every person, who should be about to lend to the government, would demand a compensation; and would add to the actual difference, between the nominal and the market value, and equivalent for the chance of greater decrease; which, in a precarious state of public credit, is always to be taken into the account.

Every compensation of this sort, it is evident, would be an absolute loss to the government.

In the preceding discussion of the impolicy of a discrimination, the injurious tendency of it to those, who continue to be the holders of the securities, they received from the government, has been explained. Nothing need be added, on this head, except that this is an additional and interesting light, in which the injustice of the measure may be seen. It would not only divest present proprietors by purchase, of the rights they had acquired under the sanction of public faith, but it would depreciate the property of the remaining original holders.

It is equally unnecessary to add any thing to what has been already said to demonstrate the fatal influence, which the principle of discrimination would have on the public credit.

But there is still a point in view in which it will appear perhaps even more exceptionable, than in either of the former. It would be repugnant to an express provision of the Constitution of the United States. This provision is, that "all debts contracted and engagements entered into before the adoption of that Constitution shall be as valid against the United States under it, as under the confederation," which amounts to a constitutional ratification of the contracts respecting the debt, in the state in which they existed under the confederation. And resorting to that standard, there can be no doubt, that the rights of assignees and original holders, must be considered as equal.

In exploding thus fully the principle of discrimination, the Secretary is happy in reflecting, that he is the only advocate of what has been already sanctioned by the formal and express authority of the government of the Union, in these emphatic terms—"The remaining class of creditors (say Congress in their circular address to the states, of the 26th of April 1783) is composed, partly of such of our fellow-citizens as originally lent to the public the use of their funds, or have since manifested *most confidence* in their country, by receiving transfers from the lenders; and partly of those, whose property has been either advanced or assumed for the public service. To *discriminate* the merits of these several descriptions of creditors, would be a task equally unnecessary and invidious. If the voice of humanity plead more loudly in favor of some than of others, the voice of policy, no less than of justice, pleads in favor of all. A WISE NATION will never permit those who relieve the wants of their country, or who *rely most* on its *faith*, its *firmness*, and its *resources*, when either of them is distrusted, to suffer by the event."

The Secretary concluding, that a discrimination, between the different classes of creditors of the United States, cannot with propriety be *made*, proceeds to examine whether a difference ought to be permitted to *remain* between them, and another description of public creditors—Those of the states individually.

The Secretary, after mature reflection on this point, entertains a full conviction, that an assumption of the debts of the particular states by the union, and a like provision for them, as for those of the union, will be a measure of sound policy and substantial justice.

It would, in the opinion of the Secretary, contribute, in an eminent degree, to an orderly, stable and satisfactory arrangement of the national finances.

Admitting, as ought to be the case, that a provision must be made in some way or other, for the entire debt; it will follow, that no greater revenues will be required, whether that provision be made wholly by the United States, or partly by them, and partly by the states separately.

The principal question then must be, whether such a provision cannot be more conveniently and effectually made, by one general plan issuing from one authority, than by different plans originating in different authorities.

In the first case there can be no competition for resources; in the last, there must be such a competition. The consequences of this, without the greatest caution on both sides, might be interfering regulations, and thence collision and confusion. Particular branches of industry might also be oppressed by it. The most productive objects of revenue are not numerous. Either these must be wholly engrossed by one side, which might lessen the efficacy of the provisions by the other; or both must have recourse to the same objects in different modes, which might occasion an accumulation upon them, beyond what they could properly bear. If this should not happen, the caution requisite to avoiding it, would prevent the revenue's deriving the full benefit of each object. The danger of interference and of excess would be apt to impose restraints very unfriendly to the complete command of those resources, which are the most convenient; and to compel the having recourse to others, less eligible in themselves, and less agreeable to the community.

The difficulty of an effectual command of the public resources, in case of separate provisions for the debt, may be seen in another, and perhaps more striking light. It would naturally happen that different states, from local considerations, would in some instances have recourse to different objects, in others, to the same objects, in different degrees, for procuring the funds of which they stood in need. It is easy to conceive how this diversity would affect the aggregate revenue of the country. By the supposition, articles which yielded a full supply in some states, would yield nothing, or an insufficient product, in others. And hence the public revenue would not derive the full benefit of those articles, from state regulations. Neither could the deficiencies be made good by those of the union. It is a provision of the national constitution, that "all duties, imposts and excises, shall be uniform throughout the United States." And as the general government would be under a necessity from motives of policy, of paying regard to the duty, which may have been previously imposed upon any article, though but in a single state, it would be constrained, either to refrain wholly from any further imposition, upon such article, where it had been already rated as high as was proper, or to confine itself to the difference between the existing rate, and what the article would reasonably bear. Thus the pre-occupancy of an article by a single state, would tend to arrest or abridge the impositions of the union on that article. And as it is supposeable, that a great variety of articles might be placed in this situation, by dissimilar arrangements of the particular states, it is evident, that the aggregate revenue of the country would be likely to be very materially contracted by the plan of separate provisions.

If all the public creditors receive their dues from one source, distributed with an equal hand, their interest will be the same. And having the same interests, they will unite in the support of the fiscal arrangements of the government: As these, too, can be made with more convenience, where there is no competition: These circumstances combined will insure to the revenue laws a more ready and more satisfactory execution.

If on the contrary there are distinct provisions, there will be distinct interests, drawing different ways. That union and concert of views, among the creditors, which in every government is of great importance to their security, and to that of public credit, will not only not exist, but will be likely to give place to mutual jealousy and opposition. And from this cause, the operation of the systems which may be adopted, both by the particular states, and by the union, with relation to their respective debts, will be in danger of being counteracted.

There are several reasons, which render it probable, that the situation of the state creditors would be worse, than that of the creditors of the union, if there be not a national assumption of the state debts. Of these it will be sufficient to mention two; one, that a principal branch of revenue is exclusively vested in the union; the other, that a state must always be checked in the imposition of taxes on articles of consumption, from the want of power to extend the same regulation to the other states, and from the tendency of partial duties to injure its industry and commerce. Should the state creditors stand upon a less eligible footing than the others, it is unnatural to expect they would see with pleasure a provision for them. The influence which their dissatisfaction might have, could not but operate injuriously, both for the creditors, and the credit, of the United States.

Hence it is even the interest of the creditors of the union, that those of the individual states should be comprehended in a general provision. Any attempt to secure to the former either exclusive or peculiar advantages, would materially hazard their interests.

Neither would it be just, that one class of the public creditors should be more favoured than the other. The objects for which both descriptions of the debt were contracted, are in the main the same. Indeed a great part of the particular debts of the States has arisen from assumptions by them on account of the union. And it is most equitable, that there should be the same measure of retribution for all.

There is an objection, however, to an assumption of the state debts, which deserves particular notice. It may be supposed, that it would increase the difficulty of an equitable settlement between them and the United States.

The principles of that settlement, whenever they shall be discussed, will require all the moderation and wisdom of the government. In the opinion of the Secretary, that discussion, till further lights are obtained, would be premature.

All therefore which he would now think adviseable on the point in question, would be, that the amount of the debts assumed and provided for, should be charged to the respective states, to abide an eventual arrangement. This, the United States, as assignees to the creditors, would have an indisputable right to do.

# Opinion on the Constitutionality of an Act to Establish a Bank

The Secretary of the Treasury having perused with attention the papers containing the opinions of the Secretary of State and Attorney General concerning the constitutionality of the bill for establishing a National Bank proceeds according to the order of the President to submit the reasons which have induced him to entertain a different opinion.

It will naturally have been anticipated that, in performing this task he would feel uncommon solicitude. Personal considerations alone arising from the reflection that the measure originated with him would be sufficient to produce it: The sense which he has manifested of the great importance of such an institution to the successful administration of the department under his particular care; and an expectation of serious ill consequences to result from a failure of the measure, do not permit him to be without anxiety on public accounts. But the chief solicitude arises from a firm persuasion, that principles of construction like those espoused by the Secretary of State and the Attorney General would be fatal to the just & indispensible authority of the United States.

In entering upon the argument it ought to be premised, that the objections of the Secretary of State and Attorney General are founded on a general denial of the authority of the United States to erect corporations. The latter indeed expressly admits, that if there be any thing in the bill which is not warranted by the constitution, it is the clause of incorporation.

Now it appears to the Secretary of the Treasury, that this *general principle* is *inherent* in the very *definition* of *Government* and *essential* to every step of the progress to be made by that of the United States; namely—that every power vested in a Government is in its nature *sovereign*, and includes by *force* of the *term*, a right to employ all the *means* requisite, and fairly *applicable* to the attainment of the *ends* of such power; and which are not precluded by restrictions & exceptions specified in the constitution; or not immoral, or not contrary to the essential ends of political society.

This principle in its application to Government in general would be admitted as an axiom. And it will be incumbent upon those, who may incline to deny it, to *prove* a distinction; and to shew that a rule which in the general system of things is essential to the preservation of the social order is inapplicable to the United States.

The circumstances that the powers of sovereignty are in this country divided between the National and State Governments, does not afford the distinction required. It does not follow from this, that each of the *portions* of powers delegated to the one or to the other is not sovereign *with regard to its proper objects*. It will only *follow* from it, that each has sovereign power as to *certain things*, and not as to *other things*. To deny that the Government of the United States has sovereign power as to its declared purposes & trusts, because its power does not extend to all cases, would be equally to deny, that the State Governments have sovereign power in any case; because their power does not extend to every case. The tenth section of the first article of the constitution exhibits a long list of very important things which they may not do. And thus the United States would furnish the singular spectacle of a *political society* without *sovereignty,* or of a people *governed* without *government.*

If it would be necessary to bring proof to a proposition so clear as that which affirms that the powers of the fœderal government, *as to its objects*, are sovereign, there is a clause of its constitution which would be decisive. It is that which declares, that the constitution and the laws of the United States made in pursuance of it, and all treaties made or which shall be made under their authority shall be the supreme law of the land. The power which can create the *Supreme law* of the land, in any case, is doubtless sovereign *as to such case*.

This general & indisputable principle puts at once an end to the *abstract* question—Whether the United States have power to *erect a corporation?* that is to say, to give a *legal* or *artificial* capacity to one or more persons, distinct from the natural. For it is unquestionably incident to *sovereign power* to erect corporations, and consequently to *that* of the United States, in *relation to the objects* intrusted to the management of the government. The difference is this—where the authority of the government is general, it can create corporations in *all cases*; where it is confined to certain branches of legislation, it can create corporations only in those cases.

Here then as far as concerns the reasonings of the Secretary of State & the Attorney General, the affirmative of the constitutionality of the bill might be permitted to rest. It will occur to the President that the principle here advanced has been untouched by either of them.

For a more complete elucidation of the point nevertheless, the arguments which they have used against the power of the government to erect corporations, however foreign they are to the great & fundamental rule which has been stated, shall be particularly examined. And after shewing that they do not tend to impair its force, it shall also be shewn, that the power of incorporation incident to the government in certain cases, does fairly extend to the particular case which is the object of the bill.

The first of these arguments is, that the foundation of the constitution is laid on this ground "that all powers not delegated to the United States by the Constitution nor prohibited to it by the States are reserved to the States or to the people", whence it is meant to be inferred, that congress can in no case exercise any power not included in those enumerated in the constitution. And it is affirmed that the power of erecting a corporation is not included in any of the enumerated powers.

The main proposition here laid down, in its true signification is not to be questioned. It is nothing more than a consequence of this republican maxim, that all government is a delegation of power. But how much is delegated in each case, is a question of fact to be made out by fair reasoning & construction upon the particular provisions of the constitution—taking as guides the general principles & general ends of government.

It is not denied, that there are *implied*, as well as *express* powers, and that the former are as effectually delegated as the latter. And for the sake of accuracy it shall be mentioned, that there is another class of powers, which may be properly denominated *resulting* powers. It will not be doubted that if the United States should make a conquest of any of the territories of its neighbours, they would possess sovereign jurisdiction over the conquered territory. This would rather be a result from the whole mass of the powers of the government & from the nature of political society, than a consequence of either of the powers specially enumerated.

But be this as it may, it furnishes a striking illustration of the general doctrine contended for. It shews an extensive case, in which a power of erecting corporations is either implied in, or would result from some or all of the powers, vested in the National Government. The jurisdiction acquired over such conquered territory would certainly be competent to every species of legislation.

To return—It is conceded, that implied powers are to be considered as delegated equally with express ones.

Then it follows, that as a power of erecting a corporation may as well be *implied* as any other thing; it may as well be employed as an *instrument* or *mean* of carrying into execution any of the specified powers, as any other instrument or mean whatever. The only question must be, in this as in every other case, whether the mean to be employed, or in this instance the corporation to be erected, has a natural relation to any of the acknowledged objects or lawful ends of the government. Thus a corporation may not be erected by congress, for superintending the police of the city of Philadelphia because they are not authorised to *regulate* the *police* of that city; but one may be erected in relation to the collection of the taxes, or to the trade with foreign countries, or to the trade between the States, or with the Indian Tribes, because it is the province of the fœderal government to regulate those objects & because it is incident to a general *sovereign* or *legislative power* to *regulate* a thing, to employ all the means which relate to its regulation to the *best & greatest advantage*.

A strange fallacy seems to have crept into the manner of thinking & reasoning upon the subject. Imagination appears to have been unusually busy concerning it. An incorporation seems to have been regarded as some great, independent, substantive thing—as a political end of peculiar magnitude & moment; whereas it is truly to be considered as a *quality*, *capacity*, or *mean* to an end. Thus a mercantile company is formed with a certain capital for the purpose of carrying on a particular branch of business. Here the business to be prosecuted is the *end*; the association in order to form the requisite capital is the primary mean. Suppose that an incorporation were added to this; it would only be to add a new *quality* to that association; to give it an artificial capacity by which it would be enabled to prosecute the business with more safety & convenience.

That the importance of the power of incorporation has been exaggerated, leading to erroneous conclusions, will further appear from tracing it to its origin. The roman law is the source of it, according to which a *voluntary* association of individuals at *any time* or *for any purpose* was capable of producing it. In England, whence our notions of it are immediately borrowed, it forms a part of the executive authority, & the exercise of it has been often *delegated* by that authority. Whence therefore the ground of the supposition, that it lies beyond the reach of all those very important portions of sovereign power, legislative as well as executive, which belong to the government of the United States?

To this mode of reasoning respecting the right of employing all the means requisite to the execution of the specified powers of the Government, it is objected that none but *necessary* & proper means are to be employed, & the Secretary of State maintains, that no means are to be considered as *necessary*, but those without which the grant of the power would be *nugatory*. Nay so far does he go in his restrictive interpretation of the word, as even to make the case of *necessity* which shall warrant the constitutional exercise of the power to depend on *casual* & *temporary* circumstances, an idea which alone refutes the construction. The *expediency* of exercising a particular power, at a particular time, must indeed depend on *circumstances*; but the constitutional right of exercising it must be uniform & invariable— the same to day, as to morrow.

All the arguments therefore against the constitutionality of the bill derived from the accidental existence of certain State-banks: institutions which *happen* to exist to day, & for ought that concerns the government of the United States, may disappear to morrow, must not only be rejected as fallacious, but must be viewed as demonstrative, that there is a *radical* source of error in the reasoning.

It is essential to the being of the National government, that so erroneous a conception of the meaning of the word *necessary*, should be exploded.

It is certain, that neither the grammatical, nor popular sense of the term requires that construction. According to both, *necessary* often means no more than *needful*, *requisite*, *incidental*, *useful*, or *conducive to*. It is a common mode of expression to say, that it is *necessary* for a government or a person to do this or that thing, when nothing more is intended or understood, than that the interests of the government or person require, or will be promoted, by the doing of this or that thing. The imagination can be at no loss for exemplifications of the use of the word in this sense.

And it is the true one in which it is to be understood as used in the constitution. The whole turn of the clause containing it, indicates, that it was the intent of the convention, by that clause to give a liberal latitude to the exercise of the specified powers. The expressions have peculiar comprehensiveness. They are—"to make *all laws*, necessary & proper for *carrying into execution* the foregoing powers & all *other powers* vested by the constitution in the *government* of the United States, or in any *department* or *officer* thereof." To understand the word as the Secretary of State does, would be to depart from its obvious & popular sense, and to give it a *restrictive* operation; an idea never before entertained. It would be to give it the same force as if the word *absolutely* or *indispensibly* had been prefixed to it.

Such a construction would beget endless uncertainty & embarassment. The cases must be palpable & extreme in which it could be pronounced with certainty, that a measure was absolutely necessary, or one without which the exercise of a given power would be nugatory. There are few measures of any government, which would stand so severe a test. To insist upon it, would be to make the criterion of the exercise of any implied power a *case of extreme necessity*; which is rather a rule to justify the overleaping of the bounds of constitutional authority, than to govern the ordinary exercise of it.

It may be truly said of every government, as well as of that of the United States, that it has only a right, to pass such laws as are necessary & proper to accomplish the objects intrusted to it. For no government has a right to do *merely what it pleases*. Hence by a process of reasoning similar to that of the Secretary of State, it might be proved, that neither of the State governments has a right to incorporate a bank. It might be shewn, that all the public business of the State, could be performed without a bank, and inferring thence that it was unnecessary it might be argued that it could not be done, because it is against the rule which has been just mentioned. A like mode of reasoning would prove, that there was no power to incorporate the Inhabitants of a town, with a view to a more perfect police: For it is certain, that an incorporation may be dispensed with, though it is better to have one. It is to be remembered, that there is no *express* power in any State constitution to erect corporations.

The *degree* in which a measure is necessary, can never be a test of the *legal* right to adopt it. That must ever be a matter of opinion; and can only be a test of expediency. The *relation* between the *measure* and the *end*, between the *nature* of *the mean* employed towards the execution of a power and the object of that power, must be the criterion of constitutionality not the more or less of *necessity* or *utility*.

The practice of the government is against the rule of construction advocated by the Secretary of State. Of this the act concerning light houses, beacons, buoys & public piers, is a decisive example. This doubtless must be referred to the power of regulating trade, and is fairly relative to it. But it cannot be affirmed, that the exercise of that power, in this instance, was strictly necessary; or that the power itself would be *nugatory* without that of regulating establishments of this nature.

This restrictive interpretation of the word *necessary* is also contrary to this sound maxim of construction namely, that the powers contained in a constitution of government, especially those which concern the general administration of the affairs of a country, its finances, trade, defence &c ought to be construed liberally, in advancement of the public good. This rule does not depend on the particular form of a government or on the particular demarkation of the boundaries of its powers, but on the nature and objects of government itself. The means by which national exigencies are to be provided for, national inconveniencies obviated, national prosperity promoted, are of such infinite variety, extent and complexity, that there must, of necessity, be great latitude of discretion in the selection & application of those means. Hence consequently, the necessity & propriety of exercising the authorities intrusted to a government on principles of liberal construction.

The Attorney General admits the *rule*, but takes a distinction between a State, and the fœderal constitution. The latter, he thinks, ought to be construed with greater strictness, because there is more danger of error in defining partial than general powers.

But the reason of the *rule* forbids such a distinction. This reason is—the variety & extent of public exigencies, a far greater proportion of which and of a far more critical kind, are objects of National than of State administration. The greater danger of error, as far as it is supposeable, may be a prudential reason for caution in practice, but it cannot be a rule of restrictive interpretation.

In regard to the clause of the constitution immediately under consideration, it is admitted by the Attorney General, that no *restrictive* effect can be ascribed to it. He defines the word necessary thus. "To be necessary is to be *incidental*, and may be denominated the natural means of executing a power."

But while, on the one hand, the construction of the Secretary of State is deemed inadmissible, it will not be contended on the other, that the clause in question gives any *new* or *independent* power. But it gives an explicit sanction to the doctrine of *implied* powers, and is equivalent to an admission of the proposition, that the government, *as to its specified powers* and *objects*, has plenary & sovereign authority, in some cases paramount to that of the States, in others coordinate with it. For such is the plain import of the declaration, that it may pass *all laws* necessary & proper to carry into execution those powers.

It is no valid objection to the doctrine to say, that it is calculated to extend the powers of the general government throughout the entire sphere of State legislation. The same thing has been said, and may be said with regard to every exercise of power by *implication* or *construction*. The moment the literal meaning is departed from, there is a chance of error and abuse. And yet an adherence to the letter of its powers would at once arrest the motions of the government. It is not only agreed, on all hands, that the exercise of constructive powers is indispensible, but every act which has been passed is more or less an exemplification of it. One has been already mentioned, that relating to light houses &c. That which declares the power of the President to remove officers at pleasure, acknowlidges the same truth in another, and a signal instance.

The truth is that difficulties on this point are inherent in the nature of the fœderal constitution. They result inevitably from a division of the legislative power. The consequence of this division is, that there will be cases clearly within the power of the National Government; others clearly without its power; and a third class, which will leave room for controversy & difference of opinion, & concerning which a reasonable latitude of judgment must be allowed.

But the doctrine which is contended for is not chargeable with the consequence imputed to it. It does not affirm that the National government is sovereign in all respects, but that it is sovereign to a certain extent: that is, to the extent of the objects of its specified powers.

It leaves therefore a criterion of what is constitutional, and of what is not so. This criterion is the *end* to which the measure relates as a *mean*. If the end be clearly comprehended within any of the specified powers, & if the measure have an obvious relation to that end, and is not forbidden by any particular provision of the constitution—it may safely be deemed to come within the compass of the national authority. There is also this further criterion which may materially assist the decision. Does the proposed measure abridge a preexisting right of any State, or of any individual? If it does not, there is a strong presumption in favour of its constitutionality; & slighter relations to any declared object of the constitution may be permitted to turn the scale.

The general objections which are to be inferred from the reasonings of the Secretary of State and of the Attorney General to the doctrine which has been advanced, have been stated and it is hoped satisfactorily answered. Those of a more particular nature shall now be examined.

The Secretary of State introduces his opinion with an observation, that the proposed incorporation undertakes to create certain capacities properties or attributes which are *against* the laws of *alienage*, *descents*, *escheat* and *forfeiture*, *distribution* and *monopoly*, and to confer a power to make laws paramount to those of the States. And nothing says he, in another place, but a *necessity invincible by other means* can justify such a *prostration* of *laws* which constitute the pillars of our whole system of jurisprudence, and are the foundation laws of the State Governments.

If these are truly the foundation laws of the several states, then have most of them subverted their own foundations. For there is scarcely one of them which has not, since the establishment of its particular constitution, made material alterations in some of those branches of its jurisprudence especially the law of descents. But it is not conceived how any thing can be called the fundamental law of a State Government which is not established in its constitution unalterable by the ordinary legislature. And with regard to the question of necessity it has been shewn, that this can only constitute a question of expediency, not of right.

To erect a corporation is to substitute a *legal* or *artificial* to a *natural* person, and where a number are concerned to give them *individuality*. To that legal or artificial person once created, the common law of every state of itself *annexes* all those incidents and attributes, which are represented as a prostration of the main pillars of their jurisprudence. It is certainly not accurate to say, that the erection of a corporation is *against* those different *heads* of the State laws; because it is rather to create a kind of person or entity, to which *they* are inapplicable, and to which the general rule of those laws assign a different regimen. The laws of alienage cannot apply to an artificial person, because it can have no country. Those of descent cannot apply to it, because it can have no heirs. Those of escheat are foreign from it for the same reason. Those of forfeiture, because it cannot commit a crime. Those of distribution, because, though it may be dissolved, it cannot die. As truly might it be said, that the exercise of the power of prescribing the rule by which foreigners shall be naturalised, is *against* the law of alienage; while it is in fact only to put them in a situation to cease to be the subject of that law. To do a thing which is *against* a law, is to do something which it forbids or which is a violation of it.

But if it were even to be admitted that the erection of a corporation is a direct alteration of the State laws in the enumerated particulars; it would do nothing towards proving, that the measure was unconstitutional. If the government of the United States can do no act, which amounts to an alteration of a State law, all its powers are nugatory. For almost every new law is an alteration, in some way or other of an old *law*, either *common*, or *statute*.

There are laws concerning bankruptcy in some states—some states have laws regulating the values of foreign coins. Congress are empowered to establish uniform laws concerning bankruptcy throughout the United States, and to regulate the values of foreign coins. The exercise of either of these powers by Congress necessarily involves an alteration of the laws of those states.

Again: Every person by the common law of each state may export his property to foreign countries, at pleasure. But Congress, in pursuance of the power of regulating trade, may prohibit the exportation of commodities: in doing which, they would alter the common law of each state in abridgement of individual rights.

It can therefore never be good reasoning to say—this or that act is unconstitutional, because it alters this or that law of a State. It must be shewn, that the act which makes the alteration is unconstitutional on other accounts, not *because* it makes the alteration.

There are two points in the suggestions of the Secretary of State which have been noted that are peculiarly incorrect. One is, that the proposed incorporation is against the laws of monopoly, because it stipulates an exclusive right of banking under the national authority. The other that it gives power to the institution to make laws paramount to those of the states.

But with regard to the first point, the bill neither prohibits any State from erecting as many banks as they please, nor any number of

Individuals from associating to carry on the business: & consequently is free from the charge of establishing a monopoly: for monopoly implies a *legal impediment* to the carrying on of the trade by others than those to whom it is granted.

And with regard to the second point, there is still less foundation. The bye-laws of such an institution as a bank can operate only upon its own members; can only concern the disposition of its own property and must essentially resemble the rules of a private mercantile partnership. They are expressly not to be contrary to law; and law must here mean the law of a State as well as of the United States. There never can be a doubt, that a law of the corporation, if contrary to a law of a state, must be overruled as void; unless the law of the State is contrary to that of the United States; and then the question will not be between the law of the State and that of the corporation, but between the law of the State and that of the United States.

Another argument made use of by the Secretary of State, is, the rejection of a proposition by the convention to empower Congress to make corporations, either generally, or for some special purpose.

What was the precise nature or extent of this proposition, or what the reasons for refusing it, is not ascertained by any authentic document, or even by accurate recollection. As far as any such document exists, it specifies only canals. If this was the amount of it, it would at most only prove, that it was thought inexpedient to give a power to incorporate for the purpose of opening canals, for which purpose a special power would have been necessary; except with regard to the Western Territory, there being nothing in any part of the constitution respecting the regulation of canals. It must be confessed however, that very different accounts are given of the import of the proposition and of the motives for rejecting it. Some affirm that it was confined to the opening of canals and obstructions in rivers; others, that it embraced banks; and others, that it extended to the power of incorporating generally. Some again alledge, that it was disagreed to, because it was thought improper to vest in Congress a power of erecting corporations—others, because it was thought unnecessary to *specify* the power, and inexpedient to furnish an additional topic of objection to the constitution. In this state of the matter, no inference whatever can be drawn from it.

But whatever may have been the nature of the proposition or the reasons for rejecting it concludes nothing in respect to the real merits of the question. The Secretary of State will not deny, that whatever may have been the intention of the framers of a constitution, or of a law, that intention is to be sought for in the instrument itself, according to the usual & established rules of construction. Nothing is more common than for laws to *express* and *effect*, more or less than was intended. If then a power to erect a corporation, in any case, be deducible by fair inference from the whole or any part of the numerous provisions of the constitution of the United States, arguments drawn from extrinsic circumstances, regarding the intention of the convention, must be rejected.

Most of the arguments of the Secretary of State which have not been considered in the foregoing remarks, are of a nature rather to apply to the expediency than to the constitutionality of the bill. They will however be noticed in the discussions which will be necessary in reference to the particular heads of the powers of the government which are involved in the question.

Those of the Attorney General will now properly come under review.

His first observation is, that the power of incorporation is not *expressly* given to congress. This shall be conceded, but in *this sense* only, that it is not declared in *express terms* that congress may erect a *corporation*. But this cannot mean, that there are not certain *express* powers, which *necessarily* include it.

For instance, Congress have express power "to exercise exclusive legislation in all cases whatsoever, over such *district* (not exceeding ten miles square) as may by cession of particular states, & the acceptance of Congress become the seat of the government of the United states; and to exercise *like authority* over all places purchased by consent of the legislature of the State in which the same shall be for the erection of forts, arsenals, dock yards & other needful buildings."

Here then is express power to exercise *exclusive legislation in all cases whatsoever over certain places*; that is to do in respect to those places, all that any government whatever may do: For language does not afford a more complete designation of sovereign power, than in those comprehensive terms. It is in other words a power to pass all laws whatsoever, & consequently to pass laws for erecting corporations, as well as for any other purpose which is the proper object of law in a free government. Surely it can never be believed, that Congress with *exclusive power of legislation in all cases whatsoever*, cannot erect a corporation within the district which shall become the seat of government, for the better regulation of its police. And yet there is an unqualified denial of the power to erect corporations in every case on the part both of the Secretary of State and of the Attorney General. The former indeed speaks of that power in these emphatical terms, that it is *a right remaining exclusively with the states*.

As far then as there is an express power to do any *particular act of legislation*, there is an express one to erect corporations in the cases above described. But accurately speaking, no *particular power* is more than *implied* in a *general one*. Thus the power to lay a duty on a *gallon of rum*, is only a particular *implied* in the general power to lay and collect taxes, duties, imposts and excises. This serves to explain in what sense it may be said, that congress have not an express power to make corporations.

This may not be an improper place to take notice of an argument which was used in debate in the House of Representatives. It was there urged, that if the constitution intended to confer so important a power as that of erecting corporations, it would have been expressly mentioned. But the case which has been noticed is clearly one in which such a power exists, and yet without any specification or express grant of it, further than as every *particular implied* in a general power, can be said to be so granted.

But the argument itself is founded upon an exaggerated and erroneous conception of the nature of the power. It has been shewn, that it is not of so transcendent a kind as the reasoning supposes; and that viewed in a just light it is a mean which ought to have been left to *implication*, rather than an end which ought to have been *expressly* granted.

Having observed, that the power of erecting corporations is not expressly granted to Congress, the Attorney General proceeds thus . . .

"If it can be exercised by them, it must be

1. because the nature of the fœderal government implies it.
2. because it is involved in some of the specified powers of legislation or
3. because it is necessary & proper to carry into execution some of the specified powers."

To be implied in the *nature of the fœderal government*, says he, would beget a doctrine so indefinite, as to grasp every power.

This proposition it ought to be remarked is not precisely, or even substantially, that, which has been relied upon. The proposition relied upon is, that the *specified powers* of Congress are in their nature sovereign—that it is incident to sovereign power to erect corporations; & that therefore Congress have a right within the *sphere* & *in relation to the objects of their power, to erect corporations.*

It shall however be supposed, that the Attorney General would consider the two propositions in the same light, & that the objection made to the one, would be made to the other.

To this objection an answer has been already given. It is this; that the doctrine is stated with this express *qualification*, that the right to erect corporations does *only* extend to *cases* & *objects* within the *sphere* of the *specified powers* of the government. A general legislative authority implies a power to erect corporations *in all cases*—a particular legislative power implies authority to erect corporations, in relation to cases arising under that power only. Hence the affirming, that as an *incident* to sovereign power, congress may erect a corporation in relation to the *collection* of their taxes, is no more than to affirm that they may do whatever else they please; than the saying that they have a power to regulate trade would be to affirm that they have a power to regulate religion: or than the maintaining that they have sovereign power as to taxation, would be to maintain that they have sovereign power as to every thing else.

The Attorney General undertakes, in the next place, to shew, that the power of erecting corporations is not involved in any of the specified powers of legislation confided to the National government.

In order to this he has attempted an enumeration of the particulars which he supposes to be comprehended under the several heads of the *powers* to lay & collect taxes &c—to borrow money on the credit of the United States—to regulate commerce with foreign nations—between the states, and with the Indian Tribes—to dispose of and make all needful rules & regulations respecting the territory or other property belonging to the United States; the design of which enumeration is to shew *what is* included under those different heads of power, & *negatively*, that the power of erecting corporations is not included.

The truth of this inference or conclusion must depend on the accuracy of the enumeration. If it can be shewn that the enumeration is *defective*, the inference is destroyed. To do this will be attended with no difficulty.

The heads of the power to lay & collect taxes, he states to be

1. To ascertain the subject of taxation &c

2. to declare the quantum of taxation &c

3. to prescribe the *mode* of *collection*.

4. to ordain the manner of accounting for the taxes &c

The defectiveness of this enumeration consists in the generality of the third division "*to prescribe the mode* of collection"; which is in itself an immense chapter. It will be shewn hereafter, that, among a vast variety of particulars, it comprises the very power in question; namely to *erect corporations*.

The heads of the power to borrow money are stated to be

1. to stipulate the sum to be lent.

2. an interest or no interest to be paid.

3. the time & manner of repaying, unless the loan be placed on an irredeemable fund.

This enumeration is liable to a variety of objections. It omits, in the first place, the *pledging* or *mortgaging* of a fund for the security of the money lent, an usual and in most cases an essential ingredient.

The idea of a stipulation of *an interest or no interest* is too confined. It should rather have been said, to stipulate the *consideration* of the loan. Individuals often borrow upon considerations other than the payment of interest. So may government; and so they often find it necessary to do. Every one reCollects the lottery tickets & other douceurs often given in Great Britain, as collateral inducements to the lending of money to the Government.

There are also frequently collateral conditions, which the enumeration does not contemplate. Every contract which has been made for monies borrowed in Holland includes stipulations that the sum due shall be *free from taxes*, and from sequestration in time of war, and mortgages all the land & property of the United States for the reimbursement.

It is also known, that a lottery is a common expedient for borrowing money, which certainly does not fall under either of the enumerated heads.

The heads of the power to regulate commerce with foreign nations are stated to be

1. to prohibit them or their commodities from our ports.

2. to impose duties on *them* where none existed before, or to increase existing duties on them.

3. to subject *them* to any species of custom house regulation
4. to grant *them* any exemptions or privileges which policy may suggest.

This enumeration is far more exceptionable than either of the former. It omits *every thing* that relates to the *citizens vessels* or *commodities* of the United States. The following palpable omissions occur at once.

1. Of the power to prohibit the exportation of commodities which not only exists at all times, but which in time of war it would be necessary to exercise, particularly with relation to naval and warlike stores.
2. Of the power to prescribe rules concerning the *characteristics* & *priviledges* of an american bottom—how she shall be navigated, as whether by citizens or foreigners, or by a proportion of each.
3. Of the power of regulating the manner of contracting with seamen, the police of ships on their voyages &c of which the act for the government & regulation of seamen in the merchants service is a specimen.

That the three preceding articles are omissions, will not be doubted. There is a long list of items in addition, which admit of little, if any question; of which a few samples shall be given.

1. The granting of bounties to certain kinds of vessels, & certain species of merchandise. Of this nature is the allowance on dried & pickled fish & salted provisions.
2. The prescribing of rules concerning the *inspection* of commodities to be exported. Though the states individually are competent to this regulation, yet there is no reason, in point of authority at least, why a general system might not be adopted by the United States.
3. The regulation of policies of insurance; of salvage upon goods found at sea, and the disposition of such goods.
4. The regulation of pilots.
5. The regulation of bills of exchange drawn by a merchant of *one state* upon a merchant of *another state*. This last rather belongs to the regulation of trade between the states, but is equally omitted in the specification under that head.

The last enumeration relates to the power "to dispose of & make *all needful rules and regulations* respecting the territory *or other property* belonging to the United States."

The heads of this power are said to be

1. to exert an ownership over the territory of the United States, which may be properly called the property of the United States, as in the Western Territory, and to *institute a government therein*: or

2. to exert an ownership over the other property of the United States.

This idea of exerting an ownership over the Territory or other property of the United States, is particularly indefinite and vague. It does not at all satisfy the conception of what must have been intended by a power, to make all needful *rules* and *regulations*; nor would there have been any use for a special clause which authorised nothing more. For the right of exerting an ownership is implied in the very definition of property.

It is admitted that in regard to the western territory some thing more is intended—even the institution of a government; that is the creation of a body politic, or corporation of the highest nature; one, which in its maturity, will be able itself to create other corporations. Why then does not the same clause authorise the erection of a corporation in respect to the regulation or disposal of any other of the property of the United States? This idea will be enlarged upon in another place.

Hence it appears, that the enumerations which have been attempted by the Attorney General are so imperfect, as to authorise no conclusion whatever. They therefore have no tendency to disprove, that each and every of the powers to which they relate, includes that of erecting corporations; which they certainly do, as the subsequent illustrations will more & more evince.

It is presumed to have been satisfactorily shewn in the course of the preceding observations

1. That the power of the government, *as to* the objects intrusted to its management, is in its nature sovereign.

2. That the right of erecting corporations is one, inherent in & inseparable from the idea of sovereign power.

3. That the position, that the government of the United States can exercise no power but such as is delegated to it by its constitution, does not militate against this principle.

4. That the word *necessary* in the general clause can have no

*restrictive* operation, derogating from the force of this principle, indeed, that the degree in which a measure is, or is not necessary, cannot be a *test* of *constitutional* right, but of expediency only.

5. That the power to erect corporations is not to be considered, as an *independent* & *substantive* power but as an *incidental* & *auxiliary* one; and was therefore more properly left to implication, than expressly granted.

6. that the principle in question does not extend the power of the government beyond the prescribed limits, because it only affirms a power to *incorporate* for *purposes within the sphere of the specified powers*.

And lastly that the right to exercise such a power, in certain cases, is unequivocally granted in the most *positive* & *comprehensive* terms.

To all which it only remains to be added that such a power has actually been exercised in two very eminent instances: namely in the erection of two governments, One, northwest of the river Ohio, and the other south west—*the last, independent of any antecedent compact.*

And there results a full & complete demonstration, that the Secretary of State & Attorney General are mistaken, when they deny generally the power of the National government to erect corporations.

It shall now be endeavoured to be shewn that there is a power to erect one of the kind proposed by the bill. This will be done, by tracing a natural & obvious relation between the institution of a bank, and the objects of several of the enumerated powers of the government; and by shewing that, *politically* speaking, it is necessary to the effectual execution of one or more of those powers. In the course of this investigation, various instances will be stated, by way of illustration, of a right to erect corporations under those powers.

Some preliminary observations maybe proper.

The proposed bank is to consist of an association of persons for the purpose of creating a joint capital to be employed, chiefly and essentially, in loans. So far the object is not only lawful, but it is the mere exercise of a right, which the law allows to every individual. The bank of New York which is not incorporated, is an example of such an association. The bill proposes in addition, that the government shall become a joint proprietor in this undertaking, and that it shall permit the bills of the company payable on demand to be receivable in its revenues & stipulates that it shall not grant privileges similar to those which are to be allowed to this company, to any others. All this is in controvertibly within the compass of the discretion of the government. The only question is, whether it has a right to incorporate this company, in order to enable it the more effectually to accomplish *ends*, which are in themselves lawful.

To establish such a right, it remains to shew the relation of such an institution to one or more of the specified powers of the government.

Accordingly it is affirmed, that it has a relation more or less direct to the power of collecting taxes; to that of borrowing money; to that of regulating trade between the states; and to those of raising, supporting & maintaining fleets & armies. To the two former, the relation may be said to be *immediate*.

And, in the last place, it will be argued, that it is, *clearly*, within the provision which authorises the making of all *needful* rules & *regulations* concerning the *property* of the United States, as the same has been practiced upon by the Government.

A Bank relates to the collection of taxes in two ways; *indirectly*, by increasing the quantity of circulating medium & quickening circulation, which facilitates the means of paying—*directly*, by creating a *convenient species* of *medium* in which they are to be paid.

To designate or appoint the money or *thing* in which taxes are to be paid, is not only a proper, but a necessary *exercise* of the power of collecting them. Accordingly congress in the law concerning the collection of the duties on imports & tonnage, have provided that they shall be payable in gold & silver. But while it was an indispensible part of the work to say in what they should be paid, the choice of the specific thing was mere matter of discretion. The payment might have been required in the commodities themselves. Taxes in kind, however ill judged, are not without precedents, even in the United States. Or it might have been in the paper money of the several states; or in the bills of the bank of North America, New York and Massachusetts, all or either of them: or it might have been in bills issued under the authority of the United States.

No part of this can, it is presumed, be disputed. The appointment, then, of the *money* or *thing*, in which the taxes are to be paid, is an incident to the power of collection. And among the expedients which may be adopted, is that of bills issued under the authority of the United States.

Now the manner of issuing these bills is again matter of discretion. The government might, doubtless, proceed in the following manner. It might provide, that they should be issued under the direction of certain officers, payable on demand; and in order to support their credit & give them a ready circulation, it might, besides giving them a currency in its taxes, set apart out of any monies in its Treasury, a given sum and appropriate it under the direction of those officers as a fund for answering the bills as presented for payment.

The constitutionality of all this would not admit of a question. And yet it would amount to the institution of a bank, with a view to the more convenient collection of taxes. For the simplest and most precise idea of a bank, is, a deposit of coin or other property, as a fund for *circulating* a *credit* upon it, which is to answer the purpose of money. That such an arrangement would be equivalent to the establishment of a bank would become obvious, if the place where the fund to be set apart was kept should be made a receptacle of the monies of all other persons who should incline to deposit them there for safe keeping; and would become still more so, if the Officers charged with the direction of the fund were authorised to make discounts at the usual rate of interest, upon good security. To deny the power of the government to add these ingredients to the plan, would be to refine away all government.

This process serves to exemplify the natural & direct relation which may subsist between the institution of a bank and the collection of taxes. It is true that the species of bank which has been designated, does not include the idea of incorporation. But the argument intended to be founded upon it, is this: that the institution comprehended in the idea of a bank being one immediately relative to the collection of taxes, *in regard to the appointment* of *the money or thing* in which they are to be paid; the sovereign power of providing for the collection of taxes necessarily includes the right of granting a corporate capacity to such an institution, as a requisite to its greater security, utility and more convenient management.

A further process will still more clearly illustrate the point. Suppose, when the species of bank which has been described was about to be instituted, it were to be urged, that in order to secure to it a due degree of confidence the fund ought not only to be set apart & appropriated generally, but ought to be specifically vested in the officers who were to have the direction of it, and in their *successors* in office, to the end that it might acquire the character of *private property* incapable of being resumed without a violation of the sanctions by which the rights of property are protected & occasioning more serious & general alarm, the apprehension of which might operate as a check upon the government—such a proposition might be opposed by arguments against the expediency of it or the solidity of the reason assigned for it, but it is not conceivable what could be urged against its constitutionality.

And yet such a disposition of the thing would amount to the erection of a corporation. For the true definition of a corporation seems to be this. It is a *legal* person, or a person created by act of law, consisting of one or more natural persons authorised to hold property or a franchise in succession in a legal as contradistinguished from a natural capacity.

Let the illustration proceed a step further. Suppose a bank of the nature which has been described with or without incorporation, had been instituted, & that experience had evinced as it probably would, that being wholly under public direction it possessed not the confidence requisite to the credit of its bills—Suppose also that by some of those adverse conjunctures which occasionally attend nations, there had been a very great drain of the specie of the country, so as not only to cause general distress for want of an adequate medium of circulation, but to produce, in consequence of that circumstance, considerable defalcations in the public revenues—suppose also, that there was no bank instituted in any State—in such a posture of things, would it not be most manifest that the incorporation of a bank, like that proposed by the bill, would be a measure immediately relative to the *effectual collection* of the taxes and completely within the province of the sovereign power of providing by all laws necessary & proper for that collection?

If it be said, that such a state of things would render that necessary & therefore constitutional, which is not so now—the answer to this, and a solid one it doubtless is, must still be, that which has been already stated—Circumstances may affect the expediency of the measure, but they can neither add to, nor diminish its constitutionality.

A Bank has a direct relation to the power of borrowing money, because it is an usual and in sudden emergencies an essential instrument in the obtaining of loans to Government.

A nation is threatened with a war. Large sums are wanted, on a sudden, to make the requisite preparations. Taxes are laid for the purpose, but it requires time to obtain the benefit of them. Anticipation is indispensible. If there be a bank, the supply can, at once be had; if there be none loans from Individuals must be sought. The progress of these is often too slow for the exigency: in some situations they are not practicable at all. Frequently when they are, it is of great consequence to be able to anticipate the product of them by advances from a bank.

The essentiality of such an institution as an instrument of loans is exemplified at this very moment. An Indian expedition is to be prosecuted. The only fund out of which the money can arise consistently with the public engagements, is a tax which will only begin to be collected in July next. The preparations, however, are instantly to be made. The money must therefore be borrowed. And of whom could it be borrowed; if there were no public banks?

It happens, that there are institutions of this kind, but if there were none, it would be indispensible to create one.

Let it then be supposed, that the necessity existed, (as but for a casualty would be the case) that proposals were made for obtaining a loan; that a number of individuals came forward and said, we are willing to accommodate the government with this money; with what we have in hand and the credit we can raise upon it we doubt not of being able to furnish the sum required: but in order to this, it is indispensible, that we should be incorporated as a bank. This is essential towards putting it in our power to do what is desired and we are obliged on that account to make it the *consideration* or condition of the loan.

Can it be believed, that a compliance with this proposition would be unconstitutional? Does not this alone evince the contrary? It is a necessary part of a power to borrow to be able to stipulate the consideration or conditions of a loan. It is evident, as has been remarked elsewhere, that this is not confined to the mere stipulation of a sum of money by way of interest—why may it not be deemed to extend, where a government is the contracting party, to the stipulation of a *franchise*? If it may, & it is not perceived why it may not, then the grant of a corporate capacity may be stipulated as a consideration of the loan? There seems to be nothing unfit, or foreign from the nature of the thing in giving individuality or a corporate capacity to a number of persons who are willing to lend a sum of money to the government, the better to enable them to do it, and make them an ordinary instrument of loans in future emergencies of the state.

But the more general view of the subject is still more satisfactory.

The legislative power of borrowing money, & of making all laws necessary & proper for carrying into execution that power, seems obviously competent to the appointment of the *organ* through which the abilities and wills of individuals may be most efficaciously exerted, for the accommodation of the government by loans.

The Attorney General opposes to this reasoning, the following observation. "To borrow money presupposes the accumulation of a fund to be lent, and is secondary to the creation of an ability to lend." This is plausible in theory, but it is not true in fact. In a great number of cases, a previous accumulation of a fund equal to the whole sum required, does not exist. And nothing more can be actually presupposed, than that there exist resources, which put into activity to the greatest advantage by the nature of the operation with the government, will be equal to the effect desired to be produced. All the provisions and operations of government must be presumed to contemplate things as they *really* are.

The institution of a bank has also a natural relation to the regulation of trade between the States: in so far as it is conducive to the creation of a convenient medium of *exchange* between them, and to the keeping up a full circulation by preventing the frequent displacement of the metals in reciprocal remittances. Money is the very hinge on which commerce turns. And this does not mean merely gold & silver, many other things have served the purpose with different degrees of utility. Paper has been extensively employed.

It cannot therefore be admitted with the Attorney General, that the regulation of trade between the States, as it concerns the medium of circulation & exchange ought to be considered as confined to coin. It is even supposeable in argument, that the whole, or the greatest part of the coin of the country, might be carried out of it.

The Secretary of State objects to the relation here insisted upon, by the following mode of reasoning—"To erect a bank, says he, & to regulate commerce, are very different acts. He who erects a bank, creates a subject of commerce, so does he, who makes a bushel of wheat, or digs a dollar out of the mines. Yet neither of these persons regulates commerce thereby. To make a thing which may be bought & sold is not to *prescribe* regulations for *buying* & *selling*: thus making the regulation of commerce to consist in prescribing rules for *buying* & *selling*.

This indeed is a species of regulation of trade; but is one which falls more aptly within the province of the local jurisdictions than within that of the general government, whose care must be presumed to have been intended to be directed to those general political arrangements concerning trade on which its aggregate interests depend, rather than to the details of buying and selling.

Accordingly such only are the regulations to be found in the laws of the United States; whose objects are to give encouragement to the entreprise of our own merchants, and to advance our navigation and manufactures.

And it is in reference to these general relations of commerce, that an establishment which furnishes facilities to circulation and a convenient medium of exchange & alienation, is to be regarded as a regulation of trade.

The Secretary of State further argues, that if this was a regulation of commerce, it would be void, *as extending as much to the internal commerce of every state as to its external.* But what regulation of commerce does not extend to the internal commerce of every state? What are all the duties upon imported articles amounting to prohibitions, but so many bounties upon domestic manufactures affecting the interests of different classes of citizens in different ways? What are all the provisions in the coasting act, which relate to the trade between district and district of the same State? In short what regulation of trade between the States, but must affect the internal trade of each State? What can operate upon the whole but must extend to every part!

The relation of a bank to the execution of the powers, that concern the common defence, has been anticipated. It has been noted, that at this very moment the aid of such an institution is essential to the measures to be pursued for the protection of our frontier.

It now remains to shew, that the incorporation of a bank is within the operation of the provision which authorises Congress to make all needful rules & regulations concerning the property of the United States. But it is previously necessary to advert to a distinction which has been taken by the Attorney General.

He admits, that the word *property* may signify personal property however acquired. And yet asserts, that it cannot signify money arising from the sources of revenue pointed out in the constitution; because, says he, "the disposal & regulation of money is the final cause for raising it by taxes."

But it would be more accurate to say, that the *object* to which money is intended to be applied is the *final cause* for raising it, than that the disposal and regulation of it is *such*. The support of Government; the support of troops for the common defence; the payment of the public debt, are the true *final causes* for raising money. The disposition & regulation of it when raised, are the steps by which it is applied to the *ends* for which it was raised, not the ends themselves. Hence therefore the money to be raised by taxes as well as any other personal property, must be supposed to come within the meaning as they certainly do within the letter of the authority, to make all needful rules & regulations concerning the property of the United States.

A case will make this plainer: suppose the public debt discharged, and the funds now pledged for it liberated. In some instances it would be found expedient to repeal the taxes, in others, the repeal might injure our own industry, our agriculture and manufactures. In these cases they would of course be retained. Here then would be monies arising from the authorised sources of revenue which would not fall within the rule by which the Attorney General endeavours to except them from other personal property, & from the operation of the clause in question.

The monies being in the coffers of the government, what is to hinder such a disposition to be made of them as is contemplated in the bill or what an incorporation of the parties concerned under the clause which has been cited.

It is admitted that with regard to the Western territory they give a power to erect a corporation—that is to institute a government. And by what rule of construction can it be maintained, that the same words in a constitution of government will not have the same effect when applied to one species of property, as to another, as far as the subject is capable of it? or that a legislative power to make all needful rules & regulations, or to pass all laws necessary & proper concerning the public property which is admitted to authorise an incorporation in one case will not authorise it in another? will justify the institution of a government over the western territory & will not justify the incorporation of a bank, for the more useful management of the money of the nation? If it will do the last, as well as the first, then under this provision alone the bill is constitutional, because it contemplates that the United States shall be joint proprietors of the stock of the bank.

There is an observation of the secretary of state to this effect, which may require notice in this place. Congress, says he, are not to lay taxes *ad libitum for any purpose they please*, but only to pay the debts, or provide for the *welfare* of the Union. Certainly no inference can be drawn from this against the power of applying their money for the institution of a bank. It is true, that they cannot without breach of trust, lay taxes for any other purpose than the general welfare but so neither can any other government. The welfare of the community is the only legitimate end for which money can be raised on the community. Congress can be considered as under only one restriction, which does not apply to other governments—They cannot rightfully apply the money they raise to any purpose *merely* or purely local. But with this exception they have as large a discretion in relation to the *application* of money as any legislature whatever. The constitutional *test* of a right application must always be whether it be for a purpose of *general* or *local* nature. If the former, there can be no want of constitutional power. The quality of the object, as how far it will really promote or not the welfare of the union, must be matter of conscientious discretion. And the arguments for or against a measure in this light, must be arguments concerning expediency or inexpediency, not constitutional right. Whatever relates to the general order of the finances, to the general interests of trade &c being general objects are constitutional ones for *the application* of *money*.

A Bank then whose bills are to circulate in all the revenues of the country, is *evidently* a general object, and for that very reason a constitutional one as far as regards the appropriation of money to it. Whether it will really be a beneficial one, or not, is worthy of careful examination, but is no more a constitutional point, in the particular referred to; than the question whether the western lands shall be sold for twenty or thirty cents ℔ acre.

A hope is entertained, that it has by this time been made to appear, to the satisfaction of the President, that a bank has a natural relation to the power of collecting taxes; to that of borrowing money; to that of regulating trade; to that of providing for the common defence: and that as the bill under consideration contemplates the government in the light of a joint proprietor of the stock of the bank, it brings the case within the provision of the clause of the constitution which immediately respects the property of the United States.

Under a conviction that such a relation subsists, the Secretary of the Treasury, with all deference conceives, that it will result as a necessary consequence from the position, that all the specified powers of the government are sovereign as to the proper objects; that the incorporation of a bank is a constitutional measure, and that the objections taken to the bill, in this respect, are ill founded.

But from an earnest desire to give the utmost possible satisfaction to the mind of the President, on so delicate and important a subject, the Secretary of the Treasury will ask his indulgence while he gives some additional illustrations of cases in which a power of erecting corporations may be exercised, under some of those heads of the specified powers of the Government, which are alledged to include the right of incorporating a bank.

1. It does not appear susceptible of a doubt, that if Congress had thought proper to provide in the collection law, that the bonds to be given for the duties should be given to the collector of each district in the name of the collector of the district A. or B. as the case might require, to enure to him & his successors in office, in trust for the United States, that it would have been consistent with the constitution to make such an arrangement. And yet this it is conceived would amount to an incorporation.

2. It is not an unusual expedient of taxation to farm particular branches of revenue, that is to mortgage or sell the product of them for certain definite sums, leaving the collection to the parties to whom they are mortgaged or sold. There are even examples of this in the United States. Suppose that there was any particular branch of revenue which it was manifestly expedient to place on this footing, & there were a number of persons willing to engage with the Government, upon condition, that they should be incorporated & the funds vested in them, as well for their greater safety as for the more convenient recovery & management of the taxes. Is it supposeable, that there could be any constitutional obstacle to the measure? It is presumed that there could be none. It is certainly a mode of collection which it would be in the discretion of the Government to adopt; though the circumstances must be very extraordinary, that would induce the Secretary to think it expedient.

3. suppose a new & unexplored branch of trade should present itself with some foreign country. Suppose it was manifest, that, to undertake it with advantage, required an union of the capitals

of a number of individuals; & that those individuals would not be disposed to embark without an incorporation, as well to obviate that consequence of a private partnership, which makes every individual liable in his whole estate for the debts of the company to their utmost extent, as for the more convenient management of the business—what reason can there be to doubt, that the national government would have a constitutional right to institute and incorporate such a company? None.

They possess a general authority to regulate trade with foreign countries. This is a mean which has been practiced to that end by all the principal commercial nations; who have trading companies to this day which have subsisted for centuries. Why may not the United States *constitutionally* employ the means usual in other countries for attaining the ends entrusted to them?

A power to make all needful rules & regulations concerning territory has been construed to mean a power to erect a government. A power to *regulate* trade is a power to make all needful rules & regulations concerning trade. Why may it not then include that of erecting a trading company as well as in the other case to erect a Government?

It is remarkable, that the State Conventions who have proposed amendments in relation to this point, have most, if not all of them, expressed themselves nearly thus—"Congress shall not grant monopolies, nor *erect any company* with exclusive advantages of commerce;" thus at the same time expressing their sense, that the power to erect trading companies or corporations, was inherent in Congress, & objecting to it no further, than as to the grant of *exclusive* priviledges.

The Secretary entertains all the doubts which prevail concerning the utility of such companies; but he cannot fashion to his own mind a reason to induce a doubt, that there is a constitutional authority in the United States to establish them. If such a reason were demanded, none could be given unless it were this—that congress cannot erect a corporation; which would be no better than to say they cannot do it, because they cannot do it: first presuming an inability, without reason, & then assigning that *inability* as the cause of itself.

Illustrations of this kind might be multiplied without end. They shall however be pursued no further.

There is a sort of evidence on this point, arising from an aggregate view of the constitution, which is of no inconsiderable weight. The very general power of laying & collecting taxes & appropriating their proceeds—that of borrowing money indefinitely—that of coining money & regulating foreign coins—that of making all needful rules and regulations respecting the property of the United States—these powers combined, as well as the reason & nature of the thing speak strongly this language: That it is the manifest design and scope of the constitution to vest in congress all the powers requisite to the effectual administration of the finances of the United States. As far as concerns this object, there appears to be no parsimony of power.

To suppose then, that the government is precluded from the employment of so usual as well as so important an instrument for the administration of its finances as that of a bank, is to suppose, what does not coincide with the general tenor & complexion of the constitution, and what is not agreeable to impressions that any mere spectator would entertain concerning it. Little less than a prohibitory clause can destroy the strong presumptions which result from the general aspect of the government. Nothing but demonstration should exclude the idea, that the power exists.

In all questions of this nature the practice of mankind ought to have great weight against the theories of Individuals.

The fact, for instance, that all the principal commercial nations have made use of trading corporations or companies for the purposes of *external commerce*, is a satisfactory proof, that the Establishment of them is an incident to the regulation of that commerce.

This other fact, that banks are an usual engine in the administration of national finances, & an ordinary & the most effectual instrument of loans & one which in this country has been found essential, pleads strongly against the supposition, that a government clothed with most of the most important prerogatives of sovereignty in relation to the revenues, its debts, its credit, its defence, its trade, its intercourse with foreign nations—is forbidden to make use of that instrument as an appendage to its own authority.

It has been stated as an auxiliary test of constitutional authority, to try, whether it abridges any preexisting right of any state, or any Individual. The proposed incorporation will stand the most severe examination on this point. Each state may still erect as many banks as it pleases; every individual may still carry on the banking business to any extent he pleases.

Another criterion may be this, whether the institution or thing has a more direct relation as to its uses, to the objects of the reserved powers of the State Governments, than to those of the powers delegated by the United States. This rule indeed is less precise than the former, but it may still serve as some guide. Surely a bank has more reference to the objects entrusted to the national government, than to those, left to the care of the State Governments. The common defence is decisive in this comparison.

It is presumed, that nothing of consequence in the observations of the Secretary of State and Attorney General has been left unnoticed.

There are indeed a variety of observations of the Secretary of State designed to shew that the utilities ascribed to a bank in relation to the collection of taxes and to trade, could be obtained without it, to analyse which would prolong the discussion beyond all bounds. It shall be forborne for two reasons—first because the report concerning the Bank may speak for itself in this respect; and secondly, because all those observations are grounded on the erroneous idea, that the *quantum* of necessity or utility is the test of a constitutional exercise of power.

One or two remarks only shall be made: one is that he has taken no notice of a very essential advantage to trade in general which is mentioned in the report, as peculiar to the existence of a bank circulation equal, in the public estimation to Gold & silver. It is this, that it renders it unnecessary to *lock* up the money of the country to accumulate for months successively in order to the periodical payment of interest. The other is this; that his arguments to shew that treasury orders & bills of exchange from the course of trade will prevent any considerable displacement of the metals, are founded on a partial view of the subject. A case will prove this: The sums collected in a state may be small in comparison with the debt due to it. The balance of its trade, direct & circuitous, with the seat of government may be even or nearly so. Here then without bank bills, which in that state answer the purpose of coin, there must be a displacement of the coin, in proportion to the difference between the sum collected in the State and that to be paid in it. With bank bills no such displacement would take place, or, as far as it did, it would be gradual & insensible. In many other ways also, would there be at least a temporary & inconvenient displacement of the coin, even where the course of trade would eventually return it to its proper channels.

The difference of the two situations in point of convenience to the Treasury can only be appreciated by one, who experiences the embarassments of making provision for the payment of the interest on a stock continually changing place in thirteen different places.

One thing which has been omitted just occurs, although it is not very material to the main argument. The Secretary of State affirms, that the bill only contemplates a re-payment, not a loan to the government. But here he is, certainly mistaken. It is true, the government invests in the stock of the bank a sum equal to that which it receives on loan. But let it be remembered, that it does not, therefore, cease to be a proprietor of the stock; which would be the case, if the money received back were in the nature of a repayment. It remains a proprietor still, & will share in the profit, or loss, of the institution, according as the dividend is more or less than the interest it is to pay on the sum borrowed. Hence that sum is manifestly, and, in the strictest sense, a loan.

*Philadelphia February 23d. 1791.*

## *To Philip A. Hamilton*

*Philadelphia December 5*
*1791*

I received with great pleasure My Dear Philip the letter which you wrote me last week. Your Mama and myself were very happy to learn that you are pleased with your situation and content to stay as long as shall be thought for your good. We hope and believe that nothing will happen to alter this disposition.

Your Master also informs me that you recited a lesson the first day you began, very much to his satisfaction. I expect every letter from him will give me a fresh proof of your progress. For I know that you can do a great deal, if you please, and I am sure you have too much spirit not to exert yourself, that you may make us every day more and more proud of you.

Your Mama has got an Ovid for you and is looking up your Mairs introduction. If it cannot be found tomorrow another will be procured and the books with the other articles she promised to send you will be forwarded in two or three days.

You remember that I engaged to send for you next Saturday and I will do it, unless you request me to put it off. For a promise must never be broken; and I never will make you one, which I will not fulfil as far as I am able. But it has occurred to me that the Christmas holidays are near at hand, and I suppose your school will then break up for some days and give you an opportunity of coming to stay with us for a longer time than if you should come on Saturday. Will it not be best for you, therefore, to put off your journey till the holidays? But determine as you like best and let me know what will be most pleasing to you.

A good night to my darling son. Adieu

A HAMILTON

## To Edward Carrington

*Philadelphia May 26th, 1792*

MY DEAR SIR

Believing that I possess a share of your personal friendship and confidence and yielding to that which I feel towards you—persuaded also that our political creed is the same on *two essential points*, 1st the necessity of *Union* to the respectability and happiness of this Country and 2 the necessity of an *efficient* general government to maintain that Union—I have concluded to unbosom myself to you on the present state of political parties and views. I ask no reply to what I shall say. I only ask that you will be persuaded, the representations I shall make are agreable to the real and sincere impressions of my mind. You will make the due allowances for the influence of circumstances upon it—you will consult your own observations and you will draw such a conclusion as shall appear to you proper.

When I accepted the Office, I now hold, it was under a full persuasion, that from similarity of thinking, conspiring with personal goodwill, I should have the firm support of Mr. Madison, in the *general course* of my administration. Aware of the intrinsic difficulties of the situation and of the powers of Mr. Madison, I do not believe I should have accepted under a different supposition.

I have mentioned the similarity of thinking between that Gentleman and myself. This was relative not merely to the general principles of National Policy and Government but to the leading points which were likely to constitute questions in the administration of the finances. I mean  1 the expediency of *funding* the debt  2 the inexpediency of *discrimination* between original and present holders    3 The expediency of *assuming* the state Debts.

As to the first point, the evidence of Mr. Madisons sentiments at one period is to be found in the address of Congress of April 26th 1783, which was planned by him in conformity to his own ideas and without any previous suggestions from the Committee and with his hearty cooperation in every part of the business. His conversations upon various occasions since have been expressive of a continuance in the same sentiment, nor indeed, has he yet contradicted it by any part of his official conduct. How far there is reason to apprehend a change in this particular will be stated hereafter.

As to the second part, the same address is an evidence of Mr. Madison's sentiments at the same period. And I had been informed that at a later period he had been in the Legislature of Virginia a strenuous and successful opponent of the principle of discrimination. Add to this that a variety of conversations had taken place between him and myself respecting the public debt down to the commencement of the New Government in none of which had he glanced at the idea of a change of opinion. I wrote him a letter after my appointment in the recess of Congress to obtain his sentiments on the subject of the Finances. In his answer there is not a lisp of his new system.

As to the third point, the question of an assumption of the state Debts by the U States was in discussion when the Convention that framed the present Government was sitting at Philadelphia; and in a long conversation, which I had with Mr. Madison in an afternoon's walk I well remember that we were perfectly agreed in the expediency and propriety of such a measure, though we were both of opinion that it would be more adviseable to make it a measure of administration than an article of constitution; from the impolicy of multiplying obstacles to its reception on collateral details.

Under these circumstances, you will naturally imagine that it must have been matter of surprize to me, when I was apprised, that it was Mr. Madison's intention to oppose my plan on both the last mentioned points.

Before the debate commenced, I had a conversation with him on my report, in the course of which I alluded to the calculation I had made of his sentiments and the grounds of that calculation. He did not deny them, but alledged in his justification that the very considerable alienation of the debt, subsequent to the periods at which he had opposed a discrimination, had essentially changed the state of the question—and that as to the assumption, he had contemplated it to take place *as matters stood at the peace*.

While the change of opinion avowed on the point of discrimination diminished my respect for the force of Mr. Madison's mind and the soundness of his judgment—and while the idea of reserving and setting afloat a vast mass of already extinguished debt as the condition of a measure the leading objects of which were an accession of strength to the National Government and an assurance of order and vigour in the national finances by doing away the necessity of thirteen complicated and conflicting systems of finance—appeared to me somewhat extraordinary: Yet my previous impressions of the fairness of Mr. Madison's character and my reliance on his good will towards me disposed me to believe that his suggestions were sincere; and even, on the point of an assumption of the debts of the States as they stood at the peace, to lean towards a cooperation in his view; 'till on feeling the ground I found the thing impracticable, and on further reflection I thought it liable to immense difficulties. It was tried and failed with little countenance.

At this time and afterwards repeated intimations were given to me that Mr. Madison, from a spirit of rivalship or some other cause had become personally unfriendly to me; and one Gentleman in particular, whose honor I have no reason to doubt, assured me, that Mr. Madison in a conversation with him had made a pretty direct attempt to insinuate unfavourable impressions of me.

Still I suspended my opinion on the subject. I knew the malevolent officiousness of mankind too well to yield a very ready acquiescence to the suggestions which were made, and resolved to wait 'till time and more experience should afford a solution.

It was not 'till the last session that I became unequivocally convinced of the following truth—*"That Mr. Madison cooperating with Mr. Jefferson is at the head of a faction decidedly hostile to me and my administration, and actuated by views in my judgment subversive of the principles of good government and dangerous to the union, peace and happiness of the Country."*

These are strong expressions; they may pain your friendship for one or both of the Gentlemen whom I have named. I have not lightly resolved to hazard them. They are the result of a *Serious alarm* in my mind for the public welfare, and of a full conviction that what I have alledged is a truth, and a truth, which ought to be told and well attended to, by all the friends of Union and efficient National Government. The suggestion will, I hope, at least awaken attention, free from the byass of former prepossessions.

This conviction in my mind is the result of a long train of circumstances; many of them minute. To attempt to detail them all would fill a volume. I shall therefore confine myself to the mention of a few.

First—As to the point of opposition to me and my administration.

Mr. Jefferson with very little reserve manifests his dislike of the funding system generally; calling in question the expediency of funding a debt at all. Some expressions which he has dropped in my own presence (sometimes without sufficient attention to delicacy) will not permit me to doubt on this point, representations, which I have had from various respectable quarters. I do not mean, that he advocates directly the undoing of what has been done, but he censures the whole on principles, which if they should become general, could not but end in the subversion of the system.

In various conversations with *foreigners* as well as citizens, he has thrown censure on my *principles* of government and on my measures of administration. He has predicted that the people would not long tolerate my proceedings & that I should not long maintain my ground. Some of those, whom he *immediately* and *notoriously* moves, have *even* whispered suspicions of the rectitude of my motives and conduct. In the question concerning the Bank he not only delivered an opinion in writing against its constitutionality & expediency; but he did it *in a stile and manner* which I felt as partaking of asperity and ill humour towards me. As one of the trustees of the sinking fund, I have experienced in almost every leading question opposition from him. When any turn of things in the community has threatened either odium or embarrassment to me, he has not been able to suppress the satisfaction which it gave him.

A part of this is of course information, and might be misrepresentation. But it comes through so many channels and so well accords with what falls under my own observation that I can entertain no doubt.

I find a strong confirmation in the following circumstances. *Freneau* the present Printer of the National Gazette, who was a journeyman with Childs & Swain at New York, was a known anti-federalist. It is reduced to a certainty that he was brought to Philadelphia by Mr. Jefferson to be the conductor of a News Paper. It is notorious that cotemporarily with the commencement of his paper he was a Clerk in the department of state for foreign languages. Hence a clear inference that his paper has been set on foot and is conducted under the patronage & not against the views of Mr. Jefferson. What then is the complexion of this paper? Let any impartial man peruse all the numbers down to the present day; and I never was more mistaken, if he does not pronounce that it is a paper devoted to the subversion of me & the measures in which I have had an Agency; and I am little less mistaken if he do not pronounce that it is a paper of a tendency *generally unfriendly* to the Government of the U States.

It may be said, that a News Paper being open to all the publications, which are offered to it, its complexion may be influenced by other views than those of the Editor. But the fact here is that wherever the Editor appears it is in a correspondent dress. The paragraphs which appear as his own, the publications, not original which are selected for his press, are of the same malignant and unfriendly aspect, so as not to leave a doubt of the temper which directs the publication.

Again *Brown*, who publishes an Evening paper called *The Federal Gazette* was originally a zealous federalist and personally friendly to me. He has been employed by Mr. Jefferson as a Printer to the Government for the publication of the laws; and for some time past 'till lately the complexion of his press was equally bitter and unfriendly to me & to the Government.

Lately, Col Pickering in consequence of certain attacks upon him, got hold of some instances of malconduct of his which have served to hold him in Check and seemed to have varied his tone a little. I dont lay so much stress on this last case as on the former. There, I find an internal evidence which is as conclusive as can be expected in any similar case. Thus far, as to Mr. Jefferson.

With regard to Mr. Madison—the matter stands thus. I have not heard, but in the one instance to which I have alluded, of his having held language unfriendly to me in private conversation. But in his public conduct there has been a more uniform & persevering opposition than I have been able to resolve into a sincere difference of opinion. I cannot persuade myself that Mr. Madison and I, whose politics had formerly so much the *same point of departure*, should now diverge so widely in our opinions of the measures which are proper to be pursued. The opinion I once entertained of the candour and simplicity and fairness of Mr. Madisons character has, I acknowledge, given way to a decided opinion that *it is one of a peculiarly artificial and complicated kind*.

For a considerable part of the last session, Mr. Madison lay in a great measure *perdu*. But it was evident from his votes & a variety of little movements and appearances, that he was the prompter of Mr. Giles & others, who were the open instruments of opposition. Two facts occurred, in the course of the session, which I view as unequivocal demonstrations of his disposition towards me. In one, a direct and decisive blow was aimed. When the department of the Treasury was established Mr. Madison was an unequivocal advocate of the principles which prevailed in it and of the powers and duties which were assigned by it to the head of the department. This appeared both from his private and public discourses; and I will add, that I have personal evidence that Mr. Madison is as well convinced as any man in the U States of the necessity of the arrangement which characterizes that establishment to the orderly conducting of the business of the Finances.

Mr. Madison nevertheless opposed directly a reference to me to report *ways* & *means* for the Western expedition, & combatted *on principle* the propriety of such references.

He well knew, that, if he had prevailed, a certain consequence was, my *resignation*—that I would not be fool enough to make pecuniary sacrifices and endure a life of extreme drudgery without opportunity either to do material good or to acquire reputation; and frequently with a responsibility in reputation for measures in which I had no hand, and in respect to which, the part I had acted, if any, could not be known.

To accomplish this point, an effectual train, as was supposed, was laid. Besides those who ordinarily acted under Mr. Madison's banners, several, who had generally acted with me from various motives, vanity, self importance, &c. &c. were enlisted.

My overthrow was anticipated as certain and Mr. Madison, *laying aside his wonted caution*, boldly led his troops as he imagined to a certain victory. He was disappointed. Though, *late* I became apprized of the danger. Measures of counteraction were adopted, & when the Question was called, Mr. Madison was confounded to find characters voting against him, whom he had counted upon as certain.

Towards the close of the Session, another, though a more covert, attack was made. It was in the shape of a proposition to insert in the supplementary Act respecting the public Debt something by way of instruction to the Trustees "to make their purchases of the debt at the *lowest* market price." In the course of the discussion of this point, Mr. Madison dealt much in *insidious insinuations* calculated to give an impression that the public money under my particular direction had been unfaithfully applied to put undue advantages in the pockets of speculators, & to support the debt at an *artificial* price for their benefit. The whole manner of this transaction left no doubt in any ones mind that Mr. Madison was actuated by *personal* & political animosity.

As to this last instance, it is but candid to acknowledge, that Mr. Madison had a better right to act the enemy than on any former occasion. I had some short time before, subsequent to his conduct respecting the reference, declared openly my opinion of the views, by which he was actuated towards me, & my determination to consider & treat him as a political enemy.

An intervening proof of Mr. Madisons unfriendly intrigues to my disadvantage is to be found in the following incident which I relate to you upon my honor but from the nature of it, you will perceive in the *strictest confidence*. The president having prepared his speech at the commencement of the ensuing session communicated it to Mr. Madison for his remarks. It contained among other things a *clause* concerning weights & measures, hinting the advantage of an invariable standard, which *preceded*, in the original state of the speech, a clause concerning the Mint. Mr. Madison suggested a transposition of these clauses & the addition of certain words, which I now forget importing an *immediate connection* between the two subjects. You may recollect that Mr. Jefferson proposes that the *unit of weight* & the *unit in the coins* shall be the same, & that my propositions are to preserve the Dollar as the Unit, adhering to its present quantity of Silver, & establishing the same proportion of alloy in the silver as in the gold Coins. The evident design of this manoeuvre was to connect the Presidents opinion in favour of Mr. Jefferson's idea, in contradiction to mine, &, the worst of it is, *without his being aware of the tendency of the thing*. It happened, that the President shewed me the Speech, altered in conformity to Mr. Madisons suggestion, just before it was copied for the purpose of being delivered. I remarked to him the tendency of the alteration. *He declared that he had not been aware of it & had no such intention; & without hesitation agreed to expunge the words which were designed to connect the two subjects.*

This transaction, in my opinion, not only furnishes a proof of Mr. Madisons *intrigues*, in opposition to my measures, but charges him with an *abuse* of the Presidents confidence in him, by endeavouring to make him, without his knowledge, take part with one officer against another, in a case in which they had given different opinions to the Legislature of the Country. *I forbore to awaken the President's mind to this last inference;* but it is among the circumstances which have convinced me that Mr. Madisons true character is the reverse of that *simple, fair, candid one,* which he has assumed.

I have informed you, that Mr. Freneau was brought to Philadelphia, by Mr. Jefferson, to be the Conductor of a News Paper. My information announced Mr. Madison as the mean of negotiation while he was at New York last summer. This and the general coincidence & close intimacy between the two Gentlemen leave no doubt that their views are substantially the same.

Secondly As to the tendency of the views of the two Gentlemen who have been named.

Mr. Jefferson is an avowed enemy to a funded debt. Mr. Madison disavows in public any intention to *undo* what has been done; but in a private conversation with Mr. Charles Carroll (Senator), this Gentlemans name I mention confidentially though he mentioned the matter to Mr. King & several other Gentlemen as well as myself; & if any chance should bring you together you would easily bring him to repeat it to you, he favoured the sentiment in Mr. Mercers speech that a Legislature had no right to *fund* the debt by mortgaging permanently the public revenues because they had no right to bind posterity. The inference is that what has been unlawfully done may be undone.

The discourse of partizans in the Legislature & the publications in the party news-papers direct their main battery against the *principle* of a funded debt, & represent it in the most odious light as a perfect *Pandoras box*.

If Mr. Barnewell of St. Carolina, who appears to be a man of nice honor, may be credited, Mr. Giles declared in a conversation with him that if there was a question for reversing the funding system on the abstract point of the right of pledging & the futility of preserving public faith, he should be for reversal; merely to demonstrate his sense of the defect of right & the inutility of the thing. If positions equally extravagant were not publicly advanced by some of the party & secretly countenanced by the most guarded & *discreet* of them, one would be led, from the absurdity of the declaration, to suspect misapprehension. But from what is *known* any thing may be *believed*.

Whatever were the original merits of the funding system, after having been so solemly adopted, & after so great a transfer of property under it, what would become of the Government should it be reversed? What of the National Reputation? Upon what system of morality can so atrocious a doctrine be maintained? In me, I confess it excites *indignation* & *horror*!

What are we to think of those maxims of Government by which the power of a Legislature is denied to bind the Nation by a *Contract* in an affair of *property* for twenty four years? For this is precisely the case of the debt. What are to become of all the legal rights of property, of all charters to corporations, nay, of all grants to a man his heirs & assigns for ever, if this doctrine be true? What is the term for which a government is in capacity to *contract*? Questions might be multiplied without end to demonstrate the perniciousness & absurdity of such a doctrine.

In almost all the questions great & small which have arisen, since the first session of Congress, Mr. Jefferson & Mr. Madison have been found among those who were disposed to narrow the Federal authority. The question of a National Bank is one example. The question of bounties to the Fisheries is another. Mr. Madison resisted it on the ground of constitutionality, 'till it was evident, by the intermediate questions taken, that the bill would pass & he then under the wretched subterfuge of a change of a single word "bounty" for "allowance" went over to the Majority & voted for the bill. In the Militia bill & in a variety of minor cases he has leaned to abridging the exercise of foederal authority, & leaving as much as possible to the States & he has lost no opportunity of *sounding the alarm* with great affected solemnity at encroachments meditated on the rights of the States, & of holding up the bugbear of a faction in the Government having designs unfriendly to Liberty.

This kind of conduct has appeared to me the more extraordinary on the part of Mr. Madison as I know for a certainty it was a primary article in his Creed that the real danger in our system was the subversion of the

National authority by the preponderancy of the State Governments. All his measures have proceeded on an opposite supposition.

I recur again to the instance of Freneaus paper. In matters of this kind one cannot have direct proof of men's latent views; they must be inferred from circumstances. As the coadjutor of Mr. Jefferson in the establishment of this paper, I include Mr. Madison in the consequences imputable to it.

In respect to our foreign politics the views of these Gentlemen are in my judgment equally unsound & dangerous. *They have a womanish attachment to France and a womanish resentment against Great Britain.* They would draw us into the closest embrace of the former & involve us in all the consequences of her politics, & they would risk the peace of the country in their endeavours to keep us at the greatest possible distance from the latter. This disposition goes to a length particularly in Mr. Jefferson of which, till lately, I had no adequate Idea. Various circumstances prove to me that if these Gentlemen were left to pursue their own course there would be in less than six months *an open War between the U States & Great Britain.*

I trust I have a due sense of the conduct of France towards this Country in the late Revolution, & that I shall always be among the foremost in making her every suitable return; but there is a wide difference between this & implicating ourselves in all her politics; between bearing good will to her, & hating and wranggling with all those whom she hates. The Neutral & the Pacific Policy appear to me to mark the true path to the U States.

Having now delineated to you what I conceive to be the true complexion of the politics of these Gentlemen, I will now attempt a solution of these strange appearances.

Mr. Jefferson, it is known, did not in the first instance cordially acquiesce in the new constitution for the U States; he had many doubts & reserves. He left this Country before we had experienced the imbicillities of the former.

In France he saw government only on the side of its abuses. He drank deeply of the French Philosophy, in Religion, in Science, in politics. He came from France in the moment of a fermentation which he had had a share in exciting, & in the passions and feelings of which he shared both from temperament and situation.

He came here probably with a too partial idea of his own powers, and with the expectation of a greater share in the direction of our councils than he has in reality enjoyed. I am not sure that he had not peculiarly marked out for himself the department of the Finances.

He came electrified *plus* with attachment to France and with the project of knitting together the two Countries in the closest political bands.

Mr. Madison had always entertained an exalted opinion of the talents, knowledge and virtues of Mr. Jefferson. The sentiment was probably reciprocal. A close correspondence subsisted between them during the time of Mr. Jefferson's absence from this country. A close intimacy arose upon his return.

Whether any peculiar opinions of Mr. Jefferson concerning the public debt wrought a change in the sentiments of Mr. Madison (for it is certain that the former is more radically wrong than the latter) or whether Mr. Madison seduced by the expectation of popularity and possibly by the calculation of advantage to the state of Virginia was led to change his own opinion—certain it is, that a very material change took place, & that the two Gentlemen were united in the new ideas. Mr. Jefferson was indiscreetly open in his approbation of Mr. Madison's principles, upon his first coming to the seat of Government. I say indiscreetly, because a Gentleman in the administration in one department ought not to have taken sides against another, in another department.

The course of this business & a variety of circumstances which took place left Mr. Madison a very discontented & chagrined man and begot some degree of ill humour in Mr. Jefferson.

Attempts were made by these Gentlemen in different ways to produce a Commercial Warfare with Great Britain. In this too they were disappointed. And as they had the liveliest wishes on the subject their dissatisfaction has been proportionally great; and as I had not favoured the project, I was comprehended in their displeasure.

These causes and perhaps some others created, much sooner than I was aware of it, a systematic opposition to me on the part of those Gentlemen. My subversion, I am now satisfied, has been long an object with them.

Subsequent events have encreased the Spirit of opposition and the feelings of personal mortification on the part of these Gentlemen.

A mighty stand was made on the affair of the Bank. There was much *commitment* in that case. I prevailed.

On the Mint business I was opposed from the same Quarter, & with still less success. In the affair of ways & means for the Western expedition—on the supplementary arrangements concerning the debt except as to the additional assumption, my views have been equally prevalent in opposition to theirs. This current of success on one side & defeat on the other have rendered the Opposition furious, & have produced a disposition to subvert their Competitors even at the expence of the Government.

Another circumstance has contributed to widening the breach. 'Tis evident beyond a question, from every movement, that Mr Jefferson aims with ardent desire at the Presidential Chair. This too is an important object of the party-politics. It is supposed, from the nature of my former personal & political connexions, that I may favour some other candidate more than Mr. Jefferson when the Question shall occur by the retreat of the present Gentleman. My influence therefore with the Community becomes a thing, on ambitious & personal grounds, to be resisted & destroyed.

You know how much it was a point to establish the Secretary of State as the Officer who was to administer the Government in defect of the President & Vice President. Here I acknowledge, though I took far less part than was supposed, I run counter to Mr. Jefferson's wishes; but if I had had no other reason for it, I had already *experienced opposition* from him which rendered it a measure of *self defence*.

It is possible too (for men easily heat their imaginations when their passions are heated) that they have by degrees persuaded themselves of what they may have at first only sported to influence others—namely that there is some dreadful combination against State Government & republicanism; which according to them, are convertible terms. But there is so much absurdity in this supposition, that the admission of it tends to apologize for their hearts, at the expence of their heads.

Under the influence of all these circumstances, the attachment to the Government of the U States originally weak in Mr Jeffersons mind has given way to something very like dislike; in Mr. Madisons, it is so counteracted by personal feelings, as to be more an affair of the head than of the heart—more the result of a conviction of the necessity of Union than of cordiality to the thing itself. I hope it does not stand worse than this with him.

In such a state of mind, both these Gentlemen are prepared to hazard a great deal to effect a change. Most of the important measures of every Government are connected with the Treasury. To subvert the present head of it they deem it expedient to risk rendering the Government itself odious; perhaps foolishly thinking that they can easily recover the lost affections & confidence of the people, and not appreciating as they ought to do the natural resistance to Government which in every community results from the human passions, the degree to which this is strengthened by the *organised rivality* of State Governments, & the infinite danger that the National Government once rendered odious will be kept so by these powerful & indefatigable enemies.

They forget an old but a very just, though a coarse saying—That it is much easier to raise the Devil than to lay him.

Poor *Knox* has come in for a share of their persecution as a man who generally thinks with me & who has a portion of the Presidents good Will & confidence.

In giving you this picture of political parties, my design is I confess, to awaken your attention, if it has not yet been awakened to the conduct of the Gentlemen in question. If my opinion of them is founded, it is certainly of great moment to the public weal that they should be understood. I rely on the strength of your mind to appreciate men as they merit—when you have a clue to their real views.

A word on another point. I am told that serious apprehensions are disseminated in your state as to the existence of a Monarchical party meditating the destruction of State & Republican Government. If it is possible that so absurd an idea can gain ground it is necessary that it should be combatted. I assure you on my *private faith* and *honor* as a Man that there is not in my judgment a shadow of foundation of it. A very small number of men indeed may entertain theories less republican than Mr Jefferson & Mr. Madison; but I am persuaded there is not a Man among them who would not regard as both *criminal* & *visionary* any attempt to subvert the republican system of the Country. Most of these men rather *fear* that it may not justify itself by its fruits, than feel a predilection for a different form; and their fears are not diminished by the factions & fanatical politics which they find prevailing among a certain set of Gentlemen and threatening to disturb the tranquillity and order of the Government.

As to the destruction of State Governments, the *great* and *real* anxiety is to be able to preserve the National from the too potent and counteracting influence of those Governments. As to my own political Creed, I give it to you with the utmost sincerity. I am *affectionately* attached to the Republican theory. I desire *above all things* to see the *equality* of political rights exclusive of all *hereditary* distinction firmly established by a practical demonstration of its being consistent with the order and happiness of society.

As to State Governments, the prevailing byass of my judgment is that if they can be circumscribed within bounds consistent with the preservation of the National Government they will prove useful and salutary. If the States were all of the size of Connecticut, Maryland or New Jersey, I should decidedly regard the local Governments as both safe & useful. As the thing now is, however, I acknowledge the most serious apprehensions that the Government of the U States will not be able to maintain itself against their influence. I see that influence already penetrating into the National Councils & preverting their direction.

Hence a disposition on my part towards a liberal construction of the powers of the National Government and to erect every fence to guard it from depredations, which is, in my opinion, consistent with constitutional propriety.

As to any combination to prostrate the State Governments I disavow and deny it. From an apprehension lest the Judiciary should not work efficiently or harmoniously I have been desirous of seeing some rational scheme of connection adopted as an amendment to the constitution, otherwise I am for maintaining things as they are, though I doubt much the possibility of it, from a tendency in the nature of things towards the preponderancy of the State Governments.

I said, that I was *affectionately* attached to the Republican theory. This is the real language of my heart which I open to you in the sincerity of friendship; & I add that I have strong hopes of the success of that theory; but in candor I ought also to add that I am far from being without doubts. I consider its success as yet a problem.

It is yet to be determined by experience whether it be consistent with that *stability* and *order* in Government which are essential to public strength & private security and happiness. On the whole, the only enemy which Republicanism has to fear in this Country is in the Spirit of faction and anarchy. If this will not permit the ends of Government to be attained under it—if it engenders disorders in the community, all regular & orderly minds will wish for a change—and the demagogues who have produced the disorder will make it for their own aggrandizement. This is the old Story.

If I were disposed to promote Monarchy & overthrow State Governments, I would mount the hobby horse of popularity—I would cry out usurpation—danger to liberty &c. &c—I would endeavour to prostrate the National Government—raise a ferment—and then "ride in the Whirlwind and direct the Storm." That there are men acting with Jefferson & Madison who have this in view I verily believe. I could lay my finger on some of them. That Madison does *not* mean it I also verily believe, and I rather believe the same of Jefferson; but I read him upon the whole thus—"A man of profound ambition & violent passions."

You must be by this time tired of my epistle. Perhaps I have treated certain characters with too much severity. I have however not meant to do them injustice—and from the bottom of my soul believe I have drawn them truly and that it is of the utmost consequence to the public weal they should be viewed in their true colors. I yield to this impression. I will only add that I make no clandestine attacks on the gentlemen concerned. They are both apprized indirectly from myself of the opinion I entertain of their views. With the truest regard and esteem.

## *An American No. I*

For the Gazette of the United States

Mr. Fenno

It was easy to foresee, when the hint appeared in your Gazette of [     ] that the Editor of the National Gazette received a salary from the General Government, advantage would be taken of its want of explicitness and particularity to make the circumstance matter of merit in Mr. Freneau and an argument of his independent disinterestedness. Such a turn of the thing cannot be permitted to succeed. It is now necessary that the whole truth should be told, and that the real state of the affair should be well understood.

Mr. Freneau before he came to this City to conduct the National Gazette was employed by Childs & Swaine Printers of the Dayly Advertiser in the City of New York in capacity of [     ]. A paper more devoted to the views of a certain party of which Mr. Jefferson is the head than any to be found in this City was wanted. Mr. Freneau was thought a fit instrument. His talents for invective and abuse had before been tried as Conductor of the Freemans Journal in this City. A negotiation was opened with him, which ended in the establishment of the National Gazette under his direction. There is good ground to believe that Mr. Madison while in New York in the summer of [    ] was the medium of that Negotiation.

Mr. Freneau came here at once Editor of the National Gazette and Clerk for foreign languages in the department of Mr. Jefferson, Secretary of State; an experiment somewhat new in the history of political manœvres in this Country; a news paper instituted by a public officer, and the Editor of it regularly pensioned with the public money, in the disposal of that officer; an example savouring not a little of that spirit, which in the enumeration of European abuses is the continual theme of declamatory censure with the party whose leader is the author of it; an example which could not have been set by any other head of a department without having long since rung throughout the UStates.

Mr. Freneau is not then, as he would have supposed, the Independent Editor of a News Paper, who though receiving a salary from Government has firmness enough to expose its maladministration. He is the faithful and devoted servant of the head of a party, from whose hand he receives the boon. The whole complexion of his paper is an exact copy of the politics of his employer foreign and domestic, and exhibits a decisive internal evidence of the influence of that patronage under which he acts.

Whether the services rendered by him are an equivalent for the compensation he receives is best known to his employer and himself. There is however some room for doubt. Tis well known that his employer is himself well acquainted with the French language; the only one of which he is the translator; and it may be a question how often his aid is necessary.

It is somewhat singular too that a man acquainted with but one foreign language engaged in a particular trade, which it may be presumed occupies his whole time and attention, the Editor of a News Paper, should be the person selected as the Clerk for foreign languages, in the department of the United States for foreign affairs. Could no person have been found acquainted with more than one foreign language, and who, in so confidential a trust, could have been regularly attached to, in the constant employ of the department and immediately under the eye of the head of it?

But it may be asked—Is it possible that Mr. Jefferson, the head of a principal department of the Government can be the Patron of a Paper, the evident object of which is to decry the Government and its measures? If he disapproves of the Government itself and thinks it deserving of opposition, could he reconcile to his own personal dignity and the principles of probity to hold an office under it and employ the means of official influence in that opposition? If he disapproves of the leading measures, which have been adopted in the course of its administration, could he reconcile it with the principles of delicacy and propriety to continue to hold a place in that administration, and at the same time to be instrumental in vilifying measures which have been adopted by majorities of both branches of the Legislature and *sanctionned by the Chief Magistrate of the Union*?

These questions would certainly be natural. An answer to them might be left to the facts which establish the relation between the Secretary of State and the Editor of the National Gazette, as the text, and to the general tenor of that paper as the Commentary. Let any intelligent man read the paper, from the commencement of it, and let him determine for himself, whether it be not a paper virulently hostile both to the Government and to its measures. Let him then ask himself, whether considering the connection which has subsisted between the Secretary of State and the Editor of that Paper, cœval with its first establishment, it be probable that the complexion of the paper is contrary to the views of that officer.

If he wishes a confirmation of the inference, which he cannot fail to draw, as a probable one, let him be informed in addition—

1 That while the Constitution of the United States was depending before the People of this Country, for their consideration and decision, Mr. Jefferson, being in France, was opposed to it, in some of its most important feautures, and wrote his objections to some of his friends in Virginia. That he, at first, went so far as to discountenance its adoption; though he afterwards recommended it, on the ground of expediency, in certain contingencies.

2 That he is the declared opponent of almost all the important measures which have been devised by the Government; more especially the provision which has been made for the public Debt, the institution

of the Bank of the United States, and such other measures as relate to the Public Credit and the Finances of the UStates.

It is proper that these facts should be known. If the People of the UStates believe, that their happiness and their safety are connected with the existence and maintenance of an efficient National or Fœderal Government—if they continue to think that, which they have created and established, worthy of their confidence, if they are willing, that the powers they have granted to it should be exercised with sufficient latitude to attain the ends they had in view in granting them and to do the essential business of the Nation—If they feel an honest pride in seeing the Credit of their country, so lately prostrate, elevated to an equal station with that of any Nation upon earth—if they are conscious that their own importance is increased by the increased respectability of their Country, which from an abject and degraded state, owing to the want of government, has, by the establishment of a wise constitution and by the measures which have been pursued under it, become a theme for the praise and admiration of mankind—if they experience that their own situation is improved and improving—that commerce and navigation have advanced—that manufactures are progressing—that agriculture is thriving—that property is more secure than it was—industry more certain of real not nominal reward, personal liberty perfectly protected—that notwithstanding the unavoidable demands upon them to satisfy the justice retrieve the reputation and answer the exigencies of the Country they are either less burthened than they were or more equal to the burthen which they have to sustain—if these are their opinions and their experience, let them know and understand, that the sentiments of the officer who has been mentioned, both as to the principles and the practice of the Constitution, which was framed by them and has been administered by their representatives, freely chosen, are essentially different from theirs.

If on the contrary—The People of the United States are of opinion that they erred in adopting their present constitution—that it contains pernicious principles and dangerous powers—that is has been administered injudiciously and wickedly—that men whose abilities and patriotism were tried in the worst of times have entered into a league to betray and oppress them—that they are really oppressed and ruined or in imminent danger of being so—If they think the preservation of National Union a matter of no or small consequence—if they are willing to return to the situation, from which they have just escaped, and to strip the government of some of the most necessary powers with which they have cloathed it—if they are desirous that those which are permitted to remain should be frittered away by a narrow timid and feeble exercise of them—If they are disposed to see the National Government transformed into the skeleton of Power—and the separate omnipotence of the state Governments exalted upon its ruins—If they are persuaded that Nations are under no ties of moral obligation that public Credit is useless or something worse—that public debts may be paid or cancelled at pleasure; that when a provision is not likely to be made for them, the discontents to be expected from the omission may honestly be transferred from a Government able to vindicate its rights to the breasts of Individuals who may first be encouraged to become the Substitutes to the Original Creditor, and afterwards defrauded without danger.* If to National Union, national respectability Public Order and public Credit they are willing to substitute National disunion, National insignificance, Public disorder and discredit—then let them unite their acclamations and plaudits in favour of Mr. Jefferson: Let him be the toast of every political club, and the theme of every popular huzza. For to those points, without examining his motives do assuredly tend the political tenets, real or pretended, of that Gentleman.

These strictures are made from a Conviction, that it is important to the People to know the characters intrusted with their public affairs.

As Mr. Jefferson is emulous of being the head of a party, whose politics have constantly aimed at elevating State-power, upon the ruins of National Authority—Let him enjoy all the glory and all the advantage of it. But Let it at the same time be understood by those, who are persuaded that the real and permanent welfare of the Country is to be promoted by other means that such are the views by which he is actuated.

AN AMERICAN
*August 4, 1792*

---

* Such was the advice given by Mr. Jefferson, when Minister Plenipotentiary to the Court of France, to Congress, respecting the debt due to France. The precise terms are not recollected but the substance may be depended upon. The poor Hollanders were to be the victims.

## To George Washington

*Philadelphia September 9*
*1792*

Sir

I have the pleasure of your private letter of the 26th of August.

The feelings and views which are manifested in that letter are such as I expected would exist. And I most sincerely regret the causes of the uneasy sensations you experience. It is my most anxious wish, as far as may depend upon me, to smooth the path of your administration, and to render it prosperous and happy. And if any prospect shall open of healing or terminating the differences which exist, I shall most chearfully embrace it; though I consider myself as the deeply injured party. The recommendation of such a spirit is worthy of the moderation and wisdom which dictated it; and if your endeavours should prove unsucessful, I do not hesitate to say that in my opinion the period is not remote when the public good will require *substitutes* for the *differing members* of your administration. The continuance of a division there must destroy the energy of Government, which will be little enough with the strictest Union. On my part there will be a most chearful acquiescence in such a result.

I trust, Sir, that the greatest frankness has always marked and will always mark every step of my conduct towards you. In this disposition, I cannot conceal from you that I have had some instrumentality of late in the retaliations which have fallen upon certain public characters and that I find myself placed in a situation not to be able to recede *for the present*.

I considered myself as compelled to this conduct by reasons public as well as personal of the most cogent nature. I know that I have been an object of uniform opposition from Mr. Jefferson, from the first moment of his coming to the City of New York to enter upon his present office. I know, from the most authentic sources, that I have been the frequent subject of the most unkind whispers and insinuating from the same quarter. I have long seen a formed party in the Legislature, under his auspices, bent upon my subversion. I cannot doubt, from the evidence I possess, that the National Gazette was instituted by him for political purposes and that one leading object of it has been to render me and all the measures connected with my department as odious as possible.

Nevertheless I can truly say, that, except explanations to confidential friends, I never directly or indirectly retaliated or countenanced retaliation till very lately. I can even assure you, that I was instrumental in preventing a very severe and systematic attack upon Mr. Jefferson, by an association of two or three individuals, in consequence of the persecution, which he brought upon the Vice President, by his indiscreet and light letter to the Printer, transmitting *Paine's* pamphlet.

As long as I saw no danger to the Government, from the machinations which were going on, I resolved to be a silent sufferer of the injuries which were done me. I determined to avoid giving occasion to any thing which could manifest to the world dissentions among the principal characters of the government; a thing which can never happen without weakening its hands, and in some degree throwing a stigma upon it.

But when I no longer doubted, that there was a formed party deliberately bent upon the subversion of measures, which in its consequences would subvert the Government—when I saw, that the undoing of the funding system in particular (which, whatever may be the original merits of that system, would prostrate the credit and the honor of the Nation, and bring the Government into contempt with that description of Men, who are in every society the only firm supporters of government) was an avowed object of the party; and that all possible pains were taking to produce that effect by rendering it odious to the body of the people—I considered it as a duty, to endeavour to resist the torrent, and as an essential mean to this end, to draw aside the veil from the principal Actors. To this strong impulse, to this decided conviction, I have yielded. And I think events will prove that I have judged rightly.

Nevertheless I pledge my honor to you Sir, that if you shall here-after form a plan to reunite the members of your administration, upon some steady principle of cooperation, I will faithfully concur in executing it during my continuance in office. And I will not directly or indirectly say or do a thing, that shall endanger a feud.

I have had it very much at heart to make an excursion to Mount Vernon, by way of the Fœderal City in the course of this Month—and have been more than once on the point of asking your permission for it. But I now despair of being able to effect it. I am nevertheless equally obliged by your kind invitation.

The subject mentioned in the Postscript of your letter shall with great pleasure be carefully attended to. With the most faithful and affectionate attachment I have the honor to remain

Sir  Your most Obed & humble servant

A HAMILTON

P.S I had written you two letters on public business, one cf which will go with this; but the other will be witheld, in consequence of a slight indisposition of the Attorney General, to be sent by express sometime in the course of tomorrow.

## *Letter to an Unknown Correspondent*

*Philadelphia Sept. 26.*
*1792*

MY DEAR SIR

Some days since, I was surprised with the following intelligence, in a letter from Mr. King (whose name I disclose to you in confidence).

"*Burr* is industrious in his Canvass and his object is well understood by our Antis. Mr. Edwards is to make interest for him in Connecticut and Mr. Dallas, who is here, and quite in the circle of the Governor and the party informs us, that Mr. Burr will be supported as Vice President in Pensylvania. Nothing which has hereto-fore happened so decisively proves the inveteracy of the opposition. Should they succeed much would be to be apprehended"

Though in my situation I deem it most proper to avoid interference in any matter relating to the elections for Members of the Government— Yet I feel reasons of sufficient force to induce a departure from that rule in the present instance.

Mr. Burr's integrity as an Individual is not unimpeached. As a public man he is one of the worst sort—a friend to nothing but as it suits his interest and ambition. Determined to climb to the highest honours of State, and as much higher as circumstances may permit—he cares nothing about the means of effecting his purpose. Tis evident that he aims at putting himself at the head of what he calls the "popular party" as affording the best tools for an ambitious man to work with. Secretly turning Liberty into ridicule, he knows as well as most men how to make use of the name. In a word, if we have an embryo-Cæsar in the United States 'tis Burr.

## *Defense of the President's Neutrality Proclamation*

1. It is a melancholy truth, which every new political occurrence more and more unfolds, that there is a discription of men in this country, irreconcileably adverse to the government of the United States; whose exertions, whatever be the springs of them, whether infatuation or depravity or both, tend to disturb the tranquillity order and prosperity of this now peaceable flourishing and truly happy land. A real and enlightened friend to public felicity cannot observe new confirmations of this fact, without feeling a deep and poignant regret, that human nature should be so refractory and perverse; that amidst a profusion of the bounties and blessings of Providence, political as well as natural, inviting to contentment and gratitude, there should still be found men disposed to cherish and propagate disquietude and alarm; to render suspected and detested the instruments of the felicity, in which they partake; to sacrifice the most substantial advantages, that ever fell to the lot of a people at the shrine of personal envy rivalship and animosity, to the instigations of a turbulent and criminal ambition, or to the treacherous phantoms of an ever craving and never to be satisfied spirit of innovation; a spirit, which seems to suggest to its votaries that the most natural and happy state of Society is a state of continual revolution and change—that the welfare of a nation is in exact ratio to the rapidity of the political vicissitudes, which it undergoes—to the frequency and violence of the tempests with which it is agitated.

2. Yet so the fact unfortunately is—such men there certainly are— and it is essential to our dearest interests to the preservation of peace and good order to the dignity and independence of our public councils— to the real and permanent security of liberty and property—that the Citizens of the UStates should open their eyes to the true characters and designs of the men alluded to—should be upon their guard against their insidious and ruinous machinations.

3. At this moment a most dangerous combination exists. Those who for some time past have been busy in undermining the constitution and government of the UStates, by indirect attacks, by labouring to render its measures odious, by striving to destroy the confidence of the people in its administration—are now meditating a more direct and destructive war against it—and embodying and arranging their forces and systematising their efforts. Secret clubs are formed and private consultations held. Emissaries are dispatched to distant parts of the United States to effect a concert of views and measures, among the members and partisans of the disorganising corps, in the several states. The language in the confidential circles is that the constitution of the United States is too complex a system—that it savours too much of the pernicious doctrine of "ballances and checks" that it requires to be simplified in its structure, to be purged of some monarchical and aristocratic ingredients which are said to have found their way into it and to be stripped of some dangerous prerogatives, with which it is pretended to be invested.

4. The noblest passion of the human soul, which no where burns with so pure and bright a flame, as in the breasts of the people of the UStates, is if possible to be made subservient to this fatal project. That zeal for the liberty of mankind, which produced so universal a sympathy in the cause of France in the first stages of its revolution, and which, it is supposed, has not yet yielded to the just reprobation, which a sober temperate and humane people, friends of religion, social order, and justice, enemies to tumult and massacre, to the wanton and lawless shedding of human blood cannot but bestow upon those extravagancies excesses and outrages, which have sullied and which endanger that cause—that laudable, it is not too much to say that holy zeal is intended by every art of misrepresentation and deception to be made the instrument first of controuling finally of overturning the Government of the Union.

5. The ground which has been so wisely taken by the Executive of the UStates, in regard to the present war of Europe against France, is to be the pretext of this mischievous attempt. The people are if possible to be made to believe, that the Proclamation of neutrality issued by the President of the US was unauthorised illegal and officious—inconsistent with the treaties and plighted faith of the Nation—inconsistent with a due sense of gratitude to France for the services rendered us in our late

contest for independence and liberty—inconsistent with a due regard for the progress and success of republican principles. Already the presses begin to groan with invective against the Chief Magistrate of the Union, for that prudent and necessary measure; a measure calculated to manifest to the World the pacific position of the Government and to caution the citizens of the UStates against practices, which would tend to involve us in a War the most unequal and calamitous, in which it is possible for a Country to be engaged—a war which would not be unlikely to prove pregnant with still greater dangers and disasters, than that by which we established our existence as an Independent Nation.

6. What is the true solution of this extraordinary appearance? Are the professed the real motives of its authors? They are not. The true object is to disparage in the opinion and affections of his fellow citizens that man who at the head of our armies fought so successfully for the Liberty and Independence, which are now our pride and our boast—who during the war supported the hopes, united the hearts and nerved the arm of his countrymen—who at the close of it, unseduced by ambition & the love of power, soothed and appeased the discontents of his suffering companions in arms, and with them left the proud scenes of a victorious field for the modest retreats of private life— who could only have been drawn out of these favourite retreats, to aid in the glorious work of ingrafting that liberty, which his sword had contributed to win, upon a stock of which it stood in need and without which it could not flourish—endure—a firm adequate national Government—who at this moment sacrifices his tranquillity and every favourite pursuit to the peremptory call of his country to aid in giving solidity to a fabric, which he has assisted in rearing—whose whole conduct has been one continued proof of his rectitude moderation disinterestedness and patriotism, who whether the evidence of a uniform course of virtuous public actions be considered, or the motives likely to actuate a man placed precisely in his situation be estimated, it may safely be pronounced, can have no other ambition than that of doing good to his Country & transmitting his fame unimpaired to posterity. For what or for whom is he to hazard that rich harvest of glory, which he has acquired that unexampled veneration and love of his fellow Citizens, which he so eminently possesses?

7. Yet the men alluded to, while they contend with affected zeal for gratitude towards a foreign Nation, which in assisting us was and ought

to have been influenced by considerations relative to its own interest—forgetting what is due to a fellow Citizen, who at every hazard rendered essential services to his Country from the most patriotic motives—insidiously endeavour to despoil him of that precious reward of his services, the confidence and approbation of his fellow Citizens.

8. The present attempt is but the renewal in another form of an attack some time since commenced, and which was only dropped because it was perceived to have excited a general indignation. Domestic arrangements of mere convenience, calculated to reconcile the œconomy of time with the attentions of decorum and civility were then the topics of malevolent declamation. A more serious article of charge is now opened and seems intended to be urged with greater earnestness and vigour. The merits of it shall be examined in one or two succeeding papers, I trust in a manner, that will evince to every candid mind to futility.

9. To be an able and firm supporter of the Government of the Union is in the eyes of the men referred to a crime sufficient to justify the most malignant persecution. Hence the attacks which have been made and repeated with such persevering industry upon more than one public Character in that Government. Hence the effort which is now going on to depreciate in the eyes and estimation of the People the man whom their unanimous suffrages have placed at the head of it.

10. Hence the pains which are taking to inculcate a discrimination between *principles* and *men* and to represent an attachment to the one as a species of war against the other; an endeavour, which has a tendency to stifle or weaken one of the best and most useful feelings of the human heart—a reverence for merit—and to take away one of the strongest incentives to public virtue—the expectation of public esteem.

11. A solicitude for the character who is attacked forms no part of the motives to this comment. He has deserved too much, and his countrymen are too sensible of it to render any advocation of him necessary. If his virtues and services do not secure his fame and ensure to him the unchangeable attachment of his fellow Citizens, twere in vain to attempt to prop them by anonymous panygeric.

12. The design of the observations which have been made is merely to awaken the public attention to the views of a party engaged in a dangerous conspiracy against the tranquillity and happiness of their country. Aware that their hostile aims against the Government can never succeed til they have subverted the confidence of the people in its present

Chief Magistrate, they have at length permitted the suggestions of their enmity to betray them into this hopeless and culpable attempt. If we can destroy his popularity (say they) our work is more than half completed.

13. In proportion as the Citizens of the UStates value the constitution on which their union and happiness depend, in proportion as they tender the blessings of peace and deprecate the calamities of War—ought to be their watchfulness against this success of the artifices which will be employed to endanger that constitution and those blessings. A mortal blow is aimed at both.

14. It imports them infinitely not to be deceived by the protestations which are made—that no harm is meditated against the Constitution—that no design is entertained to involve the peace of the Country. These appearances are necessary to the accomplishment of the plan which has been formed. It is known that the great body of the People are attached to the constitution. It would therefore defeat the intention of destroying it to avow that it exists. It is also known that the People of the UStates are firmly attached to peace. It would consequently frustrate the design of engaging them in the War to tell them that such an object is in contemplation.

15. A more artful course has therefore been adopted. Professions of good will to the Constitution are made without reserve: But every possible art is employed to render the administration and the most zealous and useful friends of the Government odious. The reasoning is obvious. If the people can be persuaded to dislike all the measures of the Government and to dislike all or the greater part of those who have been most conspicuous in establishing or conducting it—the passage from this to the dislike and change of the constitution will not be long nor difficult. The abstract idea of regard for a constitution on paper will not long resist a thorough detestation of its practice.

16. In like manner, professions of a disposition to preserve the peace of the Country are liberally made. But the means of effecting the end are condemned; and exertions are used to prejudice the community against them. A proclamation of neutrality in the most cautious form is represented as illegal—contrary to our engagements with and our duty towards one of the belligerent powers. The plain inference is that in the opinion of these characters the UStates are under obligations which do not permit them to be neutral. Of course they are in a situation to become a party in the War from duty.

17. Pains are likewise taken to inflame the zeal of the people for the cause of France and to excite their resentments against the powers at War with her. To what end all this—but to beget if possible a temper in the community which may overrule the moderate or pacific views of the Government.

*c. May 1793*

## *Pacificus No. 1*

As attempts are making very dangerous to the peace, and it is to be feared not very friendly to the constitution of the UStates—it becomes the duty of those who wish well to both to endeavour to prevent their success.

The objections which have been raised against the Proclamation of Neutrality lately issued by the President have been urged in a spirit of acrimony and invective, which demonstrates, that more was in view than merely a free discussion of an important public measure; that the discussion covers a design of weakening the confidence of the People in the author of the measure; in order to remove or lessen a powerful obstacle to the success of an opposition to the Government, which however it may change its form, according to circumstances, seems still to be adhered to and pursued with persevering Industry.

This Reflection adds to the motives connected with the measure itself to recommend endeavours by proper explanations to place it in a just light. Such explanations at least cannot but be satisfactory to those who may not have leisure or opportunity for pursuing themselves an investigation of the subject, and who may wish to perceive that the policy of the Government is not inconsistent with its obligations or its honor.

The objections in question fall under three heads—

1 That the Proclamation was without authority
2 That it was contrary to our treaties with France
3 That it was contrary to the gratitude, which is due from this to that country; for the succours rendered us in our own Revolution.
4 That it was out of time & unnecessary.

In order to judge of the solidity of the first of these objections, it is necessary to examine what is the nature and design of a proclamation of neutrality.

The true nature & design of such an act is—to *make known* to the powers at War and to the Citizens of the Country, whose Government does the Act that such country is in the condition of a Nation at Peace with the belligerent parties, and under no obligations of Treaty, to become an *associate in the war* with either of them; that this being its situation its intention is to observe a conduct conformable with it and to perform towards each the duties of neutrality; and as a consequence of this state of things, to give warning to all within its jurisdiction to abstain from acts that shall contravene those duties, under the penalties which the laws of the land (of which the law of Nations is a part) annexes to acts of contravention.

This, and no more, is conceived to be the true import of a Proclamation of Neutrality.

It does not imply, that the Nation which makes the declaration will forbear to perform to any of the warring Powers any stipulations in Treaties which can be performed without rendering it an *associate* or *party* in the War. It therefore does not imply in our case, that the UStates will not make those distinctions, between the present belligerent powers, which are stipulated in the 17th and 22d articles of our Treaty with France; because these distinctions are not incompatible with a state of neutrality; they will in no shape render the UStates an *associate* or *party* in the War. This must be evident, when it is considered, that even to furnish *determinate* succours, of a certain number of Ships or troops, to a Power at War, in consequence of *antecedent treaties having no particular reference to the existing war*, is not inconsistent with neutrality; a position well established by the doctrines of Writers and the practice of Nations.*

But no special aids, succours or favors having relation to war, not positively and precisely stipulated by some Treaty of the above description, can be afforded to either party, without a breach of neutrality.

In stating that the Proclamation of Neutrality does not imply the non performance of any stipulations of Treaties which are not of a nature to make the Nation an associate or party in the war, it is conceded that an execution of the clause of Guarantee contained in the 11th article of our Treaty of Alliance with France would be contrary to the sense and spirit of the Proclamation; because it would engage us with our whole

* See Vatel Book III Chap. VI § 101.

force as an *associate* or *auxiliary* in the War; it would be much more than the case of a definite limited succour, previously ascertained.

It follows that the Proclamation is virtually a manifestation of the sense of the Government that the UStates are, *under the circumstances of the case, not bound* to execute the clause of Guarantee.

If this be a just view of the true force and import of the Proclamation, it will remain to see whether the President in issuing it acted within his proper sphere, or stepped beyond the bounds of his constitutional authority and duty.

It will not be disputed that the management of the affairs of this country with foreign nations is confided to the Government of the UStates.

It can as little be disputed, that a Proclamation of Neutrality, where a Nation is at liberty to keep out of a War in which other Nations are engaged and means so to do, is a *usual* and a *proper* measure. *Its main object and effect are to prevent the Nation being immediately responsible for acts done by its citizens, without the privity or connivance of the Government, in contravention of the principles of neutrality.* \*

An object this of the greatest importance to a Country whose true interest lies in the preservation of peace.

The inquiry then is—what department of the Government of the UStates is the proper one to make a declaration of Neutrality in the cases in which the engagements of the Nation permit and its interests require such a declaration.

A correct and well informed mind will discern at once that it can belong neither to the Legislative nor Judicial Department and of course must belong to the Executive.

The Legislative Department is not the *organ* of intercourse between the UStates and foreign Nations. It is charged neither with *making* nor *interpreting* Treaties. It is therefore not naturally that Organ of the Government which is to pronounce the existing condition of the Nation, with regard to foreign Powers, or to admonish the Citizens of their obligations and duties as founded upon that condition of things. Still less is it charged with enforcing the execution and observance of these obligations and those duties.

It is equally obvious that the act in question is foreign to the Judiciary Department of the Government. The province of that Department is

\* See Vatel Book III Chap. VII § 113.

to decide litigations in particular cases. It is indeed charged with the interpretation of treaties; but it exercises this function only in the litigated cases; that is where contending parties bring before it a specific controversy. It has no concern with pronouncing upon the external political relations of Treaties between Government and Government. This position is too plain to need being insisted upon.

It must then of necessity belong to the Executive Department to exercise the function in Question—when a proper case for the exercise of it occurs.

It appears to be connected with that department in various capacities, as the *organ* of intercourse between the Nation and foreign Nations— as the interpreter of the National Treaties in those cases in which the Judiciary is not competent, that is in the cases between Government and Government—as that Power, which is charged with the Execution of the Laws, of which Treaties form a part—as that Power which is charged with the command and application of the Public Force.

This view of the subject is so natural and obvious—so analogous to general theory and practice—that no doubt can be entertained of its justness, unless such doubt can be deduced from particular provisions of the Constitution of the UStates.

Let us see then if cause for such doubt is to be found in that constitution.

The second Article of the Constitution of the UStates, section 1st, establishes this general Proposition, That "The EXECUTIVE POWER shall be vested in a President of the United States of America."

The same article in a succeeding Section proceeds to designate particular cases of Executive Power. It declares among other things that the President shall be Commander in Cheif of the army and navy of the UStates and of the Militia of the several states when called into the actual service of the UStates, that he shall have power by and with the advice of the senate to make treaties; that it shall be his duty to receive ambassadors and other public Ministers and to take care that the laws be faithfully executed.

It would not consist with the rules of sound construction to consider this enumeration of particular authorities as derogating from the more comprehensive grant contained in the general clause, further than as it may be coupled with express restrictions or qualifications; as in regard to the cooperation of the Senate in the appointment of Officers and the making of treaties; which are qualifications of the general executive powers of appointing officers and making treaties: Because the difficulty of a complete and perfect specification of all the cases of Executive authority would naturally dictate the use of general terms—and would render it improbable that a specification of certain particulars was designd as a substitute for those terms, when antecedently used. The different mode of expression employed in the constitution in regard to the two powers the Legislative and the Executive serves to confirm this inference. In the article which grants the legislative powers of the Governt. the expressions are— *"All Legislative powers herein granted shall be vested in a Congress of the UStates;"* in that which grants the Executive Power the expressions are, as already quoted "The EXECUTIVE POWER shall be vested in a President of the UStates of America."

The enumeration ought rather therefore to be considered as intended by way of greater caution, to specify and regulate the principal articles implied in the definition of Executive Power; leaving the rest to flow from the general grant of that power, interpreted in conformity to other parts of the constitution and to the principles of free government.

The general doctrine then of our constitution is, that the EXECUTIVE POWER of the Nation is vested in the President; subject only to the *exceptions* and *qualifications* which are expressed in the instrument.

Two of these have been already noticed—the participation of the Senate in the appointment of Officers and the making of Treaties. A third remains to be mentioned the right of the Legislature "to declare war and grant letters of marque and reprisal."

With these exceptions the EXECUTIVE POWER of the Union is completely lodged in the President. This mode of construing the Constitution has indeed been recognized by Congress in formal acts, upon full consideration and debate. The power of removal from office is an inportant instance.

And since upon general principles for reasons already given, the issuing of a proclamation of neutrality is merely an Executive Act; since also the general Executive Power of the Union is vested in the President, the conclusion is, that the step, which has been taken by him, is liable to no just exception on the score of authority.

It may be observed that this Inference would be just if the power of declaring war had not been vested in the Legislature, but that this power naturally includes the right of judging whether the Nation is under obligations to make war or not.

The answer to this is, that however true it may be, that the right of the Legislature to declare war includes the right of judging whether the Nation be under obligations to make War or not—it will not follow that the Executive is in any case excluded from a similar right of Judgment, in the execution of its own functions.

If the Legislature have a right to make war on the one hand—it is on the other the duty of the Executive to preserve Peace till war is declared; and in fulfilling that duty, it must necessarily possess a right of judging what is the nature of the obligations which the treaties of the Country impose on the Government; and when in pursuance of this right it has concluded that there is nothing in them inconsistent with a state of neutrality, it becomes both its province and its duty to enforce the laws incident to that state of the Nation. The Executive is charged with the execution of all laws, the laws of Nations as well as the Municipal law, which recognises and adopts those laws. It is consequently bound, by faithfully executing the laws of neutrality, when that is the state of the Nation, to avoid giving a cause of war to foreign Powers.

This is the direct and proper end of the proclamation of neutrality. It declares to the UStates their situation with regard to the Powers at war and makes known to the Community that the laws incident to that situation will be enforced. In doing this, it conforms to an established usage of Nations, the operation of which as before remarked is to obviate a responsibility on the part of the whole Society, for secret and unknown violations of the rights of any of the warring parties by its citizens.

Those who object to the proclamation will readily admit that it is the right and duty of the Executive to judge of, or to interpret, those articles of our treaties which give to France particular privileges, in order to the enforcement of those privileges: But the necessary consequence of this is, that the Executive must judge what are the proper bounds of those privileges—what rights are given to other nations by our treaties with them—what rights the law of Nature and Nations gives and our treaties permit, in respect to those Nations with whom we have no treaties; in fine what are the reciprocal rights and obligations of the United States & of all & each of the powers at War.

The right of the Executive to receive ambassadors and other public

Ministers may serve to illustrate the relative duties of the Executive and Legislative Departments. This right includes that of judging, in the case of a Revolution of Government in a foreign Country, whether the new rulers are competent organs of the National Will and ought to be recognised or not: And where a treaty antecedently exists between the UStates and such nation that right involves the power of giving operation or not to such treaty. For until the new Government is *acknowleged*, the treaties between the nations, as far at least as regards *public* rights, are of course suspended.

This power of determining virtually in the case supposed upon the operation of national Treaties as a consequence, of the power to receive ambassadors and other public Ministers, is an important instance of the right of the Executive to decide the obligations of the Nation with regard to foreign Nations. To apply it to the case of France, if there had been a Treaty of alliance *offensive* and defensive between the UStates and that Country, the unqualified acknowlegement of the new Government would have put the UStates in a condition to become an associate in the War in which France was engaged—and would have laid the Legislature under an obligation, if required, and there was otherwise no valid excuse, of exercising its power of declaring war.

This serves as an example of the right of the Executive, in certain cases, to determine the condition of the Nation, though it may consequentially affect the proper or improper exercise of the Power of the Legislature to declare war. The Executive indeed cannot control the exercise of that power—further than by the exercise of its general right of objecting to all acts of the Legislature; liable to being overruled by two thirds of both houses of Congress. The Legislature is free to perform its own duties according to its own sense of them—though the Executive in the exercise of its constitutional powers, may establish an antecedent state of things which ought to weigh in the legislative decisions. From the division of the Executive Power there results, in referrence to it, a *concurrent* authority, in the distributed cases.

Hence in the case stated, though treaties can only be made by the President and Senate, their activity may be continued or suspended by the President alone.

No objection has been made to the Presidents having acknowleged the Republic of France, by the Reception of its Minister, without having consulted the Senate; though that body is connected with him in the making of Treaties, and though the consequence of his act of reception is to give operation to the Treaties heretofore made with that Country: But he is censured for having declared the UStates to be in a state of peace & neutrality, with regard to the Powers at War; because the right of *changing* that state & *declaring war* belongs to the Legislature.

It deserves to be remarked, that as the participation of the senate in the making of Treaties and the power of the Legislature to declare war are exceptions out of the general "Executive Power" vested in the President, they are to be construed strictly—and ought to be extended no further than is essential to their execution.

While therefore the Legislature can alone declare war, can alone actually transfer the nation from a state of Peace to a state of War— it belongs to the "Executive Power," to do whatever else the laws of Nations cooperating with the Treaties of the Country enjoin, in the intercourse of the UStates with foreign Powers.

In this distribution of powers the wisdom of our constitution is manifested. It is the province and duty of the Executive to preserve to the Nation the blessings of peace. The Legislature alone can interrupt those blessings, by placing the Nation in a state of War.

But though it has been thought adviseable to vindicate the authority of the Executive on this broad and comprehensive ground—it was not absolutely necessary to do so. That clause of the constitution which makes it his duty to "take care that the laws be faithfully executed" might alone have been relied upon, and this simple process of argument pursued.

The President is the constitutional EXECUTOR of the laws. Our Treaties and the laws of Nations form a part of the law of the land. He who is to execute the laws must first judge for himself of their meaning. In order to the observance of that conduct, which the laws of nations combined with our treaties prescribed to this country, in reference to the present War in Europe, it was necessary for the President to judge for himself whether there was any thing in our treaties incompatible with an adherence to neutrality. Having judged that there was not, he had a right, and if in his opinion the interests of the Nation required it, it was his duty, as Executor of the laws, to proclaim the neutrality of the Nation, to exhort all persons to observe it, and to warn them of the penalties which would attend its non observance.

The Proclamation has been represented as enacting some new law.

This is a view of it entirely erroneous. It only proclaims a *fact* with regard to the *existing state* of the Nation, informs the citizens of what the laws previously established require of them in that state, & warns them that these laws will be put in execution against the Infractors of them.

*Gazette of the United States,*
*June 29, 1793*

## To Andrew G. Fraunces

Contemptible as you are, what answer could I give to your last letter?

The enclosed is a copy of what will shortly appear in one of the Gazettes of the city of New-York.

A. HAMILTON

*Albany, October 1, 1793.*

One Andrew G. Fraunces, lately a clerk in the treasury department, has been endeavoring to have it believed, that he is possessed of some facts, of a nature to criminate the official conduct of the Secretary of the Treasury; an idea to which, for obvious reasons, an extensive circulation has been given, by a certain description of persons. The Public may be assured, that the said Fraunces has been regularly and repeatedly called upon, to declare the grounds of his suggestion; that he has repeatedly evaded the enquiry; that he possesses no facts of the nature pretended; and that he is a dispicable calumniator.

## To Angelica Hamilton

I was very glad to learn, my dear daughter, that you were going to begin the study of the French language. We hope you will in every respect behave in such a manner as will secure to you the good-will and regard of all those with whom you are. If you happen to displease any of them, be always ready to make a frank apology. But the best way is to act with so much politeness, good manners, and circumspection, as never to have occasion to make any apology. Your mother joins in best love to you. Adieu, my very dear daughter.

*c. November 1793*

# *Tully No. III*

*For the American Daily Advertiser.*
*To the* PEOPLE of the UNITED STATES.

### LETTER III.

If it were to be asked, What is the most sacred duty and the greatest source of security in a Republic? the answer would be, An inviolable respect for the Constitution and Laws—the first growing out of the last. It is by this, in a great degree, that the rich and powerful are to be restrained from enterprises against the common liberty—operated upon by the influence of a general sentiment, by their interest in the principle, and by the obstacles which the habit it produces erects against innovation and encroachment. It is by this, in a still greater degree, that caballers, intriguers, and demagogues are prevented from climbing on the shoulders of faction to the tempting seats of usurpation and tyranny.

Were it not that it might require too lengthy a discussion, it would not be difficult to demonstrate, that a large and well organized Republic can scarcely lose its liberty from any other cause than that of anarchy, to which a contempt of the laws is the high road.

But, without entering into so wide a field, it is sufficient to present to your view a more simple and a more obvious truth, which is this— that a sacred respect for the constitutional law is the vital principle, the sustaining energy of a free government.

Government is frequently and aptly classed under two descriptions, a government of FORCE and a government of LAWS; the first is the definition of despotism—the last, of liberty. But how can a government of laws exist where the laws are disrespected and disobeyed? Government supposes controul. It is the power by which individuals in society are kept from doing injury to each other and are bro't to co-operate to a common end. The instruments by which it must act are either the AUTHORITY of the Laws or FORCE. If the first be destroyed, the last must be substituted; and where this becomes the ordinary instrument of government there is an end to liberty.

Those, therefore, who preach doctrines, or set examples, which undermine or subvert the authority of the laws, lead us from freedom to slavery; they incapacitate us for a GOVERNMENT OF LAWS, and consequently prepare the way for one of FORCE, for mankind MUST HAVE GOVERNMENT OF ONE SORT OR ANOTHER.

There are indeed great and urgent cases where the bounds of the constitution are manifestly transgressed, or its constitutional authorities so exercised as to produce unequivocal oppression on the community, and to render resistance justifiable. But such cases can give no colour to the resistance by a comparatively inconsiderable part of a community, of constitutional laws distinguished by no extraordinary features of rigour or oppression, and acquiesced in by the BODY OF THE COMMUNITY.

Such a resistance is treason against society, against liberty, against every thing that ought to be dear to a free, enlightened, and prudent people. To tolerate were to abandon your most precious interests. Not to subdue it, were to tolerate it. Those who openly or covertly dissuade you from exertions adequate to the occasion are your worst enemies. They treat you either as fools or cowards, too weak to perceive your interest and your duty, or too dastardly to pursue them. They therefore merit, and will no doubt meet your contempt.

To the plausible but hollow harangues of such conspirators, ye cannot fail to reply, How long, ye Catilines, will you abuse our patience.

TULLY.

*Dunlap and Claypoole's American Daily Advertiser,*
*August 28, 1794*

## *To Angelica Church*

*Bedford Pensylvania*
*October 23. 1794*
*205 Miles Westward of*
*Philadelphia*

I am thus far my dear Angelica on my way to attack and subdue the wicked insurgents of the West. But you are not to promise yourself that I shall have any trophies to lay at your feet. A large army has cooled the courage of those madmen & the only question seems now to be how to guard best aganst the return of the phrenzy.

You must not take my being here for a proof that I continue a quixot. In popular governments 'tis useful that those who propose measures should partake in whatever dangers they may involve. Twas very important there should be no mistake in the management of the affair—and I *might* contribute to prevent one. I wish to have every thing well settled for Mr. Church & you, that when you come, you may tread on safe ground. Assure him that the insurrection will do us a great deal of good and add to the solidity of every thing in this country. Say the same to Mr Jay to whom I have not time to write & to Mr Pinkney.

God bless You Dear Sister & make you as happy as I wish you. Love to Mr. Church.

A HAMILTON

## To Angelica Church

*Philadelphia, December 8, 1794.*

You say I am a politician, and good for nothing. What will you say when you learn that after January next, I shall cease to be a politician at all? So is the fact. I have formally and definitely announced my intention to resign at that period, and have ordered a house to be taken for me at New York.

My dear Eliza has been lately very ill. Thank God, she is now quite recovered, except that she continues somewhat weak. My absence on a certain expedition was the cause (with army to suppress the whisky insurrection in Pennsylvania). You will see, notwithstanding your disparagement of me, I am still of consequence to her.

Liancourt has arrived, and has delivered your letter. I pay him the attentions due to his misfortunes and his merits. I wish I was a Croesus; I might then afford solid consolations to these children of adversity, and how delightful it would be to do so. *But now*, sympathy, kind words, and *occasionally a dinner, are all I can contribute.*

Don't let Mr. Church be alarmed at my retreat—all is well with the public. Our insurrection is most happily terminated. Government has gained by it reputation and strength, and our finances are in a most flourishing condition. *Having contributed to place those of the Nation on a good footing, I go to take a little care of my own; which need my care not a little.*

Love to Mr. Church. Betsy will add a line or two. Adieu.

## The French Revolution

In the early periods of the French Revolution, a warm zeal for its success was in this Country *a sentiment truly universal.* The love of Liberty is here the ruling passion *of the Citizens of the UStates* pervading every class animating every bosom. As long therefore as the Revolution of France bore the marks of being the cause of liberty it united all hearts concentered all opinions. But this unanimity of approbation has been for a considerable time decreasing. The excesses which have constantly multiplied, with greater and greater aggravations have successively though slowly detached reflecting men from their partiality for an object which has appeared less and less to merit their regard. Their reluctance to abandon it has however been proportioned to the ardor and fondness with which they embraced it. They were willing to overlook many faults—to apologise for some enormities—to hope that better justifications existed than were seen—to look forward to more calm and greater moderation, after the first shocks of the political earthquake had subsided. But instead of this, they have been witnesses to one volcano succeeding another, the last still more dreadful than the former, spreading ruin and devastation far and wide—subverting the foundations of right security and property, of order, morality and religion—sparing neither sex nor age, confounding innocence with guilt, involving the old and the young, the sage and the madman, the long tried friend of virtue and his country and the upstart pretender to purity and patriotism—the bold projector of new treasons with the obscure in indiscriminate and profuse destruction. They have found themselves driven to the painful alternative of renouncing an object dear to their wishes or of becoming by the continuance of their affection for it accomplices with Vice Anarchy Depotism and Impiety.

But though an afflicting experience has materially lessened the number of the admirers of the French Revolution among us and has served to chill the ardor of many more, who profess still to retain their attachment to it, from what they suppose to be its ultimate tendency; yet the effect of Experience has been thus far much less than could reasonably have been expected. The predilection for it still continues extensive and ardent. And what is extraordinary it continues to comprehend men who are able to form a just estimate of the information which destroys its title to their favour.

It is not among the least perplexing phœnomina of the present times, that a people like that of the UStates—exemplary for humanity and moderation surpassed by no other in the love of order and a knowlege of the true principles of liberty, distinguished for purity of morals and a just reverence for Religion should so long perservere in partiality for a state of things the most cruel sanguinary and violent that ever stained the annuals of mankind, a state of things which annihilates the foundations of social order and true liberty, confounds all moral distinctions and *substitutes to* the mild & beneficent religion of the Gospel a gloomy persecuting and desolating atheism. To the eye of a wise man, this partiality is the most inauspicious circumstance, that has appeared in the affairs of this country. It leads involuntarily and irresistibly to apprehensions concerning the soundness of our principles and the stability of our welfare. It is natural to fear that the transition may not be difficult from the approbation of bad things to the imitation of them; a fear which can only be mitigated by a careful estimate of the extraneous causes that have served to mislead the public judgment.

But though we may find in these causes a solution of the fact calculated to abate our solicitude for the consequences; yet we can not consider the public happiness as out of the reach of danger so long as our principles continue to be exposed to the debauching influence of admiration for an example which, it will not be too strong to say, presents the caricature of human depravity. And the pride of national character at least can find no alleviation for the wound which must be inflicted by so ill-judged so unfortunate a partiality.

If there be any thing solid in virtue—the time must come when it will have been a disgrace to have advocated the Revolution of France in its late stages.

This is a language to which the ears of the people of this country have not been accustommed. Every thing has hitherto conspired to confirm the pernicious fascination by which they are enchained. There has been a positive and a negative conspiracy against the truth which has served to shut out its enlightening ray. Those who always float with the popular gale perceiving the prepossession of the people have administered to it by all the acts in their power—endeavouring to recommend themselves by an exaggerated zeal for a favourite object. Others through timidity caution or an ill-judged policy unwilling to expose themselves to the odium of resisting the general current of feeling have betrayed by silence that Truth which they were unable not to perceive. Others, whose sentiments have weight in the community have been themselves the sincere dupes of [    ]. Hence the voice of reason has been stifled and the Nation has been left unadmonished to travel on in one of the most degrading delusions that ever disparaged the understandings of an enlightened people.

To recal them from this dangerous error—to engage them to dismiss their prejudices & consult dispassionately their own good sense—to lead them to an appeal from their own enthusiasm to their reason and humanity would be the most important service that could be rendered to the UStates at the present juncture. The error entertained is not on a mere speculative question. The French Revolution is a political convulsion that in a great or less degree shakes the whole civilized world and it is of real consequence to the principles and of course to the happiness of a Nation to estimate it rightly.

*1794*

## To George Washington

*Philadelphia February 3. 1795*

SIR

My particular acknowlegements are due for your very kind letter of yesterday. As often as I may recall the vexations I have endured, your approbation will be a great and precious consolation.

It was not without a struggle, that I yielded to the very urgent motives, which impelled me to relinquish a station, in which I could hope to be in any degree instrumental in promoting the success of an administration under your direction; a struggle which would have been far greater, had I supposed that the prospect of future usefulness was proportioned to the sacrifices to be made.

Whatsoever may be my destination hereafter, I entreat you to be persuaded (not the less for my having been sparing in professions) that I shall never cease to render a just tribute to those eminent and excellent qualities which have been already productive of so many blessings to your country—that you will always have my fervent wishes for your public and personal felicity, and that it will be my pride to cultivate a continuance of that esteem regard and friendship, of which you do me the honor to assure me. With true respect and affectionate attachment I have the honor to be

Sir Your obliged & obedt servt

A HAMILTON

## To Rufus King

*Kingston Feby. 21. 1795*

MY DEAR KING

The unnecessary capricious & abominable assassination of the National honor by the rejection of the propositions respecting the unsubscribed debt in the House of Representatives haunts me every step I take, and afflicts me more than I can express. To see the character of the Government and the country so sported with, exposed to so indelible a blot puts my heart to the Torture. Am I then more of an American than those who drew their first breath on American Ground? Or What is it that thus torments me at a circumstance so calmly viewed by almost every body else? Am I a fool—a Romantic quixot—Or is there a constitutional defect in the American Mind? Were it not for yourself and a few others, I could adopt the reveries of De Paux as substantial truths, and would say with him that there is something in our climate which belittles every Animal human or brute.

I conjure you, my friend, Make a vigorous stand for the honor of your Country. Rouse all the energies of your mind, and measure swords in the Senate with the great Slayer of public faith—the hacknied *Veteran* in the violation of public engagements. Prevent him if possible from triumphing a second time over the prostrate credit* and injured interests of his Country. Unmask his false and horrid hypothesis. Display the immense difference between an able statesman and the *Man of subtilties*. Root out the distempered and noisome *weed* which is attempted to be planted in our political garden—to choak and wither in its infancy the fair plant of public credit.

I disclose to you without reserve the state of my mind. It is

---

* Witness the 40 for 1 scheme a most unskilful measure, to say the best of it.

discontented and gloomy in the extreme. I consider the cause of good government as having been put to an issue & the verdict against it.

Introduce I pray you into the Senate, when the bill comes up the clause which has been rejected freed from embarrassment by the bills of Credit bearing interest on the nominal value. Press its adoption in this the most unexceptionable shape & let the *yeas* & *nays* witness the result.

Among other reasons for this is my wish that the true friends of public credit may be distinguished from its enemies. The question is too great a one not to undergo a thorough examination before the Community. It would pain me not to be able to distinguish. Adieu.

God bless you

A HAMILTON

P.S. Do me the favour to revise carefully the course of the bill respecting the unsubscribed Debt & let me know the particulars. I wish to be able to judge more particularly of the under plot I suspect.

## *To Robert Troup*

*Albany April 13. 1795*

I should want feeling & friendship were I not penetrated by the affectionate concern you so repeatedly manifest for my interest.

Without knowing the particulars of the plan to which you refer I ought not to decide finally against it. But I very much believe that it will not comport with my general system which is to avoid large or complicated speculations especially where foreigners are concerned.

Tis not my Dear Friend that I think there is any harm or even indelicacy in the thing—I am now in no situation that restrains me— But 'tis because I think there is at present a great crisis in the affairs of mankind which may in its consequences involve this country in a sense most affecting to every true friend to it—because concerns of the nature alluded to, though very harmless in the *saints*, who may even fatten themselves on the opportunities or if you please spoils of office, as well as profit by every good thing that is going—who may [      ] agents & tools of foreign *Governments* without hazarding their popularity yet those who are not of the *regenerating* tribe may not do the most unexceptionable things without its being thundered in their ears—without being denounced as speculators peculators British Agents &c. &c. Because there must be some *public fools* who sacrifice private to public interest at the certainty of ingratitude and obloquy— because my *vanity* whispers I ought to be one of those fools and ought to keep myself in a situation the best calculated to render service— because I dont want to be rich and if I cannot live *in splendor* in Town, with a moderate fortune moderately acquired, I can at least live *in comfort* in the country and I am content to do so.

The game to be played may be a most important one. It may be for nothing less than true liberty, property, order, religion and of course *heads*. I will try Troupe if possible to guard yours & mine.

You are good enough to offer to stand between me and ostensibility. I thank you with all my soul. You cannot doubt that I should have implicit confidence in you but it has been the rule of my life to do nothing for my own emolument *undercover*—what I would not promulge I would avoid. This may be too great refinement. I know it is pride. But this pride makes it part of my plan to *appear truly what I am*.

God bless you. Always Affectionately Yrs.

A HAMILTON

## *Design for a Seal for the United States*

A Globe with Europe and part of Africa on one side—America on the other—the Atlantic Ocean between. The portion occupied by America to be larger than that occupied by Europe. A COLOSSUS to be placed on this Globe, with one foot on Europe, the other extending partly over the Atlantic towards America, having on his head a *quintuple* crown in his right hand an *Iron*-Sceptre projected but broken in the middle—in his left hand a *Pileus* reversed, the staff intwined by a snake with its head downward having the staff in its mouth and folding in its tail (as if in the act of strangling) a label with these words "Rights of Man."

Upon a base, supported by fifteen columns, erected on the Continent of America, to be placed the *Genius* of America, represented by *Pallas*—a female figure with a firm composed countenance, in an attitude of defiance, cloathed in armour with a golden breast plate, a spear in her right hand and an *Ægis* or shield in her left, decorated with the scales of Justice instead of the Medusa's head—her helmet incircled with wreaths of Olive—her spear striking upon the Sceptre of the Colussus and breaking it obliquely over her head a radiated Crown or *Glory*.

EXPLANATION

The Globe is an antient symbol of universal Dominion. This, with the Colossus alluding to the Directory, will denote the project of acquiring it—the position of one leg of the colussus will signify the *attempt* to extend it to America. The Columns will represent the American States. Pallas, as the Genius of America will denote, that though loving Peace (of which the Olive wreath is the emblem) yet guided by *Wisdom*, or an enlightened sense of her own rights and interests, she is determined to exert and does successfully exert her *valour*, in breaking the sceptre of the Tyrant. The *Glory* is the usual type of Providential interposition.

It would improve it if it did not render it too complicated to represent the Ocean in Tempest & Neptune striking with his Trident the projected leg of the Colussus.

But perhaps instead of all this it may suffice to have the figure of Pallas on horse back the harp placed on the Columns these on a small mount—her spear breaking a Sceptre projected by a *Herculean Arm*.

c. May 1796

## *To George Washington*

New York July 30. 1796

SIR

I have the pleasure to send you herewith a certain draft which I have endeavoured to make as perfect as my time and engagements would permit. It has been my object to render this act *importantly* and *lastingly* useful, and avoiding all just cause of present exception, to embrace such reflections and sentiments as will wear well, progress in approbation with time, & redound to future reputation. How far I have succeeded you will judge.

I have begun the second part of the task—the digesting the supplementary remarks to the first address which in a fortnight I hope also to send you—yet I confess the more I have considered the matter the less eligible this plan has appeared to me. There seems to me to be a certain awkwardness in the thing—and it seems to imply that there is a doubt whether the assurance without the evidence would be believed. Besides that I think that there are some ideas which will not wear well in the former address, & I do not see how any part can be omitted, if it is to be given as the thing formerly prepared. Nevertheless when you have both before you you can better judge.

If you should incline to take the draft now sent—and after perusing and noting any thing that you wish changed & will send it to me I will with pleasure shape it as you desire. This may also put it in my power to improve the expression & perhaps in some instances condense.

I rejoice that certain clouds have not lately thickened & that there is a prospect of a brighter horison.

With affectionate & respectful attachment I have the honor to be Sir Yr. Very Obed Serv

A HAMILTON

Enclosure: Draft of Washington's Farewell Address

The period for a new election of a Citizen to administer the Executive Gov of the U States being not very distant and the time actually arrived when your thoughts must be employed in designating the person who is to be cloathed with that important trust for another term, it appears to me proper, and especially as it may conduce to a more distinct expression of the public voice, that I should now apprize you of the resolution I have formed to decline being considered among the number of those out of whom a choice is to be made.

I beg you nevertheless at the same time to be assured that the resolution, which I announce, has not been taken without a strict regard to all the considerations attached to the relation which as a dutiful Citizen I bear to my Country; and that in withdrawing the tender of my service, which silence in my situation might imply, I am influenced by no diminution of zeal for its future interest nor by any deficiency of grateful respect for its past kindness, but by a full conviction that such a step is compatible with both.

The acceptance of and continuance hitherto in the office to which your suffrages have twice called me has been a uniform sacrifice of private inclination to the opinion of public duty coinciding with what appeared to be your wishes. I had constantly hoped that it would have been much earlier in my power consistently with motives which I was not at liberty to disregard to return to that retirement from which they those motives had reluctantly drawn me.

The strength of my desire to withdraw previous to the last election had even led to the preparation of an address to declare it to you—but deliberate reflection on the very critical and perplexed posture of our affairs with foreign nations and the unanimous advice of men of every way intitled to my confidence obliged me to abandon the idea.

I rejoice that the state of your national Concerns external as well as internal no longer renders the pursuit of my inclination incompatible with the sentiment of duty or propriety, and that whatever partiality any portion of You may still retain for my services, they, under the existing circumstances of our Country, will not disapprove the resolution I have formed.

The impressions under which I first accepted the arduous trust of chief Magistrate of the U States were explained on the proper occasion. In the discharge of this trust I can only say that I have with pure intentions contributed towards the organisation and administration of the Government the best exertions of which a very fallible judgment was capable. Not unconscious at the outset of the inferiority of my qualifications for the station, experience in my own eyes and perhaps still more in those of others has not diminished in me the diffidence of myself—and every day the increasing weight of years admonishes me more and more that the shade of retirement is as necessary to me as it will be welcome to me. Satisfied that if any circumstances have given a peculiar value to my services they were temporary, I have the consolation to believe that while inclination and prudence urge me to recede from the political scene patriotism does not forbid it—May I also have that of perceiving in my retreat that the involuntary errors which I have probably committed have been the causes of no serious or lasting mischief to my Country and thus be spared the anguish of regrets which would disturb the repose of my retreat and embitter the remmant of my life! I may then expect to realize without alloy the purest enjoyment of partaking, in the midst of my fellow citizens of the benign influence of good laws under a free Government; the ultimate object of all my wishes and to which

I look as the happy reward I hope of our mutual cares labours and dangers.

In looking forward to the moment which is to terminate the carreer of my public life, my sensations do not permit me to suspend the deep acknowlegements required by that debt of gratitude which I owe to my beloved country for the many honors it has conferred upon me still more for the distinguished and steadfast confidence it has reposed in me and for the opportunities it has thus afforded me of manifesting my inviolable attachment by services faithful and persevering—however the inadequateness of my faculties may have ill seconded my zeal. If benefits have resulted to you my fellow Citizens from these services, let it always be remembered to your praise and as an instructive example in our annals that the constancy of your support amidst appearances sometimes dubious vicissitudes of fortune often discouraging and in situations in which not infrequently want of success has seconded the criticisms of malevolence was the essential prop of the efforts and the guarantee of the measures by which they were atchieved. Profoundly penetrated with this idea, I shall carry it with me to my retirement and to my grave as a lively incitement to unceasing vows (the only returns I can henceforth make) that Heaven may continue to You the choicest tokens of the beneficence merited by national piety and morality—that your union and brotherly affection may be perpetual— that the free constitution, which is the work of your own hands may be sacredly maintained—that its administration in every department may be stamped with wisdom and virtue—that in fine the happiness of the People of these States under the auspices of liberty may be made complete by so careful a preservation & so prudent a use of this blessing as will acquire them the glorious satisfaction of recommending it to the affection the praise—and the adoption of every nation which is yet a stranger to it.

Here perhaps I ought to stop. But a solicitude for your welfare, which cannot end but with my life, and the fear that there may exist projects unfriendly to it against which it may be necessary you should be guarded, urge me in taking leave of you to offer to your solemn consideration and frequent review some sentiments the result of mature reflection confirmed by observation & experience which appear to me essential to the permanency of your felicity as a people. These will be offered with the more freedom as you can only see in them the disinterested advice of a parting friend who can have no personal motive to tincture or byass his counsel.

Interwoven as is the love of Liberty with every fibre of your hearts no recommendation is necessary to fortify your attachment to it. Next to this that unity of Government which constitutes you one people claims your vigilant care & guardianship—as a main pillar of your real independence of your peace safety freedom and happiness.

This being the point in your political fortress against which the batteries of internal and external enemies will be most constantly and actively however covertly and insidiously levelled, it is of the utmost importance that you should appreciate in its full force the immense value of your political Union to your national and individual happiness— that you should cherish towards it an affectionate and immoveable attachment and that you should watch for its presservation with jealous solicitude.

For this you have every motive of sympathy and interest. Children for the most part of a common country, that country claims and ought to concentrate your affections. The name of American must always gratify and exalt the just pride of patriotism more than any denomination which can be derived from local discrimination. You have with slight shades of difference the same religion manners habits & political institutions & principles. You have in a common cause fought and triumphed to gether. The independence and liberty you enjoy are the work of joint councils efforts—dangers sufferings & successes. By your Union you atchieved them, by your union you will most effectually maintain them.

The considerations which address themselves to your sensibility are greatly strengthened by those which apply to your interest. Here every portion of our Country will find the most urgent and commanding motives for guarding and preserving the Union of the Whole.

The North in a free & unfettered intercourse with the South under the equal laws of one Government will in the production of the latter many of them peculiar find vast additional resources of maritime and commercial enterprise and precious materials of their manufacturing industry. The South in the same intercourse will share in the benefits of the Agency of the North will find its agriculture promoted and its commerce extended by turning into its own channels means of Navigation which the North more abundantly affords and while it contributes to extend the national navigation will participate in the protection of a maritime strength to which itself is unequally adapted. The East in a like intercourse with the West finds and in the progressive improvement of internal navigation will more & more find, a valuable vent for the commodities which it brings from abroad or manufactures at home. The West derives through this Channel an essential supply of its wants—and what is far more important to it, it must owe the secure and permanent enjoyment of the indispensable outlets for its own productions to the weight influence & maritime resources of the Atlantic States directed by an indissoluble community of interest. The tenure by which it could hold this advantage either from its own separate strength or by an apostate and unnatural connection with any foreign Nation must be intrinsically & necessarily precarious at every moment liable to be disturbed by the fluctuating combinations of those primary European interests which constantly regulate the conduct of every portion of Europe—And where every part finds a particular interest in the Union All the parts of our Country will find in their Union greater independence from the superior abundance & variety of production incident to the diversity of soil & climate, all the parts of it must find in the aggregate assemblage & reaction of their mutual population production greater strength, proportional security from external danger, less frequent interruption of their peace with foreign nations and what is far more valuable an exemption from those broils & wars between the parts if disunited which their own rivalships fomented by foreign intrigue, or the opposite alliances with foreign nations engendered by their mutual jealousies would inevitably produce—a consequent exemption from the necessity of those military establishments upon a large scale which bear in every country so menacing an aspect toward Liberty.

These considerations speak a conclusive language to every virtuous and considerate mind. They place the continuance of our Union among the first objects of patriotic desire. Is there a doubt whether a common government can long embrace so extensive a sphere? Let Time & Experience decide the question. Speculation in such a case ought not to be listened to—And tis rational to hope that the auxiliary agency of the governments of the subdivisions, with a proper organisation of the whole will secure a favourable issue to the Experiment. Tis allowable to believe that the spirit of party the intrigues of foreign nations, the corruption & the ambition of Individuals are likely to prove more formidable adversaries to the unity of our Empire than any inherent difficulties in the scheme. Tis against these that the guards of national opinion national sympathy national prudence & virtue are to be erected. With such obvious motives to Union there will be always cause from the fact itself to distrust the <u>patriotism</u> of those who in any quarter may endeavour to weaken its bands. And by all the love I bear you My fellow Citizens I conjure you as often as it appears to frown upon the attempt.

Besides the more serious causes which have been hinted at, as endangering our Union there is another less dangerous but against which it is necessary to be on our guard. I mean the petulance collisions & disgusts of party differences of Opinion. It is not uncommon to hear the irritations which these excite vent themselves in declarations that the different parts of the Union are ill assorted and cannot remain together—in menaces from the inhabitants of one part to those of another that it will be dissolved by this or that measure. Intimations of the kind are as indiscreet as they are intemperate. Though frequently made with levity and without being in earnest they have a tendency to produce the consequence which they indicate. They teach the minds of men to consider the Union as precarious as an object to which they are not to attach their hopes and fortunes and thus weaken the sentiment in its favour. By rousing the resentment and alarming the pride of those to whom they are addressed they set ingenuity to work to depreciate the value of the object and to discover motives of Indifference to it. This is not wise. Prudence demands that we should habituate ourselves in all our words and actions to reverence the Union as a sacred and inviolable palladium of our happiness—and should discountenance whatever can lead to a suspicion that it can in any event be abandonned.

Tis matter of serious concern that parties in this Country for some time past have been too much characterised by geographical discriminations—Northern and Southern States Atlantic and Western Country. These discriminations of party which are the mere artifice of the spirit of party (always dexterous to avail itself of every source of sympathy of every handle by which the passions can be taken hold of and which has been careful to turn to account the circumstance of territorial vicinity) have furnished an argument against the Union as evidence of a real difference of local interests and views and serve to hazard it by organising large districts of country under the direction of the leaders of different factions whose passions & prejudices rather than the true interests of the Country, will be too apt to regulate the use of their influence. If it be possible to correct <u>this poison</u> in the affairs of our Country it is worthy the best endeavours of moderate & virtuous men to effect it.

One of the expedients which the partisans of Faction employ towards strengthening their influence by local discriminations is to misrepresent the opinions and views of rival districts—The People at large cannot be too much on their guard against the jealousies which grow out of these misrepresentations. They tend to render aliens to each other those who ought to be tied together by fraternal affection. The Western Country have lately had a useful lesson on this subject. They have seen in the negotiation by the Executive & in the unanimous ratification of the Treaty with Spain by the Senate & in the universal satisfaction at that event in all parts of the Country a decisive proof how unfounded have been the suspicions that have been instilled inpropagated among them of a policy in the Atlantic States & in the different departments of the General Government hostile to their interests in relation to the Mississipian. They have seen two treaties formed which secure to them every thing that they could desire to confirm their prosperity. Will they not henceforth rely for the preservation of these advantages on that union by which they were procured? Will they not reject those counsellors who would render them alien to their brethren & connect them with Aliens?

To the duration and efficacy of your Union a Government extending over the whole is indispensable. No alliances however strict between the parts could be an adequate substitute. These could not fail to be liable to the infractions and interruptions which all alliances in all times have suffered. Sensible of this important truth you have lately established a Constitution of General Government, better calculated than the former for an intimate union and more adequate to the direction of your common concerns. This Government the offspring of your own choice uninfluenced and unawed, completely free in its principles, in the distribution of its powers uniting energy with safety and containing in itself a provision for its own amendment is well entitled to your confidence and support—Respect for its authority, compliance with its laws, acquiescence in its measures, are duties dictated by the fundamental maxims of true Liberty. The basis of our political systems is the right of the people to make and to alter their constitutions of Government. But the constitution for the time, and until changed by an explicit and authentic act of the whole people, is sacredly binding upon all. The very idea of the right and power of the people to establish Government presupposes the duty of every individual to obey the established Government.

All obstructions to the execution of the laws—all <u>combinations</u> and <u>associations</u> under whatever plausible character with the real design to direct counteract countroul influence or awe the regular deliberation or action of the constituted authorities are contrary to this fundamental principle & of the most fatal tendency. They serve to organise Faction to give it an artificial force; and to put in the stead of the delegated will of the whole nation the will of a party. often a small but artful & enterprising minority of the community—and according to the alternate triumphs of different parties to make the public administration reflect the ill concerted schemes and projects of faction rather than the wholesome plans of common councils and deliberations. However combinations or associations of this description may occasionally promote popular ends and purposes they are likely to produce in the course of time and things the most effectual engines by which artful ambitious and unprincipled men will be enabled to subvert the power of the people and usurp the reins of Government.

Towards the preservation of your government and the permanency of your present happy state, it is not only requisite that you steadily discountenance irregular oppositions to its authority but that you should be upon your guard against the spirit of innovation upon its principles however specious the pretexts. One method of assault may be to effect alterations in the forms of the constitution tending to impair the energy of the system and so to undermine what cannot be directly overthrown. In all the changes to which you may be invited remember that time and habit are as necessary to fix the true character of governments as of any other human institutions, that experience is the surest standard by which the real tendency of existing constitutions of government can be tried—that changes upon the credit of mere hypothesis and opinions exposes you to perpetual change from the successive and endless variety of hypothesis and opinion—and remember also that for the efficacious management of your common interests in a country so extensive as ours a Government of as much force and strength as is consistent with the perfect security of liberty is indispensable. Liberty itself will find in such a Government, with powers properly distributed and arranged, its surest guardian—and protector. In my opinion the real danger in our system is that the General Government organised as at present will prove too weak rather than too powerful.

I have already observed the danger to be apprehended from founding our parties on Geographical discriminations. Let me now enlarge the view of this point and caution you in the most solemn manner against the baneful effects of party spirit in general. This spirit unfortunately is inseperable from human nature and has its root in the strongest passions of the human heart.—It exists under different shapes in all governments but in different degrees stifled controuled or repressed in those of the popular form it is always seen in its utmost vigour & rankness and it is their worst enemy. In republics of narrow extent, it is not difficult for those who at any time possess the reins of administration, or even for partial combinations of men, who from birth riches and other sources of distinction have an extraordinary influence by possessing or acquiring the direction of the military force or by sudden efforts of partisans & followers to overturn the established order of things and effect a usurpation. But in republics of large extent the one or the other is scarcely possible. The powers and opportunities of resistance of a numerous and wide extended nation defy the successful efforts of the ordinary military force or of any collections which wealth and patronage may call to their aid—especially if there be no city of overbearing force resources and influence. In such Republics it is perhaps safe to assert that the conflict of popular faction offer the only avenues to tyranny & usurpation. The domination of one faction over another stimulated by that spirit of Revenge which is apt to be gradually engendered and which in different ages and countries have produced the greatest enormities is itself a frightful despotism. But this leads at length to a more formal and permanent despotism. The disorders and miseries which result predispose the minds of men to seek repose & security in the absolute power of a single man. And some leader of a prevailing faction more able or more fortunate than his competitors turns this disposition to the purpose of an ambitious and criminal self aggrandisement.

Without looking forward to such an extremity (which however ought not to be out of sight) the ordinary and continual mischief of the spirit of party make it the interest and the duty of a wise people to discountenance and repress it.

It serves always to distract the Councils & enfeeble the administration of the Government. It agitates the community with ill founded jealousies and false alarms embittering one part of the community against another, & producing occasionaly riot & insurrection. It opens inlets for foreign corruption and influence—which find an easy access through the channels of party passions—and cause the true policy & interest of our own country to be made subservient to the policy and interest of one and another foreign Nation; sometimes enslaving our own Government to the will of a foreign Government.

There is an opinion that parties in free countries are salutary checks upon the administration of the Government & serve to invigorate the spirit of Liberty. This within certain limits is true and in governments of a monarchical character or byass patriotism may look with some favour on the spirit of party. But in those of the popular kind in those purely elective it is a spirit not to be fostered or encouraged. From the natural tendency of such governments, it is certain there will always be enough of it for every salutary purpose and there being constant danger of excess the effort ought to be by force of public opinion to mitigate & correct it. Tis a fire which cannot be quenched but demands a uniform vigilance to prevent its bursting into a flame—lest it should not only warm but consume.

It is important likewise that the habits of thinking of the people should tend to produce caution in their agents in the several departments of Government, to retain each within its proper sphere and not to permit one to encroach upon another—that every attempt of the kind from whatever quarter should meet with the discountenance of the community, and that in every case in which a precedent of encroachment shall have been given, a corrective be sought in (revocation be effected by) a careful attention to the next choice of public Agents. The spirit of encroachment tends to absorb & consolidate the powers of the several branches and departments into one, and thus to establish under whatever forms a despotism. A just knowlege of the human heart, of that love of power which predominates in it, is alone sufficient to establish this truth. Experiments ancient and modern—some in our own country and under our own eyes serve to confirm it. If in the public opinion the distribution of the constitutional powers be in any instance wrong or inexpedient—let it be corrected by the authority of the people in a legitimate constitutional course—Let there be no change by usurpation, for though this may be the instrument of good in one instance, it is the ordinary and natural instrument of the destruction of free Government—and the influence of the precedent is always infinitely more pernicious than any thing which it may atchieve can be beneficial.

To all those dispositions which promote political happiness prosperity, Religion and Morality are essential props. In vain does that man claim the praise of patriotism who labours to subvert or undermine these great pillars of human happiness these firmest foundations of the duties of men and citizens. The mere politician equally with the pious man ought to respect and cherish them. A volume could not trace all their connections with private and public happiness. Let it simply be asked where is the security for property for reputation for life if the sense of moral and religious obligation deserts the oaths which are administered in the instruments of Investigation Courts of Justice? Nor ought we to flatter ourselves that morality can be separated from religion. Concede as much as may be asked to the effect of refined education in minds of a peculiar structure—can we believe—can we in prudence suppose that national morality can be maintained in exclusion of religious principles? Does it not require the aid of a generally received and divinely authoritative Religion?

Tis essentially true that virtue or morality is a main & necessary spring of popular or republican Governments. The rule indeed extends with more or less force to all free Governments. Who that is a prudent & sincere friend to them can look with indifference on the ravages which are making in the foundation of the Fabric? Religion? The uncommon means which of late have been directed to this fatal end seem to make it in a particular of manner the duty of the Retiring Chief of a nation to warn his country against tasting of the poisonous draught.

Cultivate also industry and frugality. They are auxiliaries of good morals and great sources of private and national prosperity. Is there not room for regret that our propensity to expence exceeds the maturity of our Country for expense? Is there not more luxury among us, in various classes, than suits the actual period of our national progress? Whatever may be the apology for luxury in a Country mature in all the arts which are its ministers and the means of national opulence—can it promote the advantage of a young agricultural Country little advanced in manufactures and not much advanced in wealth?

Cherish public Credit as a mean of strength and security. As one method of preserving it, use it as little as possible. Avoid occasions of expence by cultivating peace— remembering always that the preparation against danger by timely and provident disbursements is often a mean of avoiding greater disbursements to repel it. Avoid the accumulation of debt by avoiding occasions of expence and by vigorous exertions in time of peace to discharge the debts which unavoidable wars may have occasionned—not transferring to posterity the burthen which we ought to bear ourselves. Recollect that towards the payment of debts there must be Revenue, that to have revenue there must be taxes, that it is impossible to devise taxes which are not more or less inconvenient and unpleasant—that they are always a choice of difficulties—that the intrinsic embarrassment which never fails to attend a selection of objects ought to be a motive for a candid construction of the conduct of the Government in making it—and that a spirit of acquiescence in those measures for obtaining revenue which the public exigencies dictate is in an especial manner the duty and interest of the citizens of every State.

Cherish good faith and Justice towards, and peace and harmony with all nations. Religion and morality enjoins this conduct And It cannot be, but that true policy equally demands it. It will be worthy of a free enlightened and at no distant period a great nation to give to mankind the magnanimous and too novel example of a people invariably governed by those exalted views. Who can doubt that in a long course of time and events the fruits of such a conduct would richly repay any temporary advantages which might be lost by a steady adherence to the plan? Can it be that Providence has not connected the permanent felicity of a nation with its virtue? The experiment is recommended by every sentiment which ennobles human nature. Alas! is it rendered impossible by its vices?

Toward the execution of such a plan <u>nothing is</u> more essential than that antipathies against particular nations and passionate attachments for others should be avoided—and that instead of them we should cultivate just and amicable feelings towards all. That nation, which indulges towards another a habitual hatred or a habitual fondness is in some degree a slave. It is a slave to its animosity or to its affection—

either of which is sufficient to lead it astray from its duty and interest. Antipathy against one nation which never fails to beget a similar sentiment in the other disposes each more readily to offer injury and insult to the other—to lay hold of slight causes of umbrage and to be haughty and intractable when accidental or trifling differences arise. Hence frequent quarrels and bitter and obstinate contests. The nation urged by resentment and rage sometimes impels the Government to War contrary to its own calculations of policy. The Government sometimes participates in this propensity & does through passion what reason would forbid—at other times it makes the animosity of the nations subservient to hostile projects which originate in ambition & other sinister motives. The peace often and sometimes the liberty of Nations has been the victim of this cause.

In like manner a passionate attachment of one nation to another produces multiplied ills. Sympathy for the favourite nations, promoting facilitating the illusion of a supposed common interest in cases where it does not exist and communicating to one the enmities of the one betrays into a participation in its quarrels & wars without adequate inducements or justifications. It leads to the concession of privileges to one nation and to the denial of them to others—which is apt doubly to injure the nation making the concession by an unnecessary yielding of what ought to have been retained and by exciting jealousy ill will and retaliation in the party from whom an equal privilege is witheld. And it gives to ambitious corrupted or deluded citizens, who devote themselves to the views of the favourite foreign power, facility in betraying or sacrificing the interests of their own country without odium & even with popularity gilding with the appearance of a virtuous impulse the base yieldings of ambition or corruption.

As avenues to foreign influence in innumerable Ways such attachments are peculiarly alarming to the enlightened independent Patriot. How many opportunities do they afford to intrigue with domestic factions to practice with success the arts of seduction—to mislead public opinion—to influence or awe the public Councils! Such an attachment of a small or weak towards a great & powerful Nation destines the former to revolve round the latter as its satellite.

Against the Mischiefs of Foreign Influence all the Jealousy of a free people ought to be constantly continually exerted. All History & Experience prove that foreign influence is one of the most baneful foes of republican Governt—but that jealousy of it to be useful must be impartial else it becomes an instrument—of the very influence to be avoided instead of a defence against it.

Excessive partiality for one foreign nation & excessive dislike of another, leads to see danger only on one side and serves to viel & second the arts of influence on the other. Real Patriots who resist the intrigues of the favorite become suspected & odious. Its tools & dupes usurp the applause & confidence of the people to betray their interests.

The great rule of conduct for us in regard to foreign Nations ought to be to have as little political connection with them as possible—so far as we have already formed engagements let them be fulfilled—with circumspection indeed but with perfect good faith. Here let us stop.

Europe has a set of primary interests which have none or a very remote relation to us. Hence she must be involved in frequent contests the causes of which will be essentially foreign to us. Hence therefore it must necessarily be unwise on our part to implicate ourselves by an artificial connection in the ordinary vicissitudes of European politics—in the combination, & collisions of her friendships or enmities.

Our detached and distant situation invites us to a different course & enables us to pursue it. If we remain a united people under an efficient Government the period is not distant when we may defy material injury from external annoyance—when we may take such an attitude as will cause the neutrality we shall at any time resolve to observe to be violated with caution—when it will be the interest of belligerent nations under the impossibility of making acquisitions upon us to be very careful how either forced us to throw our weight into the opposite scale—when we may choose peace or war as our interest guided by justice shall dictate.

Why should we forego the advantages of so felicitous a situation? Why quit our own ground to stand upon Foreign ground? Why by interweaving our destiny with any part of Europe should we intangle our prosperity and peace in the nets of European Ambition rivalship interest or Caprice?

Permanent alliance, intimate connection with any part of the foreign world is to be avoided. so far (I mean) as we are now at liberty to do it: for let me never be understood as patronising infidelity to preexisting engagements. These must be observed in their true and genuine sense. But tis not necessary nor will it be prudent to extend them. Tis our true policy as a general principle to avoid permanent or close alliance— Taking care always to keep ourselves by suitable establishments in a respectably defensive posture we may safely trust to occasional alliances for extraordinary emergencies.

Harmony liberal intercourse and commerce with all nations are recommended by justice humanity & interest. But even our commercial policy should hold an equal hand—neither seeking nor granting exclusive favours or preferences—consulting the natural course of things—<u>diffusing</u> and <u>diversifying</u> by gentle means the streams of Commerce but forcing nothing—establishing with powers so disposed in order to give to Trade a stable course, to define the rights of our Merchants and enable the Government to support them—conventional rules of intercourse the best that present circumstances and mutual opinion of interest will permit but temporary—and liable to be abandonned or varied as time experience & future circumstances may dictate—remembering alway that tis folly in one nation to expect disinterested favour in another—that to accept any thing under that character is to part with a portion of its independence—and that it may find itself in the condition of having given equivalents for nominal favours and of being reproached with ingratitude in the bargain. There can be no greater error in national policy than to desire expect or calculate upon real favours. Tis an illusion that experience must cure, that a just pride ought to discard.

In offering to you My Countrymen! these counsels of an old and affectionate friend—counsels suggested by labourious reflection and matured by a various experience—I dare not hope that they will make the strong and lasting impressions I wish—that they will controul the current of the passions or prevent our nation from running the course which has hitherto marked the destiny of all nations. But if I may flatter myself that they even produce some partial benefit, some occasional good—that they sometimes recur to moderate the violence of party spirit—to warn against the evils of foreign intrigue—to guard against the impositions of pretended patriotism—the having offered them must always afford me a precious consolation.

How far in the execution of my present Office I have been guided by the principles which have been inculcated the public records & the external evidences of my conduct must witness. My conscious assures me that I have at least believed myself to be guided by them.

In reference to the present War of Europe my Proclamation of the 22d of April 1793 is the key to my plan. Sanctioned by your approving voice and that of your representatives in Congress the spirit of that measure has continually governed me uninfluenced and unawed by the attempts of any of the warring powers their agents or partizans to deter or divert from it.

After deliberate consideration and the best lights I could obtain (and from men who did not agree in their views of the origin progress & nature of that war) I was satisfied that our Country, under all the circumstances of the case, had a right and was bound in propriety and interest to take a neutral position—And having taken it, I determined as far as should depend on me to maintain it steadily and firmly.

Though in reviewing the incidents of my administration I am unconscious of intentional error—I am yet too sensible of my own deficiencies not to think it probable that I have committed many errors. I deprecate the evils to which they may tend—and fervently implore the Almighty to avert or mitigate them. I shall carry with me nevertheless the hope that my motives will continue to be viewed by my Country with indulgence & that after forty five years of my life devoted with an upright zeal to the public service the faults of inadequate abilities will be consigned to oblivion as myself must soon be to the mansions of rest.

Neither Ambition nor interest has been the impelling cause of my actions. I never designedly misused any power confided to me. The fortune with which I came into office is not bettered otherwise than by that improvement in the value of property which the natural progress and peculiar prosperity of our country have produced. I retire without cause for a blush—with a pure heart with no alien sentiment to the ardor of those vows for the happiness of his Country which is so natural to a Citizen who sees in it vows for the native soil of himself and progenitors for four generations.

## To William Hamilton

*Albany State of New York*
*May the 2d. 1797*

My Dear Sir

Some days since I received with great pleasure your letter of the 10th. of March. The mark, it affords, of your kind attention, and the particular account it gives me of so many relations in Scotland are extremely gratifying to me. You no doubt have understood that my fathers affairs at a very early day went to wreck; so as to have rendered his situation during the greatest part of his life far from eligible. This state of things occasionned a separation between him and me, when I was very young, and threw me upon the bounty of my mothers relations, some of whom were then wealthy, though by vicissitudes to which human affairs are so liable, they have been since much reduced and broken up. Myself at about sixteen came to this Country. Having always had a strong propensity to literary pursuits, by a course of steady and laborious exertion, I was able, by the age of Ninteen to qualify myself for the degree of Batchelor of Arts in the College of New York, and to lay a foundation, by preparatory study, for the future profession of the law.

The American Revolution supervened. My principles led me to take part in it. At nineteen I entered into the American army as Captain of Artillery. Shortly after, I became by his invitation Aide De Camp to General Washington, in which station, I served till the commencement of that Campaign which ended with the seige of York, in Virginia, and the Capture of Cornwallis's Army. This Campaign I made at the head of a corps of light infantry, with which I was present at the seige of York and engaged in some interesting operations.

At the period of the peace with Great Britain, I found myself a member of Congress by appointment of the legislature of this state.

After the peace, I settled in the City of New York in the practice of the law; and was in a very lucrative course of practice, when the derangement of our public affairs, by the feebleness of the general confederation, drew me again reluctantly into public life. I became a member of the Convention which framed the present

Constitution of the U States; and having taken part in this measure, I conceived myself to be under an obligation to lend my aid towards putting the machine in some regular motion. Hence I did not hesitate to accept the offer of President Washington to undertake the office of Secretary of the Treasury.

In that office, I met with many intrinsic difficulties, and many artificial ones proceeding from passions, not very worthy, common to human nature, and which act with peculiar force in republics. The object, however, was effected, of establishing public credit and introducing order into the finances.

Public Office in this Country has few attractions. The pecuniary emolument is so inconsiderable as too amount to a sacrifice to any man who can employ his time with advantage in any liberal profession. The opportunity of doing good, from the jealousy of power and the spirit of faction, is too small in any station to warrant a long continuance of private sacrifices. The enterprises of party had so far succeeded as materially to weaken the necessary influence and energy of the Executive Authority, and so far diminish the power of doing good in that department as greatly to take the motives which a virtuous man might have for making sacrifices. The prospect was even bad for gratifying in future the love of Fame, if that passion was to be the spring of action.

The Union of these motives, with the reflections of prudence in relation to a growing family, determined me as soon as my plan had attained a certain maturity to withdraw from Office. This I did by a resignation about two years since; when I resumed the profession of the law in the City of New York under every advantage I could desire.

It is a pleasing reflection to me that since the commencement of my connection with General Washington to the present time, I have possessed a flattering share of his confidence and friendship.

Having given you a brief sketch of my political career, I proceed to some further family details.

In the year 1780 I married the second daughter of General Schuyler, a Gentleman of one of the best families of this Country; of large fortune and no less personal and public consequence. It is impossible to be happier than I am in a wife and I have five Children, four sons and a daughter, the eldest a son somewhat passed fifteen, who all promise well, as far as their years permit and yield me much satisfaction. Though I have been too much in public life to be wealthy, my situation is extremely comfortable and leaves me nothing to wish but a continuance of health. With this blessing, the profits of my profession and other prospects authorise an expectation of such addition to my resources as will render the eve of life, easy and agreeable; so far as may depend on this consideration.

It is now several months since I have heared from my father who continued at the Island of St Vincents. My anxiety at this silence would be greater than it is, were it not for the considerable interruption and precariousness of intercourse, which is produced by the War.

I have strongly pressed the old Gentleman to come to reside with me, which would afford him every enjoyment of which his advanced age is capable. But he has declined it on the ground that the advice of his Physicians leads him to fear that the change of Climate would be fatal to him. The next thing for me is, in proportion to my means to endeavour to increase his comforts where he is.

It will give me the greatest pleasure to receive your son Robert at my house in New York and still more to be of use to him; to which end my recommendation and interest will not be wanting, and, I hope, not unavailing. It is my intention to embrace the Opening which your letter affords me to extend intercourse with my relations in your Country, which will be a new source of satisfaction to me.

## The "Reynolds Pamphlet"

*Observations on Certain Documents Contained in No. V & VI of "The History of the United States for the Year 1796," In Which the Charge of Speculation against Alexander Hamilton, Late Secretary of the Treasury, is Fully Refuted. Written by Himself*

The spirit of jacobinism, if not entirely a new spirit, has at least been cloathed with a more gigantic body and armed with more powerful weapons than it ever before possessed. It is perhaps not too much to say, that it threatens more extensive and complicated mischiefs to the world than have hitherto flowed from the three great scourges of mankind, WAR, PESTILENCE and FAMINE. To what point it will ultimately lead society, it is impossible for human foresight to pronounce; but there is just ground to apprehend that its progress may be marked with calamities of which the dreadful incidents of the French revolution afford a very faint image. Incessantly busied in undermining all the props of public security and private happiness, it seems to threaten the political and moral world with a complete overthrow.

A principal engine, by which this spirit endeavours to accomplish its purposes is that of calumny. It is essential to its success that the influence of men of upright principles, disposed and able to resist its enterprises, shall be at all events destroyed. Not content with traducing their best efforts for the public good, with misrepresenting their purest motives, with inferring criminality from actions innocent or laudable, the most direct falshoods are invented and propagated, with undaunted effrontery and unrelenting perseverance. Lies often detected and refuted are still revived and repeated, in the hope that the refutation may have been forgotten or that the frequency and boldness of accusation may supply the place of truth and proof. The most profligate men are encouraged, probably bribed, certainly with patronage if not with money, to become informers and accusers. And when tales, which their characters alone ought to discredit, are refuted by evidence and facts which oblige the patrons of them to abandon their support, they still continue in corroding whispers to wear away the reputations which they could not directly subvert. If, luckily for the conspirators against honest fame, any little foible or folly can be traced out in one, whom they desire to persecute, it becomes at once in their hands a two-edged sword, by which to wound the public character and stab the private felicity of the person. With such men, nothing is sacred. Even the peace of an unoffending and amiable wife is a welcome repast to their insatiate fury against the husband.

In the gratification of this baleful spirit, we not only hear the jacobin news-papers continually ring with odious insinuations and charges against many of our most virtuous citizens; but, not satisfied with this, a measure new in this country has been lately adopted to give greater efficacy to the system of defamation—periodical pamphlets issue from the same presses, full freighted with misrepresentation and falshood, artfully calculated to hold up the opponents of the FACTION to the jealousy and distrust of the present generation and if possible, to transmit their names with dishonor to posterity. Even the great and multiplied services, the tried and rarely equalled virtues of a WASHINGTON, can secure no exemption.

How then can I, with pretensions every way inferior expect to escape? And if truly this be, as every appearance indicates, a conspiracy of vice against virtue, ought I not rather to be flattered, that I have been so long and so peculiarly an object of persecution? Ought I to regret, if there be any thing about me, so formidable to the Faction as to have made me worthy to be distinguished by the plentitude of its rancour and venom?

It is certain that I have had a pretty copious experience of its malignity. For the honor of human nature, it is to be hoped that the examples are not numerous of men so greatly calumniated and persecuted, as I have been, with so little cause.

I dare appeal to my immediate fellow citizens of whatever political party for the truth of the assertion, that no man ever carried into public life a more unblemished pecuniary reputation, than that with which I undertook the office of Secretary of the Treasury; a character marked by an indifference to the acquisition of property rather than an avidity for it.

With such a character, however natural it was to expect criticism and opposition, as to the political principles which I might manifest or be supposed to entertain, as to the wisdom or expediency of the plans, which I might propose, or as to the skill, care or diligence with which the business of my department might be executed, it was not natural to expect nor did I expect that my fidelity or integrity in a pecuniary sense would ever be called in question.

But on his head a mortifying disappointment has been experienced. Without the slightest foundation, I have been repeatedly held up to the suspicions of the world as a man directed in his administration by the most sordid views; who did not scruple to sacrifice the public to his private interest, his duty and honor to the sinister accumulation of wealth.

Merely because I *retained* an opinion once common to me and the most influencial of those who opposed me, *That the public debt ought to be provided for on the basis of the contract upon which it was created*, I have been wickedly accused with wantonly increasing the public burthen many millions, in order to promote a stock-jobbing interest of myself and friends.

Merely because a member of the House of Representatives entertained a different idea from me, as to the legal effect of appropriation laws, and did not understand accounts, I was exposed to the imputation of having committed a deliberate and criminal violation of the laws and to the suspicion of being a defaulter for millions; so as to have been driven to the painful necessity of calling for a formal and solemn inquiry.

The inquiry took place. It was conducted by a committee of fifteen members of the House of Representatives—a majority of them either my decided political enemies or inclined against me, some of them the most active and intelligent of my opponents, without a single man, who being known to be friendly to me, possessed also such knowledge and experience of public affairs as would enable him to counteract injurious intrigues. Mr. Giles of Virginia who had commenced the attack was of the committee.

The officers and books of the treasury were examined. The transactions between the several banks and the treasury were scrutinized. Even my *private accounts* with those institutions were laid open to the committee; and every possible facility given to the inquiry. The result was a complete demonstration that the suspicions which had been entertained were groundless.

Those which had taken the fastest hold were, that the public monies had been made subservient to loans, discounts and accommodations to myself and friends. The committee in reference to this point reported thus: "It appears from the affidavits of the Cashier and several officers of the bank of the United States and several of the directors, the Cashier, and other officers of the bank of New York, that the Secretary of the Treasury never has either *directly* or *indirectly*, for himself or any other person, procured any discount or credit from either of the said banks upon the basis of any public monies which at any time have been deposited therein under his direction: And the committee are *satisfied*, that *no monies* of the United States, whether *before* or *after* they have passed to the credit of the Treasurer have ever been *directly* or *indirectly* used for or applied to *any purposes* but those of the government, except so far as all monies deposited in a bank are concerned in the *general operations* thereof."

The report, which I have always understood was unanimous, contains in other respects, with considerable detail the materials of a complete exculpation. My enemies, finding no handle for their malice, abandoned the pursuit.

Yet unwilling to leave any ambiguity upon the point, when I

determined to resign my office, I gave early previous notice of it to the House of Representatives, for the declared purpose of affording an opportunity for legislative crimination, if any ground for it had been discovered. Not the least step towards it was taken. From which I have a right to infer the universal conviction of the House, that no cause existed, and to consider the result as a complete vindication.

On another occasion, a worthless man of the name of Fraunces found encouragement to bring forward to the House of Representatives a formal charge against me of unfaithful conduct in office. A Committee of the House was appointed to inquire, consisting in this case also, partly of some of my most intelligent and active enemies. The issue was an unanimous exculpation of me as will appear by the following extract from the Journals of the House of Representatives of the 19th of February 1794.

"The House resumed the consideration of the report of the Committee, to whom was referred the memorial of Andrew G. Fraunces: whereupon,

"*Resolved*, That the reasons assigned by the secretary of the treasury, for refusing payment of the warrants referred to in the memorial, are fully sufficient to justify his conduct; and that in the whole course of this transaction, the secretary and other officers of the treasury, have acted a meritorious part towards the public."

"*Resolved*, That the charge exhibited in the memorial, against the secretary of the treasury, relative to the purchase of the pension of Baron de Glaubeck is wholly illiberal and groundless*."

Was it not to have been expected that these repeated demonstrations of the injustice of the accusations hazarded against me would have abashed the enterprise of my calumniators? However natural such an expectation may seem, it would betray an ignorance of the true character of the Jacobin system. It is a maxim deeply ingrafted in that dark system, that no character, however upright, is a match for constantly reiterated attacks, however false. It is well understood by its disciples, that every calumny makes some proselites and even retains some; since justification seldom circulates as rapidly and as widely as slander. The number of those who from doubt proceed to suspicion and thence to belief of imputed guilt is continually augmenting; and

---

* Would it be believed after all this, that Mr. Jefferson Vice President of the United States would write to this Fraunces friendly letters? Yet such is the fact as will be seen in the Appendix, Nos. XLIV & XLV.

the public mind fatigued at length with resistance to the calumnies which eternally assail it, is apt in the end to sit down with the opinion that a person so often accused cannot be entirely innocent.

Relying upon this weakness of human nature, the Jacobin Scandal-Club though often defeated constantly return to the charge. Old calumnies are served up a-fresh and every pretext is seized to add to the catalogue. The person whom they seek to blacken, by dint of repeated strokes of their brush, becomes a demon in their own eyes, though he might be pure and bright as an angel but for the daubing of those wizard painters.

Of all the vile attempts which have been made to injure my character that which has been lately revived in No. V and VI, of the history of the United States for 1796 is the most vile. This it will be impossible for any *intelligent*, I will not say *candid*, man to doubt, when he shall have accompanied me through the examination.

I owe perhaps to my friends an apology for condescending to give a public explanation. A just pride with reluctance stoops to a formal vindication against so despicable a contrivance and is inclined rather to oppose to it the uniform evidence of an upright character. This would be my conduct on the present occasion, did not the tale seem to derive a sanction from the names of three men of some weight and consequence in the society: a circumstance, which I trust will excuse me for paying attention to a slander that without this prop, would defeat itself by intrinsic circumstances of absurdity and malice.

The charge against me is a connection with one James Reynolds for purposes of improper pecuniary speculation. My real crime is an amorous connection with his wife, for a considerable time with his privity and connivance, if not originally brought on by a combination between the husband and wife with the design to extort money from me.

This confession is not made without a blush. I cannot be the apologist of any vice because the ardour of passion may have made it mine. I can never cease to condemn myself for the pang, which it may inflict in a bosom eminently intitled to all my gratitude, fidelity and love. But that bosom will approve, that even at so great an expence, I should effectually wipe away a more serious stain from a name, which it cherishes with no less elevation than tenderness. The public too will I trust excuse the confession. The necessity of it to my defence against a more heinous charge could alone have extorted from me so painful an indecorum.

Before I proceed to an exhibition of the positive proof which repels the charge, I shall analize the documents from which it is deduced, and I am mistaken if with discerning and candid minds more would be necessary. But I desire to obviate the suspicions of the most suspicious.

The first reflection which occurs on a perusal of the documents is that it is morally impossible I should have been foolish as well as depraved enough to employ so vile an instrument as *Reynolds* for such *insignificant ends*, as are indicated by different parts of the story itself. My enemies to be sure have kindly pourtrayed me as another *Chartres* on the score of moral principle. But they have been ever bountiful in ascribing to me talents. It has suited their purpose to exaggerate such as I may possess, and to attribute to them an influence to which they are not intitled. But the present accusation imputes to me as much folly as wickedness. All the documents shew, and it is otherwise matter of notoriety, that Reynolds was an obscure, unimportant and profligate man. Nothing could be more weak, because nothing could be more unsafe than to make use of such an instrument; to use him too without any intermediate agent more worthy of confidence who might keep me out of sight, to write him numerous letters recording the objects of the improper connection (for this is pretended and that the letters were afterwards burnt at my request) to unbosom myself to him with a prodigality of confidence, by very unnecessarily telling him, as he alleges, of a connection in speculation between myself and Mr. Duer. It is very extraordinary, if the head of the money department of a country, being unprincipled enough to sacrifice his trust and his integrity, could not have contrived objects of profit sufficiently large to have engaged the co-operation of men of far greater importance than Reynolds, and with whom there could have been due safety, and should have been driven to the necessity of unkennelling such a reptile to be the instrument of his cupidity.

But, moreover, the scale of the concern with Reynolds, such as it is presented, is contemptibly narrow for a rapacious speculating secretary of the treasury. *Clingman, Reynolds* and his wife were manifestly in very close confidence with each other. It seems there was a free communication of secrets. Yet in clubbing their different items of information as to the supplies of money which Reynolds received from me, what do they amount to? *Clingman* states, that Mrs. Reynolds told him, that at a certain time her husband had received from me upwards of eleven hundred dollars. A note is produced which shews that at one time fifty dollars were sent to him, and another note is produced, by which and the information of Reynolds himself through Clingman, it appears that at another time 300 dollars were asked and refused. Another sum of 200 dollars is spoken of by *Clingman* as having been furnished to Reynolds at some other time. What a scale of speculation is this for the head of a public treasury, for one who in the very publication that brings forward the charge is represented as having procured to be funded at forty millions a debt which ought to have been discharged at ten or fifteen millions for the criminal purpose of enriching himself and his friends? He must have been a clumsy knave, if he did not secure enough of this excess of twenty five or thirty millions, to have taken away all inducement to risk his character in such bad hands and in so huckstering a way—or to have enabled him, if he did employ such an agent, to do it with more means and to better purpose. It is curious, that this rapacious secretary should at one time have furnished his speculating agent with the paltry sum of fifty dollars, at another, have refused him the inconsiderable sum of 300 dollars, declaring upon his honor that it was not in his power to furnish it. This declaration was true or not; if the last the refusal ill comports with the idea of a speculating connection—if the first, it is very singular that the head of the treasury engaged without scruple in schemes of profit should have been destitute of so small a sum. But if we suppose this officer to be living upon an inadequate salary, without any collateral pursuits of gain, the appearances then are simple and intelligible enough, applying to them the true key.

It appears that *Reynolds* and *Clingman* were detected by the then comptroller of the treasury, in the odious crime of suborning a witness to commit perjury, for the purpose of obtaining letters of administration on the estate of a person who was living in order to receive a small sum of money due to him from the treasury. It is certainly extraordinary that the confidential agent of the head of that department should have been in circumstances to induce a resort to so miserable an expedient. It is odd, if there was a speculating connection, that it was not more profitable both to the secretary and to his agent than are indicated by the circumstances disclosed.

It is also a remarkable and very instructive fact, that notwithstanding the great confidence and intimacy, which subsisted between *Clingman*, *Reynolds* and his wife, and which continued till after the period of the liberation of the two former from the prosecution against them, neither of them has ever specified the objects of the pretended connection in speculation between Reynolds and me. The pretext that the letters which contained the evidence were destroyed is no answer. They could not have been forgotten and might have been disclosed from memory. The total omission of this could only have proceeded from the consideration that detail might have led to detection. The destruction of letters besides is a fiction, which is refuted not only by the general improbability, that I should put myself upon paper with so despicable a person on a subject which might expose me to infamy, but by the evidence of extreme caution on my part in this particular, resulting from the laconic and disguised form of the notes which are produced. They prove incontestibly that there was an unwillingness to trust Reynolds with my hand writing. The true reason was, that I apprehended he might make use of it to impress upon others the belief of some pecuniary connection with me, and besides implicating my character might render it the engine of a false credit, or turn it to some other sinister use. Hence the disguise; for my conduct in admitting at once and without hesitation that the notes were from me proves that it was never my intention by the expedient of disguising my hand to shelter myself from any serious inquiry.

The accusation against me was never heard of 'till Clingman and Reynolds were under prosecution by the treasury for an infamous crime. It will be seen by the document No. 1 (a) that during the endeavours of *Clingman* to obtain relief, through the interposition of Mr. Mughlenberg, he made to the latter the communication of my pretended criminality. It will be further seen by document No. 2 (a) that Reynolds had while in prison conveyed to the ears of Messrs. Monroe and Venable that he could give intelligence of my being concerned in speculation, and that he also supposed that he was kept in prison by a design on my part to oppress him and drive him away. And by his letter to Clingman of the 13 of December, after he was released from prison, it also appears that he was actuated by a spirit of revenge against me; for he declares that he will have *satisfaction* from me *at all events*; adding, as addressed to *Clingman*, "And *you only I trust*."

Three important inferences flow from these circumstances—one that the accusation against me was an auxiliary to the efforts of *Clingman* and *Reynolds* to get released from a disgraceful prosecution—another that there was a vindicative spirit against me at least on the part of Reynolds—the third, that he confided in *Clingman* as a coadjutor in the plan of vengeance. These circumstances, according to every estimate of the credit due to accusers, ought to destroy their testimony. To what credit are persons intitled, who in telling a story are governed by the double motive of escaping from disgrace and punishment and of gratifying revenge? As to Mrs. Reynolds, if she was not an accomplice, as it is too probable she was, her situation would naturally subject her to the will of her husband. But enough besides will appear in the sequel to shew that her testimony merits no attention.

The letter which has been just cited deserves a more particular attention. As it was produced by Clingman, there is a chasm of three lines, which lines are manifestly essential to explain the sense. It may be inferred from the context, that these deficient lines would unfold the cause of the resentment which is expressed. 'Twas from them that might have been learnt the true nature of the transaction. The expunging of them is a violent presumption that they would have contradicted the purpose for which the letter was produced. A witness offering such a mutilated piece descredits himself. The mutilation is alone satisfactory proof of contrivance and imposition. The manner of accounting for it is frivolous.

The words of the letter are strong—satisfaction is to be had *at all events, per fas et nefas*, and *Clingman* is the chosen confidential agent of the laudable plan of vengeance. It must be confessed he was not wanting in his part.

Reynolds, as will be seen by No. II (a) alleges that a merchant came to him and offered as a volunteer to be his bail, who he suspected had been instigated to it by me, and after being decoyed to the place the merchant wished to carry him to, he refused being his bail, unless he would deposit a sum of money to some considerable amount which he could not do and was in consequence committed to prison. Clingman (No. IV a) tells the same story in substance though with some difference in form leaving to be implied what Reynolds expresses and naming *Henry Seckel* as the merchant. The deposition of this respectable citizen (No. XXIII) gives the lie to both, and shews that he was in fact the agent of *Clingman*, from motives of good will to him, as his former book-keeper, that he never had any communication with me concerning either of them till after they were both in custody, that when he came as a messenger to me from one of them, I not only declined interposing in their behalf, but informed Mr. Seckel that they had been guilty of a crime and advised him to have nothing to do with them.

This single fact goes far to invalidate the whole story. It shews plainly the disregard of truth and the malice by which the parties were actuated. Other important inferences are to be drawn from the transaction. Had I been conscious that I had any thing to fear from *Reynolds* of the nature which has been pretended, should I have warned Mr. *Seckel* against having any thing to do with them? Should I not rather have encouraged him to have come to their assistance? Should I not have been eager to promote their liberation? But this is not the only instance, in which I acted a contrary part. *Clingman* testifies in No. V. that I would not permit *Fraunces* a clerk in my office to become their bail, but signified to him that if he did it, he must quit the department.

*Clingman* states in No. IV. (a) that my note in answer to Reynolds' application for a loan towards a subscription to the *Lancaster Turnpike* was in his possession from about the time it was written (June 1792.) This circumstance, apparently trivial, is very explanatory. To what end had *Clingman* the custody of this note all that time if it was not part of a project to lay the foundation for some false accusation?

It appears from No. V. that *Fraunces* had said, or was stated to have said, something to my prejudice. If my memory serves me aright, it was that he had been my agent in some speculations. When *Fraunces* was interrogated concerning it, he absolutely denied that he had said any thing of the kind. The charge which this same *Fraunces* afterwards preferred against me to the House of Representatives, and the fate of it, have been already mentioned. It is illustrative of the nature of the combination which was formed against me.

There are other features in the documents which are relied upon to constitute the charge against me, that are of a nature to corroborate the inference to be drawn from the particulars which have been noticed. But there is no need to be over minute. I am much mistaken if the view which has been taken of the subject is not sufficient, without any thing further, to establish my innocence with every discerning and fair mind.

I proceed in the next place to offer a frank and plain solution of the enigma, by giving a history of the origin and progress of my connection with Mrs. Reynolds, of its discovery, real and pretended by the husband, and of the disagreeable embarrassments to which it exposed me. This history will be supported by the letters of Mr. and Mrs. Reynolds, which leave no room for doubt of the principal facts, and at the same time explain with precision the objects of the little notes from me which have been published, shewing clearly that such of them as have related to money had no reference to any concern in speculation. As the situation which will be disclosed, will fully explain every ambiguous appearance, and meet satisfactorily the written documents, nothing more can be requisite to my justification. For frail indeed will be the tenure by which the most blameless man will hold his reputation, if the assertions of three of the most abandoned characters in the community, two of them stigmatized by the discrediting crime which has been mentioned, are sufficient to blast it. The business of accusation would soon become in such a case, a regular trade, and men's reputations would be bought and sold like any marketable commodity.

Some time in the summer of the year 1791 a woman called at my house in the city of Philadelphia and asked to speak with me in private. I attended her into a room apart from the family. With a seeming air of affliction she informed that she was a daughter of a Mr. Lewis, sister to a Mr. G. Livingston of the State of New-York, and wife to a Mr. Reynolds whose father was in the Commissary Department during the war with Great Britain, that her husband, who for a long time had treated her very cruelly, had lately left her, to live with another woman, and in so destitute a condition, that though desirous of returning to her friends she had not the means—that knowing I was a citizen of New-York, she had taken the liberty to apply to my humanity for assistance.

I replied, that her situation was a very interesting one—that I was disposed to afford her assistance to convey her to her friends, but this at the moment not being convenient to me (which was the fact) I must request the place of her residence, to which I should bring or send a small supply of money. She told me the street and the number of the house where she lodged. In the evening I put a bank-bill in my pocket and went to the house. I inquired for Mrs. Reynolds and was shewn up stairs, at the head of which she met me and conducted me into a bed room. I took the bill out of my pocket and gave it to her. Some conversation ensued from which it was quickly apparent that other than pecuniary consolation would be acceptable.

After this, I had frequent meetings with her, most of them at my own house; Mrs. Hamilton with her children being absent on a visit to her father. In the course of a short time, she mentioned to me that her husband had solicited a reconciliation, and affected to consult me about it. I advised to it, and was soon after informed by her that it had taken place. She told me besides that her husband had been engaged in speculation, and she believed could give information respecting the conduct of some persons in the department which would be useful. I sent for Reynolds who came to me accordingly.

In the course of our interview, he confessed that he had obtained a list of claims from a person in my department which he had made use of in his speculations. I invited him, by the expectation of my friendship and good offices, to disclose the person. After some affectation of scruple, he pretended to yield, and ascribed the infidelity to Mr. Duer from whom he said he had obtained the list in New-York, while he (Duer) was in the department.

As Mr. Duer had resigned his office some time before the seat of government was removed to Philadelphia; this discovery, if it had been true, was not very important—yet it was the interest of my passions to appear to set value upon it, and to continue the expectation of friendship and good offices. Mr. Reynolds told me he was going to Virginia, and on his return would point out something in which I could serve him. I do not know but he said something about employment in a public office.

On his return he asked employment as a clerk in the treasury department. The knowledge I had acquired of him was decisive against such a request. I parried it by telling him, what was true, that there was no vacancy in my immediate office, and that the appointment of clerks in the other branches of the department was left to the chiefs of the respective branches. Reynolds alleged, as *Clingman* relates No. IV (a) as a topic of complaint against me that I had promised him *employment* and had *disappointed* him. The situation with the wife would naturally incline me to conciliate this man. It is possible I may have used vague expressions which raised expectation; but the more I learned of the person, the more inadmissible his employment in a public office became. Some material reflections will occur here to a discerning mind. Could I have preferred my private gratification to the public interest, should I not have found the employment he desired for a man, whom it was so convenient to me, on my own statement, to lay under obligations. Had I had any such connection with him, as he has since pretended, is it likely that he would have wanted other employment? Or is it likely that wanting it, I should have hazarded his resentment by a persevering refusal? This little circumstance shews at once the delicacy of my conduct, in its public relations, and the impossibility of my having had the connection pretended with Reynolds.

The intercourse with Mrs. Reynolds, in the mean time, continued; and, though various reflections, (in which a further knowledge of Reynolds' character and the suspicion of some concert between the husband and wife bore a part) induced me to wish a cessation of it; yet her conduct, made it extremely difficult to disentangle myself. All the appearances of violent attachment, and of agonizing distress at the idea of a relinquishment, were played off with a most imposing art. This, though it did not make me entirely the dupe of the plot, yet kept me in a state of irresolution. My sensibility, perhaps my vanity, admitted the possibility of a real fondness; and led me to adopt the plan of a gradual discontinuance rather than of a sudden interruption, as least calculated to give pain, if a real partiality existed.

Mrs. Reynolds, on the other hand, employed every effort to keep up my attention and visits. Her pen was freely employed, and her letters were filled with those tender and pathetic effusions which would have been natural to a woman truly fond and neglected.

One day, I received a letter from her, which is in the appendix (No. I. b) intimating a discovery by her husband. It was matter of doubt with me whether there had been really a discovery by accident, or whether the time for the catastrophe of the plot was arrived.

The same day, being the 15th of December 1791, I received from Mr. Reynolds the letter (No. II. b) by which he informs me of the detection of his wife in the act of writing a letter to me, and that he had obtained from her a discovery of her connection with me, suggesting that it was the consequence of an undue advantage taken of her distress.

In answer to this I sent him a note, or message desiring him to call upon me at my office, which I think he did the same day.

He in substance repeated the topics contained in his letter, and concluded as he had done there, that he was resolved to have satisfaction.

I replied that he knew best what evidence he had of the alleged connection between me and his wife, that I neither admitted nor denied it—that if he knew of any injury I had done him, intitling him to satisfaction, it lay with him to name it.

He travelled over the same ground as before, and again concluded with the same vague claim of satisfaction, but without specifying the kind, which would content him. It was easy to understand that he wanted money, and to prevent an explosion, I resolved to gratify him. But willing to manage his delicacy, if he had any, I reminded him that I had at our first interview made him a promise of service, that I was disposed to do it as far as might be proper, and in my power, and requested him to consider in what manner I could do it, and to write to me. He withdrew with a promise of compliance.

Two days after, the 17th of December, he wrote me the letter (No. III. b). The evident drift of this letter is to exaggerate the injury done by me, to make a display of sensibility and to magnify the atonement, which was to be required. It however comes to no conclusion, but proposes a meeting at the George Tavern, or at some other place more agreeable to me, which I should name.

On receipt of this letter, I called upon Reynolds, and assuming a decisive tone, told him, that I was tired of his indecision, and insisted upon his declaring to me explicitly what it was he aimed at. He again promised to explain by letter.

On the 19th, I received the promised letter (No. IV. b) the essence of which is that he was willing to take a thousand dollars as the plaister of his wounded honor.

I determined to give it to him, and did so in two payments, as per receipts (No. V and VI) dated the 22d of December and 3d of January. It is a little remarkable, that an avaricious speculating secretary of the treasury should have been so straitened for money as to be obliged to satisfy an engagement of this sort by two different payments!

On the 17th of January, I received the letter No. V. by which Reynolds invites me to *renew my visits to his wife*. He had before requested that I would see her no more. The motive to this step appears in the conclusion of the letter, "*I rely* upon your befriending me, *if there should any thing offer that should be to my advantage*, as you *express a wish to befriend me*." Is the pre-existence of a speculating connection reconcileable with this mode of expression?

If I recollect rightly, I did not immediately accept the invitation, nor 'till after I had received several very importunate letters from Mrs. Reynolds—See her letters No. VIII, (b) IX, X.

On the 24th of March following, I received a letter from *Reynolds*, No. XI, and on the same day one from his wife, No. XII. These letters will further illustrate the obliging co-operation of the husband with his wife to aliment and keep alive my connection with her.

The letters from Reynolds, No. XIII to XVI, are an additional comment upon the same plan. It was a persevering scheme to spare no pains to levy contributions upon my passions on the one hand, and upon my apprehensions of discovery on the other. It is probably to No. XIV that my note, in these words, was an answer; "To-morrow what is requested will be done. 'Twill hardly be possible *to-day*." The letter presses for the loan which is asked for *to-day*. A scarcity of cash, which was not very uncommon, is believed to have modelled the reply.

The letter No. XVII is a master-piece. The husband there forbids my future visits to his wife, chiefly because I was careful to avoid publicity. It was probably necessary to the project of some deeper treason against me that I should be seen at the house. Hence was it contrived, with all the caution on my part to avoid it, that *Clingman* should occasionally see me.

The interdiction was every way welcome, and was I believe, strictly observed. On the second of June following, I received the letter No. XVIII, from Mrs. Reynolds, which proves that it was not her plan yet to let me off. It was probably the prelude to the letter from Reynolds, No. XIX, soliciting a *loan* of 300 dollars towards a subscription to the Lancaster Turnpike. *Clingman's* statement, No. IV (a), admits, on the information of Reynolds, that to this letter the following note from me was an answer—"*It is utterly out of my power I assure you 'pon my honour to comply with your request. Your note is returned.*" The letter itself demonstrates, that here was no concern in speculation on my part— that the money is asked as a *favour* and as a *loan*, to be reimbursed simply and without profit *in less than a fortnight*. My answer shews that even the loan was refused.

The letter No. XX, from *Reynolds*, explains the object of my note in these words, "*Inclosed are 50 dollars, they could not be sent sooner*," proving that this sum also was begged for in a very apologetic stile as a mere loan.

The letters of the 24th and 30th of August, No. XXI and XXII, furnish the key to the affair of the 200 dollars mentioned by *Clingman* in No. IV, shewing that this sum likewise was asked by way of loan, towards furnishing a small boarding-house which Reynolds and his wife were or pretended to be about to set up.

These letters collectively, furnish a complete elucidation of the nature of my transactions with *Reynolds*. They resolve them into an amorous connection with his wife, detected, or pretended to be detected by the husband, imposing on me the necessity of a pecuniary composition with him, and leaving me afterwards under a duress for fear of disclosure, which was the instrument of levying upon me from time to time *forced loans*. They apply directly to this state of things, the notes which *Reynolds* was so careful to preserve, and which had been employed to excite suspicion.

Four, and the principal of these notes have been not only generally, but particularly explained—I shall briefly notice the remaining two.

"My dear Sir, I expected to have heard the day after I had the pleasure of seeing you." This fragment, if truly part of a letter to *Reynolds*, denotes nothing more than a disposition to be civil to a man, whom, as I said before, it was the interest of my passions to conciliate. But I verily believe it was not part of a letter to him, because I do not believe that I ever addressed him in such a stile. It may very well have been part of a letter to some other person, procured by means of which I am ignorant, or it may have been the beginning of an intended letter, torn off, thrown into the chimney in my office, which was a common practice, and there or after it had been swept out picked up by Reynolds or some coadjutor of his. There appears to have been more than one clerk in the department some how connected with him.

The endeavour shewn by the letter No. XVII, to induce me to render my visits to Mrs. Reynolds more public, and the great care with which my little notes were preserved, justify the belief that at a period, before it was attempted, the idea of implicating me in some accusation, with a view to the advantage of the accusers, was entertained. Hence the motive to pick up and preserve any fragment which might favour the idea of friendly or confidential correspondence.

2dly. "The person Mr. Reynolds inquired for on Friday waited for him all the evening at his house from a little after seven. Mr. R. may see him at any time to-day or to-morrow between the hours of two and three."

Mrs. Reynolds more than once communicated to me, that Reynolds would occasionally relapse into discontent to his situation—would treat her very ill—hint at the assassination of me—and more openly threaten, by way of revenge, to inform Mrs. Hamilton—all this naturally gave some uneasiness. I could not be absolutely certain whether it was artifice or reality. In the workings of human inconsistency, it was very possible, that the same man might be corrupt enough to compound for his wife's chastity and yet have sensibility enough to be restless in the situation and to hate the cause of it.

Reflections like these induced me for some time to use palliatives with the ill humours which were announced to me. Reynolds had called upon me in one of these discontented moods real or pretended. I was unwilling to provoke him by the appearance of neglect—and having failed to be at home at the hour he had been permitted to call, I wrote her the above note to obviate an ill impression.

The foregoing narrative and the remarks accompanying it have prepared the way for a perusal of the letters themselves. The more attention is used in this, the more entire will be the satisfaction which they will afford.

It has been seen that an explanation on the subject was had cotemporarily that is in December 1792, with three members of Congress—F. A. Muhlenberg, J. Monroe, and A. Venable. It is proper that the circumstances of this transaction should be accurately understood.

The manner in which Mr. Muhlenberg became engaged in the affair is fully set forth in the document (No. I. a). It is not equally clear how the two other gentlemen came to embark in it. The phraseology, in reference to this point in the close of (No. I. a) and beginning of (No. II. a) is rather equivocal. The gentlemen, if they please, can explain it.

But on the morning of the 15th of December 1792, the above mentioned gentlemen presented themselves at my office. Mr. Muhlenberg was then speaker. He introduced the subject by observing to me, that they *had discovered a very improper connection* between me and a Mr. Reynolds: extremely hurt by this mode of introduction, I arrested the progress of the discourse by giving way to very strong expressions of indignation. The gentlemen explained, telling me in substance that I had misapprehended them—that they did not intend to take the fact for established—that their meaning was to apprise me that unsought by them, information had been given them of an improper pecuniary connection between Mr. Reynolds and myself; that they had thought it their duty to pursue it and had become possessed of some documents of a suspicious complexion—that they had contemplated the laying the matter before the President, but before they did this, they thought it right to apprise me of the affair and to afford an opportunity of explanation; declaring at the same time that their agency in the matter was influenced solely by a sense of public duty and by no motive of personal ill will. If my memory be correct, the notes from me in a disguised hand were now shewn to me which without a moment's hesitation I acknowledged to be mine.

I replied, that the affair was now put upon a different footing—that I always stood ready to meet fair inquiry with frank communication—that it happened, in the present instance, to be in my power by written documents to remove all doubt as to the real nature of the business, and fully to convince, that nothing of the kind imputed to me did in fact exist. The same evening at my house was by mutual consent appointed for an explanation.

I immediately after saw Mr. Wolcott, and for the first time informed him of the affair and of the interview just had; and delivering into his hands for perusal the documents of which I was possessed, I engaged him to be present at the intended explanation in the evening.

In the evening the proposed meeting took place, and Mr. Wolcott according to my request attended. The information, which had been received to that time, from *Clingman*, *Reynolds* and his wife was communicated to me and the notes were I think again exhibited.

I stated in explanation, the circumstances of my affair with Mrs. Reynolds and the consequences of it and in confirmation produced the documents (No. I. b, to XXII.) One or more of the gentlemen (Mr. Wolcott's certificate No. XXIV, mentions one, Mr. Venable, but I think the same may be said of Mr. Muhlenberg) was struck with so much conviction, before I had gotten through the communication that they delicately urged me to discontinue it as unnecessary. I insisted upon going through the whole and did so. The result was a full and unequivocal acknowlegement on the part of the three gentlemen of perfect satisfaction with the explanation and expressions of regret at the trouble and embarrassment which had been occasioned to me. Mr. Muhlenberg and Mr. Venable, in particular manifested a degree of sensibility on the occasion. Mr. Monroe was more cold but intirely explicit.

One of the gentlemen, I think, expressed a hope that I also was satisfied with their conduct in conducting the inquiry. I answered, that they knew I had been hurt at the opening of the affair—that this excepted, I was satisfied with their conduct and considered myself as having been treated with candor or with fairness and liberality, I do not now pretend to recollect the exact terms. I took the next morning a memorandum of the substance of what was said to me, which will be seen by a copy of it transmitted in a letter to each of the gentlemen No. XXV.

I deny absolutely, as alleged by the editor of the publication in question, that I intreated a suspension of the communication to the President, or that from the beginning to the end of the inquiry, I asked any favour or indulgence whatever, and that I discovered any symptom different from that of a proud consciousness of innocence.

Some days after the explanation I wrote to the three gentlemen the letter No. XXVI already published. That letter evinces the light in which I considered myself as standing in their view.

I received from Mr. Muhlenberg and Mr. Monroe in answer the letters No. XXVII and XXVIII.

Thus the affair remained 'till the pamphlets No. V and VI of the history of the U. States for 1796 appeared; with the exception of some dark whispers which were communicated to me by a friend in Virginia, and to which I replied by a statement of what had passed.

When I saw No. V though it was evidence of a base infidelity somewhere, yet firmly believing that nothing more than a want of due care was chargeable upon either of the three gentlemen who had made the inquiry, I immediately wrote to each of them a letter of which No. XXV is a copy in full confidence that their answer would put the whole business at rest. I ventured to believe, from the appearances on their part at closing our former interview on the subject, that their answers would have been both cordial and explicit.

I acknowledge that I was astonished when I came to read in the pamphlet No. VI the conclusion of the document No. V, containing the equivocal phrase "*We left him under an impression our suspicions were removed*," which seemed to imply that this had been a mere piece of management, and that the impression given me had not been reciprocal.

The appearance of duplicity incensed me; but resolving to proceed with caution and moderation, I thought the first proper step was to inquire of the gentlemen whether the paper was genuine. A letter was written for this purpose the copy of which I have mislaid.

I afterwards received from Messrs. Muhlenberg and Venable the letters No. XXIX, XXX, and XXXI.

Receiving no answer from Mr. Monroe, and hearing of his arrival at New-York I called upon him. The issue of the interview was that an answer was to be given by him, in conjunction with Mr. Muhlenberg and Mr. Venable on his return to Philadelphia, he thinking that as the agency had been joint it was most proper the answer should be joint, and informing me that Mr. Venable had told him he would wait his return.

I came to Philadelphia accordingly to bring the affair to a close; but on my arrival I found Mr. Venable had left the city for Virginia.

Mr. Monroe reached Philadelphia according to his appointment. And the morning following wrote me the note No. XXXII. While this note was on its way to my lodgings I was on my way to his. I had a conversation with him from which we separated with a repetition of the assurance in the note. In the course of the interviews with Mr. Monroe, the equivoque in document No. V, (a) and the paper of January 2d, 1793, under his signature were noticed.

I received the day following the letter No. XXXIII, to which I returned the answer No. XXXIV,—accompanied with the letter No. XXXV. which was succeeded by the letters No. XXXVI—XXXVII—XXXVIII—XXXIX—XL. In due time the sequel of the correspondence will appear.

Though extremely disagreeable to me, for very obvious reasons, I at length determined in order that no cloud whatever might be left on the affair, to publish the documents which had been communicated to Messrs. Monroe, Muhlenberg and Venable, all which will be seen in the appendix from No. I, (b) to No. XXII, inclusively.

The information from *Clingman* of the 2d January 1793, to which the signature of Mr. Monroe is annexed, seems to require an observation or two in addition to what is contained in my letter to him No. XXXIX.

Clingman first suggests that he had been apprized of my vindication through Mr. Wolcott a day or two after it had been communicated. It did not occur to me to inquire of Mr. Wolcott on this point, and he being now absent from Philadelphia, I cannot do it at this moment.

Though I can have no doubt of the friendly intention of Mr. Wolcott, if the suggestion of Clingman in this particular be taken as true; yet from the condition of secrecy which was annexed to my communication, there is the strongest reason to conclude it is not true. If not true, there is besides but one of two solutions, either that he obtained the information from one of the three gentlemen who made the inquiry, which would have been a very dishonourable act in the party, or that he conjectured what my defence was from what he before knew it truly could be. For there is the highest probability, that through Reynolds and his wife, and as an accomplice, he was privy to the whole affair. This last method of accounting for his knowledge would be conclusive on the sincerity and genuineness of the defence.

But the turn which *Clingman* gives to the matter must necessarily fall to the ground. It is, that Mrs. Reynolds denied her amorous connection with me, and represented the suggestion of it as a mere contrivance between *her husband* and *myself* to cover me, alleging that there had been a fabrication of letters and receipts to countenance it. The plain answer is, that Mrs. Reynolds' own letters contradict absolutely this artful explanation of hers; if indeed she ever made it, of which *Clingman's* assertion is no evidence whatever. These letters are proved by the affidavit No. XLI, though it will easily be conceived that the proof of them was rendered no easy matter by a lapse of near five years. They shew explicitly the connection with her, the discovery of it by her husband and the pains she took to prolong it when I evidently wished to get rid of it. This cuts up, by the root, the pretence of a contrivance between the husband and myself to fabricate the evidences of it.

The variety of shapes which this woman could assume was endless. In a conversation between her and a gentleman whom I am not at liberty publicly to name, she made a voluntary confession of her belief and even knowledge, that I was innocent of all that had been laid to my charge by *Reynolds* or any other person of her acquaintance, spoke of me in exalted terms of esteem and respect, declared in the most solemn manner her extreme unhappiness lest I should suppose her accessary to the trouble which had been given me on that account, and expressed her fear that the resentment of Mr. Reynolds on *a particular score*, might have urged him to improper lengths of revenge—appearing at the same time extremely agitated and unhappy. With the gentleman who gives this information, I have never been in any relation personal or political that could be supposed to bias him. His name would evince that he is an impartial witness. And though I am not permitted to make a public use of it, I am permitted to refer any gentleman to the perusal of his letter in the hands of William Bingham, Esquire; who is also so obliging as to permit me to deposit with him for similar inspection all the original papers which are contained in the appendix to this narrative. The letter from the gentleman above alluded to has been already shewn to *Mr. Monroe*.

Let me now, in the last place, recur to some comments, in which the hireling editors of the pamphlets No. V and VI has thought fit to indulge himself.

The first of them is that the *soft* language of one of my notes addressed to a man in the habit of threatening me with disgrace, is incompatible with the idea of innocence. The threats alluded to must be those of being able to hang the Secretary of the Treasury. How does it appear that Reynolds was in such a *habit?* No otherwise than by the declaration of *Reynolds* and *Clingman.* If the assertions of these men are to condemn me, there is an end of the question. There is no need, by elaborate deductions from *parts* of their assertions, to endeavour to establish what their assertions collectively affirm in express terms. If they are worthy of credit I am guilty; if they are not, all wire-drawn inferences from parts of their story are mere artifice and nonsense. But no man, not as debauched as themselves, will believe them, independent of the positive disproof of their story in the written documents.

As to the affair of threats (except those in Reynolds letters respecting the connection with his wife, which it will be perceived were very gentle for the occasion) not the least idea of the sort ever reached me 'till after the imprisonment of Reynolds. Mr. Wolcott's certificate shews my conduct in that case—notwithstanding the powerful motives I may be presumed to have had to desire the liberation of Reynolds, on account of my situation with his wife, I cautioned Mr. Wolcott not to facilitate his liberation, till the affair of the threat was satisfactorily cleared up. The solemn denial of it in Reynold's letter No. XLII was considered by Mr. Wolcott as sufficient. This is a further proof, that though in respect to my situation with his wife, I was somewhat in Reynolds's power. I was not disposed to make any improper concession to the apprehension of his resentment.

As the threats intimated in his letters, the nature of the cause will shew that the soft tone of my note was not only compatible with them, but a natural consequence of them.

But it is observed that the dread of the disclosure of an amorous connection was not a sufficient cause for my humility, and that I had nothing to lose as to my reputation for chastity concerning which the world had fixed a previous opinion.

I shall not enter into the question what was the previous opinion entertained of me in this particular—nor how well founded, if it was indeed such as it is represented to have been. It is sufficient to say that there is a wide difference between vague rumours and suspicions and the evidence of a positive fact—no man not indelicately unprincipled, with the state of manners in this country, would be willing to have a conjugal infidelity fixed upon him with positive certainty. He would know that it would justly injure him with a considerable and respectable portion of the society—and especially no man, tender of the happiness of an excellent wife could without extreme pain look forward to the affliction which she might endure from the disclosure, especially a *public disclosure*, of the fact. Those best acquainted with the interior of my domestic life will best appreciate the force of such a consideration upon me.

The truth was, that in both relations and especially the last, I dreaded extremely a disclosure—and was willing to make large sacrifices to avoid it. It is true, that from the acquiescence of Reynolds, I had strong ties upon his secrecy, but how could I rely upon any tie upon so base a character. How could I know, but that from moment to moment he might, at the expence of his own disgrace, become the *mercenary* of a party, with whom to blast my character in *any way* is a favorite object!

Strong inferences are attempted to be drawn from the release of *Clingman* and *Reynolds* with the consent of the Treasury, from the want of communicativeness of Reynolds while in prison—from the subsequent disappearance of Reynolds and his wife, and from their not having been produced by me in order to be confronted at the time of the explanation.

As to the first, it was emphatically the transaction of Mr. Wolcott the then Comptroller of the Treasury, and was bottomed upon a very adequate motive—and one as appears from the document No. I, (a) early contemplated in this light by that officer. It was certainly of more consequence to the public to detect and expel from the bosom of the Treasury Department an unfaithful Clerk to prevent future and extensive mischief, than to disgrace and punish two worthless individuals. Besides that a powerful influence foreign to me was exerted to procure indulgence to them—that of Mr. Muhlenberg and Col. Burr—that of Col. Wadsworth, which though insidiously placed to my account was to the best of my recollection utterly unknown to me at the time, and according to the confession of Mrs. Reynolds herself, was put in motion by her entreaty. Candid men will derive strong evidence of my innocence and delicacy, from the reflection, that under circumstances so peculiar, the culprits were compelled to give a real and substantial equivalent for the relief which they obtained from a department, *over which I presided*.

The backwardness of Reynolds to enter into detail, while in jail, was an argument of nothing but that conscious of his inability to communicate any particulars which could be supported, he found it more convenient to deal in generals, and to keep up appearances by giving promises for the future.

As to the disappearance of the parties after the liberation, how am I answerable for it? Is it not presumable, that the instance discovered at the Treasury was not the only offence of the kind of which they were guilty? After one detection, is it not very probable that Reynolds fled to avoid detection in other cases? But exclusive of this, it is known and might easily be proved, that Reynolds was considerably in debt! What more natural for him than to fly from his creditors after having been once exposed by confinement for such a crime? Moreover, atrocious as his conduct had been towards me, was it not natural for him to fear that my resentment might be excited at the discovery of it, and that it might have been deemed a sufficient reason for retracting the indulgence, which was shewn by withdrawing the prosecution and for recommending it?

One or all of these considerations will explain the disappearance of Reynolds without imputing it to me as a method of getting rid of a dangerous witness.

That disappearance rendered it impracticable, if it had been desired to bring him forward to be confronted. As to *Clingman* it was not pretended that he knew any thing of what was charged upon me, otherwise than by the notes which he produced, and the information of Reynolds and his wife. As to Mrs. Reynolds, she in fact appears by *Clingman's* last story to have remained, and to have been accessible through him, by the gentlemen who had undertaken the inquiry. If they supposed it necessary to the elucidation of the affair, why did not they bring her forward? There can be no doubt of the sufficiency of Clingman's influence, for this purpose, when it is understood that Mrs. Reynolds and he afterwards lived together as man and wife. But to what purpose the confronting? What would it have availed the elucidation of truth, if Reynolds and his wife had impudently made allegations which I denied. Relative character and the written documents must still determine These could decide without it, and they were relied upon. But could it be expected, that I should so debase myself as to think it necessary to my vindication to be confronted with a person such as Reynolds? Could I have borne to suffer my veracity to be exposed to the humiliating competition?

For what?—why, it is said, to tear up the last twig of jealousy—but when I knew that I possessed written documents which were decisive, how could I foresee that any twig of jealousy would remain? When the proofs I did produce to the gentlemen were admitted by them to be completely satisfactory, and by some of them to be more than sufficient, how could I dream of the expediency of producing more—how could I imagine that every twig of jealousy was not plucked up?

If after the recent confessions of the gentlemen themselves, it could be useful to fortify the proof of the full conviction, my explanation had wrought, I might appeal to the total silence concerning this charge, when at a subsequent period, in the year 1793, there was such an active legislative persecution of me. It might not even perhaps be difficult to establish, that it came under the eye of Mr. Giles, and that he discarded it as the plain case of a private amour unconnected with any thing that was the proper subject of a public attack.

Thus has my desire to destroy this slander, completely, led me to a more copious and particular examination of it, than I am sure was necessary. The bare perusal of the letters from Reynolds and his wife is sufficient to convince my greatest enemy that there is nothing worse in the affair than an irregular and indelicate amour. For this, I bow to the just censure which it merits. I have paid pretty severely for the folly and can never recollect it without disgust and self condemnation. It might seem affectation to say more.

To unfold more clearly the malicious intent, by which the present revival of the affair must have been influenced—I shall annex an affidavit of Mr. Webster tending to confirm my declaration of the utter falsehood of the assertion, that a menace of publishing the papers which have been published had arrested the progress of an attempt to hold me up as a candidate for the office of President. Does this editor imagine that he will escape the just odium which awaits him by the miserable subterfuge of saying that he had the information from a respectable citizen of New-York? Till he names the author the inevitable inference must be that he has fabricated the tale.

ALEXANDER HAMILTON.

*Philadelphia, July, 1797.*

## *To Elizabeth Hamilton*

*Philadelphia*
*Nov 1798*

I am always very happy My Dear Eliza when I can steal a few moments to sit down and write to you. You are my good genius; of that kind which the ancient Philosophers called a *familiar;* and you know very well that I am glad to be in every way as familiar as possible with you. I have formed a sweet project, of which I will make you my confident when I come to New York, and in which I rely that you will cooperate with me chearfully.

> "You may guess and guess and guess again
> Your guessing will be still in vain."

But you will not be the less pleased when you come to understand and realize the scheme.

Adieu best of wives & best of mothers. Heaven ever bless you & me in you

A H

## *To Theodore Sedgwick*

*New York Feby 2. 1799*

What, My Dear Sir, are you going to do with Virginia? This is a very serious business, which will call for all the wisdom and firmness of the Government. The following are the ideas which occur to me on the occasion.

The first thing in all great operations of such a Government as ours is to secure the opinion of the people. To this end, the proceedings of Virginia and Kentucke with the two laws complained of should be referred to a special Committee. That Committee should make a report exhibiting with great luminousness and particularity the reasons which support the constitutionality and expediency of those laws— the tendency of the doctrines advanced by Virginia and Kentucke to destroy the Constitution of the UStates—and, with calm dignity united with pathos, the full evidence which they afford of a regular conspiracy to overturn the government. And the Report should likewise dwell upon the inevitable effect and probably the intention of these proceedings to encourage a hostile foreign power to decline accommodation and proceed in hostility. The Government must not merely defend itself but must attack and arraign its enemies. But in all this, there should be great care to distinguish the people of Virginia from the legislature and even the greater part of those who may have concurred in the legislature from the Chiefs; manifesting indeed a strong confidence in the good sense and patriotism of the people, that they will not be the dupes of an insidious plan to disunite the people of America to break down their constitution & expose them to the enterprises of a foreign power.

This Report should conclude with a declaration that there is no cause for a Repeal of the laws. If however on examination any modifications consistent with the general design of the laws, but instituting better guards, can be devised it may be well to propose them as a bridge for those who may incline to retreat over. Concessions of this kind adroitly made have a good rather than a bad effect. On a recent though hasty revision of the Alien law it seems to me deficient in precautions against abuse and for the security of Citizens. This should not be.

No pains or expence should be spared to desseminate this Report. A little pamphlet containing it should find its way into every house in Virginia.

This should be left to work and nothing to court a shock should be adopted.

In the mean time the measures for raising the Military force should proceed with activity. Tis much to be lamented that so much delay has attended the execution of this measure. In times like the present not a moment ought to have been lost to secure the Government so powerful an auxiliary. Whenever the experiment shall be made to subdue a *refractory* & powerful *state* by Militia, the event will shame the advocates of their sufficiency. In the expedition against the Western Insurgents I trembled every moment lest a great part of the Militia should take it into their heads to return home rather than go forward.

When a clever force has been collected let them be drawn towards Virginia for which there is an obvious pretext—& then let measures be taken to act upon the laws & put Virginia to the Test of resistance.

This plan will give time for the fervour of the moment to subside, for reason to resume the reins, and by dividing its enemies will enable the Government to triumph with ease.

As an auxiliary measure, it is very desireable that the Provisional Army Bill should pass & that the Executive should proceed to the appointment of the Officers. The tendency of this needs no comment.

Yrs. affecy

A HAMILTON

## To James McHenry

*New York March 18. 1799*

PRIVATE

Beware, my Dear Sir, of magnifying a riot into an insurrection, by employing in the first instance an inadequate force. Tis better far to err on the other side. Whenever the Government appears in arms it ought to appear like a *Hercules*, and inspire respect by the display of strength. The consideration of expence is of no moment compared with the advantages of energy. Tis true this is always a relative question—but tis always important to make no mistake. I only offer a *principle* and a *caution*.

A large corps of auxiliary cavalry may be had in Jersey New York Delaware Maryland without interfering with farming pursuits.

Will it be inexpedient to put under marching Orders a large force provisionally, as in eventual support of the corps to be employed—to awe the disaffected?

Let all be well considered.

Yrs. truly

A HAMILTON

## To Charles Cotesworth Pinckney

*Philadelphia Decr.*
*1799*

SIR

The death of our beloved commander in Chief was known to you before it was to me. I can be at no loss to anticipate what have been your feelings. I need not tell you what are mine. Perhaps no friend of his has more cause to lament, on personal account, than my self. The public misfortune is one which all the friends of our Government will view in the same light. I will not dwell on the subject. My Imagination is gloomy my heart sad.

Inclosed is an order relative to the occasion which speaks its own object.

With the sincerest esteem and most affectionate regard I remain Sir Yr very Obed ser

## To Martha Washington

*New York Jany. 12. 1800*

I did not think it proper, Madam, to intrude amidst the first effusions of your grief. But I can no longer restrain my sensibility from conveying to you an imperfect expression of my affectionate sympathy in the sorrows you experience. No one, better than myself, knows the greatness of your loss, or how much your excellent heart is formed to feel it in all its extent. Satisfied that you cannot receive consolation, I will attempt to offer none. Resignation to the will of Heaven, which the practice of your life ensures, can alone alleviate the sufferings of so heart-rending an affliction.

There can be few, who equally with me participate in the loss you deplore. In expressing this sentiment, I may without impropriety allude to the numerous and distinguished marks of confidence and friendship, of which you have yourself been a Witness; but I cannot say in how many ways the continuance of that confidence and friendship was necessary to me in future relations.

Vain, however, are regrets. From a calamity, which is common to a mourning nation, who can expect to be exempt? Perhaps it is even a privilege to have a claim to a larger portion of it than others.

I will only add, Madam, that I shall deem it a real and a great happiness, if any future occurrence shall enable me to give you proof of that respectful and cordial attachment with which I have the honor to be

Your obliged & very obedient servant

## *To John Jay*

*New York May 7. 1800*

Dear Sir

You have been informed of the loss of our Election in this City. It is also known that we have been unfortunate throughout Long Island & in West Chester. According to the Returns hitherto, it is too probable that we lose our Senators for this District.

The moral certainty therefore is that there will be an Anti-fœderal Majority in the Ensuing Legislature, and this very high probability is that this will bring *Jefferson* into the Chief Magistracy; unless it be prevented by the measure which I shall now submit to your consideration, namely the immediate calling together of the existing Legislature.

I am aware that there are weighty objections to the measure; but the reasons for it appear to me to outweigh the objections. And in times like these in which we live, it will not do to be overscrupulous. It is easy to sacrifice the substantial interests of society by a strict adherence to ordinary rules.

In observing this, I shall not be supposed to mean that any thing ought to be done which integrity will forbid—but merely that the scruples of delicacy and propriety, as relative to a common course of things, ought to yield to the extraordinary nature of the crisis. They ought not to hinder the taking of a *legal* and *constitutional* step, to prevent an *Atheist* in Religion and a *Fanatic* in politics from getting possession of the helm of the State.

You Sir know in a great degree the Antifœderal party, but I fear that you do not know them as well as I do. Tis a composition indeed of very incongruous materials but all tending to mischief—some of them to the overthrow of the Government by stripping it of its due energies others of them to a Revolution after the manner of Buonaparte. I speak from indubitable facts, not from conjectures & inferences.

In proportion as the true character of this party is understood is the force of the considerations which urge to every effort to disappoint it. And it seems to me that there is a very solemn obligation to employ the means in our power.

The calling of the Legislature will have for object the choosing of Electors by the people in Districts. This (as Pennsylvania will do nothing) will insure a Majority of votes in the U States for Fœderal Candidates.

The measure will not fail to be approved by all the Fœderal Party; while it will no doubt be condemned by the opposite. As to its intrinsic nature it is justified by unequivocal reasons for *public safety*.

The reasonable part of the world will I believe approve it. They will see it as a proceeding out of the common course but warranted by the particular nature of the Crisis and the great cause of social order.

If done the motive ought to be frankly avowed. In your communication to the Legislature they ought to be told that Temporary circumstances had rendered it probable that without their interposition the executive authority of the General Government would be transfered to hands hostile to the system heretofore pursued with so much success and dangerous to the peace happiness and order of the Country—that under this impression from facts convincing to your own mind you had thought it your duty to give the existing Legislature an opportunity of deliberating whether it would not be proper to interpose and endeavour to prevent so great an evil by referring the choice of Electors to the People distributed into Districts.

In weighing this suggestion you will doubtless bear in mind that Popular Governments must certainly be overturned & while they endure prove engines of mischief—if one party will call to its aid all the resources which *Vice* can give and if the other, however pressing the emergency, confines itself within all the ordinary forms of delicacy and decorum.

The legislature can be brought together in three weeks. So that there will be full time for the objects; but none ought to be lost.

Think well my Dear Sir of this proposition. Appreciate the extreme danger of the Crisis; and I am unusually mistaken in my view of the matter, if you do not see it right and expedient to adopt the measure.

Respectfully & Affecty Yrs.

A HAMILTON

## To Theodore Sedgwick

*New York May 10. 1800*

DR SIR

I am very sorry for the information contained in your letter of the 7th. But I am not intimate enough with Dexter to put myself upon Paper to him. If on his return I can catch him at New York I shall have a particular conversation with him.

He is I am persuaded much mistaken as to the opinion entertained of Mr Adams by the Fœderal party. Were I to determine from my own observation I should say, *most* of the *most influential men* of that party consider him as a very *unfit* and *incapable* character.

For my individual part my mind is made up. I will never more be responsible for him by my direct support—even though the consequence should be the election of *Jefferson*. If we must have an *enemy* at the head of the Government, let it be one whom we can oppose & for whom we are not responsible, who will not involve our party in the disgrace of his foolish and bad measures. Under *Adams* as under *Jefferson* the government will sink. The party in the hands of whose chief it shall sink will sink with it and the advantage will all be on the side of his adversaries.

Tis a notable expedient for keeping the Fœderal party together to have at the head of it a man who hates and is dispised by those men of it who in time past have been its most efficient supporters.

If the cause is to be sacrificed to a weak and perverse man, I withdraw from the party & act upon my own ground—never certainly against my principles but in pursuance of them in my own way. I am mistaken if others will not do the same.

The only way to prevent a fatal scism in the Fœderal party is to support G Pinckney in good earnest.

If I can be perfectly satisfied that Adams & Pinckney will be upheld in the East with intire good faith, on the ground of conformity I will wherever my influence may extend pursue the same plan. If not I will pursue Mr. Pinkny as my single object.

Adieu Yrs. truly

A H

## *To John Adams*

*New York August 1. 1800*

SIR

It has been repeatedly mentioned to me that you have, on different occasions, asserted the existence of a *British Faction* in this Country, embracing a number of leading or influential characters of the *Fœderal Party* (as usually denominated) and that you have sometimes named me, at other times plainly alluded to me, as one of this description of persons: And I have likewise been assured that of late some of your warm adherents, for electioneering purposes, have employed a corresponding language.

I must, Sir, take it for granted, that you cannot have made such assertions or insinuations without being willing to avow them, and to assign the reasons to a party who may conceive himself injured by them. I therefore trust that you will not deem it improper that I apply directly to yourself, to ascertain from you, in reference to your own declarations, whether the information, I have received, has been correct or not, and if correct what are the grounds upon which you have founded the suggestion.

With respect I have the honor to be Sir Your obedient servt.

ALEXANDER HAMILTON

## To William Jackson

*New-York Aug 26 1800.*

MY DEAR JACKSON.

Never was there a more ungenerous persecution of any man than of myself.—Not only the worst constructions are put upon my conduct as a public man but it seems my birth is the subject of the most humiliating criticism.

On this point as on most others which concern me, there is much mistake—though I am pained by the consciousness that it is not free from blemish.

I think it proper to confide to your bosom the real history of it, that among my friends you may if you please wipe off some part of the stain which is so industriously impressed.

The truth is that on the question who my parents were, I have better pretensions than most of those who in this Country plume themselves on Ancestry.

My Grandfather by the mothers side of the name of Faucette was a French Huguenot who emigrated to the West Indies in consequence of the revocation of the Edict of Nantz and settled in the Island of Nevis and there acquired a pretty fortune. I have been assured by persons who knew him that he was a man of letters and much of a gentleman. He practiced as a Physician, whether that was his original profession, or one assumed for livelihood after his emigration is not to me ascertained.

My father now dead was certainly of a respectable Scotch Family. His father was, and the son of his Eldest brother now is Laird of Grange. His mother was the sister of an ancient Baronet *Sir Robert Pollock*.

Himself being a younger son of a numerous family was bred to trade. In capacity of merchant he went to St Kitts, where from too generous and too easy a temper he failed in business, and at length fell into indigent circumstances. For some time he was supported by his friends in Scotland, and for several years before his death by me. It was his fault to have had too much pride and two large a portion of indolence—but his character was otherwise without reproach and his manners those of a Gentleman.

So far I may well challenge comparison, but the blemish remains to be unveiled.

A Dane a fortune-hunter of the name of *Lavine* came to Nevis bedizzened with gold, and paid his addresses to my mother then a handsome young woman having a *snug* fortune. In compliance with the wishes of her mother who was captivated by the glitter of the [    ] but against her own inclination she married Lavine. The marriage was unhappy and ended in a separation by divorce. My mother afterwards went to St Kitts, became acquainted with my father and a marriage between them ensued, followed by many years cohabitation and several children.

But unluckily it turned out that the divorce was not absolute but qualified, and thence the second marriage was not lawful. Hence when my mother died the small property which she left went to my half brother Mr Lavine who lived in South Carolina and was for a time partner with Mr Kane. He is now dead.

As to my fathers family Mr McCormick of this city, merchant, can give testimony and will corroborate what I have stated.

Yours truly and affectionately.

ALEXANDER HAMILTON

## *Rules for Philip Hamilton*

Rules for *Mr Philip Hamilton* from the first of April to the first of October he is to rise not later than Six Oclock—The rest of the year not later than Seven. If Earlier he will deserve commendation. Ten will be his hour of going to bed throughout the year.

From the time he is dressed in the morning till nine o clock (the time for breakfast Excepted) he is to read Law.

At nine he goes to the office & continues there till dinner time—he will be occupied partly in the writing and partly in reading law.

After Dinner he reads law at home till five O clock. From this hour till Seven he disposes of his time as he pleases. From Seven to ten he reads and Studies what ever he pleases.

From twelve on Saturday he is at Liberty to amuse himself.

On Sunday he will attend the morning Church. The rest of the day may be applied to innocent recreations.

He must not Depart from any of these rules without my permission.

*1800*

## *To Gouverneur Morris*

*New York 26 Decr. 1800*

Dr Sir

The post of yesterday gave me the pleasure of a letter from you. I thank you for the communication. I trust that a letter which I wrote you the day before the receipt of yours will have duly reached you as it contains some very free & confidential observations ending in two results—1 That The Convention with France ought to be ratified as the least of two evils   2 That *on the same ground Jefferson* ought to be preferred to *Burr*.

I trust the Fœderalists will not finally be so mad as to vote for the *latter*. I speak with an intimate & accurate knowlege of character. His elevation can only promote the purposes of the desperate and proflicate. If there be a man in the world I ought to hate it is Jefferson. With *Burr* I have always been personally well. But the public good must be paramount to every private consideration. My opinion may be freely used with such reserves as you shall think discreet.

Yrs.  very truly

A H

## *To John Rutledge Jr.*

*Confidential*                                           *New York Jany. 4. 1801*

My Dear Sir

My extreme anxiety about the ensuing election of President by the House of Representatives will excuse to you the liberty I take in addressing you concerning it without being consulted by you. Did you know Mr. *Burr* as well as I do, I should think it unnecessary. With your honest attachment to the Country and correctness of views, it would not then be possible for you to hesitate, *if you now do*, about the course to be taken. You would be clearly of opinion with me that Mr. Jefferson is to be preferred.

As long as the Fœderal party preserve their high ground of integrity and principle, I shall not despair of the public weal. But if they quit it and descend to be the willing instruments of the Elevation of the most unfit and most dangerous man of the Community to the highest station in the Government—I shall no longer see any anchor for the hopes of good men. I shall at once anticipate all the evils that a daring and unprincipled ambition wielding the lever of Jacobinism can bring upon an infatuated Country.

The enclosed paper exhibits a faithful sketch of Mr. Burr's character as I believe it to exist, with better opportunities than almost any other man of forming a true estimate.

The expectation, I know, is, that if Mr. Burr shall owe his elevation to the Fœderal party he will judge it his interest to adhere to that party. But it ought to be recollected, that he will owe it in the first instance to the Antifoederal party; that among these, though perhaps not in the House of Representatives, a numerous class prefers him to Mr. Jefferson as best adapted by the boldness and cunning of his temper to fulfill their mischievous views; and that it will be the interest of his Ambition to preserve and cultivate these friends.

Mr. Burr will doubtless be governed by his interest as he views it. But *stable* power and Wealth being his objects—and there being no prospect that the respectable and sober fœderalists will countenance the projects of an irregular Ambition or prodigal Cupidity, he will not long lean upon them—but selecting from among them men suited to his purpose he will seek with the aid of those and of the most unprincipled of the opposite party to accomplish his ends. At least such ought to be our calculation. From such a man as him, who practices all the maxims of a Catiline, who, while despising, has played the whole game of, democracy, what better is to be looked for. Tis not to a Chapter of Accidents, that we ought to trust the Government peace and happiness of our Country. Tis enough for us to know that Mr. Burr is one of the most unprincipled men in the UStates in order to determine us to decline being responsible for the precarious issues of his calculations of Interest.

Very different ought to be our plan. Under the uncertainty of the Event we ought to seek to obtain from Mr. Jefferson these assurances 1 That the present Fiscal System will be maintained. 2 That the present neutral plan will be adhered to. 3 That the Navy will be preserved and gradually increased. 4 That Fœderalists now in office, not being heads of the great departments, will be retained. As to the heads of Departments & other matters he ought to be free.

You cannot in my opinion render a greater service to your Country than by exerting your influence to counteract the *impolitic* and *impure* idea of raising Mr. Burr to the Chief Magistracy.

Adieu My Dear Sir    Yrs. with sincere esteem & regard

A HAMILTON

Confidential

### A Burr

1  He is in every sense a profligate; a voluptuary in the extreme, with uncommon habits of expence; in his profession extortionate to a proverb; suspected on strong grounds of having *corruptly* served the views of the Holland Company, in the capacity of a member of our legislature*; and understood to have been guilty of several breaches of probity in his pecuniary transactions. His very friends do not insist upon his integrity.

2  He is without doubt insolvent for a large *deficit*. All his visible property is deeply mortgaged, and he is known to owe other large debts, for which there is no specific security. Of the number of these is a Judgment in favour of Mr. Angerstien for a sum which with interest amounts to about 80,000 Dollars.

3  The fair emoluments of any station, under our government, will not equal his expences in that station; still less will they suffice to extricate him from his embarassments & he must therefore from the necessity of his situation have recourse to unworthy expedients. These may be a *bargain* and *sale* with some foreign power, or combinations with public agents in projects of gain by means of the public monies; perhaps and probably, to enlarge the sphere—a *War*.

4  He has no pretensions to the Station from services. He acted in different capacities in the last war finally with the rank of Lt. Col in a Regiment, and gave indications of being a good officer; but without having had the opportunity of performing any distinguished action. At a *critical period* of the War, he resigned his commission, assigning for cause ill-health, and went to reside at *Paramus* in the State of New Jersey. If his health was bad he might without difficulty have obtained a furlough and was not obliged to resign. He was afterwards seen in his usual health. The circumstance excited much jealousy of his motives. In civil life, he has never projected nor aided in producing a single measure of important public utility.

* He cooperated in obtaining a law to permit Aliens to hold & convey lands.

5 He has *constantly* sided with the party hostile to *fœderal* measures before and since the present constitution of the U States. In opposing the adoption of this constitution he was engaged covertly and insidiously; because, as he said at the time "it was too strong and too weak" and he has been uniformly the opposer of the Fœderal Administration.

6 No mortal can tell what his political principles are. He has talked *all round the compass. At times* he has dealt in all the jargon of Jacobinism; at other times he has proclaimed decidedly the total insufficiency of the Fœderal Government and the necessity of changes to one far more energetic. The truth seems to be that he has no plan but that of *getting* power by *any* means and *keeping* it by *all* means. It is probable that if he has any theory 'tis that of a simple *despotism*. He has intimated that he thinks the present French constitution not a bad one.

7 He is of a temper bold enough to think no enterprize too hazardous and sanguine enough to think none too difficult. He has censured the leaders of the Fœderal party as wanting in vigour and enterprise, for not having established a strong Government when they were in possession of the power and influence.

8 Discerning men of all parties agree in ascribing to him an irregular and inordinate ambition. Like *Catiline*, he is indefatigable in courting the *young* and the *profligate*. He knows well the weak sides of human nature, and takes care to play in with the passions of all with whom he has intercourse. By natural disposition, the haughtiest of men, he is at the same time the most creeping to answer his purposes. Cold and collected by nature and habit, he never loses sight of his object and scruples no means of accomplishing it. He is artful and intriguing to an inconceivable degree. In short all his conduct indicates that he has in view nothing less than the establishment of Supreme Power in his own person. Of this nothing can be a surer index than that having in fact high-toned notions of Government, he has nevertheless constantly opposed the *fœderal* and courted the *popular* party. As he never can effect his wish by the aid of good men, he will court and employ able and daring scoundrels of every party, and by availing himself of their assistance and of all the bad passions of the Society, he will in all likelihood attempt an usurpation.

8 Within the last three weeks at his own Table, he drank these toasts successively 1 The French Republic 2 The Commissioners who negotiated the Convention 3 *Buonaparte* 4 *La Fayette*; and he

countenanced and seconded the positions openly advanced by one of his guests that it was the interest of this Country to leave it free to the Belligerent Powers to sell their prizes in our ports and to build and equip ships for their respective uses; a doctrine which evidently aims at turning all the naval resources of the UStates into the channel of France; and which by making these states the most pernicious enemy of G Britain would compel her to go to War with us.

9 Though possessing infinite art cunning and address—he is yet to give proofs of great or solid abilities. It is certain that at the Bar he is more remarkable for ingenuity and dexterity than for sound judgment or good logic. From the character of his understanding and heart it is likely that any innovations which he may effect will be such as to serve the turn of his own power, not such as will issue in establishments favourable to the permanent security and prosperity of the Nation—founded upon the principles of a *strong free* and *regular* Government.

## To James A. Bayard

*New-York Jany. 16th. 1801.*

I was glad to find my dear sir, by your letter, that you had not yet determined to go with the current of the Fœderal Party in the support of Mr *Burr* & that you were resolved to hold yourself disengaged till the moment of final decision. Your resolution to separate yourself, in this instance, from the Fœderal Party if your conviction shall be strong of the unfitness of Mr Burr, is certainly laudable. So much does it coincide with my ideas, that if the Party Shall by supporting Mr Burr as President adopt him for their official Chief—I shall be obliged to consider myself as an *isolated* man. It will be impossible for me to reconcile with my notions of *honor* or policy, the continuing to be of a Party which according to my apprehension will have degraded itself & the country. I am sure nevertheless that the motives of many will be good, and I shall never cease to esteem the individuals, tho' I shall deplore a step which I fear experience will show to be a very fatal one. Among the letters which I receive assigning the reasons *pro* & *con* for prefering Burr to J. I observe no small exaggeration to the prejudice of the latter & some things taken for granted as to the former which are at least questionable. Perhaps myself the first, at some expence of popularity, to unfold the true character of Jefferson, it is too late for me to become his apologist. Nor can I have any disposition to do it. I admit that his politics are tinctured with fanaticism, that he is too much in earnest in his democracy, that he has been a mischevous enemy to the principle measures of our past administration, that he is crafty & persevering in his objects, that he is not scrupulous about the means of success, nor very mindful of truth, and that he is a contemptible hypocrite. But it is not true as is alleged that he is an enemy to the power of the Executive, or that he is for confounding all the powers in the House of Rs. It is a fact which I have frequently mentioned that while we were in the administration together he was generally for a large construction of the Executive authority, & not backward to act upon it in cases which coincided with his views. Let it be added, that in his theoretic Ideas he has considered as improper the participations of the Senate in the Executive Authority. I have more than once made the reflection that viewing himself as the reversioner, he was solicitous to come into possession of a Good Estate. Nor is it true that Jefferson is zealot enough to do anything in pursuance of his principles which will contravene his popularity, or his interest. He is as likely as any man I know to temporize—to calculate what will be likely to promote his own reputation and advantage; and the probable result of such a temper is the preservation of systems, though originally opposed, which being once established, could not be overturned without danger to the person who did it. To my mind a true estimate of Mr J.'s character warrants the expectation of a temporizing rather than a violent system. That Jefferson has manifested a culpable predilection for France is certainly true; but I think it a question whether it did not proceed quite as much from her *popularity* among us, as from sentiment, and in proportion as that popularity is diminished his zeal will cool. Add to this that there is no fair reason to suppose him capable of being corrupted, which is a security that he will not go beyond certain limits. It is not at all improbable that under the change of circumstances Jefferson's Gallicism has considerably abated.

As to Burr these things are admitted and indeed cannot be denied, that he is a man of *extreme* & *irregular* ambition—that he is *selfish* to a degree which excludes all social affections & that he is decidedly *profligate*. But it is said, 1st. that he is *artful* & *dexterous* to accomplish his ends—2nd. that he holds no pernicious theories, but is a mere *matter of fact* man—

3rd. that his very selfishness* is a guard against mischevous foreign predilections. 4th That his *local situation* has enabled him to appreciate the utility of our Commercial & fiscal systems, and the same quality of selfishness will lead him to support & invigorate them. 5th. that he is now disliked by the Jacobins, that his elevation will be a mortal stab to them, breed an invincible hatred to him, & compel him to lean on the Federalists. 6th. That Burr's ambition will be checked by his good sense, by the manifest impossibility of succeeding in any scheme of usurpation, & that if attempted, there is nothing to fear from the attempt. These topics are in my judgment more plausible than solid. As to the 1st point the fact must be admitted, but those qualities are objections rather than recommendations when they are under the direction of bad principles. As to the 2nd point too much is taken for granted. If Burr's conversation is to be credited he is not very far from being a visionary.† It is ascertained in some instances that he has talked perfect *Godwinism*. I have myself heard him speak with applause of the French system as unshackling the mind & leaving it to its natural energies, and I have been present when he has contended against Banking Systems‡ with earnestness & with the same arguments that Jefferson would use. The truth is that *Burr* is a man of a very subtile imagination, and a mind of this make is rarely free from ingenious whimsies. Yet I admit that he has no fixed theory & that his peculiar notions will easily give way to his interest. But is it a recommendation to have *no theory*? Can that man be a systematic or able statesman who has none? I believe not. *No general principles* will hardly work much better than erroneous ones. As to the 3rd. point— it is certain that Burr generally speaking has been as warm a partisan of France as Jefferson—that he has in some instances shewn himself to be so with passion. But if it was from calculation who will say that his calculations will not continue him so? His selfishness§ so far from being an obstacle may be a prompter. If corrupt as well as selfish he may be a partisan for gain—if ambitious as well as selfish, he may be a partisan for the sake of aid to his views. No man has trafficked more than he in the floating passions of the multitude. Hatred to G. Britain

* It is always very dangerous to look to the *vices* of men for *Good*.

† He has quoted to me Connecticut as an example of the success of the Democratic theory, and as authority, serious doubts whether it was not a good one.

‡ Yet he has lately by a trick established a *Bank*, a perfect monster in its principles; but a very convenient instrument of *profit* & *influence*.

§ Unprincipled selfishness is more apt to seek rapid gain in disorderly practices than slow advantages from orderly systems.

& attachment to France in the public mind will naturally lead a man of his selfishness, attached to place and power, to favour France & oppose G. Britain. The Gallicism of many of our patriots is to be thus resolved, & in my opinion it is morally certain that Burr will continue to be influenced by this calculation. As to the 4th point the instance I have cited with respect to Banks proves that the argument is not to be relied on. If there was much in it, why does Chancellor Livingston maintain that we ought not to cultivate navigation but ought to let foreigners be our Carriers? France is of this opinion too & Burr for some reason or other, will be very apt to be of the opinion of *France*. As to the 5th point—nothing can be more fallacious. It is demonstrated by recent facts* that Burr is *solicitous* to *keep* upon *Antifœderal ground*, to avoid compromitting himself by any engagements† with the Fœderalists. With or without such engagements he will easily persuade his former friends that he does stand on that ground, & after their first resentment they will be glad to rally under him. In the mean time he will take care not to disoblige them & he will always court those among them who are best fitted for tools. He will never choose to lean on good men because he knows that they will never support his bad projects: but instead of this he will endeavour to disorganize both parties & to form out of them a third composed of men fitted by their characters to be conspirators, & instruments of such projects. That this will be his future conduct may be inferred from his past plan, & from the admitted quality of irregular ambition. Let it be remembered that Mr Burr has never appeared solicitous for fame, & that great Ambition unchecked by principle, or the love of Glory, is an unruly Tyrant which never can keep long in a course which good men will approve. As to the last point—The propostion is against the experience of all times. Ambition without principle never was long under the guidance of good sense. Besides that, really the force of Mr Burrs understanding is much overrated. He is far more *cunning* than *wise*, far more *dexterous* than *able*. In my opinion he is inferior in real ability to Jefferson. There are also facts against the supposition. It is past all doubt that he has blamed me for not having improved the situation I once was in to change the Government. That when answered that this could not have been done without guilt—he replied—"Les grands ames se soucient peu des petits morceaux"—that

---

\* My letter to Mr Morris states some of them.

† He trusts to their *prejudices* and *hopes* for support.

when told the thing was never practicable from the genious and situation of the country, he answered, "that depends on the estimate we form of the human passions and of the means of influencing them." Does this prove that Mr Burr would consider a scheme of usurpation as visionary. The truth is with great apparent coldness he is the most sanguine man in the world. He thinks every thing possible to adventure and perseverance. And tho' I believe he will fail, I think it almost certain he will attempt usurpation. And the attempt will involve great mischief.

But there is one point of view which seems to me decisive. If the Antifœderalists who prevailed in the election are left to take their own man, they remain responsible, and the Fœderalists remain *free united* and without *stain*, in a situation to resist with effect pernicious measures. If the Fœderalists substitute Burr, they adopt him and become answerable for him. Whatever may be the theory of the case, abroad and at *home* (for so from the beginning will be taught) Mr Burr will become *in fact* the man of our party. And if he acts ill, we must share in the blame and disgrace. By adopting him we do all we can to reconcile the minds of the Fœderalists to him, and prepare them for the effectual operation of his arts. He will doubtless gain many of them, & the Fœderalists will become a disorganized and contemptible party. Can there be any serious question between the policy of leaving the Antifœderalists to be answerable for the elevation of an exceptionable man, & that of adopting ourselves & becoming answerable for a man who on all hands is acknowledged to be a complete *Cataline* in his practice & principles? 'Tis enough to state the question to indicate the answer, if reason not passion presides in the decision. You may communicate this & my former letter to discreet & confidential friends.

Your's very truly,

A H

## To Gouverneur Morris

My Dr. Sir

Your letter of the 22d is the third favour for which I am indebted to you since you left N York.

Your frankness in giving me your opinion as to the expediency of an application of our bar to Congress obliges me. But you know we are not readily persuaded to think we have been wrong. Were the matter to be done over I should pursue the same course. I did not believe the measure would be useful as a preventative, and for the people an expression of an opinion by letter would be as good as in a memorial. It appeared to me best because it saved our delicacy and because in the abstract I am not over fond of the precedent of the bar addressing Congress. But I did what I thought likely to do more good—I induced the Chamber of Commerce to send a memorial.

As to the rest, I should be a very unhappy man, if I left my tranquillity at the mercy of the misinterpretations which friends as well as foes are fond of giving to my conduct.

Mine is an odd destiny. Perhaps no man in the UStates has sacrificed or done more for the present Constitution than myself—and contrary to all my anticipations of its fate, as you know from the very begginning I am still labouring to prop the frail and worthless fabric. Yet I have the murmurs of its friends no less than the curses of its foes for my rewards. What can I do better than withdraw from the Scene? Every day proves to me more and more that this American world was not made for me.

The suggestions with which you close your letter suppose a much sounder state of the public mind than at present exists. Attempts to make a show of a general *popular* dislike of the pending measures of the Government would only serve to manifest the direct reverse. Impressions are indeed making but as yet within a very narrow sphere. The time may ere long arrive when the minds of men will be prepared to make an offer to *recover* the Constitution, but the many cannot now be brought to make a stand for its preservation. We must wait awhile.

I have read your speeches with great pleasure. They are truly worthy of you. Your real friends had many sources of satisfaction on account of them. The conspiracy of Dulness was at work. It chose to misinterpret your moderation in certain transactions of a personal reference. A public energetic display of your talents and principles was requisite to silence the Cavillers. It is now done. You, friend Morris, are by *birth* a native of this Country but by *genius* an exotic. You mistake if you fancy that you are more a favourite than myself or that you are in any sort upon a theatre suited to you.

Adieu    Yrs. ever

A H

Feby 29.

## To Benjamin Rush

*New York March 29. 1802*

Dear Sir

I felt all the weight of the obligation which I owed to you and to your amiable family, for the tender concern they manifested in an event, beyond comparison, the most afflicting of my life. But I was obliged to wait for a moment of greater calm, to express my sense of the kindness.

My loss is indeed great. The highest as well as the eldest hope of my family has been taken from me. You estimated him rightly—He was truly a fine youth. But why should I repine? It was the will of heaven; and he is now out of the reach of the seductions and calamities of a world, full of folly, full of vice, full of danger—of least value in proportion as it is best known. I firmly trust also that he has safely reached the haven of eternal repose and felicity.

You will easily imagine that every memorial of the goodness of his heart must be precious to me. You allude to one recorded in a letter to your son. If no special reasons forbid it, I should be very glad to have a copy of that letter.

Mrs. Hamilton, who has drank deeply of the cup of sorrow, joins me in affectionate thanks to Mrs. Rush and yourself. Our wishes for your happiness will be unceasing.

Very sincerely & cordially Yrs.

A Hamilton

## To James A. Bayard

*New-York April 1802*

Dear Sir.

Your letter of the 12th inst. has relieved me from some apprehension. Yet it is well that it should be perfectly understood by the truly sound part of the Fœderalists, that there do in fact exist intrigues in good earnest, between several individuals not unimportant, of the Fœderal Party, and the person in question; which are bottomed upon motives & views, by no means auspicious to the real welfare of the country. I am glad to find that it is in contemplation to adopt a plan of conduct. It is very necessary; & to be useful it must be efficient & comprehensive in the means which it embraces, at the same time that it must meditate none which are not really constitutional & patriotic. I will comply with your invitation by submitting some ideas which from time to time have passed through my mind. Nothing is more fallacious than to expect to produce any valuable or permanent results, in political projects, by relying merely on the reason of men. Men are rather reasoning than reasonable animals for the most part governed by the impulse of passion. This is a truth well understood by our adversaries who have practised upon it with no small benefit to their cause. For at the very moment they are eulogizing the reason of men & professing to appeal only to that faculty, they are courting the strongest & most active passion of the human heart—*VANITY!*

It is no less true that the Fœderalists seem not to have attended to the fact sufficiently; and that they erred in relying so much on the rectitude & utility of their measures, as to have neglected the cultivation of popular favour by fair & justifiable expedients. The observation has been repeatedly made by me to individuals with whom I particularly conversed & expedients suggested for gaining good will which were never adopted. Unluckily however for us in the competition for the passions of the people our opponents have great advantages over us; for the plain reason, that the vicious are far more active than the good passions, and that to win the latter to our side we must renounce our principles & our objects, & unite in corrupting public opinion till it becomes fit for nothing but mischief. Yet unless we can contrive to take hold of & carry along with us some strong feelings of the mind we shall in vain calculate upon any substantial or durable results. Whatever plan we may adopt, to be successful must be founded on the truth of this proposition. And perhaps it is not very easy for us to give it full effect; especially not without some deviations from what on other occasions we have maintained to be right. But in determining upon the propriety of the deviations, we must consider whether it be possible for us to succeed without in some degree employing the weapons which have been employed against us, & whether the actual state & future prospect of things, be not such as to justify the reciprocal use of them. I need not tell you that I do not mean to countenance the imitation of things intrinsically unworthy, but only of such as may be denominated irregular, such as in a sound & stable order of things ought not to exist. Neither are you to infer that any revolutionary result is contemplated. In my opinion the present Constitution is the standard to which we are to cling. Under its banners, *bona fide* must we combat our political foes—rejecting all changes but through the channel itself provides for amendments. By these general views of the subject have my reflections been guided. I now offer you the outline of the plan which they have suggested. Let an Association be formed to be denominated, "The Christian Constitutional Society." It's objects to be

1st    The support of the Christian Religion.

2nd   The support of the Constitution of the United States.

Its Organization.

1st    A directing council consisting of a President & 12 Members, of whom 4 & the President to be a quorum.

2nd   A sub-directing council in each State consisting of a Vice-President & 12 Members, of whom 4 with the Vice-President to be a quorum & 3rd As many societies in each State, as local circumstances may permit to be formed by the Sub-directing council.

The meeting at Washington to Nominate the *President* & *Vice-President* together with *4 Members of each* of the councils, who *are to complete* their own numbers respectively.

Its Means.

1st    The diffusion of information. For this purpose not only the Newspapers but pamphlets must be largely employed & to do this a fund must be created. 5 dollars annually for 8 years, to be contributed by each member who can really afford it, (taking care not to burden the less able brethren) may afford a competent fund for a competent time. It is essential to be able to disseminate *gratis* useful publications. Whenever it can be done, & there is a press, clubs should be formed to meet once a week, read the newspapers & prepare essays paragraphs &ct.

2nd   The use of all lawful means in concert to promote the election of *fit men*. A lively correspondence must be kept up between the different Societies.

3rd   The promoting of institutions of a charitable & useful nature
      in the management of Fœderalists. The populous cities ought
      particularly to be attended to. Perhaps it will be well to institute
      in such places 1st Societies for the relief of Emigrants—2nd.
      Academies each with one professor for instructing the different
      Classes of Mechanics in the principles of Mechanics & Elements
      of Chemistry. The cities have been employed by the Jacobins
      to give an impulse to the country. And it is believed to be an
      alarming fact, that while the question of Presidential Election
      was pending in the House of Rs. parties were organized in several
      of the Cities, in the event of there being no election, to cut off the
      leading Fœderalists & sieze the Government.

*especially confidential*

         An Act of association to be drawn up in concise general
      terms. It need only designate the "name" "objects" & contain
      an engagement to promote the objects by all lawful means, and
      particularly by the diffusion of Information. This act to be signed
      by every member.

The foregoing to be the principal Engine. In addition let measures
be adopted to bring as soon as possible the repeal of the Judiciary
law before the Supreme Court. Afterwards, if not before, let as many
Legislatures as can be prevailed upon, instruct their Senators to
endeavour to procure a repeal of the repealing law. The body of New-
England speaking the same language will give a powerful impulse. In
Congress our friends to *propose* little, to agree candidly to all good
measures, & to resist & expose all bad. This is a general sketch of what
has occurred to me. It is at the service of my friends for so much as it
may be worth. With true esteem & regard

   Dr Sir  Yours

                                                        AH


## To Charles Cotesworth Pinckney

                                                   *Grange (NY)*
                                                   *Decr. 29. 1802*

MY DEAR SIR

   A garden, you know, is a very usual refuge of a disappointed
politician. Accordingly, I have purchased a few acres about 9 Miles from

Town, have built a house and am cultivating a Garden. The melons in your country are very fine. Will you have the goodness to send me some seed both of the Water & Muss Melons?

My daughter adds another request, which is for three or four of your peroquets. She is very fond of birds. If there be any thing in this quarter the sending of which can give you pleasure, you have only to name them. As Farmers a new source of sympathy has risen between us; and I am pleased with every thing in which our likings and tastes can be approximated.

Amidst the triumphant reign of Democracy, do you retain sufficient interest in public affairs to feel any curiosity about what is going on? In my opinion the follies and vices of the Administration have as yet made no material impression to their disadvantage. On the contrary, I think the malady is rather progressive than upon the decline in our Northern Quarter. The last *lullaby* message, instead of inspiring contempt, attracts praise. Mankind are forever destined to be the dupes of bold & cunning imposture.

But a difficult *knot* has been twisted by the incident of the cession of Louisian and the interruption of the Deposit at New Orleans. You have seen the soft tun given to this in the message. Yet we are told the President in conversation is very stout. The great embarrassment must be how to carry on war without taxes. The pretty scheme of substituting œconomy to taxation will not do here; and a war would be a terrible comment upon the abandonment of the Internal Revenue. Yet how is popularity to be preserved with the Western partisans if their interests are tamely sacrificed? Will the artifice be for the Chief to hold a bold language and the subalters to act a public part? Time must explain.

You know my general theory as to our Western affairs. I have always held that the Unity of our empire and the best interests of our Nation require that we should annex to the UStates all the territory East of the Mississippia, New Orleans included. Of course I infer that in an emergency like the present, Energy is Wisdom.

Adieu My Dear Sir  Ever Yrs

A H


Mrs. H joins me in affectionate Compliments to Mrs. Pinckney.

## *To Elizabeth Hamilton*

*March 1803*

I thank you My Betsy for your letter from Fish Kill. I hope the subsequent part of your journey has proved less fatiguing than the two first days.

I have anticipated with dread your interview with your father. I hope your prudence and fortitude have been a match for your sensibility. Remember that the main object of visit is to console him; that his own burthen is sufficient, and that it would be too much to have it increased by the sorrows of his Children.

Arm yourself with resignation. We live in a world full of evil. In the later period of life misfortunes seem to thicken round us; and our duty and our peace both require that we should accustom ourselves to meet disasters with christian fortitude.

Kiss Kitty for me & give my love to Angelica, & all the friends & connections round you.

Adieu My excellent wife.

A H

Your Children are all well. I write your father by this oppy.

## *To Timothy Pickering*

*New York September 16*
*1803*

MY DEAR SIR

I will make no apology for my delay in answering your inquiry some time since made, because I could offer none which would satisfy myself. I pray you only to believe that it proceeded from any thing rather than want of respect or regard. I shall now comply with your request.

The highest toned propositions, which I made in the Convention, were for a President, Senate and Judges during good behaviour—a house of representatives for three years. Though I would have enlarged the Legislative power of the General Government, yet I never contemplated the abolition of the State Governments; but on the contrary, they were, in some particulars, constituent parts of my plan.

This plan was in my conception comformable with the strict theory of a Government purely republican; the essential criteria of which are that the principal organs of the Executive and Legislative departments be elected by the people and hold their offices by a *responsible* and temporary or *defeasible* tenure.

A vote was taken on the proposition respecting the Executive. Five states were in favour of it; among those Virginia; and though from the manner of voting, by delegations, individuals were not distinguished, it was morally certain, from the known situation of the Virginia members (six in number, two of them *Mason* and *Randolph* possessing popular doctrines) that *Madison* must have concurred in the vote of Virginia. Thus, if I sinned against Republicanism, Mr. Madison was not less guilty.

I may truly then say, that I never proposed either a President, or Senate for life, and that I neither recommended nor meditated the annihilation of the State Governments.

And I may add, that in the course of the discussions in the Convention, neither the propositions thrown out for debate, nor even those voted in the earlier stages of deliberation were considered as evidences of a definitive opinion, in the proposer or voter. It appeared to me to be in some sort understood, that with a view to free investigation, experimental propositions might be made, which were to be received merely as suggestions for consideration.

Accordingly, it is a fact, that my final opinion was against an Executive during good behaviour, on account of the increased danger to the public tranquility incident to the election of a Magistrate of this degree of permanency. In the plan of a Constitution, which I drew up, while the convention was sitting & which I communicated to Mr. Madison about the close of it, perhaps a day or two after, the Office of President has no greater duration than for three years.

This plan was predicated upon these bases— 1 That the political principles of the people of this country would endure nothing but republican Government. 2 That in the actual situation of the Country, it was in itself right and proper that the republican theory should have a fair and full trial— 3 That to such a trial it was essential that the

Government should be so constructed as to give it all the energy and stability reconciliable with the principles of that theory. These were the genuine sentiments of my heart, and upon them I acted.

I sincerely hope, that it may not hereafter be discovered, that through want of sufficient attention to the last idea, the experiment of Republican Government, even in this Country, has not been as complete, as satisfactory and as decisive as could be wished.

Very truly  Dear Sir Yr friend & servt

A HAMILTON

## *From Aaron Burr*

*Nyork 18 June 1804*

SIR,

I send for your perusal a letter signed Ch. D. Cooper which, though apparently published some time ago, has but very recently come to my knowledge. Mr Van Ness who does me the favor to deliver this, will point out to you that Clause of the letter to which I particularly request your attention.

You might perceive, Sir, the necessity of a prompt and unqualified acknowledgment or denial of the use of any expressions which could warrant the assertions of Dr Cooper.

I have the honor to be  Your Obt Svt

A. BURR

### Enclosure: Charles D. Cooper to Philip Schuyler

SIR,

The malignant attack which my character has sustained in an anonymous hand-bill, to which your letter of the 21st inst. directed to the chairman of the Federal electioneering committee of this city is annexed; and in which you contradict certain facts contained in a letter, said to have been written by me to ANDREW BROWN, Esq. of Bern, will be my apology for repelling the unfounded aspersions which have been thus dishonorably obtruded on the public. My letter to Mr. Brown was committed to the care of JOHAN J. DEITZ, Esq. of Bern; but to this gentleman, I hope, cannot be imputed the embezzling and breaking open of a letter, a crime which in England has met with the most ignominious punishment.

Admitting the letter published to be an exact transcript of the one intended for Mr. Brown, and which, it seems, instead of being delivered according to promise, was EMBEZZLED and BROKEN OPEN; I aver, that the assertions therein contained are substantially true, and that I can prove them by the most unquestionable testimony. I assert that Gen. HAMILTON and Judge KENT have declared, in substance, that they looked upon Mr. BURR to be a dangerous man, and one who ought not to be trusted with the reins of government. If, Sir, you attended a meeting of federalists, at the city tavern, where Gen. HAMILTON made a speech on the pending election, I might appeal to you for the truth of so much of this assertion as relates to him. I have, however, other evidence to substantiate the fact. With respect to Judge KENT's declaration, I have only to refer to THEODORUS V. W. GRAHAM, Esq. and Mr. JAMES KANE, of this city, whose veracity, I trust, will not be impeached; but should the fact have escaped their recollection, I am not in want of other evidence, equally respectable, to support it. Mr. VAN RENSSELAER, a few days before he left town for New-York, in a conversation with me, declared in substance what I communicated in the letter to Mr. BROWN, as coming from him; and I am perfectly willing to repose myself on his well-known candour for the truth of this declaration.

I asserted, in the letter which has been so disgracefully EMBEZZLED, and the BREAKING OPEN of which must be ranked with the lowest species of villainy, that many of the reflecting federalists would support Judge LEWIS. Will this be considered a rash assertion, when it is known, that two federal gentlemen, high in office in this city, have declared they would vote for him? Judge PENDLETON, of New-York, made the same declaration in this city, under the impression, however, that no federal candidate was to be offered. OLIVER PHELPS, when in this city, on his way to Canandaigua, stated, that Gen. HAMILTON, and about one hundred federalists in New-York, would not vote for Mr. Burr.

It is true, that Judge TAYLER intimated to me, the conversation Mr. VAN RENSSELAER had with him, to which you allude, but it was subsequent to my having written and dispatched the letter for Mr. BROWN.

I beg leave to remark, sir, that the anxiety you discovered, when his Honor the Chancellor was about to be nominated, induced me to believe, that you entertained a bad opinion of Mr. Burr, especially when taken in connection with General Hamilton's harangue at the city tavern; and although I have never suggested that you would act on the one side or the other in this election—yet, presuming on the correctness of your mind, and the reputation you sustain of an upright and exemplary character, I could not suppose you would support a man whom I had reason to believe, you held in the lowest estimation.

It is sufficient for me, on this occasion, to substantiate what I have asserted. I have made it an invariable rule of my life, to be circumspect in relating what I may have heard from others; and in this affair, I feel happy to think, that I have been unusually cautious—for really sir, I could detail to you a still more despicable opinion which General Hamilton has expressed of Mr. Burr.

I cannot conclude, without paying some attention to your friend, Dr. Stringer; I have to regret that this gentleman, so renowned for the Christian virtues, should have consented to dishonour your name, by connecting your letter with an anonymous production, replete with the vilest falsehood and the foulest calumny.

I am, Sir, with due respect,     Your humble servant,

CHARLES D. COOPER.

April 23, 1804.

## *To Aaron Burr*

*New York June 20. 1804*

SIR

I have maturely reflected on the subject of your letter of the 18th instant; and the more I have reflected the more I have become convinced, that I could not, without manifest impropriety, make the avowal or disavowal which you seem to think necessary.

The clause pointed out by Mr. Van Ness is in these terms "I could detail to you a *still more despicable opinion*, which General Hamilton has expressed of Mr. Burr." To endeavour to discover the meaning of this declaration, I was obliged to seek in the antecedent part of the letter, for the opinion to which it referred, as having been already disclosed. I found it in these words "General Hamilton and Judge Kent have declared, *in substance*, that they looked upon Mr. Burr to be *a dangerous man*, and one who *ought not to be trusted with the reins of Government*". The language of Doctor Cooper plainly implies, that he considered this opinion of you, which he attributes to me, as a *despicable* one; but he affirms that I have expressed some other *still more despicable;* without however mentioning to whom, when, or where. 'Tis evident, that the phrase "still more dispicable" admits of infinite shades, from very light to very dark. How am I to judge of the degree intended? Or how shall I annex any precise idea to language so indefinite?

Between Gentlemen, *despicable* and *more despicable* are not worth the pains of a distinction. When therefore you do not interrogate me, as to the opinion which is specifically ascribed to me, I must conclude, that you view it as within the limits, to which the animadversions of political opponents, upon each other, may justifiably extend; and consequently as not warranting the idea of it, which Doctor Cooper appears to entertain. If so, what precise inference could you draw as a guide for your future conduct, were I to acknowlege, that I had expressed an opinion of you, *still more despicable*, than the one which is particularised? How could you be sure, that even this opinion had exceeded the bounds which you would yourself deem admissible between political opponents?

But I forbear further comment on the embarrassment to which the requisition you have made naturally leads. The occasion forbids a more ample illustration, though nothing would be more easy than to pursue it.

Repeating, that I cannot reconcile it with propriety to make the acknowlegement, or denial, you desire—I will add, that I deem it inadmissible, on principle, to consent to be interrogated as to the justness of the *inferences*, which may be drawn by *others*, from whatever I may have said of a political opponent in the course of a fifteen years competition. If there were no other objection to it, this is sufficient, that it would tend to expose my sincerity and delicacy to injurious imputations from every person, who may at any time have conceived the import of my expressions differently from what I may then have intended, or may afterwards recollect.

I stand ready to avow or disavow promptly and explicitly any precise or definite opinion, which I may be charged with having declared of any Gentleman. More than this cannot fitly be expected from me; and especially it cannot reasonably be expected, that I shall enter into an explanation upon a basis so vague as that which you have adopted. I trust, on more reflection, you will see the matter in the same light with me. If not, I can only regret the circumstance, and must abide the consequences.

The publication of Doctor Cooper was never seen by me 'till after the receipt of your letter.

I have the honor to be  Sir  Your obed. servt

A HAMILTON

## From Aaron Burr

Nyork 21 June 1804

SIR

Your letter of the 20th. inst. has been this day received. Having Considered it attentively I regret to find in it nothing of that sincerity and delicacy which you profess to Value.

Political opposition can never absolve Gentlemen from the necessity of a rigid adherence to the laws of honor and the rules of decorum: I neither claim such priviledge nor indulge it in others.

The Common sense of Mankind affixes to the epithet adopted by Dr Cooper the idea of dishonor: it has been publicly applied to me under the Sanction of your name. The question is not whether he has understood the meaning of the word or has used it according to Syntax and with grammatical accuracy, but whether you have authorised this application either directly or by uttering expressions or opinions derogatory to my honor. The time "when" is in your own knowledge, but no way material to me, as the calumny has now first been disclosed so as to become the Subject of my Notice, and as the effect is present and palpable.

Your letter has furnished me with new reasons for requiring a definite reply.

I have the honor to be  sir  your obt st

A. BURR

## *To Aaron Burr*

*New York June 22d. 1804*

Sᴉʀ

Your first letter, in a style too peremptory, made a demand, in my opinion, unprecedented and unwarrantable. My answer, pointing out the embarrassment, gave you an opportunity to take a less exceptionable course. You have not chosen to do it, but by your last letter, received this day, containing expressions indecorous and improper, you have increased the difficulties to explanation, intrinsically incident to the nature of your application.

If by a "definite reply" you mean the direct avowal or disavowal required in your first letter, I have no other answer to give than that which has already been given. If you mean any thing different admitting of greater latitude, it is requisite you should explain.

I have the honor to be Sir Your obed servt.

A Hᴀᴍɪʟᴛᴏɴ

## *From Aaron Burr*

*Nyork June 22d. 1804*

Sᴉʀ

Mr. V Ness has this evening reported to me Verbally that you refuse to answer my last letter, that you consider the course I have taken as intemperate and unnecessary and some other conversation which it is improper that I should notice.

My request to you was in the first instance proposed in a form the most simple in order that you might give to the affair that course to which you might be induced by your temper and your knowledge of facts. I relied with unsuspecting faith that from the frankness of a Soldier and the Candor of a gentleman I might expect an ingenuous declaration; that if, as I had reason to believe, you had used expressions derogatory to my honor, you would have had the Spirit to Maintain or the Magnanimity to retract them, and, that if from your language injurious inferences had been improperly drawn, Sincerity and delicacy would have pointed out to you the propriety of correcting errors which might thus have been widely diffused.

With these impressions, I was greatly disappointed in receiving from you a letter which I could only consider as evasive and which in manner, is not altogether decorus. In one expectation however, I was not wholly deceived, for at the close of your letter I find an intimation, that if I should dislike your refusal to acknowledge or deny the charge, you were ready to meet the consequences. This I deemed a sort of defiance, and I should have been justified if I had chosen to make it the basis of an immediate message: Yet, as you had also said something (though in my opinion unfounded) of the indefiniteness of my request; as I believed that your communication was the offspring, rather of false pride than of reflection, and, as I felt the utmost reluctance to proceed to extremities while any other hope remained, my request was repeated in terms more definite. To this you refuse all reply, reposing, as I am bound to presume on the tender of an alternative insinuated in your letter.

Thus, Sir, you have invited the course I am about to pursue, and now by your silence impose it upon me. If therefore your determinations are final, of which I am not permitted to doubt, Mr. Van Ness is authorised to communicate my further expectations either to yourself or to such friend as you may be pleased to indicate.

I have the honor to be Your Ob st

A. BURR

## Remarks on a Letter from William P. Van Ness

Whether the observations in this letter are designed merely to justify the result, which is indicated in the close of the letter, or may be intended to give an opening for rendering any thing explicit which may have been deemed vague heretofore can only be judged of by the sequel. At any rate it appears to me necessary not to be misunderstood. Mr. Pendleton is therefore authorised to say that in the course of the present discussion, whether written or verbal, there has been no intention to evade defy or insult, but a sincere disposition to avoid extremities, if it could be done with propriety. With this view G H—— has been ready to enter into a frank and free explanation on any and every object of a specific nature; but not to answer a general and abstract enquiry, embracing a period too long for any accurate recollection, and exposing him to unpleasant criticisms from or unpleasant discussions with any and every person, who may have understood him in an unfavourable sense. This (admitting that he could answer in a manner the most satisfactory to Col Burr) he should deem inadmissible, in principle and precedent, and humiliating in practice. To this therefore he can never submit. Frequent allusion has been made to slanders said to be in circulation. Whether this be openly or in whispers they have a form and shape and might be specified.

If the alternative alluded to in the close of the letter is definitively tendered, it must be accepted, the time place and manner to be afterwards regulated. I should not think it right in the midst of a circuit Court to withdraw my services from those who may have confided important interests to me and expose them to the embarrassment of seeking other counsel who may not have time to be sufficiently instructed in their causes. I shall also want a little time to make some arrangements respecting my own affairs.

*June 28, 1804*

## *Alexander Hamilton's Explanation of His Financial Situation*

*New York, July 1, 1804*

Herewith is a general statement of my pecuniary affairs; in which there can be no material error. The result is that calculating my property at what it stands me in, I am now worth about Ten thousand pounds, and that estimating according to what my lands are now selling for and are likely to fetch, the surplus beyond my debts may fairly be stated at nearly double that sum. Yet I am pained to be obliged to entertain doubts whether, if an accident should happen to me, by which the sales of my property should come to be forced, it would be even sufficient to pay my debts.

In a situation like this, it is perhaps due to my reputation to explain why I have made so considerable an establishment in the country. This explanation shall be submitted.

To men, who have been so much harassed in the busy world as

myself, it is natural to look forward to a comfortable retirement, in the sequel of life, as a principal desideratum. This desire I have felt in the strongest manner; and to prepare for it has latterly been a favourite object. I thought that I might not only expect to accomplish the object, but might reasonably aim at it and pursue the preparatory measures, from the following considerations.

It has been for some time past pretty well ascertained to my mind, that the emoluments of my profession would prove equal to the maintenance of my family and the gradual discharge of my debts, within a period to the end of which my faculties, for business might be expected to extend, in full energy. I think myself warranted to estimate the annual product of those emoluments at Twelve* Dollars at the least. My expences while the first improvements of my country establishment were going on have been great; but they would this summer and fall reach the point, at which it is my intention they should stop, at least 'till I should be better able than at present to add to them; and after a fair examination founded upon an actual account of my expenditures, I am persuaded that a plan I have contemplated for the next and succeeding years would bring my expences of every kind within the compass of four thousand Dollars yearly, exclusive of the interest of my country establishment. To this limit, I have been resolved to reduce them, even though it should be necessary to lease that establishment for a few years.

In the mean time, my lands now in a course of sale & settlement would accelerate the extinguishment of my debt, and in the end leave me a handsome clear property. It was also allowable for me to take into view, collaterally, the expectations of my wife; which have been of late partly realised. She is now intitled to a property of between two and three thousand pounds (as I compute) by descent from her mother; and her father is understood to possess a large estate. I feel all the delicacy of this allusion; but the occasion I trust will plead my excuse. And that venerable father, I am sure, will pardon. He knows well all the nicety of my past conduct.

Viewing the matter in these different aspects, I trust the opinion of candid men will be, that there has been no impropriety in my conduct; especially when it is taken into the calculation that my Country establishment, though costly, promises, by the progressive rise of

* "Thousand" likely omitted in error. —ED.

property on this Island, and the felicity of its situation to become more and more valuable.

My chief apology is due to those friends, who have from mere kindness, indorsed my paper discounted at the Banks. On mature reflection I have thought it justifiable to secure them in preference to other Creditors, lest perchance there should be *a deficit*. Yet while this may save them from eventual loss, it will not exempt them from some present inconvenience. As to this I can only throw myself upon their kindness, and entreat the indulgence of the Banks for them. Perhaps this request may be supposed intitled to some regard.

In the event, which would bring this paper to the public eye, one thing at least would be put beyond a doubt. This is, that my public labours have amounted to an absolute sacrifice of the interests of my family—and that in all pecuniary concerns the delicacy, no less than the probity of my conduct in public stations, has been such as to defy even the shadow of a question.

Indeed, I have not enjoyed the ordinary advantages incident to my military services. Being a member of Congress, while the question of the commutation of the half pay of the army in a sum in gross was in debate, delicacy and a desire to be useful to the army, by removing the idea of my having an interest in the question, induced me to write to the Secretary of War and relinquish my claim to half pay; which, or the equivalent, I have accordingly never received. Neither have I ever applied for the lands allowed by the United States to Officers of my rank. Nor did I ever obtain from this state the allowance of lands made to officers of similar rank. It is true that having served through the latter period of the War on the general staff of the UStates and not in the line of this State. I could not claim that allowance as a matter of course. But having before the War resided in this State and having entered the military career at the head of a company of Artillery raised for the particular defence of this State, I had better pretensions to the allowance than others to whom it was actually made—Yet has it not been extended to me.

A H

## *To Eliʒabeth Hamilton*

This letter, my very dear Eliza, will not be delivered to you, unless I shall first have terminated my earthly career; to begin, as I humbly hope from redeeming grace and divine mercy, a happy immortality.

If it had been possible for me to have avoided the interview, my love for you and my precious children would have been alone a decisive motive. But it was not possible, without sacrifices which would have rendered me unworthy of your esteem. I need not tell you of the pangs I feel, from the idea of quitting you and exposing you to the anguish which I know you would feel. Nor could I dwell on the topic lest it should unman me.

The consolations of Religion, my beloved, can alone support you; and these you have a right to enjoy. Fly to the bosom of your God and be comforted. With my last idea; I shall cherish the sweet hope of meeting you in a better world.

Adieu best of wives and best of Women. Embrace all my darling Children for me.

Ever yours

A H

*July 4. 1804*

## *Statement on Impending Duel with Aaron Burr*

On my expected interview with Col Burr, I think it proper to make some remarks explanatory of my conduct, motives and views.

I am certainly desirous of avoiding this interview, for the most cogent reasons.

1    My religious and moral principles are strongly opposed to the practice of Duelling, and it would even give me pain to be obliged to shed the blood of a fellow creature in a private combat forbidden by the laws.

2    My wife and Children are extremely dear to me, and my life is of the utmost importance to them, in various views.

3  I feel a sense of obligation towards my creditors; who in case of accident to me, by the forced sale of my property, may be in some degree sufferers. I did not think my self at liberty, as a man of probity, lightly to expose them to this hazard.

4  I am conscious of no *ill-will* to Col Burr, distinct from political opposition, which, as I trust, has proceeded from pure and upright motives.

Lastly, I shall hazard much, and can possibly gain nothing by the issue of the interview.

But it was, as I conceive, impossible for me to avoid it. There were *intrinsick* difficulties in the thing, and *artificial* embarrassments, from the manner of proceeding on the part of Col Burr.

Intrinsick—because it is not to be denied, that my animadversions on the political principles character and views of Col Burr have been extremely severe, and on different occasions, I, in common with many others, have made very unfavourable criticisms on particular instances of the private conduct of this Gentleman.

In proportion as these impressions were entertained with sincerity and uttered with motives and for purposes, which might appear to me commendable, would be the difficulty (until they could be removed by evidence of their being erroneous), of explanation or apology. The disavowal required of me by Col Burr, in a general and indefinite form, was out of my power, if it had really been proper for me to submit to be so questionned; but I was sincerely of opinion, that this could not be, and in this opinion, I was confirmed by that of a very moderate and judicious friend whom I consulted. Besides that Col Burr appeared to me to assume, in the first instance, a tone unnecessarily peremptory and menacing, and in the second, positively offensive. Yet I wished, as far as might be practicable, to leave a door open to accommodation. This, I think, will be inferred from the written communications made by me and by my direction, and would be confirmed by the conversations between Mr van Ness and myself, which arose out of the subject.

I am not sure, whether under all the circumstances I did not go further in the attempt to accommodate, than a punctilious delicacy will justify. If so, I hope the motives I have stated will excuse me.

It is not my design, by what I have said to affix any odium on the conduct of Col Burr, in this case. He doubtless has heared of animadversions of mine which bore very hard upon him; and it is probable that as usual they were accompanied with some falshoods. He may have supposed himself under a necessity of acting as he has done. I hope the grounds of his proceeding have been such as ought to satisfy his own conscience.

I trust, at the same time, that the world will do me the Justice to believe, that I have not censured him on light grounds, or from unworthy inducements. I certainly have had strong reasons for what I may have said, though it is possible that in some particulars, I may have been influenced by misconstruction or misinformation. It is also my ardent wish that I may have been more mistaken than I think I have been, and that he by his future conduct may shew himself worthy of all confidence and esteem, and prove an ornament and blessing to his Country.

As well because it is possible that I may have injured Col Burr, however convinced myself that my opinions and declarations have been well founded, as from my general principles and temper in relation to similar affairs—I have resolved, if our interview is conducted in the usual manner, and it pleases God to give me the opportunity, to *reserve* and *throw away* my first fire, and I *have thoughts* even of *reserving* my second fire—and thus giving a double opportunity to Col Burr to pause and to reflect.

It is not however my intention to enter into any explanations on the ground. Apology, from principle I hope, rather than Pride, is out of the question.

To those, who with me abhorring the practice of Duelling may think that I ought on no account to have added to the number of bad examples—I answer that my *relative* situation, as well in public as private aspects, enforcing all the considerations which constitute what men of the world denominate honor, impressed on me (as I thought) a peculiar necessity not to decline the call. The ability to be in future useful, whether in resisting mischief or effecting good, in those crises of our public affairs, which seem likely to happen, would probably be inseparable from a conformity with public prejudice in this particular.

AH
*c. July 10, 1804*

# To Theodore Sedgwick

*New York July 10. 1804*

MY DEAR SIR

I have received two letters from you since we last saw each other— that of the latest date being the 24 of May. I have had in hand for some time a long letter to you, explaining my view of the course and tendency of our Politics, and my intentions as to my own future conduct. But my plan embraced so large a range that owing to much avocation, some indifferent health, and a growing distaste for Politics, the letter is still considerably short of being finished. I write this now to satisfy you, that want of regard for you has not been the cause of my silence.

I will here express but one sentiment, which is, that Dismemberment of our Empire will be a clear sacrifice of great positive advantages, without any counterballancing good; administering no relief to our real Disease; which is DEMOCRACY, the poison of which by a subdivision will only be the more concentered in each part, and consequently the more virulent.

*King* is on his way for Boston where you may chance to see him, and hear from himself his sentiments.

God bless you

A H

# To Elizabeth Hamilton

MY BELOVED ELIZA

Mrs. Mitchel is the person in the world to whom as a friend I am under the greatest Obligations. I have not hitherto done my duty to her. But resolved to repair my omission as much as possible, I have encouraged her to come to this Country and intend, if it shall be in my power to render the Evening of her days comfortable. But if it shall please God to put this out of my power and to inable you hereafter to be of service to her, I entreat you to do it and to treat her with the tenderness of a Sister.

This is my second letter.

The Scruples of a Christian have determined me to expose my own life to any extent rather than subject my self to the guilt of taking the life of another. This must increase my hazards & redoubles my pangs for you. But you had rather I should die innocent than live guilty. Heaven can preserve me and I humbly hope will but in the contrary event, I charge you to remember that you are a Christian. God's Will be done. The will of a merciful God must be good.

Once more Adieu My Darling darling Wife

A H
Tuesday Evening 10 oClock
*July 10, 1804*

## *Joint Statement by William P. Van Ness and Nathaniel Pendleton on the Duel*

Col: Burr arrived first on the ground as had been previously agreed. When Genl Hamilton arrived the parties exchanged salutations and the Seconds proceeded to make their arrangments. They measured the distance, ten full paces, and cast lots for the choice of positions as also to determine by whom the word should be given, both of which fell to the Second of Genl Hamilton. They then proceeded to load the pistols in each others presence, after which the parties took their stations. The Gentleman who was to give the word, then explained to the parties the rules which were to govern them in firing which were as follows: The parties being placed at their stations The Second who gives the word shall ask them whether they are ready—being answered in the affirmative, he shall say "*present*" after which the parties shall present & fire when they please. If one fires before the other the opposite second shall say one two, three, fire, and he shall fire or loose his fire. And asked if they were prepared, being answered in the affirmative he gave the word *present* as had been agreed on, and both of the parties took aim, & fired in succession, the Intervening time is not expressed as the seconds do not precisely agree on that point. The pistols were discharged within a few seconds of each other and the fire of Col: Burr took effect; Genl Hamilton almost instantly fell. Col: Burr then advanced toward Genl H———n with a manner and gesture that appeared to Genl Hamilton's friend to be expressive of regret, but without Speaking turned about

& withdrew. Being urged from the field by his friend as has been subsequently stated, with a view to prevent his being recognised by the Surgeon and Bargemen who were then approaching. No farther communications took place between the principals and the Barge that carried Col: Burr immediately returned to the City. We conceive it proper to add that the conduct of the parties in that interview was perfectly proper as suited the occasion.

*July 17, 1804*

## Nathaniel Pendleton's Amendments to the Joint Statement

The statement containing the facts that led to the interview between General Hamilton and Col. Burr, published in the Evening Post on Monday, studiously avoided mentioning any particulars of what past at the place of meeting. This was dictated by suitable considerations at the time, and with the intention, that whatever it might be deemed proper to lay before the public, should be made the subject of a future communication. The following is therefore now submitted.

In the interviews that have since taken place between the gentlemen that were present, they have not been able to agree in two important facts that passed there—for which reason nothing was said on those subjects in the paper lately published as to other particulars in which they were agreed.

Mr. P. expressed a confident opinion that General Hamilton did not fire first—and that he did not fire at all *at Col. Burr*. Mr. V. N. seemed equally confident in the opinion that Gen. H. did fire first—and of course that it must have been *at* his antagonist.

General Hamilton's friend thinks it to be a sacred duty he owes to the memory of that exalted man, to his country, and his friends, to publish to the world such facts and circumstances as have produced a decisive conviction in his own mind, that he cannot have been mistaken in the belief he has formed on these points.

1st. Besides the testimonies of Bishop Moore, and the paper containing an express declaration, under General Hamilton's own hand, enclosed to his friend in a packet, not to be delivered but in the event of his death, and which have already been published, General

Hamilton informed Mr. P. at least ten days previous to the affair, that he had doubts whether he would not receive and not return Mr. Burr's first fire. Mr. P. remonstrated against this determination, and urged many considerations against it, as dangerous to himself and not necessary in the particular case, when every ground of accommodation, not humiliating, had been proposed and rejected. He said he would not decide lightly, but take time to deliberate fully. It was incidentally mentioned again at their occasional subsequent conversations, and on the evening preceding the time of the appointed interview, he informed Mr. P. he had made up his mind *not to fire at Col. Burr the first time, but to receive his fire, and fire in the air.* Mr. P. again urged him upon this subject, and repeated his former arguments. His final answer was in terms that made an impression on Mr. P's mind which can never be effaced. "My friend, it is the effect of A RELIGIOUS SCRUPLE, and does not admit of reasoning, it is useless to say more on the subject, as my purpose is definitely fixed."

2d. His last words before he was wounded afford a proof that this purpose had not changed. When he received his pistol, after having taken his position, he was asked if he would have the hair spring set? His answer was, *"Not this time."*

3d. After he was wounded, and laid in the boat, the first words he uttered after recovering the power of speech, were, (addressing himself to a gentleman present, who perfectly well remembers it) *"Pendleton knows I did not mean to fire at Col. Burr the first time."*

4th. This determination had been communicated by Mr. P. to that gentleman that morning, before they left the city.

5th. The pistol that had been used by General Hamilton, lying loose over the other apparatus in the case which was open; after having been some time in the boat, one of the boatmen took hold of it to put it into the case. General Hamilton observing this, said *"Take care of that pistol—it is cocked. It may go off and do mischief."* This is also remembered by the gentleman alluded to.

This shews he was not sensible of having fired at all. If he had fired *previous* to receiving the wound, he would have remembered it, and therefore have known that the pistol could not go off; but if *afterwards* it must have been the effect of an involuntary exertion of the muscles produced by a mortal wound, in which case, he could not have been conscious of having fired.

6. Mr. P. having so strong a conviction that if General Hamilton had fired first, it could not have escaped his attention (all his anxiety being alive for the effect of the first fire, and having no reason to believe the friend of Col. Burr was not sincere in the contrary opinion) he determined to go to the spot where the affair took place, to see if he could not discover some traces of the course of the ball from Gen. Hamilton's pistol.

He took a friend with him the day after General Hamilton died, and after some examination they fortunately found what they were in search of. They ascertained that the ball passed through the limb of a cedar tree, at an elevation of about twelve feet and a half, perpendicularly from the ground, between thirteen and fourteen feet from the mark on which General Hamilton stood, and about four feet wide of the direct line between him and Colonel Burr, on the right side; he having fallen on the left. The part of the limb through which the ball passed was cut off and brought to this city, and is now in Mr. Church's possession.

No inferences are pointed out as resulting from these facts, nor will any comments be made. They are left to the candid judgment and feelings of the public.

*July 19, 1804*

## William P. Van Ness's Amendments to the Joint Statement

The second of G H having considered it proper to subjoin an explanatory note to the statement mutually furnished, it becomes proper for the gentleman who attended Col Burr to state also his impressions with respect to those points on which their exists a variance of opinion. In doing this he pointedly disclaims any idea disrespectful to the memory of G H, or an intention to ascribe any conduct to him that is not in his opinion perfectly honorable & correct.

The parties met as has been above related & took their respective stations as directed: the pistols were then handed to them by the seconds. Gen Hamilton elevated his, as if to try the light, & lowering it said I beg pardon for delaying you but the direction of the light renders it necessary, at the same time feeling his pockets with his left hand, & drawing forth his spectacles put them on. The second then asked if they were prepared which was replied to in the affirmative. The word *present* was then given, on which both parties took aim. The pistol of General Hamilton was first discharged, and Col Burr fired immediately after, only five or six seconds of time intervening. On this point the second of Col Burr has full & perfect reccollection. He noticed particularly the discharge of G H's pistol, & looked to his principal to ascertain whether he was hurt, he then clearly saw Col Bs pistol discharged. At this moment of looking at Col B on the discharge of G H's pistol he perceived a slight motion in his person, which induced the idea of his being struck. On this point he conversed with his principal on their return, who ascribed that circumstance to a small stone under his foot, & observed that the smoke of G Hs pistol obscured him for a moment in the interval of their firing.

When G H fell Col B advanced toward him as stated & was checked by his second who urged the importance of his immediately repairing to the barge, conceiving that G H was mortally wounded, & being desirous to secure his principal from the sight of the surgeon & bargemen who might be called in evidence. Col B complied with his request.

He shortly followed him to the boat, and Col B again expressed a wish to return, saying with an expression of much concern, I must go & speak to him. I again urged the obvious impropriety stating that the G was surrounded by the Surgeon & Bargemen by whom he must not be seen & insisted on immediate departure.

*July 21, 1804*

# Word Cloud Classics

# Word Cloud Classics

*Les Misérables*

*Little Women*

*Madame Bovary*

*Mansfield Park*

*The Merry Adventures of
Robin Hood*

*Moby-Dick*

*My Ántonia*

*Narrative of the Life of Frederick
Douglass and Other Works*

*Northanger Abbey*

*Odyssey*

*Persuasion*

*Peter Pan*

*The Phantom of the Opera*

*The Picture of Dorian Gray*

*The Poetry of Emily Dickinson*

*Pride and Prejudice*

*The Prince and Other Writings*

*The Red Badge of Courage
and Other Stories*

*The Romantic Poets*

*The Scarlet Letter*

*The Secret Garden*

*Selected Works of
Alexander Hamilton*

*Sense and Sensibility*

*Shakespeare's Sonnets and
Other Poems*

*Strange Case of Dr. Jekyll and
Mr. Hyde & Other Stories*

*Tarzan of the Apes &
The Return of Tarzan*

*The Three Musketeers*

*Treasure Island*

*Twenty Thousand Leagues
Under the Sea*

*Uncle Tom's Cabin, or Life
Among the Lowly*

*The U.S. Constitution and Other
Key American Writings*

*Walden and Civil Disobedience*

*The Wizard of Oz*

*Wuthering Heights*

permit me, as I intend

left Philadelphia. In a

it I was desirous ~~of~~ know

with regard to military

was any thing worth y

of which at the time I co

but I wished to underst

to you, with a view to t

to be seriously engaged in

compliment to you to

men who must be in

we shall want ~~one~~ men wh

but will do it with an

General Gunn

# The
# U.S. Constitution
# and Other Key
# American Writings

# The
# U.S. Constitution
# and Other Key
# American Writings

**Word Cloud Classics**
San Diego

Canterbury Classics
An imprint of Printers Row Publishing Group
10350 Barnes Canyon Road, Suite 100, San Diego, CA 92121
www.canterburyclassicsbooks.com • mail@canterburyclassicsbooks.com

Printers Row Publishing Group is a division of Readerlink Distribution Services, LLC. The Canterbury Classics and Word Cloud Classics names and logos are registered trademarks of Readerlink Distribution Services, LLC.

All correspondence concerning the content of this book should be addressed to Canterbury Classics, Editorial Department, at the above address.

*Albert Einstein's letter to Franklin D. Roosevelt is reprinted with permission from the Franklin D. Roosevelt Presidential Library and Museum, Hyde Park, New York.*

Publisher: Peter Norton
Associate Publisher: Ana Parker
Publishing/Editorial Team: April Farr, Kathryn C. Dalby
Editorial Team: JoAnn Padgett, Melinda Allman, Traci Douglas
Production/Design Team: Jonathan Lopes, Rusty von Dyl, Lidija Tomas

Spine art: Gettyimages/eyewave (statue), Gettyimages/clipartdotcom (flag)

ISBN: 978-1-64517-084-6
Printed in China
23 22 21 20 19  1 2 3 4 5

# CONTENTS

# THE MAYFLOWER COMPACT (1620)

*The Mayflower Compact was the governing charter of the English colony at Plymouth in Massachusetts. John Carver, who helped to organize the* Mayflower *voyage and became the colony's first governor, likely wrote the compact, and it was signed by the colony's forty-one free, adult men.*

In the name of God, Amen. We, whose names are underwritten, the Loyal Subjects of our dread Sovereigne Lord, King James, by the Grace of God, of Great Britaine, France, and Ireland, King, Defender of the Faith, etc.

Having undertaken for the Glory of God, and Advancement of the Christian Faith, and the Honour of our King and Country, a Voyage to plant the first colony in the Northerne Parts of Virginia; doe, by these Presents, solemnly and mutually in the Presence of God and one of another, covenant and combine ourselves together into a civill Body Politick, for our better Ordering and Preservation, and Furtherance of the Ends aforesaid; And by Virtue hereof do enact, constitute, and frame, such just and equall Laws, Ordinances, Acts, Constitutions, and Offices, from time to time, as shall be thought most meete and convenient for the Generall Good of the Colony; unto which we promise all due Submission and Obedience.

In Witness whereof we have hereunto subscribed our names at Cape Cod the eleventh of November, in the Raigne of our Sovereigne Lord, King James of England, France, and Ireland, the eighteenth, and of Scotland, the fiftie-fourth, Anno. Domini, 1620.

# "GIVE ME LIBERTY, OR GIVE ME DEATH!" (1775)

*Founding Father Patrick Henry delivered this rousing speech to encourage the colony of Virginia to send troops to fight in the Revolutionary War. He was successful and in 1784 became the first governor of the new state of Virginia.*

## ST. JOHN'S CHURCH
## RICHMOND, VIRGINIA

No man thinks more highly than I do of the patriotism, as well as abilities, of the very worthy gentlemen who have just addressed the House. But different men often see the same subject in different lights; and, therefore, I hope it will not be thought disrespectful to those gentlemen if, entertaining as I do, opinions of a character very opposite to theirs, I shall speak forth my sentiments freely, and without reserve. This is no time for ceremony. The question before the House is one of awful moment to this country. For my own part, I consider it as nothing less than a question of freedom or slavery; and in proportion to the magnitude of the subject ought to be the freedom of the debate. It is only in this way that we can hope to arrive at truth, and fulfill the great responsibility which we hold to God and our country. Should I keep back my opinions at such a time, through fear of giving offence, I should consider myself as guilty of treason towards my country, and of an act of disloyalty toward the majesty of heaven, which I revere above all earthly kings.

Mr. President, it is natural to man to indulge in the illusions of hope. We are apt to shut our eyes against a painful truth, and listen to the song of that siren till she transforms us into beasts. Is this the part of wise men, engaged in a great and arduous struggle for liberty? Are we disposed to be of the number of those who, having eyes, see not, and, having ears, hear not, the things which so nearly concern their temporal salvation? For my part, whatever anguish of spirit it may cost, I am willing to know the whole truth; to know the worst, and to provide for it.

I have but one lamp by which my feet are guided; and that is the lamp of experience. I know of no way of judging of the future but by the past. And judging by the past, I wish to know what there has been in the conduct of the British ministry for the last ten years, to justify those hopes with which gentlemen have been pleased to solace themselves, and the House. Is it that insidious smile with which our petition has been lately received? Trust it not, sir; it will prove a snare to your feet. Suffer not yourselves to be betrayed with a kiss. Ask yourselves how this gracious reception of our petition comports with these war-like preparations which cover our waters and darken our land. Are fleets and armies necessary to a work of love and reconciliation? Have we shown ourselves so unwilling to be reconciled, that force must be called in to win back our love? Let us not deceive ourselves, sir. These are the implements of war and subjugation; the last arguments to which kings resort. I ask, gentlemen, sir, what means this martial array, if its purpose be not to force us to submission? Can gentlemen assign any other possible motive for it? Has Great Britain any enemy, in this quarter of the world, to call for all this accumulation of navies and armies? No, sir, she has none. They are meant for us; they can be meant for no other. They are sent over to bind and rivet upon us those chains which the British ministry have been so long forging. And what have we to oppose to them? Shall we try argument? Sir, we have been trying that for the last ten years. Have we anything new to offer upon the subject? Nothing. We have held the subject up in every light of which it is capable; but it has been all in vain. Shall we resort to entreaty and humble supplication? What terms shall we find which have not been already exhausted? Let us not, I beseech you, sir, deceive ourselves. Sir, we have done everything that could be done to avert the storm which is now coming on. We have petitioned; we have remonstrated; we have supplicated; we have prostrated ourselves before the throne, and have implored its interposition to arrest the tyrannical hands of the ministry and Parliament. Our petitions have been slighted; our remonstrances have produced additional violence and insult; our supplications have been disregarded; and we have been spurned, with contempt, from the foot of the throne. In vain, after these things, may we indulge the fond hope of peace and reconciliation. There is no longer any room for hope. If we wish to be free if we mean to preserve inviolate those inestimable privileges for which we have been so long contending if we mean not basely to abandon the noble struggle in which we have been so long engaged, and which we have pledged ourselves never to abandon until the glorious object of our contest shall be obtained, we must fight! I repeat it, sir, we must fight! An appeal to arms and to the God of Hosts is all that is left us!

They tell us, sir, that we are weak; unable to cope with so formidable an adversary. But when shall we be stronger? Will it be the next week, or the next year? Will it be when we are totally disarmed, and when a British guard shall be stationed in every house? Shall we gather strength by irresolution and inaction? Shall we acquire the means of effectual resistance, by lying supinely on our backs, and hugging the delusive phantom of hope, until our enemies shall have bound us hand and foot? Sir, we are not weak if we make a proper use of those means which the God of nature hath placed in our power. Three millions of people, armed in the holy cause of liberty, and in such a country as that which we possess, are invincible by any force which our enemy can send against us. Besides, sir, we shall not fight our battles alone. There is a just God who presides over the destinies of nations; and who will raise up friends to fight our battles for us. The battle, sir, is not to the strong alone; it is to the vigilant, the active, the brave. Besides, sir, we have no election. If we were base enough to desire it, it is now too late to retire from the contest. There is no retreat but in submission and slavery! Our chains are forged! Their clanking may be heard on the plains of Boston! The war is inevitable—and let it come! I repeat it, sir, let it come!

It is in vain, sir, to extenuate the matter. Gentlemen may cry, "Peace, Peace"—but there is no peace. The war is actually begun! The next gale that sweeps from the north will bring to our ears the clash of resounding arms! Our brethren are already in the field! Why stand we here idle? What is it that gentlemen wish? What would they have? Is life so dear, or peace so sweet, as to be purchased at the price of chains and slavery? Forbid it, Almighty God! I know not what course others may take; but as for me, give me liberty or give me death!

# THE DECLARATION OF INDEPENDENCE (1776)

## IN CONGRESS, JULY 4, 1776

### THE UNANIMOUS DECLARATION OF THE THIRTEEN UNITED STATES OF AMERICA

When in the Course of human events, it becomes necessary for one people to dissolve the political bands which have connected them with another, and to assume, among the Powers of the earth, the separate and equal station to which the Laws of Nature and of Nature's God entitle them, a decent respect to the opinions of mankind requires that they should declare the causes which impel them to the separation.

We hold these truths to be self-evident, that all men are created equal, that they are endowed by their Creator with certain unalienable Rights, that among these are Life, Liberty, and the pursuit of Happiness. That to secure these rights, Governments are instituted among Men, deriving their just powers from the consent of the governed, That whenever any Form of Government becomes destructive of these ends, it is the Right of the People to alter or to abolish it, and to institute new Government, laying its foundation on such principles and organizing its powers in such form, as to them shall seem most likely to effect their Safety and Happiness. Prudence, indeed, will dictate that Governments long established should not be changed for light and transient causes; and accordingly all experience hath shown, that mankind are more disposed to suffer, while evils are sufferable, than to right themselves by abolishing the forms to which they are accustomed. But when a long train of abuses and usurpations, pursuing invariably the same Object evinces a design to reduce them under absolute Despotism, it is their right, it is their duty, to throw off such Government, and to provide new Guards for their future security.—Such has been the patient sufferance of these Colonies; and such is now the necessity which constrains them to alter their former Systems of Government. The history of the present King of Great Britain is a history of repeated injuries and usurpations, all having in direct object the establishment of an absolute Tyranny over these States. To prove this, let Facts be submitted to a candid world.

He has refused his Assent to Laws, the most wholesome and necessary for the public good.

He has forbidden his Governors to pass Laws of immediate and pressing importance, unless suspended in their operation till his Assent should be obtained; and when so suspended, he has utterly neglected to attend to them.

He has refused to pass other Laws for the accommodation of large districts of people, unless those people would relinquish the right of Representation in the Legislature, a right inestimable to them and formidable to tyrants only.

He has called together legislative bodies at places unusual, uncomfortable, and distant from the depository of their Public Records, for the sole purpose of fatiguing them into compliance with his measures.

He has dissolved Representative Houses repeatedly, for opposing with manly firmness his invasions on the rights of the people.

He has refused for a long time, after such dissolutions, to cause others to be elected; whereby the Legislative Powers, incapable of Annihilation, have returned to the People at large for their exercise; the State remaining in the mean time exposed to all the dangers of invasion from without, and convulsions within.

He has endeavoured to prevent the population of these States; for that purpose obstructing the Laws of Naturalization of Foreigners; refusing to pass others to encourage their migration hither, and raising the conditions of new Appropriations of Lands.

He has obstructed the Administration of Justice, by refusing his Assent to Laws for establishing Judiciary Powers.

He has made judges dependent on his Will alone, for the tenure of their offices, and the amount and payment of their salaries.

He has erected a multitude of New Offices, and sent hither swarms of Officers to harass our People, and eat out their substance.

He has kept among us, in times of peace, Standing Armies without the Consent of our legislatures.

He has affected to render the Military independent of and superior to the Civil Power.

He has combined with others to subject us to a jurisdiction foreign to our constitution, and unacknowledged by our laws; giving his Assent to their Acts of pretended legislation:

For quartering large bodies of armed troops among us:

For protecting them, by a mock Trial, from Punishment for any Murders which they should commit on the Inhabitants of these States:

For cutting off our Trade with all parts of the world:

For imposing taxes on us without our Consent:

For depriving us, in many cases, of the benefits of Trial by Jury:

For transporting us beyond Seas to be tried for pretended offences:

For abolishing the free System of English Laws in a neighbouring Province, establishing therein an Arbitrary government, and enlarging its Boundaries so as to render it at once an example and fit instrument for introducing the same absolute rule into these Colonies:

For taking away our Charters, abolishing our most valuable Laws, and altering fundamentally the Forms of our Governments:

For suspending our own Legislatures, and declaring themselves invested with Power to legislate for us in all cases whatsoever.

He has abdicated Government here, by declaring us out of his Protection and waging War against us.

He has plundered our seas, ravaged our Coasts, burnt our towns, and destroyed the lives of our people.

He is at this time transporting large armies of foreign mercenaries to compleat the works of death, desolation and tyranny, already begun with circumstances of Cruelty & perfidy scarcely paralleled in the most barbarous ages, and totally unworthy of the Head of a civilized nation.

He has constrained our fellow Citizens taken Captive on the high Seas to bear Arms against their Country, to become the executioners of their friends and Brethren, or to fall themselves by their Hands.

He has excited domestic insurrections amongst us, and has endeavoured to bring on the inhabitants of our frontiers, the merciless Indian Savages, whose known rule of warfare, is an undistinguished destruction of all ages, sexes and conditions.

In every stage of these Oppressions We have Petitioned for Redress in the most humble terms: Our repeated Petitions have been answered only by repeated injury. A Prince, whose character is thus marked by every act which may define a Tyrant, is unfit to be the ruler of a free People.

Nor have We been wanting in attention to our British brethren. We have warned them from time to time of attempts by their legislature to extend an unwarrantable jurisdiction over us. We have reminded them of the circumstances of our emigration and settlement here. We have appealed to their native justice and magnanimity, and we have conjured them by the ties of our common kindred to disavow these usurpations, which would inevitably interrupt our connections and correspondence. They too have been deaf to the voice of justice and of consanguinity.

We must, therefore, acquiesce in the necessity, which denounces our Separation, and hold them, as we hold the rest of mankind, Enemies in War, in Peace Friends.

We, therefore, the Representatives of the United States of America, in General Congress, Assembled, appealing to the Supreme Judge of the world for the rectitude of our intentions, do, in the Name, and by the Authority of the good People of these Colonies, solemnly publish and declare, That these United Colonies are, and of Right ought to be Free and Independent States; that they are Absolved from all Allegiance to the British Crown, and that all political connection between them and the State of Great Britain, is and ought to be totally dissolved; and that as Free and Independent States, they have full Power to levy War, conclude Peace, contract Alliances, establish Commerce, and to do all other Acts and Things which Independent States may of right do. And for the support of this Declaration, with a firm reliance on the Protection of Divine Providence, we mutually pledge to each other our Lives, our Fortunes and our sacred Honor.

MASSACHUSETTS:
John Hancock
Samuel Adams
John Adams
Robert Treat Paine
Elbridge Gerry

NEW YORK:
William Floyd
Philip Livingston
Francis Lewis
Lewis Morris

NEW JERSEY:
Richard Stockton
John Witherspoon
Francis Hopkinson
John Hart
Abraham Clark

PENNSYLVANIA:
Robert Morris
Benjamin Rush
Benjamin Franklin
John Morton
George Clymer
James Smith
George Taylor
James Wilson
George Ross

VIRGINIA:
George Wythe
Richard Henry Lee
Thomas Jefferson
Benjamin Harrison
Thomas Nelson, Jr.
Francis Lightfoot Lee
Carter Braxton

MARYLAND:
Samuel Chase
William Paca
Thomas Stone
Charles Carroll of Carrollton

DELAWARE:
Caesar Rodney
George Read
Thomas McKean

NEW HAMPSHIRE:
Josiah Bartlett
William Whipple
Matthew Thornton

CONNECTICUT:
Roger Sherman
Samuel Huntington
William Williams
Oliver Wolcott

RHODE ISLAND:
Stephen Hopkins
William Ellery

NORTH CAROLINA:
William Hooper
Joseph Hewes
John Penn

SOUTH CAROLINA:
Edward Rutledge
Thomas Heyward, Jr.
Thomas Lynch, Jr.
Arthur Middleton

GEORGIA:
Button Gwinnett
Lyman Hall
George Walton

# ARTICLES OF CONFEDERATION AND PERPETUAL UNION (PASSED 1777; RATIFIED 1781)

*The Articles of Confederation was the first document that detailed the rights, responsibilities, and powers of the newly independent thirteen American colonies. The Articles of Confederation proved not to be strong enough, though, and was ultimately replaced by the United States Constitution.*

Articles of Confederation and Perpetual Union between the States of New Hampshire, Massachusetts Bay, Rhode Island and Providence Plantations, Connecticut, New York, New Jersey, Pennsylvania, Delaware, Maryland, Virginia, North Carolina, South Carolina, and Georgia.

ARTICLE I. The Stile of this confederacy shall be, "The United States of America."

ART. II. Each state retains its sovereignty, freedom and independence, and every power, jurisdiction and right, which is not by this confederation expressly delegated to the United States, in Congress assembled.

ART. III. The said states hereby severally enter into a firm league of friendship with each other, for their common defence, the security of their liberties, and their mutual and general welfare, binding themselves to assist each other, against all force offered to, or attacks made upon them, or any of them, on account of religion, sovereignty, trade, or any other pretence whatever.

ART. IV. The better to secure and perpetuate mutual friendship and intercourse among the people of the different states in this union, the free inhabitants of each of these states, paupers, vagabonds and fugitives from justice excepted, shall be entitled to all privileges and immunities of free citizens in the several states; and the people of each state shall have free ingress and regress to and from any other state, and shall enjoy therein all the privileges of trade and commerce, subject to the same duties, impositions and restrictions as the inhabitants thereof respectively, provided that such restrictions shall not extend so far as to prevent the removal of property imported into any state, to any other state of which the owner is an inhabitant; provided also that no imposition, duties or restriction shall be laid by any state, on the property of the United States, or either of them.

If any person guilty of, or charged with, treason, felony, or other high misdemeanor in any state, shall flee from justice, and be found in any of the United States, he shall upon demand of the Governour or executive power of the state from which he fled, be delivered up, and removed to the state having jurisdiction of his offence.

Full faith and credit shall be given in each of these states to the records, acts and judicial proceedings of the courts and magistrates of every other state.

ART. V. For the more convenient management of the general interests of the United States, delegates shall be annually appointed in such manner as the legislature of each state shall direct, to meet in Congress on the first Monday in November, in every year, with a power reserved to each state to recall its delegates, or any of them, at any time within the year, and to send others in their stead, for the remainder of the year.

No state shall be represented in Congress by less than two, nor by more than seven members; and no person shall be capable of being delegate for more than three years, in any term of six years; nor shall any person, being a delegate, be capable of holding any office under the United States, for which he, or another for his benefit receives any salary, fees or emolument of any kind.

Each state shall maintain its own delegates in a meeting of the states, and while they act as members of the committee of the states.

In determining questions in the United States, in Congress assembled, each state shall have one vote.

Freedom of speech and debate in Congress shall not be impeached or questioned in any court, or place out of Congress, and the members of Congress shall be protected in their persons from arrests and imprisonments, during the time of their going to and from, and attendance on Congress, except for treason, felony, or breach of the peace.

Art. VI. No state, without the consent of the United States, in Congress assembled, shall send any embassy to, or receive any embassy from, or enter into any conference, agreement, alliance, or treaty, with any king, prince, or state; nor shall any person holding any office of profit or trust under the United States, or any of them, accept of any present, emolument, office, or title of any kind whatever, from any king, prince, or foreign state; nor shall the United States, in Congress assembled, or any of them, grant any title of nobility.

No two or more states shall enter into any treaty, confederation, or alliance whatever between them, without the consent of the United States, in Congress assembled, specifying accurately the purposes for which the same is to be entered into, and how long it shall continue.

No state shall lay any imposts or duties, which may interfere with any stipulations in treaties, entered into by the United States in Congress assembled, with any king, prince, or state, in pursuance of any treaties already proposed by Congress, to the courts of France and Spain.

No vessels of war shall be kept up in time of peace, by any state, except such number only, as shall be deemed necessary by the United States, in Congress assembled, for the defence of such state, or its trade; nor shall any body of forces be kept up, by any state, in time of peace, except such number only as, in the judgment of the United States, in Congress assembled, shall be deemed requisite to garrison the forts necessary for the defence of such state; but every state shall always keep up a well regulated and disciplined militia, sufficiently armed and accounted, and shall provide and constantly have ready for use, in public stores, a due number of field pieces and tents, and a proper quantity of arms, ammunition, and camp equipage.

No state shall engage in any war without the consent of the United States in Congress assembled, unless such state be actually invaded by enemies, or shall have received certain advice of a resolution being formed by some nation of Indians to invade such state, and the danger is so imminent as not to admit of a delay till the United States in Congress assembled, can be consulted: nor shall any state grant commissions to any ships or vessels of war, nor letters of marque or reprisal, except it be after a declaration of war by the United States in Congress assembled, and then only against the kingdom or state, and the subjects thereof, against which war has been so declared, and under such regulations as shall be established by the United States in

Congress assembled, unless such state be infested by pirates, in which case vessels of war may be fitted out for that occasion, and kept so long as the danger shall continue, or until the United States in Congress assembled shall determine otherwise.

ART. VII. When land forces are raised by any state, for the common defence, all officers of or under the rank of colonel, shall be appointed by the legislature of each state respectively by whom such forces shall be raised, or in such manner as such state shall direct, and all vacancies shall be filled up by the state which first made appointment.

ART. VIII. All charges of war, and all other expenses that shall be incurred for the common defence or general welfare, and allowed by the United States in Congress assembled, shall be defrayed out of a common treasury, which shall be supplied by the several states, in proportion to the value of all land within each state, granted to or surveyed for any person, as such land and the buildings and improvements thereon shall be estimated, according to such mode as the United States, in Congress assembled, shall, from time to time, direct and appoint. The taxes for paying that proportion shall be laid and levied by the authority and direction of the legislatures of the several states within the time agreed upon by the United States in Congress assembled.

ART. IX. The United States, in Congress assembled, shall have the sole and exclusive right and power of determining on peace and war, except in the cases mentioned in the sixth article—of sending and receiving ambassadors—entering into treaties and alliances, provided that no treaty of commerce shall be made, whereby the legislative power of the respective states shall be restrained from imposing such imposts and duties on foreigners, as their own people are subjected to, or from prohibiting the exportation or importation of any species of goods or commodities whatsoever—of establishing rules for deciding, in all cases, what captures on land or water shall be legal, and in what manner prizes taken by land or naval forces in the service of the United Sates, shall be divided or appropriated—of granting letters of marque and reprisal in times of peace—appointing courts for the trial of piracies and felonies committed on the high seas; and establishing courts; for receiving and determining finally appeals in all cases of captures; provided that no member of Congress shall be appointed a judge of any of the said courts.

The United States, in Congress assembled, shall also be the last resort on appeal, in all disputes and differences now subsisting, or that hereafter may arise between two or more states concerning boundary, jurisdiction, or any other cause whatever; which authority shall always be exercised in the manner following. Whenever the legislative or executive authority, or lawful agent of any state in controversy with another, shall present a petition to Congress, stating the matter in question, and praying for a hearing, notice thereof shall be given, by order of Congress, to the legislative or executive authority of the other state in controversy, and a day assigned for the appearance of the parties by their lawful agents, who shall then be directed to appoint, by joint consent, commissioners or judges to constitute a court for hearing and determining the matter in question: but if they cannot agree, Congress shall name three persons out of each of the United States, and from the list of such persons each party shall alternately strike out one, the petitioners beginning, until the number shall be reduced to thirteen; and from that number not less than seven, nor more than nine names, as Congress shall direct, shall, in the presence of Congress, be drawn out by lot, and the persons whose names shall be so drawn, or any five of them, shall be commissioners or judges, to hear and finally determine the controversy, so always as a major part of the judges, who shall hear the cause, shall agree in the determination: and if either party shall neglect to attend at the day appointed, without showing reasons which Congress shall judge sufficient, or being present, shall refuse to strike, the Congress shall proceed to nominate three persons out of each state, and the secretary of Congress shall strike in behalf of such party absent or refusing; and the judgment and sentence of the court, to be appointed in the manner before prescribed, shall be final and conclusive; and if any of the parties shall refuse to submit to the authority of such court, or to appear or defend their claim or cause, the court shall nevertheless proceed to pronounce sentence, or judgment, which shall in like manner be final and decisive; the judgment or sentence and other proceedings being in either case transmitted to Congress, and lodged among the acts of Congress, for the security of the parties concerned: provided that every commissioner, before he sits in judgment, shall take an oath to be administered by one of the judges of the supreme or superior court of the state where the cause shall be tried, "well and truly to hear and determine the matter in question, according to the best of his judgment, without favour, affection, or hope of reward." Provided, also, that no state shall be deprived of territory for the benefit of the United States.

All controversies concerning the private right of soil claimed under different grants of two or more states, whose jurisdictions as they may respect such lands, and the states which passed such grants are adjusted, the said grants or either of them being at the same time claimed to have originated antecedent to such settlement of jurisdiction, shall, on the petition of either party to the Congress of the United States, be finally determined, as near as may be, in the same manner as is before prescribed for deciding disputes respecting territorial jurisdiction between different states.

The United States, in Congress assembled, shall also have the sole and exclusive right and power of regulating the alloy and value of coin struck by their own authority, or by that of the respective states—fixing the standard of weights and measures throughout the United States—regulating the trade and managing all affairs with the Indians, not members of any of the states; provided that the legislative right of any state, within its own limits, be not infringed or violated—establishing and regulating post-offices from one state to another, throughout all the United States, and exacting such postage on the papers passing through the same, as may be requisite to defray the expenses of the said office—appointing all officers of the land forces in the service of the United States, excepting regimental officers—appointing all the officers of the naval forces, and commissioning all officers whatever in the service of the United States; making rules for the government and regulation of the said land and naval forces, and directing their operations.

The United States, in Congress assembled, shall have authority to appoint a committee, to sit in the recess of Congress, to be denominated, "*A Committee of the States*," and to consist of one delegate from each state; and to appoint such other committees and civil officers as may be necessary for managing the general affairs of the United States under their direction—to appoint one of their number to preside; provided that no person be allowed to serve in the office of president more than one year in any term of three years; to ascertain the necessary sums of money to be raised for the service of the United States, and to appropriate and apply the same for defraying the public expenses; to borrow money or emit bills on the credit of the United States, transmitting every half year to the respective states an account of the sums of money so borrowed or emitted,—to build and equip a navy—to agree upon the number of land forces, and to make requisitions from each state for its quota, in proportion to the number of white inhabitants in such state, which requisition shall be binding; and thereupon the legislature of each state shall appoint the regimental officers, raise the men, and clothe, arm, and equip them, in a soldier-like manner, at the expense of the United States; and the officers and men so clothed, armed, and equipped, shall march to the place appointed, and within the time agreed on by the United States, in Congress assembled; but if the United States, in Congress assembled, shall, on consideration of circumstances, judge proper that any state should not raise men, or should raise a smaller number than its quota, and that any other state should raise a greater number of men than the quota thereof, such extra number shall be raised, officered, clothed, armed, and equipped in the same manner as the quota of such state, unless the legislature of such state shall judge that such extra number cannot be safely spared out of the same, in which case they shall raise, officer, clothe, arm, and equip as many of such extra number as they judge can be safely spared. And the officers and men so clothed, armed, and equipped, shall march to the place appointed, and within the time agreed on by the United States in Congress assembled.

The United States, in Congress assembled, shall never engage in a war, nor grant letters of marque and reprisal in time of peace, nor enter into any treaties or alliances, nor coin money, nor regulate the value thereof nor ascertain the sums and expenses necessary for the defence and welfare of the United States, or any of them, nor emit bills, nor borrow money on the credit of the United States, nor appropriate money, nor agree upon the number of vessels of war to be built or purchased, or the number of land or sea forces to be raised, nor appoint a commander in chief of the army or navy, unless nine states assent to the same, nor shall a question on any other point, except for adjourning from day to day, be determined, unless by the votes of a majority of the United States in Congress assembled.

The Congress of the United States shall have power to adjourn to any time within the year, and to any place within the United States, so that no period of adjournment be for a longer duration than the space of six months, and shall publish the Journal of their proceedings monthly, except such parts thereof relating to treaties, alliances, or military operations, as in their judgment require secrecy; and the yeas and nays of the delegates of each state, on any question, shall be entered on the Journal, when it is desired by any delegate; and the delegates of a state, or any of them, at his or their request, shall be furnished with a transcript of the said Journal, except such parts as are above excepted, to lay before the legislatures of the several states.

ART. X. The committee of the states, or any nine of them, shall be authorized to execute, in the recess of Congress, such of the powers of Congress as the United States, in Congress assembled, by the consent of nine states, shall, from time to time, think expedient to vest them with; provided that no power be delegated to the said committee, for the exercise of which, by the articles of confederation, the voice of nine states, in the Congress of the United States assembled, is requisite.

ART. XI. Canada acceding to this confederation, and joining in the measures of the United States, shall be admitted into, and entitled to all the advantages of this union: but no other colony shall be admitted into the same, unless such admission be agreed to by nine states.

ART. XII. All bills of credit emitted, monies borrowed, and debts contracted by or under the authority of Congress, before the assembling of the United States, in pursuance of the present confederation, shall be deemed and considered as a charge against the United States, for payment and satisfaction whereof the said United States and the public faith are hereby solemnly pledged.

ART. XIII. Every state shall abide by the determinations of the United States, in Congress assembled, on all questions which by this confederation are submitted to them. And the articles of this confederation shall be inviolably observed by every state, and the union shall be perpetual; nor shall any alteration at any time hereafter be made in any of them, unless such alteration be agreed to in a Congress of the United States, and be afterwards confirmed by the legislatures of every state.

AND WHEREAS it hath pleased the Great Governor of the World to incline the hearts of the legislatures we respectively represent in Congress, to approve of, and to authorize us to ratify the said articles of confederation and perpetual union, KNOW YE, that we, the undersigned delegates, by virtue of the power and authority to us given for that purpose, do, by these presents, in the name and in behalf of our respective constituents, fully and entirely ratify and confirm each and every of the said articles of confederation and perpetual union, and all and singular the matters and things therein contained. And we do further solemnly plight and engage the faith of our respective constituents, that they shall abide by the determinations of the United States in Congress assembled, on all questions, which by the said confederation are submitted to them. And that the articles thereof shall be inviolably observed by the states we respectively represent, and that the union shall be perpetual. In Witness whereof, we have hereunto set our hands, in Congress.

DONE at Philadelphia, in the State of Pennsylvania, the ninth Day of July, in the Year of our Lord one Thousand seven Hundred and Seventy-eight, and in the third year of the Independence of America.

ON THE PART OF AND BEHALF OF THE STATE OF MASSACHUSETTS BAY:
    John Hancock
    Samuel Adams
    Elbridge Gerry
    Francis Dana
    James Lovell
    Samuel Holten

ON THE PART AND BEHALF OF THE STATE OF PENNSYLVANIA:
    Robert Morris
    Daniel Roberdeau
    John Bayard Smith
    William Clingan
    Joseph Reed; 22d July, 1778

ON THE PART AND BEHALF OF THE STATE OF VIRGINIA:
    Richard Henry Lee
    John Banister
    Thomas Adams

    John Harvie
    Francis Lightfoot Lee

ON THE PART AND BEHALF OF THE STATE OF MARYLAND:
    John Hanson; March 1, 1781
    Daniel Carroll

ON THE PART AND BEHALF OF THE STATE OF DELAWARE:
    Thomas McKean; Febr 22d, 1779
    John Dickinson; May 5th, 1779
    Nicholas Van Dyke

ON THE PART AND BEHALF OF THE STATE OF CONNECTICUT:
    Roger Sherman
    Samuel Huntington
    Oliver Wolcott
    Titus Hosmer
    Andrew Adams

On the part and behalf of the State of Rhode-Island and Providence Plantations:

William Ellery
Henry Marchant
John Collins

On the part and behalf of the State of South Carolina:

Henry Laurens
William Henry Drayton
John Mathews
Richard Hutson
Thos Heyward, Junr.

On the part and behalf of the State of New York:

James Duane
Fracis Lewis
William Duer
Gouverneur Morris

On the Part and in Behalf of the State of New Jersey, November 26th, 1778:

John Witherspoon
Nathaniel Scudder

On the part and behalf of the State of North Carolina:

John Penn; July 21st, 1778
Cornelius Harnett
John Williams

On the part and behalf of the State of Georgia:

John Walton; 24th July, 1778
Edward Telfair
Edward Langworthy

On the part of and behalf of the State of New Hampshire:

Josiah Bartlett
John Wentworth, Junior;
August 8th, 1778

# THE TREATY OF PARIS (1783)

*Signed by representatives on behalf of England's King George III and the new United States of America, the Treaty of Paris officially ended the Revolutionary War.*

## THE DEFINITIVE TREATY OF PEACE 1783

In the Name of the most Holy & undivided Trinity.

It having pleased the Divine Providence to dispose the Hearts of the most Serene and most Potent Prince George the Third, by the Grace of God, King of Great Britain, France, and Ireland, Defender of the Faith, Duke of Brunswick and Lunebourg, Arch- Treasurer and Prince Elector of the Holy Roman Empire etc.. and of the United States of America, to forget all past Misunderstandings and Differences that have unhappily interrupted the good Correspondence and Friendship which they mutually wish to restore; and to establish such a beneficial and satisfactory Intercourse between the two countries upon the ground of reciprocal Advantages and mutual Convenience as may promote and secure to both perpetual Peace and Harmony; and having for this desirable End already laid the Foundation of Peace & Reconciliation by the Provisional Articles signed at Paris on the 30th of November 1782, by the Commissioners empowered on each Part, which Articles were agreed to be inserted in and constitute the Treaty of Peace proposed to be concluded between the Crown of Great Britain and the said United States, but which Treaty was not to be concluded until Terms of Peace should be agreed upon between Great Britain & France, and his Britannic Majesty should be ready to conclude such Treaty accordingly: and the treaty between Great Britain & France having since been concluded, his Britannic Majesty & the United States of America, in Order to carry into full Effect the Provisional Articles above mentioned, according to the Tenor thereof, have constituted & appointed, that is to say his Britannic Majesty on his Part, David Hartley, Esqr., Member of the Parliament of Great Britain, and the said United States on their Part, - stop point - John Adams, Esqr., late a Commissioner of the United

States of America at the Court of Versailles, late Delegate in Congress from the State of Massachusetts, and Chief Justice of the said State, and Minister Plenipotentiary of the said United States to their High Mightinesses the States General of the United Netherlands; - stop point - Benjamin Franklin, Esqr., late Delegate in Congress from the State of Pennsylvania, President of the Convention of the said State, and Minister Plenipotentiary from the United States of America at the Court of Versailles; John Jay, Esqr., late President of Congress and Chief Justice of the state of New York, and Minister Plenipotentiary from the said United States at the Court of Madrid; to be Plenipotentiaries for the concluding and signing the Present Definitive Treaty; who after having reciprocally communicated their respective full Powers have agreed upon and confirmed the following Articles.

ARTICLE 1ST: His Britannic Majesty acknowledges the said United States, viz., New Hampshire, Massachusetts Bay, Rhode Island and Providence Plantations, Connecticut, New York, New Jersey, Pennsylvania, Delaware, Maryland, Virginia, North Carolina, South Carolina and Georgia, to be free sovereign and Independent States; that he treats with them as such, and for himself his Heirs & Successors, relinquishes all claims to the Government, Propriety, and Territorial Rights of the same and every Part thereof.

ARTICLE 2D: And that all Disputes which might arise in future on the subject of the Boundaries of the said United States may be prevented, it is hereby agreed and declared, that the following are and shall be their Boundaries, viz.; from the Northwest Angle of Nova Scotia, viz., that Angle which is formed by a Line drawn due North from the Source of St. Croix River to the Highlands; along the said Highlands which divide those Rivers that empty themselves into the river St. Lawrence, from those which fall into the Atlantic Ocean, to the northwesternmost Head of Connecticut River; Thence down along the middle of that River to the forty-fifth Degree of North Latitude; From thence by a Line due West on said Latitude until it strikes the River Iroquois or Cataraquy; Thence along the middle of said River into Lake Ontario; through the Middle of said Lake until it strikes the Communication by Water between that Lake & Lake Erie; Thence along the middle of said Communication into Lake Erie, through the middle of said Lake until it arrives at the Water Communication between that lake & Lake Huron; Thence along the middle of said Water Communication into the Lake Huron, thence through the middle of said Lake to the Water Communication between that Lake and Lake Superior; thence through Lake Superior Northward of the Isles Royal & Phelipeaux to the Long Lake; Thence through the middle of said Long Lake and the Water Communication between it & the Lake of the Woods, to the said Lake of the Woods; Thence through the said Lake to the most Northwestern Point thereof, and from thence on a due West Course to the river Mississippi; Thence by a Line to be drawn along the Middle of the said river Mississippi until it shall intersect the Northernmost Part of the thirty-first Degree of North Latitude, South, by a Line to be drawn due East from the Determination of the Line last mentioned in the Latitude of thirty-one Degrees of the Equator to the middle of the River Apalachicola or Catahouche; Thence along the middle thereof to its junction with the Flint River; Thence straight to the Head of Saint Mary's River, and thence down along the middle of Saint Mary's River to the Atlantic Ocean. East, by a Line to be drawn along the Middle of the river Saint Croix, from its Mouth in the Bay of Fundy to its Source, and from its Source directly North to the aforesaid Highlands, which divide the Rivers that fall into the Atlantic Ocean from those which fall into the river Saint Lawrence; comprehending all Islands within twenty Leagues of any Part of the Shores of the United States, and lying between Lines to be drawn due East from the Points where the aforesaid Boundaries between Nova Scotia on the one Part and East Florida on the other shall, respectively, touch the Bay of Fundy and the Atlantic Ocean, excepting such Islands as now are or heretofore have been within the limits of the said Province of Nova Scotia.

ARTICLE 3D: It is agreed that the People of the United States shall continue to enjoy unmolested the Right to take Fish of every kind on the Grand Bank and on all the other Banks of Newfoundland, also in the Gulf of Saint Lawrence and at all other Places in the Sea, where the Inhabitants of both Countries used at any time heretofore to fish. And also that the Inhabitants of the United States shall have Liberty to take Fish of every Kind on such Part of the Coast of Newfoundland as British Fishermen shall use, (but not to dry or cure the same on that Island) And also on the Coasts, Bays & Creeks of all other of his Britannic Majesty's Dominions in America; and that the American Fishermen shall have Liberty to dry and cure Fish in any of the unsettled Bays, Harbors, and Creeks of Nova Scotia, Magdalen Islands, and Labrador, so long as the same shall remain unsettled, but so soon as the same or either of them shall be settled, it shall not be lawful for the said Fishermen to dry or cure Fish at such Settlement without a previous Agreement for that purpose with the Inhabitants, Proprietors, or Possessors of the Ground.

ARTICLE 4TH: It is agreed that Creditors on either Side shall meet with no lawful Impediment to the Recovery of the full Value in Sterling Money of all bona fide Debts heretofore contracted.

ARTICLE 5TH: It is agreed that Congress shall earnestly recommend it to the Legislatures of the respective States to provide for the Restitution of all Estates, Rights, and Properties, which have been confiscated belonging to real British Subjects; and also of the Estates, Rights, and Properties of Persons resident in Districts in the Possession on his Majesty's Arms and who have not borne Arms against the said United States. And that Persons of any other Description shall have free Liberty to go to any Part or Parts of any of the thirteen United States and therein to remain twelve Months unmolested in their Endeavors to obtain the Restitution of such of their Estates, Rights & Properties as may have been confiscated. And that Congress shall also earnestly recommend to the several States a Reconsideration and Revision of all Acts or Laws regarding the Premises, so as to render the said Laws or Acts perfectly consistent not only with Justice and Equity but with that Spirit of Conciliation which on the Return of the Blessings of Peace should universally prevail. And that Congress shall also earnestly recommend to the several States that the Estates, Rights, and Properties of such last mentioned Persons shall be restored to them, they refunding to any Persons who may be now in Possession the Bona fide Price (where any has been given) which such Persons may have paid on purchasing any of the said Lands, Rights, or Properties since the Confiscation.

And it is agreed that all Persons who have any Interest in confiscated Lands, either by Debts, Marriage Settlements, or otherwise, shall meet with no lawful Impediment in the Prosecution of their just Rights.

ARTICLE 6TH: That there shall be no future Confiscations made nor any Prosecutions commenced against any Person or Persons for, or by Reason of the Part, which he or they may have taken in the present War, and that no Person shall on that Account suffer any future Loss or Damage, either in his Person, Liberty, or Property; and that those who

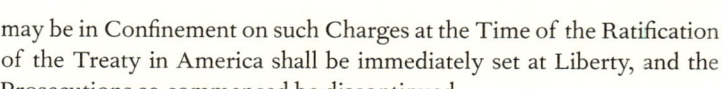

may be in Confinement on such Charges at the Time of the Ratification of the Treaty in America shall be immediately set at Liberty, and the Prosecutions so commenced be discontinued.

ARTICLE 7TH: There shall be a firm and perpetual Peace between his Britannic Majesty and the said States, and between the Subjects of the one and the Citizens of the other, wherefore all Hostilities both by Sea and Land shall from henceforth cease: All prisoners on both Sides shall be set at Liberty, and his Britannic Majesty shall with all convenient speed, and without causing any Destruction, or carrying away any Negroes or other Property of the American inhabitants, withdraw all his Armies, Garrisons & Fleets from the said United States, and from every Post, Place and Harbour within the same; leaving in all Fortifications, the American Artillery that may be therein: And shall also Order & cause all Archives, Records, Deeds & Papers belonging to any of the said States, or their Citizens, which in the Course of the War may have fallen into the hands of his Officers, to be forthwith restored and delivered to the proper States and Persons to whom they belong.

ARTICLE 8TH: The Navigation of the river Mississippi, from its source to the Ocean, shall forever remain free and open to the Subjects of Great Britain and the Citizens of the United States.

ARTICLE 9TH: In case it should so happen that any Place or Territory belonging to Great Britain or to the United States should have been conquered by the Arms of either from the other before the Arrival of the said Provisional Articles in America, it is agreed that the same shall be restored without Difficulty and without requiring any Compensation.

ARTICLE 10TH: The solemn Ratifications of the present Treaty expedited in good & due Form shall be exchanged between the contracting Parties in the Space of Six Months or sooner if possible to be computed from the Day of the Signature of the present Treaty. In witness whereof we the undersigned their Ministers Plenipotentiary have in their Name and in Virtue of our Full Powers, signed with our Hands the present Definitive Treaty, and caused the Seals of our Arms to be affixed thereto.

Done at Paris, this third day of September in the year of our Lord, one thousand seven hundred and eighty-three.

# THE VIRGINIA PLAN (1787)

*In the Virginia Plan, writer James Madison laid the foundation for our current governmental system by proposing that the United States adopt three branches of government: the legislative, judicial, and executive.*

State of the resolutions submitted to the consideration of the House by the honorable Mr. Randolph, as altered, amended, and agreed to, in a Committee of the whole House.

1. RESOLVED that it is the opinion of this Committee that a national government ought to be established consisting of a Supreme Legislative, Judiciary, and Executive.

2. RESOLVED that the national Legislature ought to consist of Two Branches.

3. RESOLVED that the members of the first branch of the national Legislature ought to be elected by the People of the several States for the term of Three years, to receive fixed stipends, by which they may be compensated for the devotion of their time to public service to be paid out of the National Treasury, to be ineligible to any Office established by a particular State or under the authority of the United-States (except those peculiarly belonging to the functions of the first branch) during the term of service, and under the national government for the space of one year after its expiration.

4. RESOLVED that the members of the second Branch of the national Legislature ought to be chosen by the individual Legislatures, to be of the age of thirty years at least, to hold their offices for a term sufficient to ensure their independency, namely seven years, to receive fixed stipends, by which they may be compensated for the devotion of their time to public service—to be paid out of the National Treasury to be ineligible to any office established by a particular State, or under the authority of the United States (except those peculiarly belonging to the functions of the second branch) during the term of service, and under the national government, for the space of one year after it's expiration.

5. RESOLVED that each branch ought to possess the right of originating acts.

6. RESOLVED that the national Legislature ought to be empowered to

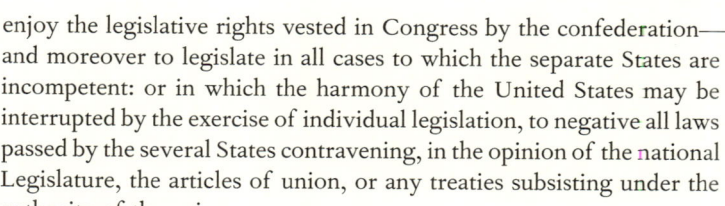

enjoy the legislative rights vested in Congress by the confederation—and moreover to legislate in all cases to which the separate States are incompetent: or in which the harmony of the United States may be interrupted by the exercise of individual legislation, to negative all laws passed by the several States contravening, in the opinion of the national Legislature, the articles of union, or any treaties subsisting under the authority of the union.

7. RESOLVED that the right of suffrage in the first branch of the national Legislature ought not to be according to the rule established in the articles of confederation: but according to some equitable ratio of representation—namely, in proportion to the whole number of white and other free citizens and inhabitants of every age, sex, and condition including those bound to servitude for a term of years, and three fifths of all other persons not comprehended in the foregoing description, except Indians, not paying taxes in each State.

8. RESOLVED that the right of suffrage in the second branch of the national Legislature ought to be according to the rule established for the first.

9. RESOLVED that a national Executive be instituted to consist of a single person, to be chosen by the National Legislature, for the term of seven years, with power to carry into execution the national Laws, to appoint to Offices in cases not otherwise provided for to be ineligible a second time, and to be removable on impeachment and conviction of mal practice or neglect of duty, to receive a fixed stipend, by which he may be compensated for the devotion of his time to public service to be paid out of the national Treasury.

10. RESOLVED that the national executive shall have a right to negative any legislative act: which shall not be afterwards passed unless by two third parts of each branch of the national Legislature.

11. RESOLVED that a national Judiciary be established to consist of One Supreme Tribunal. The Judges of which to be appointed by the second Branch of the National Legislature, to hold their offices during good behaviour to receive, punctually, at stated times, a fixed compensation for their services: in which no encrease or diminution shall be made so as to affect the persons actually in office at the time of such encrease or diminution.

12. RESOLVED that the national Legislature be empowered to appoint inferior Tribunals.

13. RESOLVED that the jurisdiction of the national Judiciary shall extend to cases which respect the collection of the national revenue; impeachments of any national officers; and questions which involve the national peace and harmony.

14. RESOLVED that provision ought to be made for the admission of States, lawfully arising within the limits of the United States, whether from a voluntary junction of government and territory, or otherwise, with the consent of a number of voices in the national Legislature less than the whole.

15. RESOLVED that provision ought to be made for the continuance of Congress and their authorities until a given day after the reform of the articles of Union shall be adopted; and for the completion of all their engagements.

16. RESOLVED that a republican constitution, and its existing laws, ought to be guaranteed to each State by the United States.

17. RESOLVED that provision ought to be made for the amendment of the articles of Union, whensoever it shall seem necessary.

18. RESOLVED that the Legislative, Executive, and Judiciary powers within the several States ought to be bound by oath to support the articles of Union.

19. RESOLVED that the amendments which shall be offered to the confederation by the Convention, ought at a proper time or times, after the approbation of Congress, to be submitted to an assembly or assemblies of representatives, recommended by the several Legislatures, to be expressly chosen by the People to consider and decide thereon.

# THE NORTHWEST ORDINANCE (1787)

*The Northwest Ordinance was an act of Congress that created the Northwest Territory, which included the modern states of Illinois, Indiana, Michigan, Minnesota, Ohio, and Wisconsin.*

An Ordinance for the government of the Territory of the United States northwest of the River Ohio

SECTION 1. Be it ordained by the United States in Congress assembled, That the said territory, for the purposes of temporary government, be one district, subject, however, to be divided into two districts, as future circumstances may, in the opinion of Congress, make it expedient.

SEC 2. Be it ordained by the authority aforesaid, That the estates, both of resident and nonresident proprietors in the said territory, dying intestate, shall descent to, and be distributed among their children, and the descendants of a deceased child, in equal parts; the descendants of a deceased child or grandchild to take the share of their deceased parent in equal parts among them: And where there shall be no children or descendants, then in equal parts to the next of kin in equal degree; and among collaterals, the children of a deceased brother or sister of the intestate shall have, in equal parts among them, their deceased parents' share; and there shall in no case be a distinction between kindred of the whole and half blood; saving, in all cases, to the widow of the intestate her third part of the real estate for life, and one third part of the personal estate; and this law relative to descents and dower, shall remain in full force until altered by the legislature of the district. And until the governor and judges shall adopt laws as hereinafter mentioned, estates in the said territory may be devised or bequeathed by wills in writing, signed and sealed by him or her in whom the estate may be (being of full age), and attested by three witnesses; and real estates may be conveyed by lease and release, or bargain and sale, signed, sealed and delivered by the person being of full age, in whom the estate may be, and attested by two witnesses, provided such wills be duly proved, and such conveyances be acknowledged, or the execution thereof duly

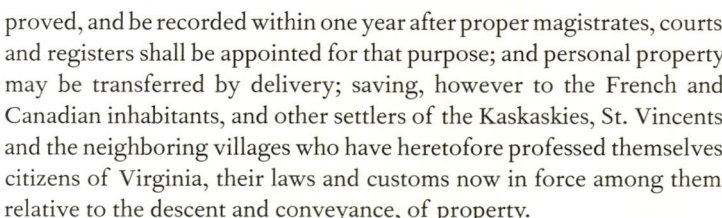

proved, and be recorded within one year after proper magistrates, courts, and registers shall be appointed for that purpose; and personal property may be transferred by delivery; saving, however to the French and Canadian inhabitants, and other settlers of the Kaskaskies, St. Vincents and the neighboring villages who have heretofore professed themselves citizens of Virginia, their laws and customs now in force among them, relative to the descent and conveyance, of property.

SEC. 3. Be it ordained by the authority aforesaid, That there shall be appointed from time to time by Congress, a governor, whose commission shall continue in force for the term of three years, unless sooner revoked by Congress; he shall reside in the district, and have a freehold estate therein in 1,000 acres of land, while in the exercise of his office.

SEC. 4. There shall be appointed from time to time by Congress, a secretary, whose commission shall continue in force for four years unless sooner revoked; he shall reside in the district, and have a freehold estate therein in 500 acres of land, while in the exercise of his office. It shall be his duty to keep and preserve the acts and laws passed by the legislature, and the public records of the district, and the proceedings of the governor in his executive department, and transmit authentic copies of such acts and proceedings, every six months, to the Secretary of Congress: There shall also be appointed a court to consist of three judges, any two of whom to form a court, who shall have a common law jurisdiction, and reside in the district, and have each therein a freehold estate in 500 acres of land while in the exercise of their offices; and their commissions shall continue in force during good behavior.

SEC. 5. The governor and judges, or a majority of them, shall adopt and publish in the district such laws of the original States, criminal and civil, as may be necessary and best suited to the circumstances of the district, and report them to Congress from time to time: which laws shall be in force in the district until the organization of the General Assembly therein, unless disapproved of by Congress; but afterwards the Legislature shall have authority to alter them as they shall think fit.

SEC. 6. The governor, for the time being, shall be commander in chief of the militia, appoint and commission all officers in the same below the rank of general officers; all general officers shall be appointed and commissioned by Congress.

SEC. 7. Previous to the organization of the general assembly, the governor shall appoint such magistrates and other civil officers in each county or township, as he shall find necessary for the preservation of the peace and good order in the same: After the general assembly shall be organized, the powers and duties of the magistrates and other civil officers shall be regulated and defined by the said assembly; but all magistrates and other civil officers not herein otherwise directed, shall during the continuance of this temporary government, be appointed by the governor.

Sec. 8. For the prevention of crimes and injuries, the laws to be adopted or made shall have force in all parts of the district, and for the execution of process, criminal and civil, the governor shall make proper divisions thereof; and he shall proceed from time to time as circumstances may require, to lay out the parts of the district in which the Indian titles shall have been extinguished, into counties and townships, subject, however, to such alterations as may thereafter be made by the legislature.

Sec. 9. So soon as there shall be five thousand free male inhabitants of full age in the district, upon giving proof thereof to the governor, they shall receive authority, with time and place, to elect a representative from their counties or townships to represent them in the general assembly: Provided, That, for every five hundred free male inhabitants, there shall be one representative, and so on progressively with the number of free male inhabitants shall the right of representation increase, until the number of representatives shall amount to twenty five; after which, the number and proportion of representatives shall be regulated by the legislature: Provided, That no person be eligible or qualified to act as a representative unless he shall have been a citizen of one of the United States three years, and be a resident in the district, or unless he shall have resided in the district three years; and, in either case, shall likewise hold in his own right, in fee simple, two hundred acres of land within the same; Provided, also, That a freehold in fifty acres of land in the district, having been a citizen of one of the states, and being resident in the district, or the like freehold and two years residence in the district, shall be necessary to qualify a man as an elector of a representative.

Sec. 10. The representatives thus elected, shall serve for the term of two years; and, in case of the death of a representative, or removal from office, the governor shall issue a writ to the county or township for which he was a member, to elect another in his stead, to serve for the residue of the term.

SEC. 11. The general assembly or legislature shall consist of the governor, legislative council, and a house of representatives. The Legislative Council shall consist of five members, to continue in office five years, unless sooner removed by Congress; any three of whom to be a quorum: and the members of the Council shall be nominated and appointed in the following manner, to wit: As soon as representatives shall be elected, the Governor shall appoint a time and place for them to meet together; and, when met, they shall nominate ten persons, residents in the district, and each possessed of a freehold in five hundred acres of land, and return their names to Congress; five of whom Congress shall appoint and commission to serve as aforesaid; and, whenever a vacancy shall happen in the council, by death or removal from office, the house of representatives shall nominate two persons, qualified as aforesaid, for each vacancy, and return their names to Congress; one of whom congress shall appoint and commission for the residue of the term. And every five years, four months at least before the expiration of the time of service of the members of council, the said house shall nominate ten persons, qualified as aforesaid, and return their names to Congress; five of whom Congress shall appoint and commission to serve as members of the council five years, unless sooner removed. And the governor, legislative council, and house of representatives, shall have authority to make laws in all cases, for the good government of the district, not repugnant to the principles and articles in this ordinance established and declared. And all bills, having passed by a majority in the house, and by a majority in the council, shall be referred to the governor for his assent; but no bill, or legislative act whatever, shall be of any force without his assent. The governor shall have power to convene, prorogue, and dissolve the general assembly, when, in his opinion, it shall be expedient.

SEC. 12. The governor, judges, legislative council, secretary, and such other officers as Congress shall appoint in the district, shall take an oath or affirmation of fidelity and of office; the governor before the president of congress, and all other officers before the Governor. As soon as a legislature shall be formed in the district, the council and house assembled in one room, shall have authority, by joint ballot, to elect a delegate to Congress, who shall have a seat in Congress, with a right of debating but not voting during this temporary government.

SEC. 13. And, for extending the fundamental principles of civil and religious liberty, which form the basis whereon these republics, their laws and constitutions are erected; to fix and establish those principles as the basis of all laws, constitutions, and governments, which forever hereafter shall be formed in the said territory: to provide also for the establishment of States, and permanent government therein, and for their admission to a share in the federal councils on an equal footing with the original States, at as early periods as may be consistent with the general interest:

SEC. 14. It is hereby ordained and declared by the authority aforesaid, That the following articles shall be considered as articles of compact between the original States and the people and States in the said territory and forever remain unalterable, unless by common consent, to wit:

ART. 1. No person, demeaning himself in a peaceable and orderly manner, shall ever be molested on account of his mode of worship or religious sentiments, in the said territory.

ART. 2. The inhabitants of the said territory shall always be entitled to the benefits of the writ of habeas corpus, and of the trial by jury; of a proportionate representation of the people in the legislature; and of judicial proceedings according to the course of the common law. All persons shall be bailable, unless for capital offenses, where the proof shall be evident or the presumption great. All fines shall be moderate; and no cruel or unusual punishments shall be inflicted. No man shall be deprived of his liberty or property, but by the judgment of his peers or the law of the land; and, should the public exigencies make it necessary, for the common preservation, to take any person's property, or to demand his particular services, full compensation shall be made for the same. And, in the just preservation of rights and property, it is understood and declared, that no law ought ever to be made, or have force in the said territory, that shall, in any manner whatever, interfere with or affect private contracts or engagements, bona fide, and without fraud, previously formed.

ART. 3. Religion, morality, and knowledge, being necessary to good government and the happiness of mankind, schools and the means of education shall forever be encouraged. The utmost good faith shall always be observed towards the Indians; their lands and property shall never be taken from them without their consent; and, in their property, rights, and liberty, they shall never be invaded or disturbed, unless in just and lawful wars authorized by Congress; but laws founded in justice and humanity, shall from time to time be made for preventing wrongs being done to them, and for preserving peace and friendship with them.

ART. 4. The said territory, and the States which may be formed therein, shall forever remain a part of this Confederacy of the United States of America, subject to the Articles of Confederation, and to such alterations therein as shall be constitutionally made; and to all the acts and ordinances of the United States in Congress assembled, conformable thereto. The inhabitants and settlers in the said territory shall be subject to pay a part of the federal debts contracted or to be contracted, and a proportional part of the expenses of government, to be apportioned on them by Congress according to the same common rule and measure by which apportionments thereof shall be made on the other States; and the taxes for paying their proportion shall be laid and levied by the authority and direction of the legislatures of the district or districts, or new States, as in the original States, within the time agreed upon by the United States in Congress assembled. The legislatures of those districts or new States, shall never interfere with the primary disposal of the soil by the United States in Congress assembled, nor with any regulations Congress may find necessary for securing the title in such soil to the bona fide purchasers. No tax shall be imposed on lands the property of the United States; and, in no case, shall nonresident proprietors be taxed higher than residents. The navigable waters leading into the Mississippi and St. Lawrence, and the carrying places between the same, shall be common highways and forever free, as well to the inhabitants of the said territory as to the citizens of the United States, and those of any other States that may be admitted into the confederacy, without any tax, impost, or duty therefor.

ART. 5. There shall be formed in the said territory, not less than three nor more than five States; and the boundaries of the States, as soon as Virginia shall alter her act of cession, and consent to the same, shall become fixed and established as follows, to wit: The western State in the said territory, shall be bounded by the Mississippi, the Ohio, and Wabash Rivers; a direct line drawn from the Wabash and Post Vincents, due North, to the territorial line between the United States and Canada; and, by the said territorial line, to the Lake of the Woods and Mississippi. The middle State shall be bounded by the said direct line, the Wabash from Post Vincents to the Ohio, by the Ohio, by a direct line, drawn due north from the mouth of the Great Miami, to the said territorial line, and by the said territorial line. The eastern State shall be bounded by the last mentioned direct line, the Ohio, Pennsylvania, and the said territorial line: Provided, however, and it is further understood and declared, that the boundaries of these three States shall be subject so far to be altered, that, if Congress shall hereafter find it expedient, they shall have authority to form one or two States in that part of the said territory which lies north of an east and west line drawn through the southerly bend or extreme of Lake Michigan. And, whenever any of the said States shall have sixty thousand free inhabitants therein, such State shall be admitted, by its delegates, into the Congress of the United States, on an equal footing with the original States in all respects whatever, and shall be at liberty to form a permanent constitution and State government: Provided, the constitution and government so to be formed, shall be republican, and in conformity to the principles contained in these articles; and, so far as it can be consistent with the general interest of the confederacy, such admission shall be allowed at an earlier period, and when there may be a less number of free inhabitants in the State than sixty thousand.

ART. 6. There shall be neither slavery nor involuntary servitude in the said territory, otherwise than in the punishment of crimes whereof the party shall have been duly convicted: Provided, always, That any person escaping into the same, from whom labor or service is lawfully claimed in any one of the original States, such fugitive may be lawfully reclaimed and conveyed to the person claiming his or her labor or service as aforesaid.

Be it ordained by the authority aforesaid, That the resolutions of the 23rd of April, 1784, relative to the subject of this ordinance, be, and the same are hereby repealed and declared null and void.

DONE by the United States, in Congress assembled, the 13th day of July, in the year of our Lord 1787, and of their sovereignty and independence the twelfth.

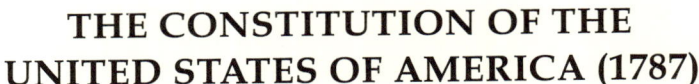 

# THE CONSTITUTION OF THE UNITED STATES OF AMERICA (1787)

We the people of the United States, in Order to form a more perfect Union, establish Justice, insure domestic Tranquility, provide for the common defence, promote the general Welfare, and secure the Blessings of Liberty to ourselves and our Posterity, do ordain and establish this Constitution for the United States of America.

## ARTICLE I

SECTION 1. All legislative Powers herein granted shall be vested in a Congress of the United States, which shall consist of a Senate and House of Representatives.

SECTION 2. The House of Representatives shall be composed of Members chosen every second Year by the People of the several States, and the electors in each State shall have the qualifications requisite for electors of the most numerous branch of the State legislature.

No Person shall be a Representative who shall not have attained to the Age of twenty five Years, and been seven Years a citizen of the United States, and who shall not, when elected, be an Inhabitant of that State in which he shall be chosen.

Representatives and direct Taxes shall be apportioned among the several States which may be included within this Union, according to their respective Numbers, which shall be determined by adding to the whole number of free Persons, including those bound to Service for a Term of Years, and excluding Indians not taxed, three fifths of all other Persons. The actual Enumeration shall be made within three Years after the first Meeting of the Congress of the United States, and within every subsequent Term of ten Years, in such Manner as they shall by law Direct. The number of Representatives shall not exceed one for every thirty Thousand, but each State shall have at least one Representative; and until such enumeration shall be made, the State of New Hampshire shall be entitled to chuse three, Massachusetts eight, Rhode Island and Providence Plantations one, Connecticut five, New York six, New Jersey four, Pennsylvania eight, Delaware one, Maryland six, Virginia ten, North Carolina five, South Carolina five, and Georgia three.

When vacancies happen in the Representation from any State, the Executive Authority thereof shall issue Writs of Election to fill such Vacancies.

The House of Representatives shall chuse their Speaker and other Officers; and shall have the sole Power of Impeachment.

SECTION 3. The Senate of the United States shall be composed of two Senators from each State, chosen by the legislature thereof, for six Years; and each Senator shall have one Vote.

Immediately after they shall be assembled in Consequence of the first Election, they shall be divided as equally as may be into three Classes. The Seats of the Senators of the first Class shall be vacated at the expiration of the second Year, of the second Class at the expiration of the fourth Year, and of the third Class at the expiration of the sixth Year, so that one third may be chosen every second Year; and if vacancies happen by Resignation, or otherwise, during the recess of the Legislature of any State, the Executive thereof may make temporary Appointments until the next meeting of the Legislature, which shall then fill such Vacancies.

No person shall be a Senator who shall not have attained to the Age of thirty Years, and been nine Years a Citizen of the United States, and who shall not, when elected, be an Inhabitant of that State for which he shall be chosen.

The Vice-President of the United States shall be President of the Senate, but shall have no Vote, unless they be equally divided.

The Senate shall choose their other Officers, and also a President pro tempore, in the Absence of the Vice-President, or when he shall exercise the Office of President of the United States.

The Senate shall have the sole Power to try all Impeachments. When sitting for that Purpose, they shall be on Oath or Affirmation. When the President of the United States is tried, the Chief Justice shall preside: And no Person shall be convicted without the Concurrence of two thirds of the Members present.

Judgment in cases of Impeachment shall not extend further than to removal from Office, and disqualification to hold and enjoy any Office of honor, Trust or Profit under the United States: but the Party

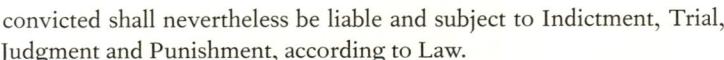

convicted shall nevertheless be liable and subject to Indictment, Trial, Judgment and Punishment, according to Law.

SECTION 4. The Times, Places and Manner of holding Elections for Senators and Representatives, shall be prescribed in each State by the Legislature thereof; but the Congress may at any time by Law make or alter such Regulations, except as to the Places of chusing Senators.

The Congress shall assemble at least once in every Year, and such Meeting shall be on the first Monday in December, unless they shall by law appoint a different Day.

SECTION 5. Each House shall be the Judge of the Elections, Returns and Qualifications of its own Members, and a Majority of each shall constitute a Quorum to do Business; but a smaller Number may adjourn from day to day, and may be authorized to compel the Attendance of absent Members, in such Manner, and under such Penalties as each House may provide.

Each house may determine the Rules of its Proceedings, punish its Members for disorderly Behavior, and, with the Concurrence of two-thirds, expel a Member.

Each house shall keep a Journal of its Proceedings, and from time to time publish the same, excepting such Parts as may in their Judgment require Secrecy; and the Yeas and Nays of the Members of either House on any question shall, at the Desire of one fifth of those Present, be entered on the Journal.

Neither House, during the Session of Congress, shall, without the Consent of the other, adjourn for more than three days, nor to any other Place than that in which the two Houses shall be sitting.

SECTION 6. The Senators and Representatives shall receive a Compensation for their Services, to be ascertained by Law, and paid out of the Treasury of the United States. They shall in all Cases, except Treason, Felony and Breach of the Peace, be privileged from Arrest during their Attendance at the Session of their respective Houses, and in going to and returning from the same; and for any Speech or Debate in either House, they shall not be questioned in any other Place.

No Senator or Representative shall, during the Time for which he was elected, be appointed to any civil Office under the authority of the United States, which shall have been created, or the Emoluments whereof shall have been increased during such time; and no Person holding any Office under the United States, shall be a Member of either House during his Continuance in Office.

SECTION 7. All Bills for raising Revenue shall originate in the House of Representatives; but the Senate may propose or concur with Amendments as on other Bills.

Every Bill which shall have passed the House of Representatives and the Senate, shall, before it become a Law, be presented to the President of the United States; If he approve he shall sign it, but if not he shall return it, with his Objections to that House in which it shall have originated, who shall enter the Objections at large on their Journal, and proceed to reconsider it. If after such Reconsideration two thirds of that house shall agree to pass the Bill, it shall be sent, together with the Objections, to the other House, by which it shall likewise be reconsidered, and if approved by two thirds of that House, it shall become a law. But in all such Cases the Votes of both Houses shall be determined by Yeas and Nays, and the Names of the Persons voting for and against the Bill shall be entered on the Journal of each House respectively. If any Bill shall not be returned by the President within ten Days (Sundays excepted) after it shall have been presented to him, the Same shall be a Law, in like Manner as if he had signed it, unless the Congress by their Adjournment prevent its Return, in which case it shall not be a Law.

Every Order, Resolution, or Vote to which the Concurrence of the Senate and House of Representatives may be necessary (except on a question of Adjournment) shall be presented to the President of the United States; and before the Same shall take Effect, shall be approved by him, or being disapproved by him, shall be repassed by two thirds of the Senate and House of Representatives, according to the Rules and Limitations prescribed in the Case of a Bill.

SECTION 8. The Congress shall have Power to lay and collect Taxes, Duties, Imposts and Excises, to pay the Debts and provide for the common Defence and general Welfare of the United States; but all Duties, Imposts and Excises shall be uniform throughout the United States;

To borrow Money on the credit of the United States;

To regulate Commerce with foreign Nations, and among the several States, and with the Indian Tribes;

To establish an uniform Rule of Naturalization, and uniform Laws on the subject of Bankruptcies throughout the United States;

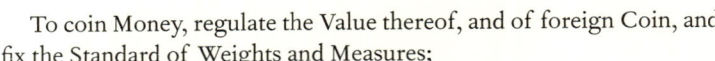

To coin Money, regulate the Value thereof, and of foreign Coin, and fix the Standard of Weights and Measures;

To provide for the Punishment of counterfeiting the Securities and current Coin of the United States;

To establish Post Offices and Post Roads;

To promote the Progress of Science and useful Arts, by securing for limited Times to Authors and Inventors the exclusive Right to their respective Writings and Discoveries;

To constitute Tribunals inferior to the supreme Court;

To define and punish Piracies and Felonies committed on the high Seas, and Offenses against the Law of Nations;

To declare War, grant Letters of Marque and Reprisal, and make Rules concerning Captures on Land and Water;

To raise and support Armies, but no Appropriation of Money to that Use shall be for a longer term than two Years;

To provide and maintain a Navy;

To make Rules for the Government and Regulation of the land and naval Forces;

To provide for calling forth the Militia to execute the Laws of the Union, suppress Insurrections and repel Invasions;

To provide for organizing, arming, and disciplining, the Militia, and for governing such Part of them as may be employed in the Service of the United States, reserving to the States respectively, the Appointment of the Officers, and the Authority of training the militia according to the discipline prescribed by Congress;

To exercise exclusive Legislation in all Cases whatsoever, over such District (not exceeding ten Miles square) as may, by Cession of particular States, and the Acceptance of Congress, become the Seat of the Government of the United States, and to exercise like Authority over all Places purchased by the Consent of the Legislature of the State in which the Same shall be, for the Erection of Forts, Magazines, Arsenals, Dockyards, and other needful Buildings;—And

To make all Laws which shall be necessary and proper for carrying into Execution the foregoing Powers, and all other Powers vested by this Constitution in the Government of the United States, or in any Department or Officer thereof.

SECTION 9. The Migration or Importation of such Persons as any of the States now existing shall think proper to admit, shall not be prohibited by the Congress prior to the Year one thousand eight hundred and eight, but a Tax or Duty may be imposed on such Importation, not exceeding ten dollars for each Person.

The Privilege of the Writ of Habeas Corpus shall not be suspended, unless when in Cases of Rebellion or Invasion the public Safety may require it.

No Bill of Attainder or ex post facto Law shall be passed.

No Capitation, or other direct, Tax shall be laid, unless in Proportion to the Census or Enumeration herein before directed to be taken.

No Tax or Duty shall be laid on Articles exported from any State.

No Preference shall be given by any Regulation of Commerce or Revenue to the Ports of one State over those of another: nor shall Vessels bound to, or from, one State, be obliged to enter, clear, or pay Duties in another.

No Money shall be drawn from the Treasury, but in Consequence of Appropriations made by Law; and a regular Statement and Account of the Receipts and Expenditures of all public Money shall be published from time to time.

No Title of Nobility shall be granted by the United States: and no Person holding any Office of Profit or Trust under them, shall, without the Consent of the Congress, accept of any present, Emolument, Office, or Title, of any kind whatever, from any King, Prince, or foreign State.

SECTION 10. No State shall enter into any Treaty, Alliance, or Confederation; grant Letters of Marque and Reprisal; coin Money; emit Bills of Credit; make any Thing but gold and silver Coin a Tender in Payment of Debts; pass any Bill of Attainder, ex post facto Law, or Law impairing the Obligation of Contracts, or grant any Title of Nobility.

No State shall, without the Consent of the Congress, lay any Imposts or Duties on Imports or Exports, except what may be absolutely necessary for executing its inspection Laws: and the net Produce of all Duties and Imposts, laid by any State on Imports or Exports, shall be for the Use of the Treasury of the United States; and all such Laws shall be subject to the Revision and Controul of the Congress.

No State shall, without the Consent of Congress, lay any Duty of Tonnage, keep Troops, or Ships of War in time of Peace, enter into any Agreement or Compact with another State, or with a foreign Power, or engage in War, unless actually invaded, or in such imminent Danger as will not admit of delay.

## Article II

SECTION 1. The executive Power shall be vested in a President of the United States of America. He shall hold his Office during the Term of four Years, and, together with the Vice President chosen for the same Term, be elected, as follows:

Each State shall appoint, in such Manner as the Legislature thereof may direct, a Number of Electors, equal to the whole Number of Senators and Representatives to which the State may be entitled in the Congress: but no Senator or Representative, or Person holding an Office of Trust or Profit under the United States, shall be appointed an Elector.

The Electors shall meet in their respective States, and vote by Ballot for two Persons, of whom one at least shall not be an Inhabitant of the same State with themselves. And they shall make a List of all the Persons voted for, and of the Number of Votes for each; which List they shall sign and certify, and transmit sealed to the Seat of the Government of the United States, directed to the President of the Senate. The President of the Senate shall, in the Presence of the Senate and House of Representatives, open all the Certificates, and the Votes shall then be counted. The Person having the greatest Number of Votes shall be the President, if such Number be a Majority of the whole Number of Electors appointed; and if there be more than one who have such Majority, and have an equal Number of votes, then the House of Representatives shall immediately chuse by Ballot one of them for President; and if no Person have a Majority, then from the five highest on the List the said House shall in like Manner chuse the President. But in chusing the President, the Votes shall be taken by States, the Representation from each State having one Vote; a Quorum for this Purpose shall consist of a Member or Members from two thirds of the States, and a Majority of all the States shall be necessary to a Choice. In every Case, after the Choice of the President, the Person having the greatest Number of Votes of the Electors shall be the Vice President. But if there should remain two or more who have equal Votes, the Senate shall chuse from them by Ballot the Vice President.

The Congress may determine the Time of chusing the Electors, and the Day on which they shall give their Votes; which Day shall be the same throughout the United States.

No Person except a natural born Citizen, or a Citizen of the United

States, at the time of the Adoption of this Constitution, shall be eligible to the Office of President; neither shall any Person be eligible to that Office who shall not have attained to the Age of thirty five Years, and been fourteen Years a Resident within the United States.

In Case of the Removal of the President from Office, or of his Death, Resignation, or Inability to discharge the Powers and Duties of the said Office, the Same shall devolve on the Vice President, and the Congress may by Law provide for the Case of Removal, Death, Resignation or Inability, both of the President and Vice President, declaring what Officer shall then act as President, and such Officer shall act accordingly, until the Disability be removed, or a President shall be elected.

The President shall, at stated Times, receive for his Services, a Compensation, which shall neither be encreased nor diminished during the Period for which he shall have been elected, and he shall not receive within that Period any other Emolument from the United States, or any of them.

Before he enter on the Execution of his Office, he shall take the following Oath or Affirmation:—"I do solemnly swear (or affirm) that I will faithfully execute the Office of President of the United States, and will to the best of my Ability, preserve, protect and defend the Constitution of the United States."

SECTION 2. The President shall be Commander in Chief of the Army and Navy of the United States, and of the Militia of the several States, when called into the actual Service of the United States; he may require the Opinion, in writing, of the principal Officer in each of the executive Departments, upon any Subject relating to the Duties of their respective Offices, and he shall have Power to grant Reprieves and Pardons for Offenses against the United States, except in Cases of impeachment.

He shall have Power, by and with the Advice and Consent of the Senate, to make Treaties, provided two thirds of the Senators present concur; and he shall nominate, and by and with the Advice and Consent of the Senate, shall appoint Ambassadors, other public Ministers and Consuls, Judges of the supreme Court, and all other Officers of the United States, whose Appointments are not herein otherwise provided for, and which shall be established by Law: but the Congress may by Law vest the Appointment of such inferior Officers, as they think

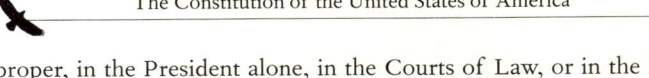

proper, in the President alone, in the Courts of Law, or in the Heads of Departments.

The President shall have Power to fill up all Vacancies that may happen during the Recess of the Senate, by granting Commissions which shall expire at the End of their next session.

SECTION 3. He shall from time to time give to the Congress Information of the State of the Union, and recommend to their Consideration such Measures as he shall judge necessary and expedient; he may, on extraordinary Occasions, convene both Houses, or either of them, and in Case of Disagreement between them, with Respect to the Time of Adjournment, he may adjourn them to such Time as he shall think proper; he shall receive Ambassadors and other public Ministers; he shall take Care that the Laws be faithfully executed, and shall Commission all the Officers of the United States.

SECTION 4. The President, Vice President and all civil Officers of the United States, shall be removed from Office on Impeachment for, and Conviction of, Treason, Bribery, or other high Crimes and Misdemeanors.

## ARTICLE III

SECTION 1. The judicial Power of the United States, shall be vested in one supreme Court, and in such inferior Courts as the Congress may from time to time ordain and establish. The Judges, both of the supreme and inferior Courts, shall hold their Offices during good behavior, and shall, at stated Times, receive for their Services, a Compensation, which shall not be diminished during their Continuance in Office.

SECTION 2. The judicial Power shall extend to all Cases, in Law and Equity, arising under this Constitution, the Laws of the United States, and Treaties made, or which shall be made, under their Authority;—to all Cases affecting Ambassadors, other public Ministers and Consuls;—to all Cases of admiralty and maritime Jurisdiction;—to Controversies to which the United States shall be a Party;—to Controversies between two or more States;—between a State and Citizens of another State;—between Citizens of different States; —between Citizens of the same State claiming Lands under Grants of different States, and between a State, or the Citizens thereof, and foreign States, Citizens or Subjects.

In all cases affecting Ambassadors, other public Ministers and Consuls, and those in which a State shall be Party, the supreme Court shall have original Jurisdiction. In all the other Cases before mentioned, the supreme Court shall have appellate Jurisdiction, both as to Law and Fact, with such Exceptions, and under such Regulations as the Congress shall make.

The Trial of all Crimes, except in Cases of Impeachment, shall be by Jury; and such Trial shall be held in the State where the said Crimes shall have been committed; but when not committed within any State, the Trial shall be at such Place or Places as the Congress may by Law have directed.

SECTION 3. Treason against the United States, shall consist only in levying War against them, or in adhering to their Enemies, giving them Aid and Comfort. No Person shall be convicted of Treason unless on the Testimony of two Witnesses to the same overt Act, or on Confession in open Court.

The Congress shall have power to declare the punishment of Treason, but no Attainder of Treason shall work Corruption of Blood, or Forfeiture except during the Life of the Person attainted.

## ARTICLE IV

SECTION 1. Full Faith and Credit shall be given in each State to the public Acts, Records, and judicial Proceedings of every other State. And the Congress may by general Laws prescribe the Manner in which such Acts, Records, and Proceedings shall be proved, and the Effect thereof.

SECTION 2. The Citizens of each State shall be entitled to all Privileges and Immunities of Citizens in the several States.

A Person charged in any State with Treason, Felony, or other Crime, who shall flee from Justice, and be found in another State, shall on Demand of the executive Authority of the State from which he fled, be delivered up, to be removed to the State having Jurisdiction of the Crime.

No person held to Service or Labor in one State, under the Laws thereof, escaping into another, shall, in Consequence of any Law or Regulation therein, be discharged from such Service or Labor, But shall be delivered up on Claim of the Party to whom such Service or Labor may be due.

SECTION 3. New States may be admitted by the Congress into this Union; but no new States shall be formed or erected within the Jurisdiction of any other State; nor any State be formed by the Junction

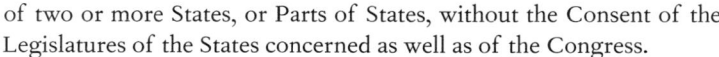

of two or more States, or Parts of States, without the Consent of the Legislatures of the States concerned as well as of the Congress.

The Congress shall have Power to dispose of and make all needful Rules and Regulations respecting the Territory or other Property belonging to the United States; and nothing in this Constitution shall be so construed as to Prejudice any Claims of the United States, or of any particular State.

SECTION 4. The United States shall guarantee to every State in this Union a Republican Form of Government, and shall protect each of them against Invasion; and on Application of the Legislature, or of the Executive (when the Legislature cannot be convened) against domestic Violence.

## ARTICLE V

The Congress, whenever two thirds of both Houses shall deem it necessary, shall propose Amendments to this Constitution, or, on the Application of the Legislatures of two thirds of the several States, shall call a Convention for proposing Amendments, which, in either Case, shall be valid to all Intents and Purposes, as Part of this Constitution, when ratified by the Legislatures of three fourths of the several States, or by Conventions in three fourths thereof, as the one or the other Mode of Ratification may be proposed by the Congress; Provided that no Amendment which may be made prior to the Year one thousand eight hundred and eight shall in any Manner affect the first and fourth Clauses in the ninth Section of the first Article; and that no State, without its Consent, shall be deprived of its equal Suffrage in the Senate.

## ARTICLE VI

All Debts contracted and Engagements entered into, before the Adoption of this Constitution, shall be as valid against the United States under this Constitution, as under the Confederation.

This Constitution, and the Laws of the United States which shall be made in Pursuance thereof; and all Treaties made, or which shall be made, under the Authority of the United States, shall be the supreme Law of the Land; and the Judges in every State shall be bound thereby, any Thing in the Constitution or Laws of any State to the Contrary notwithstanding.

The Senators and Representatives before mentioned, and the

Members of the several State Legislatures, and all executive and judicial Officers, both of the United States and of the several States, shall be bound by Oath or Affirmation, to support this Constitution; but no religious Test shall ever be required as a Qualification to any Office or public Trust under the United States.

## ARTICLE VII

The Ratification of the Conventions of nine States, shall be sufficient for the Establishment of this Constitution between the States so ratifying the Same.

DONE in Convention by the Unanimous Consent of the States present the Seventeenth Day of September in the Year of our Lord one thousand seven hundred and eighty seven and of the Independence of the United States of America the Twelfth.

IN WITNESS whereof We have hereunto subscribed our Names,

GO. WASHINGTON—
President and deputy from Virginia

NEW HAMPSHIRE
John Langdon
Nicholas Gilman

MARYLAND
James Mchenry
Dan of St Thomas Jenifer
Daniel Carroll

VIRGINIA
John Blair—
James Madison, Jr.

NORTH CAROLINA
William Blount
Richard Dobbs Spaight
Hugh Williamson

PENNSYLVANIA
Benjamin Franklin
Thomas Mifflin
Robert Morris
George Clymer
Thomas FitzSimons
Jared Ingersoll
James Wilson
Gouverneur Morris

MASSACHUSETTS
Nathaniel Gorham
Rufus King

CONNECTICUT
William Samuel Johnson
Roger Sherman

NEW JERSEY
William Livingston
David Brearley
William Paterson
Jonathan Dayton

NEW YORK
Alexander Hamilton

DELAWARE
George Read
Gunning Bedford, Jr.
John Dickinson
Richard Bassett
Jacob Broom

SOUTH CAROLINA
John Rutledge
Charles Cotesworth Pinckney
Charles Pinckney
Pierce Butler

GEORGIA
William Few
Abraham Baldwin

ATTEST:
William Jackson, Secretary

# THE FEDERALIST PAPERS (1787–88)

*To encourage New York to ratify the U.S. Constitution, founding fathers Alexander Hamilton, James Madison, and John Jay wrote* The Federalist Papers, *eighty-five essays and articles that explained the need for a Constitution and discussed many other political issues. At the time, the essays were published anonymously under the pseudonym "Publius," a popular Latin name in Ancient Rome that also gave us the word "populous."* The Federalist Papers *became the premier companion to the U.S. Constitution and are still used by federal courts today, including the U.S. Supreme Court, to interpret that document. Several of the most important papers are included here.*

## FEDERALIST NO. 1.
## GENERAL INTRODUCTION

For the Independent Journal. Saturday, October 27, 1787

### ALEXANDER HAMILTON

To the People of the State of New York:

After an unequivocal experience of the inefficacy of the subsisting Federal Government, you are called upon to deliberate on a new Constitution for the United States of America. The subject speaks its own importance; comprehending in its consequences nothing less than the existence of the Union, the safety and welfare of the parts of which it is composed, the fate of an empire in many respects the most interesting in the world. It has been frequently remarked that it seems to have been reserved to the people of this country, by their conduct and example, to decide the important question, whether societies of men are really capable or not of establishing good government from reflection and choice, or whether they are forever destined to depend for their political constitutions on accident and force. If there be

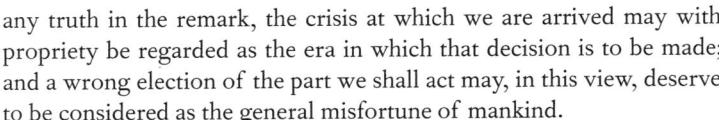 

any truth in the remark, the crisis at which we are arrived may with propriety be regarded as the era in which that decision is to be made; and a wrong election of the part we shall act may, in this view, deserve to be considered as the general misfortune of mankind.

This idea will add the inducements of philanthropy to those of patriotism, to heighten the solicitude which all considerate and good men must feel for the event. Happy will it be if our choice should be directed by a judicious estimate of our true interests, unperplexed and unbiased by considerations not connected with the public good. But this is a thing more ardently to be wished than seriously to be expected. The plan offered to our deliberations affects too many particular interests, innovates upon too many local institutions, not to involve in its discussion a variety of objects foreign to its merits, and of views, passions and prejudices little favorable to the discovery of truth.

Among the most formidable of the obstacles which the new Constitution will have to encounter may readily be distinguished the obvious interest of a certain class of men in every State to resist all changes which may hazard a diminution of the power, emolument, and consequence of the offices they hold under the State establishments; and the perverted ambition of another class of men, who will either hope to aggrandize themselves by the confusions of their country, or will flatter themselves with fairer prospects of elevation from the subdivision of the empire into several partial confederacies than from its union under one government.

It is not, however, my design to dwell upon observations of this nature. I am well aware that it would be disingenuous to resolve indiscriminately the opposition of any set of men (merely because their situations might subject them to suspicion) into interested or ambitious views. Candor will oblige us to admit that even such men may be actuated by upright intentions; and it cannot be doubted that much of the opposition which has made its appearance, or may hereafter make its appearance, will spring from sources, blameless at least, if not respectable—the honest errors of minds led astray by preconceived jealousies and fears. So numerous indeed and so powerful are the causes which serve to give a false bias to the judgment, that we, upon many occasions, see wise and good men on the wrong as well as on the right side of questions of the first magnitude to society. This circumstance, if duly attended to, would furnish a lesson of moderation to those who are ever so much persuaded of their being in the right in any controversy. And a further reason for caution, in this respect, might be drawn from the reflection that we are not always sure that those who advocate the truth are influenced by purer principles than their antagonists. Ambition, avarice, personal animosity, party opposition, and many other motives not more laudable than these, are apt to operate as well upon those who support as those who oppose the right side of a question. Were there not even these inducements to moderation, nothing could be more ill-judged than that intolerant spirit which has, at all times, characterized political parties. For in politics, as in religion, it is equally absurd to aim at making proselytes by fire and sword. Heresies in either can rarely be cured by persecution.

And yet, however just these sentiments will be allowed to be, we have already sufficient indications that it will happen in this as in all former cases of great national discussion. A torrent of angry and malignant passions will be let loose. To judge from the conduct of the opposite parties, we shall be led to conclude that they will mutually hope to evince the justness of their opinions, and to increase the number of their converts by the loudness of their declamations and the bitterness of their invectives. An enlightened zeal for the energy and efficiency of government will be stigmatized as the offspring of a temper fond of despotic power and hostile to the principles of liberty. An over-scrupulous jealousy of danger to the rights of the people, which is more commonly the fault of the head than of the heart, will be represented as mere pretense and artifice, the stale bait for popularity at the expense of the public good. It will be forgotten, on the one hand, that jealousy is the usual concomitant of love, and that the noble enthusiasm of liberty is apt to be infected with a spirit of narrow and illiberal distrust. On the other hand, it will be equally forgotten that the vigor of government is essential to the security of liberty; that, in the contemplation of a sound and well-informed judgment, their interest can never be separated; and that a dangerous ambition more often lurks behind the specious mask of zeal for the rights of the people than under the forbidden appearance of zeal for the firmness and efficiency of government. History will teach us that the former has been found a much more certain road to the introduction of despotism than the latter, and that of those men who have overturned the liberties of republics, the greatest number have begun their career by paying an obsequious court to the people; commencing demagogues, and ending tyrants.

In the course of the preceding observations, I have had an eye, my fellow-citizens, to putting you upon your guard against all attempts, from whatever quarter, to influence your decision in a matter of the utmost moment to your welfare, by any impressions other than those which may result from the evidence of truth. You will, no doubt, at the same time, have collected from the general scope of them, that they proceed from a source not unfriendly to the new Constitution. Yes, my countrymen, I own to you that, after having given it an attentive consideration, I am clearly of opinion it is your interest to adopt it. I am convinced that this is the safest course for your liberty, your dignity, and your happiness. I affect not reserves which I do not feel. I will not amuse you with an appearance of deliberation when I have decided. I frankly acknowledge to you my convictions, and I will freely lay before you the reasons on which they are founded. The consciousness of good intentions disdains ambiguity. I shall not, however, multiply professions on this head. My motives must remain in the depository of my own breast. My arguments will be open to all, and may be judged of by all. They shall at least be offered in a spirit which will not disgrace the cause of truth.

I propose, in a series of papers, to discuss the following interesting particulars:

*The utility of the Union to your political prosperity—the insufficiency of the present confederation to preserve that Union—the necessity of a government at least equally energetic with the one proposed, to the attainment of this object—the conformity of the proposed Constitution to the true principles of republican government—its analogy to your own State Constitution—and lastly, the additional security which its adoption will afford to the preservation of that species of government, to liberty, and to prosperity.*

In the progress of this discussion I shall endeavor to give a satisfactory answer to all the objections which shall have made their appearance, that may seem to have any claim to your attention.

It may perhaps be thought superfluous to offer arguments to prove the utility of the Union, a point, no doubt, deeply engraved on the hearts of the great body of the people in every State, and one, which it may be imagined, has no adversaries. But the fact is, that we already hear it whispered in the private circles of those who oppose the new Constitution, that the thirteen States are of too great extent for any general system, and that we must of necessity resort to separate confederacies of distinct portions of the whole.* This doctrine will, in all probability, be gradually propagated, till it has votaries enough to countenance an open avowal of it. For nothing can be more evident, to those who are able to take an enlarged view of the subject, than the alternative of an adoption of the new Constitution or a dismemberment of the Union. It will therefore be of use to begin by examining the advantages of that Union, the certain evils, and the probable dangers, to which every State will be exposed from its dissolution. This shall accordingly constitute the subject of my next address.

Publius

# FEDERALIST NO. 9.
## THE UNION AS A SAFEGUARD AGAINST DOMESTIC FACTION AND INSURRECTION

For the Independent Journal. Wednesday, November 21, 1787

### ALEXANDER HAMILTON

To the People of the State of New York:

A firm Union will be of the utmost moment to the peace and liberty of the States, as a barrier against domestic faction and insurrection. It is impossible to read the history of the petty republics of Greece and Italy without feeling sensations of horror and disgust at the distractions with which they were continually agitated, and at the rapid succession of revolutions by which they were kept in a state of perpetual vibration between the extremes of tyranny and anarchy. If they exhibit occasional calms, these only serve as short-lived contrast to the furious storms that are to succeed. If now and then intervals of felicity open to view, we behold them with a mixture of regret, arising from the reflection that the pleasing scenes before us are soon to be

---

* *The same idea, tracing the arguments to their consequences, is held out in several of the late publications against the new Constitution.*

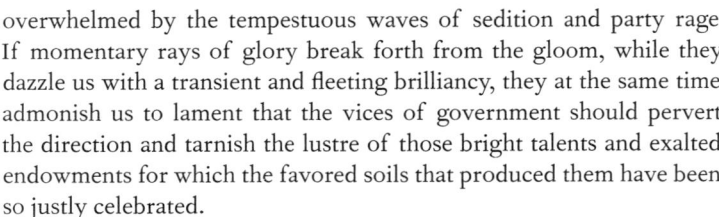

overwhelmed by the tempestuous waves of sedition and party rage. If momentary rays of glory break forth from the gloom, while they dazzle us with a transient and fleeting brilliancy, they at the same time admonish us to lament that the vices of government should pervert the direction and tarnish the lustre of those bright talents and exalted endowments for which the favored soils that produced them have been so justly celebrated.

From the disorders that disfigure the annals of those republics the advocates of despotism have drawn arguments, not only against the forms of republican government, but against the very principles of civil liberty. They have decried all free government as inconsistent with the order of society, and have indulged themselves in malicious exultation over its friends and partisans. Happily for mankind, stupendous fabrics reared on the basis of liberty, which have flourished for ages, have, in a few glorious instances, refuted their gloomy sophisms. And, I trust, America will be the broad and solid foundation of other edifices, not less magnificent, which will be equally permanent monuments of their errors.

But it is not to be denied that the portraits they have sketched of republican government were too just copies of the originals from which they were taken. If it had been found impracticable to have devised models of a more perfect structure, the enlightened friends to liberty would have been obliged to abandon the cause of that species of government as indefensible. The science of politics, however, like most other sciences, has received great improvement. The efficacy of various principles is now well understood, which were either not known at all, or imperfectly known to the ancients. The regular distribution of power into distinct departments; the introduction of legislative balances and checks; the institution of courts composed of judges holding their offices during good behavior; the representation of the people in the legislature by deputies of their own election: these are wholly new discoveries, or have made their principal progress towards perfection in modern times. They are means, and powerful means, by which the excellences of republican government may be retained and its imperfections lessened or avoided. To this catalogue of circumstances that tend to the amelioration of popular systems of civil government, I shall venture, however novel it may appear to some, to add one more, on a principle which has been made the foundation of an objection to the new Constitution; I mean the *enlargement* of the *orbit* within which such systems are to revolve, either in respect to the dimensions of a single State or to the consolidation of several smaller States into one great Confederacy. The latter is that which immediately concerns the object under consideration. It will, however, be of use to examine the principle in its application to a single State, which shall be attended to in another place.

The utility of a Confederacy, as well to suppress faction and to guard the internal tranquillity of States, as to increase their external force and security, is in reality not a new idea. It has been practiced upon in different countries and ages, and has received the sanction of the most approved writers on the subject of politics. The opponents of the plan proposed have, with great assiduity, cited and circulated the observations of Montesquieu on the necessity of a contracted territory for a republican government. But they seem not to have been apprised of the sentiments of that great man expressed in another part of his work, nor to have adverted to the consequences of the principle to which they subscribe with such ready acquiescence.

When Montesquieu recommends a small extent for republics, the standards he had in view were of dimensions far short of the limits of almost every one of these States. Neither Virginia, Massachusetts, Pennsylvania, New York, North Carolina, nor Georgia can by any means be compared with the models from which he reasoned and to which the terms of his description apply. If we therefore take his ideas on this point as the criterion of truth, we shall be driven to the alternative either of taking refuge at once in the arms of monarchy, or of splitting ourselves into an infinity of little, jealous, clashing, tumultuous commonwealths, the wretched nurseries of unceasing discord, and the miserable objects of universal pity or contempt. Some of the writers who have come forward on the other side of the question seem to have been aware of the dilemma; and have even been bold enough to hint at the division of the larger States as a desirable thing. Such an infatuated policy, such a desperate expedient, might, by the multiplication of petty offices, answer the views of men who possess not qualifications to extend their influence beyond the narrow circles of personal intrigue, but it could never promote the greatness or happiness of the people of America.

Referring the examination of the principle itself to another place, as

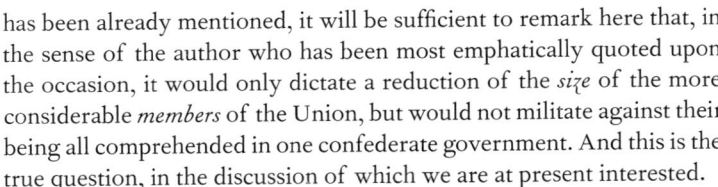

has been already mentioned, it will be sufficient to remark here that, in the sense of the author who has been most emphatically quoted upon the occasion, it would only dictate a reduction of the *size* of the more considerable *members* of the Union, but would not militate against their being all comprehended in one confederate government. And this is the true question, in the discussion of which we are at present interested.

So far are the suggestions of Montesquieu from standing in opposition to a general Union of the States, that he explicitly treats of a confederate republic as the expedient for extending the sphere of popular government, and reconciling the advantages of monarchy with those of republicanism.

"It is very probable," (says he[*]) "that mankind would have been obliged at length to live constantly under the government of a single person, had they not contrived a kind of constitution that has all the internal advantages of a republican, together with the external force of a monarchical government. I mean a *Confederate Republic*."

"This form of government is a convention by which several smaller *states* agree to become members of a larger *one*, which they intend to form. It is a kind of assemblage of societies that constitute a new one, capable of increasing, by means of new associations, till they arrive to such a degree of power as to be able to provide for the security of the united body."

"A republic of this kind, able to withstand an external force, may support itself without any internal corruptions. The form of this society prevents all manner of inconveniences."

"If a single member should attempt to usurp the supreme authority, he could not be supposed to have an equal authority and credit in all the confederate states. Were he to have too great influence over one, this would alarm the rest. Were he to subdue a part, that which would still remain free might oppose him with forces independent of those which he had usurped and overpower him before he could be settled in his usurpation."

"Should a popular insurrection happen in one of the confederate states the others are able to quell it. Should abuses creep into one part, they are reformed by those that remain sound. The state may be destroyed on one side, and not on the other; the confederacy may be dissolved, and the confederates preserve their sovereignty."

---

[*] *Spirit of Laws,"* vol. i., book ix., chap. i.

"As this government is composed of small republics, it enjoys the internal happiness of each; and with respect to its external situation, it is possessed, by means of the association, of all the advantages of large monarchies."

I have thought it proper to quote at length these interesting passages, because they contain a luminous abridgment of the principal arguments in favor of the Union, and must effectually remove the false impressions which a misapplication of other parts of the work was calculated to make. They have, at the same time, an intimate connection with the more immediate design of this paper; which is, to illustrate the tendency of the Union to repress domestic faction and insurrection.

A distinction, more subtle than accurate, has been raised between a *confederacy* and a *consolidation* of the States. The essential characteristic of the first is said to be, the restriction of its authority to the members in their collective capacities, without reaching to the individuals of whom they are composed. It is contended that the national council ought to have no concern with any object of internal administration. An exact equality of suffrage between the members has also been insisted upon as a leading feature of a confederate government. These positions are, in the main, arbitrary; they are supported neither by principle nor precedent. It has indeed happened, that governments of this kind have generally operated in the manner which the distinction taken notice of, supposes to be inherent in their nature; but there have been in most of them extensive exceptions to the practice, which serve to prove, as far as example will go, that there is no absolute rule on the subject. And it will be clearly shown in the course of this investigation that as far as the principle contended for has prevailed, it has been the cause of incurable disorder and imbecility in the government.

The definition of a *Confederate Republic* seems simply to be "an assemblage of societies," or an association of two or more states into one state. The extent, modifications, and objects of the federal authority are mere matters of discretion. So long as the separate organization of the members be not abolished; so long as it exists, by a constitutional necessity, for local purposes; though it should be in perfect subordination to the general authority of the union, it would still be, in fact and in theory, an association of states, or a confederacy. The proposed Constitution, so far from implying an abolition of the State governments, makes them constituent parts of the national sovereignty, by allowing them a direct representation in the Senate, and leaves in their possession certain exclusive and very important portions of sovereign power. This fully corresponds, in every rational import of the terms, with the idea of a federal government.

In the Lycian confederacy, which consisted of twenty-three *cities* or republics, the largest were entitled to *three* votes in the *common council*, those of the middle class to *two*, and the smallest to *one*. The *common council* had the appointment of all the judges and magistrates of the respective *cities*. This was certainly the most, delicate species of interference in their internal administration; for if there be any thing that seems exclusively appropriated to the local jurisdictions, it is the appointment of their own officers. Yet Montesquieu, speaking of this association, says: "Were I to give a model of an excellent Confederate Republic, it would be that of Lycia." Thus we perceive that the distinctions insisted upon were not within the contemplation of this enlightened civilian; and we shall be led to conclude, that they are the novel refinements of an erroneous theory.

PUBLIUS

# FEDERALIST NO. 10.
## THE SAME SUBJECT CONTINUED (THE UNION AS A SAFEGUARD AGAINST DOMESTIC FACTION AND INSURRECTION)

From the Daily Advertiser. Thursday, November 22, 1787.

### JAMES MADISON

To the People of the State of New York:

AMONG the numerous advantages promised by a well constructed Union, none deserves to be more accurately developed than its tendency to break and control the violence of faction. The friend of popular governments never finds himself so much alarmed for their character and fate, as when he contemplates their propensity to this dangerous vice. He will not fail, therefore, to set a due value on any plan which, without violating the principles to which he is attached, provides a proper cure for it. The instability, injustice, and confusion introduced into the public councils, have, in truth, been the mortal diseases under which popular governments have everywhere perished; as they continue to be the favorite and fruitful topics from which the adversaries to liberty derive their most specious declamations. The valuable improvements made by the American constitutions on the popular models, both ancient and modern, cannot certainly be too much admired; but it would be an unwarrantable partiality, to contend that they have as effectually obviated the danger on this side, as was wished and expected. Complaints are everywhere heard from our most considerate and virtuous citizens, equally the friends of public and private faith, and of public and personal liberty, that our governments are too unstable, that the public good is disregarded in the conflicts of rival parties, and that measures are too often decided, not according to the rules of justice and the rights of the minor party, but by the superior force of an interested and overbearing majority. However anxiously we may wish that these complaints had no foundation, the evidence, of known facts will not permit us to deny that they are in some degree true. It will be found, indeed, on a candid review of our situation, that some of the distresses under which we labor have been erroneously charged on the operation of our governments; but it will be found, at the same time, that other causes will not alone account for many of our heaviest misfortunes; and, particularly, for that prevailing and increasing distrust of public engagements, and alarm for private rights, which are echoed from one end of the continent to the other. These must be chiefly, if not wholly, effects of the unsteadiness and injustice with which a factious spirit has tainted our public administrations.

By a faction, I understand a number of citizens, whether amounting to a majority or a minority of the whole, who are united and actuated by some common impulse of passion, or of interest, adversed to the rights of other citizens, or to the permanent and aggregate interests of the community.

There are two methods of curing the mischiefs of faction: the one, by removing its causes; the other, by controlling its effects.

There are again two methods of removing the causes of faction: the one, by destroying the liberty which is essential to its existence; the other, by giving to every citizen the same opinions, the same passions, and the same interests.

It could never be more truly said than of the first remedy, that it was worse than the disease. Liberty is to faction what air is to fire, an aliment without which it instantly expires. But it could not be less folly to abolish liberty, which is essential to political life, because it nourishes faction, than it would be to wish the annihilation of air, which is essential to animal life, because it imparts to fire its destructive agency.

The second expedient is as impracticable as the first would be unwise. As long as the reason of man continues fallible, and he is at liberty to exercise it, different opinions will be formed. As long as the connection subsists between his reason and his self-love, his opinions and his passions will have a reciprocal influence on each other; and the former will be objects to which the latter will attach themselves. The diversity in the faculties of men, from which the rights of property originate, is not less an insuperable obstacle to a uniformity of interests. The protection of these faculties is the first object of government. From the protection of different and unequal faculties of acquiring property, the possession of different degrees and kinds of property immediately results; and from the influence of these on the sentiments and views of the respective proprietors, ensues a division of the society into different interests and parties.

The latent causes of faction are thus sown in the nature of man; and we see them everywhere brought into different degrees of activity, according to the different circumstances of civil society. A zeal for different opinions concerning religion, concerning government, and many other points, as well of speculation as of practice; an attachment to different leaders ambitiously contending for pre-eminence and power; or to persons of other descriptions whose fortunes have been interesting to the human passions, have, in turn, divided mankind into parties, inflamed them with mutual animosity, and rendered them much more disposed to vex and oppress each other than to co-operate for their common good. So strong is this propensity of mankind to fall into mutual animosities, that where no substantial occasion presents itself, the most frivolous and fanciful distinctions have been sufficient to kindle their unfriendly passions and excite their most violent conflicts. But the most common and durable source of factions has been the various and unequal distribution of property. Those who hold and those who are without property have ever formed distinct interests in society. Those who are creditors, and those who are debtors, fall under a like discrimination. A landed interest, a manufacturing interest, a mercantile interest, a moneyed interest, with many lesser interests, grow up of necessity in civilized nations, and divide them into different classes, actuated by different sentiments and views. The regulation of these various and interfering interests forms the principal task of modern legislation, and involves the spirit of party and faction in the necessary and ordinary operations of the government.

No man is allowed to be a judge in his own cause, because his interest would certainly bias his judgment, and, not improbably, corrupt his integrity. With equal, nay with greater reason, a body of men are unfit to be both judges and parties at the same time; yet what are many of the most important acts of legislation, but so many judicial determinations, not indeed concerning the rights of single persons, but concerning the rights of large bodies of citizens? And what are the different classes of legislators but advocates and parties to the causes which they determine? Is a law proposed concerning private debts? It is a question to which the creditors are parties on one side and the debtors on the other. Justice ought to hold the balance between them. Yet the parties are, and must be, themselves the judges; and the most numerous party, or, in other words, the most powerful faction must be expected to prevail. Shall domestic manufactures be encouraged, and in what degree, by restrictions on foreign manufactures? are questions which would be differently decided by the landed and the manufacturing classes, and probably by neither with a sole regard to justice and the public good. The apportionment of taxes on the various descriptions of property is an act which seems to require the most exact impartiality; yet there is, perhaps, no legislative act in which greater opportunity and temptation are given to a predominant party to trample on the rules of justice. Every shilling with which they overburden the inferior number, is a shilling saved to their own pockets.

It is in vain to say that enlightened statesmen will be able to adjust these clashing interests, and render them all subservient to the public good. Enlightened statesmen will not always be at the helm. Nor, in many cases, can such an adjustment be made at all without taking into view indirect and remote considerations, which will rarely prevail over the immediate interest which one party may find in disregarding the rights of another or the good of the whole.

The inference to which we are brought is, that the *causes* of faction cannot be removed, and that relief is only to be sought in the means of controlling its *effects*.

If a faction consists of less than a majority, relief is supplied by the republican principle, which enables the majority to defeat its sinister views by regular vote. It may clog the administration, it may convulse the society; but it will be unable to execute and mask its violence under the forms of the Constitution. When a majority is included in a faction, the form of popular government, on the other hand, enables it to sacrifice to its ruling passion or interest both the public good and the rights of other citizens. To secure the public good and private rights against the danger of such a faction, and at the same time to preserve the spirit and the form of popular government, is then the great object to which our inquiries are directed. Let me add that it is the great desideratum by which this form of government can be rescued from the opprobrium under which it has so long labored, and be recommended to the esteem and adoption of mankind.

By what means is this object attainable? Evidently by one of two only. Either the existence of the same passion or interest in a majority at the same time must be prevented, or the majority, having such coexistent passion or interest, must be rendered, by their number and local situation, unable to concert and carry into effect schemes of oppression. If the impulse and the opportunity be suffered to coincide, we well know that neither moral nor religious motives can be relied on as an adequate control. They are not found to be such on the injustice and violence of individuals, and lose their efficacy in proportion to the number combined together, that is, in proportion as their efficacy becomes needful.

From this view of the subject it may be concluded that a pure democracy, by which I mean a society consisting of a small number of citizens, who assemble and administer the government in person, can admit of no cure for the mischiefs of faction. A common passion or interest will, in almost every case, be felt by a majority of the whole; a communication and concert result from the form of government itself; and there is nothing to check the inducements to sacrifice the weaker party or an obnoxious individual. Hence it is that such democracies have ever been spectacles of turbulence and contention; have ever been found incompatible with personal security or the rights of property; and have in general been as short in their lives as they have been violent in their deaths. Theoretic politicians, who have patronized this species of government, have erroneously supposed that by reducing mankind to a perfect equality in their political rights, they would, at the same time, be perfectly equalized and assimilated in their possessions, their opinions, and their passions.

A republic, by which I mean a government in which the scheme of representation takes place, opens a different prospect, and promises the cure for which we are seeking. Let us examine the points in which it varies from pure democracy, and we shall comprehend both the nature of the cure and the efficacy which it must derive from the Union.

The two great points of difference between a democracy and a republic are: first, the delegation of the government, in the latter, to a small number of citizens elected by the rest; secondly, the greater number of citizens, and greater sphere of country, over which the latter may be extended.

The effect of the first difference is, on the one hand, to refine and enlarge the public views, by passing them through the medium of a chosen body of citizens, whose wisdom may best discern the true interest of their country, and whose patriotism and love of justice will be least likely to sacrifice it to temporary or partial considerations. Under such a regulation, it may well happen that the public voice, pronounced by the representatives of the people, will be more consonant to the public good than if pronounced by the people themselves, convened for the purpose. On the other hand, the effect may be inverted. Men of factious tempers, of local prejudices, or of sinister designs, may, by intrigue, by corruption, or by other means, first obtain the suffrages, and then betray the interests, of the people. The question resulting is, whether small or extensive republics are more favorable to the election of proper guardians of the public weal; and it is clearly decided in favor of the latter by two obvious considerations:

In the first place, it is to be remarked that, however small the republic may be, the representatives must be raised to a certain number, in order to guard against the cabals of a few; and that, however large it may be, they must be limited to a certain number, in order to guard against the confusion of a multitude. Hence, the number of representatives in the two cases not being in proportion to that of the two constituents, and being proportionally greater in the small republic, it follows that, if the proportion of fit characters be not less in the large than in the small republic, the former will present a greater option, and consequently a greater probability of a fit choice.

In the next place, as each representative will be chosen by a greater number of citizens in the large than in the small republic, it will be more difficult for unworthy candidates to practice with success the vicious arts by which elections are too often carried; and the suffrages of the people being more free, will be more likely to centre in men who possess the most attractive merit and the most diffusive and established characters.

It must be confessed that in this, as in most other cases, there is a mean, on both sides of which inconveniences will be found to lie. By enlarging too much the number of electors, you render the representatives too little acquainted with all their local circumstances and lesser interests; as by reducing it too much, you render him unduly attached to these, and too little fit to comprehend and pursue great and national objects. The federal Constitution forms a happy combination in this respect; the great and aggregate interests being referred to the national, the local and particular to the State legislatures.

The other point of difference is, the greater number of citizens and extent of territory which may be brought within the compass of republican than of democratic government; and it is this circumstance principally which renders factious combinations less to be dreaded in the former than in the latter. The smaller the society, the fewer probably will be the distinct parties and interests composing it; the fewer the distinct parties and interests, the more frequently will a majority be found of the same party; and the smaller the number of individuals composing a majority, and the smaller the compass within which they are placed, the more easily will they concert and execute their plans of oppression. Extend the sphere, and you take in a greater variety of parties and interests; you make it less probable that a majority of the whole will have a common motive to invade the rights of other citizens; or if such a common motive exists, it will be more difficult for all who feel it to discover their own strength, and to act in unison with each other. Besides other impediments, it may be remarked that, where there is a consciousness of unjust or dishonorable purposes, communication is always checked by distrust in proportion to the number whose concurrence is necessary.

Hence, it clearly appears, that the same advantage which a republic has over a democracy, in controlling the effects of faction, is enjoyed by a large over a small republic,—is enjoyed by the Union over the States composing it. Does the advantage consist in the substitution of representatives whose enlightened views and virtuous sentiments render them superior to local prejudices and schemes of injustice? It will not be denied that the representation of the Union will be most likely to possess these requisite endowments. Does it consist in the greater security afforded by a greater variety of parties, against the event of any one party being able to outnumber and oppress the rest? In an equal degree does the increased variety of parties comprised within the Union, increase this security. Does it, in fine, consist in the greater obstacles opposed to the concert and accomplishment of the secret wishes of an unjust and interested majority? Here, again, the extent of the Union gives it the most palpable advantage.

The influence of factious leaders may kindle a flame within their particular States, but will be unable to spread a general conflagration through the other States. A religious sect may degenerate into a political faction in a part of the Confederacy; but the variety of sects dispersed over the entire face of it must secure the national councils against any danger from that source. A rage for paper money, for an abolition of debts, for an equal division of property, or for any other improper or wicked project, will be less apt to pervade the whole body of the Union than a particular member of it; in the same proportion as such a malady is more likely to taint a particular county or district, than an entire State.

In the extent and proper structure of the Union, therefore, we behold a republican remedy for the diseases most incident to republican government. And according to the degree of pleasure and pride we feel in being republicans, ought to be our zeal in cherishing the spirit and supporting the character of Federalists.

PUBLIUS

# FEDERALIST NO. 14.
## OBJECTIONS TO THE PROPOSED CONSTITUTION FROM EXTENT OF TERRITORY ANSWERED

From the New York Packet. Friday, November 30, 1787.

### JAMES MADISON

To the People of the State of New York:

WE HAVE seen the necessity of the Union, as our bulwark against foreign danger, as the conservator of peace among ourselves, as the guardian of our commerce and other common interests, as the only substitute for those military establishments which have subverted the liberties of the Old World, and as the proper antidote for the diseases of faction, which have proved fatal to other popular governments, and of which alarming symptoms have been betrayed by our own. All that remains, within this branch of our inquiries, is to take notice of an objection that may be drawn from the great extent of country which the Union embraces. A few observations on this subject will be the more proper, as it is perceived that the adversaries of the new Constitution are availing themselves of the prevailing prejudice with regard to the practicable sphere of republican administration, in order to supply, by imaginary difficulties, the want of those solid objections which they endeavor in vain to find.

The error which limits republican government to a narrow district has been unfolded and refuted in preceding papers. I remark here only that it seems to owe its rise and prevalence chiefly to the confounding of a republic with a democracy, applying to the former reasonings drawn from the nature of the latter. The true distinction between these forms was also adverted to on a former occasion. It is, that in a democracy, the people meet and exercise the government in person; in a republic, they assemble and administer it by their representatives and agents. A democracy, consequently, will be confined to a small spot. A republic may be extended over a large region.

To this accidental source of the error may be added the artifice of some celebrated authors, whose writings have had a great share in forming the modern standard of political opinions. Being subjects either of an absolute or limited monarchy, they have endeavored to heighten the advantages, or palliate the evils of those forms, by placing in comparison the vices and defects of the republican, and by citing as specimens of the latter the turbulent democracies of ancient Greece and modern Italy. Under the confusion of names, it has been an easy task to transfer to a republic observations applicable to a democracy only; and among others, the observation that it can never be established but among a small number of people, living within a small compass of territory.

Such a fallacy may have been the less perceived, as most of the popular governments of antiquity were of the democratic species;

and even in modern Europe, to which we owe the great principle of representation, no example is seen of a government wholly popular, and founded, at the same time, wholly on that principle. If Europe has the merit of discovering this great mechanical power in government, by the simple agency of which the will of the largest political body may be concentred, and its force directed to any object which the public good requires, America can claim the merit of making the discovery the basis of unmixed and extensive republics. It is only to be lamented that any of her citizens should wish to deprive her of the additional merit of displaying its full efficacy in the establishment of the comprehensive system now under her consideration.

As the natural limit of a democracy is that distance from the central point which will just permit the most remote citizens to assemble as often as their public functions demand, and will include no greater number than can join in those functions; so the natural limit of a republic is that distance from the centre which will barely allow the representatives to meet as often as may be necessary for the administration of public affairs. Can it be said that the limits of the United States exceed this distance? It will not be said by those who recollect that the Atlantic coast is the longest side of the Union, that during the term of thirteen years, the representatives of the States have been almost continually assembled, and that the members from the most distant States are not chargeable with greater intermissions of attendance than those from the States in the neighborhood of Congress.

That we may form a juster estimate with regard to this interesting subject, let us resort to the actual dimensions of the Union. The limits, as fixed by the treaty of peace, are: on the east the Atlantic, on the south the latitude of thirty-one degrees, on the west the Mississippi, and on the north an irregular line running in some instances beyond the forty-fifth degree, in others falling as low as the forty-second. The southern shore of Lake Erie lies below that latitude. Computing the distance between the thirty-first and forty-fifth degrees, it amounts to nine hundred and seventy-three common miles; computing it from thirty-one to forty-two degrees, to seven hundred and sixty-four miles and a half. Taking the mean for the distance, the amount will be eight hundred and sixty-eight miles and three-fourths. The mean distance from the Atlantic to the Mississippi does not probably exceed seven hundred and fifty miles. On a comparison of this extent with that of several countries in Europe, the practicability of rendering our system commensurate to it appears to be demonstrable. It is not a great deal larger than Germany, where a diet representing the whole empire is continually assembled; or than Poland before the late dismemberment, where another national diet was the depositary of the supreme power. Passing by France and Spain, we find that in Great Britain, inferior as it may be in size, the representatives of the northern extremity of the island have as far to travel to the national council as will be required of those of the most remote parts of the Union.

Favorable as this view of the subject may be, some observations remain which will place it in a light still more satisfactory.

In the first place it is to be remembered that the general government is not to be charged with the whole power of making and administering laws. Its jurisdiction is limited to certain enumerated objects, which concern all the members of the republic, but which are not to be attained by the separate provisions of any. The subordinate governments, which can extend their care to all those other subjects which can be separately provided for, will retain their due authority and activity. Were it proposed by the plan of the convention to abolish the governments of the particular States, its adversaries would have some ground for their objection; though it would not be difficult to show that if they were abolished the general government would be compelled, by the principle of self-preservation, to reinstate them in their proper jurisdiction.

A second observation to be made is that the immediate object of the federal Constitution is to secure the union of the thirteen primitive States, which we know to be practicable; and to add to them such other States as may arise in their own bosoms, or in their neighborhoods, which we cannot doubt to be equally practicable. The arrangements that may be necessary for those angles and fractions of our territory which lie on our northwestern frontier, must be left to those whom further discoveries and experience will render more equal to the task.

Let it be remarked, in the third place, that the intercourse throughout the Union will be facilitated by new improvements. Roads will everywhere be shortened, and kept in better order; accommodations for travelers will be multiplied and meliorated; an interior navigation on our eastern side will be opened throughout, or nearly throughout, the whole extent of the thirteen States. The communication between the Western and Atlantic districts, and between different parts of each, will be rendered more and more easy by those numerous canals with which the beneficence of nature has intersected our country, and which art finds it so little difficult to connect and complete.

A fourth and still more important consideration is, that as almost every State will, on one side or other, be a frontier, and will thus find, in regard to its safety, an inducement to make some sacrifices for the sake of the general protection; so the States which lie at the greatest distance from the heart of the Union, and which, of course, may partake least of the ordinary circulation of its benefits, will be at the same time immediately contiguous to foreign nations, and will consequently stand, on particular occasions, in greatest need of its strength and resources. It may be inconvenient for Georgia, or the States forming our western or northeastern borders, to send their representatives to the seat of government; but they would find it more so to struggle alone against an invading enemy, or even to support alone the whole expense of those precautions which may be dictated by the neighborhood of continual danger. If they should derive less benefit, therefore, from the Union in some respects than the less distant States, they will derive greater benefit from it in other respects, and thus the proper equilibrium will be maintained throughout.

I submit to you, my fellow-citizens, these considerations, in full confidence that the good sense which has so often marked your decisions will allow them their due weight and effect; and that you will never suffer difficulties, however formidable in appearance, or however fashionable the error on which they may be founded, to drive you into the gloomy and perilous scene into which the advocates for disunion would conduct you. Hearken not to the unnatural voice which tells you that the people of America, knit together as they are by so many cords of affection, can no longer live together as members of the same family; can no longer continue the mutual guardians of their mutual happiness; can no longer be fellow citizens of one great, respectable, and flourishing empire. Hearken not to the voice which petulantly tells you that the form of government recommended for your adoption is a novelty in the political world; that it has never yet had a place in the theories of the wildest projectors; that it rashly attempts what it is impossible to accomplish. No, my countrymen, shut your ears against this unhallowed language. Shut your hearts against the poison which it conveys; the kindred blood which flows in the veins of American citizens, the mingled blood which they have shed in defense of their sacred rights, consecrate their Union, and excite horror at the idea of their becoming aliens, rivals, enemies. And if novelties are to be shunned, believe me, the most alarming of all novelties, the most wild of all projects, the most rash of all attempts, is that of rendering us in pieces, in order to preserve our liberties and promote our happiness. But why is the experiment of an extended republic to be rejected, merely because it may comprise what is new? Is it not the glory of the people of America, that, whilst they have paid a decent regard to the opinions of former times and other nations, they have not suffered a blind veneration for antiquity, for custom, or for names, to overrule the suggestions of their own good sense, the knowledge of their own situation, and the lessons of their own experience? To this manly spirit, posterity will be indebted for the possession, and the world for the example, of the numerous innovations displayed on the American theatre, in favor of private rights and public happiness. Had no important step been taken by the leaders of the Revolution for which a precedent could not be discovered, no government established of which an exact model did not present itself, the people of the United States might, at this moment have been numbered among the melancholy victims of misguided councils, must at best have been laboring under the weight of some of those forms which have crushed the liberties of the rest of mankind. Happily for America, happily, we trust, for the whole human race, they pursued a new and more noble course. They accomplished a revolution which has no parallel in the annals of human society. They reared the fabrics of governments which have no model on the face of the globe. They formed the design of a great Confederacy, which it is incumbent on their successors to improve and perpetuate. If their works betray imperfections, we wonder at the fewness of them. If they erred most in the structure of the Union, this was the work most difficult to be executed; this is the work which has been new modelled by the act of your convention, and it is that act on which you are now to deliberate and to decide.

PUBLIUS

# FEDERALIST NO. 39.
# THE CONFORMITY OF THE PLAN TO
# REPUBLICAN PRINCIPLES

For the Independent Journal. Wednesday, January 16, 1788

## JAMES MADISON

To the People of the State of New York:

THE last paper having concluded the observations which were meant to introduce a candid survey of the plan of government reported by the convention, we now proceed to the execution of that part of our undertaking.

The first question that offers itself is, whether the general form and aspect of the government be strictly republican. It is evident that no other form would be reconcilable with the genius of the people of America; with the fundamental principles of the Revolution; or with that honorable determination which animates every votary of freedom, to rest all our political experiments on the capacity of mankind for self-government. If the plan of the convention, therefore, be found to depart from the republican character, its advocates must abandon it as no longer defensible.

What, then, are the distinctive characters of the republican form? Were an answer to this question to be sought, not by recurring to principles, but in the application of the term by political writers, to the constitution of different States, no satisfactory one would ever be found. Holland, in which no particle of the supreme authority is derived from the people, has passed almost universally under the denomination of a republic. The same title has been bestowed on Venice, where absolute power over the great body of the people is exercised, in the most absolute manner, by a small body of hereditary nobles. Poland, which is a mixture of aristocracy and of monarchy in their worst forms, has been dignified with the same appellation. The government of England, which has one republican branch only, combined with an hereditary aristocracy and monarchy, has, with equal impropriety, been frequently placed on the list of republics. These examples, which are nearly as dissimilar to each other as to a genuine republic, show the extreme inaccuracy with which the term has been used in political disquisitions.

If we resort for a criterion to the different principles on which different forms of government are established, we may define a republic to be, or at least may bestow that name on, a government which derives all its powers directly or indirectly from the great body of the people, and is administered by persons holding their offices during pleasure, for a limited period, or during good behavior. It is *essential* to such a government that it be derived from the great body of the society, not from an inconsiderable proportion, or a favored class of it; otherwise a handful of tyrannical nobles, exercising their oppressions by a delegation of their powers, might aspire to the rank of republicans, and claim for their government the honorable title of republic. It is *sufficient* for such a government that the persons administering it be appointed, either directly or indirectly, by the people; and that they hold their appointments by either of the tenures just specified; otherwise every government in the United States, as well as every other popular government that has been or can be well organized or well executed, would be degraded from the republican character. According to the constitution of every State in the Union, some or other of the officers of government are appointed indirectly only by the people. According to most of them, the chief magistrate himself is so appointed. And according to one, this mode of appointment is extended to one of the coordinate branches of the legislature. According to all the constitutions, also, the tenure of the highest offices is extended to a definite period, and in many instances, both within the legislative and executive departments, to a period of years. According to the provisions of most of the constitutions, again, as well as according to the most respectable and received opinions on the subject, the members of the judiciary department are to retain their offices by the firm tenure of good behavior.

On comparing the Constitution planned by the convention with the standard here fixed, we perceive at once that it is, in the most rigid sense, conformable to it. The House of Representatives, like that of one branch at least of all the State legislatures, is elected immediately by the great body of the people. The Senate, like the present Congress, and the Senate of Maryland, derives its appointment indirectly from the people. The President is indirectly derived from the choice of the people, according to the example in most of the States. Even the judges, with all other officers of the Union, will, as in the several States, be the choice, though a remote choice, of the people themselves, the duration of the appointments is equally conformable to the republican standard, and to the model of State constitutions The House of Representatives is periodically elective, as in all the States; and for the period of two years, as in the State of South Carolina. The Senate is elective, for the period of six years; which is but one year more than the period of the Senate of Maryland, and but two more than that of the Senates of New York and Virginia. The President is to continue in office for the period of four years; as in New York and Delaware, the chief magistrate is elected for three years, and in South Carolina for two years. In the other States the election is annual. In several of the States, however, no constitutional provision is made for the impeachment of the chief magistrate. And in Delaware and Virginia he is not impeachable till out of office. The President of the United States is impeachable at any time during his continuance in office. The tenure by which the judges are to hold their places, is, as it unquestionably ought to be, that of good behavior. The tenure of the ministerial offices generally, will be a subject of legal regulation, conformably to the reason of the case and the example of the State constitutions.

Could any further proof be required of the republican complexion of this system, the most decisive one might be found in its absolute prohibition of titles of nobility, both under the federal and the State governments; and in its express guaranty of the republican form to each of the latter.

"But it was not sufficient," say the adversaries of the proposed Constitution, "for the convention to adhere to the republican form. They ought, with equal care, to have preserved the *federal* form, which regards the Union as a *confederacy* of sovereign states; instead of which, they have framed a *national* government, which regards the Union as a *consolidation* of the States." And it is asked by what authority this bold and radical innovation was undertaken? The handle which has been made of this objection requires that it should be examined with some precision.

Without inquiring into the accuracy of the distinction on which the objection is founded, it will be necessary to a just estimate of its force, first, to ascertain the real character of the government in question; secondly, to inquire how far the convention were authorized to propose such a government; and thirdly, how far the duty they owed to their country could supply any defect of regular authority.

First. In order to ascertain the real character of the government, it may be considered in relation to the foundation on which it is to be established; to the sources from which its ordinary powers are to be drawn; to the operation of those powers; to the extent of them; and to the authority by which future changes in the government are to be introduced.

On examining the first relation, it appears, on one hand, that the Constitution is to be founded on the assent and ratification of the people of America, given by deputies elected for the special purpose; but, on the other, that this assent and ratification is to be given by the people, not as individuals composing one entire nation, but as composing the distinct and independent States to which they respectively belong. It is to be the assent and ratification of the several States, derived from the supreme authority in each State, the authority of the people themselves. The act, therefore, establishing the Constitution, will not be a *national*, but a *federal* act.

That it will be a federal and not a national act, as these terms are understood by the objectors; the act of the people, as forming so many independent States, not as forming one aggregate nation, is obvious from this single consideration, that it is to result neither from the decision of a *majority* of the people of the Union, nor from that of a *majority* of the States. It must result from the *unanimous* assent of the several States that are parties to it, differing no otherwise from their ordinary assent than in its being expressed, not by the legislative authority, but by that of the people themselves. Were the people regarded in this transaction as forming one nation, the will of the majority of the whole people of the United States would bind the minority, in the same manner as the majority in each State must bind the minority; and the will of the majority must be determined either by a comparison of the individual votes, or by considering the will of the majority of the States as evidence of the will of a majority of the people of the United States. Neither of these rules have been adopted. Each State, in ratifying the Constitution, is considered as a sovereign body, independent of all others, and only to be bound by its own voluntary act. In this relation, then, the new Constitution will, if established, be a *federal*, and not a *national* constitution.

The next relation is, to the sources from which the ordinary powers of government are to be derived. The House of Representatives will derive its powers from the people of America; and the people will be represented in the same proportion, and on the same principle, as they are in the legislature of a particular State. So far the government is *national*, not *federal*. The Senate, on the other hand, will derive its powers from the States, as political and coequal societies; and these will be represented on the principle of equality in the Senate, as they now are in the existing Congress. So far the government is *federal*, not *national*. The executive power will be derived from a very compound source. The immediate election of the President is to be made by the States in their political characters. The votes allotted to them are in a compound ratio, which considers them partly as distinct and coequal societies, partly as unequal members of the same society. The eventual election, again, is to be made by that branch of the legislature which consists of the national representatives; but in this particular act they are to be thrown into the form of individual delegations, from so many distinct and coequal bodies politic. From this aspect of the government it appears to be of a mixed character, presenting at least as many *federal* as *national* features.

The difference between a federal and national government, as it relates to the *operation of the government*, is supposed to consist in this, that in the former the powers operate on the political bodies composing the Confederacy, in their political capacities; in the latter, on the individual citizens composing the nation, in their individual capacities. On trying the Constitution by this criterion, it falls under the *national*, not the *federal* character; though perhaps not so completely as has been understood. In several cases, and particularly in the trial of controversies to which States may be parties, they must be viewed and proceeded against in their collective and political capacities only. So far the national countenance of the government on this side seems to be disfigured by a few federal features. But this blemish is perhaps unavoidable in any plan; and the operation of the government on the people, in their individual capacities, in its ordinary and most essential proceedings, may, on the whole, designate it, in this relation, a *national* government.

But if the government be national with regard to the *operation* of its powers, it changes its aspect again when we contemplate it in relation to the *extent* of its powers. The idea of a national government involves in it, not only an authority over the individual citizens, but an indefinite supremacy over all persons and things, so far as they are objects of lawful government. Among a people consolidated into one nation, this supremacy is completely vested in the national legislature. Among communities united for particular purposes, it is vested partly in the general and partly in the municipal legislatures. In the former case, all local authorities are subordinate to the supreme; and may be controlled, directed, or abolished by it at pleasure. In the latter, the local or municipal authorities form distinct and independent portions of the supremacy, no more subject, within their respective spheres, to the general authority, than the general authority is subject to them, within its own sphere. In this relation, then, the proposed government cannot be deemed a *national* one; since its jurisdiction extends to certain enumerated objects only, and leaves to the several States a residuary and inviolable sovereignty over all other objects. It is true that in controversies relating to the boundary between the two jurisdictions, the tribunal which is ultimately to decide, is to be established under the general government. But this does not change the principle of the case. The decision is to be impartially made, according to the rules of the Constitution; and all the usual and most effectual precautions are taken to secure this impartiality. Some such tribunal is clearly essential to prevent an appeal to the sword and a dissolution of the compact; and that it ought to be established under the general rather than under the local governments, or, to speak more properly, that it could be safely established under the first alone, is a position not likely to be combated.

If we try the Constitution by its last relation to the authority by which amendments are to be made, we find it neither wholly *national* nor wholly *federal*. Were it wholly national, the supreme and ultimate authority would reside in the *majority* of the people of the Union; and this authority would be competent at all times, like that of a majority of every national society, to alter or abolish its established government. Were it wholly federal, on the other hand, the concurrence of each State in the Union would be essential to every alteration that would be binding on all. The mode provided by the plan of the convention is not founded on either of these principles. In requiring more than a majority, and principles. In requiring more than a majority, and particularly in computing the proportion by *states*, not by *citizens*, it departs from the *national* and advances towards the *federal* character; in rendering the concurrence of less than the whole number of States sufficient, it loses again the *federal* and partakes of the *national* character.

The proposed Constitution, therefore, is, in strictness, neither a national nor a federal Constitution, but a composition of both. In its foundation it is federal, not national; in the sources from which the ordinary powers of the government are drawn, it is partly federal and partly national; in the operation of these powers, it is national, not federal; in the extent of them, again, it is federal, not national; and, finally, in the authoritative mode of introducing amendments, it is neither wholly federal nor wholly national.

PUBLIUS

# FEDERALIST NO. 51.
## THE STRUCTURE OF THE GOVERNMENT MUST FURNISH THE PROPER CHECKS AND BALANCES BETWEEN THE DIFFERENT DEPARTMENTS.

For the Independent Journal. Wednesday, February 6, 1788.

### JAMES MADISON

To the People of the State of New York:

To what expedient, then, shall we finally resort, for maintaining in practice the necessary partition of power among the several departments, as laid down in the Constitution? The only answer that can be given is, that as all these exterior provisions are found to be inadequate, the defect must be supplied, by so contriving the interior structure of the government as that its several constituent parts may, by their mutual relations, be the means of keeping each other in their proper places. Without presuming to undertake a full development of this important idea, I will hazard a few general observations, which may perhaps place it in a clearer light, and enable us to form a more correct judgment of the principles and structure of the government planned by the convention.

In order to lay a due foundation for that separate and distinct exercise of the different powers of government, which to a certain extent is admitted on all hands to be essential to the preservation of liberty, it is evident that each department should have a will of its own; and consequently should be so constituted that the members of each should have as little agency as possible in the appointment of the members of the others. Were this principle rigorously adhered to, it would require that all the appointments for the supreme executive, legislative, and judiciary magistracies should be drawn from the same fountain of authority, the people, through channels having no communication whatever with one another. Perhaps such a plan of constructing the several departments would be less difficult in practice than it may in contemplation appear. Some difficulties, however, and some additional expense would attend the execution of it. Some deviations, therefore, from the principle must be admitted. In the constitution of the judiciary department in particular, it might be inexpedient to insist rigorously on the principle: first, because peculiar qualifications being essential in the members, the primary consideration ought to be to select that mode of choice which best secures these qualifications; secondly, because the permanent tenure by which the appointments are held in that department, must soon destroy all sense of dependence on the authority conferring them.

It is equally evident, that the members of each department should be as little dependent as possible on those of the others, for the emoluments annexed to their offices. Were the executive magistrate, or the judges, not independent of the legislature in this particular, their independence in every other would be merely nominal.

But the great security against a gradual concentration of the several powers in the same department, consists in giving to those who administer each department the necessary constitutional means and personal motives to resist encroachments of the others. The provision for defense must in this, as in all other cases, be made commensurate to the danger of attack. Ambition must be made to counteract ambition. The interest of the man must be connected with the constitutional rights of the place. It may be a reflection on human nature, that such devices should be necessary to control the abuses of government. But what is government itself, but the greatest of all reflections on human nature? If men were angels, no government would be necessary. If angels were to govern men, neither external nor internal controls on government would be necessary. In framing a government which is to be administered by men over men, the great difficulty lies in this: you must first enable the government to control the governed; and in the next place oblige it to control itself. A dependence on the people is, no doubt, the primary control on the government; but experience has taught mankind the necessity of auxiliary precautions.

This policy of supplying, by opposite and rival interests, the defect of better motives, might be traced through the whole system of human affairs, private as well as public. We see it particularly displayed in all the subordinate distributions of power, where the constant aim is to divide and arrange the several offices in such a manner as that each may be a check on the other—that the private interest of every individual may be a sentinel over the public rights. These inventions of prudence cannot be less requisite in the distribution of the supreme powers of the State.

But it is not possible to give to each department an equal power of self-defense. In republican government, the legislative authority necessarily predominates. The remedy for this inconveniency is to divide the legislature into different branches; and to render them, by different modes of election and different principles of action, as little connected with each other as the nature of their common functions and their common dependence on the society will admit. It may even be necessary to guard against dangerous encroachments by still further precautions. As the weight of the legislative authority requires that it should be thus divided, the weakness of the executive may require, on the other hand, that it should be fortified. An absolute negative on the legislature appears, at first view, to be the natural defense with which the executive magistrate should be armed. But perhaps it would be neither altogether safe nor alone sufficient. On ordinary occasions it might not be exerted with the requisite firmness, and on extraordinary occasions it might be perfidiously abused. May not this defect of an absolute negative be supplied by some qualified connection between this weaker department and the weaker branch of the stronger department, by which the latter may be led to support the constitutional rights of the former, without being too much detached from the rights of its own department?

If the principles on which these observations are founded be just, as I persuade myself they are, and they be applied as a criterion to the several State constitutions, and to the federal Constitution it will be found that if the latter does not perfectly correspond with them, the former are infinitely less able to bear such a test.

There are, moreover, two considerations particularly applicable to the federal system of America, which place that system in a very interesting point of view.

*First.* In a single republic, all the power surrendered by the people is submitted to the administration of a single government; and the usurpations are guarded against by a division of the government into distinct and separate departments. In the compound republic of America, the power surrendered by the people is first divided between two distinct governments, and then the portion allotted to each subdivided among distinct and separate departments. Hence a double security arises to the rights of the people. The different governments will control each other, at the same time that each will be controlled by itself.

*Second.* It is of great importance in a republic not only to guard the society against the oppression of its rulers, but to guard one part of the society against the injustice of the other part. Different interests necessarily exist in different classes of citizens. If a majority be united by a common interest, the rights of the minority will be insecure. There are but two methods of providing against this evil: the one by creating a will in the community independent of the majority—that is, of the society itself; the other, by comprehending in the society so many separate descriptions of citizens as will render an unjust combination of a majority of the whole very improbable, if not impracticable. The first method prevails in all governments possessing an hereditary or self-appointed authority. This, at best, is but a precarious security; because a power independent of the society may as well espouse the unjust views of the major, as the rightful interests of the minor party, and may possibly be turned against both parties. The second method will be exemplified in the federal republic of the United States. Whilst all authority in it will be derived from and dependent on the society, the society itself will be broken into so many parts, interests, and classes of citizens, that the rights of individuals, or of the minority, will be in little danger from interested combinations of the majority. In a free government the security for civil rights must be the same as that for religious rights. It consists in the one case in the multiplicity of interests, and in the other in the multiplicity of sects.

The degree of security in both cases will depend on the number of interests and sects; and this may be presumed to depend on the extent of country and number of people comprehended under the same government. This view of the subject must particularly recommend a proper federal system to all the sincere and considerate friends of republican government, since it shows that in exact proportion as the territory of the Union may be formed into more circumscribed Confederacies, or States oppressive combinations of a majority will be facilitated: the best security, under the republican forms, for the rights of every class of citizens, will be diminished: and consequently the stability and independence of some member of the government, the only other security, must be proportionately increased. Justice is the end of government. It is the end of civil society. It ever has been and ever will be pursued until it be obtained, or until liberty be lost in the pursuit. In a society under the forms of which the stronger faction can readily unite and oppress the weaker, anarchy may as truly be said to reign as in a state of nature, where the weaker individual is not secured against the violence of the stronger; and as, in the latter state, even the stronger individuals are prompted, by the uncertainty of their condition, to submit to a government which may protect the weak as well as themselves; so, in the former state, will the more powerful factions or parties be gradually induced, by a like motive, to wish for a government which will protect all parties, the weaker as well as the more powerful. It can be little doubted that if the State of Rhode Island was separated from the Confederacy and left to itself, the insecurity of rights under the popular form of government within such narrow limits would be displayed by such reiterated oppressions of factious majorities that some power altogether independent of the people would soon be called for by the voice of the very factions whose misrule had proved the necessity of it. In the extended republic of the United States, and among the great variety of interests, parties, and sects which it embraces, a coalition of a majority of the whole society could seldom take place on any other principles than those of justice and the general good; whilst there being thus less danger to a minor from the will of a major party, there must be less pretext, also, to provide for the security of the former, by introducing into the government a will not dependent on the latter, or, in other words, a will independent of the society itself. It is no less certain than it is

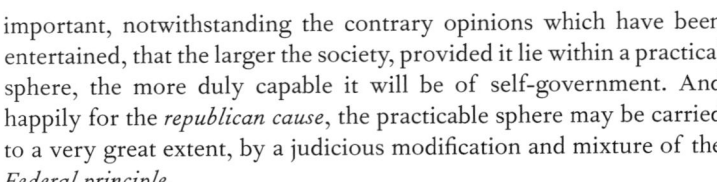

important, notwithstanding the contrary opinions which have been entertained, that the larger the society, provided it lie within a practical sphere, the more duly capable it will be of self-government. And happily for the *republican cause*, the practicable sphere may be carried to a very great extent, by a judicious modification and mixture of the *Federal principle*.

PUBLIUS

# FEDERALIST NO. 70.
# THE EXECUTIVE DEPARTMENT
# FURTHER CONSIDERED

From The Independent Journal. Saturday, March 15, 1788.

## ALEXANDER HAMILTON

To the People of the State of New York:

THERE is an idea, which is not without its advocates, that a vigorous Executive is inconsistent with the genius of republican government. The enlightened well-wishers to this species of government must at least hope that the supposition is destitute of foundation; since they can never admit its truth, without at the same time admitting the condemnation of their own principles. Energy in the Executive is a leading character in the definition of good government. It is essential to the protection of the community against foreign attacks; it is not less essential to the steady administration of the laws; to the protection of property against those irregular and high-handed combinations which sometimes interrupt the ordinary course of justice; to the security of liberty against the enterprises and assaults of ambition, of faction, and of anarchy. Every man the least conversant in Roman story, knows how often that republic was obliged to take refuge in the absolute power of a single man, under the formidable title of Dictator, as well against the intrigues of ambitious individuals who aspired to the tyranny, and the seditions of whole classes of the community whose conduct threatened the existence of all government, as against the invasions of external enemies who menaced the conquest and destruction of Rome.

There can be no need, however, to multiply arguments or examples

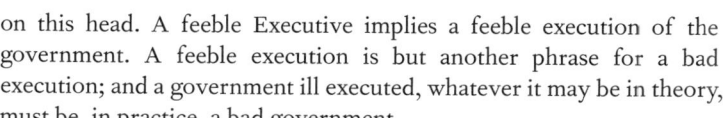

on this head. A feeble Executive implies a feeble execution of the government. A feeble execution is but another phrase for a bad execution; and a government ill executed, whatever it may be in theory, must be, in practice, a bad government.

Taking it for granted, therefore, that all men of sense will agree in the necessity of an energetic Executive, it will only remain to inquire, what are the ingredients which constitute this energy? How far can they be combined with those other ingredients which constitute safety in the republican sense? And how far does this combination characterize the plan which has been reported by the convention?

The ingredients which constitute energy in the Executive are, first, unity; secondly, duration; thirdly, an adequate provision for its support; fourthly, competent powers.

The ingredients which constitute safety in the republican sense are, first, a due dependence on the people, secondly, a due responsibility.

Those politicians and statesmen who have been the most celebrated for the soundness of their principles and for the justice of their views, have declared in favor of a single Executive and a numerous legislature. They have with great propriety, considered energy as the most necessary qualification of the former, and have regarded this as most applicable to power in a single hand, while they have, with equal propriety, considered the latter as best adapted to deliberation and wisdom, and best calculated to conciliate the confidence of the people and to secure their privileges and interests.

That unity is conducive to energy will not be disputed. Decision, activity, secrecy, and despatch will generally characterize the proceedings of one man in a much more eminent degree than the proceedings of any greater number; and in proportion as the number is increased, these qualities will be diminished.

This unity may be destroyed in two ways: either by vesting the power in two or more magistrates of equal dignity and authority; or by vesting it ostensibly in one man, subject, in whole or in part, to the control and co-operation of others, in the capacity of counsellors to him. Of the first, the two Consuls of Rome may serve as an example; of the last, we shall find examples in the constitutions of several of the States. New York and New Jersey, if I recollect right, are the only States which have intrusted the executive authority wholly to single men.* Both these

---

*New York has no council except for the single purpose of appointing to offices; New

methods of destroying the unity of the Executive have their partisans; but the votaries of an executive council are the most numerous. They are both liable, if not to equal, to similar objections, and may in most lights be examined in conjunction.

The experience of other nations will afford little instruction on this head. As far, however, as it teaches any thing, it teaches us not to be enamoured of plurality in the Executive. We have seen that the Achæans, on an experiment of two Prætors, were induced to abolish one. The Roman history records many instances of mischiefs to the republic from the dissensions between the Consuls, and between the military Tribunes, who were at times substituted for the Consuls. But it gives us no specimens of any peculiar advantages derived to the state from the circumstance of the plurality of those magistrates. That the dissensions between them were not more frequent or more fatal, is a matter of astonishment, until we advert to the singular position in which the republic was almost continually placed, and to the prudent policy pointed out by the circumstances of the state, and pursued by the Consuls, of making a division of the government between them. The patricians engaged in a perpetual struggle with the plebeians for the preservation of their ancient authorities and dignities; the Consuls, who were generally chosen out of the former body, were commonly united by the personal interest they had in the defense of the privileges of their order. In addition to this motive of union, after the arms of the republic had considerably expanded the bounds of its empire, it became an established custom with the Consuls to divide the administration between themselves by lot—one of them remaining at Rome to govern the city and its environs, the other taking the command in the more distant provinces. This expedient must, no doubt, have had great influence in preventing those collisions and rivalships which might otherwise have embroiled the peace of the republic.

But quitting the dim light of historical research, attaching ourselves purely to the dictates of reason and good sense, we shall discover much greater cause to reject than to approve the idea of plurality in the Executive, under any modification whatever.

Wherever two or more persons are engaged in any common enterprise or pursuit, there is always danger of difference of opinion. If

---

*Jersey has a council whom the governor may consult. But I think, from the terms of the constitution, their resolutions do not bind him.*

it be a public trust or office, in which they are clothed with equal dignity and authority, there is peculiar danger of personal emulation and even animosity. From either, and especially from all these causes, the most bitter dissensions are apt to spring. Whenever these happen, they lessen the respectability, weaken the authority, and distract the plans and operation of those whom they divide. If they should unfortunately assail the supreme executive magistracy of a country, consisting of a plurality of persons, they might impede or frustrate the most important measures of the government, in the most critical emergencies of the state. And what is still worse, they might split the community into the most violent and irreconcilable factions, adhering differently to the different individuals who composed the magistracy.

Men often oppose a thing, merely because they have had no agency in planning it, or because it may have been planned by those whom they dislike. But if they have been consulted, and have happened to disapprove, opposition then becomes, in their estimation, an indispensable duty of self-love. They seem to think themselves bound in honor, and by all the motives of personal infallibility, to defeat the success of what has been resolved upon contrary to their sentiments. Men of upright, benevolent tempers have too many opportunities of remarking, with horror, to what desperate lengths this disposition is sometimes carried, and how often the great interests of society are sacrificed to the vanity, to the conceit, and to the obstinacy of individuals, who have credit enough to make their passions and their caprices interesting to mankind. Perhaps the question now before the public may, in its consequences, afford melancholy proofs of the effects of this despicable frailty, or rather detestable vice, in the human character.

Upon the principles of a free government, inconveniences from the source just mentioned must necessarily be submitted to in the formation of the legislature; but it is unnecessary, and therefore unwise, to introduce them into the constitution of the Executive. It is here, too, that they may be most pernicious. In the legislature, promptitude of decision is oftener an evil than a benefit. The differences of opinion, and the jarrings of parties in that department of the government, though they may sometimes obstruct salutary plans, yet often promote deliberation and circumspection, and serve to check excesses in the majority. When a resolution too is once taken, the opposition must be at an end. That resolution is a law, and resistance to it punishable.

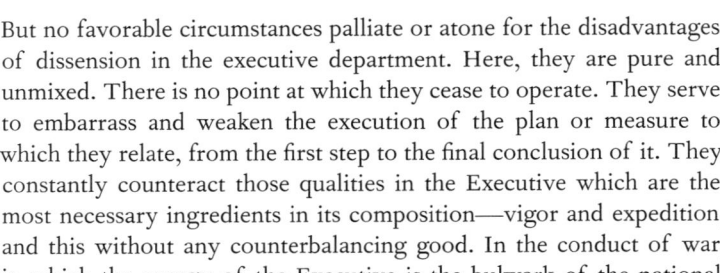

But no favorable circumstances palliate or atone for the disadvantages of dissension in the executive department. Here, they are pure and unmixed. There is no point at which they cease to operate. They serve to embarrass and weaken the execution of the plan or measure to which they relate, from the first step to the final conclusion of it. They constantly counteract those qualities in the Executive which are the most necessary ingredients in its composition—vigor and expedition, and this without any counterbalancing good. In the conduct of war, in which the energy of the Executive is the bulwark of the national security, every thing would be to be apprehended from its plurality.

It must be confessed that these observations apply with principal weight to the first case supposed—that is, to a plurality of magistrates of equal dignity and authority a scheme, the advocates for which are not likely to form a numerous sect; but they apply, though not with equal, yet with considerable weight to the project of a council, whose concurrence is made constitutionally necessary to the operations of the ostensible Executive. An artful cabal in that council would be able to distract and to enervate the whole system of administration. If no such cabal should exist, the mere diversity of views and opinions would alone be sufficient to tincture the exercise of the executive authority with a spirit of habitual feebleness and dilatoriness.

But one of the weightiest objections to a plurality in the Executive, and which lies as much against the last as the first plan, is, that it tends to conceal faults and destroy responsibility. Responsibility is of two kinds—to censure and to punishment. The first is the more important of the two, especially in an elective office. Man, in public trust, will much oftener act in such a manner as to render him unworthy of being any longer trusted, than in such a manner as to make him obnoxious to legal punishment. But the multiplication of the Executive adds to the difficulty of detection in either case. It often becomes impossible, amidst mutual accusations, to determine on whom the blame or the punishment of a pernicious measure, or series of pernicious measures, ought really to fall. It is shifted from one to another with so much dexterity, and under such plausible appearances, that the public opinion is left in suspense about the real author. The circumstances which may have led to any national miscarriage or misfortune are sometimes so complicated that, where there are a number of actors who may have had different degrees and kinds of agency, though we may clearly see upon the whole that there has been mismanagement, yet it may be impracticable to pronounce to whose account the evil which may have been incurred is truly chargeable.

"I was overruled by my council. The council were so divided in their opinions that it was impossible to obtain any better resolution on the point." These and similar pretexts are constantly at hand, whether true or false. And who is there that will either take the trouble or incur the odium, of a strict scrutiny into the secret springs of the transaction? Should there be found a citizen zealous enough to undertake the unpromising task, if there happen to be collusion between the parties concerned, how easy it is to clothe the circumstances with so much ambiguity, as to render it uncertain what was the precise conduct of any of those parties?

In the single instance in which the governor of this State is coupled with a council—that is, in the appointment to offices, we have seen the mischiefs of it in the view now under consideration. Scandalous appointments to important offices have been made. Some cases, indeed, have been so flagrant that *all parties* have agreed in the impropriety of the thing. When inquiry has been made, the blame has been laid by the governor on the members of the council, who, on their part, have charged it upon his nomination; while the people remain altogether at a loss to determine, by whose influence their interests have been committed to hands so unqualified and so manifestly improper. In tenderness to individuals, I forbear to descend to particulars.

It is evident from these considerations, that the plurality of the Executive tends to deprive the people of the two greatest securities they can have for the faithful exercise of any delegated power—first, the restraints of public opinion, which lose their efficacy, as well on account of the division of the censure attendant on bad measures among a number, as on account of the uncertainty on whom it ought to fall; and, second, the opportunity of discovering with facility and clearness the misconduct of the persons they trust, in order either to their removal from office or to their actual punishment in cases which admit of it.

In England, the king is a perpetual magistrate; and it is a maxim which has obtained for the sake of the public peace, that he is unaccountable for his administration, and his person sacred. Nothing, therefore, can be wiser in that kingdom, than to annex to the king a constitutional council, who may be responsible to the nation for the advice they give. Without this, there would be no responsibility whatever in the executive department, an idea inadmissible in a free government. But even there the king is not bound by the resolutions of his council, though they are answerable for the advice they give. He is the absolute master of his own conduct in the exercise of his office, and may observe or disregard the counsel given to him at his sole discretion.

But in a republic, where every magistrate ought to be personally responsible for his behavior in office, the reason which in the British Constitution dictates the propriety of a council, not only ceases to apply, but turns against the institution. In the monarchy of Great Britain, it furnishes a substitute for the prohibited responsibility of the chief magistrate, which serves in some degree as a hostage to the national justice for his good behavior. In the American republic, it would serve to destroy, or would greatly diminish, the intended and necessary responsibility of the Chief Magistrate himself.

The idea of a council to the Executive, which has so generally obtained in the State constitutions, has been derived from that maxim of republican jealousy which considers power as safer in the hands of a number of men than of a single man. If the maxim should be admitted to be applicable to the case, I should contend that the advantage on that side would not counterbalance the numerous disadvantages on the opposite side. But I do not think the rule at all applicable to the executive power. I clearly concur in opinion, in this particular, with a writer whom the celebrated Junius pronounces to be "deep, solid, and ingenious," that "the executive power is more easily confined when it is *one*";* that it is far more safe there should be a single object for the jealousy and watchfulness of the people; and, in a word, that all multiplication of the Executive is rather dangerous than friendly to liberty.

A little consideration will satisfy us, that the species of security sought for in the multiplication of the Executive, is unattainable. Numbers must be so great as to render combination difficult, or they are rather a source of danger than of security. The united credit and influence of several individuals must be more formidable to liberty, than the credit and influence of either of them separately. When power, therefore, is placed in the hands of so small a number of men, as to admit of their interests and views being easily combined in a common enterprise, by an artful leader, it becomes more liable to abuse, and more dangerous when abused, than if it be lodged in the hands of one

---

* *De Lolme.*

man; who, from the very circumstance of his being alone, will be more narrowly watched and more readily suspected, and who cannot unite so great a mass of influence as when he is associated with others. The Decemvirs of Rome, whose name denotes their number,* were more to be dreaded in their usurpation than any *one* of them would have been. No person would think of proposing an Executive much more numerous than that body; from six to a dozen have been suggested for the number of the council. The extreme of these numbers, is not too great for an easy combination; and from such a combination America would have more to fear, than from the ambition of any single individual. A council to a magistrate, who is himself responsible for what he does, are generally nothing better than a clog upon his good intentions, are often the instruments and accomplices of his bad and are almost always a cloak to his faults.

I forbear to dwell upon the subject of expense; though it be evident that if the council should be numerous enough to answer the principal end aimed at by the institution, the salaries of the members, who must be drawn from their homes to reside at the seat of government, would form an item in the catalogue of public expenditures too serious to be incurred for an object of equivocal utility. I will only add that, prior to the appearance of the Constitution, I rarely met with an intelligent man from any of the States, who did not admit, as the result of experience, that the *unity* of the executive of this State was one of the best of the distinguishing features of our constitution.

PUBLIUS

# FEDERALIST NO. 78.
## THE JUDICIARY DEPARTMENT

From McLean's Edition, New York. Wednesday, May 28, 1788

### ALEXANDER HAMILTON

To the People of the State of New York:

We proceed now to an examination of the judiciary department of the proposed government.

---

* *Ten.*

In unfolding the defects of the existing Confederation, the utility and necessity of a federal judicature have been clearly pointed out. It is the less necessary to recapitulate the considerations there urged, as the propriety of the institution in the abstract is not disputed; the only questions which have been raised being relative to the manner of constituting it, and to its extent. To these points, therefore, our observations shall be confined.

The manner of constituting it seems to embrace these several objects: 1st. The mode of appointing the judges. 2d. The tenure by which they are to hold their places. 3d. The partition of the judiciary authority between different courts, and their relations to each other.

FIRST. As to the mode of appointing the judges; this is the same with that of appointing the officers of the Union in general, and has been so fully discussed in the two last numbers, that nothing can be said here which would not be useless repetition.

SECOND. As to the tenure by which the judges are to hold their places; this chiefly concerns their duration in office; the provisions for their support; the precautions for their responsibility.

According to the plan of the convention, all judges who may be appointed by the United States are to hold their offices *during good behavior*; which is conformable to the most approved of the State constitutions and among the rest, to that of this State. Its propriety having been drawn into question by the adversaries of that plan, is no light symptom of the rage for objection, which disorders their imaginations and judgments. The standard of good behavior for the continuance in office of the judicial magistracy, is certainly one of the most valuable of the modern improvements in the practice of government. In a monarchy it is an excellent barrier to the despotism of the prince; in a republic it is a no less excellent barrier to the encroachments and oppressions of the representative body. And it is the best expedient which can be devised in any government, to secure a steady, upright, and impartial administration of the laws.

Whoever attentively considers the different departments of power must perceive, that, in a government in which they are separated from each other, the judiciary, from the nature of its functions, will always be the least dangerous to the political rights of the Constitution; because it will be least in a capacity to annoy or injure them. The Executive not only dispenses the honors, but holds the sword of the community. The legislature not only commands the purse, but prescribes the rules by which the duties and rights of every citizen are to be regulated. The judiciary, on the contrary, has no influence over either the sword or the purse; no direction either of the strength or of the wealth of the society; and can take no active resolution whatever. It may truly be said to have neither *force* nor *will*, but merely judgment; and must ultimately depend upon the aid of the executive arm even for the efficacy of its judgments.

This simple view of the matter suggests several important consequences. It proves incontestably, that the judiciary is beyond comparison the weakest of the three departments of power*; that it can never attack with success either of the other two; and that all possible care is requisite to enable it to defend itself against their attacks. It equally proves, that though individual oppression may now and then proceed from the courts of justice, the general liberty of the people can never be endangered from that quarter; I mean so long as the judiciary remains truly distinct from both the legislature and the Executive. For I agree, that "there is no liberty, if the power of judging be not separated from the legislative and executive powers."† And it proves, in the last place, that as liberty can have nothing to fear from the judiciary alone, but would have every thing to fear from its union with either of the other departments; that as all the effects of such a union must ensue from a dependence of the former on the latter, notwithstanding a nominal and apparent separation; that as, from the natural feebleness of the judiciary, it is in continual jeopardy of being overpowered, awed, or influenced by its co-ordinate branches; and that as nothing can contribute so much to its firmness and independence as permanency in office, this quality may therefore be justly regarded as an indispensable ingredient in its constitution, and, in a great measure, as the citadel of the public justice and the public security.

The complete independence of the courts of justice is peculiarly essential in a limited Constitution. By a limited Constitution, I understand one which contains certain specified exceptions to the legislative authority; such, for instance, as that it shall pass no bills of attainder, no ex post facto laws, and the like. Limitations of this kind

---

*The celebrated Montesquieu, speaking of them, says: "Of the three powers above mentioned, the judiciary is next to nothing."*—Spirit of Laws, *Vol. I, page 186.*
† *Idem, page 181.*

can be preserved in practice no other way than through the medium of courts of justice, whose duty it must be to declare all acts contrary to the manifest tenor of the Constitution void. Without this, all the reservations of particular rights or privileges would amount to nothing.

Some perplexity respecting the rights of the courts to pronounce legislative acts void, because contrary to the Constitution, has arisen from an imagination that the doctrine would imply a superiority of the judiciary to the legislative power. It is urged that the authority which can declare the acts of another void, must necessarily be superior to the one whose acts may be declared void. As this doctrine is of great importance in all the American constitutions, a brief discussion of the ground on which it rests cannot be unacceptable.

There is no position which depends on clearer principles, than that every act of a delegated authority, contrary to the tenor of the commission under which it is exercised, is void. No legislative act, therefore, contrary to the Constitution, can be valid. To deny this, would be to affirm, that the deputy is greater than his principal; that the servant is above his master; that the representatives of the people are superior to the people themselves; that men acting by virtue of powers, may do not only what their powers do not authorize, but what they forbid.

If it be said that the legislative body are themselves the constitutional judges of their own powers, and that the construction they put upon them is conclusive upon the other departments, it may be answered, that this cannot be the natural presumption, where it is not to be collected from any particular provisions in the Constitution. It is not otherwise to be supposed, that the Constitution could intend to enable the representatives of the people to substitute their will to that of their constituents. It is far more rational to suppose, that the courts were designed to be an intermediate body between the people and the legislature, in order, among other things, to keep the latter within the limits assigned to their authority. The interpretation of the laws is the proper and peculiar province of the courts. A constitution is, in fact, and must be regarded by the judges, as a fundamental law. It therefore belongs to them to ascertain its meaning, as well as the meaning of any particular act proceeding from the legislative body. If there should happen to be an irreconcilable variance between the two, that which has the superior obligation and validity ought, of course, to be preferred;

or, in other words, the Constitution ought to be preferred to the statute, the intention of the people to the intention of their agents.

Nor does this conclusion by any means suppose a superiority of the judicial to the legislative power. It only supposes that the power of the people is superior to both; and that where the will of the legislature, declared in its statutes, stands in opposition to that of the people, declared in the Constitution, the judges ought to be governed by the latter rather than the former. They ought to regulate their decisions by the fundamental laws, rather than by those which are not fundamental.

This exercise of judicial discretion, in determining between two contradictory laws, is exemplified in a familiar instance. It not uncommonly happens, that there are two statutes existing at one time, clashing in whole or in part with each other, and neither of them containing any repealing clause or expression. In such a case, it is the province of the courts to liquidate and fix their meaning and operation. So far as they can, by any fair construction, be reconciled to each other, reason and law conspire to dictate that this should be done; where this is impracticable, it becomes a matter of necessity to give effect to one, in exclusion of the other. The rule which has obtained in the courts for determining their relative validity is, that the last in order of time shall be preferred to the first. But this is a mere rule of construction, not derived from any positive law, but from the nature and reason of the thing. It is a rule not enjoined upon the courts by legislative provision, but adopted by themselves, as consonant to truth and propriety, for the direction of their conduct as interpreters of the law. They thought it reasonable, that between the interfering acts of an *equal* authority, that which was the last indication of its will should have the preference.

But in regard to the interfering acts of a superior and subordinate authority, of an original and derivative power, the nature and reason of the thing indicate the converse of that rule as proper to be followed. They teach us that the prior act of a superior ought to be preferred to the subsequent act of an inferior and subordinate authority; and that accordingly, whenever a particular statute contravenes the Constitution, it will be the duty of the judicial tribunals to adhere to the latter and disregard the former.

It can be of no weight to say that the courts, on the pretense of a repugnancy, may substitute their own pleasure to the constitutional intentions of the legislature. This might as well happen in the case of two contradictory statutes; or it might as well happen in every adjudication upon any single statute. The courts must declare the sense of the law; and if they should be disposed to exercise *will* instead of *judgment*, the consequence would equally be the substitution of their pleasure to that of the legislative body. The observation, if it prove any thing, would prove that there ought to be no judges distinct from that body.

If, then, the courts of justice are to be considered as the bulwarks of a limited Constitution against legislative encroachments, this consideration will afford a strong argument for the permanent tenure of judicial offices, since nothing will contribute so much as this to that independent spirit in the judges which must be essential to the faithful performance of so arduous a duty.

This independence of the judges is equally requisite to guard the Constitution and the rights of individuals from the effects of those ill humors, which the arts of designing men, or the influence of particular conjunctures, sometimes disseminate among the people themselves, and which, though they speedily give place to better information, and more deliberate reflection, have a tendency, in the meantime, to occasion dangerous innovations in the government, and serious oppressions of the minor party in the community. Though I trust the friends of the proposed Constitution will never concur with its enemies,* in questioning that fundamental principle of republican government, which admits the right of the people to alter or abolish the established Constitution, whenever they find it inconsistent with their happiness, yet it is not to be inferred from this principle, that the representatives of the people, whenever a momentary inclination happens to lay hold of a majority of their constituents, incompatible with the provisions in the existing Constitution, would, on that account, be justifiable in a violation of those provisions; or that the courts would be under a greater obligation to connive at infractions in this shape, than when they had proceeded wholly from the cabals of the representative body. Until the people have, by some solemn and authoritative act, annulled or changed the established form, it is binding upon themselves collectively, as well as individually; and no presumption, or even knowledge, of their sentiments, can warrant their representatives in a departure from it, prior to such an act. But it is easy to see, that it would require an

---

* *Vide Protest of the Minority of the Convention of Pennsylvania, Martin's Speech, etc.*

uncommon portion of fortitude in the judges to do their duty as faithful guardians of the Constitution, where legislative invasions of it had been instigated by the major voice of the community.

But it is not with a view to infractions of the Constitution only, that the independence of the judges may be an essential safeguard against the effects of occasional ill humors in the society. These sometimes extend no farther than to the injury of the private rights of particular classes of citizens, by unjust and partial laws. Here also the firmness of the judicial magistracy is of vast importance in mitigating the severity and confining the operation of such laws. It not only serves to moderate the immediate mischiefs of those which may have been passed, but it operates as a check upon the legislative body in passing them; who, perceiving that obstacles to the success of iniquitous intention are to be expected from the scruples of the courts, are in a manner compelled, by the very motives of the injustice they meditate, to qualify their attempts. This is a circumstance calculated to have more influence upon the character of our governments, than but few may be aware of. The benefits of the integrity and moderation of the judiciary have already been felt in more States than one; and though they may have displeased those whose sinister expectations they may have disappointed, they must have commanded the esteem and applause of all the virtuous and disinterested. Considerate men, of every description, ought to prize whatever will tend to beget or fortify that temper in the courts: as no man can be sure that he may not be tomorrow the victim of a spirit of injustice, by which he may be a gainer today. And every man must now feel, that the inevitable tendency of such a spirit is to sap the foundations of public and private confidence, and to introduce in its stead universal distrust and distress.

That inflexible and uniform adherence to the rights of the Constitution, and of individuals, which we perceive to be indispensable in the courts of justice, can certainly not be expected from judges who hold their offices by a temporary commission. Periodical appointments, however regulated, or by whomsoever made, would, in some way or other, be fatal to their necessary independence. If the power of making them was committed either to the Executive or legislature, there would be danger of an improper complaisance to the branch which possessed it; if to both, there would be an unwillingness to hazard the displeasure of either; if to the people, or to persons chosen by them for the special purpose, there

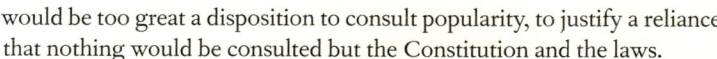

would be too great a disposition to consult popularity, to justify a reliance that nothing would be consulted but the Constitution and the laws.

There is yet a further and a weightier reason for the permanency of the judicial offices, which is deducible from the nature of the qualifications they require. It has been frequently remarked, with great propriety, that a voluminous code of laws is one of the inconveniences necessarily connected with the advantages of a free government. To avoid an arbitrary discretion in the courts, it is indispensable that they should be bound down by strict rules and precedents, which serve to define and point out their duty in every particular case that comes before them; and it will readily be conceived from the variety of controversies which grow out of the folly and wickedness of mankind, that the records of those precedents must unavoidably swell to a very considerable bulk, and must demand long and laborious study to acquire a competent knowledge of them. Hence it is, that there can be but few men in the society who will have sufficient skill in the laws to qualify them for the stations of judges. And making the proper deductions for the ordinary depravity of human nature, the number must be still smaller of those who unite the requisite integrity with the requisite knowledge. These considerations apprise us, that the government can have no great option between fit character; and that a temporary duration in office, which would naturally discourage such characters from quitting a lucrative line of practice to accept a seat on the bench, would have a tendency to throw the administration of justice into hands less able, and less well qualified, to conduct it with utility and dignity. In the present circumstances of this country, and in those in which it is likely to be for a long time to come, the disadvantages on this score would be greater than they may at first sight appear; but it must be confessed, that they are far inferior to those which present themselves under the other aspects of the subject.

Upon the whole, there can be no room to doubt that the convention acted wisely in copying from the models of those constitutions which have established good behavior as the tenure of their judicial offices, in point of duration; and that so far from being blamable on this account, their plan would have been inexcusably defective, if it had wanted this important feature of good government. The experience of Great Britain affords an illustrious comment on the excellence of the institution.

PUBLIUS

# FEDERALIST NO. 84.
## CERTAIN GENERAL AND MISCELLANEOUS OBJECTIONS TO THE CONSTITUTION CONSIDERED AND ANSWERED.

From McLean's Edition, New York. Wednesday, May 28, 1788

### ALEXANDER HAMILTON

To the People of the State of New York:

IN THE course of the foregoing review of the Constitution, I have taken notice of, and endeavored to answer most of the objections which have appeared against it. There, however, remain a few which either did not fall naturally under any particular head or were forgotten in their proper places. These shall now be discussed; but as the subject has been drawn into great length, I shall so far consult brevity as to comprise all my observations on these miscellaneous points in a single paper.

The most considerable of the remaining objections is that the plan of the convention contains no bill of rights. Among other answers given to this, it has been upon different occasions remarked that the constitutions of several of the States are in a similar predicament. I add that New York is of the number. And yet the opposers of the new system, in this State, who profess an unlimited admiration for its constitution, are among the most intemperate partisans of a bill of rights. To justify their zeal in this matter, they allege two things: one is that, though the constitution of New York has no bill of rights prefixed to it, yet it contains, in the body of it, various provisions in favor of particular privileges and rights, which, in substance amount to the same thing; the other is, that the Constitution adopts, in their full extent, the common and statute law of Great Britain, by which many other rights, not expressed in it, are equally secured.

To the first I answer, that the Constitution proposed by the convention contains, as well as the constitution of this State, a number of such provisions.

Independent of those which relate to the structure of the government, we find the following: Article 1, section 3, clause 7—"Judgment in cases of impeachment shall not extend further than to removal from office, and disqualification to hold and enjoy any office of honor, trust, or profit under the United States; but the party convicted shall, nevertheless, be liable and subject to indictment, trial, judgment, and punishment according to law." Section 9, of the same article, clause 2—"The privilege of the writ of habeas corpus shall not be suspended, unless when in cases of rebellion or invasion the public safety may require it." Clause 3—"No bill of attainder or ex-post-facto law shall be passed." Clause 7—"No title of nobility shall be granted by the United States; and no person holding any office of profit or trust under them, shall, without the consent of the Congress, accept of any present, emolument, office, or title of any kind whatever, from any king, prince, or foreign state." Article 3, section 2, clause 3—"The trial of all crimes, except in cases of impeachment, shall be by jury; and such trial shall be held in the State where the said crimes shall have been committed; but when not committed within any State, the trial shall be at such place or places as the Congress may by law have directed." Section 3, of the same article—"Treason against the United States shall consist only in levying war against them, or in adhering to their enemies, giving them aid and comfort. No person shall be convicted of treason, unless on the testimony of two witnesses to the same overt act, or on confession in open court." And clause 3, of the same section—"The Congress shall have power to declare the punishment of treason; but no attainder of treason shall work corruption of blood, or forfeiture, except during the life of the person attainted."

It may well be a question, whether these are not, upon the whole, of equal importance with any which are to be found in the constitution of this State. The establishment of the writ of habeas corpus, the prohibition of ex post facto laws, and of *titles of nobility*, to which we have no corresponding provision in our Constitution, are perhaps greater securities to liberty and republicanism than any it contains. The creation of crimes after the commission of the fact, or, in other words, the subjecting of men to punishment for things which, when they were done, were breaches of no law, and the practice of arbitrary imprisonments, have been, in all ages, the favorite and most formidable instruments of tyranny. The observations of the judicious Blackstone,* in reference to the latter, are well worthy of recital: "To bereave a man of life, (says he) or by violence to confiscate his estate, without accusation or trial, would be so gross and notorious an act of despotism, as must at once convey the alarm of tyranny throughout the whole nation; but confinement of the person, by secretly hurrying him to jail, where his sufferings are unknown or forgotten, is a less public, a less striking, and therefore a more dangerous engine of arbitrary government." And as a remedy for this fatal evil he is everywhere peculiarly emphatical in his encomiums on the habeas corpus act, which in one place he calls "the *bulwark* of the British Constitution."[†]

Nothing need be said to illustrate the importance of the prohibition of titles of nobility. This may truly be denominated the corner-stone of republican government; for so long as they are excluded, there can never be serious danger that the government will be any other than that of the people.

To the second that is, to the pretended establishment of the common and state law by the Constitution, I answer, that they are expressly made subject "to such alterations and provisions as the legislature shall from time to time make concerning the same." They are therefore at any moment liable to repeal by the ordinary legislative power, and of course have no constitutional sanction. The only use of the declaration was to recognize the ancient law and to remove doubts which might have been occasioned by the Revolution. This consequently can be considered as no part of a declaration of rights, which under our constitutions must be intended as limitations of the power of the government itself.

It has been several times truly remarked that bills of rights are, in their origin, stipulations between kings and their subjects, abridgements of prerogative in favor of privilege, reservations of rights not surrendered to the prince. Such was *Magna Charta*, obtained by the barons, sword in hand, from King John. Such were the subsequent confirmations of that charter by succeeding princes. Such was the Petition of Right assented to by Charles I, in the beginning of his reign. Such, also, was the Declaration of Right presented by the Lords and Commons to the Prince of Orange in 1688, and afterwards thrown into the form of an act of parliament called the Bill of Rights. It is evident, therefore, that,

---

*Vide Blackstone's Commentaries, *Vol. 1, p. 136.*

[†] *Idem, Vol. 4, p. 438.*

according to their primitive signification, they have no application to constitutions professedly founded upon the power of the people, and executed by their immediate representatives and servants. Here, in strictness, the people surrender nothing; and as they retain every thing they have no need of particular reservations. "*We, the People* of the United States, to secure the blessings of liberty to ourselves and our posterity, do ordain and establish this Constitution for the United States of America." Here is a better recognition of popular rights, than volumes of those aphorisms which make the principal figure in several of our State bills of rights, and which would sound much better in a treatise of ethics than in a constitution of government.

But a minute detail of particular rights is certainly far less applicable to a Constitution like that under consideration, which is merely intended to regulate the general political interests of the nation, than to a constitution which has the regulation of every species of personal and private concerns. If, therefore, the loud clamors against the plan of the convention, on this score, are well founded, no epithets of reprobation will be too strong for the constitution of this State. But the truth is, that both of them contain all which, in relation to their objects, is reasonably to be desired.

I go further, and affirm that bills of rights, in the sense and to the extent in which they are contended for, are not only unnecessary in the proposed Constitution, but would even be dangerous. They would contain various exceptions to powers not granted; and, on this very account, would afford a colorable pretext to claim more than were granted. For why declare that things shall not be done which there is no power to do? Why, for instance, should it be said that the liberty of the press shall not be restrained, when no power is given by which restrictions may be imposed? I will not contend that such a provision would confer a regulating power; but it is evident that it would furnish, to men disposed to usurp, a plausible pretense for claiming that power. They might urge with a semblance of reason, that the Constitution ought not to be charged with the absurdity of providing against the abuse of an authority which was not given, and that the provision against restraining the liberty of the press afforded a clear implication, that a power to prescribe proper regulations concerning it was intended to be vested in the national government. This may serve as a specimen of the numerous handles which would be given to the doctrine of constructive powers, by the indulgence of an injudicious zeal for bills of rights.

On the subject of the liberty of the press, as much as has been said, I cannot forbear adding a remark or two: in the first place, I observe, that there is not a syllable concerning it in the constitution of this State; in the next, I contend, that whatever has been said about it in that of any other State, amounts to nothing. What signifies a declaration, that "the liberty of the press shall be inviolably preserved"? What is the liberty of the press? Who can give it any definition which would not leave the utmost latitude for evasion? I hold it to be impracticable; and from this I infer, that its security, whatever fine declarations may be inserted in any constitution respecting it, must altogether depend on public opinion, and on the general spirit of the people and of the government.* And here, after all, as is intimated upon another occasion, must we seek for the only solid basis of all our rights.

There remains but one other view of this matter to conclude the point. The truth is, after all the declamations we have heard, that the Constitution is itself, in every rational sense, and to every useful purpose, *a Bill of Rights*. The several bills of rights in Great Britain form its Constitution, and conversely the constitution of each State is its bill of rights. And the proposed Constitution, if adopted, will be the bill of rights of the Union. Is it one object of a bill of rights to declare and specify the political privileges of the citizens in the structure and

---

* *To show that there is a power in the Constitution by which the liberty of the press may be affected, recourse has been had to the power of taxation. It is said that duties may be laid upon the publications so high as to amount to a prohibition. I know not by what logic it could be maintained, that the declarations in the State constitutions, in favor of the freedom of the press, would be a constitutional impediment to the imposition of duties upon publications by the State legislatures. It cannot certainly be pretended that any degree of duties, however low, would be an abridgment of the liberty of the press. We know that newspapers are taxed in Great Britain, and yet it is notorious that the press nowhere enjoys greater liberty than in that country. And if duties of any kind may be laid without a violation of that liberty, it is evident that the extent must depend on legislative discretion, respecting the liberty of the press, will give it no greater security than it will have without them. The same invasions of it may be effected under the State constitutions which contain those declarations through the means of taxation, as under the proposed Constitution, which has nothing of the kind. It would be quite as significant to declare that government ought to be free, that taxes ought not to be excessive, etc., as that the liberty of the press ought not to be restrained.*

administration of the government? This is done in the most ample and precise manner in the plan of the convention; comprehending various precautions for the public security, which are not to be found in any of the State constitutions. Is another object of a bill of rights to define certain immunities and modes of proceeding, which are relative to personal and private concerns? This we have seen has also been attended to, in a variety of cases, in the same plan. Adverting therefore to the substantial meaning of a bill of rights, it is absurd to allege that it is not to be found in the work of the convention. It may be said that it does not go far enough, though it will not be easy to make this appear; but it can with no propriety be contended that there is no such thing. It certainly must be immaterial what mode is observed as to the order of declaring the rights of the citizens, if they are to be found in any part of the instrument which establishes the government. And hence it must be apparent, that much of what has been said on this subject rests merely on verbal and nominal distinctions, entirely foreign from the substance of the thing.

Another objection which has been made, and which, from the frequency of its repetition, it is to be presumed is relied on, is of this nature: "It is improper (say the objectors) to confer such large powers, as are proposed, upon the national government, because the seat of that government must of necessity be too remote from many of the States to admit of a proper knowledge on the part of the constituent, of the conduct of the representative body." This argument, if it proves any thing, proves that there ought to be no general government whatever. For the powers which, it seems to be agreed on all hands, ought to be vested in the Union, cannot be safely intrusted to a body which is not under every requisite control. But there are satisfactory reasons to show that the objection is in reality not well founded. There is in most of the arguments which relate to distance a palpable illusion of the imagination. What are the sources of information by which the people in Montgomery County must regulate their judgment of the conduct of their representatives in the State legislature? Of personal observation they can have no benefit. This is confined to the citizens on the spot. They must therefore depend on the information of intelligent men, in whom they confide; and how must these men obtain their information? Evidently from the complexion of public measures, from the public prints, from correspondences with their representatives, and with other persons who reside at the place of their deliberations. This does not apply to Montgomery County only, but to all the counties at any considerable distance from the seat of government.

It is equally evident that the same sources of information would be open to the people in relation to the conduct of their representatives in the general government, and the impediments to a prompt communication which distance may be supposed to create, will be overbalanced by the effects of the vigilance of the State governments. The executive and legislative bodies of each State will be so many sentinels over the persons employed in every department of the national administration; and as it will be in their power to adopt and pursue a regular and effectual system of intelligence, they can never be at a loss to know the behavior of those who represent their constituents in the national councils, and can readily communicate the same knowledge to the people. Their disposition to apprise the community of whatever may prejudice its interests from another quarter, may be relied upon, if it were only from the rivalship of power. And we may conclude with the fullest assurance that the people, through that channel, will be better informed of the conduct of their national representatives, than they can be by any means they now possess of that of their State representatives.

It ought also to be remembered that the citizens who inhabit the country at and near the seat of government will, in all questions that affect the general liberty and prosperity, have the same interest with those who are at a distance, and that they will stand ready to sound the alarm when necessary, and to point out the actors in any pernicious project. The public papers will be expeditious messengers of intelligence to the most remote inhabitants of the Union.

Among the many curious objections which have appeared against the proposed Constitution, the most extraordinary and the least colorable is derived from the want of some provision respecting the debts due to the United States. This has been represented as a tacit relinquishment of those debts, and as a wicked contrivance to screen public defaulters. The newspapers have teemed with the most inflammatory railings on this head; yet there is nothing clearer than that the suggestion is entirely void of foundation, the offspring of extreme ignorance or extreme dishonesty. In addition to the remarks I have made upon the subject in another place, I shall only observe that as it is a plain dictate of common-sense, so it is also an established doctrine of political law,

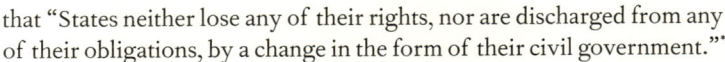

that "States neither lose any of their rights, nor are discharged from any of their obligations, by a change in the form of their civil government."*

The last objection of any consequence, which I at present recollect, turns upon the article of expense. If it were even true, that the adoption of the proposed government would occasion a considerable increase of expense, it would be an objection that ought to have no weight against the plan.

The great bulk of the citizens of America are with reason convinced, that Union is the basis of their political happiness. Men of sense of all parties now, with few exceptions, agree that it cannot be preserved under the present system, nor without radical alterations; that new and extensive powers ought to be granted to the national head, and that these require a different organization of the federal government—a single body being an unsafe depositary of such ample authorities. In conceding all this, the question of expense must be given up; for it is impossible, with any degree of safety, to narrow the foundation upon which the system is to stand. The two branches of the legislature are, in the first instance, to consist of only sixty-five persons, which is the same number of which Congress, under the existing Confederation, may be composed. It is true that this number is intended to be increased; but this is to keep pace with the progress of the population and resources of the country. It is evident that a less number would, even in the first instance, have been unsafe, and that a continuance of the present number would, in a more advanced stage of population, be a very inadequate representation of the people.

Whence is the dreaded augmentation of expense to spring? One source indicated, is the multiplication of offices under the new government. Let us examine this a little.

It is evident that the principal departments of the administration under the present government, are the same which will be required under the new. There are now a Secretary of War, a Secretary of Foreign Affairs, a Secretary for Domestic Affairs, a Board of Treasury, consisting of three persons, a Treasurer, assistants, clerks, etc. These officers are indispensable under any system, and will suffice under the new as well as the old. As to ambassadors and other ministers and agents in foreign countries, the proposed Constitution can make no other difference than

---

*Vide Rutherford's Institutes, *Vol. 2, Book II, Chapter X, Sections XIV and XV.*
Vide also Grotius, *Book II, Chapter IX, Sections VIII and IX.*

to render their characters, where they reside, more respectable, and their services more useful. As to persons to be employed in the collection of the revenues, it is unquestionably true that these will form a very considerable addition to the number of federal officers; but it will not follow that this will occasion an increase of public expense. It will be in most cases nothing more than an exchange of State for national officers. In the collection of all duties, for instance, the persons employed will be wholly of the latter description. The States individually will stand in no need of any for this purpose. What difference can it make in point of expense to pay officers of the customs appointed by the State or by the United States? There is no good reason to suppose that either the number or the salaries of the latter will be greater than those of the former.

Where then are we to seek for those additional articles of expense which are to swell the account to the enormous size that has been represented to us? The chief item which occurs to me respects the support of the judges of the United States. I do not add the President, because there is now a president of Congress, whose expenses may not be far, if any thing, short of those which will be incurred on account of the President of the United States. The support of the judges will clearly be an extra expense, but to what extent will depend on the particular plan which may be adopted in regard to this matter. But upon no reasonable plan can it amount to a sum which will be an object of material consequence.

Let us now see what there is to counterbalance any extra expense that may attend the establishment of the proposed government. The first thing which presents itself is that a great part of the business which now keeps Congress sitting through the year will be transacted by the President. Even the management of foreign negotiations will naturally devolve upon him, according to general principles concerted with the Senate, and subject to their final concurrence. Hence it is evident that a portion of the year will suffice for the session of both the Senate and the House of Representatives; we may suppose about a fourth for the latter and a third, or perhaps half, for the former. The extra business of treaties and appointments may give this extra occupation to the Senate. From this circumstance we may infer that, until the House of Representatives shall be increased greatly beyond its present number, there will be a considerable saving of expense from the difference between the constant session of the present and the temporary session of the future Congress.

But there is another circumstance of great importance in the view of economy. The business of the United States has hitherto occupied the State legislatures, as well as Congress. The latter has made requisitions which the former have had to provide for. Hence it has happened that the sessions of the State legislatures have been protracted greatly beyond what was necessary for the execution of the mere local business of the States. More than half their time has been frequently employed in matters which related to the United States. Now the members who compose the legislatures of the several States amount to two thousand and upwards, which number has hitherto performed what under the new system will be done in the first instance by sixty-five persons, and probably at no future period by above a fourth or fifth of that number. The Congress under the proposed government will do all the business of the United States themselves, without the intervention of the State legislatures, who thenceforth will have only to attend to the affairs of their particular States, and will not have to sit in any proportion as long as they have heretofore done. This difference in the time of the sessions of the State legislatures will be clear gain, and will alone form an article of saving, which may be regarded as an equivalent for any additional objects of expense that may be occasioned by the adoption of the new system.

The result from these observations is that the sources of additional expense from the establishment of the proposed Constitution are much fewer than may have been imagined; that they are counterbalanced by considerable objects of saving; and that while it is questionable on which side the scale will preponderate, it is certain that a government less expensive would be incompetent to the purposes of the Union.

PUBLIUS

# GEORGE WASHINGTON'S FIRST INAUGURAL ADDRESS APRIL 30, 1789

Fellow-Citizens of the Senate and of the House of Representatives: Among the vicissitudes incident to life no event could have filled me with greater anxieties than that of which the notification was transmitted by your order, and received on the 14th day of the present month. On the one hand, I was summoned by my country, whose voice I can never hear but with veneration and love, from a retreat which I had chosen with the fondest predilection, and, in my flattering hopes, with an immutable decision, as the asylum of my declining years—a retreat which was rendered every day more necessary as well as more dear to me by the addition of habit to inclination, and of frequent interruptions in my health to the gradual waste committed on it by time. On the other hand, the magnitude and difficulty of the trust to which the voice of my country called me, being sufficient to awaken in the wisest and most experienced of her citizens a distrustful scrutiny into his qualifications, could not but overwhelm with despondence one who (inheriting inferior endowments from nature and unpracticed in the duties of civil administration) ought to be peculiarly conscious of his own deficiencies. In this conflict of emotions all I dare aver is that it has been my faithful study to collect my duty from a just appreciation of every circumstance by which it might be affected. All I dare hope is that if, in executing this task, I have been too much swayed by a grateful remembrance of former instances, or by an affectionate sensibility to this transcendent proof of the confidence of my fellow-citizens, and have thence too little consulted my incapacity as well as disinclination for the weighty and untried cares before me, my error will be palliated by the motives which mislead me, and its consequences be judged by my country with some share of the partiality in which they originated.

Such being the impressions under which I have, in obedience to the public summons, repaired to the present station, it would be peculiarly improper to omit in this first official act my fervent supplications to that Almighty Being who rules over the universe, who presides in

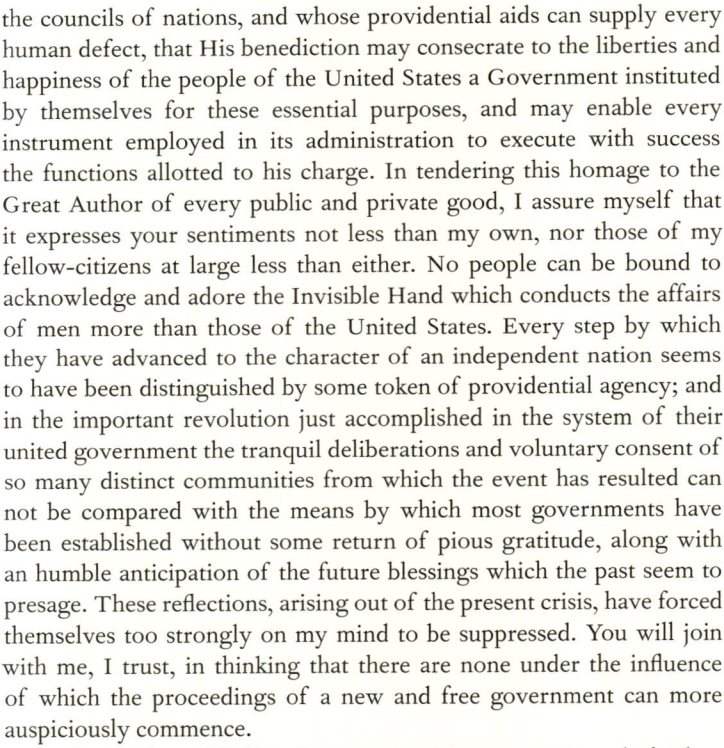

the councils of nations, and whose providential aids can supply every human defect, that His benediction may consecrate to the liberties and happiness of the people of the United States a Government instituted by themselves for these essential purposes, and may enable every instrument employed in its administration to execute with success the functions allotted to his charge. In tendering this homage to the Great Author of every public and private good, I assure myself that it expresses your sentiments not less than my own, nor those of my fellow-citizens at large less than either. No people can be bound to acknowledge and adore the Invisible Hand which conducts the affairs of men more than those of the United States. Every step by which they have advanced to the character of an independent nation seems to have been distinguished by some token of providential agency; and in the important revolution just accomplished in the system of their united government the tranquil deliberations and voluntary consent of so many distinct communities from which the event has resulted can not be compared with the means by which most governments have been established without some return of pious gratitude, along with an humble anticipation of the future blessings which the past seem to presage. These reflections, arising out of the present crisis, have forced themselves too strongly on my mind to be suppressed. You will join with me, I trust, in thinking that there are none under the influence of which the proceedings of a new and free government can more auspiciously commence.

By the article establishing the executive department it is made the duty of the President "to recommend to your consideration such measures as he shall judge necessary and expedient." The circumstances under which I now meet you will acquit me from entering into that subject further than to refer to the great constitutional charter under which you are assembled, and which, in defining your powers, designates the objects to which your attention is to be given. It will be more consistent with those circumstances, and far more congenial with the feelings which actuate me, to substitute, in place of a recommendation of particular measures, the tribute that is due to the talents, the rectitude, and the patriotism which adorn the characters selected to devise and adopt them. In these honorable qualifications I behold the surest pledges that as on one side no local prejudices or attachments, no separate views nor party animosities, will misdirect the comprehensive and equal eye which ought to watch over this great assemblage of communities and interests, so, on another, that the foundation of our national policy will be laid in the pure and immutable principles of private morality, and the preeminence of free government be exemplified by all the attributes which can win the affections of its citizens and command the respect of the world. I dwell on this prospect with every satisfaction which an ardent love for my country can inspire, since there is no truth more thoroughly established than that there exists in the economy and course of nature an indissoluble union between virtue and happiness; between duty and advantage; between the genuine maxims of an honest and magnanimous policy and the solid rewards of public prosperity and felicity; since we ought to be no less persuaded that the propitious smiles of Heaven can never be expected on a nation that disregards the eternal rules of order and right which Heaven itself has ordained; and since the preservation of the sacred fire of liberty and the destiny of the republican model of government are justly considered, perhaps, as deeply, as finally, staked on the experiment entrusted to the hands of the American people.

Besides the ordinary objects submitted to your care, it will remain with your judgment to decide how far an exercise of the occasional power delegated by the fifth article of the Constitution is rendered expedient at the present juncture by the nature of objections which have been urged against the system, or by the degree of inquietude which has given birth to them. Instead of undertaking particular recommendations on this subject, in which I could be guided by no lights derived from official opportunities, I shall again give way to my entire confidence in your discernment and pursuit of the public good; for I assure myself that whilst you carefully avoid every alteration which might endanger the benefits of an united and effective government, or which ought to await the future lessons of experience, a reverence for the characteristic rights of freemen and a regard for the public harmony will sufficiently influence your deliberations on the question how far the former can be impregnably fortified or the latter be safely and advantageously promoted.

To the foregoing observations I have one to add, which will be most properly addressed to the House of Representatives. It concerns myself, and will therefore be as brief as possible. When I was first honored with a call into the service of my country, then on the eve of an arduous struggle for its liberties, the light in which I contemplated my duty required that I should renounce every pecuniary compensation. From this resolution I have in no instance departed; and being still under the impressions which produced it, I must decline as inapplicable to myself any share in the personal emoluments which may be indispensably included in a permanent provision for the executive department, and must accordingly pray that the pecuniary estimates for the station in which I am placed may during my continuance in it be limited to such actual expenditures as the public good may be thought to require.

Having thus imparted to you my sentiments as they have been awakened by the occasion which brings us together, I shall take my present leave; but not without resorting once more to the benign Parent of the Human Race in humble supplication that, since He has been pleased to favor the American people with opportunities for deliberating in perfect tranquillity, and dispositions for deciding with unparalleled unanimity on a form of government for the security of their union and the advancement of their happiness, so His divine blessing may be equally conspicuous in the enlarged views, the temperate consultations, and the wise measures on which the success of this Government must depend.

# THE UNITED STATES' BILL OF RIGHTS (PASSED 1789; RATIFIED 1791)

Congress of the United States begun and held at the City of New York on Wednesday the fourth of March, one thousand seven hundred and eighty nine

THE Conventions of a number of the States, having at the time of their adopting the Constitution, expressed a desire, in order to prevent misconstruction or abuse of its powers, that further declaratory and restrictive clauses should be added: And as extending the ground of public confidence in the Government, will best ensure the beneficent ends of its institution.

RESOLVED by the Senate and House of Representatives of the United States of America, in Congress assembled, two thirds of both Houses concurring, that the following Articles be proposed to the Legislatures of the several States, as amendments to the Constitution of the United States, all, or any of which Articles, when ratified by three fourths of the said Legislatures, to be valid to all intents and purposes, as part of the said Constitution; viz.

ARTICLES in addition to, and Amendment of the Constitution of the United States of America, proposed by Congress, and ratified by the Legislatures of the several States, pursuant to the fifth Article of the original Constitution.

## AMENDMENT I

Congress shall make no law respecting an establishment of religion, or prohibiting the free exercise thereof; or abridging the freedom of speech, or of the press, or the right of the people peaceably to assemble, and to petition the Government for a redress of grievances.

## AMENDMENT II

A well-regulated militia, being necessary to the security of a free State, the right of the people to keep and bear arms, shall not be infringed.

## AMENDMENT III

No soldier shall, in time of peace be quartered in any house, without the consent of the owner, nor in time of war, but in a manner to be prescribed by law.

## AMENDMENT IV

The right of the people to be secure in their persons, houses, papers, and effects, against unreasonable searches and seizures, shall not be violated, and no Warrants shall issue, but upon probable cause, supported by oath or affirmation, and particularly describing the place to be searched, and the persons or things to be seized.

## AMENDMENT V

No person shall be held to answer for a capital, or otherwise infamous crime, unless on a presentment or indictment of a Grand Jury, except in cases arising in the land or naval forces, or in the Militia, when in actual service in time of War or public danger; nor shall any person be subject for the same offense to be twice put in jeopardy of life or limb; nor shall be compelled in any criminal case to be a witness against himself, nor be deprived of life, liberty, or property, without due process of law; nor shall private property be taken for public use without just compensation.

## AMENDMENT VI

In all criminal prosecutions, the accused shall enjoy the right to a speedy and public trial, by an impartial jury of the State and district wherein the crime shall have been committed, which district shall have been previously ascertained by law, and to be informed of the nature and cause of the accusation; to be confronted with the witnesses against him; to have compulsory process for obtaining witnesses in his favor, and to have the assistance of counsel for his defense.

## AMENDMENT VII

In suits at common law, where the value in controversy shall exceed twenty dollars, the right of trial by jury shall be preserved, and no fact tried by a jury shall be otherwise re-examined in any court of the United States, than according to the rules of the common law.

## AMENDMENT VIII

Excessive bail shall not be required nor excessive fines imposed, nor cruel and unusual punishments inflicted.

## AMENDMENT IX

The enumeration in the Constitution, of certain rights, shall not be construed to deny or disparage others retained by the people.

## AMENDMENT X

The powers not delegated to the United States by the Constitution, nor prohibited by it to the States, are reserved to the States respectively, or to the people.

# THOMAS JEFFERSON'S
# FIRST INAUGURAL ADDRESS
# MARCH 4, 1801

Friends and Fellow-Citizens:

Called upon to undertake the duties of the first executive office of our country, I avail myself of the presence of that portion of my fellow-citizens which is here assembled to express my grateful thanks for the favor with which they have been pleased to look toward me, to declare a sincere consciousness that the task is above my talents, and that I approach it with those anxious and awful presentiments which the greatness of the charge and the weakness of my powers so justly inspire. A rising nation, spread over a wide and fruitful land, traversing all the seas with the rich productions of their industry, engaged in commerce with nations who feel power and forget right, advancing rapidly to destinies beyond the reach of mortal eye—when I contemplate these transcendent objects, and see the honor, the happiness, and the hopes of this beloved country committed to the issue, and the auspices of this day, I shrink from the contemplation, and humble myself before the magnitude of the undertaking. Utterly, indeed, should I despair did not the presence of many whom I here see remind me that in the other high authorities provided by our Constitution I shall find resources of wisdom, of virtue, and of zeal on which to rely under all difficulties. To you, then, gentlemen, who are charged with the sovereign functions of legislation, and to those associated with you, I look with encouragement for that guidance and support which may enable us to steer with safety the vessel in which we are all embarked amidst the conflicting elements of a troubled world.

During the contest of opinion through which we have passed, the animation of discussions and of exertions has sometimes worn an aspect which might impose on strangers unused to think freely and to speak and to write what they think; but this being now decided by the voice of the nation, announced according to the rules of the Constitution, all will, of course, arrange themselves under the will of the law, and unite in common efforts for the common good. All, too, will bear in mind this sacred principle, that though the will of the majority is in all cases to prevail, that will to be rightful must be reasonable; that the minority possess their equal rights, which equal law must protect, and to violate would be oppression. Let us, then, fellow-citizens, unite with one heart and one mind. Let us restore to social intercourse that harmony and affection without which liberty and even life itself are but dreary things. And let us reflect that, having banished from our land that religious intolerance under which mankind so long bled and suffered, we have yet gained little if we countenance a political intolerance as despotic, as wicked, and capable of as bitter and bloody persecutions. During the throes and convulsions of the ancient world, during the agonizing spasms of infuriated man, seeking through blood and slaughter his long-lost liberty, it was not wonderful that the agitation of the billows should reach even this distant and peaceful shore; that this should be more felt and feared by some and less by others, and should divide opinions as to measures of safety. But every difference of opinion is not a difference of principle. We have called by different names brethren of the same principle. We are all Republicans, we are all Federalists. If there be any among us who would wish to dissolve this Union or to change its republican form, let them stand undisturbed as monuments of the safety with which error of opinion may be tolerated where reason is left free to combat it. I know, indeed, that some honest men fear that a republican government can not be strong, that this Government is not strong enough; but would the honest patriot, in the full tide of successful experiment, abandon a government which has so far kept us free and firm on the theoretic and visionary fear that this Government, the world's best hope, may by possibility want energy to preserve itself? I trust not. I believe this, on the contrary, the strongest Government on earth. I believe it the only one where every man, at the call of the law, would fly to the standard of the law, and would meet invasions of the public order as his own personal concern. Sometimes it is said that man can not be trusted with the government of himself. Can he, then, be trusted with the government of others? Or have we found angels in the forms of kings to govern him? Let history answer this question.

Let us, then, with courage and confidence pursue our own Federal and Republican principles, our attachment to union and representative government. Kindly separated by nature and a wide ocean from the exterminating havoc of one quarter of the globe; too high-minded to endure the degradations of the others; possessing a chosen country, with room enough for our descendants to the hundredth and thousandth generation; entertaining a due sense of our equal right to the use of our own faculties, to the acquisitions of our own industry, to honor and confidence from our fellow-citizens, resulting not from birth, but from our actions and their sense of them; enlightened by a benign religion, professed, indeed, and practiced in various forms, yet all of them inculcating honesty, truth, temperance, gratitude, and the love of man; acknowledging and adoring an overruling Providence, which by all its dispensations proves that it delights in the happiness of man here and his greater happiness hereafter—with all these blessings, what more is necessary to make us a happy and a prosperous people? Still one thing more, fellow-citizens—a wise and frugal Government, which shall restrain men from injuring one another, shall leave them otherwise free to regulate their own pursuits of industry and improvement, and shall not take from the mouth of labor the bread it has earned. This is the sum of good government, and this is necessary to close the circle of our felicities.

About to enter, fellow-citizens, on the exercise of duties which comprehend everything dear and valuable to you, it is proper you should understand what I deem the essential principles of our Government, and consequently those which ought to shape its Administration. I will compress them within the narrowest compass they will bear, stating the general principle, but not all its limitations. Equal and exact justice to all men, of whatever state or persuasion, religious or political; peace, commerce, and honest friendship with all nations, entangling alliances with none; the support of the State governments in all their rights, as the most competent administrations for our domestic concerns and the surest bulwarks against anti-republican tendencies; the preservation of the General Government in its whole constitutional vigor, as the sheet anchor of our peace at home and safety abroad; a jealous care of the right of election by the people—a mild and safe corrective of abuses which are lopped by the sword of revolution where peaceable remedies are unprovided; absolute acquiescence in the decisions of the majority, the vital principle of republics, from which there is no appeal but to force, the vital principle and immediate parent of despotism; a well-disciplined militia, our best reliance in peace and for the first moments of war, till regulars may relieve them; the supremacy of the civil over the military authority; economy in the public expense, that labor may be lightly burthened; the honest payment of our debts and sacred preservation of the public faith; encouragement of agriculture, and of commerce as its handmaid; the diffusion of information and arraignment of all abuses at the bar of the public reason; freedom of religion; freedom of the press, and freedom of person under the protection of the habeas corpus, and trial by juries impartially selected. These principles form the bright constellation which has gone before us and guided our steps through an age of revolution and reformation. The wisdom of our sages and blood of our heroes have been devoted to their attainment. They should be the creed of our political faith, the text of civic instruction, the touchstone by which to try the services of those we trust; and should we wander from them in moments of error or of alarm, let us hasten to retrace our steps and to regain the road which alone leads to peace, liberty, and safety.

I repair, then, fellow-citizens, to the post you have assigned me. With experience enough in subordinate offices to have seen the difficulties of this the greatest of all, I have learnt to expect that it will rarely fall to the lot of imperfect man to retire from this station with the reputation and the favor which bring him into it. Without pretensions to that high confidence you reposed in our first and greatest revolutionary character, whose preeminent services had entitled him to the first place in his country's love and destined for him the fairest page in the volume of faithful history, I ask so much confidence only as may give firmness and effect to the legal administration of your affairs. I shall often go wrong through defect of judgment. When right, I shall often be thought wrong by those whose positions will not command a view of the whole ground. I ask your indulgence for my own errors, which will never be intentional, and your support against the errors of others, who may condemn what they would not if seen in all its parts. The approbation implied by your suffrage is a great consolation to me for the past, and my future solicitude will be to retain the good opinion of those who have bestowed it in advance, to conciliate that of others by doing them all the good in my power, and to be instrumental to the happiness and freedom of all.

Relying, then, on the patronage of your good will, I advance with obedience to the work, ready to retire from it whenever you become sensible how much better choice it is in your power to make. And may that Infinite Power which rules the destinies of the universe lead our councils to what is best, and give them a favorable issue for your peace and prosperity.

# THE LOUISIANA PURCHASE TREATY (1803)

*The Louisiana Purchase Treaty consisted of three separate documents: an agreement between France and the United States called the Treaty of Cession and two conventions. With the Louisiana Purchase, the United States paid just $15 million (or, 4¢ per acre) to double its size and expand west of the Mississippi River.*

## TREATY BETWEEN
## THE UNITED STATES OF AMERICA
## AND THE FRENCH REPUBLIC

The President of the United States of America and the First Consul of the French Republic, in the name of the French People, desiring to remove all Source of misunderstanding relative to objects of discussion mentioned in the second and fifth articles of the Convention of the 8th Vendémiaire an 9 (30 September 1800) relative to the rights claimed by the United States in virtue of the Treaty concluded at Madrid the 27 of October 1795, between His Catholic Majesty & the Said United States, & willing to Strengthen the union and friendship which at the time of the said Convention was happily reestablished between the two nations have respectively named their Plenipotentiaries, to wit, the President of the United States, by and with the advice and consent of the Senate of the said States; Robert R. Livingston Minister Plenipotentiary of the United States; and James Monroe Minister Plenipotentiary and Envoy extraordinary of the said States near the Government of the French Republic; and the First Consul in the name of the French people, Citizen Francis Barbé Marbois Minister of the public treasury who after having respectively exchanged their full powers have agreed to the following Articles.

### ARTICLE I

Whereas by the Article the third of the Treaty concluded at St. Ildefonso the 9th Vendémiaire an 9 (1st October) 1800 between the

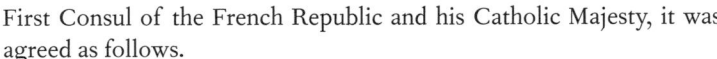 

First Consul of the French Republic and his Catholic Majesty, it was agreed as follows.

"His Catholic Majesty promises and engages on his part to cede to the French Republic six months after the full and entire execution of the conditions and Stipulations herein relative to his Royal Highness the Duke of Parma, the Colony or Province of Louisiana with the Same extent that it now has in the hand of Spain, & that it had when France possessed it; and Such as it Should be after the Treaties subsequently entered into between Spain and other States."

And whereas in pursuance of the Treaty and particularly of the third article the French Republic has an incontestible title to the domain and to the possession of the said Territory—The First Consul of the French Republic desiring to give to the United States a strong proof of his friendship doth hereby cede to the United States in the name of the French Republic for ever and in full Sovereignty the said territory with all its rights and appurtenances as fully and in the Same manner as they have been acquired by the French Republic in virtue of the above mentioned Treaty concluded with his Catholic Majesty.

## Art: II

In the cession made by the preceeding article are included the adjacent Islands belonging to Louisiana all public lots and Squares, vacant lands and all public buildings, fortifications, barracks and other edifices which are not private property.—The Archives, papers & documents relative to the domain and Sovereignty of Louisiana and its dependences will be left in the possession of the Commissaries of the United States, and copies will be afterwards given in due form to the Magistrates and Municipal officers of such of the said papers and documents as may be necessary to them.

## Art: III

The inhabitants of the ceded territory shall be incorporated in the Union of the United States and admitted as soon as possible according to the principles of the federal Constitution to the enjoyment of all the rights, advantages and immunities of citizens of the United States, and in the mean time they shall be maintained and protected in the free enjoyment of their liberty, property and the Religion which they profess.

## Art: IV

There shall be sent by the Government of France a Commissary to Louisiana to the end that he do every act necessary as well to receive from the Officers of his Catholic Majesty the said country and its dependances in the name of the French Republic if it has not been already done as to transmit it in the name of the French Republic to the Commissary or agent of the United States.

## Art: V

Immediately after the ratification of the present Treaty by the President of the United States and in case that of the first Consul's shall have been previously obtained, the commissary of the French Republic shall remit all military posts of New Orleans and other parts of the ceded territory to the Commissary or Commissaries named by the President to take possession—the troops whether of France or Spain who may be there shall cease to occupy any military post from the time of taking possession and shall be embarked as soon as possible in the course of three months after the ratification of this treaty.

## Art: VI

The United States promise to execute such treaties and articles as may have been agreed between Spain and the tribes and nations of Indians until by mutual consent of the United States and the said tribes or nations other suitable articles shall have been agreed upon.

## Art: VII

As it is reciprocally advantageous to the commerce of France and the United States to encourage the communication of both nations for a limited time in the country ceded by the present treaty until general arrangements relative to commerce of both nations may be agreed on; it has been agreed between the contracting parties that the French ships coming directly from France or any of her colonies loaded only with the produce and manufactures of France or her said Colonies; and the ships of Spain coming directly from Spain or any of her colonies loaded only with the produce or manufactures of Spain or her Colonies shall be admitted during the space of twelve years in the Port of New-Orleans and in all other legal ports-of-entry within the ceded territory in the same manner as the ships of the United States coming directly from France or Spain or any of their Colonies without being subject to any other or greater duty on merchandize [merchandise] or other or greater tonnage than that paid by the citizens of the United States.

During that space of time above mentioned no other nation shall have a right to the same privileges in the Ports of the ceded territory—the twelve years shall commence three months after the exchange of ratifications if it shall take place in France or three months after it shall have been notified at Paris to the French Government if it shall take place in the United States; It is however well understood that the object of the above article is to favour the manufactures, Commerce, freight and navigation of France and of Spain So far as relates to the importations that the French and Spanish shall make into the said Ports of the United States without in any sort affecting the regulations that the United States may make concerning the exportation of the produce and merchandize of the United States, or any right they may have to make such regulations.

## ART: VIII

In future and for ever after the expiration of the twelve years, the ships of France shall be treated upon the footing of the most favoured nations in the ports above mentioned.

## ART: IX

The particular Convention Signed this day by the respective Ministers, having for its object to provide for the payment of debts due to the Citizens of the United States by the French Republic prior to the 30th Sept. 1800 (8th Vendémiaire an 9) is approved and to have its execution in the same manner as if it had been inserted in this present treaty, and it shall be ratified in the same form and in the same time so that the one shall not be ratified distinct from the other.

Another particular Convention signed at the same date as the present treaty relative to a definitive rule between the contracting parties is in the like manner approved and will be ratified in the same form, and in the same time and jointly.

## ART: X

The present treaty shall be ratified in good and due form and the ratifications shall be exchanged in the space of six months after the date of the signature by the Ministers Plenipotentiary or sooner if possible.

In faith whereof the respective Plenipotentiaries have signed these articles in the French and English languages; declaring nevertheless that the present Treaty was originally agreed to in the French language; and have thereunto affixed their Seals.

Done at Paris the tenth day of Floreal in the eleventh year of the French Republic; and the 30th of April 1803.

# A CONVENTION BETWEEN
# THE UNITED STATES OF AMERICA
# AND THE FRENCH REPUBLIC

The President of the United States of America and the First Consul of the French Republic in the name of the French people, in consequence of the treaty of cession of Louisiana which has been signed this day; wishing to regulate definitively every thing which has relation to the said cession have authorized to this effect the Plenipotentiaries, that is to say the President of the United States has, by and with the advice and consent of the Senate of the said States, nominated for their Plenipotentiaries, Robert R. Livingston, Minister Plenipotentiary of the United States, and James Monroe, Minister Plenipotentiary and Envoy-Extraordinary of the said United States, near the Government of the French Republic; and the First Consul of the French Republic, in the name of the French people, has named as Pleniopotentiary of the said Republic the citizen Francis Barbé Marbois: who, in virtue of their full powers, which have been exchanged this day, have agreed to the following articles:

## ART: 1

The Government of the United States engages to pay to the French government in the manner specified in the following article the sum of sixty millions of francs independent of the sum which shall be fixed by another Convention for the payment of the debts due by France to citizens of the United States.

## ART: 2

For the payment of the sum of sixty millions of francs mentioned in the preceeding article the United States shall create a stock of eleven million, two hundred and fifty thousand dollars bearing an interest of Six percent per annum payable half yearly in London Amsterdam or Paris amounting by the half year to three hundred and thirty seven thousand five hundred Dollars, according to the proportions which shall be determined by the French Govenment to be paid at either place: The principal of the said stock to be reimbursed at the treasury of the United States in annual payments of not less than three millions of dollars each; of which the first payment shall commence fifteen years after the date of the exchange of ratifications:—this stock shall be transferred to the government of France or to such person or persons as Shall be authorized to receive it in three months at most after the exchange of ratifications of this treaty and after Louisiana shall be taken possession of the name of the Government of the United States.

It is further agreed that if the French Government should be desirous of disposing of the said stock to receive the capital in Europe at shorter terms that its measures for that purpose shall be taken so as to favour in the greatest degree possible the credit of the United States, and to raise to the highest price the said stock.

## Art: 3

It is agreed that the Dollar of the United States specified in the present Convention shall be fixed at five francs 3333/100000 or five livres eight Sous tournois.

The present Convention shall be ratified in good and due form, and the ratifications shall be exchanged the space of six months to date from this day or sooner it possible.

In faith of which the respective Plenipotentiaries have signed the above articles both in the French and English languages, declaring nevertheless that the present treaty has been originally agreed on and written in the French language; to which they have hereunto affixed their Seals.

Done at Paris the tenth of Floreal eleventh year of the French Republic; 30th April 1803.

# A CONVENTION BETWEEN
# THE UNITED STATES OF AMERICA
# AND THE FRENCH REPUBLIC

The President of the United States of America and the First Consul of the French Republic in the name of the French People having by a Treaty of this date terminated all difficulties relative to Louisiana, and established on a solid foundation the friendship which unites the two nations and being desirous in complyance with the Second and fifth Articles of the Convention of the 8th Vendémiaire ninth year of the French Republic (30th September 1800) to secure the payment of the Sums due by France to the citizens of the United States have respectively nominated as Plenipotentiaries that is to say the President of the United States of America by and with the advise and consent of their Senate Robert R. Livingston Minister Plenipotentiary and James Monroe Minister Plenipotentiary and Envoy Extraordinary of the said States near the Government of the French Republic: and the First Consul in the name of the French People the Citizen Francis Barbé Marbois Minister of the Public Treasury; who after having exchanged their full powers have agreed to the following articles.

## Art: 1

The debts due by France to citizens of the United States contracted before the 8th Vendémiaire ninth year of the French Republic (30th September 1800) shall be paid according to the following regulations with interest at Six per cent; to commence from the period when the accounts and vouchers were presented to the French Government.

## Art: 2

The debts provided for by the preceeding Article are those whose result is comprised in the conjectural note annexed to the present Convention and which, with the interest cannot exceed the Sum of twenty millions of Francs. The claims comprised in the said note which fall within the exceptions of the following articles, shall not be admitted to the benefit of this provision.

## Art: 3

The principal and interests of the said debts shall be discharged by the United States, by orders drawn by their Minister Plenipotentiary on their treasury, these orders shall be payable Sixty days after the exchange of ratifications of the Treaty and the Conventions signed this day, and after possession shall be given of Louisiana by the Commissaries of France to those of the United States.

## Art: 4

It is expressly agreed that the preceding articles shall comprehend no debts but such as are due to citizens of the United States who have been and are yet creditors of France for Supplies for embargoes and prizes made at sea, in which the appeal has been properly lodged within the time mentioned in the said Convention 8th Vendémiaire ninth year, (30th Sept 1800)

## Art: 5

The preceding Articles shall apply only, First: to captures of which the council of prizes shall have ordered restitution, it being well understood that the claimant cannot have recourse to the United States otherwise than he might have had to the Government of the French republic, and only in case of insufficiency of the captors—2d the debts mentioned in the Said fifth Article of the Convention contracted before the 8th Vendémiaire an 9 (30th September 1800) the payment of which has been heretofore claimed of the actual Government of France and for which the creditors have a right to the protection of the United States;—the said 5th Article does not comprehend prizes whose condemnation has been or shall be confirmed: it is the express intention of the contracting parties not to extend the benefit of the present Convention to reclamations of American citizens who Shall have established houses of Commerce in France, England or other countries than the United States in partnership with foreigners, and who by that reason and the nature of their commerce ought to be regarded as domiciliated in the places where such house exist.—All agreements and bargains concerning merchandize [merchandise], which shall not be the property of American citizens, are equally excepted from the benefit of the said Conventions, saving however to such persons their claims in like manner as if this Treaty had not been made.

## Art: 6

And that the different questions which may arise under the preceding article may be fairly investigated, the Ministers Plenipotentiary of the United States Shall name three persons, who Shall act from the present and provisionally, and who shall have full power to examine, without removing the documents, all the accounts of the different claims already liquidated by the Bureaus established for this purpose by the French Republic, and to ascertain whether they belong to the classes designated by the present Convention and the principles established in it or if they are not in one of its exceptions and on their Certificate, declaring that the debt is due to an American Citizen or his representative and that it existed before the 8th Vendémiaire 9th year (30 September 1800) the debtor shall be entitled to an order on the Treasury of the United States in the manner prescribed by the 3d Article.

## Art: 7

The same agents shall likewise have power, without removing the documents, to examine the claims which are prepared for verification, and to certify those which ought to be admitted by uniting the necessary qualifications, and not being comprised in the exceptions contained in the present Convention.

## Art: 8

The same agents shall likewise examine the claims which are not prepared for liquidation, and certify in writing those which in their judgement ought to be admitted to liquidation.

## Art: 9

In proportion as the debts mentioned in these articles shall be admitted they shall be discharged with interest at six per cent: by the Treasury of the United States.

## Art: 10

And that no debt shall not have the qualifications above mentioned and that no unjust or exorbitant demand may be admitted, the Commercial agent of the United States at Paris or such other agent as the Minister Plenipotentiary or the United States shall think proper to nominate shall assist at the operations of the Bureaus and cooperate in the examinations of the claims; and if this agent shall be of the opinion that any debt is not completely proved, or if he shall judge that it is not comprised in the principles of the fifth article above mentioned, and if notwithstanding his opinion the Bureaus established by the French Government should think that it ought to be liquidated, he shall transmit his observations to the board established by the United States, who, without removing documents, shall make a complete examination of the debt and vouchers which support it, and report the result to the Minister of the United States.——The Minister of the United States shall transmit his observations in all such cases to the Minister of the treasury of the French Republic, on whose report the French Government shall decide definitively in every case.

The rejection of any claim shall have no other effect than to exempt the United States from the payment of it, the French Government reserving to itself, the right to decide definitively on such claim so far as it concerns itself.

## Art: 11

Every necessary decision shall be made in the course of a year to commence from the exchange of ratifications, and no reclamation shall be admitted afterwards.

## Art: 12

In case of claims for debts contracted by the Government of France with citizens of the United States since the 8th Vendémiaire 9th year/30 September 1800 not being comprised in this Convention may be pursued, and the payment demanded in the Same manner as if it had not been made.

## Art: 13

The present convention shall be ratified in good and due form and the ratifications shall be exchanged in six months from the date of the Signature of the Ministers Plenipotentiary, or sooner if possible.

In faith of which, the respective Ministers Plenipotentiary have signed the above Articles both in the French and English languages, declaring nevertheless that the present treaty has been originally agreed on and written in the French language, to which they have hereunto affixed their Seals.

Done at Paris, the tenth of Floreal, eleventh year of the French Republic.

# "THE STAR-SPANGLED BANNER" (1814)

*Francis Scott Key wrote the "Star-Spangled Banner" during the War of 1812, but it didn't become the country's official anthem until 1931.*

O say can you see, by the dawn's early light,
What so proudly we hail'd at the twilight's last gleaming,
Whose broad stripes and bright stars through the perilous fight
O'er the ramparts we watched were so gallantly streaming?
And the rocket's red glare, the bombs bursting in air,
Gave proof through the night that our flag was still there,
O say does that star-spangled banner yet wave
O'er the land of the free and the home of the brave?

On the shore dimly seen through the mists of the deep
Where the foe's haughty host in dread silence reposes,
What is that which the breeze, o'er the towering steep,
As it fitfully blows, half conceals, half discloses?
Now it catches the gleam of the morning's first beam,
In full glory reflected now shines in the stream,
'Tis the star-spangled banner—O long may it wave
O'er the land of the free and the home of the brave!

And where is that band who so vauntingly swore,
That the havoc of war and the battle's confusion
A home and a country should leave us no more?
Their blood has washed out their foul footstep's pollution.
No refuge could save the hireling and slave
From the terror of flight or the gloom of the grave,
And the star-spangled banner in triumph doth wave
O'er the land of the free and the home of the brave.

O thus be it ever when freemen shall stand
Between their loved home and the war's desolation!
Blest with victory and peace may the heaven-rescued land
Praise the power that hath made and preserved us a nation!
Then conquer we must, when our cause it is just,
And this be our motto—"In God is our trust,"
And the star-spangled banner in triumph shall wave
O'er the land of the free and the home of the brave.

# THE MONROE DOCTRINE (1823)

*During his seventh annual message to Congress in December 1823, President James Monroe laid out the principle of American foreign policy that became known as the Monroe Doctrine, which said that European countries no longer had any right to colonize land or otherwise interfere in the western hemisphere.*

At the proposal of the Russian Imperial Government, made through the minister of the Emperor residing here, a full power and instructions have been transmitted to the minister of the United States at St. Petersburg to arrange by amicable negotiation the respective rights and interests of the two nations on the northwest coast of this continent. A similar proposal has been made by His Imperial Majesty to the Government of Great Britain, which has likewise been acceded to. The Government of the United States has been desirous by this friendly proceeding of manifesting the great value which they have invariably attached to the friendship of the Emperor and their solicitude to cultivate the best understanding with his Government. In the discussions to which this interest has given rise and in the arrangements by which they may terminate the occasion has been judged proper for asserting, as a principle in which the rights and interests of the United States are involved, that the American continents, by the free and independent condition which they have assumed and maintain, are henceforth not to be considered as subjects for future colonization by any European powers.

It was stated at the commencement of the last session that a great effort was then making in Spain and Portugal to improve the condition of the people of those countries, and that it appeared to be conducted with extraordinary moderation. It need scarcely be remarked that the results have been so far very different from what was then anticipated. Of events in that quarter of the globe, with which we have so much intercourse and from which we derive our origin, we have always been anxious and interested spectators. The citizens of the United States cherish sentiments the most friendly in favor of the liberty and happiness of their fellow-men on that side of the Atlantic. In the wars of the European powers in matters relating to themselves we have never taken any part, nor does it comport with our policy to do so. It is only when our rights are invaded or seriously menaced that we resent injuries or make preparation for our defense. With the movements in this hemisphere we are of necessity more immediately connected, and by causes which must be obvious to all enlightened and impartial observers. The political system of the allied powers is essentially different in this respect from that of America. This difference proceeds from that which exists in their respective Governments; and to the defense of our own, which has been achieved by the loss of so much blood and treasure, and matured by the wisdom of their most enlightened citizens, and under which we have enjoyed unexampled felicity, this whole nation is devoted. We owe it, therefore, to candor and to the amicable relations existing between the United States and those powers to declare that we should consider any attempt on their part to extend their system to any portion of this hemisphere as dangerous to our peace and safety. With the existing colonies or dependencies of any European power we have not interfered and shall not interfere. But with the Governments who have declared their independence and maintain it, and whose independence we have, on great consideration and on just principles, acknowledged, we could not view any interposition for the purpose of oppressing them, or controlling in any other manner their destiny, by any European power in any other light than as the manifestation of an unfriendly disposition toward the United States. In the war between those new Governments and Spain we declared our neutrality at the time of their recognition, and to this we have adhered, and shall continue to adhere, provided no change shall occur which, in the judgement of the competent authorities of this Government, shall make a corresponding change on the part of the United States indispensable to their security.

The late events in Spain and Portugal shew that Europe is still unsettled. Of this important fact no stronger proof can be adduced than that the allied powers should have thought it proper, on any principle satisfactory to themselves, to have interposed by force in the internal concerns of Spain. To what extent such interposition may be carried, on the same principle, is a question in which all independent powers whose governments differ from theirs are interested, even those most remote, and surely none of them more so than the United States. Our policy in regard to Europe, which was adopted at an early stage of the wars which have so long agitated that quarter of the globe, nevertheless remains the same, which is, not to interfere in the internal concerns of any of its powers; to consider the government de facto as the legitimate government for us; to cultivate friendly relations with it, and to preserve those relations by a frank, firm, and manly policy, meeting in all instances the just claims of every power, submitting to injuries from none. But in regard to those continents circumstances are eminently and conspicuously different.

It is impossible that the allied powers should extend their political system to any portion of either continent without endangering our peace and happiness; nor can anyone believe that our southern brethren, if left to themselves, would adopt it of their own accord. It is equally impossible, therefore, that we should behold such interposition in any form with indifference. If we look to the comparative strength and resources of Spain and those new Governments, and their distance from each other, it must be obvious that she can never subdue them. It is still the true policy of the United States to leave the parties to themselves, in hope that other powers will pursue the same course.

# ON INDIAN REMOVAL (1830)

*President Andrew Jackson used his first annual message to Congress to discuss the "successes" of the Indian Removal Act of 1830, which called for the removal of Native Americans located in the southeastern states. The act relocated tribes to areas west of the Mississippi River, thereby opening up the land in the South for white settlement. The Indian Removal Act was not the first attempt to take control of Native American land—the U.S. government had been negotiating treaties, fighting wars, and forcing Native Americans to move since the country was founded. But it was the first time the government officially called for complete removal and relocation. It also laid the foundation for much of the country's subsequent relationships with Native Americans and led to tragedy, including the 1838–39 Trail of Tears, during which more than 4,000 of about 15,000 Cherokees died during a forced, 800-mile march from their homes in Georgia to Oklahoma's Indian Territory.*

It gives me pleasure to announce to Congress that the benevolent policy of the Government, steadily pursued for nearly thirty years, in relation to the removal of the Indians beyond the white settlements is approaching to a happy consummation. Two important tribes have accepted the provision made for their removal at the last session of Congress, and it is believed that their example will induce the remaining tribes also to seek the same obvious advantages.

The consequences of a speedy removal will be important to the United States, to individual States, and to the Indians themselves. The pecuniary advantages which it promises to the Government are the least of its recommendations. It puts an end to all possible danger of collision between the authorities of the General and State Governments on account of the Indians. It will place a dense and civilized population in large tracts of country now occupied by a few savage hunters. By opening the whole territory between Tennessee on the north and Louisiana on the south to the settlement of the whites it will incalculably strengthen the southwestern frontier and render the adjacent States strong enough to repel future invasions without remote

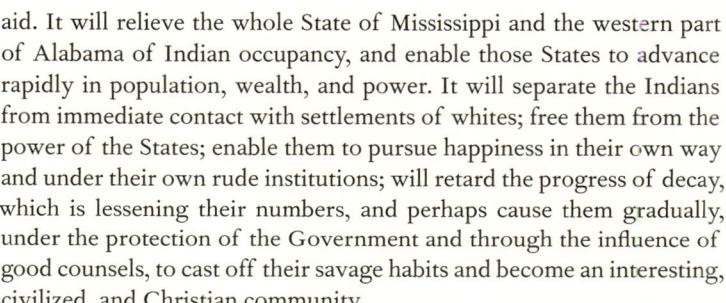

aid. It will relieve the whole State of Mississippi and the western part of Alabama of Indian occupancy, and enable those States to advance rapidly in population, wealth, and power. It will separate the Indians from immediate contact with settlements of whites; free them from the power of the States; enable them to pursue happiness in their own way and under their own rude institutions; will retard the progress of decay, which is lessening their numbers, and perhaps cause them gradually, under the protection of the Government and through the influence of good counsels, to cast off their savage habits and become an interesting, civilized, and Christian community.

What good man would prefer a country covered with forests and ranged by a few thousand savages to our extensive Republic, studded with cities, towns, and prosperous farms embellished with all the improvements which art can devise or industry execute, occupied by more than 12,000,000 happy people, and filled with all the blessings of liberty, civilization and religion?

The present policy of the Government is but a continuation of the same progressive change by a milder process. The tribes which occupied the countries now constituting the Eastern States were annihilated or have melted away to make room for the whites. The waves of population and civilization are rolling to the westward, and we now propose to acquire the countries occupied by the red men of the South and West by a fair exchange, and, at the expense of the United States, to send them to land where their existence may be prolonged and perhaps made perpetual. Doubtless it will be painful to leave the graves of their fathers; but what do they more than our ancestors did or than our children are now doing? To better their condition in an unknown land our forefathers left all that was dear in earthly objects. Our children by thousands yearly leave the land of their birth to seek new homes in distant regions. Does Humanity weep at these painful separations from everything, animate and inanimate, with which the young heart has become entwined? Far from it. It is rather a source of joy that our country affords scope where our young population may range unconstrained in body or in mind, developing the power and facilities of man in their highest perfection. These remove hundreds and almost thousands of miles at their own expense, purchase the lands they occupy, and support themselves at their new homes from the moment of their arrival. Can it be cruel in this Government when, by events which it can not control, the Indian is made discontented in his ancient home to purchase his lands, to give him a new and extensive territory, to pay the expense of his removal, and support him a year in his new abode? How many thousands of our own people would gladly embrace the opportunity of removing to the West on such conditions! If the offers made to the Indians were extended to them, they would be hailed with gratitude and joy.

And is it supposed that the wandering savage has a stronger attachment to his home than the settled, civilized Christian? Is it more afflicting to him to leave the graves of his fathers than it is to our brothers and children? Rightly considered, the policy of the General Government toward the red man is not only liberal, but generous. He is unwilling to submit to the laws of the States and mingle with their population. To save him from this alternative, or perhaps utter annihilation, the General Government kindly offers him a new home, and proposes to pay the whole expense of his removal and settlement.

# RULES AND REGULATIONS OF THE KNICKERBOCKER BASE BALL CLUB (1845)

*Playing baseball was a popular pastime for men during the 19th century, but the game had no formal or universal rules. In 1845, a bank clerk from New York named Alexander Cartwright Jr. formed the Knickerbocker Base Ball Club with some friends, and they played regular games at a park in Hoboken, New Jersey. Cartwright and his club created the Knickerbocker Rules, a list of twenty guidelines that formed the foundation for "America's game" as we know it today.*

For many years the games of Town ball, Rounders and old Cat have been the sport of young boys. Recently, they have, in one form or another, been much enjoyed by gentlemen seeking wholesome American exercise. In 1845 Alexander Cartwright and other members of the Knickerbocker Base Ball Club of New York codified the unwritten rules of these boys' games into one, and so made the game of Base Ball a sport worthy of attention by adults. We have little doubt but that this gentlemanly pastime will capture the interest and imagination of sportsman and spectator alike throughout this country. Herewith are offered the first and complete rules of the game of Base Ball as played by the Knickerbocker Base Ball Club:

RULES AND REGULATIONS

1st. Member must strictly observe the time agreed upon for exercise, and be punctual in their attendance.

2nd. When assembled for exercise, the President, or in his absence the Vice-President, shall appoint an Umpire, who shall keep the game in a book provided for that purpose, and note violations of the By-Laws and Rules during the time of exercise.

3rd. The presiding officer shall designate two members as Captains, who shall retire and make the match to be played, observing at the same time that the players put opposite to each other should be nearly as equal as possible; the choice of sides to be then tossed for, and the first in hand to be decided in like manner.

4th. The bases shall be from "home" to second base, forty-two paces; from first to third base, forty-two paces equidistant.

5th. No stump match shall be played on a regular day of exercise.

6th If there should not be a sufficient number of members of the Club present at the time agreed upon to commence exercise, gentlemen not members may be chosen in to make up the match, which shall not be broken up to take in members that may afterward appear; but, in all cases, members shall have the preference, when present, at the making of a match.

7th. If members appear after the game is commenced they may be chosen in if mutually agreed upon.

8th. The game to consist of twenty-one counts, or aces; but at the conclusion an equal number of hands must be played.

9th. The ball must be pitched, and not thrown, for the bat.

10th. A ball knocked out of the field or outside the range of the first or third base, is foul.

11th. Three balls being struck at and missed and the last one caught, is a hand out; if not caught is considered fair, and the striker is bound to run.

12th. If a ball be struck, or tipped, and caught, either flying or on the first bound, it is a hand out.

13th. A player running the bases shall be out, if the ball is in the hands of an adversary on the base, or the runner is touched with it before he makes base; it being understood, however, that in no instance is a ball to be thrown at him.

14th. A player running who shall prevent an adversary from catching or getting the ball before making his base, is hand out.

15th. Three hands out, all out.

16th. Players must take their strike in regular turn.

17th. All disputes and differences relative to the game, to be decided by the Umpire, from which there is no appeal.

18th. No ace or base can be made on a foul strike.

19th. A runner cannot be put out in making one base, when a balk is made by the pitcher.

20th. But one base allowed when a ball bound out of the field when struck.

# "A HOUSE DIVIDED" (1858)

*On June 16, 1858, Abraham Lincoln, then a candidate for the U.S. Senate, delivered a powerful (and many said, radical) speech before the Illinois Republican National Convention. In the speech, Lincoln argued that the United States could not last much longer divided among free and slave states, nor would the issue of slavery be solved by allowing new states to choose a side, the most popular political approach at the time. Instead, the United States would ultimately have to become either all slave or all free. Lincoln lost that Senate election to Stephen A. Douglas, his Democratic opponent who supported allowing new states to decide if they would be free or slave-holding. But two years later, Lincoln won the Republican party's nomination for president and then won the election, setting into motion events that would end the practice of slavery in the United States.*

If we could first know where we are and whither we are tending, we could better judge what to do and how to do it. We are now far into the fifth year since a policy was initiated with the avowed object and confident promise of putting an end to slavery agitation. Under the operation of that policy, that agitation has not only not ceased but has constantly augmented. In my opinion, it will not cease until a crisis shall have been reached and passed. "A house divided against itself cannot stand." I believe this government cannot endure, permanently, half slave and half free. I do not expect the Union to be dissolved; I do not expect the house to fall; but I do expect it will cease to be divided. It will become all one thing, or all the other. Either the opponents of slavery will arrest the further spread of it and place it where the public mind shall rest in the belief that it is in the course of ultimate extinction, or its advocates will push it forward till it shall become alike lawful in all the states, old as well as new, North as well as South.

Have we no tendency to the latter condition?

Let anyone who doubts carefully contemplate that now almost complete legal combination—piece of machinery, so to speak—compounded of the Nebraska doctrine and the Dred Scott decision. Let him consider, not only what work the machinery is adapted to do, and how well adapted, but also let him study the history of its construction and trace, if he can, or rather fail, if he can, to trace the evidences of design and concert of action among its chief architects, from the beginning.

The new year of 1854 found slavery excluded from more than half the states by state constitutions and from most of the national territory by congressional prohibition. Four days later commenced the struggle which ended in repealing that congressional prohibition. This opened all the national territory to slavery and was the first point gained.

But, so far, Congress only had acted; and an endorsement by the people, real or apparent, was indispensable to save the point already gained and give chance for more.

This necessity had not been overlooked, but had been provided for, as well as might be, in the notable argument of "squatter sovereignty," otherwise called "sacred right of self-government," which latter phrase, though expressive of the only rightful basis of any government, was so perverted in this attempted use of it as to amount to just this: That if any one man choose to enslave another, no third man shall be allowed to object. That argument was incorporated into the Nebraska Bill itself, in the language which follows:

> It being the true intent and meaning of this act not to legislate slavery into an territory or state, nor to exclude it therefrom, but to leave the people there-of perfectly free to form and regulate their domestic institutions in their own way, subject only to the Constitution of the United States.

Then opened the roar of loose declamation in favor of "squatter sovereignty" and "sacred right of self-government." "But," said opposition members, "let us amend the bill so as to expressly declare that the people of the territory may exclude slavery." "Not we," said the friends of the measure; and down they voted the amendment.

While the Nebraska Bill was passing through Congress, a law case, involving the question of a Negro's freedom, by reason of his owner having voluntarily taken him first into a free state and then into a territory covered by the congressional prohibition, and held him as a slave for a long time in each, was passing through the United States Circuit Court for the district of Missouri; and both Nebraska Bill and lawsuit were brought to a decision in the same month of May 1854. The Negro's name was Dred Scott, which name now designates the decision finally made in the case. Before the then next presidential election, the law case came to, and was argued in, the Supreme Court of the United States; but the decision of it was deferred until after the election. Still, before the election, Senator Trumbull, on the floor of the Senate, requested the leading advocate of the Nebraska Bill to state his opinion whether the people of a territory can constitutionally exclude slavery from their limits; and the latter answers: "That is a question for the Supreme Court."

The election came. Mr. Buchanan was elected, and the endorsement, such as it was, secured. That was the second point gained. The endorsement, however, fell short of a clear popular majority by nearly 400,000 votes, and so, perhaps, was not overwhelmingly reliable and satisfactory. The outgoing President, in his last annual message, as impressively as possible echoed back upon the people the weight and authority of the endorsement. The Supreme Court met again, did not announce their decision, but ordered a reargument.

The presidential inauguration came, and still no decision of the Court; but the incoming President, in his inaugural address, fervently exhorted the people to abide by the forthcoming decision, whatever it might be. Then, in a few days, came the decision.

The reputed author of the Nebraska Bill finds an early occasion to make a speech at this capital endorsing the Dred Scott decision, and vehemently denouncing all opposition to it. The new President, too, seizes the early occasion of the Silliman letter to endorse and strongly construe that decision, and to express his astonishment that any different view had ever been entertained!

At length a squabble springs up between the President and the author of the Nebraska Bill, on the mere question of fact, whether the Lecompton constitution was or was not in any just sense made by the people of Kansas; and in that quarrel the latter declares that all he wants is a fair vote for the people, and that he cares not whether slavery be voted down or voted up. I do not understand his declaration, that he cares not whether slavery be voted down or voted up, to be intended by him other than as an apt definition of the policy he would impress upon the public mind—the principle for which he declares he has suffered so much and is ready to suffer to the end. And well may he cling to that principle! If he has any parental feeling, well may he cling to it. That principle is the only shred left of his original Nebraska doctrine.

Under the Dred Scott decision, "squatter sovereignty" squatted out of existence, tumbled down like temporary scaffolding; like the mold at the foundry, served through one blast and fell back into loose sand; helped to carry an election and then was kicked to the winds. His late joint struggle with the Republicans against the Lecompton constitution involves nothing of the original Nebraska doctrine. That struggle was made on a point—the right of a people to make their own constitution —upon which he and the Republicans have never differed.

The several points of the Dred Scott decision, in connection with Senator Douglas' "care not" policy, constitute the piece of machinery in its present state of advancement. This was the third point gained. The working points of that machinery are:

First, that no Negro slave, imported as such from Africa, and no descendant of such slave can ever be a citizen of any state in the sense of that term as used in the Constitution of the United States. This point is made in order to deprive the Negro, in every possible event, of the benefit of that provision of the United States Constitution which declares that "the citizens of each state shall be entitled to all the privileges and immunities of citizens in the several states."

Second, that, "subject to the Constitution of the United States," neither Congress nor a territorial legislature can exclude slavery from any United States territory. This point is made in order that individual men may fill up the territories with slaves, without danger of losing them as property, and thus enhance the chances of permanency to the institution through all the future.

Third, that whether the holding a Negro in actual slavery in a free state makes him free, as against the holder, the United States courts will not decide, but will leave to be decided by the courts of any slave state the Negro may be forced into by the master. This point is made, not to be pressed immediately but, if acquiesced in for awhile, and apparently endorsed by the people at an election, then to sustain the logical conclusion that what Dred Scott's master might lawfully do with Dred Scott in the free state of Illinois, every other master may lawfully do with any other one, or 1,000 slaves, in Illinois or in any other free state.

Auxiliary to all this, and working hand in hand with it, the Nebraska doctrine, or what is left of it, is to educate and mold public opinion, at least Northern public opinion, not to care whether slavery is voted down or voted up. This shows exactly where we now are; and partially, also, whither we are tending.

It will throw additional light on the latter to go back and run the mind over the string of historical facts already stated. Several things will now appear less dark and mysterious than they did when they were transpiring. The people were to be left "perfectly free," "subject only to the Constitution." What the Constitution had to do with it, outsiders could not then see. Plainly enough, now, it was an exactly fitted niche for the Dred Scott decision to afterward come in and declare the perfect freedom of the people to be just no freedom at all.

Why was the amendment expressly declaring the right of the people voted down? Plainly enough, now, the adoption of it would have spoiled the niche for the Dred Scott decision. Why was the Court decision held up? Why even a senator's individual opinion withheld till after the presidential election? Plainly enough, now, the speaking out then would have damaged the "perfectly free" argument upon which the election was to be carried. Why the outgoing President's felicitation on the endorsement? Why the delay of a reargument? Why the incoming President's advance exhortation in favor of the decision? These things look like the cautious patting and petting of a spirited horse preparatory to mounting him when it is dreaded that he may give the rider a fall. And why the hasty after-endorsement of the decision by the President and others?

We cannot absolutely know that all these exact adaptations are the result of preconcert. But when we see a lot of framed timbers, different portions of which we know have been gotten out at different times and places and by different workmen—Stephen, Franklin, Roger, and James, for instance—and when we see these timbers joined together and see they exactly make the frame of a house or a mill, all the tenons and mortises exactly fitting, and all the lengths and proportions of the different pieces exactly adapted to their respective places, and not a piece too many or too few, not omitting even scaffolding, or, if a single piece be lacking, we see the place in the frame exactly fitted and prepared yet to bring such piece in—in such a case, we find it impossible not to believe that Stephen and Franklin and Roger and James all understood one another from the beginning, and all worked upon a common plan or draft drawn up before the first blow was struck.

# THE EMANCIPATION PROCLAMATION (1862–63)

*President Abraham Lincoln's Emancipation Proclamation—drafted in 1862 and delivered on January 1 of the next year—officially freed all slaves in states rebelling against the Union. As Northern troops assumed control of Southern areas, the proclamation took effect.*

By the President of the United States of America:

## A Proclamation

Whereas on the 22nd day of September, A.D. 1862, a proclamation was issued by the President of the United States, containing, among other things, the following, to wit:

"That on the 1st day of January, A.D. 1863, all persons held as slaves within any State or designated part of a State the people whereof shall then be in rebellion against the United States shall be then, thenceforward, and forever free; and the executive government of the United States, including the military and naval authority thereof, will recognize and maintain the freedom of such persons and will do no act or acts to repress such persons, or any of them, in any efforts they may make for their actual freedom.

"That the executive will on the 1st day of January aforesaid, by proclamation, designate the States and parts of States, if any, in which the people thereof, respectively, shall then be in rebellion against the United States; and the fact that any State or the people thereof shall on that day be in good faith represented in the Congress of the United States by members chosen thereto at elections wherein a majority of the qualified voters of such States shall have participated shall, in the absence of strong countervailing testimony, be deemed conclusive evidence that such State and the people thereof are not then in rebellion against the United States."

Now, therefore, I, Abraham Lincoln, President of the United States, by virtue of the power in me vested as Commander-In-Chief of the Army and Navy of the United States in time of actual armed rebellion against the authority and government of the United States, and as a fit and necessary war measure for suppressing said rebellion, do, on this 1st day of January, A.D. 1863, and in accordance with my purpose so to do, publicly proclaimed for the full period of one hundred days from the first day above mentioned, order and designate as the States and parts of States wherein the people thereof, respectively, are this day in rebellion against the United States the following, to wit:

Arkansas, Texas, Louisiana (except the parishes of St. Bernard, Plaquemines, Jefferson, St. John, St. Charles, St. James, Ascension, Assumption, Terrebone, Lafourche, St. Mary, St. Martin, and Orleans, including the city of New Orleans), Mississippi, Alabama, Florida, Georgia, South Carolina, North Carolina, and Virginia (except the forty-eight counties designated as West Virginia, and also the counties of Berkeley, Accomac, Northhampton, Elizabeth City, York, Princess Anne, and Norfolk, including the cities of Norfolk and Portsmouth), and which excepted parts are for the present left precisely as if this proclamation were not issued.

And by virtue of the power and for the purpose aforesaid, I do order and declare that all persons held as slaves within said designated States and parts of States are, and henceforward shall be, free; and that the Executive Government of the United States, including the military and naval authorities thereof, will recognize and maintain the freedom of said persons.

And I hereby enjoin upon the people so declared to be free to abstain from all violence, unless in necessary self-defence; and I recommend to them that, in all cases when allowed, they labor faithfully for reasonable wages.

And I further declare and make known that such persons of suitable condition will be received into the armed service of the United States to garrison forts, positions, stations, and other places, and to man vessels of all sorts in said service.

And upon this act, sincerely believed to be an act of justice, warranted by the Constitution upon military necessity, I invoke the considerate judgment of mankind and the gracious favor of Almighty God.

# THE HOMESTEAD ACT (1862)

*In an effort to encourage settlement of the American West, President Abraham Lincoln signed the Homestead Act into law in 1862. For the first time in history, nearly any American who was a head of household or older than twenty-one—from farmers and immigrants to newly freed slaves and even some women—could claim 160 acres of once-public land as his own after paying only an $18 filing fee. The law has long been considered one of the most important pieces of American legislation, and it transformed the landscape of the western United States.*

## AN ACT TO SECURE HOMESTEADS TO ACTUAL SETTLERS ON THE PUBLIC DOMAIN

Be it enacted by the Senate and House of Representatives of the United States of America in Congress assembled, That any person who is the head of a family, or who has arrived at the age of twenty-one years, and is a citizen of the United States, or who shall have filed his declaration of intention to become such, as required by the naturalization laws of the United States, and who has never borne arms against the United States Government or given aid and comfort to its enemies, shall, from and after the first January, eighteen hundred and sixty-three, be entitled to enter one quarter section or a less quantity of unappropriated public lands, upon which said person may have filed a preemption claim, or which may, at the time the application is made, be subject to preemption at one dollar and twenty-five cents, or less, per acre; or eighty acres or less of such unappropriated lands, at two dollars and fifty cents per acre, to be located in a body, in conformity to the legal subdivisions of the public lands, and after the same shall have been surveyed: Provided, That any person owning and residing on land may, under the provisions of this act, enter other land lying contiguous to his or her said land, which shall not, with the land so already owned and occupied, exceed in the aggregate one hundred and sixty acres.

SEC. 2. And be it further enacted, That the person applying for the benefit of this act shall, upon application to the register of the land office in which he or she is about to make such entry, make affidavit before the said register or receiver that he or she is the head of a family, or is twenty-one years or more of age, or shall have performed service in the army or navy of the United States, and that he has never borne arms against the Government of the United States or given aid and comfort to its enemies, and that such application is made for his or her exclusive use and benefit, and that said entry is made for the purpose of actual settlement and cultivation, and not either directly or indirectly for the use or benefit of any other person or persons whomsoever; and upon filing the said affidavit with the register or receiver, and on payment of ten dollars, he or she shall thereupon be permitted to enter the quantity of land specified: Provided, however, That no certificate shall be given or patent issued therefore until the expiration of five years from the date of such entry ; and if, at the expiration of such time, or at any time within two years thereafter, the person making such entry ; or, if he be dead, his widow; or in case of her death, his heirs or devisee; or in case of a widow making such entry, her heirs or devisee, in case of her death; shall prove by two credible witnesses that he, she, or they have resided upon or cultivated the same for the term of five years immediately succeeding the time of filing the affidavit aforesaid, and shall make affidavit that no part of said land has been alienated, and that he has borne true allegiance to the Government of the United States; then, in such case, he, she, or they, if at that time a citizen of the United States, shall be entitled to a patent, as in other cases provided for by law: And provided, further, That in case of the death of both father and mother, leaving an Infant child, or children, under twenty-one years of age, the right and fee shall ensure to the benefit of said infant child or children ; and the executor, administrator, or guardian may, at any time within two years after the death of the surviving parent, and in accordance with the laws of the State in which such children for the time being have their domicil, sell said land for the benefit of said infants, but for no other purpose; and the purchaser shall acquire the absolute title by the purchase, and be entitled to a patent from the United States, on payment of the office fees and sum of money herein specified.

SEC. 3. And be it further enacted, That the register of the land office shall note all such applications on the tract books and plats of his office, and keep a register of all such entries, and make return thereof to the General Land Office, together with the proof upon which they have been founded.

Sec. 4. And be it further enacted, That no lands acquired under the provisions of this act shall in any event become liable to the satisfaction of any debt or debts contracted prior to the issuing of the patent therefor.

Sec. 5. And be it further enacted, That if, at any time after the filing of the affidavit, as required in the second section of this act, and before the expiration of the five years aforesaid, it shall be proven, after due notice to the settler, to the satisfaction of the register of the land office, that the person having filed such affidavit shall have actually changed his or her residence, or abandoned the said land for more than six months at any time, then and in that event the land so entered shall revert to the government.

Sec. 6. And be it further enacted, That no individual shall be permitted to acquire title to more than one quarter section under the provisions of this act; and that the Commissioner of the General Land Office is hereby required to prepare and issue such rules and regulations, consistent with this act, as shall be necessary and proper to carry its provisions into effect; and that the registers and receivers of the several land offices shall be entitled to receive the same compensation for any lands entered under the provisions of this act that they are now entitled to receive when the same quantity of land is entered with money, one half to be paid by the person making the application at the time of so doing, and the other half on the issue of the certificate by the person to whom it may be issued; but this shall not be construed to enlarge the maximum of compensation now prescribed by law for any register or receiver: Provided, That nothing contained in this act shall be so construed as to impair or interfere in any manner whatever with existing preemption rights: And provided, further, That all persons who may have filed their applications for a preemption right prior to the passage of this act, shall be entitled to all privileges of this act: Provided, further, That no person who has served, or may hereafter serve, for a period of not less than fourteen days in the army or navy of the United States, either regular or volunteer, under the laws thereof, during the existence of an actual war, domestic or foreign, shall be deprived of the benefits of this act on account of not having attained the age of twenty-one years.

SEC 7. And be it further enacted, That the fifth section of the act entitled "An act in addition to an act more effectually to provide for the punishment of certain crimes against the United States, and for other purposes," approved the third of March, in the year eighteen hundred and fifty-seven, shall extend to all oaths, affirmations, and affidavits, required or authorized by this act.

SEC. 8. And be it further enacted, That nothing in this act shall be so construed as to prevent any person who has availed him or herself of the benefits of the first section of this act, from paying the minimum price, or the price to which the same may have graduated, for the quantity of land so entered at any time before the expiration of the five years, and obtaining a patent therefore from the government, as in other cases provided by law, on making proof of settlement and cultivation as provided by existing laws granting preemption rights.

# ABRAHAM LINCOLN'S
# GETTYSBURG ADDRESS (1863)

*More than 51,000 Union and Confederate soldiers were killed, wounded, or missing after the Battle of Gettysburg (July 1–3, 1863). In memory of that loss, President Abraham Lincoln delivered the following speech four months later when he visited the battlefield.*

## GIVEN ON THE BATTLEFIELD NEAR GETTYSBURG, PENNSYLVANIA

Four score and seven years ago, our fathers brought forth upon this continent a new nation: conceived in liberty, and dedicated to the proposition that all men are created equal.

Now we are engaged in a great civil war, testing whether that nation, or any nation so conceived and so dedicated, can long endure. We are met on a great battlefield of that war. We have come to dedicate a portion of that field as a final resting place for those who here gave their lives that this nation might live. It is altogether fitting and proper that we should do this. But, in a larger sense, we cannot dedicate—we cannot consecrate—we cannot hallow this ground. The brave men, living and dead, who struggled here have consecrated it, far above our poor power to add or detract. The world will little note, nor long remember, what we say here, but it can never forget what they did here.

It is for us the living, rather, to be dedicated here to the unfinished work which they who fought here have thus far so nobly advanced. It is rather for us to be here dedicated to the great task remaining before us—that from these honored dead we take increased devotion to that cause for which they gave the last full measure of devotion—that we here highly resolve that these dead shall not have died in vain; that this nation, under God, shall have a new birth of freedom, and that government of the people by the people for the people shall not perish from this earth.

# ABRAHAM LINCOLN'S
# SECOND INAUGURAL ADDRESS
# MARCH 4, 1865

At this second appearing to take the oath of the Presidential office, there is less occasion for an extended address than there was at the first. Then a statement somewhat in detail of a course to be pursued seemed fitting and proper. Now, at the expiration of four years, during which public declarations have been constantly called forth on every point and phase of the great contest which still absorbs the attention and engrosses the energies of the nation, little that is new could be presented. The progress of our arms, upon which all else chiefly depends, is as well known to the public as to myself, and it is, I trust, reasonably satisfactory and encouraging to all. With high hope for the future, no prediction in regard to it is ventured.

On the occasion corresponding to this four years ago all thoughts were anxiously directed to an impending civil war. All dreaded it, all sought to avert it. While the inaugural address was being delivered from this place, devoted altogether to saving the Union without war, insurgent agents were in the city seeking to destroy it without war— seeking to dissolve the Union and divide effects by negotiation. Both parties deprecated war, but one of them would make war rather than let the nation survive, and the other would accept war rather than let it perish, and the war came.

One-eighth of the whole population were colored slaves, not distributed generally over the Union, but localized in the southern part of it. These slaves constituted a peculiar and powerful interest. All knew that this interest was somehow the cause of the war. To strengthen, perpetuate, and extend this interest was the object for which the insurgents would rend the Union even by war, while the Government claimed no right to do more than to restrict the territorial enlargement of it. Neither party expected for the war the magnitude or the duration which it has already attained. Neither anticipated that the cause of the conflict might cease with or even before the conflict itself should cease. Each looked for an easier triumph, and a result less fundamental and astounding. Both read the same Bible and pray to the same God, and each invokes His aid against the other. It may seem strange that any men should dare to ask a just God's assistance in wringing their bread from the sweat of other men's faces, but let us judge not, that we be not judged. The prayers of both could not be answered. That of neither has been answered fully. The Almighty has His own purposes. "Woe unto the world because of offenses; for it must needs be that offenses come, but woe to that man by whom the offense cometh." If we shall suppose that American slavery is one of those offenses which, in the providence of God, must needs come, but which, having continued through His appointed time, He now wills to remove, and that He gives to both North and South this terrible war as the woe due to those by whom the offense came, shall we discern therein any departure from those divine attributes which the believers in a living God always ascribe to Him? Fondly do we hope, fervently do we pray, that this mighty scourge of war may speedily pass away. Yet, if God wills that it continue until all the wealth piled by the bondsman's two hundred and fifty years of unrequited toil shall be sunk, and until every drop of blood drawn with the lash shall be paid by another drawn with the sword, as was said three thousand years ago, so still it must be said "the judgments of the Lord are true and righteous altogether."

With malice toward none, with charity for all, with firmness in the right as God gives us to see the right, let us strive on to finish the work we are in, to bind up the nation's wounds, to care for him who shall have borne the battle and for his widow and his orphan, to do all which may achieve and cherish a just and lasting peace among ourselves and with all nations.

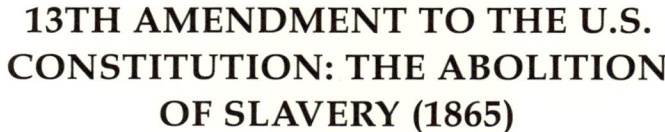

# 13TH AMENDMENT TO THE U.S. CONSTITUTION: THE ABOLITION OF SLAVERY (1865)

## AMENDMENT XIII

### SECTION 1.

Neither slavery nor involuntary servitude, except as a punishment for crime whereof the party shall have been duly convicted, shall exist within the United States, or any place subject to their jurisdiction.

### SECTION 2.

Congress shall have power to enforce this article by appropriate legislation.

# THE PURCHASE OF ALASKA (1867)

*The United States bought the territory of Alaska from Russia in 1867 for $7.2 million, the result of a treaty negotiated by U.S. Secretary of State William Seward. At the time, many critics called the purchase "Seward's Folly" and considered it a waste of money. But when the Klondike Gold Rush began in Canada in 1896, miners and others streamed into the new territory, boosting its economy and proving the purchase worthwhile. Alaska became the forthy-ninth state in 1959.*

Treaty concerning the Cession of the Russian Possessions in North America by his Majesty the Emperor of all the Russias to the United States of America; Concluded March 30, 1867; Ratified by the United States May 28, 1867; Exchanged June 20, 1867; Proclaimed by the United States June 20, 1867.

## BY THE PRESIDENT OF THE UNITED STATES OF AMERICA.

## A PROCLAMATION.

Whereas a treaty between the United States of America and his Majesty the Emperor of all the Russias was concluded and signed by their respective plenipotentiaries at the city of Washington, on the thirtieth day of March, last, which treaty, being in English and French languages, is, word for word as follows:

[The French version is omitted for brevity.]

The United States of America and His Majesty the Emperor of all the Russias, being desirous of strengthening, if possible, the good understanding which exists between them, have, for that purpose, appointed as their Plenipotentiaries: the President of the United States, William H. Seward, Secretary of State; and His Majesty the Emperor of all the Russias, the Privy Councillor Edward de Stoeckl, his Envoy Extraordinary and Minister Plenipotentiary to the United States.

And the said Plenipotentiaries, having exchanged their full powers, which were found to be in due form, have agreed upon and signed the following articles:

## Article I.

His Majesty the Emperor of all the Russias agrees to cede to the United States, by this convention, immediately upon the exchange of the ratifications thereof, all the territory and dominion now possessed by his said Majesty on the continent of America and in the adjacent islands, the same being contained within the geographical limits herein set forth, to wit: The eastern limit is the line of demarcation between the Russian and the British possessions in North America, as established by the convention between Russia and Great Britain, of February 28 - 16, 1825, and described in Articles III and IV of said convention, in the following terms:

"Commencing from the southernmost point of the island called Prince of Wales Island, which point lies in the parallel of 54 degrees 40 minutes north latitude, and between the 131st and the 133d degree of west longitude, (meridian of Greenwich,) the said line shall ascend to the north along the channel called Portland channel, as far as the point of the continent where it strikes the 56th degree of north latitude; from this last-mentioned point, the line of demarcation shall follow the summit of the mountains situated parallel to the coast as far as the point of intersection of the 141st degree of west longitude, (of the same meridian;) and finally, from the said point of intersection, the said meridian line of the 141st degree, in its prolongation as far as the Frozen ocean.

"IV. With reference to the line of demarcation laid down in the preceding article, it is understood—

"1st. That the island called Prince of Wales Island shall belong wholly to Russia," (now, by this cession, to the United States.)

"2d. That whenever the summit of the mountains which extend in a direction parallel to the coast from the 56th degree of north latitude to the point of intersection of the 141st degree of west longitude shall prove to be at the distance of more than ten marine leagues from the ocean, the limit between the British possessions and the line of coast which is to belong to Russia as above mentioned (that is to say, the limit to the possessions ceded by this convention) shall be formed by a line parallel to the winding of the coast, and which shall never exceed the distance of ten marine leagues therefrom."

The western limit within which the territories and dominion conveyed, are contained, passes through a point in Behring's straits on the parallel of sixty-five degrees thirty minutes north latitude, at its intersection by the meridian which passes midway between the islands of Krusenstern, or Ignalook, and the island of Ratmanoff, or Noonarbook, and proceeds due north, without limitation, into the same Frozen ocean. The same western limit, beginning at the same initial point, proceeds thence in a course nearly southwest through Behring's straits and Behring's sea, so as to pass midway between the northwest point of the island of St. Lawrence and the southeast point of Cape Choukotski, to the meridian of one hundred and seventy-two west longitude; thence, from the intersection of that meridian, in a southwesterly direction, so as to pass midway between the island of Attou and the Copper island of the Kormandorski couplet or group in the North Pacific ocean, to the meridian of one hundred and ninety-three degrees west longitude, so as to include in the territory conveyed the whole of the Aleutian islands east of that meridian.

## ARTICLE II.

In the cession of territory and dominion made by the preceding article are included the right of property in all public lots and squares, vacant lands, and all public buildings, fortifications, barracks, and other edifices which are not private individual property. It is, however, understood and agreed, that the churches which have been built in the ceded territory by the Russian government, shall remain the property of such members of the Greek Oriental Church resident in the territory, as may choose to worship therein. Any government archives, papers, and documents relative to the territory and dominion aforesaid, which may be now existing there, will be left in the possession of the agent of the United States; but an authenticated copy of such of them as may be required, will be, at all times, given by the United States to the Russian government, or to such Russian officers or subjects as they may apply for.

## ARTICLE III.

The inhabitants of the ceded territory, according to their choice, reserving their natural allegiance, may return to Russia within three years; but if they should prefer to remain in the ceded territory, they, with the exception of uncivilized native tribes, shall be admitted to the enjoyment of all the rights, advantages, and immunities of citizens of the United States, and shall be maintained and protected in the free enjoyment of their liberty, property, and religion. The uncivilized tribes will be subject to such laws and regulations as the United States may, from time to time, adopt in regard to aboriginal tribes of that country.

## ARTICLE IV.

His Majesty the Emperor of all the Russias shall appoint, with convenient despatch, an agent or agents for the purpose of formally delivering to a similar agent or agents appointed on behalf of the United States, the territory, dominion, property, dependencies and appurtenances which are ceded as above, and for doing any other act which may be necessary in regard thereto. But the cession, with the right of immediate possession, is nevertheless to be deemed complete and absolute on the exchange of ratifications, without waiting for such formal delivery.

## ARTICLE V.

Immediately after the exchange of the ratifications of this convention, any fortifications or military posts which may be in the ceded territory shall be delivered to the agent of the United States, and any Russian troops which may be in the territory shall be withdrawn as soon as may be reasonably and conveniently practicable.

## ARTICLE VI.

In consideration of the cession aforesaid, the United States agree to pay at the treasury in Washington, within ten months after the exchange of the ratifications of this convention, to the diplomatic representative or other agent of his Majesty the Emperor of all the Russias, duly authorized to receive the same, seven million two hundred thousand dollars in gold. The cession of territory and dominion herein made is hereby declared to be free and unencumbered by any reservations, privileges, franchises, grants, or possessions, by any associated companies, whether corporate or incorporate, Russian or any other, or by any parties, except merely private individual property holders; and the cession hereby made, conveys all the rights, franchises, and privileges now belonging to Russia in the said territory or dominion, and appurtenances thereto.

## ARTICLE VII.

When this convention shall have been duly ratified by the President of the United States, by and with the advice and consent of the Senate, on the one part, and on the other by his Majesty the Emperor of all the Russias, the ratifications shall be exchanged at Washington within three months from the date hereof, or sooner if possible.

In faith whereof, the respective plenipotentiaries have signed this convention, and thereto affixed the seals of their arms.

Done at Washington, the thirtieth day of March, in the year of our Lord one thousand eight hundred and sixty-seven.

# ACT ESTABLISHING YELLOWSTONE NATIONAL PARK (1872)

*President Ulysses S. Grant signed this law establishing Yellowstone National Park on March 1, 1872. It was the first national park in the world.*

Forty-Second Congress of the United States of America;
At the Second Session, Begun and held at the City of Washington, on Monday, the Fourth day of December, one thousand eight hundred and seventy-one.

An act to set apart a certain tract of land lying near the headwaters of the Yellowstone River as a public park.

Be it enacted by the Senate and House of Representatives of the United States of America in Congress assembled, That the tract of land in the Territories of Montana and Wyoming, lying near the headwaters of the Yellowstone River, and described as follows, to wit, commencing at the junction of Gardiner's river with the Yellowstone river, and running east to the meridian passing ten miles to the eastward of the most eastern point of Yellowstone lake; thence south along said meridian to the parallel of latitude passing ten miles south of the most southern point of Yellowstone lake; thence west along said parallel to the meridian passing fifteen miles west of the most western point of Madison lake; thence north along said meridian to the latitude of the junction of Yellowstone and Gardiner's rivers; thence east to the place of beginning, is hereby reserved and withdrawn from settlement, occupancy, or sale under the laws of the United States, and dedicated and set apart as a public park or pleasuring-ground for the benefit and enjoyment of the people; and all persons who shall locate or settle upon or occupy the same, or any part thereof, except as hereinafter provided, shall be considered trespassers and removed therefrom.

SEC 2. That said public park shall be under the exclusive control of the Secretary of the Interior, whose duty it shall be, as soon as practicable, to make and publish such rules and regulations as he may deem necessary or proper for the care and management of the same. Such regulations shall provide for the preservation, from injury or spoliation, of all timber, mineral deposits, natural curiosities, or wonders within said park, and their retention in their natural condition. The Secretary may in his discretion, grant leases for building purposes for terms not exceeding ten years, of small parcels of ground, at such places in said park as shall require the erection of buildings for the accommodation of visitors; all of the proceeds of said leases, and all other revenues that may be derived from any source connected with said park, to be expended under his direction in the management of the same, and the construction of roads and bridle-paths therein. He shall provide against the wanton destruction of the fish and game found within said park, and against their capture or destruction for the purposes of merchandise or profit. He shall also cause all persons trespassing upon the same after the passage of this act to be removed therefrom, and generally shall be authorized to take all such measures as shall be necessary or proper to fully carry out the objects and purposes of this act.

# SUSAN B. ANTHONY ON WOMEN'S SUFFRAGE (1873)

*In 1872, activist Susan B. Anthony cast an illegal vote in the presidential election. She was arrested and put on trial the next year, where she delivered a rousing speech about the injustice of the ban on women voting. Ultimately, Anthony was found guilty and fined $100, which she refused to pay. Throughout her life, she remained an advocate for many issues, including women's suffrage. Susan B. Anthony died in 1906 . . . fourteen years before the U.S. government amended the Constitution to give women the right to vote.*

## DELIVERED IN TWENTY-NINE OF THE POST OFFICE DISTRICTS OF MONROE, AND TWENTY-ONE OF ONTARIO, IN HER CANVASS OF THOSE COUNTIES, PRIOR TO HER TRIAL IN JUNE, 1873.

Friends and Fellow-citizens: I stand before you tonight, under indictment for the alleged crime of having voted at the last Presidential election, without having a lawful right to vote. It shall be my work this evening to prove to you that in thus voting, I not only committed no crime, but, instead, simply exercised my citizen's right, guaranteed to me and all United States citizens by the National Constitution, beyond the power of any State to deny.

Our democratic-republican government is based on the idea of the natural right of every individual member thereof to a voice and a vote in making and executing the laws. We assert the province of government to be to secure the people in the enjoyment of their unalienable rights. We throw to the winds the old dogma that governments can give rights. Before governments were organized, no one denies that each individual possessed the right to protect his own life, liberty and property. And when 100 or 1,000,000 people enter into a free government, they do not barter away their natural rights; they simply pledge themselves to protect each other in the enjoyment of them, through prescribed judicial and legislative tribunals. They agree to abandon the methods of brute force in the adjustment of their differences, and adopt those of civilization.

Nor can you find a word in any of the grand documents left us by the fathers that assumes for government the power to create or to confer rights. The Declaration of Independence, the United States Constitution, the constitutions of the several states and the organic laws of the territories, all alike propose to protect the people in the exercise of their God-given rights. Not one of them pretends to bestow rights.

> All men are created equal, and endowed by their Creator
> with certain unalienable rights. Among these are life,
> liberty and the pursuit of happiness. That to secure these,
> governments are instituted among men, deriving their just
> powers from the consent of the governed.

Here is no shadow of government authority over rights, nor exclusion of any class from their full and equal enjoyment. Here is pronounced the right of all men, and "consequently," as the Quaker preacher said, "of all women," to a voice in the government. And here, in this very first paragraph of the declaration, is the assertion of the natural right of all to the ballot; for, how can "the consent of the governed" be given, if the right to vote be denied. Again:

> That whenever any form of government becomes
> destructive of these ends, it is the right of the people to alter
> or abolish it, and to institute a new government, laying its
> foundations on such principles, and organizing its powers in
> such forms as to them shall seem most likely to effect their
> safety and happiness.

Surely, the right of the whole people to vote is here clearly implied. For however destructive to their happiness this government might become, a disfranchised class could neither alter nor abolish it, nor institute a new one, except by the old brute force method of insurrection and rebellion. One-half of the people of this nation today are utterly powerless to blot from the statute books an unjust law, or to write there a new and a just one. The women, dissatisfied as they are with this form of government, that enforces taxation without representation,— that compels them to obey laws to which they have never given their consent,—that imprisons and hangs them without a trial by a jury of their peers, that robs them, in marriage, of the custody of their own persons, wages and children,—are this half of the people left wholly at the mercy of the other half, in direct violation of the spirit and letter of the declarations of the framers of this government, every one of which was based on the immutable principle of equal rights to all. By those declarations, kings, priests, popes, aristocrats, were all alike dethroned, and placed on a common level, politically, with the lowliest born subject or serf. By them, too, men, as such, were deprived of their divine right to rule, and placed on a political level with women. By the practice of those declarations all class and caste distinction will be abolished; and slave, serf, plebeian, wife, woman, all alike, bound from their subject position to the proud platform of equality.

The preamble of the federal constitution says:

> We, the people of the United States, in order to form a more perfect union, establish justice, insure domestic tranquility, provide for the common defence, promote the general welfare and secure the blessings of liberty to ourselves and our posterity, do ordain and establish this constitution for the United States of America.

It was we, the people, not we, the white male citizens, nor yet we, the male citizens; but we, the whole people, who formed this Union. And we formed it, not to give the blessings of liberty, but to secure them; not to the half of ourselves and the half of our posterity, but to the whole people—women as well as men. And it is downright mockery to talk to women of their enjoyment of the blessings of liberty while they are denied the use of the only means of securing them provided by this democratic-republican government—the ballot.

The early journals of Congress show that when the committee reported to that body the original articles of confederation, the very first article which became the subject of discussion was that respecting equality of suffrage. Article 4th said:

> The better to secure and perpetuate mutual friendship and intercourse between the people of the different States of this Union, the free inhabitants of each of the States, (paupers, vagabonds and fugitives from justice excepted,) shall be

entitled to all the privileges and immunities of the free
citizens of the several States.

Thus, at the very beginning, did the fathers see the necessity of
the universal application of the great principle of equal rights to all—
in order to produce the desired result—a harmonious union and a
homogeneous people.

Luther Martin, attorney-general of Maryland, in his report to the
Legislature of that State of the convention that framed the United
States Constitution, said:

Those who advocated the equality of suffrage took the
matter up on the original principles of government: that
the reason why each individual man in forming a State
government should have an equal vote, is because each
individual, before he enters into government, is equally free
and equally independent.

James Madison said:

Under every view of the subject, it seems indispensable
that the mass of the citizens should not be without a voice
in making the laws which they are to obey, and in choosing
the magistrates who are to administer them." Also, "Let it
be remembered, finally, that it has ever been the pride and
the boast of America that the rights for which she contended
were the rights of human nature.

And these assertions of the framers of the United States Constitution
of the equal and natural rights of all the people to a voice in the
government, have been affirmed and reaffirmed by the leading statesmen
of the nation, throughout the entire history of our government.

Thaddeus Stevens, of Pennsylvania, said in 1866:

I have made up my mind that the elective franchise is one of
the inalienable rights meant to be secured by the declaration
of independence.

B. Gratz Brown, of Missouri, in the three days' discussion in the
United States Senate in 1866, on Senator Cowan's motion to strike
"male" from the District of Columbia suffrage bill, said:

Mr. President, I say here on the floor of the American
Senate, I stand for universal suffrage; and as a matter of
fundamental principle, do not recognize the right of society
to limit it on any ground of race or sex. I will go farther
and say, that I recognize the right of franchise as being
intrinsically a natural right. I do not believe that society
is authorized to impose any limitations upon it that do not
spring out of the necessities of the social state itself. Sir,
I have been shocked, in the course of this debate, to hear
Senators declare this right only a conventional and political
arrangement, a privilege yielded to you and me and others;
not a right in any sense, only a concession! Mr. President, I
do not hold my liberties by any such tenure. On the contrary,
I believe that whenever you establish that doctrine, whenever
you crystalize that idea in the public mind of this country,
you ring the death-knell of American liberties.

Charles Sumner, in his brave protests against the fourteenth
and fifteenth amendments, insisted that, so soon as by the thirteenth
amendment the slaves became free men, the original powers of the
United States Constitution guaranteed to them equal rights—the right
to vote and to be voted for. In closing one of his great speeches he said:

I do not hesitate to say that when the slaves of our country
became 'citizens' they took their place in the body politic as
a component part of the 'people,' entitled to equal rights,
and under the protection of these two guardian principles:
First—That all just governments stand on the consent of the
governed; and second, that taxation without representation
is tyranny; and these rights it is the duty of Congress to
guarantee as essential to the idea of a Republic.

The preamble of the Constitution of the State of New York declares
the same purpose. It says:

We, the people of the State of New York, grateful to
Almighty God for our freedom, in order to secure its
blessings, do establish this Constitution.

Here is not the slightest intimation, either of receiving freedom
from the United States Constitution, or of the State conferring the
blessings of liberty upon the people; and the same is true of every

one of the thirty-six State Constitutions. Each and all, alike declare rights God-given, and that to secure the people in the enjoyment of their inalienable rights, is their one and only object in ordaining and establishing government. And all of the State Constitutions are equally emphatic in their recognition of the ballot as the means of securing the people in the enjoyment of these rights.

Article 1 of the New York State Constitution says:

> No member of this State shall be disfranchised or deprived
> of the rights or privileges secured to any citizen thereof,
> unless by the law of the land, or the judgment of his peers.

And so carefully guarded is the citizen's right to vote, that the Constitution makes special mention of all who may be excluded. It says:

> Laws may be passed excluding from the right of suffrage
> all persons who have been or may be convicted of bribery,
> larceny or any infamous crime.

In naming the various employments that shall not affect the residence of voters—the 3d section of article 2d says "that being kept at any alms house, or other asylum, at public expense, nor being confined at any public prison, shall deprive a person of his residence," and hence his vote. Thus is the right of voting most sacredly hedged about. The only seeming permission in the New York State Constitution for the disfranchisement of women is in section 1st of article 2d, which says:

> Every male citizen of the age of twenty-one years, &c., shall
> be entitled to vote.

But I submit that in view of the explicit assertions of the equal right of the whole people, both in the preamble and previous article of the constitution, this omission of the adjective "female" in the second, should not be construed into a denial; but, instead, counted as of no effect. Mark the direct prohibition: "No member of this State shall be disfranchised, unless by the 'law of the land,' or the judgment of his peers." "The law of the land," is the United States Constitution: and there is no provision in that document that can be fairly construed into a permission to the States to deprive any class of their citizens of their right to vote. Hence New York can get no power from that source to disfranchise one entire half of her members. Nor has "the judgment of their peers" been pronounced against women exercising their right to vote; no disfranchised person is allowed to be judge or juror—and none but disfranchised persons can be women's peers; nor has the legislature passed laws excluding them on account of idiocy or lunacy; nor yet the courts convicted them of bribery, larceny, or any infamous crime. Clearly, then, there is no constitutional ground for the exclusion of women from the ballot-box in the State of New York. No barriers whatever stand to-day between women and the exercise of their right to vote save those of precedent and prejudice.

The clauses of the United States Constitution, cited by our opponents as giving power to the States to disfranchise any classes of citizens they shall please, are contained in sections 2d and 4th of article 1st. The second says:

> The House of Representatives shall be composed of members chosen every second year by the people of the several States; and the electors in each State shall have the qualifications requisite for electors of the most numerous branch of the State Legislature.

This cannot be construed into a concession to the States of the power to destroy the right to become an elector, but simply to prescribe what shall be the qualifications, such as competency of intellect, maturity of age, length of residence, that shall be deemed necessary to enable them to make an intelligent choice of candidates. If, as our opponents assert, the last clause of this section makes it the duty of the United States to protect citizens in the several States against higher or different qualifications for electors for representatives in Congress, than for members of Assembly, then must the first clause make it equally imperative for the national government to interfere with the States, and forbid them from arbitrarily cutting off the right of one-half of the people to become electors altogether. Section 4th says:

> The times, places and manner of holding elections for Senators and Representatives shall be prescribed in each State by the Legislature thereof; but Congress may at any time, by law, make or alter such regulations, except as to the places of choosing Senators.

Here is conceded the power only to prescribe times, places and manner of holding the elections; and even with these Congress may interfere, with all excepting the mere place of choosing Senators. Thus you see, there is not the slightest permission in either section for the States to discriminate against the right of any class of citizens to vote. Surely, to regulate cannot be to annihilate! nor to qualify to wholly deprive. And to this principle every true Democrat and Republican said amen, when applied to black men by Senator Sumner in his great speeches for *equal rights to all* from 1865 to 1869; and when, in 1871, I asked that Senator to declare the power of the United States Constitution to protect women in their right to vote—as he had done for black men—he handed me a copy of all his speeches during that reconstruction period, and said:

> Miss Anthony, put 'sex' where I have 'race' or 'color,' and you have here the best and strongest argument I can make for woman. There is not a doubt but women have the constitutional right to vote, and I will never vote for a sixteenth amendment to guarantee it to them. I voted for both the fourteenth and fifteenth under protest; would never have done it but for the pressing emergency of that hour; would have insisted that the power of the original Constitution to protect all citizens in the equal enjoyment of their rights should have been vindicated through the courts. But the newly made freedmen had neither the intelligence, wealth nor time to wait that slow process. Women possess all these in an eminent degree, and I insist that they shall appeal to the courts, and through them establish the powers of our American magna charta, to protect every citizen of the Republic. But, friends, when in accordance with Senator Summer's counsel, I went to the ballot-box, last November, and exercised my citizen's right to vote, the courts did not wait for me to appeal to them—they appealed to me, and indicted me on the charge of having voted illegally.

Senator Sumner, putting sex where he did color, said:

> Qualifications cannot be in their nature permanent or insurmountable. Sex cannot be a qualification any more than size, race, color, or previous condition of servitude. A permanent or insurmountable qualification is equivalent to a

deprivation of the suffrage. In other words, it is the tyranny of taxation without representation, against which our revolutionary mothers, as well as fathers, rebelled.

For any State to make sex a qualification that must ever result in the disfranchisement of one entire half of the people, is to pass a bill of attainder, or an ex post facto law, and is therefore a violation of the supreme law of the land. By it, the blessings of liberty are forever withheld from women and their female posterity. To them, this government has no just powers derived from the consent of the governed. To them this government is not a democracy. It is not a republic. It is an odious aristocracy; a hateful obligarchy of sex. The most hateful aristocracy ever established on the face of the globe. An obligarchy of wealth, where the rich govern the poor; an obligarchy of learning, where the educated govern the ignorant; or even an obligarchy of race, where the Saxon rules the African, might be endured; but this obligarchy of sex, which makes father, brothers, husband, sons, the obligarchs over the mother and sisters, the wife and daughters of every household; which ordains all men sovereigns, all women subjects, carries dissension, discord and rebellion into every home of the nation. And this most odious aristocracy exists, too, in the face of Section 4, of Article 4, which says:

> The United States shall guarantee to every State in the Union a republican form of government.

What, I ask you, is the distinctive difference between the inhabitants of a monarchical and those of a republican form of government, save that in the monarchical the people are subjects, helpless, powerless, bound to obey laws made by superiors—while in the republican, the people are citizens, individual sovereigns, all clothed with equal power, to make and unmake both their laws and law makers, and the moment you deprive a person of his right to a voice in the government, you degrade him from the status of a citizen of the republic, to that of a subject, and it matters very little to him whether his monarch be an individual tyrant, as is the Czar of Russia, or a 15,000,000 headed monster, as here in the United States; he is a powerless subject, serf or slave; not a free and independent citizen in any sense.

But, it is urged, the use of the masculine pronouns he, his and him, in all the constitutions and laws, is proof that only men were meant to be included in their provisions. If you insist on this version of the letter of the law, we shall insist that you be consistent, and accept the other horn of the dilemma, which would compel you to exempt women from taxation for the support of the government, and from penalties for the violation of laws.

A year and a half ago I was at Walla Walla, Washington Territory. I saw there a theatrical company, called the "Pixley Sisters," playing before crowded houses, every night of the whole week of the territorial fair. The eldest of those three fatherless girls was scarce eighteen. Yet every night a United States officer stretched out his long fingers, and clutched six dollars of the proceeds of the exhibitions of those orphan girls, who, but a few years before, were half starvelings in the streets of Olympia, the capital of that far-off north-west territory. So the poor widow, who keeps a boarding house, manufactures shirts, or sells apples and peanuts on the street corners of our cities, is compelled to pay taxes from her scanty pittance. I would that the women of this republic, at once, resolve, never again to submit to taxation, until their right to vote be recognized.

Miss Sarah E. Wall, of Worcester, Mass., twenty years ago, took this position. For several years, the officers of the law distrained her property, and sold it to meet the necessary amount; still she persisted, and would not yield an iota, though every foot of her lands should be struck off under the hammer. And now, for several years, the assessor has left her name off the tax list, and the collector passed her by without a call.

Mrs. J. S. Weeden, of Viroqua, Wis., for the past six years, has refused to pay her taxes, though the annual assessment is $75.

Mrs. Ellen Van Valkenburg, of Santa Cruz, Cal., who sued the County Clerk for refusing to register her name, declares she will never pay another dollar of tax until allowed to vote; and all over the country, women property holders are waking up to the injustice of taxation without representation, and ere long will refuse, en masse, to submit to the imposition.

There is no she, or her, or hers, in the tax laws.

The statute of New York reads:

> Every person shall be assessed in the town or ward where
> he resides when the assessment is made, for the lands owned
> by him, &c. . . . Every collector shall call at least once on

> the person taxed, or at his usual place of residence, and shall
> demand payment of the taxes charged on him. If any one
> shall refuse to pay the tax imposed on him, the collector shall
> levy the same by distress and sale of his property.

The same is true of all the criminal laws: "No person shall be compelled to be a witness against himself, &c."

The same with the law of May 31st, 1870, the 19th section of which I am charged with having violated; not only are all the pronouns in it masculine, but everybody knows that that particular section was intended expressly to hinder the rebels from voting. It reads "If any person shall knowingly vote without his having a lawful right," &c. Precisely so with all the papers served on me—the U.S. Marshal's warrant, the bail-bond, the petition for habeas corpus, the bill of indictment—not one of them had a feminine pronoun printed in it; but, to make them applicable to me, the Clerk of the Court made a little carat at the left of "he" and placed an "s" over it, thus making she out of he. Then the letters "is" were scratched out, the little carat under and "er" over, to make her out of his, and I insist if government officials may thus manipulate the pronouns to tax, fine, imprison and hang women, women may take the same liberty with them to secure to themselves their right to a voice in the government.

So long as any classes of men were denied their right to vote, the government made a show of consistency, by exempting them from taxation. When a property qualification of $250 was required of black men in New York, they were not compelled to pay taxes, so long as they were content to report themselves worth less than that sum; but the moment the black man died, and his property fell to his widow or daughter, the black woman's name would be put on the assessor's list, and she be compelled to pay taxes on the same property exempted to her husband. The same is true of ministers in New York. So long as the minister lives, he is exempted from taxation on $1,500 of property, but the moment the breath goes out of his body, his widow's name will go down on the assessor's list, and she will have to pay taxes on the $1,500. So much for the special legislation in favor of women.

In all the penalties and burdens of the government, (except the military,) women are reckoned as citizens, equally with men. Also, in all the privileges and immunities, save those of the jury box and ballot box, the two fundamental privileges on which rest all the others. The

United States government not only taxes, fines, imprisons and hangs women, but it allows them to pre-empt lands, register ships, and take out passport and naturalization papers. Not only does the law permit single women and widows to the right of naturalization, but Section 2 says: "A married woman may be naturalized without the concurrence of her husband." (I wonder the fathers were not afraid of creating discord in the families of foreigners); and again: "When an alien, having complied with the law, and declared his intention to become a citizen, dies before he is actually naturalized, his widow and children shall be considered citizens, entitled to all rights and privileges as such, on taking the required oath." If a foreign born woman by becoming a naturalized citizen, is entitled to all the rights and privileges of citizenship, is not a native born woman, by her national citizenship, possessed of equal rights and privileges?

The question of the masculine pronouns, yes and nouns, too, has been settled by the United States Supreme Court, in the Case of Silver versus Ladd, December, 1868, in a decision as to whether a woman was entitled to lands, under the Oregon donation law of 1850. Elizabeth Cruthers, a widow, settled upon a claim, and received patents. She died, and her son was heir. He died. Then Messrs. Ladd & Nott took possession, under the general pre-emption law, December, 1861. The administrator, E.P. Silver, applied for a writ of ejectment at the land office in Oregon City. Both the Register and Receiver decided that an unmarried woman could not hold land under that law. The Commissioner of the General Land Office, at Washington, and the Secretary of the Interior, also gave adverse opinions. Here patents were issued to Ladd & Nott, and duly recorded. Then a suit was brought to set aside Ladd's patent, and it was carried through all the State Courts and the Supreme Court of Oregon, each, in turn, giving adverse decisions. At last, in the United States Supreme Court, Associate Justice Miller reversed the decisions of all the lower tribunals, and ordered the land back to the heirs of Mrs. Cruthers. The Court said:

> In construing a benevolent statute of the government, made for the benefit of its own citizens, inviting and encouraging them to settle on its distant public lands, the words 'single man,' and 'unmarried man' may, especially if aided by the context and other parts of the statute, be taken in a generic sense. Held, accordingly, that the Fourth Section of the Act

of Congress, of September 27th, 1850, granting by way of donation, lands in Oregon Territory, to every white settler or occupant, American half-breed Indians included, embraced within the term single man an unmarried woman.

And the attorney, who carried this question to its final success, is now the United States senator elect from Oregon, Hon. J.H. Mitchell, in whom the cause of equal rights to women has an added power on the floor of the United States Senate.

Though the words persons, people, inhabitants, electors, citizens, are all used indiscriminately in the national and state constitutions, there was always a conflict of opinion, prior to the war, as to whether they were synonymous terms, as for instance:

> No person shall be a representative who shall not have been seven years a citizen, and who shall not, when elected, be an inhabitant of that state in which he is chosen. No person shall be a senator who shall not have been a citizen of the United States, and an inhabitant of that state in which he is chosen.

But, whatever room there was for a doubt, under the old regime, the adoption of the fourteenth amendment settled that question forever, in its first sentence: "All persons born or naturalized in the United States and subject to the jurisdiction thereof, are citizens of the United States and of the state wherein they reside."

And the second settles the equal status of all persons—all citizens:

> No state shall make or enforce any law which shall abridge the privileges or immunities of citizens; nor shall any state deprive any person of life, liberty or property, without due process of law, nor deny to any person within its jurisdiction the equal protection of the laws.

The only question left to be settled, now, is: Are women persons? And I hardly believe any of our opponents will have the hardihood to say they are not. Being persons, then, women are citizens, and no state has a right to make any new law, or to enforce any old law, that shall abridge their privileges or immunities. Hence, every discrimination against women in the constitutions and laws of the several states, is today null and void, precisely as is every one against negroes.

Is the right to vote one of the privileges or immunities of citizens? I think the disfranchised ex-rebels, and the ex-state prisoners will all agree with me, that it is not only one of them, but the one without which all the others are nothing. Seek first the kingdom of the ballot, and all things else shall be given thee, is the political injunction.

Webster, Worcester and Bouvier all define citizen to be a person, in the United States, entitled to vote and hold office.

Prior to the adoption of the thirteenth amendment, by which slavery was forever abolished, and black men transformed from property to persons, the judicial opinions of the country had always been in harmony with these definitions. To be a person was to be a citizen, and to be a citizen was to be a voter.

Associate Justice Washington, in defining the privileges and immunities of the citizen, more than fifty years ago, said: "they included all such privileges as were fundamental in their nature. And among them is the right to exercise the elective franchise, and to hold office."

Even the "Dred Scott" decision, pronounced by the abolitionists and republicans infamous, because it virtually declared "black men had no rights white men were bound to respect," gave this true and logical conclusion, that to be one of the people was to be a citizen and a voter.

Chief Judge Daniels said:

> There is not, it is believed, to be found in the theories
> of writers on government, or in any actual experiment
> heretofore tried, an exposition of the term citizen, which has
> not been considered as conferring the actual possession and
> enjoyment of the perfect right of acquisition and enjoyment
> of an entire equality of privileges, civil and political.

Associate Justice Taney said:

> The words 'people of the United States,' and 'citizens,' are
> synonymous terms, and mean the same thing. They both
> describe the political body, who, according to our republican
> institutions, form the sovereignty, and who hold the power
> and conduct the government, through their representatives.
> They are what we familiarly call the sovereign people, and
> every citizen is one of this people, and a constituent member
> of this sovereignty.

Thus does Judge Taney's decision, which was such a terrible ban to the black man, while he was a slave, now, that he is a person, no longer property, pronounce him a citizen, possessed of an entire equality of privileges, civil and political. And not only the black man, but the black woman, and all women as well.

And it was not until after the abolition of slavery, by which the negroes became free men, hence citizens, that the United States Attorney, General Bates, rendered a contrary opinion. He said:

> The constitution uses the word 'citizen' only to express the political quality, (not equality mark,) of the individual in his relation to the nation; to declare that he is a member of the body politic, and bound to it by the reciprocal obligations of allegiance on the one side, and protection on the other. The phrase, 'a citizen of the United States,' without addition or qualification, means neither more nor less than a member of the nation.

Then, to be a citizen of this republic, is no more than to be a subject of an empire. You and I, and all true and patriotic citizens must repudiate this base conclusion. We all know that American citizenship, without addition or qualification, means the possession of equal rights, civil and political. We all know that the crowning glory of every citizen of the United States is, that he can either give or withhold his vote from every law and every legislator under the government.

Did "I am a Roman citizen," mean nothing more than that I am a "member" of the body politic of the republic of Rome, bound to it by the reciprocal obligations of allegiance on the one side, and protection on the other? Ridiculously absurd question, you say. When you, young man, shall travel abroad, among the monarchies of the old world, and there proudly boast yourself an "American citizen," will you thereby declare yourself neither more nor less than a "member" of the American nation?

And this opinion of Attorney General Bates, that a black citizen was not a voter, made merely to suit the political exigency of the republican party, in that transition hour between emancipation and enfranchisement, was no less infamous, in spirit or purpose, than was the decision of Judge Taney, that a black man was not one of the people, rendered in the interest and at the behest of the old democratic party, in its darkest hour of subjection to the slave power. Nevertheless, all of the adverse arguments, adverse congressional reports and judicial opinions, thus far, have been based on this purely partisan, time-serving opinion of General Bates, that the normal condition of the citizen of the United States is that of disfranchisement. That only such classes of citizens as have had special legislative guarantee have a legal right to vote.

And if this decision of Attorney General Bates was infamous, as against black men, but yesterday plantation slaves, what shall we pronounce upon Judge Bingham, in the house of Representatives, and Carpenter, in the Senate of the United States, for citing it against the women of the entire nation, vast numbers of whom are the peers of those honorable gentlemen, themselves, in morals!! intellect, culture, wealth, family—paying taxes on large estates, and contributing equally with them and their sex, in every direction, to the growth, prosperity and well-being of the republic? And what shall be said of the judicial opinions of Judges Carter, Jameson, McKay and Sharswood, all based upon this aristocratic, monarchial idea, of the right of one class to govern another?

I am proud to mention the names of the two United States Judges who have given opinions honorable to our republican idea, and honorable to themselves—Judge Howe, of Wyoming Territory, and Judge Underwood, of Virginia.

The former gave it as his opinion a year ago, when the Legislature seemed likely to revoke the law enfranchising the women of that territory, that, in case they succeeded, the women would still possess the right to vote under the fourteenth amendment.

Judge Underwood, of Virginia, in noticing the recent decision of Judge Carter, of the Supreme Court of the District of Columbia, denying to women the right to vote, under the fourteenth and fifteenth amendment, says;

> If the people of the United States, by amendment of their constitution, could expunge, without any explanatory or assisting legislation, an adjective of five letters from all state and local constitutions, and thereby raise millions of our most ignorant fellow-citizens to all of the rights and privileges of electors, why should not the same people, by the same amendment, expunge an adjective of four letters

from the same state and local constitutions, and thereby
raise other millions of more educated and better informed
citizens to equal rights and privileges, without explanatory
or assisting legislation?

If the fourteenth amendment does not secure to all citizens the right
to vote, for what purpose was that grand old charter of the fathers
lumbered with its unwieldy proportions? The republican party, and
Judges Howard and Bingham, who drafted the document, pretended
it was to do something for black men; and if that something was not
to secure them in their right to vote and hold office, what could it have
been? For, by the thirteenth amendment, black men had become people,
and hence were entitled to all the privileges and immunities of the
government, precisely as were the women of the country, and foreign
men not naturalized. According to Associate Justice Washington, they
already had the

Protection of the government, the enjoyment of life and
liberty, with the right to acquire and possess property of
every kind, and to pursue and obtain happiness and safety,
subject to such restraints as the government may justly
prescribe for the general welfare of the whole; the right
of a citizen of one state to pass through or to reside in any
other state for the purpose of trade, agriculture, professional
pursuit, or otherwise; to claim the benefit of the writ of
habeas corpus, to institute and maintain actions of any
kind in the courts of the state; to take, hold, and dispose of
property, either real or personal, and an exemption from
higher taxes or impositions than are paid by the other citizens
of the state.

Thus, you see, those newly freed men were in possession of every
possible right, privilege and immunity of the government, except that
of suffrage, and hence, needed no constitutional amendment for any
other purpose. What right, I ask you, has the Irishman the day after
he receives his naturalization papers that he did not possess the day
before, save the right to vote and hold office? And the Chinamen, now
crowding our Pacific coast, are in precisely the same position. What
privilege or immunity has California or Oregon the constitutional right
to deny them, save that of the ballot? Clearly, then, if the fourteenth

amendment was not to secure to black men their right to vote, it did nothing for them, since they possessed everything else before. But, if it was meant to be a prohibition of the states, to deny or abridge their right to vote—which I fully believe—then it did the same for all persons, white women included, born or naturalized in the United States; for the amendment does not say all male persons of African descent, but all persons are citizens.

The second section is simply a threat to punish the states, by reducing their representation on the floor of Congress, should they disfranchise any of their male citizens, on account of color, and does not allow of the inference that the states may disfranchise from any, or all other causes; nor in any wise weaken or invalidate the universal guarantee of the first section. What rule of law or logic would allow the conclusion, that the prohibition of a crime to one person, on severe pains and penalties, was a sanction of that crime to any and all other persons save that one?

But, however much the doctors of the law may disagree, as to whether people and citizens, in the original constitution, were one and the same, or whether the privileges and immunities in the fourteenth amendment include the right of suffrage, the question of the citizen's right to vote is settled forever by the fifteenth amendment. "The citizen's right to vote shall not be denied by the United States, nor any state thereof; on account of race, color, or previous condition of servitude." How can the state deny or abridge the right of the citizen, if the citizen does not possess it? There is no escape from the conclusion, that to vote is the citizen's right, and the specifications of race, color, or previous condition of servitude can, in no way, impair the force of the emphatic assertion, that the citizen's right to vote shall not be denied or abridged.

The political strategy of the second section of the fourteenth amendment, failing to coerce the rebel states into enfranchising their negroes, and the necessities of the republican party demanding their votes throughout the South, to ensure the re-election of Grant in 1872, that party was compelled to place this positive prohibition of the fifteenth amendment upon the United States and all the states thereof.

If we once establish the false principle, that United States citizenship does not carry with it the right to vote in every state in this Union, there is no end to the petty freaks and cunning devices, that will be resorted to, to exclude one and another class of citizens from the right of suffrage.

It will not always be men combining to disfranchise all women; native born men combining to abridge the rights of all naturalized citizens, as in Rhode Island. It will not always be the rich and educated who may combine to cut off the poor and ignorant; but we may live to see the poor, hardworking, uncultivated day laborers, foreign and native born, learning the power of the ballot and their vast majority of numbers, combine and amend state constitutions so as to disfranchise the Vanderbilts and A.T. Stewarts, the Conklings and Fentons. It is a poor rule that won't work more ways than one. Establish this precedent, admit the right to deny suffrage to the states, and there is no power to foresee the confusion, discord and disruption that may await us. There is, and can be, but one safe principle of government—equal rights to all. And any and every discrimination against any class, whether on account of color, race, nativity, sex, property, culture, can but imbitter and disaffect that class, and thereby endanger the safety of the whole people.

Clearly, then, the national government must not only define the rights of citizens, but it must stretch out its powerful hand and protect them in every state in this Union.

But if you will insist that the fifteenth amendment's emphatic interdiction against robbing United States citizens of their right to vote, "on account of race, color, or previous condition of servitude," is a recognition of the right, either of the United States, or any state, to rob citizens of that right, for any or all other reasons, I will prove to you that the class of citizens for which I now plead, and to which I belong, may be, and are, by all the principles of our government, and many of the laws of the states, included under the term "previous condition of servitude."

First.—The married women and their legal status. What is servitude? "The condition of a slave." What is a slave? "A person who is robbed of the proceeds of his labor; a person who is subject to the will of another."

By the law of Georgia, South Carolina, and all the states of the South, the negro had no right to the custody and control of his person. He belonged to his master. If he was disobedient, the master had the right to use correction. If the negro didn't like the correction, and attempted to run away, the master had a right to use coercion to bring him back.

By the law of every state in this Union to-day, North as well as South, the married woman has no right to the custody and control of her person. The wife belongs to her husband; and if she refuses obedience to his will, he may use moderate correction, and if she doesn't like his moderate correction, and attempts to leave his "bed and board," the husband may use moderate coercion to bring her back. The little word "moderate," you see, is the saving clause for the wife, and would doubtless be overstepped should her offended husband administer his correction with the "cat-o'-nine-tails," or accomplish his coercion with blood-hounds.

Again, the slave had no right to the earnings of his hands, they belonged to his master; no right to the custody of his children, they belonged to his master; no right to sue or be sued, or testify in the courts. If he committed a crime, it was the master who must sue or be sued.

In many of the states there has been special legislation, giving to married women the right to property inherited, or received by bequest, or earned by the pursuit of any avocation outside of the home; also, giving her the right to sue and be sued in matters pertaining to such separate property; but not a single state of this Union has ever secured the wife in the enjoyment of her right to the joint ownership of the joint earnings of the marriage copartnership. And since, in the nature of things, the vast majority of married women never earn a dollar, by work outside of their families, nor inherit a dollar from their fathers, it follows that from the day of their marriage to the day of the death of their husbands, not one of them ever has a dollar, except it shall please her husband to let her have it.

In some of the states, also, there have been laws passed giving to the mother a joint right with the father in the guardianship of the children. But twenty years ago, when our woman's rights movement commenced, by the laws of the State of New York, and all the states, the father had the sole custody and control of the children. No matter if he were a brutal, drunken libertine, he had the legal right, without the mother's consent, to apprentice her sons to rumsellers, or her daughters to brothel keepers. He could even will away an unborn child, to some other person than the mother. And in many of the states the law still prevails, and the mothers are still utterly powerless under the common law.

I doubt if there is, to-day, a State in this Union where a married woman can sue or be sued for slander of character, and until quite recently there was not one in which she could sue or be sued for injury of person. However damaging to the wife's reputation any slander may be, she is wholly powerless to institute legal proceedings against her accuser, unless her husband shall join with her; and how often have we heard of the husband conspiring with some outside barbarian to blast the good name of his wife? A married woman cannot testify in courts in cases of joint interest with her husband. A good farmer's wife near Earlville, Ill., who had all the rights she wanted, went to a dentist of the village and had a full set of false teeth, both upper and under. The dentist pronounced them an admirable fit, and the wife declared they gave her fits to wear them; that she could neither chew nor talk with them in her mouth. The dentist sued the husband; his counsel brought the wife as witness; the judge ruled her off the stand, saying "a married woman cannot be a witness in matters of joint interest between herself and her husband." Think of it, ye good wives, the false teeth in your mouths are joint interest with your husbands, about which you are legally incompetent to speak!! If in our frequent and shocking railroad accidents a married woman is injured in her person, in nearly all of the States, it is her husband who must sue the company, and it is to her husband that the damages, if there are any, will be awarded. In Ashfield, Mass., supposed to be the most advanced of any State in the Union in all things, humanitarian as well as intellectual, a married woman was severely injured by a defective sidewalk. Her husband sued the corporation and recovered $13,000 damages. And those $13,000 belong to him bona fide; and whenever that unfortunate wife wishes a dollar of it to supply her needs she must ask her husband for it; and if the man be of a narrow, selfish, niggardly nature, she will have to hear him say, every time, "What have you done, my dear, with the twenty-five cents I gave you yesterday?" Isn't such a position, I ask you, humiliating enough to be called "servitude?" That husband, as would any other husband, in nearly every State of this Union, sued and obtained damages for the loss of the services of his wife, precisely as the master, under the old slave regime, would have done, had his slave been thus injured, and precisely as he himself would have done had it been his ox, cow or horse instead of his wife.

There is an old saying that "a rose by any other name would smell as sweet," and I submit if the deprivation by law of the ownership of one's own person, wages, property, children, the denial of the right as an individual, to sue and be sued, and to testify in the courts, is not a condition of servitude most bitter and absolute, though under the sacred name of marriage?

Does any lawyer doubt my statement of the legal status of married women? I will remind him of the fact that the old common law of England prevails in every State in this Union, except where the Legislature has enacted special laws annulling it. And I am ashamed that not one State has yet blotted from its statute books the old common law of marriage, by which Blackstone, summed up in the fewest words possible, is made to say, "husband and wife are one, and that one is the husband."

Thus may all married women, wives and widows, by the laws of the several States, be technically included in the fifteenth amendment's specification of "condition of servitude," present or previous. And not only married women, but I will also prove to you that by all the great fundamental principles of our free government, the entire womanhood of the nation is in a "condition of servitude" as surely as were our revolutionary fathers, when they rebelled against old King George. Women are taxed without representation, governed without their consent, tried, convicted and punished without a jury of their peers. And is all this tyranny any less humiliating and degrading to women under our democratic-republican government to-day than it was to men under their aristocratic, monarchical government one hundred years ago? There is not an utterance of old John Adams, John Hancock or Patrick Henry, but finds a living response in the soul of every intelligent, patriotic woman of the nation. Bring to me a common-sense woman property holder, and I will show you one whose soul is fired with all the indignation of 1776 every time the tax-gatherer presents himself at her door. You will not find one such but feels her condition of servitude as galling as did James Otis when he said:

> The very act of taxing exercised over those who are not
> represented appears to me to be depriving them of one of
> their most essential rights, and if continued, seems to be in
> effect an entire disfranchisement of every civil right. For,
> what one civil right is worth a rush after a man's property is

subject to be taken from him at pleasure without his consent? If a man is not his own assessor in person, or by deputy, his liberty is gone, or he is wholly at the mercy of others.

What was the three-penny tax on tea, or the paltry tax on paper and sugar to which our revolutionary fathers were subjected, when compared with the taxation of the women of this Republic? The orphaned Pixley sisters, six dollars a day, and even the women, who are proclaiming the tyranny of our taxation without representation, from city to city throughout the country, are often compelled to pay a tax for the poor privilege of defending our rights. And again, to show that disfranchisement was precisely the slavery of which the fathers complained, allow me to cite to you old Ben. Franklin, who in those olden times was admitted to be good authority, not merely in domestic economy, but in political as well; he said:

> Every man of the commonalty, except infants, insane persons and criminals, is of common right and the law of God, a freeman and entitled to the free enjoyment of liberty. That liberty or freedom consists in having an actual share in the appointment of those who are to frame the laws, and who are to be the guardians of every man's life, property and peace. For the all of one man is as dear to him as the all of another; and the poor man has an equal right, but more need to have representatives in the Legislature than the rich one. That they who have no voice or vote in the electing of representatives, do not enjoy liberty, but are absolutely enslaved to those who have votes and their representatives; for to be enslaved is to have governors whom other men have set over us, and to be subject to laws made by the representatives of others, without having had representatives of our own to give consent in our behalf.

Suppose I read it with the feminine gender:

> That women who have no voice nor vote in the electing of representatives, do not enjoy liberty, but are absolutely enslaved to men who have votes and their representatives; for to be enslaved is to have governors whom men have set over us, and to be subject to the laws made by the

representatives of men, without having representatives of our own to give consent in our behalf.

And yet one more authority; that of Thomas Paine, than whom not one of the Revolutionary patriots more ably vindicated the principles upon which our government is founded:

> The right of voting for representatives is the primary right by which other rights are protected. To take away this right is to reduce man to a state of slavery; for slavery consists in being subject to the will of another; and he that has not a vote in the election of representatives is in this case. The proposal, therefore, to disfranchise any class of men is as criminal as the proposal to take away property.

Is anything further needed to prove woman's condition of servitude sufficiently orthodox to entitle her to the guaranties of the fifteenth amendment?

Is there a man who will not agree with me, that to talk of freedom without the ballot, is mockery—is slavery—to the women of this Republic, precisely as New England's orator Wendell Phillips, at the close of the late war, declared it to be to the newly emancipated black men?

I admit that prior to the rebellion, by common consent, the right to enslave, as well as to disfranchise both native and foreign born citizens, was conceded to the States. But the one grand principle, settled by the war and the reconstruction legislation, is the supremacy of national power to protect the citizens of the United States in their right to freedom and the elective franchise, against any and every interference on the part of the several States. And again and again, have the American people asserted the triumph of this principle, by their overwhelming majorities for Lincoln and Grant.

The one issue of the last two Presidential elections was, whether the fourteenth and fifteenth amendments should be considered the irrevocable will of the people; and the decision was, they shall be—and that it is not only the right, but the duty of the National Government to protect all United States citizens in the full enjoyment and free exercise of all their privileges and immunities against any attempt of any State to deny or abridge.

And in this conclusion Republicans and Democrats alike agree. Senator Frelinghuysen said:

> The heresy of State rights has been completely buried in these amendments, that as amended, the Constitution confers not only national but State citizenship upon all persons born or naturalized within our limits.

The Call for the national Republican convention said:

> Equal suffrage has been engrafted on the national Constitution; the privileges and immunities of American citizenship have become a part of the organic law.

The national Republican platform said:

> Complete liberty and exact equality in the enjoyment of all civil, political and public rights, should be established and maintained throughout the Union by efficient and appropriate State and federal legislation.

If that means anything, it is that Congress should pass a law to require the States to protect women in their equal political rights, and that the States should enact laws making it the duty of inspectors of elections to receive women's votes on precisely the same conditions they do those of men.

Judge Stanley Mathews—a substantial Ohio democrat—in his preliminary speech at the Cincinnati convention, said most emphatically:

> The constitutional amendments have established the political equality of all citizens before the law.

President Grant, in his message to Congress March 30th, 1870, on the adoption of the fifteenth amendment, said:

> A measure which makes at once four millions of people voters, is indeed a measure of greater importance than any act of the kind from the foundation of the Government to the present time.

How could four millions negroes be made voters if two millions were not included?

The California State Republican convention said:

> Among the many practical and substantial triumphs of the
> principles achieved by the Republican party during the past
> twelve years, it enumerated with pride and pleasure, the
> prohibiting of any State from abridging the privileges of any
> citizen of the Republic, the declaring the civil and political
> equality of every citizen, and the establishing all these
> principles in the federal constitution by amendments thereto,
> as the permanent law.

Benjamin F. Butler, in a recent letter to me, said:

> I do not believe anybody in Congress doubts that the
> Constitution authorizes the right of women to vote,
> precisely as it authorizes trial by jury and many other like
> rights guaranteed to citizens.

And again, General Butler said:

> It is not laws we want; there are plenty of laws—good
> enough, too. Administrative ability to enforce law is the
> great want of the age, in this country especially. Everybody
> talks of law, law. If everybody would insist on the
> enforcement of law, the government would stand on a firmer
> basis, and questions would settle themselves.

And it is upon this just interpretation of the United States Constitution
that our National Woman Suffrage Association which celebrates the
twenty-fifth anniversary of the woman's rights movement in New York
on the 6th of May next, has based all its arguments and action the past
five years.

We no longer petition Legislature or Congress to give us the right
to vote. We appeal to the women everywhere to exercise their too
long neglected "citizen's right to vote." We appeal to the inspectors of
election everywhere to receive the votes of all United States citizens
as it is their duty to do. We appeal to United States commissioners and
marshals to arrest the inspectors who reject the names and votes of
United States citizens, as it is their duty to do, and leave those alone
who, like our eighth ward inspectors, perform their duties faithfully
and well.

We ask the juries to fail to return verdicts of "guilty" against honest, law-abiding, tax-paying United States citizens for offering their votes at our elections. Or against intelligent, worthy young men, inspectors of elections, for receiving and counting such citizens' votes.

We ask the judges to render true and unprejudiced opinions of the law, and wherever there is room for a doubt to give its benefit on the side of liberty and equal rights to women, remembering that "the true rule of interpretation under our national constitution, especially since its amendments, is that anything for human rights is constitutional, everything against human rights unconstitutional."

And it is on this line that we propose to fight our battle for the ballot—all peaceably, but nevertheless persistently through to complete triumph, when all United States citizens shall be recognized as equals before the law.

# CHIEF JOSEPH OF THE NEZ PERCE SURRENDERS (1877)

*In 1877, the U.S. government broke its peace treaty with the Wallowa Valley, Oregon, band of the Nez Perce and demanded that they move to a reservation in Idaho. When the tribe refused, the government sent 2,000 soldiers to force them to move. Led by Chief Joseph, the 750 or so Nez Perce went looking for asylum: first with the Crow in Montana, and then when the Crow refused protection, they headed for Canada and Sitting Bull's Sioux tribe. Along the way, they fought and held off the pursuing American army and earned a reputation for benevolence, treating prisoners humanely and buying, rather than stealing, supplies. However, after chasing them more than 1,000 miles, the Americans caught up with Chief Joseph on October 5, 1877, just forty miles from the Canadian border. Chief Joseph and his men were captured, and he delivered an eloquent speech of surrender that earned him a place in history. Chief Joseph was sent first to reservations in Oklahoma and Kansas before being allowed to return home to the Pacific Northwest. He died in 1904.*

Tell General Howard I know his heart. What he told me before, I have it in my heart. I am tired of fighting. Our Chiefs are killed; Looking Glass is dead, Ta Hool Hool Shute is dead. The old men are all dead. It is the young men who say yes or no. He who led on the young men is dead. It is cold, and we have no blankets; the little children are freezing to death. My people, some of them, have run away to the hills, and have no blankets, no food. No one knows where they are—perhaps freezing to death. I want to have time to look for my children, and see how many of them I can find. Maybe I shall find them among the dead. Hear me, my Chiefs! I am tired; my heart is sick and sad. From where the sun now stands I will fight no more forever.

# THE DAWES ACT (1887)

*In 1887, President Grover Cleveland signed the Dawes Act into law. Named for Henry Dawes, the Massachusetts senator who wrote it, the act divided up the land on Native American reservations into smaller parcels that would then be owned by individual members of the tribes. Cleveland's hope was that by breaking up the reservations and making Native Americans landowners, they would become self-sufficient farmers and assimilate into white culture. However, many of the reservations were in desert or semi-desert areas and, therefore, unsuitable for farming. Plus, certain provisions in the law (including one that said any Native American who failed at farming lost his allotment to the federal government) led to the amount of tribal land in the United States shrinking from 138 million acres in 1887 to just 78 million acres thirteen years later. The Dawes Act remained in effect until 1934, when President Franklin D. Roosevelt signed the Indian Reorganization Act, which, among other things, restored communal reservation land to Native American tribes.*

An Act to provide for the allotment of lands in severalty to Indians on the various reservations, and to extend the protection of the laws of the United States and the Territories over the Indians, and for other purposes.

Be it enacted by the Senate and House of Representatives of the United States of America in Congress assembled, That in all cases where any tribe or band of Indians has been, or shall hereafter be, located upon any reservation created for their use, either by treaty stipulation or by virtue of an act of Congress or executive order setting apart the same for their use, the President of the United States be, and he hereby is, authorized, whenever in his opinion any reservation or any part thereof of such Indians is advantageous for agricultural and grazing purposes, to cause said reservation, or any part thereof, to be surveyed, or resurveyed if necessary, and to allot the lands in said reservation in severalty to any Indian located thereon in quantities as follows:

To each head of a family, one-quarter of a section;

To each single person over eighteen years of age, one-eighth of a section;

To each orphan child under eighteen years of age, one-eighth of a section; and

To each other single person under eighteen years now living, or who may be born prior to the date of the order of the President directing an allotment of the lands embraced in any reservation, one-sixteenth of a section:

Provided, That in case there is not sufficient land in any of said reservations to allot lands to each individual of the classes above named in quantities as above provided, the lands embraced in such reservation or reservations shall be allotted to each individual of each of said classes pro rata in accordance with the provisions of this act: And provided further, That where the treaty or act of Congress setting apart such reservation provides the allotment of lands in severalty in quantities in excess of those herein provided, the President, in making allotments upon such reservation, shall allot the lands to each individual Indian belonging thereon in quantity as specified in such treaty or act: And provided further, That when the lands allotted are only valuable for grazing purposes, an additional allotment of such grazing lands, in quantities as above provided, shall be made to each individual.

SEC. 2. That all allotments set apart under the provisions of this act shall be selected by the Indians, heads of families selecting for their minor children, and the agents shall select for each orphan child, and in such manner as to embrace the improvements of the Indians making the selection, where the improvements of two or more Indians have been made on the same legal subdivision of land, unless they shall otherwise agree, a provisional line may be run dividing said lands between them, and the amount to which each is entitled shall be equalized in the assignment of the remainder of the land to which they are entitled under his act: Provided, That if any one entitled to an allotment shall fail to make a selection within four years after the President shall direct that allotments may be made on a particular reservation, the Secretary of the Interior may direct the agent of such tribe or band, if such there be, and if there be no agent, then a special agent appointed for that purpose, to make a selection for such Indian, which selection shall be allotted as in cases where selections are made by the Indians, and patents shall issue in like manner.

SEC. 3. That the allotments provided for in this act shall be made by special agents appointed by the President for such purpose, and the agents in charge of the respective reservations on which the allotments are directed to be made, under such rules and regulations as the Secretary of the Interior may from time to time prescribe, and shall be certified by such agents to the Commissioner of Indian Affairs, in duplicate, one copy to be retained in the Indian Office and the other to be transmitted to the Secretary of the Interior for his action, and to be deposited in the General Land Office.

SEC. 4. That where any Indian not residing upon a reservation, or for whose tribe no reservation has been provided by treaty, act of Congress, or executive order, shall make settlement upon any surveyed or unsurveyed lands of the United States not otherwise appropriated, he or she shall be entitled, upon application to the local land-office for the district in which the lands are located, to have the same allotted to him or her, and to his or her children, in quantities and manner as provided in this act for Indians residing upon reservations; and when such settlement is made upon unsurveyed lands, the grant to such Indians shall be adjusted upon the survey of the lands so as to conform thereto; and patents shall be issued to them for such lands in the manner and with the restrictions as herein provided. And the fees to which the officers of such local land-office would have been entitled had such lands been entered under the general laws for the disposition of the public lands shall be paid to them, from any moneys in the Treasury of the United States not otherwise appropriated, upon a statement of an account in their behalf for such fees by the Commissioner of the General Land Office, and a certification of such account to the Secretary of the Treasury by the Secretary of the Interior.

SEC. 5. That upon the approval of the allotments provided for in this act by the Secretary of the Interior, he shall cause patents to issue therefor in the name of the allottees, which patents shall be of the legal effect, and declare that the United States does and will hold the land thus allotted, for the period of twenty-five years, in trust for the sole use and benefit of the Indian to whom such allotment shall have been made, or, in case of his decease, of his heirs according to the laws of the State or Territory where such land is located, and that at the expiration of said period the United States will convey the same by patent to said Indian, or his heirs as aforesaid, in fee, discharged of said trust and free of all charge or incumbrance whatsoever: Provided, That the President of the United States may in any case in his discretion extend the period. And if any conveyance shall be made of the lands set apart and allotted as herein provided, or any contract made touching the same, before the expiration of the time above mentioned, such conveyance or contract shall be absolutely null and void: Provided, That the law of descent and partition in force in the State or Territory where such lands are situate shall apply thereto after patents therefor have been executed and delivered, except as herein otherwise provided; and the laws of the State of Kansas regulating the descent and partition of real estate shall, so far as practicable, apply to all lands in the Indian Territory which may be allotted in severalty under the provisions of this act: And provided further, That at any time after lands have been allotted to all the Indians of any tribe as herein provided, or sooner if in the opinion of the President it shall be for the best interests of said tribe, it shall be lawful for the Secretary of the Interior to negotiate with such Indian tribe for the purchase and release by said tribe, in conformity with the treaty or statute under which such reservation is held, of such portions of its reservation not allotted as such tribe shall, from time to time, consent to sell, on such terms and conditions as shall be considered just and equitable between the United States and said tribe of Indians, which purchase shall not be complete until ratified by Congress, and the form and manner of executing such release prescribed by Congress: Provided however, That all lands adapted to agriculture, with or without irrigation so sold or released to the United States by any Indian tribe shall be held by the United States for the sole purpose of securing homes to actual settlers and shall be disposed of by the United States to actual and bona fide settlers only tracts not exceding one hundred and sixty acres to any one person, on such terms as Congress shall prescribe, subject to grants which Congress may make in aid of education: And provided further, That no patents shall issue therefor except to the person so taking the same as and homestead, or his heirs, and after the expiration of five years occupancy therof as such homestead; and any conveyance of said lands taken as a homestead, or any contract touching the same, or lieu thereon, created prior to the date of such patent, shall be null and void. And the sums agreed to be paid by the United States as purchase money for any portion of any such reservation shall be held in the Treasury of the United States for the sole use of the tribe or tribes Indians; to whom such reservations belonged; and the same, with interest thereon at three per cent per annum, shall be at all times subject to appropriation by Congress for the education and civilization of such tribe or tribes of Indians or the members thereof. The patents aforesaid shall be recorded in the General Land Office, and afterward delivered, free of charge, to the allottee entitled thereto. And if any religious society or other organization is now occupying any of the public lands to which this act is applicable, for religious or educational work among the Indians, the Secretary of the Interior is hereby authorized to confirm such occupation to such society or organization, in quantity not exceeding one hundred and sixty acres in any one tract, so long as the same shall be so occupied, on such terms as he shall deem just; but nothing herein contained shall change or alter any claim of such society for religious or educational purposes heretofore granted by law. And hereafter in the employment of Indian police, or any other employes in the public service among any of the Indian tribes or bands affected by this act, and where Indians can perform the duties required, those Indians who have availed themselves of the provisions of this act and become citizens of the United States shall be preferred.

SEC. 6. That upon the completion of said allotments and the patenting of the lands to said allottees, each and every member of the respective bands or tribes of Indians to whom allotments have been made shall have the benefit of and be subject to the laws, both civil and criminal, of the State or Territory in which they may reside; and no Territory shall pass or enforce any law denying any such Indian within its jurisdiction the equal protection of the law. And every Indian born within the territorial limits of the United States to whom allotments shall have been made under the provisions of this act, or under any law or treaty, and every Indian born within the territorial limits of the United States who has voluntarily taken up, within said limits, his residence separate and apart from any tribe of Indians therein, and has adopted the habits of civilized life, is hereby declared to be a citizen of the United States, and is entitled to all the rights, privileges, and immunities of such citizens, whether said Indian has been or not, by birth or otherwise, a member of any tribe of Indians within the territorial limits of the United States without in any manner affecting the right of any such Indian to tribal or other property.

SEC. 7. That in cases where the use of water for irrigation is necessary to render the lands within any Indian reservation available for agricultural purposes, the Secretary of the Interior be, and he is hereby, authorized to prescribe such rules and regulations as he may deem necessary to secure a just and equal distribution thereof among the Indians residing upon any such reservation; and no other appropriation or grant of water by any riparian proprietor shall permitted to the damage of any other riparian proprietor.

Sec. 8. That the provisions of this act shall not extend to the territory occupied by the Cherokees, Creeks, Choctaws, Chickasaws, Seminoles, and Osage, Miamies and Peorias, and Sacs and Foxes, in the Indian Territory, nor to any of the reservations of the Seneca Nation of New York Indians in the State of New York, nor to that strip of territory in the State of Nebraska adjoining the Sioux Nation on the south added by executive order.

Sec. 9. That for the purpose of making the surveys and resurveys mentioned in section two of this act, there be, and hereby is, appropriated, out of any moneys in the Treasury not otherwise appropriated, the sum of one hundred thousand dollars, to be repaid proportionately out of the proceeds of the sales of such land as may be acquired from the Indians under the provisions of this act.

Sec. 10. That nothing in this act contained shall be so construed to affect the right and power of Congress to grant the right of way through any lands granted to an Indian, or a tribe of Indians, for railroads or other highways, or telegraph lines, for the public use, or condemn such lands to public uses, upon making just compensation.

Sec. 11. That nothing in this act shall be so construed as to prevent the removal of the Southern Ute Indians from their present reservation in Southwestern Colorado to a new reservation by and with consent of a majority of the adult male members of said tribe.

# JOINT RESOLUTION TO PROVIDE FOR ANNEXING THE HAWAIIAN ISLANDS TO THE UNITED STATES (1898)

*The story of Hawaiian annexation began in 1893 when the kingdom's Queen Lili'uokalani drafted a constitution meant to restore governance of the islands to the native Hawaiians, rather than the constitutional government supported by non-native businessmen (primarily the islands' sugar barons) and politicians. In response, the businessmen and politicians, with the support of the U.S. military, deposed Lili'uokalani in a nonviolent coup and placed her under house arrest. They also instituted a provisional government that petitioned the U.S. government for annexation. Congress passed a resolution, but President Grover Cleveland opposed annexation and refused to sign it. It wasn't until 1898 that pro-annexation William McKinley was elected president, and he signed a new Congressional order to annex the islands.*

Whereas, the Government of the Republic of Hawaii having, in due form, signified its consent, in the manner provided by its constitution, to cede absolutely and without reserve to the United States of America, all rights of sovereignty of whatsoever kind in and over the Hawaiian Islands and their dependencies, and also to cede and transfer to the United States, the absolute fee and ownership of all public, Government, or Crown lands, public buildings or edifices, ports, harbors, military equipment, and all other public property of every kind and description belonging to the Government of the Hawaiian Islands, together with every right and appurtenance thereunto appertaining: Therefore,

Resolved by the Senate and House of Representatives of the United States of America in Congress assembled, That said cession is accepted, ratified, and confirmed, and that the said Hawaiian Islands and their dependencies be, and they are hereby, annexed as a part of the territory of the United States and are subject to the sovereign dominion thereof, and that all and singular the property and rights hereinbefore mentioned are vested in the United States of America.

The existing laws of the United States relative to public lands shall not apply to such lands in the Hawaiian Islands; but the Congress of the United States shall enact special laws for their management and disposition: Provided, That all revenue from or proceeds of the same, except as regards such part thereof as may be used or occupied for the civil, military, or naval purposes of the United States, or may be assigned for the use of the local government, shall be used solely for the benefit of the inhabitants of the Hawaiian Islands for educational and other public purposes.

Until Congress shall provide for the government of such islands all the civil, judicial, and military powers exercised by the officers of the existing government in said islands shall be vested in such person or persons and shall be exercised in such manner as the President of the United States shall direct; and the President shall have power to remove said officers and fill the vacancies so occasioned.

The existing treaties of the Hawaiian Islands with foreign nations shall forthwith cease and determine, being replaced by such treaties as may exist, or as may be hereafter concluded, between the United States and such foreign nations. The municipal legislation of the Hawaiian Islands, not enacted for the fulfillment of the treaties so extinguished, and not inconsistent with this joint resolution nor contrary to the Constitution of the United States nor to any existing treaty of the United States, shall remain in force until the Congress of the United States shall otherwise determine.

Until legislation shall be enacted extending the United States customs laws and regulations to the Hawaiian Islands the existing customs relations of the Hawaiian Islands with the United States and other countries shall remain unchanged.

The public debt of the Republic of Hawaii, lawfully existing at the date of the passage of this joint resolution, including the amounts due to depositors in the Hawaiian Postal Savings Bank, is hereby assumed by the Government of the United States; but the liability of the United States in this regard shall in no case exceed four million dollars. So long, however, as the existing Government and the present commercial relations of the Hawaiian Islands are continued as hereinbefore, provided said Government shall continue to pay the interest on said debt.

There shall be no further immigration of Chinese into the Hawaiian Islands, except upon such conditions as are now or may hereafter be allowed by the laws of the United States; and no Chinese, by reason of anything herein contained, shall be allowed to enter the United States from the Hawaiian Islands.

SEC. 1. The President shall appoint five commissioners, at least two of whom shall be residents of the Hawaiian Islands, who shall, as soon as reasonably practicable, recommend to Congress such legislation concerning the Hawaiian Islands as they shall deem necessary or proper.

SEC. 2. That the commissioners hereinbefore provided for shall be appointed by the President, by and with the advice and consent of the Senate.

SEC. 3. That the sum of one hundred thousand dollars, or so much thereof as may be necessary, is hereby appropriated, out of any money in the Treasury not otherwise appropriated, and to be immediately available, to be expended at the discretion of the President of the United States of America, for the purpose of carrying this joint resolution into effect.

# LETTER OF PROTEST FROM QUEEN LILI'UOKALANI OF HAWAII TO THE HOUSE OF REPRESENTATIVES (1898)

*In 1898, Hawaii's last queen, Lili'uokalani, traveled to Washington, D.C., to ask President William McKinley, the U.S. Congress, and the American people to restore governance of the Hawaiian islands to the native monarchy. Her efforts failed, but she continued to lobby for Hawaiian independence until her death in 1917.*

The House of Representatives of the United States:

I, Lili'uokalani of Hawaii, named heir apparent on the 10th day of April, 1877, and proclaimed Queen of the Hawaiian Islands on the 29th day of January, 1891, do hereby earnestly and respectfully protest against the assertion of ownership by the United States of America of the so-called Hawaiian Crown Islands amounting to about one million acres and which are my property, and I especially protest against such assertion of ownership as a taking of property without due process of law and without just or other compensation.

Therefore, supplementing my protest of June 17, 1897, I call upon the President and the National Legislature and the People of the United States to do justice in this matter and to restore to me this property, the enjoyment of which is being withheld from me by your Government under what must be a misapprehension of my right and title.

Done at Washington, District of Columbia, United States of America, this nineteenth day of December, in the year one thousand eight hundred and ninety-eight.

# THEODORE ROOSEVELT'S INAUGURAL ADDRESS MARCH 4, 1905

My fellow-citizens, no people on earth have more cause to be thankful than ours, and this is said reverently, in no spirit of boastfulness in our own strength, but with gratitude to the Giver of Good who has blessed us with the conditions which have enabled us to achieve so large a measure of well-being and of happiness. To us as a people it has been granted to lay the foundations of our national life in a new continent. We are the heirs of the ages, and yet we have had to pay few of the penalties which in old countries are exacted by the dead hand of a bygone civilization. We have not been obliged to fight for our existence against any alien race; and yet our life has called for the vigor and effort without which the manlier and hardier virtues wither away. Under such conditions it would be our own fault if we failed; and the success which we have had in the past, the success which we confidently believe the future will bring, should cause in us no feeling of vainglory, but rather a deep and abiding realization of all which life has offered us; a full acknowledgment of the responsibility which is ours; and a fixed determination to show that under a free government a mighty people can thrive best, alike as regards the things of the body and the things of the soul.

Much has been given us, and much will rightfully be expected from us. We have duties to others and duties to ourselves; and we can shirk neither. We have become a great nation, forced by the fact of its greatness into relations with the other nations of the earth, and we must behave as beseems a people with such responsibilities. Toward all other nations, large and small, our attitude must be one of cordial and sincere friendship. We must show not only in our words, but in our deeds, that we are earnestly desirous of securing their good will by acting toward them in a spirit of just and generous recognition of all their rights. But justice and generosity in a nation, as in an individual, count most when shown not by the weak but by the strong. While ever careful to refrain from wrongdoing others, we must be no less insistent that we are not wronged ourselves. We wish peace, but we wish the peace of justice, the peace of righteousness. We wish it because we think it is right and not because we are afraid. No weak nation that acts manfully and justly should ever have cause to fear us, and no strong power should ever be able to single us out as a subject for insolent aggression.

Our relations with the other powers of the world are important; but still more important are our relations among ourselves. Such growth in wealth, in population, and in power as this nation has seen during the century and a quarter of its national life is inevitably accompanied by a like growth in the problems which are ever before every nation that rises to greatness. Power invariably means both responsibility and danger. Our forefathers faced certain perils which we have outgrown. We now face other perils, the very existence of which it was impossible that they should foresee. Modern life is both complex and intense, and the tremendous changes wrought by the extraordinary industrial development of the last half century are felt in every fiber of our social and political being. Never before have men tried so vast and formidable an experiment as that of administering the affairs of a continent under the forms of a Democratic republic. The conditions which have told for our marvelous material well-being, which have developed to a very high degree our energy, self-reliance, and individual initiative, have also brought the care and anxiety inseparable from the accumulation of great wealth in industrial centers. Upon the success of our experiment much depends, not only as regards our own welfare, but as regards the welfare of mankind. If we fail, the cause of free self-government throughout the world will rock to its foundations, and therefore our responsibility is heavy, to ourselves, to the world as it is to-day, and to the generations yet unborn. There is no good reason why we should fear the future, but there is every reason why we should face it seriously, neither hiding from ourselves the gravity of the problems before us nor fearing to approach these problems with the unbending, unflinching purpose to solve them aright.

Yet, after all, though the problems are new, though the tasks set before us differ from the tasks set before our fathers who founded and preserved this Republic, the spirit in which these tasks must be undertaken and these problems faced, if our duty is to be well done, remains essentially unchanged. We know that self-government is difficult. We know that no people needs such high traits of character as that people which seeks to govern its affairs aright through the freely expressed will of the freemen who compose it. But we have faith that we shall not prove false to the memories of the men of the mighty past. They did their work, they left us the splendid heritage we now enjoy. We in our turn have an assured confidence that we shall be able to leave this heritage unwasted and enlarged to our children and our children's children. To do so we must show, not merely in great crises, but in the everyday affairs of life, the qualities of practical intelligence, of courage, of hardihood, and endurance, and above all the power of devotion to a lofty ideal, which made great the men who founded this Republic in the days of Washington, which made great the men who preserved this Republic in the days of Abraham Lincoln.

# 16TH AMENDMENT TO THE U.S. CONSTITUTION: FEDERAL INCOME TAX (PASSED 1909, RATIFIED 1913)

Sixty-first Congress of the United States of America, At the First Session,

Begun and held at the City of Washington on Monday, the fifteenth day of March, one thousand nine hundred and nine.

### JOINT RESOLUTION

Proposing an amendment to the Constitution of the United States.

RESOLVED by the Senate and House of Representatives of the United States of America in Congress assembled (two-thirds of each House concurring therein), That the following article is proposed as an amendment to the Constitution of the United States, which, when ratified by the legislature of three-fourths of the several States, shall be valid to all intents and purposes as a part of the Constitution:

"ARTICLE XVI. The Congress shall have power to lay and collect taxes on incomes, from whatever source derived, without apportionment among the several States, and without regard to any census or enumeration."

# WOODROW WILSON'S FOURTEEN POINTS (1918)

*In January 1918, President Woodrow Wilson delivered a speech to Congress in which he outlined "fourteen points" that he believed were needed to achieve peace after the fighting in World War I. He intended for the fourteen points to be used as a framework for the treaty that ended the war, but during the negotiations, Wilson discovered that America's allies in that war (England, France, and Italy) instead wanted to punish their enemies (Germany and Austria–Hungary). In the end, Wilson's suggestions were abandoned in favor of a more punitive treaty, but the fourteenth point, which called for a world organization dedicated to maintaining world peace, led to the creation of the League of Nations. The United States never joined the League, but thirty years later, the country did join its successor: the United Nations.*

Once more, as repeatedly before, the spokesmen of the Central Empires have indicated their desire to discuss the objects of the war and the possible basis of a general peace. Parleys have been in progress at Brest-Litovsk between Russian representatives and representatives of the Central Powers to which the attention of all the belligerents has been invited for the purpose of ascertaining whether it may be possible to extend these parleys into a general conference with regard to terms of peace and settlement. The Russian representatives presented not only a perfectly definite statement of the principles upon which they would be willing to conclude peace but also an equally definite program of the concrete application of those principles. The representatives of the Central Powers, on their part, presented an outline of settlement which, if much less definite, seemed susceptible of liberal interpretation until their specific program of practical terms was added. That program proposed no concessions at all either to the sovereignty of Russia or to the preferences of the populations with whose fortunes it dealt, but meant, in a word, that the Central Empires were to keep every foot of territory their armed forces had occupied,—every province, every city, every point of vantage,—as a permanent addition to their territories and their power. It is a reasonable conjecture that the general principles of settlement which they at first suggested originated with the more liberal statesmen of Germany and Austria, the men who have begun to feel the force of their own peoples' thought and purpose, while the concrete terms of actual settlement came from the military leaders who have no thought but to keep what they have got. The negotiations have been broken off. The Russian representatives were sincere and in earnest. They cannot entertain such proposals of conquest and domination.

The whole incident is full of significance. It is also full of perplexity. With whom are the Russian representatives dealing? For whom are the representatives of the Central Empires speaking? Are they speaking for the majorities of their respective parliaments or for the minority parties, that military and imperialistic minority which has so far dominated their whole policy and controlled the affairs of Turkey and of the Balkan states which have felt obliged to become their associates in this war? The Russian representatives have insisted, very justly, very wisely, and in the true spirit of modern democracy, that the conferences they have been holding with the Teutonic and Turkish statesmen should be held within open, not closed, doors, and all the world has been audience, as was desired. To whom have we been listening, then? To those who speak the spirit and intention of the Resolutions of the German Reichstag of the ninth of July last, the spirit and intention of the liberal leaders and parties of Germany, or to those who resist and defy that spirit and intention and insist upon conquest and subjugation? Or are we listening, in fact, to both, unreconciled and in open and hopeless contradiction? These are very serious and pregnant questions. Upon the answer to them depends the peace of the world.

But, whatever the results of the parleys at Brest-Litovsk, whatever the confusions of counsel and of purpose in the utterances of the spokesmen of the Central Empires, they have again attempted to acquaint the world with their objects in the war and have again challenged their adversaries to say what their objects are and what sort of settlement they would deem just and satisfactory. There is no good reason why that challenge should not be responded to, and responded to with the utmost candor. We did not wait for it. Not once, but again and again, we have laid our whole thought and purpose before the world, not in general terms only, but each time with sufficient definition to make it clear what sort of definitive terms of settlement must necessarily spring out of them. Within the last week Mr. Lloyd George has spoken with admirable candor and in admirable spirit for the people and Government of Great Britain. There is no confusion of counsel among the adversaries of the Central Powers, no uncertainty of principle, no vagueness of detail. The only secrecy of counsel, the only lack of fearless frankness, the only failure to make definite statement of the objects of the war, lies with Germany and her Allies. The issues of life and death hang upon these definitions. No statesman who has the least conception of his responsibility ought for a moment to permit himself to continue this tragical and appalling outpouring of blood and treasure unless he is sure beyond a peradventure that the objects of the vital sacrifice are part and parcel of the very life of society and that the people for whom he speaks think them right and imperative as he does.

There is, moreover, a voice calling for these definitions of principle and of purpose which is, it seems to me, more thrilling and more compelling than any of the many moving voices with which the troubled air of the world is filled. It is the voice of the Russian people. They are prostrate and all but helpless, it would seem, before the grim power of Germany, which has hitherto known no relenting and no pity. Their power, apparently, is shattered. And yet their soul is not subservient. They will not yield either in principle or in action. Their conception of what is right, of what it is humane and honorable for them to accept, has been stated with a frankness, a largeness of view, a generosity of spirit, and a universal human sympathy which must challenge the admiration of every friend of mankind; and they have refused to compound their ideals or desert others that they themselves may be safe. They call to us to say what it is that we desire, in what, if in anything, our purpose and our spirit differ from theirs; and I believe that the people of the United States would wish me to respond, with utter simplicity and frankness. Whether their present leaders believe it or not, it is our heartfelt desire and hope that some way may be opened whereby we may be privileged to assist the people of Russia to attain their utmost hope of liberty and ordered peace.

It will be our wish and purpose that the processes of peace, when they are begun, shall be absolutely open and that they shall involve and permit henceforth no secret understandings of any kind. The day of conquest and aggrandizement is gone by; so is also the day of secret covenants entered into in the interest of particular governments and likely at some unlooked-for moment to upset the peace of the world. It is this happy fact, now clear to the view of every public man whose thoughts do not still linger in an age that is dead and gone, which makes it possible for every nation whose purposes are consistent with justice and the peace of the world to avow now or at any other time the objects it has in view.

We entered this war because violations of right had occurred which touched us to the quick and made the life of our own people impossible unless they were corrected and the world secured once for all against their recurrence. What we demand in this war, therefore, is nothing peculiar to ourselves. It is that the world be made fit and safe to live in; and particularly that it be made safe for every peace-loving nation which, like our own, wishes to live its own life, determine its own institutions, be assured of justice and fair dealing by the other peoples of the world as against force and selfish aggression. All the peoples of the world are in effect partners in this interest, and for our own part we see very clearly that unless justice be done to others it will not be done to us. The program of the world's peace, therefore, is our program; and that program, the only possible program, as we see it, is this:

I. Open covenants of peace, openly arrived at, after which there shall be no private international understandings of any kind, but diplomacy shall proceed always frankly and in the public view.

II. Absolute freedom of navigation upon the seas, outside territorial waters, alike in peace and in war, except as the seas may be closed in whole or in part by international action for the enforcement of international covenants.

III. The removal, so far as possible, of all economic barriers and the establishment of an equality of trade conditions among all the nations consenting to the peace and associating themselves for its maintenance.

IV. Adequate guarantees given and taken that national armaments will be reduced to the lowest point consistent with domestic safety.

V. A free, open-minded, and absolutely impartial adjustment of all colonial claims, based upon a strict observance of the principle that in determining all such questions of sovereignty the interests of the populations concerned must have equal weight with the equitable claims of the government whose title is to be determined.

VI. The evacuation of all Russian territory and such a settlement of all questions affecting Russia as will secure the best and freest cooperation of the other nations of the world in obtaining for her an unhampered and unembarrassed opportunity for the independent determination of her own political development and national policy and assure her of a sincere welcome into the society of free nations under institutions of her own choosing; and, more than a welcome, assistance also of every kind that she may need and may herself desire. The treatment accorded Russia by her sister nations in the months to come will be the acid test of their good will, of their comprehension of her needs as distinguished from their own interests, and of their intelligent and unselfish sympathy.

VII. Belgium, the whole world will agree, must be evacuated and restored, without any attempt to limit the sovereignty which she enjoys in common with all other free nations. No other single act will serve as this will serve to restore confidence among the nations in the laws which they have themselves set and determined for the government of their relations with one another. Without this healing act the whole structure and validity of international law is forever impaired.

VIII. All French territory should be freed and the invaded portions restored, and the wrong done to France by Prussia in 1871 in the matter of Alsace-Lorraine, which has unsettled the peace of the world for nearly fifty years, should be righted, in order that peace may once more be made secure in the interest of all.

IX. A readjustment of the frontiers of Italy should be effected along clearly recognizable lines of nationality.

X. The peoples of Austria–Hungary, whose place among the nations we wish to see safeguarded and assured, should be accorded the freest opportunity of autonomous development.

XI. Romania, Serbia, and Montenegro should be evacuated; occupied territories restored; Serbia accorded free and secure access to the sea; and the relations of the several Balkan states to one another determined by friendly counsel along historically established lines of allegiance and nationality; and international guarantees of the political and economic independence and territorial integrity of the several Balkan states should be entered into.

XII. The Turkish portions of the present Ottoman Empire should be assured a secure sovereignty, but the other nationalities which are now under Turkish rule should be assured an undoubted security of life and an absolutely unmolested opportunity of autonomous development and the Dardanelles should be permanently opened as a free passage to the ships and commerce of all nations under international guarantees.

XIII. An independent Polish state should be erected which should include the territories inhabited by indisputably Polish populations, which should be assured a free and secure access to the sea, and whose political and economic independence and territorial integrity should be guaranteed by international covenant.

XIV. A general association of nations must be formed under specific covenants for the purpose of affording mutual guarantees of political independence and territorial integrity to great and small states alike.

In regard to these essential rectifications of wrong and assertions of right we feel ourselves to be intimate partners of all the governments and peoples associated together against the Imperialists. We cannot be separated in interest or divided in purpose. We stand together until the end.

For such arrangements and covenants we are willing to fight and to continue to fight until they are achieved; but only because we wish the right to prevail and desire a just and stable peace such as can be secured only by removing the chief provocations to war, which this program does remove. We have no jealousy of German greatness, and there is nothing in this program that impairs it. We grudge her no achievement or distinction of learning or of pacific enterprise such as have made her record very bright and very enviable. We do not wish to injure her or to block in any way her legitimate influence or power. We do not wish to fight her either with arms or with hostile arrangements of trade if she is willing to associate herself with us and the other peace-loving nations of the world in covenants of justice and law and fair dealing. We wish her only to accept a place of equality among the peoples of the world,—the new world in which we now live,—instead of a place of mastery.

Neither do we presume to suggest to her any alteration or modification of her institutions. But it is necessary, we must frankly say, and necessary as a preliminary to any intelligent dealings with her on our part, that we should know whom her spokesmen speak for when they speak to us, whether for the Reichstag majority or for the military party and the men whose creed is imperial domination.

We have spoken now, surely, in terms too concrete to admit of any further doubt or question. An evident principle runs through the whole program I have outlined. It is the principle of justice to all peoples and nationalities, and their right to live on equal terms of liberty and safety with one another, whether they be strong or weak. Unless this principle be made its foundation no part of the structure of international justice can stand. The people of the United States could act upon no other principle; and to the vindication of this principle they are ready to devote their lives, their honor, and everything that they possess. The moral climax of this the culminating and final war for human liberty has come, and they are ready to put their own strength, their own highest purpose, their own integrity and devotion to the test.

# 19TH AMENDMENT TO THE U.S. CONSTITUTION: WOMEN'S RIGHT TO VOTE (1920)

Sixty-sixth Congress of the United States of America; At the First Session,

Begun and held at the City of Washington on Monday, the nineteenth day of May, one thousand nine hundred and nineteen.

### JOINT RESOLUTION

Proposing an amendment to the Constitution extending the right of suffrage to women.

RESOLVED by the Senate and House of Representatives of the United States of America in Congress assembled (two-thirds of each House concurring therein), That the following article is proposed as an amendment to the Constitution, which shall be valid to all intents and purposes as part of the Constitution when ratified by the legislature of three-fourths of the several States.

"ARTICLE ————.

"The right of citizens of the United States to vote shall not be denied or abridged by the United States or by any State on account of sex.

Congress shall have power to enforce this article by appropriate legislation."

# FRANKLIN D. ROOSEVELT'S FIRST INAUGURAL ADDRESS MARCH 4, 1933

I am certain that my fellow Americans expect that on my induction into the Presidency I will address them with a candor and a decision which the present situation of our Nation impels. This is preeminently the time to speak the truth, the whole truth, frankly and boldly. Nor need we shrink from honestly facing conditions in our country today. This great Nation will endure as it has endured, will revive and will prosper.

So, first of all, let me assert my firm belief that the only thing we have to fear is fear itself—nameless, unreasoning, unjustified terror which paralyzes needed efforts to convert retreat into advance. In every dark hour of our national life a leadership of frankness and vigor has met with that understanding and support of the people themselves which is essential to victory. I am convinced that you will again give that support to leadership in these critical days.

In such a spirit on my part and on yours we face our common difficulties. They concern, thank God, only material things. Values have shrunken to fantastic levels; taxes have risen; our ability to pay has fallen; government of all kinds is faced by serious curtailment of income; the means of exchange are frozen in the currents of trade; the withered leaves of industrial enterprise lie on every side; farmers find no markets for their produce; the savings of many years in thousands of families are gone. More important, a host of unemployed citizens face the grim problem of existence, and an equally great number toil with little return. Only a foolish optimist can deny the dark realities of the moment.

Yet our distress comes from no failure of substance. We are stricken by no plague of locusts. Compared with the perils which our forefathers conquered because they believed and were not afraid, we have still much to be thankful for. Nature still offers her bounty and human efforts have multiplied it. Plenty is at our doorstep, but a generous use of it languishes in the very sight of the supply. Primarily this is because the rulers of the exchange of mankind's goods have failed, through their own stubbornness and their own incompetence, have admitted their failure, and abdicated. Practices of the unscrupulous money changers stand indicted in the court of public opinion, rejected by the hearts and minds of men.

True they have tried, but their efforts have been cast in the pattern of an outworn tradition. Faced by failure of credit they have proposed only the lending of more money. Stripped of the lure of profit by which to induce our people to follow their false leadership, they have resorted to exhortations, pleading tearfully for restored confidence. They know only the rules of a generation of self-seekers. They have no vision, and when there is no vision the people perish.

The money changers have fled from their high seats in the temple of our civilization. We may now restore that temple to the ancient truths. The measure of the restoration lies in the extent to which we apply social values more noble than mere monetary profit.

Happiness lies not in the mere possession of money; it lies in the joy of achievement, in the thrill of creative effort. The joy and moral stimulation of work no longer must be forgotten in the mad chase of evanescent profits. These dark days, my friends, will be worth all they cost us if they teach us that our true destiny is not to be ministered unto but to minister to ourselves and to our fellow men.

Recognition of the falsity of material wealth as the standard of success goes hand in hand with the abandonment of the false belief that public office and high political position are to be valued only by the standards of pride of place and personal profit; and there must be an end to a conduct in banking and in business which too often has given to a sacred trust the likeness of callous and selfish wrongdoing. Small wonder that confidence languishes, for it thrives only on honesty, on honor, on the sacredness of obligations, on faithful protection, on unselfish performance; without them it cannot live.

Restoration calls, however, not for changes in ethics alone. This Nation asks for action, and action now.

Our greatest primary task is to put people to work. This is no unsolvable problem if we face it wisely and courageously. It can be accomplished in part by direct recruiting by the Government itself, treating the task as we would treat the emergency of a war, but at the same time, through this employment, accomplishing greatly needed projects to stimulate and reorganize the use of our natural resources.

Hand in hand with this we must frankly recognize the overbalance of population in our industrial centers and, by engaging on a national scale in a redistribution, endeavor to provide a better use of the land for those best fitted for the land. The task can be helped by definite efforts to raise the values of agricultural products and with this the power to purchase the output of our cities. It can be helped by preventing realistically the tragedy of the growing loss through foreclosure of our small homes and our farms. It can be helped by insistence that the Federal, State, and local governments act forthwith on the demand that their cost be drastically reduced. It can be helped by the unifying of relief activities which today are often scattered, uneconomical, and unequal. It can be helped by national planning for and supervision of all forms of transportation and of communications and other utilities which have a definitely public character. There are many ways in which it can be helped, but it can never be helped merely by talking about it. We must act and act quickly.

Finally, in our progress toward a resumption of work we require two safeguards against a return of the evils of the old order. There must be a strict supervision of all banking and credits and investments; there must be an end to speculation with other people's money, and there must be provision for an adequate but sound currency.

There are the lines of attack. I shall presently urge upon a new Congress in special session detailed measures for their fulfillment, and I shall seek the immediate assistance of the several States.

Through this program of action we address ourselves to putting our own national house in order and making income balance outgo. Our international trade relations, though vastly important, are in point of time and necessity secondary to the establishment of a sound national economy. I favor as a practical policy the putting of first things first. I shall spare no effort to restore world trade by international economic readjustment, but the emergency at home cannot wait on that accomplishment.

The basic thought that guides these specific means of national recovery is not narrowly nationalistic. It is the insistence, as a first consideration, upon the interdependence of the various elements in all parts of the United States—a recognition of the old and permanently important manifestation of the American spirit of the pioneer. It is the way to recovery. It is the immediate way. It is the strongest assurance that the recovery will endure.

In the field of world policy I would dedicate this Nation to the policy of the good neighbor—the neighbor who resolutely respects himself and, because he does so, respects the rights of others—the neighbor who respects his obligations and respects the sanctity of his agreements in and with a world of neighbors.

If I read the temper of our people correctly, we now realize as we have never realized before our interdependence on each other; that we can not merely take but we must give as well; that if we are to go forward, we must move as a trained and loyal army willing to sacrifice for the good of a common discipline, because without such discipline no progress is made, no leadership becomes effective. We are, I know, ready and willing to submit our lives and property to such discipline, because it makes possible a leadership which aims at a larger good. This I propose to offer, pledging that the larger purposes will bind upon us all as a sacred obligation with a unity of duty hitherto evoked only in time of armed strife.

With this pledge taken, I assume unhesitatingly the leadership of this great army of our people dedicated to a disciplined attack upon our common problems.

Action in this image and to this end is feasible under the form of government which we have inherited from our ancestors. Our Constitution is so simple and practical that it is possible always to meet extraordinary needs by changes in emphasis and arrangement without loss of essential form. That is why our constitutional system has proved itself the most superbly enduring political mechanism the modern world has ever seen. It has met every stress of vast expansion of territory, of foreign wars, of bitter internal strife, of world relations.

It is to be hoped that the normal balance of executive and legislative authority may be wholly adequate to meet the unprecedented task before us. But it may be that an unprecedented demand and need for undelayed action may call for temporary departure from that normal balance of public procedure.

I am prepared under my constitutional duty to recommend the measures that a stricken nation in the midst of a stricken world may require. These measures, or such other measures as the Congress may build out of its experience and wisdom, I shall seek, within my constitutional authority, to bring to speedy adoption.

But in the event that the Congress shall fail to take one of these two

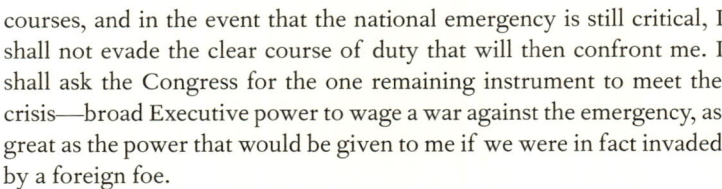 

courses, and in the event that the national emergency is still critical, I shall not evade the clear course of duty that will then confront me. I shall ask the Congress for the one remaining instrument to meet the crisis—broad Executive power to wage a war against the emergency, as great as the power that would be given to me if we were in fact invaded by a foreign foe.

For the trust reposed in me I will return the courage and the devotion that befit the time. I can do no less.

We face the arduous days that lie before us in the warm courage of the national unity; with the clear consciousness of seeking old and precious moral values; with the clean satisfaction that comes from the stern performance of duty by old and young alike. We aim at the assurance of a rounded and permanent national life.

We do not distrust the future of essential democracy. The people of the United States have not failed. In their need they have registered a mandate that they want direct, vigorous action. They have asked for discipline and direction under leadership. They have made me the present instrument of their wishes. In the spirit of the gift I take it.

In this dedication of a Nation we humbly ask the blessing of God. May He protect each and every one of us. May He guide me in the days to come.

# THE SOCIAL SECURITY ACT (1935)

An act to provide for the general welfare by establishing a system of Federal old-age benefits, and by enabling the several States to make more adequate provision for aged persons, blind persons, dependent and crippled children, maternal and child welfare, public health, and the administration of their unemployment compensation laws; to establish a Social Security Board; to raise revenue; and for other purposes.

Be it enacted by the Senate and House of Representatives of the United States of America in Congress assembled,

## Title I
## Grants to States for Old-Age Assistance

APPROPRIATION

SECTION 1. For the purpose of enabling each State to furnish financial assistance, as far as practicable under the conditions in such State, to aged needy individuals, there is hereby authorized to be appropriated for the fiscal year ended June 30, 1936, the sum of $49,750,000, and there is hereby authorized to be appropriated for each fiscal year thereafter a sum sufficient to carry out the purposes of this title. The sums made available under this section shall be used for making payments to States which have submitted, and had approved by the Social Security Board established by Title VII (hereinafter referred to as the Board ), State plans for old-age assistance.

STATE OLD-AGE ASSISTANCE PLANS

SEC. 2. (a) A State plan for old-age assistance must

(1) provide that it shall be in effect in all political subdivisions of the State, and, if administered by them, be mandatory upon them;

(2) provide for financial participation by the State;

(3) either provide for the establishment or designation of a single State agency to administer the plan, or provide for the establishment or designation of a single State agency to supervise the administration of the plan;

(4) provide for granting to any individual, whose claim for old-age assistance is denied, an opportunity for a fair hearing before such State agency;

(5) provide such methods of administration (other than those relating to selection, tenure of office, and compensation of personnel) as are found by the Board to be necessary for the efficient operation of the plan;

(6) provide that the State agency will make such reports, in such form and containing such information, as the Board may from time to time require, and comply with such provisions as the Board may from time to time find necessary to assure the correctness and verification of such reports; and

(7) provide that, if the State or any of its political subdivisions collects from the estate of any recipient of old-age assistance any amount with respect to old-age assistance furnished him under the plan, one-half of the net amount so collected shall be promptly paid to the United States. Any payment so made shall be deposited in the Treasury to the credit of the appropriation for the purposes of this title.

(b) The Board shall approve any plan which fulfills the conditions specified in subsection (a), except that it shall not approve any plan which imposes, as a condition of eligibility for old-age assistance under the plan—

(1) An age requirement of more than sixty-five years, except that the plan may impose, effective until January 1, 1940, an age requirement of as much as seventy years; or

(2) Any residence requirement which excludes any resident of the State who has resided therein five years during the nine years immediately preceding the application for old-age assistance and has resided therein continuously for one year immediately preceding the application; or (3) Any citizenship requirement which excludes any citizen of the United States.

PAYMENT TO STATES

SEC. 3. (a) From the sums appropriated therefor, the Secretary of the Treasury shall pay to each State which has an approved plan for old-age assistance, for each quarter, beginning with the quarter commencing July 1, 1935,

(1) an amount, which shall be used exclusively as old-age assistance,

equal to one-half of the total of the sums expended during such quarter as old-age assistance under the State plan with respect to each individual who at the time of such expenditure is sixty-five years of age or older and is not an inmate of a public institution, not counting so much of such expenditure with respect to any individual for any month as exceeds $30, and

(2) 5 per centum of such amount, which shall be used for paying the costs of administering the State plan or for old-age assistance, or both, and for no other purpose: Provided, That the State plan, in order to be approved by the Board, need not provide for financial participation before July 1, 1937, by the State, in the case of any State which the Board, upon application by the State and after reasonable notice and opportunity for hearing to the State, finds is prevented by its constitution from providing such financial participation.

(b) The method of computing and paying such amounts shall be as follows:

(1) The Board shall, prior to the beginning of each quarter, estimate the amount to be paid to the State for such quarter under the provisions of clause (1) of subsection (a), such estimate to be based on

(A) a report filed by the State containing its estimate of the total sum to be expended in such quarter in accordance with the provisions of such clause, and stating the amount appropriated or made available by the State and its political subdivisions for such expenditures in such quarter, and if such amount is less than one-half of the total sum of such estimated expenditures, the source or sources from which the difference is expected to be derived,

(B) records showing the number of aged individuals in the State, and

(C) such other investigation as the Board may find necessary.

(2) The Board shall then certify to the Secretary of the Treasury the amount so estimated by the Board, reduced or increased, as the case may be, by any sum by which it finds that its estimate for any prior quarter was greater or less than the amount which should have been paid to the State under clause (1) of subsection (a) for such quarter, except to the extent that such sum has been applied to make the amount certified for any prior quarter greater or less than the amount estimated by the Board for such prior quarter.

(3) The Secretary of the Treasury shall thereupon, through the

Division of Disbursement of the Treasury Department and prior to audit or settlement by the General Accounting Office, pay to the State, at the time or times fixed by the Board, the amount so certified, increased by 5 per centum.

OPERATION OF STATE PLANS

SEC. 4. In the case of any State plan for old-age assistance which has been approved by the Board, if the Board, after reasonable notice and opportunity for hearing to the State agency administering or supervising the administration of such plan, finds—

(1) that the plan has been so changed as to impose any age, residence, or citizenship requirement prohibited by section 2 (b), or that in the administration of the plan any such prohibited requirement is imposed, with the knowledge of such State agency, in a substantial number of cases; or

(2) that in the administration of the plan there is a failure to comply substantially with any provision required by section 2 (a) to be included in the plan; the Board shall notify such State agency that further payments will not be made to the State until the Board is satisfied that such prohibited requirement is no longer so imposed, and that there is no longer any such failure to comply. Until it is so satisfied it shall make no further certification to the Secretary of the Treasury with respect to such State.

ADMINISTRATION

SEC. 5. There is hereby authorized to be appropriated for the fiscal year ending June 30, 1936, the sum of $250,000, for all necessary expenses of the Board in administering the provisions of this title.

DEFINITION

SEC. 6. When used in this title the term old age assistance means money payments to aged individuals.

## TITLE II
### FEDERAL OLD-AGE BENEFITS
### OLD-AGE RESERVE ACCOUNT

SECTION 201. (a) There is hereby created an account in the Treasury of the United States to be known as the Old-Age Reserve Account hereinafter in this title called the Account. There is hereby authorized to be appropriated to the Account for each fiscal year, beginning with the fiscal year ending June 30, 1937, an amount sufficient as an annual premium to provide for the payments required under this title, such amount to be determined on a reserve basis in accordance with accepted actuarial principles, and based upon such tables of mortality as the Secretary of the Treasury shall from time to time adopt, and upon an interest rate of 3 per centum per annum compounded annually. The Secretary of the Treasury shall submit annually to the Bureau of the Budget an estimate of the appropriations to be made to the Account.

(b) It shall be the duty of the Secretary of the Treasury to invest such portion of the amounts credited to the Account as is not, in his judgment, required to meet current withdrawals. Such investment may be made only in interest-bearing obligations of the United States or in obligations guaranteed as to both principal and interest by the United States. For such purpose such obligations may be acquired

(1) on original issue at par, or

(2) by purchase of outstanding obligations at the market price. The purposes for which obligations of the United States may be issued under the Second Liberty Bond Act, as amended, are hereby extended to authorize the issuance at par of special obligations exclusively to the Account. Such special obligations shall bear interest at the rate of 3 per centum per annum. Obligations other than such special obligations may be acquired for the Account only on such terms as to provide an investment yield of not less than 3 per centum per annum.

(c) Any obligations acquired by the Account (except special obligations issued exclusively to the Account) may be sold at the market price, and such special obligations may be redeemed at par plus accrued interest.

(d) The interest on, and the proceeds from the sale or redemption of, any obligations held in the Account shall be credited to and form a part of the Account.

(e) All amounts credited to the Account shall be available for making payments required under this title.

(f) The Secretary of the Treasury shall include in his annual report the actuarial status of the Account.

OLD–AGE BENEFIT PAYMENTS

SEC. 202. (a) Every qualified individual (as defined in section 210) shall be entitled to receive, with respect to the period beginning on the date he attains the age of sixty-five, or on January 1, 1942, whichever is the later, and ending on the date of his death, an old-age benefit (payable as nearly as practicable in equal monthly installments) as follows:

(1) If the total wages (as defined in section 210) determined by the Board to have been paid to him, with respect to employment (as defined in section 210) after December 31, 1936, and before he attained the age of sixty-five, were not more than $3,000, the old-age benefit shall be at a monthly rate of one-half of 1 per centum of such total wages;

(2) If such total wages were more than $3,000, the old-age benefit shall be at a monthly rate equal to the sum of the following:

(A) One-half of 1 per centum of $3,000; plus

(B) One-twelfth of 1 per centum of the amount by which such total wages exceeded $3,000 and did not exceed $45,000; plus

(C) One-twenty-fourth of 1 per centum of the amount by which such total wages exceeded $45,000.

(b) In no case shall the monthly rate computed under subsection (a) exceed $85.

(c) If the Board finds at any time that more or less than the correct amount has theretofore been paid to any individual under this section, then, under regulations made by the Board, proper adjustments shall be made in connection with subsequent payments under this section to the same individual.

(d) Whenever the Board finds that any qualified individual has received wages with respect to regular employment after he attained the age of sixty-five, the old-age benefit payable to such individual shall be reduced, for each calendar month in any part of which such regular employment occurred, by an amount equal to one month's benefit. Such reduction shall be made, under regulations prescribed by the Board, by deductions from one or more payments of old-age benefit to such individual.

PAYMENTS UPON DEATH

SEC. 203. (a) If any individual dies before attaining the age of sixty-five, there shall be paid to his estate an amount equal to 3 « per centum of the total wages determined by the Board to have been paid to him, with respect to employment after December 31, 1936.

(b) If the Board finds that the correct amount of the old-age benefit payable to a qualified individual during his life under section 202 was less than 3 « per centum of the total wages by which such old-age benefit was measurable, then there shall be paid to his estate a sum equal to the amount, if any, by which such 3 « per centum exceeds the amount (whether more or less than the correct amount) paid to him during his life as old-age benefit.

(c) If the Board finds that the total amount paid to a qualified individual under an old-age benefit during his life was less than the correct amount to which he was entitled under section 202, and that the correct amount of such old-age benefit was 3 per centum or more of the total wages by which such old-age benefit was measurable, then there shall be paid to his estate a sum equal to the amount, if any, by which the correct amount of the old-age benefit exceeds the amount which was so paid to him during his life.

PAYMENTS TO AGED INDIVIDUALS NOT QUALIFIED FOR BENEFITS

SEC. 204. (a) There shall be paid in a lump sum to any individual who, upon attaining the age of sixty-five, is not a qualified individual, an amount equal to 3 « per centum of the total wages determined by the Board to have been paid to him, with respect to employment after December 31, 1936, and before he attained the age of sixty-five.

(b) After any individual becomes entitled to any payment under subsection (a), no other payment shall be made under this title in any manner measured by wages paid to him, except that any part of any payment under subsection (a) which is not paid to him before his death shall be paid to his estate.

AMOUNTS OF $500 OR LESS PAYABLE TO ESTATES.

SEC. 205. If any amount payable to an estate under section 203 or 204 is $500 or less, such amount may, under regulations prescribed by the Board, be paid to the persons found by the Board to be entitled thereto under the law of the State in which the deceased was domiciled, without the necessity of compliance with the requirements of law with respect to the administration of such estate.

OVERPAYMENTS DURING LIFE

SEC. 206. If the Board finds that the total amount paid to a qualified

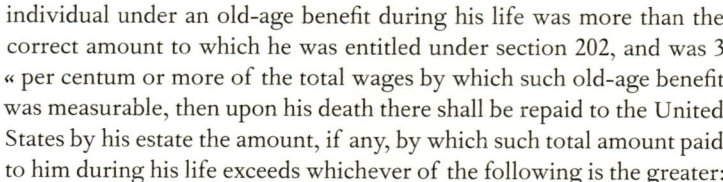

individual under an old-age benefit during his life was more than the correct amount to which he was entitled under section 202, and was 3 « per centum or more of the total wages by which such old-age benefit was measurable, then upon his death there shall be repaid to the United States by his estate the amount, if any, by which such total amount paid to him during his life exceeds whichever of the following is the greater:

(1) Such 3 per centum, or

(2) the correct amount to which he was entitled under section 202.

METHOD OF MAKING PAYMENTS

SEC. 207. The Board shall from time to time certify to the Secretary of the Treasury the name and address of each person entitled to receive a payment under this title, the amount of such payment, and the time at which it should be made, and the Secretary of the Treasury through the Division of Disbursement of the Treasury Department, and prior to audit or settlement by the General Accounting Office, shall make payment in accordance with the certification by the Board.

ASSIGNMENT

SEC. 208. The right of any person to any future payment under this title shall not be transferable or assignable, at law or in equity, and none of the moneys paid or payable or rights existing under this title shall be subject to execution, levy, attachment, garnishment, or other legal process, or to the operation of any bankruptcy or insolvency law.

PENALTIES

SEC. 209. Whoever in any application for any payment under this title makes any false statement as to any material fact, knowing such statement to be false, shall be fined not more than $1,000 or imprisoned for not more than one year, or both.

DEFINITIONS

SEC. 210. When used in this title— (a) The term wages means all remuneration for employment, including the cash value of all remuneration paid in any medium other than cash; except that such term shall not include that part of the remuneration which, after remuneration equal to $3,000 has been paid to an individual by an employer with respect to employment during any calendar year, is paid to such employer with respect to employment during such calendar year.

(b) The term employment means any service, of whatever nature, performed within the United States by an employee for his employer, except—

(1) Agricultural labor;

(2) Domestic service in a private home;

(3) Casual labor not in the course of the employer's trade or business;

(4) Service performed as an officer or member of the crew of a vessel documented under the laws of the United States or of any foreign country;

(5) Service performed in the employ of the United States Government or of an instrumentality of the United States;

(6) Service performed in the employ of a State, a political subdivision thereof, or an instrumentality of one or more States or political subdivisions;

(7) Service performed in the employ of a corporation, community chest, fund, or foundation, organized and operated exclusively for religious, charitable, scientific, literary, or educational purposes, or for the prevention of cruelty to children or animals, no part of the net earnings of which inures to the benefit of any private shareholder or individual.

(c) The term qualified individual means any individual with respect to whom it appears to the satisfaction of the Board that—

(1) He is at least sixty-five years of age; and

(2) The total amount of wages paid to him, with respect to employment after December 31, 1936, and before he attained the age of sixty-five, was not less than $2,000; and

(3) Wages were paid to him, with respect to employment on some five days after December 31, 1936, and before he attained the age of sixty-five, each day being in a different calendar year.

## Title III
### Grants to States for Unemployment Compensation Administration Appropriation

SECTION 301. For the purpose of assisting the States in the administration of their unemployment compensation laws, there is hereby authorized to be appropriated, for the fiscal year ending June 30, 1936, the sum of $4,000,000, and for each fiscal year thereafter the sum of $49,000,000, to be used as hereinafter provided.

PAYMENTS TO STATES

SEC. 302. (a) The Board shall from time to time certify to the Secretary of the Treasury for payment to each State which has an unemployment compensation law approved by the Board under Title IX, such amounts as the Board determines to be necessary for the proper administration of such law during the fiscal year in which such payment is to be made. The Board's determination shall be based on

(1) the population of the State;

(2) an estimate of the number of persons covered by the State law and of the cost of proper administration of such law; and

(3) such other factors as the Board finds relevant. The Board shall not certify for payment under this section in any fiscal year a total amount in excess of the amount appropriated therefor for such fiscal year.

(b) Out of the sums appropriated therefor, the Secretary of the Treasury shall, upon receiving a certification under subsection (a), pay, through the Division of Disbursement of the Treasury Department and prior to audit or settlement by the General Accounting Office, to the State agency charged with the administration of such law the amount so certified.

PROVISIONS OF STATE LAWS

SEC. 303. (a) The Board shall make no certification for payment to any State unless it finds that the law of such State, approved by the Board under Title IX, includes provisions for—

(1) Such methods of administration (other than those relating to selection, tenure of office, and compensation of personnel) as are found by the Board to be reasonably calculated to insure full payment of unemployment compensation when due; and

(2) Payment of unemployment compensation solely through public employment offices in the State or such other agencies as the Board may approve; and

(3) Opportunity for a fair hearing, before an impartial tribunal, for all individuals whose claims for unemployment compensation are denied; and

(4) The payment of all money received in the unemployment fund of such State, immediately upon such receipt, to the Secretary of the Treasury to the credit of the Unemployment Trust Fund established by section 904; and

(5) Expenditure of all money requisitioned by the State agency from the Unemployment Trust Fund, in the payment of unemployment compensation, exclusive of expenses of administration; and

(6) The making of such reports, in such form and containing such information, as the Board may from time to time require, and compliance with such provisions as the Board may from time to time find necessary to assure the correctness and verification of such reports; and

(7) Making available upon request to any agency of the United States charged with the administration of public works or assistance through public employment, the name, address, ordinary occupation, and employment status of each recipient of unemployment compensation, and a statement of such recipient's rights to further compensation under such law.

(b) Whenever the Board, after reasonable notice and opportunity for hearing to the State agency charged with the administration of the State law finds that in the administration of the law there is—

(1) a denial, in a substantial number of cases, of unemployment compensation to individuals entitled thereto under such law; or

(2) a failure to comply substantially with any provision specified in subsection (a); the Board shall notify such State agency that further payments will not be made to the State until the Board is satisfied that there is no longer any such denial or failure to comply. Until it is so satisfied it shall make no further certification to the Secretary of the Treasury with respect to such State.

## TITLE IV
### GRANTS TO STATES FOR AID TO DEPENDENT CHILDREN
### APPROPRIATION

SECTION 401. For the purpose of enabling each State to furnish financial assistance, as far as practicable under the conditions in such State, to needy dependent children, there is hereby authorized to be appropriated for the fiscal year ending June 30, 1936, the sum of

$24,750,000, and there is hereby authorized to be appropriated for each fiscal year thereafter a sum sufficient to carry out the purposes of this title. The sums made available under this section shall be used for making payments to States which have submitted, and had approved by the Board, State plans for aid to dependent children.

STATE PLANS FOR AID TO DEPENDENT CHILDREN

SEC. 402. (a) A State plan for aid to dependent children must

(1) provide that it shall be in effect in all political subdivisions of the State, and, if administered by them, be mandatory upon them;

(2) provide for financial participation by the State;

(3) either provide for the establishment or designation of a single State agency to administer the plan, or provide for the establishment or designation of a single State agency to supervise the administration of the plan;

(4) provide for granting to any individual, whose claim with respect to aid to a dependent child is denied, an opportunity for a fair hearing before such State agency;

(5) provide such methods of administration (other than those relating to selection, tenure of office, and compensation of personnel) as are found by the Board to be necessary for the efficient operation of the plan; and

(6) provide that the State agency will make such reports, in such form and containing such information, as the Board may from time to time require, and comply with such provisions as the Board may from time to time find necessary to assure the correctness and verification of such reports.

(b) The Board shall approve any plan which fulfills the conditions specified in subsection (a) except that it shall not approve any plan which imposes as a condition of eligibility for aid to dependent children, a residence requirement which denies aid with respect to any child residing in the State

(1) who has resided in the State for one year immediately preceding the application for such aid or

(2) who was born within the State within one year immediately preceding the application, if its mother has resided in the State for one year immediately preceding the birth.

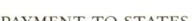

PAYMENT TO STATES

SEC. 403. (a) From the sums appropriated therefor, the Secretary of the Treasury shall pay to each State which has an approved plan for aid to dependent children, for each quarter, beginning with the quarter commencing July 1, 1935, an amount, which shall be used exclusively for carrying out the State plan, equal to one-third of the total of the sums expended during such quarter under such plan, not counting so much of such expenditure with respect to any dependent child for any month as exceeds $18, or if there is more than one dependent child in the same home, as exceeds $18 for any month with respect to one such dependent child and $12 for such month with respect to each of the other dependent children.

(b) The method of computing and paying such amounts shall be as follows:

(1) The Board shall, prior to the beginning of each quarter, estimate the amount to be paid to the State for such quarter under the provisions of subsection

(a), such estimate to be based on

(A) a report filed by the State containing its estimate of the total sum to be expended in such quarter in accordance with the provisions of such subsection and stating the amount appropriated or made available by the State and its political subdivisions for such expenditures in such quarter, and if such amount is less than two-thirds of the total sum of such estimated expenditures, the source or sources from which the difference is expected to be derived,

(B) records showing the number of dependent children in the State, and

(C) such other investigation as the Board may find necessary.

(2) The Board shall then certify to the Secretary of the Treasury the amount so estimated by the Board, reduced or increased, as the case may be, by any sum by which it finds that its estimate for any prior quarter was greater or less than the amount which should have been paid to the State for such quarter, except to the extent that such sum has been applied to make the amount certified for any prior quarter greater or less than the amount estimated by the Board for such prior quarter.

(3) The Secretary of the Treasury shall thereupon, through the Division of Disbursement of the Treasury Department and prior to

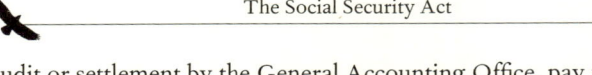

audit or settlement by the General Accounting Office, pay to the State, at the time or times fixed by the Board, the amount so certified.

OPERATION OF STATE PLANS

SEC. 404. In the case of any State plan for aid to dependent children which has been approved by the Board, if the Board, after reasonable notice and opportunity for hearing to the State agency administering or supervising the administration of such plan, finds—

(1) that the plan has been so changed as to impose any residence requirement prohibited by section 402 (b), or that in the administration of the plan any such prohibited requirement is imposed, with the knowledge of such State agency, in a substantial number of cases; or

(2) that in the administration of the plan there is a failure to comply substantially with any provision required by section 402 (a) to be included in the plan; the Board shall notify such State agency that further payments will not be made to the State until the Board is satisfied that such prohibited requirement is no longer so imposed, and that there is no longer any such failure to comply. Until it is so satisfied it shall make no further certification to the Secretary of the Treasury with respect to such State.

ADMINISTRATION

SEC. 405. There is hereby authorized to be appropriated for the fiscal year ending June 30, 1936, the sum of $250,000 for all necessary expenses of the Board in administering the provisions of this title.

DEFINITIONS

SEC. 406. When used in this title—

(a) The term dependent child means a child under the age of sixteen who has been deprived of parental support or care by reason of the death, continued absence from the home, or physical or mental incapacity of a parent, and who is living with his father, mother, grandfather, grandmother, brother, sister, stepfather, stepmother, stepbrother, stepsister, uncle, or aunt, in a place of residence maintained by one or more of such relatives as his or their own home;

(b) The term aid to dependent children means money payments with respect to a dependent child or dependent children.

# Title V
# Grants to States for Maternal and Child Welfare

## Part 1—Maternal and Child Health Services

### APPROPRIATION

SECTION 501. For the purpose of enabling each State to extend and improve, as far as practicable under the conditions in such State, services for promoting the health of mothers and children, especially in rural areas and in areas suffering from severe economic distress, there is hereby authorized to be appropriated for each fiscal year, beginning with the fiscal year ending June 30, 1936, the sum of $3,800,000. The sums made available under this section shall be used for making payments to States which have submitted, and had approved by the Chief of the Children's Bureau, State plans for such services.

### ALLOTMENTS TO STATES

SEC. 502. (a) Out of the sums appropriated pursuant to section 501 for each fiscal year the Secretary of Labor shall allot to each State $20,000, and such part of $1,800,000 as he finds that the number of live births in such State bore to the total number of live births in the United States, in the latest calendar year for which the Bureau of the Census has available statistics.

(b) Out of the sums appropriated pursuant to section 501 for each fiscal year the Secretary of Labor shall allot to the States $980,000 (in addition to the allotments made under subsection (a)), according to the financial need of each State for assistance in carrying out its State plan, as determined by him after taking into consideration the number of live births in such State.

(c) The amount of any allotment to a State under subsection (a) for any fiscal year remaining unpaid to such State at the end of such fiscal year shall be available for payment to such State under section 504 until the end of the second succeeding fiscal year. No payment to a State under section 504 shall be made out of its allotment for any fiscal year until its allotment for the preceding fiscal year has been exhausted or has ceased to be available.

### APPROVAL OF STATE PLANS

SEC. 503. (a) A State plan for maternal and child-health services

must (1) provide for financial participation by the State;

(2) provide for the administration of the plan by the State health agency or the supervision of the administration of the plan by the State health agency;

(3) provide such methods of administration (other than those relating to selection, tenure of office, and compensation of personnel) as are necessary for the efficient operation of the plan;

(4) provide that the State health agency will make such reports, in such form and containing such information, as the Secretary of Labor may from time to time require, and comply with such provisions as he may from time to time find necessary to assure the correctness and verification of such reports;

(5) provide for the extension and improvement of local maternal and child-health services administered by local child health units;

(6) provide for cooperation with medical, nursing, and welfare groups and organizations; and

(7) provide for the development of demonstration services in needy areas and among groups in special need.

(b) The Chief of the Children's Bureau shall approve any plan which fulfills the conditions specified in subsection (a) and shall thereupon notify the Secretary of Labor and the State health agency of his approval.

PAYMENT TO STATES

Sec. 504. (a) From the sums appropriate therefor and the allotments available under section 502 (a), the Secretary of the Treasury shall pay to each State which has an approved plan for maternal and child-health services, for each quarter beginning with the quarter commencing July 1935, an amount, which shall be used exclusively for carrying out the State plan, equal to one-half of the total sum expended during such quarter for carrying out such plan.

(b) The method of computing and paying such amounts shall be as follows:

(1) The Secretary of Labor shall, prior the beginning of each quarter, estimate the amount to be paid to the State for such quarter under the provisions of subsection (a), such estimate to be based on

(A) a report filed by the State containing its estimate of the total sum to be expended in such quarter in accordance with the provisions of such subsection and stating the amount appropriated or made available by the State and its political subdivisions for such expenditures in such quarter, and if such amount is less than one-half of the total sum of such estimated expenditures, the source or sources from which the difference is expected to be derived, and

(B) such investigation as he may find necessary.

(2) The Secretary of Labor shall then certify the amount so estimated by him to the Secretary of the Treasury, reduced or increased, as the case may be, by any sum by which the Secretary of Labor finds that his estimate for any prior quarter was greater or less than the amount, which should have been paid to the State for such quarter, except to the extent that such sum has been applied to make the amount certified for any prior quarter greater or less than the amount, estimated by the Secretary of Labor for such prior quarter.

(3) The Secretary of the Treasury shall thereupon, through the Division of Disbursement of the Treasury Department and prior to audit or settlement by the General Accounting Office, pay to the State, at the time or times fixed by the Secretary of Labor, the amount so certified.

(c) The Secretary of Labor shall from time to time certify to the Secretary of the Treasury the amounts to be paid to the States from the allotments available under section 502 (b), and the Secretary of the Treasury shall, through the Division of Disbursement of the Treasury Department and prior to audit or settlement by the General Accounting Office, make payments of such amounts from such allotments at the time or times specified by the Secretary of Labor.

OPERATION OF STATE PLANS

SEC. 505. In the case of any State plan for maternal and child-health services which has been approved by the Chief of the Children's Bureau, if the Secretary of Labor, after reasonable notice and opportunity for hearing to the State agency administering or supervising the administration of such plan, finds that in the administration of the plan there is a failure to comply substantially with any provision required by section 503 to be included in the plan, he shall notify such State agency that further payments will not be made to the State until he is satisfied that there is no longer any such failure to comply. Until he is so satisfied he shall make no further certification to the Secretary of the Treasury with respect to such State.

## PART 2—SERVICES FOR CRIPPLED CHILDREN

### APPROPRIATION

SEC. 511. For the purpose of enabling each State to extend and improve (especially in rural areas and in areas suffering from severe economic distress), as far as practicable under the conditions in such State, services for locating crippled children and for providing medical, surgical, corrective, and other services and care, and facilities for diagnosis, hospitalization, and aftercare, for children who are crippled or who are suffering from conditions which lead to crippling, there is hereby authorized to be appropriated for each fiscal year beginning with the fiscal year ending June 30, 1936, the sum of $2,850,000. The sums made available under this section shall be used for making payments to States which have submitted, and had approved by the Chief of the Children's Bureau, State plans for such services.

### ALLOTMENTS TO STATES

SEC. 512. (a) Out of the sums appropriated pursuant to section 511 for each fiscal year the Secretary of Labor shall allot to each State $20,000, and the remainder to the States according to the need of each State as determined by him after taking into consideration the number of crippled children in such State in need of the services referred to section 511 and the cost of furnishing such service to them

(b) The amount of any allotment to a State under subsection (a) for any fiscal year remaining unpaid to such State at the end of such fiscal year shall be available for payment to such State under section 514 until the end of the second succeeding fiscal year. No payment to a State under section 514 shall be made out of its allotment for any fiscal year until its allotment for the preceding fiscal year has been exhausted or has ceased to be available.

### APPROVAL OF STATE PLANS

SEC. 513. (a) A State plan for services for crippled children must

(1) provide for financial participation by the State;

(2) provide for the administration of the plan by a State agency or the supervision of the administration of the plan by a State agency;

(3) provide such methods of administration (other than those relating to selection, tenure of office, and compensation of personnel) as are necessary for the efficient operation of the plan;

(4) provide that the State agency will make such reports, in such form and containing such information, as the Secretary of Labor may from time to time require, and comply with such provisions as he may from time to time find necessary to assure the correctness and verification of such reports;

(5) provide for carrying out the purposes specified in section 511; and

(6) provide for cooperation with medical, health, nursing, and welfare groups and organizations and with any agency in such State charged with administering State laws providing for vocational rehabilitation of physically handicapped children.

(b) The Chief of the Children's Bureau shall approve any plan which fulfills the conditions specified in subsection (a) and shall thereupon notify the Secretary of Labor and the State agency of his approval.

PAYMENT TO STATES

Sec. 514. (a) From the sums appropriated therefor and the allotments available under section 512, the Secretary of the Treasury shall pay to each State which has an approved plan for services for crippled children, for each quarter, beginning the quarter commencing July 1, 1935, an amount which shall be used exclusively for carrying out the State plan, equal to one-half of the total sum expended during such quarter for carrying out such plan.

(b) The method of computing and paying such amounts shall be as follows:

(1) The Secretary of Labor shall, prior the beginning of each quarter, estimate the amount to be paid to the State for such quarter under the provisions of subsection (a), such estimate to be based on

(A) a report filed by the State containing its estimate of the total sum to be expended in such quarter in accordance with the provisions of such subsection and stating the amount appropriated or made available by the State and its political subdivisions for such expenditures in such quarter and if such amount is less than one-half of the total sum of such estimated expenditures the source or sources from which the difference is expected to be derived, and

(B) such investigation as he may find necessary.

(2) The Secretary of Labor shall then certify the amount so estimated by him to the Secretary of the Treasury, reduced or increased as the

case may be, by any sum by which the Secretary of Labor finds that his estimate for any prior quarter was greater or less than the amount which should have been paid to the State for such quarter, except to the extent that such sum has been applied to make the amount certified for any prior quarter greater or less than the amount estimated by the Secretary of Labor for such prior quarter.

(3) The Secretary of the Treasury shall thereupon, through the Division of Disbursement of the Treasury Department and prior to audit or settlement by the General Accounting Office, pay to the State, at the time or times fixed by the Secretary of Labor, the amount so certified.

OPERATION OF STATE PLANS

SEC. 515. In the case of any State plan for services for crippled children which has been approved by the Chief of the Children's Bureau, if the Secretary of Labor, after reasonable notice and opportunity for hearing to the State agency administering or supervising the administration of such plan finds that in the administration of the plan there a failure to comply substantially with any provision required by section 513 to be included in the plan, he shall notify such State agency that further payments will not be made to the State until he is satisfied that there is no longer any such failure to comply. Until he is so satisfied he shall make no further certification to the Secretary of the Treasury with respect to such State.

PART 3—CHILD WELFARE SERVICES

SEC. 521. (a) For the purpose of enabling the United States, through the Children's Bureau, to cooperate with State public-welfare agencies establishing, extending, and strengthening, especially in predominantly rural areas, public-welfare services (hereinafter in this section referred to as child-welfare services ) for the protection and care of homeless, dependent, and neglected children, and children in danger of becoming delinquent, there is hereby authorized to be appropriated for each fiscal year, beginning with the year ending June 30, 1936, the sum of $1,500,000. Such amount shall be allotted by the Secretary of Labor for use by cooperating State public-welfare agencies on the basis of plans developed jointly by the State agency and the Children's Bureau, to each State, $10,000, and the remainder to each State on the basis of such plans, not to exceed such part of the remainder as the rural population of such State bears to the total rural population of the United States. The amount so allotted shall be expended for payment of part of the cost of district, county or other local child-welfare services in areas predominantly rural, and for developing State services for the encouragement and assistance of adequate methods of community child-welfare organization in areas predominantly rural and other areas of special need. The amount of any allotment to a State under this section for any fiscal year remaining unpaid to such State at the end of such fiscal year shall be available for payment to such State under this section until the end of the second succeeding fiscal year. No payment to a State under this section shall be made out of its allotment for any fiscal year until its allotment for the preceding fiscal year has been exhausted or has ceased to be available.

(b) From the sums appropriated therefor and the allotments available under subsection (a) the Secretary of Labor shall from time to time certify to the Secretary of the Treasury the amounts to be paid to the States, and the Secretary of the Treasury shall, through the Division of Disbursement of the Treasury Department and prior to audit or settlement by the General Accounting Office, make payments of such amounts from such allotments at the time or times specified by the Secretary of Labor.

PART 4—VOCATIONAL REHABILITATION

SEC. 531. (a) In order to enable the United States to cooperate with the States and Hawaii in extending and strengthening their programs of vocational rehabilitation of the physically disabled, and to continue to carry out the provisions and purposes of the Act entitled An Act to provide for the promotion of vocational rehabilitation of persons disabled in industry or otherwise and their return to civil employment, approved June 2, 1920, as amended (U.S.C., title 29, ch. 4; U.S.C., Supp. VII title 29, secs. 31, 32, 34, 35, 37, 39, and 40), there is hereby authorized to be appropriated for the fiscal years ending June 30, 1936, and June 30, 1937, the sum of $841,000 for each such fiscal year in addition to the amount of the existing authorization, and for each fiscal year thereafter the sum of $1,938,000. Of the sums appropriated pursuant to such authorization for each fiscal year, $5,000 shall be apportioned to the Territory of Hawaii and the remainder shall be apportioned among the several States in the manner provided in such Act of June 2, 1920, as amended.

(b) For the administration of such Act of June 2, 1920, as amended, by the Federal agency authorized to administer it, there is hereby authorized to be appropriated for the fiscal years ending June 30, 1936, and June 30, 1937, the sum of $22,000 for each such fiscal year in addition to the amount of the existing authorization, and for each fiscal year thereafter the sum of $102,000.

PART 5—ADMINISTRATION

SEC. 541. (a) There is hereby authorized to be appropriated for the fiscal year ending June 30, 1936, the sum of $425,000, for all necessary expenses of the Children's Bureau in administering the provisions of this title, except section 531.

(b) The Children's Bureau shall make such studies and investigations as will promote the efficient administration of this title, except section 531.

(c) The Secretary of Labor shall include in his annual report to Congress a full account of the administration of this title, except section 531.

## TITLE VI
## PUBLIC HEALTH WORK APPROPRIATION

SECTION 601. For the purpose of assisting States, counties, health districts, and other political subdivisions of the States in establishing and maintaining adequate public-health services, including the training of personnel for State and local health work, there is hereby authorized to be appropriated for each fiscal year, beginning with the fiscal year ending June 30, 1936, the sum of $8,000,000 to be used as hereinafter provided.

STATE AND LOCAL PUBLIC HEALTH SERVICES

SEC. 602. (a) The Surgeon General of the Public Health Service, with the approval of the Secretary of the Treasury, shall, at the beginning of each fiscal year, allot to the States the total of (1) the amount appropriated for such year pursuant to section 601; and (2) the amounts of the allotments under this section for the preceding fiscal year remaining unpaid to the States at the end of such fiscal year. The amounts of such allotments shall be determined on the basis of (1) the population; (2) the special health problems; and (3) the financial needs; of the respective States. Upon making such allotments the Surgeon General of the Public Health Service shall certify the amounts thereof to the Secretary of the Treasury.

(b) The amount of an allotment to any State under subsection (a) for any fiscal year, remaining unpaid at the end of such fiscal year, shall be available for allotment to States under subsection (a) for the succeeding fiscal year, in addition to the amount appropriated for such year.

(c) Prior to the beginning of each quarter of the fiscal year, the Surgeon General of the Public Health Service shall, with the approval of the Secretary of the Treasury, determine in accordance with rules and regulations previously prescribed by such Surgeon General after consultation with a conference of the State and Territorial health authorities, the amount to be paid to each State for such quarter from the allotment to such State, and shall certify the amount so determined to the Secretary of the Treasury. Upon receipt of such certification, the Secretary of the Treasury shall, through the Division of Disbursement of the Treasury Department and prior to audit or settlement by the General Accounting Office, pay in accordance with such certification.

(d) The moneys so paid to any State shall be expended solely in carrying out the purposes specified in section 601, and in accordance with plans presented by the health authority of such State and approved by the Surgeon General of the Public Health Service.

INVESTIGATIONS

SEC. 603. (a) There is hereby authorized to be appropriated for each fiscal year, beginning with the fiscal year ending June 30, 1936, the sum of $2,000,000 for expenditure by the Public Health Service for investigation of disease and problems of sanitation (including the printing and binding of the findings of such investigations), and for the pay and allowances and traveling expenses of personnel of the Public Health Service, including commissioned officers, engaged in such investigations or detailed to cooperate with the health authorities of any State in carrying out the purposes specified in section 601: Provided, That no personnel of the Public Health Service shall be detailed to cooperate with the health authorities of any State except at the request of the proper authorities of such State.

(b) The personnel of the Public Health Service paid from any appropriation not made pursuant to subsection (a) may be detailed to assist in carrying out the purposes of this title. The appropriation from which they are paid shall be reimbursed from the appropriation made pursuant to subsection (a) to the extent of their salaries and allowances for services performed while so detailed.

(c) The Secretary of the Treasury shall include in his annual report to Congress a full account of the administration of this title.

# Title VII
## Social Security Board Establishment

SECTION 701. There is hereby established a Social Security Board (in this Act referred to as the Board ) to be composed of three members to be appointed by the President, by and with the advice and consent of the Senate. During his term of membership on the Board , no member shall engage in any other business, vocation, or employment. Not more than two of the members of the Board shall be members of the same political party. Each member shall receive a salary at the rate of $10,000 a year and shall hold office for a term of six years, except that

(1) any member appointed to fill a vacancy occurring prior to the expiration of the term for which his predecessor was appointed, shall be appointed for the remainder of such term; and

(2) the terms of office of the members first taking office after the date of the enactment of this Act shall expire, as designated by the President at the time of appointment, one at the end of two years, one at the end of four years, and one at the end of six years, after the date of the enactment of this Act. The President shall designate one of the members as the chairman of the Board.

DUTIES OF THE SOCIAL SECURITY BOARD

SEC. 702. The Board shall perform the duties imposed upon it by this Act and shall also have the duty of studying and making recommendations as to the most effective methods of providing economic security through social insurance, and as to legislation and matters of administrative policy concerning old-age pensions, unemployment compensation, accident compensation, and related subjects.

EXPENSES OF THE BOARD

SEC. 703. The Board is authorized to appoint and fix the compensation of such officers and employees, and to make such expenditures, as may be necessary for carrying out its functions under this Act. Appointments of attorneys and experts may be made without regard to the civil-service laws.

REPORTS

SEC. 704. The Board shall make a full report to Congress, at the beginning of each regular session, of the administration of the functions with which it is charged.

# TITLE VIII
## TAXES WITH RESPECT TO EMPLOYMENT

INCOME TAX ON EMPLOYEES

SECTION 801. In addition to other taxes, there shall be levied, collected, and paid upon the income of every individual a tax equal to the following percentages of the wages (as defined in section 811) received by him after December 31, 1936, with respect to employment (as defined in section 811) after such date:

(1) With respect to employment during the calendar years 1937, 1938, and 1939, the rate shall be 1 per centum.

(2) With respect to employment during the calendar years 1940, 1941, and 1942, the rate shall 1 « per centum.

(3) With respect to employment during the calendar years 1943, 1944, and 1945, the rate shall be 2 per centum.

(4) With respect to employment during the calendar years 1946, 1947, and 1948, the rate shall be 2 « per centum.

(5) With respect to employment after December 31, 1948, the rate shall be 3 per centum.

DEDUCTION OF TAX FROM WAGES

SEC. 802. (a) The tax imposed by section 801 shall be collected by the employer of the taxpayer by deducting the amount of the tax from the wages as and when paid. Every employer required so to deduct the tax is hereby made liable for the payment of such tax, and is hereby indemnified against the claims and demands of any person for the amount of any such payment made by such employer.

(b) If more or less than the correct amount of tax imposed by section 801 is paid with respect to any wage payment, then, under regulations made under this title, proper adjustments, with respect both to the tax and the amount to be deducted, shall be made, without interest, in connection with subsequent wage payments to the same individual by the same employer.

DEDUCTIBILITY FROM INCOME TAX

SEC. 803. For the purposes of the income tax imposed by Title I of the Revenue Act of 1934 or by any Act of Congress in substitution therefor, the tax imposed by section 801 shall not be allowed as a deduction to the taxpayer in computing his net income for the year in which such tax is deducted from his wages.

EXCISE TAX ON EMPLOYERS

SEC. 804. In addition to other taxes, every employer shall pay an excise tax, with respect to having individuals in his employ, equal to the following percentages of the wages (as defined in section 811) paid by him after December 31, 1936, with respect to employment (as defined in section 811) after such date:

(1) With respect to employment during the calendar years 1937, 1938, and 1939, the rate shall be 1 per centum.

(2) With respect to employment during the calendar years 1940, 1941, and 1942, the rate shall be 1 « per centum.

(3) With respect to employment during the calendar years 1943, 1944, and 1945, the rate shall be 2 per centum.

(4) With respect to employment during the calendar years 1946, 1947, and 1948, the rate shall be 2 « per centum.

(5) With respect to employment after December 31, 1948, the rate shall be 3 per centum.

ADJUSTMENT OF EMPLOYERS TAX

SEC. 805. If more or less than the correct amount of tax imposed by section 804 is paid with respect to any wage payment, then, under regulations made under this title, proper adjustments with respect the tax shall be made, without interest, in connection with subsequent wage payments to the same individual by the same employer.

REFUNDS AND DEFICIENCIES

SEC. 806. If more or less than the correct amount of tax imposed by section 801 or 804 is paid or deducted with respect to any wage payment and the overpayment or underpayment of tax cannot be adjusted under section 802 (b) or 805 the amount of the overpayment shall be refunded and the amount of the underpayment shall be collected in such manner and at such times (subject to the statutes of limitations properly applicable thereto) as may be prescribed by regulations made under this title.

COLLECTION AND PAYMENT OF TAXES

SEC. 807. (a) The taxes imposed by this title shall be collected by the Bureau of Internal Revenue under the direction of the Secretary of the Treasury and shall be paid into the Treasury of the United States as internal-revenue collections. If the tax is not paid when due, there shall be added as part of the tax interest (except in the case of adjustments made in accordance with the provisions of sections 802 (b) and 805) at the rate of one-half of 1 per centum per month from the date the tax became due until paid.

(b) Such taxes shall be collected and paid in such manner, at such times, and under such conditions, not inconsistent with this title (either by making and filing returns, or by stamps, coupons, tickets, books, or other reasonable devices or methods necessary or helpful in securing a complete and proper collection and payment of the tax or in securing proper identification of the taxpayer), as may be prescribed by the Commissioner of Internal Revenue, with the approval of the Secretary of the Treasury.

(c) All provisions of law, including penalties, applicable with respect to any tax imposed by section 600 or section 800 of the Revenue Act of 1926 and the provisions of section 607 of the Revenue Act of 1934, shall, insofar as applicable and not inconsistent with the provisions of this title, be applicable with respect to the taxes imposed by this title.

(d) In the payment of any tax under this title a fractional part of a cent shall be disregarded unless it amounts to one-half cent or more, in which case it shall be increased to 1 cent.

RULES AND REGULATIONS

SEC. 808. The Commissioner of Internal Revenue, with the approval

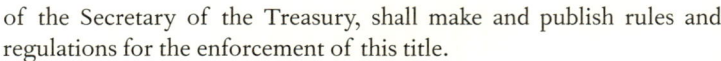 

of the Secretary of the Treasury, shall make and publish rules and regulations for the enforcement of this title.

SALE OF STAMPS BY POSTMASTERS

SEC. 809. The Commissioner of Internal Revenue shall furnish to the Postmaster General without prepayment a suitable quantity of stamps, coupons, tickets, books, or other devices prescribed by the Commissioner under SECTION 807 for the collection or payment of any tax imposed by this title, to be distributed to, and kept on sale by, all post offices of the first and second classes, and such post offices of the third and fourth classes as

(1) are located in county seats, or

(2) are certified by the Secretary of the Treasury to the Postmaster General as necessary to the proper administration of this title. The Postmaster General may require each such postmaster to furnish bond in such increased amount as he may from time to time determine, and each such postmaster shall deposit the receipts from the sale of such stamps, coupons, tickets, books, or other devices, to the credit of, and render accounts to, the Postmaster General at such times and in such form as the Postmaster General may by regulations prescribe. The Postmaster General shall at least once a month transfer to the Treasury, as internal-revenue collections all receipts so deposited together with a statement of the additional expenditures in the District of Columbia and elsewhere incurred by the Post Office Department in performing the duties imposed upon said Department by this Act, and the Secretary of the Treasury is hereby authorized and directed to advance from time to time to the credit of the Post Office Department from appropriations made for the collection of the taxes imposed by this title, such sums as may be required for such additional expenditures incurred by the Post Office Department.

PENALTIES

SEC. 810. (a) Whoever buys, sells, offers for sale, uses, transfers, takes or gives in exchange, or pledges or gives in pledge, except as authorized in this title or in regulations made pursuant thereto, any stamp, coupon, ticket, book, or other device, prescribed by the Commissioner of Internal Revenue under section 807 for the collection or payment of any tax imposed by this title, shall be fined not more than $1,000 or imprisoned for not more than six months, or both.

(b) Whoever, with intent to defraud, alters, forges, makes, or counterfeits any stamp, coupon, ticket, book, or other device prescribed by the Commissioner of Internal Revenue under section 807 for the collection or payment of any tax imposed by this title, or uses, sells, lends, or has in his possession any such altered, forged, or counterfeited stamp, coupon, ticket, book, or other device, or makes, uses, sells, or has in his possession any material in imitation of the material used in the manufacture of such stamp, coupon, ticket, book, or other device, shall be fined not more than $5,000 or imprisoned not more than five years, or both.

DEFINITIONS

SEC. 811. When used in this title- (a) The term wages means all remuneration for employment, including the cash value of all remuneration paid in any medium other than cash; except that such term shall not include that part of the remuneration which, after remuneration equal to $3,000 has been paid to an individual by an employer with respect to employment during any calendar year, is paid to such individual by such employer with respect to employment during such calendar year.

(b) The term employment means any service, of whatever nature, performed within the United States by an employee for his employer, except—

(1) Agricultural labor;

(2) Domestic service in a private home;

(3) Casual labor not in the course of the employer's trade or business;

(4) Service performed by an individual who has attained the age of sixty-five;

(5) Service performed as an officer or member of the crew of a vessel documented under the laws of the United States or of any foreign country;

(6) Service performed in the employ of the United States Government or of an instrumentality of the United States;

(7) Service performed in the employ of a State, a political subdivision thereof, or an instrumentality of one or more States or political subdivisions;

(8) Service performed in the employ of a corporation, community chest, fund, or foundation, organized and operated exclusively for

religious, charitable, scientific, literary, or educational purposes, or for the prevention of cruelty to children or animals, no part of the net earnings of which inures to the benefit of any private shareholder or individual.

# TITLE IX
## TAX ON EMPLOYERS OF EIGHT OR MORE

IMPOSITION OF TAX

SECTION 901. On and after January 1, 1936, every employer (as defined in section 907) shall pay for each calendar year an excise tax, with respect to having individuals in his employ, equal to the following percentages of the total wages (as defined in section 907) payable by him (regardless of the time of payment) with respect to employment (as defined in section 907) during such calendar year:

(1) With respect to employment during the calendar year 1936 the rate shall be 1 per centum;

(2) With respect to employment during the calendar year 1937 the rate shall be 2 per centum;

(3) With respect to employment after December 31, 1937, the rate shall be 3 per centum.

CREDIT AGAINST TAX

SEC. 902. The taxpayer may credit against the tax imposed by section 901 the amount of contributions, with respect to employment during the taxable year, paid by him (before the date of filing of his return for the taxable year) into an unemployment fund under a State law. The total credit allowed to a taxpayer under this section for all contributions paid into unemployment funds with respect to employment during such taxable year shall not exceed 90 per centum of the tax against which it is credited, and credit shall be allowed only for contributions made under the laws of States certified for the taxable year as provided in section 903.

CERTIFICATION OF STATE LAWS

SEC. 903 (a) The Social Security Board shall approve any State law submitted to it, within thirty days of such submission, which it finds provides that—

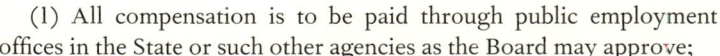

(1) All compensation is to be paid through public employment offices in the State or such other agencies as the Board may approve;

(2) No compensation shall be payable with respect to any day of unemployment occurring within two years after the first day of the first period with respect to which contributions are required;

(3) All money received in the unemployment fund shall immediately upon such receipt be paid over to the Secretary of the Treasury to the credit of the Unemployment Trust Fund established by section 904;

(4) All money withdrawn from the Unemployment Trust Fund by the State agency shall be used solely in the payment of compensation, exclusive of expenses of administration;

(5) Compensation shall not be denied in such State to any otherwise eligible individual for refusing to accept new work under any of the following conditions:

(A) If the position offered is vacant due directly to a strike, lockout, or other labor dispute;

(B) if the wages, hours, or other conditions of the work offered are substantially less favorable to the individual than those prevailing for similar work in the locality;

(C) if as a condition of being employed the individual would be required to join a company union or to resign from or refrain from joining any bona-fide labor organization;

(6) All the rights, privileges, or immunities conferred by such law or by acts done pursuant thereto shall exist subject to the power of the legislature to amend or repeal such law at any time. The Board shall, upon approving such law, notify the Governor of the State of its approval.

(b) On December 31 in each taxable year the Board shall certify to the Secretary of the Treasury each State whose law it has previously approved, except that it shall not certify any State which, after reasonable notice and opportunity for hearing to the State agency, the Board finds has changed its law so that it no longer contains the provisions specified in subsection (a) or has with respect to such taxable year failed to comply substantially with any such provision.

(c) If, at any time during the taxable year, the Board has reason to believe that a State whose law it has previously approved, may not be certified under subsection (b), it shall promptly so notify the Governor of such State.

UNEMPLOYMENT TRUST FUND

Sec. 904. (a) There is hereby established in the Treasury of the United States a trust fund to be known as the Unemployment Trust Fund , hereinafter in this title called the Fund. The Secretary of the Treasury is authorized and directed to receive and hold in the Fund all moneys deposited therein by a State agency from a State unemployment fund. Such deposit may be made directly with the Secretary of the Treasury or with any Federal reserve bank or member bank of the Federal Reserve System designated by him for such purpose.

(b) It shall be the duty of the Secretary of the Treasury to invest such portion of the Fund as is not, in his judgment, required to meet current withdrawals. Such investment may be made only in interest-bearing obligations of the United States or in obligations guaranteed as to both principal and interest by the United States. For such purpose such obligations may be acquired

(1) on original issue at par, or

(2) by purchase of outstanding obligations at the market price. The purposes for which obligations of the United States may be is- sued under the Second Liberty Bond Act, as amended, are hereby extended to authorize the issuance at par of special obligations exclusively to the Fund. Such special obligations shall bear interest at a rate equal to the average rate of interest, computed as of the end of the calendar month next preceding the date of such issue, borne by all interest-bearing obligations of the United States then forming part of the public debt; except that where such average rate is not a multiple of one eighth of 1 per centum, the rate of interest of such special obligations shall be the multiple of one-eighth of 1 per centum next lower than such average rate. Obligations other than such special obligations may be acquired for the Fund only on such terms as to provide an investment yield not less than the yield which would be required in the case of special obligations if issued to the Fund upon the date of such acquisition.

(c) Any obligations acquired by the Fund (except special obligations issued exclusively to the Fund) may be sold at the market price, and such special obligations may be redeemed at par plus accrued interest.

(d) The interest on, and the proceeds from the sale or redemption of, any obligations held in the Fund shall be credited to and form a part of the Fund.

(e) The Fund shall be invested as a single fund, but the Secretary of the Treasury shall maintain a separate book account for each State agency and shall credit quarterly on March 31, June 30, September 30, and December 31, of each year, to each account, on the basis of the average daily balance of such account, a proportionate part of the earnings of the Fund for the quarter ending on such date.

(f) The Secretary of the Treasury is authorized and directed to pay out of the Fund to any State agency such amount as it may duly requisition, not exceeding the amount standing to the account of such State agency at the time of such payment.

ADMINISTRATION, REFUNDS, AND PENALTIES

SEC. 905. (a) The tax imposed by this title shall be collected by the Bureau of Internal Revenue under the direction of the Secretary of the Treasury and shall be paid into the Treasury of the United States as internal-revenue collections. If the tax is not paid when due, there shall be added as part of the tax interest at the rate of one-half of 1 per centum per month from the date the tax became due until paid.

(b) Not later than January 31, next following the close of the taxable year, each employer shall make a return of the tax under this title for such taxable year. Each such return shall be made under oath, shall be filed with the collector of internal revenue for the district in which is located the principal place of business of the employer, or, if he has no principal place of business in the United States, then with the collector at Baltimore, Maryland, and shall contain such information and be made in such manner as the Commissioner of Internal Revenue, with the approval of the Secretary of the Treasury, may by regulations prescribe. All provisions of law (including penalties) applicable in respect of the taxes imposed by section 600 of the Revenue Act of 1926, shall, insofar as not inconsistent with this title, be applicable in respect of the tax imposed by this title. The Commissioner may extend the time for filing the return of the tax imposed by this title, under such rules and regulations as he may prescribe with the approval of the Secretary of the Treasury, but no such extension shall be for more than sixty days.

(c) Returns filed under this title shall be open to inspection in the same manner, to the same extent, and subject to the same provisions of law, including penalties, as returns made under Title II of the Revenue Act of 1926.

(d) The taxpayer may elect to pay the tax in four equal installments instead of in a single payment, in which case the first installment shall be paid not later than the last day prescribed for the filing of returns, the second installment shall be paid on or before the last day of the third month, the third installment on or before the last day of the sixth month, and the fourth installment on or before the last day of the ninth month, after such last day. If the tax or any installment thereof is not paid on or before the last day of the period fixed for its payment, the whole amount of the tax unpaid shall be paid upon notice and demand from the collector.

(e) At the request of the taxpayer the time for payment of the tax or any installment thereof may be extended under regulations prescribed by the Commissioner with the approval of the Secretary of the Treasury, for a period not to exceed six months from the last day of the period prescribed for the payment of the tax or any installment thereof. The amount of the tax in respect of which any extension is granted shall be paid (with interest at the rate of one-half of 1 per centum per month) on or before the date of the expiration of the period of the extension.

(f) In the payment of any tax under this title a fractional part of a cent shall be disregarded unless it amounts to one-half cent or more, in which case it shall be increased to 1 cent.

INTERSTATE COMMERCE

Sec. 906. No person required under a State law to make payments to an unemployment fund shall be relieved from compliance therewith on the ground that he is engaged in interstate commerce, or that the State law does not distinguish between employees engaged in interstate commerce and those engaged in intrastate commerce.

DEFINITIONS

Sec. 907. When used in this title — (a) The term employer does not include any person unless on each of some twenty days during the taxable year, each day being in a different calendar week, the total number of individuals who were in his employ for some portion of the day (whether or not at the same moment of time) was eight or more.

(b) The term wages means all remuneration for employment, including the cash value of all remuneration paid in any medium other than cash.

(c) The term employment means any service, of whatever nature, performed within the United States by an employee for his employer, except—

(1) Agricultural labor;

(2) Domestic service in a private home;

(3) Service performed as an officer or member of a crew of a vessel on the navigable waters of the United States;

(4) Service performed by an individual in the employ of his son, daughter, or spouse, and service performed by a child under the age of twenty-one in the employ of his father or mother;

(5) Service performed in the employ of the United States Government or of an instrumentality of the United States;

(6) Service performed in the employ of a State, a political subdivision thereof, or an instrumentality of one or more States or political subdivisions;

(7) Service performed in the employ of a corporation, community chest, fund, or foundation, organized and operated exclusively for religious, charitable, scientific, literary, or educational purposes, or for the prevention of cruelty to children or animals, no part of the net earnings of which inures to the benefit of any private shareholder or individual.

(d) The term State agency means any State officer, board, or other authority, designated under a State law to administer the unemployment fund in such State.

(e) The term unemployment fund means a special fund, established under a State law and administered by a State agency, for the payment of compensation.

(f) The term contributions means payments required by a State law to be made by an employer into an unemployment fund, to the extent that such payments are made by him without any part thereof being deducted or deductible from the wages of individuals in his employ.

(g) The term compensation means cash benefits payable to individuals with respect to their unemployment.

RULES AND REGULATIONS

Sec. 908. The Commissioner of Internal Revenue, with the approval of the Secretary of the Treasury, shall make and publish rules and regulations for the enforcement of this title, except sections 903, 904, and 910.

ALLOWANCE OF ADDITIONAL CREDIT

SEC. 909. (a) In addition to the credit allowed under section 902, a taxpayer may, subject to the conditions imposed by section 910, credit against the tax imposed by section 901 for any taxable year after the taxable year 1937, an amount, with respect to each State law, equal to the amount, if any, by which the contributions, with respect to employment in such taxable year, actually paid by the taxpayer under such law before the date of filing his return for such taxable year, is exceeded by whichever of the following is the lesser— (1) The amount of contributions which he would have been required to pay under such law for such taxable year if he had been subject to the highest rate applicable from time to time throughout such year to any employer under such law; or (2) Two and seven-tenths per centum of the wages payable by him with respect to employment with respect to which contributions for such year were required under such law.

(b) If the amount of the contributions actually so paid by the taxpayer is less than the amount which he should have paid under the State law, the additional credit under subsection (a) shall be reduced proportionately.

(c) The total credits allowed to a taxpayer under this title shall not exceed 90 per centum of the tax against which such credits are taken.

CONDITIONS OF ADDITIONAL CREDIT ALLOWANCE

SEC. 910. (a) A taxpayer shall be allowed the additional credit under section 909, with respect to his contribution rate under a State law being lower, for any taxable year, than that of another employer subject to such law, only if the Board finds that under such law—

(1) Such lower rate, with respect to contributions to a pooled fund, is permitted on the basis of not less than three years of compensation experience;

(2) Such lower rate, with respect to contributions to a guaranteed employment account, is permitted only when his guaranty of employment was fulfilled in the preceding calendar year, and such guaranteed employment account amounts to not less than 7 « per centum of the total wages payable by him, in accordance with such guaranty, with respect to employment in such State in the preceding calendar year;

(3) Such lower rate, with respect to contributions to a separate reserve account, is permitted only when

(A) compensation has been payable from such account throughout the preceding calendar year, and

(B) such account amounts to not less than five times the largest amount of compensation paid from such account within any one of the three preceding calendar years, and

(C) such account amounts to not less than 7 « per centum of the total wages payable by him (plus the total wages payable by any other employers who may be contributing to such account) with respect to employment in such State in the preceding calendar year.

(b) Such additional credit shall be reduced, if any contributions under such law are made by such taxpayer at a lower rate under conditions not fulfilling the requirements of subsection (a), by the amount bearing the same ratio to such additional credit as the amount of contributions made at such lower rate bears to the total of his contributions paid for such year under such law.

(c) As used in this section—

(1) The term reserve account means a separate account in an unemployment fund, with respect to an employer or group of employers, from which compensation is payable only with respect to the unemployment of individuals who were in the employ of such employer, or of one of the employers comprising the group.

(2) The term pooled fund means an unemployment fund or any part thereof in which all contributions are mingled and undivided, and from which compensation is payable to all eligible individuals, except that to individuals last employed by employers with respect to whom reserve accounts are maintained by the State agency, it is payable only when such accounts are exhausted.

(3) The term guaranteed employment account means a separate account, in an unemployment fund, of contributions paid by an employer (or group of employers) who

(A) guarantees in advance thirty hours of wages for each of forty calendar weeks (or more, with one weekly hour deducted for each added week guaranteed) in twelve months, to all the individuals in his employ in one or more distinct establishments, except that any such individual's guaranty may commence after a probationary period (included within twelve or less consecutive calendar weeks). and

(B) gives security or assurance, satisfactory to the State agency, for the fulfillment of such guaranties, from which account compensation

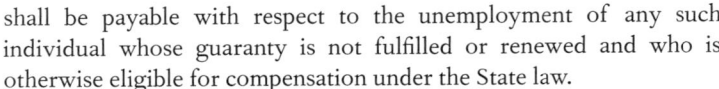
shall be payable with respect to the unemployment of any such individual whose guaranty is not fulfilled or renewed and who is otherwise eligible for compensation under the State law.

(4) The term year of compensation experience , as applied to an employer, means any calendar year throughout which compensation was payable with respect to any individual in his employ who became unemployed and was eligible for compensation.

## TITLE X
### GRANTS TO STATES FOR AID TO THE BLIND
### APPROPRIATION

SECTION 1001. For the purpose of enabling each State to furnish financial assistance, as far as practicable under the conditions in such State, to needy individuals who are blind, there is hereby authorized to be appropriated for the fiscal year ending June 30, 1936, the sum of $3,000,000, and there is hereby authorized to be appropriated for each fiscal year thereafter a sum sufficient to carry out the purposes of this title. The sums made available under this section shall be used for making payments to States which have submitted, and had approved by the Social Security Board, State plans for aid to the blind.

STATE PLANS FOR AID TO THE BLIND

SEC. 1002. (a) A State plan for aid to the blind must

(1) provide that it shall be in effect in all political subdivisions of the State, and, if administered by them, be mandatory upon them;

(2) provide for financial participation by the State;

(3) either provide for the establishment or designation of a single State agency to administer the plan, or provide for the establishment or designation of a single State agency to supervise the administration of the plan;

(4) provide for granting to any individual, whose claim for aid is denied, an opportunity for a fair hearing before such State agency;

(5) provide such methods of administration (other than those relating to selection, tenure of office, and compensation of personnel) as are found by the Board to be necessary for the efficient operation of the plan;

(6) provide that the State agency will make such reports, in such

form and containing such information, as the Board may from time to time require, and comply with such provisions as the Board may from time to time find necessary to assure the correctness and verification of such reports; and

(7) provide that no aid will be furnished any individual under the plan with respect to any period with respect to which he is receiving old-age assistance under the State plan approved under section 2 of this Act.

(b) The Board shall approve any plan which fulfills the conditions specified in subsection (a), except that it shall not approve any plan which imposes, as a condition of eligibility for aid to the blind under the plan—

(1) Any residence requirement which excludes any resident of the State who has resided therein five years during the nine years immediately preceding the application for aid and has resided therein continuously for one year immediately preceding the application or

(2) Any citizenship requirement which excludes any citizen of the United States.

PAYMENT TO STATES

SEC. 1003. (a) From the sums appropriated therefor, the Secretary of the Treasury shall pay to each State which has an approved plan for aid to the blind, for each quarter, beginning with the quarter commencing July 1, 1935,

(1) an amount which shall be used exclusively as aid to the blind equal to one-half of the total of the sums expended during such quarter as aid to the blind under the State plan with respect to each individual who is blind and is not an inmate of a public institution not counting so much of such expenditure with respect to any individual for any month as exceeds $30, and

(2) 5 per centum of such amount, which shall be used for paying the costs of administering the State plan or for aid to the blind, or both, and for no other purpose.

(b) The method of computing and paying such amounts shall be as follows:

(1) The Board shall, prior to the beginning of each quarter, estimate the amount to be paid to the State for such quarter under provisions of clause (1) of subsection (a), such estimate to be based on

(A) a report filed by the State containing its estimate of the total sum to be expended in such quarter in accordance with the provisions of such clause, and stating the amount appropriated or made available by the State and its political subdivisions for such expenditures in such quarter, and if such amount is less than one-half of the total sum of such estimated expenditures, the source or sources from which the difference is expected to be derived,

(B) records showing the number of blind individuals in the State, and

(C) such other investigation as the Board may find necessary.

(2) The Board shall then certify to the Secretary of the Treasury the amount so estimated by the Board, reduced or increased, as the case may be, by any sum by which it finds that its estimate for any prior quarter was greater or less than the amount which should have been paid to the State under clause (1) of subsection (a) for such quarter, except to the extent that such sum has been applied to make the amount certified for any prior quarter greater or less than the amount estimated by the Board for such prior quarter.

(3) The Secretary of the Treasury shall thereupon, through the Division of Disbursement of the Treasury Department and prior to audit or settlement by the General Accounting Office, pay to the State, at the time or times fixed by the Board, the amount so certified, increased by 5 per centum.

OPERATION OF STATE PLANS

Sec. 1004. In the case of any State plan for aid to the blind which has been approved by the Board, if the Board, after reasonable notice and opportunity for hearing to the State agency administering or supervising the administration of such a plan, finds—

(1) that the plan has been so changed as to impose any residence or citizenship requirement prohibited by section 1002 (b), or that in the administration of the plan any such prohibited requirement is imposed, with the knowledge of such State agency, in a substantial number of cases; or

(2) that in the administration of the plan there is a failure to comply substantially with any provision required by section 1002 (a) be included in the plan; the Board shall notify such State agency that further payments will not be made to the State until the Board is satisfied that such prohibited

requirement is no longer so imposed, and that there is no longer any such failure to comply. Until it is satisfied it shall make no further certification to the Secretary of the Treasury with respect to such State.

SEC. 1005. There is hereby authorized to be appropriated for the fiscal year ending June 30, 1936 the sum of $30,000, for all necessary expenses of the Board in administering the provisions of this title.

SEC. 1006. When used in this title the term aid to the blind means money payments to blind individuals.

# TITLE XI
## GENERAL PROVISIONS

SECTION 1101. (a) When used in this Act—

(1) The term State (except when used in section 531) includes Alaska, Hawaii, and the District of Columbia.

(2) The term United States when used in a geographical sense means the States, Alaska, Hawaii, and the District of Columbia.

(3) The term person means an individual, a trust or estate, a partnership, or a corporation.

(4) The term corporation includes associations, joint-stock companies, and insurance companies.

(5) The term shareholder includes a member in an association, joint-stock company, or insurance company.

(6) The term employee includes an officer of a corporation.

(b) The terms includes and including when used in a definition contained in this Act shall not be deemed to exclude other things otherwise within the meaning of the term defined.

(c) Whenever under this Act or any Act of Congress, or under the law of any State, an employer is required or permitted to deduct any amount from the remuneration of an employee and to pay the amount deducted to the United States, a State, or any political subdivision thereof, then for the purposes of this Act the amount so deducted shall be considered to have been paid to the employee at the time of such deduction.

(d) Nothing in this Act shall be construed as authorizing any Federal official, agent, or representative, in carrying out any of the provisions of this Act, to take charge of any child over the objection of either of the parents of such child, or of the person standing in loco parentis to such child.

RULES AND REGULATIONS

Sec. 1102. The Secretary of the Treasury, the Secretary of Labor, and the Social Security Board respectively, shall make and publish such rules and regulations, not inconsistent with this Act, as may be necessary to the efficient administration of the functions with which each is charged under this Act.

SEPARABILITY

Sec. 1103. If any provision of this Act, or the application thereof to any person or circumstance is held invalid, the remainder of the Act, and the application of such provision to other persons or circumstances shall not be affected thereby.

RESERVATION OF POWER

Sec. 1104. The right to alter, amend, or repeal any provision of this Act is hereby reserved to the Congress.

SHORT TITLE

Sec. 1105. This Act may be cited as the Social Security Act.
Approved, August 14, 1935.

# ALBERT EINSTEIN'S LETTER TO PRESIDENT FRANKLIN D. ROOSEVELT ABOUT THE ATOMIC BOMB (1939)

*On August 2, 1939, physicist Albert Einstein sent a letter to President Franklin D. Roosevelt warning of a new and dangerous weapon, the atomic bomb. Einstein's letter was the result of a meeting that included several well-known scientists, some of whom had fled Nazi Germany and feared that the Germans were close to creating an atomic bomb themselves. In response, Roosevelt called for action on the part of the U.S. government and created what became known as the Manhattan Project, a top-secret military operation that built the world's first nuclear weapons. America's two atomic bombs were used against Japan in 1945, prompting a surrender and an end to World War II. Einstein never worked on the development of the atom bomb; the U.S. government refused him the needed security clearance because his politics skewed too leftist.*

Sir:

Some recent work by E. Fermi and L. Szilard, which has been communicated to me in manuscript, leads me to expect that the element uranium may be turned into a new and important source of energy in the immediate future. Certain aspects of the situation which has arisen seem to call for watchfulness and, if necessary, quick action on the part of the administration. I believe therefore that it is my duty to bring to your attention the following facts and recommendations:

In the course of the last four months it has been made probable—through the work of Joliot [Jean Frédéric Joliot-Curie] in France as well as Fermi and Szilard in America—that it may become possible to set up a nuclear chain reaction in a large mass of uranium, by which vast amounts of power and large quantities of new radium like elements would be generated. Now it appears almost certain that this could be achieved in the immediate future.

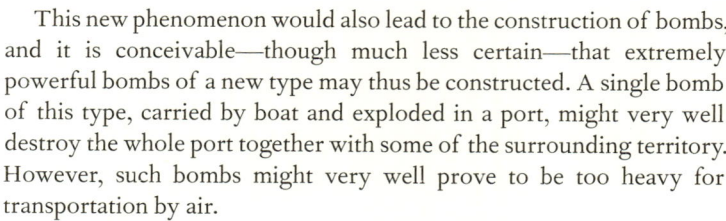

This new phenomenon would also lead to the construction of bombs, and it is conceivable—though much less certain—that extremely powerful bombs of a new type may thus be constructed. A single bomb of this type, carried by boat and exploded in a port, might very well destroy the whole port together with some of the surrounding territory. However, such bombs might very well prove to be too heavy for transportation by air.

The United States has only very poor ores of uranium in moderate quantities. There is some good ore in Canada and the former Czechoslovakia, while the most important source of uranium is Belgian Congo.

In view of this situation you may think it desirable to have some permanent contact maintained between the Administration and the group of physicists working on chain reactions in America. One possible way of achieving this might be for you to entrust with this task a person who has your confidence and who could perhaps serve in an unofficial capacity. His task might comprise the following:

a) To approach Government Departments, keep them informed of the further development, and out forward recommendations for Government action, giving particular attention to the problem of uranium ore for the United States;

b) To speed up the experimental work, which is at present being carried on within the limits of the budgets of University laboratories, by providing funds, if such funds be required, through his contacts with private persons who are willing to make a contribution for this cause, and perhaps also by obtaining the co-operation of industrial laboratories which have the necessary equipment.

I understand that Germany has actually stopped the sale of uranium from the Czechoslovakian mines, which she has taken over. That she should have taken such early action might perhaps be understood on the ground that the son of the German Under-Secretary of State, von Weizsächer, is attached to the Kaiser Wilheim Institute in Berlin where some of the American work on uranium is now being repeated.

Yours very truly,
Albert Einstein

# FRANKLIN D. ROOSEVELT'S STATE OF THE UNION ADDRESS JANUARY 6, 1941

Mr. President, Mr. Speaker, Members of the Seventy-seventh Congress:

I address you, the Members of the Seventy-seventh Congress, at a moment unprecedented in the history of the Union. I use the word "unprecedented," because at no previous time has American security been as seriously threatened from without as it is today.

Since the permanent formation of our Government under the Constitution, in 1789, most of the periods of crisis in our history have related to our domestic affairs. Fortunately, only one of these—the four-year War Between the States—ever threatened our national unity. Today, thank God, one hundred and thirty million Americans, in forty-eight States, have forgotten points of the compass in our national unity.

It is true that prior to 1914 the United States often had been disturbed by events in other Continents. We had even engaged in two wars with European nations and in a number of undeclared wars in the West Indies, in the Mediterranean and in the Pacific for the maintenance of American rights and for the principles of peaceful commerce. But in no case had a serious threat been raised against our national safety or our continued independence.

What I seek to convey is the historic truth that the United States as a nation has at all times maintained clear, definite opposition, to any attempt to lock us in behind an ancient Chinese wall while the procession of civilization went past. Today, thinking of our children and of their children, we oppose enforced isolation for ourselves or for any other part of the Americas.

That determination of ours, extending over all these years, was proved, for example, during the quarter century of wars following the French Revolution. While the Napoleonic struggles did threaten interests of the United States because of the French foothold in the West Indies and in Louisiana, and while we engaged in the War of 1812 to vindicate our right to peaceful trade, it is nevertheless clear that

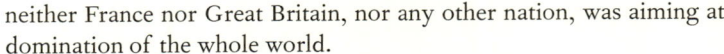 

neither France nor Great Britain, nor any other nation, was aiming at domination of the whole world.

In like fashion from 1815 to 1914—ninety-nine years—no single war in Europe or in Asia constituted a real threat against our future or against the future of any other American nation.

Except in the Maximilian interlude in Mexico, no foreign power sought to establish itself in this Hemisphere; and the strength of the British fleet in the Atlantic has been a friendly strength. It is still a friendly strength.

Even when the World War broke out in 1914, it seemed to contain only small threat of danger to our own American future. But, as time went on, the American people began to visualize what the downfall of democratic nations might mean to our own democracy.

We need not overemphasize imperfections in the Peace of Versailles. We need not harp on failure of the democracies to deal with problems of world reconstruction. We should remember that the Peace of 1919 was far less unjust than the kind of "pacification" which began even before Munich, and which is being carried on under the new order of tyranny that seeks to spread over every continent today. The American people have unalterably set their faces against that tyranny.

Every realist knows that the democratic way of life is at this moment being directly assailed in every part of the world—assailed either by arms, or by secret spreading of poisonous propaganda by those who seek to destroy unity and promote discord in nations that are still at peace.

During sixteen long months this assault has blotted out the whole pattern of democratic life in an appalling number of independent nations, great and small. The assailants are still on the march, threatening other nations, great and small.

Therefore, as your President, performing my constitutional duty to "give to the Congress information of the state of the Union," I find it, unhappily, necessary to report that the future and the safety of our country and of our democracy are overwhelmingly involved in events far beyond our borders.

Armed defense of democratic existence is now being gallantly waged in four continents. If that defense fails, all the population and all the resources of Europe, Asia, Africa and Australasia will be dominated by the conquerors. Let us remember that the total of those populations and their resources in those four continents greatly exceeds the sum total of the population and the resources of the whole of the Western Hemisphere—many times over.

In times like these it is immature—and incidentally, untrue—for anybody to brag that an unprepared America, single-handed, and with one hand tied behind its back, can hold off the whole world.

No realistic American can expect from a dictator's peace international generosity, or return of true independence, or world disarmament, or freedom of expression, or freedom of religion—or even good business.

Such a peace would bring no security for us or for our neighbors. Those who would give up essential liberty to purchase a little temporary safety deserve neither liberty nor safety.

As a nation, we may take pride in the fact that we are softhearted; but we cannot afford to be soft-headed.

We must always be wary of those who with sounding brass and a tinkling cymbal preach the "ism" of appeasement.

We must especially beware of that small group of selfish men who would clip the wings of the American eagle in order to feather their own nests.

I have recently pointed out how quickly the tempo of modern warfare could bring into our very midst the physical attack which we must eventually expect if the dictator nations win this war.

There is much loose talk of our immunity from immediate and direct invasion from across the seas. Obviously, as long as the British Navy retains its power, no such danger exists. Even if there were no British Navy, it is not probable that any enemy would be stupid enough to attack us by landing troops in the United States from across thousands of miles of ocean, until it had acquired strategic bases from which to operate.

But we learn much from the lessons of the past years in Europe—particularly the lesson of Norway, whose essential seaports were captured by treachery and surprise built up over a series of years.

The first phase of the invasion of this Hemisphere would not be the landing of regular troops. The necessary strategic points would be occupied by secret agents and their dupes—and great numbers of them are already here, and in Latin America.

As long as the aggressor nations maintain the offensive, they—not we—will choose the time and the place and the method of their attack.

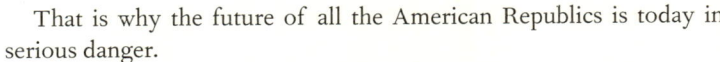 

That is why the future of all the American Republics is today in serious danger.

That is why this Annual Message to the Congress is unique in our history.

That is why every member of the Executive Branch of the Government and every member of the Congress faces great responsibility and great accountability.

The need of the moment is that our actions and our policy should be devoted primarily—almost exclusively—to meeting this foreign peril. For all our domestic problems are now a part of the great emergency.

Just as our national policy in internal affairs has been based upon a decent respect for the rights and the dignity of all our fellow men within our gates, so our national policy in foreign affairs has been based on a decent respect for the rights and dignity of all nations, large and small. And the justice of morality must and will win in the end.

Our national policy is this:

First, by an impressive expression of the public will and without regard to partisanship, we are committed to all-inclusive national defense.

Second, by an impressive expression of the public will and without regard to partisanship, we are committed to full support of all those resolute peoples, everywhere, who are resisting aggression and are thereby keeping war away from our Hemisphere. By this support, we express our determination that the democratic cause shall prevail; and we strengthen the defense and the security of our own nation.

Third, by an impressive expression of the public will and without regard to partisanship, we are committed to the proposition that principles of morality and considerations for our own security will never permit us to acquiesce in a peace dictated by aggressors and sponsored by appeasers. We know that enduring peace cannot be bought at the cost of other people's freedom.

In the recent national election there was no substantial difference between the two great parties in respect to that national policy. No issue was fought out on this line before the American electorate. Today it is abundantly evident that American citizens everywhere are demanding and supporting speedy and complete action in recognition of obvious danger.

Therefore, the immediate need is a swift and driving increase in our armament production.

Leaders of industry and labor have responded to our summons. Goals of speed have been set. In some cases these goals are being reached ahead of time; in some cases we are on schedule; in other cases there are slight but not serious delays; and in some cases—and I am sorry to say very important cases—we are all concerned by the slowness of the accomplishment of our plans.

The Army and Navy, however, have made substantial progress during the past year. Actual experience is improving and speeding up our methods of production with every passing day. And today's best is not good enough for tomorrow.

I am not satisfied with the progress thus far made. The men in charge of the program represent the best in training, in ability, and in patriotism. They are not satisfied with the progress thus far made. None of us will be satisfied until the job is done.

No matter whether the original goal was set too high or too low, our objective is quicker and better results. To give you two illustrations:

We are behind schedule in turning out finished airplanes; we are working day and night to solve the innumerable problems and to catch up.

We are ahead of schedule in building warships but we are working to get even further ahead of that schedule.

To change a whole nation from a basis of peacetime production of implements of peace to a basis of wartime production of implements of war is no small task. And the greatest difficulty comes at the beginning of the program, when new tools, new plant facilities, new assembly lines, and new ship ways must first be constructed before the actual materiel begins to flow steadily and speedily from them.

The Congress, of course, must rightly keep itself informed at all times of the progress of the program. However, there is certain information, as the Congress itself will readily recognize, which, in the interests of our own security and those of the nations that we are supporting, must of needs be kept in confidence.

New circumstances are constantly begetting new needs for our safety. I shall ask this Congress for greatly increased new appropriations and authorizations to carry on what we have begun.

I also ask this Congress for authority and for funds sufficient to

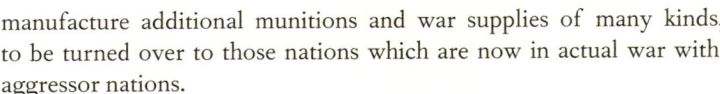

manufacture additional munitions and war supplies of many kinds, to be turned over to those nations which are now in actual war with aggressor nations.

Our most useful and immediate role is to act as an arsenal for them as well as for ourselves. They do not need manpower, but they do need billions of dollars worth of the weapons of defense.

The time is near when they will not be able to pay for them all in ready cash. We cannot, and we will not, tell them that they must surrender, merely because of present inability to pay for the weapons which we know they must have.

I do not recommend that we make them a loan of dollars with which to pay for these weapons—a loan to be repaid in dollars.

I recommend that we make it possible for those nations to continue to obtain war materials in the United States, fitting their orders into our own program. Nearly all their materiel would, if the time ever came, be useful for our own defense.

Taking counsel of expert military and naval authorities, considering what is best for our own security, we are free to decide how much should be kept here and how much should be sent abroad to our friends who by their determined and heroic resistance are giving us time in which to make ready our own defense.

For what we send abroad, we shall be repaid within a reasonable time following the close of hostilities, in similar materials, or, at our option, in other goods of many kinds, which they can produce and which we need.

Let us say to the democracies: "We Americans are vitally concerned in your defense of freedom. We are putting forth our energies, our resources and our organizing powers to give you the strength to regain and maintain a free world. We shall send you, in ever-increasing numbers, ships, planes, tanks, guns. This is our purpose and our pledge."

In fulfillment of this purpose we will not be intimidated by the threats of dictators that they will regard as a breach of international law or as an act of war our aid to the democracies which dare to resist their aggression. Such aid is not an act of war, even if a dictator should unilaterally proclaim it so to be.

When the dictators, if the dictators, are ready to make war upon us, they will not wait for an act of war on our part. They did not wait for Norway or Belgium or the Netherlands to commit an act of war.

Their only interest is in a new one-way international law, which lacks mutuality in its observance, and, therefore, becomes an instrument of oppression.

The happiness of future generations of Americans may well depend upon how effective and how immediate we can make our aid felt. No one can tell the exact character of the emergency situations that we may be called upon to meet. The Nation's hands must not be tied when the Nation's life is in danger.

We must all prepare to make the sacrifices that the emergency—almost as serious as war itself—demands. Whatever stands in the way of speed and efficiency in defense preparations must give way to the national need.

A free nation has the right to expect full cooperation from all groups. A free nation has the right to look to the leaders of business, of labor, and of agriculture to take the lead in stimulating effort, not among other groups but within their own group.

The best way of dealing with the few slackers or trouble-makers in our midst is, first, to shame them by patriotic example, and, if that fails, to use the sovereignty of Government to save Government.

As men do not live by bread alone, they do not fight by armaments alone. Those who man our defenses, and those behind them who build our defenses, must have the stamina and the courage which come from unshakable belief in the manner of life which they are defending. The mighty action that we are calling for cannot be based on a disregard of all things worth fighting for.

The Nation takes great satisfaction and much strength from the things which have been done to make its people conscious of their individual stake in the preservation of democratic life in America. Those things have toughened the fiber of our people, have renewed their faith and strengthened their devotion to the institutions we make ready to protect.

Certainly this is no time for any of us to stop thinking about the social and economic problems which are the root cause of the social revolution which is today a supreme factor in the world.

For there is nothing mysterious about the foundations of a healthy and strong democracy. The basic things expected by our people of their political and economic systems are simple. They are:

Equality of opportunity for youth and for others.

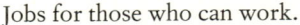
Jobs for those who can work.

Security for those who need it.

The ending of special privilege for the few.

The preservation of civil liberties for all.

The enjoyment of the fruits of scientific progress in a wider and constantly rising standard of living.

These are the simple, basic things that must never be lost sight of in the turmoil and unbelievable complexity of our modern world. The inner and abiding strength of our economic and political systems is dependent upon the degree to which they fulfill these expectations.

Many subjects connected with our social economy call for immediate improvement.

As examples:

We should bring more citizens under the coverage of old-age pensions and unemployment insurance.

We should widen the opportunities for adequate medical care.

We should plan a better system by which persons deserving or needing gainful employment may obtain it.

I have called for personal sacrifice. I am assured of the willingness of almost all Americans to respond to that call.

A part of the sacrifice means the payment of more money in taxes. In my Budget Message I shall recommend that a greater portion of this great defense program be paid for from taxation than we are paying today. No person should try, or be allowed, to get rich out of this program; and the principle of tax payments in accordance with ability to pay should be constantly before our eyes to guide our legislation.

If the Congress maintains these principles, the voters, putting patriotism ahead of pocketbooks, will give you their applause.

In the future days, which we seek to make secure, we look forward to a world founded upon four essential human freedoms.

The first is freedom of speech and expression—everywhere in the world.

The second is freedom of every person to worship God in his own way—everywhere in the world.

The third is freedom from want—which, translated into world terms, means economic understandings which will secure to every nation a healthy peacetime life for its inhabitants—everywhere in the world.

The fourth is freedom from fear—which, translated into world terms, means a world-wide reduction of armaments to such a point and in such a thorough fashion that no nation will be in a position to commit an act of physical aggression against any neighbor—anywhere in the world.

That is no vision of a distant millennium. It is a definite basis for a kind of world attainable in our own time and generation. That kind of world is the very antithesis of the so-called new order of tyranny which the dictators seek to create with the crash of a bomb.

To that new order we oppose the greater conception—the moral order. A good society is able to face schemes of world domination and foreign revolutions alike without fear.

Since the beginning of our American history, we have been engaged in change—in a perpetual peaceful revolution—a revolution which goes on steadily, quietly adjusting itself to changing conditions—without the concentration camp or the quick-lime in the ditch. The world order which we seek is the cooperation of free countries, working together in a friendly, civilized society.

This nation has placed its destiny in the hands and heads and hearts of its millions of free men and women; and its faith in freedom under the guidance of God. Freedom means the supremacy of human rights everywhere. Our support goes to those who struggle to gain those rights or keep them. Our strength is our unity of purpose. To that high concept there can be no end save victory.

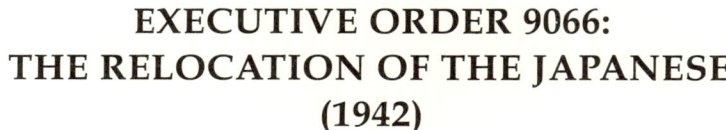 

# EXECUTIVE ORDER 9066:
# THE RELOCATION OF THE JAPANESE
# (1942)

*Amid the fear and hysteria over a possible Japanese attack on the continental United States during World War II, President Franklin D. Roosevelt issued Executive Order 9066 in 1942, authorizing the forced relocation of thousands of people of Japanese descent (mostly U.S. citizens) from the western United States. More than 120,000 people were moved into government-run internment camps and kept there until 1944 when Roosevelt rescinded the order. In 1982, a government committee ruled that the internment of the Japanese during World War II had been unnecessary and based on both racism and hysteria. In 1988, President Ronald Reagan issued a public apology to on behalf of the country, and the next year, President George H. W. Bush authorized that the United States pay reparations to former internees.*

### EXECUTIVE ORDER
### AUTHORIZING THE SECRETARY OF WAR
### TO PRESCRIBE MILITARY AREAS

Whereas the successful prosecution of the war requires every possible protection against espionage and against sabotage to national-defense material, national-defense premises, and national-defense utilities as defined in Section 4, Act of April 20, 1918, 40 Stat. 533, as amended by the Act of November 30, 1940, 54 Stat. 1220, and the Act of August 21, 1941, 55 Stat. 655 (U.S.C., Title 50, Sec. 104);

Now, therefore, by virtue of the authority vested in me as President of the United States, and Commander in Chief of the Army and Navy, I hereby authorize and direct the Secretary of War, and the Military Commanders whom he may from time to time designate, whenever he or any designated Commander deems such action necessary or desirable, to prescribe military areas in such places and of such extent as he or the appropriate Military Commander may determine, from which any or all persons may be excluded, and with respect to which, the right of any person to enter, remain in, or leave shall be subject to whatever restrictions the Secretary of War or the appropriate Military Commander may impose in his discretion. The Secretary of War is hereby authorized to provide for residents of any such area who are excluded therefrom, such transportation, food, shelter, and other accommodations as may be necessary, in the judgment of the Secretary of War or the said Military Commander, and until other arrangements are made, to accomplish the purpose of this order. The designation of military areas in any region or locality shall supersede designations of prohibited and restricted areas by the Attorney General under the Proclamations of December 7 and 8, 1941, and shall supersede the responsibility and authority of the Attorney General under the said Proclamations in respect of such prohibited and restricted areas.

I hereby further authorize and direct the Secretary of War and the said Military Commanders to take such other steps as he or the appropriate Military Commander may deem advisable to enforce compliance with the restrictions applicable to each Military area hereinabove authorized to be designated, including the use of Federal troops and other Federal Agencies, with authority to accept assistance of state and local agencies.

I hereby further authorize and direct all Executive Departments, independent establishments and other Federal Agencies, to assist the Secretary of War or the said Military Commanders in carrying out this Executive Order, including the furnishing of medical aid, hospitalization, food, clothing, transportation, use of land, shelter, and other supplies, equipment, utilities, facilities, and services.

This order shall not be construed as modifying or limiting in any way the authority heretofore granted under Executive Order No. 8972, dated December 12, 1941, nor shall it be construed as limiting or modifying the duty and responsibility of the Federal Bureau of Investigation, with respect to the investigation of alleged acts of sabotage or the duty and responsibility of the Attorney General and the Department of Justice under the Proclamations of December 7 and 8, 1941, prescribing regulations for the conduct and control of alien enemies, except as such duty and responsibility is superseded by the designation of military areas hereunder.

Franklin D. Roosevelt
The White House,
February 19, 1942.

# FRANKLIN D. ROOSEVELT'S SPEECH UPON SIGNING THE G.I. BILL OF RIGHTS (1944)

*Best known as the G.I. Bill, the Servicemen's Readjustment Act of 1944 authorized millions of dollars in benefits to American soldiers returning from World War II. Grants for college tuition, low-interest mortgages, small-business loans, and job training were just some of the benefits included in the act. By 1956 more than 7.5 million people had used the G.I. Bill, and it continues to assist veterans today.*

This bill, which I have signed today, substantially carries out most of the recommendations made by me in a speech on July 28, 1943, and more specifically in messages to the Congress dated October 27, 1943, and November 23, 1943:

It gives servicemen and women the opportunity of resuming their education or technical training after discharge, or of taking a refresher or retrainer course, not only without tuition charge up to $500 per school year, but with the right to receive a monthly living allowance while pursuing their studies.

It makes provision for the guarantee by the Federal Government of not to exceed 50 percent of certain loans made to veterans for the purchase or construction of homes, farms, and business properties.

It provides for reasonable unemployment allowances payable each week up to a maximum period of one year, to those veterans who are unable to find a job.

It establishes improved machinery for effective job counseling for veterans and for finding jobs for returning soldiers and sailors.

It authorizes the construction of all necessary additional hospital facilities.

It strengthens the authority of the Veterans Administration to enable it to discharge its existing and added responsibilities with promptness and efficiency.

With the signing of this bill a well-rounded program of special veterans' benefits is nearly completed. It gives emphatic notice to the men and women in our armed forces that the American people do not intend to let them down.

By prior legislation, the Federal Government has already provided for the armed forces of this war: adequate dependency allowances; mustering-out pay; generous hospitalization, medical care, and vocational rehabilitation and training; liberal pensions in case of death or disability in military service; substantial war risk life insurance, and guaranty of premiums on commercial policies during service; protection of civil rights and suspension of enforcement of certain civil liabilities during service; emergency maternal care for wives of enlisted men; and reemployment rights for returning veterans.

This bill therefore and the former legislation provide the special benefits which are due to the members of our armed forces—for they "have been compelled to make greater economic sacrifice and every other kind of sacrifice than the rest of us, and are entitled to definite action to help take care of their special problems." While further study and experience may suggest some changes and improvements, the Congress is to be congratulated on the prompt action it has taken.

# THE UNITED NATIONS CHARTER (1945)

We the people of the United Nations determined to save succeeding generations from the scourge of war, which twice in our lifetime has brought untold sorrow to mankind, and to reaffirm faith in fundamental human rights, in the dignity and worth of the human person, in the equal rights of men and women and of nations large and small, and to establish conditions under which justice and respect for the obligations arising from treaties and other sources of international law can be maintained, and to promote social progress and better standards of life in larger freedom, and *for these ends* to practice tolerance and live together in peace with one another as good neighbours, and to unite our strength to maintain international peace and security, and to ensure, by the acceptance of principles and the institution of methods, that armed force shall not be used, save in the common interest, and to employ international machinery for the promotion of the economic and social advancement of all peoples, *have resolved to combine our efforts to accomplish these aims*. Accordingly, our respective Governments, through representatives assembled in the city of San Francisco, who have exhibited their full powers found to be in good and due form, have agreed to the present Charter of the United Nations and do hereby establish an international organization to be known as the United Nations.

## CHAPTER I
## PURPOSES AND PRINCIPLES

### ARTICLE 1

The Purposes of the United Nations are:

1. To maintain international peace and security, and to that end: to take effective collective measures for the prevention and removal of threats to the peace, and for the suppression of acts of aggression or other breaches of the peace, and to bring about by peaceful means, and in conformity with the principles of justice and international law,

adjustment or settlement of international disputes or situations which might lead to a breach of the peace;

2. To develop friendly relations among nations based on respect for the principle of equal rights and self-determination of peoples, and to take other appropriate measures to strengthen universal peace;

3. To achieve international co-operation in solving international problems of an economic, social, cultural, or humanitarian character, and in promoting and encouraging respect for human rights and for fundamental freedoms for all without distinction as to race, sex, language, or religion; and

4. To be a centre for harmonizing the actions of nations in the attainment of these common ends.

## ARTICLE 2

The Organization and its Members, in pursuit of the Purposes stated in Article 1, shall act in accordance with the following Principles.

1. The Organization is based on the principle of the sovereign equality of all its Members.

2. All Members, in order to ensure to a of them the rights and benefits resulting from membership, shall fulfill in good faith the obligations assumed by them in accordance with the present Charter.

3. All Members shall settle their international disputes by peaceful means in such a manner that international peace and security, and justice, are not endangered.

4. All Members shall refrain in their international relations from the threat or use of force against the territorial integrity or political independence of any state, or in any other manner inconsistent with the Purposes of the United Nations.

5. All Members shall give the United Nations every assistance in any action it takes in accordance with the present Charter, and shall refrain from giving assistance to any state against which the United Nations is taking preventive or enforcement action.

6. The Organization shall ensure that states which are not Members of the United Nations act in accordance with these Principles so far as may be necessary for the maintenance of international peace and security.

7. Nothing contained in the present Charter shall authorize the United Nations to intervene in matters which are essentially within the domestic

jurisdiction of any state or shall require the Members to submit such matters to settlement under the present Charter; but this principle shall not prejudice the application of enforcement measures under Chapter VII.

## CHAPTER II
## MEMBERSHIP

### ARTICLE 3

The original Members of the United Nations shall be the states which, having participated in the United Nations Conference on International Organization at San Francisco, or having previously signed the Declaration by United Nations of 1 January 1942, sign the present Charter and ratify it in accordance with Article 110.

### ARTICLE 4

1. Membership in the United Nations is open to a other peace-loving states which accept the obligations contained in the present Charter and, in the judgment of the Organization, are able and willing to carry out these obligations.

2. The admission of any such state to membership in the United Nations will be effected by a decision of the General Assembly upon the recommendation of the Security Council.

### ARTICLE 5

A Member of the United Nations against which preventive or enforcement action has been taken by the Security Council may be suspended from the exercise of the rights and privileges of membership by the General Assembly upon the recommendation of the Security Council. The exercise of these rights and privileges may be restored by the Security Council.

### ARTICLE 6

A Member of the United Nations which has persistently violated the Principles contained in the present Charter may be expelled from the Organization by the General Assembly upon the recommendation of the Security Council.

## CHAPTER III
## ORGANS

### ARTICLE 7

1. There are established as the principal organs of the United Nations: a General Assembly, a Security Council, an Economic and Social Council, a Trusteeship Council, an International Court of Justice, and a Secretariat.

2. Such subsidiary organs as may be found necessary may be established in accordance with the present Charter.

### ARTICLE 8

The United Nations shall place no restrictions on the eligibility of men and women to participate in any capacity and under conditions of equality in its principal and subsidiary organs.

## CHAPTER IV
## THE GENERAL ASSEMBLY

#### COMPOSITION

### ARTICLE 9

1. The General Assembly shall consist of all the Members of the United Nations.

2. Each Member shall have not more than five representatives in the General Assembly.

#### FUNCTIONS AND POWERS

### ARTICLE 10

The General Assembly may discuss any questions or any matters within the scope of the present Charter or relating to the powers and functions of any organs provided for in the present Charter, and, except as provided in Article 12, may make recommendations to the Members of the United Nations or to the Security Council or to both on any such questions or matters.

## ARTICLE 11

1. The General Assembly may consider the general principles of co-operation in the maintenance of international peace and security, including the principles governing disarmament and the regulation of armaments, and may make recommendations with regard to such principles to the Members or to the Security Council or to both.

2. The General Assembly may discuss any questions relating to the maintenance of international peace and security brought before it by any Member of the United Nations, or by the Security Council, or by a state which is not a Member of the United Nations in accordance with Article 35, paragraph 2, and, except as provided in Article 12, may make recommendations with regard to any such questions to the state or states concerned or to the Security Council or to both. Any such question on which action is necessary shall be referred to the Security Council by the General Assembly either before or after discussion.

3. The General Assembly may call the attention of the Security Council to situations which are likely to endanger international peace and security.

4. The powers of the General Assembly set forth in this Article shall not limit the general scope of Article 10.

## ARTICLE 12

1. While the Security Council is exercising in respect of any dispute or situation the functions assigned to it in the present Charter, the General Assembly shall not make any recommendation with regard to that dispute or situation unless the Security Council so requests.

2. The Secretary-General, with the consent of the Security Council, shall notify the General Assembly at each session of any matters relative to the maintenance of international peace and security which are being dealt with by the Security Council and similarly notify the General Assembly, or the Members of the United Nations if the General Assembly is not in session, immediately the Security Council ceases to deal with such matters.

## ARTICLE 13

1. The General Assembly shall initiate studies and make recommendations for the purpose of:

a. promoting international co-operation in the political field and encouraging the progressive development of international law and its codification;

b. promoting international co-operation in the economic, social, cultural, educational, and health fields, and assisting in the realization of human rights and fundamental freedoms for all without distinction as to race, sex, language, or religion.

2. The further responsibilities, functions and powers of the General with respect to matters mentioned in paragraph 1) above are set forth in Chapters IX and X.

## ARTICLE 14

Subject to the provisions of Article 12, the General Assembly may recommend measures for the peaceful adjustment of any situation, regardless of origin, which it deems likely to impair the general welfare or friendly relations among nations, including situations resulting from a violation of the provisions of the present Charter setting forth the Purposes and Principles of the United Nations.

## ARTICLE 15

1. The General Assembly shall receive and consider annual and special reports from the Security Council; these reports shall include an account of the measures that the Security Council has decided upon or taken to maintain international peace and security.

2. The General Assembly shall receive and consider reports from the other organs of the United Nations.

## ARTICLE 16

The General Assembly shall perform such functions with respect to the international trusteeship system as are assigned to it under Chapters XII and XIII, including the approval of the trusteeship agreements for areas not designated as strategic.

## ARTICLE 17

1. The Genera Assembly shall consider and approve the budget of the Organization.

2. The expenses of the Organization shall be borne by the Members as apportioned by the General Assembly.

3. The Assembly shall consider and approve any financial and budgetary arrangements with specialized agencies referred to in Article 57 and shall examine the administrative budgets of such specialized agencies with a view to making recommendations to the agencies concerned.

VOTING

## ARTICLE 18

1. Each member of the General Assembly shall have one vote.

2. Decisions of the General Assembly on important questions shall be made by a two-thirds majority of the members present and voting. These questions shall include: recommendations with respect to the maintenance of international peace and security, the election of the non-permanent members of the Security Council, the election of the members of the Economic and Social Council, the election of members of the Trusteeship Council in accordance with paragraph 1 (c) of Article 86, the admission of new Members to the United Nations, the suspension of the rights and privileges of membership, the expulsion of Members, questions relating to the operation of the trusteeship system, and budgetary questions.

3. Decisions on other questions, including the determination of additional categories of questions to be decided by a two-thirds majority, shall be made by a majority of the members present and voting.

## ARTICLE 19

A Member of the United Nations which is in arrears in the payment of its financial contributions to the Organization shall have no vote in the General Assembly if the amount of its arrears equals or exceeds the amount of the contributions due from it for the preceding two full years. The General Assembly may, nevertheless, permit such a Member to vote if it is satisfied that the failure to pay is due to conditions beyond the of the Member.

PROCEDURE

## ARTICLE 20

The General Assembly shall meet in regular annual sessions and in such special sessions as occasion may require. Special sessions shall be convoked by the Secretary-General at the request of the Security Council or of a majority of the Members of the United Nations.

### ARTICLE 21

The General Assembly shall adopt its own rules of procedure. It shall elect its President for each session.

### ARTICLE 22

The General Assembly may establish such subsidiary organs as it deems necessary for the performance of its functions.

## CHAPTER V
## THE SECURITY COUNCIL

COMPOSITION

### ARTICLE 23

1. The Security Council shall consist of fifteen Members of the United Nations. The Republic of China, France, the Union of Soviet Socialist Republics, the United Kingdom of Great Britain and Northern Ireland, and the United States of America shall be permanent members of the Security Council. The General Assembly shall elect ten other Members of the United Nations to be non-permanent members of the Security Council, due regard being specially paid, in the first instance to the contribution of Members of the United Nations to the maintenance of international peace and security and to the other purposes of the Organization, and also to equitable geographical distribution.

2. The non-permanent members of the Security Council shall be elected for a term of two years. In the first election of the non-permanent members after the increase of the membership of the Security Council from eleven to fifteen, two of the four additional members shall be chosen for a term of one year. A retiring member shall not be eligible for immediate re-election.

3. Each member of the Security Council shall have one representative.

FUNCTIONS AND POWERS

## ARTICLE 24

1. In order to ensure prompt and effective action by the United Nations, its Members confer on the Security Council primary responsibility for the maintenance of international peace and security, and agree that in carrying out its duties under this responsibility the Security Council acts on their behalf.

2. In discharging these duties the Security Council shall act in accordance with the Purposes and Principles of the United Nations. The specific powers granted to the Security Council for the discharge of these duties are laid down in Chapters VI, VII, VIII, and XII.

3. The Security Council shall submit annual and, when necessary, special reports to the General Assembly for its consideration.

## ARTICLE 25

The Members of the United Nations agree to accept and carry out the decisions of the Security Council in accordance with the present Charter.

## ARTICLE 26

In order to promote the establishment and maintenance of international peace and security with the least diversion for armaments of the world's human and economic resources, the Security Council shall be responsible for formulating, with the assistance of the Military Staff Committee referred to in Article 47, plans to be submitted to the Members of the United Nations for the establishment of a system for the regulation of armaments.

VOTING

## ARTICLE 27

1. Each member of the Security Council shall have one vote.

2. Decisions of the Security Council on procedural matters shall be made by an affirmative vote of nine members.

3. Decisions of the Security Council on all other matters shall be made by an affirmative vote of nine members including the concurring votes of the permanent members; provided that, in decisions under

Chapter VI, and under paragraph 3 of Article 52, a party to a dispute shall abstain from voting.

PROCEDURE

## ARTICLE 28

1. The Security Council shall be so organized as to be able to function continuously. Each member of the Security Council shall for this purpose be represented at times at the seat of the Organization.

2. The Security Council shall hold meetings at which each of its members may, if it so desires, be represented by a member of the government or by some other specially designated representative.

3. The Security Council may hold meetings at such places other than the seat of the Organization as in its judgment will best facilitate its work.

## ARTICLE 29

The Security Council may establish such subsidiary organs as it deems necessary for the performance of its functions.

## ARTICLE 30

The Security Council shall adopt its own rules of procedure, including the method of selecting its President.

## ARTICLE 31

Any Member of the United Nations which is not a member of the Security Council may participate, without vote, in the discussion of any question brought before the Security Council whenever the latter considers that the interests of that Member are specially affected.

## ARTICLE 32

Any Member of the United Nations which is not a member of the Security Council or any state which is not a Member of the United Nations, if it is a party to a dispute under consideration by the Security Council, shall be invited to participate, without vote, in the discussion relating to the dispute. The Security Council shall any down such conditions as it deems just for the participation of a state which is not a Member of the United Nations.

## CHAPTER VI
## PACIFIC SETTLEMENT OF DISPUTES

### ARTICLE 33

1. The parties to any dispute, the continuance of which is likely to endanger the maintenance of international peace and security, shall, first of all, seek a solution by negotiation, enquiry, mediation, conciliation, arbitration, judicial settlement, resort to regional agencies or arrangements, or other peaceful means of their own choice.

2. The Security Council shall, when it deems necessary, call upon the parties to settle their dispute by such means.

### ARTICLE 34

The Security Council may investigate any dispute, or any situation which might lead to international friction or give rise to a dispute, in order to determine whether the continuance of the dispute or situation is likely to endanger the maintenance of international peace and security.

### ARTICLE 35

1. Any Member of the United Nations may bring any dispute, or any situation of the nature referred to in Article 34, to the attention of the Security Council or of the General Assembly.

2. A state which is not a Member of the United Nations may bring to the attention of the Security Council or of the General Assembly any dispute to which it is a party if it accepts in advance, for the purposes of the dispute, the obligations of pacific settlement provided in the present Charter.

3. The proceedings of the General Assembly in respect of matters brought to its attention under this Article will be subject to the provisions of Articles 11 and 12.

### ARTICLE 36

1. The Security Council may, at any stage of a dispute of the nature referred to in Article 33 or of a situation of like nature, recommend appropriate procedures or methods of adjustment.

2. The Security Council should take into consideration any procedures for the settlement of the dispute which have already been adopted by the parties.

3. In making recommendations under this Article the Security Council should also take into consideration that legal disputes should as a general rule be referred by the parties to the International Court of Justice in accordance with the provisions of the Statute of the Court.

## ARTICLE 37

1. Should the parties to a dispute of the nature referred to in Article 33 fail to settle it by the means indicated in that Article, they shall refer it to the Security Council.

2. If the Security Council deems that the continuance of the dispute is in fact likely to endanger the maintenance of international peace and security, it shall decide whether to take action under Article 36 or to recommend such terms of settlement as it may consider appropriate.

## ARTICLE 38

Without prejudice to the provisions of Articles 33 to 37, the Security Council may, if all the parties to any dispute so request, make recommendations to the parties with a view to a pacific settlement of the dispute.

### CHAPTER VII
### ACTION WITH RESPECT TO THREATS TO THE PEACE, BREACHES OF THE PEACE, AND ACTS OF AGGRESSION

## ARTICLE 39

The Security Council shall determine the existence of any threat to the peace, breach of the peace, or act of aggression and shall make recommendations, or decide what measures shall be taken in accordance with Articles 4 and 42, to maintain or restore international peace and security.

## ARTICLE 40

In order to prevent an aggravation of the situation, the Security Council may, before making the recommendations or deciding upon the measures provided for in Article 39, call upon the parties concerned to comply with such provisional measures as it deems necessary or desirable. Such provisional measures shall be without prejudice to the rights, claims, or position of the parties concerned. The Security Council shall duly take account of failure to comply with such provisional measures.

## ARTICLE 41

The Security Council may decide what measures not involving the use of armed force are to be employed to give effect to its decisions, and it may call upon the Members of the United Nations to apply such measures. These may include complete or partial interruption of economic relations and of rail, sea, air, postal, telegraphic, radio, and other means of communication, and the severance of diplomatic relations.

## ARTICLE 42

Should the Security Council consider that measures provided for in Article 41 would be inadequate or have proved to be inadequate, it may take such action by air, sea, or land forces as may be necessary to maintain or restore international peace and security. Such action may include demonstrations, blockade, and other operations by air, sea, or land forces of Members of the United Nations.

## ARTICLE 43

1. All Members of the United Nations, in order to contribute to the maintenance of international peace and security, undertake to make available to the Security Council, on its call and in accordance with a special agreement or agreements, armed forces, assistance, and facilities, including rights of passage, necessary for the purpose of maintaining international peace and security.

2. Such agreement or agreements shall govern the numbers and types of forces, their degree of readiness and general location, and the nature of the facilities and assistance to be provided.

3. The agreement or agreements shall be negotiated as soon as possible on the initiative of the Security Council. They shall be concluded between the Security Council and Members or between the Security Council and groups of Members and shall be subject to ratification by the signatory states in accordance with their respective constitutional processes.

## ARTICLE 44

When Security Council has decided to use force it shall, before calling upon a Member not represented on it to provide armed forces in fulfilment of the obligations assumed under Article 43, invite that Member, if the Member so desires, to participate in the decisions of the Security Council concerning the employment of contingents of that Member's armed forces.

## ARTICLE 45

In order to enable the Nations to take urgent military measures, Members shall hold immediately available national air-force contingents for combined international enforcement action. The strength and degree of readiness of these contingents and plans for their combined action shall be determined within the limits laid down in the special agreement or agreements referred to in Article 43, by the Security Council with the assistance of the Military Committee.

## ARTICLE 46

Plans for the application of armed force shall be made by the Security Council with the assistance of the Military Staff Committee.

## ARTICLE 47

1. There shall be established a Military Staff Committee to advise and assist the Security Council on questions relating to the Security Council's military requirements for the maintenance of international peace and security, the employment and command of forces placed at its disposal, the regulation of armaments, and possible disarmament.

2. The Military Staff Committee consist of the Chiefs of Staff of the permanent members of the Security Council or their representatives. Any Member of the United Nations not permanently represented on the Committee shall be invited by the Committee to be associated with it when the efficient discharge of the Committee's responsibilities requires the participation of that Member its work.

3. The Military Staff Committee be responsible under the Security Council for the strategic direction of any armed forces placed at the disposal of the Security Council. Questions relating to the command of such forces shall be worked out subsequently.

4. The Military Staff Committee, with the authorization of the

Security Council and after consultation with appropriate regional agencies, may establish sub-committees.

## ARTICLE 48

1. The action required to carry out the decisions of the Security Council for the maintenance of international peace and security shall be taken by all the Members of the United Nations or by some of them, as the Security Council may determine.

2. Such decisions shall be carried out by the Members of the United Nations directly and through their action in the appropriate international agencies of which they are members.

## ARTICLE 49

The Members of the United Nations shall join in affording mutual assistance in carrying out the measures decided upon by the Security Council.

## ARTICLE 50

If preventive or enforcement measures against any state are taken by the Security Council, any other state, whether a Member of the United Nations or not, which finds itself confronted with special economic problems arising from the carrying out of those measures shall have the right to consult the Security Council with regard to a solution of those problems.

## ARTICLE 51

Nothing in the present Charter shall impair the inherent right of individual or collective self-defence if an armed attack occurs against a Member of the United Nations, until the Security Council has taken measures necessary to maintain international peace and security. Measures taken by Members in the exercise of this right of self-defence shall be immediately reported to the Security Council and shall not in any way affect the authority and responsibility of the Security Council under the present Charter to take at any time such action as it deems necessary in order to maintain or restore international peace and security.

## CHAPTER VIII
## REGIONAL ARRANGEMENTS

### ARTICLE 52

1. Nothing in the present Charter precludes the existence of regional arrangements or agencies for dealing with such matters relating to the maintenance of international peace and security as are appropriate for regional action provided that such arrangements or agencies and their activities are consistent with the Purposes and Principles of the United Nations.

2. The Members of the United Nations entering into such arrangements or constituting such agencies shall make every effort to achieve pacific settlement of local disputes through such regional arrangements or by such regional agencies before referring them to the Security Council.

3. The Security Council shall encourage the development of pacific settlement of local disputes through such regional arrangements or by such regional agencies either on the initiative of the states concerned or by reference from the Security Council.

4. This Article in no way the application of Articles 34 and 35.

### ARTICLE 53

1. The Security Council shall, where appropriate, utilize such regional arrangements or agencies for enforcement action under its authority. But no enforcement action shall be taken under regional arrangements or by regional agencies without the authorization of the Security Council, with the exception of measures against any enemy state, as defined in paragraph 2 of this Article, provided for pursuant to Article 107 or in regional arrangements directed against renewal of aggressive policy on the part of any such state, until such time as the Organization may, on request of the Governments concerned, be charged with the responsibility for preventing further aggression by such a state.

2. The term enemy state as used in paragraph 1 of this Article applies to any state which during the Second World War has been an enemy of any signatory of the present Charter.

## ARTICLE 54

The Security Council shall at all times be kept fully informed of activities undertaken or in contemplation under regional arrangements or by regional agencies for the maintenance of international peace and security.

## CHAPTER IX
## INTERNATIONAL ECONOMIC AND
## SOCIAL CO-OPERATION

## ARTICLE 55

With a view to the creation of conditions of stability and well-being which are necessary for peaceful and friendly relations among nations based on respect for the principle of equal rights and self-determination of peoples, the United Nations shall promote:

a. higher standards of living, full employment, and conditions of economic and social progress and development;

b. solutions of international economic, social, health, and related problems; and international cultural and educational co-operation; and

c. universal respect for, and observance of, human rights and fundamental freedoms for all without distinction as to race, sex, language, or religion.

## ARTICLE 56

All Members pledge themselves to take joint and separate action in co-operation with the Organization for the achievement of the purposes set forth in Article 55.

## ARTICLE 57

1. The various specialized agencies, established by intergovernmental agreement and having wide international responsibilities, as defined in their basic instruments, in economic, social, cultural, educational, health, and related fields, shall be brought into relationship with the United Nations in accordance with the provisions of Article 63.

2. Such agencies thus brought into relationship with the United Nations are hereinafter referred to as specialized agencies.

## ARTICLE 58

The Organization shall make recommendations for the co-ordination of the policies and activities of the specialized agencies.

## ARTICLE 59

The Organization shall, where appropriate, initiate negotiations among the states concerned for the creation of any new specialized agencies required for the accomplishment of the purposes set forth in Article 55.

## ARTICLE 60

Responsibility for the discharge of the functions of the Organization set forth in this Chapter shall be vested in the General Assembly and, under the authority of the General Assembly, in the Economic and Social Council, which shall have for this purpose the powers set forth in Chapter X.

## CHAPTER X
## THE ECONOMIC AND SOCIAL COUNCIL

### COMPOSITION

## ARTICLE 61

1. The Economic and Social Council shall consist of fifty-four Members of the United Nations elected by the General Assembly.

2. Subject to the provisions of paragraph 3, eighteen members of the Economic and Social Council shall be elected each year for a term of three years. A retiring member shall be eligible for immediate re-election.

3. At the first election after the increase in the membership of the Economic and Social Council from twenty-seven to fifty-four members, in addition to the members elected in place of the nine members whose term of office expires at the end of that year, twenty-seven additional members shall be elected. Of these twenty-seven additional members, the term of office of nine members so elected shall expire at the end of one year, and of nine other members at the end of two years, in accordance with arrangements made by the General Assembly.

4. Each member of the Economic and Social Council shall have one representative.

FUNCTIONS AND POWERS

## ARTICLE 62

1. The Economic and Social Council may make or initiate studies and reports with respect to international economic, social, cultural, educational, health, and related matters and may make recommendations with respect to any such matters to the General Assembly to the Members of the United Nations, and to the specialized agencies concerned.

2. It may make recommendations for the purpose of promoting respect for, and observance of, human rights and fundamental freedoms for all.

3. It may prepare draft conventions for submission to the General Assembly, with respect to matters falling within its competence.

4. It may call, in accordance with the rules prescribed by the United Nations, international conferences on matters falling within its competence.

## ARTICLE 63

1. The Economic and Social Council may enter into agreements with any of the agencies referred to in Article 57, defining the terms on which the agency concerned shall be brought into relationship with the United Nations. Such agreements shall be subject to approval by the General Assembly.

2. It may co-ordinate the activities of the specialized agencies through consultation with and recommendations to such agencies and through recommendations to the General Assembly and to the Members of the United Nations.

## ARTICLE 64

1. The Economic and Social Council may take appropriate steps to obtain regular reports from the specialized agencies. It may make arrangements with the Members of the United Nations and with the specialized agencies to obtain reports on the steps taken to give effect to its own recommendations and to recommendations on matters falling within its competence made by the General Assembly.

2. It may communicate its observations on these reports to the General Assembly.

## ARTICLE 65

The Economic and Social Council may furnish information to the Security Council and shall assist the Security Council upon its request.

## ARTICLE 66

1. The Economic and Social Council shall perform such functions as fall within its competence in connection with the carrying out of the recommendations of the General Assembly.

2. It may, with the approval of the General Assembly, perform services at the request of Members of the United Nations and at the request of specialized agencies.

3. It shall perform such other functions as are specified elsewhere in the present Charter or as may be assigned to it by the General Assembly.

### VOTING

## ARTICLE 67

1. Each member of the Economic and Social Council shall have one vote.

2. Decisions of the Economic and Social Council shall be made by a majority of the members present and voting.

### PROCEDURE

## ARTICLE 68

The Economic and Social Council shall set up commissions in economic and social fields and for the promotion of human rights, and such other commissions as may be required for the performance of its functions.

## ARTICLE 69

The Economic and Social Council shall invite any Member of the United Nations to participate, without vote, in its deliberations on any matter of particular concern to that Member.

## ARTICLE 70

The Economic and Social Council may make arrangements for representatives of the specialized agencies to participate, without vote,

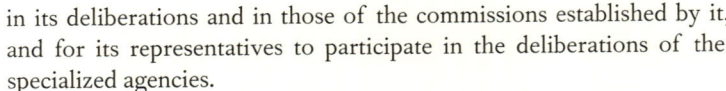

in its deliberations and in those of the commissions established by it, and for its representatives to participate in the deliberations of the specialized agencies.

## ARTICLE 71

The Economic and Social Council may make suitable arrangements for consultation with non-governmental organizations which are concerned with matters within its competence. Such arrangements may be made with international organizations and, where appropriate, with national organizations after consultation with the Member of the United Nations concerned.

## ARTICLE 72

1. The Economic and Social Council shall adopt its own rules of procedure, including the method of selecting its President.

2. The Economic and Social Council shall meet as required in accordance with its rules, which shall include provision for the convening of meetings on the request of a majority of its members.

## CHAPTER XI
## DECLARATION REGARDING
## NON-SELF-GOVERNING TERRITORIES

## ARTICLE 73

Members of the United Nations which have or assume responsibilities for the administration of territories whose peoples have not yet attained a full measure of self-government recognize the principle that the interests of the inhabitants of these territories are paramount, and accept as a sacred trust the obligation to promote to the utmost, within the system of international peace and security established by the present Charter, the well-being of the inhabitants of these territories, and, to this end:

   a. to ensure, with due respect for the culture of the peoples concerned, their political, economic, social, and educational advancement, their just treatment, and their protection against abuses;

   b. to develop self-government, to take due account of the political aspirations of the peoples, and to assist them in the progressive development of their free political institutions, according to the particular circumstances of each territory and its peoples and their varying stages of advancement;

c. to further international peace and security;

d. to promote constructive measures of development, to encourage research, and to co-operate with one another and, when and where appropriate, with specialized international bodies with a view to the practical achievement of the social, economic, and scientific purposes set forth in this Article; and

e. to transmit regularly to the Secretary-General for information purposes, subject to such limitation as security and constitutional considerations may require, statistical and other information of a technical nature relating to economic, social, and educational conditions in the territories for which they are respectively responsible other than those territories to which Chapters XII and XIII apply.

## ARTICLE 74

Members of the United Nations also agree that their policy in respect of the territories to which this Chapter applies, no less than in respect of their metropolitan areas, must be based on the general principle of good-neighbourliness, due account being taken of the interests and well-being of the rest of the world, in social, economic, and commercial matters.

## CHAPTER XII
## INTERNATIONAL TRUSTEESHIP SYSTEM

## ARTICLE 75

The United Nations shall establish under its authority an international trusteeship system for the administration and supervision of such territories as may be placed thereunder by subsequent individual agreements. These territories are hereinafter referred to as trust territories.

## ARTICLE 76

The basic objectives of the trusteeship system, in accordance with the Purposes of the United Nations laid down in Article 1 of the present Charter, shall be:

a. to further international peace and security;

b. to promote the political, economic, social, and educational advancement of the inhabitants of the trust territories, and their progressive development towards self-government or independence as may be appropriate to the particular circumstances of each territory and its peoples and the freely expressed wishes of the peoples concerned, and as may be provided by the terms of each trusteeship agreement;

c. to encourage respect for human rights and for fundamental freedoms for all without distinction as to race, sex, language, or religion, and to encourage recognition of the interdependence of the peoples of the world; and

d. to ensure equal treatment in social, economic, and commercial matters for all Members of the United Nations and their nationals, and also equal treatment for the latter in the administration of justice, without prejudice to the attainment of the foregoing objectives and subject to the provisions of Article 80.

## ARTICLE 77

1. The trusteeship system shall apply to such territories in the following categories as may be placed thereunder by means of trusteeship agreements:

a. territories now held under mandate;

b. territories which may be detached from enemy states as a result of the Second World War; and

c. territories voluntarily placed under the system by states responsible for their administration.

2. It will be a matter for subsequent agreement as to which territories in the foregoing categories will be brought under the trusteeship system and upon what terms.

## ARTICLE 78

The trusteeship system shall not apply to territories which have become Members of the United Nations, relationship among which shall be based on respect for the principle of sovereign equality.

## ARTICLE 79

The terms of trusteeship for each territory to be placed under the trusteeship system, including any alteration or amendment, shall be agreed upon by the states directly concerned, including the mandatory power in the case of territories held under mandate by a Member of the United Nations, and shall be approved as provided for in Articles 83 and 85.

## ARTICLE 80

1. Except as may be agreed upon in individual trusteeship agreements, made under Articles 77, 79, and 81, placing each territory under the trusteeship system, and until such agreements have been concluded, nothing in this Chapter shall be construed in or of itself to alter in any manner the rights whatsoever of any states or any peoples or the terms of existing international instruments to which Members of the United Nations may respectively be parties.

2. Paragraph 1 of this Article shall not be interpreted as giving grounds for delay or postponement of the negotiation and conclusion of agreements for placing mandated and other territories under the trusteeship system as provided for in Article 77.

## ARTICLE 81

The trusteeship agreement shall in each case include the terms under which the trust territory will be administered and designate the authority which will exercise the administration of the trust territory. Such authority, hereinafter called the administering authority, may be one or more states or the Organization itself.

## ARTICLE 82

There may be designated, in any trusteeship agreement, a strategic area or areas which may include part or all of the trust territory to which the agreement applies, without prejudice to any special agreement or agreements made under Article 43.

## ARTICLE 83

1. All functions of the United Nations relating to strategic areas, including the approval of the terms of the trusteeship agreements and of their alteration or amendment, shall be exercised by the Security Council.

2. he basic objectives set forth in Article 76 shall be applicable to the people of each strategic area.

3. The Security Council shall, subject to the provisions of the trusteeship agreements and without prejudice to security considerations, avail itself of the assistance of the Trusteeship Council to perform those functions of the United Nations under the trusteeship system relating to political, economic, social, and educational matters in the strategic areas.

## ARTICLE 84

It shall be the duty of the administering authority to ensure that the trust territory shall play its part in the maintenance of international peace and security. To this end the administering authority may make use of volunteer forces, facilities, and assistance from the trust territory in carrying out the obligations towards the Security Council undertaken in this regard by the administering authority, as well as for local defence and the maintenance of law and order within the trust territory.

## ARTICLE 85

1. The functions of the United Nations with regard to trusteeship agreements for all areas not designated as strategic, including the approval of the terms of the trusteeship agreements and of their alteration or amendment, shall be exercised by the General Assembly.

2. The Trusteeship Council, operating under the authority of the General Assembly, shall assist the General Assembly in carrying out these functions.

## CHAPTER XIII
## THE TRUSTEESHIP COUNCIL

### COMPOSITION

## ARTICLE 86

1. The Trusteeship Council shall consist of the following Members of the United Nations:

a. those Members administering trust territories;

b. such of those Members mentioned by name in Article 23 as are not administering trust territories; and

c. as many other Members elected for three-year terms by the

General Assembly as may be necessary to ensure that the total number of members of the Trusteeship Council is equally divided between those Members of the United Nations which administer trust territories and those which do not.

2. Each member of the Trusteeship Council shall designate one specially qualified person to represent it therein.

Functions and Powers

## Article 87

The General Assembly and, under its authority, the Trusteeship Council, in carrying out their functions, may:

a. consider reports submitted by the administering authority;

b. accept petitions and examine them in consultation with the administering authority;

c. provide for periodic visits to the respective trust territories at times agreed upon with the administering authority; and

d. take these and other actions in conformity with the terms of the trusteeship agreements.

## Article 88

The Trusteeship Council shall formulate a questionnaire on the political, economic, social, and educational advancement of the inhabitants of each trust territory, and the administering authority for each trust territory within the competence of the General Assembly shall make an annual report to the General Assembly upon the basis of such questionnaire.

Voting

## Article 89

1. Each member of the Trusteeship Council shall have one vote.

2. Decisions of the Trusteeship Council shall be made by a majority of the members present and voting.

PROCEDURE

## ARTICLE 90

1. The Trusteeship Council shall adopt its own rules of procedure, including the method of selecting its President.

2. The Trusteeship Council shall meet as required in accordance with its rules, which shall include provision for the convening of meetings on the request of a majority of its members.

## ARTICLE 91

The Trusteeship Council shall, when appropriate, avail itself of the assistance of the Economic and Social Council and of the specialized agencies in regard to matters with which they are respectively concerned.

## CHAPTER XIV
## THE INTERNATIONAL COURT OF JUSTICE

## ARTICLE 92

The International Court of Justice shall be the principal judicial organ of the United Nations. It shall function in accordance with the annexed Statute, which is based upon the Statute of the Permanent Court of International Justice and forms an integral part of the present Charter.

## ARTICLE 93

1. All Members of the United Nations are *ipso facto* parties to the Statute of the International Court of Justice.

2. A state which is not of the United Nations may become a party to the Statute of the International Court of Justice on to be determined in each case by the General Assembly upon the recommendation of the Security Council.

## ARTICLE 94

1. Each Member of the United Nations undertakes to comply with the decision of the International Court of Justice in any case to which it is a party.

2. If any party to a case fails to perform the obligations incumbent

upon it under a judgment rendered by the Court, the other party may have recourse to the Security Council, which may, if it deems necessary, make recommendations or decide upon measures to be taken to give effect to the judgment.

## ARTICLE 95

Nothing in the present Charter shall prevent Members of the United Nations from entrusting the solution of their differences to other tribunals by virtue of agreements already in existence or which may be concluded in the future.

## ARTICLE 96

1. The General Assembly or the Security Council may request the International Court of Justice to give an advisory opinion on any legal question.

2. Other organs of the United Nations and specialized agencies, which may at any time be so authorized by the General Assembly, may also request advisory opinions of the Court on legal questions arising within the scope of their activities.

### CHAPTER XV
### THE SECRETARIAT

## ARTICLE 97

The Secretariat shall comprise a Secretary-General and such staff as the Organization may require. The Secretary-General shall be appointed by the General Assembly upon the recommendation of the Security Council. He shall be the chief administrative officer of the Organization.

## ARTICLE 98

The Secretary-General shall act in that capacity in all meetings of the General Assembly, of the Security Council, of the Economic and Social Council, and of the Trusteeship Council, and shall perform such other functions as are entrusted to him by these organs. The Secretary-General shall make an annual report to the General Assembly on the work of the Organization.

## ARTICLE 99

The Secretary-General may bring to the attention of the Security Council any matter which in his opinion may threaten the maintenance of international peace and security.

## ARTICLE 100

1. In the performance of their duties the Secretary-General and the staff shall not seek or receive instructions from any government or from any other authority external to the Organization. They shall refrain from any action which might reflect on their position as international officials responsible only to the Organization.

2. Each Member of the United Nations undertakes to respect the exclusively international character of the responsibilities of the Secretary-General and the staff and not to seek to influence them in the discharge of their responsibilities.

## ARTICLE 101

1. The staff shall be appointed by the Secretary-General under regulations established by the General Assembly.

2. Appropriate staffs shall be permanently assigned to the Economic and Social Council, the Trusteeship Council, and, as required, to other organs of the United Nations. These staffs shall form a part of the Secretariat.

3. The paramount consideration in the employment of the staff and in the determination of the conditions of service shall be the necessity of securing the highest standards of efficiency, competence, and integrity. Due regard shall be paid to the importance of recruiting the staff on as wide a geographical basis as possible.

## CHAPTER XVI
## MISCELLANEOUS PROVISIONS

## ARTICLE 102

1. Every treaty and every international agreement entered into by any Member of the United Nations after the present Charter comes into force shall as soon as possible be registered with the Secretariat and published by it.

2. No party to any such treaty or international agreement which has not been registered in accordance with the provisions of paragraph I of this Article may invoke that treaty or agreement before any organ of the United Nations.

## ARTICLE 103

In the event of a conflict between the obligations of the Members of the United Nations under the present Charter and their obligations under any other international agreement, their obligations under the present Charter shall prevail.

## ARTICLE 104

The Organization shall enjoy in the territory of each of its Members such legal capacity as may be necessary for the exercise of its functions and the fulfilment of its purposes.

## ARTICLE 105

1. The Organization shall enjoy in the territory of each of its Members such privileges and immunities as are necessary for the fulfilment of its purposes.

2. Representatives of the Members of the United Nations and officials of the Organization shall similarly enjoy such privileges and immunities as are necessary for the independent exercise of their functions in connexion with the Organization.

3. The General Assembly may make recommendations with a view to determining the details of the application of paragraphs 1 and 2 of this Article or may propose conventions to the Members of the United Nations for this purpose.

## CHAPTER XVII
## TRANSITIONAL SECURITY ARRANGEMENTS

## ARTICLE 106

Pending the coming into force of such special agreements referred to in Article 43 as in the opinion of the Security Council enable it to begin the exercise of its responsibilities under Article 42, the parties to the Four-Nation Declaration, signed at Moscow, 30 October 1943, and

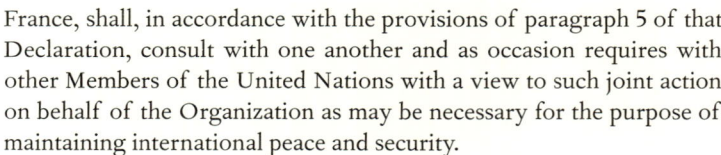

France, shall, in accordance with the provisions of paragraph 5 of that Declaration, consult with one another and as occasion requires with other Members of the United Nations with a view to such joint action on behalf of the Organization as may be necessary for the purpose of maintaining international peace and security.

### ARTICLE 107

Nothing in the present Charter shall invalidate or preclude action, in relation to any state which during the Second World War has been an enemy of any signatory to the present Charter, taken or authorized as a result of that war by the Governments having responsibility for such action.

### CHAPTER XVIII
### AMENDMENTS

### ARTICLE 108

Amendments to the present Charter shall come into force for all Members of the United Nations when they have been adopted by a vote of two thirds of the members of the General Assembly and ratified in accordance with their respective constitutional processes by two thirds of the Members of the United Nations, including all the permanent members of the Security Council.

### ARTICLE 109

1. A General Conference of the Members of the United Nations for the purpose of reviewing the present Charter may be held at a date and place to be fixed by a two-thirds vote of the members of the General Assembly and by a vote of any nine members of the Security Council. Each Member of the United Nations shall have one vote in the conference.

2. Any alteration of the present Charter recommended by a two-thirds vote of the conference shall take effect when ratified in accordance with their respective constitutional processes by two thirds of the Members of the United Nations including the permanent members of the Security Council.

3. If such a conference has not been held before the tenth annual session of the General Assembly following the coming into force of the present

Charter, the proposal to call such a conference shall be placed on the agenda of that session of the General Assembly, and the conference shall be held if so decided by a majority vote of the members of the General Assembly and by a vote of any seven members of the Security Council.

## CHAPTER XIX
## RATIFICATION AND SIGNATURE

### ARTICLE 110

1. The present Charter shall be ratified by the signatory states in accordance with their respective constitutional processes.

2. The ratifications shall be deposited with the Government of the United States of America, which shall notify all the signatory states of each deposit as well as the Secretary-General of the Organization when he has been appointed.

3. The present Charter shall come into force upon the deposit of ratifications by the Republic of China, France, the Union of Soviet Socialist Republics, the United Kingdom of Great Britain and Northern Ireland, and the United States of America, and by a majority of the other signatory states. A protocol of the ratifications deposited shall thereupon be drawn up by the Government of the United States of America which shall communicate copies thereof to all the signatory states.

4. The states signatory to the present Charter which ratify it after it has come into force will become original Members of the United Nations on the date of the deposit of their respective ratifications.

### ARTICLE 111

The present Charter, of which the Chinese, French, Russian, English, and Spanish texts are equally authentic, shall remain deposited in the archives of the Government of the United States of America. Duly certified copies thereof shall be transmitted by that Government to the Governments of the other signatory states.

IN FAITH WHEREOF the representatives of the Governments of the United Nations have signed the present Charter.

DONE at the city of San Francisco the twenty-sixth day of June, one thousand nine hundred and forty-five.

# HARRY S. TRUMAN'S
# INAUGURAL ADDRESS
# JANUARY 20, 1949

Mr. Vice President, Mr. Chief Justice, and fellow citizens, I accept with humility the honor which the American people have conferred upon me. I accept it with a deep resolve to do all that I can for the welfare of this Nation and for the peace of the world.

In performing the duties of my office, I need the help and prayers of every one of you. I ask for your encouragement and your support. The tasks we face are difficult, and we can accomplish them only if we work together.

Each period of our national history has had its special challenges. Those that confront us now are as momentous as any in the past. Today marks the beginning not only of a new administration, but of a period that will be eventful, perhaps decisive, for us and for the world.

It may be our lot to experience, and in large measure to bring about, a major turning point in the long history of the human race. The first half of this century has been marked by unprecedented and brutal attacks on the rights of man, and by the two most frightful wars in history. The supreme need of our time is for men to learn to live together in peace and harmony.

The peoples of the earth face the future with grave uncertainty, composed almost equally of great hopes and great fears. In this time of doubt, they look to the United States as never before for good will, strength, and wise leadership.

It is fitting, therefore, that we take this occasion to proclaim to the world the essential principles of the faith by which we live, and to declare our aims to all peoples.

The American people stand firm in the faith which has inspired this Nation from the beginning. We believe that all men have a right to equal justice under law and equal opportunity to share in the common good. We believe that all men have the right to freedom of thought and expression. We believe that all men are created equal because they are created in the image of God.

From this faith we will not be moved.

The American people desire, and are determined to work for, a world in which all nations and all peoples are free to govern themselves as they see fit, and to achieve a decent and satisfying life. Above all else, our people desire, and are determined to work for, peace on earth—a just and lasting peace—based on genuine agreement freely arrived at by equals.

In the pursuit of these aims, the United States and other like-minded nations find themselves directly opposed by a regime with contrary aims and a totally different concept of life.

That regime adheres to a false philosophy which purports to offer freedom, security, and greater opportunity to mankind. Misled by this philosophy, many peoples have sacrificed their liberties only to learn to their sorrow that deceit and mockery, poverty and tyranny, are their reward.

That false philosophy is communism.

Communism is based on the belief that man is so weak and inadequate that he is unable to govern himself, and therefore requires the rule of strong masters.

Democracy is based on the conviction that man has the moral and intellectual capacity, as well as the inalienable right, to govern himself with reason and justice.

Communism subjects the individual to arrest without lawful cause, punishment without trial, and forced labor as the chattel of the state. It decrees what information he shall receive, what art he shall produce, what leaders he shall follow, and what thoughts he shall think.

Democracy maintains that government is established for the benefit of the individual, and is charged with the responsibility of protecting the rights of the individual and his freedom in the exercise of his abilities.

Communism maintains that social wrongs can be corrected only by violence.

Democracy has proved that social justice can be achieved through peaceful change.

Communism holds that the world is so deeply divided into opposing classes that war is inevitable.

Democracy holds that free nations can settle differences justly and maintain lasting peace.

These differences between communism and democracy do not concern the United States alone. People everywhere are coming to realize that what is involved is material well-being, human dignity, and the right to believe in and worship God.

I state these differences, not to draw issues of belief as such, but because the actions resulting from the Communist philosophy are a threat to the efforts of free nations to bring about world recovery and lasting peace.

Since the end of hostilities, the United States has invested its substance and its energy in a great constructive effort to restore peace, stability, and freedom to the world.

We have sought no territory and we have imposed our will on none. We have asked for no privileges we would not extend to others.

We have constantly and vigorously supported the United Nations and related agencies as a means of applying democratic principles to international relations. We have consistently advocated and relied upon peaceful settlement of disputes among nations.

We have made every effort to secure agreement on effective international control of our most powerful weapon, and we have worked steadily for the limitation and control of all armaments.

We have encouraged, by precept and example, the expansion of world trade on a sound and fair basis.

Almost a year ago, in company with 16 free nations of Europe, we launched the greatest cooperative economic program in history. The purpose of that unprecedented effort is to invigorate and strengthen democracy in Europe, so that the free people of that continent can resume their rightful place in the forefront of civilization and can contribute once more to the security and welfare of the world.

Our efforts have brought new hope to all mankind. We have beaten back despair and defeatism. We have saved a number of countries from losing their liberty. Hundreds of millions of people all over the world now agree with us, that we need not have war—that we can have peace.

The initiative is ours.

We are moving on with other nations to build an even stronger structure of international order and justice. We shall have as our partners countries which, no longer solely concerned with the problem of national survival, are now working to improve the standards of living of all their people. We are ready to undertake new projects to strengthen the free world.

In the coming years, our program for peace and freedom will emphasize four major courses of action.

First, we will continue to give unfaltering support to the United Nations and related agencies, and we will continue to search for ways to strengthen their authority and increase their effectiveness. We believe that the United Nations will be strengthened by the new nations which are being formed in lands now advancing toward self-government under democratic principles.

Second, we will continue our programs for world economic recovery.

This means, first of all, that we must keep our full weight behind the European recovery program. We are confident of the success of this major venture in world recovery. We believe that our partners in this effort will achieve the status of self-supporting nations once again.

In addition, we must carry out our plans for reducing the barriers to world trade and increasing its volume. Economic recovery and peace itself depend on increased world trade.

Third, we will strengthen freedom-loving nations against the dangers of aggression.

We are now working out with a number of countries a joint agreement designed to strengthen the security of the North Atlantic area. Such an agreement would take the form of a collective defense arrangement within the terms of the United Nations Charter.

We have already established such a defense pact for the Western Hemisphere by the treaty of Rio de Janeiro.

The primary purpose of these agreements is to provide unmistakable proof of the joint determination of the free countries to resist armed attack from any quarter. Each country participating in these arrangements must contribute all it can to the common defense.

If we can make it sufficiently clear, in advance, that any armed attack affecting our national security would be met with overwhelming force, the armed attack might never occur.

I hope soon to send to the Senate a treaty respecting the North Atlantic security plan.

In addition, we will provide military advice and equipment to free nations which will cooperate with us in the maintenance of peace and security.

Fourth, we must embark on a bold new program for making the benefits of our scientific advances and industrial progress available for the improvement and growth of underdeveloped areas.

More than half the people of the world are living in conditions approaching misery. Their food is inadequate. They are victims of disease. Their economic life is primitive and stagnant. Their poverty is a handicap and a threat both to them and to more prosperous areas.

For the first time in history, humanity possesses the knowledge and the skill to relieve the suffering of these people.

The United States is pre-eminent among nations in the development of industrial and scientific techniques. The material resources which we can afford to use for the assistance of other peoples are limited. But our imponderable resources in technical knowledge are constantly growing and are inexhaustible.

I believe that we should make available to peace-loving peoples the benefits of our store of technical knowledge in order to help them realize their aspirations for a better life. And, in cooperation with other nations, we should foster capital investment in areas needing development.

Our aim should be to help the free peoples of the world, through their own efforts, to produce more food, more clothing, more materials for housing, and more mechanical power to lighten their burdens.

We invite other countries to pool their technological resources in this undertaking. Their contributions will be warmly welcomed. This should be a cooperative enterprise in which all nations work together through the United Nations and its specialized agencies wherever practicable. It must be a worldwide effort for the achievement of peace, plenty, and freedom.

With the cooperation of business, private capital, agriculture, and labor in this country, this program can greatly increase the industrial activity in other nations and can raise substantially their standards of living.

Such new economic developments must be devised and controlled to benefit the peoples of the areas in which they are established. Guarantees to the investor must be balanced by guarantees in the interest of the people whose resources and whose labor go into these developments.

The old imperialism—exploitation for foreign profit—has no place in our plans. What we envisage is a program of development based on the concepts of democratic fair-dealing.

All countries, including our own, will greatly benefit from a constructive program for the better use of the world's human and natural resources. Experience shows that our commerce with other countries expands as they progress industrially and economically.

Greater production is the key to prosperity and peace. And the key to greater production is a wider and more vigorous application of modern scientific and technical knowledge.

Only by helping the least fortunate of its members to help themselves can the human family achieve the decent, satisfying life that is the right of all people.

Democracy alone can supply the vitalizing force to stir the peoples of the world into triumphant action, not only against their human oppressors, but also against their ancient enemies—hunger, misery, and despair.

On the basis of these four major courses of action we hope to help create the conditions that will lead eventually to personal freedom and happiness for all mankind.

If we are to be successful in carrying out these policies, it is clear that we must have continued prosperity in this country and we must keep ourselves strong.

Slowly but surely we are weaving a world fabric of international security and growing prosperity.

We are aided by all who wish to live in freedom from fear—even by those who live today in fear under their own governments.

We are aided by all who want relief from the lies of propaganda— who desire truth and sincerity.

We are aided by all who desire self-government and a voice in deciding their own affairs.

We are aided by all who long for economic security—for the security and abundance that men in free societies can enjoy.

We are aided by all who desire freedom of speech, freedom of religion, and freedom to live their own lives for useful ends.

Our allies are the millions who hunger and thirst after righteousness.

In due time, as our stability becomes manifest, as more and more nations come to know the benefits of democracy and to participate in growing abundance, I believe that those countries which now oppose us will abandon their delusions and join with the free nations of the world in a just settlement of international differences.

Events have brought our American democracy to new influence and new responsibilities. They will test our courage, our devotion to duty, and our concept of liberty.

But I say to all men, what we have achieved in liberty, we will surpass in greater liberty.

Steadfast in our faith in the Almighty, we will advance toward a world where man's freedom is secure.

To that end we will devote our strength, our resources, and our firmness of resolve. With God's help, the future of mankind will be assured in a world of justice, harmony, and peace.

# THE NORTH ATLANTIC TREATY (1949)

*Drafted in Washington, D.C., the North Atlantic Treaty established the North Atlantic Treaty Organization (NATO), a peacetime military alliance that initially included twelve countries: the United States, Canada, and ten Western European nations. NATO's goals included rebuilding Western Europe after the devastation of World War II, protecting Western Europe from another attack or invasion, and guarding against the spread of communism. Today, NATO includes twenty-eight nations and is the world's largest peacetime military alliance.*

The Parties to this Treaty reaffirm their faith in the purposes and principles of the Charter of the United Nations and their desire to live in peace with all peoples and all governments.

They are determined to safeguard the freedom, common heritage and civilisation of their peoples, founded on the principles of democracy, individual liberty and the rule of law. They seek to promote stability and well-being in the North Atlantic area.

They are resolved to unite their efforts for collective defence and for the preservation of peace and security. They therefore agree to this North Atlantic Treaty :

### ARTICLE 1

The Parties undertake, as set forth in the Charter of the United Nations, to settle any international dispute in which they may be involved by peaceful means in such a manner that international peace and security and justice are not endangered, and to refrain in their international relations from the threat or use of force in any manner inconsistent with the purposes of the United Nations.

### ARTICLE 2

The Parties will contribute toward the further development of peaceful and friendly international relations by strengthening their free institutions, by bringing about a better understanding of the principles upon which these institutions are founded, and by promoting conditions of stability and well-being. They will seek to eliminate conflict in their international economic policies and will encourage economic collaboration between any or all of them.

## ARTICLE 3

In order more effectively to achieve the objectives of this Treaty, the Parties, separately and jointly, by means of continuous and effective self-help and mutual aid, will maintain and develop their individual and collective capacity to resist armed attack.

## ARTICLE 4

The Parties will consult together whenever, in the opinion of any of them, the territorial integrity, political independence or security of any of the Parties is threatened.

## ARTICLE 5

The Parties agree that an armed attack against one or more of them in Europe or North America shall be considered an attack against them all and consequently they agree that, if such an armed attack occurs, each of them, in exercise of the right of individual or collective self-defence recognised by Article 51 of the Charter of the United Nations, will assist the Party or Parties so attacked by taking forthwith, individually and in concert with the other Parties, such action as it deems necessary, including the use of armed force, to restore and maintain the security of the North Atlantic area.

Any such armed attack and all measures taken as a result thereof shall immediately be reported to the Security Council. Such measures shall be terminated when the Security Council has taken the measures necessary to restore and maintain international peace and security .

## ARTICLE 6 (1)

For the purpose of Article 5, an armed attack on one or more of the Parties is deemed to include an armed attack:
  • on the territory of any of the Parties in Europe or North America, on the Algerian Departments of France (2), on the territory of or on the Islands under the jurisdiction of any of

the Parties in the North Atlantic area north of the Tropic of Cancer;

• on the forces, vessels, or aircraft of any of the Parties, when in or over these territories or any other area in Europe in which occupation forces of any of the Parties were stationed on the date when the Treaty entered into force or the Mediterranean Sea or the North Atlantic area north of the Tropic of Cancer.

## ARTICLE 7

This Treaty does not affect, and shall not be interpreted as affecting in any way the rights and obligations under the Charter of the Parties which are members of the United Nations, or the primary responsibility of the Security Council for the maintenance of international peace and security.

## ARTICLE 8

Each Party declares that none of the international engagements now in force between it and any other of the Parties or any third State is in conflict with the provisions of this Treaty, and undertakes not to enter into any international engagement in conflict with this Treaty.

## ARTICLE 9

The Parties hereby establish a Council, on which each of them shall be represented, to consider matters concerning the implementation of this Treaty. The Council shall be so organised as to be able to meet promptly at any time. The Council shall set up such subsidiary bodies as may be necessary; in particular it shall establish immediately a defence committee which shall recommend measures for the implementation of Articles 3 and 5.

## ARTICLE 10

The Parties may, by unanimous agreement, invite any other European State in a position to further the principles of this Treaty and to contribute to the security of the North Atlantic area to accede to this Treaty. Any State so invited may become a Party to the Treaty by depositing its instrument of accession with the Government of the United States of America. The Government of the United States of America will inform each of the Parties of the deposit of each such instrument of accession.

## ARTICLE 11

This Treaty shall be ratified and its provisions carried out by the Parties in accordance with their respective constitutional processes. The instruments of ratification shall be deposited as soon as possible with the Government of the United States of America, which will notify all the other signatories of each deposit. The Treaty shall enter into force between the States which have ratified it as soon as the ratifications of the majority of the signatories, including the ratifications of Belgium, Canada, France, Luxembourg, the Netherlands, the United Kingdom and the United States, have been deposited and shall come into effect with respect to other States on the date of the deposit of their ratifications. (3)

## ARTICLE 12

After the Treaty has been in force for ten years, or at any time thereafter, the Parties shall, if any of them so requests, consult together for the purpose of reviewing the Treaty, having regard for the factors then affecting peace and security in the North Atlantic area, including the development of universal as well as regional arrangements under the Charter of the United Nations for the maintenance of international peace and security.

## ARTICLE 13

After the Treaty has been in force for twenty years, any Party may cease to be a Party one year after its notice of denunciation has been given to the Government of the United States of America, which will inform the Governments of the other Parties of the deposit of each notice of denunciation.

## ARTICLE 14

This Treaty, of which the English and French texts are equally authentic, shall be deposited in the archives of the Government of the United States of America. Duly certified copies will be transmitted by that Government to the Governments of other signatories.

1. The definition of the territories to which Article 5 applies was revised by Article 2 of the Protocol to the North Atlantic Treaty on the accession of Greece and Turkey signed on 22 October 1951.

2. On January 16, 1963, the North Atlantic Council noted that insofar as the former Algerian Departments of France were concerned, the relevant clauses of this Treaty had become inapplicable as from July 3, 1962.

3. The Treaty came into force on 24 August 1949, after the deposition of the ratifications of all signatory states.

# BROWN V. BOARD OF EDUCATION (1954)

*Despite winning emancipation after the Civil War, African Americans in the United States continued to face discrimination. An 1896 Supreme Court decision called Plessy v. Ferguson made the discrimination legal. After Homer Plessy, an African American man, was arrested for riding in a whites-only train car in New Orleans, he appealed all the way to the Supreme Court, arguing that segregating black passengers violated the 14th Amendment. In an 8–1 decision, the Court ruled against Plessy, saying that as long as "equal" accommodations were provided, "separate" facilities were lawful. This lead to a rash of new laws in the South segregating African Americans and whites in everything from restaurants to buses to schools. The laws, called Jim Crow laws, remained in place well into the twentieth century. But in the 1950s, another case made it to the Supreme Court. The child named in the lawsuit, eight-year-old Linda Brown, represented five African American families whose children were forced to endure unsafe and substandard conditions at segregated black schools. This time, the Court, led by Justice Earl Warren, rendered a unanimous decision that struck down the concept of "separate but equal" and ultimately led to the integration of America's public schools.*

SUPREME COURT OF THE UNITED STATES
Brown v. Board of Education, 347 U.S. 483 (1954) (USSC+)
Argued December 9, 1952
Reargued December 8, 1953
Decided May 17, 1954

## APPEAL FROM THE UNITED STATES DISTRICT COURT FOR THE DISTRICT OF KANSAS*

* *Together with No. 2, Briggs et al. v. Elliott et al., on appeal from the United States District Court for the Eastern District of South Carolina, argued December 9–10,*

S egregation of white and Negro children in the public schools of a State solely on the basis of race, pursuant to state laws permitting or requiring such segregation, denies to Negro children the equal protection of the laws guaranteed by the Fourteenth Amendment — even though the physical facilities and other "tangible" factors of white and Negro schools may be equal.

(a) The history of the Fourteenth Amendment is inconclusive as to its intended effect on public education.

(b) The question presented in these cases must be determined not on the basis of conditions existing when the Fourteenth Amendment was adopted, but in the light of the full development of public education and its present place in American life throughout the Nation.

(c) Where a State has undertaken to provide an opportunity for an education in its public schools, such an opportunity is a right which must be made available to all on equal terms.

(d) Segregation of children in public schools solely on the basis of race deprives children of the minority group of equal educational opportunities, even though the physical facilities and other "tangible" factors may be equal.

(e) The "separate but equal" doctrine adopted in Plessy v. Ferguson, 163 U.S. 537, has no place in the field of public education.

(f) The cases are restored to the docket for further argument on specified questions relating to the forms of the decrees.

OPINION

*Mr. Chief Justice Earl Warren* delivered the opinion of the Court.

These cases come to us from the States of Kansas, South Carolina, Virginia, and Delaware. They are premised on different facts and different local conditions, but a common legal question justifies their consideration together in this consolidated opinion.

---

*1952, reargued December 7–8, 1953; No. 4, Davis et al. v. County School Board of Prince Edward County, Virginia, et al., on appeal from the United States District Court for the Eastern District of Virginia, argued December 10, 1952, reargued December 7–8, 1953, and No. 10, Gebhart et al. v. Belton et al., on certiorari to the Supreme Court of Delaware, argued December 11, 1952, reargued December 9, 1953.*

In each of the cases, minors of the Negro race, through their legal representatives, seek the aid of the courts in obtaining admission to the public schools of their community on a nonsegregated basis. In each instance, they had been denied admission to schools attended by white children under laws requiring or permitting segregation according to race. This segregation was alleged to deprive the plaintiffs of the equal protection of the laws under the Fourteenth Amendment. In each of the cases other than the Delaware case, a three-judge federal district court denied relief to the plaintiffs on the so-called "separate but equal" doctrine announced by this Court in Plessy v. Ferguson, 163 U.S. 537. Under that doctrine, equality of treatment is accorded when the races are provided substantially equal facilities, even though these facilities be separate. In the Delaware case, the Supreme Court of Delaware adhered to that doctrine, but ordered that the plaintiffs be admitted to the white schools because of their superiority to the Negro schools.

The plaintiffs contend that segregated public schools are not "equal" and cannot be made "equal," and that hence they are deprived of the equal protection of the laws. Because of the obvious importance of the question presented, the Court took jurisdiction. Argument was heard in the 1952 Term, and reargument was heard this Term on certain questions propounded by the Court.

Reargument was largely devoted to the circumstances surrounding the adoption of the Fourteenth Amendment in 1868. It covered exhaustively consideration of the Amendment in Congress, ratification by the states, then-existing practices in racial segregation, and the views of proponents and opponents of the Amendment. This discussion and our own investigation convince us that, although these sources cast some light, it is not enough to resolve the problem with which we are faced. At best, they are inconclusive. The most avid proponents of the post-War Amendments undoubtedly intended them to remove all legal distinctions among "all persons born or naturalized in the United States." Their opponents, just as certainly, were antagonistic to both the letter and the spirit of the Amendments and wished them to have the most limited effect. What others in Congress and the state legislatures had in mind cannot be determined with any degree of certainty.

An additional reason for the inconclusive nature of the Amendment's history with respect to segregated schools is the status of public education at that time. In the South, the movement toward free common schools, supported by general taxation, had not yet taken hold. Education of white children was largely in the hands of private groups. Education of Negroes was almost nonexistent, and practically all of the race were illiterate. In fact, any education of Negroes was forbidden by law in some states. Today, in contrast, many Negroes have achieved outstanding success in the arts and sciences, as well as in the business and professional world. It is true that public school education at the time of the Amendment had advanced further in the North, but the effect of the Amendment on Northern States was generally ignored in the congressional debates. Even in the North, the conditions of public education did not approximate those existing today. The curriculum was usually rudimentary; ungraded schools were common in rural areas; the school term was but three months a year in many states, and compulsory school attendance was virtually unknown. As a consequence, it is not surprising that there should be so little in the history of the Fourteenth Amendment relating to its intended effect on public education.

In the first cases in this Court construing the Fourteenth Amendment, decided shortly after its adoption, the Court interpreted it as proscribing all state-imposed discriminations against the Negro race. The doctrine of "separate but equal" did not make its appearance in this Court until 1896 in the case of Plessy v. Ferguson, supra, involving not education but transportation. American courts have since labored with the doctrine for over half a century. In this Court, there have been six cases involving the "separate but equal" doctrine in the field of public education. In Cumming v. County Board of Education, 175 U.S. 528, and Gong Lum v. Rice, 275 U.S. 78, the validity of the doctrine itself was not challenged. In more recent cases, all on the graduate school level, inequality was found in that specific benefits enjoyed by white students were denied to Negro students of the same educational qualifications. Missouri ex rel. Gaines v. Canada, 305 U.S. 337; Sipuel v. Oklahoma, 332 U.S. 631; Sweatt v. Painter, 339 U.S. 629; McLaurin v. Oklahoma State Regents, 339 U.S. 637. In none of these cases was it necessary to reexamine the doctrine to grant relief to the Negro plaintiff. And in Sweatt v. Painter, supra, the Court expressly reserved decision on the question whether Plessy v. Ferguson should be held inapplicable to public education.

In the instant cases, that question is directly presented. Here, unlike

Sweatt v. Painter, there are findings below that the Negro and white schools involved have been equalized, or are being equalized, with respect to buildings, curricula, qualifications and salaries of teachers, and other "tangible" factors. Our decision, therefore, cannot turn on merely a comparison of these tangible factors in the Negro and white schools involved in each of the cases. We must look instead to the effect of segregation itself on public education.

In approaching this problem, we cannot turn the clock back to 1868, when the Amendment was adopted, or even to 1896, when Plessy v. Ferguson was written. We must consider public education in the light of its full development and its present place in American life throughout the Nation. Only in this way can it be determined if segregation in public schools deprives these plaintiffs of the equal protection of the laws.

Today, education is perhaps the most important function of state and local governments. Compulsory school attendance laws and the great expenditures for education both demonstrate our recognition of the importance of education to our democratic society. It is required in the performance of our most basic public responsibilities, even service in the armed forces. It is the very foundation of good citizenship. Today it is a principal instrument in awakening the child to cultural values, in preparing him for later professional training, and in helping him to adjust normally to his environment. In these days, it is doubtful that any child may reasonably be expected to succeed in life if he is denied the opportunity of an education. Such an opportunity, where the state has undertaken to provide it, is a right which must be made available to all on equal terms.

We come then to the question presented: Does segregation of children in public schools solely on the basis of race, even though the physical facilities and other "tangible" factors may be equal, deprive the children of the minority group of equal educational opportunities? We believe that it does.

In Sweatt v. Painter, supra, in finding that a segregated law school for Negroes could not provide them equal educational opportunities, this Court relied in large part on "those qualities which are incapable of objective measurement but which make for greatness in a law school." In McLaurin v. Oklahoma State Regents, supra, the Court, in requiring that a Negro admitted to a white graduate school be treated like all other students, again resorted to intangible considerations: ". . . his ability to study, to engage in discussions and exchange views with other students, and, in general, to learn his profession." Such considerations apply with added force to children in grade and high schools. To separate them from others of similar age and qualifications solely because of their race generates a feeling of inferiority as to their status in the community that may affect their hearts and minds in a way unlikely ever to be undone. The effect of this separation on their educational opportunities was well stated by a finding in the Kansas case by a court which nevertheless felt compelled to rule against the Negro plaintiffs:

Segregation of white and colored children in public schools has a detrimental effect upon the colored children. The impact is greater when it has the sanction of the law, for the policy of separating the races is usually interpreted as denoting the inferiority of the negro group. A sense of inferiority affects the motivation of a child to learn. Segregation with the sanction of law, therefore, has a tendency to [retard] the educational and mental development of negro children and to deprive them of some of the benefits they would receive in a racial[ly] integrated school system.

Whatever may have been the extent of psychological knowledge at the time of Plessy v. Ferguson, this finding is amply supported by modern authority. Any language in Plessy v. Ferguson contrary to this finding is rejected.

We conclude that, in the field of public education, the doctrine of "separate but equal" has no place. Separate educational facilities are inherently unequal. Therefore, we hold that the plaintiffs and others similarly situated for whom the actions have been brought are, by reason of the segregation complained of, deprived of the equal protection of the laws guaranteed by the Fourteenth Amendment. This disposition makes unnecessary any discussion whether such segregation also violates the Due Process Clause of the Fourteenth Amendment.

Because these are class actions, because of the wide applicability of this decision, and because of the great variety of local conditions, the formulation of decrees in these cases presents problems of considerable complexity. On reargument, the consideration of appropriate relief was necessarily subordinated to the primary question — the constitutionality of segregation in public education. We have now announced that such segregation is a denial of the equal protection of the laws. In order that

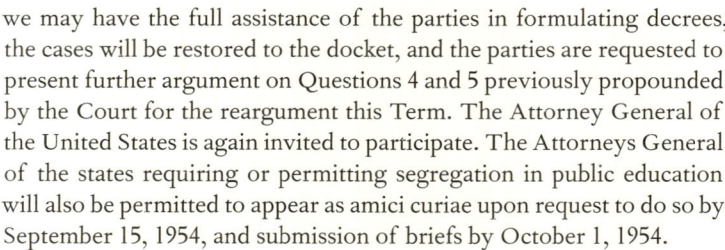

we may have the full assistance of the parties in formulating decrees, the cases will be restored to the docket, and the parties are requested to present further argument on Questions 4 and 5 previously propounded by the Court for the reargument this Term. The Attorney General of the United States is again invited to participate. The Attorneys General of the states requiring or permitting segregation in public education will also be permitted to appear as amici curiae upon request to do so by September 15, 1954, and submission of briefs by October 1, 1954.

It is so ordered.

1. In the Kansas case, Brown v. Board of Education, the plaintiffs are Negro children of elementary school age residing in Topeka. They brought this action in the United States District Court for the District of Kansas to enjoin enforcement of a Kansas statute which permits, but does not require, cities of more than 15,000 population to maintain separate school facilities for Negro and white students. Kan. Gen.Stat. § 72-1724 (1949). Pursuant to that authority, the Topeka Board of Education elected to establish segregated elementary schools. Other public schools in the community, however, are operated on a nonsegregated basis. The three-judge District Court, convened under 28 U.S.C. §§ 2281 and 2284, found that segregation in public education has a detrimental effect upon Negro children, but denied relief on the ground that the Negro and white schools were substantially equal with respect to buildings, transportation, curricula, and educational qualifications of teachers. 98 F.Supp. 797. The case is here on direct appeal under 28 U.S.C. § 1253.

In the South Carolina case, Briggs v. Elliott, the plaintiffs are Negro children of both elementary and high school age residing in Clarendon County. They brought this action in the United States District Court for the Eastern District of South Carolina to enjoin enforcement of provisions in the state constitution and statutory code which require the segregation of Negroes and whites in public schools. S.C.Const., Art. XI, § 7; S.C.Code § 5377 (1942). The three-judge District Court, convened under 28 U.S.C. §§ 2281 and 2284, denied the requested relief. The court found that the Negro schools were inferior to the white schools, and ordered the defendants to begin immediately to equalize the facilities. But the court sustained the validity of the contested provisions and denied the plaintiffs admission to the white schools during the equalization program. 98 F.Supp. 529. This Court vacated the District Court's judgment and remanded the case for the purpose of obtaining the court's views on a report filed by the defendants concerning the progress made in the equalization program. 342 U.S. 350. On remand, the District Court found that substantial equality had been achieved except for buildings and that the defendants were proceeding to rectify this inequality as well. 103 F.Supp. 920. The case is again here on direct appeal under 28 U.S.C. § 1253.

In the Virginia case, Davis v. County School Board, the plaintiffs are Negro children of high school age residing in Prince Edward County. They brought this action in the United States District Court for the Eastern District of Virginia to enjoin enforcement of provisions in the state constitution and statutory code which require the segregation of Negroes and whites in public schools. Va.Const., § 140; Va.Code § 22-221 (1950). The three-judge District Court, convened under 28 U.S.C. §§ 2281 and 2284, denied the requested relief. The court found the Negro school inferior in physical plant, curricula, and transportation, and ordered the defendants forthwith to provide substantially equal curricula and transportation and to "proceed with all reasonable diligence and dispatch to remove" the inequality in physical plant. But, as in the South Carolina case, the court sustained the validity of the contested provisions and denied the plaintiffs admission to the white schools during the equalization program. 103 F.Supp. 337. The case is here on direct appeal under 28 U.S.C. § 1253.

In the Delaware case, Gebhart v. Belton, the plaintiffs are Negro children of both elementary and high school age residing in New Castle County. They brought this action in the Delaware Court of Chancery to enjoin enforcement of provisions in the state constitution and statutory code which require the segregation of Negroes and whites in public schools. Del.Const., Art. X, § 2; Del.Rev.Code § 2631 (1935). The Chancellor gave judgment for the plaintiffs and ordered their immediate admission to schools previously attended only by white children, on the ground that the Negro schools were inferior with respect to teacher training, pupil-teacher ratio, extracurricular activities, physical plant, and time and distance involved in travel. 87

A.2d 862. The Chancellor also found that segregation itself results in an inferior education for Negro children (see note 10, infra), but did not rest his decision on that ground. Id. at 865. The Chancellor's decree was affirmed by the Supreme Court of Delaware, which intimated, however, that the defendants might be able to obtain a modification of the decree after equalization of the Negro and white schools had been accomplished. 91 A.2d 137, 152. The defendants, contending only that the Delaware courts had erred in ordering the immediate admission of the Negro plaintiffs to the white schools, applied to this Court for certiorari. The writ was granted, 344 U.S. 891. The plaintiffs, who were successful below, did not submit a cross-petition.

2. 344 U.S. 1, 141, 891.

3. 345 U.S. 972. The Attorney General of the United States participated both Terms as amicus curiae.

4. For a general study of the development of public education prior to the Amendment, see Butts and Cremin, A History of Education in American Culture (1953), Pts. I, II; Cubberley, Public Education in the United States (1934 ed.), cc. II-XII. School practices current at the time of the adoption of the Fourteenth Amendment are described in Butts and Cremin, supra, at 269-275; Cubberley, supra, at 288-339, 408-431; Knight, Public Education in the South (1922), cc. VIII, IX. See also H. Ex.Doc. No. 315, 41st Cong., 2d Sess. (1871). Although the demand for free public schools followed substantially the same pattern in both the North and the South, the development in the South did not begin to gain momentum until about 1850, some twenty years after that in the North. The reasons for the somewhat slower development in the South (e.g., the rural character of the South and the different regional attitudes toward state assistance) are well explained in Cubberley, supra, at 408-423. In the country as a whole, but particularly in the South, the War virtually stopped all progress in public education. Id. at 427-428. The low status of Negro education in all sections of the country, both before and immediately after the War, is described in Beale, A History of Freedom of Teaching in American Schools (1941), 112-132, 175-195. Compulsory school attendance laws were not generally adopted until after the ratification of the Fourteenth Amendment, and it was not until

1918 that such laws were in force in all the states. Cubberley, supra, at 563-565.

5. Slaughter-House Cases, 16 Wall. 36, 67-72 (1873); Strauder v. West Virginia, 100 U.S. 303, 307-308 (1880): It ordains that no State shall deprive any person of life, liberty, or property, without due process of law, or deny to any person within its jurisdiction the equal protection of the laws. What is this but declaring that the law in the States shall be the same for the black as for the white; that all persons, whether colored or white, shall stand equal before the laws of the States, and, in regard to the colored race, for whose protection the amendment was primarily designed, that no discrimination shall be made against them by law because of their color? The words of the amendment, it is true, are prohibitory, but they contain a necessary implication of a positive immunity, or right, most valuable to the colored race — the right to exemption from unfriendly legislation against them distinctively as colored — exemption from legal discriminations, implying inferiority in civil society, lessening the security of their enjoyment of the rights which others enjoy, and discriminations which are steps towards reducing them to the condition of a subject race. See also Virginia v. Rives, 100 U.S. 313, 318 (1880); Ex parte Virginia, 100 U.S. 339, 344-345 (1880).

6. The doctrine apparently originated in Roberts v. City of Boston, 59 Mass.198, 206 (1850), upholding school segregation against attack as being violative of a state constitutional guarantee of equality. Segregation in Boston public schools was eliminated in 1855. Mass. Acts 1855, c. 256. But elsewhere in the North, segregation in public education has persisted in some communities until recent years. It is apparent that such segregation has long been a nationwide problem, not merely one of sectional concern.

7. See also Berea College v. Kentucky, 211 U.S. 45 (1908).

8. In the Cummin case, Negro taxpayers sought an injunction requiring the defendant school board to discontinue the operation of a high school for white children until the board resumed operation of a high school for Negro children. Similarly, in the Gong Lum case,

the plaintiff, a child of Chinese descent, contended only that state authorities had misapplied the doctrine by classifying him with Negro children and requiring him to attend a Negro school.

9. In the Kansas case, the court below found substantial equality as to all such factors. 98 F.Supp. 797, 798. In the South Carolina case, the court below found that the defendants were proceeding "promptly and in good faith to comply with the court's decree." 103 F.Supp. 920, 921. In the Virginia case, the court below noted that the equalization program was already "afoot and progressing" (103 F.Supp. 337, 341); since then, we have been advised, in the Virginia Attorney General's brief on reargument, that the program has now been completed. In the Delaware case, the court below similarly noted that the state's equalization program was well under way. 91 A.2d 137, 149.

10. A similar finding was made in the Delaware case: I conclude from the testimony that, in our Delaware society, State-imposed segregation in education itself results in the Negro children, as a class, receiving educational opportunities which are substantially inferior to those available to white children otherwise similarly situated.87 A.2d 862, 865.

11. K.B. Clark, Effect of Prejudice and Discrimination on Personality Development (Mid-century White House Conference on Children and Youth, 1950); Witmer and Kotinsky, Personality in the Making (1952), c. VI; Deutscher and Chein, The Psychological Effects of Enforced Segregation A Survey of Social Science Opinion, 26 J.Psychol. 259 (1948); Chein, What are the Psychological Effects of Segregation Under Conditions of Equal Facilities?, 3 Int.J.Opinion and Attitude Res. 229 (1949); Brameld, Educational Costs, in Discrimination and National Welfare (MacIver, ed., 1949), 44-48; Frazier, The Negro in the United States (1949), 674-681. And see generally Myrdal, An American Dilemma (1944).

12. See Bolling v. Sharpe, post, p. 497, concerning the Due Process Clause of the Fifth Amendment.

13.

4. Assuming it is decided that segregation in public schools violates the Fourteenth Amendment(a) would a decree necessarily follow providing that, within the limits set by normal geographic school districting. Negro children should forthwith be admitted to schools of their choice, or(b) may this Court, in the exercise of its equity powers, permit an effective gradual adjustment to be brought about from existing segregated systems to a system not based on color distinctions?

5. On the assumption on which questions 4(a) and (b) are based, and assuming further that this Court will exercise its equity powers to the end described in question 4(b),(a) should this Court formulate detailed decrees in these cases;(b) if so, what specific issues should the decrees reach;(c) should this Court appoint a special master to hear evidence with a view to recommending specific terms for such decrees;(d) should this Court remand to the courts of first instance with directions to frame decrees in these cases and, if so, what general directions should the decrees of this Court include and what procedures should the courts of first instance follow in arriving at the specific terms of more detailed decrees?

14. See Rule 42, Revised Rules of this Court (effective July 1, 1954).

# SENATE RESOLUTION 301: CENSURE OF SENATOR JOSEPH MCCARTHY (1954)

*The Cold War was in full swing by the early 1950s, and many in the United States feared the influx of communist sympathizers in all walks of American life. This fear—called the Red Scare— dominated politics at the time, and no one better represented the hysteria than Wisconsin senator Joseph McCarthy. In 1950, McCarthy announced that he had a list of 205 members of the U.S. State Department who were working with the Communist Party. Despite the fact that a Senate panel found no evidence of subversive activity, McCarthy spent the next four years accusing various government employees of being communist sympathizers. It wasn't until 1953, when McCarthy accused the U.S. Army of being overrun by communists, that the media and government really began to condemn McCarthy's crusade. Finally, in 1954, the U.S. Senate issued an official document of censure.*

Resolved, that the Senator from Wisconsin, Mr. McCarthy, failed to cooperate with the Subcommittee on Privileges and Elections of the Senate Committee on Rules and Administration in clearing up matters referred to that subcommittee which concerned his conduct as a Senator and affected the honor of the Senate and, instead, repeatedly abused the subcommittee and its members who were trying to carry out assigned duties, thereby obstructing the constitutional processes of the Senate, and that this conduct of the Senator from Wisconsin, Mr. McCarthy, is contrary to senatorial traditions and is hereby condemned.

SEC 2. The Senator from Wisconsin, Mr. McCarthy, in writing to the chairman of the Select Committee to Study Censure Charges (Mr. Watkins) after the Select Committee had issued its report and before the report was presented to the Senate charging three members of the Select Committee with "deliberate deception" and "fraud" for failure to disqualify themselves; in stating to the press on November 4, 1954, that the special Senate session that was to begin November 8, 1954, was a "lynch-party"; in repeatedly describing this special Senate session as a "lynch bee" in a nationwide television and radio show on November 7, 1954; in stating to the public press on November 13, 1954, that the chairman of the Select Committee (Mr. Watkins) was guilty of "the most unusual, most cowardly things I've ever heard of" and stating further: "I expected he would be afraid to answer the questions, but didn't think he'd be stupid enough to make a public statement"; and in characterizing the said committee as the "unwitting handmaiden," "involuntary agent" and "attorneys-in-fact" of the Communist Party and in charging that the said committee in writing its report "imitated Communist methods — that it distorted, misrepresented, and omitted in its effort to manufacture a plausible rationalization" in support of its recommendations to the Senate, which characterizations and charges were contained in a statement released to the press and inserted in the Congressional Record of November 10, 1954, acted contrary to senatorial ethics and tended to bring the Senate into dishonor and disrepute, to obstruct the constitutional processes of the Senate, and to impair its dignity; and such conduct is hereby condemned.

# DWIGHT D. EISENHOWER'S FAREWELL ADDRESS JANUARY 17, 1961

My fellow Americans:

Three days from now, after half a century in the service of our country, I shall lay down the responsibilities of office as, in traditional and solemn ceremony, the authority of the Presidency is vested in my successor.

This evening I come to you with a message of leave-taking and farewell, and to share a few final thoughts with you, my countrymen.

Like every other citizen, I wish the new President, and all who will labor with him, Godspeed. I pray that the coming years will be blessed with peace and prosperity for all.

Our people expect their President and the Congress to find essential agreement on issues of great moment, the wise resolution of which will better shape the future of the Nation.

My own relations with the Congress, which began on a remote and tenuous basis when, long ago, a member of the Senate appointed me to West Point, have since ranged to the intimate during the war and immediate post-war period, and, finally, to the mutually interdependent during these past eight years.

In this final relationship, the Congress and the Administration have, on most vital issues, cooperated well, to serve the national good rather than mere partisanship, and so have assured that the business of the Nation should go forward. So, my official relationship with the Congress ends in a feeling, on my part, of gratitude that we have been able to do so much together.

## II

We now stand ten years past the midpoint of a century that has witnessed four major wars among great nations. Three of these involved our own country. Despite these holocausts, America is today the strongest, the most influential and most productive nation in the world. Understandably proud of this pre-eminence, we yet realize that America's leadership and prestige depend, not merely upon our unmatched material progress, riches and military strength, but on how we use our power in the interests of world peace and human betterment.

## III

Throughout America's adventure in free government, our basic purposes have been to keep the peace; to foster progress in human achievement, and to enhance liberty, dignity and integrity among people and among nations. To strive for less would be unworthy of a free and religious people. Any failure traceable to arrogance, or our lack of comprehension or readiness to sacrifice would inflict upon us grievous hurt both at home and abroad.

Progress toward these noble goals is persistently threatened by the conflict now engulfing the world. It commands our whole attention, absorbs our very beings. We face a hostile ideology—global in scope, atheistic in character, ruthless in purpose, and insidious in method. Unhappily, the danger it poses promises to be of indefinite duration. To meet it successfully, there is called for, not so much the emotional and transitory sacrifices of crisis, but rather those which enable us to carry forward steadily, surely, and without complaint the burdens of a prolonged and complex struggle—with liberty at stake. Only thus shall we remain, despite every provocation, on our charted course toward permanent peace and human betterment.

Crises there will continue to be. In meeting them, whether foreign or domestic, great or small, there is a recurring temptation to feel that some spectacular and costly action could become the miraculous solution to all current difficulties. A huge increase in newer elements of our defense; development of unrealistic programs to cure every ill in agriculture; a dramatic expansion in basic and applied research—these and many other possibilities, each possibly promising in itself, may be suggested as the only way to the road we which to travel.

But each proposal must be weighed in the light of a broader consideration: the need to maintain balance in and among national programs, balance between the private and the public economy, balance between cost and hoped for advantage, balance between the clearly necessary and the comfortably desirable, balance between our essential requirements as a nation and the duties imposed by the nation upon the individual, balance between action of the moment and the national

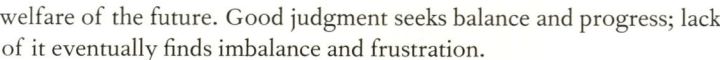 

welfare of the future. Good judgment seeks balance and progress; lack of it eventually finds imbalance and frustration.

The record of many decades stands as proof that our people and their government have, in the main, understood these truths and have responded to them well, in the face of stress and threat. But threats, new in kind or degree, constantly arise. I mention two only.

## IV

A vital element in keeping the peace is our military establishment. Our arms must be mighty, ready for instant action, so that no potential aggressor may be tempted to risk his own destruction.

Our military organization today bears little relation to that known by any of my predecessors in peace time, or indeed by the fighting men of World War II or Korea.

Until the latest of our world conflicts, the United States had no armaments industry. American makers of plowshares could, with time and as required, make swords as well. But now we can no longer risk emergency improvisation of national defense; we have been compelled to create a permanent armaments industry of vast proportions. Added to this, three and a half million men and women are directly engaged in the defense establishment. We annually spend on military security more than the net income of all United States corporations.

This conjunction of an immense military establishment and a large arms industry is new in the American experience. The total influence— economic, political, even spiritual—is felt in every city, every state house, every office of the Federal government. We recognize the imperative need for this development. Yet we must not fail to comprehend its grave implications. Our toil, resources and livelihood are all involved; so is the very structure of our society.

In the councils of government, we must guard against the acquisition of unwarranted influence, whether sought or unsought, by the military—industrial complex. The potential for the disastrous rise of misplaced power exists and will persist.

We must never let the weight of this combination endanger our liberties or democratic processes. We should take nothing for granted. Only an alert and knowledgeable citizenry can compel the proper meshing of huge industrial and military machinery of defense with our peaceful methods and goals, so that security and liberty may prosper together.

Akin to, and largely responsible for the sweeping changes in our industrial-military posture, has been the technological revolution during recent decades.

In this revolution, research has become central; it also becomes more formalized, complex, and costly. A steadily increasing share is conducted for, by, or at the direction of, the Federal government.

Today, the solitary inventor, tinkering in his shop, has been over-shadowed by task forces of scientists in laboratories and testing fields. In the same fashion, the free university, historically the fountainhead of free ideas and scientific discovery, has experienced a revolution in the conduct of research. Partly because of the huge costs involved, a government contract becomes virtually a substitute for intellectual curiosity. For every old blackboard there are now hundreds of new electronic computers.

The prospect of domination of the nation's scholars by Federal employment, project allocations, and the power of money is ever present and is gravely to be regarded.

Yet, in holding scientific research and discovery in respect, as we should, we must also be alert to the equal and opposite danger that public policy could itself become the captive of a scientific-technological elite.

It is the task of statesmanship to mold, to balance, and to integrate these and other forces, new and old, within the principles of our democratic system—ever aiming toward the supreme goals of our free society.

## V

Another factor in maintaining balance involves the element of time. As we peer into society's future, we—you and I, and our government—must avoid the impulse to live only for today, plundering, for our own ease and convenience, the precious resources of tomorrow. We cannot mortgage the material assets of our grandchildren without risking the loss also of their political and spiritual heritage. We want democracy to survive for all generations to come, not to become the insolvent phantom of tomorrow.

## VI

Down the long lane of the history yet to be written America knows that this world of ours, ever growing smaller, must avoid becoming a community of dreadful fear and hate, and be, instead, a proud confederation of mutual trust and respect.

Such a confederation must be one of equals. The weakest must come to the conference table with the same confidence as do we, protected as we are by our moral, economic, and military strength. That table, though scarred by many past frustrations, cannot be abandoned for the certain agony of the battlefield.

Disarmament, with mutual honor and confidence, is a continuing imperative. Together we must learn how to compose differences, not with arms, but with intellect and decent purpose. Because this need is so sharp and apparent I confess that I lay down my official responsibilities in this field with a definite sense of disappointment. As one who has witnessed the horror and the lingering sadness of war—as one who knows that another war could utterly destroy this civilization which has been so slowly and painfully built over thousands of years—I wish I could say tonight that a lasting peace is in sight.

Happily, I can say that war has been avoided. Steady progress toward our ultimate goal has been made. But, so much remains to be done. As a private citizen, I shall never cease to do what little I can to help the world advance along that road.

## VII

So—in this my last good night to you as your President—I thank you for the many opportunities you have given me for public service in war and peace. I trust that in that service you find something worthy; as for the rest of it, I know you will find ways to improve performance in the future.

You and I—my fellow citizens—need to be strong in our faith that all nations, under God, will reach the goal of peace with justice. May we be ever unswerving in devotion to principle, confident but humble with power, diligent in pursuit of the Nation's great goals.

To all the peoples of the world, I once more give expression to America's prayerful and continuing aspiration:

We pray that peoples of all faiths, all races, all nations, may have their great human needs satisfied; that those now denied opportunity shall come to enjoy it to the full; that all who yearn for freedom may experience its spiritual blessings; that those who have freedom will understand, also, its heavy responsibilities; that all who are insensitive

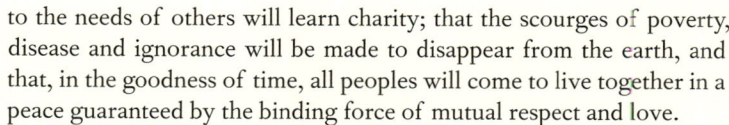

to the needs of others will learn charity; that the scourges of poverty, disease and ignorance will be made to disappear from the earth, and that, in the goodness of time, all peoples will come to live together in a peace guaranteed by the binding force of mutual respect and love.

# JOHN F. KENNEDY'S INAUGURAL ADDRESS JANUARY 20, 1961

Vice President Johnson, Mr. Speaker, Mr. Chief Justice, President Eisenhower, Vice President Nixon, President Truman, reverend clergy, fellow citizens, we observe today not a victory of party, but a celebration of freedom—symbolizing an end, as well as a beginning—signifying renewal, as well as change. For I have sworn before you and Almighty God the same solemn oath our forebears prescribed nearly a century and three quarters ago.

The world is very different now. For man holds in his mortal hands the power to abolish all forms of human poverty and all forms of human life. And yet the same revolutionary beliefs for which our forebears fought are still at issue around the globe—the belief that the rights of man come not from the generosity of the state, but from the hand of God.

We dare not forget today that we are the heirs of that first revolution. Let the word go forth from this time and place, to friend and foe alike, that the torch has been passed to a new generation of Americans—born in this century, tempered by war, disciplined by a hard and bitter peace, proud of our ancient heritage—and unwilling to witness or permit the slow undoing of those human rights to which this Nation has always been committed, and to which we are committed today at home and around the world.

Let every nation know, whether it wishes us well or ill, that we shall pay any price, bear any burden, meet any hardship, support any friend, oppose any foe, in order to assure the survival and the success of liberty.

This much we pledge—and more.

To those old allies whose cultural and spiritual origins we share, we pledge the loyalty of faithful friends. United, there is little we cannot do in a host of cooperative ventures. Divided, there is little we can do—for we dare not meet a powerful challenge at odds and split asunder.

To those new States whom we welcome to the ranks of the free, we pledge our word that one form of colonial control shall not have passed away merely to be replaced by a far more iron tyranny. We shall not always expect to find them supporting our view. But we shall always hope to find them strongly supporting their own freedom—and to remember that, in the past, those who foolishly sought power by riding the back of the tiger ended up inside.

To those peoples in the huts and villages across the globe struggling to break the bonds of mass misery, we pledge our best efforts to help them help themselves, for whatever period is required—not because the Communists may be doing it, not because we seek their votes, but because it is right. If a free society cannot help the many who are poor, it cannot save the few who are rich.

To our sister republics south of our border, we offer a special pledge—to convert our good words into good deeds—in a new alliance for progress—to assist free men and free governments in casting off the chains of poverty. But this peaceful revolution of hope cannot become the prey of hostile powers. Let all our neighbors know that we shall join with them to oppose aggression or subversion anywhere in the Americas. And let every other power know that this Hemisphere intends to remain the master of its own house.

To that world assembly of sovereign states, the United Nations, our last best hope in an age where the instruments of war have far outpaced the instruments of peace, we renew our pledge of support—to prevent it from becoming merely a forum for invective—to strengthen its shield of the new and the weak—and to enlarge the area in which its writ may run.

Finally, to those nations who would make themselves our adversary, we offer not a pledge but a request: that both sides begin anew the quest for peace, before the dark powers of destruction unleashed by science engulf all humanity in planned or accidental self-destruction.

We dare not tempt them with weakness. For only when our arms are sufficient beyond doubt can we be certain beyond doubt that they will never be employed.

But neither can two great and powerful groups of nations take comfort from our present course—both sides overburdened by the cost of modern weapons, both rightly alarmed by the steady spread of the deadly atom, yet both racing to alter that uncertain balance of terror that stays the hand of mankind's final war.

So let us begin anew—remembering on both sides that civility is

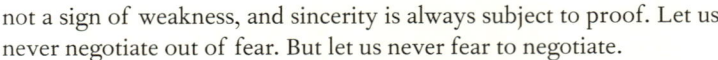

not a sign of weakness, and sincerity is always subject to proof. Let us never negotiate out of fear. But let us never fear to negotiate.

Let both sides explore what problems unite us instead of belaboring those problems which divide us.

Let both sides, for the first time, formulate serious and precise proposals for the inspection and control of arms—and bring the absolute power to destroy other nations under the absolute control of all nations.

Let both sides seek to invoke the wonders of science instead of its terrors. Together let us explore the stars, conquer the deserts, eradicate disease, tap the ocean depths, and encourage the arts and commerce.

Let both sides unite to heed in all corners of the earth the command of Isaiah—to "undo the heavy burdens . . . and to let the oppressed go free."

And if a beachhead of cooperation may push back the jungle of suspicion, let both sides join in creating a new endeavor, not a new balance of power, but a new world of law, where the strong are just and the weak secure and the peace preserved.

All this will not be finished in the first 100 days. Nor will it be finished in the first 1,000 days, nor in the life of this Administration, nor even perhaps in our lifetime on this planet. But let us begin.

In your hands, my fellow citizens, more than in mine, will rest the final success or failure of our course. Since this country was founded, each generation of Americans has been summoned to give testimony to its national loyalty. The graves of young Americans who answered the call to service surround the globe.

Now the trumpet summons us again—not as a call to bear arms, though arms we need; not as a call to battle, though embattled we are—but a call to bear the burden of a long twilight struggle, year in and year out, "rejoicing in hope, patient in tribulation"—a struggle against the common enemies of man: tyranny, poverty, disease, and war itself.

Can we forge against these enemies a grand and global alliance, North and South, East and West, that can assure a more fruitful life for all mankind? Will you join in that historic effort?

In the long history of the world, only a few generations have been granted the role of defending freedom in its hour of maximum danger. I do not shrink from this responsibility—I welcome it. I do not believe that any of us would exchange places with any other people or any

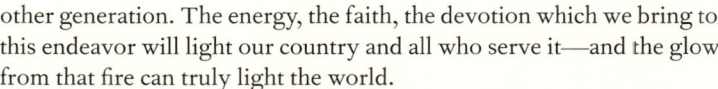

other generation. The energy, the faith, the devotion which we bring to this endeavor will light our country and all who serve it—and the glow from that fire can truly light the world.

And so, my fellow Americans: ask not what your country can do for you—ask what you can do for your country.

My fellow citizens of the world: ask not what America will do for you, but what together we can do for the freedom of man.

Finally, whether you are citizens of America or citizens of the world, ask of us the same high standards of strength and sacrifice which we ask of you. With a good conscience our only sure reward, with history the final judge of our deeds, let us go forth to lead the land we love, asking His blessing and His help, but knowing that here on earth God's work must truly be our own.

# THE LIMITED NUCLEAR TEST BAN TREATY (1963)

*After the United States used atomic bombs during World War II, the Soviet Union ramped up its own nuclear weapons program, exploding its first atomic bomb in 1949. Other countries around the world, including Great Britain, also began to create and test their own nuclear weapons. All this led to an arms race between the East and West, but as scientists became concerned about the effects that nuclear weapons' testing had on air, soil, and water supplies, calls began to impose limits. In 1963, after much negotiation, the United States, the Soviet Union, and Great Britain signed the first international treaty aimed at limiting nuclear weapons testing.*

TREATY banning nuclear weapon tests in the atmosphere, in outer space and under water.

The Governments of the United States of America, the United Kingdom of Great Britain and Northern Ireland, and the Union of Soviet Socialist Republics, hereinafter referred to as the "Original Parties,"

Proclaiming as their principal aim the speediest possible achievement of an agreement on general and complete disarmament under strict international control in accordance with the objectives of the United Nations which would put an end to the armaments race and eliminate the incentive to the production and testing of all kinds of weapons, including nuclear weapons,

Seeking to achieve the discontinuance of all test explosions of nuclear weapons for all time, determined to continue negotiations to this end, and desiring to put an end to the contamination of man's environment by radioactive substances,

Have agreed as follows:

## ARTICLE I

1. Each of the Parties to this Treaty undertakes to prohibit, to

prevent, and not to carry out any nuclear weapon test explosion, or any other nuclear explosion, at any place under its jurisdiction or control:

(a) in the atmosphere; beyond its limits, including outer space; or under water, including territorial waters or high seas; or

(b) in any other environment if such explosion causes radioactive debris to be present outside the territorial limits of the State under whose jurisdiction or control such explosion is conducted. It is understood in this connection that the provisions of this subparagraph are without prejudice to the conclusion of a Treaty resulting in the permanent banning of all nuclear test explosions, including all such explosions underground, the conclusion of which, as the Parties have stated in the Preamble to this Treaty, they seek to achieve.

2. Each of the Parties to this Treaty undertakes furthermore to refrain from causing, encouraging, or in any way participating in, the carrying out of any nuclear weapon test explosion, or any other nuclear explosion, anywhere which would take place in any of the environments described, or have the effect referred to, in paragraph 1 of this Article.

## ARTICLE II

1. Any Party may propose amendments to this Treaty. The text of any proposed amendment shall be submitted to the Depositary Governments which shall circulate it to all Parties to this Treaty. Thereafter, if requested to do so by one-third or more of the Parties, the Depositary Governments shall convene a conference, to which they shall invite all the Parties, to consider such amendment.

2. Any amendment to this Treaty must be approved by a majority of the votes of all the Parties to this Treaty, including the votes of all of the Original Parties. The amendment shall enter into force for all Parties upon the deposit of instruments of ratification by a majority of all the Parties, including the instruments of ratification of all of the Original Parties.

## ARTICLE III

1. This Treaty shall be open to all States for signature. Any State which does not sign this Treaty before its entry into force in accordance with paragraph 3 of this Article may accede to it at any time.

2. This Treaty shall be subject to ratification by signatory States. Instruments of ratification and instruments of accession shall be

deposited with the Governments of the Original Parties — the United States of America, the United Kingdom of Great Britain and Northern Ireland, and the Union of Soviet Socialist Republics — which are hereby designated the Depositary Governments.

3. This Treaty shall enter into force after its ratification by all the Original Parties and the deposit of their instruments of ratification.

4. For States whose instruments of ratification or accession are deposited subsequent to the entry into force of this Treaty, it shall enter into force on the date of the deposit of their instruments of ratification or accession.

5. The Depositary Governments shall promptly inform all signatory and acceding States of the date of each signature, the date of deposit of each instrument of ratification of and accession to this Treaty, the date of its entry into force, and the date of receipt of any requests for conferences or other notices.

6. This Treaty shall be registered by the Depositary Governments pursuant to Article 102 of the Charter of the United Nations.

## ARTICLE IV

This Treaty shall be of unlimited duration.

Each Party shall in exercising its national sovereignty have the right to withdraw from the Treaty if it decides that extraordinary events, related to the subject matter of this Treaty, have jeopardized the supreme interests of its country. It shall give notice of such withdrawal to all other Parties to the Treaty three months in advance.

## ARTICLE V

This Treaty, of which the English and Russian texts are equally authentic, shall be deposited in the archives of the Depositary Governments. Duly certified copies of this Treaty shall be transmitted by the Depositary Governments to the Governments of the signatory and acceding States.

# THE CIVIL RIGHTS ACT (1964)

*In June 1963, President John F. Kennedy proposed that the United States adopt a sweeping civil rights law that would prohibit segregation in all public places and of all public facilities, would prohibit restrictions to voting rights, and would prohibit employment discrimination based on race, color, sex, religion, or national origin. After Kennedy's assassination in 1963, President Lyndon B. Johnson continued to fight for the legislation. He faced much opposition in Congress, including a Senate filibuster, but the Civil Rights Act finally became law on July 2, 1964.*

A n act
To enforce the constitutional right to vote, to confer jurisdiction upon the district courts of the United States to provide injunctive relief against discrimination in public accommodations, to authorize the Attorney General to institute suits to protect constitutional rights in public facilities and public education, to extend the Commission on Civil Rights, to prevent discrimination in federally assisted programs, to establish a Commission on Equal Employment Opportunity, and for other purposes.

Be it enacted by the Senate and House of Representatives of the United States of America in Congress assembled, That this Act may be cited as the "Civil Rights Act of 1964".

## Title I
### Voting Rights

Sec. 101. Section 2004 of the Revised Statutes (42 U.S.C. 1971), as amended by section 131 of the Civil Rights Act of 1957 (71 Stat. 637), and as further amended by section 601 of the Civil Rights Act of 1960 (74 Stat. 90), is further amended as follows:

(a) Insert "1" after "(a)" in subsection (a) and add at the end of subsection (a) the following new paragraphs:

"(2) No person acting under color of law shall—

"(A) in determining whether any individual is qualified under State law or laws to vote in any Federal election, apply any standard, practice, or procedure different from the standards, practices, or procedures applied under such law or laws to other individuals within the same county, parish, or similar political subdivision who have been found by State officials to be qualified to vote;

"(B) deny the right of any individual to vote in any Federal election because of an error or omission on any record or paper relating to any application, registration, or other act requisite to voting, if such error or omission is not material in determining whether such individual is qualified under State law to vote in such election; or

"(C) employ any literacy test as a qualification for voting in any Federal election unless (i) such test is administered to each individual and is conducted wholly in writing, and (ii) a certified copy of the test and of the answers given by the individual is furnished to him within twenty-five days of the submission of his request made within the period of time during which records and papers are required to be retained and preserved pursuant to title III of the Civil Rights Act of 1960 (42 U.S.C. 1974–74e; 74 Stat. 88): *Provided, however,* That the Attorney General may enter into agreements with appropriate State or local authorities that preparation, conduct, and maintenance of such tests in accordance with the provisions of applicable State or local law, including such special provisions as are necessary in the preparation, conduct, and maintenance of such tests for persons who are blind or otherwise physically handicapped, meet the purposes of this subparagraph and constitute compliance therewith.

"(3) For purposes of this subsection—

"(A) the term 'vote' shall have the same meaning as in subsection (e) of this section;

"(B) the phrase 'literacy test' includes any test of the ability to read, write, understand, or interpret any matter."

(b) Insert immediately following the period at the end of the first sentence of subsection (c) the following new sentence: "If in any such proceeding literacy is a relevant fact there shall be a rebuttable presumption that any person who has not been adjudged an incompetent and who has completed the sixth grade in a public school in, or a private school accredited by, any State or territory, the District of Columbia, or the Commonwealth of Puerto Rico where instruction is carried on predominantly in the English language, possesses sufficient literacy, comprehension, and intelligence to vote in any Federal election."

(c) Add the following subsection "(f)" and designate the present subsection "(f)" as subsection "(g)": "(f) When used in subsection (a) or (c) of this section, the words 'Federal election' shall mean any general, special, or primary election held solely or in part for the purpose of electing or selecting any candidate for the office of President, Vice President, presidential elector, Member of the Senate, or Member of the House of Representatives."

(d) Add the following subsection "(h)":

"(h) In any proceeding instituted by the United States in any district court of the United States under this section in which the Attorney General requests a finding of a pattern or practice of discrimination pursuant to subsection (e) of this section the Attorney General, at the time he files the complaint, or any defendant in the proceeding, within twenty days after service upon him of the complaint, may file with the clerk of such court a request that a court of three judges be convened to hear and determine the entire case. A copy of the request for a three-judge court shall be immediately furnished by such clerk to the chief judge of the circuit (or in his absence, the presiding circuit judge of the circuit) in which the case is pending. Upon receipt of the copy of such request it shall be the duty of the chief justice of the circuit or the presiding circuit judge, as the case may be, to designate immediately three judges in such circuit, of whom at least one shall be a circuit judge and another of whom shall be a district judge of the court in which the proceeding was instituted, to hear and determine such case, and it shall be the duty of the judges so designated to assign the case for hearing at the earliest practicable date, to participate in the hearing and determination thereof, and to cause the case to be in every way expedited.

An appeal from the final judgment of such court will lie to the Supreme Court.

"In any proceeding brought under subsection (c) of this section to enforce subsection (b) of this section, or in the event neither the Attorney General nor any defendant files a request for a three-judge court in any proceeding authorized by this subsection, it shall be the duty of the chief judge of the district (or in his absence, the acting chief judge) in which the case is pending immediately to designate a judge in such district to hear and determine the case. In the event that no judge in the district is available to hear and determine the case, the chief judge of the district, or the acting chief judge, as the case may be, shall certify this fact to the chief judge of the circuit (or, in his absence, the acting chief judge) who shall then designate a district or circuit judge of the circuit to hear and determine the case.

"It shall be the duty of the judge designated pursuant to this section to assign the case for hearing at the earliest practicable date and to cause the case to be in every way expedited."

## TITLE II
### INJUNCTIVE RELIEF AGAINST DISCRIMINATION IN PLACES OF PUBLIC ACCOMMODATION

SEC. 201. (a) All persons shall be entitled to the full and equal enjoyment of the goods, services, facilities, and privileges, advantages, and accommodations of any place of public accommodation, as defined in this section, without discrimination or segregation on the ground of race, color, religion, or national origin.

(b) Each of the following establishments which serves the public is a place of public accommodation within the meaning of this title if its operations affect commerce, or if discrimination or segregation by it is supported by State action:

(1) any inn, hotel, motel, or other establishment which provides lodging to transient guests, other than an establishment located within a building which contains not more than five rooms for rent or hire and which is actually occupied by the proprietor of such establishment as his residence;

(2) any restaurant, cafeteria, lunchroom, lunch counter, soda fountain, or other facility principally engaged in selling food for consumption on the premises, including, but not limited to, any such facility located on the premises of any retail establishment; or any gasoline station;

(3) any motion picture house, theater, concert hall, sports arena, stadium or other place of exhibition or entertainment; and

(4) any establishment (A)(i) which is physically located within the premises of any establishment otherwise covered by this subsection, or (ii) within the premises of which is physically located any such covered establishment, and (B) which holds itself out as serving patrons of such covered establishment.

(c) The operations of an establishment affect commerce within the meaning of this title if (1) it is one of the establishments described in paragraph (1) of subsection (b); (2) in the case of an establishment described in paragraph (2) of subsection (b), it serves or offers to serve interstate travelers or a substantial portion of the food which it serves, or gasoline or other products which it sells, has moved in commerce; (3) in the case of an establishment described in paragraph (3) of subsection (b), it customarily presents films, performances, athletic teams, exhibitions, or other sources of entertainment which move in commerce; and (4) in the case of an establishment described in paragraph (4) of subsection (b), it is physically located within the premises of, or there is physically located within its premises, an establishment the operations of which affect commerce within the meaning of this subsection. For purposes of this section, "commerce" means travel, trade, traffic, commerce, transportation, or communication among the several States, or between the District of Columbia and any State, or between any foreign country or any territory or possession and any State or the District of Columbia, or between points in the same State but through any other State or the District of Columbia or a foreign country.

(d) Discrimination or segregation by an establishment is supported by State action within the meaning of this title if such discrimination or segregation (1) is carried on under color of any law, statute, ordinance, or regulation; or (2) is carried on under color of any custom or usage required or enforced by officials of the State or political subdivision thereof; or (3) is required by action of the State or political subdivision thereof.

(e) The provisions of this title shall not apply to a private club or other establishment not in fact open to the public, except to the extent that the facilities of such establishment are made available to the customers or patrons of an establishment within the scope of subsection (b).

SEC. 202. All persons shall be entitled to be free, at any establishment or place, from discrimination or segregation of any kind on the ground of race, color, religion, or national origin, if such discrimination or segregation is or purports to be required by any law, statute, ordinance, regulation, rule, or order of a State or any agency or political subdivision thereof.

SEC. 203. No person shall (a) withhold, deny, or attempt to withhold or deny, or deprive or attempt to deprive, any person of any right or privilege secured by section 201 or 202, or (b) intimidate, threaten, or coerce, or attempt to intimidate, threaten, or coerce any person with the purpose of interfering with any right or privilege secured by section 201 or 202, or (c) punish or attempt to punish any person for exercising or attempting to exercise any right or privilege secured by section 201 or 202.

Sec. 204. (a) Whenever any person has engaged or there are reasonable grounds to believe that any person is about to engage in any act or practice prohibited by section 203, a civil action for preventive relief, including an application for a permanent or temporary injunction, restraining order, or other order, may be instituted by the person aggrieved and, upon timely application, the court may, in its discretion, permit the Attorney General to intervene in such civil action if he certifies that the case is of general public importance. Upon application by the complainant and in such circumstances as the court may deem just, the court may appoint an attorney for such complainant and may authorize the commencement of the civil action without the payment of fees, costs, or security.

(b) In any action commenced pursuant to this title, the court, in its discretion, may allow the prevailing party, other than the United States, a reasonable attorney's fee as part of the costs, and the United States shall be liable for costs the same as a private person.

(c) In the case of an alleged act or practice prohibited by this title which occurs in a State, or political subdivision of a State, which has a State or local law prohibiting such act or practice and establishing or authorizing a State or local authority to grant or seek relief from such practice or to institute criminal proceedings with respect thereto upon receiving notice thereof, no civil action may be brought under subsection (a) before the expiration of thirty days after written notice of such alleged act or practice has been given to the appropriate State or local authority by registered mail or in person, provided that the court may stay proceedings in such civil action pending the termination of State or local enforcement proceedings.

(d) In the case of an alleged act or practice prohibited by this title which occurs in a State, or political subdivision of a State, which has no State or local law prohibiting such act or practice, a civil action may be brought under subsection (a): *Provided*, That the court may refer the matter to the Community Relations Service established by title X of this Act for as long as the court believes there is a reasonable possibility of obtaining voluntary compliance, but for not more than sixty days: *Provided further*, That upon expiration of such sixty-day period, the court may extend such period for an additional period, not to exceed a cumulative total of one hundred and twenty days, if it believes there then exists a reasonable possibility of securing voluntary compliance.

SEC. 205. The Service is authorized to make a full investigation of any complaint referred to it by the court under section 204(d) and may hold such hearings with respect thereto as may be necessary. The Service shall conduct any hearings with respect to any such complaint in executive session, and shall not release any testimony given therein except by agreement of all parties involved in the complaint with the permission of the court, and the Service shall endeavor to bring about a voluntary settlement between the parties.

SEC. 206. (a) Whenever the Attorney General has reasonable cause to believe that any person or group of persons is engaged in a pattern or practice of resistance to the full enjoyment of any of the rights secured by this title, and that the pattern or practice is of such a nature and is intended to deny the full exercise of the rights herein described, the Attorney General may bring a civil action in the appropriate district court of the United States by filing with it a complaint (1) signed by him (or in his absence the Acting Attorney General), (2) setting forth facts pertaining to such pattern or practice, and (3) requesting such preventive relief, including an application for a permanent or temporary injunction, restraining order or other order against the person or persons responsible for such pattern or practice, as he deems necessary to insure the full enjoyment of the rights herein described.

(b) In any such proceeding the Attorney General may file with the clerk of such court a request that a court of three judges be convened to hear and determine the case. Such request by the Attorney General shall be accompanied by a certificate that, in his opinion, the case is of general public importance. A copy of the certificate and request for a three-judge court shall be immediately furnished by such clerk to the chief judge of the circuit (or in his absence, the presiding circuit judge of the circuit) in which the case is pending. Upon receipt of the copy of such request it shall be the duty of the chief judge of the circuit or the presiding circuit judge, as the case may be, to designate immediately three judges in such circuit, of whom at least one shall be a circuit judge and another of whom shall be a district judge of the court in which the proceeding was instituted, to hear and determine such case, and it shall be the duty of the judges so designated to assign the case for hearing at the earliest practicable date, to participate in the hearing and determination thereof, and to cause the case to be in every way expedited. An appeal from the final judgment of such court will lie to the Supreme Court.

In the event the Attorney General fails to file such a request in any such proceeding, it shall be the duty of the chief judge of the district (or in his absence, the acting chief judge) in which the case is pending immediately to designate a judge in such district to hear and determine the case. In the event that no judge in the district is available to hear and determine the case, the chief judge of the district, or the acting chief judge, as the case may be, shall certify this fact to the chief judge of the circuit (or in his absence, the acting chief judge) who shall then designate a district or circuit judge of the circuit to hear and determine the case.

It shall be the duty of the judge designated pursuant to this section to assign the case for hearing at the earliest practicable date and to cause the case to be in every way expedited.

SEC. 207. (a) The district courts of the United States shall have jurisdiction of proceedings instituted pursuant to this title and shall exercise the same without regard to whether the aggrieved party shall have exhausted any administrative or other remedies that may be provided by law.

(b) The remedies provided in this title shall be the exclusive means of enforcing the rights based on this title, but nothing in this title shall preclude any individual or any State or local agency from asserting any right based on any other Federal or State law not inconsistent with this title, including any statute or ordinance requiring nondiscrimination in public establishments or accommodations, or from pursuing any remedy, civil or criminal, which may be available for the vindication or enforcement of such right.

# TITLE III
## DESEGREGATION OF PUBLIC FACILITIES

SEC. 301. (a) Whenever the Attorney General receives a complaint in writing signed by an individual to the effect that he is being deprived of or threatened with the loss of his right to the equal protection of the laws, on account of his race, color, religion, or national origin, by being denied equal utilization of any public facility which is owned, operated, or managed by or on behalf of any State or subdivision thereof, other than a public school or public college as defined in section 401 of title IV hereof, and the Attorney General believes the complaint is meritorious and certifies that the signer or signers of such complaint are unable, in his judgment, to initiate and maintain appropriate legal proceedings for relief and that the institution of an action will materially further the orderly progress of desegregation in public facilities, the Attorney General is authorized to institute for or in the name of the United States a civil action in any appropriate district court of the United States against such parties and for such relief as may be appropriate, and such court shall have and shall exercise jurisdiction of proceedings instituted pursuant to this section. The Attorney General may implead as defendants such additional parties as are or become necessary to the grant of effective relief hereunder.

(b) The Attorney General may deem a person or persons unable to initiate and maintain appropriate legal proceedings within the meaning of subsection (a) of this section when such person or persons are unable, either directly or through other interested persons or organizations, to bear the expense of the litigation or to obtain effective legal representation; or whenever he is satisfied that the institution of such litigation would jeopardize the personal safety, employment, or economic standing of such person or persons, their families, or their property.

Sec. 302. In any action or proceeding under this title the United States shall be liable for costs, including a reasonable attorney's fee, the same as a private person.

Sec. 303. Nothing in this title shall affect adversely the right of any person to sue for or obtain relief in any court against discrimination in any facility covered by this title.

Sec. 304. A complaint as used in this title is a writing or document within the meaning of section 1001, title 18, United States Code.

## TITLE IV
## DESEGREGATION OF PUBLIC EDUCATION

DEFINITIONS

Sec. 401. As used in this title—

(a) "Commissioner" means the Commissioner of Education.

(b) "Desegregation" means the assignment of students to public schools and within such schools without regard to their race, color, religion, or national origin, but "desegregation" shall not mean the assignment of students to public schools in order to overcome racial imbalance.

(c) "Public school" means any elementary or secondary educational institution, and "public college" means any institution of higher education or any technical or vocational school above the secondary school level, provided that such public school or public college is operated by a State, subdivision of a State, or governmental agency within a State, or operated wholly or predominantly from or through the use of governmental funds or property, or funds or property derived from a governmental source.

(d) "School board" means any agency or agencies which administer a system of one or more public schools and any other agency which is responsible for the assignment of students to or within such system.

SURVEY AND REPORT OF EDUCATIONAL OPPORTUNITIES

SEC. 402. The Commissioner shall conduct a survey and make a report to the President and the Congress, within two years of the enactment of this title, concerning the lack of availability of equal educational opportunities for individuals by reason of race, color, religion, or national origin in public educational institutions at all levels in the United States, its territories and possessions, and the District of Columbia.

TECHNICAL ASSISTANCE

SEC. 403. The Commissioner is authorized, upon the application of any school board, State, municipality, school district, or other governmental unit legally responsible for operating a public school or schools, to render technical assistance to such applicant in the preparation, adoption, and implementation of plans for the desegregation of public schools. Such technical assistance may, among other activities, include making available to such agencies information regarding effective methods of coping with special educational problems occasioned by desegregation, and making available to such agencies personnel of the Office of Education or other persons specially equipped to advise and assist them in coping with such problems.

TRAINING INSTITUTES

SEC. 404. The Commissioner is authorized to arrange, through grants or contracts, with institutions of higher education for the operation of short-term or regular session institutes for special training designed to improve the ability of teachers, supervisors, counselors, and other elementary or secondary school personnel to deal effectively with special educational problems occasioned by desegregation. Individuals who attend such an institute on a full-time basis may be paid stipends for the period of their attendance at such institute in amounts specified by the Commissioner in regulations, including allowances for travel to attend such institute.

GRANTS

SEC. 405. (a) The Commissioner is authorized, upon application of a school board, to make grants to such board to pay, in whole or in part, the cost of—

(1) giving to teachers and other school personnel inservice training in dealing with problems incident to desegregation, and

(2) employing specialists to advise in problems incident to desegregation.

(b) In determining whether to make a grant, and in fixing the amount thereof and the terms and conditions on which it will be made, the Commissioner shall take into consideration the amount available for grants under this section and the other applications which are pending before him; the financial condition of the applicant and the other resources available to it; the nature, extent, and gravity of its problems incident to desegregation; and such other factors as he finds relevant.

PAYMENTS

SEC. 406. Payments pursuant to a grant or contract under this title may be made (after necessary adjustments on account of previously made overpayments or underpayments) in advance or by way of reimbursement, and in such installments, as the Commissioner may determine.

SUITS BY THE ATTORNEY GENERAL

SEC. 407. (a) Whenever the Attorney General receives a complaint in writing—

(1) signed by a parent or group of parents to the effect that his or their minor children, as members of a class of persons similarly situated, are being deprived by a school board of the equal protection of the laws, or

(2) signed by an individual, or his parent, to the effect that he has been denied admission to or not permitted to continue in attendance at a public college by reason of race, color, religion, or national origin, and the Attorney General believes the complaint is meritorious and certifies that the signer or signers of such complaint are unable, in his judgment, to initiate and maintain appropriate legal proceedings for relief and that the institution of an action will materially further the orderly achievement of desegregation in public education, the Attorney General is authorized, after giving notice of such complaint to the appropriate school board or college authority and after certifying that he is satisfied that such board or authority has had a reasonable time to adjust the conditions alleged in such complaint, to institute for or in the name of the United States a civil action in any appropriate district court of the United States against such parties and for such relief as may be appropriate, and such court shall have and shall exercise jurisdiction of proceedings instituted pursuant to this section, provided that nothing herein shall empower any official or court of the United States to issue any order seeking to achieve a racial balance in any school by requiring the transportation of pupils or students from one school to another or one school district to another in order to achieve such racial balance, or otherwise enlarge the existing power of the court to insure compliance with constitutional standards. The Attorney General may implead as defendants such additional parties as are or become necessary to the grant of effective relief hereunder.

(b) The Attorney General may deem a person or persons unable to initiate and maintain appropriate legal proceedings within the meaning of subsection (a) of this section when such person or persons are unable, either directly or through other interested persons or organizations, to bear the expense of the litigation or to obtain effective legal representation; or whenever he is satisfied that the institution of such litigation would jeopardize the personal safety, employment, or economic standing of such person or persons, their families, or their property.

(c) The term "parent" as used in this section includes any person standing in loco parentis. A "complaint" as used in this section is a writing or document within the meaning of section 1001, title 18, United States Code.

SEC. 408. In any action or proceeding under this title the United States shall be liable for costs the same as a private person.

SEC. 409. Nothing in this title shall affect adversely the right of any person to sue for or obtain relief in any court against discrimination in public education.

SEC. 410. Nothing in this title shall prohibit classification and assignment for reasons other than race, color, religion, or national origin.

## TITLE V
## COMMISSION ON CIVIL RIGHTS

SEC. 501. Section 102 of the Civil Rights Act of 1957 (42 U.S.C. 1975a; 71 Stat. 634) is amended to read as follows:

### RULES OF PROCEDURE OF THE COMMISSION HEARINGS

"SEC. 102. (a) At least thirty days prior to the commencement of any hearing, the Commission shall cause to be published in the Federal Register notice of the date on which such hearing is to commence, the place at which it is to be held and the subject of the hearing. The Chairman, or one designated by him to act as Chairman at a hearing of the Commission, shall announce in an opening statement the subject of the hearing.

"(b) A copy of the Commission's rules shall be made available to any witness before the Commission, and a witness compelled to appear before the Commission or required to produce written or other matter shall be served with a copy of the Commission's rules at the time of service of the subpoena.

"(c) Any person compelled to appear in person before the Commission shall be accorded the right to be accompanied and advised by counsel, who shall have the right to subject his client to reasonable examination, and to make objections on the record and to argue briefly the basis for such objections. The Commission shall proceed with reasonable dispatch to conclude any hearing in which it is engaged. Due regard shall be had for the convenience and necessity of witnesses.

"(d) The Chairman or Acting Chairman may punish breaches of order and decorum by censure and exclusion from the hearings.

"(e) If the Commission determines that evidence or testimony at any hearing may tend to defame, degrade, or incriminate any person, it shall receive such evidence or testimony or summary of such evidence or testimony in executive session. The Commission shall afford any person defamed, degraded, or incriminated by such evidence or testimony an opportunity to appear and be heard in executive session, with a reasonable number of additional witnesses requested by him, before deciding to use such evidence or testimony. In the event the Commission determines to release or use such evidence or testimony in such manner as to reveal publicly the identity of the person defamed, degraded, or incriminated, such evidence or testimony, prior to such public release or use, shall be given at a public session, and the Commission shall afford such person an opportunity to appear as a voluntary witness or to file a sworn statement in his behalf and to submit brief and pertinent sworn statements of others. The Commission shall receive and dispose of requests from such person to subpoena additional witnesses.

"(f) Except as provided in sections 102 and 105 (f) of this Act, the Chairman shall receive and the Commission shall dispose of requests to subpoena additional witnesses.

"(g) No evidence or testimony or summary of evidence or testimony taken in executive session may be released or used in public sessions without the consent of the Commission. Whoever releases or uses in public without the consent of the Commission such evidence or testimony taken in executive session shall be fined not more than $1,000, or imprisoned for not more than one year.

"(h) In the discretion of the Commission, witnesses may submit brief and pertinent sworn statements in writing for inclusion in the record. The Commission shall determine the pertinency of testimony and evidence adduced at its hearings.

"(i) Every person who submits data or evidence shall be entitled to retain or, on payment of lawfully prescribed costs, procure a copy or transcript thereof, except that a witness in a hearing held in executive session may for good cause be limited to inspection of the official transcript of his testimony. Transcript copies of public sessions may be obtained by the public upon the payment of the cost thereof. An accurate transcript shall be made of the testimony of all witnesses at all hearings, either public or executive sessions, of the Commission or of any subcommittee thereof.

"(j) A witness attending any session of the Commission shall receive $6 for each day's attendance and for the time necessarily occupied in going to and returning from the same, and 10 cents per mile for going from and returning to his place of residence. Witnesses who attend at points so far removed from their respective residences as to prohibit return thereto from day to day shall be entitled to an additional allowance of $10 per day for expenses of subsistence including the time necessarily occupied in going to and returning from the place of attendance. Mileage payments shall be tendered to the witness upon service of a subpoena issued on behalf of the Commission or any subcommittee thereof.

"(k) The Commission shall not issue any subpoena for the attendance and testimony of witnesses or for the production of written or other matter which would require the presence of the party subpoenaed at a hearing to be held outside of the State wherein the witness is found or resides or is domiciled or transacts business, or has appointed an agent for receipt of service of process except that, in any event, the Commission may issue subpoenas for the attendance and testimony of witnesses and the production of written or other matter at a hearing held within fifty miles of the place where the witness is found or resides or is domiciled or transacts business or has appointed an agent for receipt of service of process.

"(l) The Commission shall separately state and currently publish in the Federal Register (1) descriptions of its central and field organization including the established places at which, and methods whereby, the public may secure information or make requests; (2) statements of the general course and method by which its functions are channeled and determined, and (3) rules adopted as authorized by law. No person shall in any manner be subject to or required to resort to rules, organization, or procedure not so published."

SEC. 502. Section 103(a) of the Civil Rights Act of 1957 (42 U.S.C. 1975b(a); 71 Stat. 634) is amended to read as follows:

"SEC. 103. (a) Each member of the Commission who is not otherwise in the service of the Government of the United States shall receive the sum of $75 per day for each day spent in the work of the Commission, shall be paid actual travel expenses, and per diem in lieu of subsistence expenses when away from his usual place of residence, in accordance with section 5 of the Administrative Expenses Act of 1946, as amended (5 U.S.C 73b-2; 60 Stat. 808)."

SEC. 503. Section 103(b) of the Civil Rights Act of 1957 (42 U.S.C. 1975(b); 71 Stat. 634) is amended to read as follows:

"(b) Each member of the Commission who is otherwise in the service of the Government of the United States shall serve without compensation in addition to that received for such other service, but while engaged in the work of the Commission shall be paid actual travel expenses, and per diem in lieu of subsistence expenses when away from his usual place of residence, in accordance with the provisions of the Travel Expenses Act of 1949, as amended (5 U.S.C. 835–42; 63 Stat. 166)."

SEC. 504. (a) Section 104(a) of the Civil Rights Act of 1957 (42 U.S.C. 1975c(a); 71 Stat. 635), as amended, is further amended to read as follows:

### DUTIES OF THE COMMISSION

"SEC. 104. (a) The Commission shall—

"(1) investigate allegations in writing under oath or affirmation that certain citizens of the United States are being deprived of their right to vote and have that vote counted by reason of their color, race, religion, or national origin; which writing, under oath or affirmation, shall set forth the facts upon which such belief or beliefs are based;

"(2) study and collect information concerning legal developments constituting a denial of equal protection of the laws under the Constitution because of race, color, religion or national origin or in the administration of justice;

"(3) appraise the laws and policies of the Federal Government with respect to denials of equal protection of the laws under the Constitution because of race, color, religion or national origin or in the administration of justice;

"(4) serve as a national clearinghouse for information in respect to denials of equal protection of the laws because of race, color, religion or national origin, including but not limited to the fields of voting, education, housing, employment, the use of public facilities, and transportation, or in the administration of justice;

"(5) investigate allegations, made in writing and under oath or affirmation, that citizens of the United States are unlawfully being accorded or denied the right to vote, or to have their votes properly counted, in any election of presidential electors, Members of the United States Senate, or of the House of Representatives, as a result of any patterns or practice of fraud or discrimination in the conduct of such election; and

"(6) Nothing in this or any other Act shall be construed as authorizing the Commission, its Advisory Committees, or any person under its supervision or control to inquire into or investigate any membership practices or internal operations of any fraternal organization, any college or university fraternity or sorority, any private club or any religious organization."

(b) Section 104(b) of the Civil Rights Act of 1957 (42 U.S.C. 1975c(b); 71 Stat. 635), as amended, is further amended by striking out the present subsection "(b)" and by substituting therefor:

"(b) The Commission shall submit interim reports to the President and to the Congress at such times as the Commission, the Congress or the President shall deem desirable, and shall submit to the President and to the Congress a final report of its activities, findings, and recommendations not later than January 31, 1968."

SEC. 505. Section 105(a) of the Civil Rights Act of 1957 (42 U.S.C. 1975d(a); 71 Stat. 636) is amended by striking out in the last sentence thereof "$50 per diem" and inserting in lieu thereof "$75 per diem."

SEC. 506. Section 105(f) and section 105(g) of the Civil Rights Act of 1957 (42 U.S.C. 1975d (f) and (g); 71 Stat. 636) are amended to read as follows:

"(f) The Commission, or on the authorization of the Commission any subcommittee of two or more members, at least one of whom shall be of each major political party, may, for the purpose of carrying out the provisions of this Act, hold such hearings and act at such times and places as the Commission or such authorized subcommittee may deem advisable. Subpoenas for the attendance and testimony of witnesses or the production of written or other matter may be issued in accordance with the rules of the Commission as contained in section 102 (j) and (k) of this Act, over the signature of the Chairman of the Commission or of such subcommittee, and may be served by any person designated by such Chairman. The holding of hearings by the Commission, or the appointment of a subcommittee to hold hearings pursuant to this subparagraph, must be approved by a majority of the Commission, or by a majority of the members present at a meeting at which at least a quorum of four members is present.

"(g) In case of contumacy or refusal to obey a subpoena, any district court of the United States or the United States court of any territory or possession, or the District Court of the United States for the District of Columbia, within the jurisdiction of which the inquiry is carried on or within the jurisdiction of which said person guilty of contumacy or refusal to obey is found or resides or is domiciled or transacts business, or has appointed an agent for receipt of service of process, upon application by the Attorney General of the United States shall have jurisdiction to issue to such person an order requiring such person to appear before the Commission or a subcommittee thereof, there to produce pertinent, relevant and nonprivileged evidence if so ordered, or there to give testimony touching the matter under investigation; and any failure to obey such order of the court may be punished by said court as a contempt thereof."

Sec. 507. Section 105 of the Civil Rights Act of 1957 (42 U.S.C. 1975d; 71 Stat. 636), as amended by section 401 of the Civil Rights Act of 1960 (42 U.S.C. 1975d(h); 74 Stat. 89), is further amended by adding a new subsection at the end to read as follows:

"(i) The Commission shall have the power to make such rules and regulations as are necessary to carry out the purposes of this Act."

## Title VI
### Nondiscrimination in Federally Assisted Programs

Sec. 601. No person in the United States shall, on the ground of race, color, or national origin, be excluded from participation in, be denied the benefits of, or be subjected to discrimination under any program or activity receiving Federal financial assistance.

Sec. 602. Each Federal department and agency which is empowered to extend Federal financial assistance to any program or activity, by way of grant, loan, or contract other than a contract of insurance or guaranty, is authorized and directed to effectuate the provisions of section 601 with respect to such program or activity by issuing rules, regulations, or orders of general applicability which shall be consistent with achievement of the objectives of the statute authorizing the financial assistance in connection with which the action is taken. No such rule, regulation, or order shall become effective unless and until approved by the President. Compliance with any requirement adopted pursuant to this section may be effected (1) by the termination of or refusal to grant or to continue assistance under such program or activity to any recipient as to whom there has been an express finding on the record, after opportunity for hearing, of a failure to comply with such requirement, but such termination or refusal shall be limited to the particular political entity, or part thereof, or other recipient as to whom such a finding has been made and, shall be limited in its effect to the particular program, or part thereof, in which such non-compliance has been so found, or (2) by any other means authorized by law: *Provided, however,* That no such action shall be taken until the department or agency concerned has advised the appropriate person or persons of the failure to comply with the requirement and has determined that compliance cannot be secured by voluntary means. In the case of any action terminating, or refusing to grant or continue, assistance because of failure to comply with a requirement imposed pursuant to this section, the head of the federal department or agency shall file with the committees of the House and Senate having legislative jurisdiction over the program or activity involved a full written report of the circumstances and the grounds for such action. No such action shall become effective until thirty days have elapsed after the filing of such report.

Sec. 603. Any department or agency action taken pursuant to section 602 shall be subject to such judicial review as may otherwise be provided by law for similar action taken by such department or agency on other grounds. In the case of action, not otherwise subject to judicial review, terminating or refusing to grant or to continue financial assistance upon a finding of failure to comply with any requirement imposed pursuant to section 602, any person aggrieved (including any State or political subdivision thereof and any agency of either) may obtain judicial review of such action in accordance with section 10 of the Administrative Procedure Act, and such action shall not be deemed committed to unreviewable agency discretion within the meaning of that section.

Sec. 604. Nothing contained in this title shall be construed to authorize action under this title by any department or agency with respect to any employment practice of any employer, employment agency, or labor organization except where a primary objective of the Federal financial assistance is to provide employment.

SEC. 605. Nothing in this title shall add to or detract from any existing authority with respect to any program or activity under which Federal financial assistance is extended by way of a contract of insurance or guaranty.

# TITLE VII
## EQUAL EMPLOYMENT OPPORTUNITY

DEFINITIONS

SEC. 701. For the purposes of this title—

(a) The term "person" includes one or more individuals, labor unions, partnerships, associations, corporations, legal representatives, mutual companies, joint-stock companies, trusts, unincorporated organizations, trustees, trustees in bankruptcy, or receivers.

(b) The term "employer" means a person engaged in an industry affecting commerce who has twenty-five or more employees for each working day in each of twenty or more calendar weeks in the current or preceding calendar year, and any agent of such a person, but such term does not include (1) the United States, a corporation wholly owned by the Government of the United States, an Indian tribe, or a State or political subdivision thereof, (2) a bona fide private membership club (other than a labor organization) which is exempt from taxation under section 501(c) of the Internal Revenue Code of 1954: *Provided*, That during the first year after the effective date prescribed in subsection (a) of section 716, persons having fewer than one hundred employees (and their agents) shall not be considered employers, and, during the second year after such date, persons having fewer than seventy-five employees (and their agents) shall not be considered employers, and, during the third year after such date, persons having fewer than fifty employees (and their agents) shall not be considered employers: *Provided further*, That it shall be the policy of the United States to insure equal employment opportunities for Federal employees without discrimination because of race, color, religion, sex or national origin and the President shall utilize his existing authority to effectuate this policy.

(c) The term "employment agency" means any person regularly

undertaking with or without compensation to procure employees for an employer or to procure for employees opportunities to work for an employer and includes an agent of such a person; but shall not include an agency of the United States, or an agency of a State or political subdivision of a State, except that such term shall include the United States Employment Service and the system of State and local employment services receiving Federal assistance.

(d) The term "labor organization" means a labor organization engaged in an industry affecting commerce, and any agent of such an organization, and includes any organization of any kind, any agency, or employee representation committee, group, association, or plan so engaged in which employees participate and which exists for the purpose, in whole or in part, of dealing with employers concerning grievances, labor disputes, wages, rates of pay, hours, or other terms or conditions of employment, and any conference, general committee, joint or system board, or joint council so engaged which is subordinate to a national or international labor organization.

(e) A labor organization shall be deemed to be engaged in an industry affecting commerce if (1) it maintains or operates a hiring hall or hiring office which procures employees for an employer or procures for employees opportunities to work for an employer, or (2) the number of its members (or, where it is a labor organization composed of other labor organizations or their representatives, if the aggregate number of the members of such other labor organization) is (A) one hundred or more during the first year after the effective date prescribed in subsection (a) of section 716, (B) seventy-five or more during the second year after such date or fifty or more during the third year, or (C) twenty-five or more thereafter, and such labor organization—

(1) is the certified representative of employees under the provisions of the National Labor Relations Act, as amended, or the Railway Labor Act, as amended;

(2) although not certified, is a national or international labor organization or a local labor organization recognized or acting as the representative of employees of an employer or employers engaged in an industry affecting commerce; or

(3) has chartered a local labor organization or subsidiary body which is representing or actively seeking to represent employees of employers within the meaning of paragraph (1) or (2); or

(4) has been chartered by a labor organization representing or actively seeking to represent employees within the meaning of paragraph (1) or (2) as the local or subordinate body through which such employees may enjoy membership or become affiliated with such labor organization; or

(5) is a conference, general committee, joint or system board, or joint council subordinate to a national or international labor organization, which includes a labor organization engaged in an industry affecting commerce within the meaning of any of the preceding paragraphs of this subsection.

(f) The term "employee" means an individual employed by an employer.

(g) The term "commerce" means trade, traffic, commerce, transportation, transmission, or communication among the several States; or between a State and any place outside thereof; or within the District of Columbia, or a possession of the United States; or between points in the same State but through a point outside thereof.

(h) The term "industry affecting commerce" means any activity, business, or industry in commerce or in which a labor dispute would hinder or obstruct commerce or the free flow of commerce and includes any activity or industry "affecting commerce" within the meaning of the Labor-Management Reporting and Disclosure Act of 1959.

(i) The term "State" includes a State of the United States, the District of Columbia, Puerto Rico, the Virgin Islands, American Samoa, Guam, Wake Island, The Canal Zone, and Outer Continental Shelf lands defined in the Outer Continental Shelf Lands Act.

EXEMPTION

SEC. 702. This title shall not apply to an employer with respect to the employment of aliens outside any State, or to a religious corporation, association, or society with respect to the employment of individuals of a particular religion to perform work connected with the carrying on by such corporation, association, or society of its religious activities or to an educational institution with respect to the employment of individuals to perform work connected with the educational activities of such institution.

## DISCRIMINATION BECAUSE OF RACE, COLOR, RELIGION, SEX, OR NATIONAL ORIGIN

Sec. 703. (a) It shall be an unlawful employment practice for an employer—

(1) to fail or refuse to hire or to discharge any individual, or otherwise to discriminate against any individual with respect to his compensation, terms, conditions, or privileges of employment, because of such individual's race, color, religion, sex, or national origin; or

(2) to limit, segregate, or classify his employees in any way which would deprive or tend to deprive any individual of employment opportunities or otherwise adversely affect his status as an employee, because of such individual's race, color, religion, sex, or national origin.

(b) It shall be an unlawful employment practice for an employment agency to fail or refuse to refer for employment, or otherwise to discriminate against, any individual because of his race, color, religion, sex, or national origin, or to classify or refer for employment any individual on the basis of his race, color, religion, sex, or national origin.

(c) It shall be an unlawful employment practice for a labor organization—

(1) to exclude or to expel from its membership, or otherwise to discriminate against, any individual because of his race, color, religion, sex, or national origin;

(2) to limit, segregate, or classify its membership, or to classify or fail or refuse to refer for employment any individual, in any way which would deprive or tend to deprive any individual of employment opportunities, or would limit such employment opportunities or otherwise adversely affect his status as an employee or as an applicant for employment, because of such individual's race, color, religion, sex, or national origin; or

(3) to cause or attempt to cause an employer to discriminate against an individual in violation of this section.

(d) It shall be an unlawful employment practice for any employer, labor organization, or joint labor-management committee controlling apprenticeship or other training or retraining, including on-the-job training programs to discriminate against any individual because of his race, color, religion, sex, or national origin in admission to, or employment in, any program established to provide apprenticeship or other training.

(e) Notwithstanding any other provision of this title, (1) it shall not be an unlawful employment practice for an employer to hire and employ employees, for an employment agency to classify, or refer for employment any individual, for a labor organization to classify its membership or to classify or refer for employment any individual, or for an employer, labor organization, or joint labor-management committee controlling apprenticeship or other training or retraining programs to admit or employ any individual in any such program, on the basis of his religion, sex, or national origin in those certain instances where religion, sex, or national origin is a bona fide occupational qualification reasonably necessary to the normal operation of that particular business or enterprise, and (2) it shall not be an unlawful employment practice for a school, college, university, or other educational institution or institution of learning to hire and employ employees of a particular religion if such school, college, university, or other educational institution or institution of learning is, in whole or in substantial part, owned, supported, controlled, or managed by a particular religion or by a particular religious corporation, association, or society, or if the curriculum of such school, college, university, or other educational institution or institution of learning is directed toward the propagation of a particular religion.

(f) As used in this title, the phrase "unlawful employment practice" shall not be deemed to include any action or measure taken by an employer, labor organization, joint labor-management committee, or employment agency with respect to an individual who is a member of the Communist Party of the United States or of any other organization required to register as a Communist-action or Communist-front organization by final order of the Subversive Activities Control Board pursuant to the Subversive Activities Control Act of 1950.

(g) Notwithstanding any other provision of this title, it shall not be an unlawful employment practice for an employer to fail or refuse to hire and employ any individual for any position, for an employer to discharge any individual from any position, or for an employment agency to fail or refuse to refer any individual for employment in any position, or for a labor organization to fail or refuse to refer any individual for employment in any position, if—

(1) the occupancy of such position, or access to the premises in or upon which any part of the duties of such position is performed or is to

be performed, is subject to any requirement imposed in the interest of the national security of the United States under any security program in effect pursuant to or administered under any statute of the United States or any Executive order of the President; and

(2) such individual has not fulfilled or has ceased to fulfill that requirement.

(h) Notwithstanding any other provision of this title, it shall not be an unlawful employment practice for an employer to apply different standards of compensation, or different terms, conditions, or privileges of employment pursuant to a bona fide seniority or merit system, or a system which measures earnings by quantity or quality of production or to employees who work in different locations, provided that such differences are not the result of an intention to discriminate because of race, color, religion, sex, or national origin, nor shall it be an unlawful employment practice for an employer to give and to act upon the results of any professionally developed ability test provided that such test, its administration or action upon the results is not designed, intended or used to discriminate because of race, color, religion, sex or national origin. It shall not be an unlawful employment practice under this title for any employer to differentiate upon the basis of sex in determining the amount of the wages or compensation paid or to be paid to employees of such employer if such differentiation is authorized by the provisions of section 6(d) of the Fair Labor Standards Act of 1938, as amended (29 U.S.C. 206(d)).

(i) Nothing contained in this title shall apply to any business or enterprise on or near an Indian reservation with respect to any publicly announced employment practice of such business or enterprise under which a preferential treatment is given to any individual because he is an Indian living on or near a reservation.

(j) Nothing contained in this title shall be interpreted to require any employer, employment agency, labor organization, or joint labor-management committee subject to this title to grant preferential treatment to any individual or to any group because of the race, color, religion, sex, or national origin of such individual or group on account of an imbalance which may exist with respect to the total number or percentage of persons of any race, color, religion, sex, or national origin employed by any employer, referred or classified for employment by any employment agency or labor organization, admitted to membership or classified by any labor organization, or admitted to, or employed in, any apprenticeship or other training program, in comparison with the total number or percentage of persons of such race, color, religion, sex, or national origin in any community, State, section, or other area, or in the available work force in any community, State, section, or other area.

## OTHER UNLAWFUL EMPLOYMENT PRACTICES

SEC. 704. (a) It shall be an unlawful employment practice for an employer to discriminate against any of his employees or applicants for employment, for an employment agency to discriminate against any individual, or for a labor organization to discriminate against any member thereof or applicant for membership, because he has opposed any practice made an unlawful employment practice by this title, or because he has made a charge, testified, assisted, or participated in any manner in an investigation, proceeding, or hearing under this title.

(b) It shall be an unlawful employment practice for an employer, labor organization, or employment agency to print or publish or cause to be printed or published any notice or advertisement relating to employment by such an employer or membership in or any classification or referral for employment by such a labor organization, or relating to any classification or referral for employment by such an employment agency, indicating any preference, limitation, specification, or discrimination, based on race, color, religion, sex, or national origin, except that such a notice or advertisement may indicate a preference, limitation, specification, or discrimination based on religion, sex, or national origin when religion, sex, or national origin is a bona fide occupational qualification for employment.

## EQUAL EMPLOYMENT OPPORTUNITY COMMISSION

SEC. 705. (a) There is hereby created a Commission to be known as the Equal Employment Opportunity Commission, which shall be composed of five members, not more than three of whom shall be members of the same political party, who shall be appointed by the President by and with the advice and consent of the Senate. One of the original members shall be appointed for a term of one year, one for a term of two years, one for a term of three years, one for a term of four years, and one for a term of five years, beginning from the date of enactment of this title, but their successors shall be appointed for terms of five years each, except that any individual chosen to fill a vacancy shall be appointed only for the unexpired term of the member whom he shall succeed. The President shall designate one member to serve as Chairman of the Commission, and one member to serve as Vice Chairman. The Chairman shall be responsible on behalf of the Commission for the administrative operations of the Commission, and shall appoint, in accordance with the civil service laws, such officers, agents, attorneys, and employees as it deems necessary to assist it in the performance of its functions and to fix their compensation in accordance with the Classification Act of 1949, as amended. The Vice Chairman shall act as Chairman in the absence or disability of the Chairman or in the event of a vacancy in that office.

(b) A vacancy in the Commission shall not impair the right of the remaining members to exercise all the powers of the Commission and three members thereof shall constitute a quorum.

(c) The Commission shall have an official seal which shall be judicially noticed.

(d) The Commission shall at the close of each fiscal year report to the Congress and to the President concerning the action it has taken; the names, salaries, and duties of all individuals in its employ and the moneys it has disbursed; and shall make such further reports on the cause of and means of eliminating discrimination and such recommendations for further legislation as may appear desirable.

(e) The Federal Executive Pay Act of 1956, as amended (5 U.S.C. 2201-2209), is further amended—

(1) by adding to section 105 thereof (5 U.S.C. 2204) the following clause:

"(32) Chairman, Equal Employment Opportunity Commission"; and

(2) by adding to clause (45) of section 106(a) thereof (5 U.S.C. 2205(a)) the following: "Equal Employment Opportunity Commission (4)."

(f) The principal office of the Commission shall be in or near the District of Columbia, but it may meet or exercise any or all its powers at any other place. The Commission may establish such regional or State offices as it deems necessary to accomplish the purpose of this title.

(g) The Commission shall have power—

(1) to cooperate with and, with their consent, utilize regional, State, local, and other agencies, both public and private, and individuals;

(2) to pay to witnesses whose depositions are taken or who are summoned before the Commission or any of its agents the same witness and mileage fees as are paid to witnesses in the courts of the United States;

(3) to furnish to persons subject to this title such technical assistance as they may request to further their compliance with this title or an order issued thereunder;

(4) upon the request of (i) any employer, whose employees or some of them, or (ii) any labor organization, whose members or some of them, refuse or threaten to refuse to cooperate in effectuating the provisions of this title, to assist in such effectuation by conciliation or such other remedial action as is provided by this title;

(5) to make such technical studies as are appropriate to effectuate the purposes and policies of this title and to make the results of such studies available to the public;

(6) to refer matters to the Attorney General with recommendations for intervention in a civil action brought by an aggrieved party under section 706, or for the institution of a civil action by the Attorney General under section 707, and to advise, consult, and assist the Attorney General on such matters.

(h) Attorneys appointed under this section may, at the direction of the Commission, appear for and represent the Commission in any case in court.

(i) The Commission shall, in any of its educational or promotional activities, cooperate with other departments and agencies in the performance of such educational and promotional activities.

(j) All officers, agents, attorneys, and employees of the Commission shall be subject to the provisions of section 9 of the Act of August 2, 1939, as amended (the Hatch Act), notwithstanding any exemption contained in such section.

### PREVENTION OF UNLAWFUL EMPLOYMENT PRACTICES

SEC. 706. (a) Whenever it is charged in writing under oath by a person claiming to be aggrieved, or a written charge has been filed by a member of the Commission where he has reasonable cause to believe a violation of this title has occurred (and such charge sets forth the facts upon which it is based) that an employer, employment agency, or labor organization has engaged in an unlawful employment practice, the Commission shall furnish such employer, employment agency, or labor organization (hereinafter referred to as the "respondent") with a copy of such charge and shall make an investigation of such charge, provided that such charge shall not be made public by the Commission. If the Commission shall determine, after such investigation, that there is reasonable cause to believe that the charge is true, the Commission shall endeavor to eliminate any such alleged unlawful employment practice by informal methods of conference, conciliation, and persuasion. Nothing said or done during and as a part of such endeavors may be made public by the Commission without the written consent of the parties, or used as evidence in a subsequent proceeding. Any officer or employee of the Commission, who shall make public in any manner whatever any information in violation of this subsection shall be deemed guilty of a misdemeanor and upon conviction thereof shall be fined not more than $1,000 or imprisoned not more than one year.

(b) In the case of an alleged unlawful employment practice occurring in a State, or political subdivision of a State, which has a State or local law prohibiting the unlawful employment practice alleged and establishing or authorizing a State or local authority to grant or seek relief from such practice or to institute criminal proceedings with respect thereto upon receiving notice thereof, no charge may be filed under subsection (a) by the person aggrieved before the expiration of sixty days after proceedings have been commenced under the State or local law, unless such proceedings have been earlier terminated, provided that such sixty-day period shall be extended to one hundred and twenty days during the first year after the effective date of such State or local law. If any requirement for the commencement of such proceedings is imposed by a State or local authority other than a requirement of the filing of a written and signed statement of the facts upon which the proceeding is based, the proceeding shall be deemed to have been commenced for the purposes of this subsection at the time such statement is sent by registered mail to the appropriate State or local authority.

(c) In the case of any charge filed by a member of the Commission alleging an unlawful employment practice occurring in a State or political subdivision of a State, which has a State or local law prohibiting the practice alleged and establishing or authorizing a State or local authority to grant or seek relief from such practice or to institute criminal proceedings with respect thereto upon receiving notice thereof, the Commission shall, before taking any action with respect to such charge, notify the appropriate State or local officials and, upon request, afford them a reasonable time, but not less than sixty days (provided that such sixty-day period shall be extended to one hundred and twenty days during the first year after the effective day of such State or local law), unless a shorter period is requested, to act under such State or local law to remedy the practice alleged.

(d) A charge under subsection (a) shall be filed within ninety days after the alleged unlawful employment practice occurred, except that in the case of an unlawful employment practice with respect to which the person aggrieved has followed the procedure set out in subsection (b), such charge shall be filed by the person aggrieved within two hundred and ten days after the alleged unlawful employment practice occurred, or within thirty days after receiving notice that the State or local agency has terminated the proceedings under the State or local, law, whichever is earlier, and a copy of such charge shall be filed by the Commission with the State or local agency.

(e) If within thirty days after a charge is filed with the Commission or within thirty days after expiration of any period of reference under subsection (c) (except that in either case such period may be extended to not more than sixty days upon a determination by the Commission that further efforts to secure voluntary compliance are warranted), the Commission has been unable to obtain voluntary compliance with this title, the Commission shall so notify the person aggrieved and a civil action may, within thirty days thereafter, be brought against the respondent named in the charge (1) by the person claiming to be aggrieved, or (2) if such charge was filed by a member of the Commission, by any person whom the charge alleges was aggrieved by the alleged unlawful employment practice. Upon application by the complainant and in such circumstances as the court may deem just, the court may appoint an attorney for such complainant and may authorize the commencement of the action without the payment of fees, costs, or security. Upon timely application, the court may, in its discretion, permit the Attorney General to intervene in such civil action if he certifies that the case is of general public importance. Upon request, the court may, in its discretion, stay further proceedings for not more than sixty days pending the termination of State or local proceedings described in subsection (b) or the efforts of the Commission to obtain voluntary compliance.

(f) Each United States district court and each United States court of a place subject to the jurisdiction of the United States shall have jurisdiction of actions brought under this title. Such an action may be brought in any judicial district in the State in which the unlawful employment practice is alleged to have been committed, in the judicial district in which the employment records relevant to such practice are maintained and administered, or in the judicial district in which the plaintiff would have worked but for the alleged unlawful employment practice, but if the respondent is not found within any such district, such an action may be brought within the judicial district in which the respondent has his principal office. For purposes of sections 1404 and 1406 of title 28 of the United States Code, the judicial district in which the respondent has his principal office shall in all cases be considered a district in which the action might have been brought.

(g) If the court finds that the respondent has intentionally engaged in or is intentionally engaging in an unlawful employment practice charged in the complaint, the court may enjoin the respondent from engaging in such unlawful employment practice, and order such affirmative action as may be appropriate, which may include reinstatement or hiring of employees, with or without back pay (payable by the employer, employment agency, or labor organization, as the case may be, responsible for the unlawful employment practice). Interim earnings or amounts earnable with reasonable diligence by the person or persons discriminated against shall operate to reduce the back pay otherwise allowable. No order of the court shall require the admission or reinstatement of an individual as a member of a union or the hiring, reinstatement, or promotion of an individual as an employee, or the payment to him of any back pay, if such individual was refused admission, suspended, or expelled or was refused employment or advancement or was suspended or discharged for any reason other than discrimination on account of race, color, religion, sex or national origin or in violation of section 704(a).

(h) The provisions of the Act entitled "An Act to amend the Judicial Code and to define and limit the jurisdiction of courts sitting in equity, and for other purposes," approved March 23, 1932 (29 U.S.C. 101–

115),—shall not apply with respect to civil actions brought under this section.

(i) In any case in which an employer, employment agency, or labor organization fails to comply with an order of a court issued in a civil action brought under subsection (e), the Commission may commence proceedings to compel compliance with such order.

(j) Any civil action brought under subsection (e) and any proceedings brought under subsection (i) shall be subject to appeal as provided in sections 1291 and 1292, title 28, United States Code.

(k) In any action or proceeding under this title the court, in its discretion, may allow the prevailing party, other than the Commission or the United States, a reasonable attorney's fee as part of the costs, and the Commission and the United States shall be liable for costs the same as a private person.

SEC. 707. (a) Whenever the Attorney General has reasonable cause to believe that any person or group of persons is engaged in a pattern or practice of resistance to the full enjoyment of any of the rights secured by this title, and that the pattern or practice is of such a nature and is intended to deny the full exercise of the rights herein described, the Attorney General may bring a civil action in the appropriate district court of the United States by filing with it a complaint (1) signed by him (or in his absence the Acting Attorney General), (2) setting forth facts pertaining to such pattern or practice, and (3) requesting such relief, including an application for a permanent or temporary injunction, restraining order or other order against the person or persons responsible for such pattern or practice, as he deems necessary to insure the full enjoyment of the rights herein described.

(b) The district courts of the United States shall have and shall exercise jurisdiction of proceedings instituted pursuant to this section, and in any such proceeding the Attorney General may file with the clerk of such court a request that a court of three judges be convened to hear and determine the case. Such request by the Attorney General shall be accompanied by a certificate that, in his opinion, the case is of general public importance. A copy of the certificate and request for a three-judge court shall be immediately furnished by such clerk to the chief judge of the circuit (or in his absence, the presiding circuit judge of the circuit) in which the case is pending. Upon receipt of such request it shall be the duty of the chief judge of the circuit or the presiding circuit judge, as the case may be, to designate immediately three judges in such circuit, of whom at least one shall be a circuit judge and another of whom shall be a district judge of the court in which the proceeding was instituted, to hear and determine such case, and it shall be the duty of the judges so designated to assign the case for hearing at the earliest practicable date, to participate in the hearing and determination thereof, and to cause the case to be in every way expedited. An appeal from the final judgment of such court will lie to the Supreme Court.

In the event the Attorney General fails to file such a request in any such proceeding, it shall be the duty of the chief judge of the district (or in his absence, the acting chief judge) in which the case is pending immediately to designate a judge in such district to hear and determine the case. In the event that no judge in the district is available to hear and determine the case, the chief judge of the district, or the acting chief judge, as the case may be, shall certify this fact to the chief judge of the circuit (or in his absence, the acting chief judge) who shall then designate a district or circuit judge of the circuit to hear and determine the case.

It shall be the duty of the judge designated pursuant to this section to assign the case for hearing at the earliest practicable date and to cause the case to be in every way expedited.

**EFFECT ON STATE LAWS**

SEC. 708. Nothing in this title shall be deemed to exempt or relieve any person from any liability, duty, penalty, or punishment provided by any present or future law of any State or political subdivision of a State, other than any such law which purports to require or permit the doing of any act which would be an unlawful employment practice under this title.

**INVESTIGATIONS, INSPECTIONS, RECORDS, STATE AGENCIES**

SEC. 709. (a) In connection with any investigation of a charge filed under section 706, the Commission or its designated representative shall at all reasonable times have access to, for the purposes of examination, and the right to copy any evidence of any person being investigated or proceeded against that relates to unlawful employment practices covered by this title and is relevant to the charge under investigation.

(b) The Commission may cooperate with State and local agencies charged with the administration of State fair employment practices laws and, with the consent of such agencies, may for the purpose of carrying out its functions and duties under this title and within the limitation of funds appropriated specifically for such purpose, utilize the services of such agencies and their employees and, notwithstanding any other provision of law, may reimburse such agencies and their employees for services rendered to assist the Commission in carrying out this title. In furtherance of such cooperative efforts, the Commission may enter into written agreements with such State or local agencies and such agreements may include provisions under which the Commission shall refrain from processing a charge in any cases or class of cases specified in such agreements and under which no person may bring a civil action under section 706 in any cases or class of cases so specified, or under which the Commission shall relieve any person or class of persons in such State or locality from requirements imposed under this section. The Commission shall rescind any such agreement whenever it determines that the agreement no longer serves the interest of effective enforcement of this title.

(c) Except as provided in subsection (d), every employer, employment agency, and labor organization subject to this title shall (1) make and keep such records relevant to the determinations of whether unlawful employment practices have been or are being committed, (2) preserve such records for such periods, and (3) make such reports therefrom, as the Commission shall prescribe by regulation or order, after public hearing, as reasonable, necessary, or appropriate for the enforcement of this title or the regulations or orders thereunder. The Commission shall, by regulation, require each employer, labor organization, and joint labor-management committee subject to this title which controls an apprenticeship or other training program to maintain such records as are reasonably necessary to carry out the purpose of this title, including, but not limited to, a list of applicants who wish to participate in such program, including the chronological order in which such applications were received, and shall furnish to the Commission, upon request, a detailed description of the manner in which persons are selected to participate in the apprenticeship or other training program. Any employer, employment agency, labor organization, or joint labor-management committee which believes that the application to it of any regulation or order issued under this section would result in undue hardship may (1) apply to the Commission for an exemption from the application of such regulation or order, or (2) bring a civil action in the United States district court for the district where such records are kept. If the Commission or the court, as the case may be, finds that the application of the regulation or order to the employer, employment agency, or labor organization in question would impose an undue hardship, the Commission or the court, as the case may be, may grant appropriate relief.

(d) The provisions of subsection (c) shall not apply to any employer, employment agency, labor organization, or joint labor-management committee with respect to matters occurring in any State or political subdivision thereof which has a fair employment practice law during any period in which such employer, employment agency, labor organization, or joint labor-management committee is subject to such law, except that the Commission may require such notations on records which such employer, employment agency, labor organization, or joint labor-management committee keeps or is required to keep as are necessary because of differences in coverage or methods of enforcement between the State or local law and the provisions of this title. Where an employer is required by Executive Order 10925, issued March 6, 1961, or by any other Executive order prescribing fair employment practices for Government contractors and subcontractors, or by rules or regulations issued thereunder, to file reports relating to his employment practices with any Federal agency or committee, and he is substantially in compliance with such requirements, the Commission shall not require him to file additional reports pursuant to subsection (c) of this section.

(e) It shall be unlawful for any officer or employee of the Commission to make public in any manner whatever any information obtained by the Commission pursuant to its authority under this section prior to the institution of any proceeding under this title involving such information. Any officer or employee of the Commission who shall make public in any manner whatever any information in violation of this subsection shall be guilty of a misdemeanor and upon conviction thereof, shall be fined not more than $1,000, or imprisoned not more than one year.

### INVESTIGATORY POWERS

SEC. 710. (a) For the purposes of any investigation of a charge filed under the authority contained in section 706, the Commission shall have authority to examine witnesses under oath and to require the production of documentary evidence relevant or material to the charge under investigation.

(b) If the respondent named in a charge filed under section 706 fails or refuses to comply with a demand of the Commission for permission to examine or to copy evidence in conformity with the provisions of section 709(a), or if any person required to comply with the provisions of section 709 (c) or (d) fails or refuses to do so, or if any person fails or refuses to comply with a demand by the Commission to give testimony under oath, the United States district court for the district in which such person is found, resides, or transacts business, shall, upon application of the Commission, have jurisdiction to issue to such person an order requiring him to comply with the provisions of section 709 (c) or (d) or to comply with the demand of the Commission, but the attendance of a witness may not be required outside the State where he is found, resides, or transacts business and the production of evidence may not be required outside the State where such evidence is kept.

(c) Within twenty days after the service upon any person charged under section 706 of a demand by the Commission for the production of documentary evidence or for permission to examine or to copy evidence in conformity with the provisions of section 709(a), such person may file in the district court of the United States for the judicial district in which he resides, is found, or transacts business, and serve upon the Commission a petition for an order of such court modifying or setting aside such demand. The time allowed for compliance with the demand in whole or in part as deemed proper and ordered by the court shall not run during the pendency of such petition in the court. Such petition shall specify each ground upon which the petitioner relies in seeking such relief, and may be based upon any failure of such demand to comply with the provisions of this title or with the limitations generally applicable to compulsory process or upon any constitutional or other legal right or privilege of such person. No objection which is not raised by such a petition may be urged in the defense to a proceeding initiated by the Commission under subsection (b) for enforcement of such a demand unless such proceeding is commenced by the Commission prior to the expiration of the twenty-day period, or unless the court determines that the defendant could not reasonably have been aware of the availability of such ground of objection.

(d) In any proceeding brought by the Commission under subsection (b), except as provided in subsection (c) of this section, the defendant may petition the court for an order modifying or setting aside the demand of the Commission.

### NOTICES TO BE POSTED

Sec. 711. (a) Every employer, employment agency, and labor organization, as the case may be, shall post and keep posted in conspicuous places upon its premises where notices to employees, applicants for employment, and members are customarily posted a notice to be prepared or approved by the Commission setting forth excerpts from or, summaries of, the pertinent provisions of this title and information pertinent to the filing of a complaint.

(b) A willful violation of this section shall be punishable by a fine of not more than $100 for each separate offense.

### VETERANS' PREFERENCE

Sec. 712. Nothing contained in this title shall be construed to repeal or modify any Federal, State, territorial, or local law creating special rights or preference for veterans.

### RULES AND REGULATIONS

Sec. 713. (a) The Commission shall have authority from time to time to issue, amend, or rescind suitable procedural regulations to carry out the provisions of this title. Regulations issued under this section shall be in conformity with the standards and limitations of the Administrative Procedure Act.

(b) In any action or proceeding based on any alleged unlawful employment practice, no person shall be subject to any liability or punishment for or on account of (1) the commission by such person of an unlawful employment practice if he pleads and proves that the act or omission complained of was in good faith, in conformity with, and in reliance on any written interpretation or opinion of the Commission, or (2) the failure of such person to publish and file any information required by any provision of this title if he pleads and proves that he failed to publish and file such information in good faith, in conformity with the instructions of the Commission issued under this title regarding the filing of such information. Such a defense, if established, shall be a bar to the action or proceeding, notwithstanding that (A) after such act or omission, such interpretation or opinion is modified or rescinded or is determined by judicial authority to be invalid or of no legal effect, or (B) after publishing or filing the description and annual reports, such publication or filing is determined by judicial authority not to be in conformity with the requirements of this title.

### FORCIBLY RESISTING THE COMMISSION OR ITS REPRESENTATIVES

SEC. 714. The provisions of section 111, title 18, United States Code, shall apply to officers, agents, and employees of the Commission in the performance of their official duties.

### SPECIAL STUDY BY SECRETARY OF LABOR

SEC. 715. The Secretary of Labor shall make a full and complete study of the factors which might tend to result in discrimination in employment because of age and of the consequences of such discrimination on the economy and individuals affected. The Secretary of Labor shall make a report to the Congress not later than June 30, 1965, containing the results of such study and shall include in such report such recommendations for legislation to prevent arbitrary discrimination in employment because of age as he determines advisable.

### EFFECTIVE DATE

SEC. 716. (a) This title shall become effective one year after the date of its enactment.

(b) Notwithstanding subsection (a), sections of this title other than sections 703, 704, 706, and 707 shall become effective immediately.

(c) The President shall, as soon as feasible after the enactment of this title, convene one or more conferences for the purpose of enabling the leaders of groups whose members will be affected by this title to become familiar with the rights afforded and obligations imposed by its provisions, and for the purpose of making plans which will result in the fair and effective administration of this title when all of its provisions become effective. The President shall invite the participation in such conference or conferences of (1) the members of the President's Committee on Equal Employment Opportunity, (2) the members of the Commission on Civil Rights, (3) representatives of State and local agencies engaged in furthering equal employment opportunity, (4) representatives of private agencies engaged in furthering equal employment opportunity, and (5) representatives of employers, labor organizations, and employment agencies who will be subject to this title.

## TITLE VIII
### REGISTRATION AND VOTING STATISTICS

Sec. 801. The Secretary of Commerce shall promptly conduct a survey to compile registration and voting statistics in such geographic areas as may be recommended by the Commission on Civil Rights. Such a survey and compilation shall, to the extent recommended by the Commission on Civil Rights, only include a count of persons of voting age by race, color, and national origin, and determination of the extent to which such persons are registered to vote, and have voted in any statewide primary or general election in which the Members of the United States House of Representatives are nominated or elected, since January 1, 1960. Such information shall also be collected and compiled in connection with the Nineteenth Decennial Census, and at such other times as the Congress may prescribe. The provisions of section 9 and chapter 7 of title 13, United States Code, shall apply to any survey, collection, or compilation of registration and voting statistics carried out under this title: *Provided, however,* That no person shall be compelled to disclose his race, color, national origin, or questioned about his political party affiliation, how he voted, or the reasons therefore, nor shall any penalty be imposed for his failure or refusal to make such disclosure. Every person interrogated orally, by written survey or questionnaire or by any other means with respect to such information shall be fully advised with respect to his right to fail or refuse to furnish such information.

## TITLE IX
### INTERVENTION AND PROCEDURE AFTER REMOVAL IN CIVIL RIGHTS CASES

Sec. 901. Title 28 of the United States Code, section 1447(d), is amended to read as follows:

"An order remanding a case to the State court from which it was removed is not reviewable on appeal or otherwise, except that an order remanding a case to the State court from which it was removed pursuant to section 1443 of this title shall be reviewable by appeal or otherwise."

SEC. 902. Whenever an action has been commenced in any court of the United States seeking relief from the denial of equal protection of the laws under the fourteenth amendment to the Constitution on account of race, color, religion, or national origin, the Attorney General for or in the name of the United States may intervene in such action upon timely application if the Attorney General certifies that the case is of general public importance. In such action the United States shall be entitled to the same relief as if it had instituted the action.

## TITLE X
### ESTABLISHMENT OF COMMUNITY RELATIONS SERVICE

SEC. 1001. (a) There is hereby established in and as a part of the Department of Commerce a Community Relations Service (hereinafter referred to as the "Service"), which shall be headed by a Director who shall be appointed by the President with the advice and consent of the Senate for a term of four years. The Director is authorized to appoint, subject to the civil service laws and regulations, such other personnel as may be necessary to enable the Service to carry out its functions and duties, and to fix their compensation in accordance with the Classification Act of 1949, as amended. The Director is further authorized to procure services as authorized by section 15 of the Act of August 2, 1946 (60 Stat. 810; 5 U.S.C. 55(a)), but at rates for individuals not in excess of $75 per diem.

(b) Section 106(a) of the Federal Executive Pay Act of 1956, as amended (5 U.S.C. 2205(a)), is further amended by adding the following clause thereto:

"(52) Director, Community Relations Service."

SEC. 1002. It shall be the function of the Service to provide assistance to communities and persons therein in resolving disputes, disagreements, or difficulties relating to discriminatory practices based on race, color, or national origin which impair the rights of persons in such communities under the Constitution or laws of the United States or which affect or may affect interstate commerce. The Service may offer its services in cases of such disputes, disagreements, or difficulties whenever, in its judgment, peaceful relations among the citizens of the community involved are threatened thereby, and it may offer its services either upon its own motion or upon the request of an appropriate State or local official or other interested person.

Sec. 1003. (a) The Service shall, whenever possible, in performing its functions, seek and utilize the cooperation of appropriate State or local, public, or private agencies.

(b) The activities of all officers and employees of the Service in providing conciliation assistance shall be conducted in confidence and without publicity, and the Service shall hold confidential any information acquired in the regular performance of its duties upon the understanding that it would be so held. No officer or employee of the Service shall engage in the performance of investigative or prosecuting functions of any department or agency in any litigation arising out of a dispute in which he acted on behalf of the Service. Any officer or other employee of the Service, who shall make public in any manner whatever any information in violation of this subsection, shall be deemed guilty of a misdemeanor and, upon conviction thereof, shall be fined not more than $1,000 or imprisoned not more than one year.

Sec. 1004. Subject to the provisions of sections 205 and 1003(b), the Director shall, on or before January 31 of each year, submit to the Congress a report of the activities of the Service during the preceding fiscal year.

## Title XI
### Miscellaneous

Sec. 1101. In any proceeding for criminal contempt arising under title II, III, IV, V, VI, or VII of this Act, the accused, upon demand therefor, shall be entitled to a trial by jury, which shall conform as near as may be to the practice in criminal cases. Upon conviction, the accused shall not be fined more than $1,000 or imprisoned for more than six months.

This section shall not apply to contempts committed in the presence of the court, or so near thereto as to obstruct the administration of justice, nor to the misbehavior, misconduct, or disobedience of any officer of the court in respect to writs, orders, or process of the court. No person shall be convicted of criminal contempt hereunder unless the act or omission constituting such contempt shall have been intentional, as required in other cases of criminal contempt.

Nor shall anything herein be construed to deprive courts of their power, by civil contempt proceedings, without a jury, to secure compliance with or to prevent obstruction of, as distinguished from punishment for violations of, any lawful writ, process, order, rule, decree, or command of the court in accordance with the prevailing usages of law and equity, including the power of detention.

SEC. 1102. No person should be put twice in jeopardy under the laws of the United States for the same act or omission. For this reason, an acquittal or conviction in a prosecution for a specific crime under the laws of the United States shall bar a proceeding for criminal contempt, which is based upon the same act or omission and which arises under the provisions of this Act; and an acquittal or conviction in a proceeding for criminal contempt, which arises under the provisions of this Act, shall bar a prosecution for a specific crime under the laws of the United States based upon the same act or omission.

SEC. 1103. Nothing in this Act shall be construed to deny, impair, or otherwise affect any right or authority of the Attorney General or of the United States or any agency or officer thereof under existing law to institute or intervene in any action or proceeding.

SEC. 1104. Nothing contained in any title of this Act shall be construed as indicating an intent on the part of Congress to occupy the field in which any such title operates to the exclusion of State laws on the same subject matter, nor shall any provision of this Act be construed as invalidating any provision of State law unless such provision is inconsistent with any of the purposes of this Act, or any provision thereof.

SEC. 1105. There are hereby authorized to be appropriated such sums as are necessary to carry out the provisions of this Act.

SEC. 1106. If any provision of this Act or the application thereof to any person or circumstances is held invalid, the remainder of the Act and the application of the provision to other persons not similarly situated or to other circumstances shall not be affected thereby.

# LYNDON B. JOHNSON'S SPECIAL MESSAGE TO CONGRESS: THE AMERICAN PROMISE (1965)

*President Lyndon B. Johnson addressed Congress on March 15, 1965, to urge the legislature to pass the Voting Rights Act, which he calls a "civil rights bill." Johnson was successful—Congress passed the Voting Rights Act in August of that year.*

I speak tonight for the dignity of man and the destiny of democracy. I urge every member of both parties, Americans of all religions and of all colors, from every section of this country, to join me in that cause.

At times history and fate meet at a single time in a single place to shape a turning point in man's unending search for freedom. So it was at Lexington and Concord. So it was a century ago at Appomattox. So it was last week in Selma, Alabama.

There, long-suffering men and women peacefully protested the denial of their rights as Americans. Many were brutally assaulted. One good man, a man of God, was killed.

There is no cause for pride in what has happened in Selma. There is no cause for self-satisfaction in the long denial of equal rights of millions of Americans. But there is cause for hope and for faith in our democracy in what is happening here tonight.

For the cries of pain and the hymns and protests of oppressed people have summoned into convocation all the majesty of this great Government—the Government of the greatest Nation on earth.

Our mission is at once the oldest and the most basic of this country: to right wrong, to do justice, to serve man.

In our time we have come to live with moments of great crisis. Our lives have been marked with debate about great issues; issues of war and peace, issues of prosperity and depression. But rarely in any time does an issue lay bare the secret heart of America itself. Rarely are we met with a challenge, not to our growth or abundance, our welfare or our security, but rather to the values and the purposes and the meaning of our beloved Nation.

The issue of equal rights for American Negroes is such an issue. And should we defeat every enemy, should we double our wealth and conquer the stars, and still be unequal to this issue, then we will have failed as a people and as a nation.

For with a country as with a person, "What is a man profited, if he shall gain the whole world, and lose his own soul?"

There is no Negro problem. There is no Southern problem. There is no Northern problem. There is only an American problem. And we are met here tonight as Americans—not as Democrats or Republicans—we are met here as Americans to solve that problem.

This was the first nation in the history of the world to be founded with a purpose. The great phrases of that purpose still sound in every American heart, North and South: "All men are created equal"—"government by consent of the governed"—"give me liberty or give me death." Well, those are not just clever words, or those are not just empty theories. In their name Americans have fought and died for two centuries, and tonight around the world they stand there as guardians of our liberty, risking their lives.

Those words are a promise to every citizen that he shall share in the dignity of man. This dignity cannot be found in a man's possessions; it cannot be found in his power, or in his position. It really rests on his right to be treated as a man equal in opportunity to all others. It says that he shall share in freedom, he shall choose his leaders, educate his children, and provide for his family according to his ability and his merits as a human being.

To apply any other test—to deny a man his hopes because of his color or race, his religion or the place of his birth—is not only to do injustice, it is to deny America and to dishonor the dead who gave their lives for American freedom.

THE RIGHT TO VOTE

Our fathers believed that if this noble view of the rights of man was to flourish, it must be rooted in democracy. The most basic right of all was the right to choose your own leaders. The history of this country, in large measure, is the history of the expansion of that right to all of our people.

Many of the issues of civil rights are very complex and most difficult. But about this there can and should be no argument. Every American citizen must have an equal right to vote. There is no reason which can excuse the denial of that right. There is no duty which weighs more heavily on us than the duty we have to ensure that right.

Yet the harsh fact is that in many places in this country men and women are kept from voting simply because they are Negroes.

Every device of which human ingenuity is capable has been used to deny this right. The Negro citizen may go to register only to be told that the day is wrong, or the hour is late, or the official in charge is absent. And if he persists, and if he manages to present himself to the registrar, he may be disqualified because he did not spell out his middle name or because he abbreviated a word on the application.

And if he manages to fill out an application he is given a test. The registrar is the sole judge of whether he passes this test. He may be asked to recite the entire Constitution, or explain the most complex provisions of State law. And even a college degree cannot be used to prove that he can read and write.

For the fact is that the only way to pass these barriers is to show a white skin.

Experience has clearly shown that the existing process of law cannot overcome systematic and ingenious discrimination. No law that we now have on the books—and I have helped to put three of them there—can ensure the right to vote when local officials are determined to deny it.

In such a case our duty must be clear to all of us. The Constitution says that no person shall be kept from voting because of his race or his color. We have all sworn an oath before God to support and to defend that Constitution. We must now act in obedience to that oath.

GUARANTEEING THE RIGHT TO VOTE

Wednesday I will send to Congress a law designed to eliminate illegal barriers to the right to vote.

The broad principles of that bill will be in the hands of the Democratic and Republican leaders tomorrow. After they have reviewed it, it will come here formally as a bill. I am grateful for this opportunity to come here tonight at the invitation of the leadership to reason with my friends, to give them my views, and to visit with my former colleagues.

I have had prepared a more comprehensive analysis of the legislation which I had intended to transmit to the clerk tomorrow but which I will

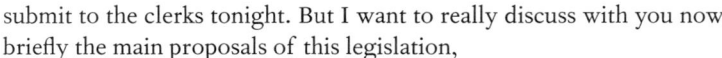

submit to the clerks tonight. But I want to really discuss with you now briefly the main proposals of this legislation,

This bill will strike down restrictions to voting in all elections—Federal, State, and local—which have been used to deny Negroes the right to vote.

This bill will establish a simple, uniform standard which cannot be used, however ingenious the effort, to flout our Constitution.

It will provide for citizens to be registered by officials of the United States Government if the State officials refuse to register them.

It will eliminate tedious, unnecessary lawsuits which delay the right to vote.

Finally, this legislation will ensure that properly registered individuals are not prohibited from voting.

I will welcome the suggestions from all of the Members of Congress—I have no doubt that I will get some—on ways and means to strengthen this law and to make it effective. But experience has plainly shown that this is the only path to carry out the command of the Constitution.

To those who seek to avoid action by their National Government in their own communities; who want to and who seek to maintain purely local control over elections, the answer is simple:

Open your polling places to all your people.

Allow men and women to register and vote whatever the color of their skin.

Extend the rights of citizenship to every citizen of this land.


THE NEED FOR ACTION

There is no constitutional issue here. The command of the Constitution is plain.

There is no moral issue. It is wrong—deadly wrong—to deny any of your fellow Americans the right to vote in this country.

There is no issue of States rights or national rights. There is only the struggle for human rights.

I have not the slightest doubt what will be your answer.

The last time a President sent a civil rights bill to the Congress it contained a provision to protect voting rights in Federal elections. That civil rights bill was passed after 8 long months of debate. And when that bill came to my desk from the Congress for my signature, the heart of the voting provision had been eliminated.

This time, on this issue, there must be no delay, no hesitation and no compromise with our purpose.

We cannot, we must not, refuse to protect the right of every American to vote in every election that he may desire to participate in. And we ought not and we cannot and we must not wait another 8 months before we get a bill. We have already waited a hundred years and more, and the time for waiting is gone.

So I ask you to join me in working long hours—nights and weekends, if necessary—to pass this bill. And I don't make that request lightly. For from the window where I sit with the problems of our country I recognize that outside this chamber is the outraged conscience of a nation, the grave concern of many nations, and the harsh judgment of history on our acts.

WE SHALL OVERCOME

But even if we pass this bill, the battle will not be over. What happened in Selma is part of a far larger movement which reaches into every section and State of America. It is the effort of American Negroes to secure for themselves the full blessings of American life.

Their cause must be our cause too. Because it is not just Negroes, but really it is all of us, who must overcome the crippling legacy of bigotry and injustice.

And we shall overcome.

As a man whose roots go deeply into Southern soil I know how agonizing racial feelings are. I know how difficult it is to reshape the attitudes and the structure of our society.

But a century has passed, more than a hundred years, since the Negro was freed. And he is not fully free tonight.

It was more than a hundred years ago that Abraham Lincoln, a great President of another party, signed the Emancipation Proclamation, but emancipation is a proclamation and not a fact.

A century has passed, more than a hundred years, since equality was promised. And yet the Negro is not equal.

A century has passed since the day of promise. And the promise is unkept.

The time of justice has now come. I tell you that I believe sincerely that no force can hold it back. It is right in the eyes of man and God that it should come. And when it does, I think that day will brighten the lives of every American.

For Negroes are not the only victims. How many white children have gone uneducated, how many white families have lived in stark poverty, how many white lives have been scarred by fear, because we have wasted our energy and our substance to maintain the barriers of hatred and terror?

So I say to all of you here, and to all in the Nation tonight, that those who appeal to you to hold on to the past do so at the cost of denying you your future.

This great, rich, restless country can offer opportunity and education and hope to all: black and white, North and South, sharecropper and city dweller. These are the enemies: poverty, ignorance, disease. They are the enemies and not our fellow man, not our neighbor. And these enemies too, poverty, disease and ignorance, we shall overcome.

AN AMERICAN PROBLEM

Now let none of us in any sections look with prideful righteousness on the troubles in another section, or on the problems of our neighbors. There is really no part of America where the promise of equality has been fully kept. In Buffalo as well as in Birmingham, in Philadelphia as well as in Selma, Americans are struggling for the fruits of freedom.

This is one Nation. What happens in Selma or in Cincinnati is a matter of legitimate concern to every American. But let each of us look within our own hearts and our own communities, and let each of us put our shoulder to the wheel to root out injustice wherever it exists.

As we meet here in this peaceful, historic chamber tonight, men from the South, some of whom were at Iwo Jima, men from the North who have carried Old Glory to far corners of the world and brought it back without a stain on it, men from the East and from the West, are all fighting together without regard to religion, or color, or region, in Vietnam. Men from every region fought for us across the world 20 years ago.

And in these common dangers and these common sacrifices the South made its contribution of honor and gallantry no less than any other region of the great Republic—and in some instances, a great many of them, more.

And I have not the slightest doubt that good men from everywhere in this country, from the Great Lakes to the Gulf of Mexico, from the Golden Gate to the harbors along the Atlantic, will rally together now in this cause to vindicate the freedom of all Americans. For all of us owe this duty; and I believe that all of us will respond to it.

Your President makes that request of every American.

### PROGRESS THROUGH THE DEMOCRATIC PROCESS

The real hero of this struggle is the American Negro. His actions and protests, his courage to risk safety and even to risk his life, have awakened the conscience of this Nation. His demonstrations have been designed to call attention to injustice, designed to provoke change, designed to stir reform.

He has called upon us to make good the promise of America. And who among us can say that we would have made the same progress were it not for his persistent bravery, and his faith in American democracy.

For at the real heart of battle for equality is a deep-seated belief in the democratic process. Equality depends not on the force of arms or tear gas but upon the force of moral right; not on recourse to violence but on respect for law and order.

There have been many pressures upon your President and there will be others as the days come and go. But I pledge you tonight that we intend to fight this battle where it should be fought: in the courts, and in the Congress, and in the hearts of men.

We must preserve the right of free speech and the right of free assembly. But the right of free speech does not carry with it, as has been said, the right to holler fire in a crowded theater. We must preserve the right to free assembly, but free assembly does not carry with it the right to block public thoroughfares to traffic.

We do have a right to protest, and a right to march under conditions that do not infringe the constitutional rights of our neighbors. And I intend to protect all those rights as long as I am permitted to serve in this office.

We will guard against violence, knowing it strikes from our hands the very weapons which we seek—progress, obedience to law, and belief in American values.

In Selma as elsewhere we seek and pray for peace. We seek order. We seek unity. But we will not accept the peace of stifled rights, or the order imposed by fear, or the unity that stifles protest. For peace cannot be purchased at the cost of liberty.

In Selma tonight, as in every—and we had a good day there—as in every city, we are working for just and peaceful settlement. We must all remember that after this speech I am making tonight, after the police and the FBI and the Marshals have all gone, and after you have promptly passed this bill, the people of Selma and the other cities of the Nation must still live and work together. And when the attention of the Nation has gone elsewhere they must try to heal the wounds and to build a new community.

This cannot be easily done on a battleground of violence, as the history of the South itself shows. It is in recognition of this that men of both races have shown such an outstandingly impressive responsibility in recent days—last Tuesday, again today,

## Rights Must Be Opportunities

The bill that I am presenting to you will be known as a civil rights bill. But, in a larger sense, most of the program I am recommending is a civil rights program. Its object is to open the city of hope to all people of all races.

Because all Americans just must have the right to vote. And we are going to give them that right.

All Americans must have the privileges of citizenship regardless of race. And they are going to have those privileges of citizenship regardless of race.

But I would like to caution you and remind you that to exercise these privileges takes much more than just legal right. It requires a trained mind and a healthy body. It requires a decent home, and the chance to find a job, and the opportunity to escape from the clutches of poverty.

Of course, people cannot contribute to the Nation if they are never taught to read or write, if their bodies are stunted from hunger, if their sickness goes untended, if their life is spent in hopeless poverty just drawing a welfare check.

So we want to open the gates to opportunity. But we are also going to give all our people, black and white, the help that they need to walk through those gates.

## The Purpose of this Government

My first job after college was as a teacher in Cotulla, Tex., in a small Mexican-American school. Few of them could speak English, and I couldn't speak much Spanish. My students were poor and they often came to class without breakfast, hungry. They knew even in their youth the pain of prejudice. They never seemed to know why people disliked them. But they knew it was so, because I saw it in their eyes. I often walked home late in the afternoon, after the classes were finished, wishing there was more that I could do. But all I knew was to teach them the little that I knew, hoping that it might help them against the hardships that lay ahead.

Somehow you never forget what poverty and hatred can do when you see its scars on the hopeful face of a young child.

I never thought then, in 1928, that I would be standing here in 1965. It never even occurred to me in my fondest dreams that I might have the chance to help the sons and daughters of those students and to help people like them all over this country.

But now I do have that chance—and I'll let you in on a secret—I mean to use it. And I hope that you will use it with me.

This is the richest and most powerful country which ever occupied the globe. The might of past empires is little compared to ours. But I do not want to be the President who built empires, or sought grandeur, or extended dominion.

I want to be the President who educated young children to the wonders of their world. I want to be the President who helped to feed the hungry and to prepare them to be taxpayers instead of taxeaters.

I want to be the President who helped the poor to find their own way and who protected the right of every citizen to vote in every election.

I want to be the President who helped to end hatred among his fellow men and who promoted love among the people of all races and all regions and all parties.

I want to be the President who helped to end war among the brothers of this earth.

And so at the request of your beloved Speaker and the Senator from Montana; the majority leader, the Senator from Illinois; the minority leader, Mr. McCulloch, and other Members of both parties, I came here tonight—not as President Roosevelt came down one time in person to veto a bonus bill, not as President Truman came down one time to urge the passage of a railroad bill—but I came down here to ask you to share this task with me and to share it with the people that we both work for. I want this to be the Congress, Republicans and Democrats alike, which did all these things for all these people.

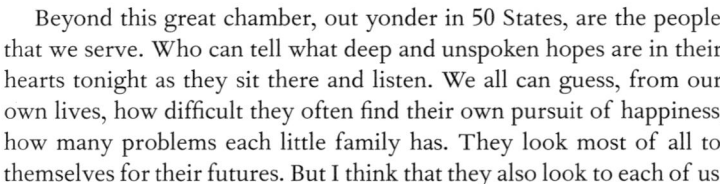 

Beyond this great chamber, out yonder in 50 States, are the people that we serve. Who can tell what deep and unspoken hopes are in their hearts tonight as they sit there and listen. We all can guess, from our own lives, how difficult they often find their own pursuit of happiness, how many problems each little family has. They look most of all to themselves for their futures. But I think that they also look to each of us.

Above the pyramid on the great seal of the United States it says—in Latin—"God has favored our undertaking."

God will not favor everything that we do. It is rather our duty to divine His will. But I cannot help believing that He truly understands and that He really favors the undertaking that we begin here tonight.

# RONALD REAGAN'S FIRST INAUGURAL ADDRESS JANUARY 20, 1981

Senator Hatfield, Mr. Chief Justice, Mr. President, Vice President Bush, Vice President Mondale, Senator Baker, Speaker O'Neill, Reverend Moomaw, and my fellow citizens: To a few of us here today, this is a solemn and most momentous occasion; and yet, in the history of our Nation, it is a commonplace occurrence. The orderly transfer of authority as called for in the Constitution routinely takes place as it has for almost two centuries and few of us stop to think how unique we really are. In the eyes of many in the world, this every-four-year ceremony we accept as normal is nothing less than a miracle.

Mr. President, I want our fellow citizens to know how much you did to carry on this tradition. By your gracious cooperation in the transition process, you have shown a watching world that we are a united people pledged to maintaining a political system which guarantees individual liberty to a greater degree than any other, and I thank you and your people for all your help in maintaining the continuity which is the bulwark of our Republic.

The business of our nation goes forward. These United States are confronted with an economic affliction of great proportions. We suffer from the longest and one of the worst sustained inflations in our national history. It distorts our economic decisions, penalizes thrift, and crushes the struggling young and the fixed-income elderly alike. It threatens to shatter the lives of millions of our people.

Idle industries have cast workers into unemployment, causing human misery and personal indignity. Those who do work are denied a fair return for their labor by a tax system which penalizes successful achievement and keeps us from maintaining full productivity.

But great as our tax burden is, it has not kept pace with public spending. For decades, we have piled deficit upon deficit, mortgaging our future and our children's future for the temporary convenience of the present. To continue this long trend is to guarantee tremendous social, cultural, political, and economic upheavals.

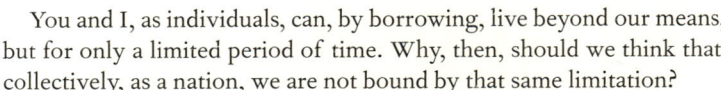

You and I, as individuals, can, by borrowing, live beyond our means, but for only a limited period of time. Why, then, should we think that collectively, as a nation, we are not bound by that same limitation?

We must act today in order to preserve tomorrow. And let there be no misunderstanding—we are going to begin to act, beginning today.

The economic ills we suffer have come upon us over several decades. They will not go away in days, weeks, or months, but they will go away. They will go away because we, as Americans, have the capacity now, as we have had in the past, to do whatever needs to be done to preserve this last and greatest bastion of freedom.

In this present crisis, government is not the solution to our problem.

From time to time, we have been tempted to believe that society has become too complex to be managed by self-rule, that government by an elite group is superior to government for, by, and of the people. But if no one among us is capable of governing himself, then who among us has the capacity to govern someone else? All of us together, in and out of government, must bear the burden. The solutions we seek must be equitable, with no one group singled out to pay a higher price.

We hear much of special interest groups. Our concern must be for a special interest group that has been too long neglected. It knows no sectional boundaries or ethnic and racial divisions, and it crosses political party lines. It is made up of men and women who raise our food, patrol our streets, man our mines and our factories, teach our children, keep our homes, and heal us when we are sick—professionals, industrialists, shopkeepers, clerks, cabbies, and truck drivers. They are, in short, "We the people," this breed called Americans.

Well, this administration's objective will be a healthy, vigorous, growing economy that provides equal opportunity for all Americans, with no barriers born of bigotry or discrimination. Putting America back to work means putting all Americans back to work. Ending inflation means freeing all Americans from the terror of runaway living costs. All must share in the productive work of this "new beginning" and all must share in the bounty of a revived economy. With the idealism and fair play which are the core of our system and our strength, we can have a strong and prosperous America at peace with itself and the world.

So, as we begin, let us take inventory. We are a nation that has a government—not the other way around. And this makes us special among the nations of the Earth. Our Government has no power except that granted it by the people. It is time to check and reverse the growth of government which shows signs of having grown beyond the consent of the governed.

It is my intention to curb the size and influence of the Federal establishment and to demand recognition of the distinction between the powers granted to the Federal Government and those reserved to the States or to the people. All of us need to be reminded that the Federal Government did not create the States; the States created the Federal Government.

Now, so there will be no misunderstanding, it is not my intention to do away with government. It is, rather, to make it work—work with us, not over us; to stand by our side, not ride on our back. Government can and must provide opportunity, not smother it; foster productivity, not stifle it.

If we look to the answer as to why, for so many years, we achieved so much, prospered as no other people on Earth, it was because here, in this land, we unleashed the energy and individual genius of man to a greater extent than has ever been done before. Freedom and the dignity of the individual have been more available and assured here than in any other place on Earth. The price for this freedom at times has been high, but we have never been unwilling to pay that price.

It is no coincidence that our present troubles parallel and are proportionate to the intervention and intrusion in our lives that result from unnecessary and excessive growth of government. It is time for us to realize that we are too great a nation to limit ourselves to small dreams. We are not, as some would have us believe, doomed to an inevitable decline. I do not believe in a fate that will fall on us no matter what we do. I do believe in a fate that will fall on us if we do nothing. So, with all the creative energy at our command, let us begin an era of national renewal. Let us renew our determination, our courage, and our strength. And let us renew our faith and our hope.

We have every right to dream heroic dreams. Those who say that we are in a time when there are no heroes just don't know where to look. You can see heroes every day going in and out of factory gates. Others, a handful in number, produce enough food to feed all of us and then the world beyond. You meet heroes across a counter—and they are on both sides of that counter. There are entrepreneurs with faith in themselves and faith in an idea who create new jobs, new wealth and opportunity. They are individuals and families whose taxes support the Government and whose voluntary gifts support church, charity, culture, art, and education. Their patriotism is quiet but deep. Their values sustain our national life.

I have used the words "they" and "their" in speaking of these heroes. I could say "you" and "your" because I am addressing the heroes of whom I speak—you, the citizens of this blessed land. Your dreams, your hopes, your goals are going to be the dreams, the hopes, and the goals of this administration, so help me God.

We shall reflect the compassion that is so much a part of your makeup. How can we love our country and not love our countrymen, and loving them, reach out a hand when they fall, heal them when they are sick, and provide opportunities to make them self-sufficient so they will be equal in fact and not just in theory?

Can we solve the problems confronting us? Well, the answer is an unequivocal and emphatic "yes." To paraphrase Winston Churchill, I did not take the oath I have just taken with the intention of presiding over the dissolution of the world's strongest economy.

In the days ahead I will propose removing the roadblocks that have slowed our economy and reduced productivity. Steps will be taken aimed at restoring the balance between the various levels of government. Progress may be slow—measured in inches and feet, not miles—but we will progress. Is it time to reawaken this industrial giant, to get government back within its means, and to lighten our punitive tax burden. And these will be our first priorities, and on these principles, there will be no compromise.

On the eve of our struggle for independence a man who might have been one of the greatest among the Founding Fathers, Dr. Joseph Warren, President of the Massachusetts Congress, said to his fellow Americans, "Our country is in danger, but not to be despaired of ... On you depend the fortunes of America. You are to decide the important questions upon which rests the happiness and the liberty of millions yet unborn. Act worthy of yourselves."

Well, I believe we, the Americans of today, are ready to act worthy of ourselves, ready to do what must be done to ensure happiness and liberty for ourselves, our children and our children's children.

And as we renew ourselves here in our own land, we will be seen as having greater strength throughout the world. We will again be the exemplar of freedom and a beacon of hope for those who do not now have freedom.

To those neighbors and allies who share our freedom, we will strengthen our historic ties and assure them of our support and firm commitment. We will match loyalty with loyalty. We will strive for mutually beneficial relations. We will not use our friendship to impose on their sovereignty, for our own sovereignty is not for sale.

As for the enemies of freedom, those who are potential adversaries, they will be reminded that peace is the highest aspiration of the American people. We will negotiate for it, sacrifice for it; we will not surrender for it—now or ever.

Our forbearance should never be misunderstood. Our reluctance for conflict should not be misjudged as a failure of will. When action is required to preserve our national security, we will act. We will maintain sufficient strength to prevail if need be, knowing that if we do so we have the best chance of never having to use that strength.

Above all, we must realize that no arsenal, or no weapon in the arsenals of the world, is so formidable as the will and moral courage of free men and women. It is a weapon our adversaries in today's world do not have. It is a weapon that we as Americans do have. Let that be understood by those who practice terrorism and prey upon their neighbors.

I am told that tens of thousands of prayer meetings are being held on this day, and for that I am deeply grateful. We are a nation under God, and I believe God intended for us to be free. It would be fitting and good, I think, if on each Inauguration Day in future years it should be declared a day of prayer.

This is the first time in history that this ceremony has been held, as you have been told, on this West Front of the Capitol. Standing here, one faces a magnificent vista, opening up on this city's special beauty and history. At the end of this open mall are those shrines to the giants on whose shoulders we stand.

Directly in front of me, the monument to a monumental man: George Washington, Father of our country. A man of humility who came to greatness reluctantly. He led America out of revolutionary victory into infant nationhood. Off to one side, the stately memorial to Thomas Jefferson. The Declaration of Independence flames with his eloquence.

And then beyond the Reflecting Pool the dignified columns of the Lincoln Memorial. Whoever would understand in his heart the meaning of America will find it in the life of Abraham Lincoln.

Beyond those monuments to heroism is the Potomac River, and on the far shore the sloping hills of Arlington National Cemetery with its row on row of simple white markers bearing crosses or Stars of David. They add up to only a tiny fraction of the price that has been paid for our freedom.

Each one of those markers is a monument to the kinds of hero I spoke of earlier. Their lives ended in places called Belleau Wood, The Argonne, Omaha Beach, Salerno and halfway around the world on Guadalcanal, Tarawa, Pork Chop Hill, the Chosin Reservoir, and in a hundred rice paddies and jungles of a place called Vietnam.

Under one such marker lies a young man—Martin Treptow—who left his job in a small town barber shop in 1917 to go to France with the famed Rainbow Division. There, on the western front, he was killed trying to carry a message between battalions under heavy artillery fire.

We are told that on his body was found a diary. On the flyleaf under the heading, "My Pledge," he had written these words: "America must win this war. Therefore, I will work, I will save, I will sacrifice, I will endure, I will fight cheerfully and do my utmost, as if the issue of the whole struggle depended on me alone."

The crisis we are facing today does not require of us the kind of sacrifice that Martin Treptow and so many thousands of others were called upon to make. It does require, however, our best effort, and our willingness to believe in ourselves and to believe in our capacity to perform great deeds; to believe that together, with God's help, we can and will resolve the problems which now confront us.

And, after all, why shouldn't we believe that? We are Americans. God bless you, and thank you.

# GERALDINE FERRARO ACCEPTS THE VICE PRESIDENTIAL NOMINATION (1984)

*In July 1984, Geraldine Ferraro, a Congressional representative from New York, became the first female vice-presidential candidate from a major American political party. However, she and her running mate, Walter Mondale, lost to Ronald Reagan in the election that year.*

Ladies and gentlemen of the convention: My name is Geraldine Ferraro. I stand before you to proclaim tonight: America is the land where dreams can come true for all of us.

As I stand before the American people and think of the honor this great convention has bestowed upon me, I recall the words of Dr. Martin Luther King Jr., who made America stronger by making America more free. He said: "Occasionally in life there are moments which cannot be completely explained by words. Their meaning can only be articulated by the inaudible language of the heart."

Tonight is such a moment for me.

My heart is filled with pride.

My fellow citizens, I proudly accept your nomination for vice president of the United States.

And I am proud to run with a man who will be one of the great presidents of this century, Walter F. Mondale.

Tonight, the daughter of a woman whose highest goal was a future for her children talks to our nation's oldest party about a future for us all.

Tonight, the daughter of working Americans tells all Americans that the future is within our reach—if we're willing to reach for it.

Tonight, the daughter of an immigrant from Italy has been chosen to run for [vice] president in the new land my father came to love.

Our faith that we can shape a better future is what the American dream is all about. The promise of our country is that the rules are fair. If you work hard and play by the rules, you can earn your share of America's blessings. Those are the beliefs I learned from my parents.

And those are the values I taught my students as a teacher in the public schools of New York City.

At night, I went to law school. I became an assistant district attorney, and I put my share of criminals behind bars. I believe: If you obey the law, you should be protected. But if you break the law, you must pay for your crime.

When I first ran for Congress, all the political experts said a Democrat could not win my home district in Queens. I put my faith in the people and the values that we shared. Together, we proved the political experts wrong.

In this campaign, Fritz Mondale and I have put our faith in the people. And we are going to prove the experts wrong again. We are going to win. We are going to win because Americans across this country believe in the same basic dream.

Last week, I visited Elmore, Minnesota, the small town where Fritz Mondale was raised. And soon Fritz and Joan will visit our family in Queens. Nine hundred people live in Elmore. In Queens, there are 2,000 people on one block. You would think we would be different, but we're not. Children walk to school in Elmore past grain elevators; in Queens, they pass by subway stops. But, no matter where they live, their future depends on education, and their parents are willing to do their part to make those schools as good as they can be.

In Elmore, there are family farms; in Queens, small businesses. But the men and women who run them all take pride in supporting their families through hard work and initiative.

On the Fourth of July in Elmore, they hang flags out on Main Street; in Queens, they fly them over Grand Avenue. But all of us love our country, and stand ready to defend the freedom that it represents.

Americans want to live by the same set of rules. But under this administration, the rules are rigged against too many of our people. It isn't right that every year, the share of taxes paid by individual citizens is going up, while the share paid by large corporations is getting smaller and smaller. The rules say: Everyone in our society should contribute their fair share.

It isn't right that this year Ronald Reagan will hand the American people a bill for interest on the national debt larger than the entire cost of the federal government under John F. Kennedy. Our parents left us a growing economy. The rules say: We must not leave our kids a mountain of debt.

It isn't right that a woman should get paid 59 cents on the dollar for the same work as a man. If you play by the rules, you deserve a fair day's pay for a fair day's work.

It isn't right that—that if trends continue—by the year 2000, nearly all of the poor people in America will be women and children. The rules of a decent society say, when you distribute sacrifice in times of austerity, you don't put women and children first.

It isn't right that young people today fear they won't get the Social Security they paid for, and that older Americans fear that they will lose what they have already earned. Social Security is a contract between the last generation and the next, and the rules say: You don't break contracts. We're going to keep faith with older Americans.

We hammered out a fair compromise in the Congress to save Social Security. Every group sacrificed to keep the system sound. It is time Ronald Reagan stopped scaring our senior citizens.

It isn't right that young couples question whether to bring children into a world of 50,000 nuclear warheads. That isn't the vision for which Americans have struggled for more than two centuries. And our future doesn't have to be that way.

Change is in the air, just as surely as when John Kennedy beckoned America to a new frontier, when Sally Ride rocketed into space, and when Reverend Jesse Jackson ran for the office of president of the United States. By choosing a woman to run for our nation's second-highest office, you sent a powerful signal to all Americans. There are no doors we cannot unlock. We will place no limits on achievement. If we can do this, we can do anything.

Tonight, we reclaim our dream. We're going to make the rules of American life work fairly for all Americans again. To an administration that would have us debate all over again whether the Voting Rights Act should be renewed and whether segregated schools should be tax exempt, we say, Mr. President: Those debates are over.

On the issue of civil rights, voting rights, and affirmative action for minorities, we must not go backwards. We must—and we will— move forward to open the doors of opportunity.

To those who understand that our country cannot prosper unless we draw on the talents of all Americans, we say: We will pass the Equal Rights Amendment. The issue is not what America can do for women, but what women can do for America.

To the Americans who will lead our country into the 21st century, we say: We will not have a Supreme Court that turns the clock back to the 19th century.

To those concerned about the strength of American family values, as I am, I say: We are going to restore those values—love, caring, partnership—by including, and not excluding, those whose beliefs differ from our own. Because our own faith is strong, we will fight to preserve the freedom of faith for others.

To those working Americans who fear that banks, utilities, and large special interests have a lock on the White House, we say: Join us; let's elect a people's president; and let's have government by and for the American people again.

To an administration that would savage student loans and education at the dawn of a new technological age, we say: You fit the classic definition of a cynic; you know the price of everything, but the value of nothing.

To our students and their parents, we say: We will insist on the highest standards of excellence because the jobs of the future require skilled minds.

To young Americans who may be called to our country's service, we say: We know your generation will proudly answer our country's call, as each generation before you. This past year, we remembered the bravery and sacrifice of Americans at Normandy. And we finally paid tribute—as we should have done years ago—to that unknown soldier who represents all the brave young Americans who died in Vietnam.

Let no one doubt, we will defend America's security and the cause of freedom around the world. But we want a president who tells us what America is fighting for, not just what we are fighting against.

We want a president who will defend human rights—not just where it is convenient—but wherever freedom is at risk—from Chile to Afghanistan, from Poland to South Africa.

To those who have watched this administration's confusion in the Middle East, as it has tilted first toward one and then another of Israel's longtime enemies and wonder, "Will America stand by her friends and sister democracy?" We say: America knows who her friends are in the Middle East and around the world. America will stand with Israel always.

Finally, we want a president who will keep America strong, but use that strength to keep America and the world at peace. A nuclear freeze is not a slogan: It is a tool for survival in the nuclear age. If we leave our children nothing else, let us leave them this earth as we found it—whole and green and full of life.

I know in my heart that Walter Mondale will be that president.

A wise man once said, "Every one of us is given the gift of life, and what a strange gift it is. If it is preserved jealously and selfishly, it impoverishes and saddens. But if it is spent for others, it enriches and beautifies." My fellow Americans: We can debate policies and programs. But in the end what separates the two parties in this election campaign is whether we use the gift of life—for others or only ourselves.

Tonight, my husband, John, and our three children are in this hall with me. To my daughters, Donna and Laura, and my son, John Jr., I say: My mother did not break faith with me . . . and I will not break faith with you.

To all the children of America, I say: The generation before ours kept faith with us, and like them, we will pass on to you a stronger, more just America.

Thank you.

# RONALD REAGAN'S REMARKS ON EAST–WEST RELATIONS AT THE BRANDENBURG GATE IN WEST BERLIN (1987)

*In one of the most famous speeches in American history, President Ronald Reagan challenged Soviet leader Mikhail Gorbachev to "tear down this wall," referring to the cement barrier that had separated East (communist) and West (democratic) Berlin since 1961. The speech didn't get much of a reaction at the time, but two years later, as reforms spread throughout the Soviet Union and Eastern Europe, the speech took on new importance. Demolition on the Berlin Wall began in November 1989.*

Thank you very much. Chancellor Kohl, Governing Mayor Diepgen, ladies and gentlemen: Twenty four years ago, President John F. Kennedy visited Berlin, speaking to the people of this city and the world at the city hall. Well, since then two other presidents have come, each in his turn, to Berlin. And today I, myself, make my second visit to your city.

We come to Berlin, we American Presidents, because it's our duty to speak, in this place, of freedom. But I must confess, we're drawn here by other things as well: by the feeling of history in this city, more than 500 years older than our own nation; by the beauty of the Grunewald and the Tiergarten; most of all, by your courage and determination. Perhaps the composer, Paul Lincke, understood something about American presidents. You see, like so many presidents before me, I come here today because wherever I go, whatever I do: *Ich hab noch einen Koffer in Berlin.*\*

Our gathering today is being broadcast throughout Western Europe and North America. I understand that it is being seen and heard as well in the East. To those listening throughout Eastern Europe, I extend my warmest greetings and the good will of the American people. To those listening in East Berlin, a special word: Although I cannot be with you,

---

\**I still have a suitcase in Berlin.*

I address my remarks to you just as surely as to those standing here before me. For I join you, as I join your fellow countrymen in the West, in this firm, this unalterable belief: *Es gibt nur ein Berlin.**

Behind me stands a wall that encircles the free sectors of this city, part of a vast system of barriers that divides the entire continent of Europe. From the Baltic, south, those barriers cut across Germany in a gash of barbed wire, concrete, dog runs, and guard towers. Farther south, there may be no visible, no obvious wall. But there remain armed guards and checkpoints all the same—still a restriction on the right to travel, still an instrument to impose upon ordinary men and women the will of a totalitarian state. Yet it is here in Berlin where the wall emerges most clearly; here, cutting across your city, where the news photo and the television screen have imprinted this brutal division of a continent upon the mind of the world. Standing before the Brandenburg Gate, every man is a German, separated from his fellow men. Every man is a Berliner, forced to look upon a scar.

President von Weizsacker has said: "The German question is open as long as the Brandenburg Gate is closed." Today I say: As long as this gate is closed, as long as this scar of a wall is permitted to stand, it is not the German question alone that remains open, but the question of freedom for all mankind. Yet I do not come here to lament. For I find in Berlin a message of hope, even in the shadow of this wall, a message of triumph.

In this season of spring in 1945, the people of Berlin emerged from their air-raid shelters to find devastation. Thousands of miles away, the people of the United States reached out to help. And in 1947 Secretary of State—as you've been told—George Marshall announced the creation of what would become known as the Marshall plan. Speaking precisely 40 years ago this month, he said: "Our policy is directed not against any country or doctrine, but against hunger, poverty, desperation, and chaos."

In the Reichstag a few moments ago, I saw a display commemorating this 40th anniversary of the Marshall plan. I was struck by the sign on a burnt-out, gutted structure that was being rebuilt. I understand that Berliners of my own generation can remember seeing signs like it dotted throughout the Western sectors of the city. The sign read simply: "The Marshall plan is helping here to strengthen the free world." A strong,

---

*There is only one Berlin.*

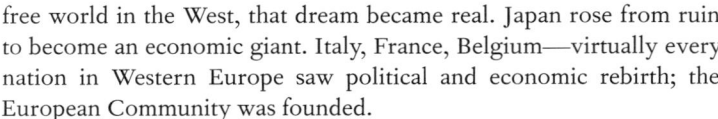 

free world in the West, that dream became real. Japan rose from ruin to become an economic giant. Italy, France, Belgium—virtually every nation in Western Europe saw political and economic rebirth; the European Community was founded.

In West Germany and here in Berlin, there took place an economic miracle, the Wirtschaftswunder. Adenauer, Erhard, Reuter, and other leaders understood the practical importance of liberty—that just as truth can flourish only when the journalist is given freedom of speech, so prosperity can come about only when the farmer and businessman enjoy economic freedom. The German leaders reduced tariffs, expanded free trade, lowered taxes. From 1950 to 1960 alone, the standard of living in West Germany and Berlin doubled.

Where four decades ago there was rubble, today in West Berlin there is the greatest industrial output of any city in Germany—busy office blocks, fine homes and apartments, proud avenues, and the spreading lawns of parkland. Where a city's culture seemed to have been destroyed, today there are two great universities, orchestras and an opera, countless theaters, and museums. Where there was want, today there's abundance—food, clothing, automobiles—the wonderful goods of the Ku'damm. From devastation, from utter ruin, you Berliners have, in freedom, rebuilt a city that once again ranks as one of the greatest on Earth. The Soviets may have had other plans. But, my friends, there were a few things the Soviets didn't count on: *Berliner herz, Berliner humor, ja, und Berliner schnauze.*\*

In the 1950s, Khrushchev predicted: "We will bury you." But in the West today, we see a free world that has achieved a level of prosperity and well-being unprecedented in all human history. In the Communist world, we see failure, technological backwardness, declining standards of health, even want of the most basic kind—too little food. Even today, the Soviet Union still cannot feed itself. After these four decades, then, there stands before the entire world one great and inescapable conclusion: Freedom leads to prosperity. Freedom replaces the ancient hatreds among the nations with comity and peace. Freedom is the victor.

And now the Soviets themselves may, in a limited way, be coming to understand the importance of freedom. We hear much from Moscow about a new policy of reform and openness. Some political prisoners have been released. Certain foreign news broadcasts are no longer being

---

\**Berliner hearts, Berliner humor, and yes, a Berliner schnauze.*

jammed. Some economic enterprises have been permitted to operate with greater freedom from state control. Are these the beginnings of profound changes in the Soviet state? Or are they token gestures, intended to raise false hopes in the West, or to strengthen the Soviet system without changing it? We welcome change and openness; for we believe that freedom and security go together, that the advance of human liberty can only strengthen the cause of world peace.

There is one sign the Soviets can make that would be unmistakable, that would advance dramatically the cause of freedom and peace. General Secretary Gorbachev, if you seek peace, if you seek prosperity for the Soviet Union and Eastern Europe, if you seek liberalization: Come here to this gate! Mr. Gorbachev, open this gate! Mr. Gorbachev, tear down this wall!

I understand the fear of war and the pain of division that afflict this continent —and I pledge to you my country's efforts to help overcome these burdens. To be sure, we in the West must resist Soviet expansion. So we must maintain defenses of unassailable strength. Yet we seek peace; so we must strive to reduce arms on both sides. Beginning 10 years ago, the Soviets challenged the Western alliance with a grave new threat, hundreds of new and more deadly SS-20 nuclear missiles, capable of striking every capital in Europe. The Western alliance responded by committing itself to a counter-deployment unless the Soviets agreed to negotiate a better solution; namely, the elimination of such weapons on both sides. For many months, the Soviets refused to bargain in earnestness. As the alliance, in turn, prepared to go forward with its counter-deployment, there were difficult days—days of protests like those during my 1982 visit to this city—and the Soviets later walked away from the table.

But through it all, the alliance held firm. And I invite those who protested then—I invite those who protest today—to mark this fact: Because we remained strong, the Soviets came back to the table. And because we remained strong, today we have within reach the possibility, not merely of limiting the growth of arms, but of eliminating, for the first time, an entire class of nuclear weapons from the face of the Earth. As I speak, NATO ministers are meeting in Iceland to review the progress of our proposals for eliminating these weapons. At the talks in Geneva, we have also proposed deep cuts in strategic offensive weapons. And the Western allies have likewise made far-reaching proposals to reduce the danger of conventional war and to place a total ban on chemical weapons.

While we pursue these arms reductions, I pledge to you that we will maintain the capacity to deter Soviet aggression at any level at which it might occur. And in cooperation with many of our allies, the United States is pursuing the Strategic Defense Initiative—research to base deterrence not on the threat of offensive retaliation, but on defenses that truly defend; on systems, in short, that will not target populations, but shield them. By these means we seek to increase the safety of Europe and all the world. But we must remember a crucial fact: East and West do not mistrust each other because we are armed; we are armed because we mistrust each other. And our differences are not about weapons but about liberty. When President Kennedy spoke at the City Hall those 24 years ago, freedom was encircled, Berlin was under siege. And today, despite all the pressures upon this city, Berlin stands secure in its liberty. And freedom itself is transforming the globe.

In the Philippines, in South and Central America, democracy has been given a rebirth. Throughout the Pacific, free markets are working miracle after miracle of economic growth. In the industrialized nations, a technological revolution is taking place—a revolution marked by rapid, dramatic advances in computers and telecommunications.

In Europe, only one nation and those it controls refuse to join the community of freedom. Yet in this age of redoubled economic growth, of information and innovation, the Soviet Union faces a choice: It must make fundamental changes, or it will become obsolete. Today thus represents a moment of hope. We in the West stand ready to cooperate with the East to promote true openness, to break down barriers that separate people, to create a safer, freer world.

And surely there is no better place than Berlin, the meeting place of East and West, to make a start. Free people of Berlin: Today, as in the past, the United States stands for the strict observance and full implementation of all parts of the Four Power Agreement of 1971. Let us use this occasion, the 750th anniversary of this city, to usher in a new era, to seek a still fuller, richer life for the Berlin of the future. Together, let us maintain and develop the ties between the Federal Republic and the Western sectors of Berlin, which is permitted by the 1971 agreement.

And I invite Mr. Gorbachev: Let us work to bring the Eastern and

Western parts of the city closer together, so that all the inhabitants of all Berlin can enjoy the benefits that come with life in one of the great cities of the world. To open Berlin still further to all Europe, East and West, let us expand the vital air access to this city, finding ways of making commercial air service to Berlin more convenient, more comfortable, and more economical. We look to the day when West Berlin can become one of the chief aviation hubs in all central Europe.

With our French and British partners, the United States is prepared to help bring international meetings to Berlin. It would be only fitting for Berlin to serve as the site of United Nations meetings, or world conferences on human rights and arms control or other issues that call for international cooperation. There is no better way to establish hope for the future than to enlighten young minds, and we would be honored to sponsor summer youth exchanges, cultural events, and other programs for young Berliners from the East. Our French and British friends, I'm certain, will do the same. And it's my hope that an authority can be found in East Berlin to sponsor visits from young people of the Western sectors.

One final proposal, one close to my heart:

Sport represents a source of enjoyment and ennoblement, and you many have noted that the Republic of Korea—South Korea—has offered to permit certain events of the 1988 Olympics to take place in the North. International sports competitions of all kinds could take place in both parts of this city. And what better way to demonstrate to the world the openness of this city than to offer in some future year to hold the Olympic games here in Berlin, East and West?

In these four decades, as I have said, you Berliners have built a great city. You've done so in spite of threats—the Soviet attempts to impose the East-mark, the blockade. Today the city thrives in spite of the challenges implicit in the very presence of this wall. What keeps you here? Certainly there's a great deal to be said for your fortitude, for your defiant courage. But I believe there's something deeper, something that involves Berlin's whole look and feel and way of life—not mere sentiment. No one could live long in Berlin without being completely disabused of illusions. Something instead, that has seen the difficulties of life in Berlin but chose to accept them, that continues to build this good and proud city in contrast to a surrounding totalitarian presence that refuses to release human energies or aspirations. Something that

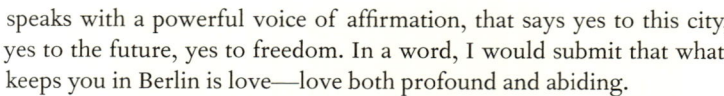 

speaks with a powerful voice of affirmation, that says yes to this city, yes to the future, yes to freedom. In a word, I would submit that what keeps you in Berlin is love—love both profound and abiding.

Perhaps this gets to the root of the matter, to the most fundamental distinction of all between East and West. The totalitarian world produces backwardness because it does such violence to the spirit, thwarting the human impulse to create, to enjoy, to worship. The totalitarian world finds even symbols of love and of worship an affront. Years ago, before the East Germans began rebuilding their churches, they erected a secular structure: the television tower at Alexander Platz. Virtually ever since, the authorities have been working to correct what they view as the tower's one major flaw, treating the glass sphere at the top with paints and chemicals of every kind. Yet even today when the Sun strikes that sphere—that sphere that towers over all Berlin—the light makes the sign of the cross. There in Berlin, like the city itself, symbols of love, symbols of worship, cannot be suppressed.

As I looked out a moment ago from the Reichstag, that embodiment of German unity, I noticed words crudely spray-painted upon the wall, perhaps by a young Berliner, "This wall will fall. Beliefs become reality." Yes, across Europe, this wall will fall. For it cannot withstand faith; it cannot withstand truth. The wall cannot withstand freedom.

And I would like, before I close, to say one word. I have read, and I have been questioned since I've been here about certain demonstrations against my coming. And I would like to say just one thing, and to those who demonstrate so. I wonder if they have ever asked themselves that if they should have the kind of government they apparently seek, no one would ever be able to do what they're doing again.

Thank you and God bless you all.

# BILL CLINTON ANNOUNCES THE MILITARY POLICY "DON'T ASK, DON'T TELL" (1993)

*Before 1993, homosexuals were not allowed to serve in the U.S. Armed Forces. President Bill Clinton campaigned on a promise to lift the ban. He was unsuccessful, but settled for a compromise: the policy of "don't ask, don't tell," which said that military personnel could not be asked to disclose their sexual preference. The law stood until 2010, when Congress passed and President Barack Obama signed a repeal. Today, gay men and women can serve openly in the U.S. military.*

Thank you very much. Secretary Aspin, General Powell, members of the Joint Chiefs, Admiral Kime; to our host, Admiral Smith, ladies and gentlemen.

I have come here today to discuss a difficult challenge and one which has received an enormous amount of publicity and public and private debate over the last several months—our nation's policy toward homosexuals in the military.

I believe the policy I am announcing today represents a real step forward. But I know it will raise concerns in some of your minds. So I wanted you to hear my thinking and my decision directly and in person, because I respect you and because you are among the elite who will lead our Armed Forces into the next century, and because you will have to put this policy into effect and I expect your help in doing it.

The policy I am announcing today is, in my judgment, the right thing to do and the best way to do it. It is right because it provides greater protection to those who happen to be homosexual and want to serve their country honorably in uniform, obeying all the military's rules against sexual misconduct.

It is the best way to proceed because it provides a sensible balance between the rights of the individual and the needs of our military to remain the world's number one fighting force. As President of all the

American people, I am pledged to protect and to promote individual rights. As Commander in Chief, I am pledged to protect and advance our security. In this policy, I believe we have come close to meeting both objectives.

Let me start with this clear fact: Our military is one of our greatest accomplishments and our most valuable assets. It is the world's most effective and powerful fighting force, bar none. I have seen proof of this fact almost every day since I became President. I saw it last week when I visited Camp Casey along the DMZ in Korea. I witnessed it at our military academies at Annapolis and West Point when I visited there. And I certainly relied on it three weeks ago when I ordered an attack on Iraq after that country's leadership attempted to assassinate President Bush.

We owe a great deal to the men and women who protect us through their service, their sacrifice and their dedication. And we owe it to our own security to listen hard to them and act carefully as we consider any changes in the military. A force ready to fight must maintain the highest priority under all circumstances.

Let me review the events which bring us here today. Before I ran for President, this issue was already upon us. Some of the members of the military returning from the Gulf War announced their homosexuality in order to protest the ban. The military's policy has been questioned in college ROTC programs. Legal challenges have been filed in court, including one that has since succeeded. In 1991, the Secretary of Defense Dick Cheney was asked about reports that the Defense Department spent an alleged $500 million to separate and replace about 17,000 homosexuals from the military service during the 1980s, in spite of the findings of a government report saying there was no reason to believe that they could not serve effectively and with distinction.

Shortly thereafter, while giving a speech at the Kennedy School of Government at Harvard, I was asked by one of the students what I thought of this report and what I thought of lifting the ban. This question had never before been presented to me, and I had never had the opportunity to discuss it with anyone. I stated then what I still believe: that I thought there ought to be a presumption that people who wish to do so should be able to serve their country if they are willing to conform to the high standards of the military, and that the emphasis should be always on people's conduct, not their status.

For me, and this is very important, this issue has never been one of group rights, but rather of individual ones—of the individual opportunity to serve and the individual responsibility to conform to the highest standards of military conduct. For people who are willing to play by the rules, able to serve, and make a contribution, I believe then and I believe now we should give them the chance to do so.

The central facts of this issue are not much in dispute. First, notwithstanding the ban, there have been and are homosexuals in the military service who serve with distinction. I have had the privilege of meeting some of these men and women, and I have been deeply impressed by their devotion to duty and to country.

Second, there is no study showing them to be less capable or more prone to misconduct than heterosexual soldiers. Indeed, all the information we have indicates that they are not less capable or more prone to misbehavior.

Third, misconduct is already covered by the laws and rules which also cover activities that are improper by heterosexual members of the military.

Fourth, the ban has been lifted in other nations and in police and fire departments in our country with no discernible negative impact on unit cohesion or capacity to do the job, though there is, admittedly, no absolute analogy to the situation we face and no study bearing on this specific issue.

Fifth, even if the ban were lifted entirely, the experience of other nations and police and fire departments in the United States indicates that most homosexuals would probably not declare their sexual orientation openly, thereby, making an already hard life even more difficult in some circumstances.

But as the sociologist, Charles Moskos, noted after spending many years studying the American military, the issue may be tougher to resolve here in the United States than in Canada, Australia, and in some other nations because of the presence in our country of both vocal gay rights groups and equally vocal antigay rights groups, including some religious groups who believe that lifting the ban amounts to endorsing a lifestyle they strongly disapprove of.

Clearly, the American people are deeply divided on this issue, with most military people opposed to lifting the ban because of the feared impact on unit cohesion, rooted in disapproval of homosexual lifestyles, and the fear of invasion of privacy of heterosexual soldiers who must live and work in close quarters with homosexual military people.

However, those who have studied this issue extensively have discovered an interesting fact. People in this country who are aware of having known homosexuals are far more likely to support lifting the ban. In other words, they are likely to see this issue in terms of individual conduct and individual capacity instead of the claims of a group with which they do not agree; and also to be able to imagine how this ban could be lifted without a destructive impact on group cohesion and morale.

Shortly after I took office and reaffirmed my position, the foes of lifting the ban in the Congress moved to enshrine the ban in law. I asked that congressional action be delayed for six months while the Secretary of Defense worked with the Joint Chiefs to come up with a proposal for changing our current policy. I then met with the Joint Chiefs to hear their concerns and asked them to try to work through the issue with Secretary Aspin. I wanted to handle the matter in this way on grounds of both principle and practicality.

As a matter of principle, it is my duty as Commander in Chief to uphold the high standards of combat readiness and unit cohesion of the world's finest fighting force, while doing my duty as President to protect the rights of individual Americans and to put to use the abilities of all the American people. And I was determined to serve this principle as fully as possible through practical action, knowing this fact about our system of government: While the Commander in Chief and the Secretary of Defense can change military personnel policies, Congress can reverse those changes by law in ways that are difficult, if not impossible, to veto.

For months now, the Secretary of Defense and the service chiefs have worked through this issue in a highly charged, deeply emotional environment, struggling to come to terms with the competing consideration and pressures and, frankly, to work through their own ideas and deep feelings.

During this time many dedicated Americans have come forward to state their own views on this issues. Most, but not all, of the military testimony has been against lifting the ban. But support for changing the policy has come from distinguished combat veterans including Senators Bob Kerrey, Chuck Robb, and John Kerry in the United States

Congress. It has come from Lawrence Korb, who enforced the gay ban during the Reagan administration; and from former Senator Barry Goldwater, a distinguished veteran, former Chairman of the Senate Arms Services Committee, founder of the Arizona National Guard, and patron saint of the conservative wing of the Republican Party.

Senator Goldwater's statement, published in *The Washington Post* recently, made it crystal clear that when this matter is viewed as an issue of individual opportunity and responsibility rather than one of alleged group rights, this is not a call for cultural license, but rather a reaffirmation of the American value of extending opportunity to responsible individuals and of limiting the role of government over citizens, private lives.

On the other hand, those who oppose lifting the ban are clearly focused not on the conduct of individual gay service members, but on how nongay service members feel about gays in general and, in particular, those in the military service.

These past few days I have been in contact with the Secretary of Defense as he has worked through the final stages of this policy with the Joint Chiefs. We now have a policy that is a substantial advance over the one in place when I took office. I have ordered Secretary Aspin to issue a directive consisting of these essential elements:

One, servicemen and women will be judged based on their conduct, not their sexual orientation.

Two, therefore, the practice, now six months old, of not asking about sexual orientation in the enlistment procedure will continue.

Three, an open statement by a service member that he or she is a homosexual will create a rebuttable presumption that he or she intends to engage prohibited conduct, but the service member will be given an opportunity to refute that presumption; in other words, to demonstrate that he or she intends to live by the rules of conduct that apply in the military service.

And four, all provisions of the Uniform Military Justice will be enforced in an even-handed manner as regards both heterosexuals and homosexuals. And, thanks to the policy provisions agreed by the Joint Chiefs, there will be a decent regard to the legitimate privacy and associational rights of all service members.

Just as is the case under current policy, unacceptable conduct, either heterosexual or homosexual, will be unacceptable 24 hours a day, seven days a week, from the time a recruit joins the service until the day he or she is discharged. Now, as in the past, every member of our military will be required to comply with the Uniform Code of Military Justice, which is federal law and military regulations, at all times and in all places.

Let me say a few words now about this policy. It is not a perfect solution. It is not identical with some of my own goals. And it certainly will not please everyone, perhaps not anyone, and clearly not those who hold the most adamant opinions on either side of this issue.

But those who wish to ignore the issue must understand that it is already tearing at the cohesion of the military, and it is today being considered by the federal courts in ways that may not be to the liking of those who oppose any change. And those who want the ban to be lifted completely on both status and conduct must understand that such action would have faced certain and decisive reversal by the Congress and the cause for which many have fought for years would be delayed probably for years.

Thus, on grounds of both principle and practicality, this is a major step forward. It is, in my judgment, consistent with my responsibilities as President and Commander in Chief to meet the need to change current policy. It is an honorable compromise that advances the cause of people who are called to serve our country by their patriotism, the cause of our national security and our national interest in resolving an issue that has divided our military and our nation and diverted our attention from other matters for too long.

The time has come for us to move forward. As your Commander in Chief, I charge all of you to carry out this policy with fairness, with balance and with due regard for the privacy of individuals. We must and will protect unit cohesion and troop morale. We must and will continue to have the best fighting force in the world. But this is an end to witch hunts that spend millions of taxpayer dollars to ferret out individuals who have served their country well. Improper conduct, on or off base, should remain grounds for discharge. But we will proceed with an even hand against everyone regardless of sexual orientation.

Such controversies as this have divided us before. But our nation and our military have always risen to the challenge before. That was true of racial integration of the military and changes in the role of women in the military. Each of these was an issue because it was an issue for society, as well as for the military. And in each case our military was a leader in figuring out how to respond most effectively.

In the early 1970s, when President Nixon decided to transform our military into an all-volunteer force, many argued that it could not work. They said it would ruin our forces. But the leaders of our military not only made it work, they used the concept of an all-volunteer force to build the very finest fighting force our nation and the world have ever known.

Ultimately, the success of this policy will depend in large measure on the commitment it receives from the leaders of the military services.

I very much respect and commend the Joint Chiefs for the good-faith effort they have made through this whole endeavor. And I thank General Powell, the Joint Chiefs, and the Commandant of the Coast Guard for joining me here today and for their support of this policy.

I would also like to thank those who lobbied aggressively in behalf of changing the policy, including Congressman Barney Frank, Congressman Gary Studds, and the Campaign for Military Service, who worked with us and who clearly will not agree with every aspect of the policy announced today, but who should take some solace in knowing that their efforts have helped to produce a strong advance for the cause they seek to serve.

I must now look to General Powell, to the Joint Chiefs, to all the other leaders in our military to carry out this policy through effective training and leadership. Every officer will be expected to exert the necessary effort to make this policy work. That has been the key every time the military has successfully addressed a new challenge, and it will be key in this effort, too.

Our military is a conservative institution, and I say that in the very best sense, for its purpose is to conserve the fighting spirit of our troops; to conserve the resources and the capacity of our troops; to conserve the military lessons acquired during our nation's existence; to conserve our very security; and yes, to conserve the liberties of the American people. Because it is a conservative institution, it is right for the military to be wary of sudden changes. Because it is an institution that embodies the best of America and must reflect the society in which it operates, it is also right for the military to make changes when the time for change is at hand.

I strongly believe that our military, like our society, needs the talents of every person who wants to make a contribution and who is ready to live by the rules. That is the heart of the policy that I have announced today. I hope in your heart you will find the will and the desire to support it and to lead our military in incorporating it into our nation's great asset and the world's best fighting force.

Thank you very much.

# GEORGE W. BUSH ADDRESSES THE NATION AFTER THE SEPTEMBER 11 ATTACKS (2001)

Good evening. Today, our fellow citizens, our way of life, our very freedom came under attack in a series of deliberate and deadly terrorist acts. The victims were in airplanes, or in their offices; secretaries, businessmen and women, military and federal workers; moms and dads, friends and neighbors. Thousands of lives were suddenly ended by evil, despicable acts of terror.

The pictures of airplanes flying into buildings, fires burning, huge structures collapsing, have filled us with disbelief, terrible sadness, and a quiet, unyielding anger. These acts of mass murder were intended to frighten our nation into chaos and retreat. But they have failed; our country is strong.

A great people has been moved to defend a great nation. Terrorist attacks can shake the foundations of our biggest buildings, but they cannot touch the foundation of America. These acts shattered steel, but they cannot dent the steel of American resolve.

America was targeted for attack because we're the brightest beacon for freedom and opportunity in the world. And no one will keep that light from shining.

Today, our nation saw evil, the very worst of human nature. And we responded with the best of America—with the daring of our rescue workers, with the caring for strangers and neighbors who came to give blood and help in any way they could.

Immediately following the first attack, I implemented our government's emergency response plans. Our military is powerful, and it's prepared. Our emergency teams are working in New York City and Washington, D.C. to help with local rescue efforts.

Our first priority is to get help to those who have been injured, and to take every precaution to protect our citizens at home and around the world from further attacks.

The functions of our government continue without interruption. Federal agencies in Washington which had to be evacuated today are reopening for essential personnel tonight, and will be open for business tomorrow. Our financial institutions remain strong, and the American economy will be open for business, as well.

The search is underway for those who are behind these evil acts. I've directed the full resources of our intelligence and law enforcement communities to find those responsible and to bring them to justice. We will make no distinction between the terrorists who committed these acts and those who harbor them.

I appreciate so very much the members of Congress who have joined me in strongly condemning these attacks. And on behalf of the American people, I thank the many world leaders who have called to offer their condolences and assistance.

America and our friends and allies join with all those who want peace and security in the world, and we stand together to win the war against terrorism. Tonight, I ask for your prayers for all those who grieve, for the children whose worlds have been shattered, for all whose sense of safety and security has been threatened. And I pray they will be comforted by a power greater than any of us, spoken through the ages in Psalm 23: "Even though I walk through the valley of the shadow of death, I fear no evil, for You are with me."

This is a day when all Americans from every walk of life unite in our resolve for justice and peace. America has stood down enemies before, and we will do so this time. None of us will ever forget this day. Yet, we go forward to defend freedom and all that is good and just in our world.

Thank you. Good night, and God bless America.

# BARACK OBAMA'S FIRST INAUGURAL ADDRESS JANUARY 20, 2009

My fellow citizens:

I stand here today humbled by the task before us, grateful for the trust you have bestowed, mindful of the sacrifices borne by our ancestors. I thank President Bush for his service to our nation, as well as the generosity and cooperation he has shown throughout this transition.

Forty-four Americans have now taken the presidential oath. The words have been spoken during rising tides of prosperity and the still waters of peace. Yet, every so often the oath is taken amidst gathering clouds and raging storms. At these moments, America has carried on not simply because of the skill or vision of those in high office, but because we the people have remained faithful to the ideals of our forebears, and true to our founding documents.

So it has been. So it must be with this generation of Americans.

That we are in the midst of crisis is now well understood. Our nation is at war, against a far-reaching network of violence and hatred. Our economy is badly weakened, a consequence of greed and irresponsibility on the part of some, but also our collective failure to make hard choices and prepare the nation for a new age. Homes have been lost; jobs shed; businesses shuttered. Our health care is too costly; our schools fail too many; and each day brings further evidence that the ways we use energy strengthen our adversaries and threaten our planet.

These are the indicators of crisis, subject to data and statistics. Less measurable but no less profound is a sapping of confidence across our land—a nagging fear that America's decline is inevitable, and that the next generation must lower its sights.

Today I say to you that the challenges we face are real. They are serious and they are many. They will not be met easily or in a short span of time. But know this, America—they will be met.

On this day, we gather because we have chosen hope over fear, unity of purpose over conflict and discord.

On this day, we come to proclaim an end to the petty grievances and false promises, the recriminations and worn-out dogmas, that for far too long have strangled our politics.

We remain a young nation, but in the words of scripture, the time has come to set aside childish things. The time has come to reaffirm our enduring spirit; to choose our better history; to carry forward that precious gift, that noble idea, passed on from generation to generation: the God-given promise that all are equal, all are free and all deserve a chance to pursue their full measure of happiness.

In reaffirming the greatness of our nation, we understand that greatness is never a given. It must be earned. Our journey has never been one of shortcuts or settling for less. It has not been the path for the faint-hearted—for those who prefer leisure over work, or seek only the pleasures of riches and fame. Rather, it has been the risk-takers, the doers, the makers of things—some celebrated but more often men and women obscure in their labor, who have carried us up the long, rugged path towards prosperity and freedom.

For us, they packed up their few worldly possessions and traveled across oceans in search of a new life.

For us, they toiled in sweatshops and settled the West; endured the lash of the whip and plowed the hard earth.

For us, they fought and died, in places like Concord and Gettysburg; Normandy and Khe Sahn.

Time and again these men and women struggled and sacrificed and worked till their hands were raw so that we might live a better life. They saw America as bigger than the sum of our individual ambitions; greater than all the differences of birth or wealth or faction.

This is the journey we continue today. We remain the most prosperous, powerful nation on Earth. Our workers are no less productive than when this crisis began. Our minds are no less inventive, our goods and services no less needed than they were last week or last month or last year. Our capacity remains undiminished. But our time of standing pat, of protecting narrow interests and putting off unpleasant decisions—that time has surely passed. Starting today, we must pick ourselves up, dust ourselves off, and begin again the work of remaking America.

For everywhere we look, there is work to be done. The state of the economy calls for action, bold and swift, and we will act—not only to create new jobs, but to lay a new foundation for growth. We will build the roads and bridges, the electric grids and digital lines that feed our commerce and bind us together. We will restore science to its rightful place, and wield technology's wonders to raise health care's quality and lower its cost. We will harness the sun and the winds and the soil to fuel our cars and run our factories. And we will transform our schools and colleges and universities to meet the demands of a new age. All this we can do. And all this we will do.

Now, there are some who question the scale of our ambitions—who suggest that our system cannot tolerate too many big plans. Their memories are short. For they have forgotten what this country has already done; what free men and women can achieve when imagination is joined to common purpose, and necessity to courage.

What the cynics fail to understand is that the ground has shifted beneath them—that the stale political arguments that have consumed us for so long no longer apply. The question we ask today is not whether our government is too big or too small, but whether it works —whether it helps families find jobs at a decent wage, care they can afford, a retirement that is dignified. Where the answer is yes, we intend to move forward. Where the answer is no, programs will end. And those of us who manage the public's dollars will be held to account—to spend wisely, reform bad habits, and do our business in the light of day—because only then can we restore the vital trust between a people and their government.

Nor is the question before us whether the market is a force for good or ill. Its power to generate wealth and expand freedom is unmatched, but this crisis has reminded us that without a watchful eye, the market can spin out of control — and that a nation cannot prosper long when it favors only the prosperous. The success of our economy has always depended not just on the size of our gross domestic product, but on the reach of our prosperity; on our ability to extend opportunity to every willing heart—not out of charity, but because it is the surest route to our common good.

As for our common defense, we reject as false the choice between our safety and our ideals. Our founding fathers, faced with perils we can scarcely imagine, drafted a charter to assure the rule of law and the rights of man, a charter expanded by the blood of generations. Those ideals still light the world, and we will not give them up for expedience's sake. And so to all other peoples and governments who are watching today, from the grandest capitals to the small village where my father was born: know that America is a friend of each nation and every man, woman, and child who seeks a future of peace and dignity, and that we are ready to lead once more.

Recall that earlier generations faced down fascism and communism not just with missiles and tanks, but with sturdy alliances and enduring convictions. They understood that our power alone cannot protect us, nor does it entitle us to do as we please. Instead, they knew that our power grows through its prudent use; our security emanates from the justness of our cause, the force of our example, the tempering qualities of humility and restraint.

We are the keepers of this legacy. Guided by these principles once more, we can meet those new threats that demand even greater effort — even greater cooperation and understanding between nations. We will begin to responsibly leave Iraq to its people, and forge a hard-earned peace in Afghanistan. With old friends and former foes, we will work tirelessly to lessen the nuclear threat, and roll back the specter of a warming planet. We will not apologize for our way of life, nor will we waver in its defense, and for those who seek to advance their aims by inducing terror and slaughtering innocents, we say to you now that our spirit is stronger and cannot be broken; you cannot outlast us, and we will defeat you.

For we know that our patchwork heritage is a strength, not a weakness. We are a nation of Christians and Muslims, Jews and Hindus —and non-believers. We are shaped by every language and culture, drawn from every end of this Earth; and because we have tasted the bitter swill of civil war and segregation, and emerged from that dark chapter stronger and more united, we cannot help but believe that the old hatreds shall someday pass; that the lines of tribe shall soon dissolve; that as the world grows smaller, our common humanity shall reveal itself; and that America must play its role in ushering in a new era of peace.

To the Muslim world, we seek a new way forward, based on mutual interest and mutual respect. To those leaders around the globe who seek to sow conflict, or blame their society's ills on the West—know that your people will judge you on what you can build, not what you destroy. To those who cling to power through corruption and deceit and the silencing of dissent, know that you are on the wrong side of history; but that we will extend a hand if you are willing to unclench your fist.

To the people of poor nations, we pledge to work alongside you to make your farms flourish and let clean waters flow; to nourish starved bodies and feed hungry minds. And to those nations like ours that enjoy relative plenty, we say we can no longer afford indifference to suffering outside our borders; nor can we consume the world's resources without regard to effect. For the world has changed, and we must change with it.

As we consider the road that unfolds before us, we remember with humble gratitude those brave Americans who, at this very hour, patrol far-off deserts and distant mountains. They have something to tell us today, just as the fallen heroes who lie in Arlington whisper through the ages. We honor them not only because they are guardians of our liberty, but because they embody the spirit of service; a willingness to find meaning in something greater than themselves. And yet, at this moment—a moment that will define a generation—it is precisely this spirit that must inhabit us all.

For as much as government can do and must do, it is ultimately the faith and determination of the American people upon which this nation relies. It is the kindness to take in a stranger when the levees break, the selflessness of workers who would rather cut their hours than see a friend lose their job which sees us through our darkest hours. It is the firefighter's courage to storm a stairway filled with smoke, but also a parent's willingness to nurture a child, that finally decides our fate.

Our challenges may be new. The instruments with which we meet them may be new. But those values upon which our success depends— hard work and honesty, courage and fair play, tolerance and curiosity, loyalty and patriotism—these things are old. These things are true. They have been the quiet force of progress throughout our history. What is demanded then is a return to these truths. What is required of us now is a new era of responsibility—a recognition, on the part of every American, that we have duties to ourselves, our nation, and the world, duties that we do not grudgingly accept but rather seize gladly, firm in the knowledge that there is nothing so satisfying to the spirit, so defining of our character, than giving our all to a difficult task.

This is the price and the promise of citizenship.

This is the source of our confidence—the knowledge that God calls on us to shape an uncertain destiny.

This is the meaning of our liberty and our creed—why men and women and children of every race and every faith can join in celebration across this magnificent mall, and why a man whose father less than sixty years ago might not have been served at a local restaurant can now stand before you to take a most sacred oath.

So let us mark this day with remembrance, of who we are and how far we have traveled. In the year of America's birth, in the coldest of months, a small band of patriots huddled by dying campfires on the shores of an icy river. The capital was abandoned. The enemy was advancing. The snow was stained with blood. At a moment when the outcome of our revolution was most in doubt, the father of our nation ordered these words be read to the people:

"Let it be told to the future world . . . that in the depth of winter, when nothing but hope and virtue could survive . . . that the city and the country, alarmed at one common danger, came forth to meet (it)."

America, in the face of our common dangers, in this winter of our hardship, let us remember these timeless words. With hope and virtue, let us brave once more the icy currents, and endure what storms may come. Let it be said by our children's children that when we were tested we refused to let this journey end, that we did not turn back nor did we falter; and with eyes fixed on the horizon and God's grace upon us, we carried forth that great gift of freedom and delivered it safely to future generations.

# BARACK OBAMA ANNOUNCES THE DEATH OF OSAMA BIN LADEN (2011)

Good evening. Tonight, I can report to the American people and to the world that the United States has conducted an operation that killed Osama bin Laden, the leader of al Qaeda, and a terrorist who's responsible for the murder of thousands of innocent men, women, and children.

It was nearly ten years ago that a bright September day was darkened by the worst attack on the American people in our history. The images of 9/11 are seared into our national memory—hijacked planes cutting through a cloudless September sky; the Twin Towers collapsing to the ground; black smoke billowing up from the Pentagon; the wreckage of Flight 93 in Shanksville, Pennsylvania, where the actions of heroic citizens saved even more heartbreak and destruction.

And yet we know that the worst images are those that were unseen to the world. The empty seat at the dinner table. Children who were forced to grow up without their mother or their father. Parents who would never know the feeling of their child's embrace. Nearly 3,000 citizens taken from us, leaving a gaping hole in our hearts.

On September 11, 2001, in our time of grief, the American people came together. We offered our neighbors a hand, and we offered the wounded our blood. We reaffirmed our ties to each other, and our love of community and country. On that day, no matter where we came from, what God we prayed to, or what race or ethnicity we were, we were united as one American family.

We were also united in our resolve to protect our nation and to bring those who committed this vicious attack to justice. We quickly learned that the 9/11 attacks were carried out by al Qaeda—an organization headed by Osama bin Laden, which had openly declared war on the United States and was committed to killing innocents in our country and around the globe. And so we went to war against al Qaeda to protect our citizens, our friends, and our allies.

Over the last ten years, thanks to the tireless and heroic work of our military and our counterterrorism professionals, we've made great strides in that effort. We've disrupted terrorist attacks and strengthened our homeland defense. In Afghanistan, we removed the Taliban government, which had given bin Laden and al Qaeda safe haven and support. And around the globe, we worked with our friends and allies to capture or kill scores of al Qaeda terrorists, including several who were a part of the 9/11 plot.

Yet Osama bin Laden avoided capture and escaped across the Afghan border into Pakistan. Meanwhile, al Qaeda continued to operate from along that border and operate through its affiliates across the world.

And so shortly after taking office, I directed Leon Panetta, the director of the CIA, to make the killing or capture of bin Laden the top priority of our war against al Qaeda, even as we continued our broader efforts to disrupt, dismantle, and defeat his network.

Then, last August, after years of painstaking work by our intelligence community, I was briefed on a possible lead to bin Laden. It was far from certain, and it took many months to run this thread to ground. I met repeatedly with my national security team as we developed more information about the possibility that we had located bin Laden hiding within a compound deep inside of Pakistan. And finally, last week, I determined that we had enough intelligence to take action, and authorized an operation to get Osama bin Laden and bring him to justice.

Today, at my direction, the United States launched a targeted operation against that compound in Abbottabad, Pakistan. A small team of Americans carried out the operation with extraordinary courage and capability. No Americans were harmed. They took care to avoid civilian casualties. After a firefight, they killed Osama bin Laden and took custody of his body.

For over two decades, bin Laden has been al Qaeda's leader and symbol, and has continued to plot attacks against our country and our friends and allies. The death of bin Laden marks the most significant achievement to date in our nation's effort to defeat al Qaeda.

Yet his death does not mark the end of our effort. There's no doubt that al Qaeda will continue to pursue attacks against us. We must — and we will—remain vigilant at home and abroad.

As we do, we must also reaffirm that the United States is not—and never will be—at war with Islam. I've made clear, just as President

Bush did shortly after 9/11, that our war is not against Islam. Bin Laden was not a Muslim leader; he was a mass murderer of Muslims. Indeed, al Qaeda has slaughtered scores of Muslims in many countries, including our own. So his demise should be welcomed by all who believe in peace and human dignity.

Over the years, I've repeatedly made clear that we would take action within Pakistan if we knew where bin Laden was. That is what we've done. But it's important to note that our counterterrorism cooperation with Pakistan helped lead us to bin Laden and the compound where he was hiding. Indeed, bin Laden had declared war against Pakistan as well, and ordered attacks against the Pakistani people.

Tonight, I called President Zardari, and my team has also spoken with their Pakistani counterparts. They agree that this is a good and historic day for both of our nations. And going forward, it is essential that Pakistan continue to join us in the fight against al Qaeda and its affiliates.

The American people did not choose this fight. It came to our shores, and started with the senseless slaughter of our citizens. After nearly 10 years of service, struggle, and sacrifice, we know well the costs of war. These efforts weigh on me every time I, as Commander-in-Chief, have to sign a letter to a family that has lost a loved one, or look into the eyes of a service member who's been gravely wounded.

So Americans understand the costs of war. Yet as a country, we will never tolerate our security being threatened, nor stand idly by when our people have been killed. We will be relentless in defense of our citizens and our friends and allies. We will be true to the values that make us who we are. And on nights like this one, we can say to those families who have lost loved ones to al Qaeda's terror: Justice has been done.

Tonight, we give thanks to the countless intelligence and counterterrorism professionals who've worked tirelessly to achieve this outcome. The American people do not see their work, nor know their names. But tonight, they feel the satisfaction of their work and the result of their pursuit of justice.

We give thanks for the men who carried out this operation, for they exemplify the professionalism, patriotism, and unparalleled courage of those who serve our country. And they are part of a generation that has borne the heaviest share of the burden since that September day.

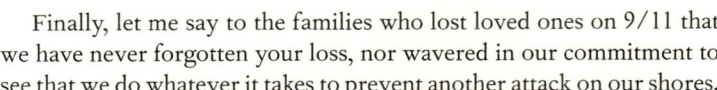 

Finally, let me say to the families who lost loved ones on 9/11 that we have never forgotten your loss, nor wavered in our commitment to see that we do whatever it takes to prevent another attack on our shores.

And tonight, let us think back to the sense of unity that prevailed on 9/11. I know that it has, at times, frayed. Yet today's achievement is a testament to the greatness of our country and the determination of the American people.

The cause of securing our country is not complete. But tonight, we are once again reminded that America can do whatever we set our mind to. That is the story of our history, whether it's the pursuit of prosperity for our people, or the struggle for equality for all our citizens; our commitment to stand up for our values abroad, and our sacrifices to make the world a safer place.

Let us remember that we can do these things not just because of wealth or power, but because of who we are: one nation, under God, indivisible, with liberty and justice for all.

Thank you. May God bless you. And may God bless the United States of America.

# Word Cloud Classics

# Word Cloud Classics

*Madame Bovary*

*Mansfield Park*

*The Merry Adventures of
Robin Hood*

*Moby-Dick*

*My Ántonia*

*Narrative of the Life of Frederick
Douglass and Other Works*

*Northanger Abbey*

*Odyssey*

*Persuasion*

*Peter Pan*

*The Phantom of the Opera*

*The Picture of Dorian Gray*

*The Poetry of Emily Dickinson*

*Pride and Prejudice*

*The Prince and Other Writings*

*The Red Badge of Courage
and Other Stories*

*The Romantic Poets*

*The Scarlet Letter*

*The Secret Garden*

*Selected Works of
Alexander Hamilton*

*Sense and Sensibility*

*Shakespeare's Sonnets and
Other Poems*

*Strange Case of Dr. Jekyll and
Mr. Hyde & Other Stories*

*Tarzan of the Apes &
The Return of Tarzan*

*The Three Musketeers*

*Treasure Island*

*Twenty Thousand Leagues
Under the Sea*

*Uncle Tom's Cabin, or Life
Among the Lowly*

*The U.S. Constitution and Other
Key American Writings*

*Walden and Civil Disobedience*

*The Wizard of Oz*

*Wuthering Heights*